MUSICIANS SINCE 1900

Performers in Concert and Opera

MUSICIANS SINCE 1900

Performers in Concert and Opera

Compiled and Edited

by

DAVID EWEN

THE H. W. WILSON COMPANY

NEW YORK

1978

Library of Congress Cataloging in Publication Data

Ewen, David, 1907–
  Musicians since 1900.

  1. Music — Bio-bibliography.   2. Opera — Bio-
bibliography.   I. Title.
ML105.E97   780'.92'2 [B]   78-12727
ISBN 0-8242-0565-0

INTRODUCTION

MUSICIANS SINCE 1900: PERFORMERS IN CONCERT AND OPERA replaces *Living Musicians* (1940) and *Living Musicians: First Supplement* (1957), both long out of print, with a work that is wider in scope than the two earlier volumes combined. The major difference is that this volume is not devoted exclusively to performing musicians still alive, as the other volumes were, but covers performers, living or dead, whose art has left a permanent impress upon the musical culture of the twentieth century. However, the fact that a distinguished performing artist of the late nineteenth century survived into the first years of the twentieth did not assure admission into these pages; only those whose art remained vital and whose performances still represented them at their prime are considered here. Jean de Reszke, for example, died in 1925, but since his last performance took place on March 29, 1901, his art had slight impact on performers of the twentieth century. Similarly, Adelina Patti died in 1919, but her scattered farewell appearances in the early twentieth century were faint reminders of her onetime glory; her contribution to music making belonged completely to the nineteenth century. The primitive recordings of the era barely suggested the quality of performances.

This volume, then, provides detailed biographical, critical, and personal information about 432 of the most distinguished performing musicians in concert and opera since 1900. Firsthand sources and recent researches and documentation have been liberally tapped to insure the accuracy of the biographical information. The cooperation of a great many musicians in the United States and in Europe is gratefully acknowledged, as well as that of managers of artists and the managers of opera houses and orchestras too numerous to single out by name.

DAVID EWEN

December 1977
Miami Beach, Florida

CONTENTS

KEY TO PRONUNCIATIONS

The pronunciation of names (when available) is indicated in footnotes to the biographies. The system of marking used follows *Webster's Biographical Dictionary*.

ā as in dāte, ā̇ as in fā̇tality, â as in hâre, ǎ as in hăt, ä as in pärt, ȧ as in bȧth, *a* as in
    *a*round
ch as in such
ē as in fēver, ė as in ėnough, ě as in měnd, *ě* as in tal*ě*nt, ẽ as in movẽr
ī as in mīce, ĭ as in wĭt, *ĭ* as in terrĭble
j as in jack
ᴋ as in German *ach*
ɴ indicates nasal tone of preceding sound
ng as in wing
ō as in vōte, ȯ as in ȯbey, ô as in ôrb, ŏ as in sŏd, *ŏ* as in bat*ŏ*n
oi as in boil
o͞o as in lo͞ose, o͝o as in fo͝ot
ou as in cow
~~th~~ as in ~~th~~an, th as in thick
ū as in cūte, u̇ as in u̇nify, û as in tûrn, ŭ as in cŭp, *ŭ* as in foc*ŭ*s, ü as in *menu* (in
    French) and *für* (in German)
y as in yen
z as in gaze
zh as in treasure
' as in battle (bat't'l)

MUSICIANS SINCE 1900

Performers in Concert and Opera

Claudio Abbado

1933–

Claudio Abbado, conductor, was born in Milan, on June 26, 1933. He was a descendant of a Moorish king, Abdul Abbad, who fled from Spain hundreds of years ago to settle in Piedmont, Italy, where he built a castle and married an Italian. In time the castle became known as Castello Abbado, and the family Italianized their name to Abbado.

For several generations the family enjoyed power and wealth until Claudio's great-grandfather squandered both in gambling. Claudio's grandfather restored the family's reputation, though not its wealth, by becoming a highly esteemed teacher of biology at the University of Turin and a much admired amateur musician. Claudio's father, Michelangelo Abbado, a professional violinist and a teacher at the Giuseppe Verdi Conservatory in Milan, and his mother, a pianist and a writer of children's books, were well able to nurture the talents of their children. One of Claudio's brothers became a concert pianist and director of the Rossini Conservatory in Pesaro; another brother, a successful architect; his sister gave up a possible career as a violinist for marriage.

From earliest childhood Claudio was influenced by the music around him. He was often taken to opera performances at La Scala, and he soon revealed a talent for music, particularly after he began taking piano lessons from his father. Claudio knew he wanted to become a conductor when, in his eighth year, he heard Debussy's *Nocturnes* performed by the La Scala Orchestra conducted by Antonio Guarnieri. Claudio made a note in his diary that this was a composition he must someday conduct.

He received his musical training at the Verdi Conservatory, from which he was graduated as a pianist in 1955. A year later he went to Vienna to attend Hans Swarowsky's class in conducting at the Vienna Academy of Music. One of his fellow students was Zubin Mehta, who eventually also became a world-famous conductor. During this period of study the two boys were able, by singing in the Musikfreunde chorus, to observe firsthand the conducting techniques of

CLAUDIO ABBADO

such masters as Bruno Walter and Herbert von Karajan.

Abbado made his conducting debut at a symphony concert in Trieste in 1958. That summer he visited the United States for the first time, to attend the Berkshire Music Center at Tanglewood, Massachusetts, where he won first prize in conducting in the Koussevitzky competition. In 1959 Abbado led his first opera performance, Prokofiev's *The Love for Three Oranges,* in Trieste. After several conducting engagements in Europe he won the Dimitri Mitropoulos International Music Competition for young conductors in 1963, a contest sponsored in the United States by the Federation of Jewish Philanthropies. Winning the contest brought Abbado a cash award of five thousand dollars and the opportunity to serve the following season as assistant conductor of the New York Philharmonic Orchestra, thus becoming an apprentice to its musical director Leonard Bernstein.

Abbado made his professional conducting debut in the United States with the New York Philharmonic Orchestra on April 7, 1963. He revealed an unusual gift for projecting his every desire to an orchestra with a minimum of body or hand movements. He possessed a well-defined beat, and he kept his emotions under control. He also showed the ability to penetrate to the details of a composition without losing sight of the overall design. "He will probably develop into an electrifying type of virtuoso conductor," wrote Harold C. Schonberg in his review in the New York *Times.* Abbado partially fulfilled this

---

Abbado: ä bä′ dô

1

prophecy—while further revealing his potential—by conducting an entire program with the New York Philharmonic Orchestra on January 30, 1964. In that concert he showed himself equally adept in the classical style of Mozart, the romanticism of Tchaikovsky, and the early twentieth century harmonic and rhythmic language of Prokofiev.

During the next year Abbado refined his technique and enriched his musical perceptiveness by conducting guest performances with some of the world's great orchestras, notably the New York Philharmonic, the Los Angeles Philharmonic, the Concertgebouw Orchestra of Amsterdam, the Berlin Philharmonic, the London Symphony, the New Philharmonia in London, and the Montreal Symphony. While performing at the RIAS Festival in Berlin in 1964 he impressed Herbert von Karajan so favorably that von Karajan invited him to conduct Mahler's Symphony No.2 (*Resurrection*) at the Salzburg Festival in 1965. "There was no doubting Abbado's control and the thoroughness of his technique," reported Michael Marcus in the Manchester *Guardian.* Abbado repeated his performance of the Mahler symphony in Vienna with the Vienna Philharmonic Orchestra, for another triumph.

Successful performances followed at the Piccola Scala in Milan on March 25, 1965, where he conducted from memory the world premiere of Giacomo Manzoni's opera *Atomtod;* at the Holland Festival in 1966 with his brilliant performance of Bellini's *I Capuletti ed i Montecchi,* a performance which he repeated at Expo '67 in Montreal with the La Scala company; at the Edinburgh Festival in 1966 with the New Philharmonia Orchestra of London; with concerts at festivals in Florence, Venice, Stresa, and Prague; with guest appearances with the New York Philharmonic Orchestra in 1967; and with other major orchestras in the United States, Europe, and Israel between 1966 and 1970.

In June 1969 Abbado became the permanent conductor of La Scala in Milan, the first musician to hold the post since Guido Cantelli nine years earlier. In 1977 he was appointed artistic director, sharing this post with Giorgio Streher and Carlo Maria Badini. From 1969 on he instituted a number of reforms, such as extending the opera season to four months, giving low-budget performances for workers and students, and vitalizing the repertory with new productions of established classics, novelties, and modern operas. One of his novelties was an opera based on Sophocles' *Oedipus Tyrannus* using the music of Andrea Gabrieli which had not received a public performance since the sixteenth century. The new operas included works by such avant-garde composers as Luigi Dallapiccola and Luigi Nono, in particular the world premiere of Nono's *Al Gran Sale Carico d'Amore* in 1975.

Abbado made his debut at the Metropolitan Opera House on October 7, 1968, with *Don Carlo* (an opera he had directed with outstanding success at Covent Garden in London the preceding June). "Conducting *Don Carlo* at the Metropolitan," said Barbara Fischer-Williams in *Opera News,* "Claudio Abbado was Orpheus incarnate, music radiating from his entire being. From his agile feet on the podium to his thick crop of black hair and to the tip of each persuasive finger he seemed totally immersed in his work. Nothing, one would say, mattered an iota to this young man in comparison with the music." In the *Saturday Review* Irving Kolodin wrote: "He asserted himself most positively as Verdi's buckler and shield. On the basis of this showing there is every reason to suppose that he can become a first rank opera conductor."

In addition to his duties at La Scala and his many appearances throughout the world in guest performances, Abbado filled the posts of permanent conductor of the Vienna Philharmonic Orchestra and principal guest conductor of the London Symphony Orchestra. In 1972–1973 he toured Australia, New Zealand, Japan, and the People's Republic of China with the Vienna Philharmonic, participating in the opening of the Sydney Opera House in Australia in 1973. For a time Abbado was subjected to severe criticism for spreading himself thin with so many performances in so many different places, particularly after he was unable to conduct the opening performance of the 1972–1973 season of La Scala because of illness. After a period of rest and medical treatment in Switzerland Abbado announced that he would curtail his guest appearances and confine his main energies to La Scala and the Vienna Philharmonic. In 1973 he toured Japan and the People's Republic of China with the Vienna Philharmonic; in 1974, the Soviet Union with the La Scala company; and in March and April of 1976, Europe and the United States with the Vienna Philharmonic. In September 1976 he conducted the La Scala company, during its American debut, in performances of *Macbeth, Simon Boccanegra* and Rossini's *La Cenerentola* in Washington, D.C., and New York in honor of the American Bicentennial.

For his operatic recordings Abbado earned many awards. Among them were the Diapason Award in 1966 and 1967, the Grand Prix du Disque in 1967, the Deutscher Schallplatten Preis in 1968, and Holland's Edison Prize. In 1973 he received the Mozart medal from the Mozart Gemeinde in Vienna.

He lives in an apartment on the Via Speronari in Milan with his wife, Gabriella (a dress designer who studied singing), their child, and Gabriella's two children from a former marriage. His political and social ideas are deeply realized and vital. To conclude the 1971–1972 season at La Scala he led a concert of "anti-fascist music" by Verdi, Beethoven, and Prokofiev, explaining that his aim was to join the world of culture with that of labor and to serve as an activist in promoting democracy and social reform.

Among his hobbies are attending theatrical performances, going to museums, and watching soccer games. He enjoys table tennis, swimming, skiing, and tennis. He is slim and wiry, has a strong chin and piercing eyes, and displays (said *Life*) "the imperious mien of a Roman dictator."

ABOUT: High Fidelity, February 1968; Life, February 1969; Newsweek, October 21, 1968; Opera News, November 13, 1968.

Licia Albanese

1913–

Licia Albanese, soprano, was born in Bari, Italy, on July 22, 1913, one of six children of Michele Albanese, a salesman for a large grocery-store chain, and Maria Rugusa Albanese. She was educated at a convent school. Though she studied the piano, her early interests were toe dancing and acting rather than music. One day when she was twelve her piano teacher heard her sing and was so impressed that he began teaching her the "Vissi d'arte" aria from *Tosca*—a providential beginning for a singer who was to gain world acclaim as Puccini's heroines. When Licia sang

---

Albanese: äl bä nā′ sä

LICIA ALBANESE

that aria at her father's birthday party, he realized she should take up singing seriously. For a time she studied voice with Emanuel De Rosa in Bari. When she was eighteen her father died and she went to live with a cousin in Milan, where she continued her vocal studies with Giuseppina Baldassare-Tedeschi for three years.

In Milan Albanese often heard opera performances at the Teatro Lirico. One evening in 1934 she attended a presentation of *Madama Butterfly* in which the singer appearing as Cio-Cio-San fell ill during the first act and could not continue. When Baldassare-Tedeschi informed the impresario that Albanese could take the role, the young singer was rushed backstage to put on the costume for the second act. She gave such a good account of herself for the remainder of that evening that she was offered a one-year contract. She turned it down (just as she had previously refused to accept a contract from La Scala after a successful audition) because she was convinced she was not yet ready to begin her professional career in opera and preferred to continue her studies with her teacher.

In 1935 Albanese was the one (among three hundred competitors) who won first prize and a gold medal in a national contest for singers sponsored by the Italian government. This award brought with it an appearance in a major opera house. In this manner Albanese finally made her official operatic debut, at the Teatro Reale in Parma on December 10, 1935, once again singing the title role of *Madama Butterfly*. She was an immediate success in a role that was to remain one of her favorites. In the years that followed she came to be regarded as one of its foremost interpreters.

Following her debut in Parma she appeared for one season at San Carlo Opera in Naples and after that was made a member of La Scala in Milan, where she gained the support of the leading tenor, Beniamino Gigli (with whom, in 1939, she recorded *La Bohème*). As her fame grew throughout Italy with appearances in other opera houses, she was made Commander of the Order of Merit in Italy and was invited to sing for King Victor Emmanuel at the royal palace. Invited to perform at the Vatican for Pope Pius XI, she became one of the few women ever so honored and the only woman asked to broadcast over the Vatican radio. The Pope decorated her with one of the Vatican's most distinguished awards: Lady Grand Cross of the Equestrian Order of the Holy Sepulchre. In 1939 she sang at a concert in Rome honoring Neville Chamberlain and Lord Halifax.

Her fame spread outside Italy, first to Paris at the Opéra, then to Covent Garden in London during the Coronation festivities in 1937, and finally to New York.

On Gigli's recommendation she was given a contract by the Metropolitan Opera and made her American debut there on February 9, 1940, in the title role of *Madama Butterfly*. Some critics remarked that her voice had technical limitations, but they acknowledged that she used that voice with sensitivity, skill, and artistry. The critics were particularly impressed by her gift for characterization, revealed later that season in her performance as Mimi in *La Bohème* and as Micaëla in *Carmen*. "The most important thing about her," said Edward Johnson, general manager of the company, "is her unlimited promise for the future. The more the public comes to know her and demand her—and it will—the more scope we can give her." Virgil Thomson became fully aware of her promise when he heard her as Violetta in *La Traviata*. Writing in the *Herald Tribune* he said: "She used her limpid voice, her delicate person, and her excellent musicianship to equal effect in creating the character. . . . She created a complete personality that lived and loved and drank champagne, and made decisions and died. She did this with skill, with art, with conviction, with beauty and with all loveliness."

During the next three decades at the Met-

ropolitan Opera her talent and flowering musicianship were given wide scope. She met all demands made upon her brilliantly. She appeared over 286 times in New York and 115 times on tour, in 17 roles, the most famous of which was Cio-Cio-San which she sang 72 times. In addition to Cio-Cio-San, Mimi, and Micaëla, she sang the roles of Susanna and the Countess in *The Marriage of Figaro*, Nedda in *I Pagliacci*, Marguerite in *Faust*, Violetta in *La Traviata*, Giorgetta in Puccini's *Il Tabarro*, Lauretta in *Gianni Schicchi*, the title role in *Manon*, Desdemona in *Otello*, Nannetta in *Falstaff*, Manon in *Manon Lescaut*, Tosca, Liù in *Turandot*, and the title role in *Adriana Lecouvreur*.

Twice she opened the Metropolitan Opera season: on November 27, 1944, as Marguerite in *Faust* and on November 29, 1948, as Desdemona in *Otello*. This performance of *Otello* was the first opera telecast from the stage of the Metropolitan. She was heard 45 times on the Metropolitan Opera Saturday afternoon broadcasts on a coast-to-coast radio network. The broadcast of January 19, 1946, when she sang Cio-Cio-San, was recorded permanently in 1975 to help raise funds for the company. "Albanese connoisseurs have always judged this 1946 broadcast—the first Metropolitan *Butterfly* since Pearl Harbor—as her best," said Peter G. Davis in the New York *Times*. "Her voice may never have been one of great natural beauty, but it had a distinctly individual timbre which Albanese always found useful in making her honest, heartfelt dramatic points. In one sense she had the perfect *Butterfly* soprano, one that could sound appealingly fragile in the score's most intimate moments, yet capable of soaring easily over Puccini's most impassioned fortissimos."

In commemoration of her twenty-five years with the Metropolitan Opera company she appeared at Carnegie Hall on February 9, 1965, in a program made up of 14 arias by Puccini, at least one from each of his operas, presented chronologically. She sang, reported Raymond Ericson in the New York *Times*, "with a fresh, luminous tone, and the sense of total involvement in the character she was portraying. . . . She has always made the most of her vocal resources through the years." After the concert she was presented with a small gold copy of the proscenium arch of the Metropolitan Opera against a red velvet background—depicted within the arch was a scene from *Madama Butterfly*.

Five years later, on February 22, 1970, she returned to Carnegie Hall to celebrate her thirtieth anniversary with the Metropolitan Opera. This time her program was devoted primarily to arias from operas she had never sung at the Metropolitan. "True," said Peter G. Davis in the New York *Times*, "the top of the voice is weak now, but the middle register retains much of its beauty, and the personal Albanese touches—direct, true and from the heart—made each aria an unmistakably individual dramatic treatment."

At sixty-two Albanese was "still something of a miracle," as John Rockwell noted in the New York *Times* following her recital at Town Hall in New York for the benefit of the Puccini Foundation, on February 5, 1975. "The color and the legato control are still there, and there is no wobble. Combined with those traditional interpretative virtues, the result can still give great pleasure indeed."

Albanese has also had a long, successful association with the San Francisco Opera where she made her debut on October 20, 1941, as Cio-Cio-San. She appeared with that company for the next nine years, and again between 1953 and 1957. When the San Francisco Opera celebrated its fiftieth anniversary with a concert at the amphitheater at Stern Grove in August 1973, Albanese participated by singing two arias from *Madama Butterfly*.

She also appeared in the first Puccini gala held at the Lincoln Center for the Performing Arts in New York for the benefit of the Puccini Foundation and its exchange program. At this concert, on December 11, 1974, she was joined by Franco Corelli, Grace Bumbry, Lucine Amara, and Eleanor Steber.

In addition to her appearances in opera and recitals in the United States and abroad, Albanese was frequently heard over American radio networks, and in the 1940s had a program of her own, "The Treasure Hour of Song." Toscanini chose her to sing the role of Mimi in his fiftieth-anniversary performance of *La Bohème* over the NBC radio network. She also sang the role of Violetta with Toscanini over the same network.

In 1945, the year she became an American citizen, she married Joseph Gimma on April 7. Gimma, a New York stockbroker, was also from Bari. "Before I leave Bari," she told an interviewer for the New York *Daily Mirror*, "his sister gives me a letter to him. The only

introduction letter I have. So he is the first I call on. No, we are not married right away. That takes five years. I work so hard I do not think of marriage until my friends say: 'Licia, you are blind for sure. Joe is in love with you.' But I say, 'Oh, no. He never tells me anything of love. It can't be.' "

A son, Joseph Jr., affectionately known as Peppino, was born in 1953. Their home, an apartment on Park Avenue in New York City, is decorated with Chinese art, metal butterflies, figurines, Nativity scenes, and objets d'art in metal, wood, and plastic. Albanese's favorite diversions have been swimming, fishing, clam digging, gardening, sailing, designing her own shoes and clothes, and cooking regional dishes.

To Howard Klein of the New York *Times* she stated her artistic creed: "Realismo!" Klein wrote: "She likes sturdy sets. . . . Props, costumes, make-up, gestures should all be real. Words should come from the heart, and diction is the key to her singing." She further revealed to Klein: "I learn the notes first, singing lightly. Then the words. To understand a musical phrase I speak the words. There are as many ways to sing words as there are ways to say them."

Licia Albanese has received honorary degrees from Seton Hall University, Manhattan College, and Fairfield (Connecticut) University.

ABOUT: Collier's Magazine, April 14, 1945; New York Times, February 7, 1965; Opera News, July 1974.

Frances Alda

1883–1952

Frances Alda (originally Frances Jeanne Davies), soprano, was born in Christchurch, New Zealand, on May 31, 1883. Her father, David, was English; her mother, Leonora, a trained singer, was Uruguayan. When Frances was four, her father died and her mother brought her two children to California. In San Francisco her mother succumbed to pneumonia and the children were brought back to New Zealand to be raised by their grandparents in St. Kilda, a suburb of Melbourne. Since the grandfather was a professional violinist who managed an Italian opera company on a world tour, Frances was brought up in a musical environment to which she responded sensitively. On her fifth birthday

Alda

FRANCES ALDA

she asked for and received a piano and piano lessons as a gift; on her seventh birthday she asked for a violin. "The piano and the violin," she once said, "remained my good friends through all the years since those childish birthdays."

When she was twelve her grandmother sent her to Miss Brown's Boarding School. Frances was unhappy there. On her grandmother's death she left the school for good, determined to make her way in music.

At seventeen, without vocal training, she auditioned for and got a job with the Williamson and Musgrave Light Opera Company that toured the Australian provinces in a repertory of Gilbert and Sullivan comic operas. She assumed the leading feminine roles in *The Mikado, The Gondoliers,* and *Iolanthe.* Then, with money from her grandmother's insurance policy she left Australia for Europe. In London she heard *La Bohème* for the first time in a performance at Covent Garden starring Melba. En route from London to Paris she met André Messager, French composer, to whom she confided her hopes of becoming a singer. Messager urged her to contact Mathilde Marchesi, a French vocal teacher who had helped to train many opera stars including Melba. Marchesi's home on the rue Jouffroy was Frances's first stop upon arriving in Paris. After an audition, Marchesi called out to her husband: "Salvatore, I've found a new Melba."

For the next ten months Marchesi took full charge of Frances. She urged her pupil to change her name from Davies to Alda. She found for Alda a pleasant apartment on the avenue Friedland and arranged for her to take lessons in Italian and French and to get coaching in acting from Victor Capoul. Through her influence Alda was invited to sing in the salons of wealthy Parisians. When Marchesi chose Massenet's *Manon* as the vehicle for Alda's debut, she asked the composer himself to coach the young singer in the title role.

Alda made her debut in the title role of *Manon* on April 15, 1904, at the Opéra-Comique in Paris, having been trained for the part by the opera's composer, Massenet. Her five appearances in this role during the season were all well received. But impatient with the restricted repertory the Opéra-Comique was assigning her, Alda left the company after one season to join the Théâtre de la Monnaie in Brussels where she made her debut as Marguerite in *Faust.* In two seasons there she appeared as Manon 52 times and as Marguerite 74 times; she was also cast as Violetta in *La Traviata,* as Marguerite de Valois in *Les Huguenots,* the Countess in *The Marriage of Figaro,* Salome in *Hérodiade,* and Ophelia in *Hamlet.*

In 1906 she performed at Covent Garden in London as Gilda in *Rigoletto,* opposite Caruso. In London, Cleofonte Campanini, the opera conductor, engaged her to appear as Gilda in a one-week festival of Verdi's operas at Parma. Soon after this appearance she went to Milan to audition for Gatti-Casazza, general manager of La Scala, at his apartment at the Hotel Milan. Gatti-Casazza was so taken with the beautiful texture of her voice that the following day he had Toscanini listen to her. The Maestro immediately engaged her for the title role in the first La Scala production of Charpentier's *Louise,* Toscanini conducting, in 1908. As Louise, and soon after that as Marguerite in Boïto's *Mefistofele,* Alda achieved a major success that immediately led to the signing of a contract with the Metropolitan Opera in New York.

After a summer of operatic appearances in Buenos Aires and Montevideo Alda went to New York to make her American debut on December 7, 1908, as Gilda, in a cast that included Caruso and Louise Homer. The critics were annihilating. "The young singer who made her debut last evening comes from the land of the sheep, and she bleated like one of them," one critic remarked acidly. H. E. Krehbiel wrote in the *Tribune:* "It cannot be said that Miss Alda's voice was uniformly agreeable in quality. Her tones were marred by a vibrato and they were often sharpened to a keen edge that cut shrilly upon the ear."

Her first reaction was to flee from New York and never again to sing at the Metropolitan. But she found some consolation in a basket of roses sent her by the diva Lillian Nordica, whom she had never met. Therein she found the following message: "There never was a young singer who appeared at the Metropolitan who wasn't severely criticized on her debut. Melba, Sembrich, Farrar, myself. . .all of us have gone through what you are going through today. Have courage. Affectionate good wishes." Going to the newspaper files in the public library, Alda found further solace in some of the reviews she read of other debuts.

At her second appearance, on December 17, the critics were kinder. This time she sang the role of Anna in the American premiere of Puccini's first opera, *Le Villi,* Toscanini conducting. "How deliciously Bonci's and Alda's voices blended in the duet," noted one of the critics, while another described her voice as "true and fresh and charming." The reviews became even more favorable later that season with her appearances as Marguerite in *Faust,* as Manon in Massenet's opera of the same name, and as Nannetta in *Falstaff.* One season later she was received triumphantly when she substituted for Geraldine Farrar as Mimi in *La Bohème,* and sang Desdemona in *Otello.*

On April 3, 1910, in a quiet ceremony in her apartment, Alda married Giulio Gatti-Casazza, who had become the general manager of the Metropolitan Opera. She was seventeen years younger than he. He had been in love with her for several years, had bombarded her with flowers, gifts, and love letters, and had repeatedly proposed to her. She finally accepted him, as she reveals in her autobiography, not because she was in love with him but because she respected him, had been touched by his overpowering demonstrations of love, and had been proposed to a final time when she felt particularly lonely. This marriage, she said frankly, was "on my part at least, a marriage after the European pattern: a sensible arrangement between a man and a woman who liked and respected each other and who would be mutually benefited by sharing the same name and home." In New York they lived

at the Knickerbocker Hotel where Caruso lived; in Paris, in an apartment on the Champs de Mars. Early in World War I they permanently closed down their Parisian home and brought all their furnishings to an apartment on Fifty-eighth Street in New York.

Feeling that it might prove embarrassing for the wife of the general manager to be a member of the company, Alda resigned from the Metropolitan Opera after the 1909–1910 season. During 1910–1911 she was heard in opera performances in Boston and Chicago. She also embarked on the first of the national tours in song recitals that she would make regularly for the next fifteen years. It was mainly through her persistent performances that "The Bells of St. Mary's" became successful, and it was for her that Charles Wakefield Cadman wrote "From the Land of the Sky-Blue Water" which Alda lifted to world popularity.

She made the first of her yearly recitals at Carnegie Hall in New York on March 3, 1911. Following one such appearance on November 14, 1916, Richard Aldrich wrote in the New York *Times:* "She did a good deal of fine singing of that type where vocal qualities are distinguished above the desire to portray the deeper moods or express strongly marked feeling. This seems to be her forte as a lyric soprano, and one within which she consciously holds herself for the present if one may judge of her intentions by the program, an excellent one. When her voice is at its best it has an evenness and flexibility in the upper portions that is capable of producing excellent results, and this was often in evidence. . . .Her style was tasteful and effective in producing the results required."

She was on tour in January 1912 when she received a wire from Otto H. Kahn, chairman of the board of the Metropolitan Opera, reading: "Come back. Your place at the Metropolitan is waiting for you." She returned as Desdemona on February 21, 1912, and remained one of the stars of the company for a quarter of a century, singing over twenty-four roles. She was heard most frequently as Marguerite in *Faust,* Mimi, Manon in *Manon Lescaut,* Marguerite in *Mefistofele,* Nannetta in *Falstaff,* and Lady Harriet in *Martha.* She appeared in several American premieres as Jaroslavna in *Prince Igor* (December 30, 1915), in the title role of Zandonai's *Francesca da Rimini* (December 22, 1916), and as the Princess in Rabaud's *Mârouf* (December 19, 1917).

She was in the first Metropolitan Opera production of Giordano's *La Cena della Beffe* as Ginevra (January 2, 1926). When she was cast as Rozenn in the first New York production of Lalo's *Le Roi d'Ys* on January 5, 1921, she prevailed on the composer to write for her a new aria for the third act.

She was also starred in the world premieres of several American operas: as Roxanne in Walter Damrosch's *Cyrano de Bergerac* (February 27, 1913), in the title role of Victor Herbert's *Madeleine* (January 24, 1914), and as Cleopatra in Henry Hadley's *Cleopatra's Night* (January 31, 1920). Her other Metropolitan Opera roles were Giulietta in *The Tales of Hoffmann,* Suzanne in *The Secret of Suzanne,* Micaëla in *Carmen,* Aida, and the title role in Catalani's *Loreley.* Reginald de Koven pleaded with her to take on the role of the Wife of Bath in the world premiere of his opera *The Canterbury Pilgrims.* Since De Koven had been one of the critics who had treated her harshly at her American debut she turned down his request.

Her favorite role was Mimi. During her years at the Metropolitan she sang Mimi to the Rodolfo of nearly every distinguished tenor appearing in New York.

During World War I she was often called upon to sing for war charities, in hospitals, for the Red Cross, for the sale of Liberty Bonds, and to raise money to provide men of the Navy with music and instruments. She sang "The Star-Spangled Banner" for numerous patriotic events, and on November 24, 1918, she participated in the Victory Peace Festival at the Hippodrome by singing several popular patriotic songs.

In the post–World War I era she eventually combined her career in the opera house and in concert halls with performances over the radio. In 1925 she became the first major opera singer to give a recital over the air. Later on she was the star of the "Atwater Kent Hour" and appeared in a series of radio programs devoted to Puccini's operas and sponsored by the American Radiator Company.

In 1928, after several years of a nonpublicized separation, Alda was divorced from Gatti-Casazza. "I was not happy in my marriage," she revealed. "As years went on the differences in age and temperament between Gatti and myself did not lessen. They increased." She felt she could no longer remain with a company managed by her ex-husband. On December 28, 1929, she made her farewell appearance at the Metropolitan Opera in the title role of *Manon Lescaut.* It was an occasion filled with sentiment. At the end of the second act she received fifteen curtain calls and more than fifty bouquets of flowers, wreaths from the company's management and board of directors, and an illuminated scroll signed by all her colleagues. "I am overwhelmed," Alda told her audience. "My heart is too full for speech." She had appeared 266 times in New York and 82 times on tour.

She then devoted herself mainly to recitals, to performances over the radio, and to teaching. In 1939 she became an American citizen. Two years later, on April 14, 1941, in Charleston, South Carolina, she married Ray Vir Den, an advertising executive. With her husband she made her home at Casa Mia, an estate in Great Neck, Long Island, which she had acquired in 1926 and where she had ten servants in attendance. "In her lemon-colored drawing room hung the vibrant Halmi portrait of Alda," wrote Gordon M. Eby in *Opera News,* "and nearby at least twenty-five Caruso caricatures. Scattered about the room were inscribed portraits of her teacher, Mathilde Marchesi . . . King Edward VII, Elsa Maxwell on the Lido, the Duke of Windsor, Marconi, the Agha Khan . . . a tender postcard message from Toscanini and a citation-letter from Secretary of the Navy Franklin D. Roosevelt commending her for services during World War I. . . . Rare jade, fabulous oils, lustrous petit-point chairs and stools, bibelots and curios filled every room, and there was an eye-filling view eastward over Long Island Sound."

During World War II she again devoted herself to war-relief work. She was on vacation in Venice with her husband, when she died of a cerebral hemorrhage on September 18, 1952.

From childhood she had been an active sportswoman, equally adept at tennis, swimming, croquet, and cricket. In her later years her greatest pleasure came from collecting antiques and autographs of famous musicians and officiating as a hostess at Casa Mia at her celebrated Sunday suppers, as popular for their lively conversation on music and politics as for their gourmet dishes and champagne. She often said that she had a temperament to match her red hair. Her tempestuous outbursts, her professional quarrels, and her frank and provocative statements provided considerable grist for the newspaper mills during her prima-donna years, and at times even carried her into the law courts. "She was," says Gordon M. Eby, "an extravagant woman—in her talent, taste, transgression and intolerance."

During her retirement years she completed an autobiography, *Men, Women and Tenors* (1937).

ABOUT: Alda, F. Men, Women and Tenors. Periodicals—Opera News, May 4, 1963.

Paul Althouse

1889–1954

Paul Shearer Althouse, tenor, was the first American-born singer to achieve international renown as a Wagnerian *Heldentenor;* he was also one of the handful of American-born and American-trained singers to assume principal roles at the Metropolitan Opera in New York at a time when the company was dominated by European artists.

Althouse was born on December 2, 1889, in Reading, Pennsylvania, to Harry Althouse, a manufacturer, and Laura Shearer Althouse. Paul was educated in the Reading public schools where Evelyn Essick, a supervisor of music, first noticed his superior voice. Essick persuaded Althouse's father to allow him to join the boys' choir of the Christ Episcopal Church, with which Paul remained for several years. When Paul's voice changed from boy soprano to tenor, Evelyn Essick began to give him systematic training.

After completing his academic education at Bucknell University in Lewisburg, Pennsylvania, Althouse went to New York. He received advanced instruction in concert music, oratorio, and opera from Perley Dunn Aldrich, Oscar Saenger, and Percy Rector Stephens before beginning his professional career as a member of the Hammerstein Opera Company in Philadelphia.

On March 19, 1913, Althouse made his debut at the Metropolitan Opera as Dimitri in the American premiere of *Boris Godunov.* Though interest that evening was focused on the opera itself and on the conductor in the pit (Toscanini), the debut of Paul Althouse did not pass unnoticed. In the *Sun* W. J. Henderson wrote: "At present it remains only to make note of the

PAUL ALTHOUSE

fact, an important one, that in Paul Althouse, a young American tenor in his first season on the stage, the Metropolitan has made an important acquisition. His impersonation of the false Dimitri showed much beauty of voice, good theatrical instincts, and natural vigor. He will surely be heard from in the future if he pursues his career with good judgment."

During the next six years Althouse appeared in numerous Italian, French, Russian, and German roles: Walther in *Tannhäuser,* the Singer in *Der Rosenkavalier,* the First Guard in *The Magic Flute,* Neipperg in *Madame Sans-Gêne,* Froh in *Das Rheingold,* Vladimir in *Prince Igor,* Pinkerton in *Madama Butterfly,* Turiddu in *Cavalleria Rusticana,* Cavaradossi in *Tosca,* Win-San-Luy in Leoni's *L'Oracolo,* the title role in *Oberon,* and Nicias in *Thaïs.* In addition he was heard in the world premieres of several American operas: as François in Victor Herbert's *Madeleine* (January 24, 1914), as the Squire in Reginald de Koven's *The Canterbury Pilgrims* (March 8, 1917), as Lionel in Charles Wakefield Cadman's *Shanewis* (March 23, 1918), and as Stephen in Joseph Breil's *The Legend* (March 12, 1919).

On the evening of December 7, 1917, Althouse appeared as Turiddu in a bill that included *I Pagliacci,* with Caruso. Backstage, Caruso took exception to Althouse's costume and immediately dispatched a messenger for his own costume. "Here," he told Althouse, "you will wear it tonight, and you can keep it as a souvenir of your first performance in this opera." Caruso became one of Althouse's admirers and is re-

9

ported to have said: "That young man will be my successor. He has a voice just like mine, only a little smaller."

During his first years at the Metropolitan Opera Althouse extended his activities with annual tours of the United States and appearances in the United States, Australia, and New Zealand, not only in operas but also in recitals and oratorios.

Althouse left the Metropolitan Opera after the 1922–1923 season. On September 23, 1926, he made his debut with the San Francisco Opera in the title role of Gounod's *Faust.* He returned to that company in 1933, after several years of giving recitals, performing in oratorios, and appearing as soloist with symphony orchestras. During this period he also sang with the Chicago Civic Opera.

On visiting Bayreuth for the Wagner festival Althouse was so deeply moved by what he heard that he decided to become a Wagnerian tenor. It is generally believed that his one-time teacher, Evelyn Essick, played an important role in this decision. In any event, between concert engagements during the next nine years, Althouse studied the Wagnerian roles, first performing some of them in Berlin, Stuttgart, and Stockholm.

In 1932, Toscanini invited Althouse to be a soloist with the New York Philharmonic Orchestra in an all-Wagner program. The critical and public response proved so enthusiastic that the Metropolitan Opera reengaged him, this time to fill leading parts in the Wagnerian repertory. On February 3, 1934, Althouse made what he called his second Metropolitan debut as Siegmund in *Die Walküre.* "Althouse sounded younger than when he left," said Olin Downes in the New York *Times,* "younger in the quality of tone and in his interpretative spirit, but much more mature and authoritative in his treatment of the melodic phrase, and in diction and dramatic conception."

On March 16 of the same year Althouse appeared as Tristan in *Tristan and Isolde,* the first time in Metropolitan Opera history that an American-born singer had assumed this role. In 1935 Althouse sang Siegmund in the performance of *Die Walküre* in which Kirsten Flagstad made her American debut. He was also heard as Parsifal, Siegfried in *Die Götterdämmerung,* Walther in *Die Meistersinger,* Tannhäuser, Lohengrin, and Loge in *Das Rheingold.* On January 7, 1938, he took the part of Aegisthus in Strauss's *Elektra.*

He continued to appear in the concert hall. Before Toscanini retired as music director of the New York Philharmonic, Althouse had sung under his baton in such masterworks as Beethoven's Symphony No.9 and *Missa Solemnis,* and in all-Wagner programs. Althouse was also a soloist with the New York Philharmonic under Artur Rodzinski and Bruno Walter. He sang in Mahler's *Das Lied von der Erde* with the Boston Symphony under Koussevitzky and with the St. Louis Symphony in a festival presentation of Berlioz' *The Damnation of Faust.* For several consecutive years he was a featured artist at the Worcester Festival.

In 1940 Althouse appeared in ceremonies attending the opening of the World's Fair in New York. He left the Metropolitan Opera permanently, following the 1939–1940 season, after singing in 170 performances in New York and 34 on tour and devoted himself to teaching and coaching young singers at a studio on West Seventy-second Street in New York City. When he went into total retirement as a singer in 1943, teaching became his full-time activity. He limited his teaching schedule to ten students, to whom he devoted himself conscientiously and completely. His students were given songs and arias to learn, poetry and prose to read, operas, concerts, and dramatic plays to attend. Althouse became one of America's foremost voice teachers. Among the many students who studied with him were Richard Tucker and Eleanor Steber.

Althouse and his first wife, Elizabeth Breen, whom he married on June 20, 1914, had two daughters. His second wife, the former Cecilia Glynn, survived him. Paul Althouse died at his home in New York City on February 6, 1954.

ABOUT: Musical America, March 1954.

Lucine Amara

1927–

Lucine Amara (originally Lucine Tockqui Armaganian), soprano, was born in Hartford, Connecticut, on March 1, 1927. Her parents, George and Adrine Kazanjian Armaganian, came to the United States from Armenia where her mother had survived the Armenian massacre. Her father

Amara: ä mä′ rä

LUCINE AMARA

was the proprietor of a small shoe repair shop.

When her family moved to Pontiac, Michigan, in her early years, Lucine took violin lessons with Bertha Roth. She continued her violin studies in San Francisco, when her family moved there. Before long she was a member of several orchestras.

Her career as a singer began in an Armenian church. In 1945–1946 she sang in the chorus of the San Francisco Opera.

At the suggestion of a cousin, Amara began studying voice with Stella Eisner-Eyn, a voice teacher in San Francisco. She continued vocal lessons at the Music Academy of the West at Santa Barbara in 1947, and between 1949 and 1950 at the University of Southern California, both times on scholarships.

After winning the first prize of two thousand dollars in a national competition conducted by the Atwater Kent Company among fifteen hundred contestants, Amara was engaged in 1948 as soloist at the Hollywood Bowl in a concert conducted by Eugene Ormandy. During the next year she was heard in the title role in *Ariadne auf Naxos* at the University of Southern California and as soloist with the San Francisco Symphony under Pierre Monteux.

She made her debut at the Metropolitan Opera on November 6, 1950 (the opening night of the season), as the Celestial Voice in *Don Carlo*. To Max de Schauensee, writing in the Philadelphia *Bulletin*, her "tones did not seem sufficiently ethereal for a 'celestial voice.'" During the remainder of that season she appeared over

70 times in minor roles. On December 14, 1951, she scored such a success as Nedda in *I Pagliacci* that, even while continuing in small parts, she was also given the roles of Micaëla in *Carmen* on December 6, 1952, Mimi in *La Bohème* on February 13, 1953, and Donna Elvira in *Don Giovanni* on February 6, 1954. She opened the 1955–1956 season on November 14, 1955, as Antonia in *The Tales of Hoffmann* and again on October 28, 1957, as Tatiana in a new production of *Eugene Onegin*.

In a quarter of a century she appeared in about 450 performances in New York and 210 performances on tour in 42 roles in 36 operas. Among her most celebrated roles were Desdemona in *Otello*, Tosca, Euridice in Gluck's *Orfeo ed Euridice*, Liù in *Turandot*, Nedda, Donna Elvira, Antonia, Aida, Fiordiligi in *Così fan Tutte*, Micaëla, Tatiana, Cio-Cio-San in *Madama Butterfly*, Leonora in *Il Trovatore*, Leonora in *La Forza del Destino*, Pamina in *The Magic Flute*, the Countess in *The Marriage of Figaro*, Eva in *Die Meistersinger*, the title role in *Ariadne auf Naxos*, Marguerite in *Faust*, Ellen in Britten's *Peter Grimes*, Luisa in *Luisa Miller*, Maddalena in *Andrea Chénier*, Alice Ford in *Falstaff*, and the title role in *Manon Lescaut*. Winthrop Sargeant in the *New Yorker* described her voice as "wonderfully limpid and expressive," and a critic for the Boston *Herald* said she brought to the stage a blending "of voice and passion into a single tightly unified performance. You live with her, soar with her voice and her feelings and weep when she sings."

Amara made her first appearance at the Glyndebourne Festival in 1954; three years later she enjoyed a major success there in the title role of *Ariadne auf Naxos*. At the Caracalla Baths in Rome in 1954 she sang the title role in *Aida*. That year she also participated in the Edinburgh Festival. In 1955 she made her debut with the Royal Stockholm Opera and in 1961 with the Stuttgart Opera. In 1968 came her first world tour, with particularly successful performances in the Soviet Union, Israel, and the Far East. She appeared in a new role when she made her debut with the Canadian Opera in Toronto, in 1975, as Giorgetta in Puccini's *Il Tabarro*.

She has appeared many times with major American and European opera companies, in recitals, and as soloist with major orchestras. Her first New York recital took place in September 1967 at Carnegie Hall. Irving Kolodin reported in the *Saturday Review:* "Assuming that Miss Amara has a serious interest in this kind of singing, it may be said that she has an ample voice for it, but not as yet the control, refinement, or variety of insights the literature requires."

For five consecutive years she was a featured soloist on the "Bell Telephone Hour" over radio. She also performed on television with the "Bell Telephone Hour," on "Opera Cameos" in New York, and "Opera" on Educational Television in California. She was heard in several opera scenes with Mario Lanza in the motion picture *The Great Caruso* (1951).

Lucine Amara lives in an apartment in San Francisco. She was married on January 1, 1961, and divorced three years later. A gifted linguist, she speaks eight languages in addition to English.

ABOUT: Kutsch, K. J. and Riemens, L. A Concise Biographical Dictionary of Singers.

Pasquale Amato

1878–1942

Pasquale Amato, baritone, a descendant of one of the venerable families of Naples, was born in that city on March 21, 1878. As a boy he often attracted attention with his singing in the church choir. In 1896 he entered the Conservatorio San Pietro a Majella in Naples for vocal training, graduating three years later. He made his operatic debut as the elder Germont in *La Traviata* at the Teatro Bellini in Naples in 1900.

His first successes came in 1902 with guest appearances at the Teatro dal Verme in Milan and the Genoa Opera. In 1903 he sang in opera houses in Monte Carlo, Nuremberg, Leipzig, and Odessa; and in 1904 at the Teatro Costanzi in Rome, Teatro Massimo in Palermo, and Covent Garden in London. He made a particularly good impression at Covent Garden as Escamillo in *Carmen.*

These and other appearances brought him a contract for La Scala, but before this debut could take place he fell ill and lost his voice. A period of despair ensued during which Amato was convinced his career was at an end, and even

Amato: ä mä′ tō

PASQUALE AMATO

contemplated suicide. Toscanini often visited him to bring words of hope and consolation. Amato eventually accepted an engagement in Germany where his voice returned to its full splendor. He finally arrived at the stage of La Scala in 1907 as Golaud in the Italian premiere of *Pelléas and Mélisande,* Toscanini conducting.

Gatti-Casazza engaged him for the Metropolitan Opera, and Amato made his debut on November 20, 1908, as the elder Germont. "Of the newcomers in last night's performance," wrote H. E. Krehbiel in the *Tribune,* "Signor Amato, the representative of Giorgio Germont, made the finest impression, one that promises to be lasting; for though he appeared as a singer of the old conventional Italian order, he displayed an ample voice of excellent quality and a convincing style."

This debut was the prelude to a long, rich career at the Metropolitan Opera, extending to 1921. In that time Amato was heard in almost every important baritone role in the French and Italian repertory. Above and beyond the role of the elder Germont his specialties were Valentin in *Faust,* Rigoletto, Amfortas in *Parsifal,* Figaro in *The Barber of Seville,* Scarpia in *Tosca,* Sharpless in *Madama Butterfly,* Iago in *Otello,* Barnaba in *La Gioconda,* Amonasro in *Aida,* Renato in *Un Ballo in Maschera,* Sir Henry Ashton in *Lucia di Lammermoor,* Marcello in *La Bohème,* Count di Luna in *Il Trovatore,* Escamillo in *Carmen,* Jack Rance in *The Girl of the Golden West,* and Manfredo in *L'Amore dei Tre Re.* He appeared in the world premieres of *The Girl of the*

Golden West (December 10, 1910), Walter Damrosch's *Cyrano de Bergerac* in the title role (February 27, 1913), and Giordano's *Madame Sans-Gêne* in the role of Napoleon (January 25, 1915). He was cast in the following American premieres: Catalani's *La Wally* as Vincenzo Gellner (January 6, 1909); Franchetti's *Germania* as Carlo Worms (January 22, 1910); Montemezzi's *L'Amore dei Tre Re* as Manfredo (January 2, 1914); and Zandonai's *Francesca da Rimini* as Giovanni (December 22, 1916). He also appeared as Athanaël in the first Metropolitan production of *Thaïs*. He participated in seven opening night performances: as Barnaba in *La Gioconda,* 1909–1910; Hidroat in Gluck's *Armide,* 1911–1912; Amonasro in *Aida,* 1913–1914; Barnaba, 1914–1915; Renato in *Un Ballo in Maschera,* 1915–1916; the High Priest in *Samson and Delilah,* 1915–1916; and Amonasro, 1917–1918.

Illness checked his career at its high point in 1924. Amato spent the next few years in retirement, mostly in Italy. On February 26, 1933, after a ten-year absence, he returned to the Metropolitan Opera to help celebrate the silver jubilee of Gatti-Casazza as general manager. This Sunday evening gala concert in which he participated was a presentation of the third act of *Falstaff.*

On November 20, 1933, Amato celebrated the twenty-fifth anniversary of his operatic debut in the United States with a guest appearance at the Hippodrome Theater in New York–his role, the elder Germont, in which he had made his Metropolitan Opera debut. Upon his entrance in the second act the audience of five thousand, including many stars from the Metropolitan Opera, stood up in tribute. At the end of the act Amato was presented with a gold medal.

On April 1, 1934, Amato became director of the Hippodrome Opera Company, a post he held only briefly. Going into retirement as a professional singer, he opened a vocal studio in New York City. He later became the director of operatic productions at the University of Louisiana in Baton Rouge. He died in Jackson Heights, New York City, on August 12, 1942.

ABOUT: Kutsch, K. J. and Riemens. L. A Concise Biographical Dictionary of Singers.

Marian Anderson

1902–

As the first black singer to appear in a major role at the Metropolitan Opera Marian Anderson helped open a door for other black artists who in time became leading performers. She was the greatest box-office attraction of any black concert singer up to her time.

Marian Anderson, contralto, was born in South Philadelphia, Pennsylvania, on February 17, 1902, the oldest of three daughters. Her father, John Berkeley Anderson, dealt in ice and coal; her mother, Anna, who had been a schoolteacher in Lynchburg, Virginia, supplemented the family income by taking in wash. Her father was a special officer in charge of ushers at the Union Baptist Church in South Philadelphia to which young Marian was often brought for the services. When she was six she joined the junior choir and sang her first solo, the hymn "Dear to the Heart of the Shepherd."

From savings she accumulated by scrubbing the steps of her neighbors' houses and by running errands, she bought a violin for $3.45 in a pawnshop. "I was extremely happy the first time I held it in my hands," she once recalled, "and started at once to learn how to play it by myself. I played it a long time in fact, until the strings gave way. But by then it had served its purpose."

Her greatest joy came from singing, which seemed to come to her as naturally as breathing, and which her relatives and friends early came to recognize and admire. When she was eight she received her first fee (fifty cents) for a performance at church. From then on she often sang at church affairs and local clubs.

Her father died when she was ten, and the family went to live with Marian's grandparents who supervised her religious training and education. After completing grammar school, she took a commercial course at the William Penn High School to prepare herself for a business career that would enable her to support her family while she continued with music study. Her sole interest in school was the once-a-week music period and the assemblies where she was occasionally asked to perform. A stranger, hearing her sing one day at an assembly, persuaded the school principal to allow her to give up a commercial course for an academic one and at the

MARIAN ANDERSON

same time to give her enough time for music study. She was transferred to the South Philadelphia High School. During her years there she sang with the senior choir at the Union Baptist Church and at concerts in nearby black communities. With several members of this group she paid her first visit to New York, appearing at the Abyssinian Baptist Church in Harlem.

After giving up the violin she studied the piano, which she mastered sufficiently to accompany herself in her singing. Singing had become the focal point of her life. When she was sixteen she gave her first concert, at a black school in Atlanta, Georgia. More concerts followed, sometimes for a tiny fee, sometimes for no payment at all. As a member of the Philadelphia Choral Society she performed out of town at black colleges and churches.

A vivid and ugly experience with racism occurred when she tried to enroll in one of Philadelphia's leading music schools. "This beautiful young blonde girl behind the window ignored me when it got to be my turn in line," she recalled. "I thought, at first, it was because she didn't notice me. But when I was the only one left, she tossed her head in delight and told me, 'We don't take coloreds.' You might expect this sort of thing at a place where pugilists are fighting. But at a Conservatory it was absolutely a jolt to me."

In her third year at the South Philadelphia High School she began to study voice with Mary Saunders Patterson. With funds raised at a benefit by the Philadelphia Choral Society she

soon progressed to more advanced instruction with Agnes Reifsnyder. In 1919 the principal of South Philadelphia High School persuaded Giuseppe Boghetti to give her singing lessons, lessons paid for out of six hundred dollars raised for her at a benefit concert at the Union Baptist Church. Boghetti never forgot the evening Marian Anderson auditioned for him. It was dusk, the end of a long and arduous day of teaching. Sinking into an armchair he motioned to her to begin. She sang "Deep River" and, as he recalls it, "it was as if the sun had suddenly flooded the room."

While working with Boghetti after graduation from high school she made concert tours, earning between fifty and one hundred dollars an appearance. Two of these concerts were in New York City. Generally she received unfavorable reviews. One critic remarked: "Marian Anderson sang her Brahms as if by rote." "I felt lost and defeated," she remembers. "The dream was over." For a time she refused to make public appearances, preferring to study languages (particularly French and German) and to work on vocal exercises and her repertory. Then she slowly drifted back to concert work, gaining self-assurance with each new tour.

In 1923 she won first prize in a singing contest held by the Philharmonic Society of Philadelphia. Two years later she entered a contest held by the New York Philharmonic Orchestra at Lewisohn Stadium. Three hundred singers competed. Singing "O mio Fernando" from *La Favorita,* Anderson captured first prize, which brought her a guest appearance with the New York Philharmonic on August 27, 1925. Her success led to an appearance with the Philadelphia Orchestra, then to a recital in New York which attracted critical interest and enthusiasm for the first time. A critic for the New York *Times* said: "She is endowed by nature with a voice of unusual compass, color and dramatic capacity. The lower tones have a warm contralto quality, but this voice has the range and the resources of a mezzo soprano. In passages of sustained melody, the singer showed a feeling for melodic lines, while in the aria 'O mio Fernando' she gave evidence of instructive dramatic impulse."

When Arthur Judson became her manager he urged her to continue working on her repertory with Frank La Forge in New York, then had her appear in a recital in Carnegie Hall in 1929.

Since major engagements were not readily available at the time for black artists, she left for London in 1930 to study the German *Lied* with Raimund von Zur Mühlen and to make public appearances at Wigmore Hall and as a soloist at a Promenade concert conducted by Sir Henry J. Wood.

On her return to the United States, she made a nineteen-concert tour. Then she went to Europe on a Julius Rosenwald Fellowship for additional study of German *Lieder* with Michael Raucheisen and vocal training with Sverre Jordan. In 1933 she made her debut in Berlin. The audience was particularly enthusiastic after her rendition of several spirituals, and the reviews were flattering. A tour of Scandinavia followed immediately with two concerts each in Oslo, Stockholm, and Helsinki. "It made me realize that the time and energy invested in seeking to become an artist were worth while, and that what I had dared to aspire to was not impossible."

Later in 1933 a second Julius Rosenwald Fellowship provided her with the means for another extended visit to Europe. Within the next year she gave 142 concerts in large cities and small outlying communities. In Finland she sang some of his songs for Sibelius. He advised her to be "more Marian Anderson and less Sibelius" and dedicated to her his song "Solitude." Her concert orbit widened to include the Salle Gaveau in Paris, the Konzerthaus in Vienna, and the principal concert halls of Brussels, Geneva, Hungary, Salzburg, Italy, Spain, the Baltic countries, and the Soviet Union. Because of the antireligious policy of the Soviet government, Schubert's "Ave Maria" was identified on the program as an aria and any religious connotations in the titles of spirituals were carefully deleted.

Sol Hurok, the impresario, heard her sing in Paris, went backstage, and offered her a contract. For the rest of her career her artistic life was shaped by Hurok, who was largely responsible for developing her into one of the greatest box-office attractions in music.

Her international fame received a powerful boost in the summer of 1935 at a private gathering in Salzburg during the festival season. In *Between the Thunder and the Sun* Vincent Sheean described what happened: "A musical hostess, Mrs. Moulton, invited three or four hundred people to an afternoon of songs at the Hotel de l'Europe. The guests included Toscanini, Lotte Lehmann, Bruno Walter and practically all the other musical powers of Salzburg. The artist was Marian Anderson. I do not think anybody there had heard her before. She sang Bach, Schubert and Schumann, with a final group of Negro spirituals. . . . The Archbishop was sitting in the front row, and at his insistence she repeated the Schubert 'Ave Maria.' In the last group she sang a spiritual, 'They Crucified My Lord, and He Never Said a Mumblin' Word.' Hardly anybody in the audience understood English well enough to follow what she was saying, and yet the immense sorrow—something more than the sorrow of a single person— that weighed her tones and lay over her dusky, angular face was enough. At the end of the spiritual, there was no applause at all—a silence, instinctive, natural, and intense, so that you were afraid to breathe." Toscanini is reputed to have said to her: "A voice like yours is heard only once in a hundred years."

She returned to America to make a historic appearance at Town Hall, New York, on November 30, 1935, a concert which established her as one of the foremost American concert singers of all time. She gave that performance suffering pain: A few days earlier, aboard the Île de France, she had fractured a bone in her foot, and she was forced to appear in a cast, of which the audience was unaware. She sang beautifully and her concert was a triumph. "She was the mistress of all she surveyed," reported a critic for the New York *Times*. Her reaction to the concert was: "If there has been one appearance that seemed like a leap forward this Town Hall event was it. I resolved to make myself equal to the challenge."

A second New York appearance followed on January 30, 1936, this time in Carnegie Hall. "The voice is a rare one," wrote Olin Downes in the New York *Times*. An American tour and appearances on major network radio programs came next. Then she embarked on a new European tour. She had planned to stay just one month in the Soviet Union but was compelled to remain three. In Vienna she was a soloist at a concert conducted by Bruno Walter, followed by concerts in Madrid just before the outbreak of the civil war, and in Switzerland, Monte Carlo, and Scandinavia. Then she swung back to the United States for more concerts, followed by a tour of the Near East and South America. In

Buenos Aires she gave 12 concerts to capacity houses.

In February 1939 Anderson became the center of controversy in the United States when the Daughters of the American Revolution canceled her concert appearance at Constitution Hall, in Washington, D.C., because she was black. This action precipitated a storm of protest from leading musicians, clergymen, political figures, writers, and welfare workers. Eleanor Roosevelt resigned from the DAR to express her personal opposition to bigotry. Secretary of the Interior Harold L. Ickes invited Anderson to give her concert at the Lincoln Memorial on Easter Sunday, April 9. She consented, refusing a fee so that anybody could come. (Since no hotel would accommodate her, she was a house guest of Gifford Pinchot, a former governor of Pennsylvania.) An audience of 85,000 assembled before the Memorial, including Supreme Court judges, congressmen, and cabinet ministers. Another audience of several millions heard the concert over the radio. She sang *Lieder* and spirituals. Behind her loomed the massive, benign statue of Abraham Lincoln. (This scene was the inspiration for a mural decorating the Department of the Interior building in Washington.) The enthusiastic response of the audience to each of her numbers was merely the preface to the ovation accorded her after her last spiritual. She made a brief speech: "I am overwhelmed. I just can't talk. I can't tell you what you have done for me today. I thank you from the bottom of my heart again and again."

A few days later, on April 16, she appeared in Carnegie Hall to receive one of the greatest ovations experienced by any artist in that auditorium. On July 2 she was awarded the Spingarn Award for "highest and noblest achievement by an American Negro during the preceding year." In 1941 she received the ten-thousand-dollar Bok Award from the city of Philadelphia, which she used to establish the Marian Anderson Award for the promotion of the careers of struggling young artists.

By 1939 she had arrived at her fullest powers as an interpretative artist and was in complete command of her vocal resources. The three-octave span of her voice appeared to be flawless. "In sheer beauty of tonal production, in variety of colors, from the deep purple of her low tones to the bright crimson of her falsetto, her voice is like a Stradivarius in the hands of Heifetz. . . .

She fashions a lyric line the way Casals did on the cello, each note having its precise role to fill, and assuming its inevitable place in the overall design. She achieves drama and tragedy with the most economical use of shade and nuance." (D. Ewen. *Men and Women Who Make Music.* Merlin, 1949) And in her rendition of spirituals, for which she always had a particular affinity, she had few rivals. "To these songs she brings the full tragedy of a race despised and rejected. 'Nobody Knows de Trouble I've Seen'—the expression of sorrow becomes more poignant and heartbreaking because of the restraint with which she speaks her woe. 'Were You There When They Crucified My Lord?'—she brings the immense and shattering sorrow of one who knows what it means to be crucified. 'Deep River'—with those incomparable low tones of hers, luscious in texture, the melody acquires wings and soars as never before." (D. Ewen. *ibid.*)

To commemorate the tenth anniversary of her concert debut in New York a testimonial dinner was given for her in December 1945. By that time her career had accumulated impressive statistics. She had given over 700 concerts in 289 cities throughout the world and before audiences numbering about 4 million. For five consecutive years she had been selected by national polls as the foremost female concert singer over the radio.

On January 7, 1955, Anderson contributed to both the social and the operatic history of America by becoming the first black singer to assume a major role at the Metropolitan Opera: Ulrica in *Un Ballo in Maschera.* Though the opera boasted an all-star cast that included Richard Tucker, Zinka Milanov, Leonard Warren, and Roberta Peters, with Dimitri Mitropoulos conducting, it was Anderson who stole the spotlight that evening. As Howard Taubman reported in a front-page story in the New York *Times:* "The excitement in the opera house had an opening-night quality, plus an extra emotional impact. Many in the audience knew that Miss Anderson—like Joshua, but more quietly—had fought the battle of Jericho and at last the walls had come tumbling down." Anderson described her own reactions to this evening: "I trembled and when the audience applauded and applauded before I could sing a note I felt myself tightening into a knot. . . . With all my experience I had behind me, I should have been firm and secure, but my emotions were too strong. . . . I know I tried too hard; I know I overdid. I was not pleased with the first performance; I know it was not the best I could do." Reviewing the performance, Olin Downes thought otherwise in the New York *Times:* "She proceeded with her first aria, 'Re dell' abisso.' The passage suited well the dark and rich color of the voice, as the simplicity and eloquence of Miss Anderson's singing graced the song. . . . Before the air was finished the singer had demonstrated the same musicianship and instinct for dramatic communication she had long since demonstrated on the concert stage. As the act proceeded and the voice warmed it gained in sonority and concentrated resonance. . . . There was no moment in which Miss Anderson's interpretation was commonplace or repetitive in effect. . . . Miss Anderson stamped herself in the memory and the lasting esteem of those who listened."

One week later she repeated her performance in Philadelphia during a visit by the Metropolitan Opera company. "The Philadelphia performance for me went better," she said. "I felt happier about it, and securer."

Anderson remained with the Metropolitan Opera for a second season. "The chance to be a member of the Metropolitan," she wrote, "has been a highlight of my life. It has meant much to me and to my people. If I have been privileged to serve as a symbol, to be the first Negro to sing as a regular member of the company, I take greater pride from knowing that it has encouraged other singers of my group to realize that the doors everywhere may open increasingly to those who have prepared themselves well."

Though abandoning opera, she continued to pursue an active and worldwide career as a concert singer. It was interrupted in 1957 and 1958 to allow her to fulfill her duties as a delegate appointed by President Eisenhower to the thirteenth General Assembly of the United Nations. She began her last world tour in 1965 and gave her final concert at Carnegie Hall, in New York, on Easter Sunday 1967.

On July 24, 1943, she married Orpheus H. Fisher, an architect, who designed and built for her Mariana Farm, a one-hundred-and-five-acre hillside property outside Danbury, Connecticut. Upon their first appearance at the farm, Fisher gathered his staff to warn them: "The first person who calls my wife Miss Anderson is going to be fired." Publicly she has always referred to

him as "Mr. Fisher" and privately as "the king."

At her farm she was able to renew her energies and refresh her spirits after the strains of her concert tours. Since her retirement she has lived there quietly, jealously guarding her privacy and refusing to see any but her closest friends. Her time is taken up with helping with the housework, sewing, occasionally cooking, and undemonstratively helping to advance the cause and interests of her people (children particularly) in any way she can. She almost never listens to her own recordings. "I always feel that somehow had I been given one more chance I could have done better," she says.

Hers is a lifetime crowded with honors. She has received twenty-three honorary degrees from educational institutions in the United States, including Princeton, Smith, and New York University. She has received from Sweden the Litteris and Artibus medal, from Finland the Order of the White Rose (conferred on her by Field Marshal Mannerheim), from Japan the Yukusho medal, and from President Lyndon B. Johnson the American Freedom Medal. She has been decorated by the Philippines, Liberia, Haiti, and France. Upon three occasions she has sung at the White House: the first time at the invitation of President Roosevelt, becoming the first black person ever to entertain there; the second time, for England's King George VI and his daughter, Elizabeth, who later became Queen of England. She was invited to sing the national anthem at the V-E day ceremonies for General Dwight D. Eisenhower and later on for his second inauguration as President in 1957. She also sang it at the inaugural ball for President Kennedy in 1961.

Marian Anderson emerged from her retirement for a single day on October 29, 1976, appearing as the narrator for Aaron Copland's *Lincoln Portrait* with the National Symphony Orchestra of Washington, D.C. (Antal Dorati conducting) at the Grand Assembly, United Nations, in New York. This was done as part of the ceremonies commemorating United Nations Day.

Her seventy-fifth birthday was celebrated at Carnegie Hall, New York, on February 27, 1977, by a concert featuring such outstanding performers as Leontyne Price and Pinchas Zukerman among others. Mrs. Rosalynn Carter, the wife of the President, attended—this was her first official visit away from Washington, D.C., and was made to honor Anderson. She praised Anderson for her "untiring and unselfish devotion to the promotion of the arts in this country [during] a distinguished and impressive career [spanning] more than half a century." A gold medal, which the United States Congress voted to award her, was presented as part of these ceremonies together with the United Nations Peace Prize and the New York City Handel Medallion. Leontyne Price not only sang but also spoke. "Dear Marian Anderson," she said in part, "because of you I am."

Also in honor of Anderson's birthday were a radio program, "Once in a Century," broadcast nationwide over the National Public Radio network on February 25 and the *Ladies' Home Journal* "Women of the Year Award" on May 23.

ABOUT: Anderson, M. My Lord, What a Morning; Truman, M. Women of Courage; Vehanen, K. Marian Anderson: A Portrait. *Periodicals*—Musical America, September 1964; New York Times, January 8, 1954, February 28, 1972; New York Times Magazine, December 30, 1945, February 26, 1977; Time, December 30, 1946.

Victoria de los Angeles

1923–

Victoria de los Angeles (originally Victoria Gómez Cima), soprano, was born in Barcelona, Spain, on November 1, 1923. Her father, Bernardo López Gómez, was caretaker at the University of Barcelona; her mother, Victoria García Cima, an amateur singer, encouraged music at home. While Victoria was still a child her uncle presented her with a guitar which she soon learned to use in accompanying herself in her singing. Revealing a gift for music at the Instituto Balmes, where she delighted her fellow students with her singing in class, she was sent to the Conservatorio del Liceo when she was sixteen. There she studied voice with Dolores Frau, completing a six-year course in three years. At the Conservatory her singing attracted the interest of a group of seven amateur musicians who called themselves Ars Musica and who devoted themselves to the performance of old, neglected Spanish music. This group adopted her as their protégée and financed her until she could support herself as a professional sing-

VICTORIA DE LOS ANGELES

er. Studying by herself over a five-year period, she developed her repertory and technique until she felt she was prepared to begin her career in earnest.

In 1944 she made her concert debut at the Barcelona Conservatory; in 1946, as the Countess in *The Marriage of Figaro,* she made her opera debut at the Teatro Lirico in Barcelona, where she also sang the principal female roles in *The Secret of Suzanne* and *La Serva Padrona.*

Her career leaped forward in 1947 when she won first prize among one hundred and twenty contestants at the International Singing Contest in Geneva. There followed opera appearances in Barcelona as Elsa in *Lohengrin,* Eva in *Die Meistersinger,* Elisabeth in *Tannhäuser,* Manon in Massenet's opera, Marguerite in *Faust,* Agathe in *Der Freischütz,* and other roles. In 1948 she sang in Manuel de Falla's *La Vida Breve* on the London radio. A year later she made a successful debut at the Paris Opéra as Marguerite in *Faust* and went on a concert tour of South America. In 1950 she extended her successes to Scandinavia, to Covent Garden where she made her debut as Mimi in *La Bohème,* and to La Scala where she assumed the title role in *Ariadne auf Naxos.*

Appearances in other distinguished opera houses of Europe, South America, and Scandinavia, and at some of Europe's important festivals preceded her American debut at Carnegie Hall, New York, on October 24, 1950. Her voice, reported Virgil Thomson in the *Herald Tribune,* was "one of rare natural beauty," her

18

schooling "impeccable," and her artistry "first class." Louis Biancolli, in the *World-Telegram and Sun,* called her "one of the greatest vocal talents since Claudia Muzio."

On March 17, 1951, she made her debut at the Metropolitan Opera as Marguerite in *Faust.* Virgil Thomson reported: "She projected the text as clearly as she did the musical line, and she acted the role with a delicate intensity all unusual to that stage. Her vocalism, beautifully schooled and in every way secure, was marked by a similar concentration on excellence and an abstention from broad effects. As in her recitals, she worked quietly, behaved lovingly toward the music, showed no hard edges, never forced a tone or made any effort to dazzle. The effect was delightful. . . . I think she has the makings of a great star—voice, schooling, musicianship, sincerity and a stage personality that is strong and warm."

During her initial season at the Metropolitan Opera she was also acclaimed as Cio-Cio-San in *Madama Butterfly* and as Mimi. In the *Saturday Review* Irving Kolodin called her Butterfly "certainly the most interesting new one we have heard since Licia Albanese first sang the part here in the late 1930s," and her Mimi was praised by Robert Bagar in the *World-Telegram and Sun* for its "lightness and tenderness." In subsequent seasons she enhanced her reputation with performances as Mélisande in *Pelléas and Mélisande,* Desdemona in *Otello,* the Countess in *The Marriage of Figaro,* Rosina in *The Barber of Seville,* Eva in *Die Meistersinger,* Micaëla in *Carmen,* Violetta in *La Traviata,* Manon in Massenet's opera of the same name, Elisabeth in *Tannhäuser* and Harriet in *Martha.* Olin Downes, in the New York *Times,* described her as "the most eloquent, moving Manon we have seen and heard, singularly expressive in facial play, gesture, irresistible in song."

In 1953 she made her first tour of South Africa, and in 1956, of Australia. In 1957 she scored a triumph at the Vienna State Opera, and in the festivals of 1961 and 1962 at Bayreuth she was praised for her Elisabeth in *Tannhäuser.* At Covent Garden in June 1961 she gave a command performance as Santuzza in *Cavalleria Rusticana* and as Nedda in *I Pagliacci* on the same evening, in productions designed and staged by Franco Zeffirelli.

She undertook a new role—the Marschallin in *Der Rosenkavalier*—in a concert performance in Cincinnati on May 13, 1977, and later the same year she recorded Vivaldi's *Orlando Furioso* and Granados's *Goyescas* for London Records.

As she devoted herself more to the concert platform than to the operatic stage, she became established as one of the greatest recitalists of her time. At her concerts she sometimes accompanied herself on the guitar in her renditions of Spanish flamenco folk songs. Reviewing one of her recitals in Carnegie Hall, Raymond Ericson wrote in the New York *Times* that "the voice and art of Victoria de los Angeles grows more distilled with the passage of time. . . . The exquisite voice, spinning out a convoluting melody with the most delicate gradations in tone, provided about as beautiful a sound as the human voice could experience."

On November 28, 1948, Victoria de los Angeles married Enrique Magriñá Mir, an impresario whom she had met in Barcelona seven years earlier. After the marriage he became her manager. They live in Barcelona where as a respite from singing she enjoys knitting, cooking, and playing the guitar. Her honors include the Cross of Lazo de Dama of the Order of Isabel the Catholic in Spain, the Condecoración Banda de la Orden Civil de Alfonso X in Spain, a gold and silver medal from Barcelona, and the Medal Premio Roma from Italy.

ABOUT: Musical America, January 1, 1952; New York Times, March 12, 1961; Time, November 6, 1950.

Ernest Ansermet

1883–1969

Ernest Alexandre Ansermet, conductor, was born on November 11, 1883, in Vevey, Switzerland, in the French-speaking canton of Vaud. His father, Gabriel A. Ansermet, was a mathematician skilled in geometry. Since Ernest Ansermet's grandfather and mother were both trained musicians, music played an important role in the life of the family. Ernest received his first musical training in piano and violin. He played in local orchestras in Vevey, sang with a local choir, and did some composing. But music was only a diversion because both he and his family believed that the opportunities for profes-

Ansermet: än ser me′

Ansermet

ERNEST ANSERMET

sional musicians in Switzerland were few. Following in the footsteps of his father, Ernest became interested in mathematics. He received his academic education in secondary schools and graduated from the University of Lausanne.

His main interest along with mathematics was the theater. Failing to find a place for himself as an actor after several unsuccessful auditions, he became a teacher of mathematics in Vevey. He later completed a graduate course in mathematics at the Sorbonne in Paris and occupied a teaching post at the Gymnasium in Lausanne until 1909.

Although settled down to a secure and seemingly permanent academic life, married and the father of a child, Ansermet found that music was becoming increasingly important to him. In his leisure hours he continued to study the piano, the violin, theory, and composition with Otto Barblan, André Gédalge, and Ernest Bloch. He also studied conducting with Francisco de Lacerda at the Schola Cantorum in Paris and with Arthur Nikisch and Felix Weingartner in Germany.

By 1910 he had decided to abandon mathematics for music and to try to develop himself as a conductor. His first opportunity came in 1911 when he stepped in as a substitute conductor at the Kursaal in Montreux in a program including Beethoven's Symphony No.5. He performed so well that in the same year he was made conductor of the Kursaal orchestra. During the next three years the orchestra under Ansermet developed into a well-known Swiss symphonic organization. However, with the outbreak of World War I it was disbanded.

Then Ansermet went to Geneva to succeed Bernhard Stavenhagen as the conductor of its principal symphony orchestra. At this time he met and became a friend of Igor Stravinsky. On Stravinsky's recommendation he was made principal conductor of Diaghilev's Ballet Russe de Monte Carlo in performances in France, Italy, England, Buenos Aires, and New York. With this organization he first revealed his affinity for twentieth century music with brilliant performances of scores by Stravinsky, Ravel, Manuel de Falla, Erik Satie, and others. Early in 1916 he made his American debut in New York City as a conductor of the Ballet Russe.

In 1918 Ansermet founded the Orchestre de la Suisse Romande in Geneva. Its first concert took place on November 30, 1918, at Victoria Hall in Geneva in a program made up of works by Handel, Mozart, Rimsky-Korsakov, and Émile Jaques-Dalcroze. He remained the orchestra's principal conductor until 1967, and during this period he elevated it to a position of international prominence. An undemonstrative conductor, avoiding podium histrionics and resorting to the most elementary and unobtrusive gestures, Ansermet's sole concern was the translation of the subtlest demands of the composer as faithfully as possible. His was basically the intellectual approach, in which every detail of a score was dissected and analyzed, and in which emotional responses were kept in strict control. His forte was the music of the twentieth century, and his performances of the music of Stravinsky, Debussy, Ravel, Manuel de Falla, and Honegger remained the yardstick by which all other such performances were measured. He was responsible for many notable world premieres in Geneva among which were Conrad Beck's *Innominata* (January 14, 1932), Britten's *Cantata Misericordium* (September 1, 1963), Frank Martin's opera *Monsieur de Pourceaugnac* (April 28, 1963), and Stravinsky's *Le Chant du Rossignol* (December 6, 1919).

In addition to his involvement with the Orchestre de la Suisse Romande, with which he made numerous tours (including those to the United States and Japan in 1966 and to Expo '67 in Montreal in June 1967) and with which he made numerous recordings, Ansermet was a frequent visitor to Europe's symphony orchestras, often bringing with him new works. In Lausanne, Switzerland, he gave the world premieres of Honegger's *Horace Victorieux* (October 30, 1921), Milhaud's opera *Christophe Colomb* (April 17, 1940), and Stravinsky's *L'Histoire du Soldat* (September 28, 1918). In Paris he conducted the first performances of Stravinsky's Capriccio, for piano and orchestra (December 6, 1929), *Pulcinella* (May 15, 1920), and the ballet *Le Rossignol* (May 26, 1914). In Brussels he led the premiere of Stravinsky's *Symphony of Psalms* (December 13, 1930); in Milan, Stravinsky's *Mass* (October 27, 1948); in London, William Walton's *Sinfonia Concertante* (January 5, 1928).

In 1934 he returned to the United States for the first time in eighteen years to conduct a concert over network radio, and in 1936 he was again heard in the United States at the Hollywood Bowl and at Ravinia Park near Chicago. In 1937 he again returned to the United States for additional symphony performances, after which he stayed away for ten years.

In January 1946 Ansermet became the first non-French conductor invited to Paris to lead a symphony concert. He also performed in Brussels, London, The Hague, and Prague. He made his first extended tour of the United States in 1947 beginning with a four-week engagement with the NBC Symphony Orchestra over the NBC radio network at the invitation of Arturo Toscanini. With this orchestra he introduced in the United States Ernest Bloch's *Concerto Symphonique* and Frank Martin's *Petite Symphonie Concertante*. In the same season he appeared with the Chicago and Dallas symphony orchestras. He expanded his activity in the United States one season later with appearances with the NBC Symphony, the Cleveland Orchestra, the Philadelphia Orchestra, the Boston Symphony, and the Dallas Symphony.

In 1953, on his seventieth birthday, Ansermet received the "citizenship of honor of the State and City of Geneva." His fame had become worldwide, and he was a frequent visitor to the United States. "He is a conductor of the very first rank," wrote Robert A. Hague in *PM* after one of Ansermet's concerts with the NBC Symphony, "a brilliant orchestral technician and an interpreter of extraordinary intelligence, sensibility, insight and power." In the *Herald Tribune,* Virgil Thomson called him "one of the half-dozen greatest living orchestral workers and interpreters."

On September 29, 1962, Ansermet conducted the American premiere of parts of Manuel de Falla's last work, the scenic cantata *La Atlántida,* in a concert performance at the Lincoln Center for the Performing Arts in New York. Two months later, on November 30, Ansermet made his debut at the Metropolitan Opera in New York conducting *Pelléas and Mélisande.* In the *New Yorker* Winthrop Sargeant wrote that "the performance . . . owed most of its distinction to the conducting of Ernest Ansermet, a maestro who understands all the opera's subtleties but whose understanding never leads to forgetfulness of the grand line. . . . His was an unusually vertebrate *Pelléas,* constructed with complete intellectual control from start to finish, and building to what in this work may be regarded as some pretty smashing climaxes."

Ansermet was responsible for the world premieres of more Stravinsky compositions than any other conductor. For many years he and Stravinsky maintained not only a close musical relationship but a profound friendship. However, in 1961 after Ansermet had published *Les Fondements de la musique dans la conscience humaine,* a book condemning serial music, Stravinsky became alienated from him. What upset Stravinsky, an avowed serialist, was the blanket indictment not only of that avant-garde idiom but also of Stravinsky himself. At one point in the book Ansermet commented that though Vincent Youmans's popular tune "Tea for Two" was sublime, the serial music of Stravinsky was not.

When Ansermet was invited by the New York Philharmonic Orchestra to participate in a Stravinsky festival at the Lincoln Center for the Performing Arts in 1965, he accepted eagerly because he hoped it would help bring about a reconciliation with his friend. "I hope we can make peace," he told Stravinsky. "We are too old to fight." But Stravinsky was too ill to attend any of these performances and a final meeting between the two men never came to pass.

Ansermet resigned as principal conductor of the Orchestre de la Suisse Romande in 1967 but remained its musical adviser. He continued to make guest appearances in and out of Switzerland and gave his last performance in Geneva on December 18, 1967. He died in Geneva on February 20, 1969.

France made him Commander of the Legion of Honor, and Belgium, Commandeur Légion d'Honneur et Étoile. Greece bestowed on him the Order of the Golden Phoenix. He also received honorary doctorates from the universities of Neuchâtel and Lausanne.

Ansermet orchestrated Debussy's *Six Épigraphes Antiques* and was the composer of a tone poem, a ballade for piano and orchestra, and other compositions. In addition to the work *Les Fondements de la musique dans la conscience humaine* mentioned earlier, he was the author of *Le Geste du chef d'orchestre* (1943).

Ansermet lived on the rue Bellot in Geneva. After music, mathematics, philosophy and the theater were his main interests.

ABOUT: Blaukopf, K. Great Conductors; Gelatt, R. Music Makers. *Periodicals*—New York Times, February 21, 1969; Newsweek, January 1, 1949; Opera News, December 29, 1962, April 5, 1969; Time, February 2, 1948.

CLAUDIO ARRAU

Claudio Arrau

1903–

Claudio Arrau, pianist, was born in Chillán, Chile, on February 6, 1903. His father, Carlos, an oculist, died before Claudio reached his first birthday. He and his two brothers were raised by their mother, Lucrecia Leon Arrau, a piano teacher. Claudio was about four when he was attracted to the piano and began to teach himself to read music. Though largely self-taught, except for some guidance by his mother, he was able to make his debut in a small local auditorium when he was five. A year later he performed in Santiago, and when he was seven, in Buenos Aires. His talent drew official recognition when he was eight: The Chilean congress established a ten-year endowment to enable him to study abroad.

When the family moved to Berlin, Claudio came under the influence of Martin Krause, a pupil of Liszt. When Krause heard Claudio audition he remarked: "This child will be my masterpiece." For six years Claudio lived with Krause and took lessons from him daily. "Krause was terribly demanding," recalls Arrau. "He escorted me to museums, guided my reading, found other children with whom I

Arrau: är rä′ o͞o

could play. He taught me that an artist cannot be a great artist without interest in all the arts, in all of life."

He was eleven when, on December 10, 1914, he made his debut in Berlin, dressed in a Buster Brown suit with lace collar. "The child's playing is marvelous," wrote one Berlin critic, "impossible to understand and more impossible to explain." Claudio followed this debut with recitals throughout Germany and Scandinavia, playing for the king of Saxony, the king of Bavaria, the queen of Romania, and in various ducal courts. In 1917 he received the Ilbach Prize.

Arrau remembered these years as "fairyland." But fairyland evaporated when, in August 1918, Krause died of pneumonia. "Now I was inconsolably alone," Arrau says. Having lost not only a teacher and an inspiration but also a substitute father, Claudio was seized with a melancholia that played havoc with his progress as a pianist. "I made mistakes," he recalls. "Then I could no longer play certain works. People repeated the fallacy people always repeat about a prodigy: 'He was only a *wunderkind,* already spent.' In 1919 my career was gone, and now I thought of, perhaps longed for, my own death."

He sought the help of Dr. Hubert Abrahamson, a psychoanalyst who had studied with Carl Jung. "I had to clear a psyche jungle," says Arrau. "With Abrahamson, layer after layer of covering was stripped away. My mother's ambitions for me were intense. She expected divinity from her son. So did Martin Krause, who was really my second father. Slowly, I was brought to realize a terrible weakness in myself. Vanity. I was playing for my own glory."

It took several years for Arrau to free himself of his psychological problems and to rehabilitate himself professionally. He supported himself in Berlin teaching the piano. Without any formal guidance he began working again on his technique and repertory determined to renew his virtuoso career, to revive in himself the artist that he had come to believe was dead.

After World War I he returned to the concert stage. In 1921 he gave successful performances in Argentina and Chile. On February 4, 1924, he made his debut in the United States as a guest artist with the Boston Symphony Orchestra, Pierre Monteux conducting, following it with an appearance with the Chicago Symphony under Frederick Stock. These American appearances attracted little attention. After a tour of South America in 1924 he gave concerts throughout Europe. In 1927 he captured the first prize in the International Geneva Concours for pianists. In 1929 and 1930 he toured the Soviet Union.

Resettling in Berlin in 1925, he became a member of the faculty of the Stern Conservatory and slowly began to reestablish his reputation and to acquire a large following. Much of his later fame rested on the cycles of concerts he began giving at that time. In 1935 he presented twelve successive concerts, in both Berlin and Vienna, devoted to the complete keyboard music of Johann Sebastian Bach. Then, in five concerts, he played Mozart's solo piano compositions, following these with cycles of all Beethoven's piano sonatas, the five Beethoven concertos, and other comprehensive series concentrating on the piano music of Schumann, Liszt, Schubert, or Chopin.

On July 8, 1938, he married Ruth Schneider, a soprano from Frankfort. They had two children, a son, Mario, and a daughter, Carmen.

After the outbreak of World War II in Europe Arrau and his family settled permanently in the United States. In 1941 with a successful recital in Carnegie Hall he began to lay the groundwork for his immense prestige in America. Since then he has toured the United States annually and in addition has performed in nearly every music center of the world, giving over one hundred concerts a year. He made his first tour of Australia in 1947 and of South Africa two years later.

By his sixtieth birthday he was acknowledged one of the living giants of the keyboard. In his sixtieth year he gave twelve concerts in fifteen days in Israel, performed nine concertos in three concerts with the London Philharmonic in London, and became the first pianist since Artur Schnabel to perform all five Beethoven piano concertos with the Concertgebouw Orchestra of Amsterdam.

Neville Cardus, English musicologist, wrote in *Full Score:* "Claudio Arrau is the complete pianist. He can revel in the keyboard for its pianistic sake, presenting to us the instrument's range, its power to mingle song, percussion, depth of harmony and rhythmic fluency; but also he can go beyond piano playing, taking us into the world of music, into the mind of a composer, so searchingly that we are free to forget his technical scope; we take it for granted as we are led by his art to the secret chambers of creative imagination."

When the Beethoven International Festival in Bonn initiated bicentennial celebrations of Beethoven's birth in 1970, Arrau was heard in an all-Beethoven recital and in a performance of the *Emperor* Concerto. At that time Arrau received one of West Germany's highest honors, the Bundes Verdienst Kreuz. As a further commemoration of the two-hundredth anniversary of Beethoven's birth Arrau published a new edition of all Beethoven's sonatas and performed them in one hundred concerts in seventy major cities. He also recorded all the sonatas on thirteen disks for Philips Records. Reviewing this release, Richard Osborne said in the New York *Times:* "Everywhere ... Arrau commands the elements of the music, physically and psychologically, with a concentration few can match. His stamina is amazing. In the entire cycle there is not a chord muddied, not a single flight of sixteenth notes that isn't colored, weighted and shaped to illustrate precisely the truth of the moment as formally, intellectually, and intuitively as Arrau perceived it."

Arrau maintains his winter home in Douglaston, New York, where he keeps a vast library of books in many languages and his collection of rare jewelry and art objects gathered from all over the world, including Chinese figurines, Russian icons, pre-Columbian vases, old Incan jewelry, modern paintings, African statues. He also maintains a summer home in Chester, Vermont. He is an avid reader in four languages, and likes both ballet and social dancing. Despite his American residence he has remained a citizen of Chile where he is regarded as a national hero, with streets named after him in Santiago and Chillán.

In 1936 Arrau appeared as Liszt in a Spanish-made motion picture, *Sueño de Amore.*

ABOUT: Cardus, N. Full Score. *Periodicals*—Life, August 1972; Musical America, April 1, 1953, March 1963; New York Times, November 23, 1975; New Yorker, November 15, 1941; Time, March 23, 1942.

MARTINA ARROYO

Martina Arroyo

1940–

Martina Arroyo, soprano, was born in New York City's Harlem on February 2, 1940. Her father, Demetrio, was of Spanish origin and had been raised in Puerto Rico. He was a mechanical engineer at the Navy Yard in Brooklyn. Her mother, Lucille Washington Arroyo, came from Charleston, South Carolina. The Arroyo family which, in addition to Martina and her parents, included her brother (sixteen years her senior), lived comfortably. When as a child Martina revealed an interest in music and the ballet, the Arroyos bought her a piano and paid for ballet lessons. Periodically the mother would take her two children downtown to enlarge their cultural horizon through attendance at concerts, plays, and movies. When Martina saw screen musicals in which Kathryn Grayson or Jane Powell sang opera arias, she felt the first stirrings of an ambition to become a singer.

Her parents were determined to give their two children a sound education. Martina's brother was directed to the ministry and ultimately became the pastor of the St. Augustine Baptist Church in New York. She was encouraged to become a schoolteacher. She attended public schools in Harlem where she was always an outstanding student. While there she studied the piano with her mother, sang in the choir of the Baptist Church, and appeared in school productions. After graduating from junior high school she passed the entrance examinations for Hunter College High School, a school for superior students. Her interest in opera was developed through her occasional attendance at the opera workshop of Joseph Turnau at Hunter College.

Arroyo: är rō′ yō

One day, hearing her sing the "Jewel Song" from *Faust* (which she had learned by listening to a recording), Turnau recognized her talent. He introduced her to Marinka Gurewich, a voice teacher who took her in hand and helped develop her voice. "I didn't have many bad habits to unlearn," Arroyo recalls. "What she did was refine my voice without taking away its freedom. She taught me how it should come out and how to shade it." Gurewich remained the only voice teacher Arroyo ever had.

From Hunter High School Arroyo progressed to Hunter College. She became a permanent and active member of the opera workshop, even though undergraduates were not usually admitted. Her daily schedule was a taxing one with college classes from nine to three, the opera workshop from four to eight and, after that, voice lessons and practicing. When free from her normal routine she attended performances at the Metropolitan Opera. Despite the scattering of her energies she completed the four-year college course in three years, specializing in Romance languages and comparative literature as a preparation for a possible career in opera. Then she attended New York University for graduate work in Romance languages. While there she finally fulfilled her mother's ambition for her by teaching in the Bronx for one year. But she soon recognized that the demands made upon her by her teaching duties seriously interfered with her work in music, and she gave up the classroom for good. To support herself she worked for two years as a social investigator for the Welfare Department.

She was now being groomed for a professional career in music not only by her teacher, Gurewich, but also by Thea Dispeaker, an artist's representative who offered to work for her without compensation as long as necessary. In 1958 Arroyo entered the Metropolitan Auditions of the Air, sang "O mia patria" from *Aida,* and became one of the four finalists to receive a prize of one thousand dollars, a guest contract with the Metropolitan Opera company, and a scholarship for the Kathryn Long School sponsored by the Metropolitan Opera for the study of languages, drama, and diction.

Before making her debut at the Metropolitan, Arroyo appeared in a concert in Central Park, New York City, on September 9, 1958. A week later, on September 17, she made her debut at Carnegie Hall as Corifea in a semistaged production of Ildebrando Pizzetti's opera *Assassinio nella Cattedrale,* then receiving its American premiere. In the New York *Times* Harold Schonberg reported that she was gifted "with a voice of amplitude and lovely color."

In 1959 Arroyo traveled to Europe as a member of a tour sponsored by the United States Information Service. She made several concert appearances, including one in Perugia, Italy, in a performance of Handel's oratorio *Solomon.* She made her bow at the Metropolitan Opera on March 14, 1959, as the offstage Celestial Voice in *Don Carlo,* a part too insignificant to draw attention to her. The following season she was heard again in minor parts, this time in the Wagnerian *Ring* cycle: Woglinde in *Das Rheingold* and *Die Götterdämmerung,* Ortlinde in *Die Walküre,* the Third Norn in *Die Götterdämmerung,* and the Forest Bird in *Siegfried.* On May 10, 1960, she was a soloist in Bach's B minor Mass at Carnegie Hall. She gave a recital at the National Gallery in Washington, D.C., on December 5, 1960, and on February 17, 1961, made her first New York recital appearance at Town Hall.

She left the Metropolitan Opera after the 1961–1962 season to advance her career elsewhere. In 1963 she became a permanent member of the Zurich Opera where she was assigned principal roles. She also made noteworthy appearances with the Vienna State Opera and the Berlin Deutsche Staatsoper.

On April 4, 1963, she was heard in the world premiere of Samuel Barber's *Andromache's Farewell* as a soloist with the New York Philharmonic Orchestra under Thomas Schippers. Within the next few years she appeared as soloist with other major American orchestras in performances of such choral masterworks as Beethoven's Ninth Symphony, Dvořák's Requiem, Verdi's Requiem, and Berlioz' *The Damnation of Faust.*

When she returned to the Metropolitan Opera it was more through chance than design. Birgit Nilsson was scheduled to sing the title role in *Aida* but was suddenly taken ill. Rudolf Bing, general manager of the Metropolitan Opera, aware of Arroyo's enormous success as Aida at the Vienna State Opera and other European opera houses, asked her to take over the role with the performance just two days off. Without any rehearsal with the orchestra or the rest of the cast she stepped in for Nilsson on February 6, 1965, to receive a standing ovation. One day later Rudolf Bing offered her a star's contract.

She has remained a star at the Metropolitan Opera. She opened three consecutive seasons there, an honor without precedent for a leading soprano: as Elvira in a new production of *Ernani* in 1971, as Elisabetta in *Don Carlo* in 1972, and as Leonora in *Il Trovatore* in 1973. Her other roles have been Elsa in *Lohengrin* (her first leading role in a Wagnerian opera), Amelia in *Un Ballo in Maschera,* Donna Anna in *Don Giovanni,* Liù in *Turandot,* Maddalena in *Andrea Chénier,* Santuzza in *Cavalleria Rusticana,* Lady Macbeth in *Macbeth,* Cio-Cio-San in *Madama Butterfly,* Aida, Leonore in *Fidelio,* the Countess in *The Marriage of Figaro.* In *Newsweek* Hubert Saal called her "the reigning queen of Verdi opera, a dramatic soprano with a voice capable of expanding to slingshot power and diminishing to kittenish pathos." Her versatility has made her equally at home in the works of other composers, to whose leading soprano parts she brings a voice of refulgent beauty and varied color together with discipline and authority. Hers is "one of the most gorgeous voices before the public today," wrote Raymond Ericson in the New York *Times.* In the London *Times* William Mann said: "She can move an audience perceptibly by a single note or gesture."

Each year Arroyo makes between sixty and seventy appearances. She has been heard with the world's leading opera companies, including La Scala in Milan, the Vienna State Opera, the Berlin Deutsche Oper, the Paris Opéra, Teatro

Colón in Buenos Aires, Rome Opera, the Verona Arena, and the San Francisco Opera. On October 25, 1977, she undertook a new major Wagnerian role when she was heard as Senta in *The Flying Dutchman* with the Philadelphia Opera. She has also appeared in concerts where she has distinguished herself both in the standard repertory and in such avant-garde compositions as Edgard Varèse's *Offrande,* Luigi Dallapiccola's *An Mathilde,* and Karlheinz Stockhausen's *Momente.* Stockhausen himself selected Arroyo for the world premiere of the revised version of his *Momente,* her performance leading Eric Salzman to state in *Stereo Review:* "She is simply sensational and must be heard to be believed."

When she made her first trip to Europe in 1959 she met, in Perugia, Emilio Poggioni, a violist with the Societa Cameristica Italiana, who performed in the orchestra when she sang in *Solomon.* They fell in love and two years later were married in New York City. Since his musical duties were concentrated in Europe and hers in America, they managed to spend only a few months a year together. "Being in the same profession but in different parts of it, and sometimes in different parts of the world," she said, "demands a great deal of marriage. It's not easy for either of us. We've had to work at making it a success." Nevertheless, after a decade of marriage, they were legally separated. "Our situations clashed," she explained to Stephen E. Rubin in *Opera News.* "His career took him into the chamber music area where the whole way of life is different. We had everything working against us except our love."

While still married, they owned a six-room house in Perugia, the base of Emilio Poggioni's musical activities. Arroyo has since occupied a seven-room apartment in New York City during her commitments to the Metropolitan Opera, and an apartment in Zurich. For relaxation she reads mystery novels, cooks Italian dishes, or listens to jazz. She has been described by one interviewer as "about as fragile as a cyclone."

ABOUT: Jacobson, R. Reverberations. *Periodicals*—High Fidelity, June 1968; New York Sunday News Magazine, November 8, 1970; New York Times Magazine, May 14, 1972; Opera News, November 1971, May 1977; Time, September 28, 1970.

Vladimir Ashkenazy

1937–

Vladimir Ashkenazy, pianist, was born in Gorki, twenty miles from Moscow, on July 6, 1937. Both his father, David, and his mother, Evstolia Plotnovna Ashkenazy, were pianists, and Vladimir began piano lessons when he was six. At the age of eight he was admitted to the Central Music School in Moscow where for ten years he studied piano with Anaida Sumbatian. During his first year he made his initial public appearance performing Haydn's D major Piano Concerto with the school orchestra. In his last school year he entered the fifth International Chopin Competition in Warsaw and won second prize. Later the same year (1955) he enrolled in the Moscow State Conservatory as a piano student of Lev Oborin.

Ashkenazy achieved international prominence in 1956 when he captured the first prize in the Queen Elisabeth Competition in Brussels, selected by a thirteen-member jury as the winner from among fifty-nine competing pianists from twenty countries. One of the requirements was to play a modern unpublished work which the contestant was required to learn in a week. In this instance the composition was a piano concerto by René Defossez. "Vladimir Ashkenazy," reported *Time* Magazine, "stupefied . . . his colleagues by memorizing the Defossez in two days."

The victory in Brussels brought Ashkenazy to the attention of the impresario Sol Hurok, who became his manager. After a tour of Belgium, Holland, East and West Germany, and Poland, Ashkenazy was brought to the United States for his first American tour. His American debut took place in Washington, D.C., on October 14, 1958, when he played Chopin's Second Piano Concerto with the National Symphony Orchestra under Howard Mitchell. "Here was Chopin in the old tradition," said Theodore Schaeffer in *Musical America,* "almost understated yet so exquisitely proportioned and perfectly paced that the capacity audience in the vast hall seemed caught in the spell of finely wrought chamber music."

On October 24 Ashkenazy gave his first recit-

Ashkenazy: ŭsh kĕn ä′ zē

VLADIMIR ASHKENAZY

al at Carnegie Hall, New York, in a program of music by Chopin, Rachmaninoff, Liszt, and Brahms. "Mr. Ashkenazy," wrote Howard Taubman in the New York *Times,* "is a young poet of the piano. He is no thunderer. He does not seek to overpower with speed or brilliance. Though he has all the technique he needs, he chooses to phrase with refinement and perception. His tone, never too big, is always under sensitive control. And whatever music he undertakes he performs with individuality."

In 1958 Ashkenazy met a young pianist, Thorunn Sofia Johannsdottir, a native of Iceland, at the first International Tchaikovsky Competition in Moscow. A friendship began that year and in 1960 it grew when she returned to the Soviet Union to attend the Moscow State Conservatory as a pupil of Lev Oborin. They were married on February 25, 1961, and she became a Soviet citizen. In 1962 their first child, Vladimir, was born. A daughter, Nadia, followed in 1963, and another son, Dimitri Thor, in 1969.

In 1962 the Soviet authorities entered Ashkenazy in the second Tchaikovsky Competition. He did not wish to compete since he felt that such contests should be reserved for unknowns making a first bid for a career and not for one whose reputation as a virtuoso was already firmly established. Moreover, having won first prize in the Queen Elisabeth Competition he was convinced he had already proved his ability to win contests. Finally, he did not want to go through the harrowing grind involved in such an undertaking. But the authorities were insistent.

Ashkenazy submitted, and he shared the first prize with John Ogdon of England.

The difference of opinion between Ashkenazy and the Soviet authorities over his entering the Tchaikovsky Competition was not the first conflict to cool the relationship between government and virtuoso. Soviet officialdom did not look favorably upon the fact that in 1960 Ashkenazy attended the funeral of Boris Pasternak. Ashkenazy did more than that: He also visited the home of the deceased author and played upon his upright piano. Pasternak, of course, had been in disrepute with the government and any homage bestowed on him was regarded as criticism of authority. The authorities were also displeased by the way in which Ashkenazy's wife often spoke her mind openly in criticism of the Soviet system. Despite these differences, the government made no attempt to discipline Ashkenazy.

In 1963 he made his first appearance in England. He had gone with his wife, pregnant with their second child, and his son. At this time the Ashkenazys decided to establish their permanent home outside the Soviet Union—at first, in England. When this news was publicized in the Western world on April 16, 1963, the story was circulated that Ashkenazy was defecting from the Soviet Union for political reasons. But in a press conference in Liverpool on April 17, and in several subsequent interviews, Ashkenazy insisted that he never concerned himself with political matters, that he was not anti-Soviet, and that he was grateful to his country for the many opportunities it had given him. He did not, however, clarify why he had made this decision. There was good reason to believe that he had been swayed by his wife, whose long residence in England had made her an Anglophile, and by her wish to raise her children in the Western world. In May 1963 Ashkenazy returned with his family to the Soviet Union for a two-month visit and made appearances there in duo recitals with the American pianist Malcolm Frager. He was allowed to retain his Soviet citizenship and was permitted to travel on a Soviet passport.

From his base in London Ashkenazy made tours throughout the world and his eminence as an interpreter of Beethoven, Brahms, Rachmaninoff, Scriabin, and Prokofiev was universally recognized. On several occasions in Europe and in the United States he gave cycles of all five Beethoven piano concertos, performances that elicited high praise from the critics. (His record-ing of the concertos with the Chicago Sym-phony Orchestra conducted by Sir Georg Solti received a Grammy award from the National Academy of Recording Arts and Sciences in 1974. In 1968 he performed a cycle of the four Rachmaninoff piano concertos on four succes-sive nights with the London Symphony Orches-tra, Daniel Barenboim conducting, at Carnegie Hall, New York. In September 1971 he was solo-ist with the Chicago Symphony Orchestra at the Edinburgh Festival, during its first concert tour of Europe. In 1973, to commemorate the cente-nary of Scriabin's birth he devoted many of his concerts entirely to the music of that Russian master. He has also performed and recorded all five of Prokofiev's piano concertos.

In addition to solo appearances, Ashkenazy has performed chamber music publicly with Jacqueline du Pré, Pinchas Zukerman, and Itz-hak Perlman. He has also ventured into con-ducting, making his baton debut in 1973–1974 at a symphonic concert in Iceland. In March 1975 he conducted the National Arts Centre Orches-tra in Ottawa.

Since 1968 the Ashkenazys have lived in Reykjavík, Iceland. In 1972 Ashkenazy became an Icelandic citizen by an act of the Icelandic parliament. Icelandic citizens are required to as-sume Icelandic names, but this requirement was waived for Ashkenazy after considerable parlia-mentary debate. The Ashkenazys also have a summer home in Greece, at Savinka on the edge of the Aegean Sea, where they spend about six weeks each year.

Ashkenazy speaks English fluently, the lan-guage used in his home. His four children also speak Icelandic, but no Russian. Short and slight of build, Ashkenazy is a diffident and retiring person. Filling about one hundred engagements a year, fifty of them in the United States, keeps him away from home a good part of the year, but his wife invariably travels with him, and some-times the children as well. "On tour," he re-vealed to Faubion Bowers of the New York *Times*, "I divide my day into half work, half travel. In Iceland, it's all work. I have no exer-cises, practise no technical routines. I just main-tain my repertoire of big pieces ... anywhere where I really have to move my fingers—as op-posed to Mozart sonatas. ... Basically what I try to do with myself in the West is to get rid of affectedness. I want to get to the core, to achieve

simplicity combined with inner energy that is inherent in great music like Beethoven's and Mozart's, to have absolute honesty, to under-stand what they mean by such few notes and not try to introduce a meaning which isn't there. I don't want music to be pretty. I want it to be true."

Ashkenazy was awarded the Icelandic Order of the Falcon in 1971. In 1972 he was made an honorary member of the Royal Academy of Mu-sic in London.

ABOUT: Musical America, May 1970; New York Times, February 21, 1972.

Salvatore Baccaloni

1900–1969

Salvatore Baccaloni, basso buffo, was born in Rome on April 14, 1900, the son of Joaquin and Ferminia Desideri Baccaloni. His father was a building contractor. When he was five Salvatore began his musical training at the San Salvatore in Lauro school established in Rome by St. Francis de Sales. Two years later Salvatore became a chorister at the Sistine Chapel at St. Peter's where he remained five years. When his voice broke and he thought his singing days were over he was encouraged by his father to enroll in the Academy of Fine Arts for the study of archi-tecture. These studies were interrupted by World War I. Drafted into military service, he saw action as a member of the signal corps divi-sion of the 211th regiment shock troops of the Fifth Italian Army. When the war ended, he returned to the Academy, graduating with a de-gree in architecture in 1920.

By this time his singing voice had developed into a robust basso, and he began giving perfor-mances at parties and musicales. At one of these he was heard by Giuseppe Kaschmann, a bari-tone who had sung with the Metropolitan Opera company during its first season in 1883. Kasch-mann persuaded Baccaloni to forget architec-ture and specialize in singing. After studying with Kaschmann for two years, Baccaloni made his opera debut at the Teatro Adriano in Rome in April 1922, as Bartolo in *The Barber of Se-ville*. During the next four years Baccaloni

---

Baccaloni: bäk kä lō′ ne

28

SALVATORE BACCALONI

gained valuable experience by appearing in many of Italy's small opera houses in basso serio roles, sometimes earning as little as twenty-five lire per performance. This was a time of intense poverty; often he did not have the price of a meal.

In 1925 he appeared as the father in a performance of *Louise* which was heard by Toscanini, then musical director of La Scala. Toscanini arranged for Baccaloni to join La Scala in 1926, and there he remained for thirteen years. For the first three years, Baccaloni was cast solely in basso serio roles. Then, upon the death of one of the principals who had specialized in buffo parts, Toscanini advised Baccaloni to abandon serio for buffo parts. Toscanini told him: "Comic roles in opera are always played by old men who have lost their voices. I should like to have a young man in full voice play them. You have a fine voice and an aptitude for comedy. You should become a specialist in comic roles."

Concentrating on buffo parts Baccaloni was heard not only at La Scala but in other major European opera houses, both in principal and minor roles (which in time numbered 170 parts in five languages). In roles such as Don Pasquale, Falstaff, Dulcamara in *L'Elisir d'Amore*, Bartolo in both *The Barber of Seville* and *The Marriage of Figaro*, and Leporello in *Don Giovanni*, Baccaloni combined a finely disciplined, sonorous voice with brilliant acting that included a special gift for projecting broad humor and burlesque. Some historians came to regard him as the best basso buffo since Luigi

Lablache (1794–1858). In 1934 Baccaloni was decorated Knight of the Crown of Italy.

Baccaloni married Elena Svilarova, a Bulgarian, in 1930, and in that same year made his first tour of South America. During the 1930–1931 season he made his American debut with the Chicago Opera. He returned to the United States in 1938 to appear as Leporello with the San Francisco Opera on October 10. During that season he was also heard as the Sheriff in *Martha,* and as Don Pasquale and Melitone in *La Forza del Destino.* During the years 1936–1939 he appeared annually at the Glyndebourne Festival in England where he was acclaimed as Bartolo in *The Marriage of Figaro* and as Osmin in *The Abduction from the Seraglio.*

On December 3, 1940, in Philadelphia, Baccaloni made his first appearance with the Metropolitan Opera as Bartolo in *The Marriage of Figaro.* He repeated this performance in New York on December 7. His first personal triumph came three weeks later, on December 21, when he assumed what many critics came to regard as his finest role: Don Pasquale in Donizetti's opera of the same name. Virgil Thomson described his performance in the *Herald Tribune* as "the finest piece of lyric acting in the comic vein I have ever seen, not excepting Chaliapin." In the New York *Times* Olin Downes wrote: "His story was so plain, in characterization, diction, the inflection, and the coloring of the voice, that everyone understood it, whether or not the Italian words were comprehended. Everything was droll, lively, significant. But the greatest of all—having made the world laugh with him—Mr. Baccaloni provided astonishingly and memorably the moment of pathos which must touch comedy to complete it. . . . But Mr. Baccaloni is not only an actor, comedian and clever diseur. He sings with admirable ease and variety of effect, and the voice is a very fine one. His recitative is a wonder of clarity and declamation."

He gathered more praise when he appeared as Sulpice in *The Daughter of the Regiment* on December 28, 1940; as Bartolo in *The Barber of Seville* on February 19, 1941; and as Leporello on March 7, 1941. "Not in memory has the company possessed a basso buffo of the gifts and personality of Salvatore Baccaloni," wrote Oscar Thompson in *Musical America.*

For more than two decades Baccaloni remained the principal basso buffo of the Metropolitan Opera. For Baccaloni the Metropolitan Opera restored to *The Barber of Seville* the aria "A un dottore," which long had been deleted because it could not be properly rendered. So completely did Baccaloni dominate every performance of *The Barber of Seville* that one New York music critic remarked facetiously that the opera should now be renamed *The Bartolo of Seville.*

Baccaloni's famous buffo roles included Leporello in *Don Giovanni,* Dulcamara, Uberto in Pergolesi's *La Serva Padrona,* and the title role in *Gianni Schicchi.* He was also heard in serio roles: Melitone, the Sacristan in *Tosca,* Geronte in *Manon Lescaut,* Benoit and Alcindoro in *La Bohème,* Varlaam in *Boris Godunov,* and Mathieu in *Andrea Chénier.* The total number of his appearances with the Metropolitan Opera were 297 in New York and 146 on tour.

Baccaloni's last performance at the Metropolitan Opera took place on February 14, 1962, in *La Forza del Destino,* after which he devoted himself to motion pictures. He made his debut in 1957 in a nonsinging role in *Full of Life* starring Judy Holliday. Subsequently he took on character roles in *Merry Andrews* (1957), *Rock-a-bye Baby* (1958), *Fanny* (1961), and *The Pigeon That Took Rome* (1962).

A huge man weighing over three hundred pounds, Baccaloni often said that he was happy with his rotund figure because it was his stock in trade. His wife helped to keep that figure ample by preparing for him rich dishes from her native Bulgaria and special sauces for his favorite dish of spaghetti.

The Baccalonis, who were childless, lived during the opera season in a three-room apartment on West Fifty-fifth Street, New York, with their French poodle, Menelik. Home, off season, was a fourteen-room house at Sea Cliff, Long Island. For his pastimes Baccaloni favored sketching and etching, designing costumes, reading history and philosophy, playing gin rummy or poker, eating good food, and puffing cigars. Maurice Zolotow in the *Saturday Evening Post* described him in 1947: "He has a solid, squat, ponderous appearance, like a baby elephant standing on its hind legs. His face is large and plump and his hazel eyes are small and gleaming. His face always bears a half-smiling expression of blandness and great imperturbability.... In his style of dressing, Baccaloni is casually florid. He likes to wear preposterous combinations of hound's tooth brown slacks, plaid coats and bizarre plaid

shirts. ... Over his suit he will wear a sealskin lined overcoat with a beaver collar. Regardless of any temporarily warm variations in the weather, Baccaloni wears this heavy coat from October first until April first."

Baccaloni died in St. Clare's Hospital in New York City on December 31, 1969.

ABOUT: New York Times, November 24, 1940; Opera News, December 2, 1940; Saturday Evening Post, November 29, 1947; Time, January 6, 1941.

Gina Bachauer

1913–1976

Gina Bachauer, pianist, was born in a suburb of Athens on May 21, 1913. Her father, Jean, who was of Austrian descent, was a dealer in foreign cars; her mother, Ersilia Marostica Bachauer, was of Italian lineage. "My first inspiration," she revealed, "was a beautiful song sung by my mother. The second was a toy piano given me for Christmas when I was five years old. I learned to play mother's songs on it, and kept begging for a real piano till I got it." When she was eight she gave her first public recital in Athens to help raise money for a charity for wounded soldiers. Intensive music study followed with Ariadne Casasis and Waldemar Freeman at the Athens Conservatory from which she was graduated in 1929 with a gold medal. Despite her obvious talent and her dedication to music, her father insisted that a professional career in music was too competitive for a woman and persuaded her to turn elsewhere for her life's work. After graduating from high school in Athens, Gina attended the University of Athens for two years to study law. However, she continued her piano study all this time without outside instruction. Then, finally determined to make music and not law her profession, she left Athens for Paris where she attended the École Normale de Musique as a piano pupil of Alfred Cortot. From 1932 to 1935 she also studied intermittently with Serge Rachmaninoff, following him all over Europe during his tours in order to take these lessons.

In 1933 she won the Gold Medal of Honor in an international competition for pianists and

Bachauer: bäch′ ou ĕr

GINA BACHAUER

singers held in Vienna. A financial crisis in her family compelled her to return to Greece and to help out by teaching the piano at the Athens Conservatory. She taught all day; and through much of the night she practiced and worked on her repertory. In 1935, returning to a virtuoso career, she made her official debut in Greece as a soloist with the Athens Symphony Orchestra, Dimitri Mitropoulos conducting, in a performance of Tchaikovsky's First Piano Concerto. On this occasion King Paul and Queen Frederika presented her with a platinum vanity box inlaid with sapphires and diamonds. In 1937 she returned to Paris to make her debut there in a recital and an appearance with the Paris Symphony Orchestra under Monteux. She followed this with a tour of Italy, Yugoslavia, Austria, and Egypt.

En route to Italy for her third tour of that country she heard that her native land had plunged into World War II. She immediately canceled her Italian appearances and returned home. When the Nazis invaded Greece all the members of her immediate family were killed and all her possessions were confiscated. She fled to Egypt, devoting her talent to war work by making some 600 appearances for armed forces personnel. Her programs included not only the classics but even popular songs and boogie-woogie. She became known as "the Myra Hess of the Middle East." (The celebrated English pianist Dame Myra Hess was honored for her service to music and the public during World War II.)

After the war she went to London with the

hope of resuming her professional career, but she was unknown and for a time was unable to interest either managers or agents. One evening she performed privately at the salon of a distinguished Englishwoman who became so enthusiastic over her playing that she persuaded Alec Sherman, the conductor, to feature Bachauer as a soloist at one of his concerts. This English debut took place on January 21, 1946, with a performance at the Royal Albert Hall of Grieg's A minor Piano Concerto with the New London Symphony, Alec Sherman conducting. Bachauer's vigor, orchestral-like sonorities, and rhythmic vitality drew favorable responses from the English critics. Appearances throughout Europe and the Near East soon carried her to the front rank of women pianists. Some critics called her a second Teresa Carreño.

Her American debut took place at Town Hall, New York, on October 15, 1950. "I was completely terrified," she said in recalling the event. "The piano seemed two miles away when I went on stage and I thought I would never reach it." Writing in the *Herald Tribune,* Jerome D. Bohm said she performed "miracles of virtuosity," and in the New York *Times* Harold C. Schonberg described her playing as "large and authoritative." She achieved an even greater success a few months later as soloist with the New York Philharmonic under Mitropoulos in Tchaikovsky's First Piano Concerto. Later that year she made two more appearances with the New York Philharmonic. In 1951–1952 she returned once more to the United States to fill engagements. After 1952 Bachauer concertized throughout the world. During the summer of 1955 she appeared with the National Symphony Orchestra of Athens, Alec Sherman conducting, in a command performance before King Paul and Queen Frederika. Bachauer also became the first pianist to play before that royal pair in the ancient open-air theater constructed in the hollow of the hill on which the Parthenon stands. Subsequently she performed for Norway's King Olaf, Britain's Princess Margaret, and Princesses Birgitte and Désirée of Sweden. Twice she was decorated by King Paul of Greece for her services to Greek Relief: with the Order of the Golden Phoenix in 1948 and as Commander, Order of Welfare, in 1951.

In reviewing one of her concerts in New York in 1964, Harold C. Schonberg said in the New

York *Times:* "She is one of today's pianistic originals. That means her technique and her interpretations are *sui generis.* One does not have to see her to recognize her playing. Ten measures should be enough for any trained listener to put his finger on what constitutes a Bachauer performance. . . . There is the enormous technical solidity, including a bravura when necessary that is hair raising. . . . There is the curiously penetrating tone, a tone not so large as most people seem to think, but a tone so well weighted and measured that it sounds enormous. Above all there is her choice of tempos. . . . So secure is Miss Bachauer's technique, so perfect her articulation, and so steady her rhythm, that the music almost never sounds rushed. She feels it way and is able to make it sound logical."

Ke 1971 she became a founding artist of the Wa Center for the Performing Arts in pian on, D.C., presenting the first solo same al given in that auditorium. In the ate in e was awarded an honorary doctor-Utah. umanities from the University of

On Nov Alec Sherma 21, 1951, Bachauer married riage in 1937 e conductor. An earlier marended with his hn Christodoulo in Greece end of World W en death shortly after the Cumberland Terra The Shermans resided at and maintained a se Regent's Park, London, chauer's interests incl home in Athens. Bacooking, and flower ar reading, swimming,

On August 22, 1976 ng. scheduled to perform with na Bachauer was Symphony Orchestra of Wa visiting National der Antal Dorati, at the open gton, D.C., un-Theater at the foot of the Acr Herod Atticus Just before her appearance on th is in Athens. cumbed to a fatal heart attack. A ge she sucwas announced to the audience, Dor her death ed in her memory the Funeral March onduct-thoven's *Eroica* Symphony. m Bee-

ABOUT: High Fidelity, November 1963, Fe 1977; Musical America, February 1, 1954; News ary February 5, 1951; Time, February 5, 1951. k,

Wilhelm Backhaus

1884–1969

Wilhelm Backhaus (or Bachaus), pianist, was born in Leipzig, on March 26, 1884, to Guido and Clara Backhaus. From 1891 to 1898 he studied the piano with A. Rackendorf, at first privately, then for five years at the Leipzig Conservatory. In his eighth year Wilhelm made his concert debut in Leipzig. Three years later, when Brahms came to Leipzig to conduct both of his piano concertos with the Gewandhaus Orchestra, with Eugène d'Albert as soloist, the young Backhaus met the master and received from him the gift of a candy bar which Backhaus treasured and preserved for a number of years. Upon completing his studies with Rackendorf, Wilhelm went to Frankfort to become a pupil of Eugène d'Albert. D'Albert's methods did not appeal to him and after a few lessons he abandoned the teacher, ending his formal musical education. Thereafter he studied the piano by himself, depending exclusively on self-criticism to improve technically and artistically.

In 1900 he began a concert tour which was only moderately successful. Five years later, after settling in London, he received the Rubinstein Prize for piano playing. That same year he was appointed professor of the piano at the Royal College of Music at Manchester, beginning a long and successful teaching career. During the years 1907–1909 he conducted master classes in piano at the Sonderhausen Conservatory.

In continual appearances in recitals and as soloist with symphony orchestras his fame grew gradually in Europe, particularly in the works of Beethoven on which he was accepted as an authority. By the time he first visited the United States he was recognized throughout Europe as one of the outstanding interpreters of the classic and romantic piano literature. In 1909 he made his first recording, and in 1910 the first recording of a concerto in disk history.

However impressive his fame in Europe he was almost unknown when he made his first appearance in the United States on January 5, 1912, as soloist with the New York Symphony ociety, Walter Damrosch conducting, in Beethoven's *Emperor* Concerto. "He played the

Backhaus: bä′ ᴋous

WILHELM BACKHAUS

concerto with a remarkable freshness and buoyancy," wrote Richard Aldrich in the New York *Times,* "with true poetical feeling, with brilliant, crisp and clear-cut technique. . . . But the most significant feature of his performance was its deep musical quality. He approached the concerto not as a medium for the exploitation of skill gained by sore toil, but as a work of art which through skill was privileged to assist in the exposition. Mr. Backhaus' performance was thus that of a true artist, unassuming and forgetful of himself in the presence of a masterpiece."

For the remainder of the season and during the following one Backhaus toured America in recitals, as soloist with symphony orchestras, and in joint concerts with the violinists Jan Kubelik and Kathleen Parlow. By 1914 his reputation as a virtuoso was as solidly entrenched in the United States as it had been in Europe. Critics spoke repeatedly about his "virility, boldness, solidity, and breadth of style." Maurice Rosenfeld, the Chicago critic, called him "a pianist on the order of Moriz Rosenthal. He has that absolute command of the keyboard."

During World War I Backhaus served garrison duty in the German army. At periodic intervals he received official leaves to give concerts. With the war over, he continued his concert tours on a more extensive scale, making several visits to the United States from 1923 to 1926. He specialized in Beethoven and often gave recitals made up exclusively of Beethoven's sonatas. His recording of all the Beethoven sonatas was one of the glories of the monaural era in recorded music.

In 1930 Backhaus made his home with his wife, the former Alma Herzberg (a Brazilian), in a villa in Lugano, Switzerland, where he became a Swiss citizen and devoted himself to teaching. Though he continued to concertize, he did not return to the United States for twenty-eight years. When he reappeared in America with a recital at Carnegie Hall in New York on March 20, 1954, he proved himself an artist of undiminished interpretative powers, still in command of his technique though he was seventy years old. Olin Downes, reviewing that concert in the New York *Times,* called his interpretation of Beethoven "one of the greatest . . . heard here in a long time." When he gave two all-Beethoven concerts in New York in 1956, Carnegie Hall was crowded with pianists who came to learn some of the secrets of his Beethoven interpretations. Harold C. Schonberg, in the New York *Times,* wrote: "His playing is immense, monolithic, carved out of granite. . . . When Mr. Backhaus goes about his work the music emerges in gigantic proportions." Backhaus gave his last recital in New York in 1962.

In 1964, at the age of eighty, Backhaus once again launched the monumental recording project of performing on disks all thirty-two Beethoven piano sonatas, this time in stereo, for London Records. By the time he died this venture was completed, except for one sonata, the *Hammerklavier,* Op. 106. "Comparing the latest stereo performances with Backhaus' own mono versions," reported Donal Henahan in the New York *Times,* "the listener is struck immediately with the unmistakable authority of the man's playing in old age."

Wilhelm Backhaus died on July 5, 1969, in a hospital in the Austrian resort town of Villach, where he had gone for a concert appearance.

Backhaus enjoyed playing bridge, taking long walks, and motoring in the country, but his favorite hobby was the collection of autographs. He has written: "I began to collect autographs when I was a student at the Leipzig Conservatory. I remember at one time that I was especially anxious to obtain an autograph of Joachim, who acceded to my request by practically kicking me out of the artist's room in the hall in which he was appearing. His autograph therefore is missing from my collection. I am especially proud of Brahms' signature which is on the front page of my book with the words, 'for a jolly start,' and a few bars from Brahms' B-flat major Concerto. I remember calling once on the celebrated Gustav Mahler, who looked at me with a frown and asked what in the world I wanted his signature for. I was so amazed at the question that I could not find an adequate reply. However, he suddenly smiled, much to my amazement, and obligingly signed my book adding the beautiful words: 'The further you go, the less you must hurry.' "

ABOUT: New York Times, July 6, 1969.

Dame Janet Baker

1933–

DAME JANET BAKER

Janet Abbott Baker, mezzo-soprano, was born in York, England, on August 21, 1933. Her musical talents were nurtured and encouraged by her parents, Robert Abbott Baker and May Pollard Baker, both of whom were music lovers. Janet's first memory of a musical experience was an orchestral concert heard over the radio when she was four. She was also brought into contact with the theater early, since her mother, a devotee of the stage, used to take her regularly to performances of the York repertory theater.

Since the family could not afford to pay for it, Janet did not receive any musical training until her ninth year when she joined the church choir in York. Sometimes, as she sang a hymn, she felt as if the heavens were opening up; and invariably the piece of music she was then singing turned out to be a Bach chorale. "I came to measure everything by the sounds I heard in Bach," she says, "and everything that didn't come up to that was no good."

When her family finally acquired a piano she was given some instruction, most of which she now remembers as inadequate. Much more valuable to her musical development was her attendance at the annual Diocesan Choir Meetings in York conducted by Sir Edward Bairstow. "They dominated our lives in a special way," she recalls. "It was a fabulous place and a great sound. Things that we in our own choir had been working on for weeks suddenly came together." She also looks back to the concerts of the Madrigal Society attached to the church choir in Grimsby, the town to which her family moved when Janet was fourteen.

After leaving the College for Girls in York when she was seventeen, Baker worked in a bank in Leeds to pay for singing lessons. At this time she made her first public appearance, substituting for the solo soprano in a performance of Haydn's Lord Nelson Mass. When her voice broke she was fortunate in getting the advice of Ruth Railton, who encouraged her to stop all singing for a time and later on had her study in London with Helene Isepp and Meriel St. Clair. Winning the London Daily Mail Kathleen Ferrier Prize in 1956 enabled Baker to study at the Mozarteum in Salzburg and later to attend a master class under Lotte Lehmann in London.

Baker soon began to make significant appearances as a singer: first in recitals sponsored by the Arts Council in towns in England and Wales; then in the chorus of the Glyndebourne Festival in 1956; and in 1957 in a performance of Smetana's opera The Secret by the Oxford Opera Club. By 1959 she had to her credit performances in Purcell's Dido and Aeneas (in the minor role of the Sorceress) conducted by Colin Davis, and appearances in a Sadler's Wells production of Handel's Rodelinda in which Joan Sutherland was starred and in a presentation of Rossini's La Gazza Ladra.

In 1960 Baker gave a recital at the Edinburgh Festival and was a soloist at a Promenade Concert in London, making a highly favorable impression on both occasions. Her talent was further recognized through the award of the

Queen's Prize from the Royal College of Music and through a grant from the Arts Council.

Appearances in the years 1961–1963 in Bach's *St. John* Passion in Copenhagen, in Mahler's Second Symphony under Otto Klemperer at the Edinburgh Festival, and in Bach's B minor Mass under Klemperer in Zurich added appreciably to her rapidly expanding fame in the concert auditorium. She was also gaining ground in the opera house beginning with 1960 as a member of the English Opera Group directed by Benjamin Britten, with whom she assumed the principal female role in Purcell's *Dido and Aeneas,* in Britten's *The Rape of Lucretia,* and in Britten's adaptation of *The Beggar's Opera.* Some years later Britten wrote for her the exacting role of Kate in his television opera *Owen Wingrave,* which received its premiere simultaneously on the television screens of about a dozen countries on May 16, 1971.

In the spring of 1966 Baker made her American debut as soloist with the San Francisco Symphony under Josef Krips in Mahler's *Das Lied von der Erde.* Later the same year she was heard in Donizetti's *Anna Bolena* in a concert presentation at Carnegie Hall, New York, by the American Opera Society, and in Handel's *Xerxes* offered by the Handel Society. On December 2, 1966, she gave a recital at Town Hall, New York. The ease with which she used her vocal resources, her perfect diction, exquisite phrasing, and perceptive musicianship inspired an extraordinary ovation from the audience. "She can do just about anything vocally and dramatically in a variety of contexts," wrote Howard Klein in the New York *Times,* "and she does it all with a communicative radiance and a personal warmth that borders on magic."

After her 1975 New York recital Harold C. Schonberg reported in the New York *Times:* "As usual the British mezzo-soprano came, sang and conquered. . . . Already she is an object of veneration with international audiences, and the audience last night washed her with waves of adulation. . . . Miss Baker, with her rich voice, her dignity of presentation and her sensitive musicianship, made everything her own."

In 1967 Baker made her first appearance at Covent Garden in the role of Hermia in Benjamin Britten's *A Midsummer Night's Dream.* She returned to Covent Garden in the fall of 1969 to substitute for Josephine Veasey, on a few hours' notice, as Dido in Berlioz' *Les Troyens.* When she sang that role with the Scottish Opera in Edinburgh in the spring of 1969, Desmond Shawe-Taylor, critic of the London *Sunday Times,* wrote: "Not even her finest achievements . . . had prepared us for the dramatic fire and intensity of her Dido."

Baker has continued to distinguish herself in recitals, oratorios, operas, and as a soloist with major symphony orchestras. In 1970 she appeared as Diana in Cavalli's *La Calisto* at the Glyndebourne Festival, and in 1971 in Berlioz' *The Damnation of Faust* at Sadler's Wells in London. She was soloist with the New Philharmonia Orchestra under John Barbirolli when it visited Japan during Expo '70. In 1971, during a six-week tour of the United States, she appeared in a joint recital with Dietrich Fischer-Dieskau, accompanied by Daniel Barenboim. In 1974 she gave six performances of Mahler's *Der Kindertotenlieder* with the Israel Philharmonic in Israel under Leonard Bernstein. In 1975 she sang the role of Vittelia in a new production of Mozart's *La Clemenza di Tito* at Covent Garden, a performance she later repeated at La Scala in Milan. With the Scottish Opera, on November 12, 1976, she assumed for the first time the role of the Composer in *Ariadne auf Naxos.* In 1976, at Covent Garden, she was heard as Cressida in the revised version of Sir William Walton's *Troilus and Cressida* in which the composer lowered some of the voice parts of that role to suit her range better. In June of the same year she presented the premiere of Britten's last completed composition, a cantata based on monologues from Racine's *Phèdre.* And when Mozart's *Idomeneo* received its first production at Covent Garden—in 1977–1978—she was heard as Idamante.

Gerald Moore, who has served as piano accompanist to some of the world's greatest singers, has written: "My idea of a great singer is one who can do everything: baroque, modern, Italian, German opera, oratorio. Janet Baker can do all that with absolute ease and conviction. She and baritone Dietrich Fischer-Dieskau are the two greatest singers in the world today."

In 1957 Baker married James Keith Shelley, an executive who gave up business to manage her career. They have a cottage at Harrow-on-the-Hill, just outside London. When she is not occupied professionally, she indulges in her favorite pastimes of playing tennis, taking long walks, and reading books on history and philosophy.

In 1970 she was designated Commander of the Order of the British Empire; in 1975 she was named Dame of the British Empire by Queen Elizabeth II. She has also received honorary doctorates in music from the University of Birmingham, Oxford University, and the University of London.

In 1975 her recording, in a Philips release, of Handel's *Cantata Lucretia* and several Handel arias was awarded first prize in the eighth annual Montreux International Record Awards.

ABOUT: Blythe, A. Janet Baker. *Periodicals*—High Fidelity/Musical America, February 1975; New York Times, January 28, 1970; Opera News, March 7, 1970, July 1977; Time, September 21, 1970.

ROSE BAMPTON

Rose Bampton

1909–

Rose Elizabeth Bampton, soprano, was born in Cleveland, Ohio, on November 28, 1909. She was the only girl among three children. Her father, Samuel W. Bampton, was a businessman of English birth; her mother, Henrietta, was an American whose family had lived in America for several generations. Rose spent her early years in Buffalo, New York, where she attended the public schools. At six she began piano study; her singing career was initiated at South Park High School in Buffalo when she filled a role as coloratura soprano in a Christmas pageant.

She received her basic musical training at the Curtis Institute of Music in Philadelphia where she spent five years on a scholarship, four of them studying voice with Horatio Connell and the fifth with Queena Mario, who had sung at the Metropolitan Opera.

Initially she was a coloratura soprano. While attending the Curtis Institute she was engaged for a concert appearance in Buffalo. At that time she suffered laryngitis and consulted a throat specialist who insisted she was a contralto and not a soprano. Her singing teacher at Curtis confirmed this diagnosis and began training her within the mezzo-soprano and contralto range. It was as a mezzo-soprano that Bampton made her debut in opera in 1929, in the role of Siebel in *Faust*, with the Chautauqua Opera Company.

An engagement as soloist with the Worcester Festival followed that same year. From 1929 to 1932 she was a member of the Philadelphia Opera Company performing in mezzo-soprano and contralto roles. During this period she attracted the interest of Leopold Stokowski, the musical director of the Philadelphia Orchestra, who engaged her to sing the part of the Wood Dove in the American premiere of Arnold Schoenberg's *Gurre-Lieder* in Philadelphia and New York in 1932 and also for a concert performance of the original version of Mussorgsky's *Boris Godunov*. At this time she also appeared at the Bethlehem Bach Festival and as a soloist with several principal American orchestras, including the New York Philharmonic under Toscanini. On March 5, 1933, she sang in the world premiere of Samuel Barber's *Dover Beach* in New York with the New York String Quartet.

Encouraged by these successes, Bampton decided to audition for the Metropolitan Opera. She made a good impression and was asked to return for a second hearing at which time she was offered a contract. She says: "At that moment, with pen in hand, a great wave of doubt swept over me. I was suddenly overcome by all my inadequacies and shortcomings. Perhaps I was not ready? Perhaps I would be a failure? I left without signing. It was only a few weeks later, with my morale restored, that I returned and signed the contract."

Bampton made her Metropolitan Opera debut as Laura in *La Gioconda* on November 22, 1932, while the company was on tour. Six days later, on her twenty-third birthday, she sang the same role at the Metropolitan in New York. "In appearance and in song, the young mezzo-soprano made a highly favorable impression," wrote Francis D. Perkins in the *Herald Tribune.* "The vocal range was generous, the quality usually warm, smooth and even, marked by a certain opulent duskiness of hue in middle and lower notes. Her top notes proved full and resonant." In the New York *Times,* Hubbard Hutchinson said: "Miss Bampton brought to . . . Laura . . . most of the qualities desirable for operatic work —a charming unaffected presence admirably sustained throughout the nerve-racking ordeal of a debut; the uncommon contralto virtues of slender good looks and a voice of operatic dimensions and beauty."

For three seasons Bampton continued to sing mezzo-soprano and contralto roles, the most important of which was Amneris in *Aida* on March 24, 1933. As a mezzo-soprano, she made her first trip abroad in 1935 as an official artist representative of the English-Speaking Union to London, where she was received at court and was heard by millions throughout the British Isles in special broadcasts. The following fall she made her first tour of Scandinavia and Central Europe. At that time she was beginning to retrain her voice to a higher range and to assume principal soprano parts. In 1937 she made her debut at Covent Garden in London.

Her American debut as a soprano took place with a recital at Town Hall, New York, in March 1937. Commenting upon her change of voice, Olin Downes wrote in the New York *Times:* "The voice, which is of unusual range . . . sounds like a true soprano. It was full, free, clear in color. The singing was flexible, brilliant, dramatic by turns."

On May 7, 1937, Bampton sang her first leading soprano role at the Metropolitan Opera, Leonora in *Il Trovatore.* As a soprano she gathered more praise than she had earned in the lower range: as Donna Anna in *Don Giovanni,* as Aida, and as Alceste in Gluck's opera of the same name.

As a principal soprano she first ventured into Wagnerian roles in 1939 when she was heard as Sieglinde in *Die Walküre* with the Chicago Opera. That same role was her first principal Wagnerian assignment with the Metropolitan Opera, on tour on April 17, 1941, and in New York on December 12, 1941. Other major Wagnerian

roles at the Metropolitan Opera were Elsa in *Lohengrin,* Elisabeth in *Tannhäuser,* and Kundry in *Parsifal.* It was in a Wagnerian role— Kundry—that she made her farewell appearance at the Metropolitan, on April 5, 1950.

In 1938 Bampton was chosen from a long list of distinguished singers to appear at the May Day Music Festival, the 1938 preview of the 1939 New York World's Fair, before an audience of over a hundred thousand. On April 30, 1939, she inaugurated the New York World's Fair by singing the national anthem before an audience that included the President of the United States.

During the years 1942–1947 she appeared almost annually at the Teatro Colón in Buenos Aires. In 1946 she was heard at the Teatro Municipal in Rio de Janeiro. She made her debut with the San Francisco Opera on September 27, 1949, as Donna Anna.

In addition to her appearances in opera and concerts both in the United States and abroad, Bampton carved for herself an impressive career in radio with regularly scheduled programs over the National Broadcasting System. After she left the Metropolitan Opera in 1950, she appeared with the New York City Opera. Subsequently she concentrated on concerts and television appearances.

On May 24, 1937, Bampton married Wilfrid Pelletier, conductor at the Metropolitan Opera during the seasons between 1921 and 1950. Their apartment in New York City overflowed with musical mementos: inscribed pictures of Bampton's colleagues lined the walls; trophies and reminders of her many concert and opera appearances filled nooks and corners.

Rose Bampton has interested herself in many things: politics, cooking, current events, and sports (mainly swimming and horseback riding). She has confessed a weakness for rich Renaissance colors, old fabrics, medieval sleeves, large hats, and antique earrings. Playing charades at parties has been a favorite diversion and going to the movies her preferred way of relaxing.

She always carried a frayed handkerchief in her hands when she sang, a handkerchief her mother gave her before her first public concert. She recalls: "I was so nervous then that I practically pulled it apart as I sang. It brought me luck, and I have always kept it with me since." She also considered it good luck to whistle while

Barbieri

applying makeup, thereby flouting an old theatrical superstition.

ABOUT: Musician, March 1940; Newsweek, March 13, 1957; Opera News, January 15, 1940; Time, May 17, 1937.

Fedora Barbieri

1919–

Fedora Barbieri, mezzo-soprano and contralto, was born on June 4, 1919, in Trieste, where her parents, Rafaele and Ida Barbieri, were shopkeepers. She attended the local public schools and did not receive any music instruction until her eighteenth year. During her school years she worked in her parents' shop, singing continually "to make the days pass faster," she says. One day a customer heard her sing and urged her to cultivate her voice. She became a pupil of Federico Bugamelli, with whom she studied in Trieste for two years, following this with nine months of training with Luigi Toffolo. She made her first public appearance as a soloist in the church of San Giusto in Trieste where she had been baptized.

On a scholarship she attended the Centro Amiamento Teatro Lirico in Florence as a pupil of Giacomo Armani in voice and of Armani's wife, Giulia Tess, in stagecraft.

On November 4, 1940, Barbieri made her opera debut at the Teatro Comunale in Florence as Fidalma in Cimarosa's *Il Matrimonio Segreto.* Her physical stamina received almost as much attention as her voice, for the day following her debut she was heard as Azucena in *Il Trovatore,* and on the next day she reappeared as Fidalma. A few months later, on May 10, 1941, at the Florence May Music Festival, she sang the role of Dariola in the world premiere of Alfano's *Don Juan de Mañara.* In 1942 she made her debut at La Scala as Dame Quickly in *Falstaff,* then toured Germany, Belgium, and Holland.

After marrying Luigi Barlozzetti, administrative director of the Florence May Music Festival, in 1943, Barbieri went into a one-year retirement. Her "second debut" took place at the Teatro Verdi in Florence in 1945 when she was acclaimed for her performance of Amneris

---

Barbieri: bär byâ′ rẽ

FEDORA BARBIERI

in *Aida.* From this point on she was considered an important Italian mezzo-soprano. In December 1946 she appeared at La Scala in Verdi's *Nabucco,* which reopened the theater rebuilt following World War II.

Her recordings helped to bring her international renown. The wide range of her voice (from low E to high C) enabled her to appear in many works long neglected because suitable mezzo-sopranos were not available. These works included lesser-known operas by Rossini together with rarely performed operas by Monteverdi. In 1949 she appeared at the Florence May Music Festival in the title role of Monteverdi's *Orfeo.*

In 1950 she made her first appearance in England, as a member of the visiting La Scala company, winning praise for her performance both as Dame Quickly in *Falstaff* and, in the concert hall, as the contralto soloist in Verdi's Requiem. The following fall she went for the first time to the United States to make her debut at the Metropolitan Opera. She was detained on Ellis Island because she revealed she had attended an Italian school that was Fascist. She insisted that she had never had any affiliation with the Fascist party and was finally cleared by the federal authorities.

Her Metropolitan Opera debut took place on November 6, 1950, as Princess Eboli in *Don Carlo.* This opera not only opened the new Metropolitan Opera season but also was the first performance under the new directorial regime of Rudolf Bing. Since she was already known to American audiences through her recordings, she was given a warm welcome, which her persuasive vocal and dramatic performance well deserved. In the *Saturday Review* Irving Kolodin spoke of her "flaming temperament" and her "decidedly interesting vocal instrument." In the *Herald Tribune* Virgil Thomson wrote: "She exposed a ringing contralto voice with a bravura style that should be of sound service to the company." When later that season she was heard as Azucena, Louis Biancolli in the *World-Telegram and Sun* wrote about "the massive impact of her voice and interpretation."

Barbieri remained with the Metropolitan Opera through the 1953–1954 season, then returned in 1956–1957. Her roles there, in addition to Princess Eboli, were Santuzza in *Cavalleria Rusticana,* Laura in *La Gioconda,* Amneris in *Aida,* Carmen, Mistress Quickly in *Falstaff,* Adalgisa in *Norma* and the Princess in *Suor Angelica* and Zita in *Gianni Schicchi* in Puccini's *Il Trittico.* When she sang Adalgisa on October 29, the opening night of the Metropolitan Opera season of 1956–1957, Maria Callas was making her Metropolitan debut in the title role. At that time Paul Henry Lang commented in the *Herald Tribune* that her voice was "bigger and more shining than Miss Callas's." After that season Barbieri did not return to the Metropolitan until October 5, 1967, when she again sang the role of Dame Quickly.

In the summer of 1956 Barbieri scored a great success at both the Arena in Verona and the Baths of Caracalla in Rome. She was starred as Cornelia in a noteworthy revival of Handel's *Giulio Cesare* in Rome in January 1956. Guest appearances at the Teatro Colón in Buenos Aires and in the leading opera houses of Italy, London, Paris, Vienna, San Francisco, and Chicago added further to her international stature. In her later years she added to her repertory by appearing in the world premieres of new Italian operas: Flavio Testi's *La Celestina* at the Florence May Music Festival on May 28, 1963; Renzo Rossellini's *Linguággio dei Fiori* at La Scala, also in 1963; Luciano Chailly's *L'Idiota* in Rome on February 13, 1970; and Ennio Porrino's *Esculapio al Neon* at Cagliari in 1972.

She has also been heard frequently in recitals and has participated in performances of choral masterworks with major symphony orchestras.

As the mother of two sons and the wife of Luigi Barlozzetti, who has served as her manager, Fedora Barbieri has combined a successful artistic career with the life of a homemaker, *una donna di casa* as she phrases it, at her house on the Viale Belfiore in Florence, and at her suite on Central Park West in New York.

ABOUT: Opera (London), September 1950; Opera News, November 8, 1950, February 26, 1977.

Sir John Barbirolli

1899–1970

John Barbirolli, conductor, was born above a baker's shop in Southampton Row, London, on December 2, 1899, and baptized Giovanni Battista Barbirolli by his Italian father (Lorenzo) and French mother (Louise Ribeyrol Barbirolli). He came from a family of musicians. Both his father and grandfather were violinists who played in the opera orchestra of La Scala at the world premiere of *Otello.* One of Barbirolli's ancestors had been the organist of the Il Santo church in Padua.

When Barbirolli was a child his father and grandfather were employed at the Empire Theatre in London and would sometimes bring the three-year-old John to listen to rehearsals. When he was seven, John asked for a musical instrument and was presented with a violin. Before long he exchanged the violin for a cello. As he often liked to explain later, he used to pace the floor so nervously while practicing the violin that his father decided to have him study the cello so that he would stay in one place during a performance. His academic schooling was at the St. Clement Danes and Holborn Estate Grammar School, which he entered in 1907, the Dane House in the senior school where he remained from 1909 to 1914, and Trinity College in 1911 and 1912. At the same time his musical education was proceeding at the Royal Academy of Music in London, which he entered when he was thirteen and where he remained on a scholarship until 1917. On December 16, 1911, John made his debut as a cellist in a performance of a concerto by Saint-Saëns at Queen's Hall. At about this time he also made his first recordings, four compositions for cello and piano in which he was accompanied by his sister, Rosa.

At sixteen he was the youngest member of the

Barbirolli: bär bĭ rŏl′ ĭ

Barbirolli

SIR JOHN BARBIROLLI

Promenade Concerts orchestra conducted by Sir Henry J. Wood. His work there was combined with performances in theater pits, movie houses, dance halls, restaurants, and cafés. "I have played everywhere except in the street," he later recalled. On July 13, 1917, he gave his first recital at Aeolian Hall in London. A critic for the *Times* found his performance of a composition by Locatelli "masterly."

When he was eighteen he joined the orchestra of the Carl Rosa Opera at the Shaftesbury Theatre. Shortly after that he played in the orchestra of the Beecham Opera Company, and on November 26, 1917, he was a member of the Royal Philharmonic Orchestra in a concert conducted by Sir Thomas Beecham.

Once he reached his eighteenth birthday he was eligible for conscription into the army, but late in 1917 he volunteered as a private in the First Reserve Garrison Battalion of the Suffolk Regiment stationed on the Isle of Grain. In the army he helped form an orchestra and made his first attempt at conducting. "From the first time I picked up a baton," he told an interviewer many years later, "I had the same facility as I have now. . . . I'm speaking of the physical side of conducting, of course."

About a year after Barbirolli entered the service the war ended. Back in London he once again played the cello wherever he could find an opening: with Diaghilev's Ballet Russe in London, the London Symphony Orchestra at the Three Choirs Festival in London, the orchestra accompanying Anna Pavlova and her troupe,

and the orchestra of the Beecham Opera Company.

From 1923 to 1926, Barbirolli was a member of the International String Quartet which toured Great Britain, France, Belgium, Germany, and Spain. In 1924 he joined the Kutcher Quartet which gave concerts in England. One year later he founded the Barbirolli String Orchestra of twelve musicians, which contributed a series of concerts at the Chenil Galleries in Chelsea, London, and with them Barbirolli made his professional bow as a conductor. Among those who admired these concerts was Frederick Austin, head of the British National Opera Company. Austin engaged Barbirolli to conduct a series of opera performances with his company. In 1926 Barbirolli's debut as an opera conductor took place at Newcastle-on-Tyne in performances of *Romeo and Juliet, Madama Butterfly,* and *Aida,* all in a single week, and each for him for the first time. "If I hadn't been a born conductor I shouldn't have survived one aft," he has stated. He repeated these performances in London in January before going on a tour of the provinces. He remained with the British National Opera Company until its demise in 1928 and then conducted the opera company of Covent Garden both in London and on tour.

He was also beginning to demonstrate a gift for conducting symphony concerts. On December 12, 1927, when Sir Thomas Beecham was indisposed for a performance of the London Symphony Orchestra at Queen's Hall, he called on Barbirolli to substitute for him. Despite an exacting program that included Elgar's Second Symphony, Barbirolli gave an excellent account of himself, particularly in the Elgar symphony. "Mr. Barbirolli," reported a critic for the *Daily Telegraph,* "came through the ordeal successfully, moments of special beauty being the brilliant climax of the first movement and the diminuendo which marks the coda of the finale. His skill in keeping his forces in control also showed up well in the third movement. . . . Mr. Barbirolli has few personal idiosyncrasies, and his beat is always indicated in a straightforward way." This success brought him engagements with the London Symphony Orchestra, the Royal Philharmonic (with which he presented the world premiere of Vaughan Williams's *Fantasia on Sussex* on March 13, 1930), the BBC, the Hallé in Manchester, the Liverpool Philharmonic, as well as with foreign orchestras, including the

Leningrad Symphony, the National Finnish Orchestra of Helsingfors, and the Residentie Orchestra at The Hague. During this period, in June 1932, Barbirolli married Marjorie Perry, a singer who had appeared under his direction in opera performances; they settled down in Woburn Court, off Russell Square, in London.

In November 1933, Barbirolli was appointed permanent conductor of the Scottish Orchestra in Glasgow and remained with that group three years. Then in 1936 one of the most desirable conducting posts in the world unexpectedly came to him. Arturo Toscanini, the very popular and highly esteemed music director of the New York Philharmonic, was leaving his post, and Wilhelm Furtwängler was chosen as a replacement. Because of Furtwängler's involvements with Nazi Germany a furor arose in New York over his selection, and he discreetly withdrew. At this juncture Toscanini recommended Barbirolli, about whom little was known in the United States except for a few recordings. Though some of the world's greatest conductors had been eyeing this post covetously, Barbirolli was chosen. "I forced myself to forget that I was supposed to succeed Mr. Toscanini," Barbirolli told an interviewer. "I said to myself: Look here, you've been hired to do a job. Do it as well as you can and let the devil take the hindmost."

His debut in New York on November 5, 1936, made an excellent impression in a program that included the Fourth Symphony of Brahms, Arnold Bax's *The Tale the Pine Trees Knew,* and the *Roman Carnival Overture* of Berlioz. Lawrence Gilman reported in the *Herald Tribune:* "He has disclosed himself to be a musician of taste and fire and intensity, electric, vital, sensitive, dynamic, experienced: an artist who knows his way with the scores he elects to set before us, who has mastered not only his temperament but his trade. He is already, at thirty-six, a conductor of impressive authority, delicacy, and imagination, with a power of control and stimulus before an orchestra that exerts itself wholly upon the music to be revealed."

His first season in New York proved so successful that Barbirolli was given a three-year contract as permanent conductor, the youngest in the world to hold such a post with an orchestra of first importance. In 1940 the contract was renewed for an additional two years.

Benjamin Britten (then in his mid-twenties) was introduced to the American public on the programs of the New York Philharmonic under Barbirolli with the world premieres of Britten's Violin Concerto (March 28, 1940) and his *Sinfonia da Requiem* (March 29, 1941). Other New York Philharmonic world premieres under Barbirolli were those of Castelnuovo-Tedesco's *King John* (March 15, 1942) and his Piano Concerto No. 2 (November 2, 1939); Bernard Herrmann's *Moby Dick* (April 11, 1940); Daniel Gregory Mason's *A Lincoln Symphony* (November 17, 1937); Milhaud's *Philharmonic Overture* (December 3, 1936); Gardner Read's Symphony No.1 (November 4, 1937); and Jaromir Weinberger's *Under the Spreading Chestnut Tree* (October 12, 1939).

However, the years with the New York Philharmonic were not always a time of triumph for Barbirolli. Comparison with his predecessor was inevitable, and it was not always favorable. At his best Barbirolli revealed musicianship and talent, but he did not possess the studied repertory or the experience to cope with the heavy burdens of conducting so great an orchestra for so many concerts each year.

Barbirolli's marriage to Marjorie Perry was dissolved in 1939, and on July 5, 1939, he married Evelyn Rothwell, who had been the first oboist of the Scottish Orchestra when Barbirolli was its principal conductor, and who had sometimes appeared as a soloist under his direction with other orchestras.

In March 1943 Barbirolli conducted his last concert with the New York Philharmonic Orchestra. One month later he was appointed music director of the Hallé Orchestra in Manchester, the fourth permanent conductor since its founding in 1858. A formidable assignment faced him. World War II had reduced this once great orchestra to just twenty-three musicians. The concert auditorium in which it performed had been bombed into rubble. Barbirolli hurled his enormous energies and talent into the job of rebuilding the orchestra and re-creating its impressive image. Within a month the orchestra was increased to seventy musicians and in only a few years after the end of World War II its former status as one of Europe's finest symphonic organizations was regained. His dedication and devotion to this orchestra were emphasized in 1946 when he refused an appointment as music director of the BBC Symphony Orchestra at twice the salary he was drawing in Manchester. The offer was repeated in 1950 and

41

once again turned down. In recognition of his achievements in Manchester, which had a powerful impact on the musical culture of England in the first postwar years, Barbirolli was named conductor laureate for life in 1967 (the orchestra's silver jubilee celebration), the only conductor of this orchestra to receive such an appointment. A grateful kingdom had previously honored him in June 1948 with a knighthood, and in 1950 he was awarded the gold medal of the Royal Philharmonic Society.

The Hallé Orchestra celebrated its centenary on October 16, 1957, with the premiere of Vaughan Williams's *Flourish for Glorious John,* composed in Barbirolli's honor. Barbirolli had given the world premieres of two of Vaughan Williams's symphonies with this orchestra: the *Sinfonia Antarctica* (January 14, 1953) and the Symphony No.8 (May 2, 1956).

During his fifteen years as music director of the Hallé Orchestra Barbirolli matured as a performing artist, developing into one of the world's great conductors, an interpreter of a large repertory. The United States became aware of this growth in 1959 when he returned to the New York Philharmonic for guest appearances. In 1960 he was appointed music director of the Houston Symphony in Texas, succeeding Leopold Stokowski. In the years between 1961 and 1967 he divided his activities between Houston and Manchester. On October 3, 1966, he conducted the first concert in Houston's new auditorium, the Jesse H. Jones Hall, presenting the world premiere of Alan Hovhaness's *Ode to the Temple of Sound* written for this occasion. When he resigned from the Houston Symphony in 1967 he was made conductor emeritus.

After leaving Texas, Barbirolli remained active not only in Manchester but throughout Europe with guest performances with some of Europe's most important orchestras and opera houses. On his seventieth birthday in October 1969 the Queen made him Companion of Honor. Other honors came from other countries: Commendatore of the Order of Merit of the Italian Republic, Commander First Class of the White Rose of Finland, and Honorary Academician of the Santa Cecilia Academy in Rome.

He was rehearsing the New Philharmonia Orchestra at Croydon, England, on May 29, 1970, in preparation for a tour of Japan, when he suddenly collapsed. He died in a hospital in London of coronary thrombosis on July 29, 1970.

Barbirolli was short and stocky. He was English by birth and speech (when excited he sometimes lapsed into Cockney), and with his swarthy complexion and dark intense eyes Italian in name and appearance. In choice of food, too, he seemed more Italian than English, preferring for his one meal a day Italian recipes (which he sometimes prepared himself).

Napoleonic in size, he was, as Neville Cardus, the English musicologist, said: "Napoleonic, too, in his imperiousness, his uncompromising exercise of his own will, his unhesitating trust in his intuitions." Cardus described him as "an egoist, terrifically so, but in a way that is endearing." He further stated that the secret of Barbirolli's "universal range as interpreter" lay in "the complex in Sir John of austerity and sensuous love of life, of Spartan and Epicure, of kindly consideration and ruthless integrity."

Barbirolli had great interest in reading and in collecting medical books, old English glass, and eighteenth century English furniture. His favorite spectator sport was cricket. He was superstitious and never began a venture on a Friday. He made orchestral transcriptions of the music of Henry Purcell which he gathered into several suites and he composed a concerto for oboe and orchestra, based on themes by Pergolesi, which he dedicated to his second wife.

ABOUT: Reid, C. John Barbirolli; Rigby, C. John Barbirolli. *Periodicals*—Hi Fi, October 1961, August 1968, November 1970; Musical America, July 1964; Newsweek, August 10, 1970; Opera News, December 6, 1969; Saturday Review, October 28, 1967.

Daniel Barenboim

1942–

Daniel Barenboim, pianist and conductor, was born in Buenos Aires on November 15, 1942. His parents, Enrique and Aïda Schuster Barenboim, were piano teachers who went to Argentina from Russia. "I was listening to music practically before I was born," he says. "For several years I didn't meet anyone who didn't play an instrument. When I was four my father played a duet with a violinist. In my childish way I thought I would have to play a violin in order to be able to play a duet with my father. But I was so small that they couldn't get a violin little enough. Finally, another pianist played a

DANIEL BARENBOIM

duet with my father and I discovered that I didn't have to be a violinist."

He received his first instruction on the piano from his parents when he was five. Two years later he gave a recital in Buenos Aires that was so well received that he had to give seven encores, only stopping then because he had exhausted his repertory. After several more appearances in Buenos Aires and other South American cities Daniel was encouraged by Igor Markevitch, the distinguished French conductor and composer, to go to Salzburg, Austria, to attend the Mozarteum. There he studied piano with Edwin Fischer, chamber music with Enrico Mainardi, and conducting with Markevitch. Though only ten years old, Daniel made a profound impression at the Mozarteum, performing Mozart's Concerto in D Minor. Wilhelm Furtwängler said of him after hearing a recital in which he performed Bach's *Italian Concerto* and sonatas by Beethoven and Mozart: "Daniel Barenboim is a phenomenon. His musical and technical capacities are equally amazing." At the Mozarteum he was also given his first opportunity to conduct: he led the student orchestra in a performance of Brahms's *Variations on a Theme by Haydn*. In recognition of Daniel's exceptional gifts the city officials of Salzburg permitted him to give a concert on Mozart's own spinet—the first time in twenty-five years that anyone had been allowed to play on that instrument.

In 1952 the Barenboim family moved to Israel and became Israeli citizens. On a scholarship from the American-Israel Cultural Foundation, Daniel continued his music studies in Europe: composition with Nadia Boulanger in Paris; conducting at the Accademia Chigiana in Siena; theory and composition at the Santa Cecilia Academy in Rome. In 1956 he became the youngest musician in the history of Santa Cecilia to receive its diploma.

In January 1956, Daniel made his debut in England, as soloist with the Royal Philharmonic Orchestra, Josef Krips conducting, in Mozart's A major Concerto, K.488. The critic of the *Times* wrote: "There is no doubt about his pianistic ability, which is prodigious for his age, nor about his musicality." Appearances throughout Europe as a concert pianist followed. In Vienna he was heard in an all-American music concert. During a tour of Italy he made his first recordings. In Italy in 1956 he won first prize in the Alfredo Casella competition for pianists.

On Arthur Rubinstein's recommendation, Sol Hurok, the American impresario, put Daniel under contract to make his first American tour. The tour began at Carnegie Hall, New York, on January 20, 1957, with a performance of Prokofiev's First Piano Concerto, Leopold Stokowski conducting the Symphony of the Air. The *Herald Tribune* described him as "every inch a miniature master," and the New York *Post* spoke of him as a "remarkable young artist." After Daniel gave his first recital in the United States, in New York City on January 17, 1958, Howard Taubman wrote in the New York *Times:* "His future can be as big as he chooses to make it. Already exceptional as a teenager he could become one of the major virtuosos of tomorrow."

In 1958 Barenboim received the Beethoven medal; and in 1963, the Harriet Cohen Paderewski Centenary Prize.

Barenboim did not live the part of a *wunderkind,* nor did he behave like one. With his concert appearances limited to three months to permit a normal development, he pursued his academic education in Israeli schools, learned to speak five languages fluently, and was encouraged by his parents to box and play soccer without concern about his hands, to seek out recreation in chess and stamp collecting, and to go out on dates.

His powers as a piano virtuoso in an extensive repertory, particularly in the music of Beethoven, were universally recognized in performances around the world. Besides appearing many times in the United States, he toured South America, Europe, the Near East, Australia, New Zealand, and the Soviet Union. When he was seventeen, he performed in Tel Aviv his first cycle of the thirty-two sonatas of Beethoven (which he had committed to memory when he was fourteen). He repeated this performance in London (inaugurating the new Queen Elizabeth Hall), Buenos Aires, Vienna, New York, and on Angel records. After a concert made up of three of these sonatas (including the formidable *Hammerklavier*, Op.106), Howard Klein commented in the New York *Times:* "It may be premature to call a twenty-two-year-old a master pianist, but the kind of artistry Daniel Barenboim demonstrated . . . was so impressive there is no alternative." Later, in 1975, he performed a cycle of all of Mozart's piano concertos in seven concerts in Tel Aviv, repeating this performance later in London and Paris with the English Chamber Orchestra, and recording the cycle for Angel. On several occasions he has performed cycles of the five Beethoven concertos, the only artist to record these five concertos both as a pianist and as a conductor: as pianist, for EMI, with Otto Klemperer conducting; as conductor, for RCA, with Arthur Rubinstein as soloist. For recording he not only conducted the Beethoven Violin Concerto but also performed the piano arrangement made by the composer. Because of Barenboim's extensive representation on disks, the English record critic Edward Greenfield has remarked that "in a hundred years' time people will see this as the period of Barenboim."

When the Six Day War erupted in the Middle East in June 1967, Barenboim canceled his engagements in Europe to return to Israel to serve the country through his music. With him went his fiancée, Jacqueline du Pré, the cellist. They had met in London at the home of a mutual friend. "When I met him," she said, "I was very huge; I weighed 180 pounds and I felt like a great lump. I had been in Russia for five months eating potatoes. We were all drinking coffee when this dynamic small thing burst into the room. Being a shy and somewhat insecure person at that time, the only thing I could do was get up and play." About two weeks later Barenboim proposed marriage and, since she was then on tour, he kept hounding her with telephone calls at each of her stops, even beyond the Iron Curtain.

They were married in Jerusalem on June 15, 1967, three days after the end of the Six Day War, after du Pré had undergone all the preliminaries of conversion to Judaism as required by Israeli law. Since then she has often shared the concert platform with her husband: in sonata recitals; in trio concerts with her husband and either Itzhak Perlman or Pinchas Zukerman as violinist; and in performances of works for cello and orchestra with her husband conducting.

They have homes in London (an apartment near Baker Street) and in Israel. Both places are crowded with books and music. They are a highly gregarious pair who love the companionship of their musician friends and who, when they have time from their concert activities, enjoy entertaining and being entertained. It is not unusual before one of Barenboim's concerts to find his dressing room overflowing with people nor for Barenboim to invite thirty or forty friends to a late dinner after the concert. With his closest friends—including Zubin Mehta, the conductor; Vladimir Ashkenazy, the pianist; and Itzhak Perlman, the violinist—Barenboim gives free rein to his penchant for playing practical jokes or for telling stories.

He enjoys good food and good friends, a good Havana cigar, and champagne. But what he enjoys most of all is working; he sometimes works for several years without taking a single vacation.

Since 1962 Barenboim has combined his career as piano virtuoso with that of conductor. "To the best of my knowledge," he once said, "I am the only musician currently active who is listed both as a pianist and as a conductor." He has divided his well-over-one-hundred appearances each year equally between the piano and the baton. Although his first attempt at conducting took place in Salzburg when he was ten years old, he did not engage in it professionally until 1962 when, during a tour of Australia, he conducted the symphony orchestras of Melbourne and Sydney in several performances. In 1964 his career as a conductor was further advanced when he led the English Chamber Orchestra in London for the first time. He appeared as the conductor of this group in festivals in Lucerne, Stresa, Prague, and Athens, and in the United States at the Lincoln Center for the Performing

Arts on July 9, 1968. In the New York *Times* Harold Schonberg described this performance: "There was no question of who was in charge. For better or for worse, the ideas were his, the tempos were his, the phrasing and shadings were his. . . . He is a born conductor, one with authority, a clear and logical beat and a strong musicality. Any performance he conducts is going to be his performance." This appearance, with the English Chamber Orchestra, followed his conducting debut in the United States two months earlier, in April, when István Kertész was unable to appear as conductor of the visiting London Symphony Orchestra and Barenboim was called in as a replacement for four concerts. He has since conducted the Israel Philharmonic, the New York Philharmonic, the Boston Symphony, and the Philadelphia Orchestra, among other major orchestras. In 1973 he made his debut as a conductor of opera with a performance of *Don Giovanni* at the Edinburgh Festival (recorded on the Angel label); he returned to Edinburgh in 1975 to direct *The Marriage of Figaro*. In 1974 he was appointed principal conductor of the Orchestre de Paris, to succeed Sir Georg Solti, beginning with the 1975–1976 season. In April and May 1976, at Carnegie Hall in New York, Barenboim appeared in the dual role of conductor and pianist with the English Chamber Orchestra in a cycle of all of Mozart's piano concertos. This series was presented as "A British Salute to the American Bicentennial" through a grant by the National Westminster Bank of England.

"Barenboim's manner on the podium is much like his manner offstage," wrote Martin Mayer in the New York *Times,* "brisk and very intelligent. He is a small man with black hair which grows in a straight line on his forehead, giving him a squared-off and deceptively serious look. He walks quickly, and talks quickly, always alert, radiating energy and confidence; he can be patient when necessary, but it takes work. Rehearsing an orchestra he tends to run through a largish section of a piece, and he works backwards over the mistakes. Surprisingly for a pianist, whose life is spent amidst the approximations of tempered tuning, he takes a good deal of time on questions of intonation."

Barenboim has made numerous appearances over television both as a pianist and as a conductor, including a series of master classes. He collaborated with the Greater London Council in the presentation of a festival of summer music on the South Bank of London from 1969 to 1970. From 1971 to 1974 he was artistic adviser for the Israel Festival. As pianist and as conductor he has made over one hundred recordings.

ABOUT: Jacobson, R. Reverberations. *Periodicals*—Hi Fi, July 1965, March 1973; New York Times, June 30, 1968, January 24, 1971, May 7, 1976; New York Times Magazine, March 16, 1969; Saturday Evening Post, September 7, 1968; Time, August 11, 1967.

David Bar-Illan

1930–

David Bar-Illan, pianist, born in Haifa, Palestine (now Israel), on February 7, 1930, is a third-generation Palestinian. Music was integral to the Bar-Illan household. David's grandfather, Reuven Beilin, was a composer of liturgical music. David's father, Aaron, though a graduate in piano of the Tel Aviv Conservatory, never pursued a career as a piano virtuoso. Instead he turned to electrical engineering and helped build the first high-tension line in Palestine. All his life, however, he remained a devoted and proficient amateur pianist.

"I heard piano music from birth and probably before," says Bar-Illan. "My parents say that I showed interest in music when I was an infant." However, he does recall that when he was five he heard a concert of the newly founded Palestine Symphony Orchestra (later to become the Israel Philharmonic) with Toscanini conducting. "I was hypnotized by that concert and immediately begged my parents to let me begin lessons."

While receiving his academic education at the Hebrew Gymnasium in Haifa, David studied the piano with Elisheva Segal, a graduate of the Paris Conservatory, and Hans Neumann, a concert pianist who had emigrated from Prague. A scholarship brought Bar-Illan to the Juilliard School of Music in New York in 1947, but when the Israel War of Independence broke out, he returned to Palestine to join the Haganah, the underground military force, of which he had been a member from the age of fourteen and which emerged as the Army of Israel during the War of Independence in 1947–1948. He served in Galilee during the war and was in the platoon which accepted the surrender of Nazareth. "One

Bar-Illan

DAVID BAR-ILLAN

advantage," he recalls, "of having the front line ten miles from home was that I could go home to practice whenever there was a lull in the fighting." After the war Bar-Illan returned to the Juilliard School of Music in 1949 for further piano study with Rosina Lhevinne and was graduated in 1950. He also studied theory and composition with Felix Salzer at the Mannes College of Music from 1951 to 1953 and took private lessons in piano from Hans Neumann (then teaching at the Mannes College), Constance Keene, Abram Chasins, and Dora Zaslavsky.

One of the turning points in his life came in 1950 when he auditioned for Arthur Rubinstein, who told him that the teacher he needed most was the stage. This advice encouraged Bar-Illan to begin a concert career. Two successful concerts in London in 1953 and the winning of the Coronation Year Medal in England for distinguished artistic achievement drew public attention to him. He was engaged as a soloist by the Liverpool Philharmonic and the Birmingham Orchestra.

In 1954 he returned to the United States and made his American recital debut at Carnegie Hall in New York in December before embarking on his first national tour. In 1959 he appeared as a soloist with the Israel Philharmonic in Tel Aviv in the world premiere of Robert Starer's Piano Concerto No.2, a work written for him. The conductor on this occasion, Dimitri Mitropoulos, was so taken with Bar-Illan's performance that he invited the young pianist to make his American orchestral debut with the New York Philharmonic Orchestra under his direction in January 1960. Bar-Illan's performance of Liszt's Piano Concerto in E-flat led a critic of the New York *Times* to describe him as having "the panache of an assured young virtuoso" and a critic of the *Herald Tribune* to praise his "thorough technical mastery and polish, constantly musical tone . . . and sensitive communication of mood."

He began to acquire an international reputation one season later. On September 14, 1961, he appeared as a soloist with the Berlin Philharmonic Orchestra in Berlin in Beethoven's Piano Concerto No.3, Karl Boehm conducting. This was the first time an Israeli had appeared on a German public concert stage. "He lived each phrase and illuminated the expressive value of the work with exactness and deep understanding," reported the critic of the Berlin *Kurier*. His success brought him an invitation to appear as a guest artist with the Berlin Philharmonic under Boehm during its visit to the United States in the fall of 1961. After Bar-Illan's performance of Beethoven's Piano Concerto No.3 on November 21, a critic for the *World-Telegram and Sun* reported: "Here is an attractive keyboard personality of poetic leanings and gentle fingers. . . . Mr. Bar-Illan always played like a well-bred artist who took his time and never sought to impress by the simple device of raising his voice." Earlier in 1961, on November 5, Bar-Illan was hurriedly called to Amsterdam to substitute for Emil Gilels with the Concertgebouw Orchestra under Carlo Maria Giulini in Liszt's Concerto in E-flat. Bar-Illan auditioned for Bernard Haitink, the musical director of the Concertgebouw in Amsterdam, that Wednesday, returned to the United States on Thursday, and rushed back to Holland on Friday for the concert. The *Algemeen Handesblad* called his performance "a shattering event," characterized Bar-Illan as "among the greatest of the great," and added that "no one could have imagined a worthier substitute for Gilels than Bar-Illan."

In the years between 1962 and 1964 Bar-Illan made his first appearances with a number of America's leading orchestras, including those in Philadelphia, Cleveland, Cincinnati, and Indianapolis. He also toured the West and Southwest with the San Antonio Symphony, appearing in twenty-four concerts. During the summer of 1963 he participated in an all-Mozart program of the Boston Symphony at the Berkshire Music Festival at Tanglewood, Massachusetts. In March 1964, when the Cincinnati Symphony visited Carnegie Hall, Bar-Illan was its soloist in Mendelssohn's Concerto in G minor. During this time he filled engagements in Holland, Germany, France, Denmark, and England, and he toured throughout South America.

Since 1964, Bar-Illan has frequently been heard both in the United States and in Europe in recitals and as soloist with the world's great orchestras. He taped for CBS-TV, with the CBS Orchestra under Antonini, several programs which were nationally telecast. In May 1967 he introduced Prokofiev's Piano Concerto No.4 (for the left hand) with the New York Philharmonic under Leonard Bernstein. His recording that year for RCA of Beethoven's *Eroica* Variations, Liszt's *Dante Sonata,* and Liszt's *Hungarian Rhapsody No.15* was cited by the *Saturday Review* as one of the best of the year. In 1971 he revived the Moszkowski Piano Concerto in E with the American Symphony Orchestra, Eliahu Inbal conducting, at Carnegie Hall.

The season 1971–1972 began with two "firsts": He was the soloist with the New York Philharmonic on September 23, the first Philharmonic performance under the musical directorship of Pierre Boulez; and on October 24 he became the first pianist to give a recital at the newly opened John F. Kennedy Center for the Performing Arts in Washington, D.C.

On October 9, 1974, as soloist with the Baltimore Symphony under Sergiu Comissiona, Bar-Illan presented the world premiere of Robert Starer's Piano Concerto No.3. "Performance of the concerto represents a technical tour de force," said Elliot W. Galkin in the Baltimore *Sun.* "The work requires an interpreter of unflagging verve and flexible musicianship and it could have had no more convincing a protagonist than Mr. Bar-Illan."

Bar-Illan, whose home is an apartment on West End Avenue in New York City, was married to Willetta Warberg, in 1954. Thirteen years later, after the birth of a son and a daughter, they were divorced. In 1968 Bar-Illan married Beverly Slater of Pittsburgh, Pennsylvania. His children live with them. In addition to music, his interests include mathematics, history, archeology, and writing articles on psychology and music for such American magazines as *Saturday Review, Esquire,* and *High Fidelity.* In 1973, with Patricia Barnes, he formed the ad hoc committee for the Panovs, the dancers who for a time were prevented from immigrating to Israel by the Soviet authorities. Bar-Illan is a member of the executive council of the Greater New York Conference on Soviet Jewry.

While continuing a full concert schedule in the United States and Europe and maintaining his New York residence, Bar-Illan became artist-in-residence and professor of the piano at Southern Methodist University in Dallas, Texas. In 1976 he left Dallas to occupy similar posts at the University of Cincinnati Conservatory.

ABOUT: Ewen, D. Famous Instrumentalists. *Periodicals*—Musical America, December 1961.

Georges Barrère

1876–1944

Georges Barrère, flutist, was born in Bordeaux, France, on October 31, 1876, the second of three sons of Gabriel François (a maker of furniture) and Marie Périne Barrère. His immediate family was not musical. When Georges was about three his family moved to Paris. There, as a schoolboy, Georges would pipe out tunes on a tin whistle during recess. His little friends were so enchanted with his playing that they entreated him to give them lessons, and there was a run on toy whistles in the shops. Later on Georges joined a military class at the Bataillons Scolaires, where he became sergeant of the fife and drum corps. One of his teachers, a former student of the Paris Conservatory, recognized Georges's talent for music and persuaded him to begin flute lessons in 1889. A year later, Georges became an auditor in Henri Altès's class at the Paris Conservatory. With the help of Altès he was able to pass the Conservatory entrance examinations in October 1890 and become a regular member of Altès's flute class. Three years later Barrère began studying with Claude Paul Taffanel. He called this "the turning point in my life." He added: "If it were not for Taffanel I would probably be tooting today upon what the wood-flute players so irreverently call the 'gas-pipe.'" His

Barrère: ba rar′

Barrère

GEORGES BARRÈRE

teachers in harmony were Stéphane Raoul Pugno and Xavier Leroux.

A family quarrel led Georges to leave home while he was still a Conservatory student. He rented a room in a dingy hotel, so small that he was forced, as he said, "to use my bed for a music stand and to open the windows in order to have the elbow room necessary to secure the correct position of the flute player." He supported himself by playing solo flute in the orchestra of the Folies Bergère and second flute in the Paris Opéra orchestra. He was even considering joining an act on the stage of the Folies Bergère when a reconciliation with his family brought him back home. Shortly after this he won first prize at the Conservatory for flute playing.

In 1895, after graduation from the Conservatory, he launched his professional career by reviving the Modern Society of Wind Instruments which Taffanel had organized in 1876. With this group he toured France, Spain, Portugal, Switzerland, and Belgium. The group gained such renown that it was soon subsidized by the French government. By the time the tenth anniversary of its revival was celebrated, the group could boast that it was responsible for the writing and introduction of eighty-one compositions.

Between 1899 and 1905 Barrère played the flute in the Schola Cantorum Orchestra conducted by Vincent D'Indy, and between 1900 and 1905 he was flutist of the Colonne Orchestra, rising there to the post of first flute in 1903. From 1897 to 1902 he also played the flute with the orchestra of the Paris Opéra and taught flute at the Schola Cantorum. In 1903 he was elected a member of the French Academy.

Barrère went to the United States in 1905 on the invitation of Walter Damrosch, who engaged him as first flutist of the New York Symphony Society. Describing his feelings at this time Barrère said: "I was young and eager and full of great dreams, and I was afraid and homesick, too. The thought of this adventure into a land strange to me filled me with contradictory feelings. One minute I was sure of success, and the next I seemed doomed to failure."

Barrère remained first flutist of the New York Symphony Society until 1928. During these years as an orchestral musician, he distinguished himself in recitals, in appearances with symphony orchestras, and as a guest artist with outstanding chamber music groups. In addition, he taught flute at the Institute of Musical Art in New York from 1905 to 1930 and at the Juilliard School of Music.

In 1906 Barrère formed the New York Symphony Wind Instruments Club. Four years later he organized the Barrère Ensemble of Wind Instruments (flute, oboe, clarinet, bassoon and horn), an American equivalent of the Parisian Modern Society. In 1914 he created the Barrère Little Symphony which, over a thirty-year period, gave about one hundred and fifty concerts a season in programs made up mostly of rarely heard music. At these concerts Barrère was not only the conductor but also a commentator. Sometimes he appeared also as a flute soloist. "These entertainments fill a unique place in the plethoric life of this metropolis," wrote a critic for the New York *World-Telegram*. "The charm of their informality and their intimacy, heightened by the inimitable talks with which Mr. Barrère prefaces each number that he conducts has not its equal hereabouts."

At one time the Barrère Little Symphony provided the music for the dance recitals of Isadora Duncan and her pupils. At these performances, as Isadora Duncan recalled in her autobiography, Barrère "played so divinely that I often found myself immobile on the stage, with the tears flowing from my eyes just from the ecstasy of listening to him, and the singing of the violins and the whole orchestra soaring upwards and inspired."

Barrère also helped to form the Barrère-Britt Concertino, which featured in its concerts solo

Mattia Battistini

1856–1928

appearances of Barrère as flutist and Horace Britt as cellist. He also started the Barrère-Britt-Salzedo Trio, whose other two members were Carlos Salzedo, harpist, and Horace Britt. After a series of concerts in Mexico City, the members of this trio were elected honorary professors at the Superior School of Music of the National University of Mexico.

Barrère performed on a platinum flute in preference to the wooden one favored by most of his colleagues. As a student he preferred a silver instrument which, when he became successful, he exchanged for one of gold, and still later on, for a platinum one.

In the spring of 1934 Barrère was made Chevalier of the Legion of Honor, a decoration bestowed on him by the Consul General of France in New York. At a dinner given Barrère by his friends to celebrate this event, Harold Bauer said: "In my wide acquaintance with the greatest musical artists, Georges Barrère takes his place with the highest."

Barrère married Cécile Élise Allombert on July 6, 1917. They had a son. (He had two children by an earlier marriage to Michelette Buran which ended in divorce in 1916.) The Barrère winter home, during the later years of his life, was an apartment on Riverside Drive in New York City. Summers were spent at a house in Woodstock, New York. Barrère became an American citizen in 1937.

Barrère looked "like a professor of Greek in some Wesleyan University," according to Frank Crane. He was of medium height and had sparkling eyes which often twinkled mischievously. His favorite haunt for many years was his summer house in Woodstock. There his beard was a familiar sight. One of his hobbies was to solve crossword puzzles.

On June 14, 1944, after suffering a stroke Georges Barrère died of encephalomalacia in Kingston, New York. He was buried in Woodstock.

ABOUT: De Lorenzo, L. My Complete Story of the Flute. *Periodicals*—New York Times, June 15, 1944.

Mattia Battistini, baritone, was born in Rome on February 27, 1856. He received his vocal training from Veneslao Persichini, Luigi Mancinelli, and Augusto Rotoli before making his debut at the Teatro Argentina in Rome in 1878 as Alfonso in *La Favorita*. A season in Buenos Aires was followed by further appearances in Rome and at the Teatro Regio in Turin in 1880, Covent Garden in London in 1883, and San Carlo in Naples in 1886.

His fame as one of the great baritones of his generation was established from 1888 on when he sang at La Scala in Milan. He remained there until the end of his career in 1924. His triumphs extended beyond Milan, particularly to the Imperial Opera in St. Petersburg, to Covent Garden during the seasons of 1905 and 1906, and in guest appearances in Paris, Berlin, Vienna, Monte Carlo, Lisbon, Madrid, Barcelona, Moscow, and Warsaw. His dread of sea travel kept him from going to the United States though he was repeatedly invited.

Called "the king of baritones" or "the glory of Italy," he was heard in over eighty roles, principally in the Italian repertory; he was also highly acclaimed in the roles of Don Giovanni, Werther, and Eugen Onegin. So highly did Jules Massenet regard him that he rewrote the tenor role in *Werther* for a baritone so that Battistini might star in it. The extraordinary range of his voice, flawless in the high register, and its expressiveness and beauty were widely admired as were his remarkable legato and his virtuosity in florid passages. He remained in full control of his vocal technique until his last days on the stage. When he returned to London in 1922 and 1923 for recitals after an absence of a decade, he was once again a sensation. In 1924 Battistini retired from the opera stage. He continued to give recitals until 1927, when his withdrawal from an active singing career became complete. He died on his estate at Collebaccaro, near Rome, on November 7, 1928.

Battistini recorded some one hundred sides from as early as 1903 to as late as 1924. Three albums of his recordings were re-pressed and

Battistini: bät tḕs tē′ nḕ

MATTIA BATTISTINI

re-released in 1972 by Perennial Records, the first three of a projected eight-part collection. Reviewing these recordings in *Stereo Review,* George Jellinek wrote: "He was of an earlier era; not only was his singing style different, but his performing attitude was more self-serving and autocratic." In the New York *Times* Dale Harris said: "Certainly no baritone I have encountered in the last thirty years has come anywhere near matching Battistini's combination of vocal splendor and artistic finesse. None of them has displayed the mastery of line, the purity of tone, the sheer eloquence of his 1911 'Di Provenza' from *La Traviata* in which he phrases like a noble cellist and, in response to the unfolding drama of the words, adjusts the vocal color like a great actor."

ABOUT: Kutsch, K. J. and Riemens, L. A Concise Biographical Dictionary of Singers; Monaldi, G. Cantanti Celebri, vol. 2.

Harold Bauer

1873–1951

Harold Victor Bauer, pianist, was born in Kingston-on-Thames, near London, on April 28, 1873. His father, Victor, was German; his mother, Mary Taylor Bauer, English. The whole family was musical. As a child of four, Harold Bauer revealed his own musical inclinations by composing an eight-measure polka. His aunt began teaching him the piano; and his father, the violin; it was for the violin that the boy initially showed talent. In his tenth year he made his public debut as violinist in London in a performance of Mendelssohn's Violin Concerto. A year later he played for Joseph Joachim, who was so impressed that he offered to place him in the newly established Royal College of Music in London for further training. Bauer's father disapproved, and Harold became a private pupil of Adolf Politzer, in violin. In 1891, Harold organized a string quartet in London, in which he played first violin.

In the early 1890s Bauer began studying the piano seriously with Graham Moore. Moore introduced Bauer to Paderewski who, after hearing Bauer play, remarked facetiously: "You must become a pianist because you have such beautiful hair." On Paderewski's recommendation, Daniel Mayer, a concert manager, took Bauer under his wing and arranged for him to give a piano recital at Erard Hall in London in November 1892. As Bauer himself revealed, that concert "attracted no attention and I have no record of any comment made upon it in any newspaper."

In the spring of 1893 Bauer left England for Paris where he remained for the next twenty years. There he studied the violin with Wladyslaw Gorski and piano with Paderewski. "He was wonderfully kind to me in many ways," Bauer wrote about Paderewski, "and occasionally let me play the piano for him after he had worked on the new concertos he was studying, in which I accompanied him on a second piano. I learned a great deal from my temporary association with this great man." Bauer made his debut as a pianist in Paris in 1893 when he assisted his violin teacher, Gorski, in a performance of César Franck's Violin Sonata.

Bauer was still playing both the violin and the piano and still showing greater interest in developing a career as concert violinist when, in 1894–1895, he was booked to tour Russia as an assisting artist to a singer, named Louise Nicholson. When both artists arrived in St. Petersburg they discovered that because of the recent death of the Czar no concerts were permitted in Russia's principal cities. The two artists, therefore, were compelled to appear in small towns exclusively. With no piano accompanist available in those out-of-the-way places Bauer was obliged to accompany Nicholson and fill out the program

HAROLD BAUER

with piano solos. When the ban against concerts was lifted, the manager decided to save expenses by utilizing Bauer as an accompanist as well as solo pianist. These experiences helped to develop Bauer's interest in the piano.

In Madrid in the autumn of 1895 he appeared as a soloist with a symphony orchestra in two concerts. Two successful piano recitals followed in Amsterdam. Willem Mengelberg, the distinguished conductor of the Concertgebouw Orchestra, heard Bauer and engaged him to appear as soloist with his orchestra. A performance with the Berlin Philharmonic Orchestra followed. At a festival honoring Saint-Saëns in Paris, where Bauer performed Saint-Saëns's G minor Piano Concerto, the composer was effusive in his praise and congratulations. Other concerts in Europe, in some of which Bauer was heard in joint recitals with Pablo Casals, extended his reputation. Joint recitals in Spain, Bauer recalled, "created so much interest in the provincial towns where musical events were rare that a chain of musical societies known as Philharmonic clubs, which gave an annual series of concerts on a cooperative basis, was established as a result of our visit."

On November 30, 1900, Bauer made his American debut as piano soloist with the Boston Symphony under Wilhelm Gericke in Brahms's Piano Concerto No. 1. Though this work was new to Boston, and though Philip Hale, the Boston critic, disliked it, Bauer was acclaimed for his virtuosity and his musicianship in a taxing composition that made severe demands on both.

Until World War I he appeared regularly every two years in the United States in recitals, as guest artist with orchestras, and in chamber-music performances with the Kneisel Quartet. After one of Bauer's recitals in New York City, on March 10, 1906, Richard Aldrich, in the New York *Times,* called the performance "artistically truly a rare delight." He added: "He stands apart from most virtuosos upon the piano in the profoundly artistic nature of what he does, in the high distinction of his playing, in the entire disregard of any personal display or any personal effect."

Before World War I Bauer recorded for Aeolian in the United States the Saint-Saëns Piano Concerto in G minor, one of the earliest recordings made of a concerto. After the records were released, they were heard in a special concert at the Academy of Music in Philadelphia where the Philadelphia Orchestra under Stokowski performed the accompaniment live while Bauer's playing was heard through the recording. This stunt was so successful that it was subsequently repeated by Walter Damrosch in New York City and Alfred Hertz in San Francisco.

In Europe, in addition to his recitals and appearances with orchestra, Bauer was often a participant in trio concerts with Jacques Thibaud, violinist, and Pablo Casals, cellist, and in joint recitals with the violinists Fritz Kreisler and Eugène Ysaÿe and with the pianist Ossip Gabrilowitsch.

Bauer was scheduled to make his first world tour in 1914. He gave some concerts in Honolulu and Australia. When World War I broke out in Europe, the tour ended in Adelaide where Bauer made hurried arrangements to return to the United States. During the war he was kept busy giving recitals, and on one occasion he toured with the Boston Symphony Orchestra as its soloist.

After 1914 the United States became his permanent residence, and in 1921 he became an American citizen. His performances as a soloist and with chamber-music ensembles made him one of the most highly esteemed pianists in the United States. In the *Herald Tribune* Lawrence Gilman spoke of him as "a poet and lyric rhapsodist." Henry T. Finck wrote in the New York *Post* that Bauer possessed "the absolute perfection of interpretation."

In addition to his performances as a pianist,

Bauer distinguished himself as a teacher of master classes in piano throughout the United States, as the editor of many piano works, and as the transcriber for the piano of Beethoven's *Grosse Fugue*. He founded the Beethoven Association in New York in 1919, an organization of outstanding performing artists who contributed their services for the advancement of important musical causes as well as for the performances of Beethoven's music. This organization played a major role in the musical life of New York City for twenty-one years. It suspended operations in 1940. One of its achievements was the publication of Thayer's monumental biography of Beethoven, revised by Henry E. Krehbiel.

In 1917 Bauer helped to found the Manhattan School of Music in New York. He remained affiliated with this school until his death.

Though Bauer was at the peak of his artistry at a time when the recording industry was still in its comparative infancy, he managed to record two hundred disks. He was also frequently heard over the radio in the United States and participated in what has been described as "the first demonstration ever staged of moving pictures combined with sound."

Claude Debussy, who greatly admired Bauer's performances of his piano music, dedicated *Ondine* to him. France presented Bauer with the rosette of the Legion of Honor and the London Philharmonic Orchestra awarded him its gold medal.

Bauer married Marie Knapp, a German girl from Stuttgart, in Paris in 1906. After her death Bauer married Winnie Pyle, a pianist. Neither marriage produced children.

For many years Bauer spent his winters in New York City and his summers at a country home on Long Island, where he could swim and garden. A genial, warm-hearted man, he was fond of telling stories spiced with piquant humor.

His last years were spent in Miami. Having retired from the concert stage just before World War II, he devoted himself to teaching. He died in Miami on March 12, 1951.

ABOUT: Bauer, H. Harold Bauer: His Book; Schonberg, H. C. The Great Pianists. *Periodicals*—Musical Quarterly, October 1947.

Sir Thomas Beecham

1879–1961

Godfrey Thomas Beecham, one of the greatest English conductors, was born in St. Helens, Lancashire, England, on April 29, 1879. He was the second of eight children, the oldest son of Sir Joseph and Josephine Burnett Beecham. Sir Joseph, from whom Thomas ultimately inherited both wealth and the baronetcy, was the head of Beecham, Inc. (manufacturer of Beecham's Pills), a chemical firm founded and made successful by his father. As a music lover and a collector of ancient musical instruments, Sir Joseph encouraged Thomas in his early musical interests, although he made it clear from the first that music was to remain an avocation and that Thomas was ultimately intended to enter his father's prosperous business establishment.

When Thomas was six the family moved to Huyton, six miles south of St. Helens. That year the boy heard his first concert, a piano recital. Late that night, unable to sleep, he awoke his parents to tell them he wanted to study the piano. A local organist by the name of Unsworth gave him lessons, and Thomas advanced sufficiently in two years to be able to give a piano recital in St. Helens. His musical nature was further nourished by regular visits to Liverpool to attend opera performances of the Carl Rosa Company. *Faust* was the first opera Thomas heard, followed by *Aida, Romeo and Juliet,* and *Cavalleria Rusticana.* The boy was so taken with the last of these operas that he purchased a piano score and played it continually.

From 1892 to 1897 he went to the Rossall School in Lancashire where he was given some instruction in theory. For an additional eighteen months he attended Wadham College, Oxford. Though his interests during these years were varied, including literature (he was an avid reader from early boyhood) and sports (he preferred tennis, football, and cricket), music was his passion. He played the piano at school concerts and the bass drum in the cadet corps. He wrote songs and instrumental pieces. When the Hallé Orchestra visited Lancashire in 1894, he managed to get himself placed in the percussion section.

A trip to Germany and Italy in the spring of 1898 brought him new musical experiences and persuaded him that his place was not in the halls

SIR THOMAS BEECHAM

of academe but in music. Overriding his father's objections, Thomas left Wadham College without a degree and settled at his family home in Huyton. He founded his own orchestra, the St. Helens Orchestral Society, made up of members of the Hallé Orchestra and other professional musicians from Manchester and Liverpool. The first concert, presenting music by Mendelssohn, Rossini, and Grieg, took place at the Town Hall on November 11, 1899. The orchestra gave a second concert, its last, on December 14.

Meanwhile, on December 6, 1899, the Hallé Orchestra under Hans Richter was scheduled to give a concert in Huyton to celebrate Sir Joseph Beecham's installation as mayor. When Richter was unable to appear, Thomas Beecham stepped in as a substitute, conducting from memory Beethoven's Fifth Symphony, a movement from Tchaikovsky's *Symphonie Pathétique,* and two compositions by Wagner.

Thomas's determination to pursue a career in music brought about a sharp break with his father, and he left home in 1900 to make his way in London. In 1902 he was appointed conductor of the Kelson Truman Opera Company that toured the provinces of England. On July 27, 1903, he married Utica Celestia Welles of New York. They spent their honeymoon on the Continent where Beecham enriched his musical background by attending concerts and coming into contact with many of Europe's leading musicians.

Back in England, he hired an orchestra and conducted his first concert in London at Queen's

Hall in December 1905. It was a failure and Beecham realized that he needed more study. He spent a year studying orchestral scores, memorizing treatises on conducting, and attending orchestral concerts. Then between November 1906 and January 1907 he conducted four orchestral concerts at Bechstein Hall in London which were so well regarded that Beecham was encouraged to found another symphony orchestra. The New Symphony Orchestra gave its first concert in London on November 2, 1907, and continued to give regular performances under Beecham in programs emphasizing unfamiliar music of the past and works by many still unrecognized contemporary English composers. During this period with the New Symphony Orchestra Beecham started to promote the works of Frederick Delius, whose subsequent fame owed a profound debt to Beecham's persistent performances of his compositions when Delius was still unknown.

Beecham withdrew as the conductor of the New Symphony in 1909 because the men refused to obey his order to abandon the "deputy system," which allowed them to fill other jobs and to send in substitutes at rehearsals and concerts when they found more profitable engagements elsewhere. This orchestra continued to function under the leadership of Landon Ronald; in time it became the nucleus of the Royal Albert Hall Orchestra.

In 1908 Beecham formed still another orchestra, the Beecham Orchestra, insuring each of its musicians a living wage so that they could devote themselves completely to these concerts. The first performance by this group took place on February 22, 1909. With this organization Beecham became recognized as one of the most innovative and influential English conductors of his time, and as an interpreter of uncommon penetration and powers in reading symphonic music—particularly the music of Mozart, Purcell, Handel, and Delius.

Beecham's mounting success helped to bring about a reconciliation with his father. On several occasions Sir Joseph went incognito to his son's concerts and with increasing frequency began to express pride in his son's musical achievements. The reconciliation finally took place at a gala performance of Dame Ethel Smyth's opera *The Wreckers,* which was attended by King Edward.

Sir Joseph now stood ready to place his enormous financial resources at his son's disposal.

Beecham

Thomas Beecham used those resources to form the Beecham Opera Company which performed at Covent Garden and at His Majesty's Theatre. In its first season, on February 22, 1910, Beecham gave the premiere in England of Delius's *A Village Romeo and Juliet.* In his first two seasons he spent over two hundred thousand pounds, and by 1920 the deficit had passed well beyond three hundred thousand pounds.

During this decade performances of opera in England entered a glorious new era. In the dual role of conductor and impresario Beecham was responsible for the presentation of 120 operas, nearly every important work in the repertory and some 60 that were comparative or total strangers to London operagoers. "I mounted operas more for the purpose of hearing the music myself than for giving pleasure to the public," he remarked facetiously. In 1911 Beecham brought the Diaghilev Ballet Russe to London. In another season the concentration was on Russian operas, with Feodor Chaliapin in the title role of *Boris Godunov,* and with the production of such novelties as Mussorgsky's *Khovantchina* and Rimsky-Korsakov's *Ivan the Terrible.* Other seasons were devoted either entirely or partly to comic operas, or to Wagner's music dramas. Richard Strauss's first operatic masterworks—*Salome, Elektra, Der Rosenkavalier*—received their initial English hearings. "I think," wrote the New York music critic Lawrence Gilman many years later, "that unbiased British musicians would agree with me that Beecham has done more to stimulate and enrich the musical life of England than any other musician of his time. . . . Beecham is not only the most eminent of living British musicians in the interpretative field, but he is an artistic figure of unique vitality, fascination, courage, and genius."

During World War I Beecham helped keep musical activity alive in London by directing opera performances at Drury Lane under severely inhibiting and restrictive conditions. He conducted a performance of *The Marriage of Figaro* during an air raid. In the spring of 1915 he led some of the Promenade concerts at Albert Hall. When war conditions seriously threatened the survival of the Royal Philharmonic Orchestra, he came to its financial rescue, and in addition he conducted its concerts. He also provided badly needed financial sustenance to the Hallé Orchestra in Manchester and to the London Symphony Orchestra. In the fall of 1915 he initiated the first of two seasons of opera performances using native talent exclusively.

For his services to English music Beecham was knighted on January 1, 1916. Later that year he succeeded to the title of baronet on the death of his father.

His extravagance, particularly in the field of opera, entailed a personal loss of several million dollars and brought him to bankruptcy. In 1919 a liquidator seized all the scenery, props, and wardrobe of his opera company. As a result of business and legal entanglements he was forced in the summer of 1920 to withdraw from all musical activity. But three years later he was back in the musical arena. On April 8, 1923, at the Royal Albert Hall in London he conducted the combined forces of the London Symphony Orchestra and the Royal Albert Hall Orchestra in a program made up of works by Mozart, Berlioz, Delius, and Richard Strauss. A year later he led a performance of *Die Meistersinger* at His Majesty's Theater. "Beecham," wrote Dame Ethel Smyth, "was at last master of his own soul. Up to the present, the multifariousness of his gifts, combined with his inexhaustible energy and the high tension of his spirit, had in a certain sense been his undoing. Owner and organizer of everything he touched, as well as artistic factotum, repetitor, and conductor, he had been trying to put through a task single-handed that was beyond mortal powers."

His main activity following his return to the London concert scene was to serve as conductor of the London Symphony Orchestra until 1932. In 1929 he directed a festival of Delius's music in six concerts with all of the composer's major works represented and some of his less familiar compositions included. Delius, then blind and paralyzed, heard the festival on a litter surrounded by flowers. "This festival," he told the audience, "has been the time of my life."

In 1932 Beecham again founded an orchestra, the London Philharmonic, which gave its first performance on October 7, 1932. After a season in London the London Philharmonic toured the English provinces and the Continent. In November 1936 Beecham and the London Philharmonic visited Nazi Germany, giving eight concerts in principal cities—his inaugural concert in Berlin was attended by Adolf Hitler and his cabinet. From 1933 to 1939 Beecham served as artistic director of the International Season at Covent Garden.

Beecham made his debut in the United States as guest conductor of the New York Philharmonic Orchestra on January 12, 1928, the same concert in which Vladimir Horowitz made his American bow. Reporting in the New York *Times*, Olin Downes wrote: "He always conveyed the big line and the rhythmic breadth of the music, conducting with entire authority, without affectation, with directness and vitality." From this time on, Beecham made numerous tours of the United States as guest conductor of major American orchestras. From 1941 to 1943 he served as principal conductor of the Seattle Symphony Orchestra in the state of Washington. In the years between 1942 and 1944 he was guest conductor at the Metropolitan Opera House, making his debut there on January 15, 1942, in a dual bill made up of Johann Sebastian Bach's *Phoebus and Pan* and Rimsky-Korsakov's *Le Coq d'Or*. "It was Sir Thomas' evening," wrote Oscar Thompson in the New York *Sun*. "Some of the applause directed his way was as shrill as it was voluminous." The other operas conducted by Beecham at the Metropolitan were *Faust, Carmen, Manon, Louise, Tristan and Isolde, Mignon, Falstaff*, and *The Tales of Hoffmann*.

In the United States in 1943 Beecham divorced his wife, from whom he had been separated for many years, and married Betty Humby, a concert pianist who had appeared as a soloist at several of his concerts.

The deterioration of orchestral performance in England during World War II led Beecham to organize one more new orchestra, the Royal Philharmonic, which gave its introductory performance in London on September 15, 1946. Within two years it became one of Europe's important symphonic organizations. In the fall of 1950 Beecham brought his orchestra to the United States for a 64-day tour of 43 cities in 52 concerts.

In 1951 Beecham returned to Covent Garden, after a twelve-year absence, in a performance of *Die Meistersinger*. During the summer of 1957 he was in Buenos Aires conducting operatic performances at the Teatro Colón. There his wife died of a heart attack. On August 10, 1959, Beecham, while filling conducting commitments at the Lucerne Music Festival, married his twenty-seven-year-old secretary, Shirley Hudson.

Beecham was touring the United States early in 1960 when he was stricken by virus pneumonia. He was forced to cancel his remaining American concerts and his engagement at Covent Garden for five performances of Berlioz' *Les Troyens*. By late April he had recovered sufficiently to be able to conduct a symphony concert at Festival Hall. He was scheduled for ten performances of *The Magic Flute* at the Glyndebourne Festival that summer but he suffered a heart attack. A year of rest at a nursing home seemed to promise recovery. Beecham made elaborate plans for further concert and operatic appearances and for recording sessions. Then a second heart attack proved fatal; he died at his flat in London on March 8, 1961. Two days later he was buried in Brockwood Cemetery in Surrey.

Throughout his career, Beecham was indefatigable in promoting new English music. Some of many world premieres he presented were Arnold Bax's Symphony No.5 (January 15, 1934), Havergal Brian's *Hero and Leander* (December 3, 1908), Delius's posthumous opera *Irmelin* (May 4, 1953), Delius's Mass (June 7, 1909), Cyril Scott's Piano Concerto (May 15, 1915), Cyril Scott's *Two Passacaglias* (November 3, 1914), Vaughan Williams's *In the Fen Country* (February 22, 1909), and the final version of Vaughan Williams's *A London Symphony* (February 22, 1934).

He probably made more recordings than any other conductor. His first, in 1910, was excerpts from *The Tales of Hoffmann;* his last, in 1959, was a performance of Fauré's *Dolly's Suite* with the Orchestre National de la Radiodiffusion Française. In that half century Beecham made over four hundred recordings in a repertory that included almost everything Delius ever wrote, thirteen Haydn symphonies, two Mozart operas and a dozen or so of his symphonies, oratorios by Handel, the basic symphonic repertory, and *Carmen* among other operas.

Discussing Beecham's qualities as a conductor, Robert H. Hull, the English musicologist, wrote while Beecham was still alive: "The imaginative power to search out the heart of a composer's score and the practical talents to present the resultant findings with absolute fidelity . . . these qualities are possessed by Beecham in a consummate degree. He is gifted with superlative appreciation of musical design which gives to his reading a beautiful accuracy of proportion. His phrases are exquisitely moulded with an impulse of intense vitality, and his rhythmic sense is never failing in alertness and artistic judgment. He has extraordinarily acute feeling for elegance of the melodic line."

Lawrence Gilman once described Sir Thomas's personality as follows: "He is an anomaly, a playboy who is also a profound and sensitive poet; a musician of the most exacting taste and standards who is also the acme of casualness. . . . He loves to play outrageous pranks on the unwary. His wit and his sarcasm can be devastating."

His acerbic wit was almost as famous as his conducting. About English music he said: "British composition is in a state of perpetual promise. It might be said to be one long promissory note." The invention of talking motion pictures inspired the following comment: "The movies are sheer bedlam in a madhouse. Now that silent films are through you can't go anywhere and hear nothing." When, during a rehearsal, one of the singers complained she could not synchronize her singing with that of the tenor because he insisted "on dying too soon," Beecham replied quickly: "Madam, surely you must be mistaken. No tenor can die soon enough for me." At a performance of *Aida* one of the horses in the triumphal scene yielded to physical necessity. "Upon my word," Beecham whispered to the orchestra players, "a critic."

Though he possessed extraordinary gifts at organization when he was founding and running orchestras and opera houses, he was hopelessly slipshod in his daily behavior. He habitually came to rehearsals one or more hours late. He never answered the telephone, was dilatory in replying to letters, and was irresponsible in keeping appointments. When he traveled he almost never left a forwarding address, so that even his most intimate friends were unable to get in touch with him. Though he owned several houses, he would more often than not rent a suite at a hotel, even though one of his homes was nearby. The moment he settled in a hotel his room would instantly assume a state of disorder.

He was a man of many paradoxes. He looked like a member of Parliament, but his offstage behavior was more like that of Puck. He posed as a cynic, but essentially he was a sentimentalist and an idealist. He pursued his musical career with dedication and on the highest artistic level, yet many times he did not show up at his own concerts (with an assistant conductor forced to take over at the last moment); at other times,

when a guest conductor was scheduled to perform, he would sometimes appear at the concert hall, brush the conductor aside, and take over the concert himself.

Beecham arranged music of Handel into orchestral suites which have been used for ballets. These include *The Gods Go A-Begging, The Great Elopement, The Origin of Design,* and *The Faithful Shepherd.*

ABOUT: Beecham, T. A Mingled Chime; Cardus, N. Sir Thomas Beecham: A Portrait; Geismar, B. Two Worlds of Music; Reid, C. Sir Thomas Beecham: An Independent Biography; Smyth, E. Beecham and Pharaoh. *Periodicals*—High Fidelity, June 1965; Life, January 29, 1945; Musical America, May 1961; New York Times Magazine, September 25, 1949; Saturday Review, October 28, 1950.

Eduard van Beinum

1901–1959

Eduard Alexander van Beinum, conductor, was born in Arnhem, the Netherlands, on September 3, 1901, to Eduard Alexander and Antonia Polman van Beinum. The family had produced professional musicians for generations. His grandfather and great-grandfather were musicians, his father was a bass player and assistant conductor of the Arnhem Philharmonic; his older brother was a violinist and choral conductor. Eduard received his first music instruction on the violin and piano from his brother; later he took additional piano lessons with F. Hiller. For his academic education he attended the Hoogere Burger School in Arnhem.

At sixteen, Eduard joined the viola section of the Arnhem Philharmonic (not the violin section, as is often erroneously reported). A year later, on a scholarship, he entered the Amsterdam Conservatory, a pupil of Sem Dresden, Bernard Zweers, and J. B. C. de Pauw, specializing in the piano.

After completing his conservatory studies in 1921, he made appearances both as a violinist and as a violist; he also served as piano accompanist for other artists. He conducted choirs in Schiedam and Zutphen, before his appointment as conductor of the Haarlem Orchestral Association, with which he made his debut as sym-

Beinum: bā´nŭm

EDUARD VAN BEINUM

phony conductor in 1926. On July 12, 1927, he married Josepha Antonia Anna Maria Jansen, a concert violinist, with whom he made numerous appearances in chamber music concerts. The van Beinums had two sons.

In 1931 van Beinum succeeded Cornelis Dopper as second conductor of the Concertgebouw Orchestra of Amsterdam, led by Willem Mengelberg. In 1938 ill health compelled Mengelberg to cut down his schedule, and van Beinum shared the post of first conductor with Bruno Walter. He also made guest appearances with other major European orchestras; in 1937 he toured the Soviet Union with the Leningrad Symphony.

Van Beinum abandoned his musical activities after the Nazis invaded Holland in 1940. Following Holland's liberation—and with Mengelberg discredited because he was a collaborationist—van Beinum was appointed the music director of the Concertgebouw in 1945. Only three men have held this post since the orchestra's founding in 1888, the other two being Mengelberg and Willem Kes.

As the principal conductor of the Concertgebouw (with which he toured Europe in 1945), as the sole conductor of the London Royal Philharmonic Orchestra in 1948–1949 (even while holding down his post in Amsterdam), and as a guest conductor of major symphonic organizations throughout Europe, van Beinum achieved international renown as one of Europe's top conductors. Certainly he was the foremost conductor in Holland since Mengelberg. A musician of

impeccable taste who was sparing in his gestures (dispensing with a baton) and undemonstrative in his podium behavior, he was a penetrating interpreter of an extensive repertory, ever faithful to the demands of the composer rather than concerned for personalized readings.

He made his American debut as guest conductor of the Philadelphia Orchestra in January 1954 in a program of Bruckner's Seventh Symphony and a symphony by Haydn. When the Philadelphia Orchestra under van Beinum was heard soon afterwards in New York City, Olin Downes wrote in the New York *Times* that he was "clearly a past master of his craft, being indeed one of the most skillful and polished conductors we have heard in seasons." In the *Herald Tribune* Virgil Thomson stated: "Eduard van Beinum . . . gave a performance of Bruckner's Seventh Symphony that was at once delicate and majestic. . . . This rendering enabled us to recognize in the conductor . . . a musician of taste and authority."

In the fall of 1954 van Beinum returned to the United States to tour the country with the Concertgebouw Orchestra in its first appearance in America. When the tour opened in New York City on October 13, 1954, Olin Downes reported: "It was the glory of the orchestra itself, the sincerity and passion of the players to give of their best, and the high musicianship and evident idealism of Mr. van Beinum that made the occasion a triumph of art."

During this visit to the United States van Beinum received an honorary doctorate in music from Rutgers University. He returned to America again in 1955 to conduct at the Empire State Music Festival in Ellenville, New York, as well as in New York City, Chicago, San Francisco, Cleveland, Philadelphia, Pittsburgh, and Los Angeles.

His guest appearance with the Los Angeles Philharmonic on January 12, 1956, proved so successful that he was engaged as its music director. He held this post while continuing to fulfill his commitments with the Concertgebouw Orchestra, commuting between Los Angeles and Amsterdam by air.

Eduard van Beinum suffered a fatal heart attack on April 13, 1959, while rehearsing the Concertgebouw Orchestra. The rehearsal had progressed about forty-five minutes when van Beinum suddenly asked his assistant to take

Berganza

over. Then, collapsing, he slid from the platform and died instantly.

Van Beinum was Officer and Chevalier of the French Legion of Honor and Officer of the Order of Orange-Nassau, in the Netherlands. He was also honored with the Order of the Star of the North from Sweden and the Order of Dannebrog from Denmark. After music his main interests were reading (history, philosophy, books on travel), riding horseback, and hunting.

ABOUT: Blaukopf, K. Great Conductors. *Periodicals* —New York Times, October 10, 1954; Time, January 18, 1954.

TERESA BERGANZA

Teresa Berganza

1934–

Teresa Berganza, mezzo-soprano, was born in Madrid on March 16, 1934, to Guillermo and María Ascensión Berganza. Teresa began piano study early and, as a pianist, was enrolled at the Madrid Conservatory. Since Conservatory students were required to pursue a second major subject she also began to take lessons in singing. Her singing teacher, Lola Rodriguez Aragon, a pupil of Elisabeth Schumann, was influential in redirecting Teresa from the piano to the voice. Teresa made such progress as a singing student that in 1954 she received the Conservatory's first prize at its annual competition—Premio Extraordinario Conservatorio de Madrid—together with the Premio Grande de Lucrezia Arana award. One year later she made her singing debut with a recital in Madrid. During the next two years she appeared in concerts in Spain, Portugal, France, Italy, Austria, and Germany, and won several prizes in international singing contests.

In 1957 she appeared as Dorabella in *Così fan Tutte* at the Aix-en-Provence Festival in France. Her performance was so successful that for several years she made annual appearances at this festival. She was also heard annually at the Glyndebourne Festival following her much acclaimed debut there in 1958 as Cherubino in *The Marriage of Figaro*.

In 1958 Berganza married the pianist-composer Felix Lavilla, who was her accompanist. Several months after her marriage she paid her first visit to the United States to make her American debut as Neris, in Cherubini's *Medea* (a performance in which Maria Callas sang the title role) with the Civic Opera in Dallas, Texas. Her nervousness, intensified by her first separation from her husband and her first appearance in the United States, made her lose her voice just before the debut. After intensive medical treatment the voice returned and she carried off the evening with glory. When, soon afterwards, she took on the role of Isabella in Rossini's *L'Italiana in Algieri,* John Rosenfeld, the music critic of the Dallas *Morning News,* described her performance as "an irresistible revelation."

Other successes followed. She made her debut at La Scala in Milan as Isolier in Rossini's *Le Comte Ory* and the flawless beauty of her voice and its sensuous dark-timbred sound won ovations from the audience and praise from the critics. This began a productive association with La Scala where she was highly esteemed.

In 1958 she toured England. At a reception following a recital at Leeds Festival, she met the British royal family. The Queen Mother was so taken with her singing that she attended Berganza's appearance with orchestra two days later. Then in 1959 Berganza made a triumphant debut at Covent Garden in London.

Appearances in opera, in recitals, and with orchestras throughout Europe as well as in North Africa and in Israel increased her fame. In June 1961 she achieved a personal triumph at La Piccola Scala in Milan in the title role of *L'Orontea*—the first opera of the Florentine master Cesti (first produced in Venice in 1649 and long since forgotten). Her success, reported the *Corriere Lombardo,* was on "the highest possible level."

She also began to make recordings on the London label: *Arias of the 18th Century* in 1961 and an album of Manuel de Falla's music in 1962. Both received important European awards.

After an absence of four years, Berganza returned to the United States in April 1962 to make her New York debut in the title role of Rossini's *La Cenerentola,* given a concert performance by the American Opera Society at Carnegie Hall. The critic of the *New Yorker* commented: "She revealed a voice of extraordinary qualities. ... It has an enormous range, reaching from the contralto to the high soprano register, and is produced throughout with the utmost evenness and with hauntingly expressive power of dramatic inflection. Its accuracy of intonation is virtually absolute, its flexibility is startling, and its habits of phrasing are invariably in good taste." When she gave her first American recital—at the Harvard Square series in Boston that fall—the critic of the Boston *Herald* described the concert as one "of crystalline loveliness." And he added: "Miss Berganza's voice is exceedingly pure, tonally ravishing and achieves profound communication." Three days later her first New York recital led the critic of the *Herald Tribune* to remark that "Berganza can do no wrong."

That year she made her first appearance with the Chicago Lyric Opera as Cherubino and returned to Dallas to take on the role of Rosina in *The Barber of Seville.* In 1964 she embarked on her first American coast-to-coast tour. The following season she made her first appearance over American television on the "Bell Telephone Hour." In the fall of 1966 Berganza sang Ottavia in a revival of Monteverdi's *L'Incoronazione di Poppea* by the Chicago Lyric Opera.

Her debut at the Metropolitan Opera was originally scheduled for February 1966 as Rosina. Postponed because of the birth of Berganza's third child, a daughter, that spring, the debut took place October 11, 1967, with Berganza as Cherubino in *The Marriage of Figaro.* Her petite figure, coquettish charm, and nobility and purity of classic style captured the hearts of audience and critics. When on November 7 she finally appeared as Rosina, Irving Kolodin (in the *Saturday Review*) found her to be a "performer

of cheerful charm, easy humor and appealing femininity . . . a Rosina who is a person rather than a mere purveyor of vocal tricks." That performance was recorded on tape for television.

In 1977 Berganza was heard in *La Cenerentola* at the Paris Opéra, and at the Edinburgh Festival she sang her first Carmen.

Berganza is the youngest artist ever to be honored with the Grand Cross of the Order of Isabel the Catholic by Spain. Her home is in Madrid. She absents herself from home only six weeks at a time so that she may be better able to devote herself to her family. Her favorite forms of relaxation are hunting and fishing.

ABOUT: Newsweek, December 24, 1962; Opera News, February 25, 1967; Time, June 23, 1961.

Carlo Bergonzi

1924–

Carlo Bergonzi, tenor, was born on July 13, 1924, in the small Italian town of Vidalenzo, a few miles from Busseto, where Verdi was born. He received his musical training (three years of voice and five years of piano) at the Arrigo Boïto Conservatory in Parma. His opera debut was as a baritone in Lecce in 1948, in the role of Figaro in *The Barber of Seville.* He continued to sing baritone roles for the next three years, principally Marcello in *La Bohème,* the elder Germont in *La Traviata,* the title role in *Rigoletto,* and Dr. Malatesta in *Don Pasquale.*

In 1951 he sang for the first time as a tenor, at the Teatro Petruzelli in Bari in the title role of *Andrea Chénier.* That year he also sang the leading tenor roles in a series of Verdi operas produced by RAI, the Italian radio, in commemoration of the fiftieth anniversary of the composer's death.

Following guest appearances at the San Carlo in Naples and in opera houses in Brescia and Rome, Bergonzi achieved his first successes in leading tenor roles in the Italian repertory at La Scala in Milan and he became one of its principal tenors. Engagements in Spain, Portugal, England, Monte Carlo, and South America added to his expanding reputation.

In 1955 Bergonzi made his debut in the United States with the Chicago Opera in a dual bill comprising Puccini's *Il Tabarro* (as Michele)

Bergonzi

CARLO BERGONZI

and *Cavalleria Rusticana* (as Turiddu). His first appearance at the Metropolitan Opera in New York came one year later, on April 13, 1956, in one of his finest roles, Radames in *Aida*. Three days later he appeared as Manrico in *Il Trovatore*. The critics found much to praise in the elegance of his vocal styling, the purity and texture of his voice, and the effectiveness of his characterizations. What his voice may have lacked in robustness it compensated for in subtlety of phrasing and beauty of tone. For the next two decades Bergonzi remained one of the mainstays of the Italian and French repertory at the Metropolitan Opera. Following the roles of Radames and Manrico, he was heard as Cavaradossi in *Tosca,* Rodolfo in *La Bohème,* Don José in *Carmen,* Don Alvaro in *La Forza del Destino,* the title role in *Andrea Chénier,* Edgardo in *Lucia di Lammermoor,* Pinkerton in *Madama Butterfly,* Macduff in *Macbeth,* Des Grieux in *Manon Lescaut,* Canio in *I Pagliacci,* Gabriele in *Simon Boccanegra,* Riccardo in *Un Ballo in Maschera,* the title role in *Ernani,* the Duke in *Rigoletto,* Nemorino in *L'Elisir d'Amore,* Enzo in *La Gioconda,* Alfredo in *La Traviata,* and Turiddu in *Cavalleria Rusticana.*

Following a performance as Riccardo on January 25, 1962, Winthrop Sargeant in the *New Yorker* called Bergonzi's interpretation of the role "somewhat light, but very pleasing and elegant." When Bergonzi appeared on October 14, the opening night of the 1963–1964 season, as Radames in a new production of *Aida,* Alan Rich reported in the *Herald Tribune:* "Carlo

Bergonzi, whose voice is not in itself an absorbing instrument, was nevertheless able to demonstrate in his singing the way to make a Verdian line touch the heart."

He has combined his work at the Metropolitan with regular appearances at La Scala and guest performances with the Vienna State Opera, Munich Opera, Hamburg Opera, Rome Opera, the San Carlo in Naples, the Verona Arena, the Teatro Colón in Buenos Aires, and other American and European opera companies. In Italy, Bergonzi has appeared in three of Verdi's little-known operas: as Foresto in *Attila,* as Jacopo Foscari in *I Due Foscari,* and as Carlo in *Giovanna d'Arco.*

On April 13, 1977, with the Opera Orchestra of New York, Bergonzi was heard in the title role of Puccini's early and rarely heard *Edgar* (an American premiere).

In all, his repertory embraces over sixty-five roles; in the more than a quarter of a century of operatic appearances in public and on records he has sung with every principal prima donna. He has also made successful appearances in concerts, though he waited until his fifty-third year to make his concert debut in the United States. This took place at Avery Fisher Hall at the Lincoln Center for the Performing Arts in New York on March 27, 1977.

Describing Bergonzi's vocalism, Peter G. Davis wrote in an anthology of Verdi arias: "His voice seems ideally placed to satisfy both the lyric and dramatic requirements . . . capable of spinning out graceful cavatinas as well as sounding a cry to battle. . . . Perhaps even more impressive are Mr. Bergonzi's sense of style and phrasing, his vitalization of a melody's rhythmic pulse, his unfailing instinct for proper attack."

When he is not singing he operates a small but elegant hotel-restaurant in Busseto, assisted by his wife, Adele, and their three sons. Bergonzi built the inn in 1965, after tearing down an existing hotel. Since Busseto is so near Verdi's birthplace and the Villa Sant' Agata where Verdi lived for fifty years, Bergonzi named his inn after one of Verdi's less familiar operas, *I Due Foscari.* When he finishes a performance at La Scala or when he is on vacation from the opera house, Bergonzi motors from Milan (where he maintains his permanent home) to his inn, a distance of some fifty miles, and assumes the role of restaurant proprietor. A gourmet and excellent cook, he has developed for his restaurant several culinary specialties which have won for him first prize from the Italian Culinary Society and the medal *Il Cuoco d'Oro.* Among these dishes are Chicche Verdi del Nonno Giuseppe (gnocchi made of potatoes and spinach with a secret sauce), Culatello (a delectable salami), Nido di Uova di Quaglie' Aurora (a quail's egg delicacy), and wild pheasant prepared according to his own undisclosed recipe.

ABOUT: High Fidelity/Musical America, May 1966; New York Times, April 3, 1977; Opera News, February 19, 1972.

Lazar Berman

1930–

LAZAR BERMAN

Lazar Berman, pianist, was born in Leningrad on February 26, 1930, the son of a working-class father and a mother who had been trained as a pianist by Isabelle Vengerova at the St. Petersburg Conservatory. As a child of two Lazar received piano lessons from his mother, Anna. He acquired enough of a repertory by ear to be able to make a public appearance by the time he was three. A half year later his mother tried unsuccessfully to place him in a competition for young pianists in Leningrad. She continued giving him lessons until the authorities in Leningrad took note of his talent and arranged for him to enter a special group of gifted young students at the Leningrad Conservatory, headed by Professor Samari Savshinsky.

Until his eighth year Lazar could not read or write a note of music, learning his repertory by ear while listening to his mother perform. Nevertheless, in 1937 he was able to enter a talent festival in Leningrad. Soon thereafter the authorities invited him and his family to live in Moscow so that Berman could enroll at the Central Music School. Lazar's piano teacher there, Alexander Goldenweiser, remained his piano instructor for the next eighteen years, guiding the prodigy carefully through his years not only at the Central Music School but also at the Moscow Conservatory from 1948 until his graduation in 1953 and then in graduate master classes until 1957. Meanwhile, in 1940 Lazar had made his first appearance as a soloist with orchestra, the Moscow Philharmonic under Grigori Stolyarov, in Mozart's Piano Concerto in C major, K.503. In 1942 he performed Liszt's *La Campanella* in a wartime broadcast from the Soviet Union to Great Britain.

During the early years of World War II, after the Nazis invaded the Soviet Union and menaced Moscow, the Bermans went to Penza where, for a time, Lazar studied with Theodore Gutman. On one occasion, since the Soviet government had moved to nearby Kuibyshev, Lazar was called there to perform for government officials Grieg's Piano Concerto in A minor with the Bolshoi Theater Orchestra.

In 1942 he returned to Moscow to continue his piano studies with Goldenweiser. In 1951 he won first prize at the International Youth Festival in East Germany. He also participated in two other competitions: in Budapest he earned third prize, and at the Queen Elisabeth competition in Brussels he placed fifth.

By the early 1950s Berman's phenomenal technique astonished not only his fellow students but also his teachers and the leading Soviet pianists. His name was mentioned in the same breath with that of Vladimir Horowitz for a virtuosity that seemed capable of playing faster and louder than any pianist alive. "For many years," Berman has said, "I was carried away with virtuosity, with naked technique. . . . My speed became a legend. . . . The harder a passage was the more it appealed to me. . . . I thought little about sound, only fingers, speed, perfect notes." Some of his fellow students used to clock him with a stopwatch; at one time they found he could negotiate the coda of Chopin's Sonata in

B minor in thirty seconds. "The only excuse for this was our youth—we thought music was like soccer or something," Berman explains.

Emil Gilels, the Soviet pianist, was one of those who recognized and appreciated Berman's technical powers. When Gilels paid his first visit to the United States in 1955, he singled out Sviatoslav Richter and Berman among the foremost Soviet pianists of the time. He referred to Berman—then a name totally unknown to the United States—as "a phenomenon of the music world."

Upon completing his master classes in 1956 Berman began concertizing in earnest, signing up with the Moscow Philharmonia, a concert bureau. During the next few years he covered the Soviet Union extensively; he also toured Czechoslovakia. He performed three concertos in a single evening in Brussels (the Tchaikovsky No.1, Prokofiev's No.3, and Rachmaninoff's No.3), a feat the newspapers described as "the concert of concerts." Berman's favorable impression of Brussels led him to organize the USSR-Belgium Friendship Society.

The 1960s proved for Berman a period of comparative concert inactivity. "I had no concerts at all in public," he says. "I was very much involved in contemplation and thought, and my artistic outlook changed." This was the time when he outgrew his fetish for virtuoso pyrotechnics and concerned himself with deeper musical values. Before 1968 he made some recordings for Melodiya, one of which, in 1962, introduced Berman's art to Americans. By the early 1970s his schedule of concertizing reverted to normal, but primarily in the Soviet Union. He did make a few tours of Italy, however. In 1971 his average concert audience in Italy numbered only four hundred; three years later it averaged 2,500.

By the time Berman made his debut in the United States he had become something of a legend among American musical *cognoscenti* due to the reports of his pianism filtering in from abroad and to the recordings that were being imported few though they were. Asked why it took him so long to come to the United States, Berman replied: "I was never invited."

One New York concert manager, Jacques Leiser, became interested in bringing him to America after hearing one of his recordings. "I had to keep reminding myself this wasn't some deceased giant from a golden age," Leiser has said, "but a pianist still living—I presumed—somewhere on this planet." He went to Moscow and made the necessary arrangements (often complex and difficult) with the music division of Russia's Ministry of Culture for Berman to make his first American tour, fifteen concerts covering nine states in thirty-seven days.

Arriving in the United States very much the legend come to life, Berman made his American debut with a recital in Oxford, Ohio, on January 14, 1976. His New York debut came three evenings later, as soloist with the Brooklyn Philharmonic Orchestra under Lukas Foss, in Tchaikovsky's Piano Concerto No.1. Harold C. Schonberg wrote in the New York *Times:* "Legendary? That remains to be seen. But the big Russian is indeed a pianist. . . . Mr. Berman . . . was careful to present a scrupulously note-perfect interpretation. It had a combination of power and finesse, and there never was a doubt that a master technician was at the keyboard." Berman's first New York recital on February 2, 1976, brought the following additional comment from Schonberg: "He is a big, big pianist, oriented to virtuoso Romantic music, with a big, big technique." In music by Liszt, Shostakovich, Prokofiev, and Rachmaninoff—Liszt particularly—Berman easily proved himself one of the elite of the keyboard. Reviewing Berman's performance of Liszt's Piano Concerto No.1 on February 5, 1976, with the New Jersey Symphony under Henry Lewis, Irving Kolodin wrote in the *Saturday Review:* "Berman's magnitude as a performer of Liszt . . . was his playing of the E-flat concerto, that stood out, among a hundred hearings, for being above and beyond any concern with technical difficulty and, in addition, for being musical in the extreme. Passages normally muddied or glossed over were immaculate and lovingly caressed; figurations that come from fingers of some as sequins had, in the Berman treatment, the sparkle of diamonds."

While Berman was touring the United States, his first recordings since 1968 were released in America. Two were Melodiya albums distributed by Columbia in the United States. Both carried the headings "The Legendary Lazar Berman Plays Liszt. The Phenomenon of the Music World." Two albums came from Deutsche Grammophon: the Tchaikovsky Piano Concerto No.1 with the Berlin Philharmonic under Herbert von Karajan, and an album of Prokofiev and Rachmaninoff music. Berman's first American recording, made at the Columbia studios in New York during this tour, a recording of two Beethoven sonatas (the *Appassionata* and the Op.31, No.3), was released later the same year.

Berman (affectionately known as Lialik) was described by *Time* as a "burly bear with stooped shoulders, ginger-colored beard and long brown hair that waves up at the neck." To Martin Ayer in the New York *Times* his appearance was "faintly sleepy" and his walk "lumbering." According to Barry James and Vadim Yurchenkov in *High Fidelity Magazine,* Berman's "Mephisto-type beard . . . makes him resemble a Russian Orthodox priest."

With his second wife, Valentina, and their little son, Pavel (a violin prodigy), Berman occupies a small, modest apartment on the thirteenth floor of a Moscow building housing artists and professional people. The walls of the living room are lined with original oils and photographs and filled with memorabilia of Berman's travels and nonmusical interests. His hobby is collecting stamps and coins. Each year he insists on spending four months of vacation with his family in a seaside resort. When traveling, he enjoys walking the streets aimlessly or visiting the museum in every city in which he finds himself.

Berman practices between six and seven hours every day in the week. "For me," he told Barry James and Vadim Yurchenkov, "the best style is the one with the most heart and the least possible academism. As a rule I love contrasting music—the interplay of soft and loud. For these reasons, I am more than anything a lover of the Romantics, particularly Liszt, Schumann, Rachmaninoff, the early Scriabin, Prokofiev."

ABOUT: High Fidelity, January 1976; New York Times, January 26, 1976, October 31, 1976; New York Times Magazine, October 23, 1977; Time, February 1, 1976.

Pierre Bernac

1899–

Pierre Bernac (originally Pierre Bertin), baritone, was born in Paris on January 12, 1899. He was the son of a broker prominent on the Parisian stock market. Though extremely musical, and though he received vocal training early in life, Pierre seemed headed for a career in finance;

for a time he was a member of his father's successful brokerage house. He detested the world of finance, however, and was increasingly absorbed with music. And so he used his recurrent bad health as the excuse to withdraw from the brokerage house and devote himself entirely to his musical interests.

He made his first public appearance at a charity concert in Paris. While continuing his vocal studies with various private teachers, he performed frequently as an amateur. In the winter of 1922 he gave a recital devoted exclusively to the songs of the contemporary French composer Roland-Manuel. André Caplet, French composer and conductor, came backstage to congratulate him and to urge him to consider seriously a professional career in music. Overriding his father's objections to such a move—his father wanted him to combine music with the operation of a jewelry shop—and stimulated by the guidance and interest of André Caplet and of Walther Straram, the conductor, Bertin intensified his study in preparation for a singing career. When he made his professional debut in Paris in 1926, he changed his name to Bernac to avoid confusion with the popular French actor Pierre Bertin.

On May 2, 1926, at the Salle des Agriculteurs in Paris, Bernac gave a recital in a program made up entirely of the songs of Georges Auric and Francis Poulenc. This was his first appearance as an interpreter of Poulenc's songs, with which he was to be so closely identified. He soon achieved recognition among the musical *cognoscenti* of France as an interpreter of other twentieth century French composers, notably Honegger, Milhaud, Debussy, and Ravel.

His determination to master the literature of German *Lieder* sent him to Salzburg in the summer of 1934 where he studied with Reinhold von Wahrlich. At a garden party that August in Salzburg he was invited to sing songs by Debussy. Since he did not have his accompanist with him, Francis Poulenc, one of the guests, volunteered his services. This marked the beginning of an artistic relationship between Bernac and Poulenc that lasted until the composer's death in 1963, Poulenc serving as Bernac's accompanist in song recitals in which many of Poulenc's works were heard and for which Poulenc specifically wrote numerous songs. The first such recital, at the Salzburg Festival in 1935, proved such a success that similar concerts followed throughout Europe.

As an interpreter of Poulenc's songs, with the composer as accompanist, Bernac has had few if any rivals. Poulenc's biographer, Henri Hell, wrote: "No one who has heard the legendary recitals of Bernac and Poulenc would question the contribution to their success of Poulenc's inimitable accompaniments. The partnership of the two artists was, moreover, exemplary in that each continued both to merge and to throw into relief the personality of the other."

During World War II Bernac drove a truck in the French army for three months. The French government had him give joint recitals with Poulenc in army camps and hospitals. After the fall of France in 1940—upon which a projected tour of South America was canceled—Bernac fled to southern France. But he was soon back in Paris where he remained throughout the war devoting himself to teaching as well as singing.

Bernac and Poulenc made their American debut with a joint recital at Town Hall, New York, in 1948, in a program that included German *Lieder* as well as French art songs. Despite a voice of limited range and texture, Bernac attracted considerable enthusiasm for his perceptive musicianship and his fastidious concern for the poetic texts. "Francis Poulenc is, without question, the greatest writer of concert songs," wrote Virgil Thomson in the *Herald Tribune,* and "Pierre Bernac is his authoritative interpreter. Mr. Bernac is also an interpreter of great musical power when dealing with the works of other composers." During that American tour Warren Storey of the Boston *Post* compared him to "the great Chaliapin," Claudia Cassidy in the Chicago *Tribune* referred to him as an "extraordinary interpreter . . . utterly at the service of the song," and Albert Goldberg in the Los Angeles *Times* considered his performances of Schubert's songs as "models of the most sensitive and poetic *Lieder* singing."

Henri Hell recognized Bernac as a master of German *Lieder* as well as of French art songs. "It is an interesting fact," said Hell in his biography of Poulenc, "that this distinguished French singer won wide acclaim for his authentic interpretations of Schubert and Schumann." But Hell also believed that Bernac excels in the French repertory. "The secret of his art is a manner of remarkably clear and almost penetrating verbal enunciation, peculiar to himself,

whereby the full poetic value of the text is thrown into relief without ever impairing the natural flow of the musical line. His interpretations of the French songs are thus unique, in that they are able to display the double poetic and musical origins of their inspiration."

Though Bernac continued to tour with Poulenc until the composer's death, he also devoted himself to teaching, spending the winter months in concert work and the spring and summer months with his pupils. He has conducted master classes in the United States in universities and studios; he has also been a member of the faculty at the American Conservatory at Fontainebleau, France. His book *The Interpretation of French Art Song* was published in New York in 1970 and his biography of Francis Poulenc in London in 1977.

ABOUT: Gelatt, R. Makers of Music; Hell, H. Francis Poulenc.

Leonard Bernstein

1918–

Composer of serious and popular music, pianist, conductor, lecturer, commentator, and author, Leonard Bernstein is the Renaissance man of twentieth century music. But it is his career as a performing musical artist, and particularly as a conductor, that concerns us here. In this aspect of his career Bernstein has been acclaimed over the decades as one of the most charismatic and gifted personalities in the music of our times.

Bernstein was born in Lawrenceville, Massachusetts, on August 25, 1918. He was the first child of Samuel Joseph and Jennie Resnick Bernstein, residents of Boston who had gone to Lawrenceville to visit some relatives. The father owned and operated a successful company dispensing supplies to beauty parlors and barber shops. The Bernsteins had two more children after Leonard: Shirley, born in 1924, and Burton, in 1931.

The parents had little knowledge of or interest in classical music. The only records Leonard remembers hearing on his family phonograph when he was a child were the popular hit songs of the day, such as "Barney Google" and "Oh,

Bernstein: bûrn' stĭn

LEONARD BERNSTEIN

Knowing "with finality" (his phrase) that he would someday become a musician, young Leonard sought out his first piano teacher, a neighborhood musician who charged him a dollar a lesson. When this teacher moved to California Leonard acquired a new teacher who charged three dollars. Since his father stubbornly refused to pay this fee, Leonard had to spend almost all of his allowance for piano lessons. Both these teachers left much to be desired. After more than a year of such inadequate instruction Bernstein finally acquired a new and, this time, excellent teacher in Helen Coates, under whose sensitive guidance the boy's innate musicality was finally able to surface and develop. She gave him not only intensive training on the piano but a thorough grounding in all music by having him study symphonies and operas from the printed page and by encouraging him to try his hand at composition. She also encouraged him to go to concerts. His first one, in 1934, was a recital by Rachmaninoff, an event indelibly impressed on his memory. Even more exciting was hearing the Boston Symphony Orchestra for the first time in a broadcast from Symphony Hall. The program was a modern one, Stravinsky's *The Rite of Spring* and Prokofiev's *Classical Symphony*. It made him aware not only of symphonic music but specifically of twentieth century music. "Until then," he says, "I never realized that music had a future. I always thought of it as something that had already been written." Soon he began attending the public concerts of the Boston Symphony; his desire for music was insatiable. "He was frighteningly gifted," Miss Coates recalled in later years. "He could read, sing, and memorize anything. He absorbed in one lesson an arrangement that took most of my pupils five or six lessons to learn."

by Jingo." But when he was eight another early musical experience had a much greater impact upon him: the religious music of the choir and organ in the synagogue, the beauty of which made him burst into tears.

His was an unhappy childhood for the most part. He says: "I was a miserable, terrified little child." Because his family moved frequently, he never lived in one place long enough to make close friends or to feel at home. More often than not he was the victim of the aggressions of his fellow students. In addition, he was a sickly child, from infancy a victim of chronic asthma, rose fever, and hay fever that compelled him to spend many an hour in the offices of physicians. He grew up lonely and highly introverted.

As a child, whenever he visited friends of his family who owned pianos he would invariably beat a path to the keyboard where he would experiment with making musical sounds. When he was eleven his aunt sent over to his house for storage her old weatherbeaten piano. "I made love to it right away," he recalls.

Music provided the escape he needed from boyhood frustrations and miseries. He was always at the piano, a fact that did not sit well with his parents who wanted him to spend more time on homework and who looked upon music as an impediment to the boy's eventual takeover of his father's prosperous business. Recalling his strong opposition to his son's preoccupation with music, his father remarked many years later: "How was I to know that he would someday grow up to be a Leonard Bernstein?"

He entered The Boston Latin School in his eleventh year and was graduated with honors in 1935. He received religious instruction at the Temple Mishkan Tefila where he was confirmed in a ceremony in which he delivered a speech he himself had written in Hebrew. Though he was an outstanding student—in the top ten percent of his class—he "didn't exist without music." He wrote the music for and helped to produce and direct the shows mounted in a boys' camp at Sharon, Massachusetts, where he spent several boyhood summers. On a cruise with his father through the Panama Canal soon after his thirteenth birthday, he was such a continuous source of entertainment at the piano that the director offered him a permanent job with the ship's staff.

Music brought about an extraordinary transformation in his personality and even in his health. As Bernstein recalls: "One day I was a scrawny little thing that everybody could beat up, and the next time I looked around I was the biggest boy in class. I could run faster, jump higher, dive better than anybody."

From Boston Latin School Bernstein went on to Harvard College to prepare for a career in business. In addition to the academic subjects he studied counterpoint, theory, and music history with Walter Piston and Edward Burlingame Hill, and his piano lessons were continued privately with Heinrich Gebhard. At Harvard he was always deeply involved in musical activities. He wrote for and performed in college productions. He played the piano for the glee club and provided the background music for silent motion pictures. "I remember with great nostalgia," wrote Irving Fine, who later became a recognized composer, "his appearance as piano accompanist at a series of historical films presented by the Harvard Film Society. The Battleship Potemkin rode at anchor to the accompaniment of Copland's *Piano Variations,* excerpts from Stravinsky's *Petrouchka,* and Bernstein's own paraphrases of Russian folk songs." Irving Fine also recalled Bernstein's performances at concerts of the Harvard Music Club. "Many programs would have been lost if Bernstein had not been able to tackle, almost at sight, anything from Stravinsky's Concerto for Two Solo Pianos to a work by one of his fellow students. At these club meetings he performed some of his own earliest essays." In his last year at Harvard Bernstein wrote the music for a production of Aristophanes' *The Birds,* which he himself conducted, his first such experience. Shortly afterward, he led a performance at Cambridge of Marc Blitzstein's opera *The Cradle Will Rock.*

In 1939 Bernstein was graduated from Harvard with the degree of Bachelor of Arts and a *cum laude* in music. By this time the conductor Dimitri Mitropoulos had become interested in him. He invited Bernstein to rehearsals of the Boston Symphony which Mitropoulos was then guest-conducting and encouraged him to consider becoming a conductor. Since Bernstein's father was insistent that his son enter his business,

Leonard decided to leave home and find a place for himself in music in New York City.

His first year in New York was a difficult one. Since he was not a member of the Musicians' Union he could get no employment as a pianist; even when he finally joined the Union, positions were not readily available. "There was just no place for me," he recalls. With his career at ebb tide, overwhelmed by depressions and frustrations, Bernstein suddenly found encouragement and support in Mitropoulos, who used his influence to get him a scholarship for the Curtis Institute in Philadelphia. For almost two years Bernstein studied conducting with Fritz Reiner and piano with Isabelle Vengerova. Reiner regarded him as "the most talented, all-around student I ever had."

On Reiner's recommendation Bernstein became in 1940 one of five scholarship pupils of Serge Koussevitzky at the Berkshire Music Center at Tanglewood in Massachusetts. Within a short period Bernstein became Koussevitzky's protégé as well as pupil. His demonstrations of a most extraordinary talent at conducting with the student orchestra convinced Koussevitzky that in this young man he had found his successor with the Boston Symphony. He urged Bernstein to change his name to make this eventual succession more assured, but Bernstein refused to do so.

During the summers of 1942 and 1943 Bernstein was Koussevitzky's assistant in the conducting class at the Berkshire Music Center. At this time he was beginning to emerge as a composer. His Sonata for Clarinet and Piano was performed in Boston on April 21, 1942, and repeated in New York the following February. And he also wrote, in 1942, his first work for orchestra, the symphony *Jeremiah.* In 1943 he completed and published a song cycle, *I Hate Music: Five Kid Songs,* which was performed by Jennie Tourel at Tanglewood on August 25, 1943.

The winter of 1942 was one of the bleakest times in Bernstein's life; he later often referred to it as his Valley Forge. He had returned to New York City bearing letters of recommendation from Koussevitzky and Reiner, with the hope of finding an assignment as a conductor. But worthwhile assignments could not be found. He had to do hack work to keep alive and was forced on more than one occasion to skip meals and to evade paying rent. "God, how I was miserable!" he recalls.

During the summer of 1943, on his twenty-fifth birthday, he received word in Lenox, Massachusetts, from Koussevitzky that Artur Rodzinski, the musical director of the New York Philharmonic, wanted to see him at his farm in Stockbridge, Massachusetts. There Bernstein discovered that Rodzinski was ready to offer him the post of assistant conductor of the New York Philharmonic Orchestra even though up to that time Bernstein had never led a professional symphonic organization.

He was not long in this post when he found an unexpected opportunity to reveal the full extent of his talent at conducting. The Sunday afternoon concert of the New York Philharmonic on November 14, which was broadcast on a national hookup of the Columbia Broadcasting System, was to be conducted by Bruno Walter, guest conductor. The evening before that concert Walter became too ill to perform, and Bernstein was summoned as a substitute. He had no opportunity to rehearse the orchestra and only a few hours to prepare himself in a rigorous program that included the world premiere of Miklós Rózsa's *Variations on a Hungarian Peasant Song.*

Just before performance time Bruno Zirato, the manager of the New York Philharmonic, announced from the stage of Carnegie Hall: "You are going to witness the debut of a full-fledged conductor, born, educated, and trained in this country." Bernstein then appeared wearing a gray business suit (the first time that an everyday costume was worn by a conductor at a Philharmonic concert) and proceeded to conduct the entire performance from memory, and without a baton. Even though the audience was unaware that he was performing without the benefit of a rehearsal, it was instantly made aware of Bernstein's command of the men in front of him and of the music he was conducting. They recognized that here was a young man able to charge the atmosphere with magnetic sparks and transmit electric currents throughout the auditorium.

His performance was sensational. The following morning Olin Downes wrote on the front page of the New York *Times:* "It was clear at once that he was conducting the orchestra in his own right and not the orchestra conducting him; that he had every one of the scores both in his hands and head and though he logically and inevitably conformed in broad outline, he was not following slavishly in the footsteps of his distinguished senior." The New York *Times* also discussed Bernstein's achievement in an editorial. Rodzinski, who motored in from Massachusetts to attend the performance, pronounced Bernstein "a prodigious talent." Koussevitzky, who heard him over the radio, sent congratulations by wire. That single performance made Bernstein famous overnight.

He was now in demand for guest appearances not only with the New York Philharmonic but with other major American orchestras. On February 18, 1944, he made his first appearance with the Boston Symphony, and the following May he filled the dual role of pianist and conductor with the Boston Symphony in a performance of Ravel's Concerto in G major. He also conducted in Montreal, at Chicago's Ravinia Park, at New York's Lewisohn Stadium, and in Los Angeles. In January 1944 he conducted the world premiere of his *Jeremiah* Symphony with the Pittsburgh Symphony, and the following April he directed the premiere of his ballet *Fancy Free* at the Metropolitan Opera House in a performance by the Ballet Theater. In less than a year after his professional conducting debut he had traveled over fifty thousand miles and conducted over one hundred performances.

He proved to be a born conductor with a penetrating musical intelligence, a keen insight into musical interpretation, a commanding personality, and a capacity for growth.

In 1945 Bernstein was appointed music director of the New York City Symphony, an orchestra founded one year earlier at the request of Mayor Fiorello La Guardia and conducted during that year by Leopold Stokowski. Bernstein remained with the New York City Symphony for three seasons of provocative program making, including numerous novelties and premieres, among which was the first performance of Marc Blitzstein's symphony *Airborne* (March 23, 1946).

While holding this office he continued to make appearances elsewhere. In May 1946 he was heard at the International Music Festival in Prague; that same season, on August 9, he conducted the American premiere of Britten's opera *Peter Grimes* at Tanglewood. In 1947 at the Berkshire Music Festival at Tanglewood he led two of the regular festival concerts of the Boston

Symphony (the first time Koussevitzky had permitted anybody but himself to conduct such performances). On December 2, 1949, as a guest conductor of the Boston Symphony in Boston he presented the world premiere of Olivier Messiaen's mammoth symphony *Turangalîla.*

In 1948, on his first tour of Europe and the Middle East, he enjoyed a personal triumph in Palestine as conductor of the Palestine Symphony Orchestra. "The enthusiasm of the audience at his first concert with the orchestra knew no bounds," cabled Peter Gradenwitz to the New York *Times.* "Not since the days of Arturo Toscanini . . . had a conductor been recalled so many times and given a similar ovation." Bernstein's bond with the Palestine Symphony—and with its successor, the Israel Philharmonic Orchestra which came into being after the founding of the State of Israel—remained close. During Israel's war of liberation he conducted concerts at the battlefront, his music often accompanied by the obbligato of shell explosions. After the birth of the new state he was appointed principal conductor of the Israel Philharmonic. On its first tour of the United States in 1951 Bernstein shared the dais with Koussevitzky, directing twelve concerts over a two-month period. Four years later Bernstein was once again principal conductor of the Israel Philharmonic when it made an eight-week tour of Europe. In 1957 he conducted for the opening of the Frederick R. Mann Auditorium, Tel Aviv's new concert hall. Immediately after the end of the Six Day War in 1967 he flew to Jerusalem to direct a special victory concert on recaptured Mount Scopus on July 9. That concert was the highlight of a documentary film, *Journey to Jerusalem* (1967), describing Bernstein's first visit to the reunified Jerusalem.

In 1973, when the Israel Philharmonic under Bernstein celebrated the twenty-fifth anniversary of the founding of Israel with a concert in Carnegie Hall (and simultaneously the twenty-fifth anniversary of Bernstein's affiliation with that orchestra), he was presented with the King Solomon Award by the American-Israel Cultural Foundation. A further tribute to Bernstein for his long and dedicated association with Israel and its cultural life came in March and April of 1977 when the Israel Philharmonic presented a "retrospective" two-week festival in which every major Bernstein score—except for the Mass, which was represented by just two excerpts—

was performed: the ballets, chamber music, and the music for the theater as well as the symphonic compositions. These performances were given in Tel Aviv, Jerusalem, and numerous smaller Israeli communities. Over television some of Bernstein's Harvard lectures were produced and in theaters in three cities the films *On the Waterfront* and *West Side Story* (both with Bernstein's music) were exhibited, together with installments from a then recently completed film cycle by Bernstein of Mahler's symphonies. This retrospective exhibition was repeated in August of 1977 at the Carinthian Festival at Ossiach and Villach in Austria.

Successes for Bernstein came in a seemingly endless procession. He gave his first European command performance in 1948 in Amsterdam, and later the same year he was given an ovation for his performance of his *Jeremiah* Symphony in Munich. In 1950 his performance of Mahler's Symphony No.2, the *Resurrection,* at the Holland Music Festival was described as a "revelation." In 1953 he became the first American-born conductor to appear at La Scala in Milan, when he conducted Cherubini's *Medea* with Maria Callas in the title role. That year he also directed the American premiere of Poulenc's farcical opera *Les Mamelles de Tirésias* at a festival at Brandeis University in Waltham, Massachusetts.

While achieving world renown as a conductor, Bernstein was also gathering laurels in other fields of music. As a serious composer he followed the composition of the *Jeremiah* Symphony (which was given the New York Music Critics Award) and the ballet *Fancy Free* with a second ballet, *Facsimile* (1946), a second symphony, *The Age of Anxiety* (1952), and the Serenade for Violin, Strings and Percussion (1954). For the popular musical theater he composed the scores for *On the Town* (1944) and *Wonderful Town* (1953), and for the motion picture *On the Waterfront* (1954). In 1954 he made the first of many appearances on television as a commentator and conductor, opening up new vistas for music appreciation and music education before an audience of several millions at each session.

On September 9, 1951, he married Felicia Montealegre in Boston. She was a young actress, born in Costa Rica, who had come to the United States to make a number of appearances on the stage and over television. Their home was a nine-room duplex apartment on Fifty-seventh

Street, diagonally opposite to Carnegie Hall. There they raised their first two children, a daughter, Jamie, born in 1952, and a son, Alexander Serge (named after Koussevitzky), born in 1955. Their household included Bernstein's personal secretary Helen Coates, who had been his piano teacher many years before. Bernstein once remarked that eight of those nine rooms belonged to his family. The only one exclusively his was a studio that he called his "thinking room," crowded with music scores, books, recordings, scrapbooks, sheet music, and an array of paper and pencils, furnished with a grand piano, a couch for relaxation, two telephones, a portable phonograph, and a recording apparatus.

In 1957 Dimitri Mitropoulos, music director of the New York Philharmonic, appointed Bernstein codirector for the 1957-1958 season. When that season ended, Mitropoulos withdrew to leave Bernstein as full music director. He was both the youngest man and the only American-born musician to serve in this post, and he held it for eleven years, longer than any director in the history of the organization. Under Bernstein the New York Philharmonic embarked upon a progressive and adventurous program of novelties and premieres, with frequent excursions into the world of avant-garde music; it became a box-office attraction comparable to, if not exceeding, what it had been under Toscanini. For the first time in Philharmonic history, advance sales for season tickets passed the million-dollar mark (for the 1959–1960 season), and to meet the great demand twenty additional concerts were added to the regular schedule. Bernstein's enormous personal appeal for music lovers led the CBS radio network to add seventy more stations to its hookup for the weekly Philharmonic broadcasts, brought the Lincoln Division of the Ford Motor Company to sponsor television broadcasts in 1960–1961, and greatly expanded the recording activities of both the orchestra and its conductor.

Bernstein and the New York Philharmonic made their first recording for Columbia in 1950 —Bernstein's own symphony, *The Age of Anxiety*. During the next quarter of a century Bernstein recorded for Columbia over one hundred albums with the New York Philharmonic, including complete sets of the symphonies of Beethoven, Brahms, Mahler, and Sibelius; his recording of Mahler's nine symphonies was the first such album recorded by a single conductor. His recordings of Mahler's Symphony No.8 (issued independently of the other eight symphonies) and the 1972 Metropolitan Opera production of *Carmen* won him Grammys from the National Academy of Recording Arts and Sciences.

During the years he conducted the New York Philharmonic Bernstein was prodigal in the presentation of world premieres. The tabulation of such premieres is too long for a complete listing. Only a representative selection is given here. In addition to first performances of his own works, he introduced Milton Babbitt's *Relata II* (January 16, 1969); Richard Rodney Bennett's Symphony No.2 (January 18, 1968); Mark Bucci's Concerto for Kazoo and Orchestra (March 26, 1960); Carlos Chávez' Concerto for Violin (Fall of 1965) and the Symphony No.6 (May 7, 1964); Copland's *Connotations* (September 23, 1962) and *Inscapes* (September 13, 1967); David Diamond's Symphony No.4 (January 23, 1948), Symphony No.5 (April 28, 1966), and Symphony No.8 (October 26, 1961); Lukas Foss's *Phorion* (April 27, 1967) and *Time Cycle* (October 20, 1960); Ginastera's Violin Concerto (October 3, 1963); Hans Werner Henze's Symphony No.5 (May 16, 1963); Charles Ives's Symphony No.2 (February 22, 1951); Nicolas Nabokov's Symphony No.3 (January 9, 1968); Gunther Schuller's *Spectra* (January 15, 1960); and William Schuman's Symphony No.8 (October 4, 1962) and *To Thee Old Cause* (October 3, 1968).

During his first full season as music director Bernstein took the New York Philharmonic on a fifteen-thousand-mile tour of South and Central America, with 39 concerts in 21 cities of 12 different countries. In 1959 he toured with the New York Philharmonic to Europe, the Middle East, countries behind the Iron Curtain, and the Soviet Union. "Leonard Bernstein and the New York Philharmonic showed Belgrade tonight how music can be played," cabled Paul Underwood to the New York *Times* from Yugoslavia. "In their first of two concerts in Yugoslavia, the musicians, despite the handicap of an acoustically poor hall, gave a performance of such shimmering beauty as to evoke almost awe in the hearers. 'I have never heard sound like that before; it was like crystal,' exclaimed one Belgrade music critic." The correspondent from Moscow, Max Frankel, was no less ecstatic. "It was not merely a tremendously successful performance but also one of the most exciting events in Moscow's recent musical history." That first performance in Moscow, on August 25, 1959, took place on Bernstein's forty-first birthday, and throughout that day gifts poured in to him from Soviet and American friends. But that first visit to the Soviet Union was not without controversy. Because he insisted on making a few comments on Charles Ives's *The Unanswered Question* (this was its first performance in the Soviet Union) and on Stravinsky's *The Rite of Spring* (played for the first time in the Soviet Union since the Revolution), Bernstein was called by some Soviet critics "immodest" and "conceited." Alexander Medvedev in *Sovetskaya Kultura* maintained that Bernstein had violated the traditions of music making in the Soviet Union by "presuming" to instruct a Russian audience in music. Bernstein's farewell concert in Moscow (music taken from Shostakovich's Seventh Symphony and Copland's *Billy the Kid*) was taped and telecast in the United States over the CBS television network on October 25, 1959.

While serving as the music director of the New York Philharmonic, Bernstein continued making guest appearances throughout the world, some of which had historic importance. In 1961 he made his debut at Covent Garden with Verdi's *Falstaff,* the same opera with which he would make his bow at the Metropolitan Opera on March 6, 1964, and with which he would cause a sensation at the Vienna State Opera in 1966. In the spring of 1965 he was the guest conductor of the Danish Philharmonic and was honored with the Sonning Award. In the spring of 1966 his performance of Mahler's monumental Symphony No.8, *The Symphony of a Thousand,* was acclaimed rapturously by the critics in London. In 1967 he returned to the Vienna State Opera for triumphant performances of *Der Rosenkavalier,* and two years later in Vienna he performed Beethoven's *Missa Solemnis* to commemorate the centenary of Vienna's famed opera house.

His protean intellect made it impossible for him to concentrate exclusively on conducting, however exalted his achievements in this field and however numerous the demands made upon him for appearances. He continued to develop himself as a serious composer with his third symphony, *Kaddish* (1963), dedicated to the "beloved memory" of the assassinated President

John F. Kennedy; with the *Chichester Psalms* for chorus and orchestra (1965); with the Mass, which opened the Kennedy Center for the Performing Arts in Washington, D.C., on September 8, 1971; with the ballet *The Dybbuk* (1974). For the Broadway musical theater he wrote the scores for *Candide* (1956), *West Side Story* (1957), and *1600 Pennsylvania Avenue* (1976). He extended his activities as a teacher and a commentator on music with classes at the Berkshire Music Center, Brandeis University, Harvard University (Charles Eliot Norton Professor of Poetry for 1972–1973), and Massachusetts Institute of Technology (as Institute Lecturer in 1974). The six Norton lectures at Harvard, entitled *The Unanswered Question,* were recorded in their entirety by Columbia Records: *Leonard Bernstein at Harvard,* six albums that consumed twelve hours of listening time. The lectures were also published as a book by Harvard University Press in 1976. He had already written two books: *The Joy of Music* (1959) and *The Infinite Variety of Music* (1966), both made up from his television scripts.

Just before the birth of their third child— Nina in 1962—the Bernsteins moved to a sixteen-room duplex apartment on Park Avenue. This became their winter residence. Summers were spent in a house atop a hill in Fairfield, Connecticut. (In October 1976, the Bernsteins announced that they had decided upon a legal separation. Their marriage had lasted twenty-five years. Perhaps in explanation, Bernstein told his audience at a concert at Lincoln Center for the Performing Arts in which he was appearing as a guest conductor of the New York Philharmonic: "I came to realize that, as death approaches, an artist must cast off everything that may be restraining him, and create in complete freedom." Subsequently, when Mrs. Bernstein became seriously ill, they were reconciled.)

In 1969 Bernstein resigned as music director of the New York Philharmonic to allow more time for composing. This did not end his affiliation with the orchestra—an affiliation that had lasted twenty-six years, for eleven of which he had been music director. He was given a lifetime post as "laureate conductor," an office calling for his services for a number of performances each season, for recordings and television appearances, and for foreign tours.

In June 1976 Bernstein toured Europe with the New York Philharmonic, presenting 13 concerts in 11 cities in 17 days. What distinguished this tour from all preceding ones was that every program was made up solely of American compositions, in commemoration of the United States Bicentennial. This was the first time that any American orchestra toured Europe with exclusively American music. The tour ended on June 17 in a big circus tent in the midst of the Tuileries Gardens in Paris. "The audience stomped on the plank floor built over the great round point at the entrance to the gardens," reported Flora Lewis from Paris to the New York *Times*, "and demanded more and more. Mr. Bernstein, a tired but warm smile on his face as the response grew more insistent, gave it to them."

Freedom from the taxing duties of a music director provided him with the time to perform with other orchestras and opera houses, as well as time for special occasions close to his heart. In 1970 he was chosen by the Austrian government to conduct *Fidelio* at the historic Theater-an-der-Wien, where it had been introduced, to commemorate Beethoven's two-hundredth birthday. He opened the 1972–1973 season of the Metropolitan (planned as the beginning of Göran Gentele's regime, but the plan was frustrated by Gentele's sudden tragic death) with a provocative performance of *Carmen* given in Bizet's original conception with spoken dialogue instead of recitatives and with new ideas in staging. On January 19, 1973, he performed Haydn's *Mass in Time of War* at the Washington Cathedral in Washington, D.C., as a plea for peace, in competition with other events taking place that day celebrating the inauguration of President Nixon. On June 23, 1973, he presented what he described as "a profoundly ecumenical event" when he conducted the Newark Boys Chorus, the Harvard Glee Club, and the RAI Orchestra in a performance of his own *Chichester Psalms* (sung in Hebrew) at the Vatican in Rome in honor of the tenth anniversary of Pope Paul VI's ascension to the papacy; a few days earlier Bernstein had been received in a private audience by the Pope. On July 26 and August 30, 1975, a much belated debut at the Salzburg Festival took place with two orchestral concerts, in one of which he conducted Mahler's Eighth Symphony; in the other he doubled as pianist and conductor in a Mozart piano concerto. When, early that September, a concert of Bernstein's music was given by the Hungarian Philharmon-

ic Orchestra under Janos Ferencsik at Congress Hall, in Villach, Austria, he rose from his seat in the audience to spring to the stage and give an impromptu performance of his overture to *Candide*.

In addition to honors and awards already mentioned, Bernstein has received the Albert Einstein Commemorative Award in the Arts from the Albert Einstein College of Medicine; the John H. Finley Medal for service to New York City; the Golden European trophy, an annual award given to an outstanding figure in popular music, but here given to a classical artist for the first time; the Ditson Award for "outstanding service to American music"; the Institute of International Education Award, presented by President Nixon; and citations and honors from Sylvania and the George Foster Peabody Awards for his television programs.

At the Inaugural concert for President Carter at the Kennedy Center for the Performing Arts in Washington, D.C., on January 19, 1977, two Bernstein songs were performed. One was "Take Care of This House" from Bernstein's ill-fated Broadway musical *1600 Pennsylvania Avenue,* and the other a new song, "To My Dear and Loving Wife," set to a seventeenth century text of Anne Bradstreet and dedicated by Bernstein to President Carter's wife, Rosalynn.

ABOUT: Ames, E. A Wind from the West: Bernstein and the New York Philharmonic Abroad; Briggs, J. Leonard Bernstein; Ewen, D. Leonard Bernstein; Gruen, J. The Private World of Leonard Bernstein. *Periodicals*—Harper's Magazine, May 1959; Holiday, October 1959; Life, January 7, 1957; Look, November 11, 1958; New York Times, April 17, 1977; New York Times Magazine, December 19, 1971; Reader's Digest, May 1960; Saturday Evening Post, June 16, 1956; Time, February 4, 1957.

E. Power Biggs

1906–1977

Edward George Power Biggs, organist, was born in Westcliff-on-Sea, Essex, England, on March 29, 1906, to Clarence and Alice Maud Tredgett Power-Biggs. (Edward ceased using the hyphenated form of the name.) From 1917 to 1924 he attended the Hurtspierpoint College in Sussex for the study of electrical engineering. By that time music was already a major interest and

E. POWER BIGGS

for some time he had been studying the organ. Winning the Thomas Threfall Organ Scholarship encouraged Biggs to give up the idea of becoming an engineer and enabled him to attend the Royal College of Music in London. After studying there with Sir Henry J. Wood and George D. Cunningham, among other teachers, Biggs was graduated in 1929 with highest honors in organ, piano, harmony, and counterpoint, and with the Hubert Kiver Organ Prize.

His debut as an organist in 1929 was unscheduled. Sir Henry J. Wood was conducting a Promenade concert at Queen's Hall in London that required the services of an organist. The regular organist was indisposed, and just two days before the concert Biggs was hurriedly called in as a substitute. Following this event, Biggs played in several of England's concert halls and cathedrals.

He paid his first visit to the United States in 1929 as a piano accompanist for a Welsh singer, but he soon extended the visit to a six-month tour of the country as an organist, making almost two hundred solo appearances. He returned to the United States to settle permanently, and in 1938 he became an American citizen. On March 31, 1932, he made his formal concert debut in New York City with an organ recital at Wanamaker Auditorium. Soon he was appointed choirmaster and organist of Christ Church in Cambridge, Massachusetts. He started giving impressive performances of organ music at the Harvard Memorial Church and in various auditoriums and churches

throughout the United States. He was subsequently appointed organist and music director of Harvard Church in Brookline and official organist of the Boston Symphony Orchestra. He also taught a class in organ at the Longy School of Music at Cambridge.

In 1933 he married Colette Joseph Lionne, a Boston pianist, whom he later divorced to marry Margaret Allen. They lived on Highland Street in Cambridge where Biggs indulged his love of gardening.

In 1933 he first started playing on the instrument with which he subsequently became identified: the Baroque Organ in the German Museum of Harvard. Except for its electrical action it was essentially identical with the instrument used by Johann Sebastian Bach in Weimar. When Biggs gave his first recital on this organ in April 1937, a critic for *Diapason* wrote that Biggs "more than justified his reputation in the manner in which he sensed the possibilities of the instrument. His playing was marked by beautifully defined rhythm and brilliant and clear rendition of the larger numbers, coupled with a real appreciation of the traditional manner of playing such music." Biggs's concerts at the German Museum attracted the admiration of musicians everywhere. In 1937–1938 he presented twelve recitals covering the entire organ literature of Johann Sebastian Bach (a project he repeated in 1940 at St. Paul's Chapel at Columbia University in New York City). In 1940 he dedicated the Baroque Organ at the Music Shed at Tanglewood in Lenox, Massachusetts, and in 1949 he performed a similar service for the new organ of the Boston Symphony Orchestra, celebrating the fiftieth anniversary of the orchestra.

On September 20, 1942, Biggs's fame spread from the musical specialist and the sophisticate to the general music public when he gave the first of a series of half-hour Sunday morning broadcasts over the radio network of the Columbia Broadcasting System. The first series became so popular that Biggs was permanently established in the network programming for sixteen years, nationally over CBS and in Europe by short wave; his weekly programs emanated from the Busch Reinsiger Museum in Cambridge. In 1945–1946, in commemoration of the bicentenary of Bach's birth he performed over the air for the first time anywhere all of Bach's organ works. In a national poll conducted by

Musical America in 1946 he was selected as one of the top attractions of radio.

From 1947 on Biggs recorded for Columbia an extensive and varied repertory that even embraced, in 1974, an album of ragtime music of Scott Joplin. His album of Gabrieli's *Canzoni* received a Grammy in 1968 from the National Academy of Recording Arts and Sciences. For his recordings Biggs spent the last quarter of a century of his life seeking out and performing on the old organs of Europe, particularly those that had been played upon by such masters as Bach, Handel, and Mozart. In 1970 Biggs was engaged by the East German government to record the organ music of Johann Sebastian Bach on the organ upon which Bach himself had played at the St. Thomas Church in Leipzig.

His concert tours around the world were extensive, and he was often heard as a soloist with symphony orchestras and chamber music groups. Leo Sowerby wrote the Concerto for Organ and Orchestra for him, and Biggs introduced it on April 22, 1938, with the Boston Symphony Orchestra under Koussevitzky. Walter Piston, Roy Harris, Quincy Porter, Howard Hanson, and Benjamin Britten were also composers whose organ works were given world premieres by Biggs. To a critic writing in the New York *Times* Biggs "in no small way, created a kind of musical renaissance of that great instrument—the organ."

He received honorary doctorates in music from the New England Conservatory and from Acadia University in Canada. In 1952 the National Association of Composers and Conductors presented him with a citation for his contributions to American music. He was named Knight Commander, Order of Isabella the Catholic, for his researches in Spanish organs and organ music.

E. Power Biggs made his last public appearance in Boston in June 1976 when he was a soloist with the Boston Pops Orchestra under Arthur Fiedler. Biggs died in Boston on March 10, 1977, following an operation for bleeding ulcers. A memorial service was held at the Memorial Church of Harvard University on March 27.

ABOUT: Hi-Fi Magazine, August 1972; Newsweek, April 23, 1946; New York Times, March 12, 1977; Time, March 21, 1938.

Ingrid Bjoner

1927–

Ingrid Bjoner, soprano, was born in Kråkstad, near Oslo, on November 8, 1927. She was one of nine children of Johan and Alma Bjoner, all of whom were raised on a farm. Ingrid received a degree in pharmacy from the University of Oslo in 1951 and worked in an apothecary shop before being encouraged by Kirsten Flagstad to specialize in singing. While attending the University Bjoner studied voice with Gudrun Boellemose at the Boellemose Conservatory in Oslo from 1946 to 1951, but these studies were primarily recreational. She had no thought of pursuing music as a profession. However, upon Flagstad's urging and recommendation she became a scholarship pupil in voice at the Wiesbaden Opera School in 1951. While vacationing in Sweden she sang for Paul Lohmann, professor of voice from Frankfort, Germany. He persuaded her to come to Frankfort to study with him at the High School of Music, offering lessons free of charge. While studying with Lohmann for a three-year period she supported herself by working in a drugstore.

In 1956 Flagstad invited her to appear as Gutrune in a broadcast of *Die Götterdämmerung* over Radio Oslo, a performance subsequently released on London Records. Bjoner's stage debut came in 1957 with the Norwegian Opera, as Donna Anna in *Don Giovanni.* Her performance was so successful that she was retained as leading soprano of that company from 1958 to 1960. In 1957 she also made her opera debut with the Royal Opera in Stockholm and was a participant at the Grieg Festival in Bergen.

Guest appearances with major European opera companies (including the Vienna State Opera and the Deutsche Oper in Berlin), at the Stockholm Festival, and at the Vancouver Festival in British Columbia in Canada preceded her engagement as principal soprano of the Düsseldorf Opera in 1960. During two years with the Düsseldorf Opera she also appeared in recitals and as a performing artist with orchestras throughout Europe and gave guest performances in opera in Berlin, Vienna, Hamburg, Munich, and Bayreuth. Her Bayreuth debut took place in 1960 in the roles of Freia and Gutrune in the Ring of the Nibelungs cycle.

Bjoner

INGRID BJONER

Her American debut, as Elsa in *Lohengrin* with the San Francisco Opera, came on October 21, 1960. She made her bow in the same role at the Metropolitan Opera on October 28, 1961. Douglas Watt of the *Daily News* described her performance as "stunning." He added: "She has a warm expertly produced voice. . . . She sang with increasing beauty and brilliance." As a member of the Metropolitan Opera she was subsequently acclaimed as Eva in *Die Meistersinger,* Donna Anna in *Don Giovanni,* and in the title roles of Strauss's *Ariadne auf Naxos* and *Die Frau ohne Schatten,* as well as in the *Ring* cycle. Her appearance as Eva on October 18, 1962, led Harold C. Schonberg to write in the New York *Times* that she was "a fine stylist, and not even the slight wobble that afflicts her voice when she lets it out detracted from the finish of her conception." Bjoner gave her one hundredth performance as Elsa during the 1966–1967 season of the Metropolitan Opera.

She joined the Munich Opera as principal soprano in 1961, and her performances there in the German repertory, and particularly in the dramas and operas of Wagner, Weber, Richard Strauss, and Mozart, gained her world fame. In Wagner she sang Elsa, the three Brünnhildes in the *Ring* cycle, Sieglinde in *Die Walküre,* Senta in *The Flying Dutchman,* and Isolde in *Tristan and Isolde.* When the Munich Opera celebrated its centenary with a new production of *Tristan and Isolde,* she sang Isolde. In 1967–1968 she was starred as Rezia in a new production of Weber's *Oberon,* and she was also successful in the title role of Weber's *Euryanthe.* When a new opera house was dedicated in Munich in November 1963, she sang the role of the Empress in *Die Frau ohne Schatten.* Her Strauss roles in addition to Ariadne were Chrysothemis in *Elektra,* the Gräfin in *Capriccio,* the Marschallin in *Der Rosenkavalier,* and the title roles in *Salome, Daphne,* and *Die Aegyptische Helena.* She was acclaimed as Pamina in *The Magic Flute,* the Countess in *The Marriage of Figaro,* Vitellia in *La Clemenza di Tito,* and Fiordiligi in *Così fan Tutte.*

During the two-hundredth anniversary of Beethoven's birth in 1970 she was invited to sing Leonore in *Fidelio.* She repeated this role during the anniversary year in major European opera houses, at the Teatro Colón in Buenos Aires, at the Salzburg Festival in Austria, and at the opera house in Beethoven's city of birth, Bonn. When she appeared in *Fidelio* at the Vienna State Opera with Karl Böhm conducting, the Vienna *Volksblatt* described her as "one of the most beautiful Leonores to be heard in recent times; a magnificent, powerful soprano, technically pure and with a strong tendency towards dramatic interpretation but also capable of lyrical expression."

In addition to her appearances in the German repertory, she has been successful as Aida, Tosca, Turandot, Micaëla in *Carmen,* Selika in *L'Africaine,* Amelia in *Un Ballo in Maschera,* Leonora in *La Forza del Destino,* Desdemona in *Otello,* and Elisabetta in *Don Carlo.*

In 1960 she received the Norwegian Music Critics Society Award. King Olav of Norway decorated her with the Order of St. Olav, First Class, in 1964. In 1965 she was given the honorary title *Kammersängerin* by the Bavarian State government; she has also been awarded the Bavarian Order of Merit by the Bavarian Senate.

Bjoner married Thomas Reynolds Pierpoint Jr., an executive at Boeing aircraft, on September 24, 1960. They live in Oslo.

ABOUT: Opera News, January 2, 1965.

Jussi Björling

1911–1960

JUSSI BJÖRLING

Jussi Björling (John Jonaton Björling), tenor, was born in Stora Tuna, Dalarna, Sweden, on February 2, 1911. He came from a family of singers; both parents were professionals. His father, Karl David, well-known as a tenor in Europe, is believed to have sung small parts at the Metropolitan Opera in New York though no official record of this exists. All three Björling sons were given vocal training.

When Jussi's mother died, his father was smitten with wanderlust. With his three sons he organized the Björling Quartet, and in 1919 and 1920 they toured the United States, dressed in native costume and performing in Swedish communities and churches. The tour ended with the sudden death of Jussi's father. Returning to Sweden Jussi continued his music study. At seventeen he made his first phonograph recording—an American song hit, "The Sunshine of Your Smile," which sold exceptionally well in its own time and in later years became a collector's item. In 1929 Björling entered the Royal Opera School in Stockholm as a pupil of John Forsell, the general director of the Kungsholm Opera and at one time a favorite interpreter of the role of Don Giovanni. After intensive study with Forsell and with Tullio Voghera, Björling made his opera debut in 1930 at the Royal Opera in Stockholm, as Don Ottavio in *Don Giovanni*. Guest appearances followed with opera companies in Scandinavia and Europe. In Copenhagen Björling was so successful that he was called upon to give a repeat performance. In November 1936 in Paris he was invited to appear as Rodolfo in a special performance of *La Bohème* on the occasion of the dedication of John D. Rockefeller's gift of an American wing to the Cité Universitaire. This appearance in one of his most famous roles was highly acclaimed and so were his subsequent performances at Covent Garden in London. In 1937 Toscanini chose him to appear as Don Ottavio at the Salzburg Festival and in 1938 to become the tenor soloist under his baton at the Lucerne Festival in a performance of Verdi's Requiem.

Björling: byûr′ lĭng

In the fall of 1937 Björling paid his second visit to the United States. On November 28 he made his American debut as a mature artist on a coast-to-coast radio broadcast. Four days later he gave his first American recital in Springfield, Massachusetts, where his success was so formidable that the concert was reviewed on the front pages of both city newspapers. Two nationwide broadcasts and guest appearances with the Chicago Civic Opera followed.

On January 4, 1938, Björling gave his first New York recital at Carnegie Hall to a sold-out auditorium. "The young singer achieved a success seldom paralleled in our rooms of music," wrote Pitts Sanborn in the *World-Telegram*. "Mr. Björling's voice not only has substance, sonority and compass to recommend it but it is absolutely the unspoiled voice of a young man. His breath support is truly magnificent, and he can command a flawless legato of prodigiously long sweep and spin a tone from an imposing fortissimo to a vanishing pianissimo. He possesses an extraordinarily even scale. His attack is remarkably pure, and his mezza voce is exquisite."

At this time Lucrezia Bori heard a recording of "Celeste Aida," which she identified as Caruso's. Upon discovering that the singer was Jussi Björling, she rushed to the telephone to urge Edward Johnson, general manager of the Metropolitan Opera, to consider Björling for the company. Johnson informed her that coincidentally Björling was auditioning for him the following day. That audition brought Björling a

Björling

Metropolitan Opera contract and a debut on November 24, 1938, as Rodolfo. In the New York *Times* Olin Downes described him as "a tenor of ample tone and quality for the role with a B-flat which rings and carries." In the years between 1938 and 1941 Björling was also heard as Manrico in *Il Trovatore,* as the Duke in *Rigoletto,* in the title role of *Faust,* and as Riccardo in *Un Ballo in Maschera.* On December 2, 1940, he opened the Metropolitan Opera season as Riccardo in *Un Ballo in Maschera.*

During World War II, Björling appeared with the Stockholm Opera, made recordings, and performed in Scandinavia at benefit concerts for the Red Cross and for the underground movement. For six months he was a trainee in a Swedish artillery regiment.

He returned to the Metropolitan Opera on November 29, 1945, as the Duke in *Rigoletto,* and he remained with the company as one of its principal tenors—except for the seasons of 1954 –1955, 1957–1958 and 1958–1959—up to the time of his death. He extended his Metropolitan Opera repertory with the roles of Cavaradossi in *Tosca,* Radames in *Aida,* Des Grieux in *Manon Lescaut,* Turiddu in *Cavalleria Rusticana,* and the title roles in *Romeo and Juliet* and *Don Carlo.* He opened the 1950–1951 season of the Metropolitan Opera on November 6 as Don Carlo, and that of 1953–1954, on November 16, as Faust.

Björling made his debut with the San Francisco Opera as Rodolfo on October 18, 1940. He also appeared with Europe's major opera houses. He was a concert-hall favorite, both in recitals and as soloist with symphony orchestras in performances of major choral works.

Despite his Swedish birth and training his voice was essentially Italian, and his Italian diction was perfect. The beauty of his voice, the purity of its texture, the flexibility of its range, and the brilliance of his top notes led many others besides Bori to compare him to Caruso. Caruso's widow once said that Björling sang more like her husband than any tenor she had heard. Björling's repertory was basically the same as Caruso's, with emphasis on the Italian and French repertory. His style was also frequently reminiscent of Caruso—possibly the result of Björling having been coached for several years by Tullio Voghera, whom Caruso had employed in a similar capacity during his first six years in the United States.

On June 3, 1935, Björling married one of Sweden's most beautiful women—Anna Lisa Berg, a soprano of the Stockholm Opera; one year before her marriage, she had been crowned Queen of the Santa Lucia Festival in Stockholm. They met while both were students at the Stockholm Royal Conservatory. She abandoned her own singing career after her marriage but returned to it in 1948 to appear with her husband in *La Bohème* and in 1950 they embarked on a concert tour in duo recitals.

The Björlings had three children, and lived during the winter in an apartment overlooking a garden in Stockholm. They also acquired a summer place on Siarö, an island in the Stockholm archipelago. There they followed their favorite pastimes of boating, sailing, fishing, and playing tennis.

Björling was generally a moody man, given to fits of temper and fluctuating between depression and exhilaration. Extraordinarily nervous before concert or opera time, he was known to yield to spasms of temper minutes before he stepped on the stage. He drank excessively but never at the expense of a performance.

Björling's last appearance at the Metropolitan Opera took place on December 22, 1959, in *Cavalleria Rusticana.* He was scheduled to return for the opening week of the 1960–1961 season, but he had a heart attack in his country house in Siarö on September 8, 1960. An ambulance helicopter and a physician were rushed to his island home from Stockholm but upon arrival found him dead. He had suffered other heart attacks, one just before concert time in Pasadena, California, and another during a performance of *La Bohème* at Covent Garden attended by Queen Elizabeth II and the Queen Mother. In both instances he insisted upon going through the entire performance after half an hour of rest. Björling's last appearance anywhere was in Stockholm on August 21, 1960. In all his appearances near the end of his career he was in his prime, his voice had grown in maturity and technical assurance while its beauty and purity remained unblemished.

Björling was a prolific recording artist; he made forty-three single disks and over forty albums for RCA Victor. His album *Björling in Opera* received a Grammy in 1959 from the National Academy of Recording Arts and Sciences. His last recording was Verdi's Requiem, with

Fritz Reiner conducting, made in Vienna during the summer of 1960.

Björling was made Knight, Order of Leopold II, by Belgium. His autobiography, *Med bagaget i strupen,* was published in Stockholm in 1945.

One of Björling's sons—Rolf (born in Jönköping, Sweden, on December 25, 1928)—is a successful opera and concert tenor. He made his debut as Pinkerton in *Madama Butterfly* at the Stockholm Royal Opera in 1962, and since then has been heard in opera and concerts throughout Europe and in the United States.

ABOUT: High Fidelity, January 1968; New York Times, September 10, 1960; Opera News, February 26, 1972.

JUDITH BLEGEN

Judith Blegen

1941–

Judith Eyer Blegen, soprano, was born in Missoula, Montana, on April 27, 1941. Her father, Halward Martin Blegen, was a surgeon who loved good music, and her mother, Dorothy Mae Anderson, was a teacher of the violin; both were of Norwegian descent. Since both parents regarded singers as an inferior breed ("I was brought up to hate opera," Blegen said) they gave their three children instrumental training. Judith's sister, Barbara, was a prodigy who gave piano recitals at the age of eleven and grew up to become a concert pianist; one of her brothers learned to play the viola, and another, the trumpet.

"My strongest memory of childhood," Blegen recalls, "is coming back from Sunday school every week, and there was always the smell of roast beef and potatoes, and the sound of the New York Philharmonic on the radio."

Her first music lessons were on the violin, and her first teacher was her mother. When Judith was fourteen, it became apparent that she had an attractive singing voice, and she shifted from violin to vocal lessons. Her teacher was John Lester, a member of the music faculty of the University of Montana. "I applied everything I learned on the violin to the voice, approaching it from a completely instrumental point of view." Since there was a large music library at home, and another at the University, she further enriched her musical education by sight-reading

everything she could put her hands on. Sight-reading had always been for her an "easy game," as she put it. "I just read through everything."

After graduation from Missoula High School, where she served as a cheerleader, Judith Blegen took courses in music at the University of Montana. She became a member of the choir at the local Episcopal church where her singing talent was instantly recognized by the choir director who elevated her to the position of soloist. In 1959 she passed her auditions at the Curtis Institute of Music. For the next five years she studied voice with Euphemia Gregory and violin with Toshiya Eto and Oscar Shumsky. "That girl," said Gregory, "has a wonderful ear. . . . She has absolute pitch. From the very beginning, she would stand up and all I needed to do was strike the chord. She was always there."

In her first year at the Curtis Institute she joined the Kansas City Starlight Theater in summer stock, singing in the chorus. During the summer of 1960 she was an apprentice with the Santa Fe Opera company, appearing as Barbarina in *The Marriage of Figaro*. In 1960 she made her first visit to Europe to develop fluency in foreign languages and then entered Martial Singher's opera workshop at Curtis. When Singher became head of the summer School of Arts, in Santa Barbara, California, he brought Judith to the coast to sing the title role in a school production of *Manon*.

In 1962 Blegen won the Philadelphia Orchestra Award which entitled her to make her debut with the orchestra the following season. This was her first appearance with a major orchestra. A year later, in 1963, Gian Carlo Menotti invited her to Spoleto, Italy, for his Festival of Two Worlds. She performed at Spoleto for three consecutive summers, the first two in concerts of *Lieder* and appearances with a chamber-music group, the third year as Mélisande in Menotti's new production of *Pelléas and Mélisande.* "This performance, in effect, marked her debut as a full-fledged professional," wrote Martin Mayer in *Opera News.* Meanwhile, in 1964, after receiving the Bachelor of Arts degree at Curtis, she returned to Italy on a Fulbright Fellowship to study opera with Luigi Ricci, and to Munich to work on her German repertory.

From 1965 to 1968 she was a member of the Nuremberg Opera, and made her debut as Olympia in *The Tales of Hoffmann.* She appeared there as Rosina in *The Barber of Seville* some thirty times, and in other roles ranging from Lucia in *Lucia di Lammermoor* to Zerbinetta in *Ariadne auf Naxos.* In Nuremberg in 1967 she married baritone Martial Singher's son, Peter, an airplane pilot who worked for the Aga Khan. Three years later, their son, Thomas Christopher, was born. Singher and Blegen were divorced in 1975.

Her performance as Mélisande at Spoleto in 1965 and her subsequent appearances in Nuremberg brought her to the attention of several of Europe's opera impresarios who began calling for her services. Rolf Liebermann, then general manager of the Hamburg Opera, came to Nuremberg to audition her and offered her a three-year contract with his company, to begin with a new production of Cimarosa's *Il Matrimonio Segreto.* She turned it down because she did not realize how important the Hamburg Opera was and because she had her eyes on other goals. As she put it: "By then I had heard the other girls in my *Fach,* and I said, 'By God, I'm better than they are.' I said, 'I'll bet a dollar I can get Munich or even Vienna.' And I was going to audition for Mr. Rudel and Mr. Bing in New York."

She did get a call from Vienna in 1968 where she made her debut at the Vienna State Opera as Aennchen in *Der Freischütz.* Among other roles she was heard there as Zerbinetta, Rosina, and as Adina in *L'Elisir d'Amore* and as Norina in *Don Pasquale.* She also appeared at the Volksoper in Vienna and became such a favorite there that a new production of Auber's *Fra Diavolo*

was staged for her. In addition, she made her European television debut as Blondchen in *The Abduction from the Seraglio* conducted by Georg Solti over Eurovision. She has also filmed for television the roles of Amor in Gluck's *Orfeo and Euridice* and Zdenka in Strauss's *Arabella.*

In the United States, on August 1, 1969, she sang the leading female role of Emily in the American premiere of Menotti's children's opera *Help, Help, the Globolinks!* with the Santa Fe Opera. The role was written for Blegen who was uniquely suited for it since it called not only for singing but also for playing the violin. She appeared in this role again at the New York City Opera in December 1969.

In 1969 Rudolf Bing signed her for the Metropolitan Opera. She made her debut there on January 19, 1970, as Papagena in *The Magic Flute.* Before she had an opportunity to prove herself, she came into conflict with the Metropolitan Opera management when it wanted her to cover for Joan Sutherland in a projected production of *The Daughter of the Regiment.* "There's no way I'll do *that,*" she replied with finality. Before any ill feeling could generate, however, she became a success when she was called upon suddenly to fill in as Marzelline in a new production of *Fidelio* on December 16, mounted to commemorate the two-hundredth anniversary of Beethoven's birth. Her third role during this initial season was Zerlina in *Don Giovanni,* in which once again she reaped praise. She was cast as Sophie when *Werther* was revived in February 1971. A season later she was heard as Aennchen in *Der Freischütz* and was summoned to substitute for Teresa Stratas as Mélisande in *Pelléas and Mélisande.* Then came Nannetta in *Falstaff,* Amor in *Orfeo and Euridice,* the Forest Bird in *Siegfried,* Sophie in *Der Rosenkavalier,* Ascanius in Berlioz' *Les Troyens,* Adina in *L'Elisir d'Amore,* Lauretta in *Gianni Schicchi,* Juliet in *Romeo and Juliet,* Susanna in a new production of *The Marriage of Figaro,* and Sophie in *Werther.* Her place among the principal sopranos of the Metropolitan Opera was secure. "Her way with the music was breathtaking and exquisite; no other words will do," wrote a critic for the New York *Times* after one of her performances. "She has everything: beauty of tone, grace and ornamentation, sureness of musical instinct, conviction of personality."

In the fall of 1972 Blegen made her debut with

the San Francisco Opera as Susanna in *The Marriage of Figaro.* She returned to San Francisco in September 1973 to sing Adele to Joan Sutherland's Rosalinda in a revival of *Die Fledermaus.* When Evelyn Lear became ill, Blegen replaced her as Fulvia in a performance of Handel's *Ezio* by the Handel Society in New York in January 1973. In November 1973 she made her bow with the Chicago Lyric Opera as Sophie in *Der Rosenkavalier;* on August 10, 1974, at the Salzburg Festival as Blondchen; on June 25, 1975, at Covent Garden in London as Despina in *Così fan Tutte;* and on June 6, 1977, at the Paris Opéra in *Der Rosenkavalier.* She sang for the first time at the Edinburgh Festival in Scotland on August 25, 1976, in the role of Susanna in *The Marriage of Figaro* (which was recorded). On November 4, 1976, at the Tulsa Opera in New York, she sang professionally for the first time the title role in *Manon.*

When she first entered the concert field on January 12, 1974, in New York, a critic for the New York *Times* reported: "She is a candidate for greatness in the field." A subsequent New York recital, on November 30, 1975, led Donal Henahan to say in the New York *Times:* "Hearing a Judith Blegen song recital at this stage of her career is something akin to sampling a potentially great bottle of wine a few years before it has reached its peak. The young Metropolitan Opera soprano is always delicious in the sort of lighthearted works that made up most of her program. . . . She also sings darker music with the same purity of tone, the same intelligence, musicianship, and care." In November 1975 she was chosen to open the Great Performances series at the Lincoln Center for the Performing Arts in New York.

She appeared in joint recitals and made recordings with the soprano Frederica von Stade. She has been heard as soloist with some of America's leading orchestras, notably with the New York Philharmonic conducted by Leonard Bernstein in performances of Charles Ives's music and of Haydn's *Nelson Mass.* On July 11, 1976, she appeared at the Berkshire Music Festival at Tanglewood in Massachusetts in a program of Mozart arias. In February 1977 she was a soloist in the American premiere of Pergolesi's Mass in F in New York.

Blegen told Stephen E. Rubin of the New York *Times* that she is "driven by an artistic demon." She fears it makes her "somewhat of a bore." She added: "I'm an extremely honest musician and singer to the point of being fanatically conscientious. I'm so concerned all the time that maybe I lack a little *joie*—to be able to simply sing and be happy about it. In fact, I think I'm a hard person to rehearse with. I get tense and mad at myself because I don't feel I'm arriving at what I want. Consequently, I get snappy and impatient and hard to get along with."

Judith Blegen resides in an apartment in New York's West Side near Lincoln Center. She adorns any production in which she appears. Martin Mayer in *Esquire* called her "a classic American beauty—honey-blond hair and hazel eyes, high cheekbones, little nose, splendid symmetry, small, trim figure."

ABOUT: Esquire, July 1974; Hi-Fi Magazine, July 1971; New York Times, June 9, 1974; Opera News, January 2, 1971, December 7, 1974.

Artur Bodanzky

1877–1939

For almost a quarter of a century Artur Bodanzky was the principal conductor of German operas at the Metropolitan Opera. He was born in Vienna on December 16, 1877, the oldest of four children. His father, Carl (a manufacturer of paper), and his mother, Hanna Feuchtwang Bodanzky, wanted him to become a doctor, but from the time he was four—when he was given the gift of a toy xylophone on which he tried to produce snatches of tunes—Artur's life was dominated by music. As a child he began to study the violin at the Vienna Conservatory. In 1898 he became a violinist in the Royal Opera orchestra conducted by Gustav Mahler, and also at the Sunday evening orchestral concerts of the Gesellschaft der Musikfreunde, playing under the batons of Brahms, Dvořák, Saint-Saëns, and Anton Rubinstein.

His ambition to become a conductor was first awakened when he heard Gustav Mahler conduct *Lohengrin* at the Royal Opera. "I thought I knew *Lohengrin* by heart," he recalled in later years, "but I found I was hearing it for the first time. All the other times, I now know, it had

Bodanzky: bȯ dänts′ kĕ

Bodanzky

ARTUR BODANZKY

been stale. I suddenly realized what being a conductor meant; from that moment I changed my whole plan of life and decided to become a conductor."

After studying conducting with Alexander Zemlinsky, Bodanzky began his career by directing performances of operettas in Budweis in 1900. At this time other undistinguished assignments were undertaken, including one at the Karltheater in Vienna. But in 1902 he was appointed assistant conductor to Gustav Mahler at the Vienna Royal Opera. Two years later Bodanzky realized his first success, with *Die Fledermaus* in Paris, a performance that marked the real beginning of his successful career. He served his apprenticeships at the Theater-ander-Wien (in operettas) and in Berlin in a recently founded experimental opera house. From 1906 to 1909 Bodanzky filled his first important post, as principal conductor with the Prague Opera. An even more distinguished appointment came his way in 1909 when he was made principal conductor of opera at the Mannheim Ducal Theater. That same year he married Ada Elisa Perutz. In Mannheim, Bodanzky arrived at full maturity as a conductor, both in opera and in symphonic music. One of his chief successes outside the opera house in Mannheim came in 1912 when he conducted a festival of Mahler's music with an ensemble of fifteen hundred instrumentalists and vocalists.

In 1914 Bodanzky's success at Covent Garden in the first performance of *Parsifal* in England drew the attention and interest of Giulio Gatti-

Casazza, general manager of the Metropolitan Opera. Gatti-Casazza brought Bodanzky to New York to have him share the German repertory with Arturo Toscanini, succeeding Alfred Hertz. Bodanzky left Mannheim in 1915, became a permanent resident of the United States, and in time an American citizen.

His debut at the Metropolitan Opera took place on November 18, 1915, with *Die Götterdämmerung*. "His reading of the score," wrote Richard Aldrich in the New York *Times*, "was filled with the red blood of dramatic power, free and flexible in tempo, pulsing with the ebb and flow of passion. . . . Mr. Bodanzky is evidently one who is possessed of Wagner's idea of bringing out always the unceasing surge of significant 'melos' in the orchestra. . . . He secured a marvelous flexibility and range of dynamics and the full potency of dramatic expression entrusted to the orchestral voice without heavy-footedness or an overbearing dominance that forces the singers to shout."

During his first season at the Metropolitan Opera, Bodanzky was highly praised for his performances of *Parsifal, Lohengrin, Tristan and Isolde, Die Walküre, Siegfried, Die Meistersinger,* and—outside the Wagnerian repertory—*Der Rosenkavalier, The Magic Flute,* and Hermann Goetz's *The Taming of the Shrew*. In 1916–1917, he enlarged his repertory at the Metropolitan Opera with Gluck's *Iphigénie en Aulide, Fidelio, Das Rheingold,* and *The Marriage of Figaro*. On March 8, 1917, he conducted the world premiere of Reginald de Koven's *The Canterbury Pilgrims,* the only time in his career that he led an American opera.

The violent anti-German sentiment that developed when the United States became involved in World War I did not affect or interrupt Bodanzky's career, though most of the German repertory and all the music dramas of Wagner were proscribed. Bodanzky was called upon to take over many operas outside the German fold: *L'Africaine, Le Prophète, Prince Igor, Eugene Onegin, La Juive, Le Coq d'Or*. Some German operas were still being produced, and Bodanzky conducted *Martha, The Marriage of Figaro,* and *Oberon,* the last given in an English translation. The American premiere of Franz Liszt's *Saint Elizabeth* (January 3, 1918) was also given in English.

After World War I the bitter opposition to German operas was dissipated, and Bodanzky was able to return to his favorite territory—Wagner—beginning with *Parsifal* on February 19, 1920. *Tristan and Isolde* returned on November 20, 1920; *Lohengrin,* on February 2, 1921; *Die Walküre,* on December 16, 1921; and the complete *Ring* cycle during the 1924–1925 season. After 1925 Bodanzky led performances of the *Ring* cycle almost annually, sometimes in the cut versions sanctioned by Mahler, sometimes in the uncut presentations heard at Bayreuth.

Through the years Bodanzky was assigned important premieres: the American premieres of Karel Weis's *Der Polnische Jude* (March 9, 1920), Erich Wolfgang Korngold's *Die Tote Stadt* (November 19, 1921), Rimsky-Korsakov's *Snegurochka* (January 23, 1922), Janáček's *Jenufa* (December 6, 1924), Richard Strauss's *Die Aegyptische Helena* (November 6, 1928), Ernst Krenek's *Jonny Spielt Auf* (January 19, 1929); the New York premiere of *Così fan Tutte* in 1922; the Metropolitan Opera premiere of *Elektra* in 1932.

If he was greatly admired for his dramatic fire, dynamic shadings, precision of attack, and commanding knowledge of the scores he conducted, Bodanzky was also severely criticized for his inattention to details, his slow tempos, and his sacrifice of subtlety of expression for overall effect. The mounting criticism led to his resignation from the Metropolitan in 1929. He was replaced by Joseph Rosenstock, who met with even less favor with the Metropolitan Opera audiences. Before the season was over Bodanzky was back at his post, which he retained until his death.

In addition to conducting at the Metropolitan, Bodanzky prepared a new edition of *Oberon* and the recitatives for *Der Freischütz,* and he translated *Don Giovanni* and *Fidelio* into German.

Bodanzky was highly active as a conductor in New York outside the Metropolitan Opera House. In 1916 he helped to found the Society of Friends of Music, which he conducted in concerts of rarely heard masterworks, old and new, until its dissolution in 1931. With this organization he gave the American premieres of Mahler's *Das Lied von der Erde,* Pfitzner's *Von Deutscher Seele,* Honegger's *King David,* Bloch's *Schelomo* and *Israel Symphony,* and Pizzetti's *Abraham and Isaac.* He also conducted choral masterworks by Bach, Mozart, Haydn, and Janáček,

and operas by Purcell and Gluck in concert form. In April 1919 he was appointed principal conductor of the New (later National) Symphony Orchestra in New York. He held this post only briefly, withdrawing when the orchestra was absorbed by the New York Philharmonic.

Bodanzky's last performance at the Metropolitan was *Tristan and Isolde* on May 23, 1938. He spent a quiet summer in Vermont that year with the intention of returning to his conductor's stand at the Metropolitan to celebrate his twenty-fifth season. A severe arthritic attack frustrated such plans. Stricken by a heart attack he was hospitalized in New York on October 28, 1939, where complications brought on his death on November 23, 1939. He was buried in Sleepy Hollow Cemetery in Tarrytown, New York. His bust, the work of Malvina Hoffmann, was unveiled in the lobby of the Metropolitan Opera in 1942.

Bodanzky and his wife and two children made their home in an apartment on West One Hundredth Street in New York City. Though he was dictatorial in his manner and behavior outside the world of music as well as inside it, Bodanzky endeared himself to his many friends for his great personal charm and wit. His favorite diversion was playing pinochle or bridge.

ABOUT: New York Times, November 24, 1939; New Yorker, March 15, 1930; Opera News, January 15, 1972; Saturday Evening Post, October 26, 1929.

Karl Böhm

1894–

Karl Böhm, conductor, was born in Graz, Austria, on August 28, 1894. His father, Leopold, was a lawyer, an amateur singer, and an ardent Wagnerite. He made frequent visits to Bayreuth where he became friends with Hans Richter, the well-known conductor of Wagner, and with many Wagnerian singers. From his father Karl acquired his early reverence for Wagner's music; from his mother, a trained pianist, he received his first formal music instruction.

Since his father wanted him to become a lawyer, Karl was given an academic education in

Böhm: bûm

KARL BÖHM

the public schools of Graz before he entered the university for the study of law. But music was not neglected. At the Graz Conservatory he specialized in piano and theory, and later on, at the Vienna Conservatory, he studied theory with Eusebius Mandyczewski. Böhm never took a lesson in conducting. Throughout his career he was convinced that conductors were born and not made though he did not minimize the importance of intensive music study for the development of a conductor's art.

World War I interrupted his studies of law and music, and for a brief time he served in the army. Then, sustaining injuries from the kick of a horse and suffering from undernourishment, he was honorably discharged. Returning to Graz, he became coach and assistant conductor at the Graz Opera in 1917, and in October of that year he conducted his first opera, Victor Nessler's Der Trompeter von Säkkingen. During this time he continued his law studies at the University, receiving his doctorate in law on April 4, 1919. After being appointed principal conductor of the Graz Opera in 1920 he decided that music and not law was his lifework, a decision reaffirmed for him after he had conducted an impressive performance of The Flying Dutchman. Somewhat later a brilliant performance of Lohengrin drew the interest of Karl Muck, who volunteered to coach Böhm in the study and preparation of the Wagnerian repertory. Muck recommended Böhm to Bruno Walter, the general music director of the Munich Opera, who brought Böhm to Munich in 1921 as an assistant

conductor. During the next six years Böhm led 538 performances of 73 operas, including his first Mozart performance (The Abduction from the Seraglio), his first Tristan and Isolde, and also for the first time 2 operas which became his favorite Strauss operas, Der Rosenkavalier and Ariadne auf Naxos.

In Munich he met Thea Linhard, a seventeen-year-old soprano and pupil of Maria Ivogün, whom Bruno Walter had brought to his company. Thea Linhard made her debut in Munich as Oscar in Un Ballo in Maschera, then sang Mimi in La Bohème under Böhm's direction. A romance developed between conductor and singer, and on May 2, 1927, they were married. She gave up her career to devote herself to her husband. They lived at Casa Thea in Baldham near Munich, with their son, Karlheinz, who became a successful tenor.

In 1927 Böhm moved on to Darmstadt to become general music director of the Darmstadt Opera. He specialized in Wagner, Mozart, and Beethoven's Fidelio which he often called "my song of destiny," but he also paid special attention to twentieth century operas. In Darmstadt he produced Krenek's Jonny Spielt Auf and Das Leben des Orest, Hindemith's Neues vom Tage, Honegger's Judith, Wolf-Ferrari's Sly, and Berg's Wozzeck. After Böhm's performance of Wozzeck on February 28, 1931, Berg wrote in Böhm's score: "The Wozzeck performance in Darmstadt . . . was a great and joyful event for me, not only because it succeeded beautifully but because it brought me into contact with the dear human being and splendid musician, Dr. Karl Böhm."

From 1931 to 1934 Böhm was the general music director of the Hamburg Opera. In this post he met Richard Strauss after Strauss had come to Hamburg to supervise Böhm's rehearsals of Arabella. A deep and permanent friendship developed between these two musicians that ended only with the composer's death. Böhm became one of the world's foremost conductors of Strauss's operas. He led the world premieres of Die Schweigsame Frau on June 24, 1935, and Daphne (which Strauss dedicated to him) on October 15, 1938. His interpretations of Salome, Elektra, Der Rosenkavalier, Ariadne auf Naxos, and Die Frau ohne Schatten were acclaimed both in the United States and in Europe.

The premieres of Die Schweigsame Frau and Daphne took place in Dresden where in 1934

Karl Böhm had succeeded Fritz Busch as music director. He remained in Dresden nine years, conducting an average of one hundred performances and ten subscription orchestral concerts each year. In November 1936 the Dresden Opera under Böhm visited London for guest performances at Covent Garden.

Böhm made his first appearance at the Salzburg Festival on July 25, 1938, with a performance of *Don Giovanni*. For the next quarter of a century and more he was heard there annually in operatic and orchestral performances, scoring particular successes with his performances of *Così fan Tutte* and *Die Frau ohne Schatten*, among other Mozart and Strauss operas. In 1943 Böhm acquired one of the most coveted operatic posts in the world, the music directorship of the Vienna State Opera. He held this post just two years. In 1945 he was made director of the German repertory at the Teatro Colón in Buenos Aires.

In 1954 Böhm was reappointed music director of the Vienna State Opera on a five-year contract. He inaugurated his regime with a remarkable performance of *Fidelio* on November 5, 1955. This performance opened the rebuilt opera house on the Ringstrasse and was an event attracting world attention. It was re-created a year later by television for American audiences. In March 1956 he resigned because he was being severely criticized by the management for filling so many engagements with opera companies and orchestras outside Vienna. Though he was no longer music director, he continued to serve the company as one of its conductors throughout the years.

Böhm made his American debut on February 9, 1956, conducting the Chicago Symphony Orchestra. His American opera debut followed a year and a half later, on October 28, 1957, when he opened a new season of the Metropolitan Opera with *Don Giovanni*. In the *Herald Tribune* Paul Henry Lang called the overall performance "overwhelming" and "incredible." About Böhm's conducting, Lang said: "The supreme commander of the evening, Karl Böhm . . . offered a fully matured concept of the work which he carried out in the smallest detail. His reading of the score must be considered an extraordinary artistic achievement. . . . Mr. Böhm is a great conductor who sees the opera as a whole and vouches for the integrity of his conception." In the New York *Times* Howard

Taubman wrote: "Because he adores Mozart, Mr. Böhm has a high regard for every nuance. He has seen to it that subtle touches for voice and orchestra have their proper attention. The result is a continuous flow, not merely an emphasis on the big set numbers. *Don Giovanni* emerges as it should—an integrated music drama."

During that season at the Metropolitan Opera Böhm once again showed his remarkable interpretative powers with a performance of *Wozzeck* which drew ovations from the audience. Böhm's interpretation of *Wozzeck*, in a Berlin performance, was recorded by Deutsche Grammophon Gesellschaft and received the Grammy award in the United States from the National Academy of Recording Arts and Sciences in 1965 as the year's best opera album.

While serving with distinction at the Metropolitan Opera for seventeen years Böhm continued to gather laurels elsewhere. On December 8, 1960, he made his debut as conductor of the New York Philharmonic Orchestra. In 1961 he toured the United States with the visiting Berlin Philharmonic Orchestra; in 1963–1964 he toured Japan with that orchestra and there, in addition to orchestral performances, he also conducted *Fidelio* and *The Marriage of Figaro*. In 1962 he made his first appearance at the Bayreuth Festival in a new production of *Tristan and Isolde* staged by Wieland Wagner, and during that same year he led prodigious performances of Berg's *Lulu* at the Vienna June Festival. In 1967 Böhm conducted four concerts of the Vienna Philharmonic at Montreal's Expo '67 and brought the same orchestra to New York on September 24. Then, on October 3 he conducted the New York Philharmonic in celebration of its one-hundred-twenty-fifth anniversary. In 1972 he performed an Italian opera at the Vienna State Opera for the first time: *Otello,* which he had conducted early in his career in Germany. In 1973 he conducted for television *Salome* with Teresa Stratas. On November 16, 1975, he conducted the first of five performances of *Così fan Tutte* at the Kennedy Center in Washington, D.C., with the Deutsche Oper of Berlin in its first tour of the United States. "All of the pieces clicked together like the tumblers of a cracked safe," reported Donal Henahan in the New York *Times,* "due primarily to the expertise of Karl Böhm, whose magisterial presence in the pit gave the performance unfailing rhythmic vitality and theatrical timing." In the spring of 1976 Böhm toured the United States with the Vienna Philharmonic.

On December 1, 1977, Böhm returned to Covent Garden for the first time since 1936 to conduct a revival of *The Marriage of Figaro.* He has also conducted a taped performance of this opera for television transmission.

To Robert Breuer writing in *Opera News,* the secret of Böhm's conducting is his "sound—always soft and round and filled with inner life. He seems to be Apollo and Dionysus in one, able to lead a swirling Mozart finale of the most luminous clarity or an ecstatic *Tristan.*"

Discussing his own art Karl Böhm said: "I learned a thing or two from Strauss. You know he conducted with the greatest ease. But, believe me, it's not enough to know an orchestra and many works. The meaning of the music has to be understood and felt, and this requires self-discipline and the gift for teaching discipline to others. Again and again one is challenged to do one's very best, and even if artists always strive to do their best, the best just cannot be produced on an assembly belt." He also stated: "Conducting is a kind of hypnotism. I have a clear concept of the score, and I try to communicate this concept to the players. But I never 'strangle' them with my ideas—I leave the players freedom, too. I am also perfectly willing to discuss the music in question, and its execution, as long as I can answer for it to my artistic conscience. A conductor translates his total concept of a work into reality through gestures. . . . Every unnecessary movement is disturbing and detracts from the performance."

Böhm credits his extraordinary artistic vitality, a vitality that continued in old age, to his lifelong concern for his body. "If I had not become a lawyer or musician, I would have chosen pharmaceutics or medicine," he says. "I have always studied my own body. Since the age of twenty, there has not been a single day when I did not sleep three hours in the afternoon; this is what I need. . . . Later I found out that drinking ice-cold champagne, which I loved, was bad for the kidneys, so I gave it up, as well as smoking. I exercise every morning, stretching my arms up the walls of the room as far as possible, then half an hour of knee-bending and other gymnastics." Böhm partakes of just two meals a day, breakfast and dinner. "My favorite food is rice, lots and lots of rice. I eat few sweets and no Viennese strudels."

In 1956 the International Mozarteum Foundation in Salzburg presented Böhm with the Golden Mozart Memorial Medal. He also received the Brahms medal from Hamburg, the Bruckner Ring from the Vienna Symphony, the Schalk medal from the Vienna Philharmonic, the Honorary Mozart Ring from the city of Vienna, the Great Badge of Honor in Silver, and the Great Distinguished Service Cross in Gold with Star. In 1964, on his seventieth birthday, the Austrian government conferred on him the honorary title of General Music Director of Austria. At that time a Böhm Day was proclaimed in Vienna, and in Berlin a statue of him was commissioned by Mayor Willy Brandt. This was later placed in the foyer of the Berlin opera house. In 1970 Böhm received from Vienna the Great Golden Medal of Honor for his contributions to the cultural life of the city. His eightieth birthday was celebrated in 1974 in Salzburg and Vienna with gala performances of *Die Frau ohne Schatten.* Böhm has also been made honorary citizen of the city of Salzburg and honorary member of the Vienna Philharmonic and has been elected to the prestigious Gesellschaft der Musikfreunde in Vienna. In 1977 Böhm was named president of the London Symphony Orchestra, succeeding the late Sir Arthur Bliss.

Böhm and his wife make their home in Vienna where he houses his collection of clocks and his music memorabilia.

ABOUT: Blaukopf, K. Great Conductors. *Periodicals*—Hi-Fi Magazine, March 1960; High Fidelity, May 1977; Musical America, March 1963; New York Times, October 13, 1957, February 14, 1965; Opera (London), December 1977; Opera News, April 8, 1972, August 1974.

Michael Bohnen

1887–1965

Michael Bohnen, bass baritone, was born in Cologne, on May 2, 1887. After attending the Cologne Conservatory he made his debut with the Düsseldorf Opera as Caspar in *Der Freischütz* in 1910. From 1911 to 1914 he was a member of the Wiesbaden Opera. His first success came in

Bohnen: bōʹnʹn

MICHAEL BOHNEN

1914 when, without rehearsal, he substituted for an ailing singer as Gurnemanz in a Berlin Royal Opera production of *Parsifal*, a performance that led Kaiser Wilhelm to name him *Kammersänger*. That year Bohnen further solidified his reputation in the Wagnerian repertory with guest performances at Covent Garden and with appearances as Hans Sachs in *Die Meistersinger*, Wotan in the *Ring* cycle, and Gurnemanz.

During World War I Bohnen served for a short time in the German army. Allowed by the German government to leave military service and return to the Berlin Royal Opera, he remained there as a principal bass baritone until 1918.

Music was not his sole sphere of activity. As David E. Presser wrote in *Opera News*, by the end of World War I Bohnen had "boxed and wrestled professionally, was a swimming and billiards champion, had won eight prizes for auto racing, and was an artist in oils and watercolors of near-professional quality as well as an able sculptor." In addition, Bohnen acted in, directed, and produced several films.

Bohnen's American debut took place on March 1, 1923, at the Metropolitan Opera as Francesco and The Tourist in the American premiere of Max Schillings's *Mona Lisa*. "Mr. Bohnen," reported Henry Krehbiel in the *Tribune*, "sang in an effective bass, with much dramatic virility and command of emotional color." Two days later Bohnen made an even better impression as Gurnemanz. Later the same season he appeared as King Henry in *Lohengrin*, Amo-

nasro in *Aida*, and King Mark in *Tristan and Isolde*.

During a decade of performances at the Metropolitan Opera Bohnen was heard 175 times in New York City and 26 times on tour in 21 roles. His greatest successes came in the Wagnerian repertory. Lawrence Gilman, in the *Tribune*, called him "the greatest Wagnerian interpreter of the century." His Wagnerian repertory, besides Gurnemanz, King Henry, and King Mark, included Wotan and Hunding in *Die Walküre*, Wotan in *Das Rheingold*, the Wanderer in *Siegfried*, Hans Sachs in *Die Meistersinger*, Hagen in *Die Götterdämmerung*, Hermann in *Tannhäuser*, and Daland in *The Flying Dutchman*.

He assumed other roles as well: Caspar in *Der Freischütz*, Mephistopheles in *Faust*, Kezal in *The Bartered Bride*, Rocco in *Fidelio*, Baron Ochs in *Der Rosenkavalier*, Tonio in *I Pagliacci*, and the title role in the American premiere of Ernst Krenek's *Jonny Spielt Auf* on January 19, 1929.

Describing Bohnen's voice, Hans Borgelt wrote that it was "seductive, disquieting, appealing to the entire nervous system; it did not merely report a fact, it expressed an editorial comment." Borgelt further commented that Bohnen was "a master of gesture, movement, and mimicry, singer and actor fused into a masterful personality which held his audience in a spell of fascination." To Irving Kolodin Bohnen was "one of the truly great operatic artists of the twenties." In a Bohnen performance, Kolodin said, one could not "separate the vocal experience from the dramatic, for they were both completely interrelated."

During the 1926–1927 season Michael Bohnen married the young American soprano Mary Lewis, who made her Metropolitan Opera debut on January 28, 1926, as Mimi in *La Bohème*. Their marriage ended in divorce.

Bohnen's last appearance at the Metropolitan Opera was as the Wanderer in *Siegfried* on April 13, 1932. He returned to Europe, served as a member of the Berlin State Opera from 1934 to 1945, and made some films. Life for him in Germany was not easy since he refused to ally himself with the Nazi regime. At one point he was compelled to give up singing temporarily and work as a porter for a radio and electrical company. After the end of World War II he was made director of the Berlin City Opera, and from 1945 to 1947 he served as president of the

Bolet

Chamber of Artists, an office in which he helped to plan the rebuilding of the Berlin State Opera. During the 1950–1951 season he was heard as Baron Ochs and as Scarpia in *Tosca* at the Berlin Komische Oper. His last appearance on the stage took place at the Berlin City Opera in 1951 as Hans Sachs.

The remainder of Bohnen's life was spent in seclusion. Because he had been married to La Jana, a dancer with close affiliations with the Nazis, he spent the last years of his life under a political cloud, sometimes in dire poverty and despair. An honorary pension from the Metropolitan helped partially to alleviate his financial distress and to raise his depressed spirits. He died in Berlin on April 26, 1965.

ABOUT: Opera News, January 31, 1970.

JORGE BOLET

Jorge Bolet

1914–

Jorge Bolet, pianist, was born in Havana on November 15, 1914, to Antonio and Adelina Tremoleda Bolet. His parents, who were of Catalonian descent, were not musicians; his father held a minor post in the Cuban army. "The earliest recollection I have of life," recalls Bolet, "is hearing my sister Maria practice the piano. . . . My mother tells me that as a baby of two or three months I was quite unruly, but that whenever I heard Maria play, I would immediately quiet down and lie for hours almost as if mesmerized. Naturally, as I grew older, my dream was to become a pianist."

When Jorge was five his sister took him to a piano recital by Rudolf Ganz. "That was the moment of decision. I vowed I'd be that man up there on the stage," he has said. Jorge started piano lessons with his sister when he was six and continued for the next half dozen years. In that time he occasionally performed at soirées. At one of these a visitor from Erie, Pennsylvania, became interested in him and promised to get him an audition for the newly opened Curtis Institute of Music in Philadelphia. Funds for the Philadelphia trip were raised through a benefit concert in which Jorge played a few solos. After passing the audition, he spent the next seven years at Curtis as a pupil of David Saperton. In 1933 he made his professional debut, performing the Tchaikovsky Piano Concerto No. 1 at Carnegie Hall with Artur Rodzinski conducting. He was graduated from Curtis in 1934.

One year after graduation Bolet was financed by the Cuban government to make his first trip to Europe. "By this time," he says, "I was so sick of schools and teachers and piano lessons that I decided simply to live, to practice on my own, and to listen to a lot of music." For nine months in Paris and one in London he did just that. Refreshed by this interlude, he undertook his first concert tour, with recitals in Amsterdam, The Hague, Paris, London, Berlin, Vienna, and Milan.

Returning to the United States and to the Curtis Institute, he studied conducting with Boris Goldovsky and became a member of the piano faculty as Rudolf Serkin's assistant. In 1937 Bolet made an important forward stride in his career as virtuoso by winning the Naumburg Award which brought him a concert appearance at Town Hall, New York. One year later he was given the Josef Hofmann Award, the highest honor the Curtis Institute could bestow on one of its graduates.

When World War II broke out Bolet was called back to Cuba by President Batista. After several months of military training in Cuba, he was sent back to the United States to serve as assistant military attaché at the Cuban Embassy in Washington, D.C. When Batista lost the presidential election in Cuba in 1944, Bolet was removed from his position in Washington. He presented himself to the American draft board

86

in Philadelphia and was inducted as a private into the United States army. Upon receiving his American citizenship and completing his courses at the officers' training school, Bolet was commissioned a lieutenant and sent to join the occupation forces in Japan. He was in Special Services, in an entertainment unit for which he organized shows and did some piano playing. One of his productions was the Gilbert and Sullivan comic opera *The Mikado,* its first performance in Japan.

In 1946 Bolet returned to civilian life and to a career as a virtuoso. After one of his recitals in New York a critic for the *Herald Tribune* described him as "an artist to whom the grand manner is neither affectation nor pose. His performance [is] polished, elastic. ... Warm of tone, incisive of rhythm, he places a whirlwind technique at the service of music whose cyclonic temperament demands a masterful treatment." Though he was given engagements and was playing extraordinarily well, the going was rough. Bolet looks back to the forties and early fifties as a time of disappointments and frustrations. "Those were terrible years," he says. "There was great struggle. There was half-starvation. I would not be here if it weren't for the kindness of my friends. They saw me through those ghastly, lean years. What kept me going during that period was simply playing. ... And people kept hearing me play and they would say, 'My God! Where have you been? Why aren't you at the top?' "

He did manage to reach the top, though the ascent was slow and painful. By the late sixties he was beginning to be recognized as one of the foremost exponents of the grand piano tradition of the Romantic era; Harold C. Schonberg referred to him as "one of the great Liszt pianists of the century, with the fingers of a Horowitz and the tone of a Lhévinne." In whirlwind tours of the musical world, in recitals and appearances with symphony orchestras, Bolet became the idol of the Romantic revival in pianism. He was also heard playing Liszt's music on the soundtrack of Liszt's screen biography, *Song Without End* (1960).

He became such an attraction in the concert hall that during the 1971–1972 season he was called upon to make ten appearances with the New York Philharmonic, opening the season with Liszt's *Totentanz,* Pierre Boulez conducting. In the same period Bolet opened the season of the American Symphony Orchestra under Stokowski with Prokofiev's Piano Concerto No.2. The London *Times* called him "the Titan of the keyboard," the Munich *Presse* spoke of him as "a nobleman at the piano with the incredible dexterity of a magician," and the San Francisco *Examiner* reported that "to hear him play is one of the most sensational experiences in modern virtuoso pianism."

In 1972 Bolet signed an exclusive long-term recording contract with RCA. His album *Franz Liszt's Greatest Hits of the 1850s* became a bestseller and was chosen "Record of the Year" by *Stereo Review.* A second Liszt album sold equally well. In 1974 RCA released the album *Jorge Bolet: At Carnegie Hall,* a recording of his recital on February 25, 1974. Reviewing this album for *Stereo Review* Eric Salzman wrote: "With a certain patrician air and a sense of total command, Bolet not only gets away with all manner of pompous rhetoric and unabashed emotional display, but makes *you* believe in it. This kind of playing has been put down and buried in ignominy for years; its revival just now ... was inevitable, and Bolet is ... its outstanding exponent."

In addition to pursuing an active career as a concert artist Bolet has served as professor of the piano at Indiana University in Bloomington. In 1977 he was made head of the piano department at Curtis Institute in Philadelphia.

In a New York *Times* article, John Gruen described Bolet's appearance as follows: "Bolet, heavy-set and a towering six-foot-two, exuded the enigmatic, if not the menacing. ... The head is large, with black-brown, fiery eyes; the eyebrows are heavy—startlingly so. A moustache, thick, squarish and carefully clipped, suggests the aggressive military, as does the graying black hair, slicked down and sharply parted to the side. ... The voice is deep, resonant and decisive."

Bolet maintains two residences, one in Bloomington, Indiana, and the other in Spain. He has never married, explaining: "For me it was either marriage and a family or a career. I chose a career, and all my life has been in the pursuit of one goal: to mature as a pianist, as a musician, and as an artist."

ABOUT: Musical America, December 1, 1954; New York Times, January 28, 1973.

Alessandro Bonci

1870–1940

Alessandro Bonci, tenor, was born in Cesena, near Bologna, Italy, on February 10, 1870. He was a cobbler's apprentice when the discovery was made that he had a beautiful voice. He was then enrolled in the Rossini Conservatory in Pesaro where he studied voice with Carlo Pedrotti and Felice Coen. After five years at the Conservatory, he left for Paris for further vocal training with Enrico Delle Sedie.

In 1892 he was appointed solo vocalist with the choir at the Pilgrimage Church in Loreto. His debut in opera took place in January 1896 at the Teatro Regio in Parma as Fenton in *Falstaff*. Following this he was called upon for guest appearances, first in Leghorn, and then at La Scala in Milan where he made his debut in 1897 as Arturo in *I Puritani*. After performances in St. Petersburg, Vienna, Berlin, Lisbon, and Madrid, he went to Covent Garden in 1900 as Rodolfo in *La Bohème*. He was a prime favorite of English audiences until Caruso overshadowed him, and even then he continued making regular appearances at Covent Garden.

In the fall of 1906 Oscar Hammerstein signed Bonci for the Manhattan Opera House as a rival attraction to Caruso, and his debut took place on December 3, 1906, in *I Puritani*. He remained two years with this company, specializing in Italian roles. When Manhattan Opera closed down, Bonci made his debut at the Metropolitan Opera on November 22, 1907, as the Duke in *Rigoletto*. He remained at the Metropolitan three seasons, filling 65 engagements in New York, 11 on tour, in 14 roles. The full range of his vocal art became apparent in his initial season when he was heard as Rodolfo, Almaviva in *The Barber of Seville*, Lionel in *Martha*, Don Ottavio in *Don Giovanni*, Alfredo in *La Traviata*, Wilhelm Meister in *Mignon*, Edgardo in *Lucia di Lammermoor*, Cavaradossi in *Tosca*, Roberto in the American premiere of Puccini's first opera *Le Villi* (December 17, 1908), Nemorino in *L'Elisir d'Amore*, Ernesto in *Don Pasquale*, the title role in *Faust*, and Elvino in *La Sonnambula*.

What Bonci lacked in physical stature, power of dramatic presentation, and volume he made

Bonci: bōn' chê

ALESSANDRO BONCI

up for in the elegant beauty and sweetness of his vocal delivery, his total mastery of the *bel canto* style. In the New York *Times* Richard Aldrich analyzed Bonci's art: "There has been ample opportunity for this public to study at the two opera houses ... Mr. Bonci's delightful and finished art in vocalism, which included many of the highest attributes of style and method; fine legato, perfect finish in phrasing, management of breath, production of tone and attack, finish and flexibility of technique and excellence of diction. ... He is an operatic tenor of a type that is rapidly disappearing, and whose extinction will spell disaster for the art."

In 1910–1911 Bonci made his first transcontinental tour of the United States in song recitals. He became one of the few Italian singers able to master the art of the German *Lied*, and he was no less impressive in French, Italian, and even American song literature. "The beauty of his singing," said Richard Aldrich after Bonci's first recital at Carnegie Hall on November 22, 1910, "is of an inestimable value at the present time, when the tendency is so strong to forget how such beauty is begotten."

In 1913–1914, Bonci enjoyed major successes in Madrid and Barcelona, and in 1914 he was a member of the Chicago Opera. When the European war broke out in 1914 he joined the Italian army as an airplane pilot and mechanic. In 1918 he resumed his career with performances at the Teatro Colón in Buenos Aires. From 1919 through 1921 he appeared with the Chicago Opera and in 1922–1923 with Teatro Costanzi in Rome.

Bonci returned to the United States in 1924 to head several master classes in singing. After 1925 he devoted himself exclusively to the teaching of voice and to coaching singers in New York and Milan. In 1935 he went into total retirement in Italy. He died in Viserba, near Rimini, on August 8, 1940.

Bonci was made Knight of the Crown of Italy in 1902.

ABOUT: Kutsch, K. J. and Riemens, L. A Concise Biographical Dictionary of Singers.

Richard Bonelli

1887–

RICHARD BONELLI

Richard Bonelli (originally Richard Bunn), baritone, was born in Port Byron, New York, on February 6, 1887. He attended public schools in Port Byron and helped to support his family by working in late afternoons and evenings selling newspapers and magazine subscriptions and doing small jobs for neighbors. An excellent student, he earned a scholarship for Syracuse University where he specialized in science and mechanics as preparation for a possible career in engineering. At the university his fine singing voice attracted the interest of Dean Butler who encouraged him to study music.

After a few singing lessons Bonelli was advised by Butler to build up his physique with outdoor activities. Bonelli went west and found work first in an Arizona zinc mine and later as the manager of a hotel in Los Angeles. In Los Angeles he studied singing with Arthur Alexander. He also worked for an insurance firm, and for the telephone company, in Seattle. Alexander felt that Bonelli showed enough talent to warrant further training. On Alexander's urging, Bonelli left for Paris where he continued his vocal studies with Jean de Reszke and William Vilonat.

He returned to the United States in 1915. On April 21 of that year he made his opera debut at the Brooklyn Academy of Music in New York as Valentin in *Faust*. Several engagements in Cuba followed.

Bonelli: bô něl' ĭ

At the end of World War I Bonelli returned to Europe, and there he made his foreign opera debut in Modena, Italy, in 1923. Through the painter Léon Bakst, Bonelli met Raoul Gunsbourg, impresario of the Monte Carlo Opera, who engaged him for four performances. Bonelli's success brought him six more engagements in Monte Carlo and a contract with La Scala in Milan that he could not fulfill because of illness.

After recuperating Bonelli embarked on a tour of Europe. In Paris he sang for one season with Mary Garden at the Théâtre de la Gaîté-Lyrique. The general music director of the Chicago Opera heard him there and engaged him for his company for the 1925–1926 season. Bonelli remained in Chicago six years, distinguishing himself in the Italian and French repertory. Here Bonelli also appeared in what is generally credited as being the first opera broadcast over a nationwide radio hookup from the stage of an American opera house. This took place on January 21, 1927, when a scene from *Faust* was broadcast. On September 25, 1926, Bonelli made his first appearance with the San Francisco Opera as Figaro in *The Barber of Seville*. He returned to the San Francisco Opera for the years 1932–1935, 1937–1940, and in 1942.

He made his debut with the Metropolitan Opera on November 29, 1932, as Figaro in *The Barber of Seville* while the company was on tour. On December 1, 1932, he appeared in New York as Germont in *La Traviata*. "Mr. Bonelli's engaging and dignified presence as Germont, his big range and the full, easy utterance with which

89

he commanded the role were not alone responsible for his unqualified popular success," said Hubbard Hutchinson in the New York *Times*. "The artist supplements the vocalist, and though the scrupulous care with which he outlined Verdi's splendid phrases may have been more apparent to critical than popular ears, this very faithfulness to the composer explains his success even more than a rich timbre and the dramatic effectiveness of his upper registers. . . . On the whole his performance was remarkably fine."

Bonelli's last appearance at the Metropolitan took place on March 8, 1945, as Germont. During his thirteen years at the Metropolitan he was heard 103 times in New York and 35 times on tour in 19 roles among which were: Marcello in *La Bohème*, Valentin in *Faust*, Tonio in *I Pagliacci*, Rigoletto, Amonasro in *Aida*, Sharpless in *Madama Butterfly*, Manfredo in *L'Amore dei Tre Re*, Escamillo in *Carmen*, Barnaba in *La Gioconda*, Scarpia in *Tosca*, Figaro in *The Barber of Seville*, Ashton in *Lucia di Lammermoor*, Lescaut in *Manon*, Count di Luna in *Il Trovatore*, Wolfram in *Tannhäuser*, and Iago in *Otello*. In addition he appeared in an American opera, as Wrestling Bradford in Howard Hanson's *Merry Mount*.

While he was still at the Metropolitan, Bonelli became the head of the voice department of the Academy of the West at Santa Barbara, California, in 1943. Following his retirement from the stage in 1945 he served as chairman of the board of the Academy of the West from 1947 to 1949, and from 1950 to 1955 he taught voice at the Curtis Institute in Philadelphia.

For many years Bonelli and his wife, Pauline Curley, whom he married on October 17, 1917, lived in the town of Crystal Bay at Lake Tahoe, Nevada. More recently, however, Bonelli has been living in Los Angeles. He has never forgotten his onetime preoccupation with mechanics. He enjoys tinkering with his automobile, radio, or television set; and he once invented a new type of spark plug.

ABOUT: Kutsch, K. J. and Riemens, L. A Concise Biographical Dictionary of Singers.

Lucrezia Bori

1887–1960

Lucrezia Bori (originally Lucrecia Borja y González de Riancho), soprano, was born at Gandia, a suburb of Valencia, Spain, on December 24, 1887, to an aristocratic family. Her father, Vincenzo Borja, a descendant of the Borgia family of Italy, was a colonel in the Spanish army.

Until her eighteenth year Lucrezia was educated in a convent. She had a beautiful singing voice, and she was constantly singing. As early as her sixth year she gave a concert for charity. Though she was given musical training at the Valencia Conservatory she had little expectation of undertaking a professional career in music.

Shortly after her eighteenth birthday she began seriously considering a musical career. She found an unexpected ally in her father who took her on a trip to Italy, where for several months she studied voice with Melchior Vidal in Milan. On October 31, 1908, she made her opera debut in Rome as Micaëla in *Carmen*. It was on this occasion that she assumed the shortened and Italianized name of Lucrezia Bori because members of her family resented having the name Borja appear on billboards and in public notices. For this appearance she sewed her own costume which she wore for all her subsequent performances as Micaëla.

During several guest performances with the San Carlo Opera in Naples she was heard by Ricordi, the powerful publisher, who arranged to have her audition for Giacomo Puccini, Toscanini, and Gatti-Casazza. An engagement at La Scala in Milan resulted, and she appeared there during the years 1910–1912.

In June 1910 the Metropolitan Opera company of New York made its first tour of Europe. During its Paris engagement at the Théâtre du Chatelet, Bori was invited on June 9 to give a guest performance in the title role of *Manon Lescaut* as a last-minute replacement for Lina Cavalieri. One week later she was heard as Gilda in *Rigoletto*. Jean de Reszke said of her prophetically: "If Lucrezia Bori does not overstrain her voice while she is young, and spoil its remarkable purity, she will take her place at the top of the list of the world's great singers."

Bori: bô′ rē̄

LUCREZIA BORI

The Metropolitan Opera wanted to engage Bori immediately for the United States, but her commitments at La Scala and in South America delayed that debut until November 11, 1912 (the opening night of the season), in the title role of *Manon Lescaut.* "In the first act she was distinctly disappointing," said Henry Krehbiel in the *Tribune,* "but when her opportunity came in the second act, she surprised the audience by the real finesse of her vocal art, by an exquisite exhibition of legato singing, by exquisite diction, impeccable intonation and moving pathos." She gave even stronger evidence of her artistic potential during the rest of that season, as Nedda in *I Pagliacci,* Mimi in *La Bohème,* Norina in *Don Pasquale,* and Antonia in *The Tales of Hoffmann.*

Among the operas in which she was heard in her second season were two American premieres: *L'Amore dei Tre Re* (Fiora) on January 2, 1914, and Wolf-Ferrari's *L'Amore Medico* (Lucinda) on March 25, both conducted by Toscanini. As Fiora she experienced her first triumph. "Miss Bori must have astonished her most devoted admirers by her impersonation," wrote W. J. Henderson in the *Sun.* "To summarize briefly, it was lovely in its pictorial quality and sung almost flawlessly."

In her third season Bori added to her Metropolitan roles those of Micaëla, the title part in Mascagni's *Iris,* and Ah-Yoe in the American premiere of Leoni's *L'Oracolo* on February 4, 1915.

After her third season Bori began suffering from a throat ailment that was finally diagnosed as a growth. The surgeon's scalpel impaired her vocal chords. At one time during her convalescence she was compelled to remain totally silent for two months and it appeared that her career was over, but Bori herself never lost hope. "Never during the long dark months when I was not permitted to talk, let alone sing, did I lose faith that in the end my voice would come back. But it *was* terrible. I felt as must those stricken with sudden blindness just as the sun of spring flooded the world."

For the next few years she continued consulting voice specialists. She also visited the St. Francis Shrine continually, vowing a life of charity if her voice returned. By 1918 she had recovered sufficient voice to make an appearance in Monte Carlo. Though the Lucrezia Bori of the 1912–1915 period was hardly in evidence in 1918, she still expressed full confidence that she was well on her way to full recovery as a singer.

Finally, on January 28, 1921, she made her "second debut" at the Metropolitan Opera after an absence of six years, this time as Mimi. "Her entrance," reported Richard Aldrich in the New York *Times,* "was greeted with a long and continued demonstrative welcome. Her singing of the music that follows disclosed apparently the old quality, the old power and volume, the old style. ... But quite as valuable an element in Miss Bori's impersonation was—and is—the gracious and insinuating charm of her acting, the power of closely identifying herself with the character she represents; her mirth, gaiety and vivacity, her pathetic and poetic intensity. ... The warmth of her welcome last evening showed very clearly that she had not been forgotten, and that unfaded memories were joined with glad anticipations."

For the next fifteen years Bori was one of the glories of the Metropolitan Opera company. She sang the principal roles in the French and Italian repertory, bringing to them the lyric beauty and sensitivity of an intelligently projected voice together with a sparkling personality and dramatic appeal. On March 21, 1925, she sang Mélisande in the first Metropolitan Opera production of *Pelléas and Mélisande,* becoming the second Mélisande to be heard in New York, the first having been Mary Garden. "It is a pleasure to say that Miss Bori brought Mélisande to life —in her own way, a way that departed from traditions as we have known them here; yet in an incarnation that had unity of plan and line, sensitiveness of feeling, delicacy and vividness of deportment," wrote Lawrence Gilman in the *Herald Tribune.* On February 14, 1923, she was Consuelo in the American premiere of Vittadini's *Anima Allegra;* on November 15, 1923, she was Suzel in Mascagni's *L'Amico Fritz,* revived for her; on November 7, 1925, she was Concepción in the first Metropolitan Opera production of Ravel's *L'Heure Espagnole;* on March 6, 1926, she was Salud in the American premiere of Manuel de Falla's *La Vida Breve;* on March 10, 1928, she was Magda in the American premiere of *La Rondine;* on March 1, 1930, she assumed the title role in *Louise,* another opera revived for her; and on February 7, 1931, she created the part of Mary in the world premiere of Deems Taylor's *Peter Ibbetson.* Her other Metropolitan Opera roles were Suzanne in *The Secret of Suzanne,* Manon in Massenet's opera of the same name, the title role in Mussorgsky's *Snegurochka,* Despina in *Così fan Tutte,* Violetta in *La Traviata,* Juliet in *Romeo and Juliet,* Giulietta in *The Tales of Hoffmann,* Alice Ford in *Falstaff,* Mignon, Magda in *La Rondine,* and Madelon in Felice Lattuada's *Le Preziose Ridicole.*

In 1925 Bori was one of the first opera stars to broadcast over the radio when, with John McCormack, she was heard on a nationwide hookup.

She intended to retire from opera in 1933 after twenty-five years of service. But that year the Metropolitan Opera was gripped by one of its most critical financial crises. With the economic depression at its height the fate of the company was in doubt. Realizing that Bori was a top box-office attraction, the management urged her to reconsider her decision. She not only signed a new singing contract, but she also became the chairman of a committee formed to "save the Metropolitan Opera House." By singing, by making public speeches, and by open appeals during performances, she asked for and got the support of opera lovers. One year later she returned as the chairman of a committee to raise more funds for the company. Largely as a result of her tireless efforts more than three million dollars was raised, making it possible for the Metropolitan Opera to survive the crisis. Paul D. Cravath, president and chairman of the board of the Metropolitan Opera, recognized the importance of her fund-raising efforts by announcing from the stage of the opera house on the opening night of the 1933–1934 season that she "did more than anyone else to make opera at the Metropolitan this year a financial possibility."

In 1935, with the future of the Metropolitan Opera assured, Bori announced her retirement. On March 21, 1936, she made her last operatic appearance in New York as Magda in *La Rondine.* A week later, on March 29, a gala farewell concert was held in her honor at the Metropolitan Opera. The program was inscribed to its honored guest as follows:

As a friend—most understanding,
As a woman—adorable,
As a colleague—ideal,
As an artist—irreplaceable.

On this occasion she sang arias from *La Traviata* and *Manon.* At the conclusion of her final number the audience sprang to its feet to acclaim her and remained standing for twenty minutes. Then the curtain parted for the distribution of gifts from the patrons of the opera, fellow artists, stage hands, chorus, orchestra, and many other admirers. "My friends, my dear friends," she said at the end of the ceremony. "My heart is in such turmoil I do not know how to express the varied emotions I am feeling." The proceeds from this concert, about twenty thousand dollars, were contributed to the fund sustaining the Metropolitan Opera.

This concert was not the last time Bori sang with the Metropolitan Opera company. Her actual farewell performance took place as Mimi in Baltimore, on April 2, 1936, during the visit of the Metropolitan Opera to that city.

In all she had appeared 448 times with the Metropolitan Opera in New York and 158 times on tour, in 29 roles. As an editorial in the New York *Times* commented, she left behind her "fragrant and affectionate memories, and profound appreciation of a gracious personality, of a beautiful voice put at the service of a finely balanced artistic nature, and a rich skill and sincerity in acting. . . . She has been a brilliant figure in the operatic history of New York, and her place in the affection and admiration of the New York public is secure. It is a place won not only by artistic integrity and devotion, but by a character back of them that counts."

Following her retirement, Bori (who never married) divided her time between an apartment in the heart of New York City and a quiet country home. As a singer she occasionally made radio appearances, but for the most part her life was spent in quiet seclusion devoted to the pastimes she could now cultivate more fully: the study of philosophy and sculpture. She maintained her association with the Metropolitan Opera, becoming the first singer ever to serve on its board of directors; by serving in 1942 as chairman of the Metropolitan Opera Guild; by assuming in 1953 the co-chairmanship with George A. Sloan for the raising of a million and a half dollars for the rehabilitation of the opera house; and by retaining a permanent seat in the house—A-111—which she occupied for every important performance.

On May 14, 1960, Lucrezia Bori suffered a brain hemorrhage. Twelve days later she died at Roosevelt Hospital in New York City.

ABOUT: New York Times, May 15, 1960; Opera News, October 8, 1960.

INGE BORKH

Inge Borkh

1917–

Inge Borkh (originally Inge Simon), soprano, was born in Mannheim, Germany, on May 26, 1917. She was the daughter of a Swiss diplomat and an Austrian soprano. Several members of her family became prominent in the theater, and she too aspired to the stage and so attended the Max Reinhardt Seminar in Vienna. But she also demonstrated a gift for music and was given her first vocal lessons by her mother. When Inge was sixteen she was persuaded to attend the Vienna Academy.

She began her professional career as an actress in Linz, Austria, in 1937 and continued it in Basel, Switzerland, in 1938. Then, deciding to exchange singing for acting, she studied voice with Moratti and with Alexander Welitsch, whom she later married.

Her debut as a singer took place in Lucerne, Switzerland, in 1940 as Agathe in *Der Freischütz.* During World War II she was heard in opera performances in several other Swiss cities, including Geneva, where she appeared as Magda in Menotti's *The Consul.* Her successes in Switzerland led in 1950 to guest performances in Munich and Berlin. In 1952 she was cast as Sieglinde in *Die Walküre* at the Bayreuth Festival. In 1954 she was acclaimed at the Florence May Music Festival as Eglantine in *Euryanthe.* Appearances at the Vienna State Opera, the Hamburg Opera, Covent Garden in London, and with other important opera companies in Europe—as well as at the Salzburg Festival in Austria—brought her prominence among European sopranos. Among her roles were Santuzza in *Cavalleria Rusticana,* Leonore in *Fidelio,* Donna Anna in *Don Giovanni,* the Countess in *The Marriage of Figaro,* Pamina in *The Magic Flute,* Elektra, Salome, the Composer in *Ariadne auf Naxos,* the title roles in Gluck's *Alceste* and *Iphigénie en Aulide* and in Strauss's *Die Aegyptische Helena,* Tosca, Amelia in *Un Ballo in Maschera,* Aida, Leonora in *Il Trovatore,* Leonora in *La Forza del Destino,* Senta in *The Flying Dutchman,* Elsa in *Lohengrin,* Sieglinde in *Die Walküre,* Brünnhilde in *Siegfried,* Liù in *Turandot,* and Lady Macbeth in Verdi's *Macbeth.*

She also distinguished herself in twentieth century operas. On August 17, 1955, she created the role of Cathleen in the world premiere of Werner Egk's *Irische Legende* at the Salzburg Festival. That same year she was starred in a revival of Respighi's *La Fiamma* at La Scala in Milan. On March 1, 1962, in Frankfort, Germany, she created the role of Alceste in the world premiere of Louise Talma's *Alcestiade,* and in 1971 she was the Queen in the world premiere of Joseph Tal's *Ashmedai* with the Hamburg

Opera. Other roles in her twentieth century repertory were Marie in Berg's *Wozzeck*, Elizabeth in Britten's *Gloriana*, Dorota in Weinberger's *Schwanda*, and the title roles in Carl Orff's *Antigonae*, Janáček's *Jenufa*, and Shostakovich's *Katerina Ismailova*.

On September 25, 1953, she made her American debut with the San Francisco Opera in the title role of *Elektra*. Reporting this event for *Musical America* Marjory M. Fisher wrote: "Miss Borkh was quite superb. A handsome woman, she had a voice that sounded young, fresh, beautiful and voluminous. Her singing was mature and remarkably impressive, capable of conveying a great range of emotions. She also used her entire body as an instrument of expression, and while her actions were stylized they never became stereotyped operatic gestures. Her facial expressions were wonderful to see." During her first season with the San Francisco Opera she was also heard as Liù and Sieglinde. She returned to San Francisco annually until 1955, adding to her repertory there the roles of Salome, Senta, Leonore in *Fidelio*, Lady Macbeth, and Elsa.

On May 8, 1956, Borkh appeared in the American premiere of Britten's *Gloriana*, given a concert performance at the Cincinnati May Music Festival. At that time one of the local critics called her "one of the stars of the contemporary world . . . a singer in the heroic style."

She made her New York concert debut on November 16, 1956, at Carnegie Hall as soloist with the Pittsburgh Symphony in a performance of Alban Berg's concert aria *Der Wein* and Beethoven's *Ah, Perfido!* Hers was a voice, wrote Louis Biancolli in the *World-Telegram and Sun*, "of striking size and strength," and Howard Taubman noted in the New York *Times* that she sang "with style and vocal amplitude." Four days later, on November 20, she appeared again in New York, this time in a concert performance of *Fidelio* with the American Grand Opera Society. Howard Taubman remarked that she gave "every evidence that she knew the style of the piece. Her voice is huge. . . . Her singing of the big aria 'Abscheulicher, wo eilst du hin' had sweep as well as security."

Borkh's first appearance at the Metropolitan Opera, on January 24, 1958, was in one of her most successful roles, Salome in Strauss's opera of the same name. "Miss Borkh," wrote Robert Coleman in the *Daily Mirror*, "is a handsome figure of a woman. She's tall and lithe; she has curves that would make any Broadway musical comedy impresario seek to sign her to a contract. . . . Fortunately, Mme. Borkh has a voice to match her looks. Salome is a part to tax any singer, and she met the vocal challenge beautifully. . . . We think Mme. Borkh's Salome as thrilling pictorially and emotionally as any we've ever caught." To Irving Kolodin in the *Saturday Review*, Borkh's Salome was so well vocalized "that one's mind began placing her in this and that Wagnerian role for which her talents are suitable."

Borkh's first Wagnerian role at the Metropolitan Opera was Sieglinde in *Die Walküre* on February 5, 1958. After that season she absented herself from the Metropolitan Opera until the 1960–1961 season, returning in another of her celebrated roles, Elektra, on February 13, 1961. After leaving the Metropolitan in 1961, she became the principal soprano of the Stuttgart Opera in Germany and, in addition, made numerous guest appearances with other principal European opera companies.

Inge Borkh and Alexander Welitsch make their home in Weinacht, Switzerland. In 1963 she was named *Kammersängerin* in Bavaria, and a decade later she was awarded the Reinhardt Ring in Vienna.

ABOUT: New York Times, February 24, 1957.

Pierre Boulez

1925–

Pierre Louis Joseph Boulez, conductor, was born in Montbrison, southwest of Lyons in the Loire district of France, on March 26, 1925. Neither his father, Léon, nor his mother, Antoinette Calabre Boulez, was musical. His father, the technical director of a steel factory, wanted Pierre to be an engineer. However, Pierre and his older sister and younger brother were all given piano lessons. Of the three it was Pierre who instantly became totally absorbed in the study of the instrument. Whenever he had to be punished for derelict behavior, he was deprived of one of his lessons. He proved extraordinarily

Boulez: boo lĕz'

PIERRE BOULEZ

precocious not only in music but also in his academic studies, particularly in mathematics.

As a boy Boulez sang in the church choir. He also occasionally participated in private performances of chamber music. He heard his first live performance of a symphony orchestra at sixteen, and his first opera *(Boris Godunov)* a year later. Most of his listening experiences came from the radio since the family did not own a phonograph. He remembers that a performance of Stravinsky's *Le Chant du Rossignol* made a particularly strong impression on him at that time.

In 1943 Boulez was sent to a preparatory school in Lyons to complete mathematical studies as a preliminary to entering Polytechnical School. At the end of that year he decided to override his father's objections to a career in music and go to Paris for further music study. There he found lodgings in a two-room garret apartment atop an old house in the Marais district of Paris. The place had no running water, the bathroom was one floor below, and in the winter the place was impossible to heat. Nevertheless this remained his home for the next fourteen years.

For about two years Boulez took lessons in counterpoint from Andrée Vaurabourg, the wife of the distinguished Swiss-born French composer Arthur Honegger. "He always seemed capable of anything," she recalls. In 1944 he entered the Paris Conservatory, where for one year he attended the harmony class of Olivier Messiaen, the French avant-garde composer. Through Messiaen, Boulez was introduced to the music of

Bartók, Berg, and Schoenberg which shaped Boulez's musical thinking and tastes as well as his destiny both as composer and as conductor. Upon graduating with the first prize from Messiaen's class in 1945, Boulez continued to study composition with him for a year. Inspired and influenced by Messiaen, Boulez completed the *Three Psalmodies* for piano (1945) in which he emulated his teacher's experiments with rhythmic structures.

During his first three years in Paris Boulez lived a Spartan existence, and for the most part a solitary one. All this time he supported himself by undertaking hack assignments.

In 1945 Boulez heard a performance of Schoenberg's Wind Quintet, that composer's first large work using the twelve-tone row. This listening experience opened for Boulez a new world. He went on to study René Leibowitz's book *Schoenberg and His School,* and to become Leibowitz's pupil. Boulez (about whom Messiaen remarked that "he was against everything") now embarked upon an open and permanent rebellion against the status quo in music. He became convinced that the only way a twentieth century composer could free himself from the tyranny of past Romantic associations was by adopting Schoenberg's twelve-tone technique. Boulez did so in his own compositions in 1946—in a sonata for solo piano and another for two solo pianos. Later on, as a conductor, he would become an impassioned and dedicated advocate of the music of Schoenberg and of Schoenberg's two most celebrated disciples, Alban Berg and Anton Webern.

In 1946, on Honegger's recommendation, Boulez was appointed conductor at the Marigny Theater where the plays of Jean-Louis Barrault and Madeleine Renaud were mounted. Here for the next eight years he served his apprenticeship as a conductor. "When he first arrived," recalls Barrault, "he lived with his claws out. He was like a young cat, at once bristling and charming. He was sharp, aggressive, sometimes irritating." In 1954, with the collaboration of musicians from the Marigny theater orchestra and with Barrault's financial assistance, Boulez organized a series of avant-garde concerts in Paris. These became annual events. They were originally called the Concerts Marigny but later renamed "Domaine musicale." At these performances the most revolutionary tendencies in twentieth century music found a hearing. Success made it necessary to seek a larger auditorium, first at the Salle Gaveau and later at the Odéon.

It was at one of the "Domaine musicale" concerts that Boulez got his first opportunity to conduct serious twentieth century music. On March 21, 1956, Boulez's *Le Marteau sans Maître* was scheduled for its first Paris hearing at one of these concerts. When Hans Rosbaud, who had been assigned as its conductor, failed to make his appearance, Boulez stepped in as a substitute. Some time later Boulez once again conducted one of his own works, the *Visage Nuptial,* when he became dissatisfied with the way the conductor had rehearsed it. Having become somewhat of a luminary in advanced circles of French music, Boulez received invitations to make appearances as guest conductor at various modern-music festivals, among them Aix-en-Provence in France and at Donaueschingen in Germany.

In 1959 the Southwest German Radio in Baden-Baden offered Boulez a regular income in return for the right to first performances of his works. That year Boulez settled in Baden-Baden, planning to stay for just two years. He remained there for over a decade. Whenever Hans Rosbaud, the permanent conductor of the German Radio Orchestra, became indisposed, Boulez took his place. Although he never had a lesson in conducting, Boulez proved himself so adept that in 1961 he was asked to conduct Stravinsky's *The Rite of Spring* at the Salzburg Festival, a performance that caused a sensation. Endowed with extraordinary musical intelligence, a highly sensitized ear, an infallible gift for musical structure and style, and a particular talent for achieving transparent textures, Boulez proved himself a born conductor.

His rapid advance to the forefront of the world's conductors has few precedents. In 1963 he was invited by the Paris Opéra to conduct Berg's *Wozzeck.* His performance inspired an ovation not only from the audience but also from the men in the orchestra. In 1966 he returned to the Paris Opéra for further performances of *Wozzeck.* He subsequently recorded Berg's opera, a release that won him the Grand Prix du Disque in Paris and a Grammy award from the National Academy of Recording Arts and Sciences in the United States. The release was also selected "best recording of the year" by the magazine *Gramophone* in England.

Boulez paid his first visit to the United States in the spring of 1963 to deliver some lectures at Harvard University. On May 25 he went to New York to provide verbal commentary at a performance of his own composition *Le Marteau sans Maître.* He made his American conducting debut in March 1965 with the Cleveland Orchestra in Cleveland. The same year, on May 1, he made his New York debut as a guest conductor of the BBC Symphony Orchestra in a program of music by Webern, Berg, and Debussy, together with the New York premiere of his own *Doubles.* Oddly, he conducted the works of Webern, Berg, and Debussy from memory while using a score in the presentation of his own composition. In a review of that concert Harold C. Schonberg commented in the New York *Times* that Boulez led the orchestra "with command, flexibility and sensitivity. . . . Mr. Boulez was never rigid in his conducting. He was relaxed, his tempos sounded just right, and the Berg score [Three Fragments from *Wozzeck*] emerged with unusual color and plasticity."

In 1964 Boulez led an evening of Stravinsky's ballets at the Paris Opéra. Two years later he made his bow at the Bayreuth Festival with *Parsifal* which, as Peter Hayworth reported in the London *Observer,* emerged under his direction "as a genuinely religious work . . . a most beautiful achievement." This Bayreuth performance was recorded. In 1967 Boulez conducted the Bayreuth Festival company in performances of *Tristan and Isolde* in Japan.

Until June 1966 Boulez maintained an apartment on the Boulevard Raspail although he spent a good part of each year in Baden-Baden. In June 1966 he gave up his Paris home and broke all ties with France because he objected to a new bureau created by the French government in the cultural ministry, presided over by a reactionary musician Boulez regarded as of questionable capabilities. Boulez resigned from all French musical organizations with which he had been affiliated, including his own "Domaine musicale" group and the National Orchestra of France. He vowed never again to live or conduct in France as long as its music, as he said, rested in the hands of incompetent functionaries. However, in 1973 Boulez ended his seven-year exile by announcing that he would return to Paris in 1975 at the invitation of President Pompidou to head a new institute for the study of contemporary music, the Centre des Études de la Musique Contemporaine.

In the United States, George Szell, the music director of the Cleveland Orchestra, was so impressed with Boulez's conducting ability that he had him sign a five-year contract as principal guest conductor of the Cleveland orchestra, his duties involving six to eight weeks of performances each year. Upon Szell's death in 1970 Boulez was called upon to become the orchestra's music adviser through the 1971–1972 season.

From 1971 to 1975 Boulez was the music director of the BBC Symphony in London, succeeding Colin Davis. On March 13, 1969, Boulez made his first appearance as guest conductor of the New York Philharmonic Orchestra for the first of sixteen concerts. He returned to the New York Philharmonic for each of the next five years. In 1969, when Leonard Bernstein resigned as musical director of that orchestra, Boulez was chosen to succeed him on a three-year contract beginning with the 1971–1972 season, a contract that was renewed for an additional two seasons in 1975.

Boulez's first appearance as music director of the New York Philharmonic took place on September 21, 1971, in a program of works by Wagner, Berlioz, Liszt, Debussy, and Stravinsky. Commenting upon Boulez's performance of *The Rite of Spring,* Harold C. Schonberg wrote in the New York *Times:* "He has never conducted the work more brilliantly or with more authority in this city. It was an athletic, propulsive performance, perfectly gauged. Everything sounded alive, and the Philharmonic played it like a group of champions."

For his regime Boulez embarked upon a number of striking innovations. For his first subscription series he concentrated on "major prospectives of the music of Franz Liszt and Alban Berg." One season later the two composers chosen for detailed representation were Haydn and Stravinsky. Boulez initiated a series of intimate "Prospective Encounters." These informal concerts of avant-garde music were presented in Martinson Hall in downtown New York with Boulez conducting and discussing provocative new works in the hope of bridging the gap between the audiences and the music. Audiences were encouraged to participate in a question-and-answer period, and sometimes the composers themselves were present to discuss their methods and aims and to reply to audience queries. Boulez introduced "pre-concert recitals" in which he talked about, played, and answered questions about modern music represented on the regular program that followed. Also he introduced to Lincoln Center Rug Concerts, at which the audiences could sprawl on the floor unceremoniously and listen to the program without any of the formal trappings of a regular concert. With the financial assistance of Exxon, the National Endowment, and the State Council, these Rug Concerts grew in 1975 from six to ten performances, listened to by appreciative and sympathetic audiences not often encountered at the regular subscription series. "Not that there aren't serious listeners in subscription audiences—far from it—but the weight of collective inattention from those who are serving time for social purposes all too frequently submerges the kind of collective concentration that distinguishes the Rugs," explained David Hamilton in the New York *Times.* "That clearly is one reason Boulez likes the Rugs as much as the Ruggers like Boulez. They like the same kind of music, too, which helps along the love affair."

During the summer of 1975, on a grant from the IBM World Trade Corporation, the New York Philharmonic made its first and last tour of Europe with Boulez as its music director. Eighteen concerts were given in twelve cities, including appearances at the major festivals at Edinburgh, Berlin, Lucerne, Ghent, and Paris.

During the summer of 1975 Boulez resigned his directorship of the BBC Symphony in London. About two months earlier he had announced that after the expiration of his contract with the New York Philharmonic at the end of the 1976–1977 season he would withdraw from that post. (He made his farewell in New York with three stunning performances of Berlioz' *Damnation of Faust,* during the week of May 12, 1977.) He was planning to assume a new assignment in Paris in 1977, director of the Institut de Recherche et de Coordination Acoustique/ Musique (IRCAM). He had founded this organization to explore the resources of electronic music, specifically computer-made music. In this research center Boulez planned, as he explained, "to unleash activities that will alter the course of music for years to come."

When Bayreuth celebrated the centenary of its Wagner festival during the summer of 1976, Boulez was invited to conduct all the performances of the *Ring* cycle. This was the first time he had ever directed these four music dramas anywhere. "Everything was intelligently organized," reported Harold C. Schonberg in the New York *Times,* "the sound was luminous, the rhythms had plasticity. . . . This was masterful conducting." He returned to Bayreuth in the summer of 1977.

After receiving a Grammy award for his recording of *Wozzeck* in 1967, Boulez earned several others: for *Boulez Conducts Debussy,* volumes 1 and 2 in 1968 and 1969; for *The Rite of Spring* in 1970; for Bartók's Concerto for Orchestra in 1972; and for Ravel's *Daphnis and Chloë* in 1976. In 1976 Boulez received two top recording awards in Japan. His recording of Schoenberg's opera *Moses and Aron* brought him the Grand Prix at the National Art Festival (the first time a classical album received such an award in a dozen years); and the recording of Schoenberg's *Gurre-Lieder* earned him the Record Academy Award as the best classical album issued in Japan in 1975.

Boulez conducts without a baton, and generally from memory. Short, stocky, somewhat bald, he does not bring visual glamour to the conductor's platform. Undemonstrative in his podium behavior, he scrupulously avoids any suggestion of showmanship and conducts with businesslike precision. "Boulez," wrote Claude Samuel in *High Fidelity,* "does not overplay the dramatic side of conducting, although his movements can be brutal, and he abstains from trying to simulate nuances with clownlike mimicry. He does not, however, neglect the intensive look for he believes in the power of communication by the eye. . . . Each conductorial signal corresponds to a perfectly identified sound."

Though his brilliance as a musician and his merits as a conductor of contemporary music can never be denied, Boulez has not been beyond criticism from certain quarters. His indefatigable promotion of new music alienated some of the subscribers to the New York Philharmonic who felt that he did not seem to relate to the more traditional literature of the past as successfully as he did to present-day music. His programming, which perpetually explored the unfamiliar, was often accused of being slanted solely for an elitist rather than an average music-loving public.

Boulez never married. He maintains a Victorian mansion in Baden-Baden; during his New York years he also occupied an apartment close to Lincoln Center for the Performing Arts. He avoids social functions and rarely goes to the theater, films, or art galleries, occupying himself completely with his many musical activities, interests, and obligations.

In the liner notes to the recording of Boulez's *Le Marteau sans Maître,* Robert Craft revealed that Boulez is "without religious beliefs, is generous with money, is more attracted to Oriental and Indian cultures than to Italian and Greek and is greatly interested in the Psychological Method"; that Boulez "smokes cigars, can drink four framboises [raspberry brandy] after dinner with no decline of intellectual focus, and never eats breakfast"; and that he has "a nervous blink, doesn't date letters, sleeps five hours, is never ill, and has the tiniest handwriting in the world."

Boulez has written *Notes of an Apprenticeship* (1968) and *Boulez on Music Today* (1970), and several other books on music.

ABOUT: Boulez, P. Notes of an Apprenticeship; Golea, A. Rencontres avec Pierre Boulez; Peyser, J. Boulez: Composer, Conductor, Enigma. *Periodicals*—Esquire, February 1969; High Fidelity, March 1968; Musical America, November 1960; New York Times, June 20, 1971, May 15, 1977; New York Times Magazine, March 25, 1973; New Yorker, March 24, 31, 1973; Saturday Review, October 18, 1975; Time, November 8, 1968.

Sir Adrian Boult

1889–

Adrian Cedric Boult, conductor, was born in Chester, England, on April 8, 1889. His father, Cedric Boult, was a businessman and a justice of the peace; his mother, Katharine Florence Barman Boult, was a writer on musical subjects who translated and edited a volume of the writings of Berlioz.

Adrian received his first music lessons at the piano from his mother. When he was twelve he was enrolled in the Westminster School in London. Since music was not an important part of its curriculum, Adrian had to seek his musical experiences elsewhere. He often attended the Sunday Promenade concerts conducted by Henry J. Wood at Queen's Hall, following the music with score in hand. He used his pocket

Boult: bōlt

SIR ADRIAN BOULT

monic Orchestra. He made his London debut as conductor in February and March 1918 with four concerts at Queen's Hall, at one of which he offered the world premiere of the first revision of Vaughan Williams's *London Symphony.* During the 1918–1919 season he was one of the conductors of the Diaghilev Ballet in London.

In the years between 1919 and 1924 Boult conducted the British Symphony, an orchestra made up of ex-servicemen. On January 30, 1919, he appeared for the first time as guest conductor of the Royal Philharmonic Orchestra in London and was so successful that he conducted a second concert with that orchestra on February 17. His fame may be said to have had its roots in these two performances. During 1919 he also led concerts of the Liverpool Philharmonic and the London Symphony.

Boult was a member of the faculty of the Royal College of Music from 1919 to 1924, teaching a class in conducting. From 1924 to 1930 he conducted the senior orchestra at the college.

Guest appearances in Munich, Vienna, and Prague in the early 1920s marked the beginnings of Boult's international fame. On these occasions he became the indefatigable promoter of unfamiliar or new compositions by twentieth century English composers; many of these works were getting their first hearings on the Continent. In 1923 Pablo Casals invited Boult to direct a special concert of English music at Barcelona.

In 1924 Boult was appointed principal conductor of the Birmingham City Orchestra. Four years later he was made the music director of the British Broadcasting Company, and shortly after that he organized the BBC Symphony. As music director Boult fashioned the BBC Symphony into one of Europe's most distinguished orchestras, not only in its broadcasts but also in its public concerts. He brought the orchestra to Brussels in 1933 and to Vienna, Zurich, and Budapest in 1934. In 1942 he withdrew as music director of the British Broadcasting Company to devote his energies to its orchestra, remaining as music director until 1950.

His conducting engagements took him out of England increasingly often. In 1935 he led a concert of British music at the Salzburg Festival. That same year he made his American debut conducting the Boston Symphony Orchestra for four concerts in January. In 1937 he opened the new season for the NBC Symphony in New

money to purchase orchestral scores which he committed to memory. By the time he was eighteen he knew by heart almost every piece of important orchestral music heard at Queen's Hall. In addition, he learned some harmony, counterpoint, and fugue from a music-loving science teacher at the School.

When he was nineteen Adrian entered Christ Church, Oxford, where he came under the influence of Sir Hugh Allen, the conductor of several choral groups. Boult joined some of these and also helped to coach and rehearse performances of operas. He even sang in some of these operas, as Samiel in *Der Freischütz* and Don Fernando in *Fidelio.*

After receiving the degrees of Bachelor of Arts, Master of Arts, and a doctorate in music, Boult went to Leipzig in 1912 to attend the Leipzig Conservatory where he came under the influence of Arthur Nikisch, the conductor of the Leipzig Gewandhaus Orchestra. Boult attended not only Nikisch's concerts but also his rehearsals, and occasionally he sang in the chorus when the Gewandhaus Orchestra offered choral masterworks.

Returning to England in 1913, he worked for a year on the musical staff of Covent Garden. In 1914 he made his conducting debut with a pickup orchestra in West Kirby, near Chester.

During World War I Boult used his knowledge of German to work in the British War Ministry. However, he did not neglect music. In 1915 he became the youngest conductor ever to lead a performance by the Liverpool Philhar-

York. During the spring of 1938 he was guest conductor of several major American orchestras. The next year, on June 9 and 10, 1939, he presented two concerts of British music at the New York World's Fair in programs which featured the world premieres of Arthur Bliss's Piano Concerto, Arnold Bax's Seventh Symphony, Vaughan Williams's *Five Variants on Dives and Lazarus,* and the American premiere of Eugene Goossens' Oboe Concerto.

Boult married Mary Ann Grace Bowles in 1933. In 1937 he was knighted, and in the same year he conducted the music at the coronation of King George VI.

During World War II the BBC Symphony transferred its activities from London to Bristol and later to Bedford. Boult toured the service camps, naval centers, and factories around England with the orchestra, and in 1943 and 1944 came to London for public concerts. On several occasions these performances took place while Britain was being bombed. At one concert, as Boult himself revealed in *Musical America,* the lights were completely extinguished and the musicians had to complete their performance by candlelight and with oil lamps. "Although some of our valuable music was lost by enemy action . . . the members of the orchestra themselves stood the strain magnificently—never lowering the standard of their playing."

In May 1946 Boult helped to celebrate the fiftieth anniversary of the Czech Philharmonic Orchestra by conducting an all-British concert at the Prague Spring Festival. In 1952 he conducted the music for the coronation of Elizabeth II at Westminster Abbey.

"Boult is essentially a musician's conductor," wrote Stanley A. Bayliss in *The Chesterian.* "His instinct is to seek the purely musical *raison d'être* of a work and not to galvanize it into life by stressing the theatrical. His readings can never be called mercurial or demoniacal. In his little book . . . [on conducting] there is a sentence that admirably sums up Boult's own qualities. The conductor's work 'must be directed towards the eyes of the orchestra, and only towards the ears of the audience.'"

His gestures were economical, his bearing reserved, and his interpretations avoided personalized idiosyncrasies. "He prefers," said Bernard Shore who was in the violin section of the BBC Symphony, "to be an almost impersonal medium between the composer, orchestra, and audience rather than the central character."

Boult has been tireless in propagandizing English music both in his native land and in his guest appearances elsewhere. In addition to works already mentioned, he was responsible for the world premieres of Granville Bantock's *A Pagan Symphony* (March 8, 1936), Havergal Brian's Eighth Symphony (February 1, 1954), Gustav Holst's *The Planets* (February 17, 1919), Cyril Scott's Violin Concerto (January 27, 1928), Sir Michael Tippett's Symphony No.2 (February 5, 1958), and the following works by Vaughan Williams: Concerto Grosso (November 18, 1950), Piano Concerto (February 1, 1933), *Pastoral* Symphony (January 26, 1922), Symphony No.4 (April 10, 1935), Symphony No.6 (April 21, 1948) and Symphony No.9 (April 2, 1958).

Boult was made Companion of Honor in England in 1969. He also received the gold medal of the Royal Philharmonic Orchestra in 1944 and the gold medal of the Harvard Glee Club in 1956.

Eva Mary Grew, English writer on musical subjects, has provided the following personal information about Boult: "He likes to go for long walks and to swim every morning when possible. He rests completely between a rehearsal and the concert, and after the concert he leaves the hall alone as soon as he can, walks at least a couple of miles to his rooms, so as to calm his nerves and cool his body, and goes to bed. . . . He believes that labor is the highest lot of man, and the word that means most of all to him is Duty, his interpretation of the word covering sympathy, honorableness, kindliness and patience."

Sir Adrian Boult is the author of *A Handbook on the Technique of Conducting* (1969).

ABOUT: Blaukopf, K. Great Conductors; Brook, D. International Gallery of Conductors; Shore, B. The Orchestra Speaks. *Periodicals*—The British Musician (London), August 1933–June 1934; Musical America, April 10, 1945.

Alexander Brailowsky

1896–1976

Alexander Brailowsky, pianist, was born in Kiev, in the Ukraine, on February 16, 1896, the son of Peter and Elisabeth Rapchinsky Brailowsky. His father, who ran a music shop and gave piano lessons, was his first music teacher. "I can remember," recalled Brailowsky, "when I was only five, how my father and I used to sit at the piano and play scales together, each of us trying to see which one could get to the top of the keyboard first." Alexander's sister, Zena, was also given piano instruction by her father and, like Alexander, went on to become a concert pianist until her death just before World War I.

In his eighth year Alexander was admitted to the Kiev Conservatory. There, Serge Rachmaninoff, then the government inspector of music, heard him and prophesied an outstanding career for him as piano virtuoso. After graduating from the Conservatory with a gold medal in 1911, Alexander was given money by wealthy members of his family to go to Vienna to study with Theodor Leschetizky, the piano teacher. Leschetizky, then eighty-one years old, taught Alexander for about three years and regarded him as one of his most brilliant pupils. He made his first appearance as piano virtuoso at one of Leschetizky's house concerts.

With the outbreak of World War I Brailowsky and his family fled to Switzerland where he continued his piano study in Zurich with Ferruccio Busoni. He remained in Switzerland until the signing of the Armistice. Afterwards he made his home in Paris and in 1926 became a French citizen. After further piano study with Francis Planté, Brailowsky began his professional career in Paris with a recital at Salle Gaveau in 1920 described by the critics as sensational. Now established as one of the more popular concert pianists in Paris, he was invited to perform throughout Europe, including a command performance for Queen Elisabeth of Belgium, the consort of King Albert I.

In 1923 he decided to present all 172 of the piano works of Chopin in a series of six concerts. That summer he secluded himself in the French

Brailowsky: brī lôf′ skĭ

ALEXANDER BRAILOWSKY

Alpine city of Annecy, and for more than eight weeks lived in a peasant's cottage assembling all of Chopin's music into suitable concert programs. "It was the work of a mathematician rather than a pianist," he later explained. "They had to be arranged in such a way that they would not be monotonous. Often I spent hours trying to decide if a certain étude should go before a mazurka or after it, or whether it went better with a certain work than another sonata. I worked as though I were putting together a big puzzle. The name of each composition was written on a slip of paper, and I would then try to slip them together in the most interesting way possible. I think I pulled each program apart twenty or thirty times before I was satisfied with it."

Brailowsky's presentation of the Chopin cycle in Paris in 1924 was received so enthusiastically that the manager had to announce from the stage that a second such Chopin series would be repeated in Paris in a larger hall. Between the year 1924 and his performance of the Chopin cycle in Carnegie Hall in New York in December of 1946, Brailowsky gave the series six times: in Paris, Brussels, Zurich, Mexico City, Buenos Aires, and Montevideo. At one of the performances in Paris he played on Chopin's piano. Liszt was the only other virtuoso allowed its use since Chopin's death.

Brailowsky's first Chopin cycle in New York took place during the 1937–1938 season. The concluding concert was reviewed in the New York *Times:* "For many students who followed the program with scores, Mr. Brailowsky was the ideal pianist. For, above all else, he strives for—and attains—clarity. Neither the eye nor the ear can detect more than a few obscure notes, and the dynamics are sharply defined. Often, indeed, a yielding softness of outline might have been more to the artistic purpose than crystalline clarity. . . . Mr. Brailowsky has this music in his blood and he conveys it with integrity and stirring conviction." In spite of his concentration on Chopin's music, and in spite of the recognition by the world of music that he has been one of its outstanding interpreters, Brailowsky does not regard Chopin as his favorite composer. He prefers first Beethoven, then Mozart.

More than a dozen years before the Chopin cycle presentation, Brailowsky's American debut took place at Aeolian Hall in New York—November 19, 1924. In the New York *Times* Olin Downes called him a "born virtuoso in the highest sense of that word. He feels instinctively the resources of the piano and makes of it an instrument that sings and throbs with color." From that time on he toured the United States annually in addition to performing in music centers around the world. His pianistic mastery covered such a wide repertory from Scarlatti to Prokofiev that in a series of seventeen recitals in eight weeks in Buenos Aires he did not repeat a single number.

Commenting on Brailowsky's performances of music other than that of Chopin, Arthur V. Berger wrote in the New York *Sun:* "Brailowsky has many elements of brilliance, agility, strength, athleticism, and elan. . . . He has the further capacity of keeping a recital alive." Olin Downes in the New York *Times* spoke of Brailowsky's "singularly carrying and beautiful tone, which he can modulate exquisitely at will and the prodigious technique that is there when he wants to use it."

On November 7, 1931, Brailowsky married Felicia Karczmar, a Polish-born linguist Brailowsky had met in Warsaw in 1932. For many years they owned a manor house in Switzerland and a town house in New York City.

Brailowsky's hobbies covered a wide range: collecting railroad timetables from all over the world, dogs, clocks, books, and art works; reading history and detective stories; going to the movies (especially westerns). In his earlier years he was an avid tennis player and just as enthusiastic about racing his luxurious car at breakneck speed. During his many tours he always carried with him as mascot a doll which he had acquired in Copenhagen and which he regarded as his good-luck charm.

King Albert of Belgium honored him with the Order of the Knight, King Carol of Rumania with the Order "Pour le Mérite." Denmark awarded him the King Christian medal, and France presented him with the ribbon of the Legion of Honor and the silver medal of the City of Paris.

Alexander Brailowsky died at Lenox Hill Hospital in New York City on April 25, 1976, a victim of pneumonia and heart failure.

ABOUT: Esquire, December 1946; Musical America, January 15, 1956; Time, November 9, 1946.

Karin Branzell

1891–1974

Karin Maria Branzell, contralto, was born in Stockholm, on September 24, 1891, to Anders and Jenny Pearson Branzell. Her father, the principal of a school outside Stockholm, played the organ and led the choir in the parish church. As a child Karin revealed such delight in singing that her reward for good behavior was permission to sing for relatives or friends. She attended a private school and the Stockholm High School where she specialized in languages. Her musical activity included singing in her father's choir; in her sixteenth year she was assigned solo parts at Christmas. Among those hearing her on this occasion was the Crown Princess Margaret of Sweden who summoned the young singer and inquired if she were interested in pursuing music professionally. Receiving an affirmative response, the Crown Princess provided Karin with the funds for three years of vocal study, mostly with Thekla Hofer.

In 1911 Branzell made her debut at the Stockholm Opera in the mezzo-soprano role of Amneris in *Aida*. A fast learner (she mastered the role of Carmen in ten days) she acquired during her first season at the Stockholm Opera much of the basic repertory that would serve her for the remainder of her career. She remained in Stockholm until 1918, distinguishing herself primarily

Branzell: brän′ zĕl

KARIN BRANZELL

in Wagnerian roles, though also appearing in Italian and French operas. During this period she scored a personal triumph in Gothenburg, Sweden, as Euridice in Gluck's *Orfeo ed Euridice,* in which she appeared eleven times in thirteen days to sold-out auditoriums.

Her first appearance outside Sweden took place at a festival concert in Copenhagen at which Sibelius kissed her hand in appreciation. Visits to Berlin and London in the years preceding World War I enabled her to pursue her vocal studies further, with Louis Bachner, and to absorb musical experiences by attending opera performances.

In 1919 she auditioned for the Berlin State Opera by singing parts of the second act of *Die Walküre.* On the strength of this performance she was given a three-year contract. She remained with that company thirteen years as principal contralto, with the Wagnerian repertory as her specialty. On October 10, 1919, Richard Strauss selected her to appear in the world premiere of *Die Frau ohne Schatten* at the Vienna State Opera. While in Vienna she was also heard as Waltraute in *Die Götterdämmerung* and as Amneris.

Gatti-Casazza, general manager of the Metropolitan Opera, and Artur Bodanzky, its principal conductor of German operas, auditioned her in Vienna. She sang for them Brünnhilde's "Ho-Jo-To-Ho" from *Die Walküre,* the "Suicidio!" aria from *La Gioconda,* and several other operatic excerpts; as she herself expressed it, she sang "like a pig." A second audition was ar-

ranged for the following season, this one bringing her a five-year contract.

Her debut at the Metropolitan Opera took place on February 6, 1924, as Fricka in *Die Walküre.* "A woman of gigantic stature," wrote Olin Downes in the New York *Times,* "she loomed . . . on the stage. And not only that: her voice has the range, the power, and the quality required by Wagner's orchestra and his treatment of the ancient Nordic legend. Miss Branzell made the shrewish Fricka a character eloquent and human, and sang in the grand manner."

When two days later she appeared as Ortrud in *Lohengrin* (a role she sang reluctantly because she felt it was too soon in her Metropolitan Opera career to assume so exacting a part), Downes provided this further comment in the New York *Times:* "She is a singer to be reckoned with. . . . The opera company is fortunate indeed which possesses a young singer with the stature, the vocal range, the authority and the capacity for impersonation obviously possessed by this artist." During that first Metropolitan Opera season Branzell also appeared as Erda in *Siegfried,* Brangäne in *Tristan and Isolde* (one of her most celebrated roles), Delilah in *Samson and Delilah,* Brünnhilde in *Die Walküre,* and Azucena in *Il Trovatore.*

During the next two decades, Branzell served the Metropolitan Opera well. When Janáček's *Jenufa* was revived in 1924–1925 she appeared as the Sexton's Widow at its second presentation. At the first post–World War I production of *Die Götterdämmerung,* on January 31, 1925, she was Waltraute. She was heard as Venus in the production of *Tannhäuser* on February 27, 1926, in which Lauritz Melchior made his Metropolitan Opera debut. When Jaromir Weinberger's *Schwanda* received its American premiere on November 7, 1931, she was the Queen. On October 27, 1930, she helped open the season of 1930–1931 as Amneris. Her other Metropolitan Opera roles included Erda in *Das Rheingold,* Laura in *La Gioconda,* Klytemnestra in *Elektra,* Fides in *Le Prophète,* Magdalene in *Die Meistersinger,* Herodias in *Salome,* and Waltraute in *Die Walküre.*

What was then believed to be her last appearance at the Metropolitan Opera took place on March 18, 1944, as Erda in *Das Rheingold.* At that time she announced she was leaving the company "to make a place for some gifted American singer." But it was no secret that she was at odds with the management, specifically with Rudolf Bing who had just assumed the general managership of the company, and that she objected to the fact that she was used so rarely on Saturday afternoons when the performances were broadcast nationally. However, in 1951 Bing prevailed on her to return to the Metropolitan Opera for one more performance, that of Erda in *Siegfried* on February 7, 1951.

During her years at the Metropolitan Opera she continued her vocal studies with Enrico Rosati and Anna Schoen-René. During those years she was also making a strong impression outside the United States. At Covent Garden in London, she enlarged her repertory by appearing as Kontchakovna in Borodin's *Prince Igor.* In 1930 and 1931 she participated in the Bayreuth Festival. In 1935 she was heard at the Wagner Festival in Munich and in fifteen Wagner performances at the Teatro Colón in Buenos Aires under Fritz Busch. In 1939 she was one of the stars of the Zurich Opera Festival.

Branzell's first husband was Einar Edwardson, a Norwegian painter, whose death prevented her from appearing as Kundry in the Metropolitan Opera production of *Parsifal,* though she had rehearsed the part. On April 29, 1938, Branzell married Feja Reinshagen, who became her personal manager. They made their home in Forest Hills, New York, and spent their summers in Maine. By this time she had become an American citizen.

After studying *Lieder* with Paul Ulanovsky, Branzell embarked upon a successful career as a concert singer, a field which before 1945 she had rarely entered. Her recital at Town Hall, New York, on February 4, 1945, drew the following critical evaluation from Harriet Johnson in the *Post:* "Karin Branzell's luscious contralto has the quality of iridescence. Like a prism, its vibrations send out an abundance of beauty." In addition to the recitals she gave guest performances with major symphony orchestras, in such masterworks as Beethoven's Ninth Symphony, Mahler's *Kindertotenlieder,* and Bach's *Passion According to St. Matthew.*

From 1946 to 1950 she taught voice at the Juilliard School of Music, and for a number of years after that at Adelphi College and the Manhattan School of Music. Subsequently she devoted herself to private students.

In 1969 Branzell moved to Altadena, California, where she could pursue her hobby of raising flowers in her own garden. She was recovering from a pelvic fracture when she was stricken by a fatal embolism. She died in Altadena on December 15, 1974.

She was awarded the Litteris et Artibus decoration by the King of Sweden in 1932. In 1936, after a performance of *Carmen* in Stockholm, the King appointed her singer of the Royal Court of Sweden. In 1945 Denmark presented her with the Medal of Liberation of Christian X for her services on behalf of Danish liberation during World War II.

ABOUT: Opera News, January 31, 1944, December 26, 1964.

Sophie Braslau

1892–1935

Sophie Braslau, contralto, was born in New York City on August 16, 1892. Both her parents, Abel and Alexandra (Lascha) Goodelman Braslau, were émigrés from Russia; her father was a physician and scholar. Sophie attended the public schools in New York City and received her musical training at the Institute of Musical Art in New York, where she specialized in the piano as a pupil of Alexander Lambert. Illness prevented her from completing her course of study at the Institute.

One day she was singing while accompanying herself on the piano when Arturo Buzzi-Peccia, a teacher of the voice and a friend of the family, overheard her. He was convinced that Sophie should become a singer. Hearing a recital by Alma Gluck finally persuaded Sophie to make singing her career.

For three years she studied voice with Buzzi-Peccia. (Supplementary vocal studies were later pursued with Gabriella Sibella, Herbert Witherspoon, Marcella Sembrich and Mario Marafoti.) One evening she sang in her teacher's studio before an audience of distinguished musicians, one of whom was Arturo Toscanini, then a principal conductor at the Metropolitan Opera. He advised her to audition for that company, which she did successfully. Though she had never before appeared on the operatic stage and had no professional singing experience to speak of,

Braslau: brăs′ lou

SOPHIE BRASLAU

Braslau made her Metropolitan Opera debut as the offstage Voice in *Parsifal* on November 26, 1914. Two days later she was seen and heard on the stage proper as the Innkeeper in *Boris Godunov.*

For the next few seasons she continued to sing minor roles, such as the Shepherd in *Tosca,* Javotte in *Manon,* the Sandman in *Hansel and Gretel,* La Rossa in the world premiere of Giordano's *Madame Sans-Gêne* on January 25, 1915, the Young Woman in *L'Amore dei Tre Re,* one of the orphans in *Der Rosenkavalier,* Mercedes in a revival of *Carmen* conducted by Toscanini (November 18, 1914), Hua Qui in Leoni's *L'Oracolo,* Altichara in Zandonai's *Francesca da Rimini* and one of the pages in *The Magic Flute.* On December 29, 1917, she was given the role of Maddalena in *Rigoletto;* on March 6, 1918, she assumed the part of Amelfa in the American premiere of *Le Coq d'Or;* and on March 23, 1918, she was assigned the title role in the world premiere of Charles Wakefield Cadman's *Shanewis.* After that she was heard as Comare in the first Metropolitan Opera production of Ricci's *Crispino e la Comare.* She made her last appearance at the Metropolitan Opera on April 3, 1920, as Marina in *Boris Godunov.*

Meanwhile, in the summer of 1918 she gave her first performance anywhere of the title role of *Carmen,* at Ravinia Park, near Chicago. She never sang Carmen at the Metropolitan Opera.

It was in the concert hall, rather than in the opera house, that Braslau achieved international renown. She made her first concert appearances in Cleveland and Baltimore in 1914, and in June 1915 she gave her first performance with a symphony orchestra, substituting for Marcella Sembrich at a concert of the Philadelphia Orchestra. She followed this with her first recital in New York, at Aeolian Hall on January 13, 1916. Richard Aldrich wrote in the New York *Times:* "She met the test well. She exhibited a thoroughly musicianly attitude toward her work, displayed a sense of the correct values in *Lieder* singing, and, in general, demonstrated that she is a recital artist of personality and one with serious aims."

In 1916, Braslau was a member of the Victor Quartet which recorded operatic selections for the Victor company. On March 29, 1918, she was a soloist in the Good Friday performance of Verdi's Requiem at the Metropolitan Opera House.

After leaving the Metropolitan Opera, she devoted herself exclusively to the concert platform for the next fourteen years, in Europe as well as in the United States, as soloist with symphony orchestras as well as in recitals. An exceptional range (three octaves), a vocal sound of sensuous beauty, and a perceptive musicianship in a varied repertory combined to make her one of the most highly esteemed concert artists of her time.

A chronic illness aborted her career when she was at the peak of her fame. Her last public appearance took place at Lewisohn Stadium in New York City on July 18, 1934, when she was heard in Manuel de Falla's *El Amor Brujo* and two songs by Rachmaninoff. In June 1935 she was permanently confined to a sickbed, and on December 22, 1935, she died in New York City.

ABOUT: Thompson, O. The American Singer. *Periodicals*—Musical America, June 10, 1936; New York Times, December 23 and 25, 1935.

Julian Bream

1933–

Julian Bream, classical guitarist and lutanist, was born in London on July 15, 1933. He was the eldest son of Henry G. Bream, a commercial artist and book illustrator, who was also a versatile amateur musician. From his father, whose musical gifts included the playing of the guitar, he acquired early in life an interest in that instru-

JULIAN BREAM

ment, but his early training was on the piano which he began to study when he was ten. Soon afterwards at the Royal College of Music in London, where he also received instruction on the cello, he was given the Junior Exhibition Award.

One day his father found him trying to play the guitar. He gave his son some lessons and then had him play with his own jazz band. When Julian was eleven, his father presented him with an old gut-stringed Spanish guitar, the kind that is plucked with fingers rather than plectrum. With this instrument Julian shifted from jazz to classical music. "My father had by this time lost a great deal of his interest in the dance band and jazz, and was very keen himself to take up the classical Spanish guitar," he recalls. "We started to play the instrument, there being no source of tuition available in England at that time." Julian's interest in the classical guitar was intensified in 1945 when he heard a recording by Segovia.

His academic schooling, disrupted by conditions during World War II, ended when he was fourteen. From then on he devoted himself entirely to music. While attending a meeting of the Philharmonic Society of Guitarists, at which he was invited to perform, he met its president, Boris Perrot, who became his teacher. Through Perrot, he met Segovia personally while Segovia was touring England. From Segovia, he received only two lessons, but Julian continued studying and assimilating Segovia's style and techniques

by attending his concerts and listening to his recordings.

Julian's first appearance as guitarist took place in 1946 in a series of programs broadcast over BBC. One year later at Cheltenham, England, he gave his first recital. Determined to develop his overall musicianship, he became a full-time scholarship student at the Royal College of Music in London, attending classes in harmony, counterpoint, composition, and piano. Meanwhile he supported himself by teaching and playing the guitar.

Studies in English history awakened his interest in the Elizabethan and Jacobean eras. "The color and vitality of that period gripped me," he says. He determined to seek out the music of those times and did research in libraries and museums, consulting two musicologists, David Lumsden and Thurston Dart. Much of the music Bream helped to uncover had been written for the lute, an instrument which Bream was determined to master. In 1950 he called on Thomas Goff, a maker of harpsichords, to construct for him a lute modeled after a sixteenth century instrument in the Victoria and Albert Museum. On this instrument Bream became a virtuoso. In later years, as a successful concert artist, he often divided his programs between the guitar and the lute; it was through his efforts that the lute, so long in discard, became known to twentieth century music audiences.

In October 1950 Bream gave his first guitar recital as a mature artist. This took place at Cowdray Hall, a modest auditorium in London, and was the first time a British guitarist had presented a classical-music concert. The success of this experiment brought about a second performance, this time in the larger Wigmore Hall. The *Daily Telegraph* spoke of him as "an artist of great taste and intelligence as well as technically a master of his instrument." A tour of Great Britain, together with radio broadcasts, followed. In 1952, in collaboration with the singer Peter Pears, he appeared in concerts specializing in Elizabethan lute songs.

To extend the available repertory of the guitar, already enriched by Segovia's efforts, Bream transcribed for the guitar much forgotten or little-known keyboard music of the sixteenth, seventeenth, and eighteenth centuries together with well-known compositions by such old masters as Bach, Frescobaldi, Purcell, and Rameau. He also resurrected old guitar music that had long since been forgotten and that lay untouched in libraries and museums.

In 1952 he was called into military service. With the Royal Artillery Band he played both the cello and the guitar. Since London was his base, he was able to give public concerts there and to appear over radio and television. During one of his leaves in 1954 he embarked on his first tour outside England, with performances in Switzerland.

His service in uniform was completed in 1955 and he was then able to extend his fame in Europe with appearances at festivals in Holland, Edinburgh, Berlin, and Aldeburgh. In addition he made many recordings. His first tour of the United States occurred in 1958, his American debut taking place at Town Hall, New York, on October 30. "Each piece he touches," wrote a critic of the *Herald Tribune,* "bears the mark of a musical projection in which clarity, sensitivity, elegance and the utmost of stylistic purity are ever present."

Since then Bream has often toured the United States, making numerous appearances on college campuses where he has been a particular favorite. In 1961 he organized the Julian Bream Consort for the presentation of Elizabethan music. In 1963 an RCA Victor release of his *An Evening with Elizabethan Consort Music* received a Grammy from the National Academy of Recording Arts and Sciences as the best chamber-music album of that year. Later Grammys came to him in 1966 for *Baroque Guitar,* in 1972 for the Villa-Lobos Concerto for Guitar, and in 1973 for *Julian and John,* the last of these a duo performance with John Williams. In 1962 Bream went on a world tour. Three years later he created an international summer school for guitarists at Wiltshire, England.

In recognition of his contributions to music, Queen Elizabeth II honored him in 1964 with membership in the Order of the British Empire.

Time magazine wrote as follows about Bream's performances on guitar and lute: "Without sacrificing stylistic elegance, he draws from both instruments the rustic grace and fresh-air feeling of the English countryside, redeeming them from sentimentality as well as musicological pedantry. To make up for the narrow dynamic range of the guitar, he achieved dramatic effects with an extraordinary variety of tonal colors. Subtle, jazzlike rhythms, throbbing chords, silvery lines, harplike plinks, resonant harpsichord and piano tones—all serve not to decorate or distract but to clarify."

Julian Bream resides in a Regency house in Wiltshire where he lives eight months a year mostly in seclusion, spending from three to eight hours a day practicing, and other hours each week teaching. His concert activities are usually concentrated within a three-month period. After music his greatest interests are English history and cricket.

ABOUT: Ewen, D. Famous Instrumentalists. *Periodicals*—Hi-Fi Stereo, October 1965; Newsweek, January 8, 1962; Time, December 1, 1967.

John Browning

1933–

John Browning, pianist, was born in Denver, Colorado, on May 22, 1933. Both of his parents were musical. His father, John S. Browning, was a violin teacher, and his mother, Esther Alice Green Browning, was a professional pianist. John began to show an interest in the piano when he was three. Two years later he started formal study, and from that time on he knew that he would someday be a concert pianist.

While attending public school in Denver, John, aged ten, made his piano debut in a performance of Mozart's Piano Concerto in D major, K.537 *(Coronation)* with an orchestral group made up of members of the Denver Symphony. At about this time Rosina and Josef Lhevinne, the pianists, set up a summer school in Denver. They were so impressed by Browning's talent that they accepted him as their only child student for one summer.

When the Browning family moved to Los Angeles, John attended John Marshall High School and continued his piano study with Lee Pattison. Following his graduation from high school in 1951, he entered Occidental College in Los Angeles where he remained for two years, majoring in English literature and music. A scholarship brought him to the Juilliard School of Music in New York where he studied with Rosina Lhevinne and received his Bachelor of Science degree in 1955, after which he completed a year of graduate work. While at Juilliard, Browning won the two-thousand-dollar Stein-

Browning

JOHN BROWNING

way Centennial Award in a nationwide contest in 1954.

In 1955 the Leventritt Award in New York entitled him to solo engagements with several major American orchestras, including the New York Philharmonic. With this organization he made his New York City debut in February 1956 in a performance of Rachmaninoff's *Rhapsody on a Theme by Paganini*. On that occasion a critic of the *Herald Tribune* found him to be "a gifted pianist, boasting an excellent technique, clean articulation, and a highly refined sense of phrasing."

Later that same year Browning went to Belgium to enter the prestigious International Piano Competition founded and sponsored by Queen Elisabeth. He captured second prize, the first prize going to Vladimir Ashkenazy. In the United States other honors came his way. After six performances of Beethoven's Piano Concerto No.4 with the Los Angeles Philharmonic under Eduard van Beinum in 1957, he was presented by the Los Angeles City Council with a resolution honoring his "outstanding ability and accomplishments which have brought honor and publicity to the city of Los Angeles." That year he was also selected by the United States government to give a recital in the United States pavilion in Brussels at the World's Fair.

Following Browning's first New York recital, on November 5, 1958, Howard Taubman said of him in the New York *Times:* "Mr. Browning . . . is a prize winner who lives up to the honors that have come his way. He is . . . a credit to his country."

A gold medal in the Brussels International Piano Competition opened the doors to a virtuoso career. He was called upon to give some one hundred performances a year, both in Europe and the United States. He was also signed to a recording contract by Capitol Records. On September 24, 1962, he further attracted the interest and admiration of the music world through his performance of the world premiere of Samuel Barber's Concerto for Piano and Orchestra, one of the events during the opening week ceremonies of Philharmonic Hall at Lincoln Center for the Performing Arts. With the Boston Symphony Orchestra under Erich Leinsdorf, Browning that evening shared the honors equally with Samuel Barber for a momentous event in American music. Browning has since become the definitive interpreter of this concerto, which received the Pulitzer Prize in music in 1963 and has come to be regarded as one of the most important piano concertos by an American. Within half a dozen years Browning performed the work about 150 times, recording it with the Cleveland Symphony Orchestra under George Szell on Columbia Records. "Each day," Browning has said, "I find a new emphasis, a new meaning in a phrase, a different solution for a knotty technical passage."

In 1965, during a foreign tour by the Cleveland Orchestra under the sponsorship of the United States Department of State, Browning appeared with that orchestra in three concertos, by Brahms (No.1), Gershwin, and Barber. At this time he was also heard in recitals. This tour brought him to the major cities and festivals in Europe and behind the Iron Curtain in Poland, Czechoslovakia, and the Soviet Union. So successful were Browning's performances that he was invited to return for another tour in the spring of 1967. In November and December 1970 he paid his third visit to the Soviet Union, with recitals in most of the major cities and appearances with symphony orchestras in Moscow, Leningrad, and Kiev. In 1971 Browning made his first appearance in Japan.

When in New York, Browning (a bachelor) resides in a luxurious penthouse apartment overlooking the East River. He enjoys reading, swimming, and the companionship of his close friends. But when he takes vacations from his concert work, as he revealed in an interview, "I begin to get nervous and after a month I simply have to get back to playing again. If I don't play I'm not happy."

ABOUT: Life, November 26, 1965; New York Times, March 19, 1967; New Yorker, February 1, 1969.

Grace Bumbry

1937–

GRACE BUMBRY

Grace Melzia Bumbry (originally Grace Ann Bumbry), soprano and mezzo-soprano, was born in St. Louis, Missouri, on January 4, 1937. She was raised in a musical and religious household. Her father, Benjamin James Bumbry, handled the freight for the Cotton Belt Route railroad, and her mother, Melzia Walker Bumbry, had been a schoolteacher in Mississippi.

Grace began taking piano lessons when she was seven, but from the beginning it was the voice and not the keyboard that fascinated her. "As long as I can remember," she has said, "I was the little girl who wanted to sing." As a child she attended the rehearsals of a church choir of which her two older brothers were members. By the time she was eleven she herself had joined the Union Memorial Methodist Church choir in St. Louis. At thirteen she sang with the choir of the Sumner High School.

The choirmaster of Sumner High School noticed her voice and urged her to develop it. But even before she started studying she emerged with top prizes in several local talent competitions. After graduating from high school in 1954, she appeared on the Arthur Godfrey Talent Scouts program on which, singing the "O don fatale" aria from Don Carlo, she captured the first prize.

Her vocal studies began in St. Louis when she was fifteen. A scholarship at Boston University and later at Northwestern University enabled her to continue her music studies and to attend Lotte Lehmann's master classes at Northwestern. During the summer of 1956 she went to California to continue her vocal training with Lehmann for three and a half years at the Music Academy of the West in Santa Barbara. "Those were very fruitful and hard-working years," she recalls. While studying with Lehmann, Bumbry won several awards, the most significant of which were the Marian Anderson Scholarship and the John Hay Whitney Award in 1957, and the one-thousand-dollar prize as a semifinalist in the Metropolitan Auditions of the Air in 1958.

In 1959 Lehmann took Bumbry to Europe to seek out opportunities for developing the young artist's career. Bumbry gave her first European concert at Wigmore Hall in London in June 1959, appeared in Paris as a guest artist in performances of Handel's Messiah and Bach's Actus Tragicus, and was a soloist at concerts at the American Embassy in Paris. In Paris she was also able to pursue additional vocal study with Pierre Bernac.

Her opera debut took place at the Paris Opéra in March 1960 as Amneris in Aida. "The packed house showered her with applause," reported Edmund J. Pendleton to the New York Herald Tribune, "and at that moment one knew that Miss Bumbry has made her first step—or rather leap—in what is certain to be a far-reaching international career." This success brought her a three-year contract with the Basel Opera in Switzerland where she gained valuable experience in such roles as Azucena in Il Trovatore, Amneris, Santuzza in Cavalleria Rusticana, Orfeo in Gluck's Orfeo ed Euridice, Delilah in Samson and Delilah, and Fricka in Das Rheingold.

In Basel she met and fell in love with Erwin Andreas Jaeckel, a Polish-born tenor and impresario. They were married on July 6, 1963, and made their home in Lugano, Switzerland. Jaeckel gave up his own activities to serve as his wife's manager.

Bumbry

As a member of the Basel Opera she found opportunities to appear elsewhere. She returned to the Paris Opéra in 1961–1962 to take on the title role in *Carmen,* a performance she repeated in Japan in the fall of 1962 when the Paris Opéra toured the Orient. She also performed with the Théâtre de la Monnaie in Brussels and at the festivals at Montreux and Lucerne in Switzerland.

International renown became hers on July 23, 1961, when she made her debut at the Bayreuth Festival as Venus in *Tannhäuser.* The first black person ever to fill that role, she had been recommended for the part by the conductor Wolfgang Sawallisch to Wieland Wagner. When Wagner's selection of Bumbry became known, a furor arose in German neo-Nazi and racist circles at the casting of a black woman in the part of Venus. "I don't need any ideal Nordic figure," Wieland Wagner explained. "What I was looking for was the best Venus in voice and appearance." Despite a strong undercurrent of discontent in some areas of Germany's musical sphere, Bumbry proved a sensation, receiving forty-two curtain calls during a thirty-minute ovation. "If her performance tonight is any criterion," wrote Ronald Eyer in the New York *Herald Tribune,* "she promises to be the first great Negro Wagnerian. . . . The voice is ravishing . . . brilliant at the top, full-bodied in the best German tradition in the middle range and well supported throughout." She returned to Bayreuth in 1962 to reappear as Venus, a role she also performed that year in Lyons, France, and in 1963 with the Chicago Lyric Opera.

Jacqueline Kennedy, hearing reports of Bumbry's success in Bayreuth, invited her to the White House to sing at a State Dinner on February 20, 1962. This was one of many performances in the United States that year. Another was a recital at Carnegie Hall, her New York concert debut, that was so successful that a second concert there was arranged a few weeks later. These were the first performances in a twenty-five-concert tour in twenty-one cities.

In 1963 she was one of the vocal soloists in a performance of Beethoven's Ninth Symphony at Bayreuth celebrating the centenary of the Bayreuth Festival. In 1964 she triumphed at the Salzburg Festival as Lady Macbeth in Verdi's *Macbeth,* and in 1966 as Carmen, both under the direction of Herbert von Karajan. The performance of *Carmen* was filmed.

Bumbry made her debut at the Metropolitan Opera as Princess Eboli in *Don Carlo* on October 7, 1965. "Her voice is that of a real contralto," said Alan Rich in the New York *Herald Tribune,* "with a phenomenal range, rather than the made-over sopranos who have sung this role in recent years. It is a big voice, but flexible and beautifully focused. And she uses it for genuine dramatic, as well as musical, purposes. An exciting, magnetic, dynamic singer, Miss Bumbry."

On December 15, 1967, Bumbry was starred in a new Metropolitan Opera production of *Carmen.* "There's nothing she can't do with that lustrous, sable-colored voice, no dynamic refinement or emotional projection that isn't produced with as much ease as her sulks, her disdain, her lust, or her courage," reported *Newsweek.* She was also heard at the Metropolitan Opera as Amneris, Azucena, Delilah, Tosca, Santuzza, and as Orfeo in Gluck's *Orfeo ed Euridice.*

In June 1970, at Covent Garden in London, Bumbry made her first appearance as a soprano in the title role of *Salome,* in which she herself performed the Dance of the Seven Veils. Andrew Porter, the English critic, said of her performance: "It is rare to encounter a whole Salome so splendidly worked, so admirably sung, so lustrously played. . . . Any fears that Miss Bumbry's timbre would prove too darkly mezzo were soon allayed. She has the compass and the power for the role; the ease and smoothness of her singing, free of squalls, stridency, strain, were a constant pleasure."

On September 19, 1973, Salome became her first German role at the Metropolitan Opera. Other soprano roles included Tosca, Lady Macbeth, and Venus in *Tannhäuser* at the Metropolitan Opera, Aida in Germany, and Jenufa at La Scala. On March 25, 1973, at the Munich Opera in Germany, she took over both leading soprano roles in *Tannhäuser* in a single evening, those of Venus and Elisabeth. On July 5, 1976, she received an ovation at the Paris Opéra in the title female role of a new production of Dukas' *Ariane et Barbe-Bleue.* "She revels in Dukas' long, impassioned, soaring vocal line," reported William Mann in the London *Times,* "and in Ariane's warm heroism." Later that summer she shared the spotlight with Montserrat Caballé at the Festival of Orange in France in *Aida,* a performance that was filmed. At the Aix-en-Provence Festival in August 1977 she scored successfully as Sarah in Donizetti's *Roberto Deve-*

reux. And on August 1, 1977, at the Festival Valle d'Itria, in Italy, she was heard for the first time as Norma.

Because she has mastered both the mezzo-soprano and soprano ranges, she is that rarity among singers who has successfully negotiated both Elisabetta and Eboli in *Don Carlo,* Venus and Elisabeth in *Tannhäuser,* Aida and Amneris in *Aida;* during a BBC telecast in 1975 she assumed both of the principal female roles in *Aida.*

Commenting on the extension of her vocal range from mezzo-soprano to soprano, Bumbry explained: "My break as a mezzo used to be between A and B, but now it's higher, at F. Slowly, year to year, there has been a decided change. But it's all come about naturally. I haven't deliberately tried to push my voice higher. You don't push a voice, you just follow it. . . . The only difference between a mezzo and a soprano is that a soprano has to sustain a high tessitura. Singing mezzo is just as demanding as singing soprano. In fact, a high voice is easier to get across than a lower voice."

In addition to their villa in Lugano, Bumbry and her husband maintain an apartment overlooking Central Park in New York, a second apartment in London, and a country place in California. Husband and wife share a great enthusiasm for climbing mountains, driving high-powered sports cars, and collecting early Meissen porcelain. To these interests Grace Bumbry adds her love for animals: she owns several dogs and maintains a stable of horses in California. She also enjoys collecting expensive fur coats and capes.

Thirty-six hours before she makes an appearance on the stage she tries to remain totally silent, communicating to her full-time secretary through written notes. When the performance is over, she is so highly keyed up that when she gets home she finds herself replaying in her mind her entire performance and sometimes she finds it impossible to fall asleep until dawn.

ABOUT: Look, February 26, 1963; New York Times, December 10, 1967, January 2, 1977; Newsweek, November 19, 1962; Opera News, December 16, 1967; Stereo Review, January 1974.

Adolf Busch

1891–1952

Adolf Georg Wilhelm Busch, violinist, was born in Siegen, Westphalia, Germany, on August 8, 1891. He was one of eight children of Wilhelm and Henrietta Busch, the brother of Fritz Busch, noted conductor and violinist, and of cellist Hermann Busch.

Busch's father had hoped to become a concert artist, but financial problems compelled him to earn his living through carpentry and the construction of violins. He satisfied his own musical cravings by organizing a small orchestra which practiced regularly at his home and filled minor engagements. Adolf first revealed his love for music by listening attentively to the music of this small orchestra. He was only three years old when his father presented him with a violin and gave him some lessons. He could soon read music, and at five he gave a concert.

Because he showed such unusual talent and much love for music, at ten Adolf was sent to live with his uncle in Duisburg so that he might get better instruction. In Duisburg the state music director became interested in him and in 1902 had him enroll in the Cologne Conservatory where his teachers included Fritz Steinbach and Willy Hess. Additional music instruction was received from Bram Eldering of the University of Cologne and in 1908, following Busch's graduation from the Cologne Conservatory, from Hugo Grueters in Bonn.

Since the Busch family was in financial straits, its two oldest members, Adolf and Fritz, had to help support it by using their free evenings playing dance music, sometimes in out-of-town engagements.

When he was eighteen, Busch made his professional debut as a violinist. Other engagements followed. His teacher, Steinbach, engaged him to perform under his baton in Vienna and London. Busch performed the Max Reger Violin Concerto in Berlin with the composer conducting. In 1912 he was appointed concertmaster of the Konzertverein in Vienna, conducted by Ferdinand Loewe. On May 15, 1913, he married Frieda Grüters, the daughter of his former teacher in composition; they had one child, a daughter, Irene, who married the piano virtuoso Rudolf Serkin.

Busch

ADOLF BUSCH

In 1918 Busch succeeded Henri Marteau as head of the violin department of the High School for Music in Berlin. Four years later Busch was elevated to the post of director of the school. Meanwhile, in 1919 he founded the Busch String Quartet, in which he played first violin. The quartet toured Europe and through the years gained an international reputation among the world's chamber-music groups. Busch participated in other chamber-music performances as well: in sonata recitals with Rudolf Serkin, whose early career he helped to promote; and in performances of trios with Serkin and Hermann Busch, or with Serkin and Emanuel Feuermann.

While involved in chamber-music concerts and in teaching, Busch was also firmly establishing his reputation as a concert violinist with performances throughout Europe in recitals and as soloist with symphony orchestras. He paid his first visit to the United States in 1931, appearing in New York City as soloist with the New York Philharmonic Orchestra, Toscanini conducting, in concertos by Bach and Beethoven. Writing in the New York *Times*, Olin Downes said: "He revealed himself immediately as a consummate musician, red blooded and essentially a classicist. Mr. Busch has a clear and brilliant tone, though not one of highly sensuous quality, and a masterly technique which includes a magnificent bow arm. His sincerity and feeling did not cause him to exaggerate or become mannered."

Busch made numerous tours of the United States in recitals, as soloist with orchestras, and in chamber-music concerts. During the 1937–1938 season he was heard in a cycle of all of Beethoven's violin sonatas with Rudolf Serkin at Town Hall, New York, and in 1939–1940 these two artists presented another series of concerts of sonatas by various composers. In 1939 the Busch Quartet made its first tour of the United States.

With the rise of the Nazi government in Germany in 1933, Busch, though Aryan, renounced his German citizenship and voluntarily exiled himself. He became a Swiss citizen and established his home in Basel, in a villa adjacent to one occupied by Rudolf Serkin. In Basel, Busch founded the Busch Chamber Orchestra which toured Europe in programs specializing in performances of Bach's Brandenburg Concertos and Suites. This chamber orchestra was also heard in the United States where it recorded all of Bach's Brandenburg Concertos for Columbia and all of Bach's orchestra suites for RCA Victor.

With the outbreak of World War II, Busch made a permanent shift of residence and citizenship to the United States. For a time he and his wife Frieda occupied an apartment on East Ninety-sixth Street in New York City. Frieda died in 1946 and a year later Busch married Hedwig Fischer. They had two sons. Busch's last years were spent in Guilford, Vermont, where he helped to found the Marlboro School of Music. He died in Guilford on June 9, 1952.

Busch was a prolific composer of music for orchestra, chorus, chamber-music groups, and solo instruments. His Symphony in E minor was introduced in New York City on November 27, 1927, with his brother, Fritz Busch, conducting the New York Symphony Society; his *Capriccio*, for small orchestra, received its premiere in New York on April 14, 1935, with Werner Janssen conducting the New York Philharmonic. Among Busch's other works are *Comedy Overture* and *Variations on a Theme by Mozart*, both for orchestra, a violin concerto, a piano concerto, a string quartet, a piano quintet, and a piano sonata. In addition, he edited all the solo sonatas and partitas for violin by Bach.

In 1935 Busch received an honorary doctorate in music from Edinburgh University.

ABOUT: New York Times, June 10, 1952.

Fritz Busch

1890–1951

Fritz Busch, conductor, was born in Siegen, Westphalia, Germany, on March 13, 1890. He was the oldest of eight children of Wilhelm and Henrietta Busch. Fritz's younger brother, Adolf, became a celebrated violinist, and another brother, Hermann, distinguished himself as a cellist.

Fritz's father earned his living as a carpenter and maker of violins. A frustrated concert artist, he sublimated his ambitions by founding and conducting a small orchestra that rehearsed at home and occasionally gave concerts.

Extraordinarily musical, Fritz Busch could read music before he was able to read words. As a child he received some violin instruction from his father on a miniature instrument his father had fashioned for him. When his brother Adolf appropriated this instrument, Fritz, now almost five, started studying the piano. Two years later he began to participate in the chamber-orchestral and chamber-music concerts at home, and even gave concerts by himself. But even then he knew that some day he would be a conductor rather than a pianist. Among his prized possessions were a photograph of the conductor Felix Weingartner, which hung in the boy's room, and a baton which Weingartner had given him. To prepare himself for a possible career as a conductor, Busch began to acquaint himself with instruments other than the piano; by the time he was twelve he had received instruction on almost every instrument in the orchestra.

His academic study took place at high schools in Siegen and Sieburg. In 1906 he entered the Cologne Conservatory where he studied conducting with Fritz Steinbach, piano with Karl Boettcher and Lazzaro Uzielli, and theory and composition with Otto Klauwell. Busch's first opportunity to conduct came at the Conservatory. In 1909, he led two summer concerts at Bad Pyrmont and later that same year he was appointed conductor and chorus director of the State Theater in Riga. He left Riga in 1910 to conduct three more seasons of summer concerts at Bad Pyrmont (where in 1911 he conducted the Blüthner Orchestra of Berlin). In 1911–1912 he served as director of the Musikverein chorus in Gotha.

FRITZ BUSCH

On August 28, 1911, he married Margaret Boettcher, the niece of one of his teachers. They had three children: one, Hans, became successful as an opera stage director; another, Margareta Ruth, married the baritone Martial Singher.

Busch accepted his first important conducting post in 1912, that of musical director in Aachen, where for the next six years he conducted performances of operas and symphonic music. In June 1918 he directed the Berlin Philharmonic Orchestra in a Max Reger festival in Jena which brought him to the attention of the Stuttgart Opera, then in search of a successor to Max von Schillings as musical director. Busch's three years in Stuttgart made him well known to German music lovers. His talent at conducting opera brought him one of the most desirable appointments in Germany, that of music director of the Dresden Opera. He was appointed to this post in 1922 on a life contract to succeed Fritz Reiner. Here Busch's worldwide reputation was firmly established, not only through brilliant productions that thoroughly revitalized the standard repertory (most particularly the operas of Mozart and the music dramas of Wagner) but also through his treatment of the modern repertory for which he revealed a particular affinity. Among the world premieres conducted by Busch at the Dresden Opera were Strauss's *Intermezzo* (November 4, 1924), Busoni's *Doktor Faust* (May 21, 1925), Weill's *Der Protagonist* (March 7, 1926), Hindemith's *Cardillac* (November 9, 1926), and Strauss's *Die Aegypti-*

sche Helena (June 6, 1928). The last of these initiated a festival commemorating the fiftieth anniversary of the Dresden Opera. Among the German premieres at the Dresden Opera under Busch were *Turandot* and Strauss's ballet *Josephs Legende*. Busch's remarkable productions of *La Forza del Destino, Don Carlo*, and *Macbeth* —all three then little known in Germany—were largely responsible for creating something of a Verdi renascence in that country. In Dresden, Busch also brought his flair for innovation to the direction of symphony concerts, introducing works by Krenek, Ernest Bloch, Stravinsky, and other twentieth century composers.

During the 1927–1928 season, Busch made his first conducting appearances in the United States as guest of the New York Symphony Society. At that time Samuel Chotzinoff noted in the *World* that "the new conductor stood out as a man who is thoroughly conversant with the technique of his business. His ideas are clearcut and extremely positive, and his method of getting the ideas across to his orchestra is just as unmistakable. His control of the men is absolute. . . . His gestures are admonitory. . . . He is often perpetually unraveling orchestral strands and with this method he often gets excellent results." Busch returned the following season for additional guest performances with the New York Symphony.

For a brief period after the rise of the Nazi regime in Germany Busch remained at his post in Dresden. Though he was not a Jew, he was in disfavor with the new regime because of his outspoken opposition to Nazism and particularly to its policy of "cleansing" German musical life of Jewish influences. The Nazis had little sympathy for Busch's espousal of new music. Furthermore, they suspected that politically he had Socialist leanings. During a rehearsal of *Aida* on March 7, 1933, Nazi storm troopers invaded the opera house, occupied the front seats, and disturbed the performance with shouts of "Out with Busch!" But for the fact that Hitler had given secret orders not to harm Busch bodily (for which Busch could never find an explanation), his life might have been in danger. However, his career in Germany was over. After a violent exchange with Hermann Goering, Busch resigned from his Dresden post and vowed never to appear in Germany as long as the Nazis remained in power. When the Nazi government made an effort to bring him to the Bayreuth

Festival during the summer of 1933 (Toscanini had refused to come) Busch turned down the invitation even though its acceptance might have brought about his rehabilitation with the Nazi regime.

Busch and his family left for South America where, during the months between August 8 and October 20, he conducted the German repertory at the Teatro Colón in Buenos Aires. Busch became a naturalized Argentine citizen in 1936. In the winter of 1933 he returned to Europe to become the music director of the Statsradiofonie in Copenhagen and to conduct the Stockholm Konsertföreningen. He was heard elsewhere as well: at the Royal Opera House in Stockholm, and at the summer Glyndebourne Festival in England which he (music director from its inception in May 1934) helped to make world famous through his sensitively projected performances of Mozart's operas and of *Macbeth* and *Don Pasquale*.

When he resigned as music director of the New York Philharmonic Orchestra in 1936, Arturo Toscanini recommended Busch, first, as his successor. Busch preferred to remain with his affiliations in Scandinavia and Glyndebourne. However, when Denmark was invaded by the Nazis during World War II, Busch was once again compelled to abandon Europe. He returned to the United States in the fall of 1941 to lead performances of *Così fan Tutte* with the New Opera Company of New York, which had been founded that season. The following January and February he was a guest conductor of the New York Philharmonic, and during the next three years he was once again active in South America both in operas and in symphonic music.

On November 26, 1945, Busch made his first appearance at the Metropolitan Opera, conducting *Lohengrin*. "The point and the thrust and the inner meanings of the music were made all too clear and life-like by the assiduous, penetrating, utterly assured conducting of Fritz Busch," wrote Robert Bagar in the *World-Telegram*. "There was no mistaking the fact that although many elements entered into last evening's smoothly moving show, all emanated from a central intelligence and that intelligence was right there in the pit, waving its hand over miracles. . . . He had a supreme regard for the music in the first place. And he will not let one lyrical idea escape him, whether it is riding high on a leading singer's solo or hidden deep in the intricate maze of the orchestration."

During the remainder of that season Busch also conducted *Tannhäuser, Don Pasquale,* and *Tristan and Isolde;* and during two later seasons he added *Otello, Der Rosenkavalier, Die Meistersinger, Un Ballo in Maschera, Don Giovanni,* and *The Marriage of Figaro.* About Busch's performance of *Otello,* Francis D. Perkins wrote in the *Herald Tribune* that it "was an interpretation of a conductor who knew this music drama thoroughly and how to realize its musical and emotional resources." Noel Straus, in the New York *Times,* found Busch's interpretation of *Tristan and Isolde* "a sensuously textured, admirably adjusted account of the orchestral score." To Irving Kolodin in the *Saturday Review,* Busch's interpretation of *The Marriage of Figaro* was "an accompaniment of high style and efficiency."

The season of 1948–1949 was Busch's last at the Metropolitan Opera. After that he was heard at the Glyndebourne and Edinburgh Festivals and in opera houses in Europe and South America. He died suddenly of a heart attack in his suite at the Hotel Savoy in London on September 14, 1951.

ABOUT: Busch, F. Pages from a Musician's Life; tr. from the German by M. Strachey. *Periodicals*— Opera News, November 26, 1943.

Montserrat Caballé

1933–

Montserrat Folch Caballé, soprano, was born in Barcelona on April 12, 1933. She was one of two children of Carlos and Ana Folch Caballé. Her father was an industrial chemist. Though there were no musicians in the family, the Caballés had a healthy appreciation of good music. Despite their poverty they owned a phonograph. Recordings by opera singers provided Montserrat, during her infancy, with her first musical experiences. When she started to sing along with the recordings, her parents discovered she had an unusually attractive voice.

"From childhood on," she recalls, "I have been surrounded by wonderful people—my par-

Caballé: kä bäl yā'

MONTSERRAT CABALLÉ

ents, my brother, aunts, uncles, cousins. Good, simple working people, with true emotions. Our home in Barcelona was humble. I remember Mama had an obsession for cleaning and putting white curtains on the windows. When I'd go to school she would pull back my hair so tight with a ribbon that it hurt. My parents loved music, and when they could they went to concerts or an opera."

When Montserrat was four she heard her first opera, *Aida,* at the Gran Teatro Liceo in Barcelona, and expressed the wish to study music. A year later she heard *Manon.*

During the Civil War in Spain the Caballé house was bombed, and the family fled to the mountains. With peace the family returned to Barcelona. "Things were more difficult than ever," she remembers. "Everyone suffered, and Papa developed a serious cardiac disease. It took seven years before we could afford an operation for him. We knew privation. Mama worked like a crazy woman to support the family. In those days, when stockings had holes, people didn't throw them away, they took them to have them darned. This was Mama's job. I assisted her, and with this money we were able to survive. The Church helped many times, giving shoes to my brother, Carlos, who is nine years my junior."

Montserrat attended a convent school; and for several years she went to a school for ballet. But her love for singing and music was uppermost. At seven she sang in a performance of a Bach cantata. When she was eight, she received as a gift the complete recording of *Madama But-*

terfly, and one year later on Christmas she sang for her family the aria "Un bel dì" as it was in the recording. At nine she entered the Conservatorio del Liceo in Barcelona, where she studied for six years. "I was very shy and not popular. For years I wore the same dress, like a uniform, and this was embarrassing for a teen-ager. My long nose gave me a complex; I had no makeup and felt not very beautiful. And I was very, very thin. . . . Young people can be cruel. My classmates kidded me about my dress. It hurt, but I didn't speak back because there was no answer."

After six years she interrupted her music study at the Conservatory to find a job and help pay for an operation for her father. She worked in a handkerchief factory. "I was awful at it." After seven months, on the advice of her uncle, she wrote to an affluent Barcelona family, that of José Antonio Bertrand, for help to continue her music studies. They responded generously, providing not only the financial assistance she needed for seven more years at the Conservatory but also a piano, a radio, and a job for her father. Thus Caballé was able to complete her music study at the Liceo: voice with Eugenie Keminy, song literature with Conchita Badía, and the operatic repertory with Napoleone Annovazzi. At school she learned her first roles (Fiordiligi in Così fan Tutte, Susanna in The Marriage of Figaro, the title role in Lucia di Lammermoor, the Queen of the Night in The Magic Flute) and she gave her first concert, singing "Leise, Leise" from Der Freischütz and "Ah! non credea" from La Sonnambula.

Upon her graduation from the Liceo—after receiving in 1953 the conservatory's gold medal, the highest award given to a singer in Spain— she was sent by her patron to Italy for auditions at some of the opera houses. She did badly, her voice cracking with nervousness. An agent told her to go home and get married. When she finally did manage to get an engagement—as Salud in Manuel de Falla's La Vida Breve—at the Florence May Music Festival, the production was suddenly cancelled before she could make an appearance. In Basel, Switzerland, in 1957 she was hired on a one-year contract as a cover without any compensation whatsoever. She supported herself by working as a waitress; her mother found a factory job. In time she was allowed to fill small parts, the First Lady in The Magic Flute and Renata in Prokofiev's The Flaming Angel. For these singing parts she was paid twenty-five dollars a performance. Her first leading part came in November 1957 when the singer scheduled for Mimi in La Bohème fell ill. Caballé was received enthusiastically. Looking back on that performance, which she later was able to evaluate through tapes made at the time, she was well satisfied with the results. "I am sure it was the best I ever sang in my life. My voice was so pure, naive and innocent." As a result of this success, the Basel Opera assigned her other leading roles during the next three years: Nedda in I Pagliacci, Tosca, Aida, Donna Elvira in Don Giovanni, Violetta in La Traviata, Eva in Die Meistersinger, Marta in D'Albert's Tiefland, the three heroines in The Tales of Hoffmann, Elisabeth in Tannhäuser, Arabella in Strauss's opera of that name, Salome, Elektra, Jaraslovna in Borodin's Prince Igor, Marie in The Bartered Bride, Marie in Berg's Wozzeck. Such was her durability that in a single week she sang in The Bartered Bride, La Traviata, Tosca, Salome, and Die Fledermaus. She also made guest appearances at the Vienna State Opera, where her performance as Salome won her a gold medal as the season's finest Strauss singer. "It was a mad schedule and life," she says. "Monday Basel, Tuesday Vienna, then Thursday back in Basel."

From Basel, Caballé moved on to the Bremen Opera where her already extensive and varied repertory was enlarged through appearances in Dvořák's Rusalka and Armida (the latter revived for her) and as Tatiana in Eugene Onegin. By the time her two-year contract had been terminated she had been heard in forty-seven roles since her debut in Basel as Mimi.

Upon leaving Bremen, Caballé appeared throughout Germany and Austria. She sang in Barcelona in 1963 as Arabella. In 1964 she made her American debut in Mexico City in the title role of Manon. In the summer of 1965 she was heard at the Glyndebourne Festival as the Marschallin in Der Rosenkavalier and the Countess in The Marriage of Figaro, and in the fall of that year she was back in Mexico City.

On April 20, 1965, Marilyn Horne was scheduled to sing the title role in Donizetti's Lucrezia Borgia at Carnegie Hall in a concert-hall presentation by the American Opera Society. When Horne became unavailable, Caballé was called in as a substitute. Despite her European successes, she was still unknown in the United States, but that single performance established her reputation. As Winthrop Sargeant noted in the New

Yorker, she "caused a furor." The critics rivaled each other in their superlatives. One of them described her as "sensational," another as "the most exciting new voice of the season." Her perfect control, the beauty of her vocal sound, her agility, the way she sustained notes, and her pianissimo placed her with the great singers of the time. George R. Marek, vice president and general manager of RCA Victor Records, went to a telephone during the intermission to summon Roger Hall, the Artists and Repertory Manager for RCA Victor, to the hall. By the time the concert was over, Caballé's name was on an RCA Victor contract.

On December 14, 1965, Caballé once again triumphed in Carnegie Hall, this time in a concert presentation of Donizetti's *Roberto Devereux* in which she sang the role of Queen Elizabeth I. In the New York *Times* Harold C. Schonberg grew rhapsodic over her "incredibly beautiful pianissimo, one in which high notes are floated effortlessly and hauntingly in the Milanov manner of yore." In the *New Yorker* Sargeant described her as an actress "who can express high emotional voltage with great dignity, keeping a smooth exterior while giving the impression she is seething within."

Caballé's first appearance in a staged operatic production in the United States was as Violetta with the Dallas Civic Opera in 1965. Before 1965 ended she made her debut at the Metropolitan Opera as Marguerite in a new production of *Faust* directed by Jean-Louis Barrault on December 22, 1965. Alan Rich reported in the *Herald Tribune* that it did not take her long after her first entrance "to convince an ecstatic audience that she is the Marguerite we have been waiting for these many years."

During the 1966–1967 season, Caballé appeared at the Metropolitan as Leonora in *Il Trovatore* and Desdemona in *Otello*. She opened the 1967–1968 season of the Metropolitan Opera as Violetta. In subsequent seasons she achieved new triumphs as Liù in *Turandot,* Amelia in *Un Ballo in Maschera,* Elisabetta in *Don Carlo,* Norma, Elena in *I Vespri Siciliani,* Mimi in *La Bohème,* Aida, and the title role in *Ariadne auf Naxos.*

She assumed the role of Norma reluctantly, feeling it was still beyond her capabilities, but Joan Sutherland persuaded her that her voice was ideal for the part. After trying out Norma in Barcelona in 1970 and with the Philadelphia

Lyric Opera in 1973, she enraptured the audience of the Metropolitan Opera with it on February 12, 1973. "It was reasonable," wrote Irving Kolodin in the *Saturday Review,* "to expect that a singer of her vocal fluency would find Bellini's florid line congenial to her. What is unexpected is the serious effort she has expended to make something unusually credible of the characterization." Kolodin found that Caballé's place with the greatest Normas of all time was earned "not only by some ethereally beautiful singing but also by her disposition to the mother rather than the priestess in Norma's nature."

She gave further evidence of her remarkable art as Imogene in Bellini's *Il Pirata* and as Cleopatra in Handel's *Giulio Cesare* with the American Opera Society in 1966. In 1969 she was starred as Alaide by the American Opera Society in a rare revival of Bellini's *La Straniera,* and on March 14, 1976, in a concert presentation of Donizetti's little-known opera *Gemma di Vergy,* with Eve Queler's Opera Orchestra of New York. In other American opera houses she was hailed for her performances as Mimi, the Countess in *The Marriage of Figaro,* Salome, Pamina in *The Magic Flute,* Maddalena in *Andrea Chénier,* and the title role of *Lucrezia Borgia* in her first staged production of that opera.

Before the 1960s were over, Caballé had also made triumphant debuts at the Salzburg Festival as Donna Elvira and at La Scala in the title role of *Luisa Miller.* She has also been heard at festivals in Edinburgh, Aix-en-Provence, and Florence. She has enjoyed triumphs in the world's great opera houses, not only at the Metropolitan Opera, the Vienna State Opera, and La Scala, but also at the Deutsche Oper in Berlin, the Munich Opera, Rome Opera, San Carlo in Naples, Teatro La Fenice in Venice, Verona Arena, the Bolshoi Opera in Moscow, and the Teatro Colón in Buenos Aires among others. Her repertory, in addition to roles already mentioned, embraces Marguerite in Boïto's *Mefistofele;* the title roles in Donizetti's *Anna Bolena, Catarina Cornaro,* and *Maria Stuarda;* Marguerite in *Faust;* Fiordiligi in *Così fan Tutte;* Donna Anna in *Don Giovanni;* the title role in Rossini's *Elisabetta Regina;* Mathilde in *William Tell;* the title role in *Manon Lescaut;* Donna Elvira in *Ernani;* Leonora in *Il Trovatore;* and the title role in Verdi's *Giovanna d'Arco.*

In August 1964 Caballé married Bernabé

Marti, a tenor. She had heard him for the first time in 1962 in an open-air performance of *Rigoletto* with an all-Spanish cast. Late that summer she recommended Marti for the leading tenor role in *Madama Butterfly* in Barcelona in which she herself took on the title role. "We saw each other five or six times," she recalls, "fighting, arguing, having fun, and I was always falling more in love with him." Then, when Caballé was in Marseilles in 1964, Marti came from Paris to propose marriage. They settled in an apartment in Barcelona, where a son, Bernabé, was born in 1966, and a daughter, Montserrat, in 1971. Caballé and Marti appeared together in New York in *Il Pirata* in 1966 and gave numerous joint recitals.

Caballé is a woman of ample physical proportions. Her skin is olive, her hair and eyes jet black. Both on and off the stage she has regal bearing, with "the dark good looks of a Spanish lady and the comfortable figure of a prima donna," wrote Louis Snyder in the New York *Herald Tribune*. She confesses that her greatest weakness is her appetite for food and cigarettes.

Spain has honored her with the Cross of Isabella the Catholic and the title Most Excellent and Most Illustrious Donna.

ABOUT: Gramophone (London), May 1976; High Fidelity, October 1966; New York Times, March 4, 1973; Newsweek, December 27, 1965; Opera News, March 9, 1970, March 9, 1974; Time, December 24, 1965.

SARAH CALDWELL

Sarah Caldwell

1924–

In addition to the reputation she has acquired as the artistic director and producer of one of the most progressive small opera companies in America, Sarah Caldwell has won national fame as a conductor of both opera and symphonic music. She was born in Maryville, Missouri, on March 6, 1924—not in 1928, the date given in most reference books. Her father, a professor at the University of Arkansas, and her mother, a piano teacher, were divorced while Sarah was still an infant. She was for a time raised by relatives while her mother attended Columbia University in New York for a master's degree in music. When her mother married Henry Alexander, a teacher of political science at the University of Arkansas, and settled in Fayetteville, Arkansas, Sarah went to live with her.

During her childhood Sarah received violin lessons; she was a prodigy in music and in mathematics. By the time she was ten she was good enough to perform chamber music with adults and to give recitals not only locally but also as far away as Chicago.

Upon graduation from high school when she was fourteen, Sarah went to the University of Arkansas, where she majored in psychology. After a year and a half, she left the university to concentrate on music. At Hendrix College in Arkansas she continued her violin studies with David Robertson. After a year and a half she received a scholarship for the New England Conservatory in Boston. There she continued the study of violin with Richard Burgin, the concertmaster of the Boston Symphony, and took viola lessons with Georges Flourel and courses in conducting, opera production, and stage design. A second scholarship brought her to the Berkshire Music Center in Tanglewood, Massachusetts, in 1946. There she played the viola in the school orchestra. A year later, at Tanglewood, she staged her first opera production, Vaughan Williams's *Riders to the Sea*. Serge Koussevitzky, the director of the Center, was so impressed by her work that he invited her to return to Tanglewood the following year as a member of the faculty in the opera department and to continue her opera studies with Boris Goldovsky.

118

She turned down offers to become a violist with the Minneapolis Symphony and the Indianapolis Symphony to serve as Goldovsky's assistant with the New England Opera Theater in Boston, which he had founded and which he directed. For more than a decade she remained there, serving as a kind of factotum for the company. As conductor she made her baton debut with Mozart's *La Finta Giardiniera;* she also served as chorus director, stage director, translator of operas, and prop woman.

In 1952, she was appointed head of the opera department of Boston University. There she remained eight years. She produced familiar operas *(Carmen, Madama Butterfly),* less familiar ones (Puccini's *Il Tabarro* and *Gianni Schicchi* from his *Il Trittico*), and contemporary works (Stravinsky's *The Rake's Progress,* Jacques Ibert's *Angélique,* Bohuslav Martinů's *Comedy on the Bridge,* and on February 17, 1956, the American premiere of Hindemith's *Mathis der Maler).*

By 1957 Caldwell had crystallized her thinking about the ways the production of opera could be improved through fresh, novel, and often totally unorthodox techniques and approaches. She was determined to uncover for America a large repertory of works (particularly modern ones) which the country's major companies were avoiding. In January 1957, supported by a few friends, she raised five thousand dollars with which the Boston Opera Group (subsequently renamed the Opera Company of Boston) was formed. Utilizing local singers, a makeshift orchestra, and elementary props, the company launched its first season at the Back Bay Theater in June 1958 with a novelty: one of Offenbach's least-known opéra-bouffes, *Le Voyage dans la Lune (Voyage to the Moon),* whose incomplete score she had discovered in the Boston Public Library and reconstructed. This production was so well received that early in 1960 it went on a national tour and was presented at the White House for President and Mrs. John F. Kennedy and their guests.

When the Back Bay Theater was torn down to make way for an apartment house, Caldwell had to give her productions wherever and whenever an auditorium was available—gymnasium, hockey rink, cyclorama, converted flower stall, old movie house. Finally in 1970 she brought her productions to the Orpheum Theater. This former vaudeville house became the permanent home of her company. Herculean energy, unflagging idealism, the capacity to work around the clock if necessary, an inordinate gift for winning friends and influencing supporters, and an insatiable hunger for innovation were responsible for the development of an opera company with few rivals. Caldwell was production head, stage director, conductor, artistic and business administrator, and fund collector. She lured famous singers to join her casts in special productions (Joan Sutherland, Beverly Sills, Boris Christoff, Nicolai Gedda, Donald Gramm, Régine Crespin, Renata Tebaldi, Marilyn Horne, George London, among others). Presenting an average of seventy-five performances of four operas each season, between February and June, the company offered familiar works often in highly unorthodox stage treatments which, under her baton, maintained the highest possible musical values. What was perhaps most exciting about these productions in Boston under Caldwell was the presentation here of operas produced nowhere else in the United States: the world premiere of Gunther Schuller's children's opera, *The Fisherman and His Wife* (May 8, 1970); the American premieres of Luigi Nono's *Intolleranza 1960* (February 19, 1965), Schoenberg's *Moses und Aron* (November 2, 1966), Roger Sessions' *Montezuma* (October 19, 1969), the completely staged and uncut version of Berlioz' *Les Troyens* (August 1972) and Glinka's *Russlan and Ludmilla* (March 5, 1977); such other novelties of past and present as the original version of Mussorgsky's *Boris Godunov,* Prokofiev's *War and Peace,* Rameau's *Hippolyte et Aricie,* Alban Berg's *Lulu,* Bellini's *I Puritani* and *I Capuleti ed i Montecchi,* Rossini's *Semiramide,* Robert Kurka's *The Good Soldier Schweik,* Béla Bartók's *The Wooden Prince, The Miraculous Mandarin* and *Bluebeard's Castle,* Massenet's *Don Quichotte,* Berlioz' *Benvenuto Cellini,* and Kurt Weill's *The Rise and Fall of the City Mahagonny.*

To bring some of her productions to audiences outside the Boston area, Caldwell formed the American National Council of the Arts in 1967 with a $350,000 subsidy from the National Council of the Arts. Under the management of Sol Hurok, the company toured twenty-six cities with *Tosca, Falstaff,* and *Lulu.* The critics were generally effusive in their praise. Writing in the *New Yorker,* Winthrop Sargeant said: "Not only is she a great director, one must also place her among the finest operatic conductors currently before the public." Nevertheless, the audience response was less than enthusiastic (perhaps because there were no stars in the casts) and the venture went into bankruptcy on June 5, 1968.

Nevertheless, Caldwell succeeded in spreading her own wings outside Boston. She staged productions of Hans Werner Henze's *The Young Lord* and Strauss's *Ariadne auf Naxos* at the New York City Opera in 1973. In 1974 she brought a new staging of Prokofiev's *War and Peace* to Wolf Trap Farm Park in Vienna, Virginia, near Washington, D.C., and conducted it. In 1976 she staged a delightful new production of *The Barber of Seville* for the New York City Opera. And she has also advanced her career as a conductor nationally. She made her debut at Carnegie Hall in New York in December 1974, leading the American Symphony Orchestra in a concert performance of *War and Peace*. Her symphonic debut followed a year later, on September 6, 1975, when she was heard as guest conductor of the Milwaukee Symphony in a program made up of music by Mozart and Berlioz, and including the American premiere of Thea Musgrave's *Memento Vitae: A Concerto in Homage to Beethoven*. Her performance, reported a critic for *Musical America,* was "memorable. . . . Partially hidden behind a screen and seated on the podium, she attempted to make working in front of a symphony orchestra on stage as close as possible to operating from a familiar opera pit. Her musical perceptions are intact, wherever she sits. The sure sense of the dramatic and the skill to make that sense work . . . were brilliantly evident."

On November 10, 1975, she became the second woman ever to conduct the New York Philharmonic, when she appeared in New York in a program made up entirely of the works of women composers. "Miss Caldwell," wrote Donal Henahan in the New York *Times,* "presided over one of the most ambitious and, finally, one of the most successful concerts of unfamiliar music that New York has witnessed in some time."

Then, on January 13, 1976, she became the first woman ever to step on the conductor's dais of the Metropolitan Opera in New York. The work that evening was *La Traviata* starring Beverly Sills (who was largely responsible for bringing about Caldwell's Metropolitan Opera debut). "Everybody seemed to like her conduct-

ing, as well they should," was Harold C. Schonberg's report in the New York *Times.* "It was well organized, it was brisk but not pellmell in tempo, it was accurate in rhythm. . . . Above all, Miss Caldwell stressed clarity. . . . Miss Caldwell demonstrated that she felt the music—the drama of the last act was eloquent testimony—but she did not find it necessary to carry on high."

Many other notable guest appearances followed. Among them were the Ravinia Festival on August 3, 1976 (she was the first woman to conduct there in its forty-one-year history); the Indianapolis Symphony in December 1976, when she presented the world premiere of Alec Wilder's Concerto for Tenor Saxophone and Chamber Orchestra; the Boston Symphony on January 19, 1977. She returned to the Metropolitan Opera during the 1977–1978 season to conduct *L' Elisir d'Amore.*

As organized and disciplined as she is in her musical life, and particularly as the producer and director of her opera company, so disarrayed and unstructured is she in her everyday existence. She does not eat or sleep on schedule but only when the need for either becomes too oppressive to be ignored. A huge woman, weighing over three hundred pounds, she has long been sublimely indifferent to her appearance. The contrast between her personal and her professional characteristics prompts much comment. In the New York *Times Magazine* Donal Henahan noted: "Sarah is the despair of her associates, who describe her in varying tones of affection, amusement, and resignation as 'slovenly,' 'fearfully fat,' 'unkempt' (this from an admiring orchestra player), 'the great unwashed.' . . . It is a fact that her hair generally looks like leftover vermicelli." *Time* adds: "If a button popped on a blouse, she would simply pin it with a brooch. On really bad days she could be seen waddling through town with her entire chest hung with brooches of all descriptions."

She is inordinately absent-minded, is forever losing her pocketbooks, forgetting where she has parked her car, misplacing necessities. As might have been expected, her home—the apartment in the Back Bay of Boston which she shared with her mother for several years until the spring of 1974 when they acquired a six-room house in suburban Weston—is overcluttered. It would undoubtedly have been in a perpetual state of chaos but for the fact that her widowed mother tried as best she could to regulate not only their household but also Sarah's disoriented way of life. "Somewhere beneath this turbulent surface, however," adds Henahan, "is an organizer, someone capable of pulling together the innumerable strands of opera production into a brilliantly effective whole."

ABOUT: After Dark, May 1972; Life, March 6, 1965; New York Times, March 5, 1972, January 11, 1976; New York Times Magazine, October 5, 1975; Time, November 10, 1975.

MARIA CALLAS

Maria Callas

1924–1977

Maria Callas (originally Maria Anna Cecilia Sofia Kalogeropoulos), soprano, was born in New York City on December 3, 1924, of Greek parents, George and Evangelia Demetriadu Callas. Her father, who had been a pharmacist in Greece, came to the United States in 1923, shortened his name to Callas, and opened a drugstore. When the Depression forced him to close down, he made a living as a traveling salesman of pharmaceutical products.

Four months after the Callas family came to America, Maria was born at the Fifth Avenue Hospital. She was raised in an apartment on Manhattan's West Side. "I was the ugly duckling of the family," she once confided to an interviewer, "fat, clumsy, unpopular." She began showing an interest in opera by trying to pick out on the family piano bits and snatches of opera arias she had heard over the radio. When a phonograph came into the household, she learned arias from recordings, among the first being the "Habanera" from *Carmen* and "Je suis Titania" from *Mignon.* At eight Maria started vocal lessons; one year later she sang at assemblies at P.S. 164, which she was then attending. Driven by a relentless and overambitious mother determined to exploit her daughter's musical gift, Maria was entered in several children's contests over the radio, and she won a prize on the Major Bowes amateur hour.

On January 28, 1937, Maria was graduated from P.S. 189, appearing as a vocalist at the graduation ceremonies. A few days later the thirteen-year-old girl bade farewell to her father

and to New York. Her mother took her and her sister to Greece. That September Maria was admitted to the National Conservatory in Athens after falsifying her age as sixteen, since younger pupils were not eligible. For two years she studied voice with Maria Trivella, and in November 1938 she made her stage debut at the Conservatory as Santuzza in *Cavalleria Rusticana.*

Eager to study with Elvira de Hidalgo, former diva of the Metropolitan Opera and La Scala and the artistic adviser to the National Opera in Athens, Maria applied for admission to the Royal Conservatory, where Hidalgo was a member of the faculty. The diva's first impression of the fifteen-year-old girl was far from flattering. "The very idea of that girl wanting to become a singer was laughable. She was tall, very fat, and wore heavy glasses. Her whole being was awkward and her dress much too large, buttoned in front and quite formless." Then Maria Callas sang "Ocean, Thou Mighty Monster" from *Oberon.* Without any further preliminaries she was admitted tuition-free to the Conservatory. For the next five years she was Hidalgo's pupil. "She never flirted and nobody courted her," the teacher recalls about her pupil. "She had a real inferiority complex about everything—except her voice. . . . She would want to sing the most difficult coloratura scales and trills. Her willpower was terrific. She had a phenomenal memory and could learn the most difficult opera in eight days." At the Conservatory Callas sang the title role in Puccini's *Suor Angelica.* Soon after, she made her first professional appearance in a performance of Suppé's *Boccaccio* at the Royal Opera of Athens.

When World War II broke out, life became oppressive for all Greeks, and particularly for the Callas family. The money that had been coming to them regularly from New York was halted. Food was rationed and scarce. The Nazi troops that invaded Athens in April 1941 instituted a repressive regime. But in spite of difficulties, Callas's musical career kept progressing. Through the influence of Hidalgo, Callas became a permanent member of the Royal Opera. She made her debut there in July 1942 on twenty-four hours' notice, in the title role of *Tosca.* Her success brought her a contract with the company as one of its leading sopranos. Early in 1943 she appeared as Santuzza; in April 1944 she was assigned the leading female role of Marta in the Greek premiere of d'Albert's *Tiefland;* in September 1944, she sang Leonore in *Fidelio.* Leonore, the first role she ever sang in German (all others she performed in Greek), was her greatest triumph up to that time.

After Athens was liberated by the Greek Resistance forces and was occupied by the English, Callas worked in an English army post as interpreter and as clerk in charge of classified information. When civil war erupted, conditions in the city grew chaotic. Singers at the Royal Opera, envious of her success and talent, conspired to have her removed from the company. Hidalgo strongly recommended that she go to Italy to give her career new momentum, but she preferred returning to the United States. Sailing on the S.S. Stockholm with her mother and sister, Callas arrived in New York in September 1945. A lawyer-turned-impresario became interested in her, served as her manager, and had his wife, Louise Caselotti, coach her.

In 1946 she auditioned for the Metropolitan Opera and was offered roles in two operas. She turned down the offer because she was dissatisfied with the provisions of her contract; Edward Johnson, the general manager, later confessed that it was just "a beginner's contract." On August 3, 1947, she made her Italian debut with the first of six appearances at the Verona Arena in the title role of *La Gioconda,* Tullio Serafin conducting. She suffered a severe ankle sprain during the rehearsal and at her first performance she had to hobble around awkwardly. This may have been one reason why she was received so coolly. (The enthusiasm that

evening was reserved for Richard Tucker, also making his Italian debut.) But the conductor, Serafin, was so impressed by the brilliance and beauty of her voice that he personally coached her for several months in the role of Isolde, for performances of *Tristan and Isolde* he was to conduct at the Teatro la Fenice in Venice. On the opening night of the 1947–1948 season of La Fenice, *Tristan and Isolde* was Callas's greatest professional success up to that time. It brought her engagements to appear as Leonora in *La Forza del Destino* in Trieste, as Turandot in Verona, as Aida in Rome, and as Isolde in *Tristan and Isolde* in Genoa. She endeared herself further to Venetian opera audiences by appearing in 1948 as Elvira in *I Puritani* (a part she had to learn in six days) and as Brünnhilde in *Die Walküre* (which she was also singing for the first time).

In 1947, at a dinner party in her honor at the Pedavena Restaurant in Verona, she met Giovanni Battista Meneghini, a prosperous businessman and socialite. "I knew he was *it* five minutes after I first met him," Callas recalled. They became inseparable. On April 21, 1949, they were married at the Chiesa dei Filippini in Verona. They lived at first in Verona, moving later to the Grand Hotel in Milan (where Verdi had died) before acquiring a permanent residence in a palatial four-story town house on the Via Michelangelo Buonarotti in Milan.

Shortly after their marriage the Meneghinis set sail for South America where Callas was to sing at the Teatro Colón in Buenos Aires. She was heard as Turandot and Aida, in neither of which she was particularly successful; then, as Norma, she was a sensation.

At San Carlo in Naples she appeared on the opening night performance of its 1949–1950 season as Abigaille in *Nabucco.* At the Rome Opera she was heard not only in her familiar roles but also, for the first time, on October 19, 1950, in Rossini's comic opera *Il Turco in Italia.* At La Scala, which she joined in 1950, she became immediately one of its stars. In Mexico City during the summer of 1950 she added Leonora in *Il Trovatore* to her roles. In 1951, on the fiftieth anniversary of Verdi's death, she was heard in performances of Verdi's operas in Florence, Naples, Milan, and other major cities. She was so popular that many Italians were referring to her as "the queen of prima donnas." In Trieste she was regarded as the greatest Norma of all time, and in Genoa opera lovers carried her through the streets after one of her appearances. The *Corriere delle Sera* in Milan spoke of "the miraculous throat of Maria Meneghini Callas" and of the "prodigious extension of her tones, their phosphorescent beauty and their technical agility which is more than rare, it is unique."

She was singing in *Tosca* in Rio de Janeiro in the fall of 1951 when what later became publicized worldwide as the Callas-Tebaldi feud first erupted. At that time, Tebaldi was appearing in *Andrea Chénier* in São Paulo. When Callas left Rio de Janeiro, Tebaldi was called in from São Paulo to take on the role of Tosca. This represented to Callas a carefully devised maneuver on the part of the Teatro Colón and specifically Renata Tebaldi to displace her among prima donnas. She expressed her anger so vociferously that before long, in far-off Italy, musical Milan became split into two warring camps, the followers of Callas and the followers of Tebaldi. These warring factions made their feelings strongly felt within the opera house, creating a bitter rivalry between the two singing stars that persisted for a number of years and brought about Tebaldi's decision in 1955 to leave La Scala. In 1968 Callas attended the season's opening of the Metropolitan Opera starring Tebaldi as Adriana Lecouvreur. The two singers met backstage, embraced, and were finally reconciled.

In 1952 Callas made her debut at Covent Garden in London as a member of the visiting La Scala company in five performances of *Norma.* One London critic called her "the greatest singer, male or female, since Nordica." At La Scala in 1952–1953 she shared the throne of prima donna *assoluta* with Tebaldi, each taking over one half of the season; Callas opened that season as Lady Macbeth. In 1953–1954 she created a sensation in the title role of Cherubini's *Medea* with Leonard Bernstein conducting.

Her fame spread to the United States through her remarkable recordings on the Angel label. On the strength of this fame she again received several contractual bids from the Metropolitan Opera, all of which she turned down because no agreements could be reached on rehearsal time and repertory, and, in one instance, because her husband could not get a visa to the United States.

When she finally made her American debut it was at the newly founded Lyric Theater in Chicago, on November 1, 1954. As Norma she caused a furor. Claudia Cassidy remarked in the *Tribune:* "Her voice is more beautiful in color, more even through the range than it used to be. Her range is formidable and her technique is dazzling." When, two weeks later, she appeared there as Lucia, an ovation erupted midway in the Mad Scene. The following evening, in the same role, she received twenty-two curtain calls that lasted fifteen minutes. In March 1955 she received further acclaim for her performances in *La Sonnambula,* Leonard Bernstein conducting.

Her presence on the roster of the Metropolitan Opera had become necessary. Rudolf Bing, the general manager of the company, and his assistant, Francis Robinson, flew out to Chicago to sign her to a contract in which all of her demands were met. But before that debut took place there was Vienna to conquer. She did so on June 12, 1956, as Lucia, with Herbert von Karajan conducting. "What a voice, what art, what intensity," exclaimed the critic of the *Bild Telegraf.*

Her Metropolitan Opera debut finally took place on October 29, 1956, the opening night of the season, as Norma. The returns to the box office for that performance were the highest in Metropolitan Opera history, over seventy-five thousand dollars; fifty thousand mail requests for tickets could not be filled. If she was not in top form that evening, it was mainly because she did not come to the stage in the best of spirits. For days she had been hounded by lawyers from her one-time manager who maintained she had violated her contract with him. (The suit was settled one year later out of court.) In addition, she was violently upset by a cover story in *Time* which depicted her as instigating backstage feuds, inspiring hate among her colleagues, being difficult to work with, and behaving ruthlessly in refusing her mother's request for financial assistance. "If you can't make money to live on," she was quoted as saying to her mother, "you can jump out of the window, or drown yourself." All such allegations she denied fiercely, particularly the item about her mother.

Her depression and anger affected her singing. In the New York *Times* Howard Taubman noted that "in high fortissimos, Miss Callas is downright shrill. She also has a tendency to sing off pitch when she has no time to brace herself for a high note." Paul Henry Lang in the *Tribune* remarked that her voice "has many limitations." Yet there was also much to admire.

Taubman added that she "brought to the role the concentration of one who had studied it thoroughly. Every move, every gesture was planned. . . . She was an actress of power." And Lang found her, all in all, to be "undoubtedly a great artist, a distinguished soprano of considerable stature, with a commanding dramatic personality. She is a resolute and obviously conscientious singer who studies her part in the most minute detail, leaving nothing to chance, and she has a big voice." The audience gave her sixteen curtain calls. In her next two Metropolitan Opera roles, those of Tosca and Lucia, she was in surer control of her technical resources, combining commanding dramatic portrayals with stunning voice production. The following season she was given one of the greatest receptions ever heard at the Metropolitan Opera House when she appeared there for the first time as Violetta in *La Traviata*.

The flaming personality and temperament that made her stage presence so electrifying to audiences were also responsible for making her a highly provocative personality. Volatile in moods, irascible by nature, strong-willed to a point of intransigeance, she time and again inspired controversy that readily lent itself to newspaper headlines. Citing ill health or nervous exhaustion she canceled so many performances that the "Callas walk-out," as one British newspaperman described it, became one of her familiar offstage acts. These cancellations began to accumulate in 1957. Upon making her first return to Greece in twelve years for two concerts at the Athens Festival of Music and Drama, she announced she could not appear at the first of these because of "exhaustion." Nervous exhaustion and ill health were given as the reasons for the cancellation of appearances in Vienna, the Edinburgh Festival, and the San Francisco Opera, arousing considerable animosity against her. Her voice actually gave way during rehearsals in Rome when she was scheduled to sing Norma in 1958. That appearance had been touted as a gala affair, with the president of the Italian Republic as guest; seats were sold for as high as forty dollars apiece; and the elegant audience in the theater was supplemented by millions more listening over the Rome RAI radio network. When, early in the opera, her voice broke down, the audience began hurling invectives and shouts of disapproval at her. When Callas defiantly announced she would not return

for the second act, pandemonium reigned in the auditorium. She had to flee from the theater through an underground passage. The violent demonstration continued not only within the theater but outside her hotel as well. The opera house refused to permit her to appear for the remaining performances of her engagement. The city officials, fearing mob riots, then closed down the theater completely. The matter was even hotly discussed in the Italian parliament.

Her first appearance in Italy after this scandal took place on April 9, 1958, in the title role of Donizetti's *Anna Bolena*. Anticipating trouble, the city officials stationed two hundred policemen in the auditorium. When she made her first entrance the audience received her frigidly, but as the opera progressed, and her singing and personality exerted their magnetic spell, the audience thawed into explosions of enthusiasm.

But her troubles were not over. By now she was in conflict with Antonio Ghiringhelli, the artistic director of La Scala. When she appeared on May 31, 1958, in *I Pirata*—not only her final performance for that season but her last appearance at La Scala for an indefinite period—she brazenly pointed to Ghiringhelli's box from the stage to explain why she was leaving La Scala. Ghiringhelli ordered the curtain to be brought down without allowing her to take her final bows, and the theater was hurriedly emptied. Her fans cried out: "La Scala needs you, come back," but her enemies were no less vocal. After 157 performances in 21 roles Callas was permanently through with La Scala. "The prima donna passes," Ghiringhelli remarked, "but La Scala remains."

Other problems arose at the Metropolitan Opera. In October 1958 she came to Dallas to appear as Violetta, and as Medea in Cherubini's opera. While in Dallas there ensued a fiery exchange of letters and telegrams with Rudolf Bing regarding her plans for appearances that season at the Metropolitan. The matter had been reduced by both sides to ugliness when Bing ordered her by wire to report to the Metropolitan Opera the following morning. Angered by what she described as his "German attitude" which, she insisted, reduced those who worked under him to the status of "laborers in a concentration camp," she ignored the wire. The following day, on November 7, the newspapers carried the story that Bing had fired Callas, and that her twenty-six performances for the coming season had been canceled. It was the climax of a continuous clash between two temperamental personalities, each determined to have the upper hand. Public reaction was mixed. Paul Hume, the music critic in Washington, D.C., insisted that Rudolf Bing should resign. *Musical America* remarked: "It is clear that she is an all but impossible lady to deal with on a business basis. It is equally clear that she is one of the most incandescent and therefore fascinating artistic personalities to be visited on this glamour-starved generation."

As if all this were not enough to make Maria Callas a highly controversial personage there was also her love life, which she made no effort to conceal. Her lover was one of the world's wealthiest men, Aristotle Onassis. They met for the first time in Venice in 1959. What resulted seemed to be instantaneous combustion. He attended her performance in *Medea* in London on June 17, 1959, and gave a supper party in her honor at the Dorchester Hotel. In July, Maria Callas and her husband joined several notable guests including Sir Winston Churchill to cruise with Onassis on his yacht, the Christina, sailing from Monte Carlo. Callas and Onassis met intermittently after that. On September 11, she was his sole guest on a two-week Aegean cruise. Callas openly revealed to her husband that she was carrying on an affair with Onassis, with whom she was overwhelmingly in love; at the same time she announced that her marriage was over. After the open break between Callas and her husband in August 1959 and Onassis's divorce from his wife the following June, Callas was often observed with Onassis in many different places of the world, as well as on his yacht. The nine-year romance ended when Onassis left her for Jacqueline Kennedy, whom he married in 1968. Callas' marriage to Meneghini was finally terminated legally by a divorce decree in Brescia in 1971, following which Callas made her home in Paris.

She returned to the stage of the Metropolitan Opera for two performances of *Tosca*. Her appearance in that opera on March 25, 1965, was her last on any operatic stage for a number of years. She had been scheduled to be a soloist in Verdi's Requiem at the Dallas Civic Opera in November 1969, but she withdrew without explanation, and that concert was canceled.

A long period followed, during which she gave up performing to direct her musicianship and energies into other channels. In 1971–1972 she began conducting a twice-a-week class called The Lyric Tradition at the Juilliard School of Music, and on April 10, 1973, she made her none-too-successful debut as an opera director with a performance of *I Vespri Siciliani* at the newly rebuilt opera house in Turin. In 1973, after an absence of eight years from public singing, Callas announced she was returning to the concert stage with a world tour in joint recitals with the tenor Giuseppe di Stefano. She explained that she had gone into retirement because she had "developed some bad vocal habits," and she added that "I retired to start again." Her return concert was scheduled for London on September 22, 1973. Thirty thousand applications for tickets poured into Royal Festival Hall, but a few days before the concert it was canceled because, it was said, she had developed eye trouble. The comeback concert took place instead in Hamburg, Germany, the following month, on October 26. "It was Callas' acting above all, allied with her singing, that cast the spell, a spell that had the audience of three thousand standing and cheering for twenty-five minutes at the end." So reported Sydney Edwards to the New York *Times*. But many of the local German critics found major flaws in her technique and a marked deterioration of the texture of her voice and inaccuracy of pitch.

She made her first London return appearance on November 27 when, although she looked "beautifully grand," in the words of Philip Hope-Wallace in the *Guardian*, the top of her voice "was uncertain, weak." Her American tour (the first since 1959) began in Philadelphia on February 11, 1974, but a concert planned for Carnegie Hall, New York, on February 17 had to be canceled because she was suffering from "incipient influenza." When she finally did appear in Carnegie Hall on March 5, Harold C. Schonberg expressed the opinion in the New York *Times* that "it would be silly to pretend that Miss Callas has much voice left. But . . . she remains an artist. She gave her best, and every now and then, the old Callas sound came out."

Callas was starred in a motion picture, *Medea*, based on the Euripides tragedy, written and directed by Pier Paolo Pasolini, and released in 1971.

She died suddenly of a heart attack at her home in Paris on September 17, 1977. She had apparently been in good health up to then and

Calvé

was planning to write her autobiography for a New York publisher. Memorial services were conducted in Paris, London, New York, and Milan. Her body was taken to the Père Lachaise cemetery in Paris where it was cremated in a private ceremony.

ABOUT: Arodin, J. The Callas Legacy; Arodin, J. and Fitzgerald, G. Callas; Bing, R. 5000 Nights at the Opera; Callas, E. and Blochman, L. My Daughter Maria Callas; Fraser, N. and others. Aristotle Onassis; Jellinek, G. Callas: Portrait of a Prima Donna; Wisneski, H. Maria Callas: The Art Behind the Legend. *Periodicals*—High Fidelity, February 1965; High Fidelity/Musical America, January 1978; Life, October 31, 1955; Musical America, December 1964; New York Times, October 31, 1971, September 17, 1977; Opera (London), November 1977; Opera News, November 1977; Saturday Review, October 27, 1956.

EMMA CALVÉ

Emma Calvé

1858–1942

Emma Calvé (originally Rosa Emma Calvet), soprano, was one of the greatest Carmens of all time. She was born in Décazeville, Aveyron, France, on August 15, 1858. She attended the Convent of the Sacred Heart in Montpellier where her talent for singing was first discovered. In 1880 she was sent to Paris for musical training; for two years she studied voice with Jules Puget. Her first appearance in public took place at a charity concert in Nice. When her studies with Puget ended, she made her opera debut at the Théâtre de la Monnaie in Brussels on September 29, 1882, as Marguerite in *Faust.* She remained a member of the Théâtre de la Monnaie for one year; then, in 1882–1883 she continued her vocal studies with Mathilde Marchesi. On December 16, 1884, chosen by the French baritone Victor Maurel, she created the role of Bianca in the world premiere of Theodore Dubois's opera *Aben Hamet,* at the Théâtre des Italiens in Paris. "I have always been deeply grateful to Maurel for the lessons in lyric declamation which I received from him and which greatly influenced my career," she wrote in her autobiography.

From 1884 to 1887 she was a principal soprano of the Opéra-Comique in Paris. While there she made a guest appearance at La Scala

Calvé: kȧl vā′

in Milan in January 1887 as Ophelia in *Hamlet.* This performance went so poorly and was received by the critics with such hostility that she recognized her need for more vocal instruction. For the next eighteen months she studied with Rosine Laborde. Then she returned to La Scala, again as Ophelia, and scored a triumph. On October 31, 1891, at the Teatro Costanzi in Rome, she was heard as Suzel in the world premiere of Mascagni's *L'Amico Fritz.* Then, soon after the world premiere of *Cavalleria Rusticana* in Rome, she appeared on January 19, 1892, at the Opéra-Comique in Paris as Santuzza in the same opera. This became one of her most famous roles. "My interpretation of the role of Santuzza astonished my comrades," she recalled in her autobiography. "My spontaneous and unspoiled gestures shocked them. Even the costume, which I had brought with me from Italy, the clothes of a real peasant woman, coarse shirt, worn sandals and all were considered eccentric and ugly. . . . I went on the stage and I was . . . the naive and tragic Santuzza, the passionate, impulsive peasant girl of Italy. It was a triumph!" When she appeared in the same role in London in 1892, Bernard Shaw found her "irresistible and beautiful, and fully capable of sustaining the inevitable comparison with Duse's impersonation of the same part."

Her greatest role was Carmen. Her interpretation was the standard by which all other Carmens were henceforth to be measured. She sang it for the first time, and with sensational success, at the Opéra-Comique in Paris on November 25,

1892. Célestine Galli-Marié, who had created the role, was in the audience. She came backstage to congratulate Calvé and to herald her as a worthy successor, though how worthy not even Galli-Marié could suspect at the time. As Carmen, Calvé achieved one overwhelming success after another: in St. Petersburg, Moscow, London, Madrid, Milan, Vienna, and Berlin.

After a sensational debut at Covent Garden in London as Santuzza on May 16, 1892, Calvé went to the United States to join the Metropolitan Opera. Her debut took place on November 29, 1893, as Santuzza. "The pegs must be set high when the merits of Mme. Calvé were descanted upon," said Henry Krehbiel in the *Tribune*. "She is a singer of true dramatic instincts, unfailing musical taste and magnetic eloquence in pose, action, and vocal utterance. Her Santuzza is not one of the Continental marionettes of the operatic stage, but a dramatic creation—a woman with hot blood in her veins, whose voice takes color from the situation, and occasionally sets one's fingertips tingling. She blends declamation with singing in a manner which shows complete appreciation of the purposes of music in the modern lyric drama, yet never forgets the rights which music has, independent of the drama, in such a hybrid work as Mascagni's." One month later, on December 20, New York became acquainted with Calvé's Carmen. "Mme. Calvé," wrote W. J. Henderson in the New York *Times,* "carried out her conception of the part with the same theatrical ability she has shown in her Santuzza, and the result was that in the second act her impersonation approached the boundaries of the hazardous."

There were, however, a few who were somewhat captious in their reactions to Calvé's Carmen. These objected to her realistic costuming and even more to the dramatic truth she imparted to her interpretation. "I insisted on wearing the fringed shawl . . . instead of the bolero and short skirt in which past Carmens had always been costumed," she tells us in her autobiography. "In the matter of the dance, my ideas and those of the directors did not agree. . . . Whereupon I showed them the true dance of the gitanas, with its special use of arms and head—a manner of dancing for which the Spaniards have invented the expression of 'el bracear.' " W. J. Henderson thought that her second-act dance "brought up in many minds remembrances of the Midway Plaisance [at the Chicago World's Fair]." Her overall projection of the character of Carmen was found by some to be too sensual, passionate and uninhibited. Yet it was her acting —and principally her realistic approach to the roles, in which respect she was a pioneer—that placed Calvé with the greatest prima donnas. Minnie Maddern Fiske, one of the great actresses of her day, once said: "There are two great actresses in our time: not Duse and Bernhardt as the press would have it, but Duse and Calvé."

Following appearances at the Metropolitan Opera in 1893–1894, Calvé toured Europe, performing in Madrid, Monte Carlo, and St. Petersburg. In 1894–1895 she returned to the Opéra-Comique in Paris where, on November 27, 1897, she created the title role in Massenet's *Sapho,* which the composer had written with her in mind. On June 20, 1894, at Covent Garden, she created the role of Anita in Massenet's *La Navarraise* which had also been written for her. The season of 1895–1896 found her at the Metropolitan Opera in the roles of Ophelia in *Hamlet,* Leila in Bizet's *The Pearl Fishers,* Marguerite and Helen of Troy in Boïto's *Mefistofele,* Marguerite in *Faust,* and Anita in the American premiere of *La Navarraise.* By the time Calvé left the Metropolitan Opera, following the season of 1903–1904, she had also been heard in the title role of De Lara's *Messaline* at its American premiere on January 22, 1902.

In 1903–1904, Calvé was the principal soprano of the Opéra Municipal du Théâtre de la Gaîté in Paris. She returned to the United States in 1905 to appear in recitals. Her concert at Carnegie Hall in New York on November 4, 1905, led Richard Aldrich to say in the New York *Times:* "The voice has always been one of the most searchingly poignant in its quality, wonderfully potent in its expression of emotion and in the variety of color it could assume in heightening and enforcing the emotional significance of the music." Between 1907 and 1909 Calvé was a member of the Manhattan Opera where once again she was extremely successful.

One of the unusual qualities about her voice was the phenomenal range that allowed her to assume contralto and mezzo-soprano roles as well as soprano ones. In *The Marriage of Figaro,* at different times she sang the roles of Cherubino, Susanna, and the Countess; in Massenet's *Hérodiade* she was able at one time to sing the

Campanini

contralto role of Herodias, and at another the soprano part of Salome.

Calvé retired from the opera stage in 1910. During the decade that followed she was heard in numerous recitals in Europe and the United States. She made her last concert tour of the United States in 1923–1924 and gave her final concert in 1938.

In her closing years Calvé lived in comparative seclusion at her home, Cabières, a medieval castle near Millau, in the south central part of France in the Causses mountains. This castle was the realization of an ambition Calvé had cherished from girlhood when, seeing it for the first time, she told her friends that she would someday own it. When World War II broke out she sold it and went to live in Montpellier. A passionate French patriot, she invested all her money in French enterprises and as a result was wiped out financially by the war. She died in Millau on January 6, 1942.

ABOUT: Calvé, E. My Life; Calvé, E. Sous tous les ciels j'ai chanté; Gallus, A. Emma Calvé: Her Artistic Life.

Cleofonte Campanini

1860–1919

Cleofonte Campanini, conductor, was born in Parma, Italy, on September 1, 1860. He was the younger brother of Italo Campanini (1845–1896), an operatic tenor who sang the title role in *Faust* when the Metropolitan Opera House opened on October 22, 1883, and who later became an opera impresario.

Cleofonte received his musical training on the violin at the Parma Conservatory. After completing his musical education at the Milan Conservatory, he made his conducting debut in Parma in 1883 in *Carmen*. That year he went to the Metropolitan Opera House in New York to share the podium with Auguste Vianesi for the inaugural season. In 1883–1884 Campanini conducted performances of *Carmen, Mignon, La Sonnambula,* and Boïto's *Mefistofele.*

When Italo became an impresario at the Academy of Music in New York he called Cleofonte back to New York to direct the American premiere of *Otello* on April 16, 1888. The Desdemona that evening was Luisa Tetrazzini's sis-

CLEOFONTE CAMPANINI

ter, Eva Tetrazzini, whom Cleofonte had married in Florence on May 15, 1887.

For a dozen years beginning with 1900 Campanini conducted Italian operas at Covent Garden. Between 1888 and 1906 he conducted at La Scala and San Carlo in Italy, and also in South America.

In 1906 Oscar Hammerstein engaged him as the music director of the newly organized Manhattan Opera House in New York City. The brilliance of Campanini's overall artistic direction and conducting was largely responsible for making the Manhattan Opera a formidable artistic competitor to the Metropolitan. As a conductor, Campanini was one of the great interpreters of his generation in the Italian and French repertory. Critics eulogized his ability to concentrate on details without overlooking the overall design, his sensitivity in providing the singers an orchestral background, and his extraordinary gift in projecting an Italian singing style in the Italian repertory and a refined idiom in French operas. Among the noteworthy artistic achievements of the Manhattan Opera House under Campanini were the American premieres of *Thaïs* on November 25, 1907, *Louise* on January 3, 1908, *Pelléas and Mélisande* on February 19, 1908, and *Sapho* on November 17, 1909.

Differences with Oscar Hammerstein over the artistic program of the Manhattan Opera company, and disputes over the financial deficits Campanini was incurring with his expensive productions, led to Campanini's resignation in 1909. In 1910 he became the artistic director of

Campanini: käm pä nē′ nē̇

128

the new Philadelphia-Chicago Opera Company, a post he retained until his death. In January 1918 he took the company to New York for a four-week season.

With the Philadelphia-Chicago Opera Company Campanini conducted the world premiere of Victor Herbert's *Natoma* in Philadelphia on March 14, 1911, and the American premieres of Blockx's *La Princesse d'Auberge* (March 10, 1909), *The Secret of Suzanne* (March 14, 1911), Noguès' *Quo Vadis* (March 25, 1911), *The Jewels of the Madonna* (March 14, 1911), and Gneccho's *Cassandra* (February 26, 1914). Campanini's dedication and meticulous attention to detail in the preparation of each new opera he conducted was particularly evident in an opera such as *Natoma* which in style and subject matter differed so much from his own operatic background and experience. In a letter of gratitude, Victor Herbert wrote to Campanini after the premiere: "I desire to publicly express my deep and grateful acknowledgement to Maestro Cleofonte Campanini for his extraordinary labors in the preparation and production of our opera, *Natoma,* tonight, for his unwearying patience, for his vital interest in American opera, and . . . for his invaluable suggestions. . . . How much of its success, if any, will be due to his commanding influence, few will ever know. I can never forget his work in this production, because I can never repay him."

Cleofonte Campanini died in Chicago on December 19, 1919.

ABOUT: Baker, T. Biographical Dictionary of Musicians, completely rev. by N. Slonimsky; Grove, G. ed. Dictionary of Music and Musicians; 5th ed. edited by E. Blom.

Guido Cantelli

1920–1956

Guido Cantelli, conductor, was born in Novara, Piedmont, Italy, on April 27, 1920, to Antonio and Riccardone Angela Cantelli. His first conducting experience came in leading his father's military band when he was only five years old. "In reality," he recalled, "the band conducted me." As a child he also sang in a church choir

Cantelli: kän tĕl' lĕ

GUIDO CANTELLI

and performed children's parts in opera performances, while studying the organ with Felice Fasola and the piano with his father. He was only eleven when he began playing keyboard instruments for public performances of opera and fourteen when he gave his first piano recital.

At fourteen he went to Milan for further piano instruction. One year later he studied composition privately with Paolo Delachi. By the age of eighteen he was attending the Verdi Conservatory in Milan where his teachers in composition were Arrigo Pebrolo and Giorgio Ghedini. In his last year at the Conservatory, Cantelli conducted three orchestral concerts, one of which included his own *Theme and Variations.*

He made his professional debut as a conductor in 1941 in a performance of *La Traviata* at the Teatro Coccia in Novara (a theater which Toscanini had helped to open in 1889). For two years Cantelli, as artistic director, led many celebrated works of the Italian repertory there, including *Don Pasquale, La Bohème, Cavalleria Rusticana,* and *Andrea Chénier,* besides conducting several symphony concerts.

During World War II, in 1943, he was called into the army but refused to serve because he opposed the ideology imposed upon Italy by Nazi Germany. Because of his resistance he was imprisoned in a concentration camp in Stettin, Germany, during the years 1943–1945. His health suffered such deterioration—his weight had gone down to about eighty pounds—that he had to be sent to a hospital in Bolzano. With the help of a priest he managed to escape to Novara where he lived under an assumed name. During an involvement in the fighting between Fascists and Partisans, Cantelli was captured by the Fascists and sentenced to be shot. The liberation of Italy saved his life.

On April 28, 1945, Cantelli married his childhood sweetheart, Iris Bilucaglia, an amateur pianist. They lived in Milan. There, in July 1945 at the Castello Sforzesco (the La Scala opera house having been damaged by bombs), Cantelli made his debut as the conductor of the La Scala Orchestra. Soon after, Cantelli was asked to conduct the symphony orchestra on Radio Torino and to embark on a tour of Italy conducting operas. His appearances at the International Festival of Venice in 1946 were so successful that he received invitations to appear as guest conductor of several major orchestras, not only in Italy but in Belgium and Austria, including the Vienna Philharmonic.

The turning point in his career came in Milan on May 18, 1948, when he was rehearsing the La Scala Orchestra of which he was the permanent conductor. Toscanini, then in Milan, was so impressed at this rehearsal by Cantelli's talent that he invited Cantelli to be a guest conductor of the NBC Symphony. With this orchestra, Cantelli made his American debut on January 15, 1949, in the first of four concerts. "He is an unusually gifted musician," wrote Francis D. Perkins in the New York *Herald Tribune.* "In technique of conducting he seemed remarkably well versed: his gestures were clear and indicative and . . . told of a definite interpretative idea, an assurance based on a thorough knowledge of his scores." After attending all of the rehearsals, Toscanini called Cantelli "a real conductor" adding: "I didn't say a virtuoso conductor, either. I mean a real musician and interpreter."

During his first season in the United States Cantelli made two guest appearances with the Philadelphia Orchestra and recorded his first LP for RCA Victor (Haydn's Symphony No.93). He returned the following season to conduct four more concerts with the NBC Symphony and eight concerts the next season. He returned to Italy to lead the first performance in that country of Menotti's one-act comic opera *The Telephone,* at the International Festival in Venice in September 1949, and in 1950 and 1951 he toured Italy and England with the La Scala Or-

chestra and made noteworthy guest appearances with major European orchestras.

During the next half dozen years, Cantelli was a frequent visitor to the United States as a guest conductor of most of its principal orchestras. Until his untimely death he led a part of each season of the New York Philharmonic, beginning January 3, 1952. Abroad, he made extensive appearances both in opera and symphonic music, including performances at La Scala and at the Salzburg and Edinburgh festivals.

"Cantelli's capacity to assimilate and transmit music with the most exceptional clarity and intensity is paralleled at his best by the depth of his thinking and his powerful sense of form," wrote Olin Downes in the New York *Times.* "These are the things which set him apart from any colleague of equal years and experience."

He was en route from Italy to New York to fulfill a four-week engagement with the New York Philharmonic when, on November 24, 1956, he was killed in an airplane crash, just as his plane was taking off from Orly airfield outside Paris. "Had he lived longer," wrote Harris Goldsmith in *High Fidelity* magazine almost two decades later, "he would undoubtedly have been the preeminent conductor of the era." How great Cantelli had already become by the time of his death was remembered in 1975 when the Arturo Toscanini Society released a six-disk album called *The Cantelli Legacy,* Volume 1 comprising many of his performances with the NBC Symphony. A second volume of *The Cantelli Legacy,* made up of records he had made in Europe for EMI, was issued subsequently.

Guido Cantelli's only child—a son, Leonardo —was born in June 1956, just four months before Cantelli's fatal accident.

ABOUT: High Fidelity, April 1974, June 1975; New York Times, February 13, 1949.

Teresa Carreño

1853–1917

María Teresa Carreño, pianist, was born in Caracas, Venezuela, on December 22, 1853. She was the granddaughter of an eminent Venezuelan composer, José Cayetano Carreño, and a

---

Carreño: kär rĕ′ nyō

TERESA CARREÑO

lessons. Franz Liszt also offered to become her teacher, but she turned down the generous gesture because it necessitated following Liszt to Rome, which she refused to do. Instead, she performed extensively in England and Spain.

With some vocal training from Enrico Delle Sedie and Rossini but with no actual experience as a vocalist, she suddenly substituted for an indisposed singer in the role of the Queen in *Les Huguenots* in Edinburgh on May 24, 1872. From time to time she made other appearances as a singer and gave an excellent account of herself; she also did some further voice study in Boston in 1876. But her principal activity remained playing the piano. Grown into a woman of Amazonian proportions, she brought to her piano performances such extraordinary strength and technique, such power and passion, that she came to be known as the Brünnhilde of the piano or the Valkyrie of the piano. She developed into a pianist in the grand manner of Anton Rubinstein. In compositions of large design calling for strong romantic responses as well as physical strength, she had few rivals, even among men. Driven by her romantic impulses she did not hesitate at times to improve upon the compositions she was performing through changes in dynamics, rhythm, or tempo; at times she even rewrote passages. For such practices she was sometimes severely taken to task by musicians.

While touring the United States in the fall of 1872 as pianist with the Maurice Strakosch company, she fell in love with Émile Sauret, a violinist appearing with that group. In June 1873 she married him, and later she sometimes appeared with him in sonata recitals. This marriage was a stormy one and was dissolved by divorce about two years after the birth of two children, one of whom died in infancy. In 1876 Carreño became the wife of Giovanni Tagliapietra, a baritone. She undertook several concert tours with him in joint recitals in which she sometimes deserted the piano to join him in vocal duets. On February 25, 1876, when he appeared in the title role of *Don Giovanni* in New York she sang the role of Zerlina; and soon after that she helped her husband found an opera company touring Venezuela, making occasional appearances herself not only as a singer but also as a conductor. But this marriage, too, ended in divorce after Carreño had given birth to three more children. She returned to the concert stage as a pianist and made her German debut in Berlin on November

great-niece of María Teresa Toro, the wife of Simón Bolívar. Teresa's father, Manuel Antonio Carreño, a political figure in Venezuela who at one time had been its minister of finance, was also a well-trained musician.

Though Teresa showed unmistakable precocity in music from her third year on, she did not begin piano lessons until she was six. Her father was her first teacher; later she was given more professional training by Julius Hohenhus.

Political turmoil in Venezuela in July 1862 sent the Carreño family to the United States; they found a new home in New York. There Teresa made her piano debut at Irving Hall on November 25, 1862, and this success led to four additional concerts.

Louis Gottschalk, the American pianist-composer, heard her play in New York in 1862, pronounced her a genius, and became her teacher. On January 2, 1863, Teresa was so successful in Boston that she was called upon to give eleven additional concerts and to perform throughout New England. She was also invited to the White House to play for President Lincoln. When he asked her to perform one of his favorite songs, "Listen to the Mocking Bird," she complied, following this rendition with an improvised series of variations.

On April 7, 1866, she went to Europe, where she studied piano in Paris with Georges Mathias and Emmanuel Bazin. Following a Paris concert on May 14, 1866, she became the idol of the French music public. In London Anton Rubinstein heard her and stood ready to give her some

18, 1889. Hans von Bülow described her as "the most interesting pianist of the present age. . . . a phenomenon."

Settling in Berlin, she set forth in 1890 on her first European tour, which placed her among the great pianists of the period and earned for her the adoration of the general public and the accolades of such musicians as Grieg, Brahms and Eugène d'Albert. The last mentioned of these she married on July 27, 1892. D'Albert was eleven years younger than she, a piano virtuoso, and well-known composer. After she performed one of his piano concertos in Berlin a much-quoted remark was published by a local critic: "Frau Carreño yesterday played for the first time the second concerto of her third husband at the fourth Philharmonic concert."

During the three years this marital relationship lasted, Carreño had two more daughters. D'Albert and Carreño were sometimes heard in remarkable two-piano recitals. The marital union proved no more harmonious for Carreño than the earlier ones had been. But if she made no gain in personal happiness she did profit artistically from her intimate relationship with an artist of the caliber of d'Albert. Through him she learned to curb the strength and passion of her piano playing, to discipline her fiery temperament, and to add a sensitivity, refinement, and contemplation to her former dynamic power and emotional excesses.

In reviewing her New York recital on January 12, 1908, Richard Aldrich made this point clear when he spoke of her "great nobility and imposing breadth, contrasted with delicacy and tenderness." He added: "There was a time when her exhaustless power of arm and finger made her performances sometimes seem to fit ill in the frame of the piano. The tempestuous and mercurial characteristics that used to mark her playing have been somewhat modified by the passing years." And, following another New York recital on October 27, 1916, Aldrich wrote: "Time was when Mme. Carreño was considered a 'Valkyrie of the piano'; when tempestuous power was the distinguishing mark of her playing. It is no longer so; her art has mellowed and gained refinement in these later years. . . . Mme. Carreño cultivates now beauty of tone and some reserve in the proclamation of even the most elemental passions, and in passages of tenderer and softer emotion her tone and expression are reduced to a fine-spun thread."

She continued to concertize not only in Europe and the United States but also in Australia and New Zealand until her last days. Her final appearance with an orchestra was with the New York Philharmonic on December 6, 1916, and her last recital was in Havana on March 12, 1917. Meanwhile, on June 30, 1902, she embarked on her fourth and last marriage, the only one to turn out well. Her new husband was Arturo Tagliapietra, the younger brother of her second husband, Giovanni.

Carreño was an able teacher of the piano. One of her students was Edward MacDowell, whose piano compositions she was among the first to promote. She was also the composer of numerous pieces for the piano, one of which—the waltz "Mi Teresita"—became popular.

Teresa Carreño died in New York City of myasthenia gravis on June 12, 1917. Twenty-two years later her ashes were transferred to her native land for reburial in the poet's corner of the Cementerio del Sur in Caracas.

ABOUT: Milinowski, M. Teresa Carreño. *Periodicals* —Musical Quarterly, October 1940.

Enrico Caruso

1873–1921

There are few dissenters to the claim that Enrico (originally Errico) Caruso was one of the greatest operatic tenors of all time, possibly *the* greatest. Many attempts have been made to explain the uniqueness of the Caruso voice, beyond description of it as an incomparable instrument used with the utmost control and mastery. "No voice ever had the clarion quality of Caruso's when he sang a dramatic aria in a dramatic opera," wrote one of his biographers, T. R. Ybarra. "At such times his hearers felt that his throat must be made not of flesh and tissue but of solid, vibrant metal. Unique also . . . was the rich, deep beauty of his tones when he turned from portraying fury and vengeance to conveying the tenderness of love. . . . But who can adequately describe a thunderclap—or a nightingale? And Enrico Caruso was both."

He was born in Naples on February 25, 1873, the eighteenth of twenty-one children and the first of three to survive past infancy. His father, Marcellino, was a factory mechanic. A practical

ENRICO CARUSO

man, he was determined to have Enrico work in the factory to help out with the family finances. But his mother, Anna, was determined to have Enrico acquire an education. Somehow, from her meager funds she managed to save a dollar a month to pay for his early schooling. For two years Enrico attended kindergarten and, for a brief period after that, Father Bronzetti's Institute where he sang in the choir. Known around his neighborhood for his sweet voice, he was dubbed Carusiello and "the little diva." He was always singing Neapolitan ballads he had learned by ear. Once he was recruited to sing in Amalfi in a performance of Mercadante's Mass. At school, under Giuseppe Spasiano, young Caruso also developed a native gift for drawing.

When Enrico was twelve his father insisted he drop all formal schooling and begin to earn a living. He worked for four years as a mechanical artist and then found a job in the factory where his father worked. Singing remained a favorite avocation. In 1888 when he sang a solo at the Church of San Severino in Naples the performance was suddenly interrupted by the news that his mother had died. He left the church without finishing. Only one other time in his life did Caruso fail to complete a performance: just before his death when, on December 11, 1920, he suffered a hemorrhage during a performance of *L'Elisir d'Amore*.

Marcellino Caruso's desire to have his son specialize as a mechanic eventually conflicted sharply with Enrico's growing ambition to develop himself as a singer. After a fierce argu-

ment, Enrico at sixteen left home and found a haven with a local church organist. The organist gave the boy many opportunities to sing in church for a payment of about forty cents an appearance. Before long Caruso was also singing in Neapolitan resorts. Without any instruction or adequate preparation he applied for and got a job to sing a minor role in a performance of *Mignon* at the Teatro Fondo in Naples. He did so badly at the first rehearsal that he was instantly fired.

In 1891 Caruso began a three-year period of vocal study with Guglielmo Vergine, who took him on as a pupil only after the youth had signed a contract stipulating that, for his first five years as a professional, he would turn over twenty-five percent of his earnings. Remembering the poverty he endured during his years as Vergine's pupil, Caruso told his wife many years later: "My black suit had turned green so I bought a little bottle of dye and dyed it before I went to class. I cut my shirt fronts from paper so I would look nice. I had to walk very far every day to get there, and shoes cost money, so I sang at weddings and funerals enough to buy a pair. The soles were cardboard. Halfway to the Maestro's house came the rain. When I got there I put them by the stove to dry. They curled up and I walked home on bare feet."

At twenty-one Caruso entered military service. His commanding officer so admired his voice that he provided for Caruso's exemption from stringent military duties and subsequently arranged for Caruso's younger brother, Giovanni, to substitute for him in the army. Once out of uniform Caruso was introduced by this officer to a wealthy nobleman who was a dedicated musical amateur and a fine pianist. Through this nobleman Caruso learned his first opera role—Turiddu in *Cavalleria Rusticana*—an opera that had received a sensational world premiere four years earlier. Caruso mastered the part in five days, revealing even this early in his career a phenomenal gift for fast learning.

Caruso made his official opera debut with a touring company at the Teatro Nuovo in Naples on November 16, 1894, in *L'Amico Francesco*, a now forgotten opera by Mario Morelli, a wealthy Neapolitan amateur composer. He was paid sixteen dollars for two appearances. (Four had been scheduled, but the opera was a failure and the latter two were canceled.) As a reward for giving what Morelli regarded as an outstanding performance, Caruso was given an additional twelve dollars. Appearances in minor Italian opera houses nearby for four or five dollars a performance followed.

In 1895 Caruso gave his first performance as Turiddu, at the Cimarosa Theater in Caserta. In 1895 he added *La Traviata, La Favorita,* and *Rigoletto* to his repertory at the Teatro Fondo in Naples; on one occasion he was required to sing in *La Traviata* in the afternoon, and *Rigoletto* the same evening. After several months of coaching from Vincenzo Lombardi in 1896 he was enthusiastically received at the Massimo Theater in Palermo during the 1896–1897 season, even though Sicilians were prejudiced against foreign singers. He sang the roles of Canio in *I Pagliacci* and Enzo Grimaldo in *La Gioconda* for the first time at the Teatro Municipale in Salerno. Vincenzo Lombardi, the conductor at the Teatro Municipale, became the only vocal teacher other than Vergine that Caruso ever had.

At a performance of *La Bohème* in Leghorn in 1897 Caruso appeared with Ada Giochetti, who sang Mimi. They fell in love, but since she was a married woman and divorce was impossible, they just lived together as man and wife. Caruso had four children with Ada, two of whom (Rodolfo and Enrico Jr.) survived. After his first successes in London in 1902, Caruso established his wife and their children in a house in London. He always publicly acknowledged Rodolfo and Enrico Jr. as his sons, gave them his name, and remained throughout his life a devoted and loving father. Ada deserted him in 1908. He was appearing in *I Pagliacci* in London when just before a performance he heard the news; the singing of "Vesti la giubba" had particular meaning to him that evening. The situation was resolved by court proceedings in 1912, after much litigation.

On November 27, 1897, Caruso appeared at the Teatro Lirico in the world premiere of Francesco Cilèa's *L'Arlesiana,* learning the role of Federico in five days. A year later, again at the Teatro Lirico, he attracted international fame by creating the role of Loris in Giordano's *Fedora* on November 17, 1898.

Invitations for major appearances multiplied, and in December 1898 Caruso made his debut in St. Petersburg in *La Bohème* and *Aida* (his first Radames). After a concert at the Imperial Palace, the Czar presented him with a pair of gold cuff links set in diamonds. In 1899 he made the first of four consecutive summer tours of South America; there, on July 11, 1901, he made his first and only attempt to sing in a Wagnerian opera—as Lohengrin. In the 1899–1900 season he appeared as Osaka in Mascagni's *Iris* at the Costanzi Theater in Rome. At the same time he was chosen to create there the role of Cavaradossi in the world premiere of *Tosca,* but by the time the opera went into rehearsal Puccini had a change of heart and chose Emilio de Marchi. Caruso did sing the part soon after the opera's premiere; in fact he sang it twelve times between October 23 and November 11, 1900, at Treviso. But his disappointment in not having created the role was profound, though he accepted the loss stoically and became one of Puccini's closest friends and most illustrious interpreters.

Caruso's debut at La Scala on December 26, 1900—as Rodolfo—did not go well, since at the time he was suffering from laryngitis. On January 17, 1901, in the world premiere of Mascagni's *Le Maschere* he did far better and in a notable revival of *L'Elisir d'Amore,* with Toscanini conducting, he enjoyed a great success. On December 30, 1901, he returned to Naples to appear for the first time at the San Carlo; the opera was *L'Elisir d'Amore.* Nemorino was one of his most celebrated roles and his singing of "Una furtiva lagrima" never failed to send the house into an uproar of enthusiasm, yet this performance was received coldly. This failure, which he did not deserve, so embittered him that after finishing his commitment at the San Carlo he vowed never again to set foot on its stage.

His successes brought him to a position of first importance in the world of opera. On March 11, 1902, he participated in the world premiere of Cilèa's *Adriana Lecouvreur.* That same year he had also made a triumphant appearance at the Monte Carlo Opera, and on May 14, 1902, a sensational debut at Covent Garden, both times in *Rigoletto.*

Maurice Grau, manager of the Metropolitan Opera in New York, heard him in England and signed him to a five-year contract for fifty performances a season at an initial payment of one thousand dollars an appearance. Grau later resigned his managership, and Caruso made his debut under Heinrich Conried, on November 23, 1903, in *Rigoletto.* Henry Krehbiel in the *Tribune* called him "musically the finest Duke that New York has heard for a generation," while remarking that Caruso had "many of the tiresome Italian vocal affectations, and when he neglects to cover his tones, as he always does when he becomes strenuous, his voice becomes pallid." W. J. Henderson in the New York *Times* described Caruso's voice as "smooth and mellow," adding that "Mr. Caruso has a natural and free delivery and his voice carries well without forcing. His clear and appealing high tones set the bravos wild with delight, but connoisseurs of singing saw more promise for the season in his *mezza voce.*"

During his first six years in the United States Caruso was coached by Tullio Voghera. In his first two seasons at the Metropolitan he appeared in most of the roles for which he later was idolized: Alfredo in *La Traviata,* Enzo Grimaldo, Rodolfo, Edgar in *Lucia di Lammermoor,* Nemorino, Canio, Cavaradossi, Radames in *Aida,* Richard in *Un Ballo in Maschera.* He was also heard as Gennaro in the first Metropolitan Opera production of Donizetti's *Lucrezia Borgia,* and as Raoul in *Les Huguenots.* Each role represented another step towards his becoming the greatest box-office attraction the Metropolitan Opera had known up to that time, and possibly the most admired singer in performance history. There were other, and later, steps. Caruso sang his first Don José in *Carmen* at the Metropolitan Opera on March 5, 1906, his first Don Alvaro in *La Forza del Destino* on November 15, 1918, his first Eleazar in *La Juive* on November 22, 1919. He also appeared as Federico in the American premiere of Franchetti's *Germania* on January 22, 1910, and as Dick Johnson in the world premiere of Puccini's *The Girl of the Golden West* on December 10, 1910. The developing power, warmth, beauty of his voice, and the emotional appeal of the throb that came to be known as the "Caruso sob," kept pace with the increasing subtlety of his characterizations and the depth and power of his dramatic conceptions.

His voice, Rosa Ponselle wrote, "could caress you and soothe you. It loved you, and it excited you; every emotion you could possibly feel he gave, he was so imbued with feeling. . . . Caruso had a barrel chest, an enormous throat, a massive head with huge sinus cavities, and an unusual construction of the vocal cords. Put all this together and it was a set of physical characteristics that has never been duplicated. . . . In a way,

Caruso was a physical freak, a one-in-a-million genetic come-together."

When Puccini heard Caruso rehearsing in *Madama Butterfly* he remarked, "Caruso is singing like a god." Before Puccini, Edouard de Reszke, celebrated operatic bass, had also used the word *god* to describe Caruso's singing. Giovanni Martinelli, often considered Caruso's successor, once replied sharply when told that he sang like Caruso, "My friend, you could put me, Gigli and Lauri-Volpi together and still not get a Caruso." Geraldine Farrar was convinced that there was nobody like Caruso. "No voice was ever like his." The word used most often to describe the sounds that poured from that throat was *gold.* Caruso's own formula for the making of a great singer was: "A big chest, a big mouth, ninety percent memory, ten percent intelligence, lots of hard work and something in the heart."

By the end of his five-year contract Caruso was getting two thousand five hundred dollars a performance. When the time came to sign a new contract, the space for his fee was left blank, allowing him to write in any amount he considered reasonable. He knew he could have asked and gotten four thousand dollars an appearance. But with a generosity that was characteristic of him and indicative of how highly he regarded the Metropolitan Opera, he willingly adhered for the rest of his career to the two thousand five hundred dollar figure. Elsewhere, however, his financial returns were astronomic for those years. For each concert he was paid seven thousand five hundred dollars. In Buenos Aires he was paid seven thousand five hundred dollars for each of his operatic performances; in Cuba, ten thousand dollars a night; in Mexico, fifteen thousand dollars. At one time he was offered (and he declined) two hundred fifty thousand dollars for a two-month tour of Latin America. When he died he left an estate valued in excess of nine million dollars.

For seventeen consecutive seasons at the Metropolitan Caruso gave 626 performances in New York and 235 on tour, averaging between 40 and 50 a season. He sang on every opening night in that time, with the single exception of 1906 when he wanted the limelight to be focused on Geraldine Farrar. In New York, he sang Canio 83 times and Radames 63 times. His Metropolitan repertory of 37 operas embraced almost every famous role and some not so famous. He was also heard at the Metropolitan as Richard in *Un*

Caruso

Ballo in Maschera, Fernando in *La Favorita,* Elvino in *La Sonnambula,* Faust, Lionel in *Martha,* Loris in *Fedora,* Vasco da Gama in *L'Africaine,* Des Grieux in *Manon Lescaut,* Pinkerton in *Madama Butterfly,* Maurizio in *Adriana Lecouvreur,* Osaka in Mascagni's *Iris,* Manrico in *Il Trovatore,* Turiddu, Renaud in Gluck's *Armide,* Des Grieux in Massenet's *Manon,* the title role in Charpentier's *Julien,* Samson in *Samson and Delilah,* Nadir in *The Pearl Fishers,* Flammen in Mascagni's *Lodoletta,* John of Leyden in *Le Prophète,* and Avito in *L'Amore dei Tre Re.*

Indicative of his fame was the fact that his name was used for a race horse and a chain of Italian restaurants. A popular song, "My Cousin Carus," was written about him in Tin Pan Alley. He was starred in a motion picture, also named *My Cousin Carus* (1918), even though the silent screen did not permit his golden voice to be heard. (A second silent motion picture, *Splendid Romance,* was never released.) He had become a household name, not only because of his success in the opera house but also because of the phenomenal distribution of his phonograph recordings.

Caruso made his first records in Italy in 1902. F. W. Gaisberg, of the Gramophone and Typewriter Company, had come to Milan that year, had heard Caruso sing, and engaged him to record ten arias for a total payment of five hundred dollars. The recording was completed in a single afternoon and the finished records were rushed to London for release during Caruso's debut at Covent Garden. Their sale far exceeded Gaisberg's expectations. After the Victor Talking Machine acquired the Gramophone and Typewriter Company, it not only took over the Caruso masters but also acquired Caruso as a recording artist on a new contract. Less than three months after his Metropolitan Opera debut Caruso made his first American recordings for Victor in Carnegie Hall. Ten disks of famous arias were made, the first being "La donna è mobile" from *Rigoletto,* followed by "Vesti la giubba," "Celeste Aida," "Una furtiva lagrima," and, from *Tosca,* "E lucevan le stelle." In the ensuing years Caruso recorded every aria and almost every song from his repertory. His last recording was the "Crucifixus" from Rossini's *Petite Messe,* recorded in Camden, New Jersey, in 1920.

The enormous sale of Caruso's first American recordings ("Vesti la giubba" became the first ever to sell a million disks) was responsible not only for establishing the Victor Company as a giant industry but also for transforming the phonograph from the curiosity or toy it had been up to that time into an important medium for the dissemination of music; it commanded the interest and respect of the world's artists. In all, Caruso earned in his lifetime almost two million dollars in royalties from his records, with another two million brought into his estate since his death from numerous re-releases. On the hundredth anniversary of Caruso's birth RCA issued a commemorative album of twelve Caruso long-playing records—168 arias and songs called *The Greatest Hits of Enrico Caruso,* and a second set, *Enrico Caruso Songs and Arias,* comprising 59 other numbers, 9 of them never before released.

Caruso made his Berlin debut on October 5, 1904, at the Theater des Westens. When he invited Caruso to Potsdam, the Kaiser is reputed to have told him: "If I were not an emperor I would have liked to be your valet." In 1905 Caruso gave a command performance for the King and Queen of Spain. In April 1906 he was appearing in *The Queen of Sheba* and *Carmen* in San Francisco when the earthquake reduced much of the city to shambles. Caruso fled from San Francisco unharmed, but never again could he be induced to sing there. In 1907 he performed for Edward VII and Queen Alexandria at Buckingham Palace.

Towards the end of the 1908–1909 season his voice began to fail him, and he had to leave the Metropolitan Opera without completing the season to undergo a throat operation in Europe. He suffered a temporary loss of voice but no impairment. His voice regained its resonance and beauty.

During World War I Caruso helped raise twenty-one million dollars for the war effort by singing at benefits. This was in addition to the sizable personal contributions he himself made. He insisted on converting all of his prewar securities and assets into United States Government and Liberty Loan bonds. His contribution to the war effort also included the singing (and recording) of George M. Cohan's "Over There."

On August 20, 1918, Caruso married Dorothy Park Benjamin, a twenty-five-year-old American girl who had been trained in a convent. Her father, a business tycoon, objected to the marriage. The Carusos had a daughter, Gloria. Their permanent residence was a fourteen-room apartment on the ninth floor of the Knickerbocker Hotel on Forty-second Street and Broadway. There a small staff headed by Bruno Zirato attended them. Zirato, who was devoted to Caruso, worked practically around the clock, performing every task that might simplify the complex existence of the world's most admired singer.

Caruso was a pudgy man, standing five feet one inch and weighing 175 pounds. He dressed flamboyantly, was fanatic about cleanliness (taking two baths daily), had an enormous appetite for Italian food (specifically Neapolitan dishes, some of which he had learned to cook), and smoked incessantly (two packages of Egyptian cigarettes daily) always using a holder. His generosity to those in need was legendary. After Caruso's death his widow found a list of one hundred and twenty people in Italy whom he had been supporting, most of them people who had been kind to him when he had been most in need. His favorite pastime was to make caricatures, for which he had an unusual gift; many of these were published in *La Follia*. He had no interest in sports and never indulged in physical exercise. He rarely touched alcohol, but when he did it was usually a glass of wine or an Alexander cocktail.

He was a chronic prankster, probably because he loved to laugh and loved even more to make others laugh. Once, during a performance of *Tosca,* Antonio Scotti tried to pick up from the floor a paintbrush which had secretly been nailed down by Caruso. Sometimes Caruso would fill a hat with water and when an unsuspecting member of the cast put the hat on during a performance, the water would douse the prankster's victim.

On performance day he rarely spoke, spending the silent hours playing solitaire, drawing caricatures, or sorting his collection of gold coins. Then for about half an hour he would perform vocal exercises with his accompanist. Before leaving his apartment he would gargle with warm salt water, inhale Swedish snuff to clear his nostrils, and drink a glass of charged water or a cup of steaming coffee.

A gala performance at the Metropolitan Opera on the evening of March 22, 1919, celebrated Caruso's twenty-fifth anniversary in opera. Three operas were presented for his 550th appearance on the stage of the Metropolitan, with Caruso starring in each: *L'Elisir d'Amore* (Act 3), *I Pagliacci* (Act 1), and *Le Prophète* (Coronation Scene). When the performance ended, the curtain rose on a stage on which Caruso in evening clothes sat in a gold chair near the footlights, encircled by the entire Metropolitan Opera company. Tributes were spoken and gifts presented, one of which was a flag of the city of New York, a token of gratitude from the people of the city.

Caruso first indicated that he was not well in a letter to Bruno Zirato on August 3, 1920, in which he complained of "pain all over." Physicians diagnosed his ailment as intercostal neuralgia. In spite of the discomfort, Caruso filled twelve concert dates during a tour in late September.

On December 11, 1920, just before the curtain rose upon the Metropolitan Opera production of *L'Elisir d'Amore* at the Academy of Music in Brooklyn, Caruso coughed up blood. He insisted on beginning the performance. During the first act he continued bleeding. "His own reddened handkerchief he had discarded," reported the New York *Times* the following morning, "and one after another, members of the chorus found opportunity to come close to him and deftly give him another handkerchief and slip away. One after another he used them until they were stained scarlet, and now and then little flecks of blood would show on his lips." Though Caruso protested, the performance was ended after the first act. The physicians discovered that Caruso had suffered a broken blood vessel in his throat but thought that the condition was not serious. Indeed, Caruso showed such improvement and looked so well that he insisted on appearing at the Metropolitan Opera on Christmas Eve in *La Juive.* During the intermission, the conductor, Artur Bodanzky, visited Caruso's dressing room and found him weeping with pain.

That performance was his last. On Christmas Day, at his apartment at the Vanderbilt Hotel, he suddenly screamed with pain. A hotel physician administered codeine. It was later discovered that Caruso was suffering from acute pleurisy which developed into bronchial pneumonia. For the next five days Caruso was close to death. An operation to remove the fluid in the pleural cavity proved successful but several more operations were required. When Geraldine Farrar visited him he said, making a poignant gesture toward his throat: "I cannot sing. Geraldina, do you think I'll ever sing again?"

He recovered sufficiently to be able to go to Sorrento for further convalescence. At the Hotel Vittoria he seemed to be doing well. He swam daily, walked frequently in the hotel gardens, and seemed revivified in spirit and strength. One day a young tenor visited him and sang for him "M'appari" from *Martha*. Caruso was not satisfied with the performance and went on to demonstrate how the aria should be sung. "I heard a voice," recalls Dorothy Caruso. "I ran to the salon. There stood Enrico, singing as he had never sung before. His voice was like a shower of stars, more beautiful than it had ever been. As he finished the song he flung out his arms. His face was transfigured. 'Doro, I can sing! I can sing! I have not lost my voice.'"

But the pains returned and a new operation was needed. On July 17 Caruso lapsed into delirium. He was brought to the Hotel Vesuvio in Naples where, after considerable suffering, he died on August 2, 1921. His last words were: "Doro—I can't get my breath."

The funeral services were held on August 3 at the royal basilica of the Church of San Francisco di Paola in Naples, which up to that time had been reserved exclusively for royalty. "The life of the city stopped on the day of the funeral," recalls Dorothy Caruso. "Flags hung at half mast; the shops were closed, covered with crepe and signs—'Lutto per Caruso.' At eleven o'clock the great bell began to toll. . . . Two walls of soldiers held back the dense crowd before the church. . . . Inside the church thousands and thousands of faces turned toward me." After the service Caruso was buried in the Del Panto cemetery outside Naples, on a cypress-shaded hill overlooking the city.

During his lifetime Caruso received numerous decorations: from Italy, the Order of the Crown of Italy (all three ranks); from Germany, the Order of the Red Eagle and the Order of the Crown Eagle, of Prussia; from Spain, the Order of St. James of Compostela; from Belgium, the Order of Leopold; from Great Britain, the Order of Michael and the Order Royal Victorian; from France, the Order of the Legion of Honor and the Palmes académiques.

In 1947 Dorothy Caruso presented the Metropolitan Opera with a bust of Caruso which was placed in the foyer of the family circle. His life story, *El Cantate de Napoli,* was filmed in Italy in 1935, and in 1950 another screen biography was produced in the United States, starring Mario Lanza and called *The Great Caruso.* To commemorate the centenary of his birth, five leading tenors appeared at the San Carlo Opera in Naples on April 24, 1973, to sing the arias for which Caruso will always be remembered; Caruso himself was represented through recordings. At the Metropolitan Opera the Caruso centenary was celebrated with a display of Caruso memorabilia and a special performance of *Aida,* at which Caruso's daughter, Gloria, was the guest of honor.

ABOUT: Caruso, D. Enrico Caruso: His Life and Death; Caruso, D. and Goddard, T. Wings of Song; Key, P. and Zirato, B. Enrico Caruso; Jackson, S. Caruso; Robinson, F. (ed.) Caruso: His Life in Pictures; Ybarra, T. R. Caruso: Man of Naples and the Voice of Gold. *Periodicals*—Opera News, Caruso Issue, February 24, 1973.

Robert Casadesus

1899–1972

Robert Marcel Casadesus, pianist, was born in Paris on April 7, 1899. He was of Catalan extraction—this accounts for the pronunciation of his name (see below). Four of his uncles were celebrated professional musicians: François-Louis, conductor and composer, was the founder of the American Conservatory at Fontainebleau; Henri-Gustave organized the Society of Ancient Instruments; Marcel-Louis-Lucien was a cellist; Marius-Robert-Max was a violinist. An aunt, Rose, became a concert pianist after receiving first prize in piano at the Paris Conservatory, and one of his cousins was a violinist.

Robert's father was an actor who had achieved success under the stage name of Robert Casa. Since Robert's mother, Marie, died when he was born, he was sent to live with his grandparents. His Aunt Rose gave him his first piano lessons. He was given a violin as a gift when he was only three and a half years old and is reported to have smashed it at sight, since he preferred the piano. "I can't remember when I started to play the piano," he once said. "But I really can't remember a time when I didn't play."

When he was ten he entered the Paris Conser-

Casadesus: kä zä dĕ′so͞os

ROBERT CASADESUS

vatory in the solfeggio class. At thirteen he became a piano pupil at the Conservatory of Louis Diémer and in 1913 received first prize in piano playing.

In 1914 he was compelled to make his own living. For several years he played some percussion instruments in the orchestra of the Opéra-Comique while continuing to study the piano. In 1917 he made his debut as a concert pianist in Paris. Before World War I ended he was drafted into the French army, but the Armistice was signed before he saw service.

In 1919 he reentered the Conservatory. During the next two years he captured the first prize in harmony (which he had studied in Xavier Leroux's class) and the coveted Diémer award in piano. One day he brought to Diémer a composition he had just completed, *Six Pieces for Two Pianos,* Op.2. The teacher invited Casadesus and another of his students, Gaby L'Hôte, to perform this work for him. L'Hôte also came from a distinguished musical family, had attended the Paris Conservatory, and had received first prize in Diémer's piano class. Casadesus and Gaby L'Hôte fell in love and were married in Paris on July 16, 1921. For a time they resided in Fontainebleau where Casadesus taught the piano in the American Conservatory his uncle had founded. In 1934 he succeeded Isidor Philipp as the head of the piano department, and in 1946 he became the director of the Conservatory. He gave up all his teaching duties in 1952 to concentrate on concert work.

Through his family Casadesus met many

musicians, one of whom was Maurice Ravel. In 1922, in a recital in Paris, Casadesus's performance of Ravel's piano sonata drew high praise from the composer. Subsequently Casadesus went with Ravel to London to record some of Ravel's piano works for Aeolian Records. They often appeared in joint recitals after that—in Lyons, Brussels, Barcelona, Madrid, and in 1930 in Ravel's birthplace, Ciboure.

During the 1920s Casadesus concertized extensively throughout Europe, North Africa, and South America, not only in recitals and as a soloist with orchestras but also in two-piano recitals with Gaby. On January 20, 1935, he made his American debut, performing Mozart's Piano Concerto in D major, K.537 (*Coronation*), with the New York Philharmonic Orchestra, Hans Lange conducting. Toscanini invited him to appear as soloist with the New York Philharmonic Orchestra in a performance of Brahms's Concerto in B-flat major on January 30, 1936. After that Casadesus continued to appear throughout the United States regularly until his death. He was also featured in American telecasts.

His performances of the classical, romantic, and modern literature—and especially of the music of Mozart and the French masters—earned him praise from critics all over the world. He was extolled for the sensitivity of his musical perception, the subtlety of his colorations, the consummate mastery of his technique, and his poetic insights. "One listened with delight to performances of the most beautiful color and poetical sensibility," reported Olin Downes in the New York *Times* after one of Casadesus's appearances in New York. "Each one was a discourse of a superior artist and a distinguished musician."

When World War II broke out, Casadesus and his family went to the United States where he concentrated his musical activity not only on performing on the concert stage but also on making recordings, appearing over the radio, and teaching. After the Germans invaded France, the family found a permanent home in Princeton, New Jersey. During the summers he continued to teach the piano and direct the American Conservatory of Fontainebleau which had been transferred to the United States because of the war. In 1945–1946 Casadesus lectured at Princeton University.

One year after the war had ended in Europe Casadesus was back in France to help reestablish the American Conservatory in Fontainebleau. He maintained two homes, an apartment on the rue Vaneau in Paris and a house in Berwyn, Pennsylvania.

Casadesus made over two thousand appearances in the world's music centers. In addition, he made numerous recordings, one of which, in 1955, an album of Ravel's piano music, received the Grand Prix du Disque. He divided his musical activity between performing on the piano and composing. In time he produced seven symphonies and several concertos and sonatas, in all some fifty or so major works. Casadesus and L'Hôte introduced his Concerto for Two Pianos and Orchestra in Warsaw in 1935 before they gave its American premiere with the New York Philharmonic on November 25, 1940. His Symphony No.2 was introduced in Cincinnati on November 21, 1941. He himself gave the world premiere of his Piano Concerto, Op.37, in Minneapolis on March 21, 1947. With L'Hôte and their son, Jean, he presented the premiere of his Concerto for Three Pianos and Orchestra at Philharmonic Hall in New York on July 24, 1965.

Jean Casadesus (1927–1972) was one of three Casadesus children, the only one to become a concert performer. He died in an auto collision in Ontario, Canada, at the age of forty-four.

In June 1958 Casadesus became the only living non-German to receive from the city of Hamburg the Brahms medal. France conferred on him the title of Commander of the Legion of Honor, and the Queen of the Netherlands made him Commander of the Order of Orange-Nassau. In addition, in 1937 he was presented with a gold medal at the World's Fair in Paris, and in 1959 he received the gold medal of the city of Paris.

His seventieth birthday and the twenty-fifth anniversary of his first appearance with the New York Philharmonic were jointly celebrated in 1969 at a concert of that orchestra in which Casadesus appeared in the dual role of performer and composer. He performed the Mozart *Coronation* Concerto, and as a composer he was represented by his orchestral work the Suite No.2 in B-flat, George Szell conducting.

On September 20, 1972, Casadesus died in a hospital in Paris following an operation for cancer of the pancreas. His funeral took place at the St. Severin Church in Paris.

ABOUT: Gelatt, R. Makers of Music. *Periodicals*— Musical America, October 1953; New York Times, January 16, 1955.

Pablo Casals

1876–1973

Pablo Casals, the only musician in performing history to remain active beyond his ninetieth year, was the greatest cellist of the twentieth century and one of the greatest string instrumentalists of all time. In addition, he was, as Thomas Mann once said, "one of those artists who come to the rescue of humanity's honor."

Casals (originally Pau Carlos Salvador Defilló de Casals), cellist and conductor, was born in the Catalonian town of Vendrell, in Tarragona, Spain, on December 29, 1876. He was the second of eleven children of Carlos and Pilar Defillo de Casals. Seven of the eleven Casals children died at birth. Pablo himself almost died when the umbilical cord twisted around his neck and almost choked him. His father was the church organist in Vendrell. Casals said he "awoke in me the love of music through his lessons and example." Instruction in singing began almost in his crib; Pablo could sing in tune even before he could speak. By the time he was five he was able to join the church choir as second soprano. Gregorian chants were his first vivid musical impressions. He participated in their performance and listened to them. When Pablo was six, his father began teaching him the piano, supplementing this with lessons on the organ. Soon the boy was a good enough organist to substitute for his father at church whenever the older man fell ill. Pablo was also taught the violin; at nine he was heard as a violin soloist in a concert in Vendrell. He once said, "Music for me was a natural element, an activity as natural as breathing if you like." At this early age he was also composing music. When he was seven he helped his father write a dozen musical numbers for a pageant at church which was good enough to be repeated many times in subsequent years. A little later, Pablo completed a mazurka for piano without collaboration.

One day a group of strolling musicians came to Vendrell and one of them simulated playing

Casals: kä säls′

PABLO CASALS

Casals the cello became a solo instrument of primary importance.

To support himself during his three years at the Municipal School Pablo participated as cellist in summer festival concerts in Catalonia, which introduced him to the music of Wagner, Brahms, Richard Strauss, and other composers of note. In the winter he was a member of a trio which appeared at the Café Tost in a Barcelona suburb, playing semiclassical numbers. Once a week he introduced a program of music of higher caliber. Those evenings became famous in and around Barcelona, attracting musicians, artists, writers, and actors who made it a weekly habit to come to the café to listen to Pablo's music. One of those attending was Isaac Albéniz, the celebrated Spanish composer, who became interested in the youth's career.

A major turning point in Pablo's life came when he was about thirteen. He habitually haunted the music shops in Barcelona looking for music to feature at Café Tost. "My attention," he later recalled, "was suddenly arrested by some unaccompanied suites of Bach for the cello. I forgot entirely the reason of my visit to the shop and could only stare at this music which nobody had told me about. Sometimes even now, when I look at the covers of that old music, I see again the interior of that old and musty shop with its faint smell of the sea. I took the suites home and read and reread them. For twelve years after that I studied and worked every day at them. I was nearly twenty-five before I had the courage to play one of them in public." He added: "I discovered a new world of space and beauty—and I can now say that the feelings I experienced were among the purest and most intense of my artistic life." Unknown to the music world at large (and never before performed in public in their entirety), these cello sonatas and suites of Bach were propagandized by Casals in his concerts throughout the world until they acquired the rank they deserved among Bach's supreme instrumental compositions.

Bach became for Casals the fountainhead of his spiritual strength and musical inspiration and remained so until Casals's death. He first came to know Bach as a child when his father introduced him to the *Well-Tempered Clavier*. But it was with his discovery of the cello music that Casals first began dipping deeply into the works of one whom he always considered the

the cello by using a bent broom. When Pablo, then aged ten, expressed curiosity about the cello, his father constructed one for him, using a pumpkin as sounding board. (This instrument was exhibited at the International Exposition in Barcelona in 1929.) A year later at a chamber-music concert Pablo heard José García perform on the cello. This was the first time the boy experienced the cello sound. "I felt as if I could not breathe," he recalled. "There was something so tender, beautiful and human about the sound. A radiance filled me." He persuaded his father to buy him a real cello and to give him some lessons. He lost interest in all other musical instruments. "From that time on," he said, "I was wedded to the instrument. It would be my companion and friend for the rest of my life."

After a family conference in which the father expressed the wish to have Pablo apprenticed to a carpenter while the mother insisted that the boy be trained as a musician, the decision was finally made to send Pablo to Barcelona, forty miles away, for intensive music study. He went there in 1888 with his mother and was entered in the Municipal School where he studied harmony and counterpoint with José Rodoreda and cello with José García. As García's pupil, Pablo objected to the current method of performing on the cello, preferring a freer performing style of bowing and fingering. After many experiments, he evolved his own playing style which amazed his teachers and fellow students and helped to revolutionize the technique of cello playing. As a direct consequence of the changes effected by

141

greatest master of them all. "For me," he commented, "Bach is like Shakespeare. He has known all and felt all." For about eighty years Casals made it a practice to begin each concert by playing two preludes and fugues of Bach at the piano. "It is a sort of a benediction on the house," he said. "But this is not its only meaning for me. It is a rediscovery of the world of which I have the joy of being a part. It fills me with awareness of the wonder of life, with a feeling of the incredible marvel of being a human being. The music is never the same for me, never. Each day, it is sometimes new, fantastic, unbelievable. That is Bach, like nature, a miracle!"

Casals gave his first cello recital at the Théâtre des Nouveaux in Barcelona when he was sixteen. Increasingly persuaded of the youth's talent, Albéniz encouraged him to leave Barcelona for Madrid in 1894. Through the intervention of Count de Morphy, Casals was invited to perform at the royal palace. The Queen Regent, Doña María Cristina, developed a maternal interest in him. She arranged for him to appear regularly at palace concerts and on occasion joined him in playing piano duets. She also saw to it that he was given a scholarship for additional study with Tomás Bretón in composition and Jesús Monasterio in chamber-music performance.

After a year in Madrid, Casals was sent by Count de Morphy to Brussels with a letter of introduction to the director of the Conservatory, and with a monthly pension. Dissatisfied with the reception he received upon his audition at the Conservatory, Casals decided that Brussels was not for him. He went to Paris in 1895, a move that cost him his pension and the patronage of the Count.

In Paris Casals suffered severe poverty. He lived in a cold hovel near Porte St. Denis, and was reduced to playing the cello in the orchestra of the Folies Marigny for a dollar a day. "Every day I had to walk miles to and from work with my cello under my arms. My mother eked out a few francs with sewing. After a few weeks, I became ill with the strain and there was nothing left but to return to Spain."

In Barcelona things took a turn for the better. He found a post as professor of the cello at the Municipal School, succeeding his former teacher, García; in addition he was made principal cellist of the orchestra at the Barcelona Opera. He also organized and played with a string quar-

tet that toured Spain, and he made some solo appearances in churches and at a casino in Portugal. In Madrid he performed a cello concert publicly for the first time. The work was the Cello Concerto in D minor by Lalo, with Tomás Bretón conducting the accompaniment. This performance helped bring him the Order of Carlos III from the Queen Regent.

He made his first concert appearance in London in 1898. In 1899, just before his twenty-third birthday, he returned to Paris bearing a letter of introduction to the conductor Charles Lamoureux. "You are one of the elect," Lamoureux told him after an audition. Lamoureux arranged for Casals to appear with his orchestra in Paris as a soloist in the Lalo Concerto on November 12, 1899. This performance was a sensation and Casals was asked to return as a guest artist with the Lamoureux Orchestra. Shortly thereafter he made a triumphant reappearance in London and was invited to give a command performance for Queen Victoria.

For the next twenty years Casals traveled around the world giving concerts. He made his American debut in 1901–1902, touring the country with the soprano Emma Eames in eighty concerts. In 1903 he toured South America. In 1903–1904 he returned to the United States. At one of his American concerts he was the soloist in Strauss's *Don Quixote,* with the composer conducting. At another he performed Haydn's Cello Concerto in C major with the Sam Franko Orchestra in New York on January 12, 1904, and Richard Aldrich wrote that he showed "an extremely charming artistic capacity and exquisitely finished technique. His tone is small and his style is small, to judge from his playing of this concerto, but grace, delicacy, and a truly musical feeling were inherent in all he did." The enthusiasm of the audience encouraged Casals to play as encores two movements from Bach's unaccompanied Suite No.3.

When Casals returned to the United States in 1914, trailing behind him his European triumphs, Richard Aldrich was far more enthusiastic. Performing sonatas by Brahms and Beethoven (with Harold Bauer at the piano) and the solo Suite in C major by Bach, Casals was hailed by Aldrich as a supreme master of his instrument. "Mr. Casals's exquisite finish and grace of style, his breadth and perfection of bowing and phrasing, his subtle nuancing and his vital rhythmic feeling and his absolute certainty of intonation were put to the service of a deeply musical, intensely felt and finely poised interpretation. . . . In the solo suite by Bach he played with beautiful refinement and flexibility, with ease and with the authority of an assured master."

Other evaluations by critics, musicologists, and fellow musicians placed him with the immortals among instrumental performers. His left-hand technique and bowing reduced even the most complex compositions to elementals, while his lofty conceptions brought an incandescence to his playing, so that many of his interpretations became revelations. "As he played," the concert violinist Albert Spalding recalled, "a kind of renascent beauty flooded the . . . theater. It was achieved by an extraordinary display, a baffling simplicity to be appreciated only by those who think and feel deeply. His pulsating rhythm is a miracle in itself. It has none of the mechanical beat of the metronome; it has the elasticity of nature, and its inevitability. And Casals' technique—rarely spoken of because how he says a thing is so easily forgotten in the significance of what he has to say. All the facilities of a craft developed over a thousand years seem to have been brought to the point of effortless ease. . . . He speaks with the voice of a prophet imparting some of the wonders and mysteries of an unreachable universe."

The honors Casals gathered provided further testimony to his world fame. From Germany he received the degree of Science and Arts; from Austria-Hungary, the Cross of the Commander of Francis Joseph; from France, the Legion of Honor (Grand Officier), the Palmes académiques, and the Croix de l'Instruction Publique; from Spain, the Grand Cross; from Italy, membership in the Santa Cecilia Academy of Rome; from Portugal, the Order of Santiago de Espada; from Romania, the Commandership of the Crown; and from London the Beethoven gold medal which had previously been bestowed on Brahms, Joachim, and Liszt. Casals was also given honorary degrees from the Universities of Edinburgh, Barcelona, and Montpellier.

In addition to his worldwide successes as a solo performer, Casals distinguished himself in chamber music: in sonata recitals with Harold Bauer and Paderewski, in concerts of trios with Jacques Thibaud and Alfred Cortot, and in joint concerts with Fritz Kreisler. In 1914 Casals was appointed professor of the cello at the École Normale de Musique in Paris.

Casals's first wife was Guilhermina Suggia, a Portuguese cellist, whom he married in 1906; they were divorced in 1912. Two years later Casals married Susan Metcalfe, an American singer of *Lieder.* He sometimes acted as piano accompanist at her concerts. At one time early in his marriage Casals gave serious thought to abandoning his own career to promote that of his wife, but this idea was rejected. By 1920 the marriage had ended. Soon after the breakup, Casals went to live in Barcelona.

In 1920 he formed Barcelona's first symphony orchestra, the Orquestra Pau Casals, which he himself financed over a seven-year period at a cost of over three hundred thousand dollars. His first experience as a conductor had come when he was almost sixteen, when Enrique Granados, the Spanish composer, asked him to rehearse Granados's opera *Maria del Carmen* in Barcelona. But his career as a conductor really began when he formed his own orchestra and conducted its first concert on October 13, 1920. After seven years the orchestra finally became self-supporting.

Around 1926 Casals founded the Workmen's Concert Association which made it possible for the working man or woman to attend performances of the orchestra in return for nominal dues and provided working people with the opportunity to form little musical groups of their own.

In addition to conducting his orchestra in Barcelona, Casals began leading orchestras in Prague, Zurich, Buenos Aires, Berlin, Paris, London, and Rome. On December 28, 1922, he made his American conducting debut as a guest conductor of the New York Symphony Society.

The music critic of the London *Observer,* Fox-Strangways, wrote about Casals's conducting: "He plays as if he held a responsible trust, determined that at all costs the purity of the faith shall not suffer at his hands. He refrains from anything histrionic or ephemeral; he wants the truth of it. . . . In whatever he does, he seems to aim at some invisible and unattainable ideal, and if some part of that is reached immediately to set the standard higher."

When the Spanish Republic was proclaimed in 1931, Casals allied himself with the new democratic regime. He was appointed president of the Junta de Musica, Catalonia's music council; he traveled out of Spain to give concerts for the benefit of the Republic; and he placed his personal savings at the disposal of the government. In appreciation the government named streets and public squares after him.

When civil war broke out in Spain in the summer of 1936, friends entreated Casals to leave Barcelona and seek safety in a foreign country. But he refused to do so, maintaining that in times of duress it was imperative to provide people with the solace of great music. However, the civil war soon put an end to his music making. He conducted his last concert with his Barcelona Orchestra on July 18, 1936, a performance of Beethoven's Ninth Symphony. He told his musicians that evening: "I do not know when we shall meet again and I propose that we finish the symphony as an adieu and an au revoir for all of us."

He conducted concerts in England and France to raise money for food, clothing, and supplies for his countrymen. When the Franco forces entered Barcelona in January 1939, Casals, whose violent opposition to Fascism had been no secret, sought asylum in France. In Paris he suffered from a severe nervous depression. In the autumn of 1939 he went south to make his home in Prades, a town fronting on the sea he loved so dearly and close to the Spanish border. There he could be with other Catalonian expatriates. In Prades he organized relief for Catalonians in French camps and raised funds for other Spanish exiles. He vowed never to return to Spain as long as Franco was in power. He kept that vow to the end of his life, except for a hurried trip in 1955 to marry his longtime friend and housekeeper Francesca Vidal de Capdevila, on her deathbed.

Casals remained at the Villa Colette in Prades throughout World War II. After the French armistice he gave charity concerts in the free zone. When all of France was occupied, following the Allied invasion of North Africa, he was invited to give a public concert for Hitler and to perform for German officers in Germany and for occupying German troops in France. All this he stubbornly refused to do.

When the war ended, he resumed his concert work in Europe. In 1945 he suddenly cut short his tour of England to return to retirement in Prades. He would play in public no longer because of his bitterness that the end of the war and the defeat of the Fascists did not end the

Franco regime but instead brought it support from the victorious democracies. "I knew that in a world where cynicism held sway, my action would hardly affect the course of the nations—it was, after all, only the action of a single individual. But how else could I act? One has to live with oneself." He also maintained that he could not divorce his actions as a human being from those of an artist. "I am a man first, an artist second," he said. "As a man, my first obligation is to the welfare of fellow men. My contribution to world peace may be small. But at least I will have given all I can to an idea I hold sacred."

For about three years Casals did not perform in public, living quietly in Prades where he sometimes played for close friends and occasional visitors. But in 1950, when the bicentenary of the birth of Bach was being commemorated, Casals's friend, the violinist Alexander Schneider, prevailed on him to participate, both as a cellist and as conductor, in a Bach festival in Prades. The first Prades festival, in which many renowned musicians participated and of which Casals was artistic director, began on June 2, 1950, and continued into July at the Church of St. Pierre for an audience of music lovers from all parts of Europe and the United States. Casals conducted the six Brandenburg Concertos and played the unaccompanied cello suites and sonatas for cello and piano. The festival became an annual event, held either in Prades or nearby Perpignan, with Casals as its dominating musical personality and with its program expanded to include not only Bach but Beethoven, Mozart, Schubert, and Brahms. Instrumentalists from all over the world collaborated with Casals in these performances.

On January 28, 1956, Casals made his first concert appearance outside Prades since 1945, in a performance in Veracruz, Mexico. A three-month visit to Puerto Rico followed. During ceremonies celebrating the dedication of a bronze plaque at the house where his mother had been born in San Juan, Casals performed "Song of the Birds," a Catalan folk song his mother had taught him and which subsequently he often performed as an encore at his concerts. His accompanist in San Juan was the twenty-year-old Marta Montañez, one of his pupils. Despite the disparity in their ages, Casals and Marta were married in August 1957.

On October 10, 1956, a concert in Paris celebrated his eightieth birthday, an occasion that led him to break his vow not to perform in France as long as it recognized the Franco regime in Spain. Casals conducted two of his own works and played two minor solos on the cello.

Late in 1956 Casals announced he would make his home in Puerto Rico but would spend several months each year in Europe fulfilling various commitments there. In honor of his eightieth birthday, the government of Puerto Rico sponsored a music festival devoted to the music of Bach, Mozart, and Schubert with Casals as its central figure. This festival took place between April 22 and May 8, 1957, without Casals as a participant, because while rehearsing for it he had suffered a heart attack. Subsequently the Festival Casals became a major musical event each spring with Casals as the dominating personality, both as conductor and as cellist.

Though he was determined never to perform publicly in the United States as long as that country supported Franco, Casals allowed himself to be swayed by the advice and encouragement of several of his close friends (one of whom was Albert Schweitzer) who maintained that it was far wiser for Casals to perform *and* protest in the United States than to protest by remaining silent musically. After considerable soul-searching and reexamination of his values, Casals finally decided to return to the United States after an absence of three decades. The stage he selected was not a public concert hall but the General Assembly Hall of the United Nations in New York at a time when the United Nations was celebrating its thirteenth birthday. On October 24, 1958, he played Bach's Sonata No.2 for cello and piano (with Mieczyslaw Horszowski at the piano). "It was a beautiful performance," wrote Harold C. Schonberg in the New York *Times.* "Signor Casals used a Bergonzi cello that threw an enormous tone. Senor Casals' bow arm seemed to be as strong as ever. He took the long phrases without a tremor. The breadth of his phrasing, the rhythmic bit of the last movement, and the warm conception all were testimony of a musical heritage and a musical mind that many have called unsurpassed in this century. As an encore, Casals was heard in 'Song of the Birds.' "

Casals remained active on the American scene by giving master classes in cello, by performing at the White House for President and Mrs. John F. Kennedy and their guests in 1961, and by joining the Marlboro Festival in Vermont in 1961, conducting the orchestra and teaching the cello. On June 22, 1962, he returned to New York to conduct his own oratorio, *El Pesebre,* based on Catalan folk modes and rhythms. He had conducted the world premiere in Acapulco, Mexico, on December 17, 1960, and the American premiere on April 19, 1962 (his first appearance on the American professional stage in thirty-four years). The Puerto Rican premiere had taken place on June 20, 1962. After the New York performance Casals brought his oratorio to foreign capitals as a means of further spreading his propaganda for peace. "Never has the world been nearer to catastrophe than at this moment," he remarked sadly. "All nuclear experiments ought to be stopped altogether." Conducting his oratorio, with its message of peace, was his small way of trying to create a climate in which a nuclear war could never take place.

A concert honoring Casals, "Salud Casals," was given at the Lincoln Center for the Performing Arts on April 17, 1970. The main participants were the American Symphony Orchestra conducted by Leopold Stokowski, with Beverly Sills and Rudolf Serkin as soloists. The dramatic climax of the evening unfolded in the last composition, Casals's own *La Sardana,* a work in eight-part harmony scored for a variable number of cellos. He had composed it in 1926 and it had been performed for the first time in 1927 at Wigmore Hall in London by thirty-two of Casals's students under the direction of John Barbirolli. Groups of cellists subsequently performed this composition in Paris, Barcelona, Brussels, and Jerusalem; in 1951, to celebrate Casals' seventy-fifth birthday, it had been played by one hundred and twenty cellists in Zurich. For the New York concert in 1970 seventy cellists came from as far away as Tokyo and with thirty of Casals's former students and professional associates made up the performing ensemble for this event, conducted by the ninety-three-year-old Casals. "He may be old in years," said Harold C. Schonberg in the New York *Times,* "he may walk slowly, but once he has a baton in hand he is The Boss. At times he did everything but fly off the podium."

In New York on October 24, 1971, Casals conducted a United Nations Day Concert at the General Assembly Hall of the United Nations. His program was made up of two concertos by

Casals

Bach together with the world premiere of Casals's own Hymn to the United Nations, words by W. H. Auden. This was repeated. As an encore Casals played the "Song of the Birds" on his cello. "They virtually had to lift Pablo Casals into the conductor's chair," reported Donal Henahan in the New York *Times*, "but once there, with baton firmly in hand, any sign of weakness vanished. Mr. Casals, in an amazing display of indomitability at ninety-four years of age, led a taxing program." The Hymn to the United Nations, which Casals intended as a plea for peace, had been commissioned from Casals by U Thant, Secretary General of the United Nations. After the concert, U Thant presented Casals with the United Nations Peace Medal saying: "Don Pablo, you have devoted your life to truth, to beauty and to peace. Both as a man and as an artist you embody the ideals symbolized by the United Nations Peace Medal. I present it to you with deep respect and admiration."

In November 1972 Casals, aged ninety-five, performed the cello in Beethoven's Triple Concerto at Guadalajara, Mexico, for the benefit of an orphanage. In gratitude, the town of Guadalajara presented him with a house, which he turned down politely, maintaining he preferred spending the rest of his days in Puerto Rico. The house was later converted into a home for children.

During the summer of 1973 the ninety-six-year-old Casals arrived in Israel in ninety-degree heat. Isaac Stern, the violinist, met him at the airport and recalled how "we carried him, faint and ill, from the plane to his hotel in Jerusalem. Immediately, he demanded a piano. The only one I could find was in the hotel bar, so I had it brought up to his suite. The frail, weary old man sat down, loosened his tie, dropped his braces and started playing a Bach prelude. The color came back to his cheeks. He smiled, and everything was all right again."

When he returned to Puerto Rico, Casals was well enough to participate in the festival proceedings. But in September of the same year he was stricken by a heart attack at the home of a friend while playing dominoes. Lung complications followed. Isaac Stern tells us:"Impatient at being hospitalized, he pulled out all the intravenous tubes from his arms, flung them to the floor and told the nurses: 'Damn it, I will not die!' Incredibly he managed to survive another day."

Casals died in the hospital on October 22, 1973. After requiem services at a church in San Juan on October 23, at which the "Song of the Birds" was played as Casals had requested, Casals was buried in a small cemetery fronting on the sea. Three days of official mourning were decreed by Governor Rafael Hernandez Colon of Puerto Rico, with the flags of Puerto Rico and the United States flown at half-mast.

"Casals lived a legend and died a legend," wrote Harold C. Schonberg in an obituary tribute in the New York *Times*. "And it was a real legend, one that Casals had rightly earned. In him came together a set of attributes that few musicians have matched. The man was largely responsible for modern cello playing, was instrumental in furthering the cause of chamber music, and lived and died for music. His was an important life. And in most respects it was a beautiful life."

Casals was a short, squat man who, in his own description, was no taller than his cello. He became partially bald in his twenties, and with his gold-rimmed glasses he looked more like a bookkeeper or a bank clerk than a world-renowned musician and humanitarian. Reading, playing chess and dominoes, and chatting with his friends provided relief from the tensions of concertizing. He smoked a pipe all his life. His closing years were spent in a modest home by the sea at Santurce, Puerto Rico, with his wife, Marta.

Albert E. Kahn described a typical day for Casals at Santurce. "Each morning between seven and eight he arises . . . and carrying a black umbrella to shield his eyes from the sun, steps with his lovely wife, Marta, from the back garden onto the bordering beach. The ensuing stroll is no routine formality for him, but, rather, an essential moment of communion with nature. . . . On returning from shore he breakfasts and goes directly to the piano to start the day as he has every day for the past eighty years by playing two preludes and fugues. . . . The remainder of the morning he practises on the cello and composes at the piano. . . . After lunch the Maestro takes a siesta of an hour or so. He spends the balance of the afternoon composing or practising again, teaching a gifted pupil or distinguished musician, meeting with visitors, and going over the day's mail with Marta. . . . After supper he and Marta may visit or receive friends. One of his favorite pastimes is dominos. . . . The games often last until early morning hours. Casals plays with a passionate intensity punctuated by exuberant chortling at victorious moments. Another regular pastime of Casals is watching TV westerns. He frequently views them while eating supper at a small table; and one has the feeling that he tastes his food scarcely, if at all."

ABOUT: Casals, P. Joys and Sorrows: Reflections as Told to Albert E. Kahn; Corredor, J. M. Conversations with Casals; Kirk, H. L. Pablo Casals. *Periodicals*—Atlantic Monthly, June 1966; Hi-Fi, April 1967; Life, November 11, 1966, April 17, 1970; McCall's Magazine, May 1966, April 1970; Musical America, January 15, 1957; New Yorker, May 9, 1970; Saturday Review, December 31, 1966, June 22, 1968; Time, April 27, 1970, November 5, 1973.

BRUNA CASTAGNA

Bruna Castagna

1908–

Bruna Castagna, contralto, was born in Bari, in southern Italy, on October 15, 1908. Piano study began when she was seven. By the time she was fourteen she was recognized as a prodigy, but her own preference was for singing. After a period of vocal study with Tina Scognamiglio in Milan, Castagna made her debut at the Teatro Sociale in Mantua in 1927 as Marina in *Boris Godunov* in which Ezio Pinza sang the title role. Tullio Serafin, the conductor, invited Castagna to appear under his baton in opera performances at the Teatro Colón in Buenos Aires.

After three years of operatic appearances in South America, Castagna returned to Italy to sing in some of its opera houses. An audition before Toscanini brought her a contract with La Scala; there, in 1933, she achieved a major success as Isabella in Rossini's *L'Italiana in Algeri,* an opera that was revived for her. This and other well-received performances at La Scala brought her numerous engagements outside Italy. In Barcelona she sang the title role of *Carmen* for the first time; it became one of her most distinguished roles. She was also heard both in operas and in recitals in Australia, Egypt, Romania, France, and Germany.

In 1934 she made her first appearances in the United States as a member of an opera company, at the Hippodrome Theater in New York. Ed-

ward Johnson, general manager of the Metropolitan Opera, put her under contract and she made her debut at the Metropolitan on March 2, 1936, as Amneris in *Aida.* "Miss Castagna's voice lends itself admirably to operas of the Italian school," remarked one New York critic, "as does her style of singing. Hers is a contralto voice of fullness and agreeable quality, and she employs it musically." During the remainder of the regular season at the Metropolitan she was well received as Azucena in *Il Trovatore,* Maddalena in *Rigoletto,* and Santuzza in *Cavalleria Rusticana,* and on May 11, 1936, during the spring season, she made her first American appearance as Carmen. Writing in the *World-Telegram,* Pitts Sanborn described her Carmen as "compelling" in its "vividness" and "rich" in its "vitality." He added: "Her voice is sumptuous, a spectrum in its play of color. And always is she the accomplished musician. The mantle of the great Carmens has fallen upon her, and royally she wears it."

Castagna remained with the Metropolitan Opera company through the 1944–1945 season. During that time her roles, in addition to those already mentioned, included Laura and La Cieca in *La Gioconda,* Adalgisa in *Norma,* Delilah in *Samson and Delilah,* Dame Quickly in *Falstaff* and Ulrica in *Un Ballo in Maschera.* Her last appearance at the Metropolitan Opera was on March 31, 1945, as Azucena. She made 107 appearances in New York and 41 on tour in 11 roles.

While still with the Metropolitan Castagna

Castagna: käs tä′ nyä

made her debut at the San Francisco Opera as Carmen on November 4, 1936, following this performance ten days later with an appearance as Azucena. One season later she added Amneris, Ulrica, and Adalgisa to her San Francisco Opera repertory. In 1938 she made her debut with the Chicago Opera. During 1937–1938 she was featured in a sustaining network radio show.

For her American engagements Castagna maintained an apartment in New York City overlooking the Hudson River with a commanding view of the George Washington Bridge. She was fond of animals and owned two dogs.

After leaving the Metropolitan Opera, Bruna Castagna made several appearances in Europe. She later went into retirement in Milan to devote herself to teaching voice and coaching young singers.

ABOUT: Kutsch, K. J. and Riemens, L. A Concise Biographical Dictionary of Singers.

LINA CAVALIERI

Lina Cavalieri

1874–1944

Lina Cavalieri, soprano, was born in Viterbo, Italy, on December 25, 1874. When she was fourteen she began her singing career with appearances in cafés, after which she was heard in small theaters in Italy. A young woman of striking beauty, with a voice to match the image, she became a singing star of the Folies Bergères in Paris and of the Empire Theatre in London. In 1900 she married Prince Bariatonsky in Russia, but the marriage was ended when she decided to embark upon a career in opera. After some vocal study with Mariani-Masi in Paris, Cavalieri made her operatic debut at the Royal Theatre in Lisbon in December 1900 as Nedda in *I Pagliacci.* She scored a brilliant success in St. Petersburg in 1901, then gathered additional triumphs in Warsaw, Monte Carlo, Rome, Florence, Palermo, and Paris. Her finest roles were Thaïs, Manon in Massenet's opera, Gilda in *Rigoletto,* and Mimi in *La Bohème,* in all of which her uncommon beauty and glamour made her as attractive visually as she was aurally.

She made her American debut at the Met-

Cavalieri: kä vä lyâ' rĕ

ropolitan Opera on December 5, 1906, as Fedora in the American premiere of Giordano's opera of that name, with Caruso appearing opposite her as Loris. "Miss Cavalieri," wrote W. H. Henderson in the *Sun,* "justified her reputation as a beauty. Her figure is exquisite and her face a delight to see. Her voice is a light lyric soprano, very pretty in quality, but not rich or vibrant." On January 18, 1907, she assumed the title role in the first Metropolitan Opera presentation of *Manon Lescaut* (with Caruso as Des Grieux) and made an even stronger impression. Her singing, as some of the critics noted, had lyrical beauty rather than dramatic power, but its purity of texture and sweetness of sound were arresting. On January 25, 1907, with Emma Eames too indisposed to appear in the title role of *Tosca,* Cavalieri substituted though she had never before sung the role and had to appear without rehearsals; she brought down the house with her performance. Her subsequent roles at the Metropolitan Opera were Mimi, Nedda, and the title part in *Adriana Lecouvreur.*

Her marriage in 1907 to the American Winthrop Chandler broke up after a single week when she deserted him. The resulting scandal made it impossible for her to appear at the Metropolitan Opera. In 1908 she was heard at Covent Garden in London as Manon Lescaut, Tosca, and Fedora, and in 1909 she made several guest appearances with the Manhattan Opera Company.

A third marriage—to the tenor Lucien Muratore, who was a member of the Opéra-Comique and of the Paris Opéra for over a decade and subsequently principal tenor of the Chicago Opera for sixteen years—took place on July 10, 1913. For a number of years, until their separation in 1919, she appeared with him in joint recitals in Europe and the United States. One such performance took place at the Hippodrome Theater in New York on March 9, 1913. It marked Cavalieri's return to the city after an absence of four years. Her beauty still inspired rapturous paragraphs from the critics, but her voice now left much to be desired. "She was very nervous last night," said Richard Aldrich in the New York *Times,* "and perhaps did not do herself justice as a singer. At any rate, it did not seem as if she had improved in this direction." One of the curiosities of this concert was an encore in which she sang a popular song by Harry von Tilzer of Tin Pan Alley fame.

By 1922 she had deserted her singing career to settle down in Paris as an operator of a beauty salon. Following her divorce from Muratore in 1927, she married Giuseppe Campari. Their relationship proved both brief and stormy. Her fourth husband was Paolo D'Arvanni. She spent her last years with him at the Villa Cappucina near Florence. During World War II, on February 8, 1944, she and her husband were killed during an air raid.

Lina Cavalieri was the star of three silent films: *Manon Lescaut* (1914), *The Eternal Temptress* (1917), and *A Woman of Impulse* (1918). Her life story and romantic involvements were the subjects of a motion picture filmed in Italy in 1957: *La Donna Più Bella della Mondo,* starring Gina Lollabrigida.

ABOUT: Kutsch, K. J. and Riemens, L. A Concise Biographical Dictionary of Singers.

Aldo Ceccato

1934–

Aldo Ceccato, conductor, was born in Milan, on February 18, 1934. Precocious in music from early childhood, he was enrolled in his tenth year by his father in the Verdi Conservatory in Milan where he studied piano with Carlo Lonati and composition with Bruno Bettinelli. In 1949

Ceccato: chāk kä' tõ

ALDO CECCATO

he won first prize in piano in an international piano competition in Neuchâtel. For a number of years thereafter he made appearances as a pianist in both the classical and the jazz repertory.

Upon graduation from the conservatory with highest honors in 1955, Ceccato, then concentrating on conducting, continued his musical studies in 1958 in Holland with Albert Wolff and Willem van Otterloo and completed his musical training at the Academy of Music, once again with highest honors, in 1962. Meanwhile, from 1960 on he worked with and served as assistant to Sergiu Celibidache at the Siena Academy.

In 1964 he won first prize in the Third International Competition conducted by Italian Radio Television among young conductors. Not long after, he enjoyed his first success as a conductor, in Milan with a performance of seven Vivaldi concertos at a single concert. Engagements with leading orchestras and opera houses in Italy followed, highlighted by appearances at the Santa Cecilia Academy in Rome, La Scala in Milan, Teatro La Fenice in Venice, and the Florence May Music Festival. At the last of these he conducted the Italian premiere of Busoni's *Die Brautwahl.* At La Scala he was heard in the complete score of Beethoven's *Egmont,* in a production of the Goethe drama by Luchino Visconti.

During this period the critic of *Il Tempo* in Rome wrote of Ceccato: "His is a totally inner sensitivity, translated into interpretations of singular vividness, plenitude and coherence. His power to communicate overflows with immediacy in interpretations which merge the harmonious balance of sounds with the stirring and significant force of colors and movements. His is a unique and individual quality in that the musical vision is transformed in the vitality of performance, transfiguring and spiritualizing the sound."

His growing fame in Italy brought him engagements in Germany, France, England, and South America. At Covent Garden in London, which engaged him on the recommendation of Georg Solti, he conducted performances of *Falstaff, Simon Boccanegra, Otello,* and *La Traviata.* The last of these brought the following comment from the music critic of the London *Financial Times:* "He showed his merit in beautifully shaped preludes, played with a fine supple line, in well-chosen tempi, in a dramatic treatment of the score that never drew undue attention to himself. Naturalness, a care for details that never became fuzzy, firmness tempered by flexibility—all the attributes of a *Traviata* conductor were there." At the Glyndebourne Festival his performances of *Ariadne auf Naxos* also inspired praise.

Ceccato made his North American debut in November 1969 at the Chicago Lyric Opera with *I Puritani.* "His command was faultless," said the critic of *Chicago Today,* "his musicianship full of character, his comprehension of Bellini's strength and weakness minutely comprehensive." On November 5, 1970, Ceccato made his American debut as a symphony conductor with the New York Philharmonic. At that time a critic for the New York *Times* noted: "Ceccato is handsome, forceful and very much the virtuoso conductor. His conducting has flair, and there never for a moment was any doubt who was in full charge." On the strength of this performance he was offered the post of associate conductor of the orchestra, which he declined. He followed this appearance with performances with the Boston Symphony, the Chicago Symphony, the Cleveland Orchestra, and the Minnesota Orchestra.

In May 1972 Ceccato was engaged on a two-year contract as principal conductor of the Detroit Symphony, effective September 1973, succeeding Sixten Ehrling; the contract was renewed for an additional two years in 1975. This appointment was made before Ceccato had a single hearing in Detroit, where his debut took place on December 8, 1972. Before assuming the new post, Ceccato added to his American successes and his reputation with performances in Cleveland, Chicago, Philadelphia, Los Angeles, Pittsburgh, San Francisco, and at the Berkshire Music Festival in Massachusetts.

Because of prior commitments, Ceccato was able to conduct only nine weeks during his first year as the principal conductor of the Detroit Symphony. One season later he extended his stay in Detroit to a dozen weeks. So successful did Ceccato prove in his initial year in Detroit that in May 1974 he was made music director.

In August 1973 Ceccato and the New York Philharmonic gave a free concert in Central Park before one of the largest audiences ever to attend a symphony concert in New York—over 100,000. Some time later when Ceccato made his first appearance in New York City as music director of the Detroit Symphony, January 28, 1975, in a performance of Janáček's Mass, Harriet Johnson wrote of him in the *Post:* "While he has the superficial assets of youth and good looks, these seem incidental to his deep musicality, his perception and his ability to project a big architecture like the Mass with sweep and fire."

Ceccato was appointed general music director of the Hamburg Philharmonic in Germany beginning with the 1975-1976 season, a post he held concurrently with the one in Detroit. Then, in the fall of 1975 Ceccato announced that he was leaving Detroit at the termination of his contract in April 1977.

Ceccato is married to Eliana de Sabata. They have two sons, Francesco and Cristiano. Eliana is the daughter of the distinguished Italian composer and conductor Victor de Sabata, who was first impressed with Ceccato's conducting talent when Ceccato replaced an ailing conductor and led a brilliant performance of de Sabata's tone poem *Juventus.* "My boy," de Sabata told him, "Toscanini premiered this work. I conducted it myself. Yours is the best performance of all, because you put into it all the characteristics of *juventus* —youth."

Boyish in appearance, with piercing eyes, Ceccato is, in the words of Edward Greenfield, "the very picture of the voluble Italian musician." Given to choreographic exhibitions on the podium, Ceccato is a galvanic personality while conducting.

He received an honorary doctorate from Eastern Michigan University in 1975.

ABOUT: High Fidelity, September 1973, October 1974.

Feodor Chaliapin

1873–1938

Feodor Ivanovich Chaliapin, basso, was the first Russian singer to gain international renown, a renown second only to that of Caruso, in the world's opera houses.

Chaliapin was born to peasants in Kazan, Russia, on February 13, 1873. Singing had been a passion from childhood on. "Somehow it came naturally to me," he said in his autobiography. "Sometimes I used to sing duets with my mother, who had a charming voice. ... Any form of music pleased and delighted me." As a boy he joined the choir of the Archbishop of Kazan. Then, while still very young, Feodor saw his first theatrical performance. "I was dumbfounded with amazement," he recalled.

When he was ten he was apprenticed to a shoemaker. Then he ran away from home and joined a circus where his job was to clean oil lamps, sweep the floors, and wash and feed the animals. At fourteen he became a member of the chorus of a traveling opera company where young Maxim Gorki was also a chorister. What Feodor earned was hardly enough for existence. He was often compelled to walk the railroad tracks because he did not have the fare to get from one place to the next; and hunger was a constant companion. But there was the compensation of being able to see performances of operas; the first he saw was *Faust*.

He joined the chorus of a light opera company in southern Russia when he was seventeen. His home was a dirty underground room in a washerwoman's hovel; his bed, a mattress stuffed with straw. A cracked rubles mirror on the wall was the only luxury his salary of twenty rubles a month could afford. On the eve of a performance of Moniuszko's *Halka,* a leading member of the cast failed to show up for the role of the officer. Since none of the principals knew the part, Feodor offered to learn it. He did so well that the director of the company raised his salary by five rubles a month and from time to time called on him to appear in small roles.

Chaliapin: shŭ lyà′ pyĭn

FEODOR CHALIAPIN

During the summer of 1892 Chaliapin found a job as clerk in the accounts department of the Transcaucasian Railway; this kept him from total destitution. He became acquainted with Dmitri Ussatov, a Russian singer who was the first to recognize his talent. Ussatov not only began teaching Chaliapin but also gave him lodgings and provided him with an allowance. "He shaped my first serious ideas of the theater," Chaliapin later recalled, "gave me an insight into the nature of music, refined my taste."

In 1893 Chaliapin made his debut with a professional opera company—the Tiflis Opera—as Méphistophélès in *Faust.* He was assigned other leading roles that season among which were Tonio in *I Pagliacci* and the Singing Miller in Dargomizhsky's *Roussalka.* In 1894 he became a member of the summer opera company in St. Petersburg where he enjoyed such a success as Bertram in *Robert le Diable* that he was invited to sing at the homes of prominent government officials. One of them was the Minister of State Control, who used his influence to get Chaliapin a contract with the Imperial Opera in St. Petersburg in February 1895.

His first role there was Russlan in Glinka's *Russlan and Ludmilla.* He did not have sufficient time to prepare for this performance and consequently gave a poor account of himself. For a time only small parts were turned over to him. In one of these—that of Count Robinson in Cimarosa's *Il Matrimonio Segreto*—he was so badly miscast that he failed in the role. The consensus in the opera house, as we learn from

Chaliapin

Chaliapin's autobiography, was that "nothing could be made of Chaliapin. He has a good voice, an extraordinarily good voice, but when he is given important parts, either he makes a failure of them or he cultivates appalling affectations." Then, on the last night of his first season, one of his friends assigned to appear as Russlan feigned illness to allow Chaliapin to substitute for him. By now Chaliapin had mastered the role completely, and in it he scored a triumph.

In St. Petersburg Chaliapin had come under the influence and teachings of a celebrated actor, Mamont-Dalsky, who gave him valuable guidance in dramatic gestures, vocal inflections, and timing. Inspired by his teacher, Chaliapin haunted the theaters, studying the stage techniques of different actors and assimilating them into his own performances. When he left St. Petersburg in 1896 he had transformed himself into a singing actor who studied histrionics as much as vocalization.

With Mamontov's Opera in Moscow, which he joined in 1896, Chaliapin emerged for the first time as an original—not only a distinguished voice that was beautifully textured and pure in both the baritone and the bass range, but also an actor of power and insight and a presence which completely dominated the stage. Out of the nineteen roles he sang there fifteen were from the Russian repertory. Some of these became paragons in dramatic and musical conceptions, with which Chaliapin became fully identified as an incomparable interpreter: Boris Godunov, Ivan the Terrible in Rimsky-Korsakov's opera of the same name, Ivan Susanin in Glinka's *A Life for the Tsar,* Roussalka in Dargomizhsky's opera of that name, and Salieri in Rimsky-Korsakov's *Mozart and Salieri.* The last of these roles he created in the world premiere of the opera on December 7, 1898.

In 1901 Chaliapin appeared in his first engagement outside Russia: at La Scala in the title role of Boïto's *Mefistofele.* In the spring of 1906 he participated in a season of Russian operas in Paris where two years later, under Diaghilev's management, he caused a furor with his performances in *Boris Godunov,* an opera being heard in Paris for the first time.

Despite his formidable reputation, Chaliapin's debut in the United States, at the Metropolitan Opera House on November 20, 1907, in the title role in Boïto's *Mefistofele,* was anticlimactic. "The newcomer's impersonation of Mephistopheles," said Henry Krehbiel in the *Tribune,* "is startling in its picturesqueness, and would make a gaudy picture book for children, but with Goethe's conception of this particular devil, or even Boïto's, it has as little to do as it has with the Pater Seraphicus of Goethe's final scene. Mr. Chaliapin's notion of the devil is merely carnal. . . . When he appears among his kindred on the Brocken he is bestiality incarnate. . . . It is stupendously picturesque, of course, for the man is of marvelous stature and amazing plasticity of pose and gesture; but calls to mind, more than anything else, the vulgarity of conduct which his countryman Gorki presents with such disgusting frankness in his pictures of Russian life."

Because of the negative reactions to his performances in New York, Chaliapin remained at the Metropolitan only a single season, appearing in the additional roles of Basilio in *The Barber of Seville* and Leporello in *Don Giovanni,* and Méphistophélès in *Faust.* He did not return to the Metropolitan Opera for another fourteen years.

On February 19, 1910, Chaliapin created the role of Don Quixote in Massenet's *Don Quichotte* in Monte Carlo, and on November 20, 1911, he was Dositheus in the world premiere of Mussorgsky's *Khovantchina* at the St. Petersburg Opera. In Chaliapin's first appearances in London, in 1913 during the Thomas Beecham series of Russian operas at Covent Garden, he sang the roles of Boris Godunov, Prince Igor, and, in *Khovantchina,* Prince Ivan Khovantsky.

During World War I Chaliapin remained in Russia. After the war, with the rise of the proletariat, the Soviet government bestowed on him the rank of People's Artist. But Chaliapin had little sympathy with the new regime. He found life in Russia to be "hideously official" with "all human feelings disappeared." His wife was recruited for hard labor on the Neva in midwinter, and he himself suffered considerable deprivations in physical comfort. When the Soviet government permitted him to leave the country to help spread propaganda on behalf of the Soviet Union through his performances, he knew he was leaving his native country for good. In 1927, the Soviet Union withdrew Chaliapin's honorary title of People's Artist.

He found a new home for himself and his family in Paris; but in spite of his antagonism to the Soviets, he remained throughout his life a

Russian citizen, a fact noted on the French passport he used for travel. Only eight such passports had ever been issued by the French government, including one to Rachmaninoff and one to the painter Sorin.

Chaliapin continued to accumulate triumphs in Europe. On December 9, 1921, after a fourteen-year absence, he returned to the Metropolitan Opera for his first appearance in the United States as Boris Godunov. He sang his part in Russian while the rest of the cast used Italian. Henry Krehbiel in the *Tribune* was now made to realize "the greatness of the Russian as a dramatic singer, or a singing actor. . . . Last night, nobility of acting was paired with a beautiful nobility of voice and vocal style, and his Boris stood out of the dramatic picture like one of the old time heroes of tragedy. . . . He sang in Russian, and though it was possible even for those unfamiliar with the language to feel some of that intimacy which must exist between the original text and the music, the effect upon the Russians in the audience was akin to frenzy. All that we have heard of the greatness of his impersonation of the character of Boris was made plain. It was heartbreaking in its pathos, terrible in its vehemence and agony."

Chaliapin remained with the Metropolitan Opera company through the 1928–1929 season. On December 2, 1922, he appeared as Philip II in *Don Carlo,* once again in a production in which he sang in Russian and the remaining members of the cast in Italian. W. J. Henderson in the *Sun* called his characterization "powerful, symmetrical and convincing" and described Chaliapin as a "singer of great skill as well as an actor of the first order." Chaliapin was subsequently heard in *Mefistofele,* as Méphistophélès in *Faust,* and in the title role of Massenet's *Don Quichotte. Faust* was the opera in which Chaliapin gave his farewell performance on the stage of the Metropolitan Opera, on March 20, 1929.

While affiliated with the Metropolitan Opera Chaliapin embarked upon his first world tour in 1926. He also sang with the Chicago Opera in the years between 1922 and 1924, toured the United States at the head of his own opera troupe, and gave numerous recitals.

His first American recital took place at the Manhattan Opera House in New York on November 13, 1921. He was not heard to best advantage since he was suffering from a severe bronchial condition. Before the concert began,

an announcement was made from the stage offering to postpone the concert, but the audience proved overwhelmingly in favor of listening to Chaliapin, however indisposed. Without wishing to comment on Chaliapin's singing at this concert because its quality and power were greatly affected by his physical indisposition, Richard Aldrich in the New York *Times* found in his performance "a highly developed skill of characterization," and considered his delivery of some of the Russian songs to be "striking."

In subsequent recitals in New York and elsewhere Chaliapin proved himself as magnetic a personality and as imperial a performer in song as he was in opera. In all of these recitals he never issued a program, since he preferred to have his mood at concert time dictate what songs he would sing. In place of a program, the audience acquired a songbook with English translations for twenty-five cents. Before each of his renditions, Chaliapin himself identified each of the songs by the numbers they bore in this booklet.

After 1929 Chaliapin confined his operatic appearances to Europe and to an extended tour of the Far East in 1936. His home in Paris was a large apartment which, according to his daughter Marina, "was always full of people. We never sat down to table with less than fifteen. Anybody who came was asked to stay. To feed all these people we had two chefs. One was a Caucasian and the other a Russian."

Chaliapin was a huge man with a seemingly insatiable appetite for vodka, food, and women, about which Arthur Rubinstein has written in his autobiography, *My Young Years.* Henry Pleasants has described Chaliapin as "a primitive . . . a kind of overgrown, precocious boy— capricious, moody, impulsive and unpredictable." Chaliapin's piano accompanist, Gerald Moore, remembers him as "splendid, frightening, inspiring . . . a man of infinite charm and of quick temper, like a baby. If a door didn't open readily he'd tear the handle off." Geraldine Farrar called Chaliapin "a great blond cherub of a man." She added: "Of superb physique, he had an uncanny gift for cosmetic metamorphosis and added to dramatic gifts a magnificent voice that rolled out like melodious thunder . . . And what a fellow with the ladies! It was not easy to overlook this fascinating barbarian whose sentimental attacks were along lines quite unusual to the traditions of overpolite society, and so eminently successful."

Like Caruso, Chaliapin was a highly gifted graphic artist, with a particular bent for making striking caricatures of friends and colleagues; the one he made of himself is a gem. He also enjoyed fishing, going to museums, attending the theater, and playing card games (*belote* particularly). He was fond of dogs, keeping two or three bulldogs at a time.

On performance days he did no vocalizing whatsoever except for a few scales and ate sparingly, usually some eggs and coffee. After a performance he enjoyed his favorite dish of boiled chicken or boiled beef. On holidays he often piled some of his eight children into a car and went on drives for several days, stopping off at night at roadside inns or guest houses rather than luxury hotels. His daughter Marina remembers him as a most affectionate father. "He never raised his voice to us. When we did something wrong he would put on a sad face. And since he was a very great actor, it was the saddest face in the whole world. To see it was our greatest punishment. He would tell us stories and he made up the most wonderful fairy tales. There was one which would continue night after night, always stopping at the crucial moment. . . . Best of all we liked to hear him tell about his childhood."

Chaliapin made more than four hundred fifty recordings, beginning in 1898 with a dozen cylinders and ending in 1936; two hundred of these have been released, including an eight-record set issued posthumously by Melodiya in the Soviet Union.

In 1933 Chaliapin was starred in the French-produced motion picture *Don Quixote,* for which Jacques Ibert wrote some songs.

Feodor Chaliapin died in Paris on April 12, 1938. One of his sons, Boris, became an artist whose work often appeared on the covers of *Time* magazine. Another son, Feodor, became a successful actor, and a daughter, Lydia, a voice teacher, coached many famous singers in Russian roles for performances at the Metropolitan Opera.

ABOUT: Chaliapin, F. I. Pages of My Life; Chaliapin, F. I. Chaliapin: Man and Mask; Pleasants, H. The Great Singers; Rubinstein, A. My Young Years.

Boris Christoff

1914–

Boris Christoff, basso, was born in Plovdiv, Bulgaria, on May 14, 1914, to Kyril and Raina Christoff. While preparing for a law career he sang as a hobby, performing with the Bulgarian Gusla Choir (in which he eventually became a soloist) and with the Sofia Cathedral Choir.

Just before World War II he served in the cavalry of the Bulgarian army. Then, after receiving his law degree from the University of Sofia, he became a magistrate for the City of Sofia. The decision to make music rather than jurisprudence his permanent profession was taken in January 1942 at a festival in Sofia when he sang a Bulgarian folksong before an audience including King Boris. The king regarded Christoff's singing as the high point of the festival and urged him to leave the law for music. As an inducement, the king offered him a scholarship to study voice in Italy. There Christoff became a student of Riccardo Stracciari, an association that lasted until Stracciari's death in 1956. In 1945 Christoff went to Salzburg to study the German repertory at the Mozarteum on a scholarship. When World War II ended, he was held in a displaced persons camp in the Austrian Tyrol.

He returned to Italy early in 1945 and that same year made his professional debut with a recital at the Santa Cecilia Academy in Rome. Several other concerts and some radio appearances followed. In 1946 Christoff made his bow in opera at the Teatro La Fenice in Venice as Colline in *La Bohème*. Later that year he joined La Scala in Milan where he was first heard in the minor role of Pimenn in *Boris Godunov* and where, two years later, he assumed leading basso parts. In 1947, at La Scala, he appeared for the first time in the role which made him famous, the title part in *Boris Godunov*. Appearing in this role at Covent Garden in London in 1949, Christoff was praised for the dramatic vigor of his acting and the majesty of his vocalization, both of which reminded some of the English critics of Chaliapin. Christoff repeated his compelling interpretation of the role at the Teatro Colón in Buenos Aires and at the Opéra in Paris.

He was invited to appear with the Metropolitan Opera several times, beginning in 1950 but

BORIS CHRISTOFF

the United States State Department refused to grant him a visa because the McCarran act denied entry to "undesirable aliens," and Christoff was a native of a country that had become Communist. When this restriction was finally removed, Christoff made his American debut—not at the Metropolitan Opera but at the San Francisco Opera—on September 30, 1956, as Boris Godunov. Reporting the performance for the New York *Times,* Howard Taubman wrote: "Mr. Christoff is an outstanding singing actor and his Boris is, beyond a shadow of a doubt, the best of our generation. ... Mr. Christoff is a volcano of emotion. When he is on the stage, opera takes on an unexpected dimension. It becomes the stuff of life, but on a larger scale, as great tragedy must be." Later that season Christoff was heard as Fiesco in *Simon Boccanegra.*

In 1958 Christoff joined the Chicago Lyric Opera as its principal basso. There, in 1961, Boïto's *Mefistofele* was revived for him, the first Chicago production of that opera since the time of Chaliapin. In 1960, and again in 1961, he was hailed for his performance as Philip II in *Don Carlo* at the Salzburg Festival in Austria. In 1967 he was acclaimed as Ivan Susanin in a La Scala revival of Glinka's *A Life for the Tsar.*

Though Christoff's repertory embraces about one hundred roles, he has confined himself primarily to fifteen or so. In addition to those already mentioned the following should be noted: Tsar Ivan in Rimsky-Korsakov's *Maid of Pskov,* Dositheus in *Khovantchina,* the title role in Handel's *Julius Caesar,* Khan Kontchak and

Prince Galitzky in *Prince Igor,* Pizarro and Rocco in *Fidelio,* the title role in Massenet's *Don Quichotte,* Don Basilio in *The Barber of Seville,* Father Guardiano in *La Forza del Destino,* and the title role in *Simon Boccanegra.*

Christoff has also distinguished himself in song recitals, as a soloist with symphony orchestras, and as a recording artist. Several of his recordings have received awards from the Académie du Disque Français, and the Académie Charles Cros in France. Holland also recognized their excellence, with the Edison Prize.

He was decorated Commander of the Order of the Italian Republic and Commander of the Order of San Pietro e Paolo in Brazil. The Paris Opéra conferred on him an honorary membership.

He resides on the Via Bertolini in Rome with his wife, the former Franca de Rensis. Christoff is the brother-in-law of opera baritone Tito Gobbi.

ABOUT: Opera News, October 20, 1962.

Fausto Cleva

1902–1971

Fausto Cleva, conductor, was born in Trieste on May 17, 1902, the son of Giacomo and Fortunata Canarutto Cleva. He received his first musical training at the Trieste Conservatory and subsequently at the Verdi Conservatory in Milan. When he was seventeen, he made his conducting debut at the Teatro Carcano in Milan to which he had been appointed associate conductor. During the next two years he had an opportunity to conduct there and in other Italian opera houses and to come into personal contact with some of Italy's opera composers. His first meeting with Umberto Giordano proved a disaster. Fausto had been called in to substitute for the regular piano accompanist at a rehearsal of Giordano's *Siberia.* Never having seen the score, he had to sight-read it and, as he later confessed, "I wasn't doing very well." He went on to describe the incident that followed: "Then Giordano walked in. He listened disgustedly, came over to the piano, brushed me aside and played for the rest of the rehearsal himself. You can imagine, I felt terrible!" His next meeting with Giordano was different. Fausto had just finished

Cleva

FAUSTO CLEVA

conducting a performance of Giordano's *Andrea Chénier* when the composer came up to him to say how much he liked the conducting because it was so youthful in spirit. "I was very young when I wrote that opera," the composer added. Cleva continues: "He did not realize he had seen me before, so I reminded him of the humiliating *Siberia* rehearsal. He was astonished and amused to learn that I was the pianist he thought was so bad, and was glad to have his opinion of me corrected."

Fausto's first meeting with Puccini went very well. When the regular conductor assigned to perform *The Girl of the Golden West* at Ravenna refused to conduct at the dress rehearsal, Puccini had him dismissed and took on young Fausto Cleva, who had come to him highly recommended. Puccini expressed the highest enthusiasm for Cleva's conducting both at the dress rehearsal and at the actual performance.

In 1920, when Cleva was eighteen, Gatti-Casazza, the general manager of the Metropolitan Opera, engaged him as assistant chorus master to Giulio Setti. Setti retired in 1935 and Cleva succeeded him. In 1938 Cleva became associate conductor in addition, conducting that season all of the Sunday evening concerts beginning with December 4, 1938. He continued conducting many of the Sunday evening concerts through the spring of 1942 and a performance of *The Barber of Seville* on February 14, 1942.

Cleva resigned from the Metropolitan Opera in 1942 to advance his career elsewhere. Having made his debut with the San Francisco Opera on

October 14, 1942, with *La Traviata,* and having directed other opera performances there in the years between 1942 and 1944, he returned to San Francisco on September 20, 1949, to conduct *Tosca.* He remained for seven seasons. In addition to conducting a wide repertory of French and Italian operas, he was able to make one of his rare excursions into the Wagnerian dramas with a performance of *Lohengrin* on October 14, 1955.

From 1944 to 1946 Cleva was the music director of the Chicago Opera. For more than two decades he was also the artistic director and principal conductor of the summer Cincinnati Zoo Opera, where he had given his first performance in 1934. In Cincinnati, in addition to the French-Italian repertory he was assigned some operas in the German repertory, among them *Salome, Der Rosenkavalier, Das Rheingold,* and *Don Giovanni.*

In 1950 Rudolf Bing, the new general manager of the Metropolitan Opera, called Cleva back to New York as principal conductor. On November 18, 1950, Cleva made his reappearance there with *Manon Lescaut.* During the next two decades he became an integral part of the conducting staff of the company, directing virtually all of the principal works in the French and Italian repertory. He opened the Metropolitan seasons in 1951 (*Aida*), 1954 (Act I, *Aida*), 1956 (*Norma*), 1959 (*Il Trovatore*), 1961 (*The Girl of the Golden West*), 1962 (*The Girl of the Golden West*), 1967 (*La Traviata*), and 1968 (*Adriana Lecouvreur*).

What Howard Taubman wrote in the New York *Times* concerning Cleva's performance of *Il Trovatore* on the opening night of the 1959–1960 season applies equally to his other performances: "Under Fausto Cleva's conducting, the performance moves crisply and cleanly. His tempos, which can be metronomic, have elasticity without loss of vitality. The orchestra and chorus sounded fresh."

The fiftieth anniversary of Cleva's affiliation with the Metropolitan Opera was celebrated on April 6, 1971. By that time he had conducted 657 performances of 27 operas at the Metropolitan Opera. Lowell Wadmond, chairman of the Metropolitan board, presented Cleva with a gold cigarette case on behalf of the directors, describing that day as "the golden anniversary of a marriage to the Metropolitan Opera." Vieri Traxier, consul general of Italy, conferred on

Cleva the rank of Grand Officer of the Order of Merit. Thirteen years earlier, in 1958, between the acts of a performance of *Manon Lescaut,* Cleva had received the Order of Merit of the Republic of Italy (which carries the title Commendatore).

In addition to his association with the Metropolitan Opera, Cleva made numerous guest appearances not only with opera companies but also with orchestras, both in the United States and abroad. For several seasons he appeared regularly with the Swedish Royal Opera, and in 1959 he conducted performances with that company at the Edinburgh Festival in Scotland. Among the major opera houses in which he appeared were the Vienna State Opera, the Monte Carlo Opera, and the Teatro Colón.

In 1971 he went to Athens to conduct the National Opera Company of Greece on August 6 in a performance of Gluck's *Orfeo ed Euridice* at the ancient theater of Herod Atticus. During the overture he suffered a heart attack and collapsed. He died at the Central Athens Hospital that evening, one hour after being admitted.

Cleva became an American citizen in 1931. That same year, on June 20, he married Irene Ghedini. They had two children. The family lived in an apartment at the Hotel Ansonia on upper Broadway in New York City; but in his last years Cleva also maintained an apartment in Milan. His hobbies were fishing and ship designing.

In 1944 Cleva received an honorary doctorate in music from the College of Music in Cincinnati. A bronze bust, the work of the Hungarian sculptor George Gach, was dedicated in the Founders Hall of the Metropolitan Opera on April 10, 1974.

ABOUT: New York Times, January 6, 1961.

Van Cliburn

1934–

Van Cliburn (originally Harvey Lavan Cliburn Jr.), pianist, was born in Shreveport, Louisiana, on July 12, 1934. From childhood on he was always called Van and that is the name he took formally. His father, Harvey Lavan Cliburn Sr., was an oil company executive. His mother, Rildia Bee O'Brian Cliburn, was a concert pian-

VAN CLIBURN

ist and piano teacher. Hearing her three-year-old son picking out on the piano the music of a composition one of her pupils had played that day, she decided to give him his first lessons. At four Van made his first public appearance, his mother assisting on a second piano. By the time he was five and enrolled for public school, though still unable to read or write, he was completely literate in music.

He was six when his family moved to Kilgore, Texas, where his father found employment in a petroleum factory. By now Van and the piano were inseparable, a fact that disturbed the father no end since he wanted his son to spend more time playing with friends. To lure the boy outdoors, the father gave him roller skates, a bicycle, and a football. The child ignored all these gifts. On one occasion, when the father was particularly insistent that the boy leave the piano keyboard for outdoor games, Van cried out: "Don't say such things! I'm going to be a concert pianist."

He was making such rapid progress under his mother's guidance that in the summer of 1947 she decided to take him to New York for further music instruction. He attended the summer session at the Juilliard School of Music for classes in harmony, sight-reading, musical dictation, and keyboard harmony, in all of which he was brilliant.

Back in Kilgore for the winter, Van attended Kilgore High School, where he was an excellent student in Latin. He played the clarinet in the school band, wrote editorials and poems for the school paper, and was president of the school's Thespian Society. He also gave performances on the piano throughout Texas. In 1947 he made his debut with the Houston Symphony Orchestra in the Tchaikovsky Piano Concerto No.1 which he had learned in twenty-one days, an appearance made possible through the winning of the Texas State Prize. As the Texas winner in an interstate competition conducted by the National Music Festival Award in 1948, he repeated his performance of this Tchaikovsky concerto in Carnegie Hall, New York, where he was given an ovation.

In the summer of 1948, returning to New York for additional study of the piano, he worked with Ernest Hutcheson for five lessons. When Van proved unresponsive to his teacher's methods, these lessons were dropped; for the time being he studied with his mother.

When he came once again to New York, in 1951, he found a teacher uniquely suited to his temperament and talent: Rosina Lhevinne. At first he studied with her privately, then, on a grant from the Olga Samaroff Foundation, he was her pupil at the Juilliard School of Music. In 1952 he was awarded a Chopin scholarship of one thousand dollars by the Kosciuszko Foundation of New York and also the G. B. Dealey Memorial Award, a cash prize of five hundred dollars and an appearance with the Dallas Symphony Orchestra in MacDowell's Piano Concerto in D minor. (This award was established by the late publisher of the Dallas *Morning News.*) At the Juilliard School he received first prize for his performance of the Tchaikovsky Piano Concerto No.1. On April 9, 1953, in Kilgore, Texas, he was honored with a Van Cliburn Day, at which time the community presented him with an award of six hundred dollars. And in 1954, upon his graduation from Juilliard with highest honors he was presented with the Roeder Award for "outstanding achievement" and the Frank Damrosch Scholarship for a year of graduate work. His concert commitments in 1955, however, made it impossible for him to do the graduate work.

In 1954 Cliburn captured the important Leventritt Award which entitled him to appear as a guest artist with several major American symphony orchestras. He performed the Tchaikovsky Piano Concerto No.1 on November 15, 1954, with the New York Philharmonic, Dimitri Mitropoulos conducting. "This is one of the most genuine and refreshing keyboard talents to come out of the West—or anywhere else—in a long time," said Louis Biancolli in the New York *World-Telegram.* "Van Cliburn is obviously going places, except that he plays like he had already been there."

Cliburn made his first appearance on television on Steve Allen's "Tonight Show" on January 19; 1955, performing Ravel's Toccata and a Chopin étude before an audience estimated at several million. Such was the impact of his playing that the telephone switchboard was overloaded with congratulatory telephone calls. Steve Allen immediately engaged him for a second appearance the following April.

During the 1954–1955 season, Cliburn embarked on his first concert tour of the United States, filling eighteen engagements. The following year he gave thirty concerts, but during 1957 –1958 he could command only twenty appearances. Arthur Judson, Cliburn's manager, and Rosina Lhevinne came to realize that Cliburn's career needed a "shot in the arm" if it were not to be seriously impaired. Thus a decision was reached to have him enter the Tchaikovsky Piano Competition being initiated in Moscow in 1958, in spite of the fact that it meant canceling his first European tour. Doubt was expressed that the Soviet Union would ever allow an American to win the first prize, but it was also felt that if Cliburn could make a good showing the attendant publicity would make him more of a box-office attraction than he had thus far been.

Financed by the Mary Baird Rockefeller Foundation and the Institute of International Education, Cliburn spent three months in intensive practice to prepare for the competition. In Moscow he was one of forty-eight contestants from nineteen different countries. By the time he reached the finals he had become the darling of Moscow through his stunning performances in the first and semifinal rounds. Six pianists survived into the finals, each required to play the Tchaikovsky Piano Concerto No.1, Rachmaninoff's Concerto No.3, and a piece by Kabalevsky written for this occasion. Cliburn was the first to be heard. After he finished his performance—and though the five others were still to be heard—a clamor arose in the auditorium: "First Prize! First Prize!" Even some of the jurors joined in the demonstration for Cliburn.

Cliburn was dining with some friends at the Hotel Peking in Moscow late Sunday evening of April 13 when he was brought the news that the sixteen jurors had unanimously selected him for the top award. He made a beeline for the telephone to put through a call to his mother in Texas, but by the time the wires were cleared his mother told him she had already received the news from a representative of the Columbia Broadcasting System. Upon the official announcement the next day there was pandemonium both in Kilgore, Texas, and in Moscow. In Texas, Cliburn's home was flooded with reporters and photographers trying to get whatever material was available on Cliburn. In Moscow, Cliburn was besieged by the world's press. In addition, he had to make appearances before the television cameras, to give a special concert on April 14 attended by Premier Khrushchev, Marshal Voroshilov, and Deputy Premier Mikoyan, and to attend a post-concert reception at the Kremlin. After the reception Cliburn gave concerts in Leningrad, Riga, Kiev, and Minsk and appeared on radio and television. He was also a guest of honor at performances of operas and ballets. Wherever he went he was showered with gifts of recordings, music, books, pictures, woodcuts, medallions, tea sets, samovars, caviar, and vodka.

Returning to the United States, Cliburn became the first musician to get a ticker-tape parade in New York City. He also received the Medallion of the City of New York and the Scroll of the City "for exceptional and distinguished services." Robert F. Wagner, mayor of New York, greeted Cliburn at an official welcome, saying: "The impact of Van Cliburn's triumph in the Moscow International Competition goes far beyond music and himself as an individual and is a dramatic testimonial to American culture. . . . With his two hands Van Cliburn struck a chord which has resounded around the world, raising our prestige with artists and music lovers everywhere." At a dinner at the Waldorf Astoria Hotel Cliburn received further tributes from the elite of the musical, political, and social world. A White House meeting with President Eisenhower was arranged. Then Cliburn's first post-Russian concert was given at Carnegie Hall on May 19, 1958, drawing the largest box-office sale in the history of that auditorium up to that time. (Speculators charged as much as one hundred dollars for a pair of tickets.) Cliburn's program was made up of the two works with which he had won the competition in Moscow, concertos by Tchaikovsky and Rachmaninoff. The conductor, Kirill P. Kondrashin, had also accompanied Cliburn's performance in Moscow. "Both those who have backed him in this country and the Russians were right," wrote Ross Parmenter in the New York *Times.* "He is a major talent. . . . One was struck by the prevailing beauty of his tone, no matter how massive were the sonorities. . . . The shading was subtle and the melody was sung with lyrical sweetness."

Winning the Tchaikovsky competition in Moscow transformed Cliburn from a young artist struggling to get engagements into one of the greatest box-office attractions the concert world has known. For 1958–1959 Cliburn was getting more engagements than he could handle, and receiving between twenty-five hundred and four thousand dollars for each appearance. Recalled to the Steve Allen "Tonight Show" he was given a fee of three thousand dollars to play a few numbers, whereas in his first appearance he had been paid only seventy-five dollars. Ed Murrow invited him to appear on his "Person to Person" program over the CBS television network on May 30, 1958. RCA Victor signed him to a recording contract; his first release, the Tchaikovsky Piano Concerto No.1, sold over a million albums. His recording of Rachmaninoff's Piano Concerto No.3 brought him a Grammy from the National Academy of Recording Arts and Sciences in 1959.

He met the challenges of his newlywon fame and fortune with performances that placed him among the great piano virtuosos of the time. Endowed with a prodigious technique, his two massive hands could draw from the keyboard whispered confidences or orchestral sonorities. He brought to his music making a penetrating musical intelligence and an immaculate taste; he was a pianist in the grand manner. "There is a sweep and impetuosity to his interpretations," said Irving Lowens in the Washington, D.C., *Evening Star,* "that bring to mind such great figures as Liszt and Rachmaninoff."

His brilliant career was seriously threatened in February 1959 when a thumb infection necessitated a delicate operation involving diagonal incision and the scraping of the bone. Cliburn was compelled to cancel all performances for the next six months. But in spite of prevailing fears his recovery proved complete and he was able to resume his career.

Cliburn returned to the Soviet Union for the first time since winning the Tchaikovsky award in 1960. He was sponsored by the United States Department of State as part of a cultural exchange program. Massive crowds taxed the capacities of auditoriums in Moscow, Leningrad, Kiev, Baku, and other cities. At his final performance, at the Sports Palace in Moscow, twenty thousand were in the audience, with many more thousands unable to gain admission. At the close of that concert the audience went into such a frenzy of approval that ushers had to rush to the stage to protect Cliburn from crowds trying to throw flowers and gifts at him.

In the 1960s Cliburn branched out into conducting, first by leading individual numbers with various American orchestras. Then, on July 18, 1964, he led a full concert at the Lewisohn Stadium in New York, filling the dual role of conductor and pianist in Rachmaninoff's Third Piano Concerto. "He maneuvered the orchestra securely through the score's occasional rhythmic complexities, and at one time he did try to whip up the music simply for effect," said Raymond Ericson in the New York *Times*. "Given further experience and better acoustical conditions, Mr. Cliburn might easily become a persuasive interpreter of the orchestral repertory congenial to him."

But it is as a pianist and not as a conductor that Cliburn has continued to make his mark in the world of music. He makes some sixty appearances during the year in all parts of the music world and is among the highest paid concert performers of our time. Though his income averages several hundred thousand dollars a year, he has simple, sometimes even Spartan, habits. He maintains a modest apartment near Carnegie Hall and an equally unpretentious house in Kilgore. A man of deep religious convictions, he turns over a percentage of his earnings each year to the Baptist Church. Those religious beliefs keep him from smoking or drinking alcohol. His pastimes are reading and engaging people he admires in stimulating conversation.

In 1962 a piano competition was organized in Fort Worth, Texas, and named in his honor: the Van Cliburn International Piano Competition.

ABOUT: Chasins, A. and Stiles, V. The Van Cliburn Legend; Ewen, D. Famous Instrumentalists. *Periodicals*—Redbook, January 1962; Time, May 19, 1958, August 11, 1962, November 22, 1968.

André Cluytens

1905–1967

André Cluytens, conductor, was born in Antwerp, Belgium, on March 26, 1905, to Alphonse and Philomène Van Cauteren Cluytens. His father was the conductor of the Théâtre Royal in Antwerp. André entered the Royal Flemish Conservatory of Antwerp when he was nine to be trained as a pianist. In 1921 he received first prize in piano playing and in 1922 first prizes in harmony and counterpoint as well. Following his graduation from the Conservatory, André concertized as a pianist. In 1922 his father persuaded him to join the Théâtre Royal as coach. In addition to coaching singers and the chorus, Cluytens was a general handyman backstage. Five years of such duties provided him with the knowledge of operas and opera performances that would serve him so well when he began an active career as conductor.

He was twenty-one when the conductor for Bizet's *The Pearl Fishers* became unavailable and Cluytens substituted for him. He performed so competently that other operas were assigned to him, and in time he succeeded his father as principal conductor.

In 1932 Cluytens settled in France and became a French citizen. His first French job was as music director of the Toulouse Opera from which he progressed to the post of music director of the Lyons Opera in 1935 and the Bordeaux Opera in 1938. In 1941 in Paris he led an orchestral concert with the orchestra of the Paris Opéra, in 1944 he became one of the conductors of the Paris Opéra, and in 1947 he was appointed music director of the Opéra-Comique. In 1949 he succeeded Charles Munch as principal conductor of the Paris Conservatory Orchestra, of which he was ultimately named vice president. Subsequently Cluytens assumed the post of principal conductor of the Orchestre Nationale de France.

When the Paris Opéra celebrated the one-

Cluytens: kloi′ těn

ANDRÉ CLUYTENS

hundred-fiftieth anniversary of Berlioz' birth in 1953, Cluytens led a program of Berlioz' music that attracted national attention. One year later he enjoyed another success, at the Aix-en-Provence festival in a revival of Gounod's *Mireille*. In 1955, when Igor Markevitch was unable to conduct at the Bayreuth Festival, Cluytens was called in as his replacement, for a performance of *Tannhäuser*. As a result he was recalled to the Bayreuth Festival for other performances—*Die Meistersinger* in 1956, *Lohengrin* in 1958—becoming the first Frenchman to conduct there.

Guest appearances with the Vienna Philharmonic and the Berlin Philharmonic added further to his European reputation. In 1956 he was one of two conductors (the other was Carl Schuricht) leading the Vienna Philharmonic on its first tour of the United States. He conducted ten concerts, the first of which—on November 4, 1956, in Washington, D.C.—marked his American debut. One month later, on December 7, he took the Vienna Philharmonic to New York for his debut there in a program made up of German masterworks by Haydn, Richard Strauss, and Brahms. "Let there be no mistake about Monsieur Cluytens' technical proficiency," reported Howard Taubman in the New York *Times*. "He knows his job as a conductor. Granted that the Vienna Philharmonic is as responsive an ensemble as a conductor could encounter; the fact remains that Monsieur Cluytens had everything in hand at all times. His beat and control were sure, and he knew precisely what he wanted and how to get it from his players."

One year later, on November 7, 1957, Cluytens started a four-week engagement as guest conductor of the New York Philharmonic Orchestra. His performance of Brahms's Fourth Symphony, Taubman wrote, had "unquestionably exciting moments" but lacked "great, sustained heartbeat." Taubman found him at his best in a performance of Honegger's Symphony No.2. "Whether or not Mr. Cluytens wins everyone's suffrage, he helps to vitalize the Philharmonic's proceedings by giving them a touch of the unexpected and the unpredictable."

In 1963, after an absence of several years from the Paris Opéra, Cluytens returned to conduct memorable performances of *Tannhäuser*. In April 1967 he was engaged by the Metropolitan Opera to conduct *The Flying Dutchman* the following season, but he did not live to fill that assignment. A victim of cancer, he died in the American Hospital in Paris on June 3, 1967.

André Cluytens married Germaine Gilson on January 4, 1927. With their son, Michele, they lived in a house on the avenue Général de Gaulle, in Montmorency, Seine-et-Oise, France. His favorite exercise and diversion was swimming.

ABOUT: Gavotty, B. André Cluytens. *Periodicals* —New York Times, November 10, 1957.

Albert Coates

1882–1953

Albert Coates, conductor, was born in St. Petersburg, on April 23, 1882. His father, Charles Thomas Coates, was of English birth; he had settled in Russia and had become director of the Thornton Woollen Mills in St. Petersburg. There he married Mary Ann Gibson, whose parentage was Russian and English. Albert was the youngest of seven sons.

As a boy, Albert studied the violin, piano, and cello, and became a pupil in composition of Rimsky-Korsakov at the St. Petersburg Conservatory. "One of my earliest memories," he once recalled, "is of going to a Russian party. We were playing Russian games when suddenly I began to feel tired and bored. I hid myself in a small room where there was a piano, upon which I began to play, improvising a tune. I hardly started when the door opened and a middle-aged

Coates

ALBERT COATES

gentleman entered and asked me what I was playing. I told him I was making it up, whereupon the strange gentleman crossed the room, sat down beside me and encouraged me to continue. I did so, while he listened attentively. After he went out I asked my mother who he was. 'Why,' she said, 'that is the great composer, Tchaikovsky.' "

Five years later Albert demonstrated his admiration and respect for Tchaikovsky by tramping through the snow on foot five miles to attend the composer's funeral.

When he was fourteen, Albert was sent to a school in Buckhurst Hill, Essex, for an English education. During his one year there he was influenced by the music master, Henry Riding, who encouraged young Coates to compose.

After Buckhurst Hill, Albert went to a private school in Liverpool where his older brother was an organist. For a time he studied the organ, harmony, and composition with his brother. The sudden death of this older brother, who was only twenty, was such a blow that Albert decided to abandon music. He began studying with Sir Oliver Lodge at the University of Liverpool with the intention of becoming an industrial chemist.

Upon reaching his twentieth birthday, Coates returned to St. Petersburg to discuss his future with his father. He learned that his deceased brother had left a will urging Albert to devote himself to music. Stimulated and encouraged by this plea, and with his father's blessing, Coates went on to the Leipzig Conservatory in 1902 to study the cello with Julius Klengel and piano

with Robert Teichmüller. He made such excellent progress on the cello that he was engaged to play with the Gewandhaus Orchestra.

When Arthur Nikisch became music director of the Gewandhaus Orchestra, the Leipzig Opera, and the Conservatory, Coates concentrated on the study of conducting with Nikisch, whose dynamic personality and trenchant musicianship first ignited Coates's ambition to become a conductor.

After one year of study with Nikisch, Coates became Nikisch's assistant at the Leipzig Opera. One evening Nikisch was called to Berlin. The scheduled performance of *The Tales of Hoffmann* was taken over by Coates who demonstrated a talent for the baton. He was soon given several other opportunities to conduct operas.

In 1906, on Nikisch's recommendation, Coates was appointed principal conductor of the Elberfeld Opera. This valuable apprenticeship for a young conductor involved conducting over forty operas, particularly those of the German school of Wagner, Weber, Beethoven, Mozart, and Richard Strauss. From Elberfeld he went to Dresden in 1910 to share the chief conductor's post at the Opera there with Ernst von Schuch. Both in Dresden and at his next stepping-off place—the Mannheim Opera where he shared the conductor's post with Artur Bodanzky—Coates remained only for a short period.

In 1914 Coates gave a guest performance of *Siegfried* in St. Petersburg that was so successful that he was given a five-year contract with the Imperial Opera. In Russia, he enlarged his repertory with the works of leading Russian composers and subsequently became recognized as an authoritative interpreter of Russian works. He also came to know Scriabin well, both as a man and as a musician. Scriabin's music made a powerful impact on the young conductor. During his long residence in Russia Coates gained the unusual distinction of becoming one of the few foreign musicians able to retain success in both the Czarist and the Communist governments. He maintained cordial relations first with Czar Nicholas and later with Joseph Stalin. During the Czarist regime Coates held the title of the Czar's Opera Conductor; after the Bolshevik revolution he was elected president of the Petrograd Theatre Artists.

He made his conducting debut in London at Covent Garden in 1913 when he successfully shared the Wagnerian repertory with Arthur

Nikisch. In 1919 Sir Thomas Beecham engaged Coates as conductor and co-artistic director at Covent Garden. In addition to these duties, Coates assumed the direction of the London Symphony Orchestra. He also appeared frequently as a guest conductor of the Royal Philharmonic and led the major part of the festivals at Leeds in 1922 and 1925.

His successes in Russia and England brought him invitations for guest appearances throughout Europe; he became the first British conductor to direct opera performances in Italy and at the Paris Opéra. On December 20, 1920, he made his American debut with the New York Symphony Society. He returned for additional guest performances with this orchestra in 1921, 1922, and 1923. "He is a vigorous leader with force and authority," wrote one New York critic. "His conducting has its individual characteristics to the eye: he uses no baton but conveys his message to the players with varied, often emphatic, sometimes unusual arm gestures."

In 1923 Coates was appointed principal conductor of the newly organized Rochester (New York) Philharmonic Orchestra. While retaining this post through 1925, he also held classes in conducting at the Eastman School of Music in Rochester.

In the years between 1927 and 1929 Coates appeared as conductor in important performances at the Augusteo in Rome, La Scala in Milan, the Teatro Verdi in Trieste, and the San Carlo in Naples. During these years he was heard for five consecutive winters in a two-month season of operas in Barcelona, and in guest performances in Paris, Rotterdam, Vienna, and Stockholm.

Coates returned to the Soviet Union in June 1932 to direct operas and concerts in Moscow and Leningrad. At that time he was named music director of the leading opera houses in both cities and general music director of the United Philharmonic Orchestras of the Soviet Union. He returned to England to direct the British Opera season at Covent Garden in 1936. In 1939 he led a series of orchestral concerts at the Hollywood Bowl in Los Angeles. One year later he was appointed principal conductor of the newly formed Southern California Opera Company, which presented operas in English in Los Angeles.

Coates married twice. His first wife was Madelon Holland. They had a daughter. His second wife was Vera Joanna Netford. In 1946 he settled with her in South Africa, conducting the Johannesburg Symphony and teaching at the University of South Africa at Cape Town. In February 1953 he suffered a stroke and on December 11, 1953, he died in Milnerton, near Cape Town.

Eva Mary Grew wrote about Coates's conducting: "When he is taking an orchestra into the heart of a piece, every moment of the task is full of life and interest. To see him standing at his desk, coatless, collarless, putting every ounce of physical and mental energy into the labor of instruction—though always without extravagance—is to be stimulated to an intense degree and made aware of the technical and calisthenic qualities of force and magnetism with which a conductor of modern works has to suffuse a body of executants."

Coates's greatest interest outside conducting was to compose music. He did most of his composing at his villa on Lake Maggiore in northern Italy during vacations. He was also interested in reading, swimming, and going to the theater. He was a personal friend of George Bernard Shaw, and he considered *Back to Methuselah* one of the greatest dramas of the twentieth century. On several occasions Coates tried his hand at writing plays but with no appreciable results. Among his musical compositions are several operas, the best known of which are *Samuel Pepys,* first produced in Munich on December 21, 1929, and *Pickwick,* introduced at Covent Garden on November 20, 1936.

Coates arranged and directed the music for several Hollywood motion pictures including *Song of Russia* (1943) and *Two Girls and a Sailor* (1944).

ABOUT: Musical America, January 1, 1954.

John Coates

1865–1941

John Coates, tenor, was one of the great English-born singers in opera, oratorio, and concert in the twentieth century. He was born in Girlington, Yorkshire, England, on June 29, 1865, to Richard and Elizabeth Coates. The family was well known in Yorkshire music circles. His father was the choirmaster of the Girlington

JOHN COATES

Church, and his uncle, J. G. Walton, was the vocal teacher who gave him his first music lessons. From childhood John followed the singing tradition of his family, joining his father's choir when he was five and becoming at seven a member of the choir of St. Jude's in Bradford. There he was soon made principal soprano.

John's schooling at the Bradford Grammar School was abandoned when the boy was thirteen. The death of his father made it essential for John to begin earning a living. He found a job as an office boy in a warehouse and later worked first as a bookkeeper and then as a foreign representative for a commercial firm. Determined to become a concert singer, he studied voice with R. S. Burton and J. C. Bridge and spent nights studying foreign languages.

He made his first public appearance in the baritone role of Valentin in *Faust* with the Carl Rosa Company, in Manchester and Liverpool. In 1893 he went to London to join the D'Oyly Carte company as a baritone. He first appeared with that company in 1894 at the Savoy Theatre in *Utopia Limited* by Gilbert and Sullivan, with which he also toured the United States. Coates remained with the D'Oyly Carte troupe five years, appearing in the baritone roles of the Gilbert and Sullivan repertory throughout the United Kingdom and on tour in the United States.

Convinced that he was a tenor and not a baritone, Coates began retraining his voice. When he returned in 1899 to comic opera he began singing tenor roles. In November 1899 he appeared in *Absent-Minded Beggar,* and in 1900 he en-

joyed success in London in *The Gay Pretenders.*

After singing in Germany in 1901 at the Gürzenich concerts in Cologne, Coates graduated from comic opera to grand opera. He made his debut at Covent Garden in London on May 30, 1901, in the world premiere of *Much Ado About Nothing* by Charles Stanford, creating the principal tenor role of Claudio. That year he was also heard both at Covent Garden and at the Cologne Opera in the title roles of *Faust, Lohengrin,* and *Romeo and Juliet.* In 1902 he appeared in leading tenor roles with the Berlin Royal Opera and the Hanover Opera.

His fame as a singer of oratorios was first established in 1902 at the Worcester Festival in England where he was heard in Elgar's *The Dream of Gerontius.* At Elgar's request, Coates went to the United States in 1906 to sing in the oratorio at the Cincinnati Festival. In 1903 and again in 1906 Coates repeated his earlier successes with Elgar's music with appearances in *The Apostles* and *The Kingdom* at the Birmingham Festival.

Feeling the need of further training, Coates studied voice in Paris with Jacques Bouhy. This training completed, Coates was heard in opera, oratorio, and concerts throughout Germany and in Paris. From 1907 to 1909 he appeared in the Wagnerian repertory with the Moody-Manners Company. He returned to the Carl Rosa Company in 1909 and was heard in the premiere in England of Ethel Smyth's *The Wreckers* on June 22, 1909. He performed in the Wagnerian repertory during Thomas Beecham's winter season at Covent Garden in London in 1910, and in the years between 1911 and 1913 he toured in Wagner's music dramas as Siegfried with the Quinlan Opera Company in the United Kingdom, South Africa, and Australia.

"He appeals to your poetized intellectuality," wrote the English musicologist Sydney Grew, "and as a result you react both spiritually and sensuously. For there is ample pure beauty in his singing."

During World War I Coates ignored the fact that his age exempted him from military duty. He joined the National Reserve, received a commission in 1915, and for one year saw service on the fighting front in France with the Yorkshire Regiment. Demobilized with the rank of captain, Coates returned to his professional singing career in March 1919.

Except for occasional appearances as Don

José in *Carmen* and as Lohengrin with the Carl Rosa Opera Company he concentrated on song recitals, a field in which he was noted for the sensitivity and subtlety of his musical perception and the elegance of his singing style. He gave his first recitals at the Town Hall in Chelsea and in the period between 1920 and 1924 toured the English provinces. In April and May 1925 he gave his first recitals in the United States, returning for a second tour from January to March 1926. As a concert artist he specialized in English music of the Elizabethan and Tudor period, but he also paid considerable attention to the songs of twentieth century English composers. In May 1928 he celebrated the fiftieth anniversary of his first singing appearance, and in 1935, at the age of seventy, he became a favorite over the English radio, accompanying himself on the piano in song recitals.

Coates's permanent home was The Coterie, in Northwood, Middlesex, and it was there that he died on August 16, 1941.

ABOUT: Kutsch, K. J. and Riemens, L. A Concise Biographical Dictionary of Singers.

Harriet Cohen

1895–1967

Harriet Cohen, pianist, was born in London on December 2, 1895. Both her parents were musicians. Her father, Joseph Verney-Cohen, was a successful composer of orchestral and military music and her mother, Florence White Cohen, was an accomplished pianist. "One of my first recollections," Harriet Cohen once recalled, "is that of playing on Paderewski's knee in the artist's room of the Queen's Hall at the age of six."

Harriet took her first piano lessons from her mother. When she was thirteen she made her debut as pianist at a Chappell Sunday Evening Concert in Queen's Hall in London. From 1912 to 1917 she attended the Royal Academy of Music on a scholarship, a pupil of Tobias Matthay. In 1920 she appeared at Wigmore Hall in a joint concert with the tenor John Coates, after which she undertook tours that carried her throughout Europe. In 1922 she was appointed professor of the piano at the Royal Academy of Music. In 1924 she represented England at the International Festival of Modern Music at Salzburg.

HARRIET COHEN

She became famous in the 1920s for her researches into and performances of English keyboard music of the sixteenth and seventeenth centuries. She also became a specialist in the keyboard music of Bach. In 1925 she gave the first all-Bach program ever given at Queen's Hall, with Sir Henry J. Wood conducting. She was then heard in all-Bach programs in Barcelona in 1926 (with Pablo Casals conducting) and in London in 1929.

Her American debut took place at the Elizabeth Sprague Coolidge Festival in Chicago in October 1930. From that time on her concert appearances were worldwide, some of them of historic interest. In the 1930s the English composers Arnold Bax and Ralph Vaughan Williams presented her with a gold chain from which were suspended leaf-shaped pendants, each one representing one of her outstanding artistic achievements. These pendants commemorated her performances in 1924 in Salzburg and in 1932 at the Disarmament Conference in Geneva at the invitation of the British government, a broadcast in the Soviet Union during which she performed modern Russian compositions, her introduction to Vienna of Manuel de Falla's *Nights in the Gardens of Spain* with the Vienna Philharmonic, her broadcast in London with a jazz band during which she performed two works of Bach, and her first appearance with the Boston Symphony Orchestra.

The chain with its pendants is only a partial representation of Harriet Cohen's unique role in

English music. She was chosen to represent the British Commonwealth not only at Salzburg and Geneva but also at Strasbourg, Frankfurt-Homburg, Cheltenham, Chicago, and Washington, D.C. The outstanding composers of England composed major works for her. In 1920 in London she performed the world premiere of Arnold Bax's *Symphonic Variations;* on February 1, 1933, she presented in London the first performance anywhere of Vaughan Williams's Piano Concerto; and on July 3, 1950, she was heard at the Cheltenham Festival in the premiere of Arnold Bax's *Concertante for Left Hand and Orchestra.*

At her concerts she offered the English premieres of works by Manuel de Falla, Ernest Bloch, Sibelius, Schoenberg, Pizzetti, Ravel, Kodály, and Turina, among other twentieth century composers. To American audiences she introduced concertos by Arnold Bax, Vaughan Williams, and William Walton. She performed at the Paris Exposition of 1931 and she was invited by the Bach Gesellschaft to give a concert at Bach's birthplace, Eisenach.

Maurice Imbert, French critic, wrote of her performances: "Her playing is clear, well shaped and very varied. She has a subtle touch and a strong sense of rhythm. She plays with sympathy, yet expresses herself with authority. The delicacy, grace, playfulness and tenderness of her interpretations, which are, at the same time, of a most expressive power, full of animation, of fire, of color, prove the extent of her intelligence and convince one that she has cultivated the spirit. Everything has a personal accent."

In addition to her numerous appearances as a solo pianist in the United States, Europe, the Soviet Union, and Palestine, she joined Joseph Szigeti, violinist, and Lionel Tertis, violist, in sonata recitals and collaborated with many distinguished chamber-music groups.

For her services to British music, Harriet Cohen received from King George VI the decoration of Commander of the British Empire in 1938. Several years later the Queen of Spain presented her with a brooch of diamonds and crystals. In February 1947 she was honored by President Beneš of Czechoslovakia with the Order of White Lion (First Class), and by the Prince of Belgium with the Order of the Commander of the Crown of Belgium. After 1950 Cohen continued to amass honors and decorations: Officier d'Académie Française in 1950;

Freedom of the City of London in 1954; Cavalier of Order of Southern Cross of Brazil in 1954; Stella della Solidarietà Italiana in 1955; the medal of the Sibelius academy in 1955; Order of the Lion of Finland (the Finlandia Medal) in 1958; Lazo de Dama de la Orden Merito of Spain in 1959; and the Otto Anderson Medal of Abö Akademi of Finland in 1959.

During World War II Cohen performed in army camps, service clubs, at docks, and on troop ships. On three occasions she was hospitalized for wounds sustained during the Nazi air raids on London.

After an absence of eight years Cohen returned to the United States on February 6, 1948, appearing with the CBS Orchestra, Alfredo Antonini conducting, in a performance of Bach's Concerto in D minor over the CBS radio network. Of this and subsequent performances in the United States, Noel Straus reported in the New York *Times* that "despite the sufferings she had endured during her absence" she had retained "the same fresh, spontaneous approach to her art as of old. All of her performances were to be admired for the keen intelligence and serious musicianship that back them. They were alike remarkable for their rhythmic incisiveness, their cleanness, clarity, and precision."

Soon after her return to England from this American tour she fell in her London home while carrying a tray of glasses into the kitchen. The broken glass damaged an artery and the nerves of her right wrist; the injury caused her hand to wither. The prognosis was that never again would she be able to perform as a pianist. But two years later she made a dramatic comeback with her premiere of Arnold Bax's *Concertante for Left Hand and Orchestra* at the Cheltenham Festival. Bax had originally planned writing for Harriet Cohen a concerto for both hands but, in a concession to her infirmity, rewrote it for left hand alone.

In another two years Cohen was able to perform with both hands and presented a Handel concerto at the Town Hall in Chelsea. At that time the London critics agreed that her formerly damaged hand had lost none of its technical dexterity.

Cohen continued to concertize until 1960. Then eye trouble, followed by two operations, compelled her to abandon concert work for good. For a few years she devoted herself to lecturing about music. She died in London on November 13, 1967.

Cohen, who never married, lived at Gloucester Place Mews in London. When she sought diversion she often went to dances, but otherwise her life was preoccupied with her musical activities. She always maintained that music was far too absorbing and demanding a taskmaster to permit her many outside interests. She used to practice eight hours a day; her eye trouble in 1960 was ascribed to the strain sustained from her rigorous practice sessions. Her one hobby was to collect snuffboxes of all shapes and sizes.

Her friends included some of the intellectual and musical notables of the world. She often played the music of Bach privately for Albert Einstein, whose violin playing she accompanied on the piano in 1934 at a London concert for the benefit of German scientists seeking refuge from Nazi Germany. One of her prized possessions was a visitors' book whose signatures represented a Who's Who of celebrities. One of the inscriptions she cherished was a few bars from the *Rhapsody in Blue* penned by George Gershwin.

Harriet Cohen made arrangements for the piano of several of Bach's organ choral preludes. She was also the author of a book about piano playing—*Music's Handmaid* (1936)—and an autobiography, *A Bundle of Time,* published posthumously in London in 1967.

ABOUT: Cohen, H. A Bundle of Time.

Sergiu Comissiona

1928–

Sergiu Comissiona, conductor, was born in Bucharest, on June 16, 1928, to Jean L. and Jeanne Haufrecht Comissiona. His father was a chemical manufacturer who lost his factory and all his assets when the Communist regime came to power. Before that happened Sergiu was raised in a household that knew economic comfort. His interest in music was first awakened when he was four by the musical sounds produced outside his house by a gypsy band. "I followed them fascinated through the streets of Bucharest until I was lost," he recalls. When he was finally found and brought home he asked for and got a violin. Lessons were begun at the same time. Later he studied violin, theory, composition,

SERGIU COMISSIONA

and chamber music at the Bucharest Conservatory where he also received training in conducting from Constantin Silvestri and Edouard Lindenberg. He was graduated from the conservatory in 1947. One year earlier he played the violin with the Bucharest Radio Quartet and made his conducting debut at a symphony concert by the Bucharest Opera Orchestra.

When he was nineteen he found a permanent job as second violinist with the Romanian State Ensemble. This group included an orchestra, a chorus, and a ballet company. Looking up from the orchestra pit to the stage at one of the ballet performances, he was entranced by a young ballerina, Robinne Feldsten. "This is the girl I am going to marry," he told himself at the time. They were married on July 16, 1949.

He had been in the second violin section of the Ensemble only a short time when one of the conductors was too ill to show up for an afternoon performance and Comissiona was recruited to conduct. In 1948 he was lifted out of the orchestra pit to serve as assistant conductor, and in 1950 he was promoted to music director.

From 1955 to 1959 Comissiona was principal conductor of the Romanian State Opera. In 1956 he received second prize in an international competition for young conductors held in Besançon, France. In addition to his duties at the opera house, he was often called upon to direct the Bucharest Philharmonic Orchestra on its tours outside Romania.

He was not happy in Romania. As he told Raymond Ericson in an interview in the New

Comissiona

York *Times:* "I felt like a puppet. One night, after a performance of Enesco's *Oedipus* at the Opera, I thought about the other Jewish people flocking to Israel, and I applied for plane tickets for myself and my wife. The next day I was out of a job. It was eight or nine months before we got our papers and could start on my second life." During those trying months Comissiona had to sell practically everything he owned to stay alive—his piano, his violin, even his dress suit.

With the visas finally in hand, Sergiu and Robinne Comissiona emigrated to Israel in 1959 to find a new homeland as Israeli citizens and to enter upon a new life. "There was no red carpet out when we arrived, of course," he recalls, "and I had to pantomime to the immigration authorities what a conductor was." Robinne was the first to find a job, as a member of the ballet corps of the Tel Aviv Opera. Comissiona's first assignment in Israel was to serve as his wife's accompanist in a village performance.

His conducting career in Israel began when he substituted for an indisposed conductor at a concert of the Haifa Symphony. His performance brought him an appointment as permanent conductor and musical director of that organization. He soon became a favorite with the music-loving people of Haifa, and particularly with its young. As the Israeli writer Moshe Niv described in an article entitled *On Bread and Music in Haifa:* "Churchill Hall quickly fills with young people when they see Comissiona approaching; everyone in Haifa knows Comissiona. He leads his young and admiring musicians with his indefatigable ardor, sincere enthusiasm and profound knowledge, and as a result of Comissiona's great experience and determined dedication, he has raised the high artistic and cultural level of the orchestra and it is not surprising that he is regarded as one of Haifa's most important citizens."

In 1960 Comissiona organized and became the musical director of the Ramat Gan Chamber Orchestra with which he gave performances not only in Israel but throughout Europe on two tours and in 1963 in the United States. In 1961 he made the first of many appearances with the Israel Philharmonic, with which he directed a series of fifteen concerts in 1971.

His success outside Israel began in 1960 with guest appearances with the London Philharmonic Orchestra in England. In 1961 he made his bow in Germany with the NDR Hamburg Orchestra. In 1962 he was heard for the first time in Spain with the National Orchestra of Madrid, in Belgium with the Radio Orchestra of Brussels, and in Portugal with the National Orchestra of Lisbon; he also returned that year to England to head the Covent Garden Orchestra and the Bournemouth Symphony. He expanded his European reputation in 1964 with performances with the London Symphony, the Royal Philharmonic in London, the Scarlatti Orchestra in Naples, the Stockholm Philharmonic in Sweden, and the Barcelona Municipal Orchestra in Spain. In 1966 Comissiona was appointed musical director of the Göteborg Symphony Orchestra in Sweden where he remained four years. He then became its musical adviser. Göteborg honored him in 1970 with its award for the person who contributed most to the raising of the city's cultural standards and in 1973 with its gold medal; he was the first non-Swede to be so honored. While serving in Göteborg, Comissiona was made music adviser and conductor of the Northern Ireland Orchestra, and he toured Europe with the Residentie Orchestra of The Hague.

He gave his first performances with an American orchestra in 1964 when he appeared with the Toledo Symphony in Ohio. This engagement was followed in 1965 by his debut with the Philadelphia Orchestra. In the years between 1967 and 1969 he made guest appearances with the Denver Symphony, the Detroit Symphony, and the Baltimore Symphony Orchestra, which, in 1969, appointed him its music director.

A fiery personality, Comissiona continually charges his performances with drama and electricity. He brought to Baltimore excitement and adventure not only through his stimulating interpretations but also through his progressive programming which included much unfamiliar and much twentieth century music. He also went a long way in developing the technical virtuosity of the orchestra. In addition he extended the orchestra's repertory. In his first eight years he added almost two hundred works to the concert programs of the Baltimore Symphony, including sixty compositions by Americans. Among the latter were works commissioned by the orchestra from Lukas Foss, Elie Siegmeister, George Rochberg, Roger Sessions, and Gunther Schuller. "While any orchestra usually responds noticeably to the fresh approach of a new conductor," commented the Baltimore *Evening Sun* editorially in 1970, "the response of the Baltimore Symphony to Mr. Comissiona's leadership has been nothing short of dramatic—and not just during the initial honeymoon period. The improvement has been consistent and continuing. New musicians have been brought in to strengthen previously weak sections. The programming has been imaginative and modern. The orchestra has moved within striking distance of becoming one of the first-rank musical organizations in the country."

He has also been praised by critics outside Baltimore. After a performance of Tchaikovsky's Fifth Symphony with the New York Philharmonic Orchestra on January 10, 1975, Robert Sherman reported in the New York *Times:* "Mr. Comissiona's approach to the E minor Symphony ... highlighted the intensity and dramatic contrasts of the score, and the Philharmonic musicians responded magnificently to his search for subtleties of sonic balance within a firmly projected rhythmic framework." After one of his concerts in Brussels early in 1975, the critic of *Libre Belge* remarked: "Sergiu Comissiona is a personality musically alive and interesting. Mindful of contrasts, attentive to tone color, he transmits a rich and enthusiastic nature and a great sense of the dramatic."

Comissiona conducts about one hundred and twenty-five concerts a year in America, Europe, Israel and elsewhere. In August 1977 he directed performances of Piccini's rarely heard eighteenth century opera, *La Buona Figliuola,* at the Drottningholm Theater in Sweden and on October 16, 1977, he made his debut with the New York City Opera in *The Girl of the Golden West* which was being produced by that company for the first time. To fulfill his commitments abroad he crosses the Atlantic Ocean about a dozen times a year. His numerous engagements abroad make it necessary for him to maintain residences in Sweden and England as well as in Baltimore. When not involved in making music, Comissiona relaxes by swimming, walking, looking at paintings, and conversing with congenial friends.

In 1976 Comissiona was named music director of the Chautauqua Symphony in New York and music adviser to the Temple University Music Festival in Philadelphia; a year later he became the festival's artistic director. This was in addition to his duties with the Baltimore Symphony.

Comissiona received an honorary doctorate in music from Peabody Conservatory in 1972 and a doctorate of Humane Letters from Loyola College in Baltimore in 1973. His native country, Romania, has forgiven him his defection, and in 1969 the Romanian cultural attaché warmly congratulated him after one of his concerts in Baltimore and attended a reception in his honor. Subsequently, the Romanian government despatched a television team to Baltimore to interview Comissiona for a television show in Romania describing aspects of life in America.

Comissiona and his wife became American citizens on July 4, 1976.

ABOUT: Baltimore Sunday Sun, April 26, 1970; High Fidelity, May 1977; New York Times, March 15, 1970.

Franco Corelli

1923–

Franco Corelli, tenor, was born in Ancona, on the Adriatic coast of Italy, on April 8, 1923. He was one of four children. His father worked as a shipbuilder for the Italian navy. The Italian tradition of having the son follow in his father's profession, and Franco's own love for the sea, induced him to study naval engineering at the University of Bologna. There was no musical heritage in the Corelli family. Until he was twenty-three Franco gave no thought to a singing career, though he had always possessed an appealing voice and singing had always been a favorite pastime.

One of his friends, a musical amateur, encouraged him to study voice. In 1947 Corelli entered the Pesaro Conservatory of Music where the incompetent instruction impaired the top register of his tenor voice. He stopped these lessons abruptly, then for the next five months tried curing himself by inhaling sulphur and taking health cures. After that, for about a month, he attempted to develop himself as a baritone, was dissatisfied with the results, and decided to forget all about singing. Suddenly his top notes returned.

One day in 1952 he went to Florence with a friend who was auditioning in an amateur sing-

FRANCO CORELLI

ing contest. As a prank the friend also entered Corelli's name. Corelli captured the first prize and was thereby encouraged to undertake additional vocal study with various teachers, none of whom satisfied him. He came to the conclusion that all vocal teachers were just "a plague to singers" and decided to develop his voice in his own way without instruction. With the exception of some later coaching he was self-taught, learning the technique of singing, vocal style, and a complete operatic repertory by listening to phonograph recordings by the hour.

After a successful audition at the Spoleto Festival in Italy in 1952, Corelli made his opera debut there as Don José in *Carmen*. The success of this performance resulted in an instant demand for his services in several of Italy's opera houses. In 1953 he sang the leading tenor role of Romeo in Zandonai's *Giulietta e Romeo* at the Rome Opera; in 1954 he made his debut opposite Maria Callas as Licinio in Spontini's *La Vestale* at La Scala in Milan. During the 1953–1954 season he was also heard in Trieste (*Norma*), Naples (*Carmen*), Parma (*Aida*), San Remo (*Tosca*), Rome (*Don Carlo*), and at the Florence May Music Festival (Spontini's *Agnes von Hohenstaufen*). This swift and almost unprecedented success led some of his countrymen to refer to him as "the sputnik tenor."

His repertory grew, as did his fame. Within half a dozen years he had mastered the principal tenor roles of twenty-five operas which, in addition to those already mentioned, included the unfamiliar as well as the familiar: *Fedora, The*

Girl of the Golden West, Donizetti's *Poliuto, Les Huguenots, L'Africaine, I Pagliacci, Turandot, Andrea Chénier, Simon Boccanegra,* Verdi's *La Battaglia del Legnano,* Handel's *Giulio Cesare,* and Allegra's *Romulus.*

Corelli's first appearance outside Italy and Sicily—at Covent Garden in London on June 27, 1957—was an evening of personal triumph. Equally successful appearances were made later in the leading opera houses of Paris, Germany, Spain, Vienna, Monte Carlo, and Portugal. In 1958 he was starred in the motion picture version of *Tosca,* the first complete opera ever filmed in CinemaScope and Eastman color. By the time he signed a contract with the Metropolitan Opera he had become one of the most sought after tenors in the world.

His debut at the Metropolitan took place on January 27, 1961, as Manrico in *Il Trovatore* (a performance in which Leontyne Price also made her first Metropolitan Opera appearance). "His throat bursts with the golden tenor tones with the clarion thrusts at the top which are so ravishing to the Italian ear," wrote Ronald Eyer in the *Herald Tribune.* "It was ravishing to all ears last night." When, on February 24, 1961, Corelli, as Calaf, shared the limelight with Birgit Nilsson in the first Metropolitan Opera production of *Turandot* in thirty years (with Leopold Stokowski making his conducting debut at the Metropolitan), Winthrop Sargeant in the *New Yorker* called him "an ideal Calaf—handsome, virile and vocally splendid." During that initial season Corelli was heard in twenty performances, including the title role of *Don Carlo* on April 30. Indicative of the standing he acquired at the Metropolitan in his first year was the fact that he was called upon to open the following season, on October 15, 1962, in the title role of *Andrea Chénier.* On several occasions after that he opened Metropolitan Opera seasons. In 1968 he became the first tenor ever to open the new season of both the Metropolitan Opera and La Scala for the second time in a single career.

As one of the principal box-office attractions at the Metropolitan, Corelli sang a variety of roles in the Italian and French repertory, the principal ones—in addition to Manrico, Calaf, and Don Carlo—being Ernani, Radames in *Aida,* Rodolfo in *La Bohème,* Turiddu in *Cavalleria Rusticana,* Don Alvaro in *La Forza del Destino,* Cavaradossi in *Tosca,* Dick Johnson in *The Girl of the Golden West,* Maurizio in

Adriana Lecouvreur, Romeo in *Romeo and Juliet,* Enzo in *La Gioconda,* Andrea Chénier, Canio in *I Pagliacci,* Don José in *Carmen,* Edgardo in *Lucia di Lammermoor,* Werther, and Macduff in *Macbeth.* He was also one of the stars of the Metropolitan Opera company on tour. When the Metropolitan Opera visited Japan in June 1975, "it was Franco Corelli night at the Tokyo Bunka Kaikan," reported Richard Halloran to the New York *Times.* "Mr. Corelli as Rodolfo in *La Bohème* clearly turned on his Japanese audience with a powerful emotional performance that brought him a prolonged ovation at the end."

Not only at the Metropolitan but also in other great opera houses of the world Corelli's combustible temper made him a colorful personality. In Naples he once leaped from the stage to attack a man in the audience who had booed him. At a rehearsal in Rome he stabbed a baritone in the hand because he suspected he was being upstaged. In Boston, while touring with the Metropolitan Opera in *Turandot,* he stalked off the stage angrily when Birgit Nilsson insisted on sustaining her note while he ran out of breath. (The story that he bit her that evening is apocryphal.) He threatened critics with physical violence. On more than one occasion he canceled scheduled performances for one reason or another but always gave the pretext that he was ill. One season at the Metropolitan he absented himself from not one but several performances on the grounds that he had to be at the bedside of his sick father in Italy; but the rumor refused to die that the real cause for his absence was his pique at seeing another tenor (Placido Domingo) beginning to assume a place of importance in Metropolitan Opera productions.

His idolatrous followers tolerated his temperamental outbursts and caprices because the splendor of his vocal delivery and its expressiveness reminded them of Caruso or Björling. But some critics, while acknowledging the beauty of Corelli's voice, expressed irritation at some of his disturbing vocal mannerisms: the way he scooped, or held top notes too long; his indulgence in sobbing effects; legatos and pianissimos projected less than perfectly. "Of course he has some faults," said Rudolf Bing in *5000 Nights at the Opera.* "But I for one think . . . he is the incarnation of opera—this fantastic looking fellow who sings like that, a special timbre, a soft sound without apparent effort."

In 1958 in Milan Corelli married Loretta di Lelio, a diminutive young soprano with green eyes and red hair. They first met when she came backstage for an autograph. They live in Milan, a stone's throw from La Scala. She has acted as his secretary, translator, and business manager.

Tall (six feet two) and well built, Corelli cuts a strikingly handsome figure both on and off the stage—one of the reasons for his immense success, particularly among the younger set in Italy. His eyes are wide and brown; his hair, black and wavy. He loves cameras (of which he possesses about a dozen) and high-powered sports cars. Among other hobbies are riding horseback, going to the movies, and watching westerns on television.

His commitment to his career and to music is total. He refuses to smoke or drink any alcohol other than an occasional glass of wine, to overindulge in food, to go to late-hour parties, or to lead an intemperate life because the quality of his singing might be affected.

On performance days he will not speak above a whisper and many times he prefers maintaining a complete silence while communicating through gestures. Before the performance he eats a meal mainly of raw beefsteak. "I sleep music," he once told Rex Reed in an interview. "I see notes in my dreams. I never rest, because I am always trying to improve myself. If I have three months of absolute freedom I use them to protect my technical instrument. Without that, I am nothing."

Corelli has made numerous appearances in recitals, frequently in joint concerts with Renata Tebaldi. He has also appeared regularly on European and American television programs.

ABOUT: Breslin, H. ed. The Tenors. *Periodicals*—High Fidelity, February 1967; Musical America, May 1961; New York Times, September 17, 1967; New York Times Magazine, February 8, 1970; New Yorker, February 4, 1961; Opera News, March 4, 1961.

Fernando Corena

1916–

Fernando Corena, basso buffo, was born in Geneva on December 22, 1916, to a Turkish father (Dimitri Corena) and an Italian mother (Ugolina Albertini Corena). He was educated at

Corena

FERNANDO CORENA

the University of Fribourg in Switzerland where he specialized in Catholic theology. While attending college one summer, he heard a performance of a French operetta and fell in love with the leading soprano. When he discovered she taught singing, he decided to become her pupil. Within three months he mastered two arias (one by Pergolesi and another by Verdi) which he sang in a competition for amateurs and won first prize. Vittorio Gui, the conductor, encouraged him to consider singing as a career.

Corena left college and began studying voice with Enrico Romano in Milan. He served his singing apprenticeship at the Monte Cenerei Radio Station in Lugano. In 1947 he made his operatic debut in Trieste as Varlaam in *Boris Godunov.* One year later he auditioned for Jonel Perlea, the conductor, singing an aria from *Simon Boccanegra.* Perlea engaged him as Bartolo in a performance of *The Barber of Seville* in the Verona Arena. "I must have something comic in me," Corena has commented in recalling that debut, "because when I came out, the audience laughed. There were thirty thousand people in the audience, and when they laughed it was like a storm."

Appearances in various Italian opera houses, including La Scala in Milan, and at the Florence May Music Festival, preceded his engagement by the Metropolitan Opera in New York in 1954. Corena had been scheduled to make his debut there as Bartolo in *The Barber of Seville* on February 19, 1954, but two weeks earlier, on February 6, the artist scheduled as Leporello in

Don Giovanni fell ill, and Corena was called to fill in for him. "Mr. Corena both sings and acts well," said Ross Parmenter in the New York *Times.* "He showed a nice comic sense without resorting to exaggeration. He conveyed a sense of character in his movements and he was assured and good looking; altogether a fit serving man for the Don. Vocally, he performed with distinction, for he has a fine, resonant voice with the power to shade it with considerable subtlety." In *The Barber of Seville*—a new production mounted two weeks later on February 19—Corena, as Bartolo, was found by Louis Biancolli in the *World-Telegram* to be the "most comical" of all the performers in that cast in "a brilliant and exhilarating production."

Corena remained a principal baritone of the Metropolitan Opera for more than two decades, succeeding Salvatore Baccaloni as an interpreter of basso buffo roles. He has appeared there in about twenty roles, minor as well as major, in *opera seria* parts as well as *opera buffa* ones. When he was heard on December 23, 1955, in a new production of *Don Pasquale,* Howard Taubman said of him in the New York *Times:* "In Fernando Corena, this production had a Don Pasquale who never forgot that he was a gentleman. He managed to be amusing without benefit of horseplay. . . . Mr. Corena sang like a musician; he was on pitch and his voice had quality."

Corena's other roles at the Metropolitan Opera were Lescaut in *Manon,* the Sacristan in *Tosca,* Fra Melitone in *La Forza del Destino,* Geronte in *Manon Lescaut,* Dulcamara in *L'Elisir d'Amore,* Benoit and Alcindoro in *La Bohème,* Mathieu in *Andrea Chénier,* the title role in *Falstaff,* Dr. Bartolo in *The Marriage of Figaro,* the title role in *Gianni Schicchi,* Varlaam in *Boris Godunov,* the Bailiff in *Werther,* Don Alfonso in *Così fan Tutte,* Sulpice in *The Daughter of the Regiment.* On November 10, 1973, when Rossini's *L'Italiana in Algeri* was revived after an absence from the repertory of fifty-four years, Corena sang the comic role of Mustafa. On October 10, 1977, Corena helped to open the season of the Metropolitan Opera in *Boris Godunov.*

Corena has appeared with great success at the Berlin Deutsche Oper, the Vienna State Opera, the Munich Opera, San Carlo in Naples, La Scala, Rome Opera, Covent Garden in London, the Grand Theater in Geneva, Teatro Colón in Buenos Aires, and the San Francisco Opera, as well as in other European and American opera houses. In 1965 he was heard as Osmin in *The Abduction from the Seraglio* at the Salzburg Festival. He has also appeared at festivals in Edinburgh, Holland, Athens, and Florence.

He lives with his wife, Elisabeth, at Castagnola, Switzerland.

ABOUT: New York Times, November 4, 1973.

Alfred Cortot

1877–1962

Alfred Denis Cortot, pianist and conductor, was born in Nyon, Switzerland, on September 26, 1877, to a French father and a Swiss mother. While still a child he was taken to Paris. There he began piano lessons with his sisters as his first teachers. Later he entered the Paris Conservatory, studying the piano with Decombes, Rouguou and Louis Diémer. Decombes imbued young Cortot with his own passion for Chopin; from Rouguou Cortot received insights into the piano literature of Beethoven.

In 1896, while in Diémer's class, Cortot received first prize in piano playing. That same year he made his concert debut, appearing as a soloist with the Colonne Orchestra in Paris in Beethoven's Concerto in C minor. At further appearances with the Colonne and Lamoureux orchestras in Paris Cortot was acclaimed for the perceptiveness and musicianship of his interpretation of the Beethoven piano concertos. His fame as a virtuoso spread when he made several tours of Europe.

In 1898 Cortot went to Bayreuth to study the Wagnerian repertory with Julius Kniese. For three years he served in Bayreuth as a coach, assisting Felix Mottl and Hans Richter in the preparation of the Wagnerian music dramas. These years transformed Cortot into a confirmed and dedicated Wagnerite. He returned to Paris in 1901 determined to spread the gospel of Wagner to French audiences. In 1902 he organized the Société de Festival Lyrique with which he made his conducting debut by directing the Paris premiere of *Die Götterdämmerung* at the Théâtre du Château d'Eau in Paris on May 17, 1902. One year later he found-

Cortot: kôr tō'

ALFRED CORTOT

ed the Association des Concerts Alfred Cortot, where he conducted the French premiere of *Parsifal* as well as Brahms's Requiem, Beethoven's Mass in D, Liszt's *St. Elizabeth,* and unfamiliar works by French composers. In 1904 Cortot was appointed conductor of the orchestra of the Société Nationale, at whose concerts at the Théâtre Nouveau he led many works of young or unknown French composers. From 1904 to 1908 he was the conductor of the Concerts Populaires at Lille. On December 14, 1904, he conducted a performance in Paris of *Tristan and Isolde,* shortly after its French premiere presented by Charles Lamoureux.

In 1907 Cortot was appointed professor of piano at the Paris Conservatory; ten years later he succeeded Raoul Pugno as head of the piano division. Cortot ultimately resigned from the conservatory because the pressure of his concert work as pianist (which he had not discontinued despite his activity with the baton) grew so pressing that many other affiliations had to be excluded. In 1919 he helped found the École Normale de Musique in Paris and became its director, giving an annual summer lecture course in piano interpretation and occasionally conducting its orchestra in concerts of old music.

Cortot also distinguished himself as a performer of chamber music, as the third member of a trio that included Pablo Casals and Jacques Thibaud. They gave numerous concerts throughout Europe and made noteworthy recordings.

Cortot

During World War I Cortot officiated as head of the Ministry of Public Instruction and Beaux-Arts. After the war, though he filled occasional assignments as conductor of the Orchestre Symphonique de Paris and the Société Philharmonique, he concentrated principally on the piano. His fame rests most securely on his piano performances. His playing, as Émile Vuillermoz, the French critic, once wrote, had "lucidity and tenderness, a strength of will and emotion. Cortot always dominates over the works he interprets. . . . The Romanticism of Schumann, Liszt and Chopin—this is his intellectual preference. But the musical ideas of all types and all times always find in him an inspired priest and a convincing missionary."

On October 20, 1918, Cortot made his American debut as soloist with the visiting French Symphony Orchestra conducted by André Messager. In his performance of Saint-Saëns's Piano Concerto No.4 there was, as one American critic said of him at the time, "astonishing bravura, dash and surety. Musically he not only extracted every drop there is in the concerto, but found much more musical material in it to extract than most of us suspected of being there." Following his first piano recital in America, at Aeolian Hall, New York, on November 11, 1918, Richard Aldrich said in the New York *Times:* "He is virile. He is brilliant. And he is often as hard as nails. In Liszt, these qualities are potent factors. . . . He has muscles of steel, and his touch at times was as pointed as an icepick."

During the 1919–1920 season Cortot performed all five Beethoven piano concertos with the New York Symphony Society, Walter Damrosch conducting. From then on, Cortot toured the United States many times, in recitals, as soloist with major symphony orchestras, and in chamber-music performances. Olin Downes spoke of him in the New York *Times* as "a prophet transfigured by his theme." His last appearance in the United States took place in 1929 in a series of sonata recitals with Jacques Thibaud.

Cortot came into disrepute with many of his admirers and colleagues during World War II and the German occupation of France. He became active as a collaborator with the Vichy government's department of cultural affairs and conducted the orchestra of Radio Paris, then in Nazi hands. This sympathy with the Nazis was in sharp contrast to his reactions and responses in 1933 when the Nazis first came to power in Germany. At that time he joined a distinguished group of musicians, among whom were Thibaud, Bronislaw Hubermann and Josef Hofmann, in refusing to perform in German concert halls as long as the Nazis were in power, and in 1939 he canceled a concert in Italy in opposition to the rise of anti-Semitism there.

Late in 1944 Cortot was arrested on the charge of collaboration with the Nazis but was soon released. Returning to the concert stage in 1946 he met with such opposition from audiences and critics that he was compelled to go into comparative retirement in Lausanne, Switzerland, and to make just a few intermittent appearances. His last extensive tour in 1952 brought him from Japan to South America, but he did not set foot in North America.

In *The Great Pianists* Harold C. Schonberg described Cortot's playing as "a combination of intellectual authority, aristocracy, masculinity and poetry," even while pointing out that sometimes Cortot was guilty of technical inaccuracies and memory slips. "Cortot retained a few mannerisms of the old school, but above all he was an intellectual player—a profound musician whose fine mind came through every note he played. . . . At his best . . . he was one of the important pianists of the century—a man with a repertoire that apparently encompassed the entire history of music, an artist of formidable resource and all-embracing musical culture. Certainly no French pianist of his time approached him."

On June 15, 1962, in his eighty-fourth year, Alfred Cortot died of uremia in Lausanne. Three of his books have been translated into English: *French Piano Music* (1932), *Alfred Cortot's Studies in Musical Appreciation* (1937), and *In Search of Chopin* (1951). His diversions were skiing and collecting portraits and autographs.

Cortot was honorary professor of the Paris Conservatory. He received the gold medal of the Royal Philharmonic of London and was made Commander of the French Legion of Honor and Knight of the Order of Isabella la Católica of Spain.

ABOUT: Schonberg, H. C. The Great Pianists.

Régine Crespin

1927–

Régine Crespin, soprano, has been described as "the authoritative mistress of three repertories, the French, the Italian and the German." She was born in Marseilles, on March 23, 1927, to Henri and Marguerite Di Meirone Crespin; her father was French, her mother, Italian. She was raised in Nîmes where she attended the academic schools in preparation for a pharmaceutical career and where she pursued her initial vocal studies with a local teacher for about two years. Encouraged by the winning of several competitions for singers, she entered the Paris Conservatory to pursue vocal study more seriously with Suzanne Cesbron-Viseu and Georges Jouatte. In 1949 she won first prize in voice at the Conservatory.

In 1950 she sang at the Paris Opéra as Elsa in *Lohengrin,* with André Cluytens conducting. (Curiously enough, *Lohengrin* had been the first opera she had seen performed.) Writing for the English journal *Opera,* Jacques Chabannes reported: "A new Wagnerian singer is born." During the same year she made her debut at the Opéra-Comique in Paris as Tosca. In 1951 she made her debut at Mulhouse, again as Elsa in *Lohengrin.* A local critic reported that hers was "a magnificent debut from all points of view." Later the same year Crespin was heard in Strasbourg, Vichy, Lyons, and Marseilles.

By 1956, when she made a triumphant return to the Paris Opéra, she was recognized throughout France as one of its most gifted and versatile opera stars, her repertory having been expanded to include the Marschallin in *Der Rosenkavalier,* Leonore in *Fidelio,* Leonora in *Il Trovatore,* Desdemona in *Otello,* Sieglinde in *Die Walküre,* Rezia in *Oberon,* Marguerite in *Faust,* and Salome in *Herodiade.* In May 1956 she appeared in the world premiere of Henri Tomasi's *Sampiero Corso* at the Bordeaux Opera. She made her debut at La Scala in 1959 in Pizzetti's *Fedra* (an unusual bit of casting since French singers making their first appearances at La Scala were generally heard in the traditional French repertory). At La Scala soon afterwards she was also heard in Poulenc's *Les Dialogues des Carmélites.* In 1961, in Buenos Aires, she performed in Fauré's *Pénélope.*

RÉGINE CRESPIN

In 1958 she met Lou Bruder, whom she married on April 16, 1962. He brought new dimensions to her vocal art. An authority on German literature, theater, and diction, Bruder helped develop Crespin's interest in Wagner and greatly broadened the scope of her Wagnerian performances. These developments first became evident at the Bayreuth Festival in 1958 when she was chosen by Wieland Wagner for the role of Kundry in *Parsifal,* a performance for which one Bayreuth critic called her "the magician of the festival," placing her "among the galaxy of international stars." She returned to Bayreuth for the next two festivals, again as Kundry. In 1959 Crespin made her bow at the Vienna State Opera as Sieglinde in *Die Walküre.*

The role of the Marschallin in *Der Rosenkavalier* brought her additional triumphs at the Glyndebourne Festival in 1959 and 1960, at the Berlin State Opera with which she made her debut in 1960, and in her first appearance at Covent Garden in London in 1961. "The richtoned French soprano making her Covent Garden debut," said a critic of the London *Express,* "fully justified the reputation she made in this role. . . . Her expressive voice dominated the opera."

The opera that she sometimes referred to as one of her favorites—Berlioz' *Les Troyens*—brought her back to the Paris Opéra in 1961. She was subsequently heard in this same role with the San Francisco Opera and with the Boston Opera. Of her performance as Dido the critic of *Le Figaro* wrote that "Régine Crespin has supreme mastery of interpretation. . . . She is sublime."

Her American debut took place on October 26, 1962, as Tosca with the Chicago Lyric Opera. Writing in the Chicago *Tribune*, Claudia Cassidy said that Crespin was "a reminder that Tosca came from the Paris byways of Sarah Bernhardt." To Robert C. Marsh in the *Sun-Times*, Crespin revealed that she "has the voice, the stage sense, and the personal projection essential for any memorable realization of this role."

She appeared at the Metropolitan Opera for the first time on November 19, 1962, as the Marschallin in *Der Rosenkavalier*. At that time Harold C. Schonberg reported in the New York *Times:* "In Miss Crespin, the Metropolitan Opera and *Der Rosenkavalier* have a singer worthy of the great traditions of house and opera. She gave a simply beautiful performance. She proved a brilliant actress and handled herself with complete finesse. And vocally she was far out of the ordinary. The monumental thing about the voice was its absolute security. In matters of production and intonation, Miss Crespin was at all times a flawless technician." Paul Henry Lang further noted in the *Herald Tribune* that "she can bend a phrase upward in a fiery pianissimo and she can sing a rapid parlando in which every note is clear. And the voice has volume, too."

Later that season Crespin was heard as Senta in *The Flying Dutchman* and as Amelia in *Un Ballo in Maschera*. In 1964–1965, she sang the roles of Elsa in *Lohengrin*, Sieglinde in *Die Walküre* and Tosca. Her subsequent Metropolitan Opera roles were Kundry in *Parsifal*, Brünnhilde in *Die Walküre*, Giulietta in *The Tales of Hoffmann*, Charlotte in *Werther* and Santuzza in *Cavalleria Rusticana*.

The first time she assumed the part of Brünnhilde in *Die Walküre* was during Easter Week of 1967 in Salzburg, Herbert von Karajan conducting. Since then she has sung Sieglinde in the Georg Solti London recording of *Die Walküre* and Brünnhilde in the von Karajan Deutsche Grammophon recording. She is the first dramatic Wagnerian soprano to record both of these major soprano roles in complete recordings of *Die Walküre*.

In the early 1970s Crespin suffered a severe emotional crisis. She explained it this way to Gerald Walker in an interview in the New York *Times*. "I got divorced and I got sick. I'd found my voice getting tired. I didn't have the easy top. I didn't want to work on new parts or vocalize. I was blasé, had enough. I found my technique was not so responsive but I could not do anything at first. I had to go off the deep end." The deepening of her self-doubts and despair led her to cancel all her engagements for an entire season beginning with October 1973 and go in for some analysis. Instead of performing, she returned to vocal studies with Rudolf Bautz in Cologne, four hours a day, several days a week. Working with Bautz led her to realize that "the voice was there and not damaged at all. It was just in the brain. I also passed through analysis in the same period, over two or three years. . . . If I had not been analyzed, I would not have resumed singing, I would have stopped singing altogether and maybe be dead now. I was suicidal myself."

She made what she has since called her "comeback" with the Opéra du Rhin in Strasbourg in the title role of *Carmen* (a part she had previously sung for the first time in a concert performance with the Greater Miami Philharmonic). "I thought," she has revealed, "if I sing Carmen well, if I have a success, if it goes like I want it to go—okay, I go on. If not, I stop, because I cannot fight with myself, my voice. It was a nightmare."

It was a success, and so was her first stage appearance in the United States as Carmen. This performance, on October 30, 1975, made her the first French-born Carmen to appear at the Metropolitan Opera in many years. Writing in *Opera News*, Robert Jacobson called her performance "the most authentically French Carmen in decades. . . . Her delivery of the lines in seductive bronze tones caressed the ear. So did her pliant, lustrous voice in the arias and ensembles. Singing the role as a soprano, she did not stress heavy chest voice or big bottom tones, instead there was a lovely lyricism that created a bewitching gypsy, with strength and evenness throughout the range, filled with light and shade via exquisite phrasing."

On January 7, 1976, Crespin appeared in the title role of Massenet's sacred drama *Marie Magdeleine*, being given its American premiere in its original oratorio form at the Lincoln Center for the Performing Arts in New York by the Sacred Music Society of America. On February 5, 1977, she was heard as Mme. de Croisy (the First Prioress) in the Metropolitan Opera pro-

duction of Poulenc's *Les Dialogues des Carmélites.* "She poured out her big voice in the death
scene as though she was thinking of Brünnhilde," said Harold C. Schonberg in the New
York *Times.* "She milked it thoroughly, vocally
and dramatically." (It is of interest to note that
while Poulenc was writing his opera he consulted Crespin about singing the part of the Second
Prioress, thinking the role of the First Prioress
beyond her vocal capabilities.)

Later in 1977 Crespin sang Dido in Berlioz'
Les Troyens à Carthage when it received a concert presentation at the May Festival in Cincinnati. And on October 10 of the same year she
helped open the season of the Metropolitan Opera in *Boris Godunov.*

Régine Crespin has enjoyed a highly successful career as a recitalist and as a guest artist with
symphony orchestras. Her home is on the avenue Frochot in Paris, a "little tree-lined street
where the cars don't go," she has called it. She
also maintains a summer home on the island of
Majorca, where she can enjoy swimming and
lying in the sun. France has made her Chevalier
of the Legion of Honor, Commandeur des Arts
et des Lettres, and Chevalier de l'Ordre National
du Mérite.

Crespin conducts a master class in singing at
the Paris Conservatory.

ABOUT: High Fidelity, September 1977; New York
Times, December 7, 1975; Opera News, December 13,
1975; Stereo Review, November 1973.

Richard Crooks

1900–1972

Alexander Richard Crooks, tenor, was born in
Trenton, New Jersey, on June 26, 1900, the son
of Alexander Struthers Crooks. He received his
first music lessons from his mother, Elizabeth
Gore Crooks. When he was ten he made his first
public appearance singing several songs at the
Ocean Grove Auditorium in New Jersey. Ernestine Schumann-Heink went backstage to embrace him and to prophesy for him a rich future
in music. A few years later Crooks performed at
the Trenton Music Festival before an audience
of fourteen thousand, sharing the program and
the honors with Schumann-Heink.

Despite the family's poverty, Richard was

RICHARD CROOKS

able to acquire a comprehensive academic education at the public schools in Trenton, at Temple University in Philadelphia from which he
was graduated, and at Lafayette College in Bethlehem, Pennsylvania, where he received a doctorate in music. All this time he was working to
help his family make ends meet. At fourteen he
earned a small income by painting the great
reservoir tanks of the Trenton gas works, and
three years later he loaded ice into wagons for
twenty cents an hour.

At the outbreak of World War I he falsified
his age to join the United States Army as a member of the 626th Aero Squadron. When his true
age was discovered he was discharged from service. He went to New York to study voice with
Sydney H. Bourne and Frank La Forge. Often
he went without a real meal for days so that he
might have the price for a ticket to a Caruso
performance at the Metropolitan Opera. His
home was an overcrowded room which he
shared with four other boys. They took turns
sleeping.

He was twenty when he found his first permanent singing job, as soloist at the Fifth Avenue
Presbyterian Church in New York at a salary of
twenty-five dollars a week. One year later, on
July 23, 1921, he married a childhood sweetheart, Mildred Wallace Pine.

Shortly after the marriage he experienced
what he often referred to as one of the great
thrills of his life, his first concert engagement as
a mature singer. As he told the story: "One day
we were expecting a visit from our respective

177

families and we wanted our little flat to look extra fine. Since we were not able to afford help, we cleaned the place thoroughly ourselves. My wife was washing windows and I was down on the floor scrubbing when the telephone rang. A woman's voice came over the wire asking for Richard Crooks and offering a concert with a local woman's club at seventy-five dollars. It looked like a staggering amount to us. My hands were wet with soapsuds and I was wild with joy, but I managed to keep my balance. As calmly as I could I asked the lady to wait until I consulted my calendar to see if I were free to accept the offer. I was. I clinched the deal and told my wife I was now a professional concert singer."

Walter Damrosch was aware of Crooks's singing potential and volunteered to get him a ten-thousand-dollar loan to enable him to continue his music studies in Europe. Crooks politely turned this offer down, insisting that he must make his own way in music. In 1922 Damrosch engaged Crooks for an unprecedented number of appearances with the New York Symphony, and he made his debut performing excerpts from *Siegfried* with Florence Easton. His success was immediate, and he received other offers for concert appearances, including some in England and on the Continent.

In 1924 Crooks was offered the starring role in the Sigmund Romberg operetta *The Student Prince,* then scheduled for production on Broadway. He was offered a thousand dollars a week. Though money was still a scarce commodity in the Crooks household, Crooks refused the contract. He was afraid it would deflect him from his ambition to achieve recognition and success as a concert and operatic artist.

He concertized for the next two seasons. Then in 1927 Crooks made his opera debut in Hamburg as Cavaradossi in *Tosca.* Other opera appearances followed at the Berlin State Opera. On November 27, 1930, Crooks made his American opera debut as Cavaradossi with the Philadelphia Opera Company. The Metropolitan Opera offered him a contract, but Crooks felt he would not be ready for so important an assignment until he had gained more experience with less renowned companies.

His Metropolitan Opera debut finally took place on February 25, 1933, as Des Grieux in *Manon.* He received thirty-seven curtain calls. "The new tenor," wrote W. J. Henderson in the *Sun,* "has a voice of good quality, warm and

persuasive. The tone proved itself capable of uttering the sentimental portions of Massenet's music with feeling as well as with musical beauty. The singer revealed a serviceable technique and good breath control. Some of his phrases were long, well sustained, and made of finely spun tone."

Crooks remained with the Metropolitan Opera company through the 1942–1943 season and was assigned leading tenor roles not only in *Manon* but also in *Tosca, La Traviata, Linda di Chamounix, Mignon, Faust, Madama Butterfly, Romeo and Juliet,* and *Don Giovanni.*

He combined his appearances in opera with extensive concert tours and radio work. In 1936 he made his first tour of Australia, New Zealand, and Tasmania, singing over sixty concerts to sold-out auditoriums. For fourteen years he was featured so often as a guest artist on the "Voice of Firestone" (first over radio and later on television) that he was considered a regular member of that popular program. Because of his long and sustained success as a performer of light and popular music over radio and TV, Crooks's artistry was underestimated by many. Nevertheless, in the French and the Italian opera repertory he favored he was one of the finest tenors in the Metropolitan Opera company.

Describing him as "the American John McCormack—McCormack had also been undervalued because of his emphasis on Irish ballads and other light numbers—Harold C. Schonberg wrote in the New York *Times* on Crooks's death: "Mr. Crooks had an unusually sweet, flexible tenor voice. Singing was never work for Mr. Crooks. He had an unforced production, a smooth and even scale, and the kind of perfectly placed voice that can fill any auditorium, no matter how large. . . . His singing represented suavity with its melting legato and unfaltering breath control. . . . So beautiful was his singing that he was one of the most popular tenors in the roster of the Metropolitan Opera."

Crooks always said that when he felt he was beginning to lose his voice he would retire. He did so in the early 1950s, after many years of concertizing and of guest appearances in the world's great opera houses. For a while he spent his retirement at his home in Buck Hill Falls, Pennsylvania, where he and his wife had raised their two children, Patricia and Richard. Then he went to live on Cresta Vista Lane in Portola

Valley, California. It was there that he died of cancer on October 1, 1972.

Crooks stood six feet two in height and was of athletic build. A dedicated sportsman, he was an excellent handball player and boasted a creditable score at golf. On the day he made his debut in Carnegie Hall in New York he also won the handball championship of New York State. Fishing, both surf-casting and deep-sea, fencing, and piloting his own plane were also among his favorite pastimes.

Of his daily habits, Crooks said: "On singing days, I rise at about 8:30, breakfast on fruit juice, hot cereal and toast, rest about an hour, then vocalize for a while. If the day is not too icy, I take a brisk walk before noon. Then comes my dinner—meat, green vegetables and stewed fruit. I rest again until about four. At that time, I begin to think about getting down to the Opera House. No later than five, I have a very light lunch. I like to leave home early and arrive at my dressing room about two hours before curtain time. After the performance, I like best to go straight home. Sometimes friends come to see us, but it is best, after a taxing performance, to keep quiet. Toward midnight, I have another light meal, and then I go to sleep. Non-performance days are a very different matter. Then I try to combine business (and each day's business varies) with the things I like to do. I must rest and sleep at least eight hours a day. I must exercise, I like to see my friends, to play bridge. I enjoy reading and going to plays. I like best of all to be with my family, quietly at home."

ABOUT: Opera News, April 6, 1966.

Julia Culp

1880–1970

Julia Culp, contralto, a distinguished interpreter of *Lieder* in the early twentieth century, was born in Groningen, Holland, on October 6, 1880. She was a prodigy on the violin and early in her life appeared in violin concerts throughout Holland. In her fourteenth year she turned from violin to singing; in 1897 she entered the Conservatory of Amsterdam, a vocal student of Cornelie van Zanten. After two years of this instruction, she went to Berlin to study with Etelka Gerster.

JULIA CULP

Culp made her concert debut as a singer in a joint recital with Ferruccio Busoni, pianist, at Magdeburg, Germany, in 1901. A local critic at that time wrote with prophetic insight: "Today Julia Culp's name is printed in modest little letters on our programs, but it will soon be seen in flaming letters. For she is a singer by the Grace of God."

Success came early in her career. After a recital in Berlin that was well received, she gave several concerts in Holland where, in a single season, she became a celebrity. She was invited to perform in almost every major city in Europe, and by the time she made her first visit to the United States, she was acknowledged to be one of the great living singers of *Lieder.*

Her American debut took place in New York on January 10, 1913, in a program devoted to the *Lieder* of Schubert, Schumann, and Brahms. "Few *Lieder* singers who come to New York with a high established reputation in Europe disclose so soon and so convincingly the grounds for it," wrote Richard Aldrich in the New York *Times,* "and the grounds for the duplication of it here, as Mme. Julia Culp, who made her first appearance in Carnegie Hall yesterday afternoon. She is a Dutch artist whose voice is described as contralto, though it hardly has all the characteristic quality of a true contralto; but there will be no quarrel with the description that is applied to an organ as beautiful as hers. It has an altogether remarkable richness and silken smoothness; it is admirably equalized throughout its whole range; it has great power and fullness, which she can modulate to the extreme of pianissimo. There are many technical excellences in her employment of it, and one of the most noteworthy is her breath control, which, with her intelligence, enables her to do unusual things in the way of phrasing." An extensive American tour followed, and wherever she was heard her success at Carnegie Hall was repeated.

When Culp appeared again in Carnegie Hall, on January 5, 1915, she broke new ground for a European *Lieder* singer by including American songs on her program: three settings of Indian songs by Thurlow Lieurance and two songs by James Hotchkiss Rogers.

H. T. Parker, the Boston critic, provided the following critical evaluation of Culp's art: "First and foremost, every song brought the pleasure of Miss Culp's voice. . . . Not the least of its virtues and appeal and much of its individuality lies in its singular mingling of both the soprano and the alto quality. In its middle range, in particular, it has the rich, deep, sensuous texture and body of alto tones, and keeps them both, even in higher notes. At the same time, it has the lustrousness and the bell-like quality of a finely tempered soprano. . . . Whatever the tone, Mme. Culp keeps it flawlessly clear and beautifully rounded. Not even Dr. Muck [then the conductor of the Boston Symphony] excels Mme. Culp in the sense of the long and mounting melodic line, in instinctive and practised divination of the gradients of a long progression. And her sensibility to rhythm and her expert skill in the sustaining and the varying of it match his. And this voice and this artistry are the puissant servants of a large and fine insight and a manifold and sensitive imagination."

Though she was married to a German—Erich Merten, the personal attaché of Kaiser Wilhelm —Culp devoted herself to hospital work among the Allied troops during World War I. This divergence of political outlook was one of the reasons the marriage ended in divorce. In 1919 Culp married Wilhelm G. Ginzkey, an Austrian industrialist, with whom she lived in a castle in Mafferdorff, near Reichenberg, in the Sudeten territory of Czechoslovakia. She continued to live there after the death of her husband in 1934 and her retirement from concert work. But upon the annexation of the Sudetenland by Nazi Germany, she returned to Holland to establish residence in Amsterdam. During the Nazi occupation of Holland, in World War II, she was forced to go into hiding because she was of Jewish birth. After the war, on her seventieth birthday, in 1950, she was the recipient of many public honors. She died in Amsterdam on October 13, 1970.

ABOUT: Kutsch, K. J. and Riemens, L. A Concise Biographical Dictionary of Singers.

Phyllis Curtin

1922–

Phyllis Curtin (originally Phyllis Smith), soprano, was born on December 3, 1922, in Clarksburg, West Virginia. Her father, E. Vernon Smith, worked for a gas company. Both her parents were musical. Her mother, Betty R. Robinson Smith, was an organist and choirleader, and her father sang tenor in church. Phyllis began studying the violin when she was about seven. Later she played in her school orchestra and in a string trio. As a girl, she sang just for the fun of it.

Upon graduation from Monticello Junior College in Alton, Illinois, in 1941, she entered Wellesley College where she majored in political science. There, in her junior year, she began studying voice for the first time. Her first teacher was Olga Avierino; the first art song she learned was Fauré's "Après un rêve." Before long, Phyllis was giving song recitals which—due to the facility with which she learned new and difficult music—were already featuring works by young American composers. She was singing so much new music (for a long time she continued to do so) that as she herself has since recalled she was "doing more first and last performances of new works than anybody around."

In 1943 she was graduated from Wellesley with a Bachelor of Arts degree, and for a time she worked for the War Production Board. In 1946 she married Phillip Curtin, a student at Swarthmore College. Early in this marriage she continued her vocal studies with Joseph Regneas, to whose teaching she credits her remarkable technique. In 1946 she made several appearances at Tanglewood, in Lenox, Massachusetts, with Leonard Bernstein conducting, and with the New England Opera Theater directed by Boris Goldovsky. When her husband entered graduate school at Harvard, she went

PHYLLIS CURTIN

with him to Cambridge. She found a job singing at Temple Israel in Boston, gave some concerts, and made a few appearances with the Boston Symphony Orchestra.

Her New York concert debut took place at Town Hall in 1950. Three years later, on October 22, 1953, she made her first appearance with the New York City Opera in the American premiere of Gottfried von Einem's twentieth century opera *The Trial,* in which she performed all four of the female roles. Her success with the New York City Opera, however, did not begin until March 28, 1954, when she sang the title role in *Salome.* Her provocative dance of the seven veils, as well as her brilliant characterization and vocalization, earned her the praises of most of the critics, as well as a three-page photograph layout in *Life* on April 12.

Her versatility was demonstrated not only in subsequent seasons at the New York City Opera but elsewhere as well. In 1954 and 1955 she filled the role of Mistress Ford in two contrasting operas, *Falstaff* and *The Merry Wives of Windsor,* at the New York City Opera. On June 11, 1955, at the Festival of the Creative Arts at Brandeis University in Waltham, Massachusetts, she sang the title role in Milhaud's *Médée.* On February 24, 1955, she created the title role in Carlisle Floyd's *Susannah* in Tallahassee, Florida, a role she later sang at the New York City Opera. In March 1956 whe was heard as Cressida in the New York premiere of William Walton's *Troilus and Cressida* at the New York City Opera, and

later in 1956 she toured the United States with the NBC Opera company as the Countess Almaviva in *The Marriage of Figaro.* Of her performance as Susannah in Floyd's opera, one of her most famous roles, the critic of the New York *Herald Tribune* said: "Phyllis Curtin no longer acts the title role—she lives it now . . . . It is a stirring portrayal, fine in dramatic sense, fine in vocal sound."

Her first appearance at the Metropolitan Opera took place on November 4, 1961, as Fiordiligi in *Così fan Tutte.* "She proved," wrote Louis Biancolli in the *World-Telegram and Sun,* "that in voice and acting she is an artistic adornment to any company smart enough to negotiate for her services. Mistress of many styles from the most classic to the most modern, she was the true Mozartean . . . exquisite with word and note."

At the Metropolitan Opera in subsequent seasons, Curtin was heard in a varied repertory ranging from *The Marriage of Figaro* and *Così fan Tutte* to Britten's *Peter Grimes,* and including *Die Meistersinger, Falstaff, La Traviata,* and *Die Fledermaus,* among others. She was scheduled to appear as Agathe in *Der Freischütz* and Tatiana in *Eugene Onegin* in 1969-1970, but these productions had to be canceled when the Metropolitan Opera temporarily closed down because of a labor dispute.

Curtin possessed an extraordinary capacity to learn new roles and new scores quickly, even when they were exacting or just conceived. This gift made it possible for her to appear in more new operas than any American soprano before her, or since, and to have over fifty works written expressly for her. In addition to the world premiere of Floyd's *Susannah* she also was heard in the first performances of two more Floyd operas: *Wuthering Heights* at the Santa Fe Opera in New Mexico on July 16, 1958; *The Passion of Jonathan Wade* at the New York City Opera on October 11, 1962. She sang in two Floyd concert works: *The Mystery: Five Songs of Motherhood,* with the Pittsburgh Symphony in January 1962, and *Flower and Hawk: The Testament of a Queen* at Jacksonville, Florida, in May 1972. Darius Milhaud wrote the opera *La Mère Coupable* for her, in which she was starred in Geneva on June 13, 1966. Since the character portrayed is Countess Rosina Almaviva from Beaumarchais's *The Barber of Seville,* Curtin became the first singer ever to portray three different operatic Rosina Almavivas—Mozart's, Rossini's, and Milhaud's.

In 1967 as soloist with the Chicago Symphony Orchestra she was heard in Jean Martinon's *Rose of Sharon,* the composer conducting. In 1971 she appeared in Denver in the world premiere of Alberto Ginastera's *Milena* with the Denver Symphony, and in Washington, D.C., in the first performance of Ned Rorem's song cycle *Ariel.*

The American premieres were equally numerous. In addition to *The Trial* and *Médée* there were Poulenc's satirical opera, *Les Mamelles de Tirésias* at Waltham, Massachusetts, on June 13, 1953; Richard Strauss's *Intermezzo,* in a concert performance in New York on December 11, 1963; Britten's *A War Requiem* at the Berkshire Music Festival in Lenox, Massachusetts, on July 27, 1963; Richard Strauss's *Three Hymns* with the Boston Symphony under Leinsdorf, at the Berkshire Music Festival, in the summer of 1963; Sibelius's *Luonnotar* with the New York Philharmonic, Bernstein conducting, in 1965; and Shostakovich's Symphony No.4, with the Philadelphia Orchestra on January 1, 1971. She recorded the Shostakovich symphony with the Philadelphia Orchestra for RCA, and also the premiere performance of *Milena.*

Her repertory includes hundreds of concert works as well as over seventy operatic roles. The speed with which she can master a new role can be measured by the fact that she learned the score of *La Mère Coupable* in thirteen days, and the principal role in Vittorio Giannini's opera *The Taming of the Shrew* in a week.

On June 15, 1964, she collaborated in a Richard Strauss festival in Hamburg commemorating the centenary of his birth. At that time she received a twenty-minute ovation after her rendition of a program of Strauss's *Lieder* and arias. She was also a soloist at the Strauss Centennial Celebration in Copenhagen. She opened and closed the Edinburgh Festival in Scotland in 1958, inaugurating it with *Peter Grimes* and closing it with the rarely heard and little-known operetta of Franz Schubert *Alfonso und Estrella.* In 1969 another rarely given opera was her vehicle at the Schwetzingen Festival in Germany— Purcell's *The Fairy Queen.* When in August 1972 she was summoned to substitute for an indisposed singer in a performance of Beethoven's *Missa Solemnis* at the Berkshire Music Festival, she performed without a single rehearsal, and without having sung the music in some eight years.

On December 17, 1975, Phyllis Curtin sang Gershwin's music for the first time in her career at an all-Gershwin concert by the National Chorale at Avery Fisher Hall in New York. "I've spent my life as a song singer," she explained, "and Gershwin is one of the best writers of songs we've ever had."

Curtin made her European debut during the summer of 1958 at the World's Fair in Brussels where she appeared with the New York City Opera in the European premiere of *Susannah.* In 1959 she made her first appearance in South America, as Manon at the Teatro Colón in Buenos Aires. In 1960–1961 she received seventeen curtain calls after her debut appearance at the Vienna State Opera as Violetta in *La Traviata.* She made her Italian debut that season with the Trieste Opera as Dido in Purcell's *Dido and Aeneas.* Her introduction to Paris took place in 1965–1966 at a Festival of Contemporary Music, Gunther Schuller conducting; and her first appearance at the Glyndebourne Festival was in 1969 as Donna Anna in *Don Giovanni.*

During the 1963–1964 season in the United States she established a record for orchestral appearances by a singer: She performed in fifty-six different concerts with the major symphony orchestras, including those of Boston, Cleveland, Philadelphia, Detroit, Los Angeles, Pittsburgh, and Minneapolis. On July 15, 1976, she was invited by President and Mrs. Gerald Ford to sing at a White House dinner for Chancellor Helmut Schmidt of West Germany and his wife, Hannelore. She has also often been heard on television, not only as a guest of major sponsored network programs but also in complete opera performances with the NBC Opera. Her appearance with the NBC Opera on January 1, 1950, in *Carmen* was the first time a complete opera was telecast. She was subsequently televised as Fiordiligi in *Così fan Tutte* and Fiora in *L'Amore dei Tre Re.* At one time she was seen on the same day on the television screens of both the United States and Europe, on two different programs, and she appeared on the networks of NBC-TV and ABC-TV on two major shows within a twenty-four-hour period.

"Everything Phyllis Curtin touches," wrote Byron Belt, a nationally syndicated music critic, "is marked by the elegance of a sensitive artist and the intensity of a strong, vital and winning woman. . . . In an age when almost nobody cares, integrity and devotion are still the keys to a great career, and Phyllis Curtin is a heart-warming antidote to the sloppy get-bymanship of so many of our here today and gone tomorrow performers. . . . There is scarcely an orchestra or opera company in Europe and America that has not depended upon her innate musicianship, beautiful voice and gracious personality to high-light its season."

Following her divorce from Phillip Curtin, she married Eugene Cook, a free-lance photographer, on May 6, 1956. They have two residences: an apartment on the fifteenth floor on Riverside Drive in New York overlooking the Hudson River and a rambling old house on twelve acres of land in the Berkshire Mountains in Massachusetts. Their daughter, Claudia Madeleine (called Miss Mouse), was named after two musicians: the famous soprano Claudia Muzio and her godmother, Madeleine Milhaud, the pianist wife of the composer Darius Milhaud.

Curtin confesses to a liking for cooking. Sometimes when the professional commitments are particularly pressing she yields to an elusive dream of becoming solely a suburban housewife and mother. "But when the music begins that night on the stage," she adds hurriedly, "the feeling passes away." Whenever possible she prefers traveling with her family. "This makes us nine-tenths gypsies," she says, "which is 1000 percent better than being totally lonely." What upsets her most on her frequent trips is to have to listen to piped background music and to talk-ative air flight pilots, and to have to eat the deplorable food available at most hotels.

She has been the recipient of the Wellesley College Distinguished Alumna Award (the second time in a century it was presented). Also, she has received honorary doctorates in music from three universities, was named West Virginia's Woman of the Year and one of the two women of accomplishment for the year 1961 by the Associated Press. At the approach to the city two signs identify Clarksburg, West Virginia: one as the birthplace of Stonewall Jackson and the other as the birthplace of Phyllis Curtin.

Phyllis Curtin has taught master classes in singing at the Berkshire Music Center in Tangle-wood and elsewhere and has served as head of the voice department at Yale University.

ABOUT: Life, April 12, 1954, January 11, 1963; Musical America, September 1963; New York Times, May 14, 1972, December 17, 1975; Newsweek, January 18, 1971; Opera News, January 20, 1962; Time, December 1, 1961.

Sir Clifford Curzon

1907–

Clifford Curzon, pianist, was born in London on May 18, 1907. Both his father, Michael (an antique dealer), and his mother, Constance Young Curzon, were music lovers who encouraged their son's early interest in music. Clifford's uncle was Albert Ketelbey, the composer of such semiclassics as *In a Monastery Garden* and *In a Persian Garden.* "We lived," Curzon once disclosed to an interviewer, "in north London and my first musical memory is of my uncle Albert Ketelbey trying out his compositions at the piano. I remember being put to bed on the top floor by my nurse, but creeping out immediately to sit on the top step so as to hear him."

Clifford began violin study when he was about five. A year later Manlio di Veroli, a voice coach who taught singing to Curzon's mother, gave the boy his first piano lessons.

In his twelfth year Clifford was enrolled in the Royal Academy of Music in London, the youngest pupil to be admitted up to that time. His first important piano teacher was Charles Reddie with whom he made such progress that he won two scholarships and almost every prize open at the Academy to pianists, including the coveted McFarren Gold Medal. Later piano study took place with Tobias Matthay and Katharine Goodson.

"I think," recalls Curzon, "my father hoped I might follow in Ketelbey's footsteps, that little Clifford might make a lot of money as a composer. Instead, I worked very hard at the piano studies." Sir Henry J. Wood, the conductor of the Promenade Concerts at Queen's Hall in London, took an interest in him and had him appear at a Promenade Concert in 1923 as one of three pianists performing the Bach Concerto for Three Pianos. Somewhat later Clifford made ten appearances at the Promenade Concerts, "partly," he explains, "because I was a quick learner

Curzon: kûr′ zŏn

SIR CLIFFORD CURZON

and could take over when others fell ill. I also went with Sir Henry on several tours around the country." At one of his performances at Queen's Hall, in 1924, Clifford gave the world premiere of Germaine Tailleferre's Ballade for piano and orchestra, *Les jeux de plein air.*

In 1925 Curzon began to concertize all over England. That same year he also joined the faculty of the Royal College of Music in the piano department, remaining there until 1937 when he was made Fellow of the Academy.

After hearing a concert by Artur Schnabel, Curzon realized he needed more training before he could advance his own concert career. With money inherited from the mother of one of his colleagues at the Academy, Curzon went to Berlin in 1928 to become Schnabel's pupil. "I remember quite clearly," he has said, "that I hadn't enough money for either an overcoat or warm gloves against the freezing Berlin winters, but I was so deliriously happy to be studying with the one man I admired above all others that I didn't notice until afterwards the frostbite which marks my fingers to this day. Schnabel asked me how I was settling in, and said 'Have you got a bed and a piano?' When I said that I had both he replied, 'That's all you need, as long as they are both in the same room.'"

Work under Schnabel was arduous with daily lessons and long periods each day for practice. During the second year of study Schnabel suggested that the time had come for Curzon to give a Berlin recital. That concert, at which Curzon played sonatas by Beethoven and Liszt and some of Schubert's *Moments Musicaux,* as well as the premiere of a modern German piece, went well. But Curzon, still dissatisfied with himself, went on to Paris for further instruction with Wanda Landowska and Nadia Boulanger. Then, with a tour of the Continent in 1930 he began extensive concertizing throughout Europe, with slowly mounting success.

On July 16, 1931, in Paris, Curzon married an American-born harpsichordist, Lucille Wallace, who had studied with him under Schnabel. For a time Wallace promoted her own career as a harpsichordist, occasionally appearing with Curzon in series tracing the history of music. But after the Curzons adopted the orphaned children of the singer Maria Cebotari, Lucille decided to devote herself to her family and withdrew from the concert stage.

In addition to giving recitals and appearances with the principal European orchestras, Curzon toured Europe in 1936 with Lionel Tertis, the violist, in sonata recitals, the first continental tour of British artists under the auspices of the British Council. Two years later Curzon toured as solo pianist, once again under the auspices of the British Council.

His American debut took place at Town Hall, New York, on February 26, 1939. A few weeks later, on March 10, he was the soloist with the New York Philharmonic Orchestra, Alexander Smallens conducting, in a program made up of three concertos. Curzon made such a favorable impression that the concert manager, Arthur Judson, signed him to tour the United States the following season. The outbreak of World War II canceled this project. During the war Curzon remained in England performing for troops and civilians.

He returned to the United States in 1947, appearing on November 30 with the New York Philharmonic Orchestra under Dimitri Mitropoulos in the Tchaikovsky Concerto No.1. "This writer can remember only one previous performance, that of Rachmaninoff, which approached Mr. Curzon's incandescent intensity, technical perfection, and beauty of tonal investiture," wrote Jerome D. Boehm in the *Herald Tribune.* After Curzon's New York recital on December 20, Noel Straus wrote in the New York *Times:* "Curzon must be reckoned among the greatest keyboard artists of the time." To Olin Downes, also in the New York *Times,* Curzon was "an artist of true humbleness and a consecrated devotion to his task . . . one of the most remarkable pianists and musicians now before the public."

His appearances subsequent to 1947 along with several tours of the United States placed him with the great pianists of the time. On June 15, 1951, he gave the world premiere of Alan Rawsthorne's Piano Concerto No.2 in London, a work that had been commissioned for the Festival of Great Britain that year. In 1952 he was heard at the Edinburgh Festival in chamber-music concerts with the Edinburgh Festival Quartet, which included Joseph Szigeti, violinist, William Primrose, violist, and Pierre Fournier, cellist, in addition to Curzon. As a solo virtuoso Curzon was heard not only at the Edinburgh Festival but also at other world-famous festivals, including those at Holland, Zurich, Bergen, Munich, Salzburg, and Prades.

A Curzon recital in New York early in 1972, his first appearance in the United States in almost a decade, elicited the following report from Irving Kolodin in the *Saturday Review:* "Within a few measures, one realized that with Curzon, as with every artist of distinction, thought and sound formed a composite uniquely his." Commenting on Curzon's performance of Schubert's *Moments Musicaux,* Kolodin added: "Curzon examined each of the miniatures for its particular blend of pathos and pleasure, treating the most celebrated of all (in F minor, which is 'the' *Moment Musical* to most listeners) as one gem among the matched six. The results of this discriminating treatment nourished as well as entertained."

The Curzons have three homes: on the Attersee in Austria, an hour's distance from Salzburg; at Cumberland in England's Lake Country; and their main residence, The White House, in Highgate, a suburb of London. Incorrigible collectors of art, they store paintings, engravings, and other art works together with Curzon's extensive library of music and recordings in The White House. Summer holidays are spent either in Austria or Cumberland, and winters at The White House. In all three places the Curzons indulge in their favorite pastimes of gardening, swimming, and motoring. "If ever I fall on hard times," Curzon once said, "I would rather trim a hedge than teach." Curzon is also a compulsive reader.

He practices piano a minimum of four hours a day, and sometimes as much as eight. When he travels he makes use of a dummy keyboard. "I practice and practice and work and work," he says. "I dare not take anything for granted."

For his services to music Curzon was made a Commander of the British Empire in 1958 and was knighted in December 1976. He received an honorary doctorate in music from Leeds University in 1970 and one in humane letters from Sussex University in 1973.

ABOUT: Gramophone (London), May 1971; Musical America, March 15, 1948, January 15, 1949; New York Times, February 21, 1965; Newsweek, November 8, 1948.

Walter Damrosch

1862–1950

Walter Johannes Damrosch, conductor, was born in Breslau, Prussia (now Wroclaw, Poland), on January 30, 1862. His father, Leopold Damrosch, was one of the most influential conductors of his time in America: the founder of the Oratorio Society of New York in 1873 and the New York Symphony Society in 1878 (both of which he conducted with distinction until his death) and the conductor of the Metropolitan Opera in 1884–1885. His mother, Helene von Heimburg Damrosch, achieved recognition as a singer of *Lieder* and opera. Walter's older brother, Frank (godson of Franz Liszt), was a distinguished educator who founded the Institute of Musical Art and later the Juilliard School of Music in New York.

Many prominent German musicians came to the Leopold Damrosch home to celebrate Walter's birth. Richard Wagner had been selected as Walter's godfather, but at the last moment Wagner demurred; having christened another of Leopold's sons who died soon after birth, Wagner feared he was the carrier of misfortune. Another godfather was substituted and the boy who was to have been named Richard Wagner Damrosch was called Walter Johannes Damrosch.

In 1871 the Damrosch family went to America where the father hoped to get a desirable musical appointment. They lived in a small apartment on Twenty-third Street near Third Avenue. Shortly after his arrival in America, Walter made a somewhat inauspicious musical debut. His father was rehearsing Schubert's *Der*

Damrosch

WALTER DAMROSCH

Häusliche Krieg, in which a crash of the cymbal was called for. Since hiring a special percussionist for this passage was too expensive, Leopold enlisted the services of his son, meticulously training him when and how to crash the cymbals. When the moment arrived for the cymbal crash, the excitement immobilized the boy and he was unable to move his hands.

Walter's first music teacher was his father, who gave him lessons in harmony. In America he studied the piano with Ferdinand Von Inten, Bernardus Boekelmann and Max Pinner. Later, in Germany, he studied theory with Max Draeseke and Wilhelm Rischbieter, and conducting with Hans von Bülow.

After his return to the United States, Walter was appointed organist of the Plymouth Church in Brooklyn, New York, where Henry Ward Beecher was the pastor. He also served as the accompanist to the violin virtuoso August Wilhelmj in a tour of the southern states in 1878, played the violin in orchestras conducted by his father, and assisted his father in directing various musical organizations. Walter's first conducting assignment was with the Newark (New Jersey) Harmonic Society in 1881.

Damrosch traveled throughout Europe in 1882. In Weimar, he met Liszt, and in Bayreuth he heard *Parsifal* at its world premiere.

The sudden death of Leopold Damrosch in 1885 provided young Damrosch with his first important conducting posts. He assumed all those vacated by his father. In addition to becoming the principal conductor of the New York Symphony Society and the Oratorio Society of New York, he stepped in to complete the season at the Metropolitan Opera, beginning on February 11, 1885, with a performance of *Tannhäuser* and following that one day later with a performance of *Die Walküre.* (The latter music drama had been introduced to the United States under Leopold Damrosch's direction on January 30, 1885.) As conductor of German operas at the Metropolitan, Damrosch was responsible for the engagement there of such Wagnerian performers as the singers Lilli Lehmann, Emil Fischer, and Max Alvary, and the conductor Anton Seidl. Damrosch was assigned the American premieres of Karl Goldmark's *Merlin* on January 3, 1887, and Cornelius's *The Barber of Bagdad* on January 3, 1890. He took over the latter opera from Anton Seidl, who had fallen ill, acquitting himself, as W. J. Henderson noted in the New York *Times,* "with full credit."

As the conductor of the New York Symphony Society, Damrosch was responsible for the American premieres of Ernest Bloch's *America,* Brahms's Symphony No.4, Bruckner's Symphony No.3, Gershwin's Concerto in F, Honegger's *Pacific 231,* Liszt's oratorio *Christus,* Mahler's Symphony No.4, Ravel's *Daphnis and Chloe Suite No.2,* Sibelius's Symphony No.4 and *Tapiola,* Tchaikovsky's Symphony No.4 and the *Pathétique,* Vaughan Williams's *London* and *Pastoral* symphonies, and a concert version of *Parsifal.*

On May 5, 1891, Damrosch assisted at the opening of Carnegie Hall, conducting the New York Symphony Society. For this occasion he invited Tchaikovsky to participate in the ceremonies by leading a performance of his *Overture 1812;* this was the first time a major European composer visited the United States.

Damrosch left the Metropolitan Opera after the 1890–1891 season. In 1894 he organized the Damrosch Opera Company which opened its first season with a performance in New York of *Tristan and Isolde* and toured the United States chiefly in the Wagnerian repertory for five seasons. "I had to travel continually," he recalled in his autobiography, "and during the entire five months of a season I carried a company of one hundred and seventy people, including an orchestra of seventy men." His first season brought in a profit of fifty-three thousand dollars. "Alas! I did not retain my quickly gained fortunes long!" The second season lost forty-three thou-

186

sand dollars. In 1899 Damrosch sold his interest in the company.

From 1900 to 1902 Damrosch was back at the Metropolitan Opera. During this period he led the American premiere of Paderewski's opera *Manru* on February 14, 1902. His farewell appearance at the Metropolitan Opera took place on March 6, 1902, with *Die Götterdämmerung.*

During the season 1902–1903 Damrosch conducted the New York Philharmonic Orchestra. In 1903 his own New York Symphony Society was completely reorganized and financed on a permanent basis. For the next twenty-four years he led over a hundred concerts a season with that organization. These performances, even more than those at the Metropolitan Opera, brought Damrosch recognition as one of America's great conductors. In 1919 he became the first American invited to tour Europe with an American orchestra. On February 27, 1922, the fiftieth anniversary of his arrival in America was celebrated in Carnegie Hall with a mammoth concert in which three orchestras led by five conductors participated; the proceeds from this event helped to establish a Walter Damrosch fellowship at the American Academy in Rome.

To his regular subscription concerts with the New York Symphony Society Damrosch added annual children's concerts where he was both commentator and conductor. Initiated in 1889 these children's concerts were the first to be undertaken by a major orchestra. From time to time he gave lecture concerts for adults, the first of which took place in 1890.

During World War I Damrosch organized the American Expeditionary Forces band at the request of General Pershing. He also organized a school for bandmasters at Chaumont, France, in 1918. This school was the source of the Fontainebleau School of Music, formed immediately after the war's end in France to provide a conservatory for American musicians.

In 1926 the New York Symphony Society was dissolved, and some of its musicians were absorbed into the New York Philharmonic Orchestra. For a season Damrosch was guest conductor of the New York Philharmonic, but he then withdrew from the concert field to concentrate on radio. He had conducted his first symphony concert on radio on November 15, 1926, over the NBC network, the first such performance to receive network coverage. In 1927 Damrosch was named musical adviser to NBC.

In that capacity he directed concerts of symphonic music over the air, among the first serious orchestral concerts heard over radio. He also created the "Music Appreciation Hour" which, from its beginnings in 1928 until 1942, instructed young Americans in the appreciation of great music. It was estimated that over seven million schoolchildren heard these educational broadcasts each week.

On April 12, 1935, Damrosch conducted a festival concert at the Metropolitan Opera House in celebration of the fortieth anniversary of his first appearance as a conductor in New York City. His program was made up of the second act of *Fidelio* and the third act of *Die Meistersinger,* the latter given in his own English translation. The receipts were donated to the Musicians Emergency Fund.

He resigned as musical adviser at NBC on March 31, 1947, to go into complete retirement.

Damrosch's contributions to American music have been summed up as follows: "Walter Damrosch has sold good music to America. That has been his greatest contribution as a conductor. He has never been—not even at the height of his career—a particularly inspired, or inspiring, performer. His standards too often were lax; his readings skirted the surface; his command of the orchestra, and orchestral music, less than consummate. Yet he has been a force of incomparable significance with the baton; and—for all his inadequate performance—he has served music well." (*Dictators of the Baton*). A more specific comment on Damrosch's conducting appears in an earlier book on conductors: "His baton too often touched the surfaces of a musical work without penetrating far into the depths; and it could frequently evoke no more than a stereotyped reading from the orchestral musicians—a reading in which the inner voices, the subtle threads of sound that course and intertwine into a musical fabric, were usually absent." (*The Man With the Baton,* by D. Ewen)

Damrosch was the composer of operas, chamber music, and choral compositions. His opera *The Scarlet Letter* received its premiere with his own opera company in Boston on February 10, 1896. A comic opera, *The Dove of Peace,* was produced in Philadelphia on October 15, 1912. The Metropolitan Opera produced *Cyrano de Bergerac* on February 27, 1913, and *The Man Without a Country* on May 12, 1937. And on November 3, 1942, the New York Opera Company presented the world premiere of his one-act opera, *The Opera Cloak.* Damrosch also composed two highly popular songs: "Danny Deever" and "Death and General Putnam." During World War II he provided a musical setting for Robert Nathan's *Dunkirk,* scored for baritone solo, male chorus, and chamber orchestra, heard over the NBC network on May 2, 1943. In 1944 he wrote the music for a comic opera, *Congress and the Elephants.*

Damrosch was the author of an autobiography, *My Musical Life* (1923), and a coeditor of the *Universal Music Series.* He appeared as himself in a motion picture, *The Star Maker* (1939).

He lived in a town house on East Seventy-first Street, New York, with his wife, Margaret, the daughter of James G. Blaine, one-time secretary of state of the United States. The Damrosches were married on May 17, 1890. They had four daughters. One of them, Gretchen D. Finletter, was the wife of Secretary of the Air Force Thomas K. Finletter, and the author of a charming book of reminiscences, *From the Top of the Stairs* (1946). Another of Damrosch's daughters was married to Sidney Howard, the playwright, and a third to Robert Littell, writer and editor. Damrosch's wife died in 1949.

A genial and witty man, Damrosch, in his appearance and speech, was the image everybody carries of what a kindly grandfather should be. As a diversion from his musical activities he used to build elaborate pasteboard houses which he himself designed and decorated. At the age of eight, he had built a miniature Wagnerian theater upon which, some years later, he used puppets to enact *Das Rheingold* while he himself performed the score on the piano. His delight in pasteboard houses did not diminish with the passing of years.

Damrosch also enjoyed painting on canvas, reading (history and biography primarily), going to the theater, gardening, being a host to a small group of intimate friends, and occasionally wearing elaborate costumes at fancy-dress balls.

Damrosch was the president of the National Institute of Arts and Letters from 1937 to 1941; the Institute presented him with a gold medal in 1939. In 1941 he became president of the American Academy of Arts and Letters. He was made Chevalier of the Crown of Belgium, Officer of the French Legion of Honor, and Officer of the Crown of Italy. London presented him with the silver medal of the Worshipful Company of

Musicians, and Rome with the Banda Comunale. He received numerous honorary doctorates in music from colleges and universities, among which were Columbia, Princeton, Brown, Dartmouth, and New York University.

Walter Damrosch died of a heart attack in New York City on December 22, 1950. He was buried in Bar Harbor, Maine.

In 1959 Damrosch Park, a two-and-a-half-acre tract at Lincoln Center for the Performing Arts was established by the City of New York in honor of "the distinguished family of musicians."

ABOUT: Damrosch, W. My Musical Life; Ewen, D. Dictators of the Baton; Finletter, G. D. From the Top of the Stairs. *Periodicals*—Musical America, January 1, 1951; Musical Quarterly, January 1932; Opera News, January 27, 1962.

Colin Davis

1927–

Because of his spectacular ascent to world prominence in music at a comparatively young age, Colin (Rex) Davis, conductor, has been called "the Celtic Leonard Bernstein." Colin was born in Weybridge, Surrey, England, on September 25, 1927, the fifth in a family of seven children of Reginald George and Lillian Constance Colbran Davis. His father was a bank clerk, and the family lived in a flat above a shop. Neither parent was a musician, but each loved music deeply, and the child Colin was exposed to it through recordings.

When Colin was thirteen, the importance of music in his life became apparent to him. "Puberty burst on me," he later told an interviewer, "and music came to my rescue, and it's been with me ever since. It was a conversion—I was in it. It was Beethoven's Eighth Symphony that did it. My brother brought home a record during the holidays."

Colin was trained on the clarinet. He played it in the school band at Christ's Hospital Boys' School in Sussex. Later he studied on a scholarship at the Royal College of Music. There Colin carried about his "little secret of wanting to be a conductor. When I finally came out with it, the school said I hadn't the necessary background in piano and theory, so I never studied conduct-

COLIN DAVIS

ing." What he learned then and later about conducting came from studying manuals, memorizing scores, and acquiring his baton technique by "conducting" performances of phonograph music.

During two years of military service from 1946 to 1948 Davis played the clarinet in His Majesty's Life Guards Band. When this military service ended, he set about realizing his ambition to become a conductor. In 1949 he found his first conducting assignment with the Kalmar Chamber Orchestra, and in 1950 he served as conductor of the Chelsea Opera Group. At about this time he also conducted a performance of *Don Giovanni* in Oxford, an opera that would later provide the turning point in his career.

His conducting apprenticeship continued for a number of years: with a debut at the Royal Festival Hall in London in 1952 where he led performances of ballet; as assistant conductor of the Scottish BBC Orchestra to which he was appointed in 1957 and where he remained two years; as conductor of Sadler's Wells in London where he made his debut in 1958 with *The Abduction from the Seraglio*. Three years later he was appointed musical director of Sadler's Wells.

The attention of the English music world was first focused on him one evening in 1959 in London. Otto Klemperer was scheduled to lead a concert performance of *Don Giovanni* at the Royal Festival Hall with a cast headed by Joan Sutherland and Elisabeth Schwarzkopf. When Klemperer suddenly fell ill, Davis was called in

as replacement. "I was lucky it was *Don Giovanni*," he has commented, "because I knew it so well." That performance catapulted him to fame. One year later, when Sir Thomas Beecham became ill, Davis was again recruited as a substitute, this time for a performance of *The Magic Flute* at the Glyndebourne Festival. Once again he achieved a personal triumph. Some English critics even spoke of him as the best English-born conductor since Beecham.

At Sadler's Wells, where he became principal conductor in 1960 and music director one year later, Davis conducted an extensive and varied repertory with authority and versatility. In addition to the famous operas and musical dramas of Mozart, Verdi, Wagner, and Beethoven, Davis directed less familiar items such as Stravinsky's *Oedipus Rex* and *The Rake's Progress,* Janáček's *The Cunning Little Vixen,* Kurt Weill's *The Rise and Fall of the City Mahagonny* and, on February 24, 1965, the world premiere of Richard Rodney Bennett's *The Mines of Sulphur.*

Davis remained with Sadler's Wells until 1965. During these years he became increasingly well known worldwide. In 1959 he made his first appearance on the American continent, conducting several broadcasts of the CBC Symphony Orchestra in Canada. His debut in the United States followed in 1961 with appearances as guest conductor of the Minneapolis Symphony. He returned to the United States in 1964 to share the podium with Georg Solti and István Kertész during a world tour of the London Symphony Orchestra. After one of these concerts—at Carnegie Hall on October 23—William Bender in the *Herald Tribune* described Davis as a conductor with "a combination of orchestral skill, dramatic flair, and a sense of proportion equaled by few maestros of our day. . . . [He] built a strong performance from the very place such strength must come from—within the music itself. It is a strength born of internal meaning, of symmetry and just measure, rather than headlong movement."

In the summer of 1966 Davis conducted the London Symphony Orchestra for four weeks at the Florida International Festival at Daytona Beach.

A concert performance of Berlioz' opera *Les Troyens* at Festival Hall in London in December 1966 did much to establish Davis as an important interpreter of Berlioz' music. When Davis had conducted Berlioz' *Symphonie Fantastique* with the Philadelphia Orchestra at the Lincoln Center for the Performing Arts on January 18, 1966, Alan Rich called it in the *Herald Tribune* "one of the greatest feats of musical communication in the recent annals of New York performance." Davis has since conducted all of Berlioz' major works for Philips Records, including the complete *Les Troyens. Les Troyens* received a Grammy from the National Academy of Recording Arts and Sciences in 1970; his recording of *Benvenuto Cellini* won the Montreux International Prize in 1973.

For Davis the conducting of Berlioz is as physically demanding and exacting as it is artistically rewarding. He has described how enormous an output of energy is hurled into each of these performances. "I curse him [Berlioz] afterwards because I feel so absolutely smashed up. *The Trojans* nearly killed me. We were recording it at the same time we were performing it at Covent Garden. I always felt I wanted to shake my fist at this man. He's killing me—but I love him so."

In 1967 (a year in which Davis was awarded the Grand Prix du Disque in Paris for his recording of Handel's *Messiah*) Davis was appointed principal conductor of the BBC Symphony Orchestra, an office he held with distinction until 1971. He had become one of the lionized conductors in Britain, as Harold Rogers noted in *The Christian Science Monitor.* A year later Davis was also appointed music director of Covent Garden in London, succeeding Georg Solti, inaugurating his regime with a sensational production of *The Marriage of Figaro* (a performance recorded by Philips). With this appointment two of the most important music posts in London had fallen to a man who had just passed his forty-first birthday. A third came his way in 1969 when he was made the artistic director of the Bath Festival.

At Covent Garden Davis helped to create a new epoch for that historic opera house, highlighted by the performance in September 1969 of *Les Troyens,* presented complete on the stage for the first time as Berlioz had conceived it—and in a single evening. In recognition of his achievements, Covent Garden promoted Davis to the post of music director in 1971. Though Davis's contract as music director was to expire in 1979, Covent Garden renewed it in 1978 for an additional three years.

On November 7, 1968, Davis made his bow with the New York Philharmonic Orchestra. Since that time he has been heard with most of America's leading symphonic organizations. Early in 1972 he went for the first time to the Metropolitan Opera with a new production of *Pelléas and Mélisande.* He subsequently led other distinguished performances there, among them *Wozzeck* and *Peter Grimes.*

Davis was twice married: first, in 1949, to April Cantelo, a singer, with whom he had two children (one son, one daughter) before their divorce in 1964; second, in November 1964, to a Persian girl, Ashraf Naini, with whom he had three sons. Davis's recreations include gardening, cooking, and reading. "Music," he has said, "is not a substitute for life itself, but you must be rooted in real life." In 1965 Davis was made Commander of the Order of the British Empire.

ABOUT: Blyth, A. Colin Davis. *Periodicals*—Hi-Fi, August 1971, October 1972; New York Times, February 19, 1967, February 6, 1972; Opera News, February 11, 1967; Time, January 27, 1967, January 3, 1972.

Alicia De Larrocha

See Larrocha

Lisa Della Casa

1919–

Lisa Della Casa, soprano, was born to Swiss-Italian and German parents—Francesco Roberto and Margarete Müller Della Casa—in Burgdorf, Switzerland, on February 2, 1919. Her father, an ophthalmologist, had a pleasant baritone voice; he sang and organized performances of plays, operas, and concerts. In her fifth year Lisa made her first appearance on the stage in one of her father's productions. Playing the part of a peasant girl she was allowed one speaking line to which she introduced a note of realism by wiping her nose on her sleeve from wrist to shoulder.

Her father, determined to make her a concert singer, gave Lisa her first vocal lessons. She agreed with his wish when she was twelve, after attending a performance of *Salome.* At fifteen she began studying with Margarete Haeser in

LISA DELLA CASA

As a principal soprano of the Metropolitan Opera for almost two decades Della Casa distinguished herself as Eva, Octavian and the Marschallin, Cio-Cio-San, Zdenka, Mimi in *La Bohème,* Donna Elvira in *Don Giovanni,* Elsa in *Lohengrin,* Arabella, Ariadne in *Ariadne auf Naxos,* and Saffi in *The Gypsy Baron.* Of her performance in *Don Giovanni* on October 31, 1957, Howard Taubman said in the New York *Times:* "Donna Elvira is not a scold but an ill-used and loving woman, and her singing is pure, elegant and sensitive."

In addition to her regular appearances at the Vienna State Opera and the Metropolitan Opera, Della Casa was heard at the festivals at Edinburgh, Salzburg, Bayreuth, Zurich, Glyndebourne, Lucerne, Munich, and Bregenz. She has been a guest artist at La Scala in Milan, Covent Garden in London, Paris Opéra, Deutsche Oper in Berlin, the Vienna State Opera, Munich Opera, Cologne Opera, Théâtre de la Monnaie in Brussels, the Stockholm Royal Opera, Teatro Colón in Buenos Aires, and the San Francisco Opera. She was also heard as Marzelline in *Fidelio,* Marguerite in Berlioz' *The Damnation of Faust,* Bess in Gershwin's *Porgy and Bess,* Cleopatra in Handel's *Giulio Cesare,* Ursula in Hindemith's *Mathis der Maler,* Lucille in von Einem's *Dantons Tod,* Fiordiligi in *Così fan Tutte,* Donna Anna in *Don Giovanni,* Ilia in Mozart's *Idomeneo,* Pamina and the Queen of the Night in *The Magic Flute,* the title role in Puccini's *Suor Angelica,* Tosca, Chrysothemis in *Elektra,* Salome, and Gilda in *Rigoletto.*

On May 29, 1949, Della Casa appeared in Zurich in the world premiere of Willy Burkhard's *Die Schwarze Spinne.* This was one of many efforts on her part to promote the music of twentieth century Swiss composers.

Outside opera, she has distinguished herself as a soloist in choral masterworks by Handel, Haydn, Brahms, Bruckner, and Verdi, and in recitals.

As a young woman in Zurich Della Casa married a student, but the marriage ended after four years. In 1949, while a member of the Vienna State Opera, she met Dragan Debeljevic, a newspaperman who had reviewed her Vienna performances for a Zurich daily. They were next-door neighbors, and since both loved dogs, they took to walking together with their respective canines. Della Casa and Debeljevic were married on December 5, 1949. They have a daughter.

Zurich, the only teacher she was to have other than her father.

In 1941 Della Casa made her opera debut as Cio-Cio-San in *Madama Butterfly* in Solothurn-Biel in Switzerland. Two years later she joined the company of the Zurich Opera where she made her debut as Mimi in *La Bohème.* She remained in Zurich for seven years, acclaimed in the German repertory and particularly in the operas of Mozart and Richard Strauss. In Zurich in 1943 she appeared for the first time as Zdenka in Richard Strauss's *Arabella.* This became one of her celebrated roles. When Richard Strauss heard her, he engaged her to sing the same part at the Salzburg Festival in 1947. Her success brought invitations to appear there in subsequent years: in 1949 she achieved a brilliant success as the Countess in Richard Strauss's *Capriccio,* and on August 17, 1953, she created the three women's roles in the world premiere of Gottfried von Einem's *The Trial.*

She joined the Vienna State Opera in the fall of 1947 as leading soprano. Five years later she was heard as Eva in *Die Meistersinger* at the Bayreuth Festival.

Her debut at the Metropolitan Opera took place on November 20, 1953, as the Countess in *The Marriage of Figaro.* Henry W. Levinger described her in *Musical America* as "a beautiful woman of great dignity . . . endowed with a warm and expressive voice." He added: "She gave her part of the Countess . . . the most telling interpretation which climaxed with her rendition of 'Dove sono.' "

Del Monaco

Their home has been a thirty-room Gothic castle, Schloss Gottlieben, dating from the thirteenth century, in Thurgau, on Lake Constance, in Switzerland. Jan Huss was imprisoned there before being burned at the stake in 1415. The prison has been preserved and Czec Hussites often make pilgrimages there. Della Casa and her family also own a house in Vienna.

An attractive woman with blue-black hair and hazel eyes, Lisa Della Casa is a rarity among singers in that she never worries about her throat and often smokes cigarettes in her dressing room during a rehearsal. She avoids parties, preferring quiet evenings at home with family and friends. "A good day," she has said, "is when I can be at home and walk the garden and forget that I am a singer."

Della Casa was named Kammersängerin by the Austrian government.

ABOUT: New York Post, December 3, 1959; New York Times, December 13, 1959.

MARIO DEL MONACO

Mario Del Monaco

1915–

Mario Del Monaco, tenor, was born in Florence, on July 27, 1915. His mother was a trained singer; his father, a government official, was a music lover. Both parents directed Mario to music early in his life. Mario spent his boyhood years in Pesaro where his father had a job. When he was seven, Mario already knew that someday he would become an opera singer, and when he was thirteen he made his first public appearance in a version of Massenet's *Narcisse* at the Teatro Beniamino Gigli in Mondolfo. However, Mario found his first vocal lessons so frustrating that he abandoned them and channeled his love for music into listening to recordings, memorizing opera scores, and painting and sculpting.

At nineteen he entered the Rossini Conservatory in Pesaro, becoming a student of Luisa Melai-Palazzini and Arturo Melocchi. Once again, after just a few months of study, he was discouraged by his slow progress, and again he decided that he had had his fill of formal instruction. He never took vocal lessons again.

In 1935 Del Monaco won first prize in a sing-

Del Monaco: dĕl mŏn′ á kō

ing contest in Rome arranged by the conductor Tullio Serafin. Early in World War II Del Monaco joined the Italian army and saw service for six years. In 1941 he was given permission by the military authorities to make his professional debut at the Teatro Puccini in Milan on January 1, as Pinkerton in *Madama Butterfly*.

After the war Del Monaco pursued his singing career actively. He enjoyed his first success at La Scala in Milan, where he was heard in thirty-three leading tenor roles, mainly in the Italian repertory. He also appeared at the San Carlo in Naples, the Rome Opera, Covent Garden in London, and with companies in Barcelona, Lisbon, Stockholm and elsewhere. In 1946 his successes extended to performances at the Teatro Colón in Buenos Aires and the Teatro Municipal in Rio de Janeiro, and then in Mexico City. That summer he caused a sensation as Radames in *Aida* at the Verona Arena and later the same year as Andrea Chénier in Trieste.

He was introduced to the United States at the San Francisco Opera on the opening night of the season, September 26, 1950, as Radames. That season he also appeared there as Andrea Chénier and as Des Grieux in *Manon Lescaut*. He returned to San Francisco in 1952 and again in 1959.

Rudolf Bing, general manager of the Metropolitan Opera, heard him in San Francisco in 1950 and gave him a contract with the Metropolitan. His Metropolitan Opera debut followed on November 27, 1950, as Des Grieux in

192

Manon Lescaut. Writing in the *Herald Tribune,* Arthur Berger found that Del Monaco was the "proud possessor of a fresh and powerful voice . . . and he had the added asset of an animated and by no means reticent personality."

The following season he was made a permanent member of the Metropolitan Opera Company. In the years between 1951 and early 1954 he was heard as Radames, Turiddu in *Cavalleria Rusticana,* Edgardo in *Lucia di Lammermoor,* Otello, Don José in *Carmen,* Manrico in *Il Trovatore,* Don Alvaro in *La Forza del Destino,* Enzo in *La Gioconda,* Cavaradossi in *Tosca,* and Canio in *I Pagliacci.* In some of these performances he was criticized for overacting and for singing too loudly, but as time passed he remedied these faults. On November 16, 1954, he brought down the house as Andrea Chénier; the ovation held up the production for several minutes at one point in the performance. His later successes at the Metropolitan were as Pinkerton in *Madama Butterfly,* Pollione in a performance of *Norma* in which Maria Callas made her Metropolitan Opera debut, the title role in *Ernani,* and Samson in *Samson and Delilah.* Commenting on Del Monaco's later performances in the French and Italian repertory, Virgil Thomson called him in the *Herald Tribune* "one of the purest tenor voices lately encountered."

In 1955 and again in 1956 Del Monaco was acclaimed as Andrea Chénier and Pollione at La Scala in Milan, and in the summer of 1955 he was given an ovation for his performance as Otello at the Verona Arena. In October 1956 he appeared with the Chicago Lyric Opera as Dick Johnson in *The Girl of the Golden West* and as Andrea Chénier. During the summer of the same year he had joined former members of La Scala in a performance of *Carmen* at the Volksoper in Vienna.

Del Monaco remained with the Metropolitan Opera through the 1956–1957 season. He toured the Soviet Union in 1960 and Germany in 1961–1962 and was accepted in both places as one of the best Italian tenors to emerge since the end of World War II. The Vienna State Opera, the Paris Opera, the Deutsche Oper in Berlin, the Hamburg Opera, Teatro La Fenice in Venice, the Zurich Opera, and the Bolshoi Opera in Moscow were some of the other companies with which he made successful appearances. He has also been heard as Faust in Boïto's *Mefistofele,*

Maurizio in *Adriana Lecouvreur,* Loris in *Fedora,* Rodolfo in *La Bohème,* Calaf in *Turandot,* Ismaele in Verdi's *Nabucco,* the Duke in *Rigoletto,* and Alfredo in *La Traviata.*

Del Monaco has been starred in the following motion pictures: *The Man With the Grey Glove* (1953), *Cavalleria Rusticana* (1953), *The House of Ricordi* (1956), and *Beautiful but Dangerous* (1958). He dubbed in the singing of all the operatic arias on the sound track of *The Young Caruso* (1953).

He is married to the former Rina Fedora, a professional singer who gave up her own career to run their household in Milan and raise two sons. Del Monaco enjoys painting, sculpting, and collecting Chinese art. He has been awarded the Gold Medal of the City of Paris and the Academic Order of Lenin in the Soviet Union.

ABOUT: New York Times, November 29, 1954; Opera News, March 3, 1952.

Victoria De Los Angeles

See Angeles

Giuseppe De Luca

1876–1950

Giuseppe De Luca, baritone, was born in Rome on December 25, 1876. His father, Nicola, a blacksmith, wanted his son to learn a trade so that he might begin earning a living early. He therefore was antagonistic to music training although Giuseppe had revealed an interest in music from childhood. But his mother, the former Lucia de Filippi, who had been a professional singer, overcame her husband's objections. When Giuseppe was eight, she entered him in the Schola Cantorum in Rome which developed church singers and which prepared him to perform at St. Peter's and before Pope Leo XIII.

After receiving vocal training from Bartolini, Giuseppe entered the Santa Cecilia Academy in Rome on a scholarship in 1892. During his first year there, his father died and he had to help support the family by taking on odd jobs and

De Luca: dä lōō′ kä

De Luca

GIUSEPPE DE LUCA

occasionally singing for a fee at private parties. However he continued music study and remained at the Santa Cecilia five years, specializing in bel canto with Venceslao Persichini.

On November 6, 1897, De Luca made his opera debut in Piacenza as Valentin in *Faust*. His success brought him engagements in the early 1900s from other Italian opera companies. At the Teatro Lirico in Milan he created the role of Michonnet in Cilèa's *Adriana Lecouvreur* on November 6, 1902, Toscanini conducting. In 1903 he toured South America with a company headed by Caruso and conducted by Toscanini; in the fall he was engaged by La Scala in Milan, making his debut there as Alberich in the first Italian performance of *Das Rheingold*. While at La Scala he sang the principal baritone role in the world premiere of Giordano's *Siberia* on December 19, 1903, and on February 17, 1904, he created the role of Sharpless in the ill-fated world premiere of *Madama Butterfly*. During his eight years in many roles at La Scala De Luca was highly praised for his performances in *Rigoletto, Don Giovanni, Don Pasquale, Hamlet,* and *The Barber of Seville*.

After touring the leading cities of Italy and making noteworthy appearances in Russia and South America, De Luca made his debut at the Metropolitan Opera on November 25, 1915, as Figaro in *The Barber of Seville*. "His voice has an excellent quality and resonance," wrote Richard Aldrich in the New York *Times*. "He has the volubility and the volatile spirit, and an intelligence and comic power that made his perform-

ance acceptable, and that gave his part the value it should have in the whole."

De Luca showed to even better advantage in other appearances that first season, as Alfio in *Cavalleria Rusticana*, Marcello in *La Bohème*, Plunkett in *Martha*, the elder Germont in *La Traviata*, Scarpia in *Tosca*, Amonasro in *Aida*, Tonio in *I Pagliacci*, Sharpless, the title role in *Rigoletto*, Lescaut in *Manon Lescaut* and in *Manon*, Escamillo in *Carmen*, and Paquiro in the world premiere of Granados's *Goyescas* on January 28, 1916.

He remained the principal baritone of the Metropolitan for two decades, developing a bel canto style which for purity of texture and luxuriance of sound had few equals. He mastered about one hundred roles in the Italian and French repertory, and he made over 723 appearances in New York and 199 on tour, sometimes as many as 50 a season. At the Metropolitan Opera he created the title role in *Gianni Schicchi* on December 17, 1918, and he appeared in the American premieres of Rabaud's *Mârouf* on December 19, 1917, and Respighi's *La Campana Sommersa* on November 24, 1928. In the New York *Times*, Richard Aldrich said of De Luca's performance in the title role of *Mârouf* that he had done "nothing better than this insouciant and humorous impersonation of the adventurous cobbler," and in the *Herald Tribune* Lawrence Gilman described De Luca's interpretation of the role of the Old Man of the Well in the Respighi opera as "a masterpiece of comic grotesquerie." De Luca's other Metropolitan Opera roles were Zurga in *Les Pêcheurs de Perles*, the High Priest in *Samson and Delilah*, Figaro in *The Marriage of Figaro*, Count di Luna in *Il Trovatore*, Frédéric in *Lakmé*, Riccardo in *I Puritani*, Giannetto in Mascagni's *Lodoletta*, Don Carlo in *La Forza del Destino*, Belcore in *L'Elisir d'Amore*, Taddeo in *L'Italiana in Algeri*, the title role in *Eugene Onegin*, Cascart in *Zaza*, Rodrigo in *Don Carlo*, Valentin in *Faust*, Guglielmo in *Così fan Tutte*, Mercutio in *Romeo and Juliet*, the three principal baritone roles in *The Tales of Hoffmann*, De Siriex in *Fedora*, Hoël in *Dinorah*, Barnaba in *La Gioconda*, Nelusko in *L'Africaine*, Cinna in *La Vestale*, Sancho in *Don Quichotte*, Ping in *Turandot*, Miller in *Luisa Miller*, Kyoto in Mascagni's *Iris*, the Father in *Il Signor Bruschino*, Antonio in *Linda di Chamounix*, and Dr. Malatesta in *Don Pasquale*.

Having completed two decades at the Metropolitan Opera, De Luca announced his retirement in 1935, making what he thought would be his last appearance on that stage on March 29 as Marcello. But his career was far from over. For the next four years he continued making appearances in European opera houses, and giving recitals, and performing over the radio. Then in 1940 he returned to the Metropolitan Opera for several guest appearances, beginning February 7 when, at the age of sixty-four, he sang the part of the elder Germont. "The first five notes made the pulses beat because of the art and beauty of the song," reported Olin Downes in the New York *Times*. "The quality of the legato, the perfection of style, the sentiment which ennobled the melodic phrase, struck the whole audience. Probably many were not able to analyze their sensation, which lay in the artist's vocal skill and his lofty conception of a melody which verges so perilously close upon the sentimental, but was made on this occasion a wholly acceptable expression of genuine humanity."

Except for a few performances for wounded Italian soldiers in hospitals, De Luca refused to do any public singing during World War II, insisting he was in no mood to make music. After the war he made some appearances with the Rome Opera and gave concerts both in Europe and in America without giving the slightest indication that time and age had seriously impaired his vocal delivery. He made his last public appearance in a recital in New York on November 7, 1947, fifty years and one day after his professional debut. "Mr. De Luca shed joy as he sang," Olin Downes wrote. "The felicity of his method matched his remarkable musicianship and his capacity to make every tone and every syllable of his text instinct with meaning. . . . This was the performance of a man with the soul of a true artist, a devoted servant of his art, and a master of singing."

In retirement De Luca devoted himself to teaching voice at his apartment at the Buckingham Hotel in New York and at the Juilliard School of Music. He was planning to join the faculty of the Curtis Institute of Music in Philadelphia when he was stricken by his last illness. He died in a New York hospital on August 26, 1950, after an operation.

In half a century of worldwide successes, De Luca gathered many honors and decorations: Cavalier of the Great Cross, Crown of Italy,

Commendatore of S.S. Maurizio and Lazzaro, Donato of First Class Knights of Malta, and a decoration from the Santa Cecilia Academy in Rome.

He was twice married: in 1903 to Olimpia Fierro, who died in 1918 and with whom he had a daughter, and on October 22, 1922, to her sister, Julia. De Luca believed in physical exercise and athletics. He always rose early in the morning, regardless of the hour at which he had gone to bed the previous night, and performed setting-up exercises. He rarely used an automobile when he could get to his destination by walking. A champion swimmer, he won several prizes in competitions held in the Tiber River in Rome. In addition to athletics and music, his interests included the movies, circus performances, and occasional games of poker.

ABOUT: New York Times Magazine, November 2, 1947; New Yorker, July 6, 1946; Newsweek, March 25, 1946.

Vladimir De Pachmann

See Pachmann

Victor De Sabata

See Sabata

Emmy Destinn

1878–1930

Emmy Destinn (originally Ema Kittl), soprano, was born in Prague, Bohemia, on February 26, 1878. During her childhood she received lessons on the piano and the violin. When she was eight, she gave concerts on the latter instrument, proving herself a prodigy. Four years later she began studying singing with Marie Loewe-Destinn, a prominent vocal teacher in Prague, whose profound and decisive influence in the shaping of Emmy's career led the young student to take her teacher's name permanently.

Destinn: dĕs′ tĭn

195

Destinn

EMMY DESTINN

Destinn was twenty when she made her opera debut on July 19, 1898, at the New Opera House in Berlin, as Santuzza in *Cavalleria Rusticana.* Later she sang the role of Elisabeth in the four-hundredth performance of *Tannhäuser.* Her success brought her a five-year contract as a regular member of the Berlin Royal Opera, where she made her debut as Santuzza. There she was hailed for her performances as Mignon, as Marguerite de Valois in *Les Huguenots,* and as Diemut in the Berlin premiere of Richard Strauss's *Feuersnot* in 1901. Strauss selected her for the title role in the first presentation of *Salome* in Berlin in 1905 and invited her to come to Paris in 1907 for the French premiere of the same opera. She also reaped praise in Berlin for her performances in the Wagner repertory. She became a protégée of Cosima Wagner who, in 1901, chose her to appear as Senta in the first production of *The Flying Dutchman* at the Bayreuth Festival.

On May 2, 1904, Destinn made her initial appearance at Covent Garden in London as Donna Anna in *Don Giovanni.* After that performance she was the idol of the English opera public and was called back to Covent Garden annually until World War I. In 1905 she appeared there in the title role of the first performance in England of *Madama Butterfly,* opposite Enrico Caruso, and on July 14, 1909, in England's premiere of Baron Frederic d'Erlanger's *Tess.*

She had become a world figure in opera when she made her American debut at the Metropoli-

tan Opera on November 16, 1908 (the opening night of the season), in the title role of *Aida;* Caruso was Radames, and Toscanini, also making his American debut, was in the pit. Though attention was focused on Toscanini, Destinn did not go unnoticed. In the New York *Times* Richard Aldrich described her voice as a "voice of great power, dramatic in expression, flexible and wholly subservient to her intentions, which are those of a singer of keen musical feeling and intelligence."

She remained with the Metropolitan Opera through the 1915–1916 season, appearing as Minnie in the world premiere of *The Girl of the Golden West* on December 10, 1910, and starring in several noteworthy American premieres among which were Eugène d'Albert's *Tiefland* on November 23, 1908 (Marta), Catalani's *La Wally* on January 6, 1909 (title role), *The Bartered Bride* on February 19, 1909 (Marie), Franchetti's *Germania* on January 22, 1910 (Ricke), and Tchaikovsky's *Pique Dame* on March 5, 1910 (Lisa). As Minnie, wrote Richard Aldrich, she was "singularly delicious. . . . She acted the part with sincerity, and her singing of the music . . . was of splendid power and expressiveness."

She helped to open the following Metropolitan Opera seasons: 1909–1910 in the title role of *La Gioconda;* 1911–1912 in the title role of *Aida;* 1913–1914, again in *La Gioconda;* and 1914–1915 as Amelia in *Un Ballo in Maschera.* The last of these operas was revived on November 22, 1914, to commemorate the centenary of Verdi's birth.

Her other roles at the Metropolitan were Tosca, Santuzza, Madama Butterfly, Pamina in *The Magic Flute,* Alice Ford in *Falstaff,* Nedda in *I Pagliacci,* Eva in *Die Meistersinger,* Elsa in *Lohengrin,* Leonora in *Il Trovatore,* Elisabeth in *Tannhäuser,* Agathe in *Der Freischütz,* Valentine in *Les Huguenots,* Gerhilde in *Die Walküre,* and the Priestess in *Aida.* To each of these roles she brought dramatic power, a big voice that could also be hypersensitive, a remarkable range, and thorough musicianship. She made Tosca, as W. J. Henderson wrote in the *Sun,* "a woman of the people . . . well poised in her splendid intelligence." Of her Cio-Cio-San, in which she had proved sensational at Covent Garden in 1903 before singing the role at the Metropolitan, another critic from the *Sun* remarked: "The artistic glory of her impersonation is found . . . in wonderfully eloquent singing of the music, to which her dramatic voice is perfectly suited."

When the Metropolitan Opera made its first tour of Europe in 1910, Destinn was starred with Caruso in the opening performance at the Théâtre du Chatelet in *Aida,* Toscanini conducting.

After the 1915–1916 season of the Metropolitan Destinn returned to her native land. As a token of patriotism she adopted the Czech name of Ema Destinnová (which she soon discarded). She hurled all her energy and influence into helping promote the independence of Czechoslovakia, an activity that led the Austrian authorities to revoke her passport, thus denying her the opportunity of propagandizing for Czech liberation outside her own country. For the duration of World War I she was interned on her estate in Bohemia.

After World War I Destinn appeared at the Czechoslovakia Festival in London from May to June 1919. She returned to the Metropolitan Opera as Aida on December 8, 1919, remaining with the company through the 1920–1921 season. Her four-year layoff during the war had permanently impaired the power and brilliance of her voice and in 1926 she went into retirement. She spent her last years in a castle in Straz, Czechoslovakia, which she had purchased in 1914 and where she lived with her husband, a young captain of the Czech air force who had crashed on her property and whom she had nursed back to health. In retirement, Emmy Destinn became a writer. She was the author of a play that was produced, a novel that was published, and a considerable amount of published poetry. She died in Budějovice (Budweis), Czechoslovakia, on January 28, 1930.

In the early 1970s a 1908 recording of *Carmen* with Emmy Destinn singing the title role was re-released on the Discophilia label.

ABOUT: Opera (London), September 1955; Opera News, January 6, 1962.

Edo De Waart

See Waart

Misha Dichter

1945–

Misha Dichter, pianist, was born in Shanghai on September 27, 1945, to Leon and Lucy Lhevine Dichter. His parents, who were Polish, had stopped off in Shanghai en route to the United States. They went to Los Angeles in 1947. There Misha began his first piano lessons when he was six. In 1961 he received first prize in a competition for instrumentalists sponsored by the Music Educators National Conference, Western Division, in which sixty contestants participated. This award brought Misha his first appearance with an orchestra, a performance of Rachmaninoff's Piano Concerto No.2 at the Santa Monica Civic Auditorium.

From the time he was twelve to his eighteenth year Misha studied with Aube Tzerko, a pupil of Artur Schnabel. While attending the Beverly Hills High School, from which he was graduated in 1963, Misha made a number of public appearances. As a student at the University of California in Los Angeles, where he majored in English, he won the Atwater Kent Award in piano and was a soloist with various local orchestras, including the Los Angeles Philharmonic at a Symphonies for Youth Concert during the 1963–1964 season. He also played at an orchestral concert in Beverly Hills celebrating the fiftieth anniversary of the founding of the city.

He had gone through two semesters at the University when in June 1964 he participated in a two-week master class in piano given there by Rosina Lhevinne. She became so impressed with his talent that she urged him to join her class at the Juilliard School of Music in New York, for which he was awarded the Joseph Lhevinne scholarship. At the Juilliard School of Music Dichter received first prize in the Beethoven Concerto Contest.

In 1966 Dichter entered the third Tchaikovsky competition in Moscow and captured the silver medal (second prize). He enjoyed consid-

Didur

MISHA DICHTER

erable personal success at his concert appearances in Moscow after the competition. Returning to the United States, he made his American concert debut on August 14, 1966, at the Berkshire Music Festival, with Erich Leinsdorf conducting the Boston Symphony Orchestra, in a concert that was telecast nationally by NBC. A pianist with a fiery temperament and an effortless technique, Dichter emerged, as Hubert Saal said in *Newsweek,* as "the best of a new breed of pianists," whose specialty was Romantic literature. In quick succession after his appearance at the Berkshire Music Festival came engagements with other American orchestras, including his first New York appearance, as soloist with the New York Philharmonic Orchestra, Leonard Bernstein conducting. "A bear hug from Leonard Bernstein and an ovation from the capacity audience were Misha Dichter's rewards for a brilliant debut," reported a critic for the New York *Times.*

Since 1966 Dichter has confirmed the strong early impression that he is a pianist of extraordinary interpretative and technical endowments. He has performed throughout the world, with numerous extensive tours of the United States, Europe, Japan, and the Near East. He has been a soloist with most of the world's great orchestras and has been heard at many of Europe's music festivals. In 1969 the Soviet Ministry of Culture invited him to the Soviet Union for his first major tour of that country. He was so successful that he was invited for return tours in 1970 and 1974.

Dichter met his wife, Cipa, a Brazilian-born pianist, while both were studying with Rosina Lhevinne in New York. They were married in 1968, with the impresario Sol Hurok as best man. The Dichters and their two sons live in a seven-room apartment in New York City. They live, wrote Jane Geniesse in the New York *Times Magazine,* "surrounded by three pianos, memorabilia from countless concert tours and a hammock strung from the living room ceiling. More than anything else, this insouciant touch characterizes an easy life style that, as much as possible, puts the children first." The furnishings are eclectic, with furniture, decorations, and bric-a-brac gathered from the four corners of the world during Dichter's tours. In the studio—cluttered with two pianos, books, recording equipment, a television set, a telescope, a Chesterfield couch, numerous photographs, and objets d'art—Dichter practices between seven and eight hours a day; he is sometimes joined in his practice by his wife at the second piano. They have appeared in two-piano music at the Hollywood Bowl, the Ravinia Festival near Chicago, and the Mostly Mozart Festival in New York.

ABOUT: New York Times Magazine, April 25, 1976.

Adamo Didur

1874–1946

Adamo Didur, basso, was born in Wola Sekowa, near Sanok, Poland, on December 24, 1874. He received his academic and early musical training in Lwow (Lemberg). He began to study voice seriously in 1892 with Walery Wysocki. Then, provided with funds by a wealthy music lover, Adamo completed his vocal studies with Emerich in Milan. He made his singing debut in Milan as a soloist in Beethoven's Symphony No.9.

His opera debut took place in Rio de Janeiro in 1894. Following this he made several appearances with the Cairo Opera in Egypt. The baritone, Mattia Battistini, used his influence to advance Didur's career, which reached high ground in the years 1896–1899, when Didur was a member of La Scala in Milan, and 1899–1903, when he was the principal basso of the Warsaw Opera.

After numerous guest appearances through-

ADAMO DIDUR

out Europe, Didur made his American debut with the Manhattan Opera Company in New York as Alvise in *La Gioconda* on November 4, 1907. But it was at the Metropolitan Opera that he reached the height of his fame. His first appearance with the Metropolitan Opera company was on tour, on November 14, 1908, as Méphistophélès in *Faust*. He first came to the stage of the Metropolitan Opera House in New York on November 16, 1908, the opening night of the season, as Ramfis in *Aida*. Didur remained with the Metropolitan through the 1931–1932 season; the last time he stepped on that stage was on February 26, 1933, in a Sunday evening concert commemorating the twenty-fifth anniversary of the Gatti-Casazza regime.

Few if any artists made more appearances with the Metropolitan than Didur: 729 times in New York and 182 times on tour. Few Metropolitan Opera singers were as versatile as he. One of his great values to the company was his ability to appear in so many different roles (minor ones as well as major) with such authority both as a singer and as an actor. He sang equally well in Italian, French, German, and Russian operas—56 roles in all—to most of which he brought both musical distinction and stage authority. His most distinguished roles at the Metropolitan were: Boris Godunov, Sparafucile in *Rigoletto*, Tonio in *I Pagliacci*, Don Basilio in *The Barber of Seville*, Figaro and Count Almaviva in *The Marriage of Figaro*, Alvise, Guardiano in *La Forza del Destino*, the title role in Boïto's *Mefistofele*, Méphistophélès in *Faust*,

Archibaldo in *L'Amore dei Tre Re*, Rodolfo in *La Sonnambula*, Philip II in *Don Carlo*, Geronte in *Manon Lescaut*, Dulcamara in *L'Elisir d'Amore*, Capulet in *Romeo and Juliet*, Klingsor in *Parsifal*, Oberthal in *Le Prophète*, Don Alfonso in *Così fan Tutte*, Kezal in *The Bartered Bride*, Ottavio in Wolf-Ferrari's *Le Donne Curiose*, Gessler in *William Tell*, Don Pedro in *L'Africaine*, Cieco in Mascagni's *Iris*, Rodolfo in *Martha*, King Dodon in *Le Coq d'Or*, and Mustafa in Rossini's *L'Italiana in Algeri*.

He was cast in the following world premieres at the Metropolitan Opera: as Ashby in *The Girl of the Golden West* (December 10, 1910), as the Woodcutter in Humperdinck's *Königskinder* (December 28, 1910), and as Simone in *Gianni Schicchi* (December 14, 1918). These were his American premieres: as Count Tomsky and Plutus in Tchaikovsky's *The Queen of Spades* (March 5, 1910), as Ottavio in *Le Donne Curiose* (January 3, 1912), as Archibaldo in *L'Amore dei Tre Re* (January 2, 1914), as Galitzky and Kontchak in *Prince Igor* (December 30, 1915), and as Don Eligio in Vittadini's *Anima Allegra* (February 14, 1923). On March 6, 1926, he appeared as the Chinese Emperor in the first Metropolitan Opera production of Stravinsky's *Le Rossignol*.

Richard Aldrich in the New York *Times* described Didur's impersonation of Tomsky in *The Queen of Spades* as "gay and characteristically debonair," and H. E. Krehbiel in the *Tribune* spoke of Didur's performance in the dual role of Galitzky and Kontchak in *Prince Igor* as "admirable in the Slavic spirit." Didur's interpretation of the title role in *Boris Godunov* was regarded by Richard Aldrich as "thoughtful, eloquent, well studied."

After leaving the Metropolitan, Didur became the director of the Municipal Theater in Cracow, Poland. In 1939 he was appointed professor at the Lwow Conservatory, but the outbreak of World War II made it impossible for him to assume this post. During the war he lived in Warsaw and taught voice. In 1945 he was appointed professor of voice at the Conservatory in Katowice. He was giving a lesson there on January 7, 1946, when he suddenly announced he was not feeling well. He left the room and died in an adjoining chamber.

ABOUT: Kutsch, K. J. and Riemens, L. A Concise Biographical Dictionary of Singers.

Di Stefano

Giuseppe Di Stefano

1921–

Giuseppe Di Stefano, tenor, was born in Motta S. Anastasia, near Catania, Sicily, on July 24, 1921. He was trained for the priesthood but when he reached his sixteenth birthday he decided against entering the church and went to work at various jobs. His vocal study began with Luigi Montesanto just before the outbreak of World War II. The war interrupted these studies. Conscripted into the Italian army, Giuseppe served in the infantry and was captured. He managed an escape to Switzerland where he was interned. Despite this internment he was permitted to sing at concerts and over the radio.

GIUSEPPE DI STEFANO

After the war he returned to Italy and spent ten months of intensive study with Montesanto to prepare for a career in opera. His debut took place at Reggio Emilia in April 1946 as Des Grieux in *Manon Lescaut.* He was so successful that he was invited to appear in guest performances at Teatro Lirico in Milan. In March 1947 he made his debut at La Scala in Milan where he became a favorite in French and Italian roles.

Di Stefano made his American debut at the Metropolitan Opera as the Duke in *Rigoletto* on February 25, 1948. "There is no doubt," said a critic for the New York *Times,* "that the young man scored in a big way. Mr. Di Stefano has a lyric voice of natural beauty. It is probably the purest and freshest Italian tenor in the company." He remained at the Metropolitan until 1953 (except for the 1950–1951 season), and then had his contract terminated by Rudolf Bing, general manager, because of Di Stefano's irresponsibility in meeting his obligations with the Metropolitan, fully documented in Bing's autobiography *5000 Nights at the Opera.* There he wrote: "One of the most erratic artists with whom I had to work at the Metropolitan Opera was also one of the most gloriously talented: Giuseppe Di Stefano. The most spectacular single moment in my observation year had come when I heard his diminuendo on the high C in 'Salut! demeure' in *Faust:* I shall never so long as I live forget the beauty of that sound." A reconciliation between Di Stefano and Bing, however, enabled the tenor to return to the Metropolitan for the 1955–1956 season as Don José in *Carmen.* Then he was

gone for another decade, returning on January 27, 1965, as Hoffmann in *The Tales of Hoffmann.* The season 1964–1965 was his last at the Metropolitan. "As I had feared," Bing adds, "his lack of self-discipline soon harmed what might have been a career men would remember with Caruso's—but it was not to be."

In addition to singing the Duke, Don José, and Hoffmann, Di Stefano was heard in the following roles at the Metropolitan Opera—performances illuminated with the extraordinary brilliance and beauty of his voice: Des Grieux in *Manon,* Wilhelm Meister in *Mignon,* Alfredo in *La Traviata,* Nemorino in *L'Elisir d'Amore,* Rinuccio in *Gianni Schicchi,* Fenton in *Falstaff,* Rodolfo in *La Bohème,* the Italian Singer in *Der Rosenkavalier,* the title role in *Faust,* Count Almaviva in *The Barber of Seville,* Pinkerton in *Madama Butterfly,* and Cavaradossi in *Tosca.*

Both during his years at the Metropolitan Opera and the years that followed, Di Stefano has been heard in most of the world's great opera houses. He made his debut with the San Francisco Opera on October 8, 1950, as Rodolfo. In 1965–1966 he appeared with the Chicago Lyric Opera. Abroad, in addition to La Scala (his operatic home base in Europe), he performed at the Vienna State Opera, the Berlin State Opera, Covent Garden in London, Théâtre de la Monnaie in Brussels, the Paris Opéra, the Arena in Verona, Rome Opera, and other opera houses in Europe and Latin America. In 1967 he toured the United States and Canada with the visiting Vienna State Opera. His only roles outside the

French and Italian repertory were Rienzi, Hans in *The Bartered Bride,* Lenski in *Eugene Onegin,* and the Italian Singer in *Der Rosenkavalier.*

Di Stefano has also been heard in recitals and in Italy has combined his singing engagements with teaching voice.

While in the United States Di Stefano fell in love with Maria Girolami, a young voice student, the daughter of an engineer. They were married in New York City on May 23, 1949. They have three children. Their permanent residence is a town house in Milan.

Di Stefano has received the Mantua Award in Italy and has been made Commendatore della Repubblica Italiana.

ABOUT: Bing, R. 5000 Nights at the Opera.

MATTIWILDA DOBBS

Mattiwilda Dobbs

1925–

Mattiwilda Dobbs, soprano, was born in Atlanta, Georgia, on July 11, 1925, of partly Negro and partly American-Indian stock. She was the fifth of six children of John Wesley Dobbs and Irene Ophelia Thompson Dobbs. Her father was a railroad mail clerk who managed to see all of his children through college. At the age of seven Mattiwilda started taking piano lessons. She also revealed a gift for singing, but her native shyness prevented her from performing publicly. She was finally persuaded to join the choir of the First Congregational Church in Atlanta. While attending Spelman College she studied voice with Naomi Maise and Willis James. After her graduation from Spelman in 1946 with a Bachelor of Arts degree, as class valedictorian and with highest honors, she was taken by her father to New York for additional training in music. For four years she studied with Lotte Leonard. At the same time she received a Master's degree in Spanish at Teachers College, Columbia University.

She made her first concert appearance in 1947 at the music and drama festival at the University of Mexico. That year she won the Marian Anderson Scholarship. In 1948 and 1949 she earned two other scholarships to study opera at the David Mannes Music School in New York and at the Berkshire Music Center at Lenox, Massachusetts. The award of the John Hay Whitney

Opportunity Fellowship, amounting to three thousand dollars, enabled her to go to Paris in 1950 for two years of study with Pierre Bernac. In October 1950 she entered the International Competition for singers at Geneva, which attracted hundreds of vocalists from four continents. Though she had to compete while suffering severe pain from a sprained ankle, she captured the first prize. A concert appearance in Paris followed, attended by Sol Hurok, the American impresario, who signed her to a contract. Under Hurok's management she made her first tour of Europe in 1950–1951, giving recitals in France, Sweden, Holland, and Luxembourg. She attracted particular attention at the Holland Music Festival in the summer of 1952 as the principal soprano in a performance of Stravinsky's *Le Rossignol.*

On March 4, 1953, she made her debut at La Scala in Milan as Elvira in Rossini's *L'Italiana in Algeri.* This was the first time that a black person had sung a leading role in that theater. Later that month she was heard as the Queen of the Night in *The Magic Flute* at the Genoa Opera, and soon after that she embarked on her first concert tour of Scandinavia.

Her success at the Glyndebourne Festival in England in June 1953 as Zerbinetta in Richard Strauss's *Ariadne auf Naxos* brought her a contract from Covent Garden in London for the 1953–1954 season. There she appeared as the Queen in *Le Coq d'Or,* Gilda in *Rigoletto,* and the Forest Bird in *Siegfried.*

Her American debut took place at Town Hall

in New York on March 8, 1954, in a concert performance of *Ariadne auf Naxos* by the Little Orchestra Society, Thomas Scherman conducting. "She immediately proved herself to be one of the most gifted bravura singers now before the public," said Olin Downes in the New York *Times*. "Miss Dobbs has more than exceptional virtuosity in song. She has temperament and charm . . . and [is] a coloratura of exceptional range."

In July 1954 she appeared in a gala presentation of *Le Coq d'Or* at Covent Garden honoring King Gustav II and Queen Louise of Sweden and attended by Queen Elizabeth II of England. Dobbs made this appearance in spite of the fact that just four days earlier, on June 26, she had been stricken by tragedy: the sudden death of her husband, Louis Rodriguez, a journalist whom she had married on April 4, 1953. When her performance ended, she was summoned to the royal box to be decorated with the Order of the North Star by King Gustav II.

In 1954 Dobbs added the role of Olympia in *The Tales of Hoffmann* to her repertory at Covent Garden, and gave recitals in Paris, Holland, Belgium, and London. In the United States she gave a recital at Town Hall, New York, on January 23, 1955, an event in which, as a critic for the New York *Times* reported, she "displayed a light, beautiful voice, which was ever so agile and always fresh, clean and ravishing in tonal purity." Later that year she set forth on her first world tour.

She made her American operatic debut at the San Francisco Opera on October 11, 1955, in *Le Coq D'Or,* the first time a black person sang a major role with that company. In a communication from San Francisco to the New York *Times,* Howard Taubman wrote: "This is not the biggest nor the most exciting part in the coloratura catalogue, but Miss Dobbs, once her early nervousness had worn off, made the most of its opportunities. There is brilliance in her voice and plenty of flexibility. . . . The voice is well schooled enough for most coloratura roles."

When she made her debut at the Metropolitan Opera on November 9, 1956, as Gilda, she became the first black woman to sing a principal romantic role on that stage. "She rose to the occasion admirably," said Howard Taubman in the New York *Times.* "The young soprano has a voice of substance and quality. . . . All told, a

fine debut. It may even be that greatness is within the girl's reach."

She remained with the Metropolitan Opera company through the 1963–1964 season, singing highly acclaimed appearances as Olympia, Zerlina in *Don Giovanni,* Oscar in *Un Ballo in Maschera,* and the title role in *Lucia di Lammermoor.*

While married to her first husband, Dobbs resided in an apartment in Madrid. After marrying Bengt Janzon, a writer, on December 23, 1957, she established permanent residence in Stockholm and maintained a summer villa in Majorca. In 1961–1962 Dobbs reappeared with the Hamburg Opera where she had been a principal soprano for several years. After that she was a guest artist with the Stockholm Opera, and she gave numerous concerts and made some recordings in Europe.

She returned to the American concert stage on August 16, 1972, as soloist with the New Jersey Schola Cantorum at Alice Tully Hall in the Lincoln Center for the Performing Arts in New York. She sang, said Harriet Johnson in the *Post,* "with rare sweetness, purity and ease, and reflecting the best taste in her vocalism. She attacked high notes without forcing and in general treated her voice with a nicety of touch and phrasing that an expert violinist would employ on his instrument. Her voice isn't large but she trusts it for what it is and doesn't strain. Its carrying power is considerable."

ABOUT: Mademoiselle, January 1955; Newsweek, July 12, 1954; Time, March 16, 1953.

Ernst von Dohnányi

1877–1960

Ernst (Ernö) von Dohnányi, one of the most important composers of twentieth century Hungary, also pursued an active career as concert pianist and conductor. He was born in Pressburg (later renamed Bratislava), Hungary, on July 27, 1877. His father, Friedrich von Dohnányi—professor of physics and mathematics at the Pressburg Gymnasium—was a good amateur cellist. He gave Ernst, then six years old, his first music lessons on the piano. Only one year later

Dohnányi: dō′ nä nyĭ

ERNST VON DOHNÁNYI

Ernst made his first effort at composition. As a child he often played at being a conductor, standing on a chair, using a walking stick as a baton, and directing his little sister's musical performance at the piano, while rows of empty chairs behind him represented the audience.

In 1885, while attending public school, Ernst began studying piano and organ with Karl Forstner. A year later, he gave his first concerts. One of these, in 1888, was a performance of Schumann's Piano Quintet which led a local newspaper critic to foresee for the pianist a brilliant future as a virtuoso. In some of his later concerts he frequently performed his own compositions which by 1894 comprised a considerable repertory of piano pieces, chamber music, and songs.

In 1894 Dohnányi left Pressburg for Budapest, entering the Royal Academy of Music, where for the next three years his principal teachers were Stephan Thomán in piano and Hans Koessler in composition. After one year at the Academy he completed the Piano Quintet in C minor. Koessler thought so highly of it that he had Dohnányi mail the manuscript to Brahms in Bad Ischl, Austria. The Kneisel Quartet, then on a visit to Bad Ischl, performed it for Brahms who is reputed to have said he himself could not have written a better work. Through Brahms's influence, the Quintet received its first public performance in Vienna in November 1895 at the Tonkünstler Verein, with Dohnányi officiating at the piano. (This work was published in 1902 and was officially designated as Opus 1.) In the

following years, Dohnányi had several personal meetings with Brahms. When Brahms died in 1897, he attended the master's funeral as a student representative of the Royal Academy.

In 1896 two works by Dohnányi shared the Hungarian Millennium Prize which had been created by Emperor Franz Josef to commemorate the thousandth anniversary of Hungary's existence: the Symphony No.1 in F and the *Zrinyi Overture.*

Dohnányi was graduated from the Royal Academy of Music in 1897. That summer he took some additional piano lessons from Eugène d'Albert. It did not take d'Albert long to pronounce Dohnányi ready to start his career as a mature piano virtuoso. On October 1, 1897, Dohnányi made his debut with a recital in Berlin. On March 22, 1898, he made his first appearance in England with a performance in London of Beethoven's Piano Concerto No.4, Hans Richter conducting. And in March 1900 he made his first appearance in the United States, as a soloist with the Boston Symphony Orchestra, once again in Beethoven's Fourth Piano Concerto. When he repeated the concerto with the Boston Symphony Orchestra in New York on March 22, 1900, a critic for the New York *Times* wrote: "To please both Boston and New York falls to the lot of few pianists, and Mr. Dohnányi may account himself fortunate, or exceptionally gifted, for he achieved an immediate and well-earned respect for his art. . . . Mr. Dohnányi played the concerto beautifully. . . . He is a young man, but he is already an artist of the front rank."

Dohnányi's second American tour came during November and December 1900. Before World War I he continued to make other American tours and at the same time concertized widely throughout Europe. Both in Europe and America he came to be recognized as one of the great pianists of his time—a specialist in Mozart, Beethoven, and Brahms.

His fame as a composer was spreading with the completion of such works as the Suite in F-sharp minor, for orchestra (1909); the *Variations on a Nursery Song,* for piano and orchestra (1913)—still one of his most popular compositions; and the Piano Quintet in E-flat minor (1914).

He was also distinguishing himself as a teacher of the piano. In 1908 he was appointed to the music faculty at the Berlin High School for Music; three years later he rose to the rank of professor. In recognition of his musical achievements, Hungary bestowed on him the title of *Oberregierungsrat,* which had not been conferred on any pianist since Franz Liszt.

As an employee of the German State Dohnányi had automatically become a German subject without having to relinquish his Hungarian citizenship. During World War I Dohnányi decided to return to his native land so that, if he had to be drafted into military service, this could be done in Hungary rather than Germany. He lived in Budapest during the war years, devoting himself to teaching and concertizing. In 1918 he was made president and music director of the Budapest Philharmonic Orchestra, initiating an eventful career as conductor. He remained with the Budapest Philharmonic until 1944. In 1919 he assumed the post of associate director of the Royal Academy of Music.

He made his first postwar return to the United States in 1920–1921. After his recital at Aeolian Hall, New York, on February 25, 1921—where he performed music by Mozart, Beethoven, Mendelssohn, and some of his own compositions —Richard Aldrich wrote of him in the New York *Times:* "He showed remarkable powers as pianist yesterday; as an artist of potent but restrained temperament and insight; one who puts the music first and himself second or perhaps third; as one who illumines that music with the steady light of understanding and sympathetic imagination; as a technician of high attainments, whose command of the mechanism of the piano is comprehensive, complete and quite unusual, yet unobtrusive. While his playing is frequently brilliant and powerful, it is not brilliant for the sake of brilliancy, but as an interpretative means. He treats the piano according to its nature and character, and in the same way he treats the music."

He made annual tours of the United States as piano virtuoso between 1923 and 1928, and in 1925 he was appointed principal conductor of the New York State Symphony, an organization that enjoyed only a brief existence. After a few months as its conductor, Dohnányi confined his activities with the baton to Europe, where he served as guest of some of its principal symphonic ensembles and as the music director of the Budapest Philharmonic.

In Hungary, between the two world wars, Dohnányi became one of Hungary's most influential and most honored musicians. In 1922 he was awarded the honorary title of Doctor of Music by the Budapest Academy; in 1923 he received an honorary doctorate in philosophy from the University of Szeged in the presence of Archduke Franz Josef; and in 1929 he was given another honorary doctorate in philosophy, this time from the University of Koloszvár. In 1931, a year in which he was named general music director of the Hungarian radio, he was decorated with the Corwin Chain, the highest honor the Hungarian government could bestow in the field of arts and sciences. In 1933 he became the head of the Royal Academy of Music in Budapest. Three years later he was given an honorary membership to the Hungarian Upper House of Parliament, and he received the decoration of Officer of the Legion of Honor from France.

World War II was a time of profound emotional upheaval for Dohnányi. Both his sons died in uniform, one of them in a Nazi prison camp while awaiting execution for his alleged complicity in a plot to kill Hitler, and the other, in action with the Hungarian army. The occupation of Hungary first by the Nazis and then by the Soviets added further to his personal misfortunes. He managed to escape from Hungary on November 24, 1944, to find refuge in Austria as a displaced person with the American Army of Occupation. Before he could establish himself musically in Vienna he was hounded by false rumors that he had been pro-Nazi and anti-Semitic. His life was further complicated by the fact that the Hungarian government demanded his return for trial as a war criminal. These charges were dropped after the elections in Hungary in November 1945, and not long after that the American occupation authorities cleared Dohnányi completely of charges of any Nazi affiliations or sympathies.

Free to leave Austria, Dohnányi went to England in the winter of 1947 where he gave a series of successful concerts, in one of which he introduced his Piano Concerto No.2. The world premiere of his Symphony No.2 was given in London on November 23, 1948. In 1948 Dohnányi left Europe to concertize in Argentina, where he became the director of the music school of the University of Tucumán. He then returned to the United States to participate in the American premiere of his Second Piano Concerto, in Detroit. He also gave several piano recitals, held master classes, and delivered lectures at several universities. In October 1949 he became professor of piano and composition at Florida State University where he remained for the rest of his life. On September 7, 1955, he became an American citizen.

He went to New York on January 21, 1960, to make some recordings of his piano compositions. His last recording session took place on February 5. Stricken by a heart attack following a bout with influenza, Ernst von Dohnányi died at the Madison Avenue Hospital in New York on February 9, 1960.

Dohnányi was married three times. His first wife was Elza Kunwald; they had a son in 1902 and a daughter in 1903. After her death, Dohnányi married Elza Galafrès Huberman, who also bore him a son. They were eventually divorced. In 1949 he married his third wife, Helen (Ilona).

In addition to works already mentioned, Dohnányi composed numerous orchestral works, of which *Ruralia Hungarica* was the most celebrated, together with several operas, two piano concertos, two violin concertos, a cello concerto, and an ample library of piano, chamber, and choral music, together with songs.

Christoph Dohnányi, distinguished conductor and administrator of the Hamburg Opera, is Dohnányi's grandson.

ABOUT: Ewen, D. Composers Since 1900; Papp, V. Ernst von Dohnányi; Rueth, M. U. The Tallahassee Years of Ernst von Dohnányi. *Periodicals*—High Fidelity, December 1957; New York Times, April 20, 1947.

Paul Doktor

1919–

Paul Karl Doktor, violist, was born in Vienna on March 28, 1919. He was the son of Karl Doktor, a distinguished violist who was the cofounder of the Busch Quartet and its violist for thirty-five years. Paul's mother, Georgine Doktor, was a professional singer and singing teacher.

Paul received lessons on the violin from his father when he was five. As a boy, he often participated in chamber-music concerts at home. After several years of violin study at the Academy of Music in Vienna, where he completed a five-year course in two years, he was graduated

PAUL DOKTOR

in 1938. He then joined the violin section of the Adolf Busch Chamber Orchestra, which toured Europe.

Chance made him change from violin to viola. At a concert by the Busch Quartet in Zurich, he was called upon to substitute for his father in a performance of a Mendelssohn quintet. This concert went off so well that when the Busch Quartet performed in London he was invited to sit in the viola chair, this time in a Mozart quintet. When he won first prize at the International Music Competition in Geneva in 1942—the first time this prize went to a violist—he made the decision to change permanently to the viola. In his public appearances he concentrated solely on that instrument, reserving violin playing only for chamber-music concerts at home. Between 1940 and 1947 he was the first violist of the Lucerne Symphony and of the Collegium Musicum in Zurich.

Doktor went to the United States in 1947, established permanent residence in New York City, and became an American citizen. His American debut took place in March 1948 at the Library of Congress in Washington, D.C. "Not for many years," reported a critic for the *Times-Herald* in Washington, "has such a competent master of the viola been heard in American concert halls." On May 16, 1948, at the American Music Festival at Columbia University in New York, Doktor performed the world premiere of Quincy Porter's Concerto for Viola and Orchestra. In 1963 he introduced Walter Piston's Concerto for Viola and Orchestra, a premiere that took place not in the concert hall but in the First Edition Record Series of the Louisville Orchestra in Kentucky. In February 1972, as part of the celebration of William Walton's seventieth birthday, he performed the Walton Viola Concerto with the Royal Liverpool Philharmonic, both in a public concert and on a national radio broadcast. Reviewing Doktor's recording of the Walton concerto on the Odyssey label, Lester Trimble wrote in *Stereo Review:* "His tone is warmly handsome, robust and smooth in the lower and middle registers, and almost unbelievably sweet and refined all the way to the high pitches, where the instrument is seldom trusted to go."

Doktor has toured extensively in recitals, as guest artist with major symphony orchestras, and as a participant in chamber-music concerts. In 1963 he became the first violist to tour Alaska. In January 1965 he gave an unprecedented cycle of three concerts in New York covering the literature for the viola from the seventeenth century to the twentieth. He also appeared at the Salzburg and Edinburgh festivals.

From 1948 to 1951 Doktor taught viola and chamber music—and played the viola in a resident quartet—at the School of Music of the University of Michigan. Since then he has been on the faculties of the Mannes School of Music in New York, the summer school of Colorado College in Colorado Springs, the Juilliard School of Music in New York, the Philadelphia Music Academy, and New York University. He has also conducted master classes in various colleges and universities. Between 1952 and 1957 he was guest lecturer at the International Summer Academy at the Mozarteum in Salzburg.

Doktor founded and played in the Rococo Ensemble and the New York String Quartet. He lives with his wife, Alice, in a New York apartment where, when he is not involved with music, he seeks recreation in ceramics and photography.

ABOUT: Who's Who in Music and Musicians' International Directory.

Placido Domingo

1941–

Placido Domingo, tenor, was born in Madrid on January 21, 1941. Both his parents—Placido Domingo Sr. and Pepita Embil Domingo—were successful performers in *zarzuelas* (Spanish operettas). "My mother," he says, "could have made a career in opera, but composers wrote operettas for her, one after another; that was between 1940 and 1946, the golden time for the *zarzuela* in Spain. She and my father sang in many premieres in Madrid, and all over Latin America, too." When Placido was nine, his family toured Latin America. They settled in Mexico City where his parents organized their own company and his mother achieved such popularity that she came to be known as "the queen of *zarzuelas.* "

Placido began his musical education studying piano at the Mexico City Conservatory. Music was combined with bullfighting on an amateur level at private fiestas. His early musical ambitions reached not to the opera house but to the symphony hall—as conductor. In his teens, Placido studied conducting with Igor Markevitch.

His passion for opera was first awakened when his father came home with the gift of a complete recording of *Tosca.* "It was on that day that the world of opera was opened to me. My sister and I listened to it over and over until we had memorized all the parts and began singing them to one another. . . . What most impressed me at the time, though, was the role of Scarpia. 'If ever I should become a singer,' I told myself, 'it is the role I shall sing.' "

When he was sixteen he turned to professional singing, appearing as a baritone with his family's *zarzuela* company. For several years he not only appeared in other light stage works, including a local production of *My Fair Lady,* but also served as conductor of *zarzuelas* and played the piano in nightclubs.

He made his opera debut in 1961 in the baritone role of Gerard with the Baltimore Civic Opera in the United States. An opera company in Mexico City offered him a contract if he would change his vocal range from baritone to tenor, which he agreed to do. As a tenor, he made his debut in Monterrey in 1961, as Alfredo

PLACIDO DOMINGO

in *La Traviata*. After that he was heard as Cavaradossi in *Tosca* and as Maurizio in Cilèa's *Adriana Lecouvreur*.

Nicola Rescigno, impresario in Dallas, Texas, heard him in Mexico and brought him to Dallas in 1961 to appear as Arturo opposite Joan Sutherland in *Lucia di Lammermoor*. A year later he sang the role of Edgardo in the same opera at Fort Worth, Texas, in Lily Pons's last appearance on the operatic stage.

Domingo's first marriage, when he was sixteen, ended shortly after the birth of a son, Pepe. In 1962 he married Marta Ornelas. They had met in Carlo Morelli's class in dramatic interpretation at the Mexico City Conservatory which Placido was auditing because he could not afford to enroll as a regular student and which Ornelas was attending as a young lyric soprano. Later they met frequently, when Placido became a member of the opera company in Mexico City for which Ornelas sang leading roles; off season he often played for an opera troupe of which she was a member.

Soon after his marriage, Domingo learned that the Hebrew National Opera in Tel Aviv was looking for a leading tenor and soprano for its company. He and his wife applied for the job and were accepted at a starting salary of three hundred thirty-three dollars a month for both for ten performances. Domingo had planned to stay in Tel Aviv just six months to accumulate badly needed experience, but he remained two and a half years for what turned out to be an all-important apprenticeship. He sang 280 performances

in 12 roles, most of them in their original language, but Bizet's *The Pearl Fishers* and Tchaikovsky's *Eugene Onegin* were done in Hebrew. "It was a fantastic experience for a young singer," he recalls. "I remember a *Don Giovanni* we gave in Italian in Tel Aviv. There was a British conductor, a Japanese Zerlina, a Greek Donna Anna, an Italian Don Giovanni, and a Negro from Mississippi as Leporello. I was Don Ottavio and my wife was Donna Elvira. That *Don Giovanni* was given on and off for five months, and it was figured that in that time 120,000 people came to see it."

Returning to the United States, Domingo auditioned successfully for the New York City Opera where, in 1965, he was heard as Don José in *Carmen* and Pinkerton in *Madama Butterfly*. His performances for the most part went unnoticed. But on February 22, 1966, he became a celebrity when he sang the title role in the American premiere of Ginastera's *Don Rodrigo*, in New York City Opera's new auditorium at the Lincoln Center for the Performing Arts. Domingo at first did not know that he was supposed to sing that exacting part. It had been specified in his contract in an option clause he had never noticed. "I didn't even know what it [the opera] was or whom it was by. When they handed me the score and I looked at it, I was almost sorry—it seemed so difficult. But later I began to like it; it has a lot of melody and is theatrical."

Don Rodrigo was well received, and the principal tenor was acclaimed. "Domingo's voice is one of the best singing anywhere," said Harriet Johnson in the New York *Post*, "and the combination of his appearance and intelligence is unbeatable." "*Don Rodrigo*," wrote Winthrop Sargeant in the *New Yorker*, "was sung and acted with superb voice, bearing and intensity of feeling."

As a star at the New York City Opera, Domingo sang the leading tenor roles in *La Traviata, Madama Butterfly*, and *I Pagliacci*. In 1967 he was a guest artist at the Hamburg Opera (where he took on the role of Lohengrin for the first time), the Vienna State Opera, and the Deutsche Oper in Berlin. He joined the Metropolitan Opera while it was on tour, appearing as Turiddu in *Cavalleria Rusticana* and Canio in *I Pagliacci* on August 9, 1966. But it was more than two years before he was heard at the Metropolitan Opera in New York. On October 2,

1968, the opening night of the season, he appeared in *Adriana Lecouvreur* at only thirty-five minutes' notice, to replace Franco Corelli as Maurizio. Since then Domingo has remained one of the principal tenors of the Metropolitan Opera, distinguishing himself in the French and Italian repertory. He has appeared as Ernani, Andrea Chénier, Edgardo, Radames in *Aida,* Cavaradossi in *Tosca,* Pinkerton in *Madama Butterfly,* Manrico in *Il Trovatore,* Calaf in *Turandot,* Riccardo in *Un Ballo in Maschera,* Alfredo in *La Traviata,* Don José in *Carmen,* the title role in *Don Carlo,* Rodolfo in *Luisa Miller,* Don Alvaro in *La Forza del Destino,* the title role in *Faust,* Rodolfo in *La Bohème,* Hoffmann in *The Tales of Hoffmann,* Arrigo in *I Vespri Siciliani,* and Romeo in *Romeo and Juliet.* His performance in *La Traviata* on December 5, 1970, was his seven-hundredth operatic appearance, and when he sang in *La Forza del Destino* on April 16, 1977, it was his one-thousand-and-twelfth performance. He helped to open the 1971–1972 season for the Metropolitan Opera in the title role of *Don Carlo.* On November 3, 1972, he also helped to initiate the fiftieth season of the San Francisco Opera as Vasco da Gama in a revival of *L'Africaine.*

On December 7, 1969, the opening night of the season, he made his bow at La Scala in Milan and on October 15, 1970, he assumed the title role in a new production of Donizetti's *Roberto Devereux.* In 1977 he assumed his seventy-fourth, seventy-fifth, and seventy-sixth roles, appearing as Loris in *Fedora* in Barcelona, in the title role of *Werther* in Munich, and in the title role of *Otello* in San Francisco.

As a resident member of the Metropolitan Opera, and of La Scala in Milan, Covent Garden in London, the Paris Opéra, the Hamburg Opera, and the Teatro del Liceo in Barcelona, he was making about ninety-five operatic appearances a year, a strain that made itself felt when he developed a muscle spasm on the right side of his throat. After he canceled several appearances and underwent extensive treatment, the spasm disappeared. From then on Domingo reduced his operatic assignments to seventy-five, but he refused to pamper himself. In November 1971 he stood ready to sing in two Verdi operas—*La Forza del Destino* and *Luisa Miller*—at the Metropolitan within a forty-eight-hour period, and in one instance he took on two operas in a single day, one on Saturday afternoon and another that evening when he replaced an ailing singer.

Two important and personally significant events occurred in Domingo's career in May 1970. For the first time he was heard in his native city, Madrid, as Enzo Grimaldo in *La Gioconda.* A few days later, he sang the tenor solos in a performance of Beethoven's *Missa Solemnis* at St. Peter's in Rome before an audience that included Pope Paul. The latter performance was attended by seven thousand, but many millions more saw and heard it over television throughout Europe and the United States.

Time magazine called his "the sweetest and one of the biggest lyric-dramatic tenor voices on the operatic stage" and said, "he phrases his serenades with a taste and elegance unmatched since the days of Jussi Björling. As an actor, he is manly, confident and capable of the kind of tender gestures that can thrill girls on both sides of the footlights."

"God must have been in excellent spirits the day He created Placido," once remarked Birgit Nilsson. "He has everything needed for one of the greatest careers ever seen: an incredibly beautiful voice, great intelligence, an unbelievable musicality and acting ability, wonderful looks, a great heart, and he's a dear, dear colleague. He is almost the perfect linguist—but, alas, he has not yet learned how to say 'no' in any language!"

Domingo has recorded extensively. In 1976 eleven complete operas starring Domingo were released in as many months. His album *Placido Domingo in Romantic Arias* received the Deutsche Schallplattenpreis in 1969, and four others received Grammys from the National Academy of Recording Arts and Sciences. In one of his albums, Domingo took over the baton for opera arias sung by Sherrill Milnes. (On the reverse side, Milnes returned the compliment by conducting the accompaniment for Domingo's singing.) On November 7, 1973, he led a performance of *La Traviata* at the New York City Opera. "Let it be said immediately," noted Donal Henahan in the New York *Times,* "that he came through with considerable success in this his American conducting debut. The bearded singer plainly knew the score—not only the tenor's part either—and the orchestra responded beautifully to his strong rhythmic sense and large, clear beat."

Domingo is a huge man, standing six feet two

and weighing about two hundred and thirty pounds. While he denies being superstitious, he insists upon wearing around his neck as good-luck charms a medal of the Madonna and another bearing the likeness of Verdi. With his wife, their two sons, and his son by a previous marriage, Domingo occupies a six-bedroom house near Barcelona which he acquired in the summer of 1972; before that, they lived for five years in a modest three-bedroom home in Teaneck, New Jersey.

Just before going on the stage, Domingo sips some water from a plastic cup, clears his throat, and crosses himself. After the performance, he is so keyed up that he often does not get to bed before four or five in the morning. Following a steak dinner with his family, and before going to sleep, he records in a diary every fact and statistic about the production he appeared in that evening.

In 1971 he was awarded the International Prize Luigi Illica in Italy, and in 1972–1973, the Prize of the Teatro de España in Spain.

ABOUT: Breslin, H. ed. The Tenors. *Periodicals*—High Fidelity, October 1968; New York Times, March 13, 1977; New York Times Magazine, February 27, 1972; Opera News, October 12, 1968, March 26, 1977; Stereo Review, February 1973.

Antal Dorati

1906–

Antal Dorati, conductor, was born in Budapest on April 9, 1906. Both parents were musicians. His father, Alexander, was a violinist in the Budapest Philharmonic Orchestra, and his mother, Margit Kunwald Dorati, taught the piano. At an early age Antal was given lessons on the cello so that he might someday assist his father at his chamber-music classes. Antal entered the Royal Academy of Music in Budapest when he was fourteen; his teachers there included Bela Bartók and Zoltán Kodály. In 1924 Antal became one of the youngest persons in the history of the Academy to receive a degree.

Immediately upon leaving the Academy Antal was appointed to the staff of the Budapest Royal Opera as coach, arranger, and assistant

Dorati: dō rä′ tē

ANTAL DORATI

conductor. He held this post four years and traveled twice a week to Vienna to attend the University.

In 1928 Fritz Busch appointed Dorati his assistant conductor at the Dresden Opera, where he remained for just one season. In 1929 he was appointed music director and principal conductor of the Münster Municipal Theater. During his three years in Münster he appeared as guest conductor of orchestras and opera companies in Germany, France, Spain, and Italy.

After conducting a series of opera broadcasts over the French National Radio in Paris in 1933, Dorati was made principal conductor of the Ballet Russe de Monte Carlo, a post he retained from 1934 to 1940. With the Ballet Russe, Dorati directed performances throughout Europe, Australia, New Zealand, and the United States, and, in 1937, at the Florence May Music Festival.

In December 1937 he made his American debut as a symphony conductor when Hans Kindler invited him for a guest concert with the National Symphony Orchestra in Washington, D.C., in an all-Beethoven program. In 1939–1940 he toured Australia at the invitation of the Australian Broadcasting Commission.

Dorati made the United States his permanent home in 1941, and six years later he became an American citizen. From 1941 to 1945 he was the music director of the fledgling American Ballet Theater. In 1941–1942 he directed performances of the New Opera Company in New York. During these years he made intermittent guest-conducting appearances in Washington, New York, Minneapolis, Los Angeles, Montreal, Cuba, and South America.

When the Dallas Symphony Orchestra was reorganized in 1945, Dorati was appointed principal conductor. Under his leadership this orchestra forged ahead to a place of importance among American symphonic ensembles. At this time he began to establish his reputation as a formidable orchestra-builder. He extended the annual schedule of concerts in Dallas from forty-two to eighty-four. He inaugurated tours and broadcasts. He introduced choral festivals and cycles of orchestral literature. He made it a practice not only to emphasize new music on his programs but even to commission major composers to write works especially for his orchestra. On February 1, 1947, he presented the world premiere of Hindemith's *Sinfonia Serena* and on February 27, 1949, that of William Schuman's Symphony No.6. John Sherman, the Dallas music critic, called Dorati's regime "a love affair of four breathless seasons."

When Dimitri Mitropoulos resigned as music director of the Minneapolis Symphony in 1949, Dorati was called in as principal conductor; six years later he also became music director. Once again he expanded the music season, enriched the programming with novelties, commissioned new works, and offered vital world premieres. These world premieres included Bartók's Viola Concerto (December 2, 1949), Dohnányi's revised version of his Symphony No.2 (March 15, 1957), Walter Piston's Symphony No.4 (March 29, 1951), Harald Saeverud's *Minnesota Symphony* (October 18, 1958), Gunther Schuller's *Seven Studies on Themes of Paul Klee* (November 27, 1959), Roger Sessions' Symphony No.4 (January 2, 1960), and Ernst Toch's Symphony No.4 (November 22, 1957). On April 19, 1957, he led the orchestra in the world premiere of his own dramatic cantata, *The Way of the Cross,* and on March 18, 1960, in the premiere of his *Symphony in Five Movements.*

While fulfilling his duties in Minneapolis, Dorati continued to give guest performances elsewhere, including tours of South America and Sweden in 1953. In Sweden he led the Stockholm Philharmonic in a concert celebrating the seven-hundredth anniversary of the founding of the city.

Dorati left Minneapolis in 1960 and established his headquarters in Rome. For the next three years he remained active as a free-lance conductor in Europe and the United States. During this time he was responsible for the rehabilitation of the London Symphony Orchestra. In 1963 he was made principal conductor of the BBC Symphony Orchestra in London, with which he remained three years. On March 31, 1964, he conducted the BBC Symphony in the world premiere of Roberto Gerhard's *The Plague,* and between April 30 and May 15, 1965, he toured the United States with the orchestra, presenting a series of six concerts at Carnegie Hall, New York, devoted to the music of the twentieth century. In August and September 1966 he toured the Far East as one of three conductors of the Israel Philharmonic. During the fall of the same year he was appointed principal conductor of the Stockholm Philharmonic with which, on January 26, 1973, he conducted Mahler's Symphony No.8 at the gala inauguration of the Stockholm Concert Hall.

In the fall of 1970 Dorati was named the music director of the National Symphony Orchestra in Washington, D.C. (Acceptance of this post did not require Dorati to relinquish his duties with the Stockholm Philharmonic.) In Washington, as formerly in Dallas and London, Dorati put to valuable use his unique gift of building up an orchestra. The National Symphony was demoralized and deteriorating when he took command, but he quickly reconstructed the organization from the ground up. During his first season in Washington he brought the orchestra for a visit to New York in October 1970. Donal Henahan in the New York *Times* found that it played "with uncommon brio and purpose, and with a tonal homogeneity often missing in former years."

In June 1974 Dorati succeeded Rudolf Kempe as principal conductor of the Royal Philharmonic Orchestra of London. In 1977 he relinquished the leadership of the National Symphony of Washington, D.C., to Mstislav Rostropovich and assumed the post of music director of the Detroit Symphony. His first performance in the new post was an all-Beethoven program given on November 3, 1977.

In addition to his many year-round commitments as conductor of his own orchestras and guest conductor of other organizations and at the world's leading festivals, Dorati has made so many recordings that *Time* has referred to him as the "second most-recorded conductor in history." Dorati has produced over three hundred releases on many different labels. His monumental achievement was the recording of all 104 symphonies of Haydn with the Philharmonic Hungarica, an orchestra made up of refugee musicians who settled in West Germany after the Hungarian uprising of 1956. This Haydn release brought Dorati the coveted "gold record" in 1975 signifying that it had sold over one million copies. He had previously acquired a gold record for his recording of Tchaikovsky's *Ouverture 1812.* Four of Dorati's releases captured the Grand Prix du Disque in Paris. In 1977 he received his seventeenth prize: the Grand Prize of the City of Paris for *La Fedeltà Premiata,* the first in a series of recordings of Haydn's operas.

Dorati's first wife was Klara Korody, whom he married in Budapest on July 14, 1929, and whom he subsequently divorced. Their daughter, Antonia, is a successful stage designer. Dorati's second wife is the Austrian pianist Ilse von Alpenheim.

The Doratis own an apartment in Stockholm's well-known Wenner-Gren Center and a house on the Zugersee at St. Adrian, Switzerland. During his years in Washington they also rented a hotel apartment overlooking the Potomac, a short distance from the Kennedy Center for the Performing Arts.

When young, Dorati enjoyed playing hockey and riding horseback, but in later years his main pastimes have been sketching and entertaining friends informally at his home. About the art of conducting he has said: "Each time you conduct it is a spiritual rebirth. You unload your strength, nerves, feelings, everything. You are permitted again and again to relive a great moment."

The braid-embroidered velvet collar on the elegant dress suits worn by Dorati for concerts is the emblem of his election to the Swedish Academy, an honor enjoyed only by two other Hungarians (Liszt and Kodály). In 1973 Dorati was further honored in Sweden with the Royal Order of Wasa, Grand Commander, bestowed on him by the King for distinguished contributions to the lives of the Swedish people. France made him Chevalier des Arts et Lettres, and Macalester College in St. Paul, Minnesota, awarded him an honorary doctorate in music in 1957.

In addition to the cantata *The Way of the*

Cross and the *Symphony in Five Movements,* Dorati has composed an orchestral divertimento, a piano concerto which he and von Alpenheim introduced in Washington, D.C., on October 28, 1975, much chamber music, several pieces for the violin, and songs. In 1939 he adapted the waltzes of Johann Strauss II into a score for the ballet *Graduation Ball.*

ABOUT: High Fidelity, November 1971; New York Times, October 28, 1973, November 4, 1977.

Marcel Dupré

1886–1971

Marcel Jean Jules Dupré, organist, was born in Rouen, France, on May 3, 1886, to Albert and Alice Chauvière Dupré. For generations the Dupré family had produced professional musicians, and Marcel's father was a distinguished organist.

When he was four, Marcel began asking his father for organ lessons, having been stimulated by an organ recital by Charles Marie Widor. But organ study did not begin until he was seven. A year later he earned the high praise of Alexandre Guilmant by performing from memory Bach's organ Prelude and Fugue in E minor.

In his tenth year Marcel was a featured organist at the Rouen Exhibition, where he performed some of Bach's organ preludes and fugues, from memory. He was made first organist at the church of Saint-Vivien in Rouen in 1898, and in 1900 he completed an ambitious biblical oratorio, *The Vision of Jacob,* performed at his home under the direction of his father to celebrate Marcel's fifteenth birthday.

In 1904 Dupré was enrolled in the Paris Conservatory. There he entered the classes of Alexandre Guilmant, Charles Marie Widor, and Louis Diémer. He was given first prizes in piano playing in 1905, 1906, and 1907; in 1909, he earned first prize in fugue; and in 1914 he was awarded the Grand Prix de Rome for his cantata *Psyché.*

In 1916 he was interim organist at Notre Dame Cathedral in Paris, and in 1920 he became the assistant organist at the Saint-Sulpice Church in Paris where the largest organ in

Dupré: dü prā′

211

Dupré

MARCEL DUPRÉ

France was located. That same year Dupré attracted worldwide attention with the unprecedented feat of performing all of Bach's two hundred or so organ works from memory in ten organ recitals at the Paris Conservatory. At the last of these concerts, attended by a distinguished audience including professors from the Conservatory and members of the Institut de France, Widor said publicly: "We must all regret, my dear Dupré, the absence from our midst of the person whose name is foremost in our thoughts today—the great Johann Sebastian himself. Rest assured that if he had been here he would have embraced you and pressed you to his heart."

In December 1920 Dupré gave a concert at Albert Hall, London, before an audience of ten thousand. One year later he paid his first visit to the United States, inaugurating a new concert organ in the Wanamaker Auditorium in Philadelphia. On November 18, 1921, he made his New York debut. In Philadelphia, Dupré amazed his audience by improvising the *Symphonie-Passion,* a four-movement symphony on themes offered him by several musicians present. In the New York *Evening Post* Henry T. Finck referred to that feat as "a modern miracle." The *Symphonie-Passion* was subsequently written down and performed by Dupré in its definitive version at Westminster Cathedral in 1924. He improvised *Le Chemin de la Croix* at a Brussels concert in 1931 before writing down its final version in Paris a year later.

His formidable powers of improvisation re-mained one of the attractions of his concerts in America and abroad. During his first American tour he gave 94 recitals in 85 cities. During the next twenty-seven years, he toured the United States over a dozen times, this in addition to his exhaustive tours of Europe. On all of these occasions he aroused no little awe because he was traveling without a sheet of music, even though his concerts covered the whole range of organ literature.

In 1926 Dupré was appointed professor of organ at the Paris Conservatory, and in 1934 he succeeded Widor as the principal organist of Saint-Sulpice. In the spring of 1937 his name appeared on the front pages of the world's newspapers when he officiated as organist at the wedding of the Duke of Windsor to Wallis Warfield at the Château de Candé near Tours, France. Later that year he was heard in the United States by shortwave radio on the "Magic Key Hour," performing from his French villa.

In 1947 Dupré was made director of the American Conservatory at Fontainebleau and in 1954 he succeeded Delvincourt as director of the Paris Conservatory. Dupré gave his last organ concert two weeks before his death, at Albert Hall in London, half a century after he had given his first recital there. He died on May 30, 1971, in Meudon, France, where for many years he lived on the boulevard Anatole-France with his wife, the former Jeanne Pascouau, whom he had married on April 23, 1924, and their daughter Marguerite.

In addition to symphonies, concertos, and other compositions for the organ, and choral music, Dupré edited the organ works of Bach, Handel, Schumann, Mendelssohn, Franck, and Liszt and completed two treatises on organ playing, *Méthode d'Orgue* and *Traité d'Improvisation à l'Orgue* (1925).

He was Commander of both the French Legion of Honor and the French Ordre des Arts et des Lettres, and was decorated by France with the Croix Ordre National du Mérite. In 1961 he was elected president of the Academy of Fine Arts in France; he was also an associate of the Royal Academy of Belgium.

ABOUT: Delestre, R. L'Oeuvre de Marcel Dupré; Gavoty, B. Marcel Dupré.

Emma Eames

1865–1952

Emma Hayden Eames, soprano, was born in Shanghai on August 13, 1865, to American parents. Her father was a New England lawyer involved in business affairs in Shanghai, and her mother was an excellent musician. When she was five years old, Emma was taken to the United States to settle in her mother's native city of Bath, Maine. Her mother gave Emma her first vocal lessons. Subsequently, in 1883, she studied voice in Boston with Clara Munger. Emma started her singing career in Boston with performances in several churches and with her first appearance in opera in a school presentation of the garden scene from *Faust*.

Wilhelm Gericke, then the conductor of the Boston Symphony Orchestra, became her friend and urged her mother to take her to Paris for further musical training. After some additional study with Annie Payson Call, Eames left for Paris in 1886 to become a pupil of Mathilde Marchesi. At this time Eames tried to join the Paris Opéra but was turned down.

She worked intensively not only with Marchesi but also with Pluque who trained her in stage deportment and who helped her prepare her operatic repertory. On several occasions she was invited to make her debut with various opera houses, but always some accident intervened. She refused to admit discouragement. She finally reaped the reward of her patience by getting an engagement at the Paris Opéra. Her debut there took place on March 13, 1889, as Juliet in *Romeo and Juliet*, with Jean de Reszke singing Romeo. It was Gounod himself, the composer of *Romeo and Juliet*, who had chosen her to sing in his opera at this time. The extent of her success can be measured by the following item in the Paris *Figaro:* "Twenty years old, tall, svelte, the figure and profile of Diana, the nose fine and the nostrils quivering, the carmine mouth exhaling the breath of life, the face of a pure oval lit by big eyes full of impudence and candor at the same time, the expression astonishingly mobile, the forehead high and crowned by a mass of blond fleece, the arms superb attached to the charming shoulders—such is Mlle.

EMMA EAMES

Emma Hayden Eames . . . such is the new Juliet."

She was heard as Juliet ten times in one month and seemed to have established herself as a star of the Paris Opéra. A series of intrigues by envious singers, however, made her position at the Opéra uncomfortable and after two seasons (which she herself described as a nightmare) Eames announced her resignation. On April 7, 1891, she made a triumphant bow at Covent Garden in London as Marguerite in *Faust*. She proved such a favorite in London that from then until the end of her operatic career she appeared annually at Covent Garden and enjoyed an idolatrous following. In 1897 she gave a command performance before Queen Victoria during the Golden Jubilee Celebration, appearing as Elisabeth in *Tannhäuser*.

Before she made her debut with the Metropolitan Opera in New York, Eames was heard on tour with that company: as Elsa in *Lohengrin* on November 9, 1891, and during the following few weeks as Juliet in *Romeo and Juliet*, Marguerite in *Faust*, and Santuzza in *Cavalleria Rusticana*. Then, on December 14, 1891, she made her Metropolitan Opera debut in New York as Juliet. "Miss Eames," wrote H. E. Krehbiel in the *Tribune*, "is a singer of good intuitions and fine gifts. Her voice is scarcely large enough for a room like that in which she sang last night, but it has an individuality which marks her acting. It is a thoroughly musical voice, and its effect is lovely whenever she uses it dramatically and not merely for display."

Eames: āmz

Eames alternated between London and New York, an idol in both capitals. She boasted a wide repertory in German, French, and Italian operas. In addition to her stage presence she brought to her roles an exquisitely beautiful voice, perfectly controlled. Her Metropolitan Opera repertory (beyond those already mentioned) embraced Micaëla in *Carmen,* Eva in *Die Meistersinger,* Alice Ford in *Falstaff,* Desdemona in *Otello,* Sieglinde in *Die Walküre,* Donna Elvira and Donna Anna in *Don Giovanni,* the Countess in *The Marriage of Figaro,* Pamina in *The Magic Flute,* Aida, Charlotte in *Werther,* Elisabeth in *Tannhäuser,* Ero in Mancinelli's *Ero e Leandro,* Tosca, Amelia in *Un Ballo in Maschera,* the title role in Mascagni's *Iris,* and Leonora in *Il Trovatore.*

She made her last appearance on the stage of the Metropolitan Opera (and what she then firmly believed would be her farewell to opera) on February 15, 1909, as Tosca. It almost became a tragic occasion when the burning wax from a candle on the table in Scarpia's apartment set the cloth aflame. Without missing a note Eames extinguished the fire so skillfully and effortlessly that it all seemed part of the stage action. This performance was an evening filled with sentiment. Flowers were showered on her and a wreath from Gatti-Casazza, the general manager of the company, was presented. After the second act she told her audience: "This is goodbye. . . . You have been very kind, but you have been very exacting. You have called for the best I command, and whatever is good in me you have brought out. Therefore I owe much to you. My love I leave with you and I go."

Her resignation from the Metropolitan Opera was caused only partially by her feeling that she was past her prime. More significant in bringing about her withdrawal was her hostility to the new conductor of the Metropolitan Opera, Arturo Toscanini, whose personality clashed violently with her own. She also resented the appointment of Gatti-Casazza as general manager. "To continue at the Metropolitan under the Italian regime would have been impossible to one of my artistic ideals," she wrote. "The logical moment had come for me to say goodbye, when my public had only my success to remember."

But this was not Eames's last operatic performance. In 1911–1912 she appeared several times with the Boston Opera before going into total retirement and devoting herself to teaching.

From 1923 to 1936 she divided her year between Bath in Maine and Paris in France. In 1936 she settled permanently in New York City, where she died on June 13, 1952. She was twice married: in 1891 to the painter Julian Story, whom she divorced in 1907; and on July 13, 1911, to the baritone Emilio de Gogorza, a marriage which ended in separation. Emma Eames was decorated by the French Academy with the Order of Les Palmes Académiques, and Queen Victoria presented her with the Jubilee Medal.

ABOUT: Eames, E. Some Memories and Reflections; Lawrence, E. A Fragrance of Violets: The Life and Times of Emma Eames; Thompson, O. The American Singer.

Florence Easton

1884–1955

Florence Gertrude Easton, soprano, was born in Middlesbrough-on-Tees, Yorkshire, England, on October 25, 1884. "I began as a pianist and had no thought of singing, let alone of the opera, when I began the study of music," she once said. When she was eight she made her first public appearance as a pianist in Toronto, Canada, where her family had settled three years earlier. This debut went well, and she continued her piano study seriously. In 1898 she returned to England where she began voice training at the Royal Academy of Music. Later on, in Paris, she worked with Elliott Haslam, a coach who helped her with her tone placement. "But not long after this my father died, and my grandparents (who had good old-fashioned ideas that a woman's place to sing was in the home) discouraged my efforts. They even carried paternalism far enough to select a husband for me. When this point had been reached, I quietly disappeared and once more went back to my vocal work."

She made her debut in opera in 1903 with the Moody-Manners Company in Newcastle-on-Tyne, as the shepherd boy in *Tannhäuser.* A year later she appeared with this company at Covent Garden in London where she was heard as Inez in *Il Trovatore* and Stefano in *Romeo and Juliet.* In 1904 her American debut took place in Baltimore with the Savage Opera Com-

FLORENCE EASTON

pany as Gilda in *Rigoletto*. That year she toured with the company throughout the United States in an English production of *Parsifal*, assuming the role of Kundry, and in 1906–1907 she was starred in the title role of *Madama Butterfly*.

In 1904 she married the American singer Francis Maclennan who had appeared with her in *Parsifal*. Three years later she and her husband were engaged by the Berlin Royal Opera. They remained in Berlin six years, during which time she extended her repertory to cover a wide range of French and Italian operas and the lighter soprano roles in German works. On April 23, 1910, she created the role of Natoya in the world premiere of Arthur Finley Nevin's *Poia*. As a member of the Berlin Royal Opera she made several guest appearances at Covent Garden in London: as Cio-Cio-San in *Madama Butterfly* in 1909; in the world premiere of Edward Woodall Naylor's *The Angelus* on July 27, 1909; and in the first performance in England of *Elektra* in 1910. From 1913 to 1915 she and her husband were principals of the Hamburg Opera, where she began to take on the more demanding soprano roles in the Wagnerian repertory.

She returned to the United States in 1915 to make her debut that year with the Chicago Opera as Brünnhilde in *Siegfried*. During the next two seasons she was one of the stellar performers of this company in a repertory that included the Brünnhilde of *Die Götterdämmerung* and Sieglinde in *Die Walküre*.

On December 7, 1917, she made her first appearance at the Metropolitan Opera. As Santuz-

za in *Cavalleria Rusticana* she gave a performance which W. J. Henderson described in the New York *Times* as "of intelligent, refined and musicianly skill, never forcing but always coloring her tones to suit the emotion of the moment."

For the next dozen years Easton was one of the principal sopranos of the Metropolitan. Her versatility had few equals. Both vocally and stylistically she met every challenge offered her. She was, as Irving Kolodin said of her in *The Story of the Metropolitan Opera*, "the last mistress of so many styles the theater has known." Karl Muck, the German conductor, is said to have remarked that he could have given Easton any score at eight in the morning certain she would sing it at eight the same night. Her repertory comprised 150 roles in 4 languages, 41 of which she sang at the Metropolitan Opera. The cream of the Metropolitan Opera crop were the Brünnhildes of *Die Walküre* and *Siegfried*, Sieglinde in *Die Walküre*, the three principal female roles in Boïto's *Mefistofele* (Margherita, Elena, and Martha), Marguerite in *Faust*, La Gioconda, Fedora, Tosca, Turandot, Carmen, Isolde in *Tristan and Isolde*, Rezia in *Oberon*, Elsa in *Lohengrin*, the Marschallin in *Der Rosenkavalier*, Fiordiligi in *Così fan Tutte*, Maddalena in *Andrea Chénier*, Rachel in *La Juive*, Fiora in *L'Amore dei Tre Re*, Cio-Cio-San, Kundry, Ah-Yoe in Leoni's *L'Oracolo*, Nedda in *I Pagliacci*, Bertha in *Le Prophète*, Leonora in *Il Trovatore*, Eva in *Die Meistersinger*, Elisabeth in *Tannhäuser*, Dulcinea in *Don Quichotte*, Maliella in *The Jewels of the Madonna*, and Selika in *L'Africaine*.

At the Metropolitan Opera she created the role of Lauretta in *Gianni Schicchi* on December 14, 1918; Mother Tyl in Albert Wolff's *L'Oiseau Bleu* on December 27, 1919; the Temple Dancer in Joseph Breil's *The Legend* on March 12, 1919; and Aelfrida in Deems Taylor's *The King's Henchman* on February 17, 1927. Among the American premieres in which she participated were Franz Liszt's staged version of *Saint Elisabeth*, in the title role, and Mascagni's *Lodoletta*, also in the title role, in 1918; and, in 1929, Krenek's *Jonny Spielt Auf*, as Anita. As Saint Elisabeth she was, said Richard Aldrich in the New York *Times*, "remarkable . . . [with] a voice rich, vibrant, colorful throughout its range."

W. J. Henderson considered Easton the foremost female Mozart singer of her time, and Richard Aldrich on several occasions spoke of her as a Wagnerian soprano with few rivals. However, in *The American Singer,* Oscar Thompson carefully weighs the pros and cons of Easton's art: "Mme. Easton's was not one of the really great voices, although a very good one, often used with the most telling effect. Neither was hers an electric personality. A certain seriousness of purpose obtruded on occasions in her impersonations in a manner to suggest the most conscientious application rather than the kindling of inspiration. Her adaptability may have done her harm, so far as popularity was concerned, because of her appearances in roles that demanded quite another type of expressiveness than was hers—Carmen, for instance. But she made the most of the silvery chime of her upper notes and often demonstrated a command of vocal technique to put in the shade other singers who rode higher on the wave of public esteem. Intelligence and superior stage routine guided her in all her characterizations, a liberal number of which reached a level of distinction."

Easton bowed out of the Metropolitan Opera after the 1928–1929 season having appeared 267 times in New York and 69 times on tour. Her last appearance was on April 10, 1929, as Cio-Cio-San. She was heard at Covent Garden in 1932 as Isolde and Brünnhilde in *Siegfried,* and as Tosca at Sadler's Wells. Then, on February 29, 1936, she returned to the stage of the Metropolitan for a single appearance, as Brünnhilde in *Die Walküre.* A huge audience welcomed her enthusiastically while at the same time bidding her a permanent farewell. "There was a great outburst of applause when Miss Eaton was first glimpsed in her warrior-maiden panoply, high on the rocky eminence, at the rise of the second curtain," reported Noel Straus in the New York *Times.* "And another storm of plaudits arose at the conclusion of her brilliant negotiation of the 'Ho-yo-to-ho' which was voiced with ringing tones alive with exultation. . . . Miss Easton's singing at this point set the pace for what was to come in her sympathetic and affecting interpretation which had thrilling dramatic force, and when required, an ample fund of touching tenderness."

After that, Easton retired from the opera stage to concentrate on concert work, having long since established herself as an outstanding performer of *Lieder* in the world's concert halls. She was heard, too, in radio broadcasts. She also taught singing, first privately, then at the Juilliard School of Music.

In 1930 Florence Easton divorced her husband, operatic tenor Francis Maclennan, whom she had married in 1904, and later married Stanley Rogers. Her last years were spent in New York City, where she died on August 13, 1955.

ABOUT: Thompson, O. The American Singer. *Periodicals*—Opera News, January 13, 1968.

Sixten Ehrling

1918–

Sixten Ehrling, conductor, was born in Malmö, Sweden, on April 3, 1918, to Gunnar and Emilia Lundgren Ehrling. His grandfather was a minor conductor who migrated to New York where he became a piano tuner; his father had been a professional violinist before an accident forced him to abandon music for business.

As a boy Sixten concentrated on studying the piano, though he also took lessons on the violin and cello. He specialized in piano when he attended the Royal High School of Music in Stockholm in the years between 1936 and 1940. He hoped to become a piano virtuoso but in the end decided to become a conductor. "You need time to practice the piano," he has explained, "and this I did not have. I was living on my capital and the competition is murderous." For a time he studied conducting with Albert Wolff in Paris. While serving as a coach at the Stockholm Royal Opera, he received additional training in conducting from its music director, Nils Grevillius.

In 1940 he went to Dresden to serve as an apprentice to Karl Böhm at the Dresden State Opera, after successfully auditioning by conducting a rehearsal of *Salome* from a piano. "It was, of course, a difficult time," Ehrling recalls, "with the war and everything: I couldn't stay long. In fact I got out of Dresden the day before Germany invaded Russia in June of 1941. They invited me to go back later as assistant conductor. But that was just before the Dresden bombing of 1945 when the entire town was destroyed."

Returning to Sweden, Ehrling was made con-

Ehrling: âr′ lēng

SIXTEN EHRLING

ductor of the Stockholm Royal Opera, an affiliation that lasted twenty years. During this time he was promoted to the post of principal conductor and in 1953 to that of music director. During those two decades he conducted about two thousand performances of forty-five operas and ballets. On September 19, 1949, he directed the world premiere of Kurt Atterberg's *The Storm.* "Those were days to remember," he has said. "The working conditions were more luxurious than now, when we have zero time. For *Wozzeck* I had forty orchestral rehearsals. We traveled all over Europe." In 1951 he persuaded the management to engage Goeran Gentele as stage director. The partnership of Ehrling and Gentele brought a new era to the Royal Opera. "Our first work together was Menotti's *The Consul,* but afterwards came many dozens of other collaborations, including the world premiere of Blomdahl's *Aniara* (May 31, 1959) and the very special production of Verdi's *Un Ballo in Maschera....* Together Gentele and I worked on a *Salome* production in which Birgit Nilsson sang the role for the first time."

In official recognition of Ehrling's standing in Swedish music he was appointed honorary Court Conductor in 1953.

While affiliated with the Stockholm Royal Opera, Ehrling directed the Göteborg Orchestra in Sweden in symphony concerts in 1942 and 1943. Over a period of many years he was heard throughout Europe not only in guest appearances as conductor in opera houses and concert auditoriums but also as a concert pianist.

On September 19, 1947, Ehrling married Gunnel Lindgren, the prima ballerina of the Stockholm Royal Opera. They have two daughters.

Ehrling resigned his post in Stockholm in 1960 because of a compelling feeling that he needed a change if he was to continue growing as an artist. "I did it without any idea of what I was going to do." As a conductor, he freelanced for a time, making his American debut in December 1961 with the Detroit Symphony Orchestra. He was called back to Detroit for a six-week period of guest performances in 1962–1963, and in 1963 he was named music director of that organization.

In Detroit Ehrling increased the size of the orchestra, extended the number of concerts given each year, and amplified the repertory to include a considerable amount of twentieth century music. He also instituted coast-to-coast tours. During the ten years of his regime in Detroit he conducted 722 concerts in which 664 different compositions were heard. One hundred and four of these compositions were by twentieth century composers, and 24 of them were world premieres, including Sten Broman's Symphony No.4 (November 17, 1966), Alan Hovhaness's *Fra Angelica* (March 21, 1968), and Benjamin Lees' Symphony No.3 (January 17, 1969).

That the Detroit Symphony Orchestra was developing into one of America's great symphonic ensembles under Ehrling became apparent to Harold C. Schonberg of the New York *Times* when orchestra and conductor visited New York on November 5, 1964. "Only last season," wrote Schonberg, "the Detroit Symphony was, in a way, one of the poorer relatives in the United States symphonic family. A fine orchestra, it nevertheless was somewhat short on strings. But its new conductor, Sixten Ehrling, must be a persuasive man. The Detroit Symphony now has a full complement of players. And it achieved maturity in more ways than one. . . . There could be nothing but praise for the way he and the orchestra handled the music. Indeed, the entire program testified to the work of an orchestral conductor of considerable technique, solid musical ideals and complete integrity. The Detroit Symphony is by now one of the country's superior symphonic organizations, ready to compete in any company. . . . In short, it is as good an orchestra as one is likely to hear."

In the *Post,* Harriet Johnson described Ehrling's conducting technique as follows: "His podium technique has a directness that dismisses superfluity. His beat is consistently clear; he differentiates to a science between the functions of left and right hands."

Ehrling combined his duties in Detroit with appearances with almost every major symphony orchestra in the United States. In 1967 he became the first conductor to lead the "big five" American orchestras in a single year. He helped to found the Meadow Brook Music Festival in Michigan and served as its music director in 1964. In 1969 he led a new production of *Fidelio* at the San Francisco Opera.

He was active outside the United States as well. In 1965 he conducted the BBC Symphony in England, and a year later he was heard in London with that orchestra in a Sibelius centenary celebration. In 1967 he conducted the Stockholm Royal Opera in *Un Ballo in Maschera* and *Aniara* at Expo '67 in Montreal. In 1972 he was a guest conductor in a tour of thirty concerts in Australia and Japan, including national television concerts with the Japan Philharmonic.

In 1973 Ehrling resigned as the music director of the Detroit Symphony Orchestra. He succeeded Alfred Wallenstein as head of the orchestra department at the Juilliard School of Music and as director of its orchestral concerts. That year, on February 26, he also made his bow at the Metropolitan Opera in Britten's *Peter Grimes.* "His entire concept was musicianly," commented Harold C. Schonberg in the New York *Times.* "Mr. Ehrling got a good deal out of the orchestra, kept the music in a steady flow and worked well with the stage forces." The good impression Ehrling had made with *Peter Grimes* was strengthened by his performances of *Simon Boccanegra,* a dual bill comprising *Gianni Schicchi* and Bartók's *Bluebeard's Castle,* and, in April 1976, a revival of *Die Meistersinger.* On February 10, 1975, he led a performance of *Das Rheingold,* beginning the first of three complete cycles of the *Ring of the Nibelungs* which had not been given in its entirety on the Metropolitan Opera stage in thirteen years; Ehrling had previously conducted the *Ring* annually at the Stockholm Royal Opera in the period between 1955 and 1960. On December 19, 1975, he led a new production of Puccini's operatic trilogy *Il Trittico—Il Tabarro, Suor Angelica,* and *Gianni*

Schicchi—the first time the Metropolitan Opera had offered the three one-act operas in a single evening since their world premiere in 1918.

When, on December 3, 1975, Gennadi Rozhdestvensky was unable to appear as guest conductor of the Stockholm Philharmonic in Carnegie Hall, New York, Ehrling stepped in as a last-minute replacement. "It . . . was a tribute to Mr. Ehrling that he could carry things off so convincingly with what must have been a minimum of rehearsal," said Harold C. Schonberg in the New York *Times.*

Ehrling has made numerous recordings, including all of the Sibelius symphonies, and an album of music by Franz Berwald with the Stockholm Radio Orchestra which was selected by *Hi-Fidelity* Magazine as one of the best recordings of 1968.

In 1970 Ehrling was made Commander in the Order of the White Rose by Finland for his efforts on behalf of Sibelius's music. He has also been awarded honorary doctorates from Western Michigan University, Gustavus Adolphus College in Minnesota, University of Detroit, and Wayne State University.

ABOUT: High Fidelity/Musical America, March 1975.

Rosalind Elias

1931–

Rosalind Elias, mezzo-soprano, was born in Lowell, Massachusetts, on March 13, 1931. She was the thirteenth and youngest child of Salem and Shelahuy Rose Namy Elias, both of whom were Lebanese. Since she was also born on Friday the thirteenth and there are thirteen letters to her name she has always considered that number lucky for her. From her early days in high school she aspired to become a singer. She took vocal lessons from a local teacher, Lillian Sullivan, and appeared in school musicals. Despite parental objections to a career in singing, she entered the New England Conservatory of Music after graduation from high school, studying voice there with Gladys Miller. While still a student she appeared not only in a school production of Monteverdi's *The Coronation of Poppea* but also as a vocal soloist with the Boston Symphony Orchestra in performances of Bach's

ROSALIND ELIAS

Passion According to St. John and the *Magnificat.*

Boris Goldovsky, a member of the faculty of the New England Conservatory, encouraged her to supplement her vocal studies during the summers at the Berkshire Music Center in Tanglewood, Massachusetts. She did so for three seasons on a scholarship. Goldovsky also engaged her as a member of his New England Opera Company and she made her debut in 1948 as Maddalena in *Rigoletto.* She also sang the role of the Miller's Girl in Ibert's *Le Roi d'Yvetot* in 1950 and in 1951 the parts of Pauline in Tchaikovsky's *Pique Dame* and Dryad in *Ariadne auf Naxos.*

In 1952 Elias went to Italy. She received additional training from Luigi Ricci and Nazareno de Angelis. In Italy she made several operatic appearances in minor roles at La Scala in Milan and San Carlo in Naples.

The illness of her mother in the United States ended Elias's stay in Italy. For a brief period she attended the American Theatre Wing on a scholarship. In 1953 she entered the Metropolitan Auditions of the Air, singing the Letter Scene from *Werther* and "Stride la vampa" from *Il Trovatore.* Before she could complete her audition the Metropolitan Opera signed her to a contract for minor roles. Her Metropolitan Opera debut took place on February 23, 1954, as Grimgerde, one of the Valkyries, in *Die Walküre.* During the next few seasons she continued for the most part to sing small or secondary roles. Her most important roles in those initial

seasons were Maddalena in *Rigoletto,* Suzuki in *Madama Butterfly,* Giulietta in *The Tales of Hoffmann,* Cherubino in *The Marriage of Figaro,* and Lola in *Cavalleria Rusticana.* The critic of the *Herald Tribune* called her performance as Cherubino "a sprightly, fetching portrayal, pert, vocally rich, and dramatically endearing," and Ross Parmenter in the New York *Times* reviewed her performance of Lola saying she was "self-possessed and seductive" and that she sang the part with "fresh, clear, easy-flowing tones." On October 28, 1957, she was Olga in the season's opening performance, Tchaikovsky's *The Queen of Spades* conducted by Mitropoulos.

Her first starring role came as Erika in the world premiere of Samuel Barber's *Vanessa* on January 15, 1958. "Getting that role wasn't easy," she told an interviewer. "It's written for a soprano. I auditioned for it in the Guild Room of the Met, singing parts of Menotti's *The Saint of Bleecker Street,* both of Cherubino's arias, 'Stride la vampa,' part of Amneris's 'Judgment Scene.' Then I had to do it all on the stage. But I convinced them." As Erika, Paul Henry Lang reported in the *Herald Tribune,* "Rosalind Elias promoted herself . . . to the rank of prima donna." Howard Taubman, in the New York *Times,* said she handled the part "brilliantly . . . Erika is the most fully realized and most affecting figure in the story, and Miss Elias sings with vocal richness and musical understanding and acts with honesty." She repeated her triumph as Erika in Salzburg, Austria, during the summer of 1958 when *Vanessa* became the first American opera to be produced at that festival.

During the remainder of the 1957–1958 season, Elias was heard as Madeleine in *Andrea Chénier,* Emilia in *Otello,* and in the title role of *Carmen.* After that, she became an increasingly important member of the Metropolitan Opera company not only in the roles she had already assumed but also as Fenena in *Nabucco,* Nancy in *Martha,* Amneris in *Aida,* Dorabella in *Così fan Tutte,* Azucena in *Il Trovatore,* Prince Orlofsky in *Die Fledermaus,* Hansel in *Hansel and Gretel,* Laura and La Cieca in *La Gioconda,* Zerlina in *Don Giovanni,* Octavian in *Der Rosenkavalier,* Marina in *Boris Godunov,* Mistress Page in *Falstaff,* Pauline in Tchaikovsky's *The Queen of Spades,* Charlotte in *Werther,* and Rosina in *The Barber of Seville.* One day, before her first appearance as Octavian on December 25, 1964, she lost her voice completely. At a friend's suggestion she consulted a hypnotist who put her into a deep sleep from which she emerged fully recovered. She went through that role without any mishaps. On January 29, 1965, she became the first mezzo-soprano to sing the role of Zerlina. In the New York *Times,* Howard Klein found that her voice was "richer than most coloratura sopranos who usually sing Zerlina, and the added warmth imparted a genuine sensitivity to the peasant girl." On September 16, 1966, she participated in the opening performance of the Metropolitan Opera at its new home at the Lincoln Center for the Performing Arts by creating the role of Charmian in the world premiere of Barber's *Antony and Cleopatra.* A season later she was heard in the new production of *The Magic Flute* designed by Marc Chagall.

She paid her first visit to Lebanon, the birthplace of her parents, in 1962, a vacation that was cut short when she was called back to the United States to sing Suzuki in the RCA recording of *Madama Butterfly.* The following summer she returned to Lebanon for a vacation visit before going on to Tel Aviv and Jerusalem to perform as Dorabella in *Così fan Tutte* with Thomas Schippers conducting. In 1965 she opened the opera season in Monte Carlo as Carmen, and in the summer of 1966 she made her debut at the Teatro Colón in Buenos Aires as Laura in *La Gioconda.* She has sung over thirty-five leading mezzo-soprano roles not only at the Metropolitan Opera and Teatro Colón but also at the San Francisco Opera and the Vienna State Opera, among others. On May 26, 1974, she was starred in the world premiere of the Benjamin Lees opera *Medea in Corinth* over CBS-TV.

Elias is married to Zuhayr Moghrabi, a lawyer. They maintain an apartment on the east side of New York City. She also has a house in Lowell, Massachusetts. Her Mideast heritage clings to her in an accent that has overtones of an Arabic inflection (the first language she ever learned), in her partiality for Arabic culinary dishes, some of which she herself prepares, and in her serving of Turkish coffee to guests. On one occasion she appeared in public with a diamond ring on her toe.

She maintains many interests in addition to music, explaining: "We have to realize there's another world. If you can't grow one way, you won't grow another." She reads a great deal, harbors the ambition to do some writing, plays tennis, enjoys dancing and visiting gourmet restaurants. She insists that she is psychic, that she knows when letters will come, and that she has had prophetic dreams. "I feel I am being guided," she explains.

In addition to appearing in recitals and as guest artist with major orchestras and frequently over television in England and the United States, Elias has performed in musical comedy and operettas. At the St. Paul Opera she was starred in *Song of Norway* and at a music festival in Beverly, Massachusetts, in Noel Coward's *Bittersweet.*

She called attention to her pride in being an American in an unusual way: with a half-page advertisement in the New York *Times* on October 11, 1961. It read: "We hear of fallout shelters, of evacuation, of running away, of living underground. I shall, as an American, continue to walk upright in the open sunlight of my home. . . . My faith in God and in my country is far too great for me ever to feel anything but strong and secure. I am not afraid." For this she was given an award from the Freedom Foundation at Valley Forge.

She was awarded an honorary doctorate in music by Merrimack College in North Andover, Massachusetts.

ABOUT: High Fidelity, April 1965; Opera News, February 29, 1964.

Mischa Elman

1891–1967

Mischa Elman, violinist, was born in a ghetto of Talnoye, Russia, on January 20, 1891. His grandfather was well known in his town as a violinist. But since musicians were held in low esteem by the Jewish community, he discouraged his son, Saul—Mischa's father—from becoming seriously involved with music. Saul earned his living as a teacher of religion, but he managed to learn enough of violin playing to make it a favorite diversion. One day he found Mischa strumming on the strings of a violin and reacting painfully to discords. Saul purchased for Mischa, then four years old, a child-size instrument and began giving him some lessons. "My father had more influence on me than any other human being," Elman said in later years.

MISCHA ELMAN

and the bow slipped from my hand and fell to the floor." Nevertheless, he played so well that Auer wrote a letter to the director of the St. Petersburg Conservatory recommending that Mischa be admitted there. When objections were raised in St. Petersburg about permitting a Jewish child from the provinces to reside in that city, Auer threatened to resign his position as head of the violin department. The authorities relented but denied the boy's family the right to come with him.

The Elmans moved to St. Petersburg in 1901 in spite of this ruling. They lived as fugitives, keeping their presence a secret. The father, who found employment as a butler, hid in secluded corners of St. Petersburg during the day and at night slept in cellars to elude the police. In time the Elmans received special permission to make their home in St. Petersburg and resumed a normal life.

When he was five he was invited to play at the home of Countess Orosova who expressed her enthusiasm by engaging an experienced teacher for the prodigy.

As a child Mischa gave a recital in Talnoye outside the ghetto. None of his relatives or friends were allowed admission because they were Jewish; his father had to sneak into the auditorium and conceal himself in a dark corner.

His father, fully aware of his son's extraordinary precocity in music, took him to Odessa where, under a scholarship, he could study with Alexander Fiedelman at the Imperial Academy of Music. Racial bigotry made life hard for the Elmans. At one time Mischa's violin was destroyed by a street gang; on another occasion the father was falsely accused of having stolen a watch and would have been in danger of prolonged imprisonment if the actual criminal had not suddenly been uncovered. But nothing could impede the child's progress. Leopold Auer, on an inspection tour to Odessa, heard him. At the end of the performance he embraced Mischa and held him up to the audience exclaiming: "Look at this atom! Inside it is the most extraordinary force."

One year later Auer asked Mischa to perform for him privately. "I worried all that night," the violinist recalled later. "To face the great director and the foremost maestro of the world was to me a day of Judgment. I was to play the Wieniawski Concerto No.2 and the twenty-fourth Caprice of Paganini. As soon as I reached the professor's room I was seized with panic,

Mischa was Auer's pupil for a year and four months. Though Elman was still a youngster, Auer pronounced him ready for concert appearances. He had him appear before the nobility. The Grand Duke of Mecklenburg-Strelitz, a relative of the Czar, presented Mischa with a priceless Amati violin. A public concert at the St. Petersburg Conservatory in 1904 proved so successful that Auer decided to launch his prodigy on a professional career. It began triumphantly in Berlin on October 4, 1904, in a recital in which Mischa was heard in the Tchaikovsky Violin Concerto, the Bach Chaconne, and other compositions. That concert was almost canceled by disaster. Unfamiliar with the intricacies of manipulating the gaslight in the hotel room, his father failed to turn off the gas completely at bedtime. In his sleep Mischa was almost asphyxiated. The next day, when he was scheduled for his concert, he was ill. He managed to give the performance, but when it was over he collapsed backstage.

Following this performance Mischa played in other German cities. Arthur Nikisch, Hans Richter, and Max Fiedler praised him effusively; so did the German violinist Joseph Joachim. From Germany Mischa went on to Vienna and England. In London, in March 1905, he appeared with the London Symphony Orchestra, then gave a command performance at Buckingham Palace before King Edward VII of England and the King of Spain in a program that also featured Caruso and Melba. Within six months of his professional debut in Berlin, Mischa, though only thirteen, found himself acclaimed not only as one of the greatest violin prodigies of all time but also as one of the elect of the violinists of his day.

It was as a world-famous and highly esteemed artist, not as a prodigy, that Mischa was introduced to the United States on December 10, 1908, in New York in a performance of Tchaikovsky's Violin Concerto with the Russian Symphony Orchestra. "Elman's tone is large and is also full," wrote a critic of the *Tribune*. "His notes were produced with a precise faith to the pitch that were comforting to hear. . . . In the double stopping, the octaves, and especially his rapid passages, the violinist reached a lofty standard of proficiency, while his cantilena was admirable, full and assured." During that first season in America Mischa gave twenty-two concerts in New York alone. After a recital in Carnegie Hall on December 17, 1908, Richard Aldrich in the New York *Times* called him "without doubt one of the most talented violinists that have presented themselves in New York for a long time, highly gifted by nature and accomplishment. He has every technical advantage that training can give to natural disposition; a left hand that can do wonders, especially a bow arm so elastic, vigorous and powerful that it instills a ceaseless vitality into his play. Mr. Elman uses an instrument of great beauty, with a skill that elicits much rich mellow and rounded tone from it; a tone often of poignant and searching quality and varied expression."

Both the critics of the *Tribune* and the *Times* singled out Elman's tone for special attention, and that tone remained a hallmark of his art, a tone uniquely his in its depth and richness, described as "warm, sensuous, opulent—as vibrant as a living thing."

After that first American season Elman toured the world many times, solidifying his place with the great violinists of all time, on every continent and in every major city of the civilized world. He was the first artist of international repute to perform throughout the Far East. He boasted a repertory embracing over six hundred works, and the technical and artistic equipment to meet its every need. In 1936–1937 Elman gave a convincing demonstration of his versatility by performing a series of five concerts in New York with the National Orchestral Association, covering three centuries with fifteen concertos.

What James Gibbons Huneker wrote of Elman in *Unicorns* in 1917 had even greater validity in later years when Elman was able to free himself of the sentimentalizations and the interpretative superficialities that sometimes marred his earlier performances and when he had arrived at the discipline and insights of full maturity. Huneker said: "United to an amazing technical precision there is a still more amazing emotional temperament, all dominated by a powerful musical and mental intellect that is uncanny. In the romantic or the virtuoso realm he is a past master. His tone is lava-like in its warmth. He paints with many colors. He displays numberless nuances of feeling. . . . Hebraic, tragic, melancholy, the boisterousness of the Russian, the swift modulation from the mad caprices of Slavic despair—Elman is a magician of many moods."

On May 17, 1923, he became a naturalized American citizen, and on May 6, 1925, he married Helen Frances Katten, a San Francisco girl he had met five years before on an ocean crossing from Europe. In the interim he often included San Francisco in his concert itinerary to be near her. As a wedding gift Frances presented her husband with the Madame Récamier Stradivarius.

They lived with their two children in a duplex apartment on Central Park West, New York. When not on tour, Elman lived a disciplined life. He got up regularly before nine, ate breakfast, read the morning paper, and by nine o'clock had started practicing. At ten his pianist would arrive, and for two hours or so they would go through an entire program. The afternoon was spent with his family or attending to his business duties around town. In the evenings, after dinner, friends would frequently be entertained at the Elman home with music. "Anyone who gets tired of music," he once said, "is no friend of mine." One of his favorite diversions was chess.

In addition to pursuing his own career as a soloist Elman was for several years the first violinist of the Mischa Elman String Quartet, which he organized and with which he toured the United States.

During the 1938–1939 season Elman celebrated the thirtieth anniversary of his United States debut with a nationwide tour, contributing the entire proceeds to the relief of all faiths suffering from Nazi persecution in Germany and Austria. During World War II he contributed to the war effort by performing at many army camps.

In January 1944, with the Boston Symphony Orchestra, he gave the world premiere of Martinu's Concerto for Violin, which had been written for him. On June 30, 1965, at the Lewisohn Stadium in New York, he played his five-thousandth concert. He made his last tour of Europe and the West Coast in January 1967, and in March of that year he appeared for three days at the State University of North Carolina, giving a concert the first day, lecturing on the second, and conducting a master class in violin on the third.

Elman died of a heart attack at his home on Central Park West on April 5, 1967. That morning he had practiced for three hours with his accompanist in preparation for a scheduled concert tour. At one o'clock Elman went out for lunch, returning to his apartment three hours later complaining of difficulty in breathing. He died the same evening.

ABOUT: Elman, S. Memoirs of Mischa Elman's Father. *Periodicals*—New York Herald Tribune Magazine, April 30, 1944; New York Times Magazine, December 5, 1948; New Yorker, October 21, 1944.

GEORGES ENESCO

Georges Enesco

1881–1955

In addition to being the most important Romanian composer of the twentieth century, Georges Enesco (originally Enescu) was a violin virtuoso and a highly gifted pianist and conductor. He was born in Liveni in Moldavia, Romania, on August 19, 1881, the son of a farmer. Georges was four when he was given his first violin upon which he learned to play gypsy tunes before taking his first lesson. Nicolas Chioru, a gypsy violinist, gave the child his first lessons. By the time Georges was seven he had composed several sonatas and rondos for the piano.

He made such rapid progress on the violin with Eduardo Caudella as his teacher, that his father took him to Vienna in 1888 to enter him in the Vienna Conservatory. Joseph Hellmesberger, the Conservatory director, at first turned

the boy down because he was too young. But upon hearing him play he not only accepted him for the Conservatory but also made him a member of his own household. At the Conservatory Georges studied the violin with Sigismund Bachrich and Hellmesberger, and harmony and counterpoint with Robert Fuchs. On August 5, 1889, Georges made his formal debut at a benefit concert at Slănic Moldova. Three and a half years later, on January 26, 1892, he made his first public appearance in Vienna at a concert by conservatory students in which he was accompanied on the piano by his teacher, Hellmesberger. The following April he earned his first critical notices, all of them favorable, following his performance in Vienna of the Vieuxtemps *Fantaisie* with Hellmesberger again at the piano.

After receiving first prizes in violin and harmony in 1892, Georges was graduated from the Vienna Conservatory in July 1893 with the gold medal in violin. On March 20, 1894, he made his debut as violinist in Bucharest. Later that year, he went on to Paris to continue his music study at the Paris Conservatory. He had difficulty gaining admission because he was both too young and a foreigner. But he was finally enrolled on November 7, 1895, and during the next four years he studied the violin with Martin-Pierre-Joseph Marsick, counterpoint with André Gédalge, and composition with Massenet and Gabriel Fauré. In 1889 he captured first prizes in harmony and violin playing. By the time he left the Conservatory he had already made a strong impression as a violin virtuoso with a performance in Paris of the Beethoven Violin Concerto on March 17, 1898. He had also made his mark as a composer. An all-Enesco concert was given in Paris on June 11, 1897, and his *Poème Roumain* for orchestra was successfully introduced at a concert conducted by Édouard Colonne on February 6, 1898.

Once out of the Conservatory in 1899, he began to promote his career as a violin virtuoso, beginning with an appearance as soloist with the Colonne Orchestra in Paris on February 11, 1900, in Beethoven's Violin Concerto and Saint-Saëns's Violin Concerto No.3. He repeated his performance of these two compositions in Bucharest the following April. Other appearances in Paris, followed by concerts in Berlin, London, Brussels, Rome, Budapest, and Holland, drew attention to his aristocratic style, which adapted itself flexibly to every idiom and age, to his fine artistic taste and his penetrating musicianship. He was also an active participant in chamber-music concerts. In 1902 he formed the Enesco Trio, and in 1904, the Enesco Quartet, with both of which he gave numerous performances throughout Europe. He also appeared in sonata recitals with Alfred Cortot, Ossip Gabrilowitsch, and Alfredo Casella; and, exchanging the violin for the piano, with Jacques Thibaud and with Pablo Casals.

On January 9, 1910, Enesco conducted the Bucharest Philharmonic Orchestra in a program of his own works. He continued to conduct not only that orchestra but other symphonic organizations in Europe. He also canalized his many-faceted gifts into teaching by conducting master classes in violin at the École Normale de Musique. In 1933 and 1937 he held a series of master classes in the interpretation of violin literature at the Institut Instrumental de Paris.

Just before the outbreak of World War I, Enesco, who had made his home in Paris up to this time, settled in Bucharest where he became one of Romania's most active and highly esteemed musicians. He conducted the concerts of the Bucharest Philharmonic; he served as court violinist to the Queen of Romania; he organized concerts of new music; he established the Georges Enesco Prize for young Romanian composers. During the war he continued to concertize extensively throughout Romania. In January 1916 he gave a series of eight concerts in Bucharest tracing the history of violin music. He also performed for wounded soldiers in Romanian hospitals. In March 1917 he was sent to Russia for a series of concerts for the benefit of the Red Cross.

When the war ended, Enesco left Romania to make his home in an apartment on the rue de Clichy in Paris for the next two decades. From there he embarked on world tours as violinist, conductor, and composer.

He paid his first visit to the United States in 1923, making his American debut on January 5 with the Philadelphia Orchestra, Stokowski conducting, in the Brahms Violin Concerto. He toured the country that month, not only as a violin soloist with orchestras and in recitals but also as a guest conductor of the Philadelphia Orchestra and of orchestras in Washington, Baltimore, and Pittsburgh. In contemplating Enesco in his triple role as violinist, composer, and conductor, Olin Downes wrote in the New York *Times:* "Once in a while there steps upon the stage a man born only to be a musician, an artist in whose face and eyes and carriage is something of what he is going to do, something which connotes his own emotional high responsibility in his task, something which makes the beholder and listener immediately aware that music is to be dispensed greatly, and that is the first and last impression of Georges Enesco."

About Enesco's violin virtuosity, Richard Aldrich had this to say in the New York *Times* after a New York recital on January 22, 1923: "He established himself at once as a master of high rank, displaying qualities of a remarkable sort, and a self-contained individuality singularly engrossing. Mr. Enesco is as far as possible from being a 'virtuoso' in the more undesirable meaning of the term. He is first and last a musician and an interpreter, devoted solely to expounding music and not at all to the display of his technical powers. These are, indeed, remarkable, but they are employed entirely as a means to an end."

Both as a violinist and as a conductor Enesco continued to make numerous tours of the United States after 1923. In reviewing his first appearance as a guest conductor of the New York Philharmonic Orchestra on January 28, 1937, a New York critic spoke of his "deep human sympathy" and the "profound emotional insight which laid bare the soul of each selection." In May 1939 he was invited by the Romanian government to conduct two concerts of Romanian music with the New York Philharmonic at the

World's Fair in New York. "He is not a virtuoso conductor," said Olin Downes in the New York *Times*. "His music making is as unpretentious and as direct and as sincere as he is himself. One could say that Mr. Enesco thinks aloud, and his thought is presented with the most exceptional logic, cogency, and expressiveness. He conducts as if he were composing the music, and the hearer, so to speak, composes with him."

But it was the general consensus of American critics that it was with his violin, rather than with his baton, that Enesco was outstanding and individual as a performing musician. As one critic wrote in the New York *Times*, it is then that he succeeds in communicating "most immediately and most revealingly the searching probity of his music making. . . . There are few who can find the just color, phrasing, and accent for varied works as Mr. Enesco, and even fewer who play with such nobility."

On December 4, 1937, Enesco married Marie Rosetti-Tetcanu, a Romanian princess. They had no children. Until World War II he and his wife shared his apartment on rue de Clichy, a place of homely simplicity, whose principal embellishments were books, musical instruments, a music library, and a collection of objets d'art.

During World War II the Enescos left Paris to live on a large farm in Sinaia, near Bucharest. When Enesco was not giving performances, he helped take care of the livestock and did a considerable amount of composing. After the war, in April and May 1946 he made appearances in the Soviet Union as violinist and conductor. On November 10, 1946, he paid a return visit to the United States, the first in ten years. At that time the Romanian ambassador to the United States presented him with the Grand Cross of the Order of Loyal Service for his contributions to Romanian music. In 1948 Enesco conducted a class in the interpretation of chamber music at the Mannes College of Music in New York. On the sixtieth anniversary of his concert debut, January 21, 1950, Enesco appeared in the quadruple role of violinist, pianist, conductor, and composer in New York with the New York Philharmonic Orchestra.

A paralytic stroke suffered in Paris in July 1954 left him a permanent invalid. Though he was invited by the Romanian Embassy to return to his homeland, he stoutly refused to do so, maintaining he had no sympathy with a Communist regime. He remained in Paris until his death, on May 4, 1955.

Enesco's most celebrated composition is the *Romanian Rhapsody No.2* for orchestra which, together with his *Romanian Rhapsody No.1*, received its world premiere under his direction in Bucharest on March 8, 1903. Other works include an opera *(Oedipe)*, three symphonies, three orchestral suites, a violin concerto, three violin sonatas, two string quartets, the Octet in C major, three piano sonatas, two piano suites, and some songs.

In gratitude for Enesco's contributions to Romanian music, the government bestowed on him numerous honors, both before and after the Communist takeover. On June 8, 1916, he was elected honorary member of the Romanian Academy; on December 10, 1934, he was named honorary citizen of the city of Bucharest; on November 24, 1936, the city of Jassy followed suit. On November 5, 1945, he was made honorary president of the Bucharest Philharmonic Orchestra. After Enesco's death Romania inaugurated an international festival and competition named after him. Enesco museums were opened at his homes in Livani and Bucharest; the Bucharest Philharmonic added Georges Enesco to its name; and the town of his birth and a street in Bucharest were renamed for him.

Enesco had few interests outside music. He once told an interviewer: "I'm just a musician and a humble one. My real happiness is at the writing table, composing. Outside of music, I'm like an ostrich that hides its head under the wing. I have no hobbies. I just happened to live like a bourgeois." Up to the time of his paralytic stroke he worked continuously, getting up at about seven in the morning, working at compositions from four to five hours, and then practicing the violin and the piano for another half dozen hours. His only relaxation came from conversing with friends, not only about music but also on other cultural subjects and on politics—his usually scholarly comments tinged with a sharp-tongued irony.

ABOUT: Enesco, G. and Gavoty, B. Les Souvenirs de Georges Enesco; Ewen, D. Composers Since 1900; Kotlyarov, G. Georges Enesco.

Entremont

Philippe Entremont

1934–

Philippe Entremont, pianist, was born in Rheims, France, on June 7, 1934. His father, Jean, was a conductor; his mother, Renée Monchamps Entremont, a concert pianist. Philippe received his first piano lessons from his mother when he was six. Four years later he was brought to Paris for further instruction with Rose Aye-Lejour, and, for three years, with Marguerite Long. When he was twelve he entered the Paris Conservatory where he studied piano with Jean Doyen. In his first year there Philippe won first prize in solfeggio; two years later he was given first prize in chamber music; and when he was fifteen he captured first prize in piano.

He made his concert debut in Barcelona when he was seventeen. Less than a year later he competed and became a finalist in the Queen Elisabeth of Belgium International Competition. In 1953 he was First Laureate and Grand Prix winner of the Marguerite Long-Jacques Thibaud International Concours and the winner of the Harriet Cohen Piano Medal.

His American debut came on January 5, 1953, with a recital in Washington, D.C. The following day he made his New York debut at Carnegie Hall with the National Orchestral Association under Leon Barzin in Liszt's Piano Concerto No. 1 and the American premiere of André Jolivet's Piano Concerto. Olin Downes described his performance in the New York *Times* as "whirlwind . . . [with the] spirit and fire of youth plus a technical and musical mastery of an extremely talented musician." In 1956 Entremont made his initial appearance with the Philadelphia Orchestra, Eugene Ormandy conducting, the first of many performances Entremont has given with that symphonic organization. He grew so popular in Philadelphia that the city honored him by making him the first nonresident ever given the title Good Will Ambassador. He was also heard throughout the United States with other major orchestras, as well as in recitals. He endeared himself to audiences everywhere with the elegance of his style, fluency of technique, sensitivi-

Entremont: än trĕ môn′

ty of touch, and expressiveness of tone. He has particularly distinguished himself as an interpreter of Ravel's piano music. His recording of Ravel's Piano Concerto in G with the Philadelphia Orchestra under Ormandy received the Grand Prix du Disque in Paris, and so did his album of Ravel's complete piano works in 1975. (He received several other such awards for recordings.) He has also recorded Ravel's Concerto for piano (left hand alone) and orchestra, with the Cleveland Orchestra under Boulez. Stravinsky, Jolivet, Milhaud, and Leonard Bernstein are some of the contemporary composers who have selected Entremont to record their piano works and have themselves conducted the accompaniment. Entremont has also recorded all of Chopin's compositions. In all, his recordings are believed to have sold well over a million and a half disks.

On March 7, 1975, he helped to commemorate the centenary of Ravel's birth with an all-Ravel concert at Avery Fisher Hall in New York. "Mr. Entremont is, at his best, a persuasive interpreter of Ravel's music," reported Allen Hughes in the New York *Times*. "He negotiates complex figurations fluently, the piano tone is silvery and cool, and the playing is expressive, without becoming overwrought, and keen Gallic intelligence is in control."

In 1967 he assumed for the first time the dual role of pianist and conductor in a recording of a Mozart concerto with the Collegium Musicum in Paris. After several conducting assignments in Europe he was heard once again in the dual capacity of pianist and conductor at the Mostly Mozart Festival at the Lincoln Center for the Performing Arts in New York on August 3, 1971, in three Mozart concertos. In August 1973 and August 1975 he once again served as conductor to his own piano performances at the Mostly Mozart Festival at the Lincoln Center. He has also participated in chamber music performances with various ensembles.

On December 21, 1955, Entremont married Audrée Ragot; they have two children. An enthusiastic sportsman, Entremont enjoys driving high-powered cars. He is also fond of sailing and playing golf.

Each September Entremont teaches piano at Saint-Jean-de-Luz, France, at the Ravel Academy, of which he is president. He was made Chevalier de l'Ordre National du Mérite.

CHRISTOPH ESCHENBACH

ABOUT: American Record Guide, March 1969; Hi-Fi, November 1971; New York Times, August 5, 1973.

Christoph Eschenbach

1940–

Christoph Eschenbach (originally Christoph Ringmann), pianist, was born in Breslau, Silesia, Germany, in 1940. His mother, a professional pianist, died while giving birth, and his father, a professor of musicology at the University of Breslau, died during Christoph's infancy. Christoph was raised by his grandmother. When the Russians invaded Germany in 1944, during World War II, grandmother and grandchild fled to Czechoslovakia, then to Poland. "There was famine, epidemics," Eschenbach told John Gruen in an interview in the New York *Times.* "Then came the terrible winter of 1945–1946. Suddenly, my grandmother died. I remained completely alone. I was put on a freight train with a group of displaced persons, and placed in a refugee camp somewhere in Germany. I was six years old. Typhus broke out in the camp. The camp was put under quarantine. I nearly died of the disease and of starvation."

One of his mother's relatives who had been searching for him for months finally located him in that camp. "She found me half dead, and took me away with her to Mecklenburg, North Ger-

Eschenbach: ĕsh′ ĕn bäк

many, where she lived with her husband. They had no children. I became their son. Their name was Eschenbach."

One day, while lying ill in bed, Christoph heard his foster mother, a music teacher, giving piano lessons. Fascinated by the sound of music, he asked for music instruction. Because of a prolonged period of recuperation, he had to wait until he was eight years old for his first lesson. When his foster mother realized that Christoph had unusual talent, on the advice of the conductor Eugen Jochum she placed him with a more experienced teacher—Eliza Hansen, in Hamburg, a pupil of Artur Schnabel and Edwin Fisher. He studied with her on and off for seven years and has come to regard her as the greatest single influence in his musical development.

As a student at the Hamburg Conservatory, from which he was ultimately graduated with the highest honors, Christoph also studied the violin and conducting. "I adored the violin . . . [and] I threw myself into conducting. My conducting examination was a performance of *The Marriage of Figaro.* Suddenly, it all became too much for me. I decided to concentrate on the piano. It was, after all, my first love."

Christoph began winning prizes in piano early in his training. He was eleven when he won first prize in the Steinway Young Pianists Contest, and one year later he won it a second time. In the years between 1955 and 1959, while attending the State Conservatory of Music in Cologne as a pupil of Hans Otto Schmidt-Neuhaus, he received a special prize in the International Music Competition in Munich and first prize in a competition of German music schools in Cologne.

He returned to Hamburg in 1959 to resume his interrupted piano studies with Eliza Hansen. In 1962 he captured the first prize in the Munich International Competition. Three years later, as the winner, from among twelve finalists, of the Clara Haskil Concours in Lucerne, his career began to advance. He was invited to appear as soloist with some of the leading orchestras in Europe, including the Concertgebouw in Amsterdam, the Lamoureux Orchestra in Paris, the London Symphony, and the Berlin Philharmonic. Further recognition came in 1965 through his initial recordings for Deutsche Grammophon of Beethoven's Piano Concerto in C major, with the Berlin Philharmonic under Herbert von Karajan, and of albums of music by Mozart and Schubert. He has since recorded for Deutsche Grammophon all of Mozart's piano sonatas and, with Justus Franz, all of Mozart's four-hand piano music.

George Szell, the music director of the Cleveland Orchestra, became interested in him and invited him to be one of the soloists with the Cleveland Orchestra during its European Festival Tour in 1967. That summer, with Jörg Demus and Herbert von Karajan doubling as pianist and conductor, he performed Mozart's Concerto for Three Pianos in F, K.242, at the Salzburg and Lucerne Festivals. In October, sponsored by the German government, Eschenbach made his North American debut at Expo '67 in Montreal, the only artist representing Western Germany at the exposition. Eschenbach also became the first artist singled out for special promotion by the European Concert Managers' International Union.

His debut in the United States took place on January 16, 1969, with the Cleveland Orchestra under Szell in a performance of Mozart's Piano Concerto in F major, K.459. Szell also chose Eschenbach to perform with the orchestra on its eastern tour in February. This included Eschenbach's first appearance in New York at Carnegie Hall on February 17. "The reviews were superb," says John Gruen. "His playing was deemed fastidious, precise, delicate, transparent, virtuosic." Later in January Eschenbach gave the American premiere of Hans Werner Henze's Piano Concerto No.2, which had been written for him. Since then Eschenbach has appeared as

soloist with most of the major American orchestras as well as in recitals. Commenting on his interpretation of the Schumann Piano Concerto in New York with the visiting Cleveland Orchestra under Rafael Kubelik in 1971, Harold C. Schonberg described the performance, in the New York *Times,* as "constantly exciting, individualistic, full of reckless daring."

Eschenbach has toured Europe, South America, South Africa, the Soviet Union, Eastern Europe, Israel, and Japan and has been heard in festivals in Salzburg, Bonn, and Aix-en-Provence. In 1972 he gave a special concert in Munich in conjunction with the Olympic games.

"Speaking generally," wrote John Rockwell in the New York *Times* after Eschenbach's recital at the Lincoln Center for the Performing Arts on August 15, 1976, "Mr. Eschenbach falls into the category of modern young pianists who espouse an analytically correct, cool linearity in their playing. But what redeems him from the more clinical extremes of that category are a certain contained expressiveness within that style and a calculated willingness to indulge in melodrama when the situation seems to call for it."

Eschenbach has also made successful appearances in Europe as a conductor. On August 10, 1976, at the Mostly Mozart Festival at the Lincoln Center for the Performing Arts in New York, he conducted two Mozart symphonies and served as his own accompanist to two Mozart piano concertos. His performance, reported Donal Henahan in the New York *Times,* "showed him to be a promising conductor with a close knowledge of the score, if not yet a virtuoso technician."

Eschenbach lives in the Canary Islands. He describes himself as a "wanderer," adding, "I lead a lonely existence. . . . Basically I work. But I don't by any means lead a sheltered existence. I like encountering life. Once in a while I even throw myself into the gutter so to speak—just like that."

He described to John Gruen the way he studies his repertory and prepares it for the concert stage: "When I first look at a work, I analyze it. The page becomes a groundplan, filled with details. I study the facts. I absorb the work in a theoretical way. This leads you to the utmost understanding of a piece of music. Once I have placed this groundplan into my mind, I look at the picture again. This time, I look at it from the composer's point of view. I see it as an emotional experience. The work becomes an emotional fact, which I must now experience. ... Then comes the moment of performance. During the performance two things happen. First: I am fully conscious and aware of the over-all mechanics of a piece—the groundplan. Second: A trance-like state takes over. I am in a trance. By trance, I don't mean being *away* from the music but *inside* it. Always I try to get closer and closer to the unconscious elements revealed and disclosed by the music. Then it is that I have found the *moment*—the only moment! The music emerges. It coalesces into a true totality."

ABOUT: New York Times, February 3, 1974.

SIR GERAINT EVANS

Sir Geraint Evans

1922–

Geraint Llewellyn Evans, baritone, was born in Cilfynydd near Pontypridd, South Wales, on February 16, 1922. When Geraint was eighteen months old, his mother, Gladys May Evans, died while bearing his sister. Geraint's father, William John, a miner, consented to have the boy raised by his grandparents. As a youngster Geraint sang in the town church choir and later studied voice, although he was training for a business career. His business training was cut short during World War II when he was called into military service. In 1945 he became a singer and program arranger for the English military radio in Hamburg, while continuing vocal studies with Theo Herrman. Deciding after his demobilization to develop himself professionally as a singer, he continued his vocal studies in Geneva with Fernando Carpi and at the Guildhall School of Music and Drama in London with Walter Hyde.

Evans made his opera debut at Covent Garden in London in 1948 as the Night Watchman in *Die Meistersinger*. A year later he enjoyed his first success there as Figaro in *The Marriage of Figaro*. (This has since become one of his most celebrated roles.) He remained a principal baritone of Covent Garden for the next quarter of a century, distinguishing himself particularly in Wagnerian and Mozartean roles. He was also starred there in the world premiere of several important new English operas. Among these

were Britten's *Billy Budd* on December 1, 1951 (as John Claggart), Britten's *Gloriana* on June 8, 1953 (as Mountjoy), and William Walton's *Troilus and Cressida* on December 3, 1954 (as Antenor). In the years between 1950 and 1961 he appeared at the Glyndebourne Festival where his performances in Mozart's operas were highly acclaimed. In recognition of his status in English music, Evans was made Commander of the British Empire in 1959.

He made his American debut with the San Francisco Opera on December 6, 1959, as Beckmesser in *Die Meistersinger* and returned there on October 4, 1960, in the title role of Alban Berg's *Wozzeck*. During the next few years he made guest appearances at La Scala (where he first appeared in 1961 in *The Barber of Seville*), at the Vienna State Opera (debut also in 1961), and at the Salzburg Festival in *The Marriage of Figaro* in 1963.

On March 25, 1964, he made a triumphant debut at the Metropolitan Opera as Falstaff in Verdi's opera of that name. "Mr. Evans has a magnificent voice—a voice that can roar with drunken anger or soar with courtly elegance, according to the requirements of the moment," wrote Winthrop Sargeant in the *New Yorker*. "His Italian is beautifully enunciated, and every word can be clearly heard throughout the large auditorium. Moreover, he has created a character far above the usual slapstick one. His Falstaff is often understaged, and is no less funny for that. His stage business never seems to fall in cliches; every pantomimic motion he makes has not only a definite significance but a fresh significance, reflecting the inner psychology of the Fat Knight. . . . In short, Mr. Evans is a great actor in the British tradition as well as a greater singer in the Italian one."

As one of the principals of the Metropolitan Opera company in the ensuing years, Evans extended his American fame as Figaro in *The Marriage of Figaro,* Don Pizzaro in *Fidelio,* Leporello in *Don Giovanni,* Wozzeck, Beckmesser in *Die Meistersinger,* and Balstrode in Britten's *Peter Grimes.* He has also been acclaimed in the United States in performances away from the Metropolitan Opera—for example, as Dulcamara in a striking new production of *L'Elisir d'Amore* at the Chicago Lyric Opera on September 23, 1977.

On July 7, 1969, Evans was knighted by Queen Elizabeth II. On October 27, 1973, at the San Francisco Opera, he not only sang the leading role in *Peter Grimes* but also directed the opera. He had previously directed a performance of *Falstaff* in Buenos Aires and of *Don Pasquale* with the Welsh National Opera.

On March 27, 1948, Evans married Brenda Evans Davies, a girl who had grown up with him in his native Welsh town. Their home is in Petts Wood, Kent, England, and they have two sons. In the New York *Times,* Howard Klein described Evans's physical appearance as follows: "Evans's face is warm and sensitive, the dark brown eyes arched over by thick brows, black hair that must have been wild once but is now tamed, a quick smile that becomes grave without warning. His deep voice rolls like the hills of Wales and he speaks of simple things—the mines, the town he grew up in, how he wishes he could spend more time with his sons, how late in life success is coming to him, singing, acting."

Evans has appeared at the Vienna State Opera, the Paris Opéra, the Deutsche Oper in Berlin, the Munich Opera, La Scala in Milan, the Warsaw Opera, the Welsh National Opera (among other companies) and at festivals at Salzburg, Edinburgh, and Glyndebourne. In 1974, with the Welsh National Opera at Cardiff, he appeared as Trader Case in the world premiere of Alun Hoddinott's *Beach of Falesa.* Among his principal roles, other than those already commented upon, have been Escamillo in *Carmen,* Don Pasquale, Dulcamara in *L'Elisir d'Amore,* Enrico in *Lucia di Lammermoor,* Tonio in *I Pagliacci,* Lescaut in *Manon,* Gugliel-

mo and Alfonso in *Così fan Tutte,* Almaviva in *The Marriage of Figaro,* Papageno in *The Magic Flute,* Coppelius in *The Tales of Hoffmann,* Gianni Schicchi, Sharpless in *Madama Butterfly,* Scarpia in *Tosca,* Bartolo in *The Barber of Seville,* Kezal in *The Bartered Bride,* Amonasro in *Aida,* Rodrigo in *Don Carlo,* and Fra Melitone in *La Forza del Destino.*

Geraint Evans was awarded an honorary doctorate in music by the University of Wales in 1963 and by the University of Leicester in 1969. In 1969 he was elected an honorary member of the Royal Academy of Music in London.

ABOUT: New York Times, December 15, 1968.

Geraldine Farrar

1882–1967

Geraldine Farrar, soprano, was born in Melrose, Massachusetts, on February 28, 1882. Her father, Sidney Farrar, was a professional baseball player, a member of the Philadelphia Nationals. He was also an amateur singer—in a church choir and at concerts of the Amphion Club. Geraldine's mother, Henrietta Barnes Farrar, was the leading soprano in the church choir of which her husband was a member.

As an infant Geraldine used to play tunes by ear on the old-fashioned square piano at home. When she was three she sang a solo in a children's Sunday school class; at ten she was a vocalist at a church social; and at twelve she impersonated Jenny Lind. Meanwhile she went to public schools and began taking piano lessons.

She started her vocal studies with Mrs. J. H. Long of Boston. When Geraldine was fourteen, she received her first fee (ten dollars) as a singer for a performance at the Town Hall in Melrose. Five months later in Boston she gave her first recital. Hearing her first opera—*Carmen,* with Emma Calvé in the title role—aroused her ambition to become a singer.

Jean de Reszke heard Geraldine sing and advised her to go to New York and study with Luisa Cappiani. Though the audition with that teacher was successful, Geraldine decided to seek instruction elsewhere, since studying with Cappiani meant signing an exclusive three-year

Farrar: fǎ rär′

230

GERALDINE FARRAR

contract. Her next voice teacher was Emma Thursby. As Thursby's pupil, she attended numerous opera performances at the Metropolitan Opera, further whetting her desire to become an opera singer. She also took some lessons in elocution.

Through Thursby's influence Geraldine sang for Lillian Nordica and for Melba, both of whom were sufficiently impressed by her to offer help in her career. Then, during a social evening in New York, at the home of Dr. Holbrook Curtis, she sang several opera selections. One of those present was the wife of Maurice Grau, the managing director of the Metropolitan Opera; she invited Geraldine to sing a minor role at a benefit performance of *Mignon.* Since she was determined to accept only major soprano assignments, Geraldine politely turned down the invitation. Shortly after that Maurice Grau wanted to give her a Metropolitan Opera contract, still for minor roles. Convinced she was headed for stardom, she turned it down; she even declined to appear at one of the Sunday evening concerts at the opera house.

In Boston Geraldine gained the support of Annie Webb who arranged to underwrite all expenses necessary for living and studying in Europe. She sailed for Europe in 1899, and until 1905 Annie Webb paid over thirty thousand dollars to cover Farrar's expenses. This debt was repaid in full by 1908.

With letters of introduction from Nordica and Melba, Farrar arrived in Paris to make her home in a tiny apartment in the old Latin quarter. For two years she studied with the Spanish maestro Trabadello. Dissatisfied with her progress, she left Paris for Berlin in 1901, lived in a Potsdammerstrasse pension housing American students, and took lessons with Graziani.

She soon auditioned for Karl Muck, then the principal conductor of the Berlin Royal Opera, singing the waltz from *Romeo and Juliet,* an aria from *La Traviata,* and "Elsa's Dream" from *Lohengrin.* Muck offered her a three-year contract. On October 15, 1901, Farrar made her opera debut as Marguerite in *Faust,* Muck conducting. She was an instant sensation. The Berlin critic of the German *Times* wrote: "From the very first, Farrar established herself as a singer and an actress so gifted that she could hardly fail to conquer her audience, and an artist so independent that no degree of trickery on the stage could have shaken her confidence and repose."

During her three years with the Berlin Royal Opera Farrar sang the roles of Violetta in *La Traviata,* Juliet in *Romeo and Juliet,* Manon in Massenet's opera, Nedda in *I Pagliacci,* Zerlina in *Don Giovanni,* Leonora in *Il Trovatore,* Mignon, Gilda in *Rigoletto,* Elisabeth in *Tannhäuser,* and Angela in Auber's *Le Domino Noir.* For *Manon* (which had been revived expressly to star her) she had been coached by its composer, Massenet, and for Elisabeth she was guided by Lilli Lehmann with whom she was then studying. Farrar was one of the few prima donnas invited to give a command performance before the Kaiser and his family. A favorite of the royal family, she was said to be romantically involved with the Crown Prince, Frederick William.

Proud, headstrong, and fiercely independent, Farrar made enemies as well as admirers in Berlin. Her popularity with her audiences and critics inspired cabals and jealousies within the opera house, and her refusal to be dictated to by royal formalities or traditions aroused a good deal of antagonism outside the theater. In 1906 she decided to leave the Berlin Royal Opera. But before that, on March 10, 1904, she had made a triumphant debut at Monte Carlo as Mimi in *La Bohème,* appearing for the first time on the stage with Caruso. In October 1904 she made her bow at the Warsaw Imperial Theater as Maddalena in *Andrea Chénier,* and on April 26, 1906, she sang for the first time at the Paris Opéra in the world premiere of Camondo's *Le Clown.* She continued appearing at the Monte Carlo Opera until 1906 where her great successes came in a performance of *Don Carlo* with Chaliapin and in the world premieres of Mascagni's *Amica* on March 16, 1905, and Saint-Saëns's *L'Ancêtre* on February 24, 1906. (Substituting for Emma Calvé in *Amica,* she learned the role in five days.) At the Munich Royal Opera she sang Elisabeth in *Tannhäuser,* Richard Strauss conducting.

Her successes in Europe finally brought her a contract for starring roles at the Metropolitan Opera House. She made her first appearance there on November 26, 1906 (the opening night of the season), as Juliet. Richard Aldrich wrote in the New York *Times:* "She has a charming personality and a winning one, and her stage presence is alluring with much of the girlishness of Juliet. . . . Her voice is a full, rich soprano, lyric in its nature and flexibility, yet rather darkly colored with not a little of dramatic quality and with a power of dramatic nuance that she uses, in the main, skilfully." The critic of the *Sun* said: "Here was an actress who enters the American stage, exhibits the manners of a court, whispers a worn-out waltz song pensively . . . and suddenly finds the coldest audience in the world taking her to its heart in a storm of applause that could not, would not end."

That season Farrar was heard as Marguerite in *Faust,* Marguerite in Berlioz' *The Damnation of Faust,* Mimi in *La Bohème,* Elisabeth in *Tannhäuser,* and in what became her most famous role and almost her private property at the Metropolitan Opera during the ensuing years—Cio-Cio-San in *Madama Butterfly.* Her performance, on February 11, 1907, was the first production of the opera in America in the Italian language, and Puccini, its composer, was at hand for the rehearsals. Before assuming the role, Farrar worked for weeks with a Japanese actress to be coached in Japanese gestures, behavior, and appearance. But Puccini had his own ideas about Cio-Cio-San to which the strong-willed Farrar refused to bend. Friction between composer and prima donna developed, and Puccini went on record to say that she was somewhat less than ideal for his opera.

The Metropolitan Opera audiences, however, in and out of New York, thought otherwise. For the next sixteen years and in 136 performances they continued to applaud the glamour and exotic beauty she brought to the role. Next to Cio-Cio-San, the part for which she was most admired and in which she appeared 66 times was Carmen. Tosca (with 67 performances) and

Marguerite in *Faust* (with 62 performances) were two more of her most frequently heard roles. Other Metropolitan roles were Manon in Massenet's opera, Violetta in *La Traviata,* Mignon, Cherubino in *The Marriage of Figaro,* Charlotte in *Werther,* the title role in *Louise,* and Anita in Massenet's *La Navarraise.*

In addition, she appeared in the world premieres of Humperdinck's *Königskinder* as the Goose Girl (December 28, 1910), Giordano's *Madame Sans-Gêne* as Caterina (January 25, 1915), and in the title role of Puccini's *Suor Angelica* (December 14, 1918); the American premieres of Paul Dukas's *Ariane et Barbe-Bleue* as Ariane (March 29, 1911), Wolf-Ferrari's *Le Donne Curiose* as Rosaura (January 13, 1911), the title role in Mascagni's *Lodoletta* (January 12, 1918), and Leroux' *La Reine Fiammette* as Orlanda (January 24, 1919); and the first Metropolitan Opera productions of *Thaïs, Zaza,* and *The Secret of Suzanne,* in which she assumed the title roles.

In 1915 Farrar made her first appearance in motion pictures, in *Maria Rosa,* directed by Cecil B. De Mille. Despite the fact that the silent screen made it impossible for her to be heard as well as seen, she was starred in several more films between 1915 and 1920: *Carmen* (1915), *Temptation* (1916), *Joan the Woman* (1916), *The Woman God Forgot* (1917), *The Hell Cat* (1918), *The World and Its Women* (1919), *The Flame of the Desert* (1919), *The Woman and the Puppet* (1920) and others. In one film, *Maria Rosa,* her costar was Lou Tellegen, already a famous screen personality. Tellegen and Farrar were married on February 6, 1916. They were costarred in several films before getting a divorce in 1923.

From her autobiography we learn that where Farrar was a morning lark, Tellegen was a night owl. She would rise early in the morning and by nine would begin work on her scales. The nights when she was not performing she would be in bed by ten to store up energy for her exhausting regimen. She always required eight hours' sleep. When she and her husband gave home parties it was understood by all present that she would leave the guests early and go to bed. She detested physical exertion of any kind and had a horror of draughts, chills, snow, rain, and smoky rooms.

For a long time she insisted that she would retire from opera when she reached forty. After appearing as Anita in a revival of Massenet's *La Navarraise* on November 30, 1921, she announced that she would end her career at the Metropolitan at the termination of that season. Her final performance took place on April 22, 1922, in the title role of Leoncavallo's *Zaza*. It was, as she herself has written, a hectic affair. "It carried itself on a crescendo of frenzy, hysteria, tears and cheers." In his report to the *Sun,* W. J. Henderson went on to explain: "The celebration began mildly after the first act with paper stars marked 'G.F.' and balloons and bouquets thrown from upper boxes, and lasted till long after the performance when Miss Farrar walked out of the house not wearing the garments she had carried in, but clad in a complete outfit made by her . . . admirers." There were banners reading "Farrar, Hurrah! Hurrah! Farrar!" and speeches, as well as a concluding parade from the stage door up Broadway.

After withdrawing from the Metropolitan Opera, having been heard 517 times in New York and 147 times on tour, Farrar made concert tours as a recitalist for a number of years. On one occasion she toured the country in a condensed version of *Carmen,* giving 123 performances in 125 days. She also made appearances over the radio on the "Packard Hour" and the "General Motors Hour."

She appeared once again on the stage of the Metropolitan Opera in the early 1930s, not to sing but to make financial appeals to the audience. When the Metropolitan Opera began to broadcast under Texaco sponsorship in 1940, she served for a time as program annotator, writing all her own material.

Farrar spent her last years in retirement in a house in Ridgefield, Connecticut, devoting herself to work for the Red Cross and to various civic and community activities. She removed herself so completely from a public life in music that she even refused to make an appearance at the gala final night of the Metropolitan Opera at its old auditorium on Broadway on April 16, 1966, when nearly every surviving alumnus participated. She almost never crossed into Manhattan, having made her last visit to the Metropolitan Opera House as a member of the audience in 1951 to hear Kirsten Flagstad.

Geraldine Farrar died in Ridgefield, Connecticut, at the age of eighty-five, on March 11, 1967.

ABOUT: Farrar, G. Such Sweet Compulsion; Wagenknecht, E. Geraldine Farrar: An Authorized Record of Her Career; Thompson, O. The American Singer. *Periodicals*—Opera News, February 3, 1962, April 15, 1967.

Eileen Farrell

1920–

Eileen Farrell, soprano, was born in Willimantic, Connecticut, on February 13, 1920. Her parents, Michael John and Catherine Kennedy Farrell, were of Irish descent and had appeared as headliners in vaudeville and as performers in church entertainments, billed as "The Singing O'Farrells." They were no longer on the stage when Eileen was born. From the time Eileen began singing nursery tunes her parents recognized that she had an unusual singing voice. Her mother, who taught singing at the University of Connecticut in Storrs, gave Eileen her first vocal lessons. After the family had resettled in Woonsocket, Rhode Island, Eileen appeared as soloist in church and school performances. Originally she planned a career in the visual arts. Upon graduating from high school in 1939 she went to art school where she decided to specialize in music. She studied voice with Merle Alcock in New York, not an altogether happy experience since, together with her lessons, she was required to cook for her teacher, sew her clothes, and take care of an invalid member of the Alcock family. But these studies were musically productive. Alcock remained Eileen's only teacher until 1944 when she continued her studies with Eleanor McLellan. "The moment I heard her," McLellan has said, "I knew that this was singing in the grand old-time manner."

Early in 1940, in New York City, Farrell sang at an audition for the "Major Bowes Amateur Hour" on radio and was turned down. Discouragement sent her back to Woonsocket, where her folks were living and where, for a time, she worked in a department store. But after a few months she was back in New York, singing in choruses and ensembles over the CBS radio network.

Her professional career began on October 16, 1941, when she dubbed in for Rosa Ponselle three measures of "Home, Sweet Home" for a "March of Time" documentary over the NBC

Farrell

EILEEN FARRELL

radio network. This led to an engagement on a weekly radio program, "Songs of the Centuries." For five years she sang on radio, including a sustaining program called "Eileen Farrell Presents," then on sponsored network programs. She subsequently was a frequent guest star on several major television programs, after making her television debut on the "Milton Berle Show" in 1950.

In 1945 Edward Johnson, general manager of the Metropolitan Opera, offered her a contract which she turned down because she felt she was not yet ready. She made her first concert tour of the United States in 1947–1948 and her first South American tour in 1949. Success on the concert stage first came on October 24, 1950, with a recital at Carnegie Hall. A critic of the New York *Times* wrote: "This was great singing. The big notes soared out thrillingly, only to be followed with pianissimos of ravishing softness as the mood changed. The effortless production, the swells and diminuendos on single breaths, the purity of sound—all these were notable, and yet everything was subordinate to the interpretation, which was truly felt from the heart."

In 1950 Farrell appeared at the Roxy Theatre in New York as soloist with the New York Philharmonic Orchestra under Dimitri Mitropoulos, singing for four shows a day for two weeks (fifty-five times in all) the "Un bel di" aria from *Madama Butterfly* and "The Last Rose of Summer" from *Martha*.

Her versatility became evident during the 1950–1951 season when she made 61 appear-

ances in 5 separate engagements with the New York Philharmonic Orchestra. (No soloist had ever before appeared with the New York Philharmonic so often in a single season.) At these concerts she was heard in the American premiere of Milhaud's *Les Choëphores,* in Alban Berg's *Wozzeck,* and in an all-Wagner program. Her personal success as Marie in *Wozzeck* resulted in her recording that part for Columbia.

In 1952 Arturo Toscanini chose her as one of the soloists in his performances of Beethoven's Ninth Symphony with the NBC Symphony. A year later she became a member of William H. Scheide's Bach Aria Group that concertized throughout the United States. On November 8, 1955, she sang the title role in Cherubini's *Medea* in a concert performance by the American Opera Society in Town Hall, New York. "If a voice divested of the usual operatic paraphernalia can create the illusion of full-scale drama," said Winthrop Sargeant in *Opera News,* "Miss Farrell succeeded breathtakingly. One could hear every nuance of outraged womanhood—heartbreak, jealousy, and, finally, homicidal fury —expressed so convincingly that the performance took on an almost hypnotic power."

In 1955 Farrell was also heard on the sound track of the motion picture biography of Marjorie Lawrence, *Interrupted Melody*—she sang all the vocal selections in the film.

Her first appearance on an opera stage took place in March 1956 with the San Carlo Opera in Tampa, Florida, as Santuzza in *Cavalleria Rusticana.* Her initial performance with a major opera company followed on September 16, 1956, when she was heard as Leonora in *Il Trovatore* with the San Francisco Opera. She returned to the San Francisco Opera on September 12, 1958 (the opening night of the season), when Cherubini's *Medea* was given its first American stage production. One year later, when she sang the part of Ariadne in *Ariadne auf Naxos,* a critic of the San Francisco *Chronicle* remarked: "Miss Farrell is to singers what Niagara is to waterfalls." In 1957 she made her debut with the Chicago Lyric Opera in the title role of *La Gioconda.* Her first European appearance took place that same year when she helped to dedicate Berlin's Congress Hall. In 1959 she made a highly successful concert debut in London, gave a recital at the Festival of Two Worlds in Spoleto, Italy, and was heard at the Casals Festival in Puerto Rico.

On December 6, 1960, she came to the stage of the Metropolitan Opera in the title role of a new production of Gluck's *Alceste.* Winthrop Sargeant noted in the *New Yorker:* "Miss Farrell possesses what is, as far as I am aware, the most powerful dramatic soprano voice to be heard at the Met since Kirsten Flagstad, and it is also one of the warmest, most expressive voices to come to light during this period. . . . Miss Farrell sang with the aplomb one had expected of her, ranging from beautiful pianissimos to rich and equally beautiful fortes, and showed a command of classical style."

During five seasons at the Metropolitan Opera Farrell was also heard as Santuzza, La Gioconda, Leonora in *La Forza del Destino,* Maddalena in *Andrea Chénier,* and Ariadne.

It was no secret that Rudolf Bing, the general manager of the Metropolitan Opera, and Eileen Farrell wasted no affection upon each other. Since Bing was not particularly enthusiastic over the Wagnerian music dramas, and since Farrell wished to make Wagner her province, a parting of ways became inevitable. It took place in 1966 when the Metropolitan Opera moved to its new home at the Lincoln Center for the Performing Arts.

After leaving the Metropolitan Opera, Farrell concertized in recitals and as a guest artist with symphony orchestras. She also made numerous appearances in public and over television in performances of popular music and jazz selections. Her first important appearance in popular music took place at the Spoleto Festival of the Two Worlds in 1959. There, upon his sudden illness, she substituted for Louis Armstrong, providing a program of blues songs and other jazz pieces. This performance was shown on television and was broadcast in the United States on the "Ed Sullivan Hour." She also recorded popular selections beginning with the best-selling album *I've Got a Right to Sing the Blues,* released the same year she made her debut at the Metropolitan Opera.

When not concertizing, Farrell taught voice at the University of Indiana.

She has received several honorary degrees, conferred on her over a period of time by the University of Rhode Island, Notre Dame College in New Hampshire, and the University of Hartford in Connecticut. In 1962 she was awarded a Grammy by the National Academy of Recording Arts and Sciences for a Wagner album with the New York Philharmonic under Leonard Bernstein.

On April 4, 1946, Farrell married Robert Vincent Reagan, an amateur Irish tenor then employed on the New York City police force. Their first home was a twelve-room house on Staten Island overlooking the New York harbor; later they had an apartment in Manhattan. Later still they acquired a three-acre residence in Londonderry, New Hampshire, and a summer place on Moosehead Lake in Maine where they keep five boats. A woman of simple, down-to-earth, homespun tastes, Farrell is an excellent cook and a skilled hand at needlepoint and knitting. She often joins her husband and two children (a son and daughter) on camping trips and for boating, golfing, or fishing. For further relaxation she enjoys reading mysteries and watching boxing matches or western movies on TV.

Winthrop Sargeant described her as a "sunny-tempered, loud-laughing and obviously contented woman, untroubled by anything in the way of ambition, and eager to be accepted for what she is off stage—a diligent housewife, grateful for such homely pleasures as her situation affords."

ABOUT: Sargeant, W. Divas. *Periodicals*—Coronet, December 1960; New York Times, February 8, 1970; New Yorker, May 23, 1959; Newsweek, September 22, 1958; Opera News, December 9, 1967.

Kathleen Ferrier

1912–1953

Kathleen Ferrier, contralto, was born in Higher Walton, Lancashire, England, on April 22, 1912, to William and Alice Murray Ferrier. While still a child, she went to live in Blackburn where her father was headmaster of a boys' school. In Blackburn, Kathleen attended the public schools, at the same time studying the piano and winning first prize in a piano competition that attracted 136 contestants. In the years between 1927 and 1936 Kathleen earned her living as a piano accompanist. She had no thought of becoming a professional singer, even though she had sung in the local church choir and as soloist in nearby festivals. But in 1938, on the challenge of a bet of one shilling, she entered a

Ferrier: fĕr′ ĭ ĕr

KATHLEEN FERRIER

vocal competition in Carlisle and won first prize not only in singing but also in piano, together with a trophy for being the best all-around musician. Encouraged, she began to study voice with a local teacher and to take on singing engagements for small fees. To support herself, she worked as a telephone operator in the Blackburn Post Office.

In 1940 she went to Newcastle-on-Tyne to study voice with J. E. Hutchinson. She made her professional debut as a singer in 1942 as a soloist in a performance of Bach's *Passion According to St. Matthew.*

In December 1942 she went to London with letters of introduction from Sir Malcolm Sargent, the conductor, who had heard her sing and had been impressed by her musicianship. There she studied for a time with Roy Henderson, but before long she began appearing in recitals and as a soloist with choral groups. Her first important appearance in London was in 1943 as a soloist in the *Messiah* performed at Westminster Abbey.

During World War II Ferrier became a member of the Council for the Encouragement of Music and the Arts, a wartime agency set up to provide entertainment for both troops and civilians. She gave numerous concerts in bomb shelters, subways, factories, and hospitals.

Soon after the end of the war she was chosen for the title role in the world premiere of Britten's *The Rape of Lucretia,* given at Glyndebourne on July 12, 1946. This was the first performance by anyone at Glyndebourne since the

war. She made about sixty appearances in this opera—at Glyndebourne, Covent Garden in London, and elsewhere in England and Scotland —and later sang Orfeo in Gluck's *Orfeo ed Euridice* at the Glyndebourne Festival in 1947, a performance which brought her her first triumph. Dyneley Hussey, English musicologist, spoke of her "regal and beautiful presence" and of the beauty and power of her voice. That summer she repeated her success as Orfeo at the Edinburgh Festival. As it turned out, Lucretia and Orfeo were the only two roles she was ever destined to perform on the opera stage.

Attracting the interest of the conductor Bruno Walter, she was engaged to appear under his direction at the Edinburgh Festival of 1947 in Mahler's *Das Lied von der Erde.* "Here," said Bruno Walter, "was potentially one of the greatest singers of our time, a voice of rare beauty, warmth of expression and an innate understanding of the musical phrase."

With this Mahler composition, and under Walter's direction, Ferrier made her American debut, as soloist with the New York Philharmonic Orchestra on January 15, 1948. Herbert F. Peyser reported in *Musical America* that her voice was one "of unusual quality and texture, singularly vibrant and substantial." She toured the United States in 1948–1949 and again in 1950–1951. Among these appearances were her American debut recital at Town Hall in New York on March 29, 1949, and in the same month her first American performance as Orfeo in Gluck's opera in a concert performance. Her growing artistry as a recitalist impelled Bruno Walter to officiate as her piano accompanist when she subsequently gave a recital in New York. This was only the second time that Bruno Walter ever appeared as an accompanist; the first was for Lotte Lehmann.

In 1948 she toured Scandinavia, and in 1949 she was heard in Canada, Cuba, England, and at the Holland Music Festival where, on July 14, she sang in the world premiere of Britten's *Spring Symphony.* In addition to these appearances, she performed in Vienna, Milan, Amsterdam, Brussels, and Zurich, as well as at the Salzburg and Edinburgh festivals. She distinguished herself particularly in the music of Handel and Bach, in Mahler's *Das Lied von der Erde,* and in the repertory of art songs. "Less than five years from the time of her London debut," wrote John Culshaw, the recording executive and musicologist, "Kathleen Ferrier had been heard in all the major concert halls of the Western world, while she herself became one of the most beloved artists of our time. Beloved is the word. Beloved by audiences for the incomparable beauty of her voice, whose richness had none of the turgid quality which limits so many contraltos; and by those who knew her for her unforgettable self. She approached music with that humility and quest for understanding which together make for greatness in an artist."

In 1952 she was made Commander of the Order of the British Empire. A year later she was presented with the gold medal of the Royal Philharmonic Orchestra in London.

Suffering from cancer, Ferrier summoned her physical resources and courage to make two appearances as Orfeo in Gluck's *Orfeo ed Euridice* at Covent Garden in February 1953. She died in a hospital in London on October 8, 1953. Twenty years after her death a six-record album was released by Richmond covering a wide range of her art in opera, oratorio, art songs, and music for voice and orchestra.

She made her home in the St. John's Wood section of London. Her main diversions were playing golf, reading, and painting.

ABOUT: Cardus, N. ed. Kathleen Ferrier, a Memoir. *Periodicals*—Musical America, November 1953, April 1954; Saturday Review, October 31, 1953.

Emanuel Feuermann

1902–1942

Emanuel Feuermann, cellist, was born in Kolomea, Galicia, on November 22, 1902, to a family of musicians. His father gave him his first cello lessons; later Emanuel became a pupil of Anton Walter, cellist of the Arnold Rosé Quartet. He made such progress that in his eleventh year he was able to make his debut in Vienna as a guest artist of the Vienna Symphony Orchestra conducted by Felix Weingartner.

Emanuel continued to study the cello, in Leipzig with Julius Klengel. When he was sixteen, he was appointed professor of the cello at the Cologne Conservatory. He held this post six years before moving on to Berlin, where in 1930 he

Feuermann: foi' ĕr män

EMANUEL FEUERMANN

was made head of the cello department of the Berlin High School for Music. At the same time he made many concert appearances throughout Europe, was soloist with leading European orchestras, and participated in outstanding trio concerts with Paul Hindemith, violist, and Szymon Goldberg, violinist.

Upon the rise of the Nazi regime in Germany in 1933, Feuermann resigned from his post at the Berlin High School for Music and became a political exile. His new home was in Vienna. But with the *Anschluss* in 1938 he was forced to find another new homeland. He settled permanently in the United States, acquired a house in Scarsdale, New York, and applied for American citizenship.

Long before he made his first American concert appearance, Feuermann had established his reputation in Europe as one of the foremost cellists of his time, a virtuoso whose command of his instrument was equaled by his discerning musicianship and profound interpretative insights in an exhaustive repertory.

He paid his first visit to the United States in 1934 on an invitation from Bruno Walter to perform the Haydn Concerto in D major with the New York Philharmonic under Walter's direction on January 2, 1935. In the *Herald Tribune* Francis D. Perkins reported: "His tone was remarkably warm and mellow in texture, not, indeed, massive, but full and far-carrying and observing an unusually consistent standard in a quality eminently satisfactory to the ear. His technical skill was of a corresponding standard,

237

and his tasteful interpretation resulted in marked enthusiasm."

In the following years Feuermann gave numerous performances throughout the United States in recitals, as guest artist with America's foremost orchestras, and in trio concerts with Artur Schnabel, pianist, and Bronislaw Hubermann, violinist. In 1941 he made trio recordings for RCA Victor with Jascha Heifetz and Arthur Rubinstein. These performances reaffirmed the original impression in the United States that he was a musician of extraordinary endowments. After one of Feuermann's recitals in New York, Olin Downes referred to him in the New York *Times* as "absolutely phenomenal. . . . Difficulties do not exist for Mr. Feuermann, even difficulties that would give celebrated virtuosi pause. It would be hard to imagine a cleaner or more substantial technique which can place every resource of the instrument at the interpreter's command. And there is more than technique. There is a big tone, finely sustained in singing passages, and warm. There is palpable sincerity, earnestness and musicianship."

Feuermann performed on a Stradivarius sometimes called "The Last Cello," since it was the last instrument made by the master craftsman. His second instrument was dubbed "The Sleeping Beauty," because it had "slept" for a hundred years before Feuermann reawakened it. The latter cello was one of the finest examples of the work of Montagnana, who lived in the early eighteenth century. Whenever Feuermann was on a concert tour he always purchased an extra berth on trains for his cellos which he never permitted to leave his sight.

Emanuel Feuermann died in New York City on May 25, 1942.

ABOUT: Etude, September 1940, July 1942; Newsweek, June 8, 1942; Time, April 4, 1938.

Arthur Fiedler

1894–

During the more than four decades that Arthur Fiedler was the conductor of the Boston Pops Orchestra he made it into a national institution, not only through his annual spring concerts in

Fiedler: fē′ dlẽr

ARTHUR FIEDLER

Boston but also through his many nationwide tours, his performances on radio and television, and his recordings.

Arthur Fiedler was born in South Boston, on December 17, 1894. He was the only son and the second youngest of four children of Emanuel and Johanna Bernfeld Fiedler, Austrian-born Jews; his sisters Elsa and Rosa became, respectively, a professional violist and a cellist. His father was a violinist in the Boston Symphony Orchestra and the second violinist of the Kneisel String Quartet. One of Arthur's uncles—Bernard, known as Benny—was also a member of the violin section of the Boston Symphony, a chair he occupied for over forty years. Arthur's mother was a talented amateur pianist.

All four children received musical instruction. Piano lessons were first given to Arthur by his mother and later continued with Carl Lamson who ultimately became Fritz Kreisler's accompanist. Arthur's father taught him the violin. Arthur was no musical prodigy and practicing was a chore he detested. "It was something I had to do, like brushing my teeth." His desultory progress indicated strongly that he was not destined for a professional musical life. Actually his early ambition was to become a doctor. He went to the Prince Grammar School in Boston and the Boston Latin School. At the latter he played the drums in the school band, and on graduation day he performed some violin solos.

In 1909 his father decided to return to Europe. After a visit to his native city of Vienna, he took the family to Berlin where he had been appointed first violinist to the Berlin Philharmonic. In Berlin Arthur made it clear he had no intention of pursuing his academic education any further. "I had had it with more books and more Latin and more Greek and more algebra and I rebelled." For a time he planned a business career and found a job as office boy for a women's magazine. "I loathed it," he recalls. Only then, with apparently no other avenue open to him, did he decide to continue his musical training with the hope of becoming a professional.

For a brief period he attended the Ochs-Eichelberger Conservatory where he had his first experience at conducting, leading its orchestra in a performance of a Mozart German Dance. Then, he was one of thirteen pupils who successfully auditioned for admission to the Royal Academy of Music. There he studied the violin with Willy Hess, chamber music with Ernst von Dohnányi, and conducting with Arno Kleffel and Rudolf Krasselt. While attending the Academy he played the violin in café-houses and with the touring Blüthner Orchestra. During the summer of 1913 he played in an orchestra conducted by Johann Strauss III, the waltz king's grandson. Then, with two members of his own family Arthur formed the Fiedler Trio which gave concerts in Berlin.

The Fiedler family remained in Berlin when World War I erupted. During the early war years the Fiedler Trio gave concerts to raise money for the Red Cross and for war victims. Then when the S.S. Lusitania was sunk and American involvement in the war became a strong possibility, Fiedler was advised by his German friends to return to the United States.

In 1915 he sailed on the S.S. Rotterdam, leaving behind his parents whom he did not see again for another three and a half years. In Springfield, Massachusetts, Fiedler found a job playing the violin in a hotel orchestra. In September 1915 he was engaged for the second violin section of the Boston Symphony Orchestra, conducted by Karl Muck. In 1916–1917 Fiedler went to the viola section where he remained many years. He also served with the Boston Symphony as pianist, organist, and occasionally as percussionist.

As a violist with the Boston Symphony in 1917, Muck conducting, Fiedler participated in the first recording ever made by a symphony orchestra. In the summer of 1918 he was an assisting artist at a concert given by Caruso at Saratoga Springs, New York.

In 1924, or about that time, Fiedler was appointed conductor of the MacDowell Club Orchestra, made up of students, amateurs, and semiprofessionals. His appetite for conducting was whetted by this experience, and in 1924 he formed the Arthur Fiedler Sinfonietta with members of the Boston Symphony. The Sinfonietta gave its first concert in Plymouth, Massachusetts, on October 30, 1925. Early in January 1927 it broadcast a concert over the new Boston radio station WBET, and on January 30, 1927, the organization made its debut in Boston. "These twenty-two musicians are under as sensitive a control and are as responsive to it, as though they were under Mr. Koussevitzky himself," reported a critic for *The Christian Science Monitor*.

In 1929 Fiedler established the free Esplanade concerts on the banks of the Charles River in Boston. The first concert, on July 4, 1929, opened with Sousa's *The Stars and Stripes Forever* and ended with Victor Herbert's *American Fantasia*. Between these selections were compositions by Nicolai, Dvořák, Weber, Verdi, Wagner, Johann Strauss II, and Sigmund Romberg. Over two hundred thousand attended these concerts in their first season. Such success insured the continuation of these free performances. In 1953, commemorating the twenty-fifth anniversary of the Esplanade Concerts, a footbridge connecting the Esplanade to Beacon Hill and the Back Bay section was named after Arthur Fiedler; on both ends a plaque displayed his profile and quoted the opening measure of the Prelude to *Tristan and Isolde*—its first two notes were "A" and "F." On the thirtieth anniversary in 1959, RCA Victor presented Fiedler with a plaque dedicated "to one of the world's outstanding ambassadors of good music." The Esplanade concert on July 4, 1976, commemorating America's bicentennial, drew an audience of four hundred thousand and was an event of sufficient public interest to be covered on the nation's television news programs.

In 1929 Fiedler became the conductor of the Cecilia Society, a choral group. One year later he was appointed the eighteenth musician (and the first Boston-born) to become the conductor of the Boston Pops Orchestra which gave ten weeks of concerts each spring in Symphony Hall. When Fiedler took over, the Pops was at the lowest ebb of its popularity since its founding in 1885. But it did not take Fiedler long to restore these concerts to their one-time esteem and even to elevate them to an altogether new plane of significance. Fiedler conducted his first Boston Pops concert on May 7, 1930. His program —already a typical Fiedler musical stew—was made up of the ingredients of the standard symphonic repertory (Wagner's *Siegfried's Rhine Journey,* Richard Strauss's waltzes from *Der Rosenkavalier,* Ravel's *Bolero,* Thomas's Overture to *Mignon,* and an *Aida* fantasy) combined with semiclassics (Kreisler's *Tambourin Chinois,* Herbert's *American Fantasy*) and some popular music (Romberg's *The New Moon*). H. T. Parker reported in the *Transcript* that Fiedler "engrossed the audience. . . . Plainly, it liked his alert and business-like procedures; his swift readiness with extra numbers the moment the clapping warranted them. It took pleasure as well in his youth, pleasing manners, flowing and exuberant energy." By the end of the first Pops season both Fiedler and these concerts had completely won the hearts of Bostonians.

A man of seemingly inexhaustible energy even in his late years, the Fiedler of the early 1930s was deeply involved in many activities. From October through April he played the violin in the Boston Symphony and in the same period conducted his Sinfonietta in concerts in Boston and outlying areas in Massachusetts. For ten weeks in the spring he devoted himself to the Boston Pops; during the summer, to the Esplanade concerts. His other activities included conducting concerts of the MacDowell Club Orchestra, the Cecilia Society Chorus, and the Boston University Orchestra. Before the decade ended he also led the Men's University Glee Club in Providence, Rhode Island, and was involved with the WPA National Youth Administration Music Project helping to audition hundreds of instrumentalists trying to find a place in the All-American Youth Orchestra which Leopold Stokowski was to conduct in concerts on an international tour.

The strain of all these activities exacted their toll in 1939. Fiedler suffered his first heart attack. For six months he was confined to a hospital bed. After his recovery he refused to make any concessions to his past illness and continued to function at his former hectic pace.

On January 5, 1942, he married Ellen Bottomley, a Catholic girl from a socially elite Boston family. They met for the first time, when Ellen was seven and Fiedler twenty-three, at a concert in which Ellen's aunt was accompanied on the piano by Fiedler. They met again in 1932 when she was not yet eighteen—at that time she appeared as one of the dancers in a pageant conducted by Fiedler in Boston for the benefit of World War I veterans. After that she frequently attended his concerts.

A handsome, suave, charming, and successful artist, Fiedler had long been known throughout Boston as a lady's man. One of his more ardent romances, which began in 1919 and lasted several years, involved the actress Jeanne Eagles. Such notoriety was just one of the obstacles standing in the way of Fiedler's marriage to Ellen. Another obstacle was his Jewish heritage—though his family never actively practiced Judaism, Fiedler refused to be converted to Catholicism. After the opposition of both pairs of parents to an interreligious marriage had been overcome, Fiedler and Ellen were married in a quiet ceremony in the rectory of the Cathedral of the Holy Cross; the Cathedral itself was barred to them because Fiedler had remained Jewish.

Initially, they lived in an apartment. There their first child, Johanna, was born on September 17, 1945. In 1947 they acquired a large Georgian brick mansion on Hyslop Road in Brookline. This remained their home from that time on, and there two more children, Roberta and Peter, were born.

In the early 1940s Fiedler aspired to become the Sousa of World War II. When his musical services were turned down by the military authorities, he enlisted for active duty in the United States Coast Guard Temporary Reserve as an apprentice seaman. He often led the Coast Guard band in war-bond, Red Cross, and Victory Rally drives. He was also an active member of Boston's Concert Committee which arranged musical performances for the armed services.

In 1949 Fiedler conducted several Pop concerts over the radio in San Francisco with the San Francisco Symphony. These were so successful that he was given a regular radio program in San Francisco, "The Standard Hour," sponsored by the Standard Oil Company. In 1951 he initiated an annual series of Pop concerts with the San Francisco Symphony in its auditorium.

In addition to his activities in Boston and San Francisco, Fiedler undertook nationwide tours with the Boston Pops Orchestra beginning in

January 1953, when he led 65 concerts in 61 cities over a 10-week period. This tour was so well received that a second one was booked for February and March 1954. Since then he has made many more tours with the Boston Pops Orchestra including one in Europe in 1971. He has made numerous appearances as guest conductor of many of America's principal orchestras, and has been heard in guest concerts with orchestras in South America, Europe, Africa, Australia, Israel, and the Orient.

His remarkable drive and energy remained undiminished through the years in spite of several heart attacks and serious operations. Characteristic of the perpetual motion that so long marked his career were the events of early 1972, when he was seventy-seven. He toured Japan, returned to the United States to take the Boston Pops on a national tour (including its first appearance at Carnegie Hall, on April 6, 1972), gave two concerts with the Memphis Symphony, and conducted 8 concerts in 12 days with the Syracuse Symphony.

"Something is driving me," he told Stephen E. Rubin of the New York *Times*. "But I don't know what it is. I have that kind of nature. I just can't sit and twiddle my thumbs. I don't enjoy vacations, because I don't know what to do with myself. I don't want to lie on the beach and get sunburned. I've tried that. . . . I don't know what I would do if I retired. I'd probably just be hanging around waiting to go to the dentist or doctor or the undertaker."

One of Fiedler's distinctions is that as the head of the Boston Pops Orchestra for over four decades he has led a major American orchestra longer than any other musician. Another is that he has made more recordings than any other conductor and has enjoyed for them the largest sales of any conductor. It has been estimated that by the mid-1970s over fifty million of his records had been sold. His RCA Victor recording of Gade's *Jalousie* (a composition totally unknown before he discovered it and featured it at his Boston Pops concerts) became the first classical orchestral recording to sell over a million disks.

In reviewing some of Fiedler's recordings, Irving Kolodin wrote in the New York *Sun:* "Fiedler's feeling for period music is a long familiar fact resulting indeed in some of the most delightful records in this country. The period does not matter so long as there is style inherent in the music; he is likely to seek it out and make it live again. We have rarely heard him do anything with the care, taste and incisiveness that he applies to these minor masterpieces."

Fiedler has made innumerable appearances over television, including a series of programs sponsored by the Boston *Globe* entitled "The World of Arthur Fiedler," and taped concerts of the Boston Pops Orchestra telecast regularly over a period of many years. He also played a cameo part in the Louis de Rochemont motion picture *Windjammer.*

Fiedler celebrated his seventy-fifth birthday by conducting a gala concert with the Boston Symphony Orchestra. Governor Francis Sargent proclaimed an Arthur Fiedler Day throughout the state. Fiedler had been scheduled to make his first appearance with the Boston Symphony Orchestra during its regular season in 1944, but this engagement was canceled by Koussevitzky on the pretext that Heitor Villa-Lobos, the Brazilian conductor, was in America and eager to conduct the Boston Symphony at the time Fiedler had been scheduled. Actually, Koussevitzky is believed to have canceled Fiedler's concert because Fiedler had shortly before that conducted a concert for Frank Sinatra. Previously, when Koussevitzky fell ill, Fiedler had substituted on February 5, 1932, in a program highlighted by Beethoven's Fifth Symphony. Writing in the Boston *Post,* Warren Storey Smith said the performance was marked "by strength and sanity. . . . Certainly the performance was both stirring and satisfying." On December 16, 1955, Fiedler appeared as a guest conductor of the Boston Symphony in a program made up of music by Frescobaldi, Kodály, Beethoven (Symphony No.8), and Rachmaninoff *(Rhapsody on a Theme of Paganini)*. "Every measure . . . was sheer pleasure," wrote Cyrus Durgin in the *Globe*. "The performance *in toto* was clear and balanced, a long line of musical motion, details all in place but kept in their place and not permitted to distort the contours of the score as a whole." In the *Post* Tucker Keiser reported: "Mr. Fiedler asked for that wonderful old Koussevitzky tone and got it. So startling was this rich, gorgeous sound . . . that I bolted nearly out of my seat with surprised delight." However, when Fiedler celebrated his golden jubilee with the Boston Symphony in 1965 no effort was made to invite him to conduct a commemorative concert. The only gesture was a citation by the trustees of the orchestra presented at a dinner at the Somerset Club.

Fiedler taught conducting at the Malkin School of Music in Boston. For two decades he was a member of the music faculty of Boston University, and Boston University was one of seven educational institutions in the United States to confer on him an honorary doctorate in music. France has awarded him the Croix de l'Officier d'Académie and has named him Chevalier of the Legion of Honor. On January 4, 1977, President Gerald Ford presented him the nation's highest civilian honor, the Medal of Freedom. In addition, he has been made honorary chief of the tribe of the Otoe Indians in Stillwater, Oklahoma, with the name "Maker of Sweet Music," and in Kentucky he has been appointed honorary colonel on the governor's staff.

All his life Fiedler has been a fire buff. This passion began early in his childhood when one of his father's pupils, an engineering student at MIT, presented him with a toy replica of a Boston fire engine. Since then Fiedler has been a dedicated collector of these replicas and of helmets and fire-chief badges. He has been named honorary chief of the fire departments of almost three hundred American and foreign cities. His collection of chief's badges numbers over two hundred; of helmets, over forty. One of his automobiles comes equipped with a radio tuned to fire and police department frequencies and has an official Boston fire department plate. On his seventy-sixth birthday he received the gift of a 1936 Ford fire engine.

ABOUT: Green, C. Arthur Fiedler: Music for the Millions; Holland, J. Mr. Pops; Moore, R. Fiedler; O'Connell, C. The Other Side of the Record. *Periodicals* —Atlantic Monthly, February 1965; Musical America, July 1953; New York Times, April 2, 1972, March 29, 1977; Saturday Evening Post, September 1976; Stereo Review, February 1977.

Rudolf Firkušny

1912–

Rudolf Firkušny, pianist, was born in Napajedlá, Czechoslovakia, on February 11, 1912. His father, Rudolf, a lawyer, died when the boy was three. At that time the family moved to the larger city of Brno (Brünn). While very young Ru-

RUDOLF FIRKUŠNY

dolf began picking out melodies on the piano and improvising. Formal piano instruction began when he was four. His musical precocity led his mother, Karla Sindelarova Firkušny (who, though no professional musician, sang in church), to bring him to the distinguished Bohemian composer, Leoš Janáček, then living in Brno. Though Janáček would not teach Rudolf the piano, he agreed to give him some lessons in composition, but only on condition that at the same time Rudolf would receive a general musical education. "Janáček made a musician out of me," Firkušny recalls. "He opened for me the gates of music. I was terribly impressed by him as a person and as a composer. I was with him during years of his greatest output, from 1918 until his death in 1928. He was like a dynamo, and I felt it. I was also able to hear all his works, which came one after another."

Rudolf studied piano with local teachers. When Janáček was eighty, he had Rudolf enrolled in the Brno Conservatory where the boy studied with Ružena Kurzová, Vilém Kurz, and Janáček. On June 14, 1920, Rudolf made his concert debut as a soloist in a Mozart concerto with the Prague Philharmonic Orchestra.

He launched his professional career in Vienna in 1923 and continued for several years with appearances in different parts of Europe. He did not achieve noteworthy successes because then, as later, he was an undemonstrative performer who avoided the trappings that endear virtuosos to the general public. Provided with funds by the Czechoslovakian government through the influence of his friend and godfather Tomáš Masaryk (Czechoslovak statesman and philosopher), Rudolf returned to piano study, attending the Master School in Prague from 1927 to 1929. His teachers there included Josef Suk and Rudolf Karel. After that he continued his piano studies in Paris where Alfred Cortot told him "what you need is not a teacher but a public." In 1933 Firkušny was a pupil of Artur Schnabel in Germany and Italy. Firkušny has said of Schnabel: "He was a great influence on me, not so much pianistically as musically."

After returning to the European concert scene in the years just preceding World War II, Firkušny was able to build for himself a dedicated following and a solid reputation, particularly in his native country where he was regarded as a favorite musical son. However, in his first tour of the United States in 1938, following his American debut at Town Hall in New York, on January 13, he was not well received. "I was not very good," he confesses. "I still needed seasoning." At the end of that tour he returned to Czechoslovakia where he gave three concerts of Czech music commemorating the twentieth anniversary of the founding of the Czech Republic.

When the Nazis occupied Czechoslovakia, Firkušny hoped he could remain in his own country. But when he was ordered by the Nazis to perform in Germany—something he refused to do—he knew he could stay in Czechoslovakia no longer. He fled to Paris. When Paris fell during World War II, he went to Portugal, where the Czech government-in-exile arranged for him to travel to the United States.

He gave a recital at Town Hall, New York, in 1941, which he regards as his "real debut in the United States." One of the critics in New York remarked that whereas Firkušny had been "much too young three years earlier" he was now playing "with the poise and maturity of a master." Firkušny took root in the United States and became an American citizen. He had two residences; an apartment in New York City and a house in Staatsburg, New York.

After the Iron Curtain descended on his native land, Firkušny became *persona non grata* with the new regime in Czechoslovakia because of his past personal ties with the Masaryk family. He paid several visits to Czechoslovakia to see his family and friends, but after 1946 he refused to give any performances there.

In 1943 Firkušny toured South America, giving thirty-three concerts. He was received so enthusiastically that the original quota of four concerts scheduled for Buenos Aires had to be extended to fifteen. In 1944 he made his first tour of Mexico, Cuba, and Central America. In 1946, during a European tour, he was heard at the Prague Festival in Czechoslovakia, his last concert appearance in his native land. On November 2, 1945, he gave the world premiere of Gian Carlo Menotti's Piano Concerto and on December 31, 1948, that of Howard Hanson's Piano Concerto, in Boston. In both instances he was a soloist with the Boston Symphony Orchestra. On November 20, 1949, he introduced Bohuslav Martinu's Third Piano Concerto (which had been written for him) with the Dallas Symphony under Walter Hendl. In 1948–1949 he gave his first concerts in Israel.

His success in America really began in 1949 when he played in fifty cities and was everywhere hailed for his sensitive, poetic interpretations of the classical repertory and for the delicacy of his style. Albert Goldberg wrote in the Los Angeles *Times:* "He is one pianist who never strives for effect. He states for the composer simply, directly, and respectfully, intruding his own personality only when such comment is suitable and in good taste."

Offstage and on he has a quiet, unassuming demeanor. His gray hair is cropped short, his dress is conservative and always in good taste, and his speech is soft spoken. In appearance he might be judged a banker rather than an artist. "He is," said Stephen E. Rubin in the New York *Times,* "the quintessential understated European gentleman." "As an artist," Rubin added, "instead of capitalizing on a razzle-dazzle technique, Firkušny eschewed the obvious powerful pyrotechnics in favor of a more subtly seductive refinement. Instead of relying solely on the staples of the repertory, Firkušny concentrated on music that requires depth as well as know-how, and that is not necessarily popular."

He has been an ardent propagandist for the music of Czech composers, much of which was *terra incognita* in the United States. In 1941 he revived for America Dvořák's Piano Concerto in G minor with Beecham conducting (a work he also recorded); it had not been heard in the United States in sixty-five years. He has consistently performed little-known Czech piano music. He has even given complete Czech programs, and he has recorded for Deutsche Grammophon all the piano compositions of Janáček. On October 22, 1968, in honor of the fiftieth anniversary of the founding of the Czechoslovak Republic, he gave a concert of Czech music at Carnegie Hall, New York.

He has appeared in recitals and with major orchestras around the world. His first tour of Australia and Asia took place in 1958–1959, and his annual tours of the United States have been extensive. On October 4, 1956, he offered the first performance anywhere of Martinu's Fourth Piano Concerto with the Symphony of the Air, Stokowski conducting. He repeated this performance at the Edinburgh Festival later in 1957, as a soloist with the London Philharmonic Orchestra under Rafael Kubelik. By the time he celebrated the thirty-fifth anniversary of his debut in the United States, in 1972–1973, he had toured Europe twenty-five times, South America ten times, Mexico twelve times, Israel three times, and Australia twice.

"There is an air of unruffled perfection about his playing that is all but superhuman," wrote Harold C. Schonberg in the New York *Times*. "Mr. Firkušny's work through the years grows broader and more general, his insights deeper. And with that, one of the surest techniques of contemporary pianism plus an equally sure tonal resource. It is on Rudolf Firkušny that the mantle of Gabrilowitsch has fallen."

When he was forty-eight Firkušny married. On a visit to his family in Czechoslovakia he met and fell in love with Tatania Nevolova, a strikingly attractive young woman. They were married in Czechoslovakia in 1960.

Firkušny likes to collect manuscripts of musical masterworks and rare editions of books and music. For exercise he goes swimming and mountain climbing.

He has been decorated by King Victor Emmanuel III of Italy. The Queen Mother Elisabeth of Belgium presented him with a watch inscribed with her monogram following a command performance at Lachen Castle.

ABOUT: Musical America, June 1956; New York Times, February 2, 1964, April 8, 1973.

Edwin Fischer

1886–1960

Edwin Fischer, pianist and conductor, was born in Basel, Switzerland, on October 6, 1886. His musical training began with Hans Huber at the High School of Music in Basel, and continued in 1904 at the Stern Conservatory in Berlin with Martin Krause. In 1905 Fischer was appointed professor of piano at the Stern Conservatory, a position he retained for nine years. Subsequently, until 1935, he was professor of piano at the High School of Music in Berlin.

He first came to prominence as a pianist in Europe in 1916 when he was heard as a guest artist with orchestras directed by Arthur Nikisch, Felix Weingartner, and Willem Mengelberg. Later he gave recitals throughout Europe and appeared with almost every major orchestra. His performances, particularly of the classical literature of Bach, Beethoven, and Mozart, blended emotion with thought, power with delicacy. He combined, according to English musicologist Scott Goddard, "a fine technique with an equally comprehensive and effective interpretative insight. It is as a performer of the classics that one remembers him. He treats music with the dignity that may be expected of a sensitive artist in the presence of great art. . . . He is a particularly telling instance of music and musicians having become interpretative, both intellectually and emotionally."

Fischer was also active as a conductor: of the Musikverein of Lübeck from 1926 to 1928; of the Bachverein in Munich from 1928 to 1930; and, from 1930 to 1935, of his own chamber orchestral ensemble with which he presented forgotten or rarely heard works. From the beginning of his career as a conductor Fischer made it a practice to direct his performances from the piano in the manner of the Kapellmeisters of old. He sometimes performed the piano concerts of Bach and Mozart while conducting the accompaniment from his place at the piano.

In 1942 he returned to Switzerland and took residence in a house on the Stockerstrasse in Zurich. There he spent some of his leisure time gardening. He died in Zurich on January 24, 1960.

In the United States Fischer was known solely

EDWIN FISCHER

through his recordings of the concertos of Bach and Mozart and the complete *Well-Tempered Clavier* of Bach.

He was the author of a book on Bach, a study on the Beethoven piano sonatas, and a volume of personal musical impressions which appeared in English in 1951 as *Reflections in Music.* He also edited the piano works of Bach and Mozart.

For his service to music Fischer was awarded an honorary doctorate in music by the University at Cologne in Germany.

ABOUT: Gavoty, B. Edwin Fischer.

Dietrich Fischer-Dieskau

1925–

Dietrich Fischer-Dieskau (originally Albert Dietrich Fischer), baritone, is one of the greatest interpreters of *Lieder* of all time. Moreover, he boasts the largest repertory of any singer past or present, and he has recorded on disks more compositions and a greater variety of music than any other singer.

He was born in Zehlendorf, a suburb of Berlin, on May 28, 1925. In 1937 his grandfather added his wife's name, Dieskau, to his own and that is the name by which the family henceforth was known. Fischer-Dieskau explains: "Dieskau was the name of a little castle somewhere be-

Fischer-Dieskau: fĭsh ĕr dĕs' kou

tween Leipzig and Halle. We sold it in the 1870s or thereabouts and now it's a school for the *Volkspolizei,* but we like to remember that J. S. Bach used to stay in it and wrote some of his cantatas there." Music was a strong element in the Fischer-Dieskau household. Dietrich's father, Albert, a renowned schoolteacher who had a street in Berlin named after him, did some composing in his free time. His mother, Dora Klingelhöfer Fischer-Dieskau, from whom Dietrich inherited his love for singing *Lieder,* played the piano well and had an unfulfilled ambition to become a professional singer.

After seeing his first play, Dietrich aspired to become an actor, but soon after that, when he heard his first symphony concert, he wanted to become a conductor. And then, when he heard his first opera *(Lohengrin),* he knew he wanted to become a Wagnerian *Heldentenor.* When he was sixteen his parents and friends encouraged him to take vocal lessons. Dietrich's first vocal teacher was Georg Walter who introduced him to Bach's choral music and extended the youth's knowledge of *Lieder* repertory. Upon completing public school, Dietrich enrolled in the High School for Music in Berlin for further musical training, principally with Hermann Weissenborn. As a student, Dietrich gave a concert in Berlin, performing Schubert's complete *Die Winterreise* cycle. His studies were interrupted after three months when, in 1943, he was drafted into a cavalry unit of the *Wehrmacht,* the Nazi armed forces. His main duty was to tend to the horses in the stables. In 1945 he was captured and was interned for two years in an American prisoner-of-war camp in Italy. As a prisoner he gave recitals in various camps and became so much in demand that he was one of the last to be repatriated. "If only I can stay alive," he noted in his diary, "I have a golden future."

After his liberation in 1947, he returned to Berlin penniless. Though he had not had a music lesson for four years he remained convinced of his destiny as a singer. In Freiburg, in 1947, he made his professional debut as the solo baritone in a performance of Brahms's *A German Requiem,* substituting for an indisposed singer. He then went to Berlin for further study with Weissenborn, to whom he continually returned for coaching and singing lessons until the teacher's death in 1959.

In Berlin in 1948 he made some tape recordings of Schubert's *Die Winterreise* and several of

DIETRICH FISCHER-DIESKAU

Bach's cantatas for RIAS, the American radio station in Berlin. These tapes were broadcast so frequently that they popularized his name not only throughout West Berlin but also in other parts of Europe. When in the fall of 1948 he gave his recital debut in Berlin in the city's largest auditorium, Titania Palast, singing the Schubert cycle *Die Schöne Müllerin,* the house was completely sold out.

Heinz Tietjen, general manager of the West Berlin Municipal Opera, heard one of these broadcasts and invited Fischer-Dieskau for an audition, at the end of which Tietjen remarked casually: "You will sing Rodrigo in the premiere of our new production of *Don Carlo* in four weeks." "I felt weak at the knees," Fischer-Dieskau recalls. "I knew that my stage experience was nil, that I had no training." But with some coaching from Josef Greindl and the assistance of the conductor Ferenc Fricsay, he managed to perform the role well enough to be engaged as a principal baritone of the Berlin Municipal Opera for the next five years. There he was heard in a varied repertory that included Wolfram in *Tannhäuser,* the Count in *The Marriage of Figaro,* Jokanaan in *Salome,* Valentin in *Faust,* Don Fernando in *Fidelio,* the title role in *Rigoletto,* Falstaff in Verdi's opera, Renato in *Un Ballo in Maschera,* and minor roles in *Lohengrin, Der Freischütz,* and several other operas. The distinguished conductor Fritz Busch heard him in Berlin and later said of him: "Such a voice, such an assured technique, such musicality, such a range of interest, such an imperious intelligence!

And still in his twenties! It's phenomenal. And such a terror of performing, too! You practically need a snowplow to push him on to the stage."

World fame came to him, however, not through his operatic performances (excellent though some of these were) but from his recitals and from appearances as a guest artist with major symphony orchestras. When he sang the complete cycles *Die Schöne Müllerin* and *Die Winterreise* in London in 1950 and 1951, he inspired some of the English critics to compare him with such fabled *Lieder* singers as Elena Gerhardt and Lotte Lehmann. His first extensive concert tour, in 1951, won for him a place among the great *Lieder* singers of his time. As a soloist with orchestras, he appeared under Wilhelm Furtwängler at the Salzburg Festival in Brahms's *Four Serious Songs.* After some of his subsequent performances under Furtwängler in the music of Mahler, the conductor confessed that he was "converted" to Mahler through Fischer-Dieskau's singing.

In 1954 Fischer-Dieskau appeared at the Bayreuth Festival as Wolfram, and in 1955 he returned there as Amfortas in *Parsifal* and as Pogner in *Die Meistersinger.* He has since extended his Wagnerian repertory to become one of the most eminent interpreters of Wagnerian music. In *High Fidelity* Peter Heyworth said: "To experience Fischer-Dieskau at his greatest, one must hear him in Wagner. . . . [He is] one of the greatest living Wagnerians."

His American debut took place in Cincinnati on April 15, 1955, as soloist with the Cincinnati Symphony in a Bach cantata and Brahms's *A German Requiem.* Reporting this debut for *Musical America,* Mary Leighton wrote: "Mr. Fischer-Dieskau's voice was remarkably sonorous, his singing masterful in matters of diction, phrasing, breath control and profundity of interpretation. He impressed me as a singer of the first magnitude." About three weeks later, on May 2, he made his New York bow in a recital devoted to *Die Winterreise.* "He performed the considerable feat of holding the audience's interest and close attention throughout," wrote a critic in the New York *Times.* "Not every singer, however gifted, is capable of this feat. . . . Herr Fischer-Dieskau, in doing so, proved himself a vocalist of very unusual attainments."

In opera, as in song literature, Fischer-Dieskau has covered a wide area in his many appearances throughout the world. In addition to the more traditional German, French, and Italian repertory, he has been heard and acclaimed in twentieth century operas. On May 20, 1961, he appeared as Mittenhofer in the world premiere of Hans Werner Henze's *Elegy for Young Lovers* in Schwetzingen, Germany; in November 1963 he sang Barak in Richard Strauss's *Die Frau ohne Schatten* at the recently rebuilt National Theater in Munich where, two years later, he was heard in the title role in a highly successful revival of Hindemith's *Cardillac.* On December 1, 1964, he made his opera debut in New York as Faust in the first American performance of Busoni's *Doktor Faust,* given in a concert version. He also appeared in Berg's *Wozzeck* and *Lulu.* In the concert field, he was heard in Britten's *A War Requiem* in England in 1962 and in Stravinsky's sacred ballad for baritone and orchestra, *Abraham and Isaac,* at the Berlin Festival in 1964.

"It is not enough to say that his voice is wonderful," wrote his piano accompanist, Gerald Moore, in *Am I Too Loud?,* "that he has an incredible technique which enables him to do what he will; it is not enough that his enunciation is flawless with perfect marriage of word and tone. Temperament? Abundance of it. Passionate love for music? Of course. But there are other great singers with these virtues. If I had to put my finger on the key to Fischer-Dieskau's supremacy, setting him apart from every other singer, I would use one word, rhythm. This is the lifeblood of music and he is the master of it."

When Fischer-Dieskau sang his first Hans Sachs in *Die Meistersinger*—at the Deutsche Oper in Berlin in the spring of 1976—he scored a great success. Irving Kolodin, who attended that performance, reported to *Saturday Review:* "Fischer-Dieskau's embodiment, at long last, of the great role is not a matter of matchless singing by a performer who has some interesting ideas about the character. It is, rather, a great character study by a man who also happens to be today's outstanding singer of the whole German literature of art songs from Mozart to Mahler. ... Fischer-Dieskau's rare skill in the management of his vocal resources scored point after point in finesse, in verbal detail, in beauty of statement. ... Fischer-Dieskau is at his unique best in making every word audible, every note a contribution to meaning."

There is hardly an area of vocal music, from baroque to twentieth century, that he has not covered in public appearances and in recordings. He has impressed on disks nearly the entire literature of the German *Lied,* including a twenty-five LP, two-volume release by Deutsche Grammophon of some five hundred songs of Schubert and the complete song literature of Richard Strauss. He has recorded cantatas by Bach and Telemann, Bach's *Passion According to St. Matthew,* and Britten's *A War Requiem.* He has sung in recordings of operas ranging from *The Magic Flute* through *Tristan and Isolde* to *Wozzeck.* He has recorded less familiar songs of Haydn, Mendelssohn, Peter Cornelius, and Hans Pfitzner. With Sviatoslav Richter at the piano, he has recorded Brahms's only song cycle, *Die Schöne Magelone,* which they had presented in Menton, France, in 1969 and at the Salzburg Festival in 1970. On October 5, 1977, he was heard throughout the United States through the facilities of the Public Broadcasting Service as Count Almaviva in a taped broadcast of *The Marriage of Figaro.* All this is but a sampling of the range and diversity of his recordings, many of which have won international prizes, including the "diplôme d'honneur" from the Montreux International Record Award, the Golden Gramaphone Award in Germany in 1975, and Grammys from the National Academy of Recording Arts and Sciences in 1970 and 1972.

On February 10, 1949, Fischer-Dieskau married Irmgard Poppen, a young cellist, whom he had met while both of them were students at the High School for Music in Berlin. She died in December 1963 soon after bearing him their third son. In September 1965 he married a German film actress, Ruth Leuwerik; two years later they were divorced. His third wife is Kristina Pugell, a young American music student he met in New York and married in 1968.

For many years he made his home in the Lindenallee in Hamburg, in an old house which he had completely remodeled to his own specifications. It was surrounded by trees, was equipped with a swimming pool, and had a music room capable of accommodating a hundred people. In this room he kept his vast library of books and recordings; elsewhere in his house his collections of china, glassware, old furniture, and various musical curiosities could be found. This house was his retreat twice a year, a month each time —once in the summer and another in the winter —when he could forget about music and turn to his favorite pastimes of reading and painting. He left this house in Hamburg for a new home he had built in 1977 on the Starnbergersee near Munich. Here he had a special studio to provide him the space to indulge his interest in painting. He is a big man, standing six feet three—"big in every way," says Gerald Moore, "physically, intellectually, musically, with the commanding presence that was Chaliapin's."

When on tour, he rarely leaves his hotel room, spending his free time there reading, listening to records, and resting. He never goes to parties after concerts, preferring a full eight-hour sleep. "There are only two positions for a singer," he has said, "standing on the platform or lying in bed, studying and sleeping." He will never sing two nights consecutively, and he has made it a practice never to learn more than one new role in a single year.

On March 24, 1974, Fischer-Dieskau made his American debut as conductor, with the Los Angeles Philharmonic in an all-Schumann program. "For this writer," said Melody Peterson in *Musical America,* "one of the most unexpected aspects of the all-Schumann concert . . . was the extraordinarily mannered way in which Fischer-Dieskau communicated his intentions to his orchestra. Utilizing a vocabulary of stiff, broad, awkwardly exaggerated gestures, he frequently emphasized a heavy vertical at the expense of rhythmic flow and more than occasionally fired off cues which elicited the sound of near misses. Interpretatively, there seemed to be an ambivalence about the scope of things symphonic." By the time he was fifty, however, he decided to forget about conducting. "Two careers," he explained, "are one too many."

Among the awards and honors he has gathered through the years are the Berlin Art Prize, the Golden Orpheus of the City of Mantua, the Distinguished Service Medal First Class of the German Federal Republic, the Mozart medal, the Grosses Verdienstkreutz of the German Federal Republic, and the Sonning Prize in Copenhagen. He was named *Bayerischer Kammersänger* in 1959 and Berlin *Kammersänger* in 1963. He has been made honorary member of the Vienna Konzerthausgesellschaft, the Royal Academy of Music in London, and the Royal Swedish Academy in Stockholm.

Fischer-Dieskau is the author of *Wagner and Nietzsche* (1976), *The Fischer-Dieskau Book of Lieder* (1977), and *Schubert's Songs* (1977).

ABOUT: Moore, G. Am I Too Loud?; Rosenthal, H. Great Singers of Today. *Periodicals*—New York Times, November 29, 1964, January 17, 1971, October 31, 1976; Opera News, January 28, 1961.

Kirsten Flagstad

1895–1962

Kirsten Flagstad was one of the greatest of Wagnerian sopranos belonging in the august company of Lilli Lehmann and Olive Fremstad. In the 1930s and 1940s she had no rivals. She was born in Hamar, Norway, on July 12, 1895, to a family of musicians. Her father, Michael, was a violinist in a theater orchestra; her mother, Marie Nielsen Flagstad, played and taught the piano, conducted opera and operetta performances, and coached singers. Kirsten was the oldest of three surviving children. Her two brothers also became professional musicians, one as orchestral conductor, and the other as pianist; her sister became a singer in operetta.

Kirsten began studying the piano at an early age but showed little interest or aptitude for it. From childhood her sole love in music was singing. At her confirmation party she performed some arias from *Lohengrin* and *Aida* for her guests. A friend of the family offered to give her some practical guidance in singing since she felt that young Kirsten was abusing her voice. She undertook more intensive vocal study for three years with Ellen Schytte-Jacobsen in Oslo. At the same time Kirsten attended the public schools.

When a performance of Eugène d'Albert's *Tiefland* was scheduled in Oslo, Kirsten was chosen for the role of Nuri. In this opera debut, on December 12, 1913, she performed so well that a group of Oslo music patrons decided to finance her further music study. One year later she sang Germaine in *The Chimes of Normandy.*

Her study of voice continued, first with Albert Westwang in Oslo, then with Gillis Bratt for two and a half years in Stockholm. In 1917 she joined the company at the Mayol Theater in Oslo where for two years she appeared in a repertory of operettas.

In 1919 Flagstad married Sigurd Hall, a hardware salesman; their home was a four-room

Flagstad: fläg′ städ

KIRSTEN FLAGSTAD

hansen—on May 31, 1930. For a while after her marriage she retired from music, devoting herself to her domestic and social duties in their luxurious home in Oslo's fashionable old residential district, at their summer home in Kristiansand, and in a cabin hideaway by a lake in the Telemark hills.

Johansen persuaded her to return to opera. The Gothenburg Opera, having difficulty with casting, called her for some guest performances. Gradually Flagstad accepted more and more assignments. In 1932 a friend who was producing *Tristan and Isolde* in Oslo with a German cast prevailed upon her to take over the role of Isolde. This was her first Isolde, and the first time she sang opera in German. Her performance was so successful that she was invited to Bayreuth in the summer of 1933 as Ortlinde and the Third Norn in the *Ring* cycle—her first appearances outside Scandinavia. The following season she returned to the Bayreuth Festival as Sieglinde in *Die Walküre* and Gutrune in *Die Götterdämmerung.*

Eric Simon, a scout of the Metropolitan Opera company, heard her at Bayreuth and arranged for her to sing at a private audition in St. Moritz, Switzerland, for Artur Bodanzky, conductor, and Gatti-Casazza, the general manager of the Metropolitan Opera. This was not the first time that Flagstad had been invited to audition for the Metropolitan. In 1929 Otto H. Kahn had heard her sing in *Tosca* and suggested that the Metropolitan acquire her. The Metropolitan Opera communicated with Flagstad, asking for details of her career. Believing that the inquiry was just formal routine with the Metropolitan and finding the job of translating her Norwegian notices into English too onerous, she never answered the letter.

When she auditioned for Bodanzky and Gatti-Casazza in St. Moritz in 1934, she sang in a heavily carpeted hotel room, which disguised the true quality and resonance of her voice. Both Bodanzky and Gatti-Casazza were aware of her musicianship but felt that there was nothing extraordinary about her singing voice. However, since the resignation of Frida Leider necessitated a replacement in the Wagnerian repertory at the Metropolitan Opera, they engaged Flagstad for a single season. They did not realize that they were bringing to New York one of the greatest voices of that time. At the first rehearsal at the Metropolitan (in *Die Götterdämmerung,* since

apartment in Oslo. A daughter, Else-Marie, was born to them a year later. During her pregnancy Flagstad's voice deserted her and she thought that her singing career was over. But one day after the birth of her daughter she tried out some music by Lehár. To her amazement her voice was richer and more sensuous than before.

She returned to the stage in a leading role in a Franz Lehár operetta, and in 1921 she undertook her first concert tour, in France. Returning to Oslo she began to appear in opera, singing in thirty-eight different works including Gluck's *Orfeo ed Euridice, Faust,* and *Carmen.* Her versatility was revealed one day in Oslo when, after performing an American popular song at the Casino Theater (Harry Archer's "I Love You," a Tin Pan Alley hit in 1923), she rushed by taxi to the local concert hall to sing with the Oslo Philharmonic Orchestra in a performance of Beethoven's Ninth Symphony.

In 1928 she and her husband separated and on May 30, 1930, they were divorced. That year she joined the company of the Storm Theater in Gothenburg, Sweden, where she devoted herself exclusively to opera. Her performance there in 1930 as Elsa in *Lohengrin* drew attention for the first time to the fact that she was becoming an artist of some consequence. She was invited to a party where she met Henry Johansen, a handsome and wealthy music patron. It was a case of love at first sight. They danced all evening, met for dinner the following evening, and on the third evening became engaged. After her divorce from Sigurd Hall became final, she married Jono rehearsal had been scheduled for *Die Wal-küre,* which was to be Flagstad's introductory opera at the Metropolitan) the outburst of her golden voice startled and amazed all present. It had been some years since a voice such as this had been heard singing Wagner at the Metropolitan. For those listening to that rehearsal, it was difficult, if not impossible, to believe that this comparatively unknown artist from Norway boasted vocal equipment without comparison among the Wagnerian sopranos of the time.

Flagstad's debut at the Metropolitan Opera on February 2, 1935, as Sieglinde in *Die Wal-küre,* was a sensation. At the end of the first act the audience responded with an enthusiasm which kept growing in volume and intensity after the second act and after the final curtain. "Mme. Flagstad is that *rara avis* in the Wagnerian woods—a singer with voice, with looks, with youth," wrote Lawrence Gilman the following morning in the *Herald Tribune.* "The voice itself is rich and expressive, and yesterday it recalled to wistful Wagnerites the irrevocable magic of Olive the Immortal. The upper voice is powerful and true and does not harden under stress. The singing that we heard yesterday is that of a musician with taste and brains and sensibility, with poetic and dramatic insight. . . . Yesterday was one of those rare occasions when the exigent Richard might have witnessed with happiness an embodiment of his Sieglinde. For this was a beautiful and elusive re-creation, poignant and sensitive throughout, and crowned in its great moments with authentic exaltation."

An even greater challenge was met by Flagstad four days later, on February 6, when she sang her first Isolde in America. "She sang the part gloriously," wrote Olin Downes in the New York *Times,* "as it has not been sung here in many years, and almost immediately she captivated her audience by a beautiful stage presence, by youth, sincerity and dramatic feeling conveyed equally by acting and by song. . . . [She] brought a new vitality to this famous role, which she enacted in a noble spirit and pride, but also a womanly fire and passion which she had the vocal resource fully to convey." Lawrence Gilman wrote in the *Herald Tribune:* "Last night's performance of *Tristan* . . . was made unforgettable for its hearers by a transcendently beautiful and moving impersonation of Isolde—an embodiment so sensitively musical, so fine-grained in its imaginative and intellectual tex-ture, so lofty in its pathos and simplicity, of so memorable a loveliness that experienced operagoers sought among their memories of legendary days to find its like."

Before the season ended she was heard—and received triumphantly—as Brünnhilde in *Die Walküre* on February 15 and in *Die Götterdäm-merung* on February 28 (singing both parts for the first time in her career). She sang Elsa in *Lohengrin* on March 5 (while on tour) and Elisabeth in *Tannhäuser* on March 15. Kundry in *Parsifal* followed on April 17 (once again a new role, this one committed to memory in eighteen days). Even in her first season, she became one of the greatest box-office attractions the Metropolitan Opera had known since the days of Caruso. Whenever she sang, the house was sold out: Nine performances of *Tristan* netted more than one hundred fifty thousand dollars. Single-handed, this amazing new artist brought prosperity to an opera house during some of the leanest financial years in its history and brought back the golden age of the Wagnerian music drama performances. She remained the cornerstone of the Metropolitan repertory for the next five seasons. Her importance was made evident the season following her debut when for the first time in the thirty-five-year history of the company a German opera—*Die Walküre*—opened the season (December 21, 1936). And, the following season, once again, solely because of Flagstad, the Metropolitan Opera opened with a German opera, *Tristan and Isolde,* on November 29, 1937. Because of her popularity she was required to sing often, and she was capable of meeting this demand because of her wonderful stamina. She sang Isolde and Kundry on two successive afternoons; Brünnhilde, Isolde, and Eva in *Die Mei-stersinger* on three successive evenings. Never in that time did she betray the slightest sign of fatigue. On the contrary, with excessive use her voice kept growing in power, richness, flexibility, and intensity. In the years between 1935 and 1937 the roles of Leonore in *Fidelio,* Senta in *The Flying Dutchman,* and Brünnhilde in *Siegfried* were added to her Metropolitan Opera repertory.

Her bow at the San Francisco Opera on November 4, 1935, as Brünnhilde in *Die Wal-küre* was a spectacular success. There were triumphs in Europe as well, particularly at Covent Garden and the Vienna State Opera where she was introduced as Isolde on May 18, 1936, and

September 2, 1936, respectively. In May 1939 she was one of the central figures during the musical activities attending the New York World's Fair—she appeared in a cycle of Wagnerian music dramas in a special supplementary season of the Metropolitan Opera House. She also enjoyed enormous success as a concert singer—her fee rising from eight hundred dollars a concert to two thousand five hundred dollars just one month after her Metropolitan Opera debut, with some sixty recitals a year scheduled in nearly all the major cities of the United States and Europe.

Flagstad's art was exceptional. "Her singing is a thing of endless glory. She has great power of voice, an extraordinary compass, and unusual flexibility. Her register is equally rich in both extremes and she has a luscious tessitura. Her tones come forth fresh and easily, full of roundness and body, each tone attacked cleanly. The greatest dramatic effects in her singing are produced through the simplest of means: with a discreet use of falsetto she can voice a radiant ecstasy; with a carefully selected pause, she can dramatize an entire page of music; a subtle use of variety in her colors, and she can scorch a lyric line with the hot flame of her anger." (D. Ewen. *Men and Women Who Make Music*)

While in New York Flagstad lived in hotels. She rose early in the morning, had her masseuse put her body through a workout, then ate a breakfast consisting only of grapefruit juice. The morning was spent in relaxation unless there was a rehearsal. Her afternoons were devoted either to rehearsals or to private study of her roles. Evenings when no opera was scheduled she spent quietly at home, reading, attending to correspondence, knitting, or enjoying the company of a few close friends. She loved playing solitaire. Her accompanist, Edwin McArthur, revealed: "I have watched her playing more than twenty different, very involved games. For years, she carried a special little book with her in which she carefully put down the number of times each of these intricate bouts came out. On many occasions she would become so absorbed in a particular game that she would take the cards with her to a performance. If by chance some visitor had been admitted during the intermission, he might very well have found her completely oblivious, lost in a match with herself. Five minutes later she would be on the stage singing a great scene." If she had a performance in the evening, she

always drank a split of champagne or a large cognac when it was over. At other times she preferred a dry martini. She never touched a drop of alcohol just before singing.

After the final curtain fell on a performance of *Tristan and Isolde* on April 12, 1941, Lauritz Melchior (the *Heldentenor* who sang Tristan that evening) came before the audience to announce that Flagstad was leaving the United States the following week to return to her husband in Norway. Her decision to go home caused considerable misgiving in the United States. Norway was occupied by the Nazis. To make matters worse, her husband had made his accommodation with the Nazis, placing his entire business organization at their disposal: Johansen was a member of the infamous political party formed by Major Vidkun Quisling, the Norwegian politician who betrayed his country to the Nazis, collaborating with the invaders and eventually becoming Norway's puppet ruler. In spite of all this, Flagstad insisted that in such times her place was with her husband and family, that she was not interested in politics. Immediately following the end of the war Johansen was tried and prosecuted for treason, saved from a traitor's death only by his sudden demise in prison.

When the war was over, Flagstad resumed her career in the United States. There was considerable opposition to her return because she had lived in occupied Norway during the war years. The Metropolitan Opera refused to reengage her; she was turned down for recitals in various cities; and a major recording company would not accept her as one of its recording artists. When she did make her first American appearance—at a recital in Boston on April 6, 1947—there were pickets outside the auditorium. There were also pickets in Chicago and New York when she gave recitals in those cities; and in Philadelphia stench bombs were released in the hall. However, there could never be any question about the quality of her singing. Reporting the Boston concert to the New York *Herald Tribune,* Virgil Thomson wrote: "She sang like an angel. ... Never in this writer's concertgoing lifetime ... has there been available any other vocal artistry of such sumptuous natural acoustics, such perfect technical control and such sound musicianship."

The opposition to Flagstad's appearances soon died down and was completely forgotten.

Her first performance in opera after the war was in March 1947 at La Scala in Milan, as Isolde (her debut at that opera house). She appeared in Covent Garden in the summer of 1948 and in 1949 she was heard as Leonore in *Fidelio* at the Salzburg Festival. She made her American return to opera with an electrifying performance as Isolde at the San Francisco Opera on September 30, 1949, following it later that season with a no less sensational appearance as Brünnhilde in *Die Walküre*. In 1950 she returned to San Francisco not only as Isolde but also as Kundry. She returned to the Metropolitan Opera company on January 22, 1951, as Isolde. Her final appearance at the Metropolitan Opera—and her last opera performance in the United States—took place in the spring of 1952 in the title role of Gluck's *Alceste* which, said Olin Downes in the New York *Times,* she sang "with a simplicity and an emotion that are unforgettable and in the finest classic tradition."

In 1951 Flagstad was heard as Dido in Purcell's *Dido and Aeneas* at the Mermaid Theatre in London. She repeated this performance in that city twenty times during the Coronation year of 1953. She then returned to Norway, intending to retire permanently. But in March 1955 she came back to the United States to make two appearances with the Symphony of the Air in New York in all-Wagner programs.

During her last years she lived in Norway. There she helped to found the Norwegian State Opera, of which she became director in February 1959. Two years later ill health compelled her to withdraw completely from an active life in music. She died in Oslo on December 7, 1962.

ABOUT: Biancolli, L. ed. The Flagstad Manuscript; McArthur, E. Flagstad: A Personal Memoir; Sanborn, P. Kirsten Flagstad. *Periodicals*—Opera News, January 12, 1963.

Leon Fleisher

1928–

Leon Fleisher, pianist and conductor, was born in San Francisco, California, on July 23, 1928. His father, Isidor, who had come from Russia, was a fashion designer; his mother, Bertha, a native of Poland, had been a teacher of singing. "My mother had cultural ambitions for my old-

LEON FLEISHER

er brother and myself," he told an interviewer, "but I got out of it somehow. When I was five, I sat down at the piano because it was already there, and when I was seven my parents decided to exploit me." Once Leon revealed his talent, his mother was determined to make him one of the world's great pianists.

His first teacher was Lev Shorr with whom he made such excellent progress that in his seventh year Leon gave a recital in San Francisco and two years later was a soloist with the San Francisco Federal Symphony Orchestra. Leon was ten when Artur Schnabel heard him play and, despite Schnabel's lifelong distaste for prodigies, accepted him as a pupil. For six months he lived and studied with Schnabel at Lake Como in Italy, "the most wonderful time of my life," he later recalled. For the next decade, from time to time, Leon returned to Schnabel for additional instruction.

Just before World War II Leon returned to the United States to prepare himself for a concert career. In 1943 he was a soloist with the San Francisco Symphony conducted by Pierre Monteux, and a year later he was heard with the New York Philharmonic Orchestra, also with Monteux conducting. His success at these appearances was immediate. The critics hailed him as one of the most promising of the younger crop of American piano virtuosos. Monteux went even further and proclaimed him "the pianist find of the century." Concertizing throughout the United States, he continued to establish his fame and artistic stature even more securely.

When he was twenty he yielded to a compulsion to give up piano playing for a while. He went to Paris "to bum around," as he himself put it. "I just got sick of looking at the big black piano," he explains, "and I also wanted to get out of the house."

He resumed his career in May 1952 by entering the Queen Elisabeth of Belgium competition with seventy other pianists from all parts of the world. In the preliminary round his playing received such prolonged applause that the presiding judge had to ring a bell to restore order. In the final round, Fleisher played the Brahms Concerto in D minor among other works. Despite a mishap (one of the piano strings snapped) he was selected by the thirteen judges as the winner of the first prize, the first American to be so honored.

He returned to the United States in 1954 for a tour that included recitals in principal cities and guest performances with virtually all the major American orchestras. The critics all called him a piano virtuoso of the first rank. Reviewing his performance of Beethoven's Piano Concerto No.2 with the San Francisco Symphony under Ferenc Fricsay, Marjory M. Fisher wrote in the San Francisco *News:* "Fleisher revealed the great musical development that has come with maturity. His fleet, agile fingers moved surely and facilely over the keyboard as he sought to set forth the beauty of the piano score as he perceived it." Rudolph Elie of the Boston *Herald* said of his performance of Brahms's Concerto No.1 with the Boston Symphony under Monteux: "Fleisher is a pianist of broad musical horizons in every way suited to the hugeness of Brahms's concept and peculiarly difficult keyboard style." In the New York *Herald Tribune* Virgil Thomson wrote after Fleisher's interpretation of Brahms's Piano Concerto No.2 with the New York Philharmonic under George Szell: "This brilliant and powerful virtuoso may well be on the way to becoming a great musician. ... He is obviously a serious artist and one thoroughly prepared to communicate with the serious musical public about serious piano repertory."

Fleisher was invited to perform at the White House at a State dinner for King Baudouin during the Eisenhower Administration. He also performed extensively in Europe, Scandinavia, and South America and appeared at festivals in Berlin and Salzburg in 1958. He became such a

favorite in Buenos Aires that in 1956 an Asociación Leon Fleisher was formed there.

When the San Francisco Symphony celebrated its seventy-fifth anniversary in 1961–1962, Fleisher was one of the soloists engaged to celebrate the occasion. On October 28, 1963, he gave the world premiere of Leon Kirchner's Piano Concerto No.2 (which had been commissioned for him by the Ford Foundation) with the Seattle Symphony, the composer conducting, in Seattle, Washington; later the same year he repeated this performance with the Cleveland Orchestra under Szell. With Szell conducting the Cleveland Orchestra, Fleisher recorded for Columbia all five Beethoven piano concertos, the first virtuoso to do so since Schnabel.

He was well on his way towards establishing himself as one of the foremost pianists of the world when, in 1964, the fingers of his right hand began to fail him, with severe cramps setting in. "It was like a writer's cramp," he explains. "Nothing is known about it. Many cases are not resolved by either psychotherapy or physiotherapy." The condition worsened, making the right hand totally useless. Medical science has been unable to uncover the cause or to suggest a cure.

After a trying readjustment period, Fleisher returned to the concert stage, performing piano works exclusively for the left hand since that hand was completely unaffected. When he performed Prokofiev's Piano Concerto No.4 (for left hand) with the Baltimore Symphony Orchestra under Comissiona at Carnegie Hall in New York in February 1975, Donal Henahan said in the New York *Times* that he "gave a sure-fingered account. ... In the finale, Mr. Fleisher handled the wide leaps and other technical challenges with aplomb." Several months later, in November, Fleisher again appeared in Carnegie Hall, this time as a soloist with the Concord String Quartet in a performance of Franz Schmidt's Quintet for Left Hand Piano and Strings, following it with a presentation of Brahms's transcription for left-hand piano of Bach's Chaconne for violin.

Fleisher has also opened up for himself new horizons as a performing artist by becoming a conductor. In his conducting debut at the Lincoln Center for the Performing Arts in New York on August 24, 1970, he led a program of symphonies by Schubert and Mozart and a Mozart piano concerto with Claude Frank as soloist. Less than a year later, in July 1971, he led the Boston Symphony at the Berkshire Music Festival in Tanglewood, Massachusetts. His program—made up of works by Bartók, Mozart, and Hindemith—"made a strong impression," reported Donal Henahan in the New York *Times*. "He vaulted far out of the tyro class. His baton . . . gave clear, detailed signals and rarely beat time in a simple tactile way that betrays the amateur conductor."

He has become the conductor of the Annapolis Symphony in Maryland and the Theatre Chamber Players in Washington, D.C., the resident chamber music ensemble at the Kennedy Center. From 1973 to 1978 he was associate conductor of the Baltimore Symphony Orchestra.

Since 1959 Fleisher has taught piano at the Peabody Conservatory in Baltimore, Maryland, where he lives with his second wife and their three children. He also had three children by his first wife, the former Dorothy Druzinsky, whom he married in 1951 and from whom he was divorced in 1962. On April first of that year he married Riselle Rosenthal.

Among Fleisher's hobbies are swimming and reading. Before being disabled he was an excellent table tennis player.

ABOUT: New York Post, January 16, 1946; New York Times, August 18, 1970, October 21, 1977.

Maureen Forrester

1930–

Maureen Katherine Stewart Forrester, contralto, was born in Montreal, Canada, on July 25, 1930, the youngest of four children. Her father, Thomas, a cabinetmaker, was Scottish; her mother, Mae, Irish. As a child Maureen participated in songfests held regularly at her home. She began studying the piano when she was five. Not until her late teens did she become interested in singing. After dropping out of school in her thirteenth year she worked at various jobs, including one as a receptionist in the offices of Canada Dry Ginger Ale in Montreal and others as waitress, hatcheck girl, file clerk, and telephone operator.

She took her first singing lessons with Sally Martin when she was seventeen, and upon Mar-

MAUREEN FORRESTER

tin's retirement continued her vocal studies with Frank Rowe. Shortly after beginning vocal study, she joined the choir of the Fairmount-Taylor Presbyterian Church in Montreal where she sang solos. She also appeared in local concerts.

After attending a recital by Dutch *Lieder* singer Bernard Diamant, she was inspired to ask him for instruction. "You have a lovely voice," he told her, "but you don't know how to use it." On Diamant's urging, Forrester stopped singing in public in 1951, devoting herself to intensive vocal training which included eight hours a day of practice and two to three lessons a week. A music-loving contractor hired her to do office work three hours early each morning at forty-five dollars a week to allow her to spend the rest of the day on voice study. Diamant, who remained her only vocal teacher, described her as "a pupil such as you get once in a lifetime. She has . . . a beautiful, versatile and powerful voice, a good memory, a quick ear, musicianship, health, drive and, most unusual, a calm temperament."

Forrester's formal debut as a recitalist took place at the YWCA in Montreal in March 1953. This led to an appearance as soloist in a performance of Mendelssohn's *Elijah* at the St. James United Church in Montreal and in Beethoven's Symphony No.9 with the Montreal Symphony conducted by Otto Klemperer.

In 1955 a Montreal publisher, J. W. McConnell, financed her debut in Europe, a recital at Salle Gaveau in Paris. That year she also gained the sponsorship of Les Jeunesses Musicales du Canada which arranged for her to give sixty recitals in Quebec and Ontario and subsidized a three-month tour of Europe. Her success in Europe made it possible for her to extend her stay there for a full year, a time in which she worked extensively on German *Lieder* and the German language.

During 1955 Forrester also made her first appearances in opera, all of them in Canada: in Menotti's *The Consul,* in *Boris Godunov,* and in *Louise.* But from the beginning of her professional career her strength lay more in oratorios, recitals, and appearances with symphony orchestras than in opera.

Her first appearance in the United States was at Town Hall, New York, on November 12, 1956. Writing in the New York *Times,* Edward Downes said: "Miss Forrester has a superb voice of generous compass and volume. Its color ranges from a darkly resonant chest register to a brilliantly focused top with a middle register that she makes velvet soft or reedy according to her expressive intent."

While in New York, Forrester auditioned for Bruno Walter, who invited her to appear under his direction at a concert of the New York Philharmonic Orchestra. This appearance in February 1957 in a performance of Mahler's Symphony No.2 *(Resurrection)* was not only her American debut as soloist with a symphony orchestra but also her first appearance in Mahler's music. (She later specialized in Mahler.) Her striking success with the New York Philharmonic was followed by her triumphs as vocal soloist in Mahler's Symphony No.3 at the Holland Music Festival under Eduard van Beinum and in Mahler's *Das Lied von der Erde* with which she helped to open the 1958 season of the Berlin Philharmonic and which she frequently performed thereafter both in Europe and the United States, in addition to recording it for RCA Victor. She also recorded Mahler's *Songs of the Wayfarer* and *Kindertotenlieder* with the Boston Symphony under Charles Munch, *Des Knaben Wunderhorn* for Vanguard, and Mahler's Symphonies No.2 and No.3 for Odyssey and Philips respectively.

Her career was acquiring new dimensions with performances at the Empire State Festival in New York in 1957; the Caramoor, Ipswich, and Vancouver Festivals in 1958; and the Casals Festival in Puerto Rico in 1959. She was ac-

claimed at the Edinburgh Festival in Scotland in 1957, a year in which she toured England, Norway, Sweden, Germany, Holland, Belgium, France, and Ireland. At the Casals Festival in Puerto Rico in 1960 and in Berlin in 1961 she participated in performances of Pablo Casals' oratorio *El Pesebre,* the composer conducting. In 1961 she sang in the Soviet Union and made three tours of Israel within a nine-month period.

Her fame as an interpreter of Mahler's music has been matched by her renown as a performer of Handel. On November 18, 1958, she made her American debut in an operatic role as Cornelia in a concert version of Handel's *Giulio Cesare* performed by the American Opera Society. She made her operatic stage debut in the United States on September 27, 1966, in this same role, as a member of the New York City Opera during its first fall season at the Lincoln Center for the Performing Arts. She also sang Cornelia five times at the Teatro Colón in Buenos Aires in 1968–1969 where she was making her debut. In 1966–1967 she was heard as Rodelinda in Handel's opera of the same name and as Romilda in *Serse* at the Handel Opera Festival at the Lincoln Center for the Performing Arts. She helped to open the twentieth season of the Dallas Civic Opera on November 5, 1976, in a staged production of Handel's *Samson.* She has recorded for RCA *Giulio Cesare* in the New York City Opera production, and also *Hercules; Rodelinda* and *Serse* for Westminster; and Handel's *Theodora* and *Jephtha* for Vanguard.

Among her other opera roles have been Orfeo in Gluck's *Orfeo ed Euridice,* first sung with the Toronto Opera at O'Keefe Center in 1961–1962 produced by Donald Oenslager and staged by Hanya Holm. She made her first appearance with the San Francisco Opera in the title role of *La Gioconda* in 1967. In 1968 she sang Brangäne in a concert performance of *Tristan and Isolde* with the Montreal Symphony. (Her first staged appearance as Brangäne took place with L'Opéra du Québec in 1974 with Zubin Mehta conducting.) During 1970–1971 she appeared as the Witch in a television production of *Hansel and Gretel* shown throughout Canada and the United States. At the summer Caramoor Festival at Katonah, New York, in 1971, she appeared in Purcell's *Dido and Aeneas.* Soon after that she was heard as Marcellina in *The Marriage of Figaro* with the National Arts Center Opera Company in Canada. In 1971–1972 she took on for the first time the roles of Fricka in *Die Walküre* and Ulrica in *Un Ballo in Maschera* with the Canadian Opera Company and the Edmonton Opera Association, respectively. In 1972 Forrester also assumed the role of Arnalta in Monteverdi's *L'Incoronazione di Poppea* with the Opera Society of Washington, D.C. The summer of 1974 found her at the Stratford, Ontario, festival as Madame Flora in Menotti's *The Medium,* and that year she was cast as Dame Quickly in *Falstaff* with L'Opéra du Québec. On November 5, 1976, she sang opposite Jon Vickers in the first American staged production of Handel's *Samson* with the Dallas Civic Opera. Meanwhile, on February 11, 1975, she had made her debut at the Metropolitan Opera as Erda in *Das Rheingold,* and on March 5, 1975, she had once again been heard there as Erda, this time in *Siegfried.* In 1975–1976 she appeared at the Metropolitan Opera as Ulrica.

During the World's Fair Expo '67 in Montreal Forrester made ten appearances, including one with the visiting Concertgebouw Orchestra of Amsterdam under Bernard Haitink in Mahler's *Das Lied von der Erde,* for which she received a standing ovation. That spring she toured Europe with the Montreal Symphony conducted by Zubin Mehta. (She again toured Europe with the Montreal Symphony in May and June 1976.) During the summer of 1968 she gave a recital at the Salzburg Festival in Austria. In the summer of 1976 she participated in an almost complete performance of Bach's *Passion According to St. Matthew* at the Berkshire Music Festival at Tanglewood in Massachusetts. Donal Henahan wrote in the New York *Times:* "Miss Forrester ... provided one of the day's most moving interludes with 'Erbarme dich,' making that famous aria a pained, muted plea for mercy."

To commemorate the twentieth anniversary of her recital debut in New York, Maureen Forrester returned to Town Hall (the auditorium in which she had made her first appearance in the United States), with the same accompanist (John Newmark), to repeat the same program. This commemorative recital was given on November 12, 1976. "A pointed comparison with one's self, one's younger self, can be a risky undertaking, even when the artist has the confidence of vocal maturity, technical mastery, and twenty years' experience," commented a critic for *Musical America.* "Miss Forrester proved

that she had nothing to fear." In the New York *Times,* Allen Hughes reported: "Let us put this as plainly as possible: Maureen Forrester was triumphant."

Her native country honored her on several occasions. It presented her with the highest award it can bestow on an artist, Companion of the Order of Canada. On another occasion she was invited to sing at the House of Parliament in Ottawa before the diplomatic corps, an honor accorded to no other musician. Several colleges and universities in Canada have conferred honorary doctorates on her. In 1967 the National Film Board of Canada prepared a motion picture documentary based on her life. Forrester has served as president of Canada's Jeunesses Musicales. Outside Canada, she has been awarded the Harriet Cohen prize.

As a teacher of voice she has distinguished herself with her master classes at Aspen, Colorado.

In July 1954 she married Eugene J. Kash, a Canadian violinist and conductor; they were separated in 1975. She lives in a mansion in Toronto, with her five children. She carefully maps out her schedule of performances (consisting of over one hundred and twenty-five appearances a year) so that she can spend extended periods at home with her family between tours or engagements. At home the family is surrounded by music, with Forrester not only singing but also playing the piano and with musical friends joining in informal music-making sessions. In addition, the entire family listens continually to its extensive library of recordings. All the children are musical but, Maureen Forrester adds, "whether they will grow up and become professional musicians or not, I don't care. I want them to do whatever they want to do. But whatever work they choose for themselves, I feel sure of one thing: They will always love music."

At home her diversions are making needlepoint cushions and Christmas decorations, collecting antique thimbles, and cooking. Outdoors, her preferences are skiing and swimming.

ABOUT: Hi-Fi, July 1960; New York Times, November 12, 1976; Opera News, October 15, 1966; Reader's Digest, September 1975.

Lawrence Foster

1941–

Lawrence Foster, conductor, was born in Los Angeles, California, on October 23, 1941, of Romanian-American parentage. Neither his father, Thomas, a businessman, nor his mother, Martha Wurmbrandt Foster, was musical. Lawrence's father died when he was three, and he was subsequently adopted by his stepfather. When he was six, Lawrence was given lessons on the piano. About six years later he heard his first orchestral concert. "It was exactly at that moment," he says, "I decided I wanted to become a conductor and I never swerved from it." His subsequent musical training proceeded with Joanna Graudan (piano) and Fritz Zweig (conducting) in Los Angeles. For two seasons he attended the Bayreuth Festival Master Classes. He was originally heading for a career as a pianist, but he turned to conducting when a fall from a horse seriously injured his hand.

Among the important early musical influences upon him were the distinguished musicians from Central Europe who had found a new home in Los Angeles during the Hitler era in Germany and with whom Foster established personal contact. One of them was Karl Böhm who gave him advice and guidance; another, Bruno Walter, whose concerts and recording sessions he attended.

Lawrence made his conducting debut in 1960 with the Young Musicians Foundation Debut Orchestra. For four years he was its conductor and music director. During this period, until 1965, he also served as assistant conductor of the San Francisco Ballet, with which he made three national tours, including appearances in New York with Margot Fonteyn and Rudolf Nureyev.

In 1964 Foster went to Europe expecting to continue his apprenticeship as conductor in an opera house. But before he could find such an opening, he received and accepted in 1965 an offer from the Los Angeles Philharmonic to serve as assistant conductor to Zubin Mehta on a three-year contract. During those three years he was given numerous opportunities to conduct the orchestra at its winter subscription series, at the Hollywood Bowl during the summer, and on its world tour in 1967. In 1966 he received the

LAWRENCE FOSTER

Koussevitzky Memorial Conducting Prize and the Eleanor R. Crane Memorial Prize at the Berkshire Festival at Tanglewood, Massachusetts, where he conducted the Berkshire Music Center Orchestra and worked with Erich Leinsdorf and Sir Adrian Boult.

Foster made his European debut with the Württembergische State Opera in Stuttgart in *Aida* in 1964. In 1968 he made guest appearances with the Royal Philharmonic Orchestra in London and the Hallé Orchestra in Manchester. Though completely unknown in England at the time, he soon became so highly esteemed that in January 1969 he was made principal guest conductor of the Royal Philharmonic Orchestra, becoming one of the youngest musicians ever to hold so important a post with a London symphonic organization. After one of his concerts, Stephen Walsh wrote in the London *Times:* "Much credit for the momentous, as well as for the impressive coordination, of this performance was due to Lawrence Foster. . . . He held things together marvelously well and had the Royal Philharmonic Orchestra playing at its best." In the London *Guardian* Gerald Larner wrote: "Lawrence Foster, at the age of twenty-seven, has every chance of becoming the best of native Americans in his profession. He has a precise and effective technique, he has a sense of style, and does not distort."

With this orchestra he toured the United States in the fall of 1969, sharing the podium with its artistic director, Rudolf Kempe. A concert of the Royal Philharmonic under Foster in

Houston, Texas, made such an impression that Foster was invited to lead four subscription concerts of the Houston Symphony Orchestra during the 1970–1971 season in addition to two of three programs scheduled for Sir John Barbirolli. After these engagements he was appointed conductor-in-chief of the Houston Symphony in 1971, and one year later he became music director. After one of his concerts as the orchestra's principal conductor, Foster was described by Anna Holmes in the Houston *Chronicle:* "Already his firm beat, fine discipline and luminous sense of music in its most exciting and even theatrical aspects have done their bit to stabilize the orchestra." And in the Houston *Post,* Carl Cunningham said: "His concert Sunday restored sense and sensitivity to the Houston Symphony's turbulently rocking podium, bringing bright hopes that his era will be fully as glorious as Barbirolli's." Foster withdrew from the Houston Symphony after the 1977–1978 season.

When the Royal Philharmonic Orchestra of London toured the United States in 1972, Foster conducted twenty-three concerts. At one of these—at Carnegie Hall on October 24—he led the American premiere of Sir Michael Tippett's Symphony No.1. "Foster, new to the local scene . . . is a well-trained, modest appearing maestro, who knows how to shade, how to blend the ensemble into a unit and project the music with patrician grace," reported Harriet Johnson in the New York *Post.* "It is apparent that he knows his craft."

While holding the dual post of music director of the Houston Symphony and principal guest conductor of the Royal Philharmonic Orchestra, Foster had many opportunities to appear as guest conductor with major orchestras and opera houses in Europe and the United States. In addition, he has made noteworthy recordings for Angel, Columbia, and London Records, one of which—Beethoven's Piano Concerto No.3, with the London Symphony Orchestra and Radu Lupu as soloist—received the Grand Prix du Disque. Foster conducted the symphony orchestra in the classical repertory on the soundtrack of the motion picture *Counterpoint* (1968).

With the Royal Philharmonic in London, the Los Angeles Philharmonic, the Houston Symphony—and as a regular guest conductor for the County Art Museum's Monday Evening Concerts in Los Angeles—Foster has given numerous premiere performances. On August 3, 1967, he conducted the world premiere of Lalo Schifrin's *The Rise and Fall of the Third Reich* with the Los Angeles Philharmonic at the Hollywood Bowl. On June 1, 1972, he led in London the first performance anywhere of Harrison Birtwistle's *The Triumph of Time,* which the Royal Philharmonic Orchestra had commissioned; Foster also conducted its American premiere on September 24, 1973. He conducted what is believed to have been the American premiere of the staged production of Handel's *Rinaldo* in Houston on October 16, 1975.

On August 19, 1977, Lawrence Foster conducted an all-Mozart program at the Mostly Mozart Festival at Avery Fisher Hall in New York. His performance, reported John Rockwell in the New York *Times,* "was exemplary. The key to his success was his bravery in refusing to exaggerate. He didn't swamp the music with eccentric tempos or excessive orchestral weight. He used generally small ensembles, quick tempos and classically straightforward inflections. Yet the music was suffused with personality."

Foster married Angela Suciu, whom he met when he was conducting in Romania, on April 14, 1972. They maintain two residences, one in Houston and a second at Cap D'Ail on the French Riviera. Foster's nonmusical avocations include chess, waterskiing, tennis, and going to the movies.

ABOUT: High Fidelity/Musical America, January 1972; New York Times, August 19, 1977.

Pierre Fournier

1906–

Pierre Fournier, cellist, was born in Paris on June 24, 1906, to a distinguished family that had produced the sculptor who designed the Pont Alexandre III on the Seine River (Pierre's grandfather) and a French army general during World War I who later became governor in Corsica (Pierre's father). The musician in the family was Pierre's mother, Gabrielle, an excellent pianist. Pierre's father, Gaston, wanted him to pursue a military career, but his mother, insisting that the boy be allowed to develop his bent for music, wanted him to become a professional

Fournier: foor nyā´

PIERRE FOURNIER

musician and gave him his first piano lessons. When Pierre was nine he was stricken by poliomyelitis which made it impossible for him to use the piano pedals. He decided to take on a new instrument, the cello, which had long fascinated him. "The idea of trying to *sing* with a stringed instrument," he now explains, "captured my imagination."

At thirteen Pierre entered the Paris Conservatory. For the next few years he studied with Lucien Capet and Jean Gallon. After graduating from the Conservatory with highest honors in cello, he completed his cello study privately with Anton Hekking.

For a number of years Fournier played the cello in several orchestras and chamber-music groups in Paris. He made his concert debut there as soloist with the Colonne Orchestra in a performance that proved so successful that he was invited to perform with other European orchestras. Recitals added to his growing reputation. By 1939 Fournier had become such a favorite in Germany that to meet public demand he had to give thirty-two recitals in Berlin alone.

From 1937 to 1939 Fournier was professor of the cello and of chamber music at the École Normale de Musique in Paris. In 1941 he was appointed professor of the cello at the Paris Conservatory, a post he retained for eight years.

His career as virtuoso, temporarily interrupted during World War II, was resumed in 1945 with concerts in England. His debut in that country, as soloist with the London Philharmonic Orchestra, led the critic of the London

Times to say: "The quiet beauty of his playing seemed to create a timeless moment in which again the happy daydream of man could communicate its happiness to its auditors."

His concert work soon became worldwide. In 1947 he was heard at the Edinburgh Festival in Scotland, the first of many visits there. In 1948 he made his first tour of the United States, beginning with a recital at Town Hall, New York, where he became an immediate favorite. "Pierre Fournier," wrote Cyrus Durgin in the Boston *Globe,* "is a very great cellist and an exceptional musician. ... Technical virtuosity, mastery of style are all blended and directed toward making music. The tone is satiny. The phrasing has utmost grace. Such is the combined mastery and superior perception of this artist that everything was set forth with equal excellence." In the *Herald Tribune* Virgil Thomson said: "I do not know his superior among living cellists, nor any ... who gave one more profoundly the feeling of having been present at music-making."

His first tour of South America took place in 1949. He appeared at festivals in Edinburgh, Salzburg, and Lucerne in the years between 1948 and 1950. Tours of Europe, the Far East, South Africa, and the Soviet Union spread his fame. Indicative of his position in French music is the fact that two celebrated French writers dedicated their books to him. In one of these, Colette said that Fournier "sings better than anything sings"; in another, André Gide spoke of "vivid memories of unforgettable musical moments." Fournier was twice honored by the French government: in 1953 he was made Chevalier of the Legion of Honor; in 1963 he was cited with the higher rank of Officier.

He has collaborated in distinguished chamber-music concerts with Arthur Rubinstein and Henryk Szeryng. Their RCA recording of Schubert's Piano Trios was awarded a Grammy in 1976 by the National Academy of Recording Arts and Sciences. His other recordings cover all of Beethoven's major works for cello, the six Bach solo suites for cello, and just about every important cello concerto. On several occasions his records were awarded the Grand Prix du Disque in Paris. In 1961 his recording of Richard Strauss's *Don Quixote* with the Cleveland Orchestra under George Szell earned him a Grammy.

His repertory embraces not only the classical and romantic literature for the cello but also the music of Baroque composers and a storehouse of twentieth century compositions. He has given performances of contemporary works by Ernest Bloch, Virgil Thomson, Bohuslav Martinů, Albert Roussel, and Francis Poulenc, among many others, several of whose compositions were written for him and introduced by him. One was Martinů's Concerto for Cello and Orchestra which Fournier introduced in Basel, Switzerland, in January 1967 before presenting its American premiere in Cleveland on October 26, 1967, with the Cleveland Orchestra under Szell.

On July 16, 1936, Fournier married Lydia Antik, a concert pianist who had previously been married to Gregor Piatigorsky, the cellist. They have one son, Jean-Pierre, a piano virtuoso. Home for the Fourniers is a rambling house in Geneva, Switzerland. A collector, Fournier has overcrowded his home with paintings, jade vases, period pieces of furniture, objets d'art, and other items picked up from his travels around the world. He also collects old coins. Other interests include reading (in English and German, as well as French), playing tennis, occasionally indulging in a game of cards with friends, visiting museums, and going to the movies.

Fournier's cello playing is heard on the sound track of the motion picture *Cries and Whispers,* directed by Ingmar Bergman (1973).

ABOUT: Ewen, D. Famous Instrumentalists; Gavoty, B. Pierre Fournier.

Virgil Fox

1912–

Virgil Keel Fox, organist, was born in Princeton, Illinois, on May 3, 1912. His father, Miles, was a real estate man and theater operator who played the harmonica at barn dances; his mother, Birdie E. Nichols Fox, sang in the church choir. Beginning the study of organ early with Hugh Price, Virgil played for the services at the First Presbyterian Church in Princeton when he was ten. At fourteen he made his professional debut with a concert in Cincinnati, Ohio. Three years later, on the unanimous decision of the judges, he won a biennial contest conducted by the National Federation of Music Clubs.

VIRGIL FOX

Upon graduation from Princeton Township High School in 1930, Virgil studied the organ in Chicago with Wilhelm Middelschulte. A scholarship brought him to the Peabody Conservatory in Baltimore in 1931, where he was a student of Louis Robert. While attending the Conservatory he astonished his teachers and fellow students by giving five recitals, playing all the music from memory. In 1932 he became the first one-year student ever to graduate from that Conservatory with the artist's diploma, the school's highest honor.

In 1932 and 1933 Fox completed his organ studies in Paris with Marcel Dupré. He then embarked on a concert career, making his debut in London in 1933 and returning later the same year to the United States for his New York debut and concerts in several major American cities.

In 1938 he was appointed organist of the Brown Memorial Church in Baltimore. At the same time he succeeded Louis Robert as head of the organ department of the Peabody Conservatory, retaining this post until 1942. During World War I Fox served in the United States Army Air Force from 1942 to 1946. Stationed in Washington, D.C., he was assigned musical activities and fund-raising for the Air Force Aid Society. After separation from the Air Force, he resumed his professional life, becoming in 1946 organist of the Riverside Church in New York. This church boasted one of the finest organs in the United States—a five-manual Aeolian-Skinner instrument. He remained in this post for nineteen years, resigning in 1965 to devote more

260

of his time and energies to concert work. He returned to the concert platform in 1946, giving a series of three concerts at the Library of Congress in Washington, D.C., featuring forty-four compositions.

Since 1946 Fox has toured the world in recitals in concert halls and churches, as guest artist with major symphony orchestras, and in performances in Westminster Abbey and the Lincoln and Durham Cathedrals in England, the Dom in Berlin, the Marienkirche in Lübeck, and the Cathedral in Bern, Switzerland. He was the first American to play the organ at the Thomaskirche in Leipzig, an organ upon which Bach had performed.

In his more recent performances Fox has combined showmanship and spectacle with sound musicianship. His favored instrument is the Heavy Organ—or Rodger Tour Organ—which has an extended tonal range and dynamics and, therefore, is better able to project the current organ repertory than the baroque organ. "Once on," writes Richard Dyer in the New York *Times,* "Fox does, indeed, come across. He sways his torso and swings his hands aloft and makes a great show of changing the stops crosshanded. A spotlight on those pumps makes sure you don't forget he's moving down there, too. The swell pedal, that aural zoom lens, brings the music forward and takes it away, and the playing is alternately and in various combinations very soft and very loud and very fast and very slow. The registrations may be gaudy, the pedal . . . may honk away while the upper divisions, blowsily amplified, sometimes sound like the ultimate accordion, but no one can deny that Fox hits a powerful lot of notes, almost all of them the right ones."

Fox communicates with his audiences not only through his music but also with verbal comments, explanations, and opinions. "I've always talked to my audiences," he explains. "Years ago when I was playing a concert at a church in Augusta, Georgia, the third piece was the Fantasia and Fugue in G minor of Bach. I said to myself, 'My God, these three thousand Georgia crackers won't have the slightest idea of what's going to happen. I have to tell them. That was a milepost in my earth-existence. I even played much better. By talking, by sharing what is about to happen, an artist can rid himself of his nerves. It delivers me from the gnomes or the butterflies."

He gives about eighty concerts a year, of which fifty or so are "light shows." The latter consist of performances with the collaboration of a Revelation Lights console operated by Fox's assistant, David Snyder. The instrument throws lights, colors, clouds, and amorphous images on a huge screen in order "to further enunciate what I feel are the intentions of the composer and the style of Virgil Fox," he has explained. Michael Steinberg, the maverick music critic of the Boston *Globe,* described these light shows as "spermy," calling them a "mixture of showmanship, Bach, lights, slightly tattered virtuosity, homoerotic fantasies, animadversions on religion (pro) and drugs (contra)."

In 1955 Fox dedicated the enlarged and rebuilt organ at the Riverside Church. On December 15, 1962, with two fellow artists, he dedicated the new Aeolian-Skinner organ in Philharmonic Hall at the Lincoln Center for the Performing Arts. There, on January 7, 1963, he became the first organist to give a solo recital. In 1974 he gave the dedicatory concert on the new Rodgers electronic organ in Carnegie Hall, New York. "The organ responded nobly," said Harold C. Schonberg in the New York *Times.* "It is indeed an impressive instrument." Then in his discussion of Fox's performance, Schonberg added: "He put the organ through its paces. Mr. Fox is a romantic organist. His ideas about Bach have nothing to do with what today is considered the correct style. Indeed, there are those who would be so unkind as to call his Bach appallingly vulgar. It has not so much the romantic approach as his movie-organ mixtures, his constant breaking of the line and his tricky phrasings. . . . On the plus side, he is a superior technician, and when he came to the French music . . . there suddenly was a stylistic authority and a feeling for line that was entirely convincing. Here virtuosity and color were in secure harness."

In 1975, as head of a five-member trusteeship, Fox acquired a fifty-room Gothic castle in Gloucester, Massachusetts, for the purpose of organizing and directing an international school of the concert organ and a research center with library and museum facilities. On July 4, 1975, he began to give daily half-hour recitals for visitors touring the castle and its grounds.

Fox, who never married, occupies a twenty-six-room mansion in Englewood, New Jersey, which harbors his collection of Wedgwood and

Francescatti

Venetian glass together with memorabilia of his professional career, four thousand organ pipes from Boston's Old South Church, and a carved organ console from the home of a Cleveland oil baron. Since one of his favorite pastimes is swimming, the grounds boast an Olympic-size pool. Fox's other interests include driving his car, attending the theater, and being a host at convivial parties with congenial friends.

In 1952 Fox received the Distinguished Alumni Award from the Peabody Conservatory Alumni Association. In 1963 he was awarded an honorary doctorate in music by Bucknell University.

ABOUT: Hi-Fi, August 1963; New York Times, September 29, 1974, June 15, 1975.

ZINO FRANCESCATTI

Zino Francescatti

1902–

Zino Francescatti, violinist, was born in Marseilles, on August 9, 1902. He was christened René, but he adopted the nickname Zino which his father had given him. Both his parents were professional musicians. His father, Fortuné, an Italian, had studied with Paganini's only direct pupil, Ernesto Camillo Sivori; he played the violin in orchestras in Marseilles and also taught violin. Francescatti's mother, Ernesta Féraud, had been Fortuné Francescatti's pupil when she fell in love with him, married him, and gave up her own career. Late in her life, upon the death of one of her sons, she went back to the concert stage after an absence of several decades.

Zino began studying the violin when he was three. His only teacher was his mother, though his father contributed some coaching. He proved to be a prodigy. At five he was able to make his first public appearance, and at ten he was acclaimed for a performance of the Beethoven Violin Concerto. Since his father refused to exploit him as a prodigy—and, in fact, tried to discourage him from becoming a professional violinist—Zino was sent to academic schools in Marseilles and allowed to perform only on Sundays. When he grew older, his father directed him to the study of law. When Zino was twenty-two, his father died. It was only then that he decided to

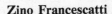

Francescatti: frăn sĕs kŏt′ tē

devote himself exclusively to playing the violin.

In 1924 he went to Paris where he auditioned for Jacques Thibaud and made a highly successful Paris debut as soloist with the Paris Conservatory Orchestra conducted by Philippe Gaubert. Further performances in recitals and as a guest artist with orchestras helped to advance his career. Upon returning to Paris, Francescatti was appointed instructor of violin at the École Normale de Musique and assistant concertmaster of the Concerts Poulet. Another member of that orchestra was the young violinist Yolande Potel de la Brière, whom Francescatti married on January 2, 1930.

At this time Francescatti was taken under the managerial wing of Léon Delort, French impresario. In the next few years his career was promoted throughout Europe. In addition to recitals, he appeared with Bruno Walter, Mengelberg, Furtwängler, and Monteux. On May 8, 1938, he made his debut in South America in a performance of the original edition of Paganini's Violin Concerto No.1 and the Bach Concerto in D minor, José Iturbi conducting. A correspondent for the New York Times reported that Francescatti received "one of the most rousing ovations seen at the Teatro Colón in many years." Success followed him that year to other cities in Brazil and to Chile and Uruguay.

His first performance in the United States took place on November 1, 1939, when he played Paganini's First Violin Concerto with the New York Philharmonic Orchestra. A tour of the United States followed, the first of many in which he appeared in recitals, with leading orchestras, over the radio (more than fifty times on the "Bell Telephone Hour"), and on records. In the United States, as well as in his performances throughout the civilized world, he came to be recognized as one of the great violinists of the time. "His playing," wrote one critic for the New York *Times,* "opens new realms of sound." A critic for the *Herald Tribune* in New York said: "His perfection, in fact, has become a habit. Virtuosity and musicianship and all the fractional distinctions between the two are his to deal with as he chooses." Virgil Thomson remarked in the *Herald Tribune:* "If violin playing is on the way to becoming a noble art again . . . this artist is one of those responsible for this change."

Francescatti has often shared the concert stage with the pianist Robert Casadesus in sonata recitals. On several occasions they gave a cycle of concerts devoted to all ten of Beethoven's violin sonatas, which they also recorded for Columbia.

Francescatti is an Officer of the French Legion of Honor and Commander of the Order of Arts and Letters in France. He is also Commander of the Order of Leopold in Belgium.

The Francescattis maintain an apartment in New York City, a second one in the rue de Faubourg St. Honoré in Paris, and a summer house in La Ciotat. Francescatti is an avid reader of travel books, biographies, adventure stories, and scientific studies. Among his pet hobbies are collecting stamps, doing crossword puzzles, playing chess, and motoring. To relieve the monotony of travel he often occupies himself by solving chess problems with a miniature chess set.

ABOUT: Musical America, November 1, 1959.

Olive Fremstad

1871–1951

Olive Fremstad, one of the greatest of Wagnerian sopranos, was born in Stockholm, on March 14, 1871. Her name at birth was Anna Olivia Rundquist. She was registered in the parish church as Anna Peterson and later was adopted by Olaf and Anna Rundquist Fremstad, a physi-

---

Fremstad: frĕm′ städ

OLIVE FREMSTAD

cian and his wife, Americans of Swedish extraction. They took her to Minnesota when she was ten. In Minneapolis, Olive studied the piano, making her public debut as pianist two years later; during this period she also played the organ in a local church. When she was sixteen she appeared as vocal soloist in church, gave public concerts, and made her stage bow in the Gilbert and Sullivan comic opera *Patience,* in the role of Lady Saphir.

She went to New York on Christmas Eve of 1890. There she received voice lessons from Frederick E. Bristol in exchange for performing on the piano for his pupils at his studio; Bristol trained her as a contralto. She was heard as the soprano soloist with the St. Patrick's Cathedral Choir in New York. Her first appearance with orchestra was in 1892 in Boston, after which she toured the eastern states with an orchestra conducted by Anton Seidl.

In 1892 she went to Berlin to continue her vocal studies with Lilli Lehmann, with whom she remained two years. Lehmann developed Fremstad into a soprano able to assume mezzo and dramatic soprano roles, of which she mastered about a dozen. In 1895 she appeared as a soloist at the Cologne Festival in Germany in a performance of Schumann's *Paradise and the Peri.* This performance brought her a contract with the Cologne Opera and she made her debut there that year as Azucena in *Il Trovatore.* During three years she was heard in some seventy roles, including Carmen, Mignon, and Prince Orlofsky in *Die Fledermaus.* While with the Cologne Opera she appeared at the Bayreuth Festival in 1896 in the minor roles of Schwertleite (a Valkyrie) in *Die Walküre* and Flosshilde in *Die Götterdämmerung* and made her debut at the Vienna Royal Opera as Brangäne in *Tristan and Isolde* in the spring of 1897 and at Covent Garden in London in 1897 as Venus in *Tannhäuser*. In 1905 she gave a command performance for King Edward VII in London, singing excerpts from *Salome*, and later the same year she created at Covent Garden the role of Iolanthe in Ethel Smyth's *Der Wald*. She was also heard as a guest artist in opera houses in Amsterdam and Antwerp.

After leaving Cologne she spent a year in Italy, following which she was a member of the Munich Royal Opera from 1900 to 1903. For her performance in Messager's *Veronique* in Munich in 1923 she received from France the order of Officier de l'Académie.

Returning to the United States in 1903, Fremstad made her debut at the Metropolitan Opera on November 25, 1903, as Sieglinde in *Die Walküre* (a performance in which the conductor, Felix Mottl, was also making his American debut). After the first act she was given an ovation. "Miss Fremstad," wrote Henry E. Krehbiel in the *Tribune*, "has everything appertaining to voice and appearance in her favor and though a tendency toward the Teutonic stride and pose which Bayreuth has encouraged militates against the sweet naturalness of which the character of Sieglinde is an index, she took rank with most of her predecessors in the part."

For a decade Fremstad's triumphs as a Wagnerian soprano continued. She sang her first Venus in *Tannhäuser* on December 4, 1903, her first Brangäne in *Tristan and Isolde* on February 13, 1904, her first Fricka in *Das Rheingold* on March 3, 1904, Kundry in *Parsifal* on December 1, 1904 (only the second artist to appear in this role outside Bayreuth), her first Brünnhilde in *Siegfried* on December 13, 1905, her first Isolde on January 1, 1908, her first Brünnhilde in *Die Götterdämmerung* on December 10, 1908, her first Elsa in *Lohengrin* (on tour) on December 14, 1909, her first Brünnhilde in *Die Walküre* on February 9, 1911, and her first Elisabeth in *Tannhäuser* (on tour) on April 17, 1911. Her conception of Kundry, said W. J. Henderson in the *Sun*, "was . . . a triumph, original, clearly drawn and convincing. . . . and her singing of the lower music such as that of the first act, was

thrilling in its beauty." Her Isolde, probably her most distinguished Wagnerian role, was, wrote H. E. Krehbiel in the *Tribune*, "imaginative and beautifully expressed in many respects," and, in the words of Richard Aldrich in the New York *Times*, "of fascinating beauty and allurement; of grave dignity, rather of gentleness than of regal imperiousness . . . a marvelously beautiful impersonation."

She also sang with success in operas outside the Wagnerian sphere. Carmen was one of her brilliant characterizations, her first appearance in that role at the Metropolitan Opera taking place on November 25, 1904, with Caruso as Don José. When *Salome* received its American premiere on January 22, 1907, she sang the title role. (She had spent a year in preparation for this but sang the part only once in New York, since *Salome* was hurriedly removed from the Metropolitan Opera repertory after a single performance because of the shock and scandal it aroused.) She sang the role again at the Théâtre du Chatelet in Paris on May 8, 1907—a performance for which the French government made her Officer of Public Instruction. At the American premiere of Gluck's *Armide* on November 14, 1910 (opening night of the season), Toscanini conducting, she created the title role. She also sang Tosca, Selika in *L'Africaine*, Santuzza in *Cavalleria Rusticana*, and Giulietta in *The Tales of Hoffmann* (in the latter, substituting for an indisposed singer).

Her farewell appearance at the Metropolitan Opera—after 205 performances in New York and 101 performances on tour—took place on April 23, 1914, in what had never been one of her strongest roles—Elsa in *Lohengrin*. Nevertheless, she received "the most remarkable demonstration ever given to an artist in the history of New York opera," as Henry E. Krehbiel reported in the *Tribune*. "Both at the end of the second act and at the close of the opera the cheers were deafening. When the curtain fell on the last act and the artist was called out, a demonstration began which lasted nineteen minutes. The asbestos curtain was lowered four times in an effort to halt the cheers and drive the audience home, but not until Mme. Fremstad had appeared and bowed more than forty times would her admirers depart from the house. From all parts of the building they streamed toward the stage, cheered and applauded, with hands and feet, and threw kisses at their favorite.

It was a farewell worthy of the place Mme. Fremstad has attained in the hearts of the music lovers of America; a superb tribute to the woman who has been one of the chief glories of the Metropolitan. With her passing, that house of song loses what it will find to replace." Fremstad made a brief speech in which she said: "I have always tried to give you my best, my very best. Goodbye, dear friends, and may we all some day meet in that land where peace and harmony reign."

This was not Fremstad's last appearance in opera. In 1912 and again in 1915 she gave guest performances with the Chicago Opera as Isolde and the three Brünnhildes. In 1913 she returned to the Munich Royal Opera as the three Brünnhildes and as Isolde. In November 1915 she appeared as Tosca at the Manhattan Opera House in New York and at the Boston Opera House. She was reengaged by the Metropolitan Opera for a three-year period in June 1917, but because of the prejudice against German-language opera during World War I she never filled this engagement.

After leaving opera, Fremstad gave recitals in 1916 and 1917. Her last appearance on any stage took place in New York on January 19, 1920, in a recital. She was a pioneer in radio broadcasting, sharing the microphone with Emmy Destinn on January 12, 1910, in New York.

After her retirement as a singer, she devoted herself to coaching young singers in New York for a few years before withdrawing into total retirement. For some months before her death she was crippled by arthritis. She died in a nursing home in Irvington-on-the-Hudson, New York, on April 21, 1951.

She was twice married: first on April 15, 1906, to Edson W. Sutphen whom she divorced in 1911; then, on November 4, 1916, to her piano accompanist, Harry Lewis Brainard. They were divorced in 1925.

Olive Fremstad was the prototype for the heroine in Willa Cather's novel *The Song of the Lark.*

ABOUT: Thompson, O. The American Singer. *Periodicals*—Musical America, May 1951.

Mirella Freni

1935–

Mirella Freni (originally Mirella Fregni), soprano, was born in Modena, Italy, on February 27, 1935, to Ennio (a civil servant) and Gianna Freni. Mirella had the same wet nurse as Luciano Pavarotti, the world-famous tenor, who was born a few months after Mirella; the mothers of Mirella and Luciano were friends, working together in the same cigarette factory.

Mirella says she cannot remember a time when she was not singing. Vocal study began early with her uncle, Dante Arcelli, in Mantua. When she was eleven she sang "Sempre libera" from *La Traviata* at a pupils' concert; her accompanist was a twelve-year-old pianist, Leone Magiera. "I thought he was terrible and ugly," she recalls. "He thought I was a monster." Some years later Magiera became her vocal teacher and coach, and in 1955 they were married.

In her thirteenth year, Mirella sang "Un bel dì" from *Madama Butterfly* in a national competition, emerging with first prize. But, on the advice of Beniamino Gigli, who feared she might strain her voice, she relaxed her singing efforts in public for a number of years, concentrating on studying singing in Bologna and learning all she could about opera by attending performances at the Teatro Comunale in Modena.

Following her marriage and the birth of a daughter, Micaëla, she gave up her ambition of becoming a professional singer to devote herself to domesticity. After about two years, however, her husband persuaded her to resume vocal study. Her teacher was Ettore Campogalliani.

On February 3, 1955, she made her opera debut at the Teatro Comunale in Modena as Micaëla in *Carmen.* "I felt no panic," she told an interviewer. "It was my town. All my friends were there. They gave me shouts and roses."

In 1958 Freni captured first prize in the Concorso Viotti in Vercelli. Her career in opera gained momentum with successful appearances at the Bologna Teatro Comunale, the Teatro Massimo in Palermo in 1958, and the Netherlands Opera at the Holland Festival of 1959. In 1960 she made her debut at San Carlo in Naples and in the summer of the same year she ap-

Freni: frā′ nē

Freni

MIRELLA FRENI

peared as Zerlina in *Don Giovanni* at the Glyndebourne Festival in England, where she was heard for three consecutive seasons. In 1961 she was acclaimed in Covent Garden in London as Zerlina and as Nannetta in *Falstaff.* She had a dual debut in Milan in 1962: At the famed La Scala she helped to open the season as Nannetta, substituting for an ailing Renata Scotto, and appearing without benefit of a single rehearsal; and at the more intimate auditorium, the Piccola Scala, as Romilda in Handel's *Serse.*

In 1962 La Scala asked her to appear the following season (on January 31, 1963) as Mimi in a new presentation of *La Bohème* produced by Franco Zeffirelli and conducted by Herbert von Karajan. "When I went for the first rehearsal, he [Herbert von Karajan] listened," she reveals. "Oh, he listened! If no good, then goodbye. But it was good." Her appearance as Mimi on January 31, 1963, brought her world fame. The day after this performance Angel Records made arrangements to record her as Mimi the following summer with Nicolai Gedda as Rodolfo and Thomas Schippers conducting. The Zeffirelli-Karajan production was filmed and circulated in theaters in Europe and the United States.

In 1963 she made guest appearances at the Vienna State Opera and the Wiesbaden Festival in Germany. In the winter of 1964 La Scala toured the Soviet Union, and Freni was heard as Liù in *Turandot* and as Mimi at the Bolshoi Theater in Moscow.

On September 29, 1965, she made her American debut at the Metropolitan Opera as Mimi. In his report to the *New Yorker,* Winthrop Sargeant said: "Miss Freni, who is small, beautiful, a good actress and certainly an ideal Mimi, has an appealing lyric voice of considerable power and range, and a personality—evident in both voice and stage bearing—that can instantly charm any audience." In the *Saturday Review* Irving Kolodin placed her in a class with Lucrezia Bori, Licia Albanese, and Bidú Sayão, stating: "Here is a singer who should have years of success before her, a good part of them, let it be hoped in New York."

Immediately following her success in New York, Freni went to the Chicago Lyric Opera, returning to the Metropolitan Opera on November 12 as Adina in *L'Elisir d'Amore.* Her subsequent Metropolitan Opera roles were Liù, Marguerite in *Faust,* Juliet in *Romeo and Juliet,* Susanna in *The Marriage of Figaro,* and Micaëla in *Carmen.*

In addition to her commitments to the Metropolitan Opera, Vienna State Opera, and La Scala, Freni has appeared at the Deutsche Oper in Berlin, Munich Opera, San Carlo in Naples, Rome Opera, Covent Garden in London, and at the Salzburg and Glyndebourne Festivals. In these and other opera houses she has been acclaimed as Marguerite in Boïto's *Mefistofele,* the title role in Bellini's *Beatrice di Tenda,* Marie in *The Daughter of the Regiment,* Zerlina in *Don Giovanni,* Susanna and the Countess in *The Marriage of Figaro,* Elvira in *I Puritani,* Adina in *L'Elisir d'Amore,* Violetta in *La Traviata,* Elisabetta in *Don Carlo,* Desdemona in *Otello,* Maria in *Simon Boccanegra,* and the title roles in *Manon* and *Madama Butterfly.*

In September 1976 the Paris Opéra paid its first visit to the United States, in celebration of America's bicentenary, and Freni was heard as Susanna (one of her greatest roles) in *The Marriage of Figaro,* conducted by Sir Georg Solti. This was her first singing appearance in New York in eight years. "She is much as she formerly was: pert, adorable and a consummate artist," reported Harold C. Schonberg in the New York *Times.*

Later in 1976 she was heard with the Paris Opéra in Paris as Susanna in *The Marriage of Figaro* and Amelia in *Simon Boccanegra.* On November 16, 1976, she returned to New York to participate in a performance of Verdi's Requiem by the Berlin Philharmonic under Herbert von Karajan at Carnegie Hall. She returned to the stage of the Metropolitan Opera after an eight-year absence on October 12, 1977, as Mimi.

Freni has appeared in recitals, has made recordings of her favorite roles for RCA, London, and Angel Records, and has appeared in filmed versions of *Madama Butterfly* with Placido Domingo and the Vienna Philharmonic conducted by von Karajan and of *The Marriage of Figaro* conducted by Karl Böhm *The Marriage of Figaro* was telecast throughout the United States through the facilities of the Public Broadcasting Service on October 5, 1977.

Mirella Freni resides in Modena, Italy, with her husband and daughter. Peter P. Jacobi has described her, in the New York *Times*, as "a quiet woman, blonde, expressive of face, and a user of hands to help conversation along. She is a pleasant woman, a gentle enchantress with a friendly manner."

She enjoys playing tennis, riding a motor scooter, going to the movies, and watching soccer games. Holidays are spent in her country home at Serramazzoni in the Appenine mountains of Italy.

ABOUT: New York Times, November 7, 1965, September 12, 1976; Newsweek, November 22, 1965; Opera News, October 1977.

Povla Frijsh

1881–1960

Povla Frijsh (originally Paula Frisch), soprano, was one of the most distinguished interpreters of song literature in her time, particularly French song literature. She was born on the island of Aero, off the coast of Denmark, on August 3, 1881. Her father, a surgeon, was an amateur singer who decided to have his daughter trained as a pianist so that she might accompany him. After attending the Copenhagen Conservatory, where she studied the piano with O. Christensen, her talent at singing was discovered. She was then sent to Paris to become a vocal student of Jean Périer and Sarah de Lalande. She attracted the interest of Raoul Pugno, the composer and piano virtuoso, who persuaded her to join him in a concert tour of France—a tour which helped to focus the interest of French music lovers on the young singer. After that, Pablo Casals

POVLA FRIJSH

also invited her to appear with him in joint recitals.

She made her debut as a solo performer in Paris in 1907, with Alfred Cortot as her accompanist, a function he would later fill for her on numerous occasions. This concert was successful, and she became one of the most highly esteemed vocal recitalists in France. In 1910 she was a soloist with an orchestra directed by Gustav Mahler, and in 1911 she performed at the Paris Conservatory in a concert commemorating the Franz Liszt centenary. She made her first appearance in Holland in 1912, and in Copenhagen in 1913.

During World War I she sang in French hospitals for wounded soldiers. She crossed the Atlantic Ocean in 1915 to make her United States debut in New York on November 10. Sigmund Spaeth in the *Evening Mail* found her to be "quite an extraordinary artist. . . . To those who enjoy a subtle and delicate art backed by thorough conviction and sincerity, Povla Frijsh may be unhesitatingly recommended." A critic for the *Tribune* wrote: "Her voice is pleasant in quality and thoroughly obedient to fine taste, instinct and knowledge; breath control is excellent; registers are admirably equalized; attack is impeccable and the phrasing is finished."

When the war ended, she made some of her rare appearances in opera in Copenhagen in 1919, and soon after that she was acclaimed for her performance in Monteverdi's *L'Incoronazione di Poppea* in Paris. But she found song literature much more appealing to her than opera and abandoned the opera house to concentrate on the concert hall. She toured the world of music, returning to the United States in 1935 after a five-year absence. At her concert in New York on November 24, she once again "demonstrated her extraordinary ability to create and sustain moods of variety," as a critic for the New York *Times* reported. "But last night there was a new depth, an added human appeal to her singing that gave it exceptional emotional intensity and warmth, even in passages of ethereal delicacy. The voice, too, had gained in opulence and was under firmer control than formerly."

While her specialty was the French art song and though she was also a master of German *Lieder,* her programs covered a wide range including American music. She introduced Negro spirituals to Paris and Copenhagen, and she gave the world premieres of many American vocal compositions, including some by Ernest Bloch, Charles Martin Loeffler, Randall Thompson, and Charles Tomlinson Griffes among others.

In addition to appearing in recitals and with orchestras, Frijsh was also a guest artist with the Casals-Thibaud-Cortot trio in France and the Flonzaley Quartet in the United States.

"A vivid figure, with her green eyes and extraordinarily mobile and expressive face and hands," wrote Robert Sabin in *Musical America,* "Mme. Frijsh exerted sheer magic in the concert hall. As she moved quietly but swiftly across the stage, clad in a black faille gown with green stockings, a green handkerchief, and a ribbon at her throat, one sensed that here was a personality of marvelous sensitivity and power, a Manet painting come to life."

From 1930 to 1940 her home was in Paris. In 1940 she established permanent residence in the United States. She left the concert stage in 1947 to teach voice for several years at the Juilliard School of Music in New York and to coach singers. She was on her customary summer vacation to Blue Hills, Maine, when she died suddenly at the home of a friend on July 10, 1960.

Her husband was Jan Posnanski, to whom she was married just two years.

ABOUT: Musical America, August 1960.

Rafael Frühbeck de Burgos

1933–

Rafael Frühbeck de Burgos, conductor, was born in Burgos, Spain, on September 15, 1933, to Wilhelm Frühbeck, a German, and Stefanie Ochs Frühbeck, a Spaniard. Rafael's musical talent was discovered early, soon after he began music lessons. He studied violin and piano, first with private teachers, then at the Bilbao Conservatory. When he was sixteen he entered the Madrid Conservatory to study harmony and composition with Don Julio Gómez. Rafael's musical training was completed at the High School for Music in Munich where he received intensive training in conducting from professors Lessing and Eichhorn. He was graduated *summa cum laude,* a distinction rarely given there. He also became the first conductor ever to receive the Richard Strauss Prize from the city of Munich.

He was twenty-six when he was appointed music director of the Bilbao Symphony Orchestra, the youngest conductor to hold a permanent post in Spain. Three years later he was appointed music director of the National Orchestra, a post he held until September 1978 with such distinction—both in Madrid and on tour throughout Europe—that he was invited to make guest appearances with Europe's major orchestras and at some of its festivals.

His recordings, released in the United States under the Angel and London labels, made him well known to American music lovers long before he made his first American tour. His American debut took place in 1969 with the Philadelphia Orchestra in Philadelphia. When he was heard for the first time in New York, on February 19, 1969, with the visiting Philadelphia Orchestra, Harold C. Schonberg found in his performance of Beethoven's music "competence rather than imagination. . . . There was nothing wrong with his ideas, and the playing was perfectly in order. What was missing was the inner tension necessary to lend character to the music." But Schonberg added that he conducted the complete score of Manuel de Falla's *The Three-Cornered Hat* "beautifully. . . . In this score he added the kind of rhythmic pliancy that a musician born to the language has mastered. With all of the steady momentum, there never

RAFAEL FRÜHBECK DE BURGOS

was a hint of a metronomic quality. Nor was there a search for anything outside the legitimate ends of the score."

Since that time Rafael Frühbeck de Burgos has often appeared as guest conductor of major American symphony orchestras. In 1974 he was appointed music director of the city of Düsseldorf and principal conductor of the Düsseldorf Symphony in Germany. In the fall of 1975 he became principal conductor of the Montreal Symphony in Canada.

He lives in Madrid. In 1959 he married María Carmen Martínez; they have two children. Spain has honored him with the decoration of the Gran Cruz al Mérito Civil, the Orden de Alfonso X, and the Orden de Isabel la Católica.

ABOUT: International Who's Who; Who's Who in the World.

Wilhelm Furtwängler

1886–1954

Wilhelm Furtwängler, conductor, was born in Berlin on January 25, 1886, to a distinguished scholarly family. His father, Adolf, was an eminent archaeologist and an authority on Greek vases and coins; his mother was a talented and recognized painter. Wilhelm was early exposed to cultural interests. While still young, he was

---

Furtwängler: foŏrt′ vĕng lēr

brought to live in Munich where his father was a professor at the University and director of one of the museums. His father became an all-important influence in Wilhelm's intellectual and cultural development. He often took Wilhelm to local museums, and occasionally he took him along on expeditions to Greece and Italy where a lifetime fascination for classical and Renaissance art was instilled in the boy. Believing strongly in the importance of physical as well as intellectual development, his father also taught him to ski, swim, ride horses, sail, and play tennis. With good music basic to the Furtwängler household, Wilhelm was often taken to symphony concerts and opera performances.

His first music study began at the piano when he was eight. He made such excellent progress that his parents gave him the best possible music instruction available in Munich: theory and composition with Josef Rheinberger, Max von Schillings, and Anton Beer-Walbrunn; conducting with Felix Mottl.

Furtwängler's conducting debut took place in 1906 with a performance of Bruckner's Ninth Symphony with the Dresden Opera Orchestra. His apprenticeship followed with minor posts in opera houses in Zurich, Strasbourg, and Lübeck. In 1915 a committee headed by Artur Bodanzky went to Lübeck to hear Furtwängler's performance of *Fidelio* and to evaluate his potential as Bodanzky's successor as music director of the Mannheim Opera. Their positive verdict was unanimous. Furtwängler made his debut in Mannheim in September 1915 with *Der Freischütz.* He also conducted in Mannheim his first orchestral concert. Both in opera and in symphonic music Furtwängler became an immediate favorite in Mannheim, where he remained four years.

In *Two Worlds of Music,* Berta Geissmar (Furtwängler's secretary) described how Mannheim saw the conductor. "Furtwängler was tall, slim and fair. The most arresting features of his fine artist's head were the high and noble forehead and the eyes. His were the eyes of a visionary, large, blue, and expressive; when he conducted . . . they were usually veiled and half closed but they were capable of widening and emitting a tremendous vitality when he entered into an argument or a conversation which interested him, and they could grow tender and radiant when he was in a softened and happy mood. His character was involved. He had a logical and

Furtwängler

persistent mind, direct and forceful; at the same time he was shy to the point of extreme sensitiveness."

In 1918 Furtwängler gave such an impressive performance of Brahms's Symphony No.3 in Vienna that he was invited to give cycles of concerts with the Tonkünstler Orchestra in 1919 and 1920. He also conducted performances at the Berlin State Opera in 1920, succeeding Richard Strauss there as first conductor. Furtwängler combined these activities with orchestral performances at the Museum Concerts in Frankfort, commuting regularly between Berlin and Frankfort; he also traveled regularly between Berlin and Vienna, having been appointed director of the Vienna Gesellschaft der Musikfreunde in 1921 following an eloquent performance of the Brahms *Requiem.*

On February 6, 1922, Furtwängler directed a memorial concert in Leipzig for Arthur Nikisch who had been the music director of the Berlin Philharmonic and the Leipzig Gewandhaus orchestras. Soon after this, he was chosen as Nikisch's successor both in Berlin and in Leipzig (an appointment believed to have been recommended by Nikisch himself just before his death).

With the principal orchestras of Leipzig and Berlin at his command, and with his first performance with the Vienna Philharmonic in 1922 commemorating the twenty-fifth anniversary of Brahms's death, Furtwängler, only thirty-six, was in the top echelon of Germany's conductors. Towards the end of May 1924 he married Zitla Lund of Denmark. During a brief honeymoon in Italy, he conducted his first concerts in that country; before 1924 was over he made a much-acclaimed debut in England with the Royal Philharmonic Orchestra.

On January 3, 1925, Furtwängler made his American bow as guest conductor of the New York Philharmonic Orchestra in a program featuring Strauss's *Don Juan,* Haydn's Concerto in C major for cello and orchestra (with Pablo Casals, soloist), and Brahms's First Symphony. This writer, who attended that performance, could never forget Furtwängler's monumental presentation of the Brahms symphony that closed the program, nor the fifteen-minute ovation that followed. Furtwängler was the romanticist who refused to be bound rigidly by the instructions of the musical score but permitted himself the luxury of molding phrases, softening the beat, and adapting the rhythmic flow to allow him to tap more deeply the poetic content of the music.

Furtwängler's triumph in New York brought him an invitation to become the music director of the New York Philharmonic. His commitments in Europe made the acceptance of such an offer impossible, but he did return to New York for two more seasons of guest performances with that orchestra.

His assignments in Europe and offers of major posts kept multiplying to make him the most idolized and sought after conductor of his time, with the single exception of Toscanini. In addition to regular assignments as music director of the Berlin Philharmonic and the Leipzig Gewandhaus Orchestra, he was given the music direction of the Vienna Philharmonic in 1927. In 1928, after his debut at the Vienna State Opera in *Das Rheingold,* he was asked to be its principal conductor. He declined the offer for the same reason that in 1928 he resigned from his post in Leipzig: The fatigue of continuous train commuting had begun to sap his energies and strength. By 1930 he had also given up the Vienna Philharmonic, preferring to concentrate on a single orchestra (the Berlin Philharmonic), to give performances at the Berlin State Opera as its music director, and to make guest appearances throughout the world.

In the spring of 1928 he toured Europe with the Berlin Philharmonic. Three years later he appeared for the first time in Bayreuth where he conducted *Tristan and Isolde* and where in 1933 he served as principal conductor. On the fiftieth anniversary of the Berlin Philharmonic in 1932 —a concert at which Furtwängler gave the world premiere of Hindemith's *Philharmonic Concerto* written for that occasion—he was presented with the Goethe Medal, a new decoration just established by President von Hindenburg and the Weimar Republic for outstanding contributions to the arts and sciences.

He was the musical idol of Germany. The reason was explained by Henry Pleasants in the New York *Times:* "Although he lives . . . in the twentieth century, he is a man of the nineteenth. This was the century of Germany's musical supremacy, and it was tempting for the Germans to see in Furtwängler a projection of that tradition into the present. They worshiped him accordingly, not just as a man or as a conductor, but as a symbol of the continuity of their musical culture."

There was an even more significant reason why Furtwängler enjoyed the adoration of his German audiences and audiences outside Germany partial to German music. In the classic and romantic literature from Haydn through Richard Strauss he had few rivals among conductors. In such music his conducting, as Harold C. Schonberg explained in *The Great Conductors,* "was marked by a feeling of space, by a bigness and nobility of concept. . . . His conducting was always dedicated to the service of the composer as he saw it; and what he was was not music in terms of historical accuracy . . . but in terms of expressive content." Schonberg then goes on to add: "One of the unforgettable things about his conducting was his ability to voice a chord, to make it ring with color and clarity . . . to float suspended and shimmering in the air. Another was his ability to phrase with an endless line without letting the rhythm sag. His was not a style that could be imitated." To Paul Hindemith, Furtwängler "possessed the great secret of proportion. . . . He understood how to interpret phrases, themes, sections, movements, entire symphonies and programs in artistic unities."

When Hitler rose to power early in 1933, Furtwängler was appointed vice-president of the Culture Chamber *(Kulturkammer)* and Hermann Goering gave him an appointment as Prussian Councilor of State *(Staatsrat).* Furtwängler indulged himself in the naive belief that coexistence between himself and the making of great music and the Nazi regime and its ideology was possible. But he was too apolitical and too little in sympathy with the Nazi racial ideals to be a Nazi. For a while his career was marked by a struggle to reconcile his own artistic integrity with that of the Nazi *Kulturkammer.* Soon after the Reichstag fire he invited world-famous Jewish-born musicians—Yehudi Menuhin, Artur Schnabel, Bronislaw Hubermann, among others —to appear as guest artists with the Berlin Philharmonic, but they refused to come. When Thomas Mann, who had voluntarily exiled himself from Germany as a protest against the Nazis though he himself was not a Jew, asked Furtwängler: "How can Beethoven be played in Himmler's Germany?" (Himmler was the head of the Gestapo), Furtwängler replied hotly, "Where is the music of Beethoven needed more than in Himmler's Germany?" He treated the Jewish musicians in his orchestra with respect, though their position in Germany was becoming increasingly insecure; and eventually when their lives were in danger, he helped some of them escape from the country.

He continued to make music in Germany and tried to ignore what was happening politically and racially. He was a vain man and proud of the fact that he was the foremost conductor in Germany; he was a German chauvinist and as such tended to minimize the atrocities perpetrated in the name of the greater glory of Germany. As an idealistic musician, he sincerely felt that it was his duty, in such difficult times, to keep on making the best possible music—that music and politics had to be kept strictly separate at all costs. He wrote to Dr. Paul Joseph Goebbels, chief Nazi propagandist, on April 12, 1933: "When the fight is directed against the real artist, it is against the interest of culture as a whole."

It was not long, however, before he was sucked into the political and social quagmire that was Nazi Germany and almost destroyed by it. Direct conflict with the Nazi authorities came in 1934 when he announced he would conduct the world premiere of Hindemith's opera *Mathis der Maler* at the Berlin State Opera. In addition to the fact that the Nazi authorities looked with disfavor upon Hindemith because he was a modernist (or, in their description, "degenerate") composer and because he was married to a Jewess, there was the delicate subject matter of the opera itself which, the Nazis felt, might prove inflammatory: the uprising of peasants against the oppressive tyranny of the Church in 1524. Nazi officials informed Furtwängler that he was not allowed to perform the opera without Hitler's personal permission. Furtwängler replied that in matters of music he and he alone must make the final decision.

Before the opera was produced, Furtwängler conducted on March 12, 1934, the world premiere of the symphony *Mathis der Maler,* whose music was derived from the operatic score. This was an open act of defiance on Furtwängler's part and the audience, who readily recognized it as such, gave him a thunderous ovation. Encouraged by this audience reaction, Furtwängler went on with his plans to stage the Hindemith opera. Meanwhile, on November 25, 1934, he published an article in the *Deutsche Allgemeine Zeitung,* "The Hindemith Case," in which he strongly espoused the cause of Hindemith and the opera. On the evening of the day on which this piece appeared, he conducted a performance of *Tristan and Isolde* at the Berlin State Opera. Once again the tumultuous reception he was given was as much testimony of the audience's appreciation of his bold opposition to the Nazi authorities as it was to the quality of his performance. Late that night Goering telephoned Hitler, insisting that Furtwängler was endangering the authority of the state, and received Hitler's direct order that the opera be banned.

With his musical authority thus compromised, Furtwängler resigned as music director of both the Berlin Philharmonic and the Berlin State Opera—hardly expecting, it must be confessed, that his resignation would be accepted. Not only was his resignation accepted, Furtwängler's passport was withdrawn, making it impossible for him to leave the country. His letters of appeal and telephone calls to the leaders of the Nazi party went unanswered. Those in power who had once fawned over him ignored him.

Furtwängler made a hasty retreat, informing Goebbels that he regretted his recent actions and that he fully recognized the right of Hitler to issue decrees on artistic as well as social and political matters. This brought about his reinstatement. By late April 1935 he was back at his post with the Berlin Philharmonic, his first return concert on April 25 attended by Hitler, Goering, Goebbels, and other high Nazi officials. He now stood ready to cooperate fully with the artistic and racial policies of the government:

When he visited Budapest with the Vienna Philharmonic in January 1936 he refused to perform a symphony by Mendelssohn because the composer had been born a Jew. This and other gestures of collaboration led the Nazi officials to restore Furtwängler to his position as music director of the Berlin State Opera in March 1936. In December 1939, after the annexation of Austria by Nazi Germany, he was appointed Director of Musical Life in Vienna in an attempt by the Nazis to rehabilitate the musical forces of the city which had been sadly depleted through Aryanization.

Because of his close ties with both the Nazi government and Nazi ideologies, Furtwängler became the center of a storm when, early in 1936, the New York Philharmonic announced that he had been appointed permanent conductor of the orchestra, succeeding Toscanini. The protests from trade unions, the American Federation of Musicians, the American Federation of Labor, and those with strong antifascist sentiments grew so vociferous and embarrassing that on March 15, 1936, Furtwängler, then on vacation in Egypt, wired the management of the Philharmonic that he could not accept the post. "Political controversy is disagreeable to me," he said. "Am not a politician but exponent of German music which belongs to all humanity regardless of politics. I propose postpone my season in interest of Philharmonic Society until the time public realizes that politics and music are apart."

The stigma of the swastika continued to haunt Furtwängler. When he conducted Beethoven's Ninth Symphony at the Salzburg Festival in the summer of 1937, Toscanini refused to have any personal contact with him. Then, when the two met at a reception, Toscanini told him: "I have always thought that a man who gives assent to a system that persecutes every independent-minded man and woman cannot interpret Beethoven's symphonies truly. You Nazis have banned all manifestations of the spirit, leaving nothing but forced rhythms and an excessive display of strength. And that is precisely what you did the other day with Beethoven's Ninth Symphony!"

During World War II Furtwängler continued conducting in Germany. With the war's end, and the occupation of Germany by the American armed forces, he still remained suspect because of his Nazi affiliations. He went to

Switzerland where he remained in temporary retirement for a year. Then, in 1946, he went back to Germany where, in December, he appeared before a seven-member board in Berlin created to decide his guilt or innocence. At these hearings it was proved that he had never been a member of the Nazi party, that he had used his influence to keep Jewish musicians in the orchestra and opera house, that he had in fact saved five of his Jewish musicians from arrest at the risk of his own safety. The board then exonerated him and the Allied denazification committee in Berlin concurred.

Now able to resume his professional life in Germany, Furtwängler conducted a concert of the Berlin Philharmonic in May 1947 under the sponsorship of the United States Government. He was given a hero's acclaim. Within a few months he was allowed to assume his post as music director of the Berlin Philharmonic, to make guest appearances with that orchestra in England and France, and to become the principal conductor of the revived Salzburg Festival.

In 1949 the Chicago Orchestra made offers to Furtwängler to become its music director. Once again the public refused to forget the past. The clamor against Furtwängler's appointment swelled to such proportions that he politely declined to go to the United States for a permanent post. He concentrated his activity in Europe for the next few years where his dominant position among the world's conductors remained undisputed.

When the Berlin Philharmonic Orchestra was scheduled to make its first tour of the United States in 1954, Furtwängler was announced as its conductor. But before the tour got under way he died of pneumonia in a sanatorium in Eberstein, near Baden-Baden, Germany, on November 30, 1954. When the orchestra made its first American appearances—in Washington, D.C., late in February 1955 and in New York on March 1—its conductor was Herbert von Karajan.

After the dissolution of his marriage to Zitla through divorce, Furtwängler married Elisabeth Albert in 1943; they had one son, Andreas. In addition to a house in Berlin, the Furtwänglers maintained a summer place on the Tegernsee in Germany and a home in Clarens, Switzerland, where Furtwängler could enjoy swimming, sailing, and riding horseback. Thoroughly disciplined in his way of life, as in music, he never

smoked or indulged in alcoholic drinks. He ate lightly, avoiding meats, and was partial to fruits and fruit juices. His passion for art invariably brought him to the leading museum of whatever city he was visiting: When he went to London for the first time, the first place he visited was the British Museum to view its collection of Greek vases and Elgin marbles.

When he went to a rehearsal, he always rushed to the stand with baton raised in hand, as if impatient to begin work. "A rehearsal with Furtwängler," said his one-time concertmaster Henry Holst, "was always a very exciting experience, partly because he demanded the utmost concentration from his players, and partly because his beat often lacked that 'flick of decisiveness' which will help enforce precision in an ensemble. That kind of precision he did not like: he wanted the precision that grew out of the orchestra, from the players' own initiative as in chamber music."

Herbert von Karajan, in an interview published in the *Saturday Review* in 1963, expressed the opinion that Furtwängler "was the first conductor who divided the responsibility for the interpretation between himself and the orchestra. Under him the Berlin Philharmonic learned to make music in the way a string quartet does. Forcing the orchestra to take the initiative and to make its own decisions in changing from one episode to the next, however, was sometimes at the risk of imperfect ensemble."

Furtwängler was the composer of four symphonies, two violin concertos, a piano concerto, and other works. A collection of his essays on music, originally published in Zurich in 1948, appeared in English in 1954 under the title *Concerning Music*. He was also the author of *Ton und Wort* (1954) and *Der Musiker und sein Publikum* (1954).

ABOUT: Blaukopf, K. Great Conductors; Geissmar, B. Two Worlds of Music; Herzfeld, F. Wilhelm Furtwängler, Weg und Wesen; Riess, C. Furtwängler, Musik und Politik; Schrenck, O. Wilhelm Furtwängler; Siebert, W. Furtwängler, Mensch und Künstler.

Gabrilowitsch

Ossip Gabrilowitsch

1878–1936

OSSIP GABRILOWITSCH

Ossip Salomonowitsch Gabrilowitsch, pianist and conductor, was born in St. Petersburg, on February 7, 1878, the youngest of four children to Solomon (a lawyer) and Rose Gabrilowitsch. His parents, both of whom had a gift for music and art, early recognized in Ossip unmistakable signs of musical talent. Ossip could sing songs in perfect pitch when he was three and at four began showing such an interest in the piano that before long his brother, George, began giving him lessons. Under George, Ossip made such rapid progress that he had to be given more experienced and advanced instruction. At ten Ossip played for Anton Rubinstein, who said: "Of course he must become a musician, for he will be among the great." At Rubinstein's recommendation, Ossip was enrolled in the St. Petersburg Conservatory in 1888. During the next six years he studied the piano with Victor Tolstov and with Rubinstein and composition and orchestration with Anatole Liadov and Alexander Glazunov, among others. His courses at the Conservatory were supplemented at home with lessons in languages, history, and mathematics. Almost as soon as he had entered the Conservatory, he was honored by being asked to give a concert, a privilege extended only to the most gifted Conservatory students; and while attending the Conservatory he gave numerous concerts at exclusive salons and social gatherings.

He was graduated from the Conservatory in 1894, with the Rubinstein Prize in piano playing. Rubinstein now suggested that he go to Vienna for further study with Theodor Leschetizky. To prepare himself, Ossip received lessons in the Leschetizky method from Anna Essipoff, a piano teacher who had formerly been married to Leschetizky.

In 1894 Ossip's mother took him to Vienna where he was Leschetizky's pupil for two years. In October 1896, in Berlin, Ossip gave his first professional concert. "A new star has arisen on the musical horizon," wrote one Berlin critic. Three more recitals followed, and then an appearance with the Leipzig Gewandhaus Orches-

---

Gabrilowitsch: gä brĭ lŭ′ vĭch

tra conducted by Arthur Nikisch. An extended tour later carried him through Austria, Russia, France, and England.

One evening in 1898 Leschetizky invited Gabrilowitsch to dine with him at the Hotel Metropole so that he might meet the American writer Mark Twain, then visiting Europe. This was Gabrilowitsch's first meeting with Mark Twain's daughter, Clara Clemens, a young and gifted singer who had gone with her father to Vienna to receive some piano instruction from Leschetizky. Clara Clemens recalled her first impression of Gabrilowitsch: "He shone like a lamp in a cave. If he laughed, one laughed, too. But I instinctively resisted his charm, his magnetism, as one shrinks from excess of anything. ... His hair was like my father's, curly and abundant, though very dark; his face and hands would please a sculptor."

Their second meeting took place at Leschetizky's class where Clara played the Mendelssohn Concerto No. 1, with Leschetizky providing an accompaniment on the piano. When the orchestral preface ended and the time came for Clara to begin playing the solo part, she froze in her seat, dropped her hands, and would not play. Her embarrassment was heightened by the outburst of laughter in the room. But she recovered and played the concerto without any lapses. Gabrilowitsch, who was in that class, told her: "You played the slow movement beautifully." He invited her to have dinner with him that evening.

For several years—since Gabrilowitsch was

274

continually on tour and Clara Clemens was located first in London and then in New York—their personal meetings were few, but they kept in touch with one another. On one occasion Gabrilowitsch sent her the gift of a song he had written for her, "Wasserfahrt," words by Heine.

Gabrilowitsch's American debut took place in New York on November 12, 1900, when he performed Tchaikovsky's Piano Concerto No.1 as soloist with the New York Symphony under Walter Damrosch. That performance was only moderately successful. To Richard Aldrich, writing in the New York *Times,* he seemed "a youth of poetic and introspective temperament somewhat too much disposed to an analytic method, to dissecting and laying bare the structure of the music that he played. His style seemed, as it were, prematurely ripened; we miss impulsiveness and turbulence of youth in the self-contained and reflective manner of the young man." But when Aldrich heard Gabrilowitsch again, this time at a recital on December 4, 1902, he noticed that the artist had developed "a freer and broader style, and he is showing the strong and vigorous promptings of a truly musical nature, that are filling his playing with life and emotional power."

That concert on December 4 took place during Gabrilowitsch's second tour of the United States. He returned to America in 1906, 1909, 1914, 1915, and 1916. By the time his 1916 tour took place he was considered by both the critics and the audiences to be among the piano virtuosos of the time. Already he was known as the "poet of the piano" because of the beauty of his tone, the sensitivity of his touch, his romantic outlook, and his ability to penetrate to the deeper content of a musical composition. Already in 1906 a critic of the *Deutsches Volksblatt* had singled out some of the qualities that endeared Gabrilowitsch to his audiences, speaking of his "singing touch, shadowlike pianissimos, and the power that never seems to force itself upon one."

In 1905 Gabrilowitsch went to Leipzig to study conducting with Arthur Nikisch. One year later the pianist served his baton apprenticeship by conducting concerts in Paris, Vienna, and Manchester. His ambition to become a conductor did not impede his progress in the concert hall as a piano virtuoso; his appearances as a recitalist and as a guest performer with orchestras were worldwide.

When Gabrilowitsch was in New York early in 1909, he had to undergo a serious operation and for a time his life was in danger. He convalesced slowly at the country home of the Mark Twains during which time a tender friendship between him and Clara blossomed into a love affair. On October 6, 1909, Gabrilowitsch and Clara Clemens were married in Redding, Connecticut. They spent their honeymoon in Atlantic City, New Jersey, before embarking for Europe. From 1910 to 1914 they lived in Munich, where Gabrilowitsch conducted the Konzertverein Orchestra. In the years 1911–1914 in Europe he performed on the piano a series of six historical concerts tracing the development of piano music from Bach to the twentieth century; he repeated this cycle in several American cities in 1914–1915. Many years later, in 1934–1935, he appeared as a soloist with the National Orchestral Association in New York in a four-concert cycle presenting sixteen piano concertos.

In 1914 the Gabrilowitsches returned to the United States, establishing permanent residence in New York with their only child, Nina. In 1921 Gabrilowitsch became an American citizen —on April 11.

He made his American debut as a conductor in New York on December 13, 1916, with a pick-up orchestra in an all-Tchaikovsky program in which he conducted the *Symphonie Pathétique* and *Francesca da Rimini* and performed and conducted the Piano Concerto No.1. "He showed," said Richard Aldrich in the New York *Times,* "that he has in him that which makes conductors of the finer grain. There is the command of the technique of the art, a full knowledge of what he wants and the ability to obtain it; a firm, decisive and significant beat, elastic and comprehensive, sometimes a beat of figures, phrases and outlines, but fitted for the end to be obtained; a full knowledge of the score, which was in his head last evening, for he conducted without the printed notes. . . . There is also a fine intelligence, musical understanding and a sense of the fitness of things."

In 1918 Gabrilowitsch was appointed principal conductor of the Detroit Symphony, which he led up to the time of his death. Under his baton, the Detroit Symphony outgrew its former provincial status to become an orchestra of technical and artistic authority. From 1928 to 1931 he also shared the podium of the Philadelphia Orchestra with Leopold Stokowski. In addition to his conducting activities, Gabrilowitsch continued to perform as a pianist. In Detroit, he made it a practice to open and close each symphony season with a concert featuring himself as the soloist, and he continued to concertize in recitals and to perform as guest soloist with other orchestras, both in the United States and in Europe. In addition, on several occasions he appeared with the Flonzaley Quartet, and he gave memorable two-piano concerts with Harold Bauer and served as accompanist at his wife's vocal recitals.

Gabrilowitsch conducted his last concert on March 14, 1935, in Detroit. The program ended with the *Symphonie Pathétique.* He suffered an intestinal hemorrhage on March 23, 1935, the night before the last of his historical concerto series in New York on March 23, 1935. In spite of this he insisted on giving that concert. Afterwards he had to be hospitalized. A scheduled performance with the New York Philharmonic under Toscanini, in which he was to perform Brahms's Concerto in B-flat major, had to be canceled.

Gabrilowitsch was operated on for cancer. He spent his last weeks learning some piano music he had never played. Just before his death he listened to a recording of Mozart's String Quartet in G major. He died on September 14, 1936. At his request the Detroit Symphony Orchestra performed Schubert's *Unfinished Symphony* and the "Liebestod" from Wagner's *Tristan and Isolde* at the funeral services. In accordance with his wishes no eulogies were given at the services. He was buried in Woodlawn Cemetery in Elmira, New York, in the plot of the Clemens family.

ABOUT: Clemens, C. My Husband Gabrilowitsch; Mason, D. G. Music in My Time; Schonberg, H. C. The Great Pianists.

Johanna Gadski

1872–1932

Johanna Emilia Agnes Gadski, Wagnerian soprano, was born in Anclam, Pomerania, Germany, on June 15, 1872. At ten she began voice study with Schroeder-Chaloupka at Stettin. There, two years later, Johanna made her sing-

Gadski: gät′ skē

JOHANNA GADSKI

ing debut at a public concert. In May 1889 she sang her first opera role at the Kroll Theatre in Berlin, the title role of Lortzing's *Undine.* She sang principal roles in *The Magic Flute, Der Freischütz,* and *Don Giovanni,* among other operas, at the Kroll during the summers of 1889–1903 and during the winters sang in opera houses in Stettin (1889–1890 and 1891–1892), Mayence (1890–1891), and Berlin (1893–1895). In 1894 she toured Germany and Holland in concerts. On November 11, 1892, she married Lieutenant Hans Tauscher, a German military man, who later became a corporation president in New York; they had one child, a daughter, Charlotte.

Walter Damrosch, then forming his own Wagnerian opera company in the United States, brought her to America as Elsa in *Lohengrin* on March 1, 1895. She continued appearing with the Damrosch company for the next three seasons, not only as Elsa but as Brünnhilde in *Die Walküre* and *Die Götterdämmerung,* Eva in *Die Meistersinger,* and Sieglinde in *Die Walküre.* On February 11, 1896, in Boston, she created the role of Hester Prynne in the world premiere of Walter Damrosch's *The Scarlet Letter.*

Her first appearance with the Metropolitan Opera company was at a Sunday evening concert on December 11, 1898. After appearing as Elisabeth in *Tannhäuser* on December 28, 1899, while the Metropolitan Opera was on tour, she sang in her first New York production at the Metropolitan Opera on January 6, 1900, as Senta in *The Flying Dutchman.* W. J. Henderson wrote in the New York *Times* that "her sincere style and her sympathetic voice gave much pleasure to the audience. . . . She sings with much tenderness at times, and her personality is pleasing." Six days later she sang the role of Elisabeth in *Tannhäuser*, then on January 31 the role of Sieglinde in *Die Walküre* and on February 2 Eva in *Die Meistersinger*. During the next three seasons she distinguished herself particularly as Brünnhilde in *Die Walküre*, on November 25, 1903 (the same performance in which Olive Fremstad made her Metropolitan Opera debut as Sieglinde); in *Siegfried* on January 18, 1904; and in *Die Götterdämmerung* (first time, on tour, on March 26, 1904). Between 1899 and 1904 she was also heard in New York as Senta in *The Flying Dutchman*, Donna Elvira in *Don Giovanni*, Elsa in *Lohengrin*, Valentine in *Les Huguenots*, Aida, Santuzza in *Cavalleria Rusticana*, Pamina in *The Magic Flute*, Ero in Mancinelli's *Ero e Leandro*, Micaëla in *Carmen*, Anna in Boieldieu's *La Dame Blanche*, and the Countess in *The Marriage of Figaro*. On March 11, 1903, she appeared as Roschen in the American premiere of Ethel Smyth's *Der Wald*. She was not at the Metropolitan from 1904 to 1907.

In 1899 she made her debut at the Bayreuth Festival as Eva, and at Covent Garden in London that same year as Elisabeth. She continued to appear at Covent Garden in major Wagnerian soprano roles through 1901. She was one of the star performers at the Wagner-Mozart Festival at the Munich Royal Opera in 1905 and 1906, and in 1906 she sang Donna Elvira at the Salzburg Festival (she returned there four years later as Pamina).

During these years she was also advancing her career as a recitalist. Between 1904 and 1906 she made two American transcontinental tours in concerts, distinguishing herself as an interpreter of *Lieder*. Her first New York recital appearance after leaving the Metropolitan Opera was at Carnegie Hall on November 10, 1904. Richard Aldrich wrote in the New York *Times*: "The qualities that have contributed to her success as a dramatic singer are also potent in giving artistic value to her singing of songs. She is, first of all, a singer in the real sense of the word; an uncommonly beautiful voice, in which the evidences of full control and skillful use are instinct, guided by intelligence and artistic understanding and she has sincere sentiment and a serious view of the artist's task."

In 1907 she returned to the Metropolitan Opera company, staying for a decade. To her Wagnerian roles she added Isolde in *Tristan and Isolde*, on February 15, 1907. In *The Story of the Metropolitan Opera: 1883–1950* Irving Kolodin writes that in her first Isolde at the Metropolitan she "hardly [had] the command of the part which was later to be hers." But in time she added dimension to her characterization and brought to it the splendor of her voice, becoming one of the great Isoldes. W. J. Henderson noted in the *Sun* that she never "sang the music with so much tenderness, with so much finish of phrase, tone and nuance" as when she appeared as Isolde on November 27, 1909, Toscanini conducting. Once again with Toscanini as conductor she was acclaimed for her performance of Euridice in Gluck's *Orfeo ed Euridice* on December 23, 1909. Her other new roles at the Metropolitan after 1907 were Marie in *The Bartered Bride*, Leonora in *Il Trovatore*, Agathe in *Der Freischütz*, the Princess in the American premiere of Ludwig Thuille's *Lobetanz* (November 18, 1911), and Frau Gertrud in the American premiere of Leo Blech's *Versiegelt* (January 20, 1912).

She announced her retirement from the Metropolitan Opera in 1917 because America's entry into World War I made her position in an American company untenable. She had previously been severely criticized for arranging a much publicized party at her home in 1915 to celebrate the sinking of the *Lusitania*, and she had often been quoted as making anti-American remarks. In addition, she was married to a reserve officer in the German army who was representing the Krupp interests and other munitions firms in the United States and who in 1916 had been accused, but acquitted of the charge, of trying to blow up the Welland Canal. (Soon after that, when the United States severed diplomatic relations with Germany, he returned to Germany under the protection of Count Johann-Heinrich von Bernstorff, who had been the German ambassador at Washington.)

Her final appearance at the Metropolitan Opera, on April 13, 1917, as Isolde, was the last presentation of a German opera at the Metropolitan for three years. W. J. Henderson, in the *Sun*, remarked that she was given "a generous but not remarkable reception." He added: "She declined to receive interviewers who wanted to ask her regarding her alleged anti-American sentiments, the word being given out that she 'maintained a dignified silence.' "

She had made 296 appearances with the Metropolitan in New York and 159 on tour. Returning to Germany, she lived in Berlin during the last years of the war. After the war she was heard for several seasons at Covent Garden. Then she toured the United States in recitals. In 1928 she formed the German Opera Company with which she returned to the American opera stage in tours between 1929 and 1931.

She died in Berlin on February 22, 1932, from complications which developed after an automobile accident.

Germany decorated Gadski with the Order of King Ludwig for Art and Science.

ABOUT: Kutsch, K. J. and Riemens, L. A Concise Biographical Dictionary of Singers.

AMELITA GALLI-CURCI

Amelita Galli-Curci

1882–1963

Amelita Galli-Curci (originally Amelita Galli), coloratura soprano, was born in Milan, Italy, on November 18, 1882. Her mother, the former Enrichetta Bellisoni, was Spanish, a descendant of the Di Luna family who are represented in *Il Trovatore.* An excellent musician from a family of musicians, Enrichetta early exposed her daughter to good music. Amelita's father, Enrico, an Italian, also saw to it that she got a well-rounded academic education at the International Institute and the Lyceum High School in Milan. As a young woman Amelita could speak five languages fluently: French, German, English, Italian, and Spanish.

She was enrolled in the Milan Conservatory where she specialized in piano as a pupil of Vincenzo Appiani. Upon graduating from the Conservatory in 1903 with the first prize in piano she was forced by her father's financial reverses to support the family by accepting a post as professor of the piano at the Conservatory instead of making plans to start a career as a virtuoso pianist.

Pietro Mascagni, composer of *Cavalleria Rusticana,* was a friend of the Galli family. One evening Amelita sang for him an aria from *I*

Puritani, and he urged her to begin thinking seriously of becoming a professional singer. Without taking any formal lessons, Amelita began to train herself vocally, recording her voice and studying her technical shortcomings. She never did have a teacher. Many years later, when she was famous, she liked to say she had learned to sing "from the birds of my Italy."

An orchestra conductor, hearing her sing "Caro Nome" from *Rigoletto,* recommended her to an impresario then looking for a competent but inexpensive singer to appear as Gilda in his forthcoming production of *Rigoletto.* She was engaged for a three-month season in Trani, southern Italy, for sixty dollars a month. There she made her operatic debut as Gilda in 1909. She went to the Teatro Costanzi in Rome the same year to repeat her performance as Gilda. In 1910 she made her debut at La Scala in Milan, and in 1912 she undertook her first tour of South America.

After completing a tour of South America in 1915, she decided to visit the United States on a sightseeing vacation. A singing teacher in New York, who had heard her in Italy, introduced her to Cleofonte Campanini, the music director of the Chicago Opera. Campanini engaged Galli-Curci for two appearances with his company at three hundred dollars a performance. She also sang for an executive of Victor Records who arranged to have her make her first American recordings.

When Galli-Curci made her American debut at the Auditorium Theater in Chicago on

Galli-Curci: gäl lē kōōr' chē

November 18, 1916, again as Gilda, few in the audience had reason to suspect that they were on the threshold of an unforgettable musical experience. As Edward Moore wrote in his history of the Chicago Opera: "We who went to the Auditorium that Saturday afternoon . . . were in an entirely calm, hopeful mood, expecting to hear just another performance of *Rigoletto*. For one scene and another ten or fifteen minutes of the next, that was all, just another performance. Then things began to happen. Suddenly a figure appeared from the stage door into the garden on the left side of the stage. An oval, medieval face, with . . . an ivory pallor, a gracious winsome manner, a throat from which poured the most entrancing tones this generation has ever heard." After singing "Caro Nome" she saw the audience rise to its feet and shout its approval. Following the performance, Campanini went to Galli-Curci's dressing room and tore up the contract she had signed. He offered her a new one for three seasons at a thousand dollars a performance.

On January 28, 1918, Galli-Curci made her New York debut, still as a member of the Chicago Opera, at the Lexington Opera House in the title role of Meyerbeer's *Dinorah*. It was a cold, snowy night, but in spite of the inclement weather the traffic to the theater jammed many streets and an extra cordon of policemen encircled the theater to keep the crowds in check. Within the theater there were boisterous ovations, especially after the rendition of the "Shadow Song." Geraldine Farrar, herself then one of the world's prima donnas, stood on her seat and cheered. The following morning some of the newspapers featured their reviews on the front page. The critic of the New York *Times* said: "The voice that this shouting audience heard for the first time is one of those voices that 'float.' At the end of its principal demonstration last night it wasn't a woman's voice but a bird's swelling throat. . . . In the limelight of the 'Shadow Song' it was bottled moonlight."

At her last appearance that season at the Lexington Opera House, "the audience refused to go home; stomping and cheering went on for thirty-two minutes," Francis Robinson reveals. "Finally, at five minutes before midnight, somewhere, somehow somebody located a battered old upright and wheeled it onto the bare stage. Mme. Galli-Curci in street clothes, seated herself at the

piano and played and sang 'Home, Sweet Home.' "

Though she had caused a sensation in New York as well as in Chicago, it took almost four years to bring Galli-Curci to the Metropolitan Opera. She was engaged after Caruso's death in August 1921 when the Metropolitan was hungry for a new box-office attraction. Her contract gave her a fee higher than that formerly earned by Caruso. And, as had previously been traditional with Caruso, she was the one who, on her debut, opened the season for the company on November 14, 1921, as Violetta in *La Traviata*. Suffering from excessive nervousness, she was not at her best that evening. The reaction of audience and critics was at best lukewarm, though W. J. Henderson in the *Sun* did notice (after pointing out her vocal defects) that her voice was "one of the most beautiful . . . this public has heard."

Three evenings later, however, she was in full command in the title role of *Lucia di Lammermoor*, and on November 26 she was a triumph as Gilda. She was subsequently heard as Rosina in *The Barber of Seville*, Mimi in *La Bohème*, the Queen in *Le Coq d'Or*, Juliet in *Romeo and Juliet*, and the title role in *Dinorah*. She had her audiences well in hand.

From 1921 to 1924 Galli-Curci was a regular member of both the Chicago Opera and the Metropolitan Opera. She resigned from the Chicago Opera in 1924 and remained at the Metropolitan as its leading coloratura soprano for the following six years. Again and again she proved to be a singer with "voice, skill, brains, and heart," as the Boston critic Philip Hale noted. In range, clarity and brilliance, and beauty of sound her voice was an incomparable instrument that, he added, "gushed forth coloratura passages. The high flute-like tones, all had warmth and a luscious quality which are personal traits of the operatic star."

"Her voice," wrote John Ardoin years later in *Musical America*, "was seamless, liquid, unforced and sweet, ranging over two octaves up to high F. . . . Technically there is no area in which Galli-Curci can be faulted. Her scales, arpeggios, trills and assorted fioriture can stand comparison with any soprano of the last fifty years and in many instances outclass the Lucias, Gildas, Aminas, and Lakmés which followed her."

She was also successful in the concert hall,

where her recitals were box-office magic. In 1925 she appeared in the Hollywood Bowl in California before twenty thousand people and her fee was one of the highest ever paid to an artist up to that time—fifteen thousand dollars. In London her first recitals were sold out months in advance. When she toured Australia and New Zealand for the first time, box-office records were continually broken.

Her recordings sold in the hundreds of thousands. When Victor issued her first two disks— the "Bell Song" from *Lakmé* and "Caro Nome" —they sold almost half a million disks in the first two months. The record sales kept swelling with each subsequent release. Among opera stars of the early 1920s only Caruso could outsell her.

On February 4, 1910, in Rome, she married Luigi Curci, Marquis of Simeri, a gifted painter. When this marriage was dissolved by divorce a decade later, Galli-Curci married her accompanist, Homer Samuels, on January 15, 1921, in Minneapolis. They built their first home, Sul Monte, in Highmount, in the Catskill Mountains of New York. There, during the summers, she delighted in gardening, mountain-climbing, and tending to her dogs and cats.

Disturbed by an ailment of the throat in 1930, Galli-Curci announced her retirement from the Metropolitan Opera. Her farewell performance took place on January 24, 1930, as Rosina in *The Barber of Seville.* She planned a two-year world tour in concerts and operas, but in Europe her throat ailment became aggravated, necessitating the cancellation of further appearances. She was operated on for a goiter of the throat in 1935 in Chicago. The operation proved successful and she announced her readiness to return to opera. On November 24, 1935, she made her second debut at the Chicago Opera, as Mimi. She was cheered but, as some critics pointed out, much more for her courage than for her singing. "It was all a sad mistake," commented Francis Robinson sadly. "The voice was thin and uncertain and many in the audience openly wept." After several appearances Galli-Curci had to concede that her career was over. She gave her last concerts in 1937. Then she went into retirement with her husband—after 1948 at Rancho Santa Fe in Westwood, California, where (as she once said) she could "converse with and caress the trees" and, on a clear day, could catch a glimpse of the distant Pacific Ocean from her patio. She and her husband became interested in metaphy-

sics, as followers of Paramhansa Yogananda, a Hindu mystic who had established an East-Indian Self-Realization Fellowship with headquarters at the Golden Lotus Temple at Encinitas.

Upon the death of her husband in 1956, Amelita Galli-Curci moved south to La Jolla, California, closer to the ocean she loved. She spent her last years in a house modeled after the Rancho Santa Fe, playing the piano and painting. Her canvases adorned the white walls of her house filled with treasures gathered over many years in different parts of the world.

She died in La Jolla on November 26, 1963, at the age of eighty-one.

ABOUT: Le Massena, C. E. Galli-Curci's Life of Song. *Periodicals*—Musical America, January 1964; Show, April 1964.

Rudolph Ganz

1877–1972

Rudolph Ganz, pianist and conductor, was born to Rudolph and Sophie Ganz in Zurich, Switzerland, on February 24, 1877. He attended the Zurich Conservatory from 1893 to 1896 studying the piano with Robert Freund and the cello and composition with Friedrich Hegar. It was as a cellist that Rudolph made his first public appearance; he was eight years old at the time. Two years later he gave his first concert as a pianist. Before continuing his concert career, he studied piano with Carl Eschmann-Dumur and composition with Ch. Blanchet in Lausanne. At seventeen, he appeared as a piano soloist with the Municipal Orchestra in Lausanne. He also studied piano with F. Blumer in Strasbourg; and, in Berlin, piano with Ferruccio Busoni and composition with Heinrich Urban.

In December 1899 he made his professional debut as a mature pianist, appearing as a soloist with the Berlin Philharmonic in three concertos: Beethoven's *Emperor,* Chopin's Concerto in E minor, and Liszt's Concerto in E-flat major. The critic of the Berliner *Morgenpost* wrote: "An even, all conquering technique, a beautiful large, warm, poetic tone, an infallible memory and absolute severity are the qualities which this great artist possesses in a most complete degree." Five

Ganz: gänts

RUDOLPH GANZ

than the qualities that penetrate into the deeper things of music."

He toured the United States in the years between 1905 and 1908, and Europe from 1908 to 1911. From 1912 on he was a familiar figure on all the major concert platforms in both the United States and Europe, an artist who kept growing in artistic stature and musicianship. His playing, one American critic said, was "characterized by clarity, the adjustment, the large cumulative effect, the weaving strand by strand, of a whole tonal web. . . . . He is not dull—far from it—to emotional content; but he also feels intellectual content. He gives music the thought that discovers and expresses the composer's thought. He does not hesitate to weigh his own playing with reflection."

In his concerts in the United States Ganz was responsible for presenting the American premieres of music by Debussy, Ravel, Bartók, Busoni, Dohnányi, Vincent d'Indy, Charles Martin Loeffler, and other twentieth century composers. His interest in contemporary music continued throughout his life. When he was seventy-five, he and his wife, Esther La Berge (a voice professor he had married on December 24, 1959, three years after the death of his first wife), performed some newly discovered songs by Anton Webern, the Austrian twelve-tone composer, at a Webern Festival in Seattle, Washington. Ganz also edited these songs for publication. Three years later in Chicago they gave a program of American songs that included compositions by the American composer John Cage. In addition to promoting new music in his own recitals and in concerts with his wife, Ganz helped to resurrect a repertory of piano music of the distant past, much of it little known to the general American music public when he reintroduced it.

In 1921 Ganz appeared as guest conductor of the St. Louis Symphony Orchestra. He made such a fine impression that in the fall of that year he was appointed its permanent conductor. He held this post six years, giving regular series of concerts in addition to children's concerts and touring with his orchestra throughout the Southwest and West.

He resigned his conducting post in St. Louis in 1927 to become vice president of the Chicago Musical College (which subsequently became a part of Roosevelt University). In 1953 he was appointed president. While holding these ad-

months later Ganz made his debut as a conductor with the same orchestra, leading the world premiere of his own Symphony No.1. He had not been scheduled to perform it, but the regular conductor of the orchestra turned his baton over to Ganz during the first rehearsal saying: "You take it. It's too modern for me."

On July 12, 1900, Ganz married an American concert singer, Mary Forrest. They went to the United States that year to live permanently. Their son, Anton, became a Swiss diplomat.

Ganz became an American citizen. On May 10, 1892, he made his American debut in Chicago with a piano recital. In 1901 he was made the head of the piano department of the Chicago Musical College, succeeding Arthur Friedheim, and for three years he withdrew from the concert scene to devote himself to teaching. But in 1904 he returned to the concert stage. Early in 1906 he appeared for the first time in New York City, as soloist with the New York Symphony Society under Walter Damrosch, in Liszt's Concerto in E-flat major. At that time, as Richard Aldrich remarked in the New York Times, Ganz "suggested powers that were quite out of the ordinary." Two months later, on March 21, he gave his first New York recital, a performance, Aldrich said, which "showed him to be possessed of a finely poetic feeling in certain ways, of a lively imagination and musical intelligence." Aldrich added: "He is more at home in music that demands primarily brilliance, speed, strength and the resources of a virtuoso rather ministrative posts he taught both piano and composition. At the same time he took on numerous assignments as a guest conductor of American orchestras, as well as of the London Symphony in England and the Paris Conservatory Orchestra in France. On May 11, 1939, he led the New York Philharmonic Orchestra in a program of Swiss music during the festivities attending the opening of the New York World's Fair. From 1938 to 1949 he led the Young People's Concerts of the New York Philharmonic, succeeding Ernest Schelling, and for a number of years up to 1949 he performed a similar service for the San Francisco Symphony.

When Ganz retired as president of the Chicago Musical College in 1954 he was named president emeritus. He continued to teach piano and composition several times a week. He suffered a stroke in the summer of 1966 but recovered sufficiently to be able to give from two to five lessons a week at his home on Lake Shore Drive in Chicago.

To celebrate his eightieth birthday in 1957, a concert hall in Chicago's Auditorium was dedicated in his name. His ninetieth birthday a decade later was commemorated with a dinner in his honor at the Chicago Musical College. When he was ninety-five, two retrospective concerts of his works were given at the Chicago Musical College. That same year, 1972, he died, in Chicago, on August 2.

For his services to French music he was made Officer of the Legion of Honor. He also received a number of honorary degrees from American universities, and Northwestern University presented him with its Centennial Award.

He was the composer of works for orchestra, piano and orchestra, solo piano, and voice. On January 19, 1933, he conducted the world premiere of his *Animal Pictures* with the Detroit Symphony, and on February 20, 1941, he performed his own Piano Concerto with the Chicago Symphony Orchestra, Frederick Stock conducting.

Late in his life Ganz updated Ernest Hutcheson's *The Literature of the Piano*. He also wrote a book of his own, *Rudolph Ganz Evaluates Modern Piano Music* (1968).

ABOUT: New York Times, February 19, 1967.

Mary Garden

1874–1967

Mary Garden, soprano, was born in Aberdeen, Scotland, on February 20, 1874. (Most reference books give 1877 as the year of her birth. But, in 1963, she was a patient at a hospital in Aberdeen and her birth year was recorded as 1874. This is the date that her closest friends have since maintained is the accurate one.) She was the daughter of Robert Davidson (a manufacturer of bicycles and an automobile salesman) and Mary Joss Garden. When she was six, Mary received her first music lessons on the violin. In 1881 her parents took her and her two sisters to Montreal, Canada, before settling in the United States—first in Chicopee, Massachusetts; then in Brooklyn, New York; and, in 1888, in Chicago. In Chicago, Mary attended the public schools and continued her music study with lessons on the piano and in voice. At fourteen she started to give vocal concerts at intimate parties. When she decided to cultivate her voice further, she became a pupil of Sarah Robinson Duff. At sixteen she participated in a performance of the Gilbert and Sullivan *Trial by Jury*.

With the financial support of both Sarah Duff and a Chicago patron, Mrs. David Mayer, Mary went to Paris in 1897 for additional vocal training. In Paris she passed restlessly from one fine teacher to another—Giovanni Sbriglia, Jules Chevallier, Jacques Joseph André Bouhy, Mathilde Marchesi, Lucien Fugère—dissatisfied with most of them, and most of all displeased with herself. When her funds were exhausted she pawned her jewels to pay for food and lodging, and it seemed that she would have to return to the United States a failure. At this point the American soprano, Sibyl Sanderson, who had created the role of *Thaïs* in Massenet's opera, became interested in her career. She invited her to live in her home and offered to sponsor her.

Through Sanderson, Garden met Albert Carré, manager of the Opéra-Comique in Paris. He recognized the charm and vitality of her personality and encouraged her to continue her vocal studies until he could find a proper opening for her in one of his productions.

That opening came on April 10, 1900, when at a scheduled performance of *Louise* the principal soprano was suddenly taken ill after the first

MARY GARDEN

two acts. Garden was called in to substitute. "My turn came and I went," she recalled later to an interviewer. "I summoned all my courage and said to myself, 'Mary, my girl, this is your chance. Take it!' I turned my back straight on the audience and waited. With the first note of 'Depuis le jour' I turned like a flash, and my first tones sang out free and clear above the orchestra. When I walked off the stage that night, I was no longer unknown."

She created a sensation not only because of the sensitive beauty of her voice but even more for her acting. She went on to appear as Louise more than a hundred times in Paris alone, as well as in London and Brussels.

She became a permanent member of the Opéra-Comique and acquired her own following in a repertory of French and Italian operas, including the world premiere of Pierné's *La Fille de Tabarin* on Febraury 20, 1901, in which she created the role of Diane, and the world premiere of Alfred Bruneau's *L'Ouragan* on April 29, 1901. Not long after that she helped shape opera history. On April 30, 1902, the Opéra-Comique presented the world premiere of *Pelléas and Mélisande*. Both Debussy and Carré had selected her for the principal female role over the violent objections of Maurice Maeterlinck, the author of the play, who wanted the French actress Georgette Leblanc for the part. When Maeterlinck first discovered that Garden had been chosen he threatened to beat Debussy and spoke of challenging him to a duel. He did none of these things, but he did everything in his power to discredit the opera and to create disturbances at the premiere.

There was, at first, mixed opinion about the opera, but not about Garden as Mélisande. She made this part her own. In spite of faulty French diction and limited vocal resources her portrayal of Mélisande, both vocally and histrionically, immediately became the yardstick by which all other Mélisandes were to be measured. Debussy wrote that during rehearsal time he rarely had to make any suggestions to her, so instinctively and completely did she understand both the music and the role. "That was the gentle voice I had been hearing within me," Debussy said, "faltering in tenderness, captivating in the charm for which I had scarcely dared to hope." In a copy of the published score which he presented to her, Debussy wrote: "You are the only Mélisande." Many years after the premiere, when Maeterlinck was induced to attend a Garden performance in this opera in New York, he told her: "You have found more in Mélisande than I ever dreamed of."

In addition to the more traditional repertory, Garden appeared in the world premieres of Massenet's *Chérubin* in Monte Carlo on February 14, 1905, and in Camille Erlanger's *Aphrodite* in Paris on March 27, 1906.

Through her appearances as Mélisande, Garden became an opera singer of international interest. Oscar Hammerstein engaged her for the Manhattan Opera House in New York, and there, on November 25, 1907, she made her American debut in the United States premiere of *Thaïs*, another role for which she will always be remembered. Some American critics hearing her for the first time complained that her voice was small and at times inadequate in technique. But they were fully aware that it had a beauty of sound and magnetic appeal all its own. As one American critic said at the time: "Through the medium of imperfect singing the natural beauty of her voice did shine forth."

Garden remained the principal soprano of the Manhattan Opera House until that company was dissolved. Vocally, some of her performances were better than others, but she never failed to make her presence in the theater felt strongly nor did she ever fail to flood the stage with glamour. One of her more striking performances was as Salome in Richard Strauss's opera on January 28, 1909, when she herself danced the Dance of the Seven Veils. Billy Sunday, the evangelist, attacked her performance as lascivious, but Garden considered it one of her best.

After the closing of the Manhattan Opera House, Garden joined the Chicago Opera in 1910, making her debut as Mélisande. Within the following few weeks she appeared as Louise and as Salome. Except for a brief interlude during World War I when she devoted herself to war work in France, Garden continued to appear at the Chicago Opera for the next nine years in a repertory covering thirty-two principal roles, thirty of which she sang in French even when the operas were Italian and the other members of the cast sang in the Italian language. She was also heard in the American premieres of Alfano's *Il Risurrezione* on December 31, 1925, and Arthur Honegger's *Judith* on January 27, 1927. On December 10, 1930, she appeared in the world premiere of Hamilton Forrest's *Camille,* an American opera which Garden had commissioned and in which she assumed the title role.

She became the artistic director of the Chicago Opera in January 1921, succeeding Cleofonte Campanini and becoming the only woman up to that time to head a major opera company. She held this post three years. Unfortunately, she allowed her personal prejudices and jealousies to dictate who should not remain with the company; this policy resulted in a major turnover of personnel. She was often accused of either favoritism or sheer caprice in her casting and of signing up more great artists than there were roles for them to perform. The opera house suffered deficits three times what it had previously known—one million dollars in a single season. The mounting criticism against her forced her resignation in 1923. At that time she said: "I am an artist and I have decided that my place is with artists, not over them." The opera company was reorganized in 1923, was renamed Chicago Civic Opera, and its artistic direction passed on to Giorgio Polacco. Garden resumed her status as a prima donna.

In 1930, Garden returned to the Opéra-Comique, where she stayed four seasons for intermittent appearances, the last in *Il Risurrezione* in 1934. After 1930 she made sporadic appearances in recitals both in Europe and the United States.

In 1935 she was appointed vocal adviser to Metro-Goldwyn-Mayer in Hollywood. In this post she was instrumental in uncovering new voices for the screen and served as technical adviser on film sequences utilizing operatic music. In 1935 she also gave master classes in voice at the Chicago Musical College. She would tell her pupils that once they had found their teacher, they must devote themselves completely to vocal study for three full years. "The first year the student is in a daze," Garden would explain. "The second year, she begins to work. The third year she is ready—or ought to be! In those three years, she must avoid gaiety, drinking, smoking and concentration on men. Friends she may have, but no marriage, no love affairs—nothing shattering. After she has arrived, she may do as she pleases; but for three years she must live as a novice to her art."

Garden returned to Aberdeen, Scotland, in 1939, intending to remain there in retirement. In 1941 she returned briefly to the stage, at Town Hall, New York, as Mélisande to Martial Singher's Pelléas, speaking (not singing) responses to his singing. In 1947 she began the first of many tours throughout the United States lecturing on opera; she also lectured at the Edinburgh Festival in Scotland in 1952. In 1954 she again visited the United States, this time to audition singers for the National Arts Foundation. The last two years of her life were spent at the House of Daviot, a nursing home in Aberdeen, where she died at the age of ninety-two on January 4, 1967.

Oscar Thompson wrote of Mary Garden in *The American Singer:* "Miss Garden's place in the hierarchy of singers remains one unique and not easily classified. . . . Histrionically, she was infallibly pictorial, sometimes devastatingly so, sometimes with an excess of pose. Again, her work was disturbingly irregular. Anyone who saw her in the same roles at intervals of several years, especially in those she had done so often as to have them become a matter of routine, must have noted the wide divergence between her best and her more commonplace performances of the same part. . . . Her Mélisande, in its early years particularly, stood alone. In *Thaïs,* she could be glamorously convincing or she could attitudinize the evening long. Her Louise was hectic and tame by turns. . . . Out of these contradictions arose an imperious something to dwarf them all. Mary Garden was Mary Garden."

Off stage as well as on it Mary Garden was *sui generis.* Though over the years she was pursued by the wealthy and the titled who showered her with jewels estimated at more than half a million dollars, and though she was often publicized for her involvements in numerous romances, she never married. To one interviewer she once disclosed that four men had been "important" in her life, but she stubbornly refused to identify them.

Her daily diet consisted of a single meal, plus twenty drops of iodine and a glass of milk before going to bed. Throughout her adult life she retained the weight of one hundred and twelve pounds because—so she said—in thirty years she had never partaken of a single supper.

She was honored by France with the ribbon of the Legion of Honor. A road over Iron Mountain to the Mt. Rushmore National Memorial in South Dakota was named the Mary Garden Way. She was starred in two silent motion pictures: *Thaïs* (1917) and *The Splendid Sinner* (1918).

ABOUT: Biancolli, L. and Garden, M. Mary Garden's Story. *Periodicals*—Etude, April 1952.

NICOLAI GEDDA

Nicolai Gedda

1925–

Nicolai H. G. Gedda (originally Nicolai Ustinov), tenor, was born in Stockholm on July 11, 1925, the only son of a Swedish mother, Olga Gedda Ustinov, and a Russian father, Michael Ustinov. (Nicolai assumed his mother's name, Gedda, out of deference to her Swedish homeland, when he began his operatic career.) His father was a schoolteacher who fought in the White Russian army and fled to Stockholm with his Swedish-born wife after the Russian revolution. In Russia he had been a baritone in the famous Don Cossack Choir, which toured the concert circuit. When Nicolai was five, his family moved to Leipzig, where his father found employment as a cantor and choirmaster of a Russian Orthodox church. Nicolai sang in the church choir and was a member of a children's vocal quintet. When his father discovered that his son had perfect pitch he gave him lessons on the piano, organ, and balalaika.

In 1934, after the Nazis came to power in Germany, the Gedda family returned to Stockholm. Nicolai became a soprano in the choir of a local Russian Orthodox church. At the same time he attended the Soedra Latin School where he had four years of Latin and a thorough grounding in French, German, and English. All this, supplemented by the Swedish and Russian he heard at home, made him a linguist. In later years he also mastered Italian and Spanish.

When he was sixteen his voice broke, and for two years he could not sing at all. Believing his future in music was gone, he went to work in a bank and was promoted to bookkeeper and administrator. Meanwhile he completed one year of military service driving a truck.

In 1948 one of the customers in his bank heard him sing and encouraged him to study with Karl-Martin Oehman. For three consecutive years Gedda won the Christine Nilsson Award. In 1950 he entered the opera school of the Stockholm Conservatory, supporting himself by working half days at the bank and then filling small-paying engagements as a singer. But even then he had no thought of becoming an opera singer. "I had a voice and I wanted to develop it," he later said. "But I wasn't thinking that I had to make a career. The talents that I had were discovered by my teachers and brought forward. That's how it started."

While still attending the Conservatory, Gedda made his opera debut on April 6, 1953, at the Stockholm Opera in the leading tenor role of Adam's *Le Postillon de Longjumeau*. At that time the British impresario and recording executive Walter Legge (husband of the singer Elisabeth Schwarzkopf) was in Stockholm to consult with Issai Dobroven, music director of the Stockholm Opera, about a Paris recording of *Boris Godunov.* While in Stockholm Legge auditioned several Swedish singers for possible roles in that recording. Legge himself told the rest of the story in a letter to *High Fidelity* magazine: "The first to sing to me (at nine thirty in the morning) was Gedda. . . . He sang the *Carmen* 'Flower Song' so tenderly, yet so passionately that I was moved almost to tears. He delivered the difficult rising scale ending with a clear and brilliant B-flat. Almost apologetically, I asked him to try to sing it as written—pianissimo, rallentando, and diminuendo. Without turning a hair he achieved the near miracle, incredibly beautifully and without effort. I asked him to come back at eight in the evening, and sent word to my wife that a great singer had fallen into my lap . . . that this twenty-three-year-old was the heaven-sent Dmitri for our *Boris.* . . . That evening Gedda sang the *Carmen* aria and two *Don Giovanni* arias for Dobroven, my wife and me, and I engaged him immediately." The *Boris Godunov* recording was the beginning of a recording career which, through the years and through more than a hundred albums, made Gedda one of the most widely recorded tenors in the world. His first albums (one of which was the Bach Mass in B minor conducted by Herbert von Karajan) helped bring him to international prominence.

Through Legge, Gedda was given an audition at La Scala. The managing director of La Scala told Legge that in all his years with that company no non-Italian singer had auditioned for him with such exquisitely clear and flawless Italian. Gedda was engaged, and in 1953 he made his La Scala debut as Ottavio in *Don Giovanni,* Herbert von Karajan conducting. On February 13 of the same year he appeared in the world premiere of Carl Orff's *Trionfo di Afrodite.* But before all this happened he had already made his debut in Rome in Stravinsky's *Oedipus Rex* over Radio Italiano.

The year 1954 saw his first appearance at the Paris Opéra, in *Faust* opposite Victoria de los Angeles. In subsequent performances at the Opéra he sang Tamino in *The Magic Flute* and Huon in Weber's *Oberon.* After signing a three-year contract with the Paris Opéra, Gedda made his home in Paris where he also appeared at the Opéra-Comique.

In 1954 Gedda gave his first performance at

Covent Garden in London in an English-language version of *Rigoletto.* Other appearances that contributed to his fame were those at the Salzburg Festival, where in the summer of 1957 he was acclaimed as Belmonte in Mozart's *The Abduction from the Seraglio* and in Rolf Liebermann's *School for Wives;* at the Aix-en-Provence festival in *The Abduction from the Seraglio, Così fan Tutte, Don Giovanni,* and a revival of Gounod's *Mireille;* and at the Vienna State Opera where he was a major success as Don José in *Carmen* in 1957.

He made his American debut with the Pittsburgh Opera on April 4, 1957, in the title role of *Faust.* During this first visit to the United States he also appeared with the Chicago Opera.

Primarily because of Gedda's excellent English diction, Rudolf Bing, general manager of the Metropolitan Opera, engaged him to assume the principal male role of Anatol in the world premiere of Samuel Barber's *Vanessa.* Gedda, however, made his Metropolitan Opera debut not in this new American opera but in the title role of Gounod's *Faust* on November 1, 1957. "A slim, personable chap with a very engaging stage presence, young Gedda revealed a pretty lyric tenor that, while essentially light in substance, was able to carry nicely to the audience," wrote Douglas Watt in the New York *Daily News.* "Best of all, he obviously enjoys singing a great deal and does so with a pleasant ease, phrasing his material in a personal but entirely musical manner." On November 13 Gedda appeared as Don Ottavio at which time Jay S. Harrison wrote in the New York *Herald Tribune:* "Nicolai Gedda was a rich-throated Ottavio, whose air ('Dalla sua pace') emerged like an endless silver thread, ready to coil with precisely the resilience demanded of the music." On January 15, 1958, Gedda created the role of Anatol in *Vanessa,* confounding "all theories," said Irving Kolodin in the *Saturday Review,* "by singing the English text more clearly than any of the natives."

Gedda's value to the Metropolitan Opera and to opera houses and festivals the world over lay not only in his beautiful voice and overall artistry but also in his versatility. He has mastered over eighty major roles, in every language in which opera has been written or translated. At the Metropolitan Opera he has performed, in perfect diction, in English-language versions of *The Magic Flute, The Gypsy Baron, Eugene One-*

gin, *Boris Godunov,* and *Alceste,* in which he has sung, respectively, Tamino, Barinkay, Lensky, Dimitri, and Admetus. Commuting between Paris and Milan he sang in *The Magic Flute* in French at the Opéra and in Italian at La Scala, in addition to performing this part just as handily in Swedish in Stockholm and English in New York. The wide range of his versatility became increasingly obvious through his years at the Metropolitan Opera where he was heard, in addition to the roles already mentioned, as the Singer in *Der Rosenkavalier,* Hoffmann in *The Tales of Hoffmann,* Des Grieux in *Manon,* Alfredo in *La Traviata,* Pinkerton in *Madama Butterfly,* Nemorino in *L'Elisir d'Amore,* Pelléas in *Pelléas and Mélisande,* Elvino in *La Sonnambula,* Kodanda in Menotti's *The Last Savage,* Don José in *Carmen,* Romeo in *Romeo and Juliet,* Edgardo in *Lucia di Lammermoor,* Rodolfo in *La Bohème,* Herman in Tchaikovsky's *The Queen of Spades,* and Arrigo in *I Vespri Siciliani.* He has sung Lohengrin in Stockholm and the title role in Berlioz' *Benvenuto Cellini* in Amsterdam, Geneva, and at Covent Garden. With the American Opera Company he has performed in concert versions of *The Merry Widow, I Puritani,* and *Benvenuto Cellini.* On March 16, 1976, he assumed for the first time the title role in *Werther,* with the Washington (D.C.) Opera Society.

He supplemented his performances at the Metropolitan Opera, La Scala, the Paris Opéra, and Covent Garden with guest performances at the Vienna State Opera, the Vienna Volksoper, the Deutsche Oper in Berlin, the Hamburg Opera, the Munich Opera, the Stuttgart Opera, the Budapest Opera, Rome Opera, San Carlo in Naples, Monte Carlo Opera—among other companies—and at festivals at Salzburg in Austria, Aix-en-Provence and Orange in France, and the Florence May Music Festival in Italy. Some of his other roles have been Tebaldo in Bellini's *I Capuleti ed i Montecchi,* Lord Arthur in *I Puritani,* Faust in Berlioz' *The Damnation of Faust,* Nadir in Bizet's *Les Pêcheurs de Perles,* Lionel in *Martha,* Sobinjin in *A Life for the Tsar,* Pylades in Gluck's *Iphigénie en Tauride,* Vincent in *Mireille,* Tristan in Frank Martin's *Le Vin Herbé,* Raoul de Nangis in *Les Huguenots,* John of Leyden in *Le Prophète,* Ferrando in *Così fan Tutte,* Belmonte in *The Abduction from the Seraglio,* Idamante and Idomeneo in Mozart's *Idomeneo,* the title role in Pfitzner's *Palestrina,*

Cavaradossi in *Tosca,* Almaviva in *The Barber of Seville,* Eisenstein in *Die Fledermaus,* Flamand in Richard Strauss's *Capriccio,* Riccardo in *Un Ballo in Maschera,* Adolar in *Euryanthe,* Max in *Der Freischütz,* and Huon in *Oberon.*

Over a period of a quarter of a century Gedda has recorded more than one hundred and fifty albums, about fifty of them complete operas.

Gedda's first marriage took place in 1952 to Nadja Nova, a French pianist of Russian parentage. The marriage ended in divorce four years later. They had one daughter, Titiana. On February 21, 1965, he married Anastasia Caraviotis. She was a typist at the office of Capitol Records when he first saw her. "I said 'hello' and looked too deeply in her eyes," he recalls. "And that was it!"

A handsome man with blue eyes, wavy brown hair combed in an upward sweep, and an athletic build, Gedda has become something of a matinee idol among operagoers everywhere. His favored pastimes are going to the movies, sailing, skiing, fencing, playing table tennis, and reading books on psychiatry, history, and philosophy. The Geddas rent an apartment in New York City and own a house at Tolochenaz, Switzerland.

Gedda was appointed Royal Court Singer of Sweden by the king and in March 1966 was made an honorary member of the Royal Academy in Stockholm. He has been awarded the Vasa Order, Litteris et Artibus, by Gustavus VI, king of Sweden. And he was named Commander, Order of Dannebrog, by Frederik IX, king of Denmark.

ABOUT: High Fidelity, March 1973; New York Times, December 10, 1972; Opera News, January 14, 1961, April 13, 1968, February 18, 1978.

Elena Gerhardt

1883–1961

In her time Elena Gerhardt, mezzo-soprano, was one of the leading interpreters of the *Lied.* She was born in Leipzig, on November 11, 1883, the only girl in a family of eight children. Both her parents were musicians. At sixteen she entered the Leipzig Conservatory where she re-

Gerhardt: gār' härt

ELENA GERHARDT

mained three years as a voice student of Marie Hedmondt. During her first year at the conservatory her singing attracted the interest of Arthur Nikisch, the conductor who was then also the director of the Conservatory. He promised to accompany her on the piano when she gave her graduation recital. This occurred in 1903. On numerous occasions after that, in public concert auditoriums, Nikisch served as Gerhardt's accompanist. He also helped to train her in the art of musical interpretation and was a significant influence in her development as a singer of *Lieder*.

On the strength of her first public recital Gerhardt was engaged by the Leipzig Opera where during 1903–1904 she appeared twenty times in *Mignon* and *Werther*. Opera, however, did not appeal to her; she felt that the concert stage offered her far greater artistic satisfaction.

She gave concerts of German art songs throughout Germany in the early 1900s and was highly acclaimed for the sensitivity and subtlety of her interpretations. On June 11, 1906, she made her debut at Queen's Hall in London, Nikisch at the piano. This concert proved so successful she had to give another only two days later. The English critics echoed the opinion of Nikisch when he said that "Miss Gerhardt is the world's greatest *Lieder* singer."

Her American debut took place with a recital in Carnegie Hall, in New York, on January 9, 1912. "She soon made it clear that she is an artist of no uncommon fiber," wrote Richard Aldrich in the New York *Times,* "and that by her intelli-

gence and understanding, her musical feeling, she penetrated deeply into the essence of the German song." Her program was made up of songs by Schubert, Brahms, Richard Strauss, Robert Franz, and Hugo Wolf in which, as Aldrich said, she was "almost uniformly successful in finding beautiful, varied and characteristic expression."

During World War I and for a while afterwards Gerhardt was in temporary retirement. She emerged in 1922 with a concert in London. "In the interval," wrote an unidentified London critic, "her style has undergone a complete change. She is no longer so lavish of her great gifts, or carries her audience away by the sheer enthusiasm of her singing, but we have instead a more deliberate and mature art in which effects are carefully graduated and the interpretations controlled by a subtle and sure instinct for artistic fitness."

She continued giving recitals in the United States and Europe until about 1930. In several respects she was a pioneer among *Lieder* singers, being one of the first to devote entire programs to a single composer, and one of the first female singers to present Schubert's cycle *Die Winterreise,* usually reserved for male voices.

After 1930 she taught voice in Leipzig and London. In 1932 in Germany she married Dr. Fritz Kohl, business manager of a German broadcasting company. Because of his liberal political leanings he was faced with arrest early during the Nazi regime and he urged his young wife to escape from Germany. She fled to Holland in 1933, carrying with her only those belongings she could carry and ten marks in cash (which she was required to spend before passing the German border) and an additional fifty marks concealed in her hair. From Holland she went on to England, which was to become her permanent home, and there she waited for news of her husband's fate. The Nazis suddenly released Kohl and gave him a passport on condition that he return to Germany to stand trial whenever summoned. It was not long after he was reunited with his wife in England that Kohl was called back to Germany. At the trial he was acquitted of everything but minor misdemeanors. He was allowed to return to London (where he remained until his death in 1947), but all his property in Germany was confiscated.

In London Gerhardt continued her activity as a teacher of singing, both privately and at the

Guildhall School of Music. During World War II she returned to concert singing to help civilian morale with performances at the National Gallery in London, still confining her programs to *Lieder.* After World War II she became a British subject.

Elena Gerhardt died in London on January 11, 1961.

She was a woman of simple character who enjoyed housekeeping, sewing, cooking, and other domestic pursuits. Her embroidery work (particularly her needlepoint designs) was almost as famous as her singing among her intimate friends. She liked to play cards (bridge mainly) and golf. She had an enormous appetite for gourmet meals, and her parties in London were famous for her lavish table, laden with succulent food and pastries crowned by mounds of whipped cream.

Gerhardt compiled the anthology *My Favorite German Songs* (1915) and edited Hugo Wolf's songs (1932). She also wrote an autobiography, *Recital,* which was published in 1953.

ABOUT: Gerhardt, E. Recital.

Nicolai Ghiaurov

1929–

Nicolai Serge Ghiaurov, basso, was born in Velingrad, Bulgaria, on September 13, 1929. His father, George, was a sacristan. Although Nicolai sang in the church choir, his study of music began first with the violin and the piano, and proceeded later on with the clarinet. Acting came naturally to him. As a member of a drama group at school he showed such acting talent that he was chosen to perform in the local theater.

Only after his voice broke did he begin to think of training it, though his ambition at that time and for some years thereafter was to become a conductor. While he was doing military service he came to the conclusion that he had a voice well worth cultivating. With the help of the Bulgarian composer Petko Stainov, he gained admission to the Academy of Music in Sofia in 1949. There he specialized in voice. His talent brought him a scholarship for the Moscow Conservatory, where he remained five years, studying both voice and conducting. He

NICOLAI GHIAUROV

was graduated with highest honors in voice in 1955. That year he won a gold medal in a vocal competition in Warsaw and the Grand Prix in an international voice competition in Paris.

On July 11, 1955, he married Zlatina Christova Michaelova, a young concert pianist who gave up her own career to devote herself to her husband and their two children. Before the year was over he made his opera debut in Sofia as Don Basilio in *The Barber of Seville.*

In 1957 he made his first appearance at the Vienna State Opera, as Ramfis in *Aida.* A year later he appeared at the Bolshoi Opera in Moscow as Méphistophélès in *Faust,* following this with appearances there as Don Basilio and as Varlaam in *Boris Godunov.* Promoted to primo basso, he began to sing leading bass roles. He was assigned leading roles at La Scala after he appeared there in 1959 as Varlaam. At the Bolshoi and at La Scala, Ghiaurov extended his repertory to embrace the roles of King Philip II in *Don Carlo,* Padre Guardiano in *La Forza del Destino,* Zaccarias in *Nabucco,* Prince Gremin in *Eugene Onegin,* Marcel in *Les Huguenots,* Creon in Cherubini's *Medea,* the title role in *Don Giovanni,* and Prince Ivan Khovantsky in Mussorgsky's *Khovantchina.*

After successful appearances with the Sofia Opera in a tour of Germany, in Paris, and at Covent Garden in London where he made his debut as Padre Guardiano, Ghiaurov made his first American appearance in 1963, with the Chicago Lyric Opera. In the title role in Boïto's

Mefistofele he made an extraordinary impression with his singing and acting.

In 1965 at the opening performance of the Salzburg Festival in Austria he assumed for the first time the title role in *Boris Godunov,* Herbert von Karajan conducting. This performance—which tempted many critics to compare him to Chaliapin and to Alexander Kipnis—was repeated at the Salzburg Festival the following summer.

When Ghiaurov sang Boris in a concert performance of the Mussorgsky opera with the New York Philharmonic, Leonard Bernstein conducting, during the 1966–1967 season, Alan Rich called the performance "magnificent." Writing in the *Herald Tribune* he added, "Ghiaurov is one of the rare musicians who can crowd the full range of dramatic experience into the sound of his voice. . . . But the remarkable thing about him is the control he exerts over it, the way he can shade it down to the smallest whisper without once losing tone, the way it rings pure and true throughout its wide range." When Ghiaurov's recording of *Boris Godunov* was released by London Records in 1971, James Ringo, writing in *Opera News,* said: "For almost seventy-five years Feodor Chaliapin has cast a mighty shadow over Mussorgsky's music drama; most recent interpreters have felt constrained to fill in the title role's outline in a way remarkably similar to his. Nicolai Ghiaurov changed all that: approaching the music with an eye to fresh detail, he has come up with an interpretation every way his own, a powerful conception of the guilt-ridden, half-crazed czar which owed little or nothing to the work of his Russian predecessor."

His debut at the Metropolitan Opera came after several years of negotiations with Rudolf Bing, general manager, were finally completed following Ghiaurov's first appearance in Chicago. The debut took place on November 8, 1965, as Méphistophélès in *Faust.* "He not only has a remarkable voice, but he is also big in every way," said Harold C. Schonberg in the New York *Times.* "He has presence, the kind that Pinza and Chaliapin had, the kind that jumps over the footlights and seizes the listener in a palpable embrace. If the voice has any defect it is in the lower range, where it sounds just a shade thin and even uncomfortable. But around a 'C' it takes on strength, and from there it is a thing of glory." About Ghiaurov's impersona-

tion of Philip II on November 16, the critic of *Newsweek* wrote: "Ghiaurov stands alone among bassos in both sheer horsepower of his voice and the ease of his performance." In 1967 Ghiaurov was heard at The Metropolitan as Guardiano, and in 1968 as Fiesco in *Simon Boccanegra.*

In the fall of 1967 he went to Montreal to appear with the La Scala company at Expo '67 and on October 18 of that year he was heard in New York with other soloists and the La Scala chorus and orchestra in Verdi's Requiem conducted by Herbert von Karajan. In October and November he made his debut with the San Francisco Opera as Méphistophélès in *Faust.*

He sang major basso parts at the principal opera houses of Europe, including the Théâtre de la Monnaie in Brussels, the Munich Opera, the Hamburg Opera, the Verona Arena, the Monte Carlo Opera, Paris Opéra, and Bolshoi Opera. His roles included Sir George in *I Puritani,* Galitzky in Borodin's *Prince Igor,* Baldassare in *La Favorita,* the title role in *Don Quichotte,* Ramfis in *Aida,* Silva in *Ernani,* and Banquo in *Macbeth.* On November 6, 1976, he was heard with the Chicago Opera in one of the infrequent productions in America of *Khovantchina.* Birgit Nilsson has called his voice "an awe-inspiring instrument in an awe-inspiring personality."

In recognition of his contributions to the Vienna State Opera and the Salzburg Festival, Ghiaurov was awarded the title of *Kammersänger* by the Austrian government in 1977.

Ghiaurov and his family have residences in Milan and Sofia. Tall, well built, handsome, standing six feet two, he is physically as impressive offstage as on. He enjoys swimming, tennis, and riding horseback. He has been named National Artist of Bulgaria.

ABOUT: New York Times, November 14, 1965; Opera (London), October 1977; Opera News, November 20, 1965.

Dusolina Giannini

1902–

Dusolina Giannini, soprano, was born in Philadelphia, on December 19, 1902. Her father, Fer-

---

Giannini: jän nē′ nē

DUSOLINA GIANNINI

ruccio Giannini, was a well-known tenor, having sung in opera with Adelina Patti and having been in 1896 one of the first singers to record the human voice for the phonograph. Her mother, Antonietta, was a violinist and pianist.

Dusolina received her first music lessons from her father, who ran a theater in Philadelphia where Dusolina played small parts when she was nine and sang opera arias when she was thirteen. Serious music study, however, was not considered until one day when Marcella Sembrich heard her sing and encouraged her to consider a professional career. Giannini went to New York, where she studied voice for four years with Sembrich. Accident, rather than calculation, gave Giannini her first major public performance, together with national attention. Anna Case, the concert and opera soprano, was scheduled to sing with the Schola Cantorum in New York on March 14, 1923, when sudden illness prevented her from appearing. Kurt Schindler, the conductor of the chorus, in his search for a substitute, was advised by Sembrich to use Giannini. The following morning Giannini was famous. The newspapers reported at length how at the last moment, called upon to replace Case, she had proved herself to be a singer with a voice of unusual quality and range and with musicianship. Henri Verbrugghen, the conductor, immediately engaged her to appear with his orchestra, the Minneapolis Symphony. Many other engagements came her way, including concerts in London in 1924 and in Berlin one year later.

Daniel Mayer, the concert manager, arranged for her to appear with the Hamburg Opera in 1927 in the title role of *Aida*. Giannini was an even greater success as Aida than she had been in her New York debut. Appearances at the Berlin State Opera followed, as well as regular performances with the Hamburg Opera. In 1930 and 1931 she sang at Covent Garden in London, where she attracted particular attention for her performances as Donna Anna in *Don Giovanni*. In the years between 1931 and 1934 she was also heard in the major opera houses of Vienna, Geneva, Oslo, Monte Carlo, Nuremberg, Prague, Zurich, Australia, and New Zealand.

One of her triumphs was realized at the Salzburg Festival in the summer of 1934 as Donna Anna with Bruno Walter conducting. The foreign correspondent of the New York *Times* reported: "Vocally and dramatically it was an extraordinarily well-rounded and finely developed performance. . . . Virtually throughout the evening the soprano's vocal accomplishment was of uncommonly high order. It was Mozart singing such as is rarely heard these times, admirably encompassing the grand manner and essential style of music." At the Salzburg Festival in 1936 she appeared as Alice Ford in *Falstaff*, Toscanini conducting.

Her successes in Vienna in 1934 and subsequent years were no less impressive. "Adelina Patti in her prime would have seen glory everlasting in the reception Dusolina Giannini harvested from press and public," reported Herbert F. Peyser from Vienna to the New York *Times*. "The opera house was jammed to the walls on the evening of her appearance. The spell which she exercises on Viennese, as upon German, audiences has something hypnotic about it. She is certain of an almost hysterical acclaim. Whenever Giannini sings the population packs the place."

On February 12, 1936, she made her American opera debut in the title role in *Aida* at the Metropolitan Opera. Olin Downes wrote in the New York *Times* the following morning: "Hers is a temperament designed for the lyric stage. . . . Giannini acts by nature and has developed herself as an actress and a dramatic interpreter by ten-odd years of experiences of the lyric theater. Her Aida immediately struck the note of passionate feeling and a proud nature and maintained this throughout the opera."

She remained with the Metropolitan Opera

until 1941, distinguishing herself as Donna Anna, Santuzza in *Cavalleria Rusticana,* and Tosca as well. When she appeared for the first time as Santuzza, on February 3, 1938, some of the critics called her performance one of the best they had witnessed since Calvé and Destinn.

At the Hamburg Opera, where she had been a principal soprano since 1930, Giannini created on June 2, 1938, the role of Hester in the world premiere of *The Scarlet Letter,* an opera by her brother, Vittorio Giannini. In May 1937, in Vienna, she had also sung in the world premiere of another of her brother's compositions, a Requiem written in memory of their mother.

Giannini married Alan Richter on December 26, 1942; they lived for some years in Upper Darby, a suburb of Philadelphia. On February 21, 1944, she sang Tosca in the first opera performance by the New York City Opera, with whom she was subsequently heard as Santuzza and Carmen. A European tour in 1947 was followed by performances at the Berlin State Opera in 1949 and the Vienna State Opera in 1950. From 1962 on Giannini resided in Zurich, Switzerland, where she conducted an opera studio.

Though comparatively short and slight—only five feet two in height—Dusolina Giannini has always been a commanding figure on the stage. She once confessed that her main weaknesses were old earrings, dolls of all nationalities (she has assembled a sizable collection), and perfumes. She enjoys reading biographies and travel books and likes to paint.

ABOUT: Opera News, April 11, 1964.

Walter Gieseking

1895–1956

Walter Wilhelm Gieseking, pianist, was born in Lyons, France, on November 5, 1895, the son of Martha Bethke Gieseking and Wilhelm Gieseking, a German physician and entomologist, who was also an excellent amateur musician. Since his father's practice was in southern France, Walter spent his early years on the French and Italian rivieras. He was educated primarily by private tutors. "At the age of five," he once said, "I discovered I could read and

Gieseking: gē' zě kǐng

WALTER GIESEKING

write. I never needed to learn anything after that." Actually, his parents, faithful to their German heritage, would not allow him to go to the French public schools. Though Walter began playing the piano when he was about four, his formal training was delayed for a number of years. In 1911 the Giesekings left France for Hanover, Germany. There Walter studied the piano for three years with Karl Leimer, his only teacher. "One of the first things I learned from Leimer," he told an interviewer, "was to practice with my head as well as with my fingers, to concentrate intently on every note of the scale or arpeggio, to play with utmost accuracy."

In 1915, while still a Conservatory student, Gieseking gave a series of six concerts in which he performed all thirty-two piano sonatas of Beethoven—probably the first time that such a feat was accomplished by a Conservatory student. A debut in Berlin scheduled for that year was canceled when Gieseking was called into the German army during World War I. He served much of the time as regimental bandsman, often entertaining fellow soldiers by giving public concerts not only on the piano but also on the violin, viola, or any other musical instrument that was at hand.

When the war ended, Gieseking had to depend exclusively upon the piano for his livelihood since the French authorities had confiscated all the property the family owned in France, leaving them destitute. In Hanover, Gieseking became a teacher of the piano, charging about forty cents a lesson. At the same time he returned to the concert stage. Having already become deeply involved in the music of Debussy and Ravel, of which he was destined to become one of the world's great interpreters, he gave a recital in Hanover devoted exclusively to these two twentieth century masters. When he finally made his debut in Berlin in 1920 it was with a Debussy-Ravel program which proved so successful that he was called upon to give six more concerts that season. His reputation grew rapidly in Germany and spread to Paris and London where, beginning with 1923, his concerts placed him among the distinguished performers of twentieth century piano music.

His first American concert took place in New York on February 22, 1926. "Mr. Gieseking is an exceptional pianist and needed only the opening measure or two of the first number to prove it," wrote Francis D. Perkins in the *Herald Tribune.* "The skill, neatness and polish of his technique are truly remarkable. He played Bach and Scarlatti with a fluent evenness, an exceptional nicety and clarity of detail producing perfect cameos of sound." Commenting in the New York *Times,* Olin Downes said: "The introspection, the poignancy, the humor, the whimsy of Schumann . . . were conveyed with the touch and technical proficiency of a true artist."

In the years between 1926 and 1938 Gieseking toured the United States annually, performing in recitals and as a guest artist with the principal American symphony orchestras. His performances of Scarlatti, Bach, Mozart, and Beethoven became almost as famous as his interpretations of Ravel and Debussy. He was a supreme musical colorist who had mastered, as few had, the secret of the pedal. As a correspondent in London wrote to the New York *Times:* "His playing was capable of unusual degrees of subtle nuances. He never attacked the keyboard; instead he drew tone from it. He was not considered one of the great pianistic technicians, but his pianistic equipment was of extremely high order—more than enough to permit him to handle some of the most difficult works in the repertory. . . . When Herr Gieseking played Debussy and other French Impressionists it was as though a new dimension had been added."

Gieseking, his wife (the former Anna Maria Haake whom he married in 1925), and their two daughters lived in Wiesbaden atop a hill in a beautiful modern house constructed of glass and steel. During the summers he conducted piano classes in Wiesbaden in collaboration with his former teacher, Karl Leimer. In appearance Gieseking resembled more the successful broker than the musician. He was six feet tall and well built, with the physique of an athlete. Among his interests were gardening, tinkering with machinery, swimming, mountain climbing, and collecting butterflies.

Late in the fall of 1939 he planned his fourteenth tour of the United States, but with the outbreak of World War II the tour was canceled. Throughout the war Gieseking toured the Continent—mostly Germany, the occupied countries, and a few neutral nations. The almost two hundred recitals he gave were endorsed by the Nazi authorities. He was also called upon by the Nazi government to give special performances as a form of propaganda, and he did so in Turkey with a series of concerts in 1944. Thus he proved himself a ready and willing collaborator with the Nazis, with whose politics he was in total sympathy. He was the sponsor and coeditor of a Nazi music magazine and had requested membership in the Nazi Militant League for German Culture as early as 1933. When the Nazis demanded that he omit the music of Ravel and Debussy from his programs, he did so without the slightest protest. He refused to maintain association with his manager who was Jewish, and he always ended his letters with "Heil Hitler."

When the war in Europe ended and the Third Reich was defeated, Gieseking was kept under surveillance at his home in Wiesbaden. For a time early in 1945 he performed for the occupation forces and for wounded soldiers and gave public concerts in the American zone. By the fall of 1945, however, the American Military Government denied him the right to give performances because "he permitted himself to be used as a cultural agent of the Nazis." This blacklisting was objected to by the Russian, French, and British authorities. An intensive investigation of Gieseking's wartime activities was made in 1946; in the course of this Gieseking protested he had never been a Nazi and was not concerned with politics. In December 1946 the blacklisting was officially lifted by the United States Information Control Division and he was cleared by a German denazification court. In 1947 he resumed his concert activity with performances in all the occupation zones of Germany, as well as in Switzerland and Italy. On December 21,

1947, he made a triumphant return to Paris, performing concertos by Mozart and Liszt with the Colonne Orchestra conducted by Paul Paray. Three weeks later, on January 17, 1948, over one thousand were turned away from the box office of the Palais de Chaillot where Gieseking was giving his first postwar recital in France. With equally successful performances in Holland, London, and South America, and with his first postwar recordings in London, his career was once again in high gear. His fourteenth tour of the United States was rescheduled—for early 1949.

However, his wartime activities had not been forgotten in the United States. In its music section the New York *Times* published a complete résumé of Gieseking's life during the war years. Just before his arrival in the United States in January 1949, anti-Nazi organizations and Jewish war veterans among others protested in all the cities where he was scheduled to appear; even in the halls of Congress, some members were lined up against him. As a result of this mounting furor, agents of the Immigration Service kept Giesking in custody upon his arrival on January 24, 1949, intending to pursue an intensive review of Gieseking's Nazi activities. Rather than face such developments he called off the scheduled Carnegie Hall concert of January 24 (which had been sold out and was being picketed) one hour and three quarters before it was to have begun, and he announced that he was heading back to Europe without further delay. "This is the first time in my life I have not been treated as an artist should be treated," he said upon boarding an Air France plane for Paris.

For the next four years Gieseking performed extensively in Europe and the Far East without incident. He was finally permitted to return to the United States in 1953 and gave his first American concert in some fifteen years in New York on April 22. Olin Downes noticed a deterioration in Gieseking's physical prowess and was convinced that the years had taken their toll of his command of the keyboard. But Downes also remarked that "this has not conditioned the distinction and beauty of his style, or his gifts as an interpreter and colorist."

In December 1953 Gieseking was in a bus accident near Stuttgart, Germany, in which his wife was killed and he himself suffered a brain concussion. He recovered from this accident and was able to resume his concert appearances in the United States in 1955, following these with a ten-week tour beginning in March 1956. "I felt that I was face to face with a survivor of the grand tradition—a man to whom musical interpretation was neither a matter of mere technique and polish nor a matter of finicky scholarship, but something involving the profound personal authority that is found only in the work of a great artist," wrote Winthrop Sargeant in the *New Yorker,* after one of Gieseking's concerts in New York in March 1956.

Late in October 1956, while in London for some recording sessions, Gieseking was hospitalized for an emergency operation to relieve pancreatitis. On October 26 he died in the hospital of a heart attack, soon after the operation.

Gieseking was the composer of several chamber-music works, piano pieces, and songs.

ABOUT: Gavotty, B. Gieseking; Gelatt, R. Makers of Music; Gieseking, W. So Warde Ich Pianist. *Periodicals*—New York Times, February 8, 1948.

Beniamino Gigli

1890–1957

Beniamino Gigli was one of the greatest Italian opera tenors in the post-Caruso era. He was born in Recanati, Italy, on March 20, 1890. His mother was Ester Magnaterra Gigli. His father, Domenico, was the town pharmacist and served as sacristan in the local church. Beniamino joined the church choir when he was seven. When his voice changed from soprano to tenor he was assigned solos in the mass.

For five of his boyhood years Beniamino worked in his father's pharmacy. During this time he received some vocal instruction from a local teacher, Lazzarini. Ambitious to get more advanced music instruction, Beniamino worked nights as assistant to the town photographer, saving his money for the time when he could go to Rome. There he tried to gain admission to the Schola Cantorum of the Sistine Chapel but failed. After additional vocal instruction from Agnese Bonucci, however, Gigli received a scholarship in 1911 for the Liceo Musicale (later renamed the Santa Cecilia Academy). There his teachers were Antonio Cotogni and Enrico Rosati.

His vocal studies were interrupted for two

Gigli: jē′ lyē

BENIAMINO GIGLI

part, and indicated assurance and experience on the stage. . . . He will no doubt be another valuable addition to the company."

That season Gigli was heard in a wide variety of Italian roles: Turiddu in *Cavalleria Rusticana,* Rodolfo in *La Bohème,* Cavaradossi in *Tosca,* Edgar in *Lucia di Lammermoor,* Avito in *L'Amore dei Tre Re,* and the title role of *Andrea Chénier* in its first Metropolitan Opera production. When Caruso died on August 2, 1921, the gap he left was filled by Gigli with ever-increasing distinction. After several seasons many critics were convinced that Gigli, more than any other tenor, had inherited Caruso's imperial position at the Metropolitan.

He remained the principal tenor of the Metropolitan Opera for twelve consecutive seasons, specializing in the French and Italian repertory. He opened the 1921–1922 season on November 14 as Alfredo in *La Traviata;* the 1925–1926 season on November 2 as Enzo; the 1929–1930 season on October 28 as Des Grieux in *Manon Lescaut.* In addition to the roles already mentioned, he assumed at the Metropolitan Opera those of Mylio in the New York premiere of Lalo's *Le Roi d'Ys,* the Duke in *Rigoletto,* Walter in the first Metropolitan Opera presentation of Catalani's *Die Loreley,* Pinkerton in *Madama Butterfly,* Romeo in *Romeo and Juliet,* Vasco da Gama in *L'Africaine,* Lionel in *Martha,* Baldo in the American premiere of Riccitelli's *I Compagnacci,* Fenton in *Falstaff,* Loris Ipanov in Giordano's *Fedora,* Gianetto in the first Metropolitan Opera production of Giordano's *La Cena delle Beffe,* Wilhelm Meister in *Mignon,* Ruggero in the American premiere of *La Rondine,* Don Ottavio in *Don Giovanni,* Radames in *Aida,* Nemorino in *L'Elisir d'Amore,* Osaka in Mascagni's *Iris,* Des Grieux in *Manon,* and Elvino in *La Sonnambula.*

During the world economic crisis in 1931, the Metropolitan Opera was compelled to make drastic financial retrenchments and called upon Gigli, then one of its highest-paid stars earning about one hundred thousand dollars a season, to take a cut in his fees. He refused to do so, even though thirty-two other leading singers willingly submitted to cuts. Gigli engaged in a bitter controversy with the director of the Metropolitan on the subject of his salary. In April 1932 many leading artists of the Metropolitan joined forces to censure him severely in a round-robin letter sent to Gatti-Casazza, the general manager. Gi-

years while he served in the army. When his service ended, he received first prize in an international competition in Parma in 1914. On October 14 of that year he made his opera debut in Rovigo as Enzo in *La Gioconda.* The beauty of his voice, the purity of its texture, its perfect control and easy delivery all made him an instant favorite not only in Rovigo but in other provincial Italian opera houses. In 1915 he was honored in Bologna and Naples for his performances as Faust in Boïto's *Mefistofele.* In 1917 he was acclaimed in Spain. On April 30, 1917, at the Teatro Costanzi in Rome, he created the role of Flammen in the world premiere of Mascagni's *Lodoletta.* On March 27, 1917, he made a successful appearance in Monte Carlo as Ruggero in the premiere of Puccini's *La Rondine.* Gigli gathered additional praise with his appearances in Berlin, Dresden, and Paris. In 1918 Toscanini selected him for the role of Faust in *Mefistofele* at the Boïto festival at La Scala; and it was on this occasion, December 26, that he made his La Scala debut. In 1919–1920 he toured South America.

On November 26, 1920, he made his American debut at the Metropolitan Opera as Faust in *Mefistofele.* Although Caruso was the reigning tenor at the Metropolitan and overshadowed most other tenors, Gigli's debut was a huge success. Writing in the New York *Times,* Richard Aldrich found him to have "a voice of really fine quality, which he does not often force, still fresh and possessed of color; and he sings not without finish and style. He was evidently at home in the gli, however, stubbornly refused to make any concessions. On April 27, 1932, he sang his farewell at the Metropolitan Opera in a performance of *Rigoletto.*

This, however, was not his last appearance at the Metropolitan. During the 1938–1939 season he returned to the United States for a concert tour and for guest appearances with several American opera houses, including the San Francisco Opera where he opened the 1938 season on October 7 as Andrea Chénier. On January 23, 1939, he returned to the Metropolitan Opera as Radames in *Aida* and received an uproarious welcome. This was his last season—in all he had sung in 375 performances in New York and 115 on tour.

Once again he became involved in bitter controversy. Upon returning to Europe in 1939, following his engagements in the United States, he was quoted in the Italian press as making scurrilous comments on the quality of the performances at the Metropolitan Opera and its singers. He was quoted as saying that he would never again return to the United States because the country had "an air of extortion and corruption." His statements inevitably aroused a storm of protest from the directors and singers of the Metropolitan. Though he denied he had ever made such comments, he was for the time being discredited in the eyes of many of his American admirers.

In Europe his popularity remained high. After his debut at Covent Garden on May 27, 1930, as Andrea Chénier, he became as much of a favorite in London as he had been in New York; in 1938 he appeared there in every Italian opera mounted on that stage. In Italy, where he was the principal tenor of La Scala, his fame and popularity were such that he had few if any rivals.

"The type of lyric-dramatic singer Gigli represents," wrote Richard Capell in Grove's *Dictionary of Music and Musicians,* "is not to be expected in his perfection more than once a generation. The natural beauty of his tone is cunningly reinforced; technically he is a master. At *fff* he gives the impression of still being within his powers. He effects pathos by pouting his lips and using the half-voice. . . . Gigli sings with the whole force of his body as naturally as a gamecock fights. . . . His temperament gives him energy; his art consists principally—since his emotional expression lies within a primitive range

and he is not an actor—in his control, which no excitement affects, of the appropriate physical tension and relaxation, resulting in open-throated singing at all dynamic degrees."

Among the many honors conferred on him was that of Grand Official Crown of Italy by King Victor Emmanuel and Commander of St. Gregory the Great by the Pope. The king of Spain made him Commander of the Royal Order of Isabella. He was also Commander Royal Order of Isabel la Católica, Commander S.S. Maurizio and Lazzaro, Chevalier of the French Legion of Honor, and a member of the Accademia Pontifica Tibernia and the Santa Cecilia Academy, both in Rome.

He starred in a number of foreign films. Among them were: *Forever Yours* (1937), *Ave Maria* (1937), *Dingehort mein Herz* (1939), *Du bist mein Glück* (1940), *Legittima Difesa* (1940), *Laugh Pagliacci* (1948), and *The Singing Taxi-Driver* (1953).

After 1928 Gigli lived at Villa Montarice, an estate built for him and his family near Recanati. This fifty-room mansion, which included a private chapel, was on top of a hill overlooking the sea, within sight of the house where Gigli was born. Villa Montarice became the tenor's favorite retreat when his season of singing was over. An excellent marksman, he went hunting in the hills that stretched beyond his house. He gave lavish fiestas for his many visitors from America and Europe. His quieter hours were spent swimming, playing his favorite card game of tressetti, and collecting rugs, paintings, rare manuscripts, and stamps.

His wife, the former Constanza Cerroni, was a Roman and of the working class. They were married in April 1915 and had two children, Enzo and Rina. Rina became an accomplished soprano and often appeared with her father in concerts and on recordings.

During and immediately after World War II, Gigli—long a favorite of Mussolini—was accused of collaboration with the Nazi-Fascist Axis. In 1944 the Allied military authorities refused to allow him to make any public appearances. After he was cleared officially of alleged pro-Fascist affiliations, Gigli returned to the opera stage in Rome in March 1945 in *Tosca,* and in November 1946 he was hailed at Covent Garden in London in *La Bohème* in which his daughter, Rina, was heard as Mimi. In extended tours of England in 1947 and 1949 and in guest performances in Europe's major opera houses, Gigli thoroughly reestablished his position as one of the great tenors of his time. In the spring of 1955 he returned to the United States for his first American tour since World War II and was given a magnificent welcome.

After 1955 Gigli went into complete retirement on his estate near Recanati. He died in Rome on November 30, 1957.

ABOUT: Gigli, B. Memoirs; Silvestrini, D. B. G. Beniamino Gigli.

EMIL GILELS

Emil Gilels

1916–

Emil Grigorevich Gilels, pianist, was born in Odessa, in the Ukraine, on October 19, 1916. His father, Grigory, was a bookkeeper in a sugar factory. Though neither of his parents were musicians, "they were musical in an amateur way," Gilels has explained, "performing on the piano. There was much singing and playing in our house." His younger sister, Elizabeth, a concert violinist, is married to the Soviet violin virtuoso Leonid Kogan.

While Gilels maintains he was never a musical prodigy, he began piano study when he was six with Yakov Tkatch. At nine he made a first public appearance and four years later a more formal debut in Odessa. After seven years with Tkatch he began in 1929 to study with Berthe Ringold. "Everything I was taught about playing I learned from her," he says.

In 1931 Emil entered the All-Ukrainian Piano Contest but failed to capture a single prize. One year later he enrolled in the Odessa Conservatory. During his first year there Arthur Rubinstein came to Odessa for a concert appearance. "I remember as if it happened yesterday," Rubinstein told Victor Seroff who in turn reported the conversation in the *Saturday Review.* "There was a boy—short, with a mass of red hair and freckles, who played. . . . I can't describe it. . . . All I can say is—if he ever comes here I might as well pack my bags and go." On Rubinstein's suggestion, Emil entered the All-Union Musicians Competition for pianists in

Gilels: gē′ lĕls

Moscow in 1933; this time he won the first prize.

Upon graduation from the Odessa Conservatory in 1935 Emil entered the Moscow Conservatory where he became a pupil of Heinrich Neuhaus. In 1936 he entered an international competition for pianists in Vienna and won the second prize. Herbert F. Peyser, the correspondent for the New York *Times,* heard him in this competition and reported back to New York: "If piano playing of utter magnificence means anything in your life, keep a sharp lookout for Emil Gilels. Up to a few days ago the name meant no more to the general run of musicians in this part of the world than it probably does to any in America, who may read these words. But I repeat, watch out for it and fix it in your minds, for sooner or later it is likely to go thundering up and down continents."

International interest was first focused on Gilels in 1938 when he emerged with the first prize in piano in the Queen Elisabeth Competition in Brussels. Also in 1938 he became assistant to his teacher, Neuhaus, at the Moscow Conservatory, and initiated an active concert career with performances throughout the Soviet Union. How highly he was regarded in the Soviet Union, from the beginning of his mature performing career, can be measured by the fact that together with the violinist David Oistrakh he was chosen to represent the Soviet Union at the New York World's Fair in 1939. This appearance never materialized because of the outbreak of World War II in Europe. Compelled to remain in their own country, both Gilels and Oistrakh concertized at the front line for Soviet troops and in occupied cities and continued their teaching chores at the Moscow Conservatory. In 1942 Gilels became a member of the Communist party.

After the war, in 1946, Gilels received the Stalin Prize of one hundred thousand rubles for his contribution to the war effort and in recognition of his high status as a piano virtuoso. Soviet honors continued to come his way. He received the Order of the Red Banner of Labor and also the Order of the Badge of Honor. In 1954 he was one of three pianists to hold the title People's Artist of the U.S.S.R.; in 1962 he was awarded the Lenin Prize; and in 1976 he was named "Hero of Socialist Labor."

His first appearance outside the Soviet Union was at the Third International Spring Festival in Prague in 1948. In his first recital there, as Seroff recalls, "it was obvious that we were in the presence of an extraordinary musical talent with supreme powers at his command." In 1951 he was one of eleven Soviet artists sent to participate at the May Music Festival in Florence, Italy, and he became the first Soviet artist sent outside the Soviet sphere after the war. In 1952 he toured Scandinavia and in February 1954 he performed at the Soviet Embassy in Berlin during a foreign ministers conference. At this time he was beginning to make recordings, some of which were distributed in the United States to bring to American attention his phenomenal technique and control and his formidable musicianship.

After a decision was reached at the Geneva Convention of 1955 for an exchange of culture between the Soviet Union and the United States —and through the personal efforts of Yehudi Menuhin and the American State Department— Gilels was invited to the United States, becoming the first major Soviet artist in thirty-five years to tour the United States. He made his American debut in Philadelphia on October 3, 1955, as soloist with the Philadelphia Orchestra under Eugene Ormandy in the Tchaikovsky Piano Concerto No.1. He was a sensation. Eugene Ormandy called him "one of the greatest." Max de Schauensee wrote in the Philadelphia *Bulletin* that he had "rarely heard playing of such beauty." When Gilels repeated this performance in New York City a day later, Howard Taubman wrote in the New York *Times:* "He is a virtuoso in the grand line. . . . Mr. Gilels has everything that it takes to be a top-grade pianist.

His tone is solid as his physique with its peasant sturdiness. His fingers have boundless agility and control. He can make the piano sing, and he can cause it to thunder; it bends to his will. Best of all he is a musician of personality." On October 11 Gilels in his first New York recital presented the American premiere of Shostakovich's Three Preludes and Fugues, and on October 24 he performed with the New York Philharmonic Orchestra at the United Nations Assembly Hall to commemorate the tenth anniversary of the United Nations.

In 1956 Gilels returned to America for a five-week coast-to-coast tour of Canada, and since then he has made many tours of the United States and has been heard in an extensive and varied repertory. When he returned to the United States for his twelfth tour in 1977, he was heard in a performance of all five Beethoven piano concertos, with the Cleveland Orchestra. Though poetic insight and sensitive reflection are not absent from his performances when called for, he has proved strongest in music of dramatic impact. He is of the Russian tradition that has produced such virtuosos in the grand manner as Anton Rubinstein in the nineteenth century and Vladimir Horowitz in the twentieth.

In 1947 Gilels married Farizet Khutsyostova, a pianist and composer who had been a student at the Moscow Conservatory when he was a pupil there. Their daughter, Elyena, a concert pianist, made her debut in the Soviet Union in 1966 and on February 15, 1969, her American debut.

Gilels, often referred to as "the little giant," is built compactly and solidly. His hands are stubby and square. A cherubic face that does not lose its boyishness is topped by a mass of reddish hair. Gilels presents, wrote Roland Gelatt in *High Fidelity,* "a curious amalgam of saturnine immobility and mercurial animation, of almost ponderous steadfastness and elfin sensitivity. Just when you are about to conclude that he is sunk in stony Russian gloom, a puckish gleam in his eye and a friendly smile offer reassurance that things are not really as bad as they seem."

When he is not on tour, Gilels devotes himself in Moscow to his duties as a full-time professor of the piano at the Moscow Conservatory. He accepts only a few students at a time (four or five) whom he teaches privately; but he also has two classes a week in piano technique.

His main diversion is spending time with family and friends in quiet social evenings at home. These invariably end up in music making or in listening to recordings.

In addition to his recordings of piano literature (among which are the five piano concertos of Beethoven with the Cleveland Orchestra under Szell) Gilels has been heard on disks in performances with Leonid Kogan, violinist, and with Mstislav Rostropovich, cellist.

ABOUT: Ewen, D. Famous Instrumentalists. *Periodicals*—Musical America, November 1, 1955; New York Times, October 23, 1955, February 11, 1977; New Yorker, October 15, 1955.

Carlo Maria Giulini

1914–

CARLO MARIA GIULINI

Carlo Maria Giulini, conductor, was born in Barletta, on the Adriatic coast of southern Italy, on March 9, 1914. He began violin lessons when he was five. At sixteen he entered the Santa Cecilia Academy in Rome where he studied composition with Alessandro Bustini and the viola with Remy Principe. While attending the Academy he joined the viola section of the Augusteo Orchestra in Rome and performed under many conductors including Richard Strauss, Mengelberg, Bruno Walter, Klemperer, and Furtwängler.

Once he decided to become a conductor, he worked with Alfredo Casella at the Chigi Academy of Siena. He received his diploma in conducting after completing postgraduate work with Bernardino Molinari, then the principal conductor of the Augusteo Orchestra.

In 1944 Giulini conducted the Augusteo Orchestra in a concert celebrating the liberation of Rome. That autumn he was appointed assistant conductor of the Radio Orchestra in Rome and became principal conductor in 1946. Four years later he founded and became the head of the Orchestra of Radio Milan.

His performance of Haydn's opera *Il Mondo della Luna* broadcast over the Milan Radio in 1951 was heard by Toscanini who was so impressed that he asked his daughter to arrange a meeting with the young conductor. This meeting marked the beginning of a friendship and a

master-disciple relationship that lasted up to the time of Toscanini's death in 1957.

The first stage performance of an opera conducted by Giulini was *La Traviata* with Renata Tebaldi at the Bergamo Festival in 1951. When the soprano became too ill to appear for a second performance she was replaced by the unknown Maria Callas. This was the beginning of a successful musical partnership between Callas and Giulini.

In 1951 Giulini was made a member of the conducting staff of La Scala in Milan, the youngest man to hold such an appointment in the history of that opera company. During the next few years—while rising to the position of principal conductor, succeeding Victor de Sabata in 1954—Giulini led performances of such brilliance that European attention was focused on him for the first time, notably *La Traviata* and *Alceste*, both stage-directed by Visconti and both presented with Callas as principal soprano.

In 1955 he made his bow at the Edinburgh Festival in a performance of *Falstaff* which Marion Harewood in *Opera* described as a "classic, like Toscanini's and de Sabata's before him." Toward the end of the year he made his American debut, as a guest conductor of the Chicago Symphony at the invitation of its music director, Fritz Reiner. "This tall, slender young Italian from Milan's La Scala," wrote a critic of the Chicago *Tribune*, "has sensitivity, imagination and skill, and he has that extra enkindling thing, the Promethean gift of fire. . . . He can make music onstage as well as in the pit. . . . The

Giulini: jē o͝o lē′ nē

performance was rich, full, utterly Italian, and with that singing darkness in the strings. . . . He works wonders." From the critic of the *Sun-Times* came the following estimate: "So highly colored and electrifying was Giulini's conception and performance that this reviewer is unable to remember any other which has been more spectacular."

During the summer of 1956 Giulini made his first appearance with the Israel Philharmonic Orchestra. This proved so successful that for the next five years he returned annually to Israel to direct that organization in series of concerts. He also conducted the orchestra on its second North American tour in 1960.

Giulini made his debut at Covent Garden in London in 1958 in *Don Carlo.* Since then he has been the music director of the Rome Opera House and has appeared as a guest conductor of Europe's principal opera companies and orchestras; he has participated in most of the important festivals in Europe, including those at Venice, Florence, Strasbourg, Prague, Holland, Edinburgh, and Aix-en-Provence. He conducted a concert inaugurating the Brucknerhaus in Linz, Austria. And, at the Edinburgh Festival, he conducted a performance of Verdi's Requiem commemorating the centenary of this masterwork.

In the United States he has led nearly every major symphony orchestra in guest appearances. His first appearance in the United States took place on November 3, 1955, when he performed as a guest conductor of the Chicago Symphony on an invitation from that orchestra's music director, Fritz Reiner. He returned to the podium of the Chicago Symphony for five subsequent seasons. In 1969 he was appointed principal guest conductor of the Chicago Symphony, in which capacity he shared the podium with Sir Georg Solti during the orchestra's spectacular tour of Europe in 1971. He left this post in 1972; one year later he was made principal conductor of the Vienna Symphony Orchestra, succeeding Wolfgang Sawallisch. In 1975 he took the Vienna orchestra on a world tour to celebrate its seventy-fifth anniversary. The tour began at the Flanders Festival, continued on to Japan, Hawaii, Canada, and the United States, and ended with a gala performance at the Musikverein in Vienna on October 30. On October 24, 1975, he brought the orchestra to New York for a nationally televised concert emanating from the United Nations.

Giulini made his operatic debut in the United States with *The Marriage of Figaro* at the Lincoln Center for the Performing Arts in New York in June 1968, during the American visit of the Rome Opera. This performance which, under Visconti's stage direction, had first been produced in Rome in 1964, had become one of the artistic triumphs of the Rome Opera.

Giulini is always meticulous about never overburdening his performing schedule. He finds that after one month of work he needs three weeks of rest to think. "I cannot be in a constant rush. I am not a machine. I give everything to music when I do it. I cannot give every day. I cannot make music the way some people make breakfast." He confines himself to a comparatively limited repertory. "If I conduct, I must be able to do it with conviction, I cannot do it otherwise. I can only make music that I understand, music that I believe, music that I love."

In 1977, Giulini was appointed music director of the Los Angeles Philharmonic, succeeding Zubin Mehta—his tenure to begin with the 1978 –1979 season. He had made his conducting debut in Los Angeles as a guest conductor of the visiting Israel Philharmonic in 1960. In 1971 he conducted the Los Angeles Philharmonic for two weeks and in 1975 for two additional weeks. In 1974, he flew into Los Angeles with the Vienna Symphony to inaugurate the auditorium at Ambassador College.

Giulini is married and has three sons. In *High Fidelity,* Dorle J. Soria has described him as "a tall man, blue-eyed with a high-bridged aristocratic nose and gentle manner." Eugene Rizzo adds in the *Opera News* that looking at Giulini closely "one thinks of the cleanness of Mozart and the vigor of Verdi—his two favorite composers for the stage."

Among Giulini's many recordings of opera and symphonic music are those of Mahler's Symphony No.1 and Symphony No.9 which earned Grammys from the National Academy of Recording Arts and Sciences in 1971 and 1978 respectively.

ABOUT: High Fidelity/Musical America, April 1975, April 1978.

Herta Glaz

1908–

Herta Glaz (originally Herta Glatz), mezzo-soprano and contralto, was born in Vienna on September 16, 1908. After attending the Vienna State Academy of Music she gave her first public performance at seventeen as a soloist with an orchestra conducted by Erich Wolfgang Korngold. That appearance, she later confided, was one of the most trying experiences of her early career. "My throat seemed to close up and I trembled from head to foot. The last thing I was conscious of was that someone pushed me on the stage. When I came to I was back in the dressing room and the director was congratulating me on the way I sang. But I had absolutely no recollection of having sung."

In 1931 Glaz was engaged by the Breslau State Opera and made her debut as Erda in *Das Rheingold.* The night after her debut she was asked to substitute for a singer who was ill. The next evening she was again recruited to meet a similar emergency. After that she was often the choice to replace indisposed mezzo-sopranos and contraltos, in addition to appearing in her own roles. As a result, in one season in Breslau she was heard in three hundred opera presentations, sometimes singing twice a day. She sang not only in the traditional repertory but also in modern stage works by Hindemith and Ernst Krenek.

Because she was of Jewish birth she had to leave Germany in 1933 with the rise of the Nazi regime. She made a concert tour of Austria, Sweden, and Russia, achieving her first successes as a singer of *Lieder.* In 1935 she was engaged as the leading contralto of the Glyndebourne Festival in England where she specialized in Mozart's operas. During the 1935–1936 season she was a member of the German Theater in Prague, mainly singing in the German repertory. She also participated in 1936 in the festival at Interlaken, Switzerland, where, with Ernst Krenek as her piano accompanist, she was heard in a series of fifteen concerts devoted to Krenek's song cycles as well as to rarely heard *Lieder* of Schubert and other German Romantic masters of song. In the summer of 1936 she became a member of the Salzburg Opera Guild where she sang in Milhaud's *Le Pauvre Matelot,* Mozart's

HERTA GLAZ

Così fan Tutte, and Monteverdi's *L'Incoronazione di Poppea.* In 1937 she participated at the Festival of Contemporary Music in Paris.

Her first appearance in the United States was in 1937 as soloist with the Los Angeles Philharmonic under Klemperer, in performances of Mahler's *Das Lied von der Erde* and Bach's *Passion According to St. Matthew.* Later she toured the country as the leading contralto of the visiting Salzburg Opera Guild, singing in more than eighty cities and giving song recitals as well. Following one of her recitals in New York City, Olin Downes wrote in the New York *Times:* "She is a musician of exceptional sincerity and intelligence. . . . In all that she did, musicianship and breadth of versatility of taste were evident. She also proved capable of stirring her audience by the feeling and dramatic impulse with which she invested certain songs."

On October 18, 1939, Glaz made her debut with the San Francisco Opera as Suzuki in *Madama Butterfly,* following this with performances as Maddalena in *Rigoletto,* Bertha in *The Barber of Seville,* and Fricka in *Die Walküre.* She returned to the San Francisco Opera in 1944, appearing regularly each year until 1951. Meanwhile, in the period between 1940 and 1942 she was heard with the Chicago Opera as Brangäne in *Tristan and Isolde* and Fricka in *Die Walküre.*

On December 25, 1942, she made her debut at the Metropolitan Opera as Amneris in *Aida.* The critic of the *World-Telegram* reported: "She sang in a truly sensuous manner. Her Amneris came mighty close to being the woman Verdi meant her to be: human, real, tragic." Later that season she sang Marcellina in *The Marriage of Figaro* and Waltraute in *Die Walküre*. She remained with the Metropolitan through the 1955 –1956 season, distinguishing herself not only in the German repertory, which was her specialty, but also in French and Italian operas.

During her many years at the Metropolitan Glaz made numerous guest appearances with leading American orchestras, including performances of Debussy's *The Blessed Demoiselle* with Toscanini conducting. She was also heard throughout the United States in recitals of *Lieder*. In 1949 she scored a major success at the Goethe Festival in Aspen, Colorado, with a *Lieder* concert. After leaving the Metropolitan Opera, Glaz taught singing at the Manhattan School of Music in New York.

She married Joseph Rosenstock, the conductor, on August 7, 1952, a marriage that ended a few years later in divorce.

One of her eccentricities was never to give a performance without first bringing to the concert hall or opera house a toy sheep which had become her good-luck charm. It was always in her dressing room when she was on the platform. Aside from music her main interest was creative writing. She produced several works of fiction and some poetry for her own pleasure, never tried to get any of it published, and refused to allow even intimate friends to read it.

ABOUT: Kutsch, K.J. and Riemens, L.A Concise Biographical Dictionary of Singers.

Alma Gluck

1884–1938

Alma Gluck (originally Reba Fiersohn), soprano, was born in Bucharest, Romania, on May 11, 1884, to parents who had emigrated from southern Russia. Her father, Israel Fiersohn, a trader in farm products, died when Alma was two. Her mother, Anna, a hunchback, raised the seven children, of whom Alma was the youngest, with most of the domestic chores assumed by the oldest sister, Cecile. When Alma was six, the family went to the United States, settling on

Gluck: glŏŏk

ALMA GLUCK

the lower East Side of New York. Alma attended the New York public schools. She received no musical training. "I didn't mean to be a singer," she later said. "But sing? Of course I sang. We all sang. The tenement was bursting with singing."

After attending grade schools, Normal School (later named Hunter College) in New York City, and Union College in Schenectady, New York, Alma took a course in typing and stenography which enabled her to work for several years in an office. On May 25, 1902, she married Bernard Glick (Gluck), an insurance agent twelve years her senior. They lived in an apartment on St. Nicholas Avenue in New York City. They had one child, Abigail, born in 1903, who became a successful writer of biography, criticism, and fiction, under the name of Marcia Davenport. Davenport's first novel, *Of Lena Geyer* (1936), was based on many incidents in her mother's professional life and her autobiography, *Too Strong for Fantasy* (1967), contains much personal and biographical material on Alma Gluck not found elsewhere.

One day Alma's husband brought home a friend who heard her singing in another room and persuaded her to begin vocal lessons. As it turned out, she required very little urging. For three years, beginning in 1906, she studied with Arturo Buzzi-Peccia. Somehow, though the financial resources at hand were most limited, she managed not only to pay for these lessons (at a reduced fee) but also to take lessons in Italian, to acquire a piano, to buy music scores, and occasionally to purchase a seat at the Metropolitan Opera. Feeling the need of foreign experience, she borrowed four hundred dollars and took off with her daughter to Paris where she learned the French language.

Soon after her return to the United States, Buzzi-Peccia arranged for her to audition for Arturo Toscanini, then principal conductor of the Metropolitan Opera, and Gatti-Casazza, its general manager. Toscanini was so impressed with her singing that he rushed over to the piano to accompany her in the aria "Regnava nel silenzio" from *Lucia di Lammermoor.* When the audition was over, Gatti-Casazza offered her a contract for the Metropolitan Opera even though up to this time she had not sung professionally, had not appeared in any opera, and had not had any dramatic training.

She made her debut with the Metropolitan Opera company not on the stage of its opera house but at the New Theater (later renamed Century Theater) in New York on November 16, 1909, as Sophie in *Werther.* Her first appearance at the Metropolitan Opera House itself was at a Sunday evening concert, on November 28, when she sang "Regnava nel silenzio." Her first appearance in an opera production came on December 23 as the Happy Shade in a revival of Gluck's *Orfeo ed Euridice,* Toscanini conducting. Writing in the *Tribune,* Henry E. Krehbiel noted that she sang the "E quest 'asilo" aria with "exquisite taste." During the rest of that season she was heard in nine other parts in three languages, and though most were minor roles, they revealed her consummate technique, exquisite intonation, beauty of vocal sound, effortlessness of production, and overall musicality. These roles were Esmeralda in *The Bartered Bride,* Freia in *Das Rheingold,* Chloë in Tchaikovsky's *The Queen of Spades,* the Flower Maiden in *Parsifal,* Leonore in Flotow's *Alessandro Stradella,* and the Priestess in *Aida.* She was also heard as Marguerite in *Faust* and Mimi in *La Bohème.* Her subsequent roles were Venus in *Tannhäuser,* the Forest Bird in *Siegfried,* Love and Lucinda in Gluck's *Armide,* Nedda in *I Pagliacci,* Amor in *Orfeo ed Euridice,* Jane in Franchetti's *Germania,* and Gilda in *Rigoletto.*

Gluck gave her first song recital on October 18, 1910, at Mendelssohn Hall in New York. "It is clear," wrote Richard Aldrich in the New York *Times,* "that she has uncommon gifts, and already has certain excellences of no mean or-der. Her diction in English and German is excellent. She has a discriminating command of broad and expressive phrasing. Much that she did was of real beauty. Such a singer is a pleasure to hear." As a result of her success at this debut concert, she was in demand for song recitals, appearances with orchestras and at festivals, and participation in the presentation of oratorios.

In 1912 she divorced her husband; she also separated herself permanently from opera to devote herself exclusively to the concert platform where she was destined to achieve her greatest renown. After some additional coaching and study in Europe with Jean de Reszke in Paris and Marcella Sembrich in Switzerland (she was Sembrich's first pupil), Gluck returned to the United States to fulfill the last year of her contract with the Metropolitan by appearing exclusively in its Sunday evening concerts. She reappeared in recital on January 10, 1914, in New York, and on January 22 she was a soloist with the Philadelphia Orchestra under young Stokowski in Blonde's aria from *The Abduction from the Seraglio,* and "Depuis le jour" from *Louise.* Reviewing the latter concert, Richard Aldrich reported: "In both she disclosed beauty of voice and vocalism; and in Mozart's air there was much of the pure style requisite for this music."

Within one year she became one of the most popular singers in America. She also became one of the best-selling vocal-recording artists of her time, outstripped only by Caruso and John McCormack; her recording of "Carry Me Back to Old Virginny" sold about two million disks, a sales record without precedent up to that time. In the years between 1914 and 1918 she is reputed to have earned well over half a million dollars in royalties from her records.

On June 15, 1914, in London, Gluck married Efrem Zimbalist, the violin virtuoso. He was five years younger than she. They first met on a ferry to New Jersey, en route to a joint concert they were to give in Morristown in 1911. With Zimbalist it was a case of love at first sight. From 1911 to 1914 he persistently proposed marriage and was just as persistently rejected. "Her reluctance," explains Marcia Davenport, "was rooted in the conviction that she could not create a real marriage whilst she was at the height of her career . . . or on the way to the height. And she wanted no less than a real marriage." But in the end she yielded to Zimbalist's urging. Their first home was a house on the West Side of New York. A few years later this was replaced by a brownstone house on Park Avenue supplemented by a summer place at Fisher's Island. They had two children, one of whom, Efrem Zimbalist Jr., became a television actor and writer-director.

Shortly before her marriage Gluck made her European debut with a recital in London that was such a huge success that plans were projected for concerts not only throughout England but also on the Continent. The outbreak of World War I frustrated these plans. From then on Gluck's career was confined exclusively to the United States.

In the early phase of World War I Gluck was subjected to severe criticism because of her open and articulate opposition to America's entry into the war. But once America became fully involved she served her country by making large donations to the Red Cross and making numerous appearances for American troops in training camps.

Until 1921 she continued to concertize extensively throughout the United States, often in joint concerts with her husband, and to make recordings. At that time she withdrew from her career, though not completely, to devote herself to her family. She gave her last concert at the Manhattan Opera House in New York in 1925.

For the remainder of her life, and in spite of rapidly failing health (ultimately diagnosed as cirrhosis of the liver), she maintained an active social life at her New York home, frequently attended concerts, the theater, and parties, and she traveled with her husband around the world on his concert tours. At home she enjoyed playing bridge or backgammon with friends or doing needlepoint. "Like all people who have made fortunes by their own powers," writes Marcia Davenport, "she had her quirks. . . . She dressed beautifully. . . . She had great style and she did everything with flair. . . . To the end of her life she kept the quality of incandescence. . . . When she was present everyone knew she was there, though she might not have made a sound or moved from one place in the room to another."

A few days before her death she attended a sonata recital by her husband in Town Hall, New York. The next day she collapsed and was rushed to the Rockefeller Institute Hospital where she died on October 27, 1938. Her ashes were interred in a cemetery on Town Hill in New Hartford, Connecticut. Five notes from Gluck's *Orfeo ed Euridice* and the line "From All My Masters Have I Learned" are engraved on her tombstone.

ABOUT: Davenport, M. Too Strong for Fantasy. *Periodicals*—Etude, February 1921; New York Times, October 28, 1938; Theatre Magazine, January 1911.

Tito Gobbi

1915–

Tito Gobbi, baritone, was born in Bassano del Grappa, Vicenza, Italy, on October 24, 1915, to Giovanni and Enrica Weiss Gobbi. His father was a successful engineer. As a boy Tito suffered from an asthmatic condition which led his father to place him under the guidance of a physical-training teacher. Tito developed so well that by the time he was eighteen he had become an excellent athlete, adept at skiing, cycling, and mountain climbing.

In his boyhood Tito showed so little talent for singing that he was dismissed from the school choir because, as he recalls, "my teacher said I had too loud a voice, and disturbed too much." He studied law at the University of Padua, but in his late teens he was advised by one of his friends to begin vocal lessons, which he did at the Opera Theatre School of La Scala on a scholarship. From 1933 to 1938 he was a pupil of Giulio Crimi with whom he made such progress that all thought of practicing law was abandoned. In 1938 Gobbi won first prize among three hundred and thirty competitors in an international voice competition in Vienna. In 1939 he made his opera debut at Teatro Adriano in Rome as the elder Germont in *La Traviata*. "I was called in as a substitute," he recalls. "I had never been on stage, never sung with another person, not even with an orchestra. I had hay fever, too. But when the costume fit I was on." Soon after that he had his first success in Rome in Wolf-Ferrari's *Le Donne Curiose*. He signed a contract for the Rome Opera as principal baritone. After 1942 he became a member of La Scala in Milan.

His popularity slowly spread not only in Italy but in Europe as well. He appeared outside Italy

Gobbi: gō′ bē

TITO GOBBI

for the first time in 1947 at the Stockholm Opera. He was a great success at the Salzburg Festival in 1950 in the title role of *Don Giovanni,* Furtwängler conducting; his reappearance at this festival in the title role of *Falstaff* in 1957 was equally memorable. His debut in London took place in September 1952 when he appeared at Covent Garden with the visiting La Scala Opera as Belcore in *L'Elisir d'Amore.* He also sang in the major opera houses of Paris, Wiesbaden, Vienna, Munich, Zurich, Barcelona, Lisbon, and London. He made extensive tours of Egypt, Israel, South America, South Africa, and the Far East.

His first appearance in the United States came on October 2, 1948, as Figaro in *The Marriage of Figaro* with the San Francisco Opera; nine days later he was heard there as Belcore. When in November 1955 he appeared in the title role of *Rigoletto* with the Chicago Lyric Opera, Claudia Cassidy called him in the *Tribune* "a crafty actor . . . and a man who knows just how to use that beautiful high baritone to full advantage."

His debut at the Metropolitan Opera followed on January 13, 1956, as Scarpia in *Tosca.* Jay Harrison wrote in the *Herald Tribune* that Gobbi's characterization was "without doubt, hesitation, or question, the finest this writer has seen." In the New York *Times,* Howard Taubman commented: "As an interpreter of Scarpia he is an expert. He understands the cruel police chief with his suave smiling surface. He plays him for all he is worth, and he is a good enough musician

to give point and emphasis to the musical aspects of a powerful role." The following season he was heard as Rigoletto, Iago in *Otello,* and the title role in Falstaff.

Gobbi's repertory covers some ninety principal baritone roles and thirty-six secondary ones. His own favorites are Tonio in *I Pagliacci,* Scarpia, Michele in *Il Tabarro,* Amonasro in *Aida,* and the title roles in *Simon Boccanegra, Nabucco, Falstaff, Wozzeck,* and *Rigoletto.* Among the other roles in which he has appeared successfully are Méphistophélès in Berlioz' *The Damnation of Faust,* Michonnet in *Adriana Lecouvreur,* Malatesta in *Don Pasquale,* Enrico in *Lucia di Lammermoor,* Gerard in *Andrea Chénier,* Sharpless in *Madama Butterfly,* Figaro in *The Barber of Seville,* Jokanaan in *Salome,* Renato in *Un Ballo in Maschera,* Germont in *La Traviata,* Rodrigo in *Don Carlo,* and the title roles in *Gianni Schicchi, William Tell,* and *Macbeth.*

Gobbi opened the season of the Rome Opera as Simon Boccanegra in November 1975 in a new production, and on New Year's Eve of the same year he was Scarpia at Dorothy Kirsten's farewell performance at the Metropolitan Opera.

He has toured the concert world in recitals, making his first swing across the American continent in 1956. His outstanding acting ability has made him almost as famous in foreign motion pictures as in the opera house. He has been starred in about thirty films, nonmusical as well as musical, in four languages. These include the screen versions of *The Barber of Seville* (1947), *La Traviata* (1948), *Rigoletto* (1949), *I Pagliacci* (1950), and *La Forza del Destino* (1952). He also starred in *The House of Ricordi* (1956) and *Verdi* (1965). In addition, Gobbi has served as a commentator for his own series of opera telecasts over BBC in London.

Gobbi has distinguished himself as a producer and stager of operas. He supervised the production of *Simon Boccanegra* at the Chicago Lyric Opera in 1965 (and somewhat later at Covent Garden), *Otello* in 1966, and *Un Ballo in Maschera* in 1976, among others. He has also produced and directed performances of *Don Giovanni, Il Tabarro, Madama Butterfly, The Barber of Seville,* and *Falstaff.* In addition to his productions for the Chicago Lyric Opera and Covent Garden, are those for the Paris Opéra, the Teatro Comunale in Florence, Rome Opera, Monte

Carlo Opera, Zurich Opera, and at the Edinburg Festival. In 1977 he held his first directing assignment in New York, a new production of *Falstaff* at the American Opera Center at the Juilliard School of Music.

Gobbi has conducted classes in opera interpretation at London's Opera Center, the Scottish Opera Center in Glasgow, Rosary College in River Forest, Vacanze Musicali in Venice, and the Santa Cecilia Academy in Rome. He founded an opera workshop at Villa Schifanoia in Florence, Italy. In 1977 he held master classes in Italian Opera at the Juilliard School of Music in New York.

On April 10, 1937, he married Matilde de Rensis, daughter of the musicologist Raffaello de Rensis; they have one daughter, Cecilia. The Gobbis reside in Rome, and they also own a cottage at the seaside near the city. Gobbi retains his early interest in sports. His major recreations are driving, shooting, tennis, and skiing. He is accomplished also in painting, sculpting, and caricaturing.

ABOUT: Davidson, G. Opera Biographies. *Periodicals* —High Fidelity, January 1972, August 1977; Opera News, October 15, 1966.

LEOPOLD GODOWSKY

Leopold Godowsky

1870–1938

Leopold Godowsky, pianist, was born in Soshly, near Vilna, Poland, on February 13, 1870, to Matthew and Anna Lewin Godowsky. His father, a physician who loved music, encouraged Leopold's marked talent which began to reveal itself in his third year. He received his first music instruction on both the piano and the violin when he was four. At seven, he began piano study in earnest in Vilna; at the same time he started composing. (Later in life, Godowsky used some of the ideas from these juvenile creative efforts for mature works.) At nine Leopold made his debut as a pianist in Vilna. Two years later he was sent on a tour of Poland and Germany. When he was thirteen, a wealthy banker in Königsberg became interested in him and provided him with the funds to go to Berlin to attend the High School of Music. For about four

---

Godowsky: gŏ dôf´ skĕ

months in 1884 he studied with Woldemar Bargiel and Ernst Friedrich Karl Rudorff at that school.

In 1884 Leopold paid his first visit to the United States, making his debut in Boston on December 7. Between 1884 and 1886 he toured the United States in joint concerts with the operatic soprano Clara Louise Kellogg, with the Belgian violinist Ovide Musin, and with the concert soprano Emma Thursby. In 1885 he appeared regularly at the New York Casino, alternating each week with the piano virtuoso Teresa Carreño; and in 1886 he toured the northeast United States and Canada with Ovide Musin.

He returned to Europe in 1886 with the intention of studying with Liszt, but Liszt's death frustrated this ambition. He earned his living playing the piano in fashionable salons in Paris and London, where he became the darling of the social elite. From 1887 to 1890 he studied composition in Paris with Camille Saint-Saëns who thought so highly of Leopold not only as a pianist but as a composer that at one time he wanted to adopt him. In 1888 he made successful concert appearances in London and gave a command performance at the British Court.

Godowsky returned to the United States in 1890. On April 30, 1891, he married an American girl, Freda Saxe, and one day later he became an American citizen. (He was naturalized a second time in 1921 because he feared he had forfeited his American citizenship a decade or so earlier by taking the oath of Königliche and Kaiserliche Professor in Austria.) In 1890 he joined the faculty of the New York College of Music, and in the years 1894–1895 he commuted regularly from New York to Philadelphia to teach the piano at the Broad Street Conservatory. From 1895 to 1900 he was head of the piano department of the Chicago Conservatory. It was during these years that he developed his pedagogic theories of "weight and relaxation." Applying them to his own piano playing he became, as Nicolas Slonimsky has remarked in *Baker's Biographical Dictionary of Musicians,* "an outstanding technician of his instrument, extending the potentialities of piano technique to the utmost, with particular attention to the left hand."

In 1900 Godowsky embarked on a European tour. His concert on December 6, 1900, was such a success in Berlin that he was called upon to give five more recitals. He settled in Berlin, where he remained until 1909, teaching the piano privately and using the city as the base from which to launch tours of Europe and the Near East. From 1909 to 1914 he was director of the master class in piano at the Akademie der Tonkunst in Vienna, succeeding Emil Sauer. Returning to the United States in 1912–1913 and again in 1913–1914, he undertook coast-to-coast tours.

After his recital in Carnegie Hall, New York, on November 27, 1912, Godowsky was called by Richard Aldrich in the New York *Times* "a technician as far as technique relates to playing many notes and combinations of notes rapidly, clearly, brilliantly." Yet Aldrich found Godowsky wanting in those compositions on the program which made "emotional and intellectual qualities demands on the performer. He is heard to less advantage in music that especially calls for these qualities and a broad and deep emotional basis, fire, imagination, poetic insight." However, to James Gibbons Huneker, Godowsky was "a pianist for pianists, as Shelley is a poet for poets. . . . Every musical person listens to the alluring playing of Godowsky quite impervious to the fact that there are aspects of his art which will always escape them."

During World War I Godowsky lived in the United States, giving master classes in piano on both coasts. After the war he resumed his concert tours with highly successful recitals and appearances with orchestras throughout Europe, South America, and Asia. He became a naturalized American citizen in 1921. In 1922 he made his last appearance in the United States.

Though he continued to perform in Europe, Central and South America, and the Near and Far East after 1922, he reduced the number of his appearances to be able to devote himself more conscientiously than before to composition, to the writing of pedagogical pieces, to the making of transcriptions for the piano, to the editing of the piano music of other composers, and to the preparation of theoretical writings on piano-playing. Among his most celebrated original compositions were the suite *Triakontameron,* made up of thirty pieces for the piano the best known of which is *Alt Wien, 53 Studies on Chopin's Etudes,* and the *Java Suite* for piano. He also wrote preludes and fugues, waltz-poems, and other items for left-hand piano alone.

While making recordings in a studio in London in 1930, Godowsky suffered a stroke which put an end to his career as concert pianist. At his home on Riverside Drive he gathered around him admiring disciples, pupils, and friends, who referred to him as Popsy and paid him homage not only for what he had accomplished as a pianist, teacher, and composer but also for the kind of wise, witty, compassionate, and cultured man he was. His wit was legendary. To a young pianist who complained of the wrong notes in a piano recital by Eugène d'Albert, Godowsky commented: "I'd rather hear d'Albert's wrong notes than your right ones." In spite of his wit, and in spite of the love and admiration of his many friends and admirers, Godowsky was embittered by his forced retirement from the concert stage. During his last years he was for the most part a man broken in spirit. He was also a lonely man after the death of his wife in 1933.

Godowsky died in a hospital in New York City on November 21, 1938, following an operation for an intestinal ailment and was buried at Mount Hope Cemetery in Westchester County in New York. He had one son and two daughters. His son, Leopold, the husband of George Gershwin's sister, Frances, was co-inventor (with Leopold Mannes) of Kodachrome. One of Godowsky's daughters was Dagmar Godowsky, an actress in silent films and on television.

Godowsky received an honorary doctorate in music from the Curtis Institute of Music in 1934.

ABOUT: Musical Courier, October 10, 1906; Musical

Golschmann

Observer, December 1916; New York Times, November 22, 1938; New Yorker, November 10, 1956; Notes, March 1957.

VLADIMIR GOLSCHMANN

Vladimir Golschmann

1893–1972

Vladimir Golschmann, conductor, was born in Paris on December 16, 1893, of Russian descent. His mother was Marie Rasumny Golschmann; his father, Leon, abandoned a career in medicine to study mathematics and literature and became the translator into French of almost one hundred books. He was also lexicographer of a French-Russian dictionary. An amateur pianist, he gave the four-year-old Vladimir his first piano lessons. Violin study soon supplemented piano study. (Boris, the other son in the family, did become a pianist.) In his early teens Vladimir gave violin recitals at the Sorbonne (University of Paris), but even then his primary ambition was to become a conductor.

He went to local schools and then to Buffon College in Paris. Later, at the Schola Cantorum, he made progress in piano and violin with Paul de Sausnières, Berthelier, and Caussade. After completing his music training, he played the violin in three of Paris's major symphony orchestras: first, the Pasdeloup; then, the Lamoureux; and then, the Paris Conservatory.

At seventeen he joined a chamber orchestra of seventeen musicians, some of whom later became world-famous: Jacques Thibaud, Lucien Capet, and José Iturbi. On one occasion the conductor was absent from a performance, and Golschmann took over the baton. Soon after that, Golschmann met Albert Verley, scientist, composer, and wealthy music amateur and patron, who in 1919 financed a symphony orchestra for Golschmann. In the next few years the Concerts Golschmann in Paris became famous for their performances of twentieth century music. Golschmann became intimately identified with the work of Les Six (a group of young French composers who made a cult of jazz and the music-hall style and became the center of many discussions) and was regarded as one of the most important early champions of the mu-

sic of Darius Milhaud, Arthur Honegger, and Francis Poulenc. On February 21, 1920, he conducted in Paris the world premiere of Milhaud's pantomime *Le Boeuf sur le Toit,* and in 1921 that of Milhaud's orchestral *Saudades do Brasil.* Five years later Golschmann identified himself with the avant-garde movement by conducting in Paris on June 19, 1926, the world premiere of George Antheil's *Ballet Mécanique,* scored for anvils, airplane propellers, electric bells, automobile horns, sixteen pianos, a player piano, and various percussion instruments.

After conducting guest performances with the Pasdeloup and the Orchestre Symphonique, in Paris, Golschmann was appointed by the French government early in the 1920s the director of the Cercle Musical of the Sorbonne, where he directed series of concerts. He arranged and conducted the Festivals of Contemporary Music in Paris featuring the music of Ravel and Stravinsky, conducted concerts at the International Festival of Music, and was music director at the Théâtre Beriza in Paris. In 1920 he conducted performances of the Diaghilev Ballet Russe. His fame was not confined to France, however. Through guest appearances in Madrid, Glasgow, Oslo, Brussels, Liège, and elsewhere in Europe, his reputation grew. In 1924 he was appointed the principal conductor of the Ballet Suédois with which he toured the United States, and for four years he led the Orquesta Sinfonica of Bilbao, Spain.

At Walter Damrosch's invitation he made his American debut as a guest conductor of the New

Golschmann: gōlsh′ màn

York Symphony Society in 1924. "His outstanding qualities," wrote Lawrence Gilman in the *Herald Tribune,* "are his vitality, his command of the orchestra, his power and intensity. He is a magnetic, stimulating conductor, unmistakably a man of talent. His reception was enthusiastic and his success was beyond question." He returned as guest conductor of the New York Symphony Society the following season.

From 1928 to 1930 he was the principal conductor of the Scottish Orchestra in Glasgow.

In 1931 Golschmann appeared as guest conductor of the St. Louis Symphony. His concerts were so successful that the following season he was appointed permanent conductor. He held that post for a quarter of a century, in which time he built the orchestra into a major symphonic ensemble ranking among the top orchestras in America and presented numerous world and American premieres. Among the world premieres heard in St. Louis under Golschmann were Morton Gould's *Harvest* (October 27, 1945), Erich Wolfgang Korngold's Violin Concerto with Jascha Heifetz as soloist (February 15, 1947), Vittorio Rieti's *Sinfonia Tripartita* (December 16, 1944), and numerous works by Alexandre Tansman including the *Rhapsodie Polonaise* (November 14, 1941), the *Ricercari* (December 22, 1949), the Symphony No.7 (October 24, 1947), *Triptyque* (November 6, 1931), and *Le Voyage de Magellan* (November 10, 1951).

In 1950, on the seventieth anniversary of the orchestra's founding, the St. Louis Orchestra under Golschmann toured the United States, making its first appearance in New York at Carnegie Hall in March of that year. Olin Downes wrote in the New York *Times* that the concert had "liveliness and musicianship under an uncommonly interesting conductor."

While fulfilling his duties in St. Louis, Golschmann appeared as guest conductor of many of the principal orchestras of the United States and Europe. Virgil Thomson, writing in the New York *Herald Tribune* about one of Golschmann's guest appearances at the Museum of Modern Art in New York in 1943, said: "For balance, precision, and authority, at once gracious and stately, we have heard no one like him here in recent years."

Upon his twenty-fifth anniversary as principal conductor of the St. Louis Symphony, Golschmann was presented with a silver plaque on which were autographed the names of twenty-four musicians who had played under him throughout the entire quarter of a century. At that time—1957—no conductor in America had held a conducting post that long.

After retiring from the St. Louis Symphony in 1957, Golschmann for a time fulfilled numerous guest engagements not only in the United States but also in Europe, Israel, and South America. In 1964 he was appointed principal conductor of the Denver Symphony where he remained until 1970. Among the last concerts he conducted were guest performances with the St. Louis Symphony on March 11 and 13, 1971.

On June 19, 1930, Golschmann married Odette le Cointe. They had no children. Their homes, first in St. Louis, then in Denver, and finally in New York City, were graced with their collections of modern French painting and African and Greek sculpture. Playing poker was one of Golschmann's favorite pastimes. He was the recipient of several French decorations: Officer of the Legion of Honor and Commander of the Order of Arts and Letters.

On March 1, 1972, Vladimir Golschmann died at his home in New York City.

ABOUT: Ewen, D. Dictators of the Baton. *Periodicals*—High Fidelity/Musical America, August, October, 1972; New York Times, July 1, 1962; Time, February 27, 1956.

Sir Eugene Goossens III

1893–1962

Eugene Goossens III, conductor, was born of Belgian ancestry in London on May 26, 1893, to a family of professional musicians. His grandfather, Eugene Goossens I, had been a well-known opera conductor in England and had directed the Liverpool premiere of *Tannhäuser* in 1882. His father, Eugene Goossens II, was also an opera conductor and had been associated with the Moody-Manners and the Carl Rosa opera companies. His mother, Annie, the daughter of opera basso Thomas Aynsley Cook, was a well-known member of the Carl Rosa Opera Company. His younger brother, Leon Goossens, became a renowned oboist. He served as first

Goossens: goo' s'nz

SIR EUGENE GOOSSENS III

oboe of the Queen's Hall Orchestra before embarking on a concert career in recitals, as soloist with orchestras, and in collaboration with chamber-music groups; he was made Commander of the British Empire. His two sisters, Marie and Sidonie, became professional harpists.

Eugene Goossens III received music lessons at an early age and at ten entered the Bruges Conservatory of Music in Belgium, where he remained three years. Returning to England in 1906, he attended the Liverpool College of Music for a year. Then he won a scholarship for the Royal College of Music in London where he studied the violin from 1907 to 1912 with Serge Rivarde, piano with Dykes, and theory with Charles Wood and composition with Sir Charles Stanford. After graduation from the Royal College in 1912, Eugene entered the ranks of professional musicians by joining the Queen's Hall Orchestra as violinist. He also became a violinist of the Philharmonic String Quartet and regularly conducted the orchestras of the Aldwych and Drury Lane Theaters in London.

In January 1916 Goossens conducted a performance of *The Critic,* an opera by Sir Charles Stanford, his formal debut as conductor. He did so well that Thomas Beecham made him his assistant with the Queen's Hall Orchestra, a post he retained until 1920. During this period he also conducted performances of the Handel Society and the Royal Choral Society, both in London. In 1921 he founded his own orchestra in London and for a single season led it in concerts of modern music. He was engaged to direct the

London performances of Diaghilev's Ballet Russe in the years between 1919 and 1923, performances of the Carl Rosa Opera Company at Covent Garden in 1922, and guest concerts with various European orchestras.

He went to the United States in 1923 when he was appointed principal conductor of the Rochester Philharmonic Orchestra in Rochester, New York. He remained there eight years, at the same time teaching classes in conducting at the Eastman School of Music. During these years he often conducted guest performances with other American orchestras. Towards the end of 1925 he led three concerts of the Boston Symphony, and on January 7, 1926, he made his New York debut with the New York Symphony Society. After his first New York concert Olin Downes described Goossens in the New York *Times* as a "definite personality [with] contagious enthusiasm." He had this to say of the performance of Stravinsky's *The Rite of Spring:* "He gave one of the clearest and most broadly effective interpretations of the score that has been heard here. ... It was this performance which promised in him a new arrival with something of his own to say." On January 24, 1926, in New York, Goossens conducted the world premiere of Carl Ruggles's *Portals,* and on January 29, 1927, also in New York, the premiere of the second movement of Charles Ives's Symphony No.4. In addition to his assignments with American orchestras, he also conducted several of Mozart's operas with the Rochester American Opera Company.

In 1931 he became permanent conductor of the Cincinnati Symphony Orchestra, succeeding Fritz Reiner. Goossens's fifteen years with this orchestra were distinguished by virtuoso performances of many modern compositions, numerous premieres, and musicianly projections of the classic and Romantic literature. Among the works that received their world premieres in Cincinnati under Goossens were Britten's *Scottish Ballad* for two pianos and orchestra, Bartlett and Robertson soloists (November 28, 1941); Paul Creston's *A Fanfare for Paratroopers* (November 27, 1942); John Haussermann's Symphony No.1 (February 21, 1941); Milhaud's *Fanfare de la Liberté* (December 11, 1942); Jaromir Weinberger's *A Lincoln Symphony* (October 17, 1941); and Emerson Whithorne's Symphony No.2 (March 19, 1937). During this time Goossens also served as the music director of many of the annual May music festivals in Cincinnati, where on May 12, 1944, he led the world premiere of Bernard Rogers's oratorio *The Passion.*

Goossens became an American citizen in 1943. He has provided the following personal information: "Outside of an occasional game of golf, I indulge in no kind of sport or sporting interest, though I formerly enjoyed fencing. Most of all I enjoy being left alone (though I am not what is known as unsociable), in preference with a good library of books. Architecture has always absorbed me and at one time I used to sketch every building I could find. I like swordfishing and anything connected with the sea. I would rather idle around a harbor than anything else I know, and can tell you the names and design of most of the trans-Atlantic liners. This comes of living my early youth in Liverpool. I also love to drive a steam locomotive and never lose an opportunity of accepting a ride.

"My secretary tells me, concerning my mannerisms and habits, that I am a telephone artist, by which she means that I must draw designs, when I speak over the telephone. . . . She also tells me that I cannot go anywhere without a cane, of which I have quite a collection. She tells me that my weaknesses are my London tailor and my Paris shirtmaker. The more decorative humanity happens to be the more partial I am towards it. I find a Tudor house with some adjoining elm trees more fascinating to keep company with than with the club bore."

After leaving Cincinnati in 1946, Goossens went to Sydney, Australia, where until 1956 he was the Conductor of the Sydney Symphony Orchestra and the director of the New South Wales Conservatory. In Sydney, Goossens led the world premieres of John Antill's *Corroborree* (August 18, 1946) and Britten's Piano Concerto with Arthur Benjamin as soloist (September 5, 1950), among other works. On March 9, 1956, Eugene Goossens was detained at the airport at Sydney and accused of trying to import to Australia over one thousand pornographic photographs. In the wake of the ensuing scandal he was forced to resign his music posts and return permanently to England.

Goossens was knighted in England in 1955. He was also made Chevalier of the French Legion of Honor. He was married three times: to Dorothy Dodsworth in 1919 (they had three daughters); to Janet Lewis in January 1930 after his divorce from Dodsworth (they had two more

daughters); and on April 18, 1946, to Marjorie Fetter Foulkrod.

Through the years Goossens also distinguished himself as a composer. His many compositions, in virtually every form of music, received major performances both in the United States and in Europe. On June 24, 1937, he conducted at Covent Garden the world premiere of his opera *Don Juan de Mañara* (libretto by Arnold Bennett), which was one of the musical events celebrating the coronation of King George VI. An earlier one-act Biblical opera, *Judith,* had been introduced at Covent Garden on June 25, 1929. Among other major Goossens compositions are his Concerto for Oboe and Orchestra, first presented in London on October 2, 1930, with Leon Goossens as soloist, and the Symphony No.1, introduced in Cincinnati under the composer's direction on April 12, 1940.

Eugene Goossens died in London on June 13, 1962.

ABOUT: Goossens, E. Overtures and Beginners: A Musical Autobiography. *Periodicals*—Music and Letters (London), December 1931; Time, July 26, 1943.

Glenn Gould

1932–

Glenn Herbert Gould, pianist, was born in Toronto, Canada, on September 25, 1932. His mother was Florence Grieg Gould. His father, Russell Robert Gould, was a furrier who played the piano well and gave Glenn his first piano lessons when he was just three. A musical prodigy, he was enrolled in the Toronto Royal Conservatory of Music in 1943. There he received his entire musical education, remaining enrolled until 1952. He studied piano mainly with Alberto Guerrero and composition with Leo Smith. At the age of twelve he was awarded the degree of Associate. While still attending the school he briefly held a post as organist at a local Episcopal Church, and on January 14, 1947, he made his concert debut performing Beethoven's Piano Concerto No.4 with the Toronto Symphony Orchestra. Upon graduation Glenn received the highest honors that the institution could bestow, both in piano and in composition. He was the youngest graduate in the history of the school.

On January 2, 1955, Gould made his first ap-

GLENN GOULD

pearance outside Canada, giving a recital in Washington, D.C. In the Washington *Post,* Paul Hume wrote: "It is unlikely that the year 1955 will bring us a finer piano recital. . . . We know of no pianist anything like him of any age." One week later Gould gave a recital in New York City. Although the critics were unanimously enthusiastic, Gould's American reputation can be said to have first been firmly established not with a public concert but through a recording, that of Bach's *Goldberg Variations* released by Columbia in January 1956. *Time* Magazine described his recording session at the Columbia studios in June 1955 as follows: "The frail-looking young pianist walked into the recording studio . . . wearing beret, coat, muffler and gloves, carrying two large bottles of spring water to drink, five small bottles of pills, and his own piano chair. Before he started to play, he soaked his hands and arms in hot water. . . . Then began a week's stint. . . . Sometimes he sang as he played, and when he finished a 'take' that particularly pleased him, he jumped up with a gleeful 'Wow!' But when a piano note sagged by a hair, a tuner was called instantly. And when the pianist made the same mistake three times, he announced desperately he must be suffering from a mental block."

In reviewing Gould's recording of the *Goldberg Variations* for the *Saturday Review,* Irving Kolodin wrote: "Here, unquestionably, is Something: a young pianist who can take such a seemingly mechanical sequence as the Bach elaborations . . . and make an absorbing, wholly

interesting experience of it. . . . Gould not only has all the finger discipline that can be taught but also the kind of darting finesse that cannot. In other words, along with learning the mechanics of his instrument thoroughly, Gould has been imbued with a considerable sense of what to do with them."

On July 9, 1956, an entire program was given over to Gould at the second annual music festival at Stratford, Ontario, in Canada, where he appeared in the triple role of composer, conductor, and pianist. He conducted Schoenberg's *Ode to Napoleon,* played the piano works of Alban Berg and Ernst Krenek, and was represented by his String Quartet No.1, Op. 1 (recorded later by Columbia in 1960).

His first tour as pianist took place during 1956 –1957 when he was heard throughout the United States and Canada both in recitals and in appearances with symphony orchestras. "He is a genius . . . one of the greatest in the world," affirmed Arthur Darack of the Cincinnati *Enquirer.* Alfred Frankenstein commented in the San Francisco *Chronicle* that Gould was "the foremost pianist this continent has produced in recent decades."

His European debut took place in the spring of 1957 when he made three appearances with the Berlin Philharmonic under Herbert von Karajan, the first on April 28. "Gould plays," said H. H. Stuckenschmidt, the Berlin critic, "as if possessed physically by a thousand passions, a young man in the strange way of a trance, an artist on the edge of dream and reality. His technical abilities are fabulous; the fluency in both hands, the manifold dynamics, and the many colors of his touch represent a degree of mastery which I have not come across since the time of Busoni." Shortly afterwards, when Gould performed at the Vienna International Music Festival, one of the Viennese critics said of him: "We do not know anyone who can equal him in the interpretation of the great master [Bach]"; another Viennese critic remarked that "Glenn Gould is possessed by Bach, under [his fingers] beats the great sensitive heart of Bach."

In May 1957 Gould became the first North American pianist invited to the Soviet Union. He gave eight concerts in Moscow and Leningrad within a two-week period, concerts that were so successful that six extra police officers had to be called to keep in check the crowds trying to gain admission. *Pravda* referred to his performances as "a bright and shining evening in the musical world," while the Soviet critic Vadim Salmanov described his playing as "veritable sorcery." Another critic, Heinrich Neuhaus, writing in *Culture and Life,* said: "He plays Bach as if he were one of the pupils of the Thomaskirche. . . . His performance is of extraordinary significance in having, as it were, bridged the distance between Bach and our own days."

After completing a sweep of Europe in 1958, Gould made his first appearance in Israel where once again the critics were rhapsodic. "Such playing," commented the critic of *Haaretz,* "moves the listener to the depths of his soul by its almost religious expression. We have never heard anything like it in one of our concerts. . . . He is a musical sensation."

In 1959 Gould played in four major festivals, including the Salzburg Festival in Austria and the Brussels World's Fair where he represented Canada. After that, for a number of years he toured Europe and the United States.

At the same time that he was becoming famous for his piano playing, he was attracting much notoriety and attention for his eccentric stage behavior. Coming out on the platform he looked ascetic and gawky in his ill-fitting formal attire and with his awkward mannerisms. He would begin to fuss endlessly with his piano stool, one of his own design which is a requisite part of the equipment he carries with him on his tours. Then he would adjust the seat higher, then lower, then higher again, seeming unable to find a comfortable position. Once this problem was solved, he would assume a posture that Richard Kostelanetz described in *Esquire* as "resembling the Australian crawl." During a performance he hums to himself and at times makes pithy comments under his breath on the quality of his performance. When during a concerto he has a long rest, he begins to conduct with one hand or both hands.

When on tour he carries with him, together with his personal belongings and his piano chair, a valise filled with medicines and his preferred brand of bottled water. He wears gloves, muffler, and a coat even in warm weather for fear of catching cold, and to prevent infection he never shakes hands with anybody.

After a recital in Chicago on March 28, 1964, Gould withdrew from concert life to become the first concert pianist to prefer reaching his public through recordings and television. He says he was seventeen when his "love affair with the microphone began." At that time he was performing some music by Hindemith and Mozart for a radio broadcast by the Canadian Broadcasting Company. Listening to a playback he discovered how he could improve his performance by making various adjustments in the sound. After his recording success with the *Goldberg Variations,* Gould devoted himself more assiduously than ever to recording sessions, feeling that here alone could he produce an art that met his most stringent demands. "Leaving the concert circuit wasn't a decision I reached overnight," he told an interviewer. "The original grand plan was to be out of the concert hall by the time I was thirty. Unfortunately, I missed the goal by two years."

It is on records, even more than on the stage, that Gould has given some of his finest performances, stripped as they are of the idiosyncrasies and mannerisms that often make his stage presence annoying. "With a piano on which the stroke of each key has been shortened a fraction of an inch to make its action more like that of a harpsichord," revealed *Time* in 1964, "Gould works tirelessly at recording sessions, positioning the microphone so close to the piano that his constant contrapuntal humming sometimes comes through on records. . . . His concert career has been made mainly notorious for flashes of eccentricity. . . . while his recording career has been a little short of genius."

Gould made his American television debut on January 31, 1960, as soloist with the New York Philharmonic under Leonard Bernstein. In 1961 he signed a contract with the Canadian Broadcasting Company, making his debut that year in a one-hour telecast, "The Subject is Beethoven," for which Gould served as narrator, pianist, and the author of the script. This program was a success and was repeated later in the season. Other one-hour telecasts followed: on Richard Strauss, on Russian composers, on Bach, on "The Anatomy of the Fugue."

He has also been a successful producer of radio and television shows for the Columbia Broadcasting Company. Over radio he experimented with a technique which he dubbed "contrapuntal radio"—documentaries in which snatches and fragments of interviews and other conversations are interwoven contrapuntally with appropriate musical excerpts. One such program was "Arnold Schoenberg: The First Hundred Years." Two others, "The Idea of North" and "The Latecomers," were concerned with his fascination with the effects of solitude in the Canadian northern regions, his first ventures with nonmusical subjects. "The point of these contrapuntal scenes," Gould has explained, "is that they test the degree to which one can listen simultaneously to more than one conversation or vocal impression."

In addition to his radio and television assignments and his prolific outpouring of recordings, Gould has devoted himself to writing book reviews and magazine articles, to interviewing himself about various musical subjects, to transcribing orchestral works for the piano, to preparing commercials, and to composing. He wrote the background music for the motion picture *Slaughterhouse Five* (1972).

Gould, who is not married, lives in a six-room apartment in Toronto. "As Gould neither cooks nor cleans," writes Richard Kostelanetz, "an occasional housekeeper fights a losing battle with the mess as well as supplies him some evenings with the one big meal he eats each day. Since he generally practices the piano less than an hour a day (touching it longer only before a recording session), and often goes for days without playing at all, he currently devotes most of his time to other activities, particularly writing and broadcasting. He entertains at home infrequently, and leaves the house as little as possible, usually either to perform work or dine with friends. . . . Although a slave to his commitments, most of which he fulfills responsibly, Gould also has the instincts of a Bohemian as well as the income to finance his several-hundred-dollar monthly telephone bill. . . . His favorite form of 'cooling off' is driving alone through the lumber towns along Lake Superior while listening to rock music on the radio. He prefers northern climates to tepid ones—London being the only city that might woo him away from Toronto; and in general he would like to spend more time in the country. 'I've got to have hills, water and leaden sky,' he says. 'My ability to work varies inversely with the niceness of the weather' "

Gould has a scholar's interest in world literature as well as in music history. He rarely attends concerts because he has a horror of drafty auditoriums. Besides, he adds, "I don't like to listen to music with thousands of people around.

I'm narcissistic about music—I like to do it alone on a phonograph, so I can think."

ABOUT: Ewen, D. Famous Instrumentalists. *Periodicals*—Esquire, November 1967; New York Times, January 5, 1974; New Yorker, May 14, 1960; Saturday Evening Post, April 3, 1959.

Gary Graffman

1928–

Gary Graffman, pianist, was born in New York City on October 14, 1928. His parents, Vladimir and Nadia Margolin Graffman, emigrated from Russia after the 1917 Revolution. His father, once a violin student of Leopold Auer at the St. Petersburg Conservatory, had served as director of a conservatory in Siberia. After going to the United States, he served for a time as concertmaster of the Minneapolis Symphony. After the family settled in New York City in October 1928, he became a member of the violin faculty at the David Mannes School of Music.

When Gary was three years old, his father began teaching him on a miniature violin, but when he had difficulty handling the instrument his father switched him to the piano. The boy's progress on the piano proved so rapid that his father turned him over to an experienced teacher, Cosby Dansby Morris, who prepared him for an audition at the Curtis Institute of Music in Philadelphia with the school's director, the piano virtuoso Josef Hofmann. Though only seven at the time, Gary was given a scholarship which continued for a decade of study, mainly with Isabelle Vengerova. Though both Gary's parents and the Curtis Institute frowned upon public appearances as a prodigy, Gary was permitted to give a few concerts in 1936 and to appear as a soloist with the Philadelphia Chamber String Sinfonietta, under Fabien Sevitzky. Two years later Sevitzky, as music director of the Indianapolis Symphony, invited the young pianist to appear with his orchestra. That same year Gary gave his first New York recital and one New York critic noted that he played "with a searching sense of style and an almost uncanny amount of musical understanding and poetry for a child of his years."

Gary continued to make intermittent appearances while devoting himself to music study at

GARY GRAFFMAN

the Curtis Institute and attending classes at the Columbia Grammar School in New York City. Despite such intense concentration on study and the demands made on him in his preparation for concert appearances, Gary pursued the usual activities of a young boy, playing baseball and football without any attempt to protect his hands.

In 1946 he was graduated from both the Curtis Institute and the Columbia Grammar School. A scholarship allowed him to continue academic studies at Columbia College for a year. In 1947 he entered the first regional competition of the Rachmaninoff competition and won a special award entitling him to appear as soloist with the Philadelphia Orchestra under Eugene Ormandy on March 28, 1947, in a performance of Rachmaninoff's Piano Concerto No.2. The critic of the *Evening Bulletin* said that he "displayed a commanding technical equipment, which combined massive power with velocity and the utmost accuracy. . . . It was apparent from the first attack of the heavy opening chords that assurance, a sound equipment, and power were among his assets." One day later this performance was broadcast throughout the United States over the coast-to-coast facilities of the Columbia Broadcasting System.

Recitals followed in Philadelphia, Washington, and Baltimore—and finally at Carnegie Hall on December 14, 1948. "What these children do!" exclaimed Olin Downes in the New York *Times*. "Mr. Graffman has extraordinary equipment and is obviously an exceptional tal-

ent. . . . This is a young pianist with a true and communicative temperament, an admirably schooled musician, and a virtuoso . . . who can give a representative performance before any audience in the world. It is not a small thing."

Winning the Edgar M. Leventritt Award in 1949 led to his first appearance with the New York Philharmonic under Leonard Bernstein, in February 1950, in the Brahms Piano Concerto No.1, and in March of the same year a performance of Beethoven's Piano Concerto No.3 with the Cleveland Orchestra under George Szell. In 1950, as a recipient of a Fulbright Award, he traveled and studied in Europe, making his home in Paris for a year. In the fall of 1951 he embarked on his first tour of the United States. In the spring of 1953 he toured with the Little Orchestra Society, Thomas Scherman conducting, in performances of five different concertos. In 1954–1955 he made his debut with the Boston Symphony, the Los Angeles Philharmonic, and several other major American orchestras. But these were also years of further music study: piano with Vladimir Horowitz and chamber music with Rudolf Serkin.

His studies concluded, Graffman put his virtuoso career into high gear. His first South American tour and his first recordings (RCA Victor) came in 1955–1956. His first full-scale tour of Europe began in the fall of 1956 with a highly praised performance of Prokofiev's Piano Concerto No.3 with the London Philharmonic. A six-month around-the-world tour in 1958–1959 covered Europe, India, Hong Kong, the Philippines, Australia, New Zealand, and the United States. In a year and a half between 1958 and 1960 he traveled about eighty-five thousand miles. His first tour of the Soviet Union took place in 1968.

He achieved top rank among concert pianists of the world in spite of the fact that he is not a charismatic personality on stage. Short, squat, compact, roundfaced, and bespectacled, he lacks glamour. As Martin Mayer said of him in the New York *Times:* "His platform manner can be described with the image Virgil Thomson once used for Jascha Heifetz—a salesman for a firm specializing in old masters." At the piano Graffman performs with professional dispatch, avoiding attitudes and pyrotechnics that have surefire audience appeal. What he has to sell, in short, is not a personality but musicianship, and it is his musicianship which has proved his most potent commodity. A pianist with a big style and an immense technique, he has earned the homage of the music world particularly in the Romantic literature of Chopin, Liszt, Tchaikovsky, Brahms, and Schumann, and in the works of such twentieth century masters as Scriabin, Rachmaninoff, Prokofiev, and Ravel. He has also served contemporary American music. On April 3, 1964, in New York he gave the premiere performance of Benjamin Lees's Piano Sonata No.4 which he had commissioned on a Ford Foundation Fellowship. Less than four years later he performed the world premiere of Benjamin Lees's Piano Concerto No.2 with the Boston Symphony in Boston under Erich Leinsdorf (March 15, 1968) and repeated the performance in New York, Kansas City, and Seattle.

On April 4, 1973, Graffman celebrated the twenty-fifth anniversary of his mature concert debut with a recital at Carnegie Hall. By then he had become the only pianist ever to record with all six principal symphony orchestras of America (Boston, Chicago, Cleveland, New York, San Francisco, and Philadelphia); the only American pianist to have recorded all three of Tchaikovsky's piano concertos; one of the few pianists to have played with twenty-two major American orchestras and to have made thirty-eight appearances with orchestras in a single season. He had averaged a hundred concerts a year over a ten-month period. Moreover, he had made a dozen or so tours of Europe and several tours of the Far East, the Soviet Union, Australia, and South America. "His has been a solid career," wrote Harold C. Schonberg in reporting the anniversary concert. "Through the years he has continually impressed as a serious, dedicated, conscientious pianist of unusual integrity."

On December 5, 1952, Graffman married Naomi Helfman who was studying composition with Wallingford Riegger and Stefan Wolpe. She always accompanies him on tours; they travel about ten months out of a year. Their home is a spacious apartment in the Osborne, a building diagonally opposite Carnegie Hall, in which they have assembled a precious collection of antique furniture and Oriental art and ceramics, including rare Chinese and Japanese paintings. Both Graffmans are excellent cooks, and both are partial to French and Oriental dishes. Graffman himself has made a specialty of mixing fruit-flavored vodka apéritifs.

Graffman is not a man to create front-page news either through word or deed, but he did so on February 27, 1964, when he refused to perform in Jackson, Mississippi, before a segregated audience. That incident was a temporary disaster, reducing the number of his engagements to just eight for the rest of that season. But he refused to retreat on his civil rights principles, and in the end he won. Not only did the number of his performing dates within the next two years increase, but when he returned to Jackson six years later, he played before an integrated audience.

ABOUT: Ewen, D. Famous Instrumentalists. *Periodicals*—High Fidelity, December 1967; New York Times, April 23, 1972, April 6, 1973; Newsweek, February 17, 1969; Time, December 29, 1967.

Donald Gramm

1927–

Donald Gramm (originally Donald Grambach), bass baritone, was born in Milwaukee, Wisconsin, on February 26, 1927, to Rinold H. and Victoria Danneker Grambach. His father was a high school teacher, and his older brother, Paul, became dean at the University of Wisconsin. "I always sang," he recalls. "I didn't know that people made a living singing, because I sang in church, and for free. When I heard someone like Dorothy Maynor sing a Sunday afternoon concert, I thought she was a housewife who sang on her day off." His love for music was acquired during his childhood through phonograph recordings. When he was eight he began piano lessons with Ruth Streeter. From 1935 to 1944 he received further music instruction, both at the piano and in voice, at the Wisconsin College of Music in Milwaukee. When his voice broke in 1940, Donald was encouraged by the choir director of the local Methodist Church to study the organ, which he did over a two-year period. In his fifteenth year with his voice changed to bass he resumed vocal study. His teacher was George Graham.

In 1943 Graham encouraged Donald to enter the Chicagoland Music Festival competition sponsored by the Chicago radio station WBN. He emerged with a medal and a contract to sing operetta and other semiclassical favorites at the Old Heidelberg restaurant in Chicago. Each

DONALD GRAMM

weekend he returned to Milwaukee to play the organ at the Sunday services of the Evangelical church. In Chicago, when he was seventeen, Donald made his appearance in opera, as Raimondo in a semiprofessional production of *Lucia di Lammermoor*.

In 1944 he entered the Chicago Musical College on a scholarship for vocal training. Later he attended Martial Singher's master classes at Santa Barbara in California and at Aspen in Colorado. During this period of study he received the Oliver Ditson Scholarship (for two years) and the Paul Lavalle Scholarship of the National Federation of Music Clubs (for three). Music study was combined with public appearances in recitals in the Chicago area as well as in Canada and Alaska in the years between 1945 and 1947.

As a result of winning the Paul Lavalle Scholarship, Gramm was invited to make his first radio appearance, on Lavalle's "Highways of Melody" program over the NBC network in May 1947. This in turn led to a job with Chicago's radio station, WGN, where over an eight-year period he was heard in such programs as "Chicago Theater of the Air," "Hymns of All Churches," "Club Time," and "The Best of All." During this time he was also appearing as a vocal soloist in churches, in recitals, and in performances of oratorios. In 1951 he made his debut in New York as a soloist with the Little Orchestra Society, Thomas Scherman conducting, in Berlioz' *L'Enfance du Christ*.

Josef Rosenstock, music director at Aspen, then about to become music director of the New York City Opera, induced Gramm to go with him to New York. "I didn't know any roles," Gramm confesses, but he went anyway. In the fall of 1952 he made his New York opera debut with the New York City Opera as Colline in *La Bohème*. Intensive study of the operatic repertory enabled Gramm to become a regular member of this company. During the next four years he was heard as Count Almaviva in *The Marriage of Figaro*, Figaro in *The Barber of Seville*, Alidoro in Rossini's *La Cenerentola*, and various other operas. He was also cast in several American premieres. Among these were Carl Orff's *Der Mond* (October 16, 1956) and Frank Martin's *The Tempest* (October 11, 1956). Elsewhere, Gramm appeared in the world premiere of Vittorio Giannini's *The Taming of the Shrew* (Cincinnati, January 31, 1953) and the American premieres of Bohuslav Martinu's *The Marriage* (NBC-TV, February 7, 1953) and Britten's *Gloriana* (Cincinnati, May 8, 1956).

Though Gramm withdrew in 1956 from the permanent cast of the New York City Opera Company, he returned intermittently in the ensuing years for guest performances. In one of these, on November 4, 1965, he appeared in the world premiere of Ned Rorem's *Miss Julie*. In the years between 1956 and 1958 he concentrated on recitals, appearances with orchestras, and performances at festivals. In 1958 he returned to opera as a member of the newly organized Boston Opera Group (later renamed Opera Company of Boston), of which Sarah Caldwell was founder and artistic director. With this group in July 1958 Gramm sang the role of the Earth King in Offenbach's rarely given opéra-bouffe *A Voyage to the Moon*. He continued to appear in many productions of the Opera Company of Boston in the years that followed. He participated in several American premieres: Schoenberg's *Moses and Aron*, as Moses (November 2, 1966); Roger Sessions' *Montezuma*, in the title role (October 19, 1969); and Prokofiev's *War and Peace*, as Dolokov and General Kutzov (May 8, 1974). He has also been heard with the Boston Company as Falstaff, as Philip II in the world premiere of the original French version of *Don Carlo*, as Sancho in *Don Quichotte*, Rocco in *Fidelio*, Bartolo in *The Barber of Seville*, Oroveso in *Norma*, Scarpia in *Tosca*, the father in *Louise*, in *Benvenuto Cellini*, and in a rare revival in America of Glinka's *Russlan and Ludmilla.*

"Donald's high level of musicianship and intelligence," Sarah Caldwell has said, "and his beautiful voice are attributes which make him the logical choice of a conductor. His remarkable ability for physical characterization and his deep interest in its development make him the logical choice of a stage director. The fusing of musical and dramatic values sets him apart as one of the most extraordinary actors of our time."

On April 7, 1963, Gramm created for the United States the role of Dr. Schoen in the American premiere of Berg's *Lulu* with the Santa Fe Opera in New Mexico. "It was the most difficult of the new music I had done," he has said, "and it also got me off on a new tangent of acting since I had preferred lighter comic roles."

Gramm made his debut at the Metropolitan Opera in New York on January 10, 1964, as Truffaldino in *Ariadne auf Naxos.* Though he himself felt he had been miscast, the critics spoke well of his performance. "The part is hardly big enough to warrant a very sophisticated judgment on how Mr. Gramm will fare in the house," said Eric Salzman in the New York *Times,* "but there was enough to suggest that the [bass baritone], familiar figure on the American musical scene, brings to the company a vocal quality and character style as well as a good musical stage presence." On February 14, 1964, Gramm took on the role of the Maharajah in Menotti's *The Last Savage* (receiving its American premiere that season). One season later Gramm was heard on the Metropolitan Opera stage in *Arabella, La Périchole,* and *Manon* and, on the spring tour of the company, as Leporello in *Don Giovanni.* Among his best roles at the Metropolitan Opera were Plunkett in *Martha,* Zuniga in *Carmen* (with which he helped to open the 1972-1973 season), Balstrode in *Peter Grimes,* Papageno in *The Magic Flute,* the doctor in *Wozzeck,* Varlaam in *Boris Godunov,* the Bailiff in *Werther,* and, on March 18, 1977, Dr. Schoen in the first Metropolitan Opera production of *Lulu.*

His career in Europe was first given momentum in 1961 with appearances at the Berlin Festwochen. In 1967 he was heard as Leporello at the Festival of Two Worlds in Spoleto, Italy. In 1969 he was Don Basilio and Leporello at the Aix-en-Provence Festival in France. In 1975 he was Nick Shadow in Stravinsky's *The Rake's Progress* at the Glyndebourne Festival. "Donald Gramm's smiling, charming, beautifully sung and enunciated Shadow effortlessly stole the show—a triumphant British debut for this excellent American baritone," reported the London *Times.* Gramm returned to Glyndebourne a year later as Falstaff. "Mr. Gramm's voice sounded immense—much bigger, more resonant and colorful, than it ever has sounded in New York or Santa Fe, New Mexico," reported Harold C. Schonberg to the New York *Times* from Glyndebourne. "He acted Falstaff as a decaying knight and even a man of feeling. Certainly his low pitched 'Va, Vecchio, John' was an example of sensitive singing that made the fat knight an object of pity rather than scorn."

Gramm has appeared with numerous opera companies in the United States besides those already mentioned. On May 8, 1970, in Boston he was cast in the world premiere of Gunther Schuller's children's opera *The Fisherman and His Wife,* and in 1973-1974 he was heard in the American premiere of Monteverdi's *The Return of Ulysses* with the Opera Society of Washington (D.C.). In 1973-1974 he appeared as Talbot in Donizetti's *Maria Stuarda,* as Des Grieux in *Manon* with the Chicago Lyric Opera, and as King Dodon in *Le Coq d'Or* with the Dallas Civic Opera. In 1974 he appeared in the Houston Opera production of *Lulu* and in the title role in *Don Giovanni.* He made his debut with the San Francisco Opera in 1975 in the title role of *Gianni Schicchi.* On February 9, 1976, at Penn State University, he assumed eight roles in the world premiere of *Be Glad Then America,* a relic from 1775 adapted by John La Montaine and conducted by Sarah Caldwell.

In 1972 Gramm appeared in miniature recitals telecast over the NET network to fill out the time for its program "Masterpiece Theater." Though he taped only ten ten-minute programs, they were repeated so often that Donald Gramm became a household name around the country. He further enhanced his reputation nationally with recitals (some of them devoted entirely to American music, with the American composer Ned Rorem at the piano), and appearances with orchestras. He has been a guest artist with almost every major American symphony orchestra in performances of choral masterworks by Bach, Handel, Haydn, Mozart, Beethoven, Berlioz, Liszt, Fauré, Stravinsky, and Walton.

His predilection for twentieth century music is indicated in the recording catalogue by such albums as *The Music of Arnold Schoenberg,* and Stravinsky's *Oedipus Rex, Renard,* and the *Requiem Canticles* (all on Columbia label), and an album of Ned Rorem's songs (on Odyssey).

Donald Gramm has never married. He maintains a town house in New York City and a country home in Brookfield, Connecticut. Both places are repositories for his collections of paintings and artifacts of the Southwest and of American pressed glass.

To Richard Dyer, reporting in the New York *Times,* Gramm described his working procedures as follows: "I tape myself and listen to what I've done with the score, to catch anything I'm not doing right—or not doing at all. My memorizing I have to do in bed, late at night. I could sit all day long repeating words, but if I were to get up and drink a cup of coffee, I'd come back and find the page looking like something I'd never seen before. . . . I don't believe for a minute in method acting; somehow a moment comes when I find something that suits me and the character, too. The problem is to get the physical appearance enough in my mind that I can do a convincing job. The details come to me from all directions. Usually I begin to concentrate on the hand, on the space between the fingers, at how that looks."

ABOUT: New York, March 21, 1977; New York Times, February 23, 1975; Opera News, December 18, 1965, December 15, 1972.

Louis Graveure

1888–1965

Louis Graveure (originally Wilfred Douthitt), baritone and tenor, was born in the Belgravia district of London on March 18, 1888. He was the son of John Read Douthitt, a master builder, and Charlotte Maria Cordelia Graveure. For many years, while pursuing a successful career as a concert singer, Graveure kept the date and place of his birth a secret. The facts were finally discovered a few years before his death.

Originally Wilfred wanted to be an architect and attended the South Kensington Art School.

Graveure: grȧ vûr´

LOUIS GRAVEURE

Then, becoming interested in singing, he studied voice with Clara Novello-Davies. As Wilfred Douthitt, he appeared on October 28, 1914, on Broadway in New York in the successful operetta *The Lilac Domino,* in which his costar was Eleanor Painter. In the fall of 1915 he returned to New York from London as Louis Graveure; he wore a Vandyke beard and maintained that he was of Belgian birth. On May 2, 1916, he married Eleanor Painter (a marriage that ended in divorce in 1930). This marriage to a star with whom he had appeared one year earlier on Broadway, and his physical resemblance to the Wilfred Douthitt of Broadway fame, led some reporters to insist that Douthitt and Graveure were one and the same person, something which Graveure consistently denied.

He achieved his first American success in the American concert field as a baritone in Portland, Maine, in 1915, as a soloist in Mendelssohn's *Elijah.* An American tour followed, the first of many that in the next dozen years placed him among the distinguished vocalists on the American concert stage. One New York critic wrote of him: "Louis Graveure is one of the great singers of the day. He has a glorious voice of wide range, he understands every nicety in the use of it, he has a great store of genuine feeling, and beyond all this he is such an enchanter with his musicianship that the effect of his singing is hypnotic; he seizes his listeners in an instant, holds them breathless, hanging on his lips until the last note of the piece is finished."

During World War I Graveure was accused of

being not only a German but a German spy. Nevertheless he still refused to acknowledge his English origin. After the war, in 1920, he gave his first recital in Berlin, following which he repeated throughout Europe the success he had previously enjoyed in the United States. He continued to maintain a permanent residence in the United States, where for some years after World War I he taught singing at the University of Michigan.

In 1928 he returned to Europe for an extended stay. When the range of his voice changed to tenor, he made his stage debut as a tenor at the Charlottenburg Opera in Berlin in 1929. For several years he continued singing in operas in Germany and also in operettas and motion pictures.

Meanwhile, on February 5, 1928, Graveure made his second concert debut in the United States, this time with a recital in New York as a tenor. "He proved," reported the critic for the *Herald Tribune,* "well able to negotiate the top notes of his arias with distinct strength of tone, although when such notes called for considerable volume there was a slight hardness in the quality of tone. . . . But there was vocal steadiness. . . . Mr. Graveure's voice had an Italianate softness, but its clarity and absence of vibrato deserved praise."

During the Nazi regime in the 1930s Graveure lived in Germany. In June 1940 he was on a French boat bound for America, but because of World War II he was removed in Bordeaux by the British consul and was evacuated to England where he remained during the war years. While in England he married the film actress Camilla Horn.

When he returned to the United States in 1947, he still refused to admit that he and Douthitt were the same person and still denied knowing where or when he was born. He lived at first in Los Angeles, then in Texas, eventually settling in Los Angeles, where he devoted himself primarily to teaching singing. He died in Los Angeles on April 27, 1965.

ABOUT: Slonimsky, N. A Thing or Two About Music.

Reri Grist

1934?–

Reri Grist, soprano, was born in a Harlem slum in New York City in or about 1934. "I never wanted a career," she told an interviewer. "I never aspired to be a singer or a dancer. I sort of just went along." In her childhood she was given some dancing lessons. She began vocal study while attending the High School of Music and Art in New York City. There, Claire Gelda, a singing teacher, asked her to sing something and was so impressed that she offered to give her lessons. "I was fascinated with it [vocal lessons]," says Grist, "because it meant learning something new . . . and so I went on studying singing. But I never really thought of making a career. Things just fell into place."

As a child she made her stage bow on Broadway in a small part in *Jeb* in 1946. Four years later she had a walk-on role on Broadway in *The Wisteria Trees,* starring Helen Hayes, and later in Jan Meyerowitz's musical drama *The Barrier.* Meanwhile her academic education proceeded without interruption, first in the public schools in New York and then at Queens College, New York, where she received a Bachelor of Arts degree in music.

In 1956–1957 she appeared as Cindy Lou in a revival of the Oscar Hammerstein II musical play *Carmen Jones* (with Bizet's music from *Carmen*) at the New York City Center. She then returned to Broadway as Phyllis in *Shinbone Alley* and as Consuelo in the Leonard Bernstein musical play *West Side Story.* While performing in *West Side Story* she won the twelfth annual Young Artists' Award in 1958 which led to a recital at the Kaufman Auditorium in New York. The same year she also won the Blanche Thebom Award.

Her opera debut took place in 1959 with the Santa Fe Opera Company as Blonde in *The Abduction from the Seraglio.* That year she also made her debut with the New York City Opera in a performance of Orff's *Carmina Burana,* Leopold Stokowski conducting, and at Carnegie Hall where she was a soloist in the world premiere of Marvin David Levy's Christmas oratorio *For the Time Being.*

In 1960 she made her first appearance with the Cologne Opera in Germany as the Queen of

RERI GRIST

the Night in *The Magic Flute* and in Stravinsky's *Le Rossignol;* she was also heard that year for the first time as a soloist with the New York Philharmonic Orchestra in Mahler's Symphony No.4, Leonard Bernstein conducting. A year later her debut followed at the Zurich Opera in Switzerland (where she sang Sophie in *Der Rosenkavalier* and Rosina in *The Barber of Seville*). Then in 1962 came her first performances at the Glyndebourne Festival in England where she appeared sixteen times as Despina in *Così fan Tutte* and four times as Zerbinetta in *Ariadne auf Naxos.* In 1963 she made her bow at the Vienna State Opera, the San Francisco Opera, and the Holland Festival. The summer of 1964 at the Salzburg Festival she appeared in *Ariadne auf Naxos,* the first of several annual performances at this Austrian festival where she distinguished herself particularly in Mozart's operas.

On February 25, 1966, she made her debut at the Metropolitan Opera, as Rosina. "Lively, pretty, petite and blessed with a bright coloratura voice," said Louis Biancolli in the *World-Telegram and Sun,* "Reri Grist won the hearts and hands of all who caught her Metropolitan Opera debut last week. Along with a cameo beauty of face and figure and a vivacious acting style, the new Rosina had what counted most, a well-placed coloratura voice which dispenses pearls instead of tones."

The ensuing seasons at the Metropolitan Opera found Grist appearing as Sophie in *Der Rosenkavalier* (a role in which she sang with

great success at the Vienna State Opera in 1967, Leonard Bernstein conducting), Zerbinetta, Olympia in *The Tales of Hoffmann,* Oscar in *Un Ballo in Maschera,* Norina in *Don Pasquale,* Adina in *L'Elisir d'Amore,* and Gilda in *Rigoletto.* Upon her first appearance in New York as Zerbinetta, Harriet Johnson wrote in the *Post:* "For the first time in coloratura soprano Reri Grist the Met has a first class Zerbinetta, that wily, wise, willful, adorable minx who sings the aria containing the most difficult pyrotechnics in the entire soprano repertory. Pretty and petite, with really wicked round eyes, Miss Grist has, better yet, the voice and technique to make sweet music out of Zerbinetta's tricky, bold adventures in the vocal ionosphere." Her Sophie was called by Douglas Watt in the *Daily News* "exquisite" and by Alan Rich in *New York Magazine* "ideal . . . a reminder of young Erna Berger." It was as Sophie that Grist returned to the stage of the Metropolitan Opera on January 7, 1978, after a five-year absence.

She has appeared at Covent Garden in London, the Deutsche Oper in Berlin, the Volksoper in Vienna, Munich Opera, La Scala in Milan, the New York City Opera, and the San Francisco Opera. Besides the roles previously mentioned, she has been heard as Micaëla in *Carmen,* Titania in Britten's *A Midsummer Night's Dream,* the title role in *Lakmé,* Norina in *Don Pasquale,* Marie in *The Daughter of the Regiment,* Amor in Gluck's *Orfeo ed Euridice,* Zerlina in *Don Giovanni,* Susanna in *The Marriage of Figaro,* Queen of the Night in *The Magic Flute,* Serpina in Pergolesi's *La Serva Padrona,* Adele in *Die Fledermaus,* Aminta in Strauss's *Die Schweigsame Frau,* and Nannetta in *Falstaff.*

She has also appeared on film for television broadcasts in *Don Pasquale, Die Schweigsame Frau, The Marriage of Figaro, The Abduction from the Seraglio, Ariadne auf Naxos, The Barber of Seville, Un Ballo in Maschera,* and Stravinsky's *Le Rossignol.*

She is married to Ulf Thomson, Estonian-born musicologist and stage director who took on the responsibilities of serving as her personal representative. With their daughter they reside in southern Germany, not far from Munich; they also rent a house in New York City.

In an interview in the New York *Times,* John Gruen described her as "all smiles and charm . . . and straightforwardness. Her hairdo is Afro, and there are pretty little earrings dangling from her ears. . . . Her speaking voice is high-pitched and melodious; it suggests the timbre of her singing voice, with its boy-soprano 'whiteness' of intonation. As she begins speaking, I note the barest suggestion of a European accent. . . . There is an almost defiant sense of self-assurance about Reri Grist—a self-confidence and open-faced candor that somehow obscure the deeper issues of her hard-earned accomplishments. The fact of her color, for example, does not seem to produce the slightest ruffle of concern. For Miss Grist, being black is merely an attribute as human and incontestable as being male or female. You live with it."

In 1976, Reri Grist was named *Kammersängerin* by the Bavarian government.

ABOUT: Esquire, February 1969; Hi-Fi, January 1970; New York Times, October 4, 1970.

ARTHUR GRUMIAUX

Arthur Grumiaux

1921–

Arthur Grumiaux, violinist, was born in Villers-Perwin, near Charleroi, Belgium, on March 21, 1921. He was just three when his grandfather, an excellent musician, noticed that he had perfect pitch and presented him with a gift of a miniature violin. He also gave Arthur his first lessons. By the time Arthur was five he was able to make his first public appearance.

At the Conservatory of Charleroi he studied violin and piano with Fernand Quinet. A year after graduation from the Conservatory at the age of eleven, Arthur was placed in the Brussels Conservatory, where he specialized in the violin with Alfred Dubois. During the next few years, Arthur captured first prizes in violin, harmony, counterpoint, and fugue, together with the Diplôme Supérieur for violin. In 1939 he captured the Vieuxtemps Prize for violin playing and in 1940 the Prix de Virtuosité from the Belgian government. Subsequently he studied composition in Paris with Georges Enesco, while completing his education at the Episcopal College where he majored in literature, languages, and history.

He first appeared as a mature artist just before World War II when he performed Vieuxtemps's Violin Concerto No.5 over the radio. Alphonse Onnou, a member of the celebrated Pro Arte

Quartet, heard that broadcast and used his influence to get the Brussels Philharmonic Orchestra to engage Grumiaux as soloist. With Charles Munch conducting, Grumiaux performed the Mendelssohn Violin Concerto and was acclaimed. This was his last public appearance for several years.

During the difficult years between 1940 and 1945 Belgium was occupied by the Nazis. Though he was unable to advance his career as a virtuoso, Grumiaux played the violin with the Artis String Quartet for four years, and taught violin at the Brussels Conservatory. The Nazis offered him the post of concertmaster with the Dresden Philharmonic, but he turned it down and then went into hiding. When Belgium was liberated, he played for the Allied troops in Belgium, Holland, France and, after VE Day, in Germany.

After the war he resumed his concert career. He was the first continental artist to appear in England since 1939, and his appearance there was the start of his international fame. He toured Europe extensively, highly regarded for the sensitivity and refinement of his performances as well as for his penetrating musicianship. He appeared with outstanding success throughout Scandinavia, Italy, France, Spain, and Switzerland, both in recitals and as soloist with principal orchestras; he was heard at festivals in Prague, Strasbourg, Glyndebourne, and Aix-en-Provence. In 1949 he was appointed professor of violin at the Brussels Conservatory, succeeding Alfred Dubois.

322

His American debut took place at the Peabody Conservatory in Baltimore on January 18, 1952. In the Baltimore *News-Post* Helen Penniman described "the magnificent texture of his tone ... like the latent shades in changeable silk" and his "admirable solo work aside from the spirited sentiment of the interpretation." Grumiaux appeared on February 1 with the Boston Symphony Orchestra, Ernest Ansermet conducting, in a concerto by Mozart. Cyrus Durgin said in the Boston *Globe* that his playing was "sheer beauty in rhythm and phrasing, sweet and rich of tone, and absolutely perfect as to style." An intensive tour of the United States followed, the first of many he would undertake in subsequent years.

His wife, the former Amanda Webb, is also a violinist. They live in a secluded part of Brussels. Grumiaux's diversions include reading books on history, cooking, playing chamber music, amateur photography, and going to the movies.

ABOUT: Who's Who in America.

Hilde Gueden

1917–

Hilde Gueden (originally Hilde Geiringer), soprano, was born in Vienna on September 15, 1917. She is of Austrian, Italian, and Hungarian descent. Her grandfather was a noted tragedian; her mother, Frida Brammer Geiringer, a professional actress; her father, Fritz Geiringer, a member of a prosperous Italian-Austrian banking family. Both parents were amateur musicians. Her musical education began at the piano when she was seven, and when she was fourteen she started studying voice.

In her sixteenth year she attracted the interest of the Viennese operetta composer Robert Stolz, who gave her a part in his musical *Goodbye, Goodbye.* Though she became an instant favorite in Vienna, she had no intention of devoting herself exclusively to the popular musical theater. During the run of the Stolz play she studied dramatics at the Max Reinhardt School, and ballet with the prima ballerina at the Vienna State Opera.

After *Goodbye, Goodbye* she starred in another operetta, *Hearts in the Snow,* her last appearance in the popular theater before World War II.

HILDE GUEDEN

When the Nazis took over Austria, she escaped to Switzerland. There she sang for Robert Denzler, the director of the Zurich Opera, who engaged her for his company. She made her operatic debut with the Zurich Opera in 1939 as Cherubino in *The Marriage of Figaro.* During the two years she remained with this company she appeared in numerous coloratura and lyric roles.

In 1941 she returned to Vienna to help her mother and sister who were being persecuted by the Nazis. Unable to escape from the Nazi orbit, she went to Munich where she appeared successfully at the Munich Opera as Zerlina in *Don Giovanni,* Clemens Krauss conducting. There she distinguished herself in a varied repertory, but principally in Mozart's operas. While appearing in *Così fan Tutte* she was heard by Richard Strauss, who visited her in her dressing room to persuade her to study the role of Sophie in his opera *Der Rosenkavalier.* She made her Italian debut in that role at the Royal Opera in Rome in December 1942 with Tullio Serafin conducting. After hearing her in this part, Strauss presented her with his photograph signed: "To my Sophie Gueden." Unwilling to return to Nazi Germany, Gueden stayed in Italy, appearing at the May Music Festival in Florence. But when Italy was occupied by Nazi troops, she retired temporarily from opera and went into seclusion, first in Venice, then in a small town near Milan.

After the war she was invited to sing at the Salzburg Festival where in 1946 she was a triumph as Zerlina. She appeared and was acclaimed at the Salzburg Festival many times after that, particularly in 1954 as Zerbinetta in *Ariadne auf Naxos,* and in 1960 when she helped to open the new Festival Theater as Sophie in *Der Rosenkavalier.* Meanwhile, in 1947 she joined the companies of the Vienna State Opera and La Scala as leading soprano, dividing her season between them and becoming a favorite in both places. In 1950 she was named by the president of Austria *Kammersängerin,* the youngest singer to be thus honored. In 1959 she received from Austria the Grand Cross for Science and Art and the Vienna Philharmonic presented her with its honorary insignia, the Silver Rose. She was also decorated by Denmark with the Cross of the Order of the Dannebrog in 1962, and in 1972 she became an honorary member of the Vienna State Opera. Other decorations and honors included the Grand Cross of Honor in 1972 and the Golden Orpheus of the Académie de Lyrique, both in Paris. For her recordings she received the Decca Golden Record in 1958, and the Golden Oscar of the Académie du Disque Français in 1961.

Her successes spanned all of Europe: Holland, Covent Garden in London, the Paris Opéra, the Glyndebourne Festival in England, the Edinburgh Festival in Scotland, and other operatic and festival centers.

When Rudolf Bing, general manager of the Metropolitan Opera, heard her in Paris during a visit to that city of the Vienna State Opera, he invited her to join the Metropolitan Opera. She made her American debut there on November 15, 1951, as Gilda in *Rigoletto.* To Louis Biancolli, writing in the *World-Telegram and Sun,* she was "lovely to look at and lovelier to listen to. The voice blossomed into rich flower, every note in its place like a petal—a voice clear, true and confident. . . . She is a welcome dish to the eye and ear."

That first season proved that she was a worthwhile addition to the Metropolitan. She was acclaimed as Rosalinda in *Die Fledermaus* on November 30, and as Susanna in *The Marriage of Figaro* on January 4, 1952. She was also heard and appreciated as Musetta in *La Bohème* and Micaëla in *Carmen.*

Hilde Gueden remained with the Metropolitan Opera company until 1960, adding to her roles those of Sophie in *Der Rosenkavalier,* Norina in *Don Pasquale,* Mimi in *La Bohème,* Zerlina, Euridice in Gluck's *Orfeo ed Euridice,* and

Marguerite in *Faust.* She was also heard in two important American premieres: as Anne in Stravinsky's *The Rake's Progress* on February 14, 1953, and as Zdenka in Strauss's *Arabella* on February 10, 1955.

Her success in *The Rake's Progress* and in the operas of Richard Strauss made her a significant interpreter of twentieth century operas. She has distinguished herself in Kurt Weill's *The Rise and Fall of the City Mahagonny,* Boris Blacher's *Romeo und Julia* (in which she created the role of Julia at the Salzburg Festival in 1950), Britten's *The Rape of Lucretia,* and Hindemith's *Mathis der Maler.*

Hilde Gueden has also performed frequently in recitals, over radio and television. On February 28, 1952, she married L. Lacey Herman; they have one son. This was her second marriage; her first husband was Robert Josef.

She acquired her large and varied repertory because of her ability to learn roles quickly. Studying a new role she often works without an accompanist, since she is a trained pianist and can well serve that function herself. After she has appeared in a part ten times or so—a period she refers to as "ripening"—she takes "a new look at it from every possible point of view and subjects it to painstaking reevaluation."

ABOUT: New York Times, December 2, 1951.

Vittorio Gui

1885–1975

Vittorio Gui, conductor, was born in Rome on September 14, 1885, to Attilio and Luigia Lupi Gui. His father was a physician. He was first taught music by his mother and then received his musical training at the Santa Cecilia Academy in Rome, mainly with Stanislao Falchi and Giacomo Setaccioli. His debut as a conductor took place at the Teatro Adriano in Rome on December 7, 1907, with *La Gioconda.* Three years later he succeeded Campanini as principal conductor of the San Carlo Opera in Naples. Gui also conducted symphony concerts at the Turin Exposition in 1911 and at the Augusteo in Rome in 1912.

His masterful conducting performances soon

Gui: gwē

placed him among Italy's brilliant younger men of the baton. Early in his career he revealed a command of a wide and varied repertory that included contemporary works, and he usually conducted from memory. The Italians soon began referring to him as "a young Toscanini." "He is of the Toscanini type," wrote one of the Italian critics, "free from mannerisms, at times elegantly reserved."

In 1924 Gui was appointed conductor of the Società dei Concerti Sinfonica in Milan. Four years later he made his debut at La Scala in Milan. Between 1925 and 1928 he was the music director of the Teatro di Torino in Turin where he inaugurated and directed an outstanding repertory. Under his direction the Turin Opera became one of the major opera companies in Italy.

He left the Turin Opera after three years, and in 1928 settled in Florence, making his home for the rest of his life at Fiesole on the outskirts of the city. In 1928 he founded the Orchestra Stabile, which he conducted for the next fifteen years. In 1933 he helped found the annual May Music Festival at which his performances were often the highlights of each season—one such was his performance of Gluck's *Alceste* in the Boboli Gardens in June 1935. Because of the high standards set by the Orchestra Stabile and the growing international fame of the May Music Festival, Florence became one of Italy's music centers, a development for which Gui deserved much of the credit. During these years he was also conducting in all parts of Italy and was a strong propagandist for the works of such twentieth century composers as Busoni, Malipiero, Ravel, and Richard Strauss.

After World War II Gui made numerous appearances in England, beginning with opera performances in 1947. In 1960 he was appointed artistic adviser of the Glyndebourne Festival at which during the next five years he gave many memorable performances. He was heard at the festivals at Salzburg and Edinburgh, and in London, Budapest, Vienna, Lisbon, Moscow, and Leningrad. He also made numerous recordings of operas and symphonic music and through these music lovers in America came to know him.

Gui remained active until the end of his life. On his ninetieth birthday, September 14, 1975, he was honored at a special celebration attended by some of the prominent cultural figures of It-aly. On that occasion he was presented with a gold medal by the regional administration of Florence, the last of a number of honors he had gathered during his lifetime. In 1923 he had been made Commander of the Crown of Italy, and in 1957 he had received the gold medal for culture from the Italian government. The city of Pesaro had made him an honorary citizen. In 1941 Sweden had made him commander of the Order of Vasa.

Gui conducted his last performance on October 4, 1975, when he led a program of symphonic works by Mozart and Brahms in Florence with the orchestra he had founded in 1928. He died two weeks later, on October 16, 1975, at his home, Villa S. Maurizio, in Fiesole.

Gui was the composer of an opera, *Fata Malerba,* which received its world premiere in Turin on May 15, 1927. He also wrote a number of symphonic works and compositions for voice and orchestra. He was the author of a monograph on Boïto's *Nerone* (1924) and a volume of critical essays, *Battute d'Aspetto* (1944).

Gui was twice married, the first time to Maria Bourbon del Monte S. Maria, and the second time to Ilda Salardi-Enriques.

ABOUT: New York Times, October 18, 1975.

Bernard Haitink

1929–

Bernard J. H. Haitink, conductor, was born in Amsterdam on March 4, 1929, to a cultured and prosperous Dutch family. He began studying violin when he was ten, then attended the Amsterdam Conservatory, where he specialized in the violin but also received instruction in conducting from Felix Hupka. In 1954 and 1955 he studied conducting with Ferdinand Leitner.

Upon graduation from the Conservatory, Haitink served his music apprenticeship as second violin with the Netherlands Radio Orchestra. In 1955 he was appointed assistant conductor to Ferdinand Leitner with the Radio Union in Hilversum. He was in charge of four orchestras and directed radio concerts.

In 1956 Carlo Giulini fell ill and could not fulfill an assignment to conduct Cherubini's Requiem at the Holland Music Festival. Haitink, then only twenty-seven, was called in as a re-

Haitink

BERNARD HAITINK

placement. He did so well that in 1957 he was appointed principal conductor of the Radio Philharmonic Orchestra in Amsterdam. Engagements as guest conductor with several major European orchestras followed. In October 1957 he made his American debut with the Los Angeles Philharmonic in California.

For five weeks in 1958–1959 Haitink served as a guest conductor of the Concertgebouw Orchestra in Amsterdam. In 1959 he toured with this orchestra in Great Britain. In 1961 he became joint conductor of the Concertgebouw with Eugen Jochum and made his first tour of the United States with the Concertgebouw in its first appearances there. He became the principal conductor of the Concertgebouw in 1964. In April of that year he toured a second time with the Concertgebouw in the United States, presenting three concerts celebrating the opening of the World's Fair. In 1965 he toured with the orchestra in Great Britain, Switzerland, and West Germany. When the Concertgebouw Orchestra made its fourth tour of the United States in May 1967, one of the highlights was Haitink's performance of Bruckner's Symphony No.7. "Haitink's carefully reasoned, deeply felt interpretation," commented *Time,* "brought out each secondary melody and delicately balanced the softer shimmer of strings with the noblest blast of brass. Yet, as he built from climax to climax, he never lost sight of the unifying line." In 1974 and again in 1977 Haitink and the Concertgebouw toured Japan.

In 1967 Haitink was appointed principal con-

ductor of the London Philharmonic Orchestra in England on a unanimous vote of its musicians. In 1970 he became artistic director. His duties required him to conduct about fourteen weeks each season in London. Since he still retained his post in Amsterdam he remained twice that time with the Concertgebouw. "It's like being married to two women," he remarked. "Like a woman, every orchestra has its own personality, that must be handled with care." With the London Philharmonic Haitink toured Japan in 1969; the United States in 1970 and 1971; Berlin in 1972; Holland, Germany, and Austria in 1973; and, in 1975, the Soviet Union. Writing in the *New Yorker,* Andrew Porter remarked: "By and large, Mr. Haitink must be the conductor most solidly esteemed in Europe today. Solti and Karajan may generate more heat; they are more extravagantly acclaimed, but often with reservations, while Haitink is simply and unanimously praised for his excellence."

Upon his first appearance in New York with the London Philharmonic in April 1970 Hubert Saal remarked in *Newsweek:* "He looked like a Hollywood version of a conductor. He has an imperious air, a ramrod-straight back, a nobly held head. But his gestures are fluid and sure. He appears to know every detail of what he wants and is prepared to fight and plead for it, visibly and emotionally, on the podium."

On this occasion Haitink's program included Bruckner's Symphony No.2. Bruckner's Symphony No.7 was the principal item in the concert with which Haitink made his bow with the New York Philharmonic in January 1975. "Mr. Haitink is submerged in this music," said Harold C. Schonberg in the New York *Times.* "Therefore the symphony emerged with a special kind of warmth, and with a great deal of personality.... Under his baton there was an organlike sonority —romantic registrations supported by marching brasses." About Haitink's conducting style, Schonberg had this to say: "As a podium figure, Mr. Haitink is not one of the glamour boys. He does not dance, he does not patronize the best tailor on the Continent. But he is a dedicated musician, always on top of the music, getting exactly what he wants from his players. He also has the technical equipment. Most of all, he seems to have a romantic impulse unusual these days."

In addition to his assignments with the Concertgebouw and the London Philharmonic, Haitink has appeared as a guest of major orchestras throughout Europe and the United States. Until 1972 he was exclusively a conductor of symphonic music. Then, in 1972, he made a highly successful debut as a conductor of opera at the Glyndebourne Festival with performances of Mozart's *The Abduction from the Seraglio.* Conducting opera for the first time was, he has said, "a ray of light." Following this debut he led performances of operas by Mozart and Wagner with the Netherlands Opera. He was a guest conductor at the Glyndebourne Festival in 1972 and 1973, and in 1978 he was appointed its musical director. At Glyndebourne, in 1976, Haitink led distinguished performances of a new production of *Pelléas and Mélisande.* In 1977 he made his opera debut at Covent Garden in London with *Lohengrin* and *Don Giovanni.*

As a specialist in Bruckner and Mahler, Haitink has recorded for Philips all the symphonies of these composers. (He was the first conductor ever to record all of Mahler's symphonies.) He has also recorded all Beethoven's symphonies and piano concertos. As of 1977 he had made more than one hundred and twenty-five recordings.

In 1969, on the occasion of the eightieth anniversary of the Concertgebouw Orchestra, Queen Juliana of the Netherlands bestowed on Haitink the Royal Order of Orange Nassau in recognition of his services to the orchestra. In 1970 he received the medal of honor of the Bruckner Society in the United States; he has also been awarded the Gold Medal of the Mahler Society. In 1972 he was named Chevalier, Ordre des Arts et des Lettres in France; and in 1973 he was made honorary member of the Royal Academy of Music in London. In 1977 he was awarded an honorary knighthood of the British Empire "in recognition of his enormous contribution to the artistic life of this country."

With his wife, Jarolein, and their children, Haitink maintains a home in Amsterdam, a cottage in Glyndebourne, and a flat in London. A man of subdued temperament, given to introspection, he is as unspectacular off stage as on. He is a quiet person, dignified and modest, and shuns any of the trappings of showmanship or artistic temperament. The activities he enjoys most are long strolls in the woods, swimming, reading, and birdwatching. "I refuse to be anything but a normal human being in a very odd profession," he says.

ABOUT: New York Times, November 21, 1976; Newsweek, May 4, 1970; Stereo Review, December 1976; Time, May 12, 1967.

Mark Hambourg

1879–1960

Mark Hambourg, pianist, was born in Bogutchar, Russia, on May 31, 1879. His father, Michael Hambourg, a professor of piano at the Moscow Conservatory, had three sons; all three became successful concert artists. Jan, a pupil of Eugène Ysaÿe, toured Europe and the United States as a concert violinist; Boris, a cellist, in addition to his concert appearances as a virtuoso was a member of the Hart House String Quartet organized in Toronto, Canada, in 1924; Mark, the oldest son, was heard throughout the world in concerts and recitals.

Mark received his first piano lessons from his aunt when he was five years old. He later confessed that he detested practicing so violently that on one occasion he ran a needle into his finger to find an excuse for staying away from the keyboard. Nevertheless he made excellent progress. When he was seven, his father became his teacher, and one year later Mark appeared as soloist with the Moscow Philharmonic Orchestra in a performance of a Mozart concerto.

When Mark was ten, the family moved to London. There, in 1890, he made his English debut with a recital at the Princess Theater. The conductor Hans Richter and the piano virtuoso Paderewski were impressed with his talent and persuaded his parents to send him to Vienna for study with Theodor Leschetizky. Mark went in 1891, working for three years with the Viennese piano master and winning the Liszt Scholarship. In his third year with Leschetizky, Mark performed for Anton Rubinstein, who immediately proclaimed him to be his own successor.

In 1894 Mark made his debut in Vienna in the Chopin Concerto in E minor, Richter conducting the Vienna Philharmonic. Both audience and critics received the performance enthusiastically. Eduard Hanslick, the Viennese critic, called him "a young Rubinstein." One year later Mark appeared as a soloist with the London Philharmonic. An Australian tour took place in

Hambourg: hăm′ bŏŏrg

MARK HAMBOURG

1895–1896, and a German tour in 1897. Indicative of his rapidly growing fame was the fact that in 1896, when Paderewski was indisposed and could not fill a London engagement, Mark was called upon as a substitute.

Hambourg's first American tour took place in 1899–1900, at which time his impressive technique, strength, and impetuosity attracted many favorable comments. Several years later his recital at Mendelssohn Hall in New York on January 13, 1902, led Richard Aldrich to say in the New York *Times:* "The storm and stress are as great as ever in what he does; and they have the same effect, at times stimulating, at times destructive of musical beauty. Mr. Hambourg has a muscular technique that is well under his control, untiring strength of finger and of arm, fluency and delicacy, and he can do what he wishes in producing dynamic gradations. He can thunder or he can lull you as gently as any suckling dove."

The growing subtlety and variety of pianistic style in Hambourg's performances became evident to Richard Aldrich at Hambourg's New York concert on November 1, 1907, the pianist's return to New York after an absence of four seasons. "He is older, portlier and has gone through what with some men is a sobering experience," wrote Aldrich, "but storm and stress still control and influence his playing, and they probably always will." However, Aldrich also noted that "in his touch and his production of tone upon the piano there are many beautiful things constantly appearing. . . . There are pas-

sages, phrases, that come forth from his hands as veritable pearls."

On June 16, 1906, Hambourg gave his one-thousandth concert. For many years after that he was heard in recitals and as guest artist with orchestras throughout the world. In addition he participated in chamber-music concerts with his two brothers and with the Kneisel Quartet. He frequently included on his recital programs new piano works which had won prizes in special competitions he himself had conducted among European composers. He also gave master classes in piano at the Hambourg Conservatory in Toronto, Canada, which his father had founded in 1911.

In 1907 Hambourg married Dorothy Mackenzie, daughter of Lord Muir Mackenzie. They lived at Langford Place, St. John's Wood, in London, with their four daughters, one of whom, Michal, also became a concert pianist. Hambourg's recreations were golf and collecting antiques.

Hambourg was the composer of many works for the piano including the *Variations on a Theme of Paganini,* the *Volkslied,* and many solo pieces. He was the author of *How to Play the Piano* (1922); an autobiography, *From Piano to Forte: A Thousand and One Notes* (1931); a second volume of memoirs, *The Eighth Octave* (1951).

Mark Hambourg died in Cambridge, England, on August 26, 1960.

ABOUT: Hambourg, M. The Eighth Octave; Hambourg, M. From Piano to Forte: A Thousand and One Notes.

Tauno Hannikainen

1896–1968

Tauno Hannikainen, conductor and a highly esteemed interpreter of the music of Jean Sibelius, came from a family of musicians. His father, Pekka Hannikainen, was a conductor, violinist, composer, teacher, and the founder of the first music journal in the Finnish language. Three of Tauno's brothers were also professional musicians: Ilmari, a pianist, composer, and professor at the Sibelius Academy in Helsinki; Arvo, a

Hannikainen: hän nǐ kǐ' nĕn

TAUNO HANNIKAINEN

In 1938 Hannikainen was invited by the Finnish government to conduct a special concert in the United States commemorating the three-hundredth anniversary of the settling of Delaware by Finns. It was on this occasion that he made his American debut, on June 30. Two years later he returned to the United States to conduct the Boston Symphony in Boston on February 2 and 3, 1940, and at Carnegie Hall in New York City on February 15, and in Brooklyn, New York, on February 17. That summer he led the Philadelphia Orchestra at Robin Hood Dell, and in December of the same year he was on the podium of the Detroit Symphony for two weeks.

violinist; and Väinö, a harpist and composer. Their mother, Laura Alfhild Nikander Hannikainen, daughter of a cantor, was a singer and teacher before her marriage.

Tauno was born in Jyväskylä, in south central Finland, on February 26, 1896. There he attended the Lyceum until his eighteenth year, and from 1914 to 1917 he was a student at the Helsinki University and the Helsinki Conservatory. At the Conservatory he specialized in cello, organ, and piano. From 1916 to 1919 he was the first cellist of the Helsinki City Symphony.

When war and revolution interrupted his musical pursuits, Hannikainen proved so active in the struggle that he was awarded the civil war medal.

After World War I Hannikainen joined his brothers, Arvo and Ilmari, in forming the Hannikainen Trio; they performed not only in Finland but also on the Continent. After serving for a time as assistant conductor of the Finnish State Opera in Helsinki, Hannikainen was promoted in 1922 to principal conductor, a post he held for five years. During this period he continued his music study: cello with André Hekking and Pablo Casals in Paris; composition in Berlin and Vienna.

In 1927 he was appointed principal conductor of the Turku Symphony in southwest Finland. While retaining this post for the next dozen years he appeared as guest conductor throughout Scandinavia and in many European cities. On June 21, 1933, he married Finnish operatic soprano Anne Arvida Niskanen.

In 1941 he was made music director of the Helsinki City Symphony, but because of the outbreak of World War II he did not fill this post at the time. Instead he settled in the United States, where in 1942 he was appointed permanent conductor of the Duluth Symphony. He remained in Duluth five years. "Schooled in the more formal traditions of Europe," wrote DeWitt John in *The Christian Science Monitor* at this time, "he insisted on strictly businesslike rehearsals and hard work." During World War II Hannikainen made frequent concert appearances to help raise funds for Finnish, Norwegian, and British war relief.

In 1946 he conducted the Chicago Symphony at Ravinia Park and occasionally over the radio. In October 1947 he became assistant conductor of the Chicago Symphony. When he was promoted to associate conductor he led the orchestra in eighty-five concerts in the 1949–1950 season. In reviewing one of his concerts, a critic for the New York *Times* described his "complete poise and control, the balancing of all elements, power held long in reserve for shattering climaxes, and reigning over all, a sovereign nobility."

In 1951 Hannikainen returned to his native country, finally assuming the post of music director of the Helsinki City Symphony which he had accepted a decade earlier. His all-Sibelius concerts and festivals with this orchestra attracted world interest.

Hannikainen was made Commander of the Order of the Finnish Lion in 1953. He died in a hospital in Helsinki on October 12, 1968.

ABOUT: Baker, T. Biographical Dictionary of Musicians; completely rev. by N. Slonimsky.

Sir Hamilton Harty

1879–1941

Herbert Hamilton Harty, conductor, was born in Hillsborough, County Down, Ireland, on December 4, 1879. His father was the organist of the Episcopal Church in Hillsborough; his mother was an excellent violinist. "I was brought up on international music, on Anglican church services and the classical and chamber music writers," he once recalled. "Music in my early impressions did not mean fiddlers at fairs, or immemorial drinking songs in taverns, or indeed anything more Bohemian or picturesque than my father's organ playing and chamber music at home where my mother led the family string quartet. I can recall hearing as a small child the sonatas of Mozart and Beethoven being played every night downstairs as I lay falling asleep. At the age of nine, I was parish organist and choirmaster at Brookmount nearby, my father helping me with the choir."

His father was his only music teacher. From him Herbert received a thorough grounding in organ, piano, viola, and counterpoint. When he was twelve he assumed the post of organist in a small church in County Antrim. From there he went on to serve as church organist in Barnabas, Belfast, and, when he was sixteen, in Bray, just outside Dublin. He gained his first orchestral experience by playing the violin in a Dublin orchestra. In Dublin he was influenced by Michele Esposito at the Royal Irish Academy of Music, who encouraged him to advance himself as a composer.

When he was twenty, Harty went to London to earn his living as a piano accompanist for concert artists. He soon came to be known as "the prince of accompanists." One of the artists for whom he worked was a singer, Agnes Nicholls, whom he married on July 15, 1904.

At this time, in addition to his work as accompanist, Harty was making progress as a composer, winning prizes for a trio in 1901 and a piano quintet in 1904. He also began to make his mark as a conductor, with guest appearances with symphony orchestras, first in London and then in other parts of Great Britain.

During World War I Harty served as lieutenant in the Naval Reserve for four years. In 1920 he was appointed permanent conductor of the

SIR HAMILTON HARTY

Hallé Orchestra in Manchester, the post in which he achieved international fame. He helped to build the orchestra into one of the foremost symphonic organizations in England, distinguished for the authority of its performances and for the wide range of its repertory which included many noteworthy premieres by English composers. In 1924 the Hallé Orchestra under Harty visited London for a series of distinguished concerts.

Harty remained at the head of the Hallé Orchestra until 1933. For his services to English music he was knighted in 1925, and in 1934 he received the gold medal of the Royal Philharmonic Society. In 1932 he became the conductor and artistic adviser of the London Symphony Orchestra, with which he performed the world premiere of Arnold Bax's Symphony No.6 (November 21, 1935) and three movements of William Walton's Symphony No.1 (December 3, 1934); Harty also conducted the world premiere of the complete four-movement symphony, this time, however, with the BBC Symphony in London (November 6, 1935).

He first visited the United States in 1931, as guest conductor with several major American orchestras. During the next few years he returned to the United States periodically to direct the major symphony orchestras of Boston, San Francisco, Chicago, Cleveland, and (at the Hollywood Bowl) Los Angeles. His musicianship and conductorial technique attracted much favorable comment. "Persuasiveness in music can scarcely rise to a higher degree than it does in his case," wrote the Chicago critic Eugene Stinson. "And all his persuasiveness is well fortified by the soundest musical judgment, the most unspoiled and eager outlook, the most inexhaustible energy of execution."

In 1934 he toured Australia, stopping off in the United States on his way back to London to conduct several concerts at the Century of Progress Exposition in Chicago.

Sir Hamilton Harty died in Brighton, England, on February 19, 1941.

He was the composer of numerous works, among them the *Irish Symphony, The Mystic Trumpeter,* and a violin concerto. He was perhaps even better known for his excellent transcriptions for the modern orchestra of Handel's *Water Music,* the *Royal Fireworks Music,* and the Concerto for Organ and Orchestra. He also transcribed for orchestra piano pieces by John Field, *A John Field Suite.*

ABOUT: Grove, G. ed. Dictionary of Music and Musicians; 5th ed. by E. Blom; Who Was Who 1941–1950.

Roland Hayes

1887–1977

Roland Hayes, tenor, was born in Curryville, Georgia, on June 3, 1887, one of three sons of Fanny and William Hayes, tenant farmers and ex-slaves. When Roland was still a young child his father was invalided by an accident. With the help of her three small sons Fanny Hayes did the farm work and kept the home together. Then, when Roland was twelve, William Hayes died. Shortly after her husband's death the widowed mother moved the family to Chattanooga, Tennessee, in the hope of bettering the future of the boys. Roland helped to support the family by working in a windowshade factory and then in a stove factory. "I happened upon a new method for making iron sashweights," he told an interviewer, "and that got me a little raise in pay and a little free time. At that time I had never heard any real music, although I had had some lessons in rhetoric from a backwoods teacher in Georgia."

Without any formal instruction he joined a church choir in Chattanooga, where he sometimes sang solos. A black teacher, W. Arthur

ROLAND HAYES

Calhoun, became interested in him and for a year and a half gave him some lessons. One day a visiting pianist heard Hayes sing in church and played for him some Caruso recordings. As Hayes has said, "That opened the heavens for me. The beauty of what could be done with the voice just overwhelmed me."

Hayes saved fifty dollars. With this money he hoped to go to Oberlin Conservatory for music study, but his money was used up long before he could reach his destination. He headed, instead, for Nashville, Tennessee, where he visited Jennie A. Robinson, director of music at Fisk University. After singing for her he was accepted on probation at the University. To support himself he became a waiter in the student dining hall. He also worked hard at his studies. At the end of his probationary period he was enrolled as a regular student. At Fisk he studied voice with Robinson for four years and became a member of the university's famed Jubilee Singers.

After leaving Fisk without completing his schooling he made his way to Louisville, Kentucky. He worked there as a waiter at an exclusive club, and sometimes he entertained the guests by singing. He also found a job singing behind the screen for silent motion-picture productions of operas. "I learned all the arias from Caruso records."

In 1911 the Jubilee Singers went to Boston for a concert, and Hayes decided to settle there permanently. He furnished a small apartment for himself and his mother, found a job as an office boy, and for eight and a half years continued his vocal studies with Arthur J. Hubbard. He went to New York as often as possible to attend performances at the Metropolitan Opera. "I wept like a child for Caruso. I came to realize what I myself had to do, and more and more I became aware that I was getting the power to do it."

On November 15, 1917, at Symphony Hall in Boston, Hayes gave his first recital. He did well enough to be encouraged to give other concerts. His formal debut in New York took place on January 30, 1919. "He is one of those natural voices," reported Richard Aldrich in the New York *Times,* "who have not lost in cultivation that rare gift of unctuous humor and pathos of his race."

Sometime in 1920 William Brennan, manager of the Boston Symphony, told Hayes, when consulted, that there just was no place in American concert auditoriums for a black singer. Hayes has said he wasn't angry but knew that he still hadn't worked hard enough. He decided to go to Europe for more musical training, working with Ira Aldridge, Victor Beigel, Dr. Theodor Lierhammer, and Sir George Henschel.

In May 1920 Hayes gave a concert at Aeolian Hall in London. One newspaper regarded this event as "sacrilege," because a black man was singing the love songs of white people. But the audience responded so favorably that Hayes was asked to give fourteen additional recitals, and in 1921 he was invited to give command performances at Buckingham Palace for King George V and Queen Mary and in Spain for Queen Mother Maria Christina.

"My first real test came in Germany," Hayes said. "When it was announced that I was going to sing there, there was a flood of outbursts in the daily papers. Well, I came out on the stage, and there was a burst of hissing that lasted about ten minutes. I just stood there, and then I decided to change my program. As soon as it was quiet, I began with Schubert's 'Du bist die Ruh.' I could see a change come over the hostile faces, and by the end of the song I knew I had won."

In France he appeared as a soloist with the Colonne Orchestra. After several more performances he came to be known as *le rage de Paris.* It is indicative of Hayes's versatility that in France he was considered an outstanding interpreter of French art songs, while in German-speaking countries he was highly praised for his interpretations of *Lieder.* And wherever he sang he was placed in a class by himself in his presentations of spirituals.

Discriminating musicians became staunch supporters. The French composer Gabriel Fauré wrote to him: "Mr. Hayes, you have a beautiful, beautiful voice, and you sing beautifully." In London Nellie Melba, the prima donna, autographed her photograph for him with the following words: "Bravo, Mr. Hayes. You are a great artist—and so says the king." In Berlin Leo Slezak, one of the great opera tenors of his generation, lifted Hayes on his own shoulders after a concert and carried him in triumph out of the hall. Fritz Kreisler, the violin virtuoso, became Hayes's friend as well as his admirer.

One English critic wrote of Hayes that he possessed "a tenor voice which he produces so well that it is resonant at all pressures and in all parts of the scale. He can command a true legato and an effective diminuendo without depreciation of tone quality, and he can also make his voice expressive of meanings of words with a variety of vocal color which many expert *Lieder* singers might envy. This, invaluable in the Negro songs, was also a constant source of pleasure in the *Lieder.*"

Hayes returned to the United States in 1923. On the recommendation of Fritz Kreisler, William Brennan signed him to a contract. Hayes's first recital in Carnegie Hall that year marked not only the start of Hayes's successful concert career in America but also the breakdown of prejudice in American concert auditoriums against black musicians. That concert was a personal triumph for Hayes, not only because of the artistry of his renditions of *Lieder* by Schubert, Brahms, and Hugo Wolf, and the songs of Monteverdi, Glinka, and others, but also his performance of spirituals which were his specialty. "From the hour of his emergence on the local stage," wrote W. J. Henderson, the New York critic, "his color was forgotten. He succeeded . . . in leaving only a conviction of beauty and persuasive eloquence."

Hayes gave thirty concerts in America that year, one hundred and twenty-five one year after that, including performances in the South before integrated audiences. He remained for many years a powerful box-office attraction, both in the United States and Europe, and was numbered among leading concert singers of his time in recitals and as a guest artist with major symphony orchestras. In 1925 he gave a second command performance for Queen Mother Maria Christina of Spain; in the United States that year he was awarded the Spingarn medal for outstanding achievement among black people. His later honors included doctorates from Fisk University and Ohio Wesleyan University in Delaware, Ohio, the Purple Ribbon from the French government for services to French music, and a Fellowship Award in 1953 from the American Academy of Arts and Sciences.

In one of his columns in the New York *World* Heywood Broun recorded his personal impressions of a Roland Hayes concert: "He sang of Jesus and it seemed to me that this was what religion ought to be. It was a mood instead of a creed, an emotion rather than a doctrine. There was nothing to define and nothing to argue. Each person took what he felt and liked, whatever he had to feel, and so there was no heresy. And as for miracles, music itself is a miracle. For that matter I saw a miracle at Town Hall. Half of the people who heard Hayes were black and half were white; and while the mood of the song held they were all the same. And at the end it was a single sob."

On June 3, 1963, Hayes at seventy-five sang in New York at a benefit for the American Missionary Association College Centennial Fund. "Surely," wrote Henry Beckett in the New York *Post,* "no singer ever did so much with a light voice, touched by age, as Hayes did. . . . Hayes sang, it seemed with his entire body and his softest note carried easily to the far reaches of the hall." In the New York *Times* Howard Klein said: "His artistic projection was magnetic." On this occasion Virgil Thomson presented Hayes with the first Amistad Award, established by the American Missionary Association to honor contributors to the betterment of human relations through the arts and sciences. "You do the human race honor to exist," Thomson told Hayes. Hayes responded to these honors by saying: "I feel very humble."

Hayes's last public appearance occurred in 1973 at the Longy School of Music in London.

With his wife, the former Helen A. Mann, and their daughter, Afrika Fanzada (a professional singer), Roland Hayes for many years lived in Brookline, a Boston suburb. Summers were spent at Angel Mo' Farm, a model farm he owned in his native city of Curryville, Georgia. To his personal life Hayes brought the same seriousness of purpose he carried into music

making. He needed few diversions, since music was his life. Outside music, his prime concern was for his race, to whose economic, social, and political advancement he devoted a lifetime of effort.

After a prolonged illness, Roland Hayes died in Boston, Massachusetts, on January 1, 1977.

ABOUT: Helm, M. Angel Mo' and Her Son, Roland. *Periodicals*—New York Times, June 3, 1962, January 2, 1977.

Jascha Heifetz

1901–

Jascha Heifetz, violinist by whom all other virtuosos are measured, was born in Vilna, Lithuania on February 2, 1901. His father, Ruvin, was a violinist in a Vilna theater orchestra. From infancy Jascha responded strongly to music, and his father purchased for him a quarter-size violin for his third birthday and gave him some lessons. When Jascha was five he was entered in the Royal School of Music as a pupil of Elias Malkin. Two years later he made his debut in Kovno, performing Mendelssohn's Violin Concerto. For the next two years he gave other concerts and grew famous as a *Wunderkind.*

When Heifetz was eight, Leopold Auer, professor of violin at the St. Petersburg Conservatory, heard him play the Mendelssohn Concerto and Paganini's Caprice No.24, in Vilna. Upon Auer's advice, Ruvin sold his belongings, resigned his post in Vilna, and brought his family to St. Petersburg so that Jascha might become Auer's pupil. The law did not permit Jews to establish residence in St. Petersburg, making an exception solely for Conservatory students, but not for their parents. The Conservatory director found a solution for the Heifetzes by also enrolling the forty-year-old father as a Conservatory student.

After six months of preparation with Johannes Nalpandian, Jascha entered Auer's class where his progress was phenomenal. Albert Spalding, American violin virtuoso, heard the boy perform in one of Auer's classes and described his reaction in his autobiography *Rise to Follow:* "A small boy stood up to play. . . . I had

Heifetz: hī′ fĕts

Heifetz

JASCHA HEIFETZ

never heard such perfect technique from a child. Jascha, they called him—Jascha Heifetz. While the boy was playing, Auer strode nervously about the room, glancing at me now and then to appraise my reactions. . . . He expected nothing less than paralyzed astonishment from me–nor was he disappointed. He would turn away with a helpless shrug of the shoulders as if to say: 'Was there ever anything like it?' Other talented students performed later, but they were eclipsed by this miniature wizard."

Jascha was subjected to a strict regimen of hard work and long hours. He recalled: "I studied at home six days a week. I took exams at school, but I worked at home, studying under my father. If we went to a play or a museum I wrote a report about it. On Sunday, I rested by reviewing all the work I had done during the week. . . . I must have resented it at the time. No youngster enjoys practicing. But when the results begin to be good, you get a satisfaction." Heifetz added "I had to wait a few years before I enjoyed a delayed childhood, when I could do all the risky and dangerous things I was forbidden as a child."

While studying under Auer, Jascha received instruction in French, German, history, geography, mathematics, and history from private tutors.

Performing at the International Exposition in Odessa, Jascha became such a public idol that police had to be called in to protect him from his admirers. His first concert in St. Petersburg on April 30, 1911, was highly acclaimed and led to equally successful performances in Austria, Germany, and Scandinavia. On May 24, 1912, Jascha gave a recital in Berlin, and ten days later he was the soloist with the Berlin Philharmonic under Arthur Nikisch. Nikisch maintained he had never heard such violin playing from one so young. Two years later Auer took Jascha to Christiania (now Oslo) for public concerts and a performance before royalty. The journey continued on to the Orient and then, by way of Siberia, to the United States.

On October 27, 1917, Jascha made his American debut at Carnegie Hall. He was a sensation. The critics rivaled each other in singing his praises. "He is a modern miracle," said Pitts Sanborn in the *Globe.* To H. E. Krehbiel, writing in the *Tribune,* he was a "modern Orpheus" capable of doing "all the things with a violin which a fabled charmer accomplished with a lyre." Sigmund Spaeth in the *Evening Mail* called him "the perfect violinist." Richard Aldrich reported in the New York *Times:* "Mr. Heifetz produces a tone of remarkable purity and beauty; a tone of power, smoothness and roundness, of searching expressiveness, of subtle modulation in power and color. . . . In his technical equipment Mr. Heifetz is unusual."

This debut inspired an oft-quoted remark. After Heifetz's performance of the Vitali Chaconne, which drew a thunderous response from the audience, Mischa Elman remarked innocently to Leopold Godowsky: "It's awfully hot here." Godowsky's dryly witty reply was: "Not for pianists."

Such was Heifetz's instant fame in the United States that in his first year there he gave no fewer than thirty concerts in New York alone, and more than a hundred on an extended tour. He then established permanent residence with his parents in an apartment on Central Park West; he became an American citizen in 1925.

In the years that followed his American debut, Heifetz held an imperial position among the world's violinists. He performed in all parts of the world. He made his first appearance in London on May 5, 1920, in Australia in 1921, the Orient in 1923, and Palestine in 1926. No violin virtuoso concertized more extensively, earned higher fees, sold more recordings, or was so universally acknowledged as a magician of the instrument. In his world tours he often gave his concerts under extraordinary circumstances. In Ireland he played during the Sinn Fein uprisings, in Japan after an earthquake, in Java during riots, in Tientsin while the Japanese were invading Manchuria, in India during uprisings following Gandhi's arrest.

As the years passed, intellect, controlled human experience, mellowness of maturity, and musical scholarship were joined to his fabulous —possibly inimitable—technique. To musicians and laymen alike the name Heifetz became a word meaning the *ne plus ultra* of violin virtuosity; to say that someone played like Heifetz was the ultimate in praise. His technical perfection once led Bernard Shaw to write to him: "Your recital filled me and my wife with anxiety. If you provoke a jealous God by playing with such superhuman perfection, you will die young. I earnestly advise you to play something badly every night before going to bed, instead of saying your prayers. No mortal should presume to play so faultlessly."

If any criticism has been leveled against Heifetz it is not for his technique, musicianship, or interpretative insights. Rather he has been accused of being aloof and cold in his performances, because he has always refused to indulge in those mannerisms with which so many other virtuosos woo their public. Deems Taylor wrote in *The Well-Tempered Listener:* "He is too Olympian, too detached they say; he touches your head too much, and your heart not enough. . . . On the platform . . . his attitude to his listeners is one of perfect, unsmiling courtesy, and when he plays he does so with such complete absorption in the music that looking at his remote, masklike face, one might make the mistake of thinking, 'Here is a cold man.' " But, Taylor adds, "it is not coldness. . . . At his best, he plays with such a complete grasp of the meaning of the music, such effortless mastery of the instrument, that you tend to forget *him.* You are no longer hearing violin playing; you are hearing the music, hearing it as the composer hoped you would hear it, unconscious of any instrumental barrier between you. It is given to only a few artists in any generation to achieve this selfless perfection of communication; and Heifetz is one of the elect few." In his autobiography, *Unfinished Journey,* Yehudi Menuhin also spoke of Heifetz's alleged coldness, commenting: "I think they misunderstood for coldness a degree of discipline and method which no other violinist of our time possessed. . . . He strove for a control so complete that each performance would be

identical—a valid, admirable approach, but not mine."

In the summer of 1934 Heifetz returned to Russia after a seventeen-year absence. Musicians came from as far away as Siberia to hear him. Music lovers sold some of their clothing and furniture to get the price for a ticket for one of his concerts. After each performance his admirers would stand three deep in the streets to shout their approval as he left the auditorium. "This was the greatest emotional experience of my life," Heifetz said at the time.

On April 29, 1936, he was the soloist in Beethoven's Violin Concerto when Toscanini gave his farewell concert as music director of the New York Philharmonic. That same year Heifetz and other musicians helped to found the American Guild of Musical Artists; he became its first vice president. In 1938 Heifetz donated a concert hall to Tel-Aviv in Palestine. A year later he was made Officier of the French Legion of Honor, thirteen years after he had been made Chevalier in 1926.

During World War II Heifetz gave over three hundred concerts for the armed forces in the three theaters of war. At the first of these appearances, at Camp Roberts in California, he told the men simply: "I don't know what you expect to hear me play, but I do know I'm going to play Bach." He did, and the GIs responded enthusiastically. Sometimes he yielded to requests to play lighter numbers as well. One of the compositions requested most often was Schubert's *Ave Maria,* which he performed sixty-three times in the course of his last sixty-five appearances.

In 1947, on the thirtieth anniversary of his American debut, Heifetz announced he was taking a sabbatical from concert work. He wanted time to reflect, to reevaluate himself, to relearn the classics he had played hundreds of times and perhaps to discard some from his repertory, and to study new music. "It will be like overhauling the engine," he said. "Some parts have to be changed and some lubricated." Then, changing the metaphor, he explained his need to "dust things off, launder them, dryclean them, and rethink some things." He was also physically and mentally tired. In those thirty years he had traveled some two million miles and had played the violin for more than one hundred thousand hours. He withdrew from the concert platform for about twenty months, returning on January

4, 1949, to begin a tour that touched fifty cities and ended on May 2.

He took another sabbatical in 1957, this time with the intention of permanently reducing the number of his public appearances and his travels to a trickle. On December 9, 1959, he returned to New York to perform at the Grand Assembly Hall of the United Nations to help commemorate the eleventh anniversary of the proclamation of the Universal Declaration of Human Rights. This was Heifetz's first appearance in New York in four years. Howard Taubman wrote in the New York *Times:* "Jascha Heifetz's return reminded us last night how much he has been missed. . . . Once he set the violin under his chin and brought his bow across the strings, he was the sovereign performer." This proved the case even though at that time Heifetz was performing under a severe handicap. Earlier in 1959 he had tripped on the wet floor of his kitchen and had fractured his hip. The infection that followed almost ended his life. Walking on the stage of the United Nations he had to use a cane for support; and he had to play on a small platform with a protective railing. "He made no concession to the difficulty," Taubman added.

On August 28, 1928, Heifetz married the motion picture actress Florence Vidor. Their first home was a penthouse apartment near Carnegie Hall. Later on, with their son and daughter, they maintained a cottage in Balboa, California, and a farmhouse near Norwalk, Connecticut. They were divorced in 1945. In January 1947 Heifetz married Frances Spiegelberg. Soon after this marriage Heifetz acquired an estate on a four-acre tract up Coldwater Canyon, overlooking Beverly Hills; the house was designed by Lloyd Wright, son of Frank Lloyd Wright. In addition to a large redwood and glass house, the estate included a swimming pool, tennis court, and a studio where Heifetz keeps his precious violins (the "Dolphin" Stradivarius of 1714, and the "David" del Gesù Guarnerius of 1742). Heifetz also acquired a beach house in Malibu. The Heifetzes, who had a son, were divorced in 1963. Since the divorce Heifetz has jealously guarded his privacy. "Even Heifetz has to make an appointment with Heifetz," one of his friends commented. But he is not a complete recluse, often having his most intimate friends or his students as guests for dinner, and for music making afterwards.

He has always enjoyed a variety of pastimes and interests. Having long since overcome his boyhood caution about hurting his hands, he has not hesitated to indulge in any number of diversions that might be considered hazardous for a violin virtuoso, such as racing sports cars, playing tennis, sportfishing, handling firearms and rapiers, tinkering with automobile engines, sailing, and driving his high-powered car at high speeds on country roads. He has also enjoyed playing table tennis, golf, and squash; tending to his garden; viewing and collecting paintings and stamps; indulging his interest in photography; and playing parlor games and, occasionally, bridge.

"Heifetz's cheekbones are prominent—Tartar cheekbones, someone called them—and his face is ruled by the eyes," wrote Roger Kahn in *Life.* "They are blue and daring and hooded. The lips are thin and the corners of the mouth turn downwards. Heifetz presents a visage that seems to say, 'What is it you want from me, and I'm certainly glad the silverware is locked.' It is a mask. Once in a while, in an old family snapshot, you can see the handsome, tender man that was. A cigarette rests on the lower lip. The face is lit with laughter. No longer. The mask has become Heifetz' norm."

Since 1960 he has frequently appeared in public in chamber music concerts with his friend Gregor Piatigorsky, the cello virtuoso. These Heifetz-Piatigorsky concerts, which recruited other musicians as well, were arranged to present chamber music other than string quartets, since string quartets received more than frequent hearings. On three occasions, recordings by Heifetz-Piatigorsky received Grammy awards from the National Academy of Recording Arts and Sciences: for the Kodály Duo for Violin and Piano coupled with Beethoven's Serenade, Op. 8, in 1961; for the album *The Heifetz-Piatigorsky Concerts* (with William Primrose, violist, and Leonard Pennario, pianist) in 1962; and for a set of Beethoven Piano Trios, Op. 1 (with Jacob Lateiner) in 1963. In public as well as on records Heifetz has given concerts of trio music with Arthur Rubinstein, pianist, and Emanuel Feuermann, cellist; later with Rubinstein and Piatigorsky. The last-mentioned group is often described as "the million dollar trio."

Heifetz served as Regents Professor of Music and artist-in-residence at the University of California in Los Angeles and later as head of master classes in violin at the University of California and the Music Center in Los Angeles.

His appearances as a solo performer since 1960 have been few. As he put it: "I've done my share of touring. I have no further interest in that kind of a career. And I can't say I admire the pace at which today's musicians travel. They move too fast; they play too often; they don't pause to reflect." But he was heard in the Beethoven Concerto on December 6, 1964, at the dedication of the new Pavilion at the Music Center for the Performing Arts in Los Angeles, a performance which the critic for the Los Angeles *Times* described as "a view from the summit." Heifetz performed the Bruch Concerto No.1 at the Hollywood Bowl in Los Angeles on August 13, 1967, as soloist with the Israel Philharmonic; this was a benefit for Israel immediately after the Six Day War in the Middle East. In May 1970 he revisited Israel, performing there several times with the Israel Philharmonic, turning over part of his fee to the orchestra's pension fund and the remainder to the Israeli Prime Minister, Golda Meir, to distribute as she deemed best. And on October 23, 1972, he gave his first recital in seventeen years—at the Dorothy Chandler Pavilion in Los Angeles—to help raise scholarship funds for the University of Southern California. This concert was recorded by Columbia.

Through the years Heifetz has commissioned numerous twentieth century composers to write violin concertos whose world premieres he then gave. These composers included Mario Castelnuovo-Tedesco (April 12, 1933), Louis Gruenberg (December 1, 1944), Erich Wolfgang Korngold (February 15, 1947), Miklós Rózsa (January 5, 1956), and William Walton (December 7, 1939).

Heifetz has appeared on television in a one-hour special sponsored by the American Telephone and Telegraph Company and telecast by NBC on April 23, 1971. Previously, Heifetz was seen on television in a series of master classes with his students. He has also performed in motion pictures: in the Samuel Goldwyn production *They Shall Have Music* (1939), in which he had a speaking part in addition to playing the violin; in the motion picture *Carnegie Hall* (1947); and in the documentary *Of Men and Music* (1951).

No violinist and few other serious musical performers have such an extended recording history as Heifetz. He made his first recordings just two weeks after his debut in the United States—at Victor's Camden studios on November 9, 1917. At that time he recorded four pieces: Schubert's *Ave Maria,* Drigo's *Valse Bluette,* Elgar's *La Capricieuse,* and Wieniawski's *Scherzo-Tarantelle.* From that time to the present he has recorded for Victor (and occasionally for Decca) virtually his entire repertory, some compositions more than once. In 1975 RCA released a retrospective in six volumes entitled *The Heifetz Collection* which begins with his first releases in 1917 and ends with recordings made in 1955. The twenty-four records in chronological sequence, covering four decades of Heifetz's career as a virtuoso, consume almost twenty-six hours of playing time and represent, as Irving Kolodin has written, "possibly the most remarkable individual recording career ever known." *The Heifetz Collection* is not the complete Heifetz discography, but about one third of it.

Though Heifetz has transcribed numerous compositions for the violin, he has done virtually no composing. Strange to report, an exception to this is not a serious work for the violin but a popular song, "When You Make Love to Me (Don't Make Believe)" written in 1946 to lyrics by Marjorie Goetschius; for this effort he took the pseudonym Jim Hoyl. The song became a hit and was recorded by many vocalists and bands, with Bing Crosby's release selling over three hundred thousand disks when first issued. "I wrote it to prove a theory," Heifetz has explained. "We were sitting around the dinner table in California . . . talking about the young American public that listens to jazz. I said that these boys and girls don't care a hoot for the names of composers. They like what they like without being overawed by tags. Some of my friends disagreed and challenged me to prove it. Well, there was one way to prove it." Heifetz also composed a few swing numbers, one of which was called *Hora Swingcato.* This was inspired by one of his most famous encore pieces, *Hora Staccato,* which he had arranged from a composition by Gheorghe Dinicu.

ABOUT: Axelrod, H.R. Heifetz; Ewen, D. Men and Women Who Make Music; Taylor, D. The Well-Tempered Listener. *Periodicals*—Coronet, August 1946; High Fidelity, August 1975; Holiday, September 1963; Life, October 31, 1969; New York Times, December 22, 1946; Saturday Evening Post, June 4, 1960; Saturday Review, April 4, 1971, September 10, 1975; Stereo Review, February 1976.

Frieda Hempel

1885–1955

Frieda Hempel, soprano, was born in Leipzig, on June 26, 1885, to Emil H. and Augusta Morler Hempel. Her background was musical, and she was given musical training from childhood on. When she was fifteen she entered the Leipzig Conservatory, specializing in the piano. Then, preferring singing to piano, she went to Berlin in 1902 to study voice for three years with Selma Nicklass-Kempner at the Stern Conservatory.

On August 28, 1905, she made her debut in *The Merry Wives of Windsor* at the Berlin Royal Opera. That summer she also appeared at the Bayreuth Festival, and from 1905 to 1907 she was a member of the Court Opera at Schwerin. Returning to the Berlin Royal Opera in 1907 she remained with that company for five years, appearing in a variety of roles, distinguishing herself particularly in Mozart's operas, and achieving a personal triumph as the Queen of the Night in *The Magic Flute*. Richard Strauss thought so highly of her that he offered her any one of three leading female roles in *Der Rosenkavalier* for its Berlin debut. She chose the Marschallin which became one of her most celebrated roles.

While with the Berlin Royal Opera (where she was given the honorary title *Kammersängerin*), Hempel began making guest appearances at Covent Garden and other major European opera houses. On December 27, 1912, she made her debut in the United States at the Metropolitan Opera as Marguerite de Valois in *Les Huguenots*. In the *Tribune* Henry E. Krehbiel wrote: "We heard a finely schooled artist, a singer with a neat and highly finished style of vocalization, a flexible voice, and good taste." But he also found that she was suffering "from the nervousness which seizes upon every singer when such a stupendous audience as that of a gala night at the Metropolitan Opera first confronts her."

Hempel soon achieved distinction at the Metropolitan. In her first season she sang Rosina in

Hempel: hĕm′ pĕl

FRIEDA HEMPEL

The Barber of Seville, the Queen of the Night, Olympia in *The Tales of Hoffmann,* Violetta in *La Traviata,* Gilda in *Rigoletto,* and the title role in *Lucia di Lammermoor.*

During the next seven seasons Hempel was one of the leading sopranos of the Metropolitan Opera company. Among her outstanding performances were Oscar in *Un Ballo in Maschera,* in which she sang opposite Caruso with Toscanini conducting; the Marschallin in the American premiere of *Der Rosenkavalier* on December 9, 1913; and the title role of Weber's *Euryanthe* at its American premiere on December 19, 1914, Toscanini conducting. Other Metropolitan Opera roles she sang were Susanna in *The Marriage of Figaro,* Eva in *Die Meistersinger,* Harriet in *Martha,* Marie in *The Daughter of the Regiment,* Leila in Bizet's *Les Pêcheurs de Perles,* Marguerite in *Faust,* Adina in *L'Elisir d'Amore,* and Annetta in Ricci's *Crispino e la Comare.* She mastered some 70 principal soprano roles in the French, Italian, and German repertories, though she appeared in only 17 with the Metropolitan. Her appearances with that company numbered 155 in New York and 32 on tour.

After leaving the Metropolitan Opera in 1919, Hempel appeared for one season with the Chicago Opera in 1920–1921.

She was also a distinguished recitalist. "Miss Hempel is one who takes thought about her art, and has raised herself to a higher artistic stature thereby," reported Richard Aldrich in the New York *Times* following her song recital in Carnegie Hall in New York on February 15, 1916.

"Her program was made up almost wholly of music particularly well adapted to her voice and style, and there was much artistic enjoyment to be derived from the way in which she presented it. . . . Nor could there be wished a greater perfection of diction than she showed in these German songs—a diction whose finish is allied with the beauty and freedom of her production of tone." Following a Carnegie Hall recital on January 5, 1921, Aldrich added: "She was in beautiful voice; in fact her voice has rarely sounded more beautiful in its rounded smoothness, its color, its equality throughout its range. Nor has she sung with a more delightful art and perfect command of the higher vocal technique."

On the centenary of the birth of Jenny Lind in 1920, Hempel appeared in Carnegie Hall on October 6 in a duplicate of Lind's first concert in the United States at Castle Garden in 1850. This became the first of more than three hundred Jenny Lind concerts that Hempel presented in Jenny Lind costume, throughout the United States and during two tours of Great Britain, singing the songs for which Lind is remembered.

In 1936 Hempel became front-page news in the United States when she instituted a lawsuit against the American philanthropist August Heckscher. In 1928 Heckscher had guaranteed Hempel an annual income of fifty thousand dollars for the remainder of her life in return for her appearances at private performances and charitable affairs. In December 1935 this income was terminated. The dispute was settled in the courts with Hempel receiving an annual income of fifteen thousand dollars a year for the rest of her life.

In 1918 Hempel married William B. Kahn; they were divorced in 1926. From 1940 to 1955 she lived on Central Park West in New York. Then, suffering from an incurable disease, she decided to return to Leipzig in 1955 where she died on October 7.

Hempel received decorations from the Emperor of Germany, the King of Belgium, the Grand Duke of Mecklenberg-Schwerin, and the Duke of Anhalt.

ABOUT: Hempel, F. Mein Leben dem Gesang.

Alfred Hertz

1872–1942

Alfred Hertz, conductor, was born in Frankfort, Germany on July 15, 1872. He was the younger of two sons of Leo Hertz, a well-to-do merchant, and Sara Koenigswerther Hertz. Though crippled in one foot through polio in his infancy, Alfred began studying the piano at the age of six. A year later he composed his first piece. The stimulus for this creative effort was a spanking he had received for being mischievous, an event that inspired him to write a funeral march.

His parents wanted him to study law, but he overcame their objections and undertook music study seriously at Hoch's Conservatory in Frankfort when he was twelve. There his teachers included Schwartz (piano), Anton Urspruch (composition), and Fleisch and Hans von Bülow (conducting). After graduation with honors at the age of nineteen, Hertz received his first conducting assignment at the Halle Stadt Theater as an assistant in 1891. He remained there a single year. Then from 1892 to 1895 he was *Hofkappelmeister* at the Altenburg Court Theater in Saxony. His work there was honored with the Order of Art and Science. At his next post, that of principal conductor at Barmen-Elberfeld from 1895 to 1899, he conducted several Wagner performances. Then, a four-year engagement at Breslau from 1899 to 1902 and his debut in London in 1899 at which he led a concert of the music of Frederick Delius, a composer then still little known and rarely performed, placed him among the leading younger German conductors.

In 1902 he went to the United States where he remained permanently and became an American citizen. He was appointed the principal conductor of German operas at the Metropolitan Opera. He was the youngest conductor ever to hold this post at the Metropolitan up to this time. On November 28, 1902, he made his debut there with *Lohengrin.* During his first season he was heard in virtually all the major Wagner dramas with the exception of *Parsifal,* which by Wagner's own request had become the exclusive property of Bayreuth. However, on December 24, 1903, overriding the objections of the Wag-

ALFRED HERTZ

ner family in Bayreuth, he conducted at the Metropolitan Opera the first staged production of *Parsifal* given outside Bayreuth. This production, which many Wagnerites regarded as heresy, provided considerable controversy. Representatives from Bayreuth went to the courts to try to prevent the performance, but they lost. The attendant publicity made *Parsifal* an artistic event attracting the interest of opera lovers throughout the United States. A special "Parsifal" train was sent from Chicago. So successful did *Parsifal* become in its first American season that its eleven performances, all of them to sold-out houses, brought in almost two hundred thousand dollars at the box office. "The musical direction," said Richard Aldrich in the New York *Times,* "was in the hands of a master conductor, thoroughly imbued with the style and significance of Wagner's music." Because of his involvement in these performances of *Parsifal,* Hertz was never again permitted to direct a Wagner opera or drama in Germany. But in 1910, when Hans Richter fell ill, Hertz was called to London to conduct *Die Götterdämmerung* and several other Wagner dramas at Covent Garden.

On January 22, 1907, Hertz conducted at the Metropolitan Opera the American premiere of another masterwork that aroused tempestuous reactions: Strauss's *Salome.* Denounced by clergy, conservative citizens, and the press as obscene, the opera had to be removed from the repertory after a single performance.

In his thirteen years at the Metropolitan Op-

era Hertz conducted twenty-seven works, eleven of them novelties. The first American opera produced by the Metropolitan Opera was assigned to him: Frederick Converse's *The Pipe of Desire* (March 18, 1910). Hertz also led the first performances of two other American operas: Walter Damrosch's *Cyrano de Bergerac* (February 27, 1912) and Horatio T. Parker's *Mona* (March 12, 1912). On December 28, 1910, he conducted the world premiere of Humperdinck's *Königskinder.* His American premieres besides *Parsifal* and *Salome* were Ethel Smyth's *Das Wald* (March 11, 1903), Eugène d'Albert's *Tiefland* (November 23, 1908), Leo Blech's *Versiegelt* (January 20, 1912), and Strauss's *Der Rosenkavalier* (December 10, 1913).

His farewell performance at the Metropolitan Opera took place on April 24, 1915, with *Der Rosenkavalier.* Otto H. Kahn presented him with a silver loving cup on behalf of the opera house directors. The artists gave him a silver wreath on each of whose leaves was engraved the title of an opera Hertz had conducted. The New York *Post* remarked editorially: "He has displayed the best traits of German musicians, besides an emotional temperament rare among them."

On July 1, 1915, Hertz directed the world premiere of Horatio T. Parker's *Fairyland* at the Panama-Pacific Exposition in Los Angeles. That fall he was appointed permanent conductor of the San Francisco Symphony. For the next fifteen years he helped raise the orchestra to a place of importance among American symphonic organizations. On July 11, 1922, Hertz conducted the first of more than one hundred concerts he gave at the Hollywood Bowl in Los Angeles; these concerts earned him the title "the father of the Hollywood Bowl."

In addition to his assignments with the San Francisco Symphony and at the Hollywood Bowl, Hertz conducted the San Francisco Municipal Orchestra. For his contributions to the cultural life of San Francisco he was named honorary citizen.

In 1930 Hertz resigned from his post with the San Francisco Symphony. He was the first American conductor to perform series of radio orchestral concerts, conducting on the "Standard Symphony Hour" from 1932 to 1936. From 1937 to 1940 he was the regional director of the Federal Music Project.

Hertz married Lilly Dorn (a Viennese *Lieder*

singer) on July 15, 1914. He lived the last 25 years of his life with his wife in a house on Camino del Mar in San Francisco; they had no children. In addition to his conducting activities, Hertz also wrote songs; at times Lilly Dorn featured them in her recitals. His favorite diversions were playing bridge and motoring. During his last five years Hertz suffered from a heart ailment. He died of pneumonia in a hospital in San Francisco on April 17, 1942.

A bequest of almost half a million dollars from Hertz's estate in 1950 was used to create an endowment for musical scholarships and to erect a music building bearing his name at the University of California in Berkeley.

During his lifetime Hertz was decorated by Saxony with the Order for Art and Science and by Romania with the Order of Merit for Art.

ABOUT: San Francisco Chronicle, May 10–July 14, 1942.

Dame Myra Hess

1890–1965

Myra Hess, pianist, was born in Hampstead, near London on February 25, 1890. She was the youngest of four children all of whom were taught Hebrew and introduced to the traditional melodies of the synagogue by their father, an Orthodox Jew. Myra early revealed her aptitude for music. When she was five she began piecing together melodies on the piano. A local piano teacher noticed her interest in music and gave her some lessons. When she was seven she successfully passed the entrance examinations for the Guildhall School of Music in London where, over a five-year period, she studied the piano with Julian Pascal and Orlando Morgan, receiving a gold medal for her piano playing. In 1902, aged twelve, she earned a scholarship for the Royal Academy of Music in London where for another five years she worked with Tobias Matthay, who was largely responsible for her development as an artist and whom she considered "the greatest inspirational teacher I know of. I had a startling awakening to all the beauties of music of which I had not even dreamed. He taught me the habit of enjoying my music as music, and that was the chief factor in finally molding me as an artist."

DAME MYRA HESS

Joseph Szigeti, the violin virtuoso, heard Myra Hess perform at a school concert in London in or about 1905. He described his impressions in his autobiography, *With Strings Attached:* "Although she was not yet sufficiently grown up for a formal hair-do at the school concert, her playing already had a mellowness, an intimate graciousness . . . which I have never since encountered in any young virtuoso, unless it may have been in the eleven or twelve-year-old Heifetz's touchingly beautiful performance of the Bruch Concerto in G minor in Berlin, some years before World War I. But in one thing Myra Hess stood alone: her playing seemed never to have gone through those unfortunate phases that mark (and mar) the development of most other virtuosos. Eloquence born of understatement, a rare gift indeed . . . was hers even in that youthful time."

She was graduated from the Royal Academy in 1907 and on November 15, 1907, she made her concert debut with the London Philharmonic Orchestra under Thomas Beecham in Beethoven's Piano Concerto No.4. A London critic then wrote prophetically: "A new star has arisen in the musical world, whose light should burn brilliantly for many a year to come." Her first recital followed on January 25, 1908, at Aeolian Hall. Then, feeling the need for further study and development, she withdrew from concert work for several years. When she finally returned to the public auditorium she was a fully mature artist whose musical insights and poetic

341

concepts won the admiration of London audiences.

Her formidable reputation in Europe can be said to have begun with appearances as guest artist with the Concertgebouw Orchestra in Amsterdam, Willem Mengelberg conducting, in 1914. Her reputation grew with recitals and performances with orchestras throughout Europe.

She made her American debut with a recital in New York on January 17, 1922, when her remarkable interpretative gifts were fully recognized. In the New York *Times* Richard Aldrich called her "an extraordinary artist . . . [who] makes her interpretations deeply engrossing through their vitality, their finesse, and subtle qualities, their intensity and glowing warmth." To W. J. Henderson, writing in the New York *Sun,* she was "a fine strong mind, capable of long perspectives and deep penetration and trained thoroughly in musicianship. She has imagination . . . and a delicate sensitivity which makes itself known in subtly wrought details of her readings."

She continued to tour the United States annually for the next sixteen seasons, becoming one of the largest box-office attractions as well as one of the most consistently acclaimed pianists of her time. "Since she first began to visit us," wrote Lawrence Gilman in the New York *Herald Tribune,* "her art has matured and deepened immeasurably. She was always a poet, sensitive and exquisite, finely touched and richly gifted, and an interpreter of the sacerdotal kind—dedicated and absorbed and self-effacing. But she has ripened from a lyric poet into an epical and dramatic one. There are splendors and immensities in her playing that were not evident before."

Her successes in Europe and elsewhere kept pace with her increasing fame in the United States. In 1936 she became the first instrumentalist ever to be decorated Commander in the Order of the British Empire, one of the last acts of George V.

She was scheduled to make her seventeenth tour of the United States in 1940, to be followed by a tour of Australia, when the outbreak of World War II in Europe compelled her to cancel all her contracted concert engagements. Initially, to help the war effort she joined the Women's Voluntary Service in London and assisted in the evacuation of the children from that city. Then, feeling that war-torn England was in greater need than ever of the solace and inspiration of

music, she gave noonday concerts five days a week in the cupola of the National Gallery in Trafalgar Square for an admission price of one shilling a performance. The first such concert took place on October 10, 1939. She clarified her aim in a brief speech in which she said: "I want to keep this little oasis of peace going in the heart of London, and although we may be a small community, the principle of not being deterred by evil forces is important." At first these concerts consisted solely of her own piano recitals. But in time she expanded her programs to include the music of other great artists. When London was ravaged by the blitzkrieg, she carried her concerts to an underground shelter, and when the National Gallery was hit by a bomb these concerts were brought to South Africa House across the way from the National Gallery. "I'll never forget," she subsequently told an interviewer, "after one of the worst raids, through which nobody slept at all, I drove to the Gallery down the streets filled with debris of all kinds. Houses were demolished everywhere. 'There'll be a small audience tonight,' I thought. But we had an overflow house of five hundred people."

These concerts continued uninterruptedly for five and a half years, the last one taking place on April 10, 1946, almost a year after V-E Day. In all, 1,698 concerts had been given, with Hess performing in 130, attending most of the others, and supervising all of them. More than a thousand artists had participated, and over a million people had attended. Through these concerts, Hess said, "taxi drivers learned to love Mozart, and cooks and waiters became friends with Beethoven's chamber music." For this monumental achievement Hess was awarded in 1941 the highest honor the British Empire could bestow on a woman: She was named Dame Commander by King George VI. She was also given the gold medal of the Royal Philharmonic Society in 1942—only the second time in the one-hundred-and-thirty-year history of this orchestra that the medal had been bestowed on a woman instrumentalist.

Dame Myra returned to the American concert scene after a seven-year absence with a recital at Town Hall, New York, on October 12, 1946. She continued concertizing for the next fifteen years. Her last public appearance took place on October 21, 1961, at the Royal Festival Hall in London at a concert commemorating the twenty-first anniversary of the end of the Battle of Britain during World War II.

A rheumatic condition of the hands brought her concert career to an end. Except for occasional visits to public auditoriums to hear performances by young and promising artists, she remained in virtual seclusion at her Georgian home in St. John's Wood in London. Several months before her death, BBC celebrated her seventy-fifth birthday with a program made up of her recordings, together with verbal tributes. Admirers and friends from all over the world sent her congratulatory greetings, including a special-broadcast performance of "Happy Birthday" by the renowned violinist Isaac Stern. After several months of failing health she died quietly in her home on November 25, 1965.

She never married. In her earlier years she enjoyed motoring and playing tennis. Later in life she preferred quieter diversions such as playing bridge and taking long walks.

She received numerous honorary degrees, principally from Manchester University in 1945, the University of London in 1946, University of Cambridge in 1949, and Leeds University in 1951. From Holland she received the decoration of Commander, Order of Orange-Nassau.

ABOUT: Brown, H. M. Modern Masters of the Keyboard; Ewen, D. Men and Women Who Make Music; Gelatt, R. Makers of Music. *Periodicals*—New York Times, June 15, 1941.

Jerome Hines

1921–

Jerome Hines (originally Jerome Heinz), bass, was born in Hollywood, California, on November 8, 1921, the son of Russell Ray Heinz and Mildred Link Heinz. His father was a motion picture executive. Jerome's introduction to music came in his fifth year, with piano lessons. Though he liked to sing, he was dismissed from the glee club at Bancroft Junior High School because he "had no voice." After graduating from Fairfax High School in Los Angeles in 1937, he entered the University of California in Los Angeles where he majored in mathematics and chemistry. One year later he auditioned for Edwin Lester, executive director of the Los Angeles Civic Light Opera Association. When

JEROME HINES

Lester advised intensive music study, Jerome became a voice pupil of Gennaro Curci. Up to the time of his death in 1955, Curci was Hines's sole music teacher. The only other person from whom he received voice coaching was Samuel Margolis of New York.

In April 1940, while attending the University, Jerome made his professional singing debut as Bill Bobstay in Gilbert and Sullivan's *Pinafore,* performed by the Los Angeles Civic Light Opera Association. On this occasion he changed his name to Hines. On October 24, 1941, he made his debut with the San Francisco Opera as Biterolf in *Tannhäuser;* later that season he also sang Monterone in *Rigoletto.* In 1942 he appeared with the San Carlo Opera as Ramfis in *Aida* and as a soloist with the Los Angeles Philharmonic and the Hollywood Bowl orchestras. In 1943 he played minor parts with the Los Angeles Opera Association.

He was graduated from UCLA in June 1943. While taking graduate courses there in physics he appeared as Méphistophélès in *Faust* with the New Orleans Opera Company in the spring of 1944. Disqualified for military service during World War II because of his height (six feet six inches), he aided the war effort in 1944 and 1945 by working as a chemist with the Union Oil Company of Los Angeles. At this time he installed a chemical laboratory in his home and did research in operational mathematics. Meanwhile he continued making random appearances in operas, including performances as Osmin in *The Abduction from the Seraglio* with the Central City Opera in Colorado in the summer of 1945, and a one-year engagement with the New Orleans Opera in 1945–1946.

His debut with the Metropolitan Opera took place on November 21, 1946, in the small role of the Sergeant in *Boris Godunov*. Hines assumed his first major part (that of Méphistophélès in *Faust*) on December 14. For several seasons he appeared in minor or secondary roles but eventually graduated to leading bass parts, the first American to do so at the Metropolitan since Herbert Witherspoon. In the more than thirty years Hines has sung with the Metropolitan Opera he has been heard in over thirty principal bass roles. He scored his greatest successes in the title roles of *Boris Godunov* and *Don Giovanni,* as Banquo in *Macbeth,* King Mark in *Tristan and Isolde,* Ramfis, Gurnemanz in *Parsifal,* Padre Guardiano in *La Forza del Destino,* Philip II in *Don Carlo,* Arkel in *Pelléas and Mélisande,* Don Basilio in *The Barber of Seville,* and Sarastro in *The Magic Flute.* He was first heard in *Boris Godunov* on February 18, 1954, as King Mark on March 3, 1955, and as Don Giovanni on March 10, 1955—in all these instances becoming the first American in thirty-nine years to be heard in these roles at the Metropolitan Opera. Jay S. Harrison reported in the New York *Herald Tribune* that as Boris, Hines "did his homeland proud and was, in addition, a credit to a role that has toppled many an older and wiser trouper." As Don Giovanni, said Howard Taubman in the New York *Times,* Hines sang "with color, smoothness and flexibility. . . . Mr. Hines sang as though he had done the part often."

Among his other roles at the Metropolitan Opera were Des Grieux in *Manon,* Ferrando in *Il Trovatore,* Raimondo in *Lucia di Lammermoor,* Sparafucile in *Rigoletto,* Don Fernando in *Fidelio,* Colline in *La Bohème,* Hermann in *Tannhäuser,* Prince Gremin in *Eugene Onegin,* Wotan in *Die Walküre,* Fiesco in *Simon Boccanegra,* Zaccaria in *Nabucco,* Wotan in *Das Rheingold,* King Henry in *Lohengrin,* Alvise in *La Gioconda,* Silva in *Ernani,* Rodolfo in *La Sonnambula,* and Walter in *Luisa Miller.* When the Metropolitan Opera revived *Le Prophète* on January 18, 1977, Hines appeared as Zacharias. He also sang this role on the Columbia recording of this opera.

At Teatro Colón in Buenos Aires Hines became the first American to sing the title role in Boïto's *Mefistofele.* When he made his debut at La Scala in 1958, he was heard in *Hercules,* a rarely performed opera by Handel. That summer he became the first American to appear as Gurnemanz at the Bayreuth Festival. Returning to Bayreuth in subsequent years he also appeared as King Mark and as Wotan in the *Ring* cycle. In addition to his appearances with major opera houses in South America and Europe, Hines was featured at festivals in Glyndebourne, Edinburgh, and Munich. In 1953 he was cast as Nick Shadow in Stravinsky's *The Rake's Progress* at both Edinburgh and Glyndebourne. At the Munich Festival one year later he was starred as Don Giovanni.

On September 23, 1962, Hines scored a spectacular success at the Bolshoi Opera in Moscow in the title role of *Boris Godunov,* the first American to sing the part in Russian. He received a standing ovation from an audience which included Premier Khrushchev and Igor Stravinsky (the latter on his first visit to his native land in half a century). This demonstration for Hines was remarkable not only because it was given to an American appearing in a Russian opera and singing in the Russian language but also because this performance took place during the Cuban missile crisis when the United States and the Soviet Union appeared to be on a collision course. After Moscow, Hines appeared with local opera companies in Leningrad, Kiev, and Tiflis.

He scored once again as Boris Godunov when the Metropolitan Opera presented for the first time the original Mussorgsky version of the opera on October 14, 1975. "The night belonged to Mr. Hines," said Donal Henahan in the New York *Times.* "At almost every moment this was a living, breathing, tormented Boris, not merely one figure in a colorful pageant. At this point in his career there are a few better singers than Mr. Hines playing Boris, but few better Borises, even now."

Between the acts of *Boris Godunov* on January 8, 1976, a ceremony took place on the stage of the Metropolitan Opera celebrating Hines's thirtieth anniversary with the company. This performance was his four hundred and fifty-fourth at the Metropolitan Opera.

Hines married soprano Lucia Evangelista, an Italian-born opera singer, on July 23, 1952. They first met while singing together at the Cincinnati Summer Opera. She gave up her career to raise their four sons.

To keep in shape Hines likes to train regularly in a gymnasium. He also enjoys such outdoor sports as horseback riding, swimming, skin diving, ice-skating, and spearfishing. He is an amateur hypnotist who enjoys entertaining his colleagues and friends with demonstrations of hypnosis. He is a partisan of opera in English when suitable translations can be had. Hines is the composer of a trilogy of operas on the life of Christ for which he wrote his own texts.

ABOUT: Musical America, November 15, 1955; New York Times, December 30, 1975.

Josef Hofmann

1876–1957

JOSEF HOFMANN

Josef Casimir Hofmann, pianist, was born in Cracow, Poland, on January 20, 1876. His father, Casimir, of Hungarian descent, was a gifted pianist and conductor; his mother was a singer at the Cracow Municipal Opera. His older sister, who was also musical, gave Josef his first piano lessons when he was four. A half year later he wrote his first composition, a mazurka, which he presented to his father as a birthday gift. By the time he was five Josef's talent for the piano was so obvious that his father took over his training and prepared him for his first concert appearance which took place in Ciechocinek, about a hundred miles from Warsaw. This performance, which occurred before Josef had reached his sixth birthday, proved so extraordinary that offers descended on his father to take him on a tour. Though his father refused to exploit Josef's talent, he did allow Josef to make several appearances. At one of these, when he was seven, Josef performed a movement from Beethoven's Piano Concerto No.1. At about this time, Anton Rubinstein heard him perform, called him "a musical phenomenon," and despite his aversion to prodigies recommended the child to Hermann Wolff, the German impresario. Through Wolff, Josef (aged ten) was engaged to perform the Beethoven Piano Concerto No.1 with the Berlin Philharmonic Orchestra under Hans von Bülow. This concert was followed by others in Denmark, Sweden, Norway, and Holland. When Josef performed in Paris, Camille Saint-Saëns is alleged to have said: "He

Hofmann: hôf' män *or* hŏf' män

is one of the greatest wonders of the present age."

Reports of the boy's ability spread across the Atlantic. "For nearly four years he has been appearing before the public as a piano virtuoso," reported *Harper's Young People* in 1887, comparing Hofmann to Mozart in an earlier paragraph, "and lately he has appeared very frequently and created what the newspapers call a 'sensation.' Never was so much written about a young man by his contemporaries as has been written about this young Hofmann. Famous musicians like Rubinstein, and callous old critics —well, most of the famous ones—have fairly gushed over him. It is a wonder that with all the attention he has received, the little fellow has not become very conceited. . . . Away from music, he is always a child, and his sense of humor is delightful. One day, his parents promised to pay him twenty-five cents for each concert and, subsequently, when encores were demanded, he said: 'No,' with a merry laugh, 'the concert is over and I have earned my quarter.' But he played encores, and upon returning to the artists' room said, 'Now in the future you may pay me by the piece—two cents for my own compositions and five cents for the others.' "

When Josef went to the United States to make his American debut at the Metropolitan Opera on November 29, 1887, the concert became the musical and social event of the New York season. Dressed in a striped sailor shirt and knee breeches, the round-faced eleven-year-old boy offered a program highlighted by Beethoven's

Piano Concerto No.1 and including pieces by Rameau, Weber, and Chopin, together with one of his own compositions and some improvisations. "When he concluded the Beethoven concerto," wrote W. J. Henderson in the New York *Times,* "a thunder of applause swept through the opera house. Many people leaped to their feet. Men shouted, 'Bravo!' and women waved their handkerchiefs. Pianists of repute were moved almost to tears. Some wiped the moisture from their eyes. The child had astonished the assembly. He was a marvel. . . . Suffice it to say for the present that Josef Hofmann as a musical phenomenon is worthy of the sensation which he created. More than that, he is an artist, and we can listen to his music without taking into consideration the fact that he is a child."

Though booked for eighty concerts in America, Josef was allowed to give just sixteen additional performances at the Metropolitan Opera and twenty-six on tour. The Society for the Prevention of Cruelty to Children had intervened and their propaganda made it necessary for him to withdraw from all further concert activity. At about this time an anonymous patron (later identified as Alfred Corning Clark of New York) provided Josef and his family with the financial means (fifty thousand dollars) to permit Josef to devote himself to study and relaxation until his eighteenth year.

An extended period of training followed in Berlin: piano with Moriz Moszkowski and musical theory and composition with Heinrich Urban. When he became sixteen, Josef was accepted as Anton Rubinstein's only private pupil. Teaching Josef proved for the master an experience that brought him no end of wonder. Rubinstein never wearied of relating the miracles performed by his pupil. "He is," said Rubinstein, who was never careless with superlatives, particularly where the playing of the piano was concerned, "the greatest genius of music the world has ever known."

After Hofmann had studied with Rubinstein for two years, the master asked his pupil to commit to memory and prepare for concert performance Rubinstein's Concerto in D minor, all in a two-day period. When Hofmann suggested that two days was too brief a time for such a formidable assignment, Rubinstein bellowed: "There is nothing formidable for *us!* " Two days later, on March 14, 1894, Hofmann performed the world premiere of this concerto in Hamburg, with the composer conducting. When Hofmann finished playing, his teacher embraced and kissed him. This Hamburg concert was the last occasion on which Hofmann collaborated publicly with his teacher. On November 20, 1894, while en route from London to Cheltenham, Hofmann learned from a newspaper headline that Rubinstein was dead. "It seemed to me that I had lost not only my greatest benefactor but also the dearest person on earth, for not only did I admire him, I had grown to love him as well." By coincidence, Hofmann was scheduled to perform the Chopin Sonata in B-flat minor (with the Funeral March) at his Cheltenham concert that evening. He played the funeral march in memory of Rubinstein. The audience sensed the significance of Hofmann's performance, and during the playing of this movement rose one by one and remained standing with bowed heads until the movement was over.

In 1895 and 1896 Hofmann toured Germany and Russia as well as England. He returned to the United States in 1898, no longer the fabled prodigy but a mature artist. "How difficult it is," he told an interviewer, "to be a prodigy and then to come back later and be accepted as a mature artist. It's like being the son of a famous father, except that in this case it is your own self they are comparing yourself with, to your disadvantage. You are the shadow of your early power and it is heartbreaking business to climb out of it into your own light."

Hofmann made the transition from prodigy to full-grown artist gracefully. In performances throughout the world he came to be accepted in the class of Busoni and Liszt, with a formidable technique matched by few and his own particular gift at tone colorations and the projection of a pure singing tone. Though he had such short and stubby fingers that he had Steinway build him a special keyboard to his own specifications with each key just a fraction of an inch narrower than usual, "there was nothing his pair of hands could not do," as Robert Jacobson noted in the *Saturday Review.* "Forte passages welled up from deep within the keyboard, filigree patterns were airborne, his dynamic range encompassed the full piano spectrum, his right hand was the executor of an exquisite singing tone, and his left hand was remarkable for its independence and staying power. . . . His security and confidence, musically and technically, were such that he could experiment with tempos, rubatos and phrasing during a performance. No work was ever played twice the same way."

In analyzing Hofmann's pianism, Samuel Chotzinoff, music critic of the New York *World,* pointed to "a tremendous digital dexterity; a command over dynamics that achieves the most delicate pianissimo and the most powerful fortissimo within the limits of beautiful sound, and a tone in cantilena in whose quality there appears to be no trace of percussion. This tone is, in fact, the mysterious element in Mr. Hofmann's pianist equipment, since its texture and quality are akin to those of a noble singing voice of many and perfectly equalized registers."

In 1924 Hofmann divorced his first wife, the former Marie C. Eustis (they had a daughter), and married Betty Short, a New York piano student. In the years that followed they had three sons.

In 1926 he became an American citizen. That year he was appointed director of the Curtis Institute of Music in Philadelphia, where for the preceding two years he had been head of the piano department and where for the next dozen years his influence was felt by an entire generation of young musicians. He announced his retirement as director in 1938 to devote more time to concert work, composition, and recording. After 1939 he became virtually a recluse at his home in Los Angeles, removing himself for the most part from the active music scene.

Before retiring to California, Hofmann occupied a suite at the Great Northern Hotel in New York City, and a house in Merion, Pennsylvania, with his wife and three sons. One son, Anton, became a nuclear physicist.

While still active as a concert artist and director of the Curtis Institute, Hofmann found relaxation in playing tennis, table tennis, chess, and poker. He enjoyed gourmet meals with fine wines and smoked Turkish cigarettes. He tinkered with inventions and mechanics and had more than sixty patents to his credit. He was the first to design a model house rotating with the sun, and he devised various forms of automobile air springs, shock absorbers, and snubbers. He built an oil-burning furnace for his home, a steam automobile for his personal use, and he constructed a collapsible piano bench whose legs were adjustable to cope with warped concert-stage floors.

As a composer, Hofmann concealed his works under the pseudonym Michel Dvorsky. For years Dvorsky's compositions were performed publicly without the identity of the composer being revealed. Finally, Hofmann emerged from his pseudonymity on January 2, 1924, when the Philadelphia Orchestra presented an entire program of his compositions, including a piano concerto, a tone poem *(The Haunted Castle),* and a "symphonic dialogue" for piano and orchestra *(Chromaticon).* In addition, Hofmann composed four other piano concertos, two piano sonatas, a symphony, and numerous short works for piano. The *Polonaise Americaine* for orchestra, written when he was ten, was revived by the Indianapolis Symphony Orchestra on April 20, 1976.

The golden jubilee of Hofmann's debut in the United States was commemorated at the Metropolitan Opera on November 28, 1937. While it was generally conceded that Hofmann was past his prime, enough of his one-time mastery and unique interpretative powers were evident to make this concert an event of special significance. The entire performance was recorded privately; part of it was issued commercially by Columbia in 1955 and all of it by International Piano Archives in 1975. International Piano Archives also released in 1975 a private recording made of Hofmann's last faculty recital at the Curtis Institute on April 7, 1938.

Hofmann's commercial recordings are few. He made his first recordings, cylinder records, at the Edison laboratories in 1887 when he was eleven, becoming the first important musician to have made a recording. In 1904 he recorded several sides in Berlin for commercial distribution. Between 1911 and 1924 he made acoustic recordings for Columbia and Brunswick. He stopped recording in 1924 because he felt the sound reproduction did not do him justice.

Hofmann gave his last New York recital at Carnegie Hall on January 16, 1946. His eightieth birthday was celebrated nationally in 1956. He died in a nursing home in Los Angeles, California, on February 16, 1957.

Hofmann was the author of a manual, *Piano-Playing With Piano-Questions Answered* (1915).

ABOUT: Chasins, A. Speaking of Pianists; Ewen, D. Men and Women Who Make Music; Schonberg, H. C. The Great Pianists. *Periodicals*—Musical America, March 1957; New York Times, April 18, 1976; Saturday Review, March 30, 1957.

Louise Homer

1871–1947

LOUISE HOMER

Louise Homer (originally Louise Dilworth Beatty), contralto, was born in Shadyside, near Pittsburgh, Pennsylvania, on April 28, 1871. She was the fourth of eight children of William Trimble Beatty, a Presbyterian minister, the founder and pastor of the Shadyside Presbyterian Church, and Sarah Colwell Beatty, one of whose ancestors was Robert Fulton.

The Beattys moved to Minneapolis when Louise was seven. Music was cultivated in their household. Together with her brothers and sisters Louise sang in the choir of her father's church. When she was eleven her father died, and her mother took the family to West Chester, Pennsylvania. At fourteen Louise made her debut as a solo vocalist in a performance of a cantata, *Ruth, the Joabitess.* Her early vocal studies for a number of years were with Abbie Whinnery and Alice Groff.

After graduation from the West Chester High School, Louise continued to study voice while supporting herself, first as a secretary at the William Penn Charter School and then as a court stenographer in Philadelphia. She also found a singing assignment as a contralto in a Philadelphia church quartet.

Determined to pursue music more actively and comprehensively, Louise went to Boston in 1894. There she enrolled at the New England Conservatory, studying voice with William L. Whitney and theory with Sidney Homer. She also joined George Chadwick's choir at the First Universalist Church.

One evening Sidney Homer took her to a performance of *Faust* given in Boston by the visiting Metropolitan Opera; the cast included Emma Eames and Édouard de Reszke. This was her introduction to opera, an experience that made her redouble her efforts as a vocal student so that she too might someday become an opera singer.

A love affair developed between Homer and Louise, and on January 9, 1895, they were married in Boston. They lived on Boylston Street and their first child was born there. One year later Sidney Homer took his young wife and their child to Paris, where she continued her vocal studies with Fidèle Koenig and Paul Lhé-

rie. A successful concert appearance in Paris, with Vincent d'Indy conducting the orchestra, proved that she was ready for opera. In 1898, she made her opera debut in Vichy as Leonora in *La Favorita.* After this debut she appeared for one season at Angers and gave several performances at Covent Garden in London. In 1899 she became a member of the Théâtre de la Monnaie Brussels, where she gave over one hundred performances in an eight-month period, her most distinguished roles being Delilah in *Samson and Delilah* and Amneris in *Aida.* She also appeared at Covent Garden in London during the spring season of 1899 with such success that she was invited to give a command performance for the King and Queen. Upon her return to Covent Garden the following spring season, she sang Wagnerian roles for the first time.

In 1900 Maurice Grau engaged her for the Metropolitan Opera in New York. On November 14 of that year she made her American opera debut with the Metropolitan Opera company during its guest season in San Francisco. Her role at that time, Amneris, was also the one that she sang in New York on December 22, 1900. The latter debut was not particularly impressive, but she began attracting interest during the season of 1900–1901 when she sang her first Wagnerian roles at the Metropolitan, Ortrud in *Lohengrin,* Venus in *Tannhäuser,* and Brangäne in *Tristan and Isolde.* She first sang Brangäne on December 3, 1901, while the company was on tour, learning the part in ten days so that she might serve as a replacement for Ernestine Schumann-Heink.

When Heinrich Conried took over the management of the Metropolitan Opera in 1903, Louise Homer was given more opportunities to extend her artistic horizon. She was capable of making the most of these opportunities, since her voice was growing richer, fuller, and more expressive, her stage poise was increasing, and her musical comprehension was deepening. She expanded her Wagnerian repertory adding the roles of Fricka and Flosshilde in *Das Rheingold,* Waltraute in *Die Walküre,* Waltraute and Flosshilde in *Die Götterdämmerung,* Erda in *Siegfried,* and Magdalena in *Die Meistersinger.* She mastered the part of Fricka in *Das Rheingold* in a single day in order to replace the ailing Olive Fremstad. When *Parsifal* received its first stage performance outside Bayreuth, at the Metropolitan Opera on December 24, 1903, she sang the small role of the Voice.

As the leading contralto of the Metropolitan Opera up through the 1918–1919 season, she played a considerable part in helping to shape some of the house's historic performances. When Enrico Caruso made his American debut in *Rigoletto* on November 24, 1903, she was Maddalena. When Arturo Toscanini made his American bow on November 16, 1908, in *Aida* she was Amneris. She was the Witch in the first Metropolitan Opera production of *Hansel and Gretel* on November 25, 1905, and she created the role of the Witch in the world premiere of Humperdinck's *Die Königskinder* on December 28, 1910. She sang Suzuki in *Madama Butterfly* on February 11, 1907, at the first Metropolitan Opera performance of Puccini's opera, with the composer himself in attendance. When Auber's *La Dame Blanche* was successfully revived on February 13, 1904, she was heard as Marguerite, and she sang the role of Czipra in the much acclaimed revival of Johann Strauss's *Der Zigeunerbaron* on February 15, 1906. She assumed the role of Hate in the historic revival of Gluck's *Armide* under Toscanini on the opening night of the 1910–1911 season (November 14). On February 14, 1902, she created for the United States the role of Hedwig in the American premiere of Paderewski's *Manru.* She also appeared in two American operas, as Naoia in Frederick Converse's *The Pipe of Desire* (March 18, 1910) and in the title role of Horatio W. Parker's *Mona* (March 14, 1912), the latter a world premiere.

She realized one of her great triumphs at the Metropolitan Opera on December 23, 1909, as Orfeo in Gluck's *Orfeo ed Euridice,* Toscanini conducting, when she revealed the full magnitude of her vocal art. As Richard Aldrich wrote in the New York *Times:* "Mme. Homer's impersonation of Orfeo was one of nobility, dignity, and plastic grace for the eye, and of full-throated and beautiful song for the ear. She was, in this, something other than a woman disguised. There was a true representation of the Greek singer, of his grief, and of the innate power that carried him through the perils and affright of his quest. It was one of the finest and most artistic as well as one of the most original impersonations that Mme. Homer has given us."

No less memorable was her performance as Delilah in Saint-Saëns's opera when she appeared opposite Caruso on March 10, 1916.

While performing at the Metropolitan Opera, Homer also made numerous appearances in the concert hall. On November 1, 1909, she appeared at the Lyceum Theatre in New York in a recital made up exclusively of the songs of her husband, Sidney Homer (who also served as her accompanist). Richard Aldrich noted in the New York *Times:* "Her voice was never more beautiful, richer, or fuller. . . . There could not have been a more favorable presentation of Mr. Homer's work than there was on this occasion."

Louise Homer left the Metropolitan Opera for a decade after the 1918–1919 season, having been heard in 468 performances in New York and 238 on tour in 42 roles. In addition to the roles already mentioned, she had been heard as Siébel in *Faust,* Martha and Pantalis in Boïto's *Mefistofele,* Lola in *Cavalleria Rusticana,* Urbain in *Les Huguenots,* Emilia in *Otello,* Ulrica in *Un Ballo in Maschera,* Azucena in *Il Trovatore,* the Second and Third Ladies in *The Magic Flute,* Laura in *La Gioconda,* Nancy in *Martha,* Dame Quickly in *Falstaff,* Marina in *Boris Godunov,* and Fides in *Le Prophète.*

Upon leaving the Metropolitan Opera company in 1919, she was heard with the Chicago Opera from 1922 to 1926 and with the Los Angeles Opera and the San Francisco Opera in 1926. She returned to the Metropolitan Opera as Amneris on December 14, 1927; and on December 6, 1927, and April 6, 1928, she was also heard there as Azucena in *Il Trovatore.*

She left the Metropolitan Opera after the 1929–1930 season to go into complete retirement, not

349

because there was any perceptible decline in her art, but because her husband was ill and she wanted to devote herself completely to her family. From this point on domesticity, as her friend, the novelist Willa Cather, once remarked, was not a role but "her real self." At her winter estate in Winter Park, Florida, and her summer residence, Homeland, at Lake George, New York, she was the total wife, mother, and housewife just as she had formerly been the total artist. "Our family life has flourished as a green bay tree," wrote Sidney Homer. "We have six children and twelve grandchildren. We are a sturdy clan of twenty-five, and frankness is our motto." One of Homer's daughters, Louise Homer Stires, became a professional singer, who occasionally shared the program with her mother on concert tours. It is interesting to note that Louise Homer was the aunt of the American composer Samuel Barber.

The death of her youngest daughter, Joy, in 1946 was a blow from which she never recovered. On May 6, 1947, Louise Homer died at her home in Winter Park, Florida, a victim of coronary thrombosis; she was buried at Bolton, New York, on Lake George. Her husband, Sidney, outlived her by about six years; he died at Winter Park, on July 10, 1953.

Between 1902 and 1929 Louise Homer made numerous recordings for Victor, many of these in collaboration with other opera stars such as Caruso, Geraldine Farrar, Emma Eames, Johanna Gadski, and Alma Gluck. She received honorary degrees from several colleges and universities including Tufts, Smith, Middlebury, and Miami University in Ohio. In 1923 a poll held by the League of Women Voters named her one of the twelve greatest living American women.

ABOUT: Homer, A. Louise Homer and the Golden Age of Opera; Homer, S. My Wife and I. *Periodicals—* McClure's Magazine, December 1913; New York Times, May 7, 1947.

Marilyn Horne

1934–

Marilyn Horne, soprano and mezzo-soprano, was born in Bradford, Pennsylvania, on January 16, 1934. She was one of four children of Bentz J. and Bernice P. Hokanson Horne. Her father, the city assessor, was also a semiprofessional singer who performed in churches and at social functions. "I can never remember a time when I did not sing," Horne told an interviewer. "My father . . . was determined that I would become a professional. He was smart enough to keep me away from opera until I was out of private schools."

When Marilyn was seven she started studying voice with Edna Luce who, Horne says, gave her a technique in breathing that has served her well in her professional career. In 1944, during the presidential campaign, the ten-year-old Marilyn sang for Franklin D. Roosevelt at a Democratic picnic at Bradford.

When Marilyn was eleven, her family moved to Long Beach, California. This was during World War II, housing was hard to come by, and for a time the entire Horne family had to live in a single room. With her sister, Gloria—billed as the Horne Sisters—Marilyn sang in churches, filled club dates, and performed at USO centers and service clubs. Upon graduating from Long Beach Polytechnic High School in 1951, she earned a voice scholarship at the University of Southern California. "I was standing by the registration desk, wondering what I should sign up for," she told Martin Mayer, who reported it in the New York *Times Magazine*. "Somebody asked me what I preferred and I said, 'Well, I'm here on a voice scholarship.' And whoever it was said to me, 'Then you ought to take a course with Bill Vennard, he's the chairman of the voice department.' That sure was a lucky moment."

While studying voice with William Vennard and subsequently attending Lotte Lehmann's master classes, Marilyn helped to support herself by imitating the voices of such popular singing stars as Patti Page and Peggy Lee on bootleg recordings distributed in supermarkets. She remained at the University two years before touring Europe as a leading singer with the Roger Wagner Chorale. Returning to California in

MARILYN HORNE

1953, she was discovered by Robert Craft, Stravinsky's collaborator and disciple, who not only invited her to sing at his Monday Evening Concerts in Los Angeles but also drew her into the Stravinsky orbit. In 1954 she gave her first recital, at the Hollywood Bowl. She also joined the Los Angeles Opera Guild, making her debut as Hata in *The Bartered Bride.* She was also heard as Hansel in *Hansel and Gretel* and in the title role in Rossini's *La Cenerentola.* Soon after that she appeared as a soloist with the Los Angeles Philharmonic. In 1955 she dubbed the singing for Dorothy Dandridge on the sound track of the motion picture *Carmen Jones.*

Her savings enabled her to return to Europe in 1956. On Stravinsky's recommendation she was invited to participate at the Venice Biennale that September, performing music by Heinrich Schütz, Giovanni Gabrieli, and Monteverdi at St. Mark's Cathedral. From Venice she went on to Vienna for a year's stay to learn German and to receive valuable coaching in opera roles from a member of the Vienna State Opera. During the year in Vienna, she performed several times over the radio and made a recording of *Cavalleria Rusticana* with the Seventh Army Symphony of Stuttgart, Germany, Henry Lewis conducting. Horne had known Lewis in Los Angeles at the University, and at that time had an on-again, off-again courtship with him. But in Europe their romance revived.

From 1957 to 1960 Horne sang with the Municipal Opera at Gelsenkirchen, a provincial company in the Ruhr Valley of Germany performing not only in Gelsenkirchen but also in outlying towns. She made her debut with this company as Giulietta in *The Tales of Hoffmann.* Her subsequent roles there included Mimi in *La Bohème,* Amelia in *Simon Boccanegra,* Tatiana in *Eugene Onegin,* Minnie in *The Girl of the Golden West,* Fulvia in Handel's *Ezio,* and Marie in *Wozzeck.*

On July 2, 1960, one day after she returned to the United States, Horne married Lewis, who at that time was assistant conductor of the Los Angeles Philharmonic. Since he was black, the marriage caused no little consternation among Horne's relatives and friends. Roger Wagner, the leader of the Chorale, thought that the marriage would permanently destroy her promising career. Her mother, as Horne herself recalls, "went all to pieces. . . . My parents had always preached tolerance, but talking and taking a step like this was pretty different." But Horne was a determined young woman who once she had decided upon a course of action refused to be deflected.

On October 4, 1960, Horne made her debut with the San Francisco Opera as Marie in *Wozzeck.* "In her beautiful voice, her sensitive face and her tremendous gifts as an actress lies a good portion of the future of American opera," wrote Alfred Frankenstein in the *Chronicle.* Her success was of such dimensions that the Los Angeles *Times* designated her "woman of the year." Kurt Adler, the general manager of the San Francisco Opera, said of her at the time, as quoted in *Newsweek,* "She's a true artist. Exceptionally sensitive, and she can learn any part quicker than almost anyone I've seen. Actually she can sing anything. It's a fabulous voice, a dramatic soprano, a mezzo-soprano, a mezzo coloratura. You don't ask what the role is, you ask if Marilyn is available." In her subsequent appearances with the San Francisco Opera, where she became a favorite performer, Horne sang Carmen, the title role of *The Daughter of the Regiment,* Nedda in *I Pagliacci,* and Isabella in *L'Italiana in Algeri.*

Her New York debut took place on February 21, 1961, as Agnese in a concert presentation of Bellini's rarely heard opera *Beatrice di Tenda,* by the American Opera Society. "I was a kid," she recalls, " and she [Joan Sutherland] was the toast of the world. I was called in to replace Giulietta Simionato and had to learn the opera in three weeks. Henry [Lewis] pounded the music at me from the piano until I threw the score at him and screamed I hated Bellini. I couldn't get the style. . . . But at the first group rehearsal everything was great."

This was the first of many times that Marilyn Horne shared top billing with Joan Sutherland. On this occasion Sutherland was also making her New York debut, and interest was for the most part focused on her performance. Nevertheless, Paul Henry Lang noted in the *Herald Tribune* that Horne was a "youthful soprano with a warm and expressive voice who handled and conveyed a positive personality," and Richard Bonynge—Sutherland's husband and the conductor of this performance—told an executive of London Records: "There's a girl here who sounds like Rosa Ponselle."

During the next three years Horne's performances led her to operatic stardom. She sang Carmen during the spring season of the San Francisco Opera in 1961, and that same year she also appeared with the Chicago Lyric Opera, where, on November 25, she was starred in the world premiere of Vittorio Giannini's *The Harvest*. After that came the lead role in Gluck's *Iphigénie en Tauride* with the American Opera Society and, with the Vancouver Opera, her first appearance as Adalgisa in *Norma* (opposite Sutherland).

The year 1964 brought a triumphant debut as Marie in *Wozzeck* at Covent Garden in London, and a spectacular performance as Arsace, opposite Sutherland, in Rossini's *Semiramide* in February in a concert performance with the Los Angeles Philharmonic in Los Angeles and later the same month in a concert performance by the American Opera Society in New York. Writing in *The Christian Science Monitor,* Miles Kastendieck pointed out the "sensational nature of the occasion developed through the singing of Marilyn Horne, whose coloratura achievements as a mezzo almost matched Miss Sutherland's soprano. To hear them together in duets was to experience one of the great moments of the music season." Concerning one of these duets, Winthrop Sargeant in the *New Yorker* said it was "as spectacular a display of trilling and cascading pyrotechnics as I have ever come across."

Two months later, on April 22, when Horne gave her first New York recital at the Lincoln Center for the Performing Arts, the start of the program had to be delayed ten minutes to allow several hundred people to get to their seats after lining up at the box office at the last possible moment. "The delay seemed to fan the already combustible air," reported Howard Klein in the New York *Times.* "Few recitals have had such expectancy. The large audience was not disappointed for it heard singing of a rare kind in any age. When she finally came out a small ovation greeted her, but when she ended her first group of Handel arias a storm of applause and cheers broke out. This continued to the end of the program." Louis Biancolli described her voice in the *World-Telegram and Sun* as "of ravishing beauty, molded by nature as a thing of unblemished purity and schooled to preserve it whatever the demands imposed upon it."

The triumphs continued in 1964: On June 21 with the San Francisco Opera as Isabella in *L'Italiana in Algeri;* at the Edinburgh Festival in Scotland that August as soloist with the Scottish National Orchestra and the French Radio Orchestra; and in the already mentioned Covent Garden debut in *Wozzeck.* On the basis of her achievements *Mademoiselle* magazine presented her with its 1964 Award of Merit.

Her debut in Italy—in Florence in 1968 as Rosina in *The Barber of Seville*—was the prelude to her first Italian tour one year later with appearances in Turin in *La Cenerentola* and her bow at La Scala in Milan on March 13, 1969, as Jocasta in Stravinsky's *Oedipus Rex.* This was followed by an appearance there as Neocle in Rossini's *The Siege of Corinth.* "What really stopped the show," reported a correspondent to the New York *Times* after her appearance in *The Siege of Corinth,* "was Marilyn Horne's gigantic, never-ending solo scene at the beginning of Act III, which the coloratura contralto tossed off as if she were singing do-re-mi. Throughout the evening, Miss Horne's musical and vocal artistry was enormously impressive—as was the huge range of her voice in the part of Neocle."

Her debut at the Metropolitan Opera took place on March 3, 1970, as Adalgisa to Sutherland's Norma. "There was screaming . . . at the Metropolitan Opera," reported Harold C. Schonberg in his review in the New York *Times.* "After each aria and ensemble of those two thoroughbreds, Sutherland and Horne, the house erupted. Miss Horne, at the end of the third act . . . received a standing ovation. People just stood, applauding and yelling. . . . She comes to the Metropolitan Opera in her vocal prime and she was in complete authority." Rudolf Bing, the general manager of the Metropolitan Opera, called the ovation given to Horne the second greatest ever experienced during his regime (the greatest having gone to Birgit Nilsson).

The Barber of Seville was added to the Metropolitan Opera repertory on January 23, 1971, to feature Marilyn Horne as Rosina. On September 19, 1972, she helped open the Metropolitan Opera season in what was expected to be the inauguration of Goeran Gentele's administration, a new production of *Carmen* conceived by Gentele and conducted by Leonard Bernstein. (Gentele died in an automobile accident in Italy and never took over the direction of the company.) That season she added to her Metropolitan Opera repertory the role of Orfeo in Gluck's *Orfeo ed Euridice;* on November 10, 1973, she was heard as Isabella in the first production of *L'Italiana in Algeri* at the Metropolitan Opera since 1920; and January 18, 1977, she was cast as Fides in the first Metropolitan Opera production of Meyerbeer's *Le Prophète* since 1928. This was the first time she sang that role. She was, said Harold C. Schonberg in the New York *Times,* "the vocal star of the evening. . . . The role of Fides is one that gives her a chance to unleash her entire range and she was in full use of her remarkable lower register. When she finally arrived at the big show-stopper, 'O prêtres de Baal,' she sounded a bit tired, but even at that it is hard to think of a mezzo-soprano today who could have duplicated this kind of vocal finesse and command."

On October 16, 1975, in the first American-staged production of Handel's *Rinaldo*—at the Houston Opera in Houston, Texas—Horne brought down the house in the title role. "She carried off the title role," wrote Carl Cunningham in *Musical America,* "with a great deal of bravura. . . . A nobly sung 'Cara sposa' and some intensely beautiful arioso passages provided Horne welcome relief from her vocal acrobatics elsewhere in the opera."

On October 13, 1977, Horne assumed the title role in Rossini's *Tancredi* with the Houston Grand Opera. Though that opera had earned for Rossini his first success, it had not been heard in the United States in more than a century and a quarter. Horne then went on to help open a new season of the Dallas Civic Opera on November 18, 1977, as Romeo (a role written for a contralto) in Bellini's *I Capuletti ed i Montecchi.*

Among her many recordings of complete operas and concert works is an album entitled *Presenting Marilyn Horne,* recorded for London Records, which received a Grammy from the National Academy of Recording Arts and Sciences.

Horne's husband, Henry Lewis, became the first black man ever to assume the direction of a major American symphony orchestra when he was appointed to that post with the New Jersey Symphony in 1968. As Horne's only vocal coach, Lewis has proved a most exacting taskmaster—he took her through the paces of most of her roles since 1960. She freely credits him with her remarkable development as a musician. "We worked together on everything. He is so thorough, always aiming at perfection, and we both love music." In Horne's own description theirs has not been an interracial marriage quite so much as an interartistic one. Race prejudice has not affected either their social or professional lives. And when marital disputes arose, they came not from differences of race but from differences of opinion on musical details and the tensions attending two successful careers. "We stay away from each other before concert time," she says. "Until we learned that, it nearly ruined us."

With their daughter, Angéla, they occupied a spacious and beautifully landscaped house in Orange, New Jersey, up to the time of their separation in 1976. Theirs was a gracious home filled with books, paintings, and sculpture. Though only five feet two and a half inches in height, "Jackie" (as all those close to Horne have called her since her childhood) presents a regal presence, offstage as well as on it, because of her robust physique and her personal dynamism. She enjoys cooking, and she has an unusual gift for mimicking the styles of other singers, popular as well as serious. A linguist, she reads extensively in several languages, particularly books providing her with additional insights into the music she is required to sing.

Marilyn Horne was awarded honorary doctorates in music from Rutgers University and Jersey City State College, both in New Jersey.

ABOUT: Sargeant, W. Divas. *Periodicals*—Ebony, May 1967; New York Times, March 1, 1970; New York Times Magazine, January 17, 1971; Opera News, January 3, 1970; Time, March 16, 1970.

Horowitz

Vladimir Horowitz

1904–

Vladimir Horowitz (originally Vladimir Gorovitz), pianist, was born in Kiev, Russia, on October 1, 1904. He was the youngest of three children, all of whom became professional musicians. Their father, Simeon, was a successful electrical engineer whose wife, Sophie Bodik Horowitz, was an amateur pianist trained at the Kiev Conservatory. Sophie gave all three children their first music instruction.

Though Vladimir revealed an interest in the piano from the time he was three, he did not get his first lessons until he was six. From the beginning he showed remarkable talent. In 1914 he began studying with Sergei Tarnowsky. Two years later he entered the Kiev Conservatory where he remained four years, studying piano and composition principally with Felix Blumenfeld, a pupil of Anton Rubinstein. At that time Horowitz wanted to become a composer. He devoured the musical literature of the great composers, even in areas outside piano music, to the point of memorizing complete opera scores. He recalls: "As a child I would go to bed with the score of Wagner's *Die Götterdämmerung* under my pillow. My mother wanted me to take Bach instead to bed. My teacher said to her, 'So let him play *Die Götterdämmerung.*'"

Since his parents had no intention of treating him as a prodigy, they insisted he get a normal education at the Kiev high school. In later years Horowitz always insisted that concert artists must be informed about and educated in subjects outside the field of music.

Vladimir was graduated from the Kiev Conservatory with highest honors when he was seventeen. For his graduation he was required to perform a long and exacting program before all the Conservatory pupils and teachers. When his performance ended with a dazzling presentation of Liszt's *Don Juan Fantasy,* everybody in the auditorium stood up and cheered.

When the revolution in Russia left the Horowitzes destitute, Vladimir supported the family by playing the piano. He became an accompanist to singers (always playing his accompaniments from memory). On several occasions the singers

VLADIMIR HOROWITZ

presented a few of his songs on their programs. Vladimir became concerned more with his progress as a pianist than as a composer since it seemed the shorter route to earning money. In 1922 his uncle, a music critic, arranged for him to make his concert debut in Kharkov. This performance was such a success that Horowitz was required to give fourteen additional concerts in that city. A tour of Russia followed one season later in which Horowitz gave seventy concerts, twenty-three of them in Leningrad alone. He performed over two hundred compositions; at that time his repertory embraced fifteen different programs.

In 1925 the Soviet government gave him official permission to leave the country for "study" abroad. Three recitals in Berlin in January 1926 marked the beginning of an extended European tour that brought him to other German cities as well as to Austria, Holland, Spain, and France, in recitals and appearances with major orchestras. On several occasions he was required to give command performances before royalty. His musical sensibility combined with a prodigious technique made European critics pour out superlatives in describing his playing. In Paris the French musicologist Henri Prunières wrote: "He is without question the greatest pianist of the rising generation. He has all the technical gifts in addition to exquisite musical sensitiveness. He excels in the interpretation of Bach and Liszt, but he can play Ravel and Debussy to perfection. From the start, this young artist has been classed among the pianists of the first rank.

Horowitz: hô′ rô vĭts

354

One can only compare him to Busoni and Paderewski. Those who heard Anton Rubinstein think they have rediscovered the Russian pianist in Horowitz."

In Paris Horowitz was heard by the American concert manager Arthur Judson, who signed him for an American tour. This contract led Horowitz to a decision he had long been pondering: He destroyed his passport with the intention of never again returning to his native land.

Horowitz made his American debut on January 12, 1928, as soloist with the New York Philharmonic Orchestra in Tchaikovsky's Piano Concerto No.1, Sir Thomas Beecham conducting. Horowitz was not heard to best advantage that evening, since he was at such odds with the conductor on matters of dynamics and tempo that from time to time soloist and conductor seemed to be competing with each other rather than collaborating. Nevertheless, Horowitz's mastery of the keyboard and his fiery personality cast a spell. In the New York *Times* Olin Downes ignored the defects of the performance to say: "It has been years since a pianist created such a furor with an audience in this city. . . . His treatment of the work was a whirlwind of virtuoso interpretation. Mr. Horowitz has amazing strength, irresistible youth, and temperament."

His worldwide fame resulted in some three hundred and fifty performances between 1928 and 1935, his fee rising from five hundred dollars an appearance to fifteen hundred dollars. In the year 1935 he gave one hundred recitals in addition to appearances with orchestras. He was universally acknowledged as the possessor of hands capable of negotiating effortlessly every possible problem or demand posed by a piece of music. It was said that nobody could play faster or louder than Horowitz. But as Horowitz was quoted by Howard Klein in the New York *Times,* "technique is not just dexterity and speed. . . . It is having a good voice, and balancing of the notes, and coloring. I try to sing with this voice. . . . Playing should be like that. It takes coordination, heart and finger. If by technique is meant the total of phrasing, shading, pedaling, then I am happy to be called the greatest technician."

In 1932 Arturo Toscanini invited Horowitz to perform Beethoven's *Emperor Concerto* with the New York Philharmonic in a Beethoven cycle conducted by Toscanini. At a supper party after the concert Horowitz met Toscanini's daughter, Wanda. Much of that evening Horowitz and Wanda sat apart from the others in intense conversation. The following day Horowitz sent her a photograph of himself inscribed simply: "To you." The following summer Horowitz visited Toscanini at his home at Lake Maggiore in northern Italy where he was welcomed almost as a member of the family. On December 17, 1933, he married Wanda Toscanini in Milan. Their first home was in Paris where Horowitz had been living since 1928. From 1938 to 1940 they lived in Switzerland. They had one child, a daughter, Sonia.

In 1935 Horowitz underwent an appendectomy and developed phlebitis. Because of his illness he decided to take a sabbatical from concert work. But there was another sound reason for Horowitz's compelling need to seclude himself from the rigors of concertizing. Always a fastidiously self-critical artist, he had become dissatisfied with his performances and wanted to take time off to reevaluate his artistry, to give piano literature renewed study, to work over his entire repertory from a fresh point of view. Additionally, the strain of continuous travel and performances had debilitated what had always been a hypersensitive nervous system. Reflecting in later years on this two-year period of rest, study, and contemplation, Horowitz has remarked: "I think I really began to live then. For years I had been playing constantly . . . played certain works so often that I couldn't hear them any more, even while my fingers were performing them. . . . I think I grew as an artist, during this long vacation. At any rate, I think I found new things in my music. I know that I learned more than I could possibly have learned if I had been continuing the exhausting rounds of practicing, rushing for trains, and giving concerts month after month."

Out of this period of rest and study emerged a new Vladimir Horowitz—still the supreme technician, but now an artist who had been spiritually enriched and revitalized. A concert in Zurich in 1938 and recitals in Paris in 1939 revealed a pianist who had grown more mellow and mature, an artist less inclined to indulge in pyrotechnics and more in profound emotional and spiritual statements. On January 31, 1940, Horowitz returned to the United States with a recital at Carnegie Hall in New York. His American audiences had not forgotten him. A full house welcomed him back enthusiastically and recognized the growth and enrichment of his art. Herbert F. Peyser wrote in the New York *Times:* "As a matter of fact a change had come over Horowitz's playing. It is not always equally noticeable, but it is more or less noticeable." And in the New York *Times Magazine,* Howard Taubman said of Horowitz: "He remains one of the greatest technicians of piano history, but his technique is no longer an end in itself. He has transformed himself from a fire-eating virtuoso into a self-critical searching artist."

With increased interpretative powers came an interest in twentieth century piano music which he had more or less sidestepped before his sabbatical. In the decade following his return to the concert platform Horowitz presented such twentieth century masterworks as Prokofiev's Piano Sonata No.7 and two other Prokofiev sonatas, two sonatas by Kabalevsky, and the world premiere of Samuel Barber's Piano Sonata on December 9, 1949.

Settling permanently in the United States in 1940, Horowitz became an American citizen in 1944. In time he acquired a town house on East Ninety-fourth Street off Fifth Avenue and an old farmhouse in New Milford, Connecticut, where the Horowitzes spent most of the year. During World War II Horowitz and Toscanini gave numerous concerts selling war bonds, on one occasion raising an estimated ten million dollars. For a patriotic rally in Central Park, New York, in 1945 Horowitz made a dazzling pyrotechnical transcription of Sousa's *The Stars and Stripes Forever,* a pianistic tour de force which he subsequently often presented as an encore at recitals.

On January 25, 1953, Horowitz celebrated the twenty-fifth anniversary of his American debut by once more performing the Tchaikovsky Piano Concerto No.1 with the New York Philharmonic. Following this concert, Horowitz again decided to remove himself from the concert platform. He had recently suffered a slight attack of influenza which made him feel he needed prolonged rest. He was also a victim of a stomach disorder that had become chronic. When his absence from the concert world extended beyond a year, false rumors began circulating that he had suffered a nervous breakdown and had been hospitalized in a mental institution. But as Horowitz himself has explained: "I stopped playing for a year and it was wonderful. I liked it so much I thought—why go

back? For over thirty-three years I traveled—thirty-three years of sitting on trains going to some small town. Believe me, I was tired of all this."

This retirement lasted a little over a dozen years. "Volodya," as Horowitz is affectionately called by his friends and relatives, spent his time reading, giving intimate chamber-music concerts with celebrated colleagues, playing canasta, watching baseball games on television, indulging his all-consuming passion for great art of which he acquired a priceless collection, and teaching privately a few carefully selected young piano students. Many an evening was spent in a motion picture theater, for Horowitz has always been a devotee of films.

To John Gruen, for the New York *Times,* Horowitz described a typical day: "First of all I go to sleep very late, and I get up very late—around 11 or 12. Then I have a breakfast which consists of a piece of chicken, three slices of bread and lots of honey. I eat no meat, only poultry or fish. I never have coffee or tea. I never touch alcohol. Before each meal I must sleep. My stomach must be very calm before I put anything into it. Every day, weather permitting, I take a very long walk—about forty blocks—two miles." Piano practicing consumed about an hour and a half after breakfast and another session of some two hours or so before dinner. Evenings were spent in the company of friends.

Though he avoided the concert platform, he continued making records, first for RCA Victor for whom he had been making recordings since 1931 when his first album, Rachmaninoff's Piano Concerto No.3, was released. There was a hiatus in his recording career for a number of years, but in 1955 he returned to the recording studio to make an album of Clementi's Piano Sonatas, which was largely responsible for lifting these little-known compositions from an undeserved obscurity. He continued making records for Victor until 1962 when he went over to Columbia. The first release for Columbia, *Columbia Presents Vladimir Horowitz,* sold one hundred and twenty thousand albums and received a Grammy from the National Academy of Arts and Sciences as the best classical album of 1962. His Columbia recordings won Grammys in 1963, 1964, 1965, 1967, 1968, 1972, 1975, and 1977.

One day in 1965 Horowitz was making some recordings from the stage of Carnegie Hall when a young critic from the New York *Times,* who had never heard Horowitz in person, went up to him and maintained passionately that recordings did not do justice to his art, that he played differently on the stage than he did in a recording studio, almost as if he were another artist. "That did it," Horowitz told Abram Chasins in an interview. "Suddenly it came to me: So that's the younger generation, that doesn't know me at all. This boy must be telling the truth. He was always complimentary about my records, and now he tells me I sound totally different. I believed him, I trusted his sincerity, and at that moment I knew I must play again."

And so, after a stage silence of about twelve years, Horowitz returned to the concert platform with a recital at Carnegie Hall on May 9, 1965 (a performance that was recorded). This return made front-page news in the New York *Times,* for it was a concert that touched off, as Murray Schumach reported, "a sustained ovation in one of the most dramatic events in recent musical history. From his first appearance on the stage . . . until half an hour after he had finished the concert, the auditorium echoed to 'bravos' as the audience rose to its feet again and again. . . . For a time it seemed that the audience would refuse to leave altogether. The house lights were turned on after four encores. But the music lovers remained firm, applauding and yelling. Then the stage lights were turned off. On the dim stage Mr. Horowitz took the last of at least a dozen bows. Finally the piano was shut, while loud groans came from the audience. And even a half hour after this, hundreds were milling in West Fifty-sixth Street at the rear of Carnegie Hall ready to give more cheers to Mr. Horowitz." As for his performance, Horowitz proved, said Harold C. Schonberg in the New York *Times,* that he was still "a monarch." The concert was "sheer magnificence."

Horowitz went into still another period of retirement in 1969 after some scattered performances in New York, Boston, Washington, and Chicago. This absence lasted five years, ending in Cleveland with a recital on May 12, 1974. Other appearances followed, at Constitution Hall in Washington, D.C., on June 2, 1974, Chicago on October 27 and November 3, and at the Metropolitan Opera House on November 17, for Horowitz's first New York recital in six years and for the first piano recital ever given in this eight-year-old auditorium.

New to his repertory was Scriabin's Fifth Piano Sonata, performed publicly for the first time by Horowitz at his Metropolitan Opera House recital. The results, said Harold C. Schonberg, were "expectedly sensational. No living pianist . . . has this kind of insight into Scriabin's music. Strength, color, phenomenal technique, a surging rhythm, an unfaltering line—everything was there. All that plus the kind of spacings that threw the varied elements into high relief."

For the above and subsequent engagements, Horowitz became the highest-paid concert artist in the world, averaging about twenty-five thousand dollars for each appearance. Since 1969, Horowitz had adopted for his concertizing a ritual all his own. From 1953 to 1978 he refused to appear with orchestras. He insisted on giving recitals only in the afternoon, generally at four o'clock on Sundays. Since he detested flying, he tried to keep to short flights between engagements, and since he detested hotel food he preferred finding an apartment with a kitchen so that he could be served meals palatable to him. "We take everything with us," Wanda Horowitz told Dorle J. Soria, "his sheets and pillows, everything except the mattress." He even travels with a special machine that purifies water. As he explains: "Every place has a different kind of water, and I don't want foreign chemicals in me."

"I am always changing," Horowitz told an interviewer in 1974. "There is never a final interpretation. . . . Maybe I was a little madman before. Now I am more quiet. . . . Before I was always thinking you have to please the public. I played a little more for the crowd. But the crowd pulls you down. Now I don't care if the public is there or not. I do my best, of course. But if the public likes it or not, it doesn't matter. That is the change. Probably I'm a little spoiled now because they are still coming."

He has also said: "I never play the same piece in the same way. When I sit down at the keyboard I never know how I will play something. I play the way I feel at *that* moment. The head—the intellect—is only the controlling factor of music making. It is not a guide. The guide is your feelings. Of course, feeling without control doesn't work at all. . . . Artists must know instinctively how to strike a balance between control and feeling."

When a gala concert was held at Carnegie

Hall in New York on May 18, 1976, to raise over a million dollars for that auditorium, Horowitz broke with his usual concert procedures. This was the first time in thirty-five years that he was willing to perform at night. It was the first time in fifty-three years that he served as an accompanist, playing for Dietrich Fischer-Dieskau in a performance of Schumann's *Dichterliebe*. It was also the first time in several decades that he participated publicly in a chamber music performance, joining with Isaac Stern and Mstislav Rostropovich in the first movement of Tchaikovsky's Piano Trio in A minor.

To commemorate the fiftieth anniversary of his American debut, Horowitz appeared as a soloist with a symphony orchestra for the first time in a quarter of a century. This event took place on January 8, 1978, when he was heard with the New York Philharmonic (the orchestra with which he had made his American bow), Eugene Ormandy conducting, in a performance of Rachmaninoff's Piano Concerto No.3. Both conductor and soloist contributed their services for the Philharmonic pension fund. "It was a triumph, of course," wrote Harold C. Schonberg in the New York *Times*. The performance was recorded live by RCA.

To commemorate further Horowitz's fiftieth anniversary in America, President and Mrs. Carter invited him to the White House on February 26, 1978, to give a recital to a specially invited audience. The concert was broadcast live over a nationwide radio network and was seen throughout the country that same evening through the facilities of the Public Broadcasting Service. In introducing Horowitz, President Carter called him "a true national treasure." This was Horowitz's second appearance at the White House; the first was in 1931 for President and Mrs. Herbert Hoover.

Horowitz broke with a lifelong precedent in 1976, consenting for the first time to join a conservatory. He agreed to teach one or two pupils of outstanding talent at the Mannes College of Music in New York without accepting a fee. "The year 1978 will be the fiftieth anniversary of my debut here," he explained, "and I wanted to contribute something to this country." Horowitz imposed two restrictions on any potential pupil. One was an agreement by the pupil never to enter a competition. "I'm absolutely against competitions," he said. "In competitions winners are chosen by elimination not by excellence

and sometimes when the winner goes out on his own there is not enough excellence. Also, sometimes it's political, it does not smell so good." The other restriction was that the pupil would have to find a sponsor willing to contribute a sizable sum of money to the Mannes College scholarship fund.

ABOUT: Chotzinoff, S. A Little Night Music; Schonberg, H. C. The Great Pianists. *Periodicals*—Collier's, April 13, 1946; High Fidelity, October 1965, February 1975; Hi Fidelity/Musical America, January 1978; Look, February 8, 1966; New York Times, May 9, 1965, November 23, 1975; New York Times Magazine, October 17, 1948, January 11, 1953, May 9, 1965, January 8, 1978; New Yorker, January 23, 1978; Newsweek, May 17, 1965, January 23, 1978; Saturday Review, April 30, 1960.

Mieczyslaw Horszowski

1892–

Mieczyslaw (Miecio) Horszowski, pianist, was born in Lwow (Lemberg), formerly Austria but now Poland, on January 23, 1892. Mieczyslaw's mother, Rose Jeanne Horszowski, gave him his first piano lessons when he was still an infant. By the time he was five he could play from memory and transpose the Inventions of Bach. Later on, at the Lwow Conservatory, he was a pupil of Mieczyslaw Soltys and Henryk Melcer; later still he studied the piano with Theodor Leschetizky in Vienna.

In 1900 Mieczyslaw made his first public appearance, performing Beethoven's Piano Concerto No.1 in Warsaw. A highly successful debut in Vienna led to a concert tour of Europe and in time to personal relationships with some of Europe's foremost musicians, among them Joachim, Arthur Rubinstein, Joseph Szigeti (then also a highly praised prodigy), Toscanini, Pablo Casals, and Gabriel Fauré. On one occasion Mieczyslaw was invited to perform at the Vatican for Pope Pius X. On December 30, 1906, aged fourteen and billed as Miecio Horszowski, he made his American debut at Carnegie Hall in New York.

His career was interrupted in 1911 to allow him to spend two years studying literature, philosophy, and the history of art in Paris. He resumed concertizing in 1913 at the insistence of Pablo Casals.

After World War I Horszowski settled in Mi-

MIECZYSLAW HORSZOWSKI

lan, where he lived until 1939. His concerts brought him to every major musical center of the world. He gained an international reputation for his interpretations of the music of Chopin, in which he was acclaimed one of the foremost authorities, but his performances of the music of Mozart and Beethoven and the works of some of the twentieth century composers were hardly less distinguished. He became an ardent propagandist for the music of twentieth century Polish composers—particularly Karol Szymanowski, whose Third Piano Sonata he introduced in 1923.

When Italy was drawn into World War II, Horszowski was touring Brazil. Instead of returning to his home in Milan he went to New York, where he established permanent residence; in 1948 he became an American citizen. His performances in the United States in the post–World War II era placed him with the great pianists of his time. Most noteworthy were his appearances with the NBC Symphony under Toscanini, his cycle of twelve recitals in New York in 1957 covering all of Beethoven's piano compositions, his cycle of all of Mozart's piano sonatas in 1960 in New York, and his cycle of Mozart's ten piano concertos in 1962 in New York. In 1961 he was invited by President and Mrs. Kennedy to the White House to perform with Pablo Casals and Alexander Schneider.

In addition to his solo recitals and appearances with orchestra, Horszowski has given joint concerts with Casals, Ravel, Szymanowski, and Szigeti. He has made numerous appearances both as a solo pianist and as a participant in chamber-music performances at the Casals Festivals in Prades, France, and in Puerto Rico. Reviewing one of his chamber-music appearances in Puerto Rico in June 1968, Irving Kolodin reported in the *Saturday Review* that "Horszowski established himself as an artist who can not only follow but lead, in the most distinguished way of all—subtly, compellingly, from the inside out. The response comes not from an imposition of will on his associates but by the insinuation that the flow of ideas emanates from where he sits. When it came to the flow of an idea from Horszowski to Casals and return, in the Schubert, his source could only be described as singular, so wholly compatible was it."

Horszowski, aged eighty-three, commemorated the seventy-fifth anniversary of his piano debut with a recital in New York on September 27, 1975. Allen Hughes in the New York *Times* found him "still in full possession of the remarkable musicality that makes the best of his playing so personal and so appealing. Mr. Horszowski applied his gentle artistry to an unusual program. . . . He is the sort of a man who, after a lifetime of association with works such as these, has very definite ideas as to how they must go to communicate his feelings about them. What he feels is not expressed by a cool, literal account of the score. So he warms the music in his hands, so to speak, and molds its phrases of subtle shadings and timings that only infrequently grow into aggressive statements. His is essentially a quiet, introspective art."

For many years Horszowski has been a member of the piano faculty of the Curtis Institute of Music, and he has been affiliated with the Marlboro School and Festival in Vermont, where a scholarship in his name was established in 1967.

In his younger years Horszowski was a mountain climber; he was made honorary member of the Zermatt Guild of Mountain Guides in Switzerland. He once compared the playing of Beethoven's music to mountain climbing by saying: "It's not to conquer but just to measure yourself, to find out if your strength is equal to the challenge."

ABOUT: Musical America, December 1960.

Huberman

Bronislaw Huberman

1882–1947

Bronislaw Huberman (or Hubermann), violinist, was born in Czestochowa, near Warsaw, December 18, 1882. His father, Jacob, a lawyer, recognized Bronislaw's early interest in music and enrolled him in the Warsaw Conservatory when he was six. There he studied the violin with Mieczyslaw Michalowicz and Isidor Lotto. When he was seven, Bronislaw performed Spohr's Violin Concerto No.2 and participated in a presentation of a string quartet by Rode. In May 1892 he went to Berlin to study with Joseph Joachim. Since he was placed not with the master himself but with one of his assistants, these lessons were soon discontinued. That year he gave his first recital, at the International Exhibition of Music in Vienna and he was commanded to appear before Emperor Franz Joseph who presented him with a precious violin.

After eight months of additional violin study in Berlin, Bronislaw went to Frankfort to become a pupil of Hugo Heermann and after that to Paris to study with Armand Marsick. At eleven he began his concert career with performances in Holland, Belgium, France, England, and Germany. In London the prima donna Adelina Patti was so impressed with him that she invited him to appear with her at her "farewell" concert in Vienna on January 12, 1895. His playing caused such a sensation that he was asked to give twelve concerts in Vienna. "The youthful artist," wrote Vienna's critic Eduard Hanslick, "achieved a success so brilliant as could not be exceeded by the brightest star in the galaxy of artists. It is not his precocity as such that characterized the display of his genius, but rather his phenomenal endowment of musical inspiration and musical capacity." At one of these concerts in Vienna, on January 29, 1896, Bronislaw performed the Brahms Violin Concerto with Brahms himself in the audience. After the concert Brahms embraced the boy and exclaimed: "This is the way the concerto appeared to me, too. My heavens! What an interpretation!" From then on and through his mature years Huberman remained a particular favorite in Vienna. The city gave him the use of the

BRONISLAW HUBERMAN

Hetzendorf Palace, former home of Emperor Karl, from 1926 to 1938. From 1934 to 1936 he taught a master class in violin at the Vienna State Academy.

Bronislaw made his American debut in 1896. Dressed in a dark velvet suit with sailor-style blouse, he offered a pretty picture on the stage, as *Harper's Weekly* noted in describing his "grave unchildish eyes, the spiritual upper half of his face and thick dark hair like a heavy silk fringe falling about his cheeks." His playing also made a highly favorable impression. One critic pointed to his "phenomenal endowment of musical inspiration and musicianly capacity."

After that first tour of the United States, he withdrew from concert activity for about half a dozen years. During much of that time he served as court violinist to the Queen of Romania. His public appearances were resumed in 1902 with a recital in Budapest. On May 16, 1909, he was invited by the city of Genoa to play on Paganini's own violin, a Guarnerius, in one of the chambers of the Town Hall.

Huberman toured many times. On several occasions he gave important series of historical concerts of violin music: eight such concerts in St. Petersburg in 1911, fourteen in Paris in 1920, ten in Vienna in 1924, and eight in Berlin in 1926. A performer whose prime concern was the penetration to the heart of the music he was playing, sometimes at the cost of beauty of violin sound, Huberman was sometimes accused of being a crude performer with technical deficiencies and a dry tone. But few could deny the majesty

Huberman: hoo' běr män

360

of his musical conceptions, particularly in the works of Bach, Mozart, Beethoven, and Brahms.

In reviewing a Huberman concert in New York on October 17, 1921, Richard Aldrich wrote in the New York *Times:* "Mr. Hubermann is an unpretentious player and makes no attempt at personal display. His mind is apparently more upon the music he is engaged with than upon himself and the effect he is making, and this predisposes to his favor. He is well equipped with technical proficiency that is expected of all violinists of reputation in these days. Yet he frequently seems to find it a severe strain to produce his effects, a laborious operation, back-bending; and the result is labored. Mr. Hubermann's tone is powerful, but it is not notable for warmth or appealing quality."

Huberman's name appeared on the front pages of newspapers from time to time. For many years he favored the Pan-European concept, expressing his ideals not only with public statements to the press and in interviews but even sometimes with comments from his concert platform. He wrote a book on the subject, *Mein Weg zu Paneuropa* (1925).

In September 1933 he became involved in political debate when he violently denounced the Nazi regime in Germany. He had been invited by Wilhelm Furtwängler to appear as a soloist with the Berlin Philharmonic in several concertos. In a forceful letter (reproduced on the front pages of several American newspapers) he wrote Furtwängler: "It is not a question of violin concertos nor even merely of the Jews; the issue is the retention of those things that our fathers achieved by blood and sacrifice, by the elementary pre-conditions of our European culture, the freedom of personality and its unconditional self-responsibility unhampered by fetters of caste or race."

In 1935 Huberman visited Palestine where he came upon many refugee musicians from Germany. These refugees inspired him to form an orchestra in Palestine made up of exiled musicians. He hurled his energies not only into the creation of the best possible symphonic ensemble but also into the business of raising funds necessary for its support. On December 26, 1936, the Palestine Symphony Orchestra (predecessor of the Israel Philharmonic) first came to life under the baton of Arturo Toscanini. In the fall of 1938 Huberman himself appeared with the Palestine Symphony Orchestra, as soloist, before an audience of thirty thousand.

Following a tour of Canada in 1941, Huberman returned to the United States, after an absence of many years, to perform throughout the country that fall. He remained in the United States during the war years, living at the Plaza Hotel in New York. His last public appearance was in New York as soloist with the New York Philharmonic in December 1945. After the war Huberman returned to Europe and spent his last year in Switzerland. He died in Nant-sur-Crosier, Switzerland, on June 15, 1947. He was cremated; his ashes repose in an urn in Israel.

Huberman divorced his wife, with whom he had a son, in or about 1916; he never remarried. He was the author of *Aus der Werkstatt des Virtuosen* (1912).

ABOUT: New York Times, March 30, 1941; Newsweek, November 3, 1934.

Eugene Istomin

1925–

Eugene Istomin, pianist, was born in New York City on November 26, 1925. In Russia his father, George T. Istomin, had been a landowner, a race horse owner, and an officer in the Czarist air force. He fled from the Soviet Union to New York where he met and married Assia Chavin. Both he and Assia were talented though untrained concert singers, specializing in Russian and Gypsy music. Their son Eugene was initiated to music through recordings at the age of four. He soon started improvising on the piano. Two years later he accompanied his mother on the piano when she gave a recital at the Academy of Music in Brooklyn, New York. Alexander Siloti, pianist and teacher, who had studied with Liszt and Tchaikovsky, was so impressed by Eugene's talent at this concert that he went backstage and urged Chavin not to allow Eugene to make any further public appearances but to have him concentrate on piano study while developing his body through physical exercises and sports. (A boyhood passion for baseball, begun when he served as bat boy for the Brooklyn Dodgers, remained with Eugene throughout his life.) Siloti's daughter, Kariena, became Eugene's teacher. Later, he was enrolled in the

Istomin

EUGENE ISTOMIN

Mannes School of Music in New York, where his teachers included Ralph Wolfe and Sascha Gorodnitzki at the piano and Constantin Svedoff in harmony and theory. At the same time he attended the Professional Children's School in Manhattan, from which he was graduated in 1939.

From 1939 to 1943 Istomin attended the Curtis Institute of Music in Philadelphia. There he received intensive training at the piano from Mieczyslaw Horszowski and Rudolf Serkin. Two important awards in 1943 preceded his official concert career. The first was the Philadelphia Youth Contest Award which brought him an appearance on November 17, 1943, with the Philadelphia Orchestra under Ormandy in Chopin's Piano Concerto No.2. The second was the Leventritt Award which brought him a guest appearance with the New York Philharmonic Orchestra, conducted by Artur Rodzinski, on November 21, 1943, in Brahms's Piano Concerto No.2. One season later the New York Philharmonic invited him to return as a guest artist. That year he also gave his first New York recital and was engaged by Adolf Busch and his Chamber Players to appear as soloist in New York and on tour.

Istomin made his first tour of Europe in 1950, performing with major orchestras in France, appearing in recitals in Italy and Switzerland, and participating at the Pablo Casals festival in Prades, France. During the next few years he continued to perform at the annual Casals festival in the south of France, often in chamber-music performance with Casals as a collaborator. In 1957 he made the first of many appearances at the Pablo Casals festival in San Juan, Puerto Rico. From Prades Howard Taubman reported to the New York *Times:* "Istomin proved to be a revelation. His piano sang; not once did he forget that he was part of an intimate chamber-music group." Pablo Casals, who became for Istomin a father figure as well as an endless source of inspiration, said of him: "He is destined for a great career."

In 1955 came Istomin's first tours of South America and South Africa, followed a year later by his first appearances in Australia and Asia. By 1962 when he took a year's sabbatical from the concert platform, he had appeared on six continents, had been heard and acclaimed at the world's foremost festivals, had made numerous recordings, and had been one of the principal artists at the World's Fair in Seattle. He had also performed at the White House before President Truman and President Kennedy.

Following his presentation of Beethoven's Piano Concerto No.4 with the San Francisco Symphony, Alfred Frankenstein said of him in the *Chronicle:* "The impression of the whole was of lyrical perfection, superbly restrained, and eloquent by virtue of rhetorical flourish." When Istomin returned to the New York concert stage, after an absence of half a dozen years, with a recital at Carnegie Hall on November 22, 1971, Harriet Johnson, writing in the New York *Post,* said he gave ample proof that he was "a master of his art. . . . His tone at the piano is more than exquisite, it is ample for all seasons of expressiveness. . . . He knows his styles. His phrasing is sensitive. Behind him is a long experience and discipline plus taste which allows him to personalize without distortion."

In addition to his appearances as a solo performer, Istomin has distinguished himself in performances of trio music throughout the United States and Europe with the Istomin-Rose-Stern Trio–the other two artists being Isaac Stern and Leonard Rose. Its debut took place in 1961 at the International Chamber Music Festival in Israel, and its New York debut came in 1962 when the trio appeared as soloists with the New York Philharmonic Orchestra in Beethoven's Triple Concerto. This trio had the distinction of being the first chamber music group heard in the opening festivities at the new Kennedy Center for the Performing Arts in

Washington, D.C., in September 1971. The group's recording of all of Beethoven's piano trios received a Grammy from the National Academy of Recording Arts and Sciences in 1971.

For a long time Istomin has cherished his privacy. His home was an apartment in a residential hotel on West Seventy-first Street in New York City; there he was surrounded by his collections of books, paintings, statues, masks, and other art objects. "I lead a life of the mind," he once told John Gruen in an interview for the New York *Times.* "I am tremendously involved mentally in so many things—from contemporary art to politics to baseball to drinking and eating. So I think I lead an enormously full life. I read a great deal, and I like to be alone a great deal."

In the early forties he was on the verge of marrying a student at the Curtis Institute. Later on his name was linked romantically with that of Princess Irene of Greece, herself a pianist. At the age of forty-nine Istomin finally abandoned his bachelorhood on February 15, 1975, to marry Marta Montañez Casals, the young widow of Pablo Casals. From 1975 through 1977 he helped her direct the annual festival in Puerto Rico founded and made famous by Casals.

ABOUT: Ewen, D. Famous Instrumentalists; Jacobson, R. Reverberations. *Periodicals*—New York Times, November 21, 1971; New York Times Magazine, October 9, 1977.

José Iturbi

1895–

José Iturbi, pianist and conductor, was born in Valencia, Spain, on November 28, 1895, one of four children of Ricardo and Teresa Baguena Iturbi. His father worked for the local gas company and, in his free hours, tuned pianos. He often took José along on his piano-tuning assignments. From earliest childhood José was attracted to the piano. He started taking lessons when he was five with María Jordan at the Escuela de Musica. By his seventh year he was helping to support himself and his family by his piano playing. He worked in Valencia's motion picture the-

---

Iturbi: ē tōōr′ bē

JOSÉ ITURBI

ater, playing with little interruption from two in the afternoon until after midnight. From there he sometimes went on to a neighborhood ball to play dance music for a few more pesetas. In early morning he attended the Conservatorio de Musica as a pupil of José Bellver. Despite this exhausting program, José developed himself as a performer of serious music and as a prodigy capable of giving several recitals.

At ten José was sent to Barcelona to continue his piano studies with Joaquín Malats. He remained in Barcelona only three months, returning to his native city to work as a café pianist. A friendly journalist there, impressed by his talent, persuaded the townspeople to subscribe fourteen hundred pesetas to enable José to go to Paris.

In Paris José entered the Conservatory as a student of Staub. He supported himself by playing in cafés at night. After graduation from the Conservatory with high honors at seventeen, he went to Zurich where he played the piano in a fashionable café. The director of the Geneva Conservatory heard him there one evening in 1919 and offered him a teaching post once held by Franz Liszt. He accepted and kept the post for four years.

On June 8, 1916, Iturbi married Maria Giner. He has survived both his wife and their daughter, Maria (who married and was divorced from the violinist Stefan Hero). Iturbi never remarried. In 1943 he became legal guardian of his two granddaughters.

Iturbi's professional career as a concert pianist began in 1923 with a highly successful debut at Queen's Hall in London. Recitals and appearances with symphony orchestras throughout Europe soon placed him in the front rank of the younger pianists of the time, particularly for his performances of Spanish music and the works of Mozart.

In 1928 Iturbi went to the United States for a three-month tour. His American debut took place in October of that year with the Philadelphia Orchestra in a performance of Beethoven's Piano Concerto No.4. Following his first performance in New York City, when he was heard as a soloist with the New York Philharmonic Orchestra in Mozart's Piano Concerto in D minor, K. 466, and Liszt's *Hungarian Fantasy,* Olin Downes said of him in the New York *Times:* "Mr. Iturbi displayed a style distinguished by the utmost clarity, a subtle use of values, and a consummate technique for the most difficult music to play well—the music of Mozart."

Iturbi's first tour of the United States proved very successful. In New York alone he was required to appear ten times, including three appearances with the New York Philharmonic and three sold-out recitals in Carnegie Hall. Outside New York, he was heard extensively in recitals and as guest artist with America's major orchestras. The critics were as one in singing his praises. Lawrence Gilman in the New York *Herald Tribune* spoke of him as "an enchanter, a superb musician, a remarkable artist," and in the New York *Sun* W. J. Henderson wrote: "He is an artist of fastidious taste and of keen understanding."

Returning for his second tour of the United States in 1930, Iturbi was heard in sixty-seven concerts, five of them in New York City to sold-out auditoriums.

Within a five-year span of concertizing in the United States, Iturbi was reported to have given about six thousand concerts, more performances than any other pianist with the exception of Paderewski. His box-office appeal remained consistently strong, not only in the United States but abroad as well. Though he radically reduced the number of his appearances, he continued through the years to give concerts intermittently. In his eightieth year he was still on the road touring several American cities. After his performance at Avery Fisher Hall in New York on March 2, 1975, Donal Henahan wrote in the New York *Times:* "The Spanish-born pianist's recital . . . again demonstrated that there is still magic in the name." Four days after his eightieth birthday, on November 24, 1975, Iturbi played concertos by Haydn, Mozart, and Mendelssohn, and César Franck's *Symphonic Variations* and conducted the Rochester Philharmonic in his own accompaniments from the piano. "None of these belong in the big bravura class nor demand excessive muscular effort," reported Raymond Ericson in the New York *Times.* "They do require agile, accurate fingers, and these the pianist supplied in full measure. He breezed through the trickier passages of the Mendelssohn and Franck pieces as if he were half his age." At intermission time Iturbi was presented with the Lincoln Center medallion and a certificate of appreciation from Mayor Beame on behalf of New York City.

Iturbi has also often appeared in concerts of two-piano music with his sister, Amparo Iturbi, who died in 1969.

He has enjoyed a long and eventful career as a conductor. His baton debut took place in Mexico City on May 25, 1933, when he led an orchestra at the Teatro Hidalgo. This performance was so well received that he was called upon to direct eleven more orchestral concerts.

Returning to New York that year, Iturbi directed two concerts at the Lewisohn Stadium in New York. In March 1934 he was a guest conductor of the Philadelphia Orchestra. After several more engagements with various orchestras in the years between 1934 and 1936, Iturbi was appointed principal conductor of the Rochester Philharmonic Orchestra in 1936. He retained this post until 1944. In those eight years, Iturbi also appeared as a guest conductor of principal orchestras in the United States and Europe as well as of symphony concerts over American network radio for the "Ford Sunday Evening Hour" and the "General Motors Hour." In 1956 Iturbi became the artistic director of the Valencia Symphony Orchestra in Spain. With this orchestra he toured Great Britain and France. In 1967 he was appointed music director of the Bridgeport Symphony in Connecticut, and a year later music director of the Calgary Philharmonic in Canada.

"Iturbi's stick technique like his piano technique serves a musical purpose," once wrote Robert A. Simon, "and that purpose is a fine respect for the composer. Iturbi knows one of the principal secrets of Toscanini: that music must sing."

He made numerous appearances in motion pictures in the 1940s, including *As Thousands Cheer* (1943), *Two Girls and a Sailor* (1944), *Music for Millions* (1944), *Anchors Aweigh* (1945), *Holiday in Mexico* (1946), and *Three Daring Daughters* (1948). In 1945 he was heard as pianist on the sound track of *A Song to Remember,* the film biography of Chopin; his performance of the Polonaise in A-flat in this motion picture was responsible for making the composition a nationwide musical rage that year, with Iturbi's own recording for RCA Victor a best seller.

During the 1930s and early 1940s Iturbi was occasionally the center of lively controversy in the United States, his provocative opinions and behavior landing him on the front pages of the newspapers. During the Spanish Civil War he antagonized antifascists in America by maintaining that what Spain needed most was a "strong man to come forward and guide us." Because of this statement, his concerts at the Lewisohn Stadium in New York during the summer of 1938 were picketed by antifascist groups. At about this time he refused to conduct the final numbers over the radio because these were popular tunes. "It is below the dignity of the orchestra to play such cheap and rotten music," he insisted. ASCAP threatened to deny Iturbi any further permission to perform music which it licensed but then relented when Iturbi apologized. In 1936 Iturbi refused to complete a program he was conducting at the Cleveland Great Lakes Exposition because he felt that the audience was too noisy. A year later he was severely criticized for his statement to an interviewer that "all women are physically limited from attaining the standards of men and are limited temperamentally as well." And in 1943 he accused his daughter Maria of being unfit to raise her two daughters and went to court to gain legal right to become their sole guardian.

Iturbi, who became an American citizen in the early 1940s, has maintained a home on North Bedford Drive in Beverly Hills, California. Short, stocky, and bullet-headed, he looks more like a bank clerk or a successful stockbroker than a musician. In earlier years his passion was speed, both in the automobiles he drove and in the planes he piloted. A sports devotee, he has enjoyed boxing exhibitions, tennis matches, and bullfights.

Before a concert he eats nothing, except possibly a raw apple followed by a cup of coffee. Several hours before concert time he slips into bed to relax. He dresses for a concert at the last possible moment, invariably arriving at the hall breathless.

Once asked by an interviewer how he studies a piece of music, he replied: "Just as a woman buys a dress. First she sees that the dress fits her ... how it is cut, the color, the line, the material. Well, first I study the score until I know it by heart, until it fits exactly—phrasing, harmony, everything. Then what must a woman do to get a dress? She must pay for it. I pay money, too. My money is practice ... mastering the technique demanded. The lady wears her dress and is proud. I wear my music and am happy."

Numerous twentieth century composers have written compositions for Iturbi which he has introduced, among them Stravinsky, Nicolas Nabokoff, Alexander Tansman, Jean Wiener, Manuel Infante, and Robert Russell Bennett.

He, himself, has written a number of compositions: *Fantasy* for piano and orchestra, *Soliloquy* for orchestra, and numerous pieces for solo piano, the most famous of which is *Pequeña Danza Española.*

Iturbi was made a member of the French Legion of Honor. He is the holder of the Order of St. Georges from Greece and of Alphonso el Sabio from Spain. Spain also awarded him one of its highest honors, the Meddia de Oro di Trabajo.

ABOUT: Ewen, D. Dictators of the Baton. *Periodicals* —Etude, April and May, 1930; Outlook, October 29, 1930.

Byron Janis

1928–

Byron Janis (originally Byron Yanks), pianist, was born in McKeesport, Pennsylvania, on March 24, 1928. When his parents, Samuel and Hattie Horelick Yankilevitch, came to the United States from Russia they contracted their name to Yanks. Byron assumed the name Janis during his adolescence.

The family settled in Pittsburgh where his fa-

Janis

BYRON JANIS

ther opened a sporting goods store. While attending kindergarten, Byron performed on a toy xylophone, revealing that he possessed perfect pitch. At five he started taking piano lessons with Abram Litow, who soon realized he had an unusual talent. Litow recommended that he be taken to New York for more comprehensive training. Byron's mother, Hattie, took him to New York when he was seven, to study piano with Adele Marcus and to take courses in composition and harmony at the Chatham School of Music as well as academic courses at the Columbia Grammar School. Samuel Chotzinoff, head of the Chatham School and director of music at NBC, soon became the boy's unofficial sponsor. In 1942 he arranged for Byron to appear over the NBC radio network both as a soloist with the NBC Symphony, Frank Black conducting, and in several recitals.

When Adele Marcus left New York for a teaching post in Texas, Byron followed her there. While continuing his piano studies with Marcus, he made a number of concert appearances. On February 20, 1944, he was heard in Rachmaninoff's Piano Concerto No.2 with the Pittsburgh Symphony Orchestra. Vladimir Horowitz was in that audience. After the concert, Horowitz offered to guide Byron's career and give him private instruction—the first time Horowitz had ever made such an offer to a young musician. He remained Horowitz's pupil for about three years.

While studying with Horowitz, Byron appeared in recitals and as guest artist with orches-

tras. Upon completing his study with Horowitz, he felt a compelling need to liberate himself from Horowitz's influence and to acquire a pianistic identity of his own. He explained his problem to an interviewer for *Musical America:* "The important thing is to say something artistically that is *you*—to learn to find yourself through making mistakes that are your mistakes. There are many ways of performing a given work, but the artist must be convinced that *his* way is right. That is what gives authority to his performance."

Janis began finding his own way as an artist in the summer of 1948 with his first tour of South America. He was so successful in Buenos Aires that his third and fourth appearances were completely sold out. Two additional concerts (also sold out) were hurriedly arranged in a larger auditorium.

Janis made his New York debut with a recital at Carnegie Hall on October 29, 1948. "Not for a long time," wrote Olin Downes in the New York *Times,* "had this writer heard such a talent allied with the musicianship, the feeling, the intelligence, and the artistic balance shown by the twenty-year-old Byron Janis." On January 27, 1949, Janis was a soloist with the New York Philharmonic under Stokowski in Gershwin's Piano Concerto in F, and Irving Kolodin wrote in the New York *Sun:* "He is certainly the finest pianist we have ever heard in this score." Two years later a music critic for the New York *Herald Tribune* remarked: "There is nothing in the literature for the piano which lies beyond the reach of his technical powers."

Janis made his bow in Europe in 1952, appearing five times as soloist with the Concertgebouw Orchestra in Amsterdam. A tour of Europe followed, the first of many. In 1958 he helped to open the American Festival Week at the World's Fair in Brussels. In 1961, in commemoration of the one hundred and fiftieth anniversary of Franz Liszt's birth, Janis performed both Liszt piano concertos at a single concert with the Boston Symphony in Boston and the Paris Conservatory Orchestra in Paris.

His fame grew in 1960 with his first tour of the Soviet Union under the auspices of the United States State Department and the Soviet Ministry of Culture. He was the first American pianist to tour the Soviet Union since Van Cliburn. Between October 7 and November 3 he was heard ten times in recitals and as a guest artist with orchestras in Moscow, Leningrad, Odessa,

366

Minsk, and Kiev. His reception by Soviet music lovers was described by a correspondent to the New York *Times* as "overwhelming." "Men and women in the audience wept," reported the same paper. One Soviet critic said of Janis that he was "not just one of those cold virtuosos that seem to be in current fashion in some places in the West, but . . . a warm and sincere, and aesthetically mature, artist."

He returned for a second tour of the Soviet Union in May and June 1962 at the invitation of the Soviet Ministry of Culture. After he had performed three concertos in a single evening as a guest of the Moscow Philharmonic (Rachmaninoff's No.1, Prokofiev's No.3, and Schumann's Concerto in A minor), following this with a repetition of the finale of Tchaikovsky's First Piano Concerto, Kiril Kondrashin, the conductor that evening, exclaimed: "I have now heard a pianist who can play three utterly different concertos with a perfect sense of style. He is one of the greatest pianists of the age." Janis subsequently performed these three concertos in a single evening in Paris, Philadelphia, Winnipeg, and Brussels.

During this visit to the Soviet Union Janis became the first American allowed to make recordings in the Soviet Union. One recording, Prokofiev's Concerto No.3, received in 1963 the French Grand Prix du Disque as the best classical recording of the year.

On November 12, 1963, Janis helped to commemorate the tenth anniversary of Prokofiev's death with Prokofiev's Concerto No.3 at a concert of the Philadelphia Orchestra. After performing in France in 1965, he was made a Chevalier des Arts et des Lettres by the French government; only two Americans before him had been similarly honored (Alexander Calder and Yehudi Menuhin).

He made front-page news in the United States in 1965 when he canceled a concert scheduled for Mobile, Alabama, on March 11. This was in protest against what he described as the "repugnant, brutal, and thoroughly un-American" racial policies of Governor George Wallace.

Janis again became news in 1967 when he helped to recover the supposedly lost manuscripts of two Chopin waltzes at Château Thoiry outside Paris, the home of the Marquis de la Panouse. In a box marked "old clothes," there were found versions of the Waltz in G-flat, Op. 70, No.1, and the Waltz in E-flat, Op.18 (the *Grande Valse Brilliante*), both dated earlier than those that were subsequently published. "My ESP, or whatever you call it, became very strong," he explained at the time. "I called Paul de la Panouse and I told him to look in the archives because I knew there would be some new Chopin material there. The point is that I knew, absolutely knew, that it would be there. Well, they looked and after six hours they found it."

About seven years later Janis's extrasensory powers once again went into operation. While visiting Yale University he asked for the Chopin file which supposedly was made up exclusively of Chopin's letters but which Janis was convinced contained some Chopin music manuscripts. Strange to say, he found there two other versions of the same waltzes that he had helped to recover in France in 1967.

Janis was married in London on November 30, 1953, to June Dickinson Wright, the daughter of the senior surgeon of St. Mary's Hospital. They had a son, Stefan. In 1965 they were divorced. Then on April 11, 1966, Janis married Maria Veronica Cooper, the socialite daughter of the motion picture star Gary Cooper.

A sports enthusiast, Janis plays tennis, badminton, and table tennis expertly. He likes to ride horseback and is a baseball fan. He enjoys driving sports cars, going to the movies, eating gourmet meals, and spending his vacations with his wife on the French Riviera.

He practices the piano from four to five hours daily. He told Harold Rogers in an interview in *The Christian Science Monitor:* "When I study a new work, I first play it through. I am excited both by its emotion and its architecture. Then I start pulling it apart, solving the technical points. During this process the emotion is gone. The technique gets in the way. Then I drop it completely for a time. When I come back to it I again find the emotion. . . . The emotional message of the music is the goal. A musician's technique is merely a means to assist him in achieving his goal."

In 1975 Byron Janis filmed a one-hour documentary on Chopin for television broadcast in Europe and the United States.

ABOUT: Musical America, October 1962; New York Times, November 3, 1960; Time, April 14, 1961.

Gundula Janowitz

1937–

GUNDULA JANOWITZ

Gundula Janowitz, soprano, was born in Berlin on August 2, 1937, to Theodor and Else Neumann Janowitz. When World War I ended, the Janowitz family left Germany for Graz, Austria, where Gundula received her earliest musical training—first violin and theory, later voice with Hubert Thöny at the Landeskonservatorium. A scholarship from the Richard Wagner Society in Graz sent her to Bayreuth in 1959 to study the Wagnerian repertory. Wieland Wagner engaged her for the 1960 festival in which she was heard as a Flower Maiden in *Parsifal* and a Rhine Maiden in the *Ring* cycle; she returned to Bayreuth for two additional seasons.

Walter Legge, executive of Angel Records, brought her to the attention of Herbert von Karajan who auditioned her in 1959 and engaged her immediately. She made her debut at the Vienna State Opera in 1959 as Barbarina in *The Marriage of Figaro*. During the next three years she appeared mainly in minor or secondary parts. After her success as Marzelline in a new production of *Fidelio* produced and conducted by Herbert von Karajan, she was assigned major roles. She soon became one of the stars of the company, a specialist in the operas and music dramas of Mozart, Wagner, and Richard Strauss. In Strauss's operas she was heard as the Empress in *Die Frau ohne Schatten,* the Countess in *Capriccio,* and the title role in *Arabella;* in Mozart, as the Countess in *The Marriage of Figaro,* Pamina in *The Magic Flute,* Fiordiligi in *Così fan Tutte,* and Donna Anna in *Don Giovanni;* in Wagner, Elsa in *Lohengrin,* Elisabeth in *Tannhäuser,* and Sieglinde in *Die Walküre.*

In 1963 Janowitz appeared as Pamina at the Aix-en-Provence festival, John Pritchard conducting. One season later she appeared for the first time at the Glyndebourne Festival in England as Ilia in *Idomeneo,* and a British critic praised her performance for its "vocal warmth, clarity, ease and great femininity." Since then she has sung at festivals in Salzburg, Lucerne, Edinburgh, and Spoleto. In addition to being a resident member of the Berlin Deutsche Oper

Janowitz: yä′ nồ vĭts

and the Vienna State Opera she has appeared with the Hamburg Opera, the Frankfort Opera, the Munich Opera, and the Paris Opéra. In September 1967, as a member of the Vienna State Opera, she made her North American debut in Montreal at Expo '67 as Donna Anna.

In March 1967 von Karajan performed *Die Walküre* in Salzburg, Austria, as the first of four annual Easter productions in which he directed, staged, and conducted the entire *Ring* cycle, one music drama a year. For the launching of this project he selected Gundula Janowitz as Sieglinde. This performance was recorded by Deutsche Grammophon. Reviewing that release in *High Fidelity,* Conrad L. Osborne said of her voice: "The instrument is exceptionally beautiful, one of its kind, and she molds phrases with an admirable care of musicality."

Von Karajan took his production of *Die Walküre* to the Metropolitan Opera in New York on November 2, 1967, and Janowitz made her debut in the United States as Sieglinde. "Hers is not a very large voice," wrote Harold C. Schonberg in the New York *Times,* "but she is a sensitive singer with an appealing vocal texture."

Her operatic roles other than those already singled out have included Euridice in *Orfeo ed Euridice,* Ighino in Pfitzner's *Palestrina,* Rosalinde in *Die Fledermaus,* Aida, Elisabetta in *Don Carlo,* Amelia in *Simon Boccanegra,* Gutrune in *Die Götterdämmerung,* Agathe in *Der Freischütz.* Early in 1978 Janowitz sang Leonore in a new production of *Fidelio* conducted by Leonard Bernstein at the Vienna State Opera and at

La Scala. At the Salzburg Festival in 1978, Janowitz assumed for the first time anywhere the role of the Marschallin in *Der Rosenkavalier.*

Janowitz has also distinguished herself in the concert auditorium in performances of major choral works. She has sung in Haydn's *The Seasons* under Karl Böhm; Beethoven's *Missa Solemnis* under Leonard Bernstein and Herbert von Karajan; Brahms's *A German Requiem,* Beethoven's Symphony No.9, Bach's *Passion According to St. Matthew,* and Haydn's *The Creation,* all under Herbert von Karajan; and Bach's *Christmas Oratorio* and Handel's *Messiah* under Karl Richter. All these performances were recorded, and *A German Requiem* received the Grand Prix du Disque in Paris. Her performance of the *Missa Solemnis* under Bernstein was a historic occasion since it took place in Vienna in 1969 during the inaugural week commemorating the bicentennial of Beethoven's birth.

In 1965 Gundula Janowitz married Wolfgang Zonner, a physician. Their home is in St. Gallen, Switzerland. They have one daughter. A vacation from music for Janowitz consists of reading books and taking long walks, sometimes as early as six in the morning. On the evenings she is scheduled to sing she refuses to speak all day. "When I sing Donna Anna, I don't even speak the day before," she has said. "In the summer of 1967 I sang Donna Anna three times in Aix-en-Provence. Six days of silence—imagine!"

In 1970 Janowitz was named *Kammersängerin* in Austria.

ABOUT: Opera News, September 9, 1967.

Maria Jeritza

1887–

Maria Jeritza (originally Maria Jedlitzka), soprano, was born in Brünn, Czechoslovakia, on October 6, 1887. In her autobiography, *Sunlight and Song,* she told how she loved to sing from infancy on and how, as a child, she preferred participating in musical performances to playing with other children. At twelve she entered the Brünn Conservatory. Two years later she began to study voice privately for several years with

Jeritza: yĕ′ rĕ tsä

MARIA JERITZA

Professor Auspitz. She served her apprenticeship by singing in the chorus of the Brünn Opera.

Maria was a shy girl, gripped with terror whenever she was required to sing a solo before an audience. For this reason she refused to listen to the advice of her teacher who urged her to audition at several opera houses. One day her teacher asked her to review several arias for him in his studio. When she finished singing, she was told that the director of the Olmütz Opera had been concealed behind the draperies. The manager emerged from hiding to engage the young singer for his opera company.

She made her debut at the Olmütz Opera as Elsa in *Lohengrin* in 1910. For five months she remained in Olmütz, gaining poise and self-assurance in such roles as Violetta in *La Traviata* and Marguerite in *Faust.* One day she paid a secret visit to Vienna to audition at the Volksoper. She had sung only a few measures of Micaëla's air from *Carmen* when she was interrupted to be told she was engaged.

In 1911 Jeritza made her first appearance at the Volksoper as Elisabeth in *Tannhäuser.* This was the beginning of a remarkable career in Vienna, where for many years she was the darling of the opera public. She stayed two seasons at the Volksoper, singing in a great variety of roles, working as an understudy, frequently substituting for absent singers, and all the while building an extraordinary repertory. During her two years at the Volksoper she made several notable guest appearances with other opera companies. On October 25, 1912, she created the title role in Richard Strauss's *Ariadne auf Naxos* at the Stuttgart Royal Opera—the beginning of her long friendship with the composer, who later frequently invited her to appear in major female roles in his operas. During the summer of 1912 she was heard in Bad Ischl as Rosalinde in Johann Strauss's *Die Fledermaus* before an audience that included Emperor Franz Josef. The Emperor was so entranced by her performance that he asked to have her join the Vienna Royal Opera. She made her debut there in 1912 as Elisabeth in *Tannhäuser* and there, later the same year, she created the title role in *Aphrodite,* an opera written for her by Max von Oberleithner.

In 1913 the Vienna Royal Opera bought out Jeritza's contract from the Volksoper to make her its sole property in Vienna. From this time on, she became one of the most glamorous stars not only in Vienna but also in guest performances with major opera companies throughout Europe. Strikingly beautiful with her crown of gold hair, possessing a personality that lit up the stage and a voice that created music with exquisite delicacy as if it were some precious filigree, Jeritza became one of the most adored prima donnas of her time. Her repertory was extraordinarily varied. She appeared successfully in several Wagnerian roles, particularly Sieglinde in *Die Walküre,* Elisabeth, and Elsa. She was one of the greatest performers of her day in the female roles in Puccini's operas; the composer himself regarded her as one of his incomparable interpreters. She scored triumphs in operas of Richard Strauss, who selected her to create the role of the Empress in the world premiere of *Die Frau ohne Schatten* in Vienna on October 10, 1919. She was heard in twentieth century operas by Erich Wolfgang Korngold, Felix Weingartner, Franz Schreker, and Leos Janáček, among others. In 1918 she created for Vienna the title role in Janáček's *Jenufa* and on December 4, 1920, in Hamburg, she appeared as Marietta in Korngold's *Die Tote Stadt.* She was also starred in many of the traditional operas of the French and Italian repertory (operas by Bizet, Massenet, and Mascagni, and Puccini), and she was a delight in operettas by Johann Strauss II and Franz von Suppé.

Vienna did not fail to honor her appropriately. In 1923 she was made honorary member of the Vienna Royal Opera and in 1935 she was presented with the Austrian Order of Knighthood, first class, one of the highest awards ever bestowed on a civilian by the Austrian government. Long after her retirement, and after many years of withdrawal from the Viennese scene, on October 23, 1967, in her eightieth year, the Austrian Consul General in New York presented her with the Golden Ring of Honor from the City of Vienna for her contributions to the artistic life of Vienna. She had previously also been decorated by the Pope, by France, and by Italy.

By 1915 her fame had crossed the Atlantic Ocean and the Metropolitan Opera House offered her a contract. Circumstances at the time prevented her from accepting it. After World War I, however, Jeritza finally made her American debut at the Metropolitan Opera as Marietta and the Apparition of Marie in the American premiere of Korngold's *Die Tote Stadt* on November 19, 1921. "Mme. Jeritza's personality is engaging and brilliant," said Richard Aldrich in the New York *Times,* "her blond piquancy undeniable. She is an actress of native ability and represented the wayward and controlled nature of the dancing woman with spirit, vivacity and full-blooded dramatic power. It seemed to be indicated that she would be a valuable addition to the company." But Aldrich had reservations about her voice which he found, at best, to be "powerful, of youthful and sympathetic quality" but which was less praiseworthy "when it was used with the power and intensity that are often required in this part. Then the voice yesterday degenerated unpleasantly into stridency."

When Jeritza appeared in the title role in *Tosca,* on December 1, she took audiences and critics by storm. "No one who saw *Tosca* last night is likely soon to forget her," wrote Deems Taylor in the New York *World.* "For last evening . . . Maria Jeritza made her first appearance in the title role of Puccini's opera and gave a performance that left a packed house alternately breathless and cheering. She gave a performance of thrilling beauty and intensity, every tone and gesture of which was instinct with authority and imagination. . . . Her voice was as beautiful as her acting." Writing in the *Herald Tribune,* Henry E. Krehbiel said that Jeritza's performance was "more than an embodiment of the operatic heroine, dramatically and musically. It was an incarnation of a woman far greater than the one conceived by the creators of the opera. . . . Pose and gesture of infinite variety and grace, vocal utterances of irresistible eloquence gave meanings to phrases of which perhaps neither dramatist nor composer had dreamed." Singing the aria "Vissi d'arte" from a prone position (which Deems Taylor called "a vocal feat as difficult as it was effective"), Jeritza created a tradition followed by several other sopranos.

As long as she remained with the Metropolitan Opera, Jeritza was one of its great prima donnas. She helped open the Metropolitan Opera season of 1922–1923 on November 13 as Tosca. On December 16, 1921, she gave a sensitive portrayal of Sieglinde. On December 14, 1922, she scored another personal triumph in still one more of her memorable impersonations: the title role in *Thaïs,* an opera revived for her. She sang Minnie in *The Girl of the Golden West* and Senta in *The Flying Dutchman* when both operas were revived for her on November 2, 1929, and November 1, 1930, respectively. She appeared in the title roles in American premieres of *Turandot* (November 16, 1926), *Jenufa* (December 6, 1924), Korngold's *Violanta* (November 5, 1927), Richard Strauss's *Die Aegyptische Helena* (November 6, 1928), and in the first Metropolitan Opera productions of Suppé's *Boccaccio* and *Donna Juanita.*

When she left the Metropolitan Opera after the 1931–1932 season she had been heard in 292 performances in New York and 56 on tour in 20 roles. Her other Metropolitan Opera roles were Elsa in *Lohengrin,* Santuzza in *Cavalleria Rusticana,* Octavian in *Der Rosenkavalier,* Elisabeth in *Tannhäuser,* Fedora, Carmen, and Maliella in *The Jewels of the Madonna.* She made a single sentimental return to the stage of the Metropolitan Opera in New York on February 22, 1951, as Rosalinde in *Die Fledermaus.*

In 1934 Jeritza toured the United States in Rudolf Friml's operetta *Music Hath Charms* (formerly entitled *Annina*). In 1953 she resigned from the Vienna State Opera. Guest appearances in several American and European opera houses followed, together with recitals and performances over the radio. Her first American tour as a recitalist began in March 1924 after she had concluded preparatory studies in song literature with Marcella Sembrich.

In 1919 Jeritza married Baron Leopold Popper de Podhurgen; they were divorced in 1935. On August 12, 1935, she married Winfield Sheehan, the motion picture executive. She withdrew from concert work to settle permanently in Hol-lywood, California, and she became an American citizen. Following her divorce from Sheehan, Jeritza married Irving F. Seery on April 10, 1948.

After World War II Jeritza involved herself in the restoration of the Vienna State Opera which had been bombed during the war. She made her return to the concert stage at that time both in New York and in Vienna to raise funds for the reconstruction of that opera house—occasions that provided her many admirers with an opportunity to reaffirm their admiration for her, even though her voice was far past its prime.

ABOUT: Decsey, E. Maria Jeritza; Jeritza, M. Sunlight and Song. *Periodicals*—New York Times, November 5, 1967.

Edward Johnson

1878–1959

Edward Johnson, tenor, was born in Guelph, Ontario, Canada, on August 22, 1878, the son of James Evans Johnson and Margaret O'Connel Johnson. His father was the proprietor of the King Edward Hotel in Guelph and operator of a grain establishment; his hobby was to play the clarinet in the local orchestra. As a boy, Edward engaged in various musical activities. He sang solo in the Presbyterian church choir, and he also served in a fife and drum corps that performed at school entertainments. His musical education began at the piano and continued on the flute; as a flutist he joined his father as a member of the local Guelph orchestra.

His parents originally planned to have him trained for the ministry, but in time law superseded religion and Edward was enrolled for law study at the University of Western Ontario. In his freshman year he was asked to substitute for an indisposed singer as soloist with a choral group. Johnson's performance of such numbers as "The Holy City" and "The Lost Chord" made a favorable impression both on his fellow performers and on the audience and this served as a stimulus to awaken Johnson's ambition to develop his voice.

He left the University before the spring examinations of his first year. In 1900 he went to New York with one hundred dollars in his pocket. To support himself while studying voice he took on

EDWARD JOHNSON

singing assignments in churches. In 1902 he was employed as an understudy in a Boston production of Reginald de Koven's operetta *Maid Marian.* In 1904, in a concert presentation of *Samson and Delilah* at the Worcester Festival in Massachusetts, he sang Samson to Louise Homer's Delilah. In 1907 he was appointed tenor soloist at the Brick Presbyterian Church in New York. That year he also sang the solo tenor part in a New York performance of Elgar's *The Apostles,* with the composer conducting.

On the recommendation of two influential singers—Herbert Witherspoon and Andreas Dippel—Johnson was chosen for the lead part of Nikki in the Broadway premiere of the Oscar Straus operetta *A Waltz Dream,* which opened on January 27, 1908. Since he was paid five hundred dollars a week (advanced to seven hundred during the run of the operetta), Johnson was able to save enough money to fulfill his dream of going to Europe to prepare himself for a career in opera. He had already served an apprenticeship in opera after the run of *A Waltz Dream* by joining a Boston company that toured several American cities in concert presentations, in English, of *Carmen, Aida,* and *The Flying Dutchman.*

In 1909 Johnson arrived in Europe where he went through a three-year period of vocal training in Florence, principally with Vincenzo Lombardi, Caruso's coach. On August 2, 1909, in London, Johnson married Beatrice d'Arniero, daughter of Viscount José d'Arniero of Lisbon; they established their home in an old castle in

Florence and had one daughter. Beatrice died in 1919; Johnson never remarried.

Johnson made his official debut in opera in January 1912 at the Verdi Theater in Padua in *Andrea Chénier;* for this appearance he was billed as Eduardo di Giovanni. As Eduardo di Giovanni he became a highly regarded tenor in Italy. After two seasons of successful appearances in various Italian cities, Johnson was engaged by La Scala in Milan, making his debut there in the first performance in Italy of *Parsifal,* Toscanini conducting. For five years Johnson remained principal tenor at La Scala. In addition to the traditional Italian and French repertory he was heard in leading tenor roles in the world premieres of Alfano's *L'Ombra di Don Giovanni* (April 2, 1914), Pizzetti's *Fedra* (March 20, 1915), Montemezzi's *La Nave* (November 1, 1918), and in the Italian premieres of Puccini's *Il Tabarro* and *Gianni Schicchi.*

During the 1919–1920 season Johnson made his professional American debut in opera as a member of the Chicago Opera. "He sang with smooth limpid tone and finished vocal art coupled with finely controlled but potent passions," reported a critic for the Chicago *Tribune.* He remained with the Chicago Opera three seasons. On November 16, 1922, he made his debut at the Metropolitan Opera as Avito in *L'Amore dei Tre Re.* At that time Richard Aldrich, writing in the New York *Times,* found him to possess "a voice of warm tenor quality which he uses with skill and with telling dramatic effect; a voice of power, but capable of reserves and subject to the discipline of musical understanding. . . . Here is a tenor who is something more than a voice, who is an artistic personality."

His success at the Metropolitan Opera grew as he sang Dmitri in *Boris Godunov,* Des Grieux in *Manon Lescaut,* Cavaradossi in *Tosca,* Don José in *Carmen,* Canio in *I Pagliacci,* Pinkerton in *Madama Butterfly,* Romeo in *Romeo and Juliet,* and the title role in *Faust.* Probably his greatest personal triumph came as Pelléas in *Pelléas and Mélisande,* a role he first sang on March 21, 1925, when the opera was given its first performance at the Metropolitan. Lawrence Gilman said in the *Herald Tribune:* "Mr. Johnson's Pelléas is a memorable performance. In no other of his roles has he made more telling use of his rare intelligence, his insight, his art as a singer and actor. He strikes the right balance between the gravity, the simplicity, the aloofness and reserve that are essential to the character and the sense of passion under difficult restraint. . . . It was a delight to hear the beautiful voice part with its infinite varieties of nuance so heedfully and so eloquently delivered as they are by Mr. Johnson."

During his thirteen years at the Metropolitan Opera Johnson appeared 163 times in New York and 45 times on tour in 23 roles. He was heard in the world premieres of several American operas: as Aethelwold in Deems Taylor's *The King's Henchman* (February 17, 1927); the title role in Taylor's *Peter Ibbetson* (February 7, 1931); and Sir Gower Lackland in Howard Hanson's *Merry Mount* (February 10, 1934). He also created for the United States the title roles in Pizzetti's *Fra Gherardo* (March 21, 1929) and Rimsky-Korsakov's *Sadko* (January 25, 1930). Other Metropolitan Opera roles were Walter in Catalani's *Loreley,* Licino in Spontini's *La Vestale,* Loris in *Fedora,* Radames in *Aida,* Calaf in *Turandot,* Lohengrin, and Dick Johnson in *The Girl of the Golden West.*

Johnson made his last appearance at the Metropolitan Opera on March 20, 1935, as Pelléas. There were no farewell ceremonies attending this performance since on that evening nobody knew that Johnson was retiring.

In the spring of 1935 Johnson was named manager of the special-priced spring season of the Metropolitan Opera. The sudden death of Herbert Witherspoon, who had been selected to succeed Gatti-Casazza as general manager of the opera company, brought Johnson to that post during the regular winter season of 1935–1936.

The Johnson regime at the Metropolitan Opera lasted until 1950 (when Rudolf Bing took over). In that time 1,800 performances of 71 operas had been given, among them the first productions by that company of *Alceste, The Abduction from the Seraglio,* and Mussorgsky's *Khovantchina.* Johnson helped develop the careers of numerous American artists, including Mimi Benzell, Jan Peerce, Dorothy Kirsten, Helen Traubel, Richard Tucker, Leonard Warren, and Eleanor Steber. He inaugurated the "Metropolitan Auditions of the Air," encouraged the founding of the Metropolitan Opera Guild, and supported performances of operas in fresh English translations. He was also responsible for bringing to the Metropolitan the conductors Bruno Walter, George Szell, Sir Thomas Beecham, Fritz Busch, and Fritz Reiner.

The fifteenth anniversary of his regime was commemorated on February 28, 1950, with a gala evening in his honor: a performance of *Tosca* followed by an opera pageant presenting the entire company, some of whose members wore costumes from roles in twelve of the most important operas produced under Johnson.

While still serving as manager of the Metropolitan Opera, Johnson was made chairman of the board of directors of the Royal Conservatory of Music of the University of Toronto. Upon his retirement from the Metropolitan, he devoted himself more assiduously to the Conservatory, helping to create their opera school and ultimately becoming chairman of the Toronto Opera Festival Association.

After suffering a coronary thrombosis while attending the opening night performance of a ballet, Edward Johnson died in a hospital in Guelph, Ontario, on April 20, 1959. Guelph remembered Johnson in May 1968 when as a part of its Spring Festival of the Arts it offered an exhibition of portraits, programs, letters, decorations, costumes, and other memorabilia of Johnson's career in opera.

Johnson became an American citizen in 1922, establishing himself in New York City where he lived in a three-room walk-up apartment on Madison Avenue at Sixty-second Street. Except for a part-time maid he had no servants. Away from opera, his main diversions were playing poker, dancing, swimming, golfing, reading biographies, and enjoying his collection of paintings, sculpture, manuscripts, objets d'art, and books. For his musical achievements he was made Commander of the British Empire and Cavaliere Ufficiale della Corona d'Italia.

ABOUT: Mercer, R. The Tenor of His Time; Thompson, O. The American Singer. *Periodicals*—American Theater Magazine, March 1940; Collier's, December 6, 1941; New York Times, December 8, 1940; New Yorker, December 14, 1935.

Gwyneth Jones

1936–

GWYNETH JONES

Gwyneth Jones, soprano, was born to Edward George and Violet Webster Jones, in Pont-newynydd, Wales, on November 7, 1936. She attended the local schools. Winning a scholarship from the County Council enabled her to enter the Royal College of Music in London where from 1956 to 1960 she studied with Arnold Smith and Ruth Packer. Her vocal training continued at the Accademia Chigiana in Siena, Italy, at Herbert Graf's International Opera Centre in Zurich, Switzerland, and with Maria Carpi in Geneva. Graf became interested in her and engaged her for the Zurich Opera in 1962; she made her debut as Annina in *Der Rosenkavalier.* At that time she was a mezzo-soprano. But soon after joining the company she began singing soprano roles since, as she explained, "the voice had been moving upward for several years, and I hadn't wanted to rush it." Her first soprano role was Amelia in *Un Ballo in Maschera.*

In 1963 she became a member of the Covent Garden company in London. In addition to the soprano roles for which she had been scheduled, she had to fill in for Leontyne Price and Regine Crespin when those singers became indisposed. Gwyneth Jones's success at Covent Garden brought her to the Vienna State Opera where she made her debut in 1966 and where she became a resident member. She also made guest appearances at La Scala in Milan, principal opera houses in Hamburg, Munich, Berlin, Paris, and Rome, and at the Bayreuth Festival. "It has given me a special thrill," she once told an interviewer, "to be accepted at the source—Verdi and Puccini at La Scala, Mozart and Beethoven in Munich and Vienna, and Wagner at Bayreuth."

To her varied repertory she brought a sensitive and perfectly controlled voice and total musicianship as well as a penetrating insight into characterization and a glamorous stage presence. Among her roles were Aida, Tosca, Leonore in *Fidelio,* Carmen, Santuzza in *Cavalleria Rusticana,* Leonora in *Il Trovatore,* Salome, Desdemona in *Otello,* Lady Macbeth in Verdi's *Macbeth,* Donna Anna in *Don Giovanni,* Cio-Cio-San in *Madama Butterfly,* Octavian and the Marschallin in *Der Rosenkavalier,* the title role in Cherubini's *Medea,* Amelia in *Un Ballo in Maschera,* Elisabetta in *Don Carlo,* the title role in Strauss's *Die Aegyptische Helena,* Sieglinde and Brünnhilde in *Die Walküre,* Brünnhilde in *Siegfried* and *Die Götterdämmerung,* Gutrune in *Die Götterdämmerung,* Ortrud in *Lohengrin,* Elisabeth and Venus in *Tannhäuser,* Senta in *The Flying Dutchman,* Kundry in *Parsifal,* and Eva in *Die Meistersinger.*

Her American debut took place in New York in 1966 in the title role of Cherubini's *Medea* at Carnegie Hall, in a concert presentation by the American Opera Society. Her popularity in the United States soared following appearances with the San Francisco Opera in *Fidelio.* She repeated her interpretation of Leonore in Beethoven's opera in May 1970 in Vienna, with Leonard Bernstein conducting, during the Beethoven centennial commemoration at the Theater-an-der-Wien, in which the opera had been introduced. The intensity of her acting, the beauty of her singing, and the nobility of her conception drew rhapsodic praise not only from the critics and audiences but also from Leonard Bernstein.

On November 26, 1972, she made a striking debut at the Metropolitan Opera as Sieglinde in *Die Walküre.* When she was heard as Leonore in a revival of *Fidelio* at the Metropolitan Opera on January 2, 1976, John Rockwell wrote in the New York *Times:* "In a few of the key dramatic climaxes she was thrilling, and there was a lovely overall warmth to her portrayal." She also made a successful appearance at the Metropolitan as the Marschallin in *Der Rosenkavalier* on December 7, 1977.

During the summer of 1975 she assumed the three Brünnhilde roles of the *Ring* cycle at the Bayreuth Festival. She did so again at the Vienna State Opera in April and May 1976 and at the Bayreuth Festival during the summer of 1976 when the centenary was commemorated.

On March 9, 1977, she appeared at the Munich State Opera in the title role of *Ariadne auf Naxos.* She sang her first Chrysothemis in *Elektra* on May 6, 1977, at Covent Garden in London. During the summer of 1977 she was busily engaged at the festivals of Vienna (Leonore in *Fidelio,* Chrysothemis, and Elisabetta), Munich (the Marschallin), and Bayreuth (the three Brünnhildes, Venus, and Elisabeth).

Gwyneth Jones married Till Haberfeld, a company director, on March 8, 1969. Their main residence is in Zurich, but they also have apartments in Vienna and Frankfort. They have one child. "My husband and I," she has said, "take regular fortnightly vacations at Christmas and March and four weeks in the summer, and I try to use another full month at least for study and preparation."

She has also been acclaimed in recitals and as a solo vocalist in the performances of great choral music with the world's great symphony orchestras. For television she has filmed *Fidelio* and *The Flying Dutchman.*

She was awarded first prize in contemporary music, the Harriet Cohen International Music Award, and she has been named Associate of the Royal College of Music and Honorary Fellow of the Royal College of Music in London. She was also named *Kammersängerin* by both the Bavarian and the Austrian governments.

ABOUT: New York Times, January 15, 1978; Opera News, December 16, 1972.

Rafael Joseffy

1852–1915

Rafael Joseffy, pianist, the only child of Vilmos Joseffy (a distinguished rabbi) and Cecilia Joseffy, was born in Hunfalu, Hungary, on July 3, 1852. He spent his early years in Miskolcz,

---

Joseffy: yŏ′ shĕf fĭ

RAFAEL JOSEFFY

near Budapest, where, when he was eight, he began studying the piano with a local teacher. He later continued piano study at the Budapest Conservatory under Brauer, who had taught Stephen Heller.

When he was fourteen Rafael entered the Leipzig Conservatory; his principal teacher was E. F. Wenzel, but he also received some random instruction from Ignaz Moscheles. From 1868 to 1870 Rafael studied the piano in Berlin with Karl Tausig, and during the summers of 1870 and 1871 he profited from the advice and guidance of Franz Liszt in Weimar. Tausig exerted a far-reaching influence on him, helping him to develop a brilliant pianistic style and a prodigious technique.

His concert debut in Berlin in 1872 was followed by several concerts in Vienna and a tour of Holland, Germany, Denmark, Sweden, and Russia. In those concerts he already gave evidence of the sensitivity of performing style and the fastidious attention to phrasing and tone color which would characterize his later performances.

In 1879 Joseffy went to live in the United States. His American debut took place at Chickering Hall in New York on October 13, 1879, in Chopin's Piano Concerto No.1 and Liszt's Piano Concerto No.1. However, before the end of the nineteenth century, he withdrew from the concert stage for five years to renew his studies of piano literature and to arrive at a deeper poetic insight. He emerged from this retirement as one of the preeminent pianists of his time. Technical powers had become subservient to details and subtlety of poetic expression. As Richard Aldrich wrote of him in the New York *Times* following his performance of Liszt's Piano Concerto No.2 on March 19, 1904: "His playing was crystal clear, delicately articulated, full of cool half tints and subtle shadings. . . . There were finish and fleetness of technique, but of technical display there was nothing." After a Joseffy performance in Carnegie Hall on April 2, 1905, Aldrich provided the following analysis of his art: "Its characteristics are restraint, a certain aloofness, a self-contained moderation. Its object is to obtain beautiful results from some of the most essential qualities of the piano as a percussive instrument, frankly accepting them and making no attempt to imitate the warmth or the color of song or the sustained power of stringed instruments. . . . It does not deeply move, but it entrances with its exquisite perfection, its cool pure sentiment, its lucidity, symmetry and delicate efflorescence."

In 1911 James Gibbons Huneker wrote as follows: "Joseffy stands today for all that is exquisite and poetic in the domain of the piano. . . . There is magic in his attack, magic and moonlight in his playing. . . . This rare combination of the virtuoso and the poet places Joseffy outside the pale of 'popular pianism.' "

In his concerts in the United States in the late nineteenth century, Joseffy became an all-important influence in propagandizing the piano music of Brahms, then not widely heard or known.

From 1888 to 1906 he was a distinguished teacher of piano at the National Conservatory of Music in New York—and privately after that. He was the author of *School of Advanced Piano Playing* (1902) and *First Studies* (1913); editor of a fifteen-volume edition of Chopin's complete works and of the études of Czerny, Moscheles, Schumann, and others; transcriber for the piano of music by Bach, Gluck, Schumann, Boccherini, and others; and composer of many pieces for the piano, the best of which were *Romance sans Paroles, Spinnlied,* and *Mazurka-Fantaisie.*

Joseffy lived many years in an apartment in New York City; he also had a summer house in Tarrytown, New York. In September 1890 he married his housekeeper, Marie Gumere. He died at his New York apartment on June 25, 1915.

ABOUT: Schonberg, H. C. The Great Pianists. *Periodicals*—Musical Observer, August 1915; Musical Quarterly, July 1916; New York Times, July 4, 1913.

Marcel Journet

1867–1933

Marcel Journet, basso, was born in Grasse, in the Alpes Maritimes section of southern France, on July 25, 1867, the son of Jule and Virginia Delphin Journet. After preliminary vocal studies in Nice he attended the Paris Conservatory, a pupil of Obin and Seghettini. His opera debut took place in Bézières in 1891, the year in which he also made his first appearances at the Théâtre de la Monnaie in Brussels where he achieved his first successes and where he remained principal basso until 1900. His debut at Covent Garden in London took place in 1893. For seven seasons he was a principal of that company; on June 20, 1894, he appeared there in the world premiere of Massenet's *La Navarraise.* During this period he was also a valued member of the Paris Opéra, remaining there many years. Among the notable world premieres in which he performed in Paris were those of *Thaïs* (March 16, 1894) and Février's *Monna Vanna* (January 13, 1909).

His American debut with the Metropolitan Opera came on tour; on November 9, 1900, as Colline in *La Bohème.* He was also heard on tour as Capulet in *Romeo and Juliet,* the king in *Aida,* Raimondo in *Lucia di Lammermoor,* Ferrando in *Il Trovatore,* Fafner in *Das Rheingold,* Sparafucile in *Rigoletto,* Marcel in *Les Huguenots,* and Méphistophélès in *Faust.* On December 22, 1900, he went to New York as Ramfis in *Aida.*

During his eight seasons at the Metropolitan Opera he proved one of the most distinguished, valuable, and versatile bassos of his time, equally gifted as an actor and as a singer. He was heard in 43 roles during 224 performances in New York and 159 on tour. He created for the United States the roles of Myrtille and Olympias in the American premiere of De Lara's *Messaline* (January 22, 1902); Titurel in the American premiere of *Parsifal* (November 24, 1903)—the first staged performance outside Bayreuth; and the Nazarene in the American premiere of *Salome* (January 22, 1907). He was also heard as

---

Journet: zhŏŏr nĕ′

MARCEL JOURNET

Narr-Havas in the New York premiere of Reyer's *Salammbô* and as Prince de Bouillon in the first Metropolitan Opera production of *Adriana Lecouvreur*. His other Metropolitan Opera roles were Zuniga and Escamillo in *Carmen*, Des Grieux in *Manon*, Friar Laurence in *Romeo and Juliet*, St. Bris in *Les Huguenots*, Lodovico in *Otello*, Oberthal and Zacharias in *Le Prophète*, Jupiter in Gounod's *Philemon et Baucis*, Schaunard in *La Bohème*, Tom in *Un Ballo in Maschera*, Silva in *Ernani*, Don Basilio in *The Barber of Seville*, Almaviva in *The Marriage of Figaro*, Fafner in *Siegfried*, Gurnemanz in *Parsifal*, King Henry in *Lohengrin*, Alvise in *La Gioconda*, Leporello in *Don Giovanni*, Plunkett in *Martha*, Nilakantha in *Lakmé*, the Grand Inquisitor and Grand Brahmin in *L'Africaine*, and Cieco in *Iris*.

When he left the Metropolitan Opera after the 1907–1908 season he continued to make appearances in Europe for the next twenty-five years. With the outbreak of World War I in Europe he returned to the United States to become a member of the Chicago Opera for two seasons. In 1918 he made his debut at La Scala in Milan, and there on May 1, 1924, he sang in the world premiere of Boïto's *Nerone*, Toscanini conducting. He continued to perform until the end of his life, with little perceptible decline in interpretative and vocal powers.

Marcel Journet died in Vittel, France, on September 5, 1933.

ABOUT: Kutsch, K. J. and Riemens, L. A Concise Biographical Dictionary of Singers.

Sena Jurinac

1921–

Sena Jurinac (originally Srebrenka Jurinac), soprano, was born in Travnik, Yugoslavia, on October 24, 1921. Her father, Ludwig Jurinac, a Croatian, was a physician; her mother, Christine Cerv Jurinac, was Viennese. After graduation from high school in Zagreb, Sena attended the Music Academy in that city as a pupil of Maria Kostrencíc. On October 15, 1942, Jurinac made her opera debut as Mimi in *La Bohème* with the Zagreb Opera. During the next two seasons she was heard there as Marguerite in *Faust*, the Countess in *The Marriage of Figaro*, Freia in *Die Walküre*, and in several Yugoslavian operas.

In 1944 she was engaged by the Vienna State Opera. Since that opera house was unable to reopen because of damage inflicted during World War II, her Viennese debut took place at the recently reopened Theater-an-der-Wien on May 1, 1945, when she sang the role of Cherubino in *The Marriage of Figaro* for the first time, Josef Krips conducting. This was the first opera performed in Vienna since the end of World War II; Vienna was then occupied by the Russians and, since a strict wartime curfew was in effect during evening hours, the performance had to take place in the afternoon. She continued to appear at the Theater-an-der-Wien as well as at the Volksoper in Vienna until 1955, expanding her repertory to include Antonia and Giulietta in *The Tales of Hoffmann*, Micaëla in *Carmen*, Marie in *The Bartered Bride*, Eva in *Die Meistersinger*, Manon in Massenet's opera of the same name, Octavian in *Der Rosenkavalier*, the Composer in *Ariadne auf Naxos*, and Ighino in Pfitzner's *Palestrina*.

She made her first appearance in London in 1947 with the visiting Vienna opera company. That summer she was also heard at the Salzburg Festival in Gluck's *Orfeo ed Euridice* and in Mozart's *The Marriage of Figaro*. She has since become a favorite at this festival; in the summer of 1960 she helped to open its new festival theater as Octavian. She was also acclaimed at festivals in Bayreuth, Glyndebourne, Edinburgh, Florence, Holland, and Wexford (Ireland).

Jurinac

SENA JURINAC

She became a resident member of the Vienna State Opera in 1955. When Herbert von Karajan became its director, he assigned to her major roles in the Italian repertory: Cio-Cio-San in *Madama Butterfly,* Elisabeth de Valois in *Don Carlo,* and Desdemona in *Otello,* among others. She also appeared as Marenka in *The Bartered Bride* and Rosalinde in *Die Fledermaus.* She became one of the world's greatest female interpreters of Mozart—often in more than one role in an opera. Besides appearing both as Cherubino and the Countess in *The Marriage of Figaro,* she was heard as Dorabella and Fiordiligi in *Così fan Tutte,* Donna Elvira and Donna Anna in *Don Giovanni,* and Ilia and Elettra in *Idomeneo.*

She has also appeared in more than one female role of *Fidelio*—first as Marzelline and in 1961 at Covent Garden as Leonore—and in *Der Rosenkavalier,* graduating from Octavian to the Marschallin at Covent Garden in 1966, Georg Solti conducting.

Among other roles in her extensive repertory are Poppea in Monteverdi's *L'Incoronazione di Poppea,* the title role in Janáček's *Jenufa,* Tosca, Elisabeth in *Tannhäuser,* Marie in Berg's *Wozzeck,* Iphigénie in Gluck's *Iphigénie en Tauride,* Nedda in *I Pagliacci,* Pamina in *The Magic Flute,* Marina in *Boris Godunov,* the title role in Puccini's *Suor Angelica,* Tatiana in *Eugene Onegin,* Amelia in *Un Ballo in Maschera,* Leonora in *La Forza del Destino,* Senta in *The Flying Dutchman,* Agathe in *Der Freischütz,* and Rosaura in Wolf-Ferrari's *Le Donne Curiose.*

She has distinguished herself as a recitalist, as a guest soloist with major orchestras, and as a solo vocalist in the choral masterworks of Haydn, Verdi, Brahms, Mozart, Beethoven, and others.

Jurinac became a familiar name and voice to American audiences, long before she made her first appearance in the United States, through her many recordings. She had been engaged by the Metropolitan Opera to create the title role in Samuel Barber's *Vanessa* in 1958, but circumstances at the time prevented her from fulfilling this commitment. Her American debut finally took place with the San Francisco Opera as Cio-Cio-San on September 22, 1959. Later the same season San Francisco heard her as Eva and Donna Anna. Her New York debut on May 16, 1968, was as guest artist with the New York Philharmonic in Richard Strauss's *Last Four Songs* and Beethoven's Symphony No.9, Leonard Bernstein conducting. Raymond Ericson reported in the New York *Times:* "She has a great deal of womanly loveliness in her appearance; she has a fine warm voice that has moments of beauty, and above all she has a purity of approach to the music she sings. ... Here and there she brought a touch of radiance to a tone or a phrase."

In May 1974 Jurinac celebrated the thirtieth anniversary of her debut in Vienna with a gala performance as the Marschallin.

Her performance of Octavian was permanently captured on films for television in a European production of *Der Rosenkavalier* in 1962 in which Elisabeth Schwarzkopf was heard as the Marschallin. Jurinac also appeared on television films in *Wozzeck* and *Otello.*

She was named *Kammersängerin* in Vienna in 1951. In 1961 she received the Ehrenkreuz für Wissenschaft und Kunst and in 1967 the Grosses Ehrenzeichen für Verdienste um die Republik Österreich. She has also been honored in Vienna with the Mozart medal, the Ehrenring der Wiener Staatsoper, the Cross of the Order Litteris et Artibus, and an honorary membership in the Vienna State Opera.

In 1953 Jurinac married Sesto Bruscantini, a baritone she had met during her appearances at the Glyndebourne Festival. Her second husband is Dr. Josef Lederle, a surgeon. They live in Augsburg, Germany.

ABOUT: Opera News, May 18, 1969.

Gertrude Kappel

1884–1971

Gertrude Kappel, soprano, was born in Halle, Germany, on September 1, 1884, daughter of Louis and Anna Dohler Kappel. At the Leipzig Conservatory she studied with Arthur Nikisch and Noe. After graduation she joined the Hanover Opera, making her debut in 1903 as Leonore in *Fidelio*. She remained with this company until 1924, attracting attention throughout Europe with her performances in the Wagnerian repertory. In 1924 she went to the Vienna State Opera where she remained for five years. Her successes there in the music dramas of Wagner and Richard Strauss made her a world figure among prima donnas, a position she maintained from 1929 to 1932 as principal dramatic soprano of the Munich State Opera and with guest appearances in Berlin, Hamburg, Amsterdam, Paris, and Madrid.

On January 16, 1928, Kappel made her American debut at the Metropolitan Opera as Isolde in *Tristan and Isolde*. Though Olin Downes, writing in the New York *Times,* found her performance "uneven," he did see much evidence "of a highly gifted artist." He further commented: "It has been many seasons since we have heard Isolde's first act delivered with such dramatic sensitiveness, proportion and distinction of style. An Isolde who did not bawl in indiscriminate fortes and fortissimos her rage and resentment against Tristan; in whose tones were to be felt every fluctuating shade of passion, feeling and embodiment of the end of all passion and desire! A woman who summoned poetic illusion as well as finely shaded song to her aid in revealing the spirit of Wagner's princess; who, in accomplishing this, matched the text with the tone and the tone with the text, and whose every act and word had significance to the audience."

During her initial season at the Metropolitan Opera, Kappel appeared five times as Isolde. She also sang the role of Brünnhilde in *Die Walküre* and *Die Götterdämmerung* and that of Kundry in *Parsifal.* Her Brünnhilde performances were, Lawrence Gilman wrote in the *Herald Tribune,* "unequalled for truth and sincerity of feeling and loveliness of song."

GERTRUDE KAPPEL

One of her triumphs at the Metropolitan Opera outside the Wagnerian repertory came with her performance as Elektra in the Metropolitan's first performance of Richard Strauss's opera on December 3, 1932. Richard Strauss had previously called her the greatest Elektra he had ever heard, and the New York music critics echoed his enthusiasm. Olin Downes commented in the New York *Times:* "The performance, as a whole, was the most eloquent interpretation that the writer remembers in eight years of listening to opera in this city." In the *World-Telegram* Pitts Sanborn exclaimed: "Altogether the Elektra of Gertrude Kappel has taken its place among the noteworthy portraits in the Metropolitan's gallery. It was vocally, however, that Mme. Kappel surpassed all competition. . . . She gave an extraordinary exhibition of accomplished and controlled art, absolutely free from forcing of tone."

Gertrude Kappel remained at the Metropolitan Opera through the 1935–1936 season. To her many roles she added that of the Marschallin in *Der Rosenkavalier.* While still a member of the Metropolitan Opera company, Kappel made her debut with the San Francisco Opera as Isolde on November 10, 1933. In 1937 she went into retirement in Berlin, and on April 3, 1971, she died in Munich.

ABOUT: Opera News, January 10, 1976.

Kappel: käp′ pĕl

Karajan

Herbert von Karajan

1908–

Herbert von Karajan, conductor and renowned orchestral technician, was born in Salzburg, Austria, on April 5, 1908, of Serbian-Greek parents. His father was Ernst von Karajan, chief medical officer in Salzburg; his mother, Martha Cosmâc von Karajan. Music was an important part of the family's life, for Ernst von Karajan loved music. He played the clarinet in an orchestra, and he began the musical education of his sons at an early age. When Herbert was three, he would listen intently to his brother taking piano lessons; then, when the lessons were over, he would try to reproduce on the piano the sounds he had heard. His own piano lessons began at about this time, and when he was five he was accomplished enough to make a public appearance. "One of my earliest recollections," he has said, "was a burning love of music which made me forget to eat or sleep. I had perfect pitch without knowing it. Wrong intonation and weak rhythm were painful to me."

He attended the Salzburg high school, and at the Mozarteum he specialized in piano. But the piano did not seem to satisfy his insatiable hunger for making music. Dr. Bernhard Paumgartner, director of the Mozarteum, who was one of his teachers, advised him to become a conductor: "Otherwise you will never be satisfied." At fifteen Herbert heard a concert of the Berlin Philharmonic and knew without a doubt that someday he would be a conductor.

He continued his music studies in Vienna at the University, where he majored in musicology and music history, and at the Vienna Music Academy, where he studied conducting with Franz Schalk. On December 17, 1928, he made his first appearance as a conductor, with the student orchestra of the Music Academy. "When I started conducting I suffered considerably because there was little opportunity for pupils to conduct," he told an interviewer. "In two years of studying, I conducted no more than thirty minutes. Consequently, some of us conducting students formed an ensemble among ourselves, and we used to perform nearly every day the opera to be given at the State Opera that

HERBERT VON KARAJAN

evening. We borrowed singers from vocal classes, two pianos, some strings, and one member sang for the choir. So, at least, we obtained knowledge of the opera. After hearing it in the evening we used to discuss it." While still a student at the Academy, Karajan made his official conducting debut in Salzburg with an orchestra hired by his father.

Hearing Toscanini conduct *Falstaff* and *Lucia di Lammermoor* in Vienna in 1929 gave Karajan his first true insight into the summits the art of conducting could scale. He later described this experience as a "revelation." And he said: "For the first time I realized the meaning of *régie* [directorial control] . . . It made me ponder for days about the secrets of musical interpretation that I could only describe as miraculous." One year later Karajan attended two concerts of the New York Philharmonic conducted by Toscanini in Vienna. "I could not discuss it with anyone, but I know that my own development now took another course: I no longer strove for the improvement of the orchestra's quality but I demanded a level of perfection beyond that which any technical improvement could reach."

In 1929 he was engaged as a conductor for the Ulm State Theater, where he first appeared as a replacement for an indisposed conductor in a performance of *Fidelio*. He remained in Ulm until 1934. "Work in Ulm was enormously difficult," explains Karajan. "The conductor was all in one—coach, chorus master, conductor. When I did not conduct I used to operate the lighting machinery to get the knowledge of everything

Karajan: kä′ rä yän

380

concerned with the production. Although artistically perhaps of limited value, my whole time in Ulm was important to me in subsequent years for I learned working from the bottom up." In summers, free from his duties in Ulm, Karajan would perform various musical jobs around the Festspielhaus in Salzburg, and thus was enabled to hear the rehearsals of Toscanini, whose methods he studied minutely.

On June 15, 1932, Karajan married Elmy Holgerloef, a soprano in the operetta division of the Aachen Opera.

Karajan's assignment after Ulm was in Aachen, where he became conductor of the opera in 1934 and then music director of both the opera company and the symphony orchestra. "With the ensemble we used to give concerts in Holland and Belgium, and as I had to conduct about forty different symphonic programs a year, I acquired an extensive repertory." In 1936 he made his first appearance in Vienna, the city with which, next to Berlin, he has since been most often identified; he introduced himself to Vienna with performances of *Tristan and Isolde* at the State Opera, performances that were highly praised.

In 1937 the Berlin Philharmonic Orchestra invited him to direct one of its concerts. He made such a good impression that he was assigned to reorganize the symphony concerts of the Berlin State Opera Orchestra. "It was a wonderful job, difficult only because I had to divide my time between Aachen and Berlin," he has said.

In 1938 Karajan went to the Berlin State Opera. There on September 30 he directed a remarkable performance of *Fidelio*. It was not long before he became known in Berlin as *das Wunder Karajan* (Karajan, the wonder), a phrase coined by a journalist for the Berlin *Zeitung*.

Karajan continued performing at the Berlin State Opera until 1945, always conducting from memory, even the music dramas of Wagner. In presentations of Bach's *Brandenburg Concertos* at symphony concerts he led the orchestra from a place at the harpsichord where he performed the continuo the way *Kapellmeisters* of old did. "Three or four times a week after a performance in Berlin I had to leave on a night plane without even having time to change my clothes. Sometimes I had to fly there and back for a single rehearsal. By the end of three years it had

become so trying that I had to resign my post in Aachen," he has commented.

At this time his fame was spreading outside Germany and Austria. In 1938 he conducted at La Scala in Milan and at the Florence May Music Festival. Other guest appearances were made in Belgium, Holland, and Scandinavia. During World War II he was the director of the Berlin Staatskapelle.

As a member of the National Socialist Party from 1935 to 1942, Karajan was in the best possible graces of the Nazi regime in Germany and, after *Anschluss,* in Austria. But his wife, Anita Gutermann, whom he married on October 2, 1942, after his divorce from Elmy Holgerloef, was a member of a German-Jewish family. This second marriage was terminated by divorce.

Because of his early Nazi affiliation and his subsequent pronounced Nazi sympathies, the United States Occupation forces refused at the end of World War II to allow him to appear as a conductor. He lived in Salzburg secluded and retired. Then a slow process of denazification began; he was permitted to resume his conducting career gradually. The first step in this reinstatement came when the United States authorities, at the request of Walter Legge, artistic director of Columbia Gramophone in England, allowed him to make recordings with the Vienna Philharmonic for that company. After being given official clearance by the denazification tribunal Karajan was allowed to conduct a public concert in Salzburg in February 1948. Later the same year he was appointed artistic director of the Gesellschaft der Musikfreunde in Vienna; his symphony concerts came to be known as "Karajan cycles." Then he made tours of Europe as well as recordings with this orchestra. His next appointment was as music director of the Vienna Symphony, which he developed from a comparatively nondescript symphonic group into a major musical organization. In 1949 he gave guest performances at the Lucerne Festival in Switzerland. One year later he was made music director at La Scala and he assumed full responsibilities for every phase of the production. That same year he led a Bach festival in Vienna; from this came an extraordinary recording of the Mass in B minor. In 1951 at the Bayreuth festival Karajan conducted the complete *Ring* cycle as well as *Die Meistersinger,* and in 1952 he was heard at Bayreuth in a new production of *Tristan and Isolde*. In addition to these activities he also served as music director of the newly founded London Philharmonic Orchestra, with which he toured Germany, Austria, Paris, and Switzerland in 1952. In 1954 he was the principal conductor of the Berlin Philharmonic Orchestra during the city's cultural festival, led a memorable performance of *Lucia di Lammermoor* at La Scala, and toured Japan under the auspices of the Japanese radio network.

Then in 1954 the Berlin Philharmonic Orchestra made its first tour of the United States. Wilhelm Furtwängler had been scheduled as its conductor, but when Furtwängler died Karajan became his replacement. Karajan's American debut took place in Washington, D.C., on February 27, 1955. A few days later, on March 1, he gave his first New York concert. "Mr. Karajan," reported Howard Taubman in the New York *Times,* "is a conductor of stature. Playing . . . solid familiar fare . . . Mr. Karajan conducted . . . from memory with very little fuss or furbelows, with a craftsman's knowledge and with an artist's understanding of the music at hand . . . He may be the best conductor in Europe as his admirers claim for him. For the moment let it be said here that he is a remarkably gifted one."

In the fall of 1955 Karajan returned to the United States for a second tour, this time at the head of the Philharmonia Orchestra of London. Following a New York concert on October 25, Howard Taubman had this to say in the New York *Times:* "He proved he is a conductor of major quality . . . a virtuoso leader. . . . The orchestra was utterly responsive to his musical requirements."

In October 1967 Karajan paid another visit to the United States, this time in his capacity as principal conductor of La Scala. On this occasion he brought to New York, from Expo '67 in Montreal, a stirring performance of Verdi's Requiem.

Meanwhile, in 1955 Karajan succeeded Furtwängler as the music director of the Berlin Philharmonic Orchestra, a lifetime appointment. (There is some irony in this succession, since Furtwängler and Karajan had been bitter rivals and outspoken antagonists.) In 1956 Karajan was also appointed artistic director of the Vienna State Opera, principal conductor of the Vienna Philharmonic Orchestra, and in 1957 artistic director of the Salzburg Festival. In addition to holding these posts, he was principal conductor at La Scala (where he was a member of the board of directors), permanent conductor of the Philharmonia Orchestra in London, and lifetime director of the Gesellschaft der Musikfreunde in Vienna.

Karajan resigned his post in Vienna in 1964 after a bitter dispute with Egon Hilbert, his codirector at the Vienna State Opera, over whose authority was primary. In an outburst of rage Karajan vowed never again to conduct in Vienna. He broke that vow six years later when he conducted the Berlin Philharmonic Orchestra there for a series of five Beethoven concerts in June 1970. Then, with a newly appointed director heading the company, Karajan finally returned to the Vienna State Opera on May 8, 1977, after a fourteen-year absence, for a two-and-a-half week series of performances of *Il Trovatore, The Marriage of Figaro,* and *La Bohème.* That return was momentarily threatened at the zero hour when an anti-Karajan poem was published; but a public apology from the author assuaged Karajan's ruffled feelings. Upon his return to the dais, reported Joseph Wechsberg in the London magazine *Opera,* "there were red roses on his stand, special floodlight and television cameras, and the house went absolutely crazy. . . . Dignified, overdressed ladies and elegant men shouted like children for minutes until the Maestro . . . with a resolute movement of his baton began conducting the music."

In Easter of 1967 Karajan not only conducted but was also responsible for the overall production of *Die Walküre* at Salzburg, Austria. This was the first of four productions, one each year, of each of the music dramas in the *Ring* cycle—*Das Rheingold* followed in 1968, *Siegfried* in 1969, and *Die Götterdämmerung* in 1970. (This was the seventeenth time Karajan conducted the entire *Ring* cycle, the first having been in Aachen [Aix-la-Chapelle] in the mid-1930s.) World-famous singers and designers joined the Berlin Philharmonic Orchestra in monumental productions which, from beginning to end, were the realizations of Karajan's overall artistic conception. "In two categories Karajan is supreme," reported George Movshon from Salzburg to *Musical America.* "As an administrator—as the man who put the whole festival together and told everybody concerned what to do—he is clearly a superman. As an orchestral technician, it is hard to imagine his peer. . . . We are hearing what Karajan wanted us to hear. There was no gap between intention and execution."

A plan was evolved in 1967 to take each of the four dramas of the *Ring* cycle from Salzburg to the Metropolitan Opera with Karajan conducting in four consecutive seasons. *Die Walküre* was heard on November 21, 1967—Karajan's American bow as an opera conductor. Harold C. Schonberg noted in the New York *Times* that Karajan's conception of *Die Walküre* was far different from "the surging romanticism of a Solti or a Böhm." And he added: "The conductor kept the dynamic level extraordinarily low and the tempos rather slow. It was an ultra-refined, chamber-music kind of sound that he drew from the orchestra." This proved more true of Act I than of the remainder of the opera in which, said Schonberg, "Karajan suddenly presented a performance ... much more conventional in tempo and dynamics. It was conducted with more finesse than almost any conductor brings to the music these days, but it was orthodox in conception. ... No Wagner conducting like it has been heard since the great old days. For in addition to the strength and surety of the conducting, there was a kind of polish, of clarity, of sheer control, not normally associated with the Metropolitan Opera orchestra."

After performances of *Das Rheingold* at the Metropolitan Opera in 1968, the Karajan *Ring* project was brought to a sudden halt in New York. A prolonged strike at the Metropolitan Opera in 1969, together with sharp differences between Karajan and the management of the company, compelled cancellation of the projected performances under Karajan of *Siegfried* and *Die Götterdämmerung*. However, Americans were not denied the privilege of hearing the entire *Ring* cycle under Karajan since the Easter season productions at Salzburg were all recorded by Deutsche Grammophon.

In 1969, in addition to all his other commitments, Karajan was made permanent music councilor and part-time conductor of the Orchestre de Paris on a three-year contract. Within a year Karajan discovered that his obligations outside Paris made it impossible for him to perform his duties with the Orchestre de Paris. In June 1970 he announced his resignation, effective in 1971.

Karajan has produced a prodigious number of recordings, committing virtually his entire repertory to records. He has also been active in filming some of his operatic and symphonic performances and these have had a wide distribution through the years over European and American televison. His American debut over television (on films) took place in November 1974 when he was heard over the Public Broadcasting Service in a musical Special.

If Karajan has become something of a cult in Europe it is not only because of his musical powers and achievements, however formidable they have been, but also because he has for years been a matinee idol (a *Kulturidol*), whose personality and comings and goings are the stuff from which innumerable magazine and newspaper stories are made. Tall, athletically built, aristocratic in manner, and strikingly handsome, he is a man who lives in the grand manner, who inspires adulation as well as emulation. "Der Chef," as his coworkers refer to him, arrives at rehearsals either in a chauffeur-driven Rolls Royce or in a red Austin which he drives himself (usually at high speed). He is an expert amateur skier, both on mountainous slopes and in the water. He pilots his own plane. He enjoys sailing his yacht, *Helisara*. Whatever he does, he cuts an elegant figure.

In 1958 Karajan married for a third time. His new wife was Eliette Mouret, a former Dior model, strikingly beautiful and always exquisitely gowned. With their two daughters, the Karajans maintain homes in St. Moritz, Switzerland; St. Tropez, France; Salzburg; and Berlin. Karajan keeps fit through yoga, swims several times a day in a pool, takes long morning and nighttime walks, and tours the Central Alps on foot. His other interests are mechanics and acoustical research.

"For the average man on the street in Central Europe," wrote the English musicologist H. C. Robbins Landon, "what is really fascinating about Karajan is that he is totally unlike an intellectual. ... As such he attracts the adulation of people who ordinarily consider conductors balding intellectuals who (in Europe) frequent coffee-houses and have soft bellies. ... All this sort of thing has inspired a curiosity about his everyday life comparable only to the public interest in personages of Hollywood—or *pace* Europe—Cannes. Karajan himself is reported to have said, 'They seem to think my conducting is only an interruption of my hobbies.'"

Rudolf Bing once said of Karajan: "Karajan is not a very cozy type of person. He doesn't lunch, doesn't drink, doesn't smoke. He is not a socially easy person; it's hard to establish friendly relations."

In commenting on his approach to music in general and conducting in particular, Karajan has said: "If you want really to say something you must forget the printed page. I try never to see the notes. The moment you are tied to seeing the notes your mind has shifted from the music. The Zen Buddhist speaks of seeing the front page of the soul and the back page—but *in satori* the two sides are one. This applies exactly to the music."

Karajan has received numerous official honors and awards. He was awarded the Mozart Ring in Vienna in 1957, and the Prix, France-Allemagne, in 1970. Finland made him Commander, First Class, Order of the White Rose. In 1973 he was made honorary citizen of Berlin.

In 1969 Karajan instituted an annual international competition for young conductors. The winners have included a Finn, a Japanese, a Russian, and an Israeli.

ABOUT: Bing, R. 5000 Nights at the Opera; Blaukopf, K. Great Conductors; Ewen, D. Famous Modern Conductors; Haeusserman, E. Herbert von Karajan; Löbl, K. Das Wunder Karajan; Robinson, P. Karajan. Spiel, C.. ed. Anekdoten um Herbert von Karajan; Witeschnik, A. Diesen Kuss der Ganzen Welt! *Periodicals*—Hi-Fi, May 1972; High Fidelity, September 1963, April 1975; New York Times, November 13, 1955, April 19, 1970; New York Times Magazine, December 3, 1967; New Yorker, November 11, 1974; Opera News, February 24, 1968, November 21, 1970; Saturday Review, June 29, 1968, June 27, 1970; Vogue, April 1973.

Rudolf Kempe

1910–1976

Rudolf Kempe, conductor, was born in Niederpoyritz, near Dresden, Germany, on June 14, 1910. Neither parent was musical. When not quite six Rudolf began to study the piano; at twelve he took lessons on the violin; and at fourteen he received instruction on the oboe. His principal musical training took place in Dresden at the Orchesterschule der Sächsischen Staatskapelle, presided over by Fritz Busch. There Rudolf specialized in the oboe.

RUDOLF KEMPE

In 1929 he was engaged as first oboist of the Leipzig Gewandhaus Orchestra, a post he retained until 1936. During these years he also served as a coach with the Leipzig Opera, where in 1936 he made his conducting debut with a performance of Lortzing's *Der Wildschütz*.

Determined to become a conductor, he resigned his orchestral post with the Gewandhaus Orchestra in 1936. His first conducting assignment was with the Chemnitz Opera. From there he went to the Weimar Opera where he directed all new productions. While performing in Weimar he made guest appearances with the Berlin State Opera and with major orchestras in Berlin, Leipzig, and Dresden.

In 1949 he was appointed principal conductor of the Dresden State Opera, and soon thereafter he was made general music director of the Dresden State Orchestra. In 1952 he took over the post of music director of the Munich State Opera. He extended his reputation at the same time with guest appearances in Vienna, Berlin, Barcelona, and Buenos Aires. He distinguished himself particularly in the operas of Richard Strauss and has since become recognized as one of the leading interpreters of Strauss. On his first visit to London, in 1953, he conducted Strauss's *Arabella* and *Die Liebe der Danae*. His success in these brought an invitation to return to London a few weeks later to conduct both *Salome* and *Elektra* at Covent Garden. One year later he was acclaimed in London for his performances of *Der Rosenkavalier*.

Immediately after the summer music festival

season of 1954 Kempe resigned as music director in Munich. He divided his activities among Covent Garden, the Vienna State Opera, and the Metropolitan Opera in New York. His Metropolitan Opera debut took place on January 26, 1955, in the Dresden version of *Tannhäuser.* "Yesterday's musical interpretation," remarked Francis D. Perkins in the *Herald Tribune,* "implied that he is a musician of experience and discernment. Musical proportion was a notable point." Douglas Watt said in the *Daily News:* "From the start of the overture it was evident that Kempe knew exactly what he wanted, possessed the means to get it, and exercised fine control. He conducted with fire and balance.... His was an impressive achievement."

That first season in New York Kempe also conducted *Tristan and Isolde* and on February 10 the American premiere of *Arabella.* Discussing Kempe's performance of the Strauss opera, Louis Biancolli wrote in the *World-Telegram and Sun:* "He showed a devotion and dedication to the task in hand that bespoke the true man of the theater." In his second and concluding season at the Metropolitan, Kempe conducted *Die Meistersinger* and *Der Rosenkavalier.*

In the spring of 1955 Kempe was acclaimed at Covent Garden for his performances of two operas of the Wagner *Ring* cycle and the following summer for his performance of Pfitzner's *Palestrina.* He made his first appearances at the Bayreuth Festival to lead the *Ring* cycle in 1960; and on numerous occasions after that he returned to Bayreuth. He was also active for a number of years at the Salzburg and Edinburgh festivals. Appearances at La Scala in Milan and extensive tours of Australia and South America added further to his prestige.

Kempe was appointed principal conductor of the Royal Philharmonic Orchestra of London in 1963, and in 1970 he was elevated to the post of artistic director, a lifetime appointment. As the head of the Royal Philharmonic he was heard in Carnegie Hall in New York on October 23, 1972. Harriet Johnson, writing in the New York *Post,* called him "one of the world's most sensitive and knowing maestros." In 1963 he was also made the principal conductor of the Tonhalle Orchestra in Zurich, but he resigned four years later to assume the post of general music director of the Munich Philharmonic. In spite of his lifetime appointment with the London Royal Philharmonic Orchestra, Kempe withdrew in

1975 to become the principal conductor of the BBC Symphony in London in September of that year, succeeding Pierre Boulez.

For many years Kempe made his home in Bavaria, at Dürnbach, Tegernsee. His wife was the former Elisabeth Lindermeier, whom he married in 1957; they had four daughters.

He received many honors, among them the Artibus et Litteris medal from Sweden, the Bayerischer Verdienstorden from Bavaria, and the Nägeli medal from Zurich.

Rudolf Kempe died in a hospital in Zurich, on May 12, 1976, following abdominal surgery.

His last record release was a complete set of Beethoven's symphonies with the Munich Philharmonic. Among his previous recordings were the complete versions of both *Lohengrin* and *Die Meistersinger.*

ABOUT: Jaeckel, H. and Schmiedel, G. Bildnis des schaffenden Künstlers.

Wilhelm Kempff

1895–

Wilhelm Walter Friedrich Kempff, pianist, was born in Jüterbog, Germany, on November 25, 1895. His father, also named Wilhelm, was a trained pianist who gave the younger Wilhelm his first piano lessons. Exceptionally precocious in music, Wilhelm at nine was able to perform Bach fugues and to transpose them to any given key. He later studied piano with Heinrich Barth, a pupil of Hans von Bülow, who gave him a solid training in the classical traditions of which Kempff was ultimately to become a master. He also studied composition in Berlin with Robert Kahn. In 1917 he received the Mendelssohn Prize for piano playing.

He began his concert career as a pianist in 1924 with a tour of Germany and Scandinavia. From the very first he drew attention to his sound interpretations of the music of the German classic and Romantic masters. He also distinguished himself for his spontaneous improvisations and these became the *tour de force* of many of his concerts. Even then Kempff belonged to what Harold C. Schonberg, in *The Great Pianists,* called a school of German pian-

Kempff: kěmpf

WILHELM KEMPFF

ism dominated by Artur Schnabel and including Wilhelm Backhaus and Rudolf Serkin. "This school," writes Schonberg, "has its roots and alliances in the German and Austrian repertoire from Bach through Brahms. The German school of piano playing is one of scrupulous musicianship, severity, strength rather than charm, solidity rather than sensuosity, intellect rather than instinct, sobriety rather than brilliance. It is a school that stresses planning and leaves nothing to chance." By World War II Kempff was recognized throughout Europe as one of the foremost living interpreters of Beethoven's sonatas, as well as a master in the piano literature of Bach, Mozart, Schubert, Schumann, and Brahms.

From 1924 to 1930 Kempff taught piano at the High School for Music in Stuttgart. After that he lived for a number of years in Potsdam before moving to Thurnau near Kulmbach in 1944. After World War II he continued to tour widely in recitals and as a guest artist with orchestras, though without going to the United States. For many years America knew him exclusively through his recordings of all of Beethoven's sonatas, major Mozart concertos, and other works by Mozart, Schumann, and Brahms.

In his sixty-ninth year Kempff finally made his American debut on October 13, 1964, with a recital in Carnegie Hall. Two days later he gave a second recital there. Critics noted imperfections in his technique, but they also found these defects inconsequential in the face of a "sane, orderly, deeply introspective involvement . . . touching in its restraint, cleansing in its serenity," in the words of a critic for *Musical America*. Another critic for *Musical America* found the performance of Brahms's Sonata in F minor at the second concert "one of the most Herculean piano performances within memory. The nobility and breadth of line Kempff brought to the music illuminated the massive architectural structure of the piece."

Since his first appearance in the United States, Kempff has recorded all the piano sonatas of Schubert in a single album and, with Pierre Fournier, all of Beethoven's works for cello and piano.

"Kempff has not squandered or lost a single nuance of the mastery he acquired early in his career," wrote Walter Deppisch in the program album accompanying the recording of the Schubert sonatas. "His style has undergone changes in some respects, but his playing . . . has lost none of the splendor, the poetry and the verve with which he enthralled his audiences long ago."

Kempff is the composer of numerous works, among them four operas (the two best known are *König Midas* and *Die Familie Gozzi*), four symphonies, concertos for piano and for violin, ballets, string quartets, a dramatic cantata *(Deutsches Schicksal)*, and pieces for solo piano. He is the author of an autobiography, *Unter dem Zimbelsterm* (1951), which was translated into English as *Under the Star of the Cymbal*.

Since 1955 Kempff has made his home in Ammerland, Oberbayern, on Starnberger See. He has received the Artibus et Litteris medal from Sweden and in 1973 was awarded the Grosses Bundesverdienstkreuz by Germany. He is a member of the Prussian Academy of Arts.

ABOUT: Gavoty, B. and Hauert, R. Wilhelm Kempff; Kempff, W. Under the Star of the Cymbal; Schonberg, H. C., The Great Pianists. *Periodicals*—Hi-Fi, June 1971; Musical America, October 1964.

István Kertész

1929–1973

István Kertész, conductor, son of Miklos and Margot Kertész, was born in Budapest on August 28, 1929. "When I was six," he told Stephen E. Rubin in an interview for *High Fidelity*, "and

ISTVÁN KERTÉSZ

started music, it was 1935 and cruel things were going on in Europe. I was affected, of course, by Nazi Germany. But whatever happened in my private life, I found my 'exile' in music, practicing the piano, the fiddle, and writing little compositions. This separated me from the problems of the world, and gave me a feeling that my real home is music."

Since one of his friends ran a concert bureau, he was provided with tickets for concerts and operas which even in his early years he attended almost nightly. "I remember that I felt I must be a conductor. . . . I asked all my teachers, 'How can I become a conductor?' 'Just practice the piano and the violin,' they said, 'read scores and go to concerts.' "

After completing high school in his sixteenth year, he entered the Academy of Music in Budapest, studying violin and composition the first year, and beginning courses in conducting in his second; among his teachers were Zoltán Kodály and Leo Weiner. It was not long before he gave up his studies of violin and composition to concentrate on conducting. Upon graduation from the Academy in 1953 he was appointed principal conductor of the Györ Philharmonic in western Hungary. After two years he returned to Budapest; there for two years more he served as one of the conductors of the Budapest Opera.

In 1957 Kertész settled permanently in Germany, and he subsequently became a citizen. He left Germany temporarily in 1958 to study conducting further with Fernando Previtali at the Santa Cecilia Academy, where he received a master's degree in conducting with highest honors *(Prèmio d'arti).*

His conducting career advanced sharply in 1958 when he was made director of the Augsburg Opera; he remained there five years. Engagements with other opera houses and orchestras in major German cities, his performance of Prokofiev's *The Flaming Angel* at the Spoleto Festival in 1960, and his first recordings for London records also in 1960, all combined to extend his fame throughout Europe. In 1961 he made his debut at the Salzburg Festival and made his first appearances in the United States as a guest conductor of the Detroit Symphony. In 1962–1963 he toured the United States with the visiting Norddeutsche Rundfunk Orchestra.

In 1964 he signed a ten-year contract as music director of the Cologne Opera; the contract was later extended to 1979. Before the end of his first contract he was also made director of the Gürzenich Orchestra, the resident symphonic ensemble of the Cologne Opera. He lived in a suburb of Cologne with his wife, the former Edith Gabry, a soprano he met when both were students at the Academy of Music in Budapest and whom he married on September 10, 1951, and their three children.

While holding down his post in Cologne, Kertész became principal conductor of the London Symphony Orchestra in April 1965, succeeding the deceased Pierre Monteux. He made his New York debut with this orchestra in 1966 in Carnegie Hall during the orchestra's second world tour. (The orchestra's first world tour, also under Kertész, had taken place during its diamond jubilee in 1964.) He resigned from the London Symphony after three years because he was impatient with his involvement in orchestral politics.

Kertész became a familiar face and his music a familiar sound in the American concert hall, since he was often called upon to serve as a guest conductor of American orchestras. His only permanent appointment in the United States was as principal conductor of the annual Ravinia festival in Chicago. When George Szell died in 1970, the members of the Cleveland Orchestra voted 96 to 2 to ask the board to favor Kertész as Szell's replacement. But the board ignored this request and selected Lorin Maazel.

In a wide repertory Kertész proved to be a conductor who continually brought drama and excitement to the podium with his intense and

high-pressured performances, always characterized by a lustrous sound and vivid contrasts.
"The sound I strive for is warm," he told Rubin,
"not *gemütlich,* but warm. Bring out, perhaps
more than necessary, the basses and cellos . . .
letting them play with a long bow, smooth and
with majesty, grandiosity, and not using a general dynamic. I make contrasts. If there is written
a true forte, it must be a true forte. This is what
I do most at rehearsals. I ask that every dynamic, every kind of characteristic, must be over-
done. Either it's fortissimo or pianissimo. Either
it's legato or staccato. This must be very clear,
even to the last row. By this kind of almost-
exaggeration the orchestra sounds alive. . . . Certainly colors improve."

His fame was worldwide. During his career,
aborted so tragically when he was only forty-
three, he led about ninety of the world's most
distinguished symphony orchestras in addition
to appearing in virtually all of Europe's opera
houses and at Europe's major festivals. He also
made over fifty recordings, including all the
symphonies of Schubert, Dvořák, and Brahms.
His recording of Bartók's music received the
Grand Prix du Disque in Paris in 1967, and an
album of Mozart's music was awarded the Edison Prize in Holland. In 1966 he earned the
Arnold Bax medal for his services to music.

For many years Kertész toured Israel as a
guest conductor of the Israel Philharmonic. He
returned to Israel for that purpose in 1973. He
was swimming in the Mediterranean off Her-
zliya on April 16, 1973, when he was caught in
a treacherous current and pulled out to sea. His
body was later recovered.

ABOUT: High Fidelity/Musical America, December
1969; Stereo Review, May 1973.

Jan Kiepura

1902–1966

Jan Wiktor Kiepura, tenor, was born in Sos-
nowiec, in southeast Poland, on May 16, 1902.
His mother, Maria Nalman Kiepura, sang
professionally when she was young, and his father, Franciszek, who owned a grocery store,
was an amateur tenor. Though both instilled a

Kiepura: kyĕ pōōr′ ä

JAN KIEPURA

love of music in Jan from childhood on, he confessed that he was a Pole before he was a singer.
In 1917–1918, while still a schoolboy, he became
a member of the PAV, a secret Polish military
organization. In 1920 he fought with Polish
volunteers against the Germans in Upper Silesia.

He had planned a law career and was graduated from the law school of the University of
Warsaw, where he was a member of the glee
club. Only after graduation did he reject law for
music. He studied voice with Tadeusz Leliwa
and W. Brzeziński in Warsaw, and for a time he
earned his living singing excerpts from Italian
opera in Polish movie theaters. In 1923 he gave
his first public recital. Soon after that the Warsaw Opera hired him for two and a half dollars
a night to appear in a ten-word role for three
nights. Then he toured with small companies in
small operatic parts.

He was substituting for an ill singer in the title
role of *Faust* in Lemberg (Lwow) when he was
heard by a scout for the Warsaw Opera. And so,
in 1925, he made his official debut as an opera
singer, appearing once again as Faust, this time
with the Warsaw Opera. His performances with
that company inspired the Warsaw critics to refer to him as "the Polish Caruso" and led to an
engagement with the Vienna State Opera. There
he made his debut as Cavaradossi in *Tosca* opposite Maria Jeritza in September 1926. He remained with the Vienna Opera until 1928,
enjoying further successes in the principal tenor
roles in *Turandot* (at its Viennese premiere) and

in Erich Wolfgang Korngold's *Die Wunder der Heliane* among other operas.

Other appearances in the French and Italian repertory took place at the Opéra-Comique in Paris, the Berlin State Opera, and La Scala in Milan. In November 1931 he made his American debut with the Chicago Civic Opera as Cavaradossi, receiving fifteen calls after the final curtain.

Kiepura made his first appearance in motion pictures in 1932 in *City of Song,* a Viennese production. His first film success came one year later in the American film *Be Mine Tonight,* which shattered a six-year attendance record in a major motion picture house in Los Angeles. During the 1930s he continued to star in films: *A Song for You* (1933), *Farewell to Love* (1933), *Give Us This Night* (1936), *Thank You, Madame* (1937), and *The Charm of La Bohème* (1938). His last motion picture, *Her Wonderful Lie,* was released in 1950.

Kiepura's debut at the Metropolitan Opera in New York took place on February 10, 1938, as Rodolfo in *La Bohème.* "Here was a Rodolfo with youth, exuberance and fervor," wrote Noel Strauss in the New York *Times,* "capped by a magnetic personality which somehow managed to give new life to the whole proceedings on the stage. It was these elements in his electrifying portrayal rather than any outstanding abilities as an actor or vocalist that counted most saliently in his victory. The voice by nature is one of unusually pure quality and evenness. At its best it possessed warmth, sensitiveness of color, and emotional urge."

Kiepura remained with the Metropolitan Opera company through the 1938–1939 season and returned for one additional season in 1941–1942, adding to his Metropolitan Opera repertory the roles of Don José in *Carmen,* Duke of Mantua in *Rigoletto,* Des Grieux in *Manon,* and Cavaradossi.

When the Nazi armies invaded Poland on September 1, 1939, Kiepura was in France working in a motion picture. He abandoned this assignment to join the Polish Legion then being formed in Paris. His government, however, urged him to abandon his uniform after the fall of Warsaw, and to continue his artistic work by singing for war workers on the German-French frontier and raising funds in the United States for Polish, British, and Russian relief.

Before sailing for the United States in 1939,

Kiepura appeared in Paris in a concert for the benefit of aged musicians. His co-artist was a soprano, Marta Eggerth, whom he had married on October 31, 1936. This concert in 1939 was Eggerth's first public appearance as a singer, and the first of many performances in which she would appear with her husband not only in concerts but also in performances of operas and operettas.

After World War II Kiepura lived in New York City. On August 4, 1943, he was costarred with his wife in a revival of Lehár's operetta *The Merry Widow* at the Majestic Theater in New York. It ran on Broadway for about a year before touring the United States for one year more.

In 1959 Kiepura returned to his native country for the first time in nineteen years to give performances in Warsaw.

To the end of his days Kiepura insisted on living in a grand baronial style. His favorite pastimes were horseback riding, tennis, and swimming. He died of a heart attack in Rye, New York, on August 15, 1966. In fulfillment of a stipulation in his will, he was buried in Poland, his funeral there attended by over one hundred thousand people. His son, also named Jan Kiepura, became a concert singer.

Kiepura was the recipient of many honors and awards. France conferred on him the ribbon of the Legion of Honor. From his native Poland he received the decoration of the Order of Polonia Restituta and the Croix de Mérite; from Sweden, the Order of the North Star; from Belgium, the Order of Leopold I. Poland also made the house of his birth a national landmark—a museum containing a detailed record of his career.

ABOUT: Waldorff, J. Jan Kiepura. *Periodicals*—Opera News, February 14, 1938, October 16, 1939.

Hans Kindler

1892–1949

Hans Kindler, cellist and conductor, was born in Rotterdam, on January 8, 1892. He was of Russian-Polish nobility and counted among the members of his family the Countess Evelina Hanska, who is reputed to have been an inspir-

Kindler: kĭn′ dlĕr

HANS KINDLER

ing influence in the life of Honoré de Balzac. Both of his parents were musical: Hans's father, Carel, played the oboe and English horn, and his mother, Jeanette Hanken Kindler, was a pianist. His sister Frieda became a concert pianist and the wife of the eminent Dutch-born composer and critic Bernard van Dieren.

Hans attended the Rotterdam Conservatory. There, in his fourteenth year, he won first prizes for piano and cello. Three years earlier he had made his first public appearance as a cellist in Rotterdam. His later study of the cello took place privately with Pablo Casals and Jean Gérardy.

When he was eighteen, Hans appeared as a solo cellist with the Berlin Philharmonic Orchestra, his offical concert debut. A year later he was appointed professor of the cello at the Klindworth-Scharwenka Conservatory. At the same time he served as first cellist of the Charlottenburg Opera orchestra in Berlin. On one occasion he was invited to make a command appearance before the Queen of Holland.

He made his first tour of Europe as a cello virtuoso in 1912–1913, in recitals, as guest performer with orchestras, and in joint concerts with such European musicians as Julia Culp, Ferruccio Busoni, and Arnold Schoenberg.

In 1914 he went to the United States, planning at that time only a brief visit. But the outbreak of World War I in Europe compelled him to extend his American stay permanently; in 1921 he became an American citizen. Until 1920 he

retained the post of first cellist with the Philadelphia Orchestra.

By 1920 the demand for his solo appearances had grown so great that he had to withdraw completely from the Philadelphia Orchestra. For the next decade he toured the United States extensively. "I do not expect in my life to hear the duplicates of an Elman or a Kreisler, a Casals or a Hans Kindler," wrote James Gibbons Huneker after one of Kindler's recitals.

In 1922 Kindler returned to Europe for the first time in eight years, performing with orchestras and appearing in recitals in London, Paris, Vienna, Amsterdam, Prague, and Rome. His success in London was such that a critic for the *Daily Telegraph* spoke of him as "the Kreisler of the violoncello."

In his recitals Kindler not only presented the masterworks of cello literature but also proved a propagandist for modern music. He introduced Ernest Bloch's *Schelomo* on May 3, 1917, and at other appearances he performed compositions by Schoenberg, Casella, Ravel, Malipiero, Pizzetti, and Leo Ornstein, many dedicated to him.

In 1927 Kindler was invited to conduct a special series of orchestral concerts in Philadelphia. He made such a favorable impression that he was invited a short time later to conduct a series of concerts of contemporary music in many of Europe's leading cities. On April 27, 1928, he conducted the world premiere of Stravinsky's ballet *Apollon Musagètes* in Washington, D.C.

At the height of his career as a solo cellist Kindler decided to abandon his concert tours so that he might establish a symphony orchestra in Washington. (He made his last tour as a virtuoso in 1929–1930, giving one hundred and ten concerts.) Though the United States was then in an economic depression, Kindler exerted a supreme effort in creating an interest in and acquiring the funds for a permanent symphonic organization in the nation's capital. He succeeded in interesting several guarantors, and in 1931 the National Symphony Orchestra entered upon its first season with Hans Kindler as conductor. The orchestra proved such a success that at the end of its first season its backers received 31 percent of their original investment. In 1938 the orchestra expanded its schedule of concerts not only in Washington, D.C., but also on its tours throughout the United States; in a nine-year period, the orchestra was heard in 263 concerts in 94 cities.

After an appearance in Boston the orchestra was said by the critic of the *Transcript* to be "in sonority, technical facility and the various essential virtues . . . approaching the standards of the best symphony orchestras in the world." While catering to the conservative musical tastes of his audiences in Washington, D.C., through the presentation of the more familiar classics, Kindler did not neglect the moderns. His programs were continually spiced with new works by such twentieth century composers as Charles Martin Loeffler, Respighi, and Malipiero.

During his nineteen years as principal conductor of the National Symphony Orchestra, Kindler made numerous guest appearances with major orchestras in the United States, Latin America, and Europe. After a performance with the Philadelphia Orchestra, the critic of the *Record* said: "Kindler sounds more like a Mozart conductor than any of his competitors heard in the Academy of Music these many seasons." In Amsterdam, Holland, a local critic wrote that Kindler was "like Mengelberg and Toscanini and other 'perfectionists' in one line or another."

Kindler was awarded the Elizabeth Sprague Coolidge medal in 1939 for "eminent services in the field of chamber music." That same year his name was inscribed on a panel at the World's Fair in New York as one of the Americans of foreign birth who made vital contributions to American culture. Queen Wilhelmina presented him with the Officer's Degree, Order of Orange-Nassau, the highest award Holland could give him.

Kindler resigned from the National Symphony Orchestra on November 30, 1948, going into total retirement at Watch Hill in Rhode Island with his wife, the former Alice Riddle, whom he had married in 1920. He died there on August 30, 1949. The Kindlers had three children. For relaxation Kindler enjoyed reading or wandering through the countryside with a rifle under his arm.

ABOUT: Ewen, D. Dictators of the Baton. *Periodicals* —Knickerbocker Weekly, March 29, 1943.

James King

1925–

James Ambros King, tenor, was born in Dodge City, Kansas, to Howard Willis and Hettie King on May 22, 1925. At nine he began study of the piano and violin, and he took his first singing lessons while attending high school. During World War II he served in the United States Naval Reserve. Released from service in 1945, he continued his music study at Louisiana State University where he studied voice with D. Draper and received his Bachelor of Music degree in 1950. He earned his master's degree in music from the University of Kansas in 1952. Then he went to New York to complete his vocal studies with Martial Singher, Ralph Errolle, Max Lorenz, Oren Brown, and William Hughes.

In 1960 King won the American Opera Auditions in Cincinnati which brought him engagements at the Teatro della Pergola in Florence. He made his opera debut at the Teatro Nuovo in Milan. He then auditioned successfully at the Deutsche Oper in Berlin. Within a few years he had become one of the company's leading dramatic tenors. His success there brought him his first engagement at the Salzburg Festival as Achille in Gluck's *Iphigénie en Aulide,* conducted by Karl Böhm. When the National Theater in Munich was rebuilt and reopened in November 1963, King was invited to sing the role of the Emperor in Strauss's *Die Frau ohne Schatten.* He further distinguished himself as a performer of other Strauss operas at the Salzburg Festival.

King's opera debut in the United States took place in 1961 with the San Francisco Opera as Don José in *Carmen.* His debut at the Metropolitan Opera in New York came on January 8, 1966, as Florestan in *Fidelio.* "King arrived unheralded," wrote Harriet Johnson in the New York *Post,* "but from the sound of things he will not remain so. . . . King has a magnificent rich tenor voice, beautiful in quality and easy in production. Such a challenging debut brought with it at some points a tentativeness, but the collective nugget shone through: sensitive artistry, musicianship, imposing stage presence, histrionic conviction, and above all, a voice of remarkable sheen."

As a principal dramatic tenor of the Metropolitan Opera, he appeared successfully in

JAMES KING

new Metropolitan Opera productions of *Die Frau ohne Schatten* as the Emperor, *Elektra* as Aegisthus, and *Lohengrin* in the title role, as well as in *Turandot* (Calaf), *Die Meistersinger* (Walther), *Die Walküre* (Siegmund), *Ariadne auf Naxos* (Bacchus), *Tosca* (Cavaradossi), *The Flying Dutchman* (Erik), and *Carmen* (Don José).

In Europe he sang in the premiere of *Die Frau ohne Schatten* at Covent Garden in London, at the Bayreuth Festival as Siegmund and Parsifal, and at the Salzburg Festival as Florestan. His other roles include Canio in *I Pagliacci*, Turiddu in *Cavalleria Rusticana*, Radames in *Aida*, Manrico in *Il Trovatore*, Des Grieux in *Manon Lescaut*, the title role in *Don Carlo*, Apollo in Strauss's *Daphne*, and the Singer in *Der Rosenkavalier*. In 1976 he was named *Kammersänger* by the Bavarian government. He has recorded *Daphne* for Deutsche Grammophon and *Die Walküre* for London. In films for television distribution he has appeared in *Daphne, Don Carlo*, and *Fidelio*.

King's appearances in opera have been with the major companies of America, Europe, and South America. He has been a resident member of the Vienna State Opera and the Bayerische Staatsoper, Munich. He has also been a frequent guest artist with symphony orchestras, with whom he performed Tristan in the second act of *Tristan and Isolde* in a concert presentation by the Boston Symphony under William Steinberg and Siegfried in the third act of *Die Götterdämmerung* under Georg Solti in Paris.

He married actress Marie-Luise Nagel on November 5, 1964; it was his second marriage. With their five children the Kings make their permanent home in a suburb of Munich.

In an interview with Speight Jenkins in *Opera News* King disclosed his schedule before a performance: "I stay in bed until about eleven in the morning, when I eat a big breakfast and go for a walk. . . . When I come back home I turn off the telephone, refuse to open telegrams or letters, don't look at television. I must have a song concentration." Lunch takes place about three o'clock. "Food is a horrible problem. I like to have at least four hours between a meal and a performance, and by ten at night I'm sure to be hungry. Should I eat and risk indigestion, or not eat and feel my strength flagging?" Jenkins then goes on to add: "The tenor prepares his voice for the evening after he eats his lunch. He begins to sing quietly to loosen up his throat. 'I treat my voice carefully; it tells me when it's ready. Of course sometimes I don't get the right message, and I go onstage needing another fifteen minutes of work.' "

ABOUT: Opera News, January 15, 1972.

Alexander Kipnis

1891–1978

Alexander Kipnis, basso, was born in the village of Zhitomir, in the Russian Ukraine, on February 1, 1891. "No one in my own family either played or sang," he told James Drake and Joseph Temesta in an interview for *High Fidelity*. "Once in a while I can remember my mother singing as she would be working around the house, and later on I was astonished to recognize what she sang was 'La donna è mobile' or Schubert's *Serenade*. Where she heard them I don't know. My father made his living by selling heavy fabrics for winter coats, and he too neither played nor sang. He died very young—I was only twelve when he died—but he was a very learned man, although music was not a part of his background." Alexander's first musical influence was the music of Russian peasants. "I would hear their songs at twilight when they would play and sing for themselves, and by the

---

Kipnis: kyĭp nyēs′ *or* kĭp′ nĭs

ALEXANDER KIPNIS

time I was four or five years old I had learned most of their songs."

He began music study not because he had any ambition to become a professional but for a very practical reason. Anticipating military service which was required of all Russians, he decided to study a brass and a string instrument so that upon being drafted he might receive the rank of officer. The specific instruments he chose were the trombone and the double bass. Later on, when he attended the Warsaw Conservatory, he specialized in conducting and was graduated in 1912 as a conductor, with honors and with a special award of a handsome gold watch on which was engraved the Czar's eagle crest inlaid with precious gems. Soon after his graduation he served in the army as a military bandmaster.

During his years in the Warsaw Conservatory he sang in the school chorus. One day the chorus master told him he had a voice that deserved training. This led him to take some voice lessons from an Italian teacher at the Conservatory. His involvement in singing sent him to the opera house to hear every opera for which he could gain admission.

After leaving military service, Kipnis decided to specialize in singing. To develop himself further in this area he decided to go either to Austria or to Germany. With all his possessions in a suitcase, he stood on the railroad station in Warsaw wondering which of these two capitals should become his destination. While he was trying to reach a decision an express train for Berlin rolled in and Kipnis allowed fate to de-

cide for him. In Berlin he studied voice with Ernst Grenzebach at the Klindworth-Scharwenka Conservatory.

While he was engaged in voice study, World War I erupted in Europe. Because he was a Russian Kipnis was arrested. A few days later a German colonel, who was a musician, heard him singing and suggested he perform for his brother, an impresario who headed the Hamburg Opera. Kipnis auditioned for the impresario while he was still in prison, and he was engaged for the Hamburg Opera where he made his debut in 1916.

Though he was under police surveillance in Hamburg, he was free to pursue his art and career. Between 1916 and 1919 he became a member of the Wiesbaden Opera. Still under police guard, he had to be confined to a hospital center whenever he was not making public appearances. It was during this period of enforced seclusion that Kipnis was able to build up his imposing operatic and song repertory. Among his principal operatic roles during these apprentice years were Titurel and Gurnemanz in *Parsifal* (both of which he sang at the Bayreuth Festival and at the Wiesbaden Opera), Colline in *La Bohème,* Kezal in *The Bartered Bride,* Sparafucile and Monterone in *Rigoletto,* Ramfis in *Aida,* Bartolo in *The Marriage of Figaro,* and Ferrando in *Il Trovatore.*

At the end of World War I Kipnis's fame was established in Germany as a member of the Charlottenburg Opera in Berlin which he joined in 1919 and with which he remained affiliated until 1930; he was also known in other European countries and in Scandinavia. In 1923 he went to the United States for the first time as a member of the visiting German Opera Company. His first American appearance was at the Manhattan Opera House in New York on February 12, 1923, as Pogner in *Die Meistersinger.* He was immediately engaged by the Chicago Civic Opera Company and remained there nine years, appearing in principal basso roles in the French, Italian, and German repertory. During these years he became an American citizen, and on April 7, 1925, he married Mildred Levy, the daughter of Heniot Levy, American concert pianist and associate director of the American Conservatory in Chicago. They had one child, a son, Igor, who achieved worldwide recognition as a harpsichordist.

Kipnis was acclaimed in the United States not

only for his operatic performances but also for his song recitals. "Kipnis," wrote a critic for the New York *Times,* "is not only one of the greatest contemporary operatic basses but also one of the foremost living masters of the *Lied.* " Mary Garden considered Kipnis the greatest male interpreter of Debussy's song literature.

He made guest appearances in most of Europe's opera houses including La Scala in Milan, Covent Garden in London, the Paris Opéra, the Vienna State Opera, and the Munich Opera. He was also a frequent participant at the Bayreuth Festival, the last time being in the summer of 1933. In 1932 he was heard for the first time at the Salzburg Festival, to which he returned for the next five years, making appearances, among other performances, as Sarastro in *The Magic Flute* with Toscanini conducting. In 1936 he appeared at the Glyndebourne Festival in England.

After leaving the Chicago Civic Opera he became the principal basso of the Berlin State Opera. He was heard there in a richly varied repertory from 1932 to 1935. In 1937 he returned to the United States as a member of the Wagnerian Festival that toured the country. Between 1938 and 1939 he once again toured the United States, this time as a recitalist.

After the rise of the Nazi regime in Germany, Kipnis transferred his principal operatic activity from Berlin to the Vienna State Opera where he had previously been heard solely in random guest appearances. Here his principal operatic characterizations were lavishly praised, particularly those of Baron Ochs in *Der Rosenkavalier,* Boris Godunov, Sarastro, Leporello in *Don Giovanni,* and Gurnemanz. Gurnemanz and Boris Godunov became recognized as his two most celebrated roles, a consensus in which Kipnis himself joined.

Such was Kipnis's popularity in Vienna that during the winter of 1937–1938 he sold out the large concert hall in Vienna for two recitals, at each of which he was compelled to repeat every number of the program because of the vociferous audience reaction.

He was en route to Australia early in 1938 when he heard that Austria had been annexed to Nazi Germany. Being an American citizen, Kipnis could have continued his activities both in Vienna and Salzburg, but he refused to have any part of the Nazi regime. He decided to make the United States his permanent residence.

On January 5, 1940, he made his debut at the Metropolitan Opera as Gurnemanz. "Mr. Kipnis," wrote Olin Downes in the New York *Times,* "immediately won the favor of his audience. He invested the role with the utmost significance. The richness of the voice made one of several fine attributes of the singer and the dramatic interpreter. The text was admirably delivered; the treatment of the melodic line was that of a true musician. The character developed with noble consistency."

During his six-year stay at the Metropolitan Opera, Kipnis further endeared himself to critics and the public with his performances as Baron Ochs, King Mark in *Tristan and Isolde,* Hermann in *Tannhäuser,* Hagen in *Die Götterdämmerung,* Arkel in *Pelléas and Mélisande,* Fasolt in *Das Rheingold,* Rocco in *Fidelio,* Hunding in *Die Walküre,* Nilakantha in *Lakmé,* Leporello, Sarastro, and most of all as Boris Godunov. His first New York appearance in the title role of Mussorgsky's opera took place on February 13, 1943. At that time Howard Taubman wrote in the New York *Times:* "Mr. Kipnis was a regal Boris in song and action. . . . Like his great Russian predecessor, Feodor Chaliapin, Mr. Kipnis sang Boris in the original language while the rest of the Metropolitan ensemble sang Italian. . . . Mr. Kipnis' portrayal was one of the best in his gallery of fine characterizations."

He made his last appearance at the Metropolitan Opera on April 19, 1946, in the same role with which he made his debut—Gurnemanz.

Kipnis was one of the most widely recorded singers of his time. His first records were made and released by German Odeon just after World War I. Afterwards he recorded the principal arias from virtually all of his principal roles and the library of vocal literature from Mozart through Richard Strauss. He was featured in the Bayreuth Festival recordings issued by Columbia. In 1928 he was chosen to record Schubert's songs in the memorial printings released by Columbia to honor the composer on the centenary of his death. Kipnis recorded the *Lieder* of Hugo Wolf in a special Society issue, and in 1937 he was selected by the Brahms Song Society for the first volume of their special recording. He regarded his recording of these Brahms songs, his release for the Hugo Wolf Society, and his reproduction of the music from Boris Godunov as his finest.

For many years Kipnis gave master classes in

voice at the Juilliard School of Music, the New York College of Music, and the Berkshire Music Center in Tanglewood.

He made his home in Westport, Connecticut, where he led a simple and secluded existence. As he once said, he could "be content with some nice walks and some good movies." He was a real camera fan; he and his cameras were inseparable companions. Sometimes he enjoyed cooking.

In an interview Kipnis described the routine he followed rigorously when he was making public appearances: "After eating lunch I would usually lie down for a time, sleeping for perhaps an hour or so. Then I would go for a long walk, possibly two miles. Later I would have one or two cups of tea and two pieces of dry toast. Then, about an hour before performance, I would be in my dressing room putting on make-up and getting into costume, vocalizing a little bit for myself, always starting lightly, and then slowly, gradually, I would be in full voice. Then I was ready."

Alexander Kipnis died on May 14, 1978, at a convalescent home in Westport, Connecticut.

ABOUT: High Fidelity, March 1976.

Igor Kipnis

1930–

Igor Kipnis, harpsichordist, was born in Berlin on September 27, 1930. He was the only child of the basso Alexander Kipnis and his wife Mildred Levy. Igor's maternal grandfather was Heniot Levy, a professional pianist and associate director of the American Conservatory in Chicago.

It was inevitable in a household as musical as that of the Kipnises that Igor be directed to music early. He told an interviewer: "Music was always a part of my life, but I really had no intention of making a career of it, except possibly in a peripheral way—maybe in radio or television programming." When Igor was eight his family settled permanently in the United States, establishing residence in Westport, Connecticut. Igor received piano instruction from his grandfather. From 1941 to 1948 he attended

Kipnis: kǐp′ nǐs

IGOR KIPNIS

the Westport School of Music, specializing in piano. In the late 1940s he served as piano accompanist for his father and his father's pupils. He explains how this chore affected his musical development: "This forced me to think about music in a vocal way. If I can be said to have any single approach to the harpsichord, it is this: Properly played, the instrument should *sing*."

In 1948 Igor matriculated at Harvard College. It was during his college years that he first became fascinated with Baroque music and with the harpsichord, influenced by Randall Thompson, a member of the Harvard music faculty, and Thompson's course on Handel. Other influences in Kipnis's growth as a harpsichord performer and as an outstanding authority on Baroque music came in later years from Melville Smith, Boston organist and harpsichordist, and from the British musicologist and harpsichordist Thurston Dart. A few lessons from Fernando Valenti were all the formal instruction Kipnis ever received on the harpsichord.

Upon graduation from Harvard with a Bachelor of Arts degree in 1952, Kipnis served for two years in the United States Army, during the Korean War, as an instructor of signal communications. After leaving the army, he supported himself by holding down a variety of jobs. He was a book salesman for Doubleday. He helped to select the top forty popular hit songs for radio station WMCA in New York. He served as art and editorial director for Westminster Records.

It was while he was employed at Westminster that he acquired his first harpsichord, which originally served solely to provide him with musical pleasure. Then, in 1959, still as an employee at Westminster, he made his debut as a harpsichord virtuoso with a performance over New York City's radio station, WNYC. Appearances with a number of ensembles, both as a soloist and as a continuo player, finally led to his first recital which took place at the Historical Society in New York City in 1961. "How can you make a career out of an ancient relic?" his father asked him. Igor Kipnis proceeded to prove that he could do just that by undertaking his first tour of the United States and Canada in 1962 and in 1964 making his first recordings. The first of several European tours (for which he received grants from the Martha Baird Rockefeller Fund for Music) took place in 1967. This was followed by his first tour of South America in 1968, Israel in 1969, and Australia in 1971. Meanwhile, during the summers of 1964 through 1967 he taught Baroque performance at the Berkshire Music Center in Lenox, Massachusetts, becoming chairman of the Baroque department for the years between 1965 and 1967. In 1968 he was appointed affiliate member of the music faculty at Temple University. For two years, beginning with 1966, he was the host of a weekly radio program over WQXR in New York called *Age of Baroque.*

In his recitals and appearances with chamber-music ensembles or symphony orchestras, as well as in his recordings, Kipnis has become recognized as one of the important harpsichordists of his time. To his performances he brings the wealth of scholarship he has accumulated through many years of intensive research into Renaissance and Baroque music and a musical style which William Bender has described in *Time* as combining "formal restraint, interpretative flair, and sheer energy." After one of Kipnis's recitals in New York City, John Rockwell wrote in the New York *Times:* "In matters musicological and musical, Mr. Kipnis is enlightened style incarnate. What is perhaps most winning about his harpsichord playing is the way he erases the line between musicology and musicality. He need bow to no one in the intelligence and scrupulousness with which he approaches the varied stylistic requirements of the Renaissance, Baroque and classical music he plays. But he manages to do so in a way that never sounds fussy or pedantic. His playing surges with a rhythmic alertness and a feeling

for line that most romantic pianists would do well to emulate."

When Kipnis made his debut as a soloist with the New York Philharmonic Orchestra, Pierre Boulez conducting, on January 1, 1975—performing the continuo in Bach's Brandenburg Concerto No.5 and the solo in Manuel de Falla's Concerto for Harpsichord and Winds and Strings—Allen Hughes remarked in the New York *Times:* "To the surprise of no one familiar with his work, Mr. Kipnis' playing was both skillful and musical."

At his recitals he has made it a practice to introduce informality by talking to his audiences about the music he is about to play. "A recital should be an entertaining affair," he says. "The benefits of a dialogue with the audience are three-fold: First of all there is the opportunity to impart information about the harpsichord and about the music. Secondly, the relaxed atmosphere tends to relax the performer. And perhaps most important of all, the informality creates a rapport with audiences—especially with the young audiences who don't like the divided auditorium with the performer on the platform and the audience in their accustomed places, all acting reverential."

Kipnis fills over sixty engagements a year. Since he insists on having his instrument accompany him on his travels—he performs on a ten-foot-long Rutkowski and Robinette harpsichord —he makes his American tours by automobile, driving thirty (or more) thousand miles a year.

Despite his active concert life he has managed to fill a full-time post as professor of music at Fairfield University in Fairfield, Connecticut, since 1971. He has lectured on Baroque music and Baroque performances at various other educational institutions as well as at many festivals. In addition to his concert work and teaching, he is also a frequent contributor to newspapers and journals of articles on Baroque music and of music reviews. He is the editor of an anthology, *A First Harpsichord Book,* as well as of compositions by Jeremiah Clarke and Jan Ladislav Dussek.

Kipnis's more than twenty record albums are devoted principally and extensively to the musical literature of the Renaissance and Baroque eras. Four times his releases have been nominated for a Grammy award by the National Academy of Recording Arts and Sciences. In 1969 he received the Deutsche Schallplatten prize and in

1971 and 1972 the *Stereo Review* Record of the Year awards.

On January 6, 1953, he married Judith Robison. With their son, Jeremy, they reside in West Redding, Connecticut.

ABOUT: American Record Guide, June 1972; Hi-Fi, May 1971; New York Times, January 5, 1975; Time, January 13, 1975.

Ralph Kirkpatrick

1911–

Few if any harpsichordists since Wanda Landowska have been more influential than Ralph Kirkpatrick in keeping the harpsichord and its music alive and vital on the twentieth century music scene. Descended from early Americans, Kirkpatrick was born in Leominster, Massachusetts, on June 10, 1911. He was one of four children of Edwin Asbury Kirkpatrick, a psychologist, and Florence May Clifford Kirkpatrick. Piano study began with his mother when he was six and was continued with private teachers while he attended public school. After graduation from Leominster High School in 1927, he entered Harvard College on a scholarship, majoring in the fine arts. During these academic years he helped to support himself by teaching the piano, giving some piano concerts, and serving as a piano accompanist. When the music department at Harvard acquired a Chickering harpsichord in 1929, he was given opportunities to learn by himself how to play it; it instantly displaced the piano as his preferred instrument. Within a few months he was able to give his first public harpsichord concert, at Paine Hall, in Cambridge, Massachusetts, in a program made up of music by Johann Sebastian Bach and Gibbons. Henry Taylor Parker gave him an enthusiastic review in the Boston *Transcript*.

In 1931 Kirkpatrick received a Bachelor of Arts degree from Harvard. Endowed by the music department with a John Knowles Paine Travelling Scholarship, he embarked upon his first trip to Europe. In Paris he studied theory with Nadia Boulanger and harpsichord with Wanda Landowska; much of his time was devoted to doing research at the Bibliothèque Nationale in the music of the distant past, which was then

RALPH KIRKPATRICK

little known. In England he continued his researches at the British Museum and studied old instruments with Arnold Dolmetsch at Haslemere. In Germany he was a pupil of Günther Ramin and Heinz Tiessen.

In January 1933 Kirkpatrick made his European concert debut as harpsichordist with a recital at the Collegium Musicum in Berlin, performing Bach's *Goldberg Variations*. Alfred Einstein, one of Germany's leading music critics, gave him a rave review. Kirkpatrick followed this concert with several appearances in Italy, including one at the villa in Florence of Bernard Berenson, the art historian. During the summers of 1933 and 1934 he was a member of the faculty at the Mozarteum in Salzburg.

Returning to the United States late in 1933, Kirkpatrick received from his friends the gift of a Chickering harpsichord that had once belonged to Busoni. He concertized in several American cities, including New York in 1934 when he was a guest artist with the Dessoff Choirs. "It was an uphill struggle in those days," he recalls, "but somehow I managed to pick up odd dates and make ends meet." In 1937, on a Guggenheim Fellowship, he was back in Europe to do research in seventeenth and eighteenth century chamber and keyboard music. In Spain he uncovered a mine of hitherto unknown sonatas by Domenico Scarlatti.

In 1938 Kirkpatrick inaugurated a festival of old American music in the ballroom of the governor's palace in Williamsburg, Virginia. For the next eight years this remained an annual event with Kirkpatrick as adviser and principal performer. Over the years he gave fifty solo and chamber-music concerts of works associated with the early history of Virginia. Reporting one of these festivals in 1939, Carleton Sprague Smith wrote in the New York *Herald Tribune:* "Ralph Kirkpatrick is undoubtedly the ablest harpsichordist in this country today. Few musicians possess thorough scholarship, virtuosity in abundance, and true musicianship, in short, a complete mastery of their métier."

In the 1940s he gave numerous recitals throughout the United States (making his first transcontinental tour in 1944), gave sonata recitals with the violinist Alexander Schneider, participated in American festivals, performed on a national radio hookup program from the Library of Congress, and made his first recordings. Following an all-Bach recital in New York, when he presented Bach's *Goldberg Variations,* Pitts Sanborn, writing in the *World-Telegram,* called him "a past master of his chosen instrument" and added: "He plays it with precision, fine command of tone and a thorough knowledge of its capacity for color and shading."

Kirkpatrick made his first concert tour of Europe in 1947, covering England, France, and Holland. In 1948 he gave concerts in Western Germany under the auspices of the United States Military Government. In 1955 he became a participant at the annual Bach Festival in Ansbach, where he was heard for many years. In January 1961 he gave the first public clavichord concert ever heard in New York (using a discreet electronic amplification to permit the baroque instrument to be better heard). This all-Bach program led his fellow harpsichordist, Igor Kipnis, to report in the New York *Times:* "Kirkpatrick's marvelous sense of rhythmic freedom, the occasional rhythmic alterations, the subtle use of 'bebung' (a method of gently alternating pressure on an already depressed key in order to produce vibrato), the improvisational but not obtrusive ornamentation . . . all combined with the expressive quality of the clavichord to provide a stimulating and enchanting evening." In a Mozart concert at the Lincoln Center for the Performing Arts in 1966, Kirkpatrick performed on both the harpsichord and the modern piano. In 1969 he helped to open the Alice Tully Hall at Lincoln Center for the Performing Arts in New York with three programs of harpsichord music.

In 1940 he was appointed visiting lecturer at Yale University. There, from 1956 to 1965, he served as associate professor of music and from 1965 on as full professor. He is a Fellow of Jonathan Edwards College. In the spring of 1964 he also served as the first Ernest Bloch Professor of Music at the University of California at Berkeley.

Kirkpatrick's researches into, and discoveries of, the music of Domenico Scarlatti have made him the greatest authority on that composer. The fruits of Kirkpatrick's scholarship were gathered in his definitive biography, *Domenico Scarlatti* (1953), and in his new edition of sixty sonatas of Scarlatti (also issued in 1953). Kirkpatrick has also edited Bach's *Goldberg Variations* and his *Klavierbüchlein vor Wilhelm Friedemann Bach.* His recordings include a monumental series of albums for Deutsche Grammophon Gesellschaft covering all of Johann Sebastian Bach's works for the clavier, a project begun in 1956 and completed in 1967. He has also recorded sixty of Scarlatti's sonatas for Columbia, together with numerous other works from the Baroque era and many of Mozart's piano sonatas and concertos.

Though Kirkpatrick has involved himself deeply in the music of the distant past, he has not sidestepped twentieth century composers. In fact, he has been responsible for the world premieres of contemporary works for the harpsichord by Stravinsky, Milhaud, Walter Piston, Henry Cowell, Quincy Porter, and Elliott Carter. On September 6, 1961, he was one of the assisting artists in the premiere in New York of Carter's *Double Concerto for Harpsichord and Piano With Two Chamber Orchestras.*

Kirkpatrick was decorated by Italy with the Order of Merit in 1954, and in 1957 he received an honorary doctorate from Oberlin College. He resides in Connecticut. He has always been partial to outdoor activities such as swimming, bricklaying, or cutting wood. Indoors he enjoys reading, gourmet cooking, and his valuable book collection.

ABOUT: Musical America, January 1963; Newsweek, November 24, 1969.

Dorothy Kirsten

1917–

Dorothy Kirsten, soprano, was born in Montclair, New Jersey, on July 6, 1917, the daughter of George W. and Margaret Beggs Kirsten. Hers was a musical background. Her grandfather, James J. Beggs, had been the conductor of the Buffalo Bill Band and an early president of the American Federation of Musicians, New York Local 802; her great aunt, Catherine Hayes, had been a European opera singer known on the continent and in England as "the Irish Jenny Lind"; and her mother was an organist and a teacher of music. While attending Montclair High School, Dorothy took lessons in drama, dancing, and voice. She also studied the piano, having taken her first lessons with her mother.

Upon graduation from high school, Dorothy worked for the New Jersey Telephone Company in Newark to pay for her voice lessons once a week with Louis Dornay in New York. She was able to increase the number of her lessons by exchanging instruction for serving as an all-around maid and secretary to her next teacher, Betsy Dornay-Culp. By getting assignments to sing over the radio and on small stations and then by getting her own five-times-a-week program in 1938, she was finally able to discontinue her menial obligations to her teacher. Subsequent vocal study took place with Ludwig Fabri, José Ruben, Ruth Moltke, and Antonietta Stabile. On December 1, 1938, she appeared on the Broadway stage in *Great Lady,* the first Broadway musical by Lerner and Loewe, which closed after only twenty performances.

A New York journalist arranged for her to audition with Grace Moore, for whom she sang "Musetta's Waltz" from *La Bohème.* Moore provided her with the funds for further music study in Italy. She went to Rome early in 1939 and began study with Astolfo Pescia, Beniamino Gigli's coach.

She planned to stay in Europe for about two years, but World War II sent her back to the United States. In the summer of 1940 she made her concert debut with a performance at the Court of Peace at New York's World's Fair, and on November 9, 1940, her opera debut followed with the Chicago Civic Opera as Pousette in *Manon.* That season she was heard in fifteen

DOROTHY KIRSTEN

minor parts. But one season later she graduated to such roles as Nedda in *I Pagliacci,* Micaëla in *Carmen,* and Musetta in *La Bohème* (in the last-mentioned Grace Moore sang the principal female role of Mimi).

Kirsten's New York operatic debut came on May 7, 1942, as Mimi with Fortune Gallo's San Carlo Opera Company. In 1942 and 1943 she gave concerts in thirty-eight states (at one time giving fifteen concerts in a single month) and appeared as guest artist on several major radio programs, such as the "Telephone Hour" and the "Prudential Family Hour"; she starred in her own regular radio series for one year, from September 1943 to September 1944, the "Keepsakes" program over the NBC network.

In the period between 1944 and 1946, she was heard as Marguerite in *Faust,* Violetta in *La Traviata,* Mimi, and the title role in *Manon Lescaut,* at the New York City Opera. Guest appearances brought her to opera houses in New Orleans, Cincinnati, Havana, Montreal, Ottawa, and Mexico City. She was also starred in operettas performed in New York and elsewhere, among which were *The Great Waltz, The New Moon,* and *Countess Maritza.*

Her debut at the Metropolitan Opera took place on December 1, 1945, as Mimi. "Her voice showed no hint of debut nerves," said Francis D. Perkins in the *Herald Tribune.* "It was satisfying in volume and consistently appealing in quality; her tones were clear and fluently produced, with well-schooled phrasing, and her singing also reflected the emotional flavor of the music." Her next role at the Metropolitan was Violetta, but her third one was new for her—Juliet in *Romeo and Juliet* on December 19, 1945. A season later she assumed the parts of Micaëla, Marguerite, and the title role in *Madama Butterfly*. And on December 12, 1947, she added further to her successes by appearing in the title role of *Louise,* a role in which she was coached by the composer himself. "Her clearly delivered high notes floated easily and her vocalism was for the most part good," wrote Miles Kastendieck in the *Journal-American.* " 'Depuis le jour' was beautifully but coolly sung." Two and a half months before this performance she had made her debut in the same role with the San Francisco Opera where she became a resident member.

Kirsten celebrated her twenty-fifth consecutive season at the Metropolitan Opera on March 3, 1971, in the role of Mimi, with which she had made her first appearance with that company, "a record unequalled by any other leading American soprano." (She was also the only leading artist to sing consecutively for twenty-five seasons at the San Francisco Opera.) To commemorate her Metropolitan Opera Anniversary, she was presented with the Handel Medal, the highest cultural award the city of New York could bestow. Speaking of her performance that evening, Raymond Ericson noted in the New York *Times:* "This is artistry more admirable and, consequently, more durable than that of more sensational singers."

When her patroness and intimate friend Grace Moore died in an airplane crash in January 1947, Kirsten sang "Ave Maria" at her memorial service at the Riverside Church in New York and at her burial in Chattanooga, Tennessee. She also appeared at the Grace Moore Memorial Night at Lewisohn Stadium in New York on July 21, 1947.

She became the first American singer to appear at the Tiflis Opera in the Soviet Union, where she was heard in the role of Violetta on January 21, 1962; she sang her part in Italian while the rest of the cast used Russian. A correspondent for the New York *Times* reported that she scored "an overwhelming success . . . At the end of the opera the audience stamped feet and shouted its approval. Miss Kirsten came out for twenty-two curtain calls. Many bouquets were thrown on the stage." She went on from Tiflis to appear with the Bolshoi Opera in Moscow, and then in Riga and Leningrad.

Having become the first leading soprano ever to complete thirty years at the Metropolitan Opera, Kirsten decided it was time to end her association with that company. Her final performance took place on New Year's Eve, 1975, as Tosca. She went out, wrote Allen Hughes in the New York *Times,* "in a blaze of glory. . . . She sang and acted the part of Tosca with the vocal control and dramatic acuity of a prima donna in mid-career." During her entire thirty-year span as a resident member of the Metropolitan Opera she had sung only leading parts—Tosca, 24 times; Mimi in *La Bohème,* 21 times; Manon in *Manon Lescaut,* 20 times. She had also been heard in the title roles of *Manon* and *The Girl of the Golden West,* Rosalinde in *Die Fledermaus,* and Nedda in *I Pagliacci.* Despite her retirement, Kirsten decided to rejoin the company for a single appearance as Mimi in a concert presentation of *La Bohème* at Central Park in New York on June 21, 1977—the audience exceeded one hundred thousand.

In San Francisco she appeared as Cressida in the American premiere of Sir William Walton's *Troilus and Cressida* on October 5, 1955.

Kirsten has also enjoyed a long and distinguished career as a recitalist. She has been the star of many prominent radio and television programs, and she was seen and heard in the motion picture *Mr. Music* (1950) that starred Bing Crosby, and in *The Great Caruso* (1951) with Mario Lanza.

On July 18, 1955, Dorothy Kirsten married John Douglas French, director of the Brain Research Institute at the University of California in Los Angeles; it was her third marriage. Her main interests have been dancing, golf, skating, swimming, and taking long walks in the country.

She has been awarded honorary doctorates by Santa Clara University in California, and Ithaca College in New York. In April 1977 she received the rank of Commander in the Order of Merit, Italy's highest cultural award, for her contributions to improving relations between Italy and the United States.

ABOUT: Life, December 10, 1946; Opera News, March 6, 1971, January 3, 1976; Time, January 13, 1975.

Erich Kleiber

1890–1956

Erich Kleiber, conductor, was born in Vienna on August 5, 1890. His father, Otto, a high school teacher, and his mother, Veronica, both died while he was still a child, and Erich was brought up by two impoverished aunts. He attended the high school where his father had been employed, and at eighteen he entered Prague University to specialize in philosophy. He also attended the Vienna Conservatory as a student of the violin. These years of boyhood and early manhood were a time of extreme poverty. He lived in a poorly lit and cold attic, often subsisting on little more than bread and water.

Kleiber conducted for the first time in 1911 at the Prague National Theater. A year later he was appointed conductor at the court theater of the Grand Duke of Hesse in Darmstadt. The six years he spent there were a valuable apprenticeship, making it possible for him to take a more ambitious post as conductor in Barmen-Elberfeld from 1919 to 1921, and in 1922 and 1923 at Düsseldorf and Mannheim. In 1923 Max von Schillings, manager of the Berlin State Opera, invited Kleiber to give several guest performances of *Fidelio* with his company. These performances were so successful that Kleiber was engaged as music director of the Berlin State Opera, a post he held with distinction for twelve years. Kleiber brought a fresh viewpoint to whatever opera he conducted. A musician of intellect and integrity, he succeeded in opening new interpretative vistas for the standard operatic repertory, particularly in works of the German school from Mozart through Wagner, in which he proved himself a master. He also became known for his interpretations of contemporary operas and was responsible for the world premieres of many provocative works which he projected with sympathy and penetration. On December 14, 1925, he introduced Berg's *Wozzeck;* his brilliant performances were largely responsible for the opera's acceptance as a masterwork. Among other world premieres conducted by Kleiber in Berlin were Ernst Krenek's *Zwingburg* (October 16, 1924), Milhaud's *Christophe Colomb* (May 5, 1930), and Karol Rat-

Kleiber: klī′ bĕr

ERICH KLEIBER

haus's *Fremde Erde* (December 10, 1930). He also led the Berlin premieres of Krenek's *Leben des Orest* and Jaromir Weinberger's *Schwanda.*

He combined his many successes in Berlin with guest appearances in Paris, Austria, South America, and the Soviet Union. While conducting in Buenos Aires in 1926 he met Ruth Goodrich, an American girl who later became his wife. When they first met neither could understand the other's language. In spite of this, romance developed. Kleiber took her to Germany and married her in December 1926.

On October 2, 1930, Kleiber made his American debut as conductor with the New York Philharmonic. "This stocky, square-shouldered, somewhat grimly earnest man is a conductor whose musicianship is secure and authoritative," wrote Lawrence Gilman in the *Herald Tribune,* "whose conceptions are definitely arrived at and a little sharp-edged, whose integrity is above suspicion. He seems to be inclined towards broad tempi and liberal breathing space, and to be perhaps a little coolly platonic in his regard for nuance."

Despite the fact that Kleiber's ancestry was not pure Aryan, the Nazi officials permitted him to retain his post with the Berlin State Opera because of his enormous popularity throughout Germany. On November 30, 1934, he conducted the first performance of the symphonic suite from Berg's opera *Lulu.* In December 1934, when Furtwängler was removed from his conducting posts in the controversy over the projected performance of Hindemith's opera *Mathis der Maler,* Kleiber handed in his resignation in protest. At first it was not accepted, but later, when Kleiber's open hostility to the Nazi regime became embarrassing, he was asked to vacate his post. He left Germany with his wife and two sons without any belongings and emigrated to South America where he arrived virtually penniless. He set up his new home in Buenos Aires and in time he became an Argentine citizen.

In 1935 he made his successful conducting debut at La Scala in Milan, and in 1936 he was made Commander of the Order of the Italian Crown. But in 1938 he refused to return to La Scala because by then the Italian government had embarked on its own anti-Semitic campaign. In the years between 1934 and 1937 Kleiber made many guest appearances in the Soviet Union. From 1936 to 1949 he was the principal conductor of German operas at the Teatro Colón in Buenos Aires. From 1944 to 1947 he served as principal conductor of the Havana Philharmonic Orchestra in Cuba.

In 1945–1946, on an invitation from Arturo Toscanini, Kleiber appeared as a guest conductor of the NBC Symphony in the United States. From 1947 on he toured Europe extensively in performances of operas and symphonic music, making noteworthy appearances at the Prague May Festival, the Zurich June Festival, and a Wagner festival in Amsterdam. In 1950 he made the first of several distinguished appearances at Covent Garden in London, where he was heard in *Wozzeck, The Magic Flute, Der Rosenkavalier,* and a new production of Tchaikovsky's *The Queen of Spades.* In June 1951 he paid his first return visit to Berlin in almost two decades, conducting performances at the Berlin State Opera, where he was given a hero's welcome.

In 1954 he was appointed principal conductor of the East Berlin State Opera. When the opera house in East Berlin was reconstructed, he was made music director. He was scheduled to open the reconstructed building with a new production of *Fidelio* on September 4, 1955, but six months before this could happen Kleiber sent in his resignation on the grounds of governmental interference with his artistic program and insistence on using art as a propaganda tool. In his letter of resignation he complained that "as in the year 1934, politics and propaganda will not halt at the doorway of this 'temple.' And so sooner or later I would have had for the second time to part company with the house for which I have longed for twenty years."

Kleiber and his family moved from East Berlin to Cologne, West Germany, from which city he sent his letter of resignation. He spent his last months in Zurich, Switzerland, where he died of a heart attack on January 27, 1956.

Kleiber was decorated by the Austrian government with the Great Silver Medal. In Belgium he was made Commander of the Order of Leopold; in Peru, Comendador, Orden del Sol Peru; and in Chile, Comendador del Merito.

Kleiber's son, Carlos, was born in Berlin on July 3, 1930. He too became a successful conductor and has served as resident conductor of the Württemberg State Opera in Stuttgart. He has made guest appearances at the Vienna State Opera, Munich Opera, Hamburg Opera, Covent Garden in London, and at the Bayreuth Festival. On September 8, 1977, he made his American debut with the San Francisco Opera in *Otello.*

ABOUT: Russell, J. Erich Kleiber: A Memoir.

Otto Klemperer

1885–1973

Otto Klemperer, conductor, was born in Breslau, Germany, on May 14, 1885. His grandfather was a Hebraic scholar. His father, Nathan, a merchant, was a music lover, and his mother, Ida Nathan Klemperer, a trained amateur pianist. When Otto was four, his family moved to Hamburg, where he began studying the piano with his mother. He entered Hoch's Conservatory in Frankfort when he was sixteen, and his music training was subsequently completed in Berlin at the Klindworth-Scharwenka Conservatory with Hans Pfitzner (composition), James Kwast (piano), and Ludwig Philipp Scharwenka (theory).

Having been trained primarily as a pianist, Otto embarked upon a career as a virtuoso as soon as he was graduated from the Klindworth-Scharwenka Conservatory. But his excessive nervousness on the stage, which impaired the quality of his piano playing, soon made him change to conducting. He served his apprentice-

Klemperer: klĕm′ pĕ rēr

OTTO KLEMPERER

marriage Klemperer was converted from Judaism to Roman Catholicism.

William Steinberg, who later became known as a conductor, played second violin in the Cologne Opera Orchestra under Klemperer in 1917. "What I thought of him at the time is what I think of him today," said Steinberg. "Klemperer has everything given him by God and Nature to make a great man." As it happened, Klemperer fired Steinberg. "I could not quarrel with his action then; from his standpoint, he certainly was right, because I was disobeying his bow markings in *Carmen;* so I was forbidden to play in the orchestra because of this unforgivable crime." But Klemperer could be as forgiving as he was strict. He later engaged Steinberg as his assistant conductor at Cologne for four years during which Steinberg first served as music coach, then as Klemperer's personal assistant, and finally as full conductor. "His colossal integrity as a musician and as a man," Steinberg said of Klemperer, "his enormous degree of erudition in many fields other than music, especially philosophy, made him a unique figure and personality."

Klemperer's fame kept growing in the early 1920s, particularly at the Wiesbaden Opera, where he assumed command in 1924 and where his energetic and perceptive interpretations not only of the standard repertory but also of modern operas attracted interest throughout Germany. Under his regime the opera house expanded its repertoire to forty-four works, from less than half that number. Klemperer's interest in modern operas intensified between 1927 and 1931 when he became the music director of the Kroll Opera in Berlin. On June 8, 1929, he led the world premiere of Hindemith's *Neues vom Tage.* Among the other twentieth century operas presented under Klemperer at the Kroll were Hindemith's *Cardillac,* Schoenberg's *Erwartung* and *Die Glückliche Hand,* Janáček's *Aus einem Totenhaus,* and Stravinsky's *Oedipus Rex* and *L'Histoire du Soldat.* Klemperer also presented regular symphony concerts in the auditorium of the Kroll Opera. His emphasis on the new and the unfamiliar made him many enemies and in 1931 resulted in the permanent closing of the Kroll Opera, at which time Klemperer went over to the Berlin State Opera to become its principal conductor.

In 1933, just before the rise of the Nazi regime, Klemperer was presented with the Goe-

ship in 1905 as an assistant to Oskar Fried in Berlin. A year later Klemperer made his conducting debut in Offenbach's *Orpheus in the Underworld,* produced and directed by Max Reinhardt. That same year Klemperer assisted Mahler in the performance of one of Mahler's symphonies. Mahler became interested in Klemperer and in 1907 recommended him for a conducting post at the German National Theater in Prague. "I do find Herr Klemperer extraordinarily good," Mahler wrote to the director of the German National Theater. "I guarantee good results in case of his appointment to the post of conductor and always stand ready personally to cooperate with him and help him."

Klemperer stayed in Prague from 1907 to 1910. In 1910, once more on Mahler's recommendation, he was called to the Hamburg Opera as principal conductor, remaining four years. From 1914 to 1917 Klemperer also served as the music director of the Strasbourg Opera and from 1917 to 1924 of the Cologne Opera. In Cologne, Klemperer conducted his first symphony concerts, an area in which he was to achieve renown second only to his fame in opera. He introduced to Cologne Mahler's Second and Seventh symphonies and his *Das Lied von der Erde.* His unusual programming and dynamic performances made his concerts events of major importance in the city.

In 1919 in Cologne Klemperer married Johanna Geissler, an opera singer who had appeared as a soloist at one of his concerts. For this ring medal for "outstanding contribution to German culture." Outside Germany he was also making his mark as a conductor, with guest appearances in England, the Soviet Union, and the United States. His American debut took place on January 24, 1926, when he conducted a program made up of three symphonies (Haydn's No.95, Mozart's *Jupiter,* and Beethoven's Seventh), with the New York Symphony Society. That performance was memorable for its striking individuality. "He was such a towering figure on the stage—standing six feet six—that he did not need a platform to elevate him above the musicians. As he conducted he crouched, stooped, swayed. At times, when he threw his arms in a broad arc, he resembled an eagle ready to swoop down on its prey. His musicianship and his knowledge of the scores could not be questioned, nor, for that matter, his ability to control the orchestra. . . . He appeared that day a diamond in the rough. He could not always keep in check the dynamic and emotional forces he released. He had power and strength in his interpretations, but he lacked sensitivity. His readings had scabrous edges. He overemphasized the significance of the double basses, brasses, and tympani. He was partial to excessive rubatos; he often disregarded fermatas; and he sometimes permitted loud or fast passages to get out of hand. There were many moments in Beethoven's Seventh Symphony, and especially in the finale, when such an approach and such methods served the music well; and at these times Klemperer was one of the most exciting conductors in the world. We knew then that he had the makings of greatness, but whether he would ever realize that greatness through discipline, sobriety and sensitivity was a question that could not be answered in 1926." (D. Ewen. *Famous Modern Conductors*)

He returned the following season for another series of guest appearances with the New York Symphony Society. In 1927 he was invited to the Soviet Union to conduct concerts commemorating the centenary of Beethoven's birth.

Soon after leaving the Kroll Opera in 1931 Klemperer was rehearsing in Leipzig. He leaned back against the railing of his podium, the rail gave way, and Klemperer fell, striking his head against the stage. He suffered severe concussion and was unconscious for hours. He remained ill for weeks and his recovery from this accident was never complete. From that time on he was victimized by severe headaches and fainting spells.

It was at this time that he was struck by a second tragedy. In 1933 the Nazis came to power in Germany. Because he was of Jewish birth he was subjected to attacks: verbally by the press, physically at the hands of Storm Troopers. His life in danger, he fled to Vienna where he conducted several concerts of the Vienna Philharmonic. Then he went to Switzerland. From there he traveled to the United States, where he applied for American citizenship.

In 1933 Klemperer was appointed music director of the Los Angeles Philharmonic. He retained this post for six years. During this period he also served as guest conductor of other major American orchestras.

In 1939 Klemperer was operated on for a brain tumor; the operation left his right side paralyzed. "He lay there in a wheelchair, his eyes glassy, not focused on anything in the world" one unidentified reporter wrote after meeting Klemperer soon after the operation. "One side of his face was dead, so was his right hand. It hung there, still and lifeless, as if it knew it could never hold a baton again."

His career seemed over, but Klemperer refused to accept what everybody else considered a fact. He learned to walk on crutches, and with indomitable will he went through the painful and enervating exercises prescribed to bring some life back to inert limbs. Then, though still for the most part incapacitated, he determined to resume his interrupted career. Since no managers or orchestras were interested in engaging him, he had to compromise on a semiprofessional orchestra in a Bach program at the New School for Social Research in 1940, his first New York appearance in five years. This was followed by an appearance with another semiprofessional organization sponsored by the New York City administration and the WPA. In the spring of 1941 he exhausted his savings to engage a seventy-five-piece symphony orchestra for a concert at Carnegie Hall. Some critics found a new richness of thought, a deeper insight, and profounder feelings in Klemperer's interpretations of music by Beethoven, Hindemith, Bach, and Mozart than he had shown previously. But in spite of such praise, there were no takers for his services. He was pushed into a retirement which everybody, including himself, thought was permanent.

He went into a deep mental depression and had to enter a private sanatorium in Rye, New York. When one morning he wanted to go out and purchase a newspaper he was denied permission. He managed to leave the sanatorium anyway, making his way to Morristown, New Jersey, where he was found after an alarm had been sent out describing him as "dangerous and insane." He called the police, who in turn summoned a psychiatrist. The latter found Klemperer "temperamental and unstrung" but by no means either insane or dangerous.

After World War II Klemperer returned to Europe. There he found some scattered assignments, among which were a symphony concert in Stockholm and a performance of Bach's *Passion According to St. Matthew* in Rome. In both performances he revealed that despite his physical disability, his power and penetration in projecting great music remained undiminished. In 1947 he became the music director of the Budapest Opera. When he went to the podium to conduct his first performance in this new post— an orchestral concert by the orchestra of the Budapest Opera—he was given an ovation. "His face has grown more haggard with the passing of time—the skin is tightly drawn over the protruding cheekbones," reported one Budapest music critic. "The light that falls on that countenance, stamped with pain untold, gives it an almost demoniac gleam. His rigid hand can no longer hold the baton. With his two arms outstretched he draws the music from the resounding depths of the orchestra. . . . His face is transformed—the tortured mouth breaks into a smile and the warm streams of music flow around the tragic profile."

Klemperer held his post in Budapest for three years, in which time he helped to restore the prestige of both the opera house and the orchestra. In 1950 he toured Australia where he led the first performance in that country of Mahler's Symphony No.2. In 1951 he directed the first two concerts of the season of the London Philharmonia Orchestra at Festival Hall. Critics and the general public were ready to accept him again when tragedy struck once more. In October 1951 he arrived in Montreal to fill the new post of music director of Les Concerts Symphoniques. In the airport he fell down a flight of stairs, shattering his left thigh in two places. His appointment as music director had to be canceled, together with other projected appearances

in the United States. For almost a year Klemperer was an invalid in a wheelchair; his physician told him he would never again conduct.

But Klemperer's determination to survive as an artist was not to be overcome. For years after that he stumbled along on crutches as he made his way to the podium. His disability compelled him for years to sit while conducting because his legs would not support him. Nevertheless he was able to produce remarkable performances annually at London's Festival Hall, including a complete cycle of Beethoven's symphonies. Equally memorable were his presentations of *Fidelio, The Magic Flute,* and *Lohengrin* at Covent Garden.

In 1965, while directing a radio performance of *Don Giovanni* in Cologne, Klemperer became so deeply involved in the music that he forgot his infirmity; for the first time in more than a decade he stood up and remained standing.

In 1959 Klemperer had been given a life appointment as principal conductor of the London Philharmonia Orchestra. When the orchestra suspended operations in March 1965, Klemperer expressed his eagerness to continue his association with it should it ever be reorganized. When the orchestra was reorganized and renamed the New Philharmonic, Klemperer was made both honorary president and (once again on a lifetime appointment) permanent conductor. The new orchestra made its debut at Royal Albert Hall with an all-Beethoven concert that drew ovations. At succeeding performances not only in London but all over Europe—in opera as well as in symphonic music, on records as well as in the concert hall—Klemperer went on to demonstrate that neither age nor crushing physical blows could blemish his intellectual powers or his profound interpretative art. "If anything," wrote Nathan Broder in reviewing one of Klemperer's recordings for *High Fidelity* in July 1965, "his performances grow even more polished, as well as more self-effacing, more completely at the service of the composer's thought. . . . At best he can reach the stars. . . . He is seldom far below that level." And in commenting on Klemperer's remarkable recording of Beethoven's Ninth Symphony, Deryck Cooke, the English critic, added: "Listening to this disc has been one of the great experiences of my life. . . . This is not only a disc of the month but a great recording of the century, indeed, the great recording of the century for me." Another of

Klemperer's recordings—the *Passion According to St. Matthew*—received in 1962 a Grammy from the National Academy of Recording Arts and Sciences.

On October 23, 1962, Klemperer made his first reappearance in the United States in a decade, leading the Philadelphia Orchestra in two symphonies by Beethoven (the Second and the *Eroica*). Harold C. Schonberg said of his performance: "He conducted from a high chair without using a podium . . . and he had the music in front of him even though he has the Beethoven symphonies memorized twenty times over. Was it music he gave us last night? Or was it a rite? Slowly, massively, deliberately, appearing to inhabit a world of his own, he went through the two symphonies. . . . He was not out to make pretty music. He was out to interpret Beethoven. One could disagree with his ideas, but one could not but bow to this kind of integrity and dedication."

Klemperer celebrated his eighty-fifth birthday in May 1970 by leading a performance of Mahler's *Das Lied von der Erde* with the New Philharmonic Orchestra at the Royal Festival Hall in London. At the conclusion of the concert, the orchestra chairman presented him with a Georgian salver, and the orchestra's chorus gave him a silver ashtray. He is, the London *Observer* said of him, "the last great survivor of the heroic age of conducting," and the *Evening Standard* referred to him as "the last of the Titans."

In 1970, Klemperer—who, in spite of his one-time conversion to Catholicism, still regarded himself as a Jew—went to Israel and asked the government to give him immigrant status. He was granted Israeli citizenship. From then on he divided his time between Israel and Zurich, attended to by his devoted daughter, Lotte (his wife had died in 1956). In January 1972 Klemperer went into total retirement in Zurich. "There will be no fuss and no farewell concert," announced a spokesman for the New Philharmonic Orchestra. "This is as Dr. Klemperer wants it." In the summer of 1973 his health began to deteriorate markedly. This lasted several weeks and for a week before his death he was unconscious. He died in his sleep at his home at the Doufourstrasse in Zurich on July 6, 1973, and was buried in Zurich's Jewish cemetery. His son Werner is an actor in motion pictures and on television.

Klemperer was the composer of two sympho-

nies, five operas, a violin concerto, a mass, string quartets, and songs. In addition to a book of memoirs, *Minor Recollections* (1964), he was the author of a book of recollections about Mahler, *Erinnerungen an Gustav Mahler* (1960).

Among the honors and decorations conferred on him were the Grand Medal of Merit with Star from the Federal Republic of Germany in 1958, the Nikisch Prize from Leipzig in 1966, and the Order of Merit in 1967. He was given an honorary doctorate by the University of California in Los Angeles in 1937. And in 1971 he was made an honorary member of the Royal Academy of Music in London. In Thomas Mann's novel about a twelve-tone composer, *Dr. Faustus,* Klemperer is mentioned as the conductor of the fictional composer's *Apocalypse.*

ABOUT: Blaukopf, K. Great Conductors; Klemperer, O. Minor Recollections. *Periodicals*—Hi-Fi, January 1959; New York Times, May 31, 1970; Opera News, September 19, 1970, September 1973; Saturday Review, May 29, 1965.

Hans Knappertsbusch

1888–1965

Known to American audiences exclusively through his recordings, Hans Knappertsbusch, conductor, was born in Elberfeld, Germany, on March 12, 1888. At the University of Bonn he specialized in philosophy. In 1909 he entered the Cologne Conservatory where, during the next three years, his principal teachers were Fritz Steinbach and Otto Lohse. From 1906 to 1911 he was a student of and assistant conductor to Hans Richter at Bayreuth.

Knappertsbusch began his conducting career in 1910 at the Mühlheim Theater, but he first attracted attention in Holland where in 1912 and 1913 he directed a festival of Wagnerian music dramas. He returned to his native city, Elberfeld, in 1913 and for five years served as music director. In 1918 he was the principal conductor at the Leipzig State Theater and from 1919 to 1922 of the Dessau Opera.

In 1922 he went to Munich on a lifelong contract as music director of the Munich Opera, succeeding Bruno Walter. Knappertsbusch

---

Knappertsbusch: k'näp′ ĕrts bŏŏsh

HANS KNAPPERTSBUSCH

became a favorite in Munich and was one of its principal drawing cards at its annual summer music festivals. His performances of Mozart, Wagner, and Richard Strauss were always characterized by authority and musicianship together with perceptive interpretations. His style was in the grand manner, with a partiality for broad sweeps of sonority, carefully planned climaxes, and a strong rhythmic pulse.

After the Nazis rose to power in Germany, Knappertsbusch came into conflict with the government authorities. On October 20, 1934, when he directed the world premiere of an American opera, Vittorio Giannini's *Lucedia,* the Nazi officials openly reprimanded him for favoring foreign musical talent at the expense of Germany. Knappertsbusch replied in defense that an opera house could retain its greatness only if it remained international rather than national in scope.

It was generally believed that the Nazis wanted to remove him from his post in Munich. The ovations greeting Knappertsbusch at each of his performances, however, made the officials cautious about taking such a step. Then, in February 1936, after Knappertsbusch refused to join the Nazi party, he was forced into retirement at the decision of Adolf Hitler.

Knappertsbusch transferred his activities to Vienna. In the summer of 1937 he participated at the Salzburg Festival, conducting newly staged productions of *The Magic Flute* and *Der Rosenkavalier.* In 1938 he became music director of the Vienna State Opera and conducted

concerts of the Vienna Philharmonic. When Austria was annexed by Germany, Knappertsbusch was once again forced to withdraw from his posts.

After World War II Knappertsbusch rose to new prominence as a conductor of Wagnerian music dramas both at Munich and at the Bayreuth Festival. His performances of *Parsifal* in 1951 both in Munich and at Bayreuth were regarded by many critics as the peak of his career. Howard Taubman reported to the New York *Times:* "His handling of the performance had a steady life-giving pulse. His pace was broad, but not excessively so. Most important he did not indulge in erratic music tricks. He conducted like a musician of integrity and he was rewarded with a fine performance from the orchestra."

Hans Knappertsbusch died at his home in Munich on October 25, 1965.

ABOUT: Opera News, December 18, 1965.

Leonid Kogan

1924–

Leonid Borisovich Kogan, violinist, was born in Dnepropetrovsk, Russia, on November 14, 1924. His father, Boris, a photographer, played the violin and gave Leonid his first lessons when the boy was seven. He proved to be a prodigy. When he was ten, his family moved to Moscow to provide him with greater opportunities for study. At the Moscow Conservatory he was a pupil of Abram Yampolsky. In 1936 Jacques Thibaud, the French violinist, heard the twelve-year-old perform and prophesied for him a rich artistic future.

Leonid made his concert debut in Moscow when he was sixteen. While continuing his music studies for another six years, he made concert appearances throughout the Soviet Union. He was heard for the first time outside his own country in Prague in 1947, when he received first prize in the International Youth Festival there. In 1948, upon his graduation, the Conservatory appointed him professor of the violin. Since then he has conducted master classes at the Conservatory.

He first attracted international interest in 1951 when he won first prize in the distinguished Concours Ysaÿe in Brussels, sponsored by

LEONID KOGAN

Queen Elisabeth. One of the judges was Jacques Thibaud, who saw the fulfillment of the prophesy he had made fifteen years earlier. The winning of that prize set in motion Kogan's career as one of the violin virtuosos of his time. Following extensive tours of the Soviet Union, he made his first appearance in England in 1955 and received a highly enthusiastic response from critics and audiences. Following his recital in Vienna in 1956, a reporter for the New York *Herald Tribune* placed him "among the greatest living violinists." At the Athens Festival that same year, a critic for the New York *Times* praised his "breath-halting technique and precision of intonation, plus a sensitivity of inflection which at times turned the dear old melodies into genuine songs without words. He is unquestionably one of the great violinists. His ovations lasted through the entire intermission, a total of eighteen minutes!"

Kogan initiated his first tour of the United States in January 1958 as a guest artist with the Boston Symphony under Pierre Monteux, in the Brahms Violin Concerto. In Boston, Cyrus Durgin of the *Daily Globe* called the debut "historic," adding that "he surely will take his place in the small but exalted group of violinists who are truly great artists." When this performance of the Brahms Concerto was repeated in New York, Irving Kolodin said in the *Saturday Review:* "He is wholly an individual as an instrumentalist, an interpreter and a platform personality. The marks of his art . . . are purity of sound and refinement of musicianship. To

those [are] added a tone of soaring lyric beauty . . . a boldness of style, and a warmth of spirit that made every note count in the total design."

In his subsequent appearances in recitals, as guest artist with orchestras, in chamber-music concerts with Emil Gilels and Mstislav Rostropovich, and in his numerous recordings, Kogan has fully justified the superlatives the critics have heaped upon him.

In 1955 he was named Honored Artist of the Russian Soviet Federated Socialist Republic. A decade later he received the Lenin Prize. He was also given the title of People's Artist of the USSR.

Kogan is married to the former Elizabeth Gilels, the sister of the celebrated Soviet pianist Emil Gilels. She is a violinist who has appeared with her husband in performances of two-violin music. They have two children, both professional musicians: Nina, a pianist who has made numerous appearances with her father in sonata recitals as well as in solo performances; Pavel, a violinist who won first prize in the Sibelius Contest in December 1970 and who made an impressive American debut as a soloist with the Philadelphia Orchestra on October 16, 1975.

Leonid Kogan's main interest away from music is in things mechanical, particularly automobile engines.

ABOUT: Crowley, E. L. and others. Prominent Personalities in the USSR.

Sándor Kónya

1923–

Sándor Kónya, tenor, was born in Sarkad, Hungary, on September 23, 1923. "Where I came from," he told an interviewer, "everybody sings or plays the fiddle without being taught. Music is just in our blood." His father, the owner of several shops, played the violin. He died when Sándor was still a child, and the family moved to Budapest where his mother married a government official.

Sándor showed unusual interest in singing from his early years, joining a children's choir and performing over the radio. However, his stepfather objected to any serious music study, insisting that the boy prepare himself for the study of medicine or law. Sándor was forced to

SÁNDOR KÓNYA

enroll secretly in the Franz Liszt Music Academy. A year later he was given a scholarship, and his stepfather waived all objections and permitted his stepson to pursue his musical inclinations freely.

During the first years of World War II Sándor was exempt from military service because of his studies. But towards the end of the war, in 1944, he was drafted into the Hungarian army and sent with his regiment to Germany. There he was captured by the British. After the war, Kónya decided to remain in Germany. He resumed his interrupted vocal studies at the Nordwestdeutsche Musikakademie in Detmold with Fred Husler, who not only gave him lessons but housed him as well. For his additional upkeep Kónya performed menial and physically taxing labors.

During this period he met Anneliese Block at a chess tournament in which both participated. When Kónya discovered she spoke English, he asked her to tutor him in that language. Romance developed quickly after that and she became his wife.

Kónya made his opera debut in 1951 at the State Opera in Bielefeld, Germany, as Turiddu in *Cavalleria Rusticana.* He made this appearance under a handicap, since his young wife was sick at the time and had to be hospitalized for months. But he did so well that he remained with the opera company for three years. Guest appearances in several German opera houses—including those in Darmstadt, Hamburg, and Stuttgart—enriched his experience; and further

study of Italian roles in Milan with Rico Lani extended his repertory.

In 1955 Kónya became the leading tenor at the State Opera in Berlin. One year later he was a visiting artist at the Edinburgh Festival, and in 1958 he made his bow as a Wagnerian tenor, as Lohengrin at the Bayreuth Festival. His success in Bayreuth encouraged him to develop himself as a *Heldentenor;* as such he has gained international renown. He appeared for the first time in the title role of *Parsifal* at La Scala in Milan, where he had made his debut in 1960 as Radames in *Aida.*

Kónya made his American debut on September 23, 1960, with the San Francisco Opera, as Dick Johnson in *The Girl of the Golden West.* Later the same season he sang Rodolfo in *La Bohème* and later the role of Lohengrin. As Lohengrin he also made his bow at the Metropolitan Opera on October 28, 1961. Douglas Watt, writing in the *Daily News,* praised his "appealing stage presence" and noted that he used his lyric voice "to fine effect." When he was heard as Walther in *Die Meistersinger* on October 18, 1962, Harold C. Schonberg reported in the New York *Times* that "as a vocalist he sang the brightest Walther heard in many a year." Within the next few years he proved to be one of the mainstays of the Metropolitan Opera company in the French, Italian, and German repertories. He was heard as Dick Johnson in *The Girl of the Golden West,* Calaf in *Turandot,* Alfredo in *La Traviata,* Radames in *Aida,* Cavaradossi in *Tosca,* Rodolfo in *Luisa Miller,* Don Alvaro in *La Forza del Destino,* the Singer in *Der Rosenkavalier,* Erik in *The Flying Dutchman,* Bacchus in *Ariadne auf Naxos,* Rodolfo in *La Bohème,* Pinkerton in *Madama Butterfly,* Edgardo in *Lucia di Lammermoor* (with which he helped to open the 1964–1965 season), Don José in *Carmen,* Lionel in *Martha,* Riccardo in *Un Ballo in Maschera,* Turiddu, Lohengrin, and Stewa Buryja in *Jenufa.*

He paid his first return visit to his native country in 1964 (after an absence of twenty years). According to the New York *Times,* "When he sang in Budapest, police had to control crowds of ticket seekers. In the audience were Mr. Kónya's mother and ninety-year-old grandmother, plus aunts, uncles and cousins from all over Hungary." In his native city, Sarkad, a street and a choir were named after him.

When Erich Leinsdorf conducted a concert

performance of *Lohengrin* in its entirety for the first time in the Western hemisphere—at the Berkshire Music Festival at Tanglewood in Massachusetts in the summer of 1965—he selected Kónya for the title role. This performance was recorded by RCA Victor. Reviewing this release for *Stereo Review* a critic said: "Kónya has done Lohengrin more than two hundred times and is generally recognized as its outstanding exponent. Now his eloquent interpretation has been preserved on records, and it is revealed here as a portrayal completely integrated in song and action, a triumph of expressiveness." He again appeared as Lohengrin in a new production of the opera mounted by the Metropolitan in 1966–1967 during the company's first season at the Lincoln Center for the Performing Arts.

Kónya has appeared with the major opera companies of the United States, Europe, and South America. His extensive repertory includes the title role in Auber's *Fra Diavolo*, Faust in Boïto's *Mefistofele*, Giasone in Cherubini's *Medea*, Paolino in Cimarosa's *Il Matrimonio Segreto*, Nureddin in Cornelius's *The Barber of Bagdad*, Boris in Janáček's *Katya Kabanova*, Canio in *I Pagliacci*, Tristan in Frank Martin's *Le Vin Herbé*, Michele in Menotti's *The Saint of Bleecker Street*, the title role in *The Tales of Hoffmann*, Des Grieux in *Manon Lescaut*, the title role in Smetana's *Dalibor*, Eisenstein and Alfred in *Die Fledermaus*, the title role in *Don Carlo*, Ismaele in *Nabucco*, Manrico in *Il Trovatore*, Otello, the Duke of Mantua in *Rigoletto*, Macduff in *Macbeth*, Siegmund in *Die Walküre*, Max in *Der Freischütz*, Huon in *Oberon*, Babinsky in Weinberger's *Schwanda*, and Filipeto in Wolf-Ferrari's *I Quattro Rusteghi*. He created the role of Leandro in the world premiere of Henze's *König Hirsch* at the Berlin State Opera (September 23, 1956), and he has appeared in a film for televison of *Un Ballo in Maschera*.

While the Kónyas maintain their official residence at Lugano, Switzerland, they also possess a home in Germany and an apartment in New York City. He and his wife are both excellent cooks and often prepare their own meals when entertaining close friends. For relaxation, Kónya tends to his garden.

ABOUT: Opera News, February 2, 1962, February 19, 1966.

André Kostelanetz

1901–

André Kostelanetz, conductor, first became prominent as a conductor of lush arrangements of popular music together with semiclassical compositions and adaptations of the classics over the radio. He has since become famous in public auditoriums for "Pop" or "Promenade" concerts. Nevertheless, as a guest conductor of many of the major orchestras of the United States and Europe he has demonstrated interpretative insight, as well as a command of baton technique, in the performances of the great literature of the classical, romantic, and modern repertory.

He was born in St. Petersburg, Russia, on December 22, 1901, one of five children of wealthy parents. Both his father, Nachman, and his mother, Rosalie Dimscha Kostelanetz, were dedicated musical amateurs. From early infancy André demonstrated a fascination for musical sounds, and his parents directed him to the study of the piano when he was only three. Two years later, in St. Petersburg, he gave a piano recital, and in his tenth year he participated in a student concert at St. Peter's School, where in the years between 1911 and 1918 he received his academic education. Early in life André became a linguist (speaking six languages), was a passionate reader of literary classics, and showed a talent for chemistry.

The Kostelanetz family often went to Germany for their summer holidays. In Germany, André, then five years old, was so fascinated by a band concert in the public park that, entranced by the music and unconscious of what he was doing, he walked to the bandstand. The conductor noticed him and playfully allowed him to lead the musicians. This, Kostelanetz has said, was one of the most thrilling experiences of his childhood.

André completed his musical training in studies at the St. Petersburg Conservatory between 1920 and 1922; in the latter year he received a doctorate in music. The revolution in Russia had depleted the Kostelanetz family fortune, compelling him to rely on music for his livelihood. When he was nineteen he found a job as assistant

---

Kostelanetz: kŏs tē lä′ nĕts

ANDRÉ KOSTELANETZ

conductor at the Grand Opera in Petrograd (St. Petersburg). The revolution had brought with it poverty and struggle, but this did not interrupt the opera performances which were given in auditoriums so cold that the singers and musicians had to rehearse wearing furs. The cold and the hunger soon drove Kostelanetz out of Russia. Leaving behind him all of his possessions, he fled to Warsaw. There in a record shop he heard Irving Berlin's "A Pretty Girl Is Like a Melody," and his lifelong love affair with American popular music began. "What I heard seemed like a new musical world to me. From that time on I was not only intrigued with American popular music but became aware of its importance as *good* music."

From Warsaw, Kostelanetz made his way to the United States, where he established permanent residence and in 1928 became a citizen. His first assignment in America was to make an arrangement of a popular song for which he was paid thirty dollars. His first job was with the Andreas Dippel Opera Company. Subsequently, over a six-year period he worked as an accompanist to singers of the Metropolitan Opera and the Chicago Opera, touring the country five times with the singers Maria Kurenko and Julia Claussen.

He made his debut over the radio in 1924, but not until 1929 did he become officially affiliated with it. In 1929 he was given a contract to conduct air concerts over the Atlantic Broadcasting Company network (the predecessor of the Columbia Broadcasting System). In 1932 Kostela-

netz acquired his first coast-to-coast sponsored program. For more than a decade afterwards his programs helped to sell automobiles, cigarettes, gasoline, soft drinks, corn syrup, and other products, and his name became a household word with radio audiences. He had the largest ensemble (forty-five men) that radio had thus far used for popular music, and for it he had arrangers contrive lush symphonic orchestrations far superior in musical interest to those previously used for popular music. "Radio," he said, "meant bringing music to millions who had never heard orchestras or symphonies before. I felt it was important that popular music be well played and that classical music be presented in a way that people's interest could be sustained. Everything was experimental: a movement from a symphony would be followed by a popular tune. That was a crossing of the boundaries, but it developed an interest in good music." While many serious musicians and critics regarded his condensations of the classics and his tendency to combine serious music with popular in a single concert as sacrilege, there could be no question that Kostelanetz became an effective missionary in converting large masses to a love for music. As Stephen E. Rubin wrote in the New York *Times* many years later (1973): "He is to music what Billy Graham is to religion. An initiator, he introduced fledglings to the felicities of 'serious' music.... In this striving he has become the High Lama of popular musical art, the quintessential middlebrow, everybody's Toscanini." In 1936 and 1937 Kostelanetz received the Radio Medal of Merit because "his program provides listeners everywhere with so much enjoyment and because it has refused to cheapen or compromise with quality." A national poll conducted by the *Motion Picture Daily* among six hundred music editors and critics gave first place to Kostelanetz's broadcasts for four years running, and in 1943 still another poll (this time among one hundred and twenty American and Canadian newspapers) gave him a place of honor in both the popular and serious music categories, the first musician ever to get such recognition. In the popular group Kostelanetz captured top honors, and in the symphonic field he took third place behind the NBC Symphony under Toscanini and the New York Philharmonic.

In 1936 he made thirteen consecutive weekend flights to California, where he had been engaged to direct the music for *I Dream Too Much,* a motion picture starring the soprano Lily Pons. Two years later, on June 2, 1938, Kostelanetz and Pons were married in her pine-covered home in Silvermine, Connecticut.

The husband and wife team of André Kostelanetz as conductor and Lily Pons as soprano soloist became in the late 1930s and early 1940s one of the leading attractions in the music business. A summer tour in five major cities in the United States in 1939, beginning at Robin Hood Dell in Philadelphia and ending at the Hollywood Bowl in California, attracted three hundred and eighty-five thousand music lovers; in one concert in Chicago they performed before two hundred and fifty thousand; this is believed to be a record turnout for a musical event up to that time. During World War II "the first family of music," as Kostelanetz and Pons were being billed, traveled seventy-eight thousand miles through all the major theaters of conflict, sometimes performing on the front lines. In recognition of their service, they were authorized by the Headquarters Army Service Forces to wear the Asiatic-Pacific campaign ribbon.

By World War II Kostelanetz was not only being heard over the radio, on recordings, and in concerts with his wife, but he was also appearing as a guest conductor of orchestras throughout North and South America. For these concerts he commissioned American composers to write new works for him. During the early war years he asked for compositions which would carry to a war-stricken country the message "of what democracy is, and what we are fighting for" and which would mirror "the magnificent spirit of our country." Toward this end Aaron Copland wrote *Lincoln Portrait,* for narrator and orchestra; Jerome Kern, *Mark Twain: A Portrait for Orchestra;* and Virgil Thomson, *The Mayor La Guardia Waltzes.* All three were given their world premieres by the Cincinnati Symphony under Kostelanetz on May 14, 1942. Among Kostelanetz's later commissions were many whose world premieres he conducted: Paul Creston's *Frontiers* (Toronto, October 14, 1943); Ferde Grofé's *Hudson River Suite* (Washington, D.C., June 26, 1955); William Schuman's *New England Triptych* (Miami, October 28, 1956); Alan Hovhaness's *Floating World—Ukiyo* (Salt Lake City, January 30, 1965); Hovhaness's *To Vishnu* (New York, June 2, 1967); Ezra Laderman's *Magic Prison* (New York, June 12, 1967);

and Copland's *Three Latin-American Sketches* (New York, June 7, 1972).

Kostelanetz's conducting assignments have been worldwide. In 1962 he initiated summer concerts at the Lincoln Center for the Performing Arts in New York with the New York Philharmonic. Called the "Promenades," they became an annual event. When he conducted the New York Philharmonic in a concert at Central Park in New York in the summer of 1975, he drew what is believed to be an all-time high in attendance at a classical concert, one hundred and fifty thousand people.

Kostelanetz and Pons were divorced in 1958. Two years later, in 1960, in San Francisco, he married Sara Gene Orcutt, a medical technician. Nine years later this marriage also ended in divorce. Kostelanetz's home is a duplex apartment in Gracie Square, New York, overlooking the East River, a place he maintained through both marriages. There he is surrounded by his collection of paintings by Renoir, Chagall, and others, and by *objets d'art* which he has gathered from all over the world.

Kostelanetz has combined his highly successful career in the concert hall with extensive recordings for Columbia. No conductor has sold more albums than he—some fifty-three million of them. He conducted the music for the motion picture *Artists and Models* (1937), was music director for the film *Hitting a New High* (1937), and made a cinematic appearance with his orchestra in *My Heart Is Full* (1941).

He received honorary doctorates in music from Albion (Michigan) College in 1939 and the Cincinnati Conservatory of Music in 1945.

ABOUT: American Magazine, May 1938, December 1941; Coronet, April 1950; Esquire, July 1939; New York Times, May 6, 1973.

Serge Koussevitzky

1874–1951

Serge Alexandrovich Koussevitzky, conductor, was a commanding figure in music not only because of his often incandescent performances of the classics and the moderns but also because of his lifelong dedication to the promotion of twen-

Koussevitzky: ko͞o sĕ vĭts' kĭ

412

SERGE KOUSSEVITZKY

tieth century music—as a conductor, as a publisher, as an educator, and as the founder of the Koussevitzky Music Foundation.

He was born in Vyshni-Volochek, Russia, on July 26, 1874. His mother, Anne Barabeitchik Koussevitzky, was a trained pianist. She died shortly after his birth. His father, Alexander, was a violin teacher who gave him his first violin lessons. These lessons were later supplemented by instruction on the piano from a local teacher and on the cello from his father. Even as a child, Serge wanted to conduct. He would line up two rows of empty chairs and imagine himself a conductor in front of an orchestra; with the score in front of him he would sing the music and go through the motions of directing an ensemble. While still a child, he played the violin in an orchestra and wrote incidental music for local theatrical productions for which he was sometimes asked to lead the orchestra. When he was twelve he became the full conductor of this troupe on its tour.

In his fourteenth year, with just three rubles in his pocket, he went to Moscow. There he entered the Moscow Philharmonic School as a scholarship student, specializing in the double bass with Joseph Rambousec and studying theory with Pavel Blaramberg and Semion Kruglikov. He supported himself by taking on odd musical jobs. He made such progress on the double bass that just one year after he had begun its study he was praised by Tchaikovsky for the way he performed some of that master's music. In the fall of 1894, still a Conservatory student,

Koussevitzky was engaged as a double bass player with the orchestra of the Bolshoi Opera.

Following his graduation from the Philharmonic School, Koussevitzky embarked on a career as a virtuoso of the double bass. He made his debut as a soloist in Moscow in 1896, then appeared in solo performances in concert halls and salons and participated in chamber-music concerts. On March 27, 1903, he gave a highly acclaimed recital in Berlin. "Listening to Koussevitzky," Vladimir Dubinsky, one of his fellow students, recalled in later years, "one would forget he was playing the double bass. It wasn't a double bass at all, it was some instrument between a cello and a bass, of unusual beauty. He possessed everything that makes a great artist—tone, technical equipment, temperament, repose, a keen sense of rhythm, and a fine conception."

In Moscow, at one of the fashionable salons in which he performed, Koussevitzky met Natalya Ushkov, the daughter of a wealthy tea merchant. On September 8, 1905, they were married. (This was Koussevitzky's second marriage. His first—to Nadezhda Galat, a ballet dancer—a few years earlier ended in divorce in 1905.) The Koussevitzkys spent their honeymoon in Berlin, where Koussevitzky attended the concerts of the Berlin Philharmonic and came to worship its conductor, Arthur Nikisch. He also studied the methods and styles of such other masterful conductors as Mahler, Mottl, Richard Strauss, and Weingartner. Koussevitzky spent many days memorizing musical scores and many hours in front of a mirror practicing the bodily and manual gestures of a conductor. On one occasion he put into practice what he had thus far been studying by conducting a student orchestra at the Berlin High School for Music. Then, with funds provided by his father-in-law, he engaged the Berlin Philharmonic with which to make his professional conducting debut on January 23, 1908, in Berlin, in an all-Russian program made up of works by Tchaikovsky and Rachmaninoff, and the world premiere of Glière's Symphony No.2. August Spanuth said in *Die Signale:* "Koussevitzky left no doubt that he is an interpreter of uncommon temperament and an effective leader. . . . He knows how to get elemental bursts of power from the orchestra, as well as the sweetest and most ingratiating sounds, and with all his energy and all his temperament he keeps authoritative control." In the spring of 1908 he conducted two concerts with the London Symphony Orchestra and one with the Konzertverein Orchestra in Vienna. In May 1909 he led orchestral concerts in Paris and London.

Returning to Moscow in 1909, Koussevitzky announced a series of eight orchestral concerts for that season with the orchestra of the Bolshoi Opera, each program of which he also performed in St. Petersburg with the Imperial Russian Music Society Orchestra. His Russian debut as conductor took place in St. Petersburg on October 27, 1909, in a program comprising Beethoven's *Egmont Overture,* Bach's *Brandenburg Concerto No.3,* Weber's *Oberon Overture,* and the Chopin Piano Concerto in E minor (with Leopold Godowsky as soloist). Nicholas Kashkin, critic of *Russkoye Slovo,* hailed this debut as a great success and spoke of Koussevitzky's signal talent and conducting ability. He prophesied that Koussevitzky would develop into an outstanding conductor. Already conscious of his obligation to Russian music—and particularly to those living composers needing promotion—Koussevitzky formed in 1909 the Éditions Russes de Musique.

"The pattern of Koussevitzky's future career was now fairly clear," notes Moses Smith in his biography of the conductor. "He was to be a sort of *grand seigneur* of Russian music, particularly symphonic music. It was to be a career of conducting and publishing, the one aiding the other quite legitimately."

From the beginning of his career in Russia Koussevitzky proved himself to be a powerful influence in developing the musical tastes of Russian audiences. At his concerts in Moscow and St. Petersburg he introduced the works of modern composers which had never, or almost never, been performed in their native country. Among his world premieres were Scriabin's *Prometheus* (March 15, 1911), Taneiev's *Upon Reading the Psalms* (April 14, 1915), and Medtner's Piano Concerto (1918). He organized festivals devoted to one composer (Bach, Beethoven, Brahms, or Wagner) which soon became the major artistic event of the season. He expanded the existing repertory of symphonic music in Russia to include many classical compositions that were still unfamiliar.

After the end of his first conducting season in Russia, he appeared as a guest conductor of the Berlin Philharmonic on March 11, 1910. At that time Arthur Nikisch told him: "You are a born conductor. Everything is there—you have the technique, you have imagination, you have temperament and you bring everything out with plasticity." The next month, on April 5, 1910, Koussevitzky gave the first performance in England of Scriabin's *Poem of Ecstasy* at a concert of the London Symphony.

In the summer of 1910 Koussevitzky formed an eighty-five-member orchestra of his own for the purpose of bringing great symphonic music on a chartered steamer to villages along the Volga that had never before heard an orchestral concert. This expedition began on May 4, 1910, at a personal expense of over one hundred thousand dollars. He traveled twenty-three hundred miles in four months, taking his music to villages and hamlets with audiences of Persians, Turks, Tartars, Armenians, Mohammedans, Buddhists, Christians, and Jews. "In Yaroslavl," Moses Smith tells us, "a woman was particularly moved by the thunderous strokes of the enthusiastic tympanist—so moved that she suffered a heart attack. In Nizhyny-Novgorod . . . several persons fainted during the climax of the slow movement of Tchaikovsky's Fifth Symphony. . . . At Simbrack . . . an old lady . . . kept her hands clasped rigidly. Tears of joy coursed intermittently down her cheeks. In Samara a gray-haired engineer was so moved by the music that he suddenly had a fit of uncontrolled sobs."

Koussevitzky made two more tours of the Volga, the second in the spring of 1912 (twenty concerts in ten cities) and the third in May 1914 (seventeen concerts in ten cities). By the time he returned to Moscow from the third and last of these musical pilgrimages he had become so famous that he received an offer to go to the United States in 1916. Because of World War I he was unable to accept. When revolution broke out in Russia, Koussevitzky's important position in his country's musical life was recognized by the Soviet Union, which made him director of the Russian State Orchestra, a post he held until 1920. But the new proletarian regime brought him misery, not only because all his Russian holdings were confiscated, but also because he became increasingly enmeshed in bureaucratic red tape in the pursuit of his art. Secretly he made plans to leave Russia, and his escape was made possible in 1920 when he received official permission to conduct in Europe. In May 1920 Koussevitzky and his wife left

Russia with only the possessions they could pack into a suitcase. They never returned.

Since the Koussevitzkys had considerable holdings outside Russia they did not experience any financial problems. They lived in the Arceuil district of Paris. Koussevitzky founded a new orchestra for the presentation of Concerts Koussevitzky which became as well known as the first one. For four years he dominated the Parisian musical scene with performances in which he introduced to France much Russian music then unknown to the French and in which he helped to promote the works of contemporary French masters. Among his world premieres were Honegger's *Chant de Joie* (May 3, 1923), Concertino for Piano (May 23, 1925), and *Pacific 231* (May 8, 1924); the Ravel transcription of Mussorgsky's *Pictures at an Exhibition* which he had commissioned (October 19, 1922); Prokofiev's Piano Concerto No.2 (May 8, 1924), Violin Concerto No.1 (October 18, 1923), *Seven Are They* (May 29, 1924), and Symphony No.2 (June 6, 1925); Roussel's Piano Concerto (June 7, 1928); Stravinsky's Piano Concerto (May 22, 1924); and Tailleferre's Piano Concerto (May 30, 1925). In addition, he formed the Éditions Russes, a new publishing house to spread further the gospel of Russian music in France.

His fame spread outside France with performances in Barcelona, Rome, London, and Berlin. In 1924 he was invited by the directors of the Boston Symphony Orchestra to become permanent conductor. The Boston Symphony had had a brilliant history in the years following its founding in 1881, but in the post–World War I era it had suffered marked artistic deterioration. The acquisition of Koussevitzky was intended to restore some of its former glory. The Koussevitzky years, from 1925 to 1949, became one of the proudest epochs in the history of this orchestra. Within the first few seasons he overhauled the personnel, training them fastidiously and autocratically, until they had become one of the great virtuoso orchestras of the world. He also revitalized the repertory—Koussevitzky had identified himself as completely with new American music and living American composers as he had previously with the Russian and the French. During his twenty-five-year regime he offered one hundred and ten world premieres of which over 70 percent were by American composers. Even a partial list of those premieres is impressive: Samuel Barber's Cello Concerto (April 5, 1946), *Knoxville: Summer of 1915* (April 9, 1948), and Symphony No.2 (March 3, 1944); Bartók's *Concerto for Orchestra* (December 1, 1944); Bax's Symphony No.2 (December 13, 1929); Leonard Bernstein's *Age of Anxiety* (April 8, 1949); John Alden Carpenter's *Patterns* (October 21, 1932); Castelnuovo-Tedesco's *Cipressi* (October 25, 1940); Copland's Piano Concerto (January 28, 1927), *Symphonic Ode* (February 19, 1932), and Symphony No.3 (October 18, 1946); David Diamond's Symphony No.2 (October 13, 1944); Vladimir Dukelsky's Cello Concerto (January 4, 1945), *Dédicaces* (December 16, 1938), and Symphony No.2 (April 25, 1930); Lukas Foss's *The Prairie,* suite (October 15, 1943), and *The Song of Songs* (March 7, 1947); Gershwin's *Second Rhapsody* (January 29, 1932); Gretchaninoff's *Missa Oecumenica* (February 25, 1944); Louis Gruenberg's Symphony No.1 (February 10, 1934); Camargo Guarnieri's Symphony No.1 (November 29, 1946); Howard Hanson's Symphony No.2 (November 28, 1930); Roy Harris's Symphony No.1 (January 26, 1934), Symphony No.3 (February 24, 1939), Symphony No.5 (February 26, 1943), and Symphony No.6 (April 14, 1944); Edward Burlingame Hill's Concertino (April 19, 1940), *Lilacs* (March 31, 1927), Symphony No.1 (March 30, 1928), Symphony No.2 (February 27, 1931), Symphony No.3 (December 3, 1937), and Violin Concerto (November 11, 1938); Hindemith's Cello Concerto (February 7, 1941) and *Konzertmusik* (April 3, 1931); Honegger's Symphony No.1 (February 13, 1931); Lopatnikoff's Symphony No.2 (December 22, 1939) and Violin Concerto (April 17, 1942); Malipiero's Symphony No.4 (February 27, 1948); Bohuslav Martinu's *La Bagarre* (November 18, 1927), Concerto Grosso (November 14, 1941), *La Symphonie* (December 14, 1928), Symphony No.1 (November 13, 1942), Symphony No.3 (October 12, 1945), and Violin Concerto (December 31, 1943); Walter Piston's Prelude and Allegro for Organ and Strings (October 29, 1943), and Symphony No.3 (January 9, 1948); Prokofiev's Symphony No.4 (November 14, 1930); Respighi's *Metamorphosen, Modi XII* (November 7, 1930) and *Vetrate di Chiesa* (February 25, 1927); Roussel's Suite in F (January 21, 1927) and Symphony in G minor (October 24, 1930); Schmitt's Symphonie Concertante, for piano and orchestra (November 25, 1932); Schoenberg's Theme and Variations (October

20, 1944); William Schuman's *American Festival Overture* (October 9, 1939), *A Free Song* (March 26, 1939), Symphony No.3 (October 17, 1941), Symphony for Strings (November 12, 1943); Roger Sessions's Symphony in E minor (April 22, 1927); Leo Sowerby's Concerto for Organ and Orchestra (April 22, 1938), Piano Concerto No.2 (November 30, 1936), and Symphony No.4 (January 7, 1949); Stravinsky's *Ode* (October 8, 1943); Alexander Tansman's Piano Concerto No.2 (December 29, 1927) and Symphony No.1 (March 18, 1927); and Emerson Whithorne's *Moon Trail* (December 15, 1933). The American premieres were also plentiful; among them were Benjamin Britten's *A Spring Symphony* (August 13, 1949), Prokofiev's Symphony No.5 (November 1945), Shostakovich's Symphony No.9 (July 25, 1946), and Stravinsky's *Symphony of Psalms* (December 19, 1930).

To further advance the cause of modern music Koussevitzky created in 1942 the Koussevitzky Music Foundation with his own personal funds. Its purpose was to commission contemporary composers everywhere to write new music. Through the years the music brought to life by this fund became a cross section of important musical creativity of the twentieth century. Among the works owing their origin to the Koussevitzky Music Foundation were Aaron Copland's Symphony No.3, Benjamin Britten's opera *Peter Grimes,* Marc Blitzstein's opera *Regina,* Arthur Honegger's Symphony No.5, Douglas Moore's opera *The Ballad of Baby Doe,* Béla Bartók's *Concerto for Orchestra,* Walter Piston's Symphony No.3, and Olivier Messiaen's *Turangalíla.*

"The history of the Koussevitzky Music Foundation is an honorable one," wrote Raymond Ericson in the New York *Times* on June 23, 1968. "It has not limited itself to composers of one clique or to works of a similar form. It has sought out young Americans as well as composers from Soviet Russia and the 'satellite' countries. By the persistence of its endeavors it has accumulated works by an impressive list of composers."

With his innovative programming and electrifying performances Koussevitzky succeeded in restoring glamour to the Boston Symphony. Discussing Koussevitzky's conducting, the English musicologist Ernest Newman wrote: "The more the artist is on fire, the cooler have to be the head and the hand that direct the fire.

Koussevitzky has the central ice to an extraordinary degree. I believe it would be hardly possible to raise some works to a higher pitch of nervous incandescence than he does; but the nervousness never gets out of hand. It is Koussevitzky's servant, not master. The excitement is always perfectly under control; one great plastic line runs round and through the work. Here, perhaps, lies the secret of Koussevitzky's unique success in the music of Ravel, Sibelius, Scriabin and Berlioz."

Of Koussevitzky's Herculean efforts as conductor of the Boston Symphony on behalf of contemporary composers, William Schuman, writing in the New York *Times,* said: "He was not alone among the conductors and solo artists of his day who cared about the composer and his problems, but, even among the most distinguished, it is difficult to cite any who made the creators of music the primary concern of their art. Serge Koussevitzky did nothing less than this. ... For Koussevitzky, the composer was ever the core. ... He talked for composers, he performed them, he commissioned works from them, he believed in them. ... There was one man, at least, whose fame and fortune as one of the great leaders of all time strengthened the primary activity which makes music endure. It all seems so simple and obvious. Perhaps that is why he was astonishing."

In the summer of 1936 Koussevitzky took the Boston Symphony to the four-hundred-acre estate Tanglewood, in Lenox, Massachusetts, which up to then had been the home of rather inconsequential summer festivals. He and the Boston Symphony transformed Tanglewood into the most important summer music festival in America, attracting pilgrims from all parts of the United States. For these concerts a special auditorium was built. On August 4, 1938, Koussevitzky conducted his first Berkshire Festival concert in the spacious newly constructed shed, a performance by the Boston Symphony of Beethoven's Symphony No.9.

Tanglewood became something more than the setting for distinguished summer music-making. In 1940, through Koussevitzky's idealism and vision, it became the home of the newly founded Berkshire Music Center, a summer school of music at which talented young musicians could mingle and work with their teachers, exchange ideas, hear lectures, participate in round table discussions, study music, and make music.

Koussevitzky was the director of the Berkshire Music Center as long as he lived. After his death he was succeeded by Aaron Copland.

With his wife, Natalya, Koussevitzky lived in Brookline, Massachusetts, where he led the life of the *grand seigneur.* In spite of the fact that he was comparatively short and of slight build, he had an impressive presence, both on and off the conductor's platform. One writer said he resembled a "diplomat of the Napoleonic era," while another said he was like "an emperor stepped out of the history book." He made his entrance in front of his orchestra—whether at a rehearsal or a concert—a kind of regal procession. As he conducted he used body, facial expressions, and eyes as instruments with which to project his intentions to his men. He was, wrote Olin Downes in the New York *Times,* "a figure to remember—erect, imperious, his face working with his emotions; a hand of which the fingers themselves are suddenly eloquent, suddenly bringing out an outburst of tone . . . ; a glance which, sweeping over the orchestra, brings suddenly dramatic results. . . . There is an authority, a quenchless enthusiasm, and a big sweep in all that he does which, if he were less sincere and individual a musician than he is, would be a compelling force for public success."

Though he could be utterly charming to those he liked or wished to please, Koussevitzky was not a man to inspire affection from the men in his orchestra. He was the total dictator, who strode imperiously into a rehearsal, wearing a cape which was removed from his shoulders as soon as he stepped on the dais. He brooked no nonsense or levity at rehearsals; and he could be merciless in his verbal attacks in the face of improper responses to his demands. He demanded at all times unquestioning obedience and discipline.

Excessively vain, he was ungracious in the face of unfavorable criticism of himself and his art and he was impatient or hostile to anyone holding an opinion differing from his. He had an explosive temper. When angry or under stress, the veins stood out prominently on his temple and his ruddy complexion became purple. He possessed the imperious nature and the snobbery of the old-world aristocrat.

Only those who stood ready to accept him on his own lofty terms could belong to his "court"; those who disagreed with him belonged, as far as he was concerned, in the enemy camp. When a critic spoke disparagingly of one of his performances he sometimes tried to use his influence (unsuccessfully) to get the man fired. When he objected to some of the opinions and observations expressed by Moses Smith in his biography of Koussevitzky, he rushed to the law courts to sue the publisher and author for "invasion of privacy"—a case he lost decisively in the court of appeals.

His wife, Natalya, died in 1942. On August 5, 1947, Koussevitzky married his niece, Olga Naumoff. In 1949, after twenty-five years of service, he announced his resignation from the Boston Symphony, feeling the post of music director should belong to a younger man. He gave his last concert with his orchestra on April 29, 1949, after which he became conductor emeritus. On May 2, Symphony Hall in Boston was converted into a banquet hall in his honor and a six-movement composition, a cantata *In Grato Jubilo,* the combined effort of a number of his former students at the Berkshire Music Center, was performed for him.

In October 1950 he emerged from retirement to help reorganize the Detroit Symphony and to conduct it. That year he also toured with the Israel Philharmonic as one of its principal conductors, and he made some guest appearances in Rio de Janeiro, Europe, and Israel.

Koussevitzky died in Boston on June 4, 1951, after a brief illness. Leonard Bernstein, his protégé, flew in to Boston in time to be with Koussevitzky just before his death. Koussevitzky presented him with his cape as a parting gift, almost with the gesture of a king turning over the royal scepter to his successor. Funeral services for Koussevitzky were held at the Protestant Episcopal Church of the Advent in Boston, and burial took place in Lenox, Massachusetts, near the grounds of Tanglewood and the Berkshire Music Center; a chamber group from the Boston Symphony provided the music.

After Koussevitzky's death, his widow, Olga, helped to administer the foundations he had established, particularly the Koussevitzky Music Foundation. She devoted herself to numerous other cultural and philanthropic causes up to the time of her death on January 5, 1978.

In 1949 Koussevitzky was appointed music consultant at Brandeis University in Waltham, Massachusetts. He was made Knight of the French Legion of Honor in 1924. In 1926 Brown University conferred on him an honorary doctorate; on the occasion he expressed his gratitude by giving a performance on the double bass. He also received an honorary doctorate in music from Harvard.

ABOUT: Leichtentritt, H. Serge Koussevitzky, the Boston Symphony Orchestra and the New American Music; Lourie, A. Serge Koussevitzky and His Epoch; Schonberg, H. C. The Great Conductors; Shore, B. The Orchestra Speaks; Smith, M. Koussevitzky. *Periodicals*—New York Times, June 23, 1968; Theatre Arts Magazine, September 1951.

Lili Kraus

1905–

LILI KRAUS

Lili Kraus, pianist, was born in Budapest on April 3, 1905. Her father, Victor, of Czechoslovakian descent, earned his living as a stone grinder, and her mother, Irene Bak Kraus, a Hungarian, was an amateur singer. Lili was six when she began to study piano, and in her eighth year she entered the Academy of Music in Budapest. There her teachers included Béla Bartók and Zoltán Kodály. In 1922 she was graduated with highest honors.

She made her concert debut with a recital in Holland in 1923. Then she went on to Vienna to attend the New Academy of Music as a student of piano with Eduard Steuermann. In 1926 she took a diploma in the master class in piano at the Vienna Conservatory where she became a professor at twenty. From 1930 to 1934 she studied piano with Artur Schnabel in Berlin.

While teaching piano at the Vienna Conservatory, she made concert appearances throughout Europe, including sonata recitals with the violinist Szymon Goldberg. "From about eighteen to twenty-three," she told Richard Freed in an interview in the New York *Times,* "I was known as a Chopin player. I had then a forest of hair on my head, and no matter how many hairpins I would use to keep it up, by the end of a big, dramatic piece—say, the F minor Fantaisie—the hairpins would all be scattered on the floor and my hair down. I'm sure the audience thought: 'If this isn't Romantic, what is?' But then I began to play Beethoven, both alone and with Szymon Goldberg (with whom I recorded all the Beethoven sonatas for violin and piano)

Kraus: krous

and for some years I was known primarily as a Beethoven pianist. After I made my first Mozart recording—the C minor Fantasy and Sonata—I was approached to do more Mozart, including the piano and violin sonatas, which I did with Goldberg. For this a Mozart Society was formed in London, and it was very successful."

In her extensive tours throughout Europe, the Orient, Australia, and South Africa, she became identified with the music of Mozart and Schubert, both as a scholar and as an interpreter. But she also played many compositions of Bach and Beethoven as well as selections from the contemporary literature. She became the first piano virtuoso of note to perform Béla Bartók's piano works at concerts, even before Bartók himself had done so.

When Nazism spread across the Continent just before World War II, Kraus established residence in London with her husband, Otto Mandl (a translator into German of the work of H. G. Wells and professor of philosophy), whom she had married on October 31, 1930, and their two children. Though Europe was embroiled in World War II in 1942, she decided to make a world tour, taking along her family. This tour—planned to end with her American debut in February 1943 with the San Francisco Symphony under Monteux—was suddenly aborted when she was captured in Java by the invading Japanese troops. For three years she was imprisoned by the Japanese in a forced labor camp. For a full year of that time she could learn nothing about the fate of her husband and her children.

Recalling this shattering experience she said: "It was the one and only time we had the kids along, then aged nine and ten. We were separated, and that was it. I was not merely interned but arrested on a trumped-up charge. A Dutch woman in trouble herself following her liaison with a Japanese officer signed a document stating that I had plotted with the American wife of the Dutch governor general to release a handful of British and Australian POWs. It was fortunate they had only this charge against me, for if they had known what my husband and I had done they probably would have killed us: we had a hidden radio, we were harboring goods for the Dutch already in prison, transporting money from camp to camp, smuggling letters from wives to husbands."

During her first year of internment she shared a filthy subterranean cell with twelve other women and was subjected to hard labor—scrubbing latrines and gutters with chemicals and strong soaps. She had to subsist on a daily ration of two cups of rice and bitter herbs. Then her presence in the camp was discovered by a Japanese symphony conductor with whom she had performed in Tokyo in 1936. He arranged to transfer her to a "privileged" camp where not only were the working conditions much better but she could finally be reunited with her family.

In October 1945 she and her family were liberated by the British who flew them to Australia. There she made two tours in 1946 and 1947. She also performed in New Zealand, on whose passport she traveled from then on. In 1948 she toured South Africa where in 1949 and 1950 she was head of the piano department at Capetown University. In 1949 she made her long-delayed debut in the United States.

By this time she was not only making appearances throughout most of the world but also making numerous recordings on the Parlaphone, Discophile Français, and Educo labels. She has since toured the world many times, achieving particular renown for her performances of Mozart's piano music. One of her recitals, in New York in the fall of 1958, led Harold C. Schonberg to write in the New York Times: "The high spot of the evening was the Mozart Fantasy and Sonata. . . . Miss Kraus is back in the form that one remembers from her pre-war recordings, which means that one of the finest classical pianists again is back in circulation." Following her performance of the Mozart

D minor Concerto with the London Mozart Players in the Royal Festival Hall in London in the spring of 1960, Neville Cardus wrote in the Guardian: "It was the piano playing of Lili Kraus that bathed and cleansed our musical sensibilities: as soloist in the D minor piano concerto of Mozart, she made the music sound as though it were coming to us unburdened of usage, beautifully poised, fine—and always the music of Mozart." Upon her return to the United States in 1966–1967, after several years' absence, she performed all of Mozart's twenty-five piano concerti in a series of nine concerts in New York, an event without precedence in that city. On this occasion Harold C. Schonberg called her "a pianist with taste, skill and heart," and in the New York Post Harriet Johnson described her as "the brightest Mozartean sage extant." She began to record all of these Mozart concertos for CBS-Epic Records with the Vienna Festival Orchestra, a project completed in 1973, and she televised a program entitled "Lili Kraus and the Mozart Piano Concerti" which was produced and released by National Educational Television Network. For the season of 1967–1968 she returned to New York for five concerts embracing all of Mozart's piano sonatas; these were also recorded by CBS-Epic. Then, almost as if to prove that Mozart was not the only composer in whom she specialized, she offered in 1968–1969 three all-Schubert concerts, in New York, as a prelude to recording for Vanguard Schubert's entire literature for the piano.

Kraus has also distinguished herself as a lecturer and teacher. In 1956 she toured the United States with "A Day with Lili Kraus," which consisted of a morning seminar, an afternoon critique of students, and an evening recital. In 1967 she was appointed artist-in-residence at Texas Christian University in Fort Worth. She has since held master classes there in piano one month a year. Her home, when she is not teaching or traveling, is a four-hundred-acre farm near Asheville, North Carolina, which she shares with her daughter and son-in-law and their three children (her husband died in 1956). Her main interests are painting, literature, yoga, and designing her own gowns. She is a devout Roman Catholic. Religion to her is "as strong in me as the necessity for survival. I cannot imagine myself outside of God even for an instant."

In 1956 Kraus visited Albert Schweitzer at Lambarene, Africa, shortly before his death, giving him private recitals every evening on the battered upright piano in the hospital's mess hall. A Lili Kraus recording of a Beethoven Piano Concerto is believed to have been the last piece of music Schweitzer heard before succumbing to his final coma. In 1970, during a tour of four continents, Kraus played at the wedding of the Shah of Iran, performed the first program of secular music heard in Canterbury Cathedral in England, gave the first concert heard during the opening of Brasilia (Brazil's new capital), was heard in a concert at Royal Festival Hall in London commemorating the ninetieth birthday of the English philosopher Bertrand Russell, and was a soloist with the Salzburg Chamber Orchestra at the Royal Moroccan Mozart Festival.

On March 4, 1978, Kraus received from the Federal Republic of Austria the Cross of Honor for Science and Art, First Class.

ABOUT: Christian Science Monitor, August 20, 1970; New York Times, February 27, 1966, October 2, 1966, August 1, 1976; Stereo Review, February 1975.

CLEMENS KRAUSS

Clemens Krauss

1893–1954

Clemens Heinrich Krauss, conductor, was born in Vienna on March 31, 1893. His father was an Austrian courtier, his mother, a successful actress. As a boy of eight, Clemens sang in the historic Imperial Chapel in Vienna which had once known the membership of the young Franz Schubert. Krauss studied music at the Vienna Conservatory with Hugo Reinhold (piano) and Hermann Grädener and Richard Heuberger (theory). He was graduated in 1912 and that year made his debut with the Brünn Opera where he had been appointed choral director.

In 1913 and 1914 Krauss served as second conductor at the Riga Opera. He held a similar post with the Nuremberg Opera in 1915–1916. In 1916 he became first conductor at the Stettin Opera, with which he remained five years. In 1921–1922 he was conductor of symphonic music in Graz.

Krauss was brought to Vienna in 1922 by Franz Schalk, conductor at the Vienna State Op-

Krauss: krous

era. In Vienna, Krauss succeeded Furtwängler as music director of the Tonkunstlerverein Orchestra, directed performances at the Vienna State Opera, and taught conducting at the Vienna Academy of Music.

His rise to eminence in Vienna brought him, in 1924, the appointment of music director of the important Museum Concerts in Frankfort, Germany, and of the Frankfort Opera. In Frankfort, Krauss married the singer Viorica Ursuleac, who had made her debut with the Frankfort Opera under Krauss's baton in 1924. In later years, Krauss often served as piano accompanist at his wife's recitals.

In Frankfort, he distinguished himself particularly in the music of Mozart and Richard Strauss. While serving in Frankfort he was also able to give guest performances elsewhere: in Munich during its festival seasons of 1925 and 1926, and in the summer of 1926 at the Salzburg Festival, where he became an important participant.

Krauss made his American debut in 1929 as a guest conductor of the Philadelphia Orchestra in Philadelphia and then in New York. After that he led some performances with the New York Philharmonic. "He is clearly a musician of sobriety and skill," said Lawrence Gilman in the New York *Herald Tribune,* "with legitimate demands upon our interest and our respect."

In December 1934 Furtwängler was compelled to leave his post as music director of the Berlin State Opera, because of his dispute with the Nazi authorities over the production of Hindemith's opera *Mathis der Maler,* and Krauss withdrew from the Vienna State Opera to succeed Furtwängler in Berlin. It was an unhappy decision. In Vienna Krauss had been highly esteemed, and he had things pretty much his own way. But during his less than two years in Berlin Krauss was continually confronted with opposition, mainly from those who resented his taking over Furtwängler's place which, they said, he did not deserve. In 1936 Krauss resigned from the post in Berlin. From 1937 to 1940 he was the music director of the Munich Opera, and in 1939 he was called upon to help reorganize the Mozarteum in Salzburg.

As Richard Strauss's friend and as one of Strauss's most highly regarded interpreters, Krauss had a long and close association with performances of Strauss's operas. For many seasons his production of *Der Rosenkavalier* was a highlight of the annual Salzburg Festival. On July 1, 1933, he led the world premiere of *Arabella* in Dresden—he also led its English premiere at Covent Garden in 1937. On July 24, 1938, he conducted the premiere of *Der Friedenstag* in Munich, an opera which Strauss dedicated jointly to Krauss and to Krauss's wife. Krauss wrote the libretto for *Capriccio* and directed its world premiere in Munich on October 28, 1942. On August 14, 1952, he presented *Der Liebe der Danae* at the Salzburg Festival in what is now considered its world premiere, though actually he had led a private performance at the Salzburg Festival in 1944 after he had prepared it under the personal supervision of Strauss himself (no further performances were given at the time because the Nazi authorities had ordered all theaters to be closed for the duration of the war).

Krauss also distinguished himself as an interpreter of the operas of other twentieth century composers, particularly those by Alban Berg, Jaromir Weinberger, Egon Wellesz, and Carl Orff.

In 1947 Krauss returned to Vienna to become principal conductor of the Vienna State Opera and the Vienna Philharmonic Orchestra. He took the Vienna Philharmonic on several European tours. He also became one of the principal conductors at the Salzburg and Bayreuth Festivals.

In 1954 he went to Mexico City to direct two weeks of concerts with the National Symphony Orchestra. After a morning performance he re-

turned to his hotel room complaining of not feeling well. He died a few hours later of a heart attack, May 16, 1954.

ABOUT: Blaukopf, K. Great Conductors; Gregor, J. Clemens Krauss, Seine Musikalische Sendung; Pander, O. von. Krauss in München.

Fritz Kreisler

1875–1962

Fritz Kreisler, violinist, was born in Vienna on February 2, 1875, the second of five children of Samuel Severein Kreisler, a distinguished physician who was also known as an amateur ichthyologist. Fritz's younger brother, Hugo, became a professional cellist. "Father was really a frustrated musician," Kreisler said. "He had begged his father, an architect, to let him choose music as his life's work, but in those days that of a musician was not considered a 'gentlemanly' profession nor a 'bread and butter' career. So my father turned to medicine." As for his own musical beginnings, Kreisler said: "I was born with music in my system. I knew musical scores instinctively before I knew my A B C. It was a gift of Providence. I did not acquire it." As a child of three he listened raptly to the Saturday performances of chamber music at his home in which his father participated as cellist. A half year later he begged his father to teach him to read music. At four Fritz received his first violin, and before long he joined in the family chamber-music concerts. One evening in his fourth year he played the Austrian national anthem in perfect tune, and a friend of the family began giving him lessons. Two years later Jacob Dont became his teacher. Fritz made such progress that three years later he was admitted to the Vienna Conservatory, the first time in the history of that institution that a child of seven was entered there. His teachers included Joseph Hellmesberger (violin) and Anton Bruckner (harmony and theory). Without any formal instruction Kreisler also began to acquire proficiency at the piano.

In the year of his enrollment in the Vienna Conservatory he also made his public debut as violinist, performing several short pieces at a

---

Kreisler: krīs' lēr

Kreisler

FRITZ KREISLER

benefit concert in Carlsbad, a concert featuring the singer Carlotta Patti; his fee was a box of chocolates.

Fritz spent three years at the Conservatory. When he was nine he was a soloist at one of its concerts. One year later he received the Conservatory gold medal for violin playing, an unprecedented award for one so young. From Vienna he was sent at age ten to Paris to become a student at the Conservatory of Joseph Massart in violin and Léo Delibes in composition. To help support himself, he played first violin with the Pasdeloup Orchestra at the Cirque d'Hiver.

Fritz received the Premier Grand Prix at the Paris Conservatory, even though the other contestants were many years older than he. After leaving the Conservatory—he was only twelve—he never again had a formal violin lesson. "But," as he has explained, "every great artist was my teacher. I gathered good impressions wherever I could, and in due time became the pupil of not only every great performer, but of the great minds in literature and art. The Bible, Homer, Goethe, Shakespeare, and Dante were my household treasures of literature."

The fourteen-year-old prodigy embarked on a tour of the United States in 1888 in joint concerts with the piano virtuoso Moriz Rosenthal. Dressed in a velvet suit, short pants, and high shining boots with tassels dangling from the top, he made his American debut in Boston on November 9, 1888, in the Mendelssohn Concerto in E minor and Heinrich Ernst's *Hungarian Airs;* Walter Damrosch conducted. Harold Mal-

colm Ticknor, writing in the *Daily Globe,* found that young Kreisler "accomplished his task creditably but gave no evidence of possessing a remarkable training. ... He plays like a nice, studious boy who has a rather musical nature ... but he cannot be ranked among prodigies or geniuses." On the other hand, in the *Daily Advertiser* Louis C. Elson felt that "young Master Kreisler is a genius who ... is destined to become a very great artist, if he does not disdain further study." One evening later, Kreisler made his New York bow at Steinway Hall in New York, once again playing the Mendelssohn Concerto, but this time as a guest artist with Anton Seidl's Orchestra. The critic of the New York *Tribune* said: "The first impression created by him was a most favorable one, and throughout the evening admiration was held by the faultless purity of his intonation; unfortunately, however, his tone is exceedingly small."

Returning to Vienna, Fritz yielded to the wishes of his father and completed his academic education. He entered the Vienna High School in preparation for a career in medicine. He completed the full course in two years and entered the medical school of the University where he went through two of the five years of required study. During all that time he almost never touched the violin. Then, abandoning medical studies, he went to Paris and Rome to study painting. When this interest palled, he returned to Vienna to complete in 1895–1896 the army service required of all Austrian citizens.

While fulfilling military duties, Kreisler resumed playing the violin. Then, once again a civilian, he made the decision to return to an active career as a violinist. He applied for a post as violinist with the Vienna Royal Opera orchestra but was turned down. This rejection led him to turn to and concentrate on a virtuoso career. Retiring to the country, he worked assiduously for eight weeks on his technique and repertory. On January 23, 1898, he was heard as soloist with the Vienna Philharmonic, Hans Richter conducting, in Bruch's Violin Concerto No.2. Eduard Hanslick reported in the *Neue Freie Presse:* "Kreisler has been putting in recent years to perfect himself, so as to enable him now to face the Vienna public as a finished master. He was recalled a number of times after having played the concerto with brilliant virtuosity. There is no doubt that this distinction was accorded his playing rather than the Bruch composition." An even greater success met Kreisler in Berlin where he gave his initial recital in March 1899 and on December 1 was soloist with the Berlin Philharmonic under Nikisch in the Mendelssohn Concerto. Eugene Ysaÿe, the violinist, was in the audience. "When I finished the last cadenza," Kreisler recalled, "Ysaÿe ostentatiously got up and applauded. That generous gesture put me over. I shall never forget it. Some papers then devoted three-quarters of a column to my appearance."

After that, between 1900 and 1902, Kreisler gave concerts in France, Italy, Germany, Austria, Spain, the Scandinavian countries, and England. In December 1900 he returned to the United States, giving his first performance in America as a mature artist with a recital at Carnegie Hall, New York, on December 7, 1900. The extended American tour that followed proved an immense success. He returned to the United States for a much longer tour in 1901–1902, appearing not only in recitals and as guest artist with orchestras, but also in chamber-music concerts with Josef Hofmann, pianist, and Jean Gérardy, cellist. "America from now on was destined to become Fritz Kreisler's habitual resort," says Kreisler's biographer, Louis P. Lochner. "The people of the United States took him to their heart as few nations did—certainly more quickly and generously than his native Austria, and not less so than Great Britain and France, in both of which countries he soon became the idol of the concertgoing public."

Returning to Europe on the *Prince Bismarck* in May 1901, Kreisler met Harriet Lies, daughter of a tobacco merchant. "I went into the barbershop of the ship where they also sold knicknacks. She was in the shop buying a small hat. . . . As I got up from the barber's chair I saw the reflection of a beautiful red-headed American girl in that mirror. I fell in love with her instantly, for she smiled at me then and there; and I smiled back. That was the beginning and the end for me." By the time the ship docked at Bremerhaven, they were totally involved emotionally with one another. Despite the prejudice of Harriet's father against Kreisler because, as Kreisler once explained, he had "a notion I was playing around at street corners fiddling," marriage became a foregone conclusion. They went through a civil marriage ceremony not once but twice: in the United States in November 1902; in London in 1903. In March 1947 they were married a third time, in a religious ceremony. Harriet, a Catholic, had been a divorcée when she married Kreisler and a religious ceremony was denied them until Harriet was permitted by the authorities to return to the Catholic Church.

She was a strong-willed, dominating woman who brought order and discipline to Kreisler's former easygoing Bohemian ways. She regulated his daily life down to details; took charge of his finances; supervised the development of his career; served as a buffer between Kreisler and the outside world. "No one will know what a blessing she has been to me," Kreisler once remarked late in life.

Kreisler's world fame was fully established by the time of World War I: one of the most highly regarded, widely admired, and highest-earning musicians of his generation; a violinist who revealed profound insights into the concertos of Mozart, Beethoven, and Brahms, and an incomparable Viennese charm and delicacy in the presentation of his own violin pieces. Already in January 1905, when Kreisler returned to New York after an absence of four years, Richard Aldrich could write in the New York *Times:* "He showed himself . . . as a true interpreter in the highest sense, standing always sincerely for the music he was engaged with and concerned not at all with that which makes for display. . . . His interpretations abound in manifold poetic touches and rarely lose the sweep of line and the larger symmetry. He possesses the indefinable quality of style, and there was stamped upon his playing always the mark of unquestionable authority."

On November 10, 1910, in London, Kreisler presented the world premiere of Edward Elgar's Violin Concerto, a work dedicated to him.

In 1914 Kreisler was on vacation in Switzerland when war broke out in Europe. He rushed back to Austria to join his regiment in Galicia. He recalled his experiences as a wartime soldier in *Four Weeks in the Trenches* (1915): "For two days I went without taking off my clothes, sleeping on wet grass, or in the mud, or in the swamps. One night, while sleeping, we were drenched to the skin by torrential rains. . . . I remember having gone for more than three days at a time without any food whatsoever, and many a time we had to lick the dew from the grass for want of water." On September 6, 1914, Kreisler's leg was pierced by a lance during a

Russian cavalry attack on Lemberg. He was discharged from the army with honors.

He was determined to help his war-stricken country as a civilian, by raising money for Austrian war charities through his extensive American concert tours. When America entered the war officially, Kreisler found himself in an untenable position in the United States. He was an ex-Austrian still helping an enemy country; he had been a soldier in the camp of the enemy; he refused to renounce his allegiance to his native land. America, gripped as it was by war fever, engaged in a fiercely hostile attack on anything or anyone German or Austrian. Abuse and antagonism, insults and hatred were showered on Kreisler from the pulpit, in the press, and at patriotic club meetings. He withdrew completely from his concert work. He left for a secluded place in Maine where he spent the rest of the war gardening, playing chess, and making music for charity.

The war over, Kreisler returned to the concert platform with a recital in Carnegie Hall on October 26, 1919. He was welcomed back enthusiastically. "He returns," reported Richard Aldrich in the New York *Times,* "with his art in all its manifestations unimpaired, in technical skill, in the plastic eloquence of his bowing, in the accuracy of his intonation, in the excellence of his tone. Above and beyond all this, which may be taken for granted, is the spiritual insight."

In 1935 Kreisler once again became the center of controversy—this time because of his admission that many of the small pieces he had been performing since the early 1900s and which he had passed off as "transcriptions" of compositions by such old masters as Pugnani, Vivaldi, Couperin, Martini, and others were actually his own. He had been brought to this confession by Olin Downes, the music critic of the New York *Times,* who asked him for the precise source of the *Praeludium and Allegro,* supposedly by Pugnani. Almost as if he were eager to come out in the open finally, Kreisler readily explained that this composition and many others were his own; that he had offered them as creations of masters because they had been written while he was still young and unknown and he wished to gain for them a wider hearing. The admission sent tremors through the music world. "We wish to apply the term discreditable to the whole transaction from start to finish," wrote one music journal editorially. Ernest Newman, in England, flayed

Kreisler for his dishonesty in a long and vitriolic article. "It is as though Mr. Keats published poems under the name of Herrick or Spenser," said Newman.

The fact that these "transcriptions" were Kreisler's own should not have caught the world by surprise. Many years earlier Kreisler had publicly revealed that his *Liebesfreud, Liebesleid,* and *Schön Rosmarin*—which had been identified on his programs as transcriptions of posthumous pieces by Josef Lanner—were in reality his own. What made Kreisler come out with this revelation was the fact that a Viennese critic had taken him severely to task for his arrogance in including with these "Lanner gems" one of Kreisler's own pieces, his *Caprice Viennois.* This disclosure should have aroused suspicion about his other transcriptions. And so might the warning that always appeared on the title page of every Kreisler publication: "The original manuscripts used for these transcriptions are the private property of Mr. Fritz Kreisler and are now published for the first time; they are, moreover, so freely treated that they constitute, in fact, original works."

But the "transcriptions" continued to be accepted as such until 1935. That Kreisler maintained his world popularity afterwards indicates the hold he had acquired on music lovers everywhere.

For a time in 1941 it seemed as if his career were over. Crossing a New York street, he was struck by a truck; he suffered a fracture of the skull and other internal injuries and for a time he lay in a coma. When he emerged from the coma, it seemed certain that he had been affected mentally and physically; he had amnesia that made him temporarily forget modern languages and enabled him to speak solely in classical Latin and Greek. But in time he responded to treatment, and eventually he was able to return to concert life and to dominate the world of music as he had previously done for four decades.

Kreisler's last public appearance was on March 6, 1950, his nineteenth appearance on the "Bell Telephone Hour" over network radio. After that, he rarely touched the violin. He sold all his precious instruments, including a Stradivarius and a Guarnerius, keeping for himself only his favorite violin, a Vuillaume.

But he was not forgotten. On his eightieth birthday, in 1955, President Eisenhower sent him a congratulatory telegram that was read at a reception for Kreisler at the Hotel St. Regis in New York. Messages also came from musicians and musical organizations the world over. When he was eighty-five, Kreisler received a scroll from Mayor Wagner and a medal from Cardinal Spellman in special ceremonies at New York City Hall. At a birthday luncheon tendered him by RCA Victor, he was given a silver pressing of his first recording, Smetana's *Aus der Heimat,* which he had made on May 11, 1910.

"I have the infirmities of eighty-five," Kreisler told an interviewer at that time. "Mostly in the ears and eyes. I can walk miles if necessary, only they won't let me. But there is no sense in my picking up a violin any more. Mostly I listen to the radio, and read whatever I can read. My ears and eyes can still do that much."

Two years later, on January 29, 1962, Kreisler died at the Columbia-Presbyterian Medical Center in New York, four days before his eighty-seventh birthday. His wife died in her apartment on East Fifty-second Street, where Kreisler had made his home for many years, on May 29, 1963. Before their respective deaths, Kreisler and his wife had set up the Fritz and Harriet Kreisler Fund for educating young musicians, a subsidiary of the Musicians Emergency Fund, Kreisler's pet charity.

Fritz Kreisler's one hundredth birthday was commemorated in New York on February 2, 1975, with a concert in Carnegie Recital Hall in New York devoted entirely to Kreisler's compositions.

At least a part of Kreisler's popularity came from the charm of his personality and his intellectual background which embraced literature, politics, philosophy, medicine, and art, as well as music. A linguist, he spoke eight languages fluently; he read books in many of these languages and collected old editions. He loved animals and owned three police dogs, several fox terriers, and an Airedale, during his long married life. He also cherished birds and provided houses for them on his estate in Switzerland. In Switzerland, Kreisler could indulge his love for the outdoors by taking long walks in the mountains. When in large cities, Kreisler was an inveterate movie- and theater-goer. His domestic pleasures included playing cards and chess. He favored Viennese cooking, but he was also partial to Italian cuisine; in his later years in New York he frequented an Italian restaurant on West Forty-sixth Street.

He was versatile as a musician, almost as gifted a pianist as he was a violinist, and a composer as adept in the light music of operettas as he was in such serious works as a string quartet, a violin concerto, or a repertory of pieces for the violin. The score of *Apple Blossoms,* an operetta produced on Broadway on October 7, 1919, was the joint effort of Victor Jacobi and Fritz Kreisler. His best-known pieces for the violin, which have become basic to the repertory, include *Caprice Viennois, Liebesfreud, Liebesleid, The Old Refrain, Praeludium and Allegro, Schön Rosmarin, Sicilienne et Rigaudon,* and *La Gitana.* For RCA Victor he recorded all of his best-known compositions and a vast literature for the violin.

When Austria was invaded by Nazi Germany in 1938, Kreisler renounced his Austrian citizenship and became a French subject. In 1943 he became an American citizen.

ABOUT: Kreisler, F. Four Weeks in the Trenches; Lochner, L. Fritz Kreisler; Taylor, D. Of Men and Music. *Periodicals*—American Magazine, February 1931; Esquire, August 1935; New Yorker, November 24, 1928; Reader's Digest, August 1944, October 1961; Saturday Evening Post, March 15, 1930; Saturday Review, February 24, 1962; Theatre Arts, January 1940; Time, February 9, 1962.

Josef Krips

1902–1974

Josef Krips, conductor, was born in Vienna on August 8, 1902, to Josef and Linse Seitz Krips. His father, a physician, was an amateur singer, a member of the Karmeliter Church choir, which young Josef joined when he was six. Though his father loved music, he did everything he could to discourage his son's interest in music, telling him: "In a career so difficult as that of a professional musician, everything should be done to prevent a child from adopting it. Then, if he still persists in spite of all obstacles, he really is fitted for it."

Josef persisted. When he was thirteen he received the birthday gift of a violin and started to take lessons, paying for them out of his own allowance. Only two years later he found employment in the orchestra of the Vienna Volksoper. When he was sixteen, he enrolled in the

Krips: krĭps

JOSEF KRIPS

val and in 1930 a Handel festival. Guest appearances in Berlin, Frankfort, Baden-Baden, Strasbourg, Cologne, and Budapest helped to solidify his reputation.

In 1933 he became the principal conductor of the Vienna State Opera. He attracted the interest and admiration of Europe through his versatility in conducting operas in the German, Italian, and French repertory with equal sympathy and skill, though his greatest strength lay in the German works. In 1935 he became affiliated for the first time with the annual Salzburg Festival in Austria, with which he continued his association, on and off, up to the time of his death. Also in 1935 he led performances of the Vienna State Opera in Rome. From 1935 to 1938 he was professor of conducting at the Vienna Music Academy.

With the Nazi occupation of Austria in 1938, Krips was removed from his music posts. "I wasn't pure enough for Hitler," he recalled later. "My mother was Catholic, so were her parents. My father was Catholic, but his parents were Jewish. So I was not allowed to conduct during the war."

For a time Krips tried to continue his profession in Belgrade, Yugoslavia, where he led performances at the Opera and the Philharmonic concerts. But with the growth of Nazi influence in Yugoslavia, Krips was forced to leave the country and return to Vienna to earn his living as a day laborer in a food processing factory. For the next few years he was unable to participate in any music performances.

After the defeat of Germany, the Soviet military government in Vienna assigned Krips the task of rebuilding the city's musical life. It was a thankless job, for he had few resources to work with. Few experienced musicians were available, and they were miserably paid and half starved. Krips had to work from morning to night in unheated halls, walking each day for two hours from his home to the rehearsal hall and back; no other mode of transportation was available to him. It was almost entirely through his Herculean efforts that Vienna finally could present its first opera performance since the beginning of World War II. This took place at the Volksoper on May 1, 1945, with *The Marriage of Figaro*. In 1946 he helped to reopen the Salzburg Festival, in which he participated successfully for the next few seasons.

As the principal conductor of both the Vienna

Vienna Academy; there his teachers were Eusebius Mandyczewski in composition and Felix Weingartner in conducting. During these years he also pursued his academic education at the local high school.

For three years Josef was employed as violinist in the Volksoper orchestra, but at the same time he served with a touring opera company as "choir conductor, stage manager, harmonium player, and at certain difficult moments even chief of claque," as he later recalled. One day when he was eighteen, the principal conductor of the Volksoper, Weingartner, asked him to serve as accompanist for auditions then being held among some singers. To Weingartner's surprise, he played all the accompaniments from memory. Weingartner promoted him to the post of chorus master and assistant conductor at the Volksoper, and Krips made his conducting debut on September 3, 1921, in a performance of *A Masked Ball*. Three months later he made another conducting debut in Vienna, this time in symphonic music, at a concert at the Redoutensaal.

After three years of conducting chores at the Volksoper, Krips was engaged as principal conductor of the Opera at Aussig-on-the-Elbe in Czechoslovakia. A year later, in 1925, he was made music director in Dortmund, Germany, and in 1926 he became general music director in Karlsruhe, one of the youngest musicians ever to fill that post. At Karlsruhe, Krips was assigned all the major operatic and symphonic performances. In 1929 he conducted a Bruckner festi-

State Opera and the Vienna Philharmonic from 1945 to 1950, Krips was responsible for rehabilitating both organizations. By 1947 both were sufficiently revitalized to be able to undertake tours of Europe for the next three consecutive seasons with Krips conducting; they also presented a cycle of Mozart operas in London in 1947.

Krips made numerous guest appearances with leading European orchestras and opera houses and toured the Soviet Union, before he was appointed principal conductor, in 1950, of the London Symphony Orchestra, with which he made numerous recordings. While holding this post for six years, Krips continued to perform seasonally in Vienna.

In 1950 Krips was invited to the United States to conduct the Chicago Orchestra at Ravinia Park. On his arrival, he was denied entrance by immigration authorities on "political grounds." After two days of detention, he decided to return to Europe without waiting for a hearing. Declaring that he had "no politics" and never had any, he insisted his difficulties must have come about because he had given performances in the Soviet Union.

He was finally permitted to enter the United States in 1953, at which time he became the music director of the May Festival in Cincinnati. On February 15, 1953, he was so well received in his American debut with the Buffalo Philharmonic that he was given a contract as music director of that orchestra. He gave his first concert in his new post on November 7, 1954. In the ensuing years he became such a favorite in Buffalo that in 1957 the Buffalo *Evening News* named him "citizen of the year" and the University of Buffalo presented him with the Chancellor's medal.

He combined his activity in Buffalo with extensive appearances in Europe. In Paris he was appointed principal guest conductor of L'Orchestre Symphonique. In 1955 he toured Australia, and in June of the same year he led performances at the Vienna State Opera, one of which (*Don Giovanni*) was recorded and was selected by the *Saturday Review* as the best operatic release of the year. Also in 1955, his performance of Bruckner's Symphony No.8 at the International Bruckner Festival in Bern, Switzerland, brought him the medal of the Bruckner Society. In the spring of 1956 he led a Beethoven cycle in London, and a few months

later he conducted a revival of Handel's *Samson* in Vienna. In 1962 Vienna recognized his contributions to the musical culture of the city by awarding him one of its highest honors, the Ring of Honor *(Ehrenring)*. He also received the Ordre de Leopold II from Belgium.

Krips made his American debut as opera conductor on March 16, 1956, with *Don Giovanni* in Buffalo. "The performance was admirable for its continuity, its proportion, and the poise and insight given it by Mr. Krips," wrote a correspondent for *Musical America.*

When Krips led a performance of Bruckner's F minor Mass at the Cincinnati May Festival on May 7, 1956, Howard Taubman reported in the New York *Times:* "Mr. Krips . . . is a real conductor. His beat is clear and decisive. He brings not only knowledge of tradition to his work . . . but also a personal point of view."

On December 18, 1956, Krips made his New York debut, appearing as a guest conductor of the Symphony of the Air. Howard Taubman wrote in the New York *Times:* "One has to admire the skill with which Mr. Krips drew from it [the orchestra] the kind of performances he wanted." In 1958 Krips led a three-day Beethoven cycle at the Lewisohn Stadium in New York and in 1961, a three-day Brahms cycle.

From 1963 to 1970 he served as the music director of the San Francisco Symphony and then was named conductor emeritus. During his tenure he launched the orchestra's first international tour, in April 1968, opening the Osaka Festival with the first of twelve successful Japanese concerts. During Leonard Bernstein's absence, Krips was asked to open the 1964–1965 season of the New York Philharmonic Orchestra.

After resigning from his post in San Francisco, Krips returned to his home in Montreux, Switzerland, with his wife, the former Baroness Marietta von Prohaska who had been his secretary and whom he married on October 9, 1969. (This was Krips's second marriage. His first wife, Maria "Mitzi" Wilheim, a singer he had coached and whom he had married in 1947, died on April 8, 1969.) The Kripses maintained a second home in Vienna.

He continued making guest appearances virtually up to the time of his death. On March 30, 1970, he made his debut at the Metropolitan Opera in *The Marriage of Figaro* and in 1972 he toured the United States at the head of the visiting Vienna Symphony. In May 1974 he prepared a new production of *Così fan Tutte* in Paris. Ill health compelled him to withdraw after seven performances. On October 12, 1974, he died of cancer at the Cantonal Hospital in Geneva, Switzerland.

In an article in the New York *Post,* Joseph Wershba described Krips as "a big man . . . with Dresden-blue eyes and a kewpie-doll face set off by wavy strands of silvery hair at the back of his head." Wershba added that Krips "carries cigars for pleasure and apples for health."

Just before his death, Krips completed an important recording project: the last twenty symphonies of Mozart with the Concertgebouw Orchestra on the Philips label. When the first three discs of this series were released in 1977 a critic for *Stereo Review* reported: "No superlatives would be excessive for them; they are an enchantment of the Mozart discography as well as of Krips's own, and would have been sufficient by themselves to identify this conductor as one of the truly great practitioners of his art."

ABOUT: Blaukopf, K. Great Conductors; Ewen, D. Modern Conductors; Stoddard, H. Symphony Conductors of the U.S.A. *Periodicals*—Musical America, March 1964, February 1967; New York Times, July 3, 1960; Opera News, November 29, 1964, December 14, 1974.

Jan Kubelik

1880–1940

Jan Kubelik, violinist, was born in Michle, near Prague, Czechoslovakia, on July 5, 1880. His father, Michle, a market gardener, was an excellent amateur musician who gave his son his first violin lessons. Jan's rapid progress made it necessary to seek out more professional teachers: first Karel Weber, later Franz Ondříček. When he was twelve, Jan entered the Prague Conservatory. For the next six years he studied the violin there with Otakar Ševčík, and composition with Josef Förster, Karel Knittl, and Karel Stecker. Occasionally Jan appeared at Conservatory concerts, which showed that he was rapidly developing into an outstanding virtuoso.

He was sent to Vienna in 1898 to advance his career. Performing at a prominent club he at-

Kubelik: kōō′ bĕ lĭk

JAN KUBELIK

tracted the interest and support of a Viennese music critic who arranged to have him give a formal recital on November 26, 1898. "Since the days of Paganini," reported the critic of the *Neue Freie Presse,* "no appearance like this has been made in the music world."

His success in Vienna led to a tour of Italy, Czechoslovakia, Moravia, Hungary, and Yugoslavia. He played before royalty in Romania and Serbia. On June 2, 1900, he made his debut in Paris, and sixteen days later in London, both occasions bringing him further triumphs. So striking was his success in London, when he performed with Hans Richter's orchestra, that he was compelled to give five recitals, all of them to sold-out auditoriums. "Society has gone mad over Kubelik," reported one London critic. "He is the new Paganini."

Within a few years he had received the Order of St. Gregory from Pope Leo XIII (1901), the Beethoven medal from the Philharmonic Society of London (1902), the Paganini medal (1905), and honorary membership in the Philharmonic Society of London (1909).

He duplicated his European triumphs in the United States, where he made the first of ten extensive tours in 1901–1902. His American debut took place in New York on December 2, 1901, when he appeared as a soloist with the New York Philharmonic Orchestra, Emil Paur conducting, in Paganini's Violin Concerto in D minor, a Spohr concerto, and Wieniawski's *Fantasy on Russian Themes.* When he returned to the United States after a four-year absence and was heard at Carnegie Hall in New York on November 30, 1905, Richard Aldrich wrote in the New York *Times:* "Mr. Kubelik, when he came four years ago, was a marvel of the highest skill in virtuosoship. . . . His performance last evening showed unmistakably that he has reached a higher standard in some things and that his artistic horizon in some respects is wider than it was. . . . There was dash and energy in his playing. . . . In brilliancy and ease of bowing, in security of technique through all the passages of octaves, thirds, leaps, arpeggios, and runs of various kinds, he was brilliantly successful. . . . He was frantically applauded."

Both in Europe and in the United States Kubelik continued to magnetize his audiences with his phenomenal technique, and with the fire and passion of his interpretations. His colorful personality inspired publicity stories by the dozen about the man who in 1903 married a Hungarian noblewoman, Countess Marianna Csáky-Széll, divorced wife of Count Csáky-Széll; who in 1904 purchased for her a castle (the estate of Býchory) near Kolín in Hungary and became a Hungarian citizen; who moved in the company of aristocrats and royalty; who by 1912 had earned well over a million dollars from his concerts . . . The Kubeliks had eight children—five daughters and three sons.

During World War I Kubelik left the concert stage to concentrate on composition. In 1916 he completed the first of his six violin concertos—the last one was completed in 1924. He also produced a library of shorter works for the violin together with cadenzas for concertos by Mozart, Beethoven, Brahms, Tchaikovsky, and Paganini. He also wrote a cadenza for a violin concerto by J. B. Förster which had been written for him.

In 1921 Kubelik returned to the concert stage, once again with tours throughout the world. His last principal tour of the United States took place in 1924. In 1922 he acquired a luxurious estate at Abbazia, then in Italy, but now in Yugoslavia; eight years later he acquired a castle in Rothenturm in the Burgenland district of Austria. Unfortunate investments in American securities and litigations over his land purchases, combined with his extravagance, resulted in his bankruptcy in 1932 with liabilities totalling one hundred and twenty-five thousand dollars.

Though he was not legally bound to do so, he insisted upon paying all his debts from the large income he could still command from his concerts. He continued to perform even though he was frequently victimized by attacks of rheumatism and though at one time he was suffering the aftermath of a serious motor accident in Paris.

Kubelik returned to the United States in 1935, intending to make America his permanent home. He appeared on the American concert stage on January 30, 1935, as a soloist in New York with an orchestra conducted by his son, Rafael Kubelik. He gave a few additional performances over the radio, and some on the stage in Cincinnati and Chicago. But on all these occasions he failed to repeat the successes of earlier years. Not even his magic name seemed able to arouse the interest of music lovers in violin playing which, sad to say, had lost much of its pyrotechnical skill and which, from an artistic point of view, proved more often than not superficial.

Jan Kubelik's closing years were spent in Prague, where he died on December 5, 1940.

In addition to decorations and honors already mentioned, Kubelik was made Chevalier of the Legion of Honor in France, Officer of the Order of the Star of the Republic in Romania, Commander of Sava Order in Serbia, and Commander of St. Anne in Russia. He was also presented with the Couronne of Romania, the Order of Art and Science in Württemberg, and the Ordre L'Instruction Publique in France.

Kubelik's son, Rafael, has become an internationally renowned conductor. Another of Kubelik's children, Anita, became a concert violinist.

ABOUT: Dostál, J. ed. Jan Kubelik; Hoffmeister, K. Jan Kubelik. *Periodicals*—Musical America, December 10, 1940.

Rafael Kubelik

1914–

Rafael Jeronym Kubelik, conductor, was one of eight children of the virtuoso Jan Kubelik and Marianna Csáky-Széll Kubelik. He was born in Býchory, Bohemia (now Czechoslovakia), on June 29, 1914. He received his earliest musical training from his father before entering the Prague Conservatory in 1928. There he studied composition with Otakar Šín, conducting with

Kubelik: kōō′ bĕ lĭk

RAFAEL KUBELIK

P. Dědeček, and violin with J. Feld. Five years later he was graduated as violinist, conductor, and composer after having composed a Fantasy for violin and orchestra, conducted Tchaikovsky's Symphony No.4, and performed Paganini's Concerto No.1 on the violin.

On January 24, 1934, Kubelik made his professional conducting debut with the Czech Philharmonic. Later the same year he toured Europe as an accompanist for his father. In the United States, between 1935 and 1936, he was heard not only in this capacity but also as a guest conductor of the Cincinnati Symphony Orchestra at the invitation of its permanent conductor, Eugene Goossens.

Upon his return to Czechoslovakia in 1936, Rafael Kubelik was appointed acting conductor of the Czech Philharmonic. With it he toured England and Belgium in 1938, and in 1942 he became its music director. Meanwhile, in 1939 he was also made first conductor of the Brünn Opera. There he made his debut with *The Bartered Bride* and there he remained until 1941, when the Nazis closed down the theater. He continued, however, as music director of the Czech Philharmonic even though during the years of Nazi occupation he refused to cooperate with the Nazis.

On June 29, 1942, Kubelik married Ludmila Bertlová, a violinist who had appeared under his direction as soloist with the Czech Philharmonic. She had studied with Karel Hoffmann in Prague and with Georges Enesco in Paris. They had one child, a son, Martin.

Soon after the end of World War II, Kubelik directed orchestral concerts in England, Belgium, Scandinavia, Austria, and Poland. Between September 1945 and January 1946 he conducted eight concerts in Moscow, and in 1947 he toured Poland, France, and Switzerland with the Czech Philharmonic.

When the Communists took over the reins of government in Czechoslovakia in 1948, Kubelik was deprived of his citizenship because of his strong anti-Communist stand. He emigrated to England and settled in London. In the summer of 1948 he conducted performances of *Don Giovanni* at the Edinburgh Festival in Scotland. One year later he proved so successful as guest conductor of the Concertgebouw Orchestra in Amsterdam that he was reengaged to conduct all thirty-six concerts of the second half of the 1949–1950 season. In 1950 he was acclaimed for his performances at the Bach festival in Zurich and in concerts in South America and Mexico. In 1951 he was heard in festivals in Salzburg, Zurich, and Brussels.

He returned to the United States in mid-November 1949 to appear as guest conductor of the Chicago Symphony. "There can be no doubt that Mr. Kubelik made a distinctly favorable impression," wrote the Chicago critic Felix Borowski in *The Christian Science Monitor.* So good an impression had Kubelik made that towards the end of the year he was engaged as principal conductor of the Chicago Symphony on a two-year contract. When he made his first appearance in his new post, in October 1950, Claudia Cassidy said in the Chicago *Tribune* that his performance "was clear and fresh and imaginative and understanding." Kubelik was only the fifth principal conductor in the fifty-nine-year history of the Chicago Symphony.

When Kubelik appeared with the Chicago Symphony in New York City on March 9, 1953, Howard Taubman reported in the New York *Times:* "It was clear last night that this conductor is a dynamic leader and a musician of character. There was a driving intensity in all that Mr. Kubelik did. ... The core of the matter was there—a vivid, personal and glowing concern for the underlying design of the music."

Despite such favorable reviews, Kubelik was the object of considerable opposition in Chicago. Many objected to his innovative procedures and, particularly, to his insistence on presenting new or unfamiliar music. In three seasons he introduced sixty new compositions, including works by Honegger, Martinu, Ernest Bloch, Copland, Schuman, Roy Harris, Lukas Foss, and Vittorio Rieti. Musical Chicago became divided into two warring camps, those who favored Kubelik and those who opposed him. The antagonists won out; in 1953 he resigned. "I never regretted Chicago," he later told Stephen Rubin in an interview in the New York *Times*. "It gave me a good lesson in how to look at the world from the other side. I came there like a fool, but I left in peace. My last concert was *Parsifal*. I did it on purpose, as an answer not only to the city but to myself. You know, I performed sixty new pieces there in three years, out of which forty were by Americans. And I don't count Stravinsky. I invited Negroes as soloists which, in those days in Orchestra Hall, was almost revolutionary. I had my enemies. I had to fight with all these ladies. But I don't regret a minute of it."

One year after this resignation, Kubelik was back in the United States, this time at the head of the Concertgebouw Orchestra which was making its first American tour. At that time he led forty-three concerts, sharing the podium with Eduard van Beinum. Since that time he has appeared as guest conductor of virtually every major American orchestra.

From 1955 to 1958 Kubelik was the music director of Covent Garden in London where he made his debut on October 17, 1955, in *Otello*. "Mr. Kubelik showed a real understanding of both the dramatic values of the score and its formal construction," reported Cecil Smith in *Musical America*. "The orchestra played clearly and beautifully; the chorus sang expertly. . . . The minor principals knew their parts more than superficially." At Covent Garden, he gave excellent performances of *The Bartered Bride,* Janáček's *Jenufa,* and, in 1957, Berlioz' *Les Troyens.* The last of these was given in English and was being heard for the first time as Berlioz intended it to be, in a single evening, rather than on two evenings as had previously been the practice. In 1960 he conducted *Les Troyens* at La Scala in Milan.

In 1961 Kubelik became the principal conductor of the Bavarian Radio Orchestra, the leading symphonic organization in Munich; with it he toured Europe for the first time in 1962, and the United States in 1968 and 1975. In 1971 he was given the newly created post of music director at the Metropolitan Opera on a three-year contract to begin in the fall of 1972, simultaneous with the new regime of Göran Gentele as general manager. The plans for that new regime were largely carried out after Gentele's tragic death in a motor accident in the summer of 1972 by Kubelik and Schuyler Chapin. Among the Gentele projects was the American premiere of *Les Troyens* in its entirety and in a single evening. This performance, on October 22, 1973, marked not only Kubelik's bow as music director of the Metropolitan Opera but also his debut in America as a conductor of operas. "This *Troyens* was worth waiting for," wrote Harold C. Schonberg in the New York *Times.* But he found much to object to in Kubelik's performance. "Often it was flabby, full of wrongly accented upbeats. Thus rhythmic groups tended to come out awry."

Though he had never before conducted the Wagner *Ring* cycle, Kubelik planned to do so at the Metropolitan Opera during the 1974–1975 season. He arrived in New York on February 10, 1974, to begin rehearsals on *Die Götterdämmerung.* Only two days after his arrival he announced he was resigning as music director, explaining: "The financial condition of the Metropolitan has unfortunately changed to such an extent that I cannot carry out the artistic ideals to which I committed myself. Relieved of certain of my artistic demands, the Metropolitan may be better able to bring its financial situation into balance." But the financial problem was not the sole explanation for Kubelik's sudden withdrawal. For a time controversy had been growing over the way he was handling his job as music director. He was accused of undertaking so many commitments in Europe that it was impossible for him to function properly in New York. When sudden decisions had to be made at the Metropolitan Opera he had to be contacted by teletype. Some critics suggested that he was far more concerned with developing himself as a star conductor than in fulfilling the duties of a music director of a major opera house, and that as a star he was spending far too much of his time away from the opera house. In spite of his resignation, Kubelik did conduct *Die Götterdämmerung* on March 8, 1974.

Despite the accusations directed at him for his handling of his post at the Metropolitan, Kubelik did not lose the prestige he had previously earned as a conductor in America and Europe. When he performed Mahler's Symphony No.9

with the visiting Bavarian Radio Orchestra in New York in May 1975, Harold C. Schonberg wrote in the New York *Times:* "As performers of Mahler under Kubelik, at least, the Bavarians can stand up against the greatest orchestras of the world. ... Mr. Kubelik's reading kept the intent of the work paramount. He did not, it seemed, confuse himself with the composer."

In 1953 he became a resident of Lucerne, Switzerland, and in 1967 he became a Swiss citizen. Following the death of his wife Ludmila in 1961, he married an Australian soprano, Elsie Morison, on January 4, 1963. She had appeared as Marie in his production of *The Bartered Bride* at Covent Garden. After the marriage she gave up her career to travel with him—her last performance was in the Kubelik recording of Mahler's Symphony No.4 (part of the recording of all of Mahler's symphonies Kubelik made for Deutsche Grammophon, released in 1971).

The Kubeliks, who have a child, live in Haus im Sand at Kastanienbaum-Lucerne, Switzerland. His diversions include tennis, chess, and composing. He has written a number of operas and several orchestral works, some chamber music, and a few concertos. His Requiem for baritone solo, chorus and orchestra—the world premiere of which he conducted in August 1962 —was written in memory of his first wife. He also directed the world premieres of his operas *Veronika* (with the Brünn Opera on April 19, 1947) and *Cornelia Faroli* (with the Augsburg Opera in 1972).

Among the honors conferred on Kubelik are the Bundesverdienstkreuz in Germany, the Bavarian Verdienstorden, the Portuguese Komturorden, the Danish Rittorden Dannebrog, the Golden Mahler medal, and the Italian Bruckner medal. He has also been named honorary member of the Royal Academy of Stockholm and the Royal Academy of London.

ABOUT: High Fidelity/Musical America, January 1974; New York Times, October 17, 1971, January 22, 1978; Stereo Review, December 1973.

Charles Kullman

1903–

Charles Kullman (originally Kullmann), tenor, was born in New Haven, Connecticut, on January 13, 1903, the son of Charles and Frances Danhauser Kullmann. He attended local public schools, sang in church choirs from his eighth year on, then attended Yale University where he sang solo parts with the Glee Club and where in his last undergraduate year he won first prize in an intercollegiate song contest. In New Haven he took some lessons in singing from Marcosano.

Upon graduation from Yale in 1924, Kullman planned a career in medicine, but financial difficulties prevented this. He then began thinking of a professional life in music for the first time. In 1924 he went to New York, sang at an audition at the Juilliard School of Music, and won a scholarship. After three years at Juilliard, he won another scholarship, this one entitling him to study at the American Conservatory at Fontainebleau, France.

In 1928 Kullman returned to the United States and joined the faculty of Smith College as a teacher of voice. There he appeared in several opera productions. His growing interest in opera compelled him to resign from Smith in order to join the American Opera Company which, under Vladimir Rosing's direction, performed opera in English. With this company, Kullman appeared in leading tenor roles.

In the fall of 1930 Kullman went to Berlin to study opera repertory. An instructor, hearing him sing, brought him to the attention of Otto Klemperer, conductor of the Kroll Opera. Klemperer engaged him for the Kroll company, and Kullman made his European opera debut at the Kroll as Pinkerton in *Madama Butterfly* on February 24, 1931.

One year later Kullman was engaged by the Berlin State Opera. Under such distinguished conductors as Furtwängler, Leo Blech, and Erich Kleiber, he was heard in the Italian repertory. He grew so popular as Pinkerton that he appeared in that role more than twenty-five times in a single season, even though *Madama Butterfly* had rarely before been performed by the Berlin State Opera more than four or five times a season.

CHARLES KULLMAN

His success in Berlin brought him engagements at the Vienna State Opera where Kullman made his debut in 1934. After that came his bow at Covent Garden in London, in Weinberger's *Schwanda.* In November 1934, Toscanini invited him to appear in a special performance of Verdi's Requiem given in memory of the assassinated Austrian Chancellor Dolfuss.

During the summers of 1934, 1935, and 1936 Kullman participated in the Salzburg Festival in Austria. In 1935 he scored a major success there as Florestan in *Fidelio,* Toscanini conducting. In 1936 he once again appeared in Salzburg under Toscanini's direction, this time as Walther in *Die Meistersinger.* "None in recent years has sung the part of Walther more musically," remarked the English music critic Richard Capell. "His singing was charmingly fresh, musical, lyric, unforced." Other roles which Kullman sang in Salzburg were Belmonte in *The Abduction from the Seraglio* and Huon in *Oberon.*

He made his debut at the Metropolitan Opera on December 19, 1935, in the title role of *Faust.* Two thousand residents from his native city of New Haven went to this premiere on special trains marked the "Charles Kullman Special." The critic of the New York *Times* reported: "His voice is a lyric tenor of equal range and agreeable texture and he employs it to admirable purpose. There was a sense of style, musicianship and authority in his work. He did not attempt to storm the heavens. . . . There is freshness not only in the young tenor's voice but in his carriage and diction."

Kullman remained two decades with the Metropolitan Opera, making 273 appearances in New York, and 119 on tour in 32 roles. How valuable he became to that company in that time can be measured by the variety of roles he assumed, to most of which he brought vocal and histrionic distinction: Alfredo in *La Traviata,* Don José in *Carmen,* the Duke in *Rigoletto,* Rodolfo in *La Bohème,* Erik in *The Flying Dutchman,* Walther in *Die Meistersinger,* Pinkerton in *Madama Butterfly,* Rinuccio in *Gianni Schicchi,* Fenton in *Falstaff,* Dimitri and Schouisky in *Boris Godunov,* Cavaradossi in *Tosca,* Julien in *Louise,* Avito in *L'Amore dei Tre Re* (with the composer conducting), Hans in *The Bartered Bride* (given in English), Don Ottavio in *Don Giovanni,* Tamino in *The Magic Flute,* Des Grieux in *Manon,* Almaviva in *The Barber of Seville,* Eisenstein and Alfred in *Die Fledermaus,* Turiddu in *Cavalleria Rusticana,* Romeo in *Romeo and Juliet,* Prince Vassily in Mussorgsky's *Khovantchina,* Parsifal, Belmonte in *The Abduction from the Seraglio,* Herod in *Salome,* Tannhäuser, Don Basilio in *The Marriage of Figaro,* Valzacchi in *Der Rosenkavalier,* and the Emperor in *The Gypsy Baron.*

While serving the Metropolitan Opera through the years, Kullman made noteworthy appearances with the Chicago Opera, the San Francisco Opera, the Teatro Colón in Buenos Aires, and other opera companies. He combined his success in opera with appearances in the concert hall, in recitals, and as a guest artist with major symphony orchestras. He also enjoyed an active career on radio and television and in motion pictures. He made his motion picture debut in *Die Sonne Geht Auf* (1935), after which he appeared in *La Paloma* (1936), the *Goldwyn Follies* (1938), and *Song of Scheherazade* (1947).

Kullman married Lisa Demander on February 14, 1928; they have a daughter. Interviewed about his hobbies and interests Kullman replied that he enjoyed boxing, wrestling, swimming, and the society of good friends. "There's nothing I'd rather see than a wrestling match or a good prize fight." He might have added that he also has enjoyed fishing. His greatest fishing coup was a striped bass weighing thirty-five pounds which took him forty-eight minutes to land.

He has always believed that the number *thirteen* is lucky for him: He was born on the 13th; he signed his Metropolitan Opera contract on the 13th; and his daughter, Elise, was born on September 13.

In 1956 Kullman became resident tenor and in 1957 professor of voice at Indiana University in Bloomington. Since then he has channeled his musical energies into teaching.

ABOUT: Kutsch, K. J. and Riemens, L. A Concise Biographical Dictionary of Singers.

ERICH KUNZ

Erich Kunz

1909–

Erich Kunz, bass, who has made a specialty of buffo roles, was born in Vienna on May 20, 1909. He was the son of Edward Kunz, an engineer, and Sophie Kunz. He studied music mainly with Theodor Lierhammer and Hans Duhan at the Vienna Academy and made his debut in 1933 as Osmin in *The Abduction from the Seraglio* with the Troppau (now Opava) Opera in Czechoslovakia. From 1933 to 1936 he was a member of the Breslau Opera, in 1936–1937 of the Plauen Opera, and from 1937 to 1941 of an opera company in Wroclaw. In 1936 he visited England where he was originally engaged as understudy at the Glyndebourne Festival but where he soon assumed minor roles.

His first success came with the Vienna State Opera which he joined in 1941 and where he soon distinguished himself, particularly in the Mozartean repertory. As an outstanding resident member of that company he achieved world recognition as Papageno in *The Magic Flute,* Figaro in *The Marriage of Figaro,* the title role and Leporello in *Don Giovanni,* and Guglielmo in *Così fan Tutte.* Between 1941 and 1944 he appeared regularly at the Salzburg Festival in Austria. In 1943 he was the youngest artist to appear up to that time in a major role at the Bayreuth Festival, where he was heard as Beckmesser in *Die Meistersinger.* In 1948 he sang at the Edinburgh Festival.

From this point on he made numerous guest appearances with such major opera companies as the Deutsche Oper in Berlin, Hamburg Opera, Munich Opera, Wiesbaden Opera, Budapest Opera, La Scala in Milan, Rome Opera, Teatro la Fenice in Venice, Monte Carlo Opera, Stock-

holm Royal Opera, Covent Garden in London, the Bolshoi Opera in Moscow, San Francisco Opera, the Chicago Opera, the Teatro Colón in Buenos Aires, and at festivals at Bregenz in Austria, Aix-en-Provence in France, Glyndebourne in England, and Florence in Italy. His roles, besides those already commented upon, were: Malatesta in *Don Pasquale,* Baculus in Lortzing's *Der Wildschütz,* van Bett in Lortzing's *Zar und Zimmermann,* Varlaam in *Boris Godunov,* Gianni Schicchi, Bartolo in *The Barber of Seville,* Kezal in *The Bartered Bride,* the Music Master in *Ariadne auf Naxos,* Fra Melitone in *La Forza del Destino,* and von Faninal in *Der Rosenkavalier.*

His American debut took place at the Metropolitan Opera in New York on November 26, 1952, as Leporello. "He is a trouper and he has a voice," wrote Jay S. Harrison in the New York *Herald Tribune.* "It makes a rich sound and is backed by a flourishing sense of dramatic fitness. The Met has itself a new bass. He is a credit to the house." Later that season Kunz was also heard as Beckmesser and Faninal and in 1953–1954 (his last year at the Metropolitan) in the title role of *The Marriage of Figaro.*

Kunz married Winifriede (Friedl) Kurzbauer, a ballerina, on June 14, 1948; they had two children. Their home is on the Grinzingerstrasse in Vienna. Kunz is an enthusiastic gardener, occasionally enjoys cooking, and relaxes by fussing around with the motor of his automobile.

In 1948 he received the honorary title of *Kammersänger* in Vienna. He has been the recipient

---

Kunz: kŏŏnts

of the Austrian Mozart medal in 1957; Order for Arts and Sciences, First Class, in 1960; and the Gold Medal of the City of Vienna in 1969. In 1968 he was named honorary member of the Vienna State Opera.

ABOUT: Kutsch, K. J. and Riemens, L. A Concise Biographical Dictionary of Singers.

Selma Kurz

1875–1933

In the first years of the twentieth century few coloratura sopranos were more highly esteemed in Europe than Selma Kurz. Few could rival the brilliance of her vocal technique or the expanse of her vocal register, which included rich mezzo tones and an incomparable trill.

She was born in Bielitz, Silesia, in Austria, on November 15, 1875. In her early years she sang in a synagogue choir in her native city where she was discovered and encouraged by its cantor. A patron was found to finance her study in Vienna with Johannes Pless. Her vocal studies were completed in Paris with Mathilde Marchesi.

Kurz made her debut at the Hamburg Opera in the title role of *Mignon* in 1895. From 1896 to 1899 she was a member of the Frankfort Opera where she appeared in lyric soprano and mezzo-soprano roles. Gustav Mahler, then the music director of the Vienna Royal Opera, heard her and bought out her contract. In 1899 she joined the Vienna Royal Opera, making her debut there as Mignon. A year later she sang the Queen of the Night in *The Magic Flute*. From then on, and for the next two decades, she was the darling of the Vienna Royal Opera and recognized throughout Europe. In 1905, when Austria celebrated the successful termination of the Russo-Japanese War, the Austrian Emperor requested that a performance of *Les Huguenots* be given at the Royal Opera, specifying that his two favorite singers—Selma Kurz and Leo Slezak—be in the cast.

She enjoyed triumphs outside Vienna as well: at Covent Garden in London where she made her debut as Gilda in *Rigoletto* on June 7, 1904, and later as Oscar in *The Masked Ball;* in opera houses in Paris, Monte Carlo, Budapest, Prague,

SELMA KURZ

Amsterdam, Warsaw, and Cairo. She received many offers from the Metropolitan Opera in New York on terms reputed to be equal to those enjoyed by Caruso, but she turned these down consistently because of her aversion both to travel and to extended guest appearances outside Vienna. Ultimately, however, she did make a few concert appearances in the United States in 1921, even though she was then suffering from the aftermath of a heart attack and was in poor physical condition. In 1922 she was heard as Constanze in *The Abduction from the Seraglio* at the Salzburg Festival.

Kurz remained with the Vienna State Opera until 1926 after which she went into retirement. In 1930 she was made an honorary member of the Vienna State Opera, an honor previously accorded to only six singers, to just one woman, and to nobody else of Jewish faith. She died in Vienna on May 10, 1933, and was given a state funeral.

She was married to Josef Halban, a distinguished Viennese gynecologist. They had two children, one of whom, Desi Kurz-Halban became a professional singer who specialized in *Lieder* and who can be heard in a recording of Mahler's Symphony No.4.

In 1976 Court Opera Classics released an album of opera arias and songs which Selma Kurz had recorded more than half a century earlier.

ABOUT: Opera News, March 11, 1962.

Kurz: kŏŏrts

Landowska

Wanda Landowska

1877–1959

WANDA LANDOWSKA

Wanda Landowska, pianist and harpsichordist, was universally recognized as the greatest harpsichordist of the twentieth century and the artist most responsible for bringing about a renascence of the harpsichord and the music written for it. She was born in Warsaw, Poland, on July 5, 1877, into a cultured household. Her father, Marjan, a lawyer, was a proficient amateur musician; her mother, Ewa, was a linguist. Informal concerts in the Landowska household were Wanda's initiation to music. She began showing an interest in the piano when she was four and soon was given lessons by Jan Kleczyński. Though her teacher, an eminent Chopin authority, emphasized Romantic literature, Wanda's preference even then leaned more heavily to the music of the baroque and classical eras—particularly to works of Bach, Haydn, and Mozart. Late in her life, Landowska told her admirers that, as a very young girl she wrote a vow on a slip of paper that she would devote her life to the forgotten music of the past, sealing the vow in an envelope marked "to be opened when I grow up."

After about two years with Kleczyński, Wanda was enrolled in the Warsaw Conservatory; her principal teacher at the piano was Aleksander Michalowski. Sympathizing with his pupil's fascination for Bach, Michalowski gave her an intensive training in Bach's keyboard music. Upon graduation from the Conservatory in her fourteenth year, Wanda gave her first public concert. It took place in Warsaw, and one of the numbers on her program was Bach's *English Suite* in E minor.

When she was seventeen, Wanda went to Berlin. There she studied composition with Heinrich Urban and Moritz Moszkowski and enjoyed the city's active musical life. In Berlin she fell in love with Henry Lew, then a student of Hebrew folklore and a fervent Zionist; in time he became a successful writer. In 1900 they went to Paris. There they were married.

In addition to playing the piano, Landowska's musical interests at this time included the writing of songs. One of these entitled "Die Weber"

had a text which revealed Landowska's social conscience. Through the years she remained partial to this piece. After the liberation of Paris, in World War II, she used its melody in *Liberation Fanfare* commemorating the historic event.

As a young musician in Paris she involved herself deeply in France's musical life, particularly with those contemporary French musicians who had done valuable researches into the French music of the seventeenth and eighteenth centuries. She became an auditor at the Bach cantata concerts of the Chanteurs de Saint-Gervais and at performances of old French music at the Schola Cantorum. This growing interest in the music of the past ignited her own interest in the keyboard instrument for which so much of it was written—the harpsichord. Borrowing a harpsichord from the Pleyel company, she moved to a village seventeen miles from Paris to devote herself to mastering the instrument.

As a harpsichordist, she made her public debut during a recital in Paris in 1903 in which she played only one composition for the harpsichord on a program otherwise devoted to piano music. She continued this practice of interpolating one or more harpsichord pieces at her piano recitals for a number of years, doling out in small doses the works of Daquin, Rameau, and Couperin, as well as Bach and Haydn. She played only a single composition on the harpsichord when, in February 1904, she offered her first all-Bach program. On March 11, 1905, when Gustave Bret offered the initial performance of his newly founded Bach Society, he invit-

Landowska: län dôf' skä

436

ed her to perform Bach's Concerto in G minor on the harpsichord. By 1905 her reputation as a harpsichordist had grown sufficiently to have Albert Schweitzer say in his book on Bach: "Anyone who has heard Wanda Landowska play the *Italian Concerto* on her wonderful Pleyel harpsichord finds it hard to understand how it could ever again be played on a modern piano."

However, before she began to dedicate herself wholly to the harpsichord, she established herself as a piano virtuoso of the first order with tours of Europe. "Wanda Landowska plays the piano in a manner uniquely hers, and inimitable," wrote the French musicologist Jean Marnold. "One would think that Wanda Landowska possesses two right hands; but her virtuosity is only the means . . . for the expression of an impeccable justice and an incorruptible truth."

As her fame, and her passion for the harpsichord, grew, Landowska decided to devote herself with an ever-increasing intensity to the study of works of the sixteenth, seventeenth, and early eighteenth centuries. The fruits of these studies can be found in two books: *Bach et Ses Interprètes* published in 1906, and *Musique Ancienne,* written in collaboration with her husband and issued in 1909. (The latter was published in New York in 1924 as *The Music of the Past.*) She also began giving concerts consisting entirely of harpsichord music—the first such concert took place in Paris. In 1910 she toured Russia and performed privately for Leo Tolstoy at his country home. She was also heard in Germany, Poland, the British Isles, and Japan. One Berlin critic wrote: "The effects she produces are subtly entrancing, the quality of her tone is fluent, and her technique, precise."

By 1912 she had become dissatisfied with the instrument on which she had been performing, convinced that it was not an authentic representation of the true eighteenth century product, and consequently inadequate for a proper performance of Bach's music. After making a comprehensive study in various museums of instruments that Bach had used, she drew up the designs for a new kind of twentieth century harpsichord, which Pleyel constructed for her. She performed on that instrument for the first time at a Bach festival in Breslau, Germany, in 1912.

In 1913 Landowska was invited to give a course on harpsichord music at the Berlin High School for Music, the first instance in modern times that such a post had been created. When World War I engulfed Europe, Landowska was in Berlin. Since she was a French citizen, she and her husband were detained throughout the war, as civil prisoners on parole. During these years of comparative isolation, totally removed from the concert stage, she was able to complete her mastery of the harpsichord and to do exhaustive researches into the music of Johann Sebastian Bach through manuscripts made available to her in German libraries.

Soon after the end of World War I, in 1918, Landowska's husband was killed in an automobile accident. Only ten days after his death, and in spite of her overwhelming grief, she participated in a performance of Bach's *Passion According to St. Matthew* in Basel, Switzerland.

She was back in Paris in 1919. From this time on her performances on the harpsichord became a kind of ritual to which music lovers came to worship, with Landowska as high priestess. Indeed, she always gave her concerts as if they were some kind of religious rite. She would walk slowly, on a darkened stage, to the harpsichord; then, sit down in front of the instrument with palms pressed and head bowed as if in prayer before beginning to play.

She made her American debut on November 20, 1923, as soloist with the Philadelphia Orchestra under Stokowski, in three concertos performed on the harpsichord (two by Handel and one by Bach) and one concerto (by Mozart) on the piano. "The daintiness and sunniness of Mme. Landowska's art lay there; the fullness of it became more apparent when she changed from the harpsichord to the piano," wrote a Philadelphia critic. This was the beginning of her first American tour, which proved so successful that she was booked for an even longer tour the following year. In 1925 she returned to the United States for a third time, this time not only to perform on both the harpsichord and the piano but also to teach the harpsichord at the Curtis Institute of Music in Philadelphia.

"Her exquisite finish is beyond description," was the way W. J. Henderson described one of her concerts in the New York *Sun.* "Its technical certainty—the sureness of the tonal response to the unerring artistic conception is something that only a musician or a very sensitive listener can perfectly appreciate. She has so thoroughly saturated herself in the spirit of seventeenth and eighteenth century music that she plays it back into vivid life and present actuality. Her interpretations are new creations of things left to perish of neglect."

In her appearances as a harpsichordist, Landowska did not confine herself exclusively to the music of the past. She was heard in contemporary works as well, some of which she had commissioned. Two important works came out of her commissions. One was Manuel de Falla's Concerto for Harpsichord, Flute, Oboe, Clarinet, Violin and Piano which she introduced in Barcelona on November 5, 1926. The other was Francis Poulenc's *Concert Champêtre,* for harpsichord and orchestra, first given in Paris on May 3, 1929.

Landowska purchased a home in Saint-Leu-la-Forêt, ten miles north of Paris, where she not only maintained a permanent residence but also established a school of harpsichord and piano playing which attracted students from all over the world. Here, too, she housed a formidable library of old music that eventually numbered ten thousand volumes together with a priceless collection of old keyboard instruments.

On July 3, 1927, Landowska inaugurated her own concert hall on the grounds of her villa at Saint-Leu-la-Forêt. Here she gave Sunday afternoon concerts on both the harpsichord and the piano. Here, too, she delivered lectures and, as had long become habitual with her, she combined her concerts with comments to the audience about the music she was about to play. To her audiences, come from far and wide, she introduced a wealth of old music that had long lain neglected and forgotten, masterworks of the seventeenth and eighteenth centuries which were revivified under her fingertips. At least once each season she performed the "Goldberg" Variations of Bach; and, proceeding to the other end of the Bach spectrum, she also habitually performed as concert pieces the two- and three-part Inventions the master had written as instruction exercises. She performed all of Scarlatti's sonatas, as well as a vast repertory of music by Couperin, Rameau, William Byrd, Thomas Morley, Bach, Haydn, and Mozart, among many other old masters.

The auditorium at Saint-Leu-la-Forêt became a summer shrine for seventeenth and eighteenth century music. As Paul Dambly, a French critic, wrote before World War II: "Her 'French Bayreuth' has become a chamber of music in which

. . . musical works, so young and so new, by the masters of old, are literally revived. . . . The profundity of her intuition, the abandon of self which often, and in spite of herself, makes her hum softly in accompaniment to the singing of her fingers, shows how music possesses her. Wanda Landowska is a priestess and a visionary."

She looked very much the priestess, dressed in her black flowing robes of severe Grecian lines which were loosely draped over her body; allowing her dark hair, which she parted in the middle and gathered into a bun in the back, to fall over her shoulders as she performed. She wore velvet ballet slippers which she discarded at concerts. She bore a striking resemblance to the ballerina Anna Pavlova. Her nose was aquiline; her eyes, dark and intense; her face lit up with radiance during a performance. Despite her diminutive size of just five feet, she managed to have regal bearing.

Landowska provided the following information about the artistic credo which dominated her life: "Since the beginning of my campaign in favor of old music, I have always compelled myself—through my concerts, writing and teaching —to focus light on the fact that this so-called 'old music' is a living force, sometimes more modern than modern music itself. Long years of battles were necessary to overcome the profound and deeply rooted prejudices against an art which was considered desiccated, naive and incapable of moving the emotions. The same prejudices prevailed for old instruments. The passionate interest which today one brings to old music and to its interpretation is an eloquent proof of the transformation which has taken place with the taste of the public and professional musicians."

When Europe was at war again, in 1939, Landowska remained at Saint-Leu-la-Forêt, using it as her citadel of peace and tranquility. But that citadel collapsed when, on the morning of May 10, 1940, the Nazis invaded France. Taking with her only a bare minimum of precious manuscripts, books, and memorabilia, she fled south to Blois, leaving behind her the inestimable treasures of her library and instruments all of which were confiscated by the Nazis. (After the war they were found in a Bavarian salt mine.) When France fell, Landowska found a home in a fishing village north of the Spanish border. She once said she managed to keep her sanity during this trying time by undertaking a comprehensive restudy of Bach's *The Well-Tempered Clavier.*

From this fishing village she managed to make her way to Switzerland, and finally to the United States, arriving in America in November 1940. She established herself in an apartment overlooking Central Park in New York City and in the main led the life of a recluse, devoting herself to studies, to self-analysis and self-criticism as a harpsichord performer. Some of her time was given over to teaching, her studio attracting students from Europe and America among whom were Clifford Curzon, Alice Ehlers, José Iturbi, and Sylvia Marlowe. She saw few people other than her most intimate friends and her students. When she desired physical movement she took a brisk walk in Central Park. She preferred a sedentary and secluded existence that precluded touring the United States or abroad. But she did give her first New York concert in fourteen years at Town Hall, New York, on February 21, 1942, performing the "Goldberg" Variations. "No matter what she plays," wrote Virgil Thomson in the *Herald Tribune,* "it is one of the richest and grandest experiences available to lovers of tonal art. . . . A performance so complete, so wholly interpreted . . . is rarely to be encountered."

Landowska concentrated her performances on recordings rather than in public appearances (though intermittently she did give some concerts in the United States). One of the first of her records since her return to the United States was the RCA Victor release of the "Goldberg" Variations, which within a few years sold over one hundred thousand albums.

In 1950 she found a new and last home: "Oak Knoll" in Lakeville, Connecticut, an old house on Millerton Road atop a hill, surrounded by trees, and with a fabulous view of a lake. The house included a fully equipped studio where she could make her Victor recordings. Among the most important made in this studio were the complete *Well-Tempered Clavier* and the Three-Part Inventions of Bach, and a set of Haydn's piano sonatas.

In his book *The Great Pianists,* Harold C. Schonberg described Landowska's art as follows: "She was a genius at underlining the dramatic and emotional content of a piece. When she held on to a fermata, worlds tottered and the sun stopped until she went on to the next phrase.

Everything she did had meaning and emotional significance. She took liberties, all kinds of liberties, but like all great artists she could get away with them. In short, her entire musical approach was romantic: intensely personal, full of light and shade, never pedantic."

"If there is one aspect of performing other than technical facility in which Landowska was supreme, it was the matter of rhythm," wrote the harpsichordist Igor Kipnis in the *Saturday Review.* "Few performers on any instrument could sound quite so rock steady, even when employing a marked rubato. When Landowska played a Bach fugue, it emerged as an edifice. Handel gigues bounced, fast Scarlatti sonatas scintillated, and her Mozart and Haydn set toes tapping. . . . In later life she could sometimes sound overly deliberate, but, as her earlier recordings attest, she was most often a rhythmically remarkable and exciting performer."

In 1948 Landowska appeared at Town Hall in New York in a series of three concerts covering the two books of *The Well-Tempered Clavier.* Her last public appearance was at the Frick Museum in New York in 1954.

She succumbed to a heart attack at her home in Lakeville, Connecticut, on August 16, 1959.

France conferred on Landowska membership in the Legion of Honor in 1925 and the Grand Prix of the Paris Exposition in 1937. She received the Hors Concours Award of the Charles Cros Academy in France for her album of Scarlatti sonatas in 1939. In 1951 the National Federation of Music Clubs gave her a citation for her recording of the complete *The Well-Tempered Clavier.*

After her death a collection and translation of her writings edited by Denise Restout and Robert Hawkins was published in the United States under the title *Landowska on Music* (1964).

ABOUT: Gavoty, B. Wanda Landowska; Gelatt, R. Makers of Music; Schonberg, H. C. The Great Pianists. *Periodicals*—New York Times, May 26, 1949; Saturday Review, October 31, 1959, November 28, 1964; Stereo Review, October 1968.

Larrocha

Alicia de Larrocha

1923–

ALICIA DE LARROCHA

Alicia de Larrocha (originally Alicia de Larrocha y de la Calle), Spanish pianist known for her interpretations of Spanish piano music (particularly that of Granados and Albéniz), was born in Barcelona, Spain, on May 23, 1923, to Eduardo de Larrocha and Maria Teresa de la Calle. Both her mother and her aunt had studied piano with Enrique Granados; her aunt taught piano at the Academia Marshall founded in 1909 by Frank Marshall, a Spaniard of English descent, who had established the school as a successor to one formerly headed by Granados.

When Alicia was two and a half, she climbed to the piano keyboard one day to play a piece a pupil of her aunt had performed. Her aunt took her to Frank Marshall who insisted that Alicia was too young to receive instruction. About a year later her aunt locked the piano because Alicia was continually using it as a plaything and as a storehouse for crayons and pencils. "I was so unhappy I cried," Alicia de Larrocha recalls. "I put my head on the floor and banged it. I was in a real temper." Once again, her aunt took her to Frank Marshall. When Alicia yelled at him, "I want to play the piano," he decided to take her on as a pupil. "The Academia Marshall," she has said, "was my home. I spent all my time there at the piano and playing games. I was never forced to play the piano, so it was never work. My toy was the piano." Frank Marshall remained the only piano teacher she ever had. (She did, however, study theory with Ricardo Lamote de Grignon.) Only one year after her piano lessons with Marshall had begun, Alicia made her debut in Barcelona with a recital. When she was nine she was a soloist with the Orquesta Sinfónica de Madrid in Mozart's *Coronation Concerto,* Enrique Fernández Arbós conducting.

She was still a child when she heard a piece by Granados for the first time, played for her by her teacher. "There opened before me a new world of poetry and dreams," she says. "I had the sensation that this music formed part of myself, and now I would never be able to free myself from its influence." But it was ten years before her teacher would allow her to play works by Granados or the piano music of any other Span-

ish composer, insisting that she must first master the classical repertory. To this day, she insists that the classical repertory is the proper preparation for the correct performance of twentieth century Spanish piano literature.

In time, Alicia became Marshall's assistant at the Academia. For a number of years the teaching of piano was her principal musical endeavor. She stayed in Barcelona during the Spanish Civil War, devoting herself to her work at the Academia. Those were difficult times. "We had no food in the last six months," she recalls. "It was a tragedy. My father went to the mountains to get greens to eat because we had no food, no bread, no oil."

When the Civil War was over, Larrocha did some concertizing in Spain and (following the termination of World War II) in Spanish Morocco and the Canary Islands as well as in several cities in Europe outside Spain. Though her concerts were well received—and though she was honored with the gold medal of the Academia Marshall in 1943—she did not consider concert work a possible career. As she put it: "Music has been the one thing of my life, and nothing else. I never thought of it as a profession."

Larrocha married Juan Torra, also a teacher of piano, on June 21, 1950. They had two children: Juan Francisco, who became a guitarist, and Alicia, who became a pianist. When Frank Marshall died in 1959, Larrocha and her husband took over the direction of the Academia, with Torra assuming all his wife's chores both at the conservatory and at home when she was touring.

In the early 1950s Alfred Wallenstein, then the music director of the Los Angeles Philharmonic, heard one of her concerts and invited her to California to appear with his orchestra. She arrived in 1954 and performed a Mozart piano concerto and Manuel de Falla's *Nights in the Gardens of Spain.* From Los Angeles she went to San Francisco to appear with the San Francisco Symphony under Enrique Jordá. A year later she gave her first American recital at Town Hall in New York in a program that included music by Granados and Albéniz as well as works in the more standard repertory. In the *Saturday Review,* Irving Kolodin noted that she played the Spanish pieces "with crisp rhythm, stylistic assurance, and the kind of flexibility in melodic statement that is hard for an outsider to simulate." But she was not yet popular. She feels her minuscule size—four feet nine, weighing less than a hundred pounds—was the drawback. "I was a little like a circus," she has said.

During the next decade she continued making appearances in Europe, teaching at the Academia, and making recordings, one of which (Albéniz's *Iberia*) gained her the Grand Prix du Disque in France and another the Edison Award in Amsterdam. Her recordings of Granados's *Spanish Dances* and the first book of *Goyescas* came to the notice of Herbert Breslin, a New York publicity man, who arranged to have her concertize in the United States (after a ten-year hiatus). In 1965 she appeared as a soloist with the New York Philharmonic, William Steinberg conducting, in Mozart's Concerto in A major, K.488; this performance was marred by a defective piano. But two weeks later she gave a recital in New York before an audience that included the pianists Arthur Rubinstein and Claudio Arrau and Harold C. Schonberg noted in the New York *Times* that her playing was "pianistically flawless, with infallible fingers, brilliant sonorities, steady rhythm, everything." During a four-and-a-half-month tour she played with half a dozen American symphony orchestras, was guest artist with the Madrid Symphony and the London Symphony on their tours, and gave about a dozen recitals. Her success placed her among the top-ranking pianists of the day. "She is a wonderful pianist," wrote Schonberg in the New York *Times* in the fall of 1966, "and more: she is an artist."

In these and later performances in the United States she continually promoted the music of Spain. In December 1966 she performed the complete four books of Albéniz's *Iberia* in a recital in New York. Though one of the keys in her piano stuck repeatedly—a circumstance she took pains to explain to her audience before beginning to play the fourth book—she was acclaimed. "She has a technique that can honestly be classified as stupendous," said Schonberg. On December 7, 1967, she commemorated the centenary of Granados's birth with a recital at Carnegie Hall in New York, devoted exclusively to his works. Granados's *Goyescas,* a fifty-minute suite, was featured at this concert, as well as at other of her recitals; she also recorded it.

After one of her performances of *Goyescas* —in New York on December 9, 1973—Robert Kimball wrote in the New York *Post*: "Larrocha, with her unassuming humility, is the quintessence of the great concert artist. Display for its own sake and personal vanity are absent when she performs the music she treasures and ennobles. She is an instrument for the expression of the music itself, which she plays with consummate dignity and total authority."

Although known as an interpreter of Spanish music, she is also a remarkable performer of the classical literature and, particularly, of the music of Mozart and Bach. Writing in *Stereo Review* Robert Offergeld described her performance of the Bach-Busoni Chaconne as "at once as vastly architectural and as full of raging turbulence as the Roman engravings of Piranesi." In her recordings of Mozart's music, Offergeld found that "what she gives us is not the radiance alone of Mozart or the darkness alone of *duende*. She gives us a darkness that is at the same time radiant. ... The only thing more striking than her deliberation is the fresh news disclosed by this unusual spacious treatment of perspectives that are, after all, familiar to every piano student. A little later, of course, after the sobriety and darkness have done their work, we begin to notice the glancing glitter of Presences gathering in the shadow. And by the time Miss de Larrocha decides to unleash the fullness of her awesome power, it is almost an act of supererogation, for we are already hopelessly spellbound."

In June 1968, in Montreal where she had come to judge a piano competition, Larrocha fractured her right thumb closing the door of a taxi. An X ray revealed that she had a growth on the bone demanding an operation. The surgery took place in Barcelona. "The possibility of never playing again was frightening," she recalls. During several months of recovery she studied the literature for piano left hand. Then, fully recovered, she resumed her concert career in Lennoxville, Quebec, on September 30. In 1969 she gave a festival of Spanish music in a three-recital series in New York, and in 1970 she recorded an album, *Spanish Piano Music of the 20th Century.*

For seven years, between 1964 and 1971, she did not give any public performances in her native city. When in April 1971 she gave two concerts in Barcelona, she was welcomed as a conquering hero. Just before her performance of Chopin's Piano Concerto No.2 she was given an ovation—something that rarely happens in Spain.

In 1961 she was given the Paderewski Memorial Award. One year later, the Spanish government decorated her with the Order of Civil Merit, and in 1972 presented her with the medal of the Order of Isabella the Catholic. She has also received the Harriet Cohen International Music Award Medal.

Larrocha is four feet nine inches tall—almost as tall sitting at the piano as she is standing up. Her hands are small and square, with an intervallic expanse of only a ninth. Her overall calm and her avoidance of dramatics in her everyday behavior make her something of a rarity among concert artists. "On tour," she says, "I relax with my job and enjoy life with friends . . . eating, sleeping, and playing. It is a job: I am a woman going to do my thing. And, thank God, I'm a pianist, because I can eat and stay out late before a concert. I couldn't do this if I were a singer." She has also said: "If I never give another recital or concert, I wouldn't die. I enjoy sitting down and playing for myself."

She fills about one hundred engagements a year, divided equally between the United States and abroad. She travels without a secretary, companion, or press agent. On tour, as at home, she practices continually—with a mute on the strings of her piano in hotels.

Alicia de Larrocha's recording of the complete *Iberia* of Albéniz received a Grammy from the National Academy of Recording Arts and Sciences in 1974, as did her recording of Ravel's two piano concertos and Fauré's *Fantaisie* in

1975. As mentioned earlier, she has also received awards in France and in the Netherlands for her recordings.

ABOUT: American Record Guide, March 1971; High Fidelity, October 1969; New York Times, September 21, 1969; New York Times Magazine, July 19, 1976; Saturday Review, October 30, 1971.

Giacomo Lauri-Volpi

1892–

Giacomo Lauri-Volpi, tenor, was born in Lanuvio, near Rome, on December 11, 1892. He studied law at the University of Rome before entering the Santa Cecilia Academy for musical training. He later continued his vocal studies privately with Enrico Rosati and Antonio Cotogni. His operatic debut took place in 1919 in Viterbo as Lord Arthur Talbot in *I Puritani,* and success first came at the Teatro Costanzi in Rome where he made his bow as Des Grieux in *Manon* in 1920. Other performances at the Teatro Costanzi and guest appearances with major companies in Genoa, Buenos Aires, and Rio de Janeiro followed. In Milan in 1922 he established himself at La Scala in the Italian and French repertory, revealing beauty and power of vocal sound combined with unusual acting ability.

On January 26, 1923, Lauri-Volpi made his debut at the Metropolitan Opera as the Duke in *Rigoletto.* He had been ill for five days before that appearance and was forced to sing with an inflamed throat. He therefore did not show himself to best advantage, performing, as one New York critic remarked, "with more fervor than freedom, more of style than substance. There were, however, happier intervals when he mastered his ailing throat and nerves and showed more than a hint of his quality." That quality became apparent later the same season when he was heard as Rodolfo in *La Bohème,* Cavaradossi in *Tosca,* Turiddu in *Cavalleria Rusticana,* Pinkerton in *Madama Butterfly,* Alfredo in *La Traviata,* and Almaviva in *The Barber of Seville.* On February 14, 1923, he sang for the first time in America the role of Pedro in Franco Vittadini's *Anima Allegra.*

Lauri-Volpi remained with the Metropolitan

Lauri-Volpi: lou′ rē vōl′ pē

GIACOMO LAURI-VOLPI

Opera for a decade, singing 238 times in New York and 61 times on tour in 29 roles. His final appearance there took place on March 11, 1932, as Edgardo in *Lucia di Lammermoor*. In that decade few tenors could rival his popularity. As a critic for the New York *Herald Tribune* remarked after one of his appearances: "Better performances have not been given since the fabulous days of Caruso. . . . His singing . . . was so spirited and white hot from the anvil of what seemed realistic passion that even the musicians in the orchestra lifted their jaded heads, and at the end of the scene rose in a body to join the general uproar of applause and cheers."

Lauri-Volpi helped open three seasons of the Metropolitan Opera: 1926–1927 as Licinio in *La Vestale* (November 1); 1927–1928 as Calaf in *Turandot* (October 31); 1931–1932 as Alfredo (November 2). On February 19, 1925, he assumed the title role in Montemezzi's *Giovanni Gallurese* at its American premiere. On November 16, 1926, he created for the United States the role of Calaf. On February 29, 1924, he was heard as Alim in the New York premiere of Massenet's *Le Roi de Lahore*.

His other roles at the Metropolitan Opera were Andrea Chénier, Radames in *Aida,* Don José in *Carmen,* Enzo in *La Gioconda,* Faust in Boïto's *Mefistofele,* Vasco da Gama in *L'Africaine,* Rinuccio in *Gianni Schicchi,* the title role in *Faust,* Pollione in *Norma,* Manrico in *Il Trovatore,* Canio in *I Pagliacci,* Rodolfo in *Luisa Miller,* Arnold in *William Tell,* Elvino in *La Sonnambula,* and Des Grieux in *Manon.*

In 1926 Lauri-Volpi made a triumphant tour of America. Five years later he initiated his first concert tour of the United States. During his years at the Metropolitan he was also heard at Covent Garden in London, the Paris Opéra, Teatro Colón in Buenos Aires, La Scala in Milan, and other major opera houses in Italy, Brussels, and Monte Carlo. After the Metropolitan Opera, his most important affiliation was with La Scala.

He was scheduled to return to the Metropolitan Opera for the 1939–1940 season after a seven-year absence, but World War II frustrated these plans. During the war he confined his appearances to Spain and Italy, while maintaining permanent residence—with his wife, the Spanish singer Maria Ros—at Berjasot, near Valencia, Spain, on an estate he had acquired in 1935.

Lauri-Volpi is the author of an autobiography, *L'Equivoco* (1930), and of *Cristali Viventi* (1948), *A Viso Aperto* (1953), and *Voci Parallele* (1955).

A singing competition in Madrid, the Lauri-Volpi International Singing Contest, has been named in his honor. During the June finals in 1977, Lauri-Volpi was serenaded by several distinguished operatic tenors, including Placido Domingo; he responded with the second verse of "La donna è mobile" from *Rigoletto.*

ABOUT: Gustarelli, A. Chi è Giacomo Lauri-Volpi?; Lauri-Volpi, G. L'Equivoco.

Marjorie Lawrence

1909–

Marjorie Florence Lawrence, soprano, was born in Dean's Marsh, Victoria, Australia, on February 17, 1909. Her parents, William and Elizabeth Smith Lawrence, were the children of pioneers who had settled in that part of Australia. The small town of Dean's Marsh numbered about one hundred and forty inhabitants, most of whom were sheep farmers. Marjorie's father owned a sheep ranch.

As a child Marjorie was often praised by friends and relatives for her singing and was sometimes referred to as "the little Melba." She sang solo parts in school entertainments and church socials and was a member of the church choir. When she was seven she began studying

MARJORIE LAWRENCE

piano and voice with the local church pastor, but her official vocal study did not begin until many years later with Ivor Boustead in Melbourne, where she worked as a seamstress and housekeeper to support herself.

"When I was eighteen," she recalls, "I went to Melbourne, about a hundred miles away from my father's sheep ranch, and entered one of the vocal competitions held regularly by a Melbourne newspaper. I won, and began to study very hard until father, who hadn't wanted me to be a singer at first, consented to send me to Paris to study."

She went to Paris on the advice of the Australian baritone John Brownlee. There she was a pupil of Cécile Gilly for three years. In 1932 Lawrence made her opera debut in Monte Carlo as Elisabeth in *Tannhäuser*. Her success in Monte Carlo earned her a contract for the Paris Opéra where, just a few weeks after her Monte Carlo debut, she appeared as Ortrud in *Lohengrin*. She followed this appearance with performances in the title roles of *Aida* and *Salome*, remaining with the Paris Opéra company until 1935.

When Edward Johnson, general manager of the Metropolitan Opera, visited Europe in 1935 he heard Lawrence at the Opéra and engaged her for his company. Her Metropolitan Opera debut took place on December 18, 1935, as Brünnhilde in *Die Walküre*. "It should be said without further ado that this newest singer of Wagner's greater heroines is discerning and vital and alert," reported Lawrence Gilman in the

Herald Tribune. "She has temperament and brains. She has a beautiful profile. She has an admirable sense of costume, a feeling for the stage, for the meaning of words and notes."

Later that season, Lawrence added to her Wagnerian repertory at the Metropolitan the roles of Ortrud and the Brünnhilde of *Siegfried* and *Die Götterdämmerung*. In addition, she proved highly effective as Rachel in *La Juive* which was "the most even accomplishment of this *La Juive*," as Irving Kolodin noted in *The Story of the Metropolitan Opera*. Her Wagnerian interpretations, to which was added Sieglinde in *Die Walküre* in 1940, continued to receive praise from the critics and from discerning opera-goers during the next few seasons, even though Kirsten Flagstad was at that time the leading Wagnerian soprano. Outside the world of Wagner, Lawrence was honored for her interpretations of Salome in Richard Strauss's opera of the same name, Thaïs, Tosca, and the title role in Gluck's *Alceste*.

Brought up in a country where children are taught to ride horses almost as soon as they learn to walk, Lawrence was an expert horsewoman. When she appeared as Brünnhilde in *Die Götterdämmerung*, she insisted on following to the letter Wagner's stage instructions which read: "Springing onto the horse with one leap he takes her into the burning pyre." Only one other singer—in Munich in 1881—had ever actually followed these stage directions so faithfully.

Lawrence added to her operatic fame in the United States with performances in Chicago, St. Louis, and San Francisco, making her debut with the San Francisco Opera on October 17, 1939, as Brünnhilde in *Die Walküre*.

On March 29, 1941, she married Thomas King, a physician. They went on their honeymoon to Mexico where Lawrence was scheduled to appear in several Wagnerian performances. During a rehearsal of *Die Walküre* in June 1941 she found herself incapable of moving her muscles or getting off the couch. At the American Hospital in Mexico City, to which she was rushed, she was found to be a victim of poliomyelitis. At first it was a question of sheer survival. Then it was feared she would be paralyzed for life.

Somehow (possibly as the consequence of an active outdoor life that had included not only horseback riding, but also swimming, tennis, and golf) she found the physical reserve with which not only to face but to fight the disease. With almost superhuman will, and with the devotion and care of her husband, she began to make slow progress. About four months after she had been stricken by the disease, she tested her voice. "I couldn't stand it any longer. I just had to know about my voice—even if what I found out was the worst. I begged for a piano and was humored. My husband strapped me to a chair and wrapped me in blankets so I could sit up, at least halfway. I wanted to sing Isolde. And I did—just a little. But enough to know deep inside of me that my voice was not impaired."

From that moment she was determined, whatever her permanent physical damage might be, to return to her career. She improvised a vocal technique enabling her to sing from a seated position. She worked over her repertory, concert as well as operatic, almost as if she were a beginner.

Her first appearance following her illness took place in a church in Florida where, on Christmas day of 1941, she sang "Ave Maria" and "The Lord's Prayer" from a wheelchair. On November 9, 1942, still seated in a wheelchair, she gave a recital in Town Hall, New York. "It is astonishing," wrote one New York critic, "that her voice . . . is just as powerful and eloquent as ever and actually more brilliant in its top level." On December 27, 1942, the Metropolitan Opera presented a concert as a tribute to her at which she sang the "Venusberg Music" from *Tannhäuser* with Lauritz Melchior. She did so well that evening that the Metropolitan Opera was encouraged to have her appear as Venus in *Tannhäuser* on January 22, 1943, her first appearance on the operatic stage since her illness. Before the opening curtain parted, she was wheeled to the stage where she was deposited on a divan on which (as the part of Venus required) she could recline for the entire act. After her performance she was given one of the most moving ovations ever to take place in the opera house —partly given to a great singer, partly to a woman of extraordinary heroism. In June 1943 she performed Isolde in Montreal in a seated position. Almost a year later, on March 24, 1944, she returned to the stage of the Metropolitan Opera as Isolde, strapped throughout the performance to a carefully camouflaged wheelchair. A year later she traveled throughout Australia, covering fifty thousand miles in army transport planes

and jeeps, singing for soldiers of the Allied nations. She made a second tour for the armed forces in England, Germany, and France in 1946; in London she sang for the king and queen of England at Buckingham Palace. On December 11, 1947, she stood throughout an entire opera performance for the first time in almost seven years when she appeared in the title role of Strauss's *Elektra*. From then on she gave a number of other performances in recitals, standing on a mobile platform.

She told the story of her illness and her return to music in an autobiography, *Interrupted Melody: The Story of My Life* (1949). In 1955 this was made into a motion picture, *Interrupted Melody,* starring Eleanor Parker as Marjorie Lawrence and with Eileen Farrell singing on the sound track.

After retiring from the stage, Lawrence served as professor of voice at Newcomb College of Tulane University in New Orleans for three years; after that, at Southern Illinois University in Carbondale.

With her husband, she spends her time at Harmony Hills, a five-hundred-acre home in the mountains of Arkansas, where she has conducted a ranch Opera Workshop for twelve to fourteen students. At the end of each course the students are presented in a public performance of scenes from operas, including such contemporary works as Carlisle Floyd's *Susannah,* Samuel Barber's *Vanessa,* and Benjamin Britten's *The Rape of Lucretia.*

Marjorie Lawrence's portrait, the work of Joseph Dickinson, was hung in Founders' Hall of the Metropolitan Opera on November 18, 1976. In 1977 she was named Commander of the British Empire by Queen Elizabeth.

ABOUT: Lawrence, M. Interrupted Melody. *Periodicals*—Coronet, August 1947; Opera News, March 18, 1961.

Evelyn Lear

1927–

Evelyn Lear (originally Evelyn Shulman), soprano, was born in Brooklyn, New York, on January 8, 1927. She came from a singing family. Her grandfather, Zavel Kwartin, was world famous as a synagogue cantor, and her mother,

EVELYN LEAR

Nina Kwartin, was trained as a professional singer. Her father, Nathan, a lawyer, was a music lover. Both her parents wanted her to receive musical training to prepare her for a future of knowledgeable listening rather than for a performing career and both were determined that she get a well-rounded academic education.

Evelyn attended the New York public schools —first, elementary schools in Brooklyn; later, George Washington High School in Manhattan (the family moved to Manhattan when Evelyn was thirteen). Her music education consisted of lessons at the piano and on the French horn. In her adolescent years she attended the Berkshire Music Center in Lenox, Massachusetts, where she played the French horn in an orchestra conducted by Leonard Bernstein. Though she aspired to become a singer from the time she was three, she did not receive any formal vocal instruction for some time; her knowledge of singing and vocal music came from listening to her mother vocalize, from concerts, and from recordings.

When she was seventeen she married Dr. Walter Lear. They made their home in Arlington, Virginia. The marriage, she later told an interviewer, was "a disaster." It ended in divorce after they had had two children. During the early years of this marriage she began studying voice with the baritone John Yard in Washington, D.C. There she also appeared as a soloist with the All Souls Unitarian Church, performed in nightclubs, gave two recitals at the Phillips Gallery, and appeared so successfully on televi-

sion on a children's program that in 1949 she was named Miss Television Queen. On November 29, 1950, she made her first appearance in opera, this time solely as an amateur, singing the leading female role of Jenny Parsons in Kurt Weill's one-act folk opera *Down in the Valley.*

After seven years of an unhappy marriage, Lear and her husband were divorced. She returned to New York with her two children. "There I was without a man," she told John Gruen in an interview for the New York *Times,* "and with two small children on my hands." She also confessed: "I resented my children terribly. I didn't give them love, I didn't give them attention. I wanted to get out of the house and leave them alone. I remember I'd get back home, in Yonkers, where we lived, and the maid was there, and I noticed that the kids had blacked up all the windows. They were very disturbed, and it was awful. Oh, I tried to give my children affection, but I wasn't loved by anybody, and when that happens it's hard to give love in return. Besides I was never the motherly type—it's not part of my nature. And I hated to be tied down, and was desperate to make a career."

During this difficult period in her life she attended the Juilliard School of Music, studying *Lieder* with Sergius Kagen and entering the school's opera workshop. The workshop enabled her to appear in several roles, including that of Despina in *Così fan Tutte.*

At Juilliard she met and fell in love with Thomas Stewart, a young baritone also studying voice there. They lived together for a year and on January 8, 1955, they were married. Running a household that included two children did not keep Lear or her husband from furthering their singing careers. In 1955 she won the Concert Artists Guild Award, which was a recital at Town Hall, New York. "I was a success with the press and the public," she recalls. "Here was the beginning, I thought, of a stupendous career. I sat waiting six months for the next big break. An appearance with the Little Orchestra Society, some television, a leading role in a Broadway show that never made it past Boston, and that was all." With the Little Orchestra Society she sang in a performance of Ravel's *L'Enfant et les Sortilèges;* the show intended for Broadway was Marc Blitzstein's *Reuben, Reuben.* She also auditioned for a part in *West Side Story* but was turned down. With her husband she appeared on the road in capsule versions of Broadway musicals, one of which was Cole Porter's *Kiss Me, Kate.* She also performed with summer stock companies and sang in choruses over radio and television.

Frederick Cohen, director of the Juilliard Opera Workshop, advised her and her husband to abandon their commercial undertakings and go to Europe for more study. They both received Fulbright grants which enabled them to go to Berlin in the fall of 1957 and enter the High School for Music. In Berlin she studied voice with Maria Ivogün and Irma Beilke. Three weeks after their arrival, Stewart was engaged by the Deutsche Oper. To Lear only the lesser opera houses seemed receptive—and exclusively for minor parts. Then she auditioned for Carl Ebert, director of the Deutsche Oper. He signed her on a three-year contract. "It was an unprecedented event, for both husband and wife (and Americans at that) to be engaged in the same opera house at the same time," she has said. She might have added that in time they also became the first husband-and-wife team ever to earn the honorary titles *Kammersänger* and *Kammersängerin.*

Lear made her professional opera debut with the Deutsche Oper in April 1959 as the Composer in Richard Strauss's *Ariadne auf Naxos.* Shortly after that she was heard as Cherubino in *The Marriage of Figaro* (her first appearance in a Mozart opera) and Octavian in *Der Rosenkavalier.* Later in 1959 she was called to London to replace an ailing singer in a performance of Richard Strauss's *Four Last Songs* with the London Symphony under Sir Adrian Boult. Over the German radio she gave performances of contemporary music, including a program devoted exclusively to modern Americans.

In 1960 the indisposition of another singer made it possible for Lear to sing in Vienna. A concert performance of Alban Berg's *Lulu* was scheduled for the Vienna June Festival, Karl Böhm conducting. When the scheduled singer fell ill, Lear was called by phone and invited to serve as a substitute. Though she had never seen the opera or even looked at the score, she accepted; she had less than three weeks to learn the complicated music. "When I opened the score and saw the twelve-tone music and dizzying tessitura I almost died on the spot, but it was learned," she has revealed. Her performance in the title role took place on May 24, 1960. She was so successful that when, less than two years

later, the first staged production of *Lulu* was given in Vienna at the recently rebuilt Theater-an-der-Wien, she was once again invited to take over the title role. She became a sensation. Elisabeth Schwarzkopf called her performance "one of the supreme achievements of the operatic stage anywhere in the world." And in a report to the New York *Times* from Vienna, Edward Downes wrote: "The seeing was almost as important as the hearing, for she not only sang the incredibly difficult part with apparent ease, she looked the part of the temptress, she acted it, and she had a stage presence."

After *Lulu* she became a specialist in modern operas. With her husband she appeared in the world premiere of Giselher Klebe's twelve-tone opera, *Alkmene,* creating the title role on September 25, 1961, during the opening-week festivities of the new auditorium of the Deutsche Oper in Berlin. On November 27, 1963, she was heard in the world premiere of Werner Egk's *Die Verlobung in San Domingo* with which the new National Theater in Munich was reopened.

In 1963 Lear presented her first European *Liederabend* (Evening of *Lieder*): an all-Strauss program at the Vienna June Festival that she later recorded for Deutsche Grammophon. One year later she made her bow at the Vienna State Opera as Fiordiligi in *Così fan Tutte* and became the first American ever to give a *Liederabend* at the Salzburg Festival. In 1965 she made her Covent Garden debut as Elvira on *Don Giovanni,* appeared as Poppea in Monteverdi's *L'Incoronazione di Poppea* in Frankfort, Germany, was heard as Lulu in Brussels, and with her husband filmed Wolf-Ferrari's *The Secret of Suzanne* for BBC Television.

Lear's American professional debut in opera took place on May 21, 1965, as Cleopatra in a revival of Handel's *Julius Caesar,* in Kansas City, Missouri, under the auspices of the Performing Arts Foundation. Writing in the New York *Times,* Harold C. Schonberg commented: "Her high clear soprano, her good looks and musical intelligence, and her ability to take those long, florid Handel phrases in stride added up to a most convincing and attractive interpretation."

In September 1965 she was heard for the first time in the United States in the role that had made her internationally famous—that of Lulu. She sang it in San Francisco, and later on in Los Angeles. In 1966 she made her debut with the

Chicago Lyric Opera in the title role of *L'Incoronazione di Poppea.*

When she finally made her debut at the Metropolitan Opera, on March 17, 1967, it was once again in a new opera: Marvin David Levy's *Mourning Becomes Electra,* in which she created the role of Lavinia. The opera itself left much to be desired according to most of the critics, but there was no question about Lear's brilliance both vocally and histrionically. "As the central figure of the play," said Miles Kastendieck in the *World Journal and Tribune,* "Miss Lear revealed histrionic ability worthy of the Broadway stage as well as a voice of exceptional purity, range and quality."

By 1968 she had experienced a vocal crisis, largely because she had devoted herself so extensively to the modern repertory, which made exacting demands on her vocal resources. "I couldn't spin pianissimi, I couldn't float high notes. I couldn't support, and I was almost hoarse," she said. In addition, she was eager to prove herself in the traditional French, Italian, and German repertories. On the advice of her manager she began a six-week period of training with Daniel Ferro at the Manhattan School of Music. "In six weeks," she noted, "Ferro relaxed my throat and my jaw so that I could sing naturally again."

She proceeded to create for herself a new musical image, this time in the more or less standard repertory. At the Metropolitan Opera she achieved noteworthy successes as Cherubino and the Countess in *The Marriage of Figaro,* the Composer in *Ariadne auf Naxos,* Donna Elvira in *Don Giovanni,* Tosca, Alice Ford in *Falstaff,* and the Marschallin in *Der Rosenkavalier.* Her appearance as the Marschallin on February 16, 1974, had been preceded one year earlier by performances in the same role at the Berlin Deutsche Oper, and in Brussels, Budapest, and Lisbon. As Donna Elvira she was assuming the part for the first time anywhere when she sang with the Metropolitan Opera company on tour on April 24, 1974, and in New York on May 29. As the Countess in *The Marriage of Figaro* on November 20, 1975, she was cast in a new production. On August 15, 1977, with the Santa Fe Opera in New Mexico, she was heard for the first time in the title role of Giordano's *Fedora.*

But she did not completely abandon modern opera. In fact, one of her greatest triumphs at the Metropolitan Opera came on April 2, 1969, when she sang there for the first time the role of Marie in Berg's *Wozzeck.* Before this she had sung Marie abroad and at the Chicago Lyric Opera; and her recording of *Wozzeck* for Deutsche Grammophon, with Karl Böhm conducting, had earned a Grammy from the National Academy of Recording Arts and Sciences in 1965. On March 5, 1974, she appeared with the Houston Opera as Irina in the world premiere of Thomas Pasatieri's *The Seagull.*

Both at the Metropolitan and elsewhere, she often shared the opera stage with her husband. In 1971 the San Francisco Opera mounted a new production of *Eugene Onegin* for them, the first time they appeared together on the American opera stage. They appeared together at the Metropolitan Opera on numerous occasions; as Count Almaviva and Cherubino in *The Marriage of Figaro* in 1971–1972, as Ford and Mistress Ford in *Falstaff,* and as Don Giovanni and Donna Elvira in *Don Giovanni,* both in 1975. In June 1974 they shared the stage of the Deutsche Oper in Berlin in *The Marriage of Figaro* and as Desdemona and Iago in *Otello.* Among the other operas in which they appeared jointly are *Die Meistersinger* (in Nuremberg in April 1972), Bartók's *Bluebeard's Castle* (in a concert performance in Miami, Florida), *Tosca* (with the Pittsburgh Opera), and Purcell's *Dido and Aeneas* (at the Lincoln Center for the Performing Arts).

They have also made many appearances in joint recitals; in August 1976 they toured South America. In addition, Lear has been heard in numerous solo concerts, both in recitals and as guest artist with major orchestras. She assumed a cameo part (that of a diva) in Robert Altman's motion picture *Buffalo Bill and the Indians* (1976).

Evelyn Lear and Thomas Stewart maintain permanent residences at Santa Fe, New Mexico, and at Fort Lauderdale, Florida. Husband and wife share an enthusiasm for golf, swimming, and cooking.

ABOUT: Esquire, August 1968; High Fidelity/Musical America, March 1967, January 1972; New York Times, February 20, 1970; New Yorker, January 22, 1972; Opera News, March 18, 1967, March 28, 1970.

Lilli Lehmann

1848–1929

LILLI LEHMANN

Lilli Lehmann, soprano, became a legend by virtue of her artistry, versatility, and performing stamina. (She was not related to the soprano Lotte Lehmann.)

Lilli was born in Würzburg, Germany, on November 24, 1848. Her mother, Marie Loewe, had sung in opera (she had been prima donna at Cassel under Ludwig Spohr), was a professional harpist, and was a friend of Richard Wagner. Lilli's father, Carl August Lehmann, was a tenor. His irresponsible ways and his weakness for alcohol led Marie to desert him in 1853, taking her two young daughters, Lilli and Marie, with her to Prague. There she found employment as a harpist in the opera orchestra and as a teacher of voice. A year after arriving in Prague, Lilli started taking piano lessons with Cölestin Müller. By the time she was twelve, she worked as her mother's accompanist. This made it possible for her to learn a sizable vocal repertory before starting to study voice with her mother, her only teacher.

On October 20, 1865, Lilli made her opera debut as the First Page in *The Magic Flute* at the Landestheater in Prague. Two weeks later, when a feud developed between a principal soprano and the conductor during the intermission of *The Magic Flute,* the soprano refused to go on with her performance. Lilli was hurriedly summoned to take over the role of Pamina. Though she had never studied the part, she went through the remainder of that performance without faltering, the first of many evidences she would give of her extraordinary ability to learn roles.

In 1868 Lehmann appeared with the Danzig Opera, and in 1869–1870 with the Leipzig Opera. For both she sang a wide variety of lyric and coloratura roles. In 1870 she joined the company of the Berlin Royal Opera, making her debut, as Vielka, on August 19 in Meyerbeer's *Ein Feldlager in Schlesien.* She remained with the Berlin Royal Opera many years to become a singing idol of the city. Her photograph bearing the caption "Our Lehmann" decorated many store windows. In 1875 she was given a life appointment

Lehmann: lä′ män

at the opera house, and one year after that she was honored with the title *Kammersängerin.*

Since Wagner was an almost daily household guest at her mother's home in Prague when he conducted in that city in 1863, Lilli came to know him well. He grew so fond of her that at one time he offered to adopt her. When he began planning his first festival for Bayreuth, in 1876, he himself coached her in minor roles in the *Ring* cycle. And so it was she who created the roles of the Forest Bird in *Siegfried,* Helmwige in *Das Rheingold* and *Die Walküre,* and Woglinde in *Die Götterdämmerung.*

In 1878 she made her debut in Stockholm, and on June 3, 1880, she appeared for the first time in London, at His Majesty's Theatre as Violetta in *La Traviata.* A few days later she sang there the role of Philine in *Mignon.* On July 2, 1884, she made her bow at Covent Garden in London. For this she appeared in the dramatic part of Isolde in *Tristan and Isolde.*

Her artistic achievements and her fame assumed even greater dimensions in the United States. Her American debut took place at the Metropolitan Opera on November 25, 1885, as Carmen. Though this was not one of her notable roles, the critics reacted favorably. In the New York *Times,* W. J. Henderson called her "the leading prima donna of the establishment," adding: "The new songstress possesses a powerful and ringing voice. . . . Considered as a vocalist, she is undoubtedly . . . the most finished songstress that has visited America in many years."

Five days later Lehmann revealed the true

range of her dramatic and vocal capabilities to a New York audience, singing for the first time in her career the role of Brünnhilde in *Die Walküre*. She was, said Henry Krehbiel in the *Tribune,* "a most statuesquely beautiful Brünnhilde and her voice glorified the music. . . . Throughout the evening, it was clear and ringing and never out of tune, and full of feeling. . . . It was a beautiful impersonation from whatever point it was viewed."

Her physical endurance caused almost as much stir as her artistry. Only one day after performing her first Brünnhilde she returned to the stage as Carmen. Two days after that, on December 2, she created for America the part of Sulamith in Karl Goldmark's *The Queen of Sheba.* On December 4 she appeared again as Sulamith; on December 5, matinee, as Brünnhilde in *Die Walküre,* and on December 9 as Bertha in Meyerbeer's *Le Prophète.* Before the season ended she was also heard as Venus in *Tannhäuser,* Marguerite in *Faust,* and Irene in *Rienzi.*

In 1889, when the Metropolitan Opera company was on tour, she appeared in the three Brünnhilde roles every week for eight consecutive weeks, and in addition she undertook another role on other nights.

Her contract with the Berlin Royal Opera allowed her leaves of absence to enable her to appear with other opera companies. In 1886, after the end of the Metropolitan Opera season, she asked for an extension of her leave, threatening to remain in America for good if her request were denied. The threat caused the authorities in Berlin not only to refuse to give her the necessary permission but also to bar her from all further appearances in German opera houses. Unable to sing in opera in her native land, Lehmann turned to the German recital halls to become one of the greatest exponents of *Lieder* of her time.

As a Wagnerian soprano, Lehmann continued to make operatic history at the Metropolitan Opera. She created for America the role of Isolde on December 1, 1886, the Brünnhilde in *Siegfried* on November 9, 1887, and the Brünnhilde in *Die Götterdämmerung* on January 25, 1888. Her first Isolde led Henry Krehbiel to write in the *Tribune:* "Vocally the performance was beyond praise. It is seldom given to the public to observe so complete a devotion of an artist to her task. From her first note to the last

she abandoned herself without reservation to a publication of the contents of the character. . . . She has grasped its passionate intensity and in a degree that was never so manifest as at this performance she disclosed the wealth of musical, vocal and histrionic gifts which qualify her to interpret the passionate heroines of Wagner." About her initial Brünnhilde in *Siegfried,* Krehbiel noted: "To Fraulein Lehmann it was reserved to fill the last scene with a musical glory which had its visual counterpart in the flood of light which filled the stage. . . . Her apostrophe to the sun was sung with thrilling power, while the struggle between pride and the dawning of love had the most eloquent exposition." And he had this to say of her Brünnhilde in *Die Götterdämmerung:* "Lehmann's portrayal of the heroine was an achievement such as it is a happiness to witness, and will remain a benediction in the memory. Here is an artist whose vocal gifts and capabilities seem as inexhaustible as her zeal."

Her other Wagner roles were Sieglinde in *Die Walküre* and Elisabeth in *Tannhäuser.* Her artistry, however, extended beyond Wagner. Other Metropolitan Opera roles (most of them given superlative performances) were Donna Anna in *Don Giovanni,* Leonora in *Il Trovatore,* the title role in Weber's *Euryanthe,* Leonore in *Fidelio,* Norma, Aida, Valentine in *Les Huguenots,* Rachel in *La Juive,* the title role in Goldmark's *The Queen of Sheba,* Philine in *Mignon,* and Selika in *L'Africaine.* She never appeared at the Metropolitan Opera as Adalgisa in *Norma,* though she had sung that role elsewhere. In the history of *Norma* she was the second artist to have sung both the title role and Adalgisa (the first being Giulia Grisi). She created for the United States the roles of Vivianne in the American premiere of Goldmark's *Merlin* (January 3, 1887) and Sulamith in the American premiere of Goldmark's *The Queen of Sheba* (December 2, 1885).

On February 24, 1888, Lehmann married the opera tenor Paul Kalisch. (A decade earlier, when she was thirty, she had been engaged to Fritz Brandt, stage director at Bayreuth. But she resented his possessiveness, felt it would infringe upon her career and her art, and broke off their relationship.) Kalisch joined the Metropolitan Opera company for the 1889–1890 season, appearing that year with his wife in *Don Giovanni, La Juive, Tristan and Isolde* (initially as the Sailor's Voice and the Shepherd), *Norma,* and *Die Walküre.* During the season of 1891–1892 he was Manrico to her Leonora in *Il Trovatore,* and Don Ottavio to her Donna Anna. On later occasions he sang Tristan to her Isolde. The marriage did not last. Though they never got a divorce, they separated permanently. From then on, marriage never again entered into Lehmann's calculations. She belonged solely to her art, confining her affections to friends and animals, whose care was one of her prime interests.

After the 1891–1892 season Lehmann absented herself from the Metropolitan Opera for seven years, returning in 1898–1899 in the roles of Donna Anna, Valentine, Brünnhilde in both *Siegfried* and *Die Götterdämmerung,* Bertha, and Sieglinde. On January 27, 1899, on several hours' notice, she took on the role of Fricka in *Das Rheingold* even though she had never before sung the part. David Bispham, who appeared in the same performance, remarked: "Let me say that there is not one artist in a thousand, perhaps not in the world, physically, nervously, mentally and musically able to perform such a feat, or, if able to perform it, willing to do so to help another artist and assist the management in its duty to the public." Her final appearance on the stage of the Metropolitan took place on March 25, 1899, in *Les Huguenots.* She had appeared in 26 roles in 203 performances in New York and 54 on tour.

In 1891 the Emperor of Germany lifted the ban against Lehmann and allowed her to return in triumph not only to the Berlin Royal Opera but also to all the other major opera houses in Germany. In 1896 she performed all three Brünnhildes at Bayreuth. She broke with Bayreuth permanently after that because she disagreed violently with the new type of production being mounted by Cosima Wagner, who had assumed the staging chores; Lehmann insisted that these new productions violated Wagner's original intentions.

During the years 1905–1910 Lehmann was both the director and the leading soprano at the Summer performances in Salzburg, Austria. Her interpretations of Mozart's heroines became the models which Salzburg henceforth aimed to emulate. More than any other single artist, Lehmann was responsible for solidifying the foundations upon which the structure of the annual summer Salzburg Festival, launched in 1920, was erected.

Lehmann gave her last performance in opera in Vienna in 1909 as Isolde when the principal soprano of that production fell ill midway in her performance; Lehmann, who was seated in Gustav Mahler's box, rushed to the stage to take over the third act (her first performance of this role in four years). After 1909 she concentrated on recitals of *Lieder* both in Europe and the United States until she was well past her seventieth year. She also devoted herself to teaching voice at the Mozarteum in Salzburg from 1926 on and for several decades during her later years privately at her home in the Grünewald section of Berlin. Among her pupils were Geraldine Farrar and Olive Fremstad.

If, as some have said, she had an almost military bearing on the stage, it was also true that offstage she had the carriage and demeanor of an empress. She strode through her long career with regal majesty, a woman of immense willpower, uncompromising ideals, thorough dedication and, where art was concerned, a dictatorial nature. Her pride, her awareness of her own greatness, and her intolerance of those who would not meet her own exacting standards bordered on arrogance. Her opinions on less than satisfactory performances were pronounced as if they were royal decrees. After the second act of an inadequate revival of *Tannhäuser* in Berlin she left the theater in open disgust. "With the air of an empress," recalled Geraldine Farrar in her autobiography, "she rose, drew her cloak about her shoulders, still statuesque, and announced in no whispered undertones—as she made her way out—'Say that Lilli Lehmann leaves her loge in disgust at the travesty they call Art in this opera house.' " On another occasion she was less than impressed by Nordica's performance as Elsa at Bayreuth. When, after the performance, Nordica asked Lilli Lehmann if she could pay a call at her home, Lehmann replied icily: "I am not taking any pupils this season."

An unidentified contemporary described her as follows: "She had a tall, regal figure, relaxed gestures, and a proud carriage. Her dark eyes had penetrating intensity. Thin lips and a slightly long nose made her face look severe, but when lit up by a smile it revealed kindness and understanding, even humor. Her speaking voice was low and ringing. Her singing voice carried crystal clear through the most tumultuous orchestra up to the highest galleries."

It took indomitable willpower, extraordinary self-discipline, and relentless perseverance to develop the power of her singing voice, since she started out with a small voice and suffered from asthma. "Nature denied her penetrating strength and sumptuousness of voice," wrote the Viennese music critic Eduard Hanslick, "and thus deprived her of her strongest, most immediate means of passionate communication, but it endowed her with a personality predestined not only for the stage, but particularly for tragic and noble roles."

She mastered 170 roles in 119 operas in the French, Italian, and German repertories. Her formidable versatility even embraced comic operas such as those of Suppé and Offenbach. Though she was probably the greatest Wagnerian soprano of her time, Brünnhilde and Isolde were not her favorite roles; she preferred Norma and Leonore in *Fidelio*. Not Wagner but Mozart was her "musical home"—as she herself said. "It took courage," says Henry Pleasants in *The Great Singers,* "and independence of mind and spirit for a great Isolde and Brünnhilde to sing not only Norma but also Lucia and Lucrezia Borgia. . . . Mme. Lehmann's distinction was in taking the big Wagnerian repertoire abroad and breaking out of it—and out of German."

Lilli Lehmann died in Berlin on May 16, 1929. She was the author of *How to Sing* (1902), a study of *Fidelio* (1904), and an autobiography, *My Path Through Life* (1914). She also edited a volume of arias by Mozart and translated into German Victor Maurel's *Dix Ans de Carrière.*

ABOUT: Lehmann, L. My Path Through Life; Pleasants, H. The Great Singers. *Periodicals*—Opera News, February 20, 1965.

LOTTE LEHMANN

Lotte Lehmann

1888–1976

No higher tribute can be paid to Lotte Lehmann, soprano, than to say she brought renewed glory to the name of Lehmann in both the opera house and the concert hall. She was not related to Lilli Lehmann, but they may be said to be of the same musical family. They both had similar high ideals, unblemished integrity, unswerving dedication to the highest principles of their art, musical penetration. Each had a voice of rare beauty.

Lotte Lehmann, soprano, was born in

Lehmann: lä′ män

Perleberg, Germany, on February 27, 1888. She was the younger of two children of Carl and Marie Schuster Lehmann. Their father, who worked as a secretary for a benevolent association, was a member of the Perleberg Singing Society. Aiming to make his daughter a schoolteacher, he saw to it that she received the advantages of a well-rounded education in elementary and secondary schools in Perleberg. But until she was sixteen she did not know a note of classical music.

In her early teens Lotte moved with her family to Berlin where she attended a high school for girls. She was a bright student, but disinterested in her studies, preferring to spend her time writing poetry. She sold one of her poems to a magazine for two dollars.

Possessing a pleasant voice, she had been singing popular and folk songs from childhood on. After receiving some coaching from Erna Tiedke she won a voice scholarship for the High School of Music in Berlin where she studied with Helene Jordan and where, strange to say, she was found to be without talent. She continued her vocal training at the Etelka Gerster School with Eva Reinhold, and completed it with Mathilde Mallinger, the Wagnerian soprano who had created the role of Eva in *Die Meistersinger* in Munich in 1868. Mallinger was the first to discover that Lehmann possessed unusual musical gifts. She devoted herself assiduously to preparing her gifted student for a professional career.

Attractive and flirtatious, Lehmann had numerous beaux. One of them asked her to marry him but only on the condition she give up all thoughts of a career and devote herself to being a wife. Though in love with the man, Lehmann unhesitatingly chose music over matrimony.

Upon completing her vocal studies, she received a three-year contract with the Hamburg Opera at a salary of about fifty dollars a month. She made her debut in 1909 as one of the pages in *The Magic Flute.* For some time she continued to fill small parts with unrewarding results. After her appearance as Freia in *Das Rheingold,* a critic of the *Hamburger Fremdenblatt* said she played with "touching awkwardness," adding that "as to the vocal qualities of the young lady, whose throat seemed constricted by excessive nervousness, we can as yet say nothing."

Then Otto Klemperer, conductor of the Hamburg Opera, decided to cast her as Elsa in *Lohengrin* when the singer scheduled for that part proved unavailable. "I had already studied the part by myself," she later recalled, "and I felt I knew every note of it. I came to the first rehearsal, therefore, somewhat sure of myself and my ground, and as proud as a peacock. But if I deluded myself into believing that I knew the role thoroughly, I was soon to see my error. Klemperer sat at the piano like some wild demon throwing his long hands, like a tiger's paws, upon the keys, guiding me by the sheer force of his fanatic will. . . . The role suddenly became the flame of my personal experience. I felt I was transfigured."

On the evening of that performance, as she added, "I did not see the audience; I did not even see the face of the director. I forgot everything—where I was, what the evening meant to me. I was Elsa, the Elsa that was first revealed to me by Klemperer, the Elsa I now fully understood for the first time. Tears came to my eyes as the chorus sang, 'Heil dir, Elsa von Brabant,' and 'Heil dir' my whole heart sings to the day of days which was the real beginning of my life."

She began to sing major roles: Anna Page in Nicolai's *The Merry Wives of Windsor,* Irene in *Rienzi,* Sophie in *Der Rosenkavalier,* as well as roles in French and Italian operas.

She was appearing as Micaëla in *Carmen* one evening in 1914 when Hans Gregor, director of the Vienna Royal Opera who had come to Hamburg to find a tenor, heard her. He engaged her

for his company where she made her debut that year as Agathe in *Der Freischütz.*

In Vienna Lehmann first achieved worldwide fame, and in Vienna she soared to greatness. She was heard as Sieglinde in *Die Walküre,* Octavian in *Der Rosenkavalier,* Leonore in *Fidelio* (which she sang for the first time in 1927 in commemoration of the centenary of Beethoven's death), Manon in Massenet's opera, Tatiana in *Eugene Onegin,* Desdemona in *Otello,* and the heroines in Puccini's greatest operas. In Vienna she emerged as one of the great interpreters of female roles in Richard Strauss's operas. Strauss chose her to create for Vienna the role of the Composer in *Ariadne auf Naxos.* "My role as the Composer . . . turned out to be decisive in determining my future success," she later wrote. "Overnight, I became a success." Strauss had her in mind when he wrote *Arabella,* though it was not until 1933 that she sang the title role in Vienna. On October 10, 1919, she created in Vienna the part of Dyer's wife (for which she had been coached by Strauss himself) in the world premiere of *Die Frau ohne Schatten.* In 1925 she appeared as Christine in the Vienna premiere of Strauss's *Intermezzo.* And, after appearing as Sophie and Octavian in *Der Rosenkavalier,* she went on to become one of the few singers to perform all three of the leading female roles and to become recognized as the most famous interpreter of the Marschallin, in which she appeared for the first time anywhere not in Vienna but at Covent Garden in London in 1924.

In Vienna she gave the first of her celebrated recitals of *Lieder,* revealing herself as one of the most eminent interpreters of the song literature of Schubert, Schumann, Brahms, and Hugo Wolf the world has known. And in Vienna, on August 28, 1926, she married Otto Krause, former officer in the Austrian army, who was an insurance executive and the father of four children. He had heard Lotte Lehmann sing and became so enchanted with her that he appeared at each of her performances after that. They met at a party and their romance developed rapidly. Theirs was an idyllic marriage. In January 1939 Otto Krause died.

Austria honored her by naming her *Kammersängerin,* making her an honorary member of the Vienna State Opera and the Academy of Music, and presenting her with the Gold Medal of Austria, the Cross of Honor (First Class), the

Ring of the City of Vienna, and the Ring of Honor of the Vienna Philharmonic. France gave her the Golden Palm and made her Chevalier of the Legion of Honor, the only woman artist of a foreign country to receive the latter decoration up to that time. Sweden presented her with the Golden Medal of Art, and the German Federal Republic with the Grand Cross of Merit. She became an honorary member of Covent Garden in London. In 1969 Salzburg presented her with the Great Silver medal. Moreover, she was awarded four honorary doctorates, in music and in humane letters.

She became as much a favorite in other opera houses as she was in Vienna. At Covent Garden she made her debut on June 2, 1914, as Sophie in *Der Rosenkavalier.* In 1922 she made a concert tour of South America. She was acclaimed in Venice, Stockholm, Istanbul, and Athens. In 1927, in Paris, in conjunction with the festivities commemorating the centenary of Beethoven's birth she sang in *Fidelio* at the Paris Opéra—this was the first time since World War I that a German opera was presented at the Opéra. It was greatly feared that Parisians, with memories of World War I still fresh in mind, would react with hostility to a German opera and a German-born singer. But Beethoven's sublime music and Lehmann's eloquent singing won the French over completely. One lady in the audience was reported to have remarked to her neighbor: "I know I should hate her, for she is a German. But who can possibly hate a person with such a heavenly voice?"

She made her first appearances at the Salzburg Festival in the summer of 1927, as the Marschallin and as Leonore in *Fidelio.* In subsequent years she sang both the role of Leonore and that of Eva in *Die Meistersinger* under the direction of Toscanini, and for many years she was an integral part of the Salzburg Festival.

Lehmann's American debut took place on October 28, 1930, as Sieglinde with the Chicago Opera. On January 11, 1934, she made her first appearance at the Metropolitan Opera, once again as Sieglinde. "If her first act was of a sort to startle the critical faculty into sharp attendance," wrote Hubbard Hutchinson in the New York *Times,* "her performance in the second had an electrifying quality that swept that faculty away for once and made even the guarded listener a breathless participant in the emotions of the anguished Sieglinde." On February 24,

Lehmann was heard as Elisabeth in *Tannhäuser,* on March 15 as Eva, and on January 4, 1935, as the Marschallin. Olin Downes had this to say in the New York *Times* about Lehmann's first appearance as the Marschallin at the Metropolitan Opera: "The Princess is a woman; when she is characterized by Lotte Lehmann she becomes the dominating and absorbing motive of a lyric drama in which the music makes us know, feel and suffer with her. Mme. Lehmann has long been famous for this characterization, which has everything—the lightness of touch, the manner and accent of the nobly born; the flaming embers of a last passion, the pathos of renunciation." Later in 1935 she appeared as Elsa in *Lohengrin* and as Tosca.

Not long after the Nazis came to power in Germany and launched their program of "cleansing" German life and art of Jewish and racial influences, Field Marshal Goering sent his private plane to bring Lehmann to Berlin to dine with him. He then offered her not only the post of *prima donna assoluta* of the Third Reich but also a munificent income and a private estate and the granting of any other personal demands she might make, on condition she appear exclusively in Germany. Lehmann refused politely; she did not wish to have any traffic with the Nazis.

When the Nazis occupied Austria, Lehmann broke her contract with the Vienna Opera, severed her ties permanently with Austria, and in 1938 went to the United States. "I who was born a German, and who was bound to Austria with the bonds of deepest love—I stand now at the door of America," she wrote at the time. "I am sure that I shall find my third home here and that I shall not again need to wander. I want to become a good American. But that which was my beloved homeland will live on for me in my songs."

Her first American home was in Riverdale, New York, not far from where Toscanini lived. In 1940 she moved permanently to Santa Barbara, California. Then, in 1945 she became an American citizen.

In 1939 Lehmann toured Australia. Her last operatic appearance at the Metropolitan Opera took place on February 23, 1945, as the Marschallin; she was given a twenty-minute ovation. She sang the Marschallin three times after that in San Francisco, in 1945 and 1946. She returned to the stage of the Metropolitan Opera on

February 17, 1946, to participate in a celebration honoring Lauritz Melchior's twentieth anniversary with that company and again in 1962, not as a singer but to serve with Ralph Herbert as coproducer of a new production of *Der Rosenkavalier.*

In the course of her career she had mastered a repertory believed to have numbered about one hundred roles. "I give myself to my part with all my soul," she once said. "I cannot think of technical matters while I sing, because I live what I sing so completely that there is no room left for anything else."

Looking back at her operatic career, Lehmann expressed two profound regrets: she had never sung Isolde, and she had never appeared in the United States as Leonore in *Fidelio.* Not often given to bitterness, Lehmann made no secret of her anger at the Metropolitan Opera management for casting Kirsten Flagstad as Leonore when, on March 7, 1936, they revived *Fidelio.* From that time on she refused to appear as Leonore on the Metropolitan stage.

After retiring from opera, Lehmann continued giving *Lieder* recitals. In song, as in opera, she was, as one New York *Times* critic wrote, "the singer who transcends mere singing, the artist with whom those of lesser vision could share exalted thought and feeling, and the woman of rare charm and warmth and human understanding."

She also devoted herself to teaching voice, primarily at the Music Academy of the West at Santa Barbara, which she helped to establish and where she became director of the vocal department and then honorary president. She also held master classes in voice at the Manhattan School of Music in New York, Northwestern University, Jordan Hall in Boston, Wigmore Hall in London, and at the University of California in Santa Barbara. Many of her pupils went on to distinguished singing careers, among them Grace Bumbry and Shirley Verrett.

At the end of the first half of her recital at Town Hall, New York, on February 16, 1951, Lehmann quietly announced that this would be her last concert, that she was going into total retirement as a performing artist. "No! No!" the audience shouted at her. She replied: "I hoped you would protest." Then she went on to quote a phrase from the famous first-act monologue of the Marschallin: "It is time." She added: "I, too, say, 'It is time.' " For her last encore, and her swan song on the stage, she performed Schubert's "An die Musik." Before she could finish it she broke down and wept, covering her face with her hands. An ovation followed which continued even after the house lights were raised and the curtains drawn. (Actually this was not her final concert appearance. That took place in Berkeley, California, later the same year.)

Recalling Lehmann's performances both in the opera house and on the concert stage, the author Vincent Sheean wrote: "The peculiar melancholy expressiveness of her voice, the beauty of her style, the general sense that her every performance was a work of art, lovingly elaborated in the secret places and brought forth with matchless authority before our eyes, made her a delight that never staled. She was like that Chinese empress of ancient days who commanded the flowers to bloom—except for Lotte they did."

The city of Santa Barbara—where she made her home on Via Huerto in Hope Ranch Park—named her woman of the year in 1958, and designated February 27, 1965, as Lotte Lehmann Day. Three years later, on February 27, 1968, her eightieth birthday was celebrated with a dinner at the Santa Barbara Music Academy of the West, attended by the Austrian consul general and many of Lehmann's friends and pupils. The cake was shaped in the form of the Vienna State Opera building. After dinner, the guests attended a concert given in her honor by the Los Angeles Philharmonic under Zubin Mehta. The program included the duet finale from the third act of *Der Rosenkavalier* sung by Lehmann's pupils. As still one more gesture of tribute on this birthday, RCA Victor reissued her recording of *Der Rosenkavalier* which had been released many years earlier and had become a collector's item.

Lehmann's personal appearance suggested not a famous prima donna or concert artist but a Viennese *Hausfrau.* Her figure was large, her face round, and she combed her hair parted in the middle and full around the ears as many Viennese housewives did. But she was far from being the traditional *Hausfrau.* She was never interested in managing a household, and she never made any attempt to learn how to cook. Nor did she display the frugality that characterized so many Viennese women. As a matter of fact, she was always extravagant, particularly in showering gifts on those she loved.

Leider

She always lived in regal style, whether in her house in Vienna (up to the time of World War II), her magnificently furnished apartment on Park Avenue in New York (for some years following the war), or her final home in Santa Barbara. When she toured at the height of her career, she traveled with two Viennese maids, a housekeeper, two Pomeranians, a white Persian cat, and huge leather folders of family pictures. These pictures were set up both in her hotel room and in her dressing room in the opera house or concert hall. Her dressing room invariably also boasted two miniature Indian totem poles, the root of a Christmas tree, three rosaries, an ancient doll, a lace handkerchief embroidered with the opening measures of her best-known operatic arias, a ring that had once belonged to Sarah Bernhardt, a fan given her by Geraldine Farrar, a wooden elephant, and an ivory squirrel. Before each of her performances she habitually kissed the pictures of her closest relatives and said the beads of one of her rosaries.

In her last months Lotte Lehmann (aged eighty-eight) suffered failing health. She died in her sleep at her home in Santa Barbara on August 26, 1976.

She was almost as devoted to literature as to music. She wrote two autobiographical volumes: *Midway in My Song* (1938) and *My Many Lives* (1948). She was also the author of a novel, *Eternal Flight* (1938), two treatises on singing— *More than Singing, the Interpretation of Songs* (1945) and *Eighteen Song Cycles* (1971)—and a book of reminiscences about Richard Strauss originally called *Five Operas and Richard Strauss* (1964) but subsequently republished as *Singing With Richard Strauss.*

Gifted also as an artist, Lehmann enjoyed painting and making sculpture and ceramics. Her paintings were exhibited at the Schaeffer Galleries in New York in 1950.

In her younger years she often went horseback riding and swimming and was very adept at both. In 1948 she played a feature role in the MGM motion picture *Big City.*

In 1977, five record companies in the United States (Angel, Columbia, Pelican, RCA, and Seraphim) issued commemorative albums of Lehmann's recordings. The album released by Seraphim covered her operatic career from 1916 to 1933. A sixth album was issued by a Canadian firm, Acquataine.

ABOUT: Lehmann, L. Midway in My Song; Lehmann, L. My Many Lives; Wessling, B. W. Lotte Lehmann, mehr als eine Sängerin. *Periodicals*—American Record Guide, June 1968; Hi-Fi, June 1968; High Fidelity/Musical America, June 1977; New York Times, August 27, 1976; Opera News, February 24, 1968, November 1976.

Frida Leider

1888–1975

Frida Leider, soprano, was born in Berlin on April 18, 1888. Before she began training her voice, she studied medicine. Then, deciding to replace science with music, she studied singing in her free time with Leo Leissner, while supporting herself by working as a bank employee. Additional vocal study took place in Milan, and her studies were completed in Berlin with Otto Schwarz.

Her debut took place at the Halle Opera in Germany in 1915, as Venus in *Tannhäuser.* From 1916 to 1919 she served an important apprenticeship with the Rostock Opera and for one year after that with the Königsberg Opera. She was then engaged by the Hamburg Opera where she distinguished herself for her interpretations of the leading Wagnerian dramatic soprano roles. In 1924 she became a permanent member of the Berlin State Opera. That same year she made her debut in London as a guest artist at Covent Garden, as Isolde in *Tristan and Isolde,* Bruno Walter conducting. Other guest appearances brought her to the front rank of Wagnerian sopranos: La Scala in Milan, the Paris Opéra, the Vienna State Opera, the Munich Opera, and opera houses in Stockholm, Stuttgart, and Brussels.

She first went to the United States in 1928, appearing with the Chicago Opera as Brünnhilde in *Die Walküre.* She continued guest appearances in Chicago for four seasons before receiving a contract from the Metropolitan Opera in New York. Her Metropolitan Opera debut came on January 16, 1933, as Isolde. "Mme. Leider's Isolde is one of singular beauty and expressiveness," wrote Lawrence Gilman in the *Herald Tribune.* "Her voice is a true Isolde voice. . . . In its middle register the voice is of

Leider: lī′ dēr

FRIDA LEIDER

rare loveliness and purity, and in mezza voce or piano passages it is often enamoring. . . . Her sense of the stage is sure and sensitive, her visual presence gracious and evocative."

She followed this impressive portrayal of Isolde with no less distinguished performances of the three Brünnhildes, that of *Siegfried* on January 20, *Die Götterdämmerung* on January 25, and *Die Walküre* on February 2. After her initial appearance in *Die Götterdämmerung,* Olin Downes reported in the New York *Times:* "Mme. Leider's Brünnhilde is a very impressive interpretation. It is by turns piteous and womanly, and very grand and prophetic in its pronouncements. The sensuous quality of tone especially needed for such a part as Isolde is less noticeable for absence in this Brünnhilde role, but in fact that voice last night was warmer, more varied in color, more passionately expressive than it had been in the performance of the other opera." On February 13, 1933, Leider made her first Metropolitan Opera appearance as Kundry in *Parsifal* and on April 4 (on tour) as Venus in *Tannhäuser.*

She remained with the Metropolitan Opera for an additional season, 1933–1934, after which she served as the leading soprano of the Vienna State Opera and the Berlin State Opera and continued to make guest appearances at other major European houses and at the Bayreuth Festival. Though the Wagnerian dramatic heroines remained her forte, she was heard in other roles as well, though often not with equal artistic conviction—notably, as Leonora in *Il Trovatore,* Don-

na Anna in *Don Giovanni,* the title role in Gluck's *Armide,* and the Marschallin in *Der Rosenkavalier.*

In Berlin, Leider married Rudolf Deman, the concertmaster of the Berlin State Opera orchestra. Before the Nazi regime, their home in Berlin was a rendezvous for famous intellectuals and well-known members of the music world such as Busoni and Einstein. Because Rudolf Deman was Jewish, he was removed from his post at the Berlin State Opera in the first years of the Third Reich. Leider was advised by the authorities that if she divorced her Jewish husband her position in the major German opera houses would remain secure. She refused and fled from Germany to Switzerland, where she spent the war years. During the war, she returned to Berlin to give concerts, the last of which took place in 1944; to stage operas at the State Opera in East Berlin; and from 1948 to 1958 to teach voice at the West Berlin Conservatory. She went into retirement in 1958, and on June 4, 1975, she died in West Berlin.

She was the author of an autobiography, *Das war mein Teil* (1959).

ABOUT: Leider, F. Das war mein Teil.

Erich Leinsdorf

1912–

Erich Leinsdorf, conductor, was born in Vienna on February 4, 1912. His father, Ludwig Julius Leinsdorf, was an amateur pianist; his mother, Charlotte Loebl Leinsdorf, a trained musician. Theirs was a musical household, with the young Erich responding sensitively to the music making. After his father died, in Erich's third year, his mother, recognizing her son's musical talent, assumed responsibility for his training. She gave him his first piano lessons when he was five, but not long after that she enrolled him at the Vienna Gymnasium, placing him in the hands of Paul Emerich and Hedwig Kammer-Rosenthal, piano teacher and wife of the piano virtuoso Moriz Rosenthal. When he was thirteen, lessons in cello (with Lilly Kosz) and in theory and composition were added to his piano studies.

Initially Erich had no ambition to become a

Leinsdorf: līns′ dõrf

457

Leinsdorf

ERICH LEINSDORF

professional musician. As he once told an interviewer: "Up to my fifteenth year I was in doubt what I was going to be. I was interested in soccer. I played left fullback, and when I was tired of running I was the goalee. I had a very good kick with my left foot." He received a comprehensive academic education as preparation for a career outside the field of music, graduating from the University of Vienna in 1930. Only then did he decide upon music as a profession. For additional music study he entered the Vienna State Academy of Music in 1930 on a scholarship and received his diploma three years later.

Upon leaving the Academy in 1933, Leinsdorf became an assistant conductor of the Vienna Workers' Chorus. Determined to find a place for himself as a conductor, he decided to go to Salzburg to seek the help of Bruno Walter. Lacking the fare, he hiked the one hundred and fifty miles, arriving tired and dusty at the Festspielhaus in Salzburg where Walter was then holding auditions for the 1934 festival. After auditioning for Walter, Leinsdorf was given a post as Walter's assistant. When a pianist was needed at the 1935 festival for a performance of Kodály's *Psalmus Hungaricus,* Leinsdorf offered his services since he knew the music from memory. Toscanini was so impressed with him that he engaged Leinsdorf to return to Salzburg in 1935 to help him prepare his performances for that summer's festival.

Leinsdorf worked as an assistant to Walter and Toscanini at Salzburg during the summers

of 1935, 1936, and 1937. He became a jack of many musical trades: practicing with the orchestra, directing the chorus, coaching singers, consulting with stage directors, playing the piano. In addition to his chores at Salzburg, he assisted Walter at the Florence May Music Festival in 1935. He also found opportunities to do some conducting on his own in 1936 at Bologna, Trieste, and San Remo.

On the recommendation of Toscanini and Lotte Lehmann, Leinsdorf was engaged by Artur Bodanzky, principal conductor of German operas at the Metropolitan Opera, to be his assistant in New York. He arrived in the United States in the fall of 1937, in time to assist Bodanzky in the preparation of *Tristan and Isolde,* with which the 1937–1938 season of the Metropolitan Opera opened. On January 21, 1938, Leinsdorf—not yet twenty-six—made his conducting debut at the Metropolitan Opera with *Die Walküre.* "He soon made it evident that he was entirely at home in the great work before him," wrote Lawrence Gilman in the *Herald Tribune,* "and that he possessed an exceptional gift for eliciting its substance from the players under his command. He knew what he wanted from his orchestra and how to get it. He was apparently without self-consciousness, wholly concerned with the music." Some months later, on March 18, Leinsdorf met and passed an even greater test. On twelve hours' notice he was called upon to conduct *Parsifal* when Bodanzky became ill. Lawrence Gilman described that performance as "one of the finest that has ever been heard at the Metropolitan."

During his first season at the Metropolitan Opera, Leinsdorf led ten performances of *Die Walküre, Parsifal,* and Strauss's *Elektra.* One season later he was heard thirty-six times, adding to his Wagnerian repertory *Das Rheingold, Siegfried, Lohengrin,* and *Tannhäuser.*

Three weeks before the opening of the 1939–1940 season Bodanzky became so ill that the burden of preparing the German repertory and other operas fell on Leinsdorf's shoulders. Bodanzky died on November 23, 1939, just six days before the season opened. Leinsdorf was instantly named his successor as principal conductor of German operas. He was only twenty-eight and his experience in the conducting of operas was limited. Nevertheless, he met the challenge with self-assurance and competence, for he knew by heart all the works he had to conduct, and he had long since carefully worked out for himself his individual concepts of interpretation.

As the principal conductor, Leinsdorf led fifty-five performances in his first season, directing not only the Wagnerian repertory (with *Tristan and Isolde, Die Götterdämmerung,* and *Die Meistersinger* already in his repertory) but also *Der Rosenkavalier, Pelléas and Mélisande,* and Gluck's *Orpheus and Eurydice,* all three operas new to him.

Leinsdorf remained with the Metropolitan Opera through the 1942–1943 season. Despite the enormous demands made upon him there, he was able to fill commitments as guest conductor with the NBC Orchestra, the Montreal Symphony, and the San Francisco Opera, making his bow with the San Francisco Opera on October 19 in *Pelléas and Mélisande.*

By 1943 Leinsdorf felt he was devoting too much of his time and energy to opera and to a single company in a circumscribed repertory. He was eager to do more conducting of symphonic music. Something else added to his restiveness. His dictatorial ways and intransigent will were resented by some members of the Metropolitan Opera company. The two principal Wagnerian singers of the Metropolitan—Kirsten Flagstad and Lauritz Melchior—openly expressed the opinion that he was too young to be conducting Wagner. Leinsdorf felt that the time had come for him to go elsewhere, to spread his wings musically.

In 1943 he was called to Cleveland to succeed Artur Rodzinski as music director of the Cleveland Orchestra, the youngest man thus far to hold such a post with a major American symphonic organization. He held this post just a few weeks, during which he was able to present the world premieres of Lopatnikoff's *Opus Sinfonicum* (December 9, 1943) and Martinu's Symphony No.2 (October 28, 1943). Then he was inducted into the United States Army since he had become a naturalized citizen in 1942. He stayed in uniform eight months, then was discharged on medical grounds. Instead of returning to Cleveland, he entered upon a three-year period as a guest conductor at the Metropolitan Opera, with the Cleveland Orchestra, and elsewhere.

His next permanent post was in Rochester, New York, where he was made music director of the Rochester Philharmonic in 1947 and where he remained nine years. In the years between 1956 and 1961 Leinsdorf was more actively involved in opera than in symphonic music. In 1956 he became the music director of the New York City Opera, leading that year the American premieres of Frank Martin's *The Tempest* and Carl Orff's *The Moon,* and the New York premiere of Carlisle Floyd's *Susannah.*

From 1957 to 1962 he was both a principal conductor and the music consultant at the Metropolitan Opera. While there he directed new productions of Gluck's *Alceste, Boris Godunov,* and *The Marriage of Figaro,* together with several cycles of the Wagner *Ring.* In 1959 he went for the first time to the Bayreuth Festival, with performances of *Die Meistersinger,* and that year he conducted Stravinsky's *The Rake's Progress* in Holland. As a guest conductor at the San Francisco Opera, where he had conducted the American premiere of Sir William Walton's *Troilus and Cressida* on October 7, 1955, he introduced to the United States Poulenc's *Les Dialogues des Carmélites* (September 20, 1957). He also conducted numerous recordings of operatic and symphonic music. In the years between 1959 and 1972 eight of his albums were awarded Grammys by the National Academy of Recording Arts and Sciences.

As a symphonic conductor he appeared as a guest of many of America's and Europe's major orchestras and also made appearances in Israel. On January 31, 1961, he conducted the Boston Symphony for the first time. "From my first second on the stage," he has remarked, "I was at home." Several months later the Boston Symphony appointed him music director, succeeding Charles Munch. Thus the Boston Symphony which had undergone a Russian era with Koussevitzky and a French one with Munch now passed on to the German regime of Leinsdorf. Precision, thoroughness of preparation, military discipline, painstaking analytical processes replaced the emotional, nervous and sometimes improvisational methods of Koussevitzky and the easy-going, genial, sometimes lackadaisical ways of Munch.

The Boston Symphony, which had known some artistic regression with Munch, began to flourish anew with Leinsdorf. After Leinsdorf's first season, Harold Rogers wrote in *The Christian Science Monitor:* "There is no gainsaying that he has done wonders with the orchestra, that he has refined its tone, adjusted its balance, polished its timbres." And in the New York

Times Harold C. Schonberg noted: "Already in the space of one season, Leinsdorf has made the Boston Symphony a more precise group. . . . Few musicians would deny that he is a steadier conductor than Munch." Yet both these critics, and others as well, sometimes took Leinsdorf severely to task for his intellectualism and pedantry at the expense of heart.

Leinsdorf remained the music director of the Boston Symphony and served in a similar capacity at the Berkshire Music Festival until 1969. In that time he directed over four hundred compositions by ninety-six composers. Among the more noteworthy world premieres he conducted were: Samuel Barber's Piano Concerto (September 24, 1962), Elliott Carter's Piano Concerto (January 6, 1967), Benjamin Lees's Piano Concerto No.2 (March 15, 1968) and Violin Concerto (February 8, 1963), Roger Sessions's *Psalm 140* (February 11, 1966), William Sydeman's *In Memoriam John F. Kennedy* (November 4, 1966) and *Study for Orchestra No.2* (November 22, 1963), and Ernst Toch's Symphony No.5 (March 13, 1964). At the Berkshire Music Festival at Tanglewood in Massachusetts on July 27, 1963, he conducted the Boston Symphony in the American premiere of Britten's *A War Requiem.* He was also responsible for highly distinguished revivals of neglected masterworks, including the complete version of *Lohengrin,* the original version of *Fidelio,* Strauss's *Ariadne auf Naxos,* and Schumann's *Scenes from Goethe's Faust.*

In announcing his retirement as music director of the Boston Symphony, Leinsdorf explained that he was leaving because the trustees had refused to lighten his work load, which he felt was far too heavy for one man to bear, and because they refused to give him the time to do more guest conducting. But it was no secret that for some time friction had developed between Leinsdorf and the orchestra men, many of whom resented his autocratic behavior.

Since 1969 Leinsdorf has been heard on every continent. He toured Australia and New Zealand with the Cleveland Orchestra; the Far East with the London Philharmonic; the Near East with the Orchestre de Paris; Israel with the Israel Philharmonic; Europe with the London Symphony, the Royal Philharmonic, and the Vienna Symphony; the United States, Scandinavia, and the Soviet Union with the New York Philharmonic; and Mexico with the London Philhar-

monic. In addition, he made guest appearances with the principal orchestras of Europe and the United States, including seasonal visits to the New York Philharmonic. He has also been active in the field of opera. In 1971, 1972, 1974, and 1976–1977 he returned to the Metropolitan to conduct new productions of *Tristan and Isolde* and *Siegfried,* as well as *Die Walküre* and *Salome.* During the summer of 1975 he appeared at the Bayreuth Festival in a new production of *Tannhäuser.* In September 1977, Leinsdorf assumed the post of principal conductor of the Radio Symphony Orchestra of West Berlin on a three-year contract.

Leinsdorf's first wife was Anne Frohnknecht, whom he married in New York City on August 3, 1939, and with whom he had five children. They were divorced after twenty-nine years. On August 5, 1968, he married Vera Graf, a young violinist from Buenos Aires. Their home for many years was an apartment in New York City; after 1977, they had one in West Berlin. Short, stocky, compactly built, Leinsdorf has been described by Milton Mayer as "aggressively bald between ear flaps of black hair; long face, large ears, huge hands. He still speaks with an accent, and his conversation is spiced with some of the choicest wit heard from a conductor since the days of Sir Thomas Beecham; like Beecham's, his wit is often coated with acid." Once an avid bridge player, Leinsdorf has outgrown games in favor of intellectual pursuits. He has said: "My greatest relaxation is moving mentally into many different directions, meeting people on a totally different 'track.'" He spends many of his leisure hours reading about politics, history, and government, or exchanging provocative ideas with interesting people. But he also enjoys photography and collecting rare stamps and vintages.

In January-February 1977, Leinsdorf led a six-day seminar for professional conductors at Avery Fisher Hall in New York City.

Leinsdorf's autobiography, *Cadenza: A Musical Career,* was published in 1976.

ABOUT: Ewen, D. Famous Modern Conductors; Leinsdorf, E. Cadenza: A Musical Career. *Periodicals* —Atlantic Monthly, September 1962; Esquire, February 1962; High Fidelity, December 1963; Musical America, December 1963; New York Times, February 16, 1969, January 2, 1977; Opera News, March 10, 1962; Time, October 5, 1962.

James Levine

1943–

JAMES LEVINE

James Lawrence Levine, pianist and conductor, was born in Cincinnati, Ohio, on June 23, 1943, the oldest of three children. He came from a musical and theatrical family. His maternal grandfather had been a cantor in a synagogue and a composer of liturgical music; his father, Lawrence, was a violinist and, in the 1930s under the stage name Larry Lee, the leader of a dance band; his mother, Helen Goldstein Levine, was an actress who played ingenue parts on Broadway.

His parents began recognizing in him signs of musical talent when James, at three, tried to pick out melodies on the piano. They started him on piano lessons one year later. Though he detested practicing, he went through the tedium and pain of exercises because he loved his piano lessons and did not want to be deprived of them. From early childhood he loved listening to music at concerts and operas. When he was nine he tried to "produce" operas at home through recordings, singing all the parts while going through the motions of conducting.

He gained such proficiency at the piano that in his tenth year he was invited to make his piano debut as a soloist with the Cincinnati Symphony Orchestra in a performance of Mendelssohn's Piano Concerto. When, as a reward for this performance, his father offered him any gift he desired, James asked for tickets to the Metropolitan Opera for one week. That year—1954 —he saw for the first time *Faust, Così fan Tutte, Cavalleria Rusticana,* and *I Pagliacci.*

He appeared more than a dozen times with the Cincinnati Symphony under the batons of Max Rudolf and Thor Johnson. In 1956 James spent the summer at Marlboro, Vermont, home of the music school and festival; there he studied the piano with Rudolf Serkin and prepared and directed the chorus for a performance of *Così fan Tutte.* In the summer of 1957 he attended the Aspen Music School in Colorado to continue his piano studies with Rosina Lhévinne. He returned to Aspen for nine consecutive summers, first as a student, later as a faculty member in the departments of piano and conducting. In addi-

Levine: lĕ vīn'

tion to his piano lessons at Aspen, he studied chamber music with members of the Juilliard String Quartet and violist Walter Trampler, the vocal repertory with Mack Harrell, Adele Addison, and Jennie Tourel, and conducting with Wolfgang Vacano. In Aspen, James was given numerous opportunities to conduct both opera and symphonic music. His first such opportunity came with a performance of Bizet's *The Pearl Fishers* in 1962. Among the other operas he conducted at Aspen were Stravinsky's *Mavra,* Strauss's *Ariadne auf Naxos,* Britten's *Albert Herring, Così fan Tutte,* and Rossini's *La Cambiale di Matrimonio.*

After graduation from high school in Cincinnati in 1961, James entered the Juilliard School of Music in September of that year. He completed its five-year undergraduate course in two years. After that he concentrated on piano with Rosina Lhévinne and conducting with Jean Morel. He stayed at the Juilliard three years, commuting each weekend from Cincinnati to New York. He was also making appearances as a piano soloist and as an assisting artist with various individual virtuosi and chamber-music groups, and he seemed headed for a successful career as a piano virtuoso.

In the spring of 1964, upon leaving Juilliard, he participated in the American Conductors Project instituted by the Ford Foundation, working with the Baltimore Symphony and studying conducting with Alfred Wallenstein, Max Rudolf, and Fausto Cleva.

On a grant from the Kulas Foundation, Levine was made an apprentice to George Szell with the Cleveland Orchestra in 1964–1965. "The funny thing," he has remarked, "was that of all the conductors in the world, he was the one I most respected and the one I most wanted to study with. My job with Szell was as an apprentice who sat in on all the rehearsals, responded to questions about balance, and rehearsed the orchestra whenever he asked me to." He also conducted a concert annually in the regular subscription series, led educational concerts, and played the piano when performances of the Cleveland Orchestra required one.

He remained four years with Szell, in that time becoming assistant conductor, the youngest ever to hold such a post with the orchestra. On Szell's suggestion he also served during this period as music director of the newly organized University Circle Orchestra, a student group administered by the Cleveland Institute of Music and Case Reserve University. "In my five years in Cleveland," Levine has said of his work with this student orchestra, "it really became a first-class ensemble capable of taking on the Mahler Fifth and winning praise from as exacting a man as Leinsdorf."

During the summers of 1967 and 1968 Levine also conducted the Meadowbrook School of Music Orchestra in Michigan in a series of symphonic and operatic performances. One Michigan critic noted that Levine was responsible for training the student orchestra "into a group that can hold its own among the finest professional orchestras." The critic also remarked that Levine was "a brilliant conductor, a super orchestral technician, and a fine musician by any standard."

Upon leaving Cleveland in 1969, Levine was invited to give guest performances with the major orchestras of Chicago, Los Angeles, Philadelphia, Atlanta, Pittsburgh, Denver, Toronto, St. Louis, and Dallas. On March 17, 1972, he conducted the New York Philharmonic for the first time. During the summer of 1972 he made his debut with the Boston Symphony Orchestra at the Berkshire Music Festival at Tanglewood in Massachusetts. In June 1973 he gave his first performance in London as guest conductor of the New Philharmonia Orchestra.

He appeared for the first time in a major opera house on June 5, 1971, during the June festival season of the Metropolitan Opera, when he directed *Tosca*. The sure control he had over the musical forces under him and his knowing musicianship, evident in *Tosca,* were further revealed the following fall when he conducted *Luisa Miller* at the Metropolitan Opera.

Rafael Kubelik, then newly appointed music director of the Metropolitan Opera (the first such in its history), chose Levine as his "right-hand man" and as principal conductor of the Metropolitan Opera, the appointment to begin with the 1973–1974 season. "I spent a long time deliberating before accepting this job," Levine has revealed, "because I feel very strongly that too many young musicians have their careers too fast nowadays." But in the end he accepted, agreeing to spend seven months of the year with the company and to conduct about forty performances of four operas, one to be a new production. Before Levine assumed this new post, he conducted during the Metropolitan Opera season of 1972–1973 an Italian repertory that included *Otello, The Barber of Seville,* and *Rigoletto. Otello,* which he first conducted on December 5, 1972, was probably his most important assignment up to that time. "When he brought down his baton," reported Harold C. Schonberg in the New York *Times,* "it was immediately apparent that we were going to be in for an exuberant evening. Exuberant it was, though not always refined. Mr. Levine has strong ideas about the score, and he wanted to achieve its mixture of strength and brooding lyricism. What with a good deal of propulsion on the upper end of the dynamic spectrum and a great deal of natural personality, he did achieve some impressive results."

In his initial year as principal conductor of the Metropolitan Opera, Levine opened the 1973–1974 season with a performance of *Il Trovatore.* Later that season he conducted *I Vespri Siciliani* and *Don Giovanni.* The next year he opened the new season 1974–1975 with *I Vespri Siciliani* and this he recorded for RCA. Among the other operas assigned to him during that and the next season were *La Forza del Destino, Aida, Ariadne auf Naxos, Der Rosenkavalier,* and *Wozzeck.*

In addition to his assignments at the Metropolitan, Levine has served as music director of the Ravinia Festival, summer home of the Chicago Symphony, to which he was appointed in 1973. Beginning with 1974 he also served as music director of the Cincinnati May Festival. He has made intermittent guest appearances with major American orchestras. In Europe he was heard with the London Symphony, the New Philharmonic, the RAI Orchestra, and the Welsh National Opera, as well as at Covent Garden in London. On July 29, 1976, he made his debut at the Salzburg Festival with a new production of Mozart's *La Clemenza di Tito.*

In May 1975 the Metropolitan Opera announced that beginning with the 1976–1977 season, Levine would be music director on a five-year contract. This was the post created for Rafael Kubelik in 1971 but left vacant after his resignation in 1974. Under this arrangement, which placed on Levine's shoulders additional responsibilities for the shaping of the company's artistic policy, Levine's services were extended over a seven-month period, and during the remaining five months of each year he was virtually in daily telephonic communication with a special liaison administrator. Between 1976 and 1978 he conducted a number of noteworthy new productions, among them the first Metropolitan Opera presentation of Berg's *Lulu, Lohengrin* (his first Wagner assignment), *Rigoletto, Tannhäuser, Pelléas and Mélisande,* and *Eugene Onegin.*

Bespectacled, short, and pudgy, Levine is far from being a charismatic figure on the podium. His platform manner is businesslike with little attention to visual appeal. His appeal has been exclusively musical and particularly to those who have worked with him. In 1972, when the announcement was made at a rehearsal of the Metropolitan Opera that Levine had been appointed principal conductor, the entire orchestra applauded enthusiastically. Sherrill Milnes, who appeared under Levine in *Don Giovanni,* said of him: "He treats you as a collaborative artist. Levine gets you to do anything he wants because he puts down the baton, runs up on the stage, and in a conversational tone, says, 'I have an idea there that I'd like. Will you try it?' He doesn't scream across the pit that you're an idiot to read a line differently from his idea."

Levine has been able to reveal a masterful hand even when he is conducting an opera for the first time, because before the performance he has absorbed the work over a period of many years and after a good deal of study and dissection. In the summer of 1971 he conducted a performance of *La Traviata* in the Hollywood Bowl. Beverly Sills, who headed the cast, said it was one of the best-conducted performances of the opera she had ever appeared in. She was amazed to discover that he had never before conducted it. "I've been living this opera since I was thirteen," Levine explained.

Levine resides in an apartment on Central Park West which is decorated with Navajo rugs and the bones of dinosaurs. He is highly gregarious and equally garrulous, describing himself as "a marathon talker." He says that the only unhappy times in his life have been when he was "musically frustrated . . . unproductive." When he is making music to his own satisfaction his personal life flourishes; when not, his personal relationships tend to deteriorate. He has a fetish for sweaters, his wardrobe including about fifty of them in all colors. When he rehearses he insists upon dressing most informally. "I cannot work in a coat and tie," he has explained.

In an interview with Stephen E. Rubin for the New York *Times,* he confided: "I have one real visionary dream, and I feel that everything I do draws me a little closer to it. Once in a while I hear a performance which is the kind of incredible thing that must have driven composers to keep on writing music despite unbelievable personal adversities. It seems to me there is a key to this which, so far, our system has not provided. I want to try and provide it."

James Levine received an honorary doctorate in music from the University of Cincinnati in 1973.

ABOUT: Rubin, S. E. The New Met in Profile. *Periodicals*—High Fidelity/Musical America, March 1974; Musical America, March 1974; New York Times, March 12, 1972, October 10, 1976; Opera News, December 11, 1971, December 9, 1972; Time, February 23, 1976.

Mischa Levitzki

1898–1941

Mischa Levitzki, pianist, was born in Kremenchug, Russia, on May 25, 1898. His parents, Jacob L. and Anna Smelanski Levitzki, were naturalized American citizens who were on an extended visit to Russia when Mischa was born. Mischa began studying the violin when he was four. When he abandoned the violin two years later, his parents thought he had no talent for music. One day, however, he visited his aunt

Levitsky: lĕ vĭts′kĭ

MISCHA LEVITZKI

who owned a piano, an instrument the boy was seeing for the first time. Drawn to it, he tried to produce melodies. Soon after that he asked for piano lessons. He made such progress with his first teacher that in 1905 he was entered in the Warsaw Conservatory, where for a year he studied with Aleksander Michalowski.

When Mischa was eight his parents returned to the United States. En route, in Antwerp in 1906, "in an unguarded moment," as Levitzki later recalled, "some enthusiastic people arranged for me to give a recital in public. According to the clippings, I was a success, but my parents prevented another scheduled concert. They did not permit me to appear again until I was sixteen."

In the United States, Mischa auditioned for Walter Damrosch, conductor of the New York Symphony Society, who encouraged him to enter the Institute of Musical Art in New York. Mischa studied at the Institute with Sigismond Stojowski from 1906 to 1911. At the same time he completed his academic studies in public schools in New York City and Brooklyn. His passion was the piano, but he was almost as devoted to baseball. Baseball, in fact, almost ended his piano career when a ball thrown at him from the outfield dislocated the tip of his third finger.

In 1911 Mischa returned to Berlin to attend the High School for Music as a piano student of Ernst von Dohnányi. Dohnányi was so prejudiced against prodigies that at first he refused to consider Mischa as a pupil. But when the boy

performed for him, Dohnányi instantly changed his mind. During the three-year period Mischa worked under Dohnányi, he was twice awarded the Mendelssohn Prize for piano playing.

Mischa's career as concert pianist was officially launched in 1912 with performances in Antwerp and Brussels, followed by a tour of Austria, Germany, Hungary, and Scandinavia. This tour was cut short by the outbreak of World War I. After an additional year in Berlin, Mischa returned to the United States to make his American debut at Aeolian Hall in New York on October 17, 1916, in a program made up mainly of works by Bach, Beethoven, Schumann, and Chopin. Reviewing that concert in the New York *Times,* Richard Aldrich wrote: "He is as little of a virtuoso as can well be imagined, and technical proficiency is to him but a means to an end. His style is, indeed, uncommonly intimate in a manner that is intensely musical. He played Liszt's arrangement of Bach's A minor fugue with full and sonorous proportion, with remarkable clearness and incisiveness, and with a firm and vital rhythmic feeling that characterized most of what he did. His treatment of Beethoven's *Waldstein Sonata* was not robustly passionate; it was poetic, intimate in feeling, not a proclamation for the market place, hardly even for the concert hall. And there was an allurement, a persuasive charm in this exposition that beguiled his listeners into unquestioned acceptance of it."

Levitzki made over twenty tours of the United States in addition to others in Europe, in Australia and New Zealand in 1921 and 1931, and in the Orient in 1925. As Richard Aldrich reported in the New York *Times* in his review of one of Levitzki's later concerts on November 8, 1922, Levitzki "steadily advanced in his own way as an artist in the years since he first appeared in New York, and in his favor with the public. . . . Mr. Levitzki is a musician of fine intimacies, delicacies and reserves. His style is individually his own, as is his technique, exceedingly finished, unfailing in its correctness, endless in its minute gradations. His tone is of an exquisite purity and pearly opalescence; he never permits the piano to utter a harshness or a tone that is out of the picture as he conceives it."

Levitzki was short and well built; his face, small, round and, until the end of his life, youthful. Powerful shoulders and strong muscles gave him the appearance of an athlete, even though he did not permit himself the pleasure of participation in strenuous sports beyond boyhood. He remained fond of baseball, but only as a spectator, and he abandoned tennis when he felt it was developing an entirely different set of muscles from those he used at the piano. Sports denied him, he found relaxation in dancing. He never assumed a snobbish attitude towards American popular music, for which he had a sincere affection. Many a time he entertained his guests by performing for them a current hit song.

Levitzki composed numerous pleasing pieces for the piano. His first published composition, the Valse in A, appeared originally in Australia but later became successful elsewhere. This and other piano compositions found their way into the repertory of concert artists. His other best-known works were the *Arabesque Valsante,* the *Valse Tzigane,* and a gavotte. He also wrote a cadenza for the first movement of Beethoven's Piano Concerto No.3 and made arrangements for the violin and piano which were performed by several violin virtuosos.

Mischa Levitzki died at Avon-by-the-Sea, New Jersey, on January 2, 1941.

In 1977, the International Piano Archives released a Levitzki disk comprising several of his all too rare recordings, all made between 1923 and 1929: shorter pieces by Chopin, Tchaikovsky, Liszt, Gluck, and Moszkowski.

ABOUT: New York Times, January 3, 1941.

Henry Lewis

1932–

Henry Lewis, conductor, made racial as well as musical history in the United States by becoming the first black man ever to conduct a major American symphony orchestra during its regular winter season; the first black man to be appointed music director of a major American symphony orchestra; and the first black man to conduct at the Metropolitan Opera.

He was born in Los Angeles on October 16, 1932, the son of Henry Lewis Sr., a well-to-do real-estate and automobile dealer, and Josephine Lewis, an administrative nurse at a Los Angeles hospital. Encouraged by his mother, Henry began taking piano lessons when he was five. During his adolescent years he also learned to play

HENRY LEWIS

some woodwind, brass, and string instruments. He attended the Roman Catholic parochial and public schools in Los Angeles.

While attending high school, he gave performances on the double bass and at his graduation he conducted the school orchestra. His free time was spent listening to recordings or going through the motions of conducting an imaginary orchestra while playing these records. His father did not look kindly upon this preoccupation with music, convinced that there just was no place for a black man in American serious music. He tried to convince Henry to pay more attention to school work in preparation for a career in business.

But Henry could not be dissuaded from advancing himself as a serious musician. When he was eighteen, he was engaged by Alfred Wallenstein, then the conductor of the Los Angeles Philharmonic, for that orchestra's double bass section. While thus employed, Lewis attended the University of Southern California in Los Angeles on a scholarship, specializing in literature and philosophy as well as advanced instrumentation. He dropped out of college because he was "bored" with the classroom, even though he had already accumulated enough credits to gain a Bachelor of Arts degree.

In 1955 he was drafted into the United States Army. For the next two years he was a member of the Seventh Army Orchestra in Germany, first as a double bassist, then as assistant conductor, and finally as full conductor. As conductor he led over a hundred and fifty public concerts not only in Germany but also elsewhere in Europe and made fifty-two recorded performances for broadcast over the United States Armed Forces network and the German radio. "It was an invaluable experience," he says. "I had an orchestra every day for rehearsals and we gave three to five concerts per week for a year." His performances attracted the interest of the European conductors Bruno Walter and Eduard van Beinum who encouraged him and became his sponsors.

One of the soloists who sang with the Seventh Army Symphony under Lewis's direction was the soprano Marilyn Horne. This was not their first meeting. They had known each other at the University of Southern California where a romantic interest had developed. They separated intending never to see each other again, but in Germany their romance was reborn.

Upon being separated from the service in 1957, Lewis returned to the double bass section of the Los Angeles Philharmonic, but before long he was promoted to the post of assistant conductor. In 1958 he founded the Los Angeles Chamber Orchestra which he conducted for several years and with which he toured Europe in 1963 under the sponsorship of the State Department. On July 2, 1960, he married Marilyn Horne in Los Angeles.

On February 9, 1961, Lewis was called upon to conduct the Los Angeles Philharmonic as a substitute for Igor Markevitch who had been taken ill. He had occasionally led the Los Angeles Philharmonic in concerts outside the city but never before at one of its regular winter subscription series. By coincidence, Marilyn Horne had been scheduled to appear as soloist for this concert. Lewis was chosen to replace Markevitch, however, not because of Horne's presence on the program but because the management had long been impressed with his conducting ability. He did so well on this occasion that he was again invited to conduct the orchestra later in its winter subscription series, as well as for six performances in other California cities. When Zubin Mehta became the music director of the Los Angeles Philharmonic in 1962 he appointed Lewis his associate, a post Lewis retained for three years. With his "quietly authoritative approach," commented a writer for *Time,* Lewis proved to be "a perfect complement to the flamboyant attack of fiery Zubin Mehta."

Lewis left his post at the Los Angeles Philharmonic in 1965. For a time he served as music director of the Los Angeles Opera Company. He also filled guest engagements with the Boston Opera and with several major orchestras in the United States, London, and Milan. In 1965 he made his debut at La Scala in Milan with a performance of *Gershwiniana,* a ballet-cantata based on the music of George Gershwin.

In February 1968 Lewis was appointed music director of the New Jersey Symphony Orchestra. At that time it was a semiprofessional organization, a "pickup group" of schoolteachers and other avocational musicians who gave twenty-two concerts a season. "That first year," Lewis recalls, "was sleight-of-hand. Everything we did was to attract attention." Horne frequently appeared as soloist in an attempt to help promote these concerts. Novelty was introduced to lure larger audiences into the concert auditorium: At one of these performances an electrically synthesized cadenza was heard between the movements of Bach's *Brandenburg Concerto No.3.*

Under Lewis the New Jersey Symphony developed into a major symphonic ensemble. Within three years the orchestra was giving over one hundred concerts during a twenty-four- to twenty-six-week season, with an orchestra of eighty-seven professional musicians. The annual budget had grown from seventy-five thousand dollars to eight hundred fifty thousand dollars. By 1975 the season was extended to thirty-eight weeks, with one hundred and twenty-five concerts a season and an annual budget exceeding one million dollars.

In the summer of 1968 Lewis brought his orchestra into those ghetto areas that had been gutted by riots. In 1971 he instituted popular-priced adult concerts (admission one dollar) and started children's concerts. "It's my job to sell classical music to ghetto kids and possibly to the adults too if they can be reached," he wrote in the New York *Times.* "It isn't a question of giving them something they *ought* to have. I'm selling them something I love, and I want everybody to love it. And I would hate to see young people deprived of it because at this stage of their lives they haven't had the opportunity to be exposed to it."

In 1971 Lewis appeared with the RAI (Radiotelevisione Italiana) Orchestra in Turin, Naples, and Rome. On October 16, 1972, he made his debut at the Metropolitan Opera in *La Bohème*. "He is a solid musician and experienced craftsman," said Harriet Johnson in the New York *Post*. "His balance between orchestra and singers was excellent. He knew when to give the singers freedom, when to support them with plenty of instrumental juice, and when to lessen the concentration. He led with taste and style." That season Lewis also directed several performances of *Carmen*. On January 18, 1977, he conducted the first Metropolitan Opera House revival of *Le Prophète* since 1928.

He has conducted opera performances elsewhere: *Il Trovatore* with the Vancouver Opera, *Tosca* and *La Traviata* with the San Francisco Opera, *Madama Butterfly* with the Los Angeles Opera, *Carmen* with the Boston Opera, *The Barber of Seville* in Montreal, *Anna Bolena* with the American Opera Society. In addition, he has led either stage or concert performances of *Don Pasquale, Romeo and Juliet, Don Giovanni, The Magic Flute*, Massenet's *La Navarraise*, Rossini's *L'Italiana in Algeri*, Gluck's *Iphigénie en Tauride, Le Prophète, La Bohème*, and *Un Ballo in Maschera*.

Lewis has served as guest conductor of many major American symphony orchestras, including the Boston Symphony, the New York Philharmonic, and the Chicago Symphony. He has also been heard in London with the London Symphony and the Royal Philharmonic.

He resigned as music director of the New Jersey Symphony in November 1975, effective the following June. It was well known that dissension had developed between conductor and orchestra. The orchestra players accused him of being too much the dictator and of abusing them verbally. In the spring of 1975 the men voted unofficially to remove Lewis, and when the orchestra went on strike to improve working conditions the following summer one of its demands was Lewis's removal. The management insisted upon its right to select conductors and the strike was settled with Lewis still in his post. But in the end Lewis decided he could no longer function in New Jersey to his fullest capabilities.

Up until his separation from his wife in 1976, the Lewises lived in a spacious Tudor-style house on a two-acre wooded lot in Orange, New Jersey. They also had a one-bedroom apartment in New York City, near Lincoln Center. Apart from music, Lewis's interests include books and art. As time goes by, he told an interviewer, he

gets less ambitious in advancing his career, adding: "I would like plenty of time to study and to be with musicians who love music."

ABOUT: New York Times, July 5, 1968, March 5, 1971; Newsweek, October 30, 1972.

Josef Lhévinne

1874–1944

Josef Lhévinne, pianist, was born in Orel, near Moscow, on December 14, 1874, the son of Arcadie and Fanny Lhévinne. His father played the trumpet in the orchestra of the Moscow Opera. The Lhévinne household did not own a piano; not until a relative sent one over for storage did Josef come into contact with the instrument. After that he spent hours at the keyboard. One day a conservatory student dropped in at the Lhévinne home and noticed Josef's interest in the piano. He offered to teach Josef the rudiments of piano playing even though the child was then only four. Somewhat later, a wealthy neighbor arranged for Josef to perform at a soiree held in honor of Grand Duke Konstantin; the Grand Duke then provided the financial backing for Josef's musical education.

Vassily Safonov, director of the Moscow Conservatory, was so impressed with Josef's talent that he insisted upon teaching him personally. In November 1888 Josef made his concert debut in the Great Hall of the Nobles in Moscow in Beethoven's *Emperor Concerto*, Anton Rubinstein conducting.

In 1891 he was graduated from the Conservatory with a virtuoso diploma and a gold medal. He embarked on a concert tour of Russia, initially as an accompanist to a baritone (sharing the program by giving some piano solos in addition to his chores as accompanist), later in recitals. During this period he pursued his piano studies with Anton Rubinstein.

In 1895 Lhévinne received first prize in the Rubinstein contest (held only once every five years)—Ferruccio Busoni served as one of the judges.

On June 20, 1898, Lhévinne married Rosina Bessie (born in Moscow in 1880), a young pianist who had just graduated from the Kiev Con-

Lhévinne: lã vēn'

467

JOSEF AND ROSINA LHÉVINNE

servatory with a gold medal. They had first met when Josef, aged fourteen, was asked to give her some piano lessons as a substitute for her teacher who had fallen ill; Rosina was then only nine. Josef remained her teacher for several months, and after that became a friend of the family. "He would come to the house many times," she later recalled, "but he would not look at me at all because . . . I was a child." One evening when Rosina was fifteen, she was a hostess at a party given by one of her teachers. When she went into the kitchen to wash the crystalware, Josef followed her. Coquettishly she inquired with whom he was in love and he responded with a description of a girl whom Rosina instantly identified as herself. The romance deepened, but it was four years before they married.

Feeling strongly that no marriage could be successful if both partners had artistic careers, Rosina, despite her impressive talent, decided to devote herself completely to her husband's development as a virtuoso. For forty years she refused to make any appearances as a solo pianist. But occasionally she did perform with her husband in two-piano concerts. The first time this took place was in the first year of their marriage, when César Cui, a friend of the Lhévinnes, urged them to appear at a charity concert in Tiflis, where they made their home. Their performance, in which they presented the world premiere of a new suite for two pianos by Arensky, went over so well that from then on they continued to play the piano together publicly. Determined that these concerts not interfere

with her husband's career as a virtuoso, she insisted that at each of their two-piano concerts Josef give at least one or two solo numbers, a practice continued through the years. These performances, therefore, were quite different from the usual run of two-piano programs in that they were concerts for one and two pianos.

In 1900 Lhévinne was appointed teacher of piano at the Tiflis Conservatory, a position he held two years. He resigned because he felt he was in a rut, and the Lhévinnes went to Berlin where he did some teaching and gave some concerts. There he and his wife moved in a circle of some of the city's leading musicians, among whom were Arthur Nikisch, young Josef Hofmann, Theodor Leschetizky, and Leopold Godowsky.

From 1902 to 1905 Lhévinne was professor of piano at the Moscow Conservatory. An American impresario signed him for his first tour of the United States in 1906. Upon arriving in New York, Lhévinne learned that his impresario was nowhere to be found. His proposed tour of America having collapsed, Lhévinne had reconciled himself to returning to Russia when Modest Altschuler, conductor of the Russian Symphony Orchestra, invited him to appear as a guest artist with his orchestra. That concert took place on January 27, 1906, with a performance of Anton Rubinstein's Piano Concerto No. 5 in E-flat. Lhévinne's former teacher, Safonov, was the conductor. Despite the fact that Lhévinne had to play with an injured finger he made an excellent impression. "He played with great brilliancy," wrote Henry E. Krehbiel in the *Tribune*, "yet with dignified and intelligent purpose, and in the slow movement with all possible appreciation of its possibilities in the way of poetical expression. His large singing tone made a deeper impression than did the dash of his bravura in the first movement, and first awakened the instructed among the listeners to a consciousness of the fact that they were in the presence of a pianist who was not only a virtuoso with an amazing skill in octave playing but also something more."

On the strength of the success of this and several more performances, the manager of the Steinway Piano Company gave Lhévinne a contract calling for one hundred and fifty concerts in America the following season. Lhévinne continued to tour the United States regularly up to the time of World War I. After a recital at

Carnegie Hall on October 31, 1908, Richard Aldrich wrote in the New York *Times:* "His tone is big and richly sonorous, with abundant modification of coloring and gradation of power. He is a conscientious and unpretending artist; he is absolutely absorbed in the music he is playing and there is no suggestion in his performance of personal display." But Aldrich did find Lhévinne "deficient in imagination, in poetical feeling."

From 1907 on, the Lhévinnes lived in Berlin where just before the outbreak of World War I they bought a forty-room house in a suburb of Berlin. Its previous owner had been the Chinese ambassador to Germany who had sold the estate at a modest price, knowing as he did that Germany would soon be involved in war.

Since the Lhévinnes were Russian citizens they were interned in Germany during the war, but Lhévinne was occasionally allowed to give concerts. When their own funds were depleted, largely through unfortunate investments in Russian government bonds, they had to borrow from their German friends to survive.

The Lhévinnes returned to the United States with their two children in 1919. His first concert of that season, at the Hippodrome in New York on October 26, drew an ovation. The Lhévinnes rented an apartment in New York, established a teaching studio, and became American citizens.

His concert tours soon brought him to the front rank of living pianists. Deeply poetic and penetrating musical values were added to his formidable technique to make his performances, particularly in the Romantic repertory, revelations. In addition to his American concerts, he toured Europe in 1926, 1929, and 1937, and performed in Mexico, Cuba, and Panama.

On the evening of January 14, 1939, the fortieth anniversary of the two-piano partnership of Josef and Rosina Lhévinne was celebrated at Carnegie Hall. For this occasion, at the urging of her husband, Rosina emerged from her forty-year retirement as a solo pianist to perform Chopin's Concerto in E minor; Josef played the Tchaikovsky Piano Concerto No.1; and both pianists joined in a performance of Mozart's Concerto in E-flat major for two pianos. Of Rosina's playing Olin Downes wrote in the New York *Times:* "The interpretation was charmingly poetic, if not particularly impassioned"; and of Josef, he "never played more magnificently or with greater virtuosity and command of tone.

Each division of the masterpieces was conceived as superbly as it was delivered." In the two-piano concerto, "the fusion of spirit and uniformity of approach resulted in ensemble of the first order," he added.

Lhévinne continued to concertize until the end of his life; from time to time he also appeared in two-piano performances with his wife. His last public appearance took place in New York City on July 31, 1944, at the Lewisohn Stadium in Tchaikovsky's Piano Concerto No.1. In August 1944 Lhévinne suffered a heart attack while visiting his daughter, Marianna, in Hollywood, California. He returned to his home in Kew Gardens, Queens, New York, only a few days before his death on December 2, 1944.

Both Josef and his wife, Rosina, enjoyed sustained and fruitful careers as teachers of piano—at their own home where they maintained a studio and at the Juilliard School of Music whose faculty they joined when the school was opened in 1924. They remained at Juilliard until the end of their lives. Rosina Lhévinne continued her career as teacher at the Juilliard School of Music after her husband's death—at that time she was the only original faculty member still alive. Until her seventy-fifth year she took on all her pupils without assistance, but after that she called upon associates to help her. In March 1976, in celebration of her ninety-sixth birthday she was made honorary chairman of the piano faculty at Juilliard. Among her most famous pupils have been Van Cliburn, John Browning, Misha Dichter, and James Levine. In 1955, when she was seventy-five, she once again returned to the concert platform, performing Mozart's Piano Concerto in C major, K.467, at Aspen, Colorado. Later she appeared as a soloist with the New York Philharmonic, Leonard Bernstein conducting, in Chopin's Piano Concerto No.1. She once again was the soloist with the New York Philharmonic in 1963. On November 9, 1976, at the age of ninety-six, she died of a stroke at Glendale, California.

In addition to their apartments in New York City (first in Manhattan and later at Kew Gardens in Queens) the Lhévinnes maintained a country place in Portage, Wisconsin. There Josef Lhévinne had built a private retreat, a converted water tower christened "Josef's Tower." At this tower, Josef indulged in his favorite avocation, astronomy, with the aid of his much prized telescope. "He adored the sky," Rosina once told an interviewer. "For him the sky was not only on the same plane as the piano, but in his heart, I think, he liked the sky more. . . . He knew every constellation with the naked eye." Besides astronomy, Lhévinne enjoyed fishing and target shooting.

ABOUT: Wallace, R.K. A Century of Music-Making. *Periodicals*—New York Times Magazine, January 8, 1939, December 3, 1944, November 21, 1976; New Yorker, January 12, 1963; Saturday Review, March 28, 1970.

EMANUEL LIST

Emanuel List

1891–1967

Emanuel List, bass, was born in Vienna on March 22, 1891, the son of Albert and Josephine List. Emanuel was a boy chorister at the historic Theater-an-der-Wien but soon left the chorus to assume small roles. Later he worked as a tailor, but singing remained a prime interest. He joined a comic vocal group which toured Europe and appeared in 1914 in a London variety theater. With World War I imminent, List decided to emigrate to the United States and arrived there late in 1914. One of his first jobs in America was singing at the Café Bismarck on East Eighty-sixth Street. An impresario engaged him for seventy-five dollars a week to tour the burlesque circuit with the Irwin Majestics for forty-six weeks. After that, he was employed at the Hippodrome in New York, appearing in some of its spectacular productions. When the United States became involved in World War I, List was dismissed from the Hippodrome company because he was Austrian. He managed to find a one-week engagement at the Rialto Theatre, a motion-picture palace in the Times Square district. Its manager, Hugo Riesenfeld, advised him to study voice seriously, something List had not done up to this time. He studied with Josiah Zuro and supported himself by appearing as a singer in motion-picture houses directed by Riesenfeld. Through Riesenfeld, he came to know Samuel L. Rothafel, popularly known as "Roxy," a director of motion-picture theaters. Rothafel encouraged him to turn to the singing of opera arias which List soon interpolated into his programs during tours of motion-picture theaters throughout the United States.

List returned to Vienna in 1920 to visit his mother. There, after a period of vocal study with Emil Steger, he made his opera debut in 1922 at the Volksoper as Méphistophélès in *Faust*. Max von Schillings, manager of the Berlin State Opera, gave him a contract to join his company in 1923. List remained as principal bass of the Berlin State Opera until 1933, specializing in Wagnerian roles and as Baron Ochs in *Der Rosenkavalier*. In 1931 he made the first of several annual visits to the Salzburg Festival, where he distinguished himself as Osmin in *The Abduction from the Seraglio*, the Commandant in *Don Giovanni*, and the Minister and Rocco in *Fidelio*. In 1933 he was heard at the Bayreuth Festival as Fafner, Hunding, and Hagen in the Wagner *Ring* cycle.

His performances as Baron Ochs at the Berlin State Opera attracted the interest of Artur Bodanzky, principal conductor of German operas at the Metropolitan Opera. As a result, List made his American operatic debut at the Metropolitan Opera on December 27, 1933, as Hermann in *Tannhäuser*. Olin Downes commented in the New York *Times:* "The depth and resonance of Mr. List's voice made his Landgrave uncommonly effective." Later the same season he was heard as Hunding in *Die Walküre*, First Nazarene in *Salome*, King Mark in *Tristan and Isolde*, the Commandant, Fafner in *Siegfried*, Pogner in *Die Meistersinger*, Fasolt in *Das Rheingold*, King Henry in *Lohengrin*, Hagen in *Die Götterdämmerung*, and Gurnemanz in *Parsifal*. On January 4, 1935, he made his first

American appearance as Baron Ochs in a revival of *Der Rosenkavalier,* a role he sang 55 times in New York and 20 times on tour with the company. As Baron Ochs he made his bow at Covent Garden in London in 1936. His debut with the San Francisco Opera took place as Hagen on November 9, 1935.

In addition to his success in opera, List enjoyed renown as a *Lieder* singer both in the United States and Europe. He made a specialty of Schubert's songs, receiving continuous praise for his all-Schubert recitals. "His singing style," wrote Leonard Liebling, the editor of *Musical Courier,* "resolves itself into a pronounced and even striking success. Assured and warm of delivery, with seriously musical foundation, and highly competent in the shading of tone, List avoids any semblance of monotony.... The experts must have been astonished at the ease with which the recitalist masters the softer episodes and more flexible passages."

Because he was a Jew, List was removed from the roster of the Berlin State Opera in 1933 when the Nazis came to power in Germany. Until the Nazi occupation of Austria, List lived in Vienna. After that he transferred his home to New York City. He remained with the Metropolitan Opera company through the 1947–1948 season, adding to his Metropolitan repertory Rocco in *Fidelio,* the Old Hebrew in *Samson and Delilah,* Daland in *The Flying Dutchman,* and Sarastro in *The Magic Flute.* From 1950 to 1952 he was once again the principal bass of the Berlin State Opera.

In the New York *Times* Ross Parmenter once described List as "a tall, commanding-looking man with black eyebrows and thick gray-white hair which he brushes back close to his head. Although he is good-humored and pink-cheeked the stamp and dignity of the Wagnerian singer are in his bearing. His colloquial speech, however, still bears many traces of the days when he was looking for jobs on Broadway."

List was a collector of precious art works that included paintings by Rembrandt, Van Dyck, Titian, and Sir Joshua Reynolds. He spent the last years of his life in Vienna with his second wife, the former Hansi Frank. On June 21, 1967, he died in a nursing home in that city.

ABOUT: Kutsch, K. J. and Riemens, L. A Concise Biographical Dictionary of Singers.

Göta Ljungberg

1893–1955

Göta Albertina Ljungberg, soprano, was born in Sundsvall, Sweden, on October 4, 1893. She showed signs of musical talent from childhood on; when she was eight she sang for the queen of Sweden.

After some preliminary music study with private teachers she entered the Royal Academy of Music in Stockholm, where she studied voice with Gillis Bratt and Sarah Walker Cahier. Her later study took place with Ferguson in London, Vittorio Vanzo in Milan, and Louis Bachner and Oscar Daniel in Berlin.

At eighteen she entered the Royal Opera School in Stockholm. There she sang the roles of Elisabeth in *Tannhäuser,* Gutrune in *Die Götterdämmerung,* and Santuzza in *Cavalleria Rusticana.* She was graduated into the regular company of the Royal Opera, making her professional opera debut in 1918 as Elsa in *Lohengrin.*

In 1922 she made her first appearance at the Salzburg Festival. Two years later she made her debut in Covent Garden in London as Salome in Strauss's opera. With the exception of 1925 she returned to that company annually until 1929, distinguishing herself not only as Salome but also as Gutrune, Sieglinde in *Die Walküre,* and several other Wagnerian roles. Eugene Goossens composed his opera *Judith* with her in mind, and she created that title role at Covent Garden on January 25, 1929.

Invited for a guest performance with the Berlin State Opera in 1926, she made such a favorable impression that she was engaged as principal soprano in the German, French, and Italian repertories. During her six-year stay in Berlin she specialized in Wagner, but she also sang Tosca, Carmen, Santuzza, Chrysothemis in *Elektra,* and the Marschallin in *Der Rosenkavalier.*

She made her debut at the Metropolitan Opera on January 20, 1932, as Sieglinde in *Die Walküre.* In the *Herald Tribune,* Lawrence Gilman commented: "She is blessed with a countenance that detains the eye. She is tall and straight and graceful, and she is admirably thin.

Ljungberg lyŏong' băr y'

London

GÖTA LJUNGBERG

... She is a singing actress of temperament and skill. She has a warm and visualizing and dramatic imagination. Her miming is fluent and expressive, contemptuous of routine. ... Her voice is a powerful one, flexible and dramatic, and Mme. Ljungberg knows how to place it at the service of the music's meaning and the text's significance." Her authority as an interpreter of Wagnerian roles became increasingly evident on February 3 when she was first heard as Isolde, on February 26 as Freia in *Das Rheingold,* on March 9 as Elsa, on March 11 as Brünnhilde in *Siegfried,* and on March 22 as Kundry in *Parsifal.*

On January 13, 1934, she appeared in the title role of the Metropolitan Opera revival of *Salome,* the first time this Strauss opera had been performed there since its disastrous American premiere in 1907. Unlike so many other famous Salomes before her, Ljungberg refused to allow a professional dancer to perform the celebrated Dance of the Seven Veils but went through the routine herself. To this role she brought her "vivid (though at times erratic) instinct for pictorial effect," wrote Lawrence Gilman in the *Herald Tribune.* "Her Salome is a fairly plausible blend of the perversely infantile and the sensual. ... Her singing of the appallingly difficult music is a courageous and creditable essay."

Previously, on December 3, 1932, she had appeared as Chrysothemis in the first production of *Elektra* at the Metropolitan Opera, and on February 10, 1934, she created the role of Lady Madrigal Sandys in the world premiere of Howard Hanson's *Merry Mount.*

Her last appearance at the Metropolitan Opera took place on March 21, 1935, as Brünnhilde in *Die Walküre.* After leaving the company, Ljungberg taught voice at the New York College of Music for several years. She subsequently returned to Sweden where she remained for the rest of her years. On June 28, 1955, she died at Lidingö near Stockholm.

Göta Ljungberg was married to Harry Stangenberg, an opera director. Tall, slender, and lithe, her supple body revealed her preoccupation with gymnastics. Daily-dozen exercises which followed her early rising each morning became something of a ritual. She disdained cosmetics. Inordinately superstitious, she insisted upon getting out of bed with right foot first and putting on her right stocking before the left. She said that she had valuable premonitions which dictated what hour or what day or what act was particularly lucky for her.

ABOUT: Kutsch, K. J. and Riemens, L. A Concise Biographical Dictionary of Singers.

George London

1920–

George London (originally George Burnstein), bass baritone, was born in Montreal, Canada, on May 30, 1920. His parents, Louis Samuel and Bertha Broad Burnstein, of Russian background, had become naturalized American citizens before settling in Canada. In 1935 his father, a manufacturer and distributor of millinery products, suffered a stroke, and the family moved to Los Angeles. Since George had no musical ambitions (he had some vague ideas of becoming a lawyer), he received no musical instruction. At Hollywood High School he began appearing in school productions of comic opera and discovered that he liked singing and had a good voice. "It was a neighbor in Los Angeles who 'discovered' me," he told an interviewer. "The neighbor heard me practice and urged my parents to have me tested by a music teacher she knew." After graduation from high school, George studied for two years (1937–1939) with Richard Lert in the opera department of the Los Angeles City College, where he assumed minor

GEORGE LONDON

roles. Further vocal studies in Los Angeles took place with Dr. Hugo Strelitzer and Nathan Stewart. He supported himself all this while by singing in synagogues, nightclubs, and churches, and having his voice dubbed on sound tracks of movies.

In 1941 Albert Coates, the conductor-composer, selected him to appear in the American premiere of his opera *Gainsborough* at a concert performance at the Hollywood Bowl. After that, London made numerous appearances with the American Music Theater which presented operas in English, and with light opera companies in Los Angeles and San Francisco. Under the name of George Burnson he appeared in the minor role of Dr. Grenvil in a performance of *La Traviata* at the Hollywood Bowl in 1941. Still as George Burnson he made his debut with the San Francisco Opera on October 24, 1943, as Monterone in *Rigoletto.*

While touring with a road company of Sigmund Romberg's operetta *The Desert Song* in 1946, London arrived in New York. There he studied voice with Paola Novikova and Enrico Rosati, changed his name to George London, and made his concert debut as soloist in Hindemith's requiem *When Lilacs Last in the Dooryard Bloom'd* at its world premiere on May 14, 1946. In 1947 he toured the United States and Europe with Mario Lanza and Frances Yeend, as the Bel Canto Trio. He also appeared as soloist with the Boston Symphony, the Chicago Symphony, and the Buffalo Philharmonic.

Convinced that opera was his career, he decided to forgo further public appearances in order to concentrate on more study. With borrowed funds he embarked for Paris in 1949. There he was coached in opera roles by Arthur Mahoney and George Doubrovsky. After a successful audition with the Vienna State Opera, he made his European debut there as Amonasro in *Aida* in 1949. He was an immediate success. In a short period of time he was heard as Escamillo in *Carmen,* Boris Godunov, Prince Galitzki in *Prince Igor,* and in all the four baritone roles in *The Tales of Hoffmann.* A correspondent for *Time* reported from Vienna: "In four months he has been the rave of Vienna." In the New York *Times* Henry Pleasants wrote: "He has an extraordinarily beautiful bass baritone, well placed, and susceptible of much dramatic coloration. He is also a gifted and accomplished actor." London remained a great favorite in Vienna; in 1954 the Austrian government gave him the honorary title *Kammersänger.* He was also awarded the Mozart Medal, City of Vienna.

In 1950 he made his debut at the Glyndebourne Festival in England as the Count in *The Marriage of Figaro,* and in 1951 he made his first appearance at the Bayreuth Festival in Germany. Rudolf Bing, general manager of the Metropolitan Opera, heard him sing Boris Godunov in Vienna and signed him to a contract. London's debut at the Metropolitan Opera took place on the opening night of the season, November 13, 1951, as Amonasro. Virgil Thomson wrote in the *Herald Tribune* that London was "one of the greatest singing actors we have any of us known or remembered." In the New York *Times* Olin Downes reported London to be "an admirably equipped baritone, capable of fine lyrical singing and of delivering with effect such passages as the earth-shaking outburst of Amonasro at the end of the Nile scene."

Hardly had the echoes of this success died down when London flew to Europe to make his first appearance at La Scala as Pizarro in *Fidelio* on January 9, 1952. After that he appeared in seven of Europe's music festivals: Salzburg, Bayreuth, Edinburgh, Glyndebourne, Munich, Aix-en-Provence, and Holland.

He scored a triumph at the Metropolitan Opera in the title role of *Boris Godunov* on March 6, 1953 (a role he had first sung in New York in a concert performance by the New York Philharmonic on October 6, 1952). The opera was being presented at the Metropolitan in what was then reputed to be Mussorgsky's original version, although it was still edited; furthermore, it was being given in English. The first American singer ever to assume the part at the Metropolitan, London received eleven curtain calls. Virgil Thomson wrote in the *Herald Tribune:* "So fine a bass handled with such art, so great a gift for drama, and so subtle a care for diction have not been met up with by this observer since the death of Chaliapin." *Time* reported: "His singing of Mussorgsky's long lines of foreboding melody had a noble air, his English diction was clear and his acting—as the czar who had murdered his way to power—swept the listeners up in the dramatic story."

Then, on September 16, 1960, London became the first American to be starred in an opera on the stage of the Bolshoi Theater in Moscow when, once again, he assumed the robes of Boris. In a front-page story in the New York *Times,* Osgood Caruthers reported: "At the end of the third act . . . the audience of more than two thousand persons rose and applauded the forty-year-old singer for eight curtain calls. Even the remainder of the all-Soviet cast that filled the stage joined in the accolade to Mr. London's stirring performance. . . . At the final curtain call, while the audience, orchestra and cast were applauding Mr. London, huge baskets of white chrysanthemums were presented to him by his fellow singers." During this visit to the Soviet Union, London gave two concerts with orchestra in Moscow, appeared in *Faust* in Leningrad, and repeated his performance of *Boris Godunov* in Riga.

For fifteen years he was a principal bass baritone of the Metropolitan Opera, making 249 appearances in New York and 54 on tour. His other Metropolitan Opera roles were Don Giovanni, Escamillo in *Carmen,* Scarpia in *Tosca,* Amfortas in *Parsifal,* Wolfram in *Tannhäuser,* Almaviva in *The Marriage of Figaro,* Méphistophélès in *Faust,* Mandryka in *Arabella,* the High Priest in *The Magic Flute,* the four principal bass-baritone roles in *The Tales of Hoffmann,* the title role in *Eugene Onegin,* Golaud in *Pelléas and Mélisande,* the Dutchman in *The Flying Dutchman,* Wotan in *Das Rheingold,* the Wanderer in *Siegfried,* Wotan in *Die Walküre.* On January 23, 1964, he created for the United States the role of Abdul in the American premiere of Menotti's *The Last Savage.*

In the spring of 1965, London once again sang Boris Godunov at the Bolshoi in Moscow and that year he appeared in the Wagner *Ring* cycle at Cologne. However, that summer he was forced to cancel all his appearances in the *Ring* cycle at the Bayreuth Festival because of a serious throat ailment. "I went through all kinds of medical attention but the doctors were unable to do anything for me," he said. By 1966, when he was scheduled to appear with the San Francisco Opera, he had reached "the stage of voicelessness." On the advice of Kurt Adler, the music director of the San Francisco Opera, London consulted a Los Angeles throat specialist who injected silicone into the withered vocal cord. Within a week London was able to do some vocalizing. After some more injections he was able to give a recital at Salzburg in February 1967. For the next two years he continued to appear in recitals, avoiding the operatic stage. At this juncture, London decided that "instead of being a hobbled George London, I'd better get out of the business and go into something my background had equipped me for." He became a guest lecturer on opera at the University of Cincinnati Conservatory of Music.

In July 1968 he accepted the post of music administrator of the John F. Kennedy Center for the Performing Arts in Washington, D.C.; his job was to develop programs for the center's opera house and concert hall then under construction. He resigned in 1971 because, as he put it, "I was more attracted to things that meant involvement in opera. It had been a good education for me, learning the administrative ropes, but not ultimately fulfilling. I think I helped to get the Center on its feet, and I left with a quiet conscience."

In 1971 he made his first attempt at stage directing with *The Magic Flute* at the Juilliard School of Music. In July of that year he was appointed general director of the Music Center Opera Association, a new company formed to present opera in Los Angeles and other parts of southern California. Just a few months later the project collapsed because of "excessive costs." London went on to become executive director, and in 1975 general director, of the Opera Society in Washington, D.C.

In the summers of 1972, 1973, and 1974, he was the stage director of Wagner's *Ring* cycle (except for *Das Rheingold),* giving one drama a year at Seattle, Washington. In June 1975 the entire *Ring* cycle was given in Seattle, one set of performances in the original German and the other in English. He has also staged operas for companies in Dallas, San Diego, and Washington, D.C., among them *Così fan Tutte, Tosca,* and *The Marriage of Figaro.*

On August 30, 1955, London married Nora Sheldon. As long as he was affiliated with the Metropolitan Opera they lived in a penthouse apartment overlooking Central Park in New York City with two children of their own and Nora's teen-aged children. "I'm a typical middle-aged husband," he told *Opera News* in 1963, "who has no time for bridge or dancing. We read—anything from historical novels to detective stories or movie magazines." He is a sports enthusiast who has kept his body in trim with daily setting-up exercises and has always enjoyed baseball as a spectator sport. His favorite dishes are bouillabaisse and apple strudel.

As general director of the Opera Society of Washington, D.C., he maintains one home on Glengalen Lane in Chevy Chase, Maryland. In addition he has a second home near Lake Lucerne in Switzerland.

George London is a member of the Opera Advisory Panel of the National Endowment for the Arts and a member of the board of directors of the New York City Center of Music and Drama.

ABOUT: Musical America, March 1953, November 1962; New York Times, November 28, 1971; New Yorker, October 26, 1957, November 2, 1957; Opera News, February 2, 1963.

CHRISTA LUDWIG

did, however, take some music courses at the High School of Music in Frankfort, Germany, and later on in her career she received some coaching from Zinka Milanov in New York.

Christa's debut took place with the Frankfort Opera in Germany in 1946 as Prince Orlofsky in *Die Fledermaus.* She remained with that company six years, attracting particular attention as Octavian in *Der Rosenkavalier* (one of her finest roles) and Cherubino in *The Marriage of Figaro.* From 1952 to 1954 she was a member of the Darmstadt Opera and in 1954–1955 she sang with the Hanover Opera. In the 1950s she added to her expanding repertory the less familiar title roles of *Judith* and *Antigone* in the operas by Arthur Honegger. In 1954 she was acclaimed at the Salzburg Festival for her performances of Dorabella in *Così fan Tutte* and in the roles of Cherubino and Octavian.

She was engaged by the Vienna State Opera in 1955. Through the years as a resident member she achieved international renown for her performances. Hers was a voice with a remarkable range and with lusciously dark colorings. In addition she had an attractive stage presence and uncommon acting ability. She was heard in a variety of roles in and out of Vienna. Her Wagnerian repertory included Kundry in *Parsifal,* Fricka in *Das Rheingold* and *Die Walküre,* Waltraute in *Die Götterdämmerung,* Magdalene in *Die Meistersinger,* Venus in *Tannhäuser,* Ortrud in *Lohengrin,* and Brangäne in *Tristan and Isolde.* In the operas of Richard Strauss she distinguished herself particularly as Octavian and

Giuseppe de Luca
See De Luca

Christa Ludwig

1928–

Christa Ludwig, mezzo-soprano, was born in Berlin, on March 16, 1928. Both her parents were professional musicians. Her father, Anton, was a tenor and opera manager, and her mother, Eugenie Besalla-Ludwig, was a contralto. Her mother was Christa's only voice teacher. Christa

Ludwig: lōōd' vĭk

as the Marschallin in *Der Rosenkavalier* (appearing in the latter role for the first time in 1968), as the Dyer's wife in *Die Frau ohne Schatten,* Ariadne and the Composer in *Ariadne auf Naxos,* Klytemnestra in *Elektra,* and Clairon in *Capriccio.* She was also hailed for her performances as Amneris in *Aida,* Lady Macbeth in Verdi's *Macbeth,* Eboli in *Don Carlo,* Preziosilla in *La Forza del Destino,* Federica in *Luisa Miller,* Charlotte in *Werther,* Carmen, Rosina in *The Barber of Seville,* Delilah in *Samson and Delilah,* Orfeo in Gluck's *Orfeo ed Euridice,* Cornelia in Handel's *Giulio Cesare,* Marina in *Boris Godunov,* Marfa in *Khovantchina,* Angelina in Rossini's *La Cenerentola,* Olga in *Eugene Onegin,* and in the Mozartean roles of Dorabella, Cherubino, and Sesto in *La Clemenza di Tito.* In June 1971, during the festival weeks in Vienna, she created the role of Claire in the world premiere of Gottfried von Einem's *Der Besuch der Alten Dame.*

In 1963 the Austrian government honored her with the title *Kammersängerin.* Four years later she was awarded the Mozart medal by the Mozart Society of Vienna and the Austrian Cross of Honor, Arts and Science, First Class.

Her American debut took place in Chicago with the Chicago Lyric Opera in 1959. Shortly after that, on December 10, 1959, she made her bow at the Metropolitan Opera as Cherubino. That premiere was not an unqualified success. She made a better impression later the same season as Amneris, Octavian, and Brangäne; but her greatest Metropolitan Opera successes were not to come for another few years.

In December 1960 she assumed the role of Dejanira in a concert presentation of Handel's opera *Hercules* in New York. Writing in the New York *Times,* Raymond Ericson described her voice as "a lovely one . . . even in texture from its lowest to its highest notes." After leaving the Metropolitan Opera in 1961, she continued to appear with the Vienna State Opera with great success. She also gave guest performances in other major European opera houses and at festivals. In 1963 she visited Tokyo with the Berlin Deutsche Oper, as Leonore in *Fidelio.* She made her debut at the Bayreuth Festival as Brangäne (a performance that was recorded by Deutsche Grammophon) and a year later she was acclaimed there for her performance of Kundry in *Parsifal.*

Between 1961 and 1963 her first significant

recordings were released by Angel: *Norma* (with Maria Callas), Bach's *Passion According to St. Matthew* (conducted by Otto Klemperer), and *Così fan Tutte.* Later she was represented in both of the major recordings of the complete *Ring* cycle issued respectively by Decca (conducted by Georg Solti) and Deutsche Grammophon (conducted by Herbert von Karajan). English musicologist Alec Robertson spoke of her "nobility" as Fricka in *Die Götterdämmerung* in the Decca recording, adding, "I have never heard so convincing an interpretation of the part." Discussing her performance of Waltraute in the Deutsche Grammophon release, Paul Hume of the Washington *Post* wrote: "Clearly Christa Ludwig is the world's reigning Waltraute. . . . She is magnificent." In 1968 her Angel recording of songs by Schubert, Brahms, Ravel, and others received a Grammy from the National Academy of Recording Arts and Sciences. In 1972 she was given the French Prix des Affaires Culturelles for her recording of the role of Venus in *Tannhäuser.* Another of her recordings received the German Orphée d'Or.

On September 29, 1957, Ludwig married Walter Berry, the Viennese-born bass who was a member of the Vienna State Opera. They met for the first time that same year when both appeared in *The Marriage of Figaro.* After their marriage, they often shared the opera stage. When Ludwig sang her first Carmen in Vienna in 1957, Berry was Escamillo. He was Bakar, the Dyer, and Ludwig was his wife in Vienna's highly successful production of *Die Frau ohne Schatten* in 1964. In March 1965 Berry was Agamemnon to her Iphigenia in a concert presentation of Gluck's *Iphigénie en Aulide* in New York and in the same month they were heard in a recital of songs and duets.

Following their marriage, Berry and Ludwig made their home in a villa in the Vienna woods overlooking the Danube. The household included Ludwig's mother, both of Berry's parents, the servants, and dogs and cats. Berry and his wife also maintained apartments in Switzerland and New York. They had one child, a son, Wolfgang, born in 1959, who was raised in Vienna by Ludwig's mother.

Die Frau ohne Schatten brought Ludwig back to the Metropolitan Opera on October 2, 1966; and in the same opera on that same evening her husband made his debut with that company. "Loudest bravos went to Christa Ludwig," reported *Time,* "whose lusty soprano and hip-swinging histrionics had bite and conviction." Two months later Ludwig sang Ortrud to her husband's Telramund in *Lohengrin,* and on November 21, 1967, Ludwig and her husband appeared in the new Herbert von Karajan production of *Die Walküre,* with which Karajan made his bow at the Metropolitan Opera. She was, noted Harold C. Schonberg in the New York *Times,* a "commanding figure who rose to real heights as her voice warmed up." Her roles at the Metropolitan that drew praise from the critics were Amneris, Kundry, Charlotte, the Marschallin, Octavian, and the Dyer's wife.

In September 1967 as a member of the visiting Vienna State Opera, Ludwig was heard as Octavian and as Marie in *Wozzeck* at Expo '67 in Montreal.

Ludwig and Berry were divorced in 1970. Nevertheless they continued to perform together from time to time both in operas and in joint concerts. Though ideally mated on the stage, their matrimonial life proved less than idyllic. As Ludwig explained to John Gruen in an interview for the New York *Times:* "We were different types. I need quiet and I need time for concentration. Walter likes to go out and be with friends and talk and laugh." In 1972 Ludwig married Paul-Emile Deiber, a French actor and stage director. Soon after her marriage she became a French citizen, though residing in Meggen, Switzerland. They have a son.

In 1971 Ludwig appeared as the Marschallin in a new production of *Der Rosenkavalier* at the Vienna State Opera with Leonard Bernstein conducting. This performance was recorded. Later that year, on April 13, she was heard in the world premiere of von Einem's *Der Besuch der Alten Dame* (*The Visit*). On March 20, 1978, at the Paris Opéra, she was heard for the first time anywhere in the title role of Monteverdi's *L'Incoronazione di Poppea.* The roles of Azucena in *Il Trovatore* and Klytemnestra in *Elektra* have also been added to her repertoire.

She has enjoyed international renown as a soloist in performances of major choral works and works for voice and orchestra. As part of the commemoration of the centenary of the Vienna State Opera she participated in a performance of Beethoven's *Missa Solemnis* conducted by Leonard Bernstein in Vienna in 1969, a performance that was televised throughout Europe. A year later, this time in commemoration of the bi-centenary of Beethoven's birth, she once again was the soloist in the *Missa Solemnis* as conducted by Wolfgang Sawallisch, broadcast from St. Peter's in Rome over the NBC-TV network. She has also excelled in performances of Bach's *Passion According to St. Matthew* and the B minor Mass; Brahms's *Alto Rhapsody;* Verdi's *Requiem;* and Mahler's *Kindertotenlieder, Das Lied von der Erde,* and Symphonies No.2 and No.3.

She is recognized as one of the world's foremost interpreters of *Lieder.* She has, said Robert Lawrence, "qualities of tone, musicianship, imagination, bound by a charisma all too rarely met with in a single artist." In 1971–1972 she gave an all-Brahms recital in Carnegie Hall, New York, with Leonard Bernstein as her accompanist. Reviewing an earlier Brahms recital, Donal Henahan reported in the New York *Times* that it was "a tour de force in every way, for in neither vocal finesse nor as a song interpreter does the Viennese mezzo-soprano have many peers. Vocally, her program was a model of the Lieder craft."

In the New York *Times,* John Gruen described Christa Ludwig: "Her tall, well-built figure immediately suggests health and generosity of spirit. . . . Her walk . . . is at once sensual and vital—a walk that invariably lends a special sexiness to her performances. Her face is not beautiful in a conventional sense. It has a pixie-ish quality—a trusting face . . . with intelligent brown eyes and flawless skin. . . . Her voice is tinged with a soft German accent. When she laughs there is music in the room."

Her main diversion is cooking, her culinary specialties being exotic flambé dishes and various types of Italian pizzas. She also enjoys swimming, walking, weaving, sewing, reading, and making home movies. An interest in archaeology led her, during her world tours, to visit excavation sites in Greece, Asia Minor, and South America. She has homes in Vienna, Paris, and Meggen, Switzerland.

ABOUT: New York Times, January 31, 1971, January 27, 1978; Opera News, December 17, 1966, March 16, 1974.

Ludwig

Leopold Ludwig

1908–

Leopold Ludwig, conductor, son of Adolf K. and Adelheid Konecny Ludwig, was born in Witkowitz, near Mährisch-Ostrau, in what was formerly Austria but is now Czechoslovakia, on January 12, 1908. He received his first musical training from local teachers, and by the time he was ten he was able to officiate as church organist. Financial support from local patrons enabled him to go to Vienna for the completion of his music studies when he was nineteen. For four years, from 1927 to 1931, he attended the Academy of Music where he specialized in piano under Emil Paur with the intention of becoming a virtuoso.

During the summer of 1931 when he heard a broadcast of *Tristan and Isolde* conducted by Wilhelm Furtwängler from the Bayreuth Festival, he decided he wanted to be a conductor. "I opened my much studied score of *Tristan*, raised my arms and began conducting along with Furtwängler," he later recalled. "By the end of the performance I had conducting fever. And when I started looking for jobs in my newly chosen field I found them."

In the years between 1931 and 1935 he served as a conductor for several minor operatic theaters in Czechoslovakia: in Gablonz, Teplitz-Schönau, and Troppau. In 1936 he became the youngest music director in the history of German musical theaters when he assumed that post with the Oldenburg Opera. Over a three-year period he did so well there and in guest performances with the Berlin State Opera that in 1939 he was engaged by the Vienna State Opera. Four years later he left Vienna to hold a similar post with the Berlin State Opera. As its principal conductor up to 1950 he became famous for his performances of the German repertory, and particularly of Wagner, and for his empathy with and understanding of contemporary operas.

His international reputation can be said to have begun building in 1951 when he was made general music director of the Hamburg State Opera. He remained nineteen years with that organization. In that time he conducted more than 1,100 performances of 60 operas, including

Ludwig: lōōd′ vĭk

LEOPOLD LUDWIG

many contemporary ones. In 1967 he went with the Hamburg Opera to Expo '67 in Montreal and to the Lincoln Center for the Performing Arts in New York, earning high praise for his brilliant performances of Alban Berg's *Lulu* and Janáček's *Jenufa*. In New York he was also heard in a concert version of *Der Freischütz*.

While holding down his post in Hamburg, Ludwig was heard at the Vienna State Opera, La Scala in Milan, at opera houses in other major cities in Europe and South America, and at festivals in Edinburgh and Glyndebourne. His American debut took place on September 30, 1958, with the San Francisco Opera in *The Bartered Bride*. He continued appearing annually with that company, celebrating his tenth consecutive season there in 1968–1969 with performances of *Die Walküre* and Berg's *Wozzeck*.

During his closing years in Hamburg he became a controversial figure. Opposing factions began attacking each other at his performances with cheers on the one hand and boos on the other. In 1968 he resigned from his post in Hamburg to become artistic director of the General Music Society in Basel and to devote himself to a greater extent than heretofore to guest appearances in Europe and the United States. On November 14, 1970, he made his debut at the Metropolitan Opera in New York in *Parsifal*, a music drama which, because of his strong religious feelings as a Catholic, was particularly close to his heart—to its performance he brought spirituality, mysticism and sound musical values. He had conducted *Parsifal* over a thirty-five-year period, the first time in 1937 with a small orchestra in the pit in Troppau. He returned to the Metropolitan Opera in the spring of 1971 to conduct *Parsifal* once again and in 1971–1972 to lead a new production of *Der Freischütz*, which had been absent from the stage of the Metropolitan Opera since 1929.

On February 23, 1946, Ludwig married Ilse Janucovec; they had two children. Among his preferences are fast cars, dogs, and the stimulation of big cities.

He received the Mozart medal from the Mozart Society of Vienna in 1941 and the Brahms medal from Hamburg in 1958. In 1968 he was named professor by the Hamburg Senate.

ABOUT: Opera News, April 3, 1971.

LORIN MAAZEL

Lorin Maazel

1930–

Lorin Maazel, conductor, was born in the Neuilly district of Paris on March 6, 1930, to Lincoln and Marie Varencove Maazel, American musicians who had gone to Paris to study. Lorin was an infant of two when his parents returned to their home in Los Angeles. There much music making took place. The fascinated response of Lorin to these performances at home and the discovery, when he was five, that he had perfect pitch were the first clues to the parents that their son was a prodigy.

Violin lessons began when Lorin was five. He was soon able to learn his lessons almost before they had been explained to him and to know a piece of music by heart after having played it through just once. He was taken to concerts and seemed to show the greatest interest in orchestral music and conductors. At seven he was found poring through the full orchestral score of Haydn's *Surprise Symphony*, singing its principal themes at the top of his voice. When his mother put a recording of the symphony on the phonograph, Lorin proceeded to conduct the music with waving arms.

In his childhood Lorin began learning the elements of conducting from Vladimir Bakaleinikov, associate conductor of the Los Angeles Philharmonic. As Bakaleinikov's pupil he was

Maazel: mā′ sĕl

allowed in 1938 to conduct a rehearsal of the Los Angeles Philharmonic and, somewhat later, a concert by the orchestra of the University of Idaho. When Bakaleinikov was appointed assistant conductor of the Pittsburgh Symphony in 1938, the Maazel family moved to Pittsburgh so that the teacher-pupil relationship might not be disturbed.

In 1939 Lorin attended the National Music Camp at Interlochen, Michigan. Olin Downes, music critic of the New York *Times*, heard him conduct an orchestral concert there and was so impressed that he used his influence to have the boy conduct the National Music Camp Orchestra at the Court of Peace at the New York World's Fair in August 1939. Lorin handled a program comprising Mendelssohn's *Italian Symphony*, Tchaikovsky's *Marche Slave*, and other orchestral pieces with technical assurance and musical understanding. After the closing measures of the Tchaikovsky composition, "the maestro toddled down ... tugged at his shorts and ran towards the waiting arms of his father and mother," reported Louis Biancolli in the *World-Telegram*. "You had to rub your eyes to believe it—this chubby little figure in a white-linen suit pace-making for an orchestra of seventy, and giving every cue on the dot."

Arthur Judson signed him to a conducting contract that brought with it assignments to lead the orchestra at Lewisohn Stadium in New York in the summer of 1940 and, a summer later, two concerts of the NBC Symphony, the latter on the personal invitation of its music director, Toscanini. At these and subsequent guest appearances with the Chicago Symphony, the Pittsburgh Symphony, and the Cleveland Orchestra, Lorin revealed that he possessed not only an unusual memory and ear but also the instincts and the personality to take command of an orchestra of experienced adult musicians.

When his prodigy years ended, and as an adolescent he had ceased to be a musical curiosity, the engagements melted away. As he put it: "I had lost my market value as a monstrosity." At fifteen Lorin had to reevaluate his career and make fresh decisions about his future. He decided to resume his academic schooling at local public schools. In 1945 he entered the University of Pittsburgh to specialize in languages, mathematics, and philosophy, while continuing his studies in violin and conducting with Bakaleinikov. When he was sixteen he made his concert debut as a violinist. In 1947 he organized and, for three years, played in the Fine Arts String Quartet. One year later he joined the second violin section of the Pittsburgh Symphony.

His conducting career was resumed in 1948 when he became an apprentice conductor of the Pittsburgh Symphony. During his three years in this post, Lorin worked hard helping to rehearse the orchestra and at the same time learning the repertory. Victor de Sabata, the Italian composer-conductor, came to Pittsburgh to make guest appearances and told him: "You will be one of the great of your generation."

In 1951 Maazel led a performance of Stravinsky's *Symphony of Psalms* at the Berkshire Music Festival at Tanglewood. In Tanglewood he met and fell in love with Miriam Sandbank, an American piano student of Brazilian background. They were married on June 18, 1952, when Maazel returned to Tanglewood as a Conducting Fellow. During that summer he also led two concerts of the Cleveland Summer Orchestra. On a Fulbright fellowship, he went to Europe in the fall of 1953 to do research in fifteenth and sixteenth century music. While in Italy he found an opportunity to conduct a symphony concert at Catania, Sicily, on Christmas eve of 1953, when the regular conductor of that orchestra became unavailable. Six months later, he conducted an orchestral concert over the radio in Rome. The directors of Rome Radio submitted to him a list of fifty works for consideration. "I told them any of these works are fine. Which was true—I didn't know any of them, so they were all the same to me." He chose Strauss's *Also Sprach Zarathustra* and Bartók's *The Wooden Prince*. "I studied the music all weekend. I didn't sleep for ninety-six hours. But when I walked in there on Monday morning I knew those scores, every note, every rehearsal letter. And things went beautifully."

More offers came from Italian musical organizations. He conducted the Scarlatti Symphony Orchestra on November 30, 1954. On February 20, 1955, he led the orchestra of the Florence May Music Festival. In June 1955 he offered two symphony concerts at La Scala in Milan.

In 1956 he toured Latin America and was awarded a citation by the Argentinean Circle of Music Critics as the year's best foreign conductor.

In 1957 he toured most of Europe, giving the opening performance of the Vienna June Festival. In 1958 he led Beethoven's *Missa Solemnis* as the initial presentation of the Edinburgh Festival. By 1960 he had become so famous throughout Europe and so highly esteemed that he was averaging fifty concerts a year and commanding fees higher than those earned by most other conductors. During the summer of 1960 he was invited to direct eight performances of *Lohengrin* at the Bayreuth Festival. Never before had an American conducted a performance there—and never before anyone so young. What made his invitation even more remarkable was the fact that up to that time Maazel had never conducted an opera in an opera house. By 1961 he had been heard in virtually every major European festival and had performed over four hundred concerts with its principal orchestras.

Reporting from Europe to the New York *Times,* Paul Moore described Maazel's conducting as follows: "Since he has the score in his head, he can devote his eyes entirely to the musicians, and he shoots his glances everywhere . . . in advance of every important entrance or tricky passage while the baton in his right hand gives a surgically exact beat and his left hand flashes signals of balance and dynamics. . . . Every movement has its motivation, and although he cuts a slimly elegant figure on the podium, his motions never became Corybantic. . . . Aside from his musical mastery, his domination of the orchestra is a matter of sheer will and forcefulness of personality, which radiates from him both on and off the podium in an almost visible aura."

In the 1950s, in the center of Rome, the Maazels and their daughter Lorian Anjali occupied an apartment in the same house Mussolini had occupied in 1922. They also had a vacation retreat, a villa on the Mediterranean coast of Italy.

Maazel made his first American appearance as a mature conductor in December 1960, as guest conductor of the Boston Symphony. On October 1, 1962, he was heard in New York as guest conductor of the visiting L'Orchestre National Français. During the orchestra's three-month tour he gave twelve concerts in twelve cities. In the New York *Times* Harold C. Schonberg noted that Maazel conducted "soberly and clearly, with plenty of strength and rhythm and thorough feeling for . . . musical organization." He added: "Mr. Maazel demonstrated that he had complete control over the orchestra, that he knew every note in the scores . . . and that he is a musician with a technique and knowledge to put his ideas into effect without any question." On November 1, 1962, Maazel made his American bow as conductor of opera at the Metropolitan Opera in a performance of *Don Giovanni* which he conducted from memory. "It was strong, logical conducting," Schonberg wrote in the New York *Times,* "superbly in balance and individual in concept."

In May and June 1963 Maazel toured the Soviet Union as a guest conductor of the Leningrad and Moscow Symphony orchestras. In 1965 he was appointed music director of the West Berlin Opera (the Deutsche Oper) and the Radio Symphony Orchestra of Berlin; at the Deutsche Oper he conducted the world premiere of Luigi Dallapiccola's *Ulysses* on September 29, 1968. The three-year agreement with both organizations (which was extended another three years upon its termination) consumed seven months of Maazel's year; during the remaining time he accepted assignments from symphony orchestras and opera houses all over the world. When Maazel resigned as music director of the West Berlin Opera in 1971, he was made a lifetime member and invited to return every year for guest performances. From 1970 to 1972 Maazel was associate principal conductor of the New Philharmonia Orchestra in London; in 1976–1977 he was appointed principal guest conductor.

In July 1971 he conducted two concerts of the Cleveland Orchestra at the Blossom Music Center, the orchestra's summer home. A few months later the management announced that he had been chosen as the orchestra's new music director to succeed the recently deceased George Szell. It was common knowledge that the members of the orchestra opposed this appointment, rejecting him by a vote of ninety-six to two and demonstrating their preference for István Kertész. But the directors of the orchestra ignored the decision of the musicians. Thus Maazel became the second American (the first having been Leonard Bernstein) to head one of the principal symphony orchestras of the United States. He was the fifth music director in the history of the Cleveland Orchestra. When he led his first concert as music director, in December 1972, his performance was cheered by the audience and well reviewed by the critics. "Throughout the program the orchestra followed Maazel's interpretative ideas to the letter," wrote Robert Finn in the *Plain Dealer,* "showing right away that they will deliver first rate playing for him."

Whatever opposition the orchestra men may have had to Maazel's appointment evaporated as he proceeded to put his enormous energies and talent into maintaining the lofty standards established by his predecessor, George Szell. He went beyond Szell in extending the repertory with numerous modern works and premieres; Szell had been more or less partial to the classical and romantic repertory. He also added to the international fame of the orchestra through extended tours: New Zealand and Australia in 1973—the orchestra under Maazel participating in the opening-week performances celebrating the inauguration of the new opera house in Sydney, Australia, the first visiting orchestra to perform there; Japan in 1974; Latin America in the spring of 1974; Europe in the fall of 1974; Latin America and Europe again, in 1975.

The international renown of the Cleveland Orchestra under Maazel was further extended through a new recording contract with London Records, calling for an initial production of thirteen disks over an eighteen-month period. Maazel himself had already been widely represented on records. He had made about one hundred recordings (including all the symphonies of Tchaikovsky and Sibelius)—conducting the Vienna Philharmonic, the Berlin Philharmonic, the Berlin Radio Symphony, the New Philharmonia Orchestra of London, and the London Symphony, and he was represented by recordings of operas made in Berlin, Vienna, and

Rome. Ten of these London releases captured the coveted Grand Prix du Disque. In his recording of *Thaïs* starring Beverly Sills, he himself performed the celebrated violin solo, "Meditation." Perhaps the most important recording the Cleveland Orchestra under Maazel made for London was the complete presentation of Gershwin's *Porgy and Bess,* released in 1976 —the first time in a forty-year history of performances on stage, in the movies, and on records that *Porgy and Bess* was done exactly the way Gershwin had written it, without any cuts. The recording earned a Grammy in 1977.

In 1975 Maazel's contract with the Cleveland Orchestra was renewed for a four-year period to end with the season of 1980–1981. In addition to conducting the Cleveland Orchestra for two thirds of its subscription series as well as for the concerts on tour and in recordings and for half of the summer season of the Blossom Festival in Cleveland, Maazel has also conceived, conducted, and narrated televised concerts transmitted through the facilities of the Public Broadcasting Service.

Maazel's duties as music director of the Cleveland Orchestra did not prevent him from making appearances with musical organizations throughout the world. Typical of his activities away from Cleveland was a two-month period between October 26 and December 28, 1974, when Maazel conducted five concerts with the New Philharmonia Orchestra of London, two with the Vienna Philharmonic, five with the Radio Symphony of Berlin, and eight performances of six operas with the Deutsche Oper, where he has continued to make annual appearances. When this company visited the United States in November 1975 as part of the American Bicentennial celebration, Maazel joined the company to direct performances of *Lohengrin* and *Tosca* at the Kennedy Center for the Performing Arts in Washington, D.C. In 1978, he returned to the Paris Opéra for a new production of *Luisa Miller.* In July of that year he was scheduled to tour Japan with the Orchestre de Paris in six programs of French music and in September to bring the Cleveland Orchestra to Japan for additional performances.

When Maazel first made his bow in Cleveland in December 1972 as music director of the Cleveland Orchestra, his soloist was his second wife, a young, dark-haired, exotic-looking Israeli pianist, Israela Margit. They had met in 1968 when she appeared as a soloist under his baton at a concert of the Berlin Radio Orchestra. At that time a romance developed between them. Following Maazel's divorce from his first wife, they were married in 1969. They had a son and a daughter, making four children in the household. (Maazel had two daughters by his first wife.) The Maazels have two homes, one in Shaker Heights outside Cleveland and the other in Monte Carlo.

When Sir Georg Solti fell ill and could not fulfill his engagement as conductor of the Paris Opéra in *Otello* at the Kennedy Center in Washington, D.C., Maazel substituted for him without having a single rehearsal. (Previously the same year, at the Orange Festival in France, Maazel's performance of *Otello* had been hailed by French critics as "definitive.") On April 1, 1977, he led *Pelléas and Mélisande* at the Paris Opéra, the first time that this masterwork had ever been performed there.

On September 1, 1977, Maazel became principal guest conductor of the Orchestre National Français in Paris. This appointment was supplementary to his duties as music director of the Cleveland Orchestra.

In his youth Maazel was interested in sports, mostly boating, tennis, swimming, horseback riding, and bicycling. In his later years, when seeking diversions he prefers exercises of the mind, such as working out problems in mathematics or reading mathematical texts, learning new languages, reading books on philosophy and history. When he feels the need for less mental activity he likes to go to the movies. A linguist, he is fluent in English, French, Spanish, Italian, German, and Portuguese. He enjoys good food and fine wines but insists he is "a gourmet and not a gourmand." He adds, "I lived a long time in Italy and I prefer North Italian cooking. Fresh food, vegetables and fruits—no rich French foods."

Maazel was awarded an honorary doctorate in music from the University of Pittsburgh in 1965 and an honorary doctorate in humanities from Beaver College in Pennsylvania in 1973. In 1975 the president of Finland made him Commander of the Order of the Lion; he had previously been awarded the Sibelius Prize in Finland. The Federal Republic of Germany decorated him with the Commander's Cross of the Order of Merit in 1977. Puebla, Mexico, named him an honorary citizen. For his recordings, Maazel has on several occasions been given the Grand Prix du Disque in Paris and the Edison Prize in Holland, in addition to a Grammy in the United States.

ABOUT: High Fidelity/Musical America, February 1972, April 1976; New York Post, April 22, 1972; New York Times, February 2, 1975, February 17, 1978; New York Times Magazine, September 30, 1962; Newsweek, October 15, 1962.

John McCormack

1884–1945

John Francis McCormack, tenor, was the most successful concert singer of his time, particularly famous for his rendition of Irish ballads. Early in his career he was an opera tenor of uncommon distinction and artistry.

Born in Athlone, Ireland, on June 14, 1884, he was the fifth of eleven children of Andrew and Hannah McCormack. The family, as he once said, was "genuinely poor as the goods of this world go, but fortunate in those things which create happiness in the home." As a pupil at the Marist Brothers School in Athlone, John, aged nine, was invited one day to sing for the entertainment of a bishop, a guest of the school. In 1896, on a scholarship, John entered the Diocesan College of the Immaculate Conception of Summer Hill, at Sligo, where one of the instructors invited him to participate as a singer in some school concerts. Upon his graduation in 1902, John captured first prizes in Latin, Greek and mathematics.

He went to Dublin in 1902 to prepare for Civil Service examinations. One day he was at his piano, accompanying himself in a song, when a neighbor stopped to listen. The neighbor took him to Vincent O'Brien, director of the choir of the Marlboro Street Cathedral. After an audition, O'Brien told him: "There's a fortune in your singing." He gave John his first instruction in voice and in 1903 engaged him to sing in the Marlboro Choir at a salary of one hundred and twenty-five dollars a year.

On May 20, 1904 McCormack won the gold medal at the Feis Ceoil, the national music festival at Dublin. That year he went for the first time to the United States with another winner of the competition—Lily Foley, a soprano—to perform at the Irish village at the Louisiana Pur-

JOHN MC CORMACK

chase Exposition in St. Louis. When he returned to Dublin, McCormack sang in the choir of the Berkeley Road Catholic Church, of which Lily Foley was also a member. He also made some song recordings on cylinders for Edison Bell and several for Gramaphone Company.

In 1905 he left for Milan to study voice with Vincenzo Sabbatini, but before he left he and Foley became engaged. When Sabbatini heard McCormack sing for the first time he exclaimed: "I cannot place that young man's voice. God has placed it already." Sabbatini helped train McCormack for the opera stage, and the young tenor made his debut on January 13, 1906, at the Teatro Chiabrera in Savona, Italy, in the title role of Mascagni's *L'Amico Fritz*. For this debut, McCormack temporarily took the stage name of Giovanni Foli.

On July 2, 1906, McCormack and Foley were married. They spent their honeymoon in London, mostly listening to opera performances at Covent Garden. This was a period of struggle, frustrations, and disappointments for McCormack. Audition followed audition; McCormack sang for concert managers, opera impresarios, and publishers, without finding an interested ear. To earn his living he was reduced to filling random engagements as a singer in hotels and cabarets.

Then a letter of introduction from Albert Vesetti of the Royal College of Music brought McCormack to the attention of Arthur Boosey, the music publisher. Boosey arranged for McCormack's London concert debut on February 17, 1907. This proved so successful that a second concert was arranged for March 15. Immediately after that came other recitals in London as well as an appearance with the Queen's Hall Orchestra directed by Henry J. Wood. Then, on October 5, 1907, McCormack made a successful debut at Covent Garden as Turiddu in *Cavalleria Rusticana* to become (at the age of twenty-three) the youngest leading singer ever engaged by that opera company. He became an immediate favorite in London, not only with that performance but later in the season as the Duke in *Rigoletto* and as Don Ottavio in *Don Giovanni*. His rendition of "Il mio tesoro" in *Don Giovanni* made even diehard Mozarteans sit up and take notice because of the purity of the vocal sound, his exquisite phrasing, and his perfect breath control.

Following his initial successes at Covent Garden, McCormack was presented to King Edward and Queen Alexandria. He returned to Covent Garden each season from 1909 through 1913 (and again in 1920). He also toured the English provinces in joint concerts with Fritz Kreisler. Meanwhile, on November 7, 1907, he made another memorable debut in London, this time as a singer in oratorios. He appeared as the tenor soloist in a performance of *Elijah*.

Oscar Hammerstein, the impresario of the Manhattan Opera House in New York, heard him in Covent Garden and brought him to the United States for his company. McCormack's American opera debut took place with the Manhattan Opera on November 10, 1909, as Alfredo in *La Traviata*. He remained only a single season with the Manhattan Opera company, for it closed down permanently in 1910. That year he toured with Melba in performances of Italian operas in Australia. On November 29, 1910, he made a guest appearance at the Metropolitan Opera as Alfredo, and H. E. Krehbiel remarked in the *Tribune* that "his delicate phrasing and the feeling and tenderness he displays in his singing were evident as ever."

That McCormack was beginning to build up a formidable following became evident on February 26, 1911, when he gave a recital in Carnegie Hall. As Richard Aldrich noted in the New York *Times,* the auditorium "could not legally hold a larger audience than was present there last evening." About his performance in a program made up partly of opera arias but mostly of Irish airs, original or arranged, Aldrich add-

ed: "Mr. McCormack's voice had all its beauty and lightness of tenor quality."

In 1910–1911 McCormack appeared for a season with the Boston Opera Company and in 1912–1913 he sang with the Chicago Opera. With the latter company, on February 25, 1911, in Philadelphia, he created the role of Lieutenant Merrill in the world premiere of Victor Herbert's *Natoma*. He returned to the Metropolitan stage for the seasons of 1912–1913 and 1913–1914, and again in 1917–1918 and 1918–1919, specializing in Puccini operas: as Rodolfo in *La Bohème,* Pinkerton in *Madama Butterfly,* and Cavaradossi in *Tosca.*

During World War I, McCormack established permanent residence in New York City; he became an American citizen on June 7, 1919.

In 1917 Olin Downes, then a music critic in Boston, wrote about McCormack as follows: "Not only is he a master of vocal difficulties, but his mastery includes the clear enunciation of the English language, and the making of this tongue beautiful in song. For vocal virtuosity alone his performance of the air of Handel would have been memorable for the control of breath, the ease of finish with which he executed the most taxing passages. At the same time, McCormack never forgot the expressive import of the music."

Reports of his success as a singer of Mozart brought him an invitation from Lilli Lehmann to appear at Salzburg in performances of *Don Giovanni* in a "dream" cast made up of Gadski, Farrar, Scotti, and herself. "Reply in whatever language you will," Lehmann wrote him, "only let it be 'yes.'" His answer was in the affirmative, but before he could make that appearance Germany declared war on England. McCormack never sang Mozart in Salzburg.

During World War I, he contributed his talent to the war effort by appearing in patriotic rallies. Through his efforts he helped raise a million dollars, including half a million dollars in the sale of Liberty Bonds.

After the war, with the exception of random guest appearances with the Monte Carlo Opera in 1921 and 1923, McCormack confined his singing activity to the concert stage where he became extremely popular. Critics and fellow musicians soon began to criticize him for stooping to conquer his audiences by pleasing them with Irish and romantic ballads rather than devoting himself extensively to great operatic and song literature. But conquer his audiences he most assuredly did, as no other singer in his time managed to do. In a single season he gave ninety-five recitals, all of them to sold-out houses; over a thirteen-year period he grossed thirteen million dollars. His popularity was such that in one season he was able to give twelve concerts in a single season in New York, alternating between the Hippodrome with its five-thousand-seat capacity and Carnegie Hall, which seated almost three thousand. The demand for tickets for his concerts proved so great that a policy was instituted to seat audiences on the stage, a practice believed to have started with him.

He was also enjoying success on records. He is said to have received an income of one hundred and eighty thousand dollars from his recordings in the single year 1918—greater than the royalties earned by any other two singers combined. In all, his income from recordings amounted to several million dollars. His best-selling record was "I Hear You Calling Me," but "Mother Machree," "Kathleen Mavourneen," and "When Irish Eyes Are Smiling" did almost as well.

Because he was an avowed Irish separatist, he was, for several years after World War I, persona non grata in the concert halls of England. But in June 1924, when he returned to London for a recital after a prolonged absence, he was received eagerly. From then on he continued to concertize extensively throughout Great Britain. When in 1932 he celebrated the twenty-fifth anniversary of his debut in England with a recital in London, he received such an ovation that he was required to give encores that doubled the length of his program.

Early in 1922 McCormack succumbed to a serious throat infection that endangered not only his career but his life as well. But in the fall of the same year he was fully recovered and able to continue his concert work.

In 1928 McCormack was raised to papal peerage and given the title of Count by Pope Pius XI. Three years later he was made vice-president of the Irish Royal Academy of Music, and in June 1933 the University of Notre Dame gave him the Laetare medal. Among his other honors and decorations were the Order of St. Gregory the Great, the Order of the Holy Sepulchre, and Chevalier of the French Legion of Honor. In 1917 he received an honorary doctorate in Letters from Holy Cross College. In 1923 he was made Freeman of the City of Dublin.

He remained active on the concert stage until 1938; up to his last concert his popularity remained undiminished. He made his last tour of the United States in 1937, giving his final American concert at Buffalo, New York, on March 6. In addition, he was often heard on American radio broadcasts, the first taking place on January 1, 1925. He was also starred in the motion picture *Song O' My Heart* (1929), for which he was paid half a million dollars. This was filmed both in Hollywood and in Ireland.

What he had planned as his permanent farewell as a singer took place in London in November 1938. Nine thousand people overtaxed the capacities of Royal Albert Hall and the demand for encores proved so insistent that he had to keep on singing until late in the night. When he delivered some of the Irish ballads with which he had become identified, some women in the audience wept. The concert over, McCormack felt he had sung his last song in public. "It is my turn to listen," he explained.

He went into retirement in Ireland, but in 1939 he returned to the concert stage to sing for the benefit of the British Red Cross. During World War II he resumed concert work, once again for the benefit of the British Red Cross. When his health broke down on one such tour, his physicians ordered him to leave the stage for good and to return to Ireland for rest and recuperation. "It was not my voice that gave out," he explained, "but my lungs." Only a week before his death, he gave a party for one of his singing protégés, Christopher Lynch, for whom he had been negotiating a recording contract. Then McCormack suddenly developed bronchial pneumonia, and on September 16, 1945, he died quietly at his home in Booterstown, outside Dublin.

The McCormacks had two children, Cyril and Gwendoline, and they raised a third child, their nephew Kevin Foley, who had become an orphan in his second year when his parents died aboard a ship torpedoed by a German U-boat during World War I. McCormack's widow, Lily, survived him by over a quarter of a century, dying in her eighty-fourth year in Dublin.

One of McCormack's greatest interests outside music was art. His personal gallery included a Rembrandt, a Frans Hals, a Gainsborough, and several Blakelocks.

In 1977 RCA released an album entitled *John McCormack, a Legendary Performer*. It included not only his favorite Irish ballads but also opera arias. Among the latter was his stunning, possibly incomparable, rendition of "Il mio tesoro" from *Don Giovanni*.

ABOUT: Foxall, R. John McCormack; Ledbetter, G. T. The Great Irish Tenor; McCormack, J. and Key, P. John McCormack: His Own Life Story; McCormack, L. I Hear You Calling; Moore, G. Am I Too Loud?; Strong, L. A. G. John McCormack; Wagner, C. L. Seeing Stars. *Periodicals*—Opera News, December 3, 1960; Time, October 1, 1945.

James McCracken

1926–

JAMES MC CRACKEN

James Eugene McCracken, tenor, was born in Gary, Indiana, on December 16, 1926. His father, John A. McCracken, was the local fire chief who sang in vocal quartets; his mother, Doris Hafey McCracken, had learned to play the piano by ear and performed for theatrical productions. As a boy, James was always singing. While attending Horace Mann High School he studied voice with Eulah Winter and also took lessons on the clarinet. In high school he was a member of the glee club with which he performed in school productions of several Gilbert and Sullivan operettas. Upon graduation from high school, he was voted by his schoolmates as the one "most likely to succeed in music."

The soprano lead in some of the high school Gilbert and Sullivan productions was Shirley Fender. After graduation, when James was eighteen, he married her. The marriage lasted half a dozen years and brought him a son.

During World War II, James enlisted in the United States Navy and was assigned to active duty as a sonarman. While training at the Great Lakes Station he joined the Blue Jacket Choir. One of the naval commanders heard him sing and urged him to consider music as a career. Upon his discharge from the Navy, James, then nineteen, enrolled at Columbia University under the GI Bill of Rights to study music for two years. There he was affiliated with the Columbia Theater Associates with whom he appeared in productions of several operas: Méhul's *Stratonice,* Otto Luening's *Evangeline,* and Douglas Moore's *White Wings.*

Upon leaving Columbia in 1948, McCracken

studied voice with Wellington Ezekiel and Mario Pagano. For the next four years he supported himself by appearing in minor roles in several Broadway musical productions, among them *A Tree Grows in Brooklyn,* a revival of *Of Thee I Sing,* and the revue *Two on the Aisle* in which he was the offstage voice for Bert Lahr singing "There Never Was a Baby Like Me." Eventually he found a steady job as a member of the Glee Club and as a vocal soloist at the Roxy Theatre in New York. "Talk about hard work," he recalls. "I sang two hundred days, four or five shows a day, without a day off, for a little over one hundred dollars a week. It would have been less than a hundred dollars a week if I hadn't worked on the seventh day."

In 1952 he made his opera debut as Rodolfo in *La Bohème* with the Central City Opera Company in Colorado. On June 13, 1953, he was heard in the American premiere of Poulenc's *Les Mamelles de Tirésias,* produced at Brandeis University in Waltham, Massachusetts

A concert performance of Saint-Saëns's *Samson and Delilah* in Norfolk, Virginia, in 1952 brought him together with Sandra Warfield, a mezzo-soprano, who was cast as Delilah. The two had met for the first time at the New York studio of the piano accompanist Emanuel Balaban, where they went over some of the music from Saint-Saëns's opera. They met daily for rehearsals and before long they realized they were in love. Since both of them were married they spent the next few months trying to avoid each other.

It was at Sandra's urging that McCracken decided to audition for the Metropolitan Opera in 1953. "I thought," McCracken says, "well, she's a bit crazy, balmy. All I knew about singing at the time were Broadway shows and the English version of a couple of operas, principally *Samson and Delilah*. Sandra said, 'No, no, it doesn't make any difference, the way you sing, they'll take you.' They did." He was given a contract and his debut took place on November 21, 1953, in the inconsequential part of Parpignol in *La Bohème* in which he was required to deliver just five words repeated twice. He appeared one hundred and twenty-six times that season (more than any other singer in the company) but always in negligible roles such as Flavio in *Norma* (with this the 1956–1957 season of the Metropolitan Opera opened on October 29).

Warfield also auditioned for the Metropolitan Opera, and she, too, landed a contract. When their respective divorces became final they were married on November 11, 1954, at the Ethical Culture Church. "After the ceremony," Sandra recalls, "we just had time for everyone to have a sip of champagne and a bite of cake, and we were off for the Met for the evening performance." That evening McCracken was appearing in the bit part of Ulrich Eisslinger in *Die Meistersinger*.

While Warfield was making notable progress at the Metropolitan and getting important roles, McCracken was standing still professionally, continually getting insignificant parts. In 1957, after he had performed in twenty-seven such roles, both he and his wife decided that the time had come for McCracken to try advancing his career in Europe. She insisted on breaking her own ties with the Metropolitan, though she was doing well, to go with him to Europe. There they encountered little but poverty and neglect for several years. "During the first three years or more in Europe," as McCracken recalls in his autobiography, *A Star in the Family,* "Sandra and I had nothing but each other. . . . In Milan we lived in an apartment without furniture. The thing I remember as the worst of bad times was the hundreds of auditions without getting a job to sing anywhere. There was one stretch in Italy of two years and two months . . . without performing anywhere. The only singing I did was to audition. Once Sandra sold her diamond ring to pay for lessons for me to learn *Andrea Chénier,*

and I did learn it, and no one would hire me to sing that either."

Finally he did get a job (paying eight dollars a day) as an understudy for Carlo Bergonzi and Franco Corelli at the Arena in Verona. Then, at long last, he was able to make his European debut—at Bonn, Germany—as Max in *Der Freischütz,* following this with appearances there as Canio in *I Pagliacci,* Manrico in *Il Trovatore,* and Radames in *Aida.*

While working as an understudy in Verona, McCracken was advised by Tullio Serafin, the conductor, to get more coaching in Italian operas. To realize this, he went to Milan to study with Marcello Conati. During this period of additional training, he received calls to make guest appearances in Bielefeld and Zurich. In Athens he sang in *Samson and Delilah*. That same year, 1959, the couple sang in the same opera company at Split in Yugoslavia—she in *Aida* and he in *Faust*.

An important turning point in his career came when the Opera Society of Washington, D.C., called upon him to assume the title role in *Otello*. Within a few weeks Conati had coached McCracken in the part "from the ground up," as McCracken put it. That performance took place on January 22, 1960, and represented the first significant success of McCracken's career—this role was soon to make him world famous.

A successful debut at the Vienna State Opera in *Ariadne auf Naxos,* with Herbert von Karajan conducting, brought him a contract with that company. Simultaneously he was engaged by the Zurich Opera. In both places he was received enthusiastically for his performances as Otello, Samson, Florestan in *Fidelio,* Canio, and Don Alvar in *L'Africaine*. At the Zurich Opera he shared a European stage for the first time with his wife in a performance of *Samson and Delilah*. He opened the Zurich season of 1961–1962 as Manrico in *Il Trovatore* with Sandra as Azucena, and later the same season he once again appeared with his wife, this time in a performance of *Le Prophète*.

He was appearing as Otello at the Zurich Festival on June 15, 1961, when Rudolf Bing, general manager of the Metropolitan Opera, heard him and signed him to a contract calling for him to repeat this performance in New York. But before this happened, McCracken made his debut with the San Francisco Opera on October 2, 1962, as Otello; he was a sensation. This was the preface to his climactic triumph as Otello in a new production of Verdi's opera at the Metropolitan Opera on March 10, 1963. He was the first American-born singer to assume that role with the company. "In singing the title role in Verdi's *Otello* last night," wrote Harriet Johnson in the New York *Post*, "thirty-five-year-old Indiana-born James McCracken has accomplished what is generally considered impossible. He left the Metropolitan in 1957 as its chief onstage tenor messenger and spear carrier and has returned in triumph in the title role of one of the greatest operas ever written." She described McCracken as "the leading protagonist of the role in the world today." The critic for the New York *Times* considered him to be the best Otello since Martinelli and commented: "His voice is as full as ever, but it is now used with finesse and style, and he produced his big sound without blasting. He is a burly, powerful Otello: powerful vocally and dramatically. He works up to convincing rages without hamming it up, and he handled the death scene with dignity." The *New Yorker* noted that his performance as Otello was "the sensation of the season."

After appearing as Manrico at the Salzburg Festival during the summer of 1964, McCracken returned to the San Francisco Opera that fall as Gherman in Tchaikovsky's *The Queen of Spades,* Amonasro in *Aida* (with his wife in the title role), and Samson. In 1964 he opened the new season in San Francisco as Otello. That year he also opened the seasons of the Zurich Opera and the Vienna State Opera and appeared with both companies during their festival weeks in *Fidelio, Aida, Il Trovatore,* and *La Forza del Destino.* His wife appeared with him in all performances of *Aida.*

In April 1964 McCracken was called to London to make an unexpected debut at Covent Garden. Del Monaco, scheduled to sing Otello there, had been in a car crash and could not appear. With only one day's notice, he became Del Monaco's replacement. "I would not have dared such a debut except that he [Solti] was musical director there. He thought I could do it, and we had just done it in New York. Luckily this impromptu debut was a triumph."

In the ensuing decade McCracken added to his already impressive reputation at the Metropolitan with highly successful appearances as Canio in *I Pagliacci,* Manrico in *Il Trovatore,* Samson in *Samson and Delilah,* Gherman in *The*

Queen of Spades, Don José in *Carmen,* Radames in *Aida,* Don Alvaro in *La Forza del Destino,* Calaf in *Turandot,* Florestan in *Fidelio* and, on January 17, 1977, John of Leyden in the first revival of *Le Prophète* at the Metropolitan Opera since 1928. His first appearance as a *Heldentenor* took place on December 22, 1977, in the role of Tannhäuser.

He made debuts in Lisbon and Israel in the spring of 1965. On April 27, 1965, he appeared with Birgit Nilsson in *Turandot* at the Hamburg Festival. His first appearance at the Berlin Deutsche Oper took place in 1966. In 1967 he helped to open the season of the Seattle Opera. Then in 1969 in Spain he appeared for the first time with the Barcelona Opera in *Carmen* and *Samson and Delilah,* in both instances opposite his wife.

He has been heard in recitals and as a guest artist with symphony orchestras as well as in opera and has performed at festivals in Salzburg, Austria; Aldeburgh, England; Athens; Edinburgh; and Hamburg.

Since 1965, when his recording of *Fidelio* in which he costarred with Birgit Nilsson was released, McCracken has made numerous operatic recordings. Reviewing his debut on disks in a major role (Florestan), Martin Mayer said in *Esquire:* "I think this the greatest performance of Beethoven's opera ever put on records, and magnificently sung, especially by Nilsson and McCracken. McCracken's explosive performance of his aria is the most overwhelming I have ever heard. It is, incidentally, McCracken's recording debut in a major role. What a way to enter!" His subsequent recording of *Otello* received the Grand Prix du Disque in Paris.

McCracken is a man of commanding presence —a huge and burly individual with brawny frame and leonine head. He stands six feet tall. His fifty-seven-inch chest is ten and a half inches greater than that of any heavyweight boxing champion. He keeps fit by maintaining a regular daily physical program that includes calisthenics and swimming. With his wife and their two children, he resides in Dübendorf, a suburb of Zurich, Switzerland, in a modest seven-room house they acquired when first they were hired by the Zurich Opera. McCracken converted an air-raid shelter into a studio and one of his garages into a storehouse for his costumes. When in New York, the McCrackens occupy a hotel suite.

He has received the Whitbread Award from Covent Garden and an honorary doctorate in music from Indiana University in Bloomington.

ABOUT: McCracken, J. and Warfield, S. A Star in the Family. *Periodicals*—Horizon, January 1978; Musical America, May 1963; New York Times, February 6, 1977; People, November 11, 1977.

Cornell MacNeil

1922–

CORNELL MAC NEIL

Cornell Hill MacNeil, baritone, was born in Minneapolis, Minnesota, on September 24, 1922. He was the youngest of three sons of Walter Hill MacNeil, a dentist, and Harriet Cornell MacNeil, a singer. In his early years Cornell had three prime interests: acting, mechanics, and singing. "I can't remember when I didn't sing," he once told an interviewer. "It was always assumed that I was going to be a singer or an actor." While attending public school, he appeared as a child actor on a radio program in St. Paul. As a high school senior he won an Apollo Club award as male vocalist and then spent a year on vocal studies. However, believing that music offered little security, he enrolled in a government training-school to learn mechanics. After graduation he worked in Connecticut as a machinist in a shop in Bridgeport, and later at the Pratt-Whitney Engine Works in Hartford. While thus employed he also made a number of appearances as an actor with local theatrical groups and over the radio.

In 1943 he won a scholarship to the Julius Hartt School of Music in Hartford where he studied voice with Friedrich Schorr. At the conclusion of these studies, he became a member in 1945 of the glee club at the Radio City Music Hall in New York and worked during the summers with stock companies, including the Paper Mill Playhouse in Millburn, New Jersey.

On January 21, 1947, he appeared on Broadway in a minor role in a revival of Victor Herbert's *Sweethearts.* Another member of this company was Margaret Gavan. A romance developed and they were married on August 24 of the same year.

While in New York he undertook vocal studies with Virgilio Lazzari, Dick Marzollo, and Otto Guth.

On March 1, 1950, he made his debut in opera in Philadelphia, creating the role of John Sorel in the world premiere of Menotti's opera *The Consul,* before it arrived on Broadway (March 15). Menotti later convinced MacNeil that he had a promising future in opera and prevailed upon him to leave the stage and devote himself to serious music study. To support himself and his family, MacNeil worked at night at the Bulova Watch Company manufacturing rocket fuses for the Korean War. He spent his days on vocal exercises and on learning the operatic repertory. In 1953 he decided to gamble on his musical future. Abandoning his job, which was paying him two hundred dollars a week, he auditioned for and was accepted by the New York City Opera. He made his debut in 1953 as the elder Germont in *La Traviata,* and for the next three years he continued to sing principal baritone roles with that company.

On October 14, 1955, he made a successful debut with the San Francisco Opera as the Herald in *Lohengrin.* Later the same season he sang the roles of Valentin in *Faust* and Escamillo in *Carmen.* Other debuts took place in Central City, Colorado, Chicago, Caracas, and Mexico City.

On March 5, 1959, he was acclaimed as Don Carlos in *Ernani* at La Scala in Milan when he replaced an indisposed singer. "MacNeil is the most promising United States baritone to frisk the operatic pea patch since George London," reported a correspondent for *Time.* "In his La Scala debut he was in typically impressive form. His rich, flexible baritone soared and swelled with enormous power. His acting had about it a quality that moved the house to bravos."

Only two and a half weeks later MacNeil made his bow at the Metropolitan Opera on March 21, 1959, in the title role of *Rigoletto,* which he took over for Leonard Warren who had fallen ill. Though he sang without any rehearsals his success was outstanding. "Mr. MacNeil," commented Eric Salzman in the New York *Times,* "came through superbly. When he cut loose, the rafters trembled. But he did not forget to sing softly and lyrically." The following season, as principal baritone of the Metropolitan Opera, he scored as Tonio in *I Pagliacci,* Scarpia in *Tosca,* Germont in *La Traviata,* and Amonasro in *Aida.*

On October 24, 1960, he opened the new season of the Metropolitan Opera with the title role in Verdi's *Nabucco.* Writing in the *Herald Tribune,* Paul Henry Lang said: "Cornell MacNeil . . . is clearly on the way to stardom." In 1973, he once again opened the Metropolitan Opera season, this time in *Il Trovatore,* and the following March he was highly praised for his performance as Guido di Monforte in the first Metropolitan Opera production of Verdi's *I Vespri Siciliani.*

Another of MacNeil's distinguished roles is that of Falstaff in Verdi's opera, in which he was heard for the first time anywhere on March 10, 1975, at the Metropolitan Opera; this was a revival of the 1964 production designed and directed by Franco Zeffirelli. In this characterization, said Harriet Johnson in the New York *Post,* he was "lusty and lustful. And with all the rowdy humor he managed a cowlike reticence, both in his wide eyes and in his approach to those two delectable ladies, Mistress Ford and Mistress Page, that made him believable as a rueful philosopher of sorts." The other roles in which MacNeil distinguished himself at the Metropolitan Opera were Renato in *Un Ballo in Maschera,* Macbeth in Verdi's opera of the same name, Iago in *Otello,* the title roles in *Simon Boccanegra* and *Gianni Schicchi,* Barnaba in *La Gioconda,* Michele in *Il Tabarro,* the Dutchman in *The Flying Dutchman,* Don Carlo in *Ernani,* Gérard in *Andrea Chénier,* Miller in *Luisa Miller,* Marcello in *La Bohème,* and Don Carlo in *La Forza del Destino.* He became universally recognized as one of the world's great interpreters of Verdi baritone roles, a worthy successor to Leonard Warren.

In addition to his successful performances at the Metropolitan Opera, MacNeil has been heard with companies throughout the United States and abroad—at La Scala in Milan, Covent Garden in London, Teatro Colón in Buenos Aires, the Vienna State Opera, the Paris Opéra, and in opera houses in many Italian cities besides Milan. He became the center of storm and controversy, and of legal action, following his appearance in 1964 in *Un Ballo in Maschera* at the Regio Theater in Parma. Infuriated at the hostile reaction of the audience to the soprano, he shouted at it: "You idiots, enough!" He then stormed off the stage and left the theater without completing the performance. The dispute ended up in the Parma court which found all parties guilty (MacNeil, the management, and the audience) and which ordered MacNeil to return to the management half of his fee.

With his first wife, Margaret, MacNeil has had five children. MacNeil's second wife, Tania, whom he married in April 1973, is a violinist. They have homes in New York and in Rome. His diversions include carpentry and, occasionally, cooking gourmet meals. Beginning in 1969 MacNeil served as president of the American Guild of Musical Artists (AGMA).

ABOUT: Opera News, December 14, 1968, April 5, 1975.

Jean Madeira

1924–1972

Jean Madeira (originally Jean Browning), contralto, was born in Centralia, Illinois, on November 14, 1924. Her father, Lee Roy Browning, who was half English and half American Indian, was a coal miner; her mother, Norma Jane Eubanks Browning, who was of English-Irish extraction, taught the piano. When she was five, Jean was given piano lessons by her mother. When her father died in 1932, the family moved to St. Louis. There, Jean, whose early interest in music had been stimulated by her mother, studied the piano for five years on a scholarship at the Leo C. Miller Music School. Winning a piano competition entitled her to appear with the St. Louis Symphony in 1936 in a performance of Beethoven's Piano Concerto No.3.

JEAN MADEIRA

With the one hundred dollars she had saved from her earnings as a piano teacher, Jean went to New York in 1941 and entered the Juilliard School of Music for further study of the piano. She fell in love with another piano student, Francis King Madeira, whom she married on June 17, 1947. "My career began," she has said, "the moment I changed my name." (Francis Madeira subsequently became the conductor of the Rhode Island Philharmonic and professor of music at Brown University.)

At the suggestion of her piano teacher, Olga Samaroff, Jean decided to concentrate on her voice rather than the piano. While involved in vocal studies she began making a number of appearances in contralto roles with the Chautauqua Opera between 1943 and 1947. In 1947 she received the Woman of Achievement Award in St. Louis. In 1947–1948 she was a member of the San Carlo Opera, and in 1948 she appeared in a performance of Menotti's *The Medium* in London.

On December 2, 1948, Madeira made her debut at the Metropolitan Opera as the First Norn in *Die Götterdämmerung*. For the remainder of that season she was called upon to fill minor roles, but during 1949–1950 she began singing the more demanding roles of Suzuki in *Madama Butterfly* and Maddalena in *Rigoletto*. By the early 1950s she had become principal contralto.

She made her debut at the Vienna State Opera on September 18, 1955, in the title role of *Carmen*. Her performance brought her forty-five

curtain calls. Police had to escort her through the crowds outside the opera house. The next day the Viennese critics were exultant. "Vienna has a new darling," reported the *Bild-Telegraf,* adding that she was the finest Carmen ever heard in Vienna.

Carmen became her most celebrated role. She was the only American ever to sing it at the Aix-en-Provence Festival, where she was heard in 1957, and she made a highly successful debut as Carmen in Spain. When she sang the part at the Metropolitan Opera on March 17, 1956, Irving Kolodin, writing in the *Saturday Review,* called her "an intelligent artist who gives close thought to what she undertakes." He continued: "Miss Madeira had prepared herself thoroughly in the dramatic as well as musical aspects of the part, utilizing her height to advantage, also a mass of dark hair that framed her face effectively. Everything had been closely worked out to a plan and found her 'doing something' almost all the time. Mostly it was done with a suggestion of youthful suppleness not often seen."

Madeira remained with the Metropolitan Opera until 1971. Her last appearance there was as Klytemnestra in *Elektra.* During her Metropolitan Opera years she was heard in 42 roles in 294 performances in New York and 83 on tour. The principal ones (in addition to Suzuki, Maddalena, Carmen, and Klytemnestra) were Amneris in *Aida,* Erda in *Das Rheingold* and *Siegfried,* Azucena in *Il Trovatore,* Lola in *Cavalleria Rusticana,* Magdalene in *Die Meistersinger,* La Cieca in *La Gioconda,* Preziosilla in *La Forza del Destino,* Ulrica in *Un Ballo in Maschera,* Waltraute in *Die Götterdämmerung,* Fricka in *Die Walküre,* Herodias in *Salome,* Madelon in *Andrea Chénier,* Orlovsky in *Die Fledermaus,* the Countess in Tchaikovsky's *The Queen of Spades,* and Mrs. Sedley in Britten's *Peter Grimes.*

She was also heard in most of the world's operatic theaters including the Paris Opéra, Covent Garden in London, the Deutsche Oper in Berlin, Teatro Colón in Buenos Aires, Théâtre de la Monnaie in Brussels, the Stockholm Royal Opera, the Munich Opera, and La Scala in Milan. In addition to the roles already mentioned she was heard as Delilah in *Samson and Delilah,* Countess Geschwitz in Berg's *Lulu* and Orfeo in Gluck's *Orfeo ed Euridice.* She created the roles of Circe and Melantho in the world premiere of Luigi Dallapiccola's *Ulisse* at the Deutsche Oper

Mahler

in Berlin on September 29, 1968, repeating these roles at La Scala when this opera received its Italian premiere in 1969. She also performed in the world's concert halls and over television in the United States.

She appeared in several of Europe's festivals, including those at Salzburg in Austria (where she was first heard in 1957), Bayreuth (from 1956 to 1958), and Munich (from 1962 to 1964). In 1958 she performed at the World's Fair in Brussels. On September 29, 1962, she assisted in the opening-week festivities at the Lincoln Center for the Performing Arts by appearing in the American premiere of Manuel de Falla's *L'Atlántida,* in a concert performance by the company of the Metropolitan Opera with Ernest Ansermet conducting.

Stricken with cancer, Jean Madeira suffered for several years and died at the Jane Brown Hospital in Providence, Rhode Island, on July 11, 1972. Her home for many years was at Warwick Neck on Narragansett Bay in Rhode Island. Cooking, swimming, canoeing, sewing, and making hats were her favorite avocations. In 1959 she was awarded an honorary master of arts degree by Brown University in Providence.

ABOUT: Musical America, December 1, 1959.

Gustav Mahler

1860–1911

That Mahler was a composer of towering significance in the German and Austrian post-Romantic movement at the end of the nineteenth century and in the first decade of the twentieth was perceived only after his death. In his lifetime he was a world-famous conductor, a sublime interpreter of a widely varied literature. But the hostility that greeted his own music caused him much pain. To meet his family obligations he constantly drove himself, in his operatic and concert work, beyond the limits of his physical endurance, hoping to gain financial independence and free his time for symphonic creation. He succeeded only in dooming himself to an early death; it was his two most devoted disciples, Willem Mengelberg and Bruno Walter, who carried his symphonic message and slowly won recognition for its greatness.

Mahler: mä′ lēr

GUSTAV MAHLER

Born in the rural Bohemian town of Kalischt, near Iglau (Jihlava), on July 7, 1860, he was the second of fourteen children (most of whom died at an early age) of Bernhard and Marie Mahler. When Gustav was born, his father owned a tavern, a distillery, and a bakery. Early in life Gustav showed signs of musical precocity. He could hum tunes before he walked, and he repeated local folk songs and peasant tunes after a first hearing. Futhermore he found endless delight in listening to the military music of the infantry regiment band in Iglau. When at three he received an accordion, he was soon able to play his favorite tunes and military marches. At six, in the attic of his grandmother's house he came upon a piano for the first time and started to play without instruction. As a parochial choirboy in Iglau, he early came to know some of the choral masterworks of Haydn, Mozart, Beethoven, and Rossini.

Piano lessons began for him when he was five and were later supplemented with the study of harmony and theory. When he was six he performed in public—a special device had to be attached to the pedals so that his legs could reach them. His appetite for music was "insatiable," as he later said. He eagerly absorbed the operas he heard in the Iglau theater. As he recalled: "Every week I came back from the library ... with a brief case full of symphonies, opera arrangements and salon pieces. All of them filled me with indescribable joy, though I was unable to say which I preferred: at that time I was peculiarly and utterly devoid of judgment.

My imagination undoubtedly filled the most junky pieces with all sorts of imaginary beauty, transforming them and perfecting them in my mind." At this time he also began to write music of his own. He was six when he put down on paper his first piece: *Polka With Introductory Funeral March,* for piano. Not long after that he composed his first *Lied,* "Die Türken," to a poem by Lessing. By the time he was fifteen he had amassed such a huge library of original compositions that upon entering the Vienna Conservatory that year he was exempted from examinations in harmony and counterpoint.

In addition to music the reading of books (which early in life had become a passion) and frequent, prolonged excursions into daydreaming were welcome escapes from an unpleasant home. There sickness was a frequent visitor; two of his brothers died before he was six. His parents were always quarreling, and his mother was in an almost perpetual state of suffering. His father made the situation even more unbearable with his dictatorial behavior.

Though his father hoped that Gustav would someday enter the world of commerce and help him out in his own business ventures, he was sympathetic to, and cooperative with, the boy's drift to music. However, he wanted Gustav to complete his academic education at the Iglau Gymnasium before deciding whether or not to become a professional musician. Gustav Schwarz, an administrator of several estates near Iglau, who was convinced of the boy's unusual musical talent, persuaded Bernhard Mahler to send him to Vienna for comprehensive musical training at the conservatory. He agreed, on condition that Julius Epstein of the Vienna Conservatory pass judgment on Gustav's abilities. In the fall of 1875 he took Gustav to Vienna and had him perform for Epstein who listened for only a few moments before announcing solemnly: "Herr Mahler, your son is a born musician."

For three years, from 1875 to 1878, Mahler attended the Vienna Conservatory, a student of Julius Epstein (piano), Robert Fuchs (harmony), and Franz Krenn (composition). In 1877 and 1878 he also attended the university for the study of history, philology, and philosophy. At a public concert by Conservatory students on October 20, 1877, Mahler performed Scharwenka's Piano Concerto No.1, which had received its world premiere two and a half years earlier.

And on July 2, 1878, he was given first prize in composition for a scherzo for piano and string quartet.

Upon graduation from the Conservatory, Mahler spent the next two years (up to 1880) writing music, supported by a small allowance sent him by his father and the money he was able to earn by giving piano lessons. One of his pupils was Josefa Poisl, with whom he fell in love. He behaved with the anguished and emotional upheavals of a true Romantic until Josefa's father put a permanent stop to their continuing relationship. Mahler found outlet for his frustration and despair in writing poems and music and launching his career as conductor.

His conducting career began in the summer of 1880 when Mahler was engaged to conduct operettas at Bad Hall, a small spa in Upper Austria. One year later he became principal conductor at the Provincial Theater in Laibach (now Ljubljana). There he was required to conduct a repertory of about a dozen operas, fifteen operettas, and various plays with incidental music. The resources available to Mahler in Laibach were limited. Yet he was able to direct such masterworks as *The Magic Flute, Der Freischütz, The Barber of Seville,* and *Il Trovatore.*

He expanded his repertory and extended his conducting experience in two other minor opera houses: Olmütz in 1883, and Kassel from 1883 to 1885. In 1885 he acquired the first post in which the musical forces at his command and the repertory were commensurate with his flowering talents. He became conductor at the Prague Opera, managed by Angelo Neumann. For his opening program on August 2, 1885, he conducted his first Wagner opera, *Lohengrin.* When Anton Seidl, the principal Wagner conductor of the Prague Opera, resigned, the entire major Wagner repertory was entrusted to Mahler. In these presentations and in Gluck's *Iphigénie en Aulide,* in *Don Giovanni* and in *Fidelio,* he proved himself a performer of penetrating musical intellect and uncommon interpretative powers. It was during his performance of *Fidelio* that Mahler adopted a practice which has since become standard procedure in many other opera houses: interpolating the *Leonore* Overture No.3 between the scenes of Act II and performing the *Fidelio Overture* before Act I.

From Prague, Mahler went to the Leipzig Opera, in 1886, as assistant to Arthur Nikisch. The rivalry that soon developed between Mahler and Nikisch was promoted by local critics who took every opportunity to deprecate Mahler's performances in order to praise Nikisch more. But when Nikisch fell suddenly ill and Mahler had to take over he did so triumphantly. Adolf Bernard Vogel, music critic for the Leipzig *Nachrichten,* called Mahler "one of the greatest conductors of the world." The premiere in Leipzig of *Siegfried* under Mahler, on May 13, 1887, drew a ten-minute ovation and unanimous approval by the critics. "I have clearly risen in the public esteem," Mahler informed his parents, "and they often call me by name at the close of the performances."

Mahler left Leipzig in 1888. As Henry Louis de La Grange wrote in *Mahler,* the two years in Leipzig "established Mahler's career and reputation more firmly than all his previous engagements; not only had Mahler acquired the technique and the rank of virtuoso conductor by competing with Nikisch on his own ground, but he had attracted the attention of the German musical world, and even of certain foreign countries."

An even more important assignment awaited Mahler in 1888, that of music director of the Budapest Opera, one of Europe's major opera companies. Now in full authority, Mahler was able during his three years in Budapest not only to maintain the lofty standards of performances in Budapest but even to elevate them to a new summit. "Such a *Don Giovanni* performance as has been heard in Budapest," said Brahms, "is not to be heard in Vienna."

At this time he was also making progress as a composer. In Kassel in 1885 he completed the *Lieder eines Fahrenden Gesellen,* written while he was once again suffering the torments of a frustrated love affair, this time with a young woman named Johanna Richter. In Budapest Mahler wrote his first symphony, the world premiere of which he conducted in that city on November 20, 1889.

After six years, 1891-1897, as principal conductor of the Hamburg Opera—the period in which he completed the writing of his second *(Resurrection)* and third symphonies—Mahler assumed in 1897 the music directorship of the Vienna Royal Opera, where he made his debut on May 7, 1897, in *Lohengrin.* Max Kalbeck, the Austrian musicologist and critic, placed Mahler among "the elect" in his review in the *Neues*

Wiener Tageblatt. In the *Fremdenblatt,* Ludwig Speidel described Mahler's performances as "full of energy and noble understanding" and noted that Mahler's gestures "characterize and embody the spiritual contents of the work." Richard Heuberger in the *Neue Freie Presse* reported that "Mahler is not only extremely self-assured and full of temperament, he is an excellent dramatic conductor and has a sense of the theater."

He was given a free hand in the administration of the opera company, and he used that hand to the utmost. His idealism would accept no compromise: The Wagnerian music dramas had to be given without any cuts. The claque had to be banished from the opera house. Latecomers were not allowed to take their seats until the end of the act. The slightest whisper caused him to turn around and glare fiercely at the audience.

Some inner demonic force drove him to try to achieve the highest possible artistic excellence. Under him the Vienna Royal Opera knew its golden age. His relentless pursuit of artistic perfection made him a despot with everybody who worked with him, but if he did not spare others he was assuredly most unsparing of himself. He hurled all of his Herculean energy and indomitable will and every ounce of physical and mental strength he could summon into the preparation of each and every performance as if it were for him a life-and-death struggle. He demanded a double cast for every opera he performed to be assured that the illness of a singer would not bring about a necessary compromise in the quality of the performance. His rehearsals were long and demanding. He was equally fastidious about every detail of the stage production—scenery, costuming, staging, acting, diction, no detail of which escaped his vigilant attention. Incompetents were dismissed to make room for the best available musicians. The masterworks, performances of which had become bogged down in a rut of mediocrity before his arrival, had to be completely restudied, and the repertory of the Vienna Royal Opera had to be expanded. Familiar masterworks emerged reborn under his direction, and unfamiliar or new works were given the same meticulous attention he brought to masterworks.

Describing Mahler's conducting, Max Graf, Viennese musicologist, wrote: "He would let his baton shoot forward suddenly, like the tongue of a poisonous serpent. With his right hand, he seemed to pull music out of the orchestra as out of the bottom of a chest of drawers. He would let his stinging glance loose on a musician who was seated far away from him and the man would quail." Guido Adler, another Viennese musicologist, noted: "When he was recreating a work of art, he exerted an irresistible power of suggestion on those who labored with him, those he led, his companions; he magnetized them to his conceptions. ... At rehearsals you could watch how the terrain was taken step by step, how he kept his eye on the cohesion of the whole, even during the punctilious polishing of the most minute detail. ... The instant he raised his baton they [the musicians] yielded to the fascination of his glance, surrendered themselves to his will. His face spoke earnestness and holy zeal; the flashing eyes cast forth light; at mystic passages they gaze dreamily before them. ... Mahler's conducting grew more and more spiritual, and his will communicated itself like an electrical discharge, remaining invisible to the observer's eye."

He was incomparable in the music of Mozart and Wagner and in Beethoven's *Fidelio,* but he was also a sublime interpreter of a varied literature that embraced Verdi, Tchaikovsky, Lortzing, Meyerbeer, Smetana, Weber, Nicolai, and Offenbach. He freshened the repertory with rarely heard novelties: Anton Rubinstein's *The Demon,* Haydn's *Der Apotheker,* Bizet's *Djamileh,* Richard Strauss's *Feuersnot,* Mozart's *Zaïde,* and Tchaikovsky's *Iolanthe.* He introduced to Vienna *The Bartered Bride, Manon, Werther,* Mascagni's *L'Amico Fritz, Louise,* and *Hansel and Gretel* among other operas.

When he could free himself from the all-demanding duties of the opera house, usually in the summertime, he was at his desk creating musical monuments of his own. But Viennese critics proved far less appreciative of the composer of the symphonies and the monumental works for voice and orchestra than they were of the general music director of the Royal Opera. The hostility that greeted Mahler's music when he conducted it caused Mahler no end of anguish.

Other serious problems beset Mahler. On March 10, 1902, he married Alma Maria Schindler, the beautiful daughter of a Viennese painter. In 1906 their daughter, born in 1903, died of scarlet fever. With Mahler, this tragedy was intensified by an overwhelming sense of guilt. In 1903 he had written a set of elegies for dead children, the *Kindertotenlieder,* and he believed that by writing these elegies he had tempted fate into robbing him of his beloved child. Added to all this, he was not well—unmistakable signs of a heart ailment were revealed not long after his daughter's death. His physicians advised him to spare his energies, but Mahler ignored their advice and defied his own physical limitations by redoubling his efforts both as conductor and as composer now that he felt he might not have long to live.

Within the opera house he was also beset by problems. Cabals and intrigues were instigated against him by his fellow workers who resented his tyrannical ways, had been victimized by his barbed criticisms, were outraged by his continual flouting of tradition, were antagonized by his arrogance, or would not forget that he had been born a Jew (though early in life he was converted to Christianity). They all joined forces to impede him in every way they could. He was also in continual conflict with the opera authorities who resented his enormous expenditures for new productions and his insistence on introducing new and unfamiliar operas. He often referred to the maneuvers of his enemies at the opera house as "a revolt of mediocrities," but in time the revolt succeeded in overthrowing his regime. By 1907 he felt unable to operate at the Vienna Royal Opera as his conscience dictated and he sent in his resignation. "I must keep to the heights," he told his friends. "I cannot let anything irritate me or drag me down." On October 15, 1907, he conducted his last performance in Vienna—*Fidelio.*

Invited to the United States to serve as principal conductor of German operas at the Metropolitan Opera, he made his debut on January 1, 1908, with *Tristan and Isolde.* "The influence of the new conductor was felt and heard in the whole spirit of the performance," wrote Richard Aldrich in the New York *Times.* "The score was revealed in all its complex beauty, with its strands of interwoven melody always clearly disposed and united with an exquisite sense of proportion and an unerring sense of the larger values. Delicacy and clearness were the characteristics of many passages, yet the climaxes were made superbly effectual. Through it all went the pulse of dramatic passion and the sense of fine musical beauty." On January 23 he conducted *Don Giovanni,* and on March 20 *Fidelio,* bringing to them an illumination that these operas had rarely if ever previously known in New York.

Mahler's stay at the Metropolitan Opera lasted just two seasons. In addition to the operas mentioned above he conducted *The Marriage of Figaro, Die Walküre, Siegfried, The Bartered Bride,* and Tchaikovsky's *Pique-Dame.* The last two operas were receiving their American premieres: *The Bartered Bride* on February 9, 1909, and *Pique-Dame* on March 5, 1910.

While still with the Metropolitan Opera, Mahler took over the music direction of the New York Philharmonic Orchestra, becoming the first conductor of that organization to have complete and final say in its artistic administration. Of the one hundred men, two thirds were newcomers who were replacements by Mahler for incompetents. Mahler abandoned the cooperative form of management under which the orchestra had been operating for sixty-seven years to provide the musicians with a regular annual income so that they could devote all their time to the Philharmonic. He discarded the policy of performing exclusively in Manhattan, taking the orchestra to Brooklyn, New York, and to Philadelphia, Boston, and other American cities. He instituted long, compulsory rehearsals and he continually sparked his programs with unfamiliar fare, including some of his own symphonies. In New York, as in Vienna, he made enemies, particularly among some of the directors of the orchestra who insisted he popularize the programs and reduce the budget.

It was not long before the dissensions and conflicts in New York drained his spirit. This, combined with overwork, damaged his ailing heart beyond repair.

His last appearance on any podium took place with the New York Philharmonic on February 21, 1911. He collapsed soon after that and had to be taken to Paris. Afterwards he entered a nursing home in Vienna. There he died on May 18, 1911. Just before he died, he moved his finger as if it were a baton directing a performance. His last word was "Mozart."

His last compositions were performed posthumously: *Das Lied von der Erde* in Munich on November 20, 1911, and the Symphony No.9 in Vienna on June 26, 1912. A half year before his death, Mahler had experienced his greatest triumph as a composer when he himself directed the highly successful premiere of his monumental Symphony No.8 *(Symphony of a Thousand)* in Munich on September 12, 1910.

His facial features gave a clue to his fanatical will and moral strength: the blazing eyes, the square jaw, the tense facial muscles. Wiry and slender, he was of medium height. "He was demonic, neurotic, demanding, selfish, noble, emotionally undisciplined, sarcastic, unpleasant and a genius," wrote Harold C. Schonberg in *The Great Conductors.* "His actions throughout his life strongly suggest those of a manic-depressive. Periods of gloom and silence alternated with periods of violence and vehemence. . . . His complicated inner life was a tortured one in which his Judaism fought with Christianity, and in which a large measure of a strange form of pantheistic mysticism contended with both."

After Mahler's death, Alma Mahler married the novelist Franz Werfel, and later the architect Walter Adolf Gropius.

ABOUT: Adler, G. Mahler; Blaukopf, K. ed. Mahler: A Documentary Study; Cardus, N. Gustav Mahler: His Mind and Music; Gartenberg, E. Mahler: The Man and His Music; La Grange, H. L. de. Mahler; Mahler, A. Gustav Mahler; Mahler, G. Memories and Letters; Walter, B. Gustav Mahler; Wiesemann, S. ed. Gustav Mahler in Vienna.

René Maison

1895–1962

René Maison, tenor, was born in Frameries, Belgium, on November 24, 1895. As a boy he sang in the town church choir. When the German army invaded Belgium during World War I, it recruited young Maison to sing for the sick and wounded and to participate in services for the dead.

After preliminary studies at the Brussels Conservatory, Maison went to Paris to attend the conservatory there. He made his opera debut in 1920 in Geneva as Rodolfo in *La Bohème.* His successes in Geneva and in Nice, France, brought him an engagement with the Monte Carlo Opera in 1922. He also gave recitals throughout Europe and South America before joining the Paris Opéra where he distinguished himself in the Wagnerian repertory and the Opéra-Comique in Paris where he scored a major

Maison: mā zôN′

RENÉ MAISON

success opposite Mary Garden in Alfano's *Resurrection.* Garden thought so highly of him that she induced the managers of the Chicago Civic Opera to place him under contract; Maison was a member of that company from 1927 to 1932.

When the Chicago Civic Opera closed down, Maison appeared in leading European and South American opera houses. He was heard regularly at the Teatro Colón in Buenos Aires from 1934 to 1937. On February 3, 1936, he made his debut at the Metropolitan Opera as Walther in *Die Meistersinger.* The first impression was not a good one; some of the critics felt that his voice was too thin and metallic and that his interpretation of the role of Walther lacked distinction. In the minority was Olin Downes, who wrote in the New York *Times* that Maison had "the routine of the part" and that he possessed "a voice of inherently fine quality." A few days after this debut, on February 6, Maison was heard to far better advantage as Loge in *Das Rheingold.* In the New York *Times* Downes described this performance as "ironical, fantastic, without exaggeration of the gestures and flirting of the red robe, significant in the treatment of the text."

Maison remained with the Metropolitan Opera as principal tenor through 1942–1943. His most distinctive roles there (besides the Wagnerian roles of Walther, Lohengrin, Loge, and Erik in *The Flying Dutchman*) were Des Grieux in *Manon,* Samson in *Samson and Delilah,* Don José in *Carmen,* Florestan in *Fidelio,* Herod in

Salome, Julien in *Louise,* and Admetus in the first Metropolitan Opera presentation of Gluck's *Alceste* on January 24, 1941.

Maison made his debut at Covent Garden in London in June 1936 as Julien. He first appeared with the San Francisco Opera during the season of 1937, making his debut there as Frédéric in *Lakmé* on October 29, and subsequently was heard there as Romeo in *Romeo and Juliet* and as Florestan and Des Grieux.

Upon leaving the Metropolitan Opera in 1943, Maison taught voice in Mexico. He returned to New York in 1945 to join the faculty of the Juilliard School of Music and remained five years. The last five years of his life were spent teaching at the Chalof School of Music in Boston.

Toward the end of his life, Maison became vice-president of the Friends of French Opera in New York. To seek out fresh talent for this company he went to France in 1962. There, for about a month, he was treated for a lung ailment at the Mont-Dore spa. He died there on July 15, 1962.

Maison became an American citizen in 1959. He was twice married, the first time in 1920 to Linette Louth, and the second time, soon after her death in 1958, to Julie Barnard. He lived in Kew Gardens, in Queens, New York, and commuted regularly to Boston to fulfill his teaching duties there.

A huge man of towering presence, six feet three and a half inches in his stocking feet, Maison is believed to have been one of the tallest singers ever to appear on the Metropolitan Opera stage. He had the physique of a wrestler. Despite his athletic build he rarely indulged in strenuous activities. Occasionally he participated in a game of tennis or in fencing, but for the most part he preferred the more sedentary pastimes of playing cards (poker or bridge), going to the movies or the circus, and fishing.

He had a wide range of interests, among which were medicine (which he had studied as a hobby), numismatics, and costuming. In the last-mentioned field he was an authority, particularly in the costumes of the Incas and of the ancient peoples of Egypt and China. He always designed his own costumes for his opera appearances.

Subject to moods, he preferred leading a more or less irregular life, rising and going to sleep, eating and drinking when the desires struck him. His one superstition was his insistence that his wife be with him in his dressing room for good luck before he appeared on the stage.

Maison was the youngest singer to have received the Order of Leopold from the Belgian government.

ABOUT: New York Times, July 17, 1962.

Witold Malcuzynski

1914–1977

Witold Malcuzynski, pianist, who made a specialty of Chopin's music, was born in Warsaw, on August 10, 1914. His family was prominent in social and financial circles in Warsaw; his father, Witold, was a member of the Warsaw Stock Exchange. Intended for law, the young Witold attended two Polish universities. At the same time he studied the piano, devoting all his free time either to making music or listening to it. When he decided upon music as a profession, he entered the Warsaw Conservatory where he studied with Jósef Turczyński. Upon being graduated from the Conservatory with honors in 1936, Malcuzynski gave a private concert arranged by his teacher and attended by Paderewski. Paderewski accepted Malcuzynski as a private pupil; for about a year, he lived with Paderewski at the latter's villa in Switzerland, working with him daily.

In 1937 Malcuzynski entered the Third Chopin Competition in Warsaw, the last held there before World War II. He won third prize among a hundred or so candidates. Another candidate was Colette Gaveau with whom Malcuzynski fell in love and whom he married in October 1939. They settled in Paris in 1939 just before the outbreak of World War II, and in 1940 Malcuzynski made his concert debut there appearing as a guest soloist with the Pasdeloup Orchestra.

During World War II the Malcuzynskis escaped from Nazi-occupied France and went to South America by way of Portugal. For the next two years he concertized extensively throughout South America, where he became a permanent favorite. There Yehudi Menuhin heard him and arranged for him to make his American debut at Carnegie Hall in New York in April 1942. "All the resources of the nineteenth century piano and the superb piano effects written for it are at his command," commented Olin Downes in the

WITOLD MALCUZYNSKI

New York *Times.* Appearances with several major American orchestras confirmed the fine impression Malcuzynski had made at his recital debut.

Before hostilities were terminated in Europe, Malcuzynski returned there aboard a troopship and made appearances in wartime England. When the war ended, he resumed a more active concert life, beginning with recitals and appearances with the London Philharmonic Orchestra, in London in April 1945, followed by an extended European tour. A year later, performing on the piano Chopin had used in London in 1848, he recorded for radio broadcast several concerts which were later relayed in the Polish and French Services of BBC.

Recognized as a Chopin specialist, Malcuzynski was chosen by the Kosciusko Foundation to inaugurate the centenary commemoration of Chopin's death with an all-Chopin recital in Carnegie Hall in February 1949. He was also one of two recitalists chosen to play in Paris on the anniversary day of Chopin's death—October 17—the concert was broadcast over the French radio. He then embarked on his first world tour, still as part of the Chopin commemoration.

From then on, Malcuzynski maintained a rigorous concert schedule in many parts of the music world. In 1949 he traveled fifty thousand miles, performing on four continents; in 1950 he made his first tour of Australia; in 1953 he gave fifty concerts in South America; in 1956 he left for his second world tour. He made numerous transcontinental tours of the United States, fourteen by 1958.

In 1958 he made his first visit to Poland since World War II and was welcomed as a national hero. The thirtieth anniversary of his first appearance in the United States was celebrated with a recital in Carnegie Hall on March 14, 1972. "He has not lost his audience," noted Raymond Ericson in the New York *Times,* "for the place was virtually full."

"If there is anything that the ten fingers of Witold Malcuzynski cannot do on the keyboard it has not yet been written," wrote Robert Bagar in the New York *World-Telegram* after one of Malcuzynski's New York recitals, "for they have the command of the technical situation. They range over the keys with confidence, whether in jet-powered fortes or in the most delicate whispers. . . . The pianist molded and shaped and worked on phrases in such an ingratiating manner that the music, as it unreeled, could hardly have communicated more."

Malcuzynski received the Officer's Cross, Order of Polonia Restituta in 1970, the highest honor that Poland bestows for cultural achievements. In 1959 he was made honorary citizen of Cracow; and the same year, honorary citizen of the State of Texas.

Malcuzynski described himself as "a romantic pianist," explaining, "This is the music I understand and feel." Though he emphasized Chopin's music at his concerts, in his later years he began to feature and to record the works of Bach, Debussy, and Liszt. He confessed he had little sympathy for or understanding of the avant-garde idiom of twentieth century music.

In 1959, Malcuzynski used his influence to restore to Poland art and national treasures that had been smuggled out of the country just before the Nazi invasion in 1939 and been given refuge with Polish and Quebec authorities in Canada.

Malcuzynski was an Argentine citizen, but his home was in Switzerland, at Chernex-sur-Montreux, where he resided with his wife, the pianist Colette Gaveau, and their two daughters. He died in Palma, Majorca, on July 17, 1977. Just before his death he was making preparations to record in Paris all of Chopin's works for solo piano.

ABOUT: Gavoty, B. Witold Malcuzynski.

Catherine Malfitano

1948–

Catherine Malfitano, soprano, was born in New York City on April 18, 1948. Her mother, the former Maria Flynn, was a dancer with the American Ballet Theater; her father, Joseph Malfitano, was a violinist in the Metropolitan Opera orchestra. Her father did not try to teach her vocal technique, preferring to concentrate on styles and song literature. Consequently, until her eighteenth year the only vocal instruction she received was group vocal techniques taught her at the High School of Music and Art. While attending high school she sang in the All-Borough Chorus (later the All-City High School Chorus).

At eighteen she enrolled at the Manhattan School of Music. Up to that time she had been interested solely in becoming a concert singer, but the advice of George Schick, president of the school, and her viewing of the TV motion pictures of *La Forza del Destino* and *The Tales of Hoffmann* persuaded her to consider opera seriously. With the school's Opera Theater she appeared in productions of *The Magic Flute,* Mascagni's *L'Amico Fritz,* Robert Ward's *The Crucible,* and in the role of Manon in Henze's *Boulevard Solitude.* After hearing her sing in *L'Amico Fritz,* Harold C. Schonberg commented in the New York *Times:* "At times, when she let loose, she sounded like a young Albanese."

Dissatisfied with the kind of vocal instruction she was getting at the Manhattan School, she turned to her father for formal training. "He worked with me every day," she says. "He did so an hour, seven days a week, for a year and a half until I began interrupting the sequence by going out of town for engagements. But by then his aim, which was to make me self-sufficient, had been accomplished." Additional training in stage deportment was acquired at the Frank Corsaro and Herbert Berghof studio and in dancing at the Alfredo Corvino and Herbert Berghof studio, both in New York.

Malfitano made her professional opera debut during the summer of 1972 as Nannetta in *Falstaff.* Thomas Pasatieri, a young composer who was on the faculty of the Manhattan School of Music and had been impressed with her performances at the school's Opera Theater, had her

Malfitano

CATHERINE MALFITANO

appear that summer as Berta in the East Coast premiere of his opera *Black Widow*, performed by the Lake George Opera Festival in New York.

She became a resident member of the Minnesota Opera Company in Minneapolis during the 1972–1973 season, assuming such varied parts as Polly Peachum in Kurt Weill's *The Threepenny Opera*, Rosina in *The Barber of Seville*, and Lady with Hand Mirror in Dominick Argento's *Postcard from Morocco*. "We rehearsed six days a week; we worked five weeks on a role; it was marvelous discipline," she has said.

That summer she was also heard at the Santa Fe Opera in New Mexico as Susanna in *The Marriage of Figaro*, at the Lake George Opera Festival as Abigail in *The Crucible*, and at Wolf Trap in Virginia as Annina in Menotti's *The Saint of Bleecker Street*. In reviewing her performance in the Menotti opera, Paul Hume wrote in the Washington *Post* that she "displayed a voice of precisely the right Italianate timbre for the role. Along with her fine full voice, Malfitano has a lovely pianissimo which gave her final scene, culminating in the arioso 'Hold back, O death' all its touching beauty."

Julius Rudel, general manager of the New York City Opera, heard that performance of *The Saint of Bleecker Street* and brought her to the New York City Opera, where she made her debut on September 7, 1974, in *La Bohème*. "The twenty-six-year-old soprano's role was that of Mimi," reported Allen Hughes in the

New York *Times,* "and her lovely voice, poised and flexible, graced the part at every turn. . . . She knew what she was doing and did it authoritatively. . . . Given the present level of her singing and interpretation, one could imagine that Miss Malfitano might just develop into a major artist if she is careful and all goes well." After that she appeared with the New York City Opera in *The Saint of Bleecker Street* (revived for her), and in the more traditional roles of Liù in *Turandot,* Micaëla in *Carmen,* and Gilda in *Rigoletto.*

Her success at the New York City Opera brought her numerous engagements elsewhere. On March 5, 1974, she sang Masha in the world premiere of Pasatieri's *The Seagull* at the Houston Opera. She subsequently returned to the Houston Opera in the title roles of Offenbach's *La Périchole* and Massenet's *Manon,* as Sophie in *Der Rosenkavalier,* and to create the role of Doll in the world premiere of Carlisle Floyd's *Bilby's Doll* on February 27, 1976. Of her performance in *Bilby's Doll* Carl Cunningham wrote in *Musical America:* "Catherine Malfitano had a noteworthy triumph with the treacherous vocal line Floyd writes for Doll Bilby, especially during a long flashback aria recalling her childhood horror at seeing her parents burned as witches on the coast of Brittany." In the spring of 1965 she made her debut at Covent Garden in London as Zerlina in *Don Giovanni.* On October 1, 1976, she created the role of Catherine Sloper in the world premiere of Pasatieri's *Washington Square,* produced by the Michigan Opera Theater. On September 22, 1977, she was heard in a new production of *The Marriage of Figaro* at the New York City Opera; and on November 15, 1977, she sang for the first time anywhere the part of Adina in *L'Elisir d'Amore* with the Opera Society of Washington in Washington, D.C.

In addition to her operatic appearances, Malfitano has been heard in song recitals and as guest artist with symphony orchestras. In April 1973, she joined her father in the Malfitano Duo and inaugurated at Carnegie Hall a new concert series of duets for soprano and violin or piano. This series, called "Three by Three," was the first of several public appearances and recordings.

Malfitano occupies an apartment in Manhattan's upper West Side in a house in which the composer Pasatieri also makes his home. Her place is decorated with an assortment of shawls about which, she confesses, she is "a freak." She received the New York *Daily News* Award in 1966 and the National Opera Institute awards in 1973 and 1974.

ABOUT: High Fidelity/Musical America, July 1975; New York Times, September 1, 1974, September 25, 1974; Opera News, March 8, 1975.

Adriana Maliponte

1942–

Adriana Maliponte, soprano, was born in Brescia, Italy, on December 26, 1942. She started to play the piano when she was five. Four years later, her family moved to Mulhouse in the Alsace region of France where she later attended the local conservatory to study piano and ballet, as well as voice with Suzanne Stappen. "I worked like a devil, busy all the time," she recalls. She made her singing debut with a performance over the radio in Mulhouse when she was fifteen. A year later an aunt who lived at Como arranged for her to audition there with Carmen Melis, prima donna and teacher. After hearing Adriana sing a few numbers, Melis said: "If this girl can't make a career, the theaters may as well shut down." Adriana lived with her grandmother, who also had a home near Como, and went three times a week to Melis's villa to study with her. "Ah," she says, "those were beautiful days."

Adriana made her first appearance on the operatic stage in 1958 at the Teatro Nuovo in Milan as Mimi in *La Bohème*. Shortly afterwards in the same year she won first prize in the International La Scala Competition. This enabled her to study stage deportment at La Scala with Claudio Frigiero. "In Milan," she recalls, "I went to the opera all the time. If Corelli sang ten *Trovatores,* I saw ten *Trovatores.* This gave me a wonderful concept of the theater, an idea of what opera is." She was also given the opportunity to gain stage experience by taking on minor roles in La Scala productions. In 1961 she won the Italian radio's RAI Trofeo Primavera, Rome.

She went to Paris in 1962 to join the Paris Opéra and made her debut there that year as Micaëla in *Carmen.* She was heard in several other roles not only at the Opéra but also at the Opéra-Comique. During her second season in

ADRIANA MALIPONTE

Paris, Menotti selected her to create the role of Sardula in the world premiere of *The Last Savage* at the Opéra-Comique on October 21, 1963. Six years later she sang Micaëla in the provocative and much-publicized production of *Carmen* by Bernard Buffet in Marseilles. In February 1970 she made her debut at La Scala in a principal role, as Manon in Massenet's opera.

When she made her first appearance in the United States it was as Leila in Bizet's *Les Pêcheurs de Perles* with the Philadelphia Lyric Opera in 1963. A Philadelphia critic called her "a consummate artist who sang like an angel." In the ensuing years she was heard in the United States in *La Traviata* in Chicago, *I Puritani* in Hartford (Connecticut), *Faust* in Philadelphia, Cherubini's *Medea* in Kansas City (Missouri), Mimi in Miami (Florida), and Massenet's *Manon* in Cincinnati. On March 19, 1971, she made her debut at the Metropolitan Opera as Mimi. Writing in the New York *Times,* Robert Sherman said: "The Metropolitan has hit the jackpot again. ... The New York debut of Adriana Maliponte was a Mimi to remember." The following season she was also heard as Micaëla (in the new 1972 production of *Carmen* conducted by Leonard Bernstein) and in the title role of *Luisa Miller,* and in subsequent seasons as Pamina in *The Magic Flute,* Juliet in *Romeo and Juliet,* Euridice in Gluck's *Orfeo ed Euridice,* Marguerite in *Faust,* Violetta in *La Traviata,* Amelia in *Simon Boccanegra,* Liù in *Turandot,* and Norina in *Don Pasquale.* Reviewing her first performance as Juliet, Robert Sherman said in the New York *Times:* "Miss Maliponte used her lovely, pure-toned voice to excellent advantage, singing with style, taste, and considerable dramatic impulse." Raymond Ericson noted in the New York *Times,* after her performance in *The Magic Flute,* that she was "a lovely musician and her Mozartean phrasing was exquisite."

She has appeared at Covent Garden in London, the Vienna State Opera, Teatro Colón in Buenos Aires, the Hamburg Opera, the San Carlo in Naples, Teatro la Fenice in Venice and at various European festivals including Glyndebourne and the Festival of Two Worlds at Spoleto. She has also toured in Japan and Australia. In 1973 she received first prize in the International Competition in Geneva. With the Vienna Volksoper she has recorded for RCA Puccini's rarely given first opera, *Le Villi,* and for Deutsche Grammophon the distinguished 1972 Metropolitan Opera production of *Carmen.* Other recordings were awarded the Grand Prix du Disque in 1965 and the Orphée d'Or in 1973.

ABOUT: New York Times, December 10, 1972; Opera News, December 11, 1971.

Vanni Marcoux

1877–1962

Vanni Marcoux (originally Jean-Émile Diogène Vanni-Marcoux), bass baritone, in private life used the name Vanni Marcoux, but professionally he preferred Vanni-Marcoux. He was born in Turin, Italy, on June 12, 1877. At the University of Turin he studied law and took singing lessons with Taverna and Collino. He made his first appearance on the stage as an actor in Turin in 1894. After additional vocal training at the Paris Conservatory with Frédéric Boyer, he made his operatic debut on January 28, 1900, at Bayonne, France, as Friar Laurence in *Romeo and Juliet.* After that he appeared with the Nice Opera as Marcel in its first production of *La Bohème* and with the Théâtre de la Monnaie in Brussels.

At Covent Garden in London he made his first appearance in the world premiere of Leoni's *L'Oracolo* on June 28, 1905, creating the role of Win-Shee. He continued making annual appearances at Covent Garden until 1915. By that time

his reputation as one of the great baritone basses of the age had become firmly established.

He made his debut at the Paris Opéra on January 13, 1909, in another world premiere, Février's *Monna Vanna* where he assumed the role of Guido Colonna. A year later, in Monte Carlo on February 19, 1910, at the personal request of the composer he created what became one of his greatest roles, the title part in Massenet's *Don Quichotte.* In all, he made well over one hundred and fifty appearances in that part in opera houses throughout Europe, and as late as 1947, when he was seventy, at the Opéra-Comique in Paris. On April 25, 1913, he created another Massenet role: Panurge in the opera of the same name at the Théâtre de la Gaîté in Paris.

Marcoux's debut in the United States took place in 1912 with the Boston Opera as Golaud in *Pelléas and Mélisande.* One year later he made his bow with the Chicago Opera as Scarpia opposite Mary Garden's *Tosca.*

When World War I broke out in Europe he returned to France. There he remained during the war years. In 1919 he made appearances at the Teatro Colón in Buenos Aires. Three years later he was heard at La Scala in the title role of *Boris Godunov,* a performance which inspired some critics to compare him favorably with Chaliapin, not only for the power and beauty of his singing but also for the depth and subtlety of his characterization.

He was heard regularly in Europe—at the Monte Carlo Opera, Covent Garden in London, and La Scala in Milan. Between 1926 and 1932 he sang regularly with the Chicago Opera and became an idol of its audiences.

From 1938 to 1943 he taught lyric declamation and stage direction at the Paris Conservatory. Upon his withdrawal from the operatic stage in 1947 he became director of the Bordeaux Opera in France, retaining this post until 1952. In the latter year he returned to Paris to spend the last decade of his life there. He died in Paris on October 21, 1962.

Marcoux boasted one of the most extensive operatic repertories of any baritone bass, comprising some two hundred and fifty roles. He also appeared successfully in films, notably in *The Miracle of the Wolves* (1925) and *Sans Famille* (1935).

Marcoux: mår kōo′

ABOUT: Kutsch, K. J. and Riemens, L. A Concise Biographical Dictionary of Singers.

Igor Markevitch

1912–

Igor Markevitch, conductor, was born in Kiev in the Ukraine on July 27, 1912, the son of Boris and Zoïa Pokitonov Markevitch. When he was a child, his family settled in Vevey, Switzerland. There he attended the academic schools and taught himself music. His talent was discovered by Alfred Cortot who gave him his first systematic musical training. When Igor was fourteen, he was sent to Paris to concentrate on music study. He studied composition with Nadia Boulanger, continuing later with Vittorio Rieti. Sergei Diaghilev, the founder-director of the Ballet Russe de Monte Carlo, was impressed by Igor's early compositions and arranged for the boy to give a piano recital in Paris. "I like his music," Diaghilev is reported to have said, "because I hear in it the quickening of a new generation." He commissioned Igor to write the music for a ballet, *Rebus,* which was not produced because of Diaghilev's death. But other Markevitch compositions attracted attention in Paris and placed him with the more promising young composers of this period. Among these works were the Concerto for Piano and Orchestra and the Concerto Grosso for orchestra, both introduced in 1929, the first in London, the other in Paris. On December 15, 1931, an orchestral suite from *Rebus* was introduced in Paris, and the French musicologist, Henri Prunières, wrote that the date of this premiere was of historic importance. *Icare,* originally composed as music for a ballet for Serge Lifar but never presented as such, added to Markevitch's growing reputation as a composer when it was introduced as a concert work in Paris in 1933. Only twenty-one years old, Igor Markevitch had become a world figure as a composer.

After studying conducting with Hermann Scherchen, Igor at eighteen launched his career as a conductor by appearing with the Concertgebouw Orchestra in Amsterdam. In 1940 he went to Italy to get material for a cantata on Lorenzo de Medici. While he was there, Italy

IGOR MARKEVITCH

became involved in World War II, and Markevitch was forced to remain in Florence for the duration. During the war years he found refuge on Bernhard Berenson's estate in Florence.

In 1944 the occupying Allied forces appointed him conductor of the orchestra of the Florence May Music Festival, a post he retained for two years. During this period his conducting began to attract attention for its vitality and perceptiveness.

After the war he served as guest conductor of major European symphony orchestras and directed special performances of operas in Vienna, London, and Naples. He also made appearances in South America and Israel and at music festivals in Salzburg, Lucerne, Vienna, Holland, and Berlin. In Salzburg, from 1947 to 1954, he taught master classes in conducting at the Mozarteum. He later taught conducting in Mexico from 1955 to 1957 and at Santiago, Chile, in 1966.

Markevitch made his American conducting debut on March 18, 1955, with the Boston Symphony in a program climaxed by Stravinsky's *Le Sacre du Printemps.* On January 4, 1957, he made his debut in New York, with the Symphony of the Air, again performing *Le Sacre du Printemps* together with compositions by Bach and Verdi. On this occasion Howard Taubman said of him in the New York *Times:* "Mr. Markevitch has personality and temperament. On the technical side he knows his business, and he brings a mind and purpose of his own to the music he undertakes. ... Markevitch's appear-

---

Markevitch: mär′ kĕ vĭch

ance is deceptive. He is slight, almost frail, and as he takes his place on the podium, he looks diffident and pallid. But once he turns his back and goes to work, he makes an entirely different impression. He conducts with concentration and energy." Concerning Markevitch's performance of *Le Sacre du Printemps,* Taubman added: "Mr. Markevitch handled its complexities as if they did not exist. This was music for which he clearly has an affinity. Under his guidance the rites of spring were celebrated with a primitive ferocity."

From 1957 to 1959 Markevitch was principal conductor of the Havana Philharmonic Orchestra. He subsequently served as the principal conductor of the Lamoureux Orchestra in Paris from 1959 to 1961; as conductor of the orchestra of Spanish Radio and Television in 1965; as musical director of the Montreal Symphony from 1955 to 1960; and beginning in 1968, as artistic director of the Monte Carlo Opera. In all these offices he distinguished himself particularly in the modern repertory. He has also been named Conductor Emeritus of the Japanese Philharmonic Orchestra.

Among his decorations are those of the Knight of the Legion of Honor and the Commander of Arts and Literature, both from France.

Markevitch was twice married, the first time in March 1936 to Kyra Nijinsky, with whom he had a son, and the second time in July 1946 to Topazia Caetani, with whom he had three more children. The Markevitches have two homes, one in France, at Saint-Cézaire, and the other at Villars-sur-Ollon in Switzerland.

ABOUT: Gavoty, B. Igor Markevitch.

Giovanni Martinelli

1885–1969

Giovanni Martinelli, tenor, sang for thirty-two years at the Metropolitan Opera, the second longest period of active service by any singer with that company. (The longest period, thirty-four years, was served by Giuseppe De Luca.)

Martinelli was born in Montagnana, near Padua, Italy, on October 22, 1885, the oldest son of fourteen children of Antonio and Lucia Bellini Martinelli. For generations his ancestors had

---

Martinelli: mär tē nĕl′ lē

GIOVANNI MARTINELLI

been cabinetmakers. Giovanni's family believed that he too would someday follow the family tradition.

As a child he played the clarinet in the town band. "I was always eager to absorb what musical knowledge I could," he later recalled, "although I never thought of myself as especially gifted. However, I heard all the music possible, attending all traveling opera performances that came to Montagnana."

At twenty Martinelli had to enter military service, as was required of all young Italians. "My ability to play the clarinet was the means of procuring me a life of comparative ease. I applied for membership in the regimental band and was accepted. Bandsmen had the privilege of officers. I was very well off."

One day his bandmaster heard him sing and told him he had "a wonderful voice." "That was all that was necessary to fire me with ambition. The bandmaster and my colonel were good friends. The latter gave me permission to go with the bandmaster to the homes of some of the prominent families of Piedmont to sing and, as they were pleased, I was granted leave to go to Milan for an audition. There I was successful!"

A sponsor was found for him. In spite of the objections of his father, Martinelli signed a contract agreeing to study music in return for financial support. When his military service ended, Martinelli studied voice seriously for the first time with Mandolini.

On December 3, 1910, Martinelli made his concert debut in Milan in a performance of Rossini's *Stabat Mater*. Two weeks later his opera debut took place at the Teatro Dal Verme in Milan in the title role of *Ernani*. "In one of the big arias I forgot the words and was obliged to ad lib. Then in the midst of a dramatic scene, I dropped my sword awkwardly. The audience roared with laughter." When he left the stage that evening he vowed never again to appear in opera, but the reviews the following morning were sufficiently favorable in spite of the mishaps to allow for the restoration of his self-confidence.

Puccini heard him and, though Martinelli had been in the public eye for only about six months and had sung in only three operas, selected him for the leading tenor role of Dick Johnson in the European premiere of *The Girl of the Golden West*. This took place in 1911 at La Scala in Milan, Toscanini conducting, and was the beginning of Martinelli's success. With the publishing house of Ricordi interested in him, Martinelli was soon heard in the principal opera houses of Italy, as well as in Budapest, Monte Carlo, and Brussels. On April 23, 1912, he made a successful debut at Covent Garden in London as Cavaradossi in *Tosca*.

Giulio Gatti-Casazza, general manager of the Metropolitan Opera company, engaged Martinelli for the opera house in 1913. Before going to America, Martinelli married Adele Previtali on August 7, 1913. Upon his arrival in the United States with his young wife, Martinelli learned that the Chicago-Philadelphia Opera Company was in desperate need of a leading tenor to replace one of its own singers for a performance of *Tosca* in Philadelphia. The director appealed to Gatti-Casazza for help and was rewarded with the services of young Martinelli, whose Metropolitan Opera debut was scheduled for later the same month. Thus Martinelli was heard for the first time in America on November 3, 1913, in Philadelphia as Cavaradossi. Then, on November 20, as Rodolfo in *La Bohème*, he finally sang at the Metropolitan Opera. "His voice is of very good quality in the higher range, which he uses naturally and easily," commented Richard Aldrich in the New York *Times*. In the *Tribune* Henry E. Krehbiel described his voice as a "splendid, clear, resonant organ." But both these critics found more deficits than credits in Martinelli's initial performance. However, in subsequent appearances that season as Pinkerton in *Madama Butterfly*, as Cavaradossi, and as

Radames in *Aida*, Martinelli gained the self-assurance and control he needed to allow his beautiful voice, with its soaring top notes, to be heard to best advantage.

Martinelli remained principal tenor of the Metropolitan Opera in the Italian and French repertories for thirty-two seasons. His last operatic appearance at the Metropolitan took place on March 8, 1945, as Pollione in *Norma*, and the last time he was heard on that stage was on March 24, 1946, in a gala benefit performance for American Relief in Italy when he participated in a performance of Act III of *La Bohème*. During those thirty-two years Martinelli appeared in thirty-seven roles (though his repertory embraced fifty-six). He was heard as Lefebvre in the world premiere of Giordano's *Madame Sans-Gêne* (January 25, 1915) and as Fernando in the world premiere of Granados's *Goyescas* (January 28, 1916). He also appeared in the following American premieres: as Paolo in Zandonai's *Francesca da Rimini* (December 22, 1916), as Lensky in *Eugene Onegin* (March 24, 1920), and as Heinrich in Respighi's *The Sunken Bell* (November 24, 1928). He was Huon in the first Metropolitan production of Weber's *Oberon*.

His other Metropolitan Opera roles were: Des Grieux in *Manon Lescaut*, Canio in *I Pagliacci*, Manrico in *Il Trovatore*, Don José in *Carmen*, Raoul in *Les Huguenots*, Riccardo in *Un Ballo in Maschera*, Edgardo in *Lucia di Lammermoor*, Gerald in *Lakmé*, the title role in *Faust*, Avito in *L'Amore dei Tre Re*, Milio in *Zaza*, the title roles in *Don Carlo* and *Ernani*, Don Alvaro in *La Forza del Destino*, Samson in *Samson and Delilah*, Arnold in *William Tell*, Loris in *Fedora*, Eleazar in *La Juive*, Gennaro in *The Jewels of the Madonna*, the title role in *Andrea Chénier*, John of Leyden in *Le Prophète*, Dick Johnson in *The Girl of the Golden West*, Gabriele in *Simon Boccanegra*, Enzo in *La Gioconda*, Vasco da Gama in *L'Africaine*, Pollione in *Norma*, and *Otello*.

His most frequent appearances were made as Radames (92 times in New York, 34 on tour), Don José (59 times in New York, 16 on tour), Canio (45 times in New York, 23 on tour) and Manrico (44 times in New York, 26 on tour). His two favorite roles were Radames and Eleazar.

During his early years at the Metropolitan Opera Martinelli was in competition with Caruso in what was basically Caruso's repertory, and this at a time when Caruso was in his fullest glory. When Caruso left, Martinelli for a short time was in the shadow of Gigli. But from both of these challenges he emerged to become Caruso's legitimate successor as the undisputed monarch of Italian tenors at the Metropolitan Opera.

He kept adding to his repertory even in his advanced years. When he was fifty-one, he sang Otello in Verdi's opera for the first time. In this opera he achieved some of his greatest triumphs, particularly at Covent Garden during the Coronation ceremonies of 1937. He appeared in the role for the first time at the Metropolitan Opera on December 22, 1937. At that time Olin Downes wrote in the New York *Times:* "This stands today as one of the finest impersonations that the Metropolitan stage now knows. It is finished and eloquent in every detail. . . . Mr. Martinelli, by carefully contrived proportion, nuance and thoroughly prepared climax, made every moment of his presence on the stage significant and . . . delivered the great monologue of the third act with such intensity, as of an elemental nature driven with despair, that the audience interrupted the opera with applause."

Still striving to broaden his repertory, Martinelli assumed his first Wagnerian role—the exacting one of Tristan to Kirsten Flagstad's Isolde—on November 24, 1939, with the Chicago Opera. He knew that the music of Wagner was not his forte, but this was a challenge he felt he had to meet.

After leaving the Metropolitan Opera, Martinelli opened a studio in New York City to teach voice and to coach young singers in the operatic repertory. In 1948 he made his last opera appearance anywhere for twenty years when he was heard as Samson opposite Blanche Thebom's Delilah in Saint-Saëns's opera in Philadelphia, the city where he had made his American debut.

When the twenty-fifth anniversary of Martinelli's affiliation with the Metropolitan Opera was commemorated on the evening of March 20, 1938, he himself was heard singing important excerpts from *La Bohème, La Juive,* and *Otello,* while the rest of the program was filled out with performances by other leading members of the company. On the fiftieth anniversary of Martinelli's Metropolitan Opera debut, commemorated on November 20, 1967, Martinelli himself did not appear on the program which,

though devoted to many of the famous arias he had sung on that stage, was taken over by the principal artists of the company in his honor. Guests from two continents were also on hand to do him honor that evening, and a leather-bound gold-stamped album of programs of each of the thirty-seven roles he had sung on that stage was presented to him.

From 1953 to 1956 Martinelli was a member of the opera department of the Benedetto Marcello Conservatory in Venice. For several years after 1956 he headed the voice department and was chief consultant in the opera workshop of the Music School Settlement in downtown New York.

In 1966 Mayor Lindsay of New York appointed Martinelli a trustee of the old Metropolitan Opera House Corporation formed to save the long-time home of the company on Broadway and Fortieth Street from destruction. The building, however, was torn down to make room for a forty-one-story office building.

In 1968, aged eighty-three, Martinelli was invited to deliver a lecture in Seattle, Washington. Glynn Ross, director of the Seattle Opera Association, prevailed on him to make an appearance as the Emperor Altoum in *Turandot* on January 31. This was Martinelli's first return to the opera stage in twenty years. He was so well received that he was induced to give two more performances—his last.

Giovanni Martinelli died at Roosevelt Hospital in New York on February 2, 1969, a victim of a circulatory ailment.

For many years Martinelli spent his winters in a seventeenth-story apartment on West Fifty-seventh Street in New York City and his summers with his two daughters and his grandchildren in a villa near Bergamo, Italy. His last years were lived in the Buckingham Hotel on West Fifty-seventh Street.

He remained almost to the end a tall, robust, spry, and handsome man whose shock of gray hair was like a crown above an attractive Italian face. Good-humored, he liked to laugh and did so frequently. His only form of exercise was to take long walks, and his favorite pastime was to partake of gourmet meals, some of which he sometimes prepared himself. His love of food almost proved the undoing of his career. On the evening of February 25, 1938, he devoured a huge seafood meal just before going on the stage of the Metropolitan Opera for a performance of

Aida. Midway in the aria "Celeste Aida" he collapsed and for one of the few occasions in the history of the Metropolitan Opera the curtain was brought down during a performance; many of the people backstage thought he was dying. But he was suffering from cramps, from which he soon recovered, though Frederick Jagel was required to take on the role for the remainder of the evening.

Martinelli was made Knight Commander of the Order of Merit by the Republic of Italy. As a further expression of the esteem in which he was held, the opera house in Martinelli's native city in Italy was named after him.

ABOUT: New York Times, November 13, 1960, January 9, 1969; Opera News, October 19, 1963.

JEAN MARTINON

Jean Martinon

1910–1976

Jean Martinon, conductor, was born in Lyons, France, on January 10, 1910, the son of Pierre and Jeanne Bidal Martinon. His father was an architect. In the years between 1918 and 1924 Martinon received his academic education at the Lycée du Parc in Lyons. He attended the National Conservatory of Lyons during 1924–1925 for musical training, specializing in the violin. In 1926 he entered the Paris Conservatory on a scholarship; two years later he was graduated with the first prize in violin. His studies at the conservatory included composition with Albert Roussel and conducting with Charles Münch and Roger Désormière. In 1952 he received the master of arts degree from the Sorbonne.

From 1934 to 1939 Martinon actively pursued a career as violinist both as a virtuoso and as a member of several French orchestras. He also began to make his mark as a composer, with the *Sinfonietta,* written in 1935 and successfully introduced in Paris, and his first symphony, in 1936.

During World War II Martinon served in the French army. He was captured in 1940 and for two years confined in a concentration camp, Stalag IX. Out of his experience as a prisoner of war came several compositions which helped place him in the vanguard of promising young French

Martinon: mår tē nôn´

composers. One of these works was *Stalag IX, ou Musique d'Exil,* an orchestral composition utilizing jazz effects; another was the motet *Absolve Domine,* which was dedicated to French musicians who had died in the war; a third was a choral work, *Psalm of the Captives,* or *Psalm 136,* which brought him the Grand Prize of the City of Paris in 1945 by a unanimous vote of the judges after it had been successfully introduced in Paris in 1943 with Charles Münch conducting.

Martinon initiated his career as conductor in the early 1940s in Paris with his own First Symphony when the scheduled conductor found he did not have the time to rehearse it properly. He did so well that soon after that he was invited to appear as guest conductor with several other orchestras. In addition, from 1944 to 1946 he was assistant to Charles Münch with the Société des Concerts du Conservatoire. In 1946 he was made a full-time conductor of the Bordeaux Symphony and in 1949 associate conductor of the London Philharmonic. Between 1951 and 1957 he firmly established himself as one of France's major conductors—and as an outstanding interpreter of the music of Debussy, Ravel, and Roussel—as principal conductor of the Lamoureux Orchestra in Paris. He also made successful tours of Europe, South America, Australia, and the Orient, establishing his reputation internationally.

After serving as music director of the Israel Philharmonic Orchestra in 1958–1959, he was appointed general music director in 1960 of the city of Düsseldorf in Germany. He thus became the first Frenchman ever to hold this post formerly held by Mendelssohn and Schumann. For three years he fulfilled with distinction his functions in Düsseldorf as conductor of symphony concerts and opera. Meanwhile, on March 29, 1957, he made a successful American debut as the guest conductor of the Boston Symphony.

In 1960 he was invited to conduct three weeks of concerts with the Chicago Symphony at its summer home in Ravinia. He returned to the Chicago Symphony in 1962 as guest conductor during its regular winter series. At that time he was acclaimed both as conductor and composer when he performed his own third symphony, the *Hymne à la Vie*.

In October 1963 Martinon was appointed music director of the Chicago Symphony, the seventh to hold this post since the founding of the orchestra in 1891. "Mr. Martinon's command of the forces arrayed before him," wrote Roger Dettmer in *Musical America* in 1963, "bespoke a thoroughness of musicianly preparation buttressed by a conducting method that in fact forbade faulty entry, uncertain release or musical indecision." After the Chicago Symphony made its first New York appearance under Martinon in the spring of 1964, Irving Kolodin reported in *Saturday Review:* "Two evenings in Carnegie Hall with Jean Martinon and the Chicago Symphony clarified a number of things about the new musical order along Lake Michigan. One immediate impression was that, in its sharpness of attack and evenness of blend, its beautifully refined solo wind playing and smooth textured transition from violins to violas to cellos and basses, this remains Reiner's orchestra, perhaps the best as well as the last creation of the life that ended last November. It embodies the flexibility as well as the strength of a master technician's ideal of orchestral culture."

Martinon remained the music director of the Chicago Symphony through the 1967–1968 season. His regime was marked by an interest in twentieth century music, of which Martinon proved himself to be an outstanding exponent. Among the works given their world premieres in Chicago by Martinon were Henze's *Muses of Sicily* (November 2, 1967) and Concerto for Double Bass and Orchestra (November 2, 1967), Ulysses Kay's Symphony (March 28, 1968), his own *Altitudes* (December 30, 1965), Roger Sessions's Symphony No.7 (October 1, 1967), and

Stravinsky's *Variations,* for orchestra (April 17, 1965). Martinon also conducted the American premiere of Carl Ruggles's *Sun Treader* on January 24, 1966.

He was responsible for creating a closer bond between the Chicago Symphony and the University of Chicago by presenting regular series of concerts at the University devoted to twentieth century music.

After leaving Chicago in 1969, Martinon returned to Paris to become music director of the Orchestre National Français with which he toured the United States on several occasions. With this orchestra, he recorded for Angel the complete orchestral music of Ravel in five albums, all the symphonies of Saint-Saëns in three LPs (including the first recordings ever made of Saint-Saëns's Symphonies in A and F), and a complete cycle of Debussy's orchestral music. He also served as principal conductor of the Hague Residentie Orchestra in Holland and led this orchestra in a concert in London in 1975, the orchestra's first appearance in that city in fourteen years.

Martinon made his home in Paris with his second wife, the former Nery Perez whom he married in 1956, and their two sons. In *Musical America,* Roger Dettmer described him as follows: "He has brush-cut, iron-gray hair and kindly eyes under bushy black brows. Away from the stage, Martinon is the polar opposite of conductors who dress in the fashion of a popular singer at a motion-picture premiere. . . . He dresses quietly in dark, durable suits, with black or brown shoes. . . . When he settles comfortably into an armchair and takes out his pipe. . . . Jean Martinon for all the world looks like a prosperous academician." A sportsman, Martinon excelled at skiing, mountain climbing, tennis, and swimming.

To Alan Blyth for an interview in the periodical *Gramophone* of London, Martinon described his philosophy of conducting as follows: "Psychology is important in concerts and recording. Perhaps it's a conductor's first requirement, and each orchestra has to be treated in a different way. Psychology and diplomacy come first—then you can think about music. But no conductor can pretend to get on with every orchestra. It's like love, you know. You cannot force a woman to love you, if she does not want to, and you cannot expect every group of players to respond to you."

Martinon was decorated with the rosette of the Legion of Honor in France in 1957. In 1960 he received the Arts and Letters Award from the Ministère des Beaux-Arts in Paris. In 1967 he became the only Frenchman ever to receive the Mahler medal.

Jean Martinon died in Paris on March 1, 1976, after a prolonged illness.

ABOUT: Machabey, A. Portraits de trente musiciens français. *Periodicals*—Musical America, November 1963.

Margarete Matzenauer

1881–1963

Margarete Matzenauer, soprano, was born in Temesvár (Timisoara), Hungary, on June 1, 1881. Since her father, Ludwig, was the director of the orchestra in the local royal theater, and her mother, Ottilie, was a dramatic soprano in the town's opera house, she grew up in a musical household. Her first ambition, however, was to become an actress. However, when it became apparent she had an exceptional voice, she began her vocal training in Graz with Georgine Neuendorf, continuing later in Berlin with Antonia Mielke and Fritz Emerich.

She made her opera debut as Puck in Weber's *Oberon* in 1901 with the Strasbourg Opera, an appearance that brought her a three-year contract. There she served a valuable apprenticeship before going in 1904 to one of Germany's leading opera companies, the Royal Opera in Munich. She remained there seven years, appearing as a contralto. While achieving fame in the Wagnerian repertory, she also distinguished herself in Italian and French operas. During these years she was invited to make guest appearances with other major European opera houses, including those in Vienna, Paris, and Germany, and in 1911 she made her debut at the Bayreuth Festival as Waltraute, Flosshilde, and the First Norn in the Wagner *Ring* cycle.

Her debut at the Metropolitan Opera took place on November 13, 1911 (opening night of the season), in the contralto role of Amneris in *Aida* in a cast that included Caruso and Destinn, Toscanini conducting. Writing in the *Tribune*,

Matzenauer: mät′ sĕ nou ēr

MARGARETE MATZENAUER

H. E. Krehbiel said she sang the part "with a large and luscious voice, with ample evidences of a fine knowledge of the art of singing, and acted it so as to make it something more than an operatic marionette." He concluded: "There must be cordial praise for her now—there will doubtless be more cordial praise for her when she takes her place in the operas in which she is to the manner born."

She proved her remarkable versatility by appearing that season in ten different roles: in the Wagnerian repertory, which was her specialty, as Brangäne in *Tristan and Isolde;* Fricka in *Das Rheingold;* Fricka, Waltraute, and Brünnhilde in *Die Walküre;* Waltraute and Flosshilde in *Die Götterdämmerung;* Ortrud in *Lohengrin;* Erda in *Siegfried;* and Kundry in *Parsifal.* In addition she assumed the parts of Orfeo in Gluck's *Orfeo ed Euridice,* Hate in Gluck's *Armide,* the Nurse in Dukas's *Ariane et Barbe-Bleue,* and La Cieca in *La Gioconda.* One of the most memorable of these performances was that in *Parsifal* on January 1, 1912, when as Kundry she substituted for Olive Fremstad without a single rehearsal. Richard Aldrich said of this appearance, in the New York *Times:* "Although Mme. Matzenauer is so much a contralto, she has in her voice the higher notes that enable her to sing the music of Kundry without obvious effort, even in the passages in the second act that are sometimes a trial. Her voice had power and significant and changing color of dramatic expression. There was unusual skill in her composition of this difficult and perplexing part. . . . There was more than routine

509

expertness, there were intelligence, insight, the comprehension gained by study."

During her next nineteen years at the Metropolitan Opera, where she later began concentrating more on soprano than on mezzo-soprano or contralto roles (after 1914 she came to regard herself solely as a soprano), she extended her repertory further to include Carmen, Laura in *La Gioconda,* Ulrica in *Un Ballo in Maschera,* Brünnhilde in *Siegfried,* Donna Elvira in *Don Giovanni,* Selika in *L'Africaine,* Delilah in *Samson and Delilah,* Isolde in *Tristan and Isolde,* Santuzza in *Cavalleria Rusticana,* Marina in *Boris Godunov,* Princess Eboli in *Don Carlo,* Venus in *Tannhäuser,* the Countess in *The Marriage of Figaro,* Leonore in *Fidelio,* Azucena in *Il Trovatore,* and Fides in *Le Prophète.* Off the beaten track were her appearances as the Landgravine Sophie in the American stage production premiere of Liszt's *Saint Elizabeth* (January 3, 1918), the Sexton's Widow in the American premiere of Janáček's *Jenufa* (December 6, 1924), and the High Priestess in the New York premiere of Spontini's *La Vestale* (September 12, 1925).

She was also a favorite in opera houses throughout Europe and South America, and a highly successful recitalist and guest soloist with major orchestras.

She left the Metropolitan Opera in 1930, making her last appearance there on February 12 as Amneris, the same role with which she had made her debut there. In 32 roles she had made 315 appearances in New York and 46 on tour. She was heard most frequently as Amneris (49 times), Ortrud (43 times), Brünnhilde in *Die Walküre* (33 times), Delilah (28 times), Venus (23 times), and Kundry (21 times).

But she did not withdraw into retirement. In 1931 she sang Klytemnestra in *Elektra* in Philadelphia. Three years later she appeared at the Lewisohn Stadium in New York in *Samson and Delilah.* And early in 1938 she bid farewell to professional singing with a last recital at Carnegie Hall in New York. "Though the once flawless voice had now certain obvious deficiencies," noted a critic for the New York *Times,* "it still possesses the sumptuous timbre and opulent resonance to distinguish her every effort. And the passing years have done nothing to detract from the force and sensitivity of her musicianship."

She spent her years of retirement in Santa Monica, California, teaching voice and coaching singers. In 1942 she came out of retirement temporarily to make a nonsinging appearance on Broadway in *Vickie,* a comedy which opened at the Plymouth Theater on September 22 and remained for forty-eight performances.

On May 19, 1963, after an illness of several months, Margarete Matzenauer died in a convalescent home in Van Nuys, California. She had been married three times: first to a singing teacher, Ernest Preuse in 1902 (divorced 1911); then to an Italian tenor, Edoardo Ferrari-Fontana (divorced in 1917); and finally to her chauffeur, Floyd Glotzbach, whom she also divorced. She had a daughter, Adrienne, the child of her second marriage, who made some appearances in light opera.

She once told an interviewer that her two greatest experiences in opera were the singing of Isolde for the first time (in Paris with Arthur Nikisch conducting) and her first performance as Brünnhilde in *Die Götterdämmerung* (in Chicago). In her younger years her diversions included mountain climbing, swimming, golfing, and motoring. In later years these interests were supplanted by two of her early interests: reading and going to the theater. She became an American citizen in 1918.

ABOUT: Opera News, November 16, 1963.

Dorothy Maynor

1910–

Dorothy Maynor was one of the most successful and brilliant sopranos of her time, though she never sang in opera and her concert career spanned just about a decade and a half. She possessed a voice of incandescent beauty and a perfect control rivaled by few. She was born in Norfolk, Virginia, on September 3, 1910. "My father, John J. Maynor, was a minister," she has said. "He was very fond of music, though he wasn't a trained musician. My sister played the piano. It was a rare day when we weren't singing in the house to her accompaniment."

As a child, Dorothy sang in the choir of her father's church. While in elementary school, she was encouraged in her singing by the school's principal.

When she was fourteen, she entered Hampton

DOROTHY MAYNOR

Institute at Hampton, Virginia, to prepare herself for a career as a schoolteacher. There she specialized in dress designing, and spent many of her free hours in the pursuit of such sports as hockey, swimming, and tennis. She also sang in the Hampton Choir. When she was sixteen she appeared as one of the soloists of this choir at Carnegie Hall, and in 1929–1930 she toured Europe with it.

On her return from Europe, Maynor became a voice student of R. Nathaniel Dett at Hampton Institute. She spent four years studying music, after which she earned a scholarship for the Westminster Choir School in Princeton, New Jersey. She spent three years at Westminster.

In 1936, financed by a Boston patron (later identified as Harriet S. Curtis), she went to New York to devote herself entirely to developing her voice. She found lodgings in a YWCA before acquiring a small apartment of her own which could accommodate a rented piano. To help support herself she led a church choir in Brooklyn, New York. For three years she studied voice, first with Wilfried Klamroth and then with John Alan Houghton. For a time, all attempts to get her singing career started by entering her in contests and by auditioning proved fruitless.

In August 1939 she visited Tanglewood, in Lenox, Massachusetts, to attend performances of the Berkshire Music Festival. One of her friends arranged for her to sing for Serge Koussevitzky who is quoted as exclaiming after hearing her: "She is a revelation—a modern Flagstad!" He arranged to have her give a recital

on the grounds of Tanglewood on August 8, during an official reception he was giving for members of his orchestra and for officials of the Berkshire Festival Committee. Singing a program that included arias by Handel, Mozart, Wagner, and Charpentier, among other items, she created such excitement that the story that a major artist had been discovered appeared in several newspapers throughout the country, as well as in *Time* Magazine.

Koussevitzky arranged for Maynor to make a recording with the Boston Symphony under his direction for an album of arias by Handel and Mozart. Then, when her concert debut was announced, it attracted considerable curiosity and interest. The debut took place in New York on November 19, 1939, and she lived up to the highest expectations of her admirers. "Miss Maynor's voice is phenomenal for its range, character and varied expressive resources," reported Olin Downes in the New York *Times*. "It is equally adapted to music of a lyric or dramatic character. The voice has power as well as rich color. The upper tones can be wildly dramatic, and need never be forced. There are many different tone qualities available, and the voice, because of the singer's sensibility, changes color constantly in response to mood and dramatic inflection."

Similar reports from other New York critics made her musical news of first importance: a black singer who had become an instant star and one who promised to measure up to the stature of Marian Anderson. She was immediately in great demand throughout the country. In her first year of concertizing, she appeared as a soloist with four of America's leading orchestras—the New York Philharmonic, the Philadelphia, the Boston Symphony, and the Chicago Symphony. She made two cross-country tours, appearing in twenty-seven states, and wherever she came to sing the auditorium was sold out. In 1940 she won the Town Hall Endowment Series Award.

On June 27, 1942, Maynor married Shelby Rooks. They met while he was teaching at Lincoln University in Pennsylvania, and they were married in the chapel of the Westminster Choir School. He subsequently became the pastor of the St. James Presbyterian Church in New York. Their first home was an apartment in Harlem. Later they moved to an apartment in the Fifty-seventh Street section of New York, and later still they acquired a nine-room house which she helped to decorate.

As one of the biggest attractions in concert music in America, Maynor made annual concert tours, filling more than a hundred engagements a year both as a recitalist and as a guest artist with established orchestras. During World War II she sang in camps and hospitals for the women and men of the armed services. In 1949 she made her first tour of South America; then in 1950 she toured Europe, appearing in Italy, Denmark, Norway, Sweden, Holland, and France; during the summer of 1951 she toured Australia.

In 1940 Maynor gave a recital at the Library of Congress in Washington, D.C., to open a festival of music dedicated to the recognition of the contributions of blacks to American culture and held to commemorate the seventy-fifth anniversary of the Thirteenth Amendment to the Constitution. In November 1944 she became the first woman ever invited to sing in the Cathedral in Washington, D.C., where she appeared in choir vestments to help celebrate the fiftieth anniversary of the YWCA.

In 1945 Maynor became the director of Bennett College in Greensboro, North Carolina. Almost twenty years later, in 1963, long after her retirement from the concert stage, she founded and became director of the Harlem School of Arts for underprivileged black children at the St. James Presbyterian Church where her husband was pastor. From a student body of about twenty children, the school grew in a decade to accommodate eight hundred students. In 1975, as executive director of that school, she was presented by New York City with a citation for her "devotion to the people of New York." The occasion included a concert of Negro spirituals by the chorus of the Harlem School of Arts given at Lincoln Center for the Performing Arts on February 25. One year later, at Lincoln Center, on March 17, 1976, at a benefit concert for the school, Arthur Rubinstein presented her with an award from Young Audiences—"in recognition of her incomparable achievement and cultural contribution to the lives of our children." He told her: "You are unique." He also said that some of his own ideas of piano phrasing were learned from her vocal artistry.

Replacing Maynor's onetime interest in sports are weaving, needlework, and petit point.

ABOUT: Collier's, March 2, 1940; New York Times, August 13, 1939, November 5, 1967; New Yorker, November 18, 1939.

Richard Mayr

1877–1935

Richard Mayr, bass, was born in Henndorf, near Salzburg, Austria, on November 18, 1877. The son of a wealthy brewer, he was encouraged to pursue a career in medicine. After finishing high school in Salzburg, he entered the University of Vienna. In Vienna, Gustav Mahler heard him sing and advised him to consider developing his voice. Although still a student of medicine at the University, Mayr enrolled at the Vienna Conservatory in 1898. For the next four years he received his musical training there. In 1902 Mahler engaged him for the Vienna Royal Opera. However, Mayr's opera debut took place not in Vienna but at the Bayreuth Festival in September 1902, where he was heard as Hagen in *Die Götterdämmerung.* "His resonant voice and splendid declamation won him an immediate success," notes Herman Klein in *Grove's Dictionary of Music and Musicians,* "but his supreme gifts as an actor were yet to be made manifest in their full maturity." Later the same year, he made his bow at the Vienna Royal Opera as Don Gomez in *Ernani.* Until his retirement, Mayr remained there as principal bass, distinguishing himself particularly in the German repertory. He became best known as Baron Ochs in *Der Rosenkavalier.* Both Richard Strauss and his librettist Hugo von Hofmannsthal wanted Mayr to create Baron Ochs when the opera received its world premiere in Dresden in 1911, but Mayr's involvements in Vienna made this impossible. However, on April 8, 1911, when *Der Rosenkavalier* was given its premiere in Vienna, Mayr sang the role which was to become so inextricably associated with him that Richard Strauss once remarked: "Richard Mayr *is* Baron Ochs." Another of Strauss's distinguished bass roles was created by Mayr, that of Barak in *Die Frau ohne Schatten* in Vienna on October 10, 1919.

For his artistic contributions to the Vienna

Mayr: mīr

RICHARD MAYR

Royal (later State) Opera, Mayr was named *Kammersänger* by the Austrian government.

Between 1906 and 1910 Mayr distinguished himself in Mozartean roles at the Salzburg festivals in Austria. When the international Salzburg Festival was officially initiated in 1922, he became one of its important participants, remaining one of the principal performers up to the time of his retirement, a favorite not only as Baron Ochs but also as Sarastro in *The Magic Flute* and Rocco in *Fidelio* (among other roles). From 1908 to 1912 Mayr appeared at the Bayreuth Festivals as Gurnemanz in *Parsifal.*

He made his debut at Covent Garden in London on May 23, 1924, as Baron Ochs. More than three years later, on November 2, 1927, he made his bow at the Metropolitan Opera in New York as Pogner in *Die Meistersinger.* Commenting in the New York *Times* on this performance, Olin Downes noted that Mayr's ability as an actor exceeded his talent as a singer. Nevertheless, Downes concluded that he "showed himself . . . [an] artist of high and deserved reputation. . . . Later performances will probably present Mr. Mayr in a different light than last night's." Mayr did reveal himself to far better advantage (as Downes took the pains to point out) in his subsequent Metropolitan Opera appearances as King Henry in *Lohengrin,* Hermann in *Tannhäuser,* Hunding in *Die Walküre* and, most of all, as Baron Ochs.

After leaving the Metropolitan Opera at the conclusion of the 1929–1930 season, Mayr was heard principally at the Vienna State Opera and the Salzburg Festival up to the time of his retirement shortly before his death. He retired at his own request and was given a life pension. He died in Vienna on December 1, 1935.

ABOUT: Holz, H. J. Richard Mayr; Kunz, O. Richard Mayr.

Zubin Mehta

1936–

Zubin Mehta, conductor, was born in Bombay, on April 29, 1936. A Parsi, he is a descendant of ancient Zoroastrian Persians who fled to India during the sixth century to escape persecution in the Middle East. His father, Mehli, was a violinist who played dinner music at the Taj Mahal Hotel in Bombay but whose heart was in serious music. He was the founder and conductor of the Bombay Symphony and he was the organizer and first violinist of the Bombay String Quartet.

There was always Western music in the Mehta home. As Zubin Mehta has said, he was "brainwashed with classical music from the cradle." As an infant he would listen with fascination to the chamber-music performances at home. "I got acquainted with Beethoven quartets before I ever heard a symphony, and I could sing all this music before I could read a note." He would also sit in whenever his father gave violin lessons. As a result, Zubin was often heard humming a Paganini caprice or some other standbys of the violin repertory while he was playing with his little friends. He was only two and a half when he received a record player of his own, and from then on he could listen to music to his heart's content.

When he was seven he began studying the violin and the piano, to both of which he was more or less indifferent. Conducting was what he wanted to do more than anything else as far back as he could remember. His father taught him some of its rudiments. In his teens Zubin applied these lessons to leading sections of the Bombay Symphony during rehearsals. When he was sixteen, his father allowed him to direct a rehearsal of the full Bombay Symphony. A cellist from that orchestra recalls that event. "The moment he got onto the podium, he instantly

Mehta: mä′ tä

Mehta

ZUBIN MEHTA

took command, gave us correct cues and put us under his spell." After that he substituted once or twice for his father as the orchestra's conductor.

Despite his complete absorption with music, he planned for a time to become a doctor. With this aim in mind he entered St. Xavier College. When, two years later, he was required to dissect a lizard in his zoology class, he walked out of college—and away from medicine—forever. He now devoted himself solely to music. In his eighteenth year he went to Vienna to complete his music study. At the Vienna Academy of Music he specialized in the double bass, on which he performed as a member of the Vienna Chamber Orchestra. He also took courses in piano, composition, and conducting, the last of these with Hans Swarowsky. "I went through the mill," he recalls. "At one time I had to take twelve courses at once." He also frequently attended concerts of the Vienna Philharmonic Orchestra, particularly when his two favorite conductors, Herbert von Karajan and Wilhelm Furtwängler, were conducting.

While still a student, Mehta organized a student orchestra, which he first conducted in 1956 at a refugee camp outside Vienna. He remained its conductor for the next two years, often embarking on the less familiar trails in music-making, such as programming an all-Schoenberg concert in 1958.

He graduated from the Vienna Academy in 1957. A year later he married Carmen Lasky, a young Canadian singer, then also studying in Vienna. This marriage did not last. Mehta's travels away from home while advancing his career in the early 1960s proved destructive to the relationship. Though by then they had two children, they were divorced in 1964. "It just happened," his wife, Carmen, has said. "I never did anything nasty to him, and he never did anything nasty to me." Two years after this divorce, Carmen married his younger brother, Zarin.

In 1958 Mehta entered a competition for conductors held in England by the Liverpool Philharmonic. He came out first among one hundred contestants and was awarded a post as assistant conductor of that orchestra for one season. In Liverpool, where he was permitted to conduct fourteen concerts, he discovered that "I just was unprepared to lead a professional orchestra. I learned at their expense—but I learned." Nevertheless, his performances were well received. For the next two seasons he gained valuable experience by serving as guest conductor in Austria, Belgium, and Yugoslavia, sometimes under the auspices of the Jeunesses Musicales. On one occasion he went to Yugoslavia to substitute for an indisposed conductor and received an ovation. On another occasion, when Eugene Ormandy was unable to fill a date with the Vienna Philharmonic, Mehta became his replacement, thus becoming the youngest man ever to lead a concert of that historic organization. "I sometimes think," he later remarked, "my success was due almost entirely to the misfortunes of my older colleagues." In 1959 he entered a conducting competition at the Berkshire Music Center at Tanglewood in Massachusetts, winning second prize and the admiration and support of Charles Münch, the music director of the Boston Symphony Orchestra and the Center.

In 1960 he was invited to direct a part of the subscription series of the Vienna Symphony Orchestra. That summer he went to New York, and on July 26 he made his New York conducting debut at Lewisohn Stadium. Later that year, on the recommendation of Münch, he was invited to conduct the Montreal Symphony for two weeks as a substitute for Igor Markevitch. He did so well that in January 1961 he was appointed music director of that orchestra. His dynamic personality, his innovative programming, and his electrifying readings brought a prestige to the Montreal Symphony it had not previously known, a prestige that extended beyond the borders of Canada. In 1962 Mehta took the orchestra to the Soviet Union for eight concerts, to Paris for two more, and to Vienna for a single performance. In Vienna the orchestra received a twenty-minute ovation and Mehta had to take fourteen bows.

Meanwhile, in 1961 he went to Los Angeles as a guest conductor of the Philharmonic Orchestra, this time as a substitute for Fritz Reiner. This concert proved so successful that Mehta was invited to give several more performances. That November he was appointed music director of the Los Angeles Philharmonic without having to relinquish his post in Montreal. Only twenty-six, he was the youngest man ever to serve in the post with the Los Angeles Philharmonic and the first conductor in America to serve as music director of two major orchestras simultaneously.

Having been without a permanent conductor for several years, the Los Angeles Philharmonic had deteriorated into a somewhat undisciplined and disorganized group. To remedy this, Mehta instituted a dictatorial regime that included long and painstaking rehearsals, an overhauling of personnel, and a revitalization of the repertory to include new and often avant-garde music. Among his world premieres were Lukas Foss's *Elytres* (December 8, 1964), Miklós Rózsa's Concerto for Piano and Orchestra (April 6, 1976), Gottfried von Einem's *Hexameron* (February 19, 1970), William Kraft's *Contextures* (April 4, 1968) and Piano Concerto (November 21, 1973), and Subotnick's *Two Butterflies, for Amplified Orchestra* (April 17, 1975) and *Before the Butterfly* (February 26, 1976).

To improve and enrich the orchestral sound, especially in the string section, he acquired precious instruments for his men—including a Stradivari violin for the concertmaster. His personality magnetized audiences as well as musicians, and his intense, dramatic readings introduced an excitement into orchestral music Los Angeles had not experienced for many years. "Showmanship," he has said, "is very important." He has also conceded to an interviewer that his gestures were directed at the audience as well as at the musicians. "For a cymbal crash," he said, "the player will come in anyway, but if I give a big gesture, it just adds to the high point. Or in the development section of Beethoven's *Eroica*, I'm not sure the audience is hearing everything—the different modulations, the canonic effects. I point to the orchestra as if to say

'Look who is playing. Now the theme is in the first violins; now it is in the basses.' "

By the time he took the Los Angeles Philharmonic to New York in 1967 for its first visit since his directorship, he was in the forefront of conductors in America and his orchestra had entered the top echelon among the country's symphonic organizations. Following his concert in Carnegie Hall in May 1967, Winthrop Sargeant wrote in the *New Yorker:* "Mehta . . . has the capacity to control every sound made by an orchestra. He has a talent for conveying a mood of serenity, or of serene grandeur, to both orchestra and audience that is rare indeed among the younger generation of conductors."

He drew superlatives from the critics when he made guest appearances in both Europe and the United States. During the summer of 1965 he made his debut at the Salzburg Festival, conducting performances of *The Abduction from the Seraglio* which several Austrian critics singled out as one of the high points of the festival. When, on November 2, 1965, he conducted the Philadelphia Orchestra in New York, Harriet Johnson, writing in the New York *Post,* extolled the performance and noted that Mehta led the orchestra "with an awareness and mastery that were more than remarkable. . . . Mehta brought something of the seer to his baton and it would be futile to deny the illumination of his crystal ball. . . . His is a spectacular gift that unites the mystery of the East with everything the West calls a great talent."

One month later, on December 29, 1965, he made his bow as an opera conductor in America with *Aida* at the Metropolitan Opera in New York. He was acclaimed for his performance not only of this opera but also of *Carmen, Tosca,* and the world premiere on March 16, 1967, of Marvin David Levy's *Mourning Becomes Electra*.

Not yet thirty, he was universally recognized as one of the world's great conductors. During a three-month period in 1964–1965 he was called upon to dedicate three new major concert auditoriums: on September 21, La Place des Arts in Montreal with a program including the world premiere of Jean Papineau-Couture's *Miroir;* on December 8, the Pavilion of the Music Center of Los Angeles with a performance of the first and ninth symphonies of Beethoven and the world premiere of Lukas Foss's *Elytres;* and the Civic Theater in San Diego. *Time* pointed to

Mehta's career as "one of the most spectacular ascents to fame in many a decade."

In Los Angeles, where at this time he preferred making his residence in a hotel rather than in an apartment or house, he came to be known as a "swinger." "His tousled sable locks, his honey-colored aquiline features and voracious energy give him the appeal of a matinee idol and make him a kind of culture hero," said *Time*. And he was receiving the matinee-idol treatment, not only from his audiences in Los Angeles but also from the media. He was the subject of an hour-long documentary over NBC-TV sponsored by Bell Telephone in 1967; and on January 19, 1968, he was the subject of the cover story in *Time*.

In the image of a matinee idol he drove a Jaguar (usually at high speed on the freeways), visited jazz clubs and discotheques, moved easily among Hollywood celebrities, and became involved in romances with beautiful women. Movies were a passion; he would sometimes go to several of them in a single evening. For exercise he preferred fencing, and for relaxation, yoga. Requiring little sleep, he spent most of his nights poring through scores that his photographic mind could remember with just a few readings.

Much of his way of life became American, but he insisted on retaining not only his Indian citizenship but also his preference for highly spiced Indian dishes. In the tradition of the Zoroastrian religion he avoided cigarettes, hard liquor, and coffee.

At Expo '67 in Montreal, Mehta led the combined forces of the Montreal Symphony and the Los Angeles Philharmonic in a performance of Berlioz' *Symphonie Fantastique*. In May of that year he resigned his post in Montreal to devote more time to Los Angeles. As part of this increased involvement he took the orchestra on an eight-week tour of Vienna, Paris, Athens, and Bombay. In November and December 1976 he toured Hungary, Poland, Yugoslavia, Czechoslovakia, Bulgaria, and Italy with the Los Angeles Philharmonic.

But his deeper involvement in Los Angeles did not preclude performances elsewhere, as demands for his services became varied and worldwide. He made recordings, filmed television programs in the United States and Italy, and made noteworthy appearances with orchestras and opera houses and at Europe's festivals. In February 1975 he made a successful debut at the Vienna State Opera conducting *Lohengrin*. On February 28, 1977, at Covent Garden in London he led *Otello*. The first performance there since 1914 of *The Girl of the Golden West* was conducted by him on May 24, 1977. And on December 31, 1977, a new production of *Die Fledermaus* was presented under his baton.

One of his affiliations outside Los Angeles was with the Israel Philharmonic, with which he made his first appearance in 1961. Since then he has conducted the orchestra not only in Israel but also in Europe, South America, the United States, and, in August 1966, in the Far East. With this organization he has made a number of recordings. He was involved with the Israel Philharmonic in some of its historic moments: its first concert in Bethlehem; its concerts during the Six-Day War when he canceled all his obligations to rush to Israel for an unscheduled visit; performances during the ceremonies attending the twenty-fifth anniversary of Israel's independence; and concerts during the Yom Kippur War. In 1969 he was appointed music adviser to the orchestra. In recognition of his contribution to Israel's cultural life he received a commendation from Prime Minister Golda Meir in July 1973, and in 1974 was given the honorary degree of Doctor of Philosophy by Tel-Aviv University. Subsequently he was made an honorary member of the Israel Philharmonic.

Mehta became a subject for bitter controversy in Israel when he tried (unsuccessfully) to program music of Wagner on one of the concerts of the Israel Philharmonic—Wagner having been boycotted by Israel from the beginning because of his identification with the Nazi regime. Mehta caused an even greater furor, in the United States, in 1967. At that time he was one of several conductors under consideration as a possible replacement for Leonard Bernstein as music director of the New York Philharmonic. Mehta let it be known that he was not interested, first because he regarded the New York Philharmonic as inferior to his own orchestra and therefore did not look upon it as a step upwards for him and secondly because he felt that the musicians in the New York Philharmonic "step over conductors." "Why not send our worst enemy to the New York Philharmonic and finish him off once and for all," he was quoted in *Newsweek*. Such remarks angered not only the men of the New York Philharmonic but also the musicians' union. He was called before the executive board of Local 802 of the American Federation of Musicians for questioning in January 1968. At that time he apologized, insisting that his remarks had been distorted and that actually he had only the highest regard for the men of the New York Philharmonic. The matter was allowed to drop, but a two-week engagement with the New York Philharmonic in 1968–1969 was canceled. Not until May 9, 1973, did he make his debut with the Philharmonic. At the first rehearsal he apologized once again. After that there was complete rapport between the musicians and their conductor. His performance at the concert was hailed. "The orchestra," wrote Speight Jenkins in the New York *Post,* "played his demanding program with verve, and the conductor . . . approached each piece with originality."

Early in 1976 the affiliation of Mehta with the New York Philharmonic became permanent—it was announced that Mehta had been appointed music director of the orchestra, succeeding Pierre Boulez, and that he would assume his new position in September 1978.

As a salute to America's Bicentennial, Mehta directed the combined forces of the Israel Philharmonic and the Los Angeles Philharmonic in a performance of Berlioz' *Symphonie Fantastique* at the Hollywood Bowl in Los Angeles on August 25, 1976. The symphony was performed as Berlioz originally conceived it: for an orchestra made up of 130 strings, 32 woodwinds, 32 basses, 4 harps, and 10 percussion instruments.

On July 20, 1969, Mehta married Nancy Kovack, a Hollywood actress, in a dual ceremony, the first taking place in Westwood United Methodist Church and the second (a Zoroastrian ritual conducted by a Parsi high priest) at the Hotel Bel-Air. Their legal residence is in Lucerne, Switzerland, but their basic home is a rambling Mediterranean villa atop a private mountain overlooking Brentwood. They have two children.

Mehta led the Los Angeles Philharmonic orchestra on October 24, 1970, in New York, in the world premiere of Penderecki's *Cosmogony.* This concert took place in the General Assembly Hall of the United Nations Building in celebration of the twenty-fifth anniversary of the United Nations. World leaders were in the audience in the hall, and since the performance was recorded on videotape for television rebroadcast through-

out the United States and abroad, the audience was also worldwide.

Mehta has been the recipient of the Padma Bhushan (Order of the Lotus), the highest cultural award India gives. Following his performance of Haydn's *Mass in Time of War* and Bruckner's *Te Deum* in May 1972 with the Rome Radio Orchestra in the Vatican's New Hall of Audiences, Pope Paul VI presented Mehta with a gold medal. In 1968 he was awarded an honorary doctorate from Occidental College and in 1970 he was given the Centennial Award by Loyola University in Chicago.

ABOUT: Ewen, D. Famous Modern Conductors. *Periodicals*—New York Times, October 18, 1970, September 5, 1976; New Yorker, December 16, 1967; Newsweek, January 10, 1967; Time, January 19, 1968.

Dame Nellie Melba

1859–1931

Nellie Melba (originally Helen Porter Mitchell), coloratura soprano, was born in Burnley, Richmond, a suburb of Melbourne, Australia, on May 19, 1859. She was the third child of David Mitchell, a Scotsman who had become prosperous in Australia as a manufacturer of bricks. He was a music lover and an amateur violinist. Her mother, Isabella Ann, was a trained pianist.

Early in her life Helen revealed a gift for singing. When she was six she appeared in a concert in Richmond's Town Hall singing "Comin' Thro' the Rye" (which remained in her repertory throughout her career) and "Shells of the Ocean."

While she was still a child, her family moved to a small county township forty-five miles from Melbourne. There Helen spent a happy childhood riding horses, fishing, and trapping through the woods. She detested school—Leigh House in Richmond and then the Presbyterian Ladies College in East Melbourne—and took flight from boredom by indulging in mischief.

Though her talent lay in singing, her father saw to it that she received a comprehensive training in piano, organ, and theory as well as in voice. In her youth she sang and played the organ in local churches.

When she was twenty-two she fell in love with Captain Charles Armstrong, son of an Irish

Melba

baronet. They were married in December 1882. It did not take them long to discover they were incompatible. They lived in a bleak and lonely house infested with insects; during their first six weeks there it rained incessantly. "I felt I should go mad unless I escaped," she later recalled. Two months after the marriage she left her husband and returned to her father's home to have her baby, a son, George. She never remarried.

It was at this juncture in her life that she decided to become a professional musician, still not certain whether she should concentrate on the piano or voice. When finally she decided in favor of voice training, she studied with Pietro Cecchi who prepared her for a concert career.

Her first appearance as a professional singer was at the Melbourne Town Hall on May 17, 1884, an occasion which she later recalled as "two hours of wonderful triumph." (At the time of this debut she had never heard an opera nor had she attended a concert by a famous singer.) A local impresario engaged her to give four concerts a week at twenty-five dollars an appearance. She was also heard as a soloist with the choir of the St. Francis Roman Catholic Church in Melbourne. In December 1885 she was a soloist in a performance of Handel's *Messiah* in Sydney.

In 1886 her father was sent to London as a commissioner to a colonial exhibition. She went with him hoping to develop her singing career in England. In London, on June 1, 1886, she gave a concert at Prince's Hall but attracted little attention. Sensing the need for more instruction, she went to Paris to audition for Mathilde Marchesi. After she had sung "Sempre libera" from *La Traviata* (Marchesi accompanying her on the piano), the teacher told her: "I shall make something extraordinary of you." To her husband, Marchesi remarked later that day: "Salvatore, at last I've found a star."

She studied with Marchesi for a year, becoming, in Marchesi's own description, "the pupil of my dreams." Two directors of the Théâtre de la Monnaie in Brussels heard her in Marchesi's studio and signed her for their company. There she made a sensational operatic debut as Gilda in *Rigoletto* on October 13, 1887. It was on this occasion that she took the name Melba by contracting the name of the Australian city near where she was born. "Within two years," prophesied the critic of *Le Patriote* after her debut, "she will be known as la Melba."

Her success in Brussels brought her an engagement with Covent Garden. There she made her first appearance on May 24, 1888, in the title role of *Lucia di Lammermoor*. This was followed by a performance as Gilda. Her first appearances at Covent Garden could hardly be classed as eventful. But a triumph came to her at the Paris Opéra at her debut there on May 8, 1889, in the role of Ophelia in Thomas's *Hamlet*, a part in which she was coached by the composer. The audience was swept by a frenzy of enthusiasm. Christine Nilsson, the Swedish soprano famous as Ophelia, went to Melba's dressing room during intermission, saying: "The old Ophelia salutes the young Ophelia." Thomas, the composer of *Hamlet*, was overcome with emotion. The critic of *Figaro* spoke rhapsodically about "the exceptional quality of that sweetly timbred voice, even, pure, brilliant and mellow, remarkably resonant in the middle register."

She remained a star at the Paris Opéra for the next two seasons. In 1890 she was acclaimed at the St. Petersburg Opera. In 1893 her successes brought her to Stockholm, Copenhagen, and La Scala in Milan, where she made her debut as Lucia. "Who else now, may we ask, can sing like Melba?" inquired Aldo Noseda in the *Corriere della Sera*.

In Paris, where she made her home in an apartment near Parc Monceau, she met and fell in love with Louis Philippe Robert, the Duke of Orleans. He was ten years younger than she—strikingly handsome as well as highborn. They became inseparable. Their romance was publicized in newspapers throughout Europe and the source of much whispered gossip. Religious and social differences doomed their relationship. In 1896 the duke married an archduchess. For Melba he remained the one man, other than her father, for whom she had an enduring love.

Promoted as "the greatest prima donna on earth," she made her American debut at the Metropolitan Opera on December 4, 1893, as Lucia. Possibly because the Metropolitan Opera audiences were faithful to Adelina Patti, she did not at first create in New York the enthusiasm she inspired elsewhere. But the critics were fully aware of her greatness. Writing in the New York *Tribune*, H. E. Krehbiel described her performance as "the finest exemplar heard on the local stage since Mme. Sembrich made her American debut ten years ago." He added: "Mme. Melba is at the zenith of her powers. Her voice is charmingly fresh, and exquisitely beautiful, and her tone production is more natural, and more spontaneous than that of the marvelous woman who so long upheld the standard of bel canto throughout the world." Later that season, she appeared as Ophelia, Nedda in *I Pagliacci*, Juliet in *Romeo and Juliet*, Gilda in *Rigoletto*, the title role in Rossini's *Semiramide*, Elsa in *Lohengrin*, Elisabeth in *Tannhäuser*, and Marguerite in *Faust*. "Since Christine Nilsson," Krehbiel said, "there has been no Marguerite the equal of Melba's."

During the next three seasons, she reigned as *prima donna assoluta* of the Metropolitan Opera. She opened the seasons of 1894–1895 and 1896–1897 as Juliet and Marguerite respectively. To her former Metropolitan Opera roles she added those of Micaëla in *Carmen*, the title role in the American premiere of Bemberg's *Elaine* (December 17, 1894), Marguerite in *Les Huguenots*, Violetta in *La Traviata*, Brünnhilde in *Siegfried*, and the title role in *Manon*. Her perfect breath control, the purity of her tones throughout the entire register, her birdlike trill were said to have had few if any rivals among prima donnas.

However, one of these roles at the Metropolitan Opera proved a disaster—that of Brünnhilde on December 30, 1896. "It may as well be said now as later," said W. J. Henderson in the New York *Times*, "that the quality of her voice and her style of singing are not suited to a complete embodiment of Brünnhilde." Adverse criticism

was not all that she had to suffer by assuming a role that was beyond her reach. Brünnhilde had proved so taxing to her vocally that after the performance she was compelled to go into temporary retirement to give her voice a prolonged rest. She announced publicly: "Tell the critics that I'm never going to do that again. It is beyond me. I have been a fool."

When her voice finally regained its pristine beauty, she toured America with the Damrosch Opera Company in 1897–1898. On December 2, 1898, she returned to the Metropolitan Opera as Juliet. At Covent Garden, on June 15, 1899, she enjoyed a spectacular success as Juliet, and later the same season went on to sing for the first time anywhere the role of Mimi in *La Bohème*, captivating her audience completely. From then on she was an idol of Covent Garden and returned annually (with the exception of 1909, 1912, and 1913) up to the end of her career. In 1900 she gave a command performance for Queen Victoria at Windsor, the first of several command performances for ruling heads of England, including Edward VII.

In September 1902, after an absence of sixteen years, Melba returned to her native land for a three-month series of concerts in Melbourne, Sydney, Brisbane, and Adelaide. The day she arrived in Melbourne the city proclaimed a public holiday. Police had to hold back the throngs, and traffic on the evening of her first concert was completely snarled. The ovations after each number reached the point of hysteria. Finally she ended her concert by sitting at the piano and accompanying herself in "Home, Sweet Home."

On February 18, 1904, Melba created the title role in Saint-Saëns's *Hélène* at the Monte Carlo Opera, a part the composer had written for her. Later that year she returned to the Metropolitan Opera for a single season, giving New York its first hearing of her Mimi (her greatest role in her later years) on December 16, 1904. In 1901 she had sung the Infanta in Massenet's *Le Cid*.

In 1906 Melba deserted the Metropolitan Opera for Oscar Hammerstein's Manhattan Opera House, receiving the highest fee ever paid to an opera star in the United States up to that time: three thousand dollars a performance. Richard Aldrich reported in the New York *Times:* "Melba's voice has its old-time lusciousness and purity, its exquisite smoothness and fullness. It poured out with all the spontaneity and freedom."

Melba

She appeared with the Manhattan Opera fifteen times, her last performance there taking place on March 25, 1907, as Mimi. There was no question that as long as she was a member of that company she was one of its mainstays. "It was Melba," says her biographer John Hetherington, "who carried the Manhattan Opera House from its ominously shaky beginnings to its first dazzling triumphs. ... Melba was the first and principal architect of Hammerstein's victory."

Her final appearance at the Manhattan Opera was one of her greatest personal triumphs. So effusive was the audience that at the end of *La Bohème* she had to come out and sing the "Mad Scene" and a few other numbers as encores. When the music was over, a festive supper in her honor was served on the stage.

In 1911 she returned to Australia to tour with the Melba-Williamson Company, and in 1913–1914 she was a member of the Chicago Opera. She spent the years of World War I partly in Australia and partly in the United States.

Her last appearance in the United States took place in the spring of 1920. After that she was a member of the newly organized British National Opera in London, and she toured Australia again with her own opera company.

On June 8, 1926, she made her last appearance at Covent Garden, singing the second act of *Romeo and Juliet,* the "Willow Song" and "Ave Maria" from *Otello,* and the last two acts of *La Bohème.* "Not even the youngest of the day is steadier in tone or hits the notes more precisely or accurately," reported the *Daily Telegraph.* "The art is still there." After the final act of *La Bohème,* the audience (which included the king and queen of England) went wild with enthusiasm. She made a brief address, saying: "There is only one word to say, and that is Farewell. I won't say goodbye, because farewell is such a beautiful word. I am sure you all know that it is part of a prayer and means Fare thee well, which I wish you all, and I feel sure that you wish me the same." The English recording company His Master's Voice recorded live her performance in *La Bohème.*

This was not her last public appearance as a singer, however. Long successful as a recitalist, with numerous American transcontinental tours behind her, she gave a concert at Royal Albert Hall in London on June 8, 1926. On December 7, 1926, she sang at a charity performance for the Sadler's Wells Theater Fund, performing the second act of *Romeo and Juliet,* the last act of *Otello,* and the last two acts of *La Bohème.* This concert was billed as her "farewell." Many came with apprehension, wondering if a sixty-seven-year-old prima donna could live up to her legendary fame. They feared her program would become her ordeal. "It didn't turn out that way," writes W. R. Moran in *High Fidelity.* "Melba's ordeal became Melba's triumph. She confounded her staunchest admirers. She sang so beautifully that years seemed to recede as in a fairy tale, and there stood again the great prima donna of a quarter of a century ago. The voice had almost a youthful charm and freshness. The heavenly legato was still there, and the wonderful technique. It was a miracle. The people who had come out of a sense of duty were in a trance. Then they went wild with excitement."

Though this was billed as her "farewell concert," Melba was heard again. After a tour of Australia, she sang on October 5, 1929, at a charity concert at the Brighton Hippodrome and again in May 1930 at a charity concert at the Hyde Park Hotel in London.

Only then was she through with her career. She returned to her native Australia and became the founder and president of the Melbourne Conservatory. Her last home was "Coombe Cottage," which she had built for her in 1923 in the Australian bush. Surrounded by gardens and equipped with a swimming pool, this "cottage" became her beloved retreat during retirement.

In 1931, suffering from a high temperature, she was brought from her cottage to St. Vincent's private hospital in Sydney. There they discovered she was suffering from paratyphoid, complicated by bacteria in her bloodstream. In February 1931 she asked for a clergyman so that she might pray. Later that day she tried to sing Gounod's "Ave Maria." She died that evening—February 23, 1931—and was buried on a hill on her farm. On her tombstone is the following inscription: "*Addio, senza rancore*—Farewell, without bitterness."

"No words can convey to a music lover who did not hear Melba any idea of the sounds with which she ravished all ears," wrote W. J. Henderson. "One could say, 'It's the unique voice of the world.' This writer never heard any other just like it. Its beauty, its clarion quality, its power differed from the fluty tones of Patti. Melba's voice has been called silvery, but what does that signify? There is one quality which it had and which may be comprehended even by those who did not hear her; it had splendor. The tones glowed with starlike brilliance. They flamed with a white flame."

At the height of her fame she lived in queenly splendor—for many years, in London, in a palatial house on Great Cumberland Place. "When she went abroad," wrote John Hetherington, "she traveled in semi-regal state. Wherever she was someone was at hand to satisfy her whims and wishes. She liked these attentions; she was a demanding woman, and often inconsiderate of the convenience or comfort of others." She could often be tactless or outright rude, but at other times she was the essence of kindliness and generosity. A strong-willed woman, she was supremely efficient both in her business affairs and in her daily life, and she needed to dominate those with whom she came in contact. "That power and money brought Melba anything but fleeting happiness is to be doubted," adds Hetherington. "She loved life and lived it vigorously and exuberantly, and her friends agree that it was impossible to be dull in her company." She was a supreme egotist, confident of her vocal powers, convinced she was irreplaceable.

In 1918 Melba was made Dame Commander of the Order of the British Empire. She published her autobiography, *Melodies and Memories,* in 1925, and in 1953 she was the subject of a motion-picture biography, *Melba,* in which Patrice Munsel was starred.

In 1976, HMV released two albums of Melba's recordings: *La Divina,* extracts from her basic repertory. "This set," reported Alan Blyth in *Opera* (London), "is required listening for any and every aspiring soprano: to learn how to produce their tone with the evenness, clarity and beauty of Melba should be an ideal ever before them."

Pêche Melba and Melba Toast were named after her. Melba Toast, a thin slice of crisp toasted bread, was marketed in 1929. Pêche Melba was the creation of Auguste Escoffier when he was the principal chef at the Savoy Hotel in London. At the time Melba was in residence, he concocted the dessert in her honor. She raved over it and Escoffier asked her permission to call it Pêche Melba. This ice cream dessert first became generally popular after the opening of the Carlton Hotel in London in 1899. There it became one of the specialties of the menu.

ABOUT: Colson, P. Melba: An Unconventional Biography; Hetherington, J. Melba; Melba, N. Melodies and Memories; Murphy, A. Melba, a Biography; Wechsberg, J. Red Plush and Black Velvet: The Story of Melba and Her Times. *Periodicals*—High Fidelity/Musical America, July 1977.

Lauritz Melchior

1890–1973

Lauritz Melchior (originally Lauritz Lebrecht Hommel Melchior), the most important *Heldentenor* since Jean de Reszke and the foremost of his own time, was born in Copenhagen on March 20, 1890. The youngest of six children, he came from a long line of clergymen and educators. His grandfather founded and directed the Melchior School for Boys, known throughout Denmark. His father, Jörgen Conradt Melchior, a schoolteacher, was also a director of the school.

Orphaned in infancy through the death of his mother, Julie Möller Melchior, Lauritz was raised by Kristine Jensen, a housekeeper, author of the celebrated Jensen cookbooks. She regarded Lauritz almost as her own son. As a boy, he attended the Melchior School, and on Sundays he sang in the choir of the English church. One day the church services were attended by the former Danish Princess Alexandra, then Queen of England, and she singled out Melchior's singing for special praise.

He was early brought into contact with opera through his blind sister, Agnes, who attended performances of the Royal Opera in a special section reserved for blind students. She took Lauritz to each of these performances and he listened with fascination. Eventually he asked to study singing so that he, too, might someday appear in operas.

With funds provided by his guardian, Kristine Jensen, Lauritz Melchior entered the Royal Opera School in 1908 and studied singing for several years with Paul Bang. In 1913 Melchior became a member of the Royal Opera House company. On April 2, 1913, substituting for a baritone who had suddenly left the company, Melchior made his opera debut at the Royal Opera in the baritone role of Silvio in *I Pagliacci*.

During World War I he was called into mili-

Melchior: měl′ kyŏr

Melchior

LAURITZ MELCHIOR

tary service in Denmark. Because of his height he was given court service in the King's Royal Guards. This limited duty allowed him time to continue with his vocal studies and to give some singing performances during the evenings.

In 1917, still as a baritone, Melchior toured Sweden as Count di Luna in *Il Trovatore*. During this tour he came under the influence of Mme. Charles Cahier (the former Sara Jane Layton Walker), one of the leading singers in that touring company and one of the renowned contraltos of the day. She recognized that Melchior's voice was placed in the wrong range, that he could perform far more effectively as a tenor, and she urged him to make this important change—no small decision for Melchior since it meant abandoning his career and returning to study.

A second all-important influence in his life carried him from Italian operas to the German repertory. On October 18, 1918, at the Royal Opera in Copenhagen, Melchior made his second debut—this time as a tenor in *Tannhäuser*. The following year he appeared as a soloist with the Queen's Hall Orchestra in London directed by Sir Henry J. Wood. The English novelist Hugh Walpole, who was in the audience, recognized in Melchior the makings of a Wagnerian *Heldentenor*. After the concert Walpole went to Melchior to place at his disposal his own influence, advice, and financial resources. He urged Melchior to begin studying German without delay and to master the *Heldentenor* roles of the Wagnerian repertory.

From 1921 to 1923 Melchior studied with Victor Beigel in London, Ernest Grenzebach in Berlin, and Anna Bahr-Mildenburg in Munich. On May 14, 1924, he emerged as an important Wagnerian tenor for the first time when he sang the role of Siegmund in *Die Walküre* at Covent Garden, Bruno Walter conducting. That debut was not without its drama. At that time Covent Garden was preparing a new production of *Der Rosenkavalier*. During that preparation it could not provide Melchior with rehearsals with orchestra, unaware that Melchior had never sung the part except to a piano accompaniment. Consequently, at the actual performance Melchior was compelled to adjust himself spontaneously to the orchestral accompaniment. He did so with confidence and without mishaps.

Two months later, on the personal invitation of Siegfried and Cosima Wagner, Melchior went to the Bayreuth Festival to appear as Siegmund on July 23, 1924, and soon after that as Parsifal. For the next seven years he returned to Bayreuth, performing all of Wagner's *Heldentenor* roles with distinction.

Melchior's debut in the United States took place at the Metropolitan Opera on February 17, 1926, as Tannhäuser. In this initial American appearance, he did not give indications of his later mature powers. He moved somewhat stiffly on the stage and his interpretation appeared self-conscious. As for his singing, in the New York *Times* Olin Downes commented that "the tone was forced and rough in quality and the melodic line suffered." But Downes did note a gradual improvement in Melchior's performance as the opera progressed. "The 'narrative' of the last act was impressively delivered. Here its singing had a quality and freedom not apparent before."

Melchior's rise to fame in the United States was gradual; his art developed and matured slowly over a period of several years. During his first Metropolitan Opera season he sang Siegmund (which W. J. Henderson in the *Sun* described as belonging "to a day of small things, daily becoming smaller"), the title role in *Siegfried* (which he had sung only twice before elsewhere), and Parsifal. He was heard intermittently during the 1926–1927 season and spent the season after that in study in Europe. Not until he was heard at the Metropolitan Opera as Siegfried in *Die Götterdämmerung* on March 14, 1929, as Tristan in *Tristan and Isolde* on March 20, 1929, and as Lohengrin on March 22, 1930, did his true caliber become apparent. Despite the musical shortcomings that remained with him throughout his career, such as his carelessness with rhythm and accentuation, it was evident his voice had acquired greater richness, power, and flexibility. He could sing "with the plenitude of noble and heroic tone . . . and also, at times, with an almost disembodied exaltation that lifts his singing into a great mood of consecrational ecstasy," wrote Lawrence Gilman in the *Herald Tribune.* After the debut of Kirsten Flagstad in 1935, the Wagner repertory began to dominate the operatic proceedings at the Metropolitan and also to draw tremendous audiences. This lasted for over a decade, and Melchior was accepted as the foremost *Heldentenor* of his time.

Though Melchior occasionally appeared as Otello, Wagner was the territory he cultivated most fully and most successfully throughout his career. In all, he appeared in 971 performances of 7 Wagner works, 476 of them at the Metropolitan Opera. He was heard as Tristan 230 times; Jean de Reszke had sung the part less than 50 times.

On February 22, 1935, Melchior's one hundredth appearance as Siegfried was celebrated at the Metropolitan. At the conclusion of that performance, he was presented with a sword forged by Kenneth Lynch after an old Viking weapon. The presentation was made by the Danish consul general in the presence of Mayor La Guardia and Gatti-Casazza, the general manager of the Metropolitan Opera. Melchior used this sword in all his subsequent appearances as Siegfried.

On February 17, 1946, Melchior once again was honored by his colleagues at the Metropolitan Opera—on the twentieth anniversary of his first appearance at the Metropolitan. The event was a special performance at which Melchior and Lotte Lehmann sang a first-act duet from *Die Walküre.* This was followed by the second act of *Tristan and Isolde* and the third act of *Lohengrin.* "At the end of each excerpt," reported the New York *Times,* "he and his colleagues were greeted with thunderous applause and bravos, and when Mr. Melchior appeared for solo curtain calls his admirers really let go with their hosannas. At the end he made a graceful little curtain speech in which he pleaded for a helping hand for young American artists in a time when a ravaged world looks to the United States for leadership in opera." Another ceremo-

ny took place backstage during which Edward Johnson, the general manager of the company, referred to Melchior as "a pillar of strength in the Wagnerian wing" and presented him with a silver bowl and plate.

Melchior's first wife was Inger Nathansen, an actress and singer in operettas, whom he married in November 1915. They had two children. They were divorced a decade later, and on May 26, 1925, Melchior married Maria Hacker, a well-known German motion-picture star sometimes described as the "Mary Pickford of Germany." Even without comparison to her husband, with his formidable physical proportions, she was pert and petite, standing five feet three and weighing just over a hundred pounds. She was always called *Kleinchen* (little one) by her husband and their friends.

Their meeting followed the lines of a romantic movie scenario. Maria was filming a picture in which she was required to parachute from a plane. The wind carried her off course and brought her into the backyard of Melchior's home in Munich. The romance began at that time. After her marriage, Maria resigned from all motion-picture duties to become her husband's secretary, business manager, and overall advisor. She accompanied him on all his tours and attended all of his performances.

Offstage, Melchior was Siegfried to the life. He was six feet three and weighed two hundred and fifty pounds. His collar was a size eighteen, his shoes a size twelve. Like Siegfried, he particularly enjoyed hunting. Every year he embarked on extended expeditions. At one time he and his friends shot 368 pheasants, at another he felled a six-hundred-pound bear in the Canadian shooting hideout of his friend, the opera tenor Richard Crooks. On still another occasion he shot a sixteen-hundred-pound American bison. In 1935 Melchior was almost killed. While hunting wild pigs in South America he turned to find a panther leaping at him; only his coolness and the accuracy of his shot saved him.

Melchior was as expansive in his personal habits as in his size. A characteristic meal included an appetizer, soup, beefsteak, potatoes, vegetables, salad, dessert, coffee, a quart of burgundy, and a Havana cigar. At other times he drank beer in great quantities. When he took a walk, it might very well turn out to be a twenty-five-mile hike. When traveling, he took along with him twenty-two trunks and sometimes his five dogs. A game of bridge or skat would often become an all-night session.

His diversions, in addition to hunting and playing cards, included fishing, hiking, boxing, watching baseball games, and cooking. He was a specialist in the preparation of oxtail soup (it required two days for cooking) and also in mixing fruit bowls. He often celebrated his birthday by preparing for his guests a smorgasbord which included one hundred and fifty varieties of food.

Melchior became an American citizen on June 13, 1947. During his later years at the Metropolitan he had two residences. One was a thirty-seventh-floor apartment in Essex House in New York City overlooking Central Park. The other was a hilltop house on Mulholland Drive in Beverly Hills, California, called The Viking.

In addition to his performances at the Metropolitan Opera, Melchior served as principal German tenor at the Berlin State Opera and was a guest artist at the world's leading opera houses.

When Rudolf Bing became the general manager of the Metropolitan Opera, he failed to contact Melchior about the renewal of his contract though he was then negotiating with other Wagnerian singers. Piqued, Melchior announced his retirement from the Metropolitan. "I would assume," he said at the time, "that the natural courtesy of the management would dictate a call to any leading artist who had appeared regularly with the company for twenty-four years." His final appearance at the Metropolitan Opera was in *Lohengrin* on February 2, 1950. In his fourteen years he had made 392 appearances in New York and 107 on tour, heard most frequently as Tristan (129 times), Siegmund (83 times), and Tannhäuser (70 times).

The hostility between Melchior and Bing was intensified in the ensuing years when Bing failed to invite Melchior to attend a single performance at the opera house during his regime. When Schuyler Chapin took over the directorial reins from Bing, he tried to make amends by inviting Melchior to be his guest at a Wagnerian performance in 1972–1973, but by then Melchior had become an invalid and could not attend.

After leaving the Metropolitan Opera, Melchior made sporadic appearances with opera companies in Europe. His principal activity, however, was limited to giving recitals and appearing as a guest star on radio and television programs. He had been a pioneer in radio broadcasting—he had performed with Melba in 1920 in the first radio transmission from the Marconi Experimental Station in England. As late as his seventieth year he sang in a performance of *Die Walküre* with the Danish State Radio Orchestra over Danish radio. He also made a number of appearances in motion pictures: *Two Sisters from Boston* (1946), *This Time for Keeps* (1947), *Luxury Liner* (1948), and *The Stars Are Singing* (1953).

The fiftieth anniversary of his bow in opera was remembered on April 18, 1963, at a concert in Garden City, Long Island, when Melchior appeared with the American Symphony Orchestra, Leopold Stokowski conducting. One month later the Royal Danish Opera in Copenhagen honored him. But the Metropolitan Opera, during the regime of Bing, ignored the occasion.

Melchior's wife died in February 1963. On May 23, 1964, he married his secretary, Mary Markham. They were divorced in 1965.

Numerous honors were bestowed upon Melchior during his career. Denmark appointed him Royal Court Singer and bestowed on him the Knighthood of Dannebrog, the Silver Cross, and the gold medal Ingenio et Arti. He was also made Commander of Order of the White Rose in Finland and Chevalier of the French Legion of Honor. Chile presented him with the El Merito award and Germany with the Grosses Verdeinstkreuz. For his services at Bayreuth he was given the Carl Eduard Medal, First Class, from Saxe-Coburg-Gotha. In 1972 he received the highest award for recordings in Germany, the Deutsche Schallplattenpreis, for a two-record album, *Melchior, The Wagner Tenor of the Century*, comprising recordings he had made in London and Berlin between 1926 and 1930 which had gone out of print.

In 1965 Melchior created the Heldentenor Foundation which provides funds for the education and support for at least a year of deserving young tenors.

Lauritz Melchior died of a liver tumor at St. John's Hospital in Santa Monica, California, on March 18, 1973, just two days short of his eighty-third birthday. His ashes, as he had requested, were taken to Copenhagen by his son, Ib, to be interred at the family site where his second wife, Maria, was buried.

A year after his death, a commemorative album of his recordings was released by RCA: a three-disk album covering performances between 1937 and 1946.

ABOUT: Ewen, D. Men and Women Who Make Music. *Periodicals*—High Fidelity/Musical America, October 1972; New York Times, December 24, 1967; Opera News, March 28, 1970, May 1973; Pathfinder, January 25, 1950; Time, April 2, 1973.

(Josef) Willem Mengelberg

1871–1951

(JOSEF) WILLEM MENGELBERG

The tragic last years of Willem Mengelberg's life, spent in exile and in disrepute, should not obscure the fact that in happier times he was one of the world's great conductors. Josef Willem Mengelberg was born in Utrecht, Holland, on March 28, 1871. He came from an old Rhineland family prominent in the arts; his father, an authority on Gothic architecture, helped restore the Cologne Cathedral. Willem attended the Conservatory of Utrecht where his teachers included Richard Hol and M. W. Petri and where he specialized in piano. When he was seventeen, he went on to the Cologne Conservatory, completing his music study with Ludwig Wüllner, Gustav Jensen, and Isidor Seiss.

In 1891 Mengelberg was chosen from among eighty candidates to fill the post of Director of Music of the City of Lucerne in Switzerland. This appointment changed the direction of his musical life, from a career as piano virtuoso for which he had been trained to that of conductor. In Lucerne for the next four years Mengelberg conducted orchestral concerts and several opera performances.

His impressive achievements in Lucerne brought him, in 1895, the post of principal conductor of the Concertgebouw of Amsterdam; three years later he combined this post with that of conductor of the Toonkunst Vereniging, a choral group in Amsterdam. Mengelberg remained the principal conductor of the Concertgebouw Orchestra for half a century. In that time he molded the orchestra to his own image, elevating it to first importance among the world's symphonic organizations and at the same time placing himself among the great conductors of his time. "The orchestra became his

Mengelberg: mĕng′ ĕl bĕrк

personal instrument; he coaxed from it a remarkable range of sounds from supple to blazingly bold, all controlled by a prodigious intellectual and technical discipline," wrote Abram Chipman in *High Fidelity* magazine. "Every interpretative 'quirk' had its organizational place in the over-all scheme. Accelerandos, ritards, pauses, and the like were always devices to accentuate an expressive or transitional point in the musical structure. ... His most romanticized ideas were delivered with astonishing tautness and precision. ... Woodwinds sound immaculately refined and limpid; the horns are full and noble without thickness; trumpets are piercing without nasality; and trombones and tubas snarl majestically. Mengelberg created in the Concertgebouw one of the world's supreme orchestral glories ... and that legacy has survived to our time."

His festivals of music by Beethoven, Mahler, or Richard Strauss—three composers for whom he had a special affinity—became musical events of prime significance. Richard Strauss considered him one of the outstanding interpreters of his symphonic music and in gratitude dedicated to him his tone poem *Ein Heldenleben*. Mengelberg was one of two or three conductors to keep Mahler's music alive in the repertory, and he espoused the post-Romantic music of Reger and avant-garde music of Schoenberg and Bartók at a time when it was rarely performed. Among his world premieres were Bartók's Violin Concerto No.2 (April 23, 1939), Hindemith's *Der Schwanendreher* (November 14, 1935), Hindemith's Violin Concerto (March 14, 1940), Kodály's *Peacock Variations,* commissioned for the fiftieth anniversary of the Concertgebouw (November 23, 1939), Willem Pijper's Symphony No.1 (April 23, 1918), Pijper's Symphony No.2 (November 2, 1922), and Lazare Saminsky's Symphony No.2 (November 16, 1922).

Invitations to appear as guest conductor of leading orchestras everywhere spread Mengelberg's fame throughout the music world. In 1903 he appeared in London for the first time to participate in a Richard Strauss festival. Two years later he made a brief visit to the United States to conduct the New York Philharmonic Orchestra, making his American debut on November 11, 1905, in a program made up of Schumann's Symphony No.4, Strauss's *Ein Heldenleben,* and Brahms's Violin Concerto. "It was in *Ein Heldenleben* that Mr. Mengelberg showed his mastery as a conductor at its highest power," wrote Richard Aldrich in the New York *Times.* "It was a truly astonishing exhibition that he gave. . . . He models all its phrases, its sections, with a wonderful plasticity, with a subtle feeling for their significance and proportions in the whole, keeping that vast maze clear and distinct, warming and coloring each after its fashion and lifting them to the high power of eloquence."

From 1907 to 1920 Mengelberg was the conductor of the Museum Concerts in Frankfort, Germany. There from 1908 to 1920 he also led the St. Cecilia Society. In Frankfort, he conducted the world premiere of Max Reger's *Konzert im Alten Stil* on October 4, 1912. During this same period he retained his post in Amsterdam. From 1911 to 1914 he was also the regular conductor of the London Symphony Orchestra and the Royal Philharmonic in London. And during these pre–World War I years he also conducted in Italy, France, and Russia.

When his twenty-fifth anniversary as principal conductor of the Concertgebouw Orchestra was commemorated in 1920, a gift of one hundred thousand gulden was raised for him by popular subscription. Mengelberg insisted on having this money used to defray the expenses of a monumental Mahler festival covering all Mahler's important symphonic works. This Mahler festival was one of the great artistic events in Europe that year; it was the subject of a book, *Das Mahlerfest in Amsterdam* (1920),

written by Mengelberg's cousin, the musicologist Rudolf Mengelberg.

In January 1921 Mengelberg returned to New York to conduct several performances of the newly organized National Symphony Orchestra in New York. He was received ecstatically by both press and audiences. One newspaper in New York described the excesses to which New York audiences went in expressing their adulation for Mengelberg. He was kissed, caressed, touched, and mobbed by swarming crowds of admirers as if he were a star of the silent screen.

When the National Symphony Orchestra was absorbed by the New York Philharmonic, Mengelberg was appointed permanent conductor. He held this post eight years, and his reign over the symphonic life of New York was brilliant. His performances of the music of Bach, Beethoven, Brahms, and Richard Strauss were regarded as the last word in authority and understanding. His presentations of Mahler's music, most of it then unknown to average New Yorkers, were revelations. In New York he offered the world premieres of Kodály's *Háry János Suite* (December 15, 1927), Milhaud's *Le Carnaval d'Aix* (December 9, 1926), Respighi's Piano Concerto (December 31, 1925), the American premieres of Kodály's *Psalmus Hungaricus* (December 19, 1927) and the three orchestral preludes to Pfitzner's opera *Palestrina* (November 11, 1926), among other works. He also conducted the New York Philharmonic in its first recording, a performance of Beethoven's *Coriolanus Overture,* released in 1922.

In recognition of his services to the musical life of New York, Columbia University conferred on him an honorary doctorate in music in 1928. Two years later Mengelberg resigned from the New York Philharmonic, leaving under a cloud. His one-time public had been wooed away by Arturo Toscanini, who had made his bow with the New York Philharmonic in 1926.

With considerable bitterness Mengelberg returned to Europe determined never to return to the United States. Back with his Concertgebouw Orchestra, where his word was the final law and where his public had remained loyal, his position as one of the world's foremost conductors remained secure.

"He is among the two or three excelling masters of orchestral technique," wrote Lawrence Gilman in the New York *Herald Tribune.* "His knowledge of sonorities, of instrumental resources, of the long and difficult path that leads from conception to realization, is unquestioned and complete. . . . When he is in the vein, his passion and energy and momentum, his amazing power, his breadth and sweep of imagination carry everything before them."

In 1933 Mengelberg was appointed professor of music at Utrecht University. Three years later the fortieth anniversary of his appointment to the Concertgebouw Orchestra was celebrated in Amsterdam with a festival of Dutch music.

As early as 1936 he was criticized in the Dutch press for his favorable opinion of the Nazi regime in Germany. These criticisms increased during World War II when Mengelberg conducted orchestras in Germany and when (in 1941) he accepted an appointment to the Nazi Culture Cabinet. He was often seen in the company of the leaders of the Nazi government. By 1945 Mengelberg knew the Nazi cause was lost. He fled to Switzerland. In July 1945, immediately after V-E day, a Dutch investigating board convicted him of complicity with the enemy during the Nazi occupation of Holland. The Netherlands Central Council of Honor for the Arts denied him forever the right to conduct in Holland. When Mengelberg appealed, the sentence was reduced to six years, but in view of Mengelberg's age and poor health it continued to be a life term in reality. In 1947 a gold medal once presented to him by Queen Wilhelmina was withdrawn, and in 1949 an annuity which had been granted him in 1939, and which he had been receiving even after the conviction, was terminated.

Willem Mengelberg died in his villa in Chur, Switzerland, on March 21, 1951, after two strokes.

In her biography of Mengelberg, Edna R. Sollitt wrote: "Mengelberg can be severe; it is even terrible to watch him in a rare moment of anger, when he maintains a silence that is absolutely thunderous. But there is always dignity, always reason and control to the fore, and he never indulges in nerves, hysteria, or temper. And never does a rehearsal finish in anger, or a player leave his presence with a weight of pain or injustice in his heart. . . .

"Never lived a man who better loved a bit of fun. Not long ago, at the end of an hour's repolishing of an overture already familiar to the players, and after allowing them to play the last section through, Mengelberg led with full vigor up to the final chords before he laid down his baton and maliciously awaited results. Anything more comic than the bewildered sheep-like confusion which followed would be hard to imagine and the rehearsal ended in gales of laughter."

He liked the simple life and the mountains. Each summer he would escape to his small chalet in Switzerland where he enjoyed taking long hikes. After a long excursion, he would relax in a soft chair, smoke Russian cigarettes, and pore over scores by contemporary composers. He was considered such an authority on paintings that he was often consulted in disputes regarding Dutch art.

In 1970 a Willem Mengelberg Society was formed in Wauwatosa, Wisconsin, to disseminate information about Mengelberg. It published a Mengelberg discography in the January 1972 issue of *Le Grand Baton.* Re-releases of several of Mengelberg's old recordings with the Concertgebouw Orchestra have helped to confirm for the present generation the high regard in which Mengelberg's conducting was held. Among these reissues have been the only Mengelberg recording of a Mahler symphony (the Fourth)—done on Turnabout, and a performance of Bach's *Passion According to St. Matthew* which Mengelberg had recorded in 1939—done on Philips.

ABOUT: Sollitt, E. R. Mengelberg and the Symphonic Epoch; Sollitt, E. R. ed. Mengelberg Spreckt. *Periodicals*—High Fidelity/Musical America, August 1975.

Yehudi Menuhin

1916–

Yehudi Menuhin, violinist, one of the prodigies of the twentieth century, became a virtuoso of international renown. Born in New York City on April 22, 1916, he was the oldest child and the only son of Moshe and Marutha Menuhin. Yehudi's two younger sisters, Hepzibah and Yaltah, eventually became concert pianists. His father was a Russian who had spent his boyhood in Palestine and later worked in the United States as a Hebrew-school teacher; his mother, though of Tartar extraction, had Jewish antecedents for several generations. When Yehudi was

Menuhin: mĕn′ ῡ ĭn

Menuhin

YEHUDI MENUHIN

an infant, the Menuhins moved to Elizabeth, New Jersey, where his father found a job as a teacher at the Jewish Community Center. He lost the job when he displeased the conservative authorities with his unusual methods of teaching Hebrew and religion. A new move was then made, with San Francisco as its destination. The Menuhins arrived there with just thirty-two cents. Yehudi was an infant of nine months. In San Francisco, Moshe soon found a job as superintendent of the Jewish Education Society. One of his duties was to establish a modern Hebrew school in that city. The salary was sufficient to provide basic necessities but not enough to permit for baby sitters. The elder Menuhins were music lovers and they took Yehudi at the age of two, in a basket, to concerts of the San Francisco Symphony. He listened to the music without making a sound, the first indication his parents had that their son was musical. Another sign came when Yehudi was four. Given a toy violin as a gift, he threw it on the floor in a rage when he discovered how incapable it was of making real music.

A year later he received a real violin, and in May 1921 he started taking lessons with Sigmund Anker.

Only six months after his first lesson, on November 26, Yehudi made his first public appearance at Anker's studio. The following February he was a soloist at a concert of the Pacific Musical Society; at that time Redford Mason predicted in the San Francisco *Examiner* that

Menuhin would "one day be a master of masters."

When Yehudi was seven, he played for Louis Persinger, the concertmaster of the San Francisco Symphony. "Quietly he put the instrument under his chin and began to play," Persinger later recalled. "He was halfway through when I stopped him. I shall never forget the fury that lit up his eyes at my interruption. It was an insult to him and his art. But I had heard enough. . . . There was a spontaneous beauty about Yehudi's playing as if from a deep, mysterious and miraculous well."

Persinger accepted Menuhin as a pupil. "He seemed to absorb everything I taught him the way a sponge absorbs water. His progress both as to the musical and technical side was very rapid." Less than a year after he had begun studying with Persinger, on February 29, 1924, Yehudi appeared as soloist with the San Francisco Symphony, Alfred Hertz conducting, in a performance of Charles de Bériot's *Scène de Ballet*. A debut recital—Menuhin's first—took place at the Scottish Rite Hall on March 25, 1925. This time Redford Mason was led to exclaim in the *Examiner:* "This is not talent; it is genius."

In 1925, when Persinger left San Francisco for New York, the Menuhins followed him. In addition to his violin lessons with Persinger, Yehudi went each Thursday morning to the Institute of Musical Art for classes in ear training, singing, and harmony—the youngest member in a class made up mainly of college students.

He made his New York debut on January 17, 1926, with a recital at the Manhattan Opera House. With Persinger as accompanist, he performed an exacting program that included a Handel sonata, Lalo's *Symphonie Espagnole,* Paganini's Concerto No.1, and some shorter pieces. The critical response was most enthusiastic. *Musical America* said that he played with "a facility and dash almost incredible for one of his years." In San Francisco, he gave a second recital at Scottish Rite Hall on March 6.

A wealthy San Francisco lawyer, Sidney Behrman, came forward as Yehudi's patron, offering to underwrite all expenses for the family for an indefinite period to allow the boy every opportunity to develop his remarkable gifts. This generosity made it possible for the Menuhins to leave for Europe in 1926. They made their home in an apartment on Rue de Sèvres in

Paris. On February 6, 1927, Menuhin made his Paris debut as soloist with the Lamoureux Orchestra in Lalo's *Symphonie Espagnole,* and one week later he performed the Tchaikovsky Violin Concerto with the same orchestra. After the performance of the Tchaikovsky Concerto, Paul Paray, the orchestra's conductor, presented Menuhin with his photograph inscribed: "To Yehudi Menuhin, to whom I owe one of the purest emotions of my life."

These two appearances helped make Yehudi a celebrity; offers for appearances came from many different places. He declined them all to devote himself to further study with Georges Enesco. Enesco prepared him for a return to the New York concert season, this time as a soloist with the New York Symphony Society on November 25, 1927, in the Beethoven Violin Concerto. The critics were beside themselves with superlatives. "Young Menuhin," said Lawrence Gilman in the *Herald Tribune,* "played . . . with a ripeness and dignity of style, a sensitive beauty of conception, an easeful brilliance of technique, which brought great names involuntarily to the tip of the listener's tongue. . . . What you hear . . . takes away the breath and leaves you groping helplessly among the mysteries of the human spirit." In the New York *Times,* Olin Downes wrote without equivocation: "A boy of eleven proved conclusively his right to be ranked with the outstanding interpreters of this music." In the *World,* Samuel Chotzinoff reported: "From the fingers of this child . . . the Beethoven Concerto flowed in all its nobility, its repose, its thoughtful and subjective beauty."

From this point on, Yehudi's march through the world of music was one of uninterrupted triumphs such as few violin prodigies before him or since have experienced. His amazing maturity in the performances of the foremost musical masterworks was a source of endless wonder. On April 12, 1929, he made his debut in Berlin as soloist with the Berlin Philharmonic under Bruno Walter in three concertos (Bach, Beethoven, Brahms). After the concert, Albert Einstein kissed him and said: "Today, Yehudi, you have once again proved to me that there is a God in heaven." Yehudi repeated this program in Dresden and Paris. On November 4, 1929, he made his debut in London with the London Symphony, performing the Brahms Violin Concerto. On November 14, 1931, he was invited by the city of Leipzig to appear with the Gewandhaus Or-

chestra on the occasion of the one hundred and fiftieth anniversary of its founding, with Bruno Walter conducting. This time he was heard in the Mendelssohn Violin Concerto at the end of which Bruno Walter cried out aloud: "This is a miracle! This is godlike! This is genius of the highest order." Yehudi also appeared in recitals, as well as in sonata concerts with his sister, Hepzibah, their first recording together receiving the Prix du Disque in Paris in 1932. In 1934 he embarked on his first world tour, filling 110 engagements in 63 cities of 13 countries.

By the time this world tour ended, he realized that he was changing from prodigy to artist, from child wonder to mature musician. To pass through this transition more gracefully he decided to spend two years of retirement at Alma, the family ranch in Los Gatos in the Santa Cruz mountains of California, to devote himself to reflection, study, and self-examination. As he explained in an interview for the *New Yorker* at the time: "Even at the risk of losing all the golden eggs of the future, I had to find out what made the goose lay those eggs. I wanted to know exactly in what way the smallest articulations of the fingers had to move, what sensation they had to evoke in the mind and in the subconscious, what feeling of ease, of balance, of facility, of strength was involved in each section and each subdivision of the intricate and complicated technique of the violin."

When Menuhin returned to the concert stage in 1937, following this hiatus, the critics unanimously greeted him as one of the foremost violinists of the twentieth century.

He had been an artist of the highest integrity, taste, and artistic ideals from his childhood on, and he remained so in full maturity. He always reached for the highest standards of which his art was capable. Frequently, in giving an encore, he selected a solo sonata or partita of Bach, or a movement from such a sonata or partita, in preference to a technical trifle. Some of his concerts with the major orchestras were made up of three concertos. With the music of Bach and Paganini's First Violin Concerto he went to the original texts *(Urtext),* refusing to follow the accepted grooves set out by all violinists using edited versions. He was always adventurous in performing works of music rarely featured. He helped to popularize Elgar's Violin Concerto, rescuing it from its undeserved neglect. He did yeoman service for rarely heard music of Bartók,

Enesco, Ernest Bloch, William Walton, and of other twentieth century composers, some of which he had commissioned and for some of which he had given the world premieres. He resurrected a concerto (the *Adelaide*) presumably written by Mozart as a child but actually the work of Mario Casadesus, and he introduced to the United States the supposedly "lost" violin concerto of Schumann. He demonstrated his profound devotion to Bach by invariably including on his concert programs, or as an encore, one of the master's works.

On May 26, 1938, Menuhin married Nola Ruby Nicholas, daughter of an Australian industrialist. They had two children before they were divorced in 1947.

During World War II he gave over five hundred concerts for the armed forces of the United States and the Allies, performing in hospitals, camps, war zones, on ships, and for various war-relief drives. In the fall of 1944 he became the first major artist to perform in liberated Paris and he used this occasion to perform the music of a Jew: Mendelssohn's Violin Concerto. He followed this with concerts in Antwerp, just a few days after that port had been freed; in Aachen, a stone's throw from the actual war front; and in the recently liberated cities of Brussels, Bucharest, and Budapest. He was the first soloist invited by the United States Military Government in Germany to perform in Berlin in the postwar period—as soloist with the Berlin Philharmonic Orchestra under Wilhelm Furtwängler in 1947. He also became the first American musician to perform in Moscow after the war's end, on invitation of the Soviet government. In 1951 he was one of the first American concert artists to perform in Japan following V-J day. And it was mainly through his influence that the first significant cultural exchange between the United States and the Soviet Union took place in 1955, with Emil Gilels and David Oistrakh concertizing in the United States and Menuhin in Moscow in May 1956.

Following his divorce from Nola, Menuhin married Diana Rosamond Gould, a successful actress and ballerina and the daughter of an official of the British Foreign Office—on October 19, 1947. They had two sons, one of whom, Jeremy, embarked upon a career as piano virtuoso. Menuhin maintained his Los Gatos ranch, Alma, and later acquired a chalet in Gstaad, Switzerland, a seventeenth century town house in the Highgate section of London, and a house on the Greek island of Mykonos.

Although in his boyhood Menuhin enjoyed such physical activities as swimming, horseback riding, bicycling, and hiking, in his mature years he has turned to more sedentary, cultural, intellectual, and metaphysical pursuits. His interests outside music are many and varied: reading (in six languages), art, sculpture, architecture, science, religion, politics. A serious student of Oriental philosophies, he has for many years practiced and been a passionate advocate of yoga. He discussed the value of yoga in general, and to his own being in particular, during a telecast over BBC in London in 1963 entitled "Yehudi Menuhin and His Guru." He has followed a health diet for many years and scrupulously avoids all white bread, white rice, white sugar, and other similar foods.

He has often allied himself with political or humanitarian causes. His liberal views and avowed humanitarianism have made him the center of considerable controversy. When he made his first tour of Israel in 1950 there was hostility at his coming since many in Israel could not forget that he had performed in Germany three years earlier. On arriving he said: "I realize that it might be asking too much of those who have suffered beyond human endurance that they share my convictions now or ever. I also realize that I may have inadvertently reopened old wounds and have caused pain. This I regret most deeply, and I offer my apologies to all those whom I may have hurt. But I cannot renounce the principles by which I live." After his first few performances in Israel, the grievance against him was completely forgotten and he was accepted as a favorite son. He duplicated the triumph of 1950 on tours in 1951 and 1952, and in 1953 he was the official guest of the Israeli government, as soloist with the Israel Philharmonic. In subsequent years, however, his independence of thought and action once again brought him into dispute with the people of Israel: after the Six-Day War when he insisted on performing charity concerts in the Arab-speaking countries for the benefit of Arab refugees; in 1975, when he spoke out in favor of Israel's exclusion from UNESCO conferences. "It was definitely the action of a Jew extending a hand of peace to the Arab," he explained about his benefit concerts in Arab countries, "an indication of compassion, if you like, and recognition of the fact that pain, suffering, misery know no boundaries."

On August 24, 1968, Menuhin joined a number of other musicians in denouncing the invasion of Czechoslovakia by the forces of the Soviet Union, Poland, Hungary, Bulgaria, and East Germany. In 1971, at a music congress in Moscow sponsored by UNESCO, he once again aroused the hostility of the Soviets by condemning (in Russian) narrow political nationalism as a destructive force in creativity and calling for open immigration policies.

Menuhin has extended his musical horizon by combining the playing of the violin with the founding and directing of music festivals, by turning to conducting, and by involving himself in music education.

In 1956 he inaugurated an annual summer festival at the church of Saanen, near his home in Gstaad, Switzerland. In 1959 he organized the Bath Festival in England, which he directed for ten years. When Menuhin withdrew from this festival in 1968 because of lack of financial support from the city, he transferred these festival activities to Windsor Castle where he formed the Menuhin Festival Orchestra. As a conductor, he made his debut with the Dallas Symphony towards the end of World War II. But he abandoned the baton until 1959 when he began leading the Bath Festival Orchestra, which toured in 1967 with performances at Expo '67 in Montreal and a series of concerts at the Lincoln Center for the Performing Arts in New York and in several other cities. Following his appearance in Montreal, Raymond Ericson reported to the New York *Times:* "It must be admitted that he was one of the most diffident conductors to be seen, looking a bit apologetic about being on the stand and waving his small baton. He seldom brought his left hand into use, and then only to emphasize a beat. . . . He is sensitive to tempo, its steadiness and its flexibility, and this he communicates clearly."

With the Menuhin Festival Orchestra he toured the United States in the spring of 1971. He also conducted opera at the Bath Festival, the first being *Così fan Tutte* in 1966. In addition to leading his own chamber orchestras, Menuhin has appeared as a guest conductor of the London Symphony, the Berlin Philharmonic, the American Symphony Orchestra, and several other established symphonic organizations. He was the conductor of the orchestra when his son,

Jeremy, made his debut as pianist in New York on December 6, 1970, performing Beethoven's Piano Concerto No.3.

As an educator, Menuhin founded in 1963 a school of music in Stoke d'Abernon, Surrey, England, where talented children between the ages of eight and fourteen could receive comprehensive training in music and academic subjects. Menuhin himself conducted master classes in violin playing. To celebrate the school's tenth anniversary, students performed for the Queen Mother at St. James's Palace. In 1973 the Ministry of Education and Science in England granted the school the same status accorded to the Royal Ballet School. Menuhin the educator was the subject of the television program "Menuhin Teaches," telecast in Europe by BBC-TV and in the United States by the NET network.

A ninety-minute television profile of Menuhin was produced in France in 1971: "Yehudi Menuhin, Chemin de Lumière." This was just one of numerous television programs on which through the years he has appeared not only as a violinist but also as a conductor and narrator.

A little less than one week short of his sixtieth birthday, on April 15, 1976, Menuhin celebrated the event with a concert in Carnegie Hall in New York where he joined his son Jeremy, Rostropovich, and Ernst Wallfisch in a performance of Fauré's Piano Quartet in C minor and Beethoven's *Archduke Trio.* The proceeds went jointly to the Jerusalem Foundation and to the Yehudi Menuhin School for Young Musicians in England. On April 23, 1976, he shared the stage of the Royal Festival Hall with his son, Jeremy, to aid Amnesty, and on May 9, with Rostropovich, he was heard in London in the Brahms *Double Concerto* for the benefit of his school. Then, fulfilling a promise he had made to his wife, Menuhin decided to celebrate his sixtieth year by taking a sabbatical from the concert stage in order to enjoy leisure, to study new works, to do much reading, and to try his hand at caricatures and painting. But this was not a total withdrawal, since a few concerts for what he regarded as good causes had to be given. During the summer of 1976 he gave performances in Gstaad as part of its twentieth anniversary celebration.

On July 3, 1976, he helped celebrate the Bicentennial of the United States by performing at Wolf Trap in Washington; that concert began at ten in the evening so that the final notes could coincide with the dawn of the Fourth of July;

and on this occasion he introduced a new violin concerto by Alan Hovhaness.

In honor of Menuhin's sixtieth birthday, HMV (the Gramophone Company) issued a commemorative album of three records made up of his early recordings between 1931 and 1938. Ten years earlier, for his fiftieth birthday, they had released a three-disk album offering a cross section of Menuhin's career as violin soloist, as a performer in chamber music, and as conductor.

Menuhin has been given the highest honor a non-British subject can receive—the Queen of England made him Honorary Knight Commander of the Order of the British Empire in 1966. He has also been awarded the Order of Merit by the German Federal Republic; the Royal Order of the Phoenix in Greece; the Legion of Honor, the Croix de Lorraine, and the Order of Arts and Letters in France; the Sonning Music Prize in Denmark; the Ordre de la Couronne and the Order of Leopold in Belgium. In 1968 he received the Jawaharlal Nehru Award for International Understanding. In addition, he has been given the gold medal of the Royal Philharmonic Society of London, the Cobbett Medal of the Worshipful Company of Musicians in England, the Freedom of Edinburgh, and an honorary Swiss citizenship. That honorary citizenship, in 1970, caused a misunderstanding with the United States State Department which informed him that as a result he had lost his American citizenship. When Menuhin wrote to the Secretary of State of his shock at this development, the Secretary sent him a personal note reversing this preliminary finding and maintaining that it had all been the result of a misunderstanding.

Menuhin is the author of *Six Lessons with Menuhin* (1972), *Theme and Variations* (1972), an autobiography, *Unfinished Journey* (1976), and (with William Primrose) *Violin and Viola* (1976). For a number of years he has served as president of the International Council of Music.

Home base for the Menuhins is their Highgate house a half hour from London; but Menuhin still maintains the ranch at Los Gatos in California where he lived with his parents and sisters for many years.

ABOUT: Fenby, E. Menuhin's House of Music; Magidoff, R. Yehudi Menuhin: The Story of the Man and the Musician; Menuhin, Y. Theme and Variations; Menuhin, Y. Unfinished Journey; Wymer, N. Yehudi Menuhin. *Periodicals*—Esquire, May 1962; Gramophone (London), April 1976; Hi-Fi, May 1971; Life, May 20, 1966; New York Times, November 27, 1966; New Yorker, October 8 and 15, 1955; Newsweek, May 9, 1966; Saturday Review, November 27, 1965, April 16, 1976.

Robert Merrill

1917–

Robert Merrill (originally Morris Miller), baritone, was born in the Williamsburg section of Brooklyn, New York, on June 4, 1917. He was the oldest of three children; the two others died in infancy from influenza. His father, Abraham Miller, was a sweatshop sewing-machine operator and later a dealer in shoes; his mother, Lillian Balaban Miller, was a frustrated soprano who had had an operatic and concert career in Poland before her marriage and who sang over local radio stations in Brooklyn. As soon as his mother discovered that Robert was blessed with a beautiful singing voice, she tried to fulfill her own ambitions through her son's career.

"From the first time I yelled 'Mama' from the courtyard on South Second Street," Merrill recalled in his autobiography, *Once More from the Beginning,* "Mama was sure of my future and called me 'singer mine.' No matter how hard I tried to hide it, to make believe that I hated it, to avoid any mention of my voice, I did love to sing. If Mama had gone about her business, I might have come around to it early; but she pressured and pushed and pulled until, in my shyness, I refused to sing for anybody." But since there was a phonograph in his home, and it was well equipped with recordings by opera stars, he learned some of the popular arias and became acquainted with the voices of the operatic greats.

When young, he had still another love: baseball. "It was like food and drink to me; and I often proved it by playing instead of having lunch, since that was the only time I could escape my mother's hawkeye."

After graduating from P.S. 19 in Brooklyn, Merrill went to New Utrecht High School where he was a member of its baseball team. "I avoided school whenever possible. With the twenty-five cents a day for lunch and the dime carfare for

ROBERT MERRILL

the elevated train, I had enough to go to the Star
Burlesque when I cut classes."

While he was in high school, his mother took
him to a singing studio in the William Fox Theater in Brooklyn where, for a dollar and a half
a lesson, he was taught "popular interpretation." Learning to sing in the style of Bing
Crosby, he found a spot over a small Brooklyn
radio station performing Crosby favorites three
times a week—for the first time using the name
of Merrill instead of Miller "to keep my musical
activities secret from the gang." This radio stint,
for which he received no payment, lasted eighteen months. Since there was no money for him
in music, he began thinking of becoming a
professional baseball player. For a time he was
a pitcher for a semiprofessional club, then had a
tryout with the Brooklyn Dodgers and was rejected.

From New Utrecht, after graduation in 1935,
Merrill went on to a trade school to learn cabi-
netmaking. "I couldn't make anything without
shedding blood. I couldn't even make a pair of
bookends that matched." He did not last long.
He then began earning his living first by working
in a shoe store in New York's Harlem, and then
in his uncle's dress manufacturing firm in New
York City. One day, while pushing the cart of
dresses along Broadway, he passed the Metropolitan Opera House from which emanated
the sounds of singing voices. He invaded the
darkened auditorium and listened to a rehearsal
of *La Traviata* by Lawrence Tibbett and
Lucrezia Bori. "It was the first time that I in-

haled the dank, glorious air that is the life's
breath of the stagestruck," he has said.

Merrill heard his first complete opera performance when he was eighteen. At that time he
was already studying voice seriously with his
first and most important teacher, Samuel Margolis. Margolis acquired for Merrill and his
mother a pair of tickets in the topmost reaches
of the opera house for a performance of *Il Trovatore.* As Merrill has said, that night changed him
from "a confused stagestruck kid to a true opera
student."

While working at his vocal studies with Margolis, Merrill supported himself by holding
down various menial jobs, including one in a
sweatshop. He also filled minor singing engagements in synagogues, at weddings and bar mitz-
vahs, and in Jewish theaters along Second
Avenue on New York's East Side. He was given
a singing stint on the *Rotterdam,* which was
cruising the Bahamas, and several others in New
York's mountain resorts. Singing the famous
"Largo al factotum" aria from *The Barber of
Seville* he won first prize on Major Bowes's ama-
teur-hour radio program. This led to Merrill's
first coast-to-coast broadcast with the NBC
Concert Orchestra, to his first sustaining program (Phil Spitalny's "Serenade to America")
and to his first sponsored radio show.

The year 1944 was an eventful one for Merrill.
He appeared for eight weeks as a principal vocalist at Radio City Music Hall in New York; he
made his first recording (an RCA Victor album
with Jeanette MacDonald of highlights from
Sigmund Romberg's musical comedy *Up in Central Park*); he was booked by the National Concerts and Artists Corporation to tour the
hinterlands in concerts; and he made his opera
debut as the elder Germont in *La Traviata* with
the Detroit Opera Company. Of his opera debut,
Merrill recalls: "Well coached for the role, I did
all right vocally, but my acting wouldn't have
won any awards. That I survived the evening's
nerves without a breakdown or heart attack was
a triumph in itself." Soon after this debut, and
still in 1944, Merrill was called upon to sing
Tonio in *I Pagliacci* in Worcester, Massachusetts, Escamillo to Gladys Swarthout's Carmen in Hartford, Connecticut, and Amonasro in
Aida in Trenton, New Jersey.

"Largo al factotum," with which Merrill was
now bringing down the house regularly almost
every time he sang it and which he sang on his

first coast-to-coast radio program, also became one of several arias he sang for the Metropolitan Opera Auditions of the Air in 1945. When Merrill first entered this competition in 1939, he failed to win. But in 1945 he captured first prize and with it an engagement at the Metropolitan Opera. His debut took place on December 15, 1945, as the elder Germont; he was the youngest man ever to sing that role at the Metropolitan. The audience welcomed him warmly, and so did the New York critics. In the New York *Times,* Olin Downes hailed the "bel canto singing of the new young baritone."

"*La Traviata* was my real beginning," Merrill says. That season he also appeared as Ashton in *Lucia di Lammermoor* and as Escamillo during the regular season. That spring he was a member of the Metropolitan Opera touring company. Later in the season he recorded his first operatic disk (the second act of *La Traviata* for RCA Victor). He was also engaged to star in and be the master of ceremonies for an RCA Victor-sponsored radio show, "Music America Loves Best," that lasted five years, supplementing his own radio program, "The Robert Merrill Show."

In 1946 Toscanini chose Merrill to appear as the elder Germont in his broadcast performance of *La Traviata* over the NBC radio network. Toscanini again selected him (this time for the role of Renato) when he conducted a radio performance of *Un Ballo in Maschera* over NBC in 1954. In July 1946 Merrill became the only singer to appear at a joint service held by both houses of Congress as a memorial to President Roosevelt. After that, he sang several times at birthday parties for President Truman and at President Truman's inauguration ceremonies in 1949. He also sang for three later American Presidents: Eisenhower, Kennedy, and Johnson.

In 1946–1947 Merrill achieved successes at the Metropolitan Opera as Amonasro, Figaro in *The Barber of Seville,* Valentin in *Faust,* and Count di Luna in *Il Trovatore.* In 1949 and 1950 he made his first appearances on television on the "Saturday Night Revue" and on "Your Show of Shows" and enjoyed a one-hundred-thousand-disk sale for his Victor recording of "The Whiffenpoof Song."

By 1950 Merrill had become such an important member of the Metropolitan Opera company that he was called upon to help open the 1950–1951 season on November 6 in the title

role of *Don Carlo.* However, in 1951 he made an unfortunate decision that almost wrecked his opera career. Offered sixty-five thousand dollars by Paramount Pictures to appear in a motion picture, he broke his contract to tour with the Metropolitan Opera so that he might go out to Hollywood. Rudolf Bing, general manager of the Metropolitan, dismissed him from the company. The picture, *Aaron Slick from Punkin Creek,* was a failure, and Merrill did not become the movie star he had dreamed of being. His troubles were compounded when Bing remained deaf to all of Merrill's entreaties, apologies, and promises and refused to reengage him.

After the completion of his stint on *Aaron Slick from Punkin Creek,* unable to get any commitment from the Metropolitan Opera, Merrill undertook a tour under the auspices of the USO to sing for American armed forces in the camps of Austria and Germany. In Salzburg, he learned that Rudolf Bing was in the city at the Goldener Hirsch. Once again Merrill put aside dignity and pride to plead with Bing for his old job, and once again Bing told him: "Never, Merrill, never as long as I am general manager." Back in New York, Merrill continued to woo Bing until, at last, Bing offered to reengage him if he stood ready to make a public apology. "Mr. Bing had demanded absolute surrender," Merrill says, "and he got it. . . . He accepted my apology in a letter—again making front-page news. Our exchange was meant to be public, my repentance well publicized. My redemption was now equally advertised." To Merrill's apologetic letter, Bing sent a succinct response: "To admit one's mistakes the way you have done is a sign of moral courage and decency. I shall be willing to forget the past." On March 11, 1952, Merrill was back on the stage of the Metropolitan as Count di Luna. His rehabilitation was further proved in 1953 when he was called upon to help open a new season (on November 16) as Valentin in *Faust.*

While overcoming his professional problem, Merrill was complicating his personal life. On March 30, 1952, he married Roberta Peters, a young and attractive soprano of the Metropolitan Opera. "Roberta was a sweet girl, and I was terribly infatuated with her," he recalls. "Our need for each other was mutual; and by the time the press got through with us we were convinced we were in love." But the marriage proved a disaster and was terminated after only ten weeks. "It was wrong from the beginning," Merrill explained to an interviewer. "I realized that with two people building a career, it's like going up to bat with two strikes on you." And in his autobiography he added: "The press had us fancied as Romeo and Juliet. I'm afraid we were more like Hansel and Gretel. ... We never should have married in the first place. I had swept her off her feet, but now we were both off balance." When, after ten weeks, Peters went to Hollywood to make a movie and Merrill embarked on a concert tour, they separated and never got together again. But they remained good friends following their divorce on June 26, 1952, and on numerous occasions they have appeared in joint recitals.

On October 31, 1970, Merrill celebrated the twenty-fifth anniversary of his debut at the Metropolitan Opera with a gala performance of the opera in which he had first been heard there—*La Traviata.* By then he had sung this role over five hundred times in opera houses the world over (sixty-four times at the Metropolitan). As part of the ceremonial that evening, eight of the sixteen sopranos who had appeared with him as Violetta through the years were gathered on the stage after the third act: Licia Albanese, Phyllis Curtin, Anna Moffo, Renata Tebaldi, Renata Scotto, Delia Rigal, Gabriella Tucci, and Joan Sutherland. After the performance, Merrill was the guest of honor at the annual Opera Ball.

During his twenty-five years at the Metropolitan, Merrill had been heard in twenty-one operas. In addition to those already mentioned were the roles of Tchelakov in *Boris Godunov,* Rigoletto, the High Priest in *Samson and Delilah,* Rodrigo in *Don Carlo,* Silvio and Tonio in *I Pagliacci,* Marcello in *La Bohème,* Renato in *Un Ballo in Maschera,* Malatesta in *Don Pasquale,* Barnaba in *La Gioconda,* Don Carlo in *La Forza del Destino,* Gérard in *Andrea Chénier,* Iago in *Otello,* and Scarpia in *Tosca.* Merrill's five-hundredth performance as Count di Luna took place on March 5, 1973. He was the only current principal at the Metropolitan to have reached such a total in any opera.

In 1976 Merrill announced that he was through with the Metropolitan Opera. He said the management refused to assign him his favorite roles. When one season they offered him the role of Ashton in *Lucia di Lammermoor,* he turned it down, explaining, "In Ashton they would be wasting me in a role other lyric baritones can do. The fact is there's no rapport at the Met anymore. They have too many people running things. There's no one top man to make decisions."

Merrill made his European debut at Teatro la Fenice in Venice in *La Traviata* in 1961. He followed this successful performance with equally acclaimed appearances at La Scala in Milan. In 1961 he made his bow at the Teatro Colón in Buenos Aires, and in 1967 he helped to open the season at Covent Garden in *La Traviata.* He has appeared in other opera houses besides touring extensively in solo recitals and in joint concerts with Richard Tucker and with Roberta Peters, and he has been a soloist with major orchestras everywhere. In 1970 he made his first appearance in the popular musical theater in the role of Teyve in *Fiddler on the Roof* in St. Louis, and after that on tour.

On May 30, 1954, he married Marion Machno, a graduate in piano of the Juilliard School of Music. At the time of her marriage she was heading for a concert career, which she then abandoned. With their two children, the Merrills live in a ten-room neo-Tudor house in New Rochelle, New York. Merrill has not lost his boyhood enthusiasm for baseball, but the sport that has engaged him most actively is golf. His indoor diversions include the preparation of exotic culinary dishes, reading anything from detective stories to philosophy, collecting paintings and etchings and practicing yoga. He is a talented painter, whose oil canvases of clowns have become famous.

In 1961 Merrill was presented with the opera medal of the Harriet Cohen International Music Award. On October 26, 1967, he received from the mayor of New York City the Handel Medallion for his contributions to the city's culture. He was also awarded an honorary doctorate in music by Gustavus Adolphus College in St. Peters, Minnesota, in 1971.

ABOUT: Merrill, R. and Dody, S. Once More from the Beginning; Merrill, R. and Saffron, R. Between the Acts. *Periodicals*—New York Times, October 25, 1967; Opera News, January 9, 1970.

Michelangeli

1920–

Arturo Benedetti Michelangeli, pianist—who uses only the family name of Michelangeli for his concert appearances—was born in Brescia, Italy, on January 6, 1920. His father, a lawyer, was an amateur musician. Music was basic to Arturo's life from earliest childhood. At the age of three he started lessons on the violin, adding instruction on the piano one year later. His musical training continued at the Venturi Institute in Brescia, mainly with Paolo Chiuieri, under whom he specialized on the violin and organ. He disliked the piano because it was, he said, "too much bim-bam banging." But in his tenth year a severe shoulder ailment forced him to give up the violin. He decided to concentrate on the piano and attended the Milan Conservatory where he was a pupil of Giovanni Anfassi. He received a piano diploma when he was thirteen. Two years later, Maurice Ravel, hearing him perform several Ravel compositions, expressed the highest enthusiasm for his performance.

Though Arturo's father recognized that his son had unusual talent for music, he objected to making music a professional career. For a while, in his late youth, Arturo began to study medicine. When he abandoned medicine, he was encouraged by his father to take on a job in the diplomatic corps. However, by this time Arturo was fully determined to make his way in life as a musician. He left home to be entirely on his own and supported himself by playing the organ. During these formative years there was a one-year lapse from music when he lived at the Laverna Monastery with the intention of becoming a Franciscan.

When he was nineteen he was appointed professor of piano at the Bologna Conservatory. That year he also won top prize in the International Piano Contest in Geneva, Switzerland. Alfred Cortot said of him at that time that he was "Liszt incarnate." But before Michelangeli could make progress as a concert pianist Europe was at war. He joined the Italian air force and reached the rank of lieutenant. Captured by the Germans, he was imprisoned for eight months and then made a daring escape.

When the war ended, Michelangeli began concertizing and soon gained a spectacular reputation for his phenomenal technique, supreme digital control, exquisite feeling for nuances and

MICHELANGELI

shadings, and luminous singing tone. However he fell seriously ill, probably from tuberculosis, and had to spend several years recuperating in a town near the Austrian-Italian border. Little is known about this part of Michelangeli's life.

Returning to the concert stage in the late 1940s, he picked up his brilliant career. In Italy he was acknowledged to be the greatest living Italian pianist and he commanded a fee of one million lire a performance, a fee with few precedents in Italy. Eventually he received the Gold Medal of the Italian Republic. He made his London debut in 1949. One year later he made his first tour of the United States and was well received by public and critics. Nevertheless the tour was broken off midway when Michelangeli could not agree with his manager as to where he was to perform or when.

His idiosyncrasies as a performing artist made him as provocative and as legendary a figure in the music world as his artistry did. At times he would refuse to appear at sold-out concerts if he were not in the mood to perform (though he always insisted that illness and not mere whim was responsible for such defection). He confined his appearances to intermittent concerts and restricted tours, and he was niggardly about making recordings. Wherever he played he had to bring with him his Steinway piano and have his personal tuner travel with him so that the instrument could always be adjusted to his most exacting and sensitive requirements before each concert. He also favored such a low piano stool that his coattails brushed the floor. He confined

536

himself to such a limited repertory that on many of his concert tours he gave only two recital programs, with only minor deviations from one performance to the next.

Despite the circumscribed area of his performances, he did manage to tour South America in the early 1960s, to enjoy success in the Soviet Union in 1964, and in January 1966 to set off for his first world tour. That tour took him back to the United States, after an absence of fifteen years—his first American return engagement taking place in January 1966 in a performance of Beethoven's *Emperor Concerto* with the New York Philharmonic Orchestra. Later the same month he gave a recital in Carnegie Hall at the end of which, as Harold C. Schonberg commented in the New York *Times,* "there was no doubt that one of the more original pianists of the day was in action. Mr. Michelangeli is one of today's great originals. . . . As an interpreter, Mr. Michelangeli suggests something of a throwback. Judging from old records and piano rolls, Busoni would appear to be his progenitor. Mr. Michelangeli strode a line between intellectualism and romanticism, veering first on one side then on the other. . . . With the force of his personality . . . he is able to drive audiences to a frenzy, taking even the doubters along with him."

In describing his own piano style, Michelangeli told John Gruen in an interview for the New York *Times:* "I found my own way of playing the piano. I discovered that the sounds made by the organ and the violin could be translated into pianistic terms. If you speak of my tone, then you must think not of the piano but a combination of the violin and organ."

Michelangeli also told Gruen: "I do not play for others—only for myself and in the service of the composer. It makes no difference to me whether there's an audience or not. When I sit at the keyboard, I am lost. And I think of what I play, and of the sound that comes forth, which is a product of the mind. . . . Before an artist can communicate anything, he must first face himself. He must know who he is. Only then can he dare to make music."

His concert repertory does not include any works by Johann Sebastian Bach (which he prefers to play solely on the organ, and then only for himself). He explains: "Bach should be played on the harpsichord. . . . It's absurd to play Bach on the piano. The piano cannot supply the necessary registrations, and they are essential."

For many years Michelangeli preferred to devote most of his musical energies not to playing the piano but to teaching it. In or about 1946 he began devoting himself to pedagogy with an almost priest-like dedication. He has taught over one thousand piano students (among whom have been Maurizio Pollini and Martha Argerich) and on numerous occasions has even helped to support some of them financially. Each year from the late 1950s until the mid-1960s he rented a villa or a palazzo in Italy, called it the International Academy, equipped it with fifteen or twenty pianos, and took on thirty students tuition free. Depending upon the mood of the teacher a lesson could be called any time of the day or night and it could last twenty minutes or three hours. The number of lessons each student received also varied. Michelangeli was the total dictator, and all students were subjected to a severe regimen requiring them to begin practicing as early as 7 A.M.

His permanent residence was a country home near Brescia and, later, one in Lugano, where he lived with his wife. There was no telephone in either place. Any communication with him is further complicated by the fact that he never writes letters. For most of his adult life, Michelangeli has been a racing-car enthusiast. He has won prizes in numerous races and has twice done the famous Mille Miglia. Occasionally he has served as his own automobile mechanic. He is also an adept skier and mountain climber. His familiar offstage uniform comprises turtleneck sweaters, a dark coat, and slacks. He smokes gold-tipped Turkish cigarettes, enjoys an occasional drink of Scotch, and detests motion pictures.

When he returned to the United States in 1966, Howard Klein, writing in the New York *Times,* described him as follows: "He is about five foot eleven inches, with a large handsome, aristocratic head, and hands that look as though they were carved out of marble. . . . He wears his blond-brown hair long, à la Liszt, and his moustache makes him resemble Claudio Arrau. His brown eyes were half-lidded, opening only after a translation to see the effect his comment had made. His thrust-out chin and tight lower lip show a defiance that could have been arrogant, supercilious or tolerant, but which seemed merely a defense."

Michelangeli is an Academician of the Santa

Milanov

Cecilia Academy in Rome and of the Accademia Cherubini in Florence.

ABOUT: High Fidelity/Musical America, January 1966; New York Times, January 16, 1966, August 21, 1977; Saturday Review, July 30, 1960.

ZINKA MILANOV

Zinka Milanov

1906–

Zinka Milanov (originally Zinka Kunc), soprano, was born in Zagreb, Yugoslavia, on May 17, 1906, the daughter of Rudolf Kunc, a banker, and Ljubica Smiciklas Kunc. Her family was musical. "My father," she revealed to Robert Jacobson in *Opera News,* "had a beautiful baritone voice, like Battistini's, and I inherited that. He put all his love into his children because he did not have a career—he wanted to, but his family prevented it. So we had music at home and worked together as children." A brother, Božidar, was a piano prodigy who became a successful singing coach and the composer of songs some of which Milanov featured in her early recitals. Zinka began studying singing when she was about four. By the time she was six she often performed at social gatherings; in her eighth year she sang the role of Carmen in a family performance of Bizet's opera. After graduation at fourteen from the Girls' Evangelical School in Zagreb, she entered the Zagreb Academy, becoming a pupil of Marija Kostrencic. One year later she gave her first recitals. Milka Ternina, Wagnerian soprano, heard her on this occasion and was so impressed by her talent that she offered to be her teacher without tuition; this was the only time Ternina accepted a pupil. Zinka was Ternina's pupil for three years. After that her vocal studies were completed with Carpi in Prague, Jacques Stückgold in Berlin, and with her brother, Božidar Kunc, in Yugoslavia.

Milanov's opera debut took place in October 1927 with the Ljubljana Opera as Leonora in *Il Trovatore.* In a short time she built up an impressive repertory, learning as many as ten roles in a single year. From 1928 to 1935 she was a principal soprano of the Zagreb National Theater where she was heard in three hundred and fifty performances, all of them sung in Croatian. Among her many roles were Minnie in *The Girl of the Golden West,* the title role in *Manon Lescaut,* Rachel in *La Juive,* Leonore in *Fidelio,* Fiora in *L'Amore dei Tre Re,* Elsa in *Lohengrin,* Sieglinde in *Die Walküre,* and the Marschallin in *Der Rosenkavalier.* During these years she also made guest appearances in Italy, Dresden, Graz in Austria, Prague, and in Brünn and Bratislava in Yugoslavia. During the 1936–1937 season she was the principal soprano of the Prague Opera.

Until 1937 she made her appearances under the name of Zinka Kunc. Then, in July of that year, she married Predrag Milanov, a Yugoslavian actor and director. From this time on she assumed the name Zinka Milanov for her professional appearances as well as for her private life.

In 1937 a soprano scheduled to sing the title role of *Aida* at the Vienna State Opera fell ill, and Milanov was called as substitute. She took twenty-five curtain calls. The conductor that evening was Bruno Walter. During intermission he went to her dressing room to inform her that Toscanini was seeking a soprano soloist for a performance of Verdi's Requiem scheduled for the Salzburg Festival. Walter offered to recommend her. Though she did not at the time know the score, she nevertheless made the trip to Salzburg for the audition. Toscanini had only to listen to her sing twenty measures before he exclaimed: *"Bene!"*

Then she appeared at the Salzburg Festival in 1937 in Verdi's Requiem under Toscanini's ba-

Milanov: mē′ lä nôf

538

ton. That year, Edward Johnson, general manager of the Metropolitan Opera, Artur Bodanzky, its conductor, and Edward Ziegler, assistant to Johnson, came to Europe to audition about one hundred and fifty singers. Milanov sang for them "In questa reggia" from *Turandot,* "Suicidio!" from *La Gioconda,* and the "Nile" aria from *Aida;* she was the only singer of those auditioned that summer to get a Metropolitan Opera contract. It specified that she had to lose twenty-five pounds and that she was to learn three major Italian operas in the original tongue (her previous performances in Italian operas had been sung either in Croatian or German). Both these conditions were met. On December 17, 1937, she made her Metropolitan Opera debut as Leonora in *Il Trovatore,* a part she had previously sung seventy-five times but which she was now singing for the first time in Italian. "She has a voice of uncommon range, flexibility and capacity for dramatic expression," wrote one New York critic. "Miss Milanov can also sing pianissimo. . . . There were however in a number of places conspicuous defects."

Milanov made a far better impression on February 2, 1938, as Aida. Another New York critic said of her: "Miss Milanov's forceful performance suggested that it will not be long before the news of her qualities spreads, for she presented a conception of the role which was at least thoroughly Italianized. . . . Miss Milanov phrased the music expertly and sang much of it with superior vocal quality."

Between 1937 and 1941 Milanov distinguished herself at the Metropolitan Opera as Amelia in *Un Ballo in Maschera* (with which she opened the season on December 2, 1940), the title role in *La Gioconda,* Santuzza in *Cavalleria Rusticana,* and Donna Anna in *Don Giovanni.* She was off the company roster in 1941–1942, but returned in 1942 for a five-year period during which she was acclaimed in the title role of *Norma* and as Leonora in *La Forza del Destino.*

Milanov divorced Predrag Milanov in 1946. A year later she married Ljubomir Ilic. The same year she left the Metropolitan Opera to visit her family in Yugoslavia for the first time since the outbreak of World War II. She was gone for three years. When she returned to the Metropolitan Opera as Santuzza on January 17, 1951, she was given such an ovation that, as she recalls, "I was moved to tears. Maybe it was good that I had been away, for when I returned I knew I had been missed."

She remained with the Metropolitan Opera for fifteen years, adding to her Metropolitan Opera repertory the roles of Maddalena in *Andrea Chénier,* Tosca, Elvira in *Ernani,* Desdemona in *Otello,* and Amelia in *Simon Boccanegra.* She opened the Metropolitan Opera seasons of 1951–1952 as Aida, 1952–1953 as Leonora in a new production of *La Forza del Destino,* 1954–1955 again as Aida, but this time only in Act 1, Scenes 1 and 2, since this was a gala evening devoted exclusively to excerpts rather than to a complete opera. Few sopranos in Metropolitan Opera history surpassed her record of opening-night performances, and none up to that time had appeared, as she had, on two consecutive opening nights.

When on November 16, 1954, she appeared as Maddalena in a new production of *Andrea Chénier,* Olin Downes noted in the New York *Times* that "for nobility of expression and complete mastery of every phase of the singer's art her plea to Gérard in Act III was the consummate artistic achievement of the evening."

Milanov celebrated the twenty-fifth anniversary of her debut at the Metropolitan Opera on December 17, 1962, as Maddalena. This was also the role in which she made her farewell Metropolitan Opera appearance on April 13, 1966. "Last night was her night," wrote Louis Snyder in the *Herald Tribune,* commenting on her final performance, "and an occasion for a bulging houseful of cheering, applauding and weeping admirers to let the illustrious Yugoslavian soprano know what she has meant to them through the past twenty-eight years. . . . She received a series of show-stopping ovations, culminating with a seven-minute outpouring of affection following her third-act aria. . . . which had few parallels in the history of the house." A silver tray was presented to her by the Metropolitan Opera Association and a Steuben glass cup from the management. Rudolf Bing, the general manager, told her: "You are a supremely great singer, and I have never known you to arrive late or unprepared, which shows your great sense of responsibility to your art, your public and to yourself." Milanov, deeply touched, replied: "I just want to say goodbye. I love you all with all my heart, and I will carry you with me as long as I live." She had given 421 performances with the company, 297 of them in New York.

Milanov made guest appearances with the Chicago Opera and the San Francisco Opera. Though her main activity was in the United States she was also a great favorite in South America at the Teatro Colón in Buenos Aires, at La Scala in Milan, at Covent Garden in London, and at the Vienna State Opera.

In addition to her performances in opera, she often sang over radio and on television and appeared in recitals and as soloist with major orchestras (fourteen times with Toscanini).

In 1977 Milanov was appointed to the voice faculty of the Curtis Institute of Music in Philadelphia. She has also taught voice at New York University in New York City.

She resides in an apartment on the west side of New York City. Her favorite pastimes have been swimming and cooking; in the latter, her specialty has been dishes native to her own country. She has been decorated with the Order of St. Stava by the Yugoslav government.

ABOUT: New Yorker, December 31, 1973; Opera News, May 1, 1965, April 9, 1977.

SHERRILL MILNES

Sherrill Milnes

1935–

Sherrill Eustace Milnes, baritone, was born in Hinsdale, Illinois, on January 10, 1935. His father, Reverend James Knowlton Milnes, was a Congregationalist minister who, for reasons of health, had to leave the ministry in 1940. He took over the management of a two-hundred-and-fifty-acre farm belonging to his wife's family in Downers Grove, twenty-eight miles from Chicago. His wife, Thelma Roe Milnes, was a pianist, voice teacher, and for thirty years director of the Downers Grove Congregational Church choir.

As a boy, Sherrill combined chores on the farm with schooling in Chicago. "Like any other farmer's son, I worked hard," he recalls. "I really was a farm boy—manure, bib overalls, pigs, milking cows before and after school, the whole works. My older brother, Roe, and I were two of only three farm kids out of twelve hundred in the school."

His lifelong interest in music came from his mother, whose rehearsals of Handel's *Messiah* and Mendelssohn's *Elijah* he attended when he was only three. She gave him his first piano lessons, then passed him on to local teachers for further music instruction. In addition to the piano he studied the violin, and he sang in his mother's church choir. "She kept playing for me, explaining the music, teaching me constantly through the general inspirational value of her musicianship."

A part of his early musical experience—and his first awareness of the magic of opera—came through records and the radio. Through recordings he came to know Kirsten Flagstad singing the "Ho yo to ho" from *Die Walküre*. "I remember when I was about five, I used to sing with her up to the high B's and C's; on an unknowing level of mind I loved it." Through radio he was brought into contact with the Saturday afternoon broadcasts from the Metropolitan Opera. "When I first found out they were live, that people were actually singing them on a stage somewhere miles away, I was excited and never missed one."

At high school in Chicago, he played the tuba in the school band and string bass in jam sessions. His versatility brought him prizes in five categories in a statewide music contest: tuba in a brass sextet; viola in a string quartet; concertmaster in an orchestra; first-chair tuba in the band; and vocal soloist.

Despite his pronounced musical proclivities, upon graduation from high school in 1952 he enrolled in North Central College in Naperville,

Illinois, as a pre-med student. He stayed there just one year before coming to the decision that music, not medicine, was his destiny.

He entered Drake University in Des Moines, Iowa, to study for a degree in music education. There he studied voice with Andrew White, took courses in harmony, counterpoint, orchestration, and composition, and was trained in the playing of a wide assortment of instruments. To pay his way through college, he played the violin with the Des Moines Symphony, sang in churches and synagogues, performed on various instruments with small combos and jazz groups, and did singing commercials for radio and television. When the Metropolitan Opera appeared in Des Moines during its spring tour he managed to find a job as a supernumerary with the company.

For a brief period after graduation from Drake University with a Bachelor's degree in music he taught voice at the New Trier High School in Winnetka, Illinois. Then he enrolled in Northwestern University for postgraduate work to fulfill requirements for a Master's degree. At Northwestern he studied voice with Hermanus Baer, who persuaded him that he had the makings of a successful singer, something which Milnes had doubted up to this time. "I was always a big vocalizer, and there I suddenly began to like what I heard. When I got my Master's I decided to get a job in Chicago and just listen how people of my own age sounded." As a member of the Northwestern opera workshop, he appeared as the Marquis in a performance of Poulenc's *Les Dialogues des Carmélites*.

He went to Chicago in 1958 and joined the chorus of the Chicago Symphony. The chorus was directed by Margaret Hillis, who taught him, as he said, "worlds about music and interpretation." He was in the chorus in the Chicago Symphony's performances of Beethoven's Ninth Symphony under Fritz Reiner and Prokofiev's *Alexander Nevsky* under Erich Leinsdorf (both recorded).

In the summer of 1959 he joined the Santa Fe Company in New Mexico to sing in its chorus and perform bit parts. Twice he entered the Metropolitan Auditions of the Air and twice the Chicago Auditions of the Air, but he failed all four times.

In 1960 Boris Goldovsky engaged him to sing with his New England Opera Company, first at the Berkshire Music Center in Tanglewood in Massachusetts, then on tour. He stayed with Goldovsky five years. In that time he sang Masetto in *Don Giovanni* fifty-five times and Scarpia in *Tosca* twenty-five times; also the title role in *Don Giovanni,* Figaro in *The Barber of Seville,* Eugene Onegin, Rigoletto, the title role in Rossini's *The Turk in Italy,* the elder Germont in *La Traviata,* and Escamillo in *Carmen.* "Those years," he recalls, "taught me to take the pace and pressure of the profession."

While serving as a member of the New England Opera Company he appeared in Baltimore in April 1961 as Charles Gérard in *Andrea Chénier,* a part in which he was coached by Rosa Ponselle; he returned a year later to Baltimore as Escamillo.

In 1962 he finally emerged as a winner in a major singing contest sponsored by the Ford Foundation. This enabled him to take further leaves from the Goldovsky troupe to make appearances with opera companies in Central City (Colorado), Pittsburgh, San Antonio, Houston, and Cincinnati—appearing in the last-named city as Count di Luna during the summer festival of 1964. Winning an award in still another competition—the 1964 American Opera Auditions—made it possible for him to make his debut in Europe on September 23, 1964, at the Teatro Nuovo in Milan, as Figaro in *The Barber of Seville.*

Returning from Europe immediately after that debut, Milnes joined the New York City Opera, making his first appearance on October 18, 1964, as Valentin in *Faust.* He remained with this company three and a half seasons, appearing as Scarpia, the elder Germont, Figaro in *The Barber of Seville,* Tonio in *I Pagliacci,* and in Menotti's *The Consul.*

While still a member of the New York City Opera, Milnes made his debut at the Metropolitan Opera on December 22, 1965, as Valentin. Montserrat Caballé was making her American bow at the same time. While Caballé was the center of interest for most critics, Milnes was not ignored. "Mr. Milnes' debut had its satisfactions, too," wrote Raymond Ericson in the New York *Times.* "The twenty-nine-year-old baritone handled himself with aplomb. . . . The rich, fresh sound of his voice . . . rang out reassuringly in his aria in the Kermesse Scene."

Though engaged to make only five appearances in his initial season (two in *Faust,* two as Yeletsky in Tchaikovsky's *The Queen of Spades,* and one as Amonasro in *Aida*), Milnes was heard eighteen times in seven operas: as Don Fernando in *Fidelio,* Charles Gérard in *Andrea Chénier,* Renato in *Un Ballo in Maschera,* Jack Rance in *The Girl of the Golden West,* Ashton in *Lucia di Lammermoor,* the High Priest in *Samson and Delilah,* and Escamillo in *Carmen.* He had to learn the part of Jack Rance in a month, and that of Renato in five weeks. While deeply involved in mastering these two new scores, he had to work on his roles in *The Consul* (New York City Opera), Verdi's *Giovanna d'Arco* (American Opera Society), and *Gianni Schicchi* (San Antonio Opera). Despite these pressures, he came through with a triumphant performance in *Un Ballo in Maschera* on March 25, 1966. "As of last night," wrote John Gruen in the *Herald Tribune,* "he stands in the major ranks of operatic baritones—the sort who can ignite the stage by the credibility of his acting and by the magnitude and control of his voice."

In his second season at the Metropolitan Opera, Milnes created the role of Adam Brant in the world premiere of Marvin David Levy's *Mourning Becomes Electra* on March 17, 1967. He further extended his Metropolitan Opera repertory that year by appearing as the Herald in *Lohengrin* and as Germont in *La Traviata.* After that he helped to fill the gap which had been created at the Metropolitan Opera through the sudden death of Leonard Warren on March 4, 1960. Milnes's later roles included Barnaba in *La Gioconda,* Miller in *Luisa Miller,* Paolo in *Simon Boccanegra,* Donner in *Das Rheingold,* Figaro in *The Barber of Seville,* Count di Luna in *Il Trovatore,* Tonio in *I Pagliacci,* Carlo in *Ernani,* Iago in *Otello,* Don Carlo in *La Forza del Destino,* Rodrigo in *Don Carlo,* Rigoletto, Macbeth in Verdi's opera, Scarpia in *Tosca,* Monforte in *I Vespri Siciliani* and the title role in *Don Giovanni.* "Mr. Milnes, young though he is, may be the finest baritone the company has at the moment," commented Raymond Ericson in the New York *Times* after a performance of *Il Trovatore.* In *I Pagliacci,* reported Winthrop Sargeant in the *New Yorker,* Milnes's performance was "a masterpiece of haunting baritone singing and a fine characterization."

One of Milnes's triumphs came on March 28, 1974, in his first appearance at the Metropolitan as Don Giovanni. "He sang beautifully," reported Harold C. Schonberg in the New York *Times,* "with good legato phrasing and firm tonal production. . . . His entire characterization was well

considered. Certainly this was another distinguished achievement from the great American baritone."

Another of Milnes's successes came on February 25, 1976, when he appeared as Sir Richard Forth in the first Metropolitan Opera production of *I Puritani* since 1918. His first appearance in New York in the title role of *Eugene Onegin* (the first time he ever sang in Russian) was at the Metropolitan Opera on October 15, 1977. On January 21, 1978, he sang Athanaël in the first Metropolitan Opera production of *Thaïs* since 1939, and on February 21, 1978, Alfonso in the first Metropolitan Opera production of *La Favorita* since 1905.

Though his principal performances have taken place at the Metropolitan Opera, Milnes has made noteworthy appearances with opera houses in Europe and Latin America. His first performance at the Vienna State Opera took place on April 18, 1970 as Macbeth. He made his Italian debut at the Macerata Festival on the Adriatic during the summer of 1974 in *Rigoletto.* In 1976 he did *Otello* in Hamburg and *Tosca* in Milan. On September 10, 1976 (the opening night of the season), he assumed a new role—that of Athanaël to Beverly Sills's Thaïs—with the San Francisco Opera.

Milnes has been heard as a soloist with major orchestras. In addition he has appeared in numerous recitals, his first such in New York City taking place at the Lincoln Center for the Performing Arts on March 18, 1973.

On several occasions Milnes has tried his hand at conducting. In 1972 he recorded an album of arias with Placido Domingo. For this recording, Milnes conducted the orchestra for Domingo's accompaniments, and Domingo did the same for Milnes. "It's a gimmick, of course," Milnes commented, "but the thing is that we can do it." This was not Milnes's first venture into conducting. In 1969 he led a performance of Mendelssohn's *Elijah* at Downers Grove in memory of his mother. He returned to Downers Grove in December 1972 to lead a performance of Handel's *Judas Maccabaeus.* In 1975 he conducted the Milwaukee Symphony Orchestra in two weekend performances.

In 1969 Milnes married Nancy Denise Stokes, an opera soprano who gave up her career as soon as their son, Shawn Edward, was born. This was Milnes's second marriage; by his first he had two children. The Milneses have a large apartment on Riverside Drive in New York City and a home in London. Milnes's interests outside music include playing table tennis and tinkering with electronic equipment and cars.

ABOUT: Hi-Fi, April 1968; New York Times, October 15, 1967, March 19, 1972; New Yorker, March 29, 1976; Opera News, January 21, 1967, February 3, 1973, March 22, 1975, January 1, 1977; Saturday Review/World, May 18, 1974; Time, May 11, 1970.

Nathan Milstein

1904–

NATHAN MILSTEIN

Nathan Milstein, violin virtuoso, was born in Odessa in the Ukraine on December 31, 1904. His father, Myron Milstein, was a prosperous importer of woolens and tweeds from England and Scotland. An unruly child who was always getting into trouble, Nathan was given his first violin by his mother, Maria Bluestein Milstein, in the hope that it would deflect his interests into more productive and less objectionable channels.

According to his own testimony, Milstein was no prodigy. He has said: "I started to play the violin not because I was drawn to it but because my mother made me. I was attracted to music, wanted to hear it. It was only when I had progressed far enough to feel the music itself in my playing that I practiced willingly and eagerly."

He revealed enough talent to be accepted as a pupil of one of Odessa's most highly respected violin teachers, Peter Stoliarsky. By the time he was nine, Nathan had a sizable repertory under the full command of his fingers. One year later, when Alexander Glazunov, the composer, visited Odessa, a concert was arranged in his honor. When one of its performers fell ill, Nathan was called in as a replacement in the performance of Glazunov's Violin Concerto, which he had already studied and mastered. The composer conducted the orchestra and expressed complete satisfaction with Nathan's performance.

Leopold Auer, Russia's foremost violin teacher and head of the violin department of the St. Petersburg Conservatory, went to Odessa in 1915 and heard Nathan play. Auer urged him to come to St. Petersburg and enter his class. Na-

Milstein: mĭl′ stīn

than arrived in that city in 1916, accompanied by his mother who, because she was Jewish, had to get special permission from the police to reside there. Before long Auer had him make his first public appearance. "I got twenty-five rubles, a box of chocolates—and applause," Milstein recalls. "I thought this the best profession. You show off, you are applauded, you get paid, and you get chocolate."

When Milstein completed his violin studies with Auer in 1917 he had received the last formal instruction he was ever to get. In 1919 he began concertizing, with his sister as piano accompanist. They gave their first concert in Odessa and then performed in Kiev. In the latter city his concert was attended by young Vladimir Horowitz, whose powers at the piano were already being talked about. After the concert, Horowitz invited Nathan to his house for tea. Horowitz played for him, and Nathan reciprocated by playing sonatas and concertos with Horowitz at the piano. "It became late," as Milstein later recalled, "and I was asked to spend the night. The next morning when I woke up I was asked to stay on. I had come for tea and I stayed three years."

Milstein and Horowitz began giving joint concerts in Russia. Occasionally, in the performance of trios, they were joined by Gregor Piatigorsky, already a fine cello virtuoso. Milstein also made solo appearances; it was not long before his fame as virtuoso began to spread throughout Russia.

When Joseph Szigeti made his first tour of the

Soviet Union in 1924 he was invited to the home of Leopold Auer's daughter to hear a "young and up and coming violinist," as Szigeti later recalled in his autobiography, *With Strings Attached.* "I heard a fabulously gifted young man, who seemed diffident about his impending first trip across the borders to Berlin. Reassuring him enthusiastically, I told him that Europa (as Russians call all countries beyond their frontier to the West) was waiting for artists of his stamp. It turned out that America was, too! The young man was Nathan Milstein and he was accompanied on the piano by Vladimir Horowitz's sister."

The party leaders in the Soviet Union felt it was excellent propaganda to send its brilliant young musicians outside Russia to demonstrate the cultural achievements of the new Communist regime. Milstein thus got permission to leave the country for two years. On Christmas Eve 1925 he left for Berlin. From there he went on to Brussels where he performed for Eugène Ysaÿe, who said that there was nothing he could teach him. Nevertheless, Milstein remained in Brussels several months and profited from the advice and guidance of Ysaÿe; he also joined Ysaÿe in performances of chamber music at the royal palace in which Queen Elisabeth of Belgium, a violist, was a participant.

After that Milstein gave a recital in Paris that proved so successful that it set the stage for conquests in other parts of Europe. Within three years, Milstein was acclaimed throughout Europe and in South America.

Milstein first went to the United States in October 1929, making his American debut that month with the Glazunov Violin Concerto, as soloist with the Philadelphia Orchestra under Stokowski. Milstein's phenomenal command of technique and his innate musicianship were highly praised. He then toured the United States in recitals and as guest artist with orchestras. This was the first of numerous such tours; they won for him a place among the elect of the violinists of the time. Lawrence Gilman described him in the New York *Herald Tribune* as "an artist of sensitive perception and adaptability. His feeling for style is unusually delicate and sure."

Since that first tour, the dimensions of Milstein's artistry have grown. His musical insight has become increasingly sharpened and penetrating; his understanding of musical values ever more profound; his style ever more subtle. The one-time phenomenal technician, in short, has become an aristocratic artist. A critic for the New York *Times* pointed this out when he wrote: "There was a time when Milstein seemed to find more satisfaction in violin playing as an unusual outlet for a spirited and . . . attractive athleticism, rather than as a means of expressing artistic thought and feeling. But now, while the muscular urgency remains evident in pleasing degree, there is plainly at work a new and deeper impulse, a probing for something far beyond the mere attractiveness of sprightly tempi, vigorous accents and bright technique."

Milstein became an American citizen in 1942. Three years later he married Thérèse Kauffman; they had one child, a daughter named Maria Bernadette. At the end of World War II Milstein acquired the Goldmann Stradivarius (named after the collector who had previously owned it); he renamed it Maria Theresa after his daughter and wife. In the early years of Milstein's marriage he occupied a one-hundred-and-fifty-year-old colonial farm in Vermont. Later on, he acquired a house in Gstaad, Switzerland. Subsequently his home has been in London, although he has also maintained an apartment in New York City.

Earlier in his life Milstein enjoyed playing bridge, chess, and table tennis, at all of which he was adept. He also devoted much time and energy to painting and drawing for both of which he demonstrated unusual talent. "On days of concerts," he once said, "I do more painting than practicing the violin." Painting and drawing have remained for him a favorite form of recreation. But, as he told Dorle J. Soria who reported for *High Fidelity*, "to me everything is recreation. If I wash my handkerchief and press it with a little iron, that is recreation. If I write a letter to my wife—I write on only one side—I draw a picture on the back. That is recreation. But if the drawing is not good I must write the letter over. The letter does not have to be good. I am not supposed to be a great writer and write only to tell my wife what happens. But if I decide the drawing is bad I make it again."

"When relaxed among friends," Dorle J. Soria wrote of Milstein, "[he] is a brilliant, amusing and non-stop talker. He is short, stocky, ebullient, looking years younger than his age. He wears horn-rimmed glasses. His gray suit, violet shirt and striped tie were quietly elegant. He complained of trouble with his back but could not sit still when launched on an idea or story. He acted as he talked, rising, pointing, lunging, illustrating his words."

Milstein is also mobile and restless when giving his master classes in violin at the Juilliard School of Music or at the Foundation for International Master Classes in Zurich. "He never would sit still for long," says Soria, who sat in on some of his classes. "He would jump to turn the pages of an accompanist or lean over the piano to demonstrate a point or phrase. He would pick up his violin to show fingering. He would hover over a student, sometimes doubling the music on his own violin. . . . His comments were always quiet, his manner friendly."

In 1976 Milstein's recording of the complete unaccompanied sonatas and partitas of Bach on Deutsche Grammophon earned a Grammy from the National Academy of Recording Arts and Sciences and the Diplôme d'Honneur at the Montreux International Awards. He had recorded these masterworks twenty years earlier, but was impelled to press them again on records after restudying the music. "This time," he said, "I must make them as good as I can. I will never do them again." To this a reviewer for *High Fidelity/Musical America* added: "He has done them colossally."

Milstein has composed numerous compositions for the violin. He has also prepared cadenzas for the violin concertos of Beethoven, Brahms, and Paganini.

ABOUT: Gavoty, B. Nathan Milstein. *Periodicals—* High Fidelity/Musical America, July 1974, November 1977; New York Times Magazine, November 13, 1949.

Dimitri Mitropoulos

1896–1960

Dimitri Mitropoulos, born in Athens on March 1, 1896, was the only conductor of world renown thus far to have been born in the Near East. Religion was a dominant influence in the Mitropoulos family. Dimitri's paternal grandfather had been a priest in the Greek Orthodox Church; two of his uncles became monks; and a

---

Mitropoulos: mē̃ trô′ poo̅ lôs

DIMITRI MITROPOULOS

granduncle was an archbishop. Dimitri's mother was Angeliki Anagnostopoulos Mitropoulos; his father, Jean, was a leather merchant. Jean passed on the profound convictions of his family to Dimitri, whose earliest ambition was to enter a monastic order. As a child, Dimitri paid frequent visits to nearby monasteries and would sometimes preach mystical sermons to his friends. All his life Mitropoulos remained a devout Greek Orthodox Catholic who wore a crucifix inside his shirt and a medallion of the Virgin Mary on the lining of his coat.

Dimitri's father hoped he would someday enter the merchant marine. But Dimitri revealed exceptional musical talents from early childhood. He began studying the piano when he was seven, continuing with private teachers while attending the public schools. By the time he was ten he was able to play the piano scores of several operas fluently and had committed some of them to memory. All this induced his father to enroll Dimitri at twelve years of age in the Odeon Conservatory in Athens instead of in a maritime school. Dimitri remained there six years, studying composition with Armand Marsick and piano with Ludwig Wassenhowen. He played percussion in the school orchestra.

Following a brief period of military service in the Balkan Army as a drummer, Mitropoulos entered the University of Athens. There, in 1919, he completed the writing of an opera, *Sister Beatrice,* based on a text by Maeterlinck. The opera was introduced at the Odeon. Camille Saint-Saëns heard it and sent a favorable report to a Paris newspaper. He also volunteered to pay Mitropoulos's expenses to Paris for additional music study. Mitropoulos did not avail himself of this generous offer because César Thomson, the Belgian violinist, had raised the funds to send him to Brussels in 1920. In Brussels, Mitropoulos studied composition with Paul Gilson. In 1921, on an endowment from the city of Athens, Mitropoulos went to Berlin and became a piano student of Ferruccio Busoni, whose influence upon his development was far-reaching. Busoni was the first to interest Mitropoulos in becoming a conductor. "From what Busoni told me," Mitropoulos later remarked, "I lost all respect for myself as a composer." After studying conducting in Berlin with Erich Kleiber, Mitropoulos was made assistant conductor of the Berlin State Opera in 1921 on Kleiber's recommendation. Mitropoulos worked for four years under Furtwängler, Kleiber, Bruno Walter, and Richard Strauss, acquiring not only baton experience but also an extensive repertory. Occasionally, when Mitropoulos was permitted to conduct a performance, he revealed a thorough grasp of the music he was performing.

Back in his native Athens in 1925, he succeeded his former teacher, Armand Marsick, as principal conductor of the Municipal Orchestra. He held this post a dozen years. At this time he began conducting without a baton and often from memory, using those contortions of body and jerky movements of hand which later became the hallmark of his technique.

Favorable reports of his good work in Athens began to filter out of Greece, and invitations came to him for guest appearances in Europe. On February 27, 1930, he conducted the Berlin Philharmonic in a concert at which Egon Petri had been scheduled to perform Prokofiev's Piano Concerto No.3. When Petri became too ill to appear, Mitropoulos took his place at the piano and conducted his own accompaniment. This tour de force made a deep impression on Berlin. He repeated this feat on February 14, 1932, when he appeared with the Orchestre Symphonique in Paris. Two weeks after this Paris debut he was heard for the first time in England. In February 1933 he toured Italy, and he visited that country again in 1934 and 1935. In May 1934 he went to the Soviet Union to conduct orchestras in Leningrad and Moscow. He was also engaged to lead three months of

symphony concerts at Monte Carlo each year from 1934 through 1937.

In 1936 Serge Koussevitzky invited him to Boston to make his American debut with the Boston Symphony on January 24. Olin Downes, the music critic of the New York *Times,* was in Boston for that concert and called Mitropoulos "more than a kindling virtuoso. He showed a microscopic knowledge . . . of strongly contrasted scores, and his temperament is that of an impetuous musician. Mitropoulos addressed himself with complete comprehension and with blazing dramatic emotion."

He returned to Boston for additional concerts in 1937. His success there brought him a call from Minneapolis in 1938 to succeed Eugene Ormandy as music director of the Minneapolis Symphony. In the twelve years Mitropoulos served in this capacity with the Minneapolis Symphony he transformed a more or less second-rate symphonic organization into one of America's finest, through his vital performances and his adventurous programming. When he presented the world premiere of Milhaud's Piano Concerto No.1 (December 2, 1938) and that of Ernst Krenek's Piano Concerto No.3 (November 22, 1946), he served in the dual role of solo pianist and conductor. Among the other works to receive a world premiere in Minneapolis under Mitropoulos were: David Diamond's Symphony No.1 (December 21, 1941) and *Rounds* (November 24, 1944); Hindemith's Symphony in E-flat (November 21, 1941); Frederick Piket's *Curtain Raiser to an American Play* (December 30, 1948); Artur Schnabel's Symphony No.1 (December 13, 1946); and Elie Siegmeister's *Ozark Set* (November 11, 1944).

A man of ascetic tastes, a mystic by nature, Mitropoulos lived in virtual monastic seclusion in Minneapolis. He occupied a dormitory in the University of Minneapolis that was furnished with just the bare necessities. He followed a Spartan diet that consisted of little more than vegetables. He never touched strong alcohol, smoked cigarettes in moderation, and pursued a rigorously disciplined existence that avoided social gatherings. Away from his orchestral duties, he spent his time in contemplation, silent prayer, reading, and the study of musical scores. His clothing, off the podium, made concessions only to comfort: baggy trousers, a polo shirt, a sweater. He not only lived the life of a man of the church but he even looked the part, with his deep-set eyes, sunken cheeks, and the short crop of frizzy hair that resembled a monk's tonsure.

In 1939 Mitropoulos appeared as a guest conductor of the NBC Symphony. When, on December 19, 1940, he made his debut with the New York Philharmonic Orchestra, Olin Downes reported in the New York *Times* that he caused so much excitement that "the subscribers did everything except steal the goalposts." Mitropoulos returned to the New York Philharmonic for several seasons after that. In 1949, when he resigned from his post in Minneapolis, he shared the podium of the New York Philharmonic with Leopold Stokowski for the season of 1949–1950. One season later he took over full command as the orchestra's music director. Meanwhile, in 1946 he had become an American citizen.

With the New York Philharmonic, even more than before, he revealed the full extent of his conducting abilities, which were formidable. His was one of the most extraordinary musical intellects and memories on the scene. When he was in his element, which was more often than not, he gave performances of uncommon brilliance. When he performed twentieth century music he was virtually in a class by himself. This was the case when he gave concert performances of *Elektra,* Alban Berg's *Wozzeck,* Ravel's *L'Heure Espagnole,* Milhaud's *Christophe Colomb* and *Les Choéphores,* Busoni's *Arlecchino,* and Schoenberg's *Erwartung*—the last four were American premieres. He made it a practice to play some twentieth century music on almost each of his programs, maintaining: "With me, playing new music is always an act of love, never just a duty." As the music director of the New York Philharmonic he was responsible for numerous world premieres of American compositions among which were: Samuel Barber's *Meditation and Dance of Vengeance* (February 2, 1954); Morton Gould's *Jekyll and Hyde Variations* (February 2, 1957) and *Variations* (October 24, 1953); Leon Kirchner's Piano Concerto (February 23, 1956); Gail Kubik's Symphony No.3 (February 28, 1957); Gunther Schuller's *Spectra* (January 14, 1960); and Howard Swanson's Symphony No.1 (November 23, 1950). Among the American premieres—besides the concert versions of operas by Busoni, Schoenberg, and Milhaud already mentioned—were Boris Blacher's *Orchestral Ornaments,*

Gottfried von Einem's *Orchestra Music,* and Shostakovich's Symphony No.10.

Mitropoulos took the New York Philharmonic Orchestra to the Edinburgh Festival in 1951 and toured Europe in 1955 and South America in 1958, with Leonard Bernstein as collaborating conductor.

While still the music director of the New York Philharmonic, Mitropoulos made his debut at the Metropolitan Opera on December 15, 1954, conducting *Salome.* "His talent for dramatic expression finds a surging outlet in opera that is not readily available in the symphonic literature," commented Jay S. Harrison in the *Herald Tribune.* "He urged sonorities and waves of sound from his crew that were downright blistering in their heat. If the reading of the occasion was a sample of what the Philharmonic Symphony maestro can do with music in the theater it is devoutly to be wished that he no longer confine his talents to the concert hall." Other operas conducted by Mitropoulos in this and subsequent seasons at the Metropolitan Opera were *Un Ballo in Maschera, Tosca, Boris Godunov, Die Walküre, Eugene Onegin,* and the world premiere of Samuel Barber's *Vanessa* (January 15, 1958). Mitropoulos's performance of *Eugene Onegin* was the opening night presentation of the 1957–1958 season, and his *Tosca* opened the season of 1958–1959.

As his appearances at the Metropolitan Opera multiplied and as he assumed additional operatic assignments at La Scala in Milan, the Vienna State Opera, and the Florence May Music Festival, the number of his appearances with the New York Philharmonic decreased. During the 1957–1958 season of that orchestra he called upon Leonard Bernstein to share the podium with him. One year later, Mitropoulos decided to devote more of his efforts to opera and to confine his symphonic appearances to guest performances. He resigned from the New York Philharmonic, turning over its music direction to Leonard Bernstein.

Mitropoulos was scheduled to direct four weeks of guest performances with the New York Philharmonic and a revival of *Macbeth* at the Metropolitan Opera in 1959 when in January of that year he suffered a severe heart attack. Despite this physical setback, Mitropoulos refused to lighten the heavy musical load he was carrying. He drove himself hard in spite of weakened physical resources to give memorable performances of Mahler's Symphony No.9 during a Mahler Festival of the New York Philharmonic Orchestra early in 1960; to conduct *Tosca, Madama Butterfly, Cavalleria Rusticana,* and a new production of *Simon Boccanegra* at the Metropolitan Opera; and to assume conducting obligations abroad. After leading a performance of Mahler's Symphony No.3 in Cologne he arrived in Milan to direct the same symphony. "I feel very fatigued," he said before his first rehearsal at La Scala on November 2, 1960. "I am an old automobile that still works." A few minutes later he fell from the conductor's stand. He died of a heart attack en route to the Polyclinic Hospital in Milan.

On the night of his death (November 2, 1960) a performance of *Boris Godunov* at the Metropolitan Opera was preceded with several words of eulogy by Rudolf Bing, general manager of the company, and by the playing of Gluck's "Dance of the Blessed Spirits" from *Orfeo ed Euridice* without a conductor. One night later the New York Philharmonic paid tribute to its former music director with the interpolation of the "Urlicht" movement from Mahler's *Resurrection Symphony,* conducted by Leonard Bernstein.

In 1951 Mitropoulos was decorated with the rosette of the French Legion of Honor. In 1956 he received the award of Orfeo d'Oro from the city of Mantua, the second conductor to be thus honored (the first was Toscanini).

As a memorial to Mitropoulos, the women's division of the Federation of Jewish Philanthropies established in 1963 the Mitropoulos Conducting Contest with Leonard Bernstein heading the jury. This was the first international annual conducting competition organized in the United States. Winners each year earn a cash award and appearances with the New York Philharmonic Orchestra.

ABOUT: Ewen, D. Famous Conductors; Gelatt, R. Music Makers. *Periodicals*—Musical America, December 1960; New York Times Magazine, October 8, 1950.

Anna Moffo

1932–

Anna Moffo, soprano, was born in Wayne, Pennsylvania, on June 27, 1932, to Italian parents, Nicholas and Regina Cinti Moffo. Her father was a shoemaker. Though she did not begin studying voice until her seventeenth year, she had been singing from childhood on, often performing at weddings and funerals, with choirs, and as a soloist in the school assembly. At Radnor High School in Wayne, from which she was graduated as valedictorian, she excelled both in scholastics and in athletics. She was the captain of the field hockey team, played on the basketball team, and was a tennis star. Since she was strikingly attractive, she was offered an opportunity to make tests for a possible career in motion pictures after graduation from high school but she turned it down in expectation of becoming a nun.

She had been studying the piano for about ten years when she finally decided to cultivate her voice. In 1951, without ever having taken a vocal lesson, possessing an operatic repertory of just one aria ("Un bel dì" from *Madama Butterfly*), she auditioned successfully for a scholarship at the Curtis Institute in Philadelphia. She stayed at the Curtis Institute four years, studying voice with Eufemia Giannini-Gregory (sister of prima donna Dusolina Giannini) and was graduated with high honors.

In 1955 she won an award from the Young Artists Auditions sponsored by the Philadelphia Orchestra. Soon after that, a Fulbright grant enabled her to continue her vocal studies in Europe. She made her home in Italy, enrolling at the Santa Cecilia Academy in Rome. To learn the Italian language she lived alone with a widow who spoke only that language. As Moffo recalls: "We played canasta every night and listened to the radio, and she wouldn't give me anything to eat unless I could ask for it."

She had made a few uneventful singing appearances over the Italian radio when in 1956 she auditioned for the role of Cio-Cio-San in a television production of *Madama Butterfly.* Though the director-producer, Mario Lanfranchi, was impressed by the beauty and purity of her tones and her natural voice placement when she sang "Un bel dì" for him, he rejected her

ANNA MOFFO

because he considered her physically too tall and statuesque to appear as the slim, frail heroine of Puccini's opera. "How can I stage *Butterfly* with her?" he inquired. "She won't fit the screen." But when a suitable Cio-Cio-San could not be found, Moffo was engaged. She proved a sensation.

On December 7, 1957, Moffo and Mario Lanfranchi were married in Milan. "We started out with only a bed and a table," she recalls. Knowledgeable in opera and voice, the son of a man who for thirty years was the general manager of the Parma Opera, Lanfranchi put his expertise at the service of his young wife. With her husband as mentor she began assuming coloratura parts, and with him as business manager she started to make operatic appearances in Italy. Her stage debut took place at the Festival of Two Worlds in Spoleto as Norina in *Don Pasquale.* This was followed by an engagement at La Scala in Milan where she sang principal soprano roles. Coached by her husband, she extended her repertory to include some eighty roles. In time, with her husband as producer, she became the star of her own television show, emanating from Rome and seen throughout southern Europe thirty-five weeks a year. She was also given a dramatic part in an Italian-made motion picture, *Austerlitz* (1962), the first of her many foreign-made films that included *The Sicilian Baroness* (1965), *Ménage Italian Style* (1965), *La Serva Padrona* (1966), *La Traviata* (1966), and *Una Storia d'Amore* or *Love Story* (1968) in which she became the first prima donna ever to

appear on the screen in the nude. Because of *Una Storia d'Amore* she was sued in Italy for indecent exposure, but after the bad publicity had died down she was given the Silver Griffo Award for her performance as well as a nomination for Italy's equivalent of the American Oscar.

She became an idol of the Italian opera public which voted her one of the ten most beautiful women in the country and referred to her as "l'Exotica" and "La Diva Imperiale." The ensuing prosperity enabled the Lanfranchis to acquire a villa near Parma, a ten-room apartment in the Palazzo del Grillo in Rome overlooking the Forum and the Palatine Hills, a *pied-à-terre* in Milan and—following her engagement by the Metropolitan Opera—an intimate two-and-a-half-room apartment in New York City.

Her successes quickly spread beyond the borders of Italy: to London, Paris, and the United States. She made her American operatic debut with the Chicago Lyric Opera on November 14, 1957, as Mimi in *La Bohème.* A debut at the Vienna State Opera in 1958 was followed by one at the Salzburg Festival in the summer of 1959.

She made her first appearance at the Metropolitan Opera on November 14, 1959, as Violetta in *La Traviata.* The critical reaction was mixed. In the *Herald Tribune,* Jay S. Harrison found that she "has every artistic grace in her favor save one: the flame of greatness which lights up a stage with its sheer incandescence." Harold C. Schonberg in the New York *Times* conceded that "at least in one respect she lived up to advance billing: she is one of the most beautiful women ever to grace the stage of an opera house." But as a singer, Schonberg added, "it is still a case of 'judgment reserved.' Miss Moffo has quite a lovely voice, she is a sensitive artist and a graceful actress. But at this stage of her career her work still seems just a shade too tentative."

In the spring of 1960 she went with the Metropolitan Opera company on its American tour as Violetta and as Marguerite in *Faust.* On October 1, 1960, she made her first appearance with the San Francisco Opera as Amina in *La Sonnambula,* and later that fall she opened the season of the Philadelphia Grand Opera as Violetta. Returning to the Metropolitan Opera House in New York in 1960–1961 she was heard in three new roles (Gilda in *Rigoletto,* Adina in *L'Elisir d'Amore,* and Liù in *Turandot*). She was beginning to reveal greater poise and self-assurance in her singing and increasing maturity in her artistry. Paul Henry Lang commented in the *Herald Tribune:* "Miss Moffo has a fine voice and excellent ear, and she knows what to do with both. She can sing a delectable pianissimo and although obviously a dramatic soprano, she is entirely at home in the coloratura passages—the staccatos were clear and on the dot."

New roles at the Metropolitan Opera have added to her reputation since 1959–1960: Gịlda in *Rigoletto,* Adina in *L'Elisir d'Amore,* Liù in *Turandot,* the four heroines in *The Tales of Hoffmann* (sung for the first time on November 11, 1961); the title roles in *La Périchole, Lucia di Lammermoor* and *Manon;* Mélisande in *Pelléas and Mélisande,* Pamina in *The Magic Flute,* Norina in *Don Pasquale,* Mimi in *La Bohème,* Cio-Cio-San in *Madama Butterfly,* Juliet in *Romeo and Juliet,* Rosina in *The Barber of Seville,* Rosalinde in *Die Fledermaus,* Nedda in *I Pagliacci.*

Among other roles in which Moffo distinguished herself, though not necessarily at the Metropolitan Opera, are Maria in *The Daughter of the Regiment,* Elvira in *I Puritani,* and Mignon. She made her first stage appearance as Thaïs (a role she had previously sung for an RCA recording) with the Seattle Opera on May 6, 1976, and the following July she assumed another role new for her, that of Fiora in *L'Amore dei Tre Re* in a performance taped in London for RCA. Her extensive repertory has also enabled her to appear in Europe in several twentieth century operas, such as Respighi's *Fiamma,* Pizzetti's *Ifigenia,* and Hindemith's *Mathis der Maler.*

In 1966–1967 she appeared with the East Berlin Komische Oper where as Violetta she proved "unforgettable" to the critic of the *Berliner Zeitung,* who called her vocal and dramatic talents "remarkable" and noted that her coloratura passages in the highest register were produced "flawlessly and without effort." She toured the German opera houses in the fall and early winter of 1969–1970 and the following spring was heard at festivals in Munich and Wiesbaden.

Moffo has been a highly successful recitalist, appearing over many years in some one hundred concerts a season in America and Europe. When in December 1969 she gave her first New York recital in six years at the Lincoln Center for the Performing Arts, a critic for the New York *Times* wrote: "Anna Moffo gave a lesson on how to put across a recital last night. . . . Her voice was pure and cool, but it was what she did with it that counted. She decorated it with an amazing array of colors, vibrato, in all degrees." In 1974 she was the only American, and the only singer, participating in the Osaka International Festival where a capacity audience gave her over a dozen curtain calls and where many of her Japanese admirers waited outside her dressing room for an hour for autographs. She followed this appearance with four other equally successful recitals in Japan.

Moffo has been heard over American television as a guest of numerous coast-to-coast sponsored programs and on innumerable talk shows. She has also appeared in an American-made star-studded film production, *The Adventurers* (1970).

In spite of her success in Japan, Anna Moffo's career began to plummet sharply in the early 1970s. Singing too often, in too many places, and through too many media had inflicted ravages on her beautiful voice. Many critics were beginning to criticize her severely. "I've been working much too hard and traveling too much," she explained to Stephen E. Rubin in the New York *Times.* "I got mixed up in TV, films, things like that. Psychologically I was miserable, *always* away, *always* alone. But I don't think I was singing *that* badly until I reached a point where I was just so tired."

An overpublicized, overpromoted, overadvertised release of *Thaïs* by RCA in 1974 (in which she assumed the title role) was a disaster. "Although the attractive timbre of Moffo's soprano is still in evidence, she has now lost all control of her middle register; following the initial attack on a note, the sound evaporates into a breathy tonelessness, a perilous wobble intrudes, the pitch sags, the phrase wilts." So wrote Peter G. Davis in the New York *Times,* adding: "Needless to say, with her voice in such shape, Miss Moffo can hardly begin to impart much sense of character to either the words or the music."

To compound her problems, both her marriage and her health were disintegrating. She straightened out her personal life by divorcing Mario Lanfranchi in the fall of 1974 and, on November 14, 1974, marrying Robert W. Sarnoff, then chairman and chief executive officer of RCA Corporation. Her health was rehabilitated through an operation.

At this time she also made a giant effort to regain both her voice and her career, through consultations with various teachers including an intensive period of study with Beverly Johnson. Moffo went on to develop a bigger, darker, richer voice than before and to learn a new dramatic repertory to suit it. Her so-called comeback came with one of these dramatic parts—Fiora in *L'Amore dei Tre Re*—in an RCA recording in May 1977. In various opera houses in the United States she undertook such new roles as Tosca, Desdemona and Adriana Lecouvreur.

She also returned successfully to the concert scene with an appearance at a Promenade concert conducted by André Kostelanetz at Avery Fisher Hall in New York on May 18, 1977. In the fall of 1977 she toured the Far East with ten recitals; in November of that year she filled orchestral dates in various European cities; and between November 1977 and May 1978 she was booked for twenty-six recitals and orchestral concerts in the United States. She was singing so much better than she had in several years—with much greater control and discipline, and with far fewer technical flaws—that there was a strong belief among critics that her professional rehabilitation had proved successful.

Except for an occasional game of tennis, Moffo has deserted sports. She has disclosed that her three main hobbies in recent years have been "hats, horses, and antiques, and not necessarily in that order." Her closets are filled with hats; her homes overflow with antiques; and her interest in horses brings her periodically to the race track.

On February 23, 1968, in Washington, D.C., the Italian government bestowed on Anna Moffo one of its highest decorations, in recognition of her achievements in Italian opera: Commendatore of the Order of Merit of the Republic of Italy.

ABOUT: Musical America, January 1963; New York Times, January 16, 1972, May 15, 1977; Opera News, March 4, 1961; Time, November 23, 1959.

Benno Moiseiwitsch

1890–1963

Benno Moiseiwitsch, pianist, was born on February 22, 1890, in Odessa in the Ukraine to David Leon and Esther Miropolsky Moiseiwitsch. His father was a timber merchant. Benno's talent for music revealed itself early, and his father enrolled him in the Imperial Music Academy where Benno studied the piano with Dimitri D. Klimoff. When he was nine, Benno won the Anton Rubinstein Prize for piano playing. Six years later, having been expelled from the Academy for mischievous behavior, he was sent to Vienna to study with Theodor Leschetizky.

Moiseiwitsch's debut took place in Town Hall, in Reading, England, on October 1, 1908. In November 1909 he realized a striking success in his first appearance in London. Within the next few years, as an exponent of the grand Russian tradition of piano playing, he acquired a considerable following not only in England but also throughout Europe. His extraordinary insight into and poetic concept of the Romantic literature of Schumann, Chopin, Brahms, and Liszt came in for special praise.

In 1914 Moiseiwitsch married Daisy Kennedy, an Australian violinist. They set up permanent residence in London, and they had two daughters, one of whom, Tanya, became a successful theatrical designer. In 1937 he became a British subject.

Following triumphant appearances throughout Europe, Moiseiwitsch made his American debut at Carnegie Hall in New York on November 29, 1919. "He is more than a technician," wrote James Gibbons Huneker, "for he has brains, a soul, as well as the fleetest of fingers." In the New York *Times* Richard Aldrich said: "His tone is not large, but it is a true piano tone, singing, delicately tinted . . . controlled with an exquisite gradation of dynamics. . . . Mr. Moiseiwitsch has a strong and elastic sense of rhythm that dominates his playing and enlivens it. . . . It seemed clear that Mr. Moiseiwitsch made a very considerable impression on his audience."

In the next few years, in repeated returns to the United States, Moiseiwitsch further endeared himself to American music audiences

---

Moiseiwitsch: moi zā′ vĭch

Monaco

BENNO MOISEIWITSCH

through his recitals and appearances with major orchestras. He made over twenty tours of the United States in all, and on several occasions he made world tours, proving himself a particular favorite in Japan and Australia. In Shanghai he met and fell in love with Annie Gensburger, a woman of French-Russian extraction. Having divorced his first wife, he married Anne Gensburger in 1929; they had a son, Boris.

During World War II, Moiseiwitsch helped the war effort in England by giving 844 concerts to sustain civilian morale and to provide entertainment for the armed forces and the wounded in hospitals. He was the last artist to perform in Queen's Hall in London before it was bombed and reduced to a shell. In Chelmsford, while performing Chopin's Sonata in B-flat minor, he recognized the sound of a buzz bomb overhead outside the auditorium. "And as I began the somber chords of the funeral march," he later recalled, "a grim thought passed through my mind—how wonderful to play one's own funeral march at one's own funeral. Suddenly, while I was playing the dirge, it whizzed overhead and a few seconds later it exploded somewhere outside the town. I have never played that piece with greater feeling."

During the war Moiseiwitsch also cooperated with Lady Churchill in raising funds for Russian relief, giving one hundred concerts and refusing either a fee or expenses. For this effort he was rewarded in 1946 with the decoration of Commander of the Order of the British Empire.

He returned to the American concert scene in 1947 after an absence of seventeen years. A year later he undertook a fresh world tour. He celebrated the fiftieth anniversary of his concert debut in the United States in 1958 with a performance in New York of three Rachmaninoff compositions for piano and orchestra as soloist with the Symphony of the Air. In 1960 he presented a cycle of three Chopin-Schumann concerts in New York. His last tour of the United States ended on February 28, 1963.

Early in 1963 Moiseiwitsch suffered a stroke. He appeared to be making a slow progress towards recuperation when he had a sudden relapse and died in a London hospital on April 9, 1963.

For relaxation Moiseiwitsch liked best of all to attend the theater, read books on history and science, and occasionally play bridge and golf. All his adult life he smoked heavily, indulged freely in hard alcohol, and had a gourmet's delight in good food. His wit was quick and sharp. While playing bridge one evening he cut a finger on his right hand. When two days later he was asked if he could play, his response was immediate: "Of course, I can deal with my left hand." When informed that a lady who had entertained him in a certain city twenty years earlier wanted to visit him backstage, he remarked: "She might at least have had the grace to send her daughter this time."

ABOUT: Moiseiwitsch, M. Benno Moiseiwitsch. *Periodicals*—Musical America, March 1962.

Mario del Monaco
See Del Monaco

Pierre Monteux

1875–1964

When, in his eighty-sixth year, Pierre Monteux was appointed principal conductor of the London Symphony Orchestra, he had known a longer period of continuous service to music than any conductor in history, a period of time spanning over half a century. The son of Gustave Monteux, a shoe salesman, Pierre was born in

Monteux: môn tû′

PIERRE MONTEUX

Paris on April 4, 1875. When he was a child he heard a Mozart violin sonata, and at that time he expressed the wish to become a violinist. Revealing unmistakable talent for music, he was enrolled in his late boyhood in the Paris Conservatory. There he studied harmony with Albert Lavignac, composition with Charles Lenepveu, and violin with Jean Pierre Maurin and Berthelier. While still attending the Conservatory, Monteux made his first public appearance as a violinist in a string quartet.

In 1896 he was graduated from the Conservatory with first prize in violin playing. He then decided to shift from the violin to the viola because (as he later confessed) he felt the viola was easier to play. Beginning in 1896 he played the viola for several years in the Colonne Orchestra and with the orchestra of the Opéra-Comique. He also organized and played the viola in a string quartet that toured Germany and performed a Brahms quartet for Brahms at his home not long before his death. "It takes Frenchmen to play my quartets," Brahms is reputed to have told the visiting musicians. "The Germans and the Austrians who play them are much too heavy-handed and slow."

With the Colonne Orchestra Monteux progressed in easy stages from his place among the violas to the positions of chorusmaster, then assistant conductor, and finally conductor. When his conducting apprenticeship was completed, he organized at the Casino de Paris in 1911 the Concerts Berlioz which specialized in the presentation of new music.

Sergei Diaghilev, founder and impresario of the Ballets Russes de Monte Carlo, was so impressed by performances of Monteux at the Concerts Berlioz that later in 1911 he engaged him to serve as principal conductor of his ballet company. With the Ballets Russes Monteux attracted world attention by directing the premieres of Stravinsky's *Petrouchka* (June 13, 1911), Ravel's *Daphnis and Chloe* (June 8, 1912), Stravinsky's *The Rite of Spring* (May 29, 1913), Debussy's *Jeux* (May 15, 1913), and Stravinsky's *Le Rossignol* (May 26, 1914). In each of these complex and provocative works he revealed himself as a musician of extraordinary musical comprehension and sympathy for the modern idiom. "He knew his job thoroughly," wrote Stravinsky in his autobiography, "and was so familiar with the surroundings from which he had risen that he knew how to get on with his musicians—a great asset for a conductor. Thus he was able to achieve a very clean and finished execution of my scores."

Monteux remained with the Ballets Russes until 1914, performing not only in Paris but also on tour. But he did not confine his conducting activity solely to the ballet company. From 1913 to 1914 he was the conductor at the Paris Opéra and Opéra-Comique. He also proved himself as adept in symphonic music as in operas and ballets by conducting the Société de Concerts Populaires (known later as Concerts Monteux) which he founded in February 1914 for the presentation of new French music and foreign works that could not easily gain a hearing in France. With this organization he presented the first concert performances of the suites derived from *Petrouchka* and *The Rite of Spring*, the former on March 1, 1914, the latter on April 5 of the same year. In addition to his appearances in Paris, he served as guest conductor at Covent Garden and Drury Lane in London, and in Berlin, Budapest, and Vienna.

With the outbreak of World War I, Monteux joined the 35th Territorial Infantry, seeing action in Rheims, Verdun, Soissons, and Argonne between August 5, 1914, and September 10, 1916. He was released from service for the purpose of spreading propaganda for the Allies in the United States. In this capacity he made a transcontinental tour of the United States in the fall of 1916 with the Ballets Russes. On this tour Monteux became involved in political controversy when on October 9 in New York he refused to conduct a ballet utilizing the music of Richard Strauss's tone poem *Till Eulenspiegel,* since its composer was a German. A compromise was reached: a substitute conductor performed the *Till Eulenspiegel* ballet and Monteux officiated for the remainder of the program.

In the summer of 1917 Monteux appeared for the first time in the United States as a symphony conductor when he led a guest performance of the New York Civic Orchestra. On November 17, 1917, he made his American debut as a conductor of opera with a performance of *Faust* at the Metropolitan Opera. For two seasons Monteux continued to conduct at the Metropolitan Opera, specializing in the French repertory: notably *Samson and Delilah,* the American premiere of Rabaud's *Mârouf* (December 19, 1917), *Thaïs,* the American premiere of Leroux's *La Reine Fiammette* (January 24, 1918), and the first New York production of Gounod's *Mireille* (February 28, 1918). He opened the 1918–1919 season with *Samson and Delilah* (November 11), and on January 20, 1919, he departed from the French repertory to lead a performance of Rimsky-Korsakov's *Le Coq d'Or.*

In 1918, when Henri Rabaud, the newly appointed music director of the Boston Symphony, was delayed in France and could not fulfill his commitments in Boston, Monteux was called upon to replace him for two weeks. He led his first concert in Boston on October 25. One season later, upon Rabaud's resignation from the Boston Symphony, Monteux became his permanent replacement. When Monteux took over the Boston Symphony it was in a state of serious deterioration; much of its personnel and repertory had been depleted by the hysteria attending America's involvement in World War I and the anti-German sentiment that fed it. Its former music director, Karl Muck, had been dismissed, and so were many other players in the orchestra who were of German origin. On assuming his post as music director, Monteux set about to rebuild the orchestra and by 1920 appeared to have gone some distance toward restoring some of the prestige the orchestra had once known under Muck. But in February 1920 the musicians embarked on a players' strike as a result of which the ranks became depleted by one half (including the concertmaster). Once again Monteux was faced with the problem of building the orchestra from the ground up. He accomplished this task so efficiently that by the time he left the

orchestra in 1924, he was able to turn over to his successor, Serge Koussevitsky, a well-trained and disciplined orchestra, technically efficient, and well able to meet every artistic demand of an exacting conductor. "From the dust and ashes of 1920," wrote the Boston critic H. T. Parker, "he [Monteux] has upreared the radiant and silken orchestra of 1924. . . . From Bach and Mozart to Strauss and Stravinsky, the whole range of music lay within the scope of the reanimated band. Ancient, classical, romantic, modernistic, at the composer's will it changed its voice. And that voice was also the voice of Pierre Monteux, fine of ear, alert of mind, many sided as is the music."

During his five years in Boston, Monteux presented a number of significant world premieres of American compositions. Among these were: the definitive version of *La Bonne Chanson* by Charles Martin Loeffler (November 1, 1918), Charles T. Griffes's *The Pleasure Dome of Kubla Khan* (November 27, 1919), Henry F. Gilbert's *Indian Sketches* (March 4, 1921), and the solo flute and string orchestra version of Arthur Foote's *A Night Piece* (November 1, 1918). He also presented American premieres of works by Stravinsky, Debussy, Ravel, Milhaud, Roger-Ducasse, and other twentieth century composers.

After leaving Boston in 1924, Monteux returned to Europe, appearing as guest conductor of major orchestras everywhere. For ten years beginning with 1924 he was co-conductor with Willem Mengelberg of the Concertgebouw Orchestra of Amsterdam. In this position he was responsible for the world premieres of Willem Pijper's Symphony No.3 which was dedicated to him (October 28, 1926) and Pijper's Piano Concerto No.2 (December 22, 1927), among other twentieth century works. In Amsterdam, he also served as the conductor of the Wagner Society.

After a four-year absence from the United States, Monteux returned in 1928 as a guest conductor of the Philadelphia Orchestra. At that time Lawrence Gilman wrote in the New York *Herald Tribune:* "He has, as a musician, sensibility and fine intelligence. He has that priceless conductorial gift, an intuitive awareness of style." Other critics, including those in Philadelphia, also found much to praise in his sensitively conceived and soberly projected performances. But Philadelphia audiences rejected him. In contrast to their own music director—the handsome, flamboyant, charismatic, and mercurial Stokowski, who was then on a leave of absence—Philadelphians found Monteux unexciting. Short and stocky, with a walrus-type moustache under his chubby cheeks, he looked far more like a French chef than a conductor. And his subdued and efficient behavior on the podium lacked dramatic interest. The audiences met his concerts with apathy, a fact that so aroused his bitterness that he vowed never to return to the United States which, he said, was concerned solely with "slim well-tailored conductors."

In 1930 Monteux took over the musical direction of the Orchestre Symphonique de Paris which had been founded two years earlier by Ernest Ansermet. He remained with this organization for a decade, vitalizing the Parisian music scene with his many world premieres, particularly of French music or music by composers residing in France. Some of these were Pierre-Octave Ferroud's Symphony (March 8, 1931), Jean Françaix' Symphony (November 6, 1932), Igor Markevitch's Piano Concerto (March 1, 1931), Nicolas Nabokov's *Symphonie Lyrique* (February 16, 1930), Francis Poulenc's *Concert Champêtre* (May 3, 1929), Prokofiev's Symphony No.3 (May 17, 1929), Jean Rivier's Symphony No.1 (January 29, 1933).

In 1935 Leonora Wood Armsby, president and director of the Musical Association of San Francisco, asked Monteux to become music director of the San Francisco Symphony which was then in financial and artistic bankruptcy. "Pierre," she told him, "there's no money. Will you take a chance?" Monteux consented on a one-year trial. He conducted his first concert in San Francisco on January 10, 1936. The following day the newspapers in San Francisco carried the following headlines: "New Conductor Works Miracles with Orchestra as Season Starts"; "Orchestra at Its Best"; "There Is a Symphony Orchestra Again in San Francisco"; and "Ovation Won by Monteux."

From an orchestra that in 1934 was made up of many incompetent musicians and had so little public support that it was able to give just four concerts a year, the San Francisco Symphony under Monteux developed into one of America's prime symphonic organizations. After a one-year trial, Monteux signed a three-year contract which was continually renewed after that. By revitalizing the orchestral personnel and the rep-

ertory, Monteux made the orchestra the backbone of the city's cultural activities. He inaugurated annual festivals devoted to a single classical or romantic program. In addition he usually interpolated at least one modern work in each of his programs. As he had done in Boston, so in San Francisco he introduced new works by Americans. Among these premieres were George Antheil's Symphony No.6 (February 10, 1949), Ernest Bloch's *Evocations* (February 11, 1938), Morton Gould's suite from the *Fall River Legend* ballet (April 22, 1948), and Ernest Schelling's *Suite Variée* (May 2, 1939). He sponsored young musical performers as soloists and initiated special concerts for students. Furthermore, he launched an ambitious recording program for RCA which within a few years saw the release of forty-one albums. Then in 1947, he took the orchestra on a fifty-three-city tour of the United States and Canada, performing fifty-six concerts in as many days.

With his wife, the former Doris Hodgkins whom he had married in Brussels on September 26, 1928, and his French poodle, Monteux spent the San Francisco winters at the Fairmount Hotel. His wife (his third) was an American, and Monteux himself became an American citizen on March 2, 1946. He became one of the city's most easily recognizable and beloved figures. *Time* magazine called him "a civic fixture" and *Life* wrote: "An open love affair has been going on between the people of San Francisco and their venerable, walrus-moustached, supremely gifted orchestral leader, Pierre Monteux." His seventy-fifth birthday in 1950 was celebrated on April 17 at the Civic Auditorium. Ten thousand admirers were present to eat birthday cake, drink champagne, and listen to a concert of light music conducted by Monteux. The California Legislature conferred on him on that evening the honorary title "Ambassador Extraordinary for the City of San Francisco."

His commitments in San Francisco did not preclude appearances elsewhere. Some had historic importance. As a guest conductor of the Berlin Philharmonic he became the first Frenchman to lead that organization before 1950. When he led the NBC Symphony on November 13, 1937, he was conducting the first concert of a new major American orchestra—an orchestra founded for Toscanini; Monteux had been called in for the first concerts to put the orchestra through its final paces before it was passed on to Toscanini.

Monteux had another commitment that was close to his heart: teaching conducting to a selected handful of students. He did so at his summer home, the Domain of the Great Pine, in Hancock, Maine, overlooking a rock-bordered tidal bay. There he established a summer school for young conductors in 1941, a renewal and extension of the conducting classes he had given for a number of years beginning with 1932 at the École Monteux in Paris. In Maine, in the most informal kind of setting, a handful of talented young musicians acquired from Monteux not only the technique but also the philosophy of the conducting art.

In 1952 Monteux resigned as music director of the San Francisco Symphony. His last concert, on April 12, 1952—a performance of Beethoven's Ninth Symphony—was an occasion for one of the most moving demonstrations by audience and orchestra men ever witnessed in that auditorium. The American Federation of Musicians presented him with its first life membership in its history; an anonymous donor contributed two hundred and fifty thousand dollars to the orchestra's pension fund in Monteux's name; the San Francisco Musical Association presented him with a silver bowl; the men and women of the orchestra gave him the gift of a high-powered pair of binoculars, having learned that he had always wanted them. After the concert, a farewell dinner was given in his honor—some of the orchestra men performed jazz and some of the ladies of the orchestra did the cancan.

After 1952, when he was not elsewhere on a conducting assignment, he lived at his estate in Maine where he entertained his friends with culinary and vintage delights of his table and with his talent as a raconteur. A fire buff who in 1963 had been presented with a helmet from and honorary membership in the London Fire Brigade, Monteux gave the town of Hanover the gift of a fire engine and a station to house it.

Refusing to make any concessions to his advancing years, he continued to fill exacting assignments in Europe and the United States that would have taxed the physical resources of men many years younger. He became an annual guest conductor of the Boston Symphony with which in 1952–1953 he made an American transcontinental and a European tour—and a second European tour in 1956 that included the first visit of that orchestra to the Soviet Union. He returned to the Metropolitan Opera on December 3, 1954, with a performance of *Manon.* During that season and the following one he was also heard in performances of *Faust, Carmen, Pelléas and Mélisande,* and Gluck's *Orfeo ed Euridice.* On September 28, 1954, he made his debut with the San Francisco Opera in *Manon;* later the same season he conducted there Honegger's *Joan of Arc at the Stake* and *Fidelio.* In the spring of 1955 he took a group of young American singers in whom he had become interested to special performances of *Pelléas and Mélisande* at the Théâtre de la Monnaie in Brussels.

All this was supplemented by guest performances the year round. And in 1961, aged eighty-six, he took on a new permanent appointment as principal conductor of the London Symphony. With this orchestra he led in Paris in May 1963 a performance of Stravinsky's *The Rite of Spring* to commemorate the fiftieth anniversary of the premiere of that work.

Even in old age there seemed little diminution in his interpretative powers. After one of Monteux's concerts in New York when he was in his eighties, Ross Parmenter wrote of him in the New York *Times:* "As he conducted one was never conscious of technique as an end in itself. Rather, the impression one gained was of being admitted into the creative mind of the composer. . . . Mr. Monteux's understanding of what he performed always seemed so profound that he seemed to reveal why the composers chose the particular instruments they did in order to give the shade of expression they wanted."

On April 4, 1955, Monteux celebrated his eightieth birthday by conducting part of a pension concert of the Boston Symphony. The second half of the program, led by Charles Münch, consisted of compositions written in honor of Monteux by Darius Milhaud and Igor Stravinsky. (Stravinsky's composition, *Greeting Prelude,* was based on the tune "Happy Birthday.") In 1960 Monteux once again celebrated his birthday (his eighty-fifth) by conducting a pension concert of the Boston Symphony, presenting Beethoven's Ninth Symphony.

He was conducting an orchestra concert at the Santa Cecilia Academy in Rome on April 1, 1964, performing Ravel's *Pavane for a Dead Princess,* when he fell off the podium and dropped six feet into the pit. Shaken, he clambered back to the platform to complete the Ravel piece and to direct Debussy's *La Mer*. From Italy he went on to conduct concerts in Amsterdam, Israel, and London. He returned to the United States in such a state of physical exhaustion that he canceled his summer conducting classes in Maine and his scheduled engagements at the Berkshire Music Festival, at Ravinia, and as guest conductor in Philadelphia, Cleveland, Pittsburgh, and New Orleans.

He died peacefully at his home in Hancock, Maine, on July 1, 1964. During more than a half century of conducting he had led over seventy symphony orchestras. For his musical achievements he was made Commander of the French Legion of Honor, a member of the French Academy, an Officer of the Crown of Romania, and Commander of Orange-Nassau in Holland. He was awarded a gold medal from the Royal Philharmonic of London, made international member of the Santa Cecilia Academy and a member of the Royal Academy of London, and awarded honorary doctorates in music by the University of California, Mills College, Oakland University in Maine, and Stanford University.

ABOUT: O'Connell, C. The Other Side of the Record. *Periodicals*—Hi-Fi, September 1964; Musical America, September 1964; New York Times, December 4, 1949; Newsweek, July 13, 1964; Opera News, September 26, 1964; Saturday Review, August 22, 1964.

Grace Moore

1901–1947

Grace Moore (originally Mary Willis Grace Moore), soprano, was born in Slabtown, in the Smoky Mountains of Tennessee, on December 5, 1901, the oldest of five children of Richard and Tessie Moore. Her father was the manager of a commissary for a lumber company. When she was five, her family moved to Jellico, Tennessee, where her father became a dry goods merchant. As a child, Grace sang in the church choir. When she was thirteen she was fired with the ambition to devote her life to missionary work in China. But that same year she changed her mind when she was taken to a recital by Mary Garden in Nashville; this inspired a new ambition, to become a professional singer. She hounded her father for vocal lessons, but he insisted that she

GRACE MOORE

first receive an academic education. For this purpose she was enrolled in the Ward-Belmont College in Nashville, but she was expelled for attending a dance without permission. Only after she had gone through what her father described as "a long period of angelic behavior" did he allow her to enter the Wilson-Greene Academy of Music in Chevy Chase, Maryland.

In 1919 Moore made her singing debut at the National Theatre in Washington, D.C., in a concert starring Giovanni Martinelli. Her own contribution was the "Ritorna vincitor" aria from *Aida*. A local reviewer wrote: "A lion and a mouse gave a concert yesterday. The lion made way for the mouse who disclosed a pretty and charming voice with a future." With borrowed funds, Moore made her way to New York City. She found her first singing job at the Black Cat, a café in Greenwich Village.

An inept singing teacher, to whom she went for instruction because the fee was modest, almost ruined her vocal cords through over-exercise. One morning Moore awoke to find that she could produce only hoarse rasping sounds. Advised by a knowledgeable voice coach, P. Mario Marafioti, she went to Canada to give her voice three months of complete rest. She used the time advantageously, to study languages.

With her voice restored, Moore returned to New York for further vocal training with Marafioti, who strengthened her voice and enriched its sound and texture. To support herself, she got a job as an ingenue lead in *Suite Sixteen*, a stage musical touring the United States. The show died on the road, leaving the company stranded in a small town in Oklahoma. Her second stage vehicle was *Just a Minute.* This also closed out of town, and a third one, *Up in the Clouds,* came no closer to Broadway than Brooklyn, New York.

But she had far better luck with Jerome Kern's musical *Hitchy Koo* (1920) in which she replaced Julia Sanderson, who had fallen ill. "A new star is born," wrote Alexander Woollcott in the New York *World.*

In 1921 Moore went to Paris to study singing with Roger Thiral. There she auditioned unsuccessfully for the Opéra-Comique. Her funds depleted, she returned to the United States and joined the cast of Irving Berlin's *Music Box Revue* in 1923. She was back with this revue for its 1924 edition. Although she had become a highly paid Broadway stage performer with a bright future ahead of her in the musical theater, her real goal was the opera house and the concert stage. Twice she auditioned for the Metropolitan Opera only to be turned down both times. Artur Bodanzky, the conductor, told her: "No matter how hard you work, you will never be an opera singer. You'll never even learn to sing on key." Giulio Gatti-Casazza, the general manager of the Metropolitan Opera, advised her to concentrate on Broadway and forget about opera.

Refusing to accept defeat and fully conscious that she needed more work on her voice, she abandoned the *Music Box Revue,* giving only twelve hours' notice to the producer, and set sail for Europe. She spent eighteen months studying voice with Richard Barthélemy and acting with Albert Carré. She also received valuable advice and guidance from Mary Garden who by this time had become her friend. In Milan she auditioned once again for Gatti-Casazza who was now sufficiently impressed with her progress to give her a Metropolitan Opera contract paying seventy-five dollars a week.

She made her Metropolitan Opera debut on February 7, 1928, as Mimi in *La Bohème.* She was so well received by the audience (which included a special delegation from Tennessee headed by its two senators) that she had to take twenty-eight curtain calls. Francis D. Perkins in the *Herald Tribune* found that her voice was "promising . . . of a smooth and pleasing quality of tone and good vocal production." Richard L. Stokes remarked in the *World Telegram* that "there were moments of softer song in which the

tendril-like phrases took on a caressing timbre."

She continued making a favorable impression, not only vocally but also as an attractive stage presence, as Lauretta in *Gianni Schicchi* and Micaëla in *Carmen* later that season. On September 29, 1928, she made an impressive debut at the Opéra-Comique in Paris. Additional appearances followed in New York and Paris in which she distinguished herself as Juliet in *Romeo and Juliet,* Manon in Massenet's opera, and Marguerite in *Faust.*

She also tried the world of motion pictures, appearing in *A Lady's Morals* (1930), a film dramatization of Jenny Lind's life. This was a failure, and so was her second film, *New Moon* (1930), in which she was costarred with Lawrence Tibbett.

In 1931, aboard a steamer bound for Europe, she met Valentin Parera, a Spanish motion picture star. Later the same year, on July 15, they were married in Cannes, France.

In 1932 Moore made a brief but none too successful return to the Broadway musical stage with *The Du Barry,* an American adaptation of Karl Millöcker's operetta. It had a run of only eighty-seven performances. In 1934 she was starred in the motion picture musical *One Night of Love.* She played the part of a prima donna, which enabled her to sing several operatic excerpts from *Madama Butterfly* and *Carmen* as well as some popular numbers including the title song and "Ciribiribin." The last of these became a favorite number in her recital repertory after that. She rarely gave a concert without featuring it either on the program or as an encore.

As a pioneer attempt to present operatic music on the screen within a popular format, *One Night of Love* took the country by storm. Overnight Moore became a motion picture star. Her performance earned a gold medal from the American Society of Arts and Sciences in 1935 for "conspicuous achievement in raising the standard of cinema entertainment." She herself knew and was proud of what she had accomplished, saying: "I am the girl who took the high hat off grand opera. . . . I made the motion picture public opera-conscious."

As the first opera singer to become an unqualified motion picture star, Moore acquired a niche all her own in the music world. She was eagerly sought after by the world's leading opera houses and for concert appearances. In July 1935 she made her debut at Covent Garden in

London as Mimi and received an ovation; outside the auditorium, after the performance, her public almost caused a riot. She was also invited to give a command performance for Queen Mary.

At the Metropolitan Opera, Moore gathered new triumphs as Tosca, Marguerite in *Faust,* Giulietta in *The Tales of Hoffmann,* Louise in Charpentier's opera, and Fiora in *L'Amore dei Tre Re.* Her first appearance as Louise (a part she had studied with the composer) took place on January 28, 1939. Olin Downes, writing in the New York *Times,* called her performance a "thoughtful, sincere and dramatically effective accomplishment. . . . The conception, dramatically as well as in song, is excellently constructed, carried out in detail." As Fiora, she was heard on February 7, 1941, in a performance led by the composer himself. (She had sung the same role in Chicago the preceding fall.) She sang, commented Olin Downes in the New York *Times,* "better than we had ever heard her sing, with freedom, and glow of color and opulent tone to cap the orchestra climaxes." However, her acting brought negative reports. Francis D. Perkins wrote in the *Herald Tribune:* "Her depiction of the part gave a certain impression of self-consciousness, a series of poses, of impersonating rather than being the character." And Olin Downes found that her "dramatic interpretation is inadequate. . . . She simulated with conspicuous unsuccess Fiora's spirit and Fiora's passion."

Some critics also found fault with her vocalizing. She had a lovely voice that flowed easily, but there were those who felt that she did not always have it under control and that her technique left much to be desired. Her own lack of confidence in her abilities, in spite of her worldwide triumphs, contributed further insecurities to her performances. Vincent Sheean, the writer, who was her close friend as well as an ardent admirer, did not hesitate to say in *Opera News:* "She always dreaded the high notes and the low notes, the quick recitatives and the staccatos and pianissimos. Nor could she be sure of the meaning of the words she sang, no matter how thoroughly she had learned them. . . . Even her memory deserted her at times. Fear, insecurity and a fundamental feeling of unfitness for what she was doing afflicted her, and in all her triumphant glory, bedizened as she was in the most precious

stones of this earth, I was always sorry for Grace."

What she did have abundantly were stage magic, the ability to make the stage glow with her physical beauty, and her inordinate personal charm.

Her successes on the concert stage were in large measure equal to those in the opera house. She toured America and Europe extensively in recitals, and wherever she went she found an idolatrous audience. She appeared frequently over the radio, both as the star of her own show and as a guest performer on principal network programs. She was a headliner in vaudeville and on the stage of motion picture palaces, filling an engagement at the Roxy Theatre in New York in 1943 that paid her ten thousand dollars a week. In explaining her performances in vaudeville and motion picture houses she said: "My greatest ambition is in reaching as many people as possible."

She continued to reach millions of admirers in her later motion pictures: *Love Me Forever* (1935), *The King Steps Out* (1936), *When You're in Love* (1937), *I'll Take Romance* (1937), and *Louise* (1940).

During World War II, Moore toured South America for the United States Department of State and made numerous appearances at bond rallies and in army camps throughout the United States. Soon after V-E Day she gave concerts for the American occupation forces in Germany.

She enjoyed the distinction of being a favorite of European royalty and of holders of high office in the United States. She was presented to six kings, sang for five American presidents, and was honored by twelve command performances. She received decorations from Norway, Sweden, Denmark, Belgium, France, Cuba, Mexico, and several other countries. Furthermore she was the only American singer to have her name appear on a golden plaque decorating the entrance to the Opéra-Comique in Paris.

She was leaving Copenhagen after giving a command performance when she met sudden death on January 26, 1947, on a KLM airliner that crashed and exploded on the snow-covered Kastrup Airport in Copenhagen. She had boarded the plane only a few minutes before she was killed.

She maintained homes in France, California, and Connecticut; her two-hundred-year-old farmhouse in Sandy Hook, Connecticut, "Far

Away Meadows," was her favorite retreat. Short, slight, blond, and attractive, she weighed about a hundred and five pounds and stood five feet four inches tall. She was one of the best-dressed opera stars in the world; famous couturiers designed clothes especially for her. Her favorite colors, blue and lavender, predominated in her wardrobe. For physical activity she preferred tennis, golf, and swimming.

She was the author of an autobiography, *You're Only Human Once* (1944). A motion picture freely based on her life and career, inspired by her autobiography, was released in 1953: *So This Is Love,* starring Kathryn Grayson.

ABOUT: Moore, G. You're Only Human Once; O'Connell, C. The Other Side of the Record. *Periodicals*— Collier's, August 21, 1937; Newsweek, April 28, 1941; New York Times, January 27, 1947; Opera News, March 31, 1941, December 20, 1969.

ERICA MORINI

Erica Morini

1904–

Erica (originally Erika) Morini, violinist, was born in Vienna on January 5, 1904. Her father, Oscar Morini, was the descendant of an Italian family of professional musicians; he himself was a professor of violin and the head of his own Conservatory in Vienna. Her mother, Amalia Weissmann Morini, was Viennese. "My destiny was mapped out for me before I was born," she recalls. "In my father's school of music, when I played with my dolls in a corner at the age of three, if any one of his pupils struck a wrong note, I would look up and frown. My baby's senses were acute with harmony. My father saw this and when I was four my musical education began. I wanted to play the piano. But my father's own talent was for the violin; and so it was the violin for me."

When she was five, she was taken to the headquarters of the Austrian General Staff to perform for Archduke Karl (later Emperor). The palace officials placed her behind a screen and told the Archduke to listen to a performance "by one of Austria's greatest artists." When the Archduke went to congratulate the violinist, he was amazed to find a child. He asked Erika to

Morini: mō rē′ nē

select any gift she wished. Her choice was modest: a large doll which throughout her life she retained as a treasured remembrance of her meeting with the Archduke.

After studying violin with her father at his Conservatory, Erika was sent to the Vienna Conservatory to become a pupil of Otakar Ševčík. Only a few lessons were required for Ševčík to realize the extent of her talent. "She knows everything that cannot be taught," he said. At the age of twelve she completed the master course at the Conservatory and that same year, on January 16, 1916, she made her concert debut in Vienna. It was so successful that six additional concerts were arranged that season in Vienna. In 1919 she made her debut with orchestra as soloist with the Leipzig Gewandhaus Orchestra under Arthur Nikisch, in the Beethoven Violin Concerto. Nikisch was so enchanted with her playing that he invited her to appear in Berlin with the Berlin Philharmonic under his direction. A recital tour then took her through Germany, Poland, Russia, and Hungary. In 1920 she was the only soloist to appear with the Vienna Philharmonic during Vienna's music festival week.

She went to the United States for the first time to appear as soloist on January 26, 1921, with the New York Philharmonic Orchestra under Artur Bodanzky, in a program made up of three concertos. The New York critics were unanimously enthusiastic. During that initial season she gave four recitals in New York within a six-week period.

After three successful tours of the United States, she toured Australia and the Orient, in addition to performing throughout Europe and Russia. When she returned to the United States in 1930 for a brief visit, and in 1935 for a prolonged tour, her place as a violin virtuoso of the first rank was universally recognized.

Following one of her appearances in New York in 1935, Olin Downes wrote in the New York *Times:* "As a young girl, Miss Morini made herself known in this city as a performer of exceptional but uneven equipment. . . . It is evident that . . . Miss Morini has made a prodigious advance. Everything . . . was done beautifully. Where the player's temperament might have run away with her, it was held in control, serving only to heighten the contagious spirit of the interpretation. Nothing was insignificant, and nothing was out of proportion."

Since her first appearance in the United States, Morini has toured the country more than twenty times, and in her engagements both in America and abroad has appeared as soloist in more than one thousand orchestral engagements. She played the standard repertory, but she was also heard in numerous new works. On January 14, 1970, as a soloist with the San Francisco Symphony under Josef Krips, she presented the world premiere of Sir William Walton's *Improvisations on an Impromptu of Benjamin Britten.*

Following her appearance with the New York Philharmonic under George Szell in the Tchaikovsky Violin Concerto, Harold C. Schonberg described her in the New York *Times* as "one of the greatest instrumentalists of the age." He added: "Miss Morini brings to her interpretations an incomparable elegance and soaring tone, plus a musicianship that provides an exquisite taper and a finish to a phrase." When she returned to the New York concert stage on February 9, 1976, after a ten-year absence, Donal Henahan, writing in the New York *Times,* called her recital "among the most musically satisfying of this season." Henahan found that though Miss Morini was now seventy-two years old her "technical equipment has held up remarkably well" and that her tone was "consistently beautiful."

Morini, who married Felice Siracusano, a jewelry merchant, on April 28, 1938, has for many years resided in an apartment on Fifth Avenue in New York City. She became an American citizen in 1945. Earlier in her life she took delight in hiking and mountain climbing; later years found her more partial to reading books, going to the theater and movies, collecting paintings, and running her household with the efficiency of a typical Viennese *Hausfrau.* Her most prized possession is a white linen handkerchief embroidered with a coronet and crest. It once belonged to Pablo de Sarasate, who bequeathed it to the Musical Society of Madrid for presentation to the violinist best able to capture the spirit of his *Spanish Dances.* She received it in Madrid in 1933.

Erica Morini was awarded honorary doctorates in music from Smith College and from the New England Conservatory of Music.

ABOUT: Etude, June 1942; New York Times, January 21, 1942.

Felix Mottl

1856–1911

Felix Mottl, Wagnerian conductor, was born in Unter-St. Veit, near Vienna, on August 24, 1856. As a boy he had a beautiful soprano voice and was entered in the Löwenburg Seminary in preparation for the boys' choir of the Imperial Court Chapel in Vienna. However, in Vienna he changed course, entering the Conservatory. There he undertook a comprehensive course of study over a period of many years, principally piano with Anton Door, theory with Anton Bruckner, composition with Otto Dessoff, and conducting with Joseph Hellmesberger. After graduation from the Conservatory with every prize it could bestow, Mottl became the president of the Richard Wagner Society in Vienna, starting his career as a conductor of Wagner's music with that organization. In 1876, when the first Bayreuth festival was launched, he went to Bayreuth to assist in the production and performance of the Wagner *Ring* cycle. There he became a member of the "Nibelungen-Kanzlei," a group of dedicated Wagnerphiles.

Upon the recommendation of Otto Dessoff, Mottl was engaged as court conductor at Karlsruhe, Germany, in 1880, and rose to the post of general music director in 1893. He ini-

Mottl: mŏt′ 'l

FELIX MOTTL

tiated a progressive repertory that included all of Wagner's principal stage works and all of the operas of Berlioz, including the first complete performance of *Les Troyens* in December 1905. He also gave the world premiere of his own edited version of Cornelius's *The Barber of Bagdad* on February 1, 1884, providing the impetus for the opera's success throughout Europe.

He returned to Bayreuth in the summer of 1886 to conduct a brilliant performance of *Tristan and Isolde.* In 1894 he led a successful Wagner concert in London, and in 1898 he directed the entire *Ring* cycle at Covent Garden.

In 1903 he went to the United States to conduct the first stage performance of *Parsifal* ever given outside Bayreuth. When the Wagner family entered into litigation to prevent this production, Mottl withdrew discreetly from that specific project and was succeeded by Alfred Hertz. Mottl made his American debut with *Die Walküre* at the Metropolitan Opera on November 25, 1903. In performances that season of *Tannhäuser, Lohengrin, Tristan and Isolde, Siegfried,* and *Das Rheingold* he was acclaimed as one of the great Wagnerian conductors of his time. He was also active at the Metropolitan Opera outside the Wagner repertory, with performances of *The Magic Flute, The Marriage of Figaro, Carmen,* Boïeldieu's *La Dame Blanche,* and *Romeo and Juliet.*

Between 1903 and 1906 Mottl alternated with Karl Muck in conducting the Vienna Philharmonic Orchestra. In 1904 he was appointed director of the Royal Academy of Music in Munich. After 1904 and up to the time of his death he was principal conductor; after 1907, he was general music director of the Munich Royal Opera. He was conducting a performance of *Tristan and Isolde* late in June 1911 when, just as Isolde sang "Death-doomed head, death-doomed heart," he collapsed. He died a few days later, on July 2, 1911, in Munich.

Mottl was the composer of three operas, the best known of which was *Agnes Bernauer,* produced in Weimar in 1880. He also wrote a string quartet and some songs. He orchestrated Wagner's *Five Wesendonk Songs,* Chabrier's *Bourée Fantasque,* and Liszt's *St. Francis of Assisi Preaching to the Birds,* and arranged several orchestral excerpts from Gluck's operas into the *Ballet Suite.* He also edited the vocal scores of all the operas and music dramas of Wagner and Berlioz.

Mottl was married to Henrietta Standthartner, a singer. For many years they made their home in Karlsruhe, Germany.

ABOUT: Baker, T. Biographical Dictionary of Musicians, completely rev. by N. Slonimsky; Grove, G. ed. Dictionary of Music and Musicians; 5th ed. by E. Blom.

Karl Muck

1859–1940

Karl Muck, conductor, was born in Darmstadt, Germany, on October 22, 1859. He was the son of a Bavarian magistrate who was also a trained musician. Before he decided to specialize in music, Karl received a comprehensive academic education and attended the universities of Heidelberg and Leipzig, where he specialized in classical philology, receiving a doctorate in philosophy from the University of Leipzig in 1880. Early in his life music became a major interest and activity. His father gave him his first piano lessons, and later he continued the study of the piano with Professor Kissner in Würzburg. In Leipzig, while attending the University, he enrolled in the Conservatory. Before his graduation from the Conservatory, he made his concert debut in 1880, appearing as a piano solo-

Muck: mŏŏk

KARL MUCK

ist with the Gewandhaus Orchestra in Leipzig.

A career as a piano virtuoso did not interest him, however. He soon found a post as chorusmaster at the Municipal Theater in Zurich, Switzerland. There he later rose to the post of conductor. Other conducting engagements in Salzburg, Brünn, and Graz followed. One of his performances in Graz was heard by the opera impresario, Angelo Neumann, who engaged him as a conductor at the Deutsches Landestheater in Prague in 1886. Sometime later, Muck succeeded Anton Seidl as principal conductor of the Neumann Nibelungen opera troupe, a traveling Wagner company.

The authority and distinction of his Wagnerian performances became recognized throughout Europe. Adding a seeming authenticity to his Wagnerian interpretations was the facial resemblance he bore to Wagner. This resemblance even led to an unfounded rumor that he was Wagner's illegitimate son. Muck's fame as a performer of Wagner brought him invitations to conduct the *Ring* cycle in London and St. Petersburg in 1889 and Moscow in 1891.

In 1892 Muck became first conductor of the Berlin Royal Opera. During the twenty years that followed he conducted in Berlin 1,071 performances of 103 different operas, 30 of them novelties; one of the last was the world premiere of Ethel Smyth's *Der Wald* (April 9, 1902). He created one of the most brilliant regimes in the history of that opera company and earned an exalted place among the conductors of his time. He was Prussian in his autocratic dominance

over his players and singers and in his demand for military discipline. The supreme master of every situation, he was thoroughly disinterested in those who worked under him as human beings but manipulated them as if they were automatons. A penetrating scholar rather than a romanticist, he brought to each of his performances a keen intellect, a well-disciplined and precise mind. His intellect was placed completely at the service of the music and its composer. He exerted prodigious effort in his own study of any given piece of music, and during rehearsals, in preparing for a performance, he expected each of his musicians to expend similar Herculean efforts. He had an acid tongue and an explosive temper and seemed incapable of any warmth of feeling, sympathy, or kindness except to those closest to him. He was an introvert who kept to himself most of the time. He did not seek affection and he did not get it. To music making he gave himself completely and in so doing he frequently transformed his performances into revelations. Artur Schnabel called him "a very great master, whose reliability, maturity and unselfish dedication are not equalled by any living artist," and Felix Weingartner described him as one of the most hard-working, conscientious conductors he had ever known.

While fulfilling his duties in Berlin, both at the Royal Opera and at the Royal Chapel where he conducted symphony concerts, Muck led annual Silesian festivals from 1891 to 1911, and from 1903 to 1906 he shared with Felix Mottl the direction of the Vienna Philharmonic. Muck also made numerous guest appearances in other principal music centers of Europe. In 1901 he conducted his first *Parsifal* at the Bayreuth Festival; for the next three decades his performances of this music drama at Bayreuth were among his highest artistic achievements. Herbert F. Peyser, the music correspondent in Europe for the New York *Times,* expressed the opinion of many authorities when he called Muck's presentations "the only and the ultimate *Parsifal;* the *Parsifal* in which every phrase was charged with infinities; the *Parsifal* which was not merely of this age but of all time."

Muck's first appearance in the United States took place on October 12, 1906, with the Boston Symphony. He led concerts in Boston for two seasons. In 1912 he resigned from his post in Berlin, his last performance there—*Tristan and Isolde*—inspiring an ovation. That same year he was made the permanent conductor of the Boston Symphony.

In Boston he scaled new heights as a symphonic conductor. His unrelenting discipline brought a new technical virtuosity to the orchestra and his genius as interpreter—as well as his involvement in the music of the twentieth century—made each of his concerts an important artistic event. In Boston, both before and after he became permanent conductor, he introduced new American works. Among these were Chadwick's *Symphonic Sketches* (February 7, 1908), Henry Hadley's *Salome* (April 12, 1907), Loeffler's *A Pagan Poem* (November 22, 1907), and Ernest Schelling's *Impressions from an Artist's Life* (December 31, 1915). On March 1, 1907, he conducted the American premiere of Debussy's *La Mer* and on December 18, 1914, Schoenberg's *Five Pieces for Orchestra.*

He was also successful in San Francisco. Beginning on May 14, 1915, he conducted thirteen daily concerts in thirteen different programs with the Boston Symphony at the Panama-Pacific International Exposition.

Under Muck the Boston Symphony became the leading symphonic organization in America —possibly in the world. There was hardly a dissenting voice to the judgment that Muck in a vast and varied repertory had few equals among the world's conductors.

But World War I changed all that. In the fall of 1915, when Muck returned from Europe to fulfill his seasonal obligations in Boston, he was interviewed by a newspaper reporter who asked him about the Belgian atrocities. Muck firmly told the reporter he could not believe that his countrymen were capable of such bestialities. This was reported in the press, but since America was then still neutral, his comment did not draw much attention. However, after America became involved in the war, this interview was remembered; so was the fact that Muck was a friend of the Kaiser. Muck, recognizing the delicacy of the situation, offered to resign but his resignation was turned down.

On October 30, 1917, shortly before an appearance of the Boston Symphony in Providence, Rhode Island, citizens and press of Providence demanded that he open his concert with "The Star-Spangled Banner." "It is as good a time as any," said the Providence *Journal* editorially, "to put Prof. Muck to the test." Muck did not play the national anthem that

evening; some say he was not told of the request until after the concert. His failure to do so, whatever the reason, brought angry protests and ugly recriminations. He was denounced not only as a sympathizer for the German cause but also as a traitor, a paid agent of Germany. He did finally perform the national anthem at his very next concert, on November 3, 1917, but the anti-Muck hysteria kept mounting. Governor Warfield of Maryland cried out in a speech that no true American could be satisfied until Muck was "mobbed" to death. Theodore Roosevelt demanded that Muck be sent back to Germany. In some places Muck was burned in effigy. Several patriotic societies banded together to institute a boycott of all Boston Symphony concerts.

Muck had completed rehearsing Bach's *Passion According to St. Matthew* on March 25, 1918, when, that evening, he was arrested at his home as an enemy alien. The newspapers implied that powerful evidence implicated Muck as a political enemy but such evidence was withheld. Eventually the government officials explained that Muck had been arrested because he had not registered as an enemy alien; and the reason Muck had not registered as such was because actually he was not a German but a Swiss citizen at the time.

Found guilty of espionage, Muck—as Prisoner 1337—was interned in Fort Oglethorpe, Georgia, where he remained fourteen months. He was released on August 12, 1919, and allowed to leave the country. Embittered, Muck told reporters on his departure that the United States was "controlled by sentiment which closely borders on mob rule."

In Germany, Muck took over the music direction of the Hamburg Symphony from 1922 to 1933; continued to give incandescent performances at Bayreuth; and from time to time made a number of guest appearances in other German cities. He conducted his last *Parsifal* in Bayreuth in 1930, and his last concert anywhere, in Leipzig in 1933. Herbert F. Peyser, who attended that Leipzig performance, reported in the New York *Times:* "A gray shadow of himself, and practically hoisted up on the podium by two stalwart attendants, the musician nevertheless struck sparks for a few brief moments. . . . Like a broken Wotan he passed from the public gaze and went off to seek the hospitality of some aloof and unpretentious Valhalla, there to await the dusk."

Muck spent his retirement in Stuttgart, where he died on March 3, 1940.

In *The Great Conductors,* Harold C. Schonberg described Muck as follows: "He was a short, slim man with a prominent hooked nose . . . a Mephistophelean expression and a fine collection of dueling scars he had picked up at Heidelberg. . . . He smoked five packs of cigarettes a day, had a hair-trigger temper and a penchant for scatological expressions, even during a concert. . . . Muck had no podium mannerisms. His bearing was erect and quiet, his beat clear, his baton describing tiny, short arcs, his elbow moving only slightly. . . . He never conducted without a score, saying that memorization was just a trick and that an orchestra was more at ease when a conductor had the music before him."

The Wagnerian soprano Frida Leider has added: "He dressed in the style prevalent at the turn of the century and never departed from it as long as I knew him. A high stiff collar, a black tie with a jeweled stickpin given to him by Emperor Wilhelm II, a plain, long black coat and stiff white cuffs with links to match the tiepin. One's first impression of him was of someone elegant, unapproachable and, in a way, belonging to a bygone age."

ABOUT: Ewen, D. Dictators of the Baton; Schonberg, H. C. The Great Conductors. *Periodicals*—Musicology, Vol. 1, No. 3, 1947.

Charles Münch

1891–1968

Charles Münch (also spelled Munch), conductor, was born in Strasbourg, Alsace (then under German rule), on September 26, 1891. His father, Ernest Münch, was director of the choir of St. Guillaume Church and a teacher at the Strasbourg Conservatory. His mother, Celestine Simon Münch, was the daughter of a French clergyman. The organist and humanitarian Albert Schweitzer was a distant relative.

There was always music at the Münch home, both in their winter residence in Strasbourg and in their summer retreat in the Vosges. The fam-

Münch: münsh

CHARLES MÜNCH

ily and its friends often congregated to sing Bach cantatas or perform chamber music.

Charles's first major interest in boyhood was not music but locomotives. When he was six he knew the exact time the European express trains came into the Strasbourg station and he was often there to await their arrival.

He received a comprehensive musical training from boyhood on. After attending the Protestant high school from 1898 to 1912 he went to the Strasbourg Conservatory where he specialized in the violin and studied composition with Hans Pfitzner. At the same time he played the violin in an orchestra conducted by his father and occasionally played the organ in church. Upon receiving his diploma in violin from the Strasbourg Conservatory in 1912, he went to Paris. There he lived in a small flat on the Île de la Cité and studied violin with Lucien Capet. He subsequently took further violin instruction from Carl Flesch in Berlin.

Just before World War I Münch gave a violin recital in Paris. He was visiting his family in Strasbourg when war broke out between Germany and France. Drafted into the German army, he saw action as a sergeant in the artillery for four years. After being gassed at Péronne and wounded at Verdun, he was demobilized.

Münch returned to Paris where he spent two years and in 1918 became a French citizen. Then, with Strasbourg once again French territory, he returned to his native city in 1919 to become professor of the violin at the Strasbourg Conservatory and concertmaster of the Municipal Orchestra. Already his ambition was veering towards conducting. To prepare himself, he spent his free time memorizing orchestral scores and studying the techniques and methods of the two conductors then active in Strasbourg, Guy Ropartz and Paul Bastide.

In 1926 Münch was engaged as violinist of the Gewandhaus Orchestra. He soon rose to the post of concertmaster, playing under Wilhelm Furtwängler and Bruno Walter. In Leipzig he got his first chance to conduct. One day the conductor for a performance of several Bach cantatas at the St. Thomas Church became ill and Münch, who was playing the violin in the orchestra, was asked to substitute. Sometime later, during a historical series of orchestral concerts by the Gewandhaus Orchestra he was called upon to lead the orchestra from his place at the concertmaster's chair, as had been the practice in the eighteenth century.

In 1929 he resigned as concertmaster of the Gewandhaus Orchestra because to hold down the post he was required to become a German citizen. He went back to Paris, where he made his conducting debut by hiring the Paris Symphony Orchestra for a concert on November 1, 1932. He later explained that the reason he turned to conducting so late in life was because "it was much easier for me to make a living as a violinist, and I just could not afford to direct an orchestra earlier."

Geneviève Aubry, granddaughter of one of the founders of the Nestlé chocolate firm, provided Münch with the funds for his conducting debut. By 1932 Münch and Geneviève were deeply involved emotionally. They had first met in Paris just before World War I. During the war they were able to communicate with each other through letters transmitted by the International Red Cross. After the war, on January 31, 1933, they were married.

Münch's wife put her considerable financial resources at the command of her husband's conducting career. She hired for him in Paris the Lamoureux and the Straram orchestras and the Orchestre de la Société Philharmonique. In 1935 Münch became the music director of the Orchestre de la Société Philharmonique, with which for three seasons he offered distinguished performances, particularly of the French repertory and of twentieth century compositions. With this orchestra, on November 26, 1936, he led the world premiere of Roussel's *Bacchus and*

Ariadne suite. In 1937 he was the principal conductor of the orchestral concerts at the Festival of International Society for Contemporary Music. All this while, from 1933 to 1940, he was studying conducting in Paris with Alfred Sendrey.

In 1938 he became the principal conductor of the oldest existing orchestra in Paris, the Paris Conservatory Orchestra, succeeding Philippe Gaubert. With this organization he introduced Poulenc's Concerto in G minor for organ, strings and tympani on June 10, 1941. His success with the Paris Conservatory Orchestra brought him invitations to appear as a guest conductor throughout Europe. He remained at his post with the Paris Conservatory Orchestra during World War II, even after the Nazis had occupied Paris, helping to sustain the morale of his countrymen with performances of French music. Whatever income he earned he turned over to the Resistance movement. He continually used his influence to protect French musicians from the Gestapo (the Nazi secret police), and on several occasions he even defied Gestapo orders to purge his orchestra of players condemned on racial or political grounds. His home became a way station in the "underground railway" devised by the Resistance to aid Frenchmen in danger from the Gestapo to flee Paris. When the Nazi officials in Paris asked him to take over the music direction of the Paris Opéra, he refused because he would not work with avowed collaborationists.

After World War II Münch became an idol of the French concert-going public not only because of his talent as a conductor but also because of his heroic stand against the Nazis. Handsome, aristocratic in manner, he was lovingly dubbed "le beau Charles" by his admirers and the younger women among his fans came to be known as "Les Münchettes." His fame spread outside France as well. He became the first French conductor to appear in England after the Germans had been driven out of France, when in 1944–1945 he led performances of the BBC Symphony and the London Philharmonic. He returned to London for more orchestral concerts in 1945–1946; in 1946 and 1947 he participated in the International Festival in Zurich. He also appeared in other places in Europe, in the Near East, and in South America.

His North American debut took place on December 27, 1946, as guest conductor of the

Boston Symphony in an all-French program that included the American premieres of Honegger's *Symphony for Strings* and Maurice Jaubert's *Sonata à Due.* During this first visit to America he also appeared as a guest conductor of the New York Philharmonic and the Chicago Symphony. "It was evident," wrote Olin Downes in the New York *Times,* "that we had with us a superb musician. . . . Back of his qualities as a conductor—his masterful treatment of phrase, his exceptional range of sonorities, from the hardly audible pianissimo to the fortissimo that is so brilliant yet not too hard, the complete flexibility of beat and capacity, when that was desirable for romantic rhetoric—are Mr. Münch's temperament and imagination."

Münch's far-reaching capabilities as a conductor were further in evidence in America in the next two seasons. In a guest appearance with the New York Philharmonic on January 1, 1948, he presented the American premiere of Honegger's *Joan of Arc at the Stake.* Later in 1948 he toured the United States with the French National Radio Orchestra. On the strength of his American successes, Münch captured the most desirable orchestral post in America in April 1948: music director of the Boston Symphony, succeeding Serge Koussevitzky. For some time it had been known that Koussevitzky was planning to retire, and in the ensuing speculation about his successor many candidates were mentioned—Leonard Bernstein most frequently—but never Münch.

Münch was Koussevitzky's opposite. Where Koussevitzky was the total autocrat who treated his men with dictatorial ruthlessness and kept himself aloof, Münch was the democrat winning over his men to his way of thinking with graciousness of manner, charm, and consideration for their feelings. Koussevitzky used to put them through grueling rehearsals in which every detail of a composition was worked over fastidiously. Münch preferred rehearsals in which the overall concept of a work was prepared and in which some of the details were left to the performance itself to allow for greater spontaneity.

A new era began for the Boston Symphony, away from the Russian traditions of Koussevitzky and back to the French traditions of Pierre Monteux. French music dominated, and it was performed superlatively. American music, however, was by no means neglected. The list of Münch's world premieres with the Boston Symphony is long and distinguished, top-heavy with French and American compositions. This is a representative list: Samuel Barber's *Prayers of Kierkegaard* (December 3, 1954) and *Die Natali* (December 22, 1960); Henri Barraud's Symphony No.3 (March 7, 1958); Easley Blackwood's Symphony No.1 (April 18, 1958); David Diamond's Symphony No.3 (November 3, 1950) and Symphony No.6 (March 8, 1957); Henri Dutilleux's Symphony No.2 (December 11, 1959); Irving Fine's Symphony (March 23, 1962); Alexei Haieff's Symphony No.2 (April 11, 1958); Howard Hanson's *Elegy* (January 20, 1956); Honegger's Symphony No.5 (March 9, 1951); Ibert's *Bostonia, Mouvement Symphonique* (January 25, 1963); Martinu's *Fantaisies Symphoniques* (January 7, 1955) and *Parables* (February 13, 1959); Milhaud's Piano Concerto No.4 (March 3, 1950) and Symphony No.6 (October 7, 1955); Nabokov's *La Vita Nuova* (March 2, 1951); Petrassi's Concerto No.5 (December 2, 1955); Piston's Symphony No.6 (November 25, 1955) and Symphony No.8 (March 5, 1965); Poulenc's Piano Concerto (January 6, 1950) and *Gloria* (January 20, 1961); William Schuman's Symphony No.7 (October 21, 1960) and Violin Concerto (February 10, 1950); Roger Sessions's Symphony No.3 (December 6, 1957); Alexander Tcherepnin's Symphony No.4 (December 5, 1958); and William Walton's Cello Concerto (January 25, 1957). Among his American premieres was that of Leonard Bernstein's *Kaddish* on January 31, 1964.

Under Münch the Boston Symphony acquired a new sound: dry, relaxed and subdued as opposed to the luscious and febrile intensity of Koussevitzky's performances. "No longer did the strings melt with Koussevitzky emotion," said Harold Rogers in the New York *Times.* "No longer did the choirs blend and swell to rotund radiance. . . . The strings were drier, brighter. Each choir spoke in its characteristic way, coexisting but not fraternizing with the orchestra. Details stood out in crystalline focus."

In Boston, Münch and his wife occupied a house on Brush Hill Road in Milton, eight miles from Boston. Each morning before breakfast he took his Welsh terrier on a stroll. This and an occasional game of golf were his sole exercise. Later in the morning he was busily occupied with rehearsals. Afternoons were spent in his second-story study on Brush Hill Road poring over orchestral scores. Evenings were spent quietly, most often with only his wife as company for dinner, but occasionally with one or two friends as well. Münch rarely went to parties and rarely gave them. Vacations were spent in Paris where he maintained a fourteen-room apartment near the Bois de Boulogne. Vacation pastimes included reading books on philosophy and classical literature, studying Egyptology, and collecting objets d'art.

In 1952 Münch took the Boston Symphony on its first European tour with performances over a four-week period in England, France, Holland, Belgium, and Germany. The high point of this tour for Münch personally was his return to his native city, Strasbourg. "When the capacity audience in Strasbourg's Salle de Palais des Fêtes let loose a storm of applause," Cyrus Durgin reported back to Boston, "that moment was perhaps the culmination of a lifetime of music-making for Charles Münch."

The Boston Symphony under Münch made its second foreign tour in 1956. At that time it was heard at the Edinburgh Festival, among other places, and it became the first American symphonic organization to perform in the Soviet Union. In 1960 the Boston Symphony and Münch toured the Far East, Australia, and New Zealand.

Münch resigned from the Boston Symphony in 1962 after thirteen seasons. This was the second longest tenure of the post of music director in the history of this orchestra, exceeded only by that of Koussevitzky. In that time Münch performed 168 compositions—36 by Americans; 39 were world premieres, 17 American premieres, and 13 Boston premieres. Under Münch the Boston Symphony received five awards from the New York Music Critics' Circle, two American-International Music Fund Awards, nine Grand Prix du Disques, two Grammys from the National Academy of Recording Arts and Sciences (one for Debussy's *Images* in 1959, the other for Ravel's *Daphnis and Chloé* in 1961), and a medal from the Vienna Mozartgemeinde.

"At his best," said Harold C. Schonberg in the New York *Times,* "he was a conductor representative of the French ideals of clarity and proportion. In many respects he also was an inspirational conductor. He always was dependable, but he inspired, and at those times he was one of the great conductors of the century."

After leaving Boston, Münch returned to France to make his home in an eighteenth century house, "La Futaie," in Louveciennes, near Versailles. In 1967 he founded the Orchestre de Paris, the first fully state-subsidized concertizing orchestra in Paris and a successor to the disbanded Paris Conservatory Orchestra. It gave its first performance, under Münch, on November 15, 1967, and in 1968 with Münch at its head it toured the United States.

While on this tour, Münch was found dead of a heart attack in the John Marshall Hotel in Richmond, Virginia, on November 5, 1968.

Münch received the decorations of Commander of the Legion of Honor from France (1952); Commander, Order of the Cedar in Lebanon (1957); Commander, Order of Arts and Letters from France. He was also the recipient of honorary doctorates in music from Harvard, Boston University, and Tufts. He was the author of *Je Suis Chef d'Orchestre* (1954) which in 1956 was translated into English as *I Am a Conductor.*

ABOUT: Gelatt, R. Music Makers; Münch, C. I Am a Conductor; Stoddard, H. Conductors of the U.S.A. *Periodicals*—New York Times, April 1, 1962, November 7, 1968; Time, December 19, 1949.

Patrice Munsel

1925–

Patrice Beverly Munsel (originally Patrice Beverly Munsil), soprano, was born in Spokane, Washington, on May 14, 1925. She was the only child of Audley Joseph Munsel, a dentist, and Eunice Ann Rasmussen Munsel, a pianist. Patrice's interest in music first revealed itself through a gift for whistling; she received lessons in rhythmic whistling from a local teacher. When she was twelve, Patrice saw her first opera—*Madama Butterfly*—and knew that someday she must become an opera singer. She began receiving vocal instruction from Charlotte Gramis Lange and Mrs. Paul Kennedy. At the Lewis and Clark High School, she appeared in a production of *The Pirates of Penzance* by Gilbert and Sullivan.

She auditioned for conductor Vladimir Bakaleinikoff, and he recognized her singing tal-

Munsel: mŭn sĕl′

PATRICE MUNSEL

ent and suggested she study more intensively. In 1940 she went to New York. There she received additional vocal lessons and coaching from William P. Herman at the William Herman School of Singing, and from Renato Bellini. She also studied acting with and received Italian lessons from Antoinette Stabile, French lessons with Maria Savage, and coaching in opera roles from Giacomo Spadoni.

Spadoni brought her to the attention of Wilfred Pelletier, conductor of the Metropolitan Auditions of the Air, through whose efforts she was able to compete in the March 1943 Auditions. Singing the "Mad Scene" from *Lucia di Lammermoor* she captured first prize, the youngest artist ever to do so.

Winning the Metropolitan Auditions of the Air not only brought her an engagement with the Metropolitan Opera (she was the youngest singer ever to receive a contract there) but also a three-year contract with the impresario Sol Hurok, who guaranteed her a minimum of one hundred and twenty thousand dollars for the next three years. Before coming to the stage of the Metropolitan Opera, Munsel (the name she now used officially) made her concert debut in Spokane, Washington, in June 1943. Her first professional appearance with a symphony orchestra came the following August as a soloist with the Utah Symphony.

On December 4, 1943, she made her debut at the Metropolitan Opera as Philine in *Mignon* —the youngest singer in the company's history

to assume a major role. The audience acclaimed her. After her aria "Je suis Titania," she received an eight-minute ovation. But the critics were less enthusiastic. In the New York *Times* Olin Downes expressed the opinion that she was miscast. However, he also pointed out that "she is comely and has charm, and has flexibility and range. But the voice will have to be treated carefully . . . before imposing on it burdens which, if permanently undertaken, can bring her disaster instead of ultimate success." And, in the *Herald Tribune,* Virgil Thomson remarked that she was "far from being prepared for present glory" though he did call her "a young woman of phenomenal talents." When later that season she was heard as Gilda in *Rigoletto* and Olympia in *The Tales of Hoffmann,* the critics still felt her singing left much to be desired.

But as a principal soprano of the Metropolitan Opera through the 1957–1958 season she eventually won the critics over. She specialized in the Italian and French repertory: the title role in *Lucia di Lammermoor,* Rosina in *The Barber of Seville,* Juliet in *Romeo and Juliet,* Norina in *Don Pasquale,* Lakmé, Adina in *L'Elisir d'Amore,* Musetta and Mimi in *La Bohème.* She was also cast in operas outside the French-Italian sphere: a Flower Maiden in *Parsifal,* the Queen in Rimsky-Korsakov's *Le Coq d'Or,* Zerlina in *Don Giovanni,* Adele in *Die Fledermaus,* Despina in *Così fan Tutte,* and the title role in *La Périchole.*

Her greatest successes, perhaps, came in those operas in which she could give full rein to her talent for comedy, as in *La Périchole, Così fan Tutte,* and *Die Fledermaus.* Her first appearance in *Die Fledermaus* on December 20, 1950, was a personal triumph and twice during the performance she stopped the show. In the *Journal-American,* Miles Kastendieck noted: "A first-rate comedienne and a first-class singer, she quite captivated her audience. It was she who injected the real champagne touch. A fetching miss, archly mischievous, and strikingly costumed, she adorned the stage and quite tickled the fancy."

Her portrayal of Despina in a new production of *Così fan Tutte* on December 28, 1951, elicited the following comment from John Briggs in the New York *Post:* "Foremost . . . is the singing and acting of Patrice Munsel as Despina. Miss Munsel, who has grown constantly in artistic stature in her years at the Metropolitan, is a genuinely gifted comedienne. Her Despina is a masterpiece of comic characterization."

Following her first appearance in the title role of *La Périchole* in its Metropolitan Opera premiere on December 21, 1956, Irving Kolodin wrote in the *Saturday Review* that she brought to her performance "a new flair for comic timing and saucy action which has, naturally, grown from her past experiences. . . . Miss Munsel contributes charm and sparkle to the enterprise. . . . In addition, her youth and ever-increasing sense of the stage give her rank as a comedienne whose future may be longer than her past as a coloratura."

In 1948 Munsel made her first tour of Europe, her European debut taking place at the Copenhagen Royal Opera as Rosina in December of that year. Soon after that she was heard at the Stockholm Royal Opera, and one critic spoke of her as "the reincarnation of Jenny Lind."

She extended the sphere of her singing activities beyond the opera house. In the recital hall she became a prime favorite and a box-office attraction. She rose to stardom over the radio. Between 1944 and 1946 she was the star of the "Prudential Family Hour" broadcasting over the CBS network. In March 1944 the "Cavalcade of America" radio program dramatized her life story. A radio poll in *Musical America* in 1944–1945 placed her with the three most prominent and popular women radio singers of that year. She then made a graceful transition to television. Her TV debut took place on the "Milton Berle Show." In 1957–1958 she was the star of the "Patrice Munsel Show" over network television. In addition, she continually appeared as a guest performer on other network television programs. She also appeared in motion pictures as the star of the motion picture *Melba* (1953).

Through the years, even while she was still at the Metropolitan Opera, she appeared in operettas. She assumed the title role in Victor Herbert's *Naughty Marietta* with the Pittsburgh Civic Opera Company in 1948, and the title role in Rudolf Friml's *Rose Marie* with the Los Angeles Civic Light Opera in 1950. In 1957 she was seen as Nellie Forbush in the Rodgers and Hammerstein musical play *South Pacific* with the Dallas Civic Light Opera Company. Between 1961 and 1963 she assumed starring roles with the Los Angeles Civic Light Opera Company in Lehár's *The Merry Widow, The Song of Norway* by Robert Wright and George Forrest, and Cole

Porter's *Kiss Me, Kate*. She toured with Cole Porter's *Can-Can* in 1963, and on August 17, 1964, she appeared in *The Merry Widow* at the New York State Theater at the Lincoln Center for the Performing Arts in New York. She assumed one of the starring roles in *A Musical Jubilee* on Broadway in 1975. Other stage musicals in which she was starred were *Hello, Dolly!; The Sound of Music; I Do, I Do; The King and I; My Fair Lady; Camelot; Applause; Do I Hear a Waltz?;* and *A Little Night Music.*

On June 10, 1952, Patrice Munsel married Robert C. Schuler, a television producer. With their four children they make their home in Brookville, Long Island, and also maintain a duplex penthouse apartment in Manhattan and a beach house in Malibu, California. From her girlhood days on, when she was a captain of a girls' football team in high school, Munsel has been adept at sports, her favorites being skiing, swimming, surfing, scuba diving, mountain climbing, and horseback riding.

In 1967 she received an honorary Doctorate of Letters from Gonzaga University at Spokane, Washington.

ABOUT: Life, February 21, 1944; Musical America, November 15, 1953; New York Times Magazine, November 21, 1943.

Lucien Muratore
1876–1954

Lucien Muratore, tenor, was born in Marseilles, on August 29, 1876. At the Marseilles Conservatory he studied the bassoon as well as singing. After graduation in 1897 with honors, he made several appearances on the stage at the Variétés in Paris and the Casino in Monte Carlo. For three years he served in the French army, after which, returning to Paris, he embarked upon a career as an actor, appearing in leading roles at the Odéon, sometimes with Sarah Bernhardt. Albert Carré, the manager of the Opéra-Comique, persuaded him to abandon the dramatic stage and embark upon a new life in opera. As preparation, Muratore attended the Paris Conservatory. On December 16, 1902, he made a highly successful opera debut at the Opéra-Comique in the world premiere of Reynaldo Hahn's *La Carmélite*. On March 19, 1903, he

---

Muratore: mü rà tôr′

LUCIEN MURATORE

it was with this company that he achieved his American triumphs. With the exception of a single season—that of 1914–1915 when he served in the French army during World War I—Muratore remained one of the stars of this company through the 1921–1922 season. He was paid two thousand eight hundred dollars a performance which was even more than Caruso was earning. One of his memorable performances was Romeo to Galli-Curci's Juliet in *Romeo and Juliet*. It was as a member of the Chicago Opera that he was heard for the first time in New York at the Metropolitan Opera, on January 28, 1914, in *Monna Vanna*.

In 1917 he achieved a personal triumph at the Teatro Colón in Buenos Aires. He combined his activity in opera with concert appearances in which he proved far less successful. When, on March 19, 1913, he appeared at the Hippodrome in New York in a joint recital with Lina Cavalieri, Richard Aldrich commented in the New York *Times:* "Mr. Muratore seems to be out of his element in concert. . . . However, it was obvious that Mr. Muratore has a good dramatic voice. Like most French singers, his enunciation was a delightful feature of his singing."

A few months after this joint appearance, on July 10, 1913, Muratore and Cavalieri were married. For Muratore this was a second marriage, his first one—with Marguerite Bériza, also an opera singer—having ended in divorce. The second marriage also terminated in divorce. Muratore's third wife was Marie Louise Brivaud, who survived him.

In 1922 Muratore returned to France. For seven years he was the mayor of the town of Le Biot. Following his retirement from the concert and operatic stage just before World War II, he made his home in Paris where he devoted himself to teaching. In 1938 he joined the faculty of the American Conservatory in Fontainebleau, France. In 1944 he took over the direction of the Opéra-Comique but held this post only one week.

Lucien Muratore died in Paris on July 16, 1954.

ABOUT: Kutsch, K. J. and Riemens, L. A Concise Biographical Dictionary of Singers.

was once again acclaimed in a world premiere, this time in Edmond Missa's *La Muguette.*

His successes at the Opéra-Comique brought him a contract from the Paris Opéra where he made his debut in 1905 as Rinaldo in Gluck's *Armide.* For the next half dozen years he was one of the stars of the company, as remarkable for his talent as an actor as for his refined and exquisitely controlled voice. He not only sang the more familiar roles in the French repertory but was often called upon to appear in world premieres. Massenet wrote the opera *Ariane* with him in mind, and Muratore created the lead role on October 31, 1906. He was later also heard at the Opéra in the world premieres of Henri Février's *Monna Vanna* (January 13, 1909) in which he created the role of Prinzivalle, Massenet's *Bacchus* (May 5, 1909), Georges Adolphe Hüe's *Le Miracle* (December 30, 1910), and in the French premieres of *Salome* and Giordano's *Siberia.*

While serving at the Paris Opéra, Muratore made many guest appearances elsewhere, most notably at Monte Carlo, Brussels, and Covent Garden in London. At Monte Carlo he appeared in several more world premieres, among these Saint-Saëns' *Déjanire* (March 14, 1911) and Massenet's *Roma* (February 17, 1912).

He made his American debut in 1913 with the Boston Opera Company and was subsequently heard there in the American premiere of *Monna Vanna* on December 4, 1913. Two weeks later, on December 15, he made his debut with the Chicago Opera as Faust in Gounod's opera, and

Riccardo Muti

1941–

RICCARDO MUTI

Riccardo Muti, conductor, was born in Naples, on July 28, 1941. His father, a physician, was a dedicated musical amateur with a fine tenor voice. Of the five sons in the family one became a doctor, another an economist, and two others, engineers. "Traditionally," Muti told an interviewer, "I should have studied law but from the time I was a child it was understood I would become a musician."

During Riccardo's childhood, his family moved to Puglia, in south Italy. There, as he has revealed, "we led disciplined lives. No sports, no television. In the evening, after studying, we would take traditional *passagiata* along the main street, talking with our friends, discussing politics and school life."

After the family returned to Naples, Muti began his musical education at the Conservatory of San Pietro a Maiella; there he specialized in the piano. When, on one occasion, he was recruited to conduct the accompaniment to two concertos by Johann Sebastian Bach he knew he wanted, above everything else, to become a conductor. With this in mind, after receiving a diploma in piano from the Conservatory, he continued his studies at the Giuseppe Verdi Conservatory in Milan: conducting with Antonino Votto, composition with Bruno Bettinelli. In 1965, while still a student, he conducted a Conservatory performance of Paisiello's little known and rarely given opera, *L'Osteria di Marechiaro.*

After graduation with honors from the Verdi Conservatory with diplomas in conducting and composition, Muti was for a time employed as pianist for the voice classes of Maria Carbone, an Italian soprano. His career as conductor took wings when, in October 1967, he became the first Italian to win first prize in the Guido Cantelli International Competition for conductors. His debut as symphonic conductor followed later that year when he was invited to serve as guest conductor of the RAI (Radiotelevisione Italiana) Orchestra in Milan. A half year later he was called to Florence to direct a concert of the Orchestra del Maggio Musicale Fiorentino in which Sviatoslav Richter was soloist. That performance was to have taken place in March 1968 but had to be cancelled on the day of the concert because of a general strike in the city. The postponement proved providential. Instead of taking place at a time when little outside interest would be focused on the event, the concert was held during the May Music Festival in Florence thus bringing Muti to world attention. "I consider this to have been my real official debut," he says.

In October 1968 Muti initiated his professional career as a conductor of opera with performances of works by Alessandro Scarlatti and Domenico Cimarosa at the Autunno Musicale Napoletano. In October 1969 he took over the post which he has since held with outstanding distinction—music director of the Orchestra del Maggio Musicale Fiorentino. As a central musical figure in Florence, he was often called upon to direct not only symphony programs with his orchestra but also performances of operas during the annual May Music Festival. In presentations of Verdi's *I Masnadieri, Macbeth, La Forza del Destino* and *Un Ballo in Maschera,* and of *L'Africaine, I Puritani, Don Pasquale, I Pagliacci, Cavalleria Rusticana,* and *William Tell* (in an uncut version), Muti proved to be a conductor of authority, scholarship, and interpretative penetration. When in 1972 Muti opened the May Music Festival with the uncut presentation of *William Tell* (a performance that lasted six hours, ending at 2 A.M.), William Weaver reported in *High Fidelity/Musical America:* "Muti's intense conviction, his subtle and accurate interpretation, made the experience memorable."

Muti has also been heard and acclaimed outside Italy: at festivals in Salzburg, Lucerne, Prague, and Montreux; in guest appearances with the Berlin Philharmonic, Vienna Philharmonic, La Scala Orchestra, and major orchestras in Budapest, Amsterdam, and Madrid; and in guest operatic performances at the Vienna State Opera, Covent Garden in London, and other distinguished European opera houses. In March 1977 he led a new production of *Norma* at the Vienna State Opera. In 1973, Muti was appointed principal conductor of the New Philharmonia Orchestra in London in succession to Otto Klemperer, without relinquishing his post in Florence.

On October 27, 1972, Muti made his American debut as a guest conductor of the Philadelphia Orchestra. His program, as a critic for *Musical America* noted, "was set forth with amazing clarity and tensile strength." When Muti visited New York with the Philadelphia Orchestra soon after that, Harriet Johnson described him in the New York *Post* as "brilliantly gifted, dynamic, but not flamboyant, fiery but not superficially theatrical, with a Roman profile and a carriage erect enough to be a ballet dancer."

Muti's success with the Philadelphia Orchestra has brought him back to its podium each season since 1972. As James Felton remarked in the Philadelphia *Evening Bulletin,* he has become "something of a matinee idol here." In the fall of 1977 he began a three-year engagement as principal guest conductor of the Philadelphia Orchestra; this was the first time such a title had been conferred on anyone by that organization. This appointment, and his continued Philadelphia successes, inspired rumors that Muti was being groomed as Eugene Ormandy's successor when Ormandy was ready to retire.

Muti has also appeared as guest conductor of most of America's distinguished symphonic organizations, including the Boston Symphony, the Chicago Symphony, the Cleveland Orchestra, and the New York Philharmonic.

When he conducted the first performance of Bruckner's Symphony No.6 ever given by the Philadelphia Orchestra, a concert heard both in Philadelphia and in New York in 1976, Robert Kimball wrote in the New York *Post:* "Muti's direction had a driving propulsiveness but was never rushed or frenzied. The Philadelphians responded most beautifully to Muti and met every challenge the symphony presented with a glow-ing, flexible performance." Following one of Muti's appearances with the Philadelphia Orchestra in New York in 1977, Harold C. Schonberg said in the New York *Times:* "Mr. Muti has plenty of glamour, plenty of talent, plenty of authority, and there never was any doubt who was in command."

In addition to winning the Guido Cantelli International Competition (1967), Muti has received the Illica-Giacosa Prize (1971) and a citation from the Accademia di Santa Cecilia in Rome (1974). His recording of Verdi's *Macbeth* brought him the André Messager Prize as "the best conductor of 1977." His recording of Mendelssohn's Symphony No.3 earned the Deutsche Schallplatten Preis as the best symphonic recording of 1977. In spite of these successes on disks, Muti is skeptical about the artistic significance of recorded music. "Records have seemed to me a betrayal of the musical fact, which must be born, go through its life, and die in a single sweeping arc," he has said. "The record cannot do this; there cannot be creative liberty, because we are so preoccupied with the perfect sound. Naturally we must try to get as close as we can to technical rightness, but if the recording becomes only a technological fact, like missiles and moon landings, then we are betraying music itself."

In 1969, Muti married Maria Cristina Mazzavillani, a trained singer who gave up her own professional career at the time of her marriage. With their two children they make their home in Florence. They also have a vacation retreat on the sea near Ravenna.

ABOUT: High Fidelity/Musical America, February 1973, March 1978; New York Times, November 7, 1976.

Claudia Muzio

1889–1936

Claudia Muzio (originally Claudina Muzzio), soprano, was born in Pavia, Italy, on February 7, 1889. Her father was an opera stage manager and in later years was employed at Covent Garden in London and at the Metropolitan Opera in New York; her mother was a professional singer

Muzio: moō′ tsyŏ

CLAUDIA MUZIO

who joined the chorus of the Metropolitan Opera. A musical child, Claudia began her training at the piano and the harp. Her piano teacher in Milan, who was also a voice coach, advised her to begin studying singing and gave her her first lessons. After further study in Turin with Mme. Casaloni, Muzio made her opera debut in the title role of *Manon Lescaut* at Arezzo on February 7, 1912. Her first success came later the same year in the same role at the Teatro dal Verme in Milan and brought her a contract for La Scala in Milan. There in 1913–1914 she was heard as Desdemona in *Otello* and Fiora in *L'Amore dei Tre Re*. In 1914 and again in 1915 she made successful guest appearances at Covent Garden in London and in France as well as in South America.

She made her debut at the Metropolitan Opera on December 4, 1916, as Tosca in a cast that included Caruso and Scotti. "In many ways," noted Richard Aldrich in the New York *Times,* "the new soprano justified the interest taken in her appearance. She is young and beautiful. It is possible to feel enthusiasm for her acting, which is composed, animated, intelligent and tasteful. She has dramatic feeling, and an individuality that governed her work. . . . Miss Muzio established the fact that her voice is of fresh and agreeable quality and that she governs it artistically."

Later that season she confirmed the good impression she had made at her debut with performances in the title role of *Manon Lescaut,* as

Nedda in *I Pagliacci,* Leonora in *Il Trovatore,* and as Aida.

Muzio remained with the Metropolitan Opera company six seasons. In that time she created the role of Giorgetta in the world premiere of Puccini's *Il Tabarro* (December 14, 1918); appeared as Tatiana in the first New York performance of *Eugene Onegin* (March 24, 1920); was heard as Maddalena and as Loreley in the first Metropolitan Opera productions of *Andrea Chénier* (March 7, 1921) and Catalani's *Loreley* (March 4, 1922) respectively; and assumed the role of Bertha in a revival of *Le Prophète,* opposite Caruso, on February 7, 1918. She opened the season of 1917–1918 on November 12 as Aida. Her other impressive roles at the Metropolitan Opera were Tosca, Fiora, Santuzza in *Cavalleria Rusticana,* Mimi in *La Bohème,* Violetta in *La Traviata,* and Cio-Cio-San in *Madama Butterfly.*

She possessed such dramatic powers both as a vocalist and as an actress that she was sometimes referred to as "the Eleanora Duse of opera." Muzio may have had limitations of voice, with an intonation that was not always precise and top notes that were not always reached securely, but it was her expression that gave her performances their uncommon distinction, the ability to carry over to a parlando passage new nuances of meaning and emotion, her exceptional diction, and the dramatic force of her musical projection.

On December 7, 1922, Muzio made her bow with the Chicago Opera as Aida. She was one of the mainstays of this company for the next eleven years, in which time she also sang in the principal operatic theaters of Italy, South America, and Havana.

She returned to the Metropolitan Opera for the single season of 1933–1934, making her first appearance on its stage in more than a decade as Violetta in *La Traviata* on January 1, 1934. She was still in full command of her dramatic powers and vocal resources. "Her convincing projection of the role," wrote Hubbard Hutchinson in the New York *Times,* "was due in part to her delightfully supple and easy playing and her beauty, but even more to the musicianship with which she endowed her portrayal. The vocal line was always clear, plastic, excellently phrased. It embodied, moreover, the grace and fluency inherent in the music and the situation and drama. The pianissimo and piano singing were particularly admirable. Mme. Muzio knows how to project a slender thread of tone through the heavier timbres of the orchestra; a tone, moreover, warmly silvery in color and delicate without fragility."

She returned to Italy in 1934, spending her last years in Rome. On February 15, 1934, she appeared there in the title role in the world premiere of Refice's *Cecilia.* In the years 1934 and 1935 she made a series of recordings for Italian Columbia which were re-released many years after her death and were largely responsible for her posthumous fame.

Claudia Muzio died in Rome on May 24, 1936.

ABOUT: Barnes, H. M. Claudia Muzio: A Biographical Sketch and Discography.

EMMA NEVADA

Emma Nevada

1859–1940

Emma Nevada (originally Emma Wixom), soprano, was born in Alpha, near Nevada City, California, on February 7, 1859. She was the only child of William Wallace Wixom, a physician of Scottish descent, and Maria Wixom, who was Irish. Emma revealed an interest in singing from the time she was three when she sang "The Star-Spangled Banner" at a benefit in Grass Valley, California. Two years later she performed for miners in Virginia City.

The family moved to Austin, Nevada, in 1864. There Emma sang in the church. Nine years later she and her father returned to California, after her mother died in 1872. At Mills Seminary (later Mills College) in Oakland, Emma received her first vocal instruction from Alfred Kelleher. Upon graduation from the Seminary in 1876 she went on a study tour to Europe. She stayed on in Europe when this tour ended, spending some time in Berlin, and three years in Vienna in vocal study with Mathilde Marchesi.

Nevada made her opera debut on May 17, 1880, with "Colonel" James Henry Mapleson's operatic troupe at Her Majesty's Theater in London, appearing as Amina in *La Sonnambula.* On this occasion she was billed for the first time as Emma Nevada, the name she henceforth retained both in her personal and professional life. She was an immediate success. After leaving the company following a dispute with Mapleson, she

appeared in operatic performances in several cities in Italy before joining the La Scala company in Milan. There she was heard in twenty-one performances.

On May 17, 1883, she made an important debut at the Opéra-Comique in Paris as Zora in a revival of Félicien David's *La Perle du Brésil.* After that she was acclaimed for her performances as Lucia in *Lucia di Lammermoor,* Lakmé, Amina, Mignon, Marguerite in *Faust,* and Elvira in *I Puritani.* In 1884 she returned to England for a tour climaxed by the performance of the oratorio *The Rose of Sharon,* which Sir Alexander Mackenzie wrote expressly for her.

She rejoined the Mapleson company later in 1884. With that company she made her American debut at the Academy of Music in New York as Amina on November 24, 1884. She alternated with Adelina Patti in the leading female roles in the French and Italian repertory in New York, and with this company she toured the eastern states. She returned the following year for another and more extended tour of the United States.

On October 1, 1885, in Paris, she married Raymond Palmer, an English physician. Ambroise Thomas, composer of *Mignon,* attended the ceremony and, upon kissing the bride, called her "my dear Mignon."

After her second American tour, in 1886, she concentrated her musical activities for many years in Europe, Scandinavia, and Russia, achieving considerable fame as a coloratura soprano, "a natural coloratura," as Thomas Beecham described her, "equal to any of her contemporaries." She made successful appearances in Belgium, Holland, France, Austria, Russia, Spain, and England. In England she gave a command performance for Queen Victoria and later for Edward VII. In Spain, following her appearance at the Royal Theater in Madrid, she became a friend of Christina, the Queen Regent. After one of Nevada's concerts in Seville, the governor of the city had the gardens stripped of their flowers so that he might present her with two thousand bouquets.

She returned to the United States for a series of concerts at the Metropolitan Opera in 1899, touring the country that year and again in 1901–1902. Still in full command of her vocal powers and at the peak of her fame, she continued to perform both in Europe and the United States in the first decade of the twentieth century, making her last tour of the United States in 1907.

After a performance of *Lakmé* in Berlin in 1910, she retired permanently from the stage to devote herself exclusively to teaching voice in England.

When Nevada's daughter, Mignon Nevada, was born in 1887, her godparents were Ambroise Thomas and Mathilde Marchesi. The younger Nevada also became an opera singer, performing at La Scala and Covent Garden among other European opera houses.

Emma Nevada spent her declining years at the home of her daughter in Liverpool, England. There she succumbed to a heart attack on June 20, 1940. She died a Catholic, having been converted to that religion in the prime of her life, with Charles Gounod as godfather.

In 1935 she was invited by the Italian government to the Bellini centennial at Catania. There a medallion of Nevada as Amina is now found on the statue of Bellini, together with medallions of Pasta as Elvira and Malibran as Norma.

ABOUT: Beecham, T. A Mingled Chime; Mapleson, J. H. The Mapleson Memoirs (ed. by H. Rosenthal); Thompson, O. The American Singer. *Periodicals*—New York Tribune Magazine, October 28, 1906; Theater Magazine, June 1916.

Arthur Nikisch

1855–1922

Arthur Nikisch, eminent conductor, was born in Szent Miklós, Hungary, on October 12, 1855. His father, August Nikisch, was the principal bookkeeper to Prince Lichtenstein. At three, Arthur revealed an unusual fascination for musical sounds. He began studying music at six—piano and theory with Franz Procházka at Butschowitz (now Bucovice, Czechoslovakia) where the Nikisch family was living. At seven, he could reproduce on paper all the notes of the *Barber of Seville Overture* and the *William Tell Overture,* which he had heard just once on an orchestrion (a mechanical musical instrument, resembling an elaborate barrel organ, capable of producing the effect of an orchestra). At eight he made his first public appearance as pianist.

In his eleventh year he enrolled in the Vienna Conservatory. He passed the entrance examinations so brilliantly that he was immediately placed in the highest class—all of his fellow students were ten years or so older than he. There he studied violin with Joseph Hellmesberger and composition with Otto Dessoff. After two years at the Conservatory, he received a gold medal for his Sextet; later he was awarded first prize for violin and second prize for piano.

While attending the Conservatory, Arthur had his first personal contact with Richard Wagner, of whose music dramas he was ultimately to become a leading interpreter. His first association with Wagner came at a concert of the Vienna Conservatory Orchestra which the master attended. After the concert, Arthur was one of three Conservatory students in the orchestra selected to present Wagner with a goblet. (The two others, Anton Seidl and Emil Paur, were also destined to become Wagnerian conductors.) In May 1872, while still a Conservatory student, Arthur played in the violin section of an orchestra directed by Wagner in a performance of Beethoven's Ninth Symphony dedicating the laying of the cornerstone of the Festival Theater in Bayreuth.

At the ceremonies for his graduation from the Conservatory in 1874, Arthur conducted a performance of his own Symphony in D minor.

Nikisch: nē′ kǐsh

ARTHUR NIKISCH

Following this he played violin in the Vienna Court Orchestra, performing under the batons of such masters as Brahms and Liszt as well as under many distinguished conductors over a three-year period.

On the recommendation of Otto Dessoff, Nikisch was engaged by Angelo Neumann in 1877 to serve as chorusmaster of the Leipzig Opera. He assumed this post on January 15, 1878, and the city of Leipzig became his permanent home and one of the principal centers of his musical activity.

Nikisch made his professional conducting debut at the Leipzig Opera in *Tannhäuser* on February 11, 1878, under dramatic circumstances. The members of the company, rebelling against performing under a conductor only twenty-three years old, threatened to resign. Neumann insisted on having Nikisch conduct that performance. As a compromise, Neumann prevailed upon the orchestra to rehearse with Nikisch merely the overture and to defer their decision about the young conductor until the rehearsal was over. It went off so brilliantly that all antagonism to Nikisch vanished and the musicians became his enthusiastic collaborators when he made his bow as a conductor of opera.

Nikisch's successful debut brought him an appointment in 1879 as first conductor of the Leipzig Opera. He became principal conductor in 1882, a post he held for seven years. Already at the Leipzig Opera his extraordinary musicianship and memory and his romantic ardor were inspiring rhapsodic comments among leading musicians. In his day book Tchaikovsky wrote in 1887: "The Leipzig Opera may well be proud of its gifted young Kapellmeister. . . . Herr Nikisch is quiet, economical in regard to superfluous movement but extraordinarily commanding, mighty and thoroughly self-controlled. He does not merely direct, but yields to a mysterious spell. One hardly notices him, for he makes no effort to attract attention to himself, and yet, nevertheless, one feels that the orchestral body, like one instrument, is in the hands of a remarkable master, is thoroughly under his control, willing and submissive."

Nikisch also made a deep impression in Leipzig as a symphonic conductor. When in 1879 he performed Schumann's Symphony No.4, Clara Schumann told him: "If only Robert could have heard your performance. He never realized that the work could sound this way!" Nikisch's performances of Liszt's *Faust* and *Dante* symphonies in Leipzig in 1885—works then completely unknown—led Franz Liszt to exclaim of him: "He is the chosen one among the elect." Brahms, who initially was taken aback when Nikisch insisted on making some revisions in one of the Brahms symphonies during rehearsals, finally had to admit after the performance: "You do it all quite differently, but you are right. It simply must be so!"

Bidding farewell to his Leipzig audiences with an eloquent performance of *Fidelio* in 1889, Nikisch paid his first visit to the United States that year to become the principal conductor of the Boston Symphony Orchestra. He remained in Boston four years, in which time he often gave fine performances, in spite of the fact that there were continual disagreements with the management over the artistic policy of the orchestra. In 1893 Nikisch felt he had had enough of petty feuds and disagreements and he returned to Europe to serve as music director of the Royal Opera in Budapest and conductor of its Philharmonic concerts from 1893 to 1895.

In 1895 Nikisch succeeded Reinecke as the music director of the Gewandhaus Orchestra in Leipzig; at the same time he also became music director of the Berlin Philharmonic. He held both posts until the end of his life. It was there that he grew world famous as one of the supremely gifted conductors of his time and one of the most glamorous. He was among the first conductors to lead performances from memory. He was also one of the first conductors to become a matinee idol. When he stood in front of his orchestra he was a portrait in elegance. His delicately poised hands, encircled at the wrists by lace cuffs that puffed foppishly out from the sleeves of his dinner jacket, inspired rhapsodic responses, as did his ever so graceful baton technique. "The expressive suppleness of his stick," commented Adrian Boult, the English conductor, "has been an example to many conductors. It seemed part of himself, and appeared to grow out of his thumb as if made of flesh and blood."

As a conductor he was the ardent romanticist who did not allow his immense intellectual powers to keep his emotions in bondage. He felt strongly that a conductor must approach his music with all the passion and fire he can summon. Thus Nikisch was at his best—perhaps inimitable—in the romantic literature of Tchaikovsky, Liszt, Brahms, and Wagner. During rehearsals he would vigorously stamp his foot on the ground and cry out: "More fire, gentlemen, more blood!" And with his powerful eyes and bold beat he would stir his men into playing with great emotional intensity.

He was a master in producing orchestral effects in dramatic passages. His crescendos rose and swelled and burst forth like volcanic eruptions. In more contemplative music, the tone of his orchestra sang with a pure and glowing tone; he could draw from the orchestra pianissimo passages that never cracked under the strain of their fragility.

Arthur Rubinstein reveals in his autobiography, *My Young Years,* the overpowering impact that Nikisch had upon his early musical growth and development. "What a wonderful, unforgettable life of music opened up to me! Nikisch's magic baton introduced me to all the Beethoven and Mozart symphonies. His performances . . . were revelations to the sensitive ears of the boy I was. Never since have I heard music played like that."

Rubinstein also described Nikisch as follows: "Nikisch was a smallish man with a shapely figure and a fine head. He was always elegantly clad, and stood motionless and erect while conducting. . . . From time to time he would raise his left hand to emphasize a phrase, pointing his little finger, a diamond ring shining on it, at one or another player. That ring on this beautiful white hand was the delight of his Berlin admirers. Such an irresistible charm and power ema-

nated from this little man that women fell in love with him, and I, too, I must confess, lived completely under his spell."

Nikisch's tours with the Berlin Philharmonic to Switzerland, and to Paris, St. Petersburg, Moscow, and other capitals made him as much an idol there, as he was in Leipzig and Berlin. In London he was also heard for many years as guest conductor of the London Symphony Orchestra, and in 1913 he conducted the Wagner *Ring* cycle at Covent Garden.

He was also the conductor of the Hamburg Philharmonic Orchestra, succeeding Hans von Bülow for a number of years beginning with 1897; was music director of the Leipzig Opera in 1905–1906; and served as director of the Leipzig Conservatory from 1902 to 1907—in 1901 he received the honorary title of Royal Professor.

He returned to the United States in 1912 to tour with the London Symphony. American newspapers spread his photograph on their front pages and referred to him as the "$1,000 a night conductor." Stories were circulated about his fabulous memory and his charismatic personality. Along the route of his tour he was stopped in the streets by admirers, some of whom tried to kiss his hand. After each of his concerts he was mobbed outside the concert auditorium by his public. Critics could not summon sufficient praise to describe his remarkable music-making. Such adulation met Nikisch wherever he raised his baton to the very end of his life—in Leipzig on January 23, 1922.

Nikisch married Amélie Heusner, an opera singer, on July 1, 1885. Their son, Mitja Nikisch, became a concert pianist and made his American debut in New York on October 23, 1923.

On several occasions Nikisch exchanged his baton for the piano to serve as an accompanist for his pupil, the *Lieder* singer Elena Gerhardt, at her recitals.

ABOUT: Chevalley, H. ed. Arthur Nikisch, Leben und Wirken; Dette, A. Nikisch; Ewen, D. The Man With the Baton; Pfohl, F. Arthur Nikisch als Mensch und als Künstler. *Periodicals*—Music and Letters (London), Vol. 3, 1922.

Elena Nikolaidi

1909–

Elena Nikolaidi, contralto, was born in Smyrna, Turkey, on June 13, 1909. Both her parents were Greek; her father, Anthony, was an authority on Byzantine music. Elena showed unusual singing ability from her childhood days on. She was only seven when she appeared as a soloist with the church choir. Eight years later she was given a six-year scholarship for the Athens Conservatory. There she received her principal vocal training from Argyri Ghini. In 1934 she was graduated with high honors. During her final year at the Conservatory she made her professional debut in Athens, appearing as a guest soloist with the State Orchestra, Dimitri Mitropoulos conducting. Soon afterwards she was engaged by the Athens Lyric Theater where she appeared in principal contralto roles in Italian and French operas including *Carmen,* the title role of which then became one of her particular specialties.

She received additional vocal instruction from Thanos Mellos, whom she married on April 27, 1936, and with whom she had a son. Soon after her marriage she received an endowment from the Greek government enabling her to go to Vienna. Not long after her arrival she won an international vocal competition that entitled her to a recital appearance at the Konzerthaus. She later auditioned for Bruno Walter, then the music director of the Vienna State Opera, who engaged her for his company. She made her Vienna opera debut on December 16, 1936, as Princess Eboli in *Don Carlo.* It was not long before she became a favorite of Viennese opera goers, and she remained so during the decade she served as leading contralto of the Vienna State Opera. In 1947 the Austrian government conferred on her the honorary title *Kammersängerin.*

In the fall of 1948 she returned to Athens to make a single appearance as Carmen, a performance that brought her seven additional appearances in that role. After that, en route to the United States, she stopped off at London where she gave a successful concert. This brought her a contract from Covent Garden.

Nikolaidi made her American debut in a recit-

Nikolaidi: nē kō li′ dē

ELENA NIKOLAIDI

al in Town Hall, New York, on January 20, 1949. "In twenty years of music reviewing and twice that number of years spent in listening to most of the world's best singers, I have encountered no greater voice or vocalist than Elena Nikolaidi," wrote Jerome D. Bohm in the *Herald Tribune.* "This personable artist is gifted with a truly phenomenal expressive medium, a true contralto of enormous range. . . . Not only, however, is her voice of exceptional range and opulence but highly individual in texture, sensuous and warm at all times, never losing quality even in the highest reaches when employed full strength, and so malleable that in the finest spun pianissimos the native beauty of her voice remains unaltered."

Her first North American tour followed this debut. She made over seventy-five appearances in recitals and as soloist with orchestras. Highlights of this tour included her debut over radio; her first recordings on the Columbia label; successful appearances with the New York Philharmonic Orchestra in concert performances of *Elektra;* appearances in San Francisco in which on successive evenings she was heard in a recital and as soloist with the San Francisco Symphony.

Her American opera debut took place with the San Francisco Opera as Amneris in *Aida* on September 26, 1950, the opening night of the season. "This artist," reported Alfred Frankenstein in the San Francisco *Chronicle,* "has enough vocal beauty, richness, color and radiance for an entire opera company and musicianship as well."

Her debut at the Metropolitan Opera followed on November 13, 1951, once again as Amneris in a new Metropolitan Opera production of Aida. Once again she helped to open a season, and once again she was an immediate success.

Nikolaidi remained with the Metropolitan Opera until 1956. She also appeared at Covent Garden in London, La Scala in Milan, the Prague Opera, the Munich Opera, and several of the festivals at Salzburg, among other music centers of the world. The King of Greece honored her with the Golden Phoenix Cross for "cementing close cultural ties between the United States and Greece and for outstanding contributions in the fields of music and art." A special bill signed by the President of the United States gave her the right to remain a permanent resident of the United States.

ABOUT: Kutsch, K. J. and Riemens, L. A Concise Biographical Dictionary of Singers.

BIRGIT NILSSON

Birgit Nilsson

1918–

In addition to being the greatest Wagnerian soprano of her generation and one of the greatest of all time, Birgit Nilsson is also one of the most versatile stars to have appeared in opera since Lilli Lehmann and Nordica.

Marta Birgit Nilsson (originally Märta Birgit Svensson), soprano, was born on a farm in Västra Karup, sixty miles north of Malmö, Sweden, on May 17, 1918. She was the only child of Nils and Justina Pålsson Svensson. At birth she was given the name *Nilsson* (her father's first name *Nils* combined with the final syllable of his last name).

When Birgit was three, her mother bought her a toy piano on which the child soon learned to pick out melodies. "They tell me," she recalls, "that I sang before I could walk. I spoke very early and sang very early—I even sang in my dreams." In public school she learned to read music at sight, and the discovery was made that she possessed perfect pitch. When she was five she performed at a Christmas concert in school, accompanying herself on the organ (while her mother lay on the floor manipulating the pedals

Nilsson: nĭls′ sôn

which the child was unable to reach). Not long after that, Birgit sang over the radio in Stockholm. Later on she was a member of the local church choir.

Her father, a farmer, had always wanted a son who could help him on the farm that had been in the family for several generations. When a daughter was born to him, he was determined to have her share the responsibilities of the farm, and for this reason he opposed developing the child's talent for music. When not at school, Birgit did some of the farm chores and helped with the cooking at home. She sought out every opportunity she could find to sing, performing for relatives, friends, and the church congregation.

She was encouraged in her musical interests by her mother, who was herself a frustrated singer. Through her mother's persistence, Birgit, aged fifteen, was sent to a resort not far from Västra Karup to audition for its choirmaster, Ragnar Blennow. He took her on as a vocal student; after the first lesson he prophesied she would someday become a great singer. Birgit remained his pupil for several years.

Recommended by Blennow, relying for financial help on five hundred dollars that her mother had been able to save from an inheritance, Nilsson went to Stockholm to enter the Royal Academy of Music. Singing "Elisabeth's Prayer" from *Tannhäuser* at her entrance examinations, she was one of two candidates chosen for a scholarship from among forty-eight applicants. After her first year at the Academy, her personal funds were spent and she had to find work to support herself while continuing with music study. "I sang at weddings and funerals, in choirs, and played small roles in films. . . . I went home in the summer to work on the farm. . . . Sometimes I would be down to my last pennies. But I was proud. I never would ask them for money."

She was graduated from the Royal Academy in 1946. The illness of a singer at the Royal Opera brought her an opportunity to appear in an opera that year, as Agathe in *Der Freischütz,* a part she had to learn in three days. She made several mistakes during the performance that aroused the anger of the conductor, Leo Blech. In later years she preferred not to think of that performance as her debut, singling out her second appearance at the Royal Opera in 1947 when she was heard as Lady Macbeth in Verdi's opera, with Fritz Busch conducting. Reporting from Stockholm to *Musical America,* a correspondent wrote: "She showed herself to be a distinguished artist from the start." That performance helped to bring her a permanent contract with the company, performing principal soprano roles in Italian and German operas. In 1950 she began undertaking Wagnerian roles, initially Woglinde in *Das Rheingold,* then such lyric roles as Senta in *The Flying Dutchman* and Sieglinde in *Die Walküre,* after that Isolde, and finally, in December 1954, her first Brünnhilde (in *Die Götterdämmerung*).

Her first significant appearance outside Sweden took place on June 20, 1951, when she was heard at the Glyndebourne Festival in England as Elettra in Mozart's *Idomeneo.* An attack of pleurisy and its aftermath then kept her off the stage for about a year. When she returned, her voice was richer in texture and fresher in sound than before. In 1953, at the Royal Opera in Sweden she sang her first Isolde (in Swedish). In 1954—the year when she was given the honorary title Court Singer at the Stockholm Royal Opera—she made her debut both at the Vienna State Opera and at the Bayreuth Festival as Elsa in *Lohengrin.* In later years she returned triumphantly to Bayreuth as Sieglinde, Brünnhilde, and Isolde. In 1956 she was acclaimed at the Florence May Music Festival for her performance of Brünnhilde in *Siegfried.* In the fall of 1957 she filled the three Brünnhilde roles in a production of the *Ring* cycle at Covent Garden in London. On that occasion William Mann, the

English authority on opera, maintained that she was "already unrivalled by the resident Queens of Wagnerland." Her first appearance at La Scala in Milan took place on the opening night of the 1958–1959 season in the title role of *Turandot.* She proved so successful in that role, and as Isolde later the same season, that she was deluged with offers for guest appearances in the major music centers of Europe. In 1959 her appearance at the Edinburgh Festival was one of its highlights.

In the western hemisphere she was first heard at the Teatro Colón in Buenos Aires, as Isolde in 1955. She returned there a year later as the Marschallin in *Der Rosenkavalier* and Donna Anna in *Don Giovanni.* On August 9, 1956, she made her first appearance in the United States as a guest artist with the Los Angeles Philharmonic at the Hollywood Bowl in California in excerpts from *Tristan and Isolde* and *Die Götterdämmerung.*

Her American opera debut followed on October 5, 1956, with the San Francisco Opera, as Brünnhilde in *Die Walküre.* Reporting from San Francisco to the New York *Times,* Howard Taubman called Nilsson "the real thing. . . . She makes it easy to grasp why she is Wotan's favorite among the Valkyries." Once again as the Brünnhilde of *Die Walküre* she sang for the first time on the stage of the Chicago Lyric Opera a few weeks after her San Francisco debut. She won praise from the critics not only in this role but also as Isolde, as Senta in *The Flying Dutchman,* and in the two Italian roles of Amelia in *Un Ballo in Maschera* and Turandot.

She was now a world figure in opera. Her extraordinary voice and dramatic characterizations were accepted as having few equals, when she finally made her first appearance at the Metropolitan Opera on December 18, 1959, as Isolde in a new production of *Tristan and Isolde.* Despite her remarkable capabilities, Rudolf Bing, the general manager of the Metropolitan Opera, had twice turned her down for the Metropolitan before finally deciding to bring her to New York. She took his long overdue invitation stoically and good-humoredly. "If Mr. Bing had hired me earlier I might not have been so expensive." Bing was soon to pay her the highest fee ever accorded to a Metropolitan Opera star, in excess of five thousand dollars an appearance.

Her performance on December 18, as Rudolf Bing remarked in his autobiography, *5000*

Nights at the Opera, "scored one of the greatest triumphs the Metropolitan Opera had ever seen." After the final curtain she received a fifteen-minute ovation, and the next morning both the New York *Times* and the *Herald Tribune* covered her appearance on their front pages as one of the most important musical events in New York in many years. "Met Has a New Isolde—and She's a True Princess," read the headline for Paul Henry Lang's report in the *Herald Tribune.* "In the new Swedish soprano, Birgit Nilsson," he wrote, "the Met has an Isolde who can overwhelm not only everyone on the stage and in the auditorium, but even the orchestra at full tilt. Such a thing, ladies and gentlemen, has not been heard since Kirsten Flagstad. Birgit Nilsson is the possessor of a magnificent voice, a clear, unobstructed, powerful soprano of extraordinary brightness that can cut through the orchestral phalanx without ever being shrill, without giving the impression of forcing, or even of an effort. . . . Her musicianship is unquestionable, as are her serious artistic attitude and careful study of her role. The new Isolde is a true princess, not only in Ireland, but in all the world of opera." The headline in the New York *Times* read: "Birgit Nilsson as Isolde Flashes Like New Star in 'Met' Heavens." Howard Taubman went on to add: "With a voice of extraordinary size, suppleness and brilliance, she dominated the stage and the performance. Isolde's fury and Isolde's passion were as consuming as cataclysms of nature."

Nilsson sang Isolde again at the Metropolitan ten days later on December 28. The singer scheduled to sing opposite her as Tristan was indisposed, and all other available substitutes were for one reason or another physically incapable of going through the entire opera. The result was that there were three different Tristans to Nilsson's Isolde that evening, one for each act: Ramón Vinay, Karl Liebl, and Alberto Da Costa.

During her initial season at the Metropolitan Opera Nilsson was also heard as Brünnhilde in *Die Walküre* and Leonore in *Fidelio.*

At the Metropolitan Opera she was heard in all the principal dramatic soprano roles of the Wagner repertory. Her first appearance as Brünnhilde in *Die Götterdämmerung* took place on December 9, 1961, and in *Siegfried* on January 2, 1962. She also assumed the lighter Wagnerian soprano roles as well. She was first heard as Elisabeth in *Tannhäuser* on January 25, 1961; on March 19, 1966, she made operatic history by taking on the roles of both Elisabeth and Venus in the same performance of *Tannhäuser,* the first time any singer ever did so. On February 20, 1975, she sang her first Sieglinde in *Die Walküre* at the Metropolitan Opera, substituting for Leonie Rysanek who had fallen ill.

Outside the Wagnerian repertory, as in it, she proved in a class by herself. In her second season at the Metropolitan Opera, on February 24, 1961, she filled the title role in a performance of *Turandot* in which Leopold Stokowski was making his conducting debut at the Metropolitan. "Her long, glorious and arduous aria, 'In questa reggia,' was the thrilling core of the performance," commented Douglas Watt in the New York *Daily News.* She was resplendent as Aida on April 14, 1961, as Tosca on January 31, 1962, as Amelia in *Un Ballo in Maschera* on January 9, 1963. She brought down the house as Lady Macbeth in Verdi's opera on March 19, 1964. In 1968–1969 a new *Tosca* was mounted for her at the Metropolitan, this being the one hundredth new production being created for her in the various opera houses of the world.

Nilsson's repertory also included Donna Anna in *Don Giovanni,* Elettra in Mozart's *Idomeneo,* the Marschallin in *Der Rosenkavalier,* Senta in *The Flying Dutchman,* Elsa in *Lohengrin,* the title role in Rolf Liebermann's *Penelope,* the title role in *Ariadne auf Naxos,* Pauline in *The Queen of Spades,* Elektra, Minnie in *The Girl of the Golden West,* and Regina in Hindemith's *Mathis der Maler.* She took on a new Richard Strauss role, that of the Dyer's Wife in *Die Frau ohne Schatten,* on December 13, 1975, at the Stockholm Royal Opera, where, a decade earlier, she had sung her first Elektra. She again appeared as the Dyer's Wife during a Richard Strauss Week at the Vienna State Opera in January 1977.

The thirtieth anniversary of her debut was celebrated on October 9, 1976, with a gala performance of *Tristan and Isolde* at the Stockholm Royal Opera. Speeches, flowers, and gifts were the order of the day.

On at least three occasions she encountered accidents during a performance, and in each instance she proved how indestructible she was. In Chicago in 1959, as Senta, while she was jumping off the cliff at the end of the opera, her wig caught on a tree and she landed off the mattress with a twisted ankle. But that did not prevent her from appearing at her next scheduled performance. In 1971, while leaping from one rock to another in *Elektra,* she pulled a muscle of her leg. Though the pain was acute she managed to finish the performance. And during a rehearsal of *Die Götterdämmerung* at the Metropolitan Opera in March 1974 a staircase on stage collapsed under her, dislocating her shoulder and bruising her face. "Nobody could touch me, it hurt so much," she revealed. She had to be rushed to a hospital. Yet just a few days later, on March 8, 1974, with her right arm strapped to her side and covered by a cape, she was able to appear as Brünnhilde in *Die Götterdämmerung* —and she sang magnificently.

On September 10, 1949, Nilsson married Bertil Niklasson, a Swedish businessman with interests in restaurants and the frozen-food industry. They met on a train while she was still a music student and he was studying to be a veterinarian. They struck up a conversation. After leaving the train, Bertil Niklasson spent six months trying to get in touch with her again. Because of his business activities, Niklasson has to stay most of the time in Sweden while his wife is circling the globe to fulfill a staggering number of commitments a year, particularly those at the Metropolitan Opera, La Scala in Milan, Covent Garden in London, the Vienna State Opera, the Deutsche Oper in West Berlin, Hamburg Opera, Munich Opera, and Bayreuth, not to mention her many recitals and performances with symphony orchestras. Only intermittently is Nilsson able to spend time with her husband at their home in Sweden and their apartment in Paris. "I do not belong to the school of prima donnas who believe that being a housewife is more important than having a career," she says. "Two intelligent people can work at separate careers and still maintain a happy marriage. I am fortunate indeed that my husband is of the same opinion. . . . Perhaps this [the separation] keeps us in a constant state of courtship, a state which makes for an even more exciting marriage."

"Physically," wrote Harold C. Schonberg in a feature article on Nilsson in the New York *Times Magazine,* "Nilsson is built on the classic lines of a Wagnerian soprano, although she is not as monumental in configuration as a Traubel or a Flagstad. She weighs about 150 pounds and is five feet, eight inches tall. Solid but not stout, she gives the impression she could carry an operatic Siegfried over each shoulder without staggering. Her chest cavity is extraordinarily large and her neck unusually thick. It is the neck of a female Caruso. Yet Nilsson, with her perfect complexion, gay smile and well-turned legs never gives the impression of masculinity."

From her early girlhood days on the farm, Nilsson has retained her love for swimming, horseback riding, and mountain climbing. In later years she has added to her list of pleasures sightseeing and shopping. But her strenuous singing program allows for few activities outside music and permits her only a few vacations, one of which she usually takes at Christmastime to return to her family farm in her native city.

Through the years many awards and honors have been given her. These include the Swedish Royal Academy of Music medal for promotion of art and music; in 1968 the decoration of Commander of the Vasa Order in Sweden and the Leonie Sonning Prize from Denmark. The Birgit Nilsson Arts Center in Steubenville, Ohio, was named after her. In 1969 she was named *Kammersängerin* by the Austrian government, and in 1970 similarly in Bavaria. She is an honorary life member of the Vienna State Opera.

ABOUT: Sargeant, W. Divas. *Periodicals*—High Fidelity Magazine, February 1965; New York Times, April 30, 1972; New York Times Magazine, January 10, 1960, October 13, 1963.

Lillian Nordica

1857–1914

Lillian Nordica (originally Lillian Bayard Norton) was the first American-born singer to achieve world renown as a Wagnerian soprano. She was born in Farmington, Maine, on May 12, 1857, the youngest of six children. Her father, Edwin Norton, was a farmer; her mother, Elizabeth Allen Norton, was the daughter of a revivalist Methodist preacher popularly known as "Camp Meeting John Allen." Her parents were descended from Thomas Mayhew, governor and owner of Martha's Vineyard.

Lillian began her vocal studies in 1874 with John O'Neill at the New England Conservatory in Boston, where her family had moved in 1864.

Nordica: nôr′ dĭ kà

Nordica

LILLIAN NORDICA

In 1874 she appeared as a soloist at the Temple Church in Boston, and a year later she was a soprano soloist in a performance of Handel's *Messiah* at Bumstead Hall. She also toured the United States with the Handel and Haydn Society conducted by Theodore Thomas.

On June 24, 1876, she was graduated from the New England Conservatory. That year she went to New York, and for a few weeks studied with Marie Maretzek. On September 30, 1876, she made her New York debut at the Madison Square Garden as soloist with Patrick Gilmore's Band. She then toured the United States and Europe with the band, making her London debut at the Crystal Palace on May 21, 1878.

With a view toward becoming an opera singer and objecting to singing outdoors, she left the Gilmore band to study drama in Paris with François Delsarte and Emilio Balari. She then settled in Milan as a student of Antonio Sangiovanni in the operatic repertory.

On March 8, 1879, she made her opera debut at the Manzoni Theatre in Milan as Donna Elvira in *Don Giovanni*. It was at this appearance that she was billed as Nordica, the name she was to use from that time on. Later the same year she sang at the Theatre Guillaume in Brescia as Violetta in *La Traviata* and inspired an ovation that lasted far into the night. The following morning a string band serenaded her under her hotel window. "I have had a grand success and no mistaking," she wrote home. "Such yelling and shouting you never heard. It makes me laugh to see men and women cry and wipe their noses in the last act."

During the summers of 1881 and 1882 she continued her vocal studies in Paris with Giovanni (Jean-Baptiste) Sbriglia. In 1880 she made her bow in St. Petersburg as Philine in *Mignon* and was also heard there as Marguerite in *Faust* (a role for which she received coaching from the composer) and as Violetta. During 1880 she also toured Germany. On April 22, 1882, she made a highly successful debut at the Paris Opéra as Marguerite.

In Paris, on January 22, 1883, she married her second cousin, Frederick A. Gower, a scientist and newspaperman. It was a marriage of convenience, entered into by Nordica so that she could purchase a fine home for her mother. Before the marriage Gower made Nordica promise she would completely withdraw from her professional career. She kept that promise eighteen months. They were separated in 1884. One year later, Gower disappeared in a balloon accident while crossing the English channel. Nordica was freed of an onerous marriage and her promise to give up singing.

"Colonel" Mapleson engaged her to appear with his opera troupe touring the United States. With that company she made her American debut at the Academy of Music in New York on November 23, 1886, as Marguerite. "She gives abundant evidence of having been admirably trained in the spirit of Gounod's music and tragedy," wrote H. E. Krehbiel in the *Tribune*. "She has a voice of fine texture and her tones are generally sympathetic."

Nordica toured with the Mapleson troupe for about four years. On March 27, 1887, while still a member of the Mapleson company, she made her debut at Covent Garden in London as Violetta. For the next five years she appeared each season in London with the Royal Italian Opera Company either at Covent Garden or Drury Lane enjoying extraordinary successes as Valentine in *Les Huguenots,* Aida, Donna Elvira, and in the title role in *Lucia di Lammermoor;* on July 26, 1893, she assumed the role of Zelica in Sir Charles Stanford's *The Veiled Prophet*.

In 1889 Nordica returned to the United States to tour with the Henry E. Abbey company, making her first appearance on December 16, 1889, as Aida. During the remainder of that tour she assumed the roles of Leonora in *Il Trovatore,* Selika in *L'Africaine,* Carmen, Valentine, Marguerite, and Desdemona in *Otello*. When Henry E. Abbey became one of the managers of the Metropolitan Opera in 1891, Nordica joined the company, making her debut on December 18, 1891, in *Les Huguenots*, taking the place of Albani who was too ill to sing Valentine. "Her performance was an extremely creditable one under the circumstances," reported H. E. Krehbiel in the *Tribune*. "She was in excellent voice and acted with great spirit." Later that season she once again made a deep impression, this time as Selika in *L'Africaine*. During the 1893–1894 season she earned further praise as Susanna in *The Marriage of Figaro*, Aida, Marguerite, Elsa in an Italian-language production of *Lohengrin*, Violetta, Venus in *Tannhäuser*, and Philine in *Mignon*. On December 31, 1894, she appeared as Donna Anna in *Don Giovanni*.

In 1894 Cosima Wagner invited Nordica to come to Bayreuth to appear as Elsa at the summer festival. After her success at Bayreuth, she undertook an extended period of study in Wagnerian roles with Julius Kniese in Bayreuth. On November 27, 1895, she emerged as a Wagnerian dramatic soprano of first importance when she appeared as Isolde at a Metropolitan Opera performance of *Tristan and Isolde* that included Jean de Reszke as Tristan, Édouard de Reszke as King Mark, with Anton Seidl conducting. "Mme. Nordica, by her performance as Isolde, amazed those who thought that they had measured the full limits of her powers," wrote W. J. Henderson in the New York *Times*. "She placed herself beside the first dramatic sopranos of her time. . . . Nothing more beautiful than the close of 'Sink hernieder' passage in the duo between her and Mr. de Reszke has been heard here, and certainly it has never been better sung anywhere." In the *Tribune*, H. E. Krehbiel remarked: "It was wonderful how Mme. Nordica rose to the opportunity which Wagner's drama opened to her. The greater the demand the larger the capacity."

Without deserting those Italian, French, and Mozartean roles with which she had achieved her fame, Nordica went on to become one of the great Wagnerian sopranos of her time. On January 2, 1896, she returned to the stage of the Metropolitan Opera as Elsa—this time in the first German production of the opera given by that company. In the period between 1898 and 1902 she sang the three Brünnhildes in the *Ring* cycle in London. She opened the Metropolitan

Opera season of 1898–1899 (November 29) as Venus in *Tannhäuser*. On December 14 and 16, 1898, she gave her first Metropolitan Opera performances in New York as the Brünnhilde in *Die Walküre* (December 14) and in *Siegfried* (two evenings later). She sang her first Metropolitan Opera Brünnhilde in *Die Götterdämmerung* on January 24, 1899, and her first Kundry in *Parsifal* on November 24, 1904. She was a member of Oscar Hammerstein's Manhattan Opera company in 1907–1908. Her last appearance on the stage of the Metropolitan Opera took place on December 8, 1909, as Isolde.

Just before leaving the Metropolitan Opera, she helped open the new Boston Opera season on November 8, 1909, in the title role of *La Gioconda*. She subsequently made other appearances with the Boston Opera Company (where she sang her last Isolde anywhere on March 26, 1913) and with Henry Russell's Opera company.

A nervous breakdown in 1913 brought her opera career to an end. From then on she concentrated on recitals. Her last appearance in New York took place at Carnegie Hall on April 24, 1913; her last in the United States came on June 12, 1913, at Reno, Nevada. She then embarked on what she planned as a world tour, but it was never completed. When the Dutch mail ship Tasman, on which she was sailing in the Pacific, struck a coral reef in Torres Strait, between Australia and New Guinea, Nordica suffered from exhaustion and exposure. When pneumonia developed, she was rushed to a hospital on Thursday Island. Without fully recovering, she insisted on continuing her voyage. She died at Batavia on the island of Java on May 10, 1914. Her funeral took place in London on July 6, 1914, after which she was cremated and buried in the New York Bay Cemetery in Jersey City, New Jersey.

She once described herself as "a poor picker of husbands." She married twice after the death of Gower. Neither of her two later marriages was any happier than the first. Her second husband was a Hungarian army officer and opera singer, Zoltan Doeme, whom she married on May 26, 1896; they were separated in 1903 and divorced a year later. On July 29, 1909, in London, she married an American banker, George W. Young; this marriage also failed.

Nordica suffered other frustrations. She never lived to see the woman suffrage movement, in which she was deeply involved, gain momentum. And she never realized a lifelong dream of establishing a Bayreuth in America near her home at Ardsley on the Hudson.

In 1927 the Nordica Memorial Association was organized to purchase and renovate her birthplace in Maine and make it into a Nordica museum.

ABOUT: Armstrong, W. Nordica: A Study; Edwards, G. T. Music and Musicians of Maine; Glackens, I. Yankee Diva: Lillian Nordica and the Golden Days of Opera; Thompson, O. The American Singer. *Periodicals*—Musical Courier, June 1914; New York Times, May 11, 1914.

JESSYE NORMAN

Jessye Norman

1945–

Jessye Norman, soprano, was born in Augusta, Georgia, on September 15, 1945, one of five children. Her father, Silas Norman, was an insurance broker; her mother, Janie King Norman, an amateur pianist. "We're all musical," she told Donal Henahan about her family in an interview for the New York *Times,* "though I'm the only professional musician. We all studied piano because our parents insisted on it. We actually all liked it." She sang from childhood on and was only seven when she entered her first competition, singing the hymn "God Will Take Care of You" at the Mount Calvary Baptist Church in Augusta. She won third prize (because she forgot the second stanza). "In fact I guess He has taken care of me," she has commented in recalling this event. "That was my last memory slip in public."

While attending public school, she sang in church, at school, and at Girl Scout and Parent-Teacher-Association meetings in Georgia and South Carolina. On Saturday afternoons she listened to the Metropolitan Opera radio broadcasts. Yet she never thought about becoming a professional singer. In fact, until her senior year at the Lucy Craft Laney High School, she planned to go to medical school and prepare for a nursing career. Then, the high school choral director, impressed with her singing talent, encouraged her to audition for a scholarship award from the Marian Anderson Foundation in Philadelphia. Jessye's fellow students in high school took up a collection to pay for her trip to Philadelphia. She made that audition in 1961, sang

arias from *Samson and Delilah* and *Il Trovatore,* but failed to make an impression.

En route back to Augusta, the choral director, who had accompanied her to Philadelphia, decided to stop off at Washington, D.C., so that Jessye might sing for Carolyn Grant, a professor of music at Howard University. Grant recommended Jessye for a full scholarship at Howard University, which she was unable to accept because she was too young. She finally went to Howard University two years later, in 1963, after graduation from high school. While attending Howard she sang in the university chorus and was a soloist at two churches in Washington. In 1965 she won first prize in a vocal competition conducted by the National Society of Arts and Letters in Washington. After four years of vocal training with Carolyn Grant, Norman was graduated in 1967 with a Bachelor of Music degree, cum laude.

She spent an unhappy summer that year studying music with Alice Duschak at the Peabody Conservatory in Baltimore. "The rat race, the terrible competitiveness there, was just not my scene at all," she has commented. She went on to the University of Michigan for a year and a half of vocal study with Pierre Bernac.

Hearing of a competition conducted by the Munich Radio, she applied in 1968 to the Institute of International Education for a scholarship to enable her to make the trip to Europe. While awaiting an answer, she went to South America on a State Department People-to-People tour. In Nicaragua she learned that the scholarship had been granted. In Munich she captured first prize in the competition and received engagements from several German opera houses as a result.

She returned to the United States and late in 1968 was a soloist in Washington, D.C., in a performance of Handel's *Messiah*. Writing in the Washington *Post*, Paul Hume spoke of her "prodigious voice" and added: "So great is the future promise in Jessye Norman that her singing, which is today immensely moving and exciting, can only be heard as the prelude to something quite extraordinary."

Norman returned to Germany in January 1969, settling in West Berlin later that year. She signed a three-year contract with the Deutsche Oper which required her to appear with that company in principal soprano roles two and a half months a year. In her debut there in December 1969 as Elisabeth in *Tannhäuser,* her sensuous voice and her musicianship drew praise from the local critics.

In the spring of 1970 she made her first appearance in Italy, at the Teatro Comunale in Florence in Handel's *Deborah*. That summer she was heard at the Festival of Two Worlds in Spoleto, Italy, in renditions of Mahler's songs. In 1971 she appeared as Idamante in a concert version of Mozart's *Idomeneo* with the RAI (Radiotelevisione Italiana) Orchestra in Rome, and she made her first recording—as the Countess in *The Marriage of Figaro*—for Philips; in both cases Colin Davis was the conductor. That year she also opened the Florence May Music Festival in the title role of *L'Africaine* and once again assumed the role of the Countess in *The Marriage of Figaro,* this time at the Berlin Festival opposite Dietrich Fischer-Dieskau. In 1972 she made her debut at Covent Garden as Cassandra in Berlioz' *Les Troyens,* Colin Davis conducting; was starred in the title role of *Aida* in a new production in Berlin under Claudio Abbado; made her debut at La Scala in Milan in *Aida,* again under Abbado; gave a recital at the Aldeburgh Festival in England; and made her debut at the Edinburgh Festival in a concert of Mahler's songs.

Norman made her professional American debut during the summer of 1972 at the Hollywood Bowl in California in a concert presentation of *Aida,* James Levine conducting. (She returned to the Hollywood Bowl in 1973 as Donna Elvira in a concert version of *Don Giovanni* conducted by Levine.) She made several other appearances in the United States during the summer of 1972, including a concert with the National Symphony Orchestra at Wolf Trap Farm Park for the Performing Arts, in Vienna, Virginia, and an appearance in an all-Wagner program at the Berkshire Music Festival in Lenox, Massachusetts, with Colin Davis conducting. "There were standing ovations and the kind of public delirium that great singing can arouse," wrote Donal Henahan in the New York *Times* in his report of her Berkshire Festival appearance.

On January 21, 1973, Norman gave her first American recital at the Lincoln Center for the Performing Arts in New York, singing *Lieder* by Brahms, Hugo Wolf, Richard Strauss, Mahler, and Wagner. "Her appearance," Donal Henahan reported in the New York *Times,* "created the electricity of great expectations, and her interpretatively poised and mature performances on the whole justified the excitement. . . . Miss Norman's recital stamped her a singer of extraordinary intelligence, taste and emotional depth."

Later in 1973 she toured Germany; appeared in Madrid under the direction of Rafael Frühbeck de Burgos; made her Holland debut as Marguerite in Berlioz' *The Damnation of Faust;* gave her first London recital and made her first Paris appearance, the latter in a concert performance of *Aida;* was one of the featured artists at the June festival weeks in Vienna and at festivals in Helsinki and Lucerne. In 1974 she made her debut in Israel in a performance of Schoenberg's *Gurre-Lieder* and also made her bow in Buenos Aires and Mexico.

ABOUT: High Fidelity/Musical America, July 1973; New York Times, January 21, 1973; Opera News, June 1973.

Guiomar Novaës

1895–

Guiomar Novaës, pianist, was born in São João da Boã Vista, in the state of São Paulo, Brazil, on February 28, 1895. She was one of nineteen children of Manoel da Cruz and Anna de Menezes Novaës. A child prodigy, Guiomar was

Novaës: nŏ′ vī ŭs

GUIOMAR NOVAËS

able to play the piano by ear when she was four. Three years later she began studying with Luigi Chiafarelli, with whom she made such progress that in 1904 she was able to make her public debut and to tour Brazil.

She was a bright child, fond not only of music but also of literature; she loved having stories told to her. While on concert tours, she would tell her manager that she would give only as many encores as the number of stories she would be told after the performance.

Brazil recognized her exceptional musical gifts. In 1909 it defrayed all her expenses for a trip to Paris. There she was one of 388 contestants in a competition for twelve available student places at the Paris Conservatory. At the second examination, her performance before a jury that included Fauré, Debussy, and Moszkowski was so outstanding that for their own listening pleasure they prevailed on her to repeat some of her numbers. This jury unanimously assigned her first place in the competition. For the next two years Guiomar studied with Isidor Philipp, winning first prize in piano playing after her second year.

When she was graduated from the Paris Conservatory with highest honors in piano in 1911, she made a highly successful debut in Paris. Two years later she toured France, England, Italy, and Switzerland. On November 11, 1915, she made her debut in the United States with a recital at Aeolian Hall in New York. "As a musician," wrote Richard Aldrich in the New York *Times,* "she does credit to her native land as well

as to the land that taught her. . . . She is well equipped with the fleet and fluent and generally accurate technique that is expected as a matter of course from public pianists these days. She has an unusual command of a richly colored tone from the instrument, in all ranges of power; and her tone is full and round, also in all ranges of power, without losing its beauty in the loudest passages."

She toured the United States that season, and again in 1916–1917, gaining a devoted following that remained faithful to her through her many years as a visiting artist. Her art grew in depth of understanding and command of technical resources until she assumed a place of first importance among the world's pianists. Reviewing one of her later American recitals, Pitts Sanborn wrote in the *Telegram:* "Looking once more at this slender, black-frocked Brazilian woman, with the soft and comely face and the black eyes and hair, you would swear she was not a day older than the young girl who made her sensational debut. And if her amazing art has grown with the years of maturity, she still weaves the exotic spell of old, as of an enchanted visitor from the strangeness of a tropic forest."

In 1922 Novaës married Octavio Ribiero Pinto, a wealthy Brazilian architectural engineer and composer. Theirs had been a long and unusual courtship. They first met when Guiomar was nine and performed at the Pinto home. They met again many years later at one of her concerts in São Paulo. After this performance the Novaës and Pinto families went on a picnic where the romance of Guiomar and Octavio is said to have begun. When Pinto finally proposed to her, he did so by sending her one of the love songs that Robert Schumann had written for Clara Wieck.

Novaës and Pinto have a home in Saõ Paulo and a summer retreat in the nearby mountains. The family includes two children, Anna Maria and Luiz Octavio, both of whom are musical; for them Villa-Lobos composed the suite *The Baby's Family,* which Novaës has featured on some of her concert programs. Anna Maria is a vocalist; Luiz, an engineer.

Whenever she went on tour, Novaës indulged her love for literature and her secret ambition to be a writer by sending her children long letters about her travels. A South American publisher offered to issue these letters as a book for children, but she refused the offer saying that they had been intended exclusively for an audience of two.

Novaës is one of the most famous performing artists to come from Brazil, and probably its greatest pianist. She has been so active in advancing the educational and cultural interests in her country that plaques in her honor adorn many theaters in Brazil's large cities—for example, the façade of the Municipal Theater at Rio de Janeiro over which is engraved in bronze: "In this theater Guiomar Novaës has played."

Under government auspices, Novaës undertook a comprehensive tour of Brazil, performing in many small cities where good music was rarely heard. This tour brought into existence the Culturas Artisticas, a government-sponsored organization with Novaës as director that arranged concerts throughout Brazil. In 1956 the Brazilian government awarded her the Order of Merit for her services as "an ambassadress of culture and good will to the United States."

After World War II Novaës drastically curtailed her concert schedule to allow herself more time with her family in São Paulo. She made one of her rare appearances in the United States with a recital in New York in December 1972. At that time Harold C. Schonberg wrote in the New York *Times:* "Many remember her well from the 1930s—the Novaës of the velvet paws, the Novaës of indescribable elegance and fluent technique, the Novaës whose body through her hands seemed welded to the keyboard. . . . Charm, style, color, intimacy—it was the kind of playing that has made Miss Novaës unique and it was present in good measure."

ABOUT: Baker, T. Biographical Dictionary of Musicians, completely rev. by N. Slonimsky; Schonberg, H. C. The Great Pianists.

Jarmila Novotna

1903–

Jarmila Novotna, soprano, was born in Prague, on September 23, 1903, the daughter of Joseph and Josepha Novotna. Her father was a banker. While attending high school in Prague, she sang at a charity concert attended by Emmy Destinn, who urged her to study music seriously. Follow-

Novotna: nō vät′ nä

JARMILA NOVOTNA

ing Destinn's advice, she attended the Prague Conservatory for a year, then studied voice privately with Destinn.

On June 27, 1926, Novotna made her opera debut with the Prague Opera as Violetta in *La Traviata.* As a member of the Prague Opera she was then heard in various roles among which were Marie in *The Bartered Bride,* Rosina in *The Barber of Seville,* the Queen of the Night in *The Magic Flute,* Tatiana in *Eugene Onegin,* and Gilda in *Rigoletto.*

In Milan she continued her vocal studies with Tenaglia, combining them with appearances at the Arena in Verona where she made her debut as Gilda, at La Scala in Milan, and at San Carlo in Naples. In 1929 she became a member of the Berlin State Opera where she caused a sensation in *Madama Butterfly* by appearing in the second act dressed in modern traveling garments "under the ingenious assumption that, according to the modern German reasoning, Butterfly wanted Pinkerton to take her with him to America and hence dressed, as the time drew near, for the journey." Her successful roles in Berlin included the title role of *Manon Lescaut,* Violetta, Marguerite de Valois in *Les Huguenots,* Cherubino in *The Marriage of Figaro,* and the leading soprano roles in several twentieth century operas among which were Ravel's *L'Heure Espagnole* and Krenek's *Leben des Orest.*

In 1929 Novotna made a guest appearance with the Vienna State Opera. She continued to appear there for many years, becoming a permanent member of the company in 1933. In Vienna she created the title role in Lehár's *Giuditta* (January 20, 1934). She scored major successes in the Mozartean roles of Cherubino, Pamina in *The Magic Flute,* Fiordiligi in *Così fan Tutte,* and Donna Elvira in *Don Giovanni.* In 1934 she was named *Kammersängerin.*

Beginning in 1935 she was a principal performer at the annual Salzburg Festival where she was heard in performances of *The Magic Flute* conducted by Toscanini, as well as in other Mozartean roles, and also as Euridice in Gluck's *Orfeo ed Euridice* and as Frasquita in Hugo Wolf's *Corregidor.*

Guest appearances at the Munich Opera, the Paris Opéra, the Florence May Music Festival, and at La Scala and San Carlo added to her European fame. In 1939 she paid her first visit to the United States in connection with a projected but never realized series of operatic performances planned for the World's Fair in New York, to be conducted by Toscanini. But her brief stay in America was not altogether fruitless, since during this time she signed a contract with the Metropolitan Opera.

Her American debut, however, did not take place at the Metropolitan Opera but with the San Francisco Opera in San Francisco on October 18, 1939, in the title role of *Madama Butterfly.* Olin Downes, music critic of the New York *Times,* was in San Francisco at the time. He sent the following report to his paper: "Miss Novotna has given proof of being not only a singer, but also a musician and interpreter of true dramatic instinct. Saying this, one is prone to add that while Miss Novotna gives much that is dramatic and vocally effective to her characterization of Butterfly, it is probably not her greatest role. The voice is a lyric soprano, capable also of brilliancy, but not a big body of tone. There is grace, warmth, communicative feeling in all that she does. She is a personality on the stage."

On January 5, 1940, Novotna made her first appearance at the Metropolitan Opera, as Mimi in *La Bohème.* Writing in the New York *Times,* Olin Downes found much to favor in her performance. "Mme. Novotna presented her character with charming simplicity, feeling and high artistic intelligence. The voice is not remarkable for opulence or sheer beauty, but it was expressively employed. It has ample range and is capable both of brilliancy and emotional expression."

With the exception of the single season of 1951–1952, Novotna remained with the Metropolitan Opera for sixteen years, through the 1955–1956 season. As a Mozart specialist, she was assigned roles in which she had distinguished herself in Europe: Cherubino, Pamina, and Donna Elvira. But she distinguished herself in other parts as well: as Euridice in Gluck's *Orfeo ed Euridice,* Violetta in *La Traviata,* the title role in *Manon,* Marie in *The Bartered Bride,* Octavian in *Der Rosenkavalier,* Manon in Massenet's opera, Antonia in *The Tales of Hoffmann,* Freia in *Das Rheingold,* Mélisande in *Pelléas and Mélisande,* and Orlofsky in *Die Fledermaus.*

After leaving the Metropolitan Opera, Novotna made guest appearances at the Volksoper in Vienna in 1957.

Over a period of many years she has appeared on stage and screen. In motion pictures she was seen in *The Beggar Student* (1933), *The Bartered Bride* (1934), *The Last Waltz* (1935), *Frasquita* (1936), *The Night of Greatest Love* (1937), *Song of the Lark* (1937), *The Search* (1948), and *The Great Caruso* (1951). She appeared on the Broadway stage in *Helen Goes to Troy* (1944) and *Sherlock Holmes* (1953).

Novotna married Baron George Daubek on July 16, 1931. They had two children. Having become an American citizen in 1946, she established permanent residence in New York City. Her avocations include golf, swimming, and embroidery.

ABOUT: Kutsch, K. J. and Riemens, L. A Concise Biographical Dictionary of Singers.

Garrick Ohlsson

1948–

Garrick Olof Ohlsson, pianist, was born in Bronxville, New York, on April 3, 1948. His father, Alvar, was a Swedish businessman who came to the United States after World War II; his mother, Paulyne Rosta Ohlsson, of Italian origin, became a travel agent. His parents presented Garrick with a piano when he was eight years old, and he began taking lessons with Thomas Lishman at the Westchester Conservatory in White Plains, New York. "Once he started," his mother recalls, "we couldn't get him away from the keyboard." When he was not

GARRICK OHLSSON

at the piano he was listening to records. "There was never a doubt about what I had to be," he has said.

In his thirteenth year he entered the preparatory division of the Juilliard School of Music in New York as a pupil of Sascha Gorodnitzki. Two years later he won first prize in a piano competition in Westchester. After graduation from White Plains High School in 1966, he went on to study the piano with Olga Barabini, whom he has identified as his most important teacher. That year he captured first prize in an international piano contest, the Busoni Competition held in Bolzano, Italy. On scholarship, he then completed his music study at the Juilliard School of Music, where for two years he was coached by Rosina Lhévinne and studied with Sascha Gorodnitzki. In 1971 he was graduated with the Bachelor of Music degree. Meanwhile in June 1968, while still in his third year at Juilliard, he was the proud winner of another international competition, the Montreal International Piano Contest, for which he performed Rachmaninoff's Piano Concerto No.3 and the works of some contemporary Canadian composers; his prize was ten thousand dollars.

He made his New York debut at the Grace Rainey Rogers Auditorium of the Metropolitan Museum of Art on January 5, 1970, and his performance of music by Ravel received a highly favorable reaction from Donal Henahan who reported the event in the New York *Times*.

A grant of five hundred and fifty dollars en-abled Ohlsson to go to Warsaw in October 1970 to compete in the Chopin International Piano Competition, an event held once every five years. There were eight more American competitors, three from the Soviet Union, (the preliminary field had numbered over six hundred candidates in Russia), and sixty-nine representatives from various European countries. When Ohlsson performed the Chopin Piano Concerto in E-flat major he received a standing ovation from the audience in the Warsaw Philharmonic Hall and responded with seven curtain calls. He won first prize—the first American to do so—and gained instant international recognition.

One week after winning the Chopin competition, he replaced Leon Fleisher (who was ill) as guest artist with the Warsaw Philharmonic in Ravel's Concerto for the Left Hand. A two-week tour of Poland followed in which Ohlsson was received with enormous enthusiasm. During this tour he received a transatlantic call from Philadelphia inviting him to appear with the Philadelphia Orchestra in a performance of the Chopin concerto with which he had captured top honors in the Warsaw competition. He made four appearances with the Philadelphia Orchestra under Eugene Ormandy "with a naturalness and simplicity that spoke volumes for his excellent training and his great instinctive musicality," wrote Donal Henahan in the New York *Times*.

In November 1970 Ohlsson performed at the White House for President and Mrs. Richard M. Nixon and the visiting English Prime Minister, Edward Heath. On November 29 he gave a recital in Washington, D.C. He returned to New York for another recital at Lincoln Center for the Performing Arts on December 13, and on February 4, 1971, he made his debut with the New York Philharmonic, Seiji Ozawa conducting, in Beethoven's Piano Concerto No.1.

Now a top-ranking virtuoso, Ohlsson made ninety-five appearances in 1971–1972 in the United States and Europe. He found continual travel so enervating and became so impatient with the restrictions of hotel rooms that the following season he reduced the number of his appearances to sixty-five and acquired a permanent *pied-à-terre* (a four-room apartment) on West End Avenue in New York City. "I found I just didn't like being on the road all the time," he told Tom Buckley in an interview for the New York *Times*. He has also said: "I've tried to go slowly. To develop more fully. I'm now exploring unfamiliar repertoire."

After Ohlsson's recital at Lincoln Center in New York early in March 1972, Harold C. Schonberg of the New York *Times* took him to task for presenting a curious program which, he felt, was "played in a rather peculiar manner." Schonberg suspected that Ohlsson was assuming affectations because "he would like to be recognized as a Deep Thinker as well as a mere pianist." But after Ohlsson's recital in New York on January 5, 1975, Schonberg swept all reservations aside. He found "a different pianist at work —a powerful technician, a strong musical mind, an interesting artist. This was not merely a good piano recital; it was an important one, and it put Mr. Ohlsson right up in the rank of major pianists."

Ohlsson has appeared as a guest with chamber music groups and has given duo recitals with Miriam Fried, violinist. He was heard on a CBS-TV Special with the Philadelphia Orchestra, on talk shows, and as a guest performer on several major-network-sponsored programs. He is a huge man, standing six feet four and weighing about two hundred pounds. Since boyhood he has enjoyed swimming and sailing. When not involved in music, he cooks, enjoys eating gourmet dishes, and reads a great deal. A linguist, he speaks four languages fluently (English, French, German, and Spanish) and three haltingly (Swedish, Polish, and Italian). He prefers attending opera performances to concerts. His principal outdoor diversions are playing tennis and swimming.

Ohlsson has conducted master classes in piano at the New England Conservatory.

ABOUT: High Fidelity/Musical America, March 1971; New York Sunday News Magazine, April 25, 1971; New York Times, September 21, 1972, April 17, 1977; New Yorker, January 2, 1971; Stereo Review, February 1977.

David Oistrakh

1908–1974

David Feodorovich Oistrakh, violinist, was born in Odessa in the Ukraine, on September 30,

---

Oistrakh: oi′ strŏk

DAVID OISTRAKH

1908. His father, Feodor, a bookkeeper, was an amateur violinist; his mother helped to support the family by singing in the Odessa Opera chorus. When David was five, his parents presented him with a violin. Pytor Stolarsky, one of Odessa's leading violin teachers and head of his own music school, gave David lessons and remained his only violin teacher. When Stolarsky was appointed director of the Odessa Musical-Dramatic Institute, Oistrakh entered his violin class there. Though revealing remarkable talent and though permitted to perform at a school concert when he was six, David was not treated as a prodigy, was never singled out from the other students in the class, and was subjected to a rigorous training not only on the violin but also in chamber music literature.

He made his first public appearance, in Odessa, when he was twelve, performing Beethoven's Violin Concerto. When the Odessa Institute held a concert in 1924 in honor of Stolarsky, David was called upon to perform Bach's Concerto in A minor and several smaller compositions.

All formal study ended for him after he was graduated from the Conservatory in 1926. For a while he supported himself by playing the violin in the villages and cities of the Soviet Union from Leningrad to Siberia. "I played with good conductors and bad," he later remarked, "but it was all a great school for me." He toured the Soviet Union again in joint performances with a ballerina. He also was a guest soloist with orchestras in Odessa and other parts of the

Ukraine. In 1926, when he performed as soloist with the symphony orchestra in Kiev in Glazunov's Violin Concerto, the composer conducting, Glazunov hailed him as an outstanding virtuoso and used his influence to advance the young artist's career. In 1928 Oistrakh settled in Moscow where he made guest appearances with the Tia Symphony, and in 1929 he gave concerts in Leningrad,

The winning of a number of violin competitions between 1930 and 1937 added appreciably to his slowly developing fame in the Soviet Union. In 1930 he received first prize in a Ukrainian contest held in Kharkov; in 1934 he gained first prize in the All-Union music competition in Leningrad; in 1935 he captured second prize at the Wieniawski Contest in Warsaw (the winner was Ginette Neveu); and in 1937 he emerged as the victor from among sixty-eight contestants in the world-famous Queen Elisabeth Competition in Brussels. This focused on him the attention of the entire music world.

In 1934 he became a lecturer at the Moscow Conservatory and rose to the post of professor in 1939. In 1935 he performed in Turkey, his first appearance outside the Soviet Union. A year later he toured the Baltic States and Sweden. In 1938 he made a much-acclaimed debut in Paris.

Plans were set in motion in 1939 to have him perform at the World's Fair in New York but the Nazi-Soviet pact and the outbreak of World War II made it impossible for Oistrakh to make the voyage. During the early part of World War II, he and his family, together with his teacher Stolarsky, were evacuated to Sverdlovsk. During most of the war he was able to concertize throughout the Soviet Union. His status as one of the leading violinists in the country was officially confirmed when in 1942 he was presented with the Stalin Prize, the highest award the Soviet Union could bestow on an artist. That year Oistrakh became a member of the Communist Party. In 1953 he was designated People's Artist of the USSR, and in 1960 he was awarded the Lenin Prize. He was subsequently decorated with the Order of Lenin.

After World War II Oistrakh divided his career between concert work and his teaching chores at the Moscow Conservatory. He gave between seventy and eighty concerts a year both inside and outside the Soviet Union. He was heard in chamber music concerts in the Soviet Union, primarily with an ensemble which he helped to organize.

His appearances outside the Soviet Union were increasingly extended. In 1946 he was heard at the Prague Festival. In 1951 he was highly successful at the Florence May Music Festival. In 1953 he gave a number of successful concerts at the Palais de Chaillot in Paris and made a remarkably well received debut in London. In 1954 he was one of four Soviet musicians selected to perform at the Soviet Embassy in East Berlin at a conference of foreign ministers. In February 1955 he became the first Soviet musician to perform in Japan since World War II, giving eleven concerts in a twenty-five-day tour. In April of the same year he toured Germany.

In addition to his public appearances he was beginning to make his mark as a recording artist outside the Soviet Union as well as in it. When his performance of the Khatchaturian Violin Concerto was released in the United States by Mercury in 1948, Irving Kolodin, writing in the *Saturday Review,* said that Oistrakh's "violinistic skill is in the true line of such Slavic fiddlers as Heifetz and Elman." Since then Oistrakh has recorded an extensive repertory on various labels, including Columbia, Angel, Deutsche Grammophon, and RCA. His recording of Brahms's *Double Concerto,* for violin, cello, and orchestra, with Rostropovich received a Grammy in 1970 from the National Academy of Recording Arts and Sciences.

Oistrakh was serving as a judge of the Queen Elisabeth Competition in Brussels in May 1955 when he expressed a wish to perform in the United States, where his recordings had already made him famous. The idea was viewed with considerable interest both by the New York *Times* and by *Pravda.* In the summer of 1955 an agreement was reached at a summit meeting in Geneva between the United States and the Soviet Union for an exchange of culture between the two countries, and Oistrakh's visit to the United States became possible. The State Department, at the insistence of the Soviet Union, even stood ready to forgo fingerprinting Oistrakh, as required by the Federal immigration law, allowing him admission as an official visitor.

Oistrakh's first appearance in the United States was to have taken place in New York City on November 13, 1955, at a concert of the London Philharmonic under Herbert von Karajan, but a sudden illness made him cancel this performance. His American debut took place one week later on November 20 with a recital at Carnegie Hall. Over seven thousand people stood in line to buy tickets for this debut; one hour after the tickets had been put on sale they were completely sold.

Short and chubby, he did not bring charisma to the stage. Furthermore, his effortless and relaxed performance and his undemonstrative stage demeanor were hardly calculated to discharge sparks into the auditorium. "He is unquestionably a violinist who does not begin by thinking how to subdue an audience through sheer brilliance," remarked Howard Taubman in his review in the New York *Times*. The interest had to lie exclusively in the sounds from his violin—the beauty of tone, the sureness of technique, the majesty of style. "He quickly proved that he belongs with the best anywhere," Taubman said. "The most impressive thing about Mr. Oistrakh was the thoughtfulness and sensitivity of his musicianship."

Three days after his debut Oistrakh gave a second Carnegie Hall recital, once again to a sold-out house and a highly demonstrative audience. "He is a master," reported Harold C. Schonberg in the New York *Times*. "The fiddle is an extension of his hands and he plays it with the ease of one slipping on a pair of gold gloves. His finger shifts are incredibly smooth, his bow seems endless, and no matter how awkward the hand position in a musical phrase, his intonation remains exact."

A six-month tour of eight major American cities followed. On December 21 he was heard with the New York Philharmonic under Mitropoulos in three concertos (the Brahms, the Tchaikovsky, and the A major Concerto of Mozart). On December 20, once again as a soloist with the New York Philharmonic, he presented the American premiere of Shostakovich's Violin Concerto in A minor, a work dedicated to him. (He had given its world premiere in Leningrad on October 29, 1955.)

Oistrakh made his second tour of the United States in 1959–1960, and several more after that. He was also heard throughout Europe, South America, and the Far East, as well as in the Soviet Union and the countries behind the Iron Curtain. A heart attack in 1964 compelled him to curtail his travels, but he continued to concertize until the end of his life. By the time of his death he had performed in 140 cities in 30 countries.

Many leading Soviet composers besides Shostakovich wrote works for him which he introduced. Among these compositions were concertos by Miaskovsky and Khatchaturian, and Prokofiev's Sonata No.2 in D major. In addition to his Violin Concerto, Shostakovich wrote a violin sonata for Oistrakh in 1968 and dedicated it to him.

Despite the exacting demands made upon him by his concert schedule throughout the world, Oistrakh managed to carry a full teaching load as violin professor at the Moscow Conservatory. He took about twenty students at a time. "He's a remarkable teacher," one of his pupils, Yuri Mazurkevich, told an interviewer. "He gives you an understanding of the music just like an artist. He's most demanding. And when he doesn't like something or if you repeat stupid mistakes or are not prepared he can be very unpleasant."

One of Oistrakh's star pupils was his son Igor, who subsequently developed into a distinguished concert artist in his own right. Like his father, he began his violin studies with Stolarsky. After attending his father's violin class, Igor went on to win first prize in a violin competition in Budapest in 1949 and the Wieniawski Contest in Warsaw in 1952. After that he forged for himself a distinguished career on the concert stage. Father and son were often heard in duo-violin recitals and in recordings, and on several occasions Igor has performed concertos with his father conducting the orchestra.

David Oistrakh first turned to conducting in 1958. After making many successful appearances as a conductor in the Soviet Union and Europe, he made his conducting bow in the United States during his third tour of the country when he led a concert of the Moscow Symphony in New York with Igor as soloist. On his fourth tour, Oistrakh conducted an American Symphony Orchestra for the first time, appearing with the Cleveland Orchestra in a dual capacity: After playing the Brahms Violin Concerto with George Szell conducting, he took over the baton for the Cleveland premiere of Shostakovich's Symphony No.10.

In October 1974 Oistrakh went to Holland to appear in Amsterdam in the dual role of violinist-conductor with the Amsterdam Philharmonic Orchestra, in a series of seven concerts devoted entirely to the music of Brahms. He was heard in six of these seven concerts, a soloist in three of them, a conductor of all six. Just before the seventh concert he died in his hotel room on October 24, 1974, presumably from a heart attack. Upon hearing of Oistrakh's death, Yehudi Menuhin said: "He was developing lately as one of the best orchestra conductors in the world. His death means a tragedy to world music."

"David Oistrakh was one of the most popular musicians of his day," said Harold C. Schonberg in an obituary piece for the New York *Times.* "Easygoing, gentle, considerate, he seemed to have no enemies. Everybody adored him. A short, portly man with a sweet smile, he looked like anything but the popular conception of a violinist. His hands were thick and spatulate, his bearing was modest, and he reserved his temperament for his playing."

Oistrakh's wife, Tamara Ivanova, was a graduate student in piano at the Moscow Conservatory before she married. She gave up her own career to devote herself to her family. When freed of his concert and teaching obligations, during the summer, Oistrakh liked to spend his vacations at a seaside resort swimming, motoring, and playing chess and tennis.

On May 25, 1967, Oistrakh received in Brussels the highest government award Belgium could bestow, the Order of Leopold. Two years later he was awarded an honorary doctorate in music from Cambridge University (an honor previously bestowed on just two Russian musicians, Tchaikovsky and Glazunov). In addition, he was elected honorary member of the Royal Academy of Music in London, the Academy of Science in Berlin, the Santa Cecilia Academy in Rome, and the American Academy of Science and Arts in the United States.

ABOUT: Bronin, V. David Oistrakh; Ewen, D. Famous Instrumentalists; Yampolsky, I. David Oistrakh. *Periodicals*—Musical America, January 1, 1956; New York Times, November 27, 1955; New Yorker, July 11, 1953; Newsweek, December 5, 1955; Time, November 28, 1955.

Magda Olivero

1913–

Magda Maddalena Olivero, soprano, was born in Saluzzo, near Turin, Italy, on March 25, 1913. A musical child, she studied piano, harmony, and counterpoint at the Turin Conservatory during her adolescent years. Later she joined a special class for solo performers conducted by the Italian Radio.

In 1933 she made her debut at the Teatro Emanuele in Turin as Lauretta in *Gianni Schicchi,* and that year she appeared for the first time at La Scala in Milan as Anna in *Nabucco.* Tullio Serafin became interested in her and gave her training in lyric and coloratura roles. For a number of years she appeared in opera houses throughout Italy in the title roles of *Lucia di Lammermoor, Manon,* and *Mignon,* as Amina in *La Sonnambula,* Gilda in *Rigoletto,* Adina in *L'Elisir d'Amore,* Margherita in *Mefistofele,* and Clorinda in Monteverdi's *Il Combattimento di Tancredi e Clorinda.* She gained a formidable following wherever she sang.

By 1937 she had come to the conclusion that her voice was best suited for *verismo* roles to which she turned with greater dedication than ever and of which she became a prime interpreter. She was a triumph in Puccini's operas, in Cilèa's *Adriana Lecouvreur* (which became one of her most celebrated vehicles), and in Alfano's *Risurrezione.* Giordano selected her for a revival of his short opera *Marcella,* at La Scala in 1938. A cult grew among record collectors for her recording of *Turandot* released by Cetra in 1938 in which she sang the part of Liù.

In 1941 she married Alfo Busch, a successful businessman who headed a prosperous lamp company. He persuaded her to withdraw from the operatic stage in spite of her popularity. After an appearance in *Adriana Lecouvreur* she went into retirement. During World War II she sang in hospitals for wounded soldiers and for benefits for the Red Cross. After the war, opera houses throughout Italy—including La Scala, then under the artistic direction of Tullio Serafin—tried in vain to lure her back to the stage.

In the spring of 1950 Cilèa wrote to Olivero entreating her to emerge from her retirement so

Olivero: ō lĕ vā' rō

595

MAGDA OLIVERO

created the role of the Mother in the world premiere of Renzo Rosselini's *La Guerra* in Naples (February 25, 1956) and that of Melibea in the world premiere of Flavio Testi's *La Celestina* at the Florence May Music Festival in Italy (May 28, 1963). Though her main sphere of activity was Italy, because she had never concerned herself with winning international fame, she made some noteworthy appearances elsewhere, such as in *La Bohème* at the Stoll Theater in London; in *Suor Angelica* at the Teatro San Carlo in Lisbon; in *Mefistofele, The Girl of the Golden West,* and *Adriana Lecouvreur* at the Teatro Municipal in Rio de Janeiro; in *Tosca* at the Vienna State Opera; and at the Paris Opéra in the first French production of *Adriana Lecouvreur.* She was also heard for the first time in Amsterdam, Lisbon, and Zagreb.

"An Italian soprano of great taste, refinement and intelligence, Magda Olivero manages to sing the Verismo repertoire and make it, paradoxically, both exquisitely musical and wildly dramatic," wrote Robert M. Connolly in *Stereo Review.* "Besides being a superb vocal technician, she is also a supreme actress, which is what Verismo calls for. . . . As with Callas, it is in the little bits of business between the arias that her superiority becomes apparent. Her singing is often disturbing, not soothing or pretty, and her performances are almost unbearably exciting. Her voice, like that of all great singers, has a unique timbre that is instantly recognizable. . . . It has a dry, even at times a hooty quality. It is perhaps like a rare vintage wine, slightly musty, but of precious bouquet, which can send the connoisseur into ecstasies."

that he might see and hear her just once more in his opera *Adriana Lecouvreur.* "Each of us has a duty which cannot be ignored," he told her. When she delayed in replying, Cilèa complained to his publisher: "I am old and sick, and could go from one day to another, why does Magda Olivero deny me this one last joy? You ask her. Ask her to let me hear *Adriana* just once more sung by her." It was this plea that finally brought Olivero back to the opera stage after an absence of a decade—on February 3, 1951, at the Teatro Grande in Brescia in *Adriana Lecouvreur.* She was a sensation, but Cilèa was not alive to enjoy this performance, for he died two months earlier.

Still in full command of the vocal and dramatic powers that had made her such a favorite, Olivero resumed her career. Her art had become richer and deeper, and her stage presence more charismatic. In the summer of 1952 she enjoyed a spectacular success in *Mefistofele* at the Verona Arena. During the next few years she graced Italian stages as Violetta in *La Traviata,* Fedora in Giordano's opera of that name, Margherita in *Mefistofele,* the title role in Massenet's *Iris,* Cio-Cio-San in *Madama Butterfly,* Minnie in *The Girl of the Golden West,* Tosca, the two Manons of Massenet and Puccini, and as Adriana Lecouvreur. She was also heard in such less familiar operas as Zandonai's *Francesca da Rimini,* Alfano's *La Leggenda di Sakuntala* and *Risurrezione,* Tchaikovsky's *Mazeppa,* Catalani's *Loreley,* Ibert's *L'Aiglon,* and Poulenc's *La Voix Humaine* and *Les Dialogues des Carmélites.* She

Her long-overdue American debut finally took place on November 4, 1967, with the Civic Opera at the State Fair Music Hall in Dallas, Texas. There she assumed the title role in Cherubini's *Medea,* a role she was singing for the first time anywhere. The audience was ecstatic, but the critics were of divided opinions. John Ardoin was rhapsodic, saying of her voice, "like no other voice. It can flutter with a poignancy which stops your breath, wrap a phrase in a caress, flash with heated brilliance or chill with an icy thrust. . . . We must also take into account the deeply sympathetic figure she creates visually. How expressive are those hands of hers as though they too could sing. And her face was a register for the myriad emotions she thought and felt as Medea. It all added up to one of the superb singing actresses to be seen today at work. Cherish her. Her breed is rare." But other critics had reservations. Reporting to the New York *Times,* Allen Hughes found her art "old fashioned by contemporary standards—very impassioned, embellished with sobs, filled with rhythmic liberties and so on." And Peter G. Davis (also in the New York *Times*) maintained: "Her voice is not a beautiful one by conventional standards. The tight vibrato, hollow chest tone and occasionally piercing upper register are qualities that one must adjust to. . . . As a stage figure, Miss Olivero moves in the grand old-fashioned manner, with broad, stylized, almost choreographic gesture. In less expert hands, this technique could be ludicrous."

In May 1968 Olivero appeared at the Kansas City Music Hall in the Dallas production of *Medea.* On October 18, 1969, she made her east coast debut in *Adriana Lecouvreur* with the Connecticut Opera Association, and on November 26, 1969, she returned to the Dallas Civic Opera as Fedora. On November 2, 1971, she made her first appearance in New York as a soloist with the Little Orchestra Society under Thomas Scherman in Poulenc's *La Voix Humaine* and several opera arias. At this time she also recorded her first complete opera since 1938—*Fedora,* a London release—and returned to La Scala as Kostelnicka in a new production of Janáček's *Jenufa.*

There was considerable anticipation and excitement attending Olivero's first appearance at the Metropolitan Opera on April 5, 1975, as *Tosca.* Her admirers, some of whom had come to New York from across the country, gathered en masse to pay tribute to their heroine. And they were hysterical in their reactions. As Harold C. Schonberg reported in his review in the New York *Times:* "They yelled and screamed when she came on. They broke into arias with bravos. They moaned orgiastically. At the end there was a twenty-minute ovation for the lady. It was one of the longest ovations in recent Metropolitan Opera history." Writing in *Stereo Review,* William Livingstone reported: "Mme. Olivero lived up to her reputation as an exceptionally powerful singing actress. . . . She was applauded not just for the arias and duets, but for certain well-delivered lines. She brought down the house in Act I with her reading of the line *'Dio mi perdona. Egli vede ch'io piango!'* The Met's executive stage manager, Osie Hawkins, is

said to have exclaimed, 'We haven't had applause on that line since Licia Albanese!' And so it went. . . . Magda had lighted a Roman candle in the tired old face of show business and the fans were delirious." Harold C. Schonberg continued his review to say: "One would have thought that a combination of Tebaldi and Callas was making her debut. Instead there was a dignified artist of uncertain age who knew how to husband what little voice she had left, and who gave a moving demonstration of how great singers of the past used to portray Tosca. . . . Holding herself back, pacing herself like the experienced artist she is, Miss Olivero got off some amazing strong high notes. There are, naturally, all kinds of holes in the voice, and there were also occasional pitch troubles. Miss Olivero must necessarily represent the art of singing rather than singing itself."

During the summer of 1976, Olivero appeared at the Spoleto Festival in Italy as the old countess in Tchaikovsky's *The Queen of Spades.* At that time she sang her part in Italian, but when she recreated this role at the first Spoleto Festival in the United States—at Charleston, South Carolina, on May 25, 1977—she sang in English. In March and April 1977 she created for Italy the principal female part in Gottfried von Einem's *Visit of the Old Lady* at the San Carlo in Naples. During the fall of 1977 she commemorated the tenth anniversary of her American debut by touring the United States in recitals, with the concert pianist Ivan Davis as her assisting artist. When she returned to the New York concert stage on December 5, 1977, after a six-year absence, Peter G. Davis in the New York *Times* found that "there's no denying that Miss Olivero was having occasional vocal difficulties." But he added that "one could still marvel at the fascinating textural nuances, the haunting pianissimo phrases, the delicate half tints and the intensely absorbed dramatic concentration she summoned up to conjure the mood of each song. This was great singing, the kind that made any intrusive technical flaws seem relatively insignificant."

Placido Domingo, one of world's leading tenors, after appearing with Olivero in *Manon Lescaut* in Verona during the summer of 1970, called her "one of a kind, whose style has all but disappeared." He added: "I was amazed at Olivero's strength. You may or may not like the voice, but as an artist she is remarkable."

Ormandy

In an interview with Howard Klein in the New York *Times*, Olivero discussed her art: "Regardless of what is going on around me during a performance—if people are shouting instead of singing—when I hear my music I am in a 'magic time.' I feel I become the character. This is effortless and natural and has always been that way. I have no choice in the matter. Becoming so identified with a tragic heroine is exhausting, since most of them die and the death scene is very involving. But I must always hold back from the emotions I have to express. I may cry during a performance, and in so doing, fail to project to the audience. But by containing them and concentrating on projecting what I feel, then the audience will cry."

She feels the emotions of each of her performances so intensely that she prefers to leave the auditorium hurriedly when the opera is over and recover by herself at her home or in a hotel room. "Once a friend saw me sobbing backstage after a performance—everyone else was happy. She said, 'Why are you crying?' I told her, 'Because I felt my own death.' "

With her husband Olivero maintains a large apartment in Milan and a country house in Rapallo. Since she returned to the opera theater, her husband has kept a low profile as far as her career is concerned. He never goes backstage after a performance, preferring to wait for her in his car.

Olivero is a gregarious person who enjoys communication with the people she likes and invariably is surrounded by her friends. She likes good conversation, good theater, good films, and good books.

ABOUT: Hi-Fi, January 1970; High Fidelity/Musical America, November 1977; Hobbies, March 1972; New York Times, November 28, 1971, December 4, 1977; Opera News, December 22, 1969, December 3, 1977; Stereo Review, November 1969, September 1975.

EUGENE ORMANDY

Eugene Ormandy

1899–

The more than forty years that Ormandy served with the Philadelphia Orchestra, first as principal conductor, then music director, is the longest

Ormandy: ôr′ măn dǐ

tenure in performing history of any conductor with a major symphonic organization. Eugene Ormandy (originally Eugene Ormandy Blau) was born in Budapest on November 18, 1899, to Benjamin and Rosalie Berger Blau. His father, a dentist, played the violin. Even before Eugene was born, his father was determined that Eugene someday become a concert violinist, and upon his birth named him Jenö (Hungarian for Eugene) after the Hungarian violinist, teacher, and composer Jenö Hubay. As an infant Eugene heard good music all the time. He was so precocious that when he was about two he could identify some fifty musical compositions after hearing just a few measures. When he was four, it was discovered that he had perfect pitch when he called out from his seat in the audience that the violinist on the stage was playing F-natural instead of F-sharp.

Eugene received his first violin lessons from his father on an eighth-size instrument when he was just four. One year later he became the youngest student ever admitted to the Budapest Royal Academy. There he made such swift progress that he was able to make his concert debut as violinist two years later. At the Academy he studied composition with Zoltán Kodály and, when he was nine, entered Hubay's master violin class. "My lessons with Hubay filled my days with work and dreams," he recalls. "My fingers were numb from the exercises of Kreutzer and Cramer and later the show pieces of Vieuxtemps and Sarasate."

At fourteen he became the youngest student

to receive a Bachelor of Music degree at the Academy—six years younger than any other recipient. In 1917 he was given a professor's diploma to teach violin there.

For a time he served as the concertmaster of the Blüthner Orchestra in Berlin, with which he made his official debut as concert violinist by performing on one program three concertos (the Mendelssohn, the Brahms, and the D minor Concerto of Vieuxtemps). He then made several moderately successful tours of Central Europe. He was also a member of an instrumental group that performed for wounded soldiers in hospitals.

In 1919 Hubay resigned as head of the master class in violin at the Academy, and Ormandy succeeded him. He kept this post two years but was then compelled to resign because his students objected violently to studying under one so young. During this time he continued to concertize. In 1921, following his successful recital in Austria, two Hungarian acquaintances offered to be his managers for a tour of the United States, promising him a fee of thirty thousand dollars for a hundred concerts. Encouraged by this offer, Ormandy sold all his belongings and went to the United States. Upon arriving he discovered that no tour had been planned for him and that the would-be impresarios were nowhere to be found. He was stranded in a foreign country whose language he did not know, without any financial resources or friends, and his future looked bleak. He auditioned for several concert managers, not one of whom offered him an engagement of any kind. The only job he could find was in vaudeville playing popular tunes on the violin for an acrobatic act at a salary of two hundred and fifty dollars a week; his pride and artistic integrity, however, did not allow him to accept it.

He was standing on the corner of Fiftieth Street and Broadway with just five cents in his pocket when he came upon Erno Rapee, an acquaintance from Budapest. Rapee was then the music director at the New York movie palace, the Capitol. When Rapee learned of Ormandy's plight he gave him some money and offered him a job in his movie orchestra. Within five days Ormandy was promoted to concertmaster. Before long he was assigned violin solos on a weekly radio program emanating from the Capitol Theater.

The Capitol Theater orchestra often offered symphonic music as a preface to the motion picture. On one such occasion David Mendoza was to conduct a movement from Tchaikovsky's Symphony No.4. When he fell ill, Rapee asked Ormandy to step in as a substitute. Conducting without a rehearsal, and from memory, in September 1924, Ormandy felt, as he later revealed, that he had discovered "a new instrument, richer and fuller than the violin—the orchestra." Ormandy's performance went over so well that he was added to the conducting staff of the Capitol Theater as an assistant in 1925 and later became full conductor. Over a four-year period he served a fruitful apprenticeship, conducting a great variety of symphonic compositions. "We played good music, movements from the great symphonies, and even such modern classics as Richard Strauss's *Till Eulenspiegel*. And, mind you, since each week we performed every work about twenty times, we had an almost incomparable opportunity to learn the music with intensive minuteness. And so, by conducting each masterpiece twenty times or so in succession over a period of several days—and doing this for years—I acquired a repertory and acquired it by learning each note in the score by heart."

His performances at the Capitol drew praise from W. J. Henderson, music critic of the New York *Times*. Ormandy's services were then recruited for radio concerts and for making recordings of semiclassical compositions. His spare time was spent in memorizing new and unfamiliar scores and in attending not only symphony concerts but also Toscanini's rehearsals at Carnegie Hall.

When Arthur Judson signed Ormandy to a contract with a view to developing him as a symphonic conductor, Ormandy resigned from the Capitol Theater in 1929. That summer he made his debut with a symphony orchestra, leading several concerts at the Lewisohn Stadium in New York. During the summers of 1930 and 1931 he was heard at Robin Hood Dell in Philadelphia with the Philadelphia Orchestra.

In 1931 Toscanini was scheduled to conduct some guest concerts with the Philadelphia Orchestra during its winter season at the Academy of Music. A sudden attack of neuritis made it necessary for him to cancel these appearances. Several conductors called upon to replace Toscanini could not accept. Leopold Stokowski, music director of the Philadelphia Orchestra, finally called Ormandy on the phone to inquire if he would be willing to take over the engagement. "I thought it was my friend, Alfred Wallenstein, playing a joke, so I said: 'Ah, cut it out, Wally.' But the voice on the phone went on in a very dignified tone: 'Would you like to conduct the Philadelphia Orchestra in view of Mr. Toscanini's illness?' I couldn't believe it."

For Ormandy to take on the Philadelphia Orchestra in view of his limited experience—and, additionally, to substitute for the most idolized conductor of the generation—was a gamble that might have spelled disaster. His friends and his manager tried to discourage him from accepting an offer which they felt might well be artistic suicide. Ormandy, however, accepted the challenge and met it successfully. He conducted the concert on October 30, 1931, from memory with such authority and solid evidence that he was a conductor to the manner born that largely on the strength of this appearance he was given, the following fall, a five-year contract as principal conductor of the Minneapolis Symphony.

During the five years Ormandy served as principal conductor of the Minneapolis Orchestra he elevated to a place among America's twenty-five or so leading symphonic organizations an organization that up to then had been regarded with no little condescension. He changed the personnel; expanded the repertory to include many twentieth century compositions, among which were the world premieres of new American compositions by Roy Harris, Aaron Copland, and others; took the orchestra on tour; and made recordings for RCA Victor. All this gained him national prominence. Already in 1932 Olin Downes could say of him in the New York *Times:* "Mr. Ormandy is a very gifted musician. . . . He is authoritative and sure in his methods. . . . He has a very healthy musical sense, much temperament, and a conductor's flair for effect."

While serving in Minneapolis, Ormandy appeared frequently as a guest conductor of the Philadelphia Orchestra in concerts that further endeared him to the audiences at the Academy of Music. In 1936 he was invited by Stokowski to share his season with the Philadelphia Orchestra. Though Ormandy's contract in Minneapolis still had a year to go, its directors generously released him to allow him to go on to Philadelphia. In 1938, when Stokowski announced his resignation as music director of the Philadelphia Orchestra, Ormandy became principal conductor.

Ormandy had no intention of becoming a carbon copy of the glamorous music director he was replacing. From his very first concert as principal conductor of the Philadelphia Orchestra he avoided spectacular or provocative methods, displays of temperament, or sensationalism. In contrast to Stokowski, Ormandy was unostentatious, reserved, devoid of postures or affectations. Where Stokowski kept himself aloof from the musicians, whom he often treated highhandedly, Ormandy helped to create a warm and personal bond between himself and his men. "I am one of you," he told them. He considers himself something of a father figure. "The musicians tell me about their personal lives and problems and I help them," he has said. At rehearsals he avoided outbursts of temper, sarcastic remarks, or annihilating criticisms, preferring geniality, courtesy, friendliness, and patience. His men soon became aware of his extraordinary memory and musicianship in a highly varied repertoire. They respected him for all this, and respecting him they gave themselves completely to their music-making.

The Ormandy sound replaced the Stokowski sound. Stokowski's had been lush, sensuous, orgiastic—given to swelling organlike sonorities (Stokowski had been an organist). Ormandy's sound emphasized the instrument on which he had been trained—the violin—and became mellow, with a polished sheen. It has, as Robert L. Sammons wrote in *Town and Country,* "the tone of a lush and beautifully tuned instrument. . . . His superb choir of string players responds to give his orchestra luxurious and velvety tone. . . . Though Stokowski instilled the Philadelphia Orchestra's sensuous warmth and depth of tone, it is Ormandy who today is responsible for its uncanny precision, opulence of sound, and balance of ensemble."

Just how fully Ormandy succeeded in replacing Stokowski became evident in the fall of 1938 when he became music director, a post endowing him with dictatorial powers. He has used those powers to keep his orchestra among the foremost in the world, placing himself among the world's leading conductors. He continued what Stokowski had begun, making the concerts of the Philadelphia Orchestra alive and exciting not only through beautifully projected performances of the familiar but also through the abundance of unfamiliar music that crowded his programs. The commissions and premieres Ormandy has given through the years represent a cross-section of symphonic writing in the twentieth century, particularly in the United States, from the post-Romantic to the avant-garde. The following listing, long as it is, is but a sample: Antheil's Symphony No.5 (December 31, 1948); Barber's *Cave of the Heart* (December 5, 1947), *Toccata Festiva* (September 30, 1960), Violin Concerto (February 7, 1941); Bartók's Piano Concerto No.3 (February 8, 1946); Leslie Bassett's *Echoes from an Invisible World* (February 27, 1976), *Variations for Orchestra* (July 6, 1963); Bloch's *Suite Symphonique* (October 26, 1945); Britten's *Diversions on a Theme* (January 16, 1942); Creston's Symphony No.3 (October 27, 1950), Symphony No.7 (January 26, 1962); Diamond's Symphony No.7 (January 26, 1962); Jean Françaix's *L'Horloge du Flore* (March 31, 1961); Gruenberg's Violin Concerto (December 1, 1944); Hanson's Symphony No.5 (February 18, 1955); Roy Harris's Symphony No.7, final version (November 20, 1952), Symphony No.9 (January 18, 1963); Hindemith's Clarinet Concerto (December 11, 1950), *Cupid and Psyche* (October 29, 1943); Martinu's Concerto for Two Pianos (November 5, 1943), Symphony No.4 (November 30, 1945); Menotti's Violin Concerto (December 5, 1962) and Symphony No.1 (August 4, 1976); Milhaud's Suite for Violin and Orchestra (November 16, 1945); Persichetti's Symphony No.3 (November 21, 1947), Symphony No.4 (December 17, 1954); Piston's Symphony No.7 (February 10, 1961); Rachmaninoff's Piano Concerto No.4, new version (October 12, 1941), *Symphonic Dances* (January 3, 1941); William Schuman's Symphony No.9 (January 10, 1969); Roger Sessions's Symphony No.5 (February 7, 1964); Virgil Thomson's Cello Concerto (March 24, 1950), *A Joyful Fugue* (February 1, 1962), *Louisiana Story* (November 26, 1948); Villa-Lobos's Symphony No.9 (May 16, 1966); Anton Webern's *Im Sommerwind* (May 25, 1962); Eugen Zádor's *Élégie* (November 11, 1960), *Five Contrasts* (January 8, 1965). The American premieres brought first hearings of works by Gottfried von Einem, Mahler (Symphony No.10), Prokofiev, Shostakovich, and Vaughan Williams among many other foreign composers.

Ormandy's empathy with new music and the modern composer led Vincent Persichetti to say: "There is virtually no one who will put so much of his heart into seeing that a new work gets off on the right foot ... insists on memorizing the composition and discusses it with you from every aspect. He invites you to rehearsals and has you sit alongside him. You are invited to interrupt at any time, to say whether something should be played faster, slower, or whether something is wanting in dynamics. Any suggestion gets his courteous consideration. It all contributes by giving the writer an inner satisfaction, a feeling that he not only has had his work played by the greatest orchestra of them all but he has found the best possible performance that the orchestra could have given it."

Ormandy has taken the Philadelphia Orchestra on numerous tours of the United States, transcontinental as well as regional. They have also been frequently heard in foreign lands. In 1944 they traveled to Australia, in 1949 to England, in 1955 to Europe, in 1958 not only to Europe but also to the Soviet Union and countries behind the Iron Curtain. The orchestra's fifth triumphal tour of Europe, in 1975, covered seventeen cities in six countries over a four-week period with twenty concerts, all of them conducted by Ormandy. Three tours covered Japan: the first, opening the Osaka Festival in 1967; the second, in 1972; and the third, in 1978. The last-mentioned tour also took in South Korea.

Undoubtedly the orchestra's most dramatic and most publicized foreign tour was the one that took place in September 1973 when the Philadelphia Orchestra under Ormandy became the first American symphonic organization to perform in China—soon after the rapprochement between the People's Republic of China and the United States during the Nixon Administration. (It was not, however, the first orchestra of international fame to play in China, having been preceded that March by the London Philharmonic under John Pritchard, and the Vienna Philharmonic under Claudio Abbado.) The Philadelphia Orchestra gave seven concerts in nine days. The first concert took place in Peking on September 14, 1973. The program comprised Mozart's *Hafner Symphony,* Roy Harris's Symphony No.3, and Brahms's Symphony No.3, with Sousa's march *The Stars and Stripes Forever* and a Chinese revolutionary song reserved as encores. Ormandy repeated this program in its entirety at his final concert in China at the auditorium of the Revolutionary Committee in Shanghai on September 21. Banquets attended by Chinese dignitaries were held for orchestra and conductor after the first and last performances, with a long drawn-out exchange of toasts. During this visit, Ormandy had the opportunity to conduct the Central Philharmonic Orchestra of Peking on September 15, when he was called upon by its regular conductor to lead the ensemble in the second movement of Beethoven's Symphony No.5. He thus became the first American conductor since the revolution to appear at the head of a Chinese orchestra.

During the summer of 1966 the Philadelphia Orchestra under Ormandy inaugurated the Saratoga Performing Arts Center in Saratoga Springs, New York—a major new summer festival of which it has since been a focal point. Under Ormandy the orchestra has also performed annually over a period of many years at its other summer home, Robin Hood Dell in Philadelphia. There, on June 14, 1976, the orchestra under Ormandy inaugurated Robin Hood Dell West, a new eight-million-dollar outdoor amphitheater that was to serve as the new summer home of the Philadelphia Orchestra.

In addition to its public concerts, the Philadelphia Orchestra under Ormandy has frequently performed over radio and television. It was the first major American symphony orchestra to be heard over television. This happened on March 20, 1948, over CBS-TV, a concert transmitted from Philadelphia to New York on a newly laid coaxial cable. Another historic television appearance took place on November 22, 1963, the day President Kennedy was assassinated. In memory of President Kennedy, the Philadelphia Orchestra under Ormandy performed the Mozart Requiem.

The Philadelphia Orchestra under Ormandy has also been one of the most highly active American symphonic organizations in the recording studios, having released over three hundred LPs since 1944, three of which topped the million-dollar mark in sales. Ormandy's recording of Orff's *Catulli Carmina* received a Grammy from the National Academy of Recording Arts and Sciences in 1967.

The honors and awards Ormandy has gathered through the decades have come from many parts of the world. He received the Order of Merit of Juan Pablo Duarte from the Dominican Republic (1945), was named Officer of the French Legion of Honor (1952) and Commander (1958), became Knight of the Order of the White Rose (1952) and a Knight of the Order of Dannebrog (1955) in Finland, and was decorated Commendatore by the Italian Republic (1972). In 1965 he received the Sibelius Medal from Finland, in 1966 the Honor Cross for Arts and Sciences from Austria, and in 1967 the golden medallion of the Vienna Philharmonic. He has been the recipient of the Philadelphia Award (1970), the National Freedom Award of the Freedoms Foundation (1970), and the gold medal of the Union League in Philadelphia (1974)—the last of these had been given only twenty-four times since the first one went to Abraham Lincoln in 1863. On January 24, 1970, in celebration of Ormandy's seventieth birthday, President Richard M. Nixon bestowed upon him on the stage of the Academy of Music in Philadelphia the country's highest civilian award, the Freedom Medal. In honor of the American Bicentenary, Ormandy was named Knight Commander of the British Empire in 1976.

He has also been awarded numerous honorary doctorates in music, including degrees from Rutgers University, the University of Pennsylvania, Temple University, and the Curtis Institute of Music.

In 1927 Ormandy became an American citizen. He was twice married: first on August 8, 1922, to Steffy Goldner, a harpist in the New York Philharmonic Orchestra; then, to Margaret Frances Hitsch on May 15, 1950. Their homes for many years were a suite at the Bellevue-Stratford Hotel in Philadelphia and a country place, Belvedere, in the Berkshires in Monterey, Massachusetts.

Though Ormandy has all his life suffered from a chronic hip condition that gave him a slight limp, he has been able to enjoy swimming and to play table tennis with professional skill. Since suffering an aggravation of his leg condition in an automobile accident, he has sought his diversions not in physical activity but in photography, reading books, and studying music scores. He rarely takes a vacation, preferring to spend his time away from his duties with the Philadelphia Orchestra in performing at European festivals or serving as guest conductor of major orchestras in America and Europe. He made one of his rare appearances as a conductor of opera on December 20, 1950, when he made his debut at the Metropolitan Opera in New York with a new production of *Die Fledermaus*.

ABOUT: Ewen, D. Dictators of the Baton; O'Connell, C. The Other Side of the Record; Stoddard, H. Symphony Conductors of the U.S.A. *Periodicals*—Hi-Fi, January 1969, November 1969; Musical America, October 1960; Time, October 15, 1965.

Seiji Ozawa

1935–

SEIJI OZAWA

Seiji Ozawa is the first Oriental to achieve international fame as a conductor and the first to assume the post of music director of a major American symphony orchestra. He was born in Hoten, in Japanese-occupied Manchuria, on September 1, 1935, the third of four sons of Kaisaku Ozawa, a dentist who was Buddhist, and Sakura Ozawa, a Christian. His father performed on native Japanese musical instruments to which Seiji was introduced in childhood. But Seiji also came into contact with Western music. As he has explained: "My mother . . . a Protestant, and my three brothers and I went to Sunday school and heard the organ and sang hymns." His interest in Western music led him to study the piano. He began lessons in his seventh year in Hoten and continued in Tokyo, where his family went to live in 1944.

In 1953 he entered the Toho School of Music in Tokyo, specializing in the piano with the hope of becoming a virtuoso. But one day, while playing soccer, he broke both index fingers. Unable to play the piano for months, he turned to the study of conducting and composition with Saito, a cellist who had once studied with Emanuel Feuermann and was able to pass on Western traditions in music to Ozawa, his sole pupil. Ozawa was required to learn two orchestral scores a week—"simple things like the *Linz Symphony* of Mozart or a Haydn symphony," he explains—and to play them from memory at the piano.

In 1959 Ozawa was graduated from the Toho School of Music with first prizes in composition and conducting. He began his conducting career by leading concerts of the NHK Orchestra (the Japanese Broadcasting Symphony) and the Japan Philharmonic. He soon demonstrated such a gift for conducting that he was named "the outstanding talent of the year" by the Japan

Ozawa: ō zä′ wä

radio orchestra and by a Japanese music magazine.

Saito urged Ozawa to leave Japan and find further opportunities for development as a symphony conductor in Europe. The only way Ozawa could make such a trip was to get a Japanese firm to provide him with a motor scooter and with free transportation, in return for helping to promote that vehicle in Europe. He took passage to Italy on a freighter. In Italy he tried to promote sales for the scooter and took on odd jobs whenever his money ran out. Then, by scooter, he traveled to France, arriving there with less than one hundred dollars. In Besançon he entered the International Competition of Orchestral Conductors in the fall of 1959 and won first prize. After that he studied conducting in Paris with Eugène Bigot.

Charles Münch, music director of the Boston Symphony and the Berkshire Music Festival, was present at the Besançon competition and invited Ozawa to Tanglewood in Massachusetts on a conducting fellowship in 1960. At the end of that summer season Ozawa was awarded the Koussevitzky Memorial Scholarship.

Once again on a scholarship, Ozawa was able to study conducting with Herbert von Karajan in West Berlin and to serve his apprenticeship by appearing before an audience every three weeks. Leonard Bernstein, then on a European tour with the New York Philharmonic, was so impressed by one of Ozawa's performances in Berlin that he invited him to become one of his three assistants in New York. Ozawa made his Ameri-

603

can debut as conductor on April 14, 1961, at a concert of the New York Philharmonic and was warmly received. Soon after that, when the New York Philharmonic went to the East-West Encounter in Tokya, Ozawa served as Bernstein's assistant. In Tokyo, Ozawa conducted a Japanese composition (Mayuzumi's *Bacchanale*) that became part of a television program, "Bernstein in Japan," transmitted throughout the United States by CBS-TV.

In Tokyo, Ozawa enjoyed such success that he was invited to return in 1962 to lead several concerts of the NHK Orchestra. When Ozawa arrived to fill this assignment, he encountered considerable opposition from members of that orchestra who resented his youth, his foreign successes, and his autocratic methods. In outright rebellion the orchestra refused to appear on the night of the first concert. In fulfillment of his contract, Ozawa appeared alone on an empty stage. He then threatened legal action against the orchestra for breaking the contract. At this point several of Ozawa's admirers arranged for him to conduct a special concert of the Japanese Symphony, which became a personal triumph for him. Ozawa withdrew his lawsuit against the NHK Orchestra, and in return the members of the orchestra submitted an apology and invited Ozawa to conduct it the following season. From then on, Ozawa's position in Japanese music was secure. His guest appearances there inspired ovations. He was appointed music director of the Nissei Theatre in Tokyo where both operas and symphonic music were presented, and in 1968 he was named music adviser to the Japan Philharmonic in which capacity he was called upon to conduct the orchestra several times a year and supervise all programs and guest-artist choices.

At this time he was also making significant strides in the United States. During the summers of 1963 and 1964 he was heard as a guest conductor at the Lewisohn Stadium in New York. During the summer of 1963, on two days' notice, he flew to Chicago to substitute for Georges Prêtre as conductor of the Chicago Symphony at the Ravinia Festival. His two appearances there had such an impact that the following summer he was appointed music director of the Ravinia Festival, a new post created expressly for him. In July 1964, when the Toho String Orchestra from the school he had attended in Tokyo visited New York for Philharmonic Hall's Japan Week cele-

bration, Ozawa led that ensemble in two performances, and that same season he conducted performances at the Berkshire Music Festival. In 1964–1965 Leonard Bernstein appointed him as his only assistant conductor with the New York Philharmonic and Ozawa was able to make a number of noteworthy appearances with that orchestra.

He gave a guest performance with the Toronto Symphony in Canada in 1964 and so endeared himself to audiences and critics that later the same year he was appointed music director beginning with the 1965–1966 season. Before Ozawa could conduct his first concert in this new post, he took the orchestra on a pre-season tour of Europe in September 1965 to participate in the Commonwealth Arts Festival in Great Britain. They were heard in London, Glasgow, and Cardiff between September 16 and October 2. A critic for the London *Sunday Times* wrote: "Under Seiji Ozawa, the Toronto Symphony gave one of the most stunning concerts I have yet heard on the South Bank. . . . [They] brought an unexpected element to a homely festival— orchestral virtuosity of international class." "It was very much Ozawa's personal character as a musician that dominated the interpretations," said Edward Greenfield in the *Guardian.* "His hands convey meaning with a clarity one normally associates with the mimes of the Japanese theater."

As the music director of the Toronto Symphony, Ozawa developed its virtuosity; extended its seasonal activities supplemented by tours outside Canada, including a visit to Japan; gave a prominent place on his programs to twentieth century music; and offered opportunities to the first-desk men to appear as soloists. He created a working relationship with his men that was described by the wife of one of them as "a most beautiful love affair . . . giving 150 per cent of themselves to each other."

Ozawa's dais behavior, like Bernstein's, proved choreographic, but his gesturing never obscured the precise clarity of his baton technique. "He seems to float above an orchestra," wrote a correspondent for *Life,* "his baton gesturing as if he were painting a silk screen. . . . He is almost disembodied." Clarity also characterized his performances noted for meticulous attention to detail, clarity of texture, lucidity, and forward rhythmic momentum. "Assertiveness seems to be a basic ingredient of Ozawa's approach to music-making," wrote William Littler in the Toronto *Star.* "When he conducts, the music always seems to be under pressure . . . the phrasing breathes tension. This has obvious advantages. It makes for focused listening."

Even while serving in Toronto, Ozawa made numerous appearances in Europe and the United States. In the summer of 1969 he made his debut as an opera conductor with Mozart's *Così fan Tutte* at the Salzburg Festival. In 1970 he was appointed coartistic director (with Gunther Schuller) of the Berkshire Music Center.

One of the many American orchestras with which Ozawa appeared as guest conductor was the San Francisco Symphony, during the 1961–1962 season. Then, and in subsequent guest appearances, he became such a favorite that when Josef Krips resigned in 1969 as the orchestra's music director, Ozawa was selected as his successor, beginning with the 1970–1971 season. Ozawa's last appearance as music director at the regular subscription series of the Toronto Symphony in April 1970 was an occasion filled with sentiment. Across the stage of Massey Hall was a banner reading: "Sayonara Seiji." After the final composition, the audience went into an uproar. But this was not Ozawa's final appearance with this orchestra. That took place the following June 9 at the opening of the fifty-million-dollar National Arts Center in Ottawa, Canada. "Seiji Ozawa closed his tenure as musical director of the Toronto Symphony with a smash-bang performance of Tchaikovsky's Symphony No.4 . . . that shot the audience from its seats like popped corn before the last drum rolls had stormed to the end," reported a Toronto music critic.

Evidence of Ozawa's popularity in San Francisco appeared during his first year there—the orchestra experienced its greatest season and the greatest single-ticket sales in its history. This record was surpassed the following season, with an overall attendance rate posted at 93 percent of capacity.

As music director of the San Francisco Symphony, Ozawa helped make the first recordings by that organization in a dozen years, with two releases on the Deutsche Grammophon label. In the spring of 1973 Ozawa headed the San Francisco Symphony on its first tour of Europe and the Soviet Union, beginning in Paris on May 15 and continuing with seventeen more concerts in fifteen other European cities. Then, in June, orchestra and conductor went to Leningrad for three concerts of a two-week tour to become the first American symphony orchestra to tour the Soviet Union in eight years. "Each night when the concert ended," Murray Seegar reported to the Los Angeles *Times* from Leningrad, "about two hundred admirers stood patiently in the street by the side door of the old Philharmonic Hall to catch a glimpse and perhaps an autograph from the orchestra's exciting young conductor. . . . Stunned by the precision and excitement which Ozawa draws from such well-worn classics as Tchaikovsky's Symphony No.4, one knowledgeable Leningrad musician commented: 'That's not how we play Tchaikovsky, but it was great.' "

In the fall of 1973 Ozawa was appointed music director of the Boston Symphony Orchestra, a post to be held concurrently with the one in San Francisco. He began his office in Boston in the grand manner in October 1973 with a brilliant performance of Berlioz' *The Damnation of Faust.* When he brought both the orchestra and the Berlioz work to New York on October 10, Miles Kastendieck wrote in the New York *Post:* "In the course of the two-and-a-quarter-hour work, he clearly defined his conductorial style as rhythm-based, energetic and brilliant." Early in 1976 Ozawa made his first tour of Europe with the Boston Symphony with three weeks of appearances in eleven cities in six countries.

With his second wife, the former Vera Ilyan, a Eurasian, and their two children, Ozawa occupied a house on San Francisco's Twin Peaks that provided a view of the city's three famous bridges. (His first wife was Kyoko Edo, concert pianist.) Besides shuttling regularly from San Francisco to Boston to fill his directorial commitments to both symphony orchestras, Ozawa continued to circle the globe in guest performances. During the summer of 1974 he made his debut at Covent Garden in London with Tchaikovsky's *Eugene Onegin.*

The responsibilities of serving as the music director of two of America's major symphony orchestras finally proved too onerous. During the summer of 1975 Ozawa announced his resignation as music director of the San Francisco Symphony. This, however, did not altogether end his affiliation with that orchestra since he accepted the post of music adviser for the 1976–1977 season and stood ready to spend ten weeks in San Francisco as guest conductor.

Pachmann

With his family expanded by the birth of a son, Ozawa found a new home in Brookline, Massachusetts, just ten minutes from Symphony Hall in Boston. Ozawa is not only tolerant to, but interested in, jazz and rock, and listens to it whenever he can, both on records and in public performances. Away from music his interests include skiing (in snow and on water), photography, golf, squash, tennis, and Italian food. In a New York *Times* article Donal Henahan described him as a "flamboyantly casual dresser, his outfits running to the turtleneck, the dashiki, the smock and the accessories popularized by the young in the nineteen-sixties."

In June 1971 the University of San Francisco awarded him an honorary doctorate in music, and in June 1972 the Japan Art Academy gave him one of its awards in recognition of his contributions to the arts.

ABOUT: Hi-Fi, May 1968; High Fidelity/Musical America, May 1968; Life, February 1969; New York Times, July 16, 1967, August 28, 1975; Saturday Review, September 27, 1969; Show, May 1963.

VLADIMIR DE PACHMANN

Vladimir de Pachmann

1848–1933

Vladimir de Pachmann, pianist, may most often be remembered for his eccentric stage behavior; but his contemporaries, while lamenting his antics and shenanigans, regarded him as second to none in the performance of Chopin's music. He was born in Odessa in the Ukraine on July 27, 1848. His father, a university professor, was an excellent amateur violinist who before settling in Russia had lived in Vienna where he had had personal contacts with some of the leading musicians, including Beethoven and Weber. From his father Vladimir received his first music instruction. He entered the Vienna Conservatory at eighteen and became a piano pupil of Joseph Dachs. For two years he remained at the conservatory and he won a gold medal. In 1869 he returned to Russia to make his first professional appearances. Though these were successful, he withdrew from the concert stage for eight years, to devote himself to an extended period of study, self-evaluation, and maturing. He resumed con-

Pachmann: pȧκ′ mȧn

cert activity in 1877 with recitals in many of Germany's principal cities, once again to receive the approbation of critics and audiences and once again to be beset by self-doubts. He went into a second period of retirement, this time for two years. Then, in 1880, with three concerts in Vienna and three more in Paris, all of them extraordinarily well received, he finally gained the assurance to continue concertizing without any further sustained interruptions until virtually the end of his life. The modesty and the lack of self-confidence of earlier years was replaced by a super-egotism. "Liszt," he once remarked, "he play very well, very well. But me, I play like a god." At a Busoni concert he called Busoni the world's greatest performer of Bach and himself the world's greatest performer of Chopin. He regarded Leopold Godowsky as the world's second greatest living pianist, leaving no doubt as to whom he placed in first position. He once insulted an interviewer who dared to remain seated during the conversation instead of being on bended knee.

On May 20, 1882, he made a sensational debut in London where many years later (1916) he was given the Beethoven medal by the Royal Philharmonic Orchestra. In Denmark in 1885 during a tour he was made Knight of the Order of Dannebrog. His first American tour took place in 1891 and he made many tours of the United States after that, the last one taking place in 1924–1925.

Glancing through the New York *Times* reviews by Richard Aldrich of de Pachmann's per-

606

formances the reader is made aware of the pianist's positive attributes. "As a worker of magical spell . . . there is no one like him," Aldrich wrote after a New York recital on November 8, 1904. Following de Pachmann's New York concert on April 14, 1908, he commented: "His tone, as it always has·been, was of a beautiful quality, and the delicacy of his playing, the shades of his pianissimos, exquisite." And a concert on October 21, 1911, led Aldrich to write: "He still commands all his old marvel of 'touch,' his old magic of delicate, filmy iridiscent tone, of sighing pianissimo, of purling, rippling passages, of clear articulation, to transform the piano into a celestial instrument."

To Arthur Symons, the English literary critic and writer, de Pachmann gives the listener "not states of soul or of temperament, not interpretations, but echoes. He gives you the notes in their own atmosphere where they live for him an individual life which has nothing to do with emotions or ideas."

But Richard Aldrich, as well as many other critics, also could find much in de Pachmann's playing to condemn. Apparently he was quixotic in the way he changed tempi, distorted rhythm, and chopped up phrases. He did not hesitate to rewrite a masterwork when it suited his fancy. "Yesterday," wrote Richard Aldrich, "he played what was called on the program Beethoven's Sonata in C major, Op.53. To those who had heard this sonata before, the music coming from under the pianist's fingers must have sounded like a novelty. In fact, Mr. de Pachmann almost composed a new andante movement out of the rondo."

Yet, when all subtractions were made, he was —when he played Chopin, and especially Chopin's miniatures—in a class all his own. "Probably nobody plays Chopin's music more nearly as Chopin himself played it, in scale of conception and quality and subtlety of tone," Richard Aldrich added.

But when audiences crowded the auditoriums to hear him play, particularly in the closing decades of his career, it was not so much to hear him play Chopin as to enjoy his eccentricities on the stage. He would grimace, make elaborate gestures of the body, and verbalize so many comments about his playing during the performance that Bernard Shaw was once led to report: "Mr. Vladimir de Pachmann gave his well-known pantomimic performance, with accompaniments by Chopin." De Pachmann was not beyond calling the audience's attention to the beauty of his tone or phrase or pianissimo without interrupting the flow of his hands on the keyboard. He even descended to vaudeville antics. Harold C. Schonberg describes one of these in *The Great Pianists:* "His struggles with the ups and downs of the piano stool were legendary. One of his tricks was to raise it, lower it, fiddle around with the controls until the audience was desperate. Then he would rush into the wings and come out with a large book, placing it on the seat. No good. Then he would rip out one page, put the book on the seat and smile beatifically at the audience. Now he was comfortable."

He carried his eccentricities into his off-stage behavior. He wore his hair in the style of Liszt and insisted that his shabby gown, socks, and gloves had once belonged to Chopin. He avoided any kind of exercise, and "all the fresh air I want comes through the window. . . . And I am seventy-seven. But I do not expect everyone to follow my example, for, after all, I am de Pachmann, the unique."

In 1884 de Pachmann married Marguerite Oakey, an Australian pianist who had studied under him and who, after her marriage, occasionally concertized. They were divorced about a decade later.

Vladimir de Pachmann died in Rome on January 6, 1933.

ABOUT: Schonberg, H. C. The Great Pianists; Sorabji, K. S. Around Music.

Ignace Jan Paderewski

1860–1941

No pianist of the early twentieth century and few pianists since Liszt have so dominated the concert stage with both art and personality as did Ignace Jan Paderewski. His very name became a synonym for the ultimate in virtuoso appeal. He was born on November 18, 1860, in Kurylówka, in Podolia (Russian Poland), formerly a province of the old Polish republic, now in the Ukraine. His family were Polish patriots who dreamed of liberating their country from

Paderewski: pä dĕ rĕf' skĕ

Paderewski

IGNACE JAN PADEREWSKI

Russian rule. His father, Jan, an administrator of large estates, was active in secret nationalistic movements; his mother, Polixena Nowicka Paderewski (who died soon after Ignace's birth), had been born in exile, the daughter of a university professor banished from Poland to Siberia. From his very beginnings Paderewski was inspired by strong nationalistic ardor.

During the Revolution of 1863 the Paderewskis lost their possessions and moved on to Volhynia. There, as a young child, Ignace revealed an interest in the piano and began piano study with W. Runowski, a local violin teacher. One year later, he became a piano pupil of Piotr Sowiński, who was quick to perceive the unusual musical talent of his pupil. Ignace not only applied himself assiduously to his piano studies but also began writing small pieces for that instrument. Even as a child, he discovered and came to love the music of Chopin. This music became for him the voice of enslaved Poland. As he later wrote: "All was forbidden us—the language and faith of our fathers, our national dress, our songs, our poets. Chopin alone was not forbidden us. . . . In him we could still find the living breath of all that was prohibited. . . . He gave all back to us, mingled with the prayers of broken hearts, the revolt of fettered souls, the pain of slavery, lost Freedom's ache, the cursing of tyrants, the exultant songs of victory."

Despite his preoccupation with music, young Paderewski had a normal interest in outdoor sports: climbing trees, swimming, and riding horseback. As he later recalled, few things gave

him more delight than playing soldiers with his friends.

When he was twelve, Ignace gave his first concert, sharing the stage with his sister. Wealthy patrons became interested in him and subsidized a trip to Kiev where he heard his first concerts. These patrons also enabled young Paderewski to enter the Warsaw Conservatory in 1872 for more intensive musical training.

His first piano teacher at the Warsaw Conservatory discouraged him from concentrating on the piano. In spite of this he worked long and hard with Schlözer, Strobl, and Janota to master technique and repertory. He also studied theory with Gustav Roguski. As a member of the school orchestra, in which he played the trombone, he became involved in a dispute over rehearsals—he preferred spending his time working on the piano rather than playing in the orchestra. This brought about his suspension from the Conservatory for a single year, even though he had already won first prizes in piano and composition. In 1877 he toured the small cities of Russia in joint recitals with a fellow student, Ignacy Cielewicz, a violinist. Then, readmitted to the Conservatory, he spent three more years—"years of toil, pain and study" he described them—as a student of the piano, counterpoint, and composition. He also made important musical contacts through his meetings with such famous musicians as Hans von Bülow, Joseph Joachim, and Henri Wieniawski, whose performances affected him profoundly. In 1878 he was graduated with honors, and that year he was appointed instructor of the piano at the Conservatory. The post paid him less than twenty-five cents an hour. But it carried with it the fulfillment of a dream. Paderewski could marry Antonina Korsak, a piano student and classmate at the Conservatory, with whom he had fallen in love in his last year there.

The first year of Paderewski's marriage in 1880 was one of the happiest of his life. Away from the Conservatory he could spend his free hours developing himself as a pianist, as well as writing music; his first published piece, an Impromptu for the piano, appeared that year. With his young wife and with his music, life was complete. Then, in 1881, his wife died in childbirth.

Unable to remain in Warsaw where he had been so happy, he decided to go to Berlin for further music study, principally composition with Friedrich Kiel. He also applied himself industriously to the piano, often working at the keyboard twelve hours a day. His nerves finally gave way. After a year in Berlin, he returned to Warsaw and to his piano post at the Conservatory.

In Berlin he had moved in the company of many distinguished musicians, among whom were Richard Strauss, Eugène d'Albert, Pablo de Sarasate, and Anton Rubinstein. For Anton Rubinstein he performed his own Variations in A minor. What impressed Rubinstein more than the composition itself was Paderewski's pianism. He advised Paderewski to consider devoting himself seriously to becoming a concert artist. After one more visit to Berlin in 1883, Paderewski decided to accept Rubinstein's judgment. But feeling the need of more preparation he went to Vienna to study with Theodor Leschetizky, with funds provided him by Helena Modjeska, the Polish actress, who became his patroness.

Paderewski arrived in Vienna early in 1884 and auditioned for Leschetizky. "It is too late," the teacher told him. "Your fingers lack discipline. You can never become a great pianist because you wasted so much of your time studying things more pleasant for yourself, such as counterpoint and orchestration." But Leschetizky allowed himself to be influenced by the young man's entreaties and finally decided to accept him as a pupil—only on condition that Paderewski follow his instruction without questioning. For the next few months, Leschetizky subjected Paderewski to a rigid technical training in simple Czerny exercises and early Beethoven sonatas in which measure after measure was dissected and analyzed. For eight to ten hours a day Paderewski worked at the piano to acquire the technical facility Leschetizky demanded. Leschetizky, Paderewski once said, taught him more in a few lessons than he had learned in the whole preceding twenty-four years of his life.

There was a brief hiatus in this period of intensive study when (on Leschetizky's advice) he became professor of the piano at the Conservatory of Strasbourg for one year. Then Paderewski was back in Vienna working again with Leschetizky. In 1887 Leschetizky told Paderewski he was ready to launch his career. That autumn Paderewski gave a concert in Vienna with the singer Pauline Lucca, performing works by Beethoven and Chopin as well his own Variations.

His first success came a few months later in Paris, with a recital at the Salle Érard attended by many musicians, including Tchaikovsky, Gounod, Saint-Saëns, and the French conductors Édouard Colonne and Charles Lamoureux. Paderewski performed Beethoven's Variations in C minor and Liszt's *Hungarian Rhapsody No. 6,* among other works, and the audience responded most enthusiastically. Lamoureux and Colonne both came backstage to invite Paderewski to appear as soloist with their respective orchestras. A critic for one of the Parisian newspapers said of the concert: "He was always a master of himself. He phrases admirably, shades with simplicity, keeps measure with rigorous exactness yet never shows stiffness. He obtains a large sonority by attack and enforcement. He knows his effects beforehand, and yet in spite of this assurance he seems to play as if by inspiration."

After a second appearance in Paris, Paderewski returned to Vienna for still more study with Leschetizky. Then, early in 1889, he gave a recital in Vienna's Bösendorfer Saal. "That concert attracted a very large audience," he later recalled. "The critics of Vienna received me with great enthusiasm. Here is perhaps the moment that I may say they hailed me as a 'great star.' My career as a pianist was launched." He was also gaining recognition in Vienna as a composer when Anna Essipova-Leschetizky performed the world premiere of his Piano Concerto in A minor with the Vienna Philharmonic, Hans Richter conducting.

In the fall of 1889 he returned to Paris to give three concerts at the Exposition. He was the sensation of musical Paris, the center of interest at fashionable salons, the object of admiration among many musicians. For the next decade in a ground-floor apartment on avenue de Victor Hugo he made Paris his home.

On May 9, 1890, billed as "the lion of Paris," he made his debut in London. It did not go well. George Bernard Shaw, who was at that time known for his brilliant music criticism, complained: "The license of his tempo rubato goes beyond all reasonable limits . . . an immensely spirited young harmonious blacksmith." But in his next three appearances he won over the London public and critics, and an all-Chopin concert after that was completely sold out. A successful tour of the English provinces helped to make him as famous in England as he had become in Paris and Vienna.

Paderewski

His American debut took place in New York on November 17, 1891, when he performed his own Concerto in A minor and the Saint-Saëns Concerto in C minor with Walter Damrosch conducting. "He is one of those virtuosi to whom the keyboard has no hidden secrets," wrote James Gibbons Huneker after hearing this performance. "His technical equipment is perfect and is used in such an exquisitely musical fashion that the virtuoso merges ever into the artist and mere brutal display and brilliant charlatanry are totally absent. His ability hinges perilously on the gates of genius. He is a veritable artistic apparition, and with that supremely magnetic personality, graceful and exotic in appearance, he naturally scored a success that was stupendous."

He gave not one but three concerts with orchestra at Carnegie Hall in New York and an additional series of performances at New York's Madison Square Garden. After that he toured the country, giving over one hundred concerts, the first of many transcontinental tours he was to make during the next forty years. By the early part of the twentieth century he was the object of a public adulation no other pianist before him had known in the United States. People mobbed him everywhere. Women were hysterical in their adoration. They lined up outside the auditorium to kiss his hand. They crowded the steamship piers whenever he went to or left America. They hounded him for autographs and photographs. "He was," said Henry Charles Lahee in *Famous Pianists of Today and Yesterday,* "the victim of a greater amount of female adulation than any pianist since Liszt."

He commanded the highest fees then paid to a concert performer: three hundred thousand dollars for a three-month tour; ten million dollars during his career. He was publicized in the press more than any musician of his time. He was even the inspiration of a popular hit song in 1902: "Since Sister Nell Heard Paderewski Play." When he traveled, it was in the style befitting an Eastern potentate. He always used a private train which had all the comforts of a palatial home, including a private lighting and heating system so that it could be sidetracked and serve as Paderewski's private hotel. His entourage was made up of a butler, a special chef, a masseur, a private physician, a piano tuner, and several servants. It sometimes also included private detectives to protect him, and extra card players to make up a bridge foursome—bridge being a game that so fascinated him that he often played it all night.

His physical features became as famous as his name. His head, said Helena Modjeska, "looked like one of Botticelli's or Fra Angelico's angels [with] its aureole of profuse golden hair and almost feminine features. It was a majestic head above an ample throat. A high brow separated his mane of hair and his gentle blue eyes. He had high cheekbones and an assertive chin, and the merest suggestion of a beard over a strong chin."

When Paderewski returned to New York on March 25, 1905, after a three-year absence, to begin his sixth American tour, Richard Aldrich noted how he continued to exert "the same fascination that has been his ever since he first came to this country. . . . Every seat was occupied and several hundred people were accommodated on the stage. . . . He was demonstratively—and, it must be confessed, somewhat indiscriminately —applauded through the course of his recital. . . . At the close the familiar scene was reenacted of a rush by the more excitable to the platform." About Paderewski's piano art, Aldrich added: "He is still a wonderworker in color when he wishes to be. His tone he can make—when he will—of entrancing loveliness, of poignant expressiveness, and his singing of a phrase still has that lyric charm and emotional power that grips the listener and tugs hard at the heart strings."

In 1898 Paderewski married Helena Górska, Baroness von Rosen. By that time a man of considerable financial means, he acquired a permanent residence in Europe, his home when he was not on tour: the twenty-six-room Châlet de Riond-Bosson on Lake Geneva near Morges. A dozen servants attended to his wants and comforts. His daily life there has been described as follows: "Rising promptly at nine in the morning, he first of all reads his daily newspaper from cover to cover. After breakfasting on a roll and tea at ten-thirty he retires to practise until two-fifteen when lunch is served. His afternoons are spent walking about the grounds, smoking a few Eygptian cigarettes, which he imports from a Manhattan tobacconist, and reading books on history, philosophy and politics. From five to eight-thirty he plays the piano, then dines, and spends the evening at the nightly ritual of a bridge game. At ten-thirty he shuffles off to bed." Besides bridge, Paderewski found diversion by playing billiards or going to the movies.

After the death of his wife in 1934, he lived in Morges with his sister, his secretary, and a dozen or so servants.

In 1905 Paderewski developed a nervous condition which not only caused him acute physical pain in playing the piano but also brought about a revulsion for that instrument. He decided to retire temporarily from the concert stage and to turn to farming. This adventure proved so costly that he was compelled to return to the stage, despite his physical and psychological ailments. He performed in Switzerland, then in America. But playing the piano proved such a harrowing experience that he had to abandon his career once more.

His restless energy soon brought him into politics. Always a passionate Polish nationalist, he hurled himself into the struggle for his country's emancipation. In 1910 he made a speech in Cracow at the ceremony for the unveiling of the bronze monument commemorating the battle of Grünwald, and it was received so enthusiastically that he realized his appeal to an audience did not rest exclusively on his piano playing. However, pressing financial difficulties brought him back to concert work. Only his iron strength of will took him through the sometimes physical torture of concert tours. He siphoned much of his enormous income into Polish nationalist causes. He contributed one hundred thousand dollars to help erect a statue of King Jagiello to commemorate the 500th anniversary of the king's victory over the Teutonic Order in 1410. In the same year he donated another sixty thousand dollars to help build Memorial Hall in Warsaw during the centenary commemoration of Chopin's birth.

He also made considerable contributions to the Polish underground. Without his knowledge some of his money was used by the underground to finance an anti-Semitic journal in Warsaw. In 1913 Paderewski was denounced by Jewish organizations in the United States as an anti-Semite and a boycott of his concerts was instigated. At first Paderewski ignored these charges. But then, at the request of President Wilson, he denied publicly under oath that he harbored ill feeling against Jews or that he had been aware of the publication of the anti-Semitic journal. For a long time after that, apparently unjustifiable charges of anti-Semitism continued to be leveled against Paderewski on the strength of this 1913 episode.

He was host at a party at his home in Switzerland in 1914 when he heard that Europe was at war. He turned his fullest resources to helping his country. He gave concerts to raise funds for Polish victims of the war and used his influence to organize committees in Paris and London in aid of Poland. In 1915 he returned to the United States to raise money for his native land and to arouse the interest of the United States in Poland's liberation. "I have to speak about a country which is not yours, in a language which is not mine," he told his American listeners. For several years, while making his home in Paso Robles in California, he was indefatigable in touring the country in concerts whose proceeds went for Polish causes. He also made more than three hundred speeches on behalf of Poland. In the end his efforts bore fruit: It was largely through him that the freedom of Poland became the thirteenth of President Wilson's Fourteen Points for a just peace as outlined in his message to Congress on January 8, 1918.

When the new Polish state came into being in 1918, Paderewski served as his country's diplomatic representative in Washington, D.C. He returned to Poland in December 1918, and soon after that he was nominated Prime Minister and Minister of Foreign Affairs. On June 28, 1919, he was a signatory for Poland of the Versailles Treaty.

Then, feeling his country needed him no longer, he left politics to return to music. In 1922 he resumed his interrupted concertizing. On November 22 of that year he returned to Carnegie Hall for his first American concert appearance in five years. He had not been forgotten. The hall overflowed with admirers and colleagues. "Would Mr. Paderewski return with his technical powers so unimpaired that his sway would suffer no diminution?" inquired Richard Aldrich in his review in the New York *Times*. And he provided his own answer. "It need not be maintained that Mr. Paderewski had achieved the impossible and presented himself as he was in the plenitude of his powers. . . . It did not appear that his technical powers were unimpaired. . . . But it is more to the purpose to think of the beautiful and characteristic features of his playing: of his remarkable management of color and rich variety of tone; of his appealing and poignant cantabile; of his molding of melody, his exquisite delivery of the singing beauty of a phrase; of his moments of grandiose and eloquent power."

He continued concertizing not only in the United States but also in Europe; in 1922–1923 he gave a series of concerts in Europe for the benefit of the victims of World War I. In the spring of 1939 Paderewski—sick and old—undertook still another tour of the United States. Illness forced him to postpone his concert in Newark, New Jersey. A performance at Madison Square Garden also had to be postponed at the last minute because of a slight heart attack. He had to cancel the rest of that tour and return to Switzerland for rest and recuperation.

When Poland was invaded by the Nazi army in September 1939, Paderewski immediately announced he was ready to help his country in any way he could. His voice was loud and clear in condemning the rape of Poland by Nazi Germany. One of his addresses was transmitted around the free world by short-wave radio. On January 23, 1940, he was named in Paris the president of Poland's National Council, the Parliament of the government in exile.

He was back in the United States on November 6, 1940, to continue his efforts on behalf of his own country and of war-stricken Great Britain and Greece.

Ignace Jan Paderewski died in New York City, at his suite in the Buckingham Hotel, on June 29, 1941. His body lay in state at St. Patrick's Cathedral after which, by order of President Roosevelt, it was placed in a crypt in the Battleship Maine Memorial in Arlington National Cemetery. Paderewski had asked to be buried in the United States, but he had also requested that his heart be removed from his body and returned to Poland when that country was again free. The heart was placed in a Brooklyn, New York, undertaking establishment where it remained until 1953 when it was removed to the Cypress Hills Abbey Mausoleum.

Paderewski appeared in the motion picture *The Moonlight Sonata* (1936). He supervised an edition of the complete works of Chopin (1935–1940) and was coauthor with Mary Lawton of an autobiography covering his life to World War I, *The Paderewski Memoirs* (1938). Among his many compositions, besides those already mentioned, were an opera, *Manru,* introduced in Dresden, Germany, on May 29, 1901, and at the Metropolitan Opera in New York on February 14, 1902; the Symphony in B minor, written to commemorate the fortieth anniversary of the 1863 Revolution in Poland, first performed by the Boston Symphony on February 12, 1909; and numerous pieces for the piano, the most celebrated of which is the *Menuet à l'Antique* in G, the first of *Six Humoresques de Concert,* Op.14.

The Polish government decorated Paderewski posthumously with the Cross of Virtuti Militari, its highest military honor. While still alive he received numerous decorations, among them Commander of the Crown of Italy; Commander of the Order of Carlos Tercero from Spain; Grand Cross of the Legion of Honor from France; Grand Cordon of the Order of Leopold from Belgium; Grand Cross of the Order of Polonia Restituta from Poland; Grand Cross of the Order of the British Empire; Grand Cross of the Order of St. Maurice and St. Lazare from Italy. He was also the recipient of many honorary doctorates in music from universities in America and Europe.

In 1900 Paderewski established a fund of ten thousand dollars, the interest from which was to provide cash prizes once every three years for outstanding compositions by native-born Americans. The first awards were presented in 1902 to Henry Hadley, Horatio W. Parker, and Arthur Bird. Among the later recipients were Gardner Read and Wallingford Riegger.

ABOUT: Gronowicz, A. Paderewski, Pianist and Patriot; Kellogg, C. Paderewski; Landau, R. Ignace Paderewski: Musician and Statesman; Opienski, H. Paderewski; Paderewski, I. J. and Lawton, M. The Paderewski Memoirs; Strakacz, A. Paderewski as I Knew Him; Wolkowicz, I. Paderewski's Diamond Jubilee.

Paul Paray

1886–

Paul Marie Adolphe Charles Paray, conductor, was born in Le Tréport, France, on May 24, 1886, to Auguste and Hortense Picard Paray. His father, a businessman, was an excellent musician who played the organ in church and was the conductor of a local band in which Paul, as a child, played the drums. Though Paul displayed unusual talent for music, so much so that

Paray: på rā′

PAUL PARAY

as an outstanding interpreter of the music of Berlioz, Ravel, and César Franck, and in the twentieth century repertory. In 1928 he supplemented his activity with the Lamoureux Orchestra by conducting a season of concerts in Monte Carlo.

"He unquestionably possesses the genius of rhythm," wrote the French critic Dominique Sordet. "He directs with irresistible force. He has authority, clarity of vision, strength of will, and bigness of scope. ... He knows what he wants and he knows how to get what he wants."

In 1932 Paray was appointed principal conductor of the Concerts Colonne in Paris, succeeding Gabriel Pierné. For the next twenty years, as head of this symphonic organization, he was placed with the leading French conductors of his time. In these years he was gaining prominence outside France as well, first in guest appearances throughout the rest of Europe and then in the United States where he made his debut on July 24, 1939, leading a concert of all-French music at the Lewisohn Stadium in New York. "He proved himself to be a conductor of outstanding capacity," said a critic in the New York *Times*.

Paray was in Paris when World War II broke out. For a while he continued his musical activities there, but after the city was occupied by the Nazis he became allied with the Resistance movement. His wife, Yolande, also worked in the French underground, but for the sake of security neither he nor his wife knew the nature of the other's involvements. When in 1940 the Nazis changed the name of the Colonne Orchestra because its founder, Édouard Colonne, had been a Jew, Paray (a Catholic) resigned his post in protest. He vowed never again to conduct in Paris until it was liberated. In Marseilles, then still unoccupied, he led radio concerts. When that city came under Nazi domination, Paray went on to Lyons where once again he stood in defiance of the Nazis. On May 16 a concert of German music was given in Lyons conducted by Clemens Krauss. The following day, in the same hall, Paray led an orchestra in a program of French music; at the end of the concert he invited the audience to join the orchestra in "The Marseillaise." After that he went into voluntary exile in Monte Carlo, where he occasionally conducted opera performances.

With Paris liberated, Paray returned to Paris and to his former post with the Colonne Orches-

he was often referred to as "another Mozart," his father objected to his receiving musical training, not wishing him to become a professional musician. But a friend of the family overcame the father's resistance. Paul was entered in the choir school in Rouen. In 1903, in Rouen, he served as church organist.

In 1904 Paray was enrolled in the Paris Conservatory. For the next seven years he was a brilliant student of Xavier Leroux, Charles Lenepveu, and Paul Vidal. He won first prize in harmony in 1908, and in 1911 he received the coveted Prix de Rome for his cantata *Yanitza*. His three years at the Villa Medici as a Prix de Rome winner were important in his musical development.

With the outbreak of World War I, Paray was drafted into the French army. He fought at the front. Captured by the Germans, he was interned as a prisoner in Darmstadt until the war's end.

After the Armistice he returned to France. For a time he conducted the orchestra at the Casino de Cauterets. One of the members of this orchestra was so impressed by Paray's talent that he arranged for him to meet Camille Chevillard, conductor of the Concerts Lamoureux in Paris. To test Paray's ability, Chevillard assigned him a concert with the Lamoureux Orchestra on February 29, 1920. This went so well that he was appointed Chevillard's assistant. When Chevillard died in 1923, Paray became full-time conductor. In this post, which he retained for five years, Paray distinguished himself tra. At his first concert on October 22, 1944, he was welcomed as a hero. He remained principal conductor of this orchestra until 1952. In 1950 he received official recognition for his contributions to French music and to the war effort: He was elected a member of the Institut de France. He was later made Commander of the Legion of Honor.

Meanwhile, in 1945 Paray returned to the United States to appear as a guest conductor of the Boston Symphony and the Cincinnati Symphony. From 1949 to 1952 he was a guest conductor of the Pittsburgh Symphony, both in Pittsburgh and on tour.

When the Detroit Symphony, which had been disbanded in 1949, was reorganized in 1951, Paray was asked to make five guest appearances. The following season he resigned as principal conductor of the Colonne Orchestra in Paris to become permanent conductor, later music director, of the Detroit Symphony. In 1954 he toured the east coast with the orchestra. On October 18, 1956, he conducted the orchestra in a concert commemorating the opening of a new concert hall, the Ford Auditorium. On his program Paray presented his own choral work, *Joan of Arc Mass,* which he had written many years earlier to commemorate the five-hundredth anniversary of the martyrdom of Joan of Arc. This composition had received its world premiere under Paray's direction in Rouen in May 1931.

When Paray resigned as music director of the Detroit Symphony in 1963, he was given the honorary title Conductor Emeritus. It was understood that he would return every year for some guest appearances, but such an invitation had to wait seven and a half years. When Paray reappeared with the Detroit Symphony for a pair of concerts on August 14 and 16, 1975, at the Meadow Brook Music Festival, he provoked, as was reported in *Musical America,* "a demonstration such as this observer has seldom witnessed at a Detroit Symphony Orchestra concert, with shouts, whistles, wild hand-clapping and an applauding orchestra." Paul Paray was deeply touched. "It was absolutely beyond expectation," he said. "These two concerts are for me among the best souvenirs of my career."

Among Paray's compositions are two symphonies; a ballet, *Artémis Troublée,* introduced at the Paris Opéra on April 28, 1922; a *Fantaisie,* for piano and orchestra, first given in Paris on

March 25, 1923; and some chamber music and piano pieces.

Paray was twice married, the first time on December 18, 1918, to Marcelle Deliry, with whom he had four children, and the second time, on August 25, 1942, to Yolande Falck. The Parays live in Monte Carlo.

France made Paray Grand Officier of the Legion of Honor and Commandeur des Arts et des Lettres. He has been awarded the Grand-Croix de l'Ordre National du Mérite.

ABOUT: Landowski, W. L. Paul Paray; Stoddard, H. Symphony Conductors of the U.S.A.

Rose Pauly

1895–1975

Rose Pauly, soprano, was born in Eperjes, Hungary (now Prešov, Czechoslovakia), on March 15, 1895. After studying voice in Vienna with Rosa Papier-Paumgartner, she made her opera debut in 1918 as Desdemona with the Vienna State Opera. After a season in Hamburg, and several more in Gera and Karlsruhe, she joined the Cologne Opera in 1923. Her successes there for the next two seasons, followed by an equally successful year with the Mannheim Opera in 1926–1927, attracted the interest of Otto Klemperer. In 1927 Klemperer brought Pauly to the Kroll Opera in Berlin where he was music director. For the next four years Pauly was heard there in numerous major roles and in practically every important premiere mounted by that company. While serving as a member of the Kroll Opera, she made guest appearances with the Berlin State Opera and opera companies in Budapest and Paris.

From 1929 to 1939 she was a leading dramatic soprano of the Vienna State Opera where she was acclaimed for her performances in operas and music dramas by Mozart, Wagner, and Richard Strauss. Her popularity in Vienna brought her the honorary title *Kammersängerin.* But after the Nazi *Anschluss,* during a performance as Senta in *The Flying Dutchman* in 1939, she was hissed and booed because she was Jewish.

In 1933 Pauly made a noteworthy appearance

Pauly: pou′ lē

ROSE PAULY

at the Salzburg Festival as the Dyer's Wife in Strauss's *Die Frau ohne Schatten.* One year later, and again in 1937, she made an unforgettable impression on the audiences at the Salzburg Festival with her performances as Elektra in Strauss's opera (probably her most famous role) and as Donna Anna in *Don Giovanni.*

In Italy, where she was heard at most of its major opera houses, including La Scala in Milan and the Rome Opera, between 1935 and 1939, she was spoken of as "La Dusa Tedesca" ("The German Duse") and in the Hall of Fame at the Verdi Opera House in Trieste her portrait was hung between those of Eleanora Duse and Alexander Moissi.

Her American debut took place in New York on March 18, 1937, when she sang Elektra in a concert performance of the Strauss opera by the New York Philharmonic under Rodzinski. The final ovation was one of the most vociferous heard in Carnegie Hall since Toscanini's farewell concert there. Backstage, musicians came to congratulate her, among them Mary Garden, Grace Moore, Fritz Reiner, José Iturbi, Artur Bodanzky, and Edward Johnson.

"Rose Pauly proved herself the greatest and most dramatic singer in this part to have been heard in this country," wrote Olin Downes in the New York *Times.* "The music has not before been sung with such grandeur and feeling in this city. No previous incumbent of the part had Miss Pauly's vocal material, which is at the disposition of an artist of the most exceptional interpretative powers." "The astonishing feat she

accomplished," said Lawrence Gilman in the *Herald Tribune,* "was to concentrate in her impersonation, without benefit of costume or make-up or settings, and with suggestions of histrionic action, not only the terrific character conceived by Strauss, but the imaginative heart and center of the drama."

Less than a year later Pauly made her bow at the Metropolitan Opera on January 7, 1938, once again as Elektra and repeated her triumph of the previous season. Hers was once again, as Lawrence Gilman noted in the *Herald Tribune,* "the superb impersonation. As before, the feature of her performance was the clarity and eloquence with which it laid bare the essential nobility of the character and the greatness of the motivation."

Still in 1938, as Elektra, she was introduced both to Covent Garden in London and, on October 24, to the San Francisco Opera. Pauly always considered Elektra not only one of her best roles but also one of the most exacting. "It takes the very heart out of me," she once explained. "There is never a light moment. All is tragedy, always the one thought to kill the mother. It is a terrific mental and physical strain when it is done right, and each time it leaves me completely *elektrisiert.*"

She also proved highly successful as Salome in Strauss's opera and was one of the first Salomes anywhere to do her own dancing. When she appeared as Salome in Cairo, a cabaret proprietor tried to engage her for his nightclub as a belly dancer and was unable to understand why she should turn down his munificent offer.

Her repertory of about forty operas included leading soprano roles in major German, French, and Italian operas. She appeared in virtually all the principal Wagnerian dramatic soprano roles, and in most of the better known Mozartean roles. (In *Don Giovanni* she sang not only the part of Donna Anna, but also the roles of Donna Elvira and Zerlina.) Besides the works in the general repertory she also appeared in such twentieth century operas as Berg's *Wozzeck,* Hindemith's *Neues vom Tage,* Max von Schillings's *Mona Lisa,* Franz Schreker's *Der Ferne Klange,* and Eugène d'Albert's *Tiefland.*

She left the Metropolitan Opera after the 1939 –1940 season. In 1939 she appeared at the Teatro Colón in Buenos Aires, and after the end of World War II she was heard not only there but also at Covent Garden and in opera houses in

Pavarotti

Germany and Austria. Her last appearance on the operatic stage was at the Teatro Colón in 1948 as the Marschallin in *Der Rosenkavalier,* a part she had never sung and which she had to learn in three days.

Following her retirement from the operatic stage, Pauly settled in Israel where for a time she taught singing and involved herself in some of Israel's musical activities, including the promotion of children's concerts. Her summers were spent in southern Germany, after 1965 usually at Baden-Baden for the water cure.

Pauly was twice married. Her first husband was a hotel proprietor. In 1931 her daughter's life was saved by a surgeon of Czech background, Dr. Fleischner, with whom she fell in love. After her divorce from her first husband, Pauly married Dr. Fleischner in 1938 in New York City. He died in 1965.

Rose Pauly died in Herzlia, Israel, on December 14, 1975.

ABOUT: Opera News, February 27, 1971, February 28, 1976.

LUCIANO PAVAROTTI

Luciano Pavarotti

1935–

Luciano Pavarotti, dubbed "the king of the high C's," is internationally recognized as one of the greatest Italian bel canto singers of our time, noted for the power and quality of his voice, its perfect pitch and purity of tone. He was born in Modena, Italy, on October 12, 1935. On the same street in Modena—as infants they shared the same wet nurse—lived Mirella Freni who also became an opera singer and sang opposite Pavarotti in many of his debuts and other performances. "Everybody in Modena sang," Pavarotti says. This included his father, Fernando, a baker who had a good tenor voice and sang in the chorus of the opera production mounted annually with local talent. The sounds of Caruso, Gigli, and Björling on records filled Pavarotti's home. "I was in the middle of it," he recalls. Luciano received his first singing lessons when he was four from his father. He sang in Modena's children's chorus and in local churches. His father dreamed of making him into a profession-

al singer, but Luciano's mother, Adele Venturi Pavarotti, who worked in the same tobacco factory as Mirella Freni's mother, wanted him to study accounting. Falling in line with his mother's thinking that he should train himself for a profession that could bring a regular income, Luciano decided to become a teacher. After completing grade school, he took the teacher-training program at the Scuolo Magistrale in Modena. At school he became an all-around athlete and was particularly interested in soccer. "I played ten hours a day, every position, from goal-keeper to forward wing." Upon graduation in 1955 he taught for two years in elementary school. "I taught everything—music, history, mathematics. I was very strict. I always loved children but they need discipline."

He had not lost his love for singing, however. While he was still teaching, he became a member of the Rossini Chorus which competed in an international choral Eisteddfodd in Wales and captured first prize. By 1957, encouraged by his father, Pavarotti decided to leave teaching to others and to begin developing his voice. While earning his living as an insurance salesman, he studied voice with Arrigo Pola and with Ettore Campogalliani. At this time he was pursuing romance as well as vocal studies—the girl was Adua Veroni, whom he had met when both were attending the Scuola Magistrale. They were married in 1961.

That same year Pavarotti won first prize in the Concorso Internationale in Reggio Emilia. This entitled him to a debut appearance in that city's

---

Pavarotti: pä vä rôt′ tē

Teatro Municipale as Rodolfo in *La Bohème*. Rodolfo has been his favorite role since then; this is the role he usually tried to choose whenever he was later called upon to make his debut in an opera house. His performance in Modena was so well received that he was invited to appear in other Italian opera houses, including major companies in Venice and Palermo.

Pavarotti made his first appearance outside Italy in 1963, as Edgardo in *Lucia di Lammermoor* in Amsterdam and several other cities in Holland. Performances as the Duke in *Rigoletto* in Vienna came after that, followed by his debut in Dublin. In September 1963 he went for the first time to the stage of Covent Garden to substitute for Giuseppe Di Stefano as Rodolfo. He was such a success that he was asked to make two major appearances over television. He was also invited to audition for Richard Bonynge, the conductor who was also Joan Sutherland's husband. Bonynge was then selecting a company to tour Australia with Sutherland. He liked Pavarotti's singing and hired him. But a back condition forced Sutherland to postpone that tour, which took place three years later. "That was my luckiest moment," he recalls. "I would not have been ready sooner."

The last months of 1963 took Pavarotti to Spain, Poland, Hungary, and Czechoslovakia. In 1964 he returned to England, this time to sing Idamante in Mozart's *Idomeneo* at the Glyndebourne Festival (one of the rare instances in which he was heard outside the Italian repertory). He was back in Covent Garden in 1965 as Alfredo in *La Traviata* opposite Renata Scotto's Violetta, and as Elvino in *La Sonnambula* to Sutherland's Amina.

He made his first appearance in the United States in 1966 in Miami, Florida, singing Edgardo to Sutherland's Lucia di Lammermoor. The postponed Sutherland tour to Australia followed. For four months during the summer of 1966 he toured with Sutherland's company in *La Sonnambula, La Traviata,* and *L'Elisir d'Amore*. In addition to gaining valuable experience in performing the roles of Elvino, Alfredo, and Nemorino, Pavarotti gained from this tour valuable hints on breathing from the diaphragm by watching and studying Sutherland's performances. Returning to Modena from this tour, he received from his native city the Principessa Carlotta Prize for his contribution to the arts and the Medaglia d'Oro Giuseppe Verdi in

Brescia. Later in 1966 he made a highly successful debut at La Scala in Milan as Rodolfo to Mirella Freni's Mimi, with Herbert von Karajan conducting, and returned to Covent Garden as Tonio in *The Daughter of the Regiment* (with Sutherland in the title role). Since the first act aria and cabaletta in *The Daughter of the Regiment* has a succession of nine high C's in a sixty-second period, every tenor since Donizetti's time has transposed this music to a lower key. Pavarotti insisted upon following the composer's written demands. At the general rehearsal he tried for the first time to negotiate the difficult aria and cabaletta in its original key. When he finished, the men in the orchestra gave him an ovation. Since then he has always sung this aria the way Donizetti wrote it.

That performance was a personal triumph for him, and so were three other appearances in Italy in 1967: at the Rome Opera where he opened the season as the Duke of Mantua in *Rigoletto;* at La Scala where he was heard as Tybaldo in Bellini's *I Capuletti ed i Montecchi;* and in Milan again when he participated in a performance of Verdi's Requiem conducted by Herbert von Karajan to commemorate the centenary of Toscanini's birth.

His first major successes in the United States took place with the San Francisco Opera, where in 1967 he made his debut as Rodolfo. With the same company he brought down the house one year later as Edgardo in *Lucia di Lammermoor.* "From the Scene two love duet, 'Ah verranno a te sull' aure,' through the explosive curse aria, to the scene in the graveyard where so many tenors lie buried, Pavarotti carried the opera on his shoulders," reported the San Francisco critic Robert Commanday, "acting with a fervor and agility that matched his vocal instrument. . . . Pavarotti is hard to believe even when you hear him—a phenomenon. Singing Edgardo's role in the original key . . . no note seems too high or phrase too demanding for him to conquer thrillingly. He colors and shapes the phrases with tremendous feeling, adding all and more of those imponderable extra qualities the performer must give to Donizetti."

On November 23, 1968, Pavarotti made his debut at the Metropolitan Opera as Rodolfo. Since he was then suffering from Hong Kong flu he wanted to postpone his performance, but Rudolf Bing, the general manager, insisted upon his appearing. Pavarotti himself was dissatisfied with his singing that evening, but the critics thought otherwise. "Pavarotti had them eating out of his hand," wrote Peter G. Davis in the New York *Times*. "Any tenor who can toss off high C's with such abandon, successfully negotiate delicate diminuendo effects and attack Puccinian phrases so fervently is going to win over any *La Bohème* audience." During his second appearance as Rodolfo, still victimized by the flu, Pavarotti knew, as he later conceded, "I was in trouble, so I stopped at the end of the second act and went home to Modena." He remained silent for two and a half months to allow his voice to recover.

He did not go back to New York for two years. He did, however, remain active in Europe, enlarging both his repertory and his fame. He opened the 1969 season of the Rome Opera in a revival of *I Lombardi*. That year he was awarded the Premio Nazionale Numero Uno in Florence and made several significant recordings, including one of the rarely heard *Beatrice di Tenda* of Bellini with Sutherland. Over the Italian radio he was heard in a performance of *Un Ballo in Maschera*.

He returned to the Metropolitan Opera as Edgardo in *Lucia di Lammermoor* on October 15, 1970. One week later he was heard as Alfredo in *La Traviata*. This time his voice was at its prime. In 1971 he appeared in the Metropolitan Opera three-week spring festival of Verdi's operas, and towards the end of the year he was heard on two successive nights, first in *Lucia di Lammermoor,* and then (as a substitute for Nicolai Gedda) in *La Bohème*. He reached a new peak in popularity on February 17, 1972, at the Metropolitan Opera as Tonio in *The Daughter of the Regiment*. "God has kissed his vocal cords," wrote Harold C. Schonberg in the New York *Times*. "This is a voice on the Gigli order, though used with more taste and musicianship. . . . Pavarotti's last act romance was as stylistic an example of bel canto as one is going to encounter from any tenor today."

Later roles at the Metropolitan Opera included the Duke in *Rigoletto,* Riccardo in *Un Ballo in Maschera,* Nemorino in *L'Elisir d'Amore,* Arturo in the first revival of *I Puritani* at the Metropolitan Opera since 1918 (February 25, 1976), and Fernando in the first Metropolitan Opera production of *La Favorita* since 1905 (February 21, 1978). He was Rodolfo when *La Bohème* became the first live performance to be telecast from the stage of the Metropolitan Opera, on March 15, 1977.

When, on October 11, 1976, Pavarotti helped to open a new season for the Metropolitan Opera as Manrico in *Il Trovatore,* he entered a new phase in his career, passing from solely lyrical roles to a dramatic one. (He had previously sung Manrico in San Francisco in the fall of 1975.) He went on from there to sing Cavaradossi in *Tosca* in Chicago in November 1976 and, later that winter, the Calaf in *Turandot* (a part he had sung for the first time anywhere on London records).

In October 1973 Pavarotti was starred in a new production of *La Favorita* at the San Francisco Opera. One month later he made his debut with the Chicago Lyric Opera as Rodolfo, and in September 1975 he made his debut at the Paris Opéra.

Pavarotti has distinguished himself in roles other than those already commented upon: Pinkerton in *Madama Butterfly,* Des Grieux in *Manon,* Rodolfo in *Luisa Miller,* and Macduff in Verdi's *Macbeth*.

He gave his first song recital anywhere at the Garden State Arts Center in New Jersey in June 1972. On February 18, 1973, he made his recital debut in New York. "Mr. Pavarotti may not be the most subtle recitalist as yet," wrote Donal Henahan in the New York *Times,* "but he is a lovable one. . . . His debut proved that he not only has the voice but also the audience-appeal to attract . . . fanatic following." Pavarotti appeared in a song recital at the Salzburg festival during the summer of 1976, and in 1977 he toured Japan in recitals. On February 12, 1978, he became the first singer to give a recital on the stage of the new Metropolitan Opera House at the Lincoln Center for the Performing Arts, a performance that was telecast live throughout the United States through the facilities of the Public Broadcasting Service. (The only other concert artist to give a recital on that stage was Vladimir Horowitz.)

Home for Pavarotti, his wife, and their three daughters is a three-family house in Modena. Because of his crowded singing-schedule he can stay there only a few weeks each year. The rest of the time the Pavarottis are traveling. While in New York they occupy a hotel suite. Vacations (usually one month a year) are spent in Pesaro, Italy, by the sea.

When Pavarotti is particularly pleased with

one of his performances he immediately telephones his parents in Modena. Pavarotti's mother has never heard him sing in an actual opera performance, since she suffers from a serious heart condition. The only time she heard him sing on the stage was at a rehearsal of *La Bohème*. The strain upon her was so severe that she had to be rushed to a hospital before the rehearsal was over.

A huge man, Pavarotti keeps physically fit by attending a gymnasium regularly when he is in New York, swimming, boating, taking long walks, bicycling, and playing tennis. He has a voracious appetite, but enjoys food best when he cooks it himself, which he does with the skill of a master chef. When he is not performing, he practices about six hours a day; and when he is learning a new part he frequently takes a tape recorder with him to bed. For diversion he watches movies on television, plays poker, studies languages, enjoys the company of his close friends, and indulges in practical jokes.

"I am the most religious man," he confided to Dorle J. Soria in an interview in *High Fidelity/ Musical America*. "Last Christmas [1975] I was near to die. My plane crashed and broke in two when it landed in Milan. It was miracle—we were all saved, saved by God. My vocal cords are His gift. I must take good care of them." He also admitted to being superstitious. Before each appearance he searches for and must find a bent nail which he then conceals in his costume. "If you see someone on the floor it is me looking for that nail. If I do not find it I do not sing. Straight nail is no good." "Pavarotti, of course, always finds his nail," adds Soria. "The management or friends or veteran stagehands see to it."

"You want to know the hardest thing about a singer?" he once asked another of his interviewers. The reply to his own query was: "It is to sacrifice yourself every moment of your life, not one exclusion. For example, if it is raining, don't go out, eat this, do this, sleep ten hours a day. It is not a very, very free life. You cannot jump on a horse. You cannot go to swim. If you are singing you cannot go on the boat. I have a beautiful boat. I cannot go on the boat."

ABOUT: Breslin, H. ed. The Tenors. *Periodicals*—Esquire, November 1972; High Fidelity/Musical America, June 1976; Life, April 1972; New York Times, February 13, 1972, October 8, 1976; New York Times Magazine, February 12, 1978; New Yorker, October 15, 1973, February 27, 1978; Opera News, December 21, 1968, January 6, 1973, October-November 1976; Saturday Review, February 9, 1973.

Sir Peter Pears

1910–

Peter Neville Luard Pears, tenor, was born at Farnham, Surrey, England, on June 22, 1910, the youngest of seven children. His father, Arthur, was a builder of roads, bridges, and canals who spent a good part of his time traveling in India, Africa, and South America; Peter did not see his father for years at a time. Peter's mother, Jessie Luard Pears, also did a good deal of traveling abroad. Denied parental supervision, he spent his boyhood years at the Grange School in Crowborough, a boarding school where he played cricket and was allowed to develop his musical ability. He had been studying the piano from the time he was five. At the Grange School he developed into a proficient performer, while at the same time revealing a marked gift for singing.

From 1923 to 1928 Peter attended Lancing College, where he played in the school orchestra. In 1928 and 1929 he concentrated on studying singing for the first time, at Keble College, Oxford. During this period he served for a time as an organist at Hertford College, Oxford. For four years, from 1929 to 1933, he was back at the Grange School, this time as director of music.

By 1933 he had permanently discarded any thoughts of satisfying his parents' desire that he become a clergyman. Instead, he entered the Royal College of Music in 1933 to study voice and to specialize in opera with Dawson Freer. At the college he made his first operatic appearance: in Delius's *A Village Romeo and Juliet* conducted by Sir Thomas Beecham, and then as Belmonte in *The Abduction from the Seraglio*.

Upon leaving the Royal College of Music, Pears continued his vocal study privately with Dawson Freer and also with a world-renowned singer of *Lieder*, Elena Gerhardt. He also received coaching in operatic roles from Clytie Hine Mundy and others.

In the mid-1930s he embarked upon a professional career as a singer, joining the BBC Singers, later becoming a member of the New

Pears: pērz

Pears

SIR PETER PEARS

English Singers which specialized in the contrapuntal music of the English Tudor period. With the New English Singers he toured Europe from 1936 to 1939 and the United States in 1936 –1937.

As a singer in oratorios, in which he later gained international fame, Pears made his first important appearance in Brighton, England, in 1935, performing the solo part of the Evangelist in *Bach's Passion According to St. Matthew* (a singing part for which he gained fame throughout Europe in later years). Three years later he gathered further praise as a recitalist in his first joint concert. with Benjamin Britten, then already one of England's most promising composers—Pears was eventually to become the foremost vocal interpreter of Britten's music. They had met for the first time as fellow students at the Royal College of Music and became close friends by the time they left the college in 1934.

Early in 1939, just before the outbreak of World War II, Britten—an avowed pacifist— went to the United States, and Pears went with him. They spent the first three years of the war in Canada, in Brooklyn, New York, in Amityville, Long Island, and in California. In New York they continued to give joint recitals, their programs ranging from old English music to the contemporary scene, including Britten's first compositions for the voice. In 1939 Pears was also heard in Carnegie Hall in a program made up of Bach cantatas conducted by Otto Klemperer.

Britten and Pears returned to England in March 1942 to help their war-stricken country in every way their pacificism would allow, but mostly through the making of music. In London in 1942 Pears made his opera debut in the title role in *The Tales of Hoffmann* with the New Opera Company. He then joined Sadler's Wells, touring the English provinces in operatic performances. With this company he was heard in a variety of roles including the Duke in *Rigoletto,* Rodolfo in *La Bohème,* Alfredo in *La Traviata,* Tamino in *The Magic Flute,* and Ferrando in *Così fan Tutte.*

When Britten returned to England he brought back with him from America a commission from the Koussevitzky Foundation to write an opera. In writing that opera, as in his subsequent ones, he had Pears in mind; and Pears was the one who sang the title role when *Peter Grimes* was introduced at Sadler's Wells in London on June 7, 1945. As the first new opera performed in London since the beginning of World War II, and as the opera which reopened the Sadler's Wells Theater after the war, *Peter Grimes* was a triumph. It established not only Britten's fame as a composer but also Pears's as a singer—and particularly as a performer in Britten's music.

In 1946, with Britten, the painter John Piper, and the author Eric Crozier, Pears helped to organize the English Opera Group to present chamber operas, past and present, in the English provinces. Britten wrote *The Rape of Lucretia* for this group, and with Pears assuming the role of Male Chorus it was introduced at Glyndebourne on July 12, 1946. On June 20, 1947, once again at Glyndebourne, the English Opera Group presented Britten's comic opera *Albert Herring,* with Pears in the title role. Besides touring England and other parts of Europe, the English Opera Group was responsible for the creation and the artistic direction of the Aldeburgh Festival in England in 1948, a summer festival on the Suffolk seacoast for which Britten served as artistic director. Both Pears and Britten made their permanent home in Aldeburgh, and to the Aldeburgh Festival they devoted a great deal of their creativity through the years.

In 1946 Pears and Britten resumed the giving of recitals of great song literature throughout Europe and repeated visits to the festivals of Salzburg, Edinburgh, and Lucerne. They also made numerous tours of the United States. These concerts revealed Pears's gift in song literature as well as the unanimity of spirit and style between Pears and Britten in the projection of this music. "His phrasing and enunciation are flawless," wrote Raymond Ericson in the New York *Times* after hearing a performance of Schumann's *Dichterliebe* in October 1969. "But these are only the parts that contribute to the whole, for it is his ability to create a dreamlike atmosphere in one song, to project the full intensity of anguish in another that makes the great interpreter." These tours had to end when Britten suffered a serious heart attack, but Pears continued his career in the concert hall with the collaboration of other artists such as Murray Perahia, pianist, and Julian Bream, guitarist.

As a performer in opera—and not exclusively in Britten's operas—Pears made his debut at Covent Garden in 1948. He appeared there in *Idomeneo, Die Meistersinger,* and Sir William Walton's *Troilus and Cressida.* Pears also made numerous guest appearances at La Scala in Milan, the Vienna State Opera, and principal opera houses in Zurich, Munich, and Rome. Among his favorite roles have been those in Mozart's operas, particularly Tamino in *The Magic Flute* and Ferrando in *Così fan Tutte.*

But it is principally with Britten's operas that the name of Peter Pears is associated. The main tenor roles in all of Britten's operas were written with Pears in mind, and Pears performed in their world premieres. After *The Rape of Lucretia* and *Albert Herring,* Pears assumed the title role in *Billy Budd* when it was produced at Covent Garden on December 1, 1951. After that Pears was heard in the world premieres of *Gloriana* (Covent Garden, June 8, 1953), *Turn of the Screw* (Venice, September 14, 1954), *A Midsummer Night's Dream,* for which Pears helped prepare the libretto (Aldeburgh Festival, June 11, 1960), *Owen Wingrave,* an opera for television (BBC-TV, May 16, 1971), and *Death in Venice* (Aldeburgh Festival, June 16, 1973).

The most exacting role Pears sang was that of Gustav von Aschenbach in *Death in Venice* which kept him on the stage throughout the entire two and a half hours of the opera and made great demands on Pears's singing and acting abilities. It was in this role that Pears, then sixty-four years old, made his debut at the Metropolitan Opera in New York on October 20, 1974, when *Death in Venice* received its American premiere. Pears's performance drew the highest praise from the New York critics. Harold C. Schonberg, writing in the New York

Times, called Pears's conception of the role of Gustav von Aschenbach "thoughtful and even noble." In *High Fidelity Magazine,* Peter G. Davis wrote: "The composer has provided his longtime friend and associate with a tour de force that Pears . . . performs with astonishing vocal virtuosity. Although the role of Aschenbach is a long one . . . he never flags or fails to project the full musical weight of the vocal line. . . . Future interpreters of Aschenbach will doubtless find themselves in the unenviable position of being compared to Pears for years to come."

Ten years before Pears achieved this, perhaps his greatest personal triumph, he had thought his career was over. He has explained: "I had a very bad season and did not sing very well, and I thought the time had come to think about stopping. But then I took a sabbatical and got a new voice teacher and things improved. I started singing again and it seemed all right, and I just kept on." The new teacher was Lucie Manen, with whom he studied for several years. "She's done wonders for me," he says.

Britten had Pears in mind when he wrote compositions for tenor, or vocal compositions utilizing a tenor voice. The most important of these is *A War Requiem,* in whose world premiere at St. Michael's Cathedral in Coventry, Pears participated on May 30, 1962. Among the many other nonoperatic compositions Britten wrote for Pears have been *Les Illuminations, Seven Sonnets of Michelangelo, Serenade for Tenor Solo, Horn and Strings, The Holy Sonnets of John Donne, Winter Words, Cantata Misericordium,* the five Canticles *Sacred and Profane,* and the three church parables *Curlew River, The Burning Fiery Furnace,* and *The Prodigal Son.*

As long as Britten was alive Pears shared the Red House in Aldeburgh with him, and an apartment in London. Pears's diversions include cooking and collecting paintings. In 1957 Queen Elizabeth II named him Commander of the Order of the British Empire and in 1977 he was knighted. He has received honorary doctorates in music from the universities of Cambridge, York, and Sussex. He is a Fellow of the Royal College of Music and the Royal Academy of Music in London, and a member of the Royal Swedish Academy.

ABOUT: White, E. W. Benjamin Britten. *Periodicals*

Peerce

—New York Times, November 13, 1974, November 2, 1975; Opera News, January 10, 1970.

Jan Peerce

1904—

Jan Peerce (originally Jacob Pincus Perelmuth), tenor, was born on New York City's East Side on June 3, 1904. He was the son of orthodox Jewish parents; his father was a caterer. Jan received his academic schooling at P.S. 62 and De Witt Clinton High School in New York. As a boy he sang in the choir of the Attorney Street Synagogue. Since the violin seemed basic to the cultural life of a Jewish family, Jan began taking lessons on it when he was nine. Music as a profession was never considered; Jan's father hoped his son would become a doctor. But music was a major preoccupation in Jan's boyhood. When he was fourteen he joined a drummer and a pianist to form a jazz trio in which he played the violin and occasionally sang the vocal solos. A year later he joined Local 802 of the Musicians Union so that he might get employment as a musician. With a three-piece combo he found a job as violinist in the Catskill Mountains of New York. For the next fourteen summers he kept returning to the so-called Borscht circuit as violinist and singer. During the winters he supported himself by performing in cabarets, with dance orchestras, in theaters, and at private concerts.

The idea of becoming a doctor was abandoned after he had spent two years in medical school. By this time Jan suspected that a richer future lay ahead for him as a singer than as a violinist. He began taking vocal lessons with Emilio Roxas, but he was still playing the violin and singing choruses with such popular orchestras as those of George Olsen and Vincent Lopez.

He was performing and singing with an orchestra at the Hotel Astor in New York for the golden anniversary dinner for Weber and Fields in September 1932 when he was heard by S. L. Rothafel, the motion picture impresario popularly known as Roxy. After hearing Peerce sing "Yours Is My Heart Alone," Roxy went backstage to offer Jan a trial contract for four weeks

Peerce: pērs

JAN PEERCE

at Radio City Music Hall for two hundred and fifty dollars a week. There were two conditions: He had to throw away his violin and concentrate solely on singing; and he had to change his name from Jacob Pincus Perelmuth to something that looked better in lights. Jan accepted both suggestions. From this point on, singing was his principal activity, and he took the name of Jan Peerce which Roxy invented for him.

At first things did not go well for Peerce at the Music Hall. On the night he was to make his debut in the stage show his song was suddenly deleted, and his debut did not take place. "I spent that evening in the wings, crying like a kid," he recalls. Then Roxy fell ill, and nobody at the theater paid much attention to Peerce or gave him opportunities to sing. The four-week trial period was rapidly ending without Peerce having proved his capabilities. One evening Erno Rapee, the music director of the Music Hall, found him backstage in a deep depression. Learning from Peerce the reasons for such a letdown, Rapee promised to help. He assigned Peerce to sing offstage "Play, Fiddle, Play" at the very next stage show. That performance drew ovations, and Peerce was engaged as a permanent member of the company.

He remained with the Music Hall eight years, until 1940, having become one of its principal singing attractions, giving on an average four complete shows a day, seven days a week. In those years he was heard by over twenty million people in more than three thousand stage appearances. Since a radio program, "Music Hall of the Air," was broadcast each Sunday morning from the Music Hall, featuring abridged versions of operas as well as concerts of orchestral and vocal music, Peerce was heard by millions more outside the theater. He grew so popular over the air that he appeared on important sponsored network programs and in time he acquired a show of his own, "Great Moments in Music." A national poll among radio artists in 1946 gave him first place among male singers.

Singing arias from operas and art songs over the radio inspired Peerce to study serious music more actively. He took voice lessons with Eleanor McLellan, and then with Giuseppe Boghetti. This training prepared him for his first major test as a serious concert singer. In January 1938 Samuel Chotzinoff, music director of the National Broadcasting Company, arranged for Peerce to audition for Arturo Toscanini. Toscanini asked Peerce to sing "Una furtiva lagrima" from *L'Elisir d'Amore* and sat down at the piano to accompany him. "It took supreme effort and will power to compel myself to forget where I was and who was sitting there at the piano playing the accompaniment," he later told an interviewer. "I looked out of the window, watched the snow fall, and sang the best I could." When Peerce finished, Toscanini exclaimed: "Che bella voce!" ("What a beautiful voice!") Peerce was engaged to sing the tenor solo in Beethoven's Symphony No.9 on February 6, 1938, at a concert of the New York Philharmonic, Toscanini conducting. This was the first of many appearances Peerce would make under Toscanini.

On May 14, 1938, Peerce made his public debut in opera with the Columbia Opera Company at the Shubert Theater in Philadelphia as the Duke of Mantua in *Rigoletto*. He repeated this performance with the same company in Baltimore. His recital debut took place in New York on November 7, 1939. Writing in the New York *World,* Samuel Chotzinoff said: "Mr. Peerce met the test most successfully, and New York can now legitimately rejoice in the possession of an exceptional tenor who can deliver both a Lied and an aria to the taste of connoisseurs of each."

Gaetano Merola, then artistic director and manager of the San Francisco Opera, asked Peerce to sing the role of Alfredo in a concert performance of *La Traviata* at the Hollywood Bowl in California in the summer of 1941. His success brought him an engagement with the San Francisco Opera where he made his debut on October 19, 1941, as the Duke in *Rigoletto* in a cast that also included Lily Pons and Lawrence Tibbett.

The next important step for Peerce—and the most significant of his career—was the Metropolitan Opera, and it did not take him long to make it. His debut took place on November 29, 1941, in *La Traviata*. "Mr. Peerce's audience . . . was delighted and with good reason by the appealing quality of his voice and his manner of using it," wrote Olin Downes in the New York *Times.*

Peerce remained with the Metropolitan Opera company for over a quarter of a century, until 1967. In that time he was heard in numerous roles, mainly in the French and Italian repertory. In New York he sang Edgardo in *Lucia di Lammermoor* forty-one times, the Duke in *Rigoletto* thirty-nine times, Alfredo in *La Traviata* thirty-four times, and Rodolfo in *La Bohème,* Don Ottavio in *Don Giovanni,* and Riccardo in *Un Ballo in Maschera* more than twenty times each. His other roles at the Metropolitan Opera were Cavaradossi in *Tosca,* Pinkerton in *Madama Butterfly,* the title role in *Faust,* Turiddu in *Cavalleria Rusticana,* and Don Alvaro in *La Forza del Destino.*

In addition to his appearances at the Metropolitan Opera Peerce was heard as a guest artist with major opera companies throughout Europe as well as in the United States. He appeared extensively as a recitalist and as a guest artist with major symphony orchestras; and he made numerous appearances both over network radio and coast-to-coast sponsored television programs. Toscanini chose him to appear in his concert performances of *La Traviata, La Bohème,* and *Un Ballo in Maschera* over the NBC radio network.

On June 6, 1956, Peerce began a concert tour of the Soviet Union, the first important American singer to appear there since World War II and the first American ever to be heard on the stage of the Bolshoi Opera. In 1963 during a tour of Europe Peerce participated in the Vienna June Festival. He filmed Verdi's *Hymn of Nations* conducted by Toscanini in 1946. After that he was seen in three full-length motion pictures: *Carnegie Hall* (1947), *Something in the Wind* (1947), and *Of Men and Music (1951).*

An eye operation in 1967, followed by a hemorrhage, compelled Peerce to leave the Metropolitan Opera for good. But this was by no means the end of his career. He was still heard in recitals, with orchestras, and in guest appearances with various opera companies. In 1968 he toured Europe and Israel, and in 1969 he filled a cameo part in the nonmusical motion picture *Goodbye, Columbus* which was directed by his son, Larry Peerce. He made his musical comedy debut on tour as Tevye in *Fiddler on the Roof* in 1971 before making his debut on Broadway in the same production in December of that year (the seventh star to have assumed that role in New York).

Peerce met his wife, the former Alice Kalmanowitz, when both were about sixteen, and it was not long afterwards that they fell in love. Since their parents objected to this romance (Alice's parents on the grounds that Jan was then unable to make a living, and Jan's parents because he was much too young to settle down to a family life) they eloped on May 10, 1929.

The Peerces, who live in New Rochelle, New York, have three children, one of whom, Larry, has become a successful motion picture producer and director. Jan Peerce has no hobbies to speak of, though at one time he tried to get interested in golf. His all-absorbing interest outside music is the land of Israel where he has appeared on numerous occasions and for whose cause he has continually donated his services. An adherent to the orthodox Jewish religion, Peerce occasionally, when on tour either in the United States or Europe, steps into the local synagogue on the Sabbath or holiday to officiate as an unpaid cantor.

ABOUT: Ewen, D. Men and Women Who Make Music (1949 ed.); Levy, A. The Bluebird of Happiness: Memoirs of Jan Peerce. *Periodicals*—Collier's, March 23, 1940; High Fidelity/Musical America, December 1971; Musical America, December 1, 1953; Opera News, November 24, 1941, January 29, 1966.

Leonard Pennario

1924–

Leonard Joseph Pennario, pianist, was born in Buffalo, New York, on July 9, 1924, the oldest son of John D. and Mary Chiarello Pennario. His father was a salesman. While attending kindergarten at the Holy Angels Parochial School

LEONARD PENNARIO

in Buffalo, Leonard revealed such an interest in the school piano and such facility in picking out tunes with a single finger that one of his teachers, Sister Macrina, suggested he begin piano lessons. He began studying with Elwood G. Fischer, under whom he made sufficient progress to be able to appear in a public concert in a Buffalo department store when he was seven.

"I was fortunate in having parents who encouraged me," he told an interviewer. "Although my parents were denied the advantages of a musical education they loved music and were happy when I showed an eagerness to learn. They bought me a piano when it was a real financial hardship for them. I never decided to become a pianist; it was just assumed that I would be by my parents and teachers, and I fell right in with the idea. I enjoyed practicing from the start."

The ambition to become a concert pianist crystallized when, in or about his eighth year, Leonard heard concerts by Serge Rachmaninoff and Paderewski. Inspired to emulation, he himself gave a recital in Buffalo that year. Two years later, the Pennario family moved to Los Angeles. While attending elementary school, Leonard was awarded the William Daniels Memorial Scholarship for piano and theory in 1934 and given a guest shot on Bing Crosby's network radio program, the "Kraft Music Hall."

After continuing piano studies with Olga Steeb and W. Samuel Ball, Leonard made his debut with orchestra in December 1936. He performed Grieg's Concerto in A minor with the

Dallas Symphony, mastering the work in six days' time. In 1939 he appeared as a soloist with the Los Angeles Philharmonic under Otto Klemperer.

After graduation from high school in 1942, Leonard enrolled in the University of Southern California in Los Angeles, majoring in music. There he studied the piano with Guy Maier, composition with Ernst Toch, and orchestration with Lucien Caillet. His piano study was ultimately completed with Isabelle Vengerova. During 1942 he made several important appearances, particularly as guest artist with the Chicago Symphony and the Minneapolis Symphony.

In the spring of 1943, during World War II, Leonard joined the Army Air Force as a private. He was assigned to the Special Service Division and allowed to give public concerts, the proceeds from which went to the Army Emergency Relief Fund. In uniform, he made his New York debut on November 17, 1943, performing Liszt's Concerto in E minor with the New York Philharmonic under Rodzinski. In the *Herald Tribune,* Virgil Thomson referred to him as "a sensationally brilliant pianist. . . . He took over the conduct of the work with a sweep and a power . . . that left the orchestra and its conductor panting behind him."

Sent by the Air Force to the China-Burma-India theater of operations, Pennario continued to give concerts in uniform in hospitals, officers' clubs, and army and air force bases, while filling the post of a clerk. He also conducted a glee club and led a class in music appreciation. By the time he was separated from the Air Corps in 1946 he had earned three bronze stars and had risen to the rank of staff sergeant.

He returned to New York to give his first recital there as a civilian, on November 6, 1946. In 1947 he gave fifty-eight concerts throughout the United States and in the spring of 1952 he made his first tour of Europe which was climaxed by a sold-out concert in Paris. A Parisian critic described him as "a phenomenon of the piano," and in London a critic for the *New Statesman and Nation* said that "nobody today plays the piano better than Pennario."

After his appearance in a New York recital on December 16, 1952, Olin Downes noted in the New York *Times* that Pennario "has wrists and fingers second to none. . . . Not many pianists

can play with the superb, transcendental virtuosity which Leonard Pennario revealed."

Since the early 1950s Pennario has confirmed these early enthusiastic estimates with performances in the United States and Europe that further demonstrated his technical powers and discerning musicianship. "Collaboration with this young musician has been one of the happiest experiences of my life," the conductor Dimitri Mitropoulos once said. "I say 'musician' because although he possesses the technique necessary to virtuosity, he possesses what is more important —a soul."

In 1961 and 1963 in Los Angeles, and in 1964 and 1966 in New York, Pennario distinguished himself in chamber music concerts in which his collaborators were Heifetz and Piatigorsky. This trio has also made recordings for RCA Victor.

In addition to his public appearances in the United States, Europe, South Africa, Australia, and New Zealand, and his numerous recordings for Capitol, Pennario was heard playing the piano on the sound track of the motion picture *September Affair* (1950). He was the composer of "Midnight on the Cliffs," the theme music for the motion picture *Julie* (1956).

His earlier interests were golf, bridge, Scrabble, and the study of languages; his more recent ones have been collecting records and playing chamber music with his musician friends.

ABOUT: Etude, June 1947; Musical America, April 1959.

Itzhak Perlman

1945–

Itzhak Perlman, violinist, was born in Tel Aviv, Israel, on August 31, 1945. His parents, Chaim and Shoshana Perlman, had emigrated to Palestine from Poland in the 1930s. They met and married in Palestine where Chaim was a barber.

When Itzhak was three, he heard a violin recital over the Israeli radio and expressed the wish to become a violinist. He was presented with a toy fiddle which so fascinated him that before long he demanded, and received, lessons on a regular instrument that cost six dollars. When he was four years and three months old he

---

Perlman: pûrl' măn

ITZHAK PERLMAN

Cultural Foundation and the Katherine Tuck Fund in Detroit, Itzhak entered the Juilliard School of Music in 1958. During the next half dozen years he was a pupil of Ivan Galamian and Dorothy DeLay. Summers were spent at the Meadowmount School of Music in upstate New York, once again on a scholarship.

Itzhak made his first New York public appearance on March 5, 1963, as a soloist in Wieniawski's Concerto No.1 with the National Orchestral Association, John Barnett conducting. Since this was a time when the New York newspapers were on strike his appearance went unnoticed by the general public—but not by Isaac Stern who used his influence to get Sol Hurok to become Perlman's concert manager.

As the youngest of nineteen contestants in the Edgar M. Leventritt contest, Perlman emerged the winner on April 21, 1964, at Carnegie Hall, New York, selected by a jury that included Isaac Stern, Lukas Foss, George Szell, William Steinberg, and Erika Morini among others. This was not the only item about Perlman to hit the newspapers the following day. Another story concerned the theft of the Guarnerius violin which the Juilliard School had loaned him for the contest. The violin was recovered one day later from a pawn shop on Eighth Avenue where it had been pawned for fifteen dollars.

Winning the Leventritt Award brought Perlman not only one thousand dollars in cash but also engagements with the New York Philharmonic Orchestra and several other major American symphonic organizations. Hurok booked him for additional appearances, and Ed Sullivan brought him back for two more performances on his television program.

The odds against his success on the concert stage seemed immeasurable. He had to stumble across the stage on metal crutches and then go into unsightly bodily contortions to ease himself into a chair where he had to perform in a seated position. To sell a crippled performer to the public seemed an impossible task, only less difficult than to have audiences accept him not as a freak but as a serious artist. But such problems, which would have destroyed the hopes for a career of most others, did not seem to disturb Perlman. He loved concertizing; playing the violin was as much a necessity as breathing. And he knew he was gifted with phenomenal talent. It did not take long for the music world to accept him on his own terms. After he performed Tchaikov-

was stricken with poliomyelitis which crippled him permanently and compelled him to use crutches. During his year of convalescence he continued to practice on the violin. After that he refused to accept the fact that his infirmity was an impediment to a professional career as virtuoso.

In early boyhood he received a scholarship from the America-Israel Cultural Foundation which enabled him to enter the Tel Aviv Academy of Music as a student of Ryvka Goldgart. A gifted student, he soon gave concerts in and around Tel Aviv. He appeared over the radio with the Broadcasting Orchestra in Jerusalem, in concerts with the Ramat-Gan Orchestra in Tel Aviv, and, at the age of ten, in his first recital.

In 1958 Ed Sullivan went to Israel to scout for new talent for his CBS-TV Sunday evening "Ed Sullivan Show." Itzhak Perlman was one of those he selected. He first appeared on the Ed Sullivan show on February 15, 1959, returning for a second appearance soon afterwards, performing a transcription of Rimsky-Korsakov's *The Flight of the Bumblebee,* Wieniawski's *Polonaise Brillante,* and a movement from Mendelssohn's Violin Concerto. After these two appearances, Itzhak decided to remain in New York where he was soon joined by his parents. Under the sponsorship of the Zionist Organization of America he embarked on a concert tour which brought him to twenty cities in the United States and Canada.

With scholarships from the America-Israel

sky's Violin Concerto in Carnegie Hall with the Israel Philharmonic Orchestra in October 1964, William Bender wrote in the *Herald Tribune:* "His flow of pure, sweet tone is unceasing. His bow arm is unfailingly strong and steady and the fingering ... is dazzlingly swift and accurate. There is a joy and bounce to his playing that had old-timers reaching back in their memories to the days of the youthful Heifetz to find a parallel."

In January 1965 Perlman returned to Israel after a seven-year absence. The highlight of this visit was his performance of concertos by Sibelius and Tchaikovsky that inspired a fifteen-minute ovation. Perlman's triumph in Israel was reported in a story in *Time* captioned "Return of the Prodigy."

In 1965–1966 Hurok booked Perlman for a coast-to-coast tour of the United States that covered thirty cities, and in 1966–1967 he toured Europe for the first time. He was well on his way towards recognition as one of the most brilliant of the younger violinists, whose technique was outstanding and whose musicianship was penetrating. He has since been heard and acclaimed in all parts of the music world, maintaining each year a rigorous schedule of more than a hundred performances. He has also recorded the basic violin repertory for RCA, Angel, and London, including the complete set of Caprices by Paganini and his own transcription of rags by Scott Joplin; also, sonatas with the pianist Vladimir Ashkenazy. In recordings, as in concerts, he sometimes collaborated with Isaac Stern or Pinchas Zukerman in two-violin music, and with Vladimir Ashkenazy in performances of violin sonatas. In 1978 Perlman received a Grammy from the National Academy of Recording Arts and Sciences for his album, Vivaldi's *The Four Seasons.*

Despite his heavy performing schedule, Perlman has found the time each year to teach the violin. For several years he has participated in the teaching and performing program of the Aspen Music Festival in Colorado, and in 1975 he was appointed to the faculty of Brooklyn College School of the Performing Arts.

Perlman married Toby Lynn Friedlander at the America-Israel Culture House in New York on January 5, 1967. Like Perlman, Toby is a violin graduate of the Juilliard School. They met at a summer camp concert in 1964 where Perlman was a performing artist. With their three children, the Perlmans occupy a nine-room apartment on Riverside Drive in New York in the same house where Pinchas Zukerman (one of his closest friends) resides with his family. Itzhak Perlman and Toby both enjoy sports as spectators, basketball particularly. In addition Itzhak particularly enjoys fishing.

ABOUT: Esquire, June 1968; Hi-Fi, November 1970; New York Times, March 8, 1970; Time, January 15, 1965.

Roberta Peters

1930–

Roberta Peters (originally Roberta Peterman), coloratura soprano, was born in New York City on May 4, 1930. Her father, Solomon, was a shoe salesman, and her mother, Ruth Hirsch Peterman, a milliner; both were of Austrian descent. As a child, Roberta revealed an unusual gift for mimicry and acting and was given many opportunities to appear in school productions at P.S. 64 and the Wade Junior High School. She was graduated from Wade in 1943. When her talent for singing became evident, her grandfather, then employed at Grossinger's, the hotel resort in the Catskill Mountains of New York, asked the tenor Jan Peerce to pass on her talent. Peerce was so impressed with her that he arranged in 1943 for her to study with William Pierce Hermann who from then on remained her sole vocal teacher.

"I was fortunate to discover at an early age what I wanted to do," she once wrote. "I wanted to become an opera singer, and I spent my entire span of teenage years preparing to do just that. From the ages of thirteen to nineteen, I didn't have dates, didn't attend parties, didn't go to proms—didn't do any of the things a normal teenage girl is supposed to do. I didn't even go to high school. I got permission from the New York Board of Education to drop out of the junior high in the Bronx I was attending to take private tutoring in academic subjects, as well as in singing, languages, dancing, and drama."

This period of study with private teachers lasted seven years. By the time she was nineteen she had learned twenty roles, including practically the entire principal coloratura repertory. When she had completed six years of concen-

ROBERTA PETERS

trated study, she auditioned for Sol Hurok, the impresario, who signed her to a contract even though she had never before made a professional appearance.

On January 23, 1950, she auditioned for the Metropolitan Opera singing a Queen of the Night aria from *The Magic Flute.* She was given a contract and was enrolled in the Kathryn Turney Long opera course. Her debut at the Metropolitan Opera was scheduled for January 1951 in *The Magic Flute.* But chance decreed otherwise. As she herself has told the story: "My mother and I were going to the Met as standees that night (November 17, 1950) to see *Don Giovanni.* At 1 P.M., Rudolf Bing, who then headed the Met, called me down and told me I would sing the part of Zerlina that night because Nadine Conner had become sick. I knew the part, but I had never sung onstage or with an orchestra before. I called my mother and said, 'We're going to the opera tonight.' She said she knew, but I said, 'But you don't know how, you'd better sit down while I tell you.'"

Thus her Metropolitan Opera debut (actually her first appearance on any professional stage) was an unscheduled one, and she had not rehearsed for it. She was given hurried instructions by Herbert Graf, the stage director, and Max Rudolf, artistic administrator. Her only contact with Fritz Reiner, the conductor that evening, was a brief meeting at seven in the evening to go over some of Zerlina's music at the piano. Nevertheless she went through the performance with such assurance that her performance was de-

scribed by Harriet Johnson in the New York *Post* as "a real tour de force." Johnson added: "She sang and acted with the ease of a veteran and with no evidence of nervousness. . . . Besides her musical success, she made a hit as a personality. Petite, slender and vivaciously pretty, she might be called an ideal Zerlina." Zerlina remained from then on one of her most celebrated roles; during the next quarter of a century she undertook it forty-two times at the Metropolitan Opera.

She early established her reputation as one of the outstanding coloratura sopranos of the Metropolitan Opera where she remained for over a quarter of a century in a large repertory. As Rosina, in a new production of *The Barber of Seville* on February 3, 1954, she added, as Louis Biancolli said in the *World-Telegram and Sun,* "another thoroughly appealing portrait to her growing gallery. This was again singing of a high order, sensitive, clear, in the best bel canto tradition—an utter delight. Her gay and exquisite acting was of the same order, and her looks doubled the attraction." Her vocal pyrotechnics gleamed and flashed in the two arias of the Queen of the Night in a new production of *The Magic Flute* on February 23, 1956. On January 23, 1964, she created for the United States the role of Kitty in the American premiere of Menotti's *The Last Savage.* Among her other distinguished roles during the quarter of a century following her debut at the Metropolitan Opera were Gilda in *Rigoletto,* Barbarina and Susanna in *The Marriage of Figaro,* Olympia in *The Tales of Hoffmann,* Norina in *Don Pasquale,* Oscar in *Un Ballo in Maschera,* Adina in *L'Elisir d'Amore,* Amina in *La Sonnambula,* Violetta in *La Traviata,* Despina in *Così fan Tutte,* Fiakermilli in *Arabella,* Zerbinetta in *Ariadne auf Naxos,* Sophie in *Der Rosenkavalier,* Lauretta in *Gianni Schicchi,* Adele in *Die Fledermaus,* Nannetta in *Falstaff,* and the title roles in *Lucia di Lammermoor, Martha,* and *Lakmé.* The roles in which she appeared most frequently during that quarter of a century, besides Zerlina, were Gilda (56), Queen of the Night (29), Rosina in *The Barber of Seville* (28), Despina (24), and Lucia (21).

On March 30, 1952, Peters married Robert Merrill, the baritone of the Metropolitan Opera. It ended just ten weeks later when they separated: Roberta, to go on a concert tour and Merrill, to do a movie in Hollywood. On June 26,

1952, they were divorced in Juarez, Mexico. They have remained good friends ever since, have visited each other's homes, and have often appeared together in joint recitals.

Her success in Europe began in 1951 when she made her debut at Covent Garden in London during the Festival of Britain in a gala performance of Balfe's *The Bohemian Girl,* conducted by Sir Thomas Beecham. She continued to appear at Covent Garden regularly after that. She had toured the Soviet Union in May and June 1950, appearing in Moscow, Leningrad, Yerevan, Baku, and Tbilisi, to one of the most enthusiastic receptions accorded an American artist up to that time. In 1963 she made a triumphant first appearance at the Vienna State Opera as Gilda, and that summer she was heard as the Queen of the Night at the Salzburg Festival. After her appearance as Violetta in *La Traviata* at the Bolshoi Opera in the Soviet Union during the late spring of 1972, she was given not only a fifteen-minute standing ovation but also the Bolshoi medal—the first American ever to receive an award reserved exclusively for Soviet artists who had been with the Bolshoi company for a quarter of a century or more.

Peters celebrated her twenty-fifth anniversary with the Metropolitan on November 17, 1975, as Despina in *Così fan Tutte.* This was her three hundred fifth appearance at the Metropolitan, and her twenty-fourth as Despina. After the first act, during a ceremony in her honor, William Rockefeller, board president, presented her with a silver bowl.

Peters has been a highly successful recitalist. In the concert hall she has created a broad base for her programming by combining opera arias and art songs with operetta arias, semiclassical and popular numbers, and songs of ethnic Jewish interest. Aram Khachaturian, Paul Creston, and Roy Harris are some of the twentieth century American composers who wrote for her songs which she has introduced; in November 1973 she presented the world premiere of a new work by Darius Milhaud at Carnegie Hall.

In addition to many appearances over television and her recordings for RCA and Deutsche Grammophon, Peters appeared in the screen biography of Sol Hurok, *Tonight We Sing* (1953). During the summer of 1975 she toured for five weeks in Noël Coward's operetta *Bittersweet,* and on November 10, 1975, she made her debut

as a dramatic actress on the "Medical Center" show over the CBS-TV network.

Peters has sung six times at the White House for four presidents—Kennedy, Johnson, Nixon, and Ford.

On April 10, 1955, Roberta Peters married Bertram Fields, an investor in hotels and real estate. They have two sons and reside in a Tudor-style house in Scarsdale, New York. She is interested in sports, tennis particularly. A highly gregarious person, she enjoys parties immensely. She has established the Roberta Peters Scholarship at Hebrew University in Jerusalem.

ABOUT: High Fidelity/Musical America, January 1976; Life, October 8, 1951; Musical America, January 15, 1955; Time, February 8, 1954.

Egon Petri

1881–1962

Egon Petri, pianist, was born in Hanover, Germany, on March 23, 1881, to a family which for several generations had produced professional musicians. His great-grandfather was an organist; his grandfather, an oboist; his father, Henri Willem Petri, an eminent violinist who at the time of Egon's birth was the concertmaster of the orchestra at the Royal Theatre in Hanover; and his mother, Katharina Tornauer Petri, was a singer who had been rewarded with a kiss by Liszt when she performed for him.

The Petri household in Hanover, and soon after that in Leipzig, was the meeting place for some of Europe's most revered musicians, including Brahms, Clara Schumann, Josef Joachim, Tchaikovsky, Grieg, Mahler, Ferruccio Busoni, and Anton Rubinstein. Egon was too young to remember all of them but in later years he said he was convinced that they exerted "a distinct influence" on his development.

When Egon was two years old, the family moved to Leipzig where his father was made concertmaster of the Gewandhaus Orchestra. In Leipzig, Petri received his first music lessons on the violin from his mother when he was five years old. Showing talent, he continued his lessons several years after that with his father. "Later on," he recalled, "I played the second

Petri: pä′ trē

EGON PETRI

violin in his [the father's] Quartet, sat at the first violin desk behind him in the Dresden Opera, and played sonatas with him in public. He was very strict about intonation, phrasing, beauty of tone, and correct rhythm and fingering." His father also insisted that Egon play other instruments, such as the piano, organ, and French horn, that he receive lessons in composition with Hermann Kretzschmar and Felix Draeseke, and that at the same time he attend the Kreuzschule in Leipzig (which Wagner had once attended) for a thorough classical education. Egon was graduated from the Kreuzschule in 1899.

After the Petris settled in Berlin in 1889 and his father took over the first-desk chair in the Dresden Opera orchestra, Egon began intensive study of the piano with Teresa Carreño. He made such excellent progress that for many years he couldn't decide whether to specialize in violin or piano, realizing that he could not try to master both instruments. Until that decision could be reached, he worked industriously on both the violin and the piano, advancing himself professionally as a violinist by occupying a chair in the Dresden Royal Opera orchestra and in his father's string quartet from 1889 to 1901.

In 1901, encouraged by his father, Petri decided the time had come for him to choose between his two favorite instruments. Paderewski had come to Dresden early that year to attend the world premiere of his opera *Manru* at the Royal Opera. At his hotel, he listened to Petri play the piano and advised him that it was with that instrument that his future belonged. Later that year, Petri entered Busoni's master class in piano in Weimar. "That," he said, "was the turning point in my development. I still tried to keep up my violin, and earned great praise from him [Busoni] for playing the violin part of his sonata at sight (it was still in manuscript). But I soon gave it up. . . . I can hardly overestimate the influence Busoni had on me. He was not only a marvelous pianist, but a great mind and a man of all-around culture. He never gave piano lessons in the accepted sense—of those I had not more than a dozen. But I saw him nearly every day when we were living in Berlin, sometimes twice a day . . . went to all his concerts, heard him practice, played under his baton or on two pianos with him, listened to his master classes . . . in short, became his friend, disciple and daily companion. He called me his 'most genuine pupil' and tried everything to further me. He recommended me to managers and conductors (generally without success), sent to me all the pupils he did not want to take, and was instrumental in getting me the appointment of professor of piano at the Royal College of Music in Manchester, England, where I remained from 1905 to 1911."

Petri made his concert debut as a pianist in 1902 in Holland. After that he toured Europe. With England as his home base, he continued to tour Europe, increasing his fame with every performance. In 1905 he married Maria Schoen. The Petris had two sons and a daughter.

Petri resigned from the Royal College of Music in 1911 and participated in the farewell concert of Hans Richter as conductor of the Hallé Orchestra in Manchester by performing Franck's *Symphonic Variations* and Liszt's *Totentanz*. He returned to Berlin where in 1911 he became Busoni's assistant. Even while pursuing a highly active career as a teacher of piano, he continued to make numerous concert tours of Germany, Austria, and Poland. From 1917 to 1920 he was professor of the piano at Zakopane, Poland; in 1920 he held a similar post at the Conservatory of Basel in Switzerland; and in 1921 he returned to Berlin to become professor of the piano at the High School for Music where he remained five years.

In November 1923 Petri became the first foreign artist since the Revolution to be invited to tour the Soviet Union. Within a forty-day period he was called upon to perform thirty-one times; on one occasion he gave three recitals in a single day. Between 1923 and 1928 he toured the Soviet Union several times more, covering not only the major cities but the smaller towns and hamlets as well.

He was a pianist of international renown when, on January 11, 1932, he made his American debut with a recital in New York. Lawrence Gilman said of him in the *Herald Tribune:* "Mr. Petri showed himself to be a musician of taste and skill and understanding, admirably modest and self-effacing, wholly absorbed in the task of re-creation. There is not a trace of the exhibitionist about him; he is a virtuoso by reason of his abilities and attainments, but he makes that tarnished word seem curiously unsuited to musicianship so genuine, and sincere and fine."

He toured the United States during the next four years, and in one of those years (1934–1935) he served as a member of the piano faculty of the Malkin Conservatory of Music in Boston.

He and his family were in their mountain retreat in Zakopane, Poland, which Petri had acquired in 1925, when the threat of war loomed over Europe in August 1939. Six days before the Germans invaded Poland, the Dutch consul in Cracow warned Petri to leave the country. With his wife and two sons and with three of his pupils, Petri took the last train to leave Poland before the Nazi invasion, leaving behind him his valuable library of books and his rare collection of manuscripts and letters. He made his way to the United States, where in February 1940 he gave an outstanding recital in New York. In September of that year he settled in Ithaca, New York, and became visiting professor of music at Cornell University. He remained at Cornell until 1946. This was a period in which he made many concert appearances in the United States, both in public auditoriums and over the radio.

A serious illness in 1945 compelled him to cut down his concert activity drastically and concentrate on teaching and the making of recordings. After leaving Cornell in 1946, he taught piano at Mills College in Oakland, California, from 1947 to 1957. In 1957 he was back in Europe conducting master classes in piano at the Academy of Music in Basel, Switzerland. After that, and up to the time of his death, he was a member of the faculty of the San Francisco Conservatory, a branch of the University of California. He died of a stroke on May 27, 1962, at the Herrick Memorial Hospital in Berkeley, California.

With Busoni and Mugellini, Petri edited Bach's piano works. He provided cadenzas for several of Mozart's piano concertos.

ABOUT: Etude, October 1940; Musical Facts, October 1940.

Gregor Piatigorsky

1903–1976

Gregor Piatigorsky, cellist, was called "the Russian Casals." He was born in Ekaterinslav (now Dnepropetrovsk) in the Ukraine, on April 17, 1903, to Paul I. and Maria Amchislawsky Piatigorsky. His father was a trained musician who had ambitions to become a concert violinist. One evening he took his son to a symphony concert, where Gregor heard and saw a cello for the first time. "I had never heard or seen anything nearly so beautiful," Piatigorsky has recalled in his autobiography, *Cellist*. "From that night on, armed with two sticks, a long one for the cello and a short one for the bow, I pretended to play the cello."

He asked for cello lessons and his father tried to give him some but soon realized that playing the cello was not like playing the violin. He turned his son over to a teacher for lessons. When Yampolsky, the teacher, had to leave town, Gubarioff, director of the local conservatory, was called in as a replacement.

Determined to pursue his own career as a violinist, and against the wishes of his own father, Gregor's father decided to leave his family and go off to St. Petersburg to study with Leopold Auer. This caused the family such financial hardship that Gregor, then only eight, had to find work to help support the family. He performed on the cello at night in a nightclub and after that in a motion-picture theater.

When his attempts to study with Auer proved a disaster, Paul Piatigorsky returned home and decided to move his family to Moscow. Gregor auditioned for Ippolitov-Ivanov, director of the Moscow Conservatory, and for Alfred von Glehn, the conservatory's cello professor, and was awarded a scholarship. Since he enjoyed practicing the cello early in the morning while others were still sleeping, he devised a "sound-

Piatigorsky: pyä tǐ gôr′ skǐ

GREGOR PIATIGORSKY

several other musicians in a public performance of Arnold Schoenberg's avant-garde composition *Pierrot Lunaire* in 1923. A flutist present at this concert was so impressed by Piatigorsky's cello playing that he suggested that Piatigorsky audition for Wilhelm Furtwängler, the principal conductor of the Berlin Philharmonic. Piatigorsky performed for Furtwängler the Schumann Cello Concerto, a movement from the Dvořák Cello Concerto, and passages from Strauss's *Don Quixote*. Furtwängler immediately engaged him as first cellist of his orchestra, a post Piatigorsky held with great honor from 1924 to 1928.

During the years in which he was a member of the Berlin Philharmonic, Piatigorsky began giving solo concerts in Berlin and made his first tour outside Germany, to the Baltic countries. In addition he collaborated with Carl Flesch and Artur Schnabel in performances of chamber music. In Berlin he also met the girl who became his first wife. He makes only passing reference to this in his autobiography: "The conductor, Efrem Kurtz, introduced me to a lady. I was very young and she was beautiful. I was shy, she was eloquent, worldly, and with the experience of a previous marriage. Her maiden name was Lydia Antik. She became my wife. Very musical and alert, she was ambitious and had great charm. My bachelorhood turned into a stormy life that, after nine childless years, ended in peaceful divorce. Faithful to the cello, she later married the eminent French cellist Pierre Fournier."

In 1926 Piatigorsky became professor of the cello at the Scharwenka Conservatory in Berlin. His fame as a virtuoso and teacher encouraged five wealthy Berlin music lovers to purchase for him the gift of an Amati cello. This was the first time he had owned a fine old instrument.

In 1928 the demands made upon him by the concert stage grew so pressing that Piatigorsky decided to resign from the Berlin Philharmonic and devote himself exclusively to a virtuoso career. In gratitude to the conductor who had opened up for him his career in Berlin, he occasionally returned to his first-desk chair with the Berlin Philharmonic when Furtwängler conducted.

He made his first tour of the United States in 1929. His American debut took place in Oberlin, Ohio, on November 5. Following this he appeared as a soloist first with the Philadelphia

less system" in which his fingers went through their routines on the fingerboard while the bow was poised in midair.

When he was fifteen, Gregor became first cellist of the orchestra at the Imperial Opera in Moscow. "My life bustled with activity," he recalls. Besides his work at the opera house he appeared in recitals and participated in chamber music performances. One summer he appeared as an assisting artist with Feodor Chaliapin in two concerts.

The Revolution brought Gregor such physical hardships that escaping from Russia almost became an obsession. In 1921 he went on a concert tour with two singers and the violinist Mischa Mischakov. In one of the small towns near the Polish border they negotiated with a band of smugglers to get across the border. "The smugglers' price was outrageous and their methods dangerous, but their terms were accepted," writes Piatigorsky. The fleeing men were fired upon as they approached the Polish border. Gregor jumped into the nearby river, struggling to keep his cello above his head. Their flight was successful, and Gregor arrived in Lwow (Lemberg) penniless and friendless. The following period of hardship finally ended when, substituting for a sick cellist, he landed a permanent job with the orchestra of the Warsaw Opera.

After almost two years in Poland, Piatigorsky went on to Berlin where he supported himself by playing the cello in cafés and theaters and where he continued his cello studies with Julius Klengel. He participated with Artur Schnabel and

Orchestra under Stokowski and then with the New York Philharmonic under Mengelberg. In the New York *World* Samuel Chotzinoff had this to say about Piatigorsky's performance of the Dvořák Cello Concerto. "In his hands, the instrument shed its reputed limitations. The lower register yielded beautiful sounds, as did the higher. . . . The technical matters that Dvořák burdened it with came through as brilliantly and as easily as they would have on a fiddle. . . . In addition, he is one of the most poetic and sensitive performers now before the public."

His later tours of the United States, together with his performances in other parts of the musical world, placed him high among the cello virtuosos of the time, possibly as the greatest since Casals. Twice in the 1930s he was called upon to perform at the White House for American presidents—for Herbert Hoover and for Franklin Roosevelt. *Newsweek* said of him: "His playing has brought about a cello renaissance." In twenty-five years of concertizing he gave over one thousand recitals and made over two hundred and fifty appearances with orchestras. Leading composers wrote major works for him as did Sir William Walton, whose Cello Concerto was introduced by Piatigorsky in Boston on January 25, 1957, with the Boston Symphony, Charles Münch conducting. Piatigorsky gave the world premieres of other cello concertos as well: those of Mario Castelnuovo-Tedesco (January 31, 1935), Hindemith (February 7, 1941), and Nicolai Berezowsky (*Concerto Lirico,* February 22, 1935).

In an analysis of Piatigorsky's cello playing for the New York *Times* Olin Downes described Piatigorsky's tone as possessing "every sonority and shading—an organ fullness and virility; lyrical beauty and intensity in passages of sustained song; or fine-spun as silk in pianissimo measures or passages of rapid ornamentation. There seems no limit to the security and agility of the left hand or the power and variety of result with which the bow was wielded. . . . The sentiment is noble, the line classic, the sense of form always present. In a word, a great virtuoso, and a greater artist."

In 1933 Piatigorsky helped to commemorate the centenary of the birth of Brahms by performing in Berlin and Hamburg all of Brahms's works for piano and strings in collaboration with Paul Hindemith (playing the viola) and Bronislaw Hubermann.

On January 26, 1937, after having divorced his first wife, Piatigorsky married Jacqueline de Rothschild, the daughter of Baron Édouard de Rothschild of Paris. She was an excellent amateur musician on the piano and the bassoon. The Piatigorskys lived in Paris until the beginning of World War II, when they moved to the United States. In 1942 he became an American citizen.

In June 1942 he became head of the cello department of the Curtis Institute of Music in Philadelphia. He held this post two years. From 1962 on he held master classes in cello at the University of California. In February 1944 he digressed temporarily and briefly from the playing of the cello to conduct a concert of the Denver Symphony Orchestra.

Beginning with the late 1940s and for some years thereafter Piatigorsky joined Jascha Heifetz in the performance of chamber music. With Arthur Rubinstein as their third partner they gave concerts of trio music to form what *Life* magazine called "The Million Dollar Trio." In 1961 the Heifetz-Piatigorsky Concerts were organized to perform throughout the United States with the collaboration of other well-known musicians, among whom were William Primrose and Leonard Pennario. RCA Victor Recordings of some of the works heard at these Heifetz-Piatigorsky concerts received Grammys from the National Academy of Recording Arts and Sciences in 1961, 1962, and 1963.

In October 1970 the fortieth anniversary of Piatigorsky's American debut was commemorated in New York with a performance of Strauss's *Don Quixote* with the New York Philharmonic under Leonard Bernstein. Two years later, on September 20, 1972, Piatigorsky returned to New York once again as guest artist with the New York Philharmonic, this time conducted by Pierre Boulez, to play the Dvořák Concerto which he had played for his first appearance with the same orchestra in 1929. In those forty-three years Piatigorsky had appeared twenty-five times with the New York Philharmonic.

On May 20, 1973, Piatigorsky was honored on his seventieth birthday by the Chamber Music Society of Lincoln Center with a gala concert in which many distinguished cellists participated (and the soprano Beverly Sills and many other artists). The program included the New York premiere of a new suite for two cellos and piano by Menotti performed by Piatigorsky and Leslie

Parnas, with Charles Wadsworth at the piano. Piatigorsky was also heard in Stravinsky's *Suite Italienne* (which many years earlier he had helped Stravinsky adapt for cello and piano from his score for *Pulcinella*) and in *Bachiana Brasileira No. 5* by Villa-Lobos. "His heart is still young even if his bow arm occasionally may falter," noted Harold C. Schonberg in the New York *Times.* "No matter what he plays, the music tends to sound the same—with a big line, the big ritard, the sentimental phrasings, the various expressive devices beloved of a previous generation."

Though he was seriously ill for a year and a half before his death, Piatigorsky continued to teach his master classes in Los Angeles and in 1976 to conduct a series of master classes in Switzerland. Occasionally he also played the cello. Six months before his death he performed at the dedication ceremonies for a school for the aging at the University of California.

Gregor Piatigorsky died at his home in Los Angeles on August 6, 1976. One evening later the Los Angeles Philharmonic performed the Verdi Requiem at the Hollywood Bowl in his honor. A public memorial service was conducted in Bovard Auditorium in Los Angeles on August 11.

For many years the Piatigorskys resided in Los Angeles. There they raised their son, Joram, and their daughter, Jephta. Six feet three inches tall, with dark eyes and sharply defined features, Piatigorsky was once called, by the sculptress Katharine Ward Lane, one of the ten most handsome men in the United States. His striking appearance made him a subject for a number of paintings, one of which won first prize in the Carnegie Institute Exhibition in Pittsburgh in 1943. He was fond of Russian food, bridge, chess, boating, swimming, writing poetry, and playing practical jokes. He performed Saint-Saëns's *The Swan* in the motion picture *Carnegie Hall* (1947) and he was the author of an autobiography, *Cellist* (1965).

ABOUT: Piatigorsky, G. Cellist. *Periodicals*—Hi-Fi, August 1973; High Fidelity/Musical America, November 1976; New York Times, August 7, 1976, September 19, 1976; Newsweek, November 9, 1970; Time, February 5, 1965.

Ezio Pinza

1892–1957

Ezio Pinza (originally Fortunio Pinza), celebrated bass whose voice was of unusual range and richness, was born in Rome on May 18, 1892. He was the seventh of nine children of Cesare Pinza, a lumber dealer, and Clelia Bulgarelli Pinza, and the first of the children to survive infancy; his younger brother and sister also survived. Ezio was not expected to live, for he was puny and sickly—two days after his birth no christening name had been chosen for him. When his survival seemed assured, the pagan name Ezio (after a family friend) was chosen, but at his baptism he was named Fortunio, in accordance with the requirement of the Catholic Church that the person being baptized be given a Christian name.

When Ezio was two years old, his family moved to Ravenna where, during his boyhood, he worked as a carpenter's helper and as a delivery boy for a bakery. His father hoped he would become a civil engineer. For this purpose Ezio started preparatory schooling. But, when in his eighteenth year he found engineering not to his taste, he abandoned his studies at the University of Ravenna to become a professional bicycle racer. He entered cross-country competitions and six-day bicycle races, winning a prize only once. "Although I did not know it at the time," he later told an interviewer, "I was developing the lung power which now makes people hear my voice in the top row of the peanut gallery."

One day after a race he was in a shower when from sheer exuberance he burst into song. A friend heard him and encouraged him to study singing. His only vocal experience up to this point had been singing in an amateur choral club, but his failures as a professional cyclist compelled him to consider the suggestion seriously. He went for an audition to Vizzani, director of the Rossini Conservatory in Bologna, but was turned down. He persisted, however, and another vocal teacher, Ruzza, accepted him. After Ruzza's death Pinza returned to Vizzani, who had become more kindly disposed toward him and arranged for him to get a small scholarship at the Rossini Conservatory. While study-

Pinza: pēnt′ sä

EZIO PINZA

ing there, Pinza supported himself by working as a handyman and carpenter.

In the fall of 1914, after two years of vocal study, he joined a small opera company in Soncino, near Milan, where he made his debut as Oroveso in *Norma*. World War I interrupted his career just as it was beginning to make some headway. Pinza enlisted as a private in the Italian army, became a member of the Italian artillery fighting in the Alps on skis, rose to the rank of captain, and received a bronze star for distinguished service. Before being demobilized in 1919 he served with the riot-prevention forces in Naples.

After his return to civilian life, he worked as a railroad brakeman while trying to resume his career. Late in 1919 he joined the company of the Teatro Reale in Rome, where in 1920 he made his bow as King Mark in *Tristan and Isolde*, receiving an ovation after the second act. He remained at the Teatro Reale for two years. Further operatic experience was gained at the Teatro Verdi in Florence and at the Teatro Regio in Turin before he went to La Scala in Milan where he was to have his first major successes. Arturo Toscanini, music director of La Scala, regarded him most highly. Under Toscanini, Pinza appeared in the world premieres of Pizzetti's *Débora e Jaéle* on December 16, 1922, and Boïto's *Nerone* on May 1, 1924.

Gatti-Casazza, general manager of the Metropolitan Opera, heard Pinza at La Scala and gave him a contract. His Metropolitan debut took place on November 1, 1926, in Spontini's

La Vestale, with Pinza assuming the role of Pontifex Maximus, the high priest. In the *Herald Tribune,* Lawrence Gilman found him to be "an imposing figure . . . [with] an excellent voice . . . he sings with brains and discretion. High priests are usually the dullest animals in the operatic herd. Mr. Pinza made this one much more tolerable." Olin Downes, writing in the New York *Times,* described Pinza as "a majestic figure on the stage; a bass of superb sonority and impressiveness."

There followed engagements with the San Francisco and Chicago Opera companies, at Covent Garden in London, the Vienna State Opera, the Paris Opéra, the Salzburg Festival, and opera companies in South America. At the Salzburg festivals in Austria, over a period of several years, he was acclaimed in the title roles of *Don Giovanni* and *The Marriage of Figaro.*

At the Metropolitan Opera, where he remained until 1948, he was regarded as one of the most accomplished and most versatile bassos in the company. He was heard in over sixty roles. Though Italian opera was his specialty, he adapted himself flexibly to the varying styles of French, German, and Russian operas as well. The first time he was fully recognized for his versatility and artistry came with the assumption of the title role of Mozart's *Don Giovanni* on November 29, 1929, in its first performance during the Gatti-Casazza regime. He appeared as Don Giovanni at the Metropolitan Opera in New York 45 times after that, a number of appearances exceeded only by those as Ramfis in *Aida* (54 times). Other roles in which he made frequent appearances were Méphistophélès in *Faust* (38), Don Basilio in *The Barber of Seville* (33), Des Grieux in *Manon* (30), Colline in *La Bohème* (28), Escamillo in *Carmen* (28), and Raimondo in *Lucia di Lammermoor* (21).

One of his greatest triumphs at the Metropolitan Opera came in a Russian masterwork, *Boris Godunov,* when he sang the title role for the first time on March 7, 1939. (He had previously sung Pimenn to Chaliapin's Boris in Europe.) "Mr. Pinza's Boris proved to be a most painstaking portrayal," commented Pitts Sanborn in the *World-Telegram,* "intelligently planned and conscientiously wrought." In the *Herald Tribune,* Francis D. Perkins extolled Pinza's characterization: "It tells of an intent and thorough study of one of the most taxing and rewarding roles in the history of opera."

Pinza

Proof of his remarkable versatility lies in the many roles he sang successfully at the Metropolitan: Alvise in *La Gioconda,* Sparafucile in *Rigoletto,* Guardiano in *La Forza del Destino,* Archibaldo in *L'Amore dei Tre Re,* Oroveso in *Norma,* Zacharias in *Le Prophète,* King Dodon in *Le Coq d'Or,* Dulcamara in *L'Elisir d'Amore,* Nilakantha ih *Lakmé,* the High Priest in *Samson and Delilah,* Sarastro in *The Magic Flute,* Hermann in *Tannhäuser,* Tcherevik in *The Fair at Sorochinsk,* Golaud in *Pelléas and Mélisande,* the father in *Louise,* the Chancellor of Ragusa in Alfano's *Madonna Imperia,* and Pastor in Respighi's *La Campana Sommersa*—the last two in their American premieres.

While occupying a dominant place in the world of opera, Pinza also distinguished himself in recitals. His first New York concert took place on January 27, 1936, when, as one New York critic noted, he exhibited "a flexibility and lyricism not always associated with singers of this type." Pinza also appeared as a guest artist with symphony orchestras and was often heard on sponsored network radio programs.

His twentieth anniversary at the Metropolitan Opera was celebrated on March 23, 1946, in *Don Giovanni.* He was presented with a silver bowl by Edward Johnson, general manager.

Pinza made his last appearance at the Metropolitan Opera on March 5, 1948, once again as Don Giovanni. He went on from the opera house to carve for himself a remarkable new career in the Broadway musical theater, starring in the Rodgers and Hammerstein musical play *South Pacific,* which opened on April 7, 1949. The musical had a New York run of almost two thousand performances. As Émile de Becque, the wealthy middle-aged owner of a large plantation in a French-run island in the Pacific during World War II, Pinza became Broadway's newest matinee idol.

In May 1950 Pinza left the cast of *South Pacific* to head for Hollywood and motion pictures. He had made his screen debut with a brief singing segment—the "Champagne Aria" from *Don Giovanni*—in *Carnegie Hall* (1947). He was now returning as a star. However, in neither *Strictly Dishonorable* nor *Mr. Imperium* (both released in 1951) was he able to approach the triumphs he had so recently enjoyed on the Broadway stage. His last motion picture assignment was in *Tonight We Sing* (1953) and in this he once again filled only a singing segment.

In 1953 Pinza returned to the stage in a non-singing role in Molnar's *The Play's the Thing,* touring New England. After 1953 he was a frequent guest on major radio and television programs. Then, after suffering a heart attack in 1956, he announced that his career was at an end.

On May 9, 1957, he died following a stroke, in Stamford, Connecticut. Funeral services were held at the Cathedral of St. John in New York with Eleanor Steber singing the "Ave Maria" from *Otello.* Pinza was buried in Putnam Cemetery in Greenwich, Connecticut.

He was twice married. His first marriage, to Augusta Cassinelli, ended in divorce. They had a daughter, Claudia Pinza, who also became an opera singer; she made her debut in a major opera house on September 12, 1947, with the San Francisco Opera, appearing as Marguerite in a performance of *Faust* in which her father was heard as Méphistophélès. In 1940 Pinza married Doris Leak, a member of the ballet corps of the Metropolitan Opera. They lived first in Rye, New York, and later in Stamford, Connecticut. They had three children.

Pinza, six feet tall and weighing almost two hundred pounds, was athletically built. Strikingly handsome, he had a finely chiseled, Roman face, dark and intense eyes, and an aquiline nose, almond-shaped eyes, and thin, firm lips. He always dressed smartly, with a preference for vivid colors and checked jackets. In 1944 a nationwide poll in *Harper's Bazaar* placed him among the fourteen most glamorous men in the world.

He enjoyed watching boxing matches, skiing, riding a bicycle, boating, fishing, driving automobiles at great speed, taking pictures, and going to the movies. He collected pipes, watches, and Roman poison rings. Superstitious, he believed that Friday and the number thirteen were lucky for him. His good-luck charm was a battered doll that for many years was his mascot wherever he went—it decorated his dressing room at the opera house. He smoked incessantly, though only half a cigarette at a time, using a holder that was stuffed with cotton in an attempt to protect himself from nicotine.

ABOUT: New York Times, September 24, 1939; Opera News, March 2, 1942; Theatre Arts, February 1938; Vogue, April 15, 1939.

Pol Plançon

1851–1914

POL PLANÇON

In the era of great casts at the Metropolitan Opera early in the twentieth century, Pol Plançon, bass, was one of the truly luminous stars. A true bass, he had an unusually high range. His voice was acclaimed for its flexibility and suavity.

Pol-Henri Plançon was born in Fumay, France, on June 12, 1851. His parents wanted him to have a business career, and early in life he received some business training. Then, discovering he had a good singing voice and driven by his love for music, he studied voice in Paris with Gilbert Louis Duprez and Giovanni Sbriglia.

In 1877 he made his debut at the Lyons Opera as St. Bris in *Les Huguenots*. For the next two years he sang major roles in Lyons, not only in the standard repertory but also in such less familiar operas as Gounod's *Cinq-Mars* and Saint-Saëns's *Étienne Marcel*. For about a year after leaving Lyons he was heard in Monte Carlo and several provincial opera houses in France. Then, on February 11, 1880, he made his opera debut in Paris at the Théâtre de la Gaîeté as Colonna in Duprat's *Pétrarque,* and soon after that his concert debut in that city as a soloist with the Lamoureux Orchestra.

His career really began on June 23, 1883, when he appeared for the first time with the Paris Opéra and brought down the house with his interpretation of the role of Méphistophélès in *Faust*. This became one of his most celebrated roles; he appeared in it over a hundred times at the Paris Opéra during the next ten years. Also at the Opéra, he created the roles of Count de Gormas and Francia in the world premieres respectively of Massenet's *Le Cid* (November 30, 1885) and Saint-Saëns's *Ascanio* (March 21, 1890), and on April 2, 1884, he was heard as Attacus in a revival of Gounod's *Sapho*.

Plançon repeated his Paris successes in London where on June 3 he made his debut as Méphistophélès. He became a favorite in London and remained so, returning each season until 1904. In London he was starred in several more world premieres, among them Massenet's *La Navarraise* on June 20, 1894, Stanford's *Much Ado About Nothing* on May 30, 1901, and on June 11, 1898, the English premiere of Mancinelli's *Ero e Leandro*.

He resigned from the Paris Opéra in 1893. On November 29 of that year he went to the United States to make his initial American appearance at the Metropolitan Opera as Jupiter in the first American production in French of Gounod's *Philémon et Baucis*. H. E. Krehbiel reported in the *Tribune* that Plançon "won the hearts of the audience with his sonorous bass and suave and finished style," and predicted that he was "destined to be a popular favorite." Later the same season he was heard as Claudius in Thomas's *Hamlet,* Capulet in *Romeo and Juliet,* Pogner in *Die Meistersinger,* King Henry in *Lohengrin,* Hermann in *Tannhäuser,* and Lothario in *Mignon*. He sang his first Méphistophélès in *Faust* on December 30, 1893, when the Metropolitan Opera was on tour; after that he was heard in that role thirty-three times in New York and fifty-one times more on tour.

With the exception of the 1897–1898 season (when no resident company occupied the Metropolitan Opera House) and the seasons of 1901–1902 and 1902–1903, Plançon remained the principal bass of the Metropolitan Opera for fifteen years. He opened the seasons of 1894–1895, 1895–1896, 1899–1900, 1900–1901, and 1906–1907 as Capulet; those of 1904–1905 and 1905–1906 as Ramfis in *Aida* and Alvise in *La Gioconda,* respectively. He created for the United States the role of Astolat in Herman Bemberg's *Elaine* (December 17, 1894), Ariofarne in *Ero e Leandro* (March 10, 1899), and Méphisto-phélès in Berlioz' *The Damnation of Faust* (December 7, 1906). He was Count des Grieux in the first American production in French of *Manon* on January 16, 1895, Gormas in the first Metropolitan Opera production of *Le Cid* on February 12, 1897, and Sarastro in the first Metropolitan Opera production of *The Magic Flute* on March 30, 1900.

He became an all-important element in the all-star casts that illuminated the stage of the Metropolitan Opera between 1903 and 1908. In *Les Huguenots* he appeared with Sembrich, Nordica, Caruso, Journet, and Scotti; in *Aida,* with Caruso, Eames, and Scotti; in *Un Ballo in Maschera,* with Caruso, Journet, Eames, Louise Homer and Scotti; in *The Magic Flute* with Eames, Sembrich, Campanari, Ternina, and Dippel.

Among the many other roles in which he distinguished himself at the Metropolitan were Gessler in *William Tell,* Oberthal in *Le Prophète,* the title role in Boïto's *Mefistofele,* Balthazar in *La Favorita,* the Grand Inquisitor in *L'Africaine,* Escamillo in *Carmen,* Plunkett in *Martha,* and Count Rodolpho in *La Sonnambula.* His extensive repertory sometimes embraced two or three roles in a single opera: for example, Don Pedro, the Grand Inquisitor, and the Grand Brahmin in *L'Africaine;* Ramfis and the King in *Aida;* Capulet and Friar Laurence in *Romeo and Juliet;* St. Bris and Marcel in *Les Huguenots;* Abimelech and the Old Hebrew in *Samson and Delilah.*

His was a rich and sonorous voice with an unusually wide range; he handled it with sensitivity and virtuosity, particularly in florid runs and trills. To his vocal attainments he contributed an impressively dignified stage presence.

While serving with the Metropolitan Opera, Plançon achieved further successes as a recitalist throughout the United States. His last appearance on any operatic stage took place with his farewell performance at the Metropolitan Opera on January 11, 1908, as Plunkett. After his retirement, he lived in Paris where he devoted himself to teaching. He died in Paris on August 12, 1914.

ABOUT: Kutsch, K. J. and Riemens, L. A Concise Biographical Dictionary of Singers.

Lily Pons

1904–1976

Lily Pons (originally Alice Joséphine Pons), soprano, was born at Draguignan, near Cannes, France, on April 12, 1904. Her father, Auguste, who was French, was an automobile engineer who made newspaper headlines when Lily was three by driving a Sizaire-Naudin car from Paris to Peking; en route he got lost in Tibet and had to be towed the last lap of his journey. Her mother, Maria Naso Pons, was of Italian extraction.

Lily did not have an unusual voice as a child. She was first trained as a pianist at the Paris Conservatory which she entered when she was thirteen and where she won some prizes. A serious illness brought her piano study to an abrupt end when her physician ordered her to stay away from the keyboard for two years.

In 1918, soon after the Armistice that ended World War I, Lily decided to help her country by touring veteran hospitals and playing the piano for wounded soldiers. It was at a soldiers' hospital in Cannes that she sang in public for the first time. She kept on singing in hospitals after she found that her singing was better received than her piano playing.

Her professional entrance into music came in 1919 when at the age of fifteen she became a singing actress at the Théâtre des Variétés in Paris. She left the stage after she married August Mesritz, a wealthy retired Dutch lawyer and newspaper publisher, on November 15, 1923. Her husband, convinced that Lily had the makings of a great singer, engaged Alberti di Gorostiaga (later known in Hollywood, California, as Señor Alberti) to teach her. For five years Lily worked daily with Gorostiaga. In 1928 she made her opera debut at Mulhouse in Alsace in the title role of *Lakmé* (this later became her most famous role). After that she toured the provincial opera houses in France for two years. While this added to her experience, it did little to enhance her fame. At a performance in Montpellier in January 1930, she was heard by opera singers Maria Gay and her husband Giovanni Zenatello, who recommended her for an audition with the Metropolitan Opera.

When she went to the United States in 1930,

Pons: pôns

LILY PONS

March 16, 1932. In each of these she achieved a triumph. Her fresh, vital, flexible, and easily projected voice, in full command of all the resources of vocal technique, brought back to Metropolitan operagoers memories of the age when the art of coloratura singing was in its heyday. In addition, she was as wonderful to look at as she was to listen to. Slender, elegant, and diminutive—standing five feet one in height and weighing about one hundred pounds—she brought to her operatic characterizations a pert, attractive, and graceful personality and an engaging charm and warmth.

She sang ten roles at the Metropolitan. In addition to Lakmé, Lucia, Rosina and Amina of *La Sonnambula,* she sang Olympia in *The Tales of Hoffmann,* Philine in *Mignon,* Gilda in *Rigoletto,* Violetta in *La Traviata,* Linda in *Linda di Chamounix,* Queen of Shemakha in *Le Coq d'Or* and Marie in *The Daughter of the Regiment.* Through the years she remained one of the Metropolitan's most popular stars. On two occasions she was called upon to open the season: as Marie on November 23, 1942, and as Lakmé on November 11, 1946. She was box-office magic abroad as well. At Covent Garden (where she made her debut in May 1935 as Rosina), at the Paris Opéra, the Opéra-Comique in Paris, Teatro Colón in Buenos Aires, and other major opera houses she was for many years a star.

She was separated from her husband in 1931; divorce followed two years later. On June 2, 1938—at La Gentilhommière, her home in Silvermine, Connecticut—she married the conductor André Kostelanetz—the climax of a transcontinental courtship in which he had proposed to her thirteen times. Geraldine Farrar was matron of honor at the wedding.

With Pons as a soloist with the orchestra conducted by Kostelanetz, the couple soon became the most successful husband-and-wife team in the music business, attracting giant-sized audiences to each of their performances: for example, at Grant Park in Chicago the size of the audience at one of their concerts was estimated at three hundred thousand. During World War II, Pons aided the war effort by traveling with Kostelanetz one hundred thousand miles, to virtually every theater of operation: Europe, North Africa, Egypt, Indochina, and China-Burma. Her first USO tour, in the summer of 1944, took her for thirteen weeks to the Middle East, North Africa, and Italy. It proved so successful that a

she had never sung with a major opera company, and in the larger cities of France she was totally unknown. Singing the "Bell Song" from *Lakmé* for Gatti-Casazza, the general manager, Tullio Serafin, conductor, and Otto H. Kahn, opera patron, she won a five-year contract at a salary of four hundred and fifty dollars a week.

Her American debut took place at the Metropolitan Opera on January 3, 1931, in the title role of *Lucia di Lammermoor.* In her rendition of the "Mad Scene" she became probably the first singer in a hundred years to render the much-discussed high note of F instead of E-flat. Donizetti himself had changed the note from E-flat to F when he discovered a singer in Paris who could negotiate it; but since then no other soprano is believed to have tried to reach this high pitch.

Of her debut Olin Downes had this to say in the New York *Times:* "Her voice has range and freshness. Certain passages were sung with marked tonal beauty and emotional color. In the 'Mad Scene' some of the bravura passages were tossed off with the best of the virtuoso spirit. . . . Miss Pons gave the impression of sincerity, intelligence and the ability to work. She never did a cheap thing and when possible subjected technical display to musical expression."

During her first season she added to her success with impressive performances as Gilda in *Rigoletto* and Rosina in *The Barber of Seville.* Her extraordinary coloratura technique soon led the Metropolitan Opera to revive *Lakmé* for her on February 19, 1932, and *La Sonnambula* on year later in December 1975 Pons canceled her performances at the Metropolitan Opera to embark on a new USO tour of the European and China-Burma-India theaters of war. For her contributions to the war effort, the commanding officer of the India-Burma Theater awarded her the Asiatic-Pacific Campaign Service Ribbon (an honor previously conferred upon only thirteen other civilians); the United States government awarded her two citations for meritorious service; and she was adopted as the official daughter of General Le Clerc's Armored Division.

Though she had become an American citizen in 1940, she also aided the French Resistance movement in whatever way she could, for which she received the Order, Cross of Lorraine from Charles de Gaulle. When Paris was liberated, she participated in a ceremony at Rockefeller Plaza in New York, singing "The Marseillaise" before an audience of twenty thousand.

Many other honors came to her for her artistic achievements: France made her Chevalier, and then Officier, of the Legion of Honor and awarded her the gold medal of the city of Paris; Belgium conferred on her the Ordre de la Couronne de Belgique and presented her with a gold medal; the City of Cannes made her honorary consul. Two American locomotives were named after her, and a town in Maryland (Lilypons); and so were the culinary dishes Sole Lily Pons at the Raleigh Hotel in Washington, D.C., Coupe Lily Pons at the Madison Hotel in New York City, and Chicken Lily Pons at the Carter Hotel in Cleveland.

During the greater part of her twenty-year marriage to Kostelanetz they occupied a duplex apartment at Gracie Square in New York City. As long as she held center stage in the opera and concert world, she led a highly disciplined, regimented life to allow her to direct her fullest energies not only to her performances, rehearsals and the study of new roles but also to costume supervision, clothes design, interviews, and business conferences. She was able to perform her many duties efficiently and energetically, with a seemingly inexhaustible storehouse of vitality. She once explained that the source of her energy was "rest, air, and a sensible diet." An hour and a half each day was reserved for deep-breathing exercises in half-hour periods. She drank six quarts of water a day, a glassful every half hour. Walking was her main form of physical exercise. Her diet consisted mainly of green vegetables, fresh fruits, and salads. A daily siesta of at least an hour's duration was essential to her health routine. When she experienced a day of hard work she revived her energy by drinking a brew composed of verbena, essence of lemon, mint, and sage prepared in an earthenware pot. After drinking this she partook of a hot tub bath followed by a cold shower.

She never touched tobacco or hard liquor and she avoided keeping late hours. She said that among her many likes were kittens, lentil soup, eighteenth century furniture, tiny fleur-de-lis designs embroidered on her clothes, and autographs. Her pet superstition was that the number thirteen was lucky for her (her automobile license plate was LP-13).

Her twenty-fifth anniversary at the Metropolitan Opera was celebrated on January 3, 1956, with a gala performance in which she appeared as Gilda in Act II of *Rigoletto,* sang the "Mad Scene" from *Lucia di Lammermoor,* and concluded with arias by Donizetti, Thomas, Delibes, and Stravinsky. "Lily Pons, petite and chic as ever," wrote Harriet Johnson in the New York *Post,* "adorned the stage of the Metropolitan Opera last night both visually and vocally at the gala event in her honor. In appearance and in song she belied the fact that she had made her debut before the Diamond Horseshoe twenty-five years to the day. The management reported that she is the first prima donna soprano ever to establish such a record." Following the "Mad Scene" she was honored in speeches and presented with many gifts. "Because Miss Pons can still command her musical abilities with first-class prowess, the event had a genuinely gala flavor," added Johnson. "We celebrated with her; we didn't commemorate something she once was."

Her last appearances at the Metropolitan Opera took place during the 1960–1961 season, after which she went into retirement. She had given 198 performances in New York with that company, and 85 on tour.

In addition to her operatic and concert appearances, and her recordings for Columbia, she was frequently heard over network radio and television. She was also starred in three screen musicals: *I Dream Too Much* (1935), *That Girl from Paris* (1936), and *Hitting a New High* (1947). She appeared as herself in a few vocal segments in the motion picture *Carnegie Hall* (1947).

Pons and Kostelanetz were divorced in 1958. In retirement she divided her year between an apartment in Dallas, Texas, and a house in Palm Springs, California.

Kostelanetz, who was conducting Prom concerts at the Lincoln Center for the Performing Arts in New York, induced her to emerge briefly from that retirement, after a ten-year hiatus, as a "surprise guest artist" at a Prom concert on May 31, 1972. She was billed as a "surprise guest" because one of her conditions in accepting was that her appearance be given no publicity whatsoever. Exquisitely groomed, and still petite and chic, she sang two Donizetti arias together with several other numbers. "It was a kind of afterglow," said Irving Kolodin in the *Saturday Review,* "a final flaring up of the barely smoldering vocal flame, a stirring about of all but exhausted embers. Miss Pons had it at twenty-six, and she still has it at sixty-eight."

This was her last public appearance. She died of cancer at St. Paul's Hospital in Dallas on February 13, 1976. In view of her superstitious belief that the number thirteen was lucky for her, it is paradoxical that her death took place on Friday the thirteenth. She was buried in Cannes, France.

"She was a diva in the old-fashioned sense of the word," the New York *Times* noted in its eulogy. "Around her always was the impression of glamour, the rich life, the beautiful people, the soft lights and champagne. Miss Pons worked hard at this image. She always was one of the most elegantly groomed women in opera, and her entrances and exits offstage as well as on stage were regal. Gifted as she was with a lovely voice and the ability to project an enchanting and glamorous personality, it was no wonder that for some two decades, she was so integral a part of operatic life in America."

In 1977, Columbia Records released a six-disk commemorative album entitled *Lily Pons: Coloratura Assoluta.*

ABOUT: Ewen, D. Men and Women Who Make Music (1949 ed.). *Periodicals*—New York Times, February 14, 1976; Opera News, April 2, 1945, February 10, 1973, April 3, 1976; Saturday Review, June 24, 1972.

Rosa Ponselle

1897–

Rosa Ponselle (originally Rosa Melba Ponzillo), soprano, was born in Meriden, Connecticut, on January 22, 1897. Her parents, Benjamin and Madalena Ponzillo, had emigrated to the United States from Caserta, a small town in southern Italy. In Meriden, her father ran a grocery store and café.

Rosa received her first vocal lessons from her mother, who had been trained as a singer. Afterwards, she studied in Meriden with Anna Ryan. At ten, she sang in the church choir while attending public school. When she was fourteen she acquired her first job—in a motion picture theater in Meriden, playing the piano—and was later similarly employed in a New Haven restaurant.

Since her older sister, Carmela, also had a talent for singing, they formed a sister act singing opera arias and semi-classics. The act made its debut in the Bronx, New York, then toured the vaudeville circuit as The Ponzillo Sisters, eventually playing the Palace Theatre in New York. The Pittsburgh *Leader* in 1916 took note of their performance: "The Ponzillo Sisters, billed as Italian girls, but possessing perfect English accents and mannerisms, received an ovation they thoroughly deserve with a song repertoire combining operatic arias, ballads, and even a syncopation or two of the better sort. . . . They possess voices of wonderful tone-sweetness, unusual range and flexibility, sufficient power for even a vaudeville stage and the ability to handle themselves in a manner that left nothing to be desired."

At the Riverside Theatre in New York, Romano Romani, a successful opera composer, heard the Ponselle sisters. He went backstage to congratulate them and to advise them to consider opera seriously. With this in mind, Rosa began to study with William Thorner, who subsequently became her manager. Thorner brought her to Enrico Caruso. "After he heard me," Ponselle told James A. Drake in *Stereo Review,* "he told me confidentially that I had everything I needed in the throat and in the heart, and that what remained for me to get was

Ponselle: pŏn sĕl′

ROSA PONSELLE

what I needed musically in my head. Then he told me flatly, 'You will sing with me.' " Caruso had her audition at the Metropolitan Opera for Gatti-Casazza, the general manager. She sang two arias from *Aida* and two from *Il Trovatore*. Gatti-Casazza was impressed, but before he would engage her he wanted her to learn two new arias: "Casta diva" from *Norma* and "Pace, pace" from *La Forza del Destino*. She returned for a second audition a few weeks later, and that day she was given a contract.

Ponselle is one of the rare examples in operatic performing history of a singer appearing for the first time in an opera and immediately becoming a prima donna. Her debut took place at the Metropolitan Opera on November 15, 1918, in the company's first production of *La Forza del Destino*. She assumed the leading female role of Leonora opposite Caruso's Don Alvaro—the only time that an American-born singer made a debut opposite Caruso.

Just before her performance Ponselle burst into tears with nervousness. Her throat became inflamed, and for a while it seemed as if her debut would have to be postponed. Caruso came to her rescue with a throat remedy which seemed to work wonders, for the inflammation was instantly relieved.

"To make matters worse," Ponselle later revealed to James A. Drake, "Thorner insisted that I vocalize in my dressing room just to make sure the voice was all right. That's when I really panicked—my voice sounded horrid, and I was sure I'd lost it. Later on I realized that I had

been vocalizing in a room that had massive drapes, heavy carpeting and every other sound-absorbing thing you could imagine. In any case, I managed to live through the first act in spite of myself, and then, wonder of wonders, I realized that I'd made it through the second act. From then on I was fairly stable, even though the soprano role in *Forza* lies high. By the last act I was totally calm, but afterward I spent several days in the hospital recuperating from the emotional drainage I experienced."

"What a promising debut!" exclaimed James Gibbons Huneker in the New York *Times*. "Added to her personal attractiveness she possesses a voice of natural beauty that may prove to be a gold mine. It is vocal gold, anyhow, with its luscious lower and middle tones, dark, rich and ductile; brilliant and flexible in the upper register. . . . After she sang the 'Addio' in Act I, she had her audience captured."

That debut made her a star, in recognition of which she was cast in two important premieres in her first season: the first Metropolitan Opera production of *Oberon* on December 28, 1918 (as Rezia), and as Carmelita in the world premiere of an American opera, Joseph Breil's *The Legend* on March 12, 1919. About her performance as Rezia, Huneker wrote: "With her dramatic temperament, musical intelligence, above all, with her beautiful, natural voice and its remarkable range from a rich velvety contralto to a vibrating, silvery soprano—well, for a newcomer on the operatic boards a few months ago, and with artistic training and antecedents, we confess our hearty admiration for her work and high hopes for her brilliant future."

She fulfilled those hopes as Rachel in *La Juive* (which had been revived for Caruso on November 22, 1919), as Norma (November 16, 1927), and as Donna Anna in *Don Giovanni* (January 2, 1930). Other roles in which she distinguished herself were Aida, Gioconda, Carmen, Luisa Miller, Selika in *L'Africaine*, Violetta in *La Traviata*, Giulia in Spontini's *La Vestale*, Santuzza in *Cavalleria Rusticana*, Elisabetta in *Don Carlo*, Maddalena in *Andrea Chénier*, Elvira in *Ernani*, and Leonora in *Il Trovatore*.

"There are voices and voices," wrote Harold C. Schonberg in the New York *Times* many years after Ponselle had sung her last performance, "and the Metropolitan Opera in the 1930s had many great ones. But there was nothing like the Ponselle sound, ever. To many of us it was the greatest single voice in any category. . . . Ponselle seemed to have everything. . . . She had the low notes of a contralto, and a knockout high C; and there were no artificial registers to the voice. . . . And that trill; that articulated br-r-r which no singer today is able to come near matching! And the emotion of her singing, withal combined with good taste! And the power when she let loose! And the delicacy of her pianissimos! And the flexibility in coloratura work! And that effortless intonation! And the handsome figure on the stage! The good fairy was very kind to Rosa Ponselle."

She made a triumphant debut at Covent Garden in May 1929 as Norma. "Nothing finer has been seen or heard at Covent Garden this season," Ernest Newman said of her performance in the London *Sunday Times.* She returned to Covent Garden the following year to make her first appearance on any stage as Violetta in June 1930. "Her Violetta," Ernest Newman wrote, "is so exquisitely sung because it is so subtly imagined. Even coloratura, as she sings it, ceases to suggest the aviary and becomes the revelation of human character." She was back in Covent Garden in 1931 and in the spring of 1933 as Leonora in *La Forza del Destino,* as Violetta, and in the title role in Romano Romani's *Fedra.* And she was heard both as Norma and as Giulia in *La Vestale* at the Florence May Music Festivals. These were her sole appearances in Europe.

In the United States, while performing at the Metropolitan Opera she was frequently heard in recitals and over the radio.

She gratified a life's ambition when on December 27, 1935, she sang Carmen for the first time. Lawrence Gilman commented in the *Herald Tribune* that "she achieved an intelligent and workmanlike performance," but most of the other critics dissented.

On December 13, 1936, Ponselle married Carl A. Jackson, an American industrialist who was the son of Baltimore's mayor. They built a five-hundred-thousand-dollar Renaissance Italian house in Green Spring Valley, twelve miles from Baltimore, and named it Villa Pace after the famous aria "Pace pace" in *La Forza del Destino,* the opera in which she had made her debut. In the first year of her marriage she asked Edward Johnson, the general manager of the Metropolitan Opera, to allow her to do a role close to her heart, that of Adriana Lecouvreur in Cilèa's opera of that name. Johnson refused, and

she handed in her resignation even though she was at the height of her fame and at the peak of her vocal powers. "I was demoralized," she explained. She made her last appearance on the stage of the Metropolitan Opera on February 15, 1937, as Carmen. Never again did she step on that or any other opera stage. She had appeared with the Metropolitan Opera 258 times in New York and 107 times on tour, in twenty-two roles.

Her retirement from an active career as a singer and her withdrawal to Villa Pace became more or less permanent when soon after her resignation she suffered a nervous breakdown. She emerged briefly from that retirement in 1952 to sing at President Eisenhower's inauguration and again in 1954 to make a few recordings which demonstrated that she was still in possession of a magnificent voice. "On this record," wrote Paul Hume, music critic in Washington, D.C., "are the sound, the quality, the timbre and the constant element of vocal style that were Ponselle's inimitable characteristics."

(Ponselle had made her first recordings in 1918, for Columbia, transferring to Victor five years later. In all she recorded over one hundred operatic and concert numbers. Columbia reissued some of these early releases, in an LP devoted entirely to Verdi, to celebrate Ponselle's seventy-fifth birthday in 1972.)

Ponselle divorced her husband in 1950. That same year she became artistic director of the Baltimore Civic Opera Company. To commemorate her seventy-fifth birthday this company presented a gala performance of the opera with which she had made her Metropolitan Opera debut, *La Forza del Destino.* A surprise party, attended by many world-famous singers, was given in celebration of her eightieth birthday in Baltimore on January 22, 1977. Ponselle responded to the warmth and affection of her guests by singing "I Love You Truly."

For many years Ponselle interested herself in designing and interior decoration. While still active in opera, she used to walk at least three miles a day, sometimes supplementing this exercise with bicycling in order to keep herself physically fit.

She meticulously followed a set routine during her years at the Metropolitan Opera: dinner at 4:30 in the afternoon, usually consisting of beef broth, steak or lamb chops, and hot Ovaltine; an early arrival at the opera house; swallowing an egg just before going on stage; and refusing to have any social contact with her colleagues at the theater before performance-time.

In 1957 Ponselle was chosen the Italian-American of the year. In 1969 she was made Commander, Order of Merit, Republic of Italy.

Her sister, Carmela, also became an opera singer, making her debut at the Metropolitan Opera on December 5, 1925, as Amneris in *Aida*. She remained in the company until 1935. On December 21, 1932, the two sisters appeared together at the Metropolitan in *La Gioconda*. After leaving the Metropolitan Opera Carmela devoted herself to radio broadcasting, to teaching, and to charity work on behalf of the underprivileged and the handicapped. Her last public appearance took place in April 1951 at a charity concert in Madison Square Garden, New York City, at which she sang "O don fatale" from *Don Carlo*.

ABOUT: Secrist, J. B. Rosa Ponselle: Biography and Discography; Thompson, O. The American Singer. *Periodicals*—Hi-Fi, September 1970; Musical America, April 1963; New York Times, January 23, 1972; Opera News, February 6, 1965, March 12, 1977; Stereo Review, April 1977.

MAUD POWELL

Maud Powell

1868–1920

Maud Powell was one of the outstanding violinists of her time. She was born in Peru, Illinois, on August 22, 1868. Her father, William Bramwell Powell, an author and superintendent of schools in Peru, had come from a Welsh background; her mother, Minnie Paul Powell, of German-Hungarian parentage, was an excellent amateur musician and composer. Her uncle, Major John Wesley Powell, was an eminent ethnologist and a pioneer explorer of the Grand Canyon.

When Maud was two years old, her family moved to Aurora, Illinois, where her father was engaged as superintendent of schools. In her fourth year she began receiving violin lessons from her mother, continuing them later with William Fickenscher while attending public school. She proved to be a prodigy performing Mozart violin sonatas when she was eight. At nine she traveled in the Midwest as a soloist with the Chicago Ladies Quartet.

In her ninth year Maud began traveling once a week to Chicago, forty miles from her home, to study violin with William Lewis and piano with Agnes Ingersoll. She continued this program for four years. By the time she was twelve, contributions from the people of Aurora made it possible for her to go to Europe for more intensive and expert training. After a year of violin study with Henry Schradieck, she received a diploma in 1881 at examinations given at the Gewandhaus. She then went to Paris where she was one of six, from a group of eighty, to gain admission to the violin class of Charles Dancla at the Paris Conservatory.

Her concert career began in her fifteenth year with performances in London and the English provinces and appearances before Queen Victoria. In London, Joseph Joachim became interested in her and encouraged her to study with him at the High School of Music in Berlin. She did so for two years. In 1885 Maud made her debut in Berlin as a soloist with the Berlin Philharmonic in a performance of Bruch's Concerto in G minor.

She returned to the United States in 1885 and appeared with the New York Philharmonic under Theodore Thomas on November 14, once again in the Bruch concerto. This was the beginning of a concert career in the United States that continued for several seasons and comprised a number of tours, including annual circuits of the country as soloist with Theodore Thomas's orchestra. A sensitive musician, more concerned with musical than with technical values, Powell was already a virtuoso of the first order. But the prevailing prejudice against women violinists precluded the acceptance she deserved, a fact that embittered her considerably. Nevertheless, she continued to forge ahead in her career, though not as successfully as was her due. In 1892 she was a soloist with the New York Arion Society, touring Austria and Germany in quadricentennial commemoration of the discovery of America. In 1893 she was invited to perform at the World's Columbian Exhibition in Chicago.

Partly through her interest in chamber music, but mainly because of her failure to gain full recognition as a virtuoso, Powell temporarily deserted solo work to form the Maud Powell Quartet which toured the United States for about four years. After the quartet was disbanded in 1898, she went to Europe, establishing her home there for several years. She made extended tours of Europe, of the United States, of Russia (in 1903 with Sousa's Band), and of South Africa (forty appearances in 1905–1906). She also gave command performances for King Edward VII, the Dukes of Cambridge and Edinburgh, and the Princess Royal of England.

On September 21, 1904, she married H. Godfrew Turner, her English manager. After the marriage he became her business manager and arranged her tours. Their home was in Great Neck, Long Island, with summers spent in Whitfield, New Hampshire. During World War I she performed and lectured for American armed forces in camps. In her late years she combined concert appearances with performances in schools and colleges in an effort to reach out to new audiences. She was on a concert tour in 1920 when she suffered a heart attack in Uniontown, Pennsylvania. She died there in her hotel room on January 8, 1920.

Maud Powell introduced to the United States many violin concertos, including those of Dvořák and Sibelius, Bruch's D minor Concerto, the Concerto No.2 of Saint-Saëns, Lalo's F minor Concerto, and various works by Rimsky-Korsakov, Arensky, Coleridge-Taylor, and others. She was also one of the first violinists to promote the Tchaikovsky Violin Concerto in America and one of the first to make recordings (for Victor Talking Machine Company). As a member of the Brooklyn Music School Settlement she encouraged young aspiring musicians, and as one of the earliest members of the Music Service League she helped bring phonographs and recordings to hospitals, prisons, and other public institutions.

She made a number of transcriptions and arrangements for violin and piano.

ABOUT: Lahee, H. C. Famous Violinists of Today and Yesterday; Martens, F. H. Violin Mastery. *Periodicals* —Etude, October 1911; Musical America, January 17, 1920; New York Times, January 9, 1920.

André Previn

1929–

André Previn, conductor and pianist, was born in Berlin on April 6, 1929. His father, Jacob, was a distinguished judge and lawyer who was also a competent pianist; his mother, Charlotte Epstein Previn, came from Alsace-Lorraine. "Our house was music every night," Previn revealed to Helen Lawrenson in an interview in *Esquire.* "The place was filled with Lieder." And not only *Lieder;* each week there were chamber music concerts.

André's interest in music revealed itself early. When he was six he asked to be given music lessons; by this time he had already shown that he had perfect pitch. His father enrolled him in the Berlin Conservatory where he received a grounding in piano, harmony, theory, and composition.

The Previns were Jewish; in spite of this they were for a time left unmolested by the Nazi regime because of the older Previn's prestige. But in 1938 André was expelled from the Conservatory because of his religion. At the same time, one of his father's former clients warned him that the Previn family was in imminent danger of arrest. The Previns fled to Paris where they lived under conditions which André has described as "squalid," waiting for a visa to the United States. They had to wait a year; during that time André attended the Paris Conservatory.

The Previns went to the United States in 1939, settling in Los Angeles. Jacob Previn, unable to pursue his profession of law, went to work as a teacher of piano, a profession he continued to pursue until the end of his life in 1963. In Los Angeles, André continued his academic and

Previn: prĕ′ vĭn

645

ANDRÉ PREVIN

musical education—at the Beverly Hills High School and by studying composition with Joseph Achron and later with Mario Castelnuovo-Tedesco. In 1943 André became an American citizen.

While attending high school he played in and sometimes conducted the California Youth Orchestra, did orchestrations for radio shows, and prepared music for the annual senior shows at Beverly Hills High School. He also became interested in American popular music in general and jazz in particular, often playing jazz pieces on the piano or participating in jazz performances with small combos. In 1945 he made some jazz recordings.

His exceptional articulateness as a popular musician and his rapidly growing reputation for producing slick arrangements and transcriptions brought him to the attention of the music department of the MGM motion picture studios. For the filming of *Holiday in Mexico,* starring José Iturbi, the studio needed a piano transcription of an improvised jazz number. Though André was not quite sixteen and was still a high school student, he was asked to do this job in 1945. He completed it with such professional dispatch that from then on the MGM studios called on him frequently to play the piano at rehearsals and to do some transcriptions and orchestrations. He was assigned to write his first motion picture score, and to conduct it, in 1949 for *The Sun Comes Up.* "It was the most inept score you ever heard," he says frankly. But he also has added: "As soon as I had conducted for

two days I realized that it was all I ever wanted to do. It was an instant and complete revelation."

In 1949 Previn was engaged by MGM studios to serve in the dual capacity of composer and conductor. He worked on some ten motion pictures within a single year. None of this music was important—in fact Previn winces whenever he remembers it—but it fully met the functional demands of the pictures for which it was intended. Measured by Hollywood standards, Previn was a success: He was being kept busy all the time, and he was making a great deal of money.

In 1950 his career was temporarily interrupted when he was called to military service. Stationed in San Francisco and eventually rising to the rank of sergeant, he remained in uniform two years, most of the time busily engaged making musical arrangements for the army. In San Francisco, Previn took one step forward in his ambition to become a conductor, by becoming one of the two private pupils of Pierre Monteux. Also in San Francisco, he met and married Betty Bennett, a young singer. They had two daughters but eventually were divorced.

After being released from the army in 1952, Previn went back to MGM studios. He became one of the top musicians in the motion picture industry both as an arranger of scores and as a creator of original music. He was also writing popular songs at this time, some of which were interpolated in his MGM motion pictures. He received Academy Awards for his scoring of the screen musicals *Kiss Me, Kate* (1953), *Kismet* (1955), *Silk Stockings* (1957), *Gigi* (1958), *Porgy and Bess* (1959), *Bells Are Ringing* (1960), *Irma la Douce* (1963), and *My Fair Lady* (1964). For his original music for Gene Kelly's *Invitation to the Dance* (1955) he was awarded a Screen Composers Association Award. Among the other motion pictures for which Previn contributed either original background music or did the scoring were *Bad Day at Black Rock* (1955), *Hot Summer Night* (1957), *The Subterraneans* (1960), *Elmer Gantry* (1960), *Long Day's Journey into Night* (1962), *Two for the Seesaw* (1962), *Harper* (1966), *Thoroughly Modern Millie* (1967), *The Graduate* (1967), *Catch 22* (1970), and *The Music Lovers* (1971)—the last of these was the screen biography of Tchaikovsky, utilizing his music. For *Rollerball* (1975) Previn conducted the orchestra.

Previn's energy and versatility did not allow

him to confine himself exclusively to the movies. He made recordings of both serious and popular music, as a solo pianist and as a member of a group; his solo piano recordings of twentieth century compositions by Samuel Barber, Poulenc, and Frank Martin, among others, have become collector's items. He performed publicly with jazz ensembles. He appeared as a piano soloist with chamber music groups and with orchestras. He wrote songs which were performed by Judy Garland and Doris Day.

By 1960 he had decided to make a serious try at becoming a symphony conductor. He confided this ambition to Schuyler Chapin, then one of the heads of Columbia Records, who put him in the hands of a manager. Because of his background both in jazz and in the Hollywood music studio Previn met considerable opposition from established orchestras who, when they were offered Previn, wanted him only for semipop or Promenade concerts of light music. As a conductor of the serious repertory, Previn had to learn his trade by conducting minor orchestral organizations. "I conducted in the sticks with semi-pro orchestras," he later recalled, "where the members all have other jobs. I'd do the concerts for like two hundred dollars. Anything. My income went plummeting right away. What you get for Mahler is not what you get for Sandra Dee. I decided it was a worthwhile trade."

A major breakthrough in his conducting career came in 1964 when he left Columbia Records, for which he had been making popular-music recordings, for RCA Victor. Victor allowed him to record at least four classical albums a year, the first two being Rachmaninoff's Symphony No.2 and Tchaikovsky's Symphony No.2. As Previn's serious-music recordings gained in acceptance, he was allowed to spread his wings considerably. On the strength of his recordings he received assignments to make conducting guest appearances with major orchestras in St. Louis, Dallas, Minneapolis, and Houston.

The Houston Symphony Orchestra liked him so well that when Sir John Barbirolli resigned as its permanent conductor in 1967 Previn was the surprise choice as his replacement. He led the first concerts of the regular subscription series in Houston on October 2, 1967 (following a tour of six Texas college towns), in a program made up of Brahms's *Academic Festival Overture*, William Schuman's Symphony No.3, and Beetho-

ven's Symphony No.5. The orchestra performed, as a critic for the Houston *Post* reported, with "uncommon brilliance." The critic added: "This first concert showed Previn capably in command of a burnished symphonic ensemble." The critic of the Houston *Chronicle* described Previn as a conductor "who is obviously going to usher in a new dynamism—his music is vividly communicative, muscular and decisive."

Previn became a dynamic force in Houston's musical life. As Martin Bernheimer, the Los Angeles music critic, remarked in 1968: "He took over from Sir John Barbirolli . . . and found himself confronted with a fine orchestra, a somewhat stodgy tradition, a new multimillion-dollar auditorium, and a slightly quizzical community. His program has been decisive. Attendance figures have risen forty-four per cent. . . . Audiences that once thought the twentieth century ended with Samuel Barber now find themselves forced to cope with Penderecki, Lukas Foss, Michael Tippett, and Richard Rodney Bennett." In addition to updating the repertory, Previn took over the direction of the children's concerts and opened up some of his rehearsals to students. To create a more tolerant climate in Houston for modern music he even stepped into the halls of academe—Houston University—to give a course on twentieth century music.

He made his first appearance in New York as symphony conductor on March 10, 1968, on the invitation of Leopold Stokowski. Leading the American Symphony Orchestra at Carnegie Hall, Previn gave a thoroughly competent account of himself in the music of Mozart, Beethoven, Nielsen, and Ravel. Later the same year he became the totally unexpected choice of the London Symphony Orchestra in England to become its principal conductor. Curiously, when Previn had been interviewed over BBC earlier in 1968 he expressed a hope that someday he might become conductor of the London Symphony. "Not for a moment did I think then that I would have a chance for years. Yet I was offered it four months later and was absolutely amazed." Previn became the eighth man to hold the position of principal conductor of this orchestra founded in 1904—Hans Richter had been its first conductor. Previn and the London Symphony, however, were no strangers in 1968. He had conducted the orchestra on records since 1964 and had made a number of guest appearances with it not only in London but also in Daytona

Beach, Florida. The London Symphony is a co-operative, self-governing symphonic organization, and it was the musicians themselves who chose Previn to succeed István Kertész on a three-year contract. Before that contract was terminated it was renewed for an indefinite period, virtually giving Previn a life appointment.

"Before André became our regular conductor," Stuart Knussen, the orchestra's first-bass player and chairman of the orchestra's board of directors, told Helen Lawrenson, "there was quite a bit of apprehension [about him]. He was American and he was from Hollywood and all that. But he won us over from the start. He won us over musically because he feels it so deeply and he knows what he's doing. And he is so great as a human being. Most conductors are very egotistical. Autocratic. Humorless. Demanding to be treated with deference, like a sultan or an emperor. André has humility and humor, both so rare as to be nonexistent in most symphony orchestra conductors."

For one year Previn commuted between Houston and London. Then in May 1969 the directors of the Houston Symphony announced that Previn's contract would not be renewed since he could not devote as much of his time and energy to Houston as was required.

Until the fall of 1976 the London Symphony remained Previn's only full-time orchestra, and at its head he rose to a place of first importance among conductors in England. He built up an extensive and progressive repertory and proved that he had all this music well in the palm of his hand and in the furthest recesses of his mind. His performances were the products of keen musicianship, immaculate good taste, the highest integrity, and penetrating interpretative insights. He played the standard repertory, to be sure, but also much of modern music—American music, his own music, avant-garde music and, to the delight of his audiences, English music. Unafraid of comparison with his distinguished English colleagues of the recent past and present who have proved themselves to be the ultimate authorities in the presentation of twentieth century English music, Previn went on to perform a cycle of Vaughan Williams's symphonies, the two symphonies of Sir Edward Elgar, and the music of Sir William Walton, Sir Michael Tippett, Benjamin Britten, and other English composers of the present and recent past.

When Previn signed a new three-year contract with the London Symphony in 1976 he became the longest-serving principal conductor in the history of that orchestra. Then, in 1977, Previn announced that this contract would be his last with the London Symphony and would terminate in August 1979.

Among Previn's extensive recordings with the London Symphony Orchestra for RCA, London, Angel, and Philips are all nine symphonies of Vaughan Williams, the nine symphonies of Dvořák, the four Rachmaninoff piano concertos (with Vladimir Ashkenazy), all the symphonies of Prokofiev, and Walton's *Belshazzar's Feast,* the last of which earned a Grammy from the National Academy of Recording Arts and Sciences in 1974.

His worldwide tours with the London Symphony and his recordings extended Previn's fame far beyond the borders of Great Britain. Between 1970 and 1976 he made three tours of the United States. With his orchestra he has performed in the Soviet Union. In 1973 the London Symphony under his direction became the first British orchestra invited to perform at the Salzburg Festival, where he offered the Austrian premiere of Shostakovich's Symphony No. 8; he and the orchestra returned to Salzburg in 1975 and 1976. During a German tour in 1972 he appeared on some of his programs as his own piano soloist in several concertos by Mozart.

Previn made numerous guest appearances with other symphonic organizations in Europe and the United States. Even in the jet age of traveling conductors, his activity through the years almost staggers the imagination. In the single year 1970–1971, for example, he made one hundred and fourteen appearances; in February 1970 he conducted every single night except four. He made his debut at the Edinburgh Festival in September 1971, and in the spring of 1972 he gave his first concerts in Israel as a guest conductor of the Israel Philharmonic. Subsequently he also made his debut as an opera conductor at Covent Garden, where he performed Sir William Walton's *Troilus and Cressida.*

Of his many guest engagements in all parts of the music world the one that touched him most personally and most poignantly was his appearance with the Berlin Philharmonic in 1969, his first return to his native country since he had been forced to leave it three decades earlier. One of his most profoundly moving childhood memories had been a concert of the Berlin Philharmonic conducted by Wilhelm Furtwängler which he had attended in his fifth year. Returning to Germany to conduct this orchestra, he presented the same program Furtwängler had performed when the young Previn had heard him: an all-Brahms concert including the *Tragic Overture,* the Violin Concerto, and the Symphony No.4. Previn's success at this concert and the adulation that attended him during his Berlin stay were sweet to one who thirty years earlier had been forced to flee from Germany because he had been born a Jew.

In addition to appearing in London with his orchestra, Previn was also heard as a pianist in chamber music performances at the South Bank Music Festival of which he was director from 1972 to 1974. Contributing further to his musical influence in England have been his regular television programs over BBC year after year. His program "André Previn's Music Night" in 1970 proved so successful that a year later BBC-TV signed him to a three-year contract (since renewed) in continuance of that show and for appearances in other BBC productions. In addition to formal concerts over television and various specials, Previn has produced and appeared in programs on specific subjects such as American music, Shostakovich, and the problems of rehearsing.

On November 7, 1959, Previn married Dory Langdon, whose specialty was the writing of song lyrics. She became his collaborator, providing words to many of Previn's popular songs which were heard in motion pictures such as *Pepe* (1960), *Two for the Seesaw* (1962), *Irma la Douce* (1963), *Goodbye, Charlie* (1964), and *The Valley of the Dolls* (1967), and which were recorded by Sammy Davis Jr., Dionne Warwick, Jack Jones, and others. Dory also provided the lyrics for the songs in Previn's debut as a composer for the Broadway musical theater: *Coco,* starring Katharine Hepburn, which opened on Broadway on December 18, 1969, and had a run of over three hundred performances. The words-and-music collaboration of husband and wife lasted a decade, and then was permanently shattered by the much publicized romance between Previn and the motion picture actress Mia Farrow, and Previn's confirmation that she was pregnant with his child. In the spring of 1969 Previn and Dory Langdon were separated, and in August 1970 they were divorced. Langdon

exposed her personal wounds publicly in a record album, *On My Way to Where,* in which she wrote the words and music for the songs, all of which were autobiographical, and sang them to her own guitar accompaniment.

On September 10, 1970, Previn and Mia Farrow were married in a small private ceremony in a Unitarian church in London; this was half a year after Farrow had given birth to twin boys, an event that made front-page news. Farrow appeared as a soloist under her husband's direction at a concert of the London Symphony on February 5, 1971, in a performance of Honegger's *Joan of Arc at the Stake* (a speaking role), a concert that was broadcast by BBC.

The Previn family which includes not only three of the children of André and Mia but also two Vietnamese children they adopted, occupies a seventeenth century farmhouse in Surrey, England, near Dawes Green. Their house is surrounded by eighteen acres of woods and is furnished with antiques the Previns picked up around the English countryside. Previn, who is small and slight and wears a Beatle-type haircut, was described by Helen Lawrenson as "something like a jaunty, amiable mouse." On the conductor's platform, with his slim stooped frame, he has the appearance of a praying mantis.

He is a man with an engaging wit who delights in exchanging stimulating ideas or light talk with his intimate friends, among whom are Daniel Barenboim, Jacqueline du Pré, Vladimir Ashkenazy, and Itzhak Perlman. He requires only five hours of sleep a night. The rest of the time he is a whirlwind of energy. Away from his music he does much reading and he collects contemporary American folk art. He wrote the music for a musical comedy, an adaptation of J. B. Priestley's *The Good Companions* (lyrics by Johnny Mercer), which had a brief run in London.

In 1975 Previn was named music director of the Pittsburgh Symphony, as a replacement for William Steinberg. Without relinquishing his post in London, he assumed the new post in the fall of 1976, directing his first concert on September 10, a program made up of music by Berlioz, Brahms, and Shostakovich. In 1978 the Pittsburgh contract was renewed for an additional three years, to end in 1982. Once again in his career he had one leg in the United States and another in England; he retained the leadership of these two world-famous orchestras until 1979.

Prey

In addition to performances at Heinz Hall for the Performing Arts in Pittsburgh, Previn and the Pittsburgh Symphony made numerous television appearances over the Public Broadcasting Service and many recordings.

Previn has composed a considerable amount of concert music: for orchestra, the *Comedy Overture, Symphony for Strings,* concertos for the violin, for cello, for guitar, and other compositions; for chamber music combinations, a wind quintet, a brass quintet, a string quintet; for piano, two sets of piano preludes for Vladimir Ashkenazy, one of which is named *The Invisible Drummer* and the other, *Pages from a Calendar.* "I'm always composing," he told Francis Crociata in an interview for the New York *Times,* "but I have no delusions. I'm a conductor who also composes. People will ask me if I expect my works to be played fifteen years from now. That question never occurs to me, and I really don't care. I only know I want them to be played now."

ABOUT: Greenfield, E. André Previn; Previn, A. and Hopkins, A. Music Face to Face; Smyth, A. ed. To Speak for Ourselves. *Periodicals*—Esquire, July 1971; Hi-Fi, November 1974; High Fidelity/Musical America, August 1968; New York Times, March 10, 1968, March 14, 1976; Saturday Evening Post, November 18, 1961, February 19, 1977; Time, April 1970, September 4, 1972.

Hermann Prey

1929–

Hermann Prey, baritone, was born in Berlin on July 11, 1929. His father, also named Hermann, was a merchant, and his mother, Anna Senkbeil Prey, had a pleasant singing voice. Early in life, revealing a gift for singing, Hermann became a member of his elementary school choir when he was nine and one year later joined the Berlin Mozart Choir. His interest in music was encouraged by his mother. "I knew music was my life," he told an interviewer about these boyhood singing experiences.

He was fifteen when the final siege of Berlin, in the closing days of World War II, took place. When he passed his physical examinations for the Nazi army, his father burned his draft card.

Prey: prī

HERMANN PREY

Hermann Prey recalls: "For three weeks we had been living in the basement of my grandfather's house, eating canned foods. We would listen in terror to the screeching of the bombs, the explosions day and night, the gunfire. Once we heard running feet. Someone looked outside and it was the SS (the *Schutzstafel,* a quasi-military unit of the Nazi party, used as special police). Another time, it was the Russians, then the SS again. Finally, the Russians came, took our food, and the wait was over. I know that the fear I learned then is the root of the icy emotions I project whenever I sing Schubert's *Die Winterreise.*"

At war's end, Prey continued his musical activities, conducting a school band that performed for the American and British occupation troops. Upon graduation from high school in 1948, he entered the Berlin Hochschul für Musik where under Günter Baum he studied voice for the first time. At the same time he took private lessons in singing from Harry Gottschalk. To support himself he organized and played in a jazz band and wrote popular songs which his band performed in nightclubs.

His musical training ended in 1952. That was the year he entered the Meistersinger competition for singers sponsored by the United States Armed Forces. Competing with twenty-five hundred other singers, Prey emerged with first prize, which entitled him to public appearances in the United States. Before embarking for America, he made his opera debut at the Hessische Staatstheater in Wiesbaden as Moruccio in Eugène d'Albert's *Tiefland* in September 1952.

About a month later he left for the United States, appearing that November and December as a soloist with the Philadelphia Orchestra under Ormandy and the National Symphony Orchestra of Washington, D.C., under Howard Mitchell. A critic in Washington wrote: "Herr Prey already possesses a gift older singers never acquire."

Upon returning to Germany, Prey became a member of the Hamburg State Opera. He remained with that company from 1953 to 1957, appearing in many Verdi roles for which he was both vocally and temperamentally unsuited, as well as in a repertory of contemporary operas by Rolf Liebermann, Gottfried von Einem, Luigi Dallapiccola, and Hans Werner Henze among others. Beginning in 1956 he appeared regularly as a guest artist with the Berlin State Opera. One year later he made his debut with the Vienna State Opera. During the summer of 1956 he made his first appearance at the Bayreuth Festival, as Wolfram in *Tannhäuser*. During these years he was also heard as a concert singer and in oratorios, two fields in which he subsequently achieved world renown.

He returned to the United States as a concert singer, making his New York City debut in the fall of 1956 with a recital in Carnegie Hall. He was heard in Schubert's *Die Schöne Müllerin* and in Beethoven's *An die Ferne Geliebte*. In the New York *Times* Ross Parmenter described Prey as "an appealing young German baritone . . . who obviously loves Lieder and . . . knew his chosen works well."

He made his debut at the Metropolitan Opera on December 17, 1960, as Wolfram. The critical reaction was mixed. He did not appear at the Metropolitan Opera for another four years. When he returned on December 2, 1964, as Count Almaviva in *The Marriage of Figaro* he won far greater approval. On February 19, 1967, he was acclaimed for what has since become one of his greatest roles, that of Papageno in the new Marc Chagall–designed *The Magic Flute*. "He has found his life's vocation in a characterization of Papageno whose like defies recollection," wrote Irving Kolodin in the *Saturday Review*. "He gives us," wrote Harold C. Schonberg in the New York *Times,* "a vital, youngish sort of birdman, natural and unforced. And he sings it beautifully." When Prey sang Figaro in *The Barber of Seville* on April 2, 1973, he became the first German-born singer to take on that role at the Metropolitan. He had previously appeared as Figaro in 1969, when he made his debut at La Scala in Milan, and there, too, he was its first German-born Figaro.

His operatic appearances also took him to Covent Garden, where he made his debut in June 1973; to the Salzburg festivals, where in 1971 he was heard in the title role of *The Marriage of Figaro* and in 1973 as Guglielmo in a new production of *Così fan Tutte;* to the Munich Opera, where in 1962 he became the youngest artist ever to be awarded the title *Kammersänger* by the Bavarian Minister and where a decade later he was starred in new productions of *The Magic Flute* and *Tannhäuser;* and to the Chicago Lyric Opera, where he sang in *The Marriage of Figaro* and *The Barber of Seville* in November and December 1971. He has appeared as Figaro in a televised production of *The Marriage of Figaro.* On New Year's Eve, December 31, 1977, he appeared as Eisenstein in a new production of *Die Fledermaus* at Covent Garden in England, the first revival of this operetta in forty years and the first opera ever transmitted live over television from Europe to the United States.

However impressive have been his operatic successes in the United States and Europe they are more than matched by his fame as a singer of *Lieder* and as a baritone soloist in performances of the great choral literature of Bach, Handel, Haydn, Mendelssohn, and Brahms. His recitals have carried him to all parts of the music world; and he has enjoyed universal acclaim for his artistry in the song literature of Schubert, Schumann, Brahms, and Hugo Wolf. His artistry has been captured in numerous recordings on London, Angel and Philips releases: in operas (*Così fan Tutte, The Marriage of Figaro, The Magic Flute, Der Freischütz,* Richard Strauss's *Ariadne auf Naxos* and *Capriccio, Martha,* Pfitzner's *Palestrina,* Lortzing's *Czar und Zimmermann,* and others); in oratorios, Masses, and Passions; and, of course, in the literature of *Lieder.* In 1974 he completed one of the most ambitious vocal recording projects ever attempted, *The Recorded History of the German Lied,* comprising twenty-seven records and covering the *Lied*'s history from Krieger and Zelter before Schubert up to Schoenberg, Alban Berg, and Henze.

In Germany, Prey has become so famous as a television personality that he is sometimes described as "Europe's Leonard Bernstein." For a number of years he was starred in his own television show in Munich. He has also appeared on television in full-length operas, in choral masterworks, and in song recitals.

On February 13, 1954, Hermann Prey married Barbara Pniok, affectionately called "Bärbel," whom he had met at the Berlin zoo. With their three children, birds, dog, and hamster, they live in Krailling, near Munich, and have a summer retreat at Amrum, an island in the North Sea off the coast of Denmark, and another retreat in the Bavarian Alps. In the New York *Times* Howard Klein described Prey as "a big man, about six feet tall, heavily built with a good physique getting a little paunch. . . . He gesticulates with operatic emphasis, smiles a great deal, but his craggy face and blue eyes, with their heavy lids and surrounding lines, give the impression of long-suffering sadness. His short, permanently rumpled blondish hair defies combing."

Prey's athletic build provides a clue to some of his extramusical diversions: swimming, horseback riding, taking long walks. Other interests include architecture, collecting antique furniture and engravings, going to the movies, watching television, listening to his collection of jazz recordings, and reading books on philosophy and parapsychology.

In May 1974 the West German government awarded him the Bundesverdienstkreuz.

ABOUT: Hi-Fi, November 1970; High Fidelity, November 1975; New York Times, January 18, 1970; Opera News, April 7, 1973.

LEONTYNE PRICE

Leontyne Price

1927–

Leontyne Price (originally Mary Leontine Price), soprano, was born in Laurel, Mississippi, on February 10, 1927. Her father, James Anthony Price, was a carpenter; her mother, Kate Baker Price, helped out with the family finances by working as a midwife. The Prices waited fourteen years for their first child and had despaired of ever having one when Kate became pregnant with Leontyne. Wishing for a son, they planned to call him Leon. When a daughter arrived, they changed the name to Leontyne, prefacing it with Mary Violet.

"I was the granddaughter of two Methodist ministers," she reveals, "one on each side." Religion ran wide and deep in the Price household, and so did music. Kate Price had a lovely soprano voice which, though untrained, gave her a place in the choir of the St. Paul Methodist Church in Laurel. As a child, Leontyne would sit in her stroller in church listening to her mother practice with the choir. When Leontyne was just three and a half, Hattie V. J. McInnis began giving her some piano lessons. Soon regarded as a prodigy, Leontyne was often called upon to perform at the homes of friends.

After graduation from Sandy Gavin School, where she received her elementary instruction, Leontyne entered the Oak Park Vocational High School in the fall of 1937. There she not only played the piano at school concerts but also became a member of the Oak Park Choral Group which performed in and about Laurel. On December 17, 1943, she gave a concert in Laurel in which she appeared in the dual role of singer and pianist.

In 1944 Leontyne was graduated from Oak Park High School with honors in music. Deciding to prepare herself as a music teacher in public schools, she entered the College of Education and Industrial Arts (now called Central State College) in Wilberforce, Ohio. There she studied voice with Catherine Van Buren, and sang in the school Glee Club, which gave concerts not only in Mississippi and neighboring states but even in

Price: prīs

such large cities as Chicago, Pittsburgh, and Columbus. At college she participated in all musical functions. Outside college she occasionally sang over the radio and gave solo performances for civic clubs and in churches.

She received her Bachelor of Arts degree in 1948 and then entered the Juilliard School of Music on a full scholarship. For four years she received vocal training from Florence Page Kimball. In New York she heard her first public opera performances: *Turandot* at the New York City Center and *Salome* at the Metropolitan Opera. (The first opera she had ever heard was a Metropolitan Opera broadcast of *Tristan and Isolde* aired while she was still in college.) Convinced that she wanted to become an opera singer, she joined the Opera Workshop at the Juilliard School. The director of the workshop, Frederic Cohen, told her: "You have the voice of the century." She appeared in several Workshop productions, beginning with the role of Nella in *Gianni Schicchi*. In her fourth year she appeared as Mistress Ford in *Falstaff*. Virgil Thomson, the composer-critic, heard her in *Falstaff* and engaged her to appear in a revival of his opera *Four Saints in Three Acts*, which was produced for two weeks on Broadway in April 1952.

When a revival of Gershwin's *Porgy and Bess* was planned for 1952, Robert Breen, the director and coproducer, auditioned Leontyne Price for the role of Bess. Upon hearing her sing "Summertime" he engaged her without further investigation. When *Porgy and Bess* opened in Dallas, Texas, on June 9, 1952, Price and William Warfield were in the title roles. During the next few weeks the production visited several cities before settling down at the Ziegfeld Theater in New York on March 10, 1953, for an eight-month run. Until June 1954 Price continued appearing as Bess as the opera traveled throughout Europe under the auspices of the Department of State. Paul Hume, the music critic of the Washington *Post*, echoed the reactions of most critics both in the United States and in Europe when he wrote: "Leontyne Price sings the most exciting and thrilling Bess we have heard. . . . Price will no doubt spend a long time in the role of Bess. But when she is available for other music she will have a dramatic career. And her acting is as fiery as her singing."

During her tenure with the *Porgy and Bess* company several important developments took place in both her personal and professional life.

On August 31, 1952, she married concert baritone William C. Warfield at the Abyssinian Baptist Church in New York. At a reception at the nearby Theresa Hotel, the wedding cake was topped by a musical staff carrying the first notes of "Bess, You Is My Woman Now."

In her professional life she was beginning to open for herself new avenues of activity. On October 30, 1953, she sang the world premiere of Samuel Barber's *Hermit Songs* at the Library of Congress in Washington, D.C. She repeated this performance in Rome at the International Conference of Contemporary Music. And on November 14, 1954, she made her New York recital debut at Town Hall with a program that included the *Hermit Songs* with Barber at the piano. At that time Jay Harrison said of her in the *Herald Tribune* that she had a personality "that literally spills over the footlights." He called her "a goddess performing before us."

Her first important concert engagement after she left the *Porgy and Bess* company took place in Boston on December 3, 1954, when she appeared as a soloist with the Boston Symphony under Charles Münch in the world premiere of Barber's *Prayers of Kierkegaard*. At this time she was also making headway in opera. On January 23, 1955, she assumed the title role of *Tosca* in a television performance by the NBC-TV Opera. Peter Herman Adler, music director of the NBC-TV Opera, chose her for the role after hearing her sing in *Porgy and Bess*. It took an act of unusual courage to cast a black woman as Tosca in a white cast on the home screen, but Adler found full support from Samuel Chotzinoff, music director of NBC, and David Sarnoff, network president. Eleven Southern affiliates of NBC refused to air the production. But Price came through with banners flying. As Olin Downes noted in the New York *Times*, she overcame all obstacles with "her remarkable voice, her native intelligence and sincerity. . . . Her voice was superbly equal to all demands made upon it, in the dramatic character of the upper register, the warmth and sensuousness of the tone throughout and the sincerity and feeling everywhere evident. The voice became freer, fuller, and richer with each scene." As a result of this performance, *Mademoiselle* magazine placed Price among the ten outstanding women of 1955.

Other leading roles in productions of the NBC-TV Opera came her way between 1956 and

1960; Pamina in *The Magic Flute* in 1956; Madame Lidoine in Poulenc's *Les Dialogues des Carmélites* in 1957; Donna Anna in *Don Giovanni* in 1960. The year 1956 also saw her as Cleopatra in a concert presentation of Handel's *Julius Caesar* by the American Opera Society in New York and brought about her debut with the San Francisco Symphony. That year she also participated in an ANTA (American National Theater & Academy) concert tour of India under the auspices of the American State Department.

Her first appearance in a major opera house took place on September 20, 1957, with the San Francisco Opera as Madame Lidoine in the American premiere of *Les Dialogues des Carmélites*. A month later, on October 18, she was called upon to assume in San Francisco the title role in *Aida* as a replacement for a soprano who became ill. Her success brought her return engagements with the San Francisco Opera: in 1958 as Leonora in *Il Trovatore*, as the Peasant's Daughter in the American premiere of Carl Orff's *Die Kluge* (October 3), and on the opening night of the 1959 season as Donna Elvira in the first production of *Don Giovanni* by this company.

In 1958 Price made her operatic debut in Europe in the title role of *Aida* at the Vienna State Opera, Herbert von Karajan conducting. Later the same year, on July 2, she received one of the most tumultuous receptions ever accorded an American-born singer at Covent Garden in London when she made her bow there as Aida. She continued her tour of Europe that year with appearances as Aida at the Verona Arena, Tullio Serafin conducting, and with concert appearances in Yugoslavia and at the World's Fair in Brussels. In 1959 she was heard as Thaïs and as Liù in *Turandot* in her first appearance with the Chicago Lyric Opera; and she was a soloist in Beethoven's *Missa Solemnis* at the Salzburg Festival, where the following summer she returned as Donna Anna and in 1962 as Leonora in *Il Trovatore*. In 1959 she made a triumphant debut at La Scala in Milan as Aida, the first time a black singer sang a major role in that opera house.

On January 21, 1961, Price went to the Metropolitan Opera as Leonora in *Il Trovatore*. "I was in the theater the night she made her debut," recalls Martina Arroyo. "And, God, was that a night! You didn't believe those sounds were coming out of a human being." Writing in

the *New Yorker,* Winthrop Sargeant called this Metropolitan Opera debut "one of the greatest operatic triumphs of recent years." Harold C. Schonberg reported in the New York *Times:* "She has matured into a beautiful singer. Her voice, warm and luscious, has enough volume to fill the house with ease, and she has a good technique to back up the voice itself. She even took trills as written, and nothing in the part as Verdi wrote it gave her the least bit of trouble."

Later the same season, over a nine-week period, she was heard as Aida, Donna Anna, Cio-Cio-San in *Madama Butterfly,* and Liù. Her position with the company was given official recognition when on October 23, 1961, she opened the Metropolitan Opera season as Minnie in *The Girl of the Golden West,* the first time a black singer was starred in a seasonal opening. When the Metropolitan Opera entered its new auditorium at the Lincoln Center for the Performing Arts on September 16, 1966, she was once again chosen to open the season, this time in the world premiere of Barber's *Antony and Cleopatra.* She opened the Metropolitan Opera season a third time in 1969.

Between 1961 and 1969 she appeared in one hundred and eighteen performances at the Metropolitan, adding to her roles those of Pamina, Tatiana in *Eugene Onegin,* Tosca, Fiordiligi in *Così fan Tutte,* Donna Elvira in *Ernani,* Leonora in *La Forza del Destino,* and Amelia in *Un Ballo in Maschera.* But in 1969–1970 her appearances at the Metropolitan dwindled to two, both times as Aida, and in 1970–1971 she made no appearances at all. When she returned to the Metropolitan Opera on September 24, 1973, as Cio-Cio-San it was only her seventh appearance in five seasons in a regularly scheduled performance.

Her absences brought to the surface not only her desire to reduce operatic performances in favor of concerts but also her dissatisfaction with Rudolf Bing, the general manager of the company. She resented that she was continually required to appear in the same roles and that just two new productions were mounted for her. "It's not exactly a thrill to go up to 63rd Street and do the same old Aida," she said. "Why shouldn't I have a new pair of pants?"

Another open sore was the dismal failure of *Antony and Cleopatra,* though she herself, as Cleopatra, received rave reviews. "That 1966 opening," she told Irving Kolodin for the *Satur-*

day Review, "was, I think, the most grueling experience of my life. It really left me almost traumatized for two and a half years. . . . So much was hanging on it. A new house, a premiere of a new work. I felt that if I caught a cold and couldn't perform, it would be worldwide news. So much to do, so much to think about, so much to cope with in so short a time." The fact that the premiere turned out to be an artistic disaster served to accentuate her torment. Then when Rudolf Bing offered her a new production of *Il Trovatore,* he wanted Franco Zeffirelli to do the staging, the same man who was largely responsible for the tragic mishaps and mistakes attending *Antony and Cleopatra.* She regarded this choice as "colossal *chutzpah*" and refused to consider it. "Anyway," she told Stephen E. Rubin in an interview for the New York *Times,* "I survived the Bing regime." After a total absence in 1972–1973 she returned the following season as Donna Anna and Cio-Cio-San. And in spite of her curtailed program of operatic appearances she made her debut at the Teatro Colón in Buenos Aires in 1969 and at the Hamburg Opera in Germany in 1970. She added a new role to her repertory in 1974—though with the San Francisco Opera rather than the Metropolitan— when she launched the company's new season in the title role of *Manon Lescaut.* She was heard in *Manon Lescaut* at the Metropolitan Opera on February 7, 1975, and on February 3, 1976, she was given a new production there of *Aida.*

Her career took a new direction when she added the title role in Strauss's *Ariadne auf Naxos* to her repertory, at the San Francisco Opera on October 19, 1977—a role she also recorded for London Records with Sir Georg Solti conducting. On this occasion, to commemorate the twentieth anniversary of her debut with the San Francisco Opera, general manager Kurt Herbert Adler presented her with the medal of the opera house. President and Mrs. Carter sent her a congratulatory letter.

Her appearances outside the opera house in recitals and as guest artist with symphony orchestras have been worldwide. Her recordings have also been extensive since her first release for Columbia in 1955 of the *Hermit Songs.* By 1976 fifteen of her albums released by RCA had received Grammys from the National Academy of Recording Arts and Sciences.

In January 1964 Price was invited to sing at the inauguration ceremonies of President Lyn-

don B. Johnson in Washington, D.C. She sang once again in his honor, this time at his funeral services at the National City Christian Church in Washington, D.C., on January 25, 1973.

Price and her husband, William Warfield, parted in 1959. The separation became legal in 1967, and in 1973 they were divorced. The three-story Dutch house they purchased in 1953 on Vandam Street in New York's Greenwich Village has remained her permanent residence (though during the 1960s she also maintained a small apartment in Rome near the Piazza Venezia). After her separation from Warfield, the Price household on Vandam Street consisted of Leontyne Price, her housekeeper-companion, Mrs. Lulu Shoemaker (whom Price often referred to as her older sister), and a German shepherd dog, Louella. Mrs. Shoemaker died in 1974, and the German shepherd dog had to be given away because he had become inconsolable over this death. Since that time Price has lived in the house by herself.

She enjoys entertaining her friends at her home where she sometimes prepares the food herself, her specialties being crab meat Imperial, stuffed eggplant casserole, and a shrimp gumbo. She drinks and smokes sparingly, her favorite alcoholic beverage being champagne. Interior decorating and record collecting, reading books, going to the movies, the theater and ballet are her favorite pastimes. She almost never attends opera performances, explaining, "I suffer along with whoever is singing." She rarely watches television because it interferes with her reading. Though she does not attend church services as often as she would like, she has remained a deeply religious woman. When she used to make regular trips to her home in Laurel while her mother was still alive, she always attended the services at the St. Paul Church and usually delighted the congregation by singing for it.

Five feet six inches tall, weighing about one hundred and thirty pounds, she is as regal in appearance offstage as she is on. She always dresses smartly in clothes designed for her in Europe.

Before her performances she eats a hearty meal late in the afternoon, then another one when the performance is over. Each performance produces such high tensions that she is unable to sleep most of the night after that. "I usually allow two days to unwind after a performance," she has said. "I do crazy things, even cleaning up, straightening my closets, anything to take my mind off what I have been doing on the stage."

Leontyne Price received the Spingarn medal from the NAACP (National Association for the Advancement of Colored People), the Order of Merit from the Republic of Italy, and the Presidential Medal of Freedom, in addition to several honorary doctorates from universities. A library at Rust College in Holly Springs, Mississippi, was named after her. Five distinguished artists have painted her portrait.

ABOUT: Lyon, H. L. Leontyne Price: Highlights of a Prima Donna; Sargeant, W. Divas. *Periodicals*— American Record Guide, January 1971; Look, January 17, 1961; Musical America, January 1962; New York Times Magazine, October 15, 1961; Opera News, February 4, 1961, February 12, 1972, April 7, 1973, March 6, 1976; Saturday Review, September 9, 1972; Stereo Review, January 1976; Time, March 10, 1961.

WILLIAM PRIMROSE

William Primrose

1903–

William Primrose, violist, was born in Glasgow, Scotland, on August 23, 1903, to John and Margaret Primrose. His father was a violinist and violist with the Scottish Symphony and London Philharmonic orchestras. He gave William his first lessons on the violin. These were followed by a ten-year period of violin study with Camillo Ritter in Glasgow; William made his debut as violinist with a concert in Glasgow. In 1920 he received a City of London grant enabling him to enter the Guildhall School of Music in London where he remained three years, a violin student of Max Mossel. In 1923 he made his London debut as concert violinist, performing Elgar's Violin Concerto with the Royal Albert Hall Orchestra.

From 1925 to 1927 Primrose continued his violin studies with Eugène Ysaÿe in Brussels. Ysaÿe persuaded him to change from the violin to the viola. It took Primrose a number of years to perfect himself on the viola. In 1930 he joined the London String Quartet as violist. Until 1935, when the Quartet was disbanded, he remained with this world-famous chamber music ensemble, touring the world with it. During this same period, he sometimes also appeared as a viola

virtuoso, though only intermittently. It was not until the London String Quartet disbanded that he devoted himself to a career as a viola virtuoso, making his debut as such in Rio de Janeiro. Then in the period between 1935 and 1937 he toured Europe and the United States in recitals and as soloist with major orchestras.

Ernest Newman, the English musicologist and critic, wrote this about one of Primrose's viola performances: "Playing so rich in subtleties and delicacies as his raises the critical listener's sensitiveness to its conceivable maximum of acuity. He treats us in abundance to the delicacy of shading and accentuation in which he specializes."

When the NBC Symphony Orchestra was founded in New York for Arturo Toscanini in 1937, Primrose was chosen as its first violist. One year later, he appeared with this same orchestra, then directed by Sir Adrian Boult, as a soloist in the American premiere of William Walton's Viola Concerto.

On April 3, 1938, he inaugurated a special radio series devoted to viola music, broadcast over the facilities of the National Broadcasting Company. He also founded the William Primrose Quartet for radio performances of great chamber music. This Quartet made its concert debut at Town Hall, New York, on November 5, 1939.

Primrose remained with the NBC Symphony until 1942. During those years he taught the viola at the Curtis Institute of Music in Philadelphia. Just before Béla Bartók's death in 1945,

Primrose commissioned him to write a viola concerto. Bartók never lived to complete it, but that chore was done for him by his friend and pupil, Tibor Serly. On December 2, 1949, Primrose presented the world premiere of the Viola Concerto in Minneapolis, Antal Dorati conducting. Primrose then performed it at the Edinburgh Festival and in London in 1950.

In 1956, following his return to England for permanent residence, Primrose became the violist of the Festival Piano Quartet in England. During the 1960s he often participated in chamber music performances of the Heifetz-Piatigorsky concerts in the United States. Two recordings of the Heifetz-Piatigorsky Concerts, with Primrose participating, released by RCA Victor, earned Grammys from the National Academy of Recording Arts and Sciences in 1961 and 1962.

On February 24, 1953, Primrose received the Order of Command of the British Empire.

With Yehudi Menuhin as collaborator, Primrose is the author of *Violin and Viola* (1976).

William Primrose married Dorothy Friend on October 2, 1928. They have two daughters. After their divorce, he married Alice Virginia French, an American, in 1952. His major pastimes have been chess, golf, and cricket.

ABOUT: Baker, T. Biographical Dictionary of Musicians, completely rev. by N. Slonimsky; Who's Who in the World, 1971/72.

Sergei Rachmaninoff

1873–1943

In addition to being one of the great composers of the twentieth century, Sergei Vassilievitch Rachmaninoff was also one of its piano virtuosos and a distinguished conductor. He was born the second son and the third of six children on April 2, 1873, at his well-to-do parents' estate, Onega, in the district of Novgorod, Russia, to a family in which music had been important for several generations. His great-grandfather had been a violinist, the founder of an orchestra and a chorus; his grandfather, Arkady, was an excellent pianist and composer; his father, Vassily, played the piano and did some composing—one

Rachmaninoff: räк mä′ nē nôf

SERGEI RACHMANINOFF

of his improvisations was used by Sergei as a theme for his own Polka, for piano; his mother, Lubov, was also a pianist.

Sergei's mother gave him his first piano lessons before she passed him on to Anna Ornazkaya for three years of more intensive training. At the same time, he received his academic education from private tutors and governesses. His mother wanted him to be a professional musician, but his father insisted he prepare himself for a military career. Destiny in the form of an economic disaster made it possible for his mother to have her way. When Sergei was nine years old, his family was ruined financially by his father's extravagance and improvidential speculations. The family had to sell its Onega estate and resettle in St. Petersburg. At that time his father deserted the family, leaving the upbringing of the children in the hands of their mother. She saw to it that Sergei was admitted to the St. Petersburg Conservatory on a scholarship in 1882, to study the piano there for three years with Demiansky.

The lack of paternal discipline was responsible for making Sergei irresponsible and indolent. He had a natural gift for music and had been born with perfect pitch; but he despised the discipline of school and the routines of practicing. He preferred to go skating or to steal rides on horse-drawn trolleys or to wander about aimlessly in the streets. When he had to bring home his Conservatory marks he would falsify them to disguise the fact that he was not doing too well in most of the major subjects. Asked to perform at his grandmother's house, he would frequently palm off his own improvisations as compositions by Chopin or Mendelssohn, having failed to commit any of the compositions of these masters to memory. None of his teachers at the Conservatory thought he had an unusual talent for music. Karl Davidov, the director of the Conservatory, called Sergei mischievous and lazy.

Sergei's mother, concerned over her son's dilatory ways, consulted her nephew, Alexander Siloti, who already was giving evidence of becoming a brilliant concert pianist. After listening to Sergei play the piano, Siloti decided that what the boy needed most was rigid discipline and that the man who could impose it upon him was Nicolai Zverev, professor of piano at the Moscow Conservatory. In 1885 young Sergei was sent to Moscow. He made his home with Zverev, and for the next three years was subjected to that teacher's program of intensive study and practicing, both at home and at the Moscow Conservatory. He thrived under this rigid course of study. His own inherent love for music, before this just a spark, burst into full flame.

In 1888 Zverev passed Sergei on to Alexander Siloti's class in piano and to the composition classes of Arensky and Taneiev at the Moscow Conservatory. Under their guidance, he developed brilliantly, both as a pianist and as a composer. He composed a scherzo for orchestra, in addition to several piano pieces and songs, in 1887. In 1891 he was graduated from the Conservatory as a pianist, and in 1892 as a composer. On the latter occasion he received the Gold Medal for his opera *Aleko,* which was produced at the Bolshoi Theater on April 23, 1893; Tchaikovsky, who was present at the performance, expressed enthusiasm. Soon after his graduation as composer, he wrote a piano piece that was to make his name known throughout the music world, the Prelude in C-sharp minor, for piano, which he introduced at a public concert in Moscow on September 26, 1892.

Sergei had made a number of appearances as pianist before that day in 1892. He had performed at student concerts at the Conservatory; he had given a recital in Moscow during the 1891 season; and he had performed his own First Piano Concerto in Moscow on March 17, 1892, with Safonov conducting. But he himself considered his concert of September 26, 1892, as the true beginning of his virtuoso career. After 1892

he concertized throughout Russia as a solo virtuoso, as a performer with orchestras, and in 1895 in joint recitals with an Italian violinist. By the time he was twenty-five he was recognized throughout Russia as a piano virtuoso of first importance. He also made his debut as a conductor, leading a performance of *Samson and Delilah* in Moscow on October 12, 1897. In 1898 he made his bow in London in the triple role of pianist, conductor, and composer by conducting his fantasy for orchestra, *The Rock,* and performing his own Piano Concerto No.1.

Though there were successes, there were also setbacks. A better integrated personality would have taken such setbacks in stride. But Rachmaninoff was a young man oppressed by insecurity, overwhelmed by spells of depression, and oversensitive to rejection. The premiere of his Symphony No.1 in St. Petersburg on March 15, 1897, was a failure. He fled from the hall in a trance. "The despair that filled my soul would not leave me," he recalled in later years. "My dreams of a brilliant career lay shattered." The despair to which Rachmaninoff succumbed deepened. For the next few years he could not summon the energy to work on his compositions. From time to time he appeared in concerts as a pianist or conducted some opera performances, but nothing could dispel his overpowering depression, his self-doubts. He has called this "the most difficult and critical period of my life." Count Leo Tolstoy tried to lift him from the abyss of his despair by telling him: "All of us have difficult moments; but this is life. Hold up your head, and keep on your appointed path."

Help, however, came from a far different quarter: from Dr. Nikolai Dahl who effected cures through autosuggestion. From consultations with Dr. Dahl, Rachmaninoff recovered hope and courage—and with these the will to create. Able to return to his working desk he completed his Piano Concerto No.2, written in a white heat of inspiration. He himself introduced it in Moscow on October 27, 1901. It was a huge success and has since become the most frequently played and the most beloved piano concerto written in the twentieth century.

Another symptom of his recovery was his marriage to his young cousin, Natalie Satina, on April 29, 1902, in an army chapel of suburban Moscow. She, too, was a pianist and had been graduated from the Moscow Conservatory. Their home was a small apartment in Moscow where a daughter, Irina, was born on May 14, 1903. A second daughter, Tatiana, came later.

In the early years of the new century, Rachmaninoff became one of the most influential and most highly admired musicians in Russia. He was concertizing more actively than ever, a performer on the piano whose profound insight into the masterworks was gaining for him an idolatrous following. He was also acclaimed as a conductor at the Bolshoi Theater where he served from 1904 to 1906 and distinguished himself in performances of Russian operas by Glinka, Borodin, Tchaikovsky, and Dargomizhsky.

Rachmaninoff's fame in Moscow made his home the natural meeting place for the city's musical and intellectual figures. His social life, he felt, was seriously interfering with his creativity as a composer, and so was the fact that he was devoting so much of his energies to performing the music of others. The time had come to concentrate on his own compositions. With this in mind, he resigned from his conducting post in 1906, left Moscow, and went to live in Dresden, Germany. There, in semiseclusion, he completed two major works: the Symphony No.2, and the tone poem *The Isle of the Dead.* He himself conducted the premieres of both works, the symphony in St. Petersburg on February 8, 1908, and the tone poem in Moscow on May 1, 1909.

He paid his first visit to the United States in 1909. His American debut took place on November 4 with a recital at Northampton, Massachusetts. Four days later he performed his Piano Concerto No.2 at a concert of the Boston Symphony in Philadelphia, Max Fiedler conducting; he also made his American bow as a conductor that evening by leading a performance of Mussorgsky's *A Night on the Bald Mountain.* He performed his concerto again with the same orchestra in Baltimore and, on November 13, in New York. Richard Aldrich noted in the New York *Times:* "He is a pianist of highly developed technique . . . and he has ample resources of expression upon the instrument, though a beautiful and varied tone is not conspicuous among them." After further appearances with this same concerto in Hartford, Boston, and Toronto he gave his first New York recital on November 20, and eight days later he presented in New York the world premiere of his Piano Concerto No.3, with Walter Damrosch conducting the New York Symphony So-

ciety. Other recitals and orchestral appearances took place in Chicago, Pittsburgh, Cincinnati, Buffalo, Boston, and New York.

Just before returning to Russia, Rachmaninoff was offered the post of principal conductor of the Boston Symphony. He turned the offer down because he did not like to stay away from Moscow for prolonged absences. He was also offered contracts to return to the United States the following season as pianist and conductor, and these, too, he refused to accept because, as he told a Russian newspaper, "America was a strain." As it turned out, he was not to return to the United States for another decade. He continued to maintain his home in Moscow where he conducted the Philharmonic Society and to concertize throughout Europe and in Russia. His fame as piano virtuoso grew to such dimensions that few pianists could compete with him as a box-office attraction.

During World War I Rachmaninoff gave concerts in Russia for soldiers and refugees. He also did much composing, including the Piano Concerto No.4, which was a rewritten version of his Piano Concerto No.1.

During the Revolution in Russia, Rachmaninoff was so unsympathetic to it that he became determined to find a permanent home in another country. He left Russia in December 1917 with just a few hundred rubles in his pocket and a single valise, ostensibly to tour Scandinavia. He never returned to Russia.

After a year in Scandinavia, Rachmaninoff returned to the United States to begin his second tour on December 8, 1918. On December 21 he gave a recital at Carnegie Hall and in the New York *Times* Richard Aldrich commented on his playing: "The same cold white light of analysis, the incisive touch, the strongly marked rhythms, the intellectual grasp of the musical ideas and the sense of the relative importance in phrase-groupings proclaimed Rachmaninoff is a cerebral, not an emotional artist."

From 1918 to 1935 Rachmaninoff lived in Switzerland, near Lake Lucerne. He went to the United States in 1935 for permanent residence, first in an apartment on Riverside Drive in New York City, then in a modest house in Beverly Hills, California. But he was a man without a home. Away from his native land he felt himself an exile incapable of adjusting to a new life and a new language. Painfully he tried to keep alive his Russian heritage by observing the holidays, speaking the language wherever possible, eating Russian dishes, drinking tea from a samovar. But all this was a poor substitute for the genuine commodity: his native land. Those who were close to him knew the extent of his homesickness and the loneliness which not even his immense success could dispel. This homesickness induced a chronic melancholy. He rarely smiled; his eyes were filled with melancholy; the creases in his face and brow deepened.

He was a methodical man who rigidly regimented his daily life. He ate at regular hours: breakfast early in the morning, lunch at one, dinner at six. Set hours were also assigned to practicing the piano, relaxing, and socializing with his friends. His preferred form of exercise was a long walk after breakfast; after lunch he refreshed himself with a nap. His only indulgence in alcohol was an occasional glass of wine, but he was a chain smoker, using a denicotined brand in a cigarette holder stuffed with absorbent cotton.

In November 1939 the thirtieth anniversary of his debut was commemorated in Philadelphia with a cycle of three concerts in which Rachmaninoff assumed the triple role of composer, conductor, and pianist. All of his major works were performed, with Rachmaninoff playing three of his concertos. About his conducting Olin Downes wrote in the New York *Times:* "Rachmaninoff . . . has proved as masterly in his control, musicianship and projective power as he is when he plays the piano. And the styles of the pianist and conductor are of a piece. There is the same complete lack of ostentation, the same dignity and apparent reserve, the same commanding, evocative power. ... From the first down-beat . . . his mastery was obvious." Later the same year he once again appeared as composer, conductor, and pianist, at Carnegie Hall in New York.

Rachmaninoff and his family settled in Beverly Hills, California, on February 1, 1943. Just before his death, he became an American citizen. He suffered from poor health in his last years. In spite of this he undertook a tour of the United States as a pianist on February 8, 1943. He collapsed in New Orleans and had to be taken back to his home in Beverly Hills. He died there on March 28, 1943, of melanoma. In his last hours he kept insisting that music was being played near his bed. When told this was not the case he remarked softly: "Then it is in my head."

He was buried in Kensico Cemetery in Valhalla, New York.

ABOUT: Bertensson, S. and Leyda, J. Rachmaninoff; Culshaw, J. Rachmaninoff: The Man and His Music; Lyle, W. Rachmaninoff: A Biography; Riesemann, O. von. Rachmaninoff's Recollections; Satin, S. ed. In Memory of Rachmaninoff; Seroff, V. Rachmaninoff; Watson, L. Rachmaninoff: A Biography. *Periodicals* —Journal of American Musicology, Spring 1968; Musical Quarterly, January–April 1944; Tempo (London), Winter 1951-1952 (Rachmaninoff issue).

Rosa Raisa

1893–1963

Rosa Raisa (originally Rosa Raisa Burchstein), soprano, was born in Bialystok, Russian Poland, on May 30, 1893. "I knew and my people knew from the time I was a child that I had an unusual voice," she once told an interviewer. "It was always understood that someday I should be a singer." As a child she made public appearances in Poland. She was fourteen when, to escape a pogrom, she and her family fled from Poland to Naples. There she was discovered by the conductor Cleofonte Campanini, whose wife, Eva Tetrazzini, began giving her singing lessons. Rosa then entered the Conservatory San Pietro a Maiello where she studied voice with Barbara Marchisio.

Raisa made her opera debut on September 6, 1913, in Verdi's *Oberto, Conte di San Bonifacio* during a Verdi festival at the Parma Opera. That same year she also made her debut at La Scala in Milan. However, her first successes came between 1914 and 1916 at the Teatro Costanzi in Rome. In 1914 she appeared for the first time at Covent Garden in London, and in 1916 at the Teatro Colón in Buenos Aires.

On November 28, 1914, she made her American debut as Aida with the Chicago Opera, at the invitation of Campanini, the music director of that company. She appeared in a number of other roles that season, then for two seasons confined her appearances to Europe. Returning to the Chicago Opera as Aida on November 13, 1916, she impressed her hearers with the dramatic power and expressiveness of her voice and her dynamic personality. From this time on until

Raisa: rä ē′ zä

ROSA RAISA

her retirement she remained a *prima donna assoluta* at the Chicago Opera. In addition to a variety of roles in the standard repertory, she appeared in Chicago in the world premiere of Franke Harling's *A Light from St. Agnes* (December 26, 1925), in the American premieres of Mascagni's *Isabeau* (November 12, 1917) and Montemezzi's *La Nave* (November 18, 1919), and in the Chicago premiere of Zandonai's *Francesca da Rimini*. With the Chicago Opera, she made her New York debut at the Lexington Theater as Maliella in *The Jewels of the Madonna* on January 24, 1917. As Aida she helped to open the new Chicago Civic Opera House in 1929, a performance that was broadcast over the NBC radio network.

In 1929 she married Giacomo Rimini, who had been a member of the Chicago Opera company since 1916. They made their home in Chicago, and both became American citizens.

As a member of the Chicago Opera company, Raisa continued to make numerous appearances at Covent Garden, La Scala, the Paris Opéra, and major opera houses of South America. Toscanini admired her greatly and selected her to create the role of Asteria in the world premiere of Boïto's *Nerone* at La Scala on May 1, 1924. Puccini was also impressed by her dramatic and vocal powers and picked her to create the title role of *Turandot*. She did so on April 25, 1926, in a performance in which her husband appeared as Ping. The performance was conducted by Toscanini.

Among her roles, other than those already touched upon, were Suor Angelica in Puccini's one-act opera of that name, the Marschallin in *Der Rosenkavalier,* Norma, Elisabeth in *Tannhäuser,* Donna Anna in *Don Giovanni,* Amelia in *Un Ballo in Maschera,* Desdemona in *Otello,* and Valentine in *Les Huguenots.*

In 1931 she was threatened by an extortion letter with death and with the kidnapping of her little daughter. She and her daughter were carefully guarded for several months, and nothing came of these threats. In 1933 she and her husband lost a fortune in investments when the utility empire of Samuel Insull collapsed.

She went into retirement in 1937, at which time her husband opened an opera studio in Chicago which she herself directed upon her husband's death. She emerged briefly from her retirement on May 6, 1938, to create for the United States the role of Leah in Ludovico Rocca's *The Dybbuk.*

Her last years were spent in ailing health in the Pacific Palisades home in California of her daughter. Rosa Raisa died in Los Angeles, on September 28, 1963.

ABOUT: Kutsch, K. J. and Riemens, L. A Concise Biographical Dictionary of Singers.

Jean-Pierre Rampal

1922–

Jean-Pierre Louis Rampal, flutist, has been a powerful force in popularizing the flute as a solo instrument in the era following World War II, in bringing to world attention many old and long-forgotten masterpieces of flute music, and in introducing many twentieth century flute compositions.

He was born in Marseilles, on July 1, 1922, the son of Andrée Roggero Rampal and Joseph Rampal, professor of flute at the Marseilles Conservatory of Music. Though his father did not want Jean-Pierre to become a professional flutist, he gave him some lessons on the instrument. "I am sure that my tone is mostly the result of listening as a child to my father," Rampal has said.

Jean-Pierre attended local schools in Marseilles and then the Lycée Thiers from which he

Rampal: rän pǎl'

JEAN-PIERRE RAMPAL

was graduated with a baccalaureate in philosophy and letters in 1939. While attending the Lycée, he continued his music study at the Marseilles Conservatory, receiving first prize in flute in 1937.

Aspiring to become a physician, Rampal obtained his degree in physics, chemistry, and biology at the University of Marseilles in 1941. Then he entered that University's school of medicine. In 1943 he was in the third year of his medical studies when, during the Nazi occupation of Paris in World War II, he was called up for military service and stationed near Paris. In order to obtain a two-week leave of absence given to enrolled students, he entered the Paris Conservatory. When his military outfit was to be sent to Germany in a labor camp, he went AWOL and fled back to Marseilles. But he was soon in Paris again, where a professor at the Conservatory persuaded him to give serious consideration to music study by attending classes in the Conservatory. Five months after he had returned to the Paris Conservatory, Rampal won first prize in flute playing.

Upon the liberation of Paris in 1945, he became a member of the Paris Opéra orchestra where from 1958 to 1964 he served as first flutist. In 1945 he made the first of his many appearances over the French radio, performing Jacques Ibert's Flute Concerto. In 1946 he signed for his first concert tour as solo flutist, forming a collaboration with pianist and harpsichordist Robert Veyron-Lacroix that continued for many years. From 1947 to 1951 Rampal was also the first flutist of the Vichy Opéra orchestra.

In addition to his performances in concerts with Veyron-Lacroix, as a soloist with orchestras, and as a member of the French Wind Quintet and the Paris Baroque Ensemble, Rampal began making recordings. It is through his recordings for Columbia and RCA, as well as other companies, that his art became known in the United States long before his first tour. No flutist has recorded more extensively than Rampal, and no flutist has sold so many of his recordings or been so highly honored. In 1954 and 1956 two of his recordings earned him the first of many Grand Prix du Disque awards in Paris, and in 1956, the Oscar du Premier Virtuose Français.

Rampal made his first tour of the United States in 1958, his American debut taking place in a duo-concert with Veyron-Lacroix at the Coolidge Auditorium of the Library of Congress in Washington, D.C. When, on February 9, 1959, he appeared with the Handel Festival Orchestra in New York, Ross Parmenter commented in the New York *Times:* "Mr. Rampal plays a golden flute, and one is tempted to say he also has a golden tone, but such a term might not do full justice to the roundness and warmth of the sound that emerges from his instrument."

In speaking of Rampal's famous tone, Hubert Saal wrote in *Newsweek,* after hearing a Rampal performance in New York late in 1967: "What puts the final eighteen-carat stamp on Rampal's musicianship is his luscious, limpid tone, brilliant without shrillness in its upper octave, resonant without weakness down below."

Since 1968 Rampal has regularly returned to the United States for appearances in recitals, with orchestras, and in chamber music concerts with Pinchas and Eugenia Zukerman, among others. He has made numerous world tours. Probably no flutist before him or since has been so popular, invariably filling to crowding every auditorium in which he appears. He gives over one hundred and fifty concerts and earns about a quarter of a million dollars a year. When not on tour he can be heard over the French radio more often than almost any instrumentalist.

As a result of Rampal's researches into the music of the past, he has succeeded in resurrecting a considerable library of Baroque music for flute long forgotten or neglected. He has also performed much twentieth century music, including that of Prokofiev, Hindemith, Khachaturian, Ibert, Martinu, and others. At The Bottom Line, a rock Greenwich Village nightclub in New York, he has performed Claude Bolling's *Suite for Flute and Jazz Piano,* and his Columbia recording of that work became a best seller.

In his attempts to enlarge the repertory of flute music he has sometimes ventured into adapting for the flute compositions originally intended for other instruments. His performance of Khachaturian's Violin Concerto, which he adapted for the flute, was performed on January 18, 1970, when he appeared with the American Symphony Orchestra, Stokowski conducting. At a Mostly Mozart concert at the Lincoln Center for the Performing Arts in New York he once gave as an encore the Adagio movement from a Mozart Violin Sonata. He has played on the flute the first violin part of Bach's Concerto for Two Violins and Orchestra with Isaac Stern as a second violinist.

In August 1973, at Lincoln Center for the Performing Arts in New York, Rampal combined the playing of the flute with conducting the orchestra, in a performance of Mozart's *Haffner Symphony.* "Rampal the musician clearly had interesting ideas as to what he wanted to accomplish," reported Allen Hughes in the New York *Times,* "but Rampal the conductor seemed not yet experienced enough to make it sound the way it should." But when Rampal conducted a Mozart program at the Mostly Mozart Festival at Lincoln Center on August 26, 1977, Joseph Horowitz remarked in the New York *Times:* "Mr. Rampal makes a vivid maestro. In fact . . . Mr. Rampal was a Mozart conductor of distinction. He evoked the composer drunk with champagne, dizzy with animation and elegance."

Rampal has edited *Ancient Music for the Flute* (1958) and collections of music for the flute by Haydn, Vivaldi, and Leclair.

He married Françoise Bacqueyrisse, a harpist, on June 7, 1947. They have two children. Their main home is in Paris, on avenue Mozart next to a bakery called *À la Flute Enchantée* (At the Magic Flute), but they also have residences in Marseilles and Corsica. A writer for a French publication, *Diapason,* has described Rampal as having "the mouth of a gourmand, the face of an epicure, and the commanding presence of a bishop." He is a sports enthusiast and enjoys swimming, tennis, and deep-sea diving. Less strenuous diversions include making amateur movies, screening his collection of Charlie Chaplin and Fred Astaire films, sampling gourmet cooking, and collecting exotic musical instruments.

France named him Chevalier de l'Ordre des Arts et des Lettres. Since 1956 his recordings have continued to be frequent recipients of the Grand Prix du Disque in Paris.

ABOUT: Hi-Fi, May 1965; New York Times Magazine, February 22, 1976; Newsweek, January 1968; People, May 6, 1977.

Nell Rankin

1926–

Nell Rankin, mezzo-soprano, was born in Montgomery, Alabama, on January 3, 1926, the daughter of Allen and Eugenia Knabe Rankin. From 1940 to 1943 she received her musical training at the Birmingham Conservatory of Music, where she studied voice with Jeanne Lorraine. From 1943 to 1949 she continued her vocal studies with Coenraad V. Bos and from 1945 to 1949 with Karin Branzell, in New York.

She made her professional debut with a recital at Town Hall in New York and then went to Europe to complete her vocal training. There, in 1950, she made her bow in opera as Ortrud in *Lohengrin* at the Zurich State Opera. In the single year that she was a member of the company she gave 126 performances in 16 roles. That same year (1950) she became the first American to capture first prize in the International Concours de la Musique in Geneva. In 1950–1951 she was a member of the Basel State Opera and in 1951 she made her debut at La Scala.

Winning the Metropolitan Opera Auditions in 1951 brought her a contract with that company, and she made her American operatic debut on November 22, 1951, as Amneris. A voice of rich and luscious texture, an arresting stage presence, and a discerning musicianship distinguished that first appearance and continued to characterize her performances over the next quarter of a century in the following roles: Maddalena in *Rigoletto,* Marina in *Boris Godunov,* Carmen, Madeleine in *Andrea Chénier,* Eboli in *Don Carlo,* Laura in *La Gioconda,* Ortrud, Azucena in *Il Trovatore,* Santuzza in *Cavalleria*

NELL RANKIN

Rusticana, Fricka in *Die Walküre,* Ulrica in *Un Ballo in Maschera,* Herodias in *Salome,* Giulietta in *The Tales of Hoffmann,* Brangäne in *Tristan and Isolde,* the Princess in *Adriana Lecouvreur,* and the Third Norn and Gutrune in *Die Götterdämmerung.* When she appeared in a new production of *Andrea Chénier* on November 16, 1954, Olin Downes wrote in the New York *Times:* "In one of the smaller parts, the greatest impression was made by Nell Rankin, in the role of the old mother who sacrificed her last son for the revolution, in a way and with a tone color that . . . made the performance pause in its progress."

Rankin made her debut at Covent Garden in London as Carmen in 1953–1954. Once again as Carmen, she made her bow with the San Francisco Opera on September 27, 1955, returning to the company one year later as Dorabella in *Così fan Tutte.* She has also made noteworthy appearances with the Teatro Colón in Buenos Aires, the Vienna State Opera, the San Carlo in Naples, and in opera houses in Bologna, Mexico City, and Barcelona. Furthermore she has appeared with virtually every opera company of note in the United States. She has in addition distinguished herself as a soloist with major orchestras in the United States and in Europe, as a recitalist, and as a teacher of voice. In March 1972 she was honored by the Birmingham Arts Festival in Alabama. Then on April 21, she was one of the soloists in a concert performance of *Tristan and Isolde* given by the Boston Symphony Orchestra under William Steinberg.

On April 6, 1951, Nell Rankin married Dr. Hugh Clark Davidson, a physician of internal medicine. Their home is an apartment in New York City. In 1972 she was elected to the American Hall of Fame.

ABOUT: Kutsch, K. J. and Riemens, L. A Concise Biographical Dictionary of Singers; Who's Who in Opera, ed. by M. F. Rich.

Judith Raskin

1928–

Judith Raskin, soprano, was born in New York City on June 21, 1928. Both her parents were educators. Her father, Harry A. Raskin, was the chairman of the music department of Evander Childs High School in the Bronx and her mother, Lillian Mendelson Raskin, was a grade school teacher.

As a child, Judith studied violin and piano, but not voice. "My parents didn't think I had it," she explains. Actually, her father did not want her to tax her voice too early and wanted her to get a solid musical background. Occasionally she did some singing accompanied on the piano by her father. At one time she made a public appearance as a singer in an amateur summer camp production. She attended concerts frequently.

At Roosevelt High School in Yonkers she sang in the glee club. Upon graduation in 1945 she went to Smith College in Northampton, Massachusetts. "Believe it or not," she says, "the same routine occurred there as at home, I wasn't allowed to study voice. Because of my extensive training in piano and violin they assumed I would fit in better as a piano student than as a voice student. Back I went to five-finger exercises until my piano teacher heard me sing. He said, 'You're in the wrong department' and promptly introduced me to my dear friend who has been my teacher ever since—Anna Hamlin." Raskin soon won a singing scholarship, the Harriet Dey Barnum Award. She became an active member of both the glee club and the Clef Club and was elected president of the college art society (Alpha).

As a senior in college, she married Dr. Raymond A. Raskin, a physician, on July 11, 1948. In 1949 she was graduated from Smith College

JUDITH RASKIN

with a Bachelor of Arts degree. (The same college awarded her an honorary doctorate in music in 1963.) Though she spent most of the next decade devoting herself to home, husband, and the raising of two children, she did not neglect music nor lose sight of a singing career. While continuing her vocal studies with Anna Hamlin, she found a regular job singing solos in synagogues. This paid her just enough to take care of a babysitter. Random engagements came her way as a soloist with the New York Oratorio Society, the Symphony of the Air, and in the summer of 1957 with the City Symphony of New York in a public concert in Central Park. That last appearance brought her a good notice from a critic of the *Herald Tribune* who said: "Had this listener cared for nothing else, he would have judged the evening well spent to have heard Judith Raskin. . . . Miss Raskin has a lovely voice as well as utter mastery of English diction."

In 1957 she auditioned for Samuel Chotzinoff, the music director of the NBC network. Favorably impressed, he turned her over to George Schick, music coordinator of NBC-TV Opera department. "You may have the voice of the decade," Schick told her. She was offered free coaching lessons in preparation for appearances with the NBC-TV Opera. At NBC she met Ludwig Donath, the actor, from whom she received coaching in acting. They became close friends.

After touring with the NBC Opera in live performances of *The Marriage of Figaro,* in which she assumed the role of Susanna, proving

herself as an excellent interpreter of Mozart, she was cast as Sister Constance in the NBC telecast of Poulenc's *Les Dialogues des Carmélites* in December 1957.

In the summer of 1958 Raskin joined the Santa Fe Opera Company, where she appeared as Despina in *Così fan Tutte* and Musetta in *La Bohème.* Later the same year she made several appearances with the American Opera Society in New York, made her debut in Dallas in a production of Cherubini's *Medea* which starred Maria Callas, and made another debut, this time in Washington, D.C., in *The Marriage of Figaro.*

After appearing as the Countess in Rossini's *Le Comte d'Ory* at the Juilliard School of Music in March 1959 and in the title role of Douglas Moore's *The Ballad of Baby Doe* in Central City, Colorado, later the same year, she was engaged by the New York City Opera. Her debut there took place in 1959 as Despina. Her success brought her other Mozart roles with the New York City Opera: Susanna in *The Marriage of Figaro* in 1961 and again (this time in an English-language production) in 1963, and Zerlina in *Don Giovanni* in 1963.

Raskin returned to television and the NBC-TV Opera as Zerlina on April 10, 1960, and on January 1, 1961, she created the role of Ann Brice in the world premiere of Leonard Kastle's *Deseret.*

She made her debut at the Metropolitan Opera as Susanna in *The Marriage of Figaro* on February 23, 1962. "Her Mozart . . . was a matter of deep study and care," said Louis Biancolli in the *World-Telegram and Sun.* "Notes and words blended easily, and she phrased exquisitely." To Raymond Ericson of the New York *Times* she was "pretty as a picture, never forcing the musical phrases, never overplaying the comedy, enunciating the Italian like a veteran."

She added to her popularity at the Metropolitan Opera on March 6, 1964, as Nannetta in Franco Zeffirelli's production of *Falstaff* conducted by Leonard Bernstein. "Judith Raskin," wrote Irving Kolodin in the *Saturday Review,* "was a sweet sounding Nannetta and a delight to watch." Further praise came when she sang Sophie in *Der Rosenkavalier* on December 19, 1965, and later on Pamina in *The Magic Flute* and Micaëla in *Carmen.*

All this time she was gaining recognition in other places as well. With the American Opera Society in New York she appeared in 1962 as

Delilah in Handel's *Samson* and as Anne True-love in Stravinsky's *The Rake's Progress,* the latter opera performed to honor the composer's eightieth birthday. Stravinsky himself selected her to repeat her performance as Anne Truelove in the Columbia recording of the opera conducted by the composer. In 1964 the American Opera Society revived for her Rossini's *Il Turco in Italia.* With the NBC-TV Opera she assumed the principal female role of the Bride in the world premiere of Menotti's *The Labyrinth* on May 3, 1963. That same year she was also featured in the soprano solo part of Bach's *Passion According to St. Matthew* in a television production. Over television she was also seen and heard as Marzelline in *Fidelio* and as Zerlina.

Raskin made her European debut at the Glyndebourne Festival in the summer of 1963 as Pamina. She repeated that role the following summer at Glyndebourne, also over BBC-TV in September 1964, and in a concert performance by the Boston Symphony at the Berkshire Music Festival during the summer of 1966.

She emerged as an interpreter of *Lieder* when she made her New York recital debut on a Ford Foundation grant at the Metropolitan Museum of Art on October 9, 1964. When in December 1965 she gave a recital in New York's Town Hall, Miles Kastendieck referred to her in the *Journal-American* as "a jewel of a recitalist." Louis Snyder, in the *Herald Tribune,* wrote: "It would take a long memory and a retentive ear to match it [Raskin's recital] in like context in this hall's annals—perhaps Elisabeth Schumann." Louis Biancolli wrote in the *World-Telegram and Sun:* "The voice was gorgeous as ever from top to bottom, one long range of smooth and sunny tone. The style was impeccable in phrase and diction, and the looks were breathtaking. Let's face it. Judith Raskin is a great American beauty blessed with a great American voice. Astonishing, too, is the brain at work behind that loveliness. Where she got all that subtlety of text and color, of mood and feeling, in fact, that is poetry become life, is her secret."

She has appeared as a soloist with most major American and European orchestras in musical masterworks ranging from Bach, Haydn, Mozart, Beethoven, and Berlioz to Mahler, Richard Strauss, and Ravel. In addition to her Columbia recording of *The Rake's Progress,* she has been heard on RCA and Columbia disks in operas by Gluck and Mozart, and choral or symphonic works by Pergolesi, Handel, Haydn, Mozart, and Mahler.

During the 1960s the Raskins occupied a five-room apartment in Queens, New York. "A different picture this: the artist as housewife, blithely humming arias as she whips up casseroles for a busy husband . . . and two children," wrote Joan Barthel in the New York *Times.* "But it remains uncomplicated, right up to the moment she glances around the casually modern living room, says she hates it there, can't wait to move to Manhattan, and describes how sometimes after a performance she comes home and compulsively scrubs the kitchen floor."

She confesses she likes good food, both to eat and to cook, reasons why it is always difficult for her to keep her weight down to about one hundred and thirty-five pounds. One of her specialties is Orange Chicken, a casserole dish, an old recipe of her mother's. "I don't smoke at all, and if I drink, it has to be forty-eight hours before a concert," she told *Opera News.* "On the day of a performance I don't talk at all—that's even better than whispering—and don't laugh, because it's the laughing that really hurts."

Raskin is on the faculty of Mannes College of Music, Manhattan College, and the City College (CUNY).

ABOUT: Esquire, April 1967; New York Times, May 8, 1966; Opera News, January 26, 1963, February 22, 1969.

John Reardon

1930–

John Robert Reardon, lyric and dramatic baritone, was born in New York City on April 8, 1930. He came from a musical family. His grandfather had led the municipal band in Waterbury, Connecticut; an uncle played the flute with the NBC Symphony under Toscanini; one aunt was a concert soprano and another a concert pianist. John's mother, Thelma Claire Fulton Reardon, was a professional singer. His father, John Joseph Reardon, the nonmusical member of this family, was an insurance salesman and factory worker.

Carrying on the musical traditions of his family, John began studying the piano when he was five. His high boy-soprano voice soon attracted

JOHN REARDON

attention, particularly when he outsang his mother and aunt in the brilliant coloratura arias of the Queen of the Night from *The Magic Flute* which he had learned by ear.

In his boyhood, he moved with his family to Lake Worth, Florida, where he attended the Lake Worth High School from which he was graduated in 1948. He entered Rollins College in Winter Park, Florida, planning to major in business administration and become a banker. But three days after school started he shifted to the college's music school, studying piano and composition, and later specializing in voice under Ross Rossazza. His first singing experience was with the college's Chapel Choir at the Winter Park Congregational Church and with the Bach Festival Choir.

In 1952 Reardon was graduated from Rollins College with a bachelor's degree in music. He spent that summer studying voice with Martial Singher at Aspen, Colorado, and then took some courses at the David Mannes College of Music in New York. He began his professional career with the Paper Mill Playhouse in Millburn, New Jersey, in the chorus in *Die Fledermaus* and, later, in small singing roles in operas and operettas. In 1954 he made his debut at the New York City Opera as Falke in *Die Fledermaus*. He soon went on to the more substantial role of Count Almaviva in *The Marriage of Figaro*. When Rolf Liebermann's *School for Wives* received its New York premiere in 1956, Reardon assumed the four baritone roles. "When I was assigned them," he wrote in *Opera News,* "I embarked on

what has become a way of life for me—singing contemporary music."

He combined his work at the New York City Opera with appearances in the popular Broadway musical theater. He was in the cast of Menotti's *The Saint of Bleecker Street* when it received its world premiere at the Broadway Theater on December 27, 1954. On June 14, 1956, he opened in the revue *New Faces of 1956.* In 1959 he sang the role of Edvard Grieg in a production of the operetta *The Song of Norway,* at the Jones Beach Marine Theatre in Long Island. He was in the cast of the Broadway musical *Do, Re, Mi* when it started a four-hundred-performance run at the St. James Theater on December 26, 1960. Still in the field of the popular musical theater he took on the role of the Count in a revival of Emmerich Kálmán's *Countess Maritza* by the American Opera Society in New York early in 1963 and was starred by the New York City Opera in its presentation of two other operettas, *Die Fledermaus* and Lehár's *The Merry Widow.*

More ambitious assignments came his way at the New York City Opera in the early 1960s: the husband in *Amelia Goes to the Ball,* Menotti's one-act *opera buffa;* one of the three principal voices in Carl Orff's *Carmina Burana;* Miles Dunster in the world premiere of Douglas Moore's *Wings of the Dove* on October 12, 1961; Olivier in Richard Strauss's *Capriccio;* Belaev in the world premiere of Lee Hoiby's *Natalia Petrovna* on October 8, 1964. With the Opera Society in Washington, D.C., he was heard as Scarpia in *Tosca* and in *Pelléas and Mélisande.* "Few other baritones successfully negotiate such dissimilar roles," reported Richard D. Fletcher in *The Christian Science Monitor.* "Reardon has done both superlatively, on the same stage."

He made his debut with the Metropolitan Opera on September 28, 1965, as Count Tomsky in Tchaikovsky's *Queen of Spades.* He was praised both for the beauty of his singing and the impact of his acting. About two weeks later, on October 14, he assumed the role of Mandryka in Strauss's *Arabella,* and Howard Klein praised him in the New York *Times* for his "smooth and velvety voice" as well as for "his rhythmic sense and his perfect timing."

During the next few years, Reardon shuttled between the Metropolitan Opera and the New York City Opera, with summer digressions to Santa Fe in New Mexico. On March 9, 1966, at the New York City Opera, he created for America the title role in Gottfried von Einem's *Dantons Tod*. To Alan Rich in the *Herald Tribune* Reardon's "masterly creation of the title role was probably the best thing the young baritone has yet accomplished." Later that year, the New York City Opera launched a Mozart festival and asked Reardon to appear as Count Almaviva in *The Marriage of Figaro* and as Papageno in *The Magic Flute*. On March 16, 1967, at the Metropolitan Opera, he created the role of Orin in the world premiere of Marvin David Levy's *Mourning Becomes Electra*. At the Metropolitan Opera Reardon was given ample opportunities through the years to display his vocal and histrionic talents in the more conventional repertory, such as Escamillo in *Carmen*, Mercutio in *Romeo and Juliet*, Belcore in *L'Elisir d'Amore*, and Sharpless in *Madama Butterfly*.

The summers of the mid- and late 1960s were spent with the Santa Fe Opera, where the adventurous modern repertory enabled him to enrich his repertoire in twentieth century music. On August 11, 1965, he appeared as Kovaliov in the American premiere of Shostakovich's satirical opera *The Nose*. On July 26, 1967, he was heard in the title role in the American premiere of the revised version of Hindemith's *Cardillac*. On August 7, 1968, he assumed the role of Pentheus in the American premiere of Hans Werner Henze's *The Bassarids*. On August 1, 1969, he appeared as Dr. Stone in the American premiere of Menotti's children's fantasy opera *Help, Help, the Globolinks!* Later the same month, on August 14, he was cast as Dr. Grandier in the American premiere of Penderecki's provocative religious opera *The Devils of Loudun*. Commenting upon Reardon's contribution to the last of these operas, *Time* reported: "As a sensual priest who is burned at the stake, Reardon gave the production just the sort of personal force it needs. He typified the new qualities necessary to survive in opera today. He is good looking. He acts superbly. He is also willing to learn the most complicated role in nothing flat." In the *Saturday Review*, Irving Kolodin noted that Reardon had reached "a career peak in his compelling portrait of Grandier."

By the time Reardon was called upon to do the role of Dr. John Buchanan Jr. in Lee Hoiby's *Summer and Smoke* (based on Tennessee Williams's play) on March 19, 1972, he had appeared in thirty contemporary operas, ten of them world premieres, and eight, American premieres. *Summer and Smoke* was introduced by the St. Paul Opera in Minnesota on June 19, 1971. In his review for the Washington *Post* Paul Hume said: "Reardon is utterly magnificent, acting and singing with a mixture of cynicism and honest sweetness that makes his work one of the outstanding portraits of any stage today. His singing is at its finest, with every word clear, and every phrase filled with meaning."

Some of the other world premieres in which Reardon has appeared were Hugo Weisgall's *Athaliah* with the Concert Opera Association in New York on February 17, 1964 (as Yehoyada); Douglas Moore's *Carry Nation*, at the University of Kansas in Lawrence on April 28, 1966 (as Alfred); and Thomas Pasatieri's *The Seagull* with the Houston Opera in Texas on March 5, 1974 (as Trigorin). Other contemporary roles in which Reardon has made noteworthy appearances are: Nick Shadow in Stravinsky's *The Rake's Progress*, Prince Andrei Bolkonsky in Prokofiev's *War and Peace*, Pantalone in Prokofiev's *Love for Three Oranges*, Heathcliff in Carlisle Floyd's *Wuthering Heights*, the Doctor in Samuel Barber's *Vanessa*, Abdul in Menotti's *The Last Savage*, and Donato in Menotti's *Maria Golovin*. Over television he has sung (among many other operas) the voice of God in the world premiere of Stravinsky's *Noah and the Flood* on June 14, 1962; the Groom in Menotti's *The Labyrinth;* and Shiskov in Janáček's *The House of the Dead*.

To *Opera News* Reardon has explained how he studies and learns a new modern role: "I begin by reading through at the piano, employing an accompanist for a particularly thorny score. Once I know the sound by looking at the page, I sit with the score and become totally involved with the vocalization; accompaniment at this point would only divide my attention. Then come the finishing touches and the staging. Especially in a modern piece, the staging is usually based so intrinsically on the music that they become reciprocal; one reminds me of the other. Consequently, if my memory fails in any spot the stage action brings it back."

Reardon's deep involvement in twentieth century operas sometimes makes it difficult to remember that he has also covered a wide range of roles in operas of the past. Some of those roles have already been mentioned. Among others have been: Guglielmo in *Così fan Tutte*, Gianni

Schicchi, Masetto and the title role in *Don Giovanni*, Schaunard and Marcello in *La Bohème*, Dandini in *La Cenerentola*, and Taddeo in Rossini's *L'Italiana in Algeri.*

In the summer of 1970 Reardon directed the student company in Sante Fe in scenes from *Così fan Tutte* and *Die Fledermaus.* In the early 1970s he spent part of each season teaching voice at the Philadelphia Musical Academy. Since the summer of 1973 he has been artistic director of the Wolf Trap Company at Wolf Trap Farm in Vienna, Virginia.

Reardon is a bachelor who lives on the upper west side of Manhattan near the Lincoln Center for the Performing Arts. His favorite hobbies are meteorology and horticulture; his favorite form of exercise, swimming. In 1976 he was awarded an honorary doctorate in music by Rollins College in Florida.

ABOUT: Hi-Fi, March 1973; New York Times, March 12, 1972; Opera News, April 1, 1972; Time, August 22, 1969.

Fritz Reiner

1888–1963

Fritz Reiner, conductor, was born in Budapest on December 19, 1888. His father, Ignaz Reiner, was a prosperous merchant who hoped his son would become a lawyer; his mother, Vilma Pollak Reiner, an excellent amateur musician, encouraged the boy's natural bent for music. As a child, Fritz expressed delight whenever a musical clock in the family sounded the tones of a melody from *Lucia di Lammermoor.* He reacted with excitement when at six he heard his first opera. At about this time he started to take piano lessons; it was not long before he could play four-hand arrangements of opera with his mother. One day he was practicing the *Tannhäuser Overture* when he was overheard by young Leo Weiner, then twelve years old. (Weiner became a distinguished Hungarian composer and teacher in his later years.) Following this incident the two boys made it a practice to play four-hand music together and this was the beginning of a friendship that lasted until Weiner's death in 1960. It was Leo who first

Reiner: rī' nĕr

FRITZ REINER

encouraged Fritz to think of becoming a conductor. "That's when I decided to go into music seriously," Reiner later recalled, adding that his own career owed far more to Leo Weiner than to any other single person.

On the urging of Leo Weiner, Fritz entered the Royal Academy of Music in Budapest in 1898. There he remained for a ten-year period, receiving training in all phases of music, particularly in piano with Stefan Thomán and in composition with Hans Koessler and Béla Bartók. Since the Conservatory had no class in conducting, Fritz devoted himself primarily to playing the piano. He made his public debut in Budapest in a performance of Mozart's *Coronation Concerto* when he was thirteen. However, in order to prepare himself for a possible conducting career he spent much time memorizing symphonic scores, studying texts on conducting, and practicing by leading a high-school orchestra. He also gained valuable experience in orchestral performance by playing the tympani in the Conservatory orchestra for five years.

Since his father was still determined that he become a lawyer, Fritz compromised by entering the University of Budapest for the study of law while continuing his musical education at the Academy. When he was graduated from the Academy in 1908 he continued his law studies for another year. Then, in 1909, upon the death of his father, he was able to devote himself completely to music.

His first music post was as a vocal coach at the Komische Oper in Budapest in 1909. One evening the regular conductor fell ill and Reiner stepped in as a substitute in a performance of *Carmen*. "It was sink or swim," was the way he later put it, "so I swam." This performance impressed the director of the Landestheater in Laibach (now Ljubljana in Yugoslavia) who engaged him in 1910 as principal conductor.

In 1911 Reiner was called back to Budapest to become principal conductor at the Volksoper. He held this post three years. In that time he conducted the first Budapest performances of *Parsifal* and *The Jewels of the Madonna*.

A more important post became his in 1914 when he was appointed royal court conductor in Dresden. His duties included conducting performances not only of operas at the Royal Opera but also of symphony concerts with the Saxon State Orchestra. This was indeed an extraordinary appointment for a non-German musician. Upon arriving in Dresden, Reiner was asked to conduct performances of Wagner's *Ring* cycle without rehearsals. He was ready for such a test, since he had long since studied the scores minutely. He remained in Dresden through the years of World War I and several years thereafter, until 1921. These were all-important years for his musical development, for he came under the influence of two of Germany's great conductors, Arthur Nikisch and Karl Muck, whose performances he attended and studied. In these years he became a close friend of Richard Strauss, of whose musical dramas he was to become an outstanding interpreter.

Reiner's performances in Dresden created so much interest all over Europe that he received invitations to appear as guest conductor in Berlin, Hamburg, and Vienna. Though he had been offered a life contract in Dresden in 1921, he turned it down when he was denied permission to conduct a performance of *Die Meistersinger* in Rome and several other performances in other parts of Europe. Leaving Dresden, he went on to Italy and Spain for guest appearances.

While performing on the island of Majorca in 1922 he received an offer to become principal conductor of the Cincinnati Symphony Orchestra, succeeding Eugène Ysaÿe. To Reiner fell the task of rebuilding that orchestra, of restoring discipline, of revitalizing the repertory. The nine years he spent in Cincinnati were stormy ones for him since he came into constant conflict with the orchestra men, who rebelled against his dictatorial ways, and with the directors of the or-

chestra who resented his partiality for twentieth century music. But, overcoming all opposition, he proceeded to make the Cincinnati Symphony a major American orchestra. Its prestige was greatly enhanced by American premieres of music by Béla Bartók and Reiner's promotion of compositions by Ravel, Respighi, and Stravinsky, among other moderns. Among his world premieres in Cincinnati were Bartók's Suite from *The Miraculous Mandarin* (November 27, 1926), Daniel Gregory Mason's Symphony No.2 (November 7, 1930), and Roger Sessions's *The Black Maskers* (December 5, 1930).

Between 1926 and 1930 Reiner made several guest appearances with the Symphony at La Scala in Milan at the invitation of Toscanini. Other European guest performances in the 1920s took place in Vienna, Budapest, Stockholm, and the principal cities of Italy.

Reiner became an American citizen in 1929. That same year he divorced his wife, the former Berta Gardini-Gerster, under circumstances that caused a considerable amount of newspaper publicity, and on April 23, 1930, he married Carlotta Irwin, a young musician performing with the Stuart Walker Players in Cincinnati.

When the Institute of Fine Arts took over the control of the Cincinnati Symphony from the private hands of Mrs. Charles Phelps Taft and demanded from Reiner a more conservative approach towards programming, Reiner resigned from his post (1931). He went to Philadelphia to head the opera and orchestral departments at the Curtis Institute of Music. In addition to teaching conducting to such pupils as Leonard Bernstein, Lukas Foss, Walter Hendl, and Vincent Persichetti, he conducted the forces of the Curtis Institute in symphonic and operatic performances, including the world premiere of *Amelia Goes to the Ball,* Menotti's one-act *opera buffa,* on April 1, 1937 (at that time the composer was only twenty-seven). Reiner also appeared as a guest conductor of the Philadelphia Orchestra and was the music director of a vital opera season presented by that orchestra in 1934–1935 —a season which included performances of *Der Rosenkavalier, The Marriage of Figaro, Falstaff, Tristan and Isolde,* and *Die Meistersinger.* On November 2, 1936, Reiner made his debut with the San Francisco Opera in *Tristan and Isolde,* following it that season with *Die Götterdämmerung* and *Die Walküre.* He returned to the San Francisco Opera in 1937 for *Tristan and*

Isolde and *Fidelio,* and in 1938 for *Don Giovanni, Die Meistersinger,* and *Elektra.* He made his first appearances at Covent Garden in London during the coronation festivities in 1936, directing *Parsifal, Der Rosenkavalier,* and *Tristan and Isolde.* And on May 18, 1939, he conducted in New York the world premiere of Douglas Moore's one-act opera *The Devil and Daniel Webster.*

Some who were close to Reiner suspected that one of the reasons he took on the post with the Curtis Institute in Philadelphia was his hope of succeeding Leopold Stokowski as music director of the Philadelphia Orchestra. These same people also thought that one of the reasons Reiner withdrew from the Curtis Institute in 1938 was that Eugene Ormandy had become the choice to replace Stokowski. In 1938 Reiner accepted an offer to become music director of the Pittsburgh Symphony. For a decade he put his talent at orchestra-building to work creating another of America's major symphonic organizations.

When Reiner took the Pittsburgh Symphony on a tour of the South and the Southwest in January and February 1947, he crossed the border into Mexico City for five concerts to become the first conductor to bring an American orchestra into that country. During these years Reiner also was a guest conductor of virtually every major orchestra in America and Europe. "Reiner has an expert knowledge of the composite instrument on which he plays," said Lawrence Gilman in the New York *Herald Tribune.* "He is a technician of uncommon adroitness and security. The orchestra is no seven-sealed book of mystery to him. . . . It is a vehicle lucidly and realistically understood, and he employs it with clear-cut imperious authority."

In baton technique Reiner was a master. His gestures were reduced to a minimum, but so articulate were the spare movements of his unusually large baton and his wrists and so communicative the expression of his eyes that any orchestra that played under him had an instant rapport with his every musical wish. As an obituary in the New York *Times* pointed out, his baton technique was "perhaps the clearest, the most precise, and the most analytical any conductor has ever had. Indeed, it was almost legendary in the music world. Mr. Reiner had no use for the flamboyant, the balletic, or consciously graceful mannerisms cultivated by many conductors to the delight of the general public."

Among the works that received their world premieres in Pittsburgh under Reiner were Paul Creston's *Threnody* (December 2, 1938), Norman Dello Joio's *Concert Music* (January 1946) and *Variations, Chaconne and Finale* (January 30, 1948), Piston's *The Incredible Flutist Suite* (November 22, 1940), and Gardner Read's *Pennsylvania Suite* (November 21, 1947).

In 1948 the Pittsburgh Symphony embarked upon a wave of economy. Personnel was reduced from ninety to eighty-five players and the season reduced from twenty-eight to twenty-five performances. Reiner would have none of these sacrifices. "I told them," he said to an interviewer, "I would take a salary cut, but I would not have the number of my musicians cut down. They did it anyway. There was nothing for me to do but to resign."

He left Pittsburgh for New York where he became a conductor at the Metropolitan Opera. There he made his debut on February 4, 1949, with *Salome.* Virgil Thomson, writing in the *Herald Tribune,* called this "one of the greatest musico-dramatic performances of our century." Reiner's reading of the score, added Olin Downes in the New York *Times,* "was exciting and symphonic, flexible and remarkably salient of detail; charged with imagination, too."

Reiner continued to conduct performances at the Metropolitan Opera during the next five seasons, among them *The Marriage of Figaro, Don Giovanni, Der Rosenkavalier, Elektra, Falstaff,* a new production of *Carmen,* and the American premiere of Stravinsky's *The Rake's Progress.* "Fritz Reiner's musical handling from the pit is a marvel of clarity and animation," said Virgil Thomson in the *Herald Tribune* about the *Carmen* production. Ronald Eyer in *Musical America* described Reiner's direction of *The Rake's Progress* as "inspired."

Objecting to the assignments to second- and third-rate conductors of operas long in Reiner's repertory, Reiner decided to withdraw from the Metropolitan Opera after the 1952–1953 season. A new post awaited him, the music directorship of the Chicago Symphony Orchestra. As in Cincinnati and Pittsburgh, Reiner found the orchestra in a technical and artistic decline; and once again he set about the onerous job of rebuilding. Irving Kolodin wrote in the *Saturday Review:* "Out of the chaos that prevailed when he took charge—a consequence of both internal and external uncertainty in the period following the retirement of Frederick Stock in 1941 after a tenure of nearly forty years—Reiner achieved not merely order, but distinction. From a position of prestige inferior to younger orchestras in smaller cities . . . the Reiner-Chicago Symphony attained a standard close to the best in America, which means the best anywhere."

On October 6, 1960, a few days before he was to begin his eighth season in Chicago, Reiner succumbed to a heart attack. Not until March 31, 1961, was he able to conduct his orchestra again—he did so for the final five pairs of subscription concerts. The following season his schedule in Chicago was reduced to ten weeks, with no more than two weeks at a stretch. Improvement in his health permitted him to fill this commitment, to make some recordings, and to appear as a guest conductor with several orchestras. He also completed arrangements to return to the Metropolitan Opera to conduct *Die Götterdämmerung* after an absence of a decade. But when he was once again hospitalized in July 1961, he realized that he could no longer properly perform his duties in Chicago. He resigned in 1962.

He was rehearsing *Die Götterdämmerung* at the Metropolitan Opera for a performance scheduled for November 14, 1963, when he was once again stricken, this time by pneumonia. On November 11, 1963, he was rushed to Mount Sinai Hospital in New York City. He died there the following Friday, November 15.

At the funeral services on November 18, composer William Schuman, who was then president of the Lincoln Center for the Performing Arts, delivered a eulogy in which he said: "Fritz Reiner, to be sure, was the virtuoso performer. But he was ever the teacher. He taught not in the classroom alone. He taught all who performed in his orchestra, all who heard him, all who saw him. Fritz was the teacher of us all through every facet of his astonishing mastery of the art he practiced. Yet these demonstrable attributes were the end result of the true example of his life in art: a complete and total commitment of self —of all his intellectual and emotional resources to the art that was his life."

Reiner was buried in Willowbrook Cemetery in Westport, Connecticut.

For the last twenty-five years of his life Reiner and his wife occupied a French provincial house, Rambleside, built for them on Davis Hill Road in Westport, Connecticut. It was equipped with a music studio, a photographic dark room, and a swimming pool. There Reiner was host to his many friends. There, too, he could indulge in his favorite hobbies: reading (mainly biographies), photography, and (occasionally) gardening. He was very interested in politics, and whenever the national or international political scene became active, could be found watching his television set for the latest news.

Reiner was made an Officer of the Crown of Italy in 1930. In 1940 and 1941 he received honorary doctorates in music from the University of Pennsylvania and the University of Pittsburgh.

ABOUT: International Musician, November 1955; Musical America, October 1963, December 1963; Saturday Review, December 28, 1963.

Maurice Renaud

1861–1933

Maurice Arnold Renaud, baritone, was born in Bordeaux, France, on July 24, 1861. He received his musical training at conservatories in Paris and Brussels. In 1883 he made his opera debut at the Théâtre de la Monnaie in Brussels. He remained its leading baritone for seven years, in which time he created the roles of the High Priest in the world premiere of Reyer's *Sigurd* on January 7, 1884, and of Hamilcar in the world premiere of Reyer's *Salammbô* on February 10, 1890. Upon leaving Brussels, he made his debut in Paris at the Opéra-Comique as Karnak in Lalo's *Le Roi d'Ys* on October 12, 1890. Nine months later, on July 17, 1891, he made his first appearance at the Paris Opéra as Nelusko in *L'Africaine*. For over a decade he remained principal baritone of the Paris Opéra, distinguishing himself particularly in the French repertory and receiving high praise for his remarkable acting ability and for his sensuous, beautifully produced vocalizations.

He made his American debut on January 4, 1893, at the French Opera House in New Orleans as Samson in *Samson and Delilah*. But it was not until more than a decade later that he repeated in the United States the triumphs he

Renaud: rē nō′

MAURICE RENAUD

had enjoyed in Europe at the Paris Opéra, La Scala in Milan, Covent Garden in London, and the Monte Carlo Opera. He made his Covent Garden debut on June 23, 1897, singing selections from *Tannhäuser* and *Les Huguenots* in a performance honoring the golden jubilee of Queen Victoria—and he continued making highly successful appearances there until 1905. In Monte Carlo he was heard in the world premieres of Massenet's *Le Jongleur de Notre-Dame* on February 18, 1902, and Massenet's *Chérubin* on February 14, 1905.

In the early 1900s he was signed by Maurice Grau to appear at the Metropolitan Opera. But when the direction of that company passed on to Heinrich Conried in 1903, Renaud abrogated his agreement, paying a penalty for breaking the contract. When he finally did appear in New York it was as a member of the Manhattan Opera House on December 6, 1906, in the title role of *Rigoletto*. He was ill at this premiere and was not heard to best advantage. But it was not long before he was fully recognized for his singing and acting, particularly when he sang the role of Athanaël in the American premiere of *Thaïs* on November 25, 1907, and was heard in the American premiere of *Le Jongleur de Notre-Dame* on November 27, 1908. Some of the other roles with which he won New York audiences were Herod in *Herodias,* Scarpia in *Tosca,* Méphistophélès in *The Damnation of Faust,* Don Giovanni, and the baritone roles in *The Tales of Hoffmann.*

When the Manhattan Opera company was disbanded, Renaud appeared for one season with the Chicago Opera. On January 10, 1911, he gave his first New York recital in Carnegie Hall. "He has inestimable power of dramatic coloring in his voice," commented Richard Aldrich in the New York *Times,* "and likewise the skill of an accomplished vocalist. ... He has a full realization of the meaning and value of legato singing, of the plastic modeling of the phrase. ... Mr. Renaud's singing ... was unmistakably the product of a fine art guided by a fine intelligence."

Finally, on November 24, 1910, Renaud appeared for the first time on the stage of the Metropolitan Opera in the title role of *Rigoletto.* "Mr. Renaud is probably the finest actor now upon the operatic stage," reported H. E. Krehbiel in the *Tribune.* "Mr. Renaud was not in his best voice yesterday, but his art in singing, his skillful use of legato, the feeling with which he informs all he utters made all defects forgivable. But best of all was the splendid power of his acting. In the part he runs practically the gamut of emotions, but instead of the bag of tricks with which the average artist composes for the role, Mr. Renaud gives forth a vital, compelling characterization, a characterization pregnant with feeling and the sense of impending tragedy."

One season later, on February 3, 1912, Renaud once again won praise, this time for his performance as Valentin in *Faust.*

After leaving the United States in 1912, Renaud limited his performances to Europe. In his later years he taught singing in Paris. There he died on October 16, 1933. Of his more than sixty roles, the ones most often referred to by opera historians as his crowning achievements are Don Giovanni, Beckmesser in *Die Meistersinger,* Athanaël, and Scarpia, none of which was sung during his brief stay at the Metropolitan Opera.

ABOUT: Kutsch, K. J. and Riemens, L. A Concise Biographical Dictionary of Singers.

Regina Resnik

1922–

Regina Resnik, mezzo-soprano, was born in the Bronx, New York City, on August 30, 1922. Her parents, Sam and Ruth Seidler Resnik, had emigrated to the United States from the Ukraine. In

REGINA RESNIK

New York, Regina's father became a manufacturer of leather.

Regina attended elementary schools in the Bronx, the Herman Ridder Junior High School, and James Monroe High School. She was graduated from the last of these in 1938. While attending high school she began taking voice lessons from Rosalie Miller, who remained her teacher even after she had achieved success. In 1942 she received a Bachelor of Arts degree from Hunter College.

On October 27, 1942, she made her concert debut at the Brooklyn Academy of Music, in New York. That same fall she was engaged as understudy for the role of Lady Macbeth in the New Opera Company of which Fritz Busch was music director and which was then giving performances on Broadway. When Florence Kirk, the principal soprano scheduled to sing the role in Verdi's *Macbeth* fell ill, Resnik was called upon to substitute for her. This was the first of several occasions when she was to be recruited as a replacement for indisposed singers. It was, then, in *Macbeth* on December 5, 1942, that she made her operatic debut. A critic for the New York *Times* took notice of her performance, commenting that she "won the audience completely . . . [with her] poise and temperament." This performance brought her an engagement with the Opera Nacional of Mexico City in 1943 when, under Erich Kleiber's direction, she was heard in the soprano roles of Leonore in *Fidelio* and Micaëla in *Carmen*.

In 1944 she became the only woman finalist in

that year's Metropolitan Auditions of the Air and received a contract with the Metropolitan Opera. Before she made that debut, however, she appeared with the New York City Opera in May 1944 as Santuzza in *Cavalleria Rusticana* and as Frasquita in *Carmen*.

She was scheduled to make her debut at the Metropolitan Opera on December 9, 1944. But a few days earlier, Zinka Milanov, scheduled to sing Leonora in *Il Trovatore,* fell ill. With no other replacement available, the Metropolitan Opera called on Resnik even though she had never appeared in that role and had not seen the score in over two years. She received just one rehearsal and had one hour and a quarter in which to learn the stage routines. From this severe challenge which she knew "could have made or broken" her she emerged successfully. Her debut on December 6, 1944, was "an auspicious one," wrote Mark A. Schubert in the New York *Times*. "She has a strong, clear soprano which, though occasionally marred by a tremolo, is both agile enough for the florid passages allotted to Leonora and forceful enough for the dramatic ones. . . . She brings to the music considerable freshness and vitality. . . . One remarkable feature of Miss Resnik's performance was the fact that despite the impromptu quality of her appearance, she handled herself on the stage with confidence and authority."

She made additional favorable impressions that season as Santuzza, Aida, and on March 17, 1945, as Leonore in the first Metropolitan Opera production in English of *Fidelio*.

For the next decade Resnik continued to sing leading soprano roles at the Metropolitan Opera: Tosca, Cio-Cio-San in *Madama Butterfly,* Donna Anna and Donna Elvira in *Don Giovanni,* Helmwige and Sieglinde in *Die Walküre,* Gutrune in *Die Götterdämmerung,* the First Lady in *The Magic Flute,* Alice Ford in *Falstaff,* Rosalinde in *Die Fledermaus,* Chrysothemus in *Elektra,* Eboli in *Don Carlo,* Musetta in *La Bohème,* Venus in *Tannhäuser,* as well as Delilah in the world premiere of Bernard Rogers's *The Warrior* on January 11, 1947, and Ellen Orford in the first Metropolitan Opera production of Britten's *Peter Grimes* on February 12, 1948. During this period she made her debut at the San Francisco Opera on October 11, 1946, as Leonore in *Fidelio* and once again was Leonore at the opera festival at Central City, Colorado, during the summer of 1947. She created the role of the "chorus" in the American premiere of Britten's *Rape of Lucretia* at the Chicago Opera in June 1947. In July 1953 she made her debut at the Bayreuth Festival as Sieglinde in *Die Walküre* and in 1957 she sang Lucretia in *Rape of Lucretia* in Stratford, Ontario.

On July 16, 1946, Resnik married Harry W. Davis, a New York attorney, who had been her first date. They have a son, Michael, affectionately known as "Mikie." She was quoted by Mary Jan Matz in the 1950s in *Opera Stars in the Sun:* "We live an informal life, so that Mikie may participate at every moment. No door is closed to him. No one ever says 'Mother has to sing' or 'Mother must rehearse.' We take all our meals together." Yet the marriage eventually ended in divorce.

After additional coaching with Giuseppe Danise, Resnik began singing mezzo-soprano roles in 1955. As a mezzo-soprano she made her debut at the Cincinnati Zoo Opera in July 1955 as Amneris in *Aida.* Her second debut at the Metropolitan Opera, this time as a mezzo-soprano, took place on February 15, 1956, as Marina in *Boris Godunov.* "Miss Resnik," wrote Harriet Johnson in the New York *Post,* "has made the change successfully, and has improved her personality stagewise along with the transformation. She looked the part of the noble, lovely Marina and sang with beauty of tone, with a vibrant dark quality in the lower voice, and with dramatic impressiveness."

On January 15, 1958, Resnik created the role of the Baroness in the world premiere of Samuel Barber's *Vanessa.* In the opinion of Irving Kolodin in the *Saturday Review* she played the role "expertly." The following March 21 she assumed what since has become one of her most celebrated roles, that of Carmen, which she has sung the world over. "Her Carmen," noted Donal Henahan in the New York *Times,* "came on like a combination of alley cat and Mae West, swaggering and blowing cigarette smoke in men's eyes. . . . She is a tough gypsy, this one. . . . Consistent with her idea of the part, she used the voice expertly as a dramatic weapon that could drip derision or suggest bottomless contempt for the sentimentalities of Don José and that prize ninny, Micaëla." When she commemorated the twenty-fifth anniversary of her Metropolitan Opera debut on June 19, 1970, it was in a gala performance of *Carmen.* By then she had been heard at the Metropolitan Opera in New York

196 times in 37 soprano and mezzo-soprano roles. On March 6, 1964, she appeared as Dame Quickly in a new production of *Falstaff* staged by Franco Zeffirelli and conducted by Leonard Bernstein; this role was the one in which she appeared most often at the Metropolitan Opera. Among her other roles were Azucena in *Il Trovatore,* Amneris in *Aida,* Laura in *La Gioconda,* Marcellina in *The Marriage of Figaro,* Herodias in *Salome,* Klytemnestra in *Elektra,* the Countess in *The Queen of Spades,* the Princess in *Adriana Lecouvreur,* Orlovsky in *Die Fledermaus,* Magdalene in *Die Meistersinger,* Ulrica in *Un Ballo in Maschera,* Czipra in *The Gypsy Baron,* Geneviève in *Pelléas et Mélisande.* On February 17, 1972, she added to her repertory the role of Marquise de Birkenfeld in a production of *The Daughter of the Regiment* that starred Sutherland and Pavarotti.

Resnik made her debut at Covent Garden in 1957 as Carmen (returning in the summer of 1958 as Amneris and in 1958–1959 opening the season as Marina). Beginning with 1958 she was for many years a guest performer at the Vienna State Opera. In 1960 she appeared at the Salzburg Festival as Eboli, and in 1961 she assumed the role of Fricka in the Wagner *Ring* cycle at the Bayreuth Festival. She has also appeared at La Scala in Milan, Munich Opera, Paris Opéra, Stuttgart State Opera, Deutsche Oper in West Berlin, Rome Opera, Teatro la Fenice in Venice, San Carlo in Naples, and Teatro Colón in Buenos Aires. On October 25, 1972, she created for the United States the role of the Old Lady in Gottfried von Einem's *The Visit* at the San Francisco Opera.

She turned her talent to stage direction in 1971 at the Hamburg Opera with *Carmen,* a performance in which she also assumed the title role. Her collaborator was the painter-sculptor and scenic designer Arbit Blatas, who designed the costumes and scenery. After that Resnik and Blatas collaborated in the production of *Elektra* in Venice and Lisbon in December 1971, with Resnik also appearing as Klytemnestra. In 1975 she and Blatas directed and designed a new *Falstaff* for the National Opera of Poland, Resnik also taking on the role of Dame Quickly. The relationship between Resnik and Blatas became personal as well as professional, and on April 6, 1975, they were married in Pawling, New York.

Resnik has also served as stage director for the Vancouver Opera in Canada and the Strasbourg

Opera in France. Some of the other operas she has directed are Menotti's *The Medium* and *The Telephone,* Tchaikovsky's *The Queen of Spades, Salome, Falstaff,* Sir William Walton's *The Bear,* and Kurt Weill's *The Rise and Fall of the City Mahagonny.*

She has given seminars on opera at the New School for Social Research in New York. Austria has given her the honorary title *Kammersängerin.* She has also been awarded the President's Medal in the United States and been made Commander of the French Academy of Arts, Sciences and Letters.

ABOUT: Matz, M. J. Opera Stars in the Sun. *Periodicals* —Musical America, April 1964.

ELISABETH RETHBERG

Elisabeth Rethberg

1894–1976

Elisabeth Rethberg (originally Lisbeth Sättler), soprano, was born in Schwarzenberg, near Dresden, in the Erz mountains of Saxony, on September 22, 1894. She was the daughter of Charles and Jenny Müller Sättler. "My father was a schoolteacher," she once revealed, "and there was plenty of music in our house. He played the piano, mother sang, one of my brothers played the organ, and I yelled folk songs when I was only two. I also had two sisters, and the five of us fought for the use of the piano. My older brother showed me how to read music by explaining what dots had to match to what keys; I bribed him by turning my piggy-bank over to him. I taught myself to play the 'three B's' at a tender age. I didn't know I was laying the foundation for my musical life."

She was so precocious that when she was seven she could sing the entire *Winterreise* cycle of Schubert. Soon after that she began studying the piano formally; by the time she was ten she had acquired such proficiency that she was in demand for concerts.

When she was sixteen, she was sent to Dresden to complete her education. She studied the piano and voice at the Conservatory in 1912–1913. Later she studied voice privately with Otto Watrin; she never had another vocal teacher.

Living in a garret and experiencing intense

Rethberg: rĕth′ bûrg *or* rĕt′ bĕrκ

poverty, she nevertheless managed to scrape together the price for tickets for opera performances, at times leaving herself only a few pennies for food. "What could one get for so little?" she later reminisced. "Roquefort cheese and bread. I loved Roquefort so I didn't mind. My friend and I owned only one good dress between us, so we could not go out together, except to the uppermost gallery of the opera house." It was during these years that she changed her name to Elisabeth Rethberg, taking the name of a woman she had met ("Reth") and adding "berg" for the mountain that reminded her of home.

In 1915 she sang at a private musicale before an audience that included Fritz Reiner, music director of the Dresden Royal Opera. He offered her a contract. Because she was still under twenty-one, her father had to make a special trip to Dresden to sign the contract for her.

She made her debut at the Dresden Royal Opera in 1915 after she was graduated from the Conservatory; her first role was Arsena in *The Gypsy Baron.* Her first success in Dresden came soon after that when she was heard as Agathe in *Der Freischütz.* For seven years she served as principal soprano of the Dresden Royal Opera. To supplement the meager income she was earning at the Royal Opera, with three of her friends she formed a singing quartet that toured Europe. But in time, invitations to make appearances in major European opera houses in Vienna and Berlin made her financially more secure. These appearances also increased her fame. Arthur Nikisch, the conductor, was so delighted with the

676

unusual beauty of her voice that he coached her for appearances under his baton with the Leipzig Gewandhaus Orchestra and the Berlin Philharmonic.

When one of her friends auditioned for Artur Bodanzky, the conductor of the Metropolitan Opera, during his visit to Dresden, she decided to go along. Almost as a challenge from Bodanzky she sang for him and found herself with a contract for the Metropolitan Opera. She made her debut there on November 22, 1922, in what was to remain her greatest role, Aida—she appeared in this role on the same stage sixteen more times. She was an instant success. Writing in the New York *Times,* Richard Aldrich spoke of her "high, clear, liquid tones of a singular brightness floating above Verdi's orchestration with unforced ease."

She had put her best foot forward in her debut. There were many other roles in which her incomparably liquid tones, which Toscanini once described as "heavenly," flooded the Metropolitan Opera stage. During her second season she appeared as Nedda in *I Pagliacci,* Sophie in *Der Rosenkavalier,* Sieglinde in *Die Walküre,* Elsa in *Lohengrin,* Maddalena in *Andrea Chénier,* Agathe in *Der Freischütz,* Eva in *Die Meistersinger,* and Anna Maria in the American premiere of Primo Riccitelli's *I Compagnacci* on January 2, 1924. On November 24, 1928, she created for the United States the role of Rautendelein in the American premiere of Respighi's *La Campana Sommersa.*

Her later roles at the Metropolitan Opera were Selika in *L'Africaine,* Margiana in *The Barber of Bagdad,* Elisabeth in *Tannhäuser,* Pamina in *The Magic Flute,* Mimi in *La Bohème,* Leonora in *Il Trovatore,* Marguerite in *Faust,* Donna Elvira and Donna Anna in *Don Giovanni,* Rachel in *La Juive,* the title role in Mascagni's *Iris,* Amelia in *Simon Boccanegra,* Desdemona in *Otello,* the Countess in *The Marriage of Figaro,* and Brünnhilde in *Siegfried.* Generally regarded as her most celebrated roles, in addition to Aida, were the Wagnerian roles of Sieglinde, Elsa, and Elisabeth; in Verdi, Desdemona; and in Mozart, the Countess in *The Marriage of Figaro.*

In addition to her appearances at the Metropolitan Opera, Rethberg was a regular visitor to the San Francisco Opera up to 1940, following her debut there as Aida on September 15, 1928.

She had pronounced successes in Europe, too.

She made her first appearance at the Salzburg Festival in 1922 as Pamina; at one of the rehearsals there, when she completed one of the arias, the men in the orchestra applauded. A decade later, in 1933, she returned to the Salzburg Festival as Leonore in *Fidelio,* and as Donna Anna. She made her debut at Covent Garden in London in 1925, at La Scala in Milan and the Rome Opera in 1929. She created the title role in Strauss's *Der Aegyptische Helena* at the Dresden Opera on June 6, 1928.

She married Ernest Albert Doman, a German businessman, in 1923 in Chicago, at a time when she was appearing at Ravinia Park. During her years at the Metropolitan Opera, they lived in Riverdale, New York, where she pursued two of her hobbies: the collection of antiques and the raising of dogs. Her antique treasures were assembled in her spacious living room and included a seventeenth century Italian chest, a Gobelin tapestry, an original Rubens, and a round Chinese rug. In the wintertime she enjoyed skiing on a ski-ride constructed on her own grounds. She became an American citizen in 1939.

In 1935 she made news when the wife of the famous Metropolitan Opera bass, Ezio Pinza, sued her for two hundred and fifty thousand dollars for alienation of affection. The suit was finally dropped.

During her many years at the Metropolitan Opera she made numerous concert appearances throughout the United States. From 1936 to 1938 she toured in joint recitals with Ezio Pinza. Her frequent appearances as soloist in performances of choral masterworks with the Society of Friends of Music in New York, of which Artur Bodanzky was conductor, were, in their time, among the highlights of the music season. She appeared as a soloist with most of the major orchestras, including the New York Philharmonic under Toscanini with whom she participated in unforgettable performances of Verdi's Requiem, Brahms's Requiem, and Beethoven's *Missa Solemnis.* Toscanini was quoted as having said that Rethberg's was the most beautiful voice he knew. Her recitals proved a musical delight. She thrilled her listeners, as Olin Downes once wrote in the New York *Times* after one of her concerts, "by truthfulness of accent and intensity of feeling that places her at the right hand of the composers. This is done without loss of tonal or dramatic proportion, by an artist who does not find it necessary to rant or to make an effect."

Her musical memory was prodigious and so was her repertoire. She was as at home in song and choral literature as in opera. She mastered the leading roles of 128 operas; most of the soprano solos of famous oratorios; Masses, Passions, and cantatas of Bach, Handel, Haydn, Mozart, and Brahms; and about a thousand songs in their original languages. She was one of the few operatic stars of her time who sang in practically every language in which operas were written.

A dispute over contract led to her resignation from the Metropolitan Opera. She made her last appearance there on March 6, 1942, as Aida. She spent the next few years on the concert stage. In 1940 she divorced her husband, and in 1956 she married George Cehanovsky, the opera tenor who had made his Metropolitan Opera debut in 1926; they had been friends for thirty years. "He was always there—like the sun, warm and soothing," she said. "He was the steady pole in my life. When I was unhappy he produced a double-sized handkerchief and cried with me. My father, who stayed with me in America for some time, knew him well. He called him 'Chek' for short. Once he said, 'If I knew you'd marry Chek, I would close my eyes in peace.' But he didn't live to see it happen."

After her retirement, Rethberg lived in a nine-room house in Yorktown Heights, in the Westchester section of New York state. The only time she came into New York City proper was to hear a concert or attend an opera. At home, as she explained, "I listen to records—Lieder and instrumental music. I play with my dog. I sit under my oak tree and look at the leaves. I take care of my plants. My deepest emotional experiences always came from nature. All my life I have had to give; I take, reflect, absorb. I have found heaven."

On April 16, 1966, at the gala farewell concert marking the closing of the auditorium of the Metropolitan Opera on Broadway and Thirty-ninth Street, she was one of the honored guests to appear on the stage. Though her role that evening was a silent one, she received one of the greatest ovations accorded to any of the artists present.

Elisabeth Rethberg died at her home in Yorktown Heights on June 6, 1976. At her funeral services in a church in Westchester, chorales from Bach's *Passion According to St. Matthew* and *Passion According to St. John* were sung.

ABOUT: Opera News, February 15, 1964, September 1976.

Ruggiero Ricci

1918–

Ruggiero Ricci, violinist, was born in San Francisco, on July 24, 1918, the second of seven children. His brother Giorgio became a prominent cellist, and his sister, Emma, a professional violinist. Their father, a day laborer, was a passionately devoted lover of music who played the trombone and the violin and at the time of Ruggiero's birth was employed as a bandmaster at a San Francisco army base. "My father was some kind of musical maniac," he told Shirley Fleming in an interview for the New York *Times*. "I started before I can remember. My father had all seven children playing an instrument. ... I wanted to be a pianist, but my parents got me off that jig. They bribed me with fiddles. I'd wake up in the morning and there would be another one. Once I had five fiddles under my bed."

Hoping that Ruggiero would emulate the achievements and the success of the young Yehudi Menuhin (who was four years older), his father was determined to make him a concert-giving prodigy. To achieve this aim, he turned Ruggiero over to Menuhin's teacher, Louis Persinger. Persinger stood ready to supervise his musical development but assigned to Mary Elizabeth Lackey the task of giving Ruggiero his preliminary instruction. So convinced was Lackey of young Ricci's talent that she offered to devote herself completely to him; she even had him live with her so that he might be continually under her personal supervision. On November 15, 1928, Ruggiero's father signed legal papers appointing Lackey the boy's guardian.

He made his concert debut in San Francisco in 1928 in a performance of the Mendelssohn Violin Concerto. On October 20, 1929, he made his New York debut with the same concerto as a soloist with the Manhattan Symphony under Henry Hadley. "Master Ricci," wrote Samuel Chotzinoff in the New York *World*, "revealed a

---

Ricci: rēt′ chē

RUGGIERO RICCI

technical mastery of the violin and a genius for interpretation which place him in a class with the handful of great living violinists." With his first New York recital at Carnegie Hall the boy's musicianship and command of violin technique drew further praise from the critics.

In 1930 Ruggiero became involved in a lawsuit in which the parents sought to regain custody of their son. The ensuing legal battle was as bitter as it was prolonged; it received considerable newspaper publicity. Social workers and editorial writers entered into the battle with accusations against his parents, his teacher, and his manager for exploiting a child for their own selfish interests. The feeling aroused by these accusations grew so intense that a scheduled concert at Carnegie Hall had to be canceled on order of Mayor James J. Walker and no further concerts were permitted until a legal decision had been arrived at.

On his own decision, Ruggiero left his teacher and returned to live with his parents even before the courts placed the custody of the boy in the hands of his father and mother. The long-drawn-out struggle had a demoralizing effect on him. His violin playing suffered additionally from the different teaching methods to which he had been subjected; the result was stylistic confusion. Persinger had been taught in the Belgian school, and this was the way young Ricci was first trained. Ruggiero then became a pupil of Mischel Piastro, who subjected the boy to the Russian tradition of violin playing. After that, George

Kulenkampff tried to wean him away from these influences to German methods.

In 1932 Ruggiero made his first tour of Europe, performing in Berlin, Vienna, and London. In Berlin the audience included some of the leading German personalities of the time, Albert Einstein, Chancellor von Papen, and the playwright Gerhart Hauptmann.

After a prolonged absence from the American concert scene, he returned to Carnegie Hall for a recital on November 24, 1934. By this time he had managed to overcome fully the emotional and musical problems that had been harassing him. "He has now the status of a young violinist of parts, brilliantly gifted, and a sincere musician," said Olin Downes in the New York *Times*.

Further appearances in the United States and a second tour of Europe in 1938 gave further proof that he had not only outgrown his earlier disturbances but had also managed to make the transition from prodigy to mature artist gracefully. After a Carnegie Hall recital on February 25, 1939, the New York *Times* reported: "More important, perhaps, than fingers or bow, is the impression that Mr. Ricci now gives of a more healthy approach to his music. He plays as if he enjoyed doing so. . . . In sum, the concert proved beyond dispute that Mr. Ricci is still unusually talented, and seemed also to indicate the pleasant prospect of natural growth."

During World War II, Ricci enlisted in the Army Air Force where, assigned to Special Services, he served for three years performing in army camps and hospitals and working with a radio production unit. Unable to get a satisfactory piano accompanist for his GI concerts, Ricci began to lean heavily in his programs on the literature for unaccompanied violin. After separation from the service, he resumed his concert work and opened for himself a new path in his violin recitals by devoting entire programs to the unaccompanied violin literature, the first virtuoso to do so.

In 1942 Ricci married Ruth Pink, a graduate in violin from the Juilliard School of Music. They lived in Teaneck, New Jersey, with their children. Eventually they were divorced, and in 1957 Ricci married Valma Rodriguez, an Argentine actress, with whom he had two daughters. Their residence for many years was an apartment in Geneva, Switzerland.

Ricci's first concert after leaving the Army

Air Force took place in November 1946 at Carnegie Hall; this was also his first public performance of a recital made up exclusively of works for unaccompanied violin. Once again both his musicianship and his technique came in for high praise. One of the New York critics called his performance "one of the finest, most sensitive and most beautiful manipulations of the violin you may expect to hear anywhere." When he paid his first visit to London in 1952, he once again was heard in a whole program of unaccompanied violin music. Five years later, in 1957, he made his first world tour. Within a few months, on one of his later tours, he gave forty-six concerts in Australia, and at the Teatro Colón in Buenos Aires he performed ten consecutive performances to standing room only. Return engagements in West Germany found the twenty concerts scheduled in several cities sold out a year in advance. He grew so popular during his first visit to the Soviet Union and to the countries behind the Iron Curtain that he was invited to make three additional tours there.

In some of his more recent concerts, Ricci has adopted a new programming format—one part of the program consists of the standard violin repertory, the second part calls for a musical collaborator (or several musical collaborators) in music more off the beaten track. Ricci has also paid considerable attention to twentieth century violin music. On October 3, 1963, for example, he presented the world premiere of Alberto Ginastera's Violin Concerto with the New York Philharmonic, Leonard Bernstein conducting.

He has made over five hundred recordings for many different companies. He was the first to record all twenty-four caprices of Paganini, and the only one to perform on disks the six solo violin sonatas of Ysaÿe. Among his other recordings are Paganini's Violin Concertos Nos.1, 2, 4, and 6, the last two of which had been totally neglected for many years. Unusual, too, is his record album *The Glory of Cremona,* in which he performs upon fifteen rare and historic instruments made by Stradivarius, Amati, and other violin-makers of the Cremona school. In his recording of Vivaldi's *The Seasons,* he plays upon four different Stradivarius violins, and the accompanying string orchestra is composed entirely of Stradivarius instruments.

Ricci is short (five feet four) and looks, as Shirley Fleming has said, "like a miniature and slightly battered boxer." He talks, adds Joseph

Wershba in the New York *Post,* "as if he could be debating baseball box scores with the fellows outside the candy store. He moves his body like a bantam boxer sparring with a partner."

Since joining the music faculty of the Juilliard School of Music in 1975, Ricci has made New York his home base. (He had previously taught a master class in violin at Indiana University in Bloomington for three years.) He makes four concert trips to Europe each year and is called upon each year to make over one hundred appearances.

ABOUT: Ewen, D. Famous Instrumentalists. *Periodicals*—Musical America, September 1954; New York Times, January 18, 1976, October 7, 1977.

Hans Richter

1843–1916

Hans Richter, known for his conducting of the music of Wagner and Brahms, was born in Raab, Hungary, on April 4, 1843. Both his parents were professional musicians—his father the Kapellmeister at the Cathedral in Raab, and his mother, Josephine Csazinsky Richter, an opera singer who had created for Vienna the role of Venus in *Tannhäuser.* Upon the death of his father in 1853, Hans was entered in the Löwenburg Seminary in Vienna. From 1855 to 1859 he was a choirboy in the Vienna court chapel. In 1860 he entered the Vienna Conservatory, where he remained five years, studying composition with Simon Sechter, violin with Heissler, and French horn with Kleinecke. At the Conservatory, he revealed himself to be a remarkably versatile musician. As his fellow music student Franz Fridberg (later one of his personal friends) recalled: "Was there no trombonist, Richter laid down his horn and seized the trombone; next time it would be the oboe, the bassoon or the trumpet, and then he would pop up among the violins. I saw him once manipulating the doublebass, and on the tympani he was unsurpassed. When we—the Conservatory orchestra—under Hellmesberger's direction, once performed a Mass in the Church of the Invalides, Richter sang. How he did sing!. ... I

Richter: rĭk′ tēr

HANS RICHTER

Royal Opera and the Vienna Philharmonic. He held both posts with extraordinary distinction until 1897 and was promoted to the post of music director of the Royal Opera in 1893. Just as he proved to be a passionate Wagnerian at the Royal Opera so did he serve as a propagandist for Brahms's music with the Vienna Philharmonic. Richter conducted the world premiere of Brahms's Second Symphony on December 30, 1877, and of the Third Symphony on December 2, 1883. He also introduced Bruckner's Symphony No.4 on February 20, 1881. In addition to his duties with the Royal Opera and the Philharmonic, Richter assumed the post of conductor of the concerts of the Gesellschaft der Musikfreunde from 1880 to 1895.

In 1876 Wagner invited Richter to Bayreuth to conduct the world premiere of the complete *Ring* cycle at the inaugural Wagner festival. At Bayreuth Richter reached the summit as a conductor. He had Wagner's music so indelibly in mind, down to the minutest details, that he never had to refer to a score. His eyes aflame, his muscles taut, singing to himself as he conducted, he electrified the musicians who worked with him. The high artistic success of that first Bayreuth festival was due in the main to Richter's efforts. This was officially recognized when at the end of that festival Richter received the Order of Maximilian from the King of Bavaria and the Falkenorden from the Duke of Weimar. He remained a principal conductor at Bayreuth until his retirement.

From May 7 to May 19, 1877, Richter visited London with Wagner, alternating with him in conducting concerts at a Wagner festival at Albert Hall. Without Wagner, Richter returned to London in 1879 from March 5 to March 12, to direct another Wagner festival. This was the beginning of England's love affair with Richter. Bernard Shaw wrote ecstatically of his "poetic creation in musical execution." His success led to the initiation of annual Richter Concerts in London in May. These continued for about twenty years. In addition, on May 30, 1882, Richter led the first performances in England of *Die Meistersinger* and on June 20, of *Tristan and Isolde,* at the Drury Lane Theatre.

In 1897 Richter settled in Manchester as principal conductor of the Hallé Orchestra. While retaining this post, he continued his Richter concerts in London each May, served as principal conductor of the Birmingham Festival from

learned to know him on that day, moreover, as an excellent organist."

From 1862 to 1866 Richter played the French horn in the orchestra of Vienna's Kärnthnerthor Theater. Recommended to Richard Wagner by a mutual friend, he went to live with Wagner at Triebschen, on Lake Lucerne, in October 1866. He remained there until December 1867, playing the piano and the organ for the master and copying out the score of *Die Meistersinger.*

On Wagner's recommendation, Richter was appointed choral director of the Munich Opera in December 1867. There, under Hans von Bülow, he assisted in the preparation of the world premiere of *Die Meistersinger* which took place on June 21, 1868. When von Bülow left the Munich Opera, Richter (once again on Wagner's recommendation) replaced him as court conductor on August 25, 1868, holding this post until September 1, 1869.

On March 22, 1870, Richter led the first Brussels performance of *Lohengrin.* That Christmas he was at Triebschen with the Wagner family, participating in the performance of the *Siegfried Idyll* which Wagner had written as a birthday gift for his wife and which was performed for Cosima at the Wagner home. That year and the following one Richter worked with Wagner preparing the scores of the *Ring* cycle.

From 1871 to 1875 Richter was the conductor of the Pest National Theater in Budapest. In January 1875 he led an orchestral concert in Vienna that proved such a success that he was appointed principal conductor of the Vienna

1885 to 1911, and conducted seasons of Wagnerian performances at Covent Garden from 1903 to 1910, including the complete *Ring* cycle in England in 1909.

He became something of a legendary figure in England, and his performances inspired adulation. "If Napoleon's presence with his army corps was worth, as Wellington said, an army of twenty thousand men, what is the value in an orchestra of this emperor of conductors?" inquired a critic for the London *Daily Telegraph.* "We cannot appraise it, but we can feel the influence of Richter's supreme mastery; of his all-embracing coup d'oeil, of his perfect resource and, no less, the confidence with which he must infuse his followers."

Richter bid farewell to London as a conductor with a concert on April 10, 1911. One day later he led his last concert with his Hallé Orchestra. His last opera performance took place at the Vienna Royal Opera in 1912, appropriately enough with a Wagnerian drama, *Die Meistersinger.* After that he went into retirement in Bayreuth, where he died on December 5, 1916.

Short and stubby, Richter presented a droll appearance. The top of his head was completely bald but from his chin flowed a luxuriant beard. The skullcap which he invariably wore contributed further to the look of a caricature. One musician who had played under him in London used to remember him as "a grumpy German, muttering in his beard, with a piercing eye that missed little. There seemed nothing about him that could endear him to anyone, and orchestras . . . . disliked him more and more."

Yet there was nothing comical once he stepped on the conductor's dais. With the most sparing use of gestures, with little physical motion to speak of, and with the controlled designs of his tiny baton, he was able to create a perfect communication with his performers. His repertory was not a large one, confined primarily to the German classics. He never played French music because he said there just was no French music. He had little interest in any music written after 1900. Despite his association with England, he did nothing to promote English music except for Elgar, whom he regarded as a master and whose *Enigma Variations,* for orchestra, and the oratorio *The Dream of Gerontius* he introduced on June 19, 1899, and October 3, 1900, respectively. Richter preferred his own sure ground—particularly Beethoven, Brahms, and Wagner—

and on that ground he was master. Few conductors had so complete a mastery of the orchestra as he; few conductors possessed his encyclopedic knowledge of the music he conducted; and few had his nobility and profundity of concept. Debussy, who attended the first Bayreuth festival, divided his adoration between Wagner and Richter. Hearing him again many years later, Debussy could still be idolatrous. He wrote: "Behind his gold spectacles his eyes still flash magnificently. They are the eyes of a prophet, and he is in fact a prophet. . . . If Richter looks like a prophet, when he conducts the orchestra he is Almighty God; and you may be sure that God Himself would have asked Richter for some hints before embarking on such an enterprise."

On two occasions Richter had been invited to the United States. When the Boston Symphony was founded, he was asked to be its first music director. He considered the offer seriously but in the end turned it down. In 1907 Oscar Hammerstein went so far as to announce that Hans Richter would be the principal conductor of the Manhattan Opera House. But Richter never went. His fear of ocean travel and his reluctance to assume a new life in a new country inhibited him.

In 1878 Richter was named Court Kapellmeister and given the Order of Franz Joseph in Austria.

ABOUT: Ewen, D. The Man With the Baton; Schonberg, H. C. The Great Conductors.

Sviatoslav Richter

1914–

Sviatoslav Teofilovich Richter, pianist, was born in Zhitomir, near Kiev, in the Ukraine on March 20, 1914. His father, Teofil Richter, who was of German extraction, was a trained musician: a pianist, organist, composer, and teacher. He taught Sviatoslav the rudiments of music. While Sviatoslav was still very young, his family moved to Odessa, where his father joined the faculty of the conservatory.

Sviatoslav's early interest was divided between music and literature. He wrote romances and literary dramas during his boyhood. At the

Richter: rĭk′ tĕr

SVIATOSLAV RICHTER

same time he pursued the study of music mostly by himself, erratically and haphazardly. One of his musical diversions was to transcribe musical masterworks for the piano.

When he was fifteen he was hired as rehearsal conductor at the Odessa Opera and Ballet Theater. In time he rose to the post of assistant conductor. He also tried his hand at composition. But he soon realized that playing the piano was his prime interest, and for its sake he gave up conducting and composition. In his twentieth year he made his public debut as pianist with an all-Chopin recital in Odessa. Up to that time he was virtually self-taught.

Feeling the need of formal training, Richter entered the Moscow Conservatory in 1937, becoming a piano pupil of Heinrich Neuhaus. "Professor Neuhaus," he later told an interviewer for the New York *Times,* "freed my hands— really liberated me." Neuhaus was continually amazed by young Richter's musical memory and his gift for adapting himself to many different styles of music, including contemporary ones.

In 1940 Neuhaus persuaded Prokofiev to entrust the concert premiere of Prokofiev's Piano Sonata No.6 to Richter. (Prokofiev had previously given the sonata its first hearing over the radio.) Richter performed it in the Small Hall of the Moscow Conservatory on November 26, 1940. His virtuoso career may be said to have begun that day. Prokofiev was delighted. He rushed backstage not only to congratulate Richter but to try to persuade him to play his

Piano Concerto No.5 which up to then had proved a failure. "Perhaps if he plays it," Prokofiev told Neuhaus, "they'll begin to like it."

Richter became one of the leading exponents of Prokofiev's piano music. He gave the world premiere of Prokofiev's Piano Sonata No.7 on January 18, 1943; in 1944 Richter gave an all-Prokofiev concert made up of the Piano Sonatas Nos. 6, 7, and 8; on April 23, 1951, he introduced Prokofiev's Piano Sonata No.9 (dedicated to him); and on February 18, 1952, he conducted the orchestral accompaniment of Prokofiev's Cello Concerto when Rostropovich gave it its world premiere in Moscow. (This was Richter's first appearance as a conductor since the early 1930s.) When the Philadelphia Orchestra toured the Soviet Union in 1958, Richter appeared as a soloist with it in Prokofiev's Piano Concerto No.5.

Richter's music studies ended in 1944. One year later he won first prize in the third USSR Competition of Executant Musicians. A broken finger that year impeded his progress as a virtuoso, but after his recovery he began touring the Soviet Union. Concentrating on subtle details and nuances rather than on the grand design and emphasizing clarity of texture and precision of tempo and rhythm, Richter gained a formidable reputation not only in the Soviet Union but also in the countries behind the Iron Curtain. V. Delson, Soviet critic, said of him in *Soviet Music:* "Richter's thoroughly emotional virtuosity recognized no compromises for the sake of technical convenience. . . . When Richter's bold probing into the heart of the music, his temperament, enthusiasm and imagination are organically united with profound concentration on design, treatment and conception, his art acquires a tremendous sweep and authority. At such times, the power of Richter's playing is limitless."

His first appearance outside the Soviet Union was at the Prague Festival in 1950. Since the Prague Festival attracted visitors from the Western world, including some from the United States, news of his extraordinary pianism began to spread beyond the Iron Curtain. Some remarkable Richter recordings, imported from the Soviet Union, further enhanced his reputation in the free world, as did reports from newspaper correspondents who had heard him play. When Howard Taubman, then the music critic of the New York *Times,* visited the Soviet Union in

1958, he attended Richter's performance of Mozart's Piano Concerto in D minor, K.466. He reported back to his newspaper: "To put it simply, he is a superb pianist. . . . His tone is pure velvet. . . . His sense of rhythm is wholly admirable—flexible, within a classic framework. His phrasing is sensitive. There is a wealth of nuance, all bent to the demands of the music. This was a radiant, searching reading of Mozart's familiar score."

Richter's first appearance outside the Iron Curtain was in Finland in May 1960. That same year, under the Soviet-American cultural exchange program, he was permitted by the Soviet Ministry of Culture to tour North America. On October 15, 1960, he made his American debut, appearing as a soloist with the Chicago Symphony Orchestra, Fritz Reiner conducting. Four days later he went to New York for the first of five recitals in Carnegie Hall given within an eleven-day period. As Harold C. Schonberg noted in the New York *Times,* every pianist in town was at hand for Richter's first New York recital which was made up of five Beethoven sonatas. "There may have been a show-me attitude at the beginning. Within fifteen minutes all was dissipated in enthusiasm. Mr. Richter proved himself to be a pianist with style, poetry and imagination; a complete artist. . . . His style is the Russian style of piano playing at its best—free, warm, romantic, without excess." In the *Journal-American* Miles Kastendieck said: "Such blending of pyrotechnical skill with velvety lyricism has perhaps never been heard." Harriet Johnson said in the New York *Post:* "As long as he plays he will make history."

So much excitement and enthusiasm were generated by Richter's five New York recitals, and so feverish was the demand for tickets, that two additional recitals were scheduled for Carnegie Hall in December, supplemented by a scheduled appearance as soloist with the New York Philharmonic on December 18 in a pension fund benefit. After all these New York appearances, Richter went on to fill thirty more engagements in the United States and Canada during a ten-week tour.

His appearances in New York revealed the wide range of his repertory; it was said that he had fifty different programs in his head. In New York his concerts covered a wide expanse of piano literature from Haydn through Scriabin, Ravel, Rachmaninoff, and Prokofiev. The gamut of his repertory, as well as his stamina, was also demonstrated one season in Berlin when he presented twenty concerts with twenty different programs.

Since the 1960s Richter has made many visits to the United States, in addition to his regular tours of Europe and other areas. He averages over one hundred performances a year. He is a temperamental artist who refuses to perform when he is not in the mood; more than one of his scheduled concerts had to be canceled for this reason. At some concerts he is extremely generous with encores, while at others he will not perform even one. Sometimes he declines to make a single public appearance within a several-week period, and at other times he assumes a backbreaking schedule. All this, he insists, is not caprice or whim, but the result of how he feels at a given time. "Good performance," he has explained, "requires the creation of a certain tension between pianist and audience. It sometimes happens that I feel too casual, too self-assured. For example, once when I was playing in the foreign capital I went right from the railroad station to the concert hall. The result was an absence of that state of tension which I require of myself if I am to play effectively."

Richter is married to the former Nina Doloyak, a well-known *Lieder* singer and a professor of voice at the Moscow Conservatory. They have a four-room apartment in Moscow, just off Gorky Street, in the building in which Leonid Kogan resides. They also own a small country home on the banks of the Oka River in the southern part of the Soviet Union. A lover of nature, he finds relaxation hiking in the country or basking in the sun. Indoors, release from tensions comes through painting (his favorite subject is landscapes in water colors) and looking at paintings, and from photography.

The Soviet Union has bestowed on him numerous honors, among them the Stalin Prize in 1949, the Lenin Prize in 1961, and the decoration of the Order of Lenin. In 1961 he was named People's Artist of the USSR, one of the highest honors given by the Soviet government.

In 1960 his recording of Brahms's Piano Concerto No.2 with the Chicago Symphony under Leinsdorf received a Grammy from the National Academy of Recording Arts and Sciences. In 1964 a Schubert album was awarded the Grand Prix du Disque in Paris as the outstanding recording of the year for piano.

ABOUT: High Fidelity, October 1958; New York Times, October 16, 1960; Newsweek, October 17, 1960; Saturday Review, October 15, 1960; Time, May 28, 1960.

Artur Rodzinski

1892–1958

ARTUR RODZINSKI

Artur Rodzinski, conductor, was born on January 2, 1892, in Spalato, Dalmatia (now Yugoslavia) to which his father, a Polish army officer, had gone for military duty. Precocious in music, Artur began to study the piano when he was six. So intense was his passion for music that, on one occasion, when his older brother objected to his continuous practicing, Artur seized a saber and slashed his brother's hand. But music was not intended as a possible profession; his father wanted him to become a lawyer, and so he was sent to Vienna to study at the University and was graduated with a doctorate in law. In Vienna, he supported himself by coaching his fellow students in mathematics and languages. His spare time was spent with music, studying theory by himself and spending many an evening at the opera house and concert hall.

Returning to Warsaw, he informed his father he was through with law and intended to become a musician. However, World War I temporarily ended any further pursuit of a musical career. Rodzinski joined the Austrian Army and in 1917 was wounded on the Russian front. Demobilized, he returned to Vienna, there to earn a living as an inspector of butcher shops and as a pianist in a cabaret. At the same time he attended the Vienna Academy of Music as a student of Franz Schalk, Emil Sauer, and Franz Schreker.

Rodzinki's first music appointment was in Lwow (Lemberg) where at first he was assigned to conduct choral music and then, later, opera performances. Recalling his first experience at conducting, Rodzinski told an interviewer that at his first rehearsal the musicians laughed at him. "You see, I did not even know the most elementary principles of conducting. Came the intermission and the very kind concertmaster showed me the rudiments of beating three-quarter and four-quarter time. While I was holding

Rodzinski: rǒ jǐn' skǐ

on to this job, I took another playing the piano in a vaudeville house. I recall with merriment now, though it was no joke then, that once a dancer gave me a round berating for spoiling her act. She called me a rotten pianist and a worse musician."

In Lwow, Rodzinski conducted performances of *Carmen, Ernani,* and a Polish opera. He apparently did well enough to be engaged as principal conductor. His experience in Lwow brought him the appointment of principal conductor of the Warsaw Opera. There he remained five years. During this period he also conducted concerts of the Warsaw Philharmonic.

On a visit to Poland, Leopold Stokowski heard Rodzinski conduct *Die Meistersinger.* Impressed by his talent, Stokowski invited him to the United States. He arrived in 1926 and for three years he was Stokowski's assistant with the Philadelphia Orchestra. He also conducted some performances of the Philadelphia Opera Company, was head of the opera and orchestral departments of the Curtis Institute of Music, and appeared as guest conductor of the New York Symphony Society, the Detroit Symphony, the Rochester Philharmonic, and the Los Angeles Philharmonic.

His guest performances with the Los Angeles Philharmonic were so well received that in 1929 he was engaged as principal conductor. He remained in Los Angeles four years, giving such a good account of himself that in 1933 (the year in which he became an American citizen) he was invited to become principal conductor of the

Cleveland Symphony. His ten-year affiliation with this organization bristled with disputes. Egocentric, arbitrary, excitable, tactless, and dictatorial, Rodzinski continually became enmeshed in dissensions: with the concertmaster, who was finally compelled to leave the orchestra; with the orchestra manager, to whom he refused to speak for two years; with members of the board of directors who questioned some of his artistic policies. Yet in spite of this never-ending friction, the orchestra flourished under his direction. Rodzinki fashioned a proficient organization from one with only semiprofessional status. He enriched the repertory with a considerable amount of new music, some of which he commissioned for his orchestra (including Jerome Kern's *Scenario,* a symphonic adaptation of music from the Kern musical play *Show Boat,* introduced on October 23, 1941). In Cleveland, Rodzinski gave the world premieres of William Schuman's Symphony No.4 (January 1, 1942) and William Walton's Violin Concerto (December 7, 1939), and the American premieres of Samuel Barber's Symphony No.1 (January 21, 1937) and Shostakovich's opera *Lady Macbeth of the Mtsensk District* (January 31, 1935). He also inaugurated the practice of staging opera performances during the symphonic season, presenting *Tristan and Isolde, Der Rosenkavalier, Elektra, Parsifal,* and *Tannhäuser.*

In 1936 Rodzinski appeared as a guest conductor at the Salzburg Festival in Austria, as well as in Vienna and in Warsaw. In 1937 he was invited to take over eight weeks of guest performances with the New York Philharmonic when he scored major successes with his concert performances of the third act of *Parsifal* and with Richard Strauss's *Elektra* in which Rose Pauly made her American debut. Speaking of Rodzinski's performance of *Elektra,* Olin Downes said in the New York *Times:* "Mr. Rodzinski has a wide range of dynamics, a subtle control of shading; a flexible and effective beat; a capacity to mold a phrase instantaneously to his heart's desire, making his thought immediately clear to the player; and he has the elasticity of beat. His interpretations are always brilliant . . . He is a leader of brilliant qualities."

When the NBC Symphony was founded in New York for Arturo Toscanini in 1937, Rodzinski (at Toscanini's request) was chosen to help select the orchestral personnel and then to whip the musicians into shape. During the 1937–1938 season Rodzinski conducted several of the orchestra's performances.

In 1937 Rodzinski led a concert of Polish music at the International Exposition in Paris. At that time he was awarded the Diplôme d'Honneur. A year later the Polish ambassador to the United States honored him with the medal of Polonia Restituta. On May 5, 1939, Rodzinski offered another program of Polish music, this time at the World's Fair in New York.

In 1943 Rodzinski was appointed music director of the New York Philharmonic Orchestra. Since the orchestra had for a number of years been deteriorating, Rodzinski proceeded to make major overhauls, beginning with the firing of fourteen of the musicians (including the concertmaster, Mishel Piastro). These dismissals were not made quietly and discreetly behind the scenes but were allowed to erupt into a news story in the New York *Times.* Accusing Rodzinski of "defamation of character and jeopardizing the livelihood of brother musicians," James Petrillo, the head of the American Federation of Musicians, forbade the entire orchestra to sign their contracts for the coming season and threatened to cancel Rodzinski's union card. The matter was finally allowed to quiet down.

During the ensuing five years, Rodzinski continually warred with Arthur Judson, the orchestra manager, because he felt that Judson, as head of the Columbia Concerts Corporation, was exploiting the orchestra to promote the careers of soloists and guest conductors under his management. When Rodzinski was denied the final say on the artistic policies of the orchestra, and when the board of directors of the orchestra gave their full support to Judson, Rodzinski turned down a new three-year contract and terminated his association with the New York Philharmonic in mid-season. "I believe I can say that my work as musical director has been a success artistically and financially," Rodzinski announced. "Critics were writing four years ago that the Philharmonic was a third-rate orchestra. Now they say it is one of the finest, if not the finest, in the United States. It was in the gutter financially. Now each concert is sold to within 95 to 99 per cent of capacity, and so far this season we are twenty-seven thousand dollars ahead of the same period a year ago." Rodzinski might have added that under his direction a wealth of new music—much of it of more than transitory interest—had been heard. Among Rodzinski's world premieres were John Alden Carpenter's *The Anxious Bugler* (November 15, 1943) and his *Seven Ages of Man* (November 28, 1945); the suite from Copland's *Appalachian Spring* (October 4, 1945); Paul Creston's Symphony No.2 (February 15, 1945); Hindemith's *Symphonic Metamorphosis on Themes by Carl Maria von Weber* (January 20, 1944); Martinu's *Memorial to Lidice* (October 28, 1943); Milhaud's Cello Concerto No.2 (November 28, 1946); Piston's *Fugue on a Victory Theme* (October 21, 1944); Bernard Rogers's *Invasion* (October 17, 1943); Manuel Rosenthal's *Musique de Table* (October 10, 1946); Schoenberg's *Ode to Napoleon* (November 23, 1944); William Schuman's *William Billings Overture* (February 17, 1944); and William Grant Still's *In Memoriam* (January 5, 1944).

The fall of 1947 found Rodzinski in a new post, that of music director of the Chicago Symphony. Here, too, life became turbulent for both the conductor and the orchestral management. Within one year the directors piled up an imposing list of grievances against their music director: he repeated numbers on his programs too often; he was quixotic in that he would not appear for a performance when he felt indisposed and turned the baton over to an assistant; his irresponsible fiscal ways brought a sharp increase in the deficit; he insisted on mounting expensive opera productions. On January 13, 1948, the Chicago Orchestral Association abruptly announced that Rodzinski would be dismissed at the end of the season.

Up to this time, and for many years, Rodzinski and his wife had been living on a farm in Stockbridge, Massachusetts, and renting a duplex apartment on Fifth Avenue for the winter season during Rodzinski's years with the New York Philharmonic. Later he had acquired a summer home in the Adirondack Mountains at Lake Placid, New York. Rodzinski's wife was Halina Wieniawska Lilpop, grandniece of the Polish composer Henri Wieniawski. They were married on July 19, 1934, and had one child, a son, Richard. (Rodzinski had another son, Witold, from an earlier marriage.) Upon leaving the Chicago scene, the Rodzinskis established their permanent home in Italy. For about a decade, he appeared as a guest conductor throughout Europe and South America. In the spring of 1953 he conducted at the Florence May Music

Festival the first performance of Prokofiev's opera *War and Peace* given outside the Soviet Union. This was also the first performance anywhere of the complete opera in its original version.

After an absence of a decade, Rodzinski returned to the United States in 1958 to conduct two productions at the Chicago Lyric Opera on November 1, 7, and 10. He was scheduled to conduct a fourth performance on November 11 but, feeling ill, he canceled that appearance to consult the Boston heart specialist Dr. Paul Dudley White. Rodzinski died at the Phillips House of the Massachusetts General Hospital on November 27, 1958.

In *Harper's Magazine* in 1943 Moses Smith described Rodzinski as "a tallish figure, with a powerful, irregular physique, and with a tendency to paunchiness. . . . His nearsighted eyes are keen and take in details that brighter ones miss. He has a powerful head and his face is quick to break into a smile which is especially infectious because it is like a grin. He is for the most part free from those annoying, often preposterous, affectations of the manner of the grand seigneur. . . . I don't say that Rodzinski does not regard himself as a grand seigneur. But if he does it is as a twentieth century model, minus the trappings of a bygone era."

In her biography of her husband, *Our Two Lives,* Halina Rodzinski has no hesitancy in confessing how quixotic, erratic, egotistical, dictatorial, and self-destructive Rodzinski was. Just before their wedding Rodzinski told her in no uncertain terms: "I come before everything and everyone else," and that is the way it was through all the years of their marriage. She also confirmed the suspicion that he used drugs and the rumor that he always came before an orchestra, whether at a concert or at a rehearsal, with a loaded gun in his hip pocket. He was ever in pursuit of some fad or fancy. At one time he became convinced that goat's milk was a panacea for all bodily ills. He devoured goat's milk by the quart. He even raised goats on his farm at Stockbridge to have an ample supply always at hand. When a severe shoulder pain was diagnosed by the physician as "spiritual" and not a physical ailment, Rodzinski turned to religion, becoming a disciple of the Buchmanites (the Oxford Group or MRA, Moral Re-Armament). He would say that he was an instrument of God. "God leads me. I don't know how He does, but

Rose

I know He does. He tells me so clearly like a bell." Each day he devoted some time to communing with God, to solitary contemplation, and to reading the Bible.

He was always interested in politics, social problems, and the international scene, keeping in touch with current events by reading books and newspapers and listening to the radio. Except for an occasional brandy he avoided strong alcohol, but he smoked cigarettes endlessly, rolling his own from specially imported Egyptian tobacco. Occasionally he went to the movies for diversion, and sometimes, too, he amused himself by listening to comedy programs over the radio.

Rodzinski's son, Richard, was appointed co-artistic administrator of the Metropolitan Opera in 1975 after having served for five years as first assistant to Kurt Herbert Adler at the San Francisco Opera.

ABOUT: Brook, Donald. International Gallery of Conductors; Rodzinski, H. Our Two Lives. *Periodicals* —Harper's Magazine, November 1943.

Leonard Rose

1918–

Leonard Rose, cellist, was born in Washington, D.C., on July 27, 1918, to Harry and Jennie Frankel Rose. His father—a designer who fashioned clothes for the wives of President Coolidge and President Harding—was an amateur cellist who even in his eightieth year was participating in amateur and semi-professional concerts in Miami Beach. When Leonard was four the family moved to Miami, Florida, where Harry Rose opened a grocery store and Leonard was raised and educated. When Leonard was ten, his father gave him his first cello lessons. A year later, the boy continued studying the cello with Walter Grossman at the Miami Conservatory. At thirteen, Rose won the Florida State High School Contest in the cello division. This brought him several concert engagements in Florida. When he was fifteen, he became a cello student of his cousin, Frank Miller (then cellist of the Philadelphia Orchestra, later first cellist of the NBC Symphony under Toscanini). In 1934, Rose won a scholarship for the Curtis Institute of Music in Philadelphia, and for four years he was a pupil

LEONARD ROSE

there of Felix Salmond and played principal cello for the Institute orchestra conducted by Fritz Reiner.

His studies completed in 1938, Rose joined the cello section of the NBC Symphony. He was with the orchestra just three weeks when he was promoted to assistant first cellist. A year later he left the NBC Symphony to become the first cellist of the Cleveland Orchestra, conducted by Artur Rodzinski. During his four years in this post he made four appearances as guest artist with that orchestra. He was also head of the cello department of the Cleveland Institute of Music and Oberlin College. In October 1943 he moved on to New York to occupy the first cello chair of the New York Philharmonic. His first appearance as guest artist with that orchestra took place on January 29, 1944, in Lalo's Concerto in D.

Rose remained with the New York Philharmonic until 1951. His last American appearance with that orchestra was on April 5, 1951, when he was the featured soloist in Bloch's *Schelomo* and the Saint-Saëns Cello Concerto in A minor. "It was in the nature of a public farewell," wrote Howard Taubman in the New York *Times.* "The truth, of course, is that Mr. Rose has been a virtuoso of the cello for some time, but his playing has always been a blend of technical musicianship and a simple, innate modesty. He may have to step out a little more in the months ahead, but it is hard to believe that his essential musical personality will change much."

Rose's last appearance as a member of the

New York Philharmonic was at the Edinburgh Festival in Scotland in September 1951. After that he launched his career as a virtuoso. His first such tour, in 1951–1952, included appearances with many major orchestras as well as numerous recitals. During 1952–1953 he gave thirteen solo performances with eleven orchestras. His first tour of Europe, in 1958, was climaxed by an appearance at the World's Fair in Brussels. In August 1961 he gave his first concerts in Israel and in 1962–1963 he performed at the White House for President and Mrs. John F. Kennedy.

Louis Biancolli wrote in the New York *World-Telegram and Sun* after one of Rose's recitals: "My guess is that Leonard Rose is the best cellist since Pablo Casals." And Bruno Walter, under whose baton Rose performed frequently, was quoted as saying: "Leonard Rose's profound musicianship, technical perfection, his emotional warmth and the rare beauty of his tone have been a source of pure joy for me in all the years of our musical association. The cause of the cello's musical literature can be in no better hands than his."

To Ronald Eyer, in *Newsday,* Rose "is the greatest American-bred cellist of this generation. The first thing that strikes you is his tremendous technical prowess and his very big and very rich tone. From the technical point of view he is complete master of one of the trickiest and most difficult of stringed instruments. . . . Aside from his artistic interpretation, there is the absolute accuracy of his intonation. He lands directly in the middle of every note no matter at what speed he is playing. The cello becomes an instrument of almost unbelievable dramatic power in Rose's hands."

In addition to his appearances as a solo virtuoso, Rose has distinguished himself as a performer of chamber music in a trio that included Isaac Stern and Eugene Istomin. Rose had begun playing chamber music privately with Stern in 1954, and in 1955 they made their first recording together—Brahms's Concerto for Violin, Cello and Orchestra, with Bruno Walter conducting, a release that received the Grand Prix du Disque in Paris. In the late 1950s Istomin began joining Stern and Rose in private presentations of trio literature. "Finally," as Rose has explained, "we decided to go public." The Istomin-Stern-Rose trio made its official debut at the first International Chamber Music

Festival in Israel in 1961, and it gave its first New York concert in 1962 as soloists with the New York Philharmonic in a performance of Beethoven's *Triple Concerto.* In the *Herald Tribune,* Paul Henry Lang called this new organization a "trio of virtuosos," adding that it provided "an evening of music-making without frills." A series of three trio concerts in New York soon after that led Irving Kolodin to say in the *Saturday Review* that their achievement was "beyond the reach of any group of players now performing." Since then the Istomin-Stern-Rose trio has performed in concerts and festivals in Europe and the United States. In 1970, during the bicentennial commemoration of Beethoven's birth, the trio gave fifty Beethoven concerts in the United States, Europe, and Israel. In September 1971 it became the first chamber music group to appear in the opening festivities of the new Kennedy Center for the Performing Arts in Washington, D.C. Later that month the trio embarked on its first tour of Japan (the first time Rose performed there). Of the one hundred and twenty concerts he gives each year, half are with the Istomin-Stern-Rose trio. The trio's recording for Columbia of all of Beethoven's trios was awarded a Grammy by the National Academy of Recording Arts and Sciences.

From 1951 to 1962 Rose taught cello at the Curtis Institute of Music. In 1962 he returned to the faculty of the Juilliard School of Music in New York where he had previously served from 1946 to 1951.

Rose has made numerous recordings for Columbia, including concertos by Schumann, Dvořák, Lalo, and Saint-Saëns, and works by Bach, Fauré, Tchaikovsky, and others. In April 1976, with the Cleveland Orchestra, Rose videotaped a performance of a work long identified with him, Bloch's *Schelomo,* and it was telecast over the network of the Public Broadcasting Service.

Leonard Rose married Minnie Knopow, a young violist, on December 1, 1938. Until her death in 1964, the Roses and their two children lived in Great Neck, Long Island. In his earlier years Rose enjoyed playing table tennis, but he subsequently found recreation in golf and in meeting with friends to exchange stimulating conversations. Occasionally he prepares special dishes for friends. "I'm good at Italian dishes and seafoods," he says.

On January 29, 1965, Rose married Xenia Rose Petschek, a schoolteacher who had written

Rosenstock

news releases for NBC-TV. They reside in a three-story English Tudor house on Overlook Road in Hastings-on-the-Hudson in New York.

ABOUT: Appelbaum, S. and Applebaum, S. The Way They Play; Ewen, D. Famous Instrumentalists. *Periodicals*—High Fidelity, May 1972; Musical America, April 1971; New York Times, April 25, 1971; Saturday Review, October 3, 1972.

Joseph Rosenstock

1895–

Joseph Rosenstock, conductor, was born in Cracow, Poland, on January 27, 1895. He was one of six children of Sabine Gelberger Rosenstock and Bernard Rosenstock, a merchant. All the children were taught a musical instrument, but Joseph was the only one to reveal talent. He was eleven when, after a few years of piano study with local teachers, he made concert appearances as a prodigy. Later he studied music at the Vienna Academy of Music from 1912 to 1919, taking composition with Franz Schreker. From 1913 to 1920 he also attended the University of Vienna, receiving a doctorate in music on the completion of his studies.

When Schreker went to Berlin in 1920 to become director of the High School of Music, Rosenstock went along with him as assistant. In Berlin, he met Fritz Busch who persuaded him to consider conducting as a career. Busch invited Rosenstock to Stuttgart to become coach and assistant conductor at the Stuttgart Opera of which Busch was then music director. Four weeks after his arrival in Stuttgart, Rosenstock made his conducting debut with a performance of *The Bartered Bride.* He conducted that performance without a single rehearsal and from memory.

From Stuttgart, he went on to Darmstadt, in 1922, to succeed George Szell as principal conductor of the Darmstadt Opera. Three years later, he was named its general music director (the youngest musician ever to hold such a position in Germany). In Darmstadt, he performed the complete version of Strauss's *Ariadne auf Naxos.* Strauss, who attended rehearsals as well as performances, expressed complete satisfaction. Then Rosenstock took over Otto Klemperer's post as principal conductor of the

JOSEPH ROSENSTOCK

Wiesbaden Opera, serving in this capacity from 1925 to 1927.

In 1929, when Artur Bodanzky resigned from the Metropolitan Opera as its principal conductor of German operas, Rosenstock was engaged to replace him. His American debut took place on October 30, 1929, in *Die Meistersinger.* The critical reaction was negative, and not much more enthusiasm was generated by his subsequent performances that season of *Der Rosenkavalier* on November 4 and *Die Walküre* on November 9. Rosenstock's inability to make a favorable impression brought about a rapprochement between Bodanzky and the Metropolitan Opera; Bodanzky was back on the podium for *Lohengrin* on December 2, 1929, and Rosenstock left the company.

Returning to Europe, Rosenstock became music director of the Mannheim Opera for the period between 1930 and 1933 and also led the orchestral concerts in that city. On the rise of the Nazi regime in 1933, Rosenstock was removed from his post because he was a Jew. He went to Berlin where he formed and was a member of the Jewish Kulturbund, a cultural organization presenting operas and dramatic performances at the Berliner Theater. "We used only actors and musicians who were Hitler victims," he told Ann M. Lingg in an interview for *Opera News.* "Even our stage hands were Jewish, and so were our subscribers, some 18,000 of them. I did *Fidelio, The Marriage of Figaro, Nabucco,* Wolf-Ferrari's *Le Donne Curiose,* among other things."

690

When the anti-Semitic program in Germany was intensified, Rosenstock departed for Japan where he lived during the next five years and led concerts of the Nippon Philharmonic Orchestra; he also became the music director of the Japanese Broadcasting Corporation. When Japan was drawn into World War II as an ally of Nazi Germany, Rosenstock's life was endangered. He fled to a primitive mountain village a hundred miles from Tokyo where he suffered indescribable hardships. To stay alive, he had to exchange his clothes for food. "We could figure our chances for survival by the number of haberdashery items in our possession," he recalls.

One September morning in 1945 a jeep with three American soldiers arrived with the news that the war was over. General Willoughby sent a request to Rosenstock to return to Tokyo to reorganize and direct the Nippon Philharmonic. At his first concert, the opening number on his program was Dvořák's *Symphony from the New World*.

In 1946 Rosenstock left Japan to conduct concerts in Havana, Palestine, and Vancouver, and then to establish permanent residence in the United States; he became an American citizen in 1949. In 1948 he was appointed conductor of the New York City Opera, making his debut there on October 14 in a new production of *The Marriage of Figaro* (given in English). "Rosenstock revealed himself not only as an excellent musician and leader," wrote Olin Downes in the New York *Times*, "but as a really sensitive artist, one who understands the opera and the essence of the score." He remained principal conductor of the New York City Opera for three years; then, in 1951, he became artistic director. His initial season was made memorable by the first repertory production in the United States of *Wozzeck* (an opera he had successfully conducted in Mannheim in the early 1930s). He also offered other twentieth century operas, among them Marc Blitzstein's *Regina*, Menotti's *Amahl and the Night Visitors*, Bartók's *Bluebeard's Castle*, Walton's *Troilus and Cressida*, Menotti's *The Consul*, and Manuel de Falla's *L'Heure Espagnole*.

In addition to his appearances with the New York City Opera, Rosenstock served as music director of the Aspen Music Festival in Aspen, Colorado, from 1949 to 1953, and appeared as a guest conductor of symphony orchestras in Europe. He made periodic returns to Japan for extended tours to conduct his former orchestra there, the Nippon Philharmonic, which made him honorary music director for life. In 1957 Japan awarded him the Third Order of the Sacred Treasure, an honor generally reserved for diplomats.

Rosenstock resigned as artistic director of the New York City Opera on December 16, 1955, but for three years he stayed on as a principal conductor. In 1956–1957 he undertook a new tour of Japan to conduct over fifty programs in the concert hall and over radio and television. On this occasion he was awarded the 1956 Cultural Award of the Japanese Broadcasting Company, the first time such an honor was conferred on a foreigner.

From 1958 to 1961 he served as general music director of the Cologne Opera in Germany. He returned to the Metropolitan Opera in New York to conduct *Tristan and Isolde* on January 31, 1961. During the next few years he was also heard and praised for his performances of *Elektra*, *Così fan Tutte*, *Lohengrin*, *Salome*, *Macbeth*, *Don Giovanni*, *Die Götterdämmerung*, *Falstaff*, *The Marriage of Figaro*, *Tannhäuser*, and a new production of *Die Meistersinger*. Of his performance of *Die Meistersinger* (the same music drama with which he had made such an unimpressive Metropolitan Opera debut many years earlier) Harold C. Schonberg wrote in the New York *Times:* "A special vote of thanks should go to Mr. Rosenstock, whose conducting had vitality and a good infusion of poetry. His is the kind of dependable musician who never is spasmodic, who is secure in the tradition of German opera and whose taste is impeccable."

Short and slight of build, Rosenstock has been described in *Theatre Arts* as a man who looks "more like an overworked schoolteacher than an impresario." His first wife was the opera singer Herta Glaz, whom he married on August 7, 1952. She was a member of the Metropolitan Opera company from 1942 to 1956. In 1958, after being divorced from Herta Glaz, he was married a second time, this time to the former Marilou Harrington. They lived in the Washington Square section of New York in an apartment cluttered with his collection of paintings and objets d'art, many of which were acquired in Japan. Rosenstock is a soccer fan who used to be an active participant in scrimmages; he has also enjoyed skiing.

Rosenthal

ABOUT: New Yorker, October 4, 1952; Opera News, March 25, 1961; Theatre Arts, May 1952.

Moriz Rosenthal

1862–1946

MORIZ ROSENTHAL

Moriz Rosenthal, pianist, was the last of the great piano students of Franz Liszt and one of the last representatives of the bravura style of pianism exemplified by Liszt. He was born in Lemberg, Austria (now Lwow, Poland), on December 19, 1862. His father, Leo Rosenthal, taught piano in the local conservatory. Moriz began studying the piano when he was eight with a local teacher named Galath. Two years later, he became a pupil of Karl Mikuli, director of the Lemberg Conservatory. That same year, he made his first public appearance in Lemberg performing Chopin's Rondo for two pianos, with his teacher at the second piano.

Moriz wanted to become a concert pianist. That ambition impelled him one day to walk from Lemberg to Vienna to play for Rafael Joseffy. Joseffy was so impressed that he induced Moriz's parents to settle permanently in Vienna so that he might take personal supervision of the boy's training. The Rosenthals went to Vienna in 1875. For an entire year Rosenthal studied with Joseffy, making such excellent progress that a year later he was able to give his first complete recital, and then to tour Romania and Russian Poland.

In 1876 Moriz's father brought him to Franz Liszt's studio in Weimar. He later recalled that first meeting. "A servant entered and brought me before the awesome presence of the most revered musical figure of the time. With aristocratic simplicity of bearing Liszt invited me to play the piano." Moriz played Liszt's *Transcendental Etudes* and *La Campanella* and Liszt's transcription of Schubert's *Der Erlkönig*. When he finished playing, Liszt turned to a concert pianist who was also in the room at that time and remarked: "That *we* cannot do, can we?"

Liszt took him on as his private pupil until 1878, both in Weimar and in Rome. As Liszt's pupil, he concertized in Warsaw, St. Petersburg, and Paris.

In 1880 he suddenly decided to abandon the

Rosenthal: rō′ zĕn täl

piano and become a student of philosophy. He qualified at the high school in Vienna to take philosophical courses at the university. While attending the university, he read voraciously. He completed his university courses in three years, having specialized in esthetics as well as in philosophy.

He returned to the concert stage in 1884 with a recital in Vienna that revealed him to be a fully mature artist, a pianist of formidable technical powers. "Through many years of acquaintance with modern piano virtuosity," wrote Eduard Hanslick, Vienna's critic, "I have almost forgotten what it is to be astonished, but I found young Rosenthal's achievements astonishing." Some of Vienna's leading musicians considered him a giant of the keyboard. One was Johannes Brahms, with whom young Rosenthal maintained a personal relationship. They visited the Viennese café-houses together, discussing music for hours. On numerous occasions Brahms would climb up four flights to Rosenthal's modest apartment to hear him play.

Rosenthal made his first tour of the United States in 1888, his American debut taking place at the Music Hall in Boston on November 9. (At that concert another artist was making his bow —fourteen-year-old Fritz Kreisler.) Three days later, Rosenthal went to Steinway Hall in New York, taking audience and critics by storm. In the *Tribune* H. E. Krehbiel wrote: "To New Yorkers there is nothing novel in brilliant pianoforte playing, but it can fairly be questioned whether an audience composed of experienced and discriminating music lovers in this city was ever before stirred to such a pitch of excitement." The critic of the *Sun* referred to Rosenthal as "a giant of ability, a demi-god, a perfect pianist."

This was the beginning of a march of triumph that was to continue for the next half century, with eleven more tours of the United States and performances in the rest of the music world. When Paderewski heard him perform Chopin he said: "I have known and played the greatest Polish music, but I have never known any Polish music as great as his." Albéniz inscribed his own photograph to Rosenthal: "The greatest of the great." The inscription Karl Goldmark put on his own photograph was: "To Moriz Rosenthal, who has no equal and no superior among pianists, dead or alive." Hans von Bülow described him as "the Jupiter of the octaves, the Pope of the scales, and the President of the Republic of staccato and legato." Young Josef Hofmann heard a Rosenthal recital in or about 1888. "He was terrific," Hofmann recalled many years later, "and we started pounding the piano at our Berlin home six hours daily trying to imitate Rosenthal." Elizabeth, Queen of Romania, who wrote under the pseudonym Carmen Sylva, appointed Rosenthal court pianist, and in 1912 so did Emperor Franz Joseph of Austria.

When Rosenthal returned to Carnegie Hall for a recital on November 7, 1906, after an eight-year absence, Richard Aldrich rhapsodized over his virtuosity in the New York *Times*. "Mr. Moriz Rosenthal stands now . . . for the extremist development of the technique of the piano. In everything that the wizards of modern technical skill have been able to exploit on the keyboard of the instrument, in all that they have been able to make the human hand, wrist, arm achieve, he stands among the chief wizards. It seemed, when he was here before, that he had no further to go. If he has moved forward in these eight years it has been in this direction."

But Rosenthal was not content being one of the greatest technicians, if not the greatest technician, the piano knew in his time. As the years progressed he added subtlety of phrasing, beauty of tonal production, and an elegance and nobility of musical concept to his whirlwind virtuosity.

In 1922 he married Hedwig Loewy Kanner, a brilliant pianist herself; as Hedwig Kanner-Rosenthal she subsequently achieved international fame as a piano teacher. Their home in Vienna became the salon where the musicians of the city gathered and where music sounded halfway through the night. The Rosenthals also established in Vienna a piano studio to which an entire generation of piano students beat a track.

After the rise of the Nazi regime in Germany, the Rosenthals left Vienna for good, went to the United States, and spent their remaining years in New York City, in an apartment at the Great Northern Hotel near Carnegie Hall.

On November 13, 1938, the golden jubilee of Rosenthal's career in the United States was commemorated in Carnegie Hall. He performed on a gilded piano built expressly for this occasion by the Baldwin Company. The musicians of the city were at hand to pay him homage. Despite old age, Rosenthal's pianism rose to the occasion. "The years have made certain inroads upon Rosenthal's physical resources," wrote Olin Downes in the New York *Times*, "but we behold him with an ever-deepening beauty and logic of thinking and the refined instinct of style."

Moriz Rosenthal died in New York City on September 3, 1946.

He was short, stocky, plump. His round cheeks supported an ample moustache trimmed in the style of Kaiser Wilhelm. His deep-set eyes twinkled as he talked. He had an exceptional wit, and his witticisms gained wide circulation among musicians. After a Paderewski recital he commented: "He's a fine musician, but he's no Paderewski." Asked for an opinion on a new composition he replied: "The fellow did very well until he came to the middle, where his memory failed him." From a "prodigy," Rosenthal inquired: "Tell me, how old are you *still?*"

In his younger years he engaged in fencing, swimming, boxing, and wrestling. At one time he swam across Lake Como to visit Anton Rubinstein at his villa fronting the water. Later in life he tried keeping fit by going through a few rounds of jiujitsu every day. Throughout his life he was preoccupied with reading books. His favorite game was chess, and he was so adept at it that he often played with José Capablanca, chess master. Rosenthal was known to begin a chess game soon after finishing one of his recitals and continue playing throughout the night.

His two favorite composers were Chopin and Beethoven. "Chopin," he once said, "was probably the most original of composers. I think that he is the great musical aristocrat and yet he never had an ancestor—by that I mean he never imitated or borrowed from early composers." He esteemed Beethoven just as highly. "Together," he said, "they are the highest summits in piano music."

ABOUT: Schonberg, H. C. The Great Pianists.

Mstislav Rostropovich

1927–

Mstislav Leopoldovich Rostropovich was universally recognized as one of the great cellists of the twentieth century before he turned to conducting. He was born in Baku, Azerbaijan, in the Soviet Union, on March 27, 1927. His grandfather, Vitold, who had been trained at the Leipzig Conservatory, had been a professional cellist and a noted teacher of the cello, and his maternal grandmother headed a music school. His father, Leopold, had studied the cello with Alexander Verzhibilovich and Pablo Casals and made his living playing and teaching the cello; his mother, Sofia Fedotova Rostropovich, was an excellent pianist; his older sister, Veronica, became a professional violinist, a member of the Moscow State Philharmonic.

From infancy on, Mstislav was surrounded by music-making in his home. When he was four he received some piano lessons from his mother; it was not long before he tried his hand at composing, completing a polka for the piano. He then continued his piano studies by himself—"without my parents' permission," he says. Without formal instruction he made sufficient headway to be able to participate in the family concerts.

When he was four he was brought by his family to Moscow. They arrived totally destitute except for a Persian rug and a Japanese ivory carving that had long been in the family. They would have been homeless had not an Armenian woman taken pity on them—she had the entire Rostropovich family come to live with her in her two-room flat; they stayed for nearly three years. Eventually, the father found a job as teacher of the cello at the Gnessin Institute and as a member of the orchestra of the All-Union Radio. In 1935, the father began teaching Mstislav the cel-

Rostropovich: rō strô pō′ vyĭch

MSTISLAV ROSTROPOVICH

lo privately before placing him in his own cello class at the Institute.

From his seventh to his fourteenth year, Mstislav attended the Preparatory Seven Years' School in Moscow. This was an elementary school providing both an academic and a musical education for children of unusual talent. In addition to such academic studies as mathematics, geography, and grammar, Mstislav was trained in music theory, music history, solfeggio, choral singing, and eurhythmics. At the same time he continued his cello studies with his father. In 1935, playing on a child's-size cello, he appeared in a concert with his sister, Veronica, a violinist, an event that led *Izvestia* to publish his photograph for the first time.

During the summers his father found employment in an orchestra in Slavyansk and Zaporozhe in the Ukraine. Listening to these performances, young Mstislav had his introduction to orchestral music. In the Ukraine, in 1940, he made his debut as a virtuoso cellist, performing Saint-Saëns's Cello Concerto in A with an orchestra in Slavyansk of which his father was a member.

In the early years of World War II, the Rostropovich family was evacuated from Moscow to Orenburg in the Urals. There his father and two friends played serious trio music in a motion picture theater before the films were viewed. "He wore gloves with holes cut out for the fingers because there was no heat," Rostropovich recalls. "I would be sick at heart when I'd stop and hear this beautiful music and see that no one in the audience was paying attention. It made me want to cry."

The death of his father from a heart attack in 1942 affected Mstislav so strongly that he fell ill. Upon recovering, inspired by a letter of guidance his father had left him, Mstislav renewed his activity in music and redoubled his efforts. Mikhail Chulaki, who had been teaching him composition, encouraged him to participate in a concert in Orenburg in which he filled the triple role of cellist, pianist, and composer. He aided the war effort by performing throughout the Soviet Union for military units and in hospitals, supplementing these appearances with other concerts in the Soviet Union in which he collaborated with singers from the Leningrad Maly Opera.

Mstislav was back in Moscow in 1943. Together with his sister, he entered the Moscow Conservatory to continue his study of the cello with Semeon Kozolupov and, in his three-year postgraduate course, to be a pupil of Vissarion Shebalin in composition and Dmitri Shostakovich in orchestration. To help support himself and his family he took on jobs as carpenter and framemaker. As a Conservatory student, he served as first cellist of the Moscow State Philharmonic, performed sonatas with young Sviatoslav Richter, and participated in trio concerts with Leonid Kogan and Emil Gilels. He was still a student at the Conservatory in 1945 when he received first prize in a cello competition in Moscow. To win that award he performed a cello concerto by the contemporary Soviet composer Miaskovsky, who was so taken with the young cellist's performance that he wrote for him, and dedicated to him, his Cello Sonata No.2, which Rostropovich introduced in 1949.

In 1946 Rostropovich appeared as a soloist with the Moscow State Philharmonic. One year later he received another first prize in a cello competition held in Prague at the World Festival of Democratic Youth.

Upon graduation from the Conservatory in 1946 (completing a five-year course in less than three), he was appointed full professor of the cello there. He completed his postgraduate course of study at the Conservatory in 1948. In 1949 he captured the top award in a cello competition held at the World Festival in Budapest and in 1950 at an International Competition in Prague. Rostropovich began to intensify his activity as a virtuoso by making numerous appearances in recitals and as guest artist with symphony orchestras throughout the Soviet Union. His phenomenal command of the cello combined with penetrating musicianship gained him a large following. He scored a major artistic success in 1951 when he performed all six of Bach's unaccompanied suites for cello at a single concert in Moscow. Two years later he was once again acclaimed in Moscow for his performance of all of Beethoven's cello sonatas on a single program both in Moscow and in Leningrad, with Sviatoslav Richter at the piano.

Rostropovich made his first appearance outside the Soviet Union in the spring of 1951 when he was one of ten musicians and dancers representing his country at the Florence May Music Festival. Howard Taubman, the music critic of the New York *Times,* heard Rostropovich on this occasion and reported back: "Rostropovich ...was ... first class. His tone ... was clean and accurate, and his musicianship was searching, particularly in Bach's unaccompanied C minor Suite. His musical style seemed to be ardent and intense, and it was only in the short encore pieces that he showed he could be light in touch." After that, Rostropovich's appearances in concerts in major European music centers brought him acceptance as the best cellist since Pablo Casals was in his prime.

When the summit meeting in Geneva brought about a detente between the Soviet Union and the United States in the summer of 1955, a cultural exchange between the two countries was agreed upon. At that time the Soviet embassy telephoned Frederick Schang of Columbia Artists, suggesting that Rostropovich tour the United States. Once the necessary clearance was obtained from the State Department, Rostropovich arrived in the United States, in 1956, making his debut at Carnegie Hall on April 4. In the New York *Times,* Howard Taubman called him "an outstanding artist. ... Mr. Rostropovitch does not stress virtuosity, though he can unleash enough to suit his purposes. He impressed with his musicianship." Writing in the *Herald Tribune,* Jay S. Harrison said: "As a cellist Mr. Rostropovitch possesses almost every skill necessary for a successful manipulation of the frequently clumsy instrument. His tone is rich, of a remarkable purity, and even in the lower strings maintains a quality all velvet and warm."

A few weeks later Rostropovich was heard as

a soloist with the New York Philharmonic, with Dimitri Mitropoulos conducting, in the American premiere of Prokofiev's second cello concerto, the *Symphony Concerto*. "He is the musician-first type of virtuoso," Paul Henry Lang wrote of this performance in the *Herald Tribune,* "consequently he went to work on the concerto without acrobatics, excessive rubatos, oversize vibrato, etc. The public sensed the devotion and gave him an ovation."

The Prokofiev *Symphony Concerto* (which Rostropovich introduced in Moscow on February 18, 1951) had been written for and dedicated to him. This was only one of many major works which twentieth century composers in general, and Soviet composers in particular, have dedicated to him—testimony to the high regard that composers everywhere have had for him and an expression of their confidence that their creations rested in the hands of a master when they entrusted them to him. As Paul Hume, the music critic of the Washington *Post,* explained: "He offers that which no composer can resist: the sure knowledge that what is written will be presented to audiences in performances that will transcend every consideration of technique and lay before the public the message of the composer as fully realized as it is humanly possible for one artist to offer the work of another."

Rostropovich's continued interest in twentieth century music for the cello and his determination to maintain the artistic importance of the cello helped him to persuade major composers to write ambitious works for it. He has said: "Although I am grateful for the attention given me, this is not the important thing. Important is the repertory for the instrument and that the cello should no longer be identified as the poor relative of violin and piano, and everything that helps along that line is good."

Among the works by Soviet composers written for and introduced by Rostropovich were: Prokofiev's Cello Concertino which Rostropovich completed when it had been left unfinished by the composer (introduced on March 18, 1960); Shostakovich's Cello Concerto No.1 (October 4, 1959) and Cello Concerto No.2 (September 25, 1966); Khrennikov's Cello Concerto (May 13, 1964); Lev Knipper's *Concerto Monologue* (February 25, 1964); and works by Khachaturian, Glière, Miaskovsky, and Kabalevsky, among others. European composers have also written important works for Rostropovich. Benjamin Britten composed the Cello Sonata which was introduced by Rostropovich at the Aldeburgh Festival in England in 1961 and the Symphony for Cello and Orchestra, introduced in Moscow on March 12, 1964, with the composer conducting. Henri Sauguet's Cello Concerto received its premiere in Moscow on February 14, 1964. Rostropovich has also given the world premieres of Lukas Foss's Cello Concerto and Walter Piston's *Variations for Cello,* in New York in March 1967.

Rostropovich's extraordinary versatility and artistry were put to the test in a series of eight concerts at Carnegie Hall between February 23 and March 12, 1967. Appearing as a soloist with the London Symphony, he performed twenty-nine major works for cello and orchestra by composers ranging from Vivaldi, Haydn, and Tartini to several moderns. Included were two world premieres (Piston's *Variations* and Foss's Cello Concerto), four American premieres (concertos by Khrennikov, André Jolivet, Shostakovich, and Boris Tchaikovsky's *Partita*), and one New York premiere (Britten's *Symphony for Cello*). This was not the first time he had assumed such a monumental undertaking. In Moscow in 1964 he had covered virtually the basic repertory of major works for the cello in a cycle that extended over a nine-month period. In 1965, at London's Royal Festival Hall, in nine concerts over a thirty-five-day period, he played thirty-one major cello works.

As his artistry continued to grow richer, deeper, and more profound, his world fame grew. As Harriet Johnson wrote when Rostropovich returned to New York in 1975 for a recital: "There is no doubt that Rostropovich is the world's greatest cellist." The Soviet Union recognized his musical preeminence by bestowing on him the State Prize in 1951 and the Lenin Prize in 1964.

Nevertheless, his worldwide success, rivaled by few other Soviet instrumentalists, did not protect Rostropovich from Soviet displeasure when in 1970 he sheltered in his country home Solzhenitsyn—the novelist whose works were prohibited in the Soviet Union and who had become persona non grata—and his family. In a letter dated October 31, 1970, Rostropovich wrote in defense of Solzhenitsyn, addressing the letter to the editors of four Soviet newspapers. The letter was never published in the Soviet Union, but it was distributed to Western correspondents and published throughout the world. "Every man must have the right fearlessly to think independently, and express his opinion," Rostropovich wrote. He also inquired: "Why is it that in our literature and our art the decisive word so often belongs to people who are absolutely incompetent in these fields?" This open defiance of Soviet authority by Rostropovich brought instant reprisal. Publication of his name in any of the media of the Soviet Union was prohibited; he was denied the right to leave the country to fulfill his concert or recording commitments; when a recording of Tchaikovsky's *Eugene Onegin* received the Jacques Rouche prize, the newspaper *Sovetskaia Kultura* reported this fact but failed to mention that Rostropovich was its conductor. All references to Rostropovich were deleted from the Great Soviet Encyclopedia and his recordings were banned from Soviet broadcasts. Appearances in the major Soviet cities and with the principal Soviet orchestras were canceled. When Rostropovich and his family were occasionally allowed to give concerts in small towns along the Volga, the concert halls in which they played were half empty because no public notice had been made of their appearance.

However, the ban against his performing outside the Soviet Union was somewhat relaxed within a year: Rostropovich's first concert outside the Soviet Union since the writing of his provocative letter took place in Paris on November 30, 1971, when he gave the world premiere of Henri Dutilleux's Cello Concerto at the Théâtre des Champs-Élysées. Further indication of Rostropovich's rehabilitation with Soviet officialdom came on June 20, 1973, when he became the first artist ever permitted to appear as a soloist with a visiting American orchestra—the San Francisco Symphony. "In a concert emotionally charged with cultural and political significance," reported a correspondent to the Los Angeles *Times* from Moscow, "the Russian cellist, Mstislav Rostropovich performed . . . before a standing-room-only crowd. . . . For Rostropovich the concert was a signal that the recent official campaign punishing him for his expressions in favor of artistic freedom may be ending."

When Rostropovich left the Soviet Union in May 1974 for a new concert tour, he decided to find for himself and his family a new home in London for a protracted stay so that he might better be able to pursue his professional life without political restraints. He had received assurances from highest political levels in the Soviet Union that his Soviet citizenship would not be revoked during his absence, and he was permitted to travel on a Soviet passport. "I will go back," Rostropovich said at the time, "when I have a firm assurance that I can give all my art and talent to my people as I see fit." Since then he has added: "One day we will go back to Russia on white stallions."

For his "courageous stand for artistic freedom" Rostropovich was given an award by the International League for the Rights of Man in New York.

While he was serving as a judge in a cello competition in Prague on May 11, 1955, Rostropovich met Galina Vishnevskaya, soprano of the Bolshoi Opera. At that time both were at the dawn of their careers. He caught a glimpse of her in his hotel and, as he confessed, fell in love at sight. For the next three days he bombarded her hotel room with gifts of flowers and candy. On the third day Vishnevskaya had to return to Moscow. Without hesitation, Rostropovich canceled all his concert engagements for the next few weeks and followed her to the Soviet capital. On the fourth day following their first meeting they were married—May 15, 1955.

Before the first year of their marriage was over, Rostropovich appeared as his wife's piano accompanist in a concert. They have since performed together publicly both in Europe and the United States; whenever Rostropovich is her accompanist he plays all the music from memory. Vishnevskaya's recording of Mussorgsky's *Songs and Dances of Death* for Philips, with Rostropovich as her accompanist, received the Grand Prix du Disque in Paris. In addition, Rostropovich earned the Diplôme d'Honneur at Montreux, Switzerland, in September 1976 for his recording of Strauss's *Don Quixote* with the Berlin Philharmonic under Herbert von Karajan. In 1976, Rostropovich recorded for EMI all the Tchaikovsky symphonies, with the London Philharmonic.

Before 1974 Rostropovich and his wife occupied a large apartment in Moscow and in Zhukovka a beautiful house in the country, equipped with a swimming pool. They owned three cars. Both their daughters are musicians—Olga, a cellist, and Yelena, a pianist. After leaving Moscow in 1974—traveling on a Soviet passport that had to be renewed every year—they lived abroad, "like gypsies," Rostropovich says. "We travel ... two days here, three days there. We are homeless." The closest thing to home has been an apartment in Paris, a place overcluttered with Russian artifacts to remind them of home. The Rostropoviches also maintain apartments in New York, at Watergate in Washington, D.C., and near Lausanne, Switzerland.

Though a voluntary exile, Rostropovich has never denied his love for his homeland. "I tell you this," he told Irving Lowens in *High Fidelity/Musical America,* "if I have a stroke, I immediately return to my home. For me, if my hand and my heart do not produce music, for me it is absolutely equal if I die in Gulag or I die in the far north with the temperature fifty degrees before zero. But I want to die in my earth."

In March 1978, Rostropovich and his wife were stripped of their Soviet citizenship. Described in *Izvestia* (the Soviet government daily newspaper) as "ideological degenerates," they were condemned for having carried on "unpatriotic activity" and for having "besmirched the Soviet social system and the status of a citizen of the U.S.S.R."

Rostropovich has distinguished himself as a conductor ever since he made his baton debut in 1968 in a performance of a new production of *Eugene Onegin* at the Bolshoi in Moscow. (This performance was recorded.) On March 6, 1975, he made his American debut as conductor in a guest appearance with the National Symphony Orchestra of Washington, D.C., at the Kennedy Center for the Performing Arts in an all-Tchaikovsky program with his wife as soloist. "Mr. Rostropovich conducts the way he plays the cello—passionately, fervently, and with a rhetoric that confounds any hint of excess," reported John Rockwell to the New York *Times.* So much excitement was generated by Rostropovich's appearance as a conductor in Washington that Irving Lowens, in the *Star-News,* suggested that "about the only thing the concert can be compared to is the Second Coming" and in the Washington *Post* Paul Hume said: "Those lucky enough to be in the Kennedy Center Concert Hall will, for years, be telling their children about the night that Mstislav Rostropovich made his conducting debut in this country." This success led the management to engage him as the music director of the National Symphony Orchestra, succeeding Antal Dorati, beginning

with the 1977–1978 season. Rostropovich gathered more praise as a conductor during the summer of 1975 at the Berkshire Music Festival where he conducted Verdi's Requiem and an orchestral concert. At the latter performance, on August 9, 1975, he was the first in America to receive the news of Shostakovich's death in the Soviet Union. As it happened, Shostakovich's Symphony No.5 was on his program that evening. Rostropovich had Seiji Ozawa come out to the platform to announce the sad news and to invite the audience to stand in silent tribute for a few moments. Then Rostropovich came out to conduct the symphony. After his eloquent performance he lifted the score of the symphony and kissed it; then he walked silently off the stage without acknowledging the audience's applause.

In the fall of 1975 Rostropovich made his American debut as an opera conductor, with a performance of Tchaikovsky's *The Queen of Spades* at the San Francisco Opera in which his wife assumed the leading female role of Lisa. He celebrated his fiftieth birthday on March 27, 1977, by conducting the National Symphony Orchestra of Washington, D.C., at Carnegie Hall in New York (his New York debut as a conductor) and by appearing in that concert as soloist in Haydn's Cello Concerto in C major. After conducting the program's last work, Prokofiev's Symphony No.3, he performed an encore: a rousing rendition of Sousa's *The Stars and Stripes Forever.* The orchestra and audience concluded the evening's proceedings by performing "Happy Birthday." After the concert a supper was held in his honor at the St. Regis Hotel.

He celebrated his fiftieth birthday in another way as well—the magnanimous gesture of gratitude of a great artist to his audiences everywhere —announcing he would give a dozen free concerts all over the world, all proceeds to go to worthwhile charities.

Rostropovich's debut as music director of the National Symphony Orchestra in Washington, D.C., on October 4, 1977, was made with a traditional program: music by Weber, Dvořák, and Beethoven. "At this concert," reported Harold C. Schonberg in the New York *Times,* "he was at home in music he understands and loves. ... Mr. Rostropovich is a hard conductor to resist." Ten days later, on October 14, Rostropovich shared the podium with Leonard Bernstein in an all-Bernstein program that included three world premieres.

Rostropovich's friends and colleagues affectionately call him Slava. He is a deeply religious man, and by nature a mystic. When he is making music, he has said, "I feel like a priest who, when he speaks, only repeats the words of God. I am not being modest here. But I consider myself a bridge between the spirit of, say, Tchaikovsky or Prokofiev and the people. I am a channel, an instrument, a transmitter. My aim is always to bring the composer as close to the public as possible."

He eats good food and imbibes vodka in copious amounts, enjoys watching sport matches on television, and does not hesitate to flirt with attractive women. Collecting antiques is a pet hobby. A dachshund, named Puks, is his constant companion.

In 1974 Rostropovich received an honorary doctorate in music from Harvard University.

ABOUT: Gaidamovich, T. Mstislav Rostropovich. *Periodicals*—High Fidelity/Musical America, October 1975, February 1978; Musical America, April 1956, February 1964; New York Times, March 23, 1975; New York Times Magazine, April 18, 1976; Newsweek, March 13, 1967; Saturday Review, March 5, 1977; Time, October 24, 1977.

Léon Rothier

1874–1951

Léon Rothier, bass, was born in Rheims, France, on December 26, 1874, the son of Antoinette Caoussin Rothier and François Rothier, a successful photographer. At six he began studying the violin; a few years later he joined the violin section of the Rheims Philharmonic Orchestra. When he was seventeen, he sang for Jean Baptiste Rouge who persuaded the young musician that his destiny lay in singing rather than in playing the violin. Rouge sent him to Théodore Dubois, director of the Paris Conservatory, who entered him in the admissions competition which Léon passed successfully. For the next few years, he attended the Conservatory as a student of Crosti (voice), Lhérie (opéra-comique), and Melchissédec (opera). During these years at the Conservatory he haunted the

Rothier: rō tyā′

LÉON ROTHIER

city's opera houses and theaters. "Those were glorious, exciting days for me," he told an interviewer. "I was privileged to meet and know Massenet, Saint-Saëns, Debussy, Charpentier, the great Sarah Bernhardt, Rodin, the de Reszkes, Victor Maurel and many many others."

In July 1899 he was graduated from the Conservatory with first prizes in voice, opéra-comique, and opera. Both the Paris Opéra and the Opéra-Comique offered him a contract. He chose the Opéra-Comique where on October 1, 1899, he made his opera debut as Jupiter in Gounod's *Philémon et Baucis*.

He remained with the Opéra-Comique until 1903. From 1903 to 1907 he appeared with the Marseilles Opera, from 1907 to 1909 with the Nice Opera, and in 1909–1910 with the Lyons Opera.

On December 10, 1910, he made his debut in the United States at the Metropolitan Opera as Méphistophélès in *Faust*. One New York critic said of him: "He has a fine physique, a good voice, and a proper understanding of the part. His acting was imbued with vigor and his singing was satisfactory." Though the initial reaction was lukewarm, enthusiasm grew during the next few years as he began giving an indication of growing artistry in such roles as Friar Laurence in *Romeo and Juliet*, Sparafucile in *Rigoletto*, Ramfis in *Aida*, Miracle in *The Tales of Hoffmann*, and Colline in *La Bohème*.

In 1914, when World War I began, Rothier returned to France to join the French army. He was at the front two months, and at one time the American newspapers reported he had been killed in action. However, after two months of service Rothier was discharged by the French army when it discovered he suffered from rheumatism of the kneecaps. He returned to the United States and later became an American citizen. Without missing a single season at the Metropolitan Opera, he opened the new season of 1914–1915 on November 16 as Tom in *Un Ballo in Maschera* conducted by Toscanini.

Rothier became one of the veterans of the Metropolitan Opera and one of its most valued performers, remaining with the company thirty years. In that time he appeared in more than twelve hundred performances in five languages. He created the role of Father Time in the world premiere of Albert Wolff's *L'Oiseau Bleu* on December 27, 1919, and that of Major Duquesnois in the first performance of Deems Taylor's *Peter Ibbetson* on February 7, 1931. He was cast in the first Metropolitan Opera productions of *Thaïs, Oberon,* and *Pelléas and Mélisande;* the first production of *Don Giovanni* during the managerial regime of Gatti-Casazza; the first post–World War I performance of *Parsifal,* in which he assumed the role of Gurnemanz; and in a significant revival of *La Juive* starring Caruso. After 1914 he helped to open five more Metropolitan Opera seasons: 1915–1916 and 1918–1919 in *Samson and Delilah;* 1916–1917, *The Pearl Fishers;* 1920–1921, *La Juive;* and 1933–1934, *Peter Ibbetson.* His last appearance on the Metropolitan Opera stage took place on February 25, 1939, as Des Grieux in *Manon.* Of one of his performances as Des Grieux, Pitts Sanborn wrote in the *World-Telegram:* "Mr. Rothier, in good voice, played and sang the part with feeling and imposing dignity, with lofty distinction of style, and of course, with a superb command of French diction."

Rothier appeared with the San Francisco Opera in 1929, making his debut as Sparafucile. Later he appeared with the summer opera at Ravinia Park in Chicago.

He also enjoyed distinction as a recitalist. Richard Aldrich commented after a recital at Aeolian Hall, New York, on February 5, 1917: "If his voice is not one of the most beautiful of its kind, he makes the most of it, and it has a noble and resonant quality, especially in the lower range. In many things he sings with fine intelligence, with discrimination and not without

distinction of style. His declamation is of the admirable sort that is one of the most valuable features of the French art of singing. They were most interestingly displayed in the French songs and operatic airs."

Upon retiring from the Metropolitan Opera, Rothier devoted himself in New York to teaching voice and coaching young students. He had previously taught voice for several years beginning with 1916 at the Volpe Institute in New York. During 1938–1939 he conducted a weekly program on opera over radio station WQXR, New York. On December 6, 1944, he made his Broadway stage debut at the Cort Theater as Father Pensovecchio in *A Bell for Adano,* a non-singing role. In 1949 he gave a recital at Town Hall, New York, celebrating the fiftieth anniversary of his singing career. A year later, at the Plymouth Rock Center of Music and Drama, he appeared in the world premiere of Florence Wickham's opera *The Legend of Hex Mountain.*

Rothier's first three marriages—to Simone Charpy de Maubourget; Marietta Mazarin, a soprano; and Maria Duchêne—terminated in divorce. A fourth marriage—to Clara Balog, manager of Rothier's voice studio—took place on August 24, 1951, less than two months before Rothier's death. He died in New York City on December 6, 1951.

Léon Rothier was named Chevalier of the Legion of Honor by France and Chevalier of the Order of Leopold II by Belgium.

ABOUT: Musical America, January 1, 1952.

Arthur Rubinstein

1887–

Arthur (Artur) Rubinstein, one of the giants of the keyboard in the twentieth century, has enjoyed the longest concert career of any pianist in performing history. He was born in Lodz, Poland, on January 28, 1887, the last of seven children of Ignace Rubinstein, a businessman who owned and operated a hand-loom textile factory, and Felicia Heyman Rubinstein. Six of their children came in quick succession; then, after an eight-year hiatus, Arthur was born. Nobody in

---

Rubinstein: roo͞′ bĭn stīn

ARTHUR RUBINSTEIN

and a performance by a visiting symphony orchestra. Upon returning home from that orchestral concert, he went to the piano and played virtually all of Grieg's *Peer Gynt Suite No. 1* from memory, even though he had heard it that evening for the first time.

He made his public debut when he was seven, on December 14, 1894, performing a sonata by Mozart and two pieces by Schubert and Mendelssohn at a charity concert. While continuing piano studies with Adolf Prechner, he was receiving his academic education in Lodz. Already he was acquiring that passion for books which remained with him for the rest of his life. He read everything within reach, not only fairy tales but biographies and books on history.

The death of his sister and grandfather brought on a period of lassitude and brooding. His parents, feeling a change of scene would prove beneficial, took him to Warsaw where he continued his piano study with Aleksander Rózycki, an old man who continually slept during lessons. Bored with the stereotyped exercises Rózycki set for him, Rubinstein spent his time at the piano improvising, playing the music he loved, and trying to do some composing. Rózycki at one time complained to Rubinstein's mother that the boy was inattentive at lesson time—he was convinced that there just was no future for Arthur in music.

At this time his family decided to take him once again to Berlin, for consultation with Joachim. Rubinstein played some music by Mozart and was once again rewarded with a kiss and a bar of chocolate. Joachim stood ready to take charge of Rubinstein's further intellectual and musical development. He raised a fund among his friends to which he himself contributed an equal share, to insure the boy's financial security while he remained in Berlin. A private tutor, Theodor Altmann, was recruited to teach him German history, geography, Latin, literature, philosophy, and mathematics (the last of which Arthur detested). Altmann carefully guided him in his reading habits, introducing him to Gogol, Maupassant, Goethe, Heine, Dostoyevsky, Tolstoy, and other literary masters as well as to the writings of the philosophers. "Yes, you treated me like a grown-up, and you listened with indulgence and apparent interest to my interjections of opinions—tolerating my sharply expressed criticism," Rubinstein wrote many decades later in his autobiography, *My Young Years.* "Thank

the Rubinstein family had ever revealed any talent for music.

The first music to interest Arthur was the songs gypsies sang in the courtyard of his home and the chants of Jewish old-clothes peddlers. When Arthur's sister began taking piano lessons, he listened with fascination, though he was just an infant at the time. Before long he learned by himself to play familiar tunes and revealed that he had been born with perfect pitch.

Though his father was not musical, he loved the sounds of the violin. When he purchased one for Arthur, the three-year-old child smashed it, insisting he wanted to play the piano. This "fixation" for the piano, as Rubinstein later described it, encouraged one of his uncles to write to Joseph Joachim in Berlin for advice. Joachim suggested that Arthur be brought to him. In Berlin, Joachim put Arthur through a series of musical tests. When all of them were performed with dispatch, Joachim kissed Arthur and rewarded him with a bar of chocolate. He then told Rubinstein's mother: "This boy may become a very great musician—he certainly has the talent for it. Let him hear some good singing, but do not force music on him. When the time comes for serious study, bring him to me, and I shall be glad to supervise his artistic education."

Arthur was about four when he started piano lessons with local teachers. While studying, he extended his musical horizon by attending an opera performance for the first time *(Aida)*, recitals by visiting artists (including one by the young violin virtuoso Bronislaw Hubermann), you for all this, my dear Theodor Altmann, from the bottom of my heart."

For his piano study he was assigned to Heinrich Barth, a pupil of Liszt, who gave him two lessons a week privately. Other music study took place at the Imperial Academy where from time to time Joachim asked him to serve as an accompanist in his violin classes, thereby introducing young Rubinstein to the basic literature for that instrument. Other musical experiences came from attending concerts, particularly those of the Berlin Philharmonic Orchestra conducted by Arthur Nikisch. These became, as he later said, "the center of my musical experiences and development," and through them he acquired an intimate knowledge of symphonic literature.

One evening, at a piano recital by Eugène d'Albert, Arthur was brought backstage and introduced to him. D'Albert asked him to come back with him on the stage and play for him. After he had performed Brahms's Rhapsody, Op.79, a few stragglers, who had lingered on in the hall, rose and cheered. D'Albert told the young pianist: "Yes, you are a true Rubinstein!"

Arthur made his formal debut in Berlin when he was thirteen, performing Mozart's Concerto in A major, K.488, at the High School for Music, Joachim conducting. "When we took our bow," he recalls, "he kissed me on both cheeks in front of the audience. This was a memorable day for me." Soon after that, in December 1900, he appeared in the Beethoven Saal in Berlin in a program that included with the Mozart A major Concerto Saint-Saëns's Concerto in G minor and Robert Schumann's *Papillons*. Joachim, Godowsky, and Max Bruch were some of the musicians in the audience who gave him an ovation. "They started to yell, and stamped their feet," Rubinstein later recalled. "I really must say it was a triumph for me." The two leading music critics in Berlin both called him an ideal interpreter of Mozart.

He began to receive calls for performances outside Berlin. The Grand Duchess of Mecklenburg invited him to perform at her palace in Schwerin and was so taken with him that she recalled him to Schwerin to appear with an orchestra in celebration of her birthday. Recitals were given in Dresden and Hamburg. In 1902, when the new Philharmonic Hall was opened in Warsaw, he was invited to appear as a soloist with the Warsaw Symphony under Emil Mlynarski and then to give a recital there.

At about this time, Joachim arranged for Arthur to play for Paderewski at the master's villa in Switzerland. Eager to impress Paderewski with his technique, Rubinstein performed for him the Brahms *Paganini Variations,* which went badly. "Don't be disheartened by a few wrong notes," Paderewski told him sympathetically. After dinner Rubinstein went back to the piano to play pieces by Brahms and Chopin which he had well in hand. "I knew right away," Paderewski said, "that you have great talent." On Paderewski's invitation, he spent one summer working with the master at the piano in regular sessions.

By 1903 Arthur, feeling he had had enough of Berlin and of Heinrich Barth's instruction, decided to dispense with the financial aid he had been getting and to go for the first time entirely on his own. First in Warsaw, then in Paris, he began to enjoy his freedom by going to concerts and the theater, attending parties, carousing a good deal, visiting good restaurants, indulging in some gambling, enjoying the companionship of close friends and falling in love with various women (including the prima donna Emmy Destinn). Then, as throughout the rest of his life, he fully enjoyed sensual as well as intellectual pleasures. That his piano playing did not suffer from all these diversions and distractions was not only due to the prodigious technique he had already developed but also to a formidable memory and a remarkable gift for sight reading.

In Paris the impresario Gabriel Astruc became his manager. He had him audition for Maurice Ravel, Paul Dukas, and Jacques Thibaud and when they expressed approval signed him to a contract. In 1904 he appeared in Paris as a soloist with the Lamoureux Orchestra conducted by Camille Chevillard, following this appearance with three more concerts. Camille Saint-Saëns, whose G minor Piano Concerto was a Rubinstein tour de force, called him "one of the greatest artists I know. I foresee for him an admirable career, and to say it all in a few words—he is worthy of the great name he bears."

A Boston music critic, who had heard Rubinstein play at Paderewski's Swiss villa, recommended the young pianist to William Knabe, head of the piano firm. Knabe signed him to make his first tour of the United States in 1906, arranging for him to give forty concerts during a three-month period. His American debut took place in Carnegie Hall, in New York, on January 8, 1906, when, as a soloist with the Philadelphia Orchestra under Fritz Scheel, he performed Saint-Saëns's G minor Concerto (following which he was heard in a solo, Liszt's *Mephisto Waltz*). While an anonymous critic for *Musical America* found him to be "one of the world's greatest pianists—great because of his stupendous technique, because of his indisputable talent, because of what he has accomplished in spite of the limitations of youth," other New York critics were less enthusiastic. The reaction of Richard Aldrich in the New York *Times* was typical of the critical consensus. Aldrich wrote: "This young Rubinstein is undoubtedly a talented youth, but his talent at present seems to reside chiefly in his fingers. . . . He is full of the exuberance and exaggeration of youth, and he is at present concerned chiefly with the exploitation of his dexterity and with impressing not only the ears but also the eyes of his hearers with his personality and the brilliancy of the effects he can produce."

After returning to Europe from his first American tour, Rubinstein decided that he needed further study of piano literature, to deepen his understanding of the masters, to enrich his interpretative responses. He reduced the number of his appearances for a number of years, while working long and hard to overcome (as he himself put it) "the greatest obstacle in the path of a prodigy, that of shedding immaturity." He did not abandon his other intellectual interests—reading, going to art museums, the theater, the study of languages, the pursuit of philosophy—nor for that matter did he sacrifice those physical pleasures he considered basic to good living. But to uncover further the secrets hidden within the pages of the music he had been playing became a prime concern.

There were periods of deep depression. In 1908 he felt all alone in the world. His funds were totally depleted, there was no woman around to love, his artistic goal seemed at the time beyond realization. One day he tried to commit suicide by hanging himself in his bathroom with his bathrobe belt. The belt broke and his life was saved. From that moment on he felt as if reborn and rededicated himself anew to his mission.

He returned to the concert stage in 1910. With performances all over Europe he proved himself not only one of the greatest living interpreters of Chopin but also an artist with a new insight into his presentation of the masters. He further enhanced his reputation in Europe by appearing in remarkable sonata recitals with Pablo Casals and Jacques Thibaud.

He was in London when World War I broke out. Determined to fight for his country, he made his way to Paris intending to join the Polish legion. When informed that there was no Polish legion, that Poles were required to fight under the Russian flag, he contributed his knowledge of languages to the war effort, becoming a civilian interpreter of letters and documents found on prisoners of war. As the Polish casualties at the hands of the Germans began mounting, his bitterness against the enemy increased. He made a vow never again to perform in Germany. He kept that vow after World War I; and when the Nazis came to power in 1933 he renewed that vow and has never set foot on German soil since then. (However, after World War II, he offered to perform for young Germans anywhere outside their own country. Such a concert was arranged in Holland near the Dutch-German border. Some one thousand five hundred young music lovers made the pilgrimage from thirty German cities and from Vienna. After the concert, Rubinstein, speaking in German, explained his position on the problem of Germany and the Jews.)

In 1915 Rubinstein returned to London to appear as soloist with the London Symphony Orchestra. In England he contributed his musical services to the war effort by performing for the Red Cross, for the Allied troops, and for various war-relief charities. Still for the war effort he gave twenty joint recitals with Eugène Ysaÿe.

In 1916 he made his debut in Spain as a soloist with the Madrid Symphony in San Sebastian, Enrique Fernández Arbós conducting. He proved so successful that he was invited to perform for María Cristina, the Queen Mother, at her summer palace. He also made twenty more appearances in Spain that season; and in 1916–1917 he gave over one hundred performances there. At some of his concerts he played twentieth century Spanish music by Albéniz and Manuel de Falla, receiving as much acclaim for his Spanish performances as for his other interpretations.

He followed these successes in Spain with his first tour of South America in the late spring of

1917. "It was at this point," he says in his autobiography, "that my young years were over. From then on my life changed color and moved forward at a more steady pace. I had gained the necessary hold on my career."

Rubinstein returned to the United States in 1919 with a Carnegie Hall recital on February 20. He still failed to make the kind of impression he was enjoying elsewhere. Richard Aldrich, writing in the New York *Times*, called his style old fashioned, in the manner of "the Viennese school, with its light action keyboard, the lack of depth in chord playing, the too rapid scales, also superficial in tone; above all, his pedaling after, instead of before, the attack."

Rubinstein did not return to the American scene for another decade. In Europe he kept accumulating successes as a virtuoso together with further intellectual, esthetic, and sensual experiences. On July 27, 1932, in London, he married Aniela Mlynarska. He credits her with bringing him a sobriety and discipline his life had never known and with inspiring him to try to develop himself further in every way in order to become the greatest possible pianist. Once again he withdrew from all concert activity to seclude himself in the Haute-Savoie region of France to work from twelve to sixteen hours a day. He studied new music and rediscovered that which he had been performing; he learned still further to harness his formidable technique and to make it the complete servant of sensitized, poetic, introspective musical declarations.

He and his wife acquired a house in Paris which they made a repository of Rubinstein's valuable collection of great paintings, countless curios, and objets d'art gathered from all over the world and his vast library that included books inscribed to him by some of the most famous writers of the twentieth century. Here they raised the first two of their four children: Eva, born in Buenos Aires in 1933, and Paul, born in Warsaw in 1935.

When, on November 21, 1937, he began his third tour of the United States, the American critics became fully aware that they were in the presence of a Titan of the keyboard. Writing in the New York *Times,* Olin Downes said: "Mr. Rubinstein played with fire and poetry. Evidently he profoundly knows the composition and loves it. The performance was distinguished by qualities of a brilliant pianist and musician who should have been heard oftener in late years on this side of the ocean."

When war came to Europe in 1939, the Rubinsteins deserted their Paris home (their treasures were soon confiscated by the Nazi invaders) and settled permanently in Beverly Hills, California. Two more children were later born here: Alina Anna in 1945; and John Arthur, a year later. In 1946 Rubinstein became an American citizen. He later acquired a second American home, a duplex apartment on Park Avenue in New York City, and later still homes in Paris and Spain.

From his base in California he continued, after the war's end, to set forth on tours that took him to every music center of the world except Germany. No performing artist ever enjoyed such a prolonged performing career—his career spanned eight decades; no performing artist was capable of maintaining such a rigorous performing schedule annually—this was true even in his octogenarian years; no performing artist was a bigger box-office attraction wherever he chose to appear; and no performing artist ever succeeded in retaining in old age so much of the technical skill, the physical stamina, and the exalted musicianship of his prime years.

In old age Rubinstein also succeeded in retaining his extraordinary zest and love for life. He told Jane Perlez in an interview in the New York *Post* on May 17, 1973: "I've never lost one second of my life with something I didn't want to do. My deepest religion is: 'You're given a short span of life, so enjoy it.' I'd rather sit at a café in Paris and look at the beautiful girls, or pick up a book, or light a cigar, than spend two days with a bore. I would have given all my money away, but not one second of my time. You can find money, you can steal it, but never can you find the time."

Few of the infirmities of advancing years have afflicted him, not arthritis, or rheumatic pains, or coronary disturbances. He has never taken pills of any kind, other than Vitamin C. To keep in shape he has devoted twenty minutes each day before breakfast to setting-up exercises. He has never lost his appetite for good wines, fine food, and expensive cigars. "He is a very easy fellow to feed," his wife has said. "Good appetite. He loves chicken, so I have a million ways to cook it. He could eat it every day and not complain."

In 1958, during a festival celebrating the tenth anniversary of the founding of Israel, Rubinstein performed fifteen concertos in five evenings. Between October 30 and December 10, 1961, he gave a cycle of ten piano recitals in Carnegie Hall in which he performed ninety works by seventeen composers ranging from Bach to Stravinsky and Szymanowski. These concerts drew a combined audience of about thirty thousand. The entire proceeds (about one hundred thousand dollars) went to eleven of his favorite charities.

On June 11, 1958, Rubinstein paid his first visit to Poland in twenty years, appearing in Philharmonic Hall in Warsaw. "This was not simply a story of a triumphal concert by a great pianist," reported A. M. Rosenthal to the New York *Times*. "It is a story of the reunion of a man and a city and of the emotions that swept them both." In 1968 Rubinstein offended the Polish authorities by printing a letter in the New York *Times* denouncing the banning in Warsaw of a play by Adam Mickiewicz, the national poet. He waited until this episode had been forgotten before returning to his native country. In Lodz, the city of his birth, on May 30, 1975, he performed with the Lodz Philharmonic in celebration of its sixtieth birthday. This event was filmed in a documentary called *The Comeback*.

He made his first appearance in the Soviet Union in nearly thirty years, in Moscow, on September 27, 1964. He was given a heroic welcome not only at this performance but also at two concerts in Leningrad and one in Kiev.

On March 15, 1976, Rubinstein commemorated the seventieth anniversary of his Carnegie Hall debut with a recital in the same hall. Eighty-nine years old, he was still, as Harold C. Schonberg remarked in the New York *Times*, "a great pianist on anybody's terms. . . . The old lion can still tear the piano apart when he desires." He was still capable of giving a remarkable performance of an exacting program even though (as he revealed at the time) his eyesight had by now become so weakened he was unable to see the keys under his fingers or read a note of music; he had been left with only peripheral vision. "I must rely entirely on my memory," he said. His hearing, he said, was also failing him.

At this commemorative concert he was given a tumultuous ovation. As Schonberg reported: "There was a rising ovation on the pianist's entrance, and a rising ovation at the end of the concert. Carnegie Hall was awash with love in all directions—love from pianist to audience, love from audience to pianist." When he had finished playing, Rubinstein told his audience: "For forty years I came every year. You listened with marvelous affection for me. I love you." A bust of Rubinstein, sculpted by Nathan Rappaport, was unveiled at Carnegie Hall to mark this historic concert.

Rubinstein has made more recordings than any other pianist, all for RCA Victor. He is believed to have sold over eight million disks. He has recorded all the works of Chopin, and on three different occasions (the last time in 1975 when he was eighty-eight) he performed on disks the five concertos of Beethoven. On several occasions he was awarded Grammys by the National Academy of Recording Arts and Sciences, the last two in 1977 and 1978—the 1977 one for his 1975 album of the five Beethoven piano concertos, the 1978 one for an album embracing Beethoven's Piano Sonata in E-flat major, Op.31, No.3 and Schumann's *Fantasiestücke*. Earlier in his career he participated with Heifetz and Piatigorsky in chamber music recordings that have become collector's items. Late in his life, in 1976, his recording of Schubert's Piano Trios with Pierre Fournier and Henryk Szeryng, received a Grammy.

As a performing artist he has remained through the years *au courant* with the music of the twentieth century and has promoted it indefatigably in his concerts. He was one of the first pianists to perform the music of twentieth century Spanish composers, that of the French Six in Paris, and major works of Poland's twentieth century composer (and Rubinstein's personal friend) Karol Szymanowski. Aware of his sympathy for their work, some of the composers of our time have written music for him and dedicated it to him, among them Prokofiev, Stravinsky, Szymanowski, Alexander Tansman, Villa-Lobos, Manuel de Falla, Milhaud, Poulenc, Manuel Ponce, and John Alden Carpenter. One of Villa-Lobos's most famous works for the piano, *Rudepoema* (1926), was intended to be a tonal portrait of Rubinstein's temperament. (The composer also orchestrated this work.)

Rubinstein appeared as himself in the motion pictures *Carnegie Hall* (1947) and *Of Men and Music* (1951). His piano playing was heard on the soundtracks of the films *I've Always Loved You* (1946), *Song of Love* (1947), and *Night Song* (1947). A full-length motion picture documentary, *Arthur Rubinstein—Love of Life,* was released early in 1975. He was also starred on numerous television specials including a ninety-minute personal profile, *The Life and Art of Arthur Rubinstein,* in 1968. This last-mentioned profile originated as a documentary for French television; it received an Oscar from the American Academy of Motion Picture Arts and Sciences in 1969.

This 1968 documentary and Rubinstein's autobiography, *My Young Years* (1973), spell his first name as Arthur; his manager, S. Hurok, preferred to use Artur for Rubinstein's American appearances. Rubinstein himself has always preferred Arthur and has used that spelling in countries outside the United States. Since the appearance of the autobiography he has also used the Arthur spelling for his American appearances.

On December 15, 1971, Rubinstein was installed in Paris as a foreign associate member of the French Académie des Beaux-Arts de l'Institut de France. This was the capstone of the innumerable honors bestowed upon him through the years, among them Commander of the Legion of Honor, France; Officer of the Order of Santiago, Portugal; Cross of Alfonso XII, Spain; Commander of the Crown and Officer, Order of Leopold I, Belgium; Order of Polonia Restituta, Poland; and Commander of the Chilean Republic. He has earned the gold medal of the Royal Philharmonic Society of London and several doctorates in music from American universities. In 1964 the Hebrew University in Jerusalem endowed an Arthur Rubinstein Chair in the department of musicology, and on January 16, 1966, the America-Israel Cultural Foundation honored him with a special concert in Carnegie Hall.

In 1946 Rubinstein organized the Frederic Chopin Fund to raise financial support for needy musicians in postwar Europe and served as its president. In September 1974 the first Arthur Rubinstein International Piano Master Competition was inaugurated in his honor in Jerusalem; Rubinstein himself donated five thousand dollars for the first prize, which went to Emanuel Ax on January 15, 1975.

ABOUT: Rubinstein, A. My Young Years. *Periodicals*—Holiday, May 1963; Life, April 5, 1948; Musical America, March 1962; New York Times Magazine, January 26, 1964, March 14, 1976; New Yorker, November 1, 1958; Show, October 1961; Time, February 25, 1966, March 29, 1976.

Julius Rudel

1921–

As the general director and principal conductor of the New York City Opera for a quarter of a century and more, Julius Rudel, conductor, raised the organization to a prestigious position among the world's opera companies. He was born in Vienna on March 6, 1921, the son of Jakob Rudel, a lawyer and insurance executive, and Josephine Sonnenblum Rudel. When Julius was three, he began playing the violin by ear. Two years later he began his formal training on the violin, and one year after that he shifted from the violin to the piano. Upon being graduated from the Realgymnasium in Vienna in 1936 he studied composition at the State Academy of Drama and Music.

His lifelong passion for music began early in life, when he attended performances at the Vienna State Opera. As a boy, his pastime was to build miniature opera houses. By the time he was sixteen he had composed two operas.

After the death of his father and the annexation of Austria by Nazi Germany, Julius emigrated to the United States in 1938 with his mother and two brothers. They settled in New York City; in 1944 Rudel became a naturalized citizen.

In New York, Julius helped to support the family by taking on all kinds of nonmusical (and sometimes menial) jobs while pursuing his musical interests at the Greenwich House Music School and the Mannes School of Music. At the latter, where he received his diploma in 1942, he studied conducting with Carl Bamberger and in 1941 served as assistant conductor in operatic and orchestral performances. For about a year after leaving the Mannes School as a student he continued to conduct there. He also played the piano for, and occasionally conducted, lesser orchestral and choral groups in New York.

When the City Center of Music and Drama was organized in 1943, Rudel applied for a job. László Halász, the conductor assigned to form the New York City Opera, hired young Rudel as an auditions and rehearsal pianist, without pay-

JULIUS RUDEL

ing him any salary. However, before long Rudel was given the salaried post of assistant conductor at rehearsals and served as coach to the singers. On November 24, 1944, he made his debut as conductor in a performance of *The Gypsy Baron,* given without any rehearsals.

Recalling those first years at the New York City Opera, Rudel told Stephen E. Rubin in an interview for the New York *Times:* "I had to hang on with my claws to the lowest rung of the ladder. People tried to kick me off several times, even Halász himself. He did give me my first chance to conduct, though. And I conducted very well. As a matter of fact, at that moment, naive as I was, I thought, my God, these marvelous reviews, I've got it made. Far from it. It was on account of those reviews that I was, for years, kept down in a most humiliating, personal way which I could only get over by swallowing and tightening up, and closing my eyes to it because I was determined not to let it upset me."

During the next decade Rudel became something of a major factotum at the New York City Opera. In addition to some conducting assignments, he was required to assist in every other department of production, including handling the props, scheduling rehearsals, assisting in the casting, helping with the stage direction, and giving a hand in the musical preparation of many operas, including ambitious productions of Alban Berg's *Wozzeck,* Britten's *The Rape of Lucretia,* Strauss's *Ariadne auf Naxos,* Rossini's *La Cenerentola, Pelléas and Mélisande,* and *Turandot.* "I was the kid who did everything backstage," he told Rubin, "who put on a costume and went on for a super because he wasn't there, or who sang a C for a bass who couldn't be found, or who pulled down the curtain to end an act. So, all of these things tended to make Rudel a good guy, a nice fellow. It's terribly tough to come through that with any aura of glamour still attached."

During these years with the New York City Opera, Rudel held various jobs outside the company. From 1945 to 1952 he was the director of the Third Street Music Settlement in New York. From 1952 to 1956 he served as the music director of summer stock theaters in Asbury Park, New Jersey, and in Hyannis and Cohasset in Massachusetts. Beginning in 1954 he served for a time as music director of the New York City Light Opera Company, directing operettas and musical comedies. In 1953 he made a guest appearance at Lewisohn Stadium in New York in a concert presentation of *Salome.* He assumed other guest-conducting assignments during the next few years: in New York, Philadelphia, Chicago. In 1956 he conducted a German-language performance of Cole Porter's *Kiss Me, Kate* at the Volksoper in Vienna.

In 1956 Rudel was offered the post of music director of the Houston Opera. At the time, this appointment would have represented a step forward in his career. He turned it down, preferring to stick it out with the New York City Opera. In sacrificing Houston for New York, he says, "instinct saved me." The Houston Opera went under, and in 1957, when Erich Leinsdorf resigned as music director of the New York City Opera, Rudel was offered the post of general director as well as that of principal conductor.

In his first season as the head of the New York City Opera, Rudel demonstrated his interest in American opera by producing and conducting the New York premiere of Carlisle Floyd's *Susannah,* which became one of the company's great artistic and commercial successes. In the summer of 1958 he took the New York City Opera production of *Susannah* to the World's Exposition in Brussels, Belgium, to represent American opera. In 1958, subsidized by the Ford Foundation, Rudel initiated five weeks of a spring season devoted to ten American operas, including the world premiere of Robert Kurka's *The Good Soldier Schweik,* which he conducted (April 23, 1958). In the spring of 1959 he presented another season of American operas, this time thirteen in number. In 1960 he took four of his American opera productions on an American tour. From this point on, Rudel continued to promote American operas. He himself led the world premieres of Douglas Moore's *Wings of the Dove* (October 12, 1961), Carlisle Floyd's *The Passion of Jonathan Wade* (October 11, 1962), Abraham Ellstein's *The Golem* (May 22, 1962), Lee Hoiby's *Natalia Petrovna* (October 8, 1964), and Vittorio Giannini's *The Servant of Two Masters* (March 9, 1967).

Rudel also brought to the New York City Opera twentieth century operas from other countries. In 1965 he presented a season of thirteen such works, among which were Shostakovich's *Katerina Ismailova*, which he both translated and conducted. He led performances of Ginastera's *Bomarzo* at the New York City Opera after having conducted its world premiere in Washington, D.C., on May 19, 1967. Among the numerous American premieres given under Rudel at the New York City Opera were Britten's *The Turn of the Screw* (October 19, 1960), Prokofiev's *The Fiery Angel* (February 22, 1966), and Ginastera's *Don Rodrigo* (March 9, 1966).

At the New York City Opera, Rudel often conducted brilliant performances of operatic masterworks of the past, many well off the beaten track. He scored one of his greatest successes with the first American-staged production of Handel's *Julius Caesar* in October 1966 (the opera which became Beverly Sills's first important step to superstardom). When Rudel took the New York City Opera for its first appearances in Los Angeles in 1967, his performance of *Julius Caesar* drew particular praise. In the Los Angeles *Times,* Martin Bernheimer wrote: "Julius Rudel's scholarly, sensitively balanced music making complements the stage picture beautifully. Rudel maintains transparent textures, strives for shimmering string tone to support the vocal flights, even pays attention to such matters as appoggiatura application and linear embellishments." Once again starring Beverly Sills, Rudel mounted in New York three rarely heard operas by Donizetti: *Roberto Devereux, Anna Bolena,* and *Maria Stuarda.* He has given special attention to the greatest operas of Mozart. And he has done all this without sidestepping the standard Italian and French repertory.

Rudel has not confined his conducting activity to the New York City Opera. From 1950 to 1959 he was the head of the Chautauqua Opera Association in Chautauqua, New York, and in 1960–1961 he formed and led the Gilbert and Sullivan company in New York. He has appeared in America, Europe, and Israel in guest performances both with orchestras and in opera houses. He opened the new season for the Festival of Two Worlds in Spoleto, Italy, with Prokofiev's *The Love for Three Oranges* in 1962, and returned there a season later with Rossini's *Il Signor Bruschino.* He directed the world premiere of Carlisle Floyd's *The Sojourner and Mollie Sinclair* in Raleigh, North Carolina, on December 2, 1963. In 1964 he staged and conducted *Faust* and *Die Fledermaus* at the Baltimore Opera. One year later he directed a Mozart orchestral cycle at Grant Park in Chicago. He made his debut with the Cologne Opera in Germany in 1966 with Henze's *Der Junge Lord.* On September 10, 1972, he directed the world premiere of Ginastera's *Beatrice Cenci* with the Washington Opera Society at the John F. Kennedy Center for the Performing Arts in Washington, D.C. For three weeks in the spring of 1973 he commuted between Paris and Hamburg to conduct *Il Trovatore* and *The Marriage of Figaro* at the Paris Opéra and a new production of Richard Strauss's *Capriccio* at the Hamburg Opera. In the spring of 1975 he conducted a new production of *La Forza del Destino* at the Paris Opéra. During the summer of 1976 he directed Mozart's *The Abduction from the Seraglio* and *Così fan Tutte* (besides preparing *Don Giovanni*) at the Paris Opéra. In addition to performances of *Die Fledermaus* he directed a new production of Mozart's *La Clemenza di Tito* at the Theater-an-der-Wien (the Vienna State Opera), Donizetti's *Roberto Devereux* at the Aix-en-Provence Festival, and *The Magic Flute* at the Paris Opéra, all in 1977. In March 1978 he led a new production of Monteverdi's *L'Incoronazione di Poppea* at the Paris Opéra. For all these performances he was acclaimed by audiences and critics. For his services to French music in general and the Paris Opéra in particular, Rudel was honored by the French government with the Croix du Chevalier in Arts and Letters in 1977.

From 1964 to 1976 Rudel was the music director of the summer Caramoor Festival in Katonah, New York. Among the novelties enlivening the proceedings at these festival performances were Mozart's *Idomeneo,* Donizetti's Requiem, Vivaldi's *Gloria,* Cherubini's *Medea,*

Monteverdi's *L'Incoronazione di Poppea,* Orff's *Die Kluge* and *Catulli Carmina,* Mahler's *Das Klagende Lied,* Debussy's *Chansons de Bilitis* presented as a ballet, and the American premieres of Britten's church parables *Curlew River* (June 26, 1961), *The Burning Fiery Furnace* (June 25, 1967), and *The Prodigal Son* (June 29, 1969).

In 1971 and 1972 Rudel served as the music director of the Cincinnati May Festival. He held a similar office at the John F. Kennedy Center for the Performing Arts in Washington, D.C., from 1971 to 1975. There he was responsible for all of the opening festivities, for the first staged performances in the United States of Handel's *Ariodante,* and for such special events as The Old and the New Festival and the comprehensive Mozart Festival. Rudel has also served as music director of the Wolf Trap Performing Arts Center at Vienna, West Virginia, and as consultant to the Philadelphia Opera.

When the twenty-fifth anniversary of the New York City Opera was commemorated in 1973, a Julius Rudel Award for Young Conductors was established. On September 1, 1976, Rudel celebrated his own twentieth anniversary with the New York City Opera by conducting *Turandot* as the season's opening night production.

On June 24, 1942, Rudel married Rita Gillis (who has since become a research neuropsychologist at the Columbia-Presbyterian Medical Center in New York). They met while both were students at the Greenwich House Music School. The Rudels, who live in a West Side apartment in New York City, have raised three children. Rudel's hobbies include snow and water skiing, swimming, and collecting paintings.

He has been awarded the Honorary Insignia of Arts and Sciences from the Austrian government and the Commander's Cross, Order of Merit, from Germany. He has also been given the Page One Award of the Newspaper Guild, the Handel Medallion from the City of New York, the Alice M. Ditson Award, and honorary doctorates in music from the University of Michigan and the University of Vermont. In 1969 the Israeli government gave him an honorary lieutenantship in the Israeli army.

ABOUT: International Musician, November 1961; New York Times, September 16, 1962, February 7, 1971, July 7, 1975; New York Times Magazine, September 29, 1963; New Yorker, October 20, 1962; Opera News, February 24, 1964.

Titta Ruffo

1877–1953

In his prime, in the decade between 1910 and 1920, Titta Ruffo was the leading baritone in opera, a box-office attraction that could command the fees of a Caruso or a Galli-Curci. Ruffo (originally Ruffo Cafiero Titta) was born in Pisa, Italy, on June 9, 1877. His father, Oreste, was a blacksmith. Though the family was extremely poor, members of the family were able to develop their musical talents. Titta's older brother, Ettore, became a composer, and his sister, Fosca, a professional singer.

Titta was being directed, however, not to music but to engineering, for which he received his training at the University of Rome. When he decided to consider singing seriously as a profession, he received some vocal lessons from his brother Ettore whom he always regarded as the most significant musical influence of his life. Then Titta studied voice with Persichini at the Santa Cecilia Academy. Since Persichini had no high opinion of his pupil—and since Titta returned the compliment by rebelling against his teacher's methods—the two soon separated. Ruffo continued his vocal studies privately with Lelio Cassini in Milan.

Even before he made his stage debut, Ruffo began to make recordings. He credited these and subsequent recordings with having been a potent force in shaping his musical development. As he told a shipboard interviewer when first he arrived in the United States: "I think I learned more from singing for the gramophone than in any other way. After I had sung for the gramophone for the first time I found defects in my voice; the second time I corrected these to some extent; the third time I found my voice quite perfect."

His opera debut took place in 1898 at the Teatro Costanzi in Rome in the minor role of the Herald in *Lohengrin.* Ruffo soon was asked to make appearances in other opera houses in Italy and in South America. He began attracting sufficient interest and attention to be invited to make guest appearances in Covent Garden in London, the Paris Opéra, the Vienna Royal Opera, and the Berlin Royal Opera. By 1910 he had become

Ruffo: rōōf′ fō

TITTA RUFFO

one of the most famous baritones of his time. His beautifully textured voice and his mastery of both powerful delivery and light *parlando* passages inspired the highest of praise not only from the critics but also from some of his most distinguished colleagues. Giuseppe De Luca said that Ruffo's voice was a miracle; Victor Maurel maintained that it was one of the most glorious baritones he had ever heard.

Ruffo made his American debut with the Chicago-Philadelphia Opera Company which was paying him the then exceptional fee of two thousand five hundred dollars a performance, the highest thus far ever given to a baritone. In this debut in Philadelphia on November 4, 1912, as Rigoletto, Ruffo was a triumph. As a member of the Chicago-Philadelphia Opera, he made his debut in New York on November 19, 1912, in the title role of *Hamlet*. During his first two seasons with the company he was acclaimed not only as Rigoletto and Hamlet but also as Tonio in *I Pagliacci*, Renato in *Un Ballo in Maschera*, Count di Luna in *Il Trovatore*, Cascart in Leoncavallo's *Zaza*, and what was probably his most celebrated role, that of Figaro in *The Barber of Seville*. At this time he also made his first American recordings (for Victor) which enjoyed such enormous sales that Victor supplemented these American releases with the distribution of Ruffo's earlier European disks.

He was in Argentina at the outbreak of World War I and returned to Italy to volunteer in the air force as a mechanic. After the war he returned to the Chicago-Philadelphia Company

for the 1919–1920 season. There, on December 13, 1920, he created the title role in Leoncavallo's one-act opera *Edipo Re,* that the composer had written for him.

Ruffo was scheduled to make his debut at the Metropolitan Opera in New York on December 8, 1921, as Don Carlos in *Ernani*. But a severe cold caused a postponement, and his debut took place several weeks later, on January 19, 1922, as Figaro in *The Barber of Seville,* in which he created a sensation (even though the years of World War I and military service had somewhat impaired the pure quality and technical perfection of his vocal delivery). "Mr. Ruffo's Figaro was pleasing in its glee, its vivacity, its genuine humor and its touches of a hitherto unrevealed skill," wrote W. J. Henderson in the New York *Sun.* "The recitativo secco as it is technically called . . . he sang with great facility, with elasticity, with unction and with color. . . . He sang some of the vocal numbers well and some more than well, though the temptation to use the full volume of his great voice in questionable places was irresistible." The music critic of the *Journal* commented: "Indubitably, his is now the biggest voice discoverable anywhere in the operatic universe . . . the loudest thing heard in the Metropolitan since Caruso departed, but its quality was rather that of brass than gold; still it is a voice, a stupendous voice."

Because of illness, Ruffo was able to appear that season at the Metropolitan Opera only once more as Figaro and once each as Don Carlos in *Ernani* and Tonio in *I Pagliacci*. But even after he was once again in good health his performances at the Metropolitan Opera during the next seven years were so few and far between (sometimes as few as only three or four times a season) that each had the aura of a special guest appearance. He never sang there two of his most famous roles (Rigoletto and Cascart), but he was heard in others for which he was also celebrated, such as Amonasro in *Aida*, Gerard in *Andrea Chénier*, Barnaba in *La Gioconda* and Neri in Giordano's *La Cena delle Beffe*. The last of these received its first Metropolitan Opera production on January 2, 1926, because of Ruffo.

He left the Metropolitan Opera in 1929 because he had received an offer of three hundred thousand dollars to appear in motion pictures which then had just recently burst into sound. Nothing tangible, however, seems to have materialized from this affiliation. Ruffo made his last public appearance on the stage of the Radio City Music Hall in New York on December 26, 1932, when he was heard as Escamillo in excerpts from *Carmen*.

After 1932 he lived in Florence. As the brother-in-law of Giacomo Matteoti, the Socialist deputy who had been assassinated by the Fascists in August of 1924, Ruffo was passionately opposed to Benito Mussolini and the Fascist regime. At one time, in 1937, he was imprisoned for a brief period because of his political stand. As an enemy of the State he was in disrepute in the years just before World War II.

He lived the last years of his life in loneliness and poverty in a small fourth-floor walk-up apartment in Florence, abandoned not only by his one-time admirers but even by members of his own family. He died of a heart attack in Florence, on July 6, 1953.

ABOUT: Barrenechea, M. A. Titta Ruffo; Pleasants, H. The Great Singers; Ruffo, T. La Mia Parabola.

LEONIE RYSANEK

Leonie Rysanek

1928–

Leonie Rysanek, soprano, was born in Vienna on November 14, 1928. She was of Czech extraction: her grandfather conducted a military band. She was the fifth of six children of Peter and Josefine Hoeberth Rysanek. Three of her brothers were killed during World War II; a sister, Lotte Rysanek, achieved success as a lyric soprano with the Vienna State Opera.

Such was the poverty of the Rysanek family that Leonie cannot remember having tasted chocolate as a child. But the house overflowed with love and with music, with all of the Rysanek children participating in home concerts. When Leonie was still a child one of her neighbors, a music teacher, predicted that she would someday become an opera singer. She showed unusual responsiveness to music. When at the age of ten she saw her first opera—a performance of *Fidelio* at the Vienna State Opera—she fainted from excitement during the performance. Her early ambition, however, was to become a dramatic actress rather than a prima donna. Music began assuming an ever-increas-

Rysanek: rē′ sån ĕk

ing importance in her life towards the end of World War II, as she told an interviewer for *The Christian Science Monitor*. "Vienna became a city without music and for over a year we were starved by silence. Not until then was I aware of my own need for music, which I had always taken for granted. When the war ended, I remember how we stood under the open sky, in our bombed-out opera house, drinking in the strains of Puccini, Verdi, Bizet, and Strauss. I then determined on a musical career."

In 1946 she entered the Austrian Academy of Music and Dramatic Arts on a scholarship for the study of voice. She was still a student at the Academy when, in 1949, she made her opera debut at Innsbruck, Austria, as Agathe in *Der Freischütz*. In Innsbruck she met Rudolf Grossmann, a baritone with the opera company. He became her coach and vocal teacher, preparing her for further operatic appearances in Germany. On August 26, 1950, he became her husband.

From 1950 to 1952 Rysanek was a member of the Saarbrücken Opera. There in 1951 she appeared as Sieglinde in *Die Walküre*. From 1952 to 1954 she was a member of the Munich Opera. During the early 1950s she appeared opposite Grossmann on numerous occasions in performances of *Arabella*, *The Flying Dutchman*, *Otello*, and *Tosca*. A performance of *Tosca* in Munich in 1954 was not only their last joint appearance but also the last time that Grossmann appeared on any stage. He then retired as a singer to devote himself to his wife's career and to coach her in new roles. Rysanek once said that there is not a single note she sang during these years that was not perfected by her husband; laughingly she referred to herself as Trilby to his Svengali.

At the Munich Opera, Rysanek appeared successfully in the works of Mozart, Beethoven, Verdi, Wagner, and Richard Strauss. She enjoyed particular distinction as an interpreter of Strauss's leading female roles, not only the more famous roles (Arabella, Chrysothemis in *Elektra,* Salome, the Marschallin in *Der Rosenkavalier,* and Ariadne in *Ariadne auf Naxos*) but also the less familiar ones (Danae in *Die Liebe der Danae,* the Empress in *Die Frau ohne Schatten,* and Helena in *Die Aegyptische Helena*). A Strauss role, that of the Empress in *Die Frau ohne Schatten,* took her for the first time to the Vienna State Opera in 1955 during the festival weeks celebrating the opening of the newly reconstructed opera house. Her success in Vienna was immediate. A correspondent for *The Christian Science Monitor* reported: "To the role of the Empress, Leonie Rysanek, really the great discovery of the Festival, gave a surpassing performance. She possesses one of the most beautiful and best trained voices among the younger generation of singers." When, a decade later, on June 11, 1964, Herbert von Karajan mounted a new production of *Die Frau ohne Schatten* at the Vienna State Opera to commemorate the centenary of Strauss's birth, he was so determined to have Rysanek as the Empress that he dispatched his private car to Stuttgart to pick her up and bring her to Vienna in time for rehearsals. "I rode all night in my costume and make-up so I could make the rehearsal in Vienna in the morning," she recalls.

She made her American debut on September 18, 1956, at the San Francisco Opera in one of her most celebrated roles, that of Senta in *The Flying Dutchman.* Two and a half weeks later, on October 5, she appeared there as Brünnhilde in *Die Walküre.* In both performances she was received with acclaim, and as a result a contract for the Metropolitan Opera was offered her. She turned it down at the time because she was dissatisfied with the roles that Rudolf Bing, the general manager, wished to assign her. The following season, on October 11, 1957, at the San Francisco Opera, she caused another sensation, this time as Lady Macbeth in Verdi's *Macbeth.* When this production moved on to Los Angeles

later the same month, Albert Goldberg noted in the Los Angeles *Times* that she received "one of the longest and stormiest ovations in local history after she had sung the sleep-walking scene." He called it "the climax of a stunning performance" and added: "When power was demanded she rose over the massed ensemble with effortless ease and the musicianly manner in which she adjusted her voice to the concert pieces was sheer delight ... and in the sleep-walking scene she produced a ravishing display of delicate coloration and an exquisite pianissimo."

Lady Macbeth was the role with which she made her New York debut on March 26, 1958, in a concert performance of Verdi's opera by the Little Orchestra Society under Thomas Scherman. And it was as Lady Macbeth that she finally made her first appearance on the stage of the Metropolitan Opera on February 5, 1959, as a replacement for Maria Callas whose contract with the Metropolitan had been summarily canceled after a dispute with Bing. To Howard Taubman, writing in the New York *Times,* her portrayal of Lady Macbeth was "beautifully schooled and controlled." He noted: "Miss Rysanek phrases with the intelligence and sensibility of a musician." She added to the success of her debut performance that season with remarkable portrayals of Aida and of Elisabetta in *Don Carlo.* Winthrop Sargeant in the *New Yorker* regarded her performance as Aida as "the most striking portrayal of the Ethiopian princess that I have witnessed on the Metropolitan's stage in many years."

Following her first season at the Metropolitan, Rysanek further distinguished herself as Senta, Leonora in *La Forza del Destino,* Leonore in *Fidelio,* Elisabeth in *Tannhäuser,* Sieglinde in *Die Walküre,* the Marschallin in *Der Rosenkavalier,* Chrysothemis in *Elektra, Salome,* Desdemona in *Otello, Tosca,* the Empress in *Die Frau ohne Schatten,* Ariadne in *Ariadne auf Naxos,* Amelia in *Un Ballo in Maschera,* Elsa in *Lohengrin* and Abigaille in *Nabucco.* In the last-named role she opened the 1960–1961 season of the Metropolitan Opera on October 24. She celebrated the twentieth anniversary of her affiliation with the Metropolitan Opera during the 1976–1977 season, with appearances as Salome and as Sieglinde in *Die Walküre.* On December 22, 1977, she was heard as Elisabeth in a new production of *Tannhäuser,* the first return of that opera to the Metropolitan in twenty-four years.

She has made numerous appearances at the Bayreuth Festival. In addition to her seasonal appearances as a principal soprano of the Vienna State Opera, where she has been a resident member, she has been heard regularly at Covent Garden in London, La Scala in Milan, the Munich Opera and the Paris Opéra, among other major European opera companies. She made her first tour of the Soviet Union in 1966–1967 with appearances in Moscow and Leningrad in *Die Walküre, Tosca, Fidelio, Otello,* and *Un Ballo in Maschera.* This tour was unusual in that it was not arranged as a cultural exchange but independently, her fees being paid in either Austrian or United States currency. In 1971 she made her debut at the Munich State Opera as Salome. On September 22, 1974, she opened the season of the San Francisco Opera as Salome; in September and October 1976 she was heard there as the Empress in *Die Frau ohne Schatten* and as Tosca and Sieglinde. She assumed for the first time in her career the role of Kundry in *Parsifal* on April 11, 1976, at the Hamburg Opera, and on July 23, 1976, she took on the title role of Cherubini's *Medea* at the Aix-en-Provence festival.

In 1956 she received the honorary title *Kammersängerin* in both Austria and Bavaria. In addition she was decorated with the Austrian Cross, First Class, for Science and Art, was given the Silver Rose of the Vienna Philharmonic, and was made an honorary member of the Vienna State Opera. In 1958 she received the Chappel gold medal for singing in London. San Francisco awarded her a medal in the fall of 1976 for her long association with the San Francisco Opera, an association that began in 1956. France presented her with the Cigale d'Or for her performance as Medea in Cherubini's opera of the same name in August 1976. She was starred in film productions of *Macbeth, Tosca,* and *Aida.*

After divorcing Rudolf Grossmann, Rysanek married musicologist Ernest Ludwig Gausmann on December 23, 1960. Their home is a fifteen-room villa in the Bavarian Alpine village of Altenbeuern, Germany, not far from the Austrian border. There, when on vacation, she indulges in her favorite hobbies of gardening and cooking Viennese delicacies.

ABOUT: New York Herald Tribune, March 5, 1959; New York Times, March 8, 1964, February 6, 1973; Opera News, February 2, 1963, February 12, 1977.

Victor de Sabata

1892–1967

Victor de Sabata, conductor, was born in Trieste on April 10, 1892, the son of the choirmaster of La Scala in Milan. His talent for music revealed itself early. He began playing the piano when he was four; two years after that he made his first attempts at composition. He entered the Milan Conservatory in 1901, remaining there a decade, a student of Michele Saladino and Giacomo Orefice among others. When he was twelve he wrote a scherzo, for orchestra, the premiere of which he himself conducted at the Conservatory.

He was graduated from the Conservatory in 1911 with a gold medal. A year later, his Suite, for orchestra, was introduced at the Augusteo in Rome. During the next three years it received performances in Paris, Brussels, and Russia.

De Sabata began his career as a conductor soon after the end of World War I, with symphonic performances in Monte Carlo, Milan, and Rome. For about a dozen years he served as principal conductor of the Monte Carlo Opera. There he led the world premiere of Ravel's *L'Enfant et les Sortilèges* on March 21, 1925.

His American debut as conductor took place in 1927, as a guest conductor of the Cincinnati Symphony. In 1930 he was appointed first conductor at La Scala in Milan. During the next twenty years he gained an international reputation for his authoritative performances of Verdi's operas, regarded as second only to performances by Toscanini. "Tall, lean and crowned with the head of a Caesar, he conducted in the heaven-storming style that recalled his friend and idol, Arturo Toscanini," commented one unidentified Milanese journalist.

In 1935 and 1936 de Sabata appeared at the June Music Weeks in performances of *Otello* and *Aida.* Reporting to the New York *Times* Herbert Peyser wrote: "De Sabata is a conductor of copious wreathing and even fantastic gestures, but with all their visual extravagance, these gestures

Sabata: sä' bä tä

VICTOR DE SABATA

are so potently evocative, so completely the mirror of the man's burning temperament and exquisite musicality, so perfectly consonant with the results they obtain, that it is impossible to take offense at them. [He] is one of those priceless regents of the operatic orchestra whose resources and routine are so sovereign that, where he controls, nothing conceivably can go wrong."

De Sabata was also heard during these years at the Florence May Music Festival. About his performance there of *Aida,* Pitts Sanborn wrote in the New York *World-Telegram:* "The first phrase of the prelude intoned with a penetrating delicacy, and a fine conduct of the line that Toscanini himself could not surpass, seemed to summon the Egyptian muse from an endless recess of time. Thenceforth, de Sabata played upon his orchestra as a supreme violinist plays upon his Strad. The same absolute control, the same inexhaustible resourcefulness, the same distinguished unerring taste marked this performance."

In the ensuing years, de Sabata conducted the Wagnerian music dramas at the Bayreuth Festival. He was also heard at the Salzburg Festival for a number of years and in guest performances with leading European symphony orchestras. He took the Augusteo Orchestra of Rome, the Berlin Philharmonic, and the London Philharmonic on several European tours.

De Sabata paid a return visit to the United States on November 12, 1948, as a guest conductor of the Pittsburgh Symphony. Indicative of his world fame as a conductor was the fact that two New York newspapers sent their critics to attend his concert. One of them, Francis D. Perkins of the *Herald Tribune,* reported: "One was conscious of a thorough musician. . . . Mr. de Sabata's leadership tonight fully justified the laudatory reports which preceded him from Europe." Olin Downes referred to de Sabata in the New York *Times* as the "foremost virtuoso conductor of today."

In 1949 de Sabata inaugurated the season of the Chicago Symphony, and in 1950 and 1951 he made appearances as a guest conductor of the New York Philharmonic and of the Boston Symphony. Reviewing de Sabata's all-Wagner concert with the New York Philharmonic in 1951, Harold C. Schonberg noted in the New York *Times* that de Sabata "likes big, colorful effects; he handles the orchestra like a primitive painter handles his palette, dabbing violent splotches in every direction."

When de Sabata appeared in London as a guest conductor of the London Philharmonic in May 1948 his performances were acclaimed as some of the greatest since Toscanini's. In October 1950 he returned to London, this time as head of the forces of La Scala in performances of *Otello, Falstaff,* and the Verdi Requiem. The last of these he had also presented earlier that year at the Edinburgh Festival. In 1951 he was named artistic director of La Scala. He retired in 1954 to spend his last years on the Italian Riviera town of Santa Margherita. He died there of a heart attack on December 11, 1967.

De Sabata was also a composer. His works included the tone poems *Juventus* and *Gethsemani.* Their world premieres were conducted by Toscanini. De Sabata's opera *Il Macigno* (later renamed *Driada*) was introduced at La Scala on March 31, 1917.

ABOUT: Mucci, R. Victor de Sabata.

Felix Salmond

1888–1952

Felix Adrian Norman Salmond, cellist, was born in London on November 19, 1888. Both his parents were musical. His father, Norman Salmond, was a well-known baritone, and his mother, a professional pianist. They started Felix's musical education early, first on the violin. Because

FELIX SALMOND

ard Aldrich called him a cellist of "high attainments and not merely in the matter of technique. He has a fervent and impressive style that often reaches a high pitch of intensity and eloquence, qualities that are not reached at the expense of repose and balance or in violation of a sense of the fitness of things."

Salmond soon established his home permanently in the United States. He married Helen Child Curtis with whom he had four children. Over the years he toured the United States frequently in recitals, as guest artist with orchestras, and in sonata recitals with such pianists as Harold Bauer, Ossip Gabrilowitsch, Artur Schnabel, Alfred Cortot, Ignace Jan Paderewski, and Josef Hofmann. In 1937 he formed the Trio of New York with Carl Friedberg and Daniel Karpilowsky.

"He is a master of the finer qualities," Philip Hale, the Boston critic, once wrote of Salmond. "He is warmly emotional without ever sinking into the slough of sentiment. He appeals to the heart as well as to the mind. Nor with all his ability does he stand between the music and his hearers."

Salmond had a long and distinguished career as a teacher of the cello. From 1925 to 1942 he was the head of the cello department at the Curtis Institute of Music in Philadelphia, and from 1925 on he also taught the cello at the Juilliard School of Music in New York. Among his many students through the years were Leonard Rose, Frank Miller, Daniel Saidenberg, Bernard Greenhouse, and Alan Shulman.

Salmond retired from the concert stage in 1949 but continued his teaching assignments at the Juilliard School of Music. He died at his home in New York City on February 19, 1952.

On February 20, 1972, the twentieth anniversary of Salmond's death was commemorated by the Violoncello Society of New York with a concert in New York City in which all the participants had been Salmond's pupils. For this occasion, Alan Shulman wrote an *Elegy,* for cello ensemble.

Apart from music, Salmond enjoyed golf and ocean bathing.

ABOUT: New York Times, February 20, 1952.

of an eye operation, Salmond had to turn to the cello, his oculist maintaining that it was better for his sight to play an instrument that required no oblique movement of the eyes.

As a holder of the all-England Opera Scholarship, Felix entered the Royal College of Music in 1905, studying the cello there with William Edward Whitehouse. After four years at the college, he continued his cello studies in Brussels with Édouard Jacobs.

In October 1909 Salmond made his concert debut in London at Bechstein Hall (later renamed Wigmore Hall), with his mother as his piano accompanist. His success brought him engagements as a soloist with England's major orchestras. These appearances and performances in chamber music concerts and recitals brought him to a top position among English cellists. He was a member of the chamber music ensemble that gave the world premieres of Elgar's String Quartet and Piano Quintet at Wigmore Hall in May 1919; and on October 27, 1919, he gave the world premiere of Elgar's Cello Concerto as a soloist of the London Symphony Orchestra, the composer conducting. From 1919 to 1921 he was the cellist of the Chamber Music Players in England. Over a period of many years he also collaborated with Lionel Tertis, Albert Sammons, and William Murdoch in performances of piano quartets.

He made his first tour of the Continent in 1921. On March 29, 1922, he made his American debut with a recital at Aeolian Hall, in New York. Reporting in the New York *Times,* Rich-

Carlos Salzedo

1885–1961

No musician of the twentieth century has been more influential in developing the harp as a solo instrument than Carlos Salzedo. He accomplished this not only as a harp virtuoso but also as a composer, transcriber, teacher, and designer of instruments.

Carlos Salzedo (originally Leon Salzédo), was born at Arcachon, France, on April 6, 1885. His father, Gaston Salzédo, was a teacher of voice who became professor at the Paris Conservatory; his mother, Anna Silva Salzédo, had been a court pianist to the Spanish royal family. Carlos began studying the piano at the age of four, and at five he began making concert appearances as a prodigy. Queen María Cristina of Spain called him "my little Mozart." His father decided to curtail Carlos's concert work to allow him to devote himself more completely to music study. From 1891 to 1894, Salzedo attended the Bordeaux Conservatory. There he received first prize in piano. He started harp lessons when he was eleven and from that time on divided his dedication and efforts equally between the harp and the piano. At the Paris Conservatory he studied the piano with Charles de Bériot and harp with Hasselmans. On graduation in 1901, he received first prizes in both harp and piano. This was said to have been unparalleled in the history of that conservatory.

He began his career as a concert harpist in 1901 with performances throughout Europe, at many of which he divided his program between the piano and the harp. From 1905 to 1909 he was the solo harpist of the Association des Premiers Prix de Paris in Monte Carlo.

In 1909 he was invited to the United States by Toscanini and by Gatti-Casazza, the general manager of the Metropolitan Opera, to become first harpist of that opera house's orchestra. He resigned from this position in 1913 to devote himself completely to a career as virtuoso, after having appeared in 1912 in a New York City concert devoted entirely to music transcribed for the harp. Soon after his resignation from the Metropolitan Opera, he helped to organize the

---

Salzedo: säl zā′ dō

CARLOS SALZEDO

Trio de Lutèce, with flutist Georges Barrère and cellist Paul Kéfer.

During World War I Salzedo served in the French army. At this time he wrote choruses for the French troops which were later performed in New York by the Schola Cantorum. Honorably discharged in 1917, he returned to the United States where he became a citizen in 1923. In 1917 he began his lifelong dedication to promoting the harp as a significant medium of solo musical expression. In recitals, as guest artist with symphony orchestras, and in chamber music concerts he emerged as a harp virtuoso with few if any rivals. Maurice Rosenfeld, the Chicago music critic, called him "a master of the purely technical aspects and dynamic resources of the harp," and added, "He has also some original ideas as to its inherent properties in regard to musical qualities and tone variants." In the Boston *Transcript,* Henry Taylor Parker maintained that "there is no harpist like Salzedo." In the New York *Times,* Olin Downes referred to him as "a miracle worker." And Walter Damrosch, who was then conductor of the New York Symphony Society, was quoted as having said: "I do not think there is a man living today who is a greater exponent of the harp than Salzedo."

Salzedo became active as a propagandist for the harp in more ways than just by performing on it. In 1917 he organized a novel type of musical organization, The Salzedo Harp Ensemble, which gave performances throughout the United States. In 1920 he was elected president of the National Association of Artists. In 1931 he organized a summer harp colony at Camden, Maine, that for many years attracted young harpists from all over the United States as well as from foreign countries. He supervised this colony in collaboration with his wife, Marjorie Call, herself a gifted harpist, whom he married in April 1939. In 1932 he organized the Barrère-Salzedo-Britt Trio which specialized in the presentation of unusual and rarely performed old and new music. With Call he formed the Salzedo Harp Duo for joint recitals.

As a teacher of the harp, his influence was felt by an entire generation of young performers, many of whom graduated into concert work to carry on his mission of extending the importance of the harp as a solo instrument. Salzedo founded and organized the harp department at the Curtis Institute of Music in Philadelphia in 1924. There, and later on at the Juilliard School of Music in New York, he taught the harp until the end of his life.

He further extended the influence of the harp by composing numerous works for it which gained wide circulation among harpists. His tone poem, *The Enchanted Isle,* has a significant harp obbligato. It was introduced by the Chicago Symphony on November 28, 1919. Another major work, the Concerto for Harp and Seven Wind Instruments, had its premiere at a concert of the League of Composers in New York on April 17, 1927. Salzedo also produced a library of shorter pieces for the harp and transcribed for that instrument compositions by Bach, Corelli, Rameau, Haydn, and Brahms, among other composers.

As a theoretician, Salzedo published *The Modern Study of the Harp* (1921) and *Method for the Harp* (1929). In collaboration with Lucile Lawrence he published the treatise *The Art of Modulating* (1950).

Salzedo was also interested in the construction of the harp. At the eighth annual National Harp Festival in Philadelphia on March 29, 1928, he demonstrated a new model he had perfected. In comparison with this new harp the old standard model was said to be "as an ox to an airplane." It was due to his efforts that the traditional gold of the instrument has been for the most part replaced by a maple with a high finish. This "Salzedo model" developed in collaboration with the designer Witold Gordon was manufactured by Lyon & Healy in Chicago from 1931 to 1954.

"Salzedo has done for the harp what Bach did for the organ, Paganini for the violin, Chopin, Liszt and Debussy for the piano," said Leopold Stokowski in 1957, "which is to enlarge the technical and expressive potentialities of their chosen instruments. This was urgently needed for the harp, because so few composers understand the true musical personalities of the harp, but write for it as if it were a piano. Salzedo's contribution to harp music for solo and symphonic music is of great aesthetic value, and so far in my opinion little understood."

Salzedo played an all-important role in providing forums for the publication, promotion, and performance of new music in the 1920s. In 1921 he was the cofounder (with Edgard Varèse) of the International Composers Guild, and in the same year he brought into being the music magazine *Eolus,* which continued publication for over a decade. He was also vice president of the International Society for Contemporary Music, organizer in 1927 of the United States section of the International Society for Contemporary Music, one of the founders of the Pan American Association of Composers (also in 1927), and a charter member of the American Composers' Alliance.

He was married three times; each marriage ended in divorce. He lived during the winter in an apartment on Riverside Drive in New York; his summers were spent in Camden, Maine. Each place showed his gift for interior decoration, and the Maine house, built for him by the architect Jules Bouy, profited greatly from Salzedo's ideas about construction. Photography was another of his hobbies.

Salzedo made his last public appearance in 1959 in New York City. In August 1961 he went to Colby College, in Waterville, Maine, to serve as a judge in the Metropolitan Auditions of the Air, New England section. He was walking to the college music building after lunch when he collapsed and died of a heart attack on August 17, 1961.

ABOUT: Harp News, Fall, 1961; International Musician, October 1961; Musical America, October 1961.

Samaroff

Olga Samaroff

1882–1948

Olga Samaroff (originally Lucie Mary Olga Agnes Hickenlooper), pianist, was born in San Antonio, Texas, on August 8, 1882, to Carlos and Jane Loening Hickenlooper. Her father was an auditor of Dutch descent, and her mother was a trained musician. On both sides, Olga's family dated back to America's colonial days. While attending the Ursuline Convent in Galveston, Texas, for her academic schooling, Olga received her first piano lessons from both her grandmother, Lucie Palmer (once a concert pianist), and her mother. Her progress convinced the composer Edward MacDowell and other well-known musicians for whom she auditioned that her talent warranted the best and most thorough training. They urged that she be sent to Europe. In 1894, in the company of her grandmother, Olga went to Paris. After a year of preliminary study with Antoine-François Marmontel, Charles-Marie Widor, and Ludovic Breitner, she became, in 1896, the first American woman ever to win a scholarship for the Paris Conservatory. When she went for her first lesson in the class of Élie Miriam Delaborde he greeted her by saying: "You are American, are you? Why do you try to play the piano? Americans are not meant to be musicians." She studied at the Paris Conservatory for about two years. Her home was the Convent of the Holy Sacrament on avenue Malakoff where she received her academic education.

Olga completed her piano studies in Berlin with Ernest Hutcheson and Ernst Jedliczka and studied organ with Hugo Riemann and composition with Otis Boise. She then faced the choice of a career in music or matrimony. "True to the psychology of my upbringing," she says in her autobiography *An American Musician's Story,* "I chose matrimony." In 1900 she married Boris Loutzky, a Russian engineer. For the next three and a half years, she and her husband lived in Berlin and St. Petersburg. Then the marriage ended in a legal divorce, followed by a papal annulment in 1904. She turned to music as a way of earning a living.

Acquiring an American manager, Henry

OLGA SAMAROFF

Wolfsohn, she resumed the name of Samaroff, making it legally hers once more, and made her American debut at Carnegie Hall in New York on January 18, 1905, as soloist with the New York Symphony Society under Walter Damrosch in a program that included two concertos (the Schumann Concerto and the Liszt Concerto in E-flat major) and a group of solo pieces. "I remember very little about the concert," she has said. "I was so dazed by nervousness that it seemed—even the following day—as though someone else had played." Nevertheless, she did remarkably well. "Mme. Samaroff showed that she possessed the endurance and the power to carry it through," wrote Richard Aldrich in the New York *Times,* "and the skill to play the music correctly. She is a painstaking and resolute player; her technique is well developed in certain lines, and she showed last evening that she has a good understanding of most of the outward requirements of the music she attempted and a sincere desire to meet them."

It took a number of years for Samaroff to mature musically and to combine her brilliant technique with a sense of poetic, dramatic, lyrical expressiveness. This maturing process took place under a new American manager, Charles A. Ellis. He shepherded her to her first European appearance (her first public recital anywhere) at Steinway Hall in London in 1905; to the performance of the Tchaikovsky Concerto with the Boston Symphony under Karl Muck in April 1906; to recitals in the United States and Europe; to sonata concerts with Fritz Kreisler

---

Samaroff: sä mä′ rŏf

718

and with Efrem Zimbalist. Her tone grew increasingly richer, the delivery of musical phrases increasingly subtle, and her concept of the musical masterworks increasingly penetrating. The years between 1906 and 1911 she has said were "happy and prosperous." She performed with virtually every major orchestra in the United States and made debuts "under the best auspices" with the Colonne Orchestra in Paris and at the Konzertverein in Vienna. She also began to make her first recordings. By 1911 she was ranked not only with the great women pianists of her time but in the top echelon of the world's virtuosos.

On April 24, 1911, she married Leopold Stokowski, then the conductor of the Cincinnati Symphony but soon to become conductor of the Philadelphia Orchestra. In order to devote herself more completely to her husband's career and to the raising of their daughter, Sonya Maria Noël, Samaroff withdrew from the concert stage for two years. But in 1913 she resumed her appearances in America and Europe.

The years of World War I were spent in Seal Harbor, Maine, in a colony of musicians that included Kreisler, Godowsky, Gabrilowitsch, Harold Bauer, and Josef Hofmann. By the time the war was over she realized that "unclouded domesticity was not to be my lot in life." In 1923 she and Stokowski were divorced. She acquired a permanent residence in Seal Harbor, Maine, a cottage perched on the side of the hill with a bungalow below that she used as her studio. Here she spent her summers. Winters were passed in a New York apartment.

She remained active as a concert pianist until 1925. At that time she injured her hand and was compelled to cancel a projected concert tour. After her recovery, rather than return to the rigors of concert life, she decided to direct her musical gifts into other channels. In 1925 she joined the piano faculty of the Juilliard School. There she continued to teach the piano for the remainder of her life; her many pupils have included William Kapell, Rosalyn Tureck, and Eugene List. In 1928 she supplemented this teaching activity in New York by becoming head of the piano department of the Philadelphia Conservatory. She held this post for a decade.

She also achieved renown as a lecturer on music appreciation, giving lectures over a period of many years under the auspices of the Layman's Music Courses, Incorporated, as well as at the David Mannes School of Music, at Town Hall in New York, and in halls in Philadelphia and Washington, D.C. She was also heard as guest lecturer on music at Harvard, Yale, University of Minnesota, Washington University, and the Curtis Institute of Music in Philadelphia. She crystallized her ideas on music appreciation in several books, the most successful of which was *The Layman's Music Book* (1935) which in its enlarged and revised edition in 1947 (retitled *The Listener's Music Book*) became a best seller. She was also the author of *The Magic World of Music* (1936), *A Musical Manual* (1937), and an autobiography, *An American Musician's Story* (1939).

For two years, from 1926 to 1928, she was the music critic of the New York *Evening Post*. In 1928, in honor of the centennial commemoration of Franz Schubert's death, she helped found the Schubert Memorial to provide funds for young artists to make their debuts with symphony orchestras. For musicians victimized by the depression years of the early 1930s she helped to form the Musicians' Emergency Fund in 1931. She was also an officer of the Beethoven Association in New York and of the International Society for Contemporary Music.

In 1936 she was selected as one of three American delegates to the International Music Education Conference in Prague. Two years later she was sent by the State Department to represent the United States at the Concours International Eugène Ysaÿe in Brussels, then recently organized by the Queen Mother Elisabeth of Belgium. She earned honorary doctorates in music from the University of Pennsylvania in 1931 and the Cincinnati Conservatory of Music in 1943.

Olga Samaroff died in her New York City apartment on May 17, 1948. Her students established the Olga Samaroff Memorial Fund in her honor to provide housing in New York for needy music students.

ABOUT: Samaroff, O. An American Musician's Story. *Periodicals*—Etude, September 1948; Musical America, June 1948; New York Times, May 18, 1948.

Sir Malcolm Sargent

1895–1967

SIR MALCOLM SARGENT

Malcolm Sargent (originally Harold Malcolm Watts Sargent), conductor, was born in Stamford, Lincolnshire, England, on April 29, 1895, the son of Henry Edward Sargent, a church organist. By the time he was ten Malcolm knew that he wanted to follow in his father's footsteps and become an organist. He began his music study in his native town while attending the Stamford School. There he made his first attempt at conducting when he replaced an indisposed director in a school production of *The Gondoliers* by Gilbert and Sullivan. His musical education was continued at the Royal College of Organists in London from which he was graduated in 1910 with the Sawyer Prize. From 1911 to 1914, he was articled to Dr. Haydn Keeton, the organist of Peterborough Cathedral.

In 1914 Malcolm was appointed organist of the Melton Mowbray Parish Church in London. He retained this post for a decade, but temporarily left it during World War I to serve with the 27th Durham Light Infantry. After the war, in 1919, he received a doctorate in music from Durham University, becoming the youngest doctor of music in Great Britain. From 1919 to 1921 he studied piano privately with Benno Moiseiwitsch.

In his autobiography, Sir Henry J. Wood reveals that in or about 1921 Sargent came to him "to ask my advice about taking up conducting. . . . I was left in no doubt that he could easily become a first rate conductor. It pleases me to think that I was right in advising him to give up the piano."

Sargent's bow as a mature conductor took place in 1921, when, through Wood's influence, he led a performance of his own composition, *Impressions on a Windy Day,* at a Promenade Concert at Queen's Hall in London. His growing interest in conducting soon led him to give it first priority in his life over and above composing or playing the piano or the organ. In 1922 he organized an orchestra in Leicester for which he served as music director for eleven years. In 1924 he was made conductor of the British National Opera company where, on July 14, 1924, he introduced Vaughan Williams's *Hugh the Drover* and, on April 3, 1925, Gustav Holst's *At*

the *Boar's Head.* These were the first of many world premieres of English music for which he was responsible.

In 1924 Sargent took over the leadership of the Robert Mayer Concerts for children in London which, because of him, generated an increased interest in good music among children. A year later he was invited by the Royal Philharmonic Orchestra of London to direct a program of English music including Vaughan Williams's *Pastoral Symphony* and the premiere of Herbert Howell's Piano Concerto No.2.

In 1926 Sargent led performances of the Gilbert and Sullivan comic operas with the D'Oyly Carte Opera Company, to which he returned for additional seasons in 1929, 1951, and 1961. In 1926 and 1927 he conducted the Llandudno Orchestra (North Wales), from 1927 to 1930 he appeared as a conductor of the Diaghilev Ballet Russe, and in 1929 he became the head of the Courtauld-Sargent concerts which gave an annual series in London for the next eleven years. In 1929 he was appointed music director of the Royal Choral Society, with which, for a number of years, he gave annual presentations of Samuel Coleridge-Taylor's *Hiawatha* as a stage pageant, as well as performances of the outstanding oratorios of the masters. In the early 1930s Artur Schnabel chose Sargent to conduct the accompaniments for his recording of the five Beethoven piano concertos.

In the 1930s Sargent began to assume the position of eminence in English music that he retained until the end of his life, becoming involved with England's orchestras and festivals and responsible for the premieres of many major new English compositions. He was heard at festivals in Edinburgh, Norwich, Bradford, and Leeds over a period of many years. At the Leeds Festival he gave the world premiere of William Walton's oratorio *Belshazzar's Feast,* on October 31, 1931. As a guest conductor of the London Philharmonic on October 10, 1932, he was heard in the premiere of Bohuslav Martinu's Quartet for Strings and Orchestra.

Sargent directed the Hallé Orchestra in Manchester from 1939 to 1943, and the Liverpool Philharmonic from 1942 to 1948. In Liverpool he offered the premiere of Vaughan Williams's Concerto for Oboe and Orchestra on September 30, 1946. From 1947 until his death, he was the principal conductor of the Promenade concerts in London, and from 1950 to 1957 he was the music director of the BBC Symphony in succession to Sir Adrian Boult. With the BBC Symphony he programmed the world premieres of Ernest Bloch's *Sinfonia Breve* and his Concerto Grosso No.2 on April 11, 1953. As a guest conductor of the London Symphony on June 17, 1951, he led the premiere of Alan Rawsthorne's Piano Concerto No.2 that had been commissioned for the Festival of Great Britain. Among Sargent's premieres after that were those of William Walton's opera *Troilus and Cressida* at Covent Garden in London on December 3, 1954, and Vaughan Williams's Symphony No.9 on April 2, 1958.

On his tours of the world Sargent was regarded as an ambassador of English music because of his lifelong dedication to it and his authority as its interpreter. From 1937 to 1939 he conducted the Palestine Symphony Orchestra in Palestine. He toured New Zealand in 1936, Australia six times between 1936 and 1962, Scandinavia and South Africa in 1956, the Soviet Union in 1957, countries behind the Iron Curtain in 1958, and South America and the Far East in 1962.

He made his first appearance in the United States as a guest conductor of the NBC Symphony on February 18, 1945. Olin Downes in the New York *Times* described his performance as "properly lusty and rhythmical.... Mr. Sargent had unmistakable orchestral control. ... The conductor's sincerity, knowledge, zest in his task were communicated."

He returned to the United States many times after that as a guest conductor of major American orchestras. In 1963 he went on a tour of the United States and Canada with the visiting Royal Philharmonic Orchestra of London. In 1964 and 1965 he was the guest conductor of the New York Philharmonic Orchestra in New York and of the Promenade concerts at the Lincoln Center for the Performing Arts. In these American appearances, Sargent proved himself a distinguished performer of a far more varied repertory than just English music. To classical literature he brought clarity of texture and sensitivity of style; to the Romantics, passionate ardor and intensity.

For many years, beginning with the early 1920s, Sargent taught conducting at the Royal College of Music. In 1923 he married Eileen Laura Harding. They lived in London and there raised their son, Peter. Sargent once revealed that his three favorite forms of recreation were to visit the zoo, attend the theater, and ride horseback.

During World War II, Sargent conducted numerous concerts for workers, frequently during air raids. When he went for the last time to the United States, in June 1966, he still appeared as the dapper, well-groomed, and spry man he had been years earlier. "Tall, slender, ramrod-straight and handsome," was the way the New York *Times* described him. A white carnation in his buttonhole was always part of his immaculate grooming.

While preparing for his twenty-first season of Promenade concerts in London during the summer of 1967, Sargent fell ill. Operated on for an acute biliary obstruction on July 26, 1967, he recovered sufficiently to be able to take a bow on the final night of the Promenade season. He died less than three months later at his home in London, on October 3, 1967.

For his services to English music he was knighted in 1947. The same year he was also presented with the St. Olav medal. In 1959 he was awarded the gold medal of the Royal Philharmonic Society. He was made Knight Commander of the Swedish Order of the Star of the North (1956), received the Finnish Star and Collar of Knight Commander of the Order of the White Rose (1965), and became Chevalier of the French Legion of Honor (1967).

ABOUT: Blaukopf, K. Great Conductors; Brook, D. International Gallery of Conductors; Reid, C. Sir Malcolm Sargent: A Biography. *Periodicals*—Newsweek,

Sawallisch

February 26, 1945; New York Times, October 4, 1967; Time, February 26, 1945.

WOLFGANG SAWALLISCH

Wolfgang Sawallisch

1923–

Wolfgang Sawallisch, conductor, was born in Munich, on August 26, 1923. He began to study the piano when he was five. At eleven he knew he wanted to become a conductor after attending a performance of *Hansel and Gretel* in Munich. What had fascinated him most during that performance was not what was happening on the stage but what was happening on the conductor's podium. He attended the Wittelsbaucher High School of Music, and later the Conservatory of Munich, from which he was graduated in 1946. There he specialized in piano and composition with Wolfgang Ruoff and Hans Sachse.

During World War II he saw military service in the German army; in the latter part of the war he was confined in Italy as a prisoner. When the war ended, he acquired a post as coach and chorusmaster at the Augsburg Stadttheater where he made his first appearance as conductor in 1947. He remained in Augsburg seven years, eventually taking on the post of principal conductor. In his last year he made a guest appearance with the Berlin Philharmonic, the youngest man to lead that organization in a major concert.

From 1953 to 1957 Sawallisch was the music director of the Aachen Opera. His performances of the Wagnerian music dramas at that theater brought him an invitation to appear at the Bayreuth Festival in 1957 in a new production of *Tristan and Isolde.* He scored a resounding success, repeating the achievement there in 1959 with his performance of a new production of *The Flying Dutchman* and in 1960 with a new production of *Tannhäuser.*

After leaving Aachen, he held the post of music director of the Wiesbaden Opera, from 1957 to 1959, and of the Cologne Opera, from 1959 to 1963. While at Cologne he also taught a conducting class at the Cologne Academy of Music.

For over a decade, beginning with 1960, Sawallisch distinguished himself in symphonic music as music director of the Hamburg Philharmonic Orchestra; and for a decade he was

principal conductor of the Vienna Symphony Orchestra.

He made his first appearances in the United States in February 1964 at the head of the visiting Vienna Symphony Orchestra, impressing American audiences during a five-week tour with his authoritative performances of the German repertory. His was a keen and incisive musical mind, a commanding and dynamic presence on the podium demonstrating a thorough mastery of conducting technique. Not until March 1966 did he appear for the first time as a guest conductor of an American symphonic organization, directing the Philadelphia Orchestra in Philadelphia and New York.

In 1969 he was appointed music director of the Munich State Opera. There, in 1972, he led the world premiere of *Sim Tjong,* an opera by the Korean composer Isang Yun. In the summer of 1976 he directed in Munich a new production of the Wagner *Ring* cycle to commemorate the centenary of its premiere.

Sawallisch's European experiences have included performances at festivals in Bayreuth, Vienna, Edinburgh, Bregenz, Salzburg, and Montreux and guest appearances with major European orchestras and with opera companies such as La Scala in Milan and the Vienna State Opera. In 1973 he was named artistic director of the Suisse Romande Orchestra in Geneva.

In addition to his conducting duties with the Munich State Opera, Sawallisch has been teaching classes in conducting at the Conservatory of Munich.

722

In recognition of his musical achievements he was awarded the Austrian Ehrenkreuz für Kunst und Wissenschaft.

With his wife, Mechthild—whom he met in 1939 when he was coaching a production of *The Magic Flute* in which she appeared as Pamina—he makes his home in Grassau, in the Federal Republic of Germany. The Sawallisches have one child. Sawallisch enjoys being a handyman around the house, fixing watches, radios, and electrical appliances.

ABOUT: New York Times, February 16, 1964.

BIDÚ SAYÃO

Bidú Sayão

1902–

Bidú Sayão (originally Balduina de Oliveira Sayão), soprano, was born in Rio de Janeiro on May 11, 1902, to Pedro de Oliveira and María José Costa Sayão. Both parents were of Brazilian birth. Her father was a successful banana planter. "As a little girl," she once recalled, "I was mad about the theater. I had an uncle, a physician, who also had a passion for the arts. He was a talented verse-maker and composer. He used to write monologues for me which I would recite at performances for charities."

The death of her father, when she was not yet five, was a traumatic experience. She became an unruly child. But her mother, a singer, did her best to control her, and to direct her to music. The first attempts to teach her the piano were unsuccessful. But she was more amenable to her uncle's suggestion that she be directed to the theater. This was vigorously rejected by the mother who considered acting a dishonorable profession. But singing was something the mother could encourage. When she was about thirteen, Bidú began studying voice with Helena Theodorini, three times a week, for four years.

When Theodorini retired from teaching and decided to go to Bucharest, she induced young Bidú Sayão to go with her to be presented to Queen Marie. In Bucharest, Sayão made her debut, singing at a reception for Queen Marie, for European royalty, and for the crown prince of Japan (who later became Emperor Hirohito). The queen presented Bidú with her signed por-

trait and a pin decorated with her crown and regimental emblem.

From Romania, Sayão went on to France where she sang for Jean de Reszke in Vichy and then studied with him at his home in Nice from 1923 to 1925. He gave her a comprehensive training in operatic literature, going through, as she has said, "entire operas, singing and acting all the parts, and even giving the illusion of a stage full of people, through dramatic power."

She made her concert debut at the Teatro Municipal in Rio de Janeiro in 1925. One year later, she made her bow in opera at the Teatro Reale in Rome as Rosina in *The Barber of Seville*. The legendary prima donna, Tetrazzini, provided Sayão with all of her own vocal cadenzas for the principal coloratura arias and was in a box at the debut. It has been rumored that when Sayão's mother discovered that her daughter was to make her opera debut, she rushed to Rome to prevent its taking place. But Bidú was adamant, and a compromise was reached. If the Rome debut proved successful, Bidú would be permitted to follow an artistic career without further interference; if not, she would have to return to Brazil and forget about a professional life in music.

Her debut was a major success and she received engagements from the Paris Opéra, La Scala in Milan, San Carlo in Naples, the Carlo Felice in Genoa, and major opera houses of Brazil and Argentina. For several seasons she was a permanent member of the Opéra-Comique in Paris. During these years she was acclaimed

Sayão: sä yä′ ō

both in bel canto operas *(Lucia di Lammermoor, The Barber of Seville, I Puritani, La Sonnambula)* and in the French repertory *(Lakmé, Manon, Romeo and Juliet).* She became a favorite in the French capital and was referred to as "the Brazilian nightingale." In 1936 the Société Française pour le Radio arranged a special broadcast of *Lakmé* for Brazil, with Sayão in the title role.

Her American debut took place with a recital at Town Hall, New York, on December 29, 1935. "Her voice, if light, was one of pronounced sweetness, silky and caressing when used at its best," noted a critic for the New York *Times.* "The tones were too small to achieve brilliance in florid passages. But the scale was one of exceptional evenness throughout its compass."

Early in 1936 Sayão returned to the United States, this time as a tourist. In New York she met Arturo Toscanini who recalled that some years earlier she had sung for him at an audition at La Scala. He informed her he was searching for a soprano to sing in a performance of Debussy's *La Damoiselle Élue* and inquired if she was interested. Told she did not know the music, Toscanini said firmly: "Then go home and learn it, and we'll begin rehearsals next week." That performance took place at a concert of the New York Philharmonic on April 16, 1936, at which time Danton Walker wrote in the *News:* "The little Brazilian soprano has not only the slim figure and cherubic face for such a role, but her voice is of an exquisitely sensuous quality."

Her debut at the Metropolitan Opera followed on February 13, 1937, in the title role of *Manon*—the first Brazilian woman to assume a major role at this opera house. "The crown of this performance . . . was the Manon of Miss Sayão," reported Olin Downes in the New York *Times.* "The tone is lovely and fresh, and the artist has genuine sensibility. She observed every nuance of expression and she made the woman real."

Since coloratura roles were the property of Lily Pons at that time, Sayão was assigned only lyric soprano roles for a while. But on March 4, 1938, she sang the role of Rosina; on December 21, 1940, the part of Norina in *Don Pasquale;* and on November 28, 1941, Adina in *L'Elisir d'Amore.* In addition, during her fourteen years at the Metropolitan Opera, she sang the following roles: Gilda in *Rigoletto,* Violetta in *La Traviata,* Mimi in *La Bohème,* Juliet in *Romeo*

and *Juliet,* Susanna in *The Marriage of Figaro,* Serpina in Pergolesi's *La Serva Padrona,* Zerlina in *Don Giovanni,* and Mélisande in *Pelléas and Mélisande.*

During her affiliation with the Metropolitan Opera, Sayão made numerous guest appearances in South America. She also gave many recitals and was often heard over the American radio. Heitor Villa-Lobos composed for her his famous *Bachianas Brasileiras No. 5,* which she introduced and which she recorded for Columbia.

In 1947 she married Giuseppe Danise, an opera tenor who was a member of the Metropolitan Opera company from 1920 to 1932. They had an apartment in New York City. Slim, short, dimpled, with dark eyes, olive-colored skin, and hair of flaming red-brown color, Sayão in the 1930s and 1940s was as much a joy to the eye as to the ear. As an escape from the rigors of a professional career she sewed and cooked. Her passion was jewelry, of which she had an excellent collection. In addition to family heirlooms and her personal acquisitions, this collection included a diamond pin presented to her by the Italian Crown Prince, a diamond-encrusted Palmes Académiques given her by the French government, and a gold insignia which was the symbol of her honorary status as a colonel in the late Queen of Romania's own regiment.

Sayão's last public appearance took place in 1957 in the concert hall, in a performance of Debussy's *La Demoiselle Élue.* "After *Demoiselle,*" she told Robert Jacobson in *Opera News,* "I cancelled everything. Suddenly you are nobody, with no interest, no glamor, and you feel emptiness around you." But she did sing once more, on records, performing Villa-Lobos' *Forest of the Amazon* at the composer's request. "It was the last thing I did—and his last work." After that she went into retirement in Maine. When her house burned down with all her belongings, she found a new home in a New York City apartment on 57th Street.

In commemoration of the thirty-fifth anniversary of her debut at the Metropolitan Opera, her Cours-la-Reine costume in *Manon* was exhibited at the Belmont Room of the Metropolitan Opera in 1972. At that time she was honored with a reception at which she was decorated Commandate by the Brazilian government. For this anniversary Odyssey Records released a commemorative disk with Sayão singing arias by Mozart, Leoncavallo, Gounod, and Puccini. "It shows," said William Livingstone in discussing this recording in *Stereo Review,* "her mastery of the beauty of tone, smooth legato and elegant phrasing that are the hallmarks of bel canto style." The four arias from *Manon* in this album "preserve the gaiety, coquettishness, fragility, and pathos she brought to one of her most beguiling impersonations."

ABOUT: Life, March 31, 1941; Opera News, November 10, 1941, March 5, 1977; Stereo Review, May 1976.

Hermann Scherchen

1891–1966

Hermann Scherchen, conductor, whose career was a lifelong crusade for twentieth century music, was born in Berlin on June 21, 1891. For the most part he was self-taught in music. When he was fifteen he was employed as a violinist in a Berlin café-house. From 1907 to 1910 he played the viola in the Berlin Philharmonic where he had an opportunity to study at first hand the techniques of some of the world's successful conductors, among whom were Arthur Nikisch and Richard Strauss. He had his first opportunity to conduct when he was twenty, leading a concert of the Berlin Philharmonic. One year later he assisted Arnold Schoenberg in the preparation and performance of Schoenberg's *Pierrot Lunaire,* a concert that took place in Berlin on October 16, 1912. This early affiliation with Schoenberg marked not only the beginnings of Scherchen's passionate advocacy of the music of the Viennese expressionist school (Schoenberg, Alban Berg, Anton Webern) but also of his total dedication to the advancement of twentieth century musical idioms and procedures.

He was conducting symphony concerts in Riga in 1914 when World War I engulfed Europe. He was interned in Russia. With the war's end, he returned to Berlin where he organized the Scherchen String Quartet which gave noteworthy concerts of chamber music. He also associated himself with many of the younger and more experimental composers of the post-World War I period and became their spokesman. In 1918 he founded the Neue Musikgesellschaft, an organization promoting and sponsoring new

Scherchen: shĕr′ kĕn

HERMANN SCHERCHEN

works by the younger school of German composers. In 1920 he brought into being *Melos,* a fortnightly magazine devoted to modern music, which he edited for a year.

In 1920 and 1925 he conducted the New Grotrian-Steinweg Orchestra in Leipzig. In 1922 he succeeded Wilhelm Furtwängler as principal conductor of the Museum Concerts in Frankfort. These programs became the forum for the younger and lesser-known composers of the twentieth century. One of Scherchen's premieres was that of *Three Fragments* from Alban Berg's expressionist opera *Wozzeck,* which he introduced on June 11, 1924. At his urging Berg had extracted three symphonic episodes from his opera for use at orchestral concerts. In Frankfort, Scherchen demonstrated his interest in American music by performing the world premiere of the *American Symphonic Suite* of Walter Stockhoff on December 10, 1924. During this period Scherchen also participated in festivals of modern music at Donaueschingen in Germany, where in 1925 he led the world premiere of Alexander Tcherepnin's *Chamber Concerto,* Op.33.

After various other appointments and assignments as conductor, Scherchen became the music director, in 1928, of the Königsberg Philharmonic Orchestra and the Königsberg Radio. Still the staunch advocate of the new in music, he affiliated himself with the International Society for Contemporary Music, at whose festivals he conducted the orchestra for many years. It was at one of these events, in Barcelona, that he directed the world premiere of Alban

Berg's Violin Concerto on April 19, 1936. At another festival, this one in Frankfort, he led a production of Luigi Dallapiccola's opera *Il Prigioniero,* on June 30, 1951.

When the Nazis came to power in 1933, Scherchen left Germany to settle in Switzerland. He conducted the concerts of the Collegium Musicum in Winterthur for six years as principal conductor, and for many years after that he served as its guest conductor. In Winterthur he introduced many new works. Among them were Miaskovsky's Symphony No.13 (October 6, 1943) and Anton Webern's *Variations for Orchestra* (March 3, 1943). With the Winterthur Orchestra he made numerous recordings of the standard Baroque, classical, and Romantic repertory which were responsible for extending his fame outside Switzerland. He also formed an orchestra of his own, called Ars Viva, dedicated mainly to modern music; it gave provocative concerts in Vienna and Italy. From 1944 to 1950 he was the music director of the Swiss Radio in Zurich and Beromünster. In 1950 in Zurich he organized a publishing house, Ars Viva, for the publication of new music.

He continued to devote himself assiduously to the music of his times during the 1950s. At the Berlin Music Festival he led a significant revival of Boris Blacher's expressionist opera *Abstract Opera No.1* in 1957, and in 1958, the world premiere of Humphrey Searle's one-act opera *The Diary of a Madman.* His performances of Schoenberg's opera *Moses and Aron* in Milan, Venice, Berlin, and Paris (following its world premiere in 1957 which he had not conducted) were largely responsible for drawing world attention to this remarkable work. In his book *On the Nature of Music,* the English musicologist Edward J. Dent maintained that to no other conductor did contemporary composers owe so profound a debt as to Scherchen.

In the early 1950s he made for himself a new home, in a seventeenth century farmhouse nestling at the foot of the mountain at Gravesano, Ticino, Switzerland. In 1954 he opened on his grounds three electronic-acoustical laboratories to explore the possibilities of electronic music. To these laboratories he invited composers, engineers, performers, and acousticians to discuss problems of electronic music. In conjunction with these studios he also created in 1954 a journal, *Gravesano Blätter,* devoted exclusively

to avant-garde music in general and electronic music in particular.

Scherchen devoted a large part of his energy to teaching conducting: at a summer school which he founded in Switzerland in 1939; and later, after World War II, in master classes in Venice. To his students, Scherchen always emphasized the importance of mastering a musical score completely—mentally, acoustically, technically—before attempting a performance. In his own case, he not only demanded of himself a complete command of the musical score but also intensive research into manuscripts, first editions, and other original sources as well as the musical findings of contemporaries to arrive at an authentic evaluation and comprehension of the composer's intentions. Thus, in 1953, in his recording of Handel's *Messiah* with the London Philharmonic Orchestra and the London Philharmonic Choir, he made the first attempt since 1742 to recreate the original Dublin performance with smaller forces than those generally employed today and following more strictly along the lines of Handel's own conception. And in his recordings of the *London* symphonies of Haydn, Scherchen took full advantage of the valuable musicological researches made by H. C. Robbins Landon.

Scherchen's fame as a voice of twentieth century music has tended to obscure the fact that he has also widely performed and recorded the classics, and with no less distinction and authority. Of the sixty or so composers on his discography, Bach, Beethoven, Handel, and Haydn are represented most often. Three of his recordings with the Ars Viva Orchestra on the Amadeo label are of Baroque composers.

Nevertheless, it was his allegiance to twentieth century music that kept him away from the American musical scene until towards the end of his life. He received repeated offers to appear as a guest conductor of major American orchestras, but he turned them all down because he was required to present only more or less conventional programs. "I do not have to conduct works I don't like," was the way he put it. "I will not conduct to order." For many years, therefore, Scherchen was known to American music lovers solely through his more than one hundred recordings.

His first visit to the United States, in 1962, was not to conduct music but to serve as chairman at the International Conference of the Association of Audio Aids for the Blind. Four years later his American conducting debut finally took place. He went to the United States in the fall of 1964 to direct five programs in New York with the New York Chamber Ensemble, an organization formed expressly for his visit. But before he made his first appearance with this group, he made his American conducting bow as a guest conductor of the Philadelphia Orchestra on October 30, 1964, in a program divided between Haydn's *La Passione* Symphony and Mahler's Symphony No.5. "A tall, gray-haired, craggy-faced man, he walked on the stage very slowly," wrote Raymond Ericson in the New York *Times.* "Once on the podium he conducted with a concentration that seemed the embodiment of energy. He did not use any score, and his baton technique varied from heaven-storming (accompanied by an audible grunt or two) to almost invisible time beating. . . . He was a very personal interpreter, which is all to the good when one has his kind of authoritativeness."

Five programs with the New York Chamber Ensemble were given at the Lincoln Center for the Performing Arts between November 8 and 22. Most of the programs were devoted to Baroque composers and to composers of the classical era. The last concert presented Mozart's Requiem as a memorial to President Kennedy. One program reflected Scherchen's interest in twentieth century music with works by Stravinsky, Alban Berg, and Anton Webern.

On June 7, 1966, Scherchen suffered a heart attack while conducting a performance of Malipiero's opera *Orpheus* at the Teatro della Pergola in Florence. He was taken to a clinic and died there on June 12.

Scherchen was married three times. He had five children with his third wife, Pia, and four others by his two earlier marriages. At his farm at Gravesano, he usually began his day by taking a swim in the pool. For many years a few select pupils in conducting lived with him; he demanded from them the utmost in work, dedication, and concentration.

Scherchen was the author of *Handbook of Conducting* (1933), *The Nature of Music* (1947), and *Musik für Jedermann* (1950).

ABOUT: New York Times, November 8, 1964; Saturday Review, October 31, 1964.

Aksel Schiøtz

1906–1975

Aksel Schiøtz, tenor, was born in Roskilde, Denmark, on September 1, 1906, to Carl and Marie Hauch Schiøtz. He was one of seven children, five boys and two girls. His father was an architect and painter. Aksel received a comprehensive academic education, earning his master's degree in languages in 1929 from the University of Copenhagen. For the next eight years he was a schoolmaster in various high schools in or near Copenhagen, teaching languages, music, and the Scriptures.

Singing had always been an avocation, and music a passion. In 1936 he gave several experimental concerts that stimulated and reinforced his ambition to involve himself in music actively and professionally. He resigned his teaching post in 1938 to enter the Danish Royal Opera School in Copenhagen. Later he took additional vocal lessons privately from the baritone John Forsell in Stockholm.

Schiøtz made his opera debut with the Royal Opera in Copenhagen in 1939 as Ferrando in *Così fan Tutte.* He made other operatic appearances that year at the Royal Opera as Faust, in addition to performing in provincial theaters in Denmark. In 1940 he was cast in a motion picture musical, *I Have Lived and Loved.*

He made his professional debut as a concert singer in Copenhagen early in April 1940, a performance that inspired such enthusiasm that a second recital was scheduled for April 10, which turned out to be one day after the Nazis had invaded Denmark. Schiøtz's concert, opening with eloquent appropriateness with Handel's "Comfort Ye, My People" from the *Messiah,* was given while Nazi troops swarmed through the streets of the city under the cover of Nazi bombers.

During World War II, Schiøtz refused to sing German *Lieder* in public, as the Nazi invaders had asked him to do, since he knew that his performances would be exploited for German propaganda. Instead, in his concerts he concentrated on Danish music, offering a rich library of Danish folk and art songs, much of it little known at that time. When Kaj Munk, the Dan-

Schiøtz: shȫtz

AKSEL SCHIØTZ

ish clergyman and playwright, was killed by the Nazis, Schiøtz sang at his funeral. After that he always volunteered his services as singer at the funeral services of any Danish patriot who had been the victim of Nazi brutality. He also involved himself in the Resistance movement in Denmark. Throughout the war years he came to be known as "the voice of Denmark." For his war services he was made a knight in 1947 by King Christian X.

When the war ended, Schiøtz toured Scandinavia in song recitals and performed as a soloist in oratorios. His extraordinary musicianship and versatility brought him a dedicated following not only in Scandinavia but also in England where he gave several recitals over the BBC network and, in public, in London and Liverpool. In the summer of 1946 he was heard at the Glyndebourne Festival in England where he alternated with Peter Pears in the role of the Male Chorus in Britten's *The Rape of Lucretia* (then receiving its first performances); Schiøtz also sang this role at the Edinburgh Festival.

By the end of 1946 Schiøtz had recorded some two hundred sides for HMV in Denmark and England, including Schubert's *Schöne Müllerin* cycle, Schumann's *Dichterliebe,* a whole repertory of Danish art and folk songs, and arias from operas and oratorios by Handel, Haydn, and Mozart. These recordings brought into being a kind of Schiøtz cult throughout Europe and the United States. When the singer Charles Panzéra heard Schiøtz's recording of *Dichterliebe* he told his wife: "This is unbelievable. I have never

heard such vocal art." Discussing this same recording in the *Stereo Review,* Irving Kolodin spoke of "a remarkable legato line throughout Schiøtz's reading of the cycle, an uncanny interrelation of word and tone, a smooth, gearless shift from piano to forte and back again. . . . One is aware of a breath support so complete, so uninterrupted, that the vocal statement sounds as effortless as it must have been effortful to master."

He had become a national hero and was well on his way towards the heights of artistic and financial success as a singer when disaster struck. In December 1946 he developed a brain tumor that affected the acoustic nerve and the nerves controlling the voice box. Surgery (known as "the Gershwin operation" since it was the same one that had taken Gershwin's life in 1937) left Schiøtz with complete paralysis of the right half of his face. After this difficult and delicate surgery, Schiøtz's physicians prescribed a long sea voyage. To further his convalescence he took a trip on a Swedish Orient steamship, a cruise from Denmark to South America, across the Pacific, and back to Europe by way of the Suez Canal. When he returned to Denmark, in spite of his infirmity Schiøtz immersed himself in music study and for a time tried to retrain his voice as a baritone. When he returned to the concert stage with a recital in Copenhagen in September 1948, it was obvious that his vocalization had been seriously impaired by his infirmity, even though his exquisite artistry remained unblemished. He thought of retiring from singing altogether, but his prolonged illness and the subsequent extended sea voyage during recuperation had completely drained his financial resources. In addition, he had to support his wife (the former Gerd Haugsted) and their five children. He gave another recital ten days later, and in 1948 he undertook his first tour of the United States. After his first recital, in Town Hall in New York, Howard Taubman commented in the New York *Times* that though his voice was "merely a shadow of what it once must have been" his musicianship remained of the highest quality and he remained "a master of style."

Schiøtz continued to give recitals from time to time, including several in the United States in 1956 and 1961. After his performance of Schubert's *Die Winterreise* on March 14, 1961, in New York, the audience gave him a standing ovation, and some in the audience cheered. "But for one listener it was a sad evening," noted Ross Parmenter in the New York *Times.* "Granted that . . . Mr. Schiøtz's performance was impressive as a display of courage. And granted, too, it had beautiful moments, it nevertheless suffered musically from the singer's vocal difficulties."

From the 1950s on, Schiøtz directed most of his energies and talent to teaching voice: in the United States at the University of Colorado and the University of Minnesota; in Canada, at the Royal Conservatory of Music at the University of Toronto.

He returned to Denmark in 1968 where he continued his singing chores at a college in Copenhagen. Leukemia and intestinal cancer claimed his life in Copenhagen on April 19, 1975.

Schiøtz was the author of *The Singer and His Art* (1969).

In 1977 the Aksel Schiøtz Memorial Fund was created in the United States "to preserve the memory and musical heritage of the great Danish tenor." The fund was to provide scholarship awards, art-song workshops, and possibly art-song contests.

ABOUT: Schiøtz, G. Kunst og Kamp: Gerd og Aksel Schiøtz. *Periodicals*—High Fidelity Magazine, July 1975; New York Times, October 24, 1948; Stereo Review, August 1975.

Tito Schipa

1889–1965

Tito Schipa (originally Raffaele Attilio Amadeo Schipa), tenor, was born in Lecce, Italy, on January 2, 1889. As a boy of seven he sang in the church choir of his native town. Six years later he entered the Seminary for Church Service Training. One day the Bishop of Lecce heard him sing and offered to pay for his musical tuition. Schipa then entered the Lecce Conservatory, receiving training in piano, theory, and composition. At fifteen he received his first vocal instruction from Alceste Gerunda with whom he studied for several years. After that, he finished his vocal studies in Milan with Emilio Piccoli.

Schipa: skē′ pä

TITO SCHIPA

Schipa made his opera debut in 1910 at Vercelli, Italy, as Alfredo in *La Traviata.* Appearances in other small opera houses during the next two years preceded his engagement as a principal tenor at Dal Verme in Milan where he made a favorable impression as Alfredo, as the Duke in *Rigoletto,* and as Elvino in *La Sonnambula.* In 1913 he made several guest appearances in Rio de Janeiro; in 1914 he made his debut at the Teatro Costanzi in Rome as Ernesto in *Don Pasquale;* and in 1915 he appeared for the first time at La Scala in Milan as Vladimir in *Prince Igor.* On August 27, 1917, he created the role of Ruggero in the world premiere of Puccini's *La Rondine* in Monte Carlo, assuming the role at the request of the composer.

In 1919 Schipa became a member of the Chicago Opera. It was with this company that he made his American debut that year. On February 2, 1920, he went to New York with the Chicago Opera in a performance of *La Sonnambula* that starred the coloratura soprano Galli-Curci. At the Chicago Opera, where he remained thirteen years, he scored major successes in lyric roles for which his light, sweet, and sensitively produced voice was particularly suited: Cavaradossi in *Tosca,* Almaviva in *The Barber of Seville,* Alfredo, and Elvino. "Such fluent, liquid singing and such a grace of carriage, refinement of manner, and dramatic fidelity in delineation of this operatic figure has not been heard or seen here in many years," wrote one Chicago critic.

In 1927 Schipa returned to Teatro Colón in Buenos Aires, and in 1929 to La Scala. He continued to appear in both houses for many years rising to heights of success equaled by few other tenors. Even his rival colleagues spoke rhapsodically about him. Beniamino Gigli said of him: "Though there were many fine tenors ... endowed with greater vocal potential than Schipa, when he sang, we all had to bow down to his greatness." Giovanni Martinelli spoke of him as "the McCormack of the Italians."

On November 23, 1932, Schipa made his debut at the Metropolitan Opera as Nemorino in *L'Elisir d'Amore.* "He had a well-deserved success," wrote Olin Downes in the New York *Times.* "The voice may be a little dryer than a decade ago, but the skill in song and the art of the musician were obvious in everything the singer accomplished. Mr. Schipa has ample bravura when that is required, but what is more to the point in this adorable opera bouffe of Donizetti is his capacity to sustain and mold beautifully a long melodic phrase. He also makes much of the text. In all these requisites of artistic singing, Mr. Schipa won the respect and enthusiasm of his audience."

He retained that respect and enthusiasm with subsequent performances as Edgardo in *Lucia di Lammermoor,* Don Ottavio in *Don Giovanni,* Almaviva in *The Barber of Seville,* Wilhelm Meister in *Mignon,* Alfredo, Des Grieux in *Manon,* Elvino, and Ernesto.

Schipa left the Metropolitan Opera in 1935 after a dispute with the management over fees. In the latter part of the 1930s he antagonized many of his American admirers by his open stance in favor of Fascism in Italy; he even was reported to have given the Fascist salute during his appearances in Australia, in defiance of the local ordinance. Answering the political charges against him, Schipa replied: "I am an artist. I am not a politician and never took any interest in politics. I am a patriot, and I love my country."

In 1937 Schipa married Rena Boratto, an Italian motion picture actress he had met while he himself was making some screen appearances in Italy. (This was his second marriage. The first, in 1920, was to Antoinette Michel, with whom he had two children.) They acquired a house in Hollywood, California. In 1941 he gave a recital in Carnegie Hall, and on March 7, 1941, he returned for a single season to the Metropolitan Opera as Don Ottavio in a performance of *Don Giovanni* conducted by Bruno Walter.

Schipa returned to Italy in 1941 at the request of Count Galeazzo Ciano, the Italian Foreign Minister. He spent the years of World War II singing in Italy and Germany. Returning to the United States for a tour in 1947 he gave a recital in Carnegie Hall, with the auditorium only half full, many avoiding the concert because of resentment at his outspoken Nazi-Fascist (Axis) allegiance before and during World War II.

After divorcing his wife in the early 1940s, Schipa married Teresa Borgna, a South American, on September 28, 1946. They had one son.

In spite of advancing years, Schipa continued making appearances at the Teatro Colón (where he was seen on the opera stage for the last time) and to give recitals throughout Europe. He made his first tour of the Soviet Union in 1957. After an absence of fifteen years from the American concert scene Schipa (age seventy-three) returned to New York with a recital at Town Hall on October 3, 1962. This time the house was packed, the audience overflowing onto the stage. "When he came forth—short, stout, dignified— it was to the accompaniment of cheers, yells and a standing ovation," reported Harold C. Schonberg in the New York *Times.* "That was the order of the evening. ... What did he have to offer after all these years? Nothing—and everything. Vocally, there is not much left. His production is unsteady, his pitch often uncertain, his breath control nil. But, and this is a big but, his singing still has style and he can communicate, even if in something close to a whisper. In short, he managed inimitably to put across song and aria, and to convince his audience that a great man was before it." An American tour (Schipa's last) followed this concert. At its termination, he went into retirement.

He spent his last years in the United States, his final home being with his niece in Forest Hills in Queens, New York. He died in New York on December 16, 1965, after suffering a cardio-circulatory failure from a diabetes condition.

Schipa composed many songs, some of which he featured at his recitals. He also wrote the music for an operetta named after his daughter, *Princess Liana.* He appeared in the Italian-made motion pictures *Vivere* (1938), *Chi' Piu Felice di Me?* (1940), and *The Life of Donizetti* (1952).

Throughout his life he showed great interest in and affection for animals. At one time he threatened to cancel a London concert because one of his pets, a marmoset, had disappeared. On

one of his return visits to the United States he took with him a nonpoisonous snake (a coral-line). A devotee of physical exercise and sports, he kept in condition for much of his adult life by playing golf and tennis and by swimming. He also enjoyed attending boxing matches and football games.

In 1955 he represented Italy in a festival of Italian operas held in the principal cities of Belgium. The Italian government made him Grande Ufficiale SS. Maurizio e Lazaro and also of the Crown of Italy. The Vatican made him Commander S. Sepulcro and S. Gregorio Magno. In Spain he became Commander of the Order Alfonso XII; in Portugal, of the Order of Christ; in Argentina, of the Order of Mercede. In France, he was made Chevalier of the Legion of Honor.

ABOUT: New York Times, September 28, 1962.

Thomas Schippers

1930–1977

Thomas Schippers, conductor, was born in Portage, Michigan, on March 9, 1930, to Peter and Anna Nanninga Schippers. His parents were of German and Dutch extraction. His father was a distributor of Westinghouse products. Thomas began to study the piano when he was four. Two years later he gave public performances on tour, and at eight he performed regularly over a local radio station. "I don't know how I could have done all the things I did as a child," he told Jim Gaines in an interview in *Saturday Review*. "I started touring when I was six and missed weeks of school every year. I practiced the church organ late at night and often so exhausted myself that I slept in the chancel. At school, the teachers liked me, but the kids didn't particularly since they thought of me as a mama's boy. To combat that, I joined the baseball team and the basketball team. It was all calculated on my part, but it worked like a charm. Soon they didn't care how many weeks I was away from school, as long as I got back for the sports season."

He was graduated from high school when he was thirteen. One year later he started earning

Schippers: shĭp' pērs

THOMAS SCHIPPERS

money by teaching the piano and accompanying artists. In 1945 he entered the Curtis Institute of Music in Philadelphia, specializing in organ and becoming the first student there to complete a four-year course in two. After a period in Yale in 1947 when he took courses in philosophy and attended Paul Hindemith's composition class, Schippers returned to the Curtis Institute to study piano with Olga Samaroff.

In 1948 he was one of five finalists, from forty contestants, in a young conductors' competition held by the Philadelphia Orchestra. He won second prize, even though his only conducting experience up to that time was to audit a class at the Berkshire Music Center at Tanglewood in Massachusetts, which he had done at Olga Samaroff's suggestion.

Schippers's father, objecting to a musical career for his son, called the boy back to Kalamazoo to try to convince him to direct his energies elsewhere. To overcome his father's objections, Thomas showed him a letter from the Village Presbyterian Church in New York offering him the post of organist. He told his father the job paid five thousand dollars a year, when actually the pay was only ten dollars a week. Getting a reluctant go-ahead from his father, Thomas returned to New York and took on the organ assignment. In the basement of the church, a neophyte opera group called the Lemonade Opera gave performances. When its conductor resigned, Thomas Schippers took over.

One day he accompanied on the piano a singer who was auditioning for a role in Menotti's opera *The Consul.* Menotti was so impressed by Schippers's musicianship that he asked him to be overall music supervisor of this production which opened in Philadelphia on March 1, 1950, before coming to New York on March 15. When, just before the New York premiere, the conductor fell ill, Schippers stepped in as substitute. After that Menotti selected Schippers to conduct *The Medium* for the screen (1951) and to direct the world premiere of his television Christmas opera *Amahl and the Night Visitors,* when it was introduced over the NBC-TV network on December 24, 1951—the latter became a television Yuletide classic.

After a brief tour of duty with the United States Army in Germany, Schippers returned to the United States to become resident conductor of the New York City Opera. He made his debut there on April 9, 1952, in a stage production of *Amahl and the Night Visitors.* During the next three years he not only conducted much of the standard operatic repertory but also such novelties as Ravel's *L'Heure Espagnole* and the world premiere of the original version of Aaron Copland's *The Tender Land* on April 1, 1954. "The measure of a conductor is his performance in unfamiliar music," said John Gurney Briggs Jr. in the New York *Times.* "By this standard, Mr. Schippers' performance was very fine indeed." In reviewing Schippers's performance in *The Tender Land,* a reviewer for the *New Yorker* found he combined "taste and energy with the rare faculty of conveying musical ideas by means of gestures that is the indispensable talent of the born conductor."

While conducting at the New York City Opera, Schippers was called upon to fill several engagements as guest conductor of major American symphony orchestras, including the Philadelphia Orchestra, the Boston Symphony, and the NBC Symphony. On December 27, 1954, he led the premiere of Menotti's *The Saint of Bleecker Street* in New York and conducted the opera during its entire New York run. In May 1955 he made a noteworthy debut at La Scala with this same opera. On March 26, 1955, he made his first appearance as conductor of the New York Philharmonic Orchestra. In the New York *Times* Olin Downes called him "a conductor of very exceptional gifts and an unusual approach to his task. . . . He seeks balance, beauty, and proportion in his readings, and this with a

highly becoming seriousness and modesty of demeanor."

During the summer of 1955 Schippers appeared at the Aix-en-Provence festival with a symphonic program made up of music by Beethoven, Bizet, and Menotti. During this same period he also conducted the Scarlatti Orchestra in Paris and appeared at the Bordeaux Festival.

On December 23, 1955, he made his conducting debut at the Metropolitan Opera in a revival of *Don Pasquale* which was preceded by the ballet *Soirée,* with music by Rossini arranged by Britten. "Mr. Schippers," reported Howard Taubman in the New York *Times,* "knows how to keep his forces together. . . . He keeps things moving but he is wise enough to give the singers a certain flexibility." This was the third time in the history of the Metropolitan Opera that an American-born conductor had been engaged by that company.

Indicative of Schippers's rapidly growing fame were the facts that the United States Junior Chamber of Commerce named him one of the nation's ten outstanding young men of 1955 and that his native city presented him with a scroll of appreciation. In 1956 he received the Award of Merit from the National Association of American Composers and Conductors for his outstanding services to American music. Soon after this, when *Life* published a list of one hundred most important young men in the United States, Schippers was the only conductor represented.

In 1956–1957, Schippers was also assigned at the Metropolitan Opera to conduct *La Bohème* and *The Tales of Hoffmann,* in 1957–1958 *Carmen,* in 1958–1959 *Un Ballo in Maschera,* and in 1959–1960 *La Forza del Destino.* On October 24, 1960, he became the first American to conduct an opening night performance of the Metropolitan Opera season, with a revival of *Nabucco* (a company premiere). After that he continued to distinguish himself at the Metropolitan Opera with performances of both the standard repertory and new or rarely heard works. On January 23, 1964, he led there the American premiere of Menotti's *The Last Savage.* He was chosen to open the new auditorium, and the new season, of the Metropolitan Opera at the Lincoln Center for the Performing Arts on September 16, 1966, with the disastrous world premiere of Samuel Barber's *Antony and Cleopatra.* On December 14, 1974, he scored perhaps the greatest operatic success of his career by performing for the first time at the Metropolitan Opera the original version of *Boris Godunov* (a combination of the first version of 1869 with the revisions of 1872), regarded as the most complete *Boris Godunov* ever heard in America and possibly in the world. On April 7, 1975, he led the American premiere of Rossini's *The Siege of Corinth,* in which Beverly Sills made her Metropolitan Opera debut. Other operas assigned to Schippers at the Metropolitan were *The Flying Dutchman, Elektra, Manon, Don Carlo, Luisa Miller, Il Trovatore, Aida, Eugene Onegin, The Queen of Spades, The Barber of Seville, Otello, Der Rosenkavalier, Lohengrin, Die Meistersinger, L' Elisir d'Amore,* and *Ernani.* In addition to opening the Metropolitan Opera season with *Nabucco* and *Antony and Cleopatra* in 1960 and 1966 respectively, Schippers performed a similar service in 1970 with *Ernani* and in 1975 with *The Siege of Corinth.* In all, his operatic repertory embraced over one hundred works.

When the New York Philharmonic toured the Soviet Union in 1959, Schippers shared the podium with Leonard Bernstein and was given an ovation after conducting a concert in Moscow. He also delivered in Moscow a lecture on the meaning of Shostakovich to Americans while performing portions of Shostakovich's Symphony No.7.

At La Scala (where he directed the world premiere of the staged presentation of Manuel de Falla's *L'Atlántida* on September 29, 1962), Schippers became one of the few non-Italians called upon regularly to direct Italian operas, including an important revival of *The Siege of Corinth* in 1970. In the summer of 1963 he made his debut at the Bayreuth Festival in a new production of *Die Meistersinger.* When the Bayreuth festival company visited Japan for the first time to participate in the Osaka Festival of 1967, he was one of its conductors. He was also one of the conductors when the Metropolitan Opera made its first tour of Europe in fifty-six years, in 1966.

In 1958 Schippers was cofounder with Menotti of the Festival of Two Worlds in Spoleto, Italy, and inaugurated the first festival season by conducting *Macbeth.* He remained the artistic director of the festival until 1976, conducting most of its orchestral and operatic performances and overseeing all the artistic and theatrical events. In this capacity he was responsible for the world premieres of American operas, pro-

duction of other twentieth century operas, and revivals of less familiar or near-forgotten operas as well as recognized masterworks. He was also responsible there for the discovery and development of new artists.

The artistic partnership of Schippers and Menotti, which spanned more than a quarter of a century, came to an abrupt end in 1976. Menotti complained to an Italian newspaper that Schippers had become too expensive for the Spoleto Festival, and Schippers countered with the accusation that Menotti was prejudiced toward big-name performers who attracted more attention than Menotti himself.

In 1970 he was named music director of the Cincinnati Symphony, replacing Max Rudolf. In Cincinnati, he introduced a number of innovations, such as presenting ballet performances during the regular subscription series, having world-famous soloists (such as Isaac Stern or André Watts) become part of the overall ensemble in performances such as Bach's *Brandenburg Concertos,* and himself accompanying on the piano in encores a singer who had been a soloist with the orchestra. In 1971 he made his first tour with the Cincinnati Orchestra as its music director, with performances in New York, Washington, D.C., and Pennsylvania.

In addition to his commitments to the Cincinnati Symphony, the Metropolitan Opera, La Scala, and the Festival of Two Worlds, Schippers made numerous guest appearances with various symphony orchestras and opera companies in the United States and Europe. His operatic commitments brought him to the Deutsche Oper in Berlin, Teatro la Fenice in Venice, Munich Opera, Rome Opera, Monte Carlo Opera, Covent Garden in London, the Athens Festival, and the Florence Music Festival. For the opening of the 1972 Venice Festival he directed a performance of the Verdi Requiem in the Throne Room of the Doges' Palace (the first time a public performance had taken place there); this concert was filmed. Subsequently, he produced a new *La Traviata* in Venice with Beverly Sills. In 1973 he toured with the Israel Philharmonic and in 1975–1976 he toured Europe and the Soviet Union. He also served as director of Special Projects for the RAI, Italy's radio and television network, and was the first foreigner to assume this post.

Victimized by lung cancer, Schippers decided to relinquish his post as music director of the

Cincinnati Symphony Orchestra in 1977 and to assume that of "conductor laureate." However he did accept an appointment as music director of the Santa Cecilia Academy Orchestra in Rome. He was scheduled to conduct his initial concerts in Rome in October 1977, but these were cancelled because of his developing illness.

In 1972 Schippers joined the faculty of the College-Conservatory of Music of the University of Cincinnati as Distinguished Professor of Music to teach orchestral conducting and interpretation. Two years later he became affiliated with the Archigiana in Siena, Italy, an international school covering all aspects of musical activity.

"On the podium," reported *Time,* "he is athletic but correct. His baton sweeps in wide, generous arcs and his left hand constantly beckons music from the air. His body dips and sways like a dancer's, and his classic profile flashes now right, now left, like a lighthouse beacon."

On days of performances Schippers kept himself in virtual isolation. "I never eat beforehand, although I drink a good deal of Coca-Cola. I arrive at the theater at the very last minute. People tell me I rub my hands a lot. Oh yes, I have a habit of tying and untying my shoelaces. Before stepping on the podium I usually pray."

On days when there was no performance, Schippers kept himself busy from six in the morning, the hour he arose. He spent the first part of the morning studying scores and practicing the piano. Then he attended to correspondence and business problems. He accepted phone calls only from twelve to one in the afternoon. After lunch, he took a nap, then returned to his studio for several more hours of study and practicing.

Thomas Schippers married Elaine ("Nonie") Phipps, the socialite daughter of the director of the W. R. Grace & Company steamship line, on April 17, 1965. Immediately after the ceremony at the Corpus Christi Roman Catholic Church in New York City, the couple left for Europe where, a week later, Schippers was scheduled to conduct the Berlin Philharmonic Orchestra. They maintained two apartments, one in New York City (in Manhattan), the other in Cincinnati. Nonie Schippers died in January 1973 after a prolonged bout with cancer. Four years later Schippers himself was similarly stricken.

Once asked by an interviewer to name his three favorite things, Schippers replied quickly:

"The ocean, the movies, and good old-fashioned, feudal, red-and-gold opera houses."

Thomas Schippers succumbed to cancer in New York City on December 16, 1977. He left the bulk of his five-million-dollar estate to the Cincinnati Symphony Orchestra.

ABOUT: High Fidelity/Musical America, April 1978; Look, June 11, 1968; New York Times, August 21, 1955, December 18, 1977; Opera News, December 1, 1962; Saturday Review, May 20, 1972.

Artur Schnabel

1882–1951

Artur Schnabel, pianist, famous as an interpreter of Beethoven's music, was born on April 17, 1882, in Lipnik, Austria (now in Czechoslovakia), where his father, Isidor Schnabel, helped to run his father-in-law's small textile firm. "When I was six," recalled Schnabel in his memoirs, "my sister got piano lessons. My mother [Ernestine Labin Schnabel]—I don't know how true this is—told me that without lessons I was much faster in learning to play than my sister. I simply went to the piano and did what was expected of her; so her teacher thought that a boy doing that must have talent, and began to teach me." In academic subjects, he was taught by a private teacher for about two years.

When Artur reached his seventh year, his teacher felt he should be tested by musical experts. He was taken to Vienna where he played for and was accepted as a pupil by Hans Schmitt. Under Schmitt's guidance, he began making public appearances as a prodigy, including an appearance with orchestra in a performance of Mozart's Concerto in D minor, K.466. However, as he later explained, "I was not exploited as a prodigy, because my parents, although ambitious, were not greedy."

After two years with Schmitt, the nine-year-old boy auditioned for Theodor Leschetizky. Leschetizky opened the piano score of *Cavalleria Rusticana* which had been published just one week earlier and asked Schnabel to play the music at sight. Satisfied with the results, Leschetizky placed him for one year with his wife,

---

Schnabel: shnä′ bĕl

ARTUR SCHNABEL

Anna Essipova, before taking him on as his own pupil. After Artur's first lessons with Leschetizky, the master told him: "You'll never be a pianist. You are a musician." Schnabel later commented: "Of course I couldn't make anything of that."

Since Leschetizky's home was the rendezvous for many of Vienna's most famous musicians, Artur came into personal and friendly contact with some of them, among whom was Brahms. On many a Sunday he went on excursions with Brahms, and on several occasions Brahms was present when he performed at private homes. "I think he never listened," Schnabel has said. Supplementing his private lessons with Leschetizky, Artur was, for a short period, given instruction in academic subjects by a private tutor before entering high school at the age of ten. "I passed somehow and attended for four or five months, studying some Latin, which turned out to be unnecessary, and seeming to fail completely in mathematics. Then I was taken out again, and I never went to another school in my life," he has said. Whatever education he received after that came from reading, going to the theater, and conversations with his intellectual superiors.

Going to the theater or to the opera meant standing in line from three o'clock in the afternoon to seven in the evening when the gates opened and a wild scramble ensued up four flights of stairs to get a seat with a good view from the fourth balcony. In later years he noted: "We had a very good time waiting; we would bring sandwiches and discuss the world and ev-

erything. There were many musicians—I often raced Arnold Schoenberg on the stairs—and we didn't see or hear too much, but I've rarely enjoyed theatrical performances as much as then."

After six years of piano study with Leschetizky and several years of theory with Eusebius Mandyczewski, Schnabel left Vienna for Berlin in 1910. He lived there for the next twenty-three years, and it was there that his professional career both as a piano virtuoso and as a teacher of the piano began to unfold. He supported himself by teaching the piano and serving for five years as a piano accompanist for several artists. One of these was the contralto Therese Behr, a *Lieder* singer. Schnabel and Behr were married in Berlin on June 9, 1905. They had two sons: Stefan and Karl Ulrich. The latter became a concert pianist and on several occasions collaborated with his father in public concerts and in recordings of two-piano music. (Schnabel had a third child—a daughter, Elisabeth—an illegitimate offspring from an early romance.)

During his first year in Germany Schnabel went on a concert tour through East Prussia. In Berlin he frequently performed at house concerts, at one of which he was joined by Karl Muck, the conductor, in the performance of Mozart's Sonata in D major, K.448, for two pianos. As a soloist with the Berlin Philharmonic, under Arthur Nikisch, he was heard and admired in concertos by Mozart, Beethoven, and Brahms. His fame spread beyond Germany when, in the early 1900s, he embarked on several tours of Spain and in 1904 made his debut in England as a soloist with the Royal Philharmonic Orchestra. Other concert engagements took him to Italy, Austria, and France, and on three occasions to Czarist Russia. In addition to his appearances as a piano virtuoso, he joined Karl Flesch in performances of violin sonatas, formed the Schnabel Trio with Alfred Wittenberg and Anton Hekking, and later gave trio performances with Karl Flesch and Jean Gerardy and with Flesch and Hugo Becker.

He spent the years of World War I in Germany. In spite of the war he was able to continue his concert work in Germany, England, and neutral European countries, though not always under favorable conditions. In neutral countries, the pro-Allied press attacked him for being a musical representative of Prussian militarism. There was hostility against him when he performed in Milan in April 1915—Italy already having decided to join the Allies in the war against Germany. But once the war was over, political biases were shelved; he was able to extend his successes throughout Europe to the point where he was recognized as one of its leading pianists, acclaimed for his penetrating performances of the music of Bach, Beethoven, Mozart, Schubert, and Brahms. In recognition of his musical achievements, the Prussian State awarded him an honorary professorship in 1919.

On Christmas Day of 1921, he made his American debut at Carnegie Hall in New York with a program made up of two sonatas (Schubert's posthumous Sonata in B major and Brahms's F minor Sonata) and Schumann's C major Fantasy. To Richard Aldrich of the New York *Times,* "Mr. Schnabel was happiest in the forthright, vigorous music of Brahms, in which his natural calm, his affectionate care for each phrase, his reserve power in larger and leisurely climaxes displayed qualities of musicianship in harmony with his reputation for twenty-five years abroad. . . . His Schubert was a more curious if not so vital miniature. . . . His Schumann, hardly the romantic Robert of some tone poets of the piano, was yet a scholarly and clarifying performance."

Despite such carefully guarded praise, Schnabel's first tour of the United States was a failure. He was unable to arouse interest in programs that sidestepped pyrotechnical displays for sound musicianship. His appearance was as unspectacular as his programs. Short (five feet four), stockily built, his hair closely cropped atop a big head, fingers short and stubby, he looked more like a Central European businessman than an artist. Furthermore, his manner at the piano was not calculated to inflame audiences with excitement. He played without flourishes of arm or body, without facial contortions or heavy breathing. Rather he performed with the quiet and efficient dispatch of a man whose sole concern was to lay bare the heart of the music he was playing.

Schnabel returned to the United States for a second tour and again failed to make a deep impression on audiences. After that he decided to confine his concert activity to Europe where his full measure as an artist was recognized and where he was not required to make concessions in his programming or assume mannerisms false to him. When in 1924 he paid his first visit to the Soviet Union, he gave a program in both Moscow and Leningrad of five sonatas of Beethoven. He returned to the Soviet Union for two years after that and again in 1935. In 1927, in honor of the centenary of Beethoven's birth, he performed in London his first complete cycle of the Beethoven sonatas stretching over seven programs, a cycle he would later repeat three times more, twice in Berlin and once in New York. In 1928 he presented another all-comprehensive cycle, this one devoted to the piano music of Schubert, to commemorate the centenary of that composer's birth.

In 1930 Koussevitzky was conducting a Brahms festival with the Boston Symphony. He invited Schnabel to America to perform with his orchestra the two Brahms concertos. It was at this time that Schnabel's immense popularity in the United States can be said to have begun. After he had been heard performing some of Beethoven's concertos with various American symphony orchestras, *Time* remarked: "There were few people in his audience who did not go away with the feeling that they had listened to the greatest of Beethoven pianists."

The full extent of his fame in the United States as a performer of Beethoven was demonstrated in January and February 1936 when he gave a series of concerts devoted to all the Beethoven piano sonatas in Carnegie Hall, a venture his manager had looked upon with considerable skepticism. Eighteen thousand people attended those seven concerts, bringing in to the box office almost twenty-five thousand dollars, a financial figure unheard of up to that time for a cycle of piano recitals. By then Schnabel had also become the first artist to record all the Beethoven sonatas, a project begun in 1931 and completed in 1935.

He was completing such a seven-concert cycle of the Beethoven sonatas in Berlin on April 28, 1933, when the Nazis came to power in Germany. Resigning from his post as professor of the piano at the High School for Music, a post he had held since 1925, he and his family left Germany to live in London during the winters and to spend their summers at Tremazzo on Lake Como in Italy. He continued his teaching chores, holding summer classes for some fifteen students. Each pupil came with his own repertory, playing it not only for Schnabel but also for the other students. Schnabel held classes for three periods three times a week. The first period began at a specific hour but ended no one could tell when. A lesson was not finished until Schnabel had made his points clear. "We have all learned some things from each other's virtues and mistakes," Schnabel said. "One thing I try to impress on my students above everything else —and that is that life is fundamentally serious, and so is study and a career. But I also warn them not to be too earnest about being serious." Among his many pupils were Leon Fleisher, Lili Kraus, André Watts, Misha Dichter, Beveridge Webster, and Claude Frank.

During the summer of 1933 Schnabel participated in the centenary festivities commemorating Brahms's birth not only by performing the Piano Concerto No.2 but also by participating in the presentation of all of Brahms's trios and piano quartets with Bronislaw Hubermann, Pablo Casals, and Paul Hindemith. After 1933 he revisited the United States annually; his artistry was given its full due wherever he appeared. "There is reason to marvel at the perfect proportion, the depth of thought and the genuineness of feeling that Schnabel conveys," wrote Olin Downes in the New York *Times*. "His is an art that recognized at the same time the grand line and the most significant finish of detail. . . . The performance is complete concentration upon the music which is projected with extraordinary significance."

He was performing with the St. Louis Symphony on March 8, 1938, when he learned that Austria had been invaded by the Nazis. Following a tour of Australia, he returned to the United States on September 2, 1939, to find a new home for himself and his family and to become an American citizen. In his apartment in New York overlooking Central Park, Schnabel continued to teach and to do some composing. In 1942 he was heard in New York City in a series of five concerts devoted entirely to Schubert.

Troubled in his last years by cataracts in both eyes and by thrombosis, Schnabel reduced the number of his public appearances drastically. His last concert took place at Hunter College in New York, on January 20, 1951. Fittingly enough, in this, his valedictory, he performed a program of Beethoven's sonatas. He died that year in the Axenstein Hotel in Canton Schwyz, in Switzerland, on August 15. His widow, Therese, outlived him by eight years.

Twenty years after his death, on August 15, 1971, a concert in his memory was held at the Lincoln Center for the Performing Arts in New York; many of his students participated, together with his son, Karl Ulrich Schnabel.

Schnabel was the composer of three symphonies, a piano concerto, a choral symphony, an orchestral rhapsody, five string quartets, a piano quintet, three piano sonatas, several piano suites, and other compositions for piano and for the voice. As a performer he was the conservative, content to dwell in the eighteenth and nineteenth centuries and never penetrating into the twentieth; as a composer he was the ultramodern whose works were dissonant and atonal, many of them influenced by Schoenberg. He never performed his own works in public.

He was the author of a two-volume annotated edition of Beethoven's sonatas published in 1935. He wrote *Reflections on Music* (1933) and *Music and the Line of Most Resistance* (1942). His reminiscences, published posthumously in 1961 as *My Life and Music,* grew out of a collection of autobiographical lectures delivered at the University of Chicago in 1945.

ABOUT: Chasins, A. Speaking of Pianists; Saerchinger, C. Artur Schnabel; Schnabel, A. My Life and Music; Wolff, K. The Teaching of Artur Schnabel. *Periodicals*—High Fidelity Magazine, November 1963; New Yorker, April 2, 1938; Time, February 10, 1936.

Friedrich Schorr

1888–1953

Friedrich Schorr, Wagnerian baritone, was born in Nagyvárad, Hungary, on September 2, 1888. His father, a lawyer, planned a legal career for him. "However," as Schorr once recalled, "Adolph Robinson, a star of the Metropolitan Opera a long time ago, heard me sing at a party in Vienna and urged me to take up the voice seriously, offering to coach me himself. My father put his foot down firmly. I must study law he insisted."

A compromise was arrived at in which Friedrich was allowed to pursue music if he studied law as well. For three years he attended Vienna University and at the same time studied voice with Adolph Robinson. After one year the manager of the Graz Opera in Austria invited

Schorr: shŏr

FRIEDRICH SCHORR

him to make his debut at his opera house. "I did not dare to tell my father. I made the trip to Graz in secret."

The opera debut in Graz took place in 1911 in what was to become one of Schorr's great roles, that of Wotan in *Die Walküre*. It proved so successful that the manager offered him a seasonal contract. Schorr took the first train to Vienna to show the contract to his father who then yielded ground and grudgingly gave his consent for Friedrich to embark on a musical career.

During 1911–1912 Schorr paid his first visit to the United States, appearing in minor roles with the Chicago Opera. The Graz Opera, however, offered him greater opportunities to develop himself in principal roles, primarily in the German repertory, and so he remained with the Graz Opera until 1916, appearing exclusively in Wagnerian roles. During this period he also made guest appearances with the Vienna State Opera where he became a favorite with the audiences. Until the annexation of Austria by the Nazis Schorr sang a season of German opera every year in Vienna.

After leaving Graz, Schorr was a member of the Prague Opera from 1916 to 1918, of the Cologne Opera from 1918 to 1923, and of the Berlin State Opera from 1923 to 1931. Each of these opera houses provided a step upward in his advance toward recognition as the most renowned Wagnerian baritone of his time.

He returned to the United States in 1923 with the Wagnerian Opera Company, appearing as Hans Sachs in *Die Meistersinger* in Baltimore and in February 1923 as Wotan at the Manhattan Opera House in New York. His American success brought him to the attention of Gatti-Casazza, general manager of the Metropolitan Opera, who offered him a contract.

Schorr made his Metropolitan Opera debut nine days earlier than scheduled. When Clarence Whitehill fell ill, Schorr was recruited for the role of Wolfram in *Tannhäuser* on February 14, 1924. His debut, commented Olin Downes in the New York *Times,* "confirmed what was expected of the admired baritone. . . . He at once took measure of the great house and sang with unforced lyric beauty not often surpassed."

Nine days later, on February 23, Schorr sang at the Metropolitan Opera the role with which he had been scheduled to make his debut—Hans Sachs. Lawrence Gilman in the *Tribune* called him "the authentic Sachs of Wagner's drama: a poet, a dreamer, a man of sorrows; but a tragedian who has mastered his grief and does not take too seriously his resignation; who is mellow without softness and noble without offense." Gilman described Schorr's voice as one "of exceptional beauty," adding that Schorr sang "like a musician. Some of his mezza-voce and pianissimo singing yesterday was of astonishing delicacy, purity and finesse." Before his first season was over, Schorr also sang Telramund in *Lohengrin,* Kurvenal in *Tristan and Isolde,* Amfortas in *Parsifal,* and on tour Wotan in *Die Walküre.*

He remained the principal Wagnerian baritone of the Metropolitan Opera through 1942–1943, making his last appearance in that auditorium on March 2, 1943, as the Wanderer in *Siegfried.* His interpretations of all the celebrated Wagnerian baritone roles became classics to be emulated. The most famous were Wotan and the Wanderer, in the *Ring* cycle, and Hans Sachs. He also gathered laurels as Telramund, Wolfram, Kurvenal, Amfortas, Gunther in *Die Götterdämmerung,* and the Dutchman in *The Flying Dutchman.* "His right to be classed among the royal line of Wagnerian singing actors" was established by Lawrence Gilman in the *Tribune.* "This magisterial artist, with his rare gifts, his technical mastery, his simplicity and dignity and integrity has brought distinction and new artistic dimensions to the Wagnerian music dramas."

Schorr did not, however, confine his wide-ranging histrionic and vocal talents exclusively to Wagner at the Metropolitan Opera. On January 19, 1929, he appeared as Daniello in the American premiere of Krenek's *Jonny Spielt Auf* and on November 7, 1931, he created for the United States the title role in Weinberger's *Schwanda.* He was cast as Orestes in the first Metropolitan Opera production of *Elektra* on December 3, 1932, and as Jokanaan in a revival of *Salome* on January 13, 1934. Other non-Wagnerian roles at the Metropolitan Opera were Amonasro in *Aida,* Don Pizarro in *Fidelio,* Faninal in *Der Rosenkavalier,* and the High Priest in *The Magic Flute.*

In 1924 Schorr made his debut at Covent Garden in London where his assumption of leading Wagnerian baritone roles under Bruno Walter's direction made him as highly esteemed in London over a period of several years as he was in New York. He was the leading Wagnerian baritone at the Bayreuth Festival in 1925, 1927, 1928, and 1930, and there he was particularly acclaimed as Wotan and the Wanderer. He was also heard in Wagnerian roles in Vienna, Paris, Prague, and Buenos Aires, among other cities.

When the Nazis took power in Germany in 1933, Schorr, a Jew, established permanent residence in the United States. In 1938 he was appointed vocal adviser in the Wagnerian department at the Metropolitan Opera, where he helped guide young American singers in the Wagnerian style and tradition. After retiring from the Metropolitan Opera, he taught voice and opera at the Hartt School in Hartford, Connecticut, where he set up an opera workshop. In 1950 he was appointed adviser on German opera at the New York City Opera.

Friedrich Schorr died in Farmington, Connecticut, on August 14, 1953.

ABOUT: Life, February 12, 1940; Musical America, March 25, 1941; New York Times, November 2, 1942; Opera News, February 10, 1941.

Elisabeth Schumann

1885–1952

Elisabeth Schumann, soprano, who distinguished herself equally in opera and as an interpreter of *Lieder,* was born in Merseburg,

---

Schumann: shoo′ män

ELISABETH SCHUMANN

Thuringia, Germany, on June 13, 1885. She was the daughter of Alfred Schumann, the organist of the Merseburg Cathedral, and Emma Sontag, a direct descendant of Henriette Sontag, the German prima donna and concert singer. Elisabeth began music study early. She received vocal training from Natalie Häuisch in Dresden, Marie Dietrich in Berlin, and Alma Schadow in Hamburg, the last of whom she always regarded as her most influential teacher.

Schumann's debut in opera took place in Hamburg in 1909 as the Shepherd in *Tannhäuser.* She remained with the Hamburg Opera for a decade, appearing in both the German and Italian repertories and enjoying particular successes in Mozart's operas, as Mignon, and as Sophie in *Der Rosenkavalier;* the last-named role, which she sang for the first time in 1911 in the Hamburg Opera premiere of that opera, became probably her most famous role. Her success as Sophie led Richard Strauss to recommend her to Gatti-Casazza, general manager of the Metropolitan Opera, when he planned an American production of *Der Rosenkavalier.* Schumann arrived in the United States in 1914, and her Metropolitan Opera debut as Sophie took place on November 20. H. E. Krehbiel reported in the *Tribune* that she "possesses a beautiful soprano voice. The role is a test of the singer's abilities. . . . Mme. Schumann, who is quite pretty, sang it with ease and displayed considerable beauty of voice, to which was added volume and character. As an actress she was eloquent."

She stayed with the Metropolitan Opera for

one season. In that time she was heard as Musetta in *La Bohème,* a Flower Maiden in *Parsifal,* Papagena in *The Magic Flute,* Gerhilde in *Die Walküre,* the Forest Bird in *Siegfried,* Wellgunde in *Das Rheingold* and *Die Götterdämmerung,* Marcellina in *Fidelio,* and Gretel in *Hansel and Gretel.* Except for one later appearance as Sophie in a Philadelphia production of *Der Rosenkavalier* under Fritz Reiner, she was not heard again in opera in the United States beyond that season.

When Richard Strauss became the music director of the Vienna State Opera, he engaged her for his company. For two decades she was one of the reigning queens of opera in Vienna. Few could match the dignity, purity, and classic simplicity of style which she brought to the Mozart roles of Despina in *Così fan Tutte,* Susanna in *The Marriage of Figaro,* Zerlina in *Don Giovanni,* Papagena in *The Magic Flute,* and Blonde in *The Abduction from the Seraglio.* Few could match the aristocratic beauty of her vocal delivery in the Italian repertory; and few if any could rival her performances in Richard Strauss's operas. She became such an authoritative performer of Strauss that when the German master arrived in the United States for a concert tour in 1921, he invited her to appear as a soloist at symphony concerts which he conducted and in recitals at which he served as her piano accompanist.

Between 1922 and 1935 she made regular appearances at the Salzburg Festival where she was acclaimed in Mozart's operas and as Sophie. In 1917 she caused a sensation at the Zurich Mozart Festival as Zerlina, with Richard Strauss conducting; she also stole the limelight at the Strauss Festival in Stuttgart where she appeared as Sophie to Richard Mayr's Baron Ochs and to Marie Gutheil-Schoder's Marschallin. When, on May 21, 1924, she sang Sophie at Covent Garden (where she had made her debut earlier that season in *Ariadne auf Naxos*), Bruno Walter, who conducted that performance, said of her: "Elisabeth Schumann was the Sophie of one's dreams"; this was the performance in which Lotte Lehmann appeared for the first time anywhere as the Marschallin. Schumann made numerous guest appearances at La Scala in Milan, the Berlin State Opera, the Munich Opera, and other companies in Europe and South America.

"It is especially with Mozart that she was associated," wrote Desmond Shawe-Taylor, the English musicologist. "She had a beautifully controlled high soprano of delicate, ringing timbre and of crystalline purity and a charming stage presence, especially in demure, mischievous parts." Then, speaking of her performances as Sophie, Shawe-Taylor added: "Few who heard her in her prime will forget her delivery of those long, soaring pianissimo phrases with which Sophie acknowledged the gift of the rose at the beginning of the second act; it seems as though the composer must have had precisely this quality in mind when writing the part."

She duplicated her triumphs in the opera house within the concert hall. It was as a recitalist that the United States came to know her best. In the world of the *Lieder* she was one of the elect. On November 8, 1931, after a ten-year absence, she returned to the American concert scene with a recital at Town Hall in New York. "She sang Schubert," wrote Olin Downes in the New York *Times,* "with a musician's regard for text and phrase, with a beautiful poetic diction. She did more than that. In most of her songs she created his spirit."

She was in France when in March 1938 the Nazis invaded and annexed Austria. Bitterly opposed to the Nazi regime, she decided to abandon her Austrian home and reestablish herself in New York City with her husband, Karl Alwin, an opera conductor, and their son, Gerd. In 1938 she joined the faculty of the Curtis Institute of Music in Philadelphia. There she remained till the end of her life, many of those years as head of the vocal department. In 1944 she became an American citizen.

When the first festival was inaugurated in Edinburgh, in 1947, Schumann appeared on the program. She gave her last recital on February 5, 1950, in New York City with Bruno Walter as her piano accompanist. Her last public appearance was at a benefit concert at the Metropolitan Opera House on January 7, 1951, when she contributed a group of Schubert songs. She died at Memorial Hospital in New York City on April 23, 1952, after several months of illness.

Elisabeth Schumann was an honorary member of the Vienna State Opera and the Vienna Philharmonic, and she was the recipient of the Ring of the Vienna Philharmonic. When Hugo Burghauser presented her with the Ring (which had previously been given to Hans Richter, Richard Strauss, Mahler, and Toscanini) he said: "The Ring is given not only to a great artist, a great musician and a beloved colleague, but to a singer who has been balm to the cast and to all of us down in the pit. In our twenty-year association, she is the only one who has never sung a note off pitch." She was also decorated by the Danish government with the High Order of Art and Science, made Chevalier of the Legion of Honor by France, and named *Kammersängerin* by Austria.

She was the author of *German Song* (1948). Her hobbies were driving cars and collecting antiques.

ABOUT: Musical America, May 1952; Opera News, December 22, 1962.

ERNESTINE SCHUMANN-HEINK

Ernestine Schumann-Heink

1861–1936

Ernestine Schumann-Heink (originally Ernestine Rössler) was one of the great contraltos of her generation. She was born in Lieben, near Prague, Bohemia, on June 15, 1861, the eldest of four children. Her father, Hans Rössler, was an officer in the Austrian army; her mother, Charlotte, an Italian and an amateur singer. Though Ernestine's maternal grandmother, Leah Kohn, was Jewish, Ernestine's mother was converted to Roman Catholicism and was educated in a convent. Ernestine herself was raised as a Catholic.

Ernestine began singing when she was three. Because of the family's poverty, a formal musical training could not be considered. When she was eleven she was sent to the Ursuline Convent in Prague, where she sang in the church choir. She received some vocal instruction from Marietta von Leclair in Graz, Austria, in 1874. In 1876, when Ernestine was fifteen, she made her debut, appearing as a soloist in a performance of Beethoven's Symphony No.9 in Graz. Nina Kienzl, mother of the German composer Wilhelm Kienzl, was impressed with her voice and got her an audition at the Vienna Royal Opera. But her unattractive appearance and her poor clothes created such a discouraging impression that she was advised to give up all thoughts of a career in music. She persevered, however, and her opera debut finally took place on October 13,

Schumann-Heink: shoo͞' măn hīngk'

1878, with the Dresden Opera, as Azucena in *Il Trovatore*. During the four years she was a member of that company, she studied with Karl Krebs and Franz Wüllner. In 1882 she married Ernst Heink, the secretary of the Dresden Opera, and both were dismissed from the company because they had married without the director's permission.

In 1883, as Ernestine Heink, she was engaged by the Hamburg Municipal Opera. There she remained sixteen years, and there she was assigned principal contralto roles in a large and varied repertory of French, Italian, and German operas. In 1887 she made her Berlin debut with the Kroll Opera, and in 1892 she made her London debut with Covent Garden. In her intermittent appearances at Covent Garden, from 1887 to 1900, she assumed Wagnerian roles, on one visit singing Erda, Fricka, and Waltraute in the *Ring* cycle, with Mahler conducting.

Having divorced Ernst Heink in 1893, she married Paul Schumann, an actor and the director of the Thalia Theater in Hamburg. From 1896 to 1906 she appeared regularly (except for the year 1904) at the Bayreuth Festival. In 1898 she signed a ten-year contract with the Berlin Royal Opera, from which she was given a leave of absence to make her first appearances in the United States. Her American debut took place with the Metropolitan Opera company during its visit to Chicago on November 7, 1898. She made her debut as Ortrud in *Lohengrin;* then, with the company still on tour, she was heard as Fricka and Waltraute in *Die Walküre*. On Janu-

741

ary 9, 1899, she made her first appearance on the New York stage of the Metropolitan Opera, this time as Erda in *Das Rheingold*. "Mme. Schumann-Heink," reported H. E. Krehbiel in the *Tribune*, "realized [the role] as it has seldom been realized in her invocation of the old Teutonic deities in the second act. ... When she wins admiration for the passages in which Wagner thought neither of contralto nor soprano, but only of his Frisian creation, half woman, half witch and all wickedness personified, she compels it by virtue of her thrilling use of tonal color, her giving out of Wagner's ideal, which she has absorbed completely. Her work last night kept the corridors buzzing."

Highly esteemed though she was in Germany and London before going to the Metropolitan Opera, Schumann-Heink rose to new heights of fame and artistry in the United States. Encouraged by her initial successes, she was led to break her contract with the Berlin Royal Opera in order to continue performing in the United States. During her initial engagement at the Metropolitan Opera that extended through the 1902–1903 season she also appeared as Flosshilde in *Das Rheingold*, Fricka in *Die Walküre*, Waltraute in *Die Götterdämmerung* and, in 1899, as Erda, Waltraute, and the Third Norn in the first "uncut" presentation of the Wagnerian *Ring* at the Metropolitan Opera. Other roles during this period were Mary in *The Flying Dutchman*, Fidès in *Le Prophète*, Magdalene in *Die Meistersinger*, Brangäne in *Tristan and Isolde*, Frau Reich in *The Merry Wives of Windsor*, the Shepherd in *Tannhäuser*, the Witch in *Hansel and Gretel*, and Prologo in Mancinelli's *Ero e Leandro*. She had previously sung the last of these roles at Covent Garden on July 11, 1898.

In 1903–1904 Schumann-Heink embarked on her first concert tour of the United States. Already recognized as a star, she was everywhere received with acclamation in auditoriums packed to overflowing. As Richard Aldrich reported in the New York *Times* following her New York recital on February 5, 1904: "There are very few people who can fill Carnegie Hall with such a throng of enthusiastic admirers by their sole unaided efforts ... as Mme. Schumann-Heink did yesterday afternoon, filling every seat in the auditorium and crowding the stage with several hundred people who could find no room elsewhere in the house. ... There

was unbounded and somewhat indiscriminate enthusiasm over everything she did, and unmistakable tokens were given of the high esteem in which the singer and her accomplishments are held by very many admirers in New York."

On October 3, 1904, Schumann-Heink appeared in New York in Julian Edward's operetta *Love's Lottery*, which then went on tour. She was back at the Metropolitan Opera for the 1906–1907 season for the *Ring* cycle. From then on, she made intermittent appearances at the Metropolitan Opera until 1932. She absented herself from the company for several seasons at a time to appear in opera houses over the world. In one of these (the Dresden Royal Opera) she created the role of Klytemnestra in the world premiere of *Elektra* on January 25, 1909.

Schumann-Heink's husband died in 1904. One year later (the year in which she became an American citizen) she married William Rapp Jr., a lawyer who had been serving as her manager; they were divorced in 1914.

During World War I, Schumann-Heink was totally involved in the Allied cause. She contributed her services freely to war rallies and Liberty Bond drives, and she often toured the army camps and hospitals. She saw her sons serve on both sides of the conflict; the oldest died in a German submarine.

Schumann-Heink celebrated the fiftieth anniversary of her singing debut with a return to the Metropolitan Opera on February 26, 1926, in *Das Rheingold*. Soon after that she appeared in a gala concert in her honor in Carnegie Hall. This was the beginning of an American tour billed as her farewell. But there were still many performances left in her and a good deal of resplendent singing still to be heard. At the age of sixty-eight she could still command the stage as Erda in *Das Rheingold* and did so when she appeared on January 21, 1929, after an absence of two seasons from the Metropolitan Opera. "Her brief address to Wotan," wrote Olin Downes in the New York *Times*, "projected itself over every other episode of the performance. ... Nothing less than a great mistress of art suffices for this passage. The consciousness that was deep in the tone itself, in its every color and inflection, so impressed the listener yesterday that it was some minutes after the disappearance of Erda that he was able to give attention again to the things transpiring before his eyes. This was the fault of Ernestine Schumann-Heink."

During 1926–1927 Schumann-Heink went on a golden jubilee concert tour of the United States. In 1930 she appeared at the Roxy Theatre in New York, a motion picture theatre featuring elaborate stage presentations. She later toured with a company of performers known as Roxy's Gang, under the aegis of Samuel L. Rothafel (Roxy), the director of the Roxy Theatre. At her last appearance at the Metropolitan Opera—on March 11, 1932, as Erda in *Siegfried*—she was still an artist in command of her dramatic and vocal powers. Once again Olin Downes could become rhapsodic over her performance. He wrote in the New York *Times:* "Her opening lines were those of a great artist gaining control of her resources. Thereafter, music and text were projected with an eloquence that took the breath away."

Between 1933 and 1935 Schumann-Heink made numerous appearances over the American radio networks. For years the playing of her recording of "Silent Night, Holy Night" became a kind of Christmas ritual over American radio.

In 1935 she appeared in a motion picture, *Here's to Romance,* that proved so successful that she was signed to a three-year contract to star in the movies. Deteriorating health made it impossible for her to fulfill this contract. She died in Hollywood on November 17, 1936.

ABOUT: Lawton, M. Schumann-Heink: The Last of the Titans. *Periodicals*—New York Times, November 18, 1936.

Carl Schuricht

1880–1967

Carl Schuricht, conductor, was born in Danzig, Germany, on July 3, 1880. His father, Carl Schuricht, was a builder of pipe organs who, with his own father, owned an organ factory in Danzig; his mother, Amanda, was an excellent pianist and singer. She was of Polish descent. As a boy, Carl attended the Berlin High School for Music where his teachers included Ernst Rudorff and Engelbert Humperdinck and where he received a scholarship in composition. He subsequently attended Max Reger's class in composition in Leipzig.

Schuricht: shŏŏ' rĭкt

CARL SCHURICHT

His studies ended, Carl served his conducting apprenticeship with various opera houses in Zwickau, Dortmund, and Weimar, among other cities. In 1909 he became the conductor of the Rühlscher-Gesangverein in Frankfort, a choral society with which he introduced to Germany many compositions of Frederick Delius. Three years later, he was appointed conductor in Wiesbaden and in 1922 became general music director. He filled that position until 1944. During these years he made numerous guest appearances throughout Europe. In 1933 he served as conductor of the Berlin Philharmonic Choir and gave impressive performances with the Concertgebouw Orchestra in Amsterdam. He became popular in Holland and in 1938 received from Queen Wilhelmina the Order of Orange-Nassau.

In 1944 Schuricht became enmeshed in difficulties with the Nazi officials, fled Germany, and settled in Switzerland. After that he held no permanent post with any opera company or symphony orchestras but made between fifty and sixty guest appearances with European orchestras each year. In 1946 he helped to reopen the Salzburg Festival in its first postwar season. He participated in other major European festivals, including those in the Netherlands, Lucerne, Aix-en-Provence, Besançon, and Montreux.

When the Vienna Philharmonic made its first tour of the United States in 1956, Schuricht was one of its two conductors. He had already made his American debut, in a single concert in St. Louis in 1927. At that time other American appearances had been projected, but sudden illness forced him to cancel all further concerts.

His second American debut took place with the Vienna Philharmonic in Washington, D.C., on November 4, 1956. Three days later he appeared with this orchestra in Carnegie Hall, New York. "There was courtliness in his manner as he came out for the first time," wrote Howard Taubman in the New York *Times*. "Once he started the program, Herr Schuricht was all artist. There were no mannerisms in his wide, dependable beat. His musicianship was to be noted at once in the phrasing of Mozart's D major Symphony." During this tour Schuricht conducted eleven concerts.

He returned to the United States one year later for four concerts at the Ravinia Festival in Chicago and for a guest appearance at the Berkshire Music Festival at Tanglewood in Massachusetts.

He died at his home at Corseaux-sur-Vevey, on Lake Geneva, in Switzerland, on January 7, 1967.

"When I was young," Schuricht told an American interviewer in 1956, "I concentrated on the moderns—Stravinsky, Bartók, Hindemith and the others. I still like them. . . . But more and more I am in demand as an interpreter of classical and romantic music. In France, I am considered a Schumann specialist. In Denmark, they call me a Brahms specialist. In Holland I am considered a Bruckner specialist." But, he added, he was essentially an exponent of "an old tradition. . . . I have nothing against what music is now, but feel it is important to pass on a sense of tradition from age to youth."

In 1944 Schuricht married Maria Martha Banz. Away from music his hobbies were reading and playing with toy soldiers. He owned a large collection of toy soldiers representing the military of the Louis XV era.

Schuricht was an honorary member of the Vienna Philharmonic and an honorary citizen of Wiesbaden; he was awarded the Grand Croix de l'Ordre, Alfonso X el Sabio.

ABOUT: Gavoty, B. Carl Schuricht. *Periodicals*—New York Times, November 4, 1956, January 8, 1967.

Elisabeth Schwarzkopf

1915–

Elisabeth Schwarzkopf, soprano, was born in Jarotschin (Jarocin), near Poznan, Poland, on December 9, 1915. Her parents, Friedrich and Elisabeth Fröhlich Schwarzkopf, were of German origin; her father was the director of a high school. When she began attending school, the family moved to Berlin where she entered the Berlin High School for Music. Her first singing teacher began training her as a contralto. After two and a half years of such misguided training, while continuing her regular curriculum at the High School, she studied privately with a Dr. Egenolf who succeeded in undoing all of the damage of her initial training. At the High School Elisabeth proved to be a brilliant student, capturing prizes in virtually every department: singing, theory, musical history, harmony, piano, and violin. She also won a League of Nations Scholarship enabling her to study English in Leicester, England.

Her student years coincided with the rise and growth of the Third Reich. As a member of the Studentenbund she allied herself with the Nazi movement. Beautiful, as well as gifted, she soon became a favorite of high Nazi officials.

Her opera debut came on Easter Day of 1938 as a Flower Maiden in *Parsifal* at the Charlottenburg Opera in Berlin. To make that appearance she had to learn her part on thirty-six hours' notice. Before her first season at Charlottenburg ended she had appeared with that company four times a week in about twenty different minor roles in *Tannhäuser, Siegfried, Rigoletto, The Magic Flute, The Merry Widow,* and *The Bartered Bride,* among other operas. She was assigned her first major roles in 1941: Oscar in *Un Ballo in Maschera,* Musetta in *La Bohème,* Lauretta in *Gianni Schicchi,* and Zerbinetta in *Ariadne auf Naxos.* Her performance as Zerbinetta made such an impression on Maria Ivogün, the concert and opera singer who had created that role, that she took Schwarzkopf on as a pupil.

One of Ivogün's accomplishments was to train Schwarzkopf as a singer of *Lieder.* Schwarzkopf's first song recital, in Vienna in November

Schwarzkopf: shvärts′ kŏpf

ELISABETH SCHWARZKOPF

1942, was so highly esteemed that Karl Böhm, principal conductor of the Vienna State Opera, invited her to appear as a guest performer with his company both as Zerbinetta and as Blonde in *The Abduction from the Seraglio.* These appearances led to her engagement as principal soprano of the Vienna State Opera. A serious illness in 1943–1944 made it impossible for her to fill this engagement. She went into complete retirement for recuperation. In 1944, however, she finally appeared with the Vienna State Opera, as Musetta, as Rosina in *The Barber of Seville,* and as Gilda in *Rigoletto.*

When the Vienna State Opera had to close down because the auditorium had been bombed during World War II, Schwarzkopf went into a second period of temporary retirement. She returned to the concert stage only after the war was over, making a triumphant appearance in Vienna in January 1946. At that time Herbert von Karajan called her "potentially the best singer we have." Already few sopranos could match the perfection of her voice production, each tone of unblemished purity and controlled by a noble musicianship. As a performer of *Lieder,* she entered the ranks of Elena Gerhardt, Lotte Lehmann, and Elisabeth Schumann, as one of the great female interpreters of German art songs. At this time she also returned to the Vienna State Opera, which had resumed performances at the Theater-an-der Wien. Within a few months she established herself there as one of the most admired members of the company. She sang for the first time the roles of Nedda in

I Pagliacci, Mimi in *La Bohème,* Violetta in *La Traviata,* Constanza in *The Abduction from the Seraglio,* Pamina in *The Magic Flute,* Susanna in *The Marriage of Figaro,* Marcelline in *Fidelio* and, subsequently, Liù in *Turandot* and Sophie in *Der Rosenkavalier.*

In 1947 she enjoyed her first success at the Salzburg Festival, appearing in a historic performance of *The Marriage of Figaro,* produced and directed by Herbert von Karajan, which later was produced intact at La Scala in Milan. This marked the beginnings of her affiliation with La Scala, where within the next few years she was acclaimed as Donna Elvira in *Don Giovanni,* Elsa in *Lohengrin,* Elisabeth in *Tannhäuser,* and the Marschallin in *Der Rosenkavalier,* the last of which she was singing for the first time in her career. At La Scala she also appeared in the first Italian production of Stravinsky's *The Rake's Progress,* in which she had created the leading female role of Annie Truelove at the Venice Festival on September 11, 1951. There too she appeared in the world premiere of Carl Orff's *Trionfo,* on February 13, 1953.

She went to London for the first time in September 1947 as a member of the Vienna State Opera. After that she was regularly invited to Covent Garden, and there she captivated her audiences as Sophie, Pamina, Mimi, Eva, and Marcelline.

When the Bayreuth Festival resumed operations in the summer of 1951 after a seven-year hiatus, Schwarzkopf sang the soprano solo in a performance of Beethoven's Symphony No.9 under Furtwängler and appeared as Eva in *Die Meistersinger* and as a Rhine maiden in the *Ring* cycle.

Her first appearance in the United States, long overdue, had to wait until her one-time unfortunate allegiance to the Nazis could be forgiven, if not altogether forgotten. Her American debut finally took place with a recital at Carnegie Hall in New York on October 25, 1953. To the audience that overcrowded the auditorium she was a legend come to life, what with reports of her European triumphs supplemented by a steady stream of remarkable recordings of *Lieder* and operas. (She had made her first recording in 1937 while still attending the High School for Music in Berlin, appearing in the cast of *The Magic Flute* performed on disks by the Mozart Society.) She won the audience and critics completely. She toured the United States that year and returned in 1954 for another three-month tour. Writing in the *Herald Tribune* about one of her American recitals, Paul Henry Lang reflected the reaction of most American music critics to her talent in *Lieder.* "The soprano does not just sing, she lives through a song, and when there is a mock dialogue or question and answer, there are two or three persons singing. She follows every turn, every nuance, her facial expression always vividly expressive." On March 13, 1960, Schwarzkopf presented in New York an all–Hugo Wolf recital to commemorate the one-hundredth anniversary of the composer's birth. "Miss Schwarzkopf reminded one that Wolf was something more than a miniaturist," noted Howard Taubman in the New York *Times,* "and the . . . soprano conveyed the tensions of these highly charged little dramas with unerring perception."

On September 20, 1955, she made her American operatic debut with the San Francisco Opera as the Marschallin. Mildred Norton reported from San Francisco that this debut presented "a poised and vibrant new personality with a vocal radiance and grace." That same season, in San Francisco, she was cast as Donna Elvira. She returned to San Francisco in 1956 as Fiordiligi in *Così fan Tutte* and in 1958 as the Countess in *The Marriage of Figaro.*

In Europe, in October 1955, she was awarded the Orfeo d'Oro award instituted that year in Mantua, Italy, for distinguished musicians; the presentation was made by Toscanini. Later the same year, in December, Schwarzkopf inaugurated the Piccolo Teatro della Scala in Milan. In the summer of 1960 she appeared as the Marschallin at the Salzburg Festival in a performance conducted by Herbert von Karajan. This production was filmed and distributed to theaters around the world.

She returned to the San Francisco Opera in 1963 as the Countess Madeleine in Strauss's *Capriccio,* an opera staged expressly for her. One year later, on October 13, 1964, she made her debut at the Metropolitan Opera as the Marschallin. "Not since the days of Lotte Lehmann have we had a Marschallin of such nuance," said Harriet Johnson in the New York *Post,* "though each was different. While Mme. Lehmann's conception was deeply reflective and philosophical, Miss Schwarzkopf's became vividly human. Onstage she was glamorous, exquisitely feminine,

voluptuous, yet aristocratic in bearing and costume—and a singer of fastidious style."

She appeared at the Metropolitan Opera for two seasons, returning in 1965–1966 to score another triumph as Donna Elvira. In 1966 she participated in the Stravinsky festival at the Lincoln Center for the Performing Arts in New York, once in a recital and a second time as a guest artist with orchestra.

She continued to appear in recitals and with symphony orchestras in the United States until 1975 when, on April 27, she made what was announced as her "farewell United States appearance" at Carnegie Hall in New York. She was still able to give a performance which, in the opinion of Donal Henahan in the New York *Times,* "few Lieder singers could equal nowadays, even though her voice had little of the sheen, range or power that one remembers from a decade ago." To Irving Kolodin in the *Saturday Review* this performance was "no caricature of greatness but a conversion of it into art by other means and methods than purely vocal."

This recital, however, was not Schwarzkopf's last public appearance. In November 1975 she substituted for Victoria de los Angeles at a recital at Covent Garden; on April 27, 1976, she gave her last New York recital and later in 1976 she was invited to assist at the five-hundredth anniversary of Uppsala University in Sweden to be celebrated in 1978.

In 1951 she decided to make London her permanent residence. There, two years later, she married Walter Legge, who in addition to being a recording executive was also the founder of the London Philharmonic Orchestra. They own a secluded estate, Le Petit Port, on the French side of Lake Geneva, an elegant house filled with books and modern Italian paintings. Schwarzkopf used to enjoy skiing, mountain climbing, and playing tennis, but in her later years she has confined her hobbies to cooking and gardening.

On June 10, 1976, she was awarded an honorary doctorate in music by the University of Cambridge in England.

With her husband, Walter Legge, Schwarzkopf conducted a series of master classes in vocal interpretation at the Juilliard School of Music in New York in November-December 1976.

ABOUT: Musical America, September 15, 1955; Opera News, July 1953, May 1975, January 22, 1977; Stereo Review, April 1975; Time, November 9, 1953; Vogue, November 15, 1954.

Albert Schweitzer

1875–1965

Albert Schweitzer, theologian and humanitarian —recipient of the Nobel Peace Prize in 1952— was also an organist and an authority on Johann Sebastian Bach.

He was born in Kaysersberg, in upper Alsace (then under German rule), on January 14, 1875, the second of five children of Adele Schillinger Schweitzer and Louis Schweitzer, a Lutheran minister. In his childhood the family moved to Gunsbach where his father became a vicar in one of the churches. In Gunsbach, Albert received his first academic schooling, going on to the preparatory school in Münster and then the gymnasium in Mulhouse. The love of music was handed down in the Schweitzer family from the maternal grandfather, who had been an organist. Albert began studying the piano when he was five, the harmonium at seven, and the organ at eight. The organ became his favorite instrument. By the time he was nine he was sufficiently proficient at it to be able to substitute for the parish organist at church services. He received his first intensive instruction at the organ from Ernst Münch, a relative. Further study took place in Paris with Charles Widor immediately after Albert had completed eight years at the Mulhouse Gymnasium in 1893. Widor was so impressed with his talent that he taught him without a fee. Later on, Widor collaborated with him in editing the first of eight volumes of the complete organ works of Johann Sebastian Bach.

In 1893 Albert entered the University of Strasbourg as a student of theology, philosophy, and musical theory. These studies were briefly interrupted in 1894 when he was called for one year of compulsory military service. This was for him a time of introspection, self-analysis, and Bible study that profoundly influenced his subsequent religious and humanitarian thinking. He returned to the University for the continuation of his studies in 1895 and one year later made a silent vow to consecrate his life for the next nine years to science and art and after that to dedicate himself to the alleviation of human suffering. Music was not forgotten, however. In

ALBERT SCHWEITZER

1896 he inaugurated a series of concerts of Bach's organ music in Strasbourg.

In 1898 Schweitzer was in Paris at the Sorbonne, writing his doctoral dissertation on the religious philosophy of Immanuel Kant. At this time he resumed organ study with Widor. One year later he received his doctorate from the University of Strasbourg and in 1900 a higher degree—that of licentiate in theology. Meanwhile, in 1899 he assumed the post of curate at the Church St. Nicholas in Strasbourg. From 1902 to 1912 he was Privatdozent in theology at the University of Strasbourg and from 1903 to 1906, principal of the Theological College of St. Thomas.

Music—specifically the playing of the organ —continued to be of prime interest. From 1905 to 1911 he was the organist of both the Société Johann Sebastian Bach in Paris (which he had helped to found with Widor) and of the Orfeó Catalá in Barcelona. During this time he also gave concerts in various European cities, slowly building for himself a reputation as an organ virtuoso and as a specialist in Bach's music. In 1911 he was a principal participant at the French Music Festival in Munich. In 1903 and 1904 he worked on a biography of Bach undertaken on the advice and encouragement of Widor. This biography was first published in French in 1905; three years later it appeared in German in a completely rewritten version; and in 1911 it was translated into English by Ernest Newman. Other musicological works appeared

---

Schweitzer: shvī′ tsēr

in the early 1900s, among them, in 1906, a treatise on organ building and playing.

By 1905 he had decided what his own specific mission would be in the service of humanity: He would bring modern medicine to Equatorial Africa. In his autobiography *Out of My Life and Thought* (1933) he revealed how on October 13, 1905, he dropped a letter in a mailbox on the avenue de la Grande Armée in Paris, informing his parents of his decision. "The plan which I meant now to put into execution had been in my mind for a long time, having been conceived so long ago as my student days. It struck me as incomprehensible that I should be allowed to lead such a happy life, while I saw so many people wrestling with care and suffering. . . . I settled with myself . . . that I would consider myself justified in living till I was thirty for science and art, in order to devote myself from that time forward to the direct service of humanity."

To fulfill this ambition he decided in 1905 to study medicine in Strasbourg. He received his medical degree in 1913; he then took courses on tropical medicine in Paris. Meanwhile, on June 18, 1912, he married Hélène Bresslau, the daughter of a professor at the University of Strasbourg, who became his collaborator in his medical and literary efforts. Their daughter, Rhena, was born in 1919.

In 1913 Schweitzer obtained from the French Missionary Society a tract of land in Lambaréné, two hundred miles within French Equatorial Africa. With funds accumulated from giving concerts with the Paris Bach Society and with contributions from various churches in Strasbourg, he left for Lambaréné early in 1914, taking with him a piano (which his friends had given him as a farewell gift). In Lambaréné he founded a hospital that in the first nine months of its existence treated over two thousand cases of almost every known disease.

During World War I he ran into difficulties because he had a German passport. He was interned as a prisoner of war for four months in Africa, then released and recalled to France where he was interned in a prison camp. After his release in July 1918, he served on the staff of the municipal hospital in Strasbourg and as a member of the faculty of the Theological College of St. Thomas. During these years he wrote a book on Africa *(On the Edge of the Primeval Forest)* and two volumes on the philosophy of civilization *(The Decay and Restoration of Civilization and Ethics)*. In 1919 he played the organ with the Orfeó Catalá in Barcelona and also performed in Sweden; in 1922 he toured Europe in organ recitals to raise money for the rebuilding of his hospital in Lambaréné which had been razed to the ground during the war years.

"Schweitzer's greatness as a performer consisted in his poetic vision," commented Rosalyn Tureck, pianist and Bach specialist, in an article in the special issue of *Saturday Review* devoted to Schweitzer. "His other work prevented him from devoting himself to music with the single-minded concentration and intensive labor that great instrumental art demands from a performer. Therefore, Schweitzer's performances were open to criticism. . . . Although I agree with the general criticism, I must urge the importance of not condemning the whole. For Schweitzer played with the spiritual vision of an artist and the man he was. Instrumental techniques and musical style form the whole of most performers' achievements. To stop here in listening to Schweitzer is to miss the distinguishing factor in his playing—the spiritual vision. I believe it is important to acknowledge this vision."

In an essay in *Europa,* Stefan Zweig recalled hearing Schweitzer perform Bach for him in a church in Alsace. "One tiny lamp alone is switched on over the keyboard of the organ; it casts its light only upon Schweitzer's hands which are now gliding over the keys. The spiritual face, leaning forward, seems bathed in an unearthly glow. And in the empty, dark church Schweitzer plays for us his favorite: Johann Sebastian Bach. Unforgettable experience! . . . Never did I sense the metaphysical might of Bach as I did here, in this little Protestant church, evoked and interpreted in utter devotion, by a truly religious man. How dreamily yet with what rhythm and precision his fingers trailed over the white keys plunged in darkness; like a human, superhuman voice, the music rose from the huge pipes and rang out mightily."

Schweitzer returned to Lambaréné in 1924 to supervise the construction of a new building and the enlargement of his hospital staff. From 1925 to 1928 he was again in Europe to give concerts in Sweden, Denmark, England, Holland, Switzerland, Germany, and Czechoslovakia to raise money for his hospital. He also lectured and completed a new book, *Mysticism of Paul the Apostle.* In 1928 the municipality of Frankfort awarded him the Goethe Prize of ten thousand marks, enabling him to build a guest house in Gunsbach to which he returned from time to time from Lambaréné for rest and contemplation.

Between continuous visits to and tours of Europe, Schweitzer spent his time in Lambaréné. There he added a plantation and built several new wards in the years between 1929 and 1932. During World War II, the Vichy French forces and the forces of the Free French fought for control of the region around Lambaréné. Schweitzer's hospital became isolated. Fortunately, Schweitzer had stored up enough food and drugs just before the outbreak of the war to take care of his three to four thousand patients from 1940 to 1942. After that, supplies were provided by the United States, England, and Sweden.

In 1949 Schweitzer went to the United States to participate in the Goethe Bicentennial ceremonies at Aspen, Colorado, and to deliver a lecture on Goethe. Two years later he was elected to the French Academy, and in 1952 he was awarded the Nobel Peace Prize. When he went to Oslo to receive the award, the King told him: "It is I who should bow to you." In 1953 Schweitzer was honored at Buckingham Palace by Queen Elizabeth with the insignia of an honorary membership in the Order of Merit—the only other non-Briton ever to receive this honor was Dwight D. Eisenhower. Schweitzer's film biography was released in the United States in 1957 and won an Academy Award in 1959. After the death of his wife in 1957, Schweitzer remained almost continuously at Lambaréné. There he celebrated his ninetieth birthday with hundreds of Africans, Europeans, and Americans who came to congratulate him. "I feel at home here," he told them. "I belong to you until my dying breath."

He suffered a stroke on August 28, 1965, after making a tour of his hospital and adjoining buildings. He lingered on for a week, dying on September 4, 1965, in his wooden hut in his jungle hospital. He died, said a medical bulletin, "quietly in peace and dignity in his bed." He was buried the following day in a brief and simple ceremony at Lambaréné next to the urn containing the ashes of his wife. His grave was marked by a cross he himself had made.

In 1967 an Albert Schweitzer Friendship House was established in Great Barrington, Massachusetts. There, in June 1971, an Albert Schweitzer Library was dedicated by Pablo Casals as an adjunct to the House.

Schweitzer's one-hundredth birthday was commemorated on January 14, 1975, with a concert at Carnegie Hall in New York with Pablo Casals and Andrés Segovia among the participants. On this occasion, the first Albert Schweitzer Award for musical and humanitarian achievements was presented to Isaac Stern.

Schweitzer was a large man: six feet tall, with well-developed physique and strong muscles. A gray moustache flowed over his fine, sensitive lips. His tastes were ascetic. When he traveled it was always as inexpensively as possible. For decades he owned the same old frock coat. This was the one he wore when he performed for the King of Spain in the 1920s and when he received the Nobel Prize three decades later. He drank nothing stronger than wine and never smoked. He refused to eat meat, fish, or even the liver dumplings he had once enjoyed, saying simply: "I can't eat anything that was alive." At Lambaréné he allowed no bird or animal to be killed for food. He had only one use for money, to pour it into his African hospital; it had no value to him for personal pleasures or comforts. Stefan Zweig spoke of Schweitzer's life as the biography of a true hero because of his "utter dogmatic immolation of the individual to the ideal, the brand of heroism which, in men like Gandhi, Romain Rolland and Albert Schweitzer, bespeaks the glory of our generation."

ABOUT: Anderson, E. The World of Albert Schweitzer; Brabazon, J. Albert Schweitzer; Hagedorn, H. Prophet in the Wilderness: The Story of Albert Schweitzer; Joy, C. R. ed. Albert Schweitzer, an Anthology; Kraus, O. Albert Schweitzer, His Work and His Philosophy; Picht, W. The Life and Thought of Albert Schweitzer; Ratter, M. C. Albert Schweitzer; Regester, J. D. Albert Schweitzer: The Man and His Music; Schweitzer, A. Out of My Life and Thought; Seaver, G. Albert Schweitzer: The Man and His Mind. *Periodicals*—Saturday Review, Schweitzer Issue, September 25, 1965.

Antonio Scotti

1866–1936

ANTONIO SCOTTI

In the era of all-star casts at the Metropolitan Opera often described as "the golden age," Antonio Scotti, baritone, played a prominent role. He performed for thirty-four seasons at the Metropolitan Opera, the longest period covered by any artist in the history of that company.

He was born in Naples, on January 25, 1866. He studied voice with Trifari Paganini, Vincenzo Lombardi, and Francesco Lamperti before making his opera debut in Malta on November 1, 1889, as Amonasro in *Aida.* For the next decade he made numerous appearances in Italy, Spain, Poland, Russia, and South America. On December 26, 1898, he made his debut at La Scala in Milan as Hans Sachs in *Die Meistersinger;* this performance also marked the first appearance at La Scala of Toscanini as conductor. On June 8, 1899, he was heard for the first time at Covent Garden in London in one of his celebrated roles, Don Giovanni. For fifteen consecutive spring seasons Scotti returned to Covent Garden, becoming one of its most esteemed baritones. There, on June 28, 1905, he created the role of Chim-Fen in the world premiere of Franco Leoni's *L'Oracolo,* a part that he made uniquely his own. As Olin Downes was to write many years later in the New York *Times:* "What is the opera without him? Of *L'Oracolo,* Mr. Scotti could well say, paraphrasing Louis XIV, 'L'opéra, c'est moi,' and he would be right."

Scotti joined the Metropolitan Opera company in the fall of 1899. His American debut took place in Chicago on November 15, 1899, as Nevers in *Les Huguenots* while the Metropolitan was on tour. Still on tour, he was heard as Don Giovanni, Valentin in *Faust,* Escamillo in *Carmen,* Rigoletto, and Amonasro. On December 27, 1899, he appeared at the Metropolitan Opera in New York as Don Giovanni. "It was speedily made plain that in Signor Scotti there had been an important acquisition made to the Metropolitan Opera's forces," wrote H. E. Krehbiel in the *Tribune.* "He possesses a beautiful baritone voice, fine and smooth in quality, fluent in execution and managed with admirable skill. . . . But still further, he is an artist in the higher sense of

the word. He sings with intelligence and discrimination, and with the accent of dramatic truthfulness."

Scotti remained with the Metropolitan Opera company 34 seasons. In that time he was heard 832 times in New York and 337 times on tour. He appeared as Scarpia in *Tosca* (probably his greatest role) 156 times; Sharpless in *Madama Butterfly* 119 times; Marcello in *La Bohème* 107 times; and performed 44 times as Tonio in *I Pagliacci* and as Chim-Fen in *L'Oracolo. Tosca* and *L'Oracolo* were American premieres, the former on February 4, 1901, and the latter on February 4, 1914. Other American premieres in which he was cast were Isidore de Lara's *Messaline* (January 22, 1902), Giordano's *Fedora* (December 5, 1906), and Wolf-Ferrari's *Le Donne Curiose* (January 3, 1912). On March 20, 1901, he was heard as Hamilcar in the first New York production of Reyer's *Salammbô.*

He appeared in the first Metropolitan Opera productions of *Ernani* (January 28, 1903), *Lucrezia Borgia* (December 5, 1904), *L'Elisir d'Amore* (January 23, 1904), *Adriana Lecouvreur* (November 18, 1907), Mascagni's *Iris* (December 6, 1907), *The Secret of Suzanne* (December 13, 1912), and Ricci's *Crispino e la Comare.*

He opened the Metropolitan Opera season eight times: 1902–1903 as Iago in *Otello;* 1903–1904 as Rigoletto; 1904–1905 and again in 1908–1909 as Amonasro; 1905–1906 as Barnaba in *La Gioconda;* 1907–1908 as Michonnet in

Scotti: skô′ tĕ

750

Adriana Lecouvreur; 1912–1913 as Lescaut in *Manon;* and 1922–1923 as Scarpia.

He was Rigoletto in the performance of November 23, 1903, when Enrico Caruso made his Metropolitan Opera debut, and he was Sharpless when, on February 11, 1907, *Madama Butterfly* was produced in Italian for the first time in the United States. He was also cast in revivals of *The Barber of Seville* in 1904, *Otello* and *Falstaff* in 1909, and *Falstaff* in 1925.

Other roles in which he distinguished himself at the Metropolitan Opera were Dr. Malatesta in *Don Pasquale,* Nelusko in *L'Africaine,* Germont in *La Traviata,* Almaviva in *The Marriage of Figaro,* Renato in *Un Ballo in Maschera,* and Count Gil in *The Secret of Suzanne.*

Scotti's twenty-fifth anniversary at the Metropolitan Opera was celebrated with a gala performance of *Tosca* on January 1, 1924. His last appearance at the Metropolitan, on January 20, 1933, was in *L'Oracolo.* What Olin Downes wrote in the New York *Times* the day after Scotti's farewell serves as a fitting evaluation of his rich career: "Mr. Scotti will have a high and lasting place in the Metropolitan history and in the history of the operatic art. He has been equal as an interpreter to the greatest parts, and he has made significant and memorable small ones. . . . The public has seen the last of this great interpreter who has taught us so much and so well. Generations to come can take example from the thorough preparation he gave himself before he began his public career; from his remarkable gift for the theater, his rare intelligence and versatility in many roles; and from his conscience as an artist, and from the simplicity, modesty, and amiability of the man. Others will come and go. There will be achievements and reputations. But we shall not see his like again."

In 1910 Scotti was acclaimed as Don Giovanni at the Salzburg Festival in Austria. Soon after World War I, he formed his own company, the Scotti Opera, with which he toured the United States for four seasons.

After retiring from the Metropolitan Opera, Scotti returned to Italy where he spent his last years in poverty and neglect. He died in Naples on February 26, 1936.

"He was a man of the world," wrote Max de Schauensee in *Opera News,* "slender and insinuating, possessed of an animal magnetism that precipitated him into love affairs with Broadway actresses, a favorite of international society. Though very serious about his career, he drew his art from the sophistication of his day."

ABOUT: Opera News, April 7, 1962.

Renata Scotto

1935–

Renata Scotto, soprano, was born in Savona, on the Ligurian coast of Italy, on February 24, 1935. "I think I was born to sing," she told Stephen E. Rubin in an interview in the New York *Times.* "I don't even remember when I started. I was too little. When I was four, my mother told me I used to go out on the terrace of our house and sing. . . . I remember, too, I used to put on my mother's clothes and go to the mirror and perform. . . . Every moment I wanted to be a star."

As a child she sang in church choirs. When she was twelve she heard her first opera—*Rigoletto*—and from then on her dream was to become a prima donna. She listened continually to opera performances over the radio and on records, singing along with the principal sopranos. She began music study when she was fourteen with lessons in voice and the piano at the Accademia Musicale Savonese. Within a short time she began to make public appearances as a mezzo-soprano, and she made a private recording of the contralto aria "Stride la vampa" from *Il Trovatore.* In her sixteenth year she moved to Milan where she studied voice more seriously with Mercedes Llopart, who changed her range from mezzo to soprano, and then helped to develop her over a two-year period into a coloratura. Further study took place at the Verdi Conservatory in Milan.

In 1953 Scotto won a singing competition in Italy which gave her an opportunity to make her opera debut in 1954 at the Teatro Nuovo in Milan, as Violetta in *La Traviata.* "I had been living in a convent with some very strict nuns. They didn't approve of my debut role, so I moved." In December 1954 she helped to open the season of La Scala in Milan in the title role of Catalani's *La Wally.* La Scala offered her a contract in secondary roles which she turned down, insisting on principal parts. She then ap-

Scotto: skô′ tô

751

RENATA SCOTTO

peared in provincial opera houses in Italy, gaining valuable experience. In the spring of 1957 she made her London debut with a visiting Italian company, appearing as Adina in *L'Elisir d'Amore.* Her successes encouraged La Scala to engage her on her own terms. When La Scala appeared at the Edinburgh Festival in early fall of 1957 for a performance of *La Sonnambula* that starred Maria Callas, it called upon Renata Scotto to replace Callas as Amina when Callas fell ill. "I didn't know the part," she recalls. "I don't know what happened, but in three days I learned it and sang it with the most success. I was very sure of myself, and I don't know why. It was the most beautiful evening of my career." The response of critics and audiences to her performance led La Scala to mount a new production of that opera for her in Milan.

In addition to appearing at La Scala, Scotto was heard in Covent Garden in London, the Vienna State Opera, the Teatro Colón in Buenos Aires, and other opera houses. In 1960 she made her American debut as Mimi in *La Bohème* with the Chicago Lyric Opera. This was also the year in which she married Lorenzo Anselmi, a first violinist at La Scala and a member of the Società Corelli, which was made up of a dozen virtuoso string performers. He gave up his own career to become her manager and coach. They acquired an apartment in Milan and a country villa at Gonzaga, Mantua. They had two children.

When La Scala paid a historic visit to the Soviet Union in September 1965, it was Scotto's performances in the title role of *Lucia di Lam-*

mermoor that aroused the most enthusiasm. Several weeks later, on October 13, came her debut at the Metropolitan Opera as Cio-Cio-San in *Madama Butterfly.* "Her strength is dramatic inflection," wrote Miles Kastendieck in the New York *Journal-American.* "She conveys more of the meaning of the text than usual. . . . Her performance may have had its share of Italian mannerisms, but it also reflected the Oriental background of the story. In short, she is an excellent actress, capable of imbuing feeling in a role. Vocally, Miss Scotto excels in pianissimos, which are quite beguiling."

The agility of her high register, the suave bel canto flow of her legato passages and her aristocratic way in molding phrases became further apparent at the Metropolitan Opera when, in her first season, she assumed the roles of Lucia in *Lucia di Lammermoor* and Adina in *L'Elisir d'Amore.* In later seasons she took on the roles of Violetta, of Gilda in *Rigoletto,* Marguerite in *Faust,* Amina in *La Sonnambula,* Mimi, and Elena in *I Vespri Siciliani.* On October 11, 1976, she opened a new season for the Metropolitan Opera as Leonora in *Il Trovatore,* and on January 18, 1977, a performance that New York critics generally agreed was a highlight of that evening.

At Expo '67 in Montreal, Scotto starred as Giulietta in a production of Bellini's *I Capuleti ed i Montecchi.* In July and August of that year she made her first appearances in the Far East in the role of Lucia. That year, again in the same role, she opened the regular season of La Scala. There in 1970 she was heard for the first time anywhere as Elena in *I Vespri Siciliani.* In 1972 she sang her first Norma in Turin and in December of the same year she appeared in a concert performance of Verdi's *I Lombardi.*

As mentioned earlier, Scotto sang Leonora in *Il Trovatore* for the opening of the 1976-1977 Metropolitan Opera season. This was her first Leonora and her first Metropolitan opening.

On January 18, 1977, Scotto appeared as Berthe in the first Metropolitan Opera production of *Le Prophète* since 1928. She was Mimi to Pavarotti's Rodolfo when *Là Bohème* became the first live performance to be telecast from the stage of the Metropolitan Opera on March 15, 1977. On June 22, 1977, she sang Norma for the first time in the United States with the Cincinnati Opera, and on September 9, 1977, she helped open a new season for the San Francisco Opera in the title role of *Adriana Lecouvreur.* In the last of these roles she was appearing publicly for the first time anywhere, though she had recorded the role for Columbia the preceding August. She opened the Florence May Music Festival in 1978 in *I Vespri Siciliani.*

In New York City she was a featured artist in the American premieres of two operas in 1976–1977: Refice's *Cecilia,* with the Sacred Music Society of America at the Lincoln Center for the Performing Arts on December 13, and Puccini's second opera, *Edgar,* with the Opera Orchestra of New York on April 13, 1977.

In 1977, Renata Scotto's Columbia recording of Puccini's *Suor Angelica,* with Lorin Maazel conducting, won the Orphée d'Or award of the Fanny Heldy Foundation in Paris.

Some of the other roles in which she has been heard include Norina in *Don Pasquale;* the title roles in Donizetti's *Linda di Chamounix, Maria di Rohan,* and *Maria Stuarda;* Lisa in Tchaikovsky's *The Queen of Spades;* Elvira in *I Puritani;* Nannetta in *Falstaff;* Desdemona in *Otello;* the title role in *Luisa Miller;* Liù in *Turandot;* Micaëla in *Carmen;* the title role in Puccini's *Suor Angelica;* Amelia in *Un Ballo in Maschera;* Donna Elvira in *Don Giovanni;* Fiordiligi in *Così fan Tutte;* the Countess in *The Marriage of Figaro;* Amelia in *Simon Boccanegra;* Leila in Bizet's *Les Pêcheurs de Perles;* the title role in *Louise;* Nedda in *I Pagliacci;* the title role in *Manon;* Antonia and Giulietta in *The Tales of Hoffmann;* and Marie in *The Bartered Bride.*

Scotto relaxes by boating, fishing, filming home movies, and listening to recordings. Both she and her husband are antique collectors. In 1975 Scotto, her husband, and their two children left their Mantua home for a cooperative apartment in New York. They now maintain a second residence in Milan.

ABOUT: New York Times, November 19, 1972, October 17, 1976; Opera News, January 1, 1966, December 17, 1977.

Irmgard Seefried

1919–

Irmgard Seefried, soprano, was born in Köngetried, Swabia, in southwest Bavaria, on October 9, 1919. Her father, Heinrich Seefried, taught music in the Gymnasium; he gave Irmgard her first lessons in singing, piano, and violin when she was five. Three years later she made her first public appearance as soloist with a choral group. When she was twelve she made her opera debut as Gretel in *Hansel and Gretel.*

She continued her musical training at a singing school in Augsburg where she remained five years. In 1935 she entered the Augsburg Conservatory. During the next four years she received vocal training from Albert Mayer, who helped her to master over twenty lyric soprano roles. When her father was killed in an accident, bringing financial distress to the family, Irmgard supported herself by singing at weddings and parties while continuing her schooling. Economic necessity finally led her to consider abandoning her musical career to become a physician. For a year and a half she attended the University of Munich for preparatory courses. During this period she also attended the State Academy of Music from which she was graduated in 1939 with a teaching license.

A successful audition with Herbert von Karajan, then music director of the Aachen State Opera, encouraged her to forget medicine and concentrate on music. She was engaged by that company for minor parts, making her debut there in 1939 as the offstage priestess in *Aida.* She followed this with an appearance as Nuri in d'Albert's *Tiefland.* During the next three years she sang more important roles: Agathe in *Der Freischütz,* Marie in *The Bartered Bride,* Pamina in *The Magic Flute,* and what was destined to become her greatest role, Susanna in *The Marriage of Figaro.*

At Aachen she also appeared in performances of oratorios with the Aachen Cathedral Choir, whose choirmaster, Theodor Bernhard Rechmann, gave her guidance and instruction.

Her performances in Aachen interested both the Dresden State Opera and the Vienna State Opera, and each offered her a contract. She

Seefried: zē′ frēt

Seefried

IRMGARD SEEFRIED

chose Vienna, and there, on May 2, 1943, she made her debut as Eva in *Die Meistersinger,* the youngest singer ever engaged by that company for leading roles. Her performance proved so extraordinary that ten years later a Viennese music critic, writing in the *Österreiche Musiker-Zeitung,* still referred to it as "spectacular."

She continued appearing with the Vienna State Opera until 1945 when the opera house had to close down after being bombed during World War II. In two years she had been heard there as Susanna in *The Marriage of Figaro,* Fiordiligi in *Così fan Tutte,* in the title role of *Carmen* and, in June 1944 in celebration of Richard Strauss's eightieth birthday, as the Composer in *Ariadne auf Naxos,* selected for that part by the composer himself.

The year 1946 was a particularly significant one for Seefried. She married Wolfgang Schneiderhan, concertmaster of the Vienna Philharmonic and subsequently founder and first violinist of the Schneiderhan String Quartet. (In later years she sometimes appeared in joint concerts with her husband.) That same year, while employed at the Vienna State Opera which had resumed operations, she made her first appearances in France and in Monte Carlo.

One year later she became affiliated for the first time with the Salzburg Festival in Austria. Her performance there as Susanna became the highlight of the season and had to be repeated the following summer. Once again as Susanna, and also as Fiordiligi, she completely won London in September 1947 when the Vienna State Opera visited Covent Garden.

Appearances throughout Europe not only in opera but also in recitals and guest performances with orchestras and as a soloist in the presentation of choral masterworks, placed her among the singers to win prominence in the post–World War II era. Recitals of *Lieder* in England, Denmark, Sweden, and Holland in 1950 and 1951 brought favorable comparisons with Lotte Lehmann and Elisabeth Schumann. "She has no competitor in Europe today," said a critic of the Stockholm *Afonbladet.* In August 1951 she earned further praise when she appeared at the Edinburgh Festival as soloist with the New York Philharmonic under Bruno Walter in a performance of Mahler's Symphony No.4.

Even before she made her American debut, Seefried was well known to American music lovers through some of her operatic and choral masterwork recordings. She made her first American appearance on October 19, 1951, as soloist with the Cincinnati Symphony Orchestra in music by Mozart. Her American tour took her through the eastern United States and Canada, and included an appearance with the Philadelphia Orchestra at the Worcester Festival in *Elijah* and three performances with the Chicago Symphony under Rafael Kubelik in Mozart's music. After her New York debut in a recital at Town Hall, Olin Downes, writing in the New York *Times,* described her voice as "of decided natural beauty. . . .The tones were well matched in quality throughout the range. They were clear, bright, and free. She used them like a real musician, keeping them true to pitch and treating the vocal line with care. She had a wide dynamic range at her disposal and with her keen intelligence knew how to reserve the full power of the voice for concluding numbers."

At the Edinburgh Festival in 1952 she was heard both in recitals and in joint concerts with the pianist Clifford Curzon and the contralto Kathleen Ferrier. She returned to Edinburgh a year later to perform with the baritone Dietrich Fischer-Dieskau.

In 1952 and 1953 she made two more tours of the United States. Early in 1953 she left for a world tour, appearing in joint concerts with her husband in Europe, India, and Australia. On November 20, 1953, she made her debut at the Metropolitan Opera. On this occasion she sang the role of Susanna in *The Marriage of Figaro* for the three-hundredth time. Olin Downes wrote in the New York *Times:* "The shining light of this performance was Miss Seefried, whose beautiful voice and brilliancy and authority of style won instant recognition for her vocal achievement. She was a finished and delightful artist throughout in every note she made." Seefried remained with the Metropolitan Opera only a single season, and Susanna was her only role there, repeated four times after her debut.

Though she was not heard in opera in the United States, Seefried continued to appear on the American music scene, making transcontinental tours in recitals and performing with symphony orchestras.

In Vienna she remained one of the standout performers of the State Opera, particularly in works of Mozart and Richard Strauss. From Austria she received several high honors. In 1947 she was named *Kammersängerin;* from the Mozart Society of Salzburg she received the Lilli Lehmann medal and from the Mozart Association of Austria, a Mozart medal; the Vienna Philharmonic named her an honorary member; and the government of Austria bestowed on her the Golden Cross for Culture and Science. From Denmark she received the Officer's Cross of the Order of the Dannebrog.

Her permanent home was in Vienna. She and her husband had two daughters.

ABOUT: Musical America, December 1, 1953; Opera News, December 21, 1953; Time, November 30, 1953.

Andrés Segovia

1893–

To Andrés Segovia goes the distinction of having raised the guitar from its former humble estate to one of artistic importance on the concert stage. As a guitar virtuoso, he has been universally acclaimed one of the elite among twentieth century instrumentalists, an artist who has made his instrument so important that leading composers have written music expressly for him and his guitar. Segovia was also responsible for the emergence in the twentieth century of a school of classic guitarists who, following his lead,

Segovia: sä gō′ vyä

ANDRÉS SEGOVIA

brought further recognition to their instrument.

Andrés Segovia was born in Linares, Andalusia, Spain, on February 21, 1893. (Various reference books give different birth dates; but Segovia himself finally pinpointed the correct one in several interviews in the United States.) His father, a lawyer, found it so difficult to support his large family that Andrés was sent to an affluent uncle and aunt in Granada. The uncle, too, was a lawyer—and a highly successful one, who later became a judge. Though he had every intention of having Andrés undertake the study of law, the uncle was also a music lover and as such introduced Andrés to good music early in life. At the Granada Musical Institute, Andrés studied the piano and the violin, neither one of which interested him greatly. One day, however, he heard a guitar at the home of a friend and knew at once that this was to be his instrument. Since, as he once explained to Samuel Chotzinoff in an interview, the guitar was then "one of the most disreputable instruments in the world, played in Spain only in taverns to accompany lascivious songs and dances," he had to keep secret from both his family and his teachers at the Institute the fact that he was trying to learn to play that instrument. He used to do his practicing hidden in a neighbor's garden. "I was my own teacher and pupil, and have been so all my life without serious quarrel with each other. I learned how to play the guitar by observing how the other artists play their instruments. For instance, I had a sweetheart who was a student of the piano. Music did not inspire her very deeply, but she inspired me strongly. By observing how she studied, I gained strength and independence to my fingers. Also I learned scales and arpeggios." He memorized manuals and texts on the guitar and before long was able to perform such literature as then existed, most of it by such Spanish masters as Fernando Sor and Francisco Tárrega Eixea.

When he was in his early teens, his uncle and aunt died, leaving him a small legacy. He decided to go to Córdoba. There his musical horizon was broadened through friendships with various musicians. One of them provided him with unpublished manuscripts of guitar music, thereby enriching his repertory; another encouraged him to think of concertizing.

The obstacles that had to be overcome before Segovia could begin a concert career seemed insurmountable. For one thing, he was trying to do what nobody had done before, give a concert of serious music on the guitar before an audience which had never before heard that instrument in a reputable auditorium. For another, very little serious-music literature existed for the guitar— too little to make his concerts appealing to a discriminating public. But from the time he made his first public appearance as a guitarist, in Granada in 1909, Segovia refused to recognize the possibility of failure. He kept on giving concerts in the smaller cities of Spain for several years, then in Madrid in 1912 and in Barcelona in 1916. Slowly he built up audiences for his kind of guitar music. All this time he was also developing his repertory, mostly by himself through the transcription of masterworks of the Renaissance and the Baroque era originally written for the lute or for the clavier. He also encouraged composers in Spain to write works for the guitar —Manuel de Falla, Joaquín Turina, Manuel Ponce, and Torroba, among others.

His first successes came in South America, which he toured for several years beginning in 1919. In 1923 he made his debut in London with a recital that attracted the inquisitive and the skeptical. A critic for the London *Times* noted: "We remained to hear the last possible note, for it was the most delightful surprise of the season." On April 7, 1924, through the influence of Pablo Casals, he gave his first concert in Paris, in the auditorium of the Conservatory to an audience that included such musicians as Paul Dukas, Albert Roussel, and Manuel de Falla. Roussel had written op.29, a solo for guitar enti-

tled, simply, *Segovia,* and it was included on that program. Recalling that performance, Segovia told Chotzinoff: "Big success, the Paris concert. The critics said Segovia discovered the guitar for them. And I have to say that the manager who organized the concert not only covered his expenses but gave me one thousand francs, and this was exceptional in the French world of music!"

Other performances in France followed, then tours of the rest of Europe, then a debut in Berlin in 1925. Later concerts took him still further afield—to Scandinavia and the Soviet Union.

Fritz Kreisler encouraged his own American manager to arrange for Segovia to make his first tour of the United States in 1928. His first American appearance took place in Proctor, Vermont, not in a formal concert hall as Segovia had a right to expect, but, to his amazement, in a one-room recreation cabin; and in place of a full-sized audience there were only a dozen people to hear him—Redfield Proctor and his sister Emily, who hosted the event, and their handpicked guests. The unique character of this debut led the New York *Times* to report it as a front-page story. (In his interviews through the years Segovia has placed the town of Proctor in Massachusetts and not in Vermont. The concert in Proctor's living room, he used to say, was played before an audience of just three people. But F. C. Schang, his manager, who was with him at the time, has since corrected these details.)

On January 8, 1928, Segovia made his first appearance in an American concert auditorium, Town Hall in New York. There his program included works by Bach and Haydn as well as Spanish guitar music. The place was half empty, but a few of New York's leading critics were present. They came out of curiosity but remained to admire. Olin Downes reported in the New York *Times:* "He belongs to the very small group of musicians who by transcendent powers of execution, by imagination and intuition create an art of their own that sometimes seems to transform the very nature of the medium. He draws the tone colors of a half a dozen instruments from the one he plays. He has an extraordinary command of nuances, he seems to discover whole planes of sonority. Although his instrument does not furnish a genuinely connected series of tones, he produced upon it very frequently the illusion of sustained song." To

Lawrence Gilman in the *Herald Tribune* Segovia's most remarkable achievement was "in the delivery of polyphonic passages, which sing from his guitar with the clarity and independence of movement that one looks for only in the performance of keyboard or vocal orchestral music, and this clarity of utterance is paired with a beauty and plasticity of nuance which could not be easily overpraised."

Such reports, together with word-of-mouth enthusiasm, brought music lovers in droves to Segovia's American concerts. Five more concerts were scheduled for New York, all sold out. Twenty-three concerts in other cities were also well attended.

With performances throughout Europe and numerous tours of the United States during the next few years, Segovia became not only one of music's major box-office attractions but an artist whose performances were being compared to those of Fritz Kreisler and Pablo Casals among instrumentalists. Segovia was also beginning to make recordings for HMV in London.

When Spain was torn apart by civil war in 1936, Segovia left his home in Madrid to live in Montevideo, Uruguay. For several years he toured South and Central America. In 1943, after a five-year absence from the American concert scene, he returned to begin his first transcontinental tour under the direction of Sol Hurok. His tours have since been worldwide (except for the Communist bloc countries), presenting about one hundred concerts a year. Among the many composers who have written music for him (in addition to the aforementioned Manuel de Falla, Turina, Ponce, Torroba, and Roussel) were Alfredo Casella, Alexander Tansman, Heitor Villa-Lobos, and Mario Castelnuovo-Tedesco. On October 28, 1939, Segovia gave the world premiere of Castelnuovo-Tedesco's Concerto in D, for guitar and orchestra, in Montevideo, and in the same city Segovia offered the premiere of Manuel Ponce's *Concierto del Sur* on October 4, 1941.

Segovia celebrated his eightieth birthday and the forty-fifth anniversary of his North American debut with a recital at the Lincoln Center for the Performing Arts in New York on February 21, 1973. The concert began, reported Donal Henahan in the New York *Times,* "with long, affectionate ovations before the Spanish guitarist had even touched finger to string. . . . With each piece, receiving a standing ovation, Mr. Segovia

responded with a bonus recital of encores." At intermission time Segovia was presented with the Lincoln Center Medal, a bronze award struck in honor of the Center's tenth anniversary in 1972 to honor distinguished musicians. He proved himself still a total master of the guitar when he was heard in New York one day after his eighty-fourth birthday as part of a seventeen-recital tour in the United States. "For this listener," wrote Raymond Ericson in the New York *Times,* "Mr. Segovia seemed to be playing better than ever." Then, on February 12, 1978, Segovia commemorated the fiftieth anniversary of his New York debut with a recital at Lincoln Center.

He has been an influential teacher, beginning in 1914 when he accepted his first pupil (Alirio Diaz) for a class in Siena. After that he taught the guitar at Santiago de Compostela in Spain and at the Accadèmia Chigi in Siena, among other schools. In 1964 at the University of California in Berkeley he gave master classes in guitar that were taped for television broadcast over the National Education Network. Of his many pupils through the years, John Williams, Christopher Parkening, Oscar Ghiglia, and Michael Lorimer became virtuosos. Segovia's example and influence were also responsible for the establishment of classes in guitar playing in Madrid, Barcelona, Florence, and London.

After leaving Uruguay, Segovia resided for many years in an old-fashioned apartment on Manhattan's East Side. In 1962, after divorcing his first wife, Segovia married Amelia Corral Sancho who was then in her early twenties. "For twelve years she was my pupil before she became my master," he says wryly. "I absorb youth from her." Soon after this marriage, the Segovias acquired a hilltop house in southern Spain between Malaga and Granada. Their son, Carlos, was born when Segovia was seventy-seven. He had two other children from his first marriage, one of whom, Andrés, became a successful painter in Paris.

Even in old age Segovia has insisted on practicing from five to six hours a day. The rest of the time, when he is not traveling or concertizing, he reads poetry, history, and philosophy, and enjoys eating gourmet dishes and participating in stimulating conversations. In earlier years he used to swim and ride horseback.

He has recorded some thirty albums, many of which have been best sellers. In 1958 his album

Segovia: Golden Jubilee received a Grammy from the National Academy of Recording Arts and Sciences. His most ambitious venture is a two-volume set entitled *The Guitar and I,* released by Decca in 1971. In these recordings he not only performs but also provides verbal commentary and reminiscences. This set was originally planned to be a forty-disk undertaking covering Segovia's entire repertory and including commentary on every phase of his life and career, but when Decca sold out to Music Corporation of America and canceled its department of classical music, the project was aborted after the initial release.

In addition to putting the guitar in schools, Segovia told Donal Henahan of the New York *Times* that he had always had three other goals: "First, to redeem my guitar from the flamenco and all those other things. Second, to create a repertory—you know that almost all good composers have written works for me and even for my pupils. Third, I wanted to create a public for the guitar."

In 1967 Spain presented Segovia with the Gold Medal for Meritorious Work. Two years later a commemorative plaque was affixed to the house of his birth describing him as the *hijo predilecto de la ciudad.* In 1972 he was awarded an honorary doctorate in music by Oxford University and in 1976 received another from Loyola University in New Orleans. He was made a member of the Royal Academy of Fine Arts in Spain, in January 1978, in a ceremony attended by King Juan Carlos and Queen Sofia.

ABOUT: Bobri, V. The Segovia Technique; Chotzinoff, S. A Little Night Music; Segovia, A. Segovia: An Autobiography; Usillos, C. Andrés Segovia. *Periodicals—* Hi-Fi, July 1961; New York Times, February 16, 1964, February 18, 1968, February 5, 1977, February 12, 1978.

Toscha Seidel

1899–1962

Toscha Seidel, violinist, was born in Odessa, in the Ukraine, on November 4, 1899. His father, Samuel Seidel, was a businessman; his mother, Tatiana, a schoolteacher. When Toscha was three, his mother presented him with a toy vio-

---

Seidel: zī′ d'l

TOSCHA SEIDEL

lin. He began studying on a regular instrument with Max Fiedelmann in Odessa when he was seven. A year later he made his first public appearance, in Odessa, performing a concerto by Charles de Bériot. Later study took place in Berlin at the Stern Conservatory with Alex Fiedelmann. Fiedelmann took his pupil to Dresden to play for Leopold Auer. After Toscha performed the Brahms Violin Concerto, Auer told him: "You are a genius. I am proud and happy to be your teacher."

From 1912 to 1915 Seidel attended St. Petersburg Conservatory as a pupil of Auer. In 1915 Auer pronounced him ready for the concert stage, and on September 1, 1915, Seidel made his official concert debut in Oslo. "Toscha Seidel is a phenomenon," wrote the critic of the Oslo *Morgenbladet.* "He possesses the qualities that distinguish the great virtuoso. He overcomes the greatest technical difficulties with consummate ease. He has a brilliant trill, a large and beautiful tone, and his cantabile is wonderful."

Other concerts in Oslo were sold out in advance with "Tosca" (as the young man was being called) the talk of the city. The story goes that two gentlemen in evening dress met one evening. "Are you going to hear the *Tosca* of Puccini?" asked one. "Oh, no!" replied the other. "I'd much rather hear the Tosca of Seidel."

At the same time that Seidel was proving so triumphant in Oslo, another phenomenal artist of the violin who was also an Auer pupil, Jascha Heifetz, was making appearances there. Musical Norway was divided between those who preferred "Tosca" and those who were more partial to Jascha. The Queen herself was eager to place the two prodigies in competition with each other. Seidel and Heifetz joined collaboratively in the Bach Concerto for Two Violins and Orchestra and each performed a set of solo numbers. When they finished, the Queen said: "Every time I hear Jascha, I am sure he is the greater. And then Toscha plays a solo and I am just as I was before."

Toscha's successes continued in other Scandinavian capitals during three tours. Then he went to the United States to make his American bow at Carnegie Hall in New York on April 14, 1918. "Of higher elements, the flawless technique, the purity of style, he is not always a master," wrote Richard Aldrich in the New York *Times,* "but he has a poet's vision. He drags out a theme, tarrying over phrases with an amazing power of sustained legato, emphasizing to the utmost every possibility of varied expression. He is never in repose, never reserved, but always vital, throwing caution to the winds in a reckless dashing off of passages of precision, yet again pouring honeyed sweetness and warmth into high harmonics that others finish with a squeak."

In the transcontinental tour that followed, Toscha was heard in recitals and as a guest artist with symphony orchestras. He appeared seven times with the Philadelphia Orchestra conducted by Stokowski; four times with the New York Symphony under Walter Damrosch. Other tours of the United States and Europe were undertaken in the ensuing years and in 1922–1923 he began his first world tour; it lasted eighteen months.

Seidel made the United States his permanent home in 1918 and became an American citizen in 1924. On January 1, 1929, he married Estelle Manheim and they established their home in Pelham Manor in New York.

From 1930 to 1932 Seidel was affiliated with the radio network of the Columbia Broadcasting System. He appeared often in radio recitals, and at one period he presented a series of radio performances devoted to the development of violin music. For a time he held the post of adviser of music at CBS.

After 1932 he continued to concertize for several years before joining the MGM motion picture studios in 1938–1939 as staff violin soloist. During World War II he served in the navy.

After his separation from the service in 1944, he went to live in Los Angeles and was employed in the music division of several major studios. In his later years he became the victim of an emotional instability that brought his professional career to an end. He died in Rosemead, California, on November 15, 1962.

Short and stocky, his hair closely cropped, always well-groomed, Toscha Seidel had the look of an American businessman. He was fond of gourmet dishes, interested in bacteriology and photography, and for exercise enjoyed swimming, sailing, and golf.

ABOUT: New York Times, November 16, 1962.

Marcella Sembrich

1858–1935

The glorious coloratura voice of Marcella Sembrich was one of the shining assets in that era at the Metropolitan Opera in New York often described as "the golden age."

Marcella Sembrich (originally Praxede Marcelline Kochańska) was born in Wisniewczyk, Galicia, Poland, on February 15, 1858. She was one of thirteen children of Kasimir Kochański, a violinist who was also adept at several other instruments, and Juliana Sembrich Kochańska. Marcella took her mother's family name when she embarked on a professional career as a singer.

Discovering in his daughter, Marcella, unmistakable signs of musical talent, Kasimir Kochański began giving her piano lessons when she was four and two years later started her on lessons on the violin. She was only ten when she made her first public appearance, performing on both instruments. At this time she was also a member of a family quartet which performed for various local entertainments.

In 1869 she was enrolled in the Lemberg (Lwow) Conservatory. She remained four years, studying the violin with Charles Mikuli and the piano with Wilhelm Stengel. The poverty of the Kochański family made it necessary for Marcella to earn her own living while attending the conservatory. She did so by playing dance music at the homes of the wealthy until the early hours

Sembrich: zĕm′ brĭk

759

MARCELLA SEMBRICH

of morning. Then she would rush home to get a few hours of sleep before going to the conservatory. During her four years at the conservatory she revealed such a talent for both piano and violin that she seemed headed for a career as an instrumentalist.

In 1874 she came to Weimar to visit Franz Liszt, for whom she played the violin and piano and sang. He urged her not to neglect her instrumental training, but at the same time he advised her to specialize in singing. Later that year she auditioned (by chance) in Vienna for Julius Epstein, piano professor at the Vienna Conservatory. Overhearing her sing, he took her to Mathilde Marchesi, the voice teacher, who encouraged her to think seriously of becoming a professional singer. Thus Marcella studied voice with Victor Rokitansky at the Vienna Conservatory in 1875–1876. While attending the conservatory she decided to specialize in singing. The added incentive was a performance at the Vienna Royal Opera where she heard Adelina Patti, an episode that made her dream of someday becoming a prima donna.

In 1875 Marcella continued her vocal studies for eight months in Milan with Giovanni Lamperti. On May 5, 1877, she married her teacher Wilhelm Stengel and he served as her manager until his death in 1917. They went to Athens, and there, on June 3, 1877, she made her opera debut as Elvira in *I Puritani.* After further study of the German repertory with Richard Lewy and dramatic interpretation with Marie Seebach in Vienna, she became a member of the Dresden Royal Opera. There in October 1878 she made her German debut in one of her most striking roles, that of Lucia in *Lucia di Lammermoor.* She and her husband set up a home in Dresden where for the next two years she continued to appear in coloratura roles at the Royal Opera.

Following a Brahms concert in Leipzig in 1879 directed by the composer and an appearance at the Lower Rhine Festival in Germany in 1880, Sembrich went to London where she auditioned for Ernest Gye, an impresario and the manager of Covent Garden. He was so taken with her voice that he signed her for five years. Her Covent Garden debut as Lucia on June 12, 1880, was the start of her success in England. Her reputation continued to grow until she was ranked among the great coloratura sopranos of her generation.

Once again as Lucia, she made her debut at the Metropolitan Opera in New York during its first season of operations, on October 24, 1883. "No singer ever won the recognition of a New York audience more easily than Mme. Sembrich did," wrote W. J. Henderson in the New York *Times.* "The very first note she uttered seemed to establish her in the favor of her hearers, and before the curtain had been lowered upon the first act the new prima donna's triumph was complete. . . . Mme. Sembrich's voice is a light soprano and, to judge by her impersonation of Lucia, she has nothing to fear from the few popular rivals she now has. The new favorite's tones are singularly clear and brilliant, and she encompasses, without seeming effort, the highest notes in the music. In addition to this, her execution is absolutely faultless and she sings with a facility of expression and a perfection that are alike most gratifying to the sensitive listener." H. E. Krehbiel was no less enthusiastic in the *Tribune:* "Her style is exquisite and plainly the outgrowth of a thoroughly musical nature. It unites some of the highest elements of art. Such reposefulness of manner, such smoothness and facility in execution, such perfect balance of tone and refinement of expression can be found only in one richly endowed with deep musical feeling and ripe artistic intelligence."

Sembrich remained just a single season with the Metropolitan Opera. In these months she gave fifty-five performances in eleven roles. In addition to Lucia, she appeared as Elvira in *I Puritani,* Violetta in *La Traviata,* Amina in *La Sonnambula,* Gilda in *Rigoletto,* Rosina in *The*

Barber of Seville, Zerlina in *Don Giovanni,* Ophelia in *Hamlet,* Harriet in *Martha,* Marguerite de Valois in *Les Huguenots,* and Juliet in *Romeo and Juliet.* That single season was enough to prove that her versatility was as phenomenal as her vocal technique and artistry. But her astonishing versatility was further demonstrated on the evening of April 21, 1884, at a gala benefit performance for Henry Eugene Abbey, the general manager of the Metropolitan Opera. After appearing in the second act of *The Barber of Seville,* Sembrich went on to perform the Adagio and Finale from Charles de Bériot's Violin Concerto No.7; after that she performed on the piano a composition of Chopin and sang "Ah! non giunge" from *La Sonnambula.* As if this were not enough, she ended up by providing the violin obbligato to Gounod's "Ave Maria" sung by Christine Nilsson.

During the summer of 1884 she received further coaching from Francesco Lamperti in Milan. For a number of years after that she toured Austria, France, Scandinavia, and Russia. In 1895 she returned to Covent Garden as Susanna in *The Marriage of Figaro,* and during the next fifteen years she appeared in opera not only in London but also with the major opera companies of Paris, Berlin, Vienna, Stockholm, and Russia. Everywhere she was idolized as a coloratura worthy to rank with Patti and Melba.

She returned to the Metropolitan Opera on November 30, 1898, as Rosina in *The Barber of Seville.* From this time on, until she retired from opera in 1909, her career as a prima donna was centered for the most part on the stage of the Metropolitan Opera. Through these years she added to her New York repertory the roles of Susanna in *The Marriage of Figaro,* Marguerite in *Faust,* Norina in *Don Pasquale,* Frau Fluth in *The Merry Wives of Windsor,* Eva in *Die Meistersinger,* the Queen of the Night in *The Magic Flute,* Elsa in *Lohengrin,* Marie in *The Daughter of the Regiment,* Mimi in *La Bohème,* Elvira in *Ernani,* Nedda in *I Pagliacci,* Adina in *L'Elisir d'Amore,* Rosalinde in *Die Fledermaus,* and Lakmé. She created for the United States Ulana in the American premiere of Paderewski's *Manru* (February 14, 1902), and on November 23, 1903, she opened the Metropolitan Opera season as Gilda.

Her final appearance in a complete opera took place in New York, on January 23, 1909, as Violetta. Her farewell appearance at the Metropolitan Opera took place on February 6, 1909, the twenty-fifth anniversary of her professional career. She was heard in Act I of *Don Pasquale,* Act II of *The Barber of Seville,* and Act I of *La Traviata.* After the final curtain of *La Traviata* a ceremony in her honor took place on the stage utilizing the scenery of Act III of *The Marriage of Figaro.* Gustav Mahler took the conductor's stand to lead the march music from *The Marriage of Figaro* as Sembrich, on the arm of Gatti-Casazza (the opera house's general manager), was followed on to the stage by the entire Metropolitan Opera company. Then she was presented with numerous gifts: flowers, loving cups, wreaths. A resolution was read making her the first honorary member of the Metropolitan Opera. "An audience of monstrous size packed the house to suffocation," reported W. J. Henderson in the New York *Sun,* "and paid to the artist a tribute beautiful enough to move even a professional watcher of operatic doings to tears."

After leaving the operatic stage, Sembrich continued to give recitals until 1917, having long before this established herself as securely in the recital hall as in the opera house. After one of her recitals, Richard Aldrich wrote in the New York *Times:* "It would be repeating a tale many times told to dwell again upon the exquisite perfection of Mme. Sembrich's voice—its sensuous charm considered purely as musical tone, its lusciousness, its perfect equality throughout its range, her beautiful legato, her complete exemplification of 'bel canto' in all its phases. Mme. Sembrich brings to her Lieder singing not only all these things but a special subjective quality. She knows how to identify herself intimately with the song, with the emotions it publishes, and to unite all her powers in enforcing the interpretation of it."

Following her complete withdrawal from her professional life when her husband died in 1917, Sembrich devoted herself to the teaching of the voice. (She had taught in Berlin and Lausanne even while she was at the height of her fame.) After 1924, with her permanent winter residence in New York City (while maintaining a summer place at Bolton Landing at Lake George, New York, after 1923), she taught voice at the Curtis Institute of Music and at the Juilliard School of Music. Among those of her pupils to achieve recognition were Alma Gluck, Dusolina Giannini, Queena Mario, Sophie Braslau, Hulda Lashanska, and Maria Jeritza.

Serafin

Marcella Sembrich died of emphysema and heart complications in New York City on January 11, 1935. Funeral services took place at St. Patrick's Cathedral in New York, and she was buried in the Stengel family mausoleum in Dresden, Germany.

In her portraits she always appeared in profile to conceal the fact that she suffered from a cast in one eye. For exercise she often went on five-mile hikes, and for relaxation she played solitaire.

ABOUT: Cooke, J. F. Great Men and Famous Musicians; Kobbe, G. Opera Singers; Owen, H. G. A Recollection of Marcella Sembrich. *Periodicals*—Munsey's Magazine, February 1909; Musical America, January 25, 1935; Musical Courier, July 1949; New York Times, January 12, 1935; Opera News, February 17, 1968.

TULLIO SERAFIN

Tullio Serafin

1878–1968

Tullio Serafin, conductor, was born in Rottanova di Cavarzere, near Venice on December 1, 1878. Most reference books place his birth date as December 8. Late in his life, however, Serafin attributed this error to a careless town clerk who smudged his birth entry to make the "one" read like "eight."

A musical child, Tullio early began to study music with private teachers. He often claimed that he began earning his living when he was seven by playing the viola. In his eleventh year he enrolled in the Milan Conservatory, remaining there nine years, and studying the violin with de Angelis and composition with Saladino and Gellio Coronaro. While still a student he toured with La Scala's orchestra as one of its violinists. In 1898 he graduated from the Conservatory with a diploma in viola, and for several years was employed as a violist with the orchestra at La Scala.

He made his conducting debut in the late 1890s with a performance of *L'Elisir d'Amore,* using an assumed name. His professional conducting debut took place at the Teatro Comunale in Ferrara in 1900 where he had been appointed conductor. Three years later and after having given guest performances in several pro-

Seraffin: sä rä fēn´

vincial opera houses in Italy, he was called to Turin to assume the post of principal conductor at the Teatro Regio. There he was assigned a large variety of operas, not only in the Italian and French repertories but also in the German; it was during this period that he began developing the versatility that would become the hallmark of his career.

In 1906 Serafin conducted at the Augusteo in Rome, and from 1907 to 1909 at the Teatro dal Verme in Milan. In 1909 he took the post of principal conductor of La Scala in Milan, remaining there many years. It was there, as well as in guest appearances in France, England, and South America, that he came to be recognized as a conductor of far-reaching talents. In 1913 he conducted a season of Italian operas in Paris and London and from 1913 to 1915 he was heard at the Teatro Colón in Buenos Aires. During this period he also led a special performance of *Parsifal* in Parma.

In 1915, en route to conducting engagements in Havana and South America, Serafin paid his first visit to the United States, where he attended a performance of *Carmen* at the Metropolitan Opera conducted by Toscanini on November 13. Almost a decade later—on November 3, 1924 (the opening night of the season)—Serafin made his first American appearance as conductor, with *Aida* at the Metropolitan Opera. He scored a striking success with a performance described by the critics as spirited and enthusiastic. After his second performance—*Tosca* on November 7—a critic for the New York *Times* spoke of his "masterly" conducting, adding: "The orchestral tone was of the most varied color: the sudden violent outbursts of the instruments were the more telling because of the way in which they were held down in other places."

During the next decade, Serafin was a mainstay of the conducting staff at the Metropolitan Opera, a musician who scrupulously avoided any displays of temperament or showmanship and whose sole concern was to bring to life the score in front of him. "There was a feeling of breathing in his conducting," wrote Harold C. Schonberg in the New York *Times.* "He never had that neurotic tension. Singers just loved to work with him. His was the style of the nineteenth century, with its long lines and long phrases; not the faster tempo of this century." He was in his element in the Italian repertory, but when he conducted American operas, Wagner *(Parsifal* and *Siegfried),* or Russian works, his performances also reached the highest possible standards. Reviewing Serafin's performance of *Siegfried,* Lawrence Gilman stated in the New York *Herald Tribune* that in Serafin's hands the music had "both power and beauty. It was pulsingly alive—and alive in all its tissues; yet it was shaped and made comely by a Latin instinct for beauty of surface and beauty of line."

No stronger indication of the importance with which the management of the Metropolitan Opera regarded Serafin could be given than by recalling that during his years with the company he was called upon to conduct the opening performance of every season. Indicative, too, of the confidence of the management in his versatility was the number of world and American premieres assigned to him. He directed the world premieres of four American operas: Deems Taylor's *The King's Henchman* (February 17, 1927) and *Peter Ibbetson* (February 7, 1931), Louis Gruenberg's *Emperor Jones* (January 7, 1933), and Howard Hanson's *Merry Mount* (February 10, 1934). His American premieres were: Montemezzi's *Giovanni Gallurese* (February 19, 1925), Falla's *La Vida Breve* (March 6, 1926), *Turandot* (November 16, 1926), Respighi's *La Campana Somersa* (November 24, 1928), Pizzetti's *Fra Gherardo* (March 21, 1929), Mussorgsky's *The Fair at Sorotchinsk* (November 29, 1930), Montemezzi's *La Notte di Zoraima* (December 2, 1931), and *Simon Boccanegra* (January 28, 1932). In addition he led the first Metropolitan Opera productions of Spontini's *La Vestale,* Giordano's *La Cena delle Beffe,* Stravinsky's *Le Rossignol,* Verdi's *Luisa Miller,* and Rimsky-Korsakov's *Sadko.*

Serafin's last appearance at the Metropolitan Opera in New York took place on March 31, 1934, with *Merry Mount,* and his final appearance with the company followed on April 12, 1934, in Rochester, New York.

For a long time it was believed that the cause of Serafin's break with the Metropolitan Opera was a salary dispute, but many years later Serafin insisted that this was not so. He had already taken two salary cuts from the fifty-eight thousand dollars a year he had been receiving when in 1934 Gatti-Casazza, the general manager, asked him to take one more cut. He would have been willing to do so, in view of the economic crisis the company was undergoing, but pressure had been put on him by Mussolini to return to Italy and stay there. Unwilling to make a permanent break with his own country he acceded to what had actually been an order.

Upon returning to Italy, Serafin became the artistic director of the Teatro Reale in Rome, retaining this post from 1934 to 1943. At this time he further demonstrated his versatility by giving the premiere performance in Italy of Alban Berg's *Wozzeck.* In 1939 he returned to La Scala and made several opera album recordings with that company. World War II brought him considerable despair since he was not a Fascist and not in sympathy with Italy's role in the war.

He returned to the United States in 1952 for a season at the New York City Opera. From 1956 to 1958 he was conductor of the Chicago Opera. In 1962 he was appointed artistic director of the Teatro dell'Opera in Rome and there, in his eighty-fourth year, he conducted four operas, including *Otello.*

Through the years Serafin helped to give form and shape to many careers, including those of Rosa Ponselle and Titta Ruffo, and he was the one who discovered Maria Callas, coached her, and was responsible for her first successes. "He was an extraordinary coach," recalled Maria Callas, "sharp as a fox. He opened a world to me, showed me there was a reason for everything. . . . He would coach us for every little detail, every movement, every word, every breath. . . . He taught me that pauses are often more important than music. . . . He taught me the proportions of recitative—how it is elastic. . . . During rehearsals he was after every detail.

Serkin

In performance . . . we would look down and feel
we had a friend there, in the pit. He was helping
you all the way . . . He was breathing with you,
living the music with you, loving it with you. It
was elastic, growing, living."

Serafin was married to the soprano Elena
Rakowska, who had sung Brünnhilde under his
direction. His last years were spent in Rome on
the Via Monti-Parioli. He died in Rome on February 2, 1968.

ABOUT: Musical America, November 1, 1952; Saturday Review, March 30, 1968.

Rudolf Serkin

1903–

RUDOLF SERKIN

Rudolf Serkin, pianist, was born in Eger,
Bohemia (now Czechoslovakia), on March 28,
1903, to Mordko and Augusta Scharg Serkin.
He was the fifth of eight children. His father was
a Russian basso who had been compelled by lack
of funds to give up music for business. He saw
to it that all of his children studied music and he
himself gave them lessons on the violin or piano.
"I hated violin since it was so close to the ear,"
Serkin recalls, "and I started to play the piano
before I can remember." He learned music
before he was able to read or write. After receiving his first lessons from his father, when he was
four he was turned over to a local teacher. He
was about five when he made his first public
appearance, performing some piano pieces by
Stephen Heller and an Impromptu by Schubert
at a concert in Franzensbad, a spa. However, his
father refused to exploit him as a prodigy and
insisted he forgo further concerts and concentrate on music study.

An attempt was made to enroll him at the
Prague Conservatory, but he was turned down
because he was too young. "About this time,"
recalls Serkin, "my father took me to hear a
concert in Pilsen by the much beloved Viennese
pianist, Alfred Grünfeld. . . . I played for Grünfeld who said I should come to Vienna to study
with a friend of his—a great teacher—Professor
Richard Robert. So my father took me to Vienna
to study privately with Professor Robert. I was
nine years old. Professor Robert put me up with

a family. I was studying, but I was very lonely."
One of his fellow students at this time was
George Szell, who later became a conductor.
"He and his family were very kind to me. We
were almost like brothers; he was fifteen, I was
nine. My friendship with Szell then and later has
been something very special."

When Rudolf was twelve he made his Viennese concert debut as soloist with the Vienna
Symphony Orchestra in Mendelssohn's Piano
Concerto in G minor, Oskar Nedbal conducting.
(Emanuel Feuermann, cellist, was also a soloist
on this same program.) Some friends convinced
Rudolf's mother that he would be more appealing on the stage if dressed in the Fauntleroy
manner, with hair arranged in curls. Before the
concert his mother sent him to a hairdresser.
When he saw himself in a mirror, he rushed out
of the hairdresser's establishment, raced home,
and put his head under a faucet until all the curls
were disarranged.

The concert proved so successful that he was
offered a tour, but his father refused to consider
the offer. In addition to his piano lessons during
the next few years Rudolf studied composition
with Joseph Marx and later with Arnold
Schoenberg. Though he was given no formal
education, he enriched his knowledge of subjects
outside music through voracious reading on literature, art, and philosophy, and through his
personal associations with some of Vienna's
leading cultural figures. He had an opportunity
to meet and become friendly with such artists as
Oskar Kokoschka and such poets as Rainer

Serkin: sĕr′ kĭn

Maria Rilke, as well as with many of Vienna's leading exponents of avant-garde music.

By 1920, his musical studies over, Rudolf was beginning to support himself by teaching the piano to children of wealthy families. At the same time he gained concert experience by giving free performances for workers. He was encouraged to go to Paris where his friends—the architect Adolf Loos and the painter Kokoschka—arranged to get him lodgings in return for giving lessons to the daughter of a Parisian hotelkeeper. Train space was at a premium in postwar Vienna, but Rudolf managed to find a seat on a Red Cross train transporting tubercular children. When he went to the railroad station he discovered that his train had already left and another reservation was not available for many weeks. Remaining in Vienna, he was introduced a few days later to Adolf Busch, the concert violinist. On the evening of their meeting Serkin and Busch played sonatas for several hours. That evening Busch urged Serkin to tour with him in sonata recitals and extended to Serkin an invitation to live with him and his family in Berlin.

In the fall of 1920 Serkin made his debut in Berlin with an all-Bach program conducted by Busch. When the audience responded enthusiastically to Serkin's playing, Busch encouraged him to give an encore. "What shall I play?" Serkin inquired. Jokingly, Busch suggested the lengthy *Goldberg Variations* of Bach. Taking him at his word, Serkin performed this fifty-five-minute composition. "When I finished there were only four people left in the hall," says Serkin with amusement. "They were Adolf Busch, Artur Schnabel, Alfred Einstein and myself."

Serkin then performed throughout Europe, not only in sonata recitals with Busch but also in solo recitals, in chamber-music concerts with the Busch Quartet, and as a soloist with the Busch Chamber Players. In the classic literature from Bach to Brahms he became identified as "the poet of the keyboard," a pianist who was a master of detail without losing sight of the overall design; in whose performances every effect was carefully planned, every nuance subtly prepared, every line fastidiously shaped. He became recognized as the outstanding exponent of German Romantic piano tradition.

In 1922 Serkin lived with the Busch family in Darmstadt, Germany; five years later they settled in Switzerland, near Basel. When Hitler came to power in Germany, both Busch (who was not a Jew) and Serkin (who was) became Swiss citizens. In 1935 Serkin married Busch's only child, Irene, then eighteen years old, and already a gifted violinist. Following this marriage, the Serkins had built for them in Switzerland a house adjoining that of the Busches, the two houses connected by a common library.

Reports of Serkin's interpretative powers began reaching America. In 1931 Herbert F. Peyser, the foreign music correspondent of the New York *Times,* reported from Berlin after hearing one of Serkin's recitals: "Before Mr. Serkin had played ten bars of the Haydn sonata music, I realized I was in the presence of something extraordinary. [I was] impressed as I have been by few pianists. I harbor the immutable conviction that under the name of Rudolf Serkin lives one of the most commanding pianists of the age."

Serkin made his first appearance in the United States in 1933 in a sonata recital with Busch at the Coolidge Festival in Washington, D.C. As a solo pianist he was first heard on February 20, 1936, in New York with the New York Philharmonic under Toscanini in Mozart's Piano Concerto in B-flat, K.595. "When a soloist of such capacity arrives," wrote Olin Downes in the New York *Times,* "it is an occasion to remember." And in the *Herald Tribune* Lawrence Gilman remarked: "Mr. Toscanini presented a new pianist and a forgotten piano concerto both charged with genius."

One year later Serkin gave his first New York recital, and it became even more apparent that he was one of the masters of the keyboard. "What Mr. Serkin did was to display a colossal art," reported Olin Downes in the New York *Times,* "which he devoted to the most idealistic purposes. He played gigantically, always with a magnificent control and with a sovereign sense of style. Richness and complexity of detail never distracted him from issues, but only added to the richness of the effect, and in lyrical passages his tone was lovely in color, in nuance, in capacity to carry, even when the key was barely pressed down by the finger, through the hall."

Since 1936 Serkin has made annual tours of the United States, in addition to his regular performances in Europe and South America. He has also given concerts in Iceland, India, Israel, and the Far East and he made a tour of the Orient in 1961 under the auspices of the State Department of the United States. His first tour of Australia and New Zealand took place in 1975. From 1950 on he was also a frequent participant at the Pablo Casals Festivals in Prades and Perpignan in France, and in Puerto Rico.

In 1937 Serkin appeared with Myra Hess in a cycle of concerts of music by Mozart and Beethoven with the National Orchestral Association in New York. In 1938, in collaboration with Busch, he presented the entire cycle of Beethoven's violin sonatas in New York. In 1939 and again in 1940 he appeared with the National Orchestral Association in cycles of major piano concertos. Subsequently he performed all of the Beethoven violin sonatas with Pina Carmirelli, an Italian violinist, and participated in a presentation of thirty-one of Haydn's trios with Alexander Schneider, violinist, and Leslie Parnas, cellist. Within the recording studio, Serkin has through the years performed an extensive repertory of piano music for Columbia.

With the coming of World War II to Europe, Serkin migrated to the United States with his family. They first made their home in an apartment in New York City and later acquired a house in Philadelphia as their winter residence. The Serkins have six children. One of them, Peter, has become a concert pianist. At the age of fourteen, he appeared with his father and the Cleveland Orchestra in a performance of Mozart's Concerto for Two Pianos and Orchestra; after that, he became a specialist in avant-garde music both in public concerts and on recordings.

Because of the emphasis that Rudolf Serkin has placed on the music of Beethoven and Schubert on his programs—and to a lesser degree on Mozart, Mendelssohn, Schumann, and Brahms—he has often been compared to Artur Schnabel. "Serkin, like Schnabel, represents the Austro-German tradition," wrote Harold C. Schonberg in the New York *Times*. "There is, however, a great deal of difference between these two pianists. Serkin's playing has a kind of tension, a nervous push, missing from Schnabel's more relaxed performances. This kind of nervousness extends to platform manners. Where Schnabel sits quietly before the keyboard, Serkin twitches, attacks, jerks up and down. He has a much more kinesthetic involvement with music than did his distinguished predecessor. He is also a stronger technician than Schnabel was."

Serkin had planned to commemorate the fortieth anniversary of his debut in America with a Carnegie Hall recital on January 28, 1976, but illness made it necessary to postpone this event. On June 9, 1976, the program was given not at Carnegie Hall or at Lincoln Center but at the intimate Theresa L. Kaufman Concert Hall in New York.

For many years Serkin directed much of his time and energy to teaching. From 1938 on he was active at the Curtis Institute of Music in Philadelphia. In 1939 he became the head of the piano department and from 1968 to 1975 served as director of the Institute, succeeding Efrem Zimbalist. Near his farm in Guilford, Vermont, which he and his family had acquired as a summer home in the late 1940s, Serkin helped to found in 1949 the Marlboro School of Music, a summer music school in the Green Mountains of Vermont for talented musicians; Serkin has served as president and artistic director of this institution. A year later he helped to organize the Marlboro Music Festival, an annual summer event on the campus of Marlboro College that has attracted music lovers from all over the country.

Both offstage and on Serkin is unprepossessing, modest, and without a suspicion of temperament. One writer has said he is about as romantic-looking as a grocery clerk. Tall and gangling, he always appears ill at ease, as his eyes look half startled through his spectacles.

At his Guilford farm Serkin maintains and is proud of his herd of Holstein cows and a menagerie of sheep, geese, dogs, and cats. In addition to farming, he has been interested in skiing and mountain climbing.

In 1963, Serkin was the recipient of the Presidential Medal of Freedom from President John F. Kennedy (it was presented to him by President Lyndon B. Johnson). In 1966 and again in 1970 he was invited to perform at the White House. In September 1967 he became the first artist to receive the newly created Governor's Award of Excellence in the Arts from the Vermont Council on the Arts. In 1971 Governor Raymond Shafer honored him with the Fifth Annual Pennsylvania Award for excellence in the performing arts, and in 1972 he received the Art Alliance Medal in Philadelphia and an honorary membership in the New York Philharmonic Orchestra to commemorate his one hundredth performance with that orchestra.

The honorary degree of Doctor of Music has been conferred on him by Harvard University, Williams College, Temple University, Oberlin,

University of Rochester, and the Curtis Institute. He has served on the Carnegie Commission on Educational Television and has been a member of the National Council of Arts and of the American Academy of Arts and Sciences.

His seventy-fifth birthday was celebrated on March 28, 1978, with a tribute televised over the facilities of the Public Broadcasting Service. On that occasion Serkin was interviewed by Isaac Stern, the first time that Serkin had been interviewed over either radio or television.

ABOUT: Ewen, D. Men and Women Who Make Music (1949 ed.); Schonberg, H. C. The Great Pianists. *Periodicals*—Hi-Fi, July 1961; Horizon, September 1961; New York Times, December 7, 1969; Newsweek, March 1, 1965.

ROBERT SHAW

Robert Shaw

1916–

Robert Lawson Shaw, choral and orchestral conductor, was born in Red Bluff, California, on April 30, 1916. His father, Reverend Shirley Richard Shaw, was a minister who himself had been the son of a clergyman; his mother, Nelle Mae Lawson Shaw, was a soloist in church choirs. Shaw's early love for music was instilled in him by his mother who often had her five children perform hymns and folk songs to entertain the neighbors. Though he revealed a gift for making music early in life, Robert initially planned to follow in the footsteps of both his grandfather and his father by becoming a minister. After attending the public schools, he enrolled in Pomona College (his father's alma mater) in Claremont, California, in 1934, specializing in philosophy and literature. All this while he supported himself by taking on odd jobs including one directing a local church choir.

At Pomona College, Shaw belonged to a glee club of which he ultimately became director. Under his guidance the glee club became known throughout the West. When the motion picture *Varsity Show* (1937) was being filmed, starring Fred Waring and his Pennsylvanians, Warner Brothers chose Pomona College as the setting. Hearing Shaw's glee club, Fred Waring was so impressed that he offered Shaw the post of choral conductor of his own organization. After receiving his Bachelor of Arts degree from

Pomona College, Shaw went to New York in 1938 to take on the job of reorganizing and leading the Fred Waring Glee Club which was affiliated with The Pennsylvanians. During the next seven years he brought it to a high degree of musical proficiency. While holding this post, he directed choral groups for several Broadway stage productions and radio programs. In 1939 he also helped to train the swimmers in their routines for the Aquacade at the New York World's Fair and at the Golden Gate International Exposition in San Francisco.

Still as Fred Waring's choral director, Shaw took on in 1941 the assignment to lead youngsters of the Marble Collegiate Church on Fifth Avenue in New York in recreational singing. Out of this endeavor came the Collegiate Chorale, an amateur, nonprofit group of one hundred and twenty-five singers. Each singer contributed ten dollars a year to help defray the expenses of the organization, the remainder of the deficit being assumed by Shaw himself. When they began giving concerts, the money from the sale of tickets was used solely for the expense account.

The Collegiate Chorale made its first professional appearance with the National Orchestral Association in Carnegie Hall in New York in March 1942 in a program made up of choral masterworks by Bach, Mozart, Beethoven, and Brahms, and several compositions by contemporary composers. A concert at Town Hall, New York, followed, and the group then toured the country and appeared in collaboration with major orchestras conducted by Stokowski, Koussevitzky, and Toscanini, among others. After performing Beethoven's Symphony No.9 with the Collegiate Chorale, Toscanini said: "The chorus was wonderful. It went through the music just once. I found nothing to criticize. As for Robert Shaw, I have at last found the maestro I have been looking for." In 1943, in recognition of his work with the Collegiate Chorale, Shaw received a citation from the National Association of American Composers and Conductors as the "year's most important American-born conductor."

From 1942 to 1945 Shaw headed the choral department of the Berkshire Music Center in Lenox, Massachusetts. In 1944 he was made choral director of the RCA Victor Chorale and received a Guggenheim Fellowship for the study of the theory and techniques of instrumental and choral conducting. In 1945 he served for several months in the navy. From 1946 to 1950 he taught choral singing at the Juilliard School of Music in New York.

In 1948 Shaw founded a new chorus, this one made up of forty-two highly trained professional singers, supplemented by a small orchestra. Named the Robert Shaw Chorale, it made its debut over the NBC radio network in 1948. From 1948 to 1956 he led this organization in distinguished choral concerts (except for a two-year period between 1949 and 1951 when he went into temporary retirement to study orchestral scores with Julius Herford, piano with Frederic Hart, and theory of conducting with George Szell). Between January and May 1952 the group presented a series of concerts of choral masterworks at Carnegie Hall, the programs encompassing choral literature from Heinrich Schütz and Josquin des Prés to Stravinsky and Poulenc. As a result of these performances a critic for *Time* called this group "one of the most highly trained and carefully blended chorus-orchestral combinations in the world, capable of far more clarity than a booming mass chorus and far more power than the usual smaller ensemble." Shaw commissioned many contemporary composers to write music for this Chorale, as a result of which the group, under Shaw, presented world premieres of works by Copland, Bartók, Milhaud, Samuel Barber, Britten and others. In the spring of 1956, under the joint auspices of ANTA (the American National Theatre and Academy) and the State Depart-

ment, the Robert Shaw Chorale performed throughout Europe and the Middle East, appearing in fifteen countries and often performing at United States Army installations. In 1962 the Robert Shaw Chorale visited the Soviet Union and countries behind the Iron Curtain, performing sixty concerts in eleven cities over a six-week period. These performances engendered tremendous enthusiasm: in Leningrad music lovers lined up through the night outside the box office to get tickets; in Lwow a riot developed outside the concert hall among those unable to gain admission. In 1964 the Chorale made a second tour sponsored by the State Department, this time to South America.

The Chorale also appeared with most major American orchestras in performances of such choral masterworks as the Mozart Requiem, the Bach Mass in B minor, the Bach *Passion According to St. John,* Beethoven's *Missa Solemnis,* Haydn's *The Creation,* and Brahms's Requiem. Additionally, the Chorale made memorable recordings for RCA Victor. Four of its releases earned Grammys from the National Academy of Recording Arts and Sciences: Bach's B minor Mass in 1961, Britten's *A Ceremony of Carols* in 1964, Stravinsky's *Symphony of Psalms* in 1965, and Handel's *Messiah* in 1966.

While becoming established as the leading choral conductor in the United States, Shaw was also beginning to make headway as an orchestral conductor, following his debut as such with the NBC Symphony in 1946. He made guest appearances with many of America's orchestras. In the years between 1953 and 1957, during the summers, he was the conductor of the San Diego Symphony in California. "I'm beginning to feel the orchestra in my fingers now," he said after his first summer in San Diego. "My fingers taste the sound; my ears taste the sound."

In October 1956 Shaw was appointed associate conductor of the Cleveland Orchestra, making his debut in his new post on December 13 in a performance of the *Missa Solemnis.* Because of the demands made upon him by this new appointment, Shaw was compelled to relinquish the leadership of the Chorale. In Cleveland his duties consisted of assisting George Szell, conducting the children's concerts and several of the season's regular programs, and directing the Cleveland Orchestra Chorus which, under him, became one of the finest choral groups in the United States affiliated with a symphony orchestra. During his eleven seasons in Cleveland, he prepared over forty choral masterworks for performances by the orchestra under Szell. "He gave a new dimension to the orchestra," George Szell once said of Shaw.

From 1956 on, for many years, Shaw was codirector with Julius Herford of the Alaska Festival of Music in Anchorage. This festival was an annual event of which, in time, Shaw became artistic director. From 1961 to 1967 he served as the Minister of Music of the First Unitarian Church of Shaker Heights in Cleveland. During the summers of 1965, 1966, and 1967, he was in residence at the Meadow Brook Music Festival in Rochester, Michigan. There he led the Cleveland Symphony in orchestral concerts and served as lecturer and director of the Institute of Choral Studies and Orchestral Institute of the Meadow Brook School of Music. In July 1968 he inaugurated the Blossom Music Festival with the Cleveland Orchestra together with the Blossom Festival School. For a number of years he lectured and conducted at the Aspen Music Festival in Colorado and at the Marlboro Music Festival in Vermont. Subsequently, he conducted a summer Robert Shaw Workshop at the University of Southern California.

In the fall of 1967 Shaw became the music director and conductor of the Atlanta Symphony Orchestra in Georgia. One year later, on October 24, 1968, conducting the Atlanta Symphony, he helped to dedicate a new symphony hall in the city—the Atlanta Memorial Arts Center. Within his first few seasons in Atlanta, he expanded the orchestra's artistic program to include ballet, oratorios, chamber music, educational concerts, and special telecasts, together with its regular symphonic fare. Another example of Shaw's path-breaking enterprise came when he applied for and got a grant from the Rockefeller Foundation to take his orchestra to the campus of Spelman College in Atlanta for a week "in residence."

In carrying out his innovative policies in Atlanta, Shaw often came into conflict with the orchestral management. When an assistant manager, described by Shaw as "a point of probity and sanity in an otherwise antagonistic atmosphere," was forced to leave in 1977, Shaw considered resigning. However, he had a change of heart and remained in his post.

Shaw married Maxine Farley on October 15, 1939; they have three children. Though he has been quoted as saying that music is his only hobby, he enjoys swimming and woodworking. He has received honorary doctorates in music from several American institutions of learning, including Michigan State University and Kenyon College.

ABOUT: Music of the West, April 1957; New York Times, February 9, 1953, October 19, 1969; Recreation, March 1949.

George Shirley

1934–

George Irving Shirley, tenor, was born in Indianapolis, Indiana, on April 18, 1934. Both parents were musical. His father, Irving Ewing Shirley, played the piano, and his mother, Daisy Bell Shirley, was a trained singer. George started singing in his infancy. His family moved to Detroit, and by the time he was six, he was giving performances of hymns at the church, accompanied by his father on the organ. Encouraged by his parents, he studied music for ten years with Amos S. Ebersole, and for a short time after that with Edward Boatner. But he planned a career as a schoolteacher, not as a singer. He attended the public schools in Detroit, and in 1955 he was graduated from Wayne State University with a Bachelor of Science degree. He then stayed on at the University for an additional year of graduate work. His first appearance in opera took place in 1955, during his senior year at the University, when he sang the title role in Stravinsky's *Oedipus Rex*.

On June 24, 1956, Shirley married Gladys Lee Ishop, then an art major at Wayne State University, later an artist and educator. One week after his marriage, he was inducted into the United States Army. While stationed at Fort Myer in Virginia he appeared as a soloist with the United States Army Chorus. While still in the army he studied voice for two years with Themy S. Georgi, who persuaded him to consider seriously a career in opera. Upon his discharge from the army in 1959, Shirley and his family, which by then included a daughter, Olwyn Elizabeth, moved to New York. There he pursued additional vocal study with Ruth Dawson and Cornelius Reid. To support his family, he worked for a time as a substitute teacher of music in the

Shirley

GEORGE SHIRLEY

city public schools. "You were lucky if you came out alive," he remembers. "You went into class and you fought for survival. There were too many students in each class and there weren't enough good teachers. The arts and music suffered first. The assembly period, once a week, was a nightmare. Kids were screaming instead of learning music."

Leaving the school system, Shirley made his professional debut as a singer in the summer of 1959 at Woodstock, New York, as a member of the Turneau Opera Players. His debut was as Eisenstein in *Die Fledermaus,* but he was also heard there in *The Abduction from the Seraglio, La Bohème,* Bizet's *Djamileh,* and Ravel's *L'Heure Espagnole.* In April 1960 he made his first appearance in New York, as Don José in a concert version of *Carmen* at the Mannes School of Music. A month later he emerged as the winner of the American Opera Auditions which enabled him to go to Italy to make his European debut at the Teatro Nuovo in Milan that year as Rodolfo in *La Bohème.* He was heard in that role three times at the Teatro della Pergola in Florence. Later in 1960 he tied for second prize in the Italian Concorso di Musica e Danza (no first prize was awarded).

He returned to the United States in 1960 with just twenty-five dollars as his total wealth. That year he won the first annual award of the National Arts Club. In January 1961 he appeared as Don José in Boston with the Goldovsky Opera Company. In the spring of the same year he was heard in New York in the American pre-

miere of Rameau's *Les Indes Galantes* and in the New York premiere of Verdi's rarely heard opera *Aroldo.* He also became a member of the San Francisco Opera Company during its spring season, singing the role of Rodolfo and that of Tamino in *The Magic Flute.*

He entered the Metropolitan Opera Auditions in the spring of 1961. Singing Calaf's aria "Nessun dorma" from *Turandot,* he was awarded a contract for the Metropolitan Opera, together with the Stuart and Irene Chambers Scholarship of two thousand dollars. But before going to the Metropolitan Opera, Shirley gained additional operatic experience that summer by traveling to Berlin with the Santa Fe Opera Company and appearing with the Opera Society of Washington, D.C., in both cases as Oedipus Rex. At the Festival of Two Worlds at Spoleto, Italy, he was Herod in *Salome.* On October 7, 1961, he made his debut with the New York City Opera as Rodolfo.

He was scheduled to make his Metropolitan Opera debut as Pinkerton in *Madama Butterfly.* "I was working away at *Butterfly* one morning," he recalls, "when the telephone call came. Mr. Bing wanted me to sing Ferrando in *Così fan Tutte* the following night. I remember how the muscles tightened up around my shoulders during that call. I knew Ferrando—all except the last ensemble. So I put on the record and played it over and over for about twenty-four hours, until the needle nearly wore through the other side. I couldn't have made a mistake that night —it came later—but that first Ferrando had every sixteenth note in place." That performance, which took place on October 24, 1961, received a highly favorable response from audience and critics. In the *Herald Tribune* Paul Henry Lang wrote: "Mr. Shirley has a nicely rounded, warm tenor, not big but remarkably suave for someone so young. He acted well and gave the impression of a promising artist."

As a member of the Metropolitan Opera company during the next decade, Shirley appeared in over twenty roles. In addition to Ferrando, there was Almaviva in *The Barber of Seville,* Pinkerton, Beppe in *I Pagliacci,* Alfredo in *La Traviata,* Rodolfo, Des Grieux in *Manon Lescaut,* Malcolm in *Macbeth,* Nemorino in *L'Elisir d'Amore,* Romeo in *Romeo and Juliet,* Fenton in *Falstaff,* Gabriele Adorno in *Simon Boccanegra,* the Singer in *Der Rosenkavalier,* the Steersman in *The Flying Dutchman,* Narraboth in *Salome,* Edgardo in *Lucia di Lammermoor,* Tamino in *The Magic Flute.* Commenting on Shirley's appearance as Gabriele Adorno in a revival of *Simon Boccanegra,* Winthrop Sargeant wrote in the *New Yorker:* "This was Mr. Shirley's first crack at one of the big tenore robusto roles, and he did it magnificently, filling the auditorium with big, breezy and expressive tone, and acting with authority and a noble stage presence. . . . In fact, I got the impression that here, at last, was a tenor who might someday aspire to the supreme place still occupied by Richard Tucker."

In 1965 Shirley made his bow at the Glyndebourne Festival as Tamino, returning there in 1968 as Riccardo in *Anna Bolena.* In July 1967 he was acclaimed at Covent Garden in London as Don Ottavio in *Don Giovanni,* and again in 1968 as David in *Die Meistersinger.* In the United States he appeared in the American premieres of *Lulu* (August 7, 1963), Richard Strauss's *Daphne* (July 29, 1964), and Henze's *The King Stag* (August 4, 1965), all three with the Santa Fe Opera in New Mexico.

In addition to recitals, Shirley has made numerous appearances with major orchestras in the United States and Europe as a soloist in the performance of choral masterworks. He has served on the music faculty of the Staten Island Community College in New York and as artist-in-residence at the Morgan State College in Baltimore, Maryland.

Shirley, his wife Gladys who is an artist and educator, and their two children occupy a house in Upper Montclair, New Jersey. On performance days he sleeps as late as possible, relaxes most of the day, takes a nap at about four, eats dinner at five, and leaves home at six to arrive at the Metropolitan Opera by seven. He enjoys athletics, both as a participant and as a spectator. He is also interested in photography and has a talent for drawing cartoons.

In 1967 Shirley received an honorary doctorate from Wilberforce University in Ohio.

ABOUT: High Fidelity/Musical America, January 1968; Musical America, December 1961.

Cesare Siepi

1923–

Cesare Siepi, bass, was born to a well-to-do family in Milan, on February 10, 1923. As a child he delighted in picking out melodies on a piano or an accordion, and he sang all the time. "With me," he once revealed, "singing came naturally. At twelve I had 'voca bianca'—a white voice. The girls liked to hear me sing popular tunes. But the summer after I turned thirteen, my voice got hoarse. I grew six feet, and that fall I could sing a low E-flat. I joined a madrigal group and learned to sing the motets of Orlando di Lasso."

Boxing was his ambition during his teen-age years, and he engaged in a number of amateur bouts in one of which his face was cut so badly that his mother made him promise never to box again. At the same time his father insisted that he become a schoolteacher. With this in mind, Cesare attended the Milan schools for an academic training. Music, for the time being, was relegated to the background, though he did receive some vocal instruction from Cesare Chiesa and sang publicly with the school chorus and with the Gruppo di Madrigalisti.

With the encouragement of his friend, Giuseppe Di Stefano (later a successful opera tenor), Cesare entered a national vocal competition in Florence when he was eighteen. Though he knew just two arias, they were enough to win him first prize. An opera impresario from a town near Venice engaged him for his company, and with this company, at Schio, Cesare made his opera debut as Sparafucile in *Rigoletto* in 1941. He was so well received that from this time on he gave serious thought to undertaking a career in opera.

World War II brought his singing career to a temporary halt. For a while he worked in a bank. In 1943, when Nazi troops entered Milan and Siepi was to be drafted into the German army, he went into hiding until he could escape from Italy into Switzerland. There, with Giuseppe Di Stefano, he gave concerts in detention camps.

He returned to Italy in 1945. At this time he participated in a benefit concert to raise funds for the rebuilding of La Scala in Milan. He also

Siepi: sē ĕ′ pē

771

CESARE SIEPI

returned to opera as Zaccaria in *Nabucco* at the Teatro la Fenice in Venice. So spectacular was his success that he was asked to help reopen the rebuilt La Scala in *Nabucco* in 1946. He continued appearing at La Scala in major bass roles, not only in the Italian repertory but also in several Wagnerian roles. On the fortieth anniversary of the death of Boïto, commemorated in 1948, Toscanini invited him to appear at La Scala in the title role of *Mefistofele* and as Simon Mago in *Nerone.*

Guest appearances in other major European opera houses together with concert appearances in Spain, Switzerland, Scandinavia, England, and Mexico spread his fame throughout most of Europe. At the Edinburgh Festival he was heard as a soloist in performances of requiems by Mozart and Verdi.

Siepi made his debut at the Metropolitan Opera as a last-minute replacement for Boris Christoff, the Bulgarian bass, who was unable to appear since he had not been cleared by the State Department. Rudolf Bing, general manager of the Metropolitan Opera, who had heard Siepi sing in Milan, reached Siepi by transatlantic telephone to make the deal. That first American appearance took place on November 6, 1950 (the opening night of the season), as Philip II in *Don Carlo.* "Mr. Siepi," reported Max de Schauensee in the Philadelphia *Bulletin,* "radiates an ease and dignity in one so young. . . . That he sings his Verdi with instinctive style was evident with his voicing of the great monologue, 'Ella giammai m'amo' which drew rounds of applause." In

the *Herald Tribune* Virgil Thomson commented that Siepi was "clearly a fine musician and artist. His rich bass voice, moreover, is both vibrant and warm. . . . It is a beautiful voice and seems to be thoroughly schooled. Mr. Siepi's dramatic performance last night was no less distinguished than his vocal work." Olin Downes described Siepi in the New York *Times* as "an admirable bass of the most accomplished mastery."

Siepi once again drew high praise, as Don Basilio, when he appeared in *The Barber of Seville* on December 6, 1950. Virgil Thomson wrote in the *Herald Tribune:* "His brilliant bass singing and pantomime of the highest comic potency united to make an effect that dominated the whole evening's performance." Later that season Siepi was further acclaimed as Méphistophélès in *Faust* and Colline in *La Bohème,* and in 1951–1952 as Figaro in *The Marriage of Figaro* and Ramfis in *Aida.* On November 10, 1952 (once again the season's opening), he was in the cast of a new production of *La Forza del Destino* as Padre Guardiano. Two of his distinguished roles were assumed for the first time at the Metropolitan before that season ended: the title parts of *Don Giovanni* on November 26, 1952, and of *Boris Godunov* on March 9, 1953. Siepi's first performance as Boris Godunov led Olin Downes to say in the New York *Times:* "Not only because of his superb voice, dark colored and well suited to the role, but also by reason of his sincerity and the dignity of his conception, Mr. Siepi now has a meritorious accomplishment to his credit; potentially it is a great one."

During his more than two decades with the Metropolitan Opera, Siepi commanded admiration in still other roles: Silva in a revival of *Ernani* on November 23, 1956; Zaccaria in the Metropolitan Opera premiere of *Nabucco* on October 24, 1960, the opening night of the season; Alvise in *La Gioconda;* Oroveso in *Norma;* Sparafucile in *Rigoletto;* Fiesco in *Simon Boccanegra;* Sarastro in *The Magic Flute;* Don Fernando in *Fidelio;* Gurnemanz in *Parsifal.* His most frequently performed roles were Figaro in *The Marriage of Figaro* (57), Méphistophélès in *Faust* (42), Basilio in *The Barber of Seville* (37), Colline in *La Bohème* (32), and Philip II in *Don Carlo* (30). When on September 27, 1965, the Metropolitan Opera opened its season for the last time at its old auditorium, Siepi was Méphistophélès in a new production of *Faust.*

On January 27, 1951, he made his American

concert debut when he appeared as soloist in a performance of Verdi's Requiem conducted by Toscanini at Carnegie Hall. This time, Olin Downes said in the New York *Times:* "Mr. Siepi has everything that the basso part requires, the noble sonorous tone, the finished technique, and beyond that, the great spirit." This performance was recorded by RCA Victor as was still another performance of the Verdi Requiem with Siepi participating, conducted by Victor de Sabata. In March 1951 Siepi was the soloist in Mozart's Requiem in Chicago with Bruno Walter conducting. In addition to such appearances with orchestras, Siepi was often heard in recitals. A recital in New York in March 1952 encouraged the critic of the *Herald Tribune* to refer to Siepi's voice as "a recital instrument," and after his recital in Vienna in June 1965, a Viennese critic called him, "Cesare the First, the Emperor of basses."

In 1951, as Don Giovanni, Siepi made his first appearance at the Salzburg Festival. Three years later he was starred in a motion picture adaptation of *Don Giovanni* filmed in Salzburg by a British company, Furtwängler conducting.

He made his debut with the San Francisco Opera on September 21, 1954, as Padre Guardiano. He returned one season later as Don Giovanni and as Méphistophélès in *Faust.*

On May 19, 1962, Siepi made his bow in the Broadway musical theater in *Bravo, Giovanni!* Since this musical had a short life (seventy-six performances) it did not require his absence from the Metropolitan Opera in the fall of 1962.

That fall Siepi married Louellen Sibley, a member of the Metropolitan Opera ballet corps. They had two children and maintained three homes—an apartment on Central Park West in New York; an apartment in Lugano, Switzerland; and a house in Milan—before establishing permanent residence in Miami, Florida. One of Siepi's chief hobbies has been social dancing; another, sailing. His strongest superstition is a good-luck charm in the shape of a little bronze pig, given him when La Scala reopened for the first time after World War II. It has stood on every table he has ever used. Otherwise, as he told Howard Klein in an interview in the New York *Times* in 1966, "I have a good mental attitude—no phobias, no manias. Singing is athletic, and I keep in training. I vocalize every day, eat only steak before singing, keep a jar of honey in the dressing room for energy. But afterwards I like parties. I like to drink beer and stay up late."

ABOUT: Hi-Fi, January 1966; New York Times, September 26, 1971; New York Times Magazine, March 20, 1966; Opera News, December 28, 1963; Time, March 19, 1951.

Beverly Sills

1929–

Beverly Sills (originally Belle Miriam Silverman), soprano—one of the world's great coloratura sopranos and an exponent of bel canto singing recalling the golden age of Adelina Patti and Melba—was born in Brooklyn, New York, on May 26, 1929. She was the youngest of three children of Morris Silverman, an insurance broker who had been born in Romania, and Shirley Bahn Silverman, who had come to the United States from Odessa in the Ukraine. Her mother was a devotee of opera. She often attended performances at the Metropolitan Opera and collected recordings of opera stars, particularly those of Galli-Curci, to which the child Beverly listened continually. These Galli-Curci records made such a deep impression on Beverly that she began imitating the diva and by the time she was seven she could sing twenty-two arias, having learned them from both sides of eleven Galli-Curci disks.

Beverly's father wanted her to become a schoolteacher. Her mother, aware of Beverly's musical nature and of her attractive shock of blond curls, had other aspirations for her. Convinced that the fates had brought her another Shirley Temple (at the time Shirley Temple was movies' greatest child star and box-office attraction), Shirley Silverman was determined that her daughter conquer the world of show business. When she was three, Beverly made her first public appearance, singing "The Wedding of Jack and Jill" in a "Miss Beautiful Baby of 1932" contest at Tompkins Park, Brooklyn—and she won first prize. At this time, the child was already receiving lessons in singing, dancing, and elocution. When she was four she joined a company of child performers appearing over radio station WOR in a Saturday morning program called "Uncle Bob's Rainbow Hour." She was billed as Bubbles Silverman. ("Bubbles" had been Beverly's nickname as a baby.) During the

BEVERLY SILLS

program "Major Bowes' Amateur Hour." The audition was successful. Beverly appeared on the program singing "Caro nome" from *Rigoletto* and won for herself a permanent place on the weekly Major Bowes show.

At ten, Beverly assumed the role of Elaine Raleigh, "the nightingale of the mountains," on the radio soap opera "Our Gal Sunday" for thirty-six weeks. She earned seven dollars and fifty cents a performance, supplementing that income by the earnings from her singing of one of radio's earliest singing commercials ("Rinso White"). She was one of the first child performers to be seen on television (on the NBC program "Stars of the Future"). She also performed on the popular Cresta Blanca Carnival radio show conducted by Morton Gould. (Young Robert Merrill was another of its performers.) In recalling this period in her life, Beverly Sills has said: "I had graduated into the Deanna Durbin era, when teenage singers imitated adults."

She went into "retirement" in her twelfth year. "I was moving into an awkward age," she explains. "I wasn't quite the *Wunderkind* I'd been. I was becoming self-conscious. To be a child prodigy you have to be a monster of insensitivity."

Her lessons with Liebling were now intensified and supplemented with piano study with Paolo Gallico, private instruction in French and Italian, and attendance at concert and opera performances. (She had seen her first opera when she was eight—*Lakmé*, starring Lily Pons, at the Metropolitan Opera.) By the time she was fifteen she had learned twenty operatic roles. All this while her academic studies went on. She was graduated from P.S. 91 in Brooklyn in 1942 (voted by her classmates the Prettiest Girl, the One Most Likely to Succeed, the Fashion Plate, and the One with the Most Personality). After a short period at Erasmus Hall High School she was enrolled at the Professional Children's School in New York City, from which she was graduated in 1945.

She decided to come out of her "retirement" in 1944, venturing into professional musical pastures. In the fall of 1945 she joined a Gilbert and Sullivan touring company, appearing in principal female parts in seven comic operas. A year later she toured with the same company in *The Merry Widow* and *Countess Maritza*, billed as "the youngest prima donna in captivity." That year, under the assumed name of Vicki Lynn,

next four years, Bubbles was called upon to do a song and a tap dance on each program. She never missed a single broadcast, even though during this period she suffered through the usual quota of childhood illnesses. At this time she also appeared live at Town Hall in New York with the "Rainbow Hour" company, singing "Il bacio," which she had learned from a Galli-Curci record.

At seven, renamed Beverly Sills, she appeared and sang in a motion picture, *Uncle Sol Solves It,* produced by Twentieth Century-Fox and starring Willie Howard.

At this point her mother decided that the time had come for Beverly to begin serious training as a singer. Estelle Liebling (who had been Galli-Curci's coach) became Beverly's teacher in 1936. Initially, Beverly took one fifteen-minute lesson a week, traveling almost two hours each Saturday from Sea Gate outside Coney Island (where her family was then living) to Estelle Liebling's New York studio. Within a few years the lessons multiplied to three or four times a week and were expanded to forty-five minutes each. Estelle Liebling remained Beverly's only voice teacher; this teacher-pupil relationship lasted thirty-four years. (In later years, Beverly Sills was also coached by Roland Gagnon.) In all that time, Liebling refused a fee for her service, even after Sills could well afford to pay it.

After Beverly had studied with Liebling for two years, the teacher decided the time had come to bring her pupil to the public. She arranged for Beverly to audition for the CBS radio she won three hundred dollars on the "Arthur Godfrey Talent Scout Show" over the radio.

Convinced by her mother that her encounters in operetta were not the right paths to take toward grand opera, Beverly left the stage to engage in more serious study with Liebling and to master more operatic roles. By her nineteenth year her repertory comprised between fifty and sixty operas. She was just over seventeen when, in February 1947, she made her entry into grand opera, appearing as Frasquita in *Carmen* with the Philadelphia Civic Opera. Then, in 1948, as a member of the Estelle Liebling Singers she toured college and university towns.

She went to Paris in the summer of 1950 to attend the acting class of Max de Rieux of the Paris Opéra and to perfect her French. Returning to the United States, she toured with the Charles L. Wagner Opera Company in 1951, singing Violetta in *La Traviata* more than forty times in one-night stands. "We covered great hunks of ground by bus," she recalls, "traveling from early morning until sometime just before a performance, usually in a high-school auditorium where we dressed outside, often in the freezing cold. . . . I came back from that first Wagner tour a far more sophisticated singer than when I had left. My voice was still that of a twenty-one-year-old girl, but the performer, the actress had matured a great deal." One year later she toured with this company again, this time singing Micaëla in *Carmen* sixty-three times. In 1953, she abandoned touring and extended her operatic experiences by appearing with the Baltimore Opera in the title role of *Manon* and with the San Francisco Opera as Elena in Boïto's *Mefistofele* (making her San Francisco Opera debut on September 15, 1953), as Donna Elvira in *Don Giovanni,* and as Gerhilde in *Die Walküre.* In 1954 she appeared in Salt Lake City in *Aida,* and during the same year she was heard on "Opera Cameos," a sponsored program on Dumont Television, singing her first Tosca and Thaïs, and also the role of Violetta.

Beginning with 1952, Sills auditioned seven times for the New York City Opera; in each instance she was turned down by the music director, Joseph Rosenstock. An eighth audition, in the fall of 1955, proved successful, bringing her the opportunity to make her debut with that company on October 29, 1955, as Rosalinde in *Die Fledermaus.* This performance led Francis D. Perkins, music critic of the *Herald Tribune,*

to remark that the New York City Opera had acquired in Sills "an accomplished singing actress." That season, when one of the singers of the New York City Opera fell ill, Sills took on the role of Oxana in Tchaikovsky's *The Golden Slippers,* learning the part in three days. She was given opportunities to sing elsewhere, too: Fiora in *L'Amore dei Tre Re* in Philadelphia (a part mastered in eight days); the title roles in *Carmen* and *Tosca* at the Music Carnival in Cleveland; Sophie in a concert presentation of *Der Rosenkavalier* in New York conducted by Leonard Bernstein.

She was appearing in *Die Fledermaus* in Cleveland with the touring New York City Opera in 1955 when she met Peter Bulkeley Greenough at a party at the Cleveland Press Club. In addition to being the club president, Greenough was associate editor of the Cleveland *Plain Dealer* (which his family owned and had founded), a financial columnist, and a wealthy socialite. Greenough and Sills met several times during the next few days. Then Greenough asked her to marry him as soon as his divorce became final. They were married on November 17, 1956, in a civil ceremony in Estelle Liebling's living room in New York. Greenough had gained the custody of his children, and Beverly Sills adopted them legally. Since they were occupying a twenty-five-room French chateau on Lake Erie in a community outside Cleveland, Sills had to commute regularly to New York for her appearances at the New York City Opera. Her expanding repertory now included Philine in *Mignon* (she brought down the house singing "Je suis Titania"), Madame Goldentrillin in Mozart's *The Impresario,* Violetta, the title role in the New York premiere of Douglas Moore's *The Ballad of Baby Doe* (April 3, 1958), the Prima Donna in the world premiere of Hugo Weisgall's *Six Characters in Search of an Author* (April 26, 1959). About her appearances as Baby Doe she has written: "If I have ever achieved definitive performances during my career thus far, Baby Doe is one of them."

In the fall of 1959, the Greenoughs moved out of Ohio to Massachusetts, settling in a nineteen-room house in Milton, ten miles south of Boston. By then, their first child had been born: Meredith, affectionately called "Muffy." A second child, Peter Jr., nicknamed "Bucky," was born in 1961. Muffy had been born deaf; Bucky was mentally retarded. This double tragedy overwhelmed Sills. "I would willingly give up my whole career," she has said, "if I could have just one normal child." Actually, in her effort to give herself completely to her afflicted children, she did seriously contemplate retiring. After appearing in the world premiere of Douglas Moore's *The Wings of the Dove* with the New York City Opera (October 12, 1961), she told Julius Rudel, the general manager of the company: "I can't sing anymore. I have too many other things on my mind."

In 1963 the persistent persuasion of Rudel brought Sills back to the stage of the New York City Opera. She enjoyed additional successes as Donna Anna in *Don Giovanni,* Louise in the opera of the same name, Constanza in *The Abduction from the Seraglio,* and in the three principal female roles in Puccini's *Il Trittico*—the last mentioned probably the first time any soprano in New York had attempted singing the three roles in the three one-act operas in a single evening. Outside New York, she assumed the part of The Queen of the Night in *The Magic Flute* at Sarah Caldwell's Opera Company in Boston. She was also heard there on February 22, 1965, in the American premiere of Luigi Nono's avant-garde opera, *Intolleranza 1960.* In the spring of 1966, Sills appeared with the same company in the first staged American production of Rameau's *Hippolyte et Aricie.*

In the fall of 1966 the New York City Opera moved to its new home at the Lincoln Center for the Performing Arts. She opened the new auditorium as Cleopatra in a gala production of Handel's infrequently staged opera, *Julius Caesar.* It was here that Beverly Sills achieved the status of a superstar. As *Newsweek* reported: "The evening belonged to Beverly Sills. . . . The tall soprano had one of those nights singers dream of. She breathed the spirit of the baroque, while her developing sparkling coloratura voice negotiated every trill and tremolo with ease, clarity and melting beauty. Her every entrance sparked a stir of excitement in the audience as she built, aria by aria, her own pyramid of Cleopatra." When, a year later, Sills appeared in this role with the visiting New York City Opera in Los Angeles, the critic of the *Examiner* wrote: "If there could ever have been any doubt that Beverly Sills is one of the greatest lyric coloraturas of this century, the Queen of the Nile dispelled it." In December 1967, RCA Victor released a recording of this performance. "*Julius*

Caesar was the turning point of my career," Sills has written in her autobiography, *Bubbles,* adding: "Of all the nights in my performing career, including the night I made my debut at the Metropolitan Opera nine years later, none will remain in my memory as long as that opening night of *Julius Caesar.* It was—and I don't mean to be immodest but after all these years I *am* a pretty good judge of performances—one of the great performances of all time in the opera house."

In performances with the New York City Opera during the following season, Sills further solidified her position as a prima donna assoluta: in a cycle of Mozart operas; as Queen of Shemakha in *Le Coq d'Or;* in the title roles of *Manon* and *Lucia di Lammermoor;* as Marguerite in *Faust.* She was continually revealing a surer control of her technique, which was becoming dazzling in its virtuosity; a richer, deeper beauty of tone; and a magnetizing stage presence. "She returned," wrote Herbert Saal in the New York *Times Magazine,* "a different artist. Even her manner was different . . . She made entrances in an aura of supreme confidence. When she sang, melody just poured out without visible breath or facial distortion."

In a further extension of her repertory and artistry, between 1967 and 1968 she assumed all three leading feminine roles in *The Tales of Hoffmann* in New Orleans and was heard as soloist with the Cleveland Orchestra in Handel's *Semele,* with the Boston Symphony in Haydn's *The Creation* and with Amor Artis in New York in Honegger's *Le Roi David.* "If I were recommending the wonders of New York to a tourist," wrote Winthrop Sargeant in the *New Yorker* on March 1, 1969, "I would place Beverly Sills at the top of the list—way ahead of such things as the Statue of Liberty and the Empire State Building."

She had become that rarity: an American-born singer who had risen to the topmost echelon of the world's foremost coloratura sopranos without having sung a note in a foreign opera house. When she finally did appear outside the United States, she was no seeker after recognition but a star of stars. In 1967 she made her debut in South America (*Tales of Hoffmann* in Santiago, *Julius Caesar* in Buenos Aires), and at the Vienna State Opera (The Queen of the Night in *The Magic Flute*). On April 11, 1969, she made a triumphant first appearance at La Scala in Milan as Pamira in Rossini's *The Siege of Corinth,* in a production commemorating the centenary of the composer's birth—La Scala's first revival of this opera since 1852. (Sills was substituting for Renata Scotto who had fallen ill.) Her flawlessly produced pyrotechnics drew thunderous responses from the men in the orchestra during rehearsals and an uproar of enthusiasm from the audience on the night of performance. "Bel Canto has returned to La Scala," noted one critic in Milan. To the Milanese, Beverly Sills became "Fenomena" (The Phenomenon) or "Il Mostro" (The Incomparable One). She again electrified the audiences at La Scala that season as Lucia. After that came her successes as Lucia in her Covent Garden debut on December 24, 1969; as Violetta at the San Carlo Opera in Naples in January 1970; as Violetta in her first appearance in Germany, at the Deutsche Oper in Berlin on January 8, 1970; as Constanza in fourteen concert performances of *The Abduction from the Seraglio,* in Israel in 1971; and, also in 1971, her bow in Paris, this time in a recital.

Between 1970 and 1973, at the New York City Opera, Beverly Sills undertook the exacting roles of the three British queens in three rarely produced Donizetti operas, each of which was revived expressly for her. She was Elizabeth I in *Roberto Devereux* on October 15, 1969; Mary Queen of Scots in *Maria Stuarda* on March 7, 1972; and Anna Bolena, in the opera of the same name, in October 1973. Sills brought "her best and most flexible soprano voice," reported Donal Henahan in the New York *Times* after hearing *Maria Stuarda,* "singing with unwavering dramatic conviction and a queenly command of her considerable vocal resources." To Harriet Johnson in the New York *Post,* the role of Anna Bolena turned out "perhaps the vehicle for her greatest singing victory because the work gives her extraordinary opportunity for the lyric bel canto in which she excels."

Reaching still further into the repertory of bel canto with which to exploit the art of Beverly Sills, the New York City Opera revived for her Bellini's *I Puritani* in 1974, an opera which had not been heard in New York since 1918. In 1974 she also assumed for the first time anywhere the part of Rosina in *The Barber of Seville,* with the Sarah Caldwell Opera Company of Boston.

While rehearsing in Donizetti's *Lucrezia Borgia* in Dallas, Texas, in October 1974, Sills discovered she was suffering from a possible malignancy in the pelvic region. She was rushed to New York for surgery; fortunately the tumor was benign. Making a remarkable recovery, she was able to fill an engagement with the San Francisco Opera beginning on November 20, as Marie in *The Daughter of the Regiment,* and to go on from there to Los Angeles with the New York City Opera in *I Puritani,* the opera in which she opened the Spring season of the company in New York City in April 1975.

On April 8, 1975, Beverly Sills finally made her long overdue debut at the Metropolitan Opera in that company's first production of *The Siege of Corinth.* For a number of years before that, Sills's inexplicable absence from the roster of the Metropolitan Opera had caused many an upraised eyebrow. "Why I haven't sung at the Met until now comes down to, basically, a clash of personalities between Rudolf Bing and myself," she explained to Joan Barthel for the New York *Times Magazine,* "partly because of the pressures of what he was doing, partly because of the pressures that were put on him to bring me in when I could no longer be called his discovery. But as Mr. Bing made it quite obvious that he didn't need me, I was also able to make it quite obvious I felt I didn't need the Met. When I was interested, he wasn't; when he became interested, it was too late. It would have been a great concession on his part." However, Sills also revealed that Bing had made some half-hearted attempts to bring her into his fold. "Pressure from the Metropolitan Opera board forced him to make some offers," she explained. "But either the operas he offered me had a performance on a night I was doing something special, such as debuting at Covent Garden, or the role would be something like Martha—very dull, just unacceptable. Had he offered me something interesting, this would never have become such a *cause célèbre.* I would probably have accepted a *Traviata* or something, and he never would have had any trouble with me again."

Rudolf Bing made no secret of his bitterness over the New York City Opera productions of the Donizetti queen-triptych with Beverly Sills, since he had planned such a venture for Montserrat Caballé at the Metropolitan. This bitterness trickled into his autobiography, *5000 Nights at the Opera,* in which he wrote: "We finally accepted the fact that Beverly Sills of the City Opera, having been born in Brooklyn, was entitled to priority in the portrayal of British royalty."

Once Bing resigned from the Metropolitan Opera as general manager, the way was clear for Sills to become a member of that company. The demand for tickets for *The Siege of Corinth,* Francis Robinson, assistant manager of the company, disclosed, was "the worst I ever remember." Though they were priced as high as five hundred dollars for the boxes, sixty dollars for the best seats in the parquet, and nine dollars in the family circle, all scheduled performances of *The Siege of Corinth* were sold out long before the opening-night performance. An outburst of cheering acclaimed her big second-act aria. After that the evening was hers. At the end of the opera she received an eighteen-minute ovation. "Miss Sills looked ravishing," reported Harriet Johnson in the New York *Post,* "slim and believable, while her lyric singing and clean fast articulation were alluring." In the New York *Times* Harold C. Schonberg wrote: "It was Miss Sills who was the center of attraction, and she obliged with some beautiful singing. ... This was the Sills everybody loves: beautiful to look at, graceful in movement, and authoritative in style."

She was called upon to open the following season of the Metropolitan Opera, on October 13, 1975, in *The Siege of Corinth.* Meanwhile, in September 1975 the New York City Opera staged for her, in English, *The Daughter of the Regiment.* Less than a year later, on March 18, 1976, the New York City Opera staged for her the first New York production since 1904 of *Lucrezia Borgia.*

She sang her first Lucia at the Metropolitan Opera on December 24, 1976, and assumed the title role of *Thaïs* in the first Metropolitan Opera production of that opera since 1939 on January 18, 1978. (She had previously sung Thaïs in 1976 with the San Francisco Opera.)

In addition to making extensive recordings which include virtually all her famous roles, Sills has often appeared on television in specials, in interview programs, and in performances of operas. She became the hostess of a weekly talk show, "Lifestyles," over WNBC-TV in New York on October 16, 1976. She has also been a highly successful recitalist and soloist with principal symphony orchestras. Her first New York recital came comparatively late in her career, on February 1, 1970, at the Lincoln Center for the Performing Arts. "The vocal qualities that have helped make Miss Sills a star," wrote Allen Hughes in the New York *Times,* "were much in evidence. ... There was the familiar agility, which enabled her to negotiate dramatic leaps between high and low registers ... and to sing roulades with astonishing smoothness and softness. There were, above all, those high pianissimos that she seems to produce so effortlessly and flawlessly."

Sills averages about one hundred appearances a year, commands a repertory of over one hundred roles, and has sung about sixty roles either in the opera house or the concert hall. "I have sung at every major opera house in the world," she wrote in her autobiography. "I have sung with all the major symphony orchestras in the country and with many abroad. ... If not the highest paid opera singer in the world, I am certainly among the top three. So what do I do for an encore? More."

Nevertheless, on January 9, 1978, at a news conference at the New State Theatre in New York Beverly Sills announced that she planned to retire from her singing career in the fall of 1980 to become codirector with Julius Rudel of the New York City Opera. "I've done everything I set out to do," she explained, "sung in every opera house I wanted to, sung every opera I wanted to. By 1980 I'll have recorded every opera I wanted to. To go on past the point where I should, I think would break my own heart. I think my voice has served me very well. I'd like to put it to bed so it would go quietly, with pride."

Her personal tragedies have failed to dim the effervescence and ebullience of her spirit or her contagiously bright humor. Her stunning successes have left unblemished a wholesome personality that has rejected prima donna eccentricities and displays of artistic temperament.

After leaving Milton, Massachusetts, Sills and her family set up home in a large apartment on Central Park West in New York City, with a house in West Chop at Martha's Vineyard on Cape Cod awaiting them during vacations. That summer place had been built as her "dream house." When it was finished, and two days before the family could move in, it burned down and had to be built all over again. She has since also acquired an apartment in Key Biscayne, Florida, which serves as a winter retreat.

When the mood strikes her, Sills enjoys gourmet cooking, an art she has learned from her husband. She is addicted to crossword and double-crostic puzzles; she is said to be able to complete the New York Sunday *Times* crossword puzzle in twenty minutes. Occasionally, she plays bridge or poker or goes fishing. She is an avid reader, a garrulous talker, and a compulsive letter-writer.

Her innate musicianship and fabulous memory have made it possible for her to know not only her own roles but usually the other principal parts of whatever opera she is doing. She is a quick learner, studying each of her parts at the piano (which she can play with professional competence). "Before she undertakes a role," Winthrop Sargeant has written in *Divas,* "Miss Sills exhausts the literature about it. If it represents a historical character, her research must be very extensive. . . . After she has absorbed all the available historical and biographical data, she starts going over the music at the piano. . . . Then she calls her coach, Roland Gagnon . . . [who] takes her through a period of intensive coaching. . . . After this she is ready for rehearsals and performances."

In 1972, Beverly Sills received an honorary doctorate in music from Temple University in Philadelphia; she has since also received honorary doctorates from Harvard, New York University, the New England Conservatory, and the California Institute of the Arts. In October 1973, Mayor John Lindsay presented her with the Handel Medallion, New York's highest cultural award. She has been invited three times to perform at the White House: the first time in February 1971 for President and Mrs. Nixon; the second, in January 1975, when President and Mrs. Ford brought her to the White House for a State dinner honoring the Prime Minister of Great Britain; the third, in 1978 for President and Mrs. Carter and their guests. In 1976 she was one of ten American women honored for outstanding achievement in their respective fields by the fourth annual *Ladies' Home Journal* Women of the Year Award, telecast over NBC-TV on April 8. In 1978 she was the only musician selected to be included in a listing of twenty-five of the most influential women in the United States published in *The World Almanac.*

Since 1972, Sills has served as national chairman of the Mothers' March on Birth Defects, helping to raise over fifty million dollars. She has

also served as a member of the Council of the National Endowment for the Arts. She was appointed to that position by President Nixon in 1971.

ABOUT: Sargeant, W. Divas; Sills, B. Bubbles: A Self Portrait. *Periodicals*—Hi-Fi, February 1969; Life, January 17, 1969; New York Times Magazine, September 17, 1967, April 6, 1975; Newsweek, April 8, 1968, April 21, 1969; Opera News, February 11, 1967, September 19, 1970; Time, November 22, 1971 (cover story), April 7, 1975.

Alexander Siloti

1863–1945

Alexander Ilyitch Siloti, pianist and conductor, was born in Kharkov, Russia, on his father's estate, on October 9, 1863. He was the fourth of five sons to Ilya Matvey Siloti (a member of nobility) and Vera Rachmaninoff Siloti, aunt of the eminent composer-pianist Sergei Rachmaninoff; both were trained musicians. Alexander Siloti's grandfather, Arkadia Rachmaninoff, had been a concert pianist.

Alexander studied the piano with Nicolai Zverev before entering the Moscow Conservatory in 1876. During the next five years he was a pupil of Zverev and Nicholas Rubinstein in piano and of Tchaikovsky in theory and composition. Upon graduation in 1881 Alexander earned a gold medal for piano playing.

His debut as pianist took place with the Moscow Musical Society in November 1880. But success did not come to him until three years later when he was acclaimed at a concert of the Tonkünstlerversammlung in Leipzig. In spite of this success, however, he was so dissatisfied with his pianism that in 1883 he abandoned concert work and went to Weimar to study with Franz Liszt for three years. The story of this experience was told in his book *My Memories of Liszt* (1913).

On February 6, 1887, Siloti married Vera Tretyakova, daughter of a wealthy art collector; they had five children. From 1887 to 1890 Siloti was professor of piano at the Moscow Conservatory. There one of his pupils was his young cousin, Sergei Rachmaninoff. Disagreement with the director of the Conservatory led to Siloti's resig-

Siloti: sē lô′ tē

ALEXANDER SILOTI

nation in 1890 and to his decision to devote himself to concert work. During the next decade he resided in various cities in Germany and Holland from which he embarked on tours of Europe. He scored brilliantly in Paris, Frankfort, Leipzig, and Berlin and was ranked with the great piano virtuosos of his time. He was one of the last exponents of the grand manner of pianism typified by the Liszt-Rubinstein school of performers.

Siloti's first visit to the United States took place in 1898, and he was welcomed as a recognized master of his instrument. One American critic said of him: "Here is a man who has brains as well as fingers and wrists, and subtle but indisputable temperament as well as brains. As a colorist, he is a master of the brush; he disdains the assistance of the palette knife. He is without affectation of any kind. ... To hear him is an education as well as a pleasure."

In 1901 Siloti returned to his native land to enter upon a new career in music—conducting. In 1901–1902 he conducted the Moscow Philharmonic Orchestra. Two years later he organized his own orchestra in St. Petersburg. The Siloti Concerts in St. Petersburg and several other Russian cities became a powerful propaganda force for younger Russian composers, many of whom were invited to conduct the orchestra in their own works, thus getting their first hearings. In addition, the Siloti Concerts introduced to Russia many foreign composers (Schoenberg, Elgar, Debussy, Ravel, Richard Strauss, Delius, Falla, Enesco, Liszt). Siloti also conducted operatic performances at the Maryinsky Opera in St. Petersburg, until 1917.

In 1918, during the revolution in Russia, Siloti escaped to England. In 1922 he went to the United States, settling permanently in New York City where he remained for the rest of his life. Though he gave concerts intermittently in the United States after 1922, his prime activity as a musician was teaching the piano, beginning in 1925 when he joined the faculty of the Juilliard School of Music where he remained until his retirement in 1942.

In 1929, at the age of sixty-six, Siloti made his first American concert appearance since 1922, at Carnegie Hall in a program made up of the Tchaikovsky Piano Concerto, the Beethoven *Emperor Concerto,* and Liszt's *Todtentanz.* "There was youth, amazing youth in the veins and in the fingers of the man of sixty-six; but there was something else that a rather puny and ungenerous present does not seem to afford, and this emanated from the days of the celebrated teachers of Mr. Siloti and the glorious past of Leipzig and Weimar," wrote Olin Downes in the New York *Times.* "It was this spirit which gave the concert its special and unforgettable significance."

During the 1930–1931 season, Siloti appeared as a guest artist with the New York Philharmonic under Toscanini—the only soloist to appear with Toscanini that season. Early in 1936 he gave a concert at the Juilliard School of Music and on November 7, 1936, he appeared with the Elizabeth Philharmonic Orchestra in New Jersey in an all-Liszt program. He announced that this would be his last public appearance as a concert pianist. In spite of the inroads made upon him by advancing years, his performances in the 1930s still showed him to be an interpreter of uncommon penetration and a performer with a noble style and taste.

On December 8, 1945, Siloti died at his home at the Hotel Ansonia in New York City after a long illness. Funeral services were conducted at the Greek Orthodox Russian Church of Christ the Savior on Madison Avenue in New York.

He edited several works of Bach, Vivaldi, and Liszt, and published a volume of piano pieces he had favored on his programs.

ABOUT: Siloti, A. My Memories of Liszt. *Periodicals—* Etude, April 1922, July 1946; New York Times, December 10, 1945.

Giulietta Simionato

1910–

Giulietta Simionato, mezzo-soprano and soprano, was born in Forlì, near Bologna, Italy, on December 15, 1910. Her father, Felice, a Sardinian, was the director of the local prison. When Giulietta was one month old, her mother, Giovanna Truddaiu Simionato, took her to the island of Sardinia, and Giulietta's home was there until she was fifteen. Giovanna, a highly devout woman, placed her daughter in a convent in Sardinia where she received her first vocal instruction. However, any singing other than of religious music was forbidden by Giovanna who hoped her daughter might someday become a nun. When Giulietta was fifteen and had found a new home in Rovigo, near Padua, her mother died. Now free to sing professionally, Giulietta began taking vocal lessons with Ettore Lucatello, a bandmaster in Rovigo. Further vocal study followed with Guido Palumbo in Padua. While studying with Palumbo, she made her opera debut in Montagnana (near Padua) as Lola in *Cavalleria Rusticana*. In 1928 she appeared with the Padua Opera as Maddalena in *Rigoletto*. "I have not stopped singing since then," she later said.

In 1933 she was one of three hundred eighty-five contestants and won first prize in the Bel Canto competition in Florence. Three years later the death of her father left her completely on her own. "I was alone and had to sing in order to live," she has said.

She assumed her first important operatic role in 1938 at the Teatro Comunale in Florence, in Pizzetti's *L'Orsèolo*. In 1936 she was engaged by La Scala in Milan for minor or secondary roles, making her first appearance there as a Flower Maiden in *Parsifal*.

The war years brought hardships and deprivations. Later she said of these years: "We lived a meaningless life. We all stayed indoors, played cards, took tea with friends, danced. I did not suffer from hunger, but the loss of my music plunged me into despair." On rare occasions she sang in opera performances hastily improvised on makeshift stages in defiance of air raids.

At La Scala, both before and after its closing during the war years, she was employed as a *comprimario* (second lead) and gained consider-

GIULIETTA SIMIONATO

able stage and vocal experience but no prospect of singing principal roles. "I was earning hardly enough to live," she recalls. "I had no satisfaction in what I was doing, and I was losing confidence in myself every day. I had to take the measure of myself and find out what I could do." One day she went into the office of the director of La Scala and informed him: "If I am going to be a comprimario all my life, tell me, and I will give up singing today." When he failed to give her assurances of promotion, she left La Scala. She then joined a touring opera company that performed for two years in major Italian cities and gave her the opportunity to appear in such major roles as Hansel in *Hansel and Gretel*, Octavian in *Der Rosenkavalier*, Cherubino in *The Marriage of Figaro*, Dorabella in *Così fan Tutte*, Carmen, Mignon, Azucena in *Il Trovatore*, and Amneris in *Aida*. Her success in these roles prompted La Scala to call her back to Milan in 1947, this time to sing the title role in *Mignon*. A year later, as Rosina in *The Barber of Seville*, she enjoyed a personal triumph. From this point on, La Scala regarded her as a *prima donna assoluta*, assigning her leading mezzo-soprano or contralto roles in Donizetti's *La Favorita* and *Anna Bolena*, Bellini's *I Capuleti ed i Montecchi*, Scarlatti's *Mitridate Eupatore*, Rossini's *L'Italiana in Algeri* and *La Cenerentola*. In 1948, Toscanini, then on one of his rare conducting assignments in post–World War II Italy, selected her to appear as Rubria in *Nerone* at La Scala.

Her success in Italy brought her important engagements at Covent Garden in London, Teatro Colón in Buenos Aires, the Paris Opéra, the Berlin State Opera, the Munich State Opera, and with companies in other European and Latin-American cities.

She had already become well known to American music lovers through her many recordings when, on September 19, 1953, Simionato made her American debut as Charlotte in *Werther* with the San Francisco Opera. Ten days later she was heard there as Marina in *Boris Godunov.* In 1954 she sang Adalgisa in *Norma* with the Chicago Lyric Opera, a performance in which Maria Callas assumed the title role.

Simionato was scheduled to make her debut at the Metropolitan Opera in 1954 as Orfeo in Gluck's *Orfeo ed Euridice,* but an attack of laryngitis compelled her to cancel this engagement. In October 1957 she made her first appearance in New York in a concert performance of *Anna Bolena* with the American Opera Society. She enjoyed such an overwhelming success that the following season the American Opera Society invited her to sing the male role of Romeo in *I Capuleti ed i Montecchi.* In November 1957 she drew critical acclaim for her performance as Isabella in *L'Italiana in Algeri* with the Dallas Civic Opera.

On October 26, 1959, the opening night of the season, she appeared at the Metropolitan Opera as Azucena in a new production of *Il Trovatore.* "The Italian mezzo-soprano," said Howard Taubman in the New York *Times,* "brings a rich, secure and cultivated voice to the Met. Her range is formidable; the high tones have accuracy and brilliance, and the low are firm and vibrant. She sings with stirring ardor and moves with intelligence. The Met has acquired a new artist of the first magnitude." She further proved herself to be an artist of considerable stature as Santuzza in *Cavalleria Rusticana* on October 31, 1959. That Santuzza, wrote Irving Kolodin in the *Saturday Review,* "was a feat to treasure in the memory—a completely realized combination of dramatic song and lyric acting, in which her vocal span provided, at both ends of the range, values to illuminate the despairing emotion Mascagni wrote into the part." One season later, on February 18, 1960, she appeared as Amneris. Then, after a one-season hiatus, she was back at the Metropolitan as Rosina in *The Barber of Seville* on November 25, 1962. On April 27, 1965, she was heard as Delilah in *Sam-son and Delilah* during an American tour made by the Metropolitan Opera company.

Though basically a mezzo, Simionato has successfully assumed soprano roles: Aennchen in *Der Freischütz,* Donna Elvira in *Don Giovanni,* Valentine in *Les Huguenots,* Dido in Berlioz' *Les Troyens,* Iphigénie in Gluck's *Iphigénie en Aulide,* the title role in *Fedora,* Leonora in *Il Trovatore,* and Santuzza in *Cavalleria Rusticana,* among others. "There were three parallel roads I followed," she says, "and I loved them all." Those roads were the coloratura repertory in Rossini and Bellini, the heavy dramatic repertory, and lyric mezzo roles.

Simionato also appeared at major European festivals, including those at Edinburgh, Salzburg, and Florence, and in Holland. She was also a guest artist with American and European symphony orchestras and a recitalist.

She decided to retire from a professional singing career, making a last appearance at La Scala exactly on the thirtieth anniversary of her debut there. The opera scheduled for that evening—February 1, 1966—was Mozart's *La Clemenza di Tito,* in which she had never sung. She consented to assume the role of Servilia, learning the part in a few days. Though this performance had not been publicized as her farewell, the audience somehow became aware of it and gave her a rousing reception at the end of the opera. "It was the only way of doing it," Simionato explains in recalling that farewell appearance. "I'm a very emotional person. I slipped out of my career almost as quietly as I entered it."

Simionato was married to one of Italy's most eminent physicians, Dr. Cesare Frugoni. "If I hadn't been married," she says, "I would have gone on singing—the voice was still in good condition. But my husband was many years older than I, and I wanted to enjoy fully his stimulating company." He died in 1977, at the age of ninety-seven.

Since her retirement, Simionato has lived in a large penthouse in Rome overlooking the gardens of Villa Savoia. Her hobbies have included the collection of fine jade and ivory objets d'art; replenishing her well-stocked wardrobe of gowns, hats, and furs; and cooking Italian dishes. Her only superstition is, for good luck, to wear as a pendant on her bracelet an old Portuguese coin on which is inscribed the Latin motto *In hoc signo vinces* (In this sign you will conquer). She has always regarded the number seven as lucky. About the pendant she has said: "When I wear it, I know all will be well."

ABOUT: High Fidelity, February 1960; Musical America, December 15, 1959; New York Times, October 25, 1959; Opera News, March 11, 1978; Saturday Review, October 31, 1959; Time, November 9, 1959.

Martial Singher

1904–

Martial Jean Paul Singher, baritone, was born in Oloron-Sainte-Marie, in the Basses Pyrénées, France, on August 14, 1904, to Joseph-Paul and Marie Dubourg Singher. Though he early revealed a talent for singing and was a member of a boys' choir in Biarritz, he was directed by his father, a civil engineer in charge of railways, toward a teaching career. He received his academic education in schools in Oloron, Bayonne, and Dax before completing his studies at the École Normale de Toulouse and the École Normale Supérieure de St.-Cloud. At the last named of these institutions he specialized in philology and was graduated with the year's highest honors.

He first began considering singing as a profession in 1924 when he appeared publicly for the first time. Three years later Édouard Herriot, Minister of Public Instruction, heard him sing and urged him to study voice. Entering the Paris Conservatory, Singher studied voice with André Gresse, stage direction with Pierre Chéreau, and repertory with Maurice Fauré. In 1929 he earned first prize in singing and in 1930 in grand opera and light opera, as well as the Grand Prix Osiris de l'Institut de France for his student performance as Iago in the second act of Verdi's *Otello,* his last assignment at the Conservatory.

Upon leaving the Conservatory in 1930, Singher was offered an engagement with the Paris Opéra. However, he felt he was not yet ready for such a test, and devoted himself to additional training with various teachers, including Juliette Fourestier, Tanara from La Scala, and Hans Bruck. His professional debut took place in Amsterdam on November 14, 1930, when, under the auspices of the Wagner Society, he was heard as Orestes in Gluck's

Singher: săN gâr'

MARTIAL SINGHER

Iphigénie en Tauride, Pierre Monteux conducting. Singher has never forgotten that debut, not because he proved such a success but because of an amusing episode. "I was in my dressing room during intermission," he told an interviewer, "wearing shorts and one sandal, when an usher came in and said something in Dutch. I didn't understand a word, but I thought, 'Ah, they told me I would be paid at intermission.' I put a towel around my shoulders and went hopping off on one sandal. Where he took me was not to the cashier, but to the royal box. Princess Juliana was there, and some other people. They were all in magnificent evening dress. The Princess did not seem to mind. She came to hear me afterwards, in London."

A month later Singher made his first appearance at the Paris Opéra as Athanaël in *Thaïs.* His success led to an engagement with the Bordeaux Opéra in the world premiere of Jean Poueigh's folk opera *Perkin* on January 16, 1931. At the Paris Opéra, Singher was for a time assigned minor roles exclusively. But in May 1931 he was called upon to replace Vanni Marcoux, leading baritone of the Paris Opéra, in a performance of *Otello.* At that time Singher was familiar only with the second act; he had to learn the rest of the opera within three days. "There were eleven curtain calls after the second act," he recalls, "only I was too bruised to enjoy them: Mr. Melchior [who sang the title role] hurled me bodily into the footlights during our passionate dialogue. He was not used to so light an Iago." After that performance Singher was given a new contract, this time as leading baritone. During the next decade he successfully sang major baritone roles in the French, Italian, and German repertories.

During the 1930s Singher's career advanced. In 1932 in a recital in Paris he performed the world premiere of Ravel's song cycle, *Don Quichotte à Dulcinée,* dedicated to him by the composer. That year too Singher appeared for the first time in a Wagnerian role: Telramund, opposite Marjorie Lawrence in her Paris debut in *Lohengrin* at the Paris Opéra. After that he was heard at the Paris Opéra as Orestes in the first Paris production of *Elektra,* and in the world premieres of Milhaud's *Maximilien* (January 4, 1932), George Witkowski's *La Princesse Lointaine* (March 26, 1933), and Reynaldo Hahn's *The Merchant of Venice* (March 25, 1935). In addition, he starred in the first production at the Paris Opéra of *The Flying Dutchman* and in a significant revival of Rameau's *Castor et Pollux.* (The latter performance was repeated in May 1935 at the Florence May Music Festival.) In Amsterdam during this period Singher assumed for the first time in his career all four baritone roles of *The Tales of Hoffmann* in a single performance, a tour de force subsequently repeated many times.

Between 1936 and 1943 Singher appeared annually at the Teatro Colón in Buenos Aires, his repertory there including *Hamlet, Werther, The Marriage of Figaro, Parsifal, Ariadne auf Naxos, Elektra, Carmen,* Gluck's *Armide,* and Rabaud's *Mârouf,* among other operas. Subsequently he was invited as guest artist to Covent Garden in London, the Glyndebourne Festival, and the Florence May Music Festival. He was affiliated with the Opéra-Comique in Paris from 1938 to 1941 and in 1937 he performed in London during the coronation ceremonies of George V.

On January 10, 1940, Singher married Margareta (Eta) Rut Busch, daughter of the conductor Fritz Busch. He first met Eta in Buenos Aires when he was appearing in a performance of *Parsifal* conducted by Busch. The Singhers were preparing to leave for South America in June 1940 when the Ministry of Fine Arts in France announced that because of war no artist would be allowed to leave. The next eighteen months were difficult for Singher—after making a number of appearances at the Paris Opéra, he was afflicted with an infection that almost paralyzed him.

In November 1941 Singher was finally given a four-month permit to visit South America. En route he went to the United States and entered the Metropolitan Opera Auditions, winning a contract. Because of difficulties with the American immigration officials, Singher's debut at the Metropolitan Opera could not take place until December 10, 1943. At that time he appeared as Dapertutto in *The Tales of Hoffmann,* giving, as Virgil Thomson noted in the *Herald Tribune,* "a stage performance of incomparable elegance ... a piece of singing that for perfection of vocal style has not been equaled since Kirsten Flagstad went away." He made an even stronger impression as Pelléas in *Pelléas and Mélisande* on January 26, 1944. This was the first time he appeared in that part; it was also the first time in the history of the Metropolitan Opera that a baritone sang that tenor role. He was, as Virgil Thomson wrote in the *Herald Tribune,* "the glory of the evening. Vocally impeccable and dramatically superb, he animated the opera personally and gave it the authority of his perfect French declamation." Commenting on the fact that a baritone was singing a tenor part, Olin Downes wrote in the New York *Times* that such casting was fully justified by the fact that Pelléas was being sung by "a fine and experienced artist, an authoritative actor, one firmly grounded in the traditions of his language and stage action, personable, if not as youthful as Pelléas of the imagination, and a potent element of the occasion." In a later performance (November 27, 1953) he sang Golaud instead of Pelléas and was the first singer to appear in both male roles.

Singher remained with the Metropolitan Opera until 1959 (except for the seasons of 1948–1949, 1950–1951, 1952–1953, and 1954–1955). He opened the Metropolitan Opera season three times: on November 17, 1944, as Valentin in *Faust;* on November 11, 1946, as Frédéric in *Lakmé;* and on November 4, 1955, in the four baritone roles of *The Tales of Hoffmann* (which he had sung at the Metropolitan Opera for the first time on January 12, 1946). The performance on November 4, 1955, commemorated the twenty-fifth anniversary of Singher's debut in opera.

Singher's other roles at the Metropolitan were Escamillo in *Carmen,* Figaro and Almaviva in *The Marriage of Figaro,* Figaro in *The Barber of Seville,* Mercutio in *Romeo and Juliet,* Wolfram in *Tannhäuser,* Scarpia in *Tosca,* Amfortas in

Parsifal, Marcello in *La Bohème,* Lescaut in *Manon,* and the High Priest in *Samson and Delilah.*

Singher has also been a distinguished recitalist and one of the world's great baritone performers in oratorios and other choral masterworks. Virgil Thomson's comments after Singher's first American recital (Town Hall, New York, January 28, 1944) applied equally to Singher's performances as baritone soloist in choral masterpieces: "A great singing style and a great musical understanding, assurance, dramatic power and impeccable taste go into all his interpretations."

From 1955 to 1968 Singher was the director of the opera department of Curtis Institute of Music in Philadelphia and also taught voice there. After 1962 he headed the opera department at Music Academy West in Santa Barbara, California, his permanent residence.

The Singhers have three sons, one of whom, Peter, was married to Judith Blegen, the opera soprano (they were divorced in 1975). Singher's interests include reading, spending social evenings with friends, enjoying family life, and watching all types of ball games. Earlier in his life he was an avid player of tennis and rugby.

Martial Singher was decorated by France with the Legion of Honor.

ABOUT: New York Herald Tribune, November 3, 1946; New York Times, October 30, 1955; Opera News, December 6, 1943.

Stanislaw Skrowaczewski

1923–

Stanislaw Skrowaczewski, conductor, was born in Lwow (Lemberg), Poland, on October 3, 1923. His father, Pawel Skrowaczewski, was a brain surgeon, and his mother, Zofia Karszniewicz Skrowaczewski, an amateur pianist. Stanislaw received his first piano lessons from his mother when he was four. Precocious, he completed the writing of his first symphony when he was eight and had an orchestral overture of his performed by the Lwow Philharmonic the same year. In 1934 he supplemented the study of the piano with that of the violin. Then, while attending secondary schools in Lwow, he divided his

Skrowaczewski: skrō vä chĕf' skē

STANISLAW SKROWACZEWSKI

musical studies equally between the piano and violin at the Lwow Music Society. When he was eleven he gave his first public piano recital, and in 1936 he filled the dual role of pianist and conductor in a performance of Beethoven's Third Piano Concerto. Upon graduation from secondary school in 1939, he received further musical training at the Lwow State Conservatory. In 1945 he earned a degree from the University of Lwow where he had specialized in physics, chemistry, and philosophy and also received diplomas in composition and conducting from the Lwow Conservatory.

After graduation he left Lwow for Cracow. There he studied composition with Roman Palester and conducting with Walerian Bierdiajew at the Cracow State Higher School of Music, receiving diplomas in both departments. He also served as an assistant professor in the department of conducting.

World War II did not end his music study, even though all types of music making in Poland had come to a virtual standstill. "We were absolutely cut off from all opportunities of study," he later told an interviewer. "It was during the occupation, but I had my library, my recordings and my piano. It is a paradox, but I could do more that way—as if in a prison where you had books and could learn more than if you had freedom."

During a bombing raid both of Skrowaczewski's hands were injured, ending any possibility of pursuing a career as virtuoso. He then concentrated on composition and on conducting. In

1946–1947 he acquired his first conducting post, music director of the Wroclaw (Breslau) Philharmonic Orchestra in Poland.

A fellowship from the French Ministry of Culture and Art took him to Paris in 1947. During the next two years he studied composition with Nadia Boulanger and conducting with Paul Kletzki. He won second prize in the Karol Szymanowski Competition with his *Overture 1947,* and in 1948 his Prelude and Fugue for Orchestra was performed over the French Radio.

Returning to Poland, he served as music director of the Katowice National Philharmonic from 1949 to 1954 and of the Cracow Philharmonic from 1954 to 1956. In 1956 he won first prize in the International Conductors Competition sponsored by the Santa Cecilia Academy in Rome.

His most important post up to that time was principal conductor of the Warsaw Philharmonic from 1956 to 1959. During these years he found numerous opportunities to tour the rest of Europe as a guest conductor.

George Szell, the music director of the Cleveland Orchestra, was in Warsaw in 1957 and heard Skrowaczewski conduct the Warsaw Philharmonic. He invited Skrowaczewski to appear as a guest conductor with the Cleveland Orchestra. This concert, on December 4, 1958, represented Skrowaczewski's American debut. Reporting from Cleveland to *The Christian Science Monitor,* Klaus Roy wrote: "His keen musicianship was enthusiastically recognized not only by the audience but by the members of the orchestra. He, in turn, was immensely pleased with the response of the orchestra. When someone said to him: 'You certainly made them sing,' he replied, 'They made *me* sing.' "

Skrowaczewski returned to the United States in 1959 to fill another engagement with the Cleveland Orchestra and again in 1960 to appear with the Pittsburgh Symphony, the Cincinnati Symphony, and the New York Philharmonic (in the last instance substituting for Dimitri Mitropoulos who had just died). He was also heard during this time with orchestras in South America and Mexico City.

In 1960 he was appointed principal conductor and music director of the Minneapolis Symphony, taking over the baton that had been held by Antal Dorati for eleven years. Skrowaczewski's debut in this post took place not in Minneapolis

but out of town, in Brainerd, Minnesota, on October 1, 1960. Writing in the Minneapolis *Star,* John K. Sherman described the debut as "one of those historical nights of excitement and revelation," while George Grim in the Minneapolis *Tribune* reported that a "new sound" had come from the orchestra . . . "a driving force the symphony has not seen since the days of Dimitri Mitropoulos." Skrowaczewski led nineteen more concerts out of town before actually appearing in Minneapolis on November 4, 1960, to inaugurate the orchestra's fifty-eighth season at the Northrop Auditorium of the University of Minnesota. A capacity audience gave him an ovation.

In the ensuing years Skrowaczewski shaped the orchestra to his own conductorial image and in doing so gave it a higher status among American symphonic orchestras than it had thus far known. As Harriet Johnson noted in the New York *Post* only two years after Skrowaczewski had assumed command: "Within a short time he has lifted the orchestra in skill and personality to a new level of performance. It sounds better than in years." In *Musical America* Everett Helm noted that same year: "He has done wonders with his orchestra, which was a good one when he took it over and is even better now."

Among the provocative new works Skrowaczewski introduced with the Minneapolis Orchestra was Penderecki's *The Passion and Death of Our Lord Jesus According to St. Luke*—he gave its American premiere. This was the composer's first work to attract attention in the United States. Skrowaczewski repeated this performance in New York City at Carnegie Hall on March 6, 1969. Other important but unfamiliar Polish works introduced to America in Minneapolis were Szymanowski's Symphony No.2 and Lutoslawski's *Funeral Music;* each of these was heard in New York when Skrowaczewski was a guest conductor of the New York Philharmonic late in 1968. At that time Irving Kolodin wrote in *Saturday Review:* "When the music director of the Minneapolis . . . first appeared with the Philharmonic as 1960 was turning into 1961, it was evident that his was a musical mentality of size, substance and unquestionable seriousness. He was then in his junior year as a conductor of American orchestras, and it was evident that he had not yet earned his letter. . . . But now, through a lengthy tour of duty in the hard school of experience, Skrowaczewski has emerged with post-graduate status in practicalities and has well earned his doctorate in the ways and means of coping with musical emergencies. He has refined his vocabulary of gesture, expanded his command of unspoken directives, and, generally, moved from the area of promise to fulfillment."

In 1968, the name of the Minneapolis Symphony was changed to Minnesota Orchestra. On November 21, 1969, Skrowaczewski celebrated the tenth anniversary of his tenure as musical director by introducing his own Concerto for English Horn. On April 21, 1972, the orchestra and conductor made their debut at the new John F. Kennedy Center for the Performing Arts in Washington, D.C., before an audience that included many Washington notables. This was part of a national tour during which Skrowaczewski presented the New York premiere of the complete *Das Klagende Lied* by Mahler (including the long neglected Part I, *Waldenmarchen*). On October 21, 1974, the Minnesota Orchestra and musical director dedicated their new home, Orchestra Hall in downtown Minneapolis.

Skrowaczewski has appeared as a guest conductor of practically every major orchestra in Europe, Canada, Mexico City, South America, and Israel. He toured with the Concertgebouw Orchestra of Amsterdam, the French National Orchestra, and the Israel Philharmonic, and in 1966 he went on a State Department tour of South America with the Philadelphia Orchestra, as coconductor with Eugene Ormandy. In 1968, he made his bow at the Salzburg Festival, conducting the Vienna Philharmonic. In the fall of 1973 he appeared as guest conductor of the Cleveland Orchestra during its first tour of Hawaii, Australia, and New Zealand.

Skrowaczewski has distinguished himself in opera too. He enjoyed a stunning success when he made his opera debut as conductor in Vienna at the State Opera in *Fidelio* in 1964. On August 14, 1969, he led the American premiere of Penderecki's *The Devils of Loudun* with the Santa Fe Opera in New Mexico. On January 8, 1970, he made his debut at the Metropolitan Opera with *The Magic Flute.* At that time Allen Hughes wrote in the New York *Times* that he "paced the opera very well, moving it briskly, while allowing the singers to sing easily and expressively. The orchestral textures were clear, and the balances between orchestra and singers made for easy listening." Later the same year, he conduct-

ed performances of the Metropolitan Opera on tour. He also appeared with the Philadelphia Orchestra in performances of *The Marriage of Figaro.*

In 1977, Skrowaczewski announced he would not renew his contract as musical director of the Minnesota Orchestra upon its expiration in 1979. He explained that he wished to be "free of the stringent demands, limitations and responsibilities of directing one orchestra." For his last season, he helped commemorate the seventy-fifth anniversary of his orchestra by presenting a Beethoven cycle that included the nine symphonies and the *Missa Solemnis,* together with the world premieres of Dominick Argento's *In Praise of Music* and Penderecki's piano concerto, *Primous Fountain.*

Skrowaczewski married Krystyna Jarosz, a philologist, on September 6, 1956. They had met six months earlier while skiing in the Carpathian mountains in Poland. They have three children. The Skrowaczewskis are both enthusiastic about sports cars and skiing. Writing in *Musical America,* Lester Trimble described Skrowaczewski as "a distinguished, even handsome, fellow, with the clearly etched features and animation of a European intellectual. . . . His eyes are a shade of blue that even dark horn-rimmed glasses cannot hide, and every gesture of head and hands betrays a kind of smooth-flowing physical vitality." Skrowaczewski speaks English fluently, having learned it by listening secretly in Poland to the forbidden broadcasts of BBC during World War II.

In 1953 he received the Polish national prize for artistic activity and in 1956 first prize in the Santa Cecilia International Competition for conductors in Rome and the Commanders Cross, Poland. He has received an honorary doctorate in music from Hamline University in St. Paul, Minnesota, and in 1973 he won Columbia University's Alice M. Ditson Conductor's Award for his efforts on behalf of American music.

ABOUT: Musical America, October 1960; High Fidelity/Musical America, March 1978; New York Times, January 25, 1959.

Leo Slezak

1873–1946

Leo Slezak, tenor, often ranked with Francesco Tamagno, who preceded him, and Enrico Caruso, who was his contemporary, was born in Mährisch-Schönberg in Moravia, on August 18, 1873. After his father had lost a family mill he had inherited, the family went to Brünn where the father found a job in a cloth factory. The family's poverty made it necessary for Leo's mother to help out with the finances by sewing and for Leo to build birdcages and make ink-wells and market them. At fourteen he left public school permanently to devote all his time to earning a living. At first he worked as a gardener's apprentice, but later he learned to be a blacksmith and a locksmith. Since he loved singing and had a good ear for music, he spent his evenings in the Brünn Opera where he was allowed to take walk-on parts in operas. Sometimes he joined the chorus in the singing. Adolph Robinson, baritone of the Brünn Opera, became interested in him and after testing his voice offered to teach him without charge. While studying with Robinson, Slezak supported himself first by working as a clerk in a lawyer's office and then by selling insurance.

Robinson arranged for Slezak to audition for the opera house in Brünn. Singing the "Vesti la giubba" aria from *I Pagliacci,* Slezak won a three-year contract, and on March 17, 1896, he made his debut in the title role of *Lohengrin.*

After three years in Brünn, he was engaged by the Berlin Royal Opera in 1899, making his debut as Lohengrin; Emmy Destinn was Elsa, and Richard Strauss conducted. The reaction was negative. One review the next day remarked sardonically: "A Mr. Slezak from the State Theater in Brünn sang Lohengrin. He did not wear a beard; he looked like a child; and he sang like an old man." Even more disheartening than the unfavorable criticisms was the fact that he could not get the roles he wanted. After a few months he asked for and got a release from his contract. He was then engaged by the Breslau Opera; his debut took place in the title role of *Tannhäuser.* In Breslau, on February 15, 1900, he married an actress, Elisabeth Wertheim, who gave up her

LEO SLEZAK

own career to devote herself completely to her husband.

Slezak appeared at Covent Garden as Lohengrin in 1900. Gustav Mahler, music director of the Vienna Royal Opera, heard him there and engaged him for his company on a seven-year contract. Slezak's first appearance in Vienna took place in 1901 in the title role of *William Tell.* He was not long with the company when he developed a hoarse condition caused by nodes on the vocal cords. After an operation he maintained three months of total silence. On the ninety-third day after the operation he tried out his voice and found that it was more beautiful than ever. Back with the Royal Opera he became an idol of the Viennese opera-going public both for his striking stage presence and for the sensuous beauty of his tone production.

Feeling the need for more vocal training, he took temporary leave from the Vienna Royal Opera in 1908 to study with Jean de Reszke in Paris. On June 2, 1909, he emerged from retirement to become a sensation at Covent Garden in the title role of *Otello.* His voice was more disciplined than before and his technique surer.

In addition to his regular appearances at the Vienna Court Opera, Slezak was heard in England, Italy, Poland, and Russia, and at the Wagner festivals in Munich. Signed to a contract with the Metropolitan Opera he went to New York in the fall of 1909 with his family and made his home in an apartment at the Hotel Ansonia. Because of his chronic fear of colds, during his years in New York he almost never left his hotel

---

Slezak: slā′ tsäk

apartment except to travel to and from the Metropolitan Opera House.

He made his American opera debut as Otello on November 17, 1909. "Despite his size," wrote H. E. Krehbiel in the *Tribune,* "his was no mountain of flesh, but such a figure as would have delighted the audience that once applauded the heroics of Tommaso Salvini. With it all, Herr Slezak showed himself a splendid actor. . . . It was an impersonation not soon to be forgotten. . . . [His was] a voice of fine power, and one used with more than ordinary discretion."

In his four seasons at the Metropolitan Opera, Slezak appeared in enough operas to prove that his extraordinary singing and acting were matched by his versatility. He sang Otello seventeen more times and in addition was heard as Manrico in *Il Trovatore,* Radames in *Aida,* Stradella in Flotow's *Alessandro Stradella,* Hermann in Tchaikovsky's *The Queen of Spades,* Walther in *Die Meistersinger,* Lohengrin, Tamino in *The Magic Flute,* and Faust. As Hermann in the American premiere of *The Queen of Spades* on March 5, 1910, he was, said Richard Aldrich in the New York *Times,* "a large part of the success the opera had yesterday. . . . He made a real personage out of a strange figure." Aldrich once again singled Slezak out for special attention in *Die Meistersinger,* in which he found Slezak to be "a superb and sympathetic figure . . . truly an aristocrat in looks and bearing. He sang with chivalrous ardor and abundant outpouring of tone and with admirable declamation of diction. There have been few Walthers who have so completely satisfied the ear and eye, and who so completely won the sympathetic appreciation of the audience." Slezak's final appearance at the Metropolitan took place on January 31, 1913, as Otello. "It was a worthy swan song to a career that left many pleasant memories in the city," wrote H. E. Krehbiel in the *Tribune.*

Slezak was also an aristocratic performer of *Lieder.* As Richard Aldrich wrote in reviewing a Slezak recital on February 3, 1912: "The remarkable beauty and power of his voice and his admirable style have often been enjoyed in lyric drama. . . . These put remarkable resources at his command as a Lieder singer. Mr. Slezak has an unusual power of giving apt and significant expression to a variety of moods, expression that is gained by subtle means in the molding of a phrase, the color of the voice, the suggestion of dramatic or emotional motive; and his singing of

Lieder is vitalized thereby in a fascinating way."

Slezak was appearing in guest performances in Russia when World War I broke out. He managed to escape to Germany where he joined the army. At one time he was reported to have been killed in action. He was demobilized in 1916 and rejoined the Vienna Royal Opera. His winter home was a fourteen-room apartment in the heart of Vienna, commanding a view of the Ringstrasse and St. Stephen's Cathedral. Summers were spent in his villa in Egern on Tegernsee in Bavaria, acquired in 1910.

During the winter season he lived an almost monastic existence. He refused to go where people smoked, though he himself smoked cigars in moderation (but never on the day of a performance). He followed a methodical schedule. Rising at seven in the morning, he took breakfast in his study and then spent several hours vocalizing with his accompanist. On performance days he never ate after a light lunch and he kept to himself, for the most part avoiding any talking. Much of the afternoon was spent in meditation. After a short nap and some tea at four in the afternoon, he reviewed in his mind the music he had to sing that evening.

At Egern in the summertime he could indulge in his favorite exercises, mainly swimming in the lake and riding a bicycle. He also relaxed by going fishing.

He began suffering from a pathological fear that he was losing his voice in 1928. He became convinced he could no longer negotiate the high notes. Each appearance became a harrowing ordeal. But with the help of a Viennese singing teacher by the name of Flamm he finally overcame his phobias and doubts and continued performing with all his former vocal splendor.

His last opera performance was in *I Pagliacci* at the Vienna State Opera on September 26, 1933. "My voice sounded as young as ever," he wrote to his son Walter. "Rarely have I had such an ovation after the aria 'Vesti la giubba'. . . . As I was waiting for my second-act entrance, I thought: Wouldn't that be a wonderful way to leave, to end my career on such a high note; maybe I will never be able to sing so well! By the time the final curtain had rung down, my mind was made up. I had sung my last opera!"

A few weeks later he received a medal from the state of Austria, the highest decoration bestowed on a civilian. The presentation was made on the stage of the opera house.

Smallens

After retiring from opera, Slezak found a new career as a motion picture actor, becoming a popular screen comedian in Austria. His first motion picture was *Ein Toller Einfall* (1934) and his last *Die Blonde Carmen* (1939). In between were almost a dozen other productions.

When Germany occupied Austria, he went to the United States, intending to stay permanently. His residence was a suite at the Beekman Hotel, in New York City. However, after a few months he decided to go home. He spent the years of World War II at his villa in Egern, years of loneliness and sometimes hardship. He died there on June 1, 1946.

Slezak's son, Walter, who was born in Vienna in 1902, became a star in Broadway musical comedies and in motion pictures. He was the author of a book of reminscences—*What Time's the Next Swan?* (1962) which provides a wealth of information about his father. The title comes from one of Leo Slezak's bon mots. He was in the wings during a performance of *Lohengrin,* when a confused stagehand started pulling the swan-drawn boat before Slezak could board it. As he watched the boat disappearing, Slezak made the mocking inquiry that has become one of the classic anecdotes on opera performances.

Leo Slezak not only boasted a quick and ready wit but was also a chronic prankster. A singer at the Vienna State Opera always wore large cotton plugs in his ears to ward off colds. On an evening when the actor was scheduled to appear as Jokanaan in *Salome* at the Vienna State Opera, Slezak sneaked into the prop room and stuffed a two-inch white earplug into each ear of the papier-mâché Jokanaan head. The sight caused so much laughter among the other singers, the musicians in the pit, and even the audience that the curtain had to be rung down.

Once, at the Metropolitan Opera, Slezak saw a venerable gray-haired gentleman in the wings during a performance of Gluck's *Armide*. At the end of the opera he pulled the man to the stage and introduced him to the audience as the composer, Gluck. After he was fined one hundred dollars, he went into the general manager's office wearing a black veil over his head; his one hundred dollars was refunded.

During World War II he sent a letter to the brewmaster of Löwenbrau beer, which had become thin because of the war. "Please send me the color," he wrote. "I have the water."

He was the author of a humorous autobiogra-phy, *Meine Sämtlichen Werke* (1922), that sold over six hundred thousand copies. He later wrote two more best sellers: *Der Wortbruch* (1927) and *Der Rückfall* (1930), and another book of reminiscences, *Mein Lebensmärchen* (1948). In 1938 an English translation of his two earliest works was published under the title *Song of Motley.*

ABOUT: Slezak, L. Mein Lebensmärchen; Slezak, L. Song of Motley: Being the Reminiscences of a Hungry Tenor; Slezak W. What Time's the Next Swan?

Alexander Smallens

1889–1972

Alexander Smallens (originally Alexander Smo-lensk), conductor, was born in St. Petersburg (now Leningrad), on January 1, 1889. His father, Pantaleimon Ossipowitch Smolensk, was a brain surgeon who left his family soon after Alexander was born. Alexander's mother, Anna Rosovski Smolensk, took her six-month-old son to the United States where their name was Americanized to Smallens. "I never saw my father," said Smallens. "Even when I was back to Russia to conduct, I didn't make any effort." In New York, Smallens received his education in the public schools and at the College of the City of New York, from which he was graduated with a Bachelor of Arts degree in 1909. His musical education, begun when he was eleven, continued at the Institute of Musical Art in New York from 1905 to 1909.

Though alienated from his father, Alexander long felt his influence, and planned on becoming a doctor. Only after he was graduated from the College of the City of New York did he turn to music. In 1909 he went to Paris, where he entered the Conservatory. As one of two foreign students there at the time, Smallens was a pupil of Paul Vidal and Paul Dukas. Since there was no conducting class at the Conservatory, Small-ens played in the school orchestra to gain experience in orchestral music.

After leaving the Conservatory in 1911, Smallens tried to make his way as a conductor. "I was getting nowhere professionally. The provincial opera houses were open only to French-men. So I marked time." One day, upon meeting Oscar Hammerstein, the opera impresario, at

ALEXANDER SMALLENS

the Café de la Paix, he summoned his courage to ask for a conducting job in New York, only to be informed that Hammerstein's Manhattan Opera House had closed down. Smallens's next move was to write to Henry Russell, who was then forming an opera company in Boston. "He hired me immediately as an audition pianist. No pay; it was considered part of my examination. I got a regular job out of it, as assistant conductor, one among thirteen, at ten dollars a week pre-season, magnificently doubled in season. One year I made $611, pieced out by coaching such singers as the elegant Edmond Clément for five dollars a lesson. Even though I never got to conduct, some of the experiences were priceless," he said.

Smallens served as assistant conductor of the Boston Opera from 1911 to 1914. In 1914 he became the conductor of the short-lived Aborn English Opera at the Century Theater in New York, and from 1915 to 1917 he was the conductor of the Boston Opera. In 1917 Anna Pavlova's husband engaged Smallens to conduct the orchestra for Pavlova's tours of South America, Central America, and the West Indies. "I think some of his finest conducting was done for Pavlova and there is no question that she danced most gloriously when Smallens was leading the orchestra," wrote Olin Downes at this time. "He seemed to possess some superlative authority that she respected." During the two years that Smallens was Pavlova's conductor he was able to direct some opera performances in Havana and at the Teatro Colón in Buenos Aires. Then, in

1919—the year in which Smallens became a naturalized American citizen—Cleofonte Campanini called him to Chicago to be assistant conductor of the Chicago Opera. After Campanini's death in 1920, Smallens took over the performances of Reginald de Koven's *Rip Van Winkle* and helped prepare the premiere of Prokofiev's *The Love for Three Oranges,* which the composer himself conducted.

Leaving Chicago in 1922, Smallens went to Europe. He replaced Leo Blech as conductor of the Italian repertory at the Berlin State Opera and gave guest performances at the Volksoper in Berlin in 1923 and in opera houses in Madrid and Barcelona. Illness took him back to the United States.

From 1924 to 1931 he was the music director of the Philadelphia Civic Opera; from 1927 to 1934, assistant conductor to Leopold Stokowski with the Philadelphia Orchestra; and from 1930 to 1935 music director for that orchestra's summer season at Robin Hood Dell. At the Philadelphia Civic Opera he directed the American premieres of Richard Strauss's *Ariadne auf Naxos* (November 1, 1928) and *Feuersnot* (December 1, 1927). When the Philadelphia Orchestra embarked upon a season of opera performances in 1934–1935, Smallens became coconductor with Fritz Reiner, presiding over five operas including Shostakovich's *Lady Macbeth of the Mtsensk District,* Gluck's *Iphigénie en Aulide,* and, on December 28, 1934, the American premiere of Stravinsky's *Mavra.* In Philadelphia, Smallens also led the Philadelphia Society for Contemporary Music in the first Philadelphia performances of Schoenberg's *Pierrot Lunaire.*

After 1934, as a free-lance conductor, Smallens appeared in many different places with many different organizations. In the summer of 1934 he was invited to stage some operas for the first time at the Lewisohn Stadium in New York. He continued appearing at the Lewisohn Stadium each summer until 1960; the last time was his twenty-seventh all-Gershwin program. In 1934 he directed the world premiere of Virgil Thomson's *Four Saints in Three Acts* in Hartford, Connecticut (February 8), and later its six-week run in New York City beginning February 21. On September 30, 1935, in Boston, he conducted the world premiere of Gershwin's *Porgy and Bess,* continuing to serve as its conductor when the folk opera went to New York City on October 10 for what proved to be a run of one hundred twenty-four performances at the Alvin Theater. Subsequently, he was the music director of *Porgy and Bess* during its world tour in the years between 1953 and 1956.

In 1939–1940 Smallens appeared as a conductor of the Ballet Theater in New York. In 1944 he was the conductor of the International Ballet and from 1947 to 1950 of the orchestra at Radio City Music Hall in New York City. During the 1940s he appeared frequently on the radio, on such programs as the "Ford Sunday Evening Hour," the "General Motors Hour" and the "Sealtest Hour." He also directed the music for several motion picture documentaries, including *The Plow that Broke the Plains* and *The River* (both with music by Virgil Thomson) and *Fight for Life* (music by Louis Gruenberg).

Writing in the *World-Telegram,* Robert Bagar once described Smallens's conducting technique as follows: "Mr. Smallens has no affectations. He does not pose, nor, by the same token, is he the diffident interpreter. . . . He devotes himself completely to [the musical work] and, to borrow a term from the lexicon of gag men, 'makes the pitch' sans fanfare, sans personalized notions and, thanks be, sans overture to the oh so pedantic ideas of the pseudo-esthetes."

Smallens's last engagement was with the Netherlands Opera Company in Holland in 1957–1958. Neuritis so crippled his hand in 1958 that he had to retire and one year later he suffered a heart attack. He spent most of his years of retirement in Taormina, Sicily. Just before his death he returned to the United States. He died at St. Joseph's Hospital in Tucson, Arizona, on November 28, 1972.

On May 15, 1935, Smallens married Ruth White, a composer, the former wife of a banker and music patron (Maurice Wertheim). They had a son. Smallens enjoyed playing chess and poker and going to the theater.

One of the movements of Virgil Thomson's *Suite for Orchestra* is a musical portrait of Smallens.

ABOUT: Ewen, D. Dictators of the Baton. *Periodicals* —Newsweek, July 14, 1947; Opera News, January 4, 1969.

Izler Solomon

1910–

Izler Solomon, conductor, was born in St. Paul, Minnesota, on January 11, 1910, to Harry Thomas Solomon and Ida Chasin Solomon. His father ran a grocery and meat market. Izler began taking violin lessons when he was six. Five years later his family moved to Kansas City, where he revealed such talent on the violin that a local organization subsidized his music education. After graduation from Manual Training High School in Kansas City in 1924, he went east, dividing his time between New York and Philadelphia for the next four years. He studied the violin with Michael Press and Myron Poliakin; and he played the violin in orchestras. He made his concert debut as violinist in Kansas City in 1925. From that time on he gave recitals, touring the Middle West. The National Federation of Music Clubs bestowed a prize on him for his violin playing.

In Philadelphia Izler decided to become a conductor after attending concerts of the Philadelphia Orchestra. He followed every performance with a pocket score and carefully studied Stokowski's conducting methods.

When Izler was eighteen, his teacher Michael Press became head of the violin department at Michigan State College in Lansing. He invited Izler to go to Lansing as his assistant. Three years later a new orchestra was formed in Lansing, and Solomon was given the post of concertmaster. The new orchestra had gone through one rehearsal when its conductor fell seriously ill; he died before the first concert could take place. Solomon replaced him and did so well without ever having taken a lesson in conducting that he remained the orchestra's conductor for five years. During this time, from 1931 to 1935, he also taught music in the public schools.

When the Music Project of the federal Works Progress Administration (later the Work Projects Administration) was organized during the depression years of the 1930s, Solomon was appointed music director for the State of Michigan. He created such a well-rounded and progressive program of musical activity that it was later adopted nationally by the WPA. Guy Maier, regional head of the WPA Federal Music Project, asked Solomon in 1936 to go to Chicago

IZLER SOLOMON

to head the American Concert Orchestra. When the national director of the Federal Music Project of the WPA, Nikolai Sokoloff, heard one of Solomon's performances with the American Concert Orchestra, he placed Solomon at the head of the Illinois Symphony, which Sokoloff had found to be in a state of disintegration. For two months Solomon rehearsed the men meticulously, whipping them into something resembling professional shape. Sokoloff, after hearing one of those rehearsals, said publicly: "After two months, the Illinois Symphony sounds better than the Cleveland Orchestra [of which Sokoloff had been principal conductor] after ten years."

The Illinois Symphony, Solomon has said, "provided me one of the most challenging musical experiences I have encountered. The one-hundred-member orchestra gave one hundred and twenty-five concerts a year. And since the orchestra was expected to do experimental work, I was able to introduce more than one hundred and fifty American compositions, as well as many works by European composers." Among the premieres he presented were Roger Sessions's Concerto for Violin and Orchestra (January 8, 1940) and Ernst Toch's *Circus* (July 8, 1954). During the five years Solomon conducted the Illinois Symphony he succeeded in making it into one of the finest WPA orchestras in the United States, good enough to attract the praise of music critic Winthrop Sargeant, who referred to it in *Time* Magazine as a major symphonic organization. After Solomon had conducted his last performance with this orchestra,

in 1941, Claudia Cassidy wrote of Solomon in the Chicago *Tribune:* "Poised over his orchestra, beckoning, persuading and shaping the music, he reminded me of a snake charmer, and the music coiled and uncoiled as if it understood and swayed to his spell. This was a superb exhibition of orchestra control in the finest sense of complete freedom within correct boundaries. It was as distinguished as it was hypnotic."

While serving with the Illinois Symphony, Solomon also conducted the Women's Symphony in Chicago for a brief period and appeared as guest conductor of the NBC Symphony, the Philadelphia Orchestra, the Chicago Symphony, and the Buffalo Philharmonic. In 1941 he began a nine-year regime as music director of the newly organized Columbus (Ohio) Philharmonic, which in a few years' time he helped to develop from a semiprofessional group giving only three concerts a season into a full-sized symphonic organization with ten subscription concerts a season, eleven "pop" concerts, five children's concerts, and performances on tour. For his efforts toward promoting new music both in Chicago and Columbus, he received a citation from the National Association of American Conductors and Composers for "understanding and intelligent interpretations of contemporary American composers." He subsequently received the Alice M. Ditson Award for distinguished services to American music and the Award of Honor from the National Music Council.

Traveling on Entry Visa No. 1 for the new state of Israel, Solomon directed concerts under bombardment during the early years of Israel's war for independence. In 1951, with Serge Koussevitzky and Leonard Bernstein, he directed concerts of the Israel Philharmonic during its tour of the United States and Canada, and in 1958 he returned to Israel to perform during ceremonies commemorating the tenth anniversary of the State.

During the 1952–1953 season he was the resident conductor of the Buffalo Philharmonic in New York. As music director of the Brandeis Festival for the Creative Arts in Waltham, Massachusetts, in 1955, he conducted the American premiere of Milhaud's opera *Medea,* and in the summer of 1956, at the Hollywood Bowl in California, the premiere of another Milhaud opera, *David.* For six summers beginning with 1956 he was the music director of the Aspen (Colorado)

Music Festival, the first American to hold this post.

In 1956 Solomon was named music director of the Indianapolis Symphony Orchestra, succeeding Fabien Sevitzky. He remained in this post twenty years, resigning in 1976. Under him the Indianapolis Symphony expanded its seasonal activities. Within a decade of his directorship attendance went up twenty-five percent, income fifty percent; the personnel of the orchestra increased from seventy-eight to eighty-six, the length of the season from twenty-two to twenty-eight weeks. Under him the orchestra embarked upon numerous national tours (including several highly praised performances at Carnegie Hall, in New York) and presented numerous world and American premieres, among them Easley Blackwood's *Symphonic Fantasy* (October 30, 1965) and William Schuman's *A Song for Orpheus* (February 17, 1962), together with compositions by George Antheil, Henry Cowell, Roy Harris, Paul Hindemith, Ernst Krenek, and Elie Siegmeister.

Since taking the post in Indianapolis, Solomon has appeared as guest conductor of many major orchestras in the United States and abroad. As a resident conductor at Indiana University in Bloomington, he directed performances there of *Turandot* in 1964. In 1966 he made successful appearances with the Berlin Philharmonic Orchestra in an avant-garde program, and in 1969 he toured Germany and Scandinavia.

Swarthy of complexion, with bushy eyebrows and an untamed hair style, Izler Solomon has been described as looking more like "a hungry Mexican Indian" than a man of Russian-Jewish ancestry. On November 26, 1931, he married Sorelle Melamed, who died in 1959. In 1961 he married again, this time to Elizabeth Weems Westfeldt; they were divorced in 1971.

ABOUT: Ewen, D. Dictators of the Baton.

Sir Georg Solti

1912–

Georg Solti, conductor, was born in Budapest on October 21, 1912, to More and Theres Rosen-

---

Solti: shōl' tē

SIR GEORG SOLTI

baum Solti. For centuries the Soltis had been bakers. To advance himself in the grain business, Solti's father left the Hungarian village where his family had lived for generations and went to Budapest. There he eventually entered the real estate business. Both parents were music lovers.

At the age of six, it was discovered that Georg had perfect pitch. That year he was recruited to serve as a piano accompanist for his sister, a voice student at the Liszt Academy. "I had to accompany her to save money," Solti told Robert Jacobson in an interview for *Opera News.* "We could not afford to have a coach. Later my parents decided it would be nice if this boy hears some operas, so I went to *Die Meistersinger*—and, of course, this was a total disaster, because in the first half of the first act I fell asleep, and I don't remember a thing! But I began to know the soprano literature, and by twelve I knew a great deal." In fact, by the time he was twelve he was already giving concerts. One year later he too entered the Liszt Academy in Budapest. Over a five-year period he specialized in piano, his principal teachers being Zoltán Kodály, Ernst von Dohnányi, and Béla Bartók. "I was recognized as a very talented young boy who played the piano. I was rather poor and had to earn some money, so I began to coach other singers and give piano lessons," he later said. When Georg was fourteen he heard an orchestral concert conducted by Erich Kleiber and realized he wanted to become a conductor.

After graduation from the Academy in 1930 with diplomas in piano and conducting, Georg found a job as a coach with the Budapest State Opera. In addition to coaching singers, he served as piano accompanist at rehearsals and helped move the scenery.

In the summer of 1936 he went to Salzburg with a letter of introduction, hoping to sit in on rehearsals during the festival season. "I arrived at the Festspielhaus," he has said, "and gave my letter, and they asked me, 'Are you able to play some rehearsals?' There was a flu epidemic—lots of coaches were ill. So I said yes, when do I start? They told me to come that afternoon. That's where I started. It was *The Magic Flute*. . . . Suddenly Toscanini stepped into the rehearsal. I was playing the piano, and from then on I just stayed." That summer and the summer after that he assisted Toscanini at rehearsals of *Falstaff, Die Meistersinger, Fidelio,* the Verdi Requiem, and *The Magic Flute.*

Solti's first opportunity to conduct an opera came on March 11, 1938—a performance of *The Marriage of Figaro* at the Budapest State Opera. "That was quite some night," Solti recalls. "All my friends and relatives left at intermission on hearing the news that Hitler had marched into Austria. They were sure he would continue his march right into Budapest. So dampened were the spirits of everybody in the opera house that nobody was much concerned about my debut, and after the performance there was no celebration."

Solti was visiting Toscanini at Lucerne in Switzerland when World War II began in Europe. Since the Hungarian government was closely allied to Nazi Germany, Solti's mother wired him to remain in Switzerland. Unable to get a work permit that would enable him to find a job in an opera house or with an orchestra, he returned to the piano, earning his keep by appearing in recitals and by teaching. In 1942 he won first prize in the International Competition at Geneva. In 1944 Ernest Ansermet gave him an opportunity to conduct concerts with the Swiss Radio Orchestra. On October 29, 1946, in Switzerland, Solti married Hedi Oechsli.

When the war ended, he got in touch with Edward Kilenyi, an American pianist of Hungarian origin who was the music control officer for the United States occupation forces in Bavaria. Through Kilenyi, Solti was given the post of principal conductor in Munich in 1946. "They were looking for a non-Nazi conductor and I was invited. No food, no light, no facilities

—but great musical enthusiasm," he says. Though his operatic repertory at that time consisted solely of *The Marriage of Figaro,* he was required to conduct numerous operas. "I took care to conceal my rather limited repertory. It was not for several years that Munich began to discover that I was conducting everything for the first time." The first opera he conducted in Munich was *Fidelio,* and the performance went off well. After two months he became music director. During the next six years he helped to reestablish the artistic importance of the Munich State Opera (which had been ravaged by the war), presenting some forty striking new productions, mainly of the Wagnerian music dramas, including the *Ring* cycle, and of operas by Mozart and by Richard Strauss. Each year he presented at least one world premiere. He was also called upon to direct from ten to twelve subscription concerts of orchestral music each season.

While he was serving in Munich, Solti was invited to give guest performances in Italy and in Vienna, and with the London Philharmonic Orchestra. He left his post in Munich in 1952 to become the general music director in Frankfort, Germany. During his nine years in Frankfort, as he later revealed, "I was dictator. I ruled the house. I made my merits and my mistakes." The Frankfort Opera under his direction put on forty-four new productions, including Hindemith's *Cardillac* and Berg's *Lulu,* neither of which had ever been given in Frankfort. Frankfort was the scene of remarkable productions of the Wagnerian music dramas and of *Elektra, Boris Godunov, Eugene Onegin, Der Rosenkavalier, The Magic Flute,* and *The Marriage of Figaro.* He also conducted the Museum Concerts, a regular series of orchestral performances. Away from Frankfort he was heard at festivals in Salzburg and Edinburgh and as a guest conductor of most of Europe's prominent orchestras.

He made his American debut on September 25, 1953, with the San Francisco Opera in *Elektra.* "His direction was always musically sensitive and finely controlled," reported *Musical America.* He was also impressive that season in performances of *Tristan and Isolde* and *Die Walküre.* The following January he made an equally successful American debut as a symphony conductor with the San Francisco Symphony.

His career in the United States during the next few years continued with appearances with the

Chicago Symphony at Ravinia and with the Los Angeles Philharmonic at the Hollywood Bowl in the summer of 1954, with the Chicago Lyric Opera in performances of *Salome* and *Die Walküre* in 1955, and with various American orchestras during the two years that followed, culminating with his debut in New York on March 14, 1957, with the New York Philharmonic Orchestra. That concert, as Howard Taubman noted in the New York *Times,* was "an impressive affair. . . . Mr. Solti left no doubt that he has the gift of leadership and a mature musical point of view." His prestige in the United States, as elsewhere, gained considerable momentum in 1957 with the release of his recording for London Records of *Die Walküre* with Kirsten Flagstad, Set Svanholm, and the Vienna Philharmonic Orchestra. Its success led London Records (English Decca in Europe) to embark upon a recording project that further enhanced his international stature: the complete *Ring* cycle, which was finally finished by 1965. *Die Walküre* from this set earned a Grammy from the National Academy of Recording Arts and Sciences in 1966. Other Solti recordings to win Grammys were *Aida* in 1962, Mahler's Symphony No.8 in 1968, Berlioz' *Benvenuto Cellini* and Mahler's Symphony No.7 in 1972, Berlioz' *Symphonie Fantastique* in 1973, the nine symphonies of Beethoven in 1976, Strauss's *Also Sprach Zarathustra* and *Classical Orchestral Performance* in 1977, and the Verdi Requiem in 1978. During his quarter-of-a-century affiliation with London Records, he became the only conductor to win the Grand Prix du Disque in Paris eleven times, winning the prize for such recordings as *Tristan and Isolde,* the Wagner *Ring* cycle, and *Salome.*

In 1960 he was engaged as music director of the Los Angeles Philharmonic Orchestra, scheduled to begin in the 1961–1962 season. "I was to be Caesar in my own orchestra, with full powers in all artistic matters," he said. But he never filled that appointment. A few months before he was to assume his duties in Los Angeles he discovered that Dorothy Buffum Chandler, music patron and chairman, Board of Governors of the Performing Arts Council of the Music Center of Los Angeles, had engaged Zubin Mehta as assistant conductor without having consulted Solti. Since he felt that his authority had been flouted, Solti sent in his resignation. "If I had given in on this one point, it would never have been the same," he explained.

On December 17, 1960, he made his debut at the Metropolitan Opera in *Tannhäuser.* During the next four years he revealed the scope of his interpretative powers and extraordinary musicianship with penetrating performances at the Metropolitan Opera of *Tristan and Isolde, Boris Godunov, Otello, Don Carlo, Aida* (with which he opened the 1963–1964 season), and *Parsifal.* Commenting upon Solti's performance of *Aida,* Alan Rich wrote in the New York *Herald Tribune:* "Georg Solti conducted a taut, alert performance that brought out lines in the orchestra that are usually submerged in mud and [he] balanced beautifully the sounds in the pit with the sounds onstage." "I was not happy at the Met," Solti reveals, "because of the rehearsal situation and the idea of changing casts. . . . When the question came to discuss the new *Peter Grimes* with Bing, he wanted a cast I did not want. That was the end of it."

In the 1960s Solti conducted so many major music organizations in Europe and the United States that he was drawing comparison with Herbert von Karajan in respect to his influence as a symphonic and operatic conductor and to the charisma he had for audiences everywhere. For ten years beginning with 1961 he was the music director of Covent Garden in London, where he had previously made an auspicious debut in 1959 in *Der Rosenkavalier.* His first performance as music director came on September 14, 1961, with Gluck's *Iphigénie en Tauride.* The excellence of his performances, many of them in new productions, attracted worldwide interest. Of particular importance during his regime were his presentations of the *Ring* cycle, *Otello, Falstaff,* Strauss's *Die Frau ohne Schatten* and *Der Rosenkavalier,* Britten's *Billy Budd* and *A Midsummer Night's Dream,* Sir Michael Tippett's *King Priam,* and Schoenberg's *Moses and Aron.* In June 1971 he made his farewell appearance as music director of Covent Garden with *Tristan and Isolde,* the first time he had ever directed this musical drama there. For his services to English music, he was made Knight Commander of the British Empire in 1972, shortly after he had become a British subject.

He left Covent Garden, where he had been happy with the results he achieved, because he was determined to pursue more actively than heretofore his career as an orchestral conductor.

"I felt strongly that if I am not stopping now, I will never go away from opera, and my symphonic music will suffer. I wanted to do a certain amount of symphony before it was too late. . . . I was already fifty-nine, and it was the latest time I could do it."

From 1971 to 1975 he was music director of the Orchestre de Paris in France. When Rolf Liebermann was made general manager and artistic director of the Paris Opéra in 1972 he asked Solti to become his music adviser and principal conductor. At the Paris Opéra in 1973 Solti conducted *The Marriage of Figaro* and *Moses and Aron* in performances which the French critics described as "monumental realizations." When the Paris Opéra visited the United States in the fall of 1976, Solti conducted it in performances of *The Marriage of Figaro* and *Otello*.

In the United States, Solti found a permanent post with the Chicago Symphony Orchestra, with which he had appeared for the first time as guest conductor on December 9, 1965. In 1968 he assumed the post of music director of that orchestra, bringing about a marriage between conductor and orchestra which was said to be the most idyllic since the days of Toscanini and the New York Philharmonic. In the fall of 1971 and again in September 1974 he toured Europe with the Chicago Symphony; there were many in Europe ready to concede that the orchestra under him was possibly the finest in the world.

"The newest culture hero among contemporary conductors is Sir Georg Solti," wrote Harold C. Schonberg in the New York *Times* in 1972, "and his appearances in New York are a phenomenon. Not even Karajan has ever evoked this kind of hysterical approval. To match it, one has to go back to the great days of Toscanini." When a replacement was sought for Pierre Boulez as music director of the New York Philharmonic Orchestra in 1976, Solti was offered the post. He turned it down, preferring to remain in Chicago, and explained: "As a close friend said to me, 'If you have a Rolls Royce, why change it?' So I said no, but I promised I would conduct the Philharmonic again and I will."

In July 1977, Solti directed two special concerts in London: one with the London Philharmonic honoring the Silver Jubilee of Queen Elizabeth II; the other, with the orchestra of Covent Garden in memory of his late assistant, Enid Blech, and to benefit the Malcolm Sargent Fund for Children. That year Solti was appointed principal conductor of the London Philharmonic. He was to assume his duties in September 1979 without relinquishing his post in Chicago.

After a separation from his wife, Hedi, Solti was divorced in 1967. "We were still young when we married," he explains, "and we just grew in different ways." During this period of separation, he met Anne Valerie Pitts, a reporter for BBC-TV who interviewed him; she was then married to a theater executive. The affair that followed between Pitts and Solti has been described by the conductor as "violent," covering the two years each had to wait for a divorce. They married on November 11, 1967, and in 1970 a daughter, Gabrielle, was born, followed by a second child in 1973.

In Chicago the Soltis live at the Drake Hotel; in Europe they have a Swiss villa; and, for two months each year, they spend their summer vacations in Italy.

Charles Reid has described Solti as follows: "He is smallish and spare of build, with quick, dark gimlets for eyes. His smile modulates from wistful to radiant, reflecting unusual mobility of mood. The baldness and sallowness are striking. . . . When in top physical form, around ten in the morning, he looks at least ten years less than his actual age. It is a different matter when a black despondency suddenly hits him. . . . Coming off the podium he takes a bath and a nibble, tumbles into bed, sleeps as if pole-axed for five hours . . . and wakes up with the music of the night before pounding away inside his temples. He is chary of sedatives."

Solti always avoids any suggestion of ostentation or the spectacular in his conducting. He comes to rehearsals in baggy pants, a loose knit shirt, and often with a towel around his neck, looking very much like "a Hungarian wrestler," as one of his musicians described him. He drives a small car, prefers mineral water to wine, and finds his greatest relaxation in such simple pleasures as playing bridge with friends or watching a soccer game over British television. He invariably rehearses and conducts a concert with a score in front of him, even though there is hardly a work he conducts that he has not committed to memory.

Solti has been decorated with the Great Cross of the German Republic and named Commander of the Legion of Honor by France. He has received doctorates in music from Oxford University, the University of Leeds in England, De Paul University in Chicago, and in 1974 from Yale University.

ABOUT: Furlong, W. B. Season With Solti. *Periodicals* —High Fidelity, January 1967, October 1969; New York Times, April 25, 1971, May 9, 1976; New York Times Magazine, December 10, 1972; Opera News, September 1976; Saturday Review, April 19, 1975; Time, May 7, 1973.

Gérard Souzay

1920–

GÉRARD SOUZAY

Gérard Marcel Souzay (originally Gérard Marcel Tisserand), baritone, was born in Angers, France, on December 8, 1920, to a musical family. His father, Victor Georges Tisserand, an army colonel, was an amateur cellist; his mother, Madeleine Hennique Tisserand, was an amateur singer. The parents and their four children often participated in chamber music concerts and songfests at home.

Though Gérard early revealed his talent for singing, his ambition at first was to become an actor. "I loved the stage," he has said, "and didn't know I loved music as much." After he was graduated from the Lycée Carnot in Paris, where he majored in philosophy, some of his friends persuaded him to abandon his academic studies and concentrate on music. For two years he studied with Pierre Bernac. In 1940 he entered the Paris Conservatory, after having studied voice with Claire Croiza and Vanni Marcoux. At the Conservatory he received first prizes in singing and vocalise, and he was graduated with high honors. He subsequently received some coaching in German *Lieder* from Lotte Lehmann.

He made his debut as a concert singer in Paris in 1945, where his talent in the French art-song repertory was immediately recognized, resulting in engagements on the Continent (including one at the Strasbourg Music Festival in 1945 commemorating the centenary of Gabriel Fauré's birth) and in North Africa. He also came to be recognized as an outstanding exponent of German *Lieder;* in 1949 he was invited to return to Strasbourg to give three concerts of German art songs.

He made his American debut on November 26, 1950, with a recital at Town Hall in New York. Though some of the critics were disturbed by some of his vocal and facial mannerisms, they praised his diction and his aristocratic style both in French and song literature. In other recitals in the United States in the 1950s he was recognized as probably the best living interpreter of Debussy, Ravel, Duparc, and Fauré, and an equally distinguished performer of *Lieder*. Though his voice was comparatively small, he handled it with consummate artistry and used an exceptional musicianship and instinct to penetrate to the core of a vast literature ranging from Lully, Rameau, and Alessandro Scarlatti to the twentieth century.

Further success came in the 1950s and 1960s at some of the world's festivals, including those at Edinburgh, Salzburg, Florence, Prades, Holland, Helsinki, Bergen, Paris, and Venice. At the Venice Festival in September 1956 he participated in the world premiere of Stravinsky's *Canticum Sacrum ad Honorem Sancti Marci Nominis,* with the composer conducting.

Though he is best known as a recitalist and as a guest artist with orchestras, he has also been acclaimed in the opera houses, beginning with engagements at the Opéra-Comique in Paris in 1947. His American operatic debut took place with the New York City Opera on September 29, 1960, in the title role of Monteverdi's *Orfeo,* Stokowski conducting. On that occasion Harold C. Schonberg noted in the New York *Times* that his singing had "style, intelligence and vocal resource." On January 18, 1962, he made his first appearance in one of his most famous roles, that of Golaud in *Pelléas and Mélisande* at the Rome Opera, repeating the same role later that year in his debuts at the Paris Opéra and at La Scala on February 2, 1973. On January 11, 1965, he assumed the role of Castor in a concert performance of Rameau's *Castor et Pollux* at the Lincoln Center for the Performing Arts. His first appearance at the Metropolitan Opera followed less than two weeks later, on January 21, 1965, in another of his favorite roles, Count Almaviva in *The Marriage of Figaro*. During the summer of 1965 he participated in the opera performances at the Glyndebourne Festival in England.

To Richard Dyer, reporting in the New York *Times,* Souzay revealed in 1975 that some years earlier he had gone through a major crisis in his life. "I was travelling all over the world and I was losing sleep. So I began taking pills, and once you do that you cannot stop. I had a real nervous breakdown because of them and it harmed several years of my career. I went to a clinic to get rid of this habit, and I went through hell." How well he succeeded in overcoming his problem became apparent on March 6, 1975, in New York when he was heard in an all-Ravel recital commemorating the centenary of that composer's birth. "Mr. Souzay," wrote Raymond Ericson in the New York *Times,* "is an ideal interpreter of this music. What sets him apart is purity of style. This does not mean that there is no color to his singing. There is a great deal. But the readings are without excess, and the vocal line is always fastidiously phrased. The style is mature and impeccable."

Souzay has recorded under various labels. His first operatic release, *Arias from the Baroque Operas,* on the Philips label, received the Grand Prix du Disque in Paris in 1964, an honor that went to him several more times for other albums including one devoted to the songs of Gabriel Fauré. His album *The World of Song* was chosen by the New York *Herald Tribune* as the best vocal recording of 1960; in this collection of folk songs he sang in seventeen different languages.

He has singled out the three elements that should go into every performance. "First there is style. Second, inspiration. Third, eloquence." Then he adds: "People want voice first of all. But soon the impact of sheer sound wears off and interpretation must create the interest. Often an ugly voice is the most interesting if the singer has a winning personality. For myself I must say that I cannot stand a flawed voice, one with a wobble or a veil, or one that makes ugly sounds. When it comes to an ugly voice I want it in the throat of genius."

A bachelor, he resides in Paris. His hobbies include playing tennis, attending soccer games, reading philosophy, and painting. France has made him Chevalier of the Legion of Honor and Chevalier de l'Ordre des Arts et des Lettres.

Souzay conducted master classes in *Lieder* singing at the Mannes College of Music in New York in 1962 and 1963.

ABOUT: Musical America, March 1963, April 1964; New York Times, January 1, 1965, February 16, 1975; Newsweek, December 4, 1950.

Albert Spalding

1888–1953

Albert Spalding was the first American-born violinist to achieve international recognition. The son of J. Walter Spalding, a partner in the sporting goods firm of A. G. Spalding, Albert was born in Chicago, on August 15, 1888. "I was an ordinary-looking child," he once recalled, "undersized for my age, but with a kind of restless and wiry energy that was always getting me into scrapes and accidents. I had asked for a violin at the age of seven. No one knows why—and I don't know myself. No one in the family played the violin. No, the likelier impulse came from a wandering street fiddler with a monkey. It thrilled me to think that perhaps with arduous work I might get to be as proficient and possibly have a monkey too. Anyway, there was the violin, dangling on the Christmas tree that year—a little half-sized violin that cost the princely sum of four dollars."

The musical member of the Spalding family was Albert's mother, Marie Boardman Spalding, who was an excellent pianist. For many years she maintained a salon in Florence, at a palace once occupied by Talleyrand, where leading musicians performed and where Albert always spent half the year. The boy's first musical experiences as a child came from listening for hours to his mother's playing. He began taking violin lessons in Florence with Ulpiano Chiti,

ALBERT SPALDING

and during the summers at Monmouth Beach, New Jersey, he studied with Juan Buitrago. "Did I like to practice? Emphatically no! I can distinctly recall shamming the practice of scales while reading a book of adventure (preferably bloody!), secretly propped upon the piano and screened by pages of music. However, I did love the violin and I loved to play; and as I soon found that you couldn't play without practicing, I did some of that, too."

After preliminary studies, Albert at fourteen applied for a diploma at the Bologna Conservatory in Italy. The Conservatory was open not only to students but also to outsiders who could pass a grueling test not only in violin playing, but also in piano, theory, harmony, and counterpoint. For his violin examinations Albert performed the Mendelssohn Violin Concerto, Tartini's *Devil's Trill Sonata,* and the E major Partita of Bach, as well as a manuscript read at sight. Fifty points was the highest mark, with thirty required for passing. He achieved forty-eight points. No other fourteen-year-old musician had earned this diploma since Mozart one hundred and thirty-three years earlier.

For two years Albert continued violin study in Paris with Lefort, and counterpoint and composition with Antonio Scontrino. On June 6, 1905, he made his concert debut in Paris at the Théâtre Nouveau, with his teacher Lefort conducting the orchestra, performing the Saint-Saëns Violin Concerto No.3 and the Bach Chaconne. "No, I did not make my debut as a prodigy. I was wearing a pair of perfectly authentic long pants. I had

a better success than I deserved, although it was not bad as debuts go." The Paris *Figaro* spoke of his "remarkable talent. . . . His playing was classically pure and noble."

Soon after this debut, at the invitation of the French actor Benoît Constant Coquelin, Spalding appeared at the Châtelet in Paris at a gala concert with many performers, one of whom was Adelina Patti. When his accompanist failed to show up, Patti kindly offered him the services of her own pianist with whom he had to play without rehearsals. "I don't know whether it was good, bad or indifferent; but somehow we got through and were greeted by what the press agent likes to call 'an ovation.' "

After these two appearances in Paris, he toured the French provinces, then gave successful performances in London and Vienna. Saint-Saëns, Joachim, and Eugène Ysaÿe were some of the musicians who hailed his talent. A London critic reported: "His fine taste is characteristic of all that this brilliant violinist does."

On November 8, 1909, he made his American debut at Carnegie Hall in New York as soloist with the New York Symphony under Walter Damrosch in the Saint-Saëns Concerto No.3. "He is assuredly a young man of talent, of high accomplishment at present and of even greater promise for the future," said Richard Aldrich in the New York *Times.* "He is well equipped with a high degree of technical skill. . . . There are energy and vitality in Mr. Spalding's playing; and this energy is dominated by a feeling of repose and poise that is altogether unusual for one of his years." A negative report was filed by H. E. Krehbiel in the *Tribune.* Krehbiel called his playing "a cacophony of rasping, raucous, snarling unmusical sounds."

A concert tour of the United States followed and also appearances with the Dresden Philharmonic which had come from Germany for American concerts in 1909. He toured Europe as a soloist with the New York Symphony when that orchestra became the first American symphonic ensemble to visit abroad.

Spalding toured extensively during the next few years, with principal visits to Russia, Scandinavia, Italy, Germany, and France. In the single season of 1913–1914 he gave eighty-one concerts in Europe. Then, when World War I began, he returned to the United States. He told American reporters on his arrival: "Like all good Americans, I am neutral and hope that right and justice will win in the unfortunate conflict now raging." However, when America was drawn into the war, he canceled more than thirty-five thousand dollars' worth of signed American contracts to enlist in the Army as a private in the air service of the U.S. Signal Corps. His first assignment was as a porter hauling the baggage of officers. He later rose to the rank of lieutenant, becoming adjutant to Major Fiorello H. La Guardia (later the mayor of New York City) at an aviation base in Italy. On one occasion he accompanied Major La Guardia on a secret mission to Spain to arrange transportation of raw materials to Italy. For his war activity Spalding was presented by the Italian government with the Cross of the Crown of Italy and by France with the rosette of an officer of the Legion of Honor.

After being demobilized in the middle of February 1919, he set out to prepare himself for the resumption of his virtuoso career. "There were stiff hinges to oil, and rigorous spring cleaning to undergo before a semblance of concert pitch could be recovered," he said. After giving twenty concerts in Italy, he returned to the United States. On July 19, 1919, he married his childhood sweetheart, Mary Vanderhef Pyle, in Ridgefield, Connecticut; at the ceremony some of the music was provided by the French violin virtuoso Jacques Thibaud, with André Benoist at the organ.

After a honeymoon in Mendon, Vermont, he began each season to average between sixty and ninety concerts in the United States and fifty more abroad, appearing with every major American orchestra and most of the principal ones in Europe. He became the only American (and one of five violinists from other countries) to be heard at La Scala in Milan, and he gave a command performance for King Edward VII of England and for the dowager Queen Margherita di Savoia of Italy. In 1920 he toured Europe as soloist with the visiting New York Symphony Society. In 1927, in commemoration of the centenary of Beethoven's birth, Karl Muck invited him to perform the Beethoven Violin Concerto with the Hamburg Philharmonic in Germany. In Hamburg there was considerable opposition to the engagement of an American violinist for such an occasion, but Karl Muck stubbornly supported "der Amerikaner" (as he called Spalding)—a remarkable attitude on Muck's part in view of his open hostility to all things American as a result of his own traumatic experiences in the United States during World War I.

In the early 1920s Spalding became one of the first concert artists to be heard over the radio in the United States. In addition to performing on the "Atwater Kent Hour," he made guest appearances on numerous other radio programs before acquiring in 1941–1942 his own coast-to-coast program, "The Pause That Refreshes," over CBS. He is reputed to have given more concerts over the radio than any other violinist.

During World War II he was commissioned colonel. Using the name of "Major Sheridan," he served in Italy with the Office of War Information, in the Psychological Warfare Branch, broadcasting instructions to the Italian partisans from the Allied command. The OWI praised his propaganda work as "unbeaten by any individual in any theater." For a few months in 1944 he was at the head of Radio Rome for the Allied forces. After the war he was decorated by the French and Italian governments, and by the United States with the Medal of Freedom.

Spalding renewed his concert career in 1945. His final appearance as a virtuoso took place on June 20, 1950, at the Lewisohn Stadium in New York in the Beethoven Concerto. In his review of that concert Olin Downes wrote in the New York Times: "His performance, as he warmed to his task and became absorbed in the noble music, became always more eloquent, more nobly in tradition, more completely representative of the special talents and the uncompromising ideals of the musician and the performer. . . . His delivery of the music gave us the true measure of his sincerity, his inalienable perception of beauty, unfaltering ideals."

Spalding then went into retirement, devoting himself to writing, teaching, and composing. He was stricken by a cerebral hemorrhage at his home on East Seventy-seventh Street in New York City on May 26, 1953, while he was getting ready to go out to dinner with his wife. He died within five minutes.

He was the composer of some sixty compositions for the violin (including two concertos), twenty-five for the piano, thirty for the voice, and four each for orchestra and for string quartet. He was the author of an autobiography, *Rise to Follow* (1943), and a novel entitled *A Sword and a Lady* (1953), based on the life of Giuseppe

Tartini, the eighteenth century Italian violinist-composer.

In 1923, Spalding became the first American to serve on the jury examinations at the Paris Conservatory. He taught master classes at the Juilliard School of Music in New York from 1933 to 1944. After his retirement from the concert stage he taught violin at Boston University College of Music in Massachusetts and at the University of Florida in Tallahassee, Florida.

Spalding made his home in New York City; summers were spent on his estate at Great Barrington, Massachusetts. For most of his adult years he was a dedicated sportsman—he held several championships in amateur tennis and he was equally adept at golf and swimming. Occasionally he would go on a collector's holiday, searching for rare pieces of Old English china or valuable first editions. His indoor hobbies were playing bridge and chess and reading. "I have a particular passion for detective stories, if they are of a nature that makes me think a bit. I am very fond of philosophy. I go back as often as possible to the Dialogues of Plato. I have read a certain amount of the more modern philosophers' works, but I must confess I never got very much out of Kant."

ABOUT: Spalding, A. Rise to Follow. *Periodicals—* Etude, August 1953; Harper's Magazine, April-June, 1942; Musical America, June 1953; New York Times, January 26, 1941, November 18, 1941, January 20, 1943, May 31, 1953; Newsweek, May 26, 1941.

Frederica von Stade
See Von Stade

Maria Stader

1915–

Maria Stader, soprano, known for her interpretations of the music of Mozart, was born in Budapest on November 5, 1915. When she was seven her father died, and she was found abandoned on a city street. The International Red Cross arranged for Hans Stader, a Swiss fisher-

Stader: shtä′ dĕr

MARIA STADER

man, to adopt her, and she was raised at his home at Lake Constance.

She began vocal study when she was sixteen. From 1933 to 1936 she was a voice student of Hans Keller at the Karlsruhe Conservatory in Germany. Later she studied with Lombardi in Milan, and with Therese Schnabel-Behr in New York.

In her late teens she gave a number of concerts in Switzerland. In 1939 she captured first prize in the International Music Competition in Geneva, as a result of which sixty concerts were arranged for her throughout Europe. But with the coming of World War II these commitments had to be canceled. During the war she made numerous concert appearances in Switzerland, and when the war ended she was able to concertize outside Switzerland.

Her reputation grew immediately after the end of World War II with appearances in leading European capitals under such conductors as Furtwängler in Berlin and Vienna, Klemperer in Amsterdam and London, and Sir Malcolm Sargent in London. In 1950 she received the Lilli Lehmann medal from the Mozarteum in Salzburg for outstanding artistic achievement, an honor that was repeated in 1956 when she became the first artist ever to receive this award twice.

Reports of her success in Europe, particularly in the music of Mozart, and many of her recordings for Decca made her name and art well known in the United States before she made her American debut in New York City on January

25, 1954. As a soloist with the Little Orchestra Society under Thomas Scherman, she was heard in the Mozart motet "Exultate, jubilate" and the American premiere of Alessandro Scarlatti's *Cantata a Voce Sola con Violini e Tromba.* Seven days later she gave her first American recital, and in February she appeared as soloist with the Cleveland Orchestra under George Szell. "Miss Stader," reported *Musical America,* "proved herself a highly accomplished and sensitive singer. She used her voice with consummate art and projected the texts with flawless clarity and emotional nuance."

In 1955 she presented a series of seven concerts with Bruno Walter in Milan, Paris, and Zurich, and in 1956 she appeared in Israel as a guest artist with the Israel Philharmonic under Ferenc Fricsay in twenty-two concert performances of Donizetti's *Lucia di Lammermoor* and Handel's *Judas Maccabaeus.* In 1956 she returned to the United States for a performance of Mozart's Mass in C minor with the Philadelphia Orchestra under Ormandy and in other programs of Mozart's works. Howard Taubman, writing in the New York *Times,* called hers "the finest Mozart singing heard in New York during the composer's bicentennial year. For this was singing released, as it were, from the bondage of flesh and blood." In 1957, among other American appearances, she sang with the New York Philharmonic under Bruno Walter in three Mahler songs and with the Philadelphia Orchestra under Ormandy in Beethoven's Symphony No.9. That year she appeared at the Berlin Festival in a concert version of Gluck's *Orfeo ed Euridice.*

Stader was a participant in numerous other festivals, offering remarkable performances of music of Bach, Mozart (and other Baroque masters), Verdi, Brahms, and Mahler at the festivals at Salzburg in Austria and at Prades in France, Milan, and Lucerne. To *Opera News* she confided that one of the most memorable experiences of her concert career took place in Einsiedeln, Switzerland, when she sang the role of the Angel in Bach's *Christmas Oratorio.* "There, in a huge church with the great Leipzig choir and everything lit by candles, they placed me twenty meters above the choir on a high balcony. When I sang the Angel's proclamation, I felt I was in heaven."

Though she appeared as the Queen of the Night in *The Magic Flute* at Covent Garden in London in 1949–1950 and made several other operatic appearances, Stader has generally avoided the opera stage, preferring to limit her appearances to concerts and recordings.

She made her last public appearance anywhere on December 7, 1969, at Carnegie Hall in New York in a performance of Mozart's Requiem. "I wanted my farewell to be Mozart," she explained. Following her retirement, she conducted master classes on the style and interpretation of concert literature at the Musical Academy in Vienna and directed other master classes in Zurich, Stuttgart, Munich, and New York.

In 1959 she married Hans Erismann, chorus master of the Zurich Opera. They have two sons. Their home is in Zurich, where she teaches at the Music Academy. In 1962 she was presented in Zurich with the Salz-Golden medal, and in 1964 Austria conferred on her the Order of Merit for Arts and Sciences.

ABOUT: Opera News, January 17, 1970.

Janos Starker

1924–

Janos Starker, cellist, was born in Budapest on July 5, 1924. Both his father, Sandor Starker, a tailor, and his mother, Margit Chajkin Starker, were music lovers. They arranged for two of their sons to study the violin, and for the third one—Janos—to take lessons on the cello. Janos was seven years old at the time. "I took to the cello supposedly like the fish to water," Starker told Stephen E. Rubin many years later in an interview for the New York *Times.* "I knew exactly what I was going to do. It astounds me today that I never wanted to have a great career or be the greatest cellist in the world. I simply wanted to play the cello as well as it's possible." While attending the local schools for his academic education, Janos specialized in the cello with Adolf Cziffer at the Franz Liszt Academy; when he was eleven, he performed there in a string quartet.

Upon graduation from the Academy, Starker began making concert appearances, but these were abruptly halted by World War II and his

Starker: shtärk′ ĕr

JANOS STARKER

service in the Hungarian Civil Defense. He recalls: "During the war years I had considerable difficulties functioning as an artist. There was a year-and-a-half period when I did not touch the cello. It was during that stretch that I decided that, as soon as I could, I would leave."

In 1945 he was appointed principal cellist of the Budapest Philharmonic Orchestra and of the orchestra of the Budapest Opera. One year later, when in Vienna for a concert appearance, he knew he had left his native country for good. For about two years after that he concertized throughout Europe. He also made some recordings, one of which—Kodály's Sonata for Unaccompanied Cello—won the Grand Prix du Disque in Paris in 1948.

In 1948 he emigrated to the United States, making it his permanent home. He was made first cellist of the Dallas Symphony in 1948–1949, and from 1949 to 1953 he was first cellist of the Metropolitan Opera orchestra. In 1953, when Fritz Reiner became the music director of the Chicago Symphony, Starker went to Chicago. He served as first cellist there for the next five years and occasionally appeared as solo artist with the orchestra. He was also heard elsewhere in the United States and in Europe during these years. At the Edinburgh Festival in Scotland in 1957, where he performed a concert devoted exclusively to Bach's unaccompanied suites, Desmond Shawe-Taylor reported in the *New Statesman and Nation:* "His masterly phrasing, pure tone, varied dynamics, and subtle rubato

confirmed an impression that he is the most notable interpreter of such music since Casals."

In 1958 Starker left his post in Chicago not only to concentrate more intensively on his virtuoso career but also to join the music faculty of Indiana University at Bloomington. He has since received the title Distinguished Professor there. Establishing permanent residence in Bloomington, Starker married Donna Rae Busch on June 22, 1960, and adopted her daughter by an earlier marriage. This was Starker's second marriage. The first, to Eva Uranyi on November 11, 1944, had ended in divorce.

Starker made his New York debut on November 14, 1960, with a sonata recital with Mieczyslaw Horszowski. Paul Henry Lang, writing in the *Tribune,* called the concert "an artistic event of the first magnitude" and referred to Starker as "a superlative cellist, equipped with an abundance of technique and magnificent tone." In the New York *Times* Harold C. Schonberg commented: "He is certainly the equal of any living cellist."

Starker's appearances have been worldwide. He gives about eighty concerts a year, both in recital and as a guest performer with major orchestras. Sometimes he combines concert work with master classes and string seminars.

During a tour embracing Germany, Scandinavia, France, Switzerland, and Turkey in the spring of 1971, Starker made his first return visit to his native Hungary, after a quarter of a century. "I was on the stage of the Franz Liszt Academy where I had played as a student," he recalls. "I went without any kind of official recognition. I went simply to another place to play a concert, and it happened to be my home town. The audience cheered, and they were maybe the best concerts I ever played in my life."

For many years Starker confined his programming primarily to the repertory of Bach, Beethoven, and Brahms. In one instance he provided a footnote to music history by introducing on July 25, 1974, a cello sonata by Brahms (D major, Op.78) that Brahms himself had adapted from his own Violin Sonata, Op.78. The existence of this sonata had long been forgotten, and the composition had long remained unknown to cellists everywhere.

Since the 1960s Starker's programming has taken a new direction and format, away from its reliance on Bach, Beethoven, and Brahms. "My acceptance came through those masterpieces," he has explained. "Then one day I woke up and realized that this was an idiotic thing to gear one's existence to the critical acceptance, while the audiences on any continent will be able to take only a certain amount of the so-called heavy pieces." He began including on his programs virtuoso pieces, transcriptions, and encore items. He also promoted new music for the cello. Miklos Rozsa and Bernhard Heiden wrote concertos for him that he has premiered. He has also introduced, and recorded, Peter Mennin's Concerto for Cello and Orchestra, performed Olivier Messiaen's *Transfiguration of Our Lord Jesus Christ,* and devoted some of his concerts exclusively to music for unaccompanied cello, including several suites by his compatriot Zoltán Kodály.

Although long recognized as one of the three or four greatest living cellists, Starker did not appear with the New York Philharmonic Orchestra until October 19, 1972, when he performed Haydn's Cello Concerto in C major, with Skrowaczewski conducting. "Mr. Starker has been regarded as one of the world's great instrumentalists," remarked Harold C. Schonberg in his review in the New York *Times,* "but for some reason he was never invited to play with the New York Philharmonic. This season the omission has been rectified, and the eminent cellist performed with all the mastery expected of him."

Supplementing his worldwide concert engagements are his many recordings; no cellist has made more recordings than he. They range chronologically from Bach and Vivaldi to Kodály, Peter Mennin, and Bartók. On three different occasions he has recorded all the unaccompanied suites for cello.

Starker has said that five musicians have had the greatest impact on his own development. They include his early teacher Adolf Cziffer, who, he has said, "never taught me anything wrong, it was always cellistically right"; Leo Weiner, a composer who taught at the Franz Liszt Academy in Budapest; Emanuel Feuermann, Jascha Heifetz, and Fritz Reiner. "Weiner taught me to hear, to apply the hearing for the sake of musical discipline, to play what's written. Feuermann was the one who showed me that the cello can be played better and better in a different and far more varied way than Casals ever did. Heifetz was the one who produced a

kind of tonal intensity plus an entire approach for the violin." He did not elaborate on how Reiner had influenced him.

Starker's home in Bloomington is an American suburban ranch house decorated, said Stephen E. Rubin in the New York *Times,* "with more warmth than style, . . . complete with vegetable garden and enormous German shepherd." He enjoys swimming, playing table tennis, writing short stories and articles, engaging in provocative conversations on current events, and eating the gourmet meals his wife prepares for students and faculty at Bloomington.

Musical life for Starker is made up of teaching and performing. "I leave Bloomington and I become a concert artist," he says. "I come back and I am the professor—equal among equals. Here there is no star system." Starker has also conducted master classes and seminars in Aspen (Colorado), at the Ravinia Festival in Chicago, in Rotterdam, and in Düsseldorf. Much of his pedagogy is based on his own book *An Organized Method of String Playing.*

He is the inventor of the so-called "Starker bridge," in which cone-shaped holes are drilled on the side of the bridge resting on the instrument; these holes, by acting like tiny megaphones, work like a miniature preamplification system. The quality of the tone produced is so improved that inexpensive instruments are made to sound like others far more expensive. *Time* has called this bridge "perhaps the most significant tonal innovation in string instruments in three hundred years."

Starker was awarded an honorary doctorate in music from the Chicago Conservatory of Music in 1961.

ABOUT: Jacobson, R. Reverberations. *Periodicals*—New York Times, October 15, 1972.

Eleanor Steber

1916–

Eleanor Steber, soprano, was born in Wheeling, West Virginia, on July 17, 1916. Her father, William Charles Steber, was a bank cashier, and her mother, Ida A. Nolte Steber, a soprano who appeared often as soloist at civic charity and

Steber: stē′ bēr

ELEANOR STEBER

church functions. She received her first singing instruction from her mother. At high school, she became interested in dramatics and dreamed for a time of becoming an actress, but even at this time singing remained an important activity. At sixteen she made her singing debut as a soloist at the Second Presbyterian Church in Wheeling. Upon graduation from high school, she entered the New England Conservatory in Boston on a scholarship. Since the scholarship provided only tuition, she took various jobs to support herself: singing in churches, playing the piano in a dancing school and for various singing groups, working as a desk attendant where she was housed, appearing as a soloist in performances of choral masterworks, and filling spots over the radio on the Fox Fur Trappers program.

Her principal vocal teacher at the New England Conservatory was William L. Whitney, whom she has acknowledged to be one of the major influences in her career. With Whitney's advice and guidance, she made several appearances in Boston with the Federal Music Project between 1935 and 1939. Her first operatic performance was given at the Boston Opera House in an English-language production of *The Flying Dutchman,* in which she was cast as Senta. She also sang the leading female role in a performance of Louis Gruenberg's fairy-tale opera *Jack and the Beanstalk,* made some guest appearances with the Commonwealth Orchestra in Boston, and sang a number of times over the Boston radio station WEEI.

After graduation from the New England Con-

servatory in 1938, Steber married Edwin L. Bilby, one of her fellow students under William Whitney, on September 25 of that year. Bilby gave up his own plans for a singing career to devote himself to that of his young wife. After fifteen years the marriage nevertheless ended in divorce.

In 1939 Steber toured the East, South, and Midwest in recitals. That spring she entered a singing contest conducted by the National Music Club League and won second prize, only a single vote away from the top award. In the fall she went to New York, where she received additional coaching from Paul Althouse while supporting herself by singing at St. Paul's and St. Andrew's churches.

Althouse prepared her for the Metropolitan Opera Auditions. In March 1940, among more than seven hundred and fifty contestants, she captured first prize after singing "Sempre libera" from *La Traviata* and Debussy's "Mandolin." In celebration of this victory, her native town of Wheeling declared an Eleanor Steber Day in her honor. This became an annual event.

She made her debut at the Metropolitan Opera on December 7, 1940, as Sophie in *Der Rosenkavalier,* a role for which she was prepared by Lotte Lehmann. "I was in another world," she said of that debut when the performance ended. "Thank Heaven, all thought of its being my debut left my mind entirely and I was caught up in the swell of the music. The real excitement came after it was over—when I realized I was in truth a full-fledged member of this historic company." That performance was received with full approval by the critics, and their enthusiasm for Steber grew during the next few seasons, particularly when she was heard in Mozart's operas. In *The Marriage of Figaro* on December 16, 1942, she made, as Howard Taubman reported in the New York *Times,* "a handsome Countess as far as sheer looks and carriage went. She also sang the part with credit." As Constanza in the first Metropolitan Opera production of *The Abduction from the Seraglio* on November 29, 1946, she "sang beautifully, sensuously, and effectively," said Robert Bagar in the *World-Telegram.* On November 29, 1944, she was heard as Donna Elvira in *Don Giovanni;* on December 20, 1947, as Pamina in *The Magic Flute;* on December 28, 1951, as Fiordiligi in *Così fan Tutte;* and on January 18, 1955, as Donna Anna in *Don Giovanni.* At the Metropolitan

Opera she sang the Countess 35 times; Donna Anna, 27 times; Fiordiligi, 23 times; Donna Elvira, 13 times; and Constanza, 4 times.

During the quarter of a century she remained at the Metropolitan she appeared 286 times in New York and 118 times on tour in 28 leading roles in the French, Italian, and German repertories, and in several minor Wagnerian parts. In addition to roles already mentioned she appeared as Micaëla in *Carmen;* Violetta in *La Traviata;* Marguerite in *Faust;* Antonia, Giulietta, and Stella in *The Tales of Hoffmann;* Alice Ford in *Falstaff;* Eva in *Die Meistersinger;* the title roles in *Manon, Tosca,* and Strauss's *Arabella;* the Marschallin in *Der Rosenkavalier;* Elisabetta in *Don Carlo;* Desdemona in *Otello;* Elsa in *Lohengrin;* Rosalinde in *Die Fledermaus;* Marie in *Wozzeck;* and Minnie in *The Girl of the Golden West.* On January 15, 1958, she created the title role in the world premiere of Samuel Barber's *Vanessa;* and she repeated her performance as Vanessa at the Salzburg Festival in Austria the following summer.

Whatever role she assumed, she invariably proved to be a singer of "élan and style," wrote John Gruen in the New York *Times.* "At its best, her voice was a refined, flowing instrument." In the San Francisco *Chronicle* Alfred Frankenstein called the timbre of her voice "of the most moving and ethereal sweetness and purity, but warm despite its delicacy. Her style of interpretation is altogether of a piece with her style of vocal production. It is simple, dignified, exquisite in its subtly achieved phrasing and magnificently just, both to the letter and the spirit of the music in hand."

Rudolf Bing, the general manager of the Metropolitan Opera, failed to renew her contract after the 1962–1963 season. "I still don't know why Bing did not reengage me," she told John Gruen of the New York *Times* in 1973. "My agents called and called. Then, finally, I faced him personally. He told me that they weren't mounting *Don Giovanni* the following season and that my size wasn't really suitable for roles like *La Traviata.* Can you believe it? He told me I wouldn't miss the Met at all, that I could still have a great career giving concerts. I tell you, I was knocked for a loop. I went into a psychological decline. I went into a depression. And there was nothing I could do about it. It was the worst moment of my life."

She was invited to return to the stage of the Metropolitan Opera for the gala performance on April 16, 1966, that closed the doors of the old opera house. And later in 1966, on two days' notice, she was called in to replace Dorothy Kirsten in *The Girl of the Golden West* for a single performance. Except for those two appearances, never again was she a member of the Metropolitan Opera company.

During her long presence on the Metropolitan Opera stage she appeared in many other places as well. She contributed her services during World War II by performing throughout the United States and Canada for the USO, for various war benefits, and for servicemen in training stations and army camps. At Fort McPherson in Canada she was made honorary colonel by the officers and men.

On September 25, 1945, she made her debut with the San Francisco Opera as Micaëla; later the same year she toured with the company. In 1946 she appeared at the Central City Opera Festival in Colorado. She was acclaimed in Europe as well: at the Glyndebourne Festival in England in 1947; as Elsa at the Bayreuth Festival in 1953; at festivals at Edinburgh, Salzburg, and Florence; in recitals; and in guest appearances with major opera companies in various capitals. In 1957 she made a world tour under the auspices of the United States Government and the American National Theater and Academy. She was also heard frequently in the United States over radio and television and on recordings.

Once she had recovered from the trauma of having been rejected by the Metropolitan Opera after her long and successful career there, she continued to perform successfully not only in recitals and intermittently in operas but also in the popular musical theater. In 1966–1967 she was starred at the Lincoln Center for the Performing Arts in a revival of Frank Loesser's musical comedy *Where's Charley?* and in the Rodgers and Hammerstein musical play *The Sound of Music.*

Between October 17, 1962, and March 10, 1963, she presented at the Lincoln Center for the Performing Arts in New York three song recitals covering a survey of German *Lieder* from 1782 to 1908. In October 1972 she once again assumed the role of the Countess in *The Marriage of Figaro* but this time in a concert presentation by the Atlanta Symphony under James Levine. In August 1973 she was heard in the

Stefano

American premiere of Britten's *Owen Wingrave* at Santa Fe, New Mexico. Between February and May 1973 she gave a series of three recitals at the Lincoln Center for the Performing Arts. At the first of these concerts, on February 26, she sang *Lieder* by Schubert, Schumann, and Richard Strauss; at the second, on March 26, thirty American songs "from the Revolution to Man in Space," and in May a program of opera arias by Mozart, Strauss, Verdi, and Puccini. She proved, said Raymond Ericson in the New York *Times* that "she can still sing quite beautifully. . . . At its best, the soprano's singing was totally as lovely and pure as it ever was."

Steber has been active as a teacher of voice. She was appointed chairman of the voice department at the Cleveland Institute of Music in 1962 and has conducted master classes in voice at the New England Conservatory in Boston and at the Juilliard School of Music in New York.

After divorcing Bilby, Steber married Colonel Gordon Andrews, but this marriage also ended in divorce after several years. "The experience of marriage was marvelous and wonderful," she has said, "but I do realize and see how difficult it is for any man to be a sort of consort to a prima donna. It was hard on those men's egos to take that—to be dedicated to me, personally, to the exclusion of anything they were doing themselves."

Eleanor Steber lives at the Ansonia Hotel in New York (next door to another diva, Teresa Stratas). She gives intimate recitals there for her friends.

In 1976 she created the Eleanor Steber Music Foundation to aid young singers in the early stages of their careers.

ABOUT: Musical America, December 1, 1952; New York Times, February 18, 1973; Newsweek, August 28, 1944; Opera News, December 23, 1940.

Giuseppe di Stefano
See Di Stefano

William Steinberg

1899–1978

William Steinberg (originally Hans Wilhelm Steinberg), conductor, was born in Cologne, on August 1, 1899. A musical prodigy on both the violin and the piano, he was encouraged in these studies by his parents, Julius and Bertha Matzdorf Steinberg. A photograph of him taken just before his first concert still exists. "I remember that picture very well," says Steinberg. "It doesn't show in the picture, but I was so nervous, I chewed a hole in the brim of the straw hat I was wearing."

When he was ten his talent as a violinist was recognized; at thirteen he made his first appearance as a conductor in a performance of one of his own compositions, a setting of a text from Ovid's *Metamorphoses* for chorus and orchestra; at fifteen he gave a public performance as virtuoso pianist.

He received his basic music training at the School of Higher Musical Studies at Cologne University from Lazzaro Uzielli (piano), Franz Bölsche (composition) and Hermann Abendroth (conducting). Upon graduation in 1920, he received from the city of Cologne the Wüllner Prize for conducting.

Otto Klemperer, music director of the Cologne Opera, engaged Steinberg in 1920 as his assistant. Within four years Steinberg had risen to the post of principal conductor. From 1925 to 1927 he was principal conductor of the German Theater in Prague, and from 1927 to 1929 he served as music director. During these years he made several guest appearances as conductor, including some at the Berlin State Opera.

His growing prestige with the baton took him in 1929 to Frankfort, were he became the music director of the Frankfort Opera and of the Museum Concerts. At the Opera he initiated a progressive repertory that included performances of Berg's *Wozzeck* and the world premieres of Schoenberg's *Von Heute auf Morgen* (February 1, 1930), Kurt Weill's *The Rise and Fall of the City Mahagonny* (March 9, 1930), and George Antheil's American opera *Transatlantic* (May 25, 1930). At the Museum Concerts, he

Steinberg: stīn′ bûrg

WILLIAM STEINBERG

provided evidence that he was as gifted in the performance of symphonic music as in operas.

The rise of the Third Reich in 1933 brought about Steinberg's dismissal from his posts in Frankfort because he was a Jew. He stayed on in Frankfort and in November 1934 he married Lotti Stern. That year he assembled many of the other Jewish musicians who had lost their positions and formed an orchestra for the Jewish Culture League; for two years this orchestra performed for Jewish audiences. Jewish-born German composers who were now denied a hearing elsewhere in Germany found performances for their works at these concerts. One of them was Ernst Toch, whose Piano Concerto No.2 was introduced on January 26, 1935.

In 1936 when the Nazi officials ordered that these concerts be given solely in secluded synagogues, Steinberg left Germany. On an invitation from Bronislaw Hubermann, who was about to organize in Palestine a symphony orchestra made up mostly of German refugees, he went to Palestine and helped to assemble and train the Palestine Symphony Orchestra for its first concerts under Toscanini in Tel Aviv. When Toscanini heard the new orchestra during his first rehearsal he smiled broadly and remarked: "Molto bene!"

After Toscanini left Palestine following the initial concerts, Steinberg took over the post of principal conductor of the Palestine Symphony Orchestra for the next two years. After the Palestine Symphony became the Israel Philharmonic, he returned to Israel periodically as guest conductor, and when this orchestra toured the United States in 1967 he served as its principal conductor. During this tour, on July 29, 1967, he performed the world premiere of Ben-Haim's *Fanfare to Israel.*

In 1937 Steinberg was invited by Toscanini to come to the United States and serve as his assistant with the NBC Symphony. Steinberg arrived that year with his wife and a son, Arturo (named after Toscanini). The Steinbergs made their home in New Rochelle, New York. He became an American citizen in 1944. On March 4, 1939, he conducted a broadcast of the NBC Symphony in what was his American debut. He led several more concerts of the NBC Symphony during the next few years. On November 9, 1940, he conducted the NBC Symphony in the world premiere of Copland's *Billy the Kid* suite.

Steinberg was also invited to appear as guest conductor of other major American orchestras as well as of orchestras in Havana and in Rio de Janeiro. On October 16, 1944, he made his American debut as a conductor of opera with a performance of *Falstaff* with the San Francisco Opera, following this with *Faust* and *A Masked Ball.* One season later he presented *Tristan and Isolde, Die Walküre,* and *Don Giovanni.* He opened the 1946 season of the San Francisco Opera with *Lohengrin* on September 17, a performance described in *The Year in American Music: 1946–1947* as "clear and masterful throughout. Orchestra, chorus and principals responded with equal fervor to it, and all elements contributed to a well-knit and thoroughly rounded performance." In later years he conducted at the San Francisco Opera *The Marriage of Figaro, Die Götterdämmerung, Otello, Falstaff, Die Meistersinger, Aida, The Flying Dutchman, Boris Godunov,* and *Ariadne auf Naxos.*

Steinberg acquired his first permanent post in the United States in 1945 when he became the music director of the Buffalo Symphony Orchestra in New York. He was responsible for increasing the annual budget, enlarging the orchestral personnel, extending the season, and enriching the repertory. In 1952 he left Buffalo for the more ambitious assignment of music director of the Pittsburgh Symphony Orchestra, a post he retained until 1976. This orchestra was totally rehabilitated under Steinberg to become one of the five or six leading American symphonic organizations. Embarking on extended tours of the United States, the Pittsburgh Symphony under Steinberg earned the admiration of music lovers everywhere. After their concert at Carnegie Hall on November 16, 1956, Howard Taubman wrote in the New York *Times:* "Under William Steinberg's leadership, the orchestra has developed into one of the most satisfying in the country, not far behind the country's best." In 1964 the orchestra under Steinberg, sponsored by the Cultural Presentations Program of the Department of State, toured fourteen European and Middle Eastern countries, covering twenty-five thousand miles in eleven weeks. His return to Berlin gave him particular satisfaction, since not only was he the first American to appear in West Berlin's new Philharmonic Hall but also he was enjoying a spectacular success in a country where he had once been regarded as undesirable. Everywhere on this tour the concerts were greeted with enthusiasm. Said the critic of the *Diario de Manha* in Lisbon: "There are no restrictions to be made concerning the quality of the orchestra; it is of the highest category and its perfection is total." As a reward for his accomplishments, the directors gave him a new contract in 1968 for an unlimited period of time—this was the first time that the orchestra had signed a conductor for more than three years.

In Pittsburgh, Steinberg presented the world premiere of the Pulitzer Prize winner, Ernst Toch's Symphony No.3, on December 2, 1955. This was just one of many premieres. Others were Lukas Foss's *Symphony of Chorales* (October 24, 1958), excerpts from Nikolai Lopatnikoff's opera *Danton* (March 25, 1967), Lopatnikoff's Concerto for Two Pianos and Orchestra (November 7, 1958) and his *Variazioni Concertante* (1958), Gardner Read's Symphony No.3 (March 2, 1962), and George Rochberg's Violin Concerto (April 4, 1975).

A serious illness requiring surgery in 1972 compelled Steinberg to curtail his activity with the Pittsburgh Symphony. When in 1976 he resigned as music director because the administrative duties had become a burden he could no longer shoulder, the orchestra conferred on him the title Conductor Emeritus and invited him to return periodically as a guest. He returned to the Pittsburgh Symphony as a guest conductor in 1976–1977 in a Beethoven cycle.

While holding the post of music director of the Pittsburgh Symphony, Steinberg, his wife, Lotti, and their two children lived in a ranch-type house in the Squirrel Hill section of Pittsburgh. His life in Pittsburgh was methodically organized. Mornings were devoted to rehearsals; afternoons to correspondence and a daily walk in Schenley Park with pipe in mouth and walking stick in hand; the rest of the day was taken up with studying scores. Before each concert he took a nap, ate a steak dinner prepared rare by his wife, and after the concert relaxed over a cup of hot chocolate.

Steinberg was a regular guest conductor with the New York Philharmonic. In 1967–1968 he was named principal guest conductor. During this period he helped commemorate the one hundred and twenty-fifth anniversary of that orchestra by performing the world premieres of Roberto Gerhard's Symphony No.4 (December 14, 1967) and Roger Sessions's Symphony No.8 (May 2, 1968), the latter specially written for the occasion. On January 2, 1965, he made his debut at the Metropolitan Opera in New York in *Aida*. That performance, said Raymond Ericson in the New York *Times*, "was always beautiful in sound, since he got the orchestra to play with unforced, smooth textures. It had the drama that comes from swift, flexible pacing."

Holding the music directorship of the Pittsburgh Symphony did not prevent him from taking on simultaneously similar posts with other orchestras. From 1958 to 1960 he served as the music director of the London Symphony. With his appointment as music director of the Boston Symphony, he became the first conductor in the history of American music to hold down simultaneously two directing posts with first-rank American orchestras. He served with the Boston Symphony from 1969 to 1973.

Of medium height and unimpressive build, Steinberg never cut a dashing figure either on or off the conductor's platform. His baton technique and movements of head and body were reserved and discreet, directed not towards the eye of the audience but solely to that of the musicians. He always preferred to operate undemonstratively and always scrupulously avoided any conductorial gimmicks. He enjoyed smoking a pipe, drinking an occasional highball, watching mystery shows on television, going to movies, the theater, and art museums.

After retiring in 1976, Steinberg moved to Atherton, California. He died in New York City on May 16, 1978.

William Steinberg earned honorary doctorates in music from Carnegie-Mellon University, Duquesne University, University of Pittsburgh, and the Westminster Choir School in Princeton, New Jersey.

ABOUT: Ewen, D. Famous Modern Conductors; Stoddard, H. Symphony Conductors of the U.S.A. *Periodicals*—New York Times, November 16, 1958, December 6, 1964.

Isaac Stern

1920–

Isaac Stern, the first world-famous violinist to have received all of his musical training in the United States, was born in Kremenets in the Ukraine, near the Polish border, on July 21, 1920. His father, Solomon Stern, was an amateur musician and his mother, Clara, had studied voice at the St. Petersburg Conservatory and was an excellent pianist. When Isaac was one year old, his family migrated to the United States, settling in San Francisco. When he was six his mother began giving him piano lessons, but he demonstrated little enthusiasm or talent for the piano. When he was eight, however, he heard one of his friends play the violin and the sounds so fascinated him that he begged for lessons. These began with a local teacher, but he was no prodigy. As he himself has good-humoredly revealed, when his parents took him to concerts he did not come home "and cry for a violin, nor did I pick up a fiddle and play from memory every note I'd heard at the concert. The idea of a career for me was always in somebody else's mind."

A San Francisco patron of the arts did believe, however, that she recognized in him signs of blossoming talent and provided the funds to enable him to enter the San Francisco Conservatory when he was ten. A year later he fulfilled her hopes by appearing as a soloist with the San Francisco Symphony under Pierre Monteux. That performance proved so successful that he was invited to perform with the Los Angeles Philharmonic and to give several recitals along the Pacific Coast.

On October 12, 1937, Isaac made his New York debut with a recital at Town Hall. He himself felt he was not sufficiently prepared for a New York test and that the concert did not go

ISAAC STERN

well. As he later explained: "I should have had a test program which I played on the road and had embedded in my fingertips." But some critics thought well of him, and one reported in the *Herald Tribune* that he was "an unusually promising young musician" and prophesied that "following the normal and judicious course of development he should become an artist of exceptional consequence."

In New York, Isaac studied with Louis Persinger. Then, convinced he needed still more training, he returned to San Francisco to work with Naoum Blinder, the concertmaster of the San Francisco Symphony. "Blinder taught me how to teach myself—the sign of a really good teacher." After two years of study with Blinder, he returned to New York for a recital in February 1939. The critic of the New York *Times* felt that with this performance he "established his title to mature artistry."

An important turning point in Stern's career came in 1940 when he acquired Alexander Zakin as his piano accompanist. Working painstakingly with Zakin day after day, sometimes for hours at a stretch, he developed his technique and repertory. As a result of this sustained period of musical give-and-take between a violinist and a sympathetic and musicianly accompanist, he grew into an artist of commanding interpretative and technical powers, as was demonstrated at a recital in Carnegie Hall, New York, on January 12, 1943. In the *Herald Tribune* Virgil Thomson described him as "one of the world's master fiddlers." Louis Biancolli, writing in the

World-Telegram and Sun, placed him in the "top rank" of living violinists, and the critic of the New York *Post* referred to him as "a master of his instrument."

During World War II he was a member of a five-man unit dispatched by the USO for a nine-month period to the South Pacific to perform for the armed forces. He also made two additional concert tours under the auspices of the USO.

When the war ended, Stern began his first tours of the United States, under the management of Sol Hurok, performing some ninety concerts a year and arousing the highest enthusiasm wherever he performed. After the first concert in Dallas, Texas, John Rosenfeld of the *Morning News* compared Stern's technique to Heifetz's, his tone to Elman's, his communicativeness to Kreisler's, and his dedication to music to Menuhin's. "Stern is one of the greatest contemporary violinists," Rosenfeld summed up, "fully entitled to a place on the bench of the mighty."

In July 1947 he toured Australia for ten weeks, and in 1948 and 1949 he made his first two sweeps of Europe and South America. Since then he has circled the music world many times, has been heard as a guest performer with every major orchestra, and has performed at all the world's best known festivals. He has made numerous appearances in chamber music concerts, particularly with the Istomin-Stern-Rose Trio which he helped to organize. This trio gave its first concerts in 1961 and has performed extensively throughout the United States, Europe, the Orient, and Israel. There have also been chamber music recitals in which Stern was heard on violin with Pinchas Zukerman as violinist or as violist. And there were the "Isaac Stern and his Friends" concerts, in which Stern joined some of his colleagues in the presentation of masterworks for unusual combinations of instruments.

Stern has recorded extensively for Columbia. His recording of the Brahms *Double Concerto* (with Leonard Rose as cellist and Bruno Walter conducting) received the Grand Prix du Disque. On several occasions he has earned Grammys from the National Academy of Recording Arts and Sciences: in 1961 with the Bartók Violin Concerto No.1, in 1964 with Prokofiev's Violin Concerto No.1, and in 1970 with the complete set of Beethoven's piano trios performed by the Istomin-Stern-Rose Trio.

In addition to being heard on numerous occasions over the radio and television networks,

Stern has performed in motion pictures. In 1947 his performance was dubbed in on the sound track for the violin playing of John Garfield in *Humoresque;* in 1952, in *Tonight We Sing* (the screen biography of the impresario Sol Hurok) not only was he heard playing on the sound track but he also appeared on the screen impersonating the Belgian violinist Eugène Ysaÿe; for the opening sequence of *Fiddler on the Roof* (1971) he performed an extended violin solo on the sound track.

As a performer he has been a human dynamo, constantly in motion, indefatigable. A twenty-two-month period between August 1953 and June 1955 saw him in a nonstop tour during which he circled the globe twice, giving some three hundred performances in all. In 1956, on his first visit to the Soviet Union, he became the first American concert artist to give concerts there after World War II and the first American violinist to be invited to broadcast over Soviet television. After completing his performances in the Soviet Union and returning to the United States, without any appreciable intermission he began a six-week tour of South American countries, at the end of which, still without a break, he entered upon a European tour climaxed with concerts at the Edinburgh Festival. In December 1959 he made twelve appearances in four days with the New York Philharmonic. During one of his world tours he gave nineteen concerts in ten Japanese cities during a two-week period. Then, at the end of this globe-circling voyage and with only a few days' respite, he embarked on a tour of the United States.

On one of many visits to Israel, he rehearsed three concertos one morning and performed them the same evening; played two more concertos the following morning at a Pension Fund concert; rehearsed later that day and then that same evening played three more concertos. The next day he repeated his three-concerto performance in Jerusalem, ending the concert by giving a fourth concerto as an encore. In 1970 he covered nine thousand miles in two months, giving concerts all the way.

His extensive repertory includes much twentieth century music for the violin and he has been responsible for the premieres of many such compositions. He has given the world premieres of Hindemith's Violin Sonata (1939), William Schuman's Violin Concerto (February 10, 1950), Leonard Bernstein's *Serenade for Violin,*

Strings and Percussion (September 12, 1954), George Rochberg's Violin Concerto (April 4, 1975), and Penderecki's Violin Concerto (January 4, 1978), among other works. And he has frequently performed, and has recorded, the violin concertos of Prokofiev, Berg, Bartók, Stravinsky, and Sibelius.

"In many respects," wrote Harold C. Schonberg in a feature article in the New York *Times Magazine,* "he is the complete violinist—that is, one who has tone, technique, musicianship, and above all the ability to project. . . . His bow arm is a legend." Schonberg has also written: "He represents the modern school of violin playing at its best, and little can be said about him that has not been said many times before. Surety and precision mark all his work, cleanly turned phrasing, strong rhythm, and impeccable technique."

His tie to Israel is strong and steadfast. It is not unusual for him, during one of his summer visits to Israel, to make from seventeen to twenty appearances within a week or two. In 1957 he helped to inaugurate the new Frederick R. Mann Auditorium in Tel Aviv. Immediately following the end of the Six-Day War in 1967 he flew to Israel to participate in a celebration concert conducted by Leonard Bernstein on July 9 on recaptured Mount Scopus. That concert was filmed in the Leonard Bernstein documentary *Journey to Jerusalem.* He has served as a tireless advocate and officer of the America-Israel Cultural Foundation which promotes cultural exchanges between Israel and the United States and has sponsored scholarship students from Israel to America's conservatories. In 1975 he helped to found the Israeli Music Center whose purpose was to break down the isolation of Israeli musicians. "My goal," he has explained, "was to find some way to give Israeli musicians exposure to the very best without forcing them to leave the country to get it. There's great potential talent here, but in the past most talented musicians always went abroad to study and few of them came back."

He has been a music benefactor in the United States as well. When in the late 1950s Carnegie Hall was threatened with demolition, Stern went into action to save that historic auditorium, persuading New York City to buy the hall and lease it to a nonprofit organization of which he assumed the presidency. In September 1961, between concert engagements in Europe, he returned to the United States for a single appearance with the New York Philharmonic to celebrate the saving of Carnegie Hall. In addition to all this he became a founder-member of the National Council of the Arts in 1965 and has campaigned actively for political candidates dedicated to helping the arts, and he was a founding member of the Kennedy Center for the Performing Arts in Washington, D.C.

He married Nora Kaye, a ballerina, on November 10, 1948, but their marriage was of short duration. In 1951 during a visit to Israel he met and fell in love with an Israeli girl, Vera Lindenblit, and married her on August 17, 1951. With their three children the Sterns occupy a ten-room duplex apartment on Central Park West. An upstairs study, isolated from the rest of the apartment, is Stern's retreat, and there he practices late into the night—sometimes even until the early hours of the morning.

Stern used to be an excellent tennis and table tennis player; now he is partial to less strenuous ways of relaxation, such as reading books, playing gin rummy, occasionally watching baseball games on the television screen, indulging his enormous appetite for gourmet food, and participating in discussions on politics and the international scene with well-informed friends.

When Albert Schweitzer's hundredth birthday was commemorated with a concert at Carnegie Hall on January 14, 1975, Isaac Stern was the recipient of the first Albert Schweitzer Award for musical and humanitarian achievements.

ABOUT: Musical America, December 15, 1954; New York Times, January 23, 1949; New York Times Magazine, December 6, 1959; Time, June 23, 1947.

Risë Stevens

1913–

Risë Stevens (originally Risë Steenberg), mezzo-soprano, was born in the Bronx, New York, on June 11, 1913. Her father, Christian Carl Steenberg, was a Lutheran from Oslo; her mother, Sadie, was Jewish. In her early childhood she revealed a lovely voice, singing such tunes as "When Irish Eyes Are Smiling" and "Sylvia" accompanied by a pianola. When she was ten, her mother took her to Orry Prado, who taught

RISË STEVENS

children to sing and arranged appearances for them on his radio program, "The Children's Hour," on WJZ. Prado accepted Risë as his pupil and as a member of his radio program, paying her five dollars an appearance to sing regularly on the Sunday morning broadcast over a period of several years.

After attending public schools in the Bronx, Risë went on to Newtown High School where she sang in the school chorus, at assemblies, and in school productions. After graduation from high school, she found a job with the New York Opéra-Comique Company as a member of the chorus and the ballet at a salary of twenty-five dollars a week. This small company performed operas and operettas at the Little Theatre in Brooklyn, New York, and at the Heckscher Theatre in New York City. Risë was soon promoted to the solo roles of Countess von Eberbach in Lortzing's *The Poacher (Der Wildschütz)* and Prince Orlofsky in *Die Fledermaus.*

When the New York Opéra-Comique folded after its second season, Stevens modeled coats in a dress house in New York City. One day Anna Schoen-René, who had heard her sing at the Opéra-Comique, got in touch with her. Schoen-René, a vocal teacher, felt that Risë had sufficient talent to warrant cultivation and she offered to teach her without a fee. Schoen-René also found Risë a singing job over the radio on the "Palmolive Show." She appeared on this show for two years, starting in the chorus and progressing to minor singing roles.

When Risë began making marked progress in her lessons, Schoen-René arranged for her to get a full scholarship to the Juilliard School of Music for instruction in languages, piano, history of music, and music theory. At the same time Risë continued voice study with Schoen-René, who was a member of the faculty. At the end of her second year at the Juilliard, Stevens was encouraged by her teacher to go to the Mozarteum in Salzburg to study one summer with Marie Gutheil-Schoder. All the while she attended Juilliard, Risë supported herself by singing, first in churches and then over the radio on Sigmund Romberg's show. At the Juilliard she appeared in the school productions of Gluck's *Orfeo ed Euridice* and Nicolai's *The Merry Wives of Windsor.*

After three years at Juilliard, she returned to Salzburg in 1935 for special classes in stage direction with Herbert Graf and for some vocal coaching with Eric Simon. She was vocalizing at Simon's house one day when she was heard by George Szell, then the conductor of the Prague Opera. He hired her as a contralto for his company. In the spring of 1936 she made her professional debut in opera in Prague in the title role of *Mignon,* following it with appearances in several other operas including *Aida* and *The Magic Flute.* Here too she received coaching, from George Schick.

In Prague, Stevens met Walter Surovy, a Czech actor. "At that time," recalls Surovy, "I was the highest-paid actor in Prague, and Risë was the lowest-paid opera singer." Romance developed quickly, but Stevens's evolving career brought about a prolonged separation. For two months she appeared in Cairo and Alexandria with a Viennese company and was heard as Octavian in *Der Rosenkavalier* and Orfeo in *Orfeo ed Euridice.* Later she made her debut with the Vienna State Opera as Octavian. Herbert F. Peyser, the American music correspondent to Europe for the New York *Times,* reported back to his newspaper: "I heard Miss Stevens in Prague, but only as one of the three ladies in *The Magic Flute.* Yet I was quite unprepared, flattering reports notwithstanding, for the big, vital impression received at the State Opera, from her Octavian in *Der Rosenkavalier.* I heard, to begin with, a lovely, blooming voice—a voice beautifully cultivated throughout its scale. Further, a skill and fastidiousness of taste in phrasing and nuance that betrayed artistry of a wholly exceptional order. And never have I seen in this opera the figure of Octavian played with such an exuberance paired with distinction or such complete credibility of boyish verisimilitude."

From Vienna Stevens went on to South America to make her debut at the Teatro Colón in Buenos Aires as Octavian and to receive, as cable dispatches reported, "one of the most enthusiastic ovations ever given a newcomer."

Her first appearance with the Metropolitan Opera company took place while it was on tour —in Philadelphia on November 22, 1938, as Octavian. One of the Philadelphia critics reported "a new star is born" and another acclaimed her for "a glorious voice, a distinguished presence, youth and beauty." On December 17, 1938, she made her New York debut with the Metropolitan Opera as Mignon. Olin Downes noted in the New York *Times:* "She is already a very accomplished and interesting singer. It is more than a voice for one or two lyrical roles, for it has unusual range, well-adjusted registers, and there are colors in it. She is pleasant to look at, and acts well. She gave the part of Mignon a dramatic substance."

Two evenings later she appeared in New York as Octavian and later the same season as Erda in *Das Rheingold* and *Siegfried,* and as Fricka in *Die Walküre.* A season later she added Cherubino in *The Marriage of Figaro* and Delilah in *Samson and Delilah* to her Metropolitan Opera roles.

On the afternoon preceding her Metropolitan Opera debut in New York Stevens received word from Walter Surovy that he had fled from Europe, following Hitler's annexation of Austria, and was in New York. They were married on January 6, 1939—legal formalities had to be sandwiched in between rehearsals at the Metropolitan and there was no time for a honeymoon. Surovy abandoned his acting career to place his theatrical know-how at his wife's disposal. As her consultant and manager he was largely responsible for persuading the Metropolitan Opera to give her those starring roles that made her an outstanding American prima donna and for extending her fame outside the opera house to the movies and on sponsored network radio programs.

In the spring and summer of 1939, Stevens appeared as Cherubino at the Glyndebourne Festival in England. She was the first American-born singer to appear there. At this time Co-lumbia Artists in the United States signed her for recitals, launching her on a career as a concert artist.

On October 12, 1940 (opening night of the season), Stevens made her debut with the San Francisco Opera as Cherubino. Her appearance with the San Francisco Opera drew the attention of officials at the MGM motion picture studios who invited her to make a screen test. She was then starred opposite Nelson Eddy in a new screen version of the operetta *The Chocolate Soldier* (1941) and in the Academy-Award-winning film *Going My Way* (1944), in which she sang the "Habanera" from *Carmen.* As a celebrity, she was able to command between two thousand five hundred and four thousand dollars for each of her concert appearances. Her Columbia album of *Carmen* became a best seller and within a few years she had signed a new recording contract with RCA Victor with an advance of two hundred thousand dollars and an assured annual income for twenty years.

Her new status compelled the Metropolitan Opera to give her a starring position with the company. She opened the 1941–1942 season on November 24 as Cherubino. On December 28, 1945, she was given the first of many opportunities to appear in what became her most famous role, Carmen. On November 21, 1949, she opened the Metropolitan Opera season as Octavian. She was assigned the leading female role of Marfa in the Metropolitan Opera premiere of Mussorgsky's *Khovantchina* (February 16, 1950). On December 20, 1950, she sang the part of Prince Orlofsky in a new English-language production of *Die Fledermaus* conducted by Eugene Ormandy. On January 31, 1952, she was starred as Carmen in a new production staged by Tyrone Guthrie, and on December 11, 1952, that production was televised over a closed circuit of thirty-one theaters in twenty-seven cities for an audience estimated in excess of seventy thousand.

Stevens remained with the Metropolitan Opera through the 1960–1961 season. By the end of the season she had appeared 220 times in New York and 117 on tour, having been heard as Carmen 75 times, Octavian 50 times, and Mignon 20 times. Her Metropolitan Opera roles also included Laura in *La Gioconda,* Hansel in *Hansel and Gretel,* and Giulietta in *The Tales of Hoffmann.*

During World War II she traveled throughout the United States singing at bond rallies and for the men in service as a member of the Hollywood Victory Caravan. In the late 1940s she became a radio star on sponsored network programs and was voted radio's leading female vocalist by *Motion Picture Daily* and by *Musical America* in 1947 and 1948 respectively. She subsequently made numerous appearances over television. In 1947 she appeared in one of the singing sequences in the motion picture *Carnegie Hall.*

Her principal European successes began in 1948 with appearances as Octavian at the Paris Opéra; she was the first foreign artist invited to that company after World War II. On March 24, 1954, she made her debut at La Scala in Milan in the world premiere of Virgilio Mortari's *La Figlia del Diavolo.* "On stage," noted the *Corriere della Sera* in Milan, "sparkled the quicksilvery and fiery Risë Stevens, with a beautiful voice and outstanding histrionic abilities." She returned to the Glyndebourne Festival as Cherubino in 1956, and that same year she was heard as Orfeo in *Orfeo ed Euridice* at the Festival of the Acropolis in Athens.

Her home for a number of years was in the Virgin Islands and after that in an apartment in the East Sixties in New York City. She and her husband had a son, Nicolas, who became an actor. Before a performance, Stevens always slept late, then had a solitary breakfast, and after that went through the score of the night's opera or concert program. She would then relax by reading a book or newspapers. At one thirty she would go to sleep for about three hours. At four she would have a steak dinner, at four thirty she would vocalize, and at five she would go to her private dressing room in her apartment to work on her hair and her makeup. She would leave for the opera house at six. An hour later Vera Schwarz, her only vocal coach after the death of Schoen-René, would arrive to go through the score with her. When Stevens left her dressing room for the stage, her husband would embrace her and, following an old Hungarian superstition, would spit three times over his left shoulder for good luck.

As one of America's best-dressed women, Risë Stevens has always shown considerable interest in her wardrobe. But she has had other interests as well: swimming and walking for exercise; collecting Wedgwood china and slim crystal glasses; going to the movies; accumulating all sorts of good-luck charms.

In 1964 she helped to open the new theater at the Lincoln Center for the Performing Arts in New York in the leading female role of the Rodgers and Hammerstein musical play *The King and I.* From 1964 to 1967 she was the general manager of the short-lived Metropolitan Opera national touring company. She joined the faculty of the Juilliard School of Music in New York in 1975. A few months later she was engaged as president of the Mannes College of Music in New York, the only woman to hold such a post with a major conservatory. She served as president for three years, resigning in June 1978 because of a dispute with some of the board members over her ambition to expand the vocal and opera departments of the college. "I have not been able to convince certain members of the board," she explained, "that this is a direction in which Mannes must expand."

ABOUT: Crichton, K. Subway to the Met: Risë Stevens' Story. *Periodicals*—High Fidelity, January 1976; New York Times, March 26, 1977; Opera News, March 7, 1964; Time, December 26, 1938.

Thomas Stewart

1928–

Thomas James Stewart Jr., baritone, was born in San Saba, Texas, on August 29, 1928, to Thomas and Gladys Reavis Stewart. His father was a highway engineer. Thomas looks back to a miserable childhood, as he once told an interviewer. "We were very poor and . . . I was an unattractive child—fat and full of complexes. I had no girl friends. I was not witty or funny. I was shy." To attract attention and interest, he started singing. As a boy soprano he sang with the local church choir. Later he began studying voice with a high school physics teacher who conducted a choir.

After his family had moved to Richmond, California, Thomas did some gospel singing, but his interest in music was soon supplemented by his fascination for electronics and engineering. After graduation from high school, he enrolled in Baylor University, in Waco, Texas, to study electronics. These studies were interrupted in 1946 when he enlisted in the United States Air

THOMAS STEWART

Force. During his three years in uniform he did mathematical-physical research at Randolph Field in San Antonio, Texas, where he worked as a statistician on an IBM prototype computer. In his free time he sang with concert groups and with the San Antonio Opera. Upon his release from the service in 1949, Stewart found employment as a civilian in the research laboratory at Randolph Field. Then he returned to Baylor University where he shifted from electronics to music, studied voice with Robert Hopkins, and received his Bachelor of Arts degree in music in 1953.

He went to New York the year of his graduation to continue his vocal studies with Mack Harrell and Frederick Cohen at the Juilliard School of Music. There he was a member of the Opera Workshop. At the Juilliard, on April 14, 1954, he appeared as La Roche in the American premiere of Strauss's *Capriccio* and came in for special praise from Olin Downes in the New York *Times* review of the performance. On November 1, 1954, he appeared with a professional opera company—the Chicago Lyric Opera—as Raimondo in a performance of *Lucia di Lammermoor* that starred Maria Callas in her American debut.

One of Stewart's fellow students at the Juilliard was Evelyn Kwartin Lear, soprano. On January 8, 1955, they were married. "We got married," Stewart recalls, "before we had time to consider the danger of having two vocal careers in one family. . . . It was a nightmare. I had a family to support—Evelyn has two children by

a previous marriage—and we were literally living from hand to mouth." For two years he took on any job he could find. He worked on "Chance of a Lifetime," a talent competition show over the radio, singing songs such as "Ol' Man River." With Evelyn Lear he toured in a condensed version of Cole Porter's musical comedy *Kiss Me, Kate.* He took on small parts in summer stock and at one time found a job with Mae West's troupe at the Latin Quarter in New York City. He even learned to play the guitar in the hope of becoming a cowboy singer but abandoned this hoped-for career when he was turned down as "too unprofessional" at an audition for the "Arthur Godfrey's Talent Scouts" radio program. "That was the rock bottom," he says.

Having come to a dead end, he eagerly accepted the advice of Frederick Cohen to apply for a Fulbright grant. When he received the grant, he and his wife went to Berlin where Stewart undertook some additional voice study with Jaro Prohaska at the Hochschule für Musik. Only three weeks after his arrival in Berlin, he was engaged by the Deutsche Oper. During the next two years he learned major roles in the standard repertory and was heard as Don Giovanni, Iago in *Otello,* Golaud in *Pelléas and Mélisande,* the Dutchman in *The Flying Dutchman,* and Doctor Falke in *Die Fledermaus.* On September 21, 1960, he created the role of William in Boris Blacher's *Rosamunde Floris,* and in 1963 he assumed the title role in the world premiere of Milhaud's *Oreste d'Eschyle.*

Evelyn Lear joined the Deutsche Oper one year after Stewart. They became the first husband-and-wife pair in the company. On September 25, 1961, during the opening-week ceremonies for the new auditorium of the Deutsche Oper they were paired in leading roles in the world premiere of Klebe's twelve-tone opera *Alkmene.* Subsequently they also became the only husband-and-wife pair to earn the honorary titles *Kammersänger* and *Kammersängerin.*

Wieland Wagner heard Stewart in 1960 and invited him to appear at Bayreuth. "He asked me," says Stewart, "what roles I preferred and I said Amfortas and Wolfram, but someone else had been assigned for *Parsifal* and there was no *Tannhäuser* that summer. So I got Gunther and Donner." Before Stewart could appear in these parts, however, George London, scheduled to sing Amfortas, fell ill, and the role went to Stewart for his Bayreuth debut. He proved so successful that he was reengaged for several succeeding seasons to perform Wolfram, the Dutchman, and Wotan. In 1970 he appeared in *Parsifal* when Pierre Boulez made his Bayreuth conducting debut. Bayreuth bestowed on Stewart the Richard Wagner medal.

His success at Bayreuth brought him engagements in Europe's major opera houses, including Covent Garden in London and the Vienna State Opera, and also at the Teatro Colón in Buenos Aires. In 1963 he made his debut with the San Francisco Opera as Prince Jeletzky in Tchaikovsky's *Queen of Spades*. At that time Harold C. Schonberg, reporting from San Francisco to the New York *Times,* described him as "a clear-voiced baritone, a fine figure of a man, and an admirable artist." In San Francisco, he was also heard as Golaud, Don Giovanni, Wolfram, and Doctor Falke.

For his debut at the Metropolitan Opera, Stewart was scheduled to appear as Wolfram. However, a change of casting in the Zeffirelli production of *Falstaff* made it necessary for him to make the debut in a different role and ten days earlier than scheduled. The debut was on March 9, 1966, in the role of Ford. The reviewer for the *Herald Tribune* said: "To the Metropolitan in triumph last night came Thomas Stewart, a tall, moustached baritone from Texas (via Europe) who seems to have just about everything going for him—good looks, a fine voice and rare operatic ability." When he appeared as Wolfram ten days later, Eric Salzman, writing in the *Herald Tribune,* called him "a consummate artist . . . able to make something strong and moving out of even such a stick as Wolfram."

The aura of success created by his initial appearances at the Metropolitan Opera was considerably magnified when he was heard there as Wotan in the new productions of *Das Rheingold* and *Die Walküre,* staged and conducted by Herbert von Karajan in 1968 and 1969 respectively. He had sung the Wotan of *Die Walküre* for the first time in the late spring of 1967 in Salzburg, when von Karajan launched his four-year project of presenting each of the dramas in the *Ring* cycle, one a year. After that Stewart sang Wotan in Paris, Bayreuth, and Berlin, and before coming to the Metropolitan Opera was already acknowledged to be one of the world's foremost *Heldenbaritons.* His first Metropolitan Opera Wotan was sung on November 21, 1967, in *Die Walküre. Time* Magazine described him

as "a Wotan of uncommon Zeus-like quality," and the New York *Times* spoke of him as "the Wotan of his generation." Subsequently, he appeared at the Metropolitan Opera as the Wanderer in *Siegfried,* Gunther in *Götterdämmerung,* Amfortas in *Parsifal,* Wolfram in *Tannhäuser,* the Dutchman in *The Flying Dutchman,* and Kurvenal (his first performance in this role) in a new production of *Tristan and Isolde.* Outside the Wagnerian repertory he was heard as Escamillo in *Carmen,* Golaud in *Pelléas and Mélisande,* Orestes in *Elektra,* Almaviva in *The Marriage of Figaro,* Jokanaan in *Salome,* Amonasro in *Aida,* Iago in *Otello,* Don Giovanni, and the four baritone roles in *The Tales of Hoffmann.*

During the 1970–1971 season Stewart appeared in three complete performances of the *Ring* cycle (in Vienna, Hamburg, and Berlin) as Wotan, the Wanderer, and Gunther; in the fall of 1972 he duplicated this performance with the San Francisco Opera when the cycle was performed twice in one season. He is the only American-born singer to appear in these three roles. He is also the only American to sing for ten consecutive seasons at the Bayreuth Festival and one of two baritones to have sung there all the principal baritone roles in the *Ring* cycle. At the Salzburg Easter Festival, in the von Karajan productions of the *Ring,* Stewart once again filled the three roles (Gunther, the Wanderer, and Wotan).

Stewart has frequently shared the stage with his wife. They did so for the first time in the United States when they were costarred by the San Francisco Opera in *Eugene Onegin* in the fall of 1971. During the 1971–1972 season at the Metropolitan Opera they performed together in *The Marriage of Figaro, Falstaff,* and *Don Giovanni.* In the first season of the experimental "Mini Met" at the Lincoln Center for the Performing Arts in 1973 they were heard in the title roles of Purcell's *Dido and Aeneas.* They also joined forces in performances of *Tosca* with the Pittsburgh Opera and in Europe, in *Otello* with the Connecticut Opera and at the Deutsche Oper in Berlin, in *Die Meistersinger* with the Nuremberg Opera in April 1972—to mention only a few of many such appearances.

They have also appeared frequently both in the United States and in Europe in joint recitals, just as individually they have given innumerable solo recitals and made many appearances with orchestras. Stewart's recital debut at the Brahmssaal in Vienna was one of the highlights of the 1970 season in that city; one of the Viennese critics called him "a brilliant new star on the concert stage, capable of communicating the subtler art of Lieder and French art songs, the humor and irony of American folk songs as well as the soaring melodies of Italian bel canto." In February 1972, when Stewart gave his first New York recital, Harriet Johnson wrote in the New York *Post:* "There is no doubt, judging by this recital, that Stewart is a natural villain—on stage, we hope—with a wicked sense of humor, all of which adds dimension to his personality."

Stewart has recorded many of his operatic portrayals for Deutsche Grammophon. These include Wotan in *Die Walküre,* the Wanderer in *Siegfried,* and Gunther in *Die Götterdämmerung* in the von Karajan productions. *Siegfried* earned a Grammy from the American Academy of Recording Arts and Sciences in 1969. In addition he has also recorded his 1970 Bayreuth performance as Amfortas. He has appeared in filmed versions of *The Secret of Suzanne* and *Die Walküre.*

Thomas Stewart and Evelyn Lear maintain two homes: one in Santa Fe, New Mexico, the other in Fort Lauderdale, Florida. They share such diversions as playing golf, swimming, and cooking.

Lear says that Stewart "constructs within his mind how a role should be sung. He'll go to the libretto first and he'll read it over and over and over again." To which Stewart adds: "I have had more experiences on the stage than in my private life."

ABOUT: High Fidelity/Musical America, January 1972; New York Times, February 20, 1970; New Yorker, January 22, 1972; Opera News, February 10, 1968, March 28, 1970.

Fritz Stiedry

1883–1968

Fritz Stiedry, conductor, was born in Vienna on October 11, 1883. While attending the University of Vienna, from which he received the degree of Doctor of Law, he also was a pupil of Eusebi-

Stiedry: shtē′ drē

FRITZ STIEDRY

us Madyczewski in composition and music history at the Vienna Conservatory. His music education was also furthered in the gallery of the Vienna Royal Opera, where he heard performances conducted by Gustav Mahler. It was here that he developed a love for Mozart's operas that remained with him for the rest of his life. To gain a more intimate knowledge of Mahler's conducting methods, he had himself smuggled into the Opera orchestra pretending he was a performer on the triangle. Mahler soon became interested in him and for a brief period in 1907 he had Stiedry serve as his assistant at the Royal Opera. That same year he used his influence to gain Stiedry a post as assistant conductor to Ernst von Schuch at the Dresden Royal Opera. Stiedry remained there for a single season. Various other engagements during the next four years gave him valuable experience as an opera conductor. From 1914 to 1923 he held his most important post up to that time, conductor at the Royal Opera in Berlin where he was required to direct an exhaustive repertory of Italian, French, and German operas.

From 1923 to 1925 Stiedry was principal conductor at the Volksoper in Vienna, succeeding Felix Weingartner. There followed a three-year period as guest conductor of operas and symphonic music in Italy, Spain, and Scandinavia. Then in 1929 he became the general music director of the newly reconstructed Berlin Municipal Opera, a post previously held by Bruno Walter. During the four years he held this post he became one of Germany's important conductors, particularly in Wagner, Verdi, and Mozart. His performance of Verdi's *Macbeth* in 1931, in a production by Carl Ebert, proved a historic event in Berlin in those years. He also served as president of the Berlin section of the International Society for Contemporary Music.

In spite of the exalted esteem in which he was held in Berlin, the Nazis did not spare him when they came to power in 1933. After directing a special performance of *The Flying Dutchman* on March 7, 1933, he was given an ovation. Goering and Goebbels, who were in the audience, were furious that such enthusiasm should be directed towards a Jew. Later that evening storm troopers broke into the auditorium and ordered Stiedry to leave. Aware that his life was in danger, he fled from Berlin to Vienna, leaving behind him all his possessions, including his valuable library of more than five thousand volumes and several thousand musical scores.

At this crucial point in his life, Stiedry received an offer from the Soviet Union to become the music director of the Leningrad Philharmonic. He was no stranger to the Soviet Union, having previously made seven trips to conduct orchestras in Leningrad, Moscow, Kiev, and other cities. For four years, given unlimited rehearsal time, he instituted a progressive repertory in Leningrad that embraced not only the Western classics but also the works of such modernists as Hindemith, Stravinsky, and Schoenberg. On October 15, 1933, he performed the premiere of Shostakovich's Piano Concerto No.1, with the composer as soloist. Under his leadership, for the first time since the Revolution, Bach's *Passion According to St. John* received a hearing, though this time in a new Russian version by Tolstoi. Stiedry was also called upon to lead new operatic productions in Moscow and Leningrad, including several operas that had been neglected in the Soviet Union but were close to Stiedry's heart, such as *Falstaff*, *The Abduction from the Seraglio*, and *The Bartered Bride*.

By 1937 the Soviet authorities had begun to condemn Shostakovich for his "Western decadence" and "bourgeois formalism." Progressive composers became unwelcome in Soviet music circles. Stiedry, who was rehearsing Shostakovich's Symphony No.4 for its premiere, was compelled to cancel this performance. In such a climate he felt he could no longer function to the best of his capacity. Though his contract was renewed, he left the Soviet Union, ostensibly on a vacation but with the intention of never returning.

He went to the United States in 1938 with his wife, the former Erica Wagner, taking with him as his only possessions the complete editions of Mozart and Bach which he treasured. A few months after his arrival he was appointed conductor of the newly organized chamber orchestra of the New Friends of Music in New York. He directed this organization for four years, including on his programs Bach's six *Brandenburg Concertos,* Bach's *Art of the Fugue* (in Stiedry's own orchestral setting), rarely heard symphonies by Haydn and Mozart (including some Haydn symphonies recently rediscovered by the musicologist Alfred Einstein that Stiedry performed for the first time in one hundred and fifty years), a cycle of Mozart's concertos, and such avant-garde music as Schoenberg's atonal *Pierrot Lunaire*. "Stiedry," wrote one New York critic following his initial concerts, "must be a phenomenal musician, and a thorough technician—for his orchestra, even though it is in its first year, has remarkable coordination, balance and evenness of execution. More important still, the orchestra played with freshness of spirit, youth and vitality."

As a guest conductor of the New Friends of Music in Los Angeles, Stiedry directed the world premiere of Schoenberg's *Chamber Symphony No.2* on October 21, 1939.

In 1946 Stiedry was engaged as a principal conductor at the Metropolitan Opera in New York, making his debut there on November 15, 1946, in *Siegfried*. "He gave an eloquent and admirably ordered reading," commented Olin Downes in the New York *Times*, "a reading characterized by sensitively modulated power and saliency of detail that enhanced but did not obscure the grand lines of the musical structure."

Stiedry's distinction as a performer of Wagner's music was enhanced that first season at the Metropolitan Opera with his performances of *Die Walküre* and *Parsifal* and, a season later, his performances of *Tannhäuser* and *Die Götterdämmerung*. He also revealed a skillful hand in *Hansel and Gretel* and *The Magic Flute*. He brought back to the stage of the Metropolitan new productions of three operas particularly close to him: *Don Carlo* on the opening night of the 1950–1951 season, *Così fan Tutte* in 1951, and *Boris Godunov* in 1953.

His last appearance at the Metropolitan Opera took place on April 8, 1958, with *Don Giovanni*. In these dozen years he had added to his Metropolitan Opera repertory *Lohengrin, Tristan and Isolde, Die Meistersinger, Siegfried, La Forza del Destino, Simon Boccanegra, Otello,* and *The Marriage of Figaro.* He directed a performance of *La Forza del Destino* on the opening night of the 1952–1953 season.

As a conductor, wrote César Saerchinger in *Saturday Review,* Stiedry conceived himself "to be simply the communicator of the music, nothing more or less. He is a master of subtle nuance rather than the overpowering effect. He employs purposely short-ranged movements and the least spectacular gestures. . . . And he is obstinately unresponsive to suggestions which aim at louder applause. As Virgil Thomson once said: 'When Stiedry conducts, the conductor disappears and we have only the music.' "

Fritz Stiedry died in Zurich, on August 9, 1968. "There are many facets to admire in his character," said Rudolf Bing, general manager of the Metropolitan Opera, "not the least of these being his fortitude in the face of ill fortune. There was a time, just before his appointment on Thirty-ninth Street, when things looked gloomy, but Stiedry was not a man to be deterred from higher goals by means of financial worries. I remember a friend telling me of a visit to Stiedry's home at a very critical moment, afraid of how he would bear up under the strain (he was no longer young even then). No reference was made to dreary problems of bread and butter; all afternoon Stiedry talked of Dostoyevsky."

ABOUT: Opera News, November 2, 1968.

Ebe Stignani

1903–

Ebe Stignani, mezzo-soprano, was born in Naples on July 10, 1903, the only child of a machinery salesman originally from Rome. Revealing early talent for music, Ebe was encouraged by her parents to begin music study. When she was ten she entered the Naples Conservatory as a

---

Stignani: stē nyä′ nē

EBE STIGNANI

student of piano. At fifteen, while singing in the Conservatory chorus she was discovered by Augustino Roche, who encouraged her to specialize in voice and became her teacher.

She was graduated from the Conservatory in 1925, and during the graduation ceremonies she sang several numbers. In the audience was the general manager of the San Carlo Opera in Naples who offered her a contract. She made her opera debut with that company as Amneris in *Aida.* She proved so successful that she was called upon to appear fifty-four times during the next few months. That same year (1925) she also appeared in Venice. There a board member of La Scala in Milan heard her and suggested she audition for Arturo Toscanini, then the artistic director of La Scala. After she had sung a few numbers for Toscanini, he nodded and dismissed her. She was convinced her audition had been a failure, but the next morning she found a contract for La Scala in her mail.

Her first appearance at La Scala took place in 1925 as Princess Eboli in *Don Carlo,* Toscanini conducting. During the next three years as a member of La Scala, she was often heard in performances conducted by Toscanini, including *Aida,* Pizzetti's *Debora e Jaele, Der Freischütz, La Gioconda, Il Trovatore, La Forza del Destino,* and *Falstaff.* Also with Toscanini she sang the soprano solo in a Milan performance of Beethoven's Symphony No.9.

In 1927 she made her debut at the Teatro Colón in Buenos Aires. When Toscanini resigned from La Scala in 1928, Stignani withdrew from the company. She made numerous appearances throughout Europe and South America, and at the Florence May Music Festival in 1940 she sang the role of Arsace in Rossini's *Semiramide.* "I have never had to struggle to succeed," she once remarked.

On October 17, 1938, she made her American debut as Santuzza in *Cavalleria Rusticana* with the San Francisco Opera. She sang so well that the San Francisco Opera gave her a contract for the following season. But the outbreak of World War II in Europe prevented her return and she did not appear again in San Francisco until September 14, 1948, when she helped to open the season in *Falstaff.* Later the same season she appeared as Santuzza and as Laura in *La Gioconda.*

In 1947 she toured South America and appeared at the Paris Opéra. In 1948 she toured the United States, covering twenty thousand miles and supplementing performances at the San Francisco Opera with recitals in leading American cities. Virgil Thomson heard her recital in October and reported back to his newspaper, the *Herald Tribune:* "Stignani's reputation as an artist appeared clearly justified. . . . There is no questioning the perfection of her style. The long-breathed phrases, the varied-at-will colorations, the lucidity of her whole linguistic projection are the work of a distinguished as well as an impeccable technician. . . . Stignani [has] a ranging top register and a deeply affecting way of projecting her chest range. . . . Her whole scale is handsomely graded. The pose of her voice throughout is impeccable; no flaw is evident in the schooling of her instrument for execution."

On December 13, 1948, she made her New York debut in recital. At that time many critics were effusive in their praises. In the New York *Times* Howard Taubman said of her voice: "It can soar well above the staff and can encompass deep chest tones. Virtually every note is produced with clarity and purity. . . . It can ring out with lavish power, and it can be refined down to a most delicate and subtly colored pianissimo." In the *World-Telegram* Robert Bagar remarked: "She sang . . . divinely."

Though her only American operatic appearances were with the San Francisco Opera in 1938 and in 1948, she continued to perform successfully in opera houses in Italy and South America. Among her finest roles, in addition to those already mentioned, were *Carmen,* Delilah in *Samson and Delilah,* Leonora in *La Favorita,* Azucena in *Il Trovatore,* Orfeo in Gluck's *Orfeo ed Euridice,* Adalgisa in *Norma,* Ortrud in *Lohengrin,* and Brangäne in *Tristan and Isolde.*

In 1940 Ebe Stignani married Alfredo Sciti, an engineer. They lived for many years on a farm in Imola, near Bologna, and maintained a residence on the Via Monteverdi in Milan. Her favorite pastime is cooking. In 1955 she was the recipient of the Orfeo d'Oro from Italy.

ABOUT: Davidson, G. Opera Biographies.

Frederick A. Stock

1872–1942

Frederick Wilhelm August Stock, conductor, was born in Jülich, Germany, a garrison town near Cologne, on November 11, 1872. His father, Friedrich Carl Stock, a bandmaster in the Prussian army, was stationed in Jülich, and Frederick was born in the fortress there. His mother, Maria, died shortly after his birth.

Frederick's early schooling took place in Rheidt, near Cologne. His academic training continued spasmodically, the poverty of his family making it impossible for him to receive a thorough education. However, his father personally saw to it that he received music lessons, which began with instruction on the violin when he was four. At eleven, he had his first opportunity to conduct when, at a rehearsal of his father's military band, one of the musicians good-humoredly offered him the baton when Frederick's father was late in arriving. He climbed the bandstand and, knowing the music by heart, went on to beat time with an accurate hand and to give a smooth account of the music.

When he was fourteen, Frederick received a scholarship for the Cologne Conservatory. During the next five years he studied the violin there with Georg Japha and theory and composition with Franz Wüllner, Gustav Jensen, and Engelbert Humperdinck.

He was graduated from the Conservatory in 1891. For the following four years he played the violin in the Cologne Municipal Orchestra un-

Stock: stŏk

FREDERICK A. STOCK

der the baton of such musicians as Tchaikovsky, Brahms, and Richard Strauss.

In 1895 Theodore Thomas invited him to the United States to become the first violist of the Chicago Symphony Orchestra. In 1901 Thomas made Stock assistant conductor; from 1903 to 1905 Stock conducted all the out-of-town concerts of the orchestra. When Thomas died on January 4, 1905, just a month after the Chicago Symphony Orchestra entered its new auditorium (Orchestra Hall), he assumed the post of principal conductor which he held up to the time of his death, except for a five-month period in 1918–1919. Because of his German origin and the war hysteria in America, Stock found it expedient to withdraw from the conducting position for those five months until his American citizenship was granted on May 22, 1919.

The Stock years in Chicago were distinguished by his progressive and innovative programming. At a time when Mahler's music was rarely heard in the United States he conducted a Mahler festival in 1917. In a survey conducted by Howard Hanson on the American orchestral repertory in 1938, the Chicago Symphony under Stock rated first place among American orchestras for the wide spectrum of its performances of American music over a twenty-year period: two hundred and seventy-two works by eighty composers. Stock probably produced more world and American premieres than any other conductor of his time. Among his world premieres were: Ernest Bloch's *Helvetia* (February 18, 1932); John Alden Carpenter's *Adventures in a*

Perambulator (March 19, 1915), *Krazy Kat,* suite (December 23, 1921), and *Sea-Drift* (November 30, 1933); Alfredo Casella's Symphony No.3 (March 27, 1941); Rudolf Ganz's Piano Concerto (February 20, 1941); Zoltán Kodály's Concerto for Orchestra (February 6, 1941); Charles Martin Loeffler's *Memories of My Childhood* (May 30, 1924); Arne Oldberg's Symphony No.3 (March 18, 1927); Prokofiev's Piano Concerto No.3 (December 17, 1921); Leo Sowerby's Symphony No.1 (April 7, 1922) and Symphony No.3 (March 6, 1941); and William Walton's *Scapino* (April 3, 1941).

"Stock was a man of modesty and rare simplicity of character. At rehearsals, for example, he resorted to no unusual antics, nor succumbed to outbursts of temper. He was soft-spoken and even tempered, knew exactly what he wanted and gave his men precise instructions. He had an extraordinary conductorial technique at his command which made it possible for him to work methodically, and with a minimum of physical effort and mental strain. Temperament he had, for his performances were alive with character; but he was no prima donna. From the humblest musician in the orchestra to its directors, it was known that he was firm on artistic standards but easy to get along with on other matters. ... He shrank from publicity, stoutly refusing to have the limelight focused on him, always deflecting it from himself to his orchestra." (D. Ewen. *Dictators of the Baton*)

Since he was determined to keep his orchestra "a home organization," he did comparatively little traveling with it. He paid only two visits to New York with the Chicago Symphony, the second time in 1940 during the orchestra's golden anniversary tour. On that occasion, Olin Downes wrote in the New York *Times:* "Dr. Stock conducted, as he always does, with a minimum of gesticulation and a technique remarkable for economy of effort, authority and conductor's skill. A wholly exceptional musician, with an abhorrence of ostentation, he achieved an exciting result in apparently the simplest manner."

On infrequent occasions Stock left Chicago to appear as a guest conductor of other American orchestras. He led the New York Philharmonic for a week in 1926 and the Lewisohn Stadium Orchestra in New York for two weeks during the summer of 1927. He was also a guest conductor of the Philadelphia Orchestra. In 1929 he served as the music director of the twenty-eighth biennial Cincinnati May Music Festival.

In Chicago he occasionally conducted concerts of organizations other than the Chicago Symphony: with the Musical Arts Club from 1907 to 1909, the Civic Music Student Orchestra after 1920, and in performances of several Wagnerian music dramas with the Chicago Civic Opera in 1923. In 1933 he served as general music director of the Century of Progress Exposition in Chicago.

On May 22, 1896, Stock married Elizabeth (Elsa) Muskulus. They lived on Astor Street, in Chicago, and had one child, a daughter. In 1910 he was elected a member of the American Institute of Arts and Letters. In 1925 he was made Chevalier of the Legion of Honor by France and in 1939 he was presented with the European medal of the Bruckner Society of America. He received honorary doctorates in music from Northwestern University (1915), the University of Michigan (1924), the University of Chicago (1925), Cornell College in Iowa (1927), and the Institute of Fine Arts in Chicago (1938).

He was the composer of numerous works for orchestra including a symphony, a violin concerto, a cello concerto, *Festival Fanfare,* and *Rhapsodic Fantasy.* He also wrote some chamber music and reorchestrated Schumann's Symphony No.4.

Stock underwent a serious operation in May 1941. In spite of this he was able to resume his duties with his orchestra. On October 15, 1942, he launched the orchestra's fifty-second season, establishing a world record of sustained conductorial service by starting his forty-eighth season with the Chicago Symphony, thirty-eight of those years as principal conductor. Only one day before his death he was at Orchestra Hall discussing plans for the season with the orchestra's business manager. Frederick Stock died of a heart attack at his home on October 20, 1942.

ABOUT: Ewen, D. Dictators of the Baton; Otis, P. A. The Chicago Symphony Orchestra; Taylor, D. Music to My Ears. *Periodicals*—New York Times, October 21, 1942, October 25, 1942.

Leopold Stokowski

1882–1977

Leopold Antoni Stanislaw Boleslawowicz Stokowski, conductor, and major influence in developing and shaping musical culture in the United States, was born in London on April 18, 1882. His father, Joseph Boleslaw Kopernik Stokowski, was a cabinetmaker from Poland; his mother, Annie Moore Stokowski, was of Irish extraction.

Though neither parent was musical, each was astute enough to recognize musical talent. They saw to it that Leopold received lessons on both the violin and the piano when he was five, and not long after that he started to learn to play the organ. Even before his feet could touch the organ pedals he was playing some of the organ music of Johann Sebastian Bach. He made his first attempt at conducting when he was twelve. At that time he was already playing the violin in an orchestra and serving as rehearsal pianist with a small London opera company. One day when the regular conductor was too ill to perform and nobody else was available as a substitute, Leopold asked for the baton and performed with the efficiency of one who knew what he was doing. From then on, though the playing of the organ remained a prime musical activity and the music of Bach virtually a fixation, he wanted to become a conductor.

He studied music mainly at the Royal College of Music in London with Charles Stanford (composition), Henry Walford Davies (counterpoint), and Stevenson Hoyte (organ), among others. For a time he also attended Queen's College at Oxford.

In 1900 he was appointed organist of St. James Church in the Piccadilly section of London. That summer he made a trip to Paris and Munich for additional music studies. The rest of that year, while attending to his organ duties in London, he learned by himself to play almost every instrument of the orchestra as preparation for a possible conducting career.

When he first went to the United States in 1905 he planned a short visit, but he stayed on to become organist and choirmaster at St. Bartholomew's in New York City. Music lovers

Stokowski: stō̇ kôf′ skē̆

LEOPOLD STOKOWSKI

during his concerts to take the audience to task for bad concert-hall manners. One evening in 1911 when he was disturbed by rustling programs during the playing of a composition, he turned sharply around and shouted: "Ple-ase, don't do *that!* We must have the proper atmosphere. We work hard all week to give you this music, but I cannot do my best, and our orchestra cannot do its best, without your help. I'll give you my best or I won't give you anything. It is for you to choose."

By 1912 Stokowski knew he had outgrown Cincinnati and that he needed a better orchestra and a somewhat more sophisticated audience for his music-making. The Philadelphia Orchestra, then just ten years old, invited him that year, and he accepted. The directors of the Cincinnati Symphony pleaded with him to reconsider his decision; they were ready, they said, to make any adjustments Stokowski felt were necessary. "Adjustments?" Stokowski replied. "What cannot be adjusted is the loss of my enthusiasm, which enthusiasm is absolutely necessary in the constructive work of building an orchestra!" At his final rehearsal in Cincinnati, a spokesman for the orchestra promised him that the men stood ready to cooperate with him more fully than ever if only he would remain. Stokowski replied: "Let's get on with our work today." Nothing and nobody could induce him to change his mind.

He conducted his first concert with the Philadelphia Orchestra at the Academy of Music on October 11, 1912. "Stokowski came forward with bowed head," reported the critic of the *Public Ledger,* "evidently pondering the content of his musical message. Those who went forth to see a hirsute eccentricity were disappointed. They beheld a surprisingly boyish and thoroughly businesslike figure who was sure of himself, yet free from conceit, who dispensed with the score by virtue of an infallible memory, and held his men and his audience from the first note to the last firmly in his grasp." The critic added further: "The new leader has been surprisingly successful in welding the several choirs into a single coherent entity. . . . He directs with a fine vigor and intensity that mount to ecstasy yet does not lose its balance or forget its sane and ordered method."

It did not take Stokowski long to establish the image he would retain throughout his years as first, principal conductor, then as music director

soon made it a habit to visit this church regularly just to hear Stokowski perform Bach. In the summer of 1908 he returned to London to make his professional debut as conductor by leading two concerts with a pickup orchestra. The violin virtuoso Joseph Szigeti was present at one of these concerts at Queen's Hall. "I still remember," he wrote, "the already then typically Stokowskian sound of the London orchestra in the concluding number—Tchaikovsky's *Marche Slave*—and the feline suppleness of the orchestral support that the young conductor gave to Efrem Zimbalist playing the Glazunov Concerto, then still a comparative novelty."

In 1909, when the Cincinnati Symphony Orchestra was being reorganized, Stokowski was engaged as its principal conductor. During his three years in Cincinnati, the world of music had glimpses of the many facets of his musicianship and personality that were to make him one of the most controversial figures in American music. Though the orchestra and its audiences were provincial—partial to the light classics and familiar masterworks—Stokowski insisted on performing new or unfamiliar compositions regularly and presented an all-American concert, a highly unusual program for those years. He took the orchestra on tours of the West, to many cities that had never before heard a symphony orchestra. In Cincinnati, he initiated lecture-concerts, an attempt to educate his audiences in music appreciation, something that no American orchestra had undertaken up to that time. He also began making short speeches of the Philadelphia Orchestra: the dictator whose autocratic control of his musicians, his audiences, and the directors of the orchestra was total; the sensationalist who did not hesitate to use Barnum-like tactics to glamorize himself and continually to make himself front-page news; the fashion plate, whose gold hair was like a crown atop his head, who on the conductor's platform was always a cynosure for the audience's eyes; and the highly dedicated, farsighted, and remarkably gifted musician who created a new luscious sound for his orchestra that became known as "the Stokowski sound," whose virtuosity placed the orchestra with the world's greatest (Rachmaninoff called it "the Stradivarius of orchestras"), and whose adventurous programming made Philadelphia one of the major music centers of the United States.

He allowed nobody to interfere with the direction he had set for himself and his orchestra. He overrode the violent objections of the orchestral management in 1916 when on March 2 he gave the American premiere of Gustav Mahler's Symphony No.8 *(Symphony of a Thousand)*, demanding extraordinarily large musical forces: a greatly augmented orchestra, a boys' choir, eight solo voices, a double chorus, and an organ. The financial expenditure involved for this performance was enormous, but this was only a minor consideration to a conductor determined to present a modern masterwork not only in Philadelphia but also in New York City.

There were also grumbles of discontent from management and audiences at the way Stokowski insisted upon playing new music. He overrode their dissent and in the process he made performing history in the United States. There was hardly a front-ranking composer in the twentieth century who did not get a hearing at Stokowski's concerts, some for the first time; there was hardly a major work written in the twentieth century that did not appear on Stokowski's programs. His premieres, world and American, virtually represent a "who's who" and a "what's what" in the music of the twentieth century. Here is a partial list of his world premieres with the Philadelphia Orchestra: Julián Carrillo's microtonal Concertino (March 4, 1927), Carlos Chavez's *H.P.* (March 31, 1932), Aaron Copland's *Dance Symphony* (March 15, 1931), Henry Cowell's Symphony No.12 (March 28, 1960), Morton Gould's *Chorale and Fugue in Jazz* (January 2, 1936), Gretchaninoff's

Symphony No.5 (April 3, 1939), Charles Tomlinson Griffes's *The White Peacock* (June 22, 1919), Alan Hovhaness's *Meditation on Zeami* (October 5, 1964), Harl McDonald's Symphony No.2 (October 4, 1935), Malipiero's *Pause del Silenzio* (April 1, 1927), Leo Ornstein's Piano Concerto No.2 (February 13, 1925), Rachmaninoff's Piano Concerto No.4 (March 18, 1927), Rachmaninoff's *Rhapsody on a Theme by Paganini* (November 7, 1934), Rachmaninoff's Symphony No.3 (November 6, 1936), Wallingford Riegger's *Study in Sonority* (October 30, 1929), Ernest Schelling's *A Victory Ball* (February 23, 1923), Schoenberg's Violin Concerto (December 6, 1940), Cyril Scott's Piano Concerto (November 5, 1920), Edgard Varèse's *Amériques* (April 9, 1926), and Varèse's *Arcana* (April 8, 1927).

The following is representative of Stokowski's many American premieres in Philadelphia: Berg's *Wozzeck* (March 9, 1931), Busoni's *Indian Fantasy* (February 19, 1915), Khachaturian's *Russian Fantasy* (April 1, 1948), Mahler's Symphony No.8 (March 2, 1916), Schoenberg's *Die Glückliche Hand* (April 11, 1930), Schoenberg's *Variations for Orchestra* (1929), Shostakovich's Symphony No.1 (November 2, 1928), Shostakovich's Symphony No.6 (March 20, 1942), Stravinsky's *The Rite of Spring* (March 3, 1922), and Szymanowski's Violin Concerto (November 28, 1924), together with other major works by Elgar, Manuel de Falla, Schoenberg, Scriabin, Sibelius, and Stravinsky.

Continuous innovation and experimentation dramatized Stokowski's concerts in Philadelphia. He was one of the first in America to conduct without a score (long before Toscanini had made it fashionable to do so) and to dispense with a baton. He did not hesitate to use his concerts as a platform from which to scold his audiences for their intolerance to modern music, for their habitual practice of coming late to concerts and leaving early, for causing disturbances during a performance. He experimented with visual colors wedded to music by flashing a series of hues on a screen from a Clavilux while the orchestra performed *Scheherazade* behind a screen. He continually introduced novel and esoteric instruments into his orchestra, such as the Thereminvox (ether music, a pioneer in the creation of electronic sounds), or a Hammond tone-sustaining piano. He was one of the first major conductors to hire women for instruments other than the harp and to take his orchestra on a coast-to-coast tour (1936). At one time he tried to dispense with applause ("the concert hall," he said, "should be like a temple—a temple of music"); on other occasions he wished to eliminate lights on the stage ("music should be heard, not seen"). He dispensed with the post of concert-master by rotating the first violins in that post to give each of them a sense of concertmaster responsibility. He tried to institute a program for the training of his orchestra men as conductors during rehearsals. He allowed his violins to bow freely in a way most natural to each individual performer. He always experimented with new musical idioms: microtonal music, Oriental music, jazz. He orchestrated the music of Johann Sebastian Bach to bring it to a larger audience than it had hitherto known, while refusing to reveal himself as the transcriber. He fashioned "orchestral syntheses" out of the Wagnerian music dramas.

He knew the full value of showmanship, and he used it fully. He adopted a phony Polish accent to accommodate his Polish name. He made himself a man of mystery who kept himself aloof from all except those closest to him. At one rehearsal he burned incense on the stage to set the mood for some Oriental music. At another he startled his musicians by rehearsing while sitting astride a hobbyhorse. One of his concerts was given on a darkened stage except for a single light suspended over his head to create a kind of halo over his golden hair. For another performance he had electricians experiment with backstage lights so that as he conducted the movement of his graceful hands might throw impressive shadows on the back of the stage.

Once he became the idol of the music world, he found his every idiosyncrasy grist for the publicity mill. Widely publicized were his food faddism, his refusal to take any stimulants (even coffee or tea), his indulgence in physical-fitness programs, and his interest in raising flowers, fruits, vegetables, and trees. His religious and nonreligious beliefs inspired comment and controversy. Baptized a Roman Catholic, he became an agnostic and later sought guidance and inspiration from philosophies and religions as varied as theosophy, Buddhism, Anglicanism, and Quaker beliefs. He once revealed that much of his inner strength came from hours of silent contemplation.

Even his marriages produced headlines. His first wife was the American concert pianist Olga Samaroff, whom he married on April 24, 1911. They had a daughter. The marriage lasted a dozen years and they were divorced in 1923. In 1926 Stokowski married an heiress, Evangeline Brewster Johnson of the pharmaceutical house of Johnson and Johnson. This marriage brought him two more daughters before it ended in divorce in 1937. One year after his divorce from his second wife, he made front-page news by going off to Europe with Greta Garbo for several weeks. On April 21, 1945, he married another heiress, Gloria Vanderbilt de Cicco. She was only twenty-one; he was sixty-three. After they had two sons, this marriage too ended in divorce, in 1955.

But in spite of publicity, shenanigans, self-glorification, and experiments that failed to have any lasting merit—and in spite of the fact that in his musical interpretations he sometimes tampered with and vulgarized masterworks—he became one of the world's great conductors, a rare and sensitive artist who brought new dimensions to performances. He had a remarkable dramatic instinct together with a Hellenic devotion to beauty, and he brought to music-making a dynamism and an incandescence that often made his performances of individual compositions unique. Olin Downes put it this way in the New York *Times:* "He may change orchestration as he likes, and in places transgress the limitations of what some consider the best taste. He may alter a tempo or a phrasing to suit himself, and not always in a manner which suits the original intentions or the best interests of the composer. He may, he does, completely bedevil a score or the actual material of a composition. But there is a great conductor, there is the resplendent hymning orchestra."

When the Depression of the early 1930s brought about a decline in income, the Philadelphia Orchestra announced that in 1932 the programs would be free of "debatable music." Stokowski at that time was on vacation. When he returned he called a press conference and said in no uncertain terms that he would "play a modern piece whenever he saw fit to do so and he would play it twice for whoever cared to listen." With the public and critics on Stokowski's side, the directors of the orchestra retreated from their position. Again, in 1934 when an explosion erupted between conductor and management over programming policies, Stokowski handed in his resignation. The ensuing outcry made the directors retreat once again. They gave Stokowski the title of music director which meant that henceforth he would have his own way without question or interference.

Two years later Stokowski resigned. He was impatient with continual disputes with the management. Moreover, he was thinking of opening for himself new areas for the spread of music culture. His resignation became effective in 1938, but he continued to make guest appearances with his orchestra each season until 1941. In 1941, his disagreements with the management grew so bitter that after conducting a performance of Bach's *Passion According to St. Matthew* he left the stage without taking any bows. He vowed never again to return to that dais. It took nineteen years to induce him to change his mind and return for guest appearances.

One of the new areas Stokowski planned to explore was motion pictures. He became the first American symphony conductor to appear on the screen. In *The Big Broadcast of 1937* (1936) he conducted a symphony orchestra in two Bach compositions. "I go to Hollywood," he said at the time, "to face a great spiritual challenge." A year later he appeared as himself in *100 Men and a Girl* starring Deanna Durbin. He not only conducted an orchestra in symphonic works but also assumed a speaking part. *Fantasia* (1940) was his most ambitious effort to bring great music to motion pictures. This was a feature-length Walt Disney cartoon in which the music of Beethoven, Dukas, Stravinsky, Mussorgsky, and Bach, among other composers, was performed on the sound track by an orchestra conducted by Stokowski while animated cartoons appeared on the screen in ballet sequences and descriptive or dramatic episodes. In 1947 Stokowski once again appeared as himself on the screen in a movie—in one sequence in *Carnegie Hall.*

Another area which he explored fully was radio broadcasting. On October 6, 1929, he had been the first major American conductor to offer a symphonic program of concert-hall standards on a coast-to-coast radio broadcast. After that concert he told the radio audience: "We have been playing good music and that is the only kind we will play. I will not play any popular music. If you do not like this, write and tell us and we will discontinue broadcasting." But he

did not discontinue broadcasting; on the contrary, he intensified his efforts to spread great symphonic music over the air. In 1953 he conducted the CBS Orchestra over the CBS network in a series called "20th Century Concert Hall."

He also intensified his efforts on recordings. He made his first recording in 1916 for RCA Victor, a single disk. His first 78 rpm album was Dvořák's *Symphony from the New World* in 1926. Throughout all the changes which affected the industry after that—electrical recording, the long-playing record, stereophonic recording—Stokowski continued to record the basic repertory of symphonic music, sometimes for RCA Victor, sometimes for Columbia. In 1971 he negotiated a new contract with RCA; his first release in 1973 under the new arrangement was Dvořák's *Symphony from the New World*—the album contained a copy of his 1926 recording of the same work. In 1976, though he was ninety-four, he signed a six-year contract with CBS; the first session was devoted to Tchaikovsky's *Aurora's Wedding*. At the signing of this contract an executive of CBS explained that plans were under way to record Stokowski's one-hundredth-birthday concert. In 1965 Stokowski's recording of Ives's Symphony No.4 for Columbia earned a Grammy from the National Academy of Recording Arts and Sciences.

In motion pictures, in radio broadcasting, and in the recording studio Stokowski worked just as long and hard in the engineer's laboratories as on the conductor's platform, always experimenting with new ways of creating a more authentic orchestral sound.

There was still one more road Stokowski wished to travel when he became free of his directorial duties in Philadelphia: He wanted to help develop young talent in music and to help train young people as orchestra players. He had revealed his interest in youngsters in Philadelphia when he inaugurated youth concerts, making the Philadelphia Orchestra one of the first of America's great symphonic organizations to do so. At those youth concerts, he had turned over the full administration of the concerts to young people: he had them help him plan his programs; he had them write the program notes, handle the publicity, and perform ushering and box-office chores.

When he left the Philadelphia Orchestra, Stokowski could have had for the asking the music directorship of any one of several of the world's great orchestras. Instead, in 1940 he hurled his remarkable energies and talent into organizing the All-American Youth Orchestra to give young people an opportunity to perform orchestral music. The average age of the musicians in this new orchestra was eighteen and two of the members were just fourteen. These players were selected by an elimination process from among fifteen thousand musicians from all states. After several preliminary concerts, Stokowski took the orchestra on a goodwill tour of South America. Upon returning to the United States the All-American Orchestra under Stokowski gave public concerts and made several recordings.

In 1944, still concerned with young people, Stokowski founded in New York City a new orchestra made up mostly of nonprofessional and inexperienced performers: the New York City Symphony. For one season he conducted its concerts, starting it off on a successful footing. Then he turned the orchestra over to the twenty-seven-year-old Leonard Bernstein.

Busy as he was in all these endeavors, Stokowski did not completely absent himself from the concert stage. From 1941 to 1944 he was coconductor of the NBC Symphony with Toscanini. In 1944 and 1945 he was the music director of the Hollywood Bowl Concerts in Los Angeles. From 1947 to 1950 he was coconductor of the New York Philharmonic. From 1955 to 1960 he was principal conductor, then music director, of the Houston Symphony. He broke his contract with the Houston Symphony over an issue concerning race, not music. Having scheduled a performance of Schoenberg's *Gurre-Lieder,* he invited a black choir to be one of the three choral groups called for by that score. When the management refused to allow black singers to mingle with whites on the stage, he refused to give any more concerts in Houston. He was never sued for breach of contract, and an explanatory letter he dispatched to a major local newspaper was never published.

He also made guest appearances both in the United States and in Europe. In 1939 he appeared as guest conductor of many European symphony orchestras. He was in Poland when Nazi Germany invaded that country to begin World War II. While he was trying to get out of Poland, his train was bombed by Nazi planes half a dozen times. However, he did finally manage to reach the United States unharmed. Dur-

ing the summer of 1958 he made his first appearances in the Soviet Union, leading three of the major Soviet orchestras. From 1959 to 1961 he was a guest conductor with the New York City Opera. There he led performances of such novelties as Orff's *Carmina Burana,* Monteverdi's *L'Orfeo,* and Luigi Dallapiccola's *Il Prigionero.* On February 24, 1961, crippled from a hip accident and forced to make his way to the orchestra pit on crutches, he made his bow at the Metropolitan Opera in *Turandot* to conduct what Douglas Watt described in the *Daily News* as "a powerful, magical performance." He returned to the Metropolitan with *Turandot* a season later. On April 16, 1966, he was one of the guest conductors at the farewell performance of the Metropolitan Opera company at its old auditorium prior to leaving for new quarters at the Lincoln Center for the Performing Arts.

In his eightieth year, in 1962, Stokowski organized a new orchestra, the American Symphony. Its first concert was held in New York City on October 15. This orchestra had been formed to afford "opportunity to highly gifted musicians regardless of age, sex, or color, and to offer concerts of great music within the means of everyone." After its first concert, one New York critic exclaimed in print: "Stokowski has done it again." Once again, as with the All-American Youth Orchestra, the emphasis was on youth; the average age of the musicians was twenty-seven. During the next decade the orchestra extended the number of its subscription concerts and often gave challenging performances of twentieth century music, performances of the highest professional standard.

Wherever he went, Stokowski was a powerful propagandist for new music. With the All-American Youth Orchestra he gave the world premiere of Henry Cowell's *Tales of Our Countryside* (May 11, 1941); with the NBC Symphony, the world premieres of George Antheil's Symphony No.4 (February 13, 1944), Schoenberg's Piano Concerto (February 1, 1944), and the American premiere of Prokofiev's *Alexander Nevsky* (March 7, 1949); with the New York City Symphony, the world premiere of Anis Fuleihan's Concerto for Thereminvox and Orchestra (February 26, 1945); with the Houston Symphony, the world premiere of Alan Hovhaness's *Mysterious Mountain* (October 31, 1955) and the American premiere of Orff's *Trionfo di Afrodite* (April 21, 1956); with the New York

Philharmonic the world premieres of Messiaen's *Hymne* (March 13, 1947), Prokofiev's Symphony No.6 (November 24, 1949), Carl Ruggles's *Organum* (November 24, 1949), Elie Siegmeister's *Prairie Legend* (January 18, 1947) and Symphony No.1 (October 30, 1947); with the American Symphony the world premieres of Charles Ives's Symphony No.4 (April 26, 1965), Panufnik's *Epitaph for the Victims of Katyn* (November 17, 1968), and Karl Weigl's Symphony No.5 (October 27, 1968). And this is only a partial listing.

Stokowski's ninetieth birthday was celebrated on April 18, 1972, at the Hotel Plaza. He came late to the reception because he had been busy that morning rehearsing Beethoven's Symphony No.9 with the American Symphony Orchestra. At the party musicians performed; Mayor John V. Lindsay presented Stokowski with the Mayor's Award (a star-shaped Steuben paperweight) and Stokowski received an additional surprise gift of a first edition (dated 1826) of Beethoven's Symphony No.9. When, following these festive proceedings, Stokowski was asked what he looked forward to most eagerly, he replied quickly: "The next rehearsal, of course."

Soon after this event, he announced his retirement as the music director of the American Symphony. Not long after his resignation, the orchestra announced it was suspending operations due to lack of financial support. (It was, however, revived a year or so later.) Stokowski left the United States for permanent residence in London. There, on June 14, 1972, he led a concert of the London Symphony at the Royal Festival Hall in a performance marking the sixtieth anniversary of his first appearance with this same orchestra in 1912—the program was a replica of the 1912 one. "Anybody can live to be ninety," wrote Peter Stadlen in the *Daily Telegraph,* "but only Leopold Stokowski will obtain quite such ravishing playing as the London Symphony Orchestra feted him with." The *Guardian* described him as "more than ever a unique, barely credible figure, controversial still, but conveying his fire, his authority with the urgency of a man half a century younger." This performance was recorded by London Records.

Stokowski's last public concert took place in London in 1974. In all he had given more than seven thousand performances during a seventy-two-year career. After that he devoted his time exclusively to recordings of major works by Brahms, Tchaikovsky, Dvořák, Rachmaninoff, and others.

In 1977, after suffering a mild virus infection, Stokowski succumbed to a heart attack at his house at Nether Wallop, a village in Hampshire, England, on September 13. Following a funeral oration by the former Prime Minister of England, Edward Heath, Stokowski was buried in St. Marylebone Cemetery in North London next to the graves of his father and sister.

France made him a Chevalier of the Legion of Honor; Poland, a Knight of Polonia Restituta; Rumania, Officer of the Crown. In 1966 he was awarded the Golden Door Award of the American Council for Nationalities Service, an award given by the Boston branch for helpfulness to new arrivals to America. At that time President Lyndon B. Johnson sent him a congratulatory message reading: "His name has become synonymous with artistic excellence in the field of music. Most of all this nation owes him its gratitude for his distinguished contributions over so many years to the life of the mind and the spirit in these United States." In 1968 he received the Gold Baton Award from the American Symphony Orchestra League "in appreciation of the imaginative leadership he has given to symphony orchestral development in America, and in recognition of his initiation and direction of the American Symphony Orchestra's program of study and career opportunities for young conductors and orchestra players." In 1972 he received the Yale University Howland Medal.

Stokowski was the composer of several compositions for orchestra and for the organ. One of these is the *Reverie,* for orchestra, which was listed on his programs as having been composed by Slavichi. At the end of a concert with the American Symphony Orchestra *da camera* at Town Hall, on March 1, 1972, after he had played it as an encore, he disclosed to his audience that it was his own piece, something he had written as a student. He was the author of *Music for All of Us* (1943).

ABOUT: Blaukopf, K. Great Conductors; Ewen, D. Dictators of the Baton; O'Connell, C. The Other Side of the Record; Robinson, P. Stokowski; Schonberg, H. C. The Great Conductors; Stoddard, H. Symphony Conductors of the U.S.A. *Periodicals*—Hi-Fi/ Stereo Review, May 1968; High Fidelity/Musical America, March 1978; Musical America, February 1959; New York Times, September 14, 1977; New York Times Magazine, December 6, 1964.

Teresa Stratas

1938–

TERESA STRATAS

Teresa Stratas (originally Anastasia Strataki), soprano, was born in Toronto, Canada, on May 26, 1938. Her parents, Emanuel and Argero Teregis Strataki, were of Greek extraction. Shortly after Teresa's birth, her father acquired a restaurant in Oshawa, a town eighteen miles from Toronto. There, when she was just four, she entertained the guests by singing such popular American tunes as "Pistol Packin' Mama," collecting as her first fees small monetary gifts the patrons gave her. In later years she said, "To keep me occupied, my parents used to pack my lunch and sit me in the movie house next door to the restaurant. I saw hundreds of pictures including every musical Betty Grable ever made. I used to memorize the songs which I sang for the customers."

When she was ten she sang in a trio made up of her brother Nick, a violinist, and her sister Mary, a pianist. She was soon performing at birthday parties and the festivals that were part of Greek tradition.

In 1953 she made her professional debut over a local Toronto radio station. She sang popular tunes over the radio for almost two years, and then in 1954 she appeared on television. A station technician advised her to cultivate her voice, suggesting she try for a scholarship at the Royal Conservatory of the University of Toronto. For the audition for this scholarship she was asked to sing an aria or *Lied*. Since she knew neither, she sang Arditi's "Il Bacio" and Jerome Kern's "Smoke Gets in Your Eyes." Her voice, in spite of her limited repertory, won her a four-year scholarship at the Royal Conservatory. There she studied voice with Irene Jessner, one-time soprano of the Metropolitan Opera. Teresa completed a four-year course in three years. "I thought I was going to learn songs I could use on TV and radio," she later said to Emily Coleman in an interview for the New York *Times.* "But for months I sang nothing but 'la,la,la,la, las.' I thought this was ridiculous. I had a low voice and I couldn't understand why she wanted me to have higher notes. I thought they were wasting their money." But when she was sixteen, she heard an opera for the first time, a performance of *La Bohème* given by the Metropolitan

Opera in Toronto in a performance starring Renata Tebaldi. She went back to her lessons "with a different attitude," as she put it. "Those years I spent in the movie house in a world of make-believe were now put together with singing and music—and all the pieces in the puzzle fell into place."

On October 16, 1958, Stratas made her opera debut with the Toronto Opera as Mimi in *La Bohème.* At that time a local Toronto critic referred to the twenty-year-old soprano as "the baby Callas." One year later she emerged successfully from the Metropolitan Opera Auditions competition with a contract. She made her debut in the minor role of Pousette in *Manon* on October 28, 1959. More important assignments for her that first season included the roles of Barberina in *The Marriage of Figaro,* a Flower Maiden in *Parsifal,* Zerlina in *Don Giovanni,* and Inez in *Il Trovatore.* But for the most part she sang, as she recalls, "every peasant girl and maid you can think of and learned what to do and what not to do. It was great experience, but I had enough of that. I needed to do something else. I was not happy, and I asked to be let out of my contract." A fortuitous accident, however, kept her at the Metropolitan Opera. Lucine Amara who was slated to appear as Liù in *Turandot* on March 9, 1961, became ill and Stratas replaced her. She gave such a striking performance that from then on she was allowed to take over major roles in the ensuing years: Mimi in *La Bohème,* Nedda in *I Pagliacci,* Yniold in *Pelléas and Mélisande,* the Composer in *Ariadne auf Naxos,* Cio-Cio-San in *Madama Butterfly,* Despina in *Così fan Tutte,* Desdemona in *Otello,* Antonia in *The Tales of Hoffmann,* Cherubino and Susanna in *The Marriage of Figaro,* Lisa in *The Queen of Spades,* Marguerite in *Faust,* the title role of *La Périchole,* Gretel in *Hansel and Gretel,* and Mélisande in *Pelléas and Mélisande.* On January 23, 1964, she created for the United States the role of Sardula in Menotti's *The Last Savage.*

"Not only does she continue to sing beautifully in each new venture," wrote Miles Kastendieck in the New York *Journal,* "but she has a knack for proving herself just right for the role. This consistent combination of vocal and dramatic excellence singles her out among the new generation of singing-actresses." In the *New Yorker* Winthrop Sargeant called Stratas "one of the most impressive finds that Mr. Bing has made. . . . It is stating the obvious to note that she has a beautiful, well-controlled voice and is an unusually gifted actress. She is more than such a statement indicates—an artist in whom the fusion of vocal gifts and personality is complete, so that every phrase is not only musical but an expression of a distinct and lively personality. Miss Stratas puts her stamp on every role she sings, and comes across the footlights with a special personal involvement."

On August 19, 1961, Stratas created the title role in Peggy Granville Hicks's *Nausicaa* at the Herod Atticus Theater in Athens. That year, too, she made her Covent Garden debut as Mimi —"one of the most touching we have heard since Albanese and Sayão were in their prime," remarked one London critic. In 1962 she made her first appearance in Moscow in a recital, inspiring a twenty-minute ovation; since then she has starred in productions at the Bolshoi Opera in Moscow and at the Leningrad Opera. On June 18, 1962, she was heard for the first time at La Scala as Queen Isabella in the world's first staged production of Manuel de Falla's *L'Atlántida.* Her debut with the Munich Opera in the spring of 1965 as Violetta in *La Traviata* "swept the packed house into a record forty-three minutes of tumultuous applause," *Time* reported.

The year 1966 saw her undertake a concert tour of the United States, give a recital of rare music with the Esterhazy Orchestra in New York, make a concert appearance in Verdi's rarely heard *Giovanna d'Arco* with the American Opera Society in New York, and sing in *The Marriage of Figaro* when the Metropolitan Opera paid a visit to Paris. Among the major opera companies, other than those already mentioned, in which she has been heard successfully are the Deutsche Oper in Berlin, the Hamburg Opera, the Frankfort Opera, the Vienna State Opera, the Paris Opéra, the Amsterdam Opera, the San Francisco Opera, and the Philadelphia Lyric Opera. She has also appeared at the Salzburg Festival and starred in motion picture productions of *Otello, Salome, Eugene Onegin, La Rondine,* and *The Bartered Bride.*

Her association with the conductor Zubin Mehta, both personal and artistic, was for a long time a close one. She appeared with him in a performance of Verdi's Requiem at the Festival of Two Worlds in Spoleto, Italy, during the summer of 1966. In 1967, under Mehta's direction, she shared the stage with Jon Vickers in a production of *Otello* at Expo '67 in Montreal.

Stratas has made numerous appearances over television networks, in recitals, and as a soloist with symphony orchestras. She makes her home in an apartment at the Ansonia Hotel in New York City, next door to another diva—Eleanor Steber. She enjoys reading, designing and sewing her own clothes, and collecting antiques.

ABOUT: New York Times, January 22, 1967; Opera News, December 25, 1965.

Richard Strauss

1864–1949

Richard Strauss's position among twentieth century composers has tended to obscure the fact that he also enjoyed a long and productive career as a conductor and that he was a remarkable interpreter of Mozart, Beethoven, Wagner, and his own masterworks.

Strauss was born to wealth and culture in Munich, on June 11, 1864. His father, Franz Strauss, was one of Germany's finest horn players; he performed in the orchestra when Richard Wagner rehearsed *Tristan and Isolde* for its premiere. An outspoken enemy of Wagner and his artistic principles, Franz Strauss participated in, and sometimes even instigated, the cabals in Munich against the master. In 1883, when Wag-

---

Strauss: shtrous

RICHARD STRAUSS

ner's death was announced to the men of the Munich Opera orchestra, all of them rose in silent tribute, but Franz Strauss remained seated. He early infected his son with his own anti-Wagner feelings, but he lived to see Richard grow into a passionate Wagnerite and, as a composer, to become an extension of Wagner's post-Romantic style.

Richard was extraordinarily precocious in music. He was four when his mother, Josephine Pschorr Strauss—daughter of the wealthy Munich brewer—gave him his first piano lessons. He proved so adept that his mother soon decided to send him for more professional instruction to August Tombo, harpist of the court orchestra. In his sixth year he was already composing; his first piece was a polka for the piano. In 1872 he began studying the violin with Benno Walter and from 1875 to 1880 he took lessons in composition with F. W. Meyer. In all his music studies he made extraordinary progress. He was composing music in many different forms, and he was doing equally well in his academic studies at the Gymnasium, which he had entered when he was ten. "Whatever he does learn gives him pleasure," reported one of his teachers, "and inspires him to greater industry. . . . There aren't many students who show as much sense of duty, talent, and liveliness as this boy."

Upon graduation from the Gymnasium in 1882, Richard entered the University of Munich. For a year he took courses in esthetics, philosophy, history of civilization, and Shakespeare. By this time he had already accumulated an impressive repertory of his own compositions. His first publication appeared in 1880: a *Festmarch* for orchestra, written when he was twelve. A few of his other works received important performances: three of his songs were sung by Cornelie Meysenheim in Munich in 1880, and a string quartet and a symphony were introduced in Munich in 1881. On December 13, 1884, his second symphony received its world premiere in the United States, conducted in New York by Theodore Thomas.

One of his works, the *Serenade for Wind Instruments,* in E-flat, attracted the interest of Hans von Bülow, who had his orchestra in Meiningen perform its premiere in 1882. Von Bülow's continued interest in Strauss led him to commission the young composer to write for the Meiningen Orchestra the *Suite for Wind Instruments,* in B-flat major. Strauss made his conducting debut performing this work in Meiningen. Soon after that von Bülow engaged him to become his assistant conductor. It was an extraordinary appointment since he thus far had had virtually no experience as a conductor. He was delighted. He considered the post "most valuable and ideal" and looked forward eagerly "to be able, by attending all . . . rehearsals, to study closely . . . [von Bülow's] interpretation of our symphonic masterpieces."

In the fall of 1885 he succeeded von Bülow as the full-time conductor of the Meiningen Orchestra, making his debut in his new post on October 18, 1885. The program was made up of Beethoven's *Coriolan Overture* and Seventh Symphony, a Mozart Piano Concerto that Strauss himself performed and in which he used his own cadenzas, and his own Symphony in F minor. Hans von Bülow expressed the opinion that he conducted "with unbelievable security." Brahms, who was in the audience, told the "young man" that his symphony was "quite pretty." During his one season in Meiningen, Strauss was given opportunities to conduct a large repertory of classical and romantic masterworks, including Mozart's Requiem, Beethoven's Symphony No.2, Schubert's *Unfinished Symphony,* and Berlioz' *Harold in Italy.*

Strauss left Meiningen in April of 1886 and the following August he was made third Kapellmeister of the Munich Royal Opera. His three years in Munich were his initiation into conducting opera, though the main repertory was assigned to the principal conductors and he was assigned such less desirable operas as Boieldieu's *Jean de Paris,* Heinrich Marschner's *Der Templer und die Jüdin,* and Cherubini's *Der Wasserträger.*

In his next post—music director of the Weimar Opera and the Weimar Court Orchestra from 1889 to 1894—Strauss was given ample opportunities to work with masterworks close to his heart: Mozart, Weber, and Wagner and, on December 31, 1893, the world premiere of *Hansel and Gretel.* He was beginning to throw upon these and other works a new illumination that gave the first indication of his coming powers as a conductor.

While all this was occurring, he was making strides as a composer that put him in the forefront of post-Romantic composers of the post-Wagnerian era. His first tone poems, with which he proved himself the most provocative composer since Wagner, were *Macbeth* (1887), *Don Juan* (1889), and *Death and Transfiguration* (1890). His first volume of songs, published in 1882, contained three masterpieces—"Allerseelen," "Zueignung," and "Die Nacht." These found worthy successors in "Morgen" and "Ständchen" in 1886. His first opera, *Guntram,* in the Wagnerian tradition, was introduced in Weimar on May 10, 1894.

In 1891 Strauss made his debut at the Bayreuth Festival with *Tannhäuser;* by this time his conversion to the cult of Wagner was complete —he remained faithful to it as long as he lived. In 1894 and again in 1895 Strauss endeared himself to Berlin music lovers by conducting the Berlin Philharmonic Orchestra.

He left Weimar in 1894 to return to Munich to become one of the two principal conductors of the Munich Royal Opera (the other was Hermann Levi). This time he was given the cream of the Mozart and Wagnerian repertory. He conducted *Die Meistersinger* for the first time and made his performances of *Così fan Tutte* so luminous and penetrating that this opera, long neglected, joined Mozart's more famous operas in general popularity. Strauss also conducted symphony concerts in Munich. Futhermore, he made numerous guest appearances as conductor not only in Berlin but outside Germany, in Switzerland, Hungary, Russia, Belgium, Holland, England, and France.

On September 10, 1894, Strauss married Pauline de Ahna, a soprano who on several occasions had appeared under his direction at the Munich Royal Opera; she had created the role of Freihild in Strauss's *Guntram.* At one of the rehearsals involving Strauss and de Ahna, they disagreed so violently about the interpretation of a certain passage in *Tannhäuser* that she threw the piano score at his head and rushed off the stage to her dressing room. Strauss, furious, followed her. When he emerged from her dressing room he calmly announced to his fellow musicians: "I have just become engaged to Fräulein de Ahna." As a woman, she was strong-willed and opinionated; as Strauss's wife she dominated his life completely, arranging his social engagements, taking care of his business affairs, assuming full charge of the family purse, and ordering him about in his daily routines as if he were a schoolboy. Strauss meekly submitted to her. Their only child, a son, was born in 1897.

Strauss reached his prime as conductor between 1898 and 1918 when, succeeding Felix Weingartner, he was appointed music director of the Royal Opera in Berlin. With his remarkable performances of Mozart and Wagner and his hardly less brilliant presentations of the Italian repertory, the Berlin Royal Opera entered upon one of its most illustrious periods. He also brought distinction to the symphony auditorium, beginning in 1901 when he became the music director of the Berlin Tonkünstler Orchestra which specialized in modern works by German and Austrian composers. Subsequently he served as music director of the Berlin Philharmonic.

As a composer he had also reached his prime, with his later tone poems—*Till Eulenspiegel's Merry Pranks* (1895), *Thus Spake Zarathustra* (1896), *Don Quixote* (1898), and *A Hero's Life* (1899)—and with his first operatic masterworks, *Salome* (1905), *Elektra* (1909), and *Der Rosenkavalier* (1911).

His first appearance in the United States occurred on February 27, 1904, when he led the Wetzler Orchestra. On March 4 he conducted *Don Quixote,* with young Pablo Casals playing the cello obbligato, and on March 31 he directed the world premiere of his own *Sinfonia Domestica.* Richard Aldrich described Strauss's conducting in the New York *Times:* "His methods . . . are extremely reserved. His beat is quiet, but firm; he has few significant gestures, except at some of the most important climaxes when he summons the power of the brass instruments through an insistent beckoning with his left hand, of which otherwise he makes but small use. . . . He evidently carries the substance of his music and all of its manifold details easily in his head, for he made only casual references to the printed pages before him. In fact, a conductor who exhibits so little of the spectacular and so much of concentration in his work has not lately been seen here."

In addition to concerts with the Wetzler Orchestra, Strauss made guest appearances with the New York Philharmonic, the Chicago Symphony, the Philadelphia Orchestra, and the Boston Symphony. He was also heard as a piano accompanist for his wife in her recitals. On April 26 Strauss and his wife were received at the White House by President and Mrs. Theodore Roosevelt.

On his fiftieth birthday, in 1914, Strauss's position as the first composer of his time was confirmed by the many honors showered on him. A street in Munich was named after him and Oxford University awarded him an honorary doctorate in music. (He had previously received an honorary doctorate from Heidelberg University in 1902.) With World War I, however, Strauss came upon far less happy times. His fortune in England, estimated at about a quarter of a million dollars, was seized; and to add to his financial difficulties, the war had greatly reduced the number of performances of his works outside Germany and greatly curtailed his travels. He had sufficient financial resources left in Germany to keep his family in style both at his home in Berlin and at his villa at Garmisch-Partenkirchen in the Bavarian Alps; but his excessive frugality, one of his less endearing qualities as a man, made any financial loss a devastating blow.

After the war, from 1919 to 1924, Strauss was the principal conductor and the music director, with Franz Schalk, of the Vienna State Opera. During his first postwar season in Vienna he conducted restudied performances of *Tristan and Isolde, Fidelio, The Magic Flute,* and his own *Ariadne auf Naxos* and *Der Rosenkavalier.* After that, as George R. Marek notes in his biography *Richard Strauss: The Life of a Non-Hero,* "he accomplished remarkable things, such as a new staging of *Lohengrin,* conceived musically as a lyrical work, free of the usual Wagnerian barking; a new *Ring* cycle; *Der Freischütz,* with Lotte Lehmann as Agathe, Elisabeth Schumann as Annchen and Michael Bohnen as Kas-

par. . . . For his favorite *Così fan Tutte* he acted as both conductor and stage director." In addition to his work at the Opera, in collaboration with Franz Schalk, he inaugurated in 1920 the Vienna Festival Weeks, which became an annual event, and in 1920 and 1923 he took contingents of the Vienna State Opera and the Vienna Philharmonic on tours of South America.

So highly was he esteemed in Vienna that the city presented him with a parcel of land from the Imperial Belvedere Palace grounds so that he might build a home where he could live four months a year. In 1924 mounting hostility between Strauss and Schalk led Strauss to hand in his resignation. However, in December 1926 he was back on the conductor's stand of the Vienna State Opera to conduct *Elektra.*

Between the two world wars Strauss continued to devote his musical activity equally to composing and conducting. As a composer, his most significant contributions were in opera, most notably *Die Frau ohne Schatten* (1917) and *Arabella* (1930). His conducting duties took him to Berlin, Budapest, and Bucharest for guest appearances. In 1921 he made his second and final tour of the United States, opening on October 31, 1921, as a guest conductor of the Philadelphia Orchestra in a program made up entirely of his own works. Richard Aldrich reported in the New York *Times:* "He was greeted with a roar of applause that persisted till he had bowed many times. . . . The applause was greater after each number; and after the second one, there were extensive tributes of flowers and a wreath tipped up with little flags of black, white and yellow laid upon the stage." During this tour he also conducted the New York Philharmonic, and he appeared with Elisabeth Schumann in an all-Strauss recital. His last American appearance was at the Hippodrome Theater in New York on New Year's Eve 1921 with the Philadelphia Orchestra. "There is no need to mention again here what was so continually evident in the concerts, Dr. Strauss' skill and authority as a conductor," wrote Richard Aldrich in the New York *Times.* "His command of the orchestra is remarkable; the influence of his beat and his indications, however conveyed, unerring. He is a conductor of great power, skill and finesse, moulding his orchestra to his wishes with an extraordinary richness and clearness of detail, subtly graded nuance, dynamic adjustment and suppleness of tempo."

With the rise of the Nazi regime in Germany in 1933, Strauss—as the foremost musician in Germany—was eagerly taken into the Nazi fold. He was appointed president of the Third Reich Music Chamber on November 15, 1933, and he was called upon to serve as president of the German Federation of Musicians. When the Nazis embarked upon their program to expunge all Jewish influences from Germany's musical life, Strauss cooperated by replacing the deposed Bruno Walter at a concert of the Leipzig Gewandhaus Orchestra and substituting for Toscanini when that conductor announced that he would not conduct at Bayreuth because of the Nazi regime. In 1934 Strauss conducted at the Salzburg Festival at a time when Austria was mourning the death of Chancellor Engelbert Dollfuss, believed to have been murdered by the Nazis. Strauss accepted with delight and gratitude the gift of the autographed photograph Hitler sent him in celebration of the composer's seventieth birthday. But George R. Marek maintains, "Strauss was not a Nazi. He was not an anti-Nazi. He was one of those who let it happen. He was one of those who played along. He was one of those who thought, 'Well they won't practice as viciously as they preach.' He thought so until the hoodlums touched him personally." Marek adds that "Strauss was politically naive, that indeed he was politically illiterate."

The marriage of convenience between Strauss and Nazi officialdom was of short duration. The Nazis were not happy at the fact that Strauss's son Franz married a Jewess. They could not forget that all the Strauss operatic masterworks that were getting such a wide circulation had librettos by a Jew—Hugo von Hofmannsthal. And they were angered when Strauss completed a new opera, *Die Schweigsame Frau,* to a libretto by still another Jew, Stefan Zweig. Hitler and Goebbels were conspicuously absent when this opera was introduced in Dresden on June 24, 1935. And the tempers of the Nazis rose further on discovering that Strauss had asked Zweig for more librettos and had told Zweig that by the time those operas were written "the gang now in power" would be out of office. *Die Schweigsame Frau* was removed from the boards. Strauss was relieved of his official positions and required to go into retirement in his Garmisch-Partenkirchen villa. There he completed a new opera, *Der Friedenstag,* which the Nazi party condemned for its antiwar stance.

During World War II Strauss lived partly at Garmisch-Partenkirchen, where he was virtually under house arrest for his antiwar statements, and partly in Switzerland. The war years were difficult for Strauss, since his royalties were choked off and his foreign income impounded. But he remained productive, completing two more operas—*Die Liebe der Danae* and *Capriccio*—and some instrumental music.

After the war Strauss visited London to conduct the Philharmonia Orchestra in a concert of his compositions at the Royal Albert Hall during a Strauss festival in 1947. A year later, on June 8, 1948, in Munich, a denazification court cleared him of all charges of having collaborated with the Nazis. He regained the position in German music that he had occupied before the war, and his eighty-fifth birthday was celebrated with festive concerts throughout the world of music. He was made honorary citizen of Bayreuth and of Garmisch, and he received an honorary doctorate in music from the University of Munich. Asked what he would most like for a birthday gift, he replied he wanted to hear a performance of his *Le Bourgeois Gentilhomme* just once more. That performance took place in Munich on June 13, 1949. A month later he conducted for the last time—a passage from his last opera, *Capriccio,* broadcast over the radio.

Richard Strauss died of uremia at his villa at Garmisch-Partenkirchen on September 8, 1949. A national day of mourning was decreed by the Bavarian government on the day Strauss was cremated. His ashes were buried in his garden in Garmisch-Partenkirchen.

As a man, Strauss left much to be desired. He was opportunistic, excessively vain, devoid of generosity, petty in his business dealings, and a notorious penny pincher. His favorite pastime was a card game called Skat at which he was so skillful that he was invariably the winner of large sums of money, sometimes at the expense of musicians who worked under him and could not afford the losses. In Bayreuth in 1933, when he insisted that the orchestral men play Skat with him and they objected, Winfried Wagner secretly told them that she would reimburse them for their losses.

Strauss was an enthusiast of the pictorial arts and of ancient Greek and Egyptian monuments. He was a prodigious reader.

The correspondence between Strauss and Hugo von Hofmannsthal, his librettist, was published in the volume *A Working Friendship* (1961).

In 1976, Vanguard reissued recordings of the Vienna Philharmonic conducted by Richard Strauss in several of his own tone poems. Writing in *Stereo Review,* Irving Kolodin reported: "This may be the most compelling effort ever recorded by a composer in his own behalf. . . . The result is the rarest kind of musical experience: an outpouring of pure artistic essence, unmarred by mannerism, ego, or intrusive, counterproductive 'personality.' "

ABOUT: Del Mar, N. Richard Strauss: A Critical Commentary of His Life and Works; Mann, W. Richard Strauss; Marek, G. R. Richard Strauss: The Life of a Non-Hero; Petzoldt, R. and Crass, E. Richard Strauss: His Life in Pictures; Rolland, R. Souvenirs sur Richard Strauss; Ronald, C. Richard Strauss.

JOAN SUTHERLAND

Joan Sutherland

1926–

Joan Sutherland, soprano acclaimed for the art of bel canto, was born in Sydney, Australia, on November 7, 1926. Her father, McDonald Sutherland, was a tailor who, as she once remarked, "was tone deaf and couldn't sing 'God Save the Queen.' " He died of a heart attack when Joan was six. But her mother, Muriel, was a trained singer who had given up a possible concert career for domesticity. Whenever her mother practised singing, Joan would sit beside her at the piano and listen raptly. "I used to copy her," she recalls. "I would do her scales and exercises with her. This formed the basis of my technique. But mother did not make me go at singing. She thought it wrong to train the voice too young."

Besides vocalizing with her mother, Joan was influenced early by the recordings of great operatic singers that her cousin, John, would bring with him whenever he visited the Sutherlands. She came to know the styles and techniques of singers such as Caruso, Melba, and Tetrazzini, and also to know many of opera's famous arias.

When she was eight she was sent to St. Catherine's Church of England School at Waverly for her academic education. She was twelve when she heard her first concert at the Town Hall in Sydney; at that time she made a personal vow that she, too, would someday sing in the same auditorium. During World War II she helped the war effort by knitting sweaters and scarves for Australian soldiers, doing volunteer work in canteens, and helping make camouflage nets. Upon graduation from St. Catherine's, she decided to complete her schooling at a secretarial school so that she might have a skill at which to earn her living; she also went to a school for tailoring to be able to make her own clothes. She got her first job in 1944 as a typist for the Council for Scientific and Industrial Research at Sydney University. Later she held other jobs, including one for a firm of country suppliers and a wholesaler of wines.

One day she read a notice that a John and Aida Dickens were offering two-year scholarships in voice for deserving students. She auditioned for them by singing "Softly Awakes My Heart" and won a scholarship. At the suggestion of the Dickenses, she attended the Rathbone Academy of Dramatic Art for the study of languages and stage deportment.

Occasionally she performed at the monthly concerts of the Affiliated Music Clubs of New South Wales. One of her accompanists was Richard Bonynge, a young pianist slated to go to England on a scholarship for the Royal College of Music in London. In later years he dramatically changed the course of both her professional and her personal life.

When the two-year free tuition with the Dickenses was over, the scholarship was extended indefinitely. Her progress allowed her in 1947 to make her debut in a concert performance of Purcell's *Dido and Aeneas.* In 1949, singing "Ritorna vincitor" from *Aida* she entered and won first prize in the *Sun* aria contest sponsored by one of Australia's newspapers. Shortly after that she captured the first prize of one thousand pounds in the Mobil Quest contest sponsored by the Vacuum Oil Company, performing "Voi lo sapete" from *Cavalleria Rusticana* and "Dich teure Halle" from *Tannhäuser.* With the money from these awards, supplemented by an additional one-thousand-pound gift from her cousin, John, she made plans to go to London for further study. Before she left, Eugene Goossens, the director of the New South Wales Conservatory in Sydney, assigned her the title role in his opera *Judith,* presented at the Conservatory. "This is Florence Austral's logical successor," he said after her performance. She also gave a concert for her own benefit at the Sydney Concert Hall, sponsored by the Vacuum Oil Company.

Sutherland arrived in London in August 1951. She entered the Opera School of the Royal College of Music as a vocal student of Clive Carey and for instruction in elementary ballet. At the College her friendship with Richard Bonynge was revived. He visited her regularly, shared the evening meal with her, and then played the piano. Before long he started to coach her. While doing so, he tried to persuade her that she was not meant to sing dramatic roles in Wagner or Puccini but that she had to develop her upper tones for coloratura singing. "We had some good rows," Bonynge recalls. "In doing her vocalizing with her, I'd make her stand on the other side of the room and get her to sing higher and higher. One day I called her over, plucked the note she had just sung, and said, 'Listen to that.' It was E-flat. She was very surprised."

She auditioned for Covent Garden three times before she was finally accepted. On October 28, 1952, she made her Covent Garden debut as the First Lady in *The Magic Flute.* Andrew Porter, the London music critic, called the singing of the three Ladies "distinctly above the average." The following November 3 she appeared as the High Priestess in *Aida,* and on November 8 as Clothilde in *Norma.*

During her first few years with Covent Garden, both in London and on tour in the provinces, Sutherland continued to sing a variety of roles. Among these were the Countess in *The Marriage of Figaro,* Amelia in *The Masked Ball,*

Frasquita in *Carmen,* Penelope Rich in Britten's *Gloriana,* Helmwige in *Die Walküre,* a Rhine maiden in *Das Rheingold,* the Woodbird in *Siegfried,* and Giulietta in *The Tales of Hoffmann.*

She gave the first indication of unusual vocal capabilities as Agathe in *Der Freischütz,* which she first sang with the Covent Garden company on tour and in London in 1954. A critic for the Manchester *Guardian* described her singing as "ravishing" and in London the Earl of Harewood, who was controller of opera planning at Covent Garden, found her performance so enchanting that he never failed to be in the auditorium when she sang this role. Having acquired a new status at Covent Garden, she was selected to create the role of Jennifer in the world premiere of Michael Tippett's *Midsummer Marriage* on January 27, 1955. In 1956 she became the first British singer to take the role of the Countess at the Glyndebourne Festival.

In 1954 Bonynge and Sutherland were married in a Spartan ceremony which had no guests, no music, and only a single bouquet of flowers sent by Covent Garden. Once Sutherland was his wife, he became more determined than ever to develop her as a coloratura soprano, particularly in the bel canto operas of Bellini, Donizetti, and Rossini, and in operas of the baroque era, in both of which he was passionately interested. Under his skillful guidance, she learned the roles of Elvira in *I Puritani,* Lucia in *Lucia di Lammermoor,* and also the title role of Handel's *Alcina.*

In March 1957 Sutherland took her audience and critics by surprise with the classical beauty and vocal perfection of her singing in *Alcina* with the Handel Opera Society. That same year she again dazzled her audience with a few arias from *Lucia di Lammermoor* sung at a concert honoring Nellie Melba. Her appearance as the Israelite woman in Handel's *Samson* in 1958 led William Mann to write in the London *Times:* "The finest singing of all came from Joan Sutherland in 'Let the Bright Seraphim'; it was worth waiting three hours to hear the liquid gold and springing mercury of her voice in this aria."

It was Bonynge's ambition to have Joan Sutherland do Lucia at Covent Garden, but it was some time before that company got around to giving her the role. Meanwhile, she was heard in various other roles at Covent Garden. Between 1957 and 1959 she sang Aida, Olympia in *The Tales of Hoffmann,* Micaëla in *Carmen,* Pamina in *The Magic Flute,* Eva in *Die Meistersinger,* Gilda in *Rigoletto,* Desdemona in *Otello,* and Madame Lidoine in the English premiere of Poulenc's *Les Dialogues des Carmélites* on January 16, 1958.

As it had on more than one occasion in operatic history, so for Sutherland *Lucia di Lammermoor* proved the making of a superstar. Sutherland made her first appearance as Lucia on February 17, 1959, in a new production at Covent Garden staged by Franco Zeffirelli and conducted by Tullio Serafin. This was the first *Lucia di Lammermoor* done in London in seventy years, except for a single presentation in 1925. What Bonynge had accomplished in preparing Sutherland's voice for the exacting demands of Lucia, the veteran conductor Serafin did in coaching her in the details of the score. In addition, Zeffirelli was responsible for transforming a formerly somewhat self-conscious and gawky stage performer into a dramatic artist of compelling magnetism. At the dress rehearsal, the orchestra applauded after Sutherland's first aria, "Regnava nel silenzio," and after the Mad Scene the orchestra exploded into shouts of bravos. Both Maria Callas and Elisabeth Schwarzkopf who were at this rehearsal were equally enthusiastic. Even greater was the excitement of the audience during and after the first performance. The uproar caused Geraint Evans, the tenor, to inquire: "My God, how far can this go?" Due to public demand, the next performance of *Lucia* with Sutherland, on February 26, had to be broadcast over BBC. The critics exhausted superlatives. Andrew Porter's report was typical: "No soprano of our century has recorded the great success of Lucia with so rare and precious a combination of marvelously accomplished singing and dramatic interpretation of the music. Miss Sutherland was spellbinding on the first night. . . . Miss Sutherland is now in the company of the most famous Donizetti singers from Pasta to Callas."

As a result of this triumph, Sutherland became a *prima donna assoluta* at Covent Garden. Her musical wishes were catered to. For her the company staged Handel's *Samson* (where once again her singing of "Let the Bright Seraphim" proved spellbinding), *Rodelinda,* and *Alcina.* Decca signed her to a recording contract; her first two releases were an operatic recital and Beethoven's Symphony No. 9. Contractual offers poured in on her from opera companies, musical organizations, and festivals. At the Teatro la Fenice in Venice she appeared on February 10, 1960, in a new Zeffirelli production of *Alcina* at which the audience shouted "La Stupenda" after the second act and showered her with flowers after the final curtain. In June 1960 she sang Elvira in *I Puritani* at the Glyndebourne Festival, a performance she repeated that year at the Edinburgh Festival. At Glyndebourne she was also cast in three Mozart operas: *The Marriage of Figaro, Don Giovanni,* and *Der Schauspieldirektor.* In her honor the Covent Garden season of 1960–1961 opened with a revival of *La Sonnambula.* And in April 1961 she joined Callas and Tebaldi as a superstar at La Scala in Milan as Lucia and in Bellini's *Beatrice di Tenda.*

The glowing reports from Europe, combined with her highly successful recordings, aroused considerable anticipation in Sutherland's American debut. This took place with the Dallas Opera in Texas on November 16, 1960, in the American premiere of *Alcina.* Reporting from Dallas to the New York *Times,* Harold C. Schonberg wrote: "As heard last night, she is probably every bit the singer advance reports say she is. . . . When she ended the opera with a fortissimo, secure, effortless high D, the audience went wild in the full realization that a great new voice has come to America. . . . What with a soaring lyric line, a superb technique, a trill that really is a trill and not a wobble, an enormous range, rapid scales and even registers, she seems equipped to handle almost any soprano role in the repertory." A few days later, still with the Dallas Opera, she proved her capability in Mozart with a stunning performance as Donna Anna in *Don Giovanni.*

Her New York debut on February 21, 1961, was a concert performance of *Beatrice di Tenda* with the American Opera Society. Her mother, to whom she had always been closely attached, had died only two days before this performance. Sutherland refused to cancel the performance and went on to prove once again that as a performer in bel canto operas she had few rivals. "She may well be the unique singer of her genre in the world today," Schonberg wrote in the New York *Times,* "a singer who can handle coloratura with complete ease, and yet whose voice is big enough to take on roles like Donna Anna and Norma. . . . In short, she is a great singer. Indeed, as the species goes these days, she is a supreme singer."

Her debut at the Metropolitan Opera in the title role of *Lucia di Lammermoor* on November 26, 1971, caused a demonstration rarely heard in that auditorium. The ovation began when she made her first-act entrance and kept mounting after that. After the Mad Scene the audience went into such an uproar that it took five minutes for the din to subside. Upon completing "Spargi d'amaro pianto" she was given a twelve-minute demonstration that brought on ten curtain calls and a standing ovation. "Those haunting curlicues of grief of the crazed Lucy, topped by one dazzling high note worked like magic," Louis Biancolli wrote in the *World-Telegram and Sun*. "At this point I am ready to concede I haven't heard a better Lucia—or seen one. The picture of the stricken girl, hair disheveled, eyes wild, voice angelic, was perfect. The crowd had every right to its own mad scene." In the New York *Post* Harriet Johnson said: "Miss Sutherland possesses the most remarkable coloratura soprano to arrive at the Metropolitan within memory and she brings with it a superb singing technique and artistry."

In her subsequent appearances at the Metropolitan Opera, Sutherland kept the fever of audience and critical enthusiasm at a high degree. She was heard as Amina in *La Sonnambula*, Norma, Donna Anna, Violetta in *La Traviata*, and the four leading female roles in *The Tales of Hoffmann*. When she filled the role of Marie in *The Daughter of the Regiment*, she revealed a new facet of her artistry, her gift for comedy. On February 25, 1976, she was Elvira in the first Metropolitan Opera revival of *I Puritani* since 1918. On November 19, 1976, she was starred in the first Metropolitan Opera production of Massenet's *Esclarmonde*, a role she had sung in 1974 when she helped inaugurate the season for the San Francisco Opera.

In 1972 Sutherland helped to open the fiftieth anniversary season of the San Francisco Opera as Norma, a role she had sung for the first time in Vancouver in 1963. A year later, on September 8, 1973, she assumed the role of Rosalinde in *Die Fledermaus* with the same company. During the summer of 1974 she made her first appearance at the new Sydney Opera House in Australia, singing the four leading roles in a new production of *The Tales of Hoffmann*. This was her first return to her native land, after an absence of nine years. Following the performances in Sydney she toured the country with her own

opera company. When her tour ended both she and her husband were elected honorary members of the Australian Opera Company.

On September 23, 1976, Sutherland appeared in a revival of Massenet's *Le Roi de Lahore* with the Vancouver Opera. A year later, she celebrated the twentieth anniversary of her debut at Covent Garden (and the thirtieth anniversary of her singing career) by appearing for the first time in London in the title role of Donizetti's *Maria Stuarda*. "She remains one of the vocal miracles of our times," reported Harold C. Schonberg to the New York *Times* from London. "She sang with a long legato line and a firmly controlled production. Scale passages were as dazzling as ever, and the high D-flats were squarely on the mark."

There are many other operas in her repertory in addition to those already mentioned. She has appeared in *Lucrezia Borgia, Semiramide,* Franz Lehár's *The Merry Widow,* and she has recorded Franco Leoni's *L'Oracolo*.

When Sutherland made her first appearance on American television she was paid seven thousand dollars to perform a single aria on a sponsored coast-to-coast program, up to then the highest fee ever paid an opera singer. Since then she has often been heard over television; she starred in a series of programs called "Who's Afraid of Opera?" and in several full length operas syndicated on Public Broadcasting Company stations throughout the United States and telecast over BBC.

Everything about Sutherland is big, in addition to her voice. She is five feet eight and a half inches tall and weighs in the neighborhood of two hundred pounds. Her hands, feet, eyes, jaw, and mouth are all oversized. Her hair is red, her eyes hazel. "I know I'm not exactly a bombshell," she says, "but one has to make the best of what one's got."

Sutherland and her husband have a son, Adam. Since stardom has enabled her to dictate her own terms, she insists on having her husband conduct at almost all of her performances. For a long time they maintained year-round an old-fashioned two-story house in Brooklyn, New York, overlooking Prospect Park, and another house in the Kensington district of London. Lately, however, they have made their principal home in Les Avants, Montreux, Switzerland.

On performance days she spends most of her time at home going over the score she is scheduled to sing, and then, to take her mind off the music, reading books on history or suspense novels, or doing needlepoint. At each performance she brings with her good-luck charms: a little rag doll; a toy bear given her by the man who took care of her costumes; a small black statue of the Madonna of Montserrat she acquired in Barcelona in 1961 during a performance of *I Puritani.*

She likes going to the movies, but does so rarely during her singing season for fear of catching cold in air-conditioned theaters. Her hobbies—in addition to needlepoint and reading —include collecting autographed opera scores, opera lithographs, and books on nineteenth century singers. Her greatest weakness is her inordinate appetite for rich foods, particularly for desserts and candy.

She was made Commander of the British Empire and has received honorary doctorates in music from Aberdeen University and Rider College in England.

ABOUT: Braddon, R. Joan Sutherland; Greenfield, E. Joan Sutherland; Sargeant, W. Divas. *Periodicals*— Musical America, February 1961; New York Times, February 19, 1961, April 12, 1970, February 22, 1976; New York Times Magazine, March 5, 1961; Opera News, December 9, 1961, April 4, 1970; Show, February 1965; Stereo Review, November 1976.

Set Svanholm

1904–1964

Set Karl Viktor Svanholm, tenor, was born in Västerås, Sweden, on September 2, 1904. Both his parents were musical. His father, Viktor, a minister, played several instruments and sang well; his mother, Beda Swanström Svanholm, a schoolteacher, played the piano and also sang. Each of their three sons was given musical training early, Set being taught the organ by his father. As a boy, he sometimes played the organ at church services. After graduation from junior college in 1922 and completion of his one-year term of military service, he was appointed organist in Tillberga. He prepared for a teaching career and took his first teaching job in 1924 in the village of Saeby, while also holding the post of organist-choirmaster at the local church. After two years in Saeby, he decided to get comprehensive musical training. To finance it, he gave

SET SVANHOLM

several organ recitals, the proceeds from which, supplemented by his savings, made it possible for him to go to Stockholm in 1927 and enter the Royal Conservatory to study piano, composition, counterpoint, and voice.

Upon graduation from the Conservatory in 1929, Svanholm held various music jobs. He directed and sang in oratorio performances, he conducted services at the St. James Church in Stockholm, and taught oratorio and singing at the Royal Conservatory. He continued his vocal training in 1930 with John Forsell who, at that time, had just three other vocal students besides Svanholm. Two of them became famous opera singers: Joel Berglund and Jussi Björling. The third was a young soprano, Ninni Högstedt, daughter of the president of the Cameral Court in Stockholm. In 1934 she gave up her own career to become Svanholm's wife and in time the mother of his six children.

Svanholm made his opera debut in a baritone role—Silvio in *I Pagliacci*—with the Stockholm Opera in 1930. For the next six years he continued appearing as a baritone. Then, persuaded by his wife that the tenor range was more natural to him, he retrained his voice, learned a new repertory, and returned to opera in 1936 as Radames in *Aida,* with the Stockholm Opera. Bruno Walter heard that performance and engaged him for the Vienna State Opera where he made his debut as Siegmund in *Die Walküre.* His successes in Wagnerian roles in Vienna led to appearances in Graz, Munich, and Prague, and finally at the festivals at Bayreuth and Salzburg.

He was scheduled to appear in the United States during the 1940–1941 season, but the outbreak of World War II compelled him to cancel this engagement. During the summer of 1942 he appeared at La Scala in Milan as Siegfried in the *Ring* cycle. But throughout most of the war he confined his performances principally to the Stockholm Opera. There he appeared not only in the Wagnerian repertory but also as Manrico in *Il Trovatore,* Florestan in *Fidelio,* Don José in *Carmen,* Bacchus in *Ariadne auf Naxos,* Calaf in *Turandot,* Vladimir in *Prince Igor,* Samson in *Samson and Delilah,* and in various operas by Meyerbeer, Janáček, Weber, and Mussorgsky. In 1946 he was appointed singer to the Swedish court.

At the end of the war, during the summer of 1946, Svanholm was acclaimed at the Teatro Colón in Buenos Aires as Tristan in *Tristan and Isolde.* He also made successful appearances at this time at the Teatro Municipal in Rio de Janeiro. Later the same year, going north to the United States, he made his American debut in the title role of *Lohengrin* in Portland, Oregon, with the San Francisco Opera; he repeated this performance on September 17, 1946, on the opening night of the company's regular fall season in San Francisco. For the next three seasons, and again in 1951, he appeared with this company, performing not only in the Wagnerian repertory but also as Otello in Verdi's opera and as Radames.

On October 5, 1946, he appeared with the Chicago Opera as Tristan. A critic for *Musical America* described his voice as "a powerful, golden tenor." Six weeks later, on November 15, he made his debut at the Metropolitan Opera in the title role of *Siegfried.* "Mr. Svanholm," reported Olin Downes in the New York *Times,* "has a fresh, brilliant, manly voice, a real 'Heldentenor' which is fully equal to all vocal requisitions. . . . He is not only an exceptionally gifted singer but also, it appears, a sound musician who sings his part accurately as it is written; who can also, by his appearance, create illusion . . . with the Siegfried role. . . . Dramatically his conception was fully rounded and always significant."

As principal tenor of the Metropolitan Opera during the next decade, Svanholm continued to distinguish himself in the Wagnerian music dramas: as Siegfried, Loge in *Das Rheingold,*

Siegmund, Walther in *Die Meistersinger,* Lohengrin, Parsifal, Tannhäuser, and Erik in *The Flying Dutchman.* But his 105 appearances at the Metropolitan Opera in New York and 27 on tour also embraced roles outside the Wagnerian sphere: Radames, Florestan, Herod in *Salome,* Eisenstein in *Die Fledermaus,* Aegisthus in *Elektra,* Admetus in *Alceste,* and Otello.

In November 1948 Covent Garden in London launched its first Wagner season in ten years and invited him to appear in the *Ring* cycle as Siegmund and Siegfried and as Walther in *Die Meistersinger.* He was also heard in other major European opera houses, among them La Scala in Milan and the Royal Opera in Stockholm.

Svanholm was also a successful recitalist. He made his New York recital debut at Town Hall in March 1948. At that time Noel Strauss, writing in the New York *Times,* described him as "an uncommonly gifted purveyor of songs . . . a rare phenomenon." One year later he presented a program of Schubert and Brahms *Lieder* at the Library of Congress in Washington, D.C.

He made numerous appearances as guest artist with symphony orchestras. In April 1949 Toscanini chose him to be one of two soloists at his last appearance of the season with the NBC Symphony in a public performance at Carnegie Hall. He was also a soloist with the New York Philharmonic, the Philadelphia Orchestra, and the Minneapolis Symphony, among other American symphonic organizations.

From 1956 to 1963 he served as the music director of the Royal Opera in Stockholm. His managerial duties compelled him to curtail greatly his career as a singer. At his home at Saltsjö-Duvnäs, near Stockholm, he found escape from managerial problems by swimming, bicycling, and playing tennis.

Set Svanholm died at Saltsjö-Duvnäs on October 4, 1964.

ABOUT: Davidson, G. Opera Biographies. *Periodicals* —Musical America, December 25, 1946; New York Times, December 8, 1946; Newsweek, November 25, 1946.

Gladys Swarthout

1904–1969

Gladys Swarthout, mezzo-soprano, was born in Deepwater, Mississippi, on December 25, 1904, to Frank Leslie and Ruth Wonser Swarthout. As a child she had a voice that was mature for her years. When, as a girl of nine, she practiced singing, people rang her doorbell to inquire who was the woman with such a beautiful voice. Upon being told that a child was singing, they refused to believe it. "It was due to the formation of my throat and vocal cords," Swarthout once explained. "I did not have to work hard to develop my voice, though I worked hard to acquire finesse."

She received her first vocal instruction from Belle Vickers, a local teacher. When she was thirteen, she pinned up her curls and applied for the job of soloist in a church in Kansas City, Missouri, to which her family had moved some years earlier. She announced she was nineteen years old. "I had been wanting that job ever since I was seven—and only because I disliked the way the incumbent contralto held her music. She held her arms rigidly stiff from her body with the sheet of music swaying up and down. I remember telling mother after one service on Sunday that I would someday be a soloist and show the woman how to hold her music." Deluded by the ripeness and fullness of Gladys's voice, the choirmaster engaged her.

At about this time she gave her first song recital in a public auditorium in Kansas City. During the recital she missed a high note in a difficult aria. With quiet aplomb, she stopped her accompanist, asked him to start the aria from its beginning and sang it through perfectly. The audience was deeply impressed; so was a wealthy Kansas City family that decided to finance her career.

In 1920 she was graduated from Central High School of Kansas City. With funds provided by her patrons she enrolled in the Bush Conservatory of Music in Chicago. Over a three-year period she received a thorough musical education there. Meanwhile she helped to support herself by singing in church. She also embarked on a concert tour with her sister, Roma, the financial

Swarthout: swôr′ thout

GLADYS SWARTHOUT

returns from which enabled her to repay her patrons completely.

In 1924 several of her friends arranged for her to audition for Herbert Johnson, the manager of the Chicago Civic Opera, even though at this time she had not yet mastered a single operatic role. Given a contract for the following season she managed within a few months' time to learn twenty-three roles.

Her debut with the Chicago Civic Opera took place during the 1924–1925 season as the off-stage shepherd in *Tosca*. During the remainder of that season she appeared in more than fifty percent of the company's performances. Towards the end of her first season in opera, on March 22, 1925, she married Harry Richmond Kern; he died six years later.

During the summers in the years between 1927 and 1929 she made several appearances with the Ravinia Opera Company in Chicago. This led to an engagement with the Metropolitan Opera; she appeared with the company on October 29, 1929, in Philadelphia as the third elf in Respighi's *The Sunken Bell.* Her Metropolitan Opera debut in New York City followed on November 15, 1929, as La Cieca in *La Gioconda.* "She showed," said Olin Downes in the New York *Times,* "a voice of good quality, depth and volume in the blind mother's air, 'Voce di donna,' and acted the character with intelligent sympathy."

She continued singing principal mezzo-soprano and contralto roles at the Metropolitan Opera until 1945, making 162 appearances in

New York and 56 on tour. Her most celebrated roles were Carmen and Mignon. On February 10, 1934, she created the role of Plentiful Tewke in the world premiere of Howard Hanson's *Merry Mount,* and she was cast as Nejata in the American premiere of *Sadko* (January 25, 1930) and in the American premiere of Felice Lattuada's *Le Preziose Ridicole* (December 10, 1930) as Cathos. Among her other roles were Stephano in *Romeo and Juliet,* Suzy in *La Rondine,* Federica in *Luisa Miller,* Lola in *Cavalleria Rusticana,* Siebel in *Faust,* Nicklausse and Giulietta in *The Tales of Hoffmann,* Maddalena in *Rigoletto,* Adalgisa in *Norma,* Preziosilla in *La Forza del Destino,* Mrs. Deane in Deems Taylor's *Peter Ibbetson,* Mallika in *Lakmé,* and Pierotto in *Linda di Chamounix.*

Swarthout became something of a national institution in American music through her frequent appearances over network radio. She made her first radio appearance on the "General Motors Hour" in 1930. After that she was heard on such major programs as "The Magic Key," "The Camel Caravan," "The Ford Symphony," and, for three years, as a star on her own show, "The Prudential Family Hour." For five consecutive years she was voted by American and Canadian critics as the leading female classical singer over the radio. She also appeared in five motion pictures during this period, though with less distinguished results: *Rose of Rancho* (1936), *Give Us This Night* (1936), *Champagne Waltz* (1937), *Romance in the Dark* (1938), *Ambush* (1939). In the last of these she had only a speaking role.

In 1932 Swarthout married Frank M. Chapman Jr., a professional singer she had met in Florence while he was a member of the Italian National Opera Company. After the marriage, Chapman continued to appear in operas, concerts, and over the radio; but his main activity was to guide his wife's career. They acquired a house in Beverly Hills, California, modeled after a French provincial manor, and maintained a second home in an apartment in New York City overlooking the East River. Subsequently they sold their California house to Greta Garbo and acquired a two-hundred-and-twenty-five-year-old farm near Redding Ridge, Connecticut.

Upon leaving the Metropolitan Opera, Swarthout made a number of appearances in American cities in her favorite role, Carmen. She was also heard in recitals. A heart attack in 1954 compelled her to retire completely. She went to Italy to live in Florence, where she died on July 7, 1969.

She was the author of a novel, *Come Soon, Tomorrow* (1943), that was mainly autobiographical. She was the only woman to become a member of Mu Pi Delta, an honorary music fraternity. She was chosen to sing before both houses of Congress, and in the presence of the President of the United States, the Supreme Court, and the diplomatic corps, on the commemoration of the one-hundred-and-fiftieth anniversary of the federal legislature.

Her interests included playing tennis, dancing, and eating gourmet food. She was several times selected as one of America's best-dressed women.

ABOUT: Opera News, April 8, 1940.

George Szell

1897–1970

George (originally Georg) Szell, conductor, was born in Budapest on June 7, 1897. He was the only child of Georg Charles Szell, a businessman and lawyer of Hungarian origin, and Margarethe Harmat Szell, who was of Slovak background. Both parents were musical. His father was a devoted operagoer and his mother a trained pianist, and consequently there was always good music at the Szell household. When George was three, he expressed indignation whenever his mother struck a wrong note on the piano by rapping her sharply on the wrist. He further revealed his musical ability during his childhood by singing in perfect pitch Hungarian, Slovak, French, and German folk songs. When a local teacher was recruited to instruct the child in the rudiments of music, he learned the treble clef in three days.

In 1903 the family moved to Vienna. There his mother gave George piano lessons. Since he showed unusual aptitude for the keyboard, he was taken to Theodor Leschetizky, the world-renowned piano teacher, who listened to the child play and expressed the opinion that he had no talent for music whatsoever. Another well-known teacher, Richard Robert, was found in

Szell: sĕl

GEORGE SZELL

Vienna and George studied the piano with him for the next ten years. To permit George to devote himself as completely to music as possible he was removed from public school and given private tutoring. "I haven't seen the inside of a classroom since," Szell later recalled. "I learned more at home from my tutors than I would have in school." For the further enrichment of his musical background he was taken to operatic and concert performances. When he was seven he heard Mahler conduct *Don Giovanni* at the Vienna State Opera and never forgot that experience. ·

In 1908 George made his debut simultaneously as pianist and composer. The Vienna Symphony under Oskar Nedbal performed at the Grosse Musikvereinssaal in Vienna a program in which the eleven-year-old prodigy was heard as soloist in Mozart's Concerto in A major, K.488, Mendelssohn's *Capriccio Brilliante,* and his own Rondo, for piano and orchestra. He was so well received that managers offered him engagements. One of these was in Dresden where he appeared as soloist with the Staatskapelle conducted by Ernest von Schuch. In London he was heard in four concerts which inspired the *Daily Mail* to devote a full-page article to him and to refer to him as "the new Mozart."

On the advice of his parents, who refused to exploit their son as a prodigy, George withdrew from the professional scene to concentrate on further music study at the Academy of Music in Vienna. After his graduation from the Academy, he continued his music training privately with Max Reger, J. B. Förster, Eusebius Mandyczewski, and Karl Prohaska. He learned symphonic literature by himself through attending concerts and performing orchestral scores on the piano.

During the summer of 1913, he and his family were vacationing in the resort town of Bad Kissingen, where orchestral concerts were given nightly. For one of these concerts the regular conductor was indisposed. George, a friend of the conductor, was asked to take his place. He was so exhilarated by this experience that from that time on he wanted to become a conductor.

In 1914 George was invited to be guest conductor of the Berlin Philharmonic Orchestra. In the triple role of conductor, pianist, and composer he was heard in a program that included Beethoven's *Emperor Concerto* (in which he was the soloist), and Richard Strauss's *Till Eulenspiegel's Merry Pranks* and his own symphony, both of which he conducted. Strauss was so taken with Szell's all-around musicianship that he engaged him as a coach with the Berlin Royal Opera. For two years, he coached singers, played the piano, and sometimes conducted at rehearsals. He did so well conducting rehearsals of *Ariadne auf Naxos* that the men of the orchestra appealed to the opera-house manager to engage Szell for the staff of conductors. The manager was ready to do so, but Strauss had other plans for Szell. He wanted Szell to gain valuable experience by taking on the job of principal conductor at the Municipal Theater in Strasbourg.

Szell went to Strasbourg in 1917, succeeding Otto Klemperer. After giving trial performances of *Carmen* and *Tannhäuser* he received a five-year contract. He remained in Strasbourg just one season; when the French troops occupied the city during World War I, the opera house closed.

For a number of years Szell was a free-lance conductor, wandering about Europe—sometimes serving as a pianist, sometimes as a conductor. Beginning in 1919 he served for two seasons as the conductor of the German Opera in Prague. In 1921–1922 he was principal conductor of the Darmstadt Court Theater, and from 1922 to 1924 he was principal conductor at the Municipal Theater in Düsseldorf.

For six years between 1924 and 1930 Szell's musical activities were confined to Berlin as principal conductor of the Berlin State Opera and the Berlin Radio Orchestra. He also took a teaching assignment at the Berlin High School for Music from 1927 to 1930.

From 1930 to 1936 he was the music director of the German Opera in Prague and the Prague Philharmonic. His performances of Mozart and Wagner attracted the interest and enthusiasm of music lovers all over Europe. His reputation throughout Europe was further enhanced with guest performances with major orchestras and opera companies in the Soviet Union, Vienna, Berlin, London, The Hague, Brussels, and Scandinavia. In 1930 he was heard for the first time in the United States—as a guest conductor of the St. Louis Symphony. In 1931 he performed once again with the St. Louis Symphony and was highly praised.

With the shadow of Nazism spreading across Central Europe, Szell knew the time had come for him to leave Czechoslovakia. In 1937 he took on two new assignments: principal conductor of the Scottish Orchestra in Glasgow succeeding John Barbirolli, and conductor of the Hague Philharmonic. While thus occupied for two years, he was able to tour Australia and conduct at the Celebrity Concerts of the Australian Broadcasting Commission in Sydney. His second Australian tour took place in 1939. En route back to Europe, he was forced to stop in New York because of the outbreak of World War II. He was accompanied by his wife, the former Helene Schulz, a young Czech woman he had married in Glasgow on January 25, 1938. (This was his second marriage; the first had ended when his young wife deserted him for the concertmaster of the orchestra Szell was then conducting.)

At this time America was overflowing with émigré European musicians. Despite his gifts and his experience, Szell was unable to get a significant conducting job during his first two years of residence in New York City. To support himself and his wife, he taught composition at the Mannes School of Music and directed an opera workshop at the New School for Social Research, both in New York. He also accepted assignments to play the piano in sonata recitals and other chamber music concerts, to conduct a few summer performances at the Hollywood Bowl in California, and to make orchestral transcriptions for a publisher.

In January 1941 Toscanini invited him to appear as a guest conductor in four concerts of the NBC Symphony over the radio network. Szell gave such striking performances that suddenly the music world focused on him. He was called to the Ravinia Festival in Chicago to direct some concerts with the Chicago Symphony that year, and he was invited to appear with the Detroit Symphony, the Los Angeles Philharmonic, and several other orchestras. In 1942 his calendar of guest performances with major American orchestras became crowded. He was also engaged as principal conductor of German opera at the Metropolitan Opera in New York. His debut there took place on December 9, 1942, in *Salome,* which, as Virgil Thomson noted in the *Herald Tribune,* was directed "with power, precision, and all imaginable exactitude of expression. Last night's revival . . . was orchestrally and vocally superb. . . . Mr. Szell did a virtuoso job on a difficult and complex work."

Szell remained three years with the Metropolitan Opera, conducting performances of the *Ring* cycle, *Die Meistersinger, Tannhäuser, Otello, Boris Godunov, Don Giovanni,* and *Der Rosenkavalier,* in addition to *Salome.* In whatever he conducted, he revealed a master's hand both in the control of the forces under him and in the depth of his musical understanding. An annual poll conducted by *Musical America* in 1945 placed him second to Bruno Walter as the most popular opera conductor in America.

Szell was back at the Metropolitan Opera for the 1953–1954 season to conduct a single performance of the "Dresden version" of *Tannhäuser,* on December 26, 1953. On that occasion, Ronald Eyer of *Musical America* called him "the hero of the evening . . . [who] achieved at a single stroke one of the most perceptive analyses and one of the most dynamic performances ever unfolded hereabouts." In January 1954 Szell announced that he would not complete his season with the Metropolitan Opera nor embark with it on a spring tour as his contract obligated him to do, because of violent disagreements with Rudolf Bing, general manager, over the staging and overall production of *Tannhäuser.*

In 1946 Szell became an American citizen. In the same year he was appointed music director of the Cleveland Orchestra which, in its preceding three years without a permanent conductor, was in a state of disintegration. "I told the board that if I had the necessary powers I would make the orchestra second to none and establish Cleveland as one of the symphony capitals of the world." Those powers were given him, and Szell went on to fulfill his end of the bargain. He dismissed twenty-two of the ninety-four musicians during his first years, and in the next few years he continued the process of replacing the less desirable with the best performers available. He increased the orchestral complement to one hundred and six men. He spared neither himself nor his musicians during grinding rehearsals during which he ruled as a total dictator and maintained a military discipline. His aim, which was fully realized within a decade, was "the supreme cultivation of ensemble playing," as he himself put it, "with the players carefully listening to one another as well as to themselves, with the most eloquent communication between the orchestra and the audience, and with the most elaborate care for proper articulation, phrasing and style, down to the subtlest inflection of every nuance."

He extended the number of subscription concerts and expanded the season. He organized a two-hundred-and-forty-voice chorus as an adjunct to the orchestra for performances of choral masterworks, placing it under the direction of Robert Shaw. He induced the management to spend over a million dollars in improving the acoustics of Severance Hall, the home of the orchestra. He engaged Pierre Boulez (then an unknown quantity as a conductor) on a five-year contract as permanent guest conductor. And he instituted a system of apprentice conductors.

In time he shaped the orchestra in his own image, to meet the severest tests of his uncompromising conscience. As Paul Hume, the music critic of the Washington *Post,* put it: "The Cleveland Orchestra . . . is wholly Szell's creation. Its members may pride themselves in being able to do anything he asks of them, for there is no finer accomplishment open to them in their profession. It is with their gifts, their technique, their tone, and above all their ability to respond to the musical intellect that Szell has fashioned them into one of the magnificent ensembles of our times. It is out of his mind and heart that the music flows in a way that no other conductor and orchestra in this country today produces it."

It became an orchestra with few rivals, a fact brought home to Europe when Szell took the Cleveland Orchestra on a tour in the spring of 1965. "I don't think I exaggerate if I say that I have never heard anything more perfect," said the critic of the *New Statesman and Nation* in London. "A magnificent orchestra, perhaps the

best that has ever visited us from abroad," remarked René Dumesnil in *Le Monde* in Paris. It proved, commented the critic of the *Stuttgarter Zeitung* in Germany "not only the equal of the star ensembles of Boston, Philadelphia and New York, but forced us to recognize the fact that it possessed more than a technical perfection, individually and collectively, namely, a certain musicianly impetus so gratifying and soothing to European musical ears."

As the music director of the Cleveland Orchestra Szell was able to fill engagements around the world as guest conductor of major orchestras and opera companies and at festivals. He was also able to hold two other permanent appointments for a number of years: permanent guest conductor of the Concertgebouw Orchestra in Amsterdam and music adviser of the New York Philharmonic.

While Szell was at his greatest in the literature from Bach through Debussy—and was one of the supreme interpreters of Haydn, Mozart, Beethoven, Schubert, Schumann, Wagner, Brahms, and Mahler—he also proved himself to be an admirable voice of twentieth century music, to which he devoted much of his efforts. On the wall of his study hung a framed letter from Sir William Walton sent to the conductor after Sir William had heard Szell perform his Second Symphony both in public and in a recording. It read: "Words fail me! It is a quite fantastic and stupendous performance from every point of view. Firstly it is absolutely right musically speaking, and the virtuosity is quite staggering."

The list of Szell's world premieres includes Easley Blackwood's Symphony No.2 (January 5, 1961), Copland's *Letter from Home* in its full orchestration (February 27, 1947), Norman Dello Joio's *Ricercari* (December 19, 1946), Henri Dutilleux's *Métaboles* (January 14, 1965), Lukas Foss's *Ode* (March 15, 1945), Hanson's *Mosaics* (January 23, 1958), Hindemith's Piano Concerto (February 27, 1947), Peter Mennin's Symphony No.7 (January 23, 1964), Walter Piston's *Symphonic Prelude* (April 20, 1961), George Rochberg's Symphony No.2 (February 26, 1959), Ernst Toch's *Hyperion* (January 8, 1948), and William Walton's *Partita* (January 30, 1958). Among his American premieres were Kodály's Symphony in C major (January 4, 1962), Frank Martin's *Concerto for Seven Wind Instruments, Percussion and Strings* (December

28, 1950), and Bohuslav Martinu's Cello Concerto (October 26, 1967).

"By and large," wrote Harold C. Schonberg in the New York *Times*, "Mr. Szell was accepted as the greatest conductor after Toscanini. . . . Like Toscanini, Mr. Szell was a precisionist and a literalist; and again like Toscanini, he never carried his literalism to the point of dogma. . . . His interpretations followed the letter of the score, but also were imbued with his own personality. It was a very strong personality, and a protean one."

In June 1970 Szell returned from a tour of the Far East with a fever. At the Hanna House of University Hospital in Cleveland it was discovered that he had suffered a heart attack and was the victim of a bone cancer. Because of his heart condition no operation for cancer was feasible. He died in University Hospital on July 30, 1970.

Szell lived in a two-story house in the Shaker Hill section of Cleveland. A methodical man, he carefully regimented his daily existence. He arose and went to sleep at the same hour each day, performed his set duties at specific times, drove his car always at the same cautious speed, registering just about the same mileage year after year. Four times a week he left his home in time to arrive at his office in Severance Hall by nine o'clock in the morning to attend to correspondence and other details. Rehearsals began at ten. When the morning rehearsal was over he drove home for lunch, then returned to the hall for afternoon rehearsal. Dinner was a gourmet repast with the proper wines. The evenings were generally spent quietly, with an early hour for bed.

On concert days Szell ate a simple lunch, had a nap in the afternoon, then dressed after a warm bath. Before concert time he studied some new orchestral score just to keep himself from worrying about the music he was conducting that evening. After the concert he generally went straight home rather than to a social gathering, allowing the entire evening's program to run through his head as he unwound from the strain of the concert.

In addition to his house in Cleveland, he maintained an apartment on Park Avenue in New York City. Every year he spent his vacations in Europe, usually going to the same resort and to the same hotel. Vacation time allowed him to indulge more freely in his passion for reading books, in playing golf and bridge, and in taking long walks. An intellectual, he possessed a wide knowledge of literature, history, painting, and current events. He spoke half a dozen languages fluently. He was as much a precisionist away from music as in it. Involved in discussions with friends, he would leap from his chair and reach to his bookshelves for an encyclopedia, dictionary, or thesaurus to check on the accuracy of what was being said.

He was an austere, arrogant, and abrasive man, whose honesty made him candid to a fault, and whose satire was stinging. He had to be in command all the time. He gave instructions to his own tailor on precisely how his clothes were to be cut. In a restaurant he instructed waiters on how dishes were to be prepared. While playing golf, even with those far more competent than he, he invariably gave instruction on how form could be improved. In the company of artists or writers he was not above giving advice on their own crafts.

His musicians called him Cyclops because of the way he would fix them with his bulging eyes framed in thick glasses. They knew him to be an authoritarian, a bully, a pedant; at times, cruel, unreasonable, and explosive in temper. While they could not give him affection, they could not deny him that which he wished most—admiration and respect. His musicianship inspired awe and because of that awe they always stood ready to give of themselves as completely as he wished.

Szell was made Chevalier of the Legion of Honor by France; he also received the Order of Orange-Nassau from the Netherlands, the Order of the British Empire from England, and the Grosses Verdienstkreuz from Germany. He received honorary doctorates in music from Western Reserve University and Oberlin College. The American Composers Alliance presented him with the Laurel Leaf Award.

For Columbia, Szell recorded a comprehensive library of symphonic music ranging from Haydn and Mozart to Samuel Barber and William Walton.

ABOUT: Ewen, D. Famous Modern Composers; Schonberg, H. C. The Great Conductors; Stoddard, H. Symphony Conductors of U.S.A. *Periodicals*—Atlantic Monthly, January 1966; Musical Courier, December 1, 1945; New York Times, August 1, 1970; New York Times Magazine, February 2, 1964; New Yorker, November 6, 1965; Time (cover story), February 22, 1963.

Henryk Szeryng

1918–

Henryk Szeryng, violinist, was born in Zelazowa Wola (the town of Chopin's birth), a suburb of Warsaw, on September 22, 1918. His father, Szymon Szeryng, was an iron and lumber magnate, and his mother, Aline Woznicka Szeryng, was an amateur pianist. Szeryng recalls that "it was only when I heard her play Chopin that I could collect my thoughts and concentrate." He was five when his mother began giving him piano lessons. Soon after that he started to study the violin, for which he immediately showed a marked preference. When he was seven, he played the Mendelssohn Violin Concerto for Bronislaw Hubermann and Hubermann, saying his talent was worth cultivating, suggested he go to Berlin to study with Carl Flesch. Henryk was taken to Berlin, where he stayed for the next six years studying with Flesch. "Everything I know, violinistically speaking, I learned from him," Szeryng has said. "Mind you, I say violinistically—not musical or interpretative."

After completing his studies with Flesch in 1931, Henryk made his first concert tour, in 1933, performing in Warsaw, Bucharest, Vienna, and Paris. In 1935 he performed the Beethoven Violin Concerto in Warsaw with Bruno Walter conducting. That same year he performed at the Romanian royal palace and was decorated by the Queen Mother of Romania with the Order of Cultural Merit.

Henryk's music studies were then continued in Paris. He attended the piano classes of Gabriel Bouillon at the Paris Conservatory and studied composition privately with Nadia Boulanger. He formed valuable friendships with two violinists then in Paris—Georges Enesco and Jacques Thibaud—who, Szeryng explains, revealed to him "that the violin could also be treated with the utmost delicacy, sweetness and even love" in contrast to the more powerful and dominating style of the Russian and German schools to which Szeryng had thus far been subjected. He left the Paris Conservatory in 1937 with first prize in violin playing. While pursuing his musical studies in Paris, Henryk spent several years at the Sorbonne University studying

Szeryng: shâr' ēng

HENRYK SZERYNG

the humanities. "I was supposed to become a scholar," he admits.

His musical and cultural pursuits were halted by World War II. When the Nazis occupied Poland in 1939, he placed his services at the command of General Sikorski, premier of the Polish government in exile and the commander in chief of the Free Polish Army. Szeryng gave over three hundred concerts for Allied troops and for wounded soldiers in hospitals in Europe, North Africa, the Near East, the United States, and Latin America. Then, as Sikorski's interpreter, he toured North and South America seeking asylum for Polish refugees.

During the war Szeryng gave a concert at Carnegie Hall in New York on November 24, 1943. The critical reaction was for the most part favorable, though not rhapsodic. He also gave two recitals in Mexico City which made a deep impression on the composers Carlos Chávez and Manuel Ponce.

In 1943, Szeryng was invited to reorganize the string department at the University of Mexico. He became so deeply involved with his teaching at the University and felt so at home with Mexico and its people that he decided to establish permanent residence in Mexico City. In 1946 he became a Mexican citizen.

Though he gave a few concerts each year, Szeryng seemed content to devote his life to teaching the violin rather than to cultivating a career as virtuoso. A meeting with Arthur Rubinstein in Mexico City in 1954 changed his mind. Rubinstein had gone to Mexico City to give a recital and Szeryng went backstage to congratulate him. Rubinstein then invited Szeryng to come to his hotel and play for him. "He played Bach sonatas," Rubinstein recalls, "and reduced me to tears."

Rubinstein urged Szeryng to consider concert work seriously. He had Szeryng record an album with him and he used his influence to get Szeryng a nine-city tour of Europe in 1956. In Paris Rubinstein introduced Szeryng to his own manager, Sol Hurok, who booked him for a twenty-concert tour of the United States that began on February 12, 1957, with a performance of the Brahms Violin Concerto with the Cleveland Orchestra at Carnegie Hall. Writing in *Musical America,* Shirley Fleming said that Szeryng performed "in a manner proclaiming a violinist of stature."

Since then, Szeryng has risen to the top among violin virtuosos. His worldwide engagements necessitate his touring ten months a year, but he insists on keeping the remaining two months not for a vacation but for supervising the master classes in violin playing which he initiated in Mexico in 1958. "He is a musician's musician," Rubinstein has said of him. "Real music lovers want emotion—great moments—which Szeryng's playing gives them." Analyzing Szeryng's violinistic style in the *American Record Guide,* Shirley Fleming has written: "Three aspects of Szeryng's art are particularly impressive: intonation which is as devastatingly accurate as any we are ever likely to hear, a healthy expressive tone, and a wonderfully controlled bow."

In addition to the well-recognized repertory of violin music, Szeryng has addressed himself to the music of the twentieth century. He presented the world premiere of the Violin Concerto by Benjamin Lees on February 8, 1963, with the Boston Symphony under Leinsdorf. Commenting upon the way Szeryng prepared this new American concerto, Lees said: "He asked endless questions pertaining to phrasing, interpretation and dynamics. He went over metronome markings, first one way, then another. He committed the orchestral score to memory—as he does with every concerto—and then learned the piano reduction. . . . He is not simply a solo artist, but a complete musician."

In both his public concerts and his recordings, Szeryng has promoted the music of twentieth century Mexican composers such as Silvestre

Revueltas, Rodolfo Halffter, and Blas Galindo. Szeryng also resurrected the long-forgotten Concerto No.3 by Paganini that had not been heard publicly since the composer's death in 1840. Only a barely legible violin part and no orchestral accompaniment existed for this. After reconstructing it Szeryng gave the first performance of this concerto in modern times in London in 1971. The audience included five direct descendants of Paganini: two granddaughters, a great-great-granddaughter and her nine-year-old daughter, and one male Paganini descendant. The North American premiere of this concerto was given by Szeryng with the Montreal Symphony in Canada in November 1971. He has also recorded it.

Szeryng has made many recordings on the RCA, Philips, CBS, and Mercury labels. He recorded the solo sonatas and partitas of Bach twice for Philips—the first recording won him the Grand Prix du Disque in Paris in 1955. During the next fourteen years he proceeded to capture the Prix du Disque five times more. In 1976 he was awarded a Grammy from the National Academy of Recording Arts and Sciences for his album of Schubert's Piano Trios performed with Arthur Rubinstein and Pierre Fournier. He also recorded Beethoven violin sonatas with Rubinstein and Mozart violin sonatas with Ingrid Haebler.

In 1956 the Mexican government appointed him Goodwill Ambassador. In 1960 he was made Mexican Cultural Ambassador, and in 1970 Cultural Adviser to the Mexican delegation to UNESCO and the Mexican Foreign Ministry. Szeryng travels on a diplomatic passport. He was made Knight Commander, Order of Polonia Restituta by Poland in 1956; Officer, Order of Arts and Letters in France in 1964; Commander, Order of the Lion in Finland in 1966. In 1963 he received the Silver Medal of the City of Paris.

He has revised concertos by Nardini, Vivaldi, and others and has composed a number of works for violin and piano as well as for chamber music groups.

In addition to the home in Mexico City which he shares with two German shepherd dogs, Szeryng maintains an apartment in Paris "so that," as he told Shirley Fleming in an interview in the New York *Times,* "I can sleep in my own bed, and read my own books and my own scores, between Helsinki and Barcelona, or Cracow and London."

His interests include linguistic research (he speaks seven languages fluently), reading books on history, philosophy, and art; and collecting rare editions. Also he is an aficionado of painting. He is inordinately generous, particularly to young musicians needing help. One of his many benefactions is an annual scholarship to the Hebrew University in Israel. In 1972, he learned that there was no Stradivarius violin in Israel, and he presented the country with his own 1734 Stradivarius to be made available to young Israeli violinists. He made the presentation on his own behalf and on behalf of the Mexican government following his concert in Jerusalem on December 24, 1972. This instrument has been named Kinor David Stradivari (the Lyre of David Stradivarius). He has also presented a Guarnerius violin to Mexico and a Vuillaume violin to the prodigy Shlomo Mintz.

ABOUT: Hi Fi, April 1963; New York Times, January 29, 1967, March 12, 1978; Time, September 3, 1965.

JOSEPH SZIGETI

Joseph Szigeti

1892–1972

Joseph ("Joska") Szigeti, violinist, was born in Budapest on September 5, 1892. His father, Adolph Szigeti, was a teacher of the violin and played in a café-house orchestra. When Joska was three, his mother, Dora Faktor Szigeti, died, and he was sent to live with his grandparents in a village in the Carpathian mountains for the next five years. When an uncle gave him the gift of a violin, he began taking lessons, making such progress that in his eighth year his father took him back to Budapest for more professional training. For a few months he attended a second-string conservatory. Then, auditioning for Jenö Hubay at the Music Academy, he was accepted for Hubay's class without being required, as was usual, to take preparatory courses with lesser teachers.

When Joseph was eleven he gave his first performance, a concert at the Music Academy. After that he made occasional appearances at school concerts, benefit and semipublic performances and, during the summer, at resorts with the Budapest Operetta Theater Orchestra.

With a letter of introduction to Hermann Wolff, the German concert manager, Joseph arrived in Berlin in 1905. Under the aegis of Wolff, he made his debut in Germany in December 1905 at Bechstein Hall at a morning concert given exclusively for the press and invited guests. Unfortunately, this debut coincided with the sensational success of another violin prodigy, Mischa Elman, a fact that robbed Joseph's performance of the limelight. Since bookings for further appearances were few and far between, Joseph performed in German vaudeville theaters, using an assumed name.

In Germany his musical horizon broadened through hearing such violinists as Kreisler and Ysaÿe for the first time. When he auditioned for Joseph Joachim, for whom he played the Beethoven Concerto (with Joachim accompanying him on the piano), Joachim offered to become his teacher and even proposed finding him a patron, but Szigeti's father decided against accepting the offer. As Szigeti explained in his autobiography, *With Strings Attached:* "My father . . . felt it would be a mistake to link my perplexed immaturity to the greatness that was already so much a part of the past." Besides both father and son were fearful that in accepting Joachim's generous offer they would offend Szigeti's teacher, Hubay.

After a year in Berlin, Szigeti moved in 1906 to London, his home for the next seven years. He made his debut and then was heard in fashiona-

Szigeti: sē gĕt′ ĭ

ble salons and at various private musicales. Occasionally he played in joint recitals with Nellie Melba, Blanche Marchesi, or Wilhelm Backhaus. He also toured the English provinces. At this time he came into personal association with the teacher-pianist-composer Ferruccio Busoni, whose influence on Szigeti's musical development was to prove far-reaching. "What worlds Busoni opened for me! Listening to him—sometimes four or five times in one week; talking to him. . . . The weeks on this tour of the provinces spent under the influence of Busoni, the man and the musician, were the ones that shook me out of my adolescent complacency," Szigeti has said, and he has admitted that before he met Busoni "music had been principally a livelihood; afterward it became a fulfillment."

In 1912 Szigeti performed the Busoni Violin Concerto for Busoni at his studio ·in London. This led to three performances of the concerto under Busoni's direction in Berlin, Paris, and London. Szigeti's performances of the Busoni Concerto, at that time and since, helped to rescue the work from total neglect.

Other experiences during these pre-World-War-I years also left their mark on Szigeti's development as an artist. In Dundee, Scotland, he performed Beethoven's Violin Sonata in C minor with young Myra Hess, with whom he was appearing in a joint recital. Myra Hess's talent made a profound impression on him and convinced him of her potential as an artist. In Neuchâtel, Switzerland, he performed with an orchestra conducted by Ernest Bloch, initiating a musical association between these two men that would continue through the years, with Szigeti serving as a promoter of Bloch's music. Szigeti made his first recordings in 1909 for HMV—an abridged version of Beethoven's *Kreutzer Sonata* and the Bach unaccompanied Prelude in E major. In 1910 he performed for the Queen of Belgium and that same year was chosen by Karl Goldmark to perform the Goldmark Violin Concerto in A minor at a concert honoring the composer on his eightieth birthday. In 1913–1914 he extended his tours as virtuoso beyond France, Germany, Austria, Hungary, and Belgium, as far north as Helsinki and Riga and as far south as Portugal; he also made his first tour of Switzerland.

For three years during World War I he was confined to a sanatorium in Davos, Switzerland, a victim of tuberculosis. Since his lung specialist

was a music lover and an amateur violinist, Szigeti was able to pay some of his bills by teaching him the violin and playing duets with him. In Davos Szigeti befriended his compatriot, Béla Bartók, who was there recovering from an attack of pneumonia. The friendship that developed continued until Bartók's death, and Szigeti continually used his own art to advance that of his colleague.

In 1917, fully recovered, he left the sanatorium. That year he became head of the violin master classes at the Geneva Conservatory, succeeding Henri Marteau. He continued his teaching chores there during the next seven years while pursuing his career as a virtuoso. Geneva became his home base. His absence from the concert stage during his prolonged stay in the sanatorium gave him a new perspective on his art and his career. He was compelled to reevaluate himself and gained the courage to strike out towards new paths. Music for him was no longer just a profession but a sacred calling demanding the highest ideals. A series of concerts in Geneva in 1919, in which he performed a cycle of all of Beethoven's violin sonatas, marked the emergence of the new Szigeti, a musician who would soon be recognized worldwide as a philosopher of the violin. So popular did he become in Switzerland that in one year he had to give forty-five recitals there. His fame was equally secure all over Europe. Eugène Ysaÿe said of him: "I found in Szigeti that rare combination of musician virtuoso. As an artist he seemed conscious of a high mission into which he put all his faith, and he placed technique entirely at the service of musical expression."

In 1919 in Geneva Szigeti married Wanda Ostrowska, a Russian girl who had been left stranded in a Geneva finishing school by the Russian revolution. They had one child, a daughter, Irene.

In 1923 Fritz Kreisler heard Szigeti at a concert of the Berlin Philharmonic Orchestra. Returning to the United States later that year, Kreisler told American journalists how highly he esteemed the artistry of Szigeti—this publicity helped to set the stage for Szigeti's American debut, a debut made possible by Leopold Stokowski for whom Szigeti had performed the Bach Chaconne in a hotel room in Zurich. Stokowski engaged him to appear with the Philadelphia Orchestra. In December 1925, playing Beethoven's Violin Concerto, Szigeti made his

American debut. A week later he repeated the concert in New York City. That season he was a guest artist with most of the major American orchestras and also appeared in recitals. The following year he returned to the United States for an even more extended tour, supplementing other performances with sonata recitals with Walter Gieseking and Ossip Gabrilowitsch. Olin Downes, writing in the New York *Times,* compared him to Ysaÿe because of his "breadth and generosity of style." Another New York music critic described him as "an individuality—a violinist whose art is more than an episode of a season."

In 1925 the Szigetis moved from Switzerland to Paris and he became a French citizen. His concert commitments were worldwide, with annual tours of the United States, eleven tours of the Soviet Union between 1924 and 1929 (and two others in 1931 and 1937), and two world tours in 1931 and 1932. In Tokyo he performed five consecutive nights, and in Buenos Aires seven nights in a row. In 1938 his reception in South Africa was so triumphant that a schedule of twelve concerts had to be expanded to nineteen.

On numerous occasions he gave cycles of concerts devoted to the six solo sonatas and partitas of Bach, to all the Beethoven and Mozart violin sonatas, and to "A Survey of Three Centuries of Violin Music." An artist of protean gifts, he gave sonata recitals with Artur Schnabel, Alfred Cortot, Carl Friedberg, and Claudio Arrau, among others, and collaborated in performances of chamber music with Pierre Fournier, William Primrose, and Artur Schnabel.

The scholarship he brought to the standard repertory and his searching interpretative gifts were also to be found in his performances of twentieth century music to which he dedicated himself throughout his career. In 1924 he performed the Prokofiev Violin Concerto No.1 at the International Society for Contemporary Music Festival at Prague; from then on he was largely responsible for making this work one of the most highly esteemed in the violin repertory of the twentieth century. On October 8, 1928, in Moscow, he gave the world premiere of Alfredo Casella's Violin Concerto in A Minor (a work dedicated to him), and in Budapest on November 22, 1929, he introduced Bartók's Rhapsody No.1, for violin and orchestra, which the composer had dedicated to him. He was responsible for the first performances of Bartók's *Contrasts*

(performed with Béla Bartók and Benny Goodman on January 9, 1939), Ernest Bloch's Violin Concerto (December 15, 1938), and the orchestral version of Bloch's *Baal Shem* Suite (October 19, 1941). He continually featured on his programs the music of Hindemith, Stravinsky, Albert Roussel, Busoni, Charles Ives, Webern, Honegger, and other composers of the twentieth century. In 1956–1957 he presented on university campuses three concerts, "Masterpieces of the Twentieth Century." When he began recording extensively in the mid-1920s he overrode the objections of recording company executives and made the earliest recordings of Prokofiev's Violin Concerto No.1, and works by Milhaud, Bloch, Bartók, and Charles Ives. Subsequently, Szigeti's exhaustive library of recordings included many more modern works such as Bloch's Violin Concerto, Busoni's Violin Concerto, Henry Cowell's First Violin Sonata, Stravinsky's Duo Concertante, Webern's *Four Pieces,* Bartók's *Rhapsody No.2,* Hindemith's Violin Sonata No.3, and violin sonatas by Prokofiev.

Many composers, esteeming him as an interpreter of their violin works, have dedicated works to him, among them Bartók, Busoni, Casella, Sir Hamilton Harty, Eugène Ysaÿe, Alexander Tansman, Prokofiev, and Ernest Bloch.

In 1933 Szigeti was invited to perform the Brahms Violin Concerto over the German radio in commemoration of the centenary of Brahms's birth. But with the rise of the Nazi regime and the takeover of the control of the German radio by Joseph Goebbels, Szigeti refused to enter Germany any longer. He concentrated his tours in the other parts of Europe and in the United States, South America, South Africa, Scandinavia, and the Middle East.

When World War II began and Paris fell, the Szigetis left Europe for permanent residence in the United States, acquiring a home at Palos Verdes Estates in California. In 1951 Szigeti became an American citizen.

In 1941 Szigeti inaugurated a series of weekly concerts of violin music over the American radio station WOR in Newark, New Jersey, and on several occasions in 1942–1943 he offered in the United States five successive evenings devoted to all the violin sonatas of Mozart. During World War II he contributed his musical services for bond drives for which he earned citations from the United States Treasury; he also performed for the USO and for veterans' organizations.

While on tour in the United States in January 1942, he was about to embark on a plane from Albuquerque, New Mexico, to California when some ferrying pilots required passage; he generously turned over his seat to one of them. That plane crashed, sending all its passengers (one of whom was the movie star Carole Lombard) to their deaths. When Artur Rodzinski, the conductor, learned that Szigeti's life had been spared, he wired him congratulations, calling that day "Szigeti's rebirthday."

At the war's end, Szigeti became the first European expatriate to resume his concert work in Europe, doing so with a tour in 1946–1947. In 1947, with Schnabel and Fournier, he gave a series of eleven chamber music concerts in London. Later that fall they helped to inaugurate the first festival at Edinburgh, with a Brahms-Schubert cycle. In 1950 Szigeti celebrated the twenty-fifth anniversary of his debut in the United States with an appearance as soloist with the New York Philharmonic. In March and April 1953 he visited Japan for the first time since the war, giving twenty-seven concerts, and in 1954 he made his first postwar tour of South America. In 1955 he conducted a Bach seminar and performed all of Bach's solo sonatas and partitas at Northwestern University. During the summer of 1957 he was a participant at the Pablo Casals Festival in Puerto Rico. Reporting to the New York *Times* from Puerto Rico, Howard Taubman wrote: "[Szigeti] understands Mozart. It is an honest Mozart. The flash and flare that young virtuosos would bring to the task are not there. Instead there is the transparent simplicity that only an experienced and subtle artist knows how to evoke."

In 1960 Szigeti left the United States to reestablish himself in Vaud, Switzerland, at Le Crépon, a modest Viennese-style villa overlooking Lake Geneva at Baugy-sur-Clarens. He was just an hour's distance from where his daughter Irene and her husband (the pianist Nikita Magaloff) resided. Withdrawing from the concert stage, he devoted himself to teaching a few select violin students. During the summer of 1965 he returned to the United States to participate in a number of musical projects at the University of Connecticut and at Harvard University. He also visited the Dartmouth Congregation of the Arts at Dartmouth College, which at that time was paying homage to the eminent eighty-two-year-old Hungarian composer Zoltán Kodály.

For his seventieth birthday in 1962, tributes poured in on him from all over the world: from Isaac Stern in New York, David Oistrakh in Moscow, Nathan Milstein in Montreux. Milstein telephoned him to play "Happy Birthday" in double and triple stops. Yehudi Menuhin gave an eloquent salute over BBC in England, saying: "We must be humbly grateful that the breed of cultured and chivalrous violin virtuosos, aristocrats as human beings and as musicians, has survived into our hostile age in the person of Joseph Szigeti. Perhaps he may be the string that will attach some chosen newborn reincarnation to his spiritual ancestor—to an Enesco, a Kreisler, a Joachim, or an Ysaÿe."

To honor Szigeti on his eightieth birthday in 1972, Columbia reissued a six-record retrospective album entitled *The Art of Joseph Szigeti,* covering some of his most popular recordings of six concertos, three sonatas, and a variety of shorter pieces.

Tall, lithe, and lean, always immaculately groomed in conservatively cut suits (usually in dark colors), Szigeti had the appearance of a diplomat. The sensitivity of his face was accentuated by his soft eyes; his forehead was high but appeared much more so because of the thin growth of hair on his head.

A highly cultured man, he had a passion for reading and learning and for visiting art museums. Walking and swimming were his preferred forms of physical exercise. His interest in bird life led to his keeping an aviary of exotic birds in Palos Verdes.

Joseph Szigeti died in a clinic in Lucerne, Switzerland, on February 20, 1973.

Among his many honors have been the decorations of Chevalier and Commander of the Legion of Honor in France, Officer of the Hungarian Order of Merit, Officer of the Belgian Order of Leopold, and the Ji Ji Shimpo Gold Medal from Japan. He received an honorary doctorate in music from Acadia University in Wolfville, Nova Scotia.

He transcribed for the violin numerous works by classical, romantic, and contemporary masters. Also, he appeared as himself in the motion picture *Hollywood Canteen* (1944). In addition to his autobiography, *With Strings Attached* (1947), he was the author of *A Violinist's Note-*

book (1965) and *Szigeti on the Violin: Improvisations on a Violinist's Themes* (1969).

ABOUT: Gelatt, R. Makers of Music; Szigeti, J. With Strings Attached. *Periodicals*—High Fidelity, November 1965; New York Times Magazine, December 17, 1950; Newsweek, January 1, 1951.

Ferruccio Tagliavini

1913–

FERRUCCIO TAGLIAVINI

Ferruccio Tagliavini, tenor, was born in Reggio Emilia, in northern Italy, on August 14, 1913, to Erasmo and Neviani Barbara Tagliavini. Since his father was the overseer of an isolated estate between Reggio Emilia and Bologna, Ferruccio had no formal schooling for his first twelve years but received tutoring in academic subjects with the children of the manor house. As a child he sang in the church choir and was known as "the little Caruso" because of his performances of several opera arias at school concerts and in the town theater. He received some training on the violin at the Conservatory in Reggio Emilia, but in spite of his talent for singing he refused to take voice lessons. His ambition was to become an electrical engineer. A maneuver by his father led him to enter a vocal competition and this in turn brought him a scholarship for the Parma Conservatory and his first singing instruction: His father had dared him to sing in a conservatory competition and on that dare Ferruccio appeared in the contest and won a scholarship, even though he had never had a lesson. He turned down the scholarship and instead studied voice privately for a time with Italo Brancucci.

After a period of military service, Tagliavini won first prize in a singing competition at the Florence May Music Festival in 1938 by performing the "O paradiso" aria from *L'Africaine.* Convinced now that his future lay with music, he took seven months of preparatory training from Amadeo Bassi and made his opera debut at the Teatro Comunale in Florence on October 28, 1939, as Rodolfo in *La Bohème.* (This was destined to become one of his most celebrated roles.) He was soon invited to appear in leading Italian opera houses, including La Scala in Milan, the Teatro Reale in Rome, and the San Car-

lo in Naples. Among his principal roles were Fritz Kobus in Mascagni's *L'Amico Fritz,* Elvino in *La Sonnambula,* Des Grieux in *Manon,* the title role in *Werther,* and Nemorino in *L'Elisir d'Amore.*

He first became known to Americans through the GIs stationed in Italy during World War II who spoke enthusiastically of his singing after his appearances at American army camps. The American music public became further acquainted with him through his many Cetra recordings imported from Italy.

In 1946 he toured South America and Mexico in *Tosca, Werther, Rigoletto,* and *La Bohème.* On October 2, 1946, he made his debut in the United States as Rodolfo with the Chicago Opera; he was subsequently heard with this company as Pinkerton in *Madama Butterfly* and Cavaradossi in *Tosca.* A few months later, on January 10, 1947, he appeared at the Metropolitan Opera, once again as Rodolfo. After Rodolfo's narrative "Che gelida manina," the performance was brought to a standstill with a storm of approving shouts and applause. Similar ovations punctuated the remainder of the performance until the final curtain when the house reverberated with bravissimos. Howard Taubman wrote in the New York *Times:* "The old house had more excitement than it has known in weeks. ... When the tenor took a solo curtain call at the end of the third act, you would have thought that a new Caruso had been discovered." Mr. Taubman went on to say: "Mr. Tagliavini is the real thing so far as a lyric voice is

Tagliavini: tä lyä vē′ nē

855

concerned. His voice is well placed and under fine control. He can sing with resounding sonority, and he can spin out a pianissimo of rare texture. . . . He sings with intelligence."

As one of the principal tenors of the Metropolitan Opera from 1946 to 1954, he earned special praise not only as Rodolfo but also as Nemorino, Count Almaviva in *The Barber of Seville,* Alfredo in *La Traviata,* the Duke of Mantua in *Rigoletto,* Edgar in *Lucia di Lammermoor,* Pinkerton, Cavaradossi, and Don Ottavio in *Don Giovanni.*

Tagliavini returned to the Metropolitan Opera for the single season of 1961–1962, as Nemorino on January 13, 1962. "It was the same old Tagliavini," wrote Harold C. Schonberg in the New York *Times,* "head atilt to the left, eyes shut as he aimed for the high notes. . . . Mr. Tagliavini's voice has not changed much, though there was a hint or two that high notes are not entirely to his liking these days. His voice is as sweet as ever, and he sang the innocent music with a good deal of grace. . . . Last night all was smooth." He was also heard that season as Rodolfo.

In the United States Tagliavini also sang with the San Francisco Opera, making his debut there as Nemorino on October 11, 1948, and with the Chicago Opera. He also appeared in recitals. When, late in his career, he gave one of his New York recitals, on October 17, 1976, Donal Henahan, writing in the New York *Times,* found that he still had a "good deal" of voice. "The tenor could sustain tones skilfully in the middle of his voice and shade with some subtlety. He also has a well-preserved sob." His radio debut took place on February 24, 1947, on the "Telephone Hour" over NBC. After this single radio appearance, a poll taken by *Musical America* among six hundred music editors of daily newspapers in the United States and Canada placed him third among the most important "occasional" male singers over the air.

Abroad, he made frequent appearances through the years with the leading opera companies of London, Paris, Buenos Aires, Italy, Brussels, and Vienna. In 1950, as a visiting member of the La Scala company, he appeared as Nemorino at La Scala.

He was starred in several motion pictures filmed in Europe: *Voglio Vivere Così* (1946), *The Barber of Seville* (1947), *The King's Jester* (1947), *Anything for a Song* (1947), *The Lady Is Fickle* (1948), *I Cadetti di Guascogna* (1952) and *My Heart Sings* (1954).

On April 30, 1941, he married Pia Tassinari, an opera singer whom he met in 1940 when both appeared in a performance of *L'Amico Fritz* at the Palermo Opera. After their marriage they sometimes appeared together on the operatic stage. Their first appearance together in the United States came when Tassinari made her Metropolitan Opera debut in the title role of *Tosca* on December 26, 1947.

For many years Tagliavini resided in an apartment on Park Avenue in New York City. He never lost his early fascination for machines and loved puttering around those in need of repair. A sportsman, he won a cup for swimming and was an avid enthusiast of football and boxing— he used to spar with the Italian middleweight champion. Many of his leisure hours have been spent painting and sculpting. He is also an ardent movie fan. Since his retirement as a singer, Tagliavini has been living in Italy.

ABOUT: New York Times, December 8, 1946, October 14, 1977; Opera News, February 10, 1947.

Martti Talvela

1935–

Martti Olavi Talvela, bass, was born in Hiitola, a coast town in the Karelia district of Finland, on February 4, 1935. He was the eighth of ten children in a family of farmers. Every member of his family sang, and there were frequent vocal concerts at home. His father, Toivo Talvela, was also an amateur violinist. When Martti was five a visitor to his home inquired if he, too, sang. "Of course," Martti replied, "but only for money." The visitor paid him five Finnish marks —this represented his first singing fee.

Martti was eight when the Soviet Union invaded Karelia. His family found a new home in a town near Helsinki where his father and older brothers continued to support themselves through farming. "On the farm," he recalls, "I was always the black sheep because I had too much temperament and did more than my share of naughty things as a boy. But my father was very strict, and often hit me with a stick or cane. I was well educated by the stick."

After graduating from high school, he worked

MARTTI TALVELA

for four years as a teacher of mathematics, languages, and history at a high school in Lahti. At that time he married Anna Kääriäinen, a schoolteacher who gave up her own profession to devote herself to being a wife, then a mother of three, and eventually even her husband's secretary.

In 1957 he studied voice with Martin Öhman. Two years later, he saw his first opera: *Boris Godunov,* in which he was eventually to enjoy some of his greatest successes. In 1960 he won first prize in a national singing contest in Finland. "It was nothing big," he told Robert Jacobson in an interview reported in the New York *Times,* "but it was important for me. It was the first time I appeared in public, and it changed my whole outlook. I then saw I could perform."

Encouraged by this award he auditioned for the Finnish National Opera but was told they had no place for another bass. With his wife and children he moved on to Stockholm where he had a successful audition with the Royal Stockholm Opera. His opera debut took place there in 1961 as the Commendatore in *Don Giovanni.* Wieland Wagner heard him in Stockholm and invited him to audition for the Berlin Deutsche Oper. In 1962 Talvela appeared for the first time in Berlin in the role of Fernando in *Fidelio;* during the same summer he was invited to Bayreuth to make his first appearance there as Titurel in *Parsifal.* "Working with Wieland Wagner changed my whole life," he told Jacobson. "He influenced me not only in singing Wagner, but in

everything I did. . . . The productions I did with him in Bayreuth, Berlin, Rome and Vienna were really the best time of my life, a time I will never forget."

He became a permanent member of the Berlin Deutsche Oper, appearing in most of the principal bass parts not only in Wagner, which was one of his specialties, but in other operas as well. The company gave him the honorary title *Kammersänger.* He often sang with the Hamburg Opera and was frequently heard at La Scala, the Vienna State Opera, the Munich Opera, the Rome Opera, at Covent Garden and Bayreuth, and with other major companies in Europe, Scandinavia, and the Soviet Union. When Herbert von Karajan launched his production of the *Ring* cycle at Salzburg with *Die Walküre,* during Easter of 1967, he engaged Talvela to appear as Hunding. In the 1968 Salzburg performance of *Das Rheingold* by von Karajan, Talvela was cast as Fasolt. Both these performances were recorded for Deutsche Grammophon, as was the 1966 Bayreuth performance of *Tristan and Isolde* conducted by Karl Böhm, in which Talvela appeared as King Mark. The recording of the 1966 performance won the Grand Prix du Disque in Paris.

Talvela made his American debut in February 1968 in a performance of Verdi's Requiem with the Cleveland Orchestra under Szell. "He is," reported a critic for the New York *Times,* "a giant of a man with an exceptionally smooth bass voice, up from the G to wherever he has to go. He has a supple technique and plenty of volume. Clearly he is one of the best living singers in his category." In the fall of 1968 he made his recital debut in New York. "Mr. Talvela's voice is immense, yes," said a critic for the New York *Times,* "but absolutely even in quality through its entire range. He can shift from sotto voce to fortissimo with the greatest facility, and the softest sounds are as true in quality and as easy to hear as the loudest ones."

On October 7, 1968 (the opening night of the season), he appeared for the first time at the Metropolitan Opera, singing the Grand Inquisitor in *Don Carlo.* "He has a big, superbly focused voice," commented the New York *Times,* "and he made a wonderfully hulking malevolent figure." Later that season he appeared at the Metropolitan Opera as Hunding and, in *Das Rheingold,* as Fasolt, both in the new von Karajan productions.

Talvela's greatest success at the Metropolitan Opera, up to that time, came on December 16, 1974, in the title role of a new production of *Boris Godunov,* the first presentation by this company of the original Mussorgsky version. He had previously sung the part over seventy times, not only abroad but at the San Francisco Opera (in 1973, also in the original Mussorgsky version). Speaking of his appearance at the Metropolitan Opera, Harriet Johnson wrote in the New York *Post:* "He is a Finn who understands the Russian psyche. He feels the terrible conflicts the Czar had and is able to project them with insight. He makes Boris a complex figure in his remorse, his driving ambition, his love for his children, his cruelty." As Boris Godunov, Talvela helped open a new season for the Metropolitan Opera on October 10, 1977; one week later he sang there for the first time anywhere the role of Gremin in *Eugene Onegin.*

In 1975–1976 he appeared in the world premiere of Joonas Kokkonen's *The Final Temptations* with the Helsinki Opera; he later repeated this performance with the Stockholm Royal Opera. He sang Sarastro in a new production of *The Magic Flute* at the Paris Opéra on May 13, 1977, and in November of that year appeared in Moscow and Leningrad as King Philip in *Don Carlo* and as Boris Godunov.

Among the roles, other than those already mentioned, in which Talvela has distinguished himself are Gurnemanz in *Parsifal,* Dositheus in *Khovantchina,* Ramfis in *Aida,* Banquo in *Macbeth,* Zaccaria in *Nabucco,* Fiesco in *Simon Boccanegra,* Padre Guardiano in *La Forza del Destino,* Daland in *The Flying Dutchman,* Hagen in *Die Götterdämmerung,* Hermann in *Tannhäuser,* and King Henry in *Lohengrin.*

The United States has come to admire Talvela outside the opera houses through his recitals, his recordings, and his appearances with major American orchestras in such works as Beethoven's *Missa Solemnis* and Symphony No.9, and the Verdi Requiem. In April 1971 he was heard as Fasolt with the Chicago Symphony under Solti in a concert version of *Das Rheingold,* and one season later he appeared as Hagen in a concert version of the third act of *Die Götterdämmerung,* once again with the Chicago Symphony under Solti.

The Talvelas maintain three homes: one in Hamburg; a second in Helsinki; and a third, called "Hunting House," in the forest region of central Finland. During his vacations at the "Hunting House," Talvela enjoys felling trees. He is also a dedicated fisherman, and pursues this hobby at one of Finland's lakes where he owns a hut. During the salmon season he not only catches salmon but also smokes it and prepares salted salmon with Swedish dill. He is, moreover, skilled in preparing other gourmet fish dishes.

Talvela's interest in art has led him to collect Finnish sculpture as well as paintings by Dali and other modernists.

He is a huge man, standing six feet seven and weighing almost three hundred pounds. "When Mr. Talvela chooses to stress a point in conversation, the effect becomes even more gigantic," says John Rockwell in the New York *Times,* "what with the cavernous speaking voice and the huge hands and arms chopping the air for emphasis."

Since 1972 he has served as the artistic director of the summer Savonlinna Opera Festival in Finland, which, in addition to its operatic productions, maintains a training program for young singers.

In 1973 Talvela was awarded the Finnish State Prize and the Pro Finlandia Prize.

ABOUT: High Fidelity/Musical America, April 1978; New York Times, November 24, 1968; Opera News, November 2, 1968, January 25, 1975.

Richard Tauber

1892–1948

Richard Tauber (originally Ernst Seiffert), tenor, was born in Linz, Austria, on May 16, 1892. His father was both a singer and one of Austria's best-known actors; his mother was a professional singer. His father's employment took the Tauber family to Berlin from 1900 to 1903, to Wiesbaden from 1903 to 1911, and after 1911 to Chemnitz where his father became the director of the State Theater. All this while Richard was growing up within the theater, watching rehearsals, learning operas and operettas through listening, and watching with fascination as the conductors worked. "I always wanted to be a conductor," Tauber later disclosed to an inter-

Tauber: tou′ bĕr

RICHARD TAUBER

viewer. "I would listen entranced to street bands and unconsciously would beat time with my hands. At school I was much more interested in the theater and in music than in grammar and arithmetic. Then I went to study music and composition at Hoch's Conservatory in Frankfort."

At eighteen he found his first post as conductor. "But I was no longer satisfied. A new ambition had come into my life. I wanted to be a singer." His father opposed a singing career for Richard since he felt that the boy was just not good enough, and he expressed the opinion that it was far better to be a good conductor than a bad singer. As Tauber recalled: "A youthful love affair was actually the cause of my going to Freiberg where I accidentally met a teacher of singing. He was Professor Karl Beines and I began a course of lessons with him."

When Richard went home for Christmas, he sang several arias for his father who expressed surprise that he had developed so well. "Perhaps there is a career in singing for you," his father told him, while advising him to return to Freiberg for another year of vocal lessons. When that additional year of training ended, Tauber's father believed that his son was ready for a career in opera. He scheduled the debut at his own State Theater in Chemnitz on March 2, 1913, with Richard singing the role of Tamino in *The Magic Flute*. Count Seebach, Intendant of the Dresden Court Theater, happened to be in the audience. After the performance he offered Richard a five-year contract for his opera house,

a contract that eventually extended to ten years.

In 1915 Tauber appeared at Salzburg, with the Berlin Royal Opera as Bacchus in *Ariadne auf Naxos*. Four years later he became a permanent member of the Berlin State Opera and concurrently, after 1925, of the Vienna State Opera. With both companies he achieved considerable renown in the German, Italian, and French repertories, but most particularly in Mozart's operas in which he distinguished himself not only with those two opera companies but at the festivals in Salzburg and Munich. He also made numerous guest appearances with other major European opera companies. In 1926 he scored a major success as the Prince (a role he learned in two days) in a new production of *Turandot* in Dresden. When he performed at the Stockholm Opera, the King of Sweden gave him the Cross of the Order of Vasa, First Class. In France he was made officer of the Legion of Honor.

In 1924 Tauber became a friend of Austria's most successful operetta composer, Franz Lehár. Lehár persuaded him to turn from opera to operetta, and wrote for him a succession of operettas which starred Tauber and made him an idol in the popular musical theater, not only in Austria but also in England. These Lehár operettas were *Paganini* (1925), *Der Zarewitsch* (1927), *Fredericke* (1928), *Das Land des Lächelns* (1929), and *Schön Ist die Welt* (1934). The most successful of these operettas, as far as Tauber was concerned, was *Das Land des Lächelns (The Land of Smiles)*, a revision of an earlier Lehár operetta, *Die Gelbe Jacke*. As Prince Sou-Chong in *Das Land des Lächelns* Tauber appeared more than twenty-five hundred times in Germany, Austria, and England. Its principal waltz, "Dein Ist Mein Ganzes Herz" ("Yours Is My Heart Alone"), became his theme song. He sang it publicly at least fifteen thousand times, not only within the operetta but also in the movies, on records, and in recitals. There probably was not a single Tauber recital, from the early 1930s on, when he did not have this song either on the program or as an encore.

Because his father was Jewish, Tauber became an undesirable in Nazi Germany in 1933, and, after the annexation of Austria by Nazi Germany in 1938, in Austria as well. In 1934 he went to London for permanent residence and in 1940 he became a British subject. In 1938 and 1939 he returned to opera with appearances in England as Tamino, Belmonte in *The Abduction from the*

Seraglio, Don Ottavio in *Don Giovanni,* and Hans in *The Bartered Bride.*

On June 20, 1936, Tauber married Diana Napier, British actress. This was his second marriage; the first one, to Carlotta Vanconti, an operetta singer, ended in divorce in 1931. Tauber met Napier while both were filming the motion picture *Heart's Desire,* and their marriage took place when the filming was completed.

During World War II he remained in England where he performed for troops, for the wounded in hospitals, and, to help sustain public morale, for civilians. He once computed that during those war years he traveled a distance equaling twice around the world though he never left the British Isles. "If they had told me that I would sing in unheated theaters, seeing my breath as I sang," he told Howard Taubman in an interview for the New York *Times,* "that I would travel in icy railroad cars, that I would sleep in rattletrap hotels, that I would miss meals, that I would put up with a thousand discomforts, any one of which would bring an eruption from a tenor, I would have said they were crazy. But I did it, enjoyed it, and didn't have a day of illness." He played one week in Coventry when the theater in which he was appearing was bombed and he was thrown down a flight of stairs by the blast, but he continued to perform. A few days later, after he left Coventry, the city was demolished by Nazi bombs.

During the war he was also starred in an operetta that he had written, *Old Chelsea.* It opened in London on February 17, 1943.

Tauber made his first tour of the United States in 1931, appearing in recitals. His American debut took place at Town Hall, New York, on October 28, 1931. Olin Downes reported in the New York *Times:* "His voice is a lyric tenor, not a large voice but one of high range, flexibility and warmth. Vocal grace and charm are its natural attributes. . . . His native sensibility, facility, and communicativeness were irresistible to the audience." He made his second American tour in 1938, and in 1946 he returned a third time—to star in a Broadway production of *Das Land des Lächelns,* renamed *Yours Is My Heart Alone* after its principal song. On opening night, September 5, 1946, the title song received such an ovation that he repeated it four times in as many languages (English, French, Italian, and German). Soon after the opening of the operetta, he fell ill and some of the performances had to

be canceled. After several weeks of uncertainty, the producer decided to close the show on October 5.

Though seriously ill, Tauber appeared at Covent Garden as Don Ottavio in 1947, and that same year he made his final tour of the United States, giving his last recital on March 30, 1947, at Carnegie Hall in New York. He died in London on January 8, 1948.

Tauber and his wife lived in London. When not involved with his career or music, he devoted himself to his hobby of making amateur color movies. Wherever he went he took his camera with him. His garage in Elstree was equipped as a small theater for the projection of his films.

He was also professionally involved in the making of motion pictures, as a singing star. He starred in *Melodie der Liebe* (1932), *Das Lockende Ziel* (1933), *Die Grosse Attraktion* (1933), *Ich Glaub' Nie Mehr an Eine Frau* (1933), *April Romance* (1937), *Heart's Desire* (1937), *A Clown Must Laugh* (1938), *Forbidden Music* (1938), *Waltz Time* (1946), and *The Lisbon Story* (1951).

ABOUT: Ludwigg, H. ed. Richard Tauber; Tauber, D. N. Richard Tauber. *Periodicals*—Gramophone (London), July 1939.

Renata Tebaldi

1922–

Renata Tebaldi, soprano, was born in Pesaro, Italy, on February 1, 1922. Her father, Teobaldo Tebaldi, was a cellist who played in orchestras in provincial opera houses. His involvement in extramarital affairs led Renata's mother, Giuseppina Barbieri Tebaldi (a nurse), to leave him and take her three-month-old child to her native town of Langhirano, where Renata was raised. There her grandfather, a dedicated music lover who played the piano and composed waltzes and mazurkas, was the first to notice that Renata had an unusually lovely voice. He consulted a piano teacher at the Parma Conservatory as to what should be done about it. Before any plans could be formed, however, her grandfather died. Renata was seven. Nothing further was done to develop her musical talents. She attended the public school at Langhirano. At that time her parents were reconciled, and her father came to Langhirano to live. This recon-

RENATA TEBALDI

ciliation ended several years later, however, when her father, serving as a captain in the Italian army during World War II, fell in love with a widow whom he ultimately married.

Renata was eight when she heard her first opera: *Lucia di Lammermoor.* Shortly thereafter she tried to sing all the parts she could remember. Before long, she learned arias from *Rigoletto, La Bohème,* and *Norma* by listening to the radio and to recordings.

Upon graduation from public school in her thirteenth year, she asked her mother for music lessons. Her mother arranged for her to receive piano instruction from Giuseppina Passani, with whom Renata made such progress during the next three years that she aspired to become a concert pianist. By the time she was sixteen, however, she began to suffer such pains of back and shoulder that she decided to channel her musicianship into singing. When her piano teacher heard her sing, she recommended that she study with Italo Branucci at the Parma Conservatory. Since the Conservatory did not allow admittance to anybody younger than eighteen, Renata falsified her age, was admitted, and was placed in the singing class of Ettore Campogalliani.

She had spent two years at the Parma Conservatory with Campogalliani when, one summer, she went with her uncle for a vacation in Pesaro. There Renata's uncle arranged for her to audition for the operatic soprano Carmen Melis, who was also a vocal teacher. After hearing the young singer perform "Mi chiamano Mimi"

from *La Bohème* and "Un bel dì" from *Madama Butterfly,* Melis offered to give her daily instruction during Renata's vacation in Pesaro. "I was impressed by her intelligence and musicianship," Melis subsequently recalled. "She grasped almost instantly everything I told her and in a few days made enormous progress."

Tebaldi decided to continue her music study at the Pesaro Conservatory where Melis was principal vocal teacher. At the Conservatory, she studied harmony, counterpoint, piano, and history of art, as well as voice. Her four half-hour lessons a week with Melis at the Conservatory were supplemented by daily hour-and-a-half lessons at Melis's apartment.

She continued her studies at the Conservatory during the first years of World War II. During this period she made her first appearance in public, in Urbino, singing an aria from Catalani's *La Wally.* In November 1942, when the Conservatory had to close down because of frequent bombing attacks, she at first continued her vocal studies privately with Melis until the teacher was compelled to leave Pesaro for Lake Como. With her mother, Renata then moved to the town of Traversetolo to continue her vocal studies by herself. There she became engaged to Antonio Pedretti, a young medical student. The romance lasted a few years before it finally broke up because Renata refused to consider trading a professional career in music for domesticity.

The war was still on when Tebaldi made her debut in opera, at Rovigo in May 1944 as Elena in Boïto's *Mefistofele.* "I was terribly nervous," she told her biographer, Victor Seroff. "I practically lost my head. It threw me in a panic. . . . I felt I couldn't endure it another minute and I was going to run away. . . . I would have fainted if at that very moment the curtain had not gone up and I had to start singing the duet with Pantalis. In a flash of a second it sobered me. I thought only of the music I was singing and the role I was playing."

She sang in *Mefistofele* three times at Rovigo. The difficulty of travel during the war arrested the development of her career at this time. "When it was possible to make a journey, I traveled in box cars," she later recalled. "Once they found out I was a singer they gave me special treatment by allowing me to sit on the bags in the mail car." In the fall of 1944 she appeared as Mimi in *La Bohème* at Parma; a year later, again at Parma, she was heard as Mimi, as Suzel in *L'Amico Fritz,* and as Maddalena in *Andrea Chénier.* In 1946 at Trieste she took on the role of Desdemona in *Otello* and achieved a personal triumph. She regards this performance as the real beginning of her operatic career. Meanwhile she continued her vocal studies with Melis and, on Melis's suggestion, with Giuseppe Pais.

In May 1946 she was engaged by the Brescia Opera to appear as Suzel. While rehearsing in Brescia she received word from Milan that Toscanini wished to hear her audition. When World War II ended, he had returned to Milan, after a seven-year absence, to conduct the concert with which the reconstructed La Scala theater, bombed during the war, was to reopen. Tebaldi later told an interviewer for the *Saturday Review* what happened: "The man who was calling out the names from a long list probably knew nothing about me for he called out Mister Tebaldi. I sang 'La Mamma Morta' from *Andrea Chénier* and then the Maestro let me sing the whole last act of *Otello.* Toscanini exclaimed, 'Bravo, bravo,' and told his son Walter to take my name and address. I was chosen." On May 11, 1946, she was one of eight soloists in a concert conducted by Toscanini. She sang "Preghiera" from Rossini's *Mosè in Egitto* and was a soloist in Verdi's Requiem.

After appearances in many of Italy's opera houses, Tebaldi once again appeared as a soloist under Toscanini at La Scala on June 26, 1949, when he directed another performance of Verdi's Requiem. At a party following the concert, Toscanini urged her to consider singing Aida, which she then felt was not for her voice. Toscanini was insistent and invited her to his house where he went through the score with her and gave her explicit instructions on how best to handle the role. And it was as Aida that she made her triumphant debut at La Scala on February 22, 1950, beginning an association with that company that saw her achieve extraordinary success and attract world interest.

In the fall of 1950 Tebaldi and the company of La Scala sang Verdi's Requiem at the Edinburgh Festival. After that she went on to London for two performances as Desdemona at Covent Garden, which inspired great excitement. From London, she proceeded to the United States, to make her American debut with the San Francisco Opera on September 26, 1950 (the opening night of the season), as Aida. *Time* reported that she was the biggest sensation in Cali-

fornia opera in twenty-eight years and that she brought down the house with the first act aria "Ritorna vincitor" and with the third-act aria "O patria mia." Arthur J. Bloomfield wrote in his history of the San Francisco Opera: "The wistful, expressive beauty of Tebaldi's voice and her attractive personality won her a fond audience immediately and deservedly. ... Merola [the general manager] had finally found a dramatic soprano for the Italian repertoire with the greatness of a Muzio or a Rethberg. Her Desdemona, which came a couple of weeks later, was, in fact, an impersonation harder to surpass than her Aida."

The year 1951 was commemorated as the fiftieth anniversary of Verdi's death, and Tebaldi was heard at La Scala as Violetta in *La Traviata.* She then assumed the title role in Verdi's *Giovanna d'Arco* at the San Carlo in Naples in the opera's first revival in about a hundred years —the opera was mounted expressly for her. Later, in Paris she made a sensational debut when, with the visiting San Carlo, she repeated her performance as Giovanna d'Arco.

But the year 1951 was also for her a time of stress and conflict. During a performance of *La Traviata* at La Scala on February 3 her voice broke badly, and for the rest of the opera she sang poorly. For this she was severely criticized and the criticism was even greater when, upon being told she required rest and treatment, she canceled all eight performances she was scheduled to give as Violetta and her scheduled performances as Aida. Then, in the fall of 1951 on a tour of South America she suffered the hostility of Maria Callas. Callas had long watched the growing fame of Renata Tebaldi with the fear of one who saw her own regal position among the prima donnas of the time endangered. When Tebaldi, then singing in *Andrea Chénier* at São Paulo, was called to Rio de Janeiro to replace Callas as Tosca, the latter saw this as a maneuver to discredit her. She expressed her anger openly, and from this time on a feud developed between the two artists. When Tebaldi returned to Milan she discovered that the city's operagoers had divided themselves into two warring camps as Tebaldiani and Callasiani. This bitter Callas-Tebaldi feud continued for several years.

Tebaldi had already appeared in virtually every major opera house in the world and been acclaimed as a star before she was finally heard at the Metropolitan Opera in New York. Actually, as early as 1948 Edward Johnson, then the general manager, offered her a contract that she turned down because she felt she was not yet ready. About two years later the new general manager, Rudolf Bing, wanted her for two performances as Donna Elvira in *Don Giovanni* and one performance as Mimi. She turned this offer down also, maintaining she could accept only if she were engaged for a full season. Finally, in the spring of 1954, Bing went to Milan to engage her for the Metropolitan Opera season of 1954–1955. Her debut took place on January 31, 1955, as Desdemona. Speaking of her performance Olin Downes called her in the New York *Times* "an artist of exceptional quality, intelligence and sincerity." He further commented: "As an actress she is a beautiful spectacle—a beautiful woman, and in appearance last night like a figure from an old Florentine painting. She is a musician, too, one of knowledge and taste." When she was heard later that season as Mimi, Downes called her interpretation "a revelation. . . . We have heard no Mimi that moved us so much by the sincerity and the gripping emotion that she gave her part." She was scheduled to sing Aida the same season, but an ear infection delayed that performance until the following year. However, she did manage to appear as Tosca and Maddalena.

When, on November 19, 1955, she was finally seen and heard as Aida at the Metropolitan Opera, Howard Taubman wrote in the New York *Times* that it "was worth waiting for." He added: "The Italian soprano has a mind and personality and leaves her own impress on whatever role she undertakes. . . . When her turn comes to sing, Miss Tebaldi does so with sovereign musicianship. Her voice has remarkable range; it can swell into a gorgeous fortissimo and it can be refined to an ethereal pianissimo. She has a way of giving individual character to a phrase, with a color or delicate regard . . . that intensifies the emotional impact."

As at La Scala, so at the Metropolitan Opera a Renata Tebaldi cult developed through the ensuing seasons as she was heard in other of her operatic characterizations: Violetta (in a new production of *La Traviata* mounted for her), Cio-Cio-San in *Madama Butterfly* (a part in which she was coached by the Japanese stage director Yoshio Aoyama), Leonora in *La Forza del Destino,* Amelia in *Simon Boccanegra,* Minnie in *The Girl of the Golden West,* Alice Ford

in *Falstaff,* the title roles in Cilèa's *Adriana Lecouvreur* and *La Gioconda* (two new productions mounted for her), and *Manon Lescaut.* In all these she was, as Alan Rich said of her in the *Herald Tribune,* "a sovereign performer . . . one of the supremely gifted singers in the canon of Italian opera. The majesty of her musical and dramatic conception, the innate feeling for lyric flow that has ennobled her art from her first appearance on the operatic stage . . . these are things to cherish." To do her the honor she deserved and to please her admirers, the Metropolitan Opera presented her on the opening night of the 1958–1959 season (October 27) as Tosca.

After the triumphs of her first Metropolitan Opera season in 1955, she returned to La Scala to fill what she thought would be her final engagements there. For a few years La Scala had tried to cool the heat of the Callas-Tebaldi rivalry by allowing them to share the position of *prima donna assoluta,* each taking over half the season. But Tebaldi began to resent increasingly the preferences given to Callas as to repertory and gala performances. In 1955, therefore, she announced she would accept such treatment no longer and would bid farewell to her La Scala audiences with a performance of *La Forza del Destino.* Her public in Milan, however, could not forget her. In 1956, when she returned to Milan to give a concert for UNICEF, the ovation of her admirers spilled over into the street where her car was surrounded and then pushed along the Via Manzoni all the way to La Scala. As the car was being pushed, her admirers shouted: "Renata, return to La Scala!"

She returned to La Scala on December 9, 1959. By then Callas, having become involved in numerous temperamental forays with the management, no longer enjoyed the same popularity, and La Scala stood ready to accept Tebaldi as its sole *prima donna assoluta.* When she went on the stage as Tosca the audience jumped to its feet shouting out her name. The ovation lasted so long that Tosca's first dialogue with Cavaradossi was completely drowned out.

Tebaldi was also a favorite at the Vienna State Opera. The month of September 1959 was set aside for her appearances as Aida, Tosca, Desdemona, Manon Lescaut (in Puccini's opera), and Cio-Cio-San, with Herbert von Karajan conducting.

She was at the height of her fame and artistry

until the early 1960s. Though she continued to appear in operas and recitals after that, critics and audiences began to recognize that her personal griefs, the overabuse of her voice, and her many severe throat ailments had left their marks on her singing. "Minor flaws in her technique opened into major fissures," said Richard Dyer in the New York *Times.* "In what became her core repertory of Verismo heroines—Tosca, Adriana, Maddalena, Fedora, later even Gioconda and Minnie—she went beyond the natural framework of her voice and sang with more abandon than skill, sacrificing warmth, poise, and control for violent accent. . . . This new brutality invaded her gentler roles (Mimi, Desdemona), rapidly making others completely inaccessible to her (Butterfly, Violetta). Too soon the abandon her roles demanded necessarily gave way to the deadening caution born of terror and one was going to a Tebaldi evening for moments, not for a performance."

Tebaldi made her first tour of the Soviet Union in the fall of 1975 with performances at the Bolshoi Opera in Moscow, in Kiev, and in Leningrad (as well as in Warsaw). She proved so successful that she was invited for a second Soviet tour in October 1976.

She has appeared in many roles other than those already mentioned: Micaëla in *Carmen,* the title role in *Fedora,* Margherita in *Mefistofele,* Cleopatra in Handel's *Giulio Cesare,* the Countess in *The Marriage of Figaro,* Mathilde in *William Tell,* Amazily in Spontini's *Fernand Cortez,* and in the Wagnerian repertory in addition to Elsa, Eva in *Die Meistersinger,* and Elisabeth in *Tannhäuser.*

She has recorded most of her famous roles as well as her song and operatic recitals. One of the latter, on the London label, received a Grammy in 1958 from the National Academy of Recording Arts and Sciences.

Tebaldi never married. Her home for many years has been a ten-room apartment in the Piazza Guastalla in Milan. She is a collector of dolls, enjoys doing crossword puzzles, finds relaxation by driving a car, and has always had a weakness for fine clothes and furs and precious jewels.

Her voice was dubbed in on the sound track of the motion pictures *Colonna Sonora* (1946) and *Aida* (1954). She appeared in the motion picture *The House of Ricordi* (1956). She has also made appearances over television.

ABOUT: Harris, K. Renata Tebaldi: An Authorized Biography; Seroff, V. Renata Tebaldi: The Woman and the Diva. *Periodicals*—New York Times, February 20, 1955, April 29, 1973; Saturday Review, February 26, 1955; Time, November 3, 1958 (cover story).

Kiri Te Kanawa

1945?–

Kiri Te Kanawa, soprano, was born in the farm and fishing port of Gisborne, on the east coast of New Zealand, on March 6 in or about 1945. Her father, a contractor who installed petrol tanks, was a Maori, a descendant of the famous warrior Te Kanawa. Her mother, an excellent amateur pianist, was white, of Irish extraction, and her family background included Sir Arthur Sullivan. Kiri was their only child.

Her mother, Te Kanawa says, "made up her mind when I was three that I would be a singer. I had only five or six notes then, but they were loud and dark colored." When Kiri was seven she began studying the piano with her mother. Four years later she was taken to Auckland where she attended the Catholic schools. "The children were cruel to me because I was different —'that Maori girl,' " she told Stephen E. Rubin in an interview for the New York *Times.* "I was the only one in the school and they picked me to pieces. I was also not a pretty child—dead ugly." Her first singing teacher was a nun, Sister Mary Leon who, Kiri recalls, "had no method or anything, just a way of bringing the voice out." Kiri was fifteen at the time.

While still in her teens, Kiri went to Australia where she sang over radio and television, winning several prizes in radio competitions and capturing the first prize in the Melbourne *Sun* aria competition. To support herself, she sang in nightclubs, for weddings and special functions, and did a recording of Maori and folk songs she later described as "stupid."

She went to London in 1966 on a grant from the New Zealand Arts Council for four years of study at the London Opera Center. There she was taught acting, fencing, languages, and repertory as well as voice. Dissatisfied with the kind of vocal instruction she was getting, in 1969 she sought out a private teacher, Vera Rozsa, without whom, she says, "I don't think I would be here now." Under Rozsa, Te Kanawa, up to

KIRI TE KANAWA

then a mezzo-soprano, began singing the soprano range.

In 1967 she married Desmond Stephen Park, a mining engineer. "I met him on a blind date in Piccadilly Circus," she admits. "My mother had warned me against blind dates. This was my first and my last. It was not love at first sight. I was engaged to someone else in New Zealand at the time. But we were married three months later." They made their home twenty miles outside London.

She returned to New Zealand in 1969 to make her opera debut as Carmen with the New Zealand Opera. That year she also auditioned successfully for Covent Garden in London. She made her Covent Garden debut during the 1970–1971 season as a Flower Maiden in *Parsifal* and after that was heard there as Xenia in *Boris Godunov.*

Assigned by Covent Garden the role of the Countess in *The Marriage of Figaro*—a part she studied not only with her own teacher but also with Colin Davis, the music director of Covent Garden, and John Copley, its stage director— she decided to prepare herself for this performance by going to the United States in the summer of 1971 to make her American debut in that role with the Santa Fe Opera. She did not attract much attention. But in December 1971 she caused such a sensation at Covent Garden as the Countess that her performance was reported in English language papers the world over. In London, Andrew Porter called her "such a Countess as I have never heard before" and Peter Hey-

worth reported that "Covent Garden here has a pearl of great price."

As the Countess she made her debut with the San Francisco Opera in the autumn of 1972 and at the Glyndebourne Festival in England the following summer with renewed success. When she assumed the role of Amelia in *Simon Boccanegra* at Covent Garden in 1973, Harold Rosenthal, the editor of *Opera,* called her performance "a revelation, Verdi singing on the highest level."

Winning the Drogheda-Mayer Fellowship enabled her to undertake some additional study of voice and repertory in Mantua, Italy. She was then scheduled to make her debut at the Metropolitan Opera in New York on March 7, 1974, as Desdemona. But Teresa Stratas, who was singing in *Otello,* fell ill, and on three hours' notice Te Kanawa was called in as a replacement on February 9, 1974, a performance that was broadcast nationally. "I got only five minutes on the set before the performance began." In the third act she suffered a cramp in the groin. In spite of all this she achieved a remarkable success. In the New York *Post,* Harriet Johnson wrote of her voice: "It is a large, full, easily produced soprano that opens up on top like a luscious rose." In the New York *Times,* Allen Hughes wrote: "She is slim and attractive and the impression she made as Desdemona was satisfying in every way." In the *New Yorker,* Andrew Porter said she sang "phrase after phrase of effortlessly spun and firmly supported tone, culminating in a last act that would have drawn tears from a stone."

She gathered more praise at the Metropolitan Opera as Donna Elvira in *Don Giovanni* on January 11, 1975. That same year she made her debut at the Paris Opéra as Donna Elvira and with the Scottish Opera in Great Britain as Mimi in *La Bohème.* At Covent Garden she sang Marguerite in a new production of *Faust.* Then she helped to open the 1975 season of the San Francisco Opera as Amelia in *Simon Boccanegra.* In 1976 she took on two more roles: Tatiana in *Eugene Onegin* at Covent Garden in April and, the following June, Fiordiligi in *Così fan Tutte* at the Paris Opéra. She also appeared in a filmed version of *The Marriage of Figaro.*

In 1975 she made a three-week tour of Australia as soloist with the New Zealand Orchestra. A year later she returned to Australia to appear with the Australian Opera in *La Bohème* and *Simon Boccanegra*. She was cast as Pamina in a new production of *The Magic Flute* at the Paris Opéra on May 13, 1977. For the first time anywhere she assumed the title role of Richard Strauss's *Arabella* at Covent Garden in London in July 1977. The following September she appeared with the Vienna Philharmonic at the Berlin Festival. Later the same year she sang Arabella for the first time in the United States, with the Houston Opera; appeared as Donna Elvira at the Mozart Festival at Cologne, Germany; and on December 31, 1977, was heard as Rosalinde in a new production of *Die Fledermaus* conducted by Zubin Mehta (the first revival of that operetta at Covent Garden and the first televised opera ever transmitted from Europe to the United States). Reporting from London to the New York *Times,* Harold C. Schonberg called Te Kanawa "by far, the vocal star of the evening. . . . Miss Te Kanawa, who is also graced with physical beauty, has a warm, sensuous, naturally produced voice of a large size. She acted with charm and sang the role in an unfaltering series of legato phrases. She has, too, a resplendent high C."

Stephen E. Rubin described Te Kanawa in the New York *Times* as "a kooky character, five feet eight and a half inches tall and sturdy, with enormous brown eyes and loosely flowing brunette hair. Her exotic good looks stem from her odd parentage."

At her home outside London, she enjoys tending to her vegetable and flower gardens. She relaxes further by sewing ("curtains and lampshades and things"). For exercise she bicycles, plays golf and squash, and goes swimming and water skiing. She rarely goes to parties (though she enjoys giving them) and is very concerned about preserving her privacy.

Kiri Te Kanawa has been decorated by England with the Order of the British Empire.

ABOUT: High Fidelity/Musical America, May 1974; New York Times, February 28, 1974, March 3, 1974; Stereo Review, March 1975.

Milka Ternina

1863–1941

Milka Ternina, Wagnerian soprano, was born in Vezisce, near Zagreb, Croatia, on December 19, 1863. Her father died when she was a child, and she was adopted by her uncle, J. Jurkovic, the Imperial State Councilor, who saw to it she received a thorough grounding in languages and music. In her twelfth year she began vocal study with Ida Winterberg, and from 1880 to 1882 she finished her vocal training in Vienna with Joseph Gänsbacher. She was still a voice student when in 1882 she made her opera debut in Zagreb (then called Agram) as Amelia in *Un Ballo in Maschera.* She followed this with appearances as Aida, Marguerite in *Faust,* and Selika in *L'Africaine.* In 1883–1884 she appeared in light opera at Leipzig and from 1884 to 1886 in the operatic repertory at Graz. Upon the recommendation of Anton Seidl, the Wagnerian conductor, she was appointed principal soprano of the Bremen Opera. She remained there from 1886 to 1889.

Her international fame as a Wagnerian soprano had its beginnings at the Munich Royal Opera where she served as principal soprano from 1890 to 1899. In Munich she was given the honorary title *Kammersängerin.* During leaves of absence from Munich she was heard in the Wagnerian repertory in many European cities. She made her London debut on April 25, 1895, in a Wagner program performed by an orchestra directed by Hermann Levi at Queen's Hall. In 1896 she was heard at a concert in Moscow given by the German ambassador to honor the coronation of Czar Nicholas II. Then in 1899 she made a triumphant bow at the Bayreuth Festival as Kundry in *Parsifal.*

She made her first appearance in the United States in February 1896 in Boston with the Damrosch Opera Company, alternating with Katharina Klafsky later that season as Isolde in *Tristan and Isolde.* Her opera debut in England followed on June 3, 1898, at Covent Garden in London as Isolde. That season at Covent Garden she duplicated her success as Isolde with performances as Brünnhilde in the *Ring* cycle and as Leonore in *Fidelio.*

Ternina: tĕr nē′ nä

MILKA TERNINA

In New York, as well as in Germany and England, Ternina's eminence as a Wagnerian soprano was fully appreciated, particularly during her years at the Metropolitan Opera. She made her debut there on January 27, 1900, as Elisabeth in *Tannhäuser,* to the approval of public and critics. In spite of her star status, she took the small part of The First Lady in the first Metropolitan Opera production of *The Magic Flute* on March 30, 1900. On February 4, 1901, she created for the United States the title role of *Tosca.* H. E. Krehbiel expressed amazement in the *Tribune* "at the tragic power disclosed by Mme. Ternina, which in its most hideous moment has had no companion on the local operatic stage since Mme. Calvé created nightmares with her impersonation of *La Navarraise*. ... Mme. Ternina's performance ... created unbounded delight." Up to 1904 (with the exception of the 1902–1903 season), Ternina was heard at the Metropolitan Opera as the three Brünnhildes, Sieglinde in *Die Walküre,* Senta in *The Flying Dutchman,* Elisabeth, Elsa in *Lohengrin,* Isolde, Kundry, Tosca, and Leonore in *Fidelio.*

She was Kundry when the Metropolitan Opera presented its highly controversial American premiere of *Parsifal* on December 24, 1903—controversial since this was the first stage performance of *Parsifal* outside Bayreuth and was given in spite of the violent objections of Cosima Wagner, who insisted that *Parsifal* could be performed only at Bayreuth. Legal representatives from Bayreuth went to the courts in New York

to prevent the performance from taking place, but they lost the suit. As Kundry, said H. E. Krehbiel in the *Tribune,* "Mme. Ternina ... is precisely what she ought to be—which is to say an enchantress, who, while feminine in all her allurements, steadily preserves that macabre quality through which Wagner lifted this character out of the ruck of operatic sirens and gave her a potent individuality. Mme. Ternina bewitched her audience, as she sought to bewitch Parsifal, with limpid song, and again she moved those who heard her by her effective use of the deeper resources she possesses." Because of her involvement in this production, Ternina was denounced in Bayreuth and never again permitted to perform there.

From 1900 to 1906 Ternina appeared regularly at Covent Garden in London. In 1900 she appeared there as Tosca in the first performance in England of the Puccini opera. Her final performance in London took place on May 28, 1906, as Elisabeth. Soon after that she was forced to go into retirement because of a paralysis of the nerves of the eye that set in after a cold contracted while climbing mountains in Switzerland. For one year after her retirement she taught voice at the Institute of Musical Art in New York. After that she returned to Zagreb where for many years she taught voice privately. One of her pupils was Zinka Milanov.

Milka Ternina died in Zagreb on May 18, 1941.

ABOUT: Kutsch, K. J. and Riemens, L. A Concise Biographical Dictionary of Singers.

Lionel Tertis

1876–1975

Lionel Tertis, violist, devoted his life and career to making the viola an important solo instrument, and he was for the most part successful in his endeavor. He became the first violist in performing history to achieve international renown as a performer both in recitals and as a guest artist with orchestras.

He was born in West Hartlepool, England, on December 29, 1876. When he was three his family took him to London. About two years later he started to study the piano, and at the age of seven he appeared in a public concert.

Tertis

LIONEL TERTIS

The poverty of his family made it impossible for him to continue studying with teachers, but he made progress by practicing on the piano without guidance. By saving his earnings, he was able to enroll at Trinity College in London, where he often appeared in performances of piano concertos. Though he demonstrated a strong talent for the piano, he ultimately began to lose his enthusiasm for that instrument. His mother, however, insisted that he continue its study, often locking him in his room to keep him at the keyboard practicing from six to eight hours a day.

The necessity of earning a living compelled him to leave Trinity College. From his thirteenth to his sixteenth years he supported himself by playing the piano. Once again he saved his money, this time with the intention of going to Leipzig, for further music study at its conservatory. At this time he began to show an interest in and started to learn to play the violin.

When he entered the Leipzig Conservatory he specialized in the study of the violin, his teacher at the time being someone who, as he later recalled, "was more interested in his stamp collection than in music." By 1894 he was back in England. Sir Alexander Mackenzie, composer and educator, arranged for Tertis to enter the Royal Academy of Music in London. It was there that Tertis finally turned from the violin to the viola. A fellow student had organized a string quartet and had difficulty finding a violist. He asked Tertis to learn to play that instrument and Tertis agreed. "From the moment I played

the first note on the viola, I loved it," he said. In three weeks' time Tertis was able to participate in his first string quartet concert, and from then on he concentrated on the viola.

He continued to study the viola with a teacher of the violin, since there were no viola instructors at the Academy, and he worked by himself to perfect his technique. He performed all the standard violin concertos on the viola, sometimes at the fortnightly concerts at the Academy.

Upon completing his studies, Tertis received an appointment at the Academy, as professor of the viola, a post he retained over a period of many years and in which he influenced an entire generation of English violists. At the same time he made a studied effort to advance himself as a virtuoso on the viola. He gave recitals which for a long time proved unsuccessful, since the prejudice against the viola as a solo instrument was too deeply entrenched to be overcome with a few performances. "Everybody seemed to be up in arms at my daring to play solos on the viola," he later recalled. "They declared it was never meant to be, and never could be a solo instrument. I was made to feel almost that I was doing something criminal."

But he refused to admit defeat. He continued to work on the viola, modeling his style of performance after that of Fritz Kreisler on the violin. He also continued to concertize. In the end, he was responsible for emancipating the viola, his perseverance combined with his artistry finally bringing about an interest in the viola as a solo instrument. His concerts became well attended, and he was called upon to appear as a soloist with many symphony orchestras. To augment the limited repertory of viola music, he made numerous transcriptions for the viola: of the Brahms Clarinet Sonata, the Bach *Chaconne,* Mozart's Clarinet Concerto, Elgar's Cello Concerto, Delius's Cello Concerto, and others. Many of England's prominent composers wrote for him, among them Arnold Bax, Frank Bridge, Cyril Scott, Eugene Goossens, and Vaughan Williams. Tertis presented the world premiere of Vaughan Williams's Suite for Viola and Orchestra in London on November 12, 1934. Though he did not introduce William Walton's Concerto for Viola and Orchestra, his influence had made it possible for Walton to write this highly successful work. Tertis performed it at a concert of the International Society for Contemporary Music at Liège on September 4, 1930.

During World War I, Tertis gave numerous concerts for the English armed forces, both as a soloist and in collaboration with other musicians. In the company of the King and Queen of Belgium he visited the front where he performed with Pablo Casals. At one time in London he participated in a performance of the Brahms Piano Quartet in C minor with Casals, Ysaÿe, and Arthur Rubinstein during a blackout.

By the time he made his first tour of the United States in 1923–1924, he was well known. In America he appeared in numerous recitals, in an all-British program with the Chicago Symphony, and in New York City in a performance of Mozart's *Sinfonie Concertante for Viola, Violin and Orchestra,* with Fritz Kreisler playing the violin.

Tertis once explained that the art of playing the viola lay in "the touch of a dove and the strength of an elephant." "Here," comments Marion M. Scott, English musicologist and critic, "lies the marvel of his playing. He can command anything of his instrument and obtain it. . . . He can express the grandeur of Bach as surely as the delicacy of Mozart, the elegance of eighteenth-century Italy, as Delius' dream quality. Wherever he finds beauty, with the true artist's instinct, he desires to share it."

In February 1937 Tertis announced that, since rheumatism of his arm had begun to affect his bowing, he was withdrawing from all concert work. "I do not wish to continue playing until the deterioration of my playing becomes apparent," he said. In that month he made his farewell appearance as soloist with the BBC Symphony in William Walton's Viola Concerto and as the viola obbligato in Berlioz' *Harold in Italy.* "Wonderfully as he has played before, even Tertis never played as he did then," commented one critic in his review. "Certainly never before has the viola proved so conclusively its claim as a solo instrument."

On June 13, 1937, some of England's leading musicians gave him a farewell dinner. Among those gathered to honor him were Sir Thomas Beecham, Felix Salmond, William Murdoch, Vaughan Williams, Sir Hugh Allen, Eugene Goossens, and Albert Sammons. "The golden tones, passionate utterances and wonderful phrases will always remain in the memory of those who heard him," said Vaughan Williams.

"And even those who have not heard him will live richer lives because he has played."

So certain was Tertis of the permanency of his retirement that he disposed of his precious Montagnana instrument. But the recovery of his health and the events of World War II eventually brought him out of retirement. He acquired a new English instrument, and with this he made several appearances in London as part of the war morale program. He performed once again, in 1949, in a recital at the Royal College of Music in London to help inaugurate a fund to encourage composers to write music for the viola.

Lionel Tertis died in London on February 22, 1975, at the age of ninety-eight. For many years, up to the time of his death, he lived at Wimbledon Commons in London. His first wife, Ada, was the daughter of Reverend Hugh Gawthrop; she died in 1931. In 1939 he married Lillian Florence Margaret Warmington, a cellist.

In 1950 he was made Commander of the British Empire and was awarded the Fritz Kreisler Award of Merit. Subsequently he was made Chevalier de l'Ordre Couronne in France and received gold medals from the Worshipful Company of Musicians and the Royal Philharmonic Society of London. He also received the Eugène Ysaÿe medal in Brussels. In 1966 he was made Honorary Fellow of Trinity College in England.

Following his retirement as a concert artist, Tertis devoted himself to experiments in designing and improving the viola. The so-called Tertis Viola, which he designed in 1956, has been adopted by many leading violists and has been manufactured in sixteen countries. Tertis also designed the Tertis Cello in 1959 and the Tertis Violin in 1962.

In addition to his autobiography, *Cinderella No More* (1953), Tertis was the author of *Beauty of Tone in String Playing* (1938).

ABOUT: Tertis, L. Cinderella No More.

Luisa Tetrazzini

1871–1940

Luisa Tetrazzini, coloratura soprano, was born in Florence, on June 28, 1871. Her father, a tailor for the military, was financially well off.

Tetrazzini: tä trät tsē' nĕ

Tetrazzini

LUISA TETRAZZINI

The Tetrazzini family was musical, and both parents encouraged their children to study music. Luisa's older sister, Eva Tetrazzini, also became a prima donna; before marrying the opera conductor Cleofonte Campanini, she had sung at the Academy of Music in New York. There on April 16, 1888, she created for the United States the role of Desdemona in *Otello*.

Eva was Luisa's first voice teacher. By the time Luisa was twelve she knew words and music of many opera arias she had heard her sister sing. Later, Luisa received vocal instruction at the Liceo Musicale in Florence with Ceccherini and Contrucci.

The inability of a scheduled singer to appear as Inez in *L'Africaine* brought Luisa to the stage of the Teatro Pagliano in 1895 for her opera debut. After that she appeared in other small opera houses in Italy and for a number of years toured South America and Mexico.

Her debut in the United States took place in 1904 at the Tivoli Opera House in San Francisco. She was so well received there that she never forgot her debt to that city. Six years later there occurred for her a conflict of dates between Manhattan Opera and San Francisco, and she told Oscar Hammerstein defiantly: "I will sing in San Francisco if I have to sing in the streets." The officials in San Francisco, informed of this remark, asked her if indeed she would be willing to sing in the streets at an open-air Christmas Eve benefit concert for the poor. She gave that performance in 1910 near the Lotta Fountain where Market, Kearney, and Geary Streets join.

A hundred thousand people came to hear her. A bronze plaque affixed to Lotta Fountain commemorated this event as "the greatest concert San Francisco or the world has ever seen." This concert became the first of such events given annually in the streets of San Francisco to raise funds for the poor.

The greatest of her initial successes were at Covent Garden in London, where she made her debut on November 2, 1907, as Violetta. She was heard later that season as Gilda in *Rigoletto* and in the title role in *Lucia di Lammermoor.* "My dear Mme. Tetrazzini," Adelina Patti wrote her after hearing her at Covent Garden. "Brava! Brava! I cannot tell you what pleasure it was for me to hear you yesterday evening, nor what joy your Italian phrasing gave me, nor how moved I was by the wonderful sensitivity and 'pathos' of your voice. You brought tears to my eyes in the last act."

After this engagement at Covent Garden, Tetrazzini was recognized, not only in England but also in Russia, Spain, Central and South America, and finally in the United States, as a prima donna with few rivals. Although she specialized in the Italian repertory, she never played any of the major opera houses in Italy and, consequently, never earned in that country the adulation that would inevitably have been hers had she been heard there in her most celebrated coloratura roles.

When Oscar Hammerstein engaged her for the Manhattan Opera House in 1907 at one of the highest fees ever given an opera performer up to then (three thousand dollars an evening) she was already a celebrity. She made her Manhattan Opera House debut on January 15, 1908, as Violetta, and was so successful that instead of the fifteen performances she had been scheduled to give that season she was heard in twenty-two. She electrified audiences with her vocal acrobatics not only as Violetta but, later on, as Rosina in *The Barber of Seville,* Ophelia in *Hamlet,* Amina in *La Sonnambula,* Lucia, and Gilda. It was true that she had a comparatively thin voice and that her lower range lacked body and expressiveness, but her trills and her virtuosity in ornamental passages were dazzling. Her high register was unfailingly brilliant; her middle register, singularly beautiful.

She continued to reign at the Manhattan Opera until it closed down in 1910. A year later she appeared for one season at the Metropolitan Opera, making her first appearance there on December 28, 1911, as Lucia. Reporting on this debut in the *Tribune,* H. E. Krehbiel wrote: "There is not much to be said of Mme. Tetrazzini's singing that has not been said over and over again in these columns—said in praise and said in mournful depreciation; in praise of her command of artistic device, in dispraise of the inequalities of her voice; in praise of the fine texture of her upper tones, in regret because of the infantile character of her lower; in laudation of skill artistically used and in denunciation of the same skill abused." During that season at the Metropolitan Opera, she was also heard as Violetta and Gilda. When she made her last appearance at the Metropolitan on February 6, 1912, as Gilda, several thousand people had to be turned away from the box office. Within the overcrowded auditorium she was given a thunderous farewell.

During the next few years Tetrazzini appeared in recitals throughout the United States. In opera, her success continued at Covent Garden and, in 1913, at the Chicago Opera where her brother-in-law, Campanini, was music director. She also appeared as a guest artist in opera houses in many foreign countries.

During World War I she devoted herself to singing in Italy for charity and for the war effort. She returned to the United States for a tour in 1919, making a return appearance in New York at the Hippodrome Theater on November 30, 1919. That audience, as Richard Aldrich remarked in the New York *Times,* was "primed for enthusiasm" and it "let loose on all occasions, principally, as was natural, after her singing of the mad scene from *Hamlet* and Benedict's Variations on *The Carnival of Venice,* the two florid numbers on her program. . . . Mme. Tetrazzini returns with her voice not only unimpaired but even in some respects improved during her absence. It seems somewhat more powerful. . . . It sounded . . . somewhat harder in its brilliancy. . . . The whole range of the voice is more nearly equalized. . . . Her delivery of florid passages of the various devices of coloratura singing . . . has the brilliance, celerity, the appearance of ease and the spontaneity that are enough to make a great effect in a day when such things are scarce. Mme. Tetrazzini is able to impart to such music the entrain and sweep that are its only reason for being."

She made front-page news in England in 1925 when she appeared in London at the first concert to be broadcast by British radio. Her last performance in the United States took place in 1931 —not in an opera house or a concert hall but in vaudeville—at the Palace Theater in New York. She bade farewell to the stage in 1934 and gave her final performance anywhere in 1938 when she made a recording to be transmitted by short wave to the United States.

Though she had earned well over five million dollars during her career, she ended up a pauper. To make ends meet she had to rent out rooms in her home in Rome to voice students, thereby supplementing whatever income she could get from teaching voice. When she died in Milan on April 28, 1940, she had become so impoverished that her funeral expenses had to be paid by the Italian government.

But as long as she was earning a fabulous income, she lived the life of the *grande dame,* spending her money with a prodigal hand. She owned a home in Rome that was furnished with regal magnificence. When she went on concert tours in the United States she always traveled in her own four-car train to accommodate two maids, a cook, a secretary, a pianist, a voice coach, and a flutist. Much of her money was spent on husbands and lovers. She was married three times. The first time, when she was quite young, was to a man named Scalaberni who became her impresario. Her second husband, J. G. Bazelli, disappeared one night never to return. In 1926 she married Pietro Vernati, who was twenty years younger than she; the relationship survived just three years. "Vernati took over his naive bride's bank account," wrote Gerald Fitzgerald in *Opera News.* "When Tetrazzini balked, he accused her of incompetence, and she was forced to sue for extortion. . . . Mystic and superstitious to a fault, Tetrazzini fell prey to more than one designing male; she often found herself involved in unpleasant litigation with swindlers, who exploited her penchant for the supernatural."

She was a woman of bountiful physical proportions, weighing over two hundred pounds. She loved good food and freely indulged herself in gourmet pasta dishes. The dish Chicken Tetrazzini (creamed chicken with baked spaghetti and mushrooms) is named for her.

In addition to her autobiography, *My Life of Song* (1921), Tetrazzini was the author of *How to Sing* (1923).

Teyte

ABOUT: Tetrazzini, L. My Life of Song. *Periodicals*—
Opera News, December 12, 1962, October 10, 1970.

Dame Maggie Teyte

1888–1976

Maggie Teyte (originally Margaret Tate), soprano, was born in Wolverhampton, Stratford-
shire, England, on April 17, 1888, of
English-Scottish-Irish descent. Both her parents
were musical. Her father, the owner of a hotel,
played the piano, and her mother was a singer.
Maggie received formal schooling at St. Joseph's
Convent at Wolverhampton. She was about
twelve when her parents, aware of her unusual
singing voice, decided she should have musical
training. They took her to London where Sir
Hubert Parry turned her down for admission to
the Royal College of Music because she was too
young but changed his mind once he heard her
sing. At the College, Maggie studied piano and
voice. In 1903 a London music patron, having
heard her sing Tosti's "Goodbye," raised a fund
to finance additional musical instruction for her
in Paris from 1903 to 1907 with Jean de Reszke
and Reynaldo Hahn.

In 1905 she made her debut in a Mozart festival in Paris as Zerlina in a concert presentation
of *Don Giovanni* conducted by Reynaldo Hahn
(a performance in which Lilli Lehmann,
Édouard de Reszke, and Mario Ancona were
also participants). Soon after this she was heard
in a joint concert with Paderewski at Monte
Carlo. There, in February 1907, she made her
formal opera debut as Zerlina.

From 1908 to 1910 she was a member of the
Opéra-Comique in Paris, where she was assigned minor roles. It was at this time that she
decided to change her name from Tate to Teyte
to forestall incorrect pronunciation by the
French public. Though up to now she had
shown little in her public performances to indicate special gifts, the Opéra-Comique chose her
to take over the role of Mélisande in *Pelléas and
Mélisande* that Mary Garden had then recently
created. She spent two hours each day for nine
months studying the role with Debussy. On June
12, 1908, she scored such a success as Mélisande

DAME MAGGIE TEYTE

that she was required to appear in it seventeen
times that season. "She added to Maeterlinck's
drama an entirely new charm," wrote the critic
of the Paris *Temps*, "and enriched the poetry of
Debussy's music with her loving and tender
touch." She told an interviewer many years
later: "I did very well. This is not conceit. I was
young and inexperienced. I didn't know what I
was doing. I just took to it as duck to water.
Perhaps it was because I was Scottish—as Mary
Garden was—that I fitted so well into the role.
You see, it needs a cool detachment that perhaps
a Scot can bring to it better than a Latin."

Teyte made her London debut in a recital in
October 1909. On December 4, 1909, she cre-
ated the role of Suzanne in Wolf-Ferrari's *The
Secret of Suzanne* at the Munich Royal Opera.
Her London opera debut followed on May 25,
1910, with the Beecham Opera Company. With
this company she was heard as Mélisande,
Cherubino in *The Marriage of Figaro*, Antonia
in *The Tales of Hoffmann*, and Marguerite in
Faust.

As Cherubino she made her American debut
on November 4, 1911, with the Philadelphia-
Chicago Opera Company. There she remained
three years. During this period her roles included the title part of Massenet's *Cendrillon*, Hansel
in *Hansel and Gretel*, Mimi in *La Bohème*, Antonia in *The Tales of Hoffmann*, Lygia in the
American premiere of Henri Cain's *Quo Vadis?*
(March 25, 1911), and Dot in Karl Goldmark's
The Cricket on the Hearth.

On November 6, 1911, she made her Ameri-

Teyte: tāt

can recital debut in New York City. Reviewing this concert, Richard Aldrich wrote in the New York *Times:* "Her voice is an almost startlingly powerful one from a person of her diminutive stature, and she showed in her singing . . . a talent and temperament of no common order. In the best tones, which were heard in her mezza voice, the voice has real beauty. . . . In certain of her songs Miss Teyte showed a command of true legato. . . . She is a singer of exceeding intelligence, of fine taste and musical feeling, of a commanding temperament that produces results sometimes unlooked for. In phrasing and in finish of style her best is of remarkable excellence."

During her first visit to the United States, she met Thomas Edison when she visited his studios in Newark, New Jersey, to hear a recording she had just made. She later recalled how Edison criticized her recording voice, particularly the way she used her top register. "I was quite sure he didn't know what he was talking about," she commented. Nevertheless, in her subsequent recordings she remembered Edison's comment and was always careful how she deployed her top notes in front of a recording microphone.

Teyte toured England and the French Riviera in 1913, and England, with Jan Kubelik, the violin virtuoso, in 1915. From 1915 to 1917 she was a member of the Boston Opera Company, and in 1917 she embarked on a concert tour of the United States.

At the end of World War I, she returned to London to appear on the popular musical stage in the operettas *Monsieur Beaucaire* on April 19, 1919, and *Little Dutch Girl* in December 1920. She also made world tours as a concert artist, achieving international recognition as an interpreter of the French art songs of Chausson, Ravel, Fauré, Berlioz, Duparc, and most particularly Debussy who, many years earlier, had been her piano accompanist in her recitals of his songs in Paris.

In 1921 she married W. S. Cottingham. This was her second marriage. Her first one—to Eugène Plumon, a Parisian, on October 16, 1909— ended in divorce. After marrying Cottingham, who was a man of considerable wealth, she went into retirement from which she emerged briefly in 1923 to appear as Mimi and Hansel with the British National Opera Company and to create the role of the Princess in the world premiere of Gustav Holst's *The Perfect Fool* on May 14,

1923. In 1930 she made a triumphant return to Covent Garden as Mélisande. After her divorce from Cottingham in 1931, she resumed her career in earnest, touring France and England in joint concerts with the piano virtuoso Alfred Cortot, appearing throughout Australia in 1932, and singing over the BBC radio, becoming one of its principal performing artists.

She returned to the United States in 1938– 1939 with the hope of resuming a concert career that had been interrupted in 1920. She found that she had been forgotten. All her efforts to interest concert managers and radio executives in her comeback proved futile.

During World War II she lived in London, experiencing the horrors of the Nazi Luftwaffe's blitz attacks on the city. For a time she drove an ambulance. When poor health compelled her to give up ambulance driving she furthered the war effort by singing for the armed forces in camps, for wounded soldiers in hospitals, and for civilians at the National Gallery in concerts organized by Myra Hess to help bolster civilian morale. Because of her continuous dedication to French music, particularly during the war, she received from France the Croix de Lorraine in 1945.

With her recordings of three albums of French songs gaining wide circulation in the United States after 1942, Teyte had little trouble getting a five-month booking in 1945. Her first program was heard over the coast-to-coast network of NBC on August 20, 1945, on the "Telephone Hour." The following November 1, in her first New York recital in over two decades, she became the first European artist to give a concert in the United States since V-E day. "Miss Teyte is fifty-six years young both vocally and artistically," reported Harriet Johnson in the New York *Post.* "She enkindles the music she sings with heartiness and warmth. . . . She is an intensely interesting artist of richly mature and remarkable talent."

On March 25, 1948, she made a reappearance on the American opera stage with several guest performances with the New York City Opera as Mélisande. Olin Downes, writing in the New York *Times,* characterized her conception of the role as "an interesting phenomenon. . . . Its eloquence, its revelation of character and emotion came with song. For Miss Teyte is not only authoritative mistress of every measure from the standpoint of musicianship and style but she colors her tones with the text and accomplishes everything that dramatic interpretation suggests by means of vocal device."

Teyte's last appearance in opera took place at the Mermaid Theater in London in 1951 as Belinda in Purcell's *Dido and Aeneas.* Her last American tour took place in 1954. After that she lived in retirement in London in an eleventh-floor apartment from whose windows she could get a breathtaking view of the city. There she did her own cooking and recorded on tape her reminiscences of great musicians. Petite in size, svelte and doll-like, she was always able to retain her slimness through her devotion to and participation in outdoor sports, particularly tennis and golf.

In 1957 she was made Chevalier of the Legion of Honor by France and Dame of the British Empire by England. In 1967 she established an annual Mozart prize for talented women students of singing, administered through the Handel and Mozart Society of London.

Maggie Teyte died in a nursing home in London on May 26, 1976. Just before her death she approved the collection of a four-record anthology covering her career from 1908, including material never before released. That album, entitled *L'Exquise,* was issued by EMI in 1976.

ABOUT: Teyte, M. Star on the Door. *Periodicals*—New York Times, September 30, 1945; Newsweek, September 3, 1945; Opera (London), April 1952; Opera News, March 21, 1970; Time, July 23, 1945.

Blanche Thebom

1918–

Blanche Thebom, mezzo-soprano and soprano, was born in Monessen, Pennsylvania, on September 19, 1918. All the men of her family were steelworkers. Her father, Carl Gustav Thebom, and her mother, Caroline Lindeberg Thebom, were of Swedish birth. Both were musical—her mother, a singer; her father, a performer on the accordion. When Blanche was young, the family moved to Canton, Ohio, where her father and two brothers found employment at the Republic Steel Mills. In Canton she began taking piano lessons while attending elementary school and

---

Thebom: tā' bōm

BLANCHE THEBOM

McKinley High School. She also sang in church choirs and glee clubs and appeared in a school production of *Martha.*

She wanted to be a schoolteacher, but her family's financial reverses compelled her to seek a shorter route to making a living. After attending a business school, from which she was graduated in 1933, she found employment as a secretary in a realty office. During the seven years she worked as a secretary she occasionally filled engagements as a singer at weddings and as a soloist with church choirs.

In 1938 she went with her parents on a trip to Sweden. Aboard the Kungsholm, en route to Europe, she appeared at the ship's concert. The audience included Kosti Vehanen, the accompanist of Marian Anderson. He was so impressed by Thebom's voice that he urged her to study singing and prepare for a professional career in music. When she returned to the United States she was aided financially by her employer, Alvin Gibbs. In 1939 she went to New York and for a few years studied voice and repertory with Edyth Walker, Margaret Matzenauer, and Lothar Wallerstein. She also took courses in languages, dramatics, and dancing.

In 1940 she auditioned for Sol Hurok, the impresario, who gave her a contract. She made her concert debut with a recital in Sheboygan, Wisconsin, in October 1941. One month later she was a soloist with the Philadelphia Orchestra under Ormandy in Brahms's *Alto Rhapsody.* For over a year after that, Hurok insisted she get further concert experience by singing in small cities throughout the United States. "I gladly went through the rigors of the 'bush circuit,' " she has said. "It was hard, but I had to become used to audiences."

Late in 1943 she appeared as soloist with the Minneapolis Symphony under Mitropoulos. On January 12, 1944, she made her concert bow in New York at Town Hall. Writing in the New York *Times,* Noel Straus commented: "The richly gifted artist disclosed the finest natural voice of any new singer heard so far this season."

When she returned to New York's Town Hall in November 1947, John Briggs said of her in the New York *Post:* "Miss Thebom's assets include a really fine voice, good looks, pleasant, reasonably unaffected stage manner, a high level of musical intelligence and (every number on her program made it obvious) the hard-working soul of a perfectionist in song." From then on, she made numerous appearances in recitals, over radio, and later over television.

During the summer of 1944 she appeared in and sang several sequences in the motion picture *When Irish Eyes Are Smiling.* That winter, on November 28, she made her debut with the Metropolitan Opera company as Brangäne in *Tristan and Isolde* during the company's visit to Philadelphia. On December 14, this time as Fricka in *Die Walküre,* she appeared for the first time on the stage of the Metropolitan Opera House. She scored "an immediate success," wrote Noel Straus. "Her gifts as vocalist were matched only by her histrionic ability in a deeply impressive portrayal, projected with the poise of a veteran artist of the lyric stage. . . . Comely, magnetic, with regal bearing befitting the goddess she impersonated, Miss Thebom was a strikingly impressive figure as she swept on the scene." When she sang her first Brangäne in New York, on February 3, 1945, Jerome D. Bohm said in the *Herald Tribune* that the music "emerged with gleaming, vibrant tonal investiture."

During the next two decades, Thebom proved to be a mainstay of the Metropolitan Opera company in the Wagnerian repertory: Ortrud in *Lohengrin,* Magdalene in *Die Meistersinger,* Erda in *Das Rheingold* and *Siegfried,* Fricka in *Das Rheingold,* Waltraute in *Die Götterdämmerung,* Venus in *Tannhäuser,* and the role of Brangäne in *Tristan and Isolde.* She distinguished herself in other operas as well—as Azucena in *Il Trovatore,* Amneris in *Aida,* Giulietta in *The Tales of Hoffmann,* Laura in *La Gioconda,* Adalgisa in *Norma,* Delilah in *Samson and Delilah,* Mignon, Carmen, Salome, Klytemnestra in *Elektra,* Princess Eboli in *Don Carlo,* Marina in *Boris Godunov,* Marfa in *Khovantchina,* Orlofsky in *Die Fledermaus,* Geneviève in *Pelléas and Mélisande,* the Countess in *The Queen of Spades,* and the Baroness in Samuel Barber's *Vanessa.* On December 28, 1951, she was Dorabella in a new Metropolitan Opera production of *Così fan Tutte;* on February 14, 1953, she was Baba in the American premiere of Stravinsky's *The Rake's Progress;* and on February 10, 1955, she created for the United States the role of Adelaide in the American premiere of Richard Strauss's *Arabella.* In all, Thebom made 236 appearances in New York and 112 on tour.

Between 1947 and 1959 she was frequently heard at the San Francisco Opera, where she had made her debut on September 30, 1947, as Laura. She was a visiting artist with leading European companies, including the Stockholm Opera, the Paris Opéra, La Scala in Milan, and the Théâtre de la Monnaie in Brussels. In the summer of 1947 she appeared at the Golden Jubilee Celebration of the Stockholm Royal Opera. She returned to the Stockholm Royal Opera in 1956 to make her debut as a soprano, in the role of Elisabeth in *Tannhäuser.* During this visit she received the Order of Vasa from the Queen, becoming the first foreign woman ever to be so honored. In 1950 she appeared as Dorabella at the Glyndebourne Festival in England.

In 1954, under the auspices of the State Department of the United States, she sang in Iceland; and in 1957 she was acclaimed for her performance as Dido in Berlioz' *Les Troyens* at Covent Garden in London. She toured the Soviet Union in 1958 as part of the Cultural Exchange Program, the first American prima donna to appear there since World War II. In addition to two recitals in Moscow, which were sold out weeks before the performances, she assumed the role of Carmen at the Bolshoi Opera. One year later she was heard in Leningrad and Kiev. She also performed as an American cultural envoy throughout South America, Romania, Yugoslavia, and the Far East, and at the Brussels World Fair in the summer of 1958 and the Osaka Festival in Japan in 1961.

After leaving the Metropolitan Opera in 1966, she supervised a production of *Aida* by the Southern Regional Opera at the Municipal Theater in Atlanta, Georgia. A year later she was appointed general manager of the company, holding this post until 1973. On July 1, 1973, she was made Distinguished Professor and director of the opera theater at the University of Arkansas in Little Rock. There she also assisted in creating and promoting the Hot Springs National Foundation for the Performing Arts.

On November 9, 1950, she married Richard E. Metz, a banker; they were divorced in 1960. She subsequently married and divorced Albert D'Errico.

Blanche Thebom was the founder and the sole contributor to the Blanche Thebom Scholarship Fund set up in 1948.

ABOUT: New York Post, April 19, 1961; Newsweek, December 2, 1946; Opera News, December 11, 1944; Time, February 12, 1945.

JACQUES THIBAUD

Jacques Thibaud

1880–1953

Jacques Thibaud, violinist, was born in Bordeaux, France, on September 27, 1880. His father, Georges Thibaud, a violinist, taught Jacques until he was thirteen. Once, when he was nine, Jacques played for Eugène Ysaÿe who patted him on the head and said: "He will be the master of us all."

From 1886 to 1894 Jacques attended the Lycée at Bordeaux. Then he was enrolled in the Paris Conservatory where he studied with Martin-Pierre-Joseph Marsick. When he was graduated from the Conservatory in 1896 he received a gold medal in violin playing.

For a time Jacques earned his living playing the violin at the Café Rouge in the Latin Quarter of Paris. There, one day, Édouard Colonne, the conductor, heard him and offered to sponsor his career. Following a debut at the annual festival at Angers in 1898, Jacques stepped in to substitute for the concertmaster of the Colonne Orchestra in Paris. He did so well that Colonne made him a soloist with his orchestra; during the winter of 1898 he was heard fifty-four times with that symphonic organization. Camille Bellaigue, the French critic and musicologist, said of him: "Thibaud has the tone and the style and these

Thibaud: tē bō′

two elements of the art of the musician are joined together in him by grace, elegance, and purity of sound."

On September 30, 1902, Thibaud married Marguerite Frankfort. They had two sons, one of whom was killed in action in 1940 during World War II.

Thibaud paid his first visit to the United States in 1903, making his American debut in New York on October 30 performing Mozart's Concerto in E-flat major, K.268, and the Concerto in B minor by Saint-Saëns, with the Wetzler Orchestra. "Mr. Thibaud's tone," wrote Richard Aldrich in the New York *Times*, "is of beautiful warmth and purity, of fine expressive potency; his style is finished, and his technical methods are admirable; especially his bowing, which is large, free and firm. The technique of his left hand is fleet and dexterous."

Despite his initial success in the United States, Thibaud did not return to the United States for another decade. In that time he performed throughout Europe and was acclaimed by musicians and critics for his performances of Mozart and the music of the French school. He became a leading exponent of the French classic school of violin playing which was less interested in bravura playing and display of technical powers than in elegance of style and emotional understatement.

In 1913, after a ten-year absence, he returned to the United States, a recognized master of his instrument. Following his first return recital—at Aeolian Hall in New York on January 5, 1914—

Richard Aldrich expressed the opinion that Thibaud had "gained artistic maturity." The review continued: "He still possesses the qualities that characterized his more youthful days, but showed perhaps something less of the youthful buoyancy and insouciance that those who heard him then will remember. His temperament still is more poetic and gracious than impassioned or impetuous. ... Elegance and refinement are clearly among his essential characteristics." After giving a single performance in New York, his projected tour of the United States was suddenly canceled (the reason was never explained), and he returned to France.

During World War I he served in the French Army, on the staff of General Gallieni. For nineteen months he was in the front battle line, seeing action at the Marne, Aisne, Ypres, Champagne, Arras, and Verdun. He was hospitalized for some time and then discharged with honors. After a period of recuperation, at which time he turned to golf and tennis to help restore the flexibility of his muscles, he visited the United States for a new concert tour, appearing first in a recital at Aeolian Hall in New York on November 16, 1916. "He was at his best in the concert yesterday," said Richard Aldrich in the New York *Times*.

Following that appearance Thibaud performed in virtually every major city of the world, in recitals, as guest artist with orchestras, and in chamber music concerts, sometimes with his two brothers (one a cellist, the other a pianist) but more often and far more significantly with Alfred Cortot and Pablo Casals.

During World War II the Germans seized his house at Saint-Jean-de-Luz, in the Basque region of France near the Spanish border, and Thibaud and his family went to Paris to occupy a top-floor apartment in a hotel. Though the hotel was commandeered by the Gestapo (secret police force of the German Nazi state), the Thibauds were permitted to remain in their apartment. Thibaud himself was allowed to give concerts in France and even in unoccupied territory and in Switzerland. The Nazis did not know that Thibaud was working for the French Resistance Movement and that his comparative freedom of movement provided him with many opportunities to be useful to the underground.

Thibaud made his last tour of the United States in 1947, after an absence of fifteen years, the first performance taking place on January 2,

1947, with the New York Philharmonic, Stokowski conducting. On September 1, 1953, while en route from Paris to French Indochina to entertain the French troops there, Thibaud was killed when the airplane in which he was traveling crashed in the French Alps.

Thibaud distinguished himself as a teacher of the violin. For many years he conducted master classes at the École Normale de Musique in Paris.

ABOUT: Dorian, J. P. ed. Un Violon Parle: Souvenirs de Jacques Thibaud.

Jess Thomas

1927–

Jess Thomas, tenor, was born in Hot Springs, South Dakota, on August 4, 1927, the only child of Charles A. Thomas, an engineer for the Army Corps, and Hatti Ellen Yocarn Thomas. His paternal ancestors had immigrated to the United States from Wales. "I earned my first five bucks when I was five," he has recalled. "A friend knew I was shy and offered me money for singing 'When I Grow Too Old to Dream.' For money it seemed like fun." As a boy, he was a member of the local church choir, and at the Hot Springs High School he won an award for singing. He was a gifted boy—excellent at his studies; active in drama and journalism; playing the piano, violin, and trumpet in the school band; and filling the position of halfback on the football team.

He hoped to become a physician, but while attending the University of Nebraska he decided to shift to psychology. At the University he participated in dramatic, choral, and operatic performances. Upon graduation with a Bachelor of Arts degree in 1949, he was for four years a guidance counselor for the public schools in Hermiston, Oregon. From 1953 to 1954 he attended Stanford University and received his Master of Arts degree. While employed as a school counselor in Alameda, California, he took further courses in psychology with the expectation of getting a doctorate.

Otto Schulmann, professor of voice at Stanford University, became so interested in Thomas's talent for singing that he had Thomas participate in the school's opera workshop and

JESS THOMAS

eventually persuaded him to consider a career as a professional singer. In 1956 Thomas resigned his post as school counselor and abandoned his doctorate in order to devote himself to vocal studies with Schulmann, supporting himself by singing in nightclubs. In 1957 he justified Schulmann's faith in him by winning the San Francisco Opera Auditions. He made his opera debut in 1957 with the San Francisco Opera as the Innkeeper in *Der Rosenkavalier.*

On Schulmann's advice, he went to Germany for further study and musical experience. In Karlsrühe he studied voice with Emmy Seiberlich and auditioned for the Badisches Staatstheater, receiving a three-year contract. He made his European opera debut at Karlsrühe in 1958 in the title role of *Lohengrin.* During his three-year engagement with the Badisches Staatstheater he sang thirty-eight roles and learned to speak German fluently.

On leave of absence from Karlsrühe, Thomas appeared with the Württemberg State Opera in Stuttgart as Bacchus in *Ariadne auf Naxos* in 1950, a role he also assumed in 1960 at the summer festival in Munich and subsequently at the Salzburg Festival in Austria. In Munich, Wieland Wagner heard him and invited him to appear at the Bayreuth Festival in 1961 in the title role of *Parsifal.* He also engaged Thomas for the role of Radames in a performance of *Aida* that opened the new Opera House in Berlin in the fall of 1961. H. H. Stuckenschmidt, music critic, found in Thomas's performance "a dramatic

power that has not been equaled since Helge Roswaenge."

In 1962 Thomas participated in the Wieland Wagner production of *Salome* at Stuttgart and was heard as Vasco da Gama in the Munich State Opera production of *L'Africaine.* By the end of that year he was back in the United States to make his debut at the Metropolitan Opera as Walther in *Die Meistersinger* on December 11, 1962. Because of the newspaper strike in New York City during this period, he was denied the press reviews that he deserved. But in the *Saturday Review,* Irving Kolodin gave Thomas's debut its due by writing: "Everything about his bearing, poise and good routine sustained the reports that had preceded him from Germany. He also has a voice of size and quality ... for a performer of German roles." *Time* Magazine commented: "Thomas may well be the Heldentenor grand opera has waited for since Melchior."

Thomas went on to fulfill the hope expressed in *Time.* His powerful dramatic voice and his commanding stage presence have placed him high among *Heldentenors* since World War II. On March 10, 1964, he made his first Metropolitan Opera appearance as Lohengrin. He sang his first Tristan in *Tristan and Isolde* in 1971, his first Siegfried in *Siegfried* and his first Siegmund in *Die Walküre* in 1972, his first Siegfried in *Die Götterdämmerung* and his first Parsifal in 1974. However, he was given the opportunity to appear in many other roles at the Metropolitan Opera, all of them performed with uncommon distinction: Bacchus in *Ariadne auf Naxos,* Radames, Florestan in *Fidelio,* Lensky in *Eugene Onegin,* Samson in *Samson and Delilah,* Calaf in *Turandot,* and Caesar in the world premiere of Samuel Barber's *Caesar and Cleopatra* (September 16, 1966).

His Wagnerian performances have been highly acclaimed in Europe. He appeared regularly at the Bayreuth Festival in the principal *Heldentenor* roles. Herbert von Karajan selected him as Siegfried for his production of *Siegfried* in 1969 and *Die Götterdämmerung* in 1970 at the Salzburg Easter festival. He was acclaimed at the Vienna State Opera in 1971 when he appeared there for the first time as Tristan. He was Tristan again when Georg Solti gave his farewell performance as the music director of Covent Garden in London in April 1971 and once again when the Vienna State Opera visited Moscow on October 9, 1971, for what is believed to have been the first staged production of *Tristan and Isolde* ever given in Russia. In an unprecedented gesture, the Vienna State Opera later created a two-month festival of performances starring him. During this time in Vienna he was heard as Parsifal, Tristan, Lohengrin, Tannhäuser, Walther, Siegmund, and Loge (in addition to Florestan).

In the United States in September 1972 Thomas sang Siegmund and Siegfried in the first complete production of the *Ring* cycle by the San Francisco Opera, appearing in two full cycles within one month.

He assumed other roles in addition to those already commented upon. When the rebuilt Munich State Opera House was opened in 1963, he sang the part of the Emperor in a new production of Richard Strauss's *Die Frau ohne Schatten.* In opera houses in Europe and the United States he has also appeared in the principal tenor roles of the traditional French and Italian repertories, as well as in Berlioz' *Les Troyens,* Eugène d'Albert's *Tiefland, The Abduction from the Seraglio, The Magic Flute, Boris Godunov, The Bartered Bride, Oberon,* Fortner's *Bluthochzeit,* and Richard Strauss's *Die Aegyptische Helena.*

Thomas has made frequent appearances as a soloist with the world's symphony orchestras. He made his debut with the New York Philharmonic and the Boston Symphony in 1967. Since then he has been heard in concert versions of *Tristan and Isolde* and *Die Götterdämmerung* with the New York Philharmonic under Leonard Bernstein; *Fidelio* with the Chicago Symphony; *Die Walküre* with the Los Angeles Philharmonic, the Detroit Symphony, the Boston Symphony, and the Chicago Symphony; *Die Götterdämmerung* with the Chicago Symphony under Solti; and *Parsifal* in London with Pierre Boulez conducting. Apart from the Wagnerian music dramas, he has appeared with the San Francisco Symphony and the New York Philharmonic in Mahler's *Das Lied von der Erde* and with the Pittsburgh Symphony in Schoenberg's *Gurre-Lieder,* to mention only two of the symphonic and choral masterworks.

On February 17, 1957, Thomas married Bettye Lee Wright, a model and choreographer he met while both were being photographed in a studio. With their two children they made their home in a villa on the outskirts of Munich. After an eighteen-year marriage and three years of litigation, they were divorced. Since then, with his second wife—the former Violeta Maria de los Angeles Rios Andino Figueroa, whom he married in 1974—he has lived in Lucerne.

Athletically inclined from boyhood, Thomas enjoys horseback riding (his horse is named Grane after the one in *Die Götterdämmerung*) and swimming. As he told Howard Klein in an interview in the New York *Times,* he also loves "to hike, camp, paint, cook, design sets and costumes (for myself), read philosophy, religion, murder mysteries, and play bridge. A dentist friend in San Francisco always arranges an all-day bridge game when I'm in town; we only stop for meals."

Jess Thomas was named *Kammersänger* by the Bavarian State Government in 1963. He received the Richard Wagner Medallion in Bayreuth that same year, and the San Francisco Opera Medallion in 1972.

ABOUT: New York Post, March 8, 1974; New York Times, December 12, 1971; Opera News, February 16, 1963; Time, December 21, 1962.

John Charles Thomas

1891–1960

John Charles Thomas, baritone, was born in Meyersdale, Pennsylvania, on September 6, 1891. His father, Reverend Milson Thomas, was an itinerant Methodist minister; his mother, Anna Dorothea Schnaebel Thomas, was a singer. When John was three he joined his parents in performing vocal trios at camp meetings where his father preached. When he was ten, he joined the choir in his father's church.

His early ambition was to become a minister. With this in mind, he attended Conway Hall in Carlisle, Pennsylvania, where he became interested in medicine. Upon graduation he enrolled in the Mount Street College of Homeopathy in Baltimore intending to become a physician. He still maintained his musical interests, however. In Baltimore he was a member of the choir of the Church of St. Michael and All Angels, earning five dollars a month in the beginning, but in two years' time receiving the highest pay ever given any singer in a Baltimore Church.

In 1910 he applied for and received a scholarship to the Peabody Conservatory in Baltimore. By this time he had decided to exchange medi-

JOHN CHARLES THOMAS

cine for music as his life's profession—he made the decision by tossing a coin.

Thomas attended the Peabody Conservatory for a single season, studying voice with Blanche Blackman. At the Conservatory he made his stage debut in a school performance of *Trial by Jury* by Gilbert and Sullivan. Later the same year he appeared there in excerpts from *Carmen* and *Martha*. After Blackman's resignation from the Conservatory, Thomas completed his vocal training with Adelin Fermin.

Upon leaving the United States, he made his professional stage debut in London, Ontario, Canada, in October 1912 as Passion in the Henry W. Savage Company production of *Everywoman*. On July 24, 1913, he made his first Broadway stage appearance at the Winter Garden in the revue *The Passing Show of 1913* and became a matinee idol. In 1914 he appeared in New York in a series of productions of Gilbert and Sullivan operettas starring DeWolf Hopper. This was the beginning of a career in the popular musical theater which saw him star in *The Peasant Girl* (1915), *Alone at Last* (1915), *Her Soldier Boy* (1916), Reginald de Koven's *The Highwayman* (1917), Sigmund Romberg's *Maytime* (1917), and Fritz Kreisler's *Apple Blossoms* (1919).

"The monotony of singing the same music day after day was unbearable to me," he later told an interviewer. "I only stayed in musical comedy to make enough money to get out and do the thing that really interests me the most—concert singing."

On December 2, 1918, he made his concert debut with a recital at Aeolian Hall in New York. "Mr. Thomas . . . scattered his vocal gold profusely, too profusely, throughout a long and often mediocre program," reported Richard Aldrich in the New York *Times.* "He was once in musical comedy, and traces persist in his style. He over-emphasizes his points; sings sentimentally and indulges in booming fortissimi; yet, his *messa di voce* is excellent, his musical feeling sound when he sings good music."

It was several years before Thomas could abandon the popular and highly lucrative Broadway stage to dedicate himself completely to serious music. On March 3, 1925, he made his debut in opera as Amonasro in *Aida* with a local company in Washington, D.C. That year he went to Europe to audition for the Théâtre de la Monnaie in Brussels. Though offered a contract, he waited three months to sign it because he was not sure he wanted to appear in opera rather than exclusively in recitals. After finally signing the contract, he made his debut at the Théâtre de la Monnaie on August 1, 1925, as Herod in *Hérodiade*. He was so successful that his contract was extended for three seasons; during this time he was heard in fifteen roles. He appeared in the world premiere of Milhaud's *Les Malheurs d'Orphée* on May 7, 1926, and was Jokanaan and Amfortas in the Brussels premieres of *Salome* and *Parsifal*.

By 1930 he was back in the United States and on September 12 he made his debut with the San Francisco Opera as Jokanaan. That season he was also heard as Tonio in *I Pagliacci* with the Chicago Civic Opera.

On February 2, 1934, he made his debut with the Metropolitan Opera in New York as the elder Germont in *La Traviata*. "It is no news to say that he sang with richness of tone, fine musicianship, intelligence and poise," commented Howard Taubman in the New York *Times.* "These qualities were present yesterday. . . . Within the frame of *Traviata*, Mr. Thomas came off with great credit. . . . The voice was big, resonant, beautifully rounded. . . . As for capturing the quality of the character, the baritone was eminently successful. He was a striking figure on the stage, warm, compassionate and dignified in action."

For nine years Thomas was a member of the Metropolitan Opera (except for the season of 1934–1935 when he was ill). He was heard thirty-five times in New York and nineteen on tour in a comparatively limited repertory of nine roles: the elder Germont, Figaro in *The Barber of Seville,* Athanaël in *Thaïs,* Renato in *Un Ballo in Maschera,* Valentin in *Faust,* Amonasro, Tonio, Rigoletto, and on tour Scarpia in *Tosca.* While a member of the Metropolitan Opera company, he made his debut at Covent Garden as Valentin and Tonio, made regular appearances with the Los Angeles Civic Opera between 1938 and 1942, and returned to the San Francisco Opera as Tonio on October 13, 1943.

Despite his success in opera, Thomas always preferred the concert stage, and he became one of the best loved concert singers in America. Each season he was heard in about sixty or seventy recitals in the United States and Europe. During 1939–1940 he presented a series of five song recitals in New York devoted to the song literature of France, England, Italy, Germany, and America. A critic for the New York *Times* said after the first of these concerts: "The event promises to be the crowning achievement of his extensive career. The artist was in superb voice from the start and husbanded his vocal resources with such admirable skill that despite the heavy demands made by the elaborate list there was no waning in freshness of his tone when the final offerings were approached." Between March 1, 1947, and April 1948 Thomas traveled forty thousand miles in the United States for one hundred and ten recitals. After that he undertook the most exhaustive tour of Australia and New Zealand ever made by an American musician, breaking all existing box-office records.

Early in his career, Thomas had appeared in the motion picture *Under the Red Robe* (1923), a silent film. He returned to the screen in *Kingdom Come* (1941). He was a frequent performer on network radio programs where he ended each of his performances (by special dispensation of the Federal Radio Commission) with the words "Goodnight, mother."

In 1951 he was appointed executive director of the Music Academy of the West at Santa Barbara, California. He made his last concert tour in 1952–1953 covering fifty cities. Following this, for a time he managed a radio station at Apple Valley, California.

On March 5, 1924, Thomas married Dorothy Mae Kaehler. For many years they owned a farm near Los Angeles on which they raised crops and livestock. In 1954 they moved to the desert community of Apple Valley, ninety miles northeast of Los Angeles. Both he and his wife were fond of boating. They owned a one-hundred-and-one-foot yacht, *The Masquerader,* and often spent their free time aboard. They also owned some smaller boats: an eighty-foot yacht called *The Memory,* runabout speedboats, a fishing skiff, and a dinghy. Thomas was prominent in American motorboat racing circles, winning many medals, cups, and other trophies.

He was an outstanding sportsman, excellent in golf and tennis, capable of running a mile in five minutes and clearing the high-jump bar at five feet ten. In addition he was an accomplished chef and a raconteur.

In 1934 John Charles Thomas was made Cavaliere of the Crown of Italy.

He died of cancer at Apple Valley on December 13, 1960.

ABOUT: Ewen, D. Men and Women Who Make Music (1949 ed.); Kaufmann, H. L. and Hansl, E. E. vom B. Artists in Music of Today; Thompson, O. The American Singer. *Periodicals*—Etude, January 1941; New York Times, November 26, 1940; Opera News, March 11, 1961.

Michael Tilson Thomas

1944–

Michael Tilson Thomas, conductor, was born in Hollywood, California, on December 21, 1944. His grandparents, Boris and Bessie Thomashefsky, were among the founders of the Yiddish theater in New York and were also two of its stars; Paul Muni, the actor, was an uncle; and his father, Theodore (Ted) Thomas, was a successful producer, director, and writer for motion pictures and television. Michael's mother, Roberta Thomas, was a teacher in the Los Angeles public school system. "I've lived a theatrical kind of life," Michael has said. "I've been used from childhood to switching roles, reacting instantly to cues. Someone would speak to me in a different accent and I'd find myself responding in kind. Los Angeles was a fantastic place to grow up in."

From childhood on, Michael divided his time between music and science. "I had played piano by ear at five, learned to read at eight, and started at U.S.C.'s [University of Southern Cali-

MICHAEL TILSON THOMAS

fornia's] prep school at ten, but I was more interested in science—mineralogy, crystallography, inorganic and then organic chemistry—than I was in music or theater. I won science prizes but the men of the arts impressed me more than the men of science, so I majored in music at the University of Southern California after high school."

He began formal piano study in his tenth year. While attending North Hollywood High School and the University of Southern California, he continued to study the piano with Muriel Kerr and John Crown, supplementing this with lessons on the harpsichord with Alice Ehlers. At the University of Southern California he studied composition with Ingolf Dahl, who exerted a particularly potent influence on his musical development. "Dahl really taught me ear training, music history, structural analysis. He was an overwhelming figure," says Thomas.

When he received his master's degree in music from the University of Southern California in 1968, he was also given an award for being one of its outstanding alumni. By that time he had already made considerable progress in his conducting career. That career began in 1963, when he was nineteen and assumed the post of conductor of the Young Musicians Foundation Debut Orchestra, a group of student musicians; he held this post for four years.

Many powerful musical forces were brought to bear on his artistic growth during those years. He worked as pianist for the master classes of Jascha Heifetz and Gregor Piatigorsky, and he

served as conductor whenever an orchestra was used for the Heifetz-Piatigorsky concerts. He appeared as conductor and pianist at the Monday Evening Concerts in Los Angeles dedicated to modern music and ultramodern compositions; there he performed compositions by Stravinsky, Boulez, Stockhausen, Lukas Foss, Ingolf Dahl, and other avant-gardists—many of the performances were premieres. He worked as assistant to Pierre Boulez at the Ojai Festival in California. Of all this he has said: "I would play the piano accompaniment of a Haydn Cello Concerto for a Piatigorsky class in the morning, then work on Haydn's Sinfonia Concertante in the afternoon with Pierre Boulez—this provides an incredible artistic shock."

When Boulez was engaged to conduct *Parsifal* at the Bayreuth Festival in the summer of 1966, he invited Thomas to go with him. In Bayreuth, Thomas attended the classes of Friedelind Wagner. When one of the coaches at the Wagner festival fell ill, Boulez summoned Thomas to assist him in the preparation of *Parsifal.* He returned to Bayreuth to assist at some of its productions the following summer and during the summers of 1968 and 1969 he served as principal conductor of the Ojai Festival.

In the summer of 1968, he attended the Berkshire Music Center at Tanglewood, Massachusetts, on a conducting fellowship. There, on August 7, 1968, he conducted the world premiere of a multimedia "occult" opera, *Elephant Steps,* by Stanley Silverman, written for Tanglewood on a commission from the Fromm Foundation; Silverman himself had selected Thomas to conduct the opera, having heard Thomas perform another of his works in California. Thomas's conducting was such a virtuoso performance that it drew praise from many discriminating musicians. Silverman said: "Michael is fantastically versatile. He has an amazing ability to get on top of a piece—it puts me in mind of Laurence Olivier in the way he shows you the work rather than the performer's personality." The following summer Erich Leinsdorf asked Thomas to assist in the preparation of Berg's *Wozzeck* for performance at the Berkshire Music Festival. At Tanglewood, Thomas won the Koussevitzky Prize for conducting and was appointed a teacher of conducting at the Berkshire Music Center.

In 1968 and 1969 he conducted the Youth Concerts of the Los Angeles Philharmonic. In the east, he appeared as guest conductor with the Boston Philharmonia, a cooperative group. William Steinberg, music director of the Boston Symphony, heard one of Thomas's concerts with the Philharmonia and was so impressed that he engaged Thomas as assistant conductor of the Boston Symphony for 1969–1970.

He made his conducting debut with the Boston Symphony soon after the season opened, in October 1969, and was cheered after his performance. On October 22, 1969, Steinberg took the Boston Symphony to New York's Lincoln Center for the Performing Arts. Falling ill at intermission time, Steinberg turned his baton over to Thomas who, without the benefit of rehearsal, conducted the familiar *Till Eulenspiegel's Merry Pranks* of Strauss and Robert Starer's new Concerto for Violin, Cello and Orchestra. "He came on the stage," wrote Harold C. Schonberg in the New York *Times,* "with an air of immense confidence and authority, and showed that his confidence was not misplaced. Mr. Thomas knows his business, and we shall be hearing from him again."

The following Saturday he conducted the entire program of the Boston Symphony at Carnegie Hall in New York, once again demonstrating that in spite of his youth and comparative inexperience he was fully able to lead one of the world's greatest orchestras.

Steinberg's illness turned out to be a heart attack; this compelled him to reduce the number of his appearances with his orchestra that season. Thomas stepped into the gap by conducting not only some thirty-seven concerts of the Boston Symphony in public but also the first recordings by that orchestra under its new affiliation with the Deutsche Grammophon Gesellschaft: Carl Ruggles's *Sun-Treader* and Ives's *Three Places in New England.* Having proved himself, he was appointed associate conductor of the Boston Symphony at the end of the season. Thomas was the first to assume that post since Richard Burgin's retirement in 1965 and the youngest ever to hold it.

Innovation became a keynote of Thomas's affiliation with the Boston Symphony. At one of his concerts he had the orchestra stand while performing a Haydn symphony because that was the way it was performed at the Esterházy palace in Eisenstadt under Haydn and that was the way Thomas felt it sounded authentic. His unorthodox programming coupled music of the distant past (for example the twelfth century organum of Perotinus Magnus) with the "music of tomorrow" (Stockhausen's *Punkte*). He initiated the Spectrum Concerts, in which he presented music for unusual combinations of instruments. "My idea of a performance," he said, "is one that presents new ideas about music." Louis Irving Snyder, writing in *The Christian Science Monitor,* commented on Thomas's unique programs as follows: "Thomas and the Boston Symphony have turned Symphony Hall into a kind of musical version of a Revere beach fun house—full of unexpected surprises and harmless jolts. . . . No sooner does the tonal floor seem comfortably firm under foot than one is plunged onto a tilting, spinning, rippling plane of sound, unfamiliar, maybe, but curiously provoking."

When Gennady Rozhdestvensky was unable to make a scheduled appearance with the London Symphony Orchestra in London in May 1970, Thomas was called in as a substitute. This was his European debut. He returned to the United States that summer to conduct at the Berkshire Music Festival, at the Ravinia Festival in Chicago, and at the Mostly Mozart Festival in New York City. The following season (1970–1971) he conducted over forty concerts with the Boston Symphony, not only in Boston and New York but also during its tour in Europe. He also appeared as a guest conductor of the Buffalo Philharmonic, the Rochester Philharmonic, and the Japan Philharmonic.

In 1971 he was appointed music director of the Buffalo Philharmonic. He continued to serve as associate conductor of the Boston Symphony, dividing his time and energies between these two organizations. At the same time he expanded his program of guest appearances, as the demands for his services began to increase. In 1971–1972 he appeared with major orchestras in London, Hamburg, Baden-Baden, Madrid, and Israel. In one seven-week period he was scheduled to give twenty-nine concerts and to fulfill two recording dates. He was looked upon as the new wonder boy of music, a "new Leonard Bernstein," for his early career and triumphs closely resembled Bernstein's. The New York *Times Magazine* devoted a cover story to him. Hamilton College conferred on him an honorary doctorate.

"In action," wrote Donal Henahan in the New York *Times Magazine,* "Thomas resembles a large, skinny bird as he stoops toward the orchestra, listening to details of voicing, intonation or instrumental blending, his long arms flapping in big, easily discernible patterns. He also is a bouncer and a pacer on the podium. . . . Like Bernstein, he seems to hear with his body, and audiences respond delightedly to his youthful brio and gift for communicating rhythmic excitement. So do orchestras."

His responsibilities in Buffalo compelled him in February 1972 to surrender his post as associate conductor of the Boston Symphony to take on a new one, that of principal guest conductor, which he retained until 1974. In 1972 he became the music director of the Ojai Festival and director and conductor of the New York Young People's Concerts which were televised nationally. On June 18, 1975, he made his bow as an opera conductor with a performance of *Faust* with the Cincinnati Opera. He has recorded for CBS Records with the Buffalo Philharmonic all of Carl Ruggles's orchestral works. In addition to his conducting assignments, Thomas has also served as visiting adjunct professor of music at the State University of New York at Buffalo.

Thomas has retained his early fascination for science. When he listens to recorded music, he avoids the repertory of the symphony hall, preferring Oriental music or rock. He is an ardent admirer of rock, his favorites being James Brown, the Rolling Stones, The Band, Bob Dylan, and the Beatles. He is an excellent dancer. "Dancing in front of others," he has confessed, "was worse than facing any of the big orchestras. But once I got started, I loved it."

ABOUT: High Fidelity/Musical America, July 1970, September 1970; New York Times, March 29, 1970, October 3, 1976; New York Times Magazine, October 24, 1971; Newsweek, March 1, 1971; Time, September 14, 1970.

Kerstin Thorborg

1896–1970

Kerstin Thorborg, Wagnerian contralto, was born in Venjan, Dalarna, Sweden, on May 19, 1896. Her father, a newspaper editor, was an amateur musician and her mother was a music lover. When they realized their daughter had an

---

Thorborg: tōōr′ bêr y′

KERSTIN THORBORG

unusual singing voice, they engaged a teacher for her. Later, Kerstin entered a competition for entrance into the Opera School of the Stockholm Royal Opera and was one of three chosen from over a thousand candidates.

She made her opera debut with the Stockholm Royal Opera in 1924 as Ortrud in *Lohengrin.* Within a year she became a permanent member of the company, remaining with it five years and appearing in principal contralto roles in the German, French, and Italian repertories. From 1930 to 1932 she was a member of the Prague Opera and from 1933 to 1935 of the Berlin State Opera. In both places her performances of the principal contralto roles in the Wagnerian repertory were greatly admired. When she made her debut at Covent Garden in London in May 1936, it was in the *Ring* cycle and she was acclaimed. From 1935 to 1938 she was a principal contralto of the Vienna State Opera. She appeared as Brangäne (one of her famous roles) in *Tristan and Isolde* in 1935 at the Salzburg Festival in Austria and returned there during the next few years as Orfeo in Gluck's *Orfeo ed Euridice,* Magdalena in *Die Meistersinger,* Eglantine in *Euryanthe,* and Frasquita in Hugo Wolf's *Der Corregidor.*

By the time she made her first appearance in the United States she was already a Wagnerian contralto of great renown. That American debut took place at the Metropolitan Opera in New York on December 21, 1936 (opening night of the season), as Fricka in *Die Walküre.* "Mme. Thorborg," reported Lawrence Gilman in the *Herald Tribune,* "is a woman of regal and distinguished beauty, stately in bearing, slender and tall and straight. She knows the significance of what she is called upon to say and do. She is clearly an actress of intelligence and skill and power. . . . Of Mme. Thorborg's power and subtlety and effectiveness in the embodiment of the character there was little question." In the New York *Times,* Olin Downes praised her for "the fire and majesty of her delivery" and commented: "These made the audience aware of one of the greatest Frickas who had graced this stage in many seasons."

Two evenings later Thorborg further distinguished herself in the role of Brangäne, and before that season was over she had also appeared as Mary in *The Flying Dutchman,* Erda in *Siegfried,* and Venus in *Tannhäuser.* By the time she left the Metropolitan Opera in 1950 she had sung other major contralto roles in the Wagnerian music dramas: Magdalene, Ortrud, Waltraute in *Die Götterdämmerung,* Fricka in *Das Rheingold,* and Kundry in *Parsifal.* She was also heard as Octavian in *Der Rosenkavalier,* Klytemnestra in *Elektra,* Salome, Orfeo, Marina in *Boris Godunov,* Ulrica in *Un Ballo in Maschera,* Amneris in *Aida,* Delilah in *Samson and Delilah,* and Azucena in *Il Trovatore.* With the Metropolitan Opera company she was heard 242 times in New York and 85 times on tour.

On October 14, 1938, Thorborg made her debut with the San Francisco Opera as Magdalena, and that season she was also heard there as Klytemnestra. She returned to San Francisco to open the 1943 season as Delilah and, two weeks later, to assume the role of Azucena. In addition to her opera appearances in the United States she made many tours of the country as a recitalist. She was also a frequent guest with major opera companies in Europe and South America.

On June 7, 1928, Thorborg married Gustav Bergmann, general manager of the Gothenburg Opera in Sweden, former stage manager and leading tenor in Berlin. He had also been a director of several motion pictures in Paris. They occupied an old farm called The Valley of the Birches, near the town of Hedemora, in Dalarna, one hundred and twenty-five miles northwest of Stockholm. When she went into retirement in 1950 she withdrew to her farm to devote herself to caring for her numerous pets, to swimming, walking, cooking, reading, and entertaining friends. Occasionally she taught voice. Her hus-

band had died a decade earlier, and she lived there with her brother.

Her one superstition at the Metropolitan Opera was to receive a penny from the stage director, Leopold Sachse, each time she was about to go on the stage. One of her prize possessions was a small doll dressed in Swedish costume, with a penny sewn on each side of her skirt; it was a gift from Sachse.

In 1944 she was appointed singer to the Swedish court. She also received the Gold Medal of Art from the King of Sweden.

Kerstin Thorborg died in Hedemora, Sweden, on April 12, 1970. She bequeathed the memorabilia of her artistic career to a music foundation; the rest of her belongings went to a foundation organized to prevent painful animal experiments.

ABOUT: American Swedish Monthly, No. 2, 1937; Opera News, November 2, 1963.

Lawrence Tibbett

1896–1960

Lawrence Mervil Tibbett, baritone, was born in Bakersfield, California, on November 16, 1896. Originally his name was spelled Tibbet. However, when he made his debut at the Metropolitan Opera in New York, a typographical error on the program placed an additional *t* at the end of his name, and Tibbett retained that spelling.

"My people came to California in the 1849 Gold Rush and settled in as pioneer farmers," Tibbett once reminisced. "My great-uncle planted the first navel orange tree in California from which sprang one of the great industries of the State. . . . Most of my forebears were sheriffs, or had something to do with the enforcement of law in a land that was almost lawless. My own father was a sheriff of Bakersfield. He might have stepped out of a Wild West novel, for those were the days of bandits and stage coach holdups, and he was constantly at war with outlaws. Later, he was shot dead by Wild Jim McKinney, one of California's famous outlaws. I was six, then, but already my father was a magnificent hero to me and remained so for many, many years."

After the death of his father, William Edward Tibbet, Lawrence was taken by his mother,

LAWRENCE TIBBETT

Frances Ellen Mackenzie Tibbet, along with his three brothers and one sister to Long Beach, California, where she ran a hotel. "Poverty struck hard at us then," Tibbett recalled. When he was twelve, his family moved to Los Angeles. "My mother and my three older brothers and sister all worked hard to keep things going. While I was growing up, I put in each summer on a cattle ranch, where I took part with the cowboys in their round-ups. I took to hunting early, and, when quite a boy, spent two years in the mountains. I remember shooting my first deer . . . with a gun not much bigger than myself. They were glorious days, good for mind and body alike."

He attended the elementary schools of Long Beach and Los Angeles before entering the Manual Arts High School in Los Angeles. From his mother, who had an excellent voice and had sung in the church choir in Bakersfield, he got his first singing lessons; he also took lessons on the piano. He acted in school plays, sang in the glee club, and earned money singing as a soloist with a church choir. But his ambition at the time was to become an actor rather than singer, and after graduation from high school in 1915, he played small parts with several professional companies in Los Angeles, including the Civic Repertory Theater and the Tyrone Power Shakespearean Players.

During World War I Tibbett served in the Navy. Four days after his discharge from service, on May 19, 1919, he married Grace Mackay Smith; twin sons were born to them a year

later. To help support his family, he formed and directed a male quartet which performed at churches, weddings, and funerals. For fifty dollars a week he was employed by the Grauman Theater in Hollywood to perform in musical prologues preceding the motion pictures shown. Later he became a member of a light opera company in Los Angeles presenting comic operas and operettas of Gilbert and Sullivan and Victor Herbert. In September 1923 he sang his first operatic role—Amonasro in *Aida*—presented at the Hollywood Bowl. All this time he was studying voice with Joseph Dupuy and Basil Ruysdael.

Encouraged by the author Rupert Hughes, and with the financial assistance of a California patron, Tibbett went to New York in 1923 for further vocal study with Frank La Forge and Ignaz Zitmorsky. He helped support himself by singing in a church in New Rochelle. His first audition with the Metropolitan Opera that fall was a failure. But the second one—when he sang the "Credo" from *Otello*—brought him a one-season contract at sixty dollars a week, with an option on his services for another three years at a slight increase of salary each year. His debut at the Metropolitan Opera took place on November 24, 1923, in the small part of Lovitsky (one of the monks) in *Boris Godunov*, a performance in which Chaliapin appeared in the title role. Six days later Tibbett was assigned the role of Valentin in *Faust* (with Chaliapin as Méphistophélès) and drew a brief comment from the New York *Times:* "As an American artist, Mr. Tibbett's Valentin had two moments in the spotlight. His French words were clear, his baritone voice of fine, fresh quality, though he may yet project it better into the far Metropolitan spaces. He looked a tall, spare figure of youth and modest demeanor."

For the next two seasons Tibbett was frequently heard, though only in minor roles in which he gave no hint that here was a star in the making. Then, on January 2, 1925, he substituted for an ailing singer as Ford in a revival of *Falstaff.* In the second act, he once recalled, "I let go with all I had. . . . I tore my heart out. Some subconscious force lifted me up." He was given a sixteen-minute ovation, one of the most tumultuous heard in that opera house in years. The New York *Times* reported this on its front page, calling the performance "without precedent in the annals of the Metropolitan" since this was the first time that an American-born singer without any foreign training had caused such a sensation and had so quickly risen to such artistic heights. In his review in the New York *Times,* Olin Downes said that "Mr. Tibbett gave a performance that was exemplary in its sincerity and dramatic feeling, its justness of accent, and its excellent vocal quality."

Tibbett proved he was not a one-role star on January 21, 1926, when he scored another triumph, this time as Neri in Giordano's *La Cena delle Beffe.* He was also heard that season as Ramiro in the first Metropolitan Opera production of Ravel's *L'Heure Espagnole.*

In the ensuing years at the Metropolitan, Tibbett repeatedly distinguished himself in the world premieres of American operas: as Eadgar in Deems Taylor's *The King's Henchman* (February 17, 1927), Colonel Ibbetson in Taylor's *Peter Ibbetson* (February 7, 1931), Brutus Jones in Gruenberg's *The Emperor Jones* (January 7, 1933), Wrestling Bradford in Howard Hanson's *Merry Mount* (February 10, 1934), the Pasha in Seymour's *In the Pasha's Garden* (January 24, 1935), and Guido in Richard Hageman's *Caponsacchi* (February 4, 1937). Speaking of Tibbett's remarkable performance as Brutus Jones, Pitts Sanborn wrote in the *World-Telegram:* "The role is one of pitiless exactions and Mr. Tibbett carried it off with intelligence and unflagging care, and a high degree of skill, from the bombast of the self-made 'emperor' through all the manifestations of terror to the utter abasement of the end." As Wrestling Bradford, Tibbett once again exhibited, said Sanborn in the *World-Telegram,* "his intelligence and skill as a singing actor, as well as splendid courage and endurance."

Tibbett was so highly esteemed in the title role of *Simon Boccanegra,* which he sang for the first time on January 28, 1932, that he was called upon to open the ensuing season on November 21, 1932, in the same role. Subsequently he opened the Metropolitan Opera season in 1934 as Amonasro, in 1935 as the elder Germont in *La Traviata,* in 1938 as Iago in *Otello,* and in 1939 as Simon Boccanegra.

Tibbett made his last appearance at the Metropolitan Opera on March 24, 1950, as Ivan in *Khovantchina.* How valuable he had been to the company in his more than a quarter of a century can be gauged by the fact that he appeared 396 times in New York and 163 on tour. His value can also be measured by the variety of parts he was called upon to sing, in addition to the world premieres of American operas and other roles already mentioned: Tonio in *I Pagliacci,* Wolfram in *Tannhäuser,* Manfredo in *L'Amore dei Tre Re,* the four leading baritone roles in *The Tales of Hoffmann,* Telramund in *Lohengrin,* Marcello in *La Bohème,* Jonny in *Jonny Spielt Auf,* Jack Rance in *The Girl of the Golden West,* Scarpia in *Tosca,* Iago in *Otello,* Don Carlo in *La Forza del Destino,* Michele in Puccini's *Il Tabarro,* Balstrode in Britten's *Peter Grimes,* and the title roles in *Rigoletto, Falstaff,* and *Gianni Schicchi.*

Tibbett made his first tour of Europe in 1937. At Covent Garden in London, he made his bow as Scarpia; at that time the first act of *Tosca* was broadcast over an international radio network. On June 24 he created the title role in the world premiere of Eugene Goossens's *Don Juan de Mañara.* During Tibbett's performances in Stockholm, King Gustav of Sweden presented him with the medal, Litteris et Artibus, rarely bestowed on a foreigner. The critics of Europe were effusive in their praise of Tibbett. One London critic wrote: "Lawrence Tibbett combines the two arts of acting and singing with a skill that made him the central figure of the performance." In Paris, a critic said of him that he "belongs to the race of grand lyric tragedians." And in Vienna, a critic remarked: "This American is a great outstanding artist, amazing in the scope of his talents."

In the United States, Tibbett's successes in opera were matched by those he enjoyed in the concert hall as a recitalist, over the radio, and in motion pictures. As a recitalist he covered some twenty-five thousand miles each year to fill his engagements. As a singer over the radio he had made his first appearance in 1922 over KHJ in Los Angeles. After he became famous later in the 1920s, he was starred for many years on leading network programs sponsored by Atwater Kent, Firestone, Packard, Chesterfield Cigarettes and the Ford Motor Company. For four years he was chosen by a poll of radio editors in the United States as the top classical singer over the radio. In 1945 he succeeded Frank Sinatra as one of the principals on the weekly radio program sponsored by Lucky Strike cigarettes, "Your Hit Parade," remaining on the show for seven months. He was also a pioneer in television opera. He produced and directed the first

opera ever given over American television—
Carmen—and he was subsequently heard in several other television operatic productions.

He was among the first opera singers to assume starring roles in American talking pictures. His first film was *The Rogue Song* (1930). After that he was starred in *New Moon* (1930), *The Southerner* (1931, also called *The Prodigal*), *Cuban Love Song* (1931), *Metropolitan* (1935), and *Under Your Spell* (1936).

In 1931 Tibbett divorced his wife, Grace, and on January 1, 1932, he married Jane Marston Burgard; they had a son. They maintained an apartment in New York City as well as Honey Hill Farm in Wilton, Connecticut, a seventy-two-acre tract of woodlands, orchards, and meadows. His favorite diversions were sports. "I love walking," he once said, "and during my season at the Metropolitan I walk from there to my New York apartment daily. I love swimming. When I am not singing in opera, I go swimming a great deal. My ambition is to climb Mount Rainier some day, or Mount Hood. When I was a boy, the mountain I climbed most was San Jacinto, eleven thousand feet high."

During World War II Tibbett was a member of the executive committee for camp shows of the United Service Organization (USO). He made many appearances in army camps, for the Red Cross, and on war bond drives. In July 1945 he embarked on an overseas USO tour.

His twenty-fifth anniversary with the Metropolitan Opera was celebrated backstage in January 1949 after a performance of *Peter Grimes*. He retired from opera completely after the spring of 1950 but continued to appear in concerts and over television. In 1956 he replaced Ezio Pinza in the role of César in the Broadway musical *Fanny*.

On June 29, 1960, Tibbett underwent an operation for an old head injury. He never recovered consciousness and on July 15, 1960, he died at Roosevelt Hospital in New York.

Tibbett was one of the organizers of AGMA in 1936, formed to protect artists who are ineligible to join a trade union. From 1940 to 1952 he was its president and from 1952 on, its honorary president. In 1955 he served on the committee to save Carnegie Hall in New York.

Tibbett sang at the inauguration ceremonies of three American presidents: Calvin Coolidge, Herbert Hoover, and Franklin D. Roosevelt. He was presented with a gold medal for diction by the American Academy of Arts and Letters in 1933. He also received an honorary Master of Music degree from the University of Southern California in 1928 and an honorary doctorate in music from New York University in 1934.

ABOUT: Ewen, D. Men and Women Who Make Music (1949 ed.); Thompson, O. The American Singer. *Periodicals*—American Magazine, August through November, 1933; Musical America, August 1960; Opera News, October 29, 1960.

Arturo Toscanini

1867–1957

Arturo Toscanini, conductor, was born in Parma, Italy, on March 25, 1867. He was the only son and the youngest of four children of Claudio, an impoverished tailor, and Paola Montani Toscanini. Though musically untutored, Claudio was a lover of grand opera and sat in the gallery of the Parma Opera whenever he could afford the price. His friends would gather at the Toscanini home to sing opera arias with him. This was the first music which Arturo heard. Since he would sit enraptured listening to the music, his father took him to an opera performance—*Un Ballo in Maschera*—where he was alleged to have cried out angrily from his seat because one of the tenors sang off-key.

While attending local grade school, Arturo received his first formal music instruction: lessons at the piano from a Signora Vernoni, one of the teachers in the school. Overwhelmed by the boy's intuition and industry, Vernoni persuaded Claudio Toscanini to send him to the Parma Conservatory for his musical education. She also arranged for a local tuba player to prepare the boy for his entrance examinations, which he passed without much difficulty.

At the Parma Conservatory, entered when he was nine, Arturo studied the cello with Carini and composition with Dacci. He soon came to be known as *il genio* (the genius). He had a phenomenal memory. He could play his exercises without consulting the printed page in front of him. To test him one of his professors showed him the full orchestral score of *Tannhäuser,* an opera then not well known in Italy. The boy read

---

Toscanini: tôs kä nē′ nē

ARTURO TOSCANINI

through the overture once, closed the score, and wrote down all the orchestral parts from memory.

His passion for music was as remarkable as his memory. When not in the classroom, he was in the library, searching for scores of symphonies and operas to take back with him to his room for private study. Sometimes he sold his precious meat coupons to buy printed music. Some of his Conservatory friends would join him in his room for musical performances, and he always looked forward impatiently to such evenings for they provided an opportunity to bring to realization the music taking shape in his mind.

Arturo remained at the Parma Conservatory nine years, seven of those on a scholarship. On July 14, 1885, he was graduated with the highest possible ratings in cello, piano, and composition, and his certificate read "with the highest distinction." A year before his graduation, on May 25, 1884, he had made his debut as conductor at the Conservatory, leading a performance of his own Andante and Scherzo, for orchestra.

During his last years at the Conservatory, he supported himself by playing the cello in local orchestras in Parma. Following his graduation, he worked for a time as a cellist in the orchestra of the Parma Opera and then with the Parma Municipal Orchestra. In 1886 a South American impresario went to Italy to form an opera company to tour his theaters. Since young Toscanini had already acquired a reputation as an orchestral musician, he was hired to play in the opera orchestra.

It was with this company that Toscanini made his professional debut as conductor, an unscheduled performance about which much has been written since that time.

For the orchestra's second performance in Rio de Janeiro on June 25, 1886, the regular conductor of the itinerant company, Leopoldo Miguez, refused to conduct *Aida,* since he had been severely criticized for his previous performance of *Faust.* When at the performance of *Aida* an assistant conductor began making his way to the podium, the Brazilian audience, in support of Miguez, began creating an uproar. With the furor refusing to die down, the assistant conductor made a hasty retreat. At this point, one of the singers suggested that young Toscanini take over the baton since he had demonstrated time and again from his chair in the cello section that he knew the opera thoroughly. Hoping that Toscanini's youth and handsome appearance would find a favorable response, the director of the company invited Toscanini to take over the performance. Apparently Toscanini's presence on the conductor's platform aroused interest and curiosity for the audience became pacified and sat back to listen. The fact that the young conductor, aged nineteen, did not consult the score in front of him during the performance was observed. More remarkable still was the fact that without a single rehearsal he managed to magnetize singers and orchestra players into a performance of *Aida* such as that audience had not heard before. After the final curtain there was an explosion of enthusiasm.

For the rest of that tour Toscanini served as principal conductor of the company. He led eighteen operas, all of them from memory, and all of them given that electric charge that moved performers and audiences.

In spite of this success Toscanini did not immediately find a conducting job when he returned to Italy. For a few months he continued playing the cello in various orchestras. Then, the composer Alfredo Catalani chose him to conduct his opera *Edmea* in Turin on November 4, 1886. This was Toscanini's professional conducting debut in Italy. One Turin critic called that performance "a splendid dawn on the horizon of music." Catalani said: "I would not have believed it if I had not heard it with my own ears."

On the strength of that appearance, Toscanini

was finally able to exchange cello for baton. The last time he occupied the cello chair was on February 5, 1887, when he participated in the world premiere of *Otello* at La Scala.

In 1887–1888 Toscanini conducted an opera troupe touring the smaller Italian cities. Already critics were beginning to take notice that something special happened whenever he conducted. After a performance of *L'Africaine,* a critic in Casale remarked: "The orchestra accomplished miracles." His performance of *Mignon* led another critic to exclaim: "Under his magic baton the orchestra was marvelous." On November 19, 1888, he led the world premiere of Antonio Cagnoni's *Francesca da Rimini* at Dal Verme. The critic of the *Gazzetta* in Milan commented on the "perfection of execution. . . . I wish many composers might have such an interpreter."

Other conducting assignments were now offered to Toscanini. At the Carlo Felice Theater in Genoa, where he was appointed principal conductor in 1891, he conducted, together with other works, Catalani's *Loreley.* "No one else can divine and interpret me the way you do," Catalani told him. When Catalani's best-known opera, *La Wally,* was scheduled for performance at Lucca in September 1892, the composer insisted that Toscanini be the conductor.

In March 1892, at Turin, Toscanini conducted his first Wagnerian opera—*The Flying Dutchman.* Two months later, on May 21, he was chosen to conduct the world premiere of *I Pagliacci* at Dal Verme. In 1895 he led a performance of *Tannhäuser* at Genoa, and that same year he inaugurated the winter season of the Teatro Regio in Turin with the first Italian production of *Die Götterdämmerung.* At Turin, on February 1, 1896, he led the world premiere of *La Bohème.* On February 1, 1897, he directed his first *Tristan and Isolde,* and a season after that, his first *Die Walküre.* All this while he was bringing to the established Italian repertory a freshness of viewpoint, a brilliance of conception, and a musical authority that placed him with the most highly esteemed conductors in Italy. At this time he also proved himself as a symphonic conductor, with a concert at Turin on March 20, 1896, when he drew a thunderous ovation after his performance of Schubert's Symphony No.9. Following this the directors of La Scala invited him to conduct four orchestral concerts in Milan with the opera house orchestra. In May 1898 at the International Exposition

at Turin he conducted forty-three orchestral concerts in a two-month period.

The most important conductorial post in Italy became his in 1898 when he was appointed principal conductor at La Scala. He inaugurated his three-year regime on December 26 with *Die Meistersinger* (given without any cuts). The selection of a Wagnerian drama in place of a beloved Italian opera as his opening production was an indication that Toscanini was determined to function on his own terms, on the highest artistic level. Those principles led him to institute rigorous rehearsals such as the opera company had never before experienced; to create a repertory that shattered the insularity of Italian opera audiences through presentations of Russian, German, and French operas in addition to the usual Italian productions. He opened the 1899–1900 season with the Italian premiere of *Siegfried* and that of 1900–1901 with *Die Walküre.* Among the non-Italian operas heard under his baton were works by Weber, Humperdinck, Karl Goldmark, Tchaikovsky, and Berlioz. Together with the more familiar Italian operas he offered the world premieres of Leoncavallo's *Zaza* (November 10, 1900), Mascagni's *Le Maschere* (January 17,1901), Dom Lorenzo Perosi's *Mosè* (November 16, 1901), and Franchetti's *Germania* (March 11, 1902).

In order to achieve fully integrated performances he was determined to destroy the star system at the cost of bruising the sensibilities of pampered prima donnas and tenors. To retain the continuity of his performances, he broke a long-standing tradition at La Scala by refusing to permit the repetition of an aria after an ovation.

His three years at La Scala brought to the opera house the first of several glorious Toscanini eras. The first regime ended abruptly after the closing performance of the 1902–1903 season. Zenatello, Milan's beloved tenor, was then appearing in *Un Ballo in Maschera,* and a highly enthusiastic audience gave him a rousing ovation after one of his arias. This enthusiasm refused to die; the audience insisted on an encore. Toscanini would not allow this, again and again raising his baton to continue with the opera. When the uproar failed to die down, he threw his baton to the floor in disgust and ran out of the opera house muttering oaths and expletives under his breath. The following morning he set sail for South America to fill some engagements there. Before departing he announced he was through with La Scala.

In time a reconciliation was effected between Toscanini and La Scala, and he returned to his old post in 1906–1907. During the next two years the rule of no encores was rigidly enforced, and other stringent demands of Toscanini were scrupulously met. During this period he gave the world premiere of Francesco Cilèa's *Gloria* (April 15, 1907) and the Italian premieres of *Salome* and *Pelléas and Mélisande*.

In 1908 Giulio Gatti-Casazza, then one of the directors of La Scala, was appointed general manager of the Metropolitan Opera in New York, and he invited Toscanini to go with him. Weary of his continuous struggles at La Scala to maintain his exacting standards, Toscanini consented. He made his Metropolitan Opera debut on the opening night of the season, with the initial performance of the Gatti-Casazza regime, *Aida* on November 16, 1908. The cast was headed by Caruso, Emmy Destinn (in her own Metropolitan Opera debut), and Louise Homer. "In the best sense," wrote H. E. Krehbiel in the *Tribune,* "he is an artist, an interpreter, a recreator. . . . Signor Toscanini brought to the understanding and emotions of the audience all of Verdi's score, body and soul, as it lives in him, mixing it with an abundance of sympathetic affection. . . . Evidently Signor Toscanini's head and heart are full of Verdi's music and his transmission of what he knows and feels is magnetic." Richard Aldrich described Toscanini in the New York *Times* as "a strenuous force, a dominating power, a man of potent authority, a musician of infinite resource."

On December 10, 1908, Toscanini conducted his first Wagnerian performance in the United States, *Die Götterdämmerung.* "He performed the remarkable feat of conducting it entirely from memory," said Aldrich in the New York *Times,* "but this is only of subsidiary importance. . . . The important thing was that he produced a fine performance of the work, and that he showed himself to be thoroughly in sympathy with the music, to understand it, and to possess in a preeminent degree the power of reproducing it in its larger sweep, its deeper significance, and its finer details. . . . He presented a performance of remarkable energy and dramatic power as well as one of great musical beauty."

For the next seven years Toscanini continued to conduct at the Metropolitan Opera performances of Italian, German, Russian, and French operas: *Madama Butterfly, Carmen, Falstaff, La Gioconda, Otello, Orfeo ed Euridice,* Gluck's *Armide, La Bohème, Tristan and Isolde, Die Meistersinger, Cavalleria Rusticana, I Pagliacci, Tosca.* He conducted two world premieres: *The Girl of the Golden West* (December 10, 1910) and Giordano's *Madame Sans-Gêne* (January 25, 1915). He also led the American premieres of Puccini's *Le Villi,* Catalani's *La Wally,* Franchetti's *Germania,* Dukas's *Ariane et Barbe-Bleue,* Wolf-Ferrari's *Le Donne Curiose* and *L'Amore Medico, Boris Godunov* and *L'Amore dei Tre Re.* For six of his seven years at the Metropolitan he was called upon to direct the season's opening performance.

His last appearance at the Metropolitan Opera took place on April 14, 1915, with Mascagni's *Iris.* He was scheduled to conduct two orchestral concerts at the Metropolitan Opera later that season but failed to do so. Rumors were beginning to circulate about a break between Toscanini and the Metropolitan Opera management, but the real cause for Toscanini's withdrawal was never disclosed. All effort to bring him back the following season proved to no avail.

In Italy during World War I, all proceeds from operas and symphonic music conducted by Toscanini were donated to war charities. He was heard at patriotic concerts and community sings helping the war effort further, and on August 31, 1916, he even led a military band on Monte Santo during an actual battle and was awarded a medal for valor under fire. At a special concert in Rome given by the Augusteo Orchestra for a soldiers' benefit, he conducted, among other works, the funeral music from Wagner's *Die Götterdämmerung.* When some in the audience shouted their resentment that Toscanini was conducting German music, Toscanini shouted back: "I am conducting music that belongs to the world." He stalked off the stage angrily and for the next three years refused to appear with the Augusteo Orchestra. When he did return he pointedly included the music of Wagner on his program.

When La Scala was reopened in 1920, after having been shut down for three years because of the war, Toscanini returned as artistic director and principal conductor. He had unlimited financial and artistic powers to carry out his program in any way he saw fit. Since every phase of the opera house's operations came under his critical scrutiny, it took eighteen months to prepare La Scala for its opening performance: the house acoustics had to be improved, costumes and scenery redone, and a new elaborate apparatus installed to facilitate scene changes—all this while the company was assembled and rehearsed. On December 26, 1921, he reopened La Scala with a performance of *Falstaff* in which completeness in every detail of stagecraft, costuming, scenery, and musical presentation had been realized. With that evening a new epoch opened for La Scala. For eight years, with Toscanini at the head of La Scala, the world's music lovers beat a path to Milan: La Scala had become the most important opera house in Europe, perhaps in the world.

The familiar operas were restudied—old conceptions were replaced by fresh ones, and errors maintained by tradition, corrected. The operas under Toscanini's baton—those of Wagner, Weber, Verdi, Mozart, Debussy, Beethoven, Gounod, Rossini—were as if reborn. There were also noteworthy premieres of works by Italy's composers: Pizzetti's *Debora e Jaele* (December 16, 1922) and *Fra Gherardo* (May 16, 1928), Boïto's *Nerone* (May 1, 1924), Giordano's *La Cena delle Beffe* (December 20, 1924), Zandonai's *I Cavalieri di Ekebu* (March 7, 1925), and Puccini's last and unfinished opera, *Turandot* (April 25, 1926). On the opening night of *Turandot,* Toscanini followed Puccini's wishes by presenting it in its unfinished state. At the point where Puccini had written his last measures, Toscanini put his baton on the stand, turned to the audience and, with tears streaming down his face, said: "Here—here—the Maestro died."

In the winter of 1920–1921 Toscanini toured the United States and Canada with La Scala's orchestra in orchestral concerts, the first of these taking place at the Metropolitan Opera House on December 28, 1920. He returned to the United States in 1926, this time as a guest conductor of the New York Philharmonic. His debut on January 14, 1926, marked the beginning of a Toscanini cult in New York—he became a legendary figure. One season later he returned to the New York Philharmonic as associate conductor; then, in 1928, after the New York Philharmonic had merged with the New York Symphony Society, he was made music director. Under him the New York Philharmonic rose to

new heights, a fact readily acknowledged abroad when he took the orchestra on its first tour of Europe in the spring of 1930. The tour began in Paris on May 3, 1930, and covered Zurich, Milan, Turin, Rome, Florence, Munich, Vienna, Budapest, Prague, Dresden, Leipzig, Berlin, Brussels, and London.

In 1929 Toscanini resigned from La Scala because the burden of personally supervising every detail of the operatic productions had become too heavy for him to bear. From this time on, his principal activity as a conductor shifted from opera to symphonic music, although opera was not neglected. In 1930 he became the first foreign conductor to be invited to the Bayreuth Festival, where he conducted *Tannhäuser* and *Tristan and Isolde;* he returned the following summer to conduct *Parsifal.* At the Salzburg festivals between 1935 and 1938 he directed performances of *Fidelio, Falstaff, The Magic Flute,* and *Die Meistersinger.*

Once freed of his obligations to La Scala, Toscanini concentrated his enormous energies on the New York Philharmonic, until 1936. With this orchestra he presented many world premieres. Among them were Samuel Barber's *First Essay for Orchestra* and *Adagio for Strings* (November 5, 1938); Castelnuovo-Tedesco's Concerto for Cello (January 31, 1935), Variazioni Sinfoniche (April 9, 1930), and Violin Concerto No.2 (April 12, 1933); *Parade* and *Three Chinese Pieces,* both by Abram Chasins (April 8, 1931); Kodály's *Summer Evening* (April 3, 1930); Pizzetti's *Concerto dell' Estate* (February 28, 1929), *Introduction to Agamemnon* (April 6, 1931), and *Rondo Veneziano* (February 27, 1930); Respighi's *Feste Romane* (February 21, 1929); Tomassini's *Il Carnevale di Venezia* (October 10, 1929); and Bernard Wagenaar's Symphony No.2 (November 10, 1932). Among the American premieres were Ravel's *Bolero,* Respighi's *Pines of Rome,* and Tansman's *Quatre Danses Polonaises.*

When Toscanini led his final concert with the New York Philharmonic on April 29, 1936, it was generally assumed that his career in the United States had ended. But in 1937 the National Broadcasting Company announced that a new symphony orchestra, the NBC Symphony, was being formed for Toscanini, to carry his music throughout the entire country by coast-to-coast radio transmission and on RCA Victor recordings. He directed his first concert with the

NBC Symphony on December 25, 1937. For the next seventeen years he remained the orchestra's music director, performing over the NBC network before the largest audience symphonic music had thus far known. During this period he also conducted the NBC Symphony in concerts for charity. On March 20, 1948, he directed a Wagner program over the NBC television network.

In 1940 he toured with the orchestra throughout South America, his first stop being Rio de Janeiro, where he had made his conducting debut. In 1950 the NBC Symphony under Toscanini toured the United States.

With the NBC Symphony in New York, he directed a number of world premieres. These included Castelnuovo-Tedesco's *A Midsummer Night's Dream Overture* (November 25, 1945), Morton Gould's *A Lincoln Legend* (November 2, 1942), Elie Siegmeister's *Western Suite* (November 25, 1945), and George Templeton Strong's *Die Nacht* (October 21, 1939). The American premieres included Kabalevsky's Symphony No.2, Kodály's *Dances of Marosszék,* and Shostakovich's Symphony No.7 (the *Leningrad*).

As passionately dedicated to democratic principles as he was to musical ones, Toscanini emerged as a valiant fighter against Fascism in the years preceding and during World War II. From the time Mussolini came to power in Italy, Toscanini made no secret of the fact that he opposed Fascist rule. He refused to join the Fascist party; he would not permit his name or his music to be used in any way to promote the Fascist regime. His hostility to Mussolini was openly and fearlessly expressed. In spite of every effort by Il Duce to win Toscanini over, never would Toscanini perform the Fascist song *Giovinezza.* After one of his concerts in Bologna on May 14, 1931, he was physically attacked by a young Fascist because he had refused to do so; four days later the Musicians Syndicate of Bologna condemned Toscanini as "absurd and unpatriotic," for refusing to play the Fascist hymn. Some years later Toscanini was placed under house arrest at his home near Stresa for once again expressing his contempt for Fascist tyranny. He was finally allowed to leave Italy and return to the United States; at that time he made a vow never to return to Italy until Fascism was overthrown.

When the Nazis came to power in Germany, he was among the first musicians to refuse to conduct there. On June 5, 1933, he announced that his scheduled appearances at the Bayreuth Festival that summer would be canceled as his protest against the Nazi persecution of Jewish musicians. In reprisal, Nazi storm troopers ransacked the record shops of Germany to seize all of Toscanini's recordings and destroy them. When a new symphony orchestra was formed in Palestine, primarily of émigrés from Germany—the Palestine Symphony Orchestra (later the Israel Philharmonic)—Toscanini offered his services, without a fee or traveling expenses, as conductor of its opening concert, which took place at Tel Aviv on December 26, 1936. During World War II, Toscanini conducted concerts in the United States, both in concert halls and over the radio, for the Red Cross, USO, War Bonds, and for the armed forces. For the Office of War Information he appeared in and conducted the music for a propaganda film distributed throughout the free world: a performance of Verdi's *Hymn of Nations* in which one of the lines of text was revised to include the phrase "Italy—Betrayed!" and into the score of which were interpolated the anthems of the principal countries in the United Nations. In commemoration of the surrender of the Italian Army he conducted a special radio concert, calling it "Victory Concert—Act I"—the second and third acts came on V-E Day and V-J Day.

When Fascism was overthrown by the Allied victory in Europe, Toscanini returned to Italy to conduct there for the first time in fifteen years, helping to reopen the partially restored La Scala auditorium that had been closed during the war. He refused payment for his services, suggesting that all the revenue from his concerts be used to complete the rehabilitation of the theater. His opening concert at La Scala, on May 11, 1946, attracted world attention; and for the Milanese it was an event of particular sentiment. When Toscanini came to the stage "the audience rose and shouted its welcome," the New York *Times* reported, "mingling in the acclaim the two names dearest to its heart—Toscanini and Italia. Many eyes, and no doubt Toscanini's eyes, were dimmed with tears."

The first indication that the Toscanini memory was beginning to falter came one morning in January 1954. A concert presentation of *Un Ballo in Maschera* had been scheduled for January 17 and 24. Just before the first rehearsal, Toscanini awoke and found he could not remember the words of the opera, though the music was still perfectly distinct in his mind. He wanted to call off the rehearsal. The following morning, however, the words all came back to his mind, and the performance could take place.

But what happened the following April 4 at an all-Wagner concert broadcast not from the NBC studio but from Carnegie Hall was far more serious. All went well that evening until the next to the last composition, the Overture and Bacchanale from *Tannhäuser*. George Marek, who was present, tells the rest of the story in his Toscanini biography: "Suddenly in the frenzied Bacchanale he seemed no longer in communication with the music. It broke away from him, as a rock, already weakened, is broken away by the impact of the next wave and is forced to bump crazily in the wash. The beat of his right arm became frail, he failed to give cues, and at one moment he pinched his eyes with the fingers of his left hand, like a man who is desperately searching for a lost thought." Suddenly Toscanini stopped conducting and the performance momentarily was a shambles. The lapse lasted only twenty-eight seconds, for thirteen measures. Then Toscanini continued conducting and put the musicians through their paces to the end of the score. The *Meistersinger* Overture, the final number on the program, went without incident. "Before the final stately chords had sounded to the end," writes Marek, "he left the podium, the baton dropped from his hand, a musician picked it up and handed it back to him, he took it indifferently and disappeared; and though the audience clamored for him, he did not show himself again."

That day the announcement was circulated that Toscanini had conducted his last concert, and copies of letters by Toscanini and David Sarnoff, president of RCA, regarding Toscanini's resignation as music director of the NBC Symphony were hastily distributed.

Only once more did he conduct after that, a recording session a few weeks later in which he redid the love duet of his recording of *Un Ballo in Maschera* and made some corrections in his recording of *Aida*. Toscanini's career ended as it had begun, with *Aida*.

After that, Toscanini went into complete retirement at his home in Riverdale, New York. He suffered a stroke on New Year's Day of 1957, and a little more than two weeks later, on January 16, 1957, he died in his sleep. Funeral services were held at St. Patrick's Cathedral in New York. His body was taken back to his native Italy for burial in the family tomb at Milan's central cemetery.

Perhaps Toscanini's greatest contribution as a conductor lay in his departure from the practices of romantic conductors who gave way to emotional excesses and did not hesitate to alter a piece of music to suit their own individual romantic leanings. He insisted on sticking not only to the spirit but also to the letter of every work he conducted. To bring to life every subtle demand of the composer he was performing, Toscanini subjected each score he conducted to continuous restudy. More than that, with a scholar's zeal he perpetually did research in manuscripts, first editions, and musicological findings to come closer to the composer's intentions by going beyond what was found in the published score.

A unique combination of gifts made Toscanini one of the immortals of the conducting world: his phenomenal memory which absorbed the entire symphonic and operatic literature, his supersensitive ear, his profound musical erudition, his unblemished integrity, his conscientious application to the job of re-creating each musical work, his freshness and youthfulness even in performances during his old age, and finally, the vibrancy of his personality. "Every musician who has been guided by the movements of his wonder-making baton will testify that, within the range of the elemental power that radiates from it, lassitude and inaccuracy are dispelled," once wrote author Stefan Zweig. "By a mysterious induction, some of his own electrical energy passes from him into every muscle and nerve, not only of the members of the orchestra, but also of all those who come to hear and to enjoy Toscanini's will; for as soon as he addresses himself to his task, each individual is inspired with the power of a divine terror, with a communicable strength, which, after an initial phase of palsied alarm, induces in those affected by it a might which greatly transcends the ordinary."

In 1897 Toscanini married Carla dei Martini, a ballerina. She gave up her own career to devote herself to her husband and to the raising of their three children: Walter, who became Toscanini's business manager; Wanda, who married Vladimir Horowitz; and Wally, who became the

Countess Castelbarco. Until just before World War II the Toscaninis maintained two homes in Italy, one in the heart of Milan and the other on an island on Lake Maggiore. When he was conducting the New York Philharmonic, Toscanini lived in a suite at the Hotel Astor in New York City. Upon giving up his homes in Italy, he established permanent residence in the United States, acquiring a two-story house, Villa Pauline, in Riverdale, a suburb of New York. Toscanini never gave up his Italian citizenship.

Away from music, Toscanini was profoundly interested in literature and painting. He could quote Shakespeare by the page, and he was thoroughly familiar with the works of Goethe, Dante, and other literary masters. He had more than the casual amateur's acquaintance with great art.

He never smoked, rarely drank anything stronger than champagne, and never participated in games of chance. His diet was Spartan, often just soup and bread as his main meal. He took delight in many trivial things, such as playing pranks on friends and relatives, toying with gadgets, and watching prizefights on television. A superstitious man, he went through a number of minor rituals before going on the concert stage, such as kissing a small crucifix or taking a last look at the portraits of great music masters arranged on a table in his dressing room. He felt that the letter *W* was lucky for him, and that is why his three children have names beginning with that letter.

ABOUT: Antek, S. This Was Toscanini; Antek, S. and Hupka, R. Toscanini; Ewen, D. The Story of Arturo Toscanini; Chotzinoff, S. Toscanini: An Intimate Portrait; Frassati, L. Il Maestro Arturo Toscanini, e il suo mondo; Gilman, L. Toscanini and Great Music; Haggin, B. H. Conversations With Toscanini; Hoeller, G. Arturo Toscanini; A Photobiography; Hughes, P. C. The Toscanini Legacy: A Critical Study of Arturo Toscanini's Performances of Beethoven, Verdi and Other Composers; Marek, G. Toscanini; Marsh, R. C. Toscanini and the Art of Orchestral Performance; Taubman, H. The Maestro: The Life of Arturo Toscanini.

Jennie Tourel

1900–1973

Until Jennie Tourel's death, the material in encyclopedias and musical dictionaries about her birth and early life was more fiction than fact. More often than not—and for reasons of her own which she never explained—Tourel herself provided this fallacious information. However, passports and other documents that surfaced soon after her death helped to correct some of these inaccuracies.

Jennie Tourel (originally Jennie Davidson), mezzo-soprano, was born not in Montreal, Canada, but in Russia (probably in St. Petersburg), and the date of her birth was not June 22, 1910, but June 22, 1900. "We lived very nicely," she once told an interviewer about her childhood years in St. Petersburg. "I was brought up by governesses, which is why I dressed in sables and chinchillas." She was only two when she began repeating the Russian songs her mother always sang to her; at six she started to learn to play the flute.

In 1918 her family fled from Communist Russia to Germany, finding for themselves a new home in or near Danzig. In Germany her family was apparently in comfortable financial circumstances. There Jennie studied piano and voice. Later she continued her piano study in Paris, showing such talent for that instrument that a concert career was planned for her, even though she detested practicing and always depended upon her sensitive musical ear to carry her through her lessons. In her twenty-sixth year she was encouraged by friends and relatives to concentrate on developing her voice, and she studied for two years in Paris with Anna El-Tour. By transposing the two syllables of El-Tour's name, Jennie coined the anagram which she used as her own professional name. She later continued her vocal studies with Marya Freund.

She appeared in several concerts in Paris before making her opera debut in 1931 at the Opéra Russe in Paris as a Polovtsian Maiden in *Prince Igor*. The conductor that evening was Emil Cooper. He invited her to the United States that year to join the Chicago Civic Opera. Tourel made her American debut with that company

Tourel: too rĕl′

JENNIE TOUREL

in Ernest Moret's *Lorenzaccio,* after which she was heard as Lola in *Cavalleria Rusticana* and in several other standard roles. It is more than probable that to facilitate her entry into the United States she created the fiction that she was born in Montreal, and having created the story she stuck to it for the rest of her life.

She returned to Paris in 1933. At a party she sang several numbers and was urged by a member of the Opéra-Comique to audition for his company. Of the thirty-two to audition, she was the only one to pass the test successfully; the manager of the Opéra-Comique offered her a single guest appearance in the title role of *Carmen.* She did so well that she was given a contract. For the next seven years, as one of the principal mezzo-sopranos, she built up an impressive repertory and a considerable reputation. She appeared more than three hundred times as Carmen and Mignon, two of her finest roles. She also was successful as Cherubino in *The Marriage of Figaro,* and in such less familiar roles as Charlotte in *Werther,* Cinderella in Rossini's *La Cenerentola,* and the title part in Bizet's *Djamileh.*

On May 15, 1937, she made her debut as Mignon at the Metropolitan Opera in New York during its supplementary spring season. She made no further appearances at the Metropolitan Opera at this time, or in the next few seasons, but continued to be heard at the Opéra-Comique in Paris.

Two days before the Nazi troops entered Paris in June 1940, Tourel escaped from France to Lisbon, leaving behind all her possessions. She intended to leave for the United States without delay, but this trip had to be postponed indefinitely because of a prolonged illness. She finally went to the United States in January 1941. An attempt to find an engagement with the Metropolitan Opera failed because the company was comparatively restricted in its operations at that time and also because her best roles had already been assigned to others. However, Wilfred Pelletier, one of the conductors of the Metropolitan Opera, offered her several appearances under his baton in Montreal as Carmen and Mignon. Later she was heard in Toronto, Havana, and several American cities, including New York where she appeared with the New Opera Company as Lisa in Tchaikovsky's *The Queen of Spades* in 1941.

Her initial success in the United States came on October 7, 1942, when she made the first of three appearances with the New York Philharmonic under Toscanini in Berlioz' *Romeo and Juliet.* "One was definitely aware when Miss Tourel sang that the house was sitting up and taking notice of some magnificent vocalism," wrote Virgil Thomson in the *Herald Tribune.* "Miss Tourel was a joy. She is a singer in the great tradition. Her voice is beautiful, her diction clear, her vocalism impeccable and her musicianship tops." On the strength of this success she was soon engaged to appear with the Boston Symphony under Koussevitzky in Debussy's *La Damoiselle Élue* and, on March 23, 1943, in the American premiere of Prokofiev's *Alexander Nevsky* conducted by Stokowski over the NBC radio network.

On August 25, 1943, she gave a concert at the Berkshire Music Festival at Tanglewood, Massachusetts, and introduced Leonard Bernstein's song cycle *I Hate Music: Five Kid Songs,* with the composer at the piano. This was the beginning of a friendship and a musical association between Bernstein and Tourel that lasted until her death. She was the vocal soloist on January 28, 1944, when Bernstein conducted the world premiere of his first orchestral work, *Jeremiah Symphony,* with the Pittsburgh Symphony Orchestra.

Tourel gave her first New York recital at Town Hall on November 13, 1943, once again including on her program Bernstein's *I Hate Music.* Virgil Thomson said of her in the *Herald Tribune:* "Miss Tourel is mistress of a wider range of coloration in all ranges at all volumes than any other singer I have ever heard. Her pitch is perfect in the most difficult modern music. Her legato skips are the kind of bel canto one dreams about. ... The musicianship in every domain is so thorough that from the whole technical and intellectual aspect her work belongs clearly with that of the great virtuosos of music."

During the inaugural season of the New York City Opera in 1944, Tourel appeared as Mignon. As Mignon she also returned to the Metropolitan Opera on March 16 the same year. A critic for *Musical America* said of her: "Her greatest accomplishments lie in exquisitely wrought detail, highly polished minutiae of musical as well as histrionic expression and sensitivity to the finer points of interpretation." Eight days later, on March 24, she assumed the role of Carmen, and Herbert F. Peyser in *Musical America* described the keynote of her impersonation as "simplicity and the avoidance of far-fetched or flamboyant effects. It has the charm of French style, of unceasing vitality, and a richness of well-conceived detail that falls effortlessly into its place in the general scheme."

In addition to singing Mignon four times and Carmen twice, Tourel was heard as Adalgisa in *Norma,* and on March 14, 1945, she became the first mezzo-soprano in Metropolitan Opera history to sing the coloratura role of Rosina in *The Barber of Seville* (Rossini originally wrote the part for a mezzo-soprano). "Last night," wrote Oscar Thompson in the *Sun,* "Jennie Tourel restored the vivacious feminine role to its original voice and the notes of the Rosina part were sung as they were written. Miss Tourel sang them very well—better, in fact, than the sopranos who have appeared in the part in recent memory."

After a lapse of one season, she returned to the Metropolitan Opera for just one season more, being heard for the last time there on April 3, 1947, as Carmen.

In the summer of 1944 Tourel made her Latin American debut with opera performances in Mexico and Brazil in *Carmen, Mignon, Norma,* and *Un Ballo in Maschera,* and in recitals. She made her first tour of Europe in 1947 beginning with an appearance at Covent Garden as Cinderella in *La Cenerentola* that led the critic of the London *Times* to call her "the greatest new singer to be heard since the war." In 1949 she made her first tour of Israel, singing in seventeen

concerts in twenty-one days. On September 11, 1951, she created the role of Baba in the world premiere of Stravinsky's *The Rake's Progress* at the Venice Festival; she was selected for the part by the composer.

From the early 1950s on Tourel concentrated on the concert stage, in recitals and as a guest artist with symphony orchestras (although on March 2, 1972, she made one of her increasingly rare appearances in opera in the world premiere of Thomas Pasatieri's *The Black Widow* in Seattle, Washington). It is perhaps in the concert area that she earned her greatest successes. As Peter Davis wrote in the New York *Times* after her New York recital of French songs in April 1972: "Miss Tourel illuminates anything she sings, no matter what the era." On December 9, 1969, she appeared in a recital at Carnegie Hall in New York with Leonard Bernstein as her accompanist, a performance that has been recorded.

She enjoyed exceptional success as an interpreter of twentieth century music. Hindemith made a special version of his monumental song cycle *Das Marienleben* for one of her concerts in New York. At a recital in New York in March 1963 she presented Poulenc's rarely given *Fiançailles pour Rire.* She also gave the first New York performance of Stravinsky's *Cantata on Four Poems by Anonymous English Poets.*

She was the soloist under Bernstein in a performance of Mahler's Symphony No.2 (*Resurrection*) given on Mt. Scopus in Israel in the spring of 1966 to celebrate Israel's victory in the Six Day War; on that occasion she used a Hebrew rather than a German text, memorizing the Hebrew part in two days.

Tourel also had a long and distinguished career as a teacher of voice. In 1957 she began her teaching career at the Aspen School in Aspen, Colorado, and at the Juilliard School of Music. In 1962 she became music director of the vocal department of the Rubin Academy of Music in Jerusalem and eight years later she founded an opera workshop there. In 1963 she gave a series of public master classes at Carnegie Hall in New York. She also gave master classes at the Julius Hartt School of Music in Hartford, Connecticut; the University of North Carolina; and Washington University in St. Louis.

Tourel died of lung cancer at Lenox Hill Hospital in New York City on November 23, 1973. At the services at Riverside Memorial Chapel on

November 27, Leonard Bernstein delivered the eulogy.

A year after her death Odyssey Records released a two-disk album, *A Tribute to Jennie Tourel,* recorded between 1944 and 1952, which contains what Richard Dyer in the New York *Times* described as "the fullest documentation of her art." Another memorial volume was released by Columbia, representing, as noted by Robert Offergeld in *Stereo Review,* "just about everything else of importance including four *Carmen* arias which, simply as examples of histrionic vocalism, recall in the context of a modern and very different vocal art the legendary dramatic force of singers like Emma Calvé, Mary Garden, and the great Spanish mezzo, Conchita Supervia."

Jennie Tourel became an American citizen in 1946. She made her home for many years in an apartment on West Fifty-eighth Street in New York City. She was married and divorced three times. Her interests included reading books, going to museums, and attending theater and motion pictures. When she went on tour her constant companion was her French poodle, Minos.

ABOUT: High Fidelity/Musical America, December 1967; Musical America, June 1963; New York Times, December 9, 1973; Stereo Review, November 1975; Time, January 27, 1947.

GIORGIO TOZZI

Giorgio Tozzi

1923–

Giorgio Tozzi, bass baritone, was born in Chicago, on January 8, 1923, the son of Enrico Tozzi, a day laborer, and Anna Bontempi Tozzi. The love of music and the ambition to become a professional singer were early instilled in Giorgio through listening to recordings of Caruso, Tetrazzini, and other opera stars. He attended a Roman Catholic school. His first voice lessons were taken when he was thirteen, and he made his first public appearance as a singer four years later in a performance of a Neapolitan opera in Chicago.

In 1940 Giorgio was graduated from De Paul Academy and entered De Paul University, majoring in biology. "My career as a singer," he once remarked whimsically, "resulted from a major contribution which I made to science by discontinuing my studies as a biologist." Those studies ended in his junior year when he was drafted into the United States Army where he served for three and a half years.

Upon being separated from the service, he found employment as a singer in nightclubs and in the chorus of the "Chicago Theater of the Air" that broadcast musical comedies and operettas from radio station WGN in Chicago. Meanwhile he continued to study voice in Chicago with Rosa Raisa and Giacomo Rimini, and subsequently with John Daggett Howell.

On December 29, 1948, he made his operatic debut in the United States as Tarquinius in the New York premiere of Britten's *The Rape of Lucretia,* which had a short run at the Ziegfeld Theater on Broadway. In 1949 he appeared for five months in *Tough at the Top,* a musical comedy produced at the Adelphi Theater in London.

Determined on a career in serious music, Tozzi went to Milan for additional vocal training with Giulio Lorandi and at the Conservatorio Giuseppe Verdi and the Scuola Musicale di Milano.

He made his European debut in 1950 at the Teatro Nuovo in Milan as Rodolfo in *La Sonnambula.* During that season he was also heard as Colline in *La Bohème.* These performances brought him to the attention of Emilio Ferone, an impresario, who booked Tozzi to appear in

Tozzi: tōt′ zĭ

provincial opera houses throughout Italy, as well as at the Royal Opera at Cairo.

In December 1953 (the opening night of the season), Tozzi made his debut at La Scala in Milan in a new production of Catalani's *La Wally* starring Renata Tebaldi and Mario del Monaco. His success that season brought him a contract for the Metropolitan Opera, where he made his bow on March 9, 1955, as Alvise in *La Gioconda.* In the *World-Telegram and Sun,* Barclay Hudson said he "revealed a strong and appealing voice . . . and a mastery of style and technique to back it up."

During the next two decades Tozzi entrenched himself as a principal bass baritone of the Metropolitan Opera. He was the Doctor in the world premiere of Samuel Barber's *Vanessa* (January 15, 1958), Fiesco in a new production of *Simon Boccanegra,* Plunkett in an English-language production of *Martha,* and Rodolfo in a new production of *La Sonnambula* starring Joan Sutherland. His other Metropolitan Opera roles were: Ramfis in *Aida,* Sparafucile in *Rigoletto,* Samuel in *Un Ballo in Maschera,* Pogner and Hans Sachs in *Die Meistersinger,* Pimen and the title role in *Boris Godunov,* Guardiano in *La Forza del Destino,* Ferrando in *Il Trovatore,* Colline in *La Bohème,* Figaro in *The Marriage of Figaro,* Raimondo in *Lucia di Lammermoor,* Gremin in *Eugene Onegin,* Commendatore and the title role in *Don Giovanni,* the Old Hebrew in *Samson and Delilah,* Don Basilio in *The Barber of Seville,* Sarastro in *The Magic Flute,* Banquo in Verdi's *Macbeth,* Philip II in *Don Carlo,* Count Des Grieux in *Manon,* Arkël in *Pelléas and Mélisande,* Daland in *The Flying Dutchman,* Don Fernando and Rocco in *Fidelio,* Zaccarias in *Nabucco,* Méphistophélès in *Faust,* Walter in *Luisa Miller,* King Mark in *Tristan and Isolde,* Gurnemanz in *Parsifal,* and Oroveso in *Norma.*

Tozzi achieved one of his greatest successes when he appeared for the first time as Hans Sachs in *Die Meistersinger* on January 14, 1967. Two years later, his performance of Hans Sachs with the Hamburg State Opera was filmed and transmitted over German television. This was not his first Wagnerian role. In 1955 Rudolf Bing had asked him to take the part of Pogner, also in *Die Meistersinger.* "I didn't want to get involved in German opera or Wagner, mainly because I didn't speak the language." But Bing insisted and on January 11, 1956, he took on that

role. "I fell in love with the music," he said. "From the beginning I had a real feeling for Wagner." On January 13, 1960, he was cast as Daland in *The Flying Dutchman.* "My Daland worked," recalls Tozzi, "and I got to perform with a great artist—George London as the Dutchman." As Hans Sachs, his most ambitious Wagnerian role up to that time, he was "one of the glories of the 1968–1969 revival," in the opinion of Irving Kolodin in the *Saturday Review.* His interpretation, Kolodin added, "now can be firmly implanted in the roster of great portrayals—he has moved from silver plate into solid sterling. With spontaneity and naturalness, with subtle unstagy touches, he encompasses Sachs's full personality; his warmth, compassion, wisdom, humor, immense humanity, and, yes, his temperament. With this characterization has come vocalism that is even riper and more settled than before." On December 9, 1971, he sang King Mark in *Tristan and Isolde* and on April 11, 1972, Gurnemanz in *Parsifal.*

In addition to his performances at the Metropolitan Opera, Tozzi has appeared regularly with the San Francisco Opera where he made his debut on September 15, 1955 (the opening night of the season), as Ramfis. Over television, on March 21, 1961, Tozzi assumed the title role of *Boris Godunov* in John Gutman's English version of the opera, produced by the NBC Opera Company.

Abroad, Tozzi was heard at the Salzburg Festival in the summer of 1958 in the European premiere of *Vanessa.* In 1962 he appeared at La Scala in a gala production of *Les Huguenots* in a cast including Joan Sutherland and Franco Corelli, and in 1966 he was heard in *Simon Boccanegra* at the Munich Opera. He has been a guest artist with other major European opera companies as well as a recitalist and soloist with major orchestras in the United States and Europe.

He has also been prominent in lighter areas of entertainment. During the summer of 1957 he appeared as Émile de Becque opposite Mary Martin in a West Coast revival of the Rodgers and Hammerstein musical play *South Pacific.* He was heard on the sound track (singing for Rossano Brazzi) in the film version of that musical in 1958. He assumed a speaking role in the motion picture *Shamus* (1973), a role he won when the producer of that motion picture happened to see a television commercial Tozzi had made for Fiat in which he spoke in a light Italian accent.

Tozzi married Catherine Dieringer, an American soprano he had met in Milan, on February 23, 1952. Until their divorce they lived in an apartment in New York City. On March 15, 1967, he married Monte Amundsen, a singer, with whom he had two children. They made their home at first in Montclair, New Jersey and later moved to Malibu, California. Tozzi's hobbies are carpentry and photography. He teaches voice and coaches repertory and has served on the faculty of the Juilliard School of Music in New York.

ABOUT: Matz, M. E. Opera Stars in the Sun. *Periodicals*—High Fidelity/Musical America, July 1972; New York Times Magazine, March 19, 1961; Opera News, December 28, 1968; Time, April 7, 1961.

WALTER TRAMPLER

Walter Trampler

1915–

Walter Trampler, violist, was born in Munich on August 25, 1915. His father, Johann Trampler, was a violinist in the Munich State Opera Orchestra and his mother, Willy Jaeger Trampler, was an excellent amateur pianist. His father initiated Walter into music with lessons on the violin when the boy was six. These continued for nine years while Walter received his academic education at the Volksschule and the Real Gymnasium, from 1920 to 1930. In 1930 he entered the State Academy of Music, specializing in the violin but also receiving training on the viola and courses in theory and music history. By the time he was graduated from the Academy in 1934, he was already playing the viola in amateur performances of string quartets. "I can't say I immediately fell in love with the viola," he told Shirley Fleming in an interview in the New York *Times*. "I began to play it because in Europe a violin student has to play viola as a second instrument. This is designed to provide violists for chamber music." He explains that he "drifted" into viola parts at the age of seventeen when he found a job as violist with the Strub Quartet which toured Europe and then in the first viola desk of the All-German Radio Symphony Orchestra. "At seventeen," he explains, "that was quite a calling."

Trampler left Germany in 1939. He went to the United States and six years later became a naturalized citizen. From 1939 to 1942 he was associate professor of music at Rollins College Conservatory of Music at Winter Park, Florida, where he taught the violin. "They never heard of a viola," he remarks wryly. During this period, in the summers of 1940 and 1941, Serge Koussevitzky invited him to perform at the Berkshire Music Festival and to teach the viola at the Berkshire Music Center at Tanglewood, Massachusetts. This affiliation with Koussevitzky brought him an invitation to join the Boston Symphony Orchestra; from 1942 to 1944 he not only played with the orchestra but also appeared as one of its soloists, gave recitals at the Gardner Museum, and performed with the Zimbler Sinfonietta.

"In the summer of 1943," Trampler told an interviewer, "I got very patriotic. I was very much a German who'd come here and wanted to do something for America. So I went to work in a factory that made cones for the propeller shafts of PT boats." In the spring of 1944 he was drafted into the United States Army. Though originally assigned to the medical corps, he was soon entertaining troops in hospital wards overseas. After serving in the Military Government Division, he was discharged in 1946.

For a time, upon his return to civilian life, Trampler wanted to become an actor; he hoped that his German accent might find him parts in films with German roles. He took some lessons in acting but "after six months I got cold feet," he said. Returning to music and the viola, he became the first violist of the New York Symphony conducted by Leonard Bernstein. In 1947 he helped organize the New Music Quartet which promoted modern music, and until the group was disbanded in 1956 Trampler was its violist. With this experience behind him he went on to participate in chamber music performances with solo virtuosos and chamber music groups. As a guest artist with the Budapest and Juilliard String Quartets and in chamber music concerts calling for an extra viola, he was heard throughout the United States. He was one of the original members of the Chamber Music Society of Lincoln Center in New York. With this group he presented the American premiere of Shostakovich's Sonata for Viola and Piano, Op.147. He was also heard in recordings, including performances of all six of Mozart's string quintets.

Trampler has performed as solo violist in a large repertory ranging from the baroque to the avant-garde. Through his musicological researches, he has brought to public attention many little-known works for the viola. He has also commissioned twentieth century composers to write works for him. Among such commissions was that of Luciano Berio to write *Chemins II* and *Chemins III* for viola and orchestra. In 1972, with the Cleveland Orchestra, he was heard in the American premiere of Henze's Concerto for Viola and Orchestra. At Trampler's instigation, the British Arts Council commissioned Simon Bainbridge to write a new viola concerto for him. As a result of all this others began writing music for the viola with Trampler in mind.

Not all his efforts met with success, however. On November 21, 1970, Trampler helped to introduce a composition which the Chamber Music Society had commissioned for him and which its composer intended to be a tonal profile of Trampler. It was *Walter* by Larry Austin, a mixed-media work calling for taped electronic music and two films in which Trampler was the subject. During the presentation of these films, Trampler changed costumes, mimed, spoke, and danced with his wife; also performed on the viola and the viola d'amore. The composition ended with a section called "Go to the Young People" in which he and his wife marched into the audience while playing on their respective violas. "*Walter* bombed," reported Allen Hughes in the New York *Times,* "because it lacked the fantasy,

the imagination, the wit, the illuminating vision that make a successful mixed-media work open up new worlds of revelation and perception and joy. . . . This was the kind of product that gives mixed-media a bad name."

But in less controversial and more formal programs Trampler has proved himself one of the great violists of his time, a musician of rare discernment, scholarship, and good taste, in total command of his instrument. In addition to his numerous performances throughout the United States, he made annual tours of Europe after 1956, and in 1963 he toured the Far East.

On the stage Trampler is a visual as well as an aural experience. As Carlie Hope Simon has noted: "His figure, graceful as a fencing master's, is strung with thin tension. Under the lights, his long hair is molten silver, spilling sparks over his ruffled shirt front to the silver buckles on his shoes. A character right out of the nineteenth century, at its most dashing."

Trampler has also taught the viola and chamber music at the Aspen Music School in Colorado from 1953 to 1956 and later from 1961 to 1962. Since 1962 he has taught at the Juilliard School of Music. In 1977 he conducted a master class in viola playing at Mannes College of Music in New York.

In December 1968 Trampler married Karen Philips, a violist who had been one of his students at the Juilliard School of Music. His first marriage, to Margaret Stark on May 15, 1959, produced two children. However, the marriage ended in divorce. The Tramplers occupy an apartment on Riverside Drive in New York City and spend their weekends and vacations in a Connecticut clapboard house. In Connecticut, he can indulge in his favorite hobby, carpentry. There, as well as in New York, he enjoys giving gourmet dinners for friends.

ABOUT: New York Times, November 15, 1970, February 20, 1977.

Helen Traubel

1903–1972

Helen Francesca Traubel, Wagnerian soprano, was born in St. Louis, Missouri, on June 20,

Traubel: trou′ běl

HELEN TRAUBEL

1903. Her parents were of German extraction. Her father, Otto Ferdinand Traubel, was a druggist; her mother, Clara Stuhr Traubel, had been a concert singer before her marriage and was a member of a church choir after that. Helen was the second of two children, preceded two years earlier by her brother Walter.

"It was music that formed the indissoluble bond of our family," she has written in her autobiography. "Music was everywhere. Stray musicians were always visiting our house and staying awhile even though we never knew some of their names. All of us could sing. . . . My mother especially loved to sit at the piano and regale us with her favorites, 'The Rosary,' 'Die Lorelei,' and 'The Sweetest Story Ever Told'. . . . I was always in the midst of any songfest."

Since her parents went often to the theater, to concerts and opera—and since they invariably took their two children with them—Helen's childhood was filled with wonderful memories of the stage. She was seven when she heard her first opera, *L'Amore dei Tre Re*. By the time she was twelve she had heard over thirty operas, including three performances at the Metropolitan Opera in New York.

She received her first music instruction during her childhood, when she took three piano lessons a week for about four years from a Mrs. Tatum. Helen was always singing. From the third grade on in elementary school she was often called upon to perform operatic and vaudeville numbers in class. While still in public school, she earned her first fee as a singer, one

hundred dollars for performing Gounod's "Ave Maria" at the Washington University auditorium. In her twelfth year she sometimes substituted for her mother in the church choir. One year later she started to study voice with Vetta Karst, who for the next seventeen years remained not only her principal teacher but also her adviser and friend.

Karst was rigid in her insistence that Helen devote herself exclusively to vocal studies. For this reason, Helen abandoned high school during her sophomore year and began to avoid making public appearances. When she was seventeen, however, she started to earn her living as a singer at the Pilgrim Congregational Church, adding two years later another job, at the United Hebrew Temple.

In 1924, Karst pronounced Traubel ready for a concert appearance, and in that year she was a soloist with the St. Louis Symphony conducted by Rudolph Ganz. Ganz thought so highly of her performance that he had her tour with his orchestra twice. He also had her appear as a soloist under his baton in the "Liebestod" from *Tristan and Isolde* (her initiation into singing Wagner publicly) when he appeared as a guest conductor at Lewisohn Stadium in New York in the summer of 1926.

On the strength of that performance, Gatti-Casazza, general manager of the Metropolitan Opera, offered her a contract which she turned down without hesitation because she felt she was not yet ready. Instead, with Arthur Judson as her manager, she went on a four-month concert tour as an assisting artist to Hans Kindler and to Wanda Landowska. She also gave a series of concerts with the Philadelphia Orchestra at the Worcester Festival in Massachusetts. And she continued to earn her living by singing in St. Louis at the Pilgrim Congregational Church and the United Temple.

When Walter Damrosch went to St. Louis to conduct at the National Saengerfest in 1935, Traubel was assigned as his soloist to sing the "Liebestod." She made such a deep impression on Damrosch that he decided to include a female role in the all-male opera he was then writing for the Metropolitan Opera—*The Man Without a Country*—and persuaded her to take the part. When the opera was auditioned at the Metropolitan Opera in 1936, she went to New York to assist. At that time she appeared as a soloist on Walter Damrosch's Music Appreciation Program over radio. Then, on May 12, 1937, during the spring season of the Metropolitan Opera, she made her debut with that company as Mary Rutledge in the world premiere of Damrosch's opera. Writing in the New York *Herald Tribune,* Lawrence Gilman called her "a woman of noble and gracious beauty, . . . [with] a voice of power and fine quality. . . . Her embodiment of the heroine was moving through its restraint and sincerity."

Traubel remained in New York about a year, appearing in the Damrosch opera three times in the late spring in 1937 and after that performing on the "Magic Key" radio program over NBC. In New York she started a period of coaching with Giuseppe Boghetti. In October 1938 she married William L. Bass, a real estate and investment broker who became her manager. This was her second marriage. Her first one, to Louis Franklin Carpenter, a car salesman, when she was nineteen, lasted only a few months.

The first years of Traubel's marriage to Bass were, as she herself put it, "the worst and the best times of our lives. . . . Our troubles and delights had begun. . . . We lived by the skin of our teeth." Their home was a cramped two-room apartment in a building situated catty-corner to Carnegie Hall in New York City. There was hardly enough money to subsist on, no money even for occasional movies. Bass tried taking on one menial job after another, failing in all of them, before he assumed the responsibility of managing his wife's career. In spite of their poverty, in 1939 Traubel turned down a fifteen-week engagement at Radio City Music Hall paying one thousand dollars a week and a ten-thousand-dollar-a-year contract with NBC, because she was determined to prepare herself as thoroughly as possible for the concert platform and the opera stage.

She made her recital debut at Town Hall in New York on October 8, 1939. A critic for the New York *Times* wrote that "a voice of remarkable beauty and eloquence was disclosed. Miss Traubel's voice is dramatic and opulent, produced with the ease of a solid technical foundation in poise and maturity. Its range in power and essential quality are truly Wagnerian though it can be modulated to the demands of phrase and color." The critic of the *Herald Tribune* said she "displayed one of the finest voices to be heard anywhere."

Such praise brought her to the notice of Edward Johnson, who had replaced Gatti-Casazza as general manager of the Metropolitan Opera. He immediately offered her a contract if she stood ready to do the role of Venus in *Tannhäuser.* She turned down the offer, insisting that Venus was not her kind of role. (In her later career as a Wagnerian soprano she never appeared as Venus.) Instead of making appearances in opera, she was heard on the "Ford Sunday Evening Hour" over the radio a few days after her recital debut and then a week later as a soloist with the New York Philharmonic under John Barbirolli in the Immolation Scene from *Die Götterdämmerung.* She brought down the house. Pitts Sanborn in the New York *Sun* reported: "Seldom, whether in the concert room or in the theater, is it one's privilege to witness so eminent an achievement in the *Götterdämmerung* finale. Of paramount importance was Miss Traubel's voice and singing. The evenness, strength and splendor of color that characterized the former had their counterpart in the grand design of her declamation and the appropriately wrought detail with which the outlines were scored. . . . It is preposterous that there should not be a more important place for so notable a voice and so good a vocal technique than America seems to have found for this singer." Spurred on by such comments, Edward Johnson once again called her to his office, and again offered her the role of Venus, and once again he was turned down. In the end he acceded to her demand that she be assigned the part of Sieglinde in *Die Walküre.*

She sang Sieglinde for the first time not in New York but in Chicago, in a cast that included Flagstad and Melchior. Later the same year, 1939, she finally made her bow on December 28 at the Metropolitan Opera in the same role. A critic for the *Herald Tribune* called hers "one of the finest voices to be heard anywhere today, exceptional for sheer loveliness of its texture. . . . Such tonal gorgeousness is in itself rare." In a review in the New York *Times* Olin Downes called her portrayal of Sieglinde "moving and piteous."

During her first season at the Metropolitan Opera she was also heard as Elisabeth in *Tannhäuser.* (At that time these were the only two Wagnerian roles she had learned.) In 1940–1941 she was again heard as Sieglinde and Elisabeth. But on December 6, 1941, she sang her first Brünnhilde in *Die Walküre.* Her first Brünnhilde in *Die Götterdämmerung* was heard on February 12, 1942; her first Isolde, on December 4, 1942; her first Brünnhilde in *Siegfried* on March 2, 1943; her first Elsa in *Lohengrin* on December 20, 1944; and her first Kundry in *Parsifal* on March 21, 1950. (Her only non-Wagnerian role after 1939 was the Marschallin in *Der Rosenkavalier* on January 3, 1951.)

When Kirsten Flagstad left the Metropolitan in 1941 (not to return for another decade), Traubel became the queen of the Wagnerian repertory. Her Brünnhilde in *Die Götterdämmerung* was described by Olin Downes in the New York *Times* as "a distinguished portrayal, histrionically as well as vocally, surpassing any previously attempted by her." Of her performance as Isolde, Downes said in the New York *Times:* "She sang it very carefully, very intelligently, always with a lofty purpose and with a sincerity that was manifest in every measure."

She made her first operatic appearance outside the United States during the summer of 1943, as Isolde, in Buenos Aires. During the summer of 1945 she was heard at the Opera Nacional in Mexico City, and in 1952 she made two world tours. On October 5, 1945, she made her first appearance at the San Francisco Opera, as Isolde.

No sooner did Rudolf Bing become general manager of the Metropolitan Opera than friction developed between Traubel and the management. Bing reengaged Kirsten Flagstad, primarily for the Wagnerian repertory, but since he was none too partial to Wagner and intended to cut down the number of Wagnerian performances, he delayed too long in sending Traubel her contract. The aggrieved soprano announced to the press that she was resigning from the Metropolitan Opera because she did not know if Bing intended to reengage her and because she wanted to arrange other commitments. The affair became such a *cause célèbre* in the press, with Bing coming in for a good deal of unfavorable criticism, that he hurriedly made an arrangement with Traubel that she not only would share the Wagnerian season with Flagstad on an equal basis but would also be given an additional plum, the role of the Marschallin.

A final break between Traubel and the management of the Metropolitan Opera came in 1953. After she made the unprecedented move (for a Wagnerian soprano) of appearing in a nightclub—Chez Paree in Chicago on September 11, 1953—Bing took her severely to task for having demeaned herself as an artist and as a member of the Metropolitan Opera company. "Mixing popular singing with the Metropolitan does not mix very well," he told her. "Perhaps you would prefer to give the Met a 'miss' for a year or so until you may possibly feel you want again to change back to the more serious aspects of your art." To this Traubel replied hotly: "To assert that art can be found at the Metropolitan Opera House but not in a nightclub is rank snobbery." Her contract that fall was not renewed, and her career as one of the world's great Wagnerian sopranos was over. She sang her last role, Isolde, on March 21, 1953.

During her fourteen years at the Metropolitan Opera she made 133 appearances in New York and 43 on the road. Her two most frequently heard roles were Brünnhilde in *Die Walküre* (44 times) and Isolde (40 times).

Traubel devoted herself to concerts, to appearances in nightclubs, and to guest performances on network television programs where she became almost as famous for her buffoonery and infectious laugh as for her rendition of popular and semiclassical songs. She was featured in two motion pictures: *Deep in My Heart* (1954), the screen biography of the operetta composer Sigmund Romberg; and *Gunn* (1967), a nonmusical film. On November 30, 1955, she made her only appearance in the Broadway musical theater when she was cast as the madam of a brothel in the Rodgers and Hammerstein musical play *Pipe Dream.*

Above and beyond such activities, she was the author of two mystery stories. One of these, *The Ptomaine Canary,* was first published privately for friends before being syndicated in newspapers in 1950. The other was a full-length mystery novel, *The Metropolitan Opera Murder* (1951). She was also the author of an autobiography, *St. Louis Woman* (1959).

She spent her last years with her husband at her home in Santa Monica, California, where she lived a domestic life, doing much of her own housework and cooking. She had never been interested in parties or social gatherings, and she avoided them now more than ever, in favor of her many interests. She was an avid baseball fan, a lifelong rooter for the St. Louis Cardinals. When she was in St. Louis she was often found at the ballpark; at one time she even had a financial share in the club. She was also enthusiastic about football, fishing (barracuda and halibut preferably), and swimming. She collected books about fairy tales. And she was a chronic shopper. For an evening's entertainment she liked to go to the movies, usually to westerns.

A simple, homespun, wholesome woman, she never assumed phony attitudes or airs. Very few things disturbed the placidity of her nature.

Traubel died of a heart attack at her home in Santa Monica, on July 28, 1972. Her last public appearance anywhere was at a resort at Lake Tahoe, California, in 1964 when she appeared in a nightclub act with Jimmy Durante.

ABOUT: O'Connell, C. The Other Side of the Record; Traubel, H. St. Louis Woman. *Periodicals*—Collier's, January 31, 1942; Saturday Evening Post, October 2, 1948; Time, November 11, 1946.

NORMAN TREIGLE

Norman Treigle

1927–1975

Norman Treigle, bass baritone, was born in New Orleans, on March 6, 1927. He was one of five children of Wilfred and Claudia Treigle. His father was a carpenter. The only musical member of his family was his mother who played the piano and organ.

Norman showed an interest in music from early childhood. While attending grammar school, he was a member of the church choir, from his ninth year on, and he became an outstanding boy soprano. At Alice Fortier High School, from which he was graduated as an honor student in 1943, he took part in all the musical activities. Not long after leaving high school, during World War II, he joined the Navy as a seaman.

After two years of naval service, he entered the business world in New Orleans, reserving music as an avocation. Then he deserted the commercial world to devote himself full time to music. He sang in local churches and synagogues and appeared with various small theater and musical groups.

Winning the New Orleans Opera Auditions of the Air in 1947 enabled him to make his opera debut that year with the New Orleans Opera Company, as Lodovico in *Otello*. From then on, throughout his career, he sang every season with the New Orleans Opera Company. During his

first years with that company he was also a member of the staff of radio station WWL in New Orleans, over whose facilities he gave numerous concerts. In 1947 he entered Loyola University on a scholarship as a voice major to begin his first professional voice studies with Elizabeth Wood, who remained his principal teacher. At Loyola, where he stayed three years, he built up his operatic and concert repertory. This enabled him to give recitals in and around New Orleans, to appear as soloist with the New Orleans Philharmonic under Massimo Freccia, and to extend the number of his appearances with the New Orleans Opera to cover virtually "every supporting role you can think of," as he later recalled.

To accumulate enough money to go to New York to further his career, Treigle took a number of engagements in supper clubs in New Orleans and Houston. In the fall of 1952 he arrived in New York and auditioned successfully for Joseph Rosenstock, the director of the New York City Opera. He made his debut on March 28, 1953, as Colline in *La Bohème*. Reporting on this debut, John Briggs wrote in the New York *Times* that he sang "with a brilliance and resonance not usual in denizens of the bass clef. His singing was warmly received in the audience."

In his first two years with the New York City Opera Treigle sang such supporting roles as Angelotti in *Tosca,* Pistol in *Falstaff,* Banquo in *Macbeth,* and Sparafucile in *Rigoletto.* He was given the lead role of Reverend Olin Blitch in the first New York City Opera production of Carlisle Floyd's *Susannah* on September 27, 1956. "He struck me," Carlisle Floyd has written, "as being completely at variance with the character of Blitch as I had originally conceived him. By the opening performance in New York Treigle had convinced me that he had everything I could possibly have wanted in the role and then some, for I was forced to admit he had enlarged the character more than I had thought possible and had invested the role with nuances that had never occurred to me." Writing in the New York *Times*, John Rockwell commented: "Mr. Treigle's portrayal of the guilt-ridden, Bible-pounding evangelist was greeted as a major interpretation of contemporary American opera." After that, Treigle appeared in the world premieres of three other Carlisle Floyd operas: *The Passion of Jonathan Wade*, with the New York City Opera on October 11, 1962; *The Sojourner and Mollie Sinclair*, performed at Raleigh, North Carolina, on December 2, 1963, during that state's Tercentenary celebration; and *Markheim*, which the composer wrote for him and which he helped to introduce in New Orleans on March 31, 1966.

For two decades he remained not only the leading bass baritone of the New York City Opera but also one of the company's cornerstones. His greatest success came in the title role of Boïto's *Mefistofele* in which (like Chaliapin before him) he sometimes made musical values subservient to dramatic ones in creating a compelling characterization. He was highly successful as Méphistophélès in *Faust;* the four villains in *The Tales of Hoffmann;* the title roles in *Gianni Schicchi, Boris Godunov* and *Don Giovanni;* Dodon in Rimsky-Korsakov's *Le Coq d'or;* Escamillo in *Carmen;* and Figaro in *The Marriage of Figaro*. He was also heard in many operas, new and old, well off the beaten track. He assumed the title role of Julius Caesar in the highly successful revival of Handel's opera of that name, produced by the company in the fall of 1966, when Beverly Sills was acclaimed a star for the first time. He also assumed the roles of the grandfather in Aaron Copland's *The Tender Land*, the vagabond in Carl Orff's *The Moon*, the title role in Luigi Dallapiccola's *The Prisoner*, and Calkas in Sir William Walton's *Troilus and Cressida*.

"In purely vocal terms," John Rockwell noted in the New York *Times*, "Mr. Treigle has one of the finest bass voices of his generation: dark-colored with a focused, cutting edge and extraordinary amplitude and resonance for a man who stood five feet eleven inches tall and weighed only one hundred forty pounds. But it was as a singing actor that Mr. Treigle was most frequently applauded."

Treigle made his first European operatic appearance in 1958 in the New York City Opera production of *Susannah* at the World's Fair at Brussels. His first performance with a European opera company, however, did not take place until November 13, 1973, when he appeared as Méphistophélès in a new production of *Faust* at Covent Garden. His main performances in opera, in over thirty roles, took place in the United States, principally at the New York City Opera and the New Orleans Opera, and in guest performances with other companies. He was also heard in recitals and as guest artist with symphony orchestras.

His final years with the New York City Opera were for him a time of disenchantment and were responsible for reducing the number of his appearances there. After the company moved to its new home at the Lincoln Center for the Performing Arts, Treigle felt it had become too star-conscious, that it had lost its one-time zest for new and unusual operas, and that the turnover of the artists in the company was too rapid to permit them time to develop as they deserved. "I guess the change in the company became a crisis to me," he said. However, just before his death the New York City Opera was renegotiating a new contract with him to go into effect in the fall of 1975.

Treigle's last appearance with the New York City Opera in New York City took place on October 19, 1972, in *The Tales of Hoffmann*. His last performance with this company anywhere followed on May 13, 1973, at the Kennedy Center for the Performing Arts in Washington, D.C.

Treigle was twice married; the first time, for eleven years. This marriage produced a son and a daughter. In 1964 he married a second time. He and his wife and their daughter made their home in the Pontchartrain section of New Orleans until they were divorced. Treigle's favorite hobby was fishing. Though a Baptist, he smoked two packs of cigarettes a day, drank Scotch whisky regularly, and often attended race tracks.

Norman Treigle died in New Orleans on February 16, 1975. A telephone, with the receiver off, was at his side. He was the victim of an overdose of sleeping pills.

After Treigle's death, the New York City Opera Guild in cooperation with the New York City Opera and the Cincinnati Conservatory of Music established the Norman Treigle Memorial Fund providing two permanent scholarships a year for young American singers.

ABOUT: New York Times, February 18, 1975.

Gabriella Tucci

1932–

Gabriella Tucci, soprano, was born in Rome on August 4, 1932. When she heard her first opera performance—*La Traviata* at the Rome Opera —she knew she wanted to become a prima donna. She studied solfeggio and piano with private teachers before entering the Santa Cecilia Academy in Rome for more intensive music instruction. Her first and only vocal teacher was Leonardo Filoni, who later became her husband.

After winning first prize in an international vocal competition at Spoleto, Italy, Gabriella made her opera debut at the Teatro Giglio in Lucca in 1951 as Violetta in *La Traviata,* a role she was to sing over three hundred times in the course of her career. In 1952 she appeared as Leonora in *La Forza del Destino* at the Festival of Two Worlds in Spoleto. Within the next few years she enjoyed major successes at La Scala in Milan, the Rome Opera, and the Verona Arena. At La Scala in 1961 she was selected to appear as Helena in the Italian premiere of Britten's *A Midsummer Night's Dream.*

She made her American debut with the San Francisco Opera on September 25, 1959, as Madeleine in *Andrea Chénier.* One year later, on October 29, 1960, she made her debut at the Metropolitan Opera in New York as Cio-Cio-San in *Madama Butterfly.* Allen Hughes, writing in the New York *Times,* called her performance "admirable. . . . The soprano has an initial advantage of an attractive voice that seems solid in all registers. She is also very attractive and a persuasive actress." She scored a striking success on March 10, 1963, as Desdemona in a new Metropolitan Opera production of *Otello.* "Her

Tucci: tōōt' chĕ

GABRIELLA TUCCI

death scene in Act IV," reported Harriet Johnson in the New York *Post,* "proved deeply touching. . . . She sang the 'Ave Maria' with beauty, climaxed by a pianissimo in high A-flat." She was cast as Alice Ford in a new production of *Falstaff* (March 6, 1964, conducted by Leonard Bernstein) and as Marguerite in a new production of *Faust* (September 27, 1965). She opened the final season at the old Metropolitan auditorium as Marguerite on September 27, 1965, and she closed it on April 16, 1966, as Mimi in *La Bohème.* That same evening she participated in the gala farewell concert.

Her other Metropolitan Opera roles were Violetta, Aida, Euridice in Gluck's *Orfeo ed Euridice,* Donna Elvira in *Don Giovanni,* Maddalena, Amelia in *Un Ballo in Maschera,* Tosca, Leonora in *Il Trovatore,* Leonora in *La Forza del Destino,* Liù in *Turandot,* Elisabetta in *Simon Boccanegra,* Gilda in *Rigoletto,* Micaëla in *Carmen,* and Luisa in *Luisa Miller.*

"She needs very little costuming," says Beni Montresor, the Metropolitan Opera stage designer, "no wigs, no fancy things on her head. Like Anna Magnani, she is enough with her own eyes, her own hands. Many performers look like plastic dolls, but she is a real woman."

Her fame has been worldwide, with highly acclaimed performances at Covent Garden in London, San Carlo in Naples, the Vienna State Opera, the Deutsche Oper in Berlin, the Rome Opera, the Munich Opera, the Bolshoi Opera in Moscow, and other major opera companies in

Europe, South America, and the United States. She has also toured the Far East.

She has been almost as highly regarded for her professionalism as for her artistry. In more than seventeen years at the Metropolitan Opera since her debut she has not missed a single performance. She always comes to rehearsals totally prepared in every detail of the score, and she works in perfect harmony and equilibrium with the conductor and other collaborators. As Bodo Igesz, stage director, once commented: "She's wonderful. You say 'A, B' and the rest of the alphabet is perfectly understood."

"Neither as an artist nor as a private person did Miss Tucci display any notable eccentricities," wrote Martin Mayer in the New York *Times,* "except perhaps an unusual taste for hard work. Her natural equipment is a striking face with naturally Roman nose and startlingly large dark eyes; a fine, none-too-large voice which grows sweeter as it goes up the scale but tends to drop below pitch if she allows her concentration to slacken; and a good musical head. Miss Tucci's phrasing, especially of longer lines, can be just exquisite."

With her husband and their two children, Gabriella Tucci resides in a duplex apartment in Rome overlooking St. Peter's; the family also maintains a summer estate at Apulia. She has been named Commendatore by the Italian Republic, Commenda by the Empress of Japan, and Gran Dama of the International Academy of Pontzen of the Order of Knights of St. Brigida.

ABOUT: New York Times, November 10, 1968; Opera News, April 16, 1966.

Richard Tucker

1913–1975

Richard Tucker (originally Reuben Ticker), one of the most beloved and highly regarded operatic tenors since Caruso, was born in Brooklyn, New York, on August 28, 1913. He was one of five children of Samuel and Fanny Chippen Ticker. His father, an emigrant from Bessarabia, was a furrier who occasionally officiated as a synagogue cantor. When Richard was six, he sang in a synagogue choir on the Lower East Side of Manhattan. "Even as a kid," Tucker

RICHARD TUCKER

once told an interviewer, "I always knew that the Metropolitan would be my goal." But at public school and at New Utrecht High School he distinguished himself far more in sports than in music. In high school he was equally proficient in baseball, basketball, and football.

His academic schooling ended with his graduation at sixteen from New Utrecht High School in Brooklyn. He first worked as a runner on Wall Street and then as an errand boy for a garment factory. Later on, with a capital of three thousand five hundred dollars, he opened a little business of his own, dyeing silk linings for fur coats. Evenings were spent in studying voice. "It was a toss-up between business and singing," he has recalled, "so I finally settled on both. That meant holding down a job and studying voice at night for years. It wasn't easy. And I kept going after athletics at the same time—baseball, football, and handball."

After some preliminary vocal studies, he embarked upon a career as a cantor in synagogues, eventually holding down a post with the Brooklyn Jewish Center on Eastern Parkway. (Even when a successful opera singer and while filling engagements all over the world, he occasionally officiated at services during important Jewish holidays either in synagogues or at resort hotels. In 1963, while touring Israel, he officiated at Sabbath morning services in a Tel Aviv synagogue, following which he led hundreds of worshipers in a procession through downtown Tel Aviv singing religious hymns.)

On February 11, 1936, he married Sara Perelmuth, the sister of Jan Peerce, a noted tenor who was to become a Metropolitan Opera star. Tucker proposed to Sara on a subway platform in Brooklyn and was accepted, even though he was hardly earning a living and had no visible prospects of financial advancement. Sara encouraged her young husband to devote himself seriously to the business of becoming a professional singer. (Up to that time Tucker had never witnessed a performance at the Metropolitan Opera.) He began vocal studies with Paul Althouse and after several years entered the Metropolitan Opera Auditions of the Air, winning second prize. He then found a job singing in condensed versions of operas and operettas over radio station WGN in Chicago. In 1939 he made his concert debut with a recital at Town Hall in New York.

In 1944, having refused to enter the Metropolitan Opera Auditions of the Air again, he persuaded Edward Johnson, general manager of the Metropolitan, to give him a private audition. Johnson consented, asking him to learn the role of Enzo in *La Gioconda*. That audition brought Tucker a contract with the Metropolitan Opera and he made his debut as Enzo on January 25, 1945. A critic for the New York *Times* reported that "he sang with warmth and expressiveness and his acting was natural and easy."

Tucker did not rush his career. Slowly and methodically he added one role after another to his repertory, consenting to appear in them only after he had fully mastered them. Enzo was his sole role in his initial season. He added Alfredo in *La Traviata* and the Duke of Mantua in *Rigoletto* in his second season, Dimitri in *Boris Godunov* and Pinkerton in *Madama Butterfly* in his third. He did not sing his first Rodolfo in *La Bohème* until November 22, 1947, his first Edgardo in *Lucia di Lammermoor* until January 14, 1949, his first Des Grieux in *Manon Lescaut* until December 26, 1949, his first Cavaradossi in *Tosca* until February 11, 1950. Not until 1963 did he assume the role of Manrico in *Il Trovatore;* not until 1970, Canio in *I Pagliacci;* and not until 1971, Samson in *Samson and Delilah.* Even at the end of his career he was adding two new roles to his repertory: Arrigo in *I Vespri Siciliani* and Eleazar in *La Juive.*

All the time his vocal art was growing; he was at the height of his artistry when he died. In the purity and brilliance of his high tones, in the smoothness of his voice production, and in his combination of sweetness and strength he was

often compared to Caruso. "Caruso, Caruso," remarked Rudolf Bing, general manager of the Metropolitan Opera, in 1965. "That's all you hear. I have an idea we're going to be proud someday to tell people we heard Richard Tucker." In 1949 Louis Biancolli, in reviewing one of Tucker's appearances at the Metropolitan, called his voice "the only voice I've heard in years that reminds me of Enrico Caruso on records. . . ."

In 1949 Toscanini selected Tucker to sing Radames in *Aida* with the NBC Symphony over the NBC network. "Not since Caruso," wrote Noel Straus in the New York *Times,* "has this reviewer heard any tenor who delivered Rodolfo's music with more fervor or greater accuracy." After Tucker's first appearance as Don José in *Carmen, Time* called him "probably the finest tenor to be heard today."

Tucker made his debut with the San Francisco Opera on the opening night of the season, September 17, 1954, as the Duke in *Rigoletto.* He was an immediate success. That season in San Francisco he was also heard as Don Alvaro in *La Forza del Destino* and a season later in the title role of *Andrea Chénier.*

His success became worldwide. In 1949 he made his debut in Europe with an appearance opposite Maria Callas in *La Gioconda* at the Verona Arena. He received one of the warmest receptions ever accorded an American singer there; at that time he was the first American tenor to appear in Italy since the end of World War II. In the spring of 1955 he made his debut at La Scala. Tucker made history there by being the first American tenor asked to make an official La Scala recording; he thus became the only tenor ever to record with both La Scala and the Metropolitan. In 1957 he became the first American tenor to tour the Orient, covering fifty thousand miles in eight weeks and performing for some quarter of a million music lovers. His debuts at Covent Garden in London and at the Paris Opéra, both in 1958 and both times as Cavaradossi, were triumphs with few if any precedents for an American-born tenor.

Only two singers had a longer association with the Metropolitan Opera than Tucker: Antonio Scotti with thirty-four years and Giovanni Martinelli with thirty-two years. Tucker remained the principal tenor of the Metropolitan Opera until his death, thirty years after his debut. In that time he performed 503 times with the company in New York and 312 times on tour and was heard in 31 leading roles, mainly in the French and Italian repertories. In addition to the roles already mentioned Tucker was heard at the Metropolitan Opera as Riccardo in *Un Ballo in Maschera,* Gabriele in *Simon Boccanegra,* Tamino in *The Magic Flute,* Alfred in *Die Fledermaus,* Ferrando in *Così fan Tutte,* Don Alvaro in *La Forza del Destino,* Lensky in *Eugene Onegin,* Lionel in *Martha,* Dick Johnson in *The Girl of the Golden West,* Calaf in *Turandot,* Radames, Rodolfo in *Luisa Miller;* the title roles in *Faust, Andrea Chénier, Tales of Hoffmann,* and *Don Carlo;* and (on tour) Turiddu in *Cavalleria Rusticana.* On six occasions—the first on November 10, 1952, as Don Alvaro—he was called upon to help open a new season for the Metropolitan Opera.

The twenty-fifth anniversary of his debut at the Metropolitan Opera was celebrated on April 11, 1970, when he was heard in a gala performance made up of acts from *La Traviata, La Gioconda,* and *Aida* and was joined in the performance by Joan Sutherland, Leontyne Price, and Renata Tebaldi. During one of the intermissions he was presented the New York City Cultural Award and during another intermission a silver bowl from his colleagues.

His last appearance at the Metropolitan took place on December 3, 1974, as Canio, only a few months before his thirtieth anniversary was to have been commemorated, an event he did not live to celebrate.

Two weeks before his death, Tucker realized an ambition of many years' standing, to sing Eleazar in *La Juive.* The opera was given at the Teatro Lirico in Barcelona. For years Tucker had tried to prevail on the Metropolitan Opera to revive the opera so that he might become the first tenor since Caruso to sing Eleazar on the Metropolitan Opera stage. When, finally, plans were being projected to revive the opera in his honor, they were aborted by his untimely death. His last operatic appearance was in Barcelona as Don José.

He returned from Europe to the United States early in January 1975 to embark on an eleven-concert tour with Robert Merrill. In Kalamazoo, Michigan, where the two singers were scheduled for an evening concert on January 8, Tucker went out to audition a young singer for a possible recommendation for a scholarship at the School of Music at Indiana University. "The weather was horrible," Robert Merrill recalls, "but he went to her house." Returning to his hotel room, Tucker collapsed with a heart attack and had to be rushed to Bronson Hospital. There he died on January 8.

Just before the performance of *Don Pasquale* on January 8, 1975, Schuyler Chapin, the general manager of the Metropolitan Opera, went on the stage to announce that Tucker had died that day. "For thirty years he was a major artist with this house," Chapin said. "He gave one hundred and seventy-five percent of himself to every operatic performance."

Funeral services took place on the stage of the Metropolitan Opera on January 10, the first time services were held in the company's new auditorium and only the third time in Metropolitan Opera history. On that evening Tucker had been scheduled to appear as Turiddu. A memorial concert for Tucker was given at Carnegie Hall on February 6 with many stars of the Metropolitan Opera participating. Later that year Columbia released a three-record album in his honor entitled *In Memoriam: Richard Tucker,* containing many of the opera arias and concert numbers for which he is most often remembered.

In December 1975 a Richard Tucker Music Foundation was formed to perpetuate his memory by helping gifted young singers. Its first project was a twenty-five-hundred-dollar Richard Tucker Memorial Award for the contract winner of the next Metropolitan Opera National Council auditions. To help provide funds for this foundation, Richard Tucker Memorial Galas were held in New York in 1976 and 1977, with leading Metropolitan Opera stars participating.

Tucker, his wife, and their three sons resided in Great Neck, Long Island. On days off from his musical commitments, Tucker often joined his boys in playing basketball or softball. His other diversions in sports were handball and golf, and his hobbies were photography, gardening, and writing comic verses.

Tucker used to get up about eight in the morning, eat a spare breakfast, and have his chauffeur drive him to his studio apartment in New York City. En route to New York he would read through the daily newspapers, with special attention to the sports page and the stock market reports. In his New York studio he would work assiduously on his repertory with his vocal coach, Joseph Garnett.

Tucker once explained the steps he took in learning a new role: "First I find out what the story means. Next I study the music, and last I put words and music together and polish. I try never to let a day in New York go by without working and learning. I wouldn't be without my coach—vocalizing is like orange juice in the morning. . . . Every time I sing a role, I sing it twice. Once on the stage, and then in the car on the way back to Great Neck. My wife and three sons always want to know, why did you do this, or why did you do that?"

Tucker was given the medal and the rank of Commander in the Order of Merit of the Italian Republic (the highest Italian civilian honor). From the State of Israel he received its first Artistic and Cultural Award; from the City of Vienna, a medal reproducing its oldest known official seal; from the University of Notre Dame, a doctorate of fine arts, the first given to a vocal artist in its one-hundred-and-twenty-three-year history. He was twice cited by the National Father's Day Committee "for outstanding service in the field of father-child relationships." He was also awarded the Justice Louis D. Brandeis medal for "service to humanity" and a gold plaque by the National Interfaith Council for "distinguished service to Israel in its formative years."

An exhibition of Richard Tucker memorabilia was held at the Lincoln Center Library in New York in the fall of 1977.

ABOUT: Breslin, H. ed. The Tenors; Rubin, S. E. The New Met in Profile. *Periodicals*—Life, November 3, 1952; Musical America, November 1961; New York Times, January 19, 1964, January 7, 1973, January 9, 1975; Opera News, April 7, 1947, April 12, 1975.

Rosalyn Tureck

1914–

Rosalyn Tureck, pianist and harpsichordist who has made the keyboard music of Johann Sebastian Bach her particular specialty, was born in Chicago, on December 14, 1914. She was one of three daughters of Samuel and Monya Lipson Turk. Her father was a Russian of Turkish descent; her mother was Russian. Upon their arrival in the United States in the early twenties, their name was changed from Turk to Tureck by an American immigration official who pro-

ROSALYN TURECK

nounced it "Turk" and wrote it down in two syllables; the new spelling was retained permanently.

"My parents came from a long line of rabbis and cantors," Tureck once told an interviewer. "My mother had a really great voice, but her father would not allow her to become a professional. The whole tradition in the family was that you didn't practice your art or your studies for money." Her mother saw to it that all three daughters received piano lessons. Rosalyn proved to be the most musical of the three, the only one who became a professional musician. At the age of four she already showed an unusual gift for music by improvising on several instruments. She began to study the piano formally at eight and one year later gave two recitals at the Lyon and Healy Hall in Chicago. In her twelfth year she appeared as a soloist with the Chicago Symphony, and in 1928 she won the first prize of five hundred dollars in a Greater Chicago Piano Tournament in which fifteen thousand students participated. After that she went on a short concert tour.

For four years she studied piano with Sophia Brilliant-Liven. From 1929 to 1931 she continued her piano studies with Jan Chiapusso, a Dutch-Italian pianist who specialized in playing the music of Johann Sebastian Bach. His passion for Bach was transmitted to his young student. Though she had studied Bach's music from the time she was ten, it was only after she had begun working with Chiapusso that she became aware of her own affinity for that master. "We immediately started doing musicological research into Bach. . . . I started studying the harpsichord, the clavichord, and the organ. By the time I was fifteen, I was already playing all-Bach concerts in Chicago."

In 1931 she entered the Juilliard School of Music on a four-year scholarship. There one of her teachers was Olga Samaroff. At this juncture, she says, the way Bach should really be performed came to her as a kind of revelation. She recalled to an interviewer for the *New Yorker:* "In early December of my first year—I remember it was just before my seventeenth birthday—I started on a Wednesday to work out the fugue in A minor from the Book I of the *Well-Tempered Clavier,* which is one of the most complicated fugues of all. I lost consciousness, and when I came to I had had a real revelation, the way great scientists have their great revelations. . . . I'd had an insight into Bach's structures, into his whole sense of form, in the biggest, deepest way. I realized that Bach had an abstract mathematical structure, which was not linked to any sonority. As a result, I realized I had to develop a whole new technique of playing Bach on the piano—new keyboard techniques of touch, phrasing and dynamics." In addition she has said: "That was the beginning. It was from those roots that I have built ever since. I had to find every inch of the way myself—a whole new pattern of thinking, an entirely different physical approach to the keyboard, entirely different ways of using the fingers, new ideas of color and articulation."

At about this time she made her debut in Carnegie Hall, New York, performing a Bach concerto not on the piano, harpsichord, or clavichord but on the Thereminvox, a pioneer electronic instrument devised by Leon Theremin.

In 1935, one year before she was graduated from Juilliard cum laude, she won first prize in each of two competitions: the Schubert Memorial Contest and the National Federation of Music Clubs Competition. On October 10 of the same year she made her recital debut in New York. "In the first place," said a critic for the New York *Times,* "her technical equipment proved a formidable one. . . . And all she accomplished was the result of a keen governing intelligence and a deep seriousness of purpose." One year later, on December 12, 1936, as a reward for winning the Schubert Memorial Contest, she was a soloist with the Philadelphia Orchestra at

Carnegie Hall in New York in a performance of Brahms's Piano Concerto No.2. Lawrence Gilman wrote in the *Herald Tribune:* "Miss Tureck played with a beauty and rectitude of feeling, a propriety of phrasing, a delicate and affectionate adjustment of dynamics and tonal values which brought us movingly close to the exquisiteness of the music's thought."

Two weeks later she gave a recital at Town Hall, New York, in which she performed the *Goldberg Variations.* This was her first important bid for acceptance as a Bach authority. More impressive still was her series of six recitals in New York initiated on November 8, 1937, covering all of Bach's keyboard compositions, including the complete *Well-Tempered Clavier.* Only Harold Samuel had ever undertaken such a project in New York. Her admirable projection of Bach's literature for the keyboard made more than one critic speak of her as one of the more important interpreters of Bach since Wanda Landowska. After the final recital on December 18, a critic for the New York *Times* wrote: "Within the knowledge of this reporter no artist of comparable years has attempted so ambitious a task." In recognition of this achievement, Tureck was awarded the first Town Hall Young Artists Award.

When Myra Hess had to cancel her American tour of 1939–1940 because of World War II, Tureck was called in as a substitute. Between 1944 and 1946 she offered several more series of Bach concerts in New York. She toured the United States annually after that, most often in Bach programs, and she appeared frequently with major American orchestras. "The secret of her work at its best," said Virgil Thomson in the *Herald Tribune* in 1945, "seems to be that her passionate nature finds its completest expression in works that demand by their own nature an objective approach."

Her first tour of Europe in Bach concerts, in 1947, caused considerable apprehension among foreign concert managers since they felt there was no large public for such performances. But the response proved overwhelming. "It was panic," recalls Tureck. "It was mad. People would run after my car and throw flowers in the window. And I'll never forget arriving in Holland one Christmas Eve and finding my room filled with gifts, many of them anonymous."

From 1951 to 1955 she was the organizer and director of Composers of Today, a society for the performance of twentieth century music. During these four seasons, the concerts given in the United States presented the first performances in this country of taped music and the New York premieres of works by Olivier Messiaen, Ernst Krenek, Alan Hovhaness, and other composers of the "new" music. Occasionally, she was heard elsewhere in performances of new American music. She has given premieres of works by William Schuman and Vittorio Giannini and of a sonata David Diamond wrote for her.

In 1947 Tureck made her first appearances in Europe, with all-Bach recitals in Copenhagen and the rest of Scandinavia. She toured the British Isles in 1953 and 1954, and all of Europe and Scandinavia in 1955. When she left for Europe in August 1955 she planned a five-month stay; instead she remained several years. From a new home she had acquired in London she made tours of Europe with noteworthy appearances at festivals in Edinburgh, Venice, and Holland, and at the Brussels World's Fair in 1958. At Copenhagen in 1958 she was the soloist with and the director of the Collegium Musicum Chamber Orchestra, and in London that year she once again filled the dual role of soloist and music director, with the Philharmonia Orchestra, presenting all of Bach's concerti for one piano. During her 1955 tour of Europe, twenty-five of her solo concerts consisted solely of a single composition—the *Goldberg Variations*.

After a three-year absence, Tureck returned to the United States for a tour that began in New York in the late fall of 1958 with a Town Hall recital and an appearance as soloist-conductor with the New York Philharmonic, in two of Bach's concertos. Since then she has made numerous appearances in both the United States and Europe. In 1963 she toured South America, and that summer she appeared as both soloist and conductor at the festival in Israel.

On December 30, 1973, at Carnegie Hall in New York, she accomplished a feat without precedent in New York: the performance of the complete *Goldberg Variations* (with all the repeats) twice the same afternoon, the first time on the harpsichord and the second time, after a fifty-minute intermission, on the piano. This concert began at two-fifteen in the afternoon and ended four hours later. "What the experience did promise, however, was the opportunity of hearing a highly admired Bach interpreter realize her individual conception of this supreme

masterpiece within two very different sonorous contexts," reported Peter G. Davis in the New York *Times*. And in the New York *Post,* Robert Eric Kimball said: "Clearly the taste and sensibility that Miss Tureck brought in abundance to her monumental feat helped sustain a consistency of interpretation on both instruments that far outweighed the differences inherent in the instruments themselves. Both performances were exhaustively prepared and rehearsed. While Miss Tureck is a more experienced pianist in public performance, she also has a formidable mastery of the harpsichord."

To commemorate the fortieth anniversary of her first all-Bach concert in New York, Rosalyn Tureck presented a series of six Bach concerts, the first of which was presented on October 11, 1977, at Carnegie Hall. At the initial concert she offered the complete *Goldberg Variations* on the harpsichord at 6 P.M. After an intermission for dinner, she repeated the work in its entirety on the piano. "I believe," she says, "there's no one else in the world who does doubleheaders quite the way I do them, and I believe there isn't anyone who plays the harpsichord, the piano, the clavichord and so forth as I do. Harpsichordists will play the clavichord now and then, or organists will play the harpsichord now and then, but there are no pianists who play both the harpsichord and clavichord in public."

As a further effort to promote Bach's music, in 1959 she formed and conducted the Tureck Bach Players, a twenty-one-member chamber orchestra, which gave performances in England. She also founded the Bach International Society in 1966 to sponsor concerts and lectures and to give technical demonstrations of Bach's music and do research. She is the author of *An Introduction to the Performance of Bach* (1960) in three volumes.

For many years Tureck was active as a teacher: at the Philadelphia Conservatory of Music from 1936 to 1942, at the David Mannes School of Music in New York from 1940 to 1944, and at the Juilliard School of Music from 1943 to 1955. In the years 1944 to 1955 she was a lecturer on music at Columbia University in New York, in 1963–1964 she was visiting professor of music at Washington University in St. Louis, and in 1966 Regent's Professor at the University of California in San Diego. In 1974 she was appointed Life Fellow at St. Hilda's College at

Oxford and since then has served as visiting Fellow at Wolfson College there.

In 1946 she was given the Phi Beta Kappa Award for Excellence in Music and the Arts. She has been awarded honorary doctorates in music from Colby College, Roosevelt University, and Wilson College. In June 1977 she became the first American woman to receive an honorary doctorate in music from Oxford University.

The sculptor Sir Jacob Epstein executed a head of Rosalyn Tureck which is exhibited in a sculpture collection at Royal Festival Hall in London.

From a publicity release we discover: "After three unsuccessful marriages, she is currently a loner ... and is rarely distracted by the mundane problems of life in the trophy-filled New York menage where attendance is danced on her by worshipful followers and where she receives visitors by dim light, sweeping into the room in exotic Oriental robe and striking a small brass gong to summon maid or secretary." Her home, a twentieth-floor apartment on New York's East Side, is cluttered wth memorabilia of her career, tapestries, masks, and various musical instruments, including a grand piano, a primitive African drum, clavichord, harpsichord, xylophone, Tibetan harp, Swedish lute, and balalaika.

ABOUT: New York Times, November 9, 1958, October 9, 1977; New Yorker, October 10, 1977; Time, July 29, 1957.

ERNEST VAN DYCK

Eduard Van Beinum
See Beinum

Ernest Van Dyck

1861–1923

Ernest Marie-Hubert Van Dyck, Wagnerian tenor, was born in Antwerp, on April 2, 1861. Originally intending to study law he attended the universities at Louvain and Brussels. However, he later earned his living not as a lawyer but as a journalist, in Antwerp and Paris.

After studying voice with Saint-Yves Bax in Paris he was recommended by Massenet as a substitute for an ailing singer (on short notice) in a performance of Vidal's cantata *Le Gladia-*

teur, in Paris in June 1883. Van Dyck's first successes came later the same year, on December 2 and 9, when he appeared as a soloist with the Lamoureux Orchestra in Paris in Bach's *Phoebus and Pan* and in Beethoven's Symphony No.9.

He made his opera debut in Antwerp one year later, in 1884. As a member of the Antwerp Opera he sang Wagnerian roles. On May 3, 1887, he was heard in the title role of *Lohengrin* at the Eden Theater in Paris in the French premiere of this opera; there were just two performances of *Lohengrin* at that time because of the open hostility in Paris to Wagner.

After being coached in the Wagnerian repertory by Felix Mottl, the Wagnerian conductor, Van Dyck made a triumphant appearance at the Bayreuth Festival in 1888 as Parsifal. He returned regularly to Bayreuth as Parsifal until 1901, then was heard once again there in 1911. In 1894 he was also heard there as Lohengrin.

In 1886 Van Dyck married Augusta Servais, sister of François Servais, Belgian cellist. In 1888 he was appointed principal tenor of the Vienna Royal Opera. A commanding figure on the stage, both dramatically and vocally, he dominated most of the performances in which he appeared, in the French repertory as well as in the Wagnerian. On February 16, 1892, he created the title role in Massenet's *Werther* at its world premiere in Vienna.

While serving for a decade at the Vienna Royal Opera, Van Dyck made regular guest appearances in the major opera houses of Paris and

914

Antwerp. In the fall of 1891 he returned to the Opéra in Paris as Lohengrin, this time earning the success previously denied him in that role in that city. He created for Paris the roles of Siegmund in *Die Walküre* in 1892 and Siegfried in *Die Götterdämmerung* in 1898. On May 19, 1891, he made his debut at Covent Garden in London as Des Grieux in *Manon.* In addition to Wagnerian roles, he was also acclaimed at Covent Garden in succeeding years as Faust in Gounod's opera and in the title role of Wilhelm Kienzl's *Der Evangelimann* upon its premiere in England on July 2, 1897.

Van Dyck made his American debut at the Metropolitan Opera on November 29, 1898 (the opening night of the season), as Tannhäuser. In the four consecutive seasons that he was a member of the Metropolitan Opera company his Wagnerian roles were Loge in *Das Rheingold,* Siegmund, Parsifal, Tristan in *Tristan and Isolde,* Lohengrin, Walther in *Die Meistersinger,* the title role in *Siegfried,* Siegfried in *Die Götterdämmerung* and *Tannhäuser.* Among his most famous roles outside the Wagnerian repertory were Des Grieux in *Manon* and Werther.

Van Dyck's subsequent operatic appearances took place mainly in major opera houses in Brussels, Amsterdam, and Bucharest. After 1906 he served as professor of voice at the conservatories in Brussels and Antwerp. In 1907 he managed a winter season of German opera at Covent Garden. A year later he was heard as Tristan, Tannhäuser, and the Siegfried of *Die Götterdämmerung* at the Paris Opéra. In 1914 he sang Parsifal in the first performance in Paris of that music drama. He also appeared that year as Parsifal in Antwerp, three years after he had sung the part for the last time at the Bayreuth Festival.

In his later years, Van Dyck was the founder of the Nouveaux Concerts in Antwerp. He died at Berlaar-lez-Lierre, Belgium, on August 31, 1923.

ABOUT: Kutsch, K. J. and Riemens, L. A Concise Biographical Dictionary of Singers.

Anton Van Rooy

1879–1932

Anton Van Rooy (originally Antonius Maria Josephus Van Rooy), Wagnerian baritone, was born in Rotterdam, on July 1, 1870. As a child he sang in the church choir, but the world of commerce, not music, was his original goal. As a young man he was involved in the business of manufacturing cigars. When he decided to cultivate his voice, he studied with Julius Stockhausen in Frankfort. In 1894 he made the first of his public appearances as a singer in recitals and as a soloist in performances of oratorios. Felix Weingartner, the conductor, heard one of his concerts and urged him to devote himself to opera. Cosima Wagner then interested him in the Wagnerian repertory.

Anton made his operatic stage debut at the Bayreuth Festival during the summer of 1897, as the three Wotans in the *Ring* cycle. He was immediately spoken of as one of the great Wagnerian baritones of his time. That winter he repeated his performance of Wotan in the *Ring* cycle in Berlin, and on May 11, 1898, he made his debut at Covent Garden in London as Wotan in *Die Walküre.* From then until 1913 he made annual appearances at Covent Garden. In 1899 he returned to the Bayreuth Festival as Hans Sachs in *Die Meistersinger.* In 1901 he was heard there as the Dutchman in *The Flying Dutchman.*

Van Rooy made his American debut on December 14, 1898, at the Metropolitan Opera as Wotan in *Die Walküre.* Writing in the *Tribune,* H. E. Krehbiel expressed his enthusiasm in no uncertain terms. "We have learned—last night's experience enforced the lesson again—that it is possible to act properly, declaim eloquently, enunciate distinctly and sing well, not only to the greater glory of Wagner, but also to the gratification of the ears and the delight of the hearts of those who listen with understanding and affection. . . . Perhaps the most complete illustration was found in Herr Van Rooy, in whose case musical and dramatic utterance seem to be so completely merged that there is no desire in the listener to differentiate between them. Moreover, he has a beautiful voice, which he emits without effort, as if it were responsive to feeling alone, as if, indeed, it were the product of that feeling and depended neither on reflection nor will."

The Metropolitan Opera fully exploited not only Van Rooy's artistry but his physical stamina as well. Two evenings after his debut he returned as the Wanderer in *Siegfried.* During the rest of that season he appeared thirteen more times, adding Wolfram in *Tannhäuser,* Kurvenal in *Tristan and Isolde,* and Escamillo in *Carmen* to his Metropolitan Opera repertory. In addition, he appeared at three Sunday evening Metropolitan Opera concerts.

He created for the United States the role of Amfortas in the highly controversial American premiere of *Parsifal* at the Metropolitan Opera on December 24, 1903. Because Cosima Wagner had objected to any performance of *Parsifal* outside Bayreuth and because she had failed in a legal action to prevent the Metropolitan Opera production, she never permitted Van Rooy to sing again at Bayreuth.

On January 22, 1907, Van Rooy participated in still another operatic *cause célèbre* at the Metropolitan Opera, when he created for the United States the role of Jokanaan in the American premiere of *Salome.* Because it outraged the morals of the times, the opera had to be withdrawn from the repertory after a single performance.

Van Rooy remained at the Metropolitan until 1908, except for the season of 1900–1901. Other roles he assumed there were Hans Sachs in *Die Meistersinger,* Telramund in *Lohengrin,* Solomon in a revival of Karl Goldmark's *Die Königin von Saba,* and Valentin in *Faust.* His last appearance at the Metropolitan Opera took place on April 16, 1908, as the Wanderer in *Siegfried.*

After leaving the Metropolitan, Van Rooy was engaged in 1908 by the Frankfort Opera in Germany, but in spite of the appointment he rarely appeared with that company. He did, however, make guest appearances with the Berlin Royal Opera, the Munich Royal Opera, the Netherlands Opera in Amsterdam, and the Théâtre de la Monnaie in Brussels. He was also heard in recitals and as a soloist with orchestra.

He spent his last years in retirement in Munich, where he died on November 28, 1932.

ABOUT: Kutsch, K. J. and Riemens, L. A Concise Biographical Dictionary of Singers.

Astrid Varnay

1918–

Astrid Ibolyka Varnay, Wagnerian soprano, was born in Stockholm, on April 25, 1918. Both her parents were of Hungarian ancestry. Opera was a way of life for the Varnay family. Astrid's mother, Maria Yavor Varnay, was an operatic coloratura soprano; her father, Alexander Varnay, was the stage director of the Stockholm Royal Opera and had established the first opera company in Oslo. Astrid was their only child.

When she was five, her family left Stockholm for South America; her parents had operatic commitments in Rio de Janeiro and Buenos Aires. Astrid began attending rehearsals and opera performances in Buenos Aires. "I think," she has said, "that during that period I must have memorized subconsciously most of the soprano roles of the standard repertory."

In 1923 the Varnays went to the United States for permanent residence—first in Manhattan; then in Brooklyn, New York; and finally in Jersey City, New Jersey. She became an American citizen in 1944.

In Jersey City she attended the public schools, and for eight years she studied the piano at the New Jersey Musical College. A few appearances as soprano in school productions at Dickinson High School, where she majored in commercial subjects, first awakened her ambition to become a singer. During her senior year she sang in the school glee club, and at her graduation ceremonies in 1935 she was a vocal soloist.

After graduation from high school, she and her mother (her father had died some years earlier) moved to New York City. To support herself while continuing her piano studies, Astrid worked as a typist in an export house and later as a clerk in a bookstore near Carnegie Hall. By then she had become convinced she did not have the talent to be a concert pianist, and she redirected her musical interests into singing. Her mother became her vocal teacher and the one who coached her in her first operatic roles.

In 1939 Varnay received additional coaching in operatic roles from Hermann O. Weigert, a conductor at the Metropolitan Opera and an authority on Wagner. Weigert brought her to

Varnay: vär' nī

ASTRID VARNAY

These two impressive performances gave her a permanent place in the Wagnerian repertory at the Metropolitan Opera. During fifteen consecutive seasons she became the only soprano up to that time to have sung eleven soprano roles and three major contralto roles in the Wagnerian repertory. She was heard as Elisabeth in *Tannhäuser* sixteen times; Sieglinde, fifteen times; Elsa in *Lohengrin,* twelve times; Kundry in *Parsifal,* eleven times. Her other Wagnerian roles were the three Brünnhildes, Isolde in *Tristan and Isolde,* Freia in *Das Rheingold,* Ortrud in *Lohengrin,* Eva in *Die Meistersinger,* Venus as well as Elisabeth in *Tannhäuser,* and Senta in *The Flying Dutchman.*

While she was essentially a Wagnerian soprano, she did not confine herself exclusively to the Wagner repertory at the Metropolitan Opera. She was a triumph in the title role of *Elektra,* which was revived expressly for her on February 18, 1952, with Fritz Reiner conducting. She was also acclaimed in the title role of *Salome* and as the Marschallin in *Der Rosenkavalier.* She was equally impressive in the Italian roles of Amelia in *Simon Boccanegra* and Santuzza in *Cavalleria Rusticana.* On February 20, 1942, she created the role of Telea in the world premiere of Menotti's *The Island God.*

On September 17, 1946 (the opening night of the season), Varnay made her debut at the San Francisco Opera as Elsa. She returned to San Francisco in 1948 as Eva and the Brünnhilde in *Siegfried,* and in 1951 as Kundry. Meanwhile, her reputation as a Wagnerian soprano was further enhanced and confirmed in South America, when she appeared in the first presentation of the complete *Ring* cycle given at the Teatro Colón in Buenos Aires. In 1948 she made her European debut at Covent Garden in London with a performance as Isolde that was regarded by Ernest Newman, the critic of the *Sunday Times,* as "one of the finest and best sung Isoldes in my experience."

Further recognition came to her in 1951—she was the first American to sing Brünnhilde at the Bayreuth Festival. She became such a mainstay of the Bayreuth Festival that in 1956 Bayreuth presented her with a special, newly instituted award, for performing at the festival for five consecutive seasons. (Varnay received this award after her forty-ninth performance.) Within a decade she had sung the roles of ten Wagnerian heroines at Bayreuth—a total of ninety-six per-

the attention of George Szell, then a conductor at the Metropolitan Opera, and he arranged for her to audition for Edward Johnson, general manager of the company. That audition in May 1941 was successful. She was engaged for the season of 1941–1942. Meanwhile, Weigert continued coaching her in the Wagnerian dramas in preparation for her debut. In 1944 he and Varnay were married.

Varnay's debut at the Metropolitan Opera came a bit earlier than she had expected. A few hours before a scheduled Saturday afternoon performance of *Die Walküre,* Lotte Lehmann, who was to have sung Sieglinde, became indisposed. Varnay was called in as a replacement, even though she had had no rehearsals and had never made an operatic appearance anywhere. Since this performance—December 6, 1941—was broadcast nationally, her debut was heard throughout the country. "Miss Varnay," reported Noel Straus in the New York *Times,* "made an instantaneous success. . . . The exceedingly comely . . . soprano acted with a skill and grace only possible to those with an inborn talent for the theater. . . . In fact, Sieglinde in Miss Varnay's hands was one of the most satisfying and convincing portrayals the season had brought."

Six days later, she again appeared on the stage of the Metropolitan as a last-minute substitute, this time for Helen Traubel scheduled to sing Brünnhilde in *Die Walküre. Time* Magazine remarked: "Astrid Varnay can just about pick up Brünnhilde's helmet where Flagstad had put it down."

formances. After World War II she became the only woman to have appeared at Bayreuth every season for well over a decade. No soprano has ever appeared there more often in the role of Brünnhilde.

In 1951 she sang Lady Macbeth in Verdi's *Macbeth* at the Florence May Music Festival, appeared as Isolde and Brünnhilde at the Allied Festival of the Arts in Berlin at the invitation of the State Department of the United States (her debut in Berlin), presented a concert at the Lucerne Festival with Furtwängler conducting, gave seven performances at Covent Garden during the Festival of Britain, and, in the United States, sang Leonore in *Fidelio* at the San Francisco Opera in a revival mounted especially for her.

On April 6, 1956, she appeared at the Metropolitan Opera as Kundry in what she thought would be her last performance there. She resigned from the company because, she said, "I seemed to be getting into a rut. My Metropolitan assignments were roles that I had already done. They were not very frequent, either, because Wagner seemed to be on the downgrade at the time, so I felt I was not moving ahead. Besides my husband had passed away [he died in 1955] and I was very unhappy. I had these European possibilities, so Mr. Bing gave me a Sabbatical for a year, keeping my name on the roster. I just never came back. I've been invited to return several times, but always it meant I would have to give up too many commitments."

However, on November 15, 1974, she did return, after an absence of almost two decades, to appear as Karolka in a revival of Janáček's *Jenufa.* And on November 25, 1975, she made her first Metropolitan Opera appearance as Klytemnestra in *Elektra.*

After 1956 Varnay appeared at La Scala, Covent Garden, the Zurich Opera, and most of the principal opera houses of Germany. In 1964 she was cast as Klytemnestra at the Salzburg Festival, with Herbert von Karajan conducting, and that same year she made her debut at the Vienna State Opera.

At this time a new career opened up for her in character roles, and in subsequent years she was heard outside the regular repertory in such roles as Claire in Gottfried von Einem's *Besuch der Alten Dame,* the Nurse in Strauss's *Die Frau ohne Schatten,* Leocadia Begbick in Kurt Weill's *Aufstieg und Fall der Stadt Mahagonny,* Jocasta

in Orff's *Oedipus der Tyrann,* and as Kabanicha in Janáček's *Katya Kabanova.* "The role that really clinched the matter for me," she informed Richard Dyer in discussing her conversion to character roles in which she emerged as a fine singing actress, "was my first Klytemnestra. I said to myself, 'If this is a success, then I will go on with it.' . . . It all went beautifully. I don't look like a juvenile anymore, and while it is very nice to be a good actress when you sing heroines, these character roles demand it." In commenting on Varnay's appearance in the role of Klytemnestra at the Metropolitan Opera, a critic for the New York *Times* remarked: "Astrid Varnay . . . confronted her deranged daughter with a demented grandeur of her own, making the old queen a kind of Pique Dame misplaced into mythological times. Her voice served surprisingly well at times, but this was fine character acting rather than first-rate singing."

When her husband was alive and while she was a regular member of the Metropolitan Opera company, Astrid Varnay made her home in an apartment on Riverside Drive in New York City. After 1956 she maintained a permanent residence in Munich. Commenting on her outside interests she has revealed: "When I am free I like to go out and enjoy life. I like to be with my godchildren. I like to take walks, to read books, I like to go to the opera. But I also like to be in my own four walls. I am a homey person. But when I work, I work."

ABOUT: Collier's, March 6, 1943; Musical America, May 1953; New York Times, November 10, 1974; Newsweek, January 2, 1950; Opera News, May 5, 1962, December 21, 1974; Time, June 14, 1948.

Shirley Verrett

1931–

Shirley Verrett, mezzo-soprano, was born in New Orleans, on May 31, 1931. She was one of six children, all of them musical, of a middle-class family. Her father, Leon Solomon Verrett, was a building contractor who owned and operated the Verrett Construction Company. "My father was choirmaster of the Ephesus Seventh-Day Adventist Church in New Orleans," she

Verrett: vĕr ĕt'

SHIRLEY VERRETT

told Winthrop Sargeant for a profile in the *New Yorker,* "and he began training me when I was five and a half years old. He was, in fact, my first voice teacher. My mother [Elvira Harris Verrett] had a beautiful voice and was interested in singing, too."

While she was still a child, her family moved to Los Angeles. There Shirley received her education in Adventist schools. She continued to receive coaching in singing from her father who also took her to concerts, including those given by Marian Anderson in Los Angeles. "He asked me if I wanted to be a concert singer," she said. "I guess that planted the seed." Her parents, as Seventh-Day Adventists, frowned on all kinds of stage productions, including opera. "You know, in that religion you're not supposed to wear bracelets or lipstick," Verrett explains. "The unexpressed idea was that if Shirley Verrett were ever to become a professional singer it would have to be a concert artist, and never in opera. There was that emphasis on the Negro as singer. Marian Anderson was my ideal. I remember gazing at her and dreaming."

Though he encouraged her in her dreams of becoming a singer—and though she sang in churches and for the Rotary and Kiwanis clubs for a small fee—her father insisted that she attend school to learn some practical trade she could fall back on if a singing career did not materialize. For a short time she attended Oakwood, an Adventist college, at Huntsville, Alabama, but the restrictions and the isolation in the South soon sent her back to California.

There she attended Ventura College, majoring in accountancy and real estate law. When she was seventeen and still in school, she won her first music award, the John Charles Thomas scholarship sponsored by Atwater Kent. This entitled her to study voice with John Charles Thomas and Lotte Lehmann. She turned down the opportunity, however, because she felt she was not yet ready. In 1951 she married a black man named Carter who was fourteen years older than she. Until 1963 she was known professionally as Shirley Verrett-Carter. The marriage ended in separation after just six months, and in divorce eight years later.

After receiving her Associate in Arts degree in 1951 Verrett acquired a realtor's license and opened a real estate office in Los Angeles. She maintained it for a year and was quite successful. "One day," as she told Winthrop Sargeant, "I woke up and thought: This is the biggest bore that I could ever have gotten myself into." Determined, at this point, to sing professionally, she took vocal instruction in Los Angeles from Anna Fitziu, a former soprano of the Metropolitan Opera. She also studied song literature with Hall Johnson, the chorus master.

In 1955 she went to New York to appear on the "Arthur Godfrey Talent Scouts" program over television, and she sang arias from *Cavalleria Rusticana, Tosca,* and *Samson and Delilah.* Marion Szekely-Freschl, a singing teacher at the Juilliard School, heard that telecast, called to say that her singing showed great talent, and offered to be her teacher. Szekely-Freschl arranged for Verrett to receive a scholarship at the Juilliard School. That scholarship plus winning the Marian Anderson award in 1955, the Walter Naumburg Award in 1958, the John Hay Whitney Fellowship in 1959, the Blanche Thebom Award in 1960, and the National Federation of Music Clubs Award in 1961, enabled her to study voice with Szekely-Freschl at Juilliard over a six-year period. There she also received training in harmony, counterpoint, solfeggio, and music literature. One summer was spent at the Berkshire Music Center at Tanglewood in Massachusetts studying opera with Boris Goldovsky on a scholarship.

Because of her outstanding scholastic record at Juilliard, she was given the privilege of making a few public appearances while working for her degree. At the Antioch College Shakespearean Festival at Yellow Springs, Ohio, she made her first professional appearance in Britten's *The Rape of Lucretia* in 1957. In 1958 she assumed the role of Irina in Kurt Weill's Broadway musical *Lost in the Stars,* then being revived by the New York City Opera. On November 4, 1958, she made her recital debut at Town Hall, New York, and a critic for the *Herald Tribune* described her voice as "predominantly dark-hued, but she can snap it bright and sunny on command" and called her "a shining promise for the future." On November 27, 1959, she appeared with the Cologne Opera in Germany in the world premiere of Nicolas Nabokov's *The Death of Gregory Rasputin,* creating the role of Zigeunerin. In 1960, when Leopold Stokowski returned to the Philadelphia Orchestra for a guest appearance after a nineteen-year absence, he selected Verrett to be his soloist in a performance of Manuel de Falla's *El Amor Brujo.*

She was graduated from Juilliard with a diploma in voice in 1961. That year Rudolf Bing, general manager of the Metropolitan Opera, offered her a contract. She turned it down, not for religious but for musical reasons. As she has explained: "My family by then had come to accept the fact that I'm my own woman and would probably sing opera some day. I said 'no' because the Met offered me only some Wagnerian roles—for contralto! Not by any stretch was I contralto then or now."

For a time she concentrated on concert rather than operatic appearances. In February 1962 she was a soloist with the New York Philharmonic Orchestra in a concert presentation of the first act of Rossini's *Le Comte Ory.* During this period she received the Ford Fellowship in 1962–1963 and the Achievement Award from Ventura College in 1963.

She returned to the opera stage in July 1962 at the Festival of Two Worlds at Spoleto, Italy, in the title role of *Carmen,* in a production by Gian-Carlo Menotti. The reaction to her performance was mixed. But the critics were enthusiastic when she was heard in Schoenberg's "Song of the Wood Dove" from the *Gurre-Lieder* at the Stratford (Ontario) Festival in July 1963. John Kraglund wrote in the Toronto *Globe and Mail:* "Miss Verrett's gloriously rich voice might have been the one Schoenberg had in mind for this song."

She was again heard as Carmen at the Bolshoi Opera in Moscow and at Kiev in September 1963 when she toured the Soviet Union. This time she was acclaimed; in Moscow she was given a twenty-minute standing ovation. This success brought her an invitation to make her television debut in 1963 on the "Ed Sullivan Show" singing the "Habanera" from *Carmen.* In 1964 she found an opportunity to present her interpretation of Carmen to New York at the New York City Opera—"the finest Carmen seen or heard in New York [in] this generation," said Alan Rich in the *Herald Tribune.* In the New York *Times* Raymond Ericson wrote: "Miss Verrett didn't portray the role. She was the role." On February 17, 1964, she assumed the title role in the world premiere of Hugo Weisgall's twelve-tone opera *Athalia* in a performance by the Concert Opera Association at the Lincoln Center for the Performing Arts.

At this time she was also making considerable headway as a concert singer, beginning with a recital at the Lincoln Center for the Performing Arts in New York on November 4, 1963. "From her total command of the subtleties of German Lieder," said Alan Rich in the *Herald Tribune,* "her future as a concert singer is assured." After that performance she continued giving recitals throughout the United States in addition to appearing as a soloist with America's principal symphony orchestras.

On May 11, 1966, Verrett made her debut at Covent Garden in London as Ulrica in *Un Ballo in Maschera,* inspiring an ovation. She returned to Covent Garden early in 1967 as Amneris in *Aida* and Princess Eboli in *Don Carlo.* Later in 1967 she was one of the highlights of the Florence May Music Festival in the soprano role of Queen Elizabeth in Donizetti's *Maria Stuarda,* a role she also sang that year at Covent Garden, where she was given an ovation. That December she was heard in a concert version of the same role presented by the American Opera Society at Carnegie Hall in New York. In 1967–1968 she was the soloist in seven performances of Verdi's Requiem in Israel, including one in Bethlehem sponsored by the city's Arab mayor and given before an audience in which Jews and Arabs were equally represented. There she shared the solo parts with another black woman (Martina Arroyo), a Jew (Richard Tucker), and an Italian (Bonaldo Giaiotti); the conductor presiding over the Israel Philharmonic was Zubin Mehta, a Parsi from India. "It said a lot," Verrett has commented on this event, "about how people can work together, and how music can help them do it."

She accepted a contract from the Metropolitan Opera in 1968 because Bing stood ready to assign her roles in which she felt she could be heard to best advantage. Her Metropolitan Opera debut took place on September 21, 1968, as Carmen, in a none too felicitous production by Jean-Louis Barrault. She detested that production from the beginning, was uncomfortable in it, and failed to demonstrate fully her vocal powers. Nevertheless, Allen Hughes was able to say in the New York *Times:* "She is good looking, and she has a beautiful voice that moves smoothly from low tones to high and plays around freely in the treacherous middle without audible shifting of vocal gears. She also has an attractive stage manner and personality. She laughs easily and convincingly, flirts beguilingly, and registers changes of attitude and feeling without hamming or posing. All these things helped to make her an admirable Carmen." Later that season she received unqualified praise for her performances as Princess Eboli and Amneris, and as Azucena in *Il Trovatore.*

But Verrett was disenchanted with the Metropolitan Opera and at odds with Bing. She left the company after that single season, explaining: "I couldn't stand the atmosphere. . . . I got the impression that they were only interested in putting bodies on the stage without regard to the human beings inside them. And that annoyed me. They didn't trouble to find out what Shirley Verrett was all about. So I decided to sing somewhere else, and if there was a change from the Bing regime, I'd come back."

She had no lack of appreciation or of successes abroad in the years that followed. Everywhere she was honored not only for the beauty of her physical presence, the sumptuous texture and resonance of her voice and her dramatic gifts, but also for an extraordinary vocal range that made it possible for her to master coloratura roles and contralto roles as easily as mezzo-soprano ones. As Queen Elizabeth in *Maria Stuarda* she enjoyed a tremendous success at the San Carlo Opera in Naples in 1969, a year in which she gathered additional triumphs as Amneris at the Florence May Music Festival, in *Maria Stuarda* at the Edinburgh Festival, and as Dido in a performance of Berlioz' *Les Troyens* over RAI, the Italian Radio in Rome. She made a momentous debut at La Scala in 1970 as Delilah

in *Samson and Delilah,* and soon after in *Maria Stuarda* and *Don Carlo.* The same year she was Adalgisa to Montserrat Caballé's Norma in a television production of Bellini's opera in Paris. In 1971 she sang Princess Eboli at the Vienna State Opera. In 1972 she made a remarkable debut at the Paris Opéra as Azucena and did equally well when she appeared that year for the first time with the San Francisco Opera as a soprano, in the role of Selika in a production of *L'Africaine* mounted for her.

When she finally returned to the Metropolitan Opera in 1973 she "blew everyone's mind" as the New York *Times* remarked. She was willing to go back because Rudolf Bing had gone and a new regime was about to be initiated under the managerial direction of Goeran Gentele. (Gentele died in an automobile accident before his regime could be launched and the management passed on to Schuyler Chapin.) She was originally scheduled to appear in the mezzo-soprano role of Dido in the first Metropolitan Opera production of *Les Troyens,* a production in which the opera was presented in its five-and-a-half-hour uncut version; the character of Dido appears in Part II of that long opera. But just before the opening night, on October 22, 1973, Christa Ludwig who was to have sung Cassandra in Part I fell ill, and Verrett (who had never before sung that part) offered to sing it too. Performing the two principal female roles over a five-and-a-half-hour period called for not only extraordinary physical stamina but also the artistic resiliency to adapt on the same evening to two strikingly contrasting roles. No other singer had ever undertaken the two roles in an uncut version of the Berlioz opera. Verrett's success became a *tour de force* with few if any parallels. "Miss Verrett had a hard night before her," wrote Harold C. Schonberg in the New York *Times,* "and she came through very well. There occasionally was a bit of forcing and pitch trouble, understandable under the circumstances. But there also was a lovely lyric line that came to its full splendor in the duets with Anna and Aeneas. Those were sung as beautifully as anybody could desire." Harriet Johnson in the New York *Post* wrote: "She triumphed. Her interpretation had vocal as well as dramatic splendor. Her voice was at its best as Dido, though Cassandra, a dramatic soprano, came through effectively, too."

On June 10, 1974, Verrett appeared as Judith

in the Metropolitan Opera premiere of Bartók's *Bluebeard's Castle.* Later that season, on April 7, 1975, when Beverly Sills made her much-publicized debut at the Metropolitan in the first production by that company of Rossini's *The Siege of Corinth,* Verrett was cast as Neocle. This was her first appearance in an opera by Rossini and represented her first incursion into the world of bel canto; she came off remarkably well. "She took on the murderously difficult third act aria, 'Non temer'—up to now the exclusive property of Marilyn Horne—and made it her own," remarked one New York critic. When, on October 13, 1975, *The Siege of Corinth* opened a new season for the Metropolitan Opera, Verrett's performance virtually "stole the show" from Sills. "The twenty-one-gun salute must go to Miss Verrett," said Donal Henahan in the New York *Times,* "whose last-act aria, 'Non temer,' was not only a vocal tour de force but the moment that blew the dramatic cork right out of the bottle." In *Variety,* Robert J. Landry reported: "Seldom indeed does an artist so absolutely 'stop the show' as she did. The outburst of the audience enthusiasm both spent itself and renewed itself. She was utterly magnificent."

Verret assumed her second Rossini role—Rosina in *The Barber of Seville*—later that season at the Metropolitan Opera. In December 1975 she opened a new season at La Scala as Lady Macbeth in Verdi's opera (a role she repeated in Boston on June 6, 1976, and with the La Scala company at the Kennedy Center for the Performing Arts in Washington, D.C., on September 7 of that year). In February 1976 she sang her first Adalgisa at the Metropolitan Opera.

When the La Scala company visited the United States in commemoration of America's Bicentenary, in the fall of 1976, Shirley Verrett assumed the soprano part in a performance of Verdi's Requiem at Carnegie Hall, New York. That same month, at a La Scala performance in Milan, she took over the soprano role of Norma (having previously sung the mezzo-soprano part of Adalgisa in the Bellini opera), becoming the first singer in the twentieth century and the third in opera history to have sung both roles and ranges. She returned to the mezzo range as Azucena when the Metropolitan Opera opened its new season with *Il Trovatore* on October 11, 1976 (her second successive Metropolitan opening-night appearance). On February 5, 1977, she

was Mme. Lidoine in the first Metropolitan Opera production of Poulenc's *Les Dialogues des Carmélites;* and on February 21, 1978, she sang Leonore in the first Metropolitan Opera production of *La Favorita* since 1905. With the Opera Company of Boston she sang her first Tosca anywhere on May 1, 1978.

On July 26, 1977, on an invitation from President Carter, Shirley Verrett sang at a state dinner at the White House honoring the visiting Premier of Italy.

"Shirley Verrett has become a diva *par excellence,"* wrote John Gruen in *Opera News.* "Not only is Verrett statuesquely beautiful but she offered the image of a woman aware of her lure and magnetism. . . . Because she is black, an added nobility and elegance inhabit her persona, intensifying and deepening her regal, exotic bearing. Her face, with its film-star symmetry, is charged with character. As she speaks (or sings) it reflects intelligence, and myriad feelings are registered in the luster of her eyes."

On December 10, 1963, Shirley Verrett married Louis LoMonaco, a painter, illustrator, and professor. With their adopted daughter, they occupy a town house in New York City. "She is every bit the *grande dame* of her profession," writes Winthrop Sargeant, "and is considered stubborn and willful by many of her colleagues. She is a proud woman, remarkably independent of coaches and conductors, sure of herself and quite unconcerned about what others may say of her singing. She is an excellent cook who enjoys preparing for her family or friends New Orleans creole specialties she had learned from her mother."

ABOUT: Esquire, May 1974; New York Times, February 24, 1974; New York Times Magazine, January 30, 1977; New Yorker, April 14, 1975; Opera News, September 21, 1968, January 17, 1976; Stereo Review, May 1975.

Jon Vickers

1926–

Jon Vickers (originally Jonathan Stewart Vickers), tenor, was born in Prince Albert, Saskatchewan, Canada, on October 29, 1926, to William and Merle Mossip Vickers. His father was a school principal. As a boy Jon sang in church

JON VICKERS

choirs and at school functions. After graduation from high school in 1945 he planned to become a doctor. Unable to gain admission to medical school, he entered the business world as the branch manager of a Safeway store in Prince Albert. Later he served as manager of several Canadian stores operated by Woolworth. While thus employed he sang in church choirs and amateur operetta productions. Upon leaving the Woolworth chain to be purchasing agent for the Hudson's Bay Company, he settled in Winnipeg, Canada, where he took the male lead in a semiprofessional production of Victor Herbert's *Naughty Marietta*. A private recording of one of his songs from this operetta brought him a scholarship for the Royal Conservatory of Music in Toronto. For three years he studied voice there with George Lambert. While attending the Conservatory he continued to appear as a singer with various theatrical groups.

After graduation from the Conservatory, Vickers made some noteworthy appearances as a soloist with the Toronto Symphony conducted by Sir Ernest MacMillan. He made his opera debut in 1952 at the Toronto Opera Festival as the Duke of Mantua in *Rigoletto*. In 1956 he appeared as the Male Chorus in Britten's *The Rape of Lucretia* at Stratford, Ontario. During this period he was heard regularly over the Canadian Radio in Wagner programs. His first appearance in the United States took place in 1956 as Florestan in a concert presentation of *Fidelio* by the American Opera Society in New York.

A successful audition at Covent Garden in London led to his European opera debut, which took place during that company's provincial tour in 1957 when he was heard as Gustavus III in *Un Ballo in Maschera*. On April 27, 1957, he appeared in the same role at Covent Garden in London. Two weeks later on June 6, 1957, he assumed at Covent Garden the role of Aeneas in Berlioz' *Les Troyens*. "The young Canadian tenor, Jon Vickers, was equal to any demand," reported J. W. Lambert from London to *The Christian Science Monitor*. "His appearance—tall, well built, slim and blond-bearded—was matched by his singing. He is that rare creature, a heroic tenor with a beautiful voice. At the moment, he does not much explore Aeneas's character; but he does command the stature to project its outline with a noble, silvered, clarion ring." This has become one of his most celebrated roles.

His success as Aeneas made his position as one of the leading tenors at Covent Garden secure. During the next year and a half he was acclaimed as Don José in *Carmen*, Radames in *Aida*, the title role in *Don Carlo*, Jason in Cherubini's *Medea*, and Siegmund in *Die Walküre*. He was also a guest artist at the Bayreuth Festival during the summer of 1958 and appeared there as Siegmund in *Die Walküre*.

In 1958 he sang the title role in a stage production of Handel's *Samson* in London and at the Leeds Festival in England. That same year he made his American debut in a staged operatic production as Jason to Maria Callas's Medea, in a presentation of the Cherubini opera at the Dallas Civic Opera in Texas. In January 1959 he made a successful debut at the Vienna State Opera, where he was heard as Siegmund, Canio in *I Pagliacci*, and Radames. On September 11 (the opening night of the season) he went to the San Francisco Opera, to make his debut as Radames.

Vickers made his bow at the Metropolitan Opera in New York on January 17, 1960, as Canio. Irving Kolodin, reporting in the *Saturday Review*, was of the conviction that Canio was not the kind of role Vickers could use to carve a career for himself in America. However, Kolodin did find that he sang "with sure control, musical intelligence and dramatic persuasion." On January 28 Vickers sang Florestan in a new Metropolitan Opera production of *Fidelio*, and Harriet Johnson, writing in the New York *Post*, found that he sang "with nobility and virility of tone." She further commented: "He managed to build his climaxes during the final poco allegro as if he had voice to spare. He also conveyed the despair of the situation with affecting emotion." (In 1970, when the Metropolitan Opera commemorated the two-hundredth anniversary of Beethoven's birth with a new production of *Fidelio,* Vickers again appeared as Florestan.)

Vickers extended his German repertory at the Metropolitan Opera on February 9, 1960, when he appeared as Siegmund. In the New York *Times* Howard Taubman reported: "The evening's unanticipated revelation was the Siegmund of Jon Vickers. The Canadian tenor sang the role better than anyone has at the Met since the days of Lauritz Melchior." On March 1, 1965, he proved impressive as Erik in *The Flying Dutchman.* He made further progress as a Metropolitan Opera *Heldentenor* when he sang Tristan in *Tristan and Isolde* on January 26, 1974—a role he had previously sung in Buenos Aires, at the Easter Festival in Salzburg, Austria, and in Orange, France.

Other roles undertaken by Vickers at the Metropolitan, invariably with distinction, were Radames, Don José, Samson in *Samson and Delilah,* Otello, Hermann in *The Queen of Spades,* Peter Grimes, Laca in *Jenufa,* and Don Alvaro in *La Forza del Destino.* When the Metropolitan Opera presented for the first time the complete version of Berlioz' *Les Troyens* on October 22, 1973, he sang Aeneas for the first time in the United States. He was, said Harold C. Schonberg in the New York *Times,* "resplendent. His voice is the voice of a champion—clarion, unforced, resonant; and the role fits him perfectly."

When the Dallas Civic Opera celebrated its twentieth anniversary on November 5, 1976, with the first American staged production of Handel's *Samson,* Vickers assumed the title role.

He made his initial appearances at La Scala in Milan in 1960–1961. In September 1975 he made his debut at the Munich Opera as Tristan (to Birgit Nilsson's Isolde) and as Otello, giving the company that season "its first moments of real luster," as a correspondent reported to *Opera News.* "Jon Vickers enthralled the audience not only with his ringing Heldentenor but with his intensely introspective interpretation." In 1976 he helped to open the season for Sarah Caldwell's Opera Company in Boston as Florestan, appeared at La Scala in a revival of *Peter*

Grimes, and was heard as Parsifal at the Paris Opéra.

Vickers made headlines in London early in 1977 when he withdrew from an announced performance of *Tannhäuser* on February 28 in which he was to have sung the title role for the first time in his career. "This decision," he informed the directors of Covent Garden, "has not been made easily. As you know, it has always been essential for me to have a point of personal contact with the personality of each role I portray. I failed completely to find any point from which to begin. I am therefore convinced of the impossibility for me to interpret Tannhäuser." He also canceled his scheduled appearance as Tannhäuser in a new production of Wagner's opera at the Metropolitan Opera on December 22, 1977.

Vickers appeared in the motion picture adaptations of *Carmen, Otello,* and *I Pagliacci.*

In 1953 Vickers married Henrietta Outerbridge. They and their five children have for many years made their home in the Knightsbridge section of London.

ABOUT: Breslin, H. ed. The Tenors. *Periodicals—* McLean's Magazine (Canada), August 27, 1960; New York Times, February 21, 1960; Saturday Review, March 18, 1978.

Galina Vishnevskaya

1926–

Galina Pavlovna Vishnevskaya, soprano, was born in Leningrad, on October 25, 1926. Both her father, Pavlov Vishnevskaya, who was a workingman, and her mother had good voices. About her mother's singing, Vishnevskaya recalls: "She would play the guitar when she sang. . . . She told me gypsy stories. I know many gypsy songs I heard her sing. . . . As far back as I can remember I sang. And I used to act out the gypsy stories."

While she was still a child her mother died, and Galina was brought up by her grandmother. Her childhood years were spent in Kronstadt where, in the first years of World War II, she sang for the wounded soldiers in port and participated in concerts put on by the Russian

Vishnevskaya: vēzh něv skī' yä

GALINA VISHNEVSKAYA

Navy. In 1943 she returned to Leningrad, and there she heard her first operas: Tchaikovsky's *The Queen of Spades* and Verdi's *La Traviata.* She looks back to her teen-age years and to the siege of Leningrad during World War II with horror. "Nine hundred days!" as she described them to Dorle J. Soria in an interview in *High Fidelity.* "The bombs and shells, the cold and starvation, but the worst year was the first. People broke down their wooden dachas for fuel. They broke up tables and chairs leg by leg. . . . We had a little stove. Into it, piece by piece, went our furniture. One day we were sitting as close to it as possible for a little warmth. My grandmother's dress caught fire. It burst into flames. I threw a blanket over her. But it was too late. She was terribly burned. Next morning when I woke up she was dead." During those terrible years she shut out reality by living in the world of her imagination. "I imagined I was on the stage, wearing warm and beautiful costumes—a great prima donna," she has said.

Galina received her first vocal lessons from a teacher named Vera Garina, who was eighty-three years old and had studied in Vienna. "My child," the teacher once told her, "you are born with a star on your brow." After two years of study, Vishnevskaya became a member of the Leningrad Light Opera Company which performed not only in Leningrad but also in many of the smaller cities of the Soviet Union. At first she was assigned minor roles exclusively. But in Kronstadt, when one of the principals fell ill, she took on the leading role of Christine in Carl

Zeller's *Der Vogelhändler* and did so well that from then on leading roles were entrusted to her.

After four years with the light opera company, she turned to more serious music, receiving further training from Vera Garina and making some appearances as guest artist with the Leningrad Philharmonic. Her teacher encouraged her in 1952 to enter a national competition in Moscow for admission to the training school of the Bolshoi Opera. She sang "O patria mia" from *Aida* and was the only candidate selected as a trainee with the Bolshoi Opera. During her first season, 1952–1953, she was given minor roles in Rimsky-Korsakov's *The Maid of Pskov,* Dargomyzhsky's *Russalka,* and Verdi's *Rigoletto.* Her first success came a season later as Tatiana in Tchaikovsky's *Eugene Onegin* and Leonore in *Fidelio.* She rose to stardom during the next few years, both in the standard repertory and in Russian operas, and soon became recognized as an outstanding interpreter. In the standard repertory she was heard as Cio-Cio-San in *Madama Butterfly,* Aida, Violetta in *La Traviata,* Desdemona in *Otello,* Alice Ford in *Falstaff,* Marguerite in *Faust,* Cherubino in *The Marriage of Figaro,* Mimi in *La Bohème,* and Tosca. Her greatest successes in Russian operas came in *Boris Godunov,* Shebalin's *The Taming of the Shrew,* Tchaikovsky's *The Queen of Spades,* Prokofiev's *War and Peace* and *The Gambler,* Rimsky-Korsakov's *Snow Maiden* and *The Tsar's Bride,* and Shostakovich's *Katerina Ismailova.*

In 1955 she toured Czechoslovakia and Yugoslavia. She was at the Prague Festival in May of that year when the Soviet cellist, Mstislav Rostropovich, caught sight of her. He said it was love at first sight. She told the rest of the story to Dorle J. Soria: "He decided on the spot that he must conquer me. He did it with a series of surprises. The next morning when I got up and opened my closet door I couldn't see my dresses—they were hidden by lilies of the valley. The day after, I found orchids in every corner of the room. The third day the floor was piled high with boxes and boxes of chocolates. That was the day I left; I had to be back in Moscow. 'Slava' [as Rostropovich is affectionately called by his intimate friends and relatives] still had concert engagements, but, without another thought, he cancelled and followed me. On the fourth day we were married." The marriage took place on May 15, 1955. They lived in a five-room apartment in Moscow. Their two daughters became well-known musicians: Olga, a violinist; Elena, a pianist.

Between 1955 and 1960 Vishnevskaya gave concerts and made opera appearances in Germany, Finland, Italy, England, and Australia. Her first appearance in the United States took place in January 1960 in New York as soloist with the visiting Moscow State Symphony Orchestra in arias from *Eugene Onegin* and *The Queen of Spades*. "In Tatiana's letter scene," wrote Howard Taubman in the New York *Times*, "she captured the doubts and ecstasy of a young girl's penning a declaration of love. In Lisa's aria there were tenderness and heartbreak. Although the soprano was standing on a concert stage, she evoked the atmosphere of the opera house. She conveyed feeling with simple gestures. If the Metropolitan Opera were fast on its feet it would invite her to make a guest appearance or two."

The invitation from the Metropolitan Opera was not slow in coming. On November 6, 1961, Vishnevskaya became the first Soviet prima donna to appear with that company, assuming the title role in *Aida*. "I cannot remember a more fiery characterization," said Robert Sabin in *Musical America*, "or one more full of original touches, revealing a high intelligence and keen musical insight. And as for her singing, it was that of a master artist." Vishnevskaya was also heard as Cio-Cio-San, on December 5, 1961. That was her only season with the Metropolitan for fifteen years.

On December 1, 1961, Vishnevskaya gave her first American recital, at Carnegie Hall in New York. She made several more tours after that in recitals, often accompanied on the piano by her husband, and also toured as a soloist with orchestra—in some cases with her husband as conductor. About this musical partnership between Vishnevskaya and Rostropovich, Louis Biancolli wrote in the *World-Telegram and Sun:* "Such teams are made in heaven."

She made her debut at Covent Garden in London in 1962. In the fall of 1964 she appeared for the first time at La Scala in Milan as a member of the visiting Bolshoi Opera in performances of *The Queen of Spades* and *War and Peace.* When La Scala opened its own season on December 7, she was a guest, singing Liù in *Turandot.* In August 1967, once again as a member of the Bolshoi Opera, she was heard at Expo '67 in Montreal, Canada, in *The Queen of Spades* and *War and Peace.*

With Vishnevskaya in mind, Benjamin Britten wrote his *War Requiem,* a choral work. Though she was unable to participate at its world premiere at Coventry Cathedral in England in 1962, she did appear in several later performances. Britten also wrote for her his song cycle based on poems of Pushkin, *The Poet's Echo,* dedicated jointly to her and to Rostropovich. With her husband at the piano, she presented the world premiere of this work in Moscow in October 1965.

When, after 1971, she and her husband, Rostropovich, came into disrepute in the Soviet Union because of Rostropovich's conflicts with Soviet authorities over the question of freedom of speech and because of his support of domestic dissidents, Vishnevskaya found her engagements at the Bolshoi Opera reduced to a trickle; on those infrequent occasions when she was allowed to appear, her name was not found in the printed program. At the same time, when her recordings were heard over the Soviet radio her name was never mentioned. "I would listen to myself being obliterated," she recalls. When she was allowed to travel outside the country, Vishnevskaya had to make a new career for herself outside her native land.

On March 24, 1975, she returned to the Metropolitan Opera as Tosca. "Miss Vishnevskaya's voice is not always pretty," wrote Raymond Ericson in the New York *Times*, "but it is dramatically effective, in its varying qualities, fiery, piercing, softly melting. . . . Dark and relatively slight, she moved around the stage gracefully, sometimes playful as a kitten, sometimes raging like a tigress."

When, two weeks later, she appeared in a recital at Carnegie Hall in New York, with her husband at the piano, Donal Henahan remarked in the New York *Times:* "Miss Vishnevskaya is quite simply one of the inspired singing actresses of the stage today, in a grand style that all singers once aimed at but that has been practically swept aside by the demand for naturalism and realism. . . . With Mr. Rostropovich . . . Mme. Vishnevskaya gave a recital that . . . provided artistic excitement on a high level."

In the summer of 1975 she filled numerous engagements—in the United States: at Wolf Trap Farm Park for the Performing Arts at Vienna in Virginia, as soloist with the National

Symphony Orchestra conducted by her husband; at the Berkshire Music Festival at Tanglewood in Massachusetts, once again with her husband conducting; at the Ravinia Festival in Chicago; and at Robin Hood Dell in Philadelphia; in Europe: at the Edinburgh Festival, in Brussels, and as a soloist with the London Symphony in London. In October 1975 she made her debut with the San Francisco Opera in *The Queen of Spades,* with her husband conducting his first opera performance in America. They subsequently recorded this opera for Deutsche Grammophon and performed it at the Paris Opéra. In October 1977 she returned to Covent Garden as Tosca, a role she also recorded for Deutsche Grammophon.

Until 1974 Vishnevskaya, her husband, and their two daughters maintained a large apartment in Moscow and a country house outside the city. In 1974, when Rostropovich decided to leave the Soviet Union, she, like her husband, traveled on a Soviet passport that had to be renewed each year. In 1978 the passports were not renewed; both Vishnevskaya and Rostropovich were stripped of their Soviet citizenship.

After leaving the Soviet Union, the Rostropovich family found a temporary home in London, spending most of the year in travel. Since then they have established residence in apartments in Paris, New York, and Washington, D.C., together with a vacation home near Lausanne, Switzerland. Vishnevskaya has said that this has not proved a happy solution. "I am not a wanderer," she says. "My clothes and costumes are now all over Europe—in London, Paris, Basel, Lausanne—and here [the United States] too." She has missed the stability her home in Moscow gave her and her family, and she has missed her precious collection of ikons and old Russian porcelain which, she says, "are close to my soul." Continuous travel also makes it more difficult for her to cook for her husband the dishes he relishes most. She hates to cook, she adds hastily, but when she wants to prepare a meal for her husband she knows how to cook well and quickly. She is an excellent seamstress and has often made her daughter's dresses.

Vishnevskaya has appeared in a cinematic adaptation of Shostakovich's opera *Katerina Ismailova.*

ABOUT: High Fidelity/Musical America, October 1975; New York Times, December 5, 1965; New York Times Magazine, April 18, 1976; Newsweek, November 1, 1965.

Herbert Von Karajan
See Karajan

Frederica Von Stade

1945–

Frederica Von Stade, mezzo-soprano, was born on June 1, 1945, in Somerville, New Jersey. Her family traces its background and heritage back to colonial Connecticut; her mother, the former Sara Clucas, was a descendant of Jonathan Trumbull, colonial governor of Connecticut. Other ancestors included socially prominent bankers, yachtsmen, and polo players. A great aunt, Leila Steele, sang with the Opéra-Comique in Paris. Her Teutonic name comes from one of her father's ancestors who was burgomaster of Stade, a town near Hamburg. Frederica's father, Charles Von Stade, was a lieutenant in the United States Army who was killed near Aachen, Germany, in one of the last battles of World War II, two months before Frederica was born.

"I never picture myself as a performer," Von Stade told Robert Jacobson in an interview in *Opera News.* "But ... I always performed as a kid, dressing up and singing, my family sitting patiently. Later, people asked me to sing."

She was fourteen when she saw her first opera (*Der Rosenkavalier* with Elisabeth Schwarzkopf at the Salzburg Festival in Austria). It was seven years before she went to another opera performance. Meanwhile she attended convent school and at eighteen went to Paris to study piano at the École Mozart and the French language. Returning to the United States, she worked for a while at Tiffany's in New York and as a secretary for the American Shakespeare Festival in Stratford, Connecticut. Her ambition then was to become a star in Broadway musicals, and her idol was Ethel Merman. "I did cattle-call auditions for summer theater. You do fifty or sixty auditions and get called back five times and maybe get one job offer—if you're lucky." Nevertheless, she did appear in a number of summer

Von Stade

FREDERICA VON STADE

stock musicals, mostly at the Long Wharf Theater in New Haven. "In summer stock you can't waste time with the singer's routines of three vitamin C pills when you get up, a steak at two o'clock, and walking to the opera house by a certain route so that you pass a certain store to give you luck," she has said. "Cold, sore throat or whatever, you have to go on. It's great training for opera."

Hoping that further study would help her achieve success she enrolled in the Mannes College of Music in New York—she was stimulated to make an audition there by a fifty-dollar bet with a friend. "I went to learn to read music, really. And I got into opera because it was the quickest way to a degree. I thought I'd never finish because I didn't have self-discipline." At the college she studied voice with Sebastian Engelberg, who has remained her only teacher. She appeared in school productions of *Hansel and Gretel* and of Chabrier's *L'Étoile.*

After graduation from Mannes College she was encouraged by Engelberg to enter the Metropolitan Opera Studio from which Rudolf Bing, general manager of the Metropolitan Opera, lifted her for secondary (*comprimario*) roles. With no previous professional opera experience, she made her Metropolitan Opera debut on January 11, 1970, as one of the three Spirits in *The Magic Flute.* During the next three seasons she was heard in some twenty roles, including such comparatively demanding parts as Nicklausse in *The Tales of Hoffmann,* Siebel in *Faust,* Hansel in *Hansel and Gretel,* Lola in Ca-

valleria Rusticana, Suzuki in *Madama Butterfly,* and the role in which she has since earned international renown, Cherubino in *The Marriage of Figaro.* On August 12, 1971, she went to the Santa Fe Opera in New Mexico to create the role of Maria in the world premiere of Villa-Lobos's *Yerma.* In 1972 she was heard in several Mozart roles at the San Francisco Opera and as Mélisande in *Pelléas and Mélisande* at Santa Fe.

She left the Metropolitan Opera after the 1971 –1972 season to make her European debut as Cherubino in the Rolf Liebermann production of *The Marriage of Figaro,* first produced in April 1973 on the stage of the Royal Theater at Versailles. She then went to the Paris Opéra for the initiation of the Liebermann regime there. Her success brought her an invitation to sing Cherubino at the Glyndebourne Festival in England, and, one summer after that, at the Salzburg Festival. Hubert Saal heard her in Salzburg and reported to *Newsweek:* "It's impossible to remember a Cherubino more breathlessly young or more passionate, or one who poured out her love in such sweet liquid tones." Von Stade has also appeared as Cherubino in a filmed version of the Mozart opera.

She returned to the Metropolitan Opera on Christmas Eve of 1973 to sing Rosina in *The Barber of Seville.* During the next few years she was also heard there as Cherubino, Zerlina in *Don Giovanni,* and as Adalgisa in *Norma.*

In January 1974 she appeared as Penelope in a revival of Monteverdi's *Il Ritorno di Ulisse* with the Washington (D.C.) Opera Society at the Kennedy Center for the Performing Arts. This was also the role with which she made her debut at the New York City Opera on February 29, 1976. Reviewing that performance, Harold C. Schonberg wrote in the New York *Times:* "She is a most artistic singer, with a voice of velvet, and her pianissimo singing was beautiful. Never was there a phrase that lacked sensitivity or understanding."

On March 5, 1974, she appeared as Nina in the world premiere of Thomas Pasatieri's *The Seagull* with the Houston Opera, which had commissioned it. In 1975 she sang her first Octavian in *Der Rosenkavalier* as a member of the Houston Opera, and on March 27 she made her debut at Covent Garden in London as Rosina in *The Barber of Seville.* In 1976–1977 she was heard as Mélisande in Geneva and Paris, and during the summer of 1976 she appeared at the

Edinburgh Festival in Scotland as Cherubino and in a performance of Mahler's Symphony No.4 with the Vienna Philharmonic under Claudio Abbado. (She had previously appeared as a soloist in this symphony with the New York Philharmonic under Pierre Boulez at Lincoln Center for the Performing Arts.)

When La Scala's company visited the Kennedy Center for the Performing Arts in Washington, D.C., on September 14, 1976, in commemoration of America's Bicentennial, Von Stade made her La Scala debut as Cherubino. Then she sang Angelina in Rossini's *La Cenerentola* (which she had previously sung in San Francisco in 1974). Her debut in Milan with La Scala followed in December 1976 as Rosina in *The Barber of Seville*. In March 1977 she appeared at the Paris Opéra as Mélisande in a new production of *Pelléas and Mélisande*. On July 2 of the same year she assumed the role of Angelina in a new production of *La Cenerentola* at the Paris Opéra.

In the fall of 1977, she decided to reduce the number of her public appearances drastically for at least two years and to remove herself as much as possible from the operatic stage in 1978 so that she could, as she told Peter J. Rosenwald in an interview in *New York* "find space to grow into music a little, or to grow with it, to learn new works with a certain calm and reexamine the works I've already sung."

Among her other roles are Belle-Mère in Massenet's *Le Cendrillon,* Sesto in Mozart's *La Clemenza di Tito,* Beatrice and Marguerite in Berlioz' *The Damnation of Faust,* and Charlotte in *Werther.*

In 1976, Von Stade received the Grand Prix du Disque in Paris, and in 1977 the High Fidelity-International Record Critics Award, for her Columbia album, *French Opera Arias.*

Affectionately known as Flicka, Frederica Von Stade lives in an apartment on the twenty-third floor of a high-rise on the west side of New York overlooking the Lincoln Center for the Performing Arts. "She has a trim (size eight) figure, an open, well-made face, with eyes that could easily be called dreamy," wrote George Movshon in the New York *Times,* "and an abundance of brown hair that can be sculpted in a score of ways." Her hobbies include playing tennis, cooking, and going to ballet performances. She married Peter Elkus, a photographer and

singer, soon after her debut in Paris in April 1973.

ABOUT: High Fidelity/Musical America, December 1973; New York, September 19, 1977; New York Times, January 13, 1974, February 29, 1976; Opera News, April 10, 1971, January 24, 1976.

Edo de Waart

1941–

Edo de Waart, conductor, was born in Amsterdam on June 1, 1941, to Marinus and Jacoba Rose de Waart. His father, for thirty years a chorister in the Netherlands Opera and a lover of *Lieder,* brought the songs of Schubert, Schumann, and Brahms into his household. Edo's love for music was stimulated early when he was taken to opera performances. His early music study took place at the Amsterdam Conservatory where he specialized in the oboe. Upon being graduated in 1962 with honors for oboe, he joined the oboe section of the Concertgebouw Orchestra under a special arrangement allowing him to spend one third of his time as an orchestral player, one third as an assistant to the conductor, and one third studying conducting with Haakon Stotijn and Rudolf Kempe and working with Jaap Spaanderman at the Amsterdam Music Lyceum.

Edo made his conducting debut in 1964 directing the Radio Philharmonic Orchestra of Amsterdam in a conductor's course with Franco Ferrara. A government subsidy enabled him to go to the United States in 1964 to enter the Mitropoulos Competition in New York. The prize, which he shared with two other winners, provided him with a year of apprenticeship in 1965–1966 with the New York Philharmonic and Leonard Bernstein. This was not altogether a happy experience. "It was cruel," he told Shirley Fleming in *Musical America.* "You do nothing. There were three of us and we are simply part of an entourage. Nobody pays attention to you, you wander these damned streets alone, and you don't conduct, you don't do anything. You go bananas." But winning that competition had compensations. "When I went back [to Holland] with the first prize—it was a time when

Waart: vàrt

929

EDO DE WAART

nothing was going on, and any news was news—I made the front page. I was a celebrity. But I was green as grass."

While still serving his apprenticeship in New York, he was given a two-week leave of absence to appear as guest conductor of the Rotterdam Philharmonic Orchestra. In the summer of 1965 he was invited to conduct at the Festival of Two Worlds at Spoleto, Italy, where he made his debut with Stravinsky's *L'Histoire du Soldat*. After his return to Holland in 1966 he founded the Netherlands Wind Ensemble, with which he remained affiliated as oboist until 1970. "It was a very democratic organization," he explains, "and in the beginning there was no money in it for any of us. We would have ten or twenty rehearsals for a difficult new work." This organization was heard not only in Holland but also in Spain, Japan, and Pakistan. It also made some Edison-prize-winning recordings for Philips.

At the same time de Waart was extending his career as conductor. Initially, in 1966, he served as assistant conductor to Bernard Haitink with the Concertgebouw Orchestra of Amsterdam, with which he toured the United States in 1967. In his first American performances he impressed critics with his total control of the orchestra in spite of his youth. In 1967 he made his debut in London as guest conductor of the London Symphony and the Royal Philharmonic. That year he was appointed one of two permanent conductors of the Rotterdam Philharmonic, with which he toured England in 1970 and 1974, the United States in 1971, 1975 and 1977, and Germany and

Austria in 1976. In 1973 he succeeded Jean Fournet as the music director of that orchestra.

In addition to his duties with the Rotterdam Philharmonic, de Waart has been a conductor of the Netherlands Opera, where he made his debut in a new production of Menotti's *The Saint of Bleecker Street*. He has since appeared regularly with this company in performances of *Fidelio, Carmen,* Stravinsky's *The Rake's Progress, Lohengrin,* Bartók's *Bluebeard's Castle, La Traviata,* and Schoenberg's *Erwartung.* With this company he was heard at the Holland Festival in *Aida* and *Der Rosenkavalier.*

He spent a month in 1968 in Cleveland on an invitation by George Szell, serving as an observer at Severance Hall at rehearsals and performances of the Cleveland Orchestra on a Kulas Foundation fellowship. De Waart's conducting career after that became as much identified with the United States as with Holland. He has appeared as a guest conductor of several of America's major symphony orchestras and at the Berkshire Music Festival at Tanglewood, Massachusetts. In 1971 he was a guest conductor of the Santa Fe Opera in New Mexico in a performance of *The Flying Dutchman,* returning in 1972 with *Don Giovanni* and in 1975 with *Falstaff.* In 1975 he conducted the Houston Opera in *Der Rosenkavalier.*

He made his debut with the San Francisco Symphony on February 27, 1974. "He is an outstanding, upcoming conductor," reported Alexander Fried in the San Francisco *Examiner.* "He commands an orchestra thoroughly, building the bones and sinews of its playing into three dimensions through all the textures of his music and with a leadership that is sharply inspiring to his musicians." De Waart's success here led to his appointment the following December as the orchestra's principal guest conductor on a three-year contract. "De Waart fully justified the wisdom of that appointment," said Heuwell Tircuit in the San Francisco *Chronicle* after de Waart had directed several concerts at the Concord Festival in San Francisco in August 1975. His performances, Tircuit added, were "judicious yet exciting." In February and March 1976 de Waart conducted for four weeks with the San Francisco Symphony at War Memorial Auditorium and in August 1976 for several more concerts at the Concord Festival. Also in 1976 he was promoted to the post of principal conductor and music director of the orchestra succeeding Seiji Ozawa on a four-year contract beginning with the fall of 1977. Under this agreement he was required to direct a minimum of thirteen weeks a season, while being permitted to retain his commitments to the Rotterdam Philharmonic and the Netherlands Opera through 1981. After a concert in March 1976, Arthur Bloomfield noted in the *Examiner:* "Seiji Ozawa is a hard act to follow at the symphonic box office, but I don't think Edo de Waart, the San Francisco Symphony's musical director-elect, is going to have too much trouble finding an audience. Last night's . . . customers greeted him warmly indeed; the applause, in fact, made a couple of crescendos, the first bringing an extra bow and a big smile, and the second a call from the podium for the orchestra to rise and share the joy." Commenting on de Waart's performance of Debussy's *La Mer* that evening, Bloomfield added: "That was by no means sensationalized, but it was full of evocations and its climaxes were very big. It was a very clean performance but not the least bit clinical; it had warmth, flow, exceptional tenderness, a real point of view."

While conducting in Santa Fe during the summer of 1975 de Waart met Ruth Welting, soprano of the New York City Opera, who sang Nannetta in de Waart's performance of *Falstaff*. On February 18, 1976, they were married. This was de Waart's second marriage; he has two children by his first marriage. The de Waarts live in San Francisco and Amsterdam. De Waart has made a hobby of toy electric trains. Occasionally he enjoys playing tennis.

ABOUT: High Fidelity/Musical America, March 1976; November 20, 1977.

Alfred Wallenstein

1898–

Alfred Franz Wallenstein, cellist and conductor, was born in Chicago, on October 7, 1898. His father, Franz Albrecht, was Austrian; his mother, Anna Klinger von Wallenstein, was German. The Wallensteins trace their lineage back to Albrecht von Wallenstein, German statesman and national hero of the Thirty Years'

Wallenstein: wäl' ĕn stīn

ALFRED WALLENSTEIN

War, who was the inspiration for Schiller's dramatic trilogy *Wallenstein.*

Franz Albrecht von Wallenstein owned a contractor's supply house in Chicago which burned down when Alfred was seven. The family then moved to Los Angeles. Alfred attended the public schools and started taking piano lessons. For his ninth birthday, he was given the choice of a bicycle or a cello. He chose the latter and began lessons with Elsa Johanna Bierlich von Grofé (mother of the popular composer and arranger Ferde Grofé), a graduate of the Leipzig conservatory and a cellist of great ability. Before he was ten, Alfred was playing the cello in the school orchestra and with several amateur orchestral groups in the Los Angeles area. Though still a child, he was given professional engagements in hotels and restaurants, was employed for the orchestra of Grauman's Chinese Theatre in Hollywood, and at one time was even employed to provide "inspirational music" during the filming of silent movies. When he was fifteen, he made his concert debut, performing at a benefit concert sponsored by the Gamut Club of Los Angeles.

Throughout southern California the fifteen-year-old musician was known as "the wonder-boy cellist." He toured throughout the United States on the Orpheum vaudeville circuit, appearing on bills starring such headliners as Will Rogers, Sophie Tucker, and Vernon and Irene Castle. After a year of such touring, he joined the cello section of the San Francisco Symphony Orchestra conducted by Alfred Hertz, for the

1916–1917 season. In 1917 he left the San Francisco Orchestra to tour as solo cellist with the ballerina Anna Pavlova through South and Central America; the tour lasted a year and a half.

In 1919 Wallenstein was engaged as cellist by the Los Angeles Philharmonic and became the youngest member of that orchestra. Then, having decided to abandon the cello for medicine, he left the Los Angeles Philharmonic after one season to return to the vaudeville circuit for the purpose of accumulating some money. In 1920 he went to Europe to begin medical studies at the University of Leipzig. While in Leipzig he studied the cello with Julius Klengel. "The decision between music and surgery as a career was the most difficult choice I ever had to make," Wallenstein later told an interviewer.

By the time he returned to the United States in 1922, music had won. In that year, he joined the Chicago Symphony, then conducted by Frederick Stock. He remained with the orchestra seven years. During that time he made a number of appearances as soloist with the orchestra (including the world premiere of Frederick Stock's Cello Concerto on January 25, 1929), gave recitals (including three over Chicago's radio station WGN in 1926), and from 1927 to 1929 was head of the cello department of the Chicago Musical College.

In 1929 Toscanini engaged Wallenstein as first cellist of the New York Philharmonic Orchestra. He retained this post until Toscanini resigned as music director in 1936. At least once each season he appeared as a soloist under Toscanini. While serving as first cellist, he also appeared in recitals throughout the country and was a guest soloist with other orchestras.

It was Toscanini who advised Wallenstein to exchange his cello for a baton. Wallenstein began conducting in 1931 when he led a thirty-five-man orchestra over the radio in the first all-classical program sponsored commercially over the air. The following summer he was one of the conductors at the Hollywood Bowl in Los Angeles. In 1933 he founded and directed the Sinfonietta, an orchestra performing programs of serious music over radio station WOR of the Mutual Broadcasting System. In February 1935 he was appointed music director of WOR. As director he initiated and conducted many music series, opening for radio a brave new world of music programming. With the Sinfonietta he presented on Sunday evenings a series of concerts devoted to the church cantatas of Johann Sebastian Bach, some of which had never been heard in the United States and most of which were little known and rarely heard. On Saturday evenings he gave performances of Mozart's operas, the little known as well as the famous. A third important series, devoted to all the piano concertos of Mozart, was undertaken with Nadia Reisenberg, the concert pianist. Still another series concentrated on contemporary American and European music. During this series three hundred first performances were given including that of Arthur Benjamin's *Jamaican Rumba* on January 21, 1942. Supplementing his activities over WOR, Wallenstein conducted the orchestra for "The Voice of Firestone" over NBC; at NBC, on February 17, 1942, he offered the world premiere of Oscar Levant's Piano Concerto with the composer at the piano. When he withdrew as music director of WOR in 1945, Wallenstein became the music director of the American Broadcasting Company. For his contributions to and achievements in radio music he was awarded the National Federation of Music Clubs prize five times; the first honors award of the National Federation of Press Women; the George Peabody Radio Award in 1942 for "pioneering in a quiet way for good music and encouraging and originating various unique broadcasts." In a nationwide poll in 1940 among radio editors to ascertain "the most eventful musical contributions to radio" he earned third place, following after Toscanini and John Barbirolli.

Wallenstein left his first-desk chair with the New York Philharmonic in 1936 to devote himself completely to conducting. During the next few years, in addition to his work over the radio, he made many appearances as a guest conductor of major American symphony orchestras.

In 1943, he was appointed music director of the Los Angeles Philharmonic, becoming the first American-born musician to head an important American symphonic organization. The orchestra was in a state of deterioration and demoralization when Wallenstein took over, but he soon built it into a symphonic organization that occupied an honorable place among American orchestras; with each passing season the music critics of Los Angeles took note of the technical and artistic improvement of the orchestra under Wallenstein. After a performance of Mahler's Symphony No.2, Albert Goldberg of the Los Angeles *Times* found that "the conductor demonstrated not only his mastery in controlling widespread forces but possession of a deep emotional power to shape a huge work into meaningful form." A performance of Beethoven's *Missa Solemnis* drew the following comment from Raymond Kendall in the *Mirror:* "Alfred Wallenstein toiled, cajoled, demanded responsiveness from his soloists, chorus and orchestra to produce the most exciting, full-of-contrasts reading of the Solemn Mass I can remember hearing."

Wallenstein initiated and built up a unique annual program in Los Angeles called Symphonies for Youth, in which the Los Angeles Philharmonic gave concerts for schoolchildren both at the Philharmonic Auditorium and, on Saturday mornings for thirteen weeks during the school year, over a nationwide radio network of the Mutual Broadcasting Company. In a further attempt to bring young people into the symphony hall, he inaugurated open rehearsals on Thursday mornings, inviting a thousand or more outstanding music students in the city public schools each week.

While occupying his post in Los Angeles, he continued to make guest appearances with other orchestras. On October 19, 1951, he made his debut in opera, conducting *Fidelio* with the San Francisco Opera. From 1952 to 1956 he was the music director of the Hollywood Bowl.

In the spring of 1956, under the auspices of the American National Theatre and Academy and of the State Department of the United States, Wallenstein toured the Far East with the Los Angeles Philharmonic. Upon his return to the United States, he resigned from his post in Los Angeles. After that he devoted himself primarily to guest performances until 1961 when, for two seasons, he served as principal conductor of the Symphony of the Air in New York with which he presented a cycle of seven all-Beethoven concerts. In March 1962 he conducted a performance of *L'Amore dei Tre Re* with the NBC-TV Opera. From 1962 to 1964 he headed the Ford Foundation Project for young American conductors. In 1966 he served as visiting conductor at the Juilliard School of Music in New York, and in 1971 he was appointed head of their orchestral department. He continued to make guest appearances for a number of years not only in auditoriums but also over television. For his services to American music he received

the Alice M. Ditson Award in 1947. France presented him with the ribbon of Commander of the Legion of Honor.

On May 10, 1924, Wallenstein married concert pianist Virginia Wilson; their home is in Palm Springs, California. His interests, other than music, include playing tennis, billiards, and poker; and going deep-sea fishing.

ABOUT: Stoddard, H. Symphony Conductors of the U.S.A. *Periodicals*—Seventeen, September 1947; Time, August 23, 1943.

Bruno Walter

1876–1962

Bruno Walter (originally Bruno Walter Schlesinger), conductor, was known especially for interpretations of the German-Viennese school of composers from Haydn and Mozart through Bruckner, Mahler, and Richard Strauss. He was born to a middle-class Jewish family in Berlin on September 15, 1876. His father was a bookkeeper in a large silk concern. "When I was a small child," Walter once recalled, "Father was in the habit of carrying me in his arms, while he hummed melodies from operas and operettas. . . . Mother had an unmistakable musical talent which she developed to a certain degree as a student at the Stern Conservatory. She played the piano nicely and sang songs by Schubert and others in an agreeable small voice. Our family was warmed by a sincere, quiet, but by no means orthodox religiousness."

Bruno's musicality revealed itself from the time he was four, as he himself has said, "through the excited fascination with which I listened to every musical sound." His mother began giving him piano lessons when he was six, then sent him to Konrad Kaiser for more professional instruction. Kaiser was so impressed with his young pupil that he had him tested by Robert Radecke, one of the directors of the Stern Conservatory. "Every inch of him is music," Radecke said.

Bruno entered the Stern Conservatory in his ninth year on a scholarship; his principal teachers there were Heinrich Ehrlich, Robert Radecke, and Ludwig Bussler. A year later he

Walter: väl′ tĕr

Walter

BRUNO WALTER

made his first appearance as a pianist at a students' concert at the Conservatory, performing music by Schubert and Mendelssohn. He also made his bow as a composer with a duet for piano and violin written as a birthday gift for his father.

His first public appearance outside the Conservatory occurred when he was thirteen, with a performance of Moscheles' Piano Concerto in E-flat major with the Berlin Philharmonic in February 1889.

While attending the Conservatory, Walter worked long hours as a singer's accompanist to earn enough money to support his needs and to purchase tickets occasionally for a concert or an opera performance. When he was not attending school, practicing the piano, or working for a living he could be found in the State Library poring over and memorizing symphonic and operatic scores. He was bent on becoming a conductor, even though his progress at the piano seemed to indicate a career as virtuoso. "My dream of a future career as a pianist," Walter has written in his autobiography, "began to fade on the day when, from a seat way up on the platform behind the kettledrums, I heard and saw Hans von Bülow conduct the Philharmonic Orchestra in a classic program. . . . I saw in von Bülow's face the glow of inspiration and the concentration of energy. I felt the compelling force of his gestures. . . . It became at once clear to me that one man was producing the music. . . . That evening decided my future. Now I

knew what I was meant for. . . . I had decided to become a conductor."

When he was seventeen he accepted a post as coach at the Cologne Opera as the first step towards a conducting career. His conducting debut came six months after he had joined the company—on March 13, 1894, with a performance of Albert Lortzing's *Der Waffenschmied.* When he failed to find any further opportunities to conduct operas, he decided to leave Cologne and find a post elsewhere. That year (1894) he became assistant conductor of the Hamburg Opera; Gustav Mahler was its principal conductor. When Bruno first arrived in Hamburg, Mahler asked him if he could play the piano. "Excellently," Bruno replied with self-assurance. Could he read music at sight? "Oh, yes! Everything!" Did he know the regular repertory? "I know it all thoroughly." At a rehearsal of *Hansel and Gretel,* Mahler asked him to take over as pianist. Before long, Mahler began giving him more ambitious assignments. Finally, Bruno was called in as a substitute to conduct a performance of *Cavalleria Rusticana;* the performance went over so well that from then on he was often required to direct light operas. When one of the principal conductors left the company in the fall of 1895, Bruno replaced him and was assigned *Aida, Tannhäuser,* and *Der Freischütz,* among many other operas.

When Mahler left Hamburg in 1896, Bruno went on to the Breslau Opera; at that time he took permanently the name Bruno Walter. After Breslau he held an appointment in Riga and then at the Berlin Royal Opera, where he was coconductor with Karl Muck and Richard Strauss.

In 1897 Mahler was appointed music director of the Vienna Royal Opera. Four years later he called Bruno Walter from Riga to become his assistant in Vienna. Walter had married Elsa Wirthschaft on May 2, 1901, and he took his young wife to the Austrian capital. They found modest lodgings on the Neustiftgasse, and later moved to larger quarters at Theobaldgasse where their two daughters, Lotte and Marguerite, were born. Working with Mahler for the next six years provided the greatest single influence in Walter's growth as an artist. Mahler was a taxing master in his indefatigable pursuit of perfection, and Walter became his willing, even idolatrous, pupil. From Mahler he learned to penetrate to the heart of every masterwork he

934

conducted in an attempt to make each performance a revelation. Mahler also inspired him
through his integrity, idealism, and the compulsion to give of himself unsparingly to the task at
hand. "I was privileged to serve a master of so
overwhelming a musical endowment and of so
powerful a personality," Walter wrote many
years later in his autobiography, "an institution
within whose walls burned a pure and strength-
irradiating flame, a temple in which indolence
and cynicism, the enemies of artistic endeavor,
were unable to gain a foothold."

Many years later Walter expressed his admiration of Mahler in a frankly adulatory biography, *Gustav Mahler* (1935). (The book was
published in English two years later.) After he
achieved world fame as a conductor, Walter
dedicated himself to the performance of Mahler's music in all the music capitals of the world,
becoming an all-powerful instrument in keeping
Mahler's masterworks alive in the concert hall.
He conducted the world premiere of Mahler's
Das Lied von der Erde in Munich on November
20, 1911, and Mahler's Symphony No.9 in Vienna on June 26, 1912, both after Mahler's death.

Walter's first success in Vienna came in 1902
with a revival of *Un Ballo in Maschera.* From
then on he was given many opportunities to conduct. When Mahler resigned from the Vienna
Royal Opera in 1907, Walter stayed on for another six years. He was assigned much of the
repertory previously belonging to Mahler and
received particular recognition for his performances of Mozart and Wagner. He also appeared frequently as conductor of the Vienna
Philharmonic Orchestra, distinguishing himself
as much in the symphonic literature as in the
operatic. His fame spread beyond Vienna, and
on March 3, 1909, he scored an outstanding
success as guest conductor of the Royal Philharmonic Society in London. Later that year he
conducted *Tristan and Isolde* and Ethel Smyth's
The Wreckers at Covent Garden. Not long after
that, he was the guest conductor of the Santa
Cecilia Orchestra in Rome, presenting the first
Italian performance of Richard Strauss's tone
poem *Don Quixote.* He also went to Moscow to
direct concerts of the Imperial Russian Musical
Society and to perform *Don Giovanni* and *The
Queen of Spades* at the Imperial Opera.

On January 1, 1913, Walter became the music
director of the Munich Royal Opera. His nine
years there added a luminous chapter to the his-

tory of that company. "My greatest gain in Munich," he later wrote, "was in the increased
depth of my relation to Mozart." His performances of Mozart's operas were, indeed, one of
the high points of his regime, but so were his
performances of the *Ring* cycle; his revivals of
Der Freischütz, Euryanthe, Gluck's *Iphigénie en
Aulide,* and Hugo Wolf's *Der Corregidor;* his
new productions of *Ariadne auf Naxos* and *Die
Frau ohne Schatten;* and the world premiere of
Pfitzner's *Palestrina* (June 12, 1917). In addition
to his performances in the opera house, he offered concerts of symphonic music with the
Odeon Symphony. He also conducted symphonic concerts with the Berlin Philharmonic, concerts which were highlights of the Berlin music
season until 1933.

During his last years in Munich, Walter was
victimized by anti-Semitic attacks instigated by
the National Socialists. However, when he decided in 1923 to leave Munich, it was not because of these attacks, which he managed to
ignore, but for personal reasons hinted at in his
autobiography, *Theme and Variations* (1946).
"Those were for me days of great and passionate
involvement, bearing the seeds of tragic development. The thought of leaving Munich, generated
by artistic considerations, offered a way out of a
tormenting situation. . . . To the day of my departure I was actually not made to suffer from
political hostility and my leaving was partly
caused by a feeling that I had completed my task
and partly by personal considerations."

He bade farewell to Munich with a performance of *Fidelio,* and once again made his home
in Vienna. In 1924 he returned to Covent Garden to conduct the first German season there
since the end of World War I. From 1924 to
1931 he was one of its conductors in the Wagnerian repertory. He was also heard in guest
performances with the Concertgebouw Orchestra in Amsterdam, in Rome, and in Moscow.
From 1925 until the occupation of Austria by
Nazi Germany he was heard regularly at the
Salzburg Festival both in opera and in symphonic music—his performances of Mozart became a
standard towards which other conductors would
later aim.

Meanwhile, on February 15, 1923, Walter
made his American debut as a guest conductor
of the New York Symphony Society. He was not
well received at the time, nor did he show himself to best advantage. Many of the men in the

orchestra were prejudiced against German conductors and he had difficulty in gaining their cooperation. His performances were below the standards to which he had long since accustomed himself. In spite of the cool reception to his concerts from American press and audiences, he returned to conduct the New York Symphony Society each season until 1926. At the same time he was heard with the major orchestras in Boston, Detroit, and Minneapolis.

En route to the United States in 1925 he received word that he had been appointed general music director of the Municipal Opera in the Charlottenburg district of Berlin. It was a second-rate company when he took charge but within five years he elevated it to an exalted place among German opera houses. He resigned in 1929 because of sharp differences with the municipal authorities over the way the company should be run. One year later he was appointed principal conductor of the Gewandhaus Orchestra in Leipzig. He continued to give concerts annually with the Berlin Philharmonic, to perform regularly at Covent Garden and at the Salzburg Festival, and to fill other engagements. In May 1927 he was invited to Paris to conduct a cycle of Mozart operas. In the summer of 1929 he returned to the United States for performances at the Hollywood Bowl in California and guest performances in Cleveland and San Francisco. In 1932 in New York he directed concerts of the New York Philharmonic and initiated an affiliation with that orchestra lasting over a quarter of a century. When he first stepped on the stage of Carnegie Hall at the head of the New York Philharmonic on January 13, 1932 (a concert in which he was also heard as piano soloist in a Mozart piano concerto), he was finally given the homage that had long been due him; from that time on he remained an idol of the New York music-going public. As Lawrence Gilman wrote in the *Herald Tribune:* "He represents with a singular completeness and authenticity what one might call . . . the great central tradition of German musical culture. . . . Here . . . are a breadth and gravity of conception, a weight of utterance, a warm and rich expansiveness relevant to an interpreter's account of that mighty flowering of the musical spirit in Central Europe which began with Beethoven and has found its end apparently in Strauss. It is of this great tradition that Mr. Walter is particularly the mouthpiece."

He returned to Germany from New York in March 1933. The Nazis were in power and had already embarked upon their program of "cleansing" German life of all Jewish influences. A concert of the Berlin Philharmonic under Walter in March 1933 was hurriedly canceled "to preserve public order and security," as the authorities explained. When Walter tried to reassume his responsibilities with the Leipzig Gewandhaus Orchestra he learned that his concert on March 16 had also been canceled. In fact he had been officially ordered to leave Germany. The Leipzig concerts too were banned because they threatened "public order and security."

He went to England where he was given a hero's welcome at his concerts in London. One London newspaper remarked: "Germany, in expelling Walter, has made a present of its greatest conductor to the rest of the world." From London he went on to Vienna to serve there as guest conductor of the Vienna Philharmonic and the Vienna State Opera and to enjoy the adulation of the Viennese. "Here," reported an American journalist after attending a Bruno Walter performance, "the town storms the halls at his approach."

When Felix Weingartner resigned as general music director of the Vienna State Opera in the fall of 1936, Walter replaced him as principal conductor and artistic adviser. He also continued to perform at the Salzburg Festival. Then, once more he was victimized by political upheaval. When the Nazi army moved into Austria in 1938, Walter was in Paris to fill some engagements. Since he could no longer return to Austria, he found a new home in France and became a French citizen. He was awarded the ribbon of Commander of the Legion of Honor. Though he could not perform in Germany and Austria, his musical presence was welcomed in all other parts of Europe.

Early in 1939 he returned to the United States as guest conductor of the NBC Symphony. Later that year he filled an intensive schedule of appearances in Europe. But political developments were moving towards a new world war. More and more the sphere of Walter's activities became restricted and his personal life was deeply affected. When Italy became a partner of Nazi Germany, forming the Axis, Walter became persona non grata in that country too. The younger of his two daughters, Lotte, was arrested in Nazi-controlled Vienna because of her anti-Nazi activities. She was, however, finally allowed to leave the country unharmed. When France fell early in World War II, Walter lost his French citizenship and his home. All his commitments in France were canceled.

Once again he uprooted himself, his wife, and daughter Lotte (his older daughter, Marguerite, had died in the summer of 1939). He found a new life in the United States in a home in the Pacific Palisades section of Los Angeles. In 1946 he became an American citizen.

Though he did not receive a permanent conducting post in the United States, he was heard frequently and in many different places. In November and December 1939 he was a guest conductor of the Los Angeles Philharmonic, to which he returned for additional concerts in the fall of 1940. In February and March 1940 he conducted concerts of the NBC Symphony. In January and February 1941 he gave guest performances with the Minneapolis Symphony and the New York Philharmonic.

On February 14, 1941, he made his opera conducting debut in the United States at the Metropolitan Opera in *Fidelio*. Beethoven's paean to liberty, his denunciation of tyranny, in *Fidelio* was a particularly timely message in 1941 and it gained in emotional appeal in the light of Bruno Walter's personal history since 1933. As the evening progressed, the applause mounted until, at the end of the opera, he was required to take thirteen curtain calls. "His feeling for every phrase of the music and his understanding of its large design were a perpetual delight," wrote Pitts Sanborn in the *World-Telegram*. "And the interval between the two scenes of the second act he filled with an overwhelmingly dramatic reading of the third Leonore Overture. Thrice familiar as that work is, this performance brought the audience to such a pitch of enthusiasm that one trembled for the safety of the august house."

Walter continued to appear at the Metropolitan Opera each season from 1940 to 1945, again in 1950–1951, from 1955 to 1957, and in 1958–1959. He was heard most often in *The Magic Flute*, which he performed twenty-nine times. In the Mozart repertory he also conducted *Don Giovanni* and *The Marriage of Figaro*. Under his baton were given Gluck's *Orfeo ed Euridice, The Bartered Bride, Un Ballo in Maschera,* and *La Forza del Destino*. His final appearance at the Metropolitan took place on March 29, 1959, with a program coupling the Convent Scene from *La Forza del Destino* with Verdi's Requiem.

In the United States, he continued to make guest appearances with symphony orchestras, most frequently with the New York Philharmonic. He directed the Philharmonic in the world premieres of Samuel Barber's *Second Essay for Orchestra* (April 16, 1942) and John Alden Carpenter's Symphony No.2 (October 22, 1942). At a concert of the New York Philharmonic in March 1944, when he performed Bruckner's *Te Deum* and Beethoven's Symphony No.9, the fiftieth anniversary of his conducting debut was commemorated. He was presented on this occasion with a hand-lettered, illuminated testimonial signed by Toscanini, Koussevitzky, Stokowski, Szell, and others, a "token of recognition to a distinguished artist who has served the cause of music nobly and faithfully for half a century." The New York *Times* took note of this event in an editorial: "Honors have been conferred upon Bruno Walter by more than one government and musical institution. Only forces of tyranny and evil have proved his enemies. These forces drove him from the lands invaded by the Nazis, first to France, where he became a citizen, and from there to America, the country to which he has given his final allegiance. He remains here, where he has been welcome for so many years, an artist for all lands and all places, where men have dreamed and served the faith—a master of his art, a citizen of the world."

In addition to filling his position as guest conductor of the New York Philharmonic in the post–World War II years, Walter took on the duties of principal conductor and music adviser from 1947 to 1949. When World War II ended, he resumed his conducting activities in Europe, making his return to Vienna with a triumphant performance of *Fidelio* at the Vienna State Opera.

In 1956, in celebration of his eightieth birthday, the Vienna Municipal Council presented him with the Honorary Ring of the City of Vienna. One year later he suffered a heart attack which compelled him to limit the number of his public appearances. He resigned as music adviser to the New York Philharmonic after the 1956–1957 season but continued to appear occasionally as guest conductor. His last appearance with the New York Philharmonic took place on April 24, 1960, with a performance of Mahler's *Das*

Lied von der Erde. This was one of several appearances by Walter in New York and Vienna commemorating the centenary of Mahler's birth.

During the next few years Walter devoted himself principally to recording sessions, putting on disks his interpretations of the music of Beethoven, Brahms, Mahler, and Bruckner, among others.

His last years were spent in a Tudor-style house in Beverly Hills. There he died of a heart attack on February 17, 1962. He was buried in Lugano, Switzerland.

Writing in the *Saturday Review,* Martin Bernheimer, Los Angeles music critic, described Walter's salient qualities: "warmth, honesty and logic." He added: "Walter was essentially a romantic; he was not afraid of slowing down a particularly tender effect, or expanding a line when the underlying emotion warranted it. Similarly, he was not averse to conveying excitement through an accelerando where none was indicated in the score, but undue haste was as foreign to him as mawkish sentimentality. All interpretative gestures came from the music. Within this framework there could be no room for ego stimulation."

John McClure, who attended Walter's last recording sessions, called the rehearsals "an education and a joy." He added: "In the four years of our association I seldom heard his voice raised in impatience, and never in anger. The men came to the sessions as if to a master class. After tapping their music stands in tribute at the conductor's entrance, their tangibly receptive silence would be broken only by his exhortation or by music. Tension was minimal; concentration was absolute. Walter was an eminently articulate man, and his guidance—now spoken, now sung in that firm . . . voice—was colorful, warm, hortatory, and unfailingly pertinent. 'Come my friends,' he would say, 'once more; trumpets a little less, violins more singing, you know? It's much better but do it again.' "

In addition to his book on Gustav Mahler, Walter was the author of an autobiography, *Theme and Variations* (1946), and a volume on music and musicians, *Von der Musik und vom Musizieren* (1959). A volume of his letters, edited by Lotte Walter Lindt, was published in 1969. He also wrote pamphlets and essays on music.

His honors included a gold medal from the Royal Philharmonic Society of London, the decoration of Grand Officer of the Dutch Order of Orange-Nassau, and honorary doctorates in music from the University of California in Los Angeles and from Edinburgh University. The centenary of his birth was remembered in September 1976 with an exhibition of memorabilia in Founders Hall of the Metropolitan Opera.

Bruno Walter had a wide cultural background. He read omnivorously—mostly the classics and poetry. He habitually visited the art galleries of the world, and he enjoyed the theater. Peace and solace came to him through long walks in the woods, on the outskirts of his beloved Vienna and later in California.

Though his heart always belonged to Vienna, he adapted himself to American ways once he became an American citizen. American food was served on his table; he spoke English in preference to German, even to the point of sometimes using slang; he read American books and attended the American theater. He never tired of singing the praises of the American way of life. But, on the other hand, he could never acquire the fascination Americans have for gadgets, mechanical appliances, and the world of electronics.

ABOUT: Blaukopf, K. Great Conductors; Brook, D. International Gallery of Conductors; Ewen, D. Famous Conductors; Gelatt, R. Music Makers; Stefan, P. Bruno Walter; Walter, B. Theme and Variations. *Periodicals*—American Record Guide, April 1962; High Fidelity Magazine, January 1964; Musical America, April 1962; Musical Quarterly, October 1946; New York Times, October 8, 1933, January 4, 1976; Opera News, March 24, 1962; Saturday Review, March 25, 1961, December 28, 1963; Theater Arts, January 1942; Time, February 24, 1941.

Leonard Warren

1911–1960

Leonard Warren (originally Leonard Varenov), baritone, was born in the Bronx, New York, on April 11, 1911, to Russian-Jewish parents. His father was a fur merchant. After becoming an American citizen he shortened the family name to Warren. His ambition was to see his son in his own business. Leonard received his early academic schooling at P.S. 11 in the Bronx. Upon graduation from Evander Childs High School he studied commerce and merchandising at night at

LEONARD WARREN

to enter the Metropolitan Opera Auditions of the Air. When he asked the management of Radio City Music Hall for two weeks' leave to allow him to prepare for these auditions he was summarily fired. Up to that time *La Traviata* was the only opera he had ever heard, he had not yet mastered a single operatic role, and his entire repertory consisted of only a few arias. But after singing the "Largo al factotum" from *The Barber of Seville* at the final auditions, he was selected from seven hundred singers for top honors and a contract.

To prepare himself for his Metropolitan Opera debut, Warren went to Italy to work on his operatic repertory with Giuseppe Pais and Riccardo Piccozi in Rome and Milan. This venture was financed by George A. Martin, president of Sherwin-Williams Company which was then sponsoring the Auditions. He mastered seven roles in seven months.

On November 27, 1938, he made his Metropolitan Opera debut at a Sunday evening concert, collaborating in a duet from *La Traviata* and performing with other Metropolitan Opera singers in excerpts from *I Pagliacci.* His first appearance in an operatic performance on the stage of the Metropolitan Opera was as Paolo in *Simon Boccanegra* on January 13, 1939. Later the same season he was given the small roles of Tchelkaloff and Rangoni in *Boris Godunov* and the important part of Count di Luna in *Il Trovatore.* Though he had already revealed a beautiful baritone voice, he was so uncomfortable on the stage, so lacking in self-assurance in his vocalization, that few could have guessed that here was a star in the making.

For a number of years he failed to attract particular attention, though he helped to open a new season for the Metropolitan on November 27, 1939, and he was given ample opportunities in his repertoire: Valentin, the Herald in *Lohengrin,* Amonasro in *Aida,* Barnaba in *La Gioconda,* Escamillo in *Carmen,* Alfio in *Cavalleria Rusticana,* the High Priest in *Samson and Delilah,* Germont in *La Traviata,* the High Priest in the first Metropolitan Opera production of *Alceste,* Ashton in *Lucia di Lammermoor,* Don Carlo in *La Forza del Destino,* Tonio in *I Pagliacci,* and Ilo in the world premiere of Menotti's *The Island God* (February 20, 1942). *Newsweek,* in looking back at this period in Warren's career, called him "the man most unreviewed at the Metropolitan." But Warren was learning all the

Columbia University and worked for his father during the day, learning the fur brokerage business. He also studied music at the Greenwich House Music School.

During the depression of the early 1930s, the fur business went into a serious slump. Leonard left his father's firm. For about a year he went from one menial job to another, including one as attendant at a service station, but he managed to continue with his music studies. Though he had a pleasant voice and had always loved singing, he had no aspiration to become a professional singer. His only contact with good music was Caruso's records; in fact, until he was twenty-two he had never heard an opera performance. When in 1933 he saw *La Traviata,* he was so moved that he "cried like a baby."

One day in 1935 he went to Radio City Music Hall where he heard a bass sing and it occurred to him that he ought to apply there for a job. He went backstage, auditioned, and was hired. During the next three years he sang in the Music Hall glee club but was never given an opportunity to perform a solo. He continued to study voice with his first important teacher, Sidney Dietch. "When I first heard his voice," Dietch later recalled, "it was of very fine basic material but the quality was not so good. A little rough. I would never have expected him to make the career he has made. But all of a sudden, after two years or so, the voice grew in size, got its characteristic color, and I realized it was a great organ."

In 1938, on Dietch's advice Warren decided

time, developing and enriching his vocal equipment and at the same time acquiring greater stage poise.

He first stepped out of this comparative neglect on December 17, 1943, when he gave a commanding performance as Renato in *Un Ballo in Maschera.* The critic for the New York *Times* called his singing "splendid" and added that Warren used his voice with "marked intelligence and with more than roaring melodrama." Fifteen hours later he was called in to replace Lawrence Tibbett in the title role of *Rigoletto.* (This became one of Warren's most famous characterizations.)

After 1943 Warren distinguished himself in other roles: Falstaff in Verdi's opera of the same name, Iago in *Otello,* the title role in *Simon Boccanegra,* Gerard in *Andrea Chénier,* Scarpia in *Tosca,* Carlo in *Ernani,* and the title role in Verdi's *Macbeth.* In the *Herald Tribune,* Virgil Thomson noted: "He is in the process of becoming one of the greatest singers in the world of Italian baritone roles," and *Newsweek* referred to him as "the world's foremost baritone." In reviewing Warren's performance as Falstaff, Olin Downes found that he had made that character "human and appealing . . . throughout. Above all, he was able to ring the changes in character whatever its interpretative problems in terms of masterly song." In the title role of *Macbeth,* reported Howard Taubman in the New York *Times,* "he evoked the troubled, terrified Macbeth, with subtle authority; as is his habit he sings with subtle art." To Winthrop Sargeant in the *New Yorker,* Warren brought to *Simon Boccanegra* "the nobility, the aristocratic sense of style and the profound dedication that characterized all his interpretations at the Metropolitan during the past two decades, in which he is one of the most memorable stars in its history and is the finest Verdi baritone of the era."

Up to his death he remained a favorite not only at the Metropolitan (where he gave 416 performances in New York and 206 on tour in 26 roles) but also at La Scala, where he made his debut in 1953 as Rigoletto. He was a frequent guest at most of the leading opera houses of Europe, Latin America, and the United States. He was also a frequent participant in major network radio and television programs.

His last complete performance in opera took place at the Metropolitan on March 1, 1960, in the title role of *Simon Boccanegra.* He was appearing as Don Carlo in *La Forza del Destino* on March 4, 1960, when, upon completing the aria "Urna fatale del mio destino," he collapsed, stricken by a cerebral hemorrhage. The curtains were hurriedly drawn and Rudolf Bing went on the stage to ask the audience to remain in the auditorium, promising that the performance would continue. But at 10:30 P.M. Bing told the patient audience that Leonard Warren was dead and asked it to stand "in memory of one of the greatest performers who died in the middle of one of his greatest performances."

Warren was survived by his wife. When he met her, in Milan in 1938, Agatha Leifflen was a voice graduate from the Juilliard School of Music. They were married on December 27, 1941. Since she was a Catholic, Warren was converted to Catholicism. Consequently, his funeral services were conducted at St. Vincent Ferrar Roman Catholic Church in New York on March 7, 1960—the requiem service offered by one of Warren's lifelong friends, Reverend Roy Gardner. At the funeral home Warren was clothed in a white robe of the Knight Commander of the Equestrian Order of the Holy Sepulchre in Jerusalem, an honor which had been bestowed on him a few months earlier by the Vatican.

During Warren's lifetime, he and his wife maintained a five-room apartment in New York City and a cottage in Greenwich, Connecticut. His diversions included fishing, sailing, gardening, tinkering with machinery, and collecting fine paintings.

He was not easy to get along with at the opera house because he was strongly opinionated, strong-willed, and very sure of himself. Dissension between him and his colleagues was frequent. As Harold C. Schonberg noted in his profile of Warren in the New York *Times Magazine* written while the baritone was still alive: "He tells other singers how to sing, conductors how to conduct, directors how to direct, photographers how to photograph, recording engineers how to engineer and costumers how to costume; and they say if Verdi were around he would tell him how to compose. One backstage worker described him as 'a pain in the neck with a great voice,' and that feeling is rather prevalent throughout the house."

ABOUT: Musical America, December 1, 1956, March

1960; New York Times Magazine, October 25, 1959; Opera News, November 23, 1942.

André Watts

1946–

André Watts, pianist, was born in Nuremberg, Germany, on June 20, 1946. His father, Sergeant Herman Watts, was a black American career soldier stationed in Germany; his mother, Maria Alexandra Gusmits Watts, was a Hungarian who lived in Germany as a displaced person. While André was still an infant, his family moved to Ulm, Germany, where his father had been transferred. His mother played the piano well, and André's first memory of anything musical was of the covers of the sheet music of Johann Strauss waltzes his mother used to play on their Blüthner piano. The first sounds he recalls were those of Liszt's Hungarian Rhapsodies. When he was six he began lessons on a miniature violin, for which he showed no special talent. Two years later his mother started to teach him the piano. He took to it instantly. "Soon I knew I preferred the piano," he recalls. "I had the hands for it and I was more at home at the keyboard."

He had been receiving piano lessons from his mother for about a year when his father was transferred back to the United States. In Philadelphia, where the Watts family made its home, André was enrolled in the Philadelphia Musical Academy, becoming a pupil of Genia Robinor, Doris Bawden, and Clement Petrillo. He made such excellent progress that when he was nine he was chosen from forty contestants to appear as soloist with the Philadelphia Orchestra at one of its children's concerts, in the performance of a Haydn concerto. One year later he returned to the Philadelphia Orchestra during its summer performances at Robin Hood Dell to play the Mendelssohn Concerto No. 1.

He was about thirteen when his parents separated (they were legally divorced in 1962). From then on he was entirely under the influence of his mother who shepherded him carefully through his studies and his early career. He had no further contact with his father. While receiving his academic education at Quaker and Roman Catholic schools and the Lincoln Preparatory

ANDRÉ WATTS

School from which he was graduated in 1963, he worked several hours each afternoon and all weekend on his piano studies. In their second-floor apartment in an old house in West Philadelphia he used to practice on an old battered piano with twenty-six of its strings missing. He never found time to make friends or to participate in boyhood games.

When he was fourteen, he was a soloist with the Philadelphia Orchestra in one of its regular subscription concerts, performing César Franck's *Symphonic Variations.* Two years later he heard that Leonard Bernstein was holding auditions for soloists to appear with the New York Philharmonic at his Young People's Concerts, which were videotaped and transmitted on a nationwide television network. When Bernstein heard him play he "flipped," as Bernstein himself said. André performed the Liszt Concerto No. 1 under Bernstein on January 15, 1963, televised over the CBS-TV network. His success that day proved so extraordinary that when he gave a student recital at the Academy of Music in Philadelphia one week later, the request for tickets far exceeded the capacity of the auditorium. "Only a prodigy," reported Samuel L. Singer in the Philadelphia *Inquirer,* "could have amassed the technique and musical insight at the age of sixteen . . . demonstrated at this recital."

When Glenn Gould was unable to appear as a guest soloist with the New York Philharmonic on January 31, 1963, Bernstein invited André to take his place. Once again he was heard in Liszt's first piano concerto. This was the first time that a black man had appeared as soloist with the New York Philharmonic at its regular subscription series since the turn of the century. André's appearance, in addition to adding a footnote to the racial history of the times, became a musical event of first importance since it placed him among the leading young pianists of his time. *Life* reported that he received "the season's wildest ovation." And *Time* said: "André approached the piece as a tone poem. In scherzo passages he had the speed and power necessary to dignify his delicately poetic ideas of the slow pianissimos. His singing tone stayed with him in every mood of his varied approach, and when he had sounded his final cadenza, the whole orchestra stood with the audience to applaud him." Bernstein called him "a natural, a real pro."

André was signed to a recording contract by Columbia and two albums were issued under the Columbia label. One of these coupled Liszt's first piano concerto with Chopin's Piano Concerto No.2; the other was called *An André Watts Recital.* On the strength of these releases, the National Academy of Recording Arts and Sciences presented him with its Grammy award as "the most promising classical artist of 1963."

In spite of his successes, André insisted on enrolling at the Peabody Conservatory in Baltimore as soon as he had graduated from high school in 1963 in order to fulfill the requirements for a Bachelor of Music degree (he succeeded in completing the requirements in the summer of 1972). At Peabody he worked under Leon Fleisher. To pursue his studies even on a part-time basis and still have enough time for practicing and enlarging his repertory, André accepted only a limited number of public appearances in spite of the heavy demand for his performances. During the next few years he was heard, however, with leading American orchestras. On June 12, 1966, he made his European debut as soloist with the London Symphony Orchestra conducted by Hans Schmidt-Isserstedt. After that he went on to Amsterdam to appear with the Concertgebouw Orchestra under Karel Ančerl. On October 26, 1966, in the United States, he made his New York recital debut with a concert at the Lincoln Center for the Performing Arts on the Great Performers series. Writing in the *New Yorker,* Winthrop Sargeant spoke of him as "a bravura pianist of stunning achievements and a romantic pianist whose style takes

one back to the great days of men like Moriz Rosenthal." André was reengaged for the Great Performers Series at the Lincoln Center for eight more successive years, and became the only artist in that time during that series to sell out the auditorium for each of his appearances. In June 1967 he embarked on a seven-week tour of Europe and Asia as soloist with the Los Angeles Philharmonic under Zubin Mehta. On this tour he played for the first time in the land of his birth and also celebrated his twenty-first birthday on June 19 and 20 with a performance of Brahms's Piano Concerto No.2, with the Berlin Philharmonic. In September 1967, he was sent by the U.S. State Department on a three-month world tour which took him to sixteen Western European and Asian countries. By 1970 he had performed with almost every great orchestra in the world. On August 14, 1970, he paid his first visit to the city of his birth, Nuremberg, with a recital, in the Hall of the Knights in the Nuremberg castle, and received a tumultuous reception.

Watts was invited to perform in 1969 at President Nixon's Inaugural in a concert at Constitution Hall in Washington, D.C. He has performed for other heads of state, among them the King and the Queen Mother of Greece, Archbishop Makarios of Cyprus, and Prince Juan Carlos de Bourbon and Princess Sophia of Spain. Watts also gave a concert in Teheran as part of the coronation festivities for the Shah of Iran. Following his appearance at the White House where he performed for President and Mrs. Mobutu of the Congo, he was presented with the Order of Zaïre, one of Africa's highest honors.

Pierre Boulez chose Watts to appear as soloist under his baton at his first concert as music director of the New York Philharmonic in 1971. Eugene Ormandy invited Watts in 1973 to perform Rachmaninoff's Piano Concerto No.3 with the Philadelphia Orchestra in commemoration of the one-hundredth anniversary of Rachmaninoff's birth. In February 1975 Watts filled the dual role of narrator and pianist in a Lincoln's Birthday concert at the historic Ford Theatre in Washington, D.C. And on November 28, 1976, he became the first solo recitalist to be televised live nationally, through the facilities of the Public Broadcasting Service, direct from Avery Fisher Hall in New York. That concert also made Watts the first artist to have appeared in ten consecutive seasons on the "Great Performers" series at Lincoln Center.

During the summer of 1976, Watts gave a recital at the Salzburg Festival in Austria: the first half of his program consisted of Schubert's music, the second half was devoted to Gershwin. In May 1978, with the collaboration of assisting artists, Watts launched a twenty-four-city tour over a period of eight months, presenting forty-four concerts devoted exclusively to the music of Franz Schubert in commemoration of the one-hundred-and-fiftieth anniversary of that composer's birth.

Watts was the subject of a one-hour documentary filmed for the NET network, a performance of a Mozart piano concerto with the Los Angeles Philharmonic under Mehta. He appeared on a television show of his own on the "Camera Three" program, performing and discussing the music of Liszt. He has also appeared on André Previn's telecasts with the London Symphony Orchestra over BBC-TV.

Though he insists on spending several months a year on study and practice, he is able to fill an average of one hundred performances a year. For many years his home was an apartment in New York City, on Seventh Avenue and Fifty-seventh Street, just a short distance from Carnegie Hall. But in his need for a more peaceful home setting he has since moved not far from New York City to a house on eight acres in a rural area in Rockland County, New York. "I was sleeping night after night with the sound of traffic and I do spend seventy-five per cent of my life as it is in big cities on the road," he told Carol Mont Parker in the New York *Times*. "I find it necessary to come home, sit on the grass, and stare at a tree."

When he is not on tour, he rises early in the morning, a little before 8 A.M., goes through a half-hour routine of yoga exercises, has an ample breakfast, and by nine in the morning gets down to the business of practicing for three or four uninterrupted hours. He has lunch at one o'clock, invariably accompanying the meal with some recorded music, because, as he has said, he does not like to live without sound. After lunch comes a brief nap, some more yoga exercises, and then several more hours of practicing. He does not have many friends because, he confesses, "individuals get on my nerves after a while." When he seeks recreation he prefers studying languages, reading books, listening to

recordings, playing chess, and occasionally participating in a low-stake poker game. He is partial to gourmet meals and cigars.

In 1973 Watts became the youngest person in over two hundred years to receive an honorary doctorate from Yale University. Two years later another honorary doctorate was conferred on him by Albright College in Reading, Pennsylvania.

ABOUT: Esquire, March 1964; High Fidelity/Musical America, February 1973; Horizon, December 1977; New York Times, October 23, 1966, October 23, 1977; New York Times Magazine, September 19, 1971; Newsweek, February 11, 1963; Saturday Review, February 16, 1963; Seventeen, January 1964; Time, February 8, 1963.

Felix Weingartner

1863–1942

Paul Felix Weingartner, Edler von Münzberg, a conductor who gained world prominence for his performance of Beethoven's symphonies, was born on the Dalmatian coast in the town of Zara (now Zadar in Yugoslavia) on June 2, 1863, to Guido and Caroline Strobl Weingartner. His father was the chief of the telegraph service.

When Felix was four his father died, and his mother took the family to the Austrian city of Graz. There Felix received his academic education at the elementary school and Gymnasium and his musical training with W. A. Remy. Felix's musical precocity expressed itself in composition. By the time he was sixteen he had published several compositions for the piano which Brahms regarded so highly that he recommended the young composer for a government stipend to enable him to continue his music studies at the Leipzig Conservatory.

In 1881 Felix went to Leipzig. At the Conservatory he was a pupil of Carl Reinecke and Salomon Jadassohn, among others. He first demonstrated his talent for conducting at a student concert when he directed the Conservatory orchestra in a performance of Beethoven's Symphony No.2, conducting from memory. For this accomplishment he received a stern rebuke from his professor, Karl Reinecke, who objected to

Weingartner: vīn′ gärt nēr

FELIX WEINGARTNER

any student dispensing with the score in directing an orchestral performance.

While attending the Conservatory, Felix took courses in philosophy for two years at the University of Leipzig. After graduation from the Conservatory in 1883 with high honors and the highly prized Mozart Award, he went to Weimar where he met and became a friend of Franz Liszt. Liszt encouraged him to compose and even used his influence to get Weingartner's opera *Sakuntala* produced at the Weimar Opera on March 23, 1884. Liszt also advised Weingartner to more actively pursue a career in conducting. On Liszt's recommendation, he was given his first conducting assignment at Königsberg in 1884.

From 1885 to 1887 Weingartner was conductor in Danzig, from 1887 to 1889 in Hamburg, and from 1889 to 1891 in Mannheim. In 1891 he was appointed first conductor of the Berlin Royal Opera and the Royal Orchestra. With the Opera he undertook an extensive repertory with professional skill. Though he had many admirers in Berlin, he antagonized many of the musicians at the Opera with his progressive methods and ideas. By 1898, no longer able to function to his fullest capacity at the opera house, he resigned; but he continued to direct the Royal Orchestra in Berlin until 1907 and toured Europe with it several times. These symphonic concerts, plus performances by the Weingartner Trio which he founded and of which he was pianist, made him known throughout Europe. In 1898 in London he made a conducting debut that proved

so successful that from then on he returned to London regularly as guest conductor of its major orchestras.

From 1898 to 1903 he was the conductor of the Kaim Orchestra in Munich. In 1908 he succeeded Gustav Mahler as music director of the Vienna Royal Opera; he also conducted symphony concerts with the Opera orchestra. He remained with the Vienna Royal Opera only two years, but he continued for some years after that to present symphony concerts with the Opera orchestra.

Weingartner made his American debut with the New York Philharmonic on February 10, 1905. He returned a year later to direct the New York Symphony Society between January and March, not only in New York but also on tour. The New York music critics hailed him. One of them wrote: "He is a commander of men, an authority, and a master." On his next visit to the United States, in 1912, he made his American opera debut directing the Boston Opera Company in *Tristan and Isolde* on February 12. "There was finesse in the working out of the detail," wrote Philip Hale, the Boston music critic, "but there was a continuous flow of musical thought with its bursts and lulls of passion, with constantly varied expression. The orchestra sang with a marvelous song."

From 1912 to 1914 Weingartner was the principal conductor of the Municipal Opera in Hamburg. For five years after that he served as conductor of the court orchestra in Darmstadt. He also became director of the Darmstadt Conservatory.

In 1919 he began a five-year tenure as principal conductor of the Vienna Volksoper and an eight-year term as conductor of the Vienna Philharmonic. During this period he made numerous appearances throughout Europe, particularly in London where he became such a favorite that he was looked upon by the English as one of their own. He was universally acknowledged to be one of the great living interpreters of Beethoven's symphonies. But whether in orchestral music or in the opera house, whether in Mozart, Beethoven, Weber, or Wagner, he proved himself to be one of the elect of the baton, a classicist by training and temperament, with an unusual capacity for seeing each musical work as a whole without losing sight of the subtlest detail and with a sure hand for architectonic structure.

When Weingartner left Vienna in 1927, he settled in Basel, Switzerland. There he became director of the Basel Conservatory and conductor of orchestral concerts at the Allgemeine Musikgesellschaft. In Basel on February 26, 1935 (eighty years after its composition), Weingartner directed the world premiere of Bizet's youthful Symphony No.1.

Early in 1935, when Clemens Krauss resigned as artistic director of the Vienna State Opera, Weingartner was called back to Vienna to replace him. During that summer he also led orchestral concerts at the Salzburg Festival. However, Weingartner did not hold his post with the Vienna State Opera long. He resigned in the fall of 1936. That year he directed several concerts in Japan, and in 1939 he performed *Parsifal* at Covent Garden. After that he went into retirement at Interlaken, Switzerland, where he established a summer school of conducting. He died in Winterthur, Switzerland, on May 7, 1942.

Weingartner composed many works in virtually every area. Among his best-known operas were *Kain und Abel* (Darmstadt, May 17, 1914) and *Dame Kobold* (Darmstadt, February 23, 1916). He also completed six symphonies, five string quartets, tone poems, concertos, choral and piano music, and violin sonatas. He was the author of a valuable treatise on conducting, *Über das Dirigieren* (1897), and one on Beethoven's symphonies (1906, translated into English in 1908), among other works. He was also the author of an autobiography published in 1923 and translated into English in 1937 as *Buffets and Rewards: a Musician's Reminiscences.*

Weingartner was one of the editors of the complete editions of Berlioz and Haydn and the editor of operas by Weber and Wagner, among others.

He was married five times: to Marie Juillerat in 1891; to Baroness Feodora von Dreifus in 1903; to Lucille Marcel, a concert singer, in 1912; to Roxo Betty Calish in 1922; and lastly to Carmen Studer.

ABOUT: Dymont, C. Felix Weingartner: Recollections and Recordings; Jacob, W. Felix Weingartner; Günther, F. Felix Weingartner; Merian, W. and others. Festschrift für Dr. Felix Weingartner zu seinem siebzigsten Geburtstag; Weingartner, F. Buffets and Rewards: A Musician's Reminiscences.

Alexis Weissenberg

1929–

Alexis Weissenberg, pianist, was born in Sofia, Bulgaria, in 1929. His mother, Lillian Phia, was a professional pianist. Since his parents were divorced when Alexis was still young, he was brought up by his mother. She was his first teacher, and piano lessons began when he was three. Later piano study in Sofia continued with Pantcho Vladigerov, Bulgarian composer.

He was eleven when the Nazis came to power in Bulgaria. During the next three years the country was alternately under the domination of Nazi or Soviet invaders. In 1944, because he was Jewish, Alexis was confined for nine months in a concentration camp. A bombing attack on Sofia by the English saved the Weissenbergs. Since several important Nazi buildings had been destroyed, Nazi troops were used to do the rebuilding, leaving the border less guarded than usual. By this time Alexis had been released from concentration camp. He and his mother made a successful plunge across the border into Turkey. From there they made their way to Palestine, where Alexis continued his piano studies with Leo Kestenberg.

In Palestine, Weissenberg took the name "Sigi" to replace Alexis; this was a pet name given him in childhood. As Sigi Weissenberg he began his virtuoso career with a recital at Tel Aviv in 1944. Jan Holcman, who heard that concert, recalled it in an article in *Saturday Review:* "He played everything, even at that stage, à la Weissenberg, with a certain elegance, his wizardly technique never reducing the artistic conception to the merely metronomic." After that recital he was a soloist with the Palestine Symphony Orchestra in a performance of Rachmaninoff's Piano Concerto No.2. The response of critics and audience was so enthusiastic that he was called upon to perform that concerto at five successive concerts. He then earned the high honor of being chosen as a permanent soloist with the Palestine Symphony Orchestra. A concert tour of South Africa followed.

He arrived in the United States in 1947 with a letter of introduction to Artur Schnabel. Schnabel told him: "You have nothing to learn,

Weissenberg: vī′ sĕn bĕrk

Weissenberg

ALEXIS WEISSENBERG

but something to develop." For that development he went for additional piano study to Olga Samaroff at the Juilliard School of Music in New York; he also profited greatly from the guidance of Wanda Landowska. Winning the Youth Contest of the Philadelphia Orchestra in 1947 brought him an opportunity to appear with that orchestra at one of its youth concerts. Later the same year he captured the Leventritt International Award, which enabled him to make his professional debut in the United States: He played Chopin's Piano Concerto No.1 with the New York Philharmonic Orchestra under George Szell on February 28, 1948. He repeated that performance the following fall with the Cleveland Orchestra under Szell.

In the United States his career moved slowly. He was booked almost exclusively in small cities and communities, and bookings with important orchestras were few. He was continually called upon to play commonplace programs, and he was kept so busy he had little time to develop himself as an artist through further study. "How many times a year can one honestly and decently play the *Liebestraum* without going nuts?" he asked Rosemarie Tauris in an interview which was published in the New York *Times.* It was all "so damaging and demoralizing," he recalled. When he finally summoned the courage to complain to his manager and to insist that he would no longer continue along such lines, his manager told him he was free to leave since he was "easily replaceable."

Weissenberg returned to Paris and became a

French citizen. With his career in a sharp decline, he withdrew completely from all concert work. "I just had to retire from the stage in order to think over things I had done well, things I could do much better, and things I should never do again," he explained to Roy Hemming in *Stereo Review.* "I had to know who I was. Every man has to know this. He has to know it as a lover. He has to know it as a musician." To earn a living, he designed Christmas cards and in 1952 he sold an ingenious sample collage to the Pepsi-Cola people. "Those were hard days," he recalls. "I never felt good until I had a place that really belonged to me."

Meanwhile he married the daughter of a Spanish diplomat and raised two daughters in Madrid. Supported by a small family allowance, he used the next few years not only to restudy his repertoire from the beginning and reappraise his musical attitudes but also to study philosophy. These were his "second formative years," as he likes to refer to them.

By 1960 he had returned to Paris and was living in an apartment that was furnished mostly in a Napoleonic style and that overlooked the Seine in full view of the Eiffel Tower. He divorced his wife at about this time and settled down to work harder than ever on his pianism and his repertory. He had been removed so long from the concert scene that he doubted if he would ever resume his career where it had been interrupted a decade earlier, but in 1966 he made a color film performing Tchaikovsky's Piano Concerto No.1 with Herbert von Karajan conducting the Berlin Philharmonic. He also recorded the concerto with the same orchestra and conductor and played it as soloist with the Berlin Philharmonic when the Philharmonic inaugurated its 1966–1967 season. This marked his return to a virtuoso career.

Ronald Wilford, an artists' manager, persuaded him to return to the United States to make a new bid for success. When Michelangeli was unable to appear as soloist with the New York Philharmonic in 1967, Weissenberg was chosen to take his place. He performed Rachmaninoff's Concerto No.3 (this became one of his specialties) with a brilliance and power that magnetized the audience. "There is no doubt about it," reported a critic for the New York *Times.* "Weissenberg is a powerhouse." An American tour in 1967–1968 began with the inaugural concert of the Great Performers Series at the Lincoln Center for the Performing Arts. Since that time Weissenberg has toured the United States annually, in addition to performing in all the major capitals of Europe and in the Far East. During the summer of 1974 he was heard at the Berkshire Music Festival at Tanglewood in Massachusetts, at the Salzburg Festival in Austria, and at the Edinburgh Festival in Scotland.

He has also proved to be a penetrating interpreter of the classical and Romantic literature, a specialist in the music of Rachmaninoff. In the *Saturday Review* Irving Kolodin spoke of the "strength of his musical character," and of the "power of artistic perfection to hold the stage and the interest." In the New York *Times* Raymond Ericson described him as a "prodigious talent [who] plays the piano as if he had been born for that alone." The critic of *Le Figaro* in Paris, Bernard Gavoty, wrote: "Weissenberg has made the composer's creative demands his own ... ever mindful of the underlying sentiment which dictates the proper approach. An extremely subtle touch and the most varied of tonal palettes permit him to make the transition from the wildest transport to the most profound sense of peace."

Weissenberg shares his second-floor apartment in a converted town house opposite the Louvre Museum in Paris with his black poodle, Tcherno, and a Spanish couple who take care of his household. He has described his life-style as "blue jeans in a seventeenth-century house." His hobby is making humorous sketches of celebrated musicians, and in the same comic vein he often entertains his friends by miming the speech and behavior of famous people. His social life is confined to conversations with intimate friends; he avoids parties and rarely attends postconcert receptions. He likes to take vacations near the sea in France or Spain or in the mountains in Switzerland, where he is sometimes joined by his two daughters.

Weissenberg has made several television films including one in which he performed Stravinsky's *Petrouchka* suite arranged for the piano; this film won several prizes after being released by the NET network. He has also conducted a musical interview program over a New York radio station. Among his recordings is a set of Beethoven's five piano concertos with the Berlin Philharmonic under Karajan.

Weissenberg fills about ninety engagements a year. Wherever he concertizes he brings with

him his own concert piano. "It is better known to custom officials than I am," he says. He calls his piano Phenomenon II. "Maybe," he explains, "because I consider myself Phenomenon I? But there is no Phenomenon I." Of his piano he adds: "I have great respect for him, and I treat him like a pharaoh."

ABOUT: New York Times, August 15, 1971; Saturday Review, September 24, 1960; Stereo Review, April 1974.

Ljuba Welitsch

1913–

Ljuba Welitsch (originally Ljuba Velitchkova), soprano, was born in Borisovo, Bulgaria, on the Black Sea, on July 10, 1913. She came from peasant stock; her father was a farmer. As a girl, she helped her two sisters till the soil on her father's land. Music study began when her oldest sister, aware of Ljuba's interest in music, gave her a violin on her eighth birthday. For the next few years Ljuba continued to study the violin. At thirteen, after completing elementary school in Borisovo, she went to a nearby town to attend high school. There one of her teachers discovered she had a voice worth cultivating and began to give her vocal lessons.

After completing high school, Ljuba entered the University of Sofia, majoring in philosophy and religion. All this while she held various jobs to support herself. In time she gave up the violin to concentrate on the voice, as a pupil of Zlateff. As a member of a local choral group she sometimes sang solo parts.

When Zlateff persuaded her to think seriously of opera as a career, Ljuba left Sofia University after two years to study opera repertory in Vienna at the State Academy of Music, principally with Theodor Lierhammer. In three years' time she finished a five-year course. In 1936 she made her opera debut as Nedda in *I Pagliacci* with the Graz Opera in Austria. She then sang other major lyric soprano parts there, among them Mimi and Musetta in *La Bohème,* Cio-Cio-San in *Madama Butterfly,* Hansel in *Hansel and Gretel,* and the title role in *Manon Lescaut.*

After four years in Graz, she appeared with

Welitsch: vā′ lĭsh

Welitsch

provincial companies in forty different roles. "I was not a fantastic Desdemona," she confessed many years later in recalling her operatic beginnings. "I was a good Puccini Manon, but not the Massenet one—two sweet." To her favorite roles she added Cherubino in *The Marriage of Figaro,* Lisa in Tchaikovsky's *The Queen of Spades,* and the Goosegirl in Humperdinck's *Königskinder.*

After two years with the Hamburg Opera (1941–1943), and guest appearances with the Berlin State Opera and the Dresden Opera, in 1943 Welitsch became a permanent member of the Munich Opera and remained there three years. In 1943 she made her debut with the Vienna State Opera as the Composer in *Ariadne auf Naxos.* One year later, during the celebration of Richard Strauss's eightieth birthday, she appeared in Vienna for the first time in the role that became her most famous one, that of Salome. Her successes in Vienna were of such magnitude that in 1946 she was engaged as a permanent member of the Vienna State Opera and soon afterward received the honorary title *Kammersängerin.*

Welitsch made the first of many appearances at Covent Garden in London when, as a member of the visiting Vienna State Opera, she was heard as Donna Anna in *Don Giovanni.* Soon after that she appeared at Covent Garden as Salome and was a sensation.

Sensational, too, was her debut at the Metropolitan Opera in New York on February 4, 1949, as Salome. "Miss Welitsch is the only soprano that the present generation of opera goers has seen on this side of the water who is equipped to give the full value to this role," wrote Olin Downes in the New York *Times.* "She has a very dramatic voice. . . . The voice has everything in it. It has the brilliance and edge needed for the Straussian climaxes. It has colors and richness of timbre in the lower registers. Miss Welitsch is a musician and an interpreter of flaming temperament, who has the part absolutely in hand. She is an actress of individuality and power." In his history of the Metropolitan Opera, Irving Kolodin maintained: "Certainly no Salome since Fremstad has sung the music with the ease and stately thrust of Welitsch, and her dance . . . was vastly effective in the sequence of the action."

Salome remained her role of roles. She appeared in it over five hundred times in some ten different productions; some seasons she was called upon to sing it twice a week. "I did not change my interpretation from production to production," she has said. "After all, I learned Salome from the composer. And Strauss said to me . . . that he never knew his score could be so well sung."

During her four seasons at the Metropolitan Opera, she also distinguished herself as Aida, Donna Anna, Tosca, Musetta, and Rosalinde in *Die Fledermaus.*

In reviewing an album of opera and operetta arias sung by Welitsch (London Records), David Hamilton wrote in *High Fidelity:* "The Welitsch sound was something rather special, not merely for its distinctive color, but because it was so needle-sharp in focus, without sacrificing span or life; this has great musical value for it permits singing of truly instrumental precision. . . . More than this, she had imagination. . . . She always trusts the composer, working out her interpretation with a framework of great literal accuracy, rather than pulling and hauling the music about to fit some personal 'idea'—and yet every note is vibrant with personality, every climax set forth with fearless thrust."

While appearing at the Metropolitan Opera, Welitsch continued to serve as guest artist at Covent Garden, La Scala in Milan, and other major European opera houses, as well as filling her commitments to the Vienna State Opera. She was also heard at the festivals at Salzburg in Austria and Edinburgh in Scotland.

She remained with the Vienna State Opera until 1964. "Then," she told Dorle J. Soria, as reported in *High Fidelity/Musical America,* "I feel my voice not the same. Tops, very well. Middle doesn't go." She handed in her resignation to the director of the Vienna State Opera, saying "I am an artist, not a businessman." Upon her retirement she was given an honorary life membership in the company.

Welitsch returned to the stage of the Metropolitan Opera on February 17, 1972. This was a sentimental rather than a musical event, since it only required her appearance in the role of the Duchess in a new production of *The Daughter of the Regiment,* a walk-on part calling for no singing and the speaking of only thirty-two words.

On August 21, 1956, Welitsch married Karl Schmalvogel, a Viennese traffic policeman; they were divorced in 1969. She has maintained an apartment in Vienna and a country house outside Vienna. Her constant companion has been her poodle, Bobi, who made six films with her. Since 1958, when she made her debut in motion pictures in a German-language version of Bernard Shaw's *Arms and the Man,* she has appeared in seventy films and thirty-five televised dramas. She has also appeared in performances of operettas and plays calling for no singing.

ABOUT: Jacobson, R. Reverberations. *Periodicals—* High Fidelity/Musical America, June 1972; New York Times, February 13, 1949; New Yorker, March 19, 1949; Newsweek, March 7, 1949; Opera News, March 25, 1972.

Clarence Whitehill

1871–1932

Clarence Eugene Whitehill, baritone, was the first American-born singer to achieve international recognition in principal Wagnerian baritone roles. He was born in Marengo, Iowa, on November 5, 1871, to William and Elizabeth Dawson McLaughlin Whitehill. His academic schooling ended with his graduation from Marengo High School in 1890. He then went on to Chicago, finding a singing post with the Fullerton Avenue Episcopal Church Choir, and studying singing with H. D. Phelps. He was working as an express clerk for Wells Fargo when Giuseppe Campanari, Metropolitan Opera baritone, heard him sing and was so impressed that he introduced Whitehill to Nellie Melba.

CLARENCE WHITEHILL

She induced him to continue his vocal studies with a view towards becoming a professional singer. The financial support of a Chicago patron made it possible for him to go to Paris in 1896, and for the next three years he studied voice there with Jean-Baptiste Sbriglia and Alfred Auguste Giraudet.

In November 1899 Whitehill made his opera debut at the Théâtre de la Monnaie in Brussels as Frère Laurent in *Romeo and Juliet,* using the stage name M. Clarence. He made such a good impression that in 1900 he was engaged by the Opéra-Comique in Paris, becoming the first American-born singer to receive a contract from that company. His debut there took place as Nilakantha in *Lakmé.*

In the fall of 1900 Henry W. Savage organized the English Grand Opera Company for performances at the Metropolitan Opera House in New York and engaged Whitehill as one of his principal baritones, assigning him nineteen roles.

Feeling the need of further training, Whitehill returned to Europe in 1902 for vocal study with Julius Stockhausen in Frankfort. He then appeared in opera houses in Lübeck and Eberfeld in Germany, and from 1903 to 1908 he was a principal at the Cologne Opera. Under the guidance of Cosima Wagner he began to study and master Wagnerian roles. In the summer of 1904 he made his debut at the Bayreuth Festival as Wolfram in *Tannhäuser.* He returned to Bayreuth in 1908 in one of his most celebrated roles —Amfortas in *Parsifal*—and was heard there the same year as Gunther in *Die Götterdämmerung*. He was also heard in Wagnerian roles at Covent Garden in London, the Munich Royal Opera, and the Paris Opéra.

His debut with the Metropolitan Opera company in New York took place on November 25, 1909, as Amfortas. He remained at the Met only one season, during which he was also heard as the Wanderer in *Siegfried*, Wotan in *Die Walküre*, Gunther, Wolfram, and The Old One in the world premiere of the first American opera produced at the Metropolitan, Frederick Converse's *The Pipe of Desire* (March 18, 1910). After his appearance as Wotan in *Die Walküre* on January 8, 1910, a critic for the Evening *Mail* wrote: "The American baritone is a rare asset to the Metropolitan stage where his Wotan was one of splendid breadth, pulsing with vital, human emotions under tremendous intellectual control, in addition to one of the most beautiful voices heard in a very long time."

From 1911 to 1916 he was the principal baritone of the Chicago Opera. As Amfortas he participated in the first Chicago production of *Parsifal* on November 25, 1911. In Chicago he also assumed the roles of Kurvenal in *Tristan and Isolde*, Wotan in *Das Rheingold* and *Die Walküre*, and Gunther.

He returned to the Metropolitan Opera on November 26, 1914, in the role with which he had made his debut there—Amfortas. By 1917 H. E. Krehbiel in the New York *Tribune* was saying that Whitehill had "no superior in the field of Wagnerian music drama." One of his greatest successes, aside from the role of Amfortas, came as Hans Sachs in *Die Meistersinger*, which he undertook for the first time anywhere at the Metropolitan Opera on March 19, 1917. He gave the character, said Krehbiel in the *Tribune*, "a warm, human and poetic creation, singing the music with delicacy and feeling. . . . It took an American to restore this spirit to *Die Meistersinger*."

Whitehill remained with the Metropolitan Opera company for eighteen seasons. His artistry enriched not only the Wagnerian music dramas but the French repertory as well, with memorable performances as the father in the first Metropolitan Opera production of *Louise*, Méphistophélès in *Faust*, the High Priest in *Samson and Delilah*, Athanaël in *Thaïs*, the elder Des Grieux in *Manon*, Capulet in *Romeo and Juliet*, Lothario in *Mignon*, and Golaud in *Pelléas and Mélisande*. When he appeared as Golaud in the first Metropolitan Opera production of *Pelléas and Mélisande*, Lawrence Gilman commented in the *Herald Tribune:* "Mr. Whitehill's Golaud is shrewdly composed and developed, a remarkable study in the progressive ravages of agony of doubt, suspicion, jealousy and at last the agony of remorse."

In addition to all the preceding roles, Whitehill created for the United States the roles of Landgrave Ludwig in Liszt's *Saint Elizabeth* (January 3, 1918), Simone Trovai in Erich Wolfgang Korngold's *Violanta* (November 5, 1927), and Altair in Strauss's *Die Aegyptische Helena* (November 6, 1928); and he appeared as Petruchio in the first Metropolitan production of Hermann Goetz's *The Taming of the Shrew*.

Because of differences with the management, Whitehill resigned from the Metropolitan Opera in 1932. He accused Gatti-Casazza, the general manager, of bias against American-born singers and Gatti-Casazza countered by insisting that Whitehill had grown bitter because he had not been assigned more roles for the 1932–1933 season. The rupture aroused a storm of protest among Whitehill's admirers and caused Gatti-Casazza considerable embarrassment. Whitehill's final appearance on the stage of the Metropolitan Opera House took place on April 9, 1932, as Capulet.

After leaving the Metropolitan, he gave recitals, an area in which he had been successful for several decades. "Mr. Whitehill showed a truly artistic conception of the task of a Lieder singer," wrote Richard Aldrich in the New York *Times* following a Whitehill recital at Mendelssohn Hall in New York on March 23, 1911, "and there were deeply poetic and dramatic traits in his interpretation of many of his songs."

Because of his resemblance to George Washington, Whitehill was called upon in 1932 to impersonate the first President of the United States in a sound film distributed nationally in commemoration of the bicentenary of Washington's birth. He was also recruited on several occasions to enact Washington in pageants.

He married Dorothea Boeckler on May 16, 1902; they had a daughter. His second marriage was to Isabelle Rush Simpson, July 26, 1912. His pet hobby was billiards, which he played expertly; he rarely failed to attend a championship match. He also enjoyed playing baseball.

Clarence Whitehill died in his sleep at his

home in New York City on December 19, 1932, only a few hours after singing at a benefit concert for the unemployed in New York City.

ABOUT: Thompson, O. The American Singer. *Periodicals*—Musical Courier, March 16, 1910; New York Times, December 20, 1932.

John Williams

1941–

John Williams, classic guitarist, was born in Melbourne, Australia, on April 24, 1941. His father, Len Williams, was a guitarist. When John was seven, his father gave him his first lessons on that instrument.

In 1952 the Williams family moved to London. There the boy played for Andrés Segovia. Segovia was so impressed by his talent that he offered to teach him and made it possible for him to receive a scholarship to the Accademia Musicale Chigiana in Siena, Italy, in 1953. John remained there five years and received the unprecedented honor of being the first student of any instrument invited to give a complete recital. John's musical training in Siena was supplemented by the study of piano and theory at the Royal College of Music in London from 1956 to 1959.

In November 1958 John made his London debut with a recital at Wigmore Hall. Following this performance, Segovia wrote: "A prince of the guitar has arrived in the musical world: John Williams. . . . God has laid a finger on his brow, and it will not be long before his name becomes a byword in England and abroad."

Since then Williams has been a favorite in England's concert halls. He has been heard in recitals and as soloist with orchestras, has appeared at the leading festivals (including those at Aldeburgh, Bath, Cheltenham, Edinburgh, City of London, and South Bank in London), and has performed with various chamber music groups, including one called The Height Below, which he founded with Brian Gascoigne. He joined Julian Bream, guitarist and lutenist, in a number of duet recitals. Also, he has made regular appearances on BBC, over both radio and television, including one series of thirteen concerts which proved so popular it had to be repeated three times. In addition he has collaborated in

JOHN WILLIAMS

mixed-media concerts and performed with popular groups at jazz clubs.

Williams has enjoyed success outside Great Britain as well. In 1960 he made a highly successful debut in Paris and Madrid. In 1962 he toured the Soviet Union. In 1963 he was heard for the first time in Japan and the United States. Since 1963 he has made numerous tours of America and has won recognition all over the world. After one of his recitals at Lincoln Center for the Performing Arts in November 1971, Allen Hughes noted in the New York *Times* that in all the music Williams performed he revealed a "superb sense of musical line and color" together with "rhythmic acuity" and an "aristocratic style." Reviewing his recital that same month in Boston, Ellen Claire Pfeiffer noted in the Boston *Globe:* "Williams must be one of the most serious of the guitar virtuosi, a no-nonsense self-effacing player whose technique is without reproach and whose musicianship is impeccable. He is not one to settle for flashiness or empty pyrotechnics."

Several composers have written compositions for him. Among them are André Previn and Stephen Dodgson, who have composed for him guitar concertos which he has introduced, and the Spanish composer Torroba whose *Aires de la Mancha* appears in Williams's record album *More Virtuoso Music for the Guitar.* Williams has also recorded numerous other LPs for RCA Victor. One of these, *Julian and John,* in which he is teamed with Julian Bream, received a

951

Windgassen

Grammy in 1973 from the American Academy of Recording Arts and Sciences.

When he is not concertizing, John Williams devotes his time to teaching guitar. He has given master classes in Spain and at the Summer School of Music at Dartington Hall in Devon, England. In 1961 he served on the jury of the Conservatory of Music International Competition for Guitar at Orense, Spain.

His interests include playing chess and table tennis and discussing politics.

ABOUT: The International Who's Who 1975–1976; Who's Who 1976–1977; Who's Who in Music (5th ed.).

WOLFGANG WINDGASSEN

Wolfgang Windgassen

1914–1974

Wolfgang Friedrich Hermann Windgassen, tenor, was one of the great Wagnerian *Heldentenors* in the post–World War II era. He was born in Annemasse, Germany, on June 26, 1914. His father, Fritz Windgassen, was the leading tenor of the Stuttgart Opera, and his mother, Vally von der Osten, was a successful coloratura soprano. Wolfgang received his first music training from his father; later he was a pupil of Maria Ranzow and Alfonso Fischer at the Württemberg Academy of Music in Stuttgart, Germany. After two years of service in the German army, from 1937 to 1939, Windgassen made his debut in 1939 at Pforzheim, Germany, as Alvaro in *La Forza del Destino.* He then joined the Stuttgart State Opera with which he remained for the rest of his life. "I worked for six years as stage technician in Stuttgart," he recalled. "My father thought it a good idea to learn a steady trade in case a singing career did not develop. So I saw and heard everything from the first minute of the first rehearsal to the premiere."

In 1950 Windgassen was invited to sing his first important Wagnerian role, that of Walther in *Die Meistersinger* in Munich. This engagement brought him into contact with Wieland Wagner who was then producing operas in Munich and was planning the reopening of the Bayreuth Festival. He invited Windgassen to appear as Parsifal in this first post–World War II festi-

Windgassen: vĭnt' gä sĕn

val to be held during the summer of 1951. Windgassen's success there marked the beginning of his international fame as a Wagnerian tenor. He became a favorite at Bayreuth and returned to the festival regularly between 1951 and 1966, making 159 appearances there. "What in the name of God would Bayreuth do without Windgassen?" the Bayreuth conductor Hans Knappertsbusch once inquired.

In the summer of 1954 at Bayreuth, Windgassen appeared for the first time opposite Birgit Nilsson with whom he was destined to enjoy some of his greatest triumphs. That year he also assumed the title role in *Lohengrin* to Nilsson's Elsa. "Those Lohengrins," Nilsson has written, "have remained unforgettable for me. I learned a lot from just listening to him. ... He never pushed, forced, sobbed or acted with false pathos. He sang the music as it was written with great musicality and marvelous phrasing. His Siegfried that same year was also a revelation. He not only sang the role in a unique way but also made an extremely handsome appearance." At Bayreuth and elsewhere Windgassen appeared ninety-seven times as Tristan to Nilsson's Isolde. "I was so spoiled by his interpretation," Nilsson has said, "that it was difficult for me to sing with anyone else. I almost felt like a wife who cheats on her husband when I was not singing with him."

Windgassen extended his fame as *Heldentenor* with his first appearances at the Vienna State Opera in 1953, and at Covent Garden in London in 1954—two opera companies with which he

952

was frequently heard thereafter. He was also a frequent guest at La Scala in Milan, the Théâtre de la Monnaie in Brussels, and other major European opera houses.

He made his first appearance in the United States, at the Metropolitan Opera, on January 22, 1957, as Siegmund in *Die Walküre.* "It is easy to understand why Windgassen is so popular in European opera houses," wrote Harriet Johnson in the New York *Post.* "Besides possessing a voice of youthful vibrancy and pleasing quality, he commands a lyric style that is priceless, considering what singing Wagner does to most tenors, or vice versa." That season (his only one at the Metropolitan Opera) he was heard six times in the *Ring* cycle; in addition to Siegmund, he sang the title role of *Siegfried* on January 30, and Siegfried in *Die Götterdämmerung* on March 2.

Though he never again appeared at the Metropolitan Opera, he was heard at the San Francisco Opera. There his last American appearance took place, in 1970, as Tristan. His fame in America never approximated the proportions it had known in Europe. He avoided going frequently to the United States because he disliked long trips and extended absences from his family in Stuttgart; even when he was making guest appearances in Europe he always managed to go home between performances.

"His voice," wrote Peter G. Davis in the New York *Times,* "may have lacked the thrusting brilliance of Lauritz Melchior and the power and size of Max Lorenz, his two immediate predecessors, but Windgassen's special strengths lay in the lyrical beauty of his unmistakably personal timbre and, when the spirit was upon him, in the passionate intensity of his declamation. What he lacked in sheer cutting volume for Siegfried's sword-forging or Tristan's delirium, he compensated for with a sturdy, poised, utterly dependable vocal line of rare expressive plasticity that could instantly communicate the delicate tenderness of Lohengrin's Farewell or the sarcasm and despair of Tannhäuser's Rome Narration."

Windgassen appeared in every principal Wagnerian tenor part, including Rienzi, and he recorded all of his major Wagnerian roles with the exception of Walther in *Die Meistersinger.*

At the State Opera in Stuttgart, where he made between thirty and forty appearances a year, and elsewhere in Europe, he was highly regarded in about fifty roles outside the Wagnerian repertory. In 1965 he gave an extraordinary performance as Otello in a Wieland Wagner production of the Verdi opera at Frankfort, and then repeated it on German television. His versatility enabled him to appear successfully in *Die Fledermaus* and *La Belle Hélène,* on the one hand, and as Florestan in *Fidelio,* Aegisthus in *Elektra,* and Tamino in *The Magic Flute,* on the other.

In his last four years Windgassen was the general manager of the Stuttgart Opera. He died in Stuttgart on September 8, 1974.

Windgassen was twice married, the first time to Charlotte Schweikher, on November 20, 1939; she died in 1961. Shortly thereafter he married Lore Wissmann, on December 29, 1961. He kept a permanent residence (with his wife and two children) in the Sillenbach suburb of Stuttgart, the city of his birth, and maintained a country home in the Upper Bavarian lake country.

Windgassen was named *Kammersänger* in Württemberg in 1951 and in Vienna in 1964. He received the Golden Orpheus medal from Italy in 1957 and, one year later, the gold medal of the Teatro Lirico in Barcelona, Spain.

ABOUT: New York Times, October 6, 1974; Opera News, March 26, 1966.

Herbert Witherspoon

1873–1935

Herbert Witherspoon, bass, was born in Buffalo, New York, on July 21, 1873, the son of Reverend Orlando Witherspoon, an Episcopalian minister. Though both the Reverend and his wife, Cora V. Taylor Witherspoon, were music lovers, their first concern for their son was to see him get a thorough academic education. As a boy, Herbert showed such a marked gift for drawing that a career as artist seemed to lie in his future. But at Yale University music took precedence over all other subjects, as he took courses with Horatio William Parker and Gustav Stoeckel and sang with the glee club, though he also studied drawing and painting at the art school.

After graduation from Yale in 1895, he made his concert debut in New Haven, Connecticut, on October 21. The debut was so successful that

HERBERT WITHERSPOON

and a style of much finish and polish. . . . He is an artist of high gifts; one of the sort who is needed and is all too rare in the ranks of American singers."

Witherspoon made his debut at the Metropolitan Opera on November 26, 1908, as Titurel in *Parsifal.* Ferrando in *Il Trovatore* and Pogner in *Die Meistersinger* were two other roles he assumed that season. On Good Friday of 1909 he was the soloist in the Metropolitan Opera performance of Verdi's Requiem conducted by Toscanini. The following November 17 he sang Lodovico in a revival of *Otello* starring Leo Slezak in his Metropolitan Opera debut, with Toscanini conducting.

Witherspoon remained with the Metropolitan Opera through the 1915–1916 season. His principal roles there, besides those already commented upon, were Gurnemanz in *Parsifal,* Hermann in *Tannhäuser,* King Mark in *Tristan and Isolde,* King Henry in *Lohengrin,* Pogner in *Die Meistersinger,* Fasolt in *Das Rheingold,* Sarastro in *The Magic Flute,* Raymond in *Lucia di Lammermoor,* and Kruschina in *The Bartered Bride.* He was cast as the first Gnome in the world premiere of Frederick Converse's *The Pipe of Desire* on March 18, 1910, the first opera by an American to be produced by the Metropolitan, and Arth in the world premiere of Horatio Parker's *Mona* on March 14, 1912. He was also heard as the Judge in the American premiere of Ludwig Thuille's *Lobetanz* on November 18, 1911.

he began to entertain ideas of becoming a professional singer. He then went to New York where he was employed by the Southford Paper Company and where he studied voice with W. J. Hall and Max Treumann and piano with Edward MacDowell. Then he went to Europe for further training in voice and repertory with Jacques Bouhy in Paris and G. B. Lamperti in Milan and received instruction in acting from Joseph Victor Capoul and Anton Fuchs in Munich.

Returning to the United States, Witherspoon was heard in 1896 as Amfortas in a concert presentation of *Parsifal* conducted by Walter Damrosch, the first time this Wagnerian consecrational play was performed in the United States. In 1898 Witherspoon joined the Castle Square Opera Company which gave performances at the American Theatre in New York and with which he made his debut as Ramfis in *Aida.* He also toured the United States as soloist with the Theodore Thomas Orchestra.

For a number of years Witherspoon distinguished himself in England and the United States as a soloist in performances of oratorios. In 1902 he appeared at the Worcester Festival in Massachusetts and was a soloist with the New York Oratorio Society. He gave a recital at Mendelssohn Hall in New York on November 6, 1902, and Richard Aldrich commented in the New York *Times:* "Few singers who appear without preliminary heralding or blowing of trumpets turn out to be so competent, to give so much genuine pleasure as Mr. Witherspoon. . . . He sings with an admirable method and delivery

After leaving the Metropolitan in 1916 he retired from opera to concentrate on recitals, teaching, lecturing, and managing opera companies. In 1922 he was instrumental in founding the American Academy of Teachers of Singing, serving as its president from 1922 to 1926. In 1925 he was appointed president of the Chicago Musical College, retaining this post four years. In 1930–1931 he was artistic director of the Chicago Civic Opera, and in 1931 president of the Cincinnati Conservatory. In 1926–1927 he embarked on a lecture tour of the United States. In 1933 he joined the voice faculty of the Juilliard Summer School of Music and served as chairman of the Century of Progress Exposition in Chicago.

When Gatti-Casazza retired as general manager of the Metropolitan Opera in 1935, Witherspoon became one of a triumvirate chosen to direct the opera company. He never lived to launch his first season. He suffered a fatal heart attack in his office at the Metropolitan Opera on May 10, 1935.

He was the author of two treatises on singing: *Singing: A Treatise for Teachers and Students* (1925) and *Thirty-Six Lessons in Singing for Teacher and Student* (1930).

Witherspoon was married three times: to Greta Hughes of Paris on September 25, 1899 (from whom he was divorced in 1915); to Florence Hinkle, a soprano, on June 22, 1916; and to Blanche Skeath on April 4, 1934. He never had children.

ABOUT: Thompson, O. The American Singer. *Periodicals*—New York Times, May 11, 1935.

SIR HENRY J. WOOD

Sir Henry J. Wood

1869–1944

Henry Joseph Wood, conductor, was born in London on March 3, 1869. His father, Henry Joseph Wood, manufactured model railway engines which he sold in a shop on Oxford Street. Both parents were musical, particularly his mother, who was an excellent pianist; she gave Henry his first musical instruction on the piano. From the time he was six he participated in family concerts. He soon supplemented the study of the piano with that of the organ, acquiring such proficiency on that instrument that by the time he was ten he served as deputy organist at St. Mary's Church at Aldermanbury and in his thirteenth year held a similar post at St. Sepulchre's in the Holborn district of London. In 1883 he appeared in recitals at the Fisheries Exhibition and in 1885 at the Inventions Exhibition.

He entered the Royal Academy of Music in 1886, remaining there six terms as a student of Ebenezer Prout, Sir George Alexander MacFarren, Charles Steggall, and Manuel García. Wood's talent, not only as organist but also as composer, was recognized at the Academy by the presentation of four medals.

When he was seventeen, he was appointed full-time organist at St. John's in Fulham. Two years later he made his first attempt at conducting with a performance of MacFarren's *May-Day Cantata* at Clapton. In 1889 he toured for four months as conductor of the Arthur Rousby

Opera Company. In 1890, after being engaged by Sir Arthur Sullivan and Richard D'Oyly Carte to supervise rehearsals, he was made assistant conductor at the Savoy Theatre in London. That same year he directed performances of *Carmen* at the Carl Rosa Opera during the farewell tour of prima donna Marie Roze. Other conducting engagements with minor opera companies in London followed, including a performance of Tchaikovsky's *Eugene Onegin* at the Olympic Theater. This was his first attempt at conducting Russian music. In 1894 Felix Mottl, the Wagnerian conductor, chose him to serve as music adviser for Wagner concerts then being organized in the newly constructed Queen's Hall in London.

When the Promenade concerts ("the Proms") were inaugurated in the new Queen's Hall by the newly founded Queen's Hall Orchestra in the fall of 1895, Wood was named conductor. He led his first Promenade concert on October 6. For the next half century he conducted nightly Promenade concerts for ten weeks each autumn and became one of England's most famous and influential musicians. Though these Promenade concerts emphasized the standard literature, they also became a medium to spread the music of twentieth century composers and, particularly, the works of English composers; between 1895 and 1919 Wood performed over two hundred works by British composers. The music of Richard Strauss, Debussy, Reger, Schoenberg, Scriabin, and many others was first heard in London at these Proms. Arnold Schoenberg's atonal *Five Pieces for Orchestra* received its world premiere at a Promenade concert under Wood on September 3, 1912. Among the many other world premieres heard at these concerts were Benjamin Britten's Piano Concerto No.1 (August 18, 1938), Delius's *Eventyr* (January 11, 1919) and *A Song of Summer* (September 17, 1931), John Ireland's *A London Symphony* (August 17, 1937), and Ernst Toch's Symphony No.2 (August 20, 1934). "Undoubtedly," wrote the English musicologist Rosa Newmarch, "when the social history of the last half century comes to be written, the sterling values of Henry Wood's influence on our aesthetic culture will be most clearly estimated by the results of this great democratic movement in music."

Even during World War I there was no interruption in these Promenade concerts; and an effort was made during World War II to continue normal operations. After Queen's Hall was destroyed by a bombing attack in 1941, the Promenades moved to Albert Hall. In 1943, because of illness, Wood could conduct only the last five weeks, and on June 30, 1944, the concerts had to be discontinued because of the intensification of the bombing raids on London. In July of that year the Promenades were heard over the radio, and on July 28, 1944, Wood conducted his last Promenade concert, during the golden anniversary of the series.

When the Queen's Hall Orchestra supplemented its activity at the Promenade Concerts with a Saturday afternoon series beginning on January 30, 1897, Wood became its conductor. In 1904, as a result of a bitter struggle within the ranks of the orchestra, the Queen's Hall Orchestra was on the verge of dissolution. But after many of the prominent orchestra men had resigned to form a competitive organization (the London Symphony), Wood's influence and directorial gifts were responsible for restoring balance, unity, and artistic importance to the Queen's Hall Orchestra; in 1915 the organization changed its name to New Queen's Hall Orchestra. With its activities further expanded, this orchestra was for many years one of the most important in London. It also participated in festivals at Norwich and Sheffield with Wood conducting, and at the London Festival of 1911. In 1927 the New Queen's Hall Orchestra was absorbed into the BBC Symphony.

Wood's activities were not confined solely to the Promenade Concerts and the Saturday concerts of the Queen's Hall Orchestra. In 1899 he founded the Nottingham Orchestra. In 1900 he was the conductor of the Wolverhampton Festival Choral Society; in 1908, conductor at the Norwich Festival; and from 1902 to 1911, conductor at the Sheffield Festival. He also appeared as a guest conductor of the London Philharmonic and other major symphonic organizations in London. As guest conductor he introduced, among many other English works, Arnold Bax's Symphony No.3 (March 14, 1930), Frank Bridge's *Rebus* (February 23, 1911) and *The Sea* (September 24, 1912), and Dame Ethel Smyth's Concerto for Violin, Horn and Orchestra (March 5, 1927).

In 1897 Wood received his first recognition from British royalty. He was invited to conduct a performance for Queen Victoria. A year later, in 1898, he married Princess Olga Urussov, a Russian singer who had been his pupil. Through her influence Wood became almost as passionate an advocate of Russian music (much of it new to London when he performed it at the Promenade concerts) as of British music. He also took a Russian pseudonym, Paul Klenovsky, for some of his orchestral transcriptions and original symphonic works. Urussov died in 1909, and in 1911 Wood married Muriel Greatorex, the daughter of a major in the British Army. They had two daughters. In 1911 he was knighted. In 1923 he was appointed professor of conducting and orchestral playing at the Royal Academy of Music.

In 1918 Wood was offered the post of music director of the Boston Symphony, to succeed Karl Muck, but he turned it down. He went to the United States in July 1925 to lead concerts at the Hollywood Bowl in Los Angeles, and to appear as guest conductor with several other American orchestras. In July 1926 he returned for more concerts in the United States. Meanwhile, in 1925, he was invited to direct a program of English music at Wiesbaden, Germany.

The fiftieth anniversary of Wood's conducting debut was celebrated on October 5, 1938, at Albert Hall. He led the combined orchestras and choirs of London in a commemorative concert that included the world premiere of Vaughan Williams's *Serenade to Music* written expressly for this occasion. This work was scored for sixteen voices as well as orchestra because Wood wanted the work to feature the sixteen singers who had been most closely identified with his own career.

Because of deteriorating health, Wood was compelled to share the annual Promenade series with Basil Cameron beginning with 1939; in 1943 he was able to perform only during the last five weeks. His condition continued to worsen and by the end of the season he was too ill to listen to the last concert, which was broadcast on August 10, 1944.

Sir Henry J. Wood died in a hospital at Hitchin, Herts, England on August 19, 1944. Funeral services were held on August 24 at St. Mary's, where as a boy he had been deputy organist, and the BBC Symphony and Chorus participated. His ashes repose in that church. A memorial window commemorating his boyhood service there was unveiled there on April 26, 1946.

In addition to his knighthood, Wood received numerous honors and awards, among them honorary doctorates in music from Oxford and the universities of Cambridge, London, Manchester, and Birmingham. In 1920 Belgium made him Chevalier of the Ordre de la Couronne; in 1921 France awarded him the ribbon of Officer of the Legion of Honor and the Royal Philharmonic Society in London presented him with its gold medal; on June 7, 1944, he was named Companion of Honor by King George VI.

He resided for many years in Hallam Street, London, a few minutes from Queen's Hall. During the concert season he rose early, attended to his correspondence, then walked to the hall for rehearsals. He worked assiduously at rehearsing, with a painstaking care for detail, yet he never allowed hard work or exhaustion to disturb his even temper or to rob him of his infectious good spirits. His favorite hobby was landscape painting, but because of the pressure of his many concert engagements he reserved this pastime for his Scottish holidays. In earlier years he was also fond of carpentry. Towards the end of his life his home was Harley House in Regent's Park.

Wood made effective orchestral transcriptions of music by Bach, Mussorgsky (*Pictures at an Exhibition*), Debussy (*La Cathédrale Engloutie*), and other composers. He was also the creator of a number of orchestral works. He wrote *The Gentle Art of Singing* (1927–1928), *About Conducting* (1945), and an autobiography, *My Life of Music* (1938).

ABOUT: Hill, R. and others. Sir Henry J. Wood: Fifty Years of the "Proms"; Pound, R. Sir Henry Wood: A Biography; Wood, H. J. My Life of Music; Wood, J. The Last Years of Sir Henry J. Wood.

Eugène Ysaÿe

1858–1931

Eugène Ysaÿe, violinist and conductor, was born in Liège, Belgium, on July 16, 1858, of Walloon extraction, to Nicholas and Theresa Sottiau Ysaÿe. His father was a conductor of theater orchestras and his younger brother, Théophile, became a violin virtuoso. Eugène was five when he received his first violin lessons from his father. Two years later he entered the Liège Conservatory. There he continued his violin studies with Désiré Heyberg and Lambert-Joseph Massart and harmony with Michel Dupuis. In 1867 he earned second prize in violin playing; in 1868, first prize in violin playing and chamber music.

While still attending the Conservatory, Eugène made his first public appearance as violinist at Montegnée near Liège, in 1865. After graduation from the Conservatory he played the violin for several years in his father's orchestras. In 1876 he won the support of Henri Vieuxtemps, who not only offered to teach him privately but also used his influence to get him a government subsidy for a three-year period of additional study at the Brussels Conservatory with Henri Wieniawski.

Ysaÿe's earliest successes as a virtuoso came in Germany in 1879 at Pauline Lucca's concerts in Cologne, at a Gürzenich concert in Cologne where he performed Mendelssohn's Violin Concerto, and at Aachen. In 1880 he was engaged as concertmaster of the Bilse Orchestra in Berlin. This engagement lasted one year and afforded Ysaÿe his first opportunity to conduct. In Germany he met and befriended Anton Rubinstein, who took him to Russia for two winters of concert appearances. In 1881 he toured Norway.

In 1883 Ysaÿe settled in Paris. He then joined the pianist Stéphane Raoul Pugno in duo recitals. Ysaÿe's reputation was further enhanced in 1886 with the founding of the Ysaÿe Quartet, which was soon recognized as one of Europe's

Ysaÿe: ē zà ē′

EUGÈNE YSAŸE

great chamber music ensembles. Debussy dedicated his celebrated String Quartet to the Ysaÿe Quartet and the group presented its world premiere at a concert of the Société Nationale in Paris on December 29, 1893.

On September 26, 1886, at Arlon, Ysaÿe married Louise Bourdeau, the daughter of an army general. At their wedding ceremony they received as a gift the manuscript of César Franck's Violin Sonata in A major. It had been inspired by Ysaÿe's artistry and was dedicated to him. Ysaÿe performed its world premiere on the afternoon of December 16, 1886, in a concert room of the Modern Museum at Brussels. No lighting was permitted in the museum. While the performance was going on the room grew so dark that it was impossible for Ysaÿe and his pianist to read the music. For a few moments it seemed as if this first performance of Franck's masterwork would be aborted. Then Ysaÿe rapped sharply on his music stand and exclaimed: "Let's continue!" The rest of the work was performed from memory in total darkness. His subsequent performances of this sonata were responsible for making it world famous.

In 1889 Ysaÿe made his debut in London performing Beethoven's Violin Concerto with the Royal Philharmonic Orchestra. After that he toured Europe extensively. He was greatly admired for the nobility of his style, the profundity of his musicianship, and his remarkable fusion of intellectualism and romanticism. In 1891 he commissioned Guillaume Lekeu to write what became his most celebrated work, the Violin

Sonata, and gave its world premiere. On December 27, 1896, he presented the first performance of Chausson's *Poème* at a private concert. (Its premiere performance at a public concert was reserved for another violinist.)

Ysaÿe made his debut in the United States, in New York, on November 16, 1894, performing Beethoven's Violin Concerto with the New York Philharmonic. He made a sensational impression. Success followed him throughout America, both on this and on subsequent tours. When he returned to New York on December 8, 1904, after a six-year absence, to perform Bach's Concerto in E major and Bruch's Concerto No.2 with the Boston Symphony under Wilhelm Gericke, Richard Aldrich wrote in the New York *Times:* "Mr. Ysaÿe returned in the plenitude of his powers, which are those of a supremely great master, an interpreter in the highest sense, who glorifies and ennobles all he touches with the communicating flame of his ardent musical temperament. Greater technicians there may be but none who have spoken with a higher and nobler eloquence, with deeper poetical insight; none who can so pluck the heart out of the mystery of great music and impart that mystery so fully and unreservedly as he." And when Ysaÿe gave a recital at Carnegie Hall on November 18, 1912, for his first return to New York in eight years, Aldrich was still rhapsodic in the New York *Times:* "The ravages of time have had little effect upon the essential qualities of his playing which make him a great master, an interpreter in the highest sense." In the United States Ysaÿe was heard not only in recitals and as guest artist with major orchestras but also in chamber music concerts with Jean Gérardy and Leopold Godowsky and in joint performances with Mischa Elman and with Pablo Casals.

In 1894 Ysaÿe founded the Ysaÿe Orchestral Concerts (Société des Concerts Ysaÿe) in Brussels. For many years this was a forum where many new French and Belgian compositions were introduced under his direction. His reputation as a conductor spread to America and in 1898 he was offered the post of music director of the New York Philharmonic succeeding Anton Seidl; he turned it down. From 1886 to 1898 he also distinguished himself in Belgium as professor of the violin at the Brussels Conservatory.

When the Germans invaded Belgium during World War I, Ysaÿe, his wife, their five children, and his brother, Théophile, fled to London. He remained in England through the war years. After the war, he returned to Belgium to resume the imperial position in its musical life that he had formerly occupied.

On April 5, 1918, he made his American debut as conductor with the Cincinnati Symphony. This appearance, and others about a month later at the Cincinnati May Music Festival, were so successful that he was appointed permanent conductor of the Cincinnati Symphony. He held this post from 1918 to 1922 and was held in high esteem among American conductors during that time.

In 1922 he resumed his activity in Belgium as the conductor of the Ysaÿe Orchestral Concerts, and he received the appointment of Maître de Chappelle to the court.

Some years after the death of his wife in 1924 Ysaÿe married Jeannette Dincin, on July 9, 1927; she was the daughter of a Brooklyn, New York, physician. In his last years he suffered severely from the ravages of diabetes, and had to have his left foot amputated. When his opera *Peter the Miner* (text written in Walloon dialect) was completed in his seventieth year and received its world premiere in Liège on March 4, 1931, he had to be carried into the auditorium in an invalid's chair. He began writing a second opera in the Walloon dialect but did not live to complete it. He died in Brussels on May 12, 1931.

Ysaÿe was also the composer of eight violin concertos, six violin sonatas, sonatas for unaccompanied violin and for unaccompanied cello, chamber music, and various compositions for solo violin including the *Chant d'Hiver, Rêve d'Enfant,* and *Lointain Passé.*

In 1937 Queen Elisabeth of Belgium established in his honor the Prix International Eugène Ysaÿe—David Oistrakh was the first recipient of this award. To commemorate the centenary of Ysaÿe's birth, the Belgian government issued on September 1, 1958, a thirty-centime Eugène Ysaÿe stamp.

ABOUT: Christen, E. Ysaÿe: Roi de l'Archet; Ysaÿe, A. and Ratcliffe, B. Ysaÿe: His Life, Work and Influence.

Nicanor Zabaleta

1907–

Since Carlos Salzedo, no harpist has done more to promote the harp as a solo instrument and to enrich its repertory than Nicanor Zabaleta. He was born in the Spanish Basque city of San Sebastian on January 7, 1907, to Pedro and Isabel Zala Zabaleta. His father was a painter and musician. Nicanor received his academic education at the Colegio del Sagrado Corazón and at the Colegio de Lecaroz, in San Sebastian, in preparation for a career in business. Music—the harp specifically—was an avocation of Nicanor's from early boyhood; he began to study the harp when he was seven. A year later he entered the Madrid Conservatory, specializing in the harp. In 1918 he made his debut as harpist with a concert in San Sebastian. Two years later he was graduated from the Madrid Conservatory with highest honors.

After completing his academic education in 1923, Nicanor decided to become a professional musician. For a while he played the harp in orchestras in San Sebastian and Madrid and continued to study that instrument with Vicenta Tormo de Calvo, Luisa Menárguez, and Pilar Michelena. He completed his harp studies with Marcel Tournier in Paris, where he went in 1925, and combined this with training in fugue and composition with Marcel Rousseau and Eugène Cools.

In or about 1929 he began his career as a concert harpist with performances in Europe and Latin America. The career was interrupted when he suffered a fungus infection of the fingers which made it impossible for him to continue playing the harp for several years. During this period of withdrawal from the concert stage he taught the harp for four years at the Caracas Conservatory in Venezuela.

Upon recovering from this ailment, Zabaleta resumed concert work. On July 5, 1934, he made his American debut as soloist with the Lewisohn Stadium Orchestra in New York, José Iturbi conducting, in a performance of Debussy's *Danse Sacrée* and *Danse Profane* and Ravel's *Introduction et Allegro,* for harp, flute and string quartet. Since then he has toured the Unit-

Zabaleta: thä bä lä' tä

Zimbalist

NICANOR ZABALETA

ed States frequently and has performed in all other parts of the music world, appearing in recitals and as a soloist with orchestras. In 1958 he embarked on an extended tour of Europe as soloist with its major symphony orchestras. In all, he has given over 2,500 recitals, has performed with 150 symphony orchestras, and has been heard at the Casals Festival in Puerto Rico and at festivals in Edinburgh, Lucerne, Berlin, Venice, and Osaka.

"Harpists of the Zabaleta stripe (which is, of course, the royal purple) do not traffic in the demonstrative, the overt or the ostentatious," wrote Irving Kolodin in the *Saturday Review.* "They are the patricians of their profession, for whom a pure harmonic, a sparkling glissando, or a glistening arabesque calls for plaudits on behalf of their deftness in the low end of the dynamic scale as a brushing fortissimo arouses the heat in piano fanciers."

In the New York *Times* Harold C. Schonberg said that Zabaleta "might be termed the Segovia of the harp, for he brings to his music the same type of dedication, style and high art that the guitarist brings to his."

To enrich a comparatively limited repertory, Zabaleta embarked upon intensive research resulting in the rediscovery of some long-forgotten music for the harp by sixteenth, seventeenth, and eighteenth century Spanish and Portuguese composers, and also by such masters as Johann Sebastian Bach, Carl Philipp Emanuel Bach, Handel, and Telemann. In addition, he has

made numerous transcriptions for the harp of musical works written for other instruments.

Zabaleta has encouraged composers to write music for the harp. Darius Milhaud, Heitor Villa-Lobos, and Joaquín Rodrigo wrote concertos for him; Germaine Tailleferre, Alan Hovhanness, and Ernst Krenek produced sonatas for him. Other composers who wrote music for him were Virgil Thomson, Walter Piston, and Alberto Ginastera.

Zabaleta married Graciela Torres Alcaide, a graduate of Wellesley College, on February 22, 1952. With their two children they reside in Puerto Rico. His main hobby is collecting coins.

Zabaleta has been awarded the Harriet Cohen International Music Prize, and, in 1969, the Grand Prix National du Disque Français for one of his recordings. During the summers he conducts a master class in harp at the Accademia Musicale Chigiana in Siena, Italy.

ABOUT: Time, December 14, 1953.

Efrem Zimbalist

1889–

Efrem Zimbalist, violinist, was born in Rostov-on-Don, Russia, on April 9, 1889. His father, Alexander Zimbalist, the conductor of the Rostov Opera orchestra, gave Efrem his first violin lessons. The boy made such progress that when he was nine he was able to fill the first violinist's chair in his father's orchestra. Sometime after that, lured by an offer of one hundred rubles a month, he ran away from home to a nearby city to become second concertmaster of an orchestra. When Efrem's mother, Maria Litvinoff Zimbalist, found him she compelled him to return home.

He was taken to St. Petersburg in 1901 to enter the Conservatory. At the Conservatory, where he remained six years, he studied with Leopold Auer. "The first time I played for him he was not very nice," Zimbalist recalled in later years. "He gave me the music of a new concerto to learn. When I came to the class next week, I was a little afraid, because I had not practiced much. I put the music on the stand and played the first movement. When I finished, the Profes-

---

Zimbalist: zĭm′ bà lĭst

960

EFREM ZIMBALIST

sor, without a word, lifted the stand and music, opened the door, and threw both out into the corridor. Then he took me by the collar and threw me out, too. . . . Believe me, after that, I took care to practice."

During his Conservatory years Efrem was sometimes invited to the home of Rimsky-Korsakov to play string quartets. The revolution of 1905 found him on the side of the revolutionists trying to stir up the Conservatory students. For this he was expelled, but a few months later, through Auer's influence, he was forgiven and readmitted. When he was graduated from the Conservatory in 1907, he was awarded a gold medal for violin playing and the Rubinstein prize of twelve hundred rubles.

On November 7, 1907, Zimbalist made his European debut performing the Brahms Violin Concerto in Berlin with the Berlin Philharmonic Orchestra. He scored a major success which was repeated the following December when he made his debut in London. Other appearances in Europe followed. His fame brought him an invitation to be the first violinist since Joachim to perform with the Gewandhaus Orchestra in Leipzig on New Year's Day; for half a century it had been traditional for Joachim to appear on that day with the orchestra.

With his reputation firmly established in Europe, Zimbalist made his American debut in Boston as a soloist with the Boston Symphony Orchestra on October 27, 1911, in the American premiere of Glazunov's Concerto in A minor. Philip Hale, the Boston music critic, reported:

"He is much more than a virtuoso . . . for he has a fine taste and musical feeling." One week later, on November 2, Zimbalist made his debut in New York as soloist with the New York Philharmonic in the Glazunov Concerto. Writing in the New York *Times,* Richard Aldrich commented: "He is already a virtuoso in the best sense of the word, of the first rank; a mature artist, who can stir feelings that it is not given to many to touch."

During that first visit to the United States, Zimbalist met Alma Gluck, soprano of the Metropolitan Opera. They were both booked to give a joint concert in New Jersey and their first meeting took place on the ferryboat. "She's very pretty for a singer, very pretty, very pretty," was Zimbalist's first reaction. They returned to New York City in each other's company, had dinner the following evening, and after that for the next three years had frequent meetings both socially and musically as coartists on the same program. Zimbalist had to propose several times before he was accepted. They were married on June 15, 1914, and had two children, one of whom, Efrem Zimbalist Jr., became an actor in motion pictures and over television. The first home of the Zimbalists was a house they purchased on New York's West Side, but a few years later they acquired a larger brownstone house on Park Avenue. They spent their summers in a cottage at Fishers Island. For many years, until her retirement in 1925, Gluck and Zimbalist appeared in joint concerts.

With his home permanently in New York and having become an American citizen, Zimbalist continued to concertize year after year throughout the United States. He also made several world tours. By the late 1930s he computed he had traveled three quarters of a million miles in giving his concerts. "An average of thirty thousand miles a year over a period of twenty-seven years is a conservative estimate," he said. "Once I covered fifty thousand miles in thirteen months, across the Pacific to Australia and up to Europe and finally across the Atlantic." He proved such a favorite in the Orient that he toured it over half a dozen times. He became one of the few Occidentals allowed, before World War II, to hear the Japanese Imperial Orchestra which had until then never appeared in public but had been assembled exclusively for the private entertainment of the Emperor.

In 1947 and 1948, in several American music

centers, Zimbalist offered a series of five recitals tracing the history of violin music.

A refined, sensitive artist who never exploited technique for its own sake and preferred understatement, Zimbalist is ranked among the great violinists of his generation. Virgil Thomson, writing in the *Herald Tribune,* said of him: "He is sound and straightforward, seldom strikingly original, never commonplace. . . . He is not obliged to substitute for clear articulation a simulation of intense personal feeling in the form of heavy vibrato. . . . Of all the fine fiddle tone, Mr. Zimbalist's is the least strained, the most pure. It is also the most human."

In 1928 Zimbalist became the head of the violin department of the Curtis Institute of Music in Philadelphia. In 1941 he was appointed director of the Curtis Institute, a post he retained twenty-seven years.

Alma Gluck died in 1938, and on July 6, 1943, Zimbalist married Mary Curtis Bok, founder of the Curtis Institute. As long as he was director of the Curtis Institute, the Zimbalists had a house on Delancey Place in Philadelphia. Following his resignation from Curtis in 1968, Zimbalist went into total retirement in Reno, Nevada. His wife died in 1970.

His broad nose and high cheekbones give Zimbalist a Slavic appearance. He is as well poised offstage as on it, a courtly mannered gentleman who is a gay companion with a keen-edged wit. He enjoys smoking good cigars and drinking fine vintage wines; his luxuries include Chinese dressing gowns and fine Japanese silk shirts. His prime enjoyment is spending a social evening with friends, or participating in performances of chamber music at home. On occasion he likes to play chess and plays a "wicked" game of poker and bridge. His passion for gambling—as well as his weakness for collecting things and for hunting for bargains at auctions—caused some apprehension with both his wives. His collections have included violins and violin bows, first editions and literary manuscripts, and curiosities ranging from Japanese medicine bottles to Chinese antique swords and snuffboxes.

Zimbalist has composed many works that have enjoyed significant performances. His opera *Landara* was performed in Philadelphia on April 6, 1956. His *American Rhapsody* for orchestra was heard in its first version in Chicago on March 3, 1936, and in a revised version in Philadelphia on February 5, 1943. *Portrait of an*

Artist, an orchestral tone poem, was introduced in Philadelphia on December 7, 1945. He has also written a violin concerto, a piano concerto, a string quartet, and a violin sonata, among other works. In a lighter vein he wrote the score for a Broadway operetta, *Honeydew,* that was produced at the Casino Theater in New York on September 6, 1920—it had a run of 231 performances.

ABOUT: Chotzinoff, S. Day's at the Morn; Davenport, M. Too Strong for Fantasy. *Periodicals*—New Yorker, December 5, 1931.

Pinchas Zukerman

1948–

Pinchas Zukerman, violinist, was born in Tel Aviv, Israel, on July 16, 1948, to Jehuda and Miriam Zukerman. About his parents, he confided to Stephen E. Rubin in an interview for the New York *Times:* "It was very difficult for them. They had gone through hell—Auschwitz and everything. They both had different marriages before the war and they lost everyone. They married after the war, and suffered through more hell in Israel. Then they had this child, a *meshugener,* like me." As a child, Zukerman's musical leanings were towards the recorder and the clarinet. But when he was seven he decided to study the violin and his father, himself a violinist, gave him his first lessons. A year later he entered the Israel Conservatory and Academy of Music in Tel Aviv where he studied with Ilona Feher. When he was eleven he began performing in public, including a performance for the Queen Mother of Belgium then visiting Israel. "My father," he says, "realized that I needed the experience of playing. So he pushed me everywhere. I became sort of a national hero. It was very bad for me."

In his thirteenth year, in 1961, Isaac Stern and Pablo Casals went to Israel to perform at Israel's first music festival. They heard Zukerman play and strongly recommended that he go to the United States for advanced study. "In twenty years of listening to young violinists," Stern said, "I have rarely heard as richly promising a talent as Pinchas Zukerman. He has an extraordinary power of communication and I fully expect him

PINCHAS ZUKERMAN

to take his rightful place among the great artists of our time."

Stern arranged for Zukerman to receive a grant from the America-Israel Cultural Foundation, enabling the boy to go to the United States in 1961. He found a home with the parents of Eugene Istomin and was enrolled at the Juilliard School of Music in New York to study with Ivan Galamian. Zukerman was then a brash, spoiled, cocksure kid, as he himself has readily confessed. He thought he had little to learn. "You have to understand that I came to America because I thought I was going to perform. . . . Ivan Galamian . . . told me 'you have to start from A-B-C.' I looked at him as if he was nuts or something. My reaction to the whole situation was that I shouldn't practice. Why should I? I was so good—I played Paganini Caprices. Of course I had no discipline. I had no idea what goes into the making of an artist."

He took to smoking and to spending day after day in the pool parlor. "I was never really good at pool, though I played day in and day out. I learned a few tricks from the hustlers. . . . On the one hand, my music teachers were trying to train me like a wild horse. On the other hand, it was the complete opposite being with these bums. . . . Now that I look back, I think I grew because of it."

Stern became a sobering influence. After Stern invited him to his house in Connecticut to play for him, Stern took him severely to task. Zukerman puts it this way: "This was the time I was going completely off the track. It was unbelieva-

ble. He had to beat me over the head. If not for him at that time, I think I would have been in a lot of trouble. I was very fortunate, though, because after that I had wonderful guidance."

Further scholarships from the Juilliard School of Music and the Helena Rubinstein Foundation enabled him to complete his music study. In 1966 he performed at the Festival of Two Worlds at Spoleto, Italy. After a brief return to Israel and a reunion with his parents, he returned to the United States. In May 1967 he captured the first prize in the Leventritt International Competition. In 1968 he was invited to appear at the Casals Festival in Puerto Rico, to return to Spoleto for additional performances, and to make his debut in Venezuela. The following season (1960–1961) under the managerial wing of Sol Hurok, he undertook his first American tour, covering thirty major cities in the United States and Canada. His New York debut came on February 6, 1969, in a performance of the Mendelssohn Concerto with the New York Philharmonic under Leonard Bernstein. "Pinchas Zukerman has a luxurious talent," reported a critic for the New York *Post*. "His command of the violin is so natural and so inborn that the most difficult passages appear one after the other easy with an easy 'hello,' a succession of conquests. At heart he is more of a dreamer than a virtuoso, and because the technique can be taken for granted, he can dream luxuriantly, too, and he did so with a wisdom beyond his years."

In 1969–1970 he was chosen by the Chamber Music Society of the Lincoln Center for the Performing Arts in New York to participate in the gala concert celebrating the opening of Alice Tully Hall. In 1970–1971 he was heard throughout Europe and Israel, including several European festivals. Everywhere he was hailed as a violinist of rare musical perception and musicianship. "Passionate conviction is already a Zukerman mark," wrote Stephen E. Rubin in the New York *Times*. "There may be fiddlers around with a bigger sound or a more bravura technique, but there are few with more soul." Commenting upon Zukerman's performance of the Tchaikovsky Concerto with the London Philharmonic at Carnegie Hall in New York in October 1971, Rubin added: "This wasn't the old warhorse, but a beautifully shaped, deeply felt, understated rendition of music obviously cherished by the performer."

A devotee of chamber music, Zukerman has

appeared in concertos of trio music with Daniel Barenboim and Jacqueline du Pré, in joint recitals with Eugenia Rich (his flutist wife), in collaboration with various artists in concerts presented by "Isaac Stern and his Friends," and in performances by the Chamber Music Society of Lincoln Center.

Zukerman has also performed on the viola both in chamber music concerts and in presentations of such works as Mozart's Sinfonia Concertante (for violin, viola, and orchestra) in which he was heard with Stern both in public appearances and in a recording.

Zukerman has also ventured into the field of conducting. His first appearance was with the English Chamber Orchestra in New York on April 26, 1974, in the dual role of violinist and conductor. This was his conducting debut in New York in a program including the Bach Concerto for Oboe, Violin and Orchestra; Mozart's Violin Concerto No.1, K.207 (in both of which he took over the violin part); and an orchestral version of Verdi's String Quartet in E minor and a Haydn symphony which he conducted. With the same organization, he also made a recording of Mozart's *Haffner Serenade*. He subsequently conducted special concerts of the Los Angeles Philharmonic. In 1975 he conducted a performance of Mozart's *Jupiter Symphony* at the opening concerts of the Mostly Mozart Festival at the Lincoln Center for the Performing Arts in New York. At that time Harold C. Schonberg called him "still a raw conductor, but one of sensitivity and ideas. . . . As it turned out, he had a natural affinity for the podium, and he should develop into one of the great conductors (if he is not already one)." At one of the Mostly Mozart concerts in July 1976 Zukerman assumed the dual role of violinist and conductor in Mozart's Rondo in C major, K.373, then conducted the orchestra in Mozart's Piano Concerto in E-flat, K.482, with Joseph Kalichstein as soloist, and in Beethoven's Symphony No.2.

Commenting on his experiences with the baton, Zukerman has said: "It's not really conducting. It's directing . . . I don't have an ambition to conduct Bruckner symphonies—at least not for the time being, for the next twenty years. But I would like to learn enough to be comfortable enough to do things like play and conduct Mozart concertos and literature like the *Haffner Serenade*. Things that basically use a

chamber orchestra. Knowing this helps me when I play with other conductors."

On May 26, 1968, Zukerman married Eugenia Rich, a flutist. They have two daughters. They met when both were attending the Juilliard School of Music and were performing in the Juilliard Orchestra. Their home is an apartment on Riverside Drive in New York, in the same building as that of his close friend Itzhak Perlman. Zukerman has a close-knit family of friends who affectionately call him Pinky. The circle includes, besides Perlman, David Barenboim, Jacqueline du Pré, Zubin Mehta, and Vladimir Ashkenazy. They often join in performances of chamber music for their own enjoyment. For relaxation, Zukerman enjoys playing tennis.

ABOUT: New York Times, November 7, 1971, February 18, 1977.

Teresa Zylis-Gara

1935–

Teresa Geralda Zylis-Gara (originally Teresa Geralda Zylis), soprano, was born in Vilno, Poland, on January 23, 1935. Both her parents were musical and so are her three brothers and one sister. "Every evening," she recalls, "there was a concert at home with the whole family." As a child, Teresa sang folk and popular songs to her own guitar accompaniment and was a soloist in church.

When she was fourteen she tried to gain admission to the Vilno Musical Academy but was turned down because she was too young. One of its professors, however, was impressed with her talent and offered to meet her once a week and give her some vocal coaching. "It was inspiring," she says, "like a sacrament, something special."

For a time she intended to study dentistry, but when at seventeen she was finally admitted to the Musical Academy, music completely displaced all thoughts of a medical career. At the Academy, where she remained for six years, she received training in voice from Olga Olgina and lessons in piano and theory. At graduation she received a special prize for having been an all-round exceptional student.

After World War II she and her family moved

TERESA ZYLIS-GARA

to Cracow where she appeared as soloist with the Cracow Philharmonic. In that city she made her opera debut in 1957 in the title role of Moniuszko's *Halka*. She then went on to Warsaw, where she won first prize in a competition which enabled her to sing in recitals and over the radio and to appear as a soloist with the Warsaw Philharmonic.

In 1960 she made her first appearance outside Poland, the result of winning first prize in a competition sponsored by the German Radio in Munich. This brought her a permanent engagement in what she has described as the smallest opera house in Germany—in Oberhausen. After that she was engaged by the Dortmund Opera. During this period of apprenticeship she was able to build up an impressive repertory that included the roles of Pamina in *The Magic Flute,* Cio-Cio-San in *Madama Butterfly,* Fiordiligi in *Così fan Tutte,* Tatiana in *Eugene Onegin,* the Composer in *Ariadne auf Naxos,* and the role to which she has since referred as her passport to success, Donna Elvira in *Don Giovanni.*

Her career began to acquire dimension and depth in 1965 when she made her debut at both Covent Garden in London and the Glyndebourne Festival as Octavian in *Der Rosenkavalier.* One year later she appeared at the Paris Opéra as Donna Elvira and was heard in Düsseldorf in Monteverdi's *L'Incoronazione di Poppea* and in the title role of *Anna Bolena.* In 1968 she scored a success at Covent Garden as Violetta and at the Salzburg Festival as Donna Elvira (a performance that was filmed). Further successes

followed—at the Vienna State Opera, the Munich Opera, and the Deutsche Oper in Berlin.

In the fall of 1968 she made her American debut, with the San Francisco Opera as Donna Elvira. This was also the role in which she first appeared at the Metropolitan Opera on December 17, 1968. The crystalline purity of her vocal production, the beauty of her vocal sound, the dramatic truth of her portrayal, and her striking stage appearance all added up to success. During the next two seasons her successes at the Metropolitan Opera continued with appearances as Pamina, the Countess in *The Marriage of Figaro,* Violetta, Fiordiligi, and Marguerite in *Faust.* Then, on March 25, 1972, her appearance as Desdemona in a new production of *Otello* made her a star. One New York critic compared her to Zinka Milanov. Since then she has also been heard at the Metropolitan and acclaimed for her performances as Mimi in *La Bohème,* Cio-Cio-San, Tosca, Liù in *Turandot,* the Marschallin in *Der Rosenkavalier,* and Tatiana in *Eugene Onegin.* Commenting on her performance as Tatiana, Harold C. Schonberg reported in the New York *Times:* "Miss Zylis-Gara, that fine artist, sang a sweet and appealing Tatiana. She molded the phrases sensitively, was youthful looking, used delicate colorations and had the lyric quality for the role." She had made her first appearance as the Marschallin at the Vienna State Opera in December 1975.

In September 1973 Zylis-Gara made her debut with the Chicago Lyric Opera in the title role of *Manon.* "This Manon," reported Robert C. Marsh in the *Sun-Times,* "brought us a Polish soprano who nearly stole the show. It must be said for Teresa Zylis-Gara in the title role that she puts the dramatic meaning of a phrase across with the consistency of a real artist. The character suits her. She captures the inconsistencies of this young woman, her selfishness and her genuine capacity for love. Most of all she sings Manon's music with taste, style and a bright and attractive tone."

After appearing in *Otello* in Vienna and Israel in 1976 Zylis-Gara sang her first Elsa in *Lohengrin* at the Orange Festival in France in August of that year. On January 13, 1977 she made her debut at La Scala in Milan as Desdemona. And the first time she sang the title role of Cilèa's *Adriana Lecouvreur* anywhere was with the Greater Miami Opera Association in Florida on March 6, 1978. "She gave," wrote James Roos in the Miami *Herald,* "just about everything, including a creamily lovely soprano with a poignant silkiness for her first-act aria and for *'Poveri fiori'* which she sang so movingly in the fourth act."

The year 1978 found her at the Salzburg Festival for *Don Giovanni,* the Hamburg Opera for a new production of *Die Fledermaus,* the Paris Opéra for a new production of *The Queen of Spades* sung in Russian, the Bolshoi Opera in Moscow for a new production of *Eugene Onegin* (also sung in Russian), and the Metropolitan Opera to open the season in a new role, that of Elisabeth in *Tannhäuser.*

She has also appeared frequently in recitals and as a soloist with major symphony orchestras in such choral masterworks as Beethoven's *Missa Solemnis,* Mahler's Symphony No.8, Verdi's Requiem, Rossini's Stabat Mater, and Dvořák's Stabat Mater, Bach's *Passion According to St. Matthew* and *Easter Oratorio,* and Mozart's Requiem. She has made many appearances on European television. Among her recordings is an album of the Salzburg Festival performance of Cavalieri's *La Rappresentazione di Anima e di Corpo* which received a German award in 1971. She has also received the Mozart Gold Medal in Mexico City and the Polish National Award for Great Distinction in Artistic Achievement.

ABOUT: New York Times, June 2, 1973; Opera News, February 4, 1969, February 8, 1975.

CLASSIFIED LIST OF MUSICIANS

BARITONES

Amato, Pasquale
Battistini, Mattia
Bernac, Pierre
Bonelli, Richard
De Luca, Giuseppe
Evans, Sir Geraint
Fischer-Dieskau, Dietrich
Ghiaurov, Nicolai
Gobbi, Tito
Graveure, Louis
MacNeil, Cornell
Merrill, Robert
Milnes, Sherrill
Prey, Hermann
Reardon, John
Renaud, Maurice
Ruffo, Titta
Schorr, Friedrich
Scotti, Antonio
Singher, Martial
Souzay, Gérard
Stewart, Thomas
Thomas, John Charles
Tibbett, Lawrence
Van Rooy, Anton
Warren, Leonard
Whitehill, Clarence

BASS-BARITONES

Bohnen, Michael
Gramm, Donald
London, George
Marcoux, Vanni
Tozzi, Giorgio
Treigle, Norman

BASSES

Baccaloni, Salvatore
Chaliapin, Feodor
Christoff, Boris
Corena, Fernando
Didur, Adamo
Hines, Jerome
Journet, Marcel
Kipnis, Alexander
Kunz, Erich
List, Emanuel
Mayr, Richard

Pinza, Ezio
Plançon, Pol
Rothier, Léon
Siepi, Cesare
Talvela, Martti
Witherspoon, Herbert

CELLISTS

Casals, Pablo
Feuermann, Emanuel
Fournier, Pierre
Kindler, Hans (also conductor)
Piatigorsky, Gregor
Rose, Leonard
Rostropovich, Mstislav (also conductor)
Salmond, Felix
Starker, Janos
Wallenstein, Alfred (also conductor)

CONDUCTORS

Abbado, Claudio
Ansermet, Ernest
Barbirolli, Sir John
Barenboim, Daniel (also pianist)
Barrère, Georges (also flutist)
Beecham, Sir Thomas
Beinum, Eduard van
Bernstein, Leonard (also pianist)
Bodanzky, Artur
Böhm, Karl
Boulez, Pierre
Boult, Sir Adrian
Busch, Fritz
Caldwell, Sarah
Campanini, Cleofonte
Cantelli, Guido
Ceccato, Aldo
Cleva, Fausto
Cluytens, André
Coates, Albert
Comissiona, Sergiu
Cortot, Alfred (also pianist)
Damrosch, Walter
Davis, Colin
Dohnányi, Ernst von (also pianist)
Dorati, Antal
Ehrling, Sixten
Enesco, Georges (also violinist)
Fiedler, Arthur

Fischer, Edwin (also pianist)
Fleisher, Leon (also pianist)
Foster, Lawrence
Frühbeck de Burgos, Rafael
Furtwängler, Wilhelm
Gabrilowitsch, Ossip (also pianist)
Ganz, Rudolph (also pianist)
Giulini, Carlo Maria
Golschmann, Vladimir
Goossens, Sir Eugene
Gui, Vittorio
Haitink, Bernard
Hannikainen, Tauno
Harty, Sir Hamilton
Hertz, Alfred
Iturbi, José (also pianist)
Karajan, Herbert von
Kempe, Rudolf
Kertész, István
Kindler, Hans (also cellist)
Kleiber, Erich
Klemperer, Otto
Knappertsbusch, Hans
Kostelanetz, André
Koussevitzky, Serge
Krauss, Clemens
Krips, Josef
Kubelik, Rafael
Leinsdorf, Erich
Levine, James
Lewis, Henry
Ludwig, Leopold
Maazel, Lorin
Mahler, Gustav
Markevitch, Igor
Martinon, Jean
Mehta, Zubin
Mengelberg, Willem
Mitropoulos, Dimitri
Monteux, Pierre
Mottl, Felix
Muck, Karl
Münch, Charles
Muti, Riccardo
Nikisch, Arthur
Ormandy, Eugene
Ozawa, Seiji
Paray, Paul
Previn, André
Rachmaninoff Sergei (also pianist)
Reiner, Fritz
Richter, Hans
Rodzinski, Artur
Rosenstock, Joseph
Rostropovich, Mstislav (also cellist)
Rudel, Julius
Sabata, Victor de
Sargent, Sir Malcolm
Sawallisch, Wolfgang

Scherchen, Hermann
Schippers, Thomas
Schuricht, Carl
Serafin, Tullio
Shaw, Robert
Skrowaczewski, Stanislaw
Smallens, Alexander
Solomon, Izler
Solti, Sir Georg
Steinberg, William
Stiedry, Fritz
Stock, Frederick A.
Stokowski, Leopold
Strauss, Richard
Szell, George
Thomas, Michael Tilson
Toscanini, Arturo
Waart, Edo de
Wallenstein, Alfred (also cellist)
Walter, Bruno
Weingartner, Felix
Wood, Sir Henry J.
Ysaÿe, Eugène (also violinist)

CONTRALTOS

Anderson, Marian
Barbieri, Fedora (also mezzo-soprano)
Branzell, Karin
Braslau, Sophie
Castagna, Bruna
Culp, Julia
Ferrier, Kathleen
Forrester, Maureen
Glaz, Hertha (also mezzo-soprano)
Homer, Louise
Madeira, Jean
Nikolaidi, Elena
Schumann-Heink, Ernestine
Simionato, Giulietta
Thorberg, Kerstin

FLUTISTS

Barrère, Georges (also conductor)
Rampal, Jean-Pierre

GUITARISTS

Bream, Julian
Segovia, Andrés
Williams, John

HARPISTS

Salzedo, Carlos
Zabaleta, Nicanor

HARPSICHORDISTS

Kipnis, Igor
Kirkpatrick, Ralph

Landowska, Wanda (also pianist)
Tureck, Rosalyn (also pianist)

MEZZO-SOPRANOS

Baker, Dame Janet
Barbieri, Fedora (also contralto)
Berganza, Teresa
Bumbry, Grace (also soprano)
Elias, Rosalind
Gerhardt, Elena
Glaz, Hertha (also contralto)
Horne, Marilyn (also soprano)
Rankin, Nell
Resnik, Regina
Stevens, Risë
Stignani, Ebe
Swarthout, Gladys
Thebom, Blanche (also soprano)
Tourel, Jennie
Verrett, Shirley
Von Stade, Frederica

ORGANISTS

Biggs, E. Power
Dupré, Marcel
Fox, Virgil
Schweitzer, Albert

PIANISTS

Arrau, Claudio
Ashkenazy, Vladimir
Bachauer, Gina
Backhaus, Wilhelm
Barenboim, Daniel (also conductor)
Bar-Illan, David
Bauer, Harold
Berman, Lazar
Bernstein, Leonard (also conductor)
Bolet, Jorge
Brailowsky, Alexander
Browning, John
Carreño, Teresa
Casadesus, Robert
Cliburn, Van
Cohen, Harriet
Cortot, Alfred (also conductor)
Curzon, Clifford
Dichter, Misha
Dohnányi, Ernst von (also conductor)
Entremont, Philippe
Eschenbach, Christoph
Firkušny, Rudolf
Fischer, Edwin (also conductor)
Fleisher, Leon (also conductor)
Gabrilowitsch, Ossip (also conductor)
Ganz, Rudolph (also conductor)
Gieseking, Walter

Gilels, Emil
Godowsky, Leopold
Gould, Glenn
Graffman, Gary
Hambourg, Mark
Hess, Dame Myra
Hofmann, Josef
Horowitz, Vladimir
Horszowski, Mieczyslaw
Istomin, Eugene
Iturbi, José (also conductor)
Janis, Byron
Joseffy, Rafael
Kempff, Wilhelm
Kraus, Lili
Landowska, Wanda (also harpsichordist)
Larrocha, Alicia de
Levitzki, Mischa
Lhévinne, Josef
Malcuzynski, Witold
Michelangeli
Moiseiwitsch, Benno
Novaës, Guiomar
Ohlsson, Garrick
Pachmann, Vladimir de
Paderewski, Ignace Jan
Pennario, Leonard
Petri, Egon
Rachmaninoff, Sergei (also conductor)
Richter, Sviatoslav
Rosenthal, Moriz
Rubinstein, Arthur
Samaroff, Olga
Schnabel, Artur
Serkin, Rudolf
Siloti, Alexander
Tureck, Rosalyn (also harpsichordist)
Watts, André
Weissenberg, Alexis

SOPRANOS

Albanese, Licia
Alda, Frances
Amara, Lucine
Angeles, Victoria de los
Arroyo, Martina
Bampton, Rose
Bjoner, Ingrid
Blegen, Judith
Bori, Lucrezia
Borkh, Inge
Bumbry, Grace (also mezzo-soprano)
Caballé, Montserrat
Callas, Maria
Calvé, Emma
Cavalieri, Lina
Crespin, Regine
Curtin, Phyllis

Della Casa, Lisa
Destinn, Emmy
Dobbs, Mattiwilda
Eames, Emma
Easton, Florence
Farrar, Geraldine
Farrell, Eileen
Flagstad, Kirsten
Fremstad, Olive
Freni, Mirella
Frijsh, Povla
Gadski, Johanna
Galli-Curci, Amelita
Garden, Mary
Giannini, Dusolina
Gluck, Alma
Grist, Reri
Gueden, Hilde
Hempel, Frieda
Horne, Marilyn (also mezzo-soprano)
Janowitz, Gundula
Jeritza, Maria
Jones, Gwyneth
Jurinac, Sena
Kappel, Gertrude
Kirsten, Dorothy
Kurz, Selma
Lawrence, Marjorie
Lear, Evelyn
Lehmann, Lilli
Lehmann, Lotte
Leider, Frida
Ljungberg, Göta
Ludwig, Christa
Malfitano, Catherine
Maliponte, Adriana
Matzenauer, Margarete
Maynor, Dorothy
Melba, Dame Nellie
Milanov, Zinka
Moffo, Anna
Moore, Grace
Munsel, Patrice
Muzio, Claudia
Nevada, Emma
Nilsson, Birgit
Nordica, Lillian
Norman, Jessye
Novotna, Jarmila
Olivero, Magda
Pauly, Rose
Peters, Roberta
Pons, Lily
Ponselle, Rosa
Price, Leontyne
Raisa, Rosa
Raskin, Judith
Rethberg, Elisabeth
Rysanek, Leonie

Sayão, Bidú
Schumann, Elisabeth
Schwarzkopf, Elisabeth
Scotto, Renata
Seefried, Irmgard
Sembrich, Marcella
Sills, Beverly
Stader, Maria
Steber, Eleanor
Stratas, Teresa
Sutherland, Joan
Tebaldi, Renata
Te Kanawa, Kiri
Ternina, Milka
Tetrazzini, Luisa
Teyte, Dame Maggie
Thebom, Blanche (also mezzo-soprano)
Traubel, Helen
Tucci, Gabriella
Varnay, Astrid
Vishnevskaya, Galina
Welitsch, Ljuba
Zylis-Gara, Teresa

TENORS

Althouse, Paul
Bergonzi, Carlo
Björling, Jussi
Bonci, Alessandro
Caruso, Enrico
Coates, John
Corelli, Franco
Crooks, Richard
Del Monaco, Mario
Di Stefano, Giuseppe
Domingo, Placido
Gedda, Nicolai
Gigli, Beniamino
Hayes, Roland
Johnson, Edward
Kiepura, Jan
King, James
Kónya, Sándor
Kullman, Charles
Lauri-Volpi, Giacomo
McCormack, John
McCracken, James
Maison, René
Martinelli, Giovanni
Melchior, Lauritz
Muratore, Lucien
Pavarotti, Luciano
Pears, Peter
Peerce, Jan
Schiøtz, Aksel
Schipa, Tito
Shirley, George
Slezak, Leo

Godowsky, Haitink, Hambourg, Horszowski, Joseffy, Journet, Kertesz, Kindler, Kraus, Kurz, Mottl, Muck, Muratore, Nevada, Nikisch, Pachmann, Powell, Previn, Renaud, Hans Richter, Samaroff, Sargent, Scotti, Siloti, Tetrazzini, Trampler, Van Dyck, Whitehill, Witherspoon, Ysaÿe; *Oggiano Ida Studio, NY:* Bonelli; *Opera News:* Baker, Bergonzi, Bodanzky, Caruso, Chaliapin, Cleva, Corelli, Davis, Della Casa, Destinn, Elias, Evans, Freni, Gadski, Gedda, Giulini, Homer, Jones, Lauri-Volpi, Lilli Lehmann, Levine, Mahler, Mayr, Melba, Milnes, Mitropoulos, Moffo, Muzio, Nordica, Pears, Pinza, Plançon, Raisa, Rankin, Rudel, Ruffo, Rysanek, Sabata, Sawallisch, Schumann-Heink, Sembrich, Simionato, Steber, Stevens, Stratas, Sutherland, Te Kanawa, Ternina, Traubel, Tucci, Vickers, Vishnevskaya, Von Stade, Windgassen; *Oscar & Associates, Chicago:* Hannikainen, Reiner; *Paramount Pictures:* Swarthout; *Pen & Lens, Kathy Wersen:* Caldwell; *Albert Petersen:* Hofmann; *Pietzner:* Kurz; *Fred Plaut:* Francescatti; *Polydor/Lauterwasser:* Jones; *RCA:* Fiedler, Ormandy; *RCA Victor Records:* Cleva; *H. Rand, Paris:* Elman; *Francesco Reale, Rome:* Ruffo; *F. vander Ryk, Rotterdam:* Godowsky; *A. Sahm:* Kappel; *John B. Sanromá:* Hayes; *Sarony, NY:* Joseffy; *Maurice Seymour, Chicago:* Schipa, John Charles Thomas; *Editta Sherman, NY:* Szell; *Adrian Siegel, Philadelphia:* Muti, Stokowski; *Christian Steiner:* Amara, Domingo, Forrester, Gramm, Horne, Ohlsson, Reardon, Ricci, Steber; *Toppo, NY:* Tureck; *H. Godfrey Turner, NY:* Powell; *Underwood & Underwood, NY:* Ganz; *Ken Veeder, Angel Records:* Igor Kipnis; *White, NY:* Destinn; *Whitestone Photo, NY:* Leinsdorf; *Wide World Studio, NY:* Johnson, Rothier; *Willinger, Vienna:* Kullman; *The World of Music Encyclopedia:* Lilli Lehmann.

974

PHOTO CREDITS

J. Abresch, NY: Baccaloni, Barbieri, Castagna, Madeira, Malcuzynski, Rosenstock; *American Studio, Prague:* Jan Kubelik; *Angel Records:* Baker, Gedda, Sawallisch; *Ray Ashman, NY:* Bampton; *Fabian Bachrach:* Ehrling; *Sophie Baker, London:* Williams; *Casa Editr. Ballerini & Fratini, Florence:* Sabata; *Barda:* Frühbeck de Burgos; *Bender:* Borkh; *Walter Bird:* Wood; *Boris:* Bar-Illan; *Breitkopf & Hartël, NY:* Pachmann; *Esther Brown, NY:* Trampler; *Brown Brothers, NY:* Casals; *Bruno of Hollywood:* Bolet, Rankin, Tebaldi, Treigle, Welitsch; *Campbell Studio:* Mengelberg; *Capitol Records:* Giulini, Klemperer; *Columbia Records:* Barbirolli, Rodzinski, Walter; *Daguerre, Chicago:* Alexander Kipnis, Leider; *Erika Davidson, NY:* Maliponte, Milnes; *De Bellis Studios, NY:* Maynor, Menuhin, Rosenthal; *Delar, NY:* Anderson, Kiepura, Rethberg; *Deutsche Grammophon/Bauer-Kempff:* Kempff; *Deutsche Grammophon/Saeger:* Kónya; *Deutsche Grammophon/Wilhelmi:* Stader; *Downey:* Eames; *M. Dührkoop:* Backhaus; *Aimé Dupont:* Didur, Gluck, Journet, Scotti, Van Dyck, Ysaye; *Verlag der Dürrschen Buchh.:* Carreño; *EG & A International,* for Netherlands Tourist Office: Haitink; *Edmond Photo:* Kreisler; *Carlo Edwards:* Bodanzky; *Elliott & Fry, London:* John Coates, Hans Richter; *Leon Elzin, NY:* Althouse, Gieseking; *Epic Records:* Entremont, Kraus; *Suzanne Estel:* Ozawa; *Mike Evans/Phonogram:* Waart; *Fayer, Vienna:* Bumbry, Corelli, Ghiaurov, Janowitz, Jurinac, Kempe, King, Kunz, Nilsson, Sawallisch; *Fred Fehl:* Browning; *Franz Fiedler:* Fritz Busch; *Trude Fleischmann:* Furtwängler, Knappertsbusch; *E.F. Foley, NY:* Tetrazzini; *Fotografic d'Arte, Milan:* Serafin; *Peter Gravina, NY:* Stewart; *Godfried de Groot, Amsterdam:* Beinum; *Senta Grüning:* Schweitzer; *Fernand de Gueldre:* Muratore; *Gyenes, Madrid:* Dobbs; *Haensel & Jones, NY:* Cavalieri; *Hague, Albany:* Hines; *Hahn:* Arroyo; *Halsman, Paris:* Brailowsky; *Peter Hastings:* Maazel; *Ibbs & Tillett:* Fischer; *Ray Lee Jackson, NY:* Boult, Feuermann, Milstein, Primrose; *Jacobi, NY:* Melchior, Scherchen, Svanholm; *Alfred Cheney Johnston:* Bori; *Kaufmann & Fabry, Chicago:* Petri; *James J. Kriegsmann, NY:* Elias, Sills, Watts; *Kubey-Rembrandt Studios, Philadelphia:* Enesco, Rachmaninoff, Smallens; *Langley Studios, Dallas:* Dorati; *Lauterwasser DG:* Berman; *A. Lavidsa, NY:* Martinelli; *Verlag Herm. Leiser, Berlin:* Battistini; *Alexander Levanton, Rochester, NY:* Goossens; *Lipnitzki, Paris:* Ansermet, Casadesus, Huberman, Landowska; *London Records:* Pears; *Lucas & Pritchard Studio, NY:* Stiedry; *Angus McBean,* for Angel Records: Leopold Ludwig; *G. Maillard Kesslère, NY:* Lotte Lehmann; *Matzene:* Garden; *Lotte Meitner-Graf, London:* Bachauer, Boulez, Comissiona, Janis, Seefried; *Louis Mélançon:* Corena; *Metropolitan Music Bureau:* Gabrilowitsch; *Metropolitan Opera Archives:* Bohnen, Braslau, Corena, Didur; *M & G Meyer-Haifa:* Moiseiwitsch; *Mishkin, NY:* Bohnen, Campanini, Chaliapin, De Luca, Fremstad, Hertz, Ponselle, Seidel, Slezak; *Herbert Mitchell, NY:* Frijsh, Pauly; *Musical America:* Ohlsson, Olivero; *Musical Courier:* Rostropovich, Schiøtz, Schuricht, Stignani, Teyte; *NBC Photo:* Toscanini; *G. Nelidoff, Chicago:* Stock; *Netherlands Information Service:* Rafael Kubelik; *Music Division, The New York Public Library at Lincoln Center, The Astor, Lenox and Tilden Foundations:* Battistini, Berman, Browning, Caldwell, Campanini, Carreño, Cavalieri, Dupré, Entremont, Fox, Gabrilowitsch, Gluck,

Svanholm, Set
Tagliavini, Ferruccio
Tauber, Richard
Thomas, Jess
Tucker, Richard
Van Dyck, Ernest
Vickers, Jon
Windgassen, Wolfgang

VIOLISTS

Doktor, Paul
Primrose, William
Tertis, Lionel
Trampler, Walter

VIOLINISTS

Busch, Adolf
Elman, Mischa
Enesco, Georges (also conductor)
Francescatti, Zino

Grumiaux, Arthur
Heifitz, Jascha
Huberman, Bronislaw
Kogan, Leonid
Kreisler, Fritz
Kubelik, Jan
Menuhin, Yehudi
Milstein, Nathan
Morini, Erica
Oistrakh, David
Perlman, Itzhak
Powell, Maud
Ricci, Ruggiero
Seidel, Toscha
Spalding, Albert
Stern, Isaac
Szeryng, Henryk
Szigeti, Joseph
Thibaud, Jacques
Ysaÿe, Eugène (also conductor)
Zimbalist, Efrem
Zukerman, Pinchas